VIEW FROM CYBERSPACE

INSIDE STORY

THE RESPONSIBLE MANAGER

Managers *and the* Legal Environment:

STRATEGIES FOR THE 21ST CENTURY

CONSTANCE E. BAGLEY
Harvard Business School

WEST

™

THOMSON LEARNING

Australia · Canada · Mexico · Singapore · Spain · United Kingdom · United States

Managers and the Legal Environment: Strategies for the 21st Century, 4e
by Constance E. Bagley

Senior Acquisitions Editor: Rob Dewey
Senior Developmental Editor: Jan Lamar
Marketing Manager: Nicole Moore
Media Technology Editor: Vicky True
Media Developmental Editor: Peggy Buskey
Media Production Editor: John Barans
Senior Production Editor: Kara ZumBahlen
Manufacturing Coordinator: Sandee Milewski
Internal Design: Ellen Pettengell Design, Chicago
Cover Design: Ramsdell Design/Craig Ramsdell, Cincinnati
Cover Images: © Peter Pearson/Stone; PhotoDisc, Inc.
Production House: WordCrafters Editorial Services, Inc.
Compositor: Parkwood Composition Service, Inc.
Printer: Courier Kendallville

Printed in the United States of America

1 2 3 4 5 04 03 02 01

For more information contact West Legal Studies in Business, South-Western, 5101
Madison Road, Cincinnati, Ohio, 45227 or find us on the Internet at
http://www.westbuslaw.com

For permission to use material from this text or product, contact us by
• **telephone: 1-800-730-2214**
• **fax: 1-800-730-2215**
• **web: http://www.thomsonrights.com**

Library of Congress Cataloging-in-Publication Data

Bagley, Constance E.
   Managers and the legal environment : strategies for the 21st century/Constance
E. Bagley.–4th ed.
      p. cm.
   Includes bibliographical references and index.
   ISBN 0-324-06187-0 (alk. paper)
   1. Business law—United States. 2. Trade regulation—United States. 3. Business
   ethics—United States. I. Title.
KF889 .B255 2002
346.7307–dc21   2001026158

Dedication

To my Son
Christoph Alexei

Contents *in* Brief

Table *of* Contents

Table *of* Cases

The principal cases are in bold type. Cases cited or discussed are in light type.

Preface

It is hard to imagine a time when law was more important to managers yet so in flux. Courts and legislatures are struggling to keep up with technological advances, especially the transformation of the Internet from a vehicle for decentralized communications among scientists and academics to an engine of global commerce. Clearly, no business curriculum today would be complete without an overview of the legal environment in which business takes place. Yet, a comprehensive and cutting-edge text about the legal environment of business must offer more. To achieve maximum effectiveness, it should provide an integrated treatment of law and management that shows how the law provides ways for managers to minimize risk and create value. It should also explain, with practical examples, how managers can use the law strategically to craft solutions to attain their core business objectives. Finally, it should highlight traps for the unwary so that managers can both spot legal issues before they become legal problems and effectively handle the inevitable legal disputes that arise in the course of doing business.

These goals have guided the writing of *Managers and the Legal Environment: Strategies for the 21st Century*, Fourth Edition. As its title implies, the text is designed as a "hands-on," transactional guide for current and future business managers and leaders, including entrepreneurs. It provides a broad and a detailed understanding of how law impacts daily management decisions and business strategies. No manager operating in the complex and ever-changing global business environment of the early twenty-first century can compete successfully without such knowledge.

The topics covered in *Managers and the Legal Environment: Strategies for the 21st Century* demonstrate its focus on meeting the needs of business managers and leaders. The text covers not only such essential legal topics as agency, contracts, torts, criminal law, antitrust, and employment law, but also others of vital concern to business managers, such as intellectual property, lending transactions, securities regulation, and environmental law. The chapter on international business transactions illustrates the overall approach of the text: It includes not only such key legal concepts as sovereign immunity and extraterritorial application of national law, but also a detailed discussion of the blend of legal, financial, operational, and logistical issues that often will determine the success or failure of an international venture.

The form of presentation is designed to convey the dynamic interplay between business decisions and the legal environment. When the most effective method of presenting the material is to demonstrate how actual business conflicts are resolved in the courts, an approach emphasizing judicial cases is used. This approach is employed in most of the chapters. However, when certain material, such as discussions of lending transactions and international trade, is best conveyed with text, this is the approach taken.

The legal topics discussed in the text are on the leading edge of business regulation. They include consumer privacy and the Internet; the World Trade Organization; copyright law in cyberspace; mandatory arbitration of employment disputes; employer liability for sexual harassment; selective disclosure of inside information to securities analysts; and the creation, sale, and patentability of genetically modified organisms.

This text is suitable for classes in the legal environment of business at the undergraduate, M.B.A., executive M.B.A., or executive education levels. It is a comprehensive and challenging, yet approachable and understandable, text that will work for those with substantial work experience as well as those who are studying business at the undergraduate level for the first time. Each chapter of *Managers and the Legal Environment: Strategies for the 21st Century* employs a wide array of effective teaching devices that reinforce the goals of the text.

⚓ Pedagogical Features

A CASE IN POINT

Each chapter presents three to nine cases, set off from the body of the text, as examples of the law in action. These cases represent crucial court decisions that have shaped important business law concepts or present key legal conflicts that managers will address in their careers. Included are many modern cases representing the most current statement of the law. These cases include, for example, the U.S. Supreme Court's 2001 decision *Whitman v. American Trucking Associations, Inc.,* which upheld the authority of the Environmental Protection Agency to promulgate air quality standards; the U.S. Court of Appeals for the District of Columbia's 2001 decision enjoining the merger of the second- and third-largest baby food manufacturers (*FTC v. H.J. Heinz Co.*); and the Second Circuit's 2000 decision limiting the liability of a securities broker-dealer's accountant for negligent misrepresentation suits brought by the broker-dealer's customers (*Securities Investor Protection Corp. v. BDO Seidman, LLP*). Traditional cases, such as *Meinhard v. Salmon* and *MacPherson v. Buick Motor Co.,* are used to show early developments in the law that remain applicable today. The selection and approach to cases is guided by the goals of the text: teaching students how to use the law strategically and how to identify legal issues before they become legal problems.

The Case in Point section is formatted to convey a detailed understanding of the cases while covering a large range of material. The case citation and facts are followed by a statement of the issue presented, which reinforces the legal principle illustrated by the case. Each case discussion then proceeds with a presentation of the court's decision and a description of the result.

The opinions in two cases in each chapter are presented in the language of the court, edited for clarity and brevity. Excerpts from dissenting opinions are used occasionally to demonstrate how reasonable people can come to different conclusions about the same facts. This is important for two reasons. First, today's dissent may be tomorrow's majority opinion. Second, comparing the arguments raised in the opinion with those of the dissent requires—and strengthens the student's ability to engage in—critical analysis. Each edited case is followed by two thought-provoking questions that challenge the student's understanding of the court's language and reasoning and encourage the student to consider the ramifications of the decision for future cases.

The opinions in the remaining cases in each chapter are summarized, which permits coverage of more cases and concepts than would be feasible if all cases were in the language of the court. Students benefit from reading a more rigorous treatment of cases than is provided by the short briefs found in many texts. Thus, this text provides a detailed recitation of the facts, the issues, the court's reasoning, and the result for each case.

Many cases also include comments, which place the case in its proper legal perspective and offer commentary on why the case is important, why the court decided it a certain way, or what the ramifications of the decision are for businesses. This explanation of the key significance of an individual case helps students understand how the case impacts the legal environment as a whole. In addition, the comments encourage students to think critically about court decisions.

ETHICAL CONSIDERATIONS

This text places great emphasis on ethical concerns, stimulating students to understand how their actions as managers and business leaders must incorporate considerations of ethics and social responsibility. Ethical considerations are emphasized in four ways. First, the opening chapter, "Ethics and the Law," includes topics such as rampant accounting fraud by companies intent on managing their earnings to meet analyst expectations, exploitation of foreign workers, racial discrimination at Coca-Cola and Texaco, and the marketing of tobacco and beer to children. Second, the text includes relevant excerpts from the *Dun & Bradstreet Code of Business Conduct* and the *American Express Company Code of Conduct*. Third, ethical considerations are highlighted throughout the text in separate boxed sections and are raised in many of the end-of-chapter Questions and Case Problems. Finally, the Manager's Dilemma question in each chapter requires students to consider how ethics factor into a managerial decision.

These ethical considerations are commentaries on how standards of ethics and social responsibility do (and sometimes do not) inform the process of lawmaking. The text discusses the ethical implications of business decisions made in response to legal rules, as well as the moral boundaries of the legal regime.

VIEW FROM CYBERSPACE

Almost every chapter includes a boxed discussion of how the laws addressed in the chapter apply to electronic commerce, the Internet, and cyberspace generally. For example, the chapter on public and private offerings of securities discusses direct initial public offerings on the World Wide Web. The constitutional law chapter discusses pornography and free speech on the Internet, and the chapter on alternate dispute resolution describes the use of ADR for online disputes. The antitrust chapter outlines the antitrust issues raised by "B2B" electronic marketplaces such as Covisint, a site major automakers are building to create an e-marketplace for trading automobile components and materials.

INTERNATIONAL CONSIDERATIONS

Two chapters cover international aspects of the legal environment. One chapter addresses international trade law, including the World Trade Organization and the European Union; the other is a transactional, integrated discussion of international business transactions, including the use of letters of credit. International considerations are also highlighted in most chapters. For example, both the product liability and the securities fraud and insider trading chapters describe the relevant European Union Directives. The chapter on civil rights and employment discrimination discusses recent amendments to Japanese law dealing with sex discrimination as well as the new European Union Directive on discrimination. Taiwanese law is discussed in the environmental law and consumer protection chapters.

ECONOMIC, HISTORICAL, AND POLITICAL PERSPECTIVES

Most chapters have a separate boxed section that puts the law into economic, historical, or political perspective. For example, the contracts chapter traces the doctrine of unconscionability from Roman law, the environmental law chapter discusses the economics of selling the right to pollute, and the torts chapter describes the politics behind efforts at tort reform.

These perspectives add a real-world dimension to the material. Too often law is presented in a vacuum, divorced from the larger political and economic context in which it is created. The goal of these sections is to heighten students' awareness of these larger forces. In addition, business managers should be made aware of the complicated interplay between economics and the law. That interplay is crucial to the operation of a business, but it is often unpredictable.

IN BRIEF

To provide a visual aid for the student, each chapter contains a boxed "In Brief" summary that breaks down into digestible pieces the key elements of material presented in that chapter. In some cases, this may be presented in the form of a flow chart; in others, it may appear as a decision tree or matrix.

AT THE TOP

Highlighted sections interspersed throughout the text reflect the importance of corporate governance, leadership, and vicarious liability in today's business and regulatory environment. These sections reflect matters that concern not only upper management and corporate officers, but also employees generally.

INSIDE STORY

Each chapter contains case summaries that present fascinating and detailed descriptions of real-world business conflicts. A strong effort has been made to include up-to-the-minute, cutting-edge business developments. The Inside Stories cover conflicts involving key-industry players, such as the *United States v. Microsoft Corp.* antitrust suit, the suit by the Recording Industry Association of America against Napster, the Firestone tire recall, and litigation against Monsanto arising out of its sale of genetically modified organisms. They describe Internet auction fraud, attempts to unionize dot-com workers, and the riots at the WTO meeting in Seattle in 1999. The Inside Stories bring the legal conflicts and developments to life and reinforce the students' appreciation for how such conflicts are played out in the real world.

DEFINED TERMS, KEY WORDS AND PHRASES, AND GLOSSARY

Throughout the text, all crucial legal terms are placed in italics and defined immediately. A list of key terms used in a chapter appears immediately before the end-of-chapter Questions and Case Problems, with a page reference to the place where that term is defined.

In addition to the page references to defined terms contained in Key Words and Phrases, there is a comprehensive glossary at the end of the text that defines the terms set in italics in the text. The definition of terms in the Glossary and the Key Words and Phrases in the text help convey the concepts and improve the students' legal and business vocabulary.

INTERNET SOURCES

Each chapter contains a list of World Wide Web sites relevant to the chapter (including their electronic addresses or URLs). These sites give students a starting point for on-line legal research. The URLs are current as of January 1, 2001. Although every attempt was made to identify Internet sites that are maintained and updated regularly, the Internet is highly dynamic, and a "hot" site today may be gone in six months.

THE RESPONSIBLE MANAGER

Each chapter concludes with a section entitled "The Responsible Manager." This section is an in-depth discussion of the crucial legal considerations that the successful manager must take into account. The Responsible Manager sections summarize each chapter, but they are far more than a mere summary. In a concise yet sophisticated manner, they alert managers to the legal issues they must spot in order to avoid violating the law or plunging the company into expensive, time-consuming litigation. In addition, these sections highlight the ethical concerns managers must confront to serve their company and community adequately.

These sections play a vital role in establishing this text as a "must-have" for upcoming and practicing business managers. In the Responsible Manager section for a particular area of the law, managers will find a wealth of practical information to bring them up to speed on the key legal issues in that area. These sections are not merely checklists; they contain a depth of analysis that is demanded by the complex, real-life nature of the problems at hand.

For example, the Responsible Manager section for the chapter on alternative dispute resolution provides a step-by-step guide to setting up an effective alternative dispute resolution procedure. The torts chapter provides a manager's guide to reducing risks of exposure for tort liability. The international business transactions chapter highlights the issues likely to arise in transactions involving more than one country and suggests strategies for managing successfully in a global setting.

END-OF-CHAPTER QUESTIONS AND THE MANAGER'S DILEMMA

Each chapter is followed by ten sophisticated and thought-provoking questions that require students to synthesize and review the material covered in the chapter. The questions are diverse. Some are imaginative hypotheticals that raise the central legal issues in a creative and sometimes humorous fashion. Others are based directly on specific cases, presenting real-world legal conflicts as opportunities for students to apply the appropriate law. For example, the bankruptcy chapter includes a question based on the attempts of a failed dot-com to transfer a below-market retail lease in New York City to another firm for $350,000. In most chapters, more than half of the questions are based on actual cases, and citations are provided for enterprising students who want to look up the cases in preparation for class. The questions that are based on actual cases often raise issues at the cutting edge of law and management. The last question in each chapter, "Manager's Dilemma," requires students to analyze the legal, business, and ethical aspects of a managerial decision.

 Changes in the Fourth Edition

The Fourth Edition represents a major revision of the text to strengthen the features that worked well in previous editions; to expand the coverage of electronic commerce and cyberlaw generally; to consolidate discussions of topics that have become more settled since the last edition (such as an employer's vicarious liability for sexual harassment); and to introduce new graphics and tables to provide clearer visual summaries of complex materials (such as a decision tree for applying the rules on insider trading and a chart of the key federal employment discrimination statutes that outlines the primary provisions and the employers covered). Finally, consistent with its reputation as a cutting-edge discussion of the intersection of law and management, the text discusses the latest cases (such as the U.S. Supreme Court's 2001 decision upholding mandatory arbitration of Title VII claims) and regulatory developments (such as the rules promulgated by the Securities and Exchange Commission in 2000 banning selective disclosure to analysts, defining what constitutes insider trading, and strengthening the requirements for auditor independence by limiting non-audit services).

More than half of the cases presented as A Case in Point and many of the end-of-chapter Questions and Case Problems are new. The text includes many cases decided in 2000 and even a few decided in 2001. Most of the Inside Stories and the Economic, Historical, and Political Perspectives are also new or have been updated to reflect the latest developments.

The chapter on contracts includes a discussion of the Uniform Electronic Transactions Act and the federal E-Sign Act, and the chapter on sales and e-commerce compares and contrasts certain key provisions in the Uniform Commercial Code, the U.N. Convention on International Sales of Goods (CISG), the Uniform Computer Information Transactions Act (UCITA), and the common law of contracts.

Several chapters have been shortened or reorganized both to reflect the relative importance of the material and to integrate recent developments. For example, the discussion of employer liability for sexual harassment in the chapter on civil rights and employment discrimination has been reworked to highlight the defense created by the U.S. Supreme Court for employers who have a reasonable sexual harassment policy in place that the employee unreasonably fails to utilize. The chapter on forms of business organizations includes an expanded discussion of franchises.

Electronic commerce is discussed extensively in an expanded chapter on sales and e-commerce and in context in many of the other chapters, with a marginal flag for the reader. For example, the torts chapter discusses the successful suit brought by eBay to stop Bidder's Edge from using "spiders" to search its site to compile comparative prices for products offered through online auctions. Cyberlaw is given an expanded treatment in a redesigned chapter entitled "Intellectual Property and Cyberlaw."

To reflect the increasingly global nature of business, the unit on international trade and business now follows the unit on the legal environment of business. New and more detailed International Considerations have been added throughout the text.

 ## Ancillary Components

ANSWERS TO END-OF-CHAPTER QUESTIONS AND CASE PROBLEMS

A complete and separate Answer Manual, prepared by the author, identifies the issues presented in each of the end-of-chapter questions and provides thorough, cogent model answers.

TEXT WEB SITE

Adopters can access the text Web site directly at <http://bagley.westbuslaw.com>.

INSTRUCTOR'S MANUAL

The Instructor's Manual was developed by Joseph A. Zavaletta, Jr. (University of Texas at Brownsville). This manual includes chapter outlines, case summaries, and teaching suggestions.

POWERPOINT PRESENTATION SLIDES

New to this edition is a set of *PowerPoint* slides developed by Joseph A. Zavaletta, Jr. (University of Texas at Brownsville). These slides can be used to enhance lectures. They are available on the text Web site <http://bagley.westbuslaw.com>.

TRANSPARENCY ACETATES

Selected figures and tables from the text are available as transparency acetates.

TEST BANK

The Test Bank was developed by Arthur M. Levine (California State University–Long Beach) and Peter M. Lee (Pacific Coast University). It contains true/false, multiple-choice, and essay test questions as well as multi-subject final exam essay questions prepared by the author.

ExamView, the computerized version of the test bank, allows instructors to create, edit, store, and print exams.

STUDY GUIDE

The Study Guide was prepared by Joseph A. Zavaletta, Jr. (University of Texas at Brownsville). It includes chapter objectives, chapter outlines, and study questions. Answers are provided at the end of the study guide.

OTHER TEACHING AIDS

West Business Law/Legal Environment Web Site: This site, available at <http://www.westbuslaw.com>, is updated regularly and offers summaries of late-breaking cases involving business law and the legal environment of business, together with links to related materials.

Web Tutor: Web Tutor (on WebCT or Blackboard) features chat, discussion groups, testing, student progress tracking, and legal environment course materials. For more information, see <http://webtutor.swcollege.com>.

Quicken® Business Lawyer 2000 CD-ROM and Applications: This booklet and CD-ROM provide your students with the opportunity to explore the law in an interactive way.

The New York Times Guide to Legal Studies in Business: *The New York Times Guide to Legal Studies in Business,* by Marianne Jennings and Jamie Murphy, is more than just a printed collection of articles. The guide gives you access, via password, to an online collection of the most current and relevant *New York Times* articles that are continually posted as news breaks. Also included are articles from *CyberTimes,* the online technology section of the *New York Times* on the Web. Correlation guides for all South-Western legal studies in business texts are available on the South-Western *New York Times* Web site at <http://nytimes.swcollege.com>. Ask your West sales representative about this great new supplement for your students.

Cutting Edge Cases in the Legal Environment of Business (2nd ed.): A collection of seventeen recent legal-environment-of-business edited cases from 1995 to 1998, using the court's own language in an expanded format, may be purchased separately.

Business Law and Legal Environment Video Library: A variety of professionally produced videos.

Ten Free Hours of WESTLAW: West's computerized legal research and Dow Jones News/Retrieval service.

PENNZOIL v. TEXACO CASE STUDY AND ACCOMPANYING VIDEO

The *Pennzoil v. Texaco* case study is the "Inside Story" for the contracts chapter (Chapter 7). It includes excerpts from the court's opinion and the legal documents so students can experience seeing such material first hand. This case study can serve as a basis for discussion or for staging a mock trial in which students can play the lawyers, executives, investment bankers, and jury. An edited videotape of the mock trial conducted by students in the author's class at the Graduate School of Business at Stanford University is also available.

 Acknowledgments

A number of professors reviewed portions of the manuscript for this and the first three editions and provided guidance, correction, and helpful commentary. I thank each of them.

Reviewers and other academics who provided insight for this edition include:

Robert W. Emerson, University of Florida, Gainesville
Joan T. A. Gabel, University of Georgia
Steven J. Green, University of California, Berkeley and Davis
Laurie A. Lucas, Arkansas Technical University
Claude Mosseri-Marlio, Schiller University and American Business School in Paris
Lynn Sharpe Paine, Harvard Business School
Arthur Segal, Harvard Business School
John A. Wrieden, Florida International University

Reviewers for the third edition include:

Royce de R. Barondes, Louisiana State University
Susan M. Denbo, Rider College
Joan T. A. Gabel, Georgia State University
Ernest W King, University of Southern Mississippi
Eugene P. O'Connor, Canisius College
Lou Ann Simpson, Drake University

Reviewers for the second edition include:

Barbara Ahna, Pacific Lutheran University
Rodolfo Camacho, Oregon State University
Kenneth D. Crews, Indiana University
James G. Frierson, East Tennessee State University
John P. Geary, Appalachian State University
David G. Jaeger, Case Western Reserve University
Arthur Levine, California State University–Long Beach
Susan L. Martin, Hofstra University
William F. Miller, Stanford University
Alan R. Thiele, University of Houston

Reviewers for the first edition include:

Thomas M. Apke, California State University, Fullerton
Dawn Bennett-Alexander, University of Georgia
Robert L. Cherry, Appalachian State University
Frank B. Cross, University of Texas, Austin
Charles J. Cunningham, University of Tampa
Michael Engber, Ball State University
Andrea Giampetro-Meyer, Loyola College, Maryland
James P. Hill, Central Michigan University
Tom Jackson, University of Vermont
Roger J. Johns, Jr., Eastern New Mexico University
Jack E. Karns, East Carolina University
Mary C. Keifer, Ohio University
Nancy Kubasek, Bowling Green University
Paul Lansing, University of Iowa
Nancy R Mansfield, Georgia State University
Arthur J. Marinelli, Ohio University
John McMahon, Stanford University
Gregory C. Mosier, Oklahoma State University
Patricia H. Nunley, Baylor University
Mark M. Phelps, University of Oregon
Michael W. Pustay, Texas A&M University
Roger Richman, University of Hartford
John C. Ruhnka, University of Colorado at Denver
Linda B. Samuels, George Mason University
Susan Samuelson, Boston University
Rudy Sandoval, University of Texas, San Antonio
John E. H. Sherry, Cornell University
S. Jay Sklar, Temple University
Larry D. Strate, University of Nevada, Las Vegas

Gary L. Tidwell, College of Charleston
William V. Vetter, Wayne State University
William H. Walker, Indiana-Purdue University, Ft. Wayne
Darryl Webb, University of Alabama

Any mistakes or inadequacies are my own.

Janet M. McGarry, a Research Associate at the Harvard Business School with a J.D. from the University of Michigan, provided invaluable assistance. Gary Bacher, who received his J.D. from Stanford Law School, took the laboring oar for Chapter 12, "International Trade." Tania Saison, an M.B.A. student at the Harvard Business School who received her J.D. from Columbia University, also helped as a research assistant. I thank each of them for their hard work, creativity, and good cheer.

Thanks to Senior Acquisitions Editor Rob Dewey and Senior Developmental Editor Jan Lamar of West Legal Studies in Business for their insightful and creative suggestions for this fourth edition. Thanks also to Senior Production Editor Kara ZumBahlen for her even temper while meeting a seemingly impossible production schedule, her tolerance of multiple missed author deadlines, and her wise decision to bring in the pros at Parkwood Composition to get the book into type.

Finally, thanks to the Division of Research at the Harvard Business School for its generous support of this edition.

Constance E. Bagley
Harvard Business School

About *the* Author

Constance E. Bagley is Associate Professor of Business Administration at the Harvard Business School. Before joining the HBS faculty in 2000, she taught for more than ten years at the Stanford University Graduate School of Business, where she received Honorable Mention (first runner-up) for the Distinguished Teaching Award and was GSB Trust Faculty Fellow for 1997–1998. Before teaching at Stanford, she was a corporate securities partner at McCutchen, Doyle, Brown & Enersen, a 250-lawyer firm based in San Francisco. Professor Bagley is the co-author of *The Entrepreneur's Guide to Business Law* (West 1998). She is also on the Editorial Board of the *Journal of Internet Law,* a staff editor of the *American Business Law Journal,* and a member of the Advisory Board for the Bureau of National Affairs Corporate Practice Series. Professor Bagley received her J.D., *magna cum laude,* from the Harvard Law School and was invited to join the *Harvard Law Review.* She received her A.B., with Honors and Distinction, from Stanford University, where she was elected to Phi Beta Kappa her junior year. She is a member of the State Bar of California and the State Bar of New York.

Foundations *of the* Legal *and* Regulatory Environment

CHAPTER 1

Ethics *and the* Law

ETHICS ARE PART OF EVERY MANAGER'S JOB

The corporate world has been rocked by a number of ethical scandals involving a variety of activities, including invasions of privacy by Internet companies, abuse of monopoly power and price-fixing, racial discrimination, cooking the books, insider trading, and use of child labor and sweatshops. New technologies continue to spawn novel ethical quandaries such as the growing and proper labeling of genetically modified food, the creation and use of large customer databases, and the cloning of animals, including humans. A Deloitte & Touche survey found that 94 percent of top corporate executives believe that the business community is troubled by ethical problems, and the *Economist* reports that "dealing with ethical issues has become part of every manager's job."[1]

Ethics can and do affect profits and even survival—as companies such as Microsoft (software giant threatened with a court-mandated breakup to remedy abuse of monopoly power), Philip Morris and the other five largest tobacco companies (against which a Florida jury awarded a $144.87 billion verdict for misleading the public about the health risks of smoking and other fraud), Informix (software company that paid $124 million to settle

1. *Business Ethics: Doing Well by Doing Good*, ECONOMIST, Apr. 22, 2000, at 65.

claims of accounting fraud), and Columbia/HCA Healthcare (hospital company expected to pay at least $1 billion in damages for Medicare fraud) can attest. An ethical manager considers not just what is best for the bottom line in the short term but also the long-term effect a particular decision will have on customers, suppliers, employees, the environment, members of the surrounding community, and other stakeholders. A manager's ethics will affect not only his or her company and its reputation and long-term viability but also the manager's personal sense of worth and accomplishment.

CHAPTER OVERVIEW

The purpose of this chapter is to provide a framework for analyzing how ethics, business, and law interact. The chapter begins with a brief overview of several theories of ethics and systems of justice. Business ethics are defined and discussed in relation to economic performance. The chapter continues with a description of notable examples of social responsibility and irresponsibility on the part of corporations. It shows how certain conduct raises ethical as well as legal issues and explains that an action may be legal yet still unethical. The chapter concludes with a perspective on the role of the corporation and its managers in ensuring ethical conduct and the evolving role of the law in this area.

Different Theories *of* Ethics

It is sometimes difficult to define what constitutes good ethical behavior. This is due in part to the fact that there are several underlying ethical theories. People, consciously or not, employ ethical theories in their decision-making processes. The important thing for a manager to remember is that there are different "ethically correct" ways of looking at a decision. As a result, a manager's constituencies may not always reach a similar decision and hence may not be as willing to accept the implications and consequences of the manager's decision.

The two main schools of ethical thought are teleological and deontological. *Teleological theory* is concerned with consequences. The ethical good of an action is to be judged by the effect of the action on others. *Deontological theory* focuses more on the motivation and principle behind an action than on the consequences.

For example, suppose that a construction company donates materials to build shelters for the homeless. In judging this action within the teleological framework, the fact that some homeless people are given housing is the important issue. Within a deontological framework, one would want to know why the company was motivated to supply the materials for the shelters. On the other hand, suppose an employer makes a promise to throw a party if the firm reaches profitability and then breaks the promise. Under teleological theory, as long as the consequences of breaking the promise are insignificant, the action of breaking the promise is not in and of itself bad. Deontological theory, however, would suggest that there is something intrinsically wrong with making a promise and breaking it, no matter what the consequences. Thus, a particular action can be evaluated differently, depending on the system under which it is examined.

For illustrative purposes, several theories within these two schools are briefly developed. *Utilitarianism* is a major teleological system of beliefs that operates under the proposition that the ideal is to maximize the total benefit for everyone involved. Under a utilitarian theory, no one person's particular interest is given more weight than another's, but rather the utility of everyone as a group is maximized.

For example, suppose that a $10,000 bonus pool is to be divided among three project managers and that their marginal benefits from receiving a portion of the money can be quantified. Imagine that the money can be allocated in either one of two ways: Under Distribution 1, the three persons benefit 6, 12, and 24 units, respectively. Under Distribution 2, the three persons benefit 8, 12,

and 16 units, respectively. A utilitarian would want Distribution 1 because the total benefit (6 + 12 + 24 = 42) is greater than under Distribution 2 (8 + 12 + 16 = 36). The utilitarian would not be concerned that the other distribution seems more equal and fair; nor would there be concern that under the benefit-maximizing utility distribution, the worst-off person has considerably less than the worst-off person in Distribution 2.

On the other hand, *Rawlsian moral theory,* a deontological theory, aims to maximize the plight of the worst-off person in society by developing principles behind a "veil of ignorance." Each person in society is to imagine that he or she does not know what his or her allotment of society's resources will be and then decide which principles should govern society's interactions. Rawls believed that behind the veil of ignorance people would create a system that benefited the least-well-off people most. According to that theory, Distribution 2 is better. Under a Rawlsian scheme, the favored distribution is the one preferred by the person who faces the possibility of getting the worst share.

Kantian theory is another main deontological line of thought. Kant's categorical imperative looks to the form of an action, rather than the intended result, in examining the ethical worth. The form of an action can be delineated into the universalizability and reversibility. *Universalizability* asks whether one would want everyone to act in this manner, and *reversibility* looks to whether one would want such a rule applied to one's self. For example, in deciding how long a break to give the workers on an assembly line, a manager might try to apply this theory. In choosing between a ten-minute break every three hours with bathroom breaks whenever necessary versus a longer lunch break, the manager might ask—under universalizability—whether he or she would like a world in which all companies applied a similar system. Under reversibility, the manager would decide whether he or she would want to be subjected to a particular break system as an employee.

The consequences of an action motivated by a certain ethical system can often be evaluated within a comparative justice framework. Such a framework allows the rights-based moral theories of Kant or Rawls to be compared with, for example, a utilitarian framework. Three main categories within the comparative justice framework are distributive, compensatory, and retributive theories of justice.

Distributive justice focuses on how the burdens and benefits of a particular system are distributed. An ideal system maximizes the overall pie by dividing it such that incentives are enough to entice persons to produce more. The system also concerns itself with a fair distribution of these goods—compensating those who contributed while still upholding a certain minimum standard. For example, the use of progressively higher income tax rates for those with more income and earned income tax credits for those earning the least can be understood within a distributive justice framework.

Compensatory justice aims at compensating people for the harm done by others. For example, if someone is found responsible for making another person miss five days of work, a compensatory system of justice would ask that the victim be somehow compensated for the lost wages.

A *retributive justice* framework may also be appropriately applied when someone does harm to another, yet the focus is more on how to deter the person from inflicting another harm. For example, suppose X steals an idea from Y and makes $10,000. If the idea had not been stolen, Y would have made $5,000. Under a compensatory framework, X would compensate Y for her thievery by paying Y $5,000. On the other hand, under a retributive framework, X should be taught that stealing an idea is wrong. X would be required to give up any benefit and pay Y closer to $10,000.

"Of course I know the difference between right and wrong. At the time, lying seemed like the right thing to do."

Business Ethics

DEFINITION OF BUSINESS ETHICS

There is more to a successful company than meeting bottom-line financial objectives. A manager concerned with ethics must consider how these financial objectives are met and what the company contributes to society. Most, if not all, business executives would agree that upholding good business ethics is essential to the success of a company and a strong economy. John Akers, former chairman of IBM, has stated: "Ethics and competitiveness are inseparable. . . . The greater the measure of mutual trust and confidence in the ethics of a society, the greater its economic strength."[2]

Despite the consensus on the importance of ethics, there is no precise definition of what constitutes good business ethics. Many decisions that at first glance may not appear to involve ethics have subsequent ethical implications.

Ethical conduct goes beyond merely complying with the law; conduct deemed legal can still be unethical. Many people associate ethics with such concepts as integrity, fairness, and honesty. For more than seventy-five years, the J.C. Penney Company has considered ethical business behavior to be that which conforms to the Golden Rule: Do unto others as you would have them do unto you.

How does a manager decide what is ethical? The chief executive officer (CEO) of a highly successful Scandinavian multinational tells his managers to conjure up the following scenario: Assume that the decision you are about to make in Timbuktu becomes public knowledge in our home country, the host country, and significant developing countries where our company is operating. Assume further that you, as the decision maker, are called upon to defend the decision on television both at home and abroad. If you think you can defend it successfully in these public forums, the probability is high that your decision is ethical.[3] Given the Internet, CNN and similar 24-hour-a-day news services, and increased scrutiny from non-governmental organizations (NGOs), it has become even more likely that bad behavior in one country will be beamed that same day to customers in the home country.[4]

2. *Good Takes on Greed*, ECONOMIST, Feb. 17, 1990, at 71.
3. Alden Lank, *The Ethical Criterion in Business Decision Making: Operational or Imperative?*, in TOUCHE ROSS AND CO., ETHICS IN AMERICAN BUSINESS: A SPECIAL REPORT 48 (1998) [hereinafter TOUCHE REPORT].
4. ECONOMIST, *supra* note 1, at 65.

Aquinas *on* Law *and* Ethics

Saint Thomas Aquinas (1225?–1274), a theologian and philosopher, believed that an unjust law could not properly be considered a law at all. The only true laws were those that followed eternal law—as far as eternal law could be discovered by the use of human reason and revelation. Eternal law is the orderly governance of the acts and movements of all creatures by God as the divine governor of the universe.

Because not every individual follows a natural inclination to do good—that is, to act virtuously in order to achieve happiness and to avoid evil—human laws are framed to train, and sometimes compel, a person to do what is right, as well as to restrain the person from doing harm to others. According to Aquinas, in order for human law to be considered law, that is, binding on human conscience, it must be just. To be just, a human law must be (1) consonant with a reasoned determination of the universal good; (2) within the power of individuals to fulfill; (3) clearly expressed by legitimate authority; (4) approved by custom, that is, the declaration of right reason by a community; and (5) widely promulgated. To the extent that human law is just, it is in concert with eternal law, as discerned through human reason, and it is binding on individuals. Human laws that promote private benefit over the common good are unjust, and individuals are bound not to obey them. Instead, individuals should "disregard them, oppose them, and do what [they] can to revoke them."[a]

Most modern legal theorists separate the question of a law's status as law from the question of its inherent morality. They argue that a law may help to resolve moral issues, punish immoral action, and serve a moral purpose (as, for example, when laws permit participation in government);

but a law need not be inherently moral to be a real law. In this so-called positive-law view, any law counts as a real law if it has been created according to recognized procedures by someone with the recognized authority to do so—for instance, a king in a monarchy or, in the U.S. system, a legislature, judge, or administrative agency. A properly created law may, of course, be criticized as immoral. Persons may even wish to disobey it. But they do so in the full knowledge that they are disobeying a valid law.

In the United States, the split between legal and moral debate has always been less clear than positive-law theorists might wish. Americans have always given their moral debates a peculiarly legal flavor, mainly because certain important but ambiguous phrases in the U.S. and state constitutions invite a person to "constitutionalize" moral questions. Moral questions are readily translatable into questions about the meaning and scope of the constitutional doctrines of due process of law, liberty, equal protection under the laws, or cruel and unusual punishment. For example, in upholding a woman's right to have an abortion, the U.S. Supreme Court stated: "At the heart of liberty is the right to define one's own concept of existence, of meaning, of the universe, and of the mystery of human life."[b]

It has become a national trait of Americans to expect their constitutions

to support their moral convictions. Just as Aquinas believed that unjust laws could not accord with eternal law, many Americans believe that unjust laws cannot be constitutional. Perhaps it is for this reason that so many of the most controversial American moral debates, such as those on slavery, segregation, student-led prayer in public school, capital punishment, the Boy Scouts' right to exclude gays, court-ordered child visitation rights for grandparents, and the right to die, have focused on the interpretation of constitutions or have been framed in terms of possible constitutional amendments. In some ways, the tendency of Americans to look to constitutions for substantiation of the just quality of law is akin to the use by theologians of the Judeo-Christian scriptures as supernatural revelation of knowledge of the universal good that is eternal law.

As this comparison of present-day constitutional analysis to thirteenth-century theology indicates, the past is often a valuable pointer to the future. At the same time, one must be able to distinguish between doctrines that prevailed in the past and those that should prevail in the future. In this regard, it is important to recall the positivists' distinction between law and morals. If a person confuses what is "allowed" with what is "right," he or she risks cutting his or her ethical discussions short and missing opportunities both for the encouragement of morality by law and for the reform of law in the light of society's morals.

a. P. GLENN, A TOUR OF THE SUMMA 170 (1978).
b. Planned Parenthood v. Casey, 505 U.S. 833 (1992).

INTERNATIONAL FOCUS: OECD CODE OF BUSINESS CONDUCT AND BRIBERY BAN

In the past, business ethics differed somewhat from culture to culture. However, as the market shifts from a domestic to an international one and as advances in technology create a greater flow of information, business ethics are becoming more standardized. In 1976, the Organization of Economic Cooperation and Development (OECD) promulgated a generalized code of business conduct for multinationals reflecting the views of government, business, labor, and consumer groups. The OECD comprises twenty-nine nations from North America, Europe, and Asia–Pacific representing more than half of the goods and services produced worldwide. Its members are committed to an open-market economy, pluralistic democracy, and respect for human rights.

The OECD code of business conduct has had a significant impact on international business practice. It requires multinational corporations to (1) act in accordance with the economic, commercial, and social goals and priorities of the host country; (2) abstain from bribery and other corrupt practices seeking favorable treatment from the host government; (3) abstain from political intervention in the host country; (4) make a positive contribution to the balance of payments of the host country; (5) abstain from borrowing from local financial institutions, so they can reserve their capital for local enterprises; (6) monitor the multinational's impact on employment, wages, labor standards, working conditions, and industrial relations; (7) protect the environment of the host country; and (8) disclose information on the multinational's activities so that the home country and the host country can formulate government policy.

In 1999, the OECD adopted a convention committing the twenty-nine OECD countries and five nonmember countries to adopt rules outlawing bribery.[5] The United States had been lobbying for such an agreement since enacting the Foreign Corrupt Practices Act (FCPA) in response to the bribery scandals of the mid-1970s. The FCPA prohibits the payment by U.S. companies of bribes to government officials. The OECD convention criminalizes bribes to government officials, and a related recommendation prohibits the tax deductibility of bribes. Also in 1999, the OECD agreed to work with the World Bank to persuade nations to reject bribery and corrupt practices.[6] As part of that agreement, the OECD will closely monitor how nations comply with the anti-bribery convention and will publicize that information.

Unfortunately, the OECD convention is unlikely to affect the business climate of the worst offenders. Among the countries that ranked highest in Transparency International's 1999 Corruption Perceptions Index were Russia, China, Argentina, Mexico, India, Indonesia, and Pakistan.[7] (Transparency International is a German NGO that fights corruption.) A Gallup poll released in January 2000 found that of the 779 multinational executives surveyed, only a quarter thought that corruption in their country had decreased in the past five years. [8]

RELATIONSHIP OF THE LAW AND ETHICS

The following case illustrates how legal liability can depend a great deal on the relationship between the parties.

5. G. Pascal Zachary, *Industrialized Countries Agree to Adopt Rules to Curb Bribery,* WALL ST. J., Feb. 16, 1999, at A18.
6. Harry Dunphy, *OECD Will Scrutinize Compliance with Anti-Bribery Treaty,* ASSOCIATED PRESS NEWSWIRES, June 23, 1999.
7. 1999 Transparency International Corruption Perceptions Index (visited Apr. 6, 2000) <http://www.transparency.de/documents>.
8. Philip Segal, *Despite Laws, Bribery Thrives, Executives Say,* INT'L HERALD TRIBUNE, Jan. 21, 2000, at 13.

A CASE IN POINT

CASE 1.1

Meinhard v. Salmon

Court of Appeals of New York
164 N.E. 545 (N.Y. 1928).

In the Language of the Court

FACTS In 1902, Louisa Gerry leased the Bristol Hotel in New York City to the defendant, Walter Salmon. The lease was for a term of twenty years, beginning in 1902 and ending in 1922. The lessee, Salmon, was to renovate the hotel building for use as shops and offices at a cost of $200,000. Salmon needed funds to complete his proposed renovations to the building, and he persuaded Morton Meinhard to act as a financial backer. Salmon and Meinhard entered into a joint venture agreement with the following terms: Meinhard agreed to pay to Salmon half of the moneys necessary to reconstruct, alter, manage, and operate the property, and Salmon agreed to pay to Meinhard 40 percent of the net profits for the first five years of the lease and 50 percent for the years thereafter. If there were losses, the parties were to bear them equally. Salmon, however, was to have sole power to "manage, lease, underlet and operate" the building.

(Continued)

(Case 1.1 continued)

In January 1922, with less than four months of the lease to run, Elbridge Gerry, who had become the owner of the property, approached the defendant, Salmon. Salmon and Gerry agreed to enter into a new twenty-year lease for not only the Bristol Hotel but also an entire tract of property surrounding it. The new lessee (the entity leasing the property) was the Midpoint Realty Company, which was owned and controlled by Salmon. Under the new lease, the Bristol Hotel would eventually be torn down, and new buildings would be built on the old Bristol site and adjacent lots at a cost of $3 million.

The lease between Gerry and the Midpoint Realty Company was signed and delivered on January 25, 1922. Salmon had not told Meinhard anything about it. Meinhard was not informed even of the existence of a new project until February, when the new lease was a done deal.

Meinhard demanded to be included in the new lease. The defendants, Salmon and Gerry, refused to do so.

Meinhard sued. A referee found in favor of Meinhard but limited his interest in (and corresponding obligations under) the lease to 25 percent. Both the plaintiff and the defendant cross-appealed to the Appellate Division of the New York court. On appeal, Meinhard was awarded one-half of the interest in (and corresponding obligations under) the lease. Salmon appealed to the New York Court of Appeals, the highest state court in New York.

ISSUE PRESENTED Did Salmon, as Meinhard's joint venturer, have a relationship of trust (or *fiduciary duty*) to Meinhard that obligated him to give Meinhard the opportunity to be included in a new lease covering property that was originally leased by Salmon on behalf of the joint venture?

OPINION CARDOZO, C.J. (later a justice of the U.S. Supreme Court), writing for the New York Court of Appeals:

Joint adventurers, like copartners, owe to one another, while the enterprise continues, the duty of the finest loyalty. Many forms of conduct permissible in a workaday world for those acting at arm's length are forbidden to those bound by fiduciary ties. A trustee is held to something stricter than the morals of the market place. Not honesty alone, but the punctilio of an honor the most sensitive, is then the standard of behavior. As to this there has developed a tradition that is unbending and inveterate. Uncompromising rigidity has been the attitude of courts of equity when petitioned to undermine the rule of undivided loyalty by the "disintegrating erosion" of particular exceptions. Only thus has the level of conduct for fiduciaries been kept at a level higher than that trodden by the crowd. It will not consciously be lowered by any judgment of this court.

The owner of the [property], Mr. Gerry, had vainly striven to find a tenant who would favor his ambitious scheme of demolition and construction. Baffled in the search, he turned to the defendant Salmon [who was] in possession of the Bristol, the keystone of the project. . . . To the eye of an observer, Salmon held the lease as owner in his own right, for himself and no one else. In fact he held it as a fiduciary, for himself and another, sharers in a common venture. If this fact had been proclaimed, if the lease by its terms had run in favor of a partnership, Mr. Gerry, we may fairly assume, would have laid before the partners, and not merely before one of them, his plan for reconstruction. . . . The trouble about [Salmon's] conduct is that he excluded his coadventurer from any chance to compete, from any chance to enjoy the opportunity for benefit that had come to him alone by virtue of his agency. This chance, if nothing more, he was under a duty to concede.

. . .

(Continued)

(Case 1.1 continued)

We have no thought to hold that Salmon was guilty of a conscious purpose to defraud. Very likely he assumed in all good faith that with the approaching end of the venture he might ignore his coadventurer and take the extension for himself. He had given to the enterprise time and labor as well as money. He had made it a success. Meinhard, who had given money, but neither time nor labor, had already been richly paid. There might seem to be something grasping in his insistence upon more. Such recriminations are not unusual when coadventurers fall out. They are not without their force if conduct is to be judged by the common standards of competitors. That is not to say that they have pertinency here. Salmon had put himself in a position in which thought of self was to be renounced, however hard the abnegation. He was much more than a coadventurer. He was a managing coadventurer. For him and for those like him the rule of undivided loyalty is relentless and supreme. . . .

RESULT The judgment for the plaintiff, Meinhard, was affirmed. He was granted one-half of the interest in (and corresponding obligations under) the new lease between Salmon and Gerry.

COMMENTS In *Meinhard v. Salmon,* the court seemed to assume without explanation that joint venturers had a fiduciary duty to one another. Judges can disagree on what types of business relations give rise to a standard that is "higher than the morals of the market place," thereby giving rise to a fiduciary duty. Furthermore, there is even disagreement as to what constitutes proper morals of the marketplace. In one recent case, decided by the New York Court of Appeals, the same court that decided *Meinhard v. Salmon,* a majority of the judges concluded that a finder of a buyer for a business did not have a fiduciary duty to disclose to the seller the unsavory reputation of the potential buyer.[9] The dissenting judge disagreed. He argued that there was a fiduciary relationship between the parties and that, even if there were not, the morals of the marketplace would require disclosure. Fiduciary duty and this case are discussed more fully in Chapter 5.

QUESTIONS

1. Would the result in this case have been different if Gerry had offered Salmon a lease on property far removed from the Bristol property that was the subject of the Salmon-Meinhard joint venture?
2. What, if any, provisions could Salmon have included in a written joint venture agreement with Meinhard that would have relieved Salmon of any obligation to Meinhard once the initial twenty-year lease ended?

9. Northeastern Gen. Corp. v. Wellington Advertising, 624 N.E.2d 129 (N.Y. 1993) (Case 5.2).

GOOD ETHICS ARE SIMPLY GOOD BUSINESS

Not only is ethical behavior good for business, but it can even improve the bottom line. This conclusion has generally been accepted by corporate America, and a number of empirical studies support it. For example, a 1997 study of sixty-seven companies rated in every corporate survey conducted by *Fortune* magazine from 1982 to 1992 found "a positive correlation between social and financial performance in large U.S. corporations," regardless of the financial performance measure (i.e., return on assets, return on equity, or return on investment).[10] A 1999 Arthur D. Little survey of 481 executives worldwide found that 95 percent of the managers believed that sustainable development (combining environmental protection and social responsibility with business strategy) offered real business value. Seventy-five percent of the managers asserted that companies needed to change their vision and strategy, although

10. *See* Lee E. Preston & Douglas P. O'Bannon, *The Corporate Social-Financial Performance Relationship,* 36 Bus. & Soc'y 419 (1997).

only 19 percent said that their companies were "well down the road" in making these changes.[11]

BUT SOMETIMES HONESTY CAN HURT

Although in many (if not most) instances a manager can both be ethical and maximize value for shareholders, it would be intellectually dishonest to pretend that honesty never hurts. Sometimes virtue must be its own reward because "[o]ne of the ethical truths of morality has been that the bad do not always do badly and the good do not always do well."[12] In other words, the sad reality is that sometimes the good guys come in last. Nonetheless, successful ethical managers strive to craft creative strategies that both are fair to all constituencies and generate maximum return to investors.

SOCIAL RESPONSIBILITY AND PROFITS

A company has an obligation to be both ethical and socially responsible, but what does it mean to be socially responsible? In his seminal article *The Social Responsibility of Business Is to Increase Its Profits*,[13] Nobel Prize winner in economics Milton Friedman asserts that the only guiding criterion for the corporation should be profitability. He argues that it is not the role of business to promote social ends in and of themselves. Friedman asserts that a corporation is an "artificial person" and therefore has no true responsibilities to any constituencies other than its owners, the shareholders. When a company makes a decision to spend money for a social cause, it is in essence making the decision for someone else and spending someone else's money for a general social interest.

Friedman argues that spending money in ways that are not consistent with shareholder wishes is tantamount to imposing a tax and unilaterally deciding where the money will be spent. Because taxation is a governmental function, and only the government has sufficient legislative and judicial provisions to ensure that taxation and expenditures fairly reflect the desires of the public, a corporation making taxation decisions on its own would render the executive "simultaneously legislator, executive and jurist."

Friedman concludes his landmark article by asserting that "social responsibility" is an inherently collectivist attitude and a "fundamentally subversive doctrine." In a free society, "there is one and only one social responsibility of business—to use its resources and engage in activities designed to increase its profits so long as it stays within the rules of the game, which is to say, engages in open and free competition without deception or fraud."

Friedman's very polemic viewpoint has not gone uncriticized.[14] Richard Nunan argues that corporations are sometimes better equipped than the government to handle certain social issues. For example, soft drink companies have a much better and more credible forum for promoting recycling of bottles than the public sector. Furthermore, corporations "have a minimal moral obligation to avoid creating social injury and to correct any past social injuries for which they can be held directly responsible."[15] Edward Simon, president of Herman Miller, goes even further and asks, "Why can't we do good works at work? . . . Business is the only institution that has a chance, as far as I can see, to fundamentally improve the injustice that exists in the world."[16]

Borg-Warner Security Corporation, a provider of consumer and business services, begins its statement of values with the following:

> Any business is a member of a social system, entitled to the rights and bound by the responsibilities of that membership.
>
> Its freedom to pursue economic goals is constrained by law and channeled by the forces of a free market. But these demands are minimal, requiring only that a business provide wanted goods and services, compete fairly, and cause no obvious harm.
>
> For some companies that is enough. It is not enough for Borg-Warner.
>
> We impose upon ourselves an obligation to reach beyond the minimal. We do so convinced that by making a larger contribution to the society that sustains us, we best assure not only its future vitality, but our own.[17]

THE TENSION: STRIDE RITE

In the early 1990s, Stride Rite shoe company found itself in the uncomfortable position of trying to balance "the demands of two masters—shareholders and society."[18] On the one hand, this nationwide company with

---

11. Konstantin Richter, *Managers & Managing: Sustainable Development Teases Consultants—Potential Looks Big, but Field Has Taken Off Slowly*, WALL ST. J. EUR, Dec. 14, 1999, at 4.

12. ECONOMIST, *supra* note 1, at 67.

13. MILTON FRIEDMAN, AN ECONOMIST'S PROTEST 177–84 (1972).

14. *See, e.g.*, Constance E. Bagley & Karen L. Page, *The Devil Made Me Do It: Replacing Corporate Directors' Veil of Secrecy with the Mantle of Stewardship*, 36 SAN DIEGO L. REV. 897 (1999).

15. Richard Nunan, *The Libertarian Conception of Corporate Property: A Critique of Milton Friedman's View on the Social Responsibility of Business*, 7 J. BUS. ETHICS 891–906 (1988).

16. *Quoted in* PETER M. SENGE, THE FIFTH DISCIPLINE: THE ART AND PRACTICE OF THE LEARNING ORGANIZATION 5 (1990).

17. *Quoted in* PATRICK E. MURPHY, EIGHTY EXEMPLARY ETHICS STATEMENTS 27 (1998).

18. Joseph Pereira, *Social Responsibility and Need for Low Cost Clash at Stride Rite*, WALL ST. J., May 28, 1993, at A1. This discussion of Stride Rite is derived from and based on this article. Reprinted by permission of *The Wall Street Journal* © 1993 Dow Jones & Company, Inc. All Rights Reserved Worldwide.

$625 million in annual sales could be seen as a paradigm of a company helping to improve the quality of life in the community while maintaining a solid financial bottom line. A favorite on the New York Stock Exchange, having almost doubled its sales within the preceding seven years, Stride Rite was also recognized for its social commitments. It had received fourteen public-service awards within the past three years from renowned institutions such as the National Women's Political Caucus and Harvard University. Among other things, the company had contributed 5 percent of pretax profits to a charitable foundation, donated sneakers, set up scholarships for inner city youths, and pioneered the effort in the corporate world to set up on-site facilities for day care and elder care.

Like other companies, Stride Rite was forced to face the issue of social responsibility versus profitability. In 1984, Stride Rite laid off 2,500 people as a result of a decision to move certain factories abroad to take advantage of lower labor costs. In May 1993, the company announced the closing of its plant in New Bedford, Massachusetts. Facing an unemployment rate of about 14 percent, residents of New Bedford did not take the news of the announced closing well; two suspicious fires caused damage estimated at $750,000.

Chairman Ervin Shames spoke in defense of the company's seemingly split personality: "Putting jobs into places where it doesn't make economic sense is a dilution of corporate and community wealth. . . . It was a difficult decision. Our hearts said, 'Stay,' but our heads said 'Move.'"[19] A former chairman of the company, Arnold Hiatt, acknowledged the inherent difficulty in this situation: "To the extent that you can stay in the city, I think you have to, [but] if it's at the expense of your business, I think you can't forget that your primary responsibility is to your stockholders."[20]

TRADE-OFF BETWEEN GOOD ETHICS AND SHORT-TERM ECONOMIC RETURN

The proposition that good ethics are good business suggests that a manager may never have to face a trade-off between what is the best behavior from an ethical point of view and what might be best for short-term economic results. As the Stride Rite example shows, this is not always the case. In today's rapidly changing business world, the success of a business is often measured by short-term results. Even though companies

may preach ethics, the managers who are promoted are generally the ones who demonstrate profitability in their units. Other employees get the message that the bottom line is what really matters. Particularly when business turns sour or becomes more competitive, companies and individuals will often turn their backs on fairness and honesty.

Cummins Engine Company acknowledges that following ethical principles may on a rare occasion mean losing some business in the short term, which it characterizes as "a regrettable, but acceptable outcome."[21] Nevertheless, Cummins asserts that "[o]ver the long haul, this type of behavior will gain us business." Heavy equipment maker Caterpillar explains that the "ethical performance of the enterprise is the sum of the ethical performance of the men and women who work here." It admonishes its employees that "any illegal act ostensibly taken to 'protect' the company is wrong. The end doesn't justify the means."[22]

BALANCE BETWEEN ECONOMIC PERFORMANCE AND ETHICS

One possible solution to the tension between economic performance and ethics is to set minimum ethical standards that all employees must meet. Managers must try to demonstrate that high ethical standards lead to business success. For example, Johnson & Johnson CEO Ralph Larsen asserted that the company's high-level executives try hard to ensure that their employees live up to the corporate credo, which stresses honesty and integrity. In the words of Larsen: "The Credo shouldn't be viewed as some kind of social welfare program. It's just plain good business."[23] When asked whether he would rather be a good corporate citizen or maximize profits, Larsen replied, "Yes."[24] He rejected what he termed the "tyranny of the 'or'" and refused to treat social responsibility and profit maximization as mutually exclusive.

And yet, in a survey done by *Industry Week,* there is evidence to suggest that the more highly compensated a manager, the more likely he or she is to compromise business ethics. Thirteen hundred managers were asked how they would handle the following situation: Their company is involved in bidding on a contract for the U.S. Navy. Although their company's price is equiva-

19. *Id*. at A5.
20. *Id*.
21. MURPHY, *supra* note 17, at 62–63.
22. *Id*. at 42.
23. Faye Rice et al., *Leaders of the Most Admired: Corporate Citizenship,* FORTUNE, Jan. 29, 1990, at 40.
24. *Quoted in* Ira M. Millstein, *The Responsible Board,* 52 BUS. LAW. 407, 408–09 (1997).

lent to that of their competitor's, company engineers say that the company will need several more months than the competitor to develop and manufacture the same output. When asked what they would tell the Navy about the company's development schedule, the more highly compensated managers were more willing to be less than frank with the Navy to get the business (see Exhibit 1.1).

Social Responsibility

The public's perception of socially responsible behavior influences the ethical decisions that businesses make. Companies have faced severe financial setbacks caused by decisions that, in hindsight, were perceived by the public as unethical. Consumer products companies are particularly sensitive to public perception, given their reliance on individual retail sales. As William D. Smithburg, chairman and CEO of the Quaker Oats Company, wrote: "[I] know ethical behavior is sound business practice because every day at the Quaker Oats Company I am reminded that we succeed or fail according to the trust consumers have in us."[25] Issues of social responsibility arise in the areas of product safety, the environment, sweatshops and underpaid foreign workers, advertising campaigns, antitrust violations, client conflicts of interest, managed earnings, and Internet companies.

CONSUMERS AND PRODUCT SAFETY

Socially responsible businesses place a heavy emphasis on the safety of their products. Huge costs have been asso-

25. TOUCHE REPORT at 45.

ciated with failure to meet the public's perception of what is safe.

Johnson & Johnson and Tylenol Johnson & Johnson's Tylenol success story is a classic illustration of socially responsible behavior. In September 1982, several Tylenol capsules were tampered with and laced with cyanide poison. As soon as the first deaths were reported, the company recalled thirty-one million bottles of Tylenol at a cost of approximately $100 million. Although the short-term economic costs of such a move were enormous, within a matter of months Johnson & Johnson was able to regain the market share it had lost. By living up to its reputation for integrity and social responsibility, Johnson & Johnson enhanced both its public image and its long-term profitability. That image was later tarnished, however, by claims that Johnson & Johnson had been slow to warn consumers that Tylenol can cause liver damage.[26]

Coca-Cola and Contaminated Product in Europe Although Coca-Cola has a reputation for attention to quality control, brand protection, and good public relations, contamination of its product in Belgium and France in June 1999 resulted in a 69 percent drop in net income for the second quarter of that year as well as a public relations disaster.[27] Two plants were responsible for the contaminated soft drink: a bottling plant in Belgium run by

26. *See* Thomas Easton, *Medicine, J&J's Dirty Little Secret, Despite Bad Publicity and Costly Legal Settlements, Johnson & Johnson Refuses to Put Ample Warnings on Its Tylenol Labels*, FORBES, Jan. 12, 1998, at 42.
27. Betsy McKay, *CCE Earnings Fall 69% in 2nd Period on Coke Recall*, WALL ST. J., July 21, 1999, at B14.

EXHIBIT 1.1	**Relationship between Compensation and Ethics**

You are a manager of a company bidding on a contract for the U.S. Navy. Although your price is the same as your competitor's, your engineers have told you that it will take your firm longer to develop and manufacture the product. What would you tell the Navy if asked about your development and manufacturing schedule? Here's how the managers in *Industry Week's* survey responded.

	Salary under $40K	Salary $40K–$80K	Salary $80K–120K	Salary over $120K
Manager indicates company can match competitor's schedule and hopes to find a solution later.	5%	12%	18%	22%
Manager describes company's production schedule as engineers outlined it.	78%	59%	51%	41%

Source: David R. Altany, *Torn Between Halo or Horns,* INDUSTRY WK., Mar. 15, 1993, at 15.

Coca-Cola Enterprises, Inc. had failed to follow quality control procedures, and fungicide sprayed on wooden pallets in a plant in France had rubbed off on the bottom of some soda cans.[28] Although no deaths were reported, Coke recalled fourteen million cases of product in five European countries.[29] In the same month, Coke also recalled bottled water in Poland after discovering 1,500 bottles with mold.

Coca-Cola was criticized for failing to follow up on warnings of potential problems reported the previous month and for bringing in the company's quality control czar so late—three days after people became ill from drinking Coke. France's health minister commented, "That a company so very expert in advertising and marketing should be so poor in communicating on this matter is astonishing."[30]

Copley Pharmaceutical In 1994, Copley Pharmaceutical (Copley) recalled one of its biggest sellers, the asthma drug albuterol, because of bacterial contamination. Lawsuits filed against Copley alleged that more than 100 deaths were caused by the contamination. Although Copley never admitted liability, the company agreed in 1995 to pay as much as $150 million to settle a class action suit. In 1997, Copley also pled guilty to criminal charges and paid the Food and Drug Administration a $10.6 million fine, the largest in the agency's history, for falsifying information about changes in manufacturing practices involving several of its other drugs.[31]

General Motors and the Chevrolet Malibu's Exploding Fuel Tank In 1999, General Motors Corporation (GM) was ordered to pay $4.8 billion in punitive damages and $107.89 million in compensatory damages to six people who were burned when their 1979 Chevrolet Malibu exploded after its fuel tank was ruptured in a crash. Internal GM memos introduced during the trial suggested that company executives had decided that redesigning the fuel system to reduce fire risk at a cost of $8.59 per car would be more expensive than paying claims for fuel-fire deaths. A key memo written by a GM engineer estimated that each death from burns from a fuel-related fire would cost the company $200,000. Based on that amount, the memo calculated that such deaths would cost $2.40 for every one of the potentially dangerous vehicles that had been sold. The memo cautioned, however, that "a human fatality is really beyond value, subjectively."[32] Subsequent to the case, GM's lawyer stated that the company had no plans to send notice to owners of cars with the same fuel system as the Malibu warning them that the system was dangerous.

The GM case is reminiscent of Ford Motor Company's ultimately very costly decision to produce the Ford Pinto without safety modifications to keep the gas tank from rupturing when rear-ended at low speeds. Ford managers relied on a classic cost–benefit analysis, which compared the $4-to-$8 cost of the alterations with the cost of defending the lawsuits from persons injured or killed by the exploding gas tanks.[33]

COMMUNITIES AND THE ENVIRONMENT

Closely akin to product safety is environmental safety. Disregard for safety has resulted in some spectacular environmental disasters that have severely hurt the surrounding communities.

Union Carbide and Bhopal The Union Carbide disaster at a pesticide factory outside Bhopal, India, in 1984 provides a vivid and still ongoing example of the failure to make the right ethical decisions. On December 3, 1984, in the most lethal industrial accident ever, forty tons of methyl isocyanate gas was emitted from the plant. At least 3,000 people died at the time of the accident; as of 2000, nearly 11,000 more had died in the following years due to illnesses related to the accident.[34] Estimates of the number of individuals who were injured and still suffer from damage to their lungs and immune system vary, but the number of victims is at least 200,000. The Indian government received 600,000 claims; as of April 2000, approximately 26,000 cases remained to be settled.[35]

Prior to the accident, a team of experts had warned Union Carbide that the plant had "serious potential for sizable releases of toxic materials."[36] In addition, six seri-

28. Mikhil Deogun et al., *Cola Stains—Anatomy of a Recall: How Coke's Controls Fizzled out in Europe—Lapses Let Contaminants into Products; PR Flubs Only Made Things Worse—Deviation in Taste and Color*, WALL ST. J., June 29, 1999, at A1.

29. *Id.*

30. *Id.*

31. William Bulkley, *Copley to Be Acquired by Israel's Teva for $220 Million, Ending Hoechst Role*, WALL ST. J., Aug. 11, 1999, at B6.

32. Jeffrey Ball & Milo Geyelin, *GM Ordered by Jury to Pay $4.9 Billion—Auto Maker Plans to Appeal Huge California Verdict in Fuel-Tank-Fire Case*, WALL ST. J., July 12, 1999, at A3.

33. *See* Grimshaw v. Ford Motor Co., 174 Cal. Rptr. 348, 361–62 (Ct. App. 1981).

34. *Faulty Design Blamed for Union Carbide Plant '84 Gas Leak*, DOW JONES BUS. NEWS, Jan. 12, 2000.

35. Sudhirak Singh, *Carbide Cash Going Abegging*, TIMES OF INDIA, April 21, 2000.

36. Robert Sherrill, *Corporate Crime and Violence: Big Business Power and the Abuse of the Public Trust*, NATION, Nov. 28, 1988, at 568.

ous accidents had occurred at the Bhopal facility during the six years that preceded the disaster. Clearly, Union Carbide had reason to believe the facility was at risk.

If this disaster had occurred in the United States, Union Carbide would have been financially crippled, if not driven into bankruptcy, by the ensuing lawsuits. In a settlement with the Indian government, however, Union Carbide—which had $5 billion in equity—agreed to pay $470 million to settle all present and future claims. In October 1991, India's Supreme Court upheld the $470 million settlement. The attorney for one of the biggest groups of victims and other opponents of the settlement had unsuccessfully argued that Union Carbide should be required to pay "First World" not "Third World" rates for the deaths and injuries.

As of March 2000, less than half of the settlement had been dispersed. More than 95 percent of those who have received payments were given approximately $600 in the case of injuries or approximately $3,000 in the case of death.[37] These amounts are low even by Indian standards.[38]

In late 1999, individual survivors and victims' organizations sued Union Carbide and its former CEO, Warren Anderson, in the U.S. federal court for the Southern District of New York for violating international law and the fundamental human rights of the victims and survivors.[39] The complaint charged that "the defendants are liable for fraud and civil contempt for their total failure to comply with the lawful orders of the courts of both the United States and India." Union Carbide argued that it was not required to provide further compensation after the 1988 settlement. As of 2000, Union Carbide and Anderson were also on trial as criminal defendants in India. Anderson and other company officials refused to subject themselves to the jurisdiction of the Bhopal district court despite orders by the Indian Supreme Court and a U.S. federal court to do so. The Indian government issued an arrest warrant for Anderson and notified Interpol that he is a fugitive. Anderson went into hiding to avoid accepting service of a summons to appear in the New York federal court, but the company accepted the summons on his behalf.[40]

Shell and Brent Spar and Nigeria In 1995, Royal Dutch/Shell oil company planned to dispose of the Brent Spar oil platform (an old offshore rig) by towing it from the North Sea and sinking it in the North Atlantic. Shell represented that it had complied with environmental regulations and that sinking was the "best practicable environmental option."[41] In April 1995, Greenpeace activists boarded the platform in protest and began a publicity campaign that resulted in consumer boycotts throughout Europe. In June 1995, Shell backed down and agreed to spend as much as $42 million to salvage the oil rig, more than twice what the company had planned to spend to sink the rig at sea.[42]

During the same year, Shell was sharply criticized for its activities in Nigeria's Niger Delta.[43] The Niger Delta, the source of most of Nigeria's oil, is home to twenty minority ethnic tribes, including the Ogoni people. In 1995, Ogoniland had approximately one thousand oil wells, including ninety-six wells owned by Shell. In the early 1990s, critics decried the adverse impact Shell's operations had on the human and ecological development of the region.

Ogoni activists protested that they were not being fairly compensated by the Nigerian government for the oil taken from their land. Tensions increased when the activists called for the Ogoni people to boycott the Nigerian election as a sign of protest. In 1994, fifteen of the activists were arrested and tried before a military tribunal regarded by many as a kangaroo court. Nine of the prisoners were found guilty and sentenced to death.

Despite requests by human rights and environmental groups for Shell to intervene and try to have the verdicts overturned, Shell refused to become involved. The company's only public statement was that the defendants were entitled to a fair trial, medical treatment, and lawyers of their own choosing. Shell's lawyers had advised the company that criticism of the trial would be contempt of court and could result in judicial sanctions. Shell executives did speak privately to Nigerian government officials but to no avail.

As a result of the media backlash from Shell's plan to sink the Brent Spar oil platform and its failure to stop the hanging of the Ogoni activists, in March 1997 Shell

---

37. Anthony Spaeth, *Court Settlement Stuns Bhopal Survivors*, WALL ST. J., Feb. 22, 1989, at A12.
38. Chris Hedges, *A Key Figure Proves Elusive in a U.S. Suit over Bhopal*, N.Y. TIMES, Mar. 5, 2000, at 4.
39. Frederick Noronha, *Union Carbide Sued in U.S. for 1984 Bhopal Gas Release*, ENV'T NEWS SERVICE, Nov. 16, 1999.
40. Devin Leonard, *Bhopal Ghosts (Still) Haunt Union Carbide, One CEO's Nightmare*, FORTUNE, Apr. 3, 2000, at 44.

41. Rubin Grove-White, *Brent Spar Rewrote the Rules (Shell Oil Co.'s Decision to Dispose of the Brent Spar Oil Platform in the North Sea)*, NEW STATESMAN, June 20, 1997, at 17.
42. *Shell Makes Move to End Dispute over Oil Platform—Plan to Cut up Brent Spar to Make a Pier in Norway Pleases Environmentalists*, WALL ST. J., Jan. 30, 1998, at B7E.
43. This discussion is based on *Royal/Dutch Shell in Nigeria* (A) & (B), HBS 399-126, 399-127 (1999), written by Mihnea C. Moldoveanu under the supervision of Professor Lynn Sharp Paine; and *Royal/Dutch Shell in Transition* (A) & (B), HBS 300-039, 300-040 (2000), written by Mihnea C. Moldoveanu under the supervision of Professor Lynn Sharp Paine.

released a new operating charter reflecting a commitment to the environment, health, safety, and human rights. Shell executives believe that the company's investment in sustainable development will give it a competitive edge over other companies facing similar challenges. Mark Wade, a manager on Shell's sustainable development team, said, "Brent Spar was our wake-up call telling us that there are heightened expectations towards corporate behavior that we hadn't recognized."[44]

In line with this new charter, Shell is taking special care to avoid harming the vulnerable Amazon rain forest while it proceeds with its $3 billion, forty-year natural-gas project in Camisea, Peru.[45] The area is accessible only by air or river, and it is unusually rich in plant and animal life. Shell is also trying to ensure that local villagers directly affected by its operations actually benefit from them. According to Thomas Lovejoy, a Smithsonian scientist and rain forest expert, big companies are finally realizing "that if you do things right from the start, it will save you a lot of money and a lot of grief in the long run."[46]

EMPLOYEES: SWEATSHOPS, CHILD LABOR, RESTRUCTURINGS, AND CONTINGENT WORKERS

Indentured Servitude in Marianas Islands In August 1999, 50,000 sweatshop laborers from the Marianas Islands demanded $1 billion from a number of U.S. corporations (including Nordstrom, Gymboree, J. Crew, and Cutter & Buck), alleging that these companies had participated in a program of indentured servitude. Ten thousand Chinese were allegedly coaxed to move to Saipan and other islands, then forced to work to pay for the trip.[47] The corporations paid $1.25 million to settle the case and agreed to allow a nonprofit organization to inspect their factories on a regular basis. Several months after this incident, Polo Ralph Lauren, Donna Karan International, and Chadwick's of Boston announced that they would begin independent monitoring of their factories.

Critics have charged the Nike athletic shoe company with using child labor and failing to pay its foreign workers a livable wage. These allegations and Nike's response are discussed in the "Inside Story" at the end of this chapter.

Child Labor at Wal-Mart In 1992, the press revealed that some of the products Wal-Mart labeled "Made in the U.S.A." were actually made in Bangladesh by child la-

borers working for pennies a day. The head of Wal-Mart's Bangladesh operation denied that they were children, saying, "The workers just look young because they are malnourished adults."[48] Wal-Mart CEO David Glass denied that the retailer misled the public with its "Buy America" campaign and stated that Wal-Mart was unable to substantiate that children were working in factories in Bangladesh. Rosalene Costa, a human rights worker in Bangladesh interviewed by NBC *Dateline,* said the children working at the factory were about twelve years old. The children told her their real ages when the supervisor was not around.[49]

Leveraged Buyouts During the 1980s (dubbed the "Decade of Greed" by *Time* magazine), managers and bankers financed hundreds of leveraged buyouts with *junk bonds*—forms of high-yield, high-risk, unsecured corporate indebtedness that are not investment grade. A *leveraged buyout (LBO)* is a takeover financed with loans secured by the acquired company's assets. Groups of investors, including management, made millions by using borrowed money along with some of their own funds to buy back the company's stock from its current shareholders.

In some cases, LBOs proved favorable for the acquired company, because a more efficient and productive organization resulted. Corporate waste, such as lazy and unproductive management, excess layers of bureaucracy, and unprofitable divisions, triggered many of the early takeovers. Yet, a number of companies (including giant retailers Macy's and Federated) declared bankruptcy when they were unable to repay the debt incurred in their LBOs. Thousands of employees of acquired companies were laid off, had their wages cut, saw their employee pension funds diminish, or had their collective bargaining or labor union agreements circumvented.

Critics claim that LBOs financed by junk bonds evolved from an important financial innovation to an extraordinarily abused one that glorified greed, manifested as short-term wealth maximization at the expense of the long term. Those profiting had a rationale for their sudden surge in wealth. As corporate raider Gordon Gekko put it in the 1987 movie *Wall Street:* "Greed, for lack of a better word, is good. Greed is right. Greed works. Greed clarifies, cuts through, and captures the essence of the evolutionary spirit. Greed, in all of its forms—greed for life, for money, for love, knowledge—has marked the upward surge of mankind."[50]

44. Richter, *supra* note 11, at 4.
45. Jonathan Friedland, *Oil Companies Strive to Turn a New Leaf to Save Rain Forest,* WALL ST. J., July 17, 1997, at A1.
46. *Id.*
47. Charlotte Houghteling, *Sweat and Tears,* HARV. INT'L REV., Oct. 1, 1999, at 16.

48. *NBC Questions Wal-Mart's "Buy America" Campaign,* UNITED PRESS INT'L, Dec. 22, 1992.
49. *Id.*
50. Quoted in Joseph Nocera, *The Decade That Got Out of Hand,* Best of Bus. Q., Winter 1989–90, at 183.

INTERNATIONAL CONSIDERATION

Firms in Japan take a pluralistic approach to corporate responsibilities, in contrast to American firms, which operate from the principle that the shareholders' interests are paramount. Indeed, the epistemological origins of *keiei,* the Japanese word for business, encompass the notion of improving society's well-being. A Japanese company concerns itself with the interests of a variety of stakeholders, including its main bank, suppliers, subcontractors, customers, and employees. When asked, "Under which of the following assumptions is a large company in your country managed?" 97 percent of Japanese firms surveyed selected, "A firm exists for the interest of all stakeholders."[a] Only 24 percent of U.S. companies, 30 percent of U.K. companies, 78 percent of French companies, and 82 percent of German companies selected this response.

In a 1987 survey by Nihon Keizai Shinbun of 113 CEOs in Japan's largest corporations, 63.2 percent of the CEOs indicated that employees were their most important source of support; only 11.5 percent identified shareholders as the most important source of support. As the Japanese economy has experienced slower growth and other changes in the 1990s and early 2000s, Japanese CEOs have had to struggle with how to keep the promise of lifetime employment or, if the promise cannot be kept, how to minimize the adverse effect on employees' trust and loyalty.

[a]. See M. Yoshimori, *Whose Company Is It? The Concept of the Corporation in Japan and the West,* 29 MGT. JAPAN 23–32 (1996).

After the 1986 LBO of Safeway supermarkets by Kohlberg Kravis & Roberts (KKR), 63,000 managers and workers were terminated through layoffs and store sales.[51] Thousands of Safeway employees wound up either unemployed or forced into the part-time work force. More than a year after the layoffs, nearly 60 percent of the former Safeway employees in Dallas still had not found full-time employment. Safeway employees were rewarded for their prior loyalty with a severance package that included one-half week's salary per year worked (up to eight weeks) and health benefits for two weeks.

Safeway's treatment of its employees sharply contrasts with that of Levi Strauss & Company, one of the industry's most benevolent employers. When Levi announced in 1999 the closing of eleven U.S. plants and layoffs of 5,900 employees because of decreased demand for its goods and its decision to move more of its manufacturing offshore, the company committed to providing a $245 million employee package. Employees were given eight months' notice, as much as three weeks of severance pay for every year of service, up to eighteen months of medical coverage, an enhanced early retirement program, and a flexible allowance of up to $6,000 for training and start-up expenses.[52]

Contingent Workers Many large companies not only substantially reduced their full-time work force in the early to mid-1990s but also hired part-time, temporary, or contract workers for many of the jobs that remained. According to the Bureau of Labor Statistics, 7.8 percent of the work force (approximately 10.2 million American workers) were employed in temporary or contract jobs or as independent contractors in 1999.[53] They earned on average 35 percent less than regular workers; only 7 percent received health-care insurance benefits from their employer; and just 4 percent were given a pension.[54]

In recent lawsuits against Microsoft and Time Warner, contingent workers claimed they were unfairly denied benefits. As explained in the "Inside Story" in Chapter 5, a federal appeals court required Microsoft to pay workers who worked at least half-time the money they had lost by not being offered company stock at a discount as full-time workers were.

Supporters of the trend to use temporary workers argue that it is necessary to give U.S. companies the flexibility to adjust their work force to reflect changing and seasonal labor demand. Critics claim that the practice saps worker morale and ultimately adversely affects worker productivity.[55] For example, Edward Hennessy, Jr., former chairman and CEO of Allied-Signal, Inc., argues:

> If we choose to deny the larger human and social impact of the corporation, if we try to reduce the company to the bare essentials of a commercial transaction, we will end up with a work force that is less capable and less dedicated over the long run. We will also cause society to be indifferent—if not completely hostile—to the interests of corporations and their shareholders.[56]

51. Susan C. Faludi, *The Reckoning: Safeway LBO Yields Vast Profits but Exacts a Heavy Human Toll,* WALL ST. J., May 16, 1990, at A1.

52. Miles Socha, *Bad Day at Levi's! 11 Plants to Close, Costing 5,900 Jobs,* WOMEN'S WEAR DAILY, Feb. 23, 1999, at 1.
53. Kirstin Downey Grimskey, *Revenge of the Temps; Independent Contractors' Victory in Microsoft Case May Have Wide Impact,* WASH. POST, Jan. 16, 2000, at H1.
54. Aaron Bernstein, *A Leg Up for the Lowly Temp: Advocates Are Lobbying for Better Benefits and an Employer's Code of Conduct,* BUSINESS WK., June 21, 1999, at 102.
55. See JEFFREY PFEFFER, THE HUMAN EQUATION: BUILDING PROFITS BY PUTTING PEOPLE FIRST 161–94 (1998).
56. TOUCHE REPORT at 44.

CONSUMERS AND ADVERTISING

Targeted Marketing In the summer of 1991, G. Heileman Brewing Company planned to release a new malt liquor called Power Master. The name and label were designed to connote the product's high alcohol content of 5.9 percent, which would have made Power Master the strongest malt liquor on the market. Through advertising and design, Power Master was targeted specifically at the African American community. African American activist groups threatened protests, including billboard whitewashing campaigns, in response to the proposed product. Michael L. Pfleger, pastor of St. Sabina Catholic Church in Chicago and one of the persons arrested for protesting outside Heileman headquarters in La Crosse, Wisconsin, stated: "We're not going to tolerate target marketing when the product is death or disease."[57] Heileman decided to withdraw the product before it was even released to the stores.

Marketing Tobacco and Beer to Children Parents and public health officials sharply criticized RJR Nabisco (maker of Camel cigarettes) for its advertisements featuring a cartoon figure, Old Joe Camel. A number of studies showed that ads involving this sharply dressed camel, who frequents pool halls and pickup bars, were tremendously successful in targeting children. In a study involving 229 children ages three to six, more than half were familiar with the figure and associated him with cigarettes. Six-year-olds were nearly as familiar with Joe Camel as they were with the Mickey Mouse logo for the Disney Channel.[58]

Faced with the Food and Drug Administration's threat to regulate nicotine as a drug and increasingly hostile public opinion, RJR voluntarily agreed in 1997 to abandon the Joe Camel ad campaign in the United States. However, Joe Camel continues to thrive outside the United States. He started showing up in other countries in 1996. Argentinian antismoking activists became incensed when Joe Camel and friends began appearing in smoking advertisements and promotional gimmicks primarily targeted at teenagers and young adults in that country.[59]

In September 1999, the Federal Trade Commission (FTC) issued a report setting forth the results of a probe prompted by concerns about alcohol advertising to children.[60] The FTC surveyed the eight largest alcoholic beverage companies (including Anheuser-Busch, Inc., Bacardi-Martini U.S.A., Inc., Miller Brewing Company, and Joseph E. Seagram & Sons, Inc.) and found that they advertised their product in media popular with children. The companies placed ads on eight of the fifteen television programs most popular with teenagers and in movies targeted at young audiences, including PG and PG-13 movies. The FTC recommended that companies impose stricter voluntary rules and establish a third-party review to ensure that they are following these codes. The FTC did not recommend government regulation of the $1 billion alcohol advertising market, however.

CUSTOMERS AND ANTITRUST

Microsoft and Abuse of Monopoly Power In April 2000, Judge Thomas Penfield Jackson ruled that Microsoft Corporation had illegally maintained and sought to extend its monopoly in the personal computer operating system markets. Two months later, after finding that Microsoft had proved "untrustworthy" in the past, he ordered the breakup of the company.[61] This is discussed in the "Inside Story" in Chapter 20.

Archer Daniels Midland and Price-Fixing In June 1995, the U.S. Justice Department charged Archer Daniels Midland (ADM), a leading agribusiness company, and several of its top executives with colluding with competitors to coordinate price increases and to allocate sales of lysine products among themselves as part of an international price-fixing scheme. Ajinomoto Company and Kyowa Hakko Kogyo Company, two Japanese companies, were also charged. Individual managers were targeted in the probe and were levied personal fines as a result of their involvement. ADM pled guilty to the price-fixing charges and paid $100 million in fines. The other companies also admitted guilt and paid fines of $10 million. Additionally, all of the companies remained subject to civil fines, as their customers filed lawsuits to recover damages for the inflated prices they paid as a result of the price-fixing. The European Commission levied additional fines of $45 million against ADM and $60 million against its Asian co-conspirators, thereby increasing ADM's total legal bill for criminal fines, civil settlements, and legal fees related to the price-fixing scheme to more than $250 million.[62]

57. Thomas Palmer, *A Target-Marketing Ploy Backfires—Malt Liquor Aimed at Blacks Dies Aborning, a Victim of Insensitivity*, BOSTON GLOBE, July 14, 1991, at 71.

58. Kathleen Deveny, *Joe Camel Is Also Pied Piper, Research Finds*, WALL ST. J., Dec. 11, 1991, at B1, B6.

59. Jonathan Friedland, *Under Siege in the U.S., Joe Camel Pops Up Alive, Well in Argentina*, WALL ST. J., Sept. 10, 1996, at B1.

60. Denise Gellene, *Leave Alcohol Ad Curbs to Industry, FTC Report Says*, L. A. TIMES, Sept. 11, 1999, at C1.

61. John R. Wilke, *For Antitrust Judge, Trust, or Lack of It, Really Was the Issue*, WALL ST. J., June 8, 2000, at A1.

62. Scott Kilman, *European Commission Sets ADM Fine*, WALL ST. J., June 8, 2000, at A4.

CLIENTS AND CONFLICTS OF INTEREST

Ernst & Young In 1998, Ernst & Young agreed to pay $185 million (one of the biggest settlements ever paid by a consulting firm) to settle a lawsuit brought by one of its clients, retailer Merry-Go-Round Enterprises, Inc. Merry-Go-Round alleged fraud, incompetence, and misrepresentation due to Ernst & Young's failure to disclose a conflict of interest.[63] In late 1993, Merry-Go-Round started having serious financial trouble and consulted top bankruptcy attorneys at the Washington, D.C., firm Swidler & Berling. The lawyers advised Merry-Go-Round to consult turnaround experts at Ernst & Young. Time is of the essence when a retailer gets in trouble, but Ernst & Young spent months conducting studies and developing proposals without taking action. When Merry-Go-Round threatened to cut back Ernst & Young's authority, Swidler & Berling intervened on its behalf. Merry-Go-Round had no idea that Swidler & Berling's advice was not completely objective, because Ernst & Young had failed to disclose to the retailer that it had a business relationship with the law firm and had paid $5.3 million in fees to it over the past seven years. In addition, Ernst & Young failed to disclose its business relationship with shopping mall company Rouse Company, one of Merry-Go-Round's main landlords. Rouse Company would have been negatively affected if Merry-Go-Round had closed many of its stores to stop losing money. Merry-Go-Round went out of business in 1996, putting thousands out of work and leaving unpaid claims of more than $200 million.

Management Buyouts Management-led buyouts present unique conflicts of interest. When management is doing the buying, it has a strong incentive to make a deal to purchase the company from the existing shareholders for the lowest possible price. This incentive conflicts with management's responsibility as a protector of the interests of the shareholders of the target company to obtain the highest price for the existing shareholders.

Morgan Bank The large fees paid advisers in mergers and acquisitions can also present conflicts of interest. For example, Sterling Drug was a longtime client of Morgan Bank of New York, one of the most prestigious commercial banks in the United States. When Hoffmann–La Roche made its surprise move to take over Sterling, Morgan Bank was not surprised—because it was the financial adviser to Hoffmann–La Roche. John M. Pietruski, Sterling's chairman, stated in a public letter to the chairman of Morgan Bank, Lewis T. Preston: "I am shocked and dismayed by what I consider to be Morgan Bank's unethical conduct in aiding and abetting a surprise raid on one of its longtime clients."[64]

Morgan Guaranty Morgan Guaranty Trust Company came under fire when it helped one client, SmithKline Beecham Corporation (the Philadelphia pharmaceutical giant), buy a firm that another client, Corning Glass Works, had agreed to purchase. Corning officials were surprised by the rival bid and outraged by Morgan Guaranty's role. When asked for a reaction, Stephen Albertalli, director of investor relations of Corning Glass, said: "You can imagine what it might be. I just don't use four-letter words over the phone."[65]

INVESTORS

Managed Earnings In an effort to meet securities analysts' earnings expectations and thereby avoid the punishing drop in stock price that usually follows a company's announcement that its earnings were below Wall Street's estimates, a number of public companies are managing earnings.[66] They use what Arthur Leavitt, chairman of the Securities and Exchange Commission (SEC), calls "accounting hocus-pocus" to recognize revenue improperly, take unjustified restructuring charges, and create "cookie-jar reserves" that can be used to smooth out earnings by making up earnings shortfalls in a later period.

Claims arising out of SEC investigations in 1998 and 1999 included misappropriation of unclaimed money from security holders that should have escheated (been forfeited) to the state (Bankers Trust); improper inflation of operating income and other accounting irregularities, which, when made known, caused the company's stock to drop by more than $14 billion in a single day (Cendant); and intentional underreporting of earnings with the excess above analysts' expectations being stuffed in a cookie-jar reserve, then fed back into earnings when needed to meet expectations (W.R. Grace). Questionable conduct ranged from making off-price deals at the end of a quarter to increase revenues (dumb but probably legal) to bill-and-hold scams whereby sales of goods are recorded but the goods are held in the seller's warehouse (probably illegal) to creation of false invoices to book fictitious sales (clearly illegal).[67]

63. Elizabeth MacDonald & Scot J. Paltrow, *Merry-Go-Round, Ernst & Young Advised the Client, but Not About Everything*, WALL ST. J., Aug. 10, 1999, at A1, A12.

64. *Quoted in* Leslie Wayne, *How the Morgan Bank Struck Out*, N.Y. TIMES, Feb. 7, 1988, at 1.

65. *Quoted in* Jed Horowitz, *Morgan's Role in Merger Pits It Against Client*, AM. BANKER, Mar. 28, 1988, at 1.

66. *See* Carol J. Loomis, *Lies, Damned Lies, and Managed Earnings*, FORTUNE, Aug. 2, 1999, at 74.

67. *Id.*

"Silicon.Valley.con" The boom in Silicon Valley, the explosion of dot.com companies engaged in electronic commerce, and the billions of dollars being made in the technology revolution have raised a number of ethical questions. Widespread practices sparking ethical concerns include accounting sleights of hand designed to inflate revenues, founders and venture capitalists unloading stock shortly after the company goes public, small corporate boards dominated by insiders, stock analysts who derive a portion of their compensation directly from the companies they cover, and the practice of giving friends-and-family stock to key employees of important customers at a low offering price prior to the company's initial public offering (IPO).[68]

Fortune magazine reporter Jerry Useem warns:

[Participants in the Internet boom] can wear a set of ethical blinders, behaving in ways that might seem perfectly acceptable within this insular context but that, when viewed with a modicum of objectivity, look borderline at best. One can already imagine the post-mortem articles that will follow any Internet crash. Silicon.Valley.con, they'll call it.[69]

Perhaps most importantly, some question the practice of creating a company for the sole purpose of making millions in an IPO rather than building a sustainable enterprise with long-term economic value. Some high-tech veterans complain that Internet entrepreneurs are primarily interested in playing the capital markets for the quick buck by hyping a concept, flipping it to an acquirer, then going on to the next hot opportunity.[70] Founders of such companies—dubbed "burgers" by some venture capitalists because they are born to be flipped—can come to expect instantaneous riches as money becomes the scorecard for success.

POSITIVE ACTION

Ford Although Ford Motor Company has been criticized in the past for its environmental practices, the company appears committed to making a change. Ford plans to start selling in 2003 a hybrid gas-and-electric-powered sports utility vehicle, which will get forty miles per gallon.[71] Honda introduced the first hybrid car (the Insight, which gets seventy miles per gallon) in the United States in 2000. However, Ford will be the first company to use the new technology on the sports utility vehicles that are so popular in America.

IN BRIEF
Making Ethical Decisions

Frequently, managers faced with ethical dilemmas do not have a clear process for evaluating and making a decision. Companies with ethical policies typically provide employees with a checklist of questions to ask themselves when pondering a situation that requires an ethical response. The following steps can also help clarify the decision-making process:

- Identify the issue and get the facts.
   Is there a conflict at the personal, interpersonal, institutional, or societal level?
   Does the issue have a moral or ethical component?
   What are the relevant facts?
   Whose interests are at stake?
   What alternative actions are available?
- Evaluate alternative actions from moral and personal points of view.
   Which alternative would do the following:
      Lead to the best overall consequences?
      Best respect and protect the moral rights of individuals?
      Treat all parties in a fair or just manner?
      Make a good general rule for people to follow in similar circumstances?
   Do any alternatives conflict with my personal ethics?
   How comfortable would I be if I had to explain my actions to shareholders, customers, family, and friends?
- Make a decision.
   Does this action best address the ethical concerns?
   Does this action have the potential to result in an outcome that I would be proud to have reported in the newspaper or on the news?
- Evaluate the consequences.
   In retrospect, were this action and outcome the best I could have achieved given the information I had available at the time?
   Which part of the decision-making process might I have approached differently?

In late 1999, Ford announced plans to spend $2 billion for a complete "green" renovation of the company's 1,200-acre Rouge manufacturing complex.[72] Under the aegis of environmental architect William McDonough (one of *Time* magazine's "Heroes for the Planet"), Ford aims to transform the complex into "a very visible testa-

---

68. *See* Jerry Useem, *New Ethics . . . or No Ethics,* FORTUNE, Mar. 20, 2000.
69. *Id.*
70. *Id.*
71. Jeffrey Ball, *Ford to Start Selling in Three Years a Gas-and-Electric Powered SUV,* WALL ST. J., Apr. 7, 2000.

72. Jim Motavalli, *Harnessing Hydrogen,* E THE ENV'T MAG, Mar.–Apr. 2000, at 34.

ment to Ford's commitment to environmental leadership and social responsibility."[73] The overhaul will include not only the site, its buildings, and the surrounding ecosystem but also the methods by which Ford designs, manufactures, and scraps its cars and trucks. Ford's Chairman William Clay Ford, Jr., the driving force behind the company's new commitment to the environment, said that he hopes the renovated Rouge site will be "the icon of 21st-century sustainable manufacturing."[74] Ford also maintains an online resource, Envirodrive, which provides consumers with specific environmental information about its vehicles, such as fuel economy, emission certification, recycled content, recyclabililty, and manufacturing plant environmental standards.[75]

At the same time Ford was touting its commitment to the environment, it came under fire for not reacting quickly enough to indications that the Firestone tires installed on Ford Explorers were, when inflated to the pressure recommended by Ford, causing fatal accidents when the tire tread separated from the rest of the tire. This is the subject of the "Inside Story" in Chapter 21.

Conoco In the wake of the environmental disaster created in 1989 when 10.1 million gallons of crude oil spilled from the tanker *Exxon Valdez* into the waters of Prince William Sound in Alaska, Conoco (one of the United States' largest oil companies) announced in April 1990 that it was ordering two new oil tankers with double hulls. Experts believe that double-hull tankers can prevent or limit spills if the tanker runs aground. Conoco president and CEO Constantine S. Nicandros stated: "We are in the business by the public's consent. We are sincere in our concern for the air, water and land of our planet as a matter of enlightened self-interest."[76]

Levi Strauss In the early 1990s, Levi Strauss learned that two of its suppliers in Bangladesh were employing children younger than fourteen. Insisting that the suppliers fire the children would have deprived their impoverished families of their wages and would not have ensured that the children would attend school. In a creative solution, Levi Strauss agreed to pay the children's tuition and to purchase books and clothes for them, and the suppliers agreed to pay their wages while they attended school and then to offer them jobs when they turned fourteen. This arrangement allowed Levi Strauss to maintain its business relationship while helping the children.[77]

Merck After the end of World War II, Merck & Company, the number-one pharmaceutical company in the world, provided medicine to treat tuberculosis in Japan. More recently, Merck developed and gave away a drug that cures river blindness, a painful parasitic infection that eventually results in loss of vision. More than one million people in developing countries have contracted the disease. Merck developed the drug expecting that governments or aid agencies would pay for and distribute the product when it was complete. When no organization did so, Merck continued development and distributed the medicine itself, at no cost to the recipients. The decision to do this was based on the company's vision and dedication to that vision: "We are in the business of preserving and improving human life. All of our actions must be measured by our success in achieving this goal."[78]

BP Amoco On May 19, 1997, Sir John Browne, chief executive of BP Amoco (BP), one of the world's largest oil companies, announced in a speech at Stanford University that BP has an obligation to help prevent global warming. Browne stated: "If we are all to take responsibility for the future of our planet, then it falls to us to begin to take precautionary action now."[79] Toward that end, BP instituted measurable objectives to ensure that it was doing what it could to create a sustainable planet. These objectives included participating in a policy debate, searching for global solutions to the problem of global warming, developing alternative fuels for the long term, funding continuing scientific research, and controlling the company's own carbon dioxide emissions. In 1999, for the first time, managers at BP were evaluated on their efforts to cut emissions as well as their financial performance.[80] A regional president of BP Amoco, Asia,

73. Jane Morley, *Former Green Dean Works for "Eco-effectiveness,"* WASH. BUS. J., Feb. 11, 2000, at 101.

74. Martha Hamilton, *Irresistibly Drawn Toward a More Hopeful Future: Architect William McDonough Tries to Combine Life's Lessons with the Designs That Are His Life's Work,* WASH. POST, Feb. 21, 2000, at F16.

75. *See* Shareholder Activism Center (visited Apr. 12, 2000) <http://www.socialfunds.com/>.

76. *Conoco Says It Will Order Oil Tankers with Double Hulls,* L.A. TIMES, Apr. 11, 1990, at D1.

77. Thomas Donaldson & Thomas W. Dunfee, *When Ethics Travel: The Promise and Peril of Global Business Ethics,* 41 CAL. MGT. REV. 45, 60 (1999) (citing J. KLINE, *Corporate Social Responsibility and Transnational Corporations, World Investment Report 1994, in* TRANSNATIONAL CORPORATIONS, EMPLOYMENT AND THE WORKPLACE 313–24 (1994)).

78. From Merck & Co., Inc., *Internal Management Guide 1989.* *quoted in* JAMES C. COLLINS & JERRY S. PORRAS, BUILT TO LAST: SUCCESSFUL HABITS OF VISIONARY COMPANIES 46–47 (1994).

79. John Browne, *Breaking Ranks,* STANFORD BUS., Sept. 1997, at 18.

80. Serna, *Companies Are Scrambling to Look a Little Greener,* WALL ST. J., Oct. 19, 1999, at B1.

stated: "As we see it, shareholder value and social responsibility support each other. We should view climate change, pollution and all the related environmental issues industry faces as another form of opportunity."[81]

McDonald's and Other Users of Packaging A number of major corporations have worked with the Alliance for Environmental Innovation, a project of the Environmental Defense Fund and the Pew Charitable Trusts, to reduce waste and pollution in their operations. For example, McDonald's Corporation, Time, Inc., United Parcel Service, Bank of America, and S.J. Johnson Wax have made innovative changes in their products and packaging to reduce the environmental impact of paper manufacturing and disposal.[82]

LESSONS

The examples in this section highlight three important needs. Companies and their managers should (1) be aware of and think critically about social, ethical, and environmental issues at all levels; (2) develop methods to evaluate and report on the social and environmental impacts of corporate activities; and (3) integrate incentives into the performance evaluation system and corporate culture to encourage employees to be responsible. The goal is to be ethical, socially responsible, and credible and to be perceived as such throughout the world.

 # Socially Responsible Investment

Individual and institutional investors are taking steps to promote more environmentally responsible behavior. In 1989, the Coalition for Environmentally Responsible Economies (CERES) promulgated investor guidelines that focus on environmental awareness and corporate activities, such as using and preserving natural resources, safely disposing of pollutants, marketing safe products, and reducing environmental risks. CERES is a diverse network of investors, environmentalists, labor unions, and community advocates collectively representing more than $270 billion in invested capital. More than fifty companies (including General Motors, American Airlines, Polaroid, and Sunoco) had endorsed the principles by 2000. In 1997, CERES convened the Global Reporting Initiative to develop glob-

ally applicable guidelines for preparing enterprise-level sustainability reports on the environmental, social, and economic aspects of enterprise performance.[83]

From 1995 to 2000, the number of ethical funds in the United Kingdom and Europe more than doubled to thirty-six.[84] Pursuant to a regulation that went into effect in July 2000, pension-fund trustees in the United Kingdom must disclose in their statement of investment principles the extent, if any, to which they consider social, environmental, or ethical factors when deciding in which companies to invest. Although the regulation does not require trustees to have a policy on these issues, they must disclose the lack of one.

Besides being concerned about product and environmental safety, the public has put pressure on corporations and institutional investors to invest responsibly, that is, in such a way as not to lend support to unjust, oppressive regimes. For instance, many companies with direct or indirect economic ties to South Africa were the subject of consumer boycotts and shareholder resolutions prohibiting investment in South Africa. South Africa's policy of racial segregation (called *apartheid*) relegated its black citizens to a second-class status in employment, housing, and opportunity. The boycotts and shareholder resolutions were critical in helping end apartheid in South Africa, a result for which Nelson Mandela and F.W. de Klerk won the Nobel Peace Prize in 1993.

As noted above, Shell has come under fire for doing business in Nigeria. The Commonwealth of Massachusetts unsuccessfully sought to preclude firms doing business in Burma (Myanmar) from bidding on government contracts.[85]

 # Promoting Ethical Behavior

THE CEO SETS THE ETHICAL TONE OF THE CORPORATION

The CEO plays the most significant role in instilling a sense of ethics throughout the organization. William F. May, chairman of the Trinity Center for Ethics and Corporate Policy, states: "The CEO has a unique responsibility; he's a role model. What he does, how he lives, and

81. *See* Shareholder Activism Center (visited Apr. 12, 2000) <http://www.socialfunds.com>.
82. The Alliance for Environmental Innovation (visited Apr. 9, 2000) <http://www.edfpewalliance.org/>.
83. *See Global Reporting Initiative, Sustainability Reporting Guidelines (March 1999 Exposure Draft)* (visited May 11, 2000) <http://www.globalreports.org/Guidelines>.
84. Sara Calian & Tamzin Booth, *Ethical-Investment Practices Expand in U.K. in Response to New Legislation*, WALL ST. J., June 19, 2000, at A15B.
85. The U.S. Supreme Court struck down the Massachusetts statute in *Crosby v. National Foreign Trade Council*, 530 U.S. 363 (2000).

the principles under which he operates become pretty much those the rest of the corporation emulate."[86] John J. Mackowski, chairman and CEO of the Atlantic Mutual Companies, states:

> I think the CEO's responsibility is to view ethics within the corporate culture, understand how its values—good or bad—come to bear upon the company, its business, and its employees. In well-run corporations, for example, the great thing is the sense the staff has of fairness. And for most things, they know enough so that they really need not go to a supervisor to find out what is right or wrong. It's there in specific statements about how they are supposed to deal with customers or one another. And that direction has to come from the top.[87]

This is not to downplay the role of middle management. Often an employee's immediate supervisor has the most direct effect on the employee. Direction from the top, however, makes middle management aware that the CEO is serious about his or her commitment to ethics. Although a corporation cannot change its corporate culture overnight, over time it can develop a sense of ethics through strong leadership and support from the CEO and the board of directors. The chairman and CEO of The Dun & Bradstreet Corporation (a global credit-rating agency) introduced his com-

pany's policy on business conduct with the letter shown in Exhibit 1.2.[88]

TREATMENT OF EMPLOYEES

Typically, corporations with high ethical standards emphasize employee self-esteem. If employees feel that they are being treated fairly, they take pride in both themselves and their company. If not, they may retaliate by stealing supplies or inventory, padding expense accounts, or calling in sick when they are not. They may simply fail to produce at their optimum level. John H. Stookey, president and chairman of Quantum Chemical Corporation, explains:

> If people work in an organization which demeans their sense of self-worth, they are humiliated by small amounts every day. But if they work for an organization that enhances their self-esteem, it is enormously valuable to them. So if by publishing a code of ethics or by setting an example you can reinforce a person's sense that he is part of an upstanding enterprise, you are reaffirming his faith in himself. He becomes prouder of who he is and of where he's working. If you understand that process, it is not difficult to raise the ethical standards of an institution, because you can play to those needs and a lot of people will work with you.[89]

---

86. TOUCHE REPORT at 28.
87. *Id.*

88. All excerpts from the *Dun & Bradstreet Corporation Policy on Business Conduct* (1998) used by permission.
89. TOUCHE REPORT at 34.

EXHIBIT 1.2   **A CEO's Message on Ethics**

Dear Associate:

For more than 155 years, The Dun & Bradstreet Corporation has carefully nurtured a reputation for integrity. As associates of this great company, we are stewards of that reputation and must act in keeping with the highest standards of fairness, honesty, and integrity in all our dealings with our fellow associates, customers, suppliers, and investors around the world. . . .

Please familiarize yourself with this document and refer to it frequently when you are presented with a complex issue or predicament in your work for The Dun & Bradstreet Corporation. If you ever have a question about proper business conduct, please consult with your manager, a Human Resources representative or a member of your unit's Legal Department before taking any action. The Dun & Bradstreet Corporation's Office of Business Protection is also available to assist you. . . .

. . .

Each and every day, it is imperative that all of our actions work to preserve and strengthen our commitment to integrity. That commitment has been a cornerstone of The Dun & Bradstreet Corporation's success for more than 155 years, and it will be a key to our success for the next 155 years and beyond.

Sincerely,

Terry Taylor
Chairman and Chief Executive Officer

Source: *Dun & Bradstreet Corporation Policy on Business Conduct* (1998). Used by permission.

MISSION STATEMENTS

Corporations sometimes include ethical language in their corporate mission statements. This language may not mention ethics by name but may stress that the corporation has responsibilities in addition to profit maximization and that it has obligations to both employees and customers. For example, Toyo Glass Company, a Japanese supplier of glass products, has the following statement:

1. Our objective is to contribute our share of work towards the happiness of the public at large.
2. Profit is not our first aim to attain, it is a natural outgrowth of successful business activities.
3. Everybody is expected to do his duty as a service to the public, individually and collectively, and thus to benefit the property of his own as well as others.[90]

CODES OF ETHICS

Codes of ethics are the most widespread means by which companies communicate their ethical standards to their employees. A code of ethics is a written set of rules or standards that states the company's principles and clarifies its expectations of employee conduct in various situations. Although these codes vary from company to company, they govern such areas as selling and marketing practices, conflict of interest, political activities, and product safety and quality.

The National Business Ethics Survey published by the Ethics Resource Center in 2000 reports that approximately 80 percent of large corporations surveyed had adopted a code of conduct. In addition, approximately 50 percent of companies provided ethics training.[91]

Business leaders consider a code of ethics to be one of the most effective measures for encouraging ethical business behavior. James Burke, chairman of Johnson & Johnson, believes that the company's code of ethics helped it survive its Tylenol-tampering crisis. Johnson & Johnson's code begins: "We believe that our first responsibility is to the doctors, nurses and patients, to mothers and fathers, and all others who use our products and services. In meeting their need, everything we do must be of high quality."[92] When it was discovered that Tylenol capsules had been tampered with, the company acted swiftly to remove the product from the shelves. "Dozens of people had to make hundreds of decisions on the fly," says Burke. "There was no doubt in their minds that the pub-

lic was going to come first in this issue because we had spelled it out [in our credo] as their responsibility."[93]

It is important to note that a company code of ethics is ineffective without proper implementation. It is not enough simply to state the rules of the company; the code must give employees an understanding of principles to guide them in making practical decisions. The code should be a living document, reviewed periodically to meet new circumstances. Managers should go over the code with personnel to ensure that they understand the company's values. The company should supplement the written code of ethics with ethics education programs conducted by professional trainers. The company should also pay increased attention to ethical standards in recruiting and hiring.

Exhibit 1.3 contains excerpts from the *American Express Company Code of Conduct* (1999).[94]

OVERSIGHT

In an effort to enforce ethical standards, some companies have set up oversight committees. As many as 20 percent of large firms have a full-time ethics officer.[95] The Ethics Officer Association grew from a dozen members in 1992 to 650 members in 2000.[96] Defense and engineering giant United Technologies has an international network of 160 business ethics officers, who distribute a code of ethics in twenty-four languages to its employees around the world.[97]

In general, ethics committees are responsible for setting standards or policy and for handling employee complaints or infractions. The membership of these committees often includes executive officers or directors of the company. Ombudspersons investigate employee complaints. Judiciary boards usually decide cases of ethics code violations.

Another method of oversight is the social audit. Increasingly, companies have been performing social audits of their activities in sensitive or controversial areas. For example, a semiconductor company might conduct an internal audit of its disposal of chemical waste, or a bank might audit the reporting practices of its securities trading division. The Body Shop retained an outsider—Kirk Hanson of the Stanford Business School—to audit the effect of its activities on the environment and the communities where it operates.

90. Robert E. Allinson, Global Disasters: Inquiries into Management Ethics (1997).
91. Interview with Jerry Brown, Program Development Manager, Ethics Resource Center, Apr. 18, 2000.
92. *Quoted in* Murphy, *supra* note 17, at 123.
93. Stanley J. Modic, *Corporate Ethics: From Commandments to Commitment*, Industry Wk., Dec. 14, 1987, at 33.
94. All excerpts from the *American Express Company Code of Conduct* (1999) used by permission.
95. Economist, *supra* note 1, at 65.
96. *Id.* at 66.
97. *Id.*

EXHIBIT 1.3	**Excerpts from the *American Express Company Code of Conduct***

Personal Responsibility

You are expected to protect and enhance the assets and reputation of American Express Company. Our business is based on a strong tradition of trust. It is the reason our customers come to us. Honesty and integrity are cornerstones of ethical behavior. Trustworthiness and dependability are essential to lasting relationships. Our continued success depends on doing what we promise—promptly, competently and fairly.

...

The Code of Conduct provides guidelines for a variety of business situations. It does not try to anticipate every ethical dilemma you may face. American Express, therefore, relies on your good judgment—your internal moral compass. When faced with a difficult ethical decision, you may find it helpful to ask yourself certain basic questions. For example:

- Am I compromising my own personal ethics in any way?
- Would I like to see my action become a general industry practice?
- How would I feel if my action were reported on the front page of the local newspaper?
- Would the Company lose customers—or shareholders—if they knew employees did this?
- Would I be comfortable explaining my action to my spouse? My parents? My children?

...

Leader's Responsibility

Managers, by virtue of their positions of authority, must be ethical role models for all employees. An important part of a leader's responsibility is to exhibit the highest standards of integrity in all dealings with fellow employees, customers, suppliers and the community at large.

Source: *American Express Company Code of Conduct (1999).* Used by permission.

A recent study of social auditing revealed that corporate financial performance typically improves with increased social responsibility. The companies studied increased their efficiency and productivity, lowered legal exposure and risk to the company's reputation, and reduced direct and overhead costs as a result of adopting socially responsible practices.[98] The financial payback to the company was between six and twenty times the audit cost over periods of six months to three years.[99]

98. Sandra Waddock & Neil Smith, *Corporate Responsibility Audits: Doing Well by Doing Good,* SLOAN MGT REV., Winter 2000, at 75.
99. *Id.* at 82.

ETHICS TRAINING

Many companies hold workshops and courses in ethics for their employees or hire ethics consultants to run training sessions. Sixty percent of the companies that provide ethics training do so during the orientation process for new employees. Companies cite two primary goals of ethics training: (1) developing a general awareness of ethics in business, and (2) drawing attention to practical ethical issues.

Some companies have developed innovative methods for educating their employees in ethics. Aircraft manufacturer Boeing offers an online quiz (with answers) to try to guide its staff through the whole gamut of moral quandaries ranging from how to deal with staff who fiddle with their expenses to suppliers who ask for kickbacks. Exhibit 1.4 provides several sample questions.

MAKING IT EASIER TO BLOW THE WHISTLE

Many employees are reluctant to "blow the whistle"—to report illegal or unethical conduct that they observe at work—for fear of being considered a troublemaker or of being fired. A number of federal, state, and local laws prohibit reprisals against employees who report activities that they believe violate a law, rule, or regulation. These whistle-blowing laws are discussed in Chapter 14.

Even with legislative and judicial protections, whistle-blowers do suffer. For example, on the eve of the space shuttle *Challenger's* takeoff in January 1986, two senior engineers from Morton Thiokol warned that the shuttle's O-ring gaskets (manufactured by Morton Thiokol) might be affected by the forecasted cold weather. The launch was not canceled, and seven astronauts died when the shuttle exploded in a ball of flame. According to the *Economist,* even though the two Morton Thiokol employees were praised for their actions, their careers suffered.[100]

Edna Ottney, a quality assurance engineer who has investigated employee concerns in the nuclear power industry since 1985, reported that 90 percent of the 1,700 whistle-blowers she interviewed had experienced negative reactions. A person who reported violations at the Comanche Peak nuclear plant in Glen Rose, Texas, warns: "Be prepared for old friends to suddenly become distant. Be prepared to change your type of job and lifestyle. Be prepared to wait years for blind justice to prevail."[101]

100. ECONOMIST, *supra* note 2, at 72.
101. Quoted in Joel Chineson, *Bureaucrats with Conscience,* LEGAL TIMES, Apr. 17, 1989, at 50.

EXHIBIT 1.4 **Sample Questions from Boeing's Online Ethics Challenge**

The Minister Drops a Hint

You are working on an important new joint venture overseas. You are asked by your boss, a vice president, to accompany him on a series of crucial meetings with the country's Minister of Transportation. During the first meeting, the Minister, who is a technology buff, admires your expensive brand new laptop computer. After the meeting, your boss tells you to have a new computer exactly like yours air shipped from the United States for presentation to the minister during the next meeting, remarking that "this is a small price to pay for landing this deal." What should you do?

Potential Answers

A Arrange to have the computer given, record it as a business expense.

B Substitute a less expensive electronic gift, like the Boeing logo watch, for the Minister.

C Tell your boss that you believe such a gift is inappropriate, and do not arrange to have the computer sent over.

D Ignore your boss's instructions and hope he forgets the matter.

Getting the Lowdown

You are a member of a sales and marketing team writing a proposal to sell a communications system to a major airline. A friend at Boeing, who previously worked for the airline, offers to have lunch with you. He tells you he can give you the "lowdown" on the decision makers at the airline, including copies of their biographical sketches. Can you accept this information?

Potential Answers

A No. It is not proper to gain this kind of inside information.

B No. You should call Boeing Security and report your friend.

C Some of it. You can have lunch and discuss your friend's former colleagues, but you should not have copies of their biographical sketches.

D Yes.

Graffiti

While washing your hands in the rest room at a company facility, you notice that a variety of abusive racial words and phrases have been written on the wall. Upon closer scrutiny, you notice that the graffiti is not targeted at just one race. It appears to have been written by different people, targeting different ethnic groups. What should you do?

Potential Answers

A Do nothing, it's not your problem.

B Try to cover up the graffiti on your own.

C Contact the Facilities Department and ask that the graffiti be removed.

D Contact your manager, the EEO People representative or your Ethics Advisor.

Racy Stickers

You are a manager. You have noticed that several members of your crew, who are avid auto racers, have placed stickers on their lunch buckets that read "The more I learn about women, the more I love my race car." Several women in your crew have complained. What should you do?

Potential Answers

A Discreetly meet with each crew member to explain that the stickers are not acceptable and they must be removed.

EXHIBIT 1.4   **Sample Questions from Boeing's Online Ethics Challenge** *(continued)*

B Call a crew meeting and review with them the Boeing policy on harassment.
C Do nothing.
D Tell the offended crew members to live with it (and ask where you can get some).

Recycling

Your machine shop shift has ended and you are no longer on company time. No night shift follows yours. You have saved some scrap materials that would otherwise be discarded. Using the large machine tools in the shop, you plan to make a few spare parts in a matter of minutes that could be used in your home bicycle shop, a side business that you run. Can you use the scrap materials to make parts, and can you use the tools?

Potential Answers

A You can use the scrap to make parts, but cannot use the tools.
B You can use the scrap to make parts, and you can use the tools.
C You cannot use the scrap to make the parts, and cannot use the tools.

Quality Quandary

While working on the assembly line, you notice that a fellow employee, who is also a close friend, has deliberately bypassed a required procedure because of schedule pressures. You have a lot of loyalty to your friend, and certainly don't want to get him in trouble. At the same time, you are concerned about the quality of the product and the possibility that safety might be compromised. What should you do?

Potential Answers

A Let it go. Friendship is the most important thing.
B Report the problem to your manager or the regulatory expert in your area.
C You are an empowered employee: use your expertise. Evaluate the procedure yourself to determine if it is really necessary. If in your judgment it is not, forget about the incident.
D Mention your concern to your friend, and ask him to follow the procedure.

Source: Used with permission of the Boeing Company. The entire quiz is available at <http://active.boeing.com/companyoffices/ethicschallenge>.

A study published in the September 1993 issue of the *British Medical Journal* shows that this problem transcends national borders. Of thirty-five Australian whistle-blowers surveyed, eight lost their jobs as a result of whistle-blowing, ten were demoted, ten resigned or retired early because of ill health related to victimization, fifteen were taking prescribed medication to deal with stress, and seventeen had considered suicide.[102]

A manager can make it easier for employees to blow the whistle by protecting them from retaliation by their immediate supervisor and coworkers. A manager provides moral and psychological support by emphasizing to coworkers the courage shown by the whistle-blower and

by providing free counseling to deal with any victimization by coworkers.

 The Law *and the* "Unethical"

ROLE OF THE LAW

The law—civil as well as criminal—plays an important part in promoting ethical conduct. Ethical behavior often requires a higher standard than that prescribed by the law; an action that is unethical may nonetheless be legal. On the other hand, unethical behavior tends to result in illegal behavior over time. Thus, Harvard Business School Professor Lynn Sharp Paine argues that creating an organization that encompasses exemplary

102. Marcy Mason, *The Curse of Whistle-Blowing*, WALL ST. J., Mar. 14, 1994, at A14.

INTERNATIONAL CONSIDERATION

There is increasing focus worldwide on ethics. In addition to the activities of the Organization of Economic Cooperation and Development mentioned earlier, individual countries are examining their business activities and assessing the need for instilling additional consideration for ethical issues in a business context. This examination often comes in the wake of scandals or other events that highlight the lack of ethical thought in business dealings.

Japan As of 1991, only about 30 percent of Japanese businesses had adopted a code of ethics. A series of major scandals in the 1990s (including illegal contributions to political parties, payment to mob figures by Nomura Securities and Mitsubishi, collusion and rigging of bids for construction contracts, and sale and distribution of HIV-infected blood products) led to the formation of the Corporate Citizenship Committee and a new focus on ethics.[a]

China The tension between *Li* (profits) and *Yi* (society's norms for distributing profits or benefits) is a long-standing one in China and is at the core of any debate about ethics. Despite recent problems U.S. companies have had with respect to their Chinese counterparts (such as massive software piracy and counterfeiting), the development of the Center for Applied Ethics in 1994 and the Beijing International Conference of Business Ethics in 1997 are signs that China is concerned about ethics.[b]

Russia Russia has been plagued with corruption as the country moves from a Communist state-controlled economy to a capitalist market. Nevertheless, the private sector has started to take steps to make business ethics a priority. In May 2000, more than 120 businesses signed the Declaration of Business Conduct designed to combat corruption and promote ethical business standards.[c] Companies signing the declaration agree to adopt an internal code of ethics and a no-bribery pledge. The Association of St. Petersburg Contractors, the St. Petersburg Chamber of Commerce and Industry, the St. Petersburg International Business Association, and the St. Petersburg Rotary Club, with a combined membership of over 1,200 companies, have supported the declaration and asked their members for signatures.[d] The Russian government has also started to combat corruption. In June 2000, President Putin announced plans to set up interregional administrations for combating economic crime.[e]

Latin America Many Latin Americans seem to view ethical behavior with a bit of disdain; materialism and selfishness guide many decisions and actions. There is a saying that captures the spirit governing many business interactions: "el que no tranza no avanza"—"one who does not act unethically does not succeed." In that environment, there is little respect for employees, who are usually poorly paid, and no attention is given to environmental issues.[f]

a. Iwao Taka, *Business Ethics in Japan,* 14 J. Bus. Ethics 1499–1508 (1997).
b. Lu Xiaohe, *Business Ethics in China,* 14 J. Bus. Ethics 1509–18 (1997).
c. Kristina Shevory, *Businessmen Sign on for Ethics,* St. Petersburg Times, May 23, 2000.
d. Matthew H. Murray, *Private Sector Ethics,* Moscow Times, Oct. 20, 1999, at 8.
e. *New Bodies in Russian Federal Districts Will Tackle Economic Crimes,* BBC Monitoring, June 7, 2000.
f. M. Cecilia Arruda, *Business Ethics in Latin America,* 14 J. Bus. Ethics 1597–1603 (1997).

conduct may be the best way to prevent damaging misconduct.[103]

When a manager breaks a law, he or she can expect to be punished. The same may not be true for those who behave unethically. Thus, frequently corporations and managers engage in conduct that may be unethical but not illegal. In finding that former executives of General Development Corporation had not violated a criminal law, the U.S. Court of Appeals for the Eleventh Circuit stated:

> Construing the evidence at its worst against defendants, it is true that these men behaved badly. We live in a fallen world. But "bad men, like good men, are entitled to be tried and sentenced in accordance with law." And, the fraud statutes, do not cover all behavior which strays from the ideal; Congress had not yet criminalized all sharp conduct, manipulative acts, or unethical transactions. . . . We might prefer that [the defendants] would have told these customers to shop around before buying. But, "there are . . . things . . . which we wish that people should do, which we like or admire them for doing, perhaps dislike or despise them for not doing, but yet admit that they are not bound to do." [104]

Another court stated: "We do not hold that the mail fraud statute criminalizes sleazy sales tactics, which abound in a free commercial society."[105]

Courts and legislatures, however, continually modify the law to take account of ethical standards. For example, scandals about American companies' payment of bribes to foreign officials led to the passage in 1977 of the Foreign

103. *See* Lynn Sharp Paine, *Managing for Organizational Integrity,* Harv. Bus. Rev., Mar.–Apr. 1994, at 106, 117.

104. United States v. Brown, 79 F.3d 1550 (11th Cir. 1996).
105. Emery v. American General Finance, Inc., 71 F.3d 1343, 1348 (7th Cir. 1995).

Corrupt Practices Act, which generally makes such payments illegal. Similarly, overbilling by defense contractors led to the passage of the False Claims Act, which gives whistle-blowers a financial reward for revealing Pentagon fraud. Medicare fraud by hospitals and physicians led to stiffer penalties and more onerous reporting requirements.

EMPLOYER'S LIABILITY FOR ACTS OF EMPLOYEES

The ethical responsibility of a company is not limited to how it provides a service or manufactures a product.

Companies have additional responsibilities to their employees and to society in general. The law enforces this responsibility by imposing liability on employers in certain instances. For example, employers are liable for any torts (civil wrongs) committed by employees acting within the scope of employment. In some states, including New Jersey and Washington, an employer may be held liable for injuries caused by an employee's drunken driving after an office party. The following case addresses the issue of whether an employer that sends an intoxicated employee home should be liable for the harm to a third party caused by the employee while driving home.

A CASE IN POINT

CASE 1.2
Riddle v. Arizona Oncology Services, Inc.
Court of Appeals of Arizona 924 P.2d 468 (Ariz. App. 1996).

Summary

FACTS In 1992, Kelly Sutton was employed as a radiology technician by Arizona Oncology Services, Inc. (AOS). AOS knew that she had a history of drug abuse. On the morning of September 21, 1992, Sutton arrived at work high on cocaine and used more cocaine while working. As a result, she was clearly intoxicated and unable to do her work. Her supervisor ordered her to leave the company's premises. After leaving AOS's premises, Sutton drove her car across the centerline of the road, crashing into the plaintiff's vehicle and seriously injuring him. The accident occurred in the afternoon during Sutton's normal work shift.

The plaintiff filed a complaint alleging that "having exercised its authority and control over Sutton by the affirmative act of ordering her from the premises under the circumstances described herein, [AOS] had a duty to act reasonably to protect third parties such as the Plaintiff from the foreseeable risk of harm." AOS moved for dismissal, arguing than an employer does not have a duty to protect a third party from injury caused by an off-duty employee away from the employer's premises. The trial court dismissed the case, and the plaintiff appealed.

ISSUE PRESENTED Does an employer that sent home an employee high on cocaine have a duty to use reasonable care to prevent harm to third-party motorists?

SUMMARY OF OPINION The Arizona Court of Appeals began by noting that although foreseeability of harm or injury is an element of duty under Arizona negligence law, foreseeability alone does not create a duty to act reasonably. Therefore, even if it was foreseeable that an impaired driver on drugs might cause an accident, that alone is not enough to impose a duty on the employer to take reasonable steps to prevent harm to third parties.

Sutton's intoxication was not caused by, contributed to, or condoned by AOS. AOS neither ordered nor required Sutton to drive and, in fact, did not take charge or have custody of her. The accident did not occur on AOS's premises nor did it involve the company's property. Therefore, AOS had no duty to use reasonable care when ordering Sutton to leave the premises.

RESULT The trial court's dismissal of the plaintiff's complaint was affirmed. AOS had no liability for the harm caused by the intoxicated employee it sent home.

COMMENTS The Arizona Court of Appeals expressly declined to follow *Otis Engineering Corp. v. Clark*,[106] in which the Texas Supreme Court held that an employer

---
106. 668 S.W.2d 307 (Tex. 1983).

(Continued)

(Case 1.2 continued)

could be held liable for injury to third parties caused by an intoxicated employee ordered home if the employer failed to use the same degree of care a reasonably prudent employer would use under the same circumstances. In imposing such a duty for the first time, the Texas Supreme Court argued that "changing social conditions lead constantly to the recognition of new duties. . . . [T]he courts will find a duty where, in general, reasonable men would recognize it and agree that it exists." A dissenting judge argued that "[in] an attempt to do justice in this one case, the majority has placed an impractical and unreasonable duty upon all employers." The dissent also charged that "the majority erodes the concept that an individual is responsible for his or her own actions." Who has the better argument, the majority or the dissent in *Otis Engineering*? Is it ethical to order a clearly intoxicated employee to leave the premises without ensuring that the employee does not drive a car? If not, what as a practical matter can an employer do to keep the employee off the road?

In another case, the West Virginia Supreme Court held the employer liable for an automobile accident caused by an employee on his way home who was not intoxicated but was exhausted from being forced to work twenty-seven consecutive hours.[107] Based on the court's reasoning in *Arizona Oncology Services*, how would you expect the Arizona court to rule on this issue?

107. Robertson v. LeMaster, 301 S.E.2d 563 (W. Va. 1983). This case is discussed in Chapter 9.

CRIMINAL LIABILITY OF MANAGER FOR ACTS OF SUBORDINATES

The law increasingly holds managers responsible both for the misdeeds of lower-level employees and for criminal violations by the employer corporation. A manager who fails to properly oversee compliance by the company can face not only civil but also criminal liability. Application of this principle in the environmental law context is discussed in Chapter 18. The following case involves the Federal Food, Drug and Cosmetic Act, which makes it a criminal offense to mislabel or adulterate food, drugs, or cosmetics that are part of interstate commerce. A CEO faced criminal charges under that act in this case.

A CASE IN POINT

CASE 1.3
United States v. Park
Supreme Court of the United States
421 U.S. 658 (1975).

Summary

FACTS John Park was the CEO of Acme Markets, Inc., a national retail food chain headquartered in Philadelphia, Pennsylvania. Acme employed 36,000 people and had 874 retail outlets and 16 warehouses. In 1971, the Food and Drug Administration (FDA) informed Park of violations by his company of the Federal Food, Drug and Cosmetic Act, including the presence of rats in one of the warehouses in which food was stored.

Park was told by employees of the company that the appropriate vice-president was looking into the matter and was taking corrective action. Park did not investigate further. Months later, in 1972, the FDA found evidence of rodent infestation in the firm's Baltimore warehouse. A letter to Park, dated January 27, 1972, included the following:

We note with much concern that the old and new warehouse areas used for food storage were actively and extensively inhabited by live rodents. Of even more concern was the observation that such reprehensible conditions obviously existed for a prolonged period of time without any detection, or were completely ignored. . . . We trust

(Continued)

(Case 1.3 continued)

> this letter will serve to direct your attention to the seriousness of the problem and formally advise you of the urgent need to initiate whatever measures are necessary to prevent recurrence and ensure compliance with the law.

A second inspection was done in March. On that occasion, the inspectors found that although the sanitary conditions had improved, there was still evidence of rodent activity in the building and in the warehouses. The inspectors also found some rodent-contaminated lots of food.

Acme and Park were charged with five criminal counts of violation of the Federal Food, Drug and Cosmetic Act by storing food shipped in interstate commerce in warehouses where it was exposed to rodent contamination. Acme, but not Park, pled guilty to the charges. At trial, Park was convicted on all five counts. He was found guilty under a theory of vicarious liability for the acts and omissions of other corporate employees. He was also found strictly liable under the statute's strict liability standard. Under strict liability, a defendant can be found guilty even without a showing of criminal intent by the defendant or any other member of the corporation.

ISSUE PRESENTED Can the CEO of a company be held vicariously and strictly criminally liable under the Federal Food, Drug and Cosmetic Act for the introduction of misbranded and adulterated articles into interstate commerce?

SUMMARY OF OPINION The U.S. Supreme Court upheld Park's conviction under both the vicarious liability and the strict liability theories. The Court stated that strict liability was applicable because "the public interest in the purity of its food is so great as to warrant the imposition of the highest standard of care on distributors." The Court reasoned that Acme's employees were in a sense under Park's general direction. By virtue of Park's position, he had authority and responsibility to maintain the physical integrity of Acme's food products. The statute makes individuals, as well as corporations, liable for violations. An individual is liable if it is clear, beyond a reasonable doubt, that the individual had a responsibility relative to the situation, even though he may not have participated personally. Thus, Park, as CEO, could be found criminally liable even if he did not consciously do wrong.

RESULT The conviction of CEO Park for causing adulteration of food held for sale was affirmed.

COMMENTS The criminal responsibility of corporate officers for misdeeds of lower-level employees is discussed further in Chapter 17.

In 1986, baby food producer Beech-Nut, its CEO Paul Andersen, its vice-president of operations Tom Storer, and its concentrate suppliers were criminally indicted after the FDA discovered that Beech-Nut's apple juice product contained colored sugar water rather than juice.[108] Beech-Nut pled guilty to willful violations of federal laws banning interstate shipment of misbranded and adulterated products, and it paid a $2 million fine plus $140,000 for reimbursement of the costs of the FDA's investigation. Beech-Nut was also suspended from federal contracting. Both Andersen and Storer were sentenced to one year and one day in jail and fined $100,000 after being found guilty of willfully violating the food and drug laws. A federal court overturned Andersen's conviction, and he later pled guilty to ten felony counts of mislabeling. He was fined $100,000 and sentenced to five years probation and six consecutive months of full-time community service.

EMPLOYER'S LIABILITY FOR RACIAL DISCRIMINATION BY EMPLOYEES

When the Civil Rights Act of 1964 was promulgated, the laws prohibiting discrimination in public accommodations,

108. Lynn Sharp Paine, *Beech-Nut Nutrition Corp.*, (A1) HBS 392-084 (1999), (A2) HBS 392-085 (1993), (A3) HBS 394-102 (1996), (B) HBS 394-103 (1995), (C) HBS 394-104 (1998), (D) HBS 394-105 (1993).

such as restaurants, were designed with Birmingham, Alabama, lunch counters in mind. Some thirty years later, in the largest settlement under the federal public-accommodation laws, Denny's Restaurants agreed to pay more than $54 million to settle two class-action lawsuits filed by African American customers. The company paid $46 million to customers and another $8.7 million to their attorneys.

Although Denny's denied that it had a policy of discrimination, African American customers had filed more than 4,300 claims of discrimination, which included not being served, having to pay a cover charge, and having to prepay for meals. Among the claims were those of six African American Secret Service agents assigned to President Bill Clinton's detail. In a Denny's in Annapolis, Maryland, fifteen white Secret Service agents were seated and served, while the African American agents were refused a table. An African American federal judge from Houston and his wife, who had been traveling for eighteen hours, were forced to wait for almost an hour at a Denny's in California, while white teenagers taunted them, calling them "niggers." Rachel Thomas, the 33-year-old vice-president of a skin-care company, recalled the incident in which she, her husband, and their three children waited for an hour and twenty minutes after a waitress took their order and never returned. About her children, she said, "Those babies don't have anything to do with this racism, and they were the ones put out by it. . . . You can't explain it to them; they don't understand."[109]

John Relman, a lawyer for the Washington Lawyers' Committee for Civil Rights, blamed Denny's management for failing to lead by example: "We believe that there was, at the company, an attitude that went into the management level, but we don't know exactly how high. This attitude at the company, at the management level and working its way down, had the effect of causing discriminatory attitudes going down to the lowest levels of the company."[110]

In 1999, Denny's corporate parent, Advantica Restaurant Group, spent millions on a publicity campaign designed to persuade minorities that Denny's had changed its policies. The corporation published statistics showing that it did $125 million worth of business (approximately 18 percent of its business) with minority-owned companies and that one-half of Denny's work force and one-third of Advantica's management team was African American. In 1993, only one Denny's franchise was owned by African Americans; in 1999, more than a dozen African Americans and other minorities owned 36 percent of Denny's franchise restaurants. In a dramatic demonstration of how a company can radically alter its culture, in 2000, the Council on Economic Priorities (a New York–based nonprofit organization promoting corporate social responsibility) named Denny's the winner of its diversity award and declared it "one of the most successfully diverse places to work in America."[111]

In 1997, Texaco agreed to pay more than $100 million to settle claims by African American employees of racial discrimination in hiring and promotion. Coca-Cola settled similar charges in 2000. This is discussed in the "Inside Story" in Chapter 15.

In a number of states, including Maryland and New Jersey, African Americans have sued the state highway patrols for singling them out to stop for possible violations of traffic laws and car registration checks based on the theory, known as racial profiling, that this practice is the most likely to yield drug arrests. In many cases, the stopped drivers were merely "Driving While Black" or DWB. Courts in Washington and New York have interpreted their state constitutions to allow suppression of evidence seized as a result of racially discriminatory traffic stops. In March 1996, the Superior Court of New Jersey found that the African Americans were stopped by the state police at a rate greatly disproportionate to the number driving on the road and the number of actual offenders. The court ruled that the state police were targeting African Americans in violation of their rights under the U.S. and state constitutions.[112] In 1999, New Jersey's attorney general admitted that racial profiling was routine for some state troopers. In December 1999, New Jersey entered into a consent decree with the U.S. Justice Department that barred state troopers from using race as a basis for making stops and required them to document the race, ethnicity, and gender of all drivers they stop.

In the summer of 1999, President Clinton issued an executive order requiring federal law enforcement agencies to gather data on the race, ethnicity, and gender of drivers subject to traffic stops. As of the middle of 2000, twenty state legislatures were considering bills to require police to collect similar data.[113]

---

109. *Id.*
110. *Id.*
111. *Business Bulletin,* WALL ST. J., Apr. 27, 2000, at A1.
112. John Lamberth, *Driving While Black; A Statistician Proves That Prejudice Still Rules the Road,* WASH. POST, Aug. 16, 1998, at C1.
113. Jeffery Channam, *Trafficking in Color,* ABA JOURNAL. May 2000, at 18.

EMPLOYEE DRUG TESTING AND E-MAIL MONITORING

Sometimes the law has to balance the conflicting interests of different groups in resolving a social issue. Employee drug testing is such an issue. The employer's interest in a drug-free workplace must be balanced against the employee's right to privacy. Employers are concerned about drug and alcohol abuse because it results in lower productivity, lower-quality output, accidents, absenteeism, tardiness, and excessive use of medical facilities. Employees, on the other hand, argue that drug testing is an invasion of their privacy, particularly when there is no objective reason to think that the employee has been using drugs.

Businesses can make and enforce rules against drug use or possession on work premises, and they can prohibit employees from being under the influence of drugs while working. They can develop drug education programs and provide drug and alcohol rehabilitation programs and counseling. In trying to deal with the problem of drug and alcohol abuse, businesses should not lose sight of their ethical responsibilities to their employees. Drug testing of employees is discussed further in Chapter 14.

Similar issues arise when an employer monitors employees' e-mail without their consent. Although such monitoring may be legal, the employer should always advise employees in advance of its intention to do so.

WHITE-COLLAR CRIME

Liability for negligent conduct that results in harm to others may sometimes be debatable. Liability for criminal conduct is not. Unfortunately, the 1980s saw white-collar crime rise to the forefront of the business agenda. White-collar crime, such as fraud and embezzlement—crimes characterized by deceit and dishonesty on the part of corporate executives and their employees—has proved quite costly. The short-term costs include lost profits. The long-term costs include erosion of the moral base of the organization, a loss of public confidence in business, and a threat to the free-enterprise system. To counteract white-collar crime, the corporate community needs to create an ethical business environment; individual businesses cannot do it alone.

The Federal Corporate Sentencing Guidelines provide a rating system, including aggravating and mitigating factors, to determine the appropriate sentence for companies convicted of federal crimes. A corporation's sentence will be reduced if it had in place an effective system designed to promote ethics and prevent violations of law. The sentencing guidelines and white-collar crime are discussed further in Chapter 17.

THE RESPONSIBLE MANAGER
Ensuring Ethical Conduct

Ethical behavior is reinforced when (1) top management exemplifies the company's values and takes a leadership role in programs to promote ethics, (2) the company creates an atmosphere of openness and trust in which employees feel comfortable in reporting violations, and (3) activities to enhance and reward ethics are part of every operational level of the company.

At the outset, a business must accept the proposition that high ethical standards and business success go hand in hand. Although ethics alone may not ensure long-term success, unethical behavior leads to illegal activity and can result in business failure. Members of top management cannot merely pay lip service to this notion. Rather, they should show a dedication and commitment to ethics. They should realize that ethical responsibility is not just a component of a successfully run business but is, in fact, a type of thinking that must permeate the entire organization.

The manager should recognize the critical importance of self-esteem at both the individual and the organizational levels. In the same way that a woman cannot be a little bit pregnant, a manager cannot be a little bit unethical. Once a person starts breaking the little rules, he or she is destined to fall into bigger ethical lapses, often culminating in illegal behavior. If a manager will cheat on the little stuff, imagine what he or she will do when the stakes really matter.

This is not to say that even the best of managers will not sometimes fail to be true to their ethical resolutions. But it is critical not to let such lapses go unnoticed. Instead, ethical managers pick themselves up from the ground and reorient their sights to the high ground. Managers who set their sights on the stars are far more likely to reach the top of the mountain than those who aim for the foothills.

A company should create a proper balance between economic performance and ethics and demonstrate that a strong ethical culture is a prerequisite to long-term profitability. In doing so, the corporation must look at itself honestly and objectively. It should ask itself what factors, either because of its industry or its internal corporate structure, inhibit it from being ethical.

A corporation needs a clearly written policy, such as a code of ethics. This policy must be legitimized and reinforced through formal and informal interaction with the entire management, beginning with the board of directors and the CEO. It should include procedural steps for reporting violations of the code of ethics and enforcing the code. The company should include a reference to the code of ethics in its employment agreements.

A company should institute ethics training, including setting up a forum to discuss ethical dilemmas. In deciding whether a decision is ethically right, a company should ask whether the decision is fair or unfair to its personnel, customers, suppliers, and the communities where it does business. Managers should consider the direct and indirect results of a particular decision, including the impact on public image. They should ask themselves how much short-term benefit they are willing to forgo for long-term gain.

Ethics are related to laws, but they are not identical. The legal thing to do is usually the right thing to do—but managers often have to go beyond their legal obligations to act ethically.

The law acknowledges that in a business deal, misunderstandings may arise, unforeseen events may occur, expected gains may disappear, or dislikes may develop that tempt one party to act in bad faith. The law, by requiring each party to act in good faith, significantly reduces the risk of a party breaking faith.[114] When reading the chapters that follow, consider whether the courts, in applying the law, are doing anything more than requiring businesspersons to do what they knew or suspected they really should have been doing all along.

114. *See* Robert S. Summers, *"Good Faith" in General Contract Law and the Sales Provisions of the Uniform Commercial Code,* 54 VA. L. REV. 195 (1968).

INSIDE STORY

Nike *and* Exploitation *of* Foreign Workers

Nike is a leading athletic footwear, apparel, and equipment company with 1999 sales of $8.8 billion. Nike designs and markets its merchandise but subcontracts the manufacturing out to roughly 600 supplier-owned factories around the world.

In June 1996, *Life* magazine featured a story about children in Pakistan who stitched leather panels together by hand for soccer balls with the Nike swoosh logo. Critics claimed that Nike was exploiting labor in developing countries in Asia and elsewhere by working with subcontractors that used child labor, paid substandard wages, and provided hazardous working conditions. Indeed, in October 1997, several members of Congress sent a public letter to Nike CEO Phil Knight stating: "As members of the United States Congress we are deeply disappointed and embarrassed that a company like Nike, headquartered in the United States, could be so directly involved in the ruthless exploitation of hundreds of thousands of desperate Third World workers, most of whom are women."[115]

At one factory producing Nike shoes, only seven toilets were available for 10,000 employees. Other factories were cited for having blocked fire exits and permitting only one bathroom break and two water breaks in an eight-hour day. Reports of abuse, both physical and verbal, were common, as were sexual harassment and corporal punishment. At one Vietnamese factory, fifty-six women were made to run laps around the building because they had not worn regulation shoes to work. They were forced to continue running even after women started to collapse; eventually, twelve of the women had to be hospitalized.

115. Bernie Sanders, *Nike Corporate Practices Come Under Attack,* CONGRESSIONAL PRESS RELEASES, Oct. 24, 1997.

Michael Jordan earned $20 million from wearing the Nike swoosh in 1996. Activist groups claimed that this is $4 million more than all the women in the subcontractors' Indonesian factories earned in one year. Activists reported that Nike's subcontractors pay its workers a regular average wage of $2.33 per day, well below the $4.25 per day estimated to be the livable wage in Indonesia in 1996. In addition, critics alleged that Nike forced its employees to work overtime. Nike stated that its workers make on average $4.67 a day with overtime, which Nike claimed is voluntary.

A 1997 Nike-commissioned study by civil rights leader Andrew Young and a group of Dartmouth College researchers concluded that workers in Nike's subcontractors' factories in Vietnam and Indonesia earned enough money to cover their basic needs and discretionary spending or savings. The report stated that although there was no grievance committee, the workers seemed satisfied with the current working conditions. Earlier reports also found that workers were satisfied with the working conditions. In September 1997, Nike ended contracts with four factories in Indonesia after discovering that they were not paying their workers the minimum wage.

Nike CEO Phil Knight maintains that Nike's presence in Indonesia and other Asian countries has done more good than harm by improving the working conditions and raising the standard of living. Knight asserts that good corporations are the ones that lead these countries out of poverty.[116] Other Nike executives have pointed out that companies such as Nike move people from farming jobs to factory jobs, a key step in industrializing farming-based economies. And Nike has some support for its point of view: dramatic declines in the percentage of people living at the lowest levels of poverty and a tripling of per capita income in the last twenty years are clear signs of economic improvement.[117]

In 1998, Nike hired Maria Eitel from Microsoft Corporation as its vice-president for corporate responsibility.

By 2000, her staff had doubled to ninety-five, one of the few areas of growth in the company.[118]

Despite its apparent efforts at reform, Nike was once again the target of student protests at college campuses in 2000. The protesters called the Fair Labor Association (a White House–backed group of human rights organizations and corporations created in 1996 to combat inhumane working conditions in factories) a sham, concerned more with public relations than with changing workers' conditions.[119] In March 2000, Nike terminated its contract to provide hockey equipment to Brown University, fearing that the school would ask it to comply with guidelines established by the Workers Right Consortium, an anti-sweatshop group without corporate board members that was founded by Brown as a rival to the Fair Labor Association.[120]

Nike's business has suffered in recent years as a result of the negative press about its human rights violations as well as shifting teen fashions and the Asian economic downturn. Nike's profits fell by 43 percent from 1997 to 1999. In early 2000, the company projected that its sales for the year would increase just 3 to 4 percent from its disappointing 1999 results.[121] Nike's payroll was reduced by 1,600 (an 8 percent reduction in the company's work force) during the period 1998 to 2000.[122]

The issues here are complex. Nike and others would say that Nike's presence in these countries is improving the lives of the workers, and there is some evidence of that. When the question of child labor, for example, is framed around Western standards, the answer seems obvious—children belong in the classroom, not in a sweatshop. But in some Asian cultures, being in a classroom is simply not an option, and the sweatshop may not look too bad when compared to the alternatives available in the reality in which those children live.

116. Keith Richburg & Anne Swardson, *US Industry Overseas: Sweatshop or Job Source?; Indonesians Praise Work at Nike Factory*, WASH. POST, July 28, 1996, at A1.

117. Associated Press, *Nike's Foreign Workers Adequately Paid, Study Says*, BUFF. NEWS, Oct. 17, 1997.

118. Louise Lee, *Can Nike Still Do It? CEO Phil Knight Is Struggling to Rebuild the Shoemaker from Top to Bottom*, BUS WK., Feb. 21, 2000, at 120.

119. David Abel, *Harvard Weighs Joining Second Sweatshop-Monitoring Gap*, BOSTON GLOBE, Mar. 2, 2000, at A25.

120. David Rising, *Nike Pulls Its Support of Brown Hockey*, ASSOCIATED PRESS NEWSWIRES, Mar. 31, 2000.

121. Jon Higerath, *Companies: Asian Suppliers Reap Profits*, WALL ST. J. EUR., Mar. 7, 2000, at 6; *see also* Lee, *supra* note 118.

122. *See* Lee, *supra* note 118.

KEY WORDS AND PHRASES

apartheid 20
compensatory justice 4
deontological theory of ethics 3
distributive justice 3
fiduciary duty 7

junk bonds 14
Kantian theory 3
leveraged buyout (LBO) 14
Rawlsian moral theory 3
retributive justice 4

reversibility 3
teleological theory of ethics 3
universalizability 3
utilitarianism 3

QUESTIONS AND CASE PROBLEMS

1. In 1993, shops began selling a line of clothes and other items depicting Charles Manson, the mass murderer whose followers killed seven persons, including actress Sharon Tate, in two Los Angeles homes in August 1969. Manson has been denied parole repeatedly and remains in prison for the gruesome murders committed by him and members of his cult. In 1993, the rock band Guns 'n' Roses included in its new release a song written and sung by Manson.

   Cesar Turner is in charge of ordering policies for Mammoth Records, a large national retail chain of stores selling compact discs, tapes, videos, and T-shirts. He has received a flood of letters and faxes from angry parent groups, church leaders, politicians, and others demanding that Mammoth pull the Guns 'n' Roses CD and tape and stop selling the Manson T-shirts. Turner knows that these are very popular items at the retail stores. If Mammoth stops selling them, its competitors will pick up the extra business, thereby reducing Mammoth's profits. What should Turner do?

   Mammoth has also come under fire from local right-to-life groups because it sells directories of physicians and clinics that will perform abortions. Should Turner stop selling the directories? Does it matter whether Turner personally views abortion as legalized murder or as a choice every woman should have?

   Finally, local police and Broad Based Apprehension Suppression Treatment and Alternatives (an anti-gang coalition) are pressuring record stores to stop carrying the CD "G.U.N. Generations of United Norteños . . . XIV Till Eternity," which includes songs exhorting members of the Norteños (a northern California gang) to kill members of the southern California gang Sureños. Lyrics include the lines, "It's up to Norteños to kill the beast. All Sureños must cease." In what ways, if any, should Turner's analysis of this request differ from his analysis of the controversies over the Guns 'n' Roses CD and tapes, the Manson T-shirts, and the abortion directories?

2. Zandra Quartney is a manager/buyer in charge of purchasing children's shoes for a large retail store chain. She's also a die-hard football fan. This year, the Super Bowl will be played in the Georgia Dome in Atlanta, Georgia, her hometown. Quartney's favorite team, the Pittsburgh Steelers, is expected to reach the Super Bowl.

   Currently, the store chain carries four brands of children's rain boots. In an effort to streamline its product line, the CEO has decided to cut back to three brands of rain boots, leaving to Quartney the decision of which brand to cut. Assume that all four brands are equally profitable. If the makers of Brand One send Quartney a pair of Super Bowl tickets, should she accept them? Does it matter whether the maker of Brand One is also a close friend of hers?

3. Assume the same facts as in Question 2, except that Brand One underperforms the other three brands. How should that affect Quartney's decision? What if it is mid-January and the Steelers are definitely in the Super Bowl? Quartney has waited her entire life to watch the Steelers play in the Super Bowl. Even if she would not accept the tickets before, should she accept them now? Can she get out of her dilemma by offering to pay the face value of the tickets? Should she accept the tickets if she has already decided to discontinue Brand One?

4. Antonio Rossati is one of two partners who own a family-style, 24-store restaurant chain in the Northeast. The restaurants have a reputation for serving quality food at bargain prices. Since the opening of the first restaurant thirty-four years ago, the restaurants have generated a loyal clientele. Many of their customers are older, however. Because the restaurant business recently took a turn for the worse, Rossati and his partner have decided to revamp the restaurants' image so that it appeals to the younger generation. Consequently, Rossati and his partner have taken on a significant amount of debt in order to remodel and renovate.

Five of the twenty-four restaurants are in Boston. In the last few days, Rossati has received seven phone calls from people who claim that they have gotten sick after eating at his restaurant in the North End. After investigating, Rossati has discovered that a shipment of frozen sausage was contaminated with *Salmonella ohio*, a rare form of food poisoning. How should Rossati respond to the seven customers who have already called? How should he respond to any further complaints? If Rossati denies that the contamination was caused by his restaurants, it is possible that no one will find out. After all, there are hundreds of restaurants and grocery stores in Boston that could have poisoned the customers.

Should Rossati pull all of the shipments of sausage from his freezers? What if he wants to compensate the victims but his partner disagrees? What if both Rossati and his partner agree to compensate the poisoned victims, but because of the recent debt this is not financially feasible? How should he balance the ethical considerations with the economic implications? Should his response vary depending on whether the restaurants are covered by liability insurance?

5. Virginia Pocock, a recent graduate of New York University, is a first-year associate with the McBain Consulting Group. The partner in charge of a major strategy study for an important new client in the shipping business has just asked Pocock to call low-level employees in competing shipping companies to gather competitive data to be used to devise a winning strategy for the client. She was instructed not to identify the client but to introduce herself as a consultant doing an analysis of the shipping industry. Assume that Pocock knows that senior managers in the competing firms would consider the data she is collecting proprietary and would not talk with her at all if they knew that she worked for a direct competitor. Is it ethical for Pocock to question the lower-level employees without revealing that she is working for a direct competitor? What should she do if after telling the partner that she considers it unethical to make the calls, she is told that consultants do this all the time and that refusal to do it would be a career-limiting move?

6. Arnita Kim is the CEO of BioDef, a biotechnology company that depends heavily on a year-to-year contract with the Department of Defense to provide antidotes for use in the event of biological warfare. Antidotes are drugs that combat the diseases spread by release of deadly biological agents. The existing product has a shelf life of one year. This creates a current stream of income for BioDef as the government must replace its supply of antidotes every year. The research director for BioDef, however, has just told Kim of a major research breakthrough that makes it possible, at little extra cost, to extend the shelf life of the antidotes from one year to four years.

The current contract with the Department of Defense will expire in two months. Assume that BioDef is not legally required to tell the government about the breakthrough and that Kim knows that the government would not be willing to buy the four-year antidotes at a price greater than two times the cost of the antidotes with the one-year shelf life. Should Kim tell the government about the breakthrough? What factors should Kim consider in making this decision?

7. After years of consulting in the beer business, three MBAs from Georgia State University decided to buy and operate a retail liquor store. When they located a target store, they sat outside to count cars and cases of beer moving out the door, looked over the seller's purchase records, talked with his major suppliers, and analyzed his prices, inventory turnovers, and competitive position. After they had agreed on terms, signed a letter of intent, and obtained bank commitments to fund the purchase of the real estate and inventory, they signed a confidentiality agreement designed to prevent them from sharing the retailer's financial information with anyone if the deal fell through. When they went to see the retailer's accountant, she checked to see that they had signed the confidentiality statement, called her client to double-check that they were the buyers, and then gave them the ledger books and tax returns for the past four years, as well as the "real" books for those four years.

The MBAs discovered that the seller was actually running his business illegally by selling part of his inventory wholesale to competing stores, rather than retail to customers. The retailer did not possess a wholesale liquor license; one cannot have both a wholesale and a retail license in the state in question. The seller was buying huge quantities of beer to gain the highest discounts from the distributors and then selling part at retail and part at wholesale. He reported his retail revenue as his gross revenue to the Internal Revenue Service, the state tax board, and the liquor board. His wholesale revenue went into the mattress.

The MBAs decided not to complete the transaction, as they had no intention of running the business that way. The store owner received an all-cash offer of $50,000 more than the MBAs had agreed on, but he liked the "young, enthusiastic guys." The MBAs told him to take the other offer, and they all parted on friendly terms.

What should the MBAs have done? Who was hurt by the retailer's illegalities?

8. DaimlerChrysler recently dropped its policy of requiring magazines in which it advertises to alert the company in advance of any editorial content that encompasses sexual, political, or social issues or any editorial that might be construed as provocative or offensive, as well as to provide DaimlerChrysler with written editorial summaries outlining major themes/articles appearing in upcoming issues. Other advertisers, including Ameritech Corporation, continue to require prenotification. What ethical and business considerations should a magazine publisher take into account when deciding whether to provide prenotification?

9. In April 1999, Tom Rudolph left the Harvard Business School to become the founder and CEO of IPO.com, a securities brokerage firm specializing in helping young companies use the Internet to raise money from the public. IPO.com went public on March 2, 2000. On September 5, 2000, Rudolph personally sold one million shares of stock for $75 million. He used $10 million of the proceeds to buy a large house in Atherton, California, an easy commute to the company's Silicon Valley offices. Rudolph still owns another four million shares.

IPO.com employs thirty senior computer programmers who are paid a starting salary of $125,000 and given stock options potentially worth millions. The company also employs five janitors who empty the trash, clean the latrines, and vacuum the senior programmers' work areas. These janitors are paid approximately $15,000 a year. Due to the astronomical cost of living in Silicon Valley, several janitors with children have second jobs and rent out space in their one-bedroom apartments to make additional money to support their families. Four of the company's janitors are non-English-speaking immigrants from Mexico who are desperate for employment and, as a result, are willing to work for the low salary.

Although there is a large pool of unskilled workers willing to work as janitors for $15,000 a year, the market for skilled programmers is so tight that IPO.com had to institute special incentives to keep the programmers happy. Most recently, one of the senior programmers was given a Hummer, the civilian version of the U.S. Army's Humvee vehicle, to celebrate completion of an important piece of code.

What ethical and business issues should a corporation and its CEO consider when setting the salaries for the different types of workers it employs?

MANAGER'S DILEMMA

10. André Gastaux is the CEO of Euro Air, a large international airline with an excellent safety record, having had only two fatal crashes in its fifty years of operations. Unfortunately, a flight from New York to Paris crashed off the coast of Canada killing all 350 passengers on board.

Gastaux has tentatively decided to compensate all of the victims' families immediately by giving each family a $150,000 check. Euro Air's insurers have complained that this payment would be overly generous and premature, and they have advised Euro Air not to make any payments until the claims are litigated in court, a process that could take several years. Euro Air's lawyers and its insurers have also advised Gastaux to offer to pay non-American passengers a smaller sum than that offered to the American passengers because only American courts award large damages to the families of airplane crash victims. Should Gastaux delay making payments to the victims' families? Should he offer every family the same amount of money even if he knows that the courts in many of the countries with citizens on the doomed plane would award far less if the claims were litigated? What factors should Gastaux consider in making these decisions?

INTERNET SOURCES

The Business Roundtable's page offers information about its efforts to affect public policy. The Business Roundtable is an association of CEOs from leading U.S. corporations committed to taking an increased role in debates about public policy.	http://www.brtable.org
The International Business Ethics Institute's page provides information about assisting corporations in establishing international ethics programs.	http://www.business-ethics.org
The Organisation for Economic Cooperation and Development provides various types of information about ethics, both in and out of business, through its searchable home page.	http://www.oecd.org
The Novartis Foundation for Sustainable Development's page provides access to a large collection of ethics articles and links to other sites addressing ethics.	http://foundation.novartis.com
The Center for Bentley College provides information about research and other activities focusing on ethics. The site has a searchable Business Ethics online library with books and journal articles on business ethics.	http://ecampusbentley.edu/dept/cbe/
The Stanford University page contains its official Code of Conduct for Business Activities.	http://www.portfolio.stanford.edu/200006
The Better Business Bureau's searchable page offers information about ethics in business.	http://www.bbb.org
The Institute for Business and Professional Ethics at DePaul University provides many resources regarding ethics including articles from the magazine *Business Ethics: Insider's Report on Corporate Responsibility.*	http://www.depaul.edu/ethics
The Ethics Officer Association's page provides links to major corporations' ethics-related Web sites and other ethics-related sites.	http://www.eoa.org
The Ethics Resource Center's site provides information about its National Business Ethics Survey, which measures business ethics at the national level.	http://www.ethics.org

CHAPTER 2

Constitutional Bases *for* Business Regulation

INTRODUCTION

EFFECT OF THE U.S. CONSTITUTION ON BUSINESS

The U.S. Constitution gives federal and state governments the power to regulate many business activities, but it also provides that certain rights cannot be taken away from individuals and organizations. Responsibility for regulating business at the federal level is allocated to the three branches of government: the legislative (the Congress, which consists of the House of Representatives and the Senate), the executive (which includes the president), and the judicial (which includes the U.S. Supreme Court).

The Constitution became effective in 1789. The first ten amendments, called the *Bill of Rights,* were added in 1791. Seventeen other amendments have subsequently been added. The most recent, the Twenty-seventh Amendment, was adopted in 1992; it prohibits changes in congressional pay from taking effect until after an intervening election of representatives.

Although this chapter focuses on the Constitution of the United States, many of the legal and policy issues discussed have analogues in the constitutions of other countries. For example, many jurisdictions afford a certain degree of protection for commercial speech and prescribe the procedures that must be followed before a person can be deprived of life, liberty, or property. Similarly, just as controversies have arisen over the allocation of power between the federal government and the states in the U.S. Constitution, the European Union and its members have struggled until now to allocate law-making authority between the European Union and its individual member states.

CHAPTER OVERVIEW

This chapter first discusses the structure of the government of the United States as established by the Constitution and the allocation of different responsibilities to the three branches of government. The scope of powers of the federal courts and the concept of judicial review are outlined, as is the Supremacy Clause. Next, the chapter details the scope of executive and legislative power. This is followed by an analysis of conflicts that can arise among the three branches.

The chapter then discusses the doctrine of *federalism,* which serves to allocate power between the federal government and the various state governments. The central importance of the Commerce Clause to this doctrine is explored. Finally, the chapter outlines the individual rights established by the Constitution and the various methods of protecting those rights. Among the various constitutional issues discussed are the rights to free speech, freedom of association and religion, and due process guaranteed under the Bill of Rights and the concepts of substantive due process, eminent domain, and equal protection.

Structure *of* Government

The Constitution divides governmental power between the state and federal governments, giving the federal government certain specified powers. Without a grant of power from the Constitution, the federal government cannot act. All powers not expressly given to the federal government in the Constitution rest with either the states or the people.

Often both the states and the federal government can regulate the same business activity. For example, there are both federal and state laws governing environmental protection, antitrust, and retail banking. If a state law conflicts with a federal law, however, then the federal law takes precedence, or *preempts,* the state law.

 # Separation *of* Powers

Within the federal government, power is divided among the judicial branch (the courts), the executive branch (the president and cabinet departments), and the legislative branch (the Congress). This division of power among the three branches is typically referred to as the *separation of powers.*

THE JUDICIAL POWER

The power of the judiciary is established in various parts of the Constitution. Articles I and III give Congress the authority to establish federal courts. Article III provides the basis for the judicial power of the federal courts.

Article III Article III of the Constitution vests judicial power in the Supreme Court of the United States and such other lower courts as Congress may from time to time establish. Federal judicial power extends to all cases or controversies:

- Arising under the Constitution, laws, or treaties of the United States
- Of admiralty and maritime jurisdiction
- In which the United States is a party
- Between two or more states
- Between a state and citizens of another state
- Between citizens of different states
- Between citizens of the same state claiming lands under grants of different states
- Between a state or citizens thereof and foreign states, citizens, or subjects.

In other words, the federal courts have *subject matter jurisdiction* to decide such cases.

Article III gives the Supreme Court *appellate jurisdiction* in all such cases. A lower court tries the case, and the Supreme Court hears only appeals from the lower court's decision. The Supreme Court also has *original jurisdiction* over cases affecting ambassadors and cases in which a state is a party. This means that such cases are tried in the Supreme Court, not in a lower court. Today, the Supreme Court's original jurisdiction is used mainly to decide controversies between states.

Congress has used its authority under Article III to establish federal district courts and courts of appeals. The structure of the federal court system is discussed in Chapter 3. All cases that fall under one of the categories listed above, except those over which the Supreme Court has original jurisdiction, are tried in federal district courts or, in some instances, in state courts with a right to remove the case to federal court.

Article I Article I allows Congress to establish special courts other than the federal district courts and the courts of appeals established under Article III. These specialized courts are often granted administrative as well as judicial powers. Examples of such courts are the U.S. Tax Court, the U.S. Bankruptcy Court, and the courts of the District of Columbia.

Judicial Review The federal courts have the power to review acts of the other two branches of the federal government to determine whether they violate the Constitution. Federal courts also have the power to review the executive, legislative, and judicial acts of the states to determine whether they violate the Constitution, federal law, or ratified treaties and are, therefore, invalid under the Supremacy Clause of the U.S. Constitution. This power of *judicial review* makes the federal judiciary a watchdog over the government.

The Constitution does not explicitly state that the federal courts have this power of review. The power was established by a landmark decision of the Supreme Court in 1803. In *Marbury v. Madison,*[1] the Supreme Court stated that it is the duty of the Supreme Court to determine what the law is. The Supreme Court held that the written Constitution must be the fundamental and paramount law of the land. Therefore, any law enacted by Congress that conflicts with the Constitution is void. The Supreme Court reiterated its ultimate authority to determine the law of the land in *City of Boerne v. Flores,*[2] when it struck down the Religious Freedom and Reformation Act (RFRA). Congress had adopted the RFRA in

1. 5 U.S. (1 Cranch) 137 (1803).
2. 521 U.S. 507 (1997).

an effort to codify a strict scrutiny standard for restrictions on religion, which the Court had rejected in favor of a new, lower standard.

THE EXECUTIVE POWER

The executive power of the president is defined in Article II, Section 1, of the Constitution. Various executive functions may be delegated within the executive branch by the president or by Congress.

Article II, Section 2, enables the president, with the advice and consent of the Senate, to appoint the justices of the U.S. Supreme Court. It also allows the president to appoint all ambassadors and consuls and all other officers of the United States whose appointments are not provided for elsewhere in the Constitution.

Article II, Section 2, also empowers the president to grant reprieves and pardons for offenses against the United States, except in cases of impeachment. President Gerald Ford invoked this section when he pardoned Richard Nixon after Nixon resigned from the presidency following the Watergate burglary scandal in the early 1970s.

Article I, Section 7, grants the president the power either to approve or to disapprove acts of Congress before they take effect. The president thus has *veto power* over laws that do not meet his or her approval. Congress can *override* a president's veto by a two-thirds vote of both the House of Representatives and the Senate.

The president has extensive power over foreign affairs. Although only Congress can formally declare war, the president may take other military action through the president's power as commander-in-chief of the armed forces under Article II, Section 2. President George Bush used this power in 1989 to invade Panama to capture General Manuel Noriega and again in 1991 to drive Iraqi forces from Kuwait during Operation Desert Storm.

The president also has the power to make treaties with the advice and consent of the Senate—that is, with two-thirds of the senators voting to ratify the treaty. The president may also make executive agreements, which do not require the advice and consent of the Senate. These agreements are superior to state law but not to federal law. Treaties and executive agreements are discussed further in Chapter 12.

THE LEGISLATIVE POWER

Article I, Section 8, of the Constitution enumerates the powers of the Congress, which consists of the House of Representatives and the Senate. Among other things, Congress has the power to (1) regulate commerce with foreign nations and among the states, (2) spend to provide for the common defense and general welfare, (3) coin money, (4) establish post offices, (5) levy and collect taxes, (6) issue patents and copyrights, (7) declare war, and (8) raise and support armies. Congress also has the power to make such laws as are "necessary and proper" to carry out any power vested in the government of the United States.

CONFLICTS BETWEEN THE BRANCHES

Inherent in this system of checks and balances is the potential for conflict between the branches of government. At times, the power of one branch of the government must be curbed to ensure the integrity of another branch.

For example, it has been inferred from the extensive impeachment proceedings outlined in the Constitution that the president is immune from criminal prosecution prior to impeachment. The president also has a type of immunity known as *executive privilege,* which protects against the forced disclosure of presidential communications made in the exercise of executive power. Yet sometimes executive privilege must give way to the judicial branch's need to obtain evidence in a criminal trial.[3] Courts are more likely to override the privilege when the president's claim of privilege is based only on a generalized interest in confidentiality and not on the need to protect military or diplomatic secrets.

Executive privilege also provides the president "absolute immunity from damages liability predicated on his official acts."[4] However, such immunity does not protect the president during his or her term of office from civil litigation over events that occurred before the president took office. In *Clinton v. Jones,*[5] the Supreme Court held that President Bill Clinton could be sued while still in office by Paula Jones, formerly an Arkansas state employee, for sexual harassment and tort claims arising from acts that allegedly took place in 1991, when Clinton was governor of Arkansas. Although conceding that the litigation would subject the president to the power of the judiciary, the Court concluded that it would not violate the separation of powers. After concluding that it was "highly unlikely" that the litigation would occupy any

---

3. United States v. Nixon, 418 U.S. 683 (1974) (President Nixon required to produce tape recordings and documents relating to confidential conversations with his advisers in a criminal case involving seven advisers charged with obstruction of justice and other offenses related to the 1973 burglary of the Democratic National Headquarters in the Watergate Hotel in Washington, D.C.).
4. Nixon v. Fitzgerald, 457 U.S. 731 (1982).
5. 520 U.S. 681 (1997).

"substantial amount" of Clinton's time, the Court rejected the argument that the litigation would impose an unacceptable burden on Clinton's time and energy and thereby impair the effective performance of his office. In fact, the case triggered special prosecutor Kenneth Starr's investigation of Clinton's sexual relations with White House intern Monica Lewinsky, and it culminated in Clinton's impeachment by the House of Representatives for perjury and obstruction of justice. Clinton was not convicted by the Senate, but the proceedings proved a major distraction.

The principle of separation of powers has also been invoked to invalidate certain legislation. In *Clinton v. City of New York*,[6] the Supreme Court struck down the line item veto given to the president by Congress. The *line item veto* allowed the president to sign a bill into law, then cancel any dollar amounts that he or she believed to be fiscally irresponsible.[7] Essentially, the veto gave the president the power to strike specific provisions from tax and spending bills, which usually include thousands of separate, discrete provisions. This made it possible for the president to shape budgetary policy without having to make the stark choice to accept or reject an entire package of provisions. Congress could effectively override any particular line item veto by adopting a disapproval bill by a two-thirds vote of both houses.

The U.S. Supreme Court, by a vote of six to three, declared the line item veto unconstitutional. The Court said that it impermissibly altered the "single, finely wrought and exhaustively considered, procedure" in Article I, Section 7, of the U.S. Constitution, which requires that laws be approved by both houses of Congress *(bicameralism)* and then presented to the president. The Court stated that the president must approve all parts of a bill or reject it in toto. The amendment and repeal of statutes must meet these same requirements. If the line item veto were valid, it would authorize the president to create a different law—one whose text was not voted on by either house of Congress or presented to the president for signature. The Court concluded that if there is to be a new procedure in which the president will play a different role in determining the final text of what may become a law, "such change must come not by legislation but through the amendment procedures set forth in Article V of the Constitution." President Clinton called the decision "a defeat for all Americans," which "deprives the president of a valuable tool for eliminating waste in the federal

"As a matter of fact, I have read the Constitution, and, frankly, I don't get it."

budget and for enlivening the public debate over how to make the best use of public funds."

Supremacy Clause *and* Preemption

The Supremacy Clause of Article VI states that the Constitution, laws, and treaties of the United States take precedence over state laws and that the judges of the state courts must follow federal law. Any federal or state laws enacted in violation of the Constitution or ratified treaties are void. State law is preempted when it directly conflicts with federal law or when Congress has manifested an intention to regulate the entire area without state participation.

For example, in *Crosby v. National Foreign Trade Council*,[8] the U.S. Supreme Court struck down a Massachusetts statute that had been enacted as a protest against human rights violations by Burma (Myanmar) and restricted the ability of Massachusetts and its agencies to purchase goods and services from companies

6. 524 U.S. 417 (1998).
7. 2 U.S.C. § 691 *et seq.* (Supp. 1997).

8. 120 S. Ct. 2288 (2000).

doing business in Burma. After the Massachusetts statute was enacted, Congress passed an act that imposed mandatory and conditional sanctions on Burma but authorized the president to (1) terminate the measures upon certifying that Burma had made progress in human rights and democracy, (2) impose new sanctions upon findings of repression, and (3) suspend the sanctions in the interest of national security. The Court concluded that the Massachusetts statute posed an obstacle to the accomplishment and execution of Congress's full purposes and objectives, in at least three respects: (1) the statute interfered with the federal act's delegation of discretion to the president to control economic sanctions against Burma; (2) by prohibiting some contracts and investments permitted under the federal act, it interfered with Congress's intention to limit economic pressure against the Burmese government to a specific range; and (3) it was at odds with the president's authority to speak for the United States among the world's nations to develop a comprehensive, multilateral Burma strategy. Accordingly, even though the federal act did not expressly preempt state legislation, the Massachusetts law was preempted by the federal act and therefore invalid under the Supremacy Clause.

In *Geier v. American Honda Motor Co.,*[9] the U.S. Supreme Court held that the National Traffic and Motor Vehicle Safety Act of 1996 (the Safety Act) preempted state product liability claims based upon a manufacturer's failure to equip a vehicle with air bags. Whereas the Safety Act deliberately provided the manufacturers of cars with a range of choices among different passive restraint devices and sought a gradual phase-in of passive restraints to give manufacturers more time to develop better systems, the state law imposed a duty to install an air bag. This presented an obstacle to the variety and mix of devices that the federal statute sought.

In an earlier case, *Medtronic, Inc. v. Lohr,*[10] the U.S. Supreme Court considered the issue of preemption with regard to claims of defective design, negligent manufacture, and failure to warn in the area of medical devices. The Medical Device Amendments (MDA) to the Food, Drug and Cosmetic Act specifically forbid states from establishing "any requirement" that is different from or in addition to those of the MDA. In *Medtronic,* a pacemaker recipient sued the device's manufacturer under state product liability law. The manufacturer argued that the state law was preempted by the MDA. Reasoning that the MDA's requirements for pacemakers were too general to preempt state law, the Court rejected the manufacturer's challenge.

Similarly, in *Duncan v. Northwest Airlines, Inc.,*[11] the U.S. Court of Appeals for the Ninth Circuit found that the Airline Deregulation Act (ADA) did not preempt a class action by flight attendants against the airline for exposure to secondhand tobacco smoke on certain flights. Under the terms of the ADA, no state can enact or enforce any law relating to the rates, routes, or service of any carrier. Northwest argued that allowing smoking on its international flights constituted or related to a "service" and was covered by the ADA. The court of appeals rejected this argument on the grounds that a "service" concerns "the frequency and scheduling of transportation, [or] the selection of markets to or from which transportation is provided," whereas a rule permitting or prohibiting smoke concerned "amenities."

Ultimately, preemption depends on the specificity of federal regulation, any statutory language addressing preemption, and the nature of the conflict between the federal and state approaches. Federal preemption of state law claims related to tobacco is discussed in Chapter 10.

Federalism

The federal government's powers are limited to those expressly granted in the Constitution. Its powers are also subject to specific restrictions, such as those in the Bill of Rights. State governments, on the other hand, have general powers not specified in the Constitution. These include the *police power* to protect the health, safety, welfare, or morals of the people of the state.

Some powers are exclusively federal because the Constitution expressly limits the states' exercise of those powers. Exclusive federal powers include the power to make treaties, to coin money, and to impose duties on imports. Other powers are inherently in the states' domain, such as the power to structure state and local governments.

THE ELEVENTH AMENDMENT

To further protect this division of power between the federal and state governments, the Eleventh Amendment was added to the Constitution in 1798. It immunizes states from lawsuits in federal court brought by citizens of another state or of another nation. Although a state may waive this sovereign immunity, it must do so voluntarily and in accordance with its own law.

In a variety of contexts, Congress has adopted legislation that purports to abrogate the states' Eleventh Amendment immunity. In reviewing the constitutionality of such legis-

9. 120 S. Ct. 1913 (2000).
10. 518 U.S. 470 (1996).

11. 208 F.3d 1112 (9th Cir. 2000).

lation, the Supreme Court has held that a state cannot be required to litigate a case involving a person from another state in federal court unless Congress (1) unequivocally expressed its intent to abrogate that immunity and (2) acted pursuant to a valid grant of constitutional authority.

The Supreme Court surprised many in 1999 when it ruled that nonconsenting states cannot be sued in federal court for patent infringement under the Patent Remedy Act even though Article I of the Constitution gives Congress the power to issue patents.[12] The Court held that Congress's powers under Article I do not include the power to subject states to suit at the hands of private individuals. The Court also ruled that Congress had not enacted the Patent Remedy Act pursuant to a valid exercise of power under Section 5 of the Fourteenth Amendment.

12. Florida Prepaid Postsecondary Educ. Expense Bd. v. College Savings Bank & United States, 527 U.S. 627 (1999).

Section 5 gives Congress the power to enforce the states' compliance with the Fourteenth Amendment, which bars states from denying any person due process or equal protection under the law. To invoke Section 5, Congress must identify conduct transgressing the Fourteenth Amendment and tailor legislation to remedy or prevent that conduct. In this case, Congress had identified neither a pattern of unremedied patent infringement by the states nor a pattern of constitutional violations. In addition, the Court found that Congress had barely considered the availability of state remedies for patent infringement despite the fact that, under the Due Process Clause, a state's infringement of a patent violates the Constitution only when the state provides no adequate remedy to injured patent owners.

In the following case, the Court considered whether a state employer could be sued in federal court for violating the federal Age Discrimination in Employment Act of 1967.

A CASE IN POINT

CASE 2.1

Kimel v. Florida Board of Regents

Supreme Court of the United States

120 S. Ct. 631 (2000).

In the Language of the Court

FACTS Three sets of plaintiffs filed suit in federal court under the Age Discrimination in Employment Act (ADEA) against their employers, two state universities and a state department of correction, seeking damages for alleged discrimination on the basis of age. In each case, the state employer moved to dismiss the suit on the basis of its Eleventh Amendment immunity. The court of appeals held that the ADEA did not validly abrogate the states' Eleventh Amendment immunity, and the plaintiffs appealed.

ISSUE PRESENTED Does the ADEA validly abrogate the states' Eleventh Amendment immunity from suits in federal court?

OPINION O'CONNOR, J., writing for the U.S. Supreme Court:

[*Ed.:* The Court first concluded that the language of the statute made it unmistakably clear that Congress intended to subject the states to suits for money damages by individual employees.]

[W]e must now determine whether Congress effectuated that abrogation pursuant to a valid exercise of constitutional authority.

. . .

. . . Congress' power "to enforce" the [Fourteenth] Amendment includes the authority both to remedy and to deter violation of rights guaranteed thereunder by prohibiting a somewhat broader swath of conduct, including that which is not itself forbidden by the Amendment's text.

Nevertheless, we have also recognized that the same language that serves as the basis for the affirmative grant of congressional power also serves to limit that power. For example, Congress cannot "decree the *substance* of the Fourteenth Amendment's restrictions on the States. . . . It has been given the power 'to enforce,' not the power to determine *what constitutes* a constitutional violation."

[T]he determination whether purportedly prophylactic legislation constitutes appropriate remedial legislation, or instead effects a substantive redefinition of the

(Continued)

(Case 2.1 continued)

Fourteenth Amendment right at issue, is often difficult. . . . "[T]here must be a congruence and proportionality between the injury to be prevented or remedied and the means adopted to that end."

. . .

[W]e conclude that the ADEA is not "appropriate legislation" under §5 of the Fourteenth Amendment. Initially, the substantive requirements the ADEA imposes on state and local governments are disproportionate to any unconstitutional conduct that conceivably could be targeted by the Act. . . . Age classifications, unlike governmental conduct based on race or gender, cannot be characterized as "so seldom relevant to the achievement of any legitimate state interest that laws grounded in such considerations are deemed to reflect prejudice and antipathy."

. . .

That the ADEA prohibits very little conduct likely to be held unconstitutional, while significant, does not alone provide the answer to our §5 inquiry. Difficult and intractable problems often require powerful remedies, and we have never held that §5 precludes Congress from enacting reasonably prophylactic legislation. Our task is to determine whether the ADEA is in fact just such an appropriate remedy or, instead, merely an attempt to substantively redefine the States' legal obligations with respect to age discrimination. . . .

. . .

A review of the ADEA's legislative record as a whole . . . reveals that Congress had virtually no reason to believe that state and local governments were unconstitutionally discriminating against their employees on the basis of age. Although that lack of support is not determinative of the §5 inquiry, . . . Congress' failure to uncover any significant pattern of unconstitutional discrimination here confirms that Congress had no reason to believe that broad prophylactic legislation was necessary in this field. In light of the indiscriminate scope of the Act's substantive requirements, and the lack of evidence of widespread and unconstitutional age discrimination by the States, we hold that the ADEA is not a valid exercise of Congress' power under §5 of the Fourteenth Amendment. The ADEA's purported abrogation of the States' sovereign immunity is accordingly invalid.

RESULT   The dismissal of the suit was affirmed. The states of Georgia and Florida were immune from suit in federal court for alleged violations of the ADEA.

QUESTIONS

1. Based on the reasoning in *Kimel,* would a private individual be allowed to sue a state in federal court for sex discrimination in violation of Title VII of the Civil Rights Act of 1964?
2. What congressional findings might have supported the application of the ADEA to the states?

In *Alden v. Maine,*[13] the Supreme Court held that the State of Maine could not be sued in *state* court by a group of employees seeking private damages for violating the overtime provisions of the Fair Labor Standards Act, a federal statute. Although the literal wording of the Eleventh Amendment refers to cases against states brought in federal court, the Court ruled that "the sovereign immunity of the States neither derives from nor is limited by the terms of the Eleventh Amendment." Due to the constitutional system recognizing the essential sov-

13. 527 U.S. 706 (1999).

ereignty of the states, nonconsenting states cannot be subject to suits in their own courts without their consent.

DUAL SOVEREIGNTY

The Supreme Court reaffirmed the system of dual sovereignty when it struck down provisions of the Brady Handgun Violence Prevention Act that required state law enforcement officers to receive reports from gun dealers regarding prospective handgun sales and to conduct background checks on prospective handgun purchasers.[14] The Court stated that "[t]he power of the Federal Government would be augmented immeasurably if it were able to impress into its service—and at no cost to itself—the police officers of the 50 States."

In *Reno v. Condon,*[15] however, the Supreme Court upheld the Driver's Privacy Protection Act of 1994, which restricts the states' ability to disclose without the driver's consent personal information contained in the records of state departments of motor vehicles. The Court rejected the contention that the Act violated the Tenth Amendment's federalism principles, and it ruled that the Act was a proper exercise of Congress's authority to regulate interstate commerce under the Commerce Clause. The Court explained:

> The motor vehicle information which the States have historically sold is used by insurers, manufacturers, direct marketers, and others engaged in interstate commerce to contact drivers with customized solicitations. The information is also used in the stream of interstate commerce by various public and private entities for matters related to interstate motoring. Because drivers' information is, in this context, an article of commerce, its sale or release into the interstate stream of business is sufficient to support congressional regulation.

 The Commerce Clause

Another boundary between federal and state powers is the Constitution's Commerce Clause. The *Commerce Clause,* contained in Article I, Section 8, gives Congress the power to regulate commerce with other nations, with Indian tribes, and between states. It is both a restraint on state action and a source of federal authority. The commerce power has been interpreted to allow federal regulation of such areas as interstate travel, labor relations, and discrimination in accommodations. As

explained below, the Supreme Court's view of what is interstate commerce subject to federal regulation has changed over time.

1824 TO 1887

The first Supreme Court discussion of the Commerce Clause was by Chief Justice John Marshall in the 1824 case *Gibbons v. Ogden.*[16] A steamboat monopoly affecting navigation between New York and New Jersey violated a federal statute regulating interstate commerce. The Court held that under the Supremacy Clause, the federal statute prevailed. In the decision, Justice Marshall discussed in detail his view that interstate commerce—which he defined as "commerce which concerns more states than one"—included every activity having any interstate impact. Therefore, Congress could regulate all such activities.

1887 TO 1937

From 1887 to 1937, the Supreme Court developed a view of the Commerce Clause quite different from Marshall's view. The Court interpreted "commerce" narrowly, holding that activities such as mining and manufacturing were not commerce and therefore could not be regulated by Congress. The Supreme Court was not persuaded by the fact that the products of these activities would later enter interstate commerce. During this period, the Court struck down various pieces of New Deal legislation, arguing that the Commerce Clause did not grant Congress the power to regulate such activities.

1937 TO 1995

A turning point in the Supreme Court's attitude came in *NLRB v. Jones & Laughlin Steel Corp.*[17] The Court held that Congress could regulate labor relations in a manufacturing plant because a work stoppage at such a plant would have a serious effect on interstate commerce; the steel manufactured by the plant was shipped across state lines.

From 1937 until 1995, virtually all federal regulation of commerce was upheld under the Commerce Clause. If legislation had a "substantial economic effect" on interstate commerce, it was held to be a valid exercise of the commerce power.

For example, in *Heart of Atlanta Motel, Inc. v. United States,*[18] the Supreme Court upheld Title II of the Civil

---

14. Printz v. United States, 521 U.S. 898 (1997).
15. 120 S. Ct. 666 (2000).

16. 22 U.S. (1 Wheat) 1 (1824).
17. 301 U.S. 1 (1937).
18. 379 U.S. 241 (1964).

Rights Act of 1964, which prohibits discrimination or segregation on the grounds of race, color, religion, or national origin in any inn, hotel, motel, or other establishment of more than five rooms that provides lodging to transient guests. The party challenging the act—the Heart of Atlanta Motel—had followed a practice of refusing to rent rooms to African Americans, and it alleged that it intended to continue to do so. The operator of the motel solicited patronage from both inside and outside the state of Georgia through billboards, signs, and various national advertising media, including magazines of national circulation. Approximately 75 percent of its registered guests were from out of state.

The Court noted that the population had become increasingly mobile, with millions of people of all races traveling from state to state. African Americans in particular were subjected to discrimination in transient accommodations, which forced them to travel great distances to secure lodging. This impaired their ability to travel to other states.

In *Katzenbach v. McClung*,[19] the Supreme Court upheld the application of the Civil Rights Act to a restaurant because a substantial portion of the food that it served had previously moved in interstate commerce. The Court reasoned that the restaurant's discrimination against African Americans, who were potential customers, resulted in its selling less food that had traveled in interstate commerce. Thus, the discrimination had a substantial effect on interstate commerce.

1995 TO 2000

In 1995, in *United States v. Lopez*,[20] the Supreme Court again changed course when it struck down a federal law

19. 379 U.S. 294 (1964).
20. 514 U.S. 549 (1995).

banning guns near schools as being beyond the power of Congress under the Commerce Clause. The Court found that the statute was neither a regulation of the use of the channels of interstate commerce, nor an attempt to prohibit the interstate transportation of a commodity through the channels of interstate commerce, nor an attempt to protect an instrumentality of interstate commerce or a thing in interstate commerce. The Court ruled that the law was not sustainable as a regulation of an activity that substantially affects interstate commerce because its terms had nothing to do with commerce or any sort of economic enterprise.

The Court rejected the government's argument that the statute was constitutional because possession of a firearm at school might result in violent crime, which in turn would (1) affect the functioning of the national economy by increasing costs and reducing people's willingness to travel to parts of the country deemed unsafe and (2) reduce national productivity by threatening the learning environment. The Court reasoned that the "cost of crime" argument would give Congress the power to regulate not only all violent crime but also all activities that might lead to violent crime. The "national productivity" argument would empower Congress to regulate any activity related to the economic productivity of individual citizens, including family law governing marriage, child support, and divorce. As a result, there would be virtually no limitations on federal power, even in areas such as criminal law and education where states historically have been sovereign, a result unacceptable to five members of the Court.

Congress had not stated any factual findings justifying its adoption of the Gun-Free School Zones Act at issue in *Lopez*. In the following case, the Court struck down the Violence Against Women Act, notwithstanding Congress's express findings about the effect of violence on the economy.

A CASE IN POINT

CASE 2.2
United States v. Morrison
Supreme Court of the United States
120 S. Ct. 1740 (2000).

In the Language of the Court

FACTS Christy Brzonkala enrolled at Virginia Polytechnic Institute where she met fellow students Antonio Morrison and James Crawford. Brzonkala claimed that within thirty minutes of meeting the two men, they assaulted her and repeatedly raped her. In the ensuing months, Morrison continued to harass Brzonkala with offensive and vulgar comments. Brzonkala became severely emotionally disturbed and depressed, then stopped attending classes, and finally withdrew from the university. Although Morrison was found guilty of sexual assault and using abusive language on two separate occasions under Virginia Tech's Assault Policy, Virginia Tech's senior vice president set aside Morrison's punishment on his appeal.

(Continued)

(Case 2.2 continued)

Brzonkala then sued Morrison, Crawford, and Virginia Tech under Section 13981 of the Violence Against Women Act of 1994, which states that "persons within the United States shall have the right to be free from crimes of violence motivated by gender."[21] After both the district court and the appeals court held that Congress lacked authority to enact Section 13981, Brzonkala appealed.

ISSUE PRESENTED Did Congress have constitutional authority to enact Section 13981 of the Violence Against Women Act of 1994, which provides a private federal civil remedy for the victims of gender-motivated violence?

OPINION REHNQUIST, C.J., writing for the U.S. Supreme Court:

Congress' commerce authority includes the power to regulate those activities having a substantial relation to interstate commerce.

...

Gender-motivated crimes of violence are not, in any sense of the phrase, economic activity. While we need not adopt a categorical rule against aggregating the effects of any noneconomic activity in order to decide these cases, thus far in our Nation's history our cases have upheld Commerce Clause regulation of interstate activity only where that activity is economic in nature.

Like the Gun-Free School Zones Act at issue in *Lopez*, section 13981 contains no jurisdictional element establishing that the federal cause of action is in pursuance of Congress' power to regulate interstate commerce. Although *Lopez* makes clear that such a jurisdictional element would lend support to the argument that section 13981 is sufficiently tied to interstate commerce, Congress elected to cast section 13981's remedy over a wider, and more purely intrastate, body of violent crime.

...

In contrast with the lack of congressional findings that we faced in *Lopez*, section 13981 is supported by numerous findings regarding the serious impact that gender-motivated violence has on victims and their families. But the existence of congressional findings is not sufficient, by itself, to sustain the constitutionality of Commerce Clause legislation. As we stated in *Lopez*, "Simply because Congress may conclude that a particular activity substantially affects interstate commerce does not necessarily make it so." Rather, "whether particular operations affect interstate commerce sufficiently to come under the constitutional power of Congress to regulate them is ultimately a judicial rather than a legislative question, and can be settled finally only by this Court."

...

[T]he concern that we expressed in *Lopez* that Congress might use the Commerce Clause to completely obliterate the Constitution's distribution between national and local authority seems well founded. . . . If accepted, petitioners' reasoning would allow Congress to regulate any crime as long as the nationwide, aggregated impact of that crime has substantial effects on employment, production, transit, or consumption.

...

We accordingly reject the argument that Congress may regulate noneconomic violent criminal conduct based solely on that conduct's aggregate effect on interstate commerce.

21. 42 U.S.C. § 13981.

(Continued)

(Case 2.2 continued)

[*Ed.:* The Court also rejected the argument that the Act should be upheld as an exercise of Congress's remedial power under Section 5 of the Fourteenth Amendment. Because the Fourteenth Amendment prohibits only state action, it cannot be the basis for a statute aimed at individuals.]

RESULT Section 13981 was struck down, and the case was dismissed.

DISSENT Souter, J., dissenting from the majority opinion:

Congress has the power to legislate with regard to activity that, in the aggregate, has a substantial effect on interstate commerce. The fact of such a substantial effect is not an issue for the courts in the first instance, but for the Congress, whose institutional capacity for gathering evidence and taking testimony far exceeds ours. . . .

One obvious difference from *United States v. Lopez* is the mountain of data assembled by Congress, here showing the effects of violence against women on interstate commerce. . . .

...

Three out of four American women will be victims of violent crimes sometime during their life. Violence is the leading cause of injuries to women ages 15 to 44. As many as 50 percent of homeless women and children are fleeing domestic violence. Since 1974, the assault rate against women has outstripped the rate for men by at least twice for some age groups and far more for others. Battering is the single largest cause of injury to women in the United States. An estimated 4 million American women are battered each year by their husbands or partners.

...

Arrest rates may be as low as 1 for every 100 domestic assaults. Partial estimates show that violent crime against women costs this country at least 3 billion—not million, but billion—dollars a year. Estimates suggest that we spend $5 to $10 billion a year on health care, criminal justice, and other social costs of domestic violence.

...

[The incidence of] rape rose four times as fast as the total national crime rate over the past 10 years. According to one study, close to half a million girls now in high school will be raped before they graduate. [One hundred twenty-five thousand] college women can expect to be raped during this—or any—year. Three-quarters of women never go to the movies alone after dark because of the fear of rape and nearly 50 percent do not use public transit alone after dark for the same reason. [Forty-one] percent of judges surveyed believed that juries give sexual assault victims less credibility than other crime victims. Less than 1 percent of all [rape] victims have collected damages. An individual who commits rape has only about 4 chances in 100 of being arrested, prosecuted, and found guilty of any offense. Almost one-quarter of convicted rapists never go to prison and another quarter received sentences in local jails where the average sentence is 11 months. Almost 50 percent of rape victims lose their jobs or are forced to quit because of the crime's severity.

...

Congress . . . explicitly stated the predicate for the exercise of its Commerce Clause power. Is its conclusion irrational in view of the data amassed?

...

Indeed, the legislative record here is far more voluminous than the record compiled by Congress and found sufficient in two prior cases upholding Title II of the

(Continued)

(Case 2.2 continued)

Civil Rights Act of 1964 against Commerce Clause challenges [*Heart of Atlanta Motel, Inc. v. United States* and *Katzenbach v. McClung*]. . . .

. . .

. . . [G]ender-based violence in the 1990's was shown to operate in a manner similar to racial discrimination in the 1960's in reducing the mobility of employees and their production and consumption of goods shipped in interstate commerce. Like racial discrimination, gender-based violence bars its most likely targets—women—from full participation in the national economy.

In 2000, the Supreme Court also ruled that Congress could not extend a federal arson statute to the burning of a private home.[22] The statute made it a federal crime for any person to damage or destroy "by means of fire or an explosive, any . . . property used in interstate or foreign commerce or in any activity affecting interstate or foreign commerce." The government argued that the burned Indiana home was used in at least three activities affecting interstate commerce: (1) the homeowner used the house as collateral to obtain a mortgage from an Oklahoma lender; (2) the house was used to obtain an insurance policy from a Wisconsin insurer; and (3) the house received natural gas from outside Indiana. The Court rejected this argument:

[H]ardly a building in the land would fall outside the federal statute's domain. Practically every building in our cities, towns, and rural areas is constructed with supplies that have moved in interstate commerce, served by utilities that have an interstate connection, financed or insured by enterprises that do business across state lines, or bears some other trace of interstate commerce.[23]

Because the private residence was used for everyday family living, not commerce or any activity affecting commerce, the federal arson law did not apply to the burning of the home.

LIMITS ON STATE POWERS

Federal powers enumerated in the Constitution impose many limits on state action. This chapter discusses only the limits on state power resulting from the commerce power, but the principles apply to other federal powers as well.

As discussed above, when Congress has indicated a policy by acting, Congress's action preempts state action because the Supremacy Clause makes federal laws supreme over state laws. Even when Congress has not taken action, the *"dormant"* or *"negative"* Commerce Clause may impose restrictions on state action.

Dormant or Negative Commerce Clause Since the mid-1930s, the Supreme Court has sought to clarify when state regulation affecting interstate commerce is valid in the absence of preempting federal regulation. State laws that regulate evenhandedly with only incidental effects on interstate commerce will generally be permitted. On the other hand, state laws that discriminate against interstate commerce, that is, that provide differential treatments of in-state and out-of-state economic interests that benefit the in-state interests and burden the out-of-state, are "virtually per se invalid."[24] Once a law has been found to be discriminatory, it will be held invalid unless its proponents "can 'sho[w]' that it advances a legitimate local purpose that cannot be adequately served by reasonable nondiscriminatory alternatives.'"[25]

The Supreme Court is clearly hostile toward state protectionism and discrimination against out-of-state interests. However, not all state regulations found invalid under the Commerce Clause are protectionist or discriminatory. The problem lies in determining the purpose of the legislation. Protectionist regulations may be explicitly discriminatory; they may be enacted for a discriminatory purpose; or they may simply have the effect of favoring local interests at the expense of out-of-state concerns.

For example, the U.S. Supreme Court invalidated a North Carolina statute that prohibited the sale of apples that bore a grade other than the applicable U.S. grade. Washington State apples bore their own state's grade on the container, a grade that was equal to or more stringent than the U.S. grade. Although neutral on its face, the effect of the statute was to discriminate against Washington apples.[26] On the other hand, a Minnesota statute banning

22. Jones v. United States, 120 S. Ct. 1904 (2000).
23. *Id.* at 1911.
24. Oregon State Waste Systems, Inc. v. Department of Envtl. Quality of Oregon, 511 U.S. 93, 98–99 (1994).
25. *Id.* at 100–101.
26. Hunt v. Washington State Apple Advertising Comm'n, 432 U.S. 333 (1997).

plastic, nonreturnable milk containers was upheld in the face of claims that it discriminated against interstate commerce.[27] The statute was not "simple protectionism"; it "regulated evenhandedly" by prohibiting all milk retailers from selling their products in the plastic containers. The regulation applied regardless of whether the milk, the containers, or the sellers were from inside or outside the state.

The U.S. Supreme Court struck down a Massachusetts law that required every milk dealer who sold milk in Massachusetts to contribute to a state fund based on the volume of milk that the dealer had sold within the state, regardless of the price the dealer paid for the milk or its point of origin.[28] Massachusetts dairy farmers received a form of subsidy because they, but not the out-of-state producers, were entitled to disbursements from the fund, based on the volume of milk they produced. In part because most of the milk sold in Massachusetts is produced by out-of-state entities, the law had the effect of enabling higher-cost Massachusetts dairy farmers to compete unfairly with lower-cost dairy farmers in other states. This "violates the principle of the unitary national market by handicapping out-of-state competitors, thus artificially encouraging in-state production even when the same goods could be produced at lower cost in other States."[29]

The California Court of Appeal struck down a California statute that required owners of automobiles last registered outside California to pay a $300 smog impact fee, even if the automobiles passed California's very stringent smog check test.[30] Although Congress had given California the power to impose higher air-quality control standards for new cars sold in the state, it had not expressly exempted California regulation and taxation of used motor vehicles from Commerce Clause analysis. Because California failed to prove that the smog impact fee advanced a legitimate California purpose that could not be served by reasonable, nondiscriminatory means, the fee was a "patent" violation of the Commerce Clause.

 Federal Fiscal Powers

Two other federal powers, the taxing and spending powers, have been invoked to regulate traditionally local "police problems" as well as purely economic problems. The Constitution grants a broad taxing power to the federal government. The only specific limitations imposed are that (1) direct taxes on anything, except in-

come and capitation (per head) taxes, must be allocated among the states in proportion to population and (2) all custom duties and excise taxes must be uniform throughout the United States. The single prohibition is that no duty shall be levied upon exports from any state. The Fifth Amendment's Due Process Clause is also a general limitation on the taxing power.

Taxes have an economic impact on business. The federal government has imposed taxes in order to affect the behavior of business as well as to raise revenues. The Supreme Court has upheld such taxes under the government's power to tax without regard to the purpose behind the tax.

Congress has the power to spend in order to provide for the common defense and general welfare. An exercise of the spending power will be upheld as long as it does not violate a specific check on federal power.

 Protection *of* Individual Liberties

The original Constitution and the Bill of Rights guarantee certain individual rights, including freedom of speech, association, and religion; due process; compensation for takings; equal protection; and the right to a jury trial.

THE CONSTITUTION

Although most explicit guarantees of individual liberty are found in the amendments to the Constitution, the original Constitution contains three specific guarantees of individual rights: the Contracts Clause, the ban on *ex post facto* laws, and the prohibition against bills of attainder.

Contracts Clause Article I, Section 10, of the Constitution specifically prohibits a state legislature from impairing the obligation of existing contracts. The Fifth Amendment imposes a similar bar on federal legislation that would retroactively impair the obligations of a contract. In *Calfarm Insurance Co. v. Deukmejian*,[31] insurance companies raised issues under the Contracts Clause in connection with insurance law changes mandated by California Proposition 103. Proposition 103, a voter initiative that made fundamental changes to the regulation of automobile and other types of insurance, included a freeze on rate increases for one year and new restrictions on an insurance company's ability to refuse to renew automobile insurance policies entered into prior to enactment of the new initia-

27. Minnesota v. Clover Leaf Creamery Co., 449 U.S. 456 (1981).
28. West Lynn Creamery, Inc. v. Healy, 512 U.S. 186 (1994).
29. *Id.*
30. Jordan v. Department of Motor Vehicles, 75 Cal. App. 4th 449, 89 Cal. Rptr. 2d 333 (1999).
31. 771 P.2d 1247 (Cal. 1989).

tive. Seven insurers and the Association of California Insurance Companies sued to invalidate the initiative as a violation of due process and an unconstitutional law impairing the obligations of contracts.

The California Supreme Court struck down the freeze on rate increases for one year as a violation of due process on the grounds that it deprived companies of their right to a reasonable return on investment. But the court upheld the nonrenewal restrictions. The decision rested in part on the fact that insurance is a highly regulated industry in which further regulation can reasonably be anticipated. In addition, the court found that the public interest in making insurance available to all Californians and the fear that insurance companies would refuse to renew in California, leaving drivers without the car insurance required by law, were sufficient, when measured against the relatively low degree of impairment of contract rights involved, to justify the nonrenewal. The court explained:

> Although the language of the Contracts Clause is facially absolute, its prohibition must be accommodated to the inherent police power of the State "to safeguard the vital interests of its people." This Court has long recognized that a statute does not violate the Contracts Clause simply because it has the effect of restricting, or even barring altogether, the performance of duties created by contracts entered into prior to its enactment. Thus, a state prohibition law may be applied to contracts for the sale of beer that were valid when entered into, a law barring lotteries may be applied to lottery tickets that were valid when issued, and workmen's compensation law may be applied to employers and employees operating under pre-existing contracts of employment that made no provision for work-related injuries.

Ex Post Facto Laws Article I, Section 9, and Article I, Section 10, prohibit *ex post facto* laws. These are laws that punish actions that were not illegal when performed. *Ex post facto* laws are discussed in greater deal in Chapter 17.

Bills of Attainder Article I, Section 9, prohibits the federal government from enacting laws to punish specific individuals. Such laws are termed *bills of attainder.*

THE BILL OF RIGHTS

The first ten amendments to the Constitution constitute the Bill of Rights. The first eight amendments contain specific guarantees of individual liberties that limit the power of the federal government. Importantly, the last two make clear that the federal government's powers are limited and enumerated, whereas the rights of the people go beyond those listed in the Constitution.

The First Amendment guarantees freedom of religion, speech, press, and assembly. The Second Amendment grants persons the right to bear arms. The Third Amendment provides that no soldier shall be quartered in any house. The Fourth Amendment prohibits unreasonable searches and seizures and requires that warrants shall be issued only upon probable cause. The Fifth Amendment (1) contains the grand jury requirements; (2) forbids double jeopardy (that is, being tried twice for the same crime); (3) prohibits forcing a person to be a witness against himself or herself; (4) prohibits the deprivation of life, liberty, or property without due process of law; and (5) requires just compensation when private property is taken for public use. The Sixth Amendment guarantees a speedy and public jury trial in all criminal prosecutions. The Seventh Amendment gives the right to a jury trial in all civil (that is, noncriminal) cases when the value in dispute is greater than $20. The Eighth Amendment prohibits excessive bails or fines as well as cruel and unusual punishment. Aspects of the Fourth, Fifth, and Sixth Amendments relevant to criminal cases are discussed in Chapter 17.

Applicability to the States The Fourteenth Amendment provides that no state shall "deprive any person of life, liberty, or property, without due process of law" (the *Due Process Clause*) and that "[n]o State shall make or enforce any law which shall abridge the privileges or immunities of citizens of the United States" (the *Privileges and Immunities Clause*). After the Fourteenth Amendment was passed, it was argued that the Due Process Clause and the Privileges and Immunities Clause made the Bill of Rights applicable to state governments.

The Supreme Court has rejected this theory. It has held that the provisions of the Bill of Rights are incorporated into the Fourteenth Amendment only if they are fundamental to the American system of law or are safeguards "essential to liberty in the American scheme of justice."[32]

Many provisions of the Bill of Rights have been held to limit the actions of state governments as well as the federal government. For example, if a state government were to abridge the freedom of speech, it would violate the First Amendment as applied to state governments through the Fourteenth Amendment.

Other provisions have been held not to apply to the states: the Second Amendment right to bear arms, the Fifth Amendment requirement of a grand jury indictment

---

32. Duncan v. Louisiana, 391 U.S. 145 (1968).

IN BRIEF
Outline of the Bill of Rights

Amendment I
Establishment Clause
Free Exercise Clause
Freedom of speech
Freedom of press
Right to assembly and petition

Amendment II
Right to keep and bear arms

Amendment III
Restrictions on quartering soldiers

Amendment IV
No unreasonable search and seizure
Requirements for warrants

Amendment V
Presentment or indictment of a grand jury required for
   capital or otherwise infamous crime
Prohibition on double jeopardy
Prohibition on compulsory self-incrimination
Due process required before taking life, liberty, or property
Just compensation for taking of private property

Amendment VI
In criminal prosecutions:
   Right to a speedy and public trial
   Right to a jury trial
   Right to confront witnesses
   Right to counsel

Amendment VII
Right to a jury trial in civil cases

Amendment VIII
No excessive bail
No excessive fines
No cruel and unusual punishment

Amendment IX
Rights of the people not limited to those listed in the
   Constitution

Amendment X
Powers not delegated to the United States in the Constitution are reserved to the states or the people, except for those
powers prohibited to the states by the Constitution, which
are reserved to the people

before any criminal prosecution, and the Seventh Amendment guarantee of a jury trial in civil cases.

The Eighth Amendment prohibition against the imposition of excessive bail has not been explicitly applied to the states, but in a number of state cases the Supreme Court has assumed that it applied. The Fifth Amendment's prohibition against the taking of property without just compensation has not been incorporated into the Fourteenth Amendment, but the due process guarantee in the Fourteenth Amendment has been interpreted to provide the same protection.

The Supreme Court has not yet determined whether the Third Amendment, which prohibits the quartering of soldiers in private houses, and the excessive-fine provision of the Eighth Amendment are applicable to state governments.

Article IV, Section 2, of the Constitution and Section 1 of the Fourteenth Amendment both guarantee the privileges and immunities of citizens of the United States, that is, the rights that go with being a citizen of the federal government, such as the right to vote in a federal election and the right to travel. Article IV provides that citizens of each state shall receive all the privileges and immunities of citizens of other states. These provisions prohibit any unreasonable discrimination between the citizens of different states. Any such discrimination must reasonably relate to legitimate state or local purposes.

 # Freedom *of* Speech *and* Press

The First Amendment states that "Congress shall make no law . . . abridging the freedom of speech, or of the press." However, the Supreme Court does not apply the First Amendment to protect all speech to the same degree. The type of speech most clearly protected is political speech, including speech critical of governmental policies and officials. Some types of expression—bribery, perjury, and obscenity—are not protected by the First Amendment at all.

A government may violate the right to free speech not only by forbidding speech but by commanding it as well. For example, the U.S. Supreme Court ruled that Massachusetts had violated the First Amendment when it ordered organizers of South Boston's St. Patrick's Day Parade to include a group of gay and lesbian Bostonians of Irish ancestry.[33] Such compulsory inclusion of a

33. Hurley v. Irish-American Gay, Lesbian & Bisexual Group of Boston, 515 U.S. 557 (1995).

group imparting a message the organizers did not wish to convey is forbidden by the Free Speech Clause.

Determining whether a type of speech is protected by the First Amendment is only the first step of the analysis. If it is determined that a certain expression is protected, it must then be determined to what extent the expression may be regulated without violating the First Amendment.

"CLEAR AND PRESENT DANGER" TEST

Throughout most of the nineteenth and early twentieth centuries, Congress followed the mandate of the First Amendment literally and made "no law" restricting freedom of speech, assembly, or the press. In response to vocal resistance to World War I, Congress passed the Espionage Act of 1917 and the Sedition Act of 1918. Charles Schenck, a dissident, was convicted under the Espionage Act for circulating to men who had been called and accepted for military service a document that stated that the draft violated the Thirteenth Amendment, which prohibits slavery or involuntary servitude. In 1919, the Supreme Court, in an opinion by Justice Oliver Wendell Holmes, first articulated the "clear and present danger" test and affirmed Schenck's conviction.[34]

The Supreme Court explained that many things that might be said in peacetime cannot be allowed in time of war:

> [T]he character of every act depends upon the circumstances in which it is done. The most stringent protection of free speech would not protect a man in falsely shouting fire in a theatre and causing a panic. [The] question in every case is whether the words used are used in such circumstances and are of such a nature as to create a *clear and present danger* that they will bring about the substantive evils that Congress has a right to prevent. (Emphasis added.)

Later, during the height of the Cold War, the clear and present danger doctrine was applied in a manner restricting First Amendment freedoms even more severely. In the 1960s, the test became stricter and more protective of free speech. In *Brandenburg v. Ohio*, the Supreme Court held that "the constitutional guarantees of free speech and free press do not permit a State to forbid or proscribe advocacy of the use of force or of law violation except where such advocacy is directed to inciting or producing imminent lawless action and is likely to incite or produce such action."[35]

In 1997, the U.S. Court of Appeals for the Fourth Circuit ruled that the First Amendment did not bar a wrongful-death action against the publisher of *Hit Man: A Technical Manual for Independent Contractors*, a 130-page manual of detailed factual instructions on how to become a professional killer.[36] A convicted murderer had used the book to commit a triple homicide. The publisher stipulated that it had targeted the market of murderers, would-be murderers, and other criminals and that it knew and intended that criminals would immediately use the book to solicit, plan, and commit murder. Rejecting the publisher's claim that this was abstract advocacy protected under *Brandenburg v. Ohio*, the court stated: "[T]his book constitutes the archetypal example of speech which, because it methodically and comprehensively prepares and steels its audience to specific criminal conduct through exhaustively detailed instructions on the planning, commission, and concealment of criminal conduct, finds no preserve in the First Amendment."

DEFAMATION OF PUBLIC FIGURES BY MEDIA

Defamatory words—words that harm a person's reputation—are protected by the First Amendment, even when they are false, if they are made by a media defendant (such as a newspaper or television network) about a public figure without knowledge they were false, that is, without actual malice. Defamation is discussed further in Chapter 9.

OBSCENITY

Obscene material does not enjoy any protection under the First Amendment. Material is obscene if it (1) appeals to a prurient or sordid and perverted interest in sex; (2) has no serious literary, artistic, political, or scientific merit; and (3) is on the whole offensive to the average person in the community. Applying this test, the U.S. Court of Appeals for the Second Circuit held that the label for Bad Frog Beer, which depicts a frog with its middle finger raised, was perhaps in bad taste, but not obscene.[37]

ACADEMIC RESEARCH

The First Amendment also protects academic research. During the U.S. government's antitrust suit against Microsoft Corporation (the "Inside Story" in Chapter 20),

---

34. Schenck v. United States, 249 F.3d 47 (1919).
35. 395 U.S. 444 (1969).

36. Rice v. Paladin Enter., Inc., 128 F.3d 233 (4th Cir. 1997), *cert. denied,* 523 U.S. 1074 (1998).
37. Bad Frog Brewery v. New York State Liquor Auth., 134 F.3d 87 (2d Cir. 1998). The Bad Frog label can be seen at <www.badfrog.com>.

Pornography *and* Free Speech *on the* Internet

Concerned with the easy availability of pornography on the Internet, Congress enacted the Communications Decency Act (CDA) in 1995. Passed in part to protect children from sexually explicit materials in cyberspace, the law criminalized the interstate and international transmission of any obscene or patently offensive communications to any person under the age of eighteen through the use of an interactive computer service giving access to the Internet, such as online service provider America Online. The CDA provided two affirmative defenses: one for those who took "good faith, reasonable, effective, and appropriate actions" to restrict access by minors to the prohibited communications, and a second for those who restricted access to covered material by requiring certain designated forms of proof of age, such as a verified credit card or an adult identification number or code.

The Supreme Court struck down much of the Act but left in place its prohibition on online transmission of obscene speech.[a] The Court rejected the government's analogy to broadcast media, which have enjoyed only limited First Amendment protection.[b] Unlike television and radio broadcasting, the Internet does not have an extensive history of government regulation; it is not a scarce resource in need of monitored allocation; and it is not intrusive into individuals' homes.

Instead, the Court viewed the Internet as analogous to a public square, a place where speech is given heightened protection:

This dynamic, multifaced category of communication includes not only traditional print and news services, but also audio, video, and still images, as well as interactive, real time dialogue. Through the use of chat rooms, any person with a phone line can become a town crier with a voice that resonates farther than it could from any soapbox. Through the use of Web pages, mail exploders, and newsgroups, the same individual can become a pamphleteer. . . . '[T]he content on the Internet is as diverse as human thought.'

Given the nature of cyberspace, the law's affirmative defenses (restricting access by minors and verifying user ages) were unworkable. Credit cards were insufficient proxies because many sites are noncommercial and many adults do not own credit cards. The Court acknowledged the government's interest in protecting children from harmful material but ruled that "the Government may not 'reduc[e] the adult population . . . to . . . only what is fit for children.' "

In 1998, in an attempt to address the specific concerns raised by the Supreme Court in invalidating the CDA, Congress enacted the Child Online Protection Act (COPA). COPA restricts its scope to material on the Web rather than the Internet as a whole, targets only Web communications made for "commercial purposes," and limits its scope to material deemed "harmful to minors." Under COPA, in determining whether material is "harmful to minors," the court is to consider contemporary community standards.

In *ACLU v. Reno,*[c] the Third Circuit found that COPA's reliance on "contemporary community standards" to identify material that was harmful to minors was overbroad and would probably lead to a finding that COPA was unconstitutional. The court argued that due to the "geography-free" nature of the Internet, a community standards test would require every Web communication to comply with the most restrictive community's standards. This would impose an overreaching burden and restriction on constitutionally protected speech.

The Child Pornography Prevention Act, enacted by Congress in 1996, criminalizes the transmission of child pornography. "Child pornography" is defined as any image that "appears to be" or "conveys the impression" of a minor engaging in sex, including computer-generated images or "virtual" child pornography. As of March 2001, the circuits were divided as to whether this provision violates the First Amendment.

The Ninth Circuit[d] struck down the ban on virtual child pornography. The court held that it was a content-based restriction on protected speech that did not further any compelling government interest because the images were not of actual children. However, the First Circuit[e] and the Eleventh Circuit[f] upheld the ban. They concluded that the statute's definition of child pornography was not overbroad; virtual pornography can be used as effectively as real pornography by pedophiles who use these images as tools to coax children to become their victims. The U.S. Supreme Court agreed to hear an appeal of the Ninth Circuit's ruling in October 2001.

a. Reno v. American Civil Liberties Union, 521 U.S. 844 (1997).
b. In *United States v. Playboy Entertainment Group, Inc.,* 120 S. Ct. 1878 (2000), the Supreme Court struck down Section 505 of the Telecommunications Act of 1996, which required cable television operators providing channels primarily dedicated to sexually-oriented programming either to fully block those channels or to limit their transmission to hours when children would be unlikely to be viewing (10 P.M. to 6 A.M.). Even though the statute did not impose a complete prohibition, the Court subjected its content-based restrictions to strict scrutiny. The Court acknowledged that Congress was legitimately concerned with shielding young viewers from unwanted, indecent speech that came into the home without parental consent, but faulted Congress for failing to use a less restrictive alternative, namely, requiring cable operators to give individual households the option to block access to the channels.
c. 217 F.3d 162 (3d Cir. 2000).
d. Free Speech Coalition v. Reno, 198 F.3d 1083 (9th Cir. 1999), *cert. granted,* 121 S. Ct. 876 (2001).
e. United States v. Hilton, 167 F.3d 61 (1st Cir. 1999), *cert. denied,* 120 S. Ct. 115 (1999).
f. United States v. Acheson, 195 F.3d 645 (11th Cir. 1999).

Microsoft sought to compel two university professors to produce notes and tape recordings of the interviews they had conducted with Netscape Communications employees while researching their book *Competing on Internet Time: Lessons from Netscape and the Battle with Microsoft*. The First Circuit denied access, reasoning that the academics, in gathering and disseminating information, were acting almost as journalists. Compelling disclosure of their research materials would "infrigidate the free flow of information to the public, thus denigrating a fundamental First Amendment value."[38] In addition, the court noted that the Netscape nondisclosure agreements signed by the authors made the information confidential and not discoverable.

COMMERCIAL SPEECH

Commercial speech, especially advertising, has always been subject to substantial regulation. The government cannot suppress commercial speech, but it can impose reasonable regulations regarding the time, place, and manner of such speech.

For example, the U.S. Court of Appeals for the Ninth Circuit upheld a municipal ordinance banning the sale of merchandise or services on the sidewalks of Waikiki, a popular tourist area in Honolulu, Hawaii.[39] The plaintiffs, sellers of T-shirts imprinted with philosophical and inspirational messages, claimed that the ordinance violated their First Amendment rights. Relying on Supreme Court precedent,[40] the court reasoned that such restrictions are valid if they (1) are content-neutral, (2) are narrowly tailored to serve a significant governmental interest, and (3) leave open ample alternative channels of communication. Because Honolulu's restriction met the three-part test, it was upheld.

Liquor and Cigarette Advertising In 1995, Coors Brewing Company successfully challenged a provision of the 1935 Federal Alcohol Administration Act that prohibited statements of alcohol content on malt beverage labels unless state law required disclosure.[41] The government's asserted goal of preventing competition based on high alcohol content was legitimate, but the Supreme Court found no evidence that the labeling restriction served the goal.

---

38. Cusamano v. Microsoft Corp., 162 F.3d 708 (1st Cir. 1998).
39. One World One Family Now v. Honolulu, 76 F.3d 1009 (9th Cir. 1996), *cert. denied*, 519 U.S. 1009 (1996).
40. *See* Ward v. Rock Against Racism, 491 U.S. 781 (1989). *See also* Clark v. Community for Creative Non-Violence, 468 U.S. 288 (1984) (defining "content neutral" as "justified without reference to the content of the regulated speech").
41. Rubin v. Coors Brewing Co., 514 U.S. 476 (1995).

INTERNATIONAL CONSIDERATION

In 1998, the head of the Internet provider CompuServe in Germany was found guilty by a Munich court of being an accomplice in spreading child pornography because the company failed to block access to sites with child pornography. The German Act on the Dissemination of Publications Morally Harmful to Youth prohibits not only obscene materials but also any materials that are harmful to minors. In November 1999, a German appeals court overturned the verdict on the grounds that the CompuServe executive was covered by a clause of a 1997 German multimedia law that states that Internet providers are not responsible for content to which they provide access.[a]

In November 2000, a French court ordered Yahoo! to prevent Internet users in France from accessing auction sites with Nazi paraphernalia.[b] A French law prohibits selling or displaying items that incite racism. Although Yahoo! had argued that it was not technologically possible to block French users from the auction sites, a court-appointed panel of experts concluded that it would be possible to prevent up to 90 percent of French Internet surfers from accessing the sites.

a. *Roundup: In Test Case, German Court Acquits Ex-CompuServe Executive of Porn Charges*, DEUTSCHE PRESSE-AGENTUR, Nov. 17, 1999.
b. John Tagliabue, *French Uphold Ruling Against Yahoo on Nazi Sites*, N.Y. TIMES, Nov. 21, 2000, at C8.

In 1996, the Court struck down a forty-year-old Rhode Island statute that prohibited the advertisement of liquor prices except at the point of sale.[42] Rhode Island asserted its interest in promoting temperance and argued that the law prevented retailers from competing on price and thereby encouraging alcohol consumption. The Court accepted that interest as legitimate but found the statute too restrictive to meet Free Speech Clause standards. Although commercial speech generally receives less protection than political speech under the First Amendment, the Court recognized a limit to that diminished standard: "[W]hen a State entirely prohibits the dissemination of truthful, nonmisleading commercial messages for reasons unrelated to the preservation of a fair bargaining process, there is far less reason to depart from the rigorous review that the First Amendment generally demands."

Gambling In the following case, the Supreme Court struck down a federal ban on radio and television advertising about privately operated casino gambling.

---

42. 44 Liquormart, Inc. v. Rhode Island, 517 U.S. 484 (1996).

A CASE IN POINT

CASE 2.3

Greater New Orleans Broadcasting Association, Inc. v. United States

Supreme Court of the United States
527 U.S. 173 (1999).

Summary

FACTS Section 1304 of the Communications Act[43] and a related Federal Communications Commission (FCC) regulation prohibited radio and television broadcasters from carrying advertising about privately operated commercial casino gambling. Advertisements for tribal casino gambling and for government-operated, nonprofit, and "occasional and ancillary" commercial casinos were permitted. An association of Louisiana broadcasters and its members wanted to run advertisements for private commercial casinos on their FCC-licensed radio and television stations in the New Orleans metropolitan area. The casinos were legal in Louisiana and Mississippi. However, broadcast signals from Louisiana stations could be heard in neighboring states, such as Texas and Arkansas, where casino gambling was unlawful. The broadcasters claimed that Section 1304 violated the First Amendment and sought an injunction preventing enforcement of the ban.

ISSUE PRESENTED Does a federal ban on radio and television advertising by privately operated commercial casinos violate the broadcasters' right to free speech?

SUMMARY OF OPINION The U.S. Supreme Court applied the four-part test established in *Central Hudson Gas & Electric Corp. v. Public Service Commercial*[44] for restrictions on "commercial" speech. The test asks (1) whether the speech at issue concerns lawful activity and is not misleading; (2) whether the asserted governmental interest is substantial; if so, (3) whether the regulation directly advances the governmental interest asserted; and (4) whether the regulation is more extensive than is necessary to serve that interest. The Court found that the first part of the test was satisfied: private casino gambling was legal in Louisiana and Mississippi, and the messages to be broadcast were not misleading. With respect to the second part of the test, the Court reluctantly accepted the argument that the government was interested in reducing the social costs associated with gambling (such as corruption and organized crime) and in assisting states that prohibit gambling. The Court noted, however, that Congress and many state legislatures have often found that the social costs of gambling are outweighed by its economic benefits.

The Court found that Section 1304 could not satisfy the third and fourth prongs of the test. The speech ban did not directly and materially further the asserted interest—alleviating the social costs of casino gambling by limiting demand:

> While it is no doubt fair to assume that more advertising would have some impact on overall demand for gambling, it is also reasonable to assume that much of that advertising would merely channel gamblers to one casino rather than another. More important, any measure of the effectiveness of the Government's attempt to minimize the social costs of gambling cannot ignore Congress' simultaneous encouragement of tribal casino gambling, which may well be growing at a rate exceeding any increase in gambling or compulsive gambling that private casino advertising could produce.

The Court concluded that "[t]he operation of §1304 and its attendant regulatory regime is so pierced by exemptions and inconsistencies that the Government cannot hope to exonerate it."

RESULT Section 1304 may not be applied to advertisements of lawful private casino gambling that are broadcast by radio or television stations located in a state where gambling is legal.

---

43. 18 U.S.C. § 1304.
44. 447 U.S. 557 (1980).

(Continued)

(Case 2.3 continued)

QUESTIONS

1. In light of the Court's reasoning, are there any restrictions on casino advertising that it would uphold?

2. What other laws could Congress enact to minimize the social costs of gambling? Would these violate any other rights under the Constitution?

Nonspeech Business The First Amendment also protects seemingly nonspeech business. The U.S. Court of Appeals for the Ninth Circuit affirmed a lower court's decision enjoining California's Santa Clara County from enforcing its ban on gun sales at the county's fairgrounds.[45] The county argued that rather than regulating speech, the ban regulated the unprotected conduct of selling guns. The trial court had found that "some type of speech is necessarily involved in the sale of any gun,"[46] and the appeals court ruled that the offer to buy constituted commercial speech. Although the county asserted an interest in curtailing gun possession, the court ruled that the ban did not directly advance that interest.

45. Nordyke v. Santa Clara County, Cal., 110 F.3d 707 (9th Cir. 1997).
46. Nordyke v. Santa Clara County, Cal., 933 F. Supp. 903 (N.D. Cal. 1996).

 INTERNATIONAL CONSIDERATION

In 1989, the Canadian Parliament responded to the anti-smoking lobby by passing the Tobacco Products Control Act, which banned all tobacco advertising and promotion and required unattributed health warnings to be printed on all tobacco products. Cigarette manufacturers challenged the law as a violation of their right to free speech, which is protected by the Canadian Charter of Rights and Freedoms. In overturning much of the Act six years later, the Supreme Court of Canada reasoned: "Smoking is a legal activity yet consumers are deprived of an important means of learning about product availability to suit their preferences and to compare brand content with an aim to reducing the risk to their health."[a] The Court stated that the Canadian Parliament does not have the right to determine unilaterally the limits of its intrusion on the rights and freedoms guaranteed by the Charter. The Court concluded that the Act's infringements on the right to free speech were neither reasonable nor "demonstrably justified in a free and democratic society."

a. RJR-MacDonald v. Attorney Gen. of Canada [1995] 127 D.L.R. 4th 1 [Can.].

Encryption In 2000, the U.S. Court of Appeals for the Sixth Circuit ruled that encryption software posted by a professor on a university Web site is entitled to First Amendment protection.[47] The appeals court reasoned: "Because computer source code is an expressive means for the exchange of information and ideas about computer programming, we hold that it is protected by the First Amendment." In January 2000, the Clinton administration published amended regulations allowing most encryption software to be exported without a license to nongovernmental entities. The professor challenged the new regulations as vague, overly broad, and an impermissible prior restraint in violation of the First and Fifth Amendments. The appeals court subjected the regulations to intermediate scrutiny, requiring the government to prove that they furthered a governmental interest that was "important" or "substantial." In addition, the government was required to prove that the regulations sought to prevent real, not conjectural, harm "in a direct and material way."

English-Only Laws Freedom of speech issues also arise in connection with "English-only" laws, requiring that all government business be conducted in English. This is discussed in Chapter 15.

PRIOR RESTRAINTS

Prior restraints of speech, such as prohibiting in advance a demonstration in a public area, are considered a more drastic infringement on free speech than permitting the speech to occur but punishing it afterward. Restrictions concerning the time, place, and manner of speech are usually acceptable under the First Amendment, but regulations that restrict speech in traditional public forums are scrutinized closely.

In 1986, the city of Dallas adopted an ordinance regulating "sexually oriented businesses," defined as any "adult arcade, adult bookstore or adult video store, adult cabaret, adult motel, adult motion picture theater, adult theater, escort agency, nude model

47. Junger v. Daley, 209 F.3d 481 (6th Cir. 2000).

studio, or sexual encounter center." The ordinance regulated such businesses through zoning, licensing, and inspections. The ordinance also banned motels that rented rooms for fewer than ten hours. The Supreme Court struck down all of the ordinance, except the ban on ten-hour motels, as a prior restraint on speech that did not comply with the procedural safeguards for that type of regulation. The Supreme Court upheld the provision prohibiting motels from renting rooms for less than ten hours. (Such rooms are often used for prostitution.) Dismissing the argument that the ordinance unconstitutionally interfered with the right of association, Justice Sandra Day O'Connor stated: "Any 'personal bonds' that are formed from the use of a motel room for less than 10 hours are not those that have 'played a critical role in the culture and traditions of the nation by cultivating and transmitting shared ideals and beliefs.'"[48] Similarly, in 2000, the Supreme Court upheld a ban on nude dancing.[49]

Prior restraints can be particularly problematic for members of the media, who may need to publish immediately or not at all. For example, during a suit by Procter & Gamble against Bankers Trust for negligent sale of financial derivative products, *Business Week* obtained confidential documents about both parties that had emerged from their court-approved secret discovery process. The trial court granted the litigants' request for a temporary restraining order (TRO) to keep *Business Week* from publishing the information and later enjoined the magazine from ever publishing it. The U.S. Court of Appeals for the Sixth Circuit struck down the injunction as a violation of the First Amendment.[50] Noting that "[a] prior restraint comes to a court 'with a heavy presumption against its constitutional validity,'" the appeals court found the trial court's grounds for granting the TRO insufficient to meet the high standard required for prior restraint.

48. FW/PBS, Inc. v. City of Dallas, 493 U.S. 215 (1990).
49. City of Erie v. Pap's A.M., 120 S. Ct. 1382 (2000).
50. Procter & Gamble v. Bankers Trust. 78 F.3d 219 (6th Cir. 1996).

 # Right *of* Association

Closely related to the right to free speech and freedom of the press is the constitutional right of association. Like freedom of speech, this right is most protected when an association is formed for political ends. In 2000, the Supreme Court struck down California's law requiring political parties to hold open primaries, in which any registered voter could vote to select that party's candidate for elected office.[51] The Court reasoned:

> Proposition 198 forces petitioners to adulterate their candidate-selection process—the 'basic function of a political party'—by opening it up to persons wholly unaffiliated with the party. Such forced association has the likely outcome—indeed, in this case the intended outcome—of changing the parties' message. We can think of no heavier burden on a political party's associational freedom.

Similar issues arise when city or state governments enact laws banning discriminatory clubs. The courts will balance the First Amendment rights of association and free speech against the government's social policy against discrimination. To increase the likelihood that such laws will be upheld, most antidiscrimination statutes apply only to clubs of a certain size where business is conducted.

In *Warfield v. Peninsula Golf Country Club*,[52] the California Supreme Court held that a private country club that allowed nonmembers, for a fee, to use its golf course, tennis courts, or dining areas was a "business establishment" and therefore subject to the state law prohibiting discrimination against women and minorities. It will generally be assumed that business is conducted in a private club if the members' employers pay for club dues, meals, or drinks or if the club is the site of company-sponsored events.

In the following case, the Supreme Court considered whether a New Jersey ban on discrimination based on sexual orientation could be constitutionally applied to the Boy Scouts.

51. California Democratic Party v. Jones, 120 S. Ct. 2402 (2000).
52. 896 P.2d 776 (Cal. 1995).

A CASE IN POINT

CASE 2.4
Boy Scouts of America v. Dale
Supreme Court of the United States
120 S. Ct. 2446 (2000).

In the Language of the Court

FACTS The Boy Scouts of America is a private, nonprofit organization engaged in instilling values in young people. James Dale became a Boy Scout when he was eight years old and remained a Scout until he turned eighteen in 1989. He was an exemplary Scout and achieved the rank of Eagle Scout, one of the organization's highest honors. In 1989, Dale was approved for adult membership with the position of assistant scoutmaster.

Around that time, he left home to attend Rutgers University and acknowledged to himself and others that he was gay. After being interviewed about the psychological and

(Continued)

(Case 2.4 continued)

health needs of gay and lesbian teenagers and having his picture in the paper, Dale received a letter from the Boy Scouts revoking his adult membership because the group forbids membership to homosexuals.

Dale filed a complaint against the Boy Scouts in New Jersey Superior Court, alleging that the Boy Scouts had violated New Jersey's public accommodations statute, which prohibits discrimination on the basis of sexual orientation in places of public accommodation. After the New Jersey Supreme Court ruled that the public accommodations statute applied to the Boy Scouts and that the First Amendment did not provide protection, the Boy Scouts appealed.

ISSUE PRESENTED Does application of New Jersey's public accommodations law prohibiting discrimination on the basis of sexual orientation violate the Boy Scouts' First Amendment right of association?

OPINION REHNQUIST, C.J., writing for the U.S. Supreme Court:

"[I]mplicit in the right to engage in activities protected by the First Amendment" is "a corresponding right to association with others in pursuit of a wide variety of political, social, economic, educational, religious, and cultural ends." This right is crucial in preventing the majority from imposing its views on groups that would rather express other, perhaps unpopular, ideas.

...

The forced inclusion of an unwanted person in a group infringes the group's freedom of expressive association if the presence of that person affects in a significant way the group's ability to advocate public or private viewpoints. But the freedom of expressive association, like many freedoms, is not absolute. We have held that the freedom could be overridden "by regulations adopted to serve compelling state interests, unrelated to the suppression of ideas, that cannot be achieved through means significantly less restrictive of associational freedoms."

...

[T]he general mission of the Boy Scouts is clear: "To instill values in young people." The Boy Scouts seeks to instill these values by having its adult leaders spend time with the youth members, instructing and engaging them in activities like camping, archery, and fishing. During the time spent with the youth members, the scoutmasters and assistant scoutmasters inculcate them with the Boy Scouts' values—both expressly and by example. It seems indisputable that an association that seeks to transmit such a system of values engages in expressive activity.

...

The Boy Scouts asserts that it "teaches that homosexual conduct is not morally straight," and that it does "not want to promote homosexual conduct as a legitimate form of behavior." We accept the Boy Scouts' assertion. We need not inquire further to determine the nature of the Boy Scouts' expression with respect to homosexuality.

...

We must then determine whether Dale's presence as an assistant scoutmaster would significantly burden the Boy Scouts' desire to not "promote homosexual conduct as a legitimate form of behavior." As we give deference to an association's assertion regarding the nature of its expression, we must also give deference to an association's view of what would impair its expression. That is not to say that an expressive association can erect a shield against antidiscrimination laws simply by asserting that mere acceptance of a member from a particular group would impair its message. But here

(Continued)

(Case 2.4 continued)

Dale, by his own admission, is one of a group of gay Scouts who have "become leaders in their community and are open and honest about their sexual orientation."

...

Having determined that the Boy Scouts is an expressive association and that the forced inclusion of Dale would significantly affect its expression, we inquire whether the application of New Jersey's public accommodations law to require that the Boy Scouts accept Dale as an assistant scoutmaster runs afoul of the Scouts' freedom of expressive association. We conclude that it does.

...

We have already concluded that a state requirement that the Boy Scouts retain Dale as an assistant scoutmaster would significantly burden the organization's right to oppose or disfavor homosexual conduct. The state interests embodied in New Jersey's public accommodations law do not justify such a severe intrusion on the Boy Scouts' rights to freedom of expressive association.

RESULT The Supreme Court reversed the New Jersey Supreme Court. The Boy Scouts were not required to admit homosexuals as members or scoutmasters.

DISSENT STEVENS, J., dissenting from the majority opinion:

Unfavorable opinions about homosexuals "have ancient roots." Like equally atavistic opinions about certain racial groups, those roots have been nourished by sectarian doctrine. Over the years, however, interaction with real people, rather than mere adherence to traditional ways of thinking about members of unfamiliar classes, have modified those opinions. A few examples: The American Psychiatric Association's and the American Psychological Association's removal of "homosexuality" from their lists of mental disorders; a move toward greater understanding within some religious communities; . . . and New Jersey's enactment of the provision at issue in this case. Indeed, the past month alone has witnessed some remarkable changes in attitudes about homosexuals [with observance of Gay Pride Day by sixty CIA workers, car manufacturers' extension of benefits to gay couples, and the acceptance of gay couples as role models at Exeter].

That such prejudices are still prevalent and that they have caused serious and tangible harm to countless members of the class New Jersey seeks to protect are established matters of fact neither the Boy Scouts nor the Court disputes. That harm can only be aggravated by the creation of a constitutional shield for a policy that is itself the product of a habitual way of thinking about strangers. As Justice Brandeis has wisely advised, "we must be ever on our guard, lest we erect our prejudices into legal principles."

If we would guide by the light of reason, we must let our minds be bold. I respectfully dissent.

 # Freedom *of* Religion

Two clauses of the First Amendment deal with religion: the Establishment Clause and the Free Exercise Clause. The Establishment Clause prohibits the establishment of a religion by the federal government. The same ban applies to state governments through the Due Process Clause of the Fourteenth Amendment. The Free Exer-

cise Clause prohibits certain, but not all, restrictions on the practice of religion.

The government must remain neutral in matters of religion. The Supreme Court has prohibited teacher- and student-led prayer (including benedictions at football games and graduations) in public schools,[53] although it

53. Santa Fe Independent School Dist. v. Doe, 120 S. Ct. 2266 (2000).

has permitted the federal government to provide secular books and other teaching materials and supplies to parochial schools on the same basis that they are given to public schools.[54] Proponents of a voucher system, which would give parents the right to use government funds to pay for the public, private, or parochial school of their choice, heralded the latter decision.

The Supreme Court upheld the imposition of general taxes on the sale of religious materials.[55] The tax was only a small fraction of any sale, and it applied neutrally to all relevant sales regardless of the nature of the seller or purchaser. Accordingly, it did not contravene the Free Exercise Clause of the First Amendment. The Court also held that the tax did not violate the Establishment Clause. There was little evidence of administrative entanglement between religion and the government; the government was not involved in the organization's day-to-day activities. The imposition of the tax did not require the state to inquire into the religious content of the items sold or the religious motivation behind selling or purchasing them.

In *Employment Division, Oregon Department of Human Resources v. Smith,*[56] the Supreme Court upheld an Oregon statute that made criminal the use of peyote, an hallucinogenic drug, even though peyote is used in Native American religious ceremonies. In deciding *Smith,* the Court overturned precedent that required courts hearing Free Exercise challenges to apply the stricter compelling-state-interest test. Instead, the Court ruled that generally applicable laws that burden but do not target religion need not be justified by a compelling state interest to pass muster under the Free Exercise Clause. Congress responded by passing the Religious Freedom and Restoration Act (RFRA), which attempted to strengthen religious freedom by codifying the prior strict scrutiny standard. The Supreme Court subsequently struck down RFRA as an unconstitutional encroachment by Congress on the powers of the judiciary to interpret the Constitution.[57]

Religion in government offices is a difficult issue that may bring the Establishment and Free Exercise Clauses into conflict. In 1996, the U.S. Court of Appeals for the Ninth Circuit ruled unconstitutional a near total ban on religious activity in the workplace imposed by the California Department of Education's Child Nutrition and Food Distribution Division.[58] Tensions arose in the di-

vision between computer analyst Monte Tucker and his supervisor after Tucker refused to stop signing office memos with his name and the acronym "SOTLJC," which stood for "Servant of the Lord Jesus Christ." After several warnings, the supervisor suspended Tucker and ordered all employees not to display religious materials outside their cubicles, not to engage in any religious advocacy, and not to put any acronym or other symbol on office communications. Although the state argued its interests in avoiding workplace disruption and the appearance of religious endorsement (which would constitute a violation of the Establishment Clause), the appeals court found such interests outweighed by Tucker's constitutional right to talk about religion. Such issues also come up in the private sector, which is regulated by various statutes barring discrimination based on religion.

Due Process

The Due Process Clauses of the Fifth Amendment (which applies to the federal government) and the Fourteenth Amendment (which applies to the states) prohibit governments from depriving any person of life, liberty, or property without due process of law. *Procedural due process* focuses on the fairness of the legal proceeding. *Substantive due process* focuses on the fundamental rights protected by the Due Process Clauses.

PROCEDURAL DUE PROCESS

Whenever a governmental action affects a person's life, liberty, or property, the due process requirement applies, and some form of notice and hearing is required. Explaining the notice requirement, the Supreme Court stated:

> An elementary and fundamental requirement of due process in any proceeding which is to be accorded finality is notice, reasonably calculated, under all the circumstances, to apprise interested parties of the pendency of the action and afford them an opportunity to present their objections. . . . The notice must be of such nature as reasonably to convey the required information, and it must afford a reasonable time for those interested to make their appearance.[59]

The type of hearing varies depending on the nature of the action, but some opportunity to be heard must be provided. In general, greater procedural protections are

54. Mitchell v. Helms, 120 S. Ct. 2530 (2000).
55. Jimmy Swaggart Ministries v. Board of Equalization, 493 U.S. 378 (1990).
56. 494 U.S. 872 (1990).
57. City of Boerne v. Flores, 521 U.S. 507 (1997).
58. Tucker v. State of Cal. Dep't of Ed., 97 F.3d 1204 (9th Cir. 1996).

59. Mullane v. Central Hanover Bank & Trust Co., 339 U.S. 306 (1950).

afforded to criminal defendants because the possibility of imprisonment and even death in capital cases is at stake.

The Due Process Clause of the Fourteenth Amendment has been interpreted to make virtually all of the procedural requirements in the Bill of Rights applicable to state criminal proceedings. These rights are discussed in Chapter 17.

SUBSTANTIVE DUE PROCESS

Disputes have raged over the years as to what fundamental rights people in our society possess, with which the government may not interfere. It has been argued that such rights and liberty interests, including the right to privacy, are guaranteed by the Due Process Clauses of the Fifth and Fourteenth Amendments. This protection of fundamental rights is known as substantive due process. The notion of substantive due process was not wholeheartedly received by the Supreme Court until the end of the nineteenth century, mainly because substantive due process rights are not specifically listed in the Constitution.

Limit on Economic Regulation The Supreme Court first invalidated a state law on substantive due process grounds in 1897.[60] A Louisiana law prohibited anyone from obtaining insurance on Louisiana property from any marine insurance company that had not complied in all respects with Louisiana law. The Court held that the statute violated the fundamental right to make contracts.

Early in the twentieth century, the concept was applied to more controversial areas, such as state statutes limiting working hours. In *Lochner v. New York*,[61] the Supreme Court struck down a New York statute that prohibited the employment of bakery employees for more than ten hours a day or sixty hours a week. The Court held that the statute interfered with the employers' and employees' fundamental right to contract with each other. Subsequently, in the period from 1905 to 1937, the Supreme Court invoked the doctrine of substantive due process to invalidate a number of laws relating to regulation of prices, labor relations, and conditions for entry into business.

In 1937, the Supreme Court reversed direction. After President Franklin Delano Roosevelt threatened to "pack" the Court (discussed in the "Inside Story"), the justices upheld a minimum wage law for women in Washington,[62] overruling an earlier decision striking down a similar statute. In 1938, the Court upheld a statute that prohibited the interstate shipment of "filled" milk (milk to which any fat or oil other than milk fat has been added).[63] The Court made clear that if any set of facts, either known or imaginable, provides a rational basis for the legislation, the legislation will not be held to violate substantive due process. Under this test, economic regulation is rarely constrained by economic liberty.

Protection of Fundamental Rights Substantive due process challenges are given more weight when fundamental rights other than the right to make contracts are at issue. Fundamental rights and liberty interests protected by the Due Process Clause include the guarantees of the Bill of Rights, the right to marry and to have children, the right to raise children, the right to travel, the right to vote, and the right to associate with other people. The Supreme Court has made clear that the fundamental rights protected by substantive due process are not limited to those specifically enumerated in the Constitution or the Bill of Rights. Legislation that limits fundamental rights violates substantive due process unless it can be shown to promote a compelling or overriding government interest.

Right to Privacy Substantive due process was extended to the right to privacy in *Griswold v. Connecticut*.[64] The executive director of the Planned Parenthood League of Connecticut and a physician who served as medical director for the league at its center in New Haven were arrested. They were charged with giving birth control advice in violation of a Connecticut statute that prohibited the use of any drug, medicinal article, or instrument for the purpose of preventing conception.

In finding that the Connecticut statute was an unconstitutional invasion of individuals' right to privacy, the Supreme Court discussed the penumbra of rights surrounding each guarantee in the Bill of Rights. The Court defined *penumbra* as the peripheral rights that are implied by the specifically enumerated rights. For example, the Court noted that the First Amendment's freedom of the press necessarily includes the right to distribute, the right to receive, the right to read, freedom of inquiry, freedom of thought, freedom to teach, and freedom of association. The Fourth Amendment, which prohibits unreasonable searches and seizures, similarly includes a "right to privacy, no less important than any other right carefully and particularly reserved to the people." The Supreme Court found that the Connecticut statute encroached on the right to privacy in marriage.

60. Allegeyer v. Louisiana, 165 U.S. 578 (1897).
61. 198 U.S. 45 (1905).
62. West Coast Hotel Co. v. Parrish, 300 U.S. 379 (1937).

63. United States v. Carolene Products Co., 304 U.S. 144 (1938).
64. 381 U.S. 479 (1965).

The right to privacy is an essential element in the debate between pro-choice and pro-life groups concerning a woman's right to an abortion. It is relevant in other areas as well. For example, the Supreme Court upheld a person's right to refuse life-sustaining treatment (such as lifesaving hydration and nutrition)[65] but declined to recognize a right to physician-assisted suicide.[66] In another case,[67] a schoolteacher successfully sued a board of education, alleging that it had not renewed her teaching contract because she was an unwed mother and her pregnancy had been by means of artificial insemination. The district court held that a woman has a constitutional privacy right to become pregnant by means of artificial insemination.

65. Cruzan v. Director, Mo. Dep't of Health, 497 U.S. 261 (1990).
66. Washington v. Glucksberg, 521 U.S. 702 (1997).
67. Cameron v. Board of Educ., 795 F. Supp. 228 (S.D. Ohio 1991).

Mandatory drug testing also presents privacy issues. The Supreme Court has upheld certain regulations concerning drug testing for public employees. This issue is discussed in Chapter 14.

Limit on Punitive Damages In certain cases involving torts, or civil wrongs, the jury is entitled to award the plaintiff not only compensatory damages equal to the plaintiff's actual loss but also punitive or exemplary damages, designed to punish and make an example of the defendant. Usually, the size of the punitive damages bears some relationship to the size of the compensatory damages and the degree of reprehensibility. The following case addressed the issue of whether an award of punitive damages that was 500 times the amount of compensatory damages was so excessive as to violate substantive due process.

A CASE IN POINT

CASE 2.5
BMW of North America, Inc. v. Gore
Supreme Court of the United States
517 U.S. 559 (1996).

In the Language of the Court

FACTS BMW of North America had a nationwide policy of not advising its dealers, and hence the ultimate customers, of predelivery damage to new cars when the cost of repair did not exceed 3 percent of the car's suggested retail price. As a result of this policy, Ira Gore, Jr., unwittingly purchased a BMW car that had been damaged in transit and then repainted. When he learned that his BMW had been repainted, Gore brought an action against BMW, BMW's American distributor, and an authorized Alabama BMW dealer based on the distributor's failure to disclose that his BMW had been repainted after being damaged prior to delivery. A jury awarded Gore compensatory damages of $4,000 and punitive damages of $4 million. The Alabama Supreme Court affirmed the judgment after reducing the punitive award to $2 million. BMW appealed.

ISSUE PRESENTED Is a $2 million punitive award arising from actions justifying only $4,000 of compensatory damages so excessive as to violate the Due Process Clause of the Fourteenth Amendment?

OPINION STEVENS, J., writing for the U.S. Supreme Court:

The Due Process Clause of the Fourteenth Amendment prohibits a State from imposing a "grossly excessive" punishment on a tort feasor. . . .

...

III

Elementary notions of fairness enshrined in our constitutional jurisprudence dictate that a person receive fair notice not only of the conduct that will subject him to punishment but also of the severity of the penalty that a State may impose. Three guideposts, each of which indicates that BMW did not receive adequate notice of the magnitude of the sanction that Alabama might impose for adhering to the nondisclosure policy adopted in 1983, lead us to the conclusion that the $2 million award against BMW is grossly excessive: the degree of reprehensibility of the nondisclosure; the disparity between the harm or potential harm suffered by Dr. Gore and his punitive

(Continued)

(Case 2.5 continued)

damages award; and the difference between this remedy and the civil penalties authorized or imposed in comparable cases. We discuss these considerations in turn.

Degree of Reprehensibility

Perhaps the most important indicium of the reasonableness of a punitive damages award is the degree of reprehensibility of the defendant's conduct.

...

In this case, none of the aggravating factors associated with particularly reprehensible conduct is present. . . .

...

Ratio

The second and perhaps most commonly cited indicium of an unreasonable or excessive punitive damages award is its ratio to the actual harm inflicted on the plaintiff. The principle that exemplary damages must bear a "reasonable relationship" to compensatory damages has a long pedigree. . . .

[T]he proper inquiry is "whether there is a reasonable relationship between the punitive damages award and the harm likely to result from the defendant's conduct as well as the harm that actually has occurred."[68] . . .

...

Of course, we have consistently rejected the notion that the constitutional line is marked by a simple mathematical formula, even one that compares actual and potential damages to the punitive award. . . . When the ratio is a breathtaking 500 to 1, however, the award must surely "raise a suspicious judicial eyebrow."

Sanctions for Comparable Misconduct

Comparing the punitive damages award and the civil or criminal penalties that could be imposed for comparable misconduct provides a third indicium of excessiveness. . . . In this case the $2 million economic sanction imposed on BMW is substantially greater than the statutory fines available in Alabama and elsewhere for similar malfeasance.

RESULT The Supreme Court reversed the judgment of the Alabama Supreme Court and ruled that the $2 million punitive damages award was so excessive as to violate the Due Process Clause of the Fourteenth Amendment. The Court remanded the case to Alabama for reconsideration of constitutional punitive damages.

COMMENTS Justice Ginsburg, dissenting from the decision, claimed that the Court "unnecessarily and unwisely ventures into territory traditionally within the States' domain" by ruling for BMW. Similarly, Justice Scalia dissented and argued: "At the time of the adoption of the Fourteenth Amendment, it was well understood that punitive damages represent the assessment by the jury, as the voice of the community, of the measure of punishment the defendant deserved."

QUESTIONS

1. What guidelines does the notion of "substantive due process" articulated by the Court give a manager contemplating a policy such as BMW's?
2. BMW deceived its customers by selling them cosmetically imperfect products. Would the result have been any different if BMW had cut costs by installing inexpensive and unreliable fuel injection systems? Air bags? Seats?

68. TXO Production Corp. v. Alliance Resources Corp., 509 U.S. 443 (1993).

Another due process concern in awarding punitive damages is the availability of judicial review of the amount. Along with the substantive due process requirement illustrated in *BMW,* there is a procedural due process requirement that such awards be subject to appellate review. In *Honda Motor Co. v. Oberg,*[69] an Oregon jury had awarded $5 million in punitive damages to a plaintiff injured in a three-wheel all-terrain vehicle accident. Although Honda wished to appeal the penalty, Oregon's constitution barred review of punitive awards unless there was no evidence to support the jury's decision. The U.S. Supreme Court found the Oregon rule in violation of due process and insufficient to protect Honda's constitutional rights.

 ## Compensation *for* Takings

One of the first provisions of the Bill of Rights incorporated into the Fourteenth Amendment was the Fifth Amendment provision that private property may not be taken for public use without just compensation. State and federal governments have the power of *eminent domain,* which is the power to take property for public uses such as building a school, park, or airport. If property is taken from a private owner for such a purpose, the owner is entitled to just compensation. A more complex situation arises when the government does not physically take the property but imposes regulations that restrict its use. If the regulation amounts to a taking of the property, the owner is entitled to just compensation. In a sense, all regulation takes some aspect of property away from the owner. The question is when does a regulation constitute a taking that requires compensation.

In one instance, the Supreme Court held that there was a taking when a homeowner was required to grant a public right-of-way through his property in order to obtain a building permit to replace his oceanfront house with a larger one.[70] Another case involved the Federal Communications Commission's regulation of the rates a utility company could charge for the attachment of television cables to the utility company's poles. The Supreme Court held that the regulation was not a taking, as long as the rates were not set so low as to be unjust and confiscatory.[71]

In another case, Penn Central Transportation Company, the owner of Grand Central Station in midtown Manhattan, was prohibited from constructing an office building above the station. The prohibition was ordered by the Landmarks Preservation Commission, which had designated the station a landmark. Under New York City law, the commission could prevent any alteration of the fundamental character of such buildings. A high-rise would arguably have altered the fundamental character of Grand Central Station. The Supreme Court found that the prohibition was not a taking.[72] This case, as well as other land-use taking cases, are discussed in Chapter 19.

In *Eastern Enterprises v. Apfel,*[73] the Supreme Court invalidated the Coal Industry Retiree Health Benefits Act of 1992 under which a former coal mine operator, Eastern Enterprises, was required to contribute an annual premium of $5 million to a health fund for coal workers. Eastern Enterprises had ceased its mine operations in 1987. The Act was enacted to remedy the shortfalls in the preexisting multi-employer benefits plans the coal industry had negotiated with the United Mine Workers union. It required all companies that had signed on to the union plans to contribute to a new health fund and to pay for their former employees even if the amount exceeded a company's obligation under the negotiated plan. The Supreme Court held that the Act was an unconstitutional "taking" of private property without compensation. The Court stated that a law violates the Fifth Amendment if "[1] it imposes a severe retroactive liability [2] on a limited class of parties that could not have anticipated the liability, and [3] the extent of the liability is substantially disproportionate to the parties' experience." Chapter 18 discusses two environmental cases in which the defendants unsuccessfully argued that, in light of *Enterprises v. Apfel,* environmental statutes imposing cleanup costs could not be applied to activities that predated the statutes' enactment.

 ## Equal Protection

The Equal Protection Clause of the Fourteenth Amendment places another limitation on the power of state governments to regulate. A comparable limitation is imposed on the federal government by the Due Process Clause of the Fifth Amendment. The Equal Protection Clause provides that no state shall "deny to any person within its jurisdiction the equal protection of the laws." The Supreme Court's interpretation of this clause continues to be the subject of much debate.

---

69. 512 U.S. 415 (1994).
70. Nollan v. California Coastal Comm'n, 483 U.S. 825 (1987).
71. FCC v. Florida Power Corp., 480 U.S. 245 (1987).

72. Penn Central Transp. Co. v. New York City, 438 U.S. 104 (1978).
73. 524 U.S. 498 (1998).

ESTABLISHING DISCRIMINATION

In order to challenge a statute on equal protection grounds, it is first necessary to establish that the statute discriminates against a class of persons. Discrimination may be found on the face of the statute, in its application, or in its purpose. The statute may (1) explicitly (on its face) treat different classes of persons differently; (2) contain no classification, but government officials may apply it differently to different classes of people; or (3) be neutral on its face and in its application but have the purpose of creating different burdens for different classes of persons.

In determining whether a facially neutral law is a device to discriminate against certain classes of people, the Supreme Court looks at three things: (1) the practical or statistical impact of the statute on different classes of persons, (2) the history of the problems that the statute seeks to solve, and (3) the legislative history of the statute. Even if a government action has a disproportionate effect on a racial minority group, it will be upheld if there was no racially discriminatory purpose or intent.[74]

VALIDITY OF DISCRIMINATION

The Supreme Court uses three tests to determine the constitutionality of various types of discrimination, depending on how the statute classifies the persons concerned.

Rational Basis Test The *rational basis test* applies to all classifications that relate to matters of economics or social welfare. Under this test, a classification will be held valid if there is any conceivable basis on which the classification might relate to a legitimate governmental interest. It is a rare regulation that cannot meet this minimal standard. For example, a system of progressive taxation, in which persons with higher income are required to pay taxes at a higher marginal rate, passes muster under this test.

Strict Scrutiny Test A classification that determines who may exercise a fundamental right or a classification based on a suspect trait, such as race, is subject to strict scrutiny. Under the *strict scrutiny test*, a classification will be held valid only if it is necessary to promote a compelling state interest and is narrowly tailored to achieve that interest. The right to privacy, the right to vote, the right to travel, and certain other guarantees in the Bill of Rights are fundamental rights. Rights such as welfare payments, housing, education, and government employment are not fundamental rights.

Substantially Related Test The Supreme Court occasionally applies a third test, which is stricter than the rational basis test but less strict than strict scrutiny. This intermediate test applies to classifications such as gender and legitimacy of birth. Under this test, a classification will be upheld if it is substantially related to an important governmental interest.

RACIAL DISCRIMINATION

Racial discrimination was the major target of the Fourteenth Amendment, so it is clear that racial classifications are suspect. Nonetheless, from 1896 to 1954, the "separate but equal" doctrine allowed governments to provide separate services for minorities as long as they were equal to the services provided for whites. For example, in *Plessy v. Ferguson*,[75] the Supreme Court upheld a law requiring all railway companies to provide separate but equal accommodations for African-American and white passengers. Fifty-eight years later, the Supreme Court held in *Brown v. Board of Education*[76] that the doctrine had no place in education. The justices unanimously ruled that the "segregation of children in public schools solely on the basis of race, even though the physical facilities and other 'tangible' factors may be equal, deprives the children of the minority group of equal educational opportunities." Supreme Court rulings following *Brown* made it clear that no governmental entity may segregate people because of their race or national origin.

Complications concerning racial classifications have arisen more recently in the area of affirmative action intended to benefit racial or ethnic minorities. A debate raged over whether strict scrutiny should be applied only to legislation that discriminates against a minority or to any legislation that generally discriminates based on race. The Supreme Court resolved that issue in *Adarand Constructors, Inc. v. Peña*,[77] when it held that all racial classifications—whether imposed by federal, state, or local government—are subject to strict scrutiny. In *Adarand,* the white owner of a construction company successfully challenged regulations adopted by the U.S. Department of Transportation that made use of race-based presumptions in awarding lucrative federal highway project contracts to economically disadvantaged businesses. The Court rejected the argument it had accepted in an earlier

---

74. Arlington Height v. Metropolitan Hous. Dev. Corp., 429 U.S. 252 (1977) (upholding a largely white suburb's refusal to rezone to permit multifamily dwellings for low- and moderate-income tenants, including members of racial minorities).

75. 163 U.S. 537 (1896).
76. 347 U.S. 483 (1954).
77. 515 U.S. 200 (1995).

case[78] that because the Equal Protection Clause was adopted after the Civil War to protect African Americans, it permits "benign" racial classifications to protect minorities as long as there is a rational basis for the classification.

78. Metro Broadcasting, Inc. v. FCC, 497 U.S. 547 (1990) (upholding two minority-preference policies mandated by Congress to achieve broadcast diversity).

A number of cases have raised the question of whether universities and schools can consider an applicant's race when deciding whether to admit the student. In the following case, the U.S. Court of Appeals for the Fourth Circuit considered a policy instituted by a public kindergarten for the purpose of creating diversity in the group of students admitted to the school.

CASE 2.6

Tuttle v. Arlington Country School Board

United States Court of Appeals for the Fourth Circuit 195 F.3d 698 (4th Cir. 1999), cert. denied, 120 S. Ct. 1552 (2000).

Summary

FACTS The Arlington Traditional School was an alternative public kindergarten in Arlington County, Virginia. In February 1998, the school board adopted a new policy with two goals: (1) "to prepare and educate students to live in a diverse, global society" by "reflecting the diversity of the community," and (2) to help the school board "serve the diverse groups of students in the district, including those from backgrounds that suggest they come to school with educational needs that are different from or greater than others." The policy defined diversity based on three weighted factors: (1) whether the applicant was from a low-income or special family background, (2) whether English was the applicant's first or second language, and (3) the racial or ethnic group to which the applicant belonged.

Admission to the school was based upon space availability not upon merit. The school accepted applications from the public without restriction, but, because the applicant pool was larger than the available number of positions, it used a lottery to choose which children to admit to fill the limited openings. The school offered admission first to applicants who had siblings attending the school. To fill the remaining positions, the school used a weighted lottery so that applicants from underrepresented groups, as defined by the policy, had a greater probability of being chosen.

Two prospective students, Tuttle and Sechler, had no increased probability of selection in the lottery based on their diversity-factor classifications, and they were not selected for admission in the lottery. They sued to force the school to abandon its weighted admission policy. The district court ruled in favor of the applicants on the grounds that "diversity was not a compelling governmental interest." The school appealed.

ISSUE PRESENTED Does the Equal Protection Clause permit a public school to give admission preference to persons based on race to achieve a diverse student body?

SUMMARY OF OPINION The U.S. Court of Appeals began by noting that the policy involved a racial classification, which is subject to strict scrutiny. The court noted that the Supreme Court has not decided whether diversity is a compelling governmental interest. So it assumed, without so holding, that diversity may be a compelling governmental interest and proceeded to examine whether the policy was narrowly tailored to achieve diversity.

In reviewing whether the state racial classification was narrowly tailored, the court considered (1) the efficacy of alternative race-neutral policies; (2) the planned duration of the policy; (3) the relationship between the numerical goal and the percentage of minority group members in the relevant population or work force; (4) the flexibility of the policy, including the provision of waivers if the goal cannot be met; and (5) the burden on innocent third parties.

The school board's own committee offered one or more race-neutral alternatives in its report to the superintendent, demonstrating that the school board had race-neutral

(Continued)

(Case 2.6 continued)

means to promote diversity. As for duration, the policy stated that the weighted lottery would be conducted "for the 1999–2000 school year and thereafter." The court stated that a racial classification cannot continue in perpetuity but must have a "logical stopping point."

The policy sought to achieve racial and ethnic diversity in the school's classes "in proportions that approximate the distribution of students from [racial] groups in the district's overall student population" by adjusting each child's probability of selection in the lottery based on his or her stated race. The policy did not treat applicants as individuals, and it burdened innocent third parties, namely, the young kindergarten-age children who did not meet any of the policy's diversity criteria. Because the policy was not narrowly tailored to further diversity, it violated the Equal Protection Clause.

The court found it ironic that a policy that seeks to teach young children to view people as individuals rather than as members of certain racial and ethnic groups directed those same children to identify themselves for admissions purposes as African American, Asian, Caucasian, or Hispanic. The court reasoned:

> If it is true that the Equal Protection Clause seeks ultimately to render the issue of race irrelevant in governmental decisionmaking, . . . it might not be overly utopian to begin by abandoning the insistence that young children categorize themselves according to race in a manner that will follow them throughout their education and, often, professional life.

RESULT The appeals court affirmed the trial court's decision that the policy was unconstitutional but ruled that the district court should have allowed an evidentiary hearing to give the school an opportunity to present alternative admissions policies. The permanent injunction was vacated, and the case was remanded for an evidentiary hearing.

COMMENTS In *Tuttle,* the Fourth Circuit left unanswered the question of whether diversity is a compelling state interest. In *Hopwell v. Texas,*[79] however, the Fifth Circuit ruled that diversity was not a compelling state interest. The court had concluded that current Supreme Court jurisprudence establishes that only remedial interests, aimed at reversing the current effects of past discrimination, justify racial classification. The court reasoned:

> The use of race, in and of itself, to choose students simply achieves a student body that looks different. Such a criterion is no more rational on its own terms than would be choices based upon the physical size or blood type of applicants. To believe that a person's race controls his point of view is to stereotype him. . . . Instead, individuals, with their own conceptions of life, further diversity of viewpoint.

79. 78 F.3d 932 (5th Cir. 1996), *cert. denied,* 116 S. Ct. 2581 (1996).

Similarly, in *Eisenberg v. Montgomery County Public Schools,*[80] the U.S. Court of Appeals for the Fourth Circuit held that a public school district with racially imbalanced schools could not use race or ethnicity as a factor in determining whether to allow transfers from one school to another. The court found that this policy was not narrowly tailored to remedy past discrimination.

Private employers are not limited by the Equal Protection Clause, which applies only to governmental actors, such as state and local governments, schools, and police departments. However, as explained in Chapter

80. 197 F.3d 123 (4th Cir. 1999), *cert. denied,* 120 S. Ct. 1420 (2000).

15, private entities are subject to the Civil Rights Act and other regulations imposed by federal and state antidiscrimination statutes.

OTHER FORMS OF DISCRIMINATION

Three classifications are subject to the intermediate-level (substantially related) test of heightened scrutiny: gender, illegitimacy, and alienage.

Gender In *United States v. Virginia*,[81] the Supreme Court ruled that the Virginia Military Academy, an all-male, state-supported military college, violated the Equal Protection Clause by excluding women. The Court held that classifications based on gender must (1) serve important governmental objectives, (2) be substantially related to achieving those objectives, and (3) rest on an "exceedingly persuasive justification." Justice Ruth Bader Ginsburg's majority opinion can be read to require gender classifications to meet a standard somewhere between intermediate and strict scrutiny. In prior cases, the Court (1) invalidated statutory provisions that gave female workers fewer benefits for their families than male workers; (2) upheld differential treatment for women when it was compensatory for past discrimination, but not when it unreasonably denied benefits to men; (3) upheld a statutory rape law that applied only to male offenders; (4) upheld exempting women from the draft; and (5) upheld disability insurance policies that excluded insurance benefits for costs relating to pregnancy but not other disabilities. Gender discrimination is discussed further in Chapter 15.

Illegitimacy Classifications based on the legitimacy of children will be held invalid unless substantially related to a proper interest of the state. The Supreme Court will usually look at the purpose behind the classification and will not uphold any law intended to punish children born out of wedlock.

Alienage Aliens, that is, persons who are not citizens of the United States, do not receive the protection of all constitutional guarantees, many of which apply only to citizens. For example, in 1990, the Supreme Court held that the Fourth Amendment prohibition of search and seizure without a warrant did not apply to a drug raid of an alien's premises in Mexico.[82] Because of Congress's plenary power over aliens, classifications imposed by the federal government based on alienage are valid if they are not arbitrary and unreasonable. State and local laws that classify on the basis of alienage are subject to strict scrutiny, however, except for state laws discriminating against alien participation in state government, which are evaluated under the rational basis test. Foreign organizations without property or presence in the United States also have no constitutional rights.[83]

Right *to* Jury Trial

The Seventh Amendment provides that "[i]n Suits at common law, where the value in controversy shall exceed twenty dollars, the right of trial by jury shall be preserved." The phrase "suits at common law" refers to suits in which legal rights are to be ascertained and monetary damages awarded, in contrast to suits where only equitable rights and remedies (such as injunctions) are recognized. To determine whether a particular action will resolve legal rights, a court must analyze both the nature of the issues involved and the remedy sought. In particular, a court will (1) compare the statutory actions to eighteenth-century actions brought before the American Revolution in the courts of England prior to the merger of the courts of law and equity and (2) examine the remedy sought to determine whether it is legal or equitable in nature.[84] In this two-part analysis, the second inquiry is more important than the first.

For example, in *GTFM, LLC v. TKN Sales, Inc.*,[85] GTFM, an apparel manufacturer in New York, successfully challenged the constitutionality of a Minnesota statute that required a non-Minnesota corporation to submit disputes with distributors in Minnesota to binding arbitration, even in the absence of an agreement or consent to arbitrate. The court analyzed the claims and the remedies sought by TKN, the Minnesota distributor, to determine whether they were legal or equitable claims. The court found that TKN's claim for breach of contract and for unpaid commissions sought clearly legal damages, which entitled GTFM to a jury trial. The fact that TKN also sought an equitable remedy, through its claim for reinstatement of the contract, did not defeat GTFM's right to a jury trial on the legal claims and issues.

81. 518 U.S. 515 (1996).
82. United States v. Verdugo-Urquidez, 494 U.S. 259 (1990).
83. People's Mojahedin Org. of Iran v. Department of State, 182 F.3d 17 (D.C. Cir. 1999), *cert. denied*, 120 S. Ct. 1846 (2000).
84. Chauffeurs, Teamsters & Helpers Local No. 391 v. Terry, 494 U.S. 588 (1990).
85. 2000 U.S. Dist. LEXIS 4488 (S.D.N.Y. 2000).

The Initiative Process

In 1898, South Dakota became the first state to establish a procedure whereby citizens could initiate change on their own without going through their elected representatives. During the next twenty years, eighteen other states adopted initiative processes; by the early 1990s, the number had grown to twenty-four. Unlike representative democracy, initiatives give direct legislative power to voters by allowing them to make new laws, either by amending the state constitution or by enacting legislation. Some states, such as California, do not allow the executive to veto initiatives (unlike legislation passed by representatives) and forbid repeal except by subsequent voter initiative.

Since 1898, the initiative process has been used by citizens seeking to change governmental policy on a wide range of topics, including child labor, women's suffrage, gambling, alcohol prohibition, prostitution, civil rights, the death penalty, environmental protection, and property taxes. Although more than a century old, the initiative has seen most of its use in recent years. For example, in California in the 1950s, only seventeen initiatives were circulated, and only ten qualified for the ballot. In the 1980s, citizens proposed more than two hundred initiatives and voted on more than forty.

In recent years, a number of major public policy battles have moved out of the state capitols and into the land of initiatives. In 1996, voters in California and Arizona legalized medical use of marijuana by ballot initiative. In that same year, Californians approved Proposition 209 to end racial preferences by state and local governments. One year later, voters in Houston turned down an initiative to end that city's affirmative action program. In 1994 and again in 1997, Oregon voters authorized physician-assisted suicide for competent, terminally ill adults.

Source: This discussion is based on K. K. DuVivier, *By Going Wrong All Things Come Right*, 63 U. CIN. L. REV. 1185 (1995); P. K. Jameson & Marsha Hosack, *Citizen Initiatives in Florida*, 23 FLA. ST. U. L. REV. 417 (1995); and David L. Callies et al., *Ballot Box Zoning*, 39 WASH. U. J. URB. & CONTEMP. L. 53 (1991).

THE RESPONSIBLE MANAGER
Preserving Constitutional Rights

Although the Constitution is directed primarily at establishing and limiting the powers of the federal and state governments, its provisions have a profound effect on private actors in society. The costs are usually high, but at times a company may find it worthwhile to challenge a regulation on constitutional grounds. This was true for the insurance companies that successfully challenged Proposition 103's freeze on rate increases for one year,[86] and for Eastern Enterprises, the former coal company that successfully challenged the $5 million assessment to fund health plans for former employees.[87] Companies engaged in advertising their products and services or in broadcasting such ads have been particularly successful in recent years in persuading the Supreme Court that the restrictions violate their rights of free speech.

Managers often have an interest in influencing legislation or other government action through direct lobbying or political action committees. When pursuing change, it is useful to know the constitutional limitations placed on different segments of the government.

Although the Constitution addresses only government actions, managers of private organizations should be aware of the societal values reflected in the Constitution. These include the right to fair and equal treatment and respect for the individual.

It may seem at times that constitutional law is far removed from the world of business. This is a misconception. Constitutional law is as close as the nearest private club that does not admit African Americans, Jews, women, or homosexuals. Such clubs may be important places for conducting business and for networking in general. A manager invited to become a member of such a club or to accompany a boss or client as a guest may face a tough choice between his or her personal values and the perceived need to "be a team player" and not challenge or embarrass an important business colleague.

86. Calfarm Ins. Co. v. Deukmejian, 771 P.2d 1247 (Cal. 1989).
87. Eastern Enterprises v. Apfel, 524 U.S. 498 (1998).

The Effect *of* Politics *on* Supreme Court Appointments

The nomination process for the U.S. Supreme Court has grown increasingly politicized and controversial over time. Being nominated to the Supreme Court now brings along with it a process of public scrutiny akin to running for national political office. Politics, however, is not new to the process.

Franklin Delano Roosevelt was probably the first president to attempt explicitly and publicly to use the power of judicial appointment to change the Court's position on the key political issues of the day. Frustrated with the Supreme Court's overturning of much of his New Deal legislation, President Roosevelt introduced his now-famous Court-packing bill. The bill would have added one justice to the Court for every sitting justice who had reached the age of seventy. The Court's membership would have increased to fifteen, of whom a majority would have been in favor of Roosevelt's policies.

Although the bill was never passed by the Senate, the threat was clear. The Court quickly capitulated and abandoned its commitment to limited government, especially regarding economic liberty. By the time of his death during his fourth term, Roosevelt had completely revamped the Court, secured passage of his New Deal legislation, and ushered in a new era of constitutional law.

Other presidents have made considerations of diversity and representation key to their selection of nominees. President Lyndon Johnson's appointment of Thurgood Marshall took into consideration the need for African Americans to be represented on the Court for the first time. Similarly, the appointments of Justices Sandra Day O'Connor (the first female member of the Court) and Clarence Thomas by Presidents Ronald Reagan and George Bush, respectively, served to expand and maintain the gender and racial diversity of the Court.

When President Dwight Eisenhower appointed Earl Warren as the Chief Justice in 1953, Warren was the Republican governor of California. He had been a critical factor in Eisenhower's 1952 bid for the presidency. Eisenhower repaid the political debt with the nomination, despite misgivings by powerful Republicans, such as Vice President Richard Nixon, about Warren's progressive stance on certain issues.

Another pivotal nomination in the recent past was President Reagan's 1987 nomination of Robert Bork, a well-known constitutional scholar. Bork was the last nominee to the Supreme Court to have a "paper trail" of opinions and writings on constitutional matters. The nightmare Senate hearings, in which Bork was forced to attempt to explain to the senators and the general public the reasoning behind some of his more radical statements over the years—of which there were many—were enough to convince any president of the impossibility today of nominating someone with that kind of record. In the end, Bork's views and the resultant political uproar across the nation led to his being denied confirmation to the Court.

More recent presidents have tended to nominate individuals who have produced few or no legal opinions on critical issues. The nomination by President Bush of David Souter, often referred to as a "stealth candidate" due to his anonymity prior to nomination, is illustrative.

The 1991 nomination of Clarence Thomas to the "black seat" on the Supreme Court, vacated by the resignation of Justice Thurgood Marshall, was supposed to be similarly quiet but resulted in another Bork-like public spectacle. Thomas seemed to be a safe bet: his writings and opinions were sparse and generally without controversy. Thomas even went so far as to deny ever having engaged in a debate on the issue of abortion:

> **Senator Leahy:** Have you [Judge Thomas] ever had discussion of *Roe v. Wade*[88] other than in this room, in the 17 or 18 years it has been there?

> **Judge Thomas:** Only, I guess, Senator, in the fact in the most general sense that other individuals express concerns one way or the other, and you listen and you try to be thoughtful. If you are asking me whether or not I have ever debated the contents of it, the answer to that is no, Senator.[89]

Even this denial, incredible as it seemed to some, did not derail Thomas's quest for a seat on this nation's highest court. Without extensive writings to defend, Thomas gained wide support in the Senate.

After completing an initial hearing, however, Thomas was called back before the Judiciary Committee to face

---

88. 410 U.S. 113 (1973).
89. *Nomination of Judge Clarence Thomas to Be Associate Justice of the Supreme Court of the United States: Hearings Before the Senate Comm. on the Judiciary,* 102d Cong., 1st. Sess. 222 (1991).

allegations of sexual harassment put forward by African-American law professor and former colleague, Anita Hill. The ensuing melee became a circus in which actors on both sides paraded before the committee, asserting their versions of the truth. Thomas, undaunted by the allegations, charged the committee with conducting a "high-tech lynching of uppity Blacks." This aggressive challenge to the senators dulled the edge of their remaining questions.

In the end, only three senators, all Democrats, admitted to changing their votes. Thomas was approved by a vote of fifty-two to forty-eight. Many members of the Senate sought to avoid the political fallout on both sides of the issue.

Though public opinion polls following the hearings found that more Americans believed Judge Thomas than Professor Hill, the image of twelve white men grilling an African-American woman about her charges of sexual harassment set in motion a political movement that resulted in the election of historic numbers of women and African Americans to both the House of Representatives and the Senate.

Two years later, in 1993, President Bill Clinton nominated Ruth Bader Ginsburg to the Court. The politics of that nomination swirled around the question of whether the Senate should apply an abortion "litmus test" to her appointment in light of the changing Supreme Court position on the pivotal issue of whether a woman has a constitutional right to an abortion. Any indication of a controversial hearing was immediately dispelled in Judge Ginsburg's opening remarks. In an effort to preempt potential litmus test–type questions, she hinted at the inappropriateness of deciding a case in advance but promised to impartially hear each case before the Court "without reaching out to cover cases not yet seen." She stated:

> You are well aware that I come to this proceeding to be judged as a judge not an advocate. . . . A judge sworn to decide impartially can offer no forecasts, no hints, for that would show not only disregard for the specifics of a partic-

ular case; it would display disdain for the entire judicial process.[90]

Judge Ginsburg's thirteen years of judicial experience on the U.S. Court of Appeals for the District of Columbia, coupled with her impressive credentials, won her nearly unanimous support from the public as well as the Judiciary Committee. She was easily confirmed by a vote of ninety-six to three, and her hearing served as an opportunity to reduce hostility in the nomination process.

One year later, President Clinton had another opportunity to nominate a justice to the Court. Having learned from his success with Justice Ginsburg and the difficulties of his predecessors, he avoided controversy and nominated "technocrat" Stephen Breyer, a judge on the U.S. Court of Appeals for the First Circuit known for his academic writings on regulatory economics. One reporter covering Breyer's nomination hearing characterized it this way:

> The most unlikely story of the moment is that the Senate Judiciary Committee's hearings on Stephen Breyer's appointment to the Supreme Court unexpectedly became a bore, albeit a pleasant bore. That is to Breyer's advantage, for it signals an overdue cooling of the passions superheated by earlier Supreme Court confirmation fights . . . .[91]

Whether these nominations signal a return to the earlier practice of polite and deliberative advice and consent by the Senate or are only a temporary respite from raging political winds remains to be seen. Court watchers expect to know soon, however, as Chief Justice William Rehnquist and Justices O'Connor and John Paul Stevens are all thought to be likely to leave the Court in the near future.

90. *Nomination of Judge Ruth Bader Ginsburg to be Associate Justice of the Supreme Court of the United States: Hearings Before the Senate Comm. on the Judiciary*, 103d Cong., 1st Sess. 222 (1993).
91. Edward M. Yoder, *Breyer's Hearings Lack Passion of Bork's*, DENVER POST, July 18, 1994, at B7.

KEY WORDS AND PHRASES

appellate jurisdiction 39	eminent domain 65	negative Commerce Clause 49
bicameralism 41	executive privilege 40	original jurisdiction 39
bill of attainder 51	*ex post facto* 50	override 40
Bill of Rights 38	federalism 38	penumbra 62
Commerce Clause 45	garnishment 73	police power 42
dormant Commerce Clause 49	judicial review 39	preempt 39
Due Process Clause 51	line item veto 41	prior restraints 57

QUESTIONS AND CASE PROBLEMS

1. Congress enacted legislation making carjacking a federal crime. The stated justifications included stopping transportation of carjacked vehicles across state lines, either in parts or intact, and the adverse effect of car theft on insurance rates. Does Congress have the power to make carjacking a federal crime? [*United States v. Oliver,* 60 F.3d 547 (9th Cir. 1995)]

2. States have adopted various strategies for dealing with hazardous waste generated within their borders or shipped in from out of state.

   a. Alabama is one of only sixteen states that have commercial hazardous-waste landfills. In the late 1980s, the annual rate of hazardous waste received by Alabama facilities more than doubled. More alarming to some Alabamans, 90 percent of the tonnage buried each year was shipped in from other states. The Alabama government reacted to this situation by passing legislation that limited the amount of hazardous wastes or substances that could be disposed of in any one-year period. The law also imposed an additional fee on waste generated outside Alabama that was disposed of at a commercial hazardous-waste site in Alabama. Chemical Waste Management, which owned and operated a hazardous-waste treatment, storage, and disposal facility in Alabama, challenged the new law as unconstitutional. Is the Alabama law constitutional? [*Chemical Waste Mgmt., Inc. v. Hunt,* 504 U.S. 334 (1992)]

   b. Instead of being alarmed over imports of waste from out of state, the municipal government of Clarkstown, New York, was concerned that too little waste was being received from anywhere to make the operation of its waste facility economical. Without the local facility, such waste might have to travel further and expose more of the state to danger from spills, leaks, and highway accidents. As a result, the town passed an ordinance requiring that all producers of nonhazardous solid waste in the town have it treated at the town's facility or pay a "tipping fee" to the town. Producers challenged the law as unconstitutional. What was the result? [*C&A Carbone v. Clarks-town, N.Y.,* 511 U.S. 383 (1994)]

3. In 1999, Illinois enacted the Illinois Wine and Spirits Industry Fair Dealing Act, which requires out-of-state suppliers to show good cause for terminating distributorships. Illinois suppliers are exempted from this requirement. After three California wineries sought to terminate contracts with Illinois distributors, the distributors filed petitions with the Illinois Liquor Control Commission alleging that the wineries had violated the Illinois statute. The wineries argued that the Illinois statute was unconstitutional.

   a. Is the Illinois legislation constitutional?

   b. If the wineries showed that the statute would have a substantial impact on interstate commerce, how could Illinois justify the legislation? [*Kendall-Jackson Winery Ltd. v. Branson,* 82 F. Supp. 2d 844 (N.D. Ill. 2000)]

4. A Wisconsin law permitted creditors to freeze the wages of a debtor (in legal terms, to *garnish* the wages) until the completion of a trial to determine the debtor's liability. Under the law, creditors' lawyers could effect a garnishment by requesting a summons from a court and serving it on the debtor's employer. No notice to the debtor was required until ten days after the summons was served. Is this procedure constitutional? Explain why or why not. [*Sniadach v. Family Fin. Corp. of Bay View,* 395 U.S. 337 (1969)]

5. An Illinois statute prohibits a motor vehicle on a highway from operating a sound amplification system, such as a radio, that can be heard outside the vehicle from seventy-five or more feet, unless the system is being operated to request assistance or to warn of a hazardous substance. In addition to exempting emergency vehicles, such as ambulances, from this prohibition, the statute also exempts vehicles engaged in advertising. Does any part of the statute violate the Constitution? Explain why or why not. [*People v. Jones,* 721 N.E.2d 546 (Ill. 1999)]

6. In an effort to protect local corporations from hostile takeover bids, a number of states have adopted antitakeover regulations.

   a. MITE Corporation, an Illinois company, initiated a *tender offer* (an offer to shareholders to buy their shares) for all the outstanding shares of Chicago River and Machine Company by filing with the Securities and Exchange Commission the schedule required by the Williams Act, which is the part of the federal Securities Exchange Act of 1934 governing tender offers. A basic purpose of the Williams Act is to place investors on an equal footing with the takeover bidder. It is based on the assumption that independent shareholders faced with tender offers are at a disadvantage. MITE did not comply with the Illinois Business Take-Over Act, which required any person or company intending to make a tender offer to notify the Illinois secretary of state and the target company of the offer twenty days before it was to become effective. During that time, the offeror could not communicate its offer to the shareholders, but the target company was free to disseminate information to its shareholders concerning the impending offer. Additionally, any takeover offer had to be registered with the Illinois secretary of state, who was authorized to hold a hearing on the fairness of the offer. Is the Illinois Business Take-Over Act constitutional? [*Edgar v. MITE Corp.*, 457 U.S. 624 (1982)]

b. Indiana's Control Share Acquisition Act provided that a "control share acquisition" that would otherwise have given an acquirer the power to vote more than specified percentages of the stock of the target (that is, 20, 33.3, or 50 percent) would not in fact result in acquisition of the commensurate voting rights unless they were conferred by a majority of the disinterested shareholders at a meeting to be held within not more than fifty days. Is the Indiana Control Share Acquisition Act constitutional? [*CTS Corp. v. Dynamics Corp. of America*, 481 U.S. 69 (1987)]

7. Terry Mitchell is a chronic alcoholic who has been unable to keep a job because of his addiction. He applied for disability insurance benefits (DIB) and supplemental security income (SSI) under the Social Security Act. Benefits were denied on the basis of Section 105 of the Contract with America Advancement Act, which prohibits the award of DIB and SSI to individuals disabled by alcoholism or drug addiction. Mitchell filed a suit alleging that Section 105 singles out alcoholics and drug addicts for unequal treatment and denies him the equal protection of the law in violation of the Fifth Amendment. What arguments can be made for striking down Section 105? What arguments can be made to justify denying DIB and SSI to alcoholics and drug addicts? [*Mitchell v. Commissioner of SSA*, 182 F.3d 272 (4th Cir. 1999), *cert. denied*, 120 S. Ct. 358 (1999)]

8. Mr. Weber, a truck driver working for a public employer, asked his employer not to assign him trucking runs that included a female partner because he was a Jehovah's Witness and his religion prohibited him from traveling overnight with a woman other than his wife. His employer informed him that the company could not make these changes to his schedule because they would unduly burden his coworkers with respect to compensation and time-off concerns. The employer had accommodated other drivers for secular reasons but only when business circumstances permitted. Has the employer violated Weber's constitutional rights? [*Weber v. Roadway Express, Inc.*, 199 F.3d 270 (5th Cir. 2000)]

9. In November 1999, San Francisco adopted a proposition prohibiting financial institutions from imposing surcharges on a customer for accessing an automated teller machine (ATM) located within San Francisco. A similar ordinance had been approved by the Santa Monica city council the prior month. Bank of America, Wells Fargo, and the California Bankers Association sued the two cities to prevent implementation of the local bans. They argued that the National Bank Act preempts the ordinances, so they could not be applied to nationally chartered banks. Attorneys general from nine states, including California and New York, filed a brief in support of San Francisco and Santa Monica, arguing that nothing in the National Bank Act regulates fees for ATM transactions and that federal laws do not preempt state or local laws enacted pursuant to the police power. They further argued that Congress had determined under the Electronic Funds Transfer Act (EFTA) that state laws are not inconsistent with the statute if they afford greater consumer protection than EFTA. How should the court rule? [*Bank of America v. City and County of San Francisco*, 2000 U.S. Dist. LEXIS 12587 (N.D. Cal. 2000)]

MANAGER'S DILEMMA

10. The federal election laws prohibit corporate contributions to political candidates but allow corporations to establish separate segregated funds known as political action committees (PACs). PACs are permitted to collect contributions from supervisory employees and management and to distribute this money to candidates. A corporation can solicit contributions from its stockholders and administrative and executive personnel and their families, the "restricted class" for its PAC. A member of a restrictive class can contribute a maximum of $5,000 to a fed-

eral PAC. Although corporations may also solicit other employees, this solicitation is highly restricted and regulated. A corporation is prohibited from giving annual bonuses to its executives with the understanding that they will contribute part of the bonus to the corporation's PAC or to a candidate.

The CEO of Techno Corporation, Sunil Zamba, is a friend and supporter of Senator Wood from Idaho, where Techno is headquartered. Zamba has sent memos to all of the executives and managers in the company reminding them that legislation pending in the Senate could negatively affect Techno's business and that Senator Wood is an opponent of the bill. Although he has not instituted a formal company policy, Zamba has strongly sug-

gested that all of the executives and managers attend a fundraising dinner for Senator Wood and persuade at least one other business associate outside Techno to attend. Attendance at the dinner requires a donation of $6,000 per person. Zamba has made it clear that Techno will reimburse the cost of the dinner for the Techno employees and their business associate guests; he claims that this dinner is an opportunity for Techno managers and executives to network with potential clients. Have Zamba and Techno Corporation violated the federal election laws? Have they acted ethically? Would your answer be different if the dinner cost only $500 per person? Should the Techno executives attend the event?

INTERNET SOURCES

The Web site for the U.S. Supreme Court offers a searchable full-text database of Supreme Court opinions. New opinions are usually posted the same day they are issued.	http://www.supremecourtus.gov/
The constitution page of the Louisiana State University's Department of Political Science contains annotated text of the U.S. Constitution, Bill of Rights, U.S. state constitutions, constitutions of other nations around the world, other founding documents, and related research.	http://www.lsu.edu/guests/poli/public_html/const.html
The Legal Information Institute page at Cornell University Law School offers a wide variety of resources related to the U.S. Constitution, including its various articles and amendments and related historical documents; state constitutions; and international constitutional law.	http://www.law.cornell.edu/topics/constitutional.html
The International Constitutional Law page at the University of Würzbug in Germany addresses constitutional law around the world and contains numerous national constitutions and related materials and links.	http://www.uni-wuerzburg.de/law
The Library of Congress's Broadside Collection offers a collection of materials concerning the formation of the U.S. Constitution.	http://lcweb2.loc.gov/ammem/bdsds/bdsdhome.html
The Constitution Society's home page offers a variety of materials about the U.S. constitutional republic, including discussions of various constitutional principles, founding documents, and related sources.	http://www.constitution.org/
Yahoo's Constitutional Law page offers links to related sites and the opportunity to search for specific items.	http://www.yahoo.com/law/constitutional
White House	http://www.whitehouse.gov
U.S. House of Representatives	http://www.house.gov
U.S. Senate	http://www.senate.gov

CHAPTER 3

Courts, Sources *of* Law, *and* Litigation

EQUAL JUSTICE UNDER THE LAW

"Equal justice under the law" is the inscription on the front of the United States Supreme Court Building in Washington, D.C. It is a reminder that the judicial system is intended to protect the legal rights of those who come before a court. In a litigation-prone society, it is important for managers to understand the judicial system and be prepared to use it, when appropriate, to protect their rights and the rights of their companies.

and choice of law. It continues with a description of the sources of law, including constitutions, statutes, regulations, and common law. The chapter then outlines the litigation process, including discovery, the attorney–client privilege, class actions, various trial strategies for companies involved in a lawsuit, and document-retention programs. Alternatives to litigation, such as mediation and arbitration, are discussed in Chapter 4.

CHAPTER OVERVIEW

This chapter begins with a discussion of the federal and state court systems, including subject matter and personal jurisdiction

How *to* Read *a* Case Citation

When an appellate court decides a case, the court writes an opinion, which is published in one or more *reporters*—collections of court opinions. Some trial courts also publish opinions. The citation of a case (the *cite*) includes the following information:

1. The plaintiff's name
2. The defendant's name
3. The volume number and title of the reporter in which the case is reported
4. The page number at which the case report begins
5. The court that decided the case (if the court is not indicated, it is understood to be the state supreme court or the U.S. Supreme Court, depending on the reporter in which the case appears)
6. The year in which the case was decided.

For example, *Bush v. Gore, Jr.,* 121 S. Ct. 525 (2000), refers to the decision rendered by the U.S. Supreme Court on December 12, 2000, in a case brought by George W. Bush against Albert Gore, Jr., to prevent manual recounts of disputed ballots for President of the United States cast by voters in Florida. (The Court held that the lack of uniform standards for determining which votes were legal violated the principle of one person, one vote mandated by the Equal Protection Clause in the Fourteenth Amendment to the U.S. Constitution.) The case is reported in volume 121 of the U.S. Supreme Court Reports on page 525. *Securities and Exchange Commission v. Current Financial Services, Inc.,* 100 F. Supp. 2d 1 (D.D.C. 2000), indicates that in 2000 an opinion was issued in a case involving the Securities and Exchange Commission as the plaintiff and Current Financial Services, Inc. as the defendant. The case was decided by the U.S. District Court for the District of Columbia. The case is reported in volume 100 of the second series of the Federal Supplement, beginning on page 1. *In re Dow Corning Corp.*, 250 B.R. 298 (Bankr. E.D. Mich. 2000), refers to the bankruptcy proceedings of silicone-breast-implant manufacturer Dow Corning Corporation. The case is reported in the Bankruptcy Reporter, volume 250, beginning on page 298. The parenthetical information indicates that this case was decided by a U.S. Bankruptcy Court sitting in the Eastern District of Michigan.

Some cases are reported in more than one reporter. For example, the famous New York taxicab case discussed in Chapter 24, *Walkovszky v. Carlton*, is cited as 18 N.Y.2d 414, 276 N.Y.S.2d 585, 223 N.E.2d 6 (N.Y. 1966). One may locate this case in volume 18 of the second series of New York Reports, in volume 276 of the second series of the New York Supplement, or in volume 223 of the second series of the North Eastern Reports.

When quoting a particular passage from an opinion, one should include the page number on which the information is found after the page number at which the case report begins. A comma should separate the two numbers. For example, suppose one wanted to quote the specific page where the Supreme Court of Delaware considered whether the lower court should have dismissed a complaint alleging that the board of directors of Walt Disney Company breached its duty of care by approving an extravagant and wasteful employment agreement with Michael Ovitz as president. The cite would read *Brehm v. Eisner*, 746 A.2d 244, 260 (Del. 2000). Thus, the case report begins on page 244 of volume 746 of the second series of the Atlantic Reporter, and the cited material is on page 260. The parenthetical information identifies the adjudicating body as the Supreme Court of Delaware and the year as 2000.

When a lawsuit is originally filed, the case name appears as *plaintiff v. defendant*. If the case is appealed, the case name usually appears as *appellant* or *petitioner* (the party who is appealing the case or seeking a writ of *certiorari*) *v. appellee* or *respondent* (the other party). So, if the defendant lost at the trial level and appealed the decision to a higher court, the name of the defendant (now the appellant) would appear first in the case citation.

 ## *The* Court System

The United States has two judicial systems: federal and state. Federal and state courts have different subject matter jurisdiction. In general, federal courts are courts of limited subject matter jurisdiction, meaning they can adjudicate only certain types of cases. The jurisdiction of the federal courts arises from the U.S. Constitution and statutes enacted by Congress. By contrast, state courts have general subject matter jurisdiction and can therefore hear any type of dispute. The jurisdiction of a state's courts arises from that state's constitution and statutes. The two coexisting judicial systems are a result of the federalism created by the U.S. Constitution, which gives certain powers to the federal government while other powers remain with the states.

The basic structure of the federal and state court systems is diagrammed in Exhibit 3.1. In practice, the structure of the U.S. court systems is more complex than the diagram indicates. For example, an applicant may appeal an adverse decision from the U.S. Patent and Trademark Office to the Board of Patent Appeals and Interferences. The person may then appeal an unfavorable ruling from this court to the Court of Appeals for the Federal Circuit. Alternatively, the applicant may appeal the unfavorable ruling of the Board of Patent Appeals and Interferences by filing a civil action, in the U.S. District Court for the District of Columbia, against the Commissioner of the U.S. Patent and Trademark Office.

 ## Federal Jurisdiction

Federal courts derive their legal power to hear civil cases from three sources: federal question jurisdiction, diversity jurisdiction, and jurisdiction when the United States is a party. As explained in Chapter 2, the Eleventh Amendment to the U.S. Constitution protects a state (or an agency thereof) from being sued without its consent in a federal court by a citizen of another state. Congress can abrogate this immunity if it unequivocally expresses its intention to do so and acts pursuant to a constitutional grant of authority, such as Section 5 of the Fourteenth Amendment.

FEDERAL QUESTION JURISDICTION

A *federal question* exists when the dispute concerns federal law, namely a legal right arising under the U.S. Constitution, a federal statute, an administrative regulation issued by a federal government agency, federal common law, or a treaty of the United States. There is no minimum monetary requirement for lawsuits involving a federal question.

DIVERSITY JURISDICTION

Diversity jurisdiction exists when a lawsuit is between citizens of two different states and the amount in controversy,

EXHIBIT 3.1 Structure of the U.S. Court Systems

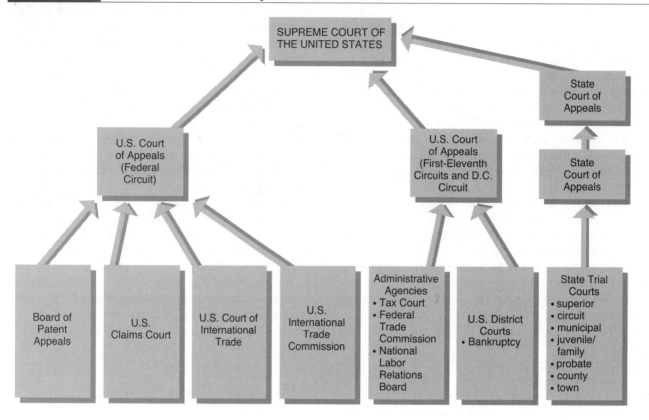

exclusive of interest and all costs, exceeds $75,000. The purpose of the monetary requirement is to prevent trivial cases from overwhelming the federal judicial system.

Diversity jurisdiction was traditionally justified by the fear that state courts might be biased against the out-of-state party. In federal district court, all litigants are in a neutral forum, and there should be no local prejudice for the home team.

Most diversity cases do not involve federal statutes or the U.S. Constitution and thus could also be resolved in state court. In the landmark case, *Erie Railroad Co. v. Tompkins*,[1] the U.S. Supreme Court addressed the question of whether state or federal law should apply to a suit brought in a federal court exercising its diversity jurisdiction. The Court held that a federal court must apply state law unless the lawsuit concerns the U.S. Constitution or a federal statute. In essence, the Supreme Court abolished the notion of federal common law in diversity cases.

1. 304 U.S. 64 (1938).

The *Erie doctrine*, as the holding of this case is known, serves an important purpose. It ensures that the outcome of a diversity case in federal court will be similar to the outcome in a state court because the same law will govern either adjudication. This prevents litigants (the parties to a lawsuit) from *forum shopping* between federal and state courts in an attempt to have the more favorable law govern their dispute.

When litigants are in federal court due to diversity jurisdiction, they cannot choose which state's law will govern the dispute. The court itself makes this decision, applying well-established *conflict-of-law rules*, which prescribe which state's law should apply to a particular kind of case. For example, a case involving a tort, such as negligent operation of a motor vehicle, is often governed by the laws of the state where the accident occurred.

Determining Citizenship An individual is a citizen of the state where the person has his or her legal residence or domicile. A person may have a house in more than one state. A person is a citizen, however, only of the state that he or she considers home.

A corporation, on the other hand, may have dual citizenship. A corporation is deemed a citizen of the state in which it has been incorporated and of the state where the company has its principal place of business. Federal courts usually apply one of three tests in determining where a company engaged in multistate operations has its principal place of business.

The first is the nerve-center test. To find the corporation's nerve center, courts consider where (1) the executive and administrative offices are located, (2) the income tax return is filed, and (3) the directors and shareholders meet. The second test focuses on the place of operations. This test requires locating the majority of the corporation's physical operations, such as manufacturing facilities or offices. The *total-activity test,* a combination of the first two tests, considers all aspects of the corporate entity, including the nature and scope of the company's activities. The total-activity test is gaining popularity among the courts.

UNITED STATES IS A PARTY

Federal courts have jurisdiction over all lawsuits in which the U.S. government, or an officer or agency thereof, is the plaintiff or the defendant. As with federal question jurisdiction, there is no minimum monetary requirement for lawsuits where the United States is a party.

Federal Courts

The main function of the federal courts is to interpret the Constitution and laws of the United States. President George Washington told the Supreme Court in 1790, "I have always been persuaded that the stability and success of the National Government, and consequently the happiness of the American people, would depend in a considerable degree on the interpretation and execution of its laws."

President Washington signed into law the Senate's first piece of legislation, entitled "An Act to Establish the Judicial Courts of the United States." This Act created the federal trial courts. Two years later, Congress created the federal courts of appeals. The three-tiered system of district courts, courts of appeals, and the Supreme Court remains today. The President of the United States nominates each judge who serves on these federal courts. The U.S. Senate, pursuant to its "advice and consent" power, then votes to approve or reject the judicial nominees. The Constitution does not impose any age or citizenship requirements on judicial candidates. Once confirmed by the Senate, federal judges have a lifetime appointment to the bench. They may be removed from office only by legislative impeachment if they violate the law. Lifetime tenure protects federal judges from public reprisal for making unpopular or difficult decisions. As a result, the federal judiciary is more independent than either the executive or the legislative branch.

U.S. DISTRICT COURTS

The U.S. district courts are the trial courts of the federal system. Currently, the country is divided into ninety-four judicial districts. Each state has at least one district, and the more populous states have as many as four. Exhibit 3.2 on page 81 shows the various districts. Many districts have two or more divisions. For example, the main location for the U.S. District Court for the Southern District of Florida is Miami. However, the Southern District of Florida also has courts in Key West, Miami/Ft. Lauderdale, West Palm Beach, and Fort Pierce. Thus, a plaintiff may file its lawsuit with the nearest federal district court, provided, of course, that the court has jurisdiction over the particular controversy.

U.S. COURTS OF APPEALS

The primary functions of a court of appeals are (1) to review decisions of the trial courts within its territory, (2) to review decisions of certain administrative agencies and commissions, and (3) to issue *writs,* or orders, to lower courts or to litigants. Only final decisions of lower courts are appealable. A decision is final if it conclusively resolves an issue in a dispute or the entire controversy.

Cases before the courts of appeals are usually presented to a panel of three judges. Occasionally, all the judges of a court of appeals will sit together to hear and decide a particularly important or close case. This is called an *en banc* (or *in banc*) *hearing*. The court of appeals can either affirm or reverse the decision of the lower court. It may also *vacate,* or nullify, the previous court's ruling and *remand* the case—send it back to the lower court for reconsideration. Frequently, the panel of judges will decide an appeal based upon the legal briefs or written memoranda submitted to the court, rather than hearing oral arguments presented by the lawyers.

There are thirteen courts of appeals, one for each of the twelve regional circuits in the United States and one for the federal circuit. The Ninth Circuit, encompassing nine states, Guam, and the Northern Mariana Islands, is the largest circuit, with twenty-eight active judges. The Court of Appeals for the First Circuit has only six active judges. Exhibit 3.2 shows the geographic boundaries of the circuits.

Partisan Foot-Dragging *on* Judicial Appointments

Due to the Republican-controlled Senate's delays in confirming judges nominated by Democratic President Bill Clinton, an unprecedented seventy-seven federal judgeships were vacant in 2000, with thirty-eight nominations pending.[a] The result was lengthy case backlogs. At the beginning of 1998, Chief Justice William Rehnquist decried the Senate's failure to vote on pending nominations and warned that "[v]acancies cannot remain at such high levels indefinitely without eroding the quality of justice."[b] Some experts blame partisan politics for the Senate's failure to act on pending nominations.[c]

A study by a nonpartisan judicial watchdog group in 1999 found that the Senate takes 163 more days to act on judicial nominations now than it did twenty years ago.[d] The study also found that President Clinton has taken seventy-five more days to nominate candidates than President Jimmy Carter did twenty years ago.[e]

Some argue that activist judges, not the Senate confirmation process, are the real problem. Senator Orrin Hatch, chairman of the Senate Judiciary Committee, asserted: "The number one problem happens to be activist judges who continue to find laws that aren't

there and expand the law beyond the intent of Congress."[f]

As of April 2000, the Administrative Office of the U.S. Courts characterized twenty of the seventy-seven vacancies as judicial emergencies.[g] The Ninth Circuit, which has jurisdiction over nine states including California and Washington, has been particularly affected by the shortage of judges. For several years, the court has been short between five and ten judges which is a substantial percentage of its allotted twenty-eight judges.[h] Due to this shortage, the average time for disposition of a case is two months longer than the national average, and Ninth Circuit court officials estimate that eight hundred appeals were not considered in 1999.[i] In an effort to deal with the crisis, the Ninth Circuit is hearing fewer oral arguments and is relying instead on short presentations by the court's staff lawyers. This new procedure has allowed the court to hear as many as

one hundred cases a day instead of six or seven.[j] In addition, the court has relied on senior judges who have no financial incentive to continue working as they receive no additional pay for working longer than their retirement age.

a. The Administrative Office of the U.S. Courts Web site (visited Apr. 30, 2000) <http://www.uscourts.gov/>.
b. David G. Savage, *Rehnquist Chides GOP for Judicial Stalling*, L.A. Times, Jan. 1, 1998, at A1. *See also Delay in Approving Judicial Nominees Angers Rehnquist*, Wall St. J., Jan. 2, 1998, at 40.
c. Francie Kiefer, *Clinton renews bid to fill empty bench; Legal analysts see partisan politics in Senate's foot-dragging on federal judges*, Christian Science Monitor, Aug. 11, 1998, at 2.
d. Marc Sandalow, *Clinton Blasts Senate over Court Delays/He calls for vote on 2 nominees for appellate judgeships in S.F.*, San Francisco Chron., Oct. 7, 1999, at A3.
e. *Id.*
f. *Chief Justice's Annual Report Criticizes Senate's Slowness in Confirming Judges*, 66 U.S.L.W. 2408 (Jan. 13, 1998).
g. The Administrative Office of the U.S. Courts Web site, *supra* note a.
h. Sandalow, *supra* note d.
i. *Id.*; Henry Weinstein, *GOP Stonewall Creates Judicial Limbo 9th Circuit: Lengthy impasse blocks Senate vote on two nominees; angering Latino and women's rights activists*, L.A. Times, Oct. 3, 1999, at B-1.
j. Kiefer, *supra* note c.

The Court of Appeals for the Federal Circuit, created in 1982, does not have jurisdiction over a specific geographic region but rather hears appeals in specialized cases (such as patent disputes) and appeals from various specialized federal courts, including the Court of Federal Claims and the Court of International Trade. Exhibit 3.3 on page 82 lists the states and territories included within each circuit.

SPECIALIZED FEDERAL COURTS

The federal system has several specialized courts that resolve legal disputes within particular subject areas.

The bankruptcy courts are units of the federal district courts that hear proceedings involving the bankruptcy laws and regulations of the United States. When Fruit of the Loom (clothing manufacturer), Filene's Basement (discount retailer), and Continental Airlines filed for protection from their creditors under Chapter 11 of the bankruptcy laws, they did so in federal bankruptcy court. (The law of bankruptcy is discussed in Chapter 26.)

The tax courts hear taxpayer petitions or appeals regarding federal income, estate, and gift taxes. The Court of International Trade has jurisdiction over disputes involving tariffs, or import taxes, and trade laws. This court also hears cases on appeal from the U.S. Interna-

EXHIBIT 3.2 **Map of Judicial Districts and Circuits**

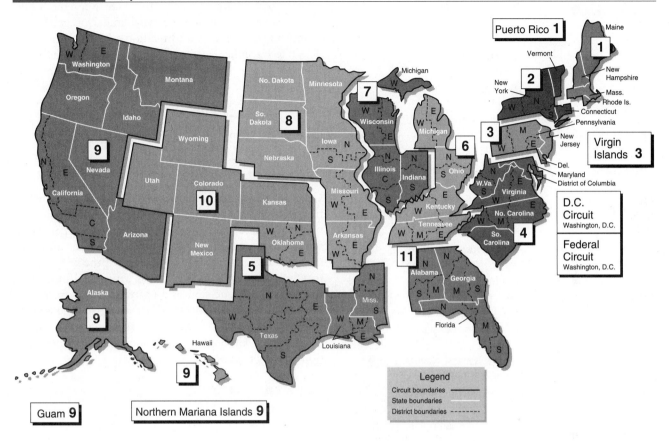

tional Trade Commission, which handles disputes involving unfair practices in import trade. The U.S. Court of Military Appeals hears cases from the lower courts and tribunals within the armed services.

U.S. SUPREME COURT

The Supreme Court consists of one chief justice and eight associate justices. At least six justices must be present to hear a case. The majority of the cases heard by the Supreme Court are on appeal from the U.S. courts of appeals. A decision by a state supreme court is also appealable to the U.S. Supreme Court, but only when the case concerns the U.S. Constitution or some other federal law. The Supreme Court may hear direct appeals from a federal district court decision if the court declared an act of the U.S. Congress unconstitutional. For example, the Supreme Court directly reviewed the invalidation of the

Line Item Veto Act by the District Court for the District of Columbia.[2]

The Supreme Court has discretionary review, meaning that it decides which cases within its jurisdiction it will adjudicate. When it decides to hear a case, the Supreme Court issues a *writ of certiorari* ordering the lower court to certify the record of proceedings below and send it up to the Court. Four justices must vote to hear a case before a writ can be issued. If a writ was sought but denied by the Supreme Court, the citation for the case will indicate *"cert. denied."*

The Supreme Court will not decide cases that involve a political question. A *political question* is defined as a conflict that should be decided by either the executive or the legislative branch of government. Under the political question doctrine, the Supreme Court identifies those disputes that are more appropriately decided by democratically

2. City of New York v. Clinton, 985 F. Supp. 168 (D.D.C. 1998).

EXHIBIT 3.3 Geographic Regions of the U.S. Courts of Appeals

Circuit	Region
District of Columbia	District of Columbia
First	Maine, Massachusetts, New Hampshire, Puerto Rico, Rhode Island
Second	Connecticut, New York, Vermont
Third	Delaware, New Jersey, Pennsylvania, Virgin Islands
Fourth	Maryland, North Carolina, South Carolina, Virginia, West Virginia
Fifth	Louisiana, Mississippi, Texas
Sixth	Kentucky, Michigan, Ohio, Tennessee
Seventh	Illinois, Indiana, Wisconsin
Eighth	Arkansas, Iowa, Minnesota, Missouri, Nebraska, North Dakota, South Dakota
Ninth	Alaska, Arizona, California, Guam, Hawaii, Idaho, Montana, Nevada, Northern Mariana Islands, Oregon, Washington
Tenth	Colorado, Kansas, New Mexico, Oklahoma, Utah, Wyoming
Eleventh	Alabama, Florida, Georgia
Federal	Based in Washington D.C., but hears specialized cases from all regions

elected officials. In the Florida manual recount case discussed above *(Bush v. Gore)*, the U.S. Supreme Court noted its consciousness of the "vital limits" on judicial authority and expressed "an admiration of the Constitution's design to leave the selection of the President to the people, through their legislatures, and to the political sphere," but went on to state that when contending parties invoke the process of the courts, "it becomes our unsought responsibility to resolve the federal and constitutional issues that the judicial system has been forced to confront."

STANDING

Courts will not hear an appeal unless a real and substantial controversy is involved and resolving the lawsuit will provide actual relief to one party. Further, the party pursuing the appeal must have standing to sue. *Standing* means that the party seeking relief (1) is the proper party to advance the litigation, (2) has a personal interest in the outcome of the suit, and (3) will benefit from a favorable ruling. The following case addressed the issue of whether commercial banks have standing to challenge the National Credit Union Administration's interpretation of the Federal Credit Union Act.

A CASE IN POINT

CASE 3.1

National Credit Union Administration v. First National Bank & Trust Company
Supreme Court of the United States
522 U.S. 479 (1998).

In the Language of the Court

FACTS Section 109 of the Federal Credit Union Act (FCUA) provides that "federal credit union membership shall be limited to groups having a common bond of occupation or association, or to groups within a well-defined neighborhood, community, or rural district." The National Credit Union Administration (NCUA), the agency responsible for administering the FCUA, interpreted Section 109 to permit federal credit unions to be composed of multiple unrelated employer groups. The NCUA later approved a series of amendments to the charter of a federal credit union that added several unrelated employer groups.

As competitors to the credit unions, five commercial banks and the American Bankers Association brought an action alleging that the new employer groups did not share the "common bond of occupation" required under Section 109. They brought their claim under Section 10 of the Administrative Procedure Act (APA), which provides that "[a] person suffering legal wrong because of agency action, or adversely affected or aggrieved by agency action within the meaning of the statute, is entitled to judicial review thereof." The district court dismissed the complaint on grounds of lack of standing. The appeals court reversed, and the defendants raised the issue again before the Supreme Court.

(Continued)

(Case 3.1 continued)

ISSUE PRESENTED Do commercial banks have standing to seek federal court review of the NCUA's interpretation of Section 109 of the FCUA?

OPINION THOMAS, J., writing for the U.S. Supreme Court:

For a plaintiff to have prudential standing under the APA, "the interest sought to be protected by the complainant [must be] arguably within the zone of interests to be protected or regulated by the statute . . . in question."

. . .

Our prior cases . . . have consistently held that for a plaintiff's interests to be arguably within the "zone of interests" to be protected by a statute, there does not have to be an "indication of congressional purpose to benefit the would-be plaintiff." The proper inquiry is simply "whether the interest sought to be protected by the complainant is arguably within the zone of interests to be protected . . . by the statute."

. . .

. . . By its express terms, §109 limits membership in every federal credit union to members of definable "groups." Because federal credit unions may, as a general matter, offer banking services only to members, §109 also restricts the markets that every federal credit union can serve. . . . [E]ven if it cannot be said that Congress had the specific purpose of benefiting commercial banks, one of the interests "arguably . . . to be protected" by §109 is an interest in limiting the markets that federal credit unions can serve. . . . [T]he NCUA's interpretation has affected that interest by allowing federal credit unions to increase their customer base.

RESULT Commercial banks have standing to challenge the NCUA's interpretation of the Federal Credit Union Act.

COMMENTS Justice O'Connor stated in a brief dissent, joined by Justices Stevens, Souter, and Breyer, that the decision of the Court "all but eviscerates the zone-of-interests requirements." Congress responded by passing legislation that expressly adopted the NCUA interpretation.

State Courts

State courts handle the bulk of legal disputes in the United States. Each state's constitution creates the judicial branch of government for that state. For example, the Constitution of Texas provides:

> [T]he judicial power of this State shall be vested in one Supreme Court, in one Court of Criminal Appeals, in Courts of Appeals, in District Courts, in County Courts, in Commissioners Courts, in Courts of Justices of the Peace, and in such other courts as may be provided by law.[3]

The various sections then provide the details of the state judicial system. These include the number of justices sitting on the state's supreme court, the jurisdiction of the state courts, the geographic districts of the various courts of appeals, the way in which justices and judges are selected or appointed, and the tenure of the justices and judges.

STATE TRIAL COURTS

At the lowest level of the state trial court system are several courts of limited jurisdiction. These courts decide minor criminal matters, small civil suits, and other specialized legal disputes. Examples include traffic courts, small claims courts, juvenile courts, and family courts. In these courts, the procedures can be informal. Parties may appear without lawyers, the court may not keep a complete transcript or recording of the proceedings, and the technical rules of evidence and formal courtroom procedures may not apply. In small claims court, the jurisdiction of the court is usually limited to disputes involving less than, for example, $5,000. Any dispute involving

---

3. Tᴇx. Cᴏɴsᴛ., Art. V, § 1.

more than this amount must be heard by a higher-level trial court.

The second level of state trial courts consists of courts of general or unlimited jurisdiction. These courts have formal courtroom procedures, apply the standard rules of evidence, and record all proceedings.

State court actions cover a broad spectrum of business activities. For example, in Vermont an employee of a ski lodge filed a claim regarding workers' compensation benefits for an injury sustained while he was skiing in his position as a "ski bum."[4] In Louisiana, a plant worker sued the chemical company Monsanto because she suffered an anxiety attack after a supervisor violently berated her for not working. In a class action brought by smokers in state court in Florida against five top tobacco companies, including Philip Morris and R.J. Reynolds, the jury awarded $6.9 million in compensatory damages and $145 billion in punitive damages.[5]

STATE APPELLATE COURTS

A state appellate court is similar to its counterpart in the federal system. It usually consists of a panel of three judges who review the lower court ruling for errors in applying the law or procedures. The appellate court usually accepts the findings of fact of the trial judge or jury, unless a particular finding is clearly unsupported by the evidence presented at trial. The appellate court is not required to accept the lower court's conclusions of law but may consider legal issues *de novo*, or anew, as if the trial court had not made any conclusions of law. An appellate court may affirm, reverse, or vacate and remand any final decision of a lower court.

STATE SUPREME COURT

Each state has one court that acts as the highest judicial authority in that state. Most states call that court the supreme court. (In New York, however, the highest state court is called the Court of Appeals; the intermediate appellate court is called the Supreme Court, Appellate Division; and the state trial courts are called supreme courts.) The number of justices on the court varies from three to nine. A state supreme court usually has discretionary jurisdiction over all decisions of a court of appeals. Further, a state supreme court may have jurisdiction over cases where a statute of the state or the United States has been ruled unconstitutional in whole or in part. A state supreme court also resolves appeals in criminal cases in which a sentence of death has been imposed.

 Personal Jurisdiction

For a state court to hear a civil case, the court must have personal jurisdiction. *Personal jurisdiction* means that the court has legal authority over the parties to the lawsuit. Personal jurisdiction may be based upon the residence or activities of the person being sued (called *in personam jurisdiction*) or upon the location of the property at issue in the lawsuit (called *in rem jurisdiction*). For example, if an individual does any business in the state, then he or she is properly within the jurisdiction of that state's courts. Owning property in a state, causing a personal injury or property damage within the state, or even paying alimony or child support to someone living within the state might justify the exercise of personal jurisdiction by that state's courts.

The Anticybersquatting Consumer Protection Act (ACPA)[6] was enacted in November 1999 to give trademark owners the ability to bring an *in rem* suit to invalidate a domain name registration by a cybersquatter when personal jurisdiction is not attainable. *In rem* jurisdiction is available only in situations where the plaintiff has "disproved" the existence of personal jurisdiction.[7]

Most states have *long-arm statutes,* which can subject an out-of-state defendant to jurisdiction in the state as long as due process requirements are met. The Due Process Clause exists, in part, to give "a degree of predictability to the legal system that allows potential defendants to structure their primary conduct with some minimum assurance as to where that conduct will and will not render them liable to suit."[8] The critical test is whether the defendant has certain *minimum contacts* with the state "such that the maintenance of the suit does not offend 'traditional notions of fair play and substantial justice.'"[9]

The courts generally require that the nonresident defendant (1) have done some act or consummated some transaction in the forum in which it is being sued, or (2) have purposefully availed itself of the privilege of conducting activities in the forum, thereby invoking the benefits and protections of the forum. Courts have held that negotiating business contracts by means of telephone calls, the mail, or even a telecopier is sufficient to provide a state court with personal jurisdiction over an individual or corporation. Personal jurisdiction may also

4. Grather v. Gables Inn, Ltd., 751 A.2d 762 (Vt. 2000).
5. Marc Kaufman, *Tobacco Suit Award: $145 Billion; Fla. Jury Hands Industry Major Setback,* Wash. Post, July 15, 2000.

6. 15 U.S.C. § 1125(d) (1999).
7. Heathmont A.E. Corp. v. Technodome.com, 106 F. Supp. 2d 860 (E.D. Va. 2000).
8. World-Wide Volkswagen Corp. v. Woodson, 444 U.S. 286, 297 (1980).
9. International Shoe Co. v. Washington, 326 U.S. 310, 316 (1945) (quoting Milliken v. Meyer, 311 U.S. 457, 463 (1940)).

E-COMMERCE

be proper over a nonresident defendant who committed an intentional tort outside the forum when the defendant aimed his or her tortious conduct at the forum and the brunt of the harm was felt by the plaintiff in the forum.[10]

10. IMO Industries, Inc. v. Kiekert AG, 155 F.3d 254 (3d Cir. 1999).

Personal Jurisdiction *and the* Web

The ability to use the Internet to conduct business throughout the world from a desktop computer has raised new issues about the permissible scope of personal jurisdiction based on Internet use. In general, "the likelihood that personal jurisdiction can be constitutionally exercised is directly proportionate to the nature and quality of commercial activity that an entity conducts over the Internet.[a] The U.S. District Court for the Western District of Pennsylvania adopted a sliding scale, stating:

At one end of the spectrum are situations where a defendant clearly does business over the Internet. If the defendant enters into contracts with residents of a foreign jurisdiction that involved the knowing and repeated transmission of computer files over the Internet, personal jurisdiction is proper. At the opposite end are situations where a defendant has simply posted information on an Internet Web site which is accessible to users in foreign jurisdictions. A passive Web site that does little more than make information available to those who are interested in it is not grounds for the exercise of personal jurisdiction. The middle ground is occupied by interactive Web sites where a user can exchange information with the host computer. In these cases, the exercise of jurisdiction is determined by examining the level of interactivity and commercial nature of the exchange of information that occurs on the Web site.[b]

Applying these principles, the Pennsylvania court held that it could assert jurisdiction over a California corporation that had a Web site accessible in Pennsylvania, 3,000 subscribers in Pennsylvania to whom it issued passwords, and seven contracts with Internet access providers to furnish its services to their customers in Pennsylvania.

The U.S. Court of Appeals for the District of Columbia rejected GTE's attempt to sue Bell South, SBC Communications, Pacific Bell, and US West Media in the District of Columbia for allegedly conspir-

ing to capture and dominate the Internet business directories market.[c] The defendants had interactive Internet Web sites accessible within the district but no physical presence there. The court rejected the argument that when a district resident accesses the defendants' Yellow Pages Web sites, the defendants are transacting business in the district, and explained:

Access to an Internet Yellow Page site is akin to searching a telephone book—the consumer pays nothing to use the search tool, and any resulting business transaction is between the consumer and a business found in the Yellow Pages, not between the consumer and the provider of the Yellow Pages.

In two defamation cases, a federal court in Virginia and a state court in California reached opposite conclusions as to whether parties could be sued in states where the defamatory statements could be read over the Internet. In *Bochan v. LaFontaine,*[d] the federal court in Virginia found that it did have jurisdiction over a defendant living in New Mexico because he "solicited business in Virginia by promoting and advertising his computer hardware company on the Internet through its website, accessible to Virginia Internet users 24 hours a day." The Web site was interactive although no sales were concluded through it. The court also found that it had jurisdiction over Texas residents who used their account with America Online (AOL) to publish allegedly defamatory statements about the plaintiff who was a Virginia resident. The Texas residents' defama-

tory statements were transmitted first to AOL's USENET server hardware located in Virginia, and the court found that use of this service was integral to the publication of the statements.

The California court ruled that contracting with Internet service providers that had databases and offices in California was not sufficient to subject defendants located in New York to California jurisdiction.[e] The plaintiff alleged that the defendants had published defamatory statements about him on their passive Web site from their New York residence. Unlike the plaintiff in *Bochan v. LaFontaine*, the plaintiff in the California case was not a resident of California and had no business interests there.

Several states have attempted to expand the scope of their courts' power to assert personal jurisdiction in cases involving the Internet. The Virginia Internet Policy Act (VIPA), enacted in March 1999, states that "for purposes of obtaining personal jurisdiction . . . , use of a computer or computer network located in Virginia . . . will constitute an act in Virginia." Because AOL, PSInet, and UUNet, as well as Network Solutions, are located in Virginia, the VIPA enables Virginia courts to issue judgments over foreign Internet users in numerous substantive legal areas. Similarly, the Attorney General of Minnesota issued a memorandum asserting jurisdiction over "[i]ndividuals and organizations outside of Minnesota which disseminate information in Minnesota via the Internet and thereby cause a result to occur in Minnesota."

a. Zippo Mfg. Co. v. Zippo Dot Com, 952 F. Supp. 1119, 1124 (W.D. Pa. 1997).
b. *Id.*
c. GTE New Media Services, Inc. v. Bell South Corp., 199 F.3d 1343 (D.C. Cir. 2000).
d. 68 F. Supp. 2d 692 (E.D. Va. 1999).
e. Jewish Defense Org. v. Superior Court, 72 Cal. App. 4th 1045 (Cal. App. 2d Dist. 1999), *review denied* (Cal. 1999).

INTERNATIONAL CONSIDERATION

Although issues of choice of law and choice of forum often arise in cases involving parties from different jurisdictions within the United States, similar issues arise when parties are from different countries. In either context, the court adjudicating the dispute must balance the competing interests of different sovereignties and resolve the conflict according to one jurisdiction's conflict-of-law rules. To avoid confusion, it is customary for a contract involving parties from different jurisdictions to specify which country's laws will govern and where any dispute will be tried.

The parties to a contract may agree in advance which law should govern their dispute in the event that one develops. This section is usually entitled "Governing Law" or "Choice of Law." Parties can also decide in advance where any disputes should be litigated. This is done by using a *choice-of-forum clause.* A contract can also provide that disputes will be decided by a method other than litigation. A common choice is arbitration, which is discussed in Chapter 4.

⬙ Choice *of* Law *and* Choice *of* Forum

The question of which jurisdiction's law to apply comes up not only in the context of diversity cases heard in federal court but also in state court actions involving the citizens of more than one state. This question is governed by a complicated set of conflict-of-law rules. In general,

the state that has the greatest governmental interest in a case will provide the governing law. Put another way, the selection of the governing law is guided by a grouping of contacts: the state with the strongest contacts with the litigants has the greatest interest in applying its law.

Sometimes a state will use formalistic rules. Some states look only to where a contract was entered into in deciding which state's contract law should govern a dispute. For example, because Pennzoil and Getty Oil Company entered into their contract in New York, the lens of New York contracts law was used to evaluate whether there was a binding contract. (Texaco's intentional interference with this contract, and the related litigation, is discussed in the "Inside Story" in Chapter 7.)

Sometimes more than one state has an interest in the outcome of a case. When that happens, under the doctrine of *depeçage,* the court is permitted to apply the laws of different states to different issues. For example, *Calhoun v. Yamaha Motor Corp.*[11] involved a suit for the wrongful death of a twelve-year-old child from Pennsylvania in a jet-ski accident in the territorial waters of Puerto Rico. The court held that Pennsylvania had an interest in securing remedies for its citizens; thus, Pennsylvania law should govern compensating damages. Because Puerto Rico had an equally strong interest in punishing wrongdoing in its territory, the court used Puerto Rico law to determine the availability of punitive damages.

A court will usually uphold the contracting parties' choice of law and forum, as happened in the following case.

11. 216 F.3d 338 (3d Cir. 2000).

A CASE IN POINT

CASE 3.2

Richards v. Lloyd's of London
United States Court of Appeals for the Ninth Circuit
(en banc)
*135 F.3d 1289
(9th Cir. 1998), cert. denied,
525 U.S. 943 (1998).*

Summary

FACTS Lloyd's of London is involved in the business of writing insurance and reinsurance. Between 1970 and 1993, Lloyd's vigorously recruited passive investors (called Names) in the United States in an attempt to increase its underwriting capacity. The information furnished by Lloyd's to potential investors did not meet the standards for prospectuses set forth by the Securities and Exchange Commission, nor were the investment contracts offered by Lloyd's registered under federal or state securities laws. As part of this campaign, Alan Richards and 573 other individuals (the plaintiffs) became passive investors in Lloyd's underwriting business, with unlimited liability.

In 1986, Lloyd's required the plaintiffs to execute a contract that included choice-of-law and forum-selection clauses. Paragraph 2.1 of the General Undertaking specified that "The rights and obligations of the parties . . . shall be governed by and construed in accordance with the laws of England." Paragraph 2.2 continued: "Each party irrevocably agrees that the courts of England shall have exclusive jurisdiction to settle any dispute and/or controversy of whatsoever nature arising out of or relating to the Member's membership of, and/or underwriting of insurance business of Lloyd's. . . ."

(Continued)

(Case 3.2 continued)

In 1994, the plaintiffs filed an amended complaint in a U.S. court alleging securities fraud under the federal securities laws and violations of RICO (Racketeer Influenced and Corrupt Organizations Act). Lloyd's argued that the suit should be dismissed on the grounds of improper venue and *forum non conveniens* (a doctrine claiming that the present suit should be dismissed because an alternative, more convenient forum should adjudicate the dispute). The trial court dismissed the suit; then a panel of the court of appeals reversed. Lloyd's requested a rehearing by the full court of appeals.

ISSUE PRESENTED Are choice-of-forum and choice-of-law clauses requiring a U.S. citizen to litigate securities fraud claims under English law in English courts valid and enforceable?

SUMMARY OF OPINION The U.S. Court of Appeals sitting *en banc* began by acknowledging that the Securities Act of 1933 and the Securities Exchange Act of 1934 both provide that contracts in violation of the acts are void. Nonetheless, in 1972, the U.S. Supreme Court ruled in *The Bremen v. Zapata Off-Shore Co.*[12] that courts should enforce choice-of-law and choice-of-forum clauses in cases of "freely negotiated private international agreement[s]." Two years later, the Supreme Court relied on *Bremen* to uphold a choice-of-forum clause in a securities transaction and characterized choice-of-forum provisions as "an almost indispensable precondition to achievement of the orderliness and predictability essential to any international business transaction." Otherwise, the scope of U.S. securities law would be boundless.

Because the Names signed a contract with English entities to participate in an English insurance market and flew to England to consummate the transaction, the appeals court ruled that the contract was international and within *Bremen*'s reach. The fact that Lloyd's solicited the Names in the United States did not change the contract's international nature.

The court identified three instances where a forum-selection clause may not be enforceable: (1) the clause was fraudulently included in the contract, (2) enforcement would deprive a party "of his day in court," and (3) enforcement would contravene a strong public policy of the forum in which suit is brought. The Names argued that the first and third grounds applied.

For the first ground to apply, the forum-selection clause itself must be induced by fraud. Alleging that the contract as a whole was entered into fraudulently is insufficient. The Names never alleged that Lloyd's misled them as to the legal effect of the choice-of-law and choice-of-forum clauses. Neither did they allege that Lloyd's fraudulently inserted the clauses without their knowledge. Hence, the first ground did not apply.

As for the third ground based on public policy, the appeals court concluded that to mandate that American standards govern such a controversy demeans the standards elsewhere and places U.S. law over that of other countries. Furthermore, it is simply not possible for the United States to trade in world markets and over international waters exclusively on its terms, governed by its laws, and resolved in its courts. As a result, the choice-of-forum and choice-of-law clauses in the contract were valid and enforceable.

RESULT The full court of appeals found that the choice-of-law and choice-of-forum clauses were enforceable and affirmed the trial court's dismissal of the federal Securities Acts claims.

COMMENTS The outcome of *Richards v. Lloyd's of London* conforms with the holdings of the U.S. Courts of Appeals for the Second, Fourth, Fifth, and Seventh Circuits.

12. 407 U.S. 1 (1972).

Sources *of the* Law

In applying the law, federal and state courts look to constitutions, statutes, regulations, and common (or case) law.

CONSTITUTIONS

Courts may be called upon to interpret the U.S. or state constitutions. For example, the First Amendment provides that Congress shall make no law abridging the freedom of speech. Incidents of flag burning have required courts to interpret just what type of conduct constitutes speech protected by the First Amendment. Lawsuits concerning random drug testing of employees have centered on whether this testing violates the Fourth Amendment ban on unreasonable searches and/or the right to privacy.

The U.S. Constitution does not expressly set forth a right to privacy. As explained in Chapter 2, such a right is found in the penumbra of other articulated rights. Some state constitutions do specifically grant a right to privacy, however. The following case addresses the issue of whether a Georgia law criminalizing the act of sodomy violates the right to privacy specified in the Georgia Constitution.

A CASE IN POINT

CASE 3.3
Powell v. Georgia
Supreme Court of Georgia
510 S.E.2d 18 (Ga. 1998).

In the Language of the Court

FACTS Powell was charged with rape and aggravated sodomy in connection with his sexual conduct with his wife's seventeen-year-old niece. The Georgia statute defined "sodomy" as "any sexual act involving the sex organs of one person and the mouth or anus of another." Powell testified that he performed the acts with the niece's consent. The jury acquitted Powell of rape and aggravated sodomy, finding that the niece had consented to the sexual conduct, but found him guilty of sodomy. Powell appealed, asserting that the statute was an unconstitutional intrusion on the right of privacy established by the Georgia Constitution.

ISSUE PRESENTED Does a Georgia statute crimininalizing the act of sodomy performed by consenting adults in private infringe upon the right of privacy guaranteed all Georgia citizens by the Georgia Constitution?

OPINION BENHAM, J., writing for the Supreme Court of Georgia:

The right of privacy has a long and distinguished history in Georgia. In 1905 [in *Pasevich v. New England Life Ins. Co.*[13]], this Court expressly recognized that Georgia citizens have a "liberty of privacy" guaranteed by the Georgia constitutional provision which declares that no person shall be deprived of liberty except by due process of law. The *Pasevich* decision constitutes the first time any court of last resort in this country recognized the right of privacy . . . making this Court a pioneer in the realm of the right of privacy. . . .

In *Pasevich,* the Court found the right of privacy to be "ancient law," . . . derived from "the Romans' conception of justice" and natural law, making it immutable and absolute. The Court described the liberty interest derived from natural law as "embrac[ing] the right of man to be free in the enjoyment of the faculties with which he has been endowed by his Creator, subject only to such restraints as are necessary for the common good." "Liberty" includes "the right to live as one will, so long as that will does not interfere with the rights of another or of the public," and the individual is "entitled to a liberty of choice as to his manner of life, and neither an individual nor the public has the right to arbitrarily take away from him his liberty." . . . Stated succinctly, the Court ringingly endorsed the "right 'to be let alone' so long as [one] was not interfering with the rights of other individuals or of the public."

Today, we are faced with whether the constitutional right of privacy screens from governmental interference a non-commercial sexual act that occurs without force in

13. 122 Ga. 190 (1905).

(Continued)

(Case 3.3 continued)

a private home between persons legally capable of consenting to the act. . . . Adults who "withdraw from the public gaze" to engage in private consensual sexual behavior are exercising a right "embraced within the right of personal liberty." We cannot think of any other activity that reasonable persons would rank as more private and more deserving of protection from governmental interference than consensual, private, adult sexual activity. We conclude that such activity is at the heart of the Georgia Constitution's protection of the right of privacy.

The State also maintains that the furtherance of "social morality," giving "due regard to the collective will of the citizens of Georgia," is a constitutional basis for legislative control of the non-commercial, unforced, private sexual activity of those legally capable of consenting to such activity. It is well within the power of the legislative branch to establish public policy through legislative enactment. . . . However, "it does not follow . . . that simply because the legislature has enacted as law what may be a moral choice of the majority, the courts are, thereafter, bound to simply acquiesce.". . .

In undertaking the judiciary's constitutional duty, it is not the prerogative of members of the judiciary to base decisions on their personal notions of morality. . . . While many believe that acts of sodomy, even those involving consenting adults, are morally reprehensible, this repugnance alone does not create a compelling justification for state regulation of the activity.

RESULT The Georgia Supreme Court found that the Georgia statute, insofar as it criminalized the performance of private, non-commercial acts of sexual intimacy between persons legally able to consent, infringed the Georgia Constitution's right of privacy. Appellant's conviction was reversed.

COMMENTS In concurring (agreeing) with the judgment of the court, Justice Sears stated:

There will, of course, be those who will criticize today's decision, and who may even seek to demonize some members of this Court for their legal analysis. This pattern of personally attacking and pillorying individuals who disagree with certain positions, rather than engaging in constructive ideological discourse with them, has regrettably become more and more prevalent in our culture. Those who would make such personal attacks, however, do not fully appreciate that all of my colleagues, those who agree with the majority as well as those who dissent, are honorable and decent jurists who struggle to fulfill their constitutional responsibilities to the people of this State.

Justice Corley stated in his dissent:

[T]he only perceptible unconstitutionality in this case is that which is evidenced by the majority's determination, acting as social engineers rather than as jurists, to elevate their notion of individual "liberty" over the collective wisdom of the people's elected representatives that a proscription on sodomy, consensual or otherwise, is "in furtherance of the moral welfare of the public."

QUESTIONS

1. Which argument do you find more persuasive, that of the majority or the dissent?
2. The U.S. Supreme Court in *Bowers v. Hardwick*[14] upheld a state ban on sodomy, after concluding that the U.S. Constitution's right of privacy did not extend to adult consensual sodomy. Given the Supremacy Clause, why wasn't the Georgia Supreme Court bound by the U.S. Supreme Court ruling in *Bowers?*

14. 478 U.S. 186 (1986).

STATUTES

Congress enacts statutes in such areas as public assistance, food and drugs, patents and copyrights, labor relations, and civil rights. For example, Title 42 of the United States Code, Section 2000(a), provides that "all persons shall be entitled to the full and equal enjoyment of the goods, services, facilities, privileges, advantages, and accommodations of any place of public accommodation . . . without discrimination or segregation on the grounds of race, color, religion or national origin." State legislatures also adopt statutes covering a broad range of topics, from requirements for a will to the formation and governance of corporations to rights of employers. For example, Section 16600[15] of the California Business and Professions Code generally invalidates employee covenants not to compete except in connection with the sale of an employee's stock in a transaction involving the sale of the corporation as a going concern.

REGULATIONS

Courts sometimes hear cases arising under regulations issued by administrative agencies and executive departments. Federal regulations and rules are printed in the multivolume *Code of Federal Regulations (CFR)*, which is revised and updated every year.

The CFR covers such varied topics as the regulations applying to federal highways issued by the Department of Transportation; the Internal Revenue Service regulations issued by the Department of the Treasury; the immigration and naturalization rules and procedures issued by the Department of Justice; the regulations governing the sale of securities issued by the Securities and Exchange Commission; and the regulations governing television, radio, and telecommunications issued by the Federal Communications Commission. Administrative rules and regulations, and the various agencies, are discussed in Chapter 6.

COMMON LAW

Common law is case law—the legal rules made by judges when they decide a case where no constitution, statute, or regulation exists to resolve the dispute. Common law originated in England, and in the United States it includes all of the case law of England and the American colonies before the American Revolution, as well as American case law since the colonial period.

15. CAL. BUS. & PROF. CODE § 16600 (2000).

INTERNATIONAL CONSIDERATION

Bulgaria's difficult struggle with both economic and political reform shows the effect of eliminating law as a means of regulation and dispute resolution. The regulations that were implemented after the breakup of the Soviet Union were "designed to protect the old order and did little to accomplish the legal reforms promised by the collapse of the former Eastern bloc."[a]

Any regulations that were passed were not enforced. Nonenforcement engendered a thriving underground economy, where intellectual property rights, including trademarks, copyrights, and related restrictions, were disregarded. The pervasive, cash-based underground economy also enabled systematic tax avoidance in both personal and business transactions. Businesses routinely violated environmental regulations, knowing the probability of enforcement to be low and believing environmental protection to be bothersome.

Due to the government's tarnished public image, Bulgarians rarely litigate when faced with a breach of contract. Rather, "the local common wisdom holds that no matter how carefully a contract may be drawn, if it is breached, most of the time the parties will settle the dispute themselves. Such an approach usually means the more powerful or ruthless party wins. . . ."[b]

a. Katherine J. Wilkinson, *A Lawyer in a World without Law: An American's Odyssey in Bulgaria*, Bus. L. TODAY, Sept.–Oct., 1997, at 41.
b. *Id.* at 44.

Stare Decisis Common law is developed through the doctrine of *stare decisis*, which translates as "to abide by decided cases." Once a court resolves a particular issue, other courts addressing a similar legal problem will generally follow that court's decision.

A legal rule established by a court's decision may be either persuasive or authoritative. A decision is *persuasive* if it reasonably and fairly resolves the dispute. Another court confronting a similar dispute will probably choose to apply the same reasoning.

An *authoritative decision*, by contrast, must be followed, regardless of its persuasive power. The U.S. Court of Appeals for the Seventh Circuit explained:

Whether a decision is authoritative depends on a variety of factors, of which the most important is the relationship between the court that decided it and the court to which it is cited later as a precedent. The simplest relationship is hierarchical: the decisions of a superior court in a unitary system bind the inferior courts. The most complex relationship is between a court and its own previous decisions.

A court must give considerable weight to its own decisions unless and until they have been overruled or undermined by the decisions of a higher court, or other supervening developments, such as a statutory overruling. But [a court] is not absolutely bound by [its previous rulings], and must give fair consideration to any substantial argument that a litigant makes for overruling a previous decision.[16]

Federal courts interpreting state law must follow that state's courts—this was the principle established in *Erie Railroad v. Tompkins,* discussed earlier in this chapter. Every court must follow a decision of the U.S. Supreme Court, unless powerfully convinced that the Supreme Court itself would change its decision at the first possible opportunity.

Although the Supreme Court rarely overrules its previous opinions, it does happen. For example, the Supreme Court rejected the "separate but equal" test adopted by *Plessy v. Ferguson*[17] in *Brown v. Board of Education,*[18] the 1954 school-desegregation case. More recently, right-to-life activists have urged the Supreme Court to reverse its 1973 holding in *Roe v. Wade*[19] that a woman has a constitutionally protected right to an abortion. The importance of the doctrine of *stare decisis* was underscored in the following case.

16. Colby v. J.C. Penney Co., 811 F.2d 1119, 1123 (7th Cir. 1987), *reh'g denied* (1987).

17. 163 U.S. 537 (1896).
18. 347 U.S. 483 (1954).
19. 410 U.S. 113 (1973).

A CASE IN POINT

CASE 3.4

Planned Parenthood of S.E. Pennsylvania v. Casey
Supreme Court of the United States
505 U.S. 833 (1992).

In the Language of the Court

FACTS The Pennsylvania Abortion Control Act requires that a woman seeking an abortion give her informed consent prior to the abortion procedure and that she be provided with certain information at least twenty-four hours before the abortion is performed. For a minor to obtain an abortion, the Act requires the informed consent of one of her parents but provides for a judicial bypass option if the minor does not wish to or cannot obtain a parent's consent. Another provision of the Act requires that, unless certain exceptions apply, a married woman seeking an abortion must sign a statement indicating that she has notified her husband of her intended abortion. The Act exempts compliance with these three requirements in the event of a medical emergency and imposes reporting requirements on facilities that provide abortion services.

Five abortion clinics and one physician, representing himself as well as a class of physicians who provide abortion services, brought suit seeking declaratory and injunctive relief. Each provision was challenged as unconstitutional on its face. Relying on *Roe v. Wade,* the district court declared all the provisions at issue unconstitutional and entered a permanent injunction against enforcing them. The appeals court upheld as constitutional all of the regulations except for the husband-notification requirement. The plaintiff appealed.

ISSUE PRESENTED In light of *Roe v. Wade* and the doctrine of *stare decisis,* should the Pennsylvania abortion regulations be upheld as constitutional?

OPINION O'CONNOR, KENNEDY, and SOUTER, JJ., writing for a plurality of the U.S. Supreme Court:

Liberty finds no refuge in a jurisprudence of doubt. Yet 19 years after our holding that the Constitution protects a woman's right to terminate her pregnancy in its early stages, *Roe v. Wade,* that definition of liberty is still questioned. Joining the respondents . . . the United States, as it has done in five other cases in the last decade, again asks us to overrule *Roe.*

. . .

After considering the fundamental constitutional questions resolved by *Roe,* principles of institutional integrity, and the rule of *stare decisis,* we are led to conclude

(Continued)

(Case 3.4 continued)

this: the essential holding of *Roe v. Wade* should be retained and once again reaffirmed.

The Court then gave a brief synopsis of the *Roe v. Wade* holding and its trimester approach to abortion regulation. Under *Roe,* a woman's right to an abortion is virtually absolute in the first trimester of pregnancy. Regulations designed to protect the woman's health, but not to further the state's interest in potential life, are permissible in the second trimester. In the third trimester, when the fetus is viable, the state may act to protect the potential life of the fetus, except when the life or health of the mother is at stake. The Court rejected the trimester framework, which it did not consider the "essential holding" of *Roe*. Instead, the Court concluded that a woman has a right to terminate her pregnancy prior to the time the fetus is viable, regardless of when that occurs.]

...

The obligation to follow precedent begins with necessity, and a contrary necessity marks its outer limit. . . . Indeed, the very concept of the rule of law underlying our own Constitution requires such continuity over time that a respect for precedent is, by definition, indispensable. At the other extreme, a different necessity would make itself felt if a prior judicial ruling should come to be seen so clearly as error that its enforcement was for that very reason doomed.

Even when the decision to overrule a prior case is not virtually foreordained, as in the rare, latter instance, it is common wisdom that the rule of *stare decisis* is not an "inexorable command," and certainly it is not such in every constitutional case. Rather, when this Court reexamines a prior holding, its judgment is customarily informed by a series of prudential and pragmatic considerations designed to test the consistency of overruling a prior decision with the ideal of the rule of law, and to gauge the respective costs of reaffirming and overruling a prior case. . . .

So, in this case, we may inquire whether *Roe's* central rule has been found unworkable; whether the rule's limitation on state power could be removed without serious inequity to those who have relied upon it or significant damage to the stability of the society governed by the rule in question; whether the law's growth in the intervening years has left *Roe's* central rule a doctrinal anachronism discounted by society; and whether *Roe's* premises of fact have so far changed in the ensuing two decades as to render its central holding somehow irrelevant or unjustifiable in dealing with the issue it addressed.

[One] comparison that 20th century history invites is with the cases employing the separate-but-equal rule for applying the Fourteenth Amendment's equal protection guarantee. They began with *Plessy v. Ferguson* holding that legislatively mandated racial segregation in public transportation works no denial of equal protection, rejecting the argument that racial separation enforced by the legal machinery of American society treats the black race as inferior. The *Plessy* Court considered "the underlying fallacy of the plaintiff's argument to consist in the assumption that the enforced separation of the two races stamps the colored race with a badge of inferiority. If this be so, it is not by reason of anything found in the act, but solely because the colored race chooses to put that construction upon it." Whether, as a matter of historical fact, the Justices in the *Plessy* majority believed this or not, this understanding of the implication of segregation was the stated justification for the Court's opinion. But this understanding of the facts and the rule it was stated to justify were repudiated in *Brown v. Board of Education.* . . .

(Continued)

(Case 3.4 continued)

The Court in *Brown* addressed these facts of life by observing that whatever may have been the understanding in *Plessy's* time of the power of segregation to stigmatize those who were segregated with a "badge of inferiority," it was clear by 1954 that legally sanctioned segregation had just such an effect, to the point that racially separate public educational facilities were deemed inherently unequal. Society's understanding of the facts upon which a constitutional ruling was sought in 1954 was thus fundamentally different from the basis claimed for the decision in 1896. While we think *Plessy* was wrong the day it was decided, . . . we must also recognize that the *Plessy* Court's explanation for its decision was so clearly at odds with the facts apparent to the Court in 1954 that the decision to reexamine *Plessy* was on this ground alone not only justified but required.

...

. . . In constitutional adjudication as elsewhere in life, changed circumstances may impose new obligations, and the thoughtful part of the Nation could accept each decision to overrule a prior case as a response to the Court's constitutional duty.

Because the case before us presents no such occasion it could be seen as no such response. Because neither the factual underpinnings of *Roe's* central holding nor our understanding of it has changed (and because no other indication of weakened precedent has been shown) the Court could not pretend to be reexamining the prior law with any justification beyond a present doctrinal disposition to come out differently from the Court of 1973. . . .

RESULT The Supreme Court upheld what it considered to be the central holding of *Roe v. Wade* under the doctrine of *stare decisis*. At the same time, the Court upheld the Pennsylvania abortion regulations as constitutional, except for the spousal-notification requirement. The regulations imposed procedural requirements that the Court did not consider central to the holding of *Roe*.

COMMENTS Chief Justice Rehnquist explicitly stated in his dissent that *Roe* was wrongly decided and could be overturned consistently with the traditional approach to *stare decisis* in constitutional cases. Justice Blackmun, author of the *Roe* opinion, strongly disagreed and argued that under the test of strict scrutiny, which he believed should be applied, all provisions of the Pennsylvania law should be struck down. He noted the slim margin behind the Court's decision to uphold *Roe*:

> In one sense, the Court's approach is worlds apart from that of the Chief Justice and Justice Scalia. And yet, in another sense, the distance between the two approaches is short—the distance is but a single vote.
>
> I am 83 years old. I cannot remain on this Court forever, and when I do step down, the confirmation process for my successor well may focus on the issue before us today. That, I regret, may be exactly where the choice between the two worlds will be made.

As discussed in the "Inside Story" for Chapter 2, Justice Ruth Bader Ginsburg refused to have an abortion litmus test applied to her nomination to the Court in 1993.

QUESTIONS

1. What factors did the Court consider in deciding whether to overturn *Roe v. Wade?*
2. Why did the Court conclude that overturning *Plessy* in *Brown v. Board of Education* was appropriate, but that overturning *Roe v. Wade* would not be?

One court of appeals does not have to follow another court of appeals. One trial court does not have to follow another trial court. It must follow the court of appeals above it but need not follow other appellate courts. Thus, if the U.S. Court of Appeals for the Tenth Circuit (based in Denver) interprets a federal air-pollution regulation in a certain way, the U.S. Court of Appeals for the Sixth Circuit (based in Cincinnati) may follow that interpretation, but it is not compelled to do so. The authority of the Tenth Circuit does not reach beyond its own geographic boundaries. However, a federal district court in Tulsa, which is within the Tenth Circuit, would be compelled to interpret the regulation in accordance with the decision of the Court of Appeals for the Tenth Circuit.

Restatements Today, many rules that originated as common law have been collected into *restatements* compiled by legal scholars, practicing attorneys, and judges. There are restatements of various areas of the law, such as torts, contracts, property, and trusts. The restatements do not compel a judge to make a particular decision unless the rule has been adopted by the state's legislature. They are persuasive rather than authoritative.

 # Civil Procedure

Civil procedure refers to the methods, procedures, and practices that govern the processing of a civil lawsuit from start to finish. The Federal Rules of Civil Procedure (FRCP) control the trial practices in all of the U.S. district courts. Each federal district court may also adopt its own local rules, applicable only within that district, to supplement the federal rules. Individual judges may even have particular rules as to how certain procedures operate in their own courts.

Each state has a set of rules governing the procedures in the state trial court system. Often, the state rules will be similar in many respects to the federal rules. Separate sets of rules govern practice before the various courts of appeals and supreme courts. These rules address every requirement, from the time deadline for filing an appeal, to the contents of the notice of appeal, to the paper size, line spacing, and type style for briefs filed with the court. Each court system has its own rules or guidelines to ensure the orderly processing of the lawsuit.

FILING AND PROSECUTING A CLAIM

Exhibit 3.4 provides a typical timeline for a suit filed in federal court.

Complaint The *complaint* briefly states a grievance and makes allegations of (1) the particular facts giving rise to the dispute; (2) the legal reason why the plaintiff is entitled to a remedy; and (3) the *prayer*, or request for relief. The complaint should also explain why this particular court has jurisdiction over the alleged dispute and indicate whether the plaintiff requests a jury trial. If the plaintiff does not request a jury trial within the time limit, that right is deemed to be waived.

Summons After the plaintiff files the complaint, the clerk of the court prepares a summons. The *summons* officially notifies the defendant that a lawsuit is pending against it in a particular court and that it must file a response to the complaint within a certain number of days. The clerk then stamps the official seal of the court on the summons. Next, the plaintiff or the clerk will serve the official summons and complaint on the defendant. Service is usually completed by sending the documents to the defendant by mail.

Answer The defendant's *answer* may admit or deny the various allegations in the complaint. If the defendant believes that it lacks sufficient information to assess the truth of an allegation, it should state this. Such a statement has the effect of a denial. The answer may also deny that the law provides relief for the plaintiff's claim regardless of whether the plaintiff's factual allegations are true.

The answer may put forth affirmative defenses to the allegations in the complaint. An *affirmative defense* admits that the defendant has acted in a certain way but claims that the defendant's conduct was not the real or legal cause of harm to the plaintiff or that the defendant's conduct is excused for some reason. An example of an affirmative defense in a contract case is the requirement under the statute of frauds (discussed in Chapter 7) that certain agreements must be in writing to be enforceable.

An answer may also include a *counterclaim,* a legal claim by the defendant against the plaintiff. The counterclaim need not be related to the plaintiff's claim.

The complaint, the answer, and any reply to the answer filed by the plaintiff are referred to as the *pleadings.*

If the defendant does not file an answer within the time required, a *default judgment* may be entered in favor of the plaintiff. The defendant, however, may ask the court to set aside the default judgment if there were extenuating circumstances for not filing the answer to the complaint on time.

PRETRIAL ACTIVITY

Before the trial begins, the attorneys and the judge usually meet to discuss certain issues.

EXHIBIT 3.4   **Typical Timeline for a Suit Filed in Federal Court**

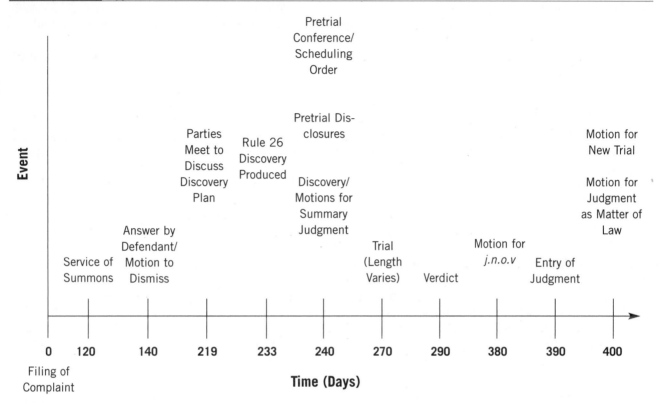

Motion to Dismiss The lawsuit may be resolved before trial by the judge granting a motion to dismiss. A motion formally requests the court to take some action. A *motion to dismiss* seeks to terminate the lawsuit on the ground that the plaintiff's claim is technically inadequate. A judge will grant a motion to dismiss if (1) the court lacks jurisdiction over the subject matter or the parties involved, (2) the plaintiff failed to properly serve the complaint on the defendant, or (3) the plaintiff has failed to state a claim on which relief can be granted.

A party may file a motion to dismiss immediately after the complaint and answer have been filed. This is known as a *motion for judgment on the pleadings.* One party, usually the defendant, argues that the complaint alone demonstrates that the action is futile.

The moving party may file *affidavits,* that is, sworn statements, or other written evidence in an attempt to show that the cause of action is without merit. When information or documents other than the pleadings are involved, the motion becomes a *motion for summary judgment.*

Summary Judgment A judge will grant *summary judgment* only if all of the written evidence before the court clearly

establishes that there are no disputed issues of material fact and that the party who requested the summary judgment is entitled to recover as a matter of law. If there is even a scintilla, that is, even the slightest bit, of evidence that casts doubt on an important fact in the lawsuit, the judge must not grant summary judgment. A judge may, however, grant summary judgment on some issues of the case and let the other issues proceed to trial. This is called a *partial summary judgment.*

Pretrial Conference Pretrial or status conferences may be held either in open court or in the judge's chambers. During these conferences, the attorneys for the litigants meet with the judge to discuss the progress of their case. Topics discussed may include (1) the issues as stated in the pleadings, (2) any amendments to the pleadings, (3) the scheduling of future discovery and a plan for the timely completion of discovery, (4) the status of pending motions or prospective motions that a party may file, (5) a schedule of the disclosure of witnesses or exhibits, and—most important—(6) the prospects for a settlement of the dispute. In the interests of promoting a settlement, the judge will often use this occasion to give each side a candid assessment of the strengths and weaknesses of its case and the likely outcome if the case goes to trial. If a settlement clearly is not feasible, then the pretrial conference will focus on formulating an efficient plan for the trial.

TRIAL

A trial usually goes through the following stages:

1. Selection of the jury (if the trial is before a jury). The judge or attorneys may question the potential jurors.
2. Opening statements, first by the plaintiff's attorney and then by the defendant's attorney.
3. Presentation of evidence and witnesses by the plaintiff's attorney. This consists of:
   a. Direct examination of witnesses by the plaintiff's attorney
   b. Cross-examination of witnesses by the defendant's attorney
   c. Redirect examination by the plaintiff's attorney
   d. Recross-examination by the defendant's attorney
   e. Redirect and recross-examination repeated until both sides have no further questions to ask
4. Presentation of evidence and witnesses by the defendant's attorney. This consists of:
   a. Direct examination of witnesses by the defendant's attorney
   b. Cross-examination of witnesses by the plaintiff's attorney
   c. Redirect and recross-examination until both sides have no further questions to ask
5. Motion for a directed verdict by either attorney.
6. Closing arguments, first by the plaintiff's attorney, then by the defendant's attorney, and then rebuttal by the plaintiff's attorney.
7. The judge's instructions to the jury.
8. Jury deliberations.
9. Announcement of the jury verdict.

Selection of Jury Each side can challenge any number of jurors for cause during the questioning of potential jurors, which is called *voir dire*. Cause includes any relationship between the juror and any of the parties or their counsel. Most jurisdictions also permit a limited number of preemptory challenges. These can be used by counsel to remove potential jurors who counsel thinks might be

"I see jury selection has begun."

inclined to decide for the other side. It is unconstitutional to use a preemptory challenge to remove a potential juror due to race or gender.[20]

Motion for a Directed Verdict At the close of the presentation of all the evidence, either attorney may ask the judge to grant a motion for a *directed verdict*. The moving party asserts that the other side has not produced enough evidence to support the legal claim or defense alleged. The motion requests that the judge take the case away from the jury and direct that a verdict be entered in favor of the party making the motion. Should the judge agree that there is not even an iota of evidence to support one party's claim or defense, the judge will issue a directed verdict. This does not happen very frequently.

Jury Verdict After both sides have presented the closing arguments, the judge instructs the jury on applicable rules of law. After deliberating in private, the jury delivers its verdict, specifying both the prevailing party and the relief to which that party is entitled. In federal court, the six-person jury verdict must be unanimous. In state courts, a unanimous jury verdict is not always required. Frequently, nine out of twelve votes is sufficient.

POSTTRIAL MOTIONS

The announcement of the jury verdict does not necessarily conclude the case. Either party may make a motion to set aside the verdict or to have the case retried.

Judgment Notwithstanding the Verdict Immediately after the jury has rendered its verdict and the jury has been excused from the courtroom, the attorney for the losing party may make a motion for a *judgment notwithstanding the verdict*. Such a judgment, also known as a *judgment n.o.v., (or j.n.o.v.)*, from the Latin *non obstante veredicto*, reverses the jury verdict on the ground that the evidence of the prevailing party was so weak that no reasonable jury could have resolved the dispute in that party's favor. If there is any reasonable possibility that the evidence could support the jury verdict, however, the judge will deny the motion.

New Trial The judge may order a new trial if there were serious errors in the trial process—such as misconduct on the part of the attorneys or the jurors, or the improper

20. *See* Batson v. Kentucky, 476 U.S. 79 (1986) (race); J.E.B. v. Alabama, 511 U.S. 127 (1994) (gender).

"And don't go whining to some higher court."

admission of evidence that severely prejudiced one party's chances for a fair trial.

APPEAL

If the trial judge does not grant the motion for a j.n.o.v. or a new trial, the losing party can appeal the decision. The appellate court will review the manner in which the trial judge applied the law to the case and conducted the trial. The appeals court can review the presentation of evidence at trial, the denial of a motion for a directed verdict, the jury instructions, and even the jury award of damages. The appellate court will not review the facts *de novo* and will reverse a judge's findings of fact only if they are clearly erroneous.

If the appellant loses before the court of appeals, it may want to have the supreme court consider the decision. Appeals are expensive, however, so the losing party should seriously evaluate the likelihood of success at the higher court before pursuing an appeal.

Discovery

Before a trial is held, the parties collect evidence to support their claims through a process called *discovery*. In general, parties may obtain discovery regarding any matter relevant to the claim or defense of any party. Discovery includes

E-COMMERCE

depositions, which are written or oral questions asked of any person who may have helpful information about the facts of the case; *interrogatories,* which are written questions to the parties in the case and their attorneys; and *requests for production of documents,* such as medical records and personal files. In addition, computer files, including electronic mail (e-mail) correspondence, are also subject to discovery and often are the source of crucial evidence.

Electronic mail has become crucial evidence in corporate litigation; it has become routine for parties to demand access to company e-mail dating back ten to twenty years.[21] The Justice Department relied upon e-mail to build its antitrust suit against Microsoft (discussed in the "Inside Story" in Chapter 18). Among these damaging e-mails were messages about rival Netscape calling for "choking off Netscape's air supply" and "knifing the baby" and an internal e-mail from AOL recounting a meeting with Microsoft CEO Bill Gates during which Gates allegedly said, "How much do we need to pay you to screw Netscape?" Most corporate executives would never write damaging statements in official company correspondence, but they often are candid or impolitic in e-mail, apparently not realizing that e-mails are evidence subject to discovery in a lawsuit. As one commentator noted, "E-mail is a truth serum."[22] Parties are frequently able to obtain e-mail messages even if they have been deleted because backup tapes and information on hard drives are also frequently subject to discovery. In fact, computer specialists can restore e-mail messages from magnetic tapes even if they have been overwritten several times.[23]

The basic purpose of discovery is to eliminate the "game" elements in a trial. If all the parties to the lawsuit have all the evidence before trial, everyone benefits. By revealing the strengths and weaknesses of the various claims, discovery frequently allows the lawsuit to be *settled*—resolved by agreement without a trial. At the least, discovery helps prevent any major surprises from occurring at trial because each side already has learned about the other's case.

Discovery serves other useful functions. First, it can preserve evidence. For example, depositions preserve the testimony of important witnesses who may otherwise be unavailable at trial. Second, discovery reduces the number of legal issues to be presented at trial because the parties can see beforehand which claims they have evidence to support and which ones are not worth pursuing.

INTERNATIONAL CONSIDERATION

Discovery rules in foreign countries are not as liberal as American discovery rules and frequently allow the parties to obtain relatively little information or none at all. As a result, if litigation in an American court concerns either an American corporation's foreign subsidiary or one of its offices located in a foreign country, it may prove difficult to obtain documents or take depositions of the employees located in the foreign country. Although litigants can obtain an order from the U.S. court that permits them to petition the court of the foreign country to obtain discovery to be used in the United States, the process is lengthy, and many countries will allow either no or very limited discovery. Even countries such as the United Kingdom, which has a legal system similar to the U.S. system, permit only limited discovery. In addition, the process for taking discovery in foreign countries is frequently different from the U.S. practice. For example, countries often require a judge to be present at depositions, making the procedure more formal and controlled than it is in the United States where only lawyers and witnesses are present.

Discovery has its drawbacks, however. The process is labor-intensive and therefore very expensive. Frequently, hours and days of depositions and hundreds of interrogatories will be undertaken. The strategy behind such a plan can be twofold: to wear down the opposing party by making the lawsuit more expensive than a victory would be worth, or to keep the papers flowing at such a rate that the other side cannot discern what all the documents really state. Taken too far, these strategies can lead to discovery abuse, which reduces the already slow pace of litigation, significantly increases costs, and can anger judges.

As discussed further in Chapter 25, the Private Securities Litigation Reform Act of 1995 severely cut back on a plaintiff's right to discovery in a securities fraud case prior to the court's ruling on the defendant's motion to dismiss. Congress intended thereby to deter plaintiffs with no evidence of wrongdoing from going on "fishing expeditions," which often proved very expensive and burdensome for the defendant and made it more likely that a defendant would settle an otherwise frivolous claim just to avoid the costs of discovery and litigation.

Rule 26 of the Federal Rules of Civil Procedure, as amended effective December 1, 2000, imposes certain mandatory disclosure requirements on parties. Prior to a discovery request, parties must produce (1) the names of individuals likely to have discoverable information that the disclosing party may use to support its claims or defenses,

21. David S. Bennahum, *Old E-mail Never Dies,* WIRED, May 1999, at 100.
22. *Id.* at 102
23. *Id.* at 109

unless solely for impeachment; (2) documents that the disclosing party may use to support its claims or defenses, unless solely for impeachment; (3) documents relating to the calculation of damages; (4) insurance agreements that may cover the claims at issue in the case; and (5) the names of expert witnesses who may testify at trial. As of December 1, 2000, Rule 30 of the Federal Rules of Civil Procedure limits parties to ten depositions per side (of not more than seven hours duration per deposition) and twenty-five interrogatories, unless the court orders otherwise.

Courts may impose penalties upon companies and their counsel for discovery abuses. In *In re E.I. DuPont de Nemours & Co.,*[24] a federal district court held that DuPont had committed fraud, abused discovery, and violated court orders by repeatedly failing to disclose test data that were critical to the plaintiff's claim that DuPont's product had damaged the plaintiff's crops. Finding that DuPont had consciously and deliberately withheld data and had presented untrue information to the court regarding the discovery requests, the court fined DuPont $6.8 million for

24. 918 F. Supp. 1524 (M.D. Ga. 1995).

discovery abuses and $100 million for civil contempt. The latter sanction could be waived by complying with the other court orders and taking out full-page ads in the *Wall Street Journal* and major papers in Georgia, Alabama, and Michigan admitting wrongdoing and describing the order of the court. For every day that DuPont did not comply with the order, it would be fined $30,000. The U.S. Court of Appeals for the Eleventh Circuit[25] overturned these fines after concluding that they were overwhelmingly punitive and therefore criminal in nature, and it remanded the case to the district court for hearings to determine the appropriate nonpunitive discovery sanctions.

Some courts have placed limitations upon deposing the most senior executives of a corporation (often referred to as *apex depositions*). In the following case, the Texas Supreme Court addressed the issue of whether senior-level executives can be deposed if other employees in the company also have knowledge of the facts in the case and could provide testimony on the issues.

25. *In re* E.I. DuPont de Nemours & Co., Belnate Litigation, 99 F.3d 363 (11th Cir. 1996), *cert. denied,* 522 U.S. 906 (1997).

A CASE IN POINT

CASE 3.5

***In re* Alcatel USA, Inc.**
Supreme Court of Texas
11 S.W.3d 173 (Tex. 2000).

In the Language of the Court

FACTS DSC Communications, Inc. (DSC) filed suit alleging that Samsung planned to steal a new DSC telecommunication technology by luring away a team of engineers from DSC and then assigning them to develop the same type of product they had developed at DSC. DSC also claimed that high-level executives at Samsung engineered this plan and were involved in its execution at all stages. DSC tried to depose two high-level Samsung executives: Jin-Ku Kang, who served as chairman of Samsung during the events that gave rise to the case and was chairman emeritus at the time that DSC filed its claim, and Kun-Hee Lee, who was chairman of the Samsung Chaebol (group of companies) during the events that gave rise to the case and was chairman and CEO of Samsung at the time the case was filed. Samsung moved to quash both depositions.

ISSUE PRESENTED Should plaintiffs be allowed to depose the senior executives of a company if there are other employees with knowledge of the facts at issue or alternative means of obtaining the information?

OPINION ABBOTT, J., writing for the Supreme Court of Texas:

This court first adopted the apex deposition guidelines in *Crown Central Petroleum Corp. v Georgia.*[26] We held that the apex deposition guidelines apply "[w]hen a party seeks to depose a corporate president or other high level corporate official. . . ."

. . . Under *Crown Central,* if the party seeking the deposition has "arguably shown that the official has any unique or superior personal knowledge of discoverable

26. 904 S.W.2d 125 (Tex. 1995).

(Continued)

(Case 3.5 continued)

information," the trial court should deny the motion for protection and the party seeking discovery should be entitled to take the apex depositions. The party seeking the apex deposition is required to pursue less intrusive means of discovering the information only when that party cannot make the requisite showing concerning unique or superior knowledge.

We consider first whether DSC arguably showed that Lee or Kang have unique or superior personal knowledge of discoverable information.

The most comprehensive discussion of Kun-Hee Lee's knowledge as it relates to this lawsuit is found in a document submitted by DSC titled: "Kun-Hee Lee's Significance and Connection to This Lawsuit." In that document, DSC urges several reasons why Lee's deposition is necessary. First, under the heading "Kun-Hee Lee Sets Samsung's Course," DSC claims that (1) Lee is the leader of the Samsung Chaebol, (2) Lee sets the overall vision for the Samsung companies, and (3) Samsung's goal is to be one of the world's top five telecommunications companies by 2005. Second, under the heading "Kun-Hee Lee's Ties To The Lead Defendant, Samsung Electronics Co., Ltd.," DSC states that Lee (1) was the chief executive officer and president of SEC, (2) was a long-standing director of SEC, and (3) is the largest single owner of Samsung and its subsidiaries.

Evidence tending to support these allegations does not satisfy the first *Crown Central* test; it merely demonstrates that Lee is a long-time company leader who sets the company vision with lofty goals. Virtually every company's CEO has similar characteristics. Allowing apex depositions merely because a high-level corporate official possesses apex-level knowledge would eviscerate the very guidelines established in *Crown Central*. Such evidence is too general to arguably show the official's knowledge is unique or superior.

…

J.K. Kang served as Chairman of defendant SEC during the earliest events that gave rise to this case and is currently Chairman Emeritus of that corporation. DSC contends that Kang's unique or superior personal knowledge is arguably shown by the deposition testimony of Dr. Joo-Hyung Lee, an SEC manager who personally oversaw the establishment of Samsung's Dallas laboratory. Contrary to DSC's contention, Joo Hyung Lee's deposition conveys that Kang may have been made aware of information contained in reports prepared by others, but still does not show why Kang's knowledge may be unique or superior.

…

[The] evidence arguably shows that Kang may have discoverable information. But the first *Crown Central* guideline requires more; it requires that the person to be deposed arguably have "unique or superior personal knowledge of discoverable information." This requirement is not satisfied by merely showing that a high-level executive has some knowledge of discoverable information. If "some knowledge" were enough, the apex deposition guidelines would be meaningless; they would be virtually indistinguishable from the scope of general discovery. Although *Crown Central* did not elaborate on what character of knowledge makes it unique or superior, there must be some showing beyond mere relevance, such as evidence that a high-level executive is the only person with personal knowledge of the information sought or that the executive arguably possesses relevant knowledge greater in quality or quantity than other available sources.

(Continued)

(Case 3.5 continued)

...

Because DSC failed to arguably show that either Kang or Lee possesses unique or superior knowledge of discoverable information, the trial court's order cannot be supported under the first *Crown Central* test. Nevertheless, DSC argues that it has pursued less intrusive means and therefore is entitled to the depositions under *Crown Central's* second guideline. From the record before us, DSC has not shown that it attempted to obtain the information it sought from Kang through less intrusive methods. DSC based its contention that Kang has unique or superior knowledge largely on his presence at a written and oral presentation concerning the next generation switching system. But, DSC was allowed to depose Joo-Hyung Lee, who presented the report to Kang and Song. Also, DSC deposed Song, the Samsung executive in charge of telecommunications, who also attended the presentation. Yet, DSC has failed to identify any relevant information that it seeks from Kang that it attempted and failed to obtain from either Joo-Hyung Lee or Song.

In addition, DSC failed to establish that it attempted to obtain the information that it sought from Lee through less intrusive methods. DSC argued that Lee has unique and superior knowledge regarding Samsung's policies. But the special master allowed DSC to depose Kim, the president and CEO of SEC during the relevant time. Yet, DSC failed to ask Kim any questions about Samsung's "vision" for telecommunications or any of the other issues DSC now contends justify an apex deposition of Lee. DSC also did not issue interrogatories, requests for admissions, or any other forms of discovery to Samsung regarding its corporate policies. The record simply does not show that the information sought from Lee was sought by less intrusive means or that the information sought was unobtainable from other sources.

RESULT The Texas Supreme Court ruled that the trial court abused its discretion when it refused to quash the depositions of Kang and Lee. DSC was not entitled to depose Kang or Lee.

DISSENT ENOCH, J., joined by BAKER, J., and O'NEILL, J., dissenting from the majority opinion:

The Court's conclusion is problematic because it would require a litigant seeking to depose a CEO regarding a board-level decision, about which all present at the board meeting have the same information, to depose a lower-level board member and not the CEO. Why should a litigant be forced to depose the least qualified witness when it could depose the most qualified if they have the same information? While the CEO and a lower-level official may have the same information, they have different levels of knowledge. As one federal court has concluded, an apex official's knowledge may be deemed unique and the deposition allowed, even if other corporate officials possess similar knowledge.

Moreover, the Court's opinion treats "knowledge" as though it were only the bare facts communicated to Kang and nothing more. But knowledge is more than mere information. The Court ignores the role that Kang's, or any apex official's, position within the corporation plays on the information received. When the policies driving corporate action and personal knowledge of actions taken in pursuit of such policies intersect, a new level of knowledge arises. When the motives behind corporate action are at issue, *arguably* the knowledge created at that intersection is unique to the corporate

(Continued)

(Case 3.5 continued)

officers. And certainly that level of knowledge is "greater in quality" than the level possessed by the individual who communicated only the bare facts.

QUESTIONS

1. Which analysis do you find more persuasive, that of the majority opinion or the dissent?
2. What public policy is served by making it harder to depose top executives than lower-level employees?

 # Attorney–Client *and* Other Privileges *and the* Attorney Work-Product Doctrine

Although generally any person with knowledge of facts relevant to a case can be required to testify in depositions or at trial, the attorney–client privilege and other privileges designed to protect certain relationships limit the introduction of certain types of evidence.

ATTORNEY–CLIENT PRIVILEGE

Perhaps the most important limitation on discovery and testimony at trial is the *attorney–client privilege*. It dates back to the sixteenth century and provides that a court cannot force the disclosure of confidential communications between a client and his or her attorney. The privilege survives the death of the client.

The attorney–client privilege is intended to promote the administration of justice. Clients are more likely to make a full and frank disclosure of the facts to an attorney if they know that the attorney cannot be compelled to pass the information on to adversary parties. An attorney is better able to advise and represent a client if the client discloses the complete facts. The privilege may also help to prevent unnecessary litigation because an attorney who knows all the facts should be better able to assess whether litigation is justified.

To be protected by the privilege, a communication must occur between the attorney and the client. The communication must also be intended to be confidential. If the client plans to relay the information to others or makes the communication in the presence of other individuals not involved in the lawsuit, there is no confidentiality.

The attorney–client privilege belongs to the client alone. The attorney, however, has an obligation to alert the client to the existence of the privilege and, if neces-

sary, to invoke it on the client's behalf. The client can waive the privilege over the attorney's objection if the client so desires.

Limitations The attorney to whom the communication is made must be a practicing attorney at the time of the communication, and the person making the communication must be a current or prospective client seeking

 ETHICAL CONSIDERATION

You are a top manager at a major corporation. The corporation has recently been sued in federal district court by an individual who was injured by one of its widgets. Your in-house counsel tells you that the plaintiff's counsel is competent but a sole practitioner specializing in family law. You discuss litigation strategy with your attorney. One tactic is to overwhelm opposing counsel through the discovery process. Your counsel provides several options: (1) delivering forty boxes of corporate documents a day for four days, of which perhaps sixty pages are relevant to the suit, then moving for dismissal on the fifth day; (2) actively mislabeling or hiding documents in the above "document dump"; (3) not providing any relevant information to opposing counsel but sending box after box of useless material; (4) stalling and delaying document requests because the corporation "is unable to locate them"; (5) accurately labeling the relevant material but including it in a "document dump"; (6) declaring that only through extensive travel would opposing counsel be able to access the relevant information (sending individuals likely to be deposed all over the world on "important projects"); (7) continuously delaying and extending the number of depositions, interrogatories, and other materials needed in order to "effectively prepare for trial"; (8) promptly providing only the relevant information in a way the opposing counsel may easily access it; and (9) lying and destroying all relevant documents. Which option should you select and why?

legal advice. A conversation between the client and the attorney about nonlegal matters is not protected. In *United States v. Frederick,*[27] the U.S. Court of Appeals for the Seventh Circuit held that neither the attorney–client privilege nor the work-product doctrine (discussed below) protected documents created by or communications with a lawyer who was acting as both an attorney and a tax preparer in preparing a client's tax returns. The court reasoned that a taxpayer "must not be allowed, by hiring a lawyer to do the work that an accountant, or other tax preparer, or the taxpayer himself, normally would do, to obtain greater protection from government investigations than a taxpayer who did not use a lawyer as his tax preparer."

In *Satcom International Group PLC v. Orbcomm International Partners LP,*[28] the district court held that Virginia's attorney–client privilege protected discussions between corporate executives and the company's lawyer at a meeting called for the purpose of making a legal decision, even if this decision also had commercial ramifications, as long as the corporation's counsel was present to provide legal advice and all discussion concerned the legal decision.

In contrast, in *United States v. Ackert,*[29] the U.S. Court of Appeals for the Second Circuit ruled that the attorney–client privilege did not protect a corporate counsel's discussion with an investment banker for the purpose of learning information to help advise the corporation on an investment decision. Paramount Corporation's tax lawyer had met with Paramount's investment banker at Goldman Sachs to discuss the legal and financial implications of an investment that could reduce Paramount's tax liability.

The attorney–client privilege does not protect client communications that are made to further a crime or other illegal act. Thus, if an executive asks his or her attorney about the best way to embezzle money, that conversation is not privileged.

In July 1997, the Florida Court of Appeal rejected the tobacco companies' claim of attorney–client privilege for eight confidential documents, including attorneys' notes from in-house meetings on legal strategy.[30] The court concluded that because the documents contained evidence that tobacco attorneys participated in an industry-wide conspiracy to defraud the public about the danger of smoking, they came within the exception for communications to further commission of fraud or a crime.

Corporate Clients With communications between a corporate client and an attorney, it is often difficult to define what element of the corporation can be considered the client. The corporation does not fit the common definition of a client because the corporation itself is unable to communicate with the attorney except through its officers, directors, agents, or employees. In *Upjohn Co. v. United States,*[31] the Supreme Court adopted a subject matter test to determine when the attorney–client privilege is available to a corporation. Under this test, the privilege protects the communications or discussions of any company employee with counsel as long as the subject matter of the communication relates to that employee's duties and the communication is made at the direction of a corporate superior. Thus, communications between a corporation's attorneys and any of its employees, not just a small, upper-level group, are protected under the attorney–client privilege as long as those communications pass the subject matter test. The Court also ruled that the attorney–client privilege extends to communications made to both in-house and outside counsel as long as the attorneys are acting in a legal capacity.

The attorney–client privilege may also extend to communications between a consultant hired by a corporation and an attorney although courts will examine the specific facts of each situation to determine whether the privilege applies. In *In re Bieter Co.,*[32] the U.S. Court of Appeals for the Eighth Circuit held that the attorney–client privilege extended to communications between a partnership's attorney and a consultant to the partnership who was the functional equivalent of an employee. Even though the consultant was an independent contractor, not an employee, he was still a representative of the client partnership. He had daily contact with the partnership's principals, had acted as the partnership's sole representative in critical meetings, and had worked with the partnership's attorneys on the lawsuit.

The decision in *Upjohn* did not resolve all of the uncertainties regarding the application of attorney–client privilege to corporations. The Supreme Court did not decide whether the privilege applies to communications with former employees. Nor did it resolve the issue of what exactly constitutes a voluntary waiver of the attorney–client privilege by a corporation. Finally, there is still uncertainty about the protection the privilege gives corporations in suits brought against them by shareholders.

Guidelines Following the Supreme Court's decision in *Upjohn,* a few guidelines can be suggested for attorneys

27. 182 F.3d 496 (7th Cir. 1999), *cert. denied,* 120 S. Ct. 1157 (2000).
28. 1999 WL 76847 (S.D.N.Y. Feb. 16, 1999).
29. 169 F.3d 136 (2d Cir. 1999).
30. 66 U.S.L.W. 1112 (Aug. 19, 1997).

31. 449 U.S. 383 (1981).
32. 16 F.3d 929 (8th Cir. 1994).

and corporations concerning the best way to keep communications within the scope of the attorney–client privilege:[33]

1. Communication between an attorney and a corporation is protected only when a client is seeking or receiving legal advice, not business advice. Thus, corporations should request legal advice in writing and assign communication with the attorney to a specific employee who has responsibility over the subject matter at issue.

2. Corporations should make sure that all communication between employees and corporate counsel is directed by senior management and that the employees know they must keep all communications confidential.

3. Corporations should deal directly with counsel (not through intermediaries) and maintain confidential files and documentation.

4. When a corporation gives a governmental agency access to its communications or files, the corporation should negotiate a written agreement of confidentiality with the agency or an agreement that the agency will not take physical possession of the documents. The corporation should also investigate the possibility of statutory protection in this situation.

OTHER PRIVILEGES

In addition to the attorney–client privilege, there are other privileges a party may assert to protect information the opposing party seeks to discover. Discussions between a physician and patient are privileged unless the patient has made his or her medical condition an issue at trial. For example, a person claiming damages for a back injury resulting from an automobile accident will be deemed to have waived the privilege at least as to any medical history relating to his or her back. The U.S. Supreme Court has recognized a privilege protecting discussions between a psychologist or licensed social worker and a patient.[34] The priest–penitent privilege protects disclosures made to a priest during confession. The Fifth Amendment to the U.S. Constitution gives any person the right to refuse to testify if it would tend to incriminate him or her.

Several courts have recognized a privilege extending to corporate "self-critical analyses," on the grounds that

the forced disclosure of such potentially negative information could deter socially beneficial investigation and evaluation. For instance, in *Tice v. American Airlines, Inc.*,[35] the plaintiffs sought to obtain American Airlines' "top-to-bottom" safety reports in connection with their claim that the forced retirement of airline pilots over the age of sixty constituted age discrimination. The court upheld American Airlines' claim of privilege, emphasizing that "the public has a strong interest in preserving the free flow of airline safety [monitoring- and improvement-] related information."

ATTORNEY WORK-PRODUCT DOCTRINE

The *attorney work-product doctrine* protects information that an attorney prepares in the course of his or her work. This information includes the private memoranda created by the attorney and his or her personal thoughts while preparing a case for trial. The rationale behind the work-product rule is that lawyers, while performing their duties, must "work with a certain degree of privacy, free from unnecessary intrusion by opposing parties and their counsel."[36] Work-product materials may be obtained only with a showing of extreme necessity, such that the failure to obtain the materials would unduly prejudice the other party's case or create hardship and injustice. The work-product doctrine is broader than the attorney–client privilege and may thus protect discovery that is not protected by the privilege. For example, in *National Education Training Group, Inc. v. SkillSoft Corp.*,[37] the court found that a corporation had waived the attorney–client privilege regarding notes summarizing its counsel's legal advice at board meetings by permitting an assistant to one of the directors to attend the meetings. However, the assistant's notes were protected by the work-product doctrine because they summarized the lawyer's advice regarding litigation against the corporation.

Class Actions

If the conduct of the defendant affected numerous persons in a common way, the case may be brought as a *class action suit* by a representative of the class of persons affected. This was done in the asbestos personal-injury cases brought against asbestos manufacturers such as GAF Corporation and Pfizer, the silicone-breast-implant cases involving Dow Corning and others, and the smoking

33. Based on Block & Remz, *After "Upjohn": The Uncertain Confidentiality of Corporate Internal Investigative Files, in* American Bar Association Section on Litigation, Recent Developments in Attorney–Client Privilege, Work-Product Doctrine and Confidentiality of Communications Between Counsel and Client (1983).

34. Jaffee v. Redmond, 518 U.S. 1 (1996).

35. 192 F.R.D. 270 (N.D. Ill. 2000).

36. Hickman v. Taylor, 329 U.S. 495, 510 (1947).

37. 1999 WL 378337 (S.D.N.Y. June 9, 1999).

cases brought against the tobacco companies. Class actions are the norm in actions alleging securities fraud.

Written notice of the formation of the class must be mailed to all potential class members. Anyone who wants to litigate separately can opt out of the class. *Business Week* estimates that 260,000 out of millions of potential claimants for asbestos-related injury elected to opt out of a $1 billion settlement reached in 1993 involving twenty of the largest asbestos manufacturers.[38] If a person does not opt out, he or she is a member of the class and will be bound by any decision or settlement reached in the class action.

Although historically corporate defendants have condemned class actions as an easy way for an eager plaintiff and his or her lawyer to get to court, this perception is changing. Some companies now view class actions as a "strategic management tool" that can end litigation nightmares and work to their advantage by avoiding potentially devastating jury awards, reducing litigation costs, and limiting long-term liability.[39] A class action can have the following advantages in a major product liability case: (1) the settlement can bind not only present class members but also future claimants; (2) standardized payment schedules avoid the risk of widely divergent jury awards; (3) some claimants who suffered less harm than others can be excluded from the settlement; and (4) the filing of suits and the settlement can occur on the same day.[40]

Any settlement of a class action requires approval by the court hearing the case. Until recently, courts were hesitant to reject a mutually agreed upon settlement. In *Amchem Products, Inc. v. Windsor,*[41] however, the U.S. Supreme Court tightened the requirements for class certification, making settlement more difficult. The named plaintiffs, nine individuals who were exposed to asbestos, filed a class-action complaint, answer, and settlement proposal with the defendant, Amchem Products. They purported to represent the class of individuals who had not previously sued asbestos manufacturers and either (1) had been exposed to asbestos attributable to petitioner through their occupations or the occupation of a household member or (2) had a spouse or family member who had been exposed to asbestos. The size of the class was indeterminate but estimated to include hundreds of thousands, perhaps millions, of individuals. Only half of the named plaintiffs alleged currently manifested medical conditions as a result of exposure, while others had not yet developed any asbestos-related medical condition.

 ETHICAL CONSIDERATION

If a product has caused harm to persons but they will not discover it until a future date, is it ethical for the product's manufacturer to enter into a class-action settlement that provides limited funds for future claimants?

The Supreme Court held that the proposed class did not satisfy Federal Rules of Civil Procedure Rule 23(b)(3)'s mandate that common questions "predominate over any question affecting only individual members." The class members' shared experience of exposure to asbestos was not sufficient because there were different categories of class members (different medical problems and the existence or absence of asbestos-related symptoms) and multiple individual differences (different medical histories, different levels and types of exposure, and varying degrees of severity of asbestos-related medical conditions). Characterizing the class as "sprawling," the Court concluded that the differences between the class members were greater than their commonalities. Therefore, the predominance requirement of Rule 23(b)(3) was not fulfilled.

The Court also found that the class failed to satisfy the Rule 23(a)(4) requirement for adequate representation. Essentially, Rule 23(a)(4) requires that the representatives of a class be part of the class and have the same interests as the class members. In this case, however, the class members had different interests. Those currently injured would seek immediate payment while exposure-only plaintiffs would seek a generous, protected fund for future compensation. Thus, it was impossible to ensure that the class representatives could adequately represent the members' interests.

The *Amchem* decision was handed down at a time when the Supreme Court's Advisory Committee on Civil Rules was considering a proposal to make settlements easier in class-action lawsuits.[42] The decision was a signal to both the Advisory Committee and the lower courts to evaluate petitions for class certification and class-action settlements more carefully. Indeed, lawyers working on lawsuits involving the so-called fen-phen diet pill (*ex post,* diet pills were linked to heart valve damage and a rare form of lung disease) indicated that class-action lawsuits "are in a new era"[43] with courts less likely to accept class certifications and settlements.

38. Catherine Yan, *Look Who's Talking Settlement,* BUS. WK., July 18, 1994, at 72.
39. Richard B. Schmitt, *The Deal Makers: Some Firms Embrace the Widely Dreaded Class-Action Lawsuit,* WALL ST. J., July 18, 1996, at A1.
40. Yan, *supra* note 38.
41. 521 U.S. 591 (1997).

42. Richard B. Schmitt, *High Court Upsets Class-Action Proposal,* WALL ST. J., July 10, 1997, at B10.
43. Richard B. Schmitt, *Thinning the Ranks: Diet-Pill Litigation Finds Courts Frowning on Mass Settlements,* WALL ST. J., Jan. 8, 1998, at A1.

INTERNATIONAL CONSIDERATION

Few countries besides the United States allow class-action suits. Changes in China's civil and administrative laws in 1991 authorized "group suits." As of 1999, at least two dozen class actions were pending before Chinese courts.[a] These cases included an action by 12,000 farmers against the local government bosses who allegedly beat the farmers and confiscated their furniture and other personal possessions when they could not pay their taxes due to the destruction of their crops by a drought followed by a flood.[b] Other class actions included claims by 200 residents against a city for evicting them from their houses to build a shopping mall, a claim by 400 shopkeepers against a government-run market for arbitrarily raising their rents, and a case brought by 1,000 farmers against a local producer of grain seeds for selling duds.[c]

a. Ian Johnson, *Class-Action Suits Let the Aggrieved in China Appeal for Rule of Law,* WALL ST. J., Mar. 24, 1999, at A1.
b. *Id.*
c. *Id.*

 Litigation Strategies
for Plaintiffs

When planning to file a lawsuit, the plaintiff must decide which legal claim is most likely to succeed. The plaintiff must also decide in which court to pursue the lawsuit.

THE DECISION TO SUE

Parties frequently file a lawsuit without giving sufficient thought to the various consequences. Before filing a lawsuit, one should consider (1) whether the likelihood of recovery and the amount of recovery are enough to justify the cost and disruption of litigation; (2) whether the defendant will be able to satisfy a judgment against it; (3) whether the defendant is likely to raise a counterclaim; (4) whether suing will cause any ill will among customers, suppliers, or other sources of corporate financing; (5) whether any publicity accompanying the suit will be harmful; and (6) whether the litigation will have a lasting adverse impact on the company's relationship with the defendant. For example, a company may be advised not to sue the manufacturer of its multimillion-dollar computer over a $50,000 software problem if the company must rely on this manufacturer for support, service, and parts for the next few years.

If a lawsuit appears inevitable, there may be some advantage to filing a claim first. The plaintiff's claim determines in which court the case will be heard. The defendant, however, may be able to remove an action from state court to federal court if there is diversity of citizenship or a federal question. Alternatively, it may be able to remove the action to a more appropriate *venue,* or location.

Parties should always consider settling the suit. Recent figures show that more than 90 percent of cases settle out of court, saving all parties the time, cost, and ill will of a trial. Filing a lawsuit can be a tactic to encourage settlement of a dispute that neither party really wishes to bring to trial. Settlement discussions usually occur during the pretrial stages.

Initiation and prosecution of a meritless and frivolous claim may result in an award of attorneys' fees. In *Kirby v. General Electric Co.,*[44] the court granted General Electric's motion for attorneys' fees after determining that a class of employees initiated a claim alleging that GE interfered with their rights under the Employee Retirement Income Security Act without inquiring into the factual or legal justification of the claim and continued to prosecute their claims even after it was clear that they were meritless and flawed. The court ordered that one-half of the attorneys' fees be assessed against the plaintiffs' counsel personally. Similarly, in *Jandrt v. Jerome Foods, Inc.,*[45] the Wisconsin Supreme Court imposed sanctions against a law firm that pursued a toxic torts case without taking any steps to investigate a critical element of the case, namely, whether the plaintiff's exposure to chemicals while working at her employer's plant was the cause of her children's birth defects; instead, the law firm had simply waited for the results of formal discovery. The court found that the law firm was, however, justified in rushing to file the lawsuit before consulting an expert about causation because a statutory change in the law could have negatively affected the plaintiff's case before the investigation was completed.

The Private Securities Reform Act of 1995, enacted to make it more difficult to initiate securities class actions, includes a provision that awards the cost of attorneys' fees to the opposing party if the court finds that a party filed a complaint, pleading, or motion that does not comply with Rule 11 of the Federal Rules of Civil Procedure. To deter frivolous actions, Rule 11 requires motions and complaints to be filed in good faith and substantiated by facts.

44. No. 5:98CV70-V (W.D.N.C. Mar. 22, 2000) (order awarding attorneys' fees).
45. 597 N.W.2d 744 (Wis. 1999), *recons. denied,* 601 N.W.2d 650 (Wis. 1999).

Parties should also consider alternatives to litigation, such as arbitration and mediation. Alternative dispute resolution techniques are discussed in Chapter 4.

Some attorneys recommend that companies construct a prelitigation "decision tree," which determines at each step of the proceeding the chances of prevailing or losing, the costs of going forward, and the potential amount of recovery. Developing a decision tree forces a company to conduct a substantial factual and legal analysis of its claim. This is in everyone's interest; courts are inclined to impose monetary penalties or "sanctions" on companies, individuals, and attorneys who file lawsuits without sufficient facts or an adequate legal basis to support their claims.

THE DECISION TO SETTLE

Some lawsuits are unlikely to settle: for example, (1) cases presenting legal questions—such as the meaning of an ambiguous term in a contract—that the court should clarify to avoid future disputes between the same parties, (2) cases that could bring a large recovery if the plaintiff wins and no great harm if it loses, and (3) cases where one side has acted so unreasonably that settlement is impossible.

Sometimes a lawsuit is worth pursuing simply to establish a company's credibility as one that will fight to support a legitimate business position. If applied too rigidly, however, such a philosophy can be expensive and may do more harm than good.

Settlement is likely in a case when pursuing the lawsuit all the way to trial is not cost efficient. For example, if a plaintiff alleges that a product is defective and caused him or her a loss of $4,500, the legal expenses will far exceed the original loss. Discovery alone is likely to cost more than $4,500. In such a case, it is in both parties' interest to settle the dispute if at all possible. However, if the plaintiff's claim is similar to many other identical claims that may be brought against the company, settling the first claim could appear to commit the defendant to paying all the other claims, too.

PRETRIAL PREPARATION

Having decided to file a lawsuit, the company should carefully select the personnel who will act as the contacts for the attorneys. These individuals should make sure that the necessary information and documents are gathered for the attorneys. They should have substantial authority in the company.

Executives or senior management who will be involved in the lawsuit or with the corporate attorneys should not

AT THE TOP

Sometimes the managers or employees intimately involved in a dispute lack the perspective and objectivity to determine the merits and the full impact a particular litigation decision will have on the company as a whole. As a result, it is important for members of higher management and, in some cases, the full board of directors to become involved in the decisions of when to sue, when to settle or dismiss, and how vigorously to defend.

handle public relations. This could lead to disputes regarding waiver of the attorney–client privilege.

The company should instruct all employees not to destroy any documents that may be relevant to the lawsuit. Destruction of these documents, particularly after the claim is filed, can be harmful and even illegal. Document-retention policies are discussed in greater detail later in this chapter.

The company should instruct employees not to discuss the lawsuit with anyone, including family or close friends. Casual comments about bankrupting the opposing party or teaching an opponent a lesson may turn up as testimony at trial, with undesirable consequences.

The company and its attorney should develop a budget for the lawsuit. Then, at each step of the case, strategic options can be discussed on the basis of cost–benefit analysis. The budget should include not only the lawyer's fees but also (1) the cost of employee time, (2) damage to company morale, (3) disruption of business, and (4) other hidden expenses. A budget will help the company manager and lawyer decide whether to pursue the lawsuit or attempt to settle.

The attorney and client should then select a court in which to file the lawsuit. Federal courts may be more accustomed to handling complex business litigation, such as that involving federal securities law or employment-discrimination laws. State courts are usually skilled in handling business disputes ranging from contract matters to personal-injury lawsuits. Other considerations about where to file include (1) the convenience and location of necessary witnesses and documents, (2) the location of trial counsel, (3) the reputation and size of the company and its opponent in a particular area, and (4) the possibility of favorable or unfavorable publicity.

All courts urge the parties to confer and settle the case if possible. The judge will act as a settlement mediator and objectively assist counsel in recognizing the strengths and weaknesses of their cases. Some state courts require a settlement conference before a specially designated settlement judge. The parties may also hire retired judges, professional mediators, law school professors, or mediators who are part of a bar association settlement program to facilitate settlement.

Litigation Strategies *for* Defendants

A defendant receiving a complaint and summons should never let the lawsuit go unattended. The defendant should plan a defense strategy and follow it step by step. Factual and legal preparation should be done promptly so that important evidence—such as the memory of key witnesses—is not lost.

When a company receives the complaint, efforts should be made to determine why the plaintiff felt it necessary to sue. Factors to consider may include (1) whether prior bargaining or negotiations with the plaintiff broke down, and why; (2) whether the company's negotiator was pursuing the wrong tactics or following an agenda inconsistent with the company's best interests; and (3) whether the lawsuit resulted from bad personnel practices that the company still needs to correct. Senior executives should also get together and decide whether it would be beneficial to discuss the lawsuit with the plaintiff.

A defendant should also promptly consider the possibility of a settlement and review the ways in which amicable negotiations could be commenced or resumed. The defendant may also want to consider mediation or arbitration as alternatives to an expensive trial. Sometimes an apology can be more important than a vigorous defense in a case where the plaintiff feels unjustly wronged.

POLITICAL PERSPECTIVE

Should *the* United States Adopt *the* British Rule That *the* Loser Pays *the* Winner's Attorneys' Fees?

The costs of litigation are spiraling, and policymakers are scrambling to find the cause. With greater frequency, informed legal commentators have fingered plaintiffs who file lawsuits to extort a settlement, even when they know that the expected return from the trial will be negative. To deter such nuisance lawsuits and lessen the tide of excessive litigation in general, scholars, politicians, and ordinary citizens have called for the United States to adopt the British rule whereby the loser of a trial must pay the legal expenses, including attorneys' fees, of the victor. Virtually every Western European country uses this rule—also known as the "loser pays" rule. The American system, by contrast, requires each litigant to bear its own attorneys' fees regardless of the trial's outcome, unless there is a contract providing that the loser must pay the winner's attorneys' fees.

In the early 1990s, these calls for legal reform entered mainstream politics. In January 1991, President George Bush's Council on Competitiveness established a working group on Federal Civil Justice Reform, which recommended adoption of a modified "loser pays" rule in cases involving state law brought under the

federal courts' diversity jurisdiction. The loser would pay the winner's costs of vindicating its prevailing position, but fee shifting would be limited to the amount of fees that the loser incurred, which could be further limited by judicial discretion. The council asserted:

Adopting a "loser pays" rule for payment of attorney's fees will provide those bringing suit with a choice of methods to finance their litigation. The rule would help fund meritorious claims not currently initiated because the cost of pursuing the claim would have exceeded the expected recovery. . . . Because the losing party will be obligated to pay the winner's fees, this approach will encourage litigants to evaluate carefully the merits of their cases before initiating a frivolous claim or adopting a spurious defense.

The proposal aroused considerable opposition, however, and was rejected by the American Bar Association (ABA). John Curtin, a former ABA president, said that the ABA had rejected the proposal for a modified British rule because it would have a "chilling effect" on the legal rights of certain individuals. He explained that execution of the "loser pays" rule would discourage potential litigants with bona fide claims from bringing suit due to trepidation over monetary ruin.

Both consumer groups and civil libertarians also attacked the proposal. On August 13, 1991, Public Citizen, a consumer advocate organization led by Ralph Nader, issued a news release calling the council's report an "anti-worker, anti-consumer, pro-corporate-wrongdoer blueprint for undermining America's system of common law." Other critics contended that the fee-shifting rule would limit access to the judiciary for the indigent and would inhibit the bringing of novel or untested legal theories. Efforts by the Republican majority in Congress in the mid-1990s to adopt the British rule as part of the "Contract With America" failed.

If the lawsuit cannot be settled, then the defendant should proceed with the same steps required of the plaintiff—plan a strategy, prepare a budget for the action, and so on. If the suit was filed in a state court, the defendant must decide whether it is possible and desirable to move the action to federal court.

Courts have imposed sanctions upon defendants for pursuing litigation in bad faith. In *Johnston v. Vendel*,[46] the Delaware Supreme Court found that the defendants' bad faith in prolonging litigation justified invoking an exception to the "American rule" that each side pays its own attorneys' fees and awarded the plaintiff $1.6 million in attorneys' fees and disbursements. The court found that the defendants misled the court in compelling unnecessary discovery, falsified evidence, and tried to justify violating a standstill agreement with the plaintiff based on changed sworn testimony.

If the plaintiff has sued in a place that is greatly inconvenient for the defendant and its witnesses, the defendant may file a motion for a change of venue. A federal district court may transfer the case to a federal district court in another state. A state court, however, can only transfer the case to another location within the state.

Document Retention

When a company is a defendant in a lawsuit, company documents, including computer files, may be used to prove liability in court. According to the *Wall Street Journal*, some companies are destroying three times as many documents as they did a decade ago. Companies have learned that nearly any corporate document can become a powerful weapon in court in the hands of opposing counsel. A well-designed and well-executed document-management program can (1) reduce corporate liability, (2) protect trade secrets and other confidential information, and, most important, (3) save on litigation costs.[47] Time and money are wasted when corporate staff and lawyers are forced to search for documents during discovery. With an organized document-management program, a company knows exactly what documents are in its possession and where they are located.

Nevertheless, most companies do not have established policies regarding document retention and destruction.

---

46. 720 A.2d 542 (Del. 1998).
47. Much of the discussion of document retention that follows is based on the work of John Ruhnka, Associate Professor at the Graduate School of Business Administration, University of Colorado at Denver, and Robert B. Austin, CRM, CSP, of Austin Associates, Denver. *See* John Ruhnka & Robert Austin, *Design Considerations for Document Retention/Destruction Programs,* 1 CORP. CONFIDENTIALITY & DISCLOSURE LETTER 2 (1988).

ETHICAL CONSIDERATION

You are a manager of Dow Chemical Company, overseeing the silicone-breast-implant litigation across the United States. Your market research tells you that most individuals distrust Big Business and that most consumers cannot identify many products of your company, except those involved in the litigation. With an upcoming trial in Louisiana, you are considering conducting a full-scale advertising campaign to boost the company's public image. The purpose is to influence public opinion in the jurisdiction of the suit, thereby creating a positive image in the minds of potential jurors. You have several options for the campaign:

1. Emphasize Dow Chemical's citizenship: employee volunteers, donations to charities, and the improvement of society as a result of Dow's products.
2. Describe the benefits of silicone products. While not mentioning the breast implant issue, tell numerous heart-wrenching tales of silicone products saving the lives of children.
3. Begin the final campaign the week before jury selection. Highlight the greed of attorneys who regularly represent plaintiffs and lament the growing litigiousness of our society. The final slogan: "You can stop the greedy lawyers!"
4. Same as 3, but also argue that silicone breast implants do no harm.[a]

What should you do? If you were the plaintiff, how would you respond to these tactics?

a. *See* Richard B. Schmitt, *Can Corporate Advertising Sway Juries?* WALL ST. J., Mar. 3, 1997, at B1.

They practice what some professionals call the "search and destroy" technique of file management: arbitrarily cleaning out file cabinets when storage space is running low.

Federal and state regulations require companies to retain certain records. The Code of Federal Regulations contains more than 2,400 regulations requiring that certain types of business records be maintained for specific periods of time. Many regulatory agencies have increased their retention requirements, forcing some companies to increase their file capacities by more than 15 percent a year.

DESIGNING A POLICY

In general, documents that a company is not required to retain for any business or legal purpose should be eliminated from company files. Documents that are kept may be obtained by opposing counsel during discovery, and they may be harmful to the company in court.

Documents containing elements of a company's decision-making process can sometimes be used out of context. A well-known example is the memorandum that was found in the files of Ford Motor Company during discovery for a 1972 trial arising out of a death caused by a Ford Pinto's allegedly defectively designed fuel tank. The memo, prepared in compliance with the regulations of a federal agency, compared the cost of design modifications to the Pinto fuel tank with the potential loss of life that might be caused by the existing design. During the trial, the plaintiff's counsel convinced the jury that the memo was proof that Ford decided to defer redesign of the fuel tanks on the basis of this cost study. The jury awarded compensatory damages of $3.5 million and punitive damages of $125 million against Ford. (Compensatory damages compensate the injured party for the harm suffered; punitive damages are intended to punish the wrongdoer for conduct that is outrageous, willful, or malicious.)

Even if a company has been careful to destroy records, duplicates may exist in an employee's personal files, where they are still subject to discovery. For example, in the mid-1970s, the Weyerhaeuser Company paid $200 million in a case after company documents were found through discovery in personal files in the home of a retired company administrative assistant.

An employee's private diaries, calendars, and notebooks are also subject to discovery. Opposing counsel could glean from them a great deal about a company's operations. Companies should therefore include this type of record in its document-management program.

CORPORATE PRIVACY

Besides protecting a company in the event of litigation, a document-management program protects corporate privacy and trade secrets. A company should destroy confidential or proprietary materials as soon as possible. It should also preserve the confidentiality of employee records and destroy these records when they are no longer necessary. If an employee sues a company for wrongful termination, the employee's file is subject to discovery, and careless or unsubstantiated information in the file may be persuasive evidence at trial. Further, cor-

porations can be liable for damages if confidential information in an employee's file, such as a medical record indicating past drug use, is made public.

NECESSARY ELEMENTS OF A DOCUMENT-RETENTION PROGRAM

Well Planned and Systematic To stand up in court, a document-retention program must be well planned and systematic. Companies usually appoint a senior officer of the organization to be responsible for supervising and auditing the document-management program. Policies should be established as to the types of documents to be destroyed, including documents stored on computer or word-processing disks. The documents should then be systematically destroyed according to an established time frame (for example, when they reach a certain age).

No Destruction in the Face of a Potential Lawsuit It is illegal to destroy documents when the company has notice of a potential lawsuit. A company cannot wait until a suit is formally filed against it to stop destroying relevant documents. A company must halt destruction as soon as it has good reason to believe that a suit is likely to be filed or an investigation started. Companies that did not halt destruction of documents have been forced to pay damages even when they acted accidentally. For example, in *Carlucci v. Piper Aircraft Corp.*,[48] flight data information essential to the case was missing. The judge did not believe Piper Aircraft's claim that it had not deliberately destroyed the relevant document. The judge issued a directed verdict for the plaintiff and rendered a $10 million judgment against Piper.

No Selective Destruction The importance of a systematic document-management program cannot be emphasized enough. The court will scrutinize whether document destruction was done in the ordinary course of business. Any hint of selective destruction jeopardizes the defensibility of a document-management program.

48. 102 F.R.D. 472 (S.D. Fla. 1984).

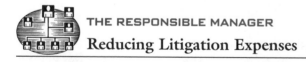

THE RESPONSIBLE MANAGER
Reducing Litigation Expenses

Legal disputes often arise in the normal course of business operations. Some may be resolved amicably, but others may require a third party to adjudicate the dis-

pute. Although the courts do provide one venue, a corporate manager should not rush to trial. The costs of effective counsel, the protracted nature of most commercial disputes, and the resultant opportunity costs can be significant. The allocation of corporate funds is one concern, but so is the distraction of corporate managers on litigation-related activities, such as depositions, interrogatories, document searches, and trial. And although most cases are settled, the settlement generally comes after hundreds of hours of pretrial activities.

To avoid these predictable pitfalls, a responsible manager seeks alternatives that maximize corporate value and interests. One solution is to engage in a continuing conversation with corporate counsel in order to find ways to reduce litigation costs.[49] In other words, find ways to settle cases cheaply and quickly. This requires identifying and overcoming litigious working assumptions of both the corporation and the lawyer. Emotions, a desire to pass the buck, and partisan bias can create a litigation trap that prevents some conflicts from being settled in a timely manner. Egos must be set aside—by both managers and lawyers—and optimal solutions to the *problem* of litigation must be pursued.

One option is for a manager to instruct corporate counsel to develop a settlement strategy in addition to a litigation strategy. In other words, while litigators are searching for ways to overcome a potential adversary, counsel should also seek ways to resolve the conflict as soon as possible. Such an organized approach enables the manager to keep the conflict in perspective by comparing the costs, advantages, and disadvantages of litigation and settlement. This approach also assists a manager in identifying those situations in which it is worthwhile to go to court, whether to establish a beneficial precedent or limit (or overturn) a disadvantageous one. Delineating specific settlement options and reviewing the results of settlement or litigation and the accuracy of cost predictions may also help reduce legal fees.

Frequent contact with counsel is also critical to reducing litigation expenses. Lack of good communication is often cited as a key problem by both managers and attorneys. Law firms often wrongly assume that they call the shots and spend more time and money on a case than the client may have intended.[50] A manager often needs legal advice to make an informed decision but should resist the temptation to just "leave it to the lawyers." Instead, the responsible manager treats legal disputes like any other business problem that requires a business solution.

49. This discussion is based on Roger Fisher, *He Who Pays the Piper,* HARV. BUS. REV., Mar.–Apr. 1985, at 150.

50. Ann Davis, *Businesses' Poor Communications with Law Firms Is Found Costly,* WALL ST. J., July 17, 1997, at B5.

The Worm Turns: Milberg Weiss Bershad Hynes & Lerach Pays $50 Million *for* Abuse *of* Legal Process

Lawyers are under an obligation to pursue cases in good faith and in an ethical manner, which includes not pursuing a case for an improper motive such as vengeance. Abuse of legal process can result in large sanctions against the lawyers. In April 1999, Milberg Weiss Bershad Hynes & Lerach, the nation's most successful securities class-action law firm, agreed to pay $50 million to settle a claim that the firm used the legal process to drive a hostile witness, Lexecon, Inc., out of business.[51] Lexecon's attorney called the settlement "an enormous victory, and a very significant case for the legal profession" that sends a message "that lawyers are not above the law, although, sometimes, they think they are."[52]

Although Milberg Weiss's profitability has been affected by securities reform legislation enacted in 1995, which makes it more difficult for lawyers to file securities class actions, the firm earned more than half a billion dollars in fees between 1988 and 1998 with the name partners, such as Bill Lerach, making $16 million apiece. Many corporations, particularly in high-tech industries, that have been sued by Milberg Weiss are extremely critical of the firm and characterize its practice as legalized extortion.

51. Richard Schmitt, *Milberg Weiss Agrees to Settle Lexecon Case,* WALL ST. J., Apr. 14, 1999, at B1.

52. *Id.*; Richard Schmitt, *Plaintiff's Lawyer Lerach and Firm Ordered to Pay $45 Million in Damages,* WALL ST. J., Apr. 13, 1999, at B5.

In 1992, the Chicago legal and economics consulting firm Lexecon sued Milberg Weiss, claiming that the law firm had seriously damaged the company by linking it with a 1980s savings and loan scandal. The principals of Lexecon were Daniel Fischel, the dean of the University of Chicago law school, and two other Chicago professors. In March 1990, Milberg Weiss had named Lexecon as a defendant in a $1.2 billion civil-racketeering class-action suit by investors involved in the Lincoln Savings & Loan failure. Lexecon had previously worked as a consultant to Lincoln and, at one point, had declared that the bank was "sound." Although Lexecon argued that it played no part in Lincoln's failure, the company agreed to settle the case and returned $700,000 in fees received from Lincoln to the class members.

Lexecon alleged that Milberg Weiss used the fact that Lexecon had been named a defendant in the Lincoln case to subsequently defame the consulting firm in other Milberg Weiss cases. Lexecon claimed that Milberg Weiss was retaliating against the firm because Lexecon had served as an expert defense witness in an earlier case brought by Milberg Weiss that the law firm lost. Lexecon claimed that it had lost profits as a result of Milberg Weiss's actions and sought damages of $209 million. In defense of its actions, Milberg Weiss claimed that it was justified in naming Lexecon as a defendant.

After a Chicago federal jury found that Milberg Weiss was liable for $45 million in compensatory damages but before the jury could begin considering punitive damages against the firm, the parties agreed to settle for $50 million. The award is one of the largest against a law firm in recent history. Because Milberg Weiss had relatively little or no liability insurance to cover this settlement, the firm indicated that the majority of the $50 million would be paid directly by the partners. In early 1999, Lexecon was acquired by a company affiliated with junk-bond king Michael Milken and Larry Ellison, chief executive of Oracle Corporation, both of whom have been previously named as defendants by Milberg Weiss.

KEY WORDS AND PHRASES

affidavit 95
affirmative defense 94
answer 94
apex deposition 99
appellant 77
appellee 77
attorney–client privilege 102
attorney work-product doctrine 104
authoritative decision 90
cert. denied 81
choice-of-forum clause 86
cite 76
civil procedure 94
class action suit 104
Code of Federal Regulations (CFR) 90
common law 90
complaint 94
conflict-of-law rules 78
counterclaim 94
default judgment 94
defendant 77
de novo 84
depeçage 86

deposition 97
directed verdict 97
discovery 97
diversity jurisdiction 77
en banc hearing 79
Erie doctrine 78
federal question 77
forum non conveniens 87
forum shopping 78
in personam jurisdiction 84
in rem jurisdiction 84
interrogatory 98
judgment notwithstanding the verdict 97
judgment n.o.v (j.n.o.v.) 97
long-arm statute 84
minimum contacts 84
motion for judgment on the pleadings 95
motion for summary judgment 95
motion to dismiss 95
non obstante veredicto 97
partial summary judgment 95
personal jurisdiction 84

persuasive 90
petitioner 77
plaintiff 77
pleadings 94
political question 81
prayer 94
remand 79
reporter 76
request for production of documents 98
respondent 77
restatement 94
settled 98
standing 82
stare decisis 90
summary judgment 95
summons 94
total-activity test 79
vacate 79
venue 106
voir dire 96
writ 79
writ of *certiorari* 77

1. Answer the following questions with regard to the case *Hudson v. United States,* 522 U.S. 93 (2000):
   a. In what year was the case decided?
   b. Which court decided the case?
   c. Can you tell from the cite which party originally brought the lawsuit or which party brought the appeal?
   d. Suppose you want to cite the following passage that appeared on page 103: "The Due Process and Equal Protection Clauses already protect individuals from sanctions which are downright irrational." Where would the page designation go?

2. Trouver Capital Partners contracted with Healthcare Acquisition, Inc. to provide financial advisory and investment banking services relating to Healthcare Acquisition's efforts to secure funding for several projects. Trouver's principal place of business is in Pennsylvania; Healthcare is headquartered in Florida. The parties had a dispute about the services performed under the contract, and Trouver sued Healthcare in federal court in Pennsylvania. Healthcare has filed a motion to dismiss the case for lack of jurisdiction. Trouver argues that the Pennsylvania court has jurisdiction over Healthcare because its president, Elizabeth Fago, visited the state on a number of occasions for business meetings regarding the contract. In addition, Fago and an executive at Trouver communicated by telephone and fax on several occasions. Are these actions by Fago sufficient to establish jurisdiction in Pennsylvania over Healthcare? [*Trouver Capital Partners v. Healthcare Acquisition, Inc.* Civil Action No. 99-3535 (E.D. Pa. Mar. 24, 2000)]

3. FC Schaffer & Associates, Inc. is an engineering firm based in Louisiana that did business with ODA Trading Agency, an Ethiopian entity that represents businesses wanting to do business in Ethiopia. Endrias, the founder and owner of ODA, employs Mesfin Gebreyes and an independent contractor, Kifle Gebre. Endrias left Ethiopia to live in the United States for five years. Shortly after Endrias's departure, Kifle learned that the Ethiopian Sugar Corporation was going to build a sugar mill and ethanol plant in Ethiopia. Kifle then contacted Schaffer about bidding on the project. Schaffer was interested and entered into a contract with ODA that provided that Schaffer would pay a commission to ODA if it was chosen as the successful bidder on the project. Schaffer was the low bidder on the project and was chosen to build the mill and plant.

   Two months after Schaffer was awarded the contract, Endrias returned to Ethiopia and contacted Schaffer to introduce himself as the owner of ODA. Schaffer had never worked with or heard of Endrias and decided to enter into a new agreement with Mesfin and Kifle. This agreement purported to supersede the prior agreement between Schaffer and ODA. Schaffer refused to pay any commission to ODA under the first agreement, and Endrias sued Schaffer for breach of contract in the U.S. District Court for the Middle District of Louisiana. Can Endrias sue Schaffer in federal court? What law will apply to the breach-of-contract claim—federal law, the state law of Louisiana, or the law of Ethiopia? [*ODA v. FC Schaffer & Associates, Inc.,* 204 F.3d 639 (5th C.R. 2000)]

4. Spalding Sports Worldwide, Inc. sued Wilson Sporting Goods Company for infringement of U.S. Patent 5,310,178 pertaining to its basketball with a polyurethane cover. During discovery, Wilson asked Spalding to produce its invention record. Invention records are standard forms used by corporations as a means for inventors to disclose to the corporation's patent attorneys that an invention has been made and to initiate patent action. They usually contain such information as the names of the inventors, descriptions and scope of the invention, closest prior art, first date of conception, and disclosure to others and dates of publications. Spalding refused to produce its invention record, asserting that it was protected by the attorney–client privilege because the record was prepared for the purpose of securing legal advice concerning the patentability of the invention and served as an aid in completing the patent application. Wilson argues that even if the invention record was submitted to Spalding's patent committee, there is no evidence that the committee "acted as a lawyer" by rendering legal advice, as opposed to making business decisions. Wilson also contends that even if a portion of the invention record was submitted for the purpose of obtaining legal advice, the portion that does not ask for legal advice but contains technical information is not protected by the attorney–client privilege and should be produced.
   a. Should Spalding be forced to produce the invention record or part of it? Explain your reasoning. Would your answer be different if the invention record was the only record that contained the technical information at issue in the case?

b. Wilson also argues that Spalding committed "fraud on the patent office" by making a material misrepresentation to the patent office and that, as a result, the attorney–client privilege was abrogated by the crime–fraud exception. Under this exception, the attorney–client privilege will be waived if the party made a communication "in furtherance of" a crime or fraud. Wilson has alleged that Spalding made a material misrepresentation but has submitted no evidence in support of this claim. Should the court find that the crime–fraud exception applies here and that Spalding has waived the attorney–client privilege? If not, what evidence would Wilson have to present to substantiate its claim that the crime–fraud exception applies in this case?

[*In Re Spalding Sports Worldwide, Inc.,* 203 F.3d 800 (Fed. Cir. 2000)]

5. DuLac Corporation, a leading U.S. manufacturer of chemicals and synthetic fabrics, is incorporated in the state of Blue Waters. All of DuLac's business is conducted within Blue Waters, and all of its offices are located within the state. Blue Waters is under the federal jurisdiction of the U.S. Court of Appeals for the Fourth Circuit. The Environmental Protection Agency (EPA) commenced an investigation of DuLac's disposal procedures for DRT, a mixture of the toxic compound DNGR and the neutralizing agent HRMLS. Upon discovering that DuLac had disposed of DRT in dump sites not approved for toxic-waste disposal, the EPA filed suit against DuLac for cleanup costs and punitive damages under a federal statute forbidding the disposal of DNGR or any derivative thereof except in approved toxic-waste-dump sites. The action was brought in a federal district court sitting in Blue Waters. DuLac's only defense to the action is that the DNGR in DRT is fully neutralized, so DRT should not be considered a derivative of DNGR for purposes of the statute. A month later, the lawyer for the EPA offers to settle the case for cleanup costs only.

a. Assume that the U.S. Court of Appeals for the Sixth Circuit recently interpreted the statute literally, upholding an award of punitive damages against a company that had disposed of fully neutralized DNGR. As DuLac's manager, would you recommend that the company accept the settlement offer?

b. Assume that another district court within the Fourth Circuit recently reached the same result as the Sixth Circuit. How would you advise DuLac regarding the settlement offer?

c. Assume that the U.S. Supreme Court recently reached the same result as the Sixth Circuit. Would your advice to DuLac remain the same?

6. AltoCom, a small software company with only twelve employees, is incorporated in California and headquartered in Silicon Valley. It develops software that is incorporated into computers, fax machines, video telephones, personal digital assistants, and other communication devices to make them run more efficiently. AltoCom licenses its softmodems to companies that manufacture these electronic devices. The softmodems are integrated into a variety of electronic products that are manufactured by corporations such as Compaq, Philips, Samsung, Sharp, and Sony. These goods are then put into worldwide distribution networks that place them for sale in retail stores such as Circuit City, Office-Max, Service Merchandise, CompUSA, and Sears, all of which have outlets in Delaware. Motorola has sued AltoCom for patent infringement in the District Court of Delaware. AltoCom has filed a motion to dismiss for lack of personal jurisdiction on the grounds that it has never had any contact with Delaware. The company ships the software code to its softmodems to its licensees' principal place of business; none of its eleven U.S.-based licensees is headquartered in Delaware, so it has never shipped its product there. In addition, AltoCom has never advertised its softmodems in Delaware, conducted any of its business there, or maintained any of its assets in that state. Does the Delaware court have jurisdiction over AltoCom because its product is a component in products that are sold there? [*Motorola, Inc. v. AltoCom, Inc.,* 58 F. Supp. 2d 349 (D. Del. 1999)]

7. Three same-sex couples who are residents of Vermont have lived together in committed relationships for a period ranging from four to twenty-five years. Two of the couples have raised children together. All three couples applied for marriage licenses and were refused a license on the grounds that they were ineligible under the state marriage laws. Plaintiffs filed a lawsuit against the state of Vermont and the towns where they lived seeking a declaratory judgment that the refusal to issue them a license violated the marriage statutes and the Vermont Constitution. Specifically, they argued that it violated the Common Benefits Clause of the Vermont Constitution, which provides "[t]hat government is, or ought to be, instituted for the common benefit, protection, and security of the people, nation, or community, and not for the particular emolument or advantage of any

single person, family, or set of persons, who are part of that community. . . ." They argued that in not having access to a civil marriage license, they are denied many legal benefits and protections incident to a marriage, including coverage under a spouse's medical, life, and disability insurance, hospital visitation and other medical decision-making privileges, and spousal support.

    a. Does Vermont's marriage license law violate same-sex couples' rights under the Vermont Constitution?

    b. Vermont claims that the state marriage laws reasonably serve the state's interest in promoting the "link between procreation and child rearing." Is this a reasonable justification for the marriage laws? Would your answer change if Vermont had a law that guarantees the right to adopt and raise children regardless of the sex or marital status of the prospective parents? [*Baker v. State,* 744 A.2d 864 (Vt. 1999)]

8. Sterling, Inc. is a manufacturer of state-of-the-art computers. For the past ten years, Sterling has acquired all of its microchips from NoBugs Corporation, the only producer of chips meeting Sterling's high specifications. The relationship has been mutually profitable: Sterling could not have built its reputation as an industry leader without NoBugs's reliability and consistently high-quality products; Sterling's business has enabled NoBugs to grow rapidly while providing its investors with an attractive rate of return.

    Some months ago, several of Sterling's computers exploded shortly after installation. Upon investigation, Sterling discovered that tiny imperfections in NoBugs's microchips had aggravated a dormant design defect in the computers, causing the explosions. Analysis of the chips indicated that they were indeed below specifications and that the imperfections were caused by a slight miscalibration of NoBugs's encoding equipment. NoBugs recalibrated the equipment and promptly resumed production of perfect chips. Sterling's losses from the explosions—lost profits, out-of-pocket costs associated with compensating customers for the explosions, and injury to business reputation—are estimated to exceed $20 million. Sterling and NoBugs disagree on the amount of the loss for which NoBugs should be responsible. Sterling's CEO is considering a lawsuit. She asks you to prepare a memo outlining the advantages and disadvantages of litigation and proposing a litigation strategy. Draft that memo.

9. In a securities case, the plaintiff sought to compel documents regarding a merger between EdgeMark Financial Corporation and Old Kent Financial Corporation. EdgeMark retained David Olson of Donaldson, Lufkin & Jenrette (DLJ) to act as its investment banker in connection with the merger. EdgeMark sent a number of documents to Olson that it claims are protected by the attorney–client privilege. The plaintiff argues that these documents are no longer protected by the privilege because disclosure to Olson resulted in waiver of the privilege. EdgeMark argues that after the plaintiff's counsel threatened the lawsuit, EdgeMark and DLJ's interests became "inextricably linked" because the litigation jeopardized the merger. As a result, EdgeMark argues, the documents are protected under the "common interest" rule, which is an exception to the general rule under the attorney–client privilege that the privilege is waived when a document is produced to a third party. The common interest rule protects from disclosure communications between one party and an attorney for another party where the parties are engaged in a joint defense effort. DLJ is not a party to the lawsuit and has not been asked to assist in the defense. Has the attorney–client privilege been waived, or does the common interest rule preserve the privilege? [*Blanchard v. EdgeMark Financial Corp.,* 192 F.R.D. 233 (N.D. Ill. 2000)]

 MANAGER'S DILEMMA

10. In response to being hit by a number of baseless suits, State Farm Insurance has become aggressive in cutting costs and defending itself in lawsuits. The insurance company bases pay raises for its claims agents on their ability to meet preset payout targets, not on the scope of claims they face during a year. In addition, the company destroys old training guides, procedure memos, claim-handling manuals, and other documents reflecting its policies that could be used against it in litigation. State Farm defends its actions by claiming that it has become the victim of tort lawyers and needs to take actions to keep costs low for policyholders. Has State Farm gone too far in its efforts to avoid paying money to settle baseless claims, or are these actions appropriate cost-cutting policies? [*See State Farm: What's Happening to the Good Neighbor,* Bus. Wk., Nov. 8, 1999, at 138.]

INTERNET SOURCES

This page offers new students of the law a variety of materials including guides to case citations and research materials.	http://www.lawlib.uh.edu/guides
Courts.net provides directory listings for courts throughout the nation on a state-by-state basis.	http://www.courts.net
The state of California's judicial system has its own home page with information about its court system, including its structure and recent decisions.	http://www.courtinfo.ca.gov
The National Center for State Courts' home page offers a variety of information pertaining to state courts, including information about court technology and administration.	http://www.ncsc.dni.us
The Cornell University Law School offers access to all U.S. Supreme Court decisions since 1990 as well as more than 600 of the most important historical decisions. It also includes the Court calendar, schedule of oral arguments, summary of questions presented in cases the Court will consider, and information about Supreme Court Justices.	http://www.law.cornell.edu/supct
Under the direction of the U.S. Department of Commerce, this page offers access to more than 7,000 U.S. Supreme Court opinions from 1937 to 1975, as well as to a wide range of information related to the federal government.	http://www.fedworld.gov/
FindLaw allows users to search for state and federal statutes, cases, and regulations.	http://www.findlaw.com/casecode
The Congressional Record Web site contains the full text of the *Congressional Record* for 1995 through 2000, which can be searched by date or keyword.	http://www.access.gpo.gov/su_docs/aces/aces150.html
Federal Web Locator is a service provided by the Center for Information Law and Policy. It provides links to federal branches of government, federal agencies, boards, organizations, and international sites.	http://www.law.vill.edu/FedAgency/fedwebloc.html
The Federal Judiciary Home Page has information about the federal court system, including information from the Administrative Office of the U.S. Courts about courts with vacancies, and provides links to the Web sites for each federal court and to PACER (Public Access to Court Electronic Records), which provides electronic public access to cases and dockets.	http://www.uscourts.gov/

CHAPTER 4

Alternative Dispute Resolution

WHY NOT JUST SUE?

Why would a manager consider alternative methods for resolving disputes when the manager has access to a judicial system provided by the government and financed through taxation? For anyone who has used litigation and the courts to resolve a business dispute, the answer is obvious. Litigation is expensive and takes a toll on management and employees. In addition to generating legal fees, lawsuits distract management from the company's business, risk damaging the firm's public image, and jeopardize relationships with the opposing party.

Instead of automatically taking legal conflicts to the courthouse, more firms than ever are using alternatives to formal litigation to settle conflicts with customers, suppliers, and employees. A recent survey of the 1,000 largest U.S. corporations found that 88 percent have used mediation and 70 percent have used arbi-

tration.[1] Eighty-four percent of these companies indicated that they were likely or very likely (46 percent) to use mediation in the future, and 71 percent were likely or very likely to use arbitration.

CHAPTER OVERVIEW

This chapter explains the manager's nonlitigation options for the resolution of business disputes. Alternative dispute resolution (ADR) methods include negotiation, mediation, and arbitration, as well as hybrids, such as minitrials, med-arb, and summary jury trials. The chapter discusses barriers to successful dispute resolution and suggests strategies for resolving disputes out of court. Finally, the chapter explains how the law views these alternatives to litigation.

1. DAVID LIPSKY & RONALD SEEBER, THE APPROPRIATE RESOLUTION OF CORPORATE DISPUTES: A REPORT ON THE GROWING USE OF ADR BY U.S. CORPORATIONS (1998).

⬧ Thinking *about* ADR

To select the best alternative to litigation, managers must be aware of their own needs and constraints. Like other business decisions, choosing a dispute resolution mechanism—including litigation—involves many trade-offs: Is the right decision more important than quick resolution, or is time of the essence? Is public attention helpful to the resolution of the conflict, or does the matter require confidentiality? Does the company need to preserve its relationship with the other party, or is this conflict the last interaction with that party? Will mutual resolution of the conflict make the company a desirable business partner, or will potential disputants seek conflict because the

company appears weak and unwilling to defend itself vigorously?

To distinguish among the alternatives, a manager should consider the following questions about dispute settlement and the possible answers:[2]

1. How are the disputants represented?
   - By lawyers
   - By persons without formal legal training
   - By themselves without any outside representation
2. Who makes the final decision?
   - A judge or other government employee with formal legal training

2. These questions and answers are based on JOHN J. COUND ET AL., CIVIL PROCEDURE: CASES AND MATERIALS 1311–13 (6th ed. 1993).

- An attorney or other legal professional
- An expert in the industry
- A representative of the community in which the company operates
- The disputants with the help of a neutral third party
- The disputants themselves

3. How are facts found and standards of judgment set?
   - The disputants or their representatives are responsible for presenting evidence of the facts and arguments to establish the standard for resolution.
   - The dispute resolver, or final decision maker, can aid the disputants in performing any of these tasks.
   - The dispute resolver alone establishes the standards and finds the facts.

4. What is the source of the standard for resolution?
   - Rules already established by legislatures and courts
   - Evolving rules and standards
   - Prior practice of those whose disputes were resolved before this one
   - Prevailing values and notions of fairness
   - The disputants themselves, as determined either before or after the dispute arises
   - A delegated third party, such as the American Arbitration Association (AAA)

5. How will any decision be enforced?
   - By a court or threat of legal action
   - By the good faith of the disputants

- By concern for reputation and future relationships

6. Who will pay for the dispute resolution procedure?
   - The losing party
   - All parties on an equal basis
   - The parties, as allocated by the dispute resolver
   - The employer (in the case of conflicts with employees) or the supplier (in the case of conflicts with customers)
   - The party bringing the dispute for resolution

Different alternatives answer these questions differently, and parties can often mix and match to suit their circumstances. Before attempting to resolve any dispute, good managers should think carefully about their own goals and the nature of dispute resolution alternatives.

"The first thing we do, let's kill all the lawyers."
—WILLIAM SHAKESPEARE, THE SECOND PART OF KING HENRY THE SIXTH Act 4, sc. 2, line 75.

 # Varieties *of* ADR

There are three basic varieties of ADR: negotiation, mediation, and arbitration. By mixing these with each other and with the formal judicial system, a manager has three more options: a minitrial, med-arb, and a summary jury trial.

HISTORICAL PERSPECTIVE

Early Binding Arbitration

In one of the earliest examples of ADR, two women brought their dispute over the maternity of an infant boy to a leading official:

Then the king [Solomon] said, "The one says, 'This is my son, who is living, and your son is the dead one;' and the other says, 'No! For your son is the dead one, and my son is the living one.'"

And the king said, "Get me a sword." So they brought a sword before the king. And the king said, "Divide the living child in two, and give half to the one and half to the other."

Then the woman whose child was the living one spoke to the king for she was deeply stirred over her son and said, "Oh my lord, give her the living child and by no means kill him."

But the other said, "He shall be neither mine nor yours; divide him!"

Then the king answered and said, "Give the first woman the living child and by no means kill him. She is his mother."

When all Israel heard of the judgment which the king had handed down, they feared the king; for they saw that the wisdom of God was in him to administer justice.[a]

a. 1 *Kings* 3: 23–28.

⬙ Negotiation

Negotiation is the give-and-take people engage in when coming to terms with each other. One can view negotiation along several different dimensions. Negotiation can be either forward looking with concern for desired relationships—*transactional negotiation*—or backward looking to address past events that have caused disagreement—*dispute negotiation*. An example of a transactional negotiation is one between two firms involved in a joint venture. An example of a dispute negotiation is one between a steel manufacturer that failed to deliver I-beams and the construction company that has already paid for them. In the former, both parties are looking to the future with positive expectations; in the latter, the parties are looking to the past and apportioning blame. Conflicts need not be simply one or the other. Labor negotiations often have elements of both transactions and disputes. The parties must work together in the future but may also feel the need to apportion blame for the event that precipitated the crisis.

Negotiation can also be viewed as involving a fixed or a growing pie. In *distributive* or *zero-sum negotiations,* the only issue is the distribution of a fixed pie. In contrast, in *integrative* or *variable-sum negotiations,* mutual gains are possible as the parties trade lower-valued resources for higher-valued ones.

For example, consider a dispute between the manufacturer of a telecommunications device and the supplier of one of the device's critical components. Although the supplier delivered the component as scheduled, the component failed to work properly in the device, causing significant friction between the manufacturer and the supplier. It is unclear which party caused the problem. In distributive negotiations, the parties would merely battle over who should absorb the resulting loss, a process that could irreversibly injure the manufacturer–supplier relationship and lead to litigation. By looking beyond the boundaries of the original transaction and dispute, however, the parties may be able to create value between them. For instance, the supplier may have the capacity to deliver a modified component at very little cost in a short period of time. The manufacturer, in turn, would highly value the ability to secure this modified component. Thus, the parties could strike a deal in which the manufacturer agrees to pay the original amount owed plus a premium for replacement in exchange for the supplier's agreement to expedite the modified component. Both parties have received more than was originally due, and their relationship has been preserved.

In the employment context, parties often expand a distributive discussion about salary to integrate issues of medical benefits, vacation days, formal titles, and other perquisites, such as parking spaces, first-class air travel, and corporate credit cards. For example, it may not cost a company anything to call a prospective employee "administrative assistant" instead of "secretary," but the title might mean enough to the employee to make up for a slightly lower cash salary.

"It's non-negotiable."

Unsurprisingly, distributive negotiations can easily become adversarial and strain even the closest relationships. With nothing to do but fight over the pie, parties are left with nothing to do but fight. Integrating other issues into the discussion creates the possibility of trade-offs that allow both parties to gain relative to their distributive starting point.

PLANNING AND PREPARATION

Professors Max Bazerman and Margaret Neale, authors of the popular book *Negotiating Rationally*, recommend asking and answering three questions before entering a negotiation (or at least before entering a negotiation one wishes to win): First, ask what is your *reservation price*, that is, the price at which you are indifferent between the success and failure of the negotiation. In their framework, a negotiator should first establish his or her *Best Alternative to a Negotiated Agreement (BATNA)*. This is the outcome a person will choose if the negotiation fails. By definition, it is the best outcome available outside the negotiation. Consequently, any settlement higher than one's BATNA is preferable to a failed negotiation. Although reservation price and BATNA are not the same, they are closely related. The transaction costs of executing the BATNA are the essential difference.

By understanding their BATNA, managers can determine the highest price they should be willing to pay. If a manager makes an offer close to his or her reservation price and the opponent refuses, the manager knows that further concessions are not in his or her interest. As Bazerman and Neale remind us, "[T]he goal of negotiating is not to reach just any agreement, but to reach an agreement that is better for you than what you would get without one."[3] Well-intentioned managers can easily get caught up in the heat of an important negotiation and mistake agreement for success.

Second, ask what are your interests, as opposed to your positions. Positions are the stated requirements that one negotiator demands of his or her opponent. Interests are what he or she actually desires, whether revealed or withheld. Knowing one's interests allows a person to fashion integrative solutions.

Third, ask how important, comparatively, each negotiation issue is to you. By establishing priorities and distinguishing between positions and interests, managers can think systematically about trade-offs that create mutual gain. Prudent negotiators ask these three questions about their opponents as well as about themselves.

Exhibit 4.1 summarizes the steps to take in preparation for a negotiation. An unprepared negotiator is a manager's favorite opponent.

Exhibit 4.2 summarizes a number of mistakes that can create barriers to a negotiation resolution.

LIABILITY FOR FAILED NEGOTIATIONS

In the United States, it is difficult to establish legal liability on the grounds that a party did not finalize a contract after a series of negotiations. As explained more fully in Chapter 7, in the United States a party is generally free to terminate negotiations at any time prior to contract formation for

---

EXHIBIT 4.1   **Negotiation Preparation**

Before embarking on a negotiation, a manager should do the following:

1. Analyze the nature of the dispute:
   - Ask why this particular constellation of actors is at the negotiating table now.
2. Specify superordinate goals and objectives:
   - Figure out what you want.
3. Outline the scope of the negotiation:
   - Identify the issues to be negotiated, both tangible and intangible.
   - Determine your reservation price.
   - Consider your alternatives to this negotiation.
   - Analyze the priorities for each issue to be negotiated.
   - Consider alternative proposals you could offer or accept.
4. Understand your opponent by asking:
   - What issues will be of concern to him or her?
   - What are his or her priorities on those issues?
   - What is his or her reservation price?
   - What are his or her alternatives to this negotiation?
   - What is the history of negotiations between you and your opponent?
   - What is your opponent's reputation?
   - Is the opponent monolithic or a group with members having differing views?
5. Understand the particular negotiation situation and ask:
   - What are the deadlines or other time constraints?
   - Who has the authority to ratify any agreement, and is that person at the negotiation?
   - Will this negotiation affect future negotiations and, if so, how?
   - How important is your relationship with the other party going forward?

Source: Based on Professor Margaret Neale's course "Conflict and Negotiation" at the Stanford University Graduate School of Business. Used by permission.

---

3. MAX H. BAZERMAN & MARGARET A. NEALE, NEGOTIATING RATIONALLY 173 (1992).

INTERNATIONAL CONSIDERATION

In negotiating across cultures or in international settings, cultural myopia is a serious barrier to success. For instance, eye contact implies dramatically different attitudes in Japan and the United States. In the United States, a negotiator who avoids eye contact will be perceived as being intimidated or shifty. In Japan, that same behavior is taken as a sign of respect. When signals are misinterpreted, complex negotiations become even more difficult. Consider the Tokyo conference room where respectful officials of Mitsubishi avoid eye contact as they begin discussions with aggressive owners of a Texas car dealership who rarely avert their eyes. What of teetotalling in Moscow? Bare heads in Jerusalem? Shoed feet in Beijing?[a]

The following excerpt from an essay written by an anonymous Japanese negotiator provides insight into how the Japanese view the American style of negotiation:

> Often they argue [the Americans] among themselves in public, so it is safe to assume that they argue even more in private. This is part of their idea of adversary proceedings and they seem to feel no shame about such embarrassing behavior.
>
> . . .
>
> Americans like to concentrate on one problem at a time. They seem not to understand that the whole picture is more important, and they spend little time on developing a general understanding of the views and interests of both sides. Since their habit of focusing on one issue often forces a direct disagreement, they often propose setting the issue aside, but they come back to it later with the same attitude and concentration. A negotiation with them may therefore become a series of small conflicts and we must always make a special effort to give proper attention to the large areas of agreement and common interest.[b]

a. For discussions of issues in cross-cultural negotiation, *see* Frank E. A. Sader & Jeffrey Z. Rubin, *Culture, Negotiation, and Eye of the Beholder,* 7 Negotiation J. 249 (1991); Stephen E. Weiss, *Negotiating with "Romans"— Part 1,* Sloan Mgmt. Rev. 51 (Winter 1994); John L. Graham, *The Japanese Negotiation Style: Characteristics of a Distinct Approach,* 9 Negotiation J. 123 (1993).
b. Yuko Yanagida, et al., Law and Investment in Japan 219–22 (1994).

EXHIBIT 4.2 | Common Negotiation Mistakes

Common negotiation mistakes include:

- Pursuing a negotiated course of action only to justify an earlier decision
- Assuming that what is good for you is necessarily bad for your opponent and vice versa
- Being irrationally affected by an initial anchor price, that is, a price that was suggested early in the negotiations and may now be an unnatural standard for evaluating other offers
- Failing to look for another frame or characterization of the issues that would put a different perspective on the negotiation
- Being affected by readily available information (such as personal experience or recent events) and ignoring other valid, but less accessible, data
- Placing too much confidence in your own fallible judgment

Source: Adapted with the permission of The Free Press, a Division of Simon & Schuster, from Negotiating Rationally by Max H. Bazerman & Margaret A. Neale. Copyright © 1992 by Max H. Bazerman and Margaret A. Neale.

any or no reason. For example, in *Apothekernes Laboratorium for Special Praeparater v. IMC Chemical Group, Inc.,*[4] IMC's board of directors rejected a negotiated deal with Apothekernes after a letter of intent had been signed and IMC's negotiator had assured Apothekernes that the board would approve the deal. Even though the negotiators had a meeting of the minds, the U.S. court held that there was no contract because the letter of intent expressly stated that the terms were "subject to our concluding an Agreement of Sale which shall be acceptable to the Boards of Directors of our respective corporations, whose discretion shall in no way be limited by this letter."

In some jurisdictions, however, a covenant of good faith and trust applies to negotiations even if they do not ripen into a contract. The following case from Japan provides an example.[5]

4. 873 F.2d 155 (7th Cir. 1989).
5. Yuko Yanagida, et al., Law and Investment in Japan 223–29 (1994).

A CASE IN POINT

CASE 4.1

D. James Wan Kim Min v. Mitsui Bussan K.K.
Tokyo High Court (1987).

Summary

FACTS D. James Wan Kim Min, a Malaysian politician and businessman, negotiated with Mitsui Bussan (Mitsui), a Japanese general trading company, to enter into a joint venture to log and develop a forested area in Indonesia. In January 1974, Min and the manager of the lumber division of Mitsui agreed upon the principal terms of the agreement, whereby Mitsui would pay $4 million by April 30, 1974, to purchase from Min

(Continued)

(Case 4.1 continued)

50 percent of the shares of a Brunei corporation that held a majority of the shares in the Indonesian corporation with the lumbering rights in Indonesia. The parties continued to negotiate, but Mitsui had neither signed the draft contract nor paid the purchase price to Min by the April 30 deadline. In July, Mitsui offered to lend $4 million to Min rather than purchase the shares in the Brunei corporation. Mitsui suspended this offer in October 1974 when Min was arrested and detained by Malaysian authorities allegedly for political reasons.

While imprisoned, Min maintained communication with Mitsui. In July 1975, Mitsui agreed by letter to use its best efforts to execute the loan after Min was released. However, when Min was released in January 1976, Mitsui refused to proceed with the loan. In May 1976, Mitsui told Min that it had no legal obligations to him. Min brought suit against Mitsui for breach of contract and violation of the principle of good faith. The trial court rejected Min's contract claim but held in his favor with respect to the principle of good faith. Both Min and Mitsui appealed.

ISSUE PRESENTED May negotiations give rise to an expectation that a contract will be formed so that if the contract is not formed, a party may recover damages from the other party?

SUMMARY OF OPINION The Japanese High Court affirmed the trial court's rejection of Min's contract claims after finding that Mitsui had not made a final and definite offer to purchase the shares. However, the High Court ruled that Mitsui was obligated under the principles of trust and good faith to conclude the contract in order not to injure Min's expectations:

> [I]n the modern world, the principles of good faith and trust govern not only contractual relationships, but also all relationships under private law, and such principles thus apply not only after conclusion of an agreement but also at the stage of preparations toward conclusion of an agreement. In the event that preparation between two parties progresses towards conclusion of an agreement and the first party comes to expect that the agreement will surely be concluded, the second party becomes obligated under the principles of good faith and trust to try to conclude the agreement, in order not to injure the expectation of the first party. Therefore, if the second party, in violation of its obligation, concludes that the agreement is undesirable [absent certain circumstances], it is liable for damages incurred by the first party as the results of its illegal acts.
>
>   . . .
>
> [T]he Letter sent by the Manager and Min's response, to which Mitsui offered no subsequent objection, caused Min to expect that the agreement would be concluded. Mitsui, therefore, should be considered to have become obligated from that time to make good faith efforts, under the principles of good faith and trust, to conclude the agreements. Absent special circumstances that justified suspension of efforts to conclude the agreements, Mitsui should not have been allowed unilaterally and unconditionally to suspend conclusion.[6]

RESULT Mitsui violated the principle of good faith and trust. The Court awarded damages for Min's expenses in preparing for the joint venture, including expenses relating to transportation, accommodations, correspondence, compensation paid to representatives

---

6. *Id.* at 227–28.

(Continued)

(Case 4.1 continued)

of the joint venture, rent for office space, expenditures for investigating lumber forests, and attorneys' fees. However, the Court held that Min's damages resulting from depreciation in the market price of the shares, mental distress, and lost profits did not reasonably relate to Mitsui's breach.

COMMENTS As explained in Chapter 7, in the United States, the doctrine of promissory estoppel can provide limited relief when a party makes promises during the course of negotiations on which the other party reasonably relies to his or her detriment.

Mediation

Litigation can turn business colleagues into bitter enemies. The win–lose nature of lawsuits usually makes it impossible for both parties to claim satisfaction, save face, or forgive-and-forget. After a lawsuit, at best one party feels vindicated and the other feels wronged. Even the ostensible winners often feel angry about having expended so much time and expense getting what they felt was their due to begin with. Mediation can be a less hostile alternative. Like negotiation, mediation can lead to joint gains. It can also help preserve relationships that might otherwise break under the strain of conflict. In a survey of 1,000 large U.S. corporations, 81 percent of the respondents said they used mediation because it provided "a more satisfactory process" than litigation; 66 percent said it provided more "satisfactory settlements"; and 59 percent asserted that it "preserves good relationships."[7]

In *mediation,* the parties agree to try to reach a solution themselves with the assistance of a neutral third party who helps them find a mutually satisfactory resolution. This third party is the *mediator.*

In many ways, mediation is an extension of the negotiation process. One can view mediation as a facilitated negotiation. The mediator/facilitator guides the parties in a structured set of discussions about the issues and alternatives. He or she confers with both parties, together and in private, and points out the elements in dispute and the areas of agreement. Sometimes the mediator helps the parties identify their own goals.

As in negotiation, parties often confuse their positions with their interests, especially after publicly stating a commitment to a position. If perceived as neutral, a mediator is better positioned to ask questions and offer suggestions without creating the suspicion of ulterior motives. Parties to mediation are less likely to ask of a

good mediator "What is she really trying to do?" Unlike the parties, a mediator can offer compromises without fear of appearing weak or too eager to settle.

A mediator's role is to suggest ways to resolve the dispute fairly and to guide the parties toward resolution. Unlike a judge, a mediator cannot enforce a solution; the parties must come to a resolution themselves and then agree to abide by it. Once agreement is reached, parties may formalize the arrangement with contracts, public statements, or letters of understanding.

HISTORY

The formal use of mediation is hardly a recent phenomenon. Early immigrant groups, including Quaker, Chinese, and Jewish communities, used mediation to resolve intragroup conflict and to avoid the American judicial system's foreign legal culture. Organized labor has used mediation since the nineteenth century. In 1926, Congress established the National Mediation Board, and in 1947 it created the Federal Mediation and Conciliation Service. These two entities remain active in dispute resolution.

Because mediators can allow parties to vent their feelings and encourage them to at least acknowledge each other's perspectives, mediation can defuse difficult interpersonal tensions. Today, violence-plagued inner city schools are experimenting with mediation programs to help students resolve conflicts with each other. Courts often mandate mediation before allowing disputes to go to trial. This is most common in family, housing, and small claims courts, which deal with the most personal of relationships.

Insurance companies have used mediation to save money, time, and other resources. The Travelers Insurance Company found that more than 85 percent of the cases it submitted to mediation were settled. Even when a settlement could not be reached, the mediation process helped the litigants focus on the most important issues, which allowed for a quicker resolution at trial. In the last few years,

7. LIPSKY & SEEBER, *supra* note 1.

thirty-seven insurance companies have entered into pacts to mediate their claims against each other. Chubb & Son, Inc., a participating insurance company, has resolved nearly a dozen disputes under mediation pacts and saved between $150,000 and $200,000 per case.[8]

In recent years, mediation has helped several companies successfully settle class-action lawsuits. In 2000, an antitrust class action against the toy company Toys 'R' Us was settled following mediation for approximately $57 million in toys and cash.[9] The same year, a class action against Toshiba America Information Systems, Inc., which involved allegations that the company manufactured and distributed faulty floppy-diskette controllers, was settled through mediation.[10] Toshiba agreed to pay approximately $2.1 billion in cash, warranty remedies, hardware replacements, and coupons to repair the allegedly defective equipment.

The Equal Employment Opportunity Commission began a pilot mediation program in 1994 in an effort to reduce its case backlog.[11] Between 1995 and 1998, the agency more than halved its backlog of pending cases; in 1999, Congress increased the agency's budget to $279 million, a $37 million increase from the prior year.

SELECTING A MEDIATOR

Although not pronouncing final judgment, a mediator can powerfully affect the outcome of the mediation. By asking some questions but not others, the mediator can move the discussion to or from an issue. By suggesting solutions and reacting to proposals, the mediator can influence both parties' attitudes toward fairness, risk aversion, and trust. A skilled mediator knows how to bring disputing parties to genuine settlement; an unskilled mediator can push parties into agreements they later regret or, worse, can inflame the situation.

In the 1980s, the Society of Professionals in Dispute Resolution (SPDR) formed a commission to study the qualifications of mediators. After concluding that performance rather than credentials should be the central qualification criterion, it determined that qualified mediators should be able to (1) understand the negotiating process and the role of advocacy; (2) earn trust and maintain acceptability; (3) convert parties' positions into needs and interests; (4) screen out nonmediable issues; (5) help parties

ETHICAL CONSIDERATION

In many businesses, volume discounts are standard practice, and large customers reasonably expect to receive favorable treatment. How should a large, international corporation with a steady stream of disputes screen prospective mediators? Is it appropriate for a manager of the corporation to make clear to prospective mediators the potential for future lucrative business "if this one goes well"?

invent creative options; (6) help parties identify principles and criteria that will guide their decision making; (7) help parties assess their nonsettlement alternatives; (8) help parties make their own informed choices; and (9) help parties assess whether their agreement can be implemented.[12] Mediation agreements may or may not specify how a mediator will be selected.

The CPR Institute for Dispute Resolution (CPR), a nonprofit alliance of 500 major corporations and law firms, offers a standard mediation clause for parties to incorporate into their contracts: "The parties shall endeavor to resolve any dispute arising out of or relating to this Agreement by mediation under the CPR Mediation Procedure. Unless otherwise agreed, the parties will select a mediator from the CPR Panels of Distinguished Neutrals." The Panels of Distinguished Neutrals are CPR's rosters of 700 attorneys, former judges, legally trained executives, and academics who can mediate disputes. CPR is a strong proponent of self-administered ADR, where the parties and the mediator manage the process themselves, because it provides parties with optimum control over the dispute resolution process and is cheaper and more efficient.

CONFIDENTIALITY

Confidentiality is central to negotiation and mediation. If parties do not feel comfortable revealing important and sensitive information, they are less likely to identify opportunities for mutual gain. Unlike negotiation, mediation allows disputants to confide in a third party without fear of being exploited. Whether the mediation process involves caucusing or shuttle diplomacy, confiding in a mediator can allow the mediator to identify potential gains and point them out to the parties. If that confidentiality is doubted, the parties will withhold useful but potentially damaging information. Even worse, if

---

8. Margaret A. Jacobs, *Industry Giants Join Movement to Mediate,* WALL ST. J., July 21, 1997, at B1.

9. *In re* Toys 'R' Us Antitrust Litig., 191 F.R.D. 347 (E.D.N.Y. 2000).

10. Shaw v. Toshiba Am. Infor. Sys., Inc., 91 F. Supp. 2d 942 (E.D. Tex. 2000).

11. Aurora Mackey, *Close Calls,* CAL. LAW., June 1999, at 36.

12. National Institute of Dispute Resolution, DISP. RESOL. F., May 9, 1989.

the promise of confidentiality is not honored, the parties will come to regret their mediation experience.

To protect such confidences, many states extend legal privileges to mediators; others do so only if the parties have agreed to keep communications with the mediator confidential. In an effort to provide some consistency in states' treatment of mediation communications, the National Conference of Commissioners of Uniform State Laws has proposed a Uniform Mediation Act that is still under consideration.[13] The revised interim draft, dated August 2000, would entitle a mediator to refuse to disclose, and prevent any other person from disclosing, a communication with the mediator in a civil proceeding before a court, administrative tribunal, or arbitrator, or in a criminal misdemeanor proceeding. Although federal law does not directly address the question, federal courts have shown a willingness to recognize a mediation privilege, even if doing so deprives a party of truthful probative evidence.[14]

WHEN TO USE MEDIATION

Mediation, like other forms of ADR, is better suited to some conflicts than to others. For mediation to be appropriate, the parties must sincerely desire to settle their dispute. If they are unwilling to compromise or seek to harm their opponents, mediation will be a frustrating waste of time. Conversely, parties who wish to preserve their relationship are best suited to mediation. Litigation is adversarial by nature and often leaves hard feelings in its wake. Arbitration can also pit one party against another such that future interactions are filled with animosity.

Mediation is often attractive because it offers resolutions that are speedy, inexpensive, and logistically simple when compared to litigation. Mediation can also be therapeutic for the parties involved if they can express their pent-up feelings of anger, frustration, or betrayal.

Legal uncertainty also makes mediation an attractive alternative. If the law is clear and one party's rights are clearly being violated, mediation will seem unnecessary. The less black-and-white the situation, the more risky legal action is. Mediation allows parties to resolve their differences more quickly and without appeal to undeveloped, ill-formed, or uncertain legal doctrine.

The need for privacy may also make some disputes more appropriate for mediation. Lawsuits require the filing of public documents and can alert the media to sensitive areas of business. Trade secrets, embryonic research, organizational structures, and internal training documents may need to be kept from the front pages of newspapers. Suppliers and customers may also become nervous if problems that could have been kept confidential are reported in the press. "Keeping it between ourselves" is much more realistic if few outsiders are involved.

THE MEDIATION PROCESS

By definition, mediation is a flexible process that allows for many different structures, rules, and procedures. Because parties are less likely to agree to anything once a dispute has arisen, mediation organizations have evolved sets of default rules to which disputants can subscribe in advance of a specific conflict or to which they can defer once a conflict has arisen. However, disputants may also agree to alternative ground rules that are specifically tailored to their particular conflict.

DANGERS

Critics of mediation point to the lack of procedural protections in the process. Some parties may be surprised to find that their legal rights are not protected in mediation even though their rights would be protected in litigation. Parties with equal bargaining power may wisely agree to trade such rights for expediency, but unequal bargainers may unfairly take advantage of each other. For example, in a conflict between a landlord and rent-controlled tenants over a rat infestation, a tenant might accept the placing of rat traps instead of the full-scale extermination that the housing code and a court would mandate.

Mediation may also effect changes in the distribution of power in a relationship. For example, introducing mediation into a nonunion plant may effectively defuse current tensions and hinder efforts to unionize the plant.[15] Before agreeing to mediation, parties should consider the possibility of such unintended consequences, including possible effects on continued adjudication of the dispute, future dealings with the opponent, and reputation with internal and external constituencies.

⚖ Arbitration

Arbitration is the resolution of a dispute by a neutral third party, called an *arbitrator*. For example, in October 1999, Gemstar International Group won a ruling in an

---

13. The revised interim draft of the Uniform Mediation Act can be found at <http://www.pon.harvard.edu/guests/uma>.
14. *See, e.g.,* NLRB v. Joseph MaCaluso, Inc., 618 F.2d 51 (9th Cir. 1980).

15. WILLIAM L. URY ET AL., GETTING DISPUTES RESOLVED 52 (1988).

ADR *for* Online Disputes

The Internet's electronic marketplace poses new challenges for resolving disputes. An October 1999 survey of online shoppers conducted by the National Consumers League found that one in five consumers had experienced a problem with transactions in the previous year.[a] The Federal Trade Commission (FTC) received 18,622 Internet-related complaints in 1999, a large increase from the 7,955 complaints received in 1998. More than half of the complaints received in 1999 involved transactions at Internet auction sites.

In December 1999, the Organization for Economic Cooperation and Development (OECD) approved Guidelines on Consumer Protection in the Context of Electronic Commerce.[b] The section on dispute resolution and redress states that "[c]onsumers should be provided meaningful access to fair and timely alternative dispute resolution and redress without undue cost or burden." The Guidelines encourage businesses, consumer representatives, and governments to "work together to continue to provide consumers with the option of alternative dispute resolution mechanisms that provide effective

resolution of the dispute in a fair and timely manner and without undue cost or burden."

On May 3, 2000, the World Intellectual Property Organization (WIPO), a United Nations agency, signed an agreement with the Application Service Provider Industry Consortium to create an international arbitration and mediation center for the application service provider (ASP) industry. The center will allow parties to resolve their disputes quickly by filing claims and supporting documents online. In addition, WIPO will select arbitrators who have the technological expertise to understand the issues in dispute. WIPO also recently began resolving domain disputes, which is discussed further in the "Inside Story" at the end of this chapter.

In September 2000, the FTC issued a report recognizing the importance of ADR to consumer protection. The report states that "[t]he same technology that enables e-commerce can provide consumers with practical access to redress without unduly burdening business."[c]

Private companies as well as consumer groups have created forums for resolving e-commerce disputes. For example, SquareTrade referees auctions at eBay in a pilot program that began in late February 2000; Cybersettle resolves disputes involving insurance settlements; and ClickNSettle allows parties to exchange settlement offers without a mediator. At Icourthouse, an online jury reads both sides of the case and then provides a verdict.

a. Michael Liedtke, *Mediators See Profit in Online Discontent/Buyer Complaints Create Opportunity,* SAN DIEGO UNION-TRIB., May 1, 2000, at A-3.
b. Text of these Guidelines can be found at the OECD Web site: <http://www.oecd.org/dsti/sti/it/ consumer/prod/ guidelines.htm>.
c. FEDERAL TRADE COMMISSION, CONSUMER PROTECTION IN THE GLOBAL ELECTRONIC MARKETPLACE (2000).

---

arbitration against General Instrument Corporation for breach of contract and misappropriation of trade secrets.[16] A panel of the American Arbitration Association found that General Instrument had breached an agreement with a Gemstar subsidiary, StarSight Telecast, Inc., and misappropriated proprietary technology that Gemstar used in cable television boxes for electronic program guides used by television viewers. Gemstar was awarded between $25 and $36 million in compensatory damages plus 50 percent of that amount for punitive damages and attorneys' fees.

In July 1999, Jeffrey Katzenberg, former chairman of Walt Disney Studios, sued the company for breach of contract, alleging that he was owed at least 2 percent of studio profits created during the ten years that he worked at Dis-

ney. The parties settled the liability portion of the case for $117 million and agreed to determine through arbitration the additional amount of money he was owed for his bonus. Although the terms of the agreement worked out in arbitration are confidential, insiders estimated that Katzenberg received an additional $150 million along with the $117 million Disney agreed to pay him.[17]

Although *nonbinding arbitration* is certainly an option, most parties enter into arbitration for its binding nature. In *final-offer arbitration,* used most notably in baseball salary disputes, each side submits its "best and final" offer to the arbitrator, who must choose one of the two proposals. Such a structure strongly encourages the parties to submit fair and reasonable offers. Otherwise, the less reasonable party is likely to lose with no chance for further conces-

16. John Lippman, *Gemstar Wins Partial Ruling on Claim General Instrument Breached Contract,* WALL ST. J., Oct. 7, 1999, at B5.

17. Janet Shprintz, *Jeff & Mickey's Odd Courtship,* VARIETY, July 12, 1999, at 1.

sions. Without its binding nature, such an exercise would be pointless. Still, some parties value the result of non-binding arbitration as a guide to what is fair. If a neutral third party has heard the strongest evidence and best arguments of both sides in a dispute, his or her opinion can serve as a baseline for what a court might decide.

THE ARBITRATION PROCESS

Arbitration is the most formalized of the ADR methods. It is unlike both negotiation, in which there is no structure unless the parties first negotiate one, and mediation, in which the mediator focuses more on creating dialogue than on enforcing a technical format. In some ways, arbitration is like a trial. The first stage is usually a *prehearing,* in which parties may submit trial-like briefs, supporting documents, and other written statements making their case. Because neither federal nor state statutes grant arbitrators the authority to use discovery devices at this stage, prehearing discovery is usually limited to what the parties voluntarily disclose.

Because the *hearing* itself (like a trial) is adversarial, the hearing is more structured than the prehearing. The precise structure varies from arbitration to arbitration, but Rule 32 of the Commercial Arbitration Rules, Conduct of Proceedings, promulgated by the American Arbitration Association, provides an illustration:

> The claimant shall present evidence to support its claim. The respondent shall then present evidence to support its defense. Witnesses for each party shall also submit to questions from the arbitrator and the adverse party. The arbitrator has the discretion to vary this procedure, provided that the parties are treated with equality and that each party has the right to be heard and is given a fair opportunity to present its case.

Although no detailed rules of evidence or procedure need apply—unlike in state and federal court, where much statutory and case law addresses fine points in exacting detail—many arbitrators believe that compliance with some of these rules is useful and necessary. Arbitrators may also subpoena documents and witnesses for the hearing.

In the final, *posthearing* phase, the arbitrator makes his or her award after considering all the evidence presented in the prehearing and the hearing itself. Often the award is unaccompanied by any discussion or explanation of the decision. "Written opinions can be dangerous because they identify targets for the losing party to attack," warns one arbitration scholar.[18] In a profession neither subject

ETHICAL CONSIDERATION

During a dispute with a competitor over copyrighted software that is similar to a competitor's products, you ask a mediator friend about his work in ADR. In the course of a few nameless anecdotes about his recent clients, you are shocked to learn how much sensitive information a skilled mediator can induce parties to share. At the same time, your attorneys tell you that without more evidence against your competitor, a lawsuit is not justified or economically prudent at this time. Should you propose mediation to the other company in the hope of learning enough information to justify legal action? If such a proposal is accepted, should you send as your representative a new employee who has no sensitive information to reveal? Should you hire a professional investigator as your representative to elicit as much damaging information as possible from your competitor?

to appeal nor constrained by precedent, arbitrators may be reluctant to give extra grist to the loser's mill. On the other hand, the U.S. Supreme Court has noted that "a well reasoned opinion tends to engender confidence in the integrity of the process and aids in clarifying the underlying agreement."[19] In some settings, such as federal labor arbitrations under the auspices of the National Labor Relations Board (NLRB), arbitrators are required to write an opinion. Also, parties can insist on such an opinion as part of their contract with the arbitrator.

CHOICE OF ARBITRATOR

The arbitrator is usually chosen by the parties to the dispute or by a third-party delegate, such as the American Arbitration Association (AAA), which represents 18,000 arbitrators. The choice of an arbitrator is crucial. Unlike a judge's decision, which can be set aside if erroneous, an arbitrator's ruling generally is binding. As New York's highest court stated nearly two decades ago: "An arbitrator's paramount responsibility is to reach an equitable result, and the courts will not assume the role of overseers to mold the award to conform to their sense of justice. Thus, an arbitrator's award will not be vacated for errors of law and fact committed by the arbitrator."[20]

An arbitration clause may list the names of potential arbitrators; if so, the parties should check the availability of these candidates before enlisting them. As with judges

---

18. R. COULSON, BUSINESS ARBITRATION—WHAT YOU NEED TO KNOW 29 (3d ed. 1986).

19. United Steelworkers of Am. v. Enterprise Wheel & Car Corp., 363 U.S. 593, 598 (1960).

20. Sprinzen v. Nomberg, 389 N.E.2d 456, 458 (N.Y. 1979).

and their courts, particular arbitrators may be too busy to provide speedy resolution. Alternatively, the arbitration clause may refer the selection of an arbitrator to the AAA or another dispute resolution organization. American Arbitration Association arbitrators are skilled, and the association makes special efforts to identify arbitrators experienced in handling particular types of disputes. The AAA decides how many arbitrators to appoint (usually from one to three) and may include arbitrators from different professions—unless the arbitration clause specifies the number and kind of arbitrators desired. Arbitration clauses often provide that each party will choose its own arbitrator and that these two will pick a third. In some states, the government itself is willing to intervene. In New York, for instance, a court may name the arbitrator upon application by either party.[21] The Federal Arbitration Act has a similar provision.[22]

The ability to select an arbitrator familiar with the industry or form of dispute further distinguishes arbitration from much of the judicial system. Judges tend to be experts in judicial procedure. Consequently, they hear cases touching on many substantive areas of the law. A federal district judge, for instance, could in a single day preside over cases ranging from felony narcotic sales to toxic tort class actions and including price-fixing cases, contract disputes between financial institutions, and racially motivated employment discrimination. Arbitrators tend to focus on business sectors or conflict types, such as labor relations or landlord–tenant disputes. To the extent one is more concerned with substance than procedure, arbitration can be an attractive alternative to litigation.

ARBITRATION CLAUSES

A common device by which parties enter into arbitration is the inclusion of an arbitration clause in a contract. An *arbitration clause* specifies that in the event of a dispute arising out of the contract, the parties will arbitrate specific issues in a stated manner. It is important that parties negotiate arbitration agreements that clearly state the types of disputes to be resolved by arbitration as well as the procedure and rules, such as discovery and types of damages to be awarded, to be used at the arbitration. The agreement should expressly state whether the arbitration is binding or nonbinding. It is far easier for parties to negotiate these terms at the beginning of their relationship than at the time a dispute arises. Arbitration clauses are especially important in international contracts when each party wishes to avoid the labyrinth of a foreign legal system and the many pitfalls awaiting a novice litigant.

When drafting a contract, managers should consider the scope of any arbitration clause. Usually, the parties to the contract are the parties to the arbitration. Sometimes, however, a dispute may arise between parties to several different contracts. For example, a dispute may arise between a construction subcontractor and an architect. The parties should ensure that each contract contains an arbitration clause and that each party agrees to a consolidated arbitration with other parties on related issues.

Foreseeing which disputes are better arbitrated than litigated is more difficult than foreseeing which parties might come into conflict. Most arbitration clauses simply state that the parties will arbitrate all disputes relating to or arising out of their contract—leaving the parties to fight over the specifics of arbitration after a dispute arises. Instead, parties should specify in the agreement the types of issues and disputes that they want to arbitrate rather than litigate.

Unfortunately, arbitration clauses often do not include details of how arbitration will proceed, when and where it will take place, and who will preside. Once again, it is better to agree upon these details before a dispute arises. Parties should agree upon a location close to their businesses and a reasonable timetable by which to settle their disputes. The arbitration clause may provide that the arbitration will commence with a prehearing conference. To minimize the conflict over such specifics, parties often designate that arbitrations will be conducted according to the rules of a third-party organization, such as the American Arbitration Association. As in mediation, such organizations have evolved rules and procedures that may serve as defaults for disputing parties. However, these rules rarely include provisions concerning the scope of discovery and limits on punitive damages. Parties are better served by including specific provisions concerning these matters. In some states, such

ETHICAL CONSIDERATION

A common premise underlying advocacy of ADR is that the parties to it have consented to the dispute resolution mechanism as opposed to the judicial system. Should the manager of a local appliance store whose sales contracts call for binding arbitration—in barely legible typeface buried in the middle of five pages of legalese—be able to enforce those arbitration clauses? Does it matter that this is the only refrigerator distributor for miles in a poor urban area? If the store serves a neighborhood where most residents speak only Chinese, should the agreement be in Chinese?

21. N.Y. C.P.L.R. 7504 (1999).
22. 9 U.S.C. § 5 (2000).

as Illinois, an arbitrator cannot award punitive damages unless the parties expressly authorize it.

FEDERAL ARBITRATION ACT

In 1920, New York enacted the first arbitration statute in the United States, giving parties the right to settle current disputes and control future ones through private arbitration. The New York act served as a model for the Uniform Arbitration Act enacted thirty-five years later. Today, most states have amended their laws to conform to the Uniform Arbitration Act, making agreements to arbitrate and arbitration awards judicially enforceable. Five years after New York blazed the trail, Congress passed what is now known as the *Federal Arbitration Act (FAA)*. Many years later, the U.S. Supreme Court proclaimed that in enacting the law, "Congress declared a national policy favoring arbitration and withdrew the power of the states to require a judicial forum for the resolution of claims which the contracting parties agreed to resolve by arbitration."[23]

The Supreme Court has enforced arbitration clauses, even when the rights at issue were protected by federal law. For example, in *Rodriguez de Quijas v. Shearson/American Express, Inc.*,[24] the Supreme Court held that a predispute agreement to submit to compulsory arbitration any controversy relating to a securities investment was enforceable even though the plaintiff alleged claims under the Securities Act of 1933. The Court noted that in recent years it had upheld agreements to arbitrate claims under the Securities Exchange Act of 1934,[25] the Racketeer Influenced and Corrupt Organizations Act (RICO),[26] and the antitrust laws.[27] By agreeing to arbitrate a statutory claim, the Court reasoned, a party does not forgo the substantive rights afforded by the statute. The agreement means only that the resolution of the dispute will be in an arbitral, rather than judicial, forum. The Supreme Court strongly endorsed statutes, such as the FAA, that favor this method of resolving disputes.

Section 2 of the FAA provides that arbitration agreements in contracts concerning interstate commerce are "valid, irrevocable, and enforceable, save upon such grounds as exist at law or in equity for the revocation of any contract." By placing arbitration agreements on the same footing as contracts, Congress precluded the states from "singling out arbitration agreements for suspect sta-

INTERNATIONAL CONSIDERATION

When parties to a contract are from different nations, disputes between the parties can lead to a collision between one party's expectations and a foreign legal regime. To avoid such difficulty, it is often helpful to include arbitration clauses in these contracts. After all, few managers would appreciate being hauled into a foreign-language court 5,000 miles from their home office and being held to unfamiliar legal standards. Many European and Asian business leaders, for example, are uncomfortable with the U.S. legal system's discovery procedures for obtaining evidence prior to trial through depositions, written interrogatories, and document production. Often the parties can draft an arbitration clause to mutual satisfaction, but even if all parties are willing to do so, the parties cannot "negotiate around" many rules of a legal system once litigation has begun.

tus."[28] For example, the Supreme Court struck down a Montana law that rendered an arbitration clause unenforceable unless "[n]otice that [the] contract is subject to arbitration" was "typed in underlined capital letters on the first page of the contract."[29] Montana's first-page notice requirement conflicted with the FAA in that it applied specifically to arbitration agreements and not to all contracts.

Nonetheless, some states have been reluctant to allow their policies regarding ADR to be preempted by the FAA. In *Sisters of the Visitation v. Cochran Plastering Co.*,[30] a Catholic religious order filed an arbitration claim against a contractor for failing to finish repairing cracks in the plaster on the ceilings and walls of a chapel and damaging paintings. The contractor filed an action in court claiming that the arbitration provision in the contract was unenforceable pursuant to an Alabama statute that prohibited the specific enforcement of a predispute arbitration agreement. Because the contract was between two Alabama residents, was performed in Alabama, and did not substantially affect interstate commerce, the Alabama Supreme Court ruled that it was not within the scope of the FAA. In rejecting application of the FAA to the case, the court stated:

> To recognize such a wide sweep of federal authority would stifle the States' interest in, or efforts toward, developing creative solutions to other common problems. Alabama has a robust alternative-dispute-resolution program whereby trial judges routinely call on the parties to a lawsuit to attempt to resolve their differences with the aid of a mediator, whose proposals are not binding on the parties.

23. Southland Corp. v. Keating, 465 U.S. 1, 2 (1984).
24. 490 U.S. 477 (1989).
25. Shearson/American Express Inc., v. McMahon, 482 U.S. 220 (1987), *reh'g denied*, 483 U.S. 1056 (1987).
26. *Id.*
27. Mitsubishi Motors Corp. v. Soler Chrysler-Plymouth, Inc., 473 U.S. 614 (1985).

28. Doctor's Assocs., Inc. v. Casarotto, 517 U.S. 681, 687 (1996).
29. *Id.*
30. Ms. 1981513 (Ala. Mar. 10, 2000).

ARBITRATION OF EMPLOYMENT DISPUTES

Individual employees are increasingly being asked to sign employment agreements with arbitration clauses. Exhibit 4.3 contains an excerpt from an arbitration agreement used by a national professional services firm. All employees were required to sign it as a condition of their employment with the firm.

In *mandatory arbitration,* one party will not do business with the other unless he or she agrees to arbitrate any future claims. In the labor context, that means that a firm will not hire an individual unless he or she agrees now to arbitrate future claims. Today, nearly all major collective-bargaining agreements include arbitration clauses.[31] The Supreme Court upheld provisions for mandatory arbitration of contract claims arising under a collective-bargaining agreement[32] but struck down a collective-bargaining agreement's provisions for mandatory arbitration of statutory Title VII claims for discrimination based on race, gender, religion, or national origin.[33] Yet seventeen years later, in *Gilmer v. Interstate/Johnson Lane Corp.*, the Court ruled that employees who had signed individual agreements to arbitrate could be required to arbitrate age discrimination claims under the Age Discrimination in Employment Act.[34] The Court also upheld a predispute agreement to arbitrate statutory claims under the Employment Retirement Income Security Act (ERISA), which governs pensions and other benefits.[35]

31. Antoine, *Arbitration and the Law, in* ARBITRATION IN PRACTICE 9 (Zack ed. 1984).
32. AT&T Techs., Inc. v. Communication Workers of Am., 475 U.S. 643 (1986).
33. Alexander v. Gardner-Denver Co., 415 U.S. 36 (1974).
34. 500 U.S. 20 (1991).
35. Shearson Lehman/American Express Inc. v. Bird, 493 U.S. 884 (1989).

| EXHIBIT 4.3 | **Sample Arbitration Clause in Employment Context** |

The Firm and I mutually consent to the resolution by final and binding arbitration of all claims or controversies, whether or not arising out of my employment (or its termination), that the Firm may have against me or that I may have against the Firm or its partners, employees or agents in their capacity as such, including, but not limited to, claims for compensation due; claims for breach of any contract or covenant (express or implied); tort claims; claims of discrimination (including, but not limited to, claims based on race, sex, sexual preference, religion, national origin, age, marital status, medical condition, handicap or disability); claims for benefits (except as set forth in paragraph 3, below [which excludes workers' compensation and unemployment benefits]); and claims alleging a violation of any federal, state or other governmental law, statute, regulation or ordinance (collectively, "Claims"), *provided however* that Claims shall not include claims excluded in [paragraph 3]. All Claims shall be arbitrated in accordance with the attached Arbitration Rules and Procedures, which are expressly incorporated herein and made part of this Agreement.

In the following case, the Supreme Court considered whether a general arbitration clause in a collective-bargaining agreement requires an employee to use arbitration for an alleged violation of the Americans with Disabilities Act.

A CASE IN POINT

CASE 4.2

Wright v. Universal Maritime Service Corp.
Supreme Court of the United States
525 U.S. 70 (1998).

In the Language of the Court

FACTS Ceasar Wright was a longshoreman and a member of the International Longshoremen's Association, AFL-CIO (Union). Through the Union, Wright was hired out to work for several stevedoring companies. Pursuant to a collective-bargaining agreement, Wright was required to follow an arbitration procedure for disputes relating to his employment.

In February 1992, while working for the Stevens Shipping and Terminal Company, Wright injured his right heel and back, and he later sought compensation for permanent disability. The claim was ultimately settled, and Wright was awarded permanent disability as well as Social Security disability benefits. In January 1995, Wright returned to the Union pool of workers and worked for several stevedoring companies with no complaint as to his performance. Nevertheless, when one company learned that Wright had previously settled a claim for permanent disability, it refused to accept him for employment

(Continued)

(Case 4.2 continued)

from the Union. Wright hired an attorney and eventually filed a claim in U.S. district court against the stevedoring companies, claiming violations of the Americans with Disabilities Act (ADA). The claim was dismissed on grounds that Wright had failed to pursue the arbitration procedure mandated by the collective-bargaining agreement. Wright appealed.

ISSUE PRESENTED Does a general arbitration clause in a collective-bargaining agreement require an employee to arbitrate claims under the ADA?

OPINION SCALIA, J., writing for the U.S. Supreme Court:

In collective-bargaining agreements, we have said, "there is a presumption of arbitrability in the sense that 'an order to arbitrate the particular grievance should not be denied unless it may be said with positive assurance that the arbitration clause is not susceptible of an interpretation that covers the asserted dispute.'"

That presumption, however, does not extend beyond the reach of the principal rationale that justifies it, which is that arbitrators are in a better position than courts to interpret the terms of a [collective-bargaining agreement]. The dispute in the present case, however, ultimately concerns not the application or interpretation of any [collective-bargaining agreement], but the meaning of a federal statute. The cause of action Wright asserts arises not out of contract, but out of the ADA, and is distinct from any right conferred by the collective-bargaining agreement.

...

Not only is petitioner's statutory claim not subject to a presumption of arbitrability; we think any CBA requirement to arbitrate it must be particularly clear. . . . "We will not infer from a general contractual provision that the parties intended to waive a statutorily protected right unless the undertaking is 'explicitly stated.' More succinctly, the waiver must be clear and unmistakable."

RESULT The Court held that the collective-bargaining agreement did not waive the right to a judicial forum for claims of employment discrimination.

QUESTIONS

1. What would have been the result if the collective-bargaining agreement had clearly required arbitration of employment discrimination claims?
2. The Court acknowledged "tension" between its holding in *Alexander v. Gardner-Denver Co.* that a collective-bargaining agreement cannot force an employee to arbitrate Title VII claims and its holding in *Gilmer v. Interstate/Johnson Lane Corp.* that an individual agreement to arbitrate can require the employee to arbitrate age discrimination claims. How, if at all, can these two cases be reconciled?

In 2001, the U.S. Supreme Court upheld an individually negotiated agreement that required the employee to arbitrate all employment disputes, including Title VII claims.[36]

Although Section 1 of the FAA excludes "contracts of employment of seamen, railroad employees, or any other class of workers engaged in foreign or interstate commerce" from the Act's requirements for judicial enforcement of arbitration agreements, the Court construed this exception narrowly to encompass only contracts with transportation workers. As discussed further in Chapter 15, there is still a split in the circuits as to how explicit and clear an employee's agreement to arbitrate statutory claims must be to compel arbitration.[37]

36. Circuit City Stores, Inc. v. Adams, 121 S.Ct. 1302 (2001).

37. *Compare* Rosenberg v. Merrill Lynch, Pierce, Fenner & Smith, Inc., 170 F.3d 1 (1st Cir. 1999) *with* Haskins v. Prudential Ins. Co. of America, 230 F.3d 231 (6th Cir. 2000).

The Equal Employment Opportunity Commission (EEOC) may file a claim in court on its own behalf against an employer, even if the employee involved has entered into an enforceable arbitration agreement, if the EEOC is seeking a permanent injunction enjoining an employer from engaging in discriminatory practices. If the EEOC is seeking monetary relief, the circuits are split on whether the EEOC must adjudicate those claims in arbitration.[38]

UNCONSCIONABLE ARBITRATION AGREEMENTS

An arbitration agreement will not be enforced if the court finds that it operates in a harsh and one-sided manner without any justification. In the following case, the California Supreme Court considered the background and educational level of the employee in determining whether the arbitration agreement was unconscionable.

38. *Compare* EEOC v. Waffle House, Inc., 193 F.3d 805 (4th Cir. 1999), *cert. granted,* 121 S.Ct. 1401 (2001) (EEOC can sue for injunctive relief but not damages) *with* EEOC v. Frank's Nursery & Crafts Inc., 177 F.3d 448 (6th Cir. 1999) (EEOC can sue for monetary or injunctive relief).

INTERNATIONAL CONSIDERATION

Throughout the 1990s, India undertook significant reforms to liberalize its economy. As part of its effort to attract international business, India enacted its Arbitration and Conciliation Act of 1996. Although India had been a signatory to the United Nations' New York Convention on the Recognition and Enforcement of Foreign Arbitral Awards since 1958, businesspeople from other nations had viewed arbitration in India with distrust. Indian courts had intervened during and after arbitrations, thus keeping parties from reliably avoiding local courts and enjoying closure to any specific dispute. The new law, based on the United Nations' Model Arbitration Law, brings international standards to both domestic and international arbitrations in India. Court interference during arbitration has been nearly eliminated, and the basis for judicial review of awards has been severely limited. India is one of the world's largest and most promising consumer markets; with a legal infrastructure better suited to resolution of commercial disputes, India is now poised to attract much commerce.

A CASE IN POINT

CASE 4.3
Armendariz v. Foundation Health Psychcare Services, Inc.
Supreme Court of California
6 P.3d 669 (Cal. 1999).

In the Language of the Court

FACTS In August 1995, the plaintiffs were hired by Foundation Health Psychcare Services, Inc. to work as employees in the "Provider Relations Group." As a condition of employment, the plaintiffs were required to sign an arbitration clause in which they agreed to arbitrate all unlawful termination claims and that their damages would not exceed an amount equal to the wages that would have been earned between the date of termination and the date of the arbitration award. Under the agreement, the employer had no reciprocal obligation to arbitrate or limit on damages.

In June 1996, the plaintiffs were informed that their positions were "being eliminated" and that they were "being terminated." The plaintiffs believed that they were the victims of same-sex discrimination and that their termination was actually due to their homosexual orientation. When the plaintiffs sued in state court alleging wrongful termination, Foundation Health moved to compel arbitration of their claims on the basis of the arbitration clause. The trial court held that the arbitration provision was an unconscionable contract. The appeals court reversed that decision.

ISSUE PRESENTED Is an arbitration contract unconscionable if it is required as a condition of employment, requires arbitration of only employee claims, and limits an employee's damages?

OPINION MOSK, J., writing for the California Supreme Court:

Unconscionability analysis begins with an inquiry into whether the contract is one of adhesion. "The term [contract of adhesion] signifies a standard contract, which, imposed and drafted by the party of superior bargaining strength, relegates the subscribing party only the opportunity to adhere to the contract or reject it." If the contract is adhesive, the court must then determine whether "other factors are present

(Continued)

(Case 4.3 continued)

which, under established legal rules—legislative or judicial—operate to render it [un-enforceable]." "Generally speaking, there are two judicially imposed limitations on the enforcement of adhesion contracts or provisions thereof. The first is that such a contract or provision which does not fall within the reasonable expectations of the weaker or 'adhering' party will not be enforced against him. The second—a principle of equity applicable to all contracts generally—is that a contract or provision, even if consistent with the reasonable expectations of the parties, will be denied enforcement if, considered in its context, it is unduly oppressive or 'unconscionable.'"

…

Applying the above principles to this case, we first determine whether the arbitration agreement is adhesive. There is little dispute that it is. It was imposed on employees as a condition of employment and there was no opportunity to negotiate.

Moreover, in the case of preemployment arbitration contracts, the economic pressure exerted by employers on all but the most sought-after employees may be particularly acute, for the arbitration agreement stands between the employee and necessary employment, and few employees are in a position to refuse a job because of an arbitration requirement.

…

Given the disadvantages that may exist for plaintiffs arbitrating disputes, it is unfairly one-sided for an employer with superior bargaining power to impose arbitration on the employee as plaintiff but not to accept such limitations when it seeks to prosecute a claim against the employee, without at least some reasonable justification for such one-sidedness based on "business realities." As has been recognized "'unconscionability turns not only on a "one-sided" result, but also on an absence of "justification" for it.'" If the arbitration system established by the employer is indeed fair, then the employer as well as the employee should be willing to submit claims to arbitration.

…

The unconscionable one-sidedness of the arbitration agreement is compounded in this case by the fact that it does not permit the full recovery of damages for employees, while placing no such restriction on the employer.

RESULT The arbitration provision was found to be an unconscionable contract. The grant of the employer's motion to compel arbitration was reversed.

QUESTIONS

1. Given the California Supreme Court's reasoning, would any mandatory arbitration agreement in the employment context be enforceable?
2. What disadvantages might exist for plaintiff–employees arbitrating disputes?

JUDICIAL REVIEW OF AWARDS

The Federal Arbitration Act lists four circumstances in which an arbitration award may be set aside by a court: (1) the award was procured by corruption, fraud, or undue means; (2) the arbitrator was demonstrably impartial or corrupt; (3) the arbitrator engaged in misconduct by refusing to postpone the hearing when given sufficient reason or by refusing to hear pertinent evidence; and (4) the arbitrator exceeded his or her powers or executed them so badly that a final award on the issue put to arbitration was not made. Acknowledging the rights of parties to agree to tailor-made procedural rules, one court held that the parties could agree to give a court the power to overturn an arbitration award if the court concluded that it was not supported by substantial evidence.[39] Overall, the courts look favorably on arbitration and favor its results.

39. LaPine Technology Corp. v. Kyocera Corp., 130 F.3d 884 (9th Cir. 1997).

Case law suggests that awards may be reversed for reasons beyond those enumerated in the FAA or provided for in the arbitration agreement itself. A court may strike down an arbitration award if it would "violate some explicit public policy that is well defined and dominant." In *Town of Groton v. United Steelworkers of America*,[40] the Supreme Court of Connecticut invalidated an arbitration

award that reinstated a union employee who had been fired after pleading *nolo contendere* and being convicted of embezzling his employer's money on the grounds that it violated the clear public policy against embezzlement.

A court might set aside an arbitrator's decision if it was "arbitrary and capricious"[41] or if the arbitrator manifestly disregarded the law.[42] In the following case, one party actively encouraged the arbitrator to disregard the law.

---

40. 757 A.2d 501 (Conn. 2000), *citing* United Paperworkers Int'l Union v. Misco, Inc., 484 U.S. 29 (1987). *But see* Eastern Associated Coal Corp. v. United Mine Workers of America, 121 S. Ct. 462 (2000) (arbitrator's decision requiring reinstatement of employee who twice tested positive for marijuana not barred by public policy) (Case 16.4).

41. Wilko v. Swan, 346 U.S. 427 (1953), *overturned by* Rodriguez de Quijas v. Shearson/American Express, Inc., 490 U.S. 477 (1989), on other grounds.

42. Greenberg v. Bear, Stearns & Co., 220 F.3d 22 (2d Cir. 2000).

A CASE IN POINT

CASE 4.4

Montes v. Shearson Lehman Brothers, Inc.
*United States
Court of Appeals for the
Eleventh Circuit
128 F.3d 1456
(11th Cir. 1997).*

Summary

FACTS Delfina Montes went to work for Shearson Lehman Brothers and signed an agreement to arbitrate any disputes arising from her employment. After the termination of her employment, Montes filed suit for allegedly unpaid overtime under the Fair Labor Standards Act (FLSA), which mandates overtime pay for certain workers. Honoring the arbitration agreement, the trial court referred the dispute to arbitration. The arbitration panel ruled that Shearson did not owe Montes any overtime pay. Montes petitioned the trial court to vacate the arbitration panel's ruling as arbitrary and capricious because the panel heeded Shearson's urging that it disregard the FLSA. In support of her claim, Montes pointed out several statements made during the arbitration hearing by Shearson's attorney, including:

> I know, as I have served many times as an arbitrator, that you as an arbitrator are not guided strictly to follow case law precedent. That you can also do what's fair and just and equitable. . . .
>
> You have to decide whether you're going to follow the statutes . . . or do what is right and just and equitable in this case.
>
> . . . in this case this law is not right.
>
> . . . I now ask you in my closing, not to follow the FLSA if you determine that she's an exempt employee.

The court denied the petition, and Montes appealed.

ISSUE PRESENTED Can a plea to deliberately disregard the relevant law provide a basis for overturning the result of an arbitration?

SUMMARY OF OPINION Although the Eleventh Circuit had never expressly adopted the "manifest disregard of the law" rationale for overturning awards, the U.S. court of appeals noted that all other circuits—except the Fifth—had done so. Furthermore, the U.S. Supreme Court had carefully distinguished between a merely erroneous interpretation of the law—which is not grounds for overturning an award—and manifest disregard of the law—which is grounds for overturning.[43] Such "manifest disregard" requires an arbitrator to be conscious of the law and to deliberately ignore it. As well, the court noted that an agreement to arbitrate statutory claims is simply an agreement to submit such claims to an arbitral, rather than judicial, forum; it is not an agreement to forfeit

---

43. Senate Comm. on the Judiciary, Fed. R. of Evid., 93d Cong., 2d sess., S. Rep. No. 1277, at 10 (1974).

(Continued)

(Case 4.4 continued)

statutory rights. Hence, manifest disregard of the law can constitute grounds for vacating an arbitration award because it can amount to a forfeiture of statutory rights.

In this case, the arbitration record and formal decision lacked supporting facts to indicate the basis for the award. Similarly, the record and decision did not indicate that the panel had rejected Shearson's plea to disregard the law. The appeals court, therefore, could not be sure that Shearson's plea went unheeded by the panel and that the arbitrators' decision was not made in manifest disregard of the law.

RESULT The appeals court reversed the district court's affirmation of the arbitration award and remanded the case for a new arbitration.

COMMENTS The appeals court's inability to understand the full basis for the arbitration award underscores the importance of a thoroughly written arbitration decision outlining the rationale for the award. Had the court been confident that the arbitration panel had rejected Shearson's plea to disregard the Fair Labor Standards Act, it would likely have upheld the award and saved the parties further uncertainty, delay, and arbitration costs. The case also points out the folly of explicitly encouraging the arbitrators to disregard the law.

Hybrids

Various hybrid forms of ADR are available, including med-arb, minitrials, and summary jury trials.

MED-ARB

Med-arb is the most obvious hybrid form of ADR. In *med-arb* the parties to a dispute enter mediation with the commitment to submit to binding arbitration if mediation fails to resolve the conflict. Typically, the same person serves as mediator and arbitrator. Delay and expense are reduced if the arbitrator is already familiar with the situation from mediation. A danger of med-arb is that honesty in mediation could become damaging revelation in arbitration, especially if the mediator then acts as arbitrator. A decision-making arbitrator cannot forget what he or she has learned confidentially in mediation caucuses with a party. Looking ahead to such a possibility, parties in the "med" stage of med-arb may be reluctant to participate openly and in good faith, thus ensuring the final "arb" stage from the beginning. In such a scenario, time and money are wasted by the doomed mediation phase. For this reason, it is usually preferable to specify that a different person will act as arbitrator if mediation fails to resolve the conflict.

MINITRIAL

In a *minitrial*, lawyers conduct discovery for a limited period, usually a few weeks. They then exchange legal briefs or memoranda of law. At this point, the top management of the two businesses hears the lawyers from each side present their case in a trial format. The presentations are moderated by a neutral third party, often an attorney or a judge.

After the minitrial, the managers of the two businesses meet to settle the case. If they are unable to reach a settlement, the presiding third party can issue a nonbinding opinion. The managers can then meet again to try to settle on the basis of the third-party opinion. For this reason, minitrials are a cross between arbitration and negotiation.

 INTERNATIONAL CONSIDERATION

The United Nations Convention on the Recognition and Enforcement of Foreign Arbitral Awards, Article III, implemented in the United States by Chapter 2 of the Federal Arbitration Act,[a] provides: "Each Contracting State shall recognize arbitral awards as binding and enforce them in accordance with the rules of procedure of the territory where the award is relied upon, under the conditions laid down in the following articles." As of 2000, over 115 countries were signatories to the convention.[b]

a. 9 U.S.C. § 201 (West Elec. Update 1997).
b. For the full text of the convention and the list of signatories, see International Alternative Dispute Resolutions Web site at <http://www.internationaladr.com>.

Minitrials have several advantages. Like litigation, they allow a thorough investigation and presentation of the parties' claims; but they give the managers the opportunity to work out their differences directly rather than through their attorneys. By shortening the time for discovery and presentation of the case, minitrials can reduce the possibility of the two sides becoming locked into opposing positions. The presence of a neutral third party gives the process an added element of discipline. Should the managers come to an impasse in their discussions, the third party can offer suggestions about a settlement. Finally, minitrials remain relatively private. This is important to parties in disputes over confidential information or trade secrets.

An example of a successful minitrial is the 1986 settlement of a dispute between Telecredit and TRW. This minitrial took place in a hotel conference room. After brief presentations by both sides, Telecredit's cofounder conferred with a vice president of TRW. Within half an hour, the two parties had agreed on the outlines of a settlement, which was negotiated over the following eleven weeks. The two companies estimated that the minitrial saved them at least $1 million in combined legal fees.

Because minitrials involve discovery, the production of briefs, oral argument, and the hiring of a third party, they can still be fairly expensive. Only when disputes are expected to involve large damage awards or protracted litigation do minitrials make economic sense.

SUMMARY JURY TRIAL

In a *summary jury trial (SJT),* parties to a dispute put their cases before a real jury, which renders a nonbinding decision. Like nonbinding arbitration, this allows the parties to assess how a decision maker might decide the case in a real trial. The result is often the basis for a negotiated settlement. Like minitrials, summary jury trials offer disputants the opportunity to present their best case in a trial-like setting. Because the SJT makes use of abbreviated procedures, the result is achieved more quickly and with less expense.

A unique feature of SJTs is their focus-group opportunity. Disputants often debrief jurors after the trial to find out how and why they reached their decision. Like discovery, this helps align the parties' information and expectations so there is less reason to go through the expense of a formal trial. For example, a car accident victim suing for $5 million may balk at the insurance company's offer of $50,000 to settle the claim. If the jury in an SJT renders an award of only $75,000, the plaintiff will be more willing to consider settlement. On the other hand, if the jury awards $3 million, the defendant insurance

company will wish to revise its settlement offer. Either way, the parties' expectations will be brought closer together, making settlement more likely.

OTHERS

Because ADR is a dynamic area, these are not the only hybrid forms. *Early Neutral Evaluation (ENE)* was created by the U.S. District Court for the Northern District of California in 1985 to help litigants honestly appreciate their position. In ENE, a neutral attorney familiar with the law in the area reviews the case and offers each side an evaluation of the strengths and weaknesses. Such early feedback by a disinterested expert can assist parties before they become engrossed in the adversarial process.

Ombudspersons are also used to help parties in conflict. Such a person hears complaints, engages in fact-finding, and generally promotes dispute resolution through information methods such as counseling or mediation. An ombudsperson allows aggrieved parties to vent their concerns and alerts *related* parties to problems before they become *opposing* parties.

As international trade grows and the resources of court systems are stretched thinner, scholars and organizations will seek new, more effective forms of ADR. What these will be, no one can say. Regardless, the need to solve disputes more efficiently will remain a strong motivation for managers to demand alternatives to litigation.

Legal Treatment *of* ADR

Although ADR is an alternative to the judicial system, the government is neither ignorant of nor indifferent to the alternatives. Federal ADR legislation has expanded significantly in recent years. One of the most comprehensive statutes, the Civil Justice Reform Act of 1990,[44] requires every federal district court to develop a civil justice expense and delay reduction plan (EDRP). The purpose of such plans is "to facilitate deliberate adjudication of civil cases on the merits, monitor discovery, improve litigation management, and ensure just, speedy, and inexpensive resolution of civil disputes." The act recommends six methods for courts to use in developing EDRPs, one of which is referring appropriate cases "to alternative dispute resolution programs . . . including mediation, minitrial, and summary jury trial." The Alternative Dispute Resolution Act of 1998[45] (ADR Act) re-

44. 28 U.S.C. §§ 471 *et seq. See also* First Options of Chicago, Inc. v. Kaplan, 514 U.S. 938, 942 (1995).
45. 28 U.S.C. § 652 (1998).

IN BRIEF

Models of Alternative Dispute Resolution

	Negotiation	Mediation	Arbitration	Med-Arb	Mini-Trial	Summary Jury Trial
How are the disputants represented?	Disputants represent themselves, or legal counsel negotiates on their behalf	By themselves	By legal counsel	By legal counsel	By legal counsel	By legal counsel
Who makes the final decision?	Disputants mutually decide	Disputants mutually decide	If binding arbitration, arbitrator(s) decides	Arbitrator(s)	Disputants mutually decide	Jury
How are the facts found and standards of judgment set?	Parties decide ad hoc	Parties decide ad hoc	Arbitrator(s) decides based on preset rules, e.g., those of the AAA	Parties and arbitrator(s) decide	Parties decide ad hoc	Rules of court
What is the source for the standard of resolution?	Mutual agreement	Mutual agreement	Arbitrator's sense of fairness	Arbitrator's sense of fairness	Mutual agreement	Jury's sense of fairness
How will the resolution be enforced?	Agreement usually turned into a contract that is enforceable by the courts	Agreement usually turned into a contract that is enforceable by the courts	By courts, according to the agreement to arbitrate the dispute	By courts, according to the agreement to arbitrate the dispute	Agreement usually turned into a contract that is enforceable by the courts	By courts
Who will pay the dispute resolution fees?	Parties decide ad hoc	Parties decide ad hoc	Parties decide before entering arbitration, often in arbitration clause	Parties decide before entering med-arb	Parties decide ad hoc	Parties decide ad hoc

quires parties in federal litigation to consider using ADR. The ADR Act requires federal trial courts to establish at least one ADR program and encourages courts to offer several choices. Federal agencies must also use ADR to resolve administrative cases; the Administrative Dispute Resolution Act of 1996[46] requires federal agencies to look at their mission to see where ADR might be effective. The U.S. Department of Justice has promulgated rules regarding consideration of ADR for many cases,

and, as noted earlier, the Equal Employment Opportunity Commission's mediation program has reduced its backlog of cases.[47]

The government, including the judicial system, promotes alternatives to litigation in a variety of ways. These include requiring pretrial settlement conferences, providing liberal discovery to reduce information asymmetry and align parties' expectations about continued litigation,

46. 5. U.S.C. §§ 571–585 (1998).

47. Eileen Barkas Hoffman, *The Impact of the ADR Act of 1998*, TRIAL, June 1, 1999.

penalizing plaintiffs who reject favorable settlement offers before trial, limiting the ability of a party to introduce willingness to negotiate as evidence of fault, and generally enforcing agreements to arbitrate.

The states also have supported efforts to use ADR rather than courts to resolve disputes. The court systems in more than half of the states now either require or encourage resolving cases through ADR in order to reduce case backlogs and provide a quicker resolution of disputes.

Parties constrained by an arbitration clause may claim that the contract itself (including its arbitration clause) is void due to force, fraud, or the like. Thus, they would argue, neither the contract nor its arbitration clause should be enforced. The U.S. Supreme Court put that issue largely to rest in the following case.

A CASE IN POINT

CASE 4.5

Prima Paint Corp. v. Flood & Conklin Manufacturing Co.
Supreme Court of the United States
388 U.S. 395 (1967).

Summary

FACTS In 1964, Prima Paint purchased Flood & Conklin's paint-selling business. As part of the overall transaction, Prima and Flood agreed that Flood would (1) provide Prima with consulting services for six years, (2) refrain for six years from selling paint and paint products in its existing sales territory and to its current customers, and (3) provide Prima with its customer list. In return for these three agreements, Prima agreed to pay Flood a percentage of its receipts during the six-year period. The agreement contained a broad arbitration clause by which the parties agreed to arbitrate all claims in New York City according to the rules of the American Arbitration Association.

Before the first payment was due, Prima concluded that Flood was insolvent and notified Flood of the discovery. Although late, Prima went ahead and made its first payment, but into escrow, not to Flood. Prima then filed a complaint against Flood in federal district court for rescission of the consulting agreement. Prima argued that it had been fraudulently induced to enter into the consulting contract, and therefore the contract was voidable. Flood responded by serving Prima with a notice to arbitrate in accordance with their contract. Prima moved to stay the arbitration pending the litigation, and Flood moved to stay the litigation pending the arbitration.

The trial court agreed with Flood and stayed the litigation pending the outcome of arbitration. Prima appealed, but the appeals court dismissed the appeal, leaving the litigation stayed pending arbitration. Prima appealed.

ISSUE PRESENTED Is it for the court or an arbitrator to resolve a claim that a party was fraudulently induced to enter into a contract containing an arbitration clause?

SUMMARY OF OPINION The U.S. Supreme Court identified the issue as one of *severability,* that is, whether an arbitration clause could be severed from the remainder of the contract or whether the clause had to stand or fall with the larger contract. If an arbitration clause were not severable, a court would be able to enforce it and require arbitration only if the court first determined in a judicial proceeding that the contract in which it appeared was valid. If the contract was voided, the arbitration clause would fall as well.

If the doctrine of severability applied, however, a court would uphold an agreement to arbitrate unless the agreement to arbitrate itself was challenged. For instance, Alpha might argue that Beta fraudulently included the arbitration clause in an otherwise valid contract by slipping it into the final draft. In that case, a court would have to consider the validity of the agreement to arbitrate. But if Alpha argued that Beta fraudulently induced it to enter into the contract as a whole, the court would sever the arbitration clause, find the agreement to arbitrate controlling on the parties, and leave the issue of the contract's validity to arbitration.

(Continued)

(Case 4.5 continued)

Looking to the exact language of the Federal Arbitration Act and the underlying congressional intent to facilitate the arbitration process, the Court adopted the doctrine of severability. Consequently, once a court is satisfied that the validity of the agreement to arbitrate is not specifically challenged, the judge must order arbitration in accordance with the clause. Unless the arbitration clause itself is challenged by a party, questions of contract validity and interpretation are properly the subject of arbitration.

Because Prima did not claim that it had intended to exclude legal issues from arbitration or that it was fraudulently induced to agree to arbitrate claims, the lower court was correct to stay Prima's lawsuit pending the outcome of arbitration.

RESULT The Supreme Court upheld the dismissal of Prima's appeal. Prima's lawsuit was stayed pending the arbitration initiated by Flood.

COMMENTS As shown in *Prima Paint,* arbitration clauses can significantly alter a company's judicial rights. Managers entering into a contract with an arbitration clause should understand that "any claims arising from this contract" may well include all claims related to the contract, including the validity of the contract itself.

TORTIOUS DISPUTE RESOLUTION

Although the law supports settlements through ADR, managers are not immune from the law simply because they pursue alternative mechanisms to resolve their disputes. The applicability of tort law is a good example.

The law of torts, which is discussed in Chapter 9, deals with civil wrongs causing injury to a person or his or her property. A claim of fraudulent misrepresentation requires proof that the defendant intentionally misled the plaintiff by making a material misrepresentation of fact upon which the plaintiff relied to his or her detriment. It is not difficult to imagine a negotiation in which one might be tempted to so mislead an opponent. Still, the law of fraud will apply, and a manager may be liable for the injury he or she causes. An overly aggressive manager attempting to "resolve" a dispute by force or threats may also be found liable for assault, intentional infliction of emotional distress, defamation, invasion of privacy, disparagement, injurious falsehood, interference with contractual obligations, or interference with prospective business advantage. Attempting to settle conflicts outside court does not exempt managers from the law.

THE RESPONSIBLE MANAGER
Staying Out *of* Court

Legal problems or disputes often arise in business, and an amicable solution to them is not always possible. Some form of dispute resolution then becomes the next step.

The courts exist to assist litigants in working out a fair solution to their dispute. But litigation is expensive, time-consuming, and disruptive to everyone involved. Consequently, all parties benefit when the courts are used as the last step in the legal process, rather than as the starting point.

Often communication, or the lack thereof, can make the difference between a minor disagreement and protracted litigation. Apologizing may be just as crucial as filing or defending a lawsuit.

A manager should decide when litigation, as opposed to a settlement or other method of resolving the dispute, is the company's best strategic move. If the problem is a recurring one, or if the opposing party is clearly making a frivolous claim or attempting to use the lawsuit as a way to extort money from the company, then the courtroom becomes the most practical alternative. Similarly, if the adverse publicity that attends a trial would be more damaging to one party than another, the party better positioned to endure the publicity may prefer to retain the right to threaten to take the dispute to court. In many cases, however, negotiation, mediation, a minitrial, or arbitration will enable the parties to conclude their dispute more quickly and with less expense and hardship.

The first step in implementing an ADR program is generating enthusiasm within the company for the program.[48] The general counsel or other appropriate person should explain to company officers and executives the benefits of an ADR program, including the savings of time and money, the decrease in disruption to employees and management, and the fact that solutions generally are more business oriented in nature. High-level management should demonstrate its commitment to an ADR program and explain the benefits to other executives who may be unfamiliar with such a program. The company needs to involve (1) in-house counsel; (2) the executives and corporate managers; (3) outside counsel; (4) the company's adversaries; and (5) certain field personnel, such as insurance industry claims personnel. Training of these various players is also essential. The company also needs to make clear that early and personal involvement by management in disputes resolved through the ADR program is crucial. Frequently, involvement by both executives and the disputants at early stages of the conflict is critical to an effective resolution of the matter.

Once a company establishes a formal program, the next step is for the general counsel and company manager to ensure that the ADR procedures are employed. Some companies negotiate ADR clauses into all of their standard business agreements or contracts. Other companies leave it to their attorneys to decide which disputes are better resolved by ADR than by litigation.

After deciding that a particular ADR method will be the best way to achieve its goal, the company must persuade the opposing party to participate in the procedure. Certain forms of ADR, such as mediation, are usually accepted readily—the proceeding is informal and can be terminated at any time, and a mediator can also protect the confidentiality of sensitive data, which might be made public during litigation.

Once a company has developed an ADR program, continuous feedback from all participants is required in order to monitor, refine, and improve the program. Constructive criticism is vital. Frequently, corporate managers or executives are in a position to discover a weakness in a particular ADR procedure that could harm the company. The company may wish to designate one employee as the ADR "point person" who monitors the program to ensure that flaws are corrected and strengths are further refined.

Establishing an ADR program has cost–benefit advantages. Valuable management time is saved by avoiding litigation. Equally important, ADR procedures help the company pursue a relationship with the opposing party and allow flexibility in resolving legal disputes.

---

48. This discussion is based on CENTER FOR PUBLIC RESOURCES, MAINSTREAMING: CORPORATE STRATEGIES FOR SYSTEMATIC ADR USE (1989).

INSIDE STORY

Uniform Domain Name Dispute Resolution Policy

On October 29, 1999, the Internet Corporation for Assigned Names and Numbers (ICANN) approved a Uniform Domain Name Dispute Resolution Policy (UDRP) and Rules for the Uniform Domain Name Dispute Resolution Policy.[49] ICANN is a quasi-governmental Internet-regulating body. Its new policy provides for an administrative proceeding for resolving disputes between domain name owners and trademark owners. The UDRP applies to every domain name registrant that registers its domain names through an ICANN-accredited registrar.

The new procedure is unusual because the filings, communications, and much of the panelists' deliberations take place online and there are no in-person hearings. The decisions are published on a readily accessible Web site and are available to the public on the Internet. The policy is incorporated by reference into every registration agreement and is directed toward allegations of bad faith registration and use of domain names.

The administrative panel must decide the dispute "in accordance with the Policy, [the] Rules and any rules and principles of law that it deems appropriate." The panel is free to select those principles of law it deems appropriate to resolve the case. The only relief available in an administrative proceeding is cancellation of the domain name registration or the transfer of that registration to the complainant. Although this relief is limited, the administrative proceeding does provide an opportunity for quick resolution of disputes.

---

49. M. Scott Donahey, *Mandatory Resolution of Domain Name Disputes*, J. INTERNET L., Jan. 2000, at 1.

ICANN has approved a list of dispute resolution providers that can resolve disputes under the UDRP. As of 2000, there were only three approved arbitration providers in the world. The only provider based in the United States is the National Arbitration Forum headquartered in Minneapolis.[50] The National Arbitration Forum was approved as a UDRP provider in December 1999 and since then has been servicing an increasingly global audience. A 2000 survey of attorneys who have filed complaints with the National Arbitration Forum under ICANN's policy indicated strong support for the program. The Arbitration and Mediation Center of the World Intellectual Property Organization (WIPO) also started handling these suits in January 2000. By May 2000, 361 cases had been filed from forty-six countries.

In January 2000, WIPO issued its first decision under the UDRP.[51] The dispute concerned The World Wrestling Foundation's (WWF) allegation of cybersquatting by a California resident Michael Bosman. Bosman had registered the domain name "www.worldwrestlingfederation.com" with an Australian domain name registrar accredited with ICANN. Three days later, he notified the WWF that his intention in registering the name was to sell it to the WWF for $1,000. The WWF alleged that Bosman had no rights or legitimate interest with respect to the domain name, which was identical to the WWF's service mark and trademark. The intellectual property lawyer appointed by WIPO to arbitrate the case found that Bosman had registered the domain name in bad faith and used it in bad faith by attempting to sell it to the WWF.

The UDRP does not prevent parties from initiating a case in court, and the language of the policy suggests that the administrative panel's decisions are not binding on federal courts. In *Weber-Stephen Products Co. v. Armitage Hardware and Building Supply, Inc.*,[52] the legal effect of a WIPO proceeding was considered for the first time in a federal court. Armitage filed a motion to declare the administrative proceeding nonbinding and to stay the court case in favor of the administrative proceeding, or alternatively—should the court find the WIPO proceeding to be binding—to stay it while the court considered whether Armitage's participation in that proceeding could be compelled. The court found that it was not bound by the outcome of the ICANN proceeding but declined to determine the standard by which it would review the panel's decision and what degree of deference it would give that decision. The court stayed the action in federal court pending the outcome of the ICANN proceedings.

50. *Test of Anti Cybersquatting Measures Reveals Preference for Arbitration at National Arbitration Forum,* PR NEWSWIRE, May 3, 2000.
51. Daniel Pruzin, *In First Cybersquatting Dispute Decision, WIPO Orders Registrant to Hand Over Name,* 68 U.S.L.W. 2430 (Jan. 25, 2000).

52. 54 U.S.P.Q.2d 1766 (N.D. Ill. May 3, 2000).

KEY WORDS AND PHRASES

arbitration 125
arbitration clause 128
arbitrator 125
Best Alternative to a Negotiated
 Agreement (BATNA) 120
dispute negotiation 119
distributive negotiations 119
Early Neutral Evaluation (ENE) 136
Federal Arbitration Act (FAA) 129
final-offer arbitration 126

hearing 127
integrative negotiations 119
mandatory arbitration 130
med-arb 135
mediation 123
mediator 123
minitrial 135
negotiation 119
nonbinding arbitration 126
ombudsperson 136

posthearing 127
prehearing 127
reservation price 120
severability 138
summary jury trial (SJT) 136
transactional negotiation 119
variable-sum negotiations 119
zero-sum negotiations 119

QUESTIONS AND CASE PROBLEMS

1. As a manager, how would you design and implement a policy to limit litigation costs by taking advantage of ADR mechanisms? Be specific in your answer. How well do your design and implementation account for strategic, structural, and psychological barriers?

2. The Securities Act of 1933 was passed to require truthful disclosure in the sale of securities in order

to promote efficient capital markets. The Age Discrimination in Employment Act was passed to protect the elderly from a culture biased toward youth and to make our culture more accepting of senior citizens. If those policies were important enough to codify into federal law, should they be left to private arbitration where only the interests of the individual parties, and not the public interest, will be represented? Does the public interest have a legitimate role in what are otherwise strictly private arbitrations? Should it have a role? If it does have a legitimate role, what procedures could be designed to ensure that that role is not neglected?

3. Rich and Enza Hill picked up the phone, ordered a computer from Gateway 2000, and gave their credit card number. Thereafter, a box arrived containing the computer and a list of terms, said to govern unless the customer returns the computer within thirty days. One of the terms was an arbitration clause requiring the arbitration of all claims against Gateway 2000 arising from the purchase of the computer. The Hills kept their computer for more than thirty days, after which they complained about its components and performance. Gateway refused to refund their money. Outraged, the Hills filed a class-action suit in federal court under the Racketeer Influenced and Corrupt Organizations Act (RICO). The Hills reasoned that Gateway had used the mail and telephone to sell the shoddy merchandise and hence committed mail and wire fraud. Can the Hills be forced to arbitrate this dispute? [*Hill v. Gateway 2000, Inc.*, 105 F.3d 1147 (7th Cir. 1997), *cert. denied*, 522 U.S. 808 (1997)]

4. In 1975, Melton Nelson began working for the Cyprus Bagdad Copper Corporation, a mining company with operations in Bagdad, Arizona. In 1993, Cyprus issued an employee handbook to all its employees that included a description of the company's mandatory grievance procedures, which culminated in binding arbitration. Nelson was required to sign an acknowledgment that stated:

> I have received a copy of the Cyprus Bagdad Copper Corporation Handbook that is effective July 1, 1993 and understand that the Handbook is a guideline to the Company's policies and procedures. I agree to read it and understand its contents. If I have any questions regarding its contents I will contact my supervisor or Human Resources Representative.

The next year, due to a corporate restructuring, Nelson's department was reorganized, and he was required to work rotating twelve-hour shifts. Concerned that his health could not tolerate rotating shifts, Nelson so notified his supervisor. After the supervisor made some initial efforts to accommodate Nelson's medical situation, Cyprus fired Nelson. Upon the advice of counsel, Nelson chose not to arbitrate his termination according to the procedures outlined in the employee handbook. Instead, he sued Cyprus for violations of the Americans with Disabilities Act and the Arizona Civil Rights Act. In response, the company argued that Nelson was bound to arbitrate his claims against the company pursuant to the terms outlined in the employee handbook. Should the court force him to arbitrate the claim? Explain. [*Nelson v. Cyprus Bagdad Copper Corp.*, 119 F.3d 756 (9th Cir. 1997), *cert. denied*, 523 U.S. 1072 (1998)]

5. Two commercial fishermen, Gill and Brook, live on the edge of a lake teeming with 10,000 pounds of fish. Each depends on the fish catch for his livelihood and has equipment to harvest immediately the lake's entire 10,000 pounds of fish, worth $10 per pound. For the population to sustain itself and offer both fishermen a lifetime of catch, no more than 4,000 pounds can be harvested in any one year. If less than 6,000 pounds are left behind to reproduce, the lake will be empty forever. But if at least 6,000 pounds are left to reproduce, a perpetual supply of 4,000 pounds, worth $40,000 now, will remain available.

If alone on the lake, Gill or Brook would happily harvest only 4,000 pounds per year and ensure a continual supply of fish. In competition with each other, however, both Gill and Brook are deeply suspicious of each other. Gill fears that Brook will harvest any fish Gill leaves behind, and Brook fears Gill will do the same if Brook limits his catch.

Without any additional information, what are the incentives for Gill and Brook to fish at various rates? What could Gill and Brook do to ensure the optimal outcome? What barriers would they face in such an attempt?

6. In January 1998, the Federal National Mortgage Association (Fannie Mae) announced that it would issue a new arbitration policy on March 16, 1998. On March 12, 1998, Emmanuel Bailey, a Fannie Mae employee, filed a memorandum with Fannie Mae's Office of Corporate Justice requesting an investigation of various allegations of race and gender discrimination. Bailey's memorandum expressly stated that he retained all redress options available with the Equal Employment Opportunity Commission (EEOC) and the federal and state court sys-

tems. On March 16, 1998, Fannie Mae issued a Dispute Resolution Policy, which required employees to pursue job-related claims internally, through arbitration, before such claims could be presented to a court of law. The Dispute Resolution Policy stated that, as of March 16, 1998:

> [T]he Policy becomes a condition of employment for all Fannie Mae employees. This means that, by starting or continuing work for Fannie Mae on or after that date, each employee is indicating that he or she accepts the Policy as a condition of employment and agrees to be bound by it.

Bailey never said anything to any official at Fannie Mae to indicate that he acceded to the Dispute Resolution Policy, and he never signed any agreement to that effect. Bailey also never did or said anything to withdraw the position stated in his March 12 complaint, in which he reserved the right to pursue statutory claims with the EEOC and in federal or state court. Can Fannie Mae require Bailey to arbitrate his claims of race and gender bias? [*Bailey v. Federal National Mortgage Assoc.*, 209 F.3d 740 (D.C. Cir. 2000). *Compare Howard v. Oakwood Homes Corp.*, 516 S.E.2d 879 (N.C. App. 1999), *cert. denied*, 120 S. Ct. 1161 (2000).]

7. Dana Bazley signed an agreement with Powertel, Inc. to purchase a cellular telephone service plan. Several months after signing the agreement, Powertel included in an envelope with Bazley's bill a pamphlet describing the terms and conditions of Powertel's service. The pamphlet restated many of the same terms and conditions outlined in the pamphlet accompanying the original service contract but included a new provision stating that all disputes would be resolved through arbitration. Nothing on the pamphlet indicated that it was a revision of the original contract except the date printed in small print below the title "Terms and Conditions of Service." The arbitration clause limited Powertel's liability to actual damages and precluded recovery of punitive damages against the company. The clause also stated that customers could neither pursue a class action against Powertel nor file claims under several statutory remedies. Dana Bazley filed a claim alleging that Powertel had wrongfully billed her and alleged as part of her claim that the arbitration clause was unconscionable. Florida courts may decline to enforce a contract on the ground that it is unconscionable if the court finds that the contract is both procedurally and substantively unconscionable. How should the court rule? What if Pow-

ertel had included the arbitration clause in the original agreement so that Bazley could have read it at the time that she purchased the service? What if the revised agreement did not limit Bazley's rights with respect to recovery of damages, class action relief, or types of claims? [*Powertel, Inc. v. Bexley*, 743 So. 2d 570 (Fl.1999)]

8. Weavers Galore, Inc., a Virginia textile manufacturer, instituted a just-in-time (JIT) inventory system to tighten its operations, reduce its working capital, and increase its lackluster profits. In such a system, the timing of supply deliveries is critical because inventories are not kept on hand but are delivered immediately prior to the time they are needed. In anticipation of the new JIT system, Weavers negotiated a supply contract with a cotton farming syndicate headquartered in Birmingham, Alabama.

In the contract, the syndicate agreed to supply Weavers with ten tons of top quality cotton on the Tuesday morning of each week for the next eighteen months. In return, Weavers agreed to pay $.65 per pound, one month in advance of each shipment. For instance, on March 15, Weavers would pay $1,300 for ten tons of cotton to be delivered by the syndicate on the morning of Tuesday, April 15. Strict adherence to the delivery schedule was of paramount importance to Weavers, the first textile manufacturer in the region and the only customer of the syndicate to implement JIT.

On October 15, six months into the agreement, the syndicate announced that it would be unable to deliver the next few shipments to Weavers on time and complete. Poor harvests and equipment failures had disrupted the syndicate's operations, and its contracts with other customers were already straining its operations. Many of them would also have to receive late and/or incomplete shipments. For the time being, the syndicate announced, Weavers would have to make do with a single ton of cotton delivered on Wednesday evenings, at best.

Christina Snow, Weavers' CEO, was livid. Without the next few shipments of cotton on time, she might well lose customers, market share, and profits. Snow's first instinct was to have Weavers' general counsel fire off a terse letter to the syndicate reminding it of its contractual obligations and Weavers' willingness to enforce its rights in court. After that, she might file a lawsuit.

Should Snow turn this matter over to Weavers' general counsel? What else could Snow do to protect and further the interests of Weavers? What are the pros and cons of these courses of actions?

9. During her second year of business school at the University of Wisconsin, Ursula learned that Freedom Consulting wanted to hire an MBA with her experience, skills, and interests to come on board as a consultant in its Boston office. After discussing Freedom with some of her classmates, Ursula discovered that the firm offered few benefits: two weeks of vacation and basic health maintenance coverage by Kaiser Permanente. To her delight, she also learned that Freedom has an office in warm and sunny San Diego, although the firm was not recruiting for that office.

   After interviewing with Freedom and feeling good about the position and the company overall, Ursula asked about compensation. Because she had a similar offer from Decisions Forever with a salary of $95,000, Ursula would not accept less than $95,000 in salary. Freedom had another candidate nearly as qualified as Ursula who was willing to work for $90,000. Freedom saw no reason to increase its offer to Ursula.

   During their discussions, Freedom explained that it was considering switching medical insurance providers to a preferred provider plan with Blue Cross and had an immediate and pressing need for MBAs to join its Chicago office. After an unusually open and honest discussion, both parties learned the value the other placed on the following issues.

Issue	Ursula's Value		Freedom's Value	
Official title	Analyst	−$1,000	Analyst	$0
	Consultant	0	Consultant	0
	Manager	2,600	Manager	−500
Number of	10	2,000	10	0
vacation days	20	4,000	20	−2,500
Medical	Blue Cross	500	Blue Cross	−3,000
insurance	Kaiser	0	Kaiser	0
provider				
Geographic	Boston	0	Boston	0
location	Chicago	−300	Chicago	2,500
	San Diego	1,000	San Diego	−5,000
Matching	Yes	2,000	Yes	−1,600
401(k)	No	0	No	0
retirement				
plan				
Start date	Immediately	−1,000	Immediately	5,000
	In 3 months	1,000	In 3 months	−1,000
Signing	Yes	5,000	Yes	−5,000
bonus of	No	0	No	0
$5,000				

Why might Ursula and Freedom place differing values on these issues? How easy would it really be for Ursula to learn fully about Freedom's values and vice versa?

Given the information above, what should a manager of Freedom who wants to hire Ursula now offer her? What should Ursula be willing to accept? How much value has been created by integration? How much value remains to be distributed?

MANAGER'S DILEMMA

10. Latisha White is director of research and development at a large pharmaceutical company, which has recently been sued by a class of persons who allege that one of the drugs the company sells causes heart problems. The suit alleges that the company was aware of these problems but didn't disclose this information to the Food and Drug Administration or the public. The parties have agreed to resolve the dispute through mediation.

   Latisha has the most knowledge about the science behind the drugs and, as a result, can provide key testimony about the issues of the case. She has been with the company since its beginning and is friends with many of the individuals on the company's board of directors. During preliminary meetings to attempt to settle the dispute, however, she has been extremely inflexible, claiming that her research was impeccable and that there is no basis for the plaintiff's claims. She regards this research as the most important of her career and has received recognition within academic circles for this work. Due in large part to her presence at the negotiations, the parties are having difficulty moving closer to settlement. As the president of the company, you must decide who will be on the team involved with reaching a settlement in this case. Other senior scientists have knowledge of the research but are junior to Latisha and have more superficial knowledge of the scientific facts at issue. Should you include Latisha on the team? If she is included, how can you minimize her negative impact on the process?

INTERNET SOURCES

The American Arbitration Association's home page offers avenues into its many services.	http://www.adr.org
The Dispute Resolution Section of the American Bar Association offers information about the law of ADR.	http://www.abanet.org/dispute/home.html
The Mediation Information Research Center offers articles and other information about mediation as well as resources concerning professional mediators.	http://www.mediate.com
JAMS/Endispute's page offers information about its many dispute resolution services.	http://www.jams-endispute.com
The Securities Law home page offers information about arbitration of disputes involving securities and securities dealers and brokers.	http://www.seclaw.com/centers/arbcent.html
The U.S. House of Representatives Internet Law Library has a large collection of ADR-related statutes, court decisions, and articles.	http://law.house.gov/314.html
The CPR Institute for Dispute Resolution Web site has information about its roster of 700 attorneys, former judges, executives, and academics who can mediate disputes and provides a standard mediation clause for parties to incorporate into their contracts.	http://www.cpradr.org
The Organization for Economic Cooperation and Development's Web site has Guidelines on Consumer Protection in the Context of Electronic Commerce and information regarding a forum on electronic commerce.	http://www.oecd.org/dsti/sti/it/consumer/prod/guidelines.htm
The World Intellectual Property Organization Electronic Commerce and Intellectual Property site provides information regarding WIPO's activities concerning intellectual property and electronic commerce, including the WIPO Arbitration and Mediation Center for the resolution of domain name disputes.	http://ecommerce.wipo.int/index-eng.html
Icourthouse	http://www.icourthouse.com
SquareTrade	http://www.squaretrade.com
Cybersettle	http://www.cybersettle.com
ClickNSettle	http://www.clicknsettle.com
International Alternative Dispute Resolutions Web site	http://www.internationaladr.com

CHAPTER 5

Agency

AGENCY AND THE CONDUCT OF BUSINESS

In an *agency* relationship, one person—the *agent*—acts for or represents another person—the *principal*. The principal delegates a portion of his or her power to the agent. The agent then manages the assigned task and exercises the discretion given by the principal. The agency relationship can be created by an express or implied agreement or by law.

Agency is perhaps the most pervasive legal relationship in the business world. Businesses of all kinds require the assistance of agents in order to conduct multiple operations in various locations. Indeed, without the law of agency, corporations could not function at all. Only through its human agents can the legal fiction of a corporation enter into any kind of binding agreement.

CHAPTER OVERVIEW

This chapter defines and discusses the central principles of agency law. First, it describes the different methods by which an agency relationship can be formed. The chapter identifies the different types of agency relationships (employer–employee and principal–independent contractor) and the consequences that flow from each. It examines the duties an agent owes to the principal and an agent's authority to enter into agreements that are binding upon the principal. Finally, the chapter discusses the extent to which a principal may be liable for the tortious or illegal conduct of an agent.

 # Formation *of an* Agency Relationship

The agency relationship is consensual in nature and is typically created by agreement of the parties. This agreement can be either written or oral. However, if the agent enters into an agreement of a type that must be in writing to be enforceable (such as an agreement for the sale of real property), then the agent's signature on the agreement will not be binding on the principal unless the agency relationship itself is evidenced by some signed writing.

An agency agreement can also be implied from conduct. For example, suppose computer maker C regularly ships inventory to distributor D with the understanding that D will sell the computers to retailers and end users,

and D regularly remits the sale proceeds to C. An agency relationship exists between C and D, even if they have not entered into a formal agreement.

Agency relationships can also be formed without agreement—by ratification or by estoppel. If a principal approves or accepts the benefits of the actions of an otherwise unauthorized agent, he or she has formed an *agency by ratification*. An *agency by estoppel* occurs when a person leads another to believe that someone else is his or her agent and is thereafter estopped (prevented) from denying it. For example, suppose Jack causes Kendra to believe that Lori is his agent, and Kendra, relying on this misrepresentation, proceeds to deal with Lori. Even if Lori is not in fact Jack's agent, Kendra's reliance creates an agency by estoppel. As a result, Lori's dealings with Kendra will be binding upon Jack.

Types *of* Agency Relationships

An agent may be either an employee of the principal or an independent contractor.

EMPLOYEE

The most common form of agency relationship is the employer–employee relationship, sometimes still referred to as the master–servant relationship. The basic characteristic of this relationship is that the employer has the right to control the conduct of the employee. The employee may have the authority to bind the employer to a contract under theories of actual or apparent authority.

INDEPENDENT CONTRACTOR

An *independent contractor,* such as a lawyer working for a client or a plumber working for a house builder, is not an employee of the person paying for the services because the independent contractor's conduct is not fully subject to that person's control. The person hiring an independent contractor bargains only for results.

An independent contractor may or may not be an agent. Generally, an agency relationship exists when the hiring person gives the independent contractor authority to enter into contracts on his or her behalf. For example, suppose a builder contracts to build a house for Ken for $200,000. Ken has no control over the builder's manner of doing the work because the house is one of a large group of houses that the builder is constructing in a housing subdivision. The builder is not Ken's agent. On the other hand, suppose Ken expressly authorizes the builder to buy redwood siding from a lumber company on his behalf. Here, the independent contractor is Ken's agent for purposes of buying the siding.

Distinguishing *between* Employees *and* Independent Contractors

Determining whether a worker is an employee or an independent contractor is a legal issue with several important consequences, including the liability of the principal for the worker's torts, as well as the principal's duty to deduct and pay certain taxes on behalf of the worker and to permit the worker to participate in employee benefit plans.

Employers are liable for the torts of their employees, as long as the employee was acting within the scope of employment. In contrast, persons hiring independent contractors are generally not liable for torts they commit.

Employers are required to deduct or pay income, Social Security, and unemployment taxes for employees but not for independent contractors, who are responsible for paying their own self-employment taxes. Moreover, independent contractors are generally not eligible for the same fringe benefits provided to employees, such as medical insurance, stock options, and 401(k) retirement plans. This was a crucial factor in the *Microsoft* case discussed in the "Inside Story" in this chapter. Because an employer does not pay employment taxes and may not provide fringe benefits for independent contractors, hiring an independent contractor may be less costly than hiring an employee to do the same work.

Although the distinction between employees and independent contractors is an important one, there is no bright-line test to distinguish one from the other. Significantly, the label used in an employment contract does not determine the employment status of a worker. The outcome turns on what one does, not on what one says. The law looks at a variety of factors, including the following:

1. How much control can the employer exercise over the details of the work?
2. Is the employed person engaged in an occupation distinct from that of the employer?
3. Is the kind of work being done usually performed under the direction of an employer or by a specialist without supervision?
4. What degree of skill does the work require?
5. Does the employer provide the worker with tools and a place of work?
6. For how long is the worker employed?
7. Is the worker paid on the basis of time or by the job?
8. Does the worker offer his or her services to the public at large?

Employee status is more likely to be found for workers who are lower paid and less skilled, lack bargaining power, and have a high degree of economic dependence on their employers.

Fiduciary Duty

In agreeing to act on behalf of the principal, the agent becomes a *fiduciary.* Loyalty and obedience are the hallmarks of the fiduciary relationship. An agent has a duty to act solely for the benefit of his or her principal in all matters directly connected with the agency undertaking. This is the *duty of loyalty.* For example, if Adrienne is entrusted with the power to buy a piece of land for Pierre, she cannot buy the best piece of land for herself instead.

An agent also has a duty to act with due care. This *duty of care* includes a duty to avoid mistakes, whether through negligence, recklessness, or intentional misconduct. Some states require an agent to exercise the same level of care a person would exercise in the conduct of his or her own affairs. Others use a comparative approach:

an agent is to exercise the same level of care a reasonable person in a like situation would exercise. Application of these duties to officers, directors, and controlling shareholders is discussed in Chapter 23.

The following case examines the contours of the duty of loyalty. Specifically, it considers the propriety of a vice president establishing a business in direct competition with that of his employer.

A CASE IN POINT

CASE 5.1

Scranton Gillette Communications, Inc. v. Dannhausen

United States District Court for the Northern District of Illinois

1999 WL 558134 (N.D. Ill. July 27, 1999).

Summary

FACTS Eugene H. McCormick was vice president of Scranton Gillette Communications and publisher of *Greenhouse Product News*. While still the publisher of *Greenhouse Product News* and advocating for its redesign, McCormick was making plans to resign and launch his own rival greenhouse publication. Not only did he not disclose this information to his employer, but he also tried to persuade several other employees to come work with him on his new venture. One of these employees was Laurie Dlugos, who worked in sales. Scranton sued McCormick and Dlugos for breach of fiduciary duty.

ISSUE PRESENTED Is an employee liable for breach of fiduciary duty if he works on a competing business venture without disclosing it to his current employer?

SUMMARY OF OPINION The U.S. district court began by noting that an agent owes the duty of fidelity and loyalty to his employer. As a result, an employee must refrain from competing with his employer. However, an employee has a right to enter into competition upon leaving his employment; an employee may even legitimately go so far as to form a rival corporation and outfit it for business while still employed by the prospective competitor. An employee is held accountable for breaching his fiduciary duty to his employer only when he goes beyond such preliminary competitive activities and commences business as a rival concern while still employed by another.

For years, McCormick held a position of confidence and trust. Thus, he had a duty (1) to treat the employer with the utmost candor, care, loyalty, and good faith; (2) to deal honestly and fairly with the employer; and (3) to disclose any conflict of interest. While he pushed for the redesign of *Greenhouse Product News,* McCormick knew that he intended to resign and launch his rival greenhouse publication, but he chose not to disclose his plans. Instead, he elected to hide his conflict of interest for months until it was too late. At the same time, while he continued to publish *Greenhouse Product News* and supervise its redesign, McCormick hired and assisted a graphic designer on the design of his future publication.

The court held that McCormick should have disclosed his conflict of interest; his failure to do so resulted in a breach of his fiduciary duty. McCormick's efforts to hire three of Scranton's employees to work for his rival greenhouse publication while he was still working for Scranton provided additional evidence of breach of his fiduciary duty. The court did note, however, that McCormick's mere planning and preparation related to the launch of his magazine did not constitute a breach of fiduciary duty.

The court held that Dlugos had also breached her fiduciary duty. Before resigning, she removed or destroyed her office files, including a database used by the company's sales associates to monitor and maintain their contacts, in an effort to hamper Scranton's ability to maintain her clients after she left the company.

RESULT McCormick and Dlugos both violated their duty of loyalty.

(Continued)

(Case 5.1 continued)

QUESTIONS

1. How could McCormick have acted differently so that he could have made plans to start a new magazine without breaching his fiduciary duty to his employer?
2. Is it realistic to think that an employee can disclose to his employer his plans to start a new business without running the risk of being fired?

Sometimes it is not clear whether a person acting on behalf of another has a fiduciary duty to the other person. This was the issue in the following case dealing with a person hired to find a buyer for a company.

A CASE IN POINT

CASE 5.2

Northeast General Corp. v. Wellington Advertising, Inc.
Court of Appeals of New York
624 N.E.2d 129 (N.Y. 1993).

In the Language of the Court

FACTS In 1988, Northeast General Corporation, through its agents Dunton and Margolis, entered into an agreement with Wellington Advertising, Inc. relating to the sale of Wellington Advertising. Northeast was to act "as a non-exclusive independent investment banker and business consultant for the purposes of finding and presenting candidates for purchase, sale, merger or other business combination." The agreement further provided that Northeast General would be entitled to a finder's fee, based on the size of the transaction, if a transaction was completed within three years of Wellington's introduction to the "found" buying party.

Margolis, one of Northeast General Corporation's agents, consulted with Northeast's new president, Dunton, then introduced Sternau to Wellington's president, Arpadi, as a potential purchaser of Wellington. Ultimately, Sternau and Wellington entered into a purchase agreement.

Before introducing Sternau to Wellington, Dunton was informed by an unidentified investment banker that Sternau had a reputation for buying companies, removing assets, rendering the companies borderline insolvent, and leaving minority investors unprotected. Dunton did not disclose this information to Wellington prior to the closing of the Wellington-Sternau deal.

After Northeast's introduction of Sternau to Wellington, but prior to the signing of the acquisition agreement, Dunton called Arpadi and offered further help with the transaction. Arpadi declined that help and discouraged Dunton from any further involvement. After the merger agreement was signed, companies controlled by Sternau purchased the controlling stock of Wellington, leaving Wellington's principals, including Arpadi, as minority investors. Ultimately, Wellington was rendered insolvent, and Arpadi and other minority investors suffered financial losses. Wellington delivered a check to Northeast for its finder services but stopped payment before the check could be negotiated.

Northeast sued Wellington to recover its finder's fee. After a trial, the jury found in favor of Northeast and awarded it the agreed-on finder's fee. The trial court judge set aside the jury's verdict. The judge's decision, which rested on arguments of public policy, imposed a fiduciary-like duty on finders to disclose adverse information to their clients. The appellate division court upheld the trial court judge's action. Northeast appealed.

ISSUE PRESENTED Does a finder–seller agreement create a relationship of trust with a "fiduciary-like" obligation on the finder to share information with the seller regarding the potential buyer's bad reputation?

(Continued)

(Case 5.2 continued)

OPINION BELLACOSA, J., writing for the New York Court of Appeals:

Before courts can infer and superimpose a duty of the finest loyalty, the contract and relationship of the parties must be plumbed. We recognize that "[m]any forms of conduct, permissible in a workaday world for those acting at arm's length, are forbidden to those bound by fiduciary ties" (*Meinhard v. Salmon*, 249 N.Y. 458, 464). Chief Judge Cardozo's oft-quoted maxim is a timeless reminder that "[a] trustee is held to something stricter than the morals of the market place. Not honesty alone, but the punctilio of an honor the most sensitive" (*id.*). If the parties find themselves or place themselves in the milieu of the "workaday" mundane market place, and if they do not create their own relationship of higher trust, courts should not ordinarily transport them to the higher realm of relationship and fashion the stricter duty for them.

The Northeast-Wellington agreement contains no cognizable fiduciary terms or relationship. The dissent ascribes inordinate weight to the titles non-exclusive "independent investment banker and business consultant." These terms in the context of this agreement are not controlling, since Dunton did not perform the services of an investment banker or consultant. Instead, Dunton's sole function was "for purposes of finding and presenting candidates." That drives the analysis of this case because he was a traditional finder functioning under a finder's agreement, and his role ceased when he found and presented someone. The finder was not described or given the function of an agent, partner or co-venturer.

. . . Probing our precedents and equitable principles unearths no supportable justification for such a judicial interposition, however highly motivated and idealistic. Indeed, responding to this fine instinct would inappropriately propel the courts into reformation of service agreements between commercially knowledgeable parties in this and perhaps countless other situations and transactions as well.

This Court may sense a sympathetic impulse to balance what it may view as the equities of a situation such as this. The hard judicial obligation, however, is to be intellectually disciplined against that tug. Instead, courts must focus on the precise law function reposed in them in such circumstances, which is to construe and enforce the meaning and thrust of the contract of the parties, not to purify their efforts.

. . . The character of the Northeast-Wellington agreement was not one of trust importing duties beyond finding a prospect. The fact that Wellington did not employ its own independent, traditional methods to check out the reputation of the prospect and accepted what turned out to be a bad prospect does not warrant this Court rescuing it from its soured deal by any post-agreement fiduciary lifeline.

. . .

The commonplace mores of the market place suffice and are appropriate to govern relationships established by a contract of the type involved here, which contemplates and asks nothing more of the parties than performance of a simple service. In sum, defendants' financial losses from their market mishap with Sternau is not reason enough to propel a sweeping new fiduciary-like doctrine into finders' agreements.

DISSENT HANCOCK, J., dissenting from the majority opinion:

A fiduciary relationship is one founded on trust or confidence reposed by one person in the integrity and fidelity of another. The term is a very broad one. It is said that the relation exists, and that relief is granted, in all cases in which influence has been acquired and abused, in which confidence has been reposed and betrayed. The origin of the confidence and the source of the influence are immaterial. The rule embraces both technical fiduciary relations and those informal relations which exist

(Continued)

(Case 5.2 continued)

whenever one man trusts in and relies upon another. Out of such a relation, the law raises the rules that neither party may exert influence or pressure upon the other.

...

The narrow question applying the above rules is whether Arpadi's and Dunton's relationship exhibits sufficient trust and de facto control upon which to ground Dunton's duty to disclose negative information regarding the very deal he was promoting. The record reveals more than enough evidence to demonstrate both elements. By imparting confidential business details as well as his personal plans and intentions [which included Arpadi's statement that he was "terrified" he "would lose everything" in a bad merger], Arpadi reposed trust in Dunton as a business counselor to find candidates likely to conform to Arpadi's investment goals. Arpadi expected Dunton to perform as a finder with Arpadi's interests at heart, i.e., not to remain silent as Wellington was being circled by a corporate predator. Dunton exerted de facto control and influence over Arpadi by fostering Arpadi's false belief that there was no reason not to accept Sternau as a suitable candidate. Dunton's review of the intimate details of Arpadi's business marked Dunton's acceptance of that trust. There is no doubt that as regards the proposed merger with [Sternau's company], Dunton and Arpadi stood in a fiduciary relation to each other.

...

There is a final point. Even if only the agreement between Northeast and Arpadi were to be considered, the law would, I submit, imply a duty on the part of Dunton to disclose critical adverse information in these circumstances. . . .

...

. . . Indeed, I believe that many would agree that even the "morals of the market place" would require it. Surely [Dunton] should not be rewarded for his failure.

RESULT The judgment for Wellington was reversed by the New York Court of Appeals, and Wellington was ordered to pay the finder's fee to Northeast General.

QUESTIONS

1. What language could Wellington have added to its contract with Northeast to ensure that it was apprised of the reputation of any proposed buyer?
2. The court stated that a broker, who helps negotiate a deal and thereby brings the parties to an agreement, has a fiduciary duty to act in the best interests of the person who hired him or her. Why should a finder, who merely introduces the parties, be governed by a lesser ethical standard?

Agent's Ability *to* Bind *the* Principal *to* Contracts Entered *into by the* Agent

An agent has the ability to bind the principal in legal relations with third parties if the agent has actual or apparent authority to do so. Even in the absence of such authority, the principal may be bound by the unauthorized acts of his or her agent if the principal subsequently ratifies those acts. A principal can be bound even if his or her identity is undisclosed to the third party.

ACTUAL AUTHORITY

The principal may give the agent *actual authority* to enter into agreements on his or her behalf; that is, the principal may give consent for the agent to act for and bind the principal. This consent (or authority) may be express or implied.

Express Authority *Express authority* may be given by the principal's actual words, for example, a request that the agent hire an architect to design a new office. Express authority may also be given by an action that indicates the principal's consent, for example, by sending the agent a check for the architect's retainer. An agent has express authority if the agent has a justifiable belief that the principal has authorized him or her to do what he or she is doing.

Implied Authority Once an agent is given express authority, the agent also has *implied authority* to do whatever is reasonable to complete the task he or she has been instructed to undertake. For example, if a principal instructs an agent to purchase a truck costing up to $20,000, the agent has implied authority to select the appropriate make and model, to negotiate the purchase price, and to finalize the sale.

Persons in certain positions or offices have implied authority to do what is reasonable for someone in that position. For example, the vice president of purchasing for a trucking business, because of his or her position, has the implied authority to engage in the activities de-

scribed in the preceding paragraph. There are limits to such implied authority, however. For example, the vice president of purchasing for a trucking division does not have the implied authority to buy an office building. Similarly, an officer of a corporation does not have the authority to bind the corporation to sell or grant rights to purchase shares of its stock; stock issuances must be approved by the corporation's board of directors.

In the following case, the court considered whether an attorney had actual authority to settle his client's claim.

"We—your agents, successors, licensees, and assigns—would like to share a few thoughts with you."

CASE 5.3

Pohl v. United Airlines, Inc.

United States Court of Appeals for the Seventh Circuit 213 F.3d 336 (7th Cir. 2000).

In the Language of the Court

FACTS Michael Pohl, an aircraft inspector for United Airlines, sued United for alleged violations of the Uniformed Services Employment and Reemployment Rights Act. He alleged discrimination based on his military status, retaliation, and failure to properly credit his employee stock ownership account. The parties entered into settlement negotiations; after a number of discussions, they informed the court that they had reached a settlement. Shortly thereafter, Pohl called the court and expressed surprise that the case had settled.

The judge convened a status conference at which Pohl refused to sign the written settlement proposal on the grounds that his attorney did not have authority to negotiate the settlement. United filed a motion to enforce the settlement, and the court entered a judgment in United's favor. Pohl appealed.

ISSUE PRESENTED Under what circumstances does an attorney have the authority to enter into a settlement agreement on behalf of his client?

OPINION ROVNER, J., writing for the U.S. Court of Appeals for the Seventh Circuit:

As the Indiana Supreme Court held in *Koval v. Simon Telelect*,[1] in order to bind a client to a settlement, an attorney must have either express, implied, or apparent authority, or must act according to the attorney's inherent agency power. . . . [R]etention of an attorney does not, in itself, confer implied or apparent authority to settle. The authority to settle, therefore, derives from other actions of the client with respect to the attorney or third parties, including but not limited to express grants of actual authority. For instance, the client may not intend for the attorney to settle a claim but may nonetheless imply that intention to the attorney. If so, the client is bound by a resulting settlement. Further, both apparent authority and inherent agency power may be created by actions of the client in its dealing with third parties even if the attorney knows there is no actual authority. Under these circumstances, the client is bound even if it is a breach of the attorney's professional obligations to make the commitment.

. . . [T]he district court rejected Pohl's claim that the settlement was reached without authority from him. The court specifically relied on the objective evidence of communications between Pohl and his counsel, which supported the testimony of Pohl's counsel that Pohl was informed of each aspect of the settlement and approved of each one. During the negotiation period from December 15 until March 8, there is an absolute correlation between phone calls by Pohl's counsel to opposing counsel, and calls by Pohl's counsel to Pohl on the same day. That supports the testimony of Pohl's counsel that he constantly communicated the proposed settlement terms to Pohl. Moreover, Pohl failed to register any objection with his counsel when informed by letter that the "case" was settled, even though he testified that when he first read the March 8 letter confirming the settlement he thought it might include the whole case. In fact, his first reaction was "okay, great, they settled it"; that is hardly the reaction one would expect of someone who has not given his attorney the authority to settle the case. Furthermore, as the court in *Koval* recognized, Pohl may be bound by the settlement if he implied an intention to settle the claim to his attorney, regardless of whether he actually intended to settle the claim. The testimony of Pohl's attorney, which the court credited, would have been enough to establish implied authority to settle, even if express authority had not been found. In light of the record, the district court certainly did not abuse its discretion in holding that the settlement was obtained with actual authority from Pohl and that Pohl was bound by it.

[1]. 693 N.E.2d 1299 (Ind. 1998).

(Continued)

(Case 5.3 continued)

RESULT The court of appeals affirmed the judgment for United. Pohl's attorney had actual authority to settle the case on his behalf.

QUESTIONS

1. What public policy is served by binding a client to a commitment made by an attorney in violation of the attorney's professional obligations to the client?
2. How could Pohl have avoided a finding of actual authority?

APPARENT AUTHORITY

Apparent authority is created when a third party reasonably believes that the agent has authority to act for and bind the principal. This belief may be based on the words or acts of the principal or on knowledge that the principal has allowed its agent to engage in certain activities on its behalf over an extended period of time.

In *Aeroquip Corp. v. Adams,*[2] Aeroquip Corporation sued two of its former distributors, alleging that they had breached their contracts with Aeroquip by improperly requesting rebates. The distributors claimed that they requested the rebates in good faith reliance on representations by Aeroquip's sales engineers who appeared to have apparent authority to modify the terms of the company's rebate program when they realized that their competitors were offering the product at a lower price. The U.S. Court of Appeals for the Ninth Circuit concluded that there was sufficient evidence for the jury to find that the sales engineers had apparent authority to modify the rebate program. The evidence showed that Aeroquip intended the sales engineers to explain the terms of the rebate programs to the distributors; the manual the company provided to its distributors contained little information, so they had to learn about the programs from the sales engineers. From the perspective of the distributors, the sales engineers appeared to have authority to modify the terms of the program in order to compete in the local market.

RATIFICATION

The principal can bind himself or herself to an agent's unauthorized acts through *ratification,* that is, affirmation, of the prior acts. When an act has been ratified, it is then treated as if the principal had originally authorized it.

Ratification, like authorization, can be either express or implied. *Express ratification* occurs when the principal, through words or behavior, manifests an intent to be bound by the agent's act. For example, a principal could ratify his or her agent's unauthorized purchase of a truck either by saying "OK" or by simply paying the bill for the vehicle. *Implied ratification* occurs when the principal, by his or her silence or failure to repudiate the agent's act, acquiesces in it.

UNDISCLOSED PRINCIPAL

An agent may lawfully conceal the principal's identity or even his or her existence. This may be desirable if, for instance, the principal is trying to buy up adjacent properties in an area before news of a business venture is made public, or if the principal's wealth would cause the seller to demand a higher price. If there is an *undisclosed principal,* that is, if the third party does not know the agent is acting for the principal, the principal will nonetheless be bound by any contract the agent enters into with actual authority. (If the agent acts without authority, the principal will not be bound; however, the agent may personally be liable on such a contract.)

Liability *for* Torts *of* Agents

A principal may be liable for not only the contracts but also the torts of his or her agents. According to the doctrine of *respondeat superior,* an agent's employer will be liable for any injuries or damage to the property of another that the agent causes while acting within the scope

 ETHICAL CONSIDERATION

Is it ethical to use an agent to enter into a contract with a third party who has made it clear that he or she is unwilling to enter into a deal with the undisclosed principal?

2. 203 F.3d 830 (9th Cir. 1999).

VIEW FROM CYBERSPACE

Intelligent Agents *and* Click-Wrap Agreements

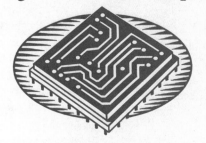

Intelligent agents are semiautonomous computer programs that can be dispatched by the user to execute certain tasks. One important type of intelligent agent can search the Internet and either retrieve relevant information or serve as a "personal shopping agent" that makes purchases on behalf of its user.[a]

A prominent feature of electronic commerce is the "click-wrap agreement,"[b] whereby computer users assent to the terms of an online contract by clicking on an acceptance box. The convergence of these two forms of cyberspace technology raises an interesting legal question: What happens when an intelligent agent comes across a click-wrap agreement?

Intelligent agents may someday have the natural language abilities to parse through contract provisions and accept only those terms their users have preprogrammed. But at least for the near term, these agents will likely be able only to accept or to reject online contracts in full. Because click-wrap agreements are so prevalent, the value of an agent that completely avoids them will be significantly reduced. The problem, however, is that traditional agency law does not offer clear guidance as to whether an

electronic device can bind an individual to a contract.

At the urging of Microsoft, the Electronic Signatures in Global and National Commerce Act, enacted in 2000, specifically recognizes the validity of contracts executed by electronic agents. Section 101(h) provides that a contract in or affecting interstate or foreign commerce may not be denied legal effect, validity, or enforceability solely because it involved the action of an electronic agent, as long as the action is "legally attributable to the person to be bound."

The Uniform Computer Information Transactions Act (UCITA), a proposed uniform commercial code for software licenses and other computer information transactions, seems to place the onus on the user of an intelligent agent. Section 107 provides that a person who uses an electronic agent is bound by its opera-

tions "even if no individual was aware of or reviewed the agent's operations or the results of the operations."[c] The Official Comment to Section 107 states:

The concept stated here embodies principles like those in agency law, but it does not depend on agency law. The electronic agent must be operating within its intended purpose. For human agents, this is often described in terms of acting within the scope of authority. Here, the focus is on whether the agent was used for the relevant purpose.[d]

a. This discussion is based in part on Stuart D. Levi & Robert Sporn, *Can Programs Bind Humans to Contracts?*, NAT'L L.J., Jan. 13, 1997, at B9.
b. The term *click-wrap agreement* is derived from shrink-wrap license. Under a *shrink-wrap license,* users are deemed to have assented to a licensing agreement with a software manufacturer by their act of tearing open the shrink wrap covering the software package. The U.S. Court of Appeals for the Seventh Circuit held that shrink-wrap licenses are generally enforceable. *See* ProCD, Inc. v. Zeidenberg, 86 F.3d 1447 (7th Cir. 1996).
c. *The Uniform Computer Information Transactions Act (UCITA): A Firestorm of Controversy,* ONLINE LIBRARIES & MICROCOMPUTERS, May 1, 2000.
d. *UCITA Online* (visited May 19, 2000) <http://www.ucitaonline.com>.

of his or her employment. As stated in *Jones v. Hart*, decided in England in 1798:

> If the servants of A with his cart run against another cart, wherein is a pipe of wine, and overturn the cart and spoil the wine, an action lieth against A. For whoever employs another is answerable for him, and undertakes for his care to all that make use of him. The act of the servant is the act of his master, where he acts by authority of the master.

If the principal is required to pay damages to a third party because of an agent's negligence, the principal has the right to demand reimbursement from the agent.

SCOPE OF EMPLOYMENT

Many cases in this area turn on whether the employee was acting within the scope of employment. (Torts of

independent contractors are discussed later in the chapter.) What constitutes scope of employment? Some of the relevant factors include (1) whether the employee's act was authorized by the employer, (2) the extent to which the employer's interests were advanced by the act, (3) whether the employer furnished the instrumentality (for example, truck or machine) that caused the injury, and (4) whether the employer had reason to know the employee would perform the act. Even an action that is a violation of the law may be within the scope of employment if the employee performed the act to serve the employer. For example, when a salesperson lies to a customer to make a sale, the tortious conduct is within the scope of employment because it benefits the employer by increasing sales, even though it may violate the employer's policy as well as the law.

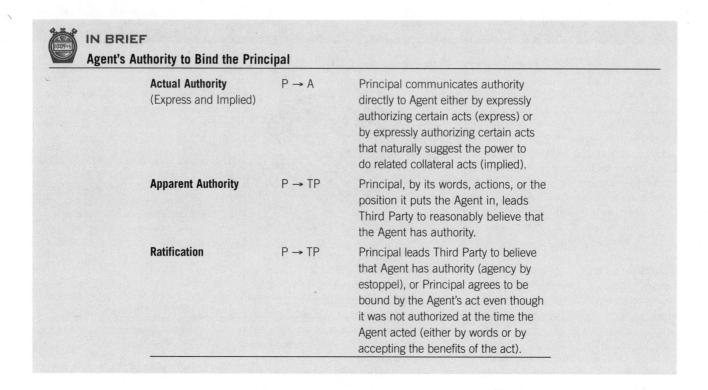

IN BRIEF

Agent's Authority to Bind the Principal

Actual Authority (Express and Implied)	P → A	Principal communicates authority directly to Agent either by expressly authorizing certain acts (express) or by expressly authorizing certain acts that naturally suggest the power to do related collateral acts (implied).
Apparent Authority	P → TP	Principal, by its words, actions, or the position it puts the Agent in, leads Third Party to reasonably believe that the Agent has authority.
Ratification	P → TP	Principal leads Third Party to believe that Agent has authority (agency by estoppel), or Principal agrees to be bound by the Agent's act even though it was not authorized at the time the Agent acted (either by words or by accepting the benefits of the act).

It is often not clear whether the agent is acting within the scope of employment. Courts tend to use the term "detour" to refer to a slight deviation from the employer's business and "frolic" to refer to conduct that in no way serves the interests of the employer. Detours are deemed to be within the scope of employment, but frolics are not. The following classic case illustrates how hard it can be to decide whether a deviation is a detour or a frolic.

A CASE IN POINT

CASE 5.4

Riley v. Standard Oil Co. of New York

Court of Appeals of New York 132 N.E. 97 (N.Y. 1921).

Summary

FACTS Arthur Riley, a child, was hit and severely injured by Million, a truck driver employed by the Standard Oil Company of New York, a large corporation even in the 1920s. Riley's mother, acting as a guardian *ad litem* (a person authorized to bring suit on behalf of a minor), sued Standard Oil. She sought to recover damages for personal injury from Standard Oil on the ground that the company was responsible for the tortious act of its truck driver.

Million had been instructed by his supervisor to drive a company truck from the Standard Oil mill to the freight yard of the Long Island Railroad, which was about two-and-a-half miles away. Million was supposed to pick up several barrels of paint at the freight yard and bring them back to the mill. Before leaving the mill, Million found some pieces of scrap wood and loaded them in the truck. As he pulled out of the mill, he did not turn in the direction of the freight yard. Instead, he drove to his sister's house, which was about four blocks in the opposite direction. After unloading the wood for his sister, he headed back toward the mill on his way to the freight yard. En route to the freight yard, but before he passed the mill, Million hit Riley. The only issue on appeal was whether Million was in fact acting as an agent for the company—that is, whether he was acting within the scope of his employment—when he hit Riley.

(Continued)

(Case 5.4 continued)

Standard Oil claimed that Million was not acting as an authorized agent of the company at the moment he hit Riley. His supervisor had told him to go to the freight yard, and he had no express or implied actual authority to go in the opposite direction to deliver the wood to his sister. The defendant argued that, at least until Million returned to his initial point of departure (the entrance to the mill), he was not acting as an agent for Standard Oil and therefore the company could not be held liable for his actions.

ISSUE PRESENTED For the purpose of determining a principal's liability for the conduct of its agent, does the scope of employment include returning to work after a diversion for a personal errand?

SUMMARY OF OPINION The New York Court of Appeals rejected Standard Oil's argument. It held that if Million had hit Riley while on the way to his sister's house, it would have been up to the jury to decide whether this side trip was a separate journey on his own business, distinct from that of his master, or a mere deviation from the general route. If the jury found it to be a new journey, Million would not have been acting as Standard Oil's agent, and the company would not be liable for his negligence. In fact, the accident occurred when Million had already completed his personal errand and was headed back in the direction of his assigned destination. The court concluded that "at some point in the route Million again engaged in the defendant's business. That point, in view of all the circumstances, we think he had reached."

RESULT Standard Oil was liable for employee Million's negligence. Million was deemed to be acting within the scope of his employment when returning from his errand.

COMMENTS Courts apply various standards in determining whether an agent is acting within the scope of his or her employment for purposes of tort liability. Most courts, however, consider such factors as when and where the tort occurred, what the employee was doing when the tort occurred, and why the employee was doing what he or she was doing.

Before the *Riley* case, there was much precedent for not holding an employer responsible for accidents caused by an employee–driver when he was using the employer's vehicle for his own purposes. The three-out-of-seven judges who dissented in *Riley* were able to cite a long list of such cases. The court could have held that Million, like the drivers in the previous cases, was still on his errand and not an agent when he hit Riley.

However, several of the judges were concerned with improving the tort system for victims of accidents. Standard Oil, as a large company, was in the best financial position to pay the damages for the serious injury caused by one of its drivers. To decide this close call the other way would have placed the financial burden on those least able to cover the loss.

LIABILITY FOR TORTS OF EMPLOYEES ACTING OUTSIDE THE SCOPE OF EMPLOYMENT

Under certain circumstances, an employer may be liable for an employee's action even if the employee was acting outside the scope of employment. The employer will be liable if (1) it intended the employee's conduct or its consequences; (2) the employee's high rank in the company makes him or her the employer's alter ego; (3) the employee's action can be attributable to the employer's own negligence or recklessness; (4) the employee uses apparent authority to act or to speak on behalf of the employer and there was reliance upon the apparent authority; or (5) the employee was aided in accomplishing the tort by the existence of the agency relationship. For example, the California Supreme Court held a city liable for a uniformed police officer who used his badge of authority to persuade a woman to get in his car and then raped her.[3]

3. Mary M. v. City of Los Angeles, 814 P.2d 1341 (Cal. 1991).

In the following case, the U.S. Supreme Court considered whether an employer could be vicariously liable for a supervisor who created a hostile work environment by sexually harassing the worker he supervised.

A CASE IN POINT

CASE 5.5

Burlington Industries, Inc. v. Ellerth

Supreme Court of the United States
524 U.S. 742 (1998).

Summary

FACTS Kimberly Ellerth worked as a salesperson at Burlington Industries, where she was subjected to constant sexual harassment by her supervisor, Ted Slowik. Slowik was a vice president and had authority to make hiring and promotion decisions subject to the approval of his supervisor. Slowik's offensive and illegal behavior included making remarks about Ellerth's breasts and warning her that he "could make [her] life very hard or very easy at Burlington." When Ellerth was being considered for a promotion, Slowik expressed reservations during an interview with her because she was not "loose enough" and then reached over and touched her knee. Burlington had a policy against sexual harassment, but Ellerth did not inform anyone in authority about Slowik's conduct.

Ellerth quit her job, then sued Burlington for sexual harassment and constructive discharge. The district court dismissed the complaint on the grounds that Burlington neither knew nor should have known about Slowik's conduct. The appeals court reversed, and Burlington appealed.

ISSUE PRESENTED Is an employer vicariously liable for a supervisor's creation of a hostile work environment when the employer neither knew nor should have known of the harassment?

SUMMARY OF OPINION The U.S. Supreme Court first noted that sexual harassment by a supervisor is generally not conduct within the scope of employment. It then cited Section 219(2)(d) of the Restatement of Agency, which provides that an employer may be subject to liability for the torts of its employees acting outside the scope of their employment if the employee was aided in accomplishing the tort by the existence of the agency relation.

The Court noted that "[i]n a sense, most workplace tortfeasors are aided in accomplishing their tortious objective by the existence of the agency relation: Proximity and regular contact may afford a captive pool of potential victims." If the employment relation itself were enough to satisfy the *aided-in-the-agency-relation standard,* then an employer would be subject to vicarious liability not only for all supervisor harassment, but also for all coworker harassment, a result enforced by neither the Equal Employment Opportunity Commission (EEOC) nor any court of appeals to have considered the issue. Therefore, there must be something more than the employment relation itself.

The Court proceeded to distinguish cases in which a supervisor takes a tangible employment action, such as denial of a raise or promotion, from the facts of this case. In the event of a tangible employment decision, it is clear that the injury could not have been inflicted absent the agency relation. As a result, a tangible employment action taken by the supervisor becomes for Title VII purposes the act of the employer, regardless of whether the employer knew or should have known of the action. The appropriate rule for supervisory harassment that does not result in a tangible employment action was less clear.

The Court noted that the aided-in–the-agency-relation standard is a developing feature of agency law but hesitated to render a definitive explanation of its understanding of the standard in an area where other important considerations must affect its judgment:

(Continued)

(Case 5.5 continued)

Title VII is designed to encourage the creation of antiharassment policies and effective grievance mechanisms. Were employer liability to depend in part on an employer's effort to create such procedures, it would effect Congress' intention to promote conciliation rather than litigation in the Title VII context . . . and the EEOC's policy of encouraging the development of grievance procedures. To the extent limiting employer liability could encourage employees to report harassing conduct before it becomes severe or pervasive, it would also serve Title VII's deterrent purpose.

In order to accommodate the agency principle of vicarious liability for harm caused by misuse of supervisory authority, as well as Title VII's equally basic policies of encouraging forethought by employers and saving action by objecting employees, the Court held that an employer may be subject to vicarious liability for a hostile environment created by a supervisor with immediate (or successively higher) authority over the victimized employee. When no tangible employment action was taken, however, a defending employer may raise an affirmative defense to liability or damages by proving by a preponderance of the evidence both that (1) the employer exercised reasonable care to prevent and correct promptly any sexually harassing behavior and that (2) the plaintiff employee unreasonably failed to take advantage of any preventive or corrective opportunities provided by the employer to avoid harm.

RESULT The Supreme Court affirmed the judgment of the U.S. court of appeals. Burlington was liable for the supervisor's harassment and could not take advantage of the possible affirmative defense because it did not have adequate policies in place to prevent sexual harassment. Burlington had no written policy prohibiting harassment and provided employees no process whereby they could complain to someone other than the immediate supervisor.

DISSENT THOMAS and SCALIA, J.J., dissenting from the majority opinion:

If a supervisor creates a hostile work environment . . . , he does not act for the employer. As the Court concedes, a supervisor's creation of a hostile work environment is neither within the scope of his employment, nor part of his apparent authority. Indeed, a hostile work environment is antithetical to the interest of the employer. In such circumstances, an employer should be liable only if it has been negligent. That is, liability should attach only if the employer either knew, or in the exercise of reasonable care should have known, about the hostile work environment and failed to take remedial action.

Sexual harassment is simply not something that employers can wholly prevent without taking extraordinary measures—constant video and audio surveillance, for example—that would revolutionize the workplace in a manner incompatible with a free society. Indeed, such measures could not even detect incidents of harassment such as the comments Slowik allegedly made to respondent in a hotel bar.

TORTS OF INDEPENDENT CONTRACTORS

The *respondeat superior* doctrine typically applies only to the action of employees. Principals may be held liable for the torts of independent contractors only in extraordinary circumstances, usually involving highly dangerous acts or nondelegable duties. For instance, if a principal hires an independent contractor to blast boulders off his or her land, the principal will be liable for any injuries or damages resulting from the blast. In other words, a principal cannot avoid liability for damages resulting from ultrahazardous activities simply by contracting out the work. Similarly, the South Carolina Supreme Court ruled that a hospital could not escape liability for the medical care provided by hiring physicians as independent contractors.[4]

Liability *of the* Principal *for* Violations *of* Law *by the* Agent

Under the theory of *vicarious liability,* a company can be held liable for violations of law by its employees even if a manager told the employee not to violate the law. The following case considers whether, under the principle of

4. Simmons v. Tuomey Regional Med. Ctr., 533 S.E.2d 312 (S.C. 2000).

apparent authority, a corporation can be held liable under the Fair Credit Reporting Act for its employee's illegal disclosure of credit records.

A CASE IN POINT

CASE 5.6
Jones v. Federated Financial Reserve Corp.
United States Court of Appeals for the Sixth Circuit
144 F.3d 961
(6th Cir. 1998).

In the Language of the Court

FACTS Karen Jones was married briefly to Randy Lind, then divorced him. Due to fear of his harassment, she refused to give him her new address or phone number. Lind obtained his ex-wife's address from his friend Janice Caylor, who had obtained this information through her employer Federated Financial Reserve Corporation. Federated, a lessor of consumer and business equipment, obtained approximately 25,000 credit reports annually through its online credit report request system, which it used for credit approval and debt collection. TRW, Inc. supplied the credit reports to Federated, which certified that it would use the reports only for specified permissible business purposes.

Caylor worked as a full-time collector for Federated and was authorized to request consumer credit reports from employees who operated Federated's credit report request system. Federated did not require her to obtain her supervisor's approval, nor did Federated determine whether she put the credit reports in customer files. Caylor obtained Jones's credit report by completing a request form and attaching the form to an unrelated business file.

Jones sued Federated for negligent and willful violation of the Fair Credit Reporting Act (FCRA), which requires that consumer reporting agencies adopt reasonable procedures for providing consumer credit information in a fair and equitable manner with respect for the consumer's right to privacy. The statute is silent as to a company's vicarious liability for its employees.

ISSUED PRESENTED May an employer be liable under the Fair Credit Reporting Act for its employee's actions under a theory of apparent authority?

OPINION COLE, J., writing for the U.S. Court of Appeals for the Sixth Circuit:

[A] principal may be vicariously liable for an agent's tortious conduct based upon an apparent authority theory, if the principal cloaked its agent with apparent authority, i.e., held the agent out to third parties as possessing sufficient authority to commit the particular act in question, and there was reliance upon the apparent authority. . . . Under an apparent authority theory, vicarious "[l]iability is based upon the fact that the agent's position facilitates the consummation of the fraud, in that from the point

(Continued)

(Case 5.6 continued)

of view of the third person the transaction seems regular on its face and the agent appears to be acting in the ordinary course of the business provided to him." Accordingly, liability may be imposed on a principal under an apparent authority theory irrespective of whether the agent acted for his own purposes, rather than those of his principal.

...

In the absence of specific language regarding the imposition of vicarious liability based on apparent authority, we must consider whether an apparent authority theory is consistent with Congress's intent behind the FCRA. Protecting consumers from the improper use of credit reports is an underlying policy of the FCRA. An apparent authority theory is in keeping with the FCRA's underlying deterrent purpose because employers are in a better position to protect consumers by use of internal safeguards. Because a company like Federated can act only through its agents, it is difficult to imagine a situation in which a company would ever be found to have willfully violated the statute directly by obtaining a credit report for an impermissible purpose. The FCRA's deterrence goal would be subverted if a corporation could escape liability for a violation that could only occur because the corporation cloaked its agent with the apparent authority to request credit reports.

RESULT The court remanded the case for a new trial on both the negligence and the willful noncompliance claims. If the jury concluded that Caylor acted willfully, then her actions and intent would be imputed to Federated, making Federated liable for willful noncompliance with the FCRA.

QUESTIONS

1. What can Federated do now to avoid liability in the future for its employees' violations of the FCRA?
2. Under the court's reasoning, would Federated still be liable if it had had adequate procedures in place to prevent violations and Caylor had managed to circumvent them?

THE RESPONSIBLE MANAGER

Working *with* Agents

The relationship between a manager and his or her employer is one of trust. As an agent, a manager owes the employer fiduciary duties, which are most often summarized as the duty of care and the duty of loyalty. The duty of care typically requires a manager to avoid grossly negligent, reckless, or intentional behavior that would harm the company. Rarely will an act of simple negligence be treated as a breach of fiduciary duty. The duty of loyalty imposes more complex obligations. It requires a manager to avoid self-dealing or for-profit activity that competes with the business of the employer. In other words, a manager has a duty to act solely for the benefit of his or her employer in all matters related to its business. This duty includes an obligation to notify the employer of all relevant facts—all that the agent knows, the principal should know.

A manager must be concerned with the scope of authority granted to the company's workers and the company's potential liability for the actions of those workers. Perhaps the most determinable aspect of this relationship is whether the worker is deemed an employee or an independent contractor. A manager may have several reasons to prefer labeling workers independent contractors rather than employees—for instance, lower tax and benefits costs or reduced exposure to liability. The manager should be aware, however, that legally the status of workers will be determined by the manner in which they are used, not by the label written into the employment agreements.

Once a manager has hired an agent, the manager must be careful to leave little doubt about the scope of the agent's authority. If the manager does not do this, he or she may find, for example, that a purchasing agent has inadvertently been given the apparent authority to bind the business to a large purchase of supplies, above the actual needs of the business. A manager can help avoid scope-of-authority problems by making explicit, unambiguous statements to third parties that specify the limits on an employee's ability to enter into a binding contract. When using an employee or other agent to deal with third parties, a manager must also monitor transactions to avoid conduct that might legally ratify an otherwise unauthorized agreement entered into by the agent.

The manager should ensure that the work environment and the machines and other equipment used in the business are safe. He or she should also stress to the employees the importance not only of complying with the law but also of being ethical and safety conscious. These concerns pertain mostly to the duties owed by employers to their employees. But an employer may owe similar duties even to workers properly termed independent contractors, depending on where they work and how much control the employer exerts over that work.

Finally, an employer must be concerned about liability for the wrongdoing of its workers. Because the employer will be liable for those torts of employees that are committed within the scope of employment, a manager should attempt to decrease the risk of such vicarious liability by defining the employees' scope of employment as narrowly as possible. In light of an employer's potential liability under the aided-in-the-agency-relation theory for acts outside the scope of employment, managers should exercise particular care when giving an employee authority that could be misused to ensure both that the employee is trustworthy and that any persons under the employee's control have the ability to complain to someone other than the supervisor. Because a company cannot avoid liability for injuries caused while it is engaged in an ultrahazardous activity, even if it is working through an independent contractor, managers should ensure that the company has adequate liability insurance. Finally, as discussed in Chapter 17, employers may be responsible for the criminal acts of employees. For example, if an employee violates an industry-related regulation during the normal course of employment, the employer could be held vicariously liable. In some situations, the supervising manager may be liable as well.

INSIDE STORY

When Are "Temporary" Workers Employees?

In an economy where many employers attempt to reduce labor costs and increase staffing flexibility by hiring temporary workers and independent contractors, the classification of workers has risen to new importance. The U.S. Court of Appeals for the Ninth Circuit caused a stir when it ordered Microsoft Corporation, the world's largest computer software company, to provide fringe benefits to certain freelance workers even though they had signed agreements expressly stating that they were independent contractors and not eligible for such benefits.[5]

Although hired to work as freelancers on specific projects, seven of the eight named plaintiffs (who sued on

their own behalf and as representatives of a class of workers) had worked on successive projects for a minimum of two years prior to the time the action was filed, while the eighth had worked for more than a year. During that time, they performed services as software testers, production editors, proofreaders, formatters, and indexers. They often worked on teams with regular employees, sharing the same supervisors, performing identical functions, and working the same core hours. However, they were not permitted to assign their work to others, were not invited to official company functions, and were not paid overtime wages. In addition, they were not paid through Microsoft's payroll department. Instead, they submitted invoices for their services, documenting their hours and the projects on which they worked, and were paid through the accounts receivable department.

5. Vizcaino v. Microsoft Corp., 97 F.3d 1187 (9th Cir. 1996), *aff'd on reh'g*, 120 F.3d 1006 (9th Cir. 1997), *cert. denied*, 522 U.S. 1099 (1998). The statement of facts that follows is excerpted from this opinion.

Even though the freelancers had agreed to be responsible for all federal and state taxes, withholding, and Social Security, the Internal Revenue Service (IRS) concluded that the freelancers were not independent contractors but employees for withholding and employment tax purposes. Microsoft therefore agreed to (1) pay overdue employer withholding taxes, (2) issue retroactive W-2 forms to allow the freelancers to recover Microsoft's share of Social Security taxes (which they had been required to pay), and (3) pay the freelancers retroactively for any overtime they had worked.

After learning of the IRS rulings, the plaintiffs sought various employee benefits, including benefits under the Employee Stock Purchase Plan (ESPP) and the Savings Plus Plan (SPP). The ESPP permitted employees to purchase company stock at 85 percent of the lower of the fair market value on the first or last day of each six-month offering period. The SPP was a retirement plan under Section 401(k) of the Internal Revenue Code, which permitted Microsoft's employees to save and invest up to 15 percent of their income through tax-deferred payroll deductions. Microsoft matched 50 percent of the employee's contribution in any year, with a maximum matching contribution of 3 percent of the employee's yearly compensation. Microsoft rejected the plaintiffs' demand for benefits on the grounds that they were independent contractors who were personally responsible for all of their own benefits.

A three-judge panel of the Ninth Circuit Court of Appeals addressed the SPP and ESPP claims separately. With respect to the ESPP claim, because Microsoft stated in the ESPP document that the plan was intended to comply with provisions of the Internal Revenue Code, Microsoft was deemed to have adopted the IRS's definition of common law employee. As a result, the ESPP expressly extended eligibility to all of the workers in the plaintiffs' class. As for the SPP claims, the court ruled that it should not address issues of plan interpretation until the plan administrator had determined whether the workers were "on the U.S. payroll" of Microsoft within the meaning of the plan.

Many companies responded to the *Microsoft* decision by leasing workers from temporary employment agencies instead of hiring them directly. This arrangement may not be fail-safe, however. The fact that leased workers are on the payroll of an employment agency does not preclude them from being considered employees of the company—the agency and company could be considered joint employers.[6]

To determine whether a company is a joint employer of leased workers, a manager should consider such factors as whether the company (1) supervises the workers, (2) has the ability to hire and fire, (3) is involved in day-to-day labor relations, (4) establishes wage rates, or (5) has the power to promote or discipline the worker. As with questions surrounding the independent contractor label, the bottom line is that if leased employees are treated the same as regular employees, they may be treated as common law employees of the company.

In January 2000, the Ninth Circuit ruled that approximately 10,000 current and former independent contractors and longtime "temporary" employees at Microsoft who had worked at least half-time, or five months a year, had become "common-law" employees of the company and thus were entitled to compensation for their exclusion from the ESPP. On December 12, 2000, the U.S. District Court for the Western District of Washington gave preliminary approval of a settlement of this litigation requiring Microsoft to pay $96.9 million to 8,000 to 12,000 class members and their attorneys.[7] The agreement acknowledged the important changes Microsoft has made in its employment practices since 1997 to ensure proper classification of workers and the fact that, in its most recent fiscal year, Microsoft had hired more than 3,000 class members as W-2 employees entitled to participate in its employee benefit plans and programs.[8]

---

6. Vizcaino v. Microsoft Corp., 173 F.3d 713, 723 (9th Cir. 1999), *cert. denied,* 120 S. Ct. 844 (2000).
7. *Microsoft to Pay $97 Million to Settle Temporary Workers' Class Action Lawsuits,* 69 U.S.L.W. 2363 (Dec. 19, 2000).
8. The settlement agreement is available at <http://www.bs-s.com>, Web site for plaintiffs' counsel.

KEY WORDS AND PHRASES

actual authority 151	agent 146	duty of care 148
agency 146	aided-in-the-agency-relation	duty of loyalty 147
agency by estoppel 146	standard 158	express authority 152
agency by ratification 146	apparent authority 154	express ratification 154

QUESTIONS AND CASE PROBLEMS

1. Singer was employed by General Automotive Manufacturing Company (GAMC) as its general manager from 1953 until 1959. He had worked in the machine-shop field for more than thirty years and enjoyed a fine reputation in machine-shop circles.

   GAMC was a small concern with only five employees and a low credit rating. Singer attracted a large volume of business to GAMC and was invaluable in bolstering the company's credit rating. At times, when collections were slow, Singer paid the customer's bill to GAMC and waited for his own reimbursement until the customer remitted. Also, when work was slack, Singer would finance the manufacture of unordered parts and wait for recoupment until the stockpiled parts were sold. Some parts were never sold, and Singer personally absorbed the loss on them.

   While working for GAMC, Singer set up his own sideline operation as a machinist–consultant. As orders came in to GAMC through him, Singer would decide that some of them required equipment GAMC lacked or that GAMC could not do the job at a competitive price. For such orders, Singer would give the customer a price, then deal with another machine shop to do the work at a lower price and pocket the difference. Singer conducted his operation without notifying GAMC of the offers that it (through Singer) did not accept. GAMC contended that this sideline business was in direct competition with its business.

   GAMC sued Singer for breach of fiduciary duty. What result? What were Singer's duties to GAMC as its agent? Was Singer's operation of a sideline business ethical? Would it have been ethical had he disclosed it to his GAMC superiors? [General Automotive Mfg. Co. v. Singer, 120 N.W.2d 659 (Wis. 1963)]

2. NTG Telecommunications, which was interested in purchasing a computer network for its office, received a promotional letter from IBM regarding IBM's PC Server 310, Small Business Solution, a computer network server designed for and marketed to small businesses. The letter stated: "When you're ready to get down to business, give us a call. . . .

We'll give you the name of the IBM business partner nearest you, as well as answer any questions you might have." The Small Business Solution was available only through an IBM business partner, which is an entity authorized to resell IBM products.

   Jud Berkowitz, president of NTG, contacted Frank Cubbage of Sun Data Services, an IBM business partner, regarding the Small Business Solution. Berkowitz decided to purchase the Small Business Solution after being informed by Cubbage that it was compatible with Windows 95, the operating system installed on each of the networked computers. After he installed the server, NTG started having serious computer problems, which were not resolved until it replaced PerfectOffice (which was sold as part of the Small Business Solution) with Lotus Smart Suite. Berkowitz sued IBM for fraud based in part on Cubbage's representation that the Small Business Solution was compatible with Windows 95. IBM argued that Cubbage's statement could not be attributed to it because a formal licensing or dealership agreement does not create an agency relationship. How should the court rule? [*NTG Telecommunications, Inc. v. IBM, Inc.*, 2000 U.S. Dist. LEXIS 6279 (E.D. Pa. May 8, 2000)]

3. Leonardo ran a small but prosperous rare-print shop. To keep the shop stocked with the finest prints, Leonardo needed to make purchases at trade shows throughout the world. When he was too busy to attend, Leonardo sometimes sent his employee, Rembrandt. On other occasions he paid for the services of an independent buyer named Rubens.

   On March 14, Leonardo sent Rembrandt to Tokyo to buy ten nineteenth-century Japanese prints. Leonardo told Rembrandt that he should use his own best judgment and buy the ten prints that he considered to be of the finest quality. Price was no concern. While at the show, Rembrandt made a written list of the finest prints. The total came to eleven. Rembrandt was unable to eliminate any from the list on the basis of quality. He closed his eyes and brought his finger down on the paper where it landed on print #4. Rembrandt purchased that print for himself and the other ten for Leonardo.

On April 14, Rubens, who had his own business buying prints for himself and other dealers, called Leonardo. Rubens said he would be attending a show in Munich and asked if Leonardo wished him to purchase a few prints on Leonardo's behalf. Leonardo replied that he was interested but only if Rubens would fax him photocopies of all prints for sale, then let Leonardo select five before Rubens bought any. Rubens usually did not make such concessions, but he agreed to do so. Rubens and Leonardo signed Rubens's standard contract, with a typed-in clause for the faxing arrangement. Once at the show, Rubens faxed the copies. Leonardo selected five prints. One of the five was a forgery, but Leonardo could not detect it in a fax. Rubens had spotted the forgery and discreetly mentioned it to the show's organizer. Not wanting to create a scandal, the organizer offered Rubens $5,000 to remain silent. Rubens accepted the bribe.

a. Leonardo believes that the print Rembrandt purchased for himself is the best of the Tokyo lot. Rembrandt refuses to sell it to Leonardo. (After he returned, Rembrandt decided his print was the finest.) Leonardo sues Rembrandt to obtain possession. Has Rembrandt violated a fiduciary duty to Leonardo?

b. Leonardo finds out about the Munich forgery. Leonardo's lawyer advises him that he cannot sue Rubens under contract law because Rubens's standard contract explicitly denies any liability for forged artwork. Does Leonardo have any other way to force Rubens to reimburse him for the loss? What can Leonardo recover in damages if he is successful?

4. Pat Skidmore worked as an inspector on a machine at Precision Printing & Packaging, Inc. Jay Mitchell worked as an operator on the same shift. During the time that they worked together, Mitchell harassed Skidmore with constant sexual remarks. Skidmore did not inform her supervisor of Mitchell's actions until an argument broke out between Skidmore and another employee who was a friend of Skidmore's husband. Skidmore wanted the friend to explain to Skidmore's husband that Mitchell was harassing her, but the friend refused. As a result of the argument, Skidmore met with her supervisor, Jim Bryan, and told him about Mitchell's offensive comments and conduct. Immediately after speaking with Skidmore, Bryan moved her to a warehouse facility for the rest of the week and instructed Mitchell to stay away from her. Three days later, Bryan returned Skidmore to her old department but as-

signed her to a different shift from Mitchell with the exception of several days when she trained her replacement. Bryan did not conduct an investigation or interview any other employees regarding Skidmore's claims until after she filed a suit against the company. Is Precision liable for Mitchell's conduct? Should the company have done anything differently? [*Skidmore v. Precision Printing & Packaging, Inc.,* 188 F.3d 606 (5th Cir. 1999)]

5. In 1987, the Leadership Council, a nonprofit fair housing corporation in the city of Chicago, suspected that the agents of Matchmaker Real Estate Sales Center were engaging in racial steering. Racial steering is an illegal practice by which real estate brokers and agents preserve and encourage patterns of racial segregation in available housing. They do this by steering prospective buyers to buildings and neighborhoods already predominantly inhabited by members of the buyers' racial or ethnic group and away from buildings and neighborhoods inhabited primarily by members of other races or groups.

Beginning in July 1987, the Leadership Council conducted a series of tests of Matchmaker's activities. In each test the Matchmaker agents engaged in blatant acts of racial steering. For example, African-American testers and white testers who contacted the agents in the same time period with very similar housing qualifications and requirements were given very different housing listings that included only houses in neighborhoods already dominated by the testers' own racial groups.

Matchmaker's sole shareholder and chief executive officer, Erwin Ernst, exercised day-to-day control over Matchmaker and its real estate agents. However, he did not engage in or condone racial steering. He had created written office policies and procedures requiring that his agents comply with fair housing laws. He was also a signatory of an agreement by a national realtors organization ordering full compliance with fair housing laws and had actively worked to get other Chicago brokers to sign the agreement. He required all his agents to attend fair housing training courses sponsored by local real estate boards. The city of Chicago, the Leadership Council, and the individual testers sued Matchmaker, Ernst, and Matchmaker's sales agents. Should the realty company, Ernst, or the agents be found liable for compensatory or punitive damages? [*Chicago v. Matchmaker Real Estate Sales Center, Inc.,* 982 F.2d 1086 (7th Cir. 1992)]

6. The president of a corporation hired an assistant to be responsible for both his personal and his business

affairs, including review of vendor invoices and credit card statements for the corporate American Express account. Without the knowledge of the president, the assistant obtained an additional credit card for the corporate account in her name. The corporation alleged that the assistant stole $412,000 via unauthorized credit card charges. The corporation sued American Express, seeking to recover $276,000 in unauthorized charges and a declaration that it was not liable for the $51,000 outstanding balance on one of the cards. The applicable federal law limits a cardholder's liability from "unauthorized" charges to $50.

American Express argued that the corporation, because of its negligence in failing to examine the credit card statements that would have revealed the assistant's fraudulent charges, had given the assistant apparent authority to make the charges. Therefore, American Express contended, the charges were not unauthorized under the meaning of the statute and the corporation was fully liable for those charges. What result? [*Minskoff v. American Express Travel Related Servs. Co.*, 98 F.3d 703 (2d Cir. 1996)]

7. Frederick Richmond agreed to sell UForma Shelby Business Forms, Inc., a business forms printing business, to Samuel Peters pursuant to a stock purchase agreement at a price of $3.6 million to be paid in annual installments. The amount of each installment was to be one-half the amount by which the profits of UForma Shelby and Miami Systems, Inc., another company owned by Peters, exceeded the 1988 and 1989 average annual profits of Miami Systems alone. The agreement stated that this formula might result in no payment being made in some years. At the time of the sale, UForma was operating at a loss. The sale agreement also stated that Peters should operate UForma according to "sound business practices." Peters paid Richmond $496,057 for 1990 and $147,368 for 1991. Because the earnings of UForma and Miami Systems were insufficient to trigger a payment under the formula set forth in the agreement, Peters paid Richmond nothing for the years 1992 through 1995. Richmond sued Peters for breach of contract and breach of fiduciary duty, alleging that he was entitled to additional payments and that Peters had not operated UForma in accordance with sound business practices. How should the court rule? [*Richmond v. Peters*, No. 97-3647 (6th Cir. Nov. 20, 1998), *reh'g denied*, 173 F.3d 429 (6th Cir. 1999)]

8. Johnson was the sole general partner of a large office building in Austin, Texas, along with several limited partners. The limited partners were also lessees of space in the office building. Each tenant of the building (including the limited partners/lessees) was responsible for the "finish-out" construction of that tenant's office space. Most of these tenants hired one of two contractors to finish out their office spaces. On most of these finish-out jobs, the contractors paid Johnson, the sole general partner, a 15 percent fee. Each contractor simply added this fee to the sum charged to the tenant. Some tenants knew about the fee, and others did not. Did Johnson owe a fiduciary duty to his limited partners (who were also his tenants) to disclose the fee? [*Johnson v. J. Hiram Moore, Ltd.*, 763 S.W.2d 496 (Tex. Ct. App. 1988), *writ denied* (Sept. 20, 1989)]

9. The plaintiffs were models in a "fitness fashion show," featured as part of the Working Women's Survival Show exhibition at a convention center in St. Louis. B.P.S., doing business as Wells Fargo Guard Service, had contracted with the city to provide guards at the center.

Security arrangements at the convention center included a number of television surveillance cameras scattered around the center, which were monitored on small screens in a central control room. The direction in which the cameras pointed could be adjusted manually or automatically in the control room. The control room also had a large screen that the guards could use to view the image from the cameras or to monitor what was being taped on the VCR. The purpose of having the VCR was to enable the guards to videotape suspicious activities. The Wells Fargo guards were told to practice taping on the VCR.

Promoters for the Working Women's Survival Show had a makeshift curtained dressing area set up near the stage for the models in the fashion shows. Unbeknown to the models, the dressing area was in a location that could be monitored by one of the surveillance cameras. That fortuity was discovered by two Wells Fargo guards, Rook and Smith. Rook had the rank of captain within Wells Fargo, denoting supervisory capacity, though there was testimony that when he worked in the control room, he had no supervisory authority. Another supervisor with disputed supervisory authority, Ramey, walked by the control room and saw the guards using the large screen to view women in a state of undress. Ramey said that he thought the guards were watching pornographic tapes that they had brought to work. (There was testimony that the guards watched their own pornographic tapes in the control room.) Either Smith or Rook (each accuses the other) focused the camera on the plaintiffs and taped them as they were changing clothes for the fashion show.

Is Wells Fargo Guard Service liable for the unauthorized actions of its agents, even if those actions were done for reasons of personal pleasure rather than for work? [*Does v. B.P.S. Guard Serv., Inc., d/b/a Wells Fargo Guard Serv.*, 945 F.2d 1422 (8th Cir. 1991)]

MANAGER'S DILEMMA

10. Stern Stewart is a leading New York boutique financial consulting firm specializing in corporate valuations and executive compensation. It uses a system called Economic Value Added; Stern Stewart has trademarked the acronym EVA. KPMG Peat Marwick (KPMG) is a Big Five accounting firm that served as Stern Stewart's auditor and tax adviser. It had access to Stern Stewart's confidential financial records and executive compensation information. While still acting in this fiduciary capacity, and without notice to Stern Stewart, KPMG decided to establish an economic consulting division that would compete with Stern Stewart. KPMG called this its Economic Value Management (EVM) unit.

Stern Stewart was not aware of KPMG's intentions until after a number of its employees had been hired by KPMG and the formation of KPMG's EVM practice was well under way. Stern Stewart sued KPMG under a variety of theories, including breach of fiduciary duty. Did KPMG's undisclosed creation of its EVM division constitute a breach of the fiduciary duty KPMG owed Stern Stewart as its accountant? If so, what should the managers at KPMG have done differently? [*Stern Stewart & Co. v. KPMG Peat Marwick LLP*, 240 A.D.2d 334, 659 N.Y.S.2d 754 (N.Y. App. Div. 1997)]

INTERNET SOURCES	
The University of Chicago offers a guide for users of independent contractors that addresses many of the distinctions between independent contractors and employees.	http://admin-www.uchicago.edu/admincompt/icug/ic-contents.html
The Independent Contractor Report provides frequent updates on rulings and other issues relevant to users of independent contractors.	http://www.workerstatus.coml
The Massachusetts Society of Certified Public Accountants, Inc. provides an online discussion of the distinction between independent contractors and employees.	http://www.mscpaonline.org/resource/cpareview/bigdif.htm

CHAPTER 6

Administrative Law

IMPORTANCE OF ADMINISTRATIVE AGENCIES

Administrative law concerns the powers and procedures of administrative agencies, such as the Internal Revenue Service, which collects taxes, and the Securities and Exchange Commission, which regulates the securities markets. The activities of administrative agencies affect nearly everyone, frequently on a daily basis. Administrative agencies set limits on pollution and emissions and regulate disposal of hazardous waste. They regulate radio and television, food and drugs, and health and safety. In a year, all of the federal courts together probably try fewer than 10,000 cases, but a single agency such as the Social Security Administration may act on millions of applications for benefits. Federal and state administrative agencies solve practical problems that cannot be handled effectively by the courts or legislatures. Agencies make rules to effectuate legislative enactments; resolve conflicts by formal adjudication, a courtlike proceeding; carry out informal discretionary actions; and conduct investigations into compliance with specific laws and regulations. Although usually part of the executive branch, administrative agencies can rightly be called a fourth branch of government.

CHAPTER OVERVIEW

This chapter discusses the various ways in which administrative agencies operate and addresses the key principles of administrative law. Constitutional issues include separation of powers, delegation of authority, and the protections afforded by the Bill of Rights. Issues arising from the judicial review of agency actions include the doctrines of ripeness and exhaustion of administrative remedies. Doctrines that limit the decision-making power of agencies include the principles that agencies are bound by their own rules and that they must explain the basis for their decisions. The chapter also describes how to find the rules of a particular agency and how to obtain documents from the government.

 How Administrative Agencies Act

An administrative agency functions in four primary ways: making rules, conducting formal adjudications, taking informal discretionary actions, and conducting investigations.

MAKING RULES

A state legislature or the Congress frequently lacks the time, human resources, and expertise to enact detailed regulations. Sometimes issues are so politically sensitive that elected officials lack the will to make the tough decisions. In such cases, the legislature will pass a law establishing general principles and guidelines and will delegate authority to an administrative agency to carry out this legislative intent. The agency will then follow a three-step procedure to promulgate appropriate rules or regulations.

Notice to the Public First, the administrative agency gives notice to the public of its intent to propose a rule. Generally, the agency publishes the proposed rule and gives the public an opportunity to submit written comments.

A written comment on a proposed rule should (1) identify the company that is concerned, (2) describe why it is concerned, (3) suggest a specific change in the language of the proposed rule, and (4) provide factual information to support its position. These kinds of comments are very helpful to an agency and can influence the final rule.

Agencies may, but are not always required to, hold a formal public hearing. They always allow people to comment on proposed rules by meeting informally or telephoning the agency personnel. If a company is particularly concerned about a proposed rule, it should both call and meet with the proposing agency about its concerns.

Evaluation Second, the administrative agency evaluates the comments, responds to them, and decides on the scope and extent of the final rule. If the comments prompt the agency to make substantial changes in the proposed rule, the agency may publish a revised proposed rule for public comment.

Adoption Third, the agency will formally adopt the rule by publishing it in the *Federal Register* along with an explanation of changes. The *Federal Register* is published daily by the U.S. Government Printing Office; rules that are not properly published there are void. The final rule will also be *codified,* that is, added to the *Code of Federal Regulations (CFR)*. The *CFR* contains more than fifty titles and includes the regulations of approximately 400 federal agencies and bureaus.

The Administrative Procedure Act (APA) requires notice to the public and an opportunity to comment before an agency can promulgate a rule. There is an exception for rules of agency procedure and general statements of policy. In the following case, the court considered whether a directive issued by the Occupational Safety and Health Administration, part of the U.S. Department of Labor, fell into either category.

A CASE IN POINT

CASE 6.1

Chamber of Commerce of the United States v. United States Department of Labor
United States Court of Appeals for the District of Columbia Circuit
174 F.3d 206
(D.C. Cir. 1999).

In the Language of the Court

FACTS The Occupational Safety and Health Administration (OSHA) issued a directive (the Directive) establishing the OSHA High Injury/Illness Rate Targeting and Cooperative Compliance Program, a new approach to the problem of work safety at dangerous workplaces. The Directive set up a procedure whereby dangerous workplaces would be placed on a "primary inspection list" and subjected to a comprehensive inspection. OSHA would remove a workplace from the list only if the employer participated in the agency's Cooperative Compliance Program (CCP), which obligated the employer to satisfy eight requirements designed to reduce dangerous conditions at the sites.

The Chamber of Commerce challenged the Directive for failure to provide notice and an opportunity to comment.

ISSUE PRESENTED Was OSHA required to provide notice and an opportunity to comment?

OPINION GINSBURG, J., writing for the U.S. Court of Appeals for the District of Columbia Circuit:

In defense of its position that the Directive is a procedural rule, the OSHA advances two arguments. First, minimizing the significance of the CCP, it asserts that the Directive is merely an inspection plan that does not put its "stamp of approval or disapproval" on any particular behavior. Then, ignoring the inspection plan, it maintains that the Directive has no "substantial impact" upon covered employers because of the voluntary nature of the CCP. But the inspection plan and the CCP are two elements of the same rule; in determining whether notice and comment were required before it could be promulgated, we must view the rule as a whole.

So viewed, it is apparent that the Directive cannot be considered procedural. If the function of the CCP were simply to provide each employer with the option of substituting self-inspection for an equivalent inspection conducted by the OSHA,

(Continued)

(Case 6.1 continued)

then the agency could make a creditable argument that the Directive does not represent the kind of normative judgment characteristic of a substantive rule. . . . The OSHA may not, however, tell employers in one breath that participation in the CCP requires more than mere compliance with the OSHA Act—which clearly ups the substantive ante—and tell us in the next that the sole purpose of the CCP is to make unnecessary the inspections it performs in order to uncover violations of the Act. At least to the extent that participation in the CCP requires more than adherence to existing law, the Directive imposes upon employers more than "the incidental inconveniences of complying with an enforcement scheme. . . ." [I]t has a substantive component.

A general statement of policy "does not establish a binding norm. It is not finally determinative of the issues or rights to which it is addressed. The agency cannot apply or rely upon [such a] policy as law because a general statement of policy only announces what the agency seeks to establish as policy." . . . The OSHA argues that the Directive meets this definition, raising once more the point that the rule imposes no formal legal obligation upon an employer that chooses not to participate in the CCP.

In this context, the agency's contention has some intuitive appeal: At first glance, one might think that a rule could not be considered a "binding norm" unless it is backed by a threat of legal sanction. Beyond that first glance, however, its appeal is fleeting. In *American Bus Association v. United States,*[1] we held that the question whether a rule is a policy statement is to be determined by whether it (1) has only a prospective effect, and (2) leaves agency decisionmakers free to exercise their informed discretion in individual cases. Both criteria lead us here to the conclusion that the Directive is a substantive rule rather than a policy statement. First, the Directive provides that every employer that does not participate in the CCP will be searched. The effect of the rule is therefore not to "announce[] the agency's tentative intentions for the future,". . . but to inform employers of a decision already made. . . . Indeed, the OSHA admits in its brief that the inspection plan "leave[s] no room for discretionary choices by inspectors in the field." And the Directive itself suggests that the agency will not remove an employer from the CCP unless the employer fails to abide by the terms of the program. Therefore, although the Directive does not impose a binding norm in the sense that it gives rise to a legally enforceable duty, neither can it be shoehorned into the exception for policy statements.

RESULT The court held that the Directive was neither a procedural rule nor a policy statement. As a result, OSHA was required to provide notice and an opportunity to comment before issuing it. The court vacated the Directive without prejudice to OSHA to re-promulgate it using the proper procedures.

QUESTIONS

1. Why should procedural rules and policy statements be exempt from the notice and comment requirements?
2. How might OSHA have modified its rule to bring it within the exceptions for procedural rules and policy statements?

1. 627 F.2d 525 (D.C. Cir. 1980).

The federal government has attempted to make the regulatory process less cumbersome and time-consuming, more informal, and less vulnerable to judicial review by applying the Japanese style of negotiating with the major affected groups in an effort to obtain a consensus on the substance of new regulations. This process is known as *regulatory negotiations* or "reg. neg." Congress facilitated this process by adopting

Compliance Assistance *or* Back-Door Rulemaking?

The Department of Labor (DOL) came under criticism at the beginning of 2000 for engaging in "back-door rulemaking" by issuing opinion letters and guidance documents in order to bypass the rulemaking process under the APA. The DOL's agencies issue hundreds of letters each year responding to questions posed to the department. These opinion letters do not create law or change existing law, and they are not legally binding. They are issued to help members of the public understand the legal requirements that apply to them in specific circumstances. Critics argue, however, that only 8 percent of the letters issued by the DOL in 1999 included an explanation of their legal effect and that only 5 percent put this explanation at the beginning of the document. In contrast, the Department of Transportation provided this explanation in 40 percent of its documents.

When agencies issue opinion letters without clearly stating whether they are binding, the public may be confused as to their legal effect. Specific opinion letters that have been criticized include a letter from the DOL's Wage and Hour Division requiring employers to pay employees for time spent putting on and taking off protective clothing and equipment and a DOL advisory stating that profits from employee stock options must be included in regular rates of pay for purposes of overtime.[a] An OSHA letter stating that safety and health regulations apply to at-home work sites is discussed in greater detail in the "Inside Story" at the end of this chapter. Michael Baroody, a senior vice president of the National Association of Manufacturers and former assistant secretary of labor for policy during the Reagan administration, claimed that this problem of back-door rulemaking was widespread in the Clinton administration: "One has the sense that the administration, perhaps having gotten in its final year an intimation of its own mortality, is in a bit of a rush to make policy by administrative fiat where it has failed to do so by legislative means or by following the regulatory order." Solicitor of Labor Henry Solano rejected accusations that the agency was engaging in inappropriate rulemaking and justified issuance of the advisory letters as a means of providing compliance assistance.[b]

a. Congress subsequently enacted legislation to exclude profits from stock options from overtime calculations.
b. Deborah Billings & Ellen Byerrum, *House Oversight Panel Levels Criticism over DOL Opinion Letters on FMLA Coverage,* U.S.L.W., Feb. 2, 2000, at 2490.

amendments to the APA entitled Negotiated Rulemaking Procedure.[2]

CONDUCTING FORMAL ADJUDICATIONS

Courts do not have the time, money, or personnel to hear all cases that might arise in the course of regulating individual and corporate behavior. Consequently, legislatures frequently give administrative agencies the responsibility for solving specific types of legal disputes, such as who is entitled to government benefits or whether civil penalties should be imposed on regulated industries.

Formal agency adjudications are courtlike proceedings that can be presided over by one or more members of the agency or by an *administrative law judge.* The presiding official is entitled to administer oaths, issue subpoenas, rule on offers of proof and relevant evidence, authorize depositions, and decide the case at hand.

These formal adjudications typically include a prehearing discovery phase. The hearing itself is conducted like a trial. Each side presents its evidence under oath, and testimony is subject to cross-examination. The main difference between administrative adjudications and courtroom trials is that there is never a jury at the administrative level.

An administrative agency's decision in a formal adjudication can be appealed to a court. Agency actions setting rates for natural gas prices or providing licenses for dams are examples of the types of cases that regularly go to court. In most instances, judicial review of an agency action is based on the *record,* that is, the oral and written evidence presented at the administrative hearing. The court's review is limited to determining whether the administrative agency acted properly based on the evidence reflected in the record. In some cases, the laws governing the administrative adjudication provide for a *de novo* (i.e., new) proceeding in court, where the entire matter is litigated from the beginning.

TAKING INFORMAL DISCRETIONARY ACTIONS

The basic role of administrative agencies is to provide a practical decision-making process for repetitive, frequent

2. 5 U.S.C. § 561 *et seq.* (2000).

actions that are inappropriate to litigate in courts. These *informal discretionary actions* have been called the lifeblood of administrative agencies. Common examples are the awarding of governmental grants and loans, workers' compensation cases, the administration of welfare benefits, the informal resolution of tax disputes, and the determination of Social Security claims. Informal discretionary action also governs most applications to governmental agencies for licenses, leases, and permits, such as driver's licenses, leases of federal lands, and the registration of securities offerings.

Informal discretionary actions also include matters such as contracting, planning, and negotiation. Thus, the process of negotiating a contract with a governmental agency to supply military parts or to build bridges or highways is within the realm of administrative law. In fact, most of what governmental agencies do falls within the category of informal discretionary action.

The most noteworthy aspect of these informal actions is their lack of clear procedural rules. In court, there is a strict set of rules and procedures to be followed, and a specific person (the judge) is assigned to hear the case. In informal discretionary actions, the agency frequently has no formal procedures, such as notice to the public, opportunity to file briefs, or opportunity to submit oral testimony. Informal agency actions can lead to quick and practical problem resolution, but they can also lead to seemingly endless administrative paper shuffling.

CONDUCTING INVESTIGATIONS

Many administrative agencies have the responsibility to determine whether a regulated company or person is complying with the laws and regulations. They can use their subpoena power to make mandatory requests for information, conduct interviews, and perform searches. Based on these investigations, the agencies may file administrative suits seeking civil penalty assessments, or they may go to court and seek civil and criminal penalties.

Since 1970, governmental agencies have increasingly relied on their investigatory and prosecutorial powers. The indictment and conviction of arbitrageur Ivan Boesky and numerous other financial figures for insider trading resulted from administrative investigations and the exercise of administrative prosecutorial powers.

The investigatory powers possessed by administrative agencies can lead to fines ranging from thousands of dollars to hundreds of millions of dollars. For example, the Securities and Exchange Commission settled its three-year securities fraud investigation of junk-bond king Michael Milken in 1990 for $600 million.

 ETHICAL CONSIDERATION

The National Highway Traffic Safety Administration (NHTSA) estimates that 20 to 30 percent of fatal accidents are due to distractions.[a] According to the Network of Employers for Traffic Safety, distracted drivers cause at least 4,000, and perhaps as many as 8,000, accidents a day. Cellular phones and other computerized gadgets used by drivers are some of the distractions that are contributing to car accidents. According to the *New England Journal of Medicine,* a driver talking on a cell phone is approximately four times as likely to get into a crash as an undistracted driver—making talking on the phone as dangerous as driving while drunk.[b]

Between 1995 and 2000, thirty-seven states considered cracking down on cell-phone use; some cities, including New York City, have already imposed restrictions. Some foreign countries, including Italy and Japan, have imposed regulations, but most still allow drivers to use hands-free phones, even though studies indicate that the main source of distraction is the conversation rather than holding the phone.

A recent NHTSA survey found that 44 percent of drivers have cell phones in their cars. General Motors Corporation claims that 70 percent of wireless calls are made from cars. Thus, large numbers of consumers purchase cell phones to use in their cars.[c]

Should the companies that produce cellular phones and other computer gadgets warn consumers about the dangers associated with driving while talking on the phone or using other devices? Should they take other measures, such as designing safer phones? What are their obligations in light of the studies that indicate that use of cell phones by drivers is as dangerous as driving while drunk? Do car manufacturers have any ethical obligations here? Or should cell-phone companies and car manufacturers wait until the government adopts regulations addressing these safety concerns?

a. Nedra Pickler, *Transportation Officials Hear About Distracted Drivers,* Associated Press, July 18, 2000.
b. Jeffrey Ball, *New Road Hazard—Driving While Cell-Phoning—Gets Federal Scrutiny,* Wall St. J., July 14, 2000, at B1.
c. Ricardo Alonso-Zaldivar, *High-Tech Users Told Not to Be Driven to Distraction,* L.A. Times, July 19, 2000, at A-1.

 Administrative Agencies *and the* Constitution

Constitutional issues raised by the creation of administrative agencies concern separation of powers, proper delegation of authority, and the limits imposed on agency actions by the Bill of Rights.

SEPARATION OF POWERS

The U.S. Constitution provides for a legislature, an executive, and a judiciary. It does not specifically provide for administrative agencies, thus raising the question of whether the delegation of legislative and judicial powers to an administrative agency is constitutional.

The few cases addressing this issue have upheld the constitutionality of this "fourth branch" of government. In 1855, the U.S. Supreme Court upheld the authority of the Department of the Treasury to audit accounts for money owed to the United States by customs collectors and to issue a warrant for the money owed. The Court rejected the argument that only the courts of the United States were empowered to perform such activities.[3]

In 1935, in a case involving the Federal Trade Commission (FTC), the Supreme Court explained with approval that the FTC was an administrative body created by Congress to carry out legislative policies in accordance with a prescribed legislative standard and to act as a legislative or judicial aide by performing rulemaking and adjudicatory functions. It found no constitutional

3. Den ex dem. Murray v. Hoboken Land & Improvement Co., 59 U.S. 272 (1856).

violation in allowing an administrative agency to perform judicial and legislative functions. It did not, however, provide much explanation as to why this was permissible.[4] Justice Jackson subsequently stated:

> [Administrative bodies] have become a veritable fourth branch of the Government which has deranged our three-branch legal theories as much as the concept of a fourth dimension unsettles our three dimensional thinking. . . . Administrative agencies have been called quasi-legislative, quasi-executive and quasi-judicial, as the occasion required. . . . The mere retreat to the qualifying "quasi". . . is a smooth cover which we draw over our confusion as we might use a counterpane to conceal a disordered bed.[5]

In *INS v. Chadha,*[6] the Supreme Court struck down a statute that gave Congress the right to overturn a decision by the Immigration and Naturalization Service. The following case addressed the issue of whether the power exercised by an administrative law judge is a violation of the separation-of-powers doctrine.

4. Humphrey's Ex'r v. United States, 295 U.S. 602 (1935).
5. FTC v. Ruberoid Co., 343 U.S. 470, 487–88 (1952).
6. 462 U.S. 919 (1983).

A CASE IN POINT

CASE 6.2

Noriega-Perez v. United States

United States Court of Appeals for the Ninth Circuit 179 F.3d 1166 (9th Cir. 1999).

Summary

FACTS Noriega-Perez was indicted in the U.S. District Court for the Southern District of California for conspiracy to possess forged, counterfeit, and false immigration documents. He entered a plea of guilty and was fined. After his plea, the Immigration and Naturalization Service (INS) filed a complaint alleging that Noriega-Perez had violated the Immigration and Nationality Act (Act) by forging immigration documents and possessing fraudulent Social Security cards and INS forms. After a number of motions, the administrative law judge (ALJ) issued an order imposing a civil fine on Noriega-Perez. Noriega-Perez appealed.

ISSUE PRESENTED Does the imposition of a fine by an ALJ, rather than a judge appointed pursuant to Article III of the U.S. Constitution with lifetime tenure, violate the separation of powers?

SUMMARY OF OPINION The U.S. Court of Appeals for the Ninth Circuit began by noting that resolution of disputes by non-Article III judges, such as ALJs, raises serious concerns regarding our constitutionally established system of checks and balances. "A judiciary free from control by the Executive and the Legislature is essential if there is a right to have claims decided by judges who are free from potential domination by other branches of government."

Yet neither the Supreme Court nor Congress has read the Constitution as requiring every federal question arising under the federal law to be tried in an Article III court. Congress began authorizing adjudication by agencies in 1789, when it empowered the Comptroller within the Treasury Department to resolve all disputes concerning claims

(Continued)

(Case 6.2 continued)

against the Treasury. Since then, a line of Supreme Court cases has developed excepting certain actions from initial adjudication by an Article III body.

In *Commodity Futures Trading Comm'n v. Schor,*[7] the Supreme Court suggested that four nondeterminative factors be balanced in determining the constitutionality of congressional delegation of matters to a non-Article III format: (1) the extent to which the "essential attributes of judicial power" are reserved to Article III courts, (2) the extent to which the non-Article III forum exercises the range of jurisdiction and powers normally vested only in Article III courts, (3) the origins and importance of the right to be adjudicated, and (4) the concerns that drove Congress to depart from the requirements of Article III.

Analyzing these four factors, the appeals court found that (1) Article III courts retained an appearance and reality of control over the interpretation of federal law as the Act provided for appellate review and imposed a *de novo* standard of review on conclusions of law; (2) the Act provided ALJs with limited jurisdiction to impose a sanction, such as a civil fine; (3) the Act involves the public right to regulate immigration, which is one of the areas best established as suitable for adjudication by an administrative agency; and (4) efficiency is a valid concern that may drive Congress to depart from the requirements of Article III and is one of the primary reasons Congress grants adjudicatory functions to non-Article III judges.

RESULT The civil fine was upheld. The Act did not impermissibly delegate Article III judicial power to a non-Article III court.

COMMENTS In a dissent from the majority opinion, Judge Ferguson stated:

> The majority's final consideration under its Article III analysis shows how little it values the principles behind an independent judiciary. Somehow the majority concludes that the compelled adjudication of this matter before an ALJ does not pose the threat of giving adjudicatory authority to judges who are "potentially dominated by other branches of the government." The majority does not explain how an ALJ who is a part of the executive branch is not dominated by that very branch. Furthermore, there is no escaping the fact that the ALJ who is deciding the case necessarily has a conflict of interest because any fine levied by the ALJ will go to the branch of government controlling the ALJ. The scheme here is exactly the type of "domination" feared by the *Schor* Court.

7. 478 U.S. 833 (1986).

DELEGATION OF AUTHORITY

The delegation of authority issue concerns the nature and degree of direction the legislature must give to administrative agencies. In only two cases has the Supreme Court refused to uphold the delegation of power to administrative agencies. One case concerned delegation of power regarding shipments of oil between states in excess of government-set quotas.[8] The second case concerned the delegation of authority to the president to determine codes of fair competition for various trades and industries.[9] In both cases, the Supreme Court held that while Congress was free to allow agencies to make rules within prescribed limits, Congress itself must lay down the policies and establish the standards. Both before and after these two cases, however, the Supreme Court has upheld vague standards, such as those requiring rules to be set "in the public interest," "for the public convenience, interest or necessity," or "to prevent unfair methods of competition."

8. Panama Ref. Co. v. Ryan, 293 U.S. 388 (1935).

9. Schechter Poultry Corp. v. United States, 295 U.S. 495 (1935).

In the following case, the U.S. Supreme Court considered whether the Clean Air Act constituted an unconstitutional delegation of legislative power to the Environmental Protection Agency.

A CASE IN POINT

CASE 6.3

Whitman v. American Trucking Associations, Inc.

Supreme Court of the United States
121 S. Ct. 903 (2001).

Summary

FACTS Sections 108 and 109 of the Clean Air Act require the Environmental Protection Agency (EPA) to promulgate national ambient air quality standards (NAAQS) for a list of air pollutants identified by the agency. The EPA sets a "primary standard," a level necessary to protect the public health with an adequate margin of safety, and a "secondary standard," a level necessary to protect the public welfare. In July 1997, the EPA issued final rules revising the primary and secondary NAAQS for particulate matter and ozone.

The National Trucking Association and a number of small business practitioners filed petitions for review of the rules on a number of grounds including that the EPA had construed Sections 108 and 109 so loosely as to render them unconstitutional delegations of legislative power.

The U.S. Court of Appeals for the District of Columbia struck down the EPA's rules, commenting:

> Here it is as though Congress commanded EPA to select "big guys," and EPA announced that it would evaluate candidates based on height and weight, but revealed no cut-off point. The announcement, though sensible in what it does say, is fatally incomplete. The reasonable person responds, "How tall? How heavy?"

SUMMARY OF OPINION The U.S. Supreme Court reversed, holding that the scope of the discretion given the EPA to establish uniform national standards at a level that is "requisite to protect public health" from the adverse effects of the pollutant in the ambient air "is . . . well within the outer limits of our nondelegation precedents." It was not necessary for Congress to specify in the statute "a 'determinate criterion' for saying 'how much [of the regulated harm] is too much.'"

RESULT The Supreme Court reversed and upheld the delegation to the EPA.

LIMITS IMPOSED BY THE BILL OF RIGHTS

There is very little limit to the investigatory powers of administrative agencies. They must, of course, comply with constitutional principles protecting freedom from self-incrimination and from unreasonable search and seizure. Over the years, however, these principles have been severely eroded.

Self-Incrimination The Fifth Amendment's protection against self-incrimination does not apply to records that the government requires to be kept. Specifically, the Fifth Amendment protections do not apply to records that are regulatory in nature, are of a kind that the party has customarily kept, and have at least some public aspect to them. In addition, the Fifth Amendment's protection against self-incrimination does not apply to corporations.

Probable Cause In carrying out their investigatory power, administrative agencies are not required to have probable cause—that is, reason to suspect a violation—before beginning an investigation. The agencies may inquire into regulated behavior merely to satisfy themselves that the law is being upheld. For example, the Internal Revenue Service needs no specific cause to order an audit of a company's tax records.

Search and Seizure In the administrative arena, the courts have largely obliterated the protection of the Fourth Amendment against unreasonable searches and seizures. Particularly for industries such as liquor and firearms, which are highly regulated, government regulators can conduct full inspections of property and records almost without restriction.

Right to Jury Trial There is no constitutional right to a jury in a formal adjudication before an administrative agency.[10] The Seventh Amendment right to a jury trial extends only to cases for which a right to trial by jury existed in common law before the enactment of the Seventh Amendment. Because administrative agencies adjudicate statutory rights that were unknown at the time the Seventh Amendment was enacted, the Supreme Court has held that the right to a jury trial does not apply.

 Principles *of* Administrative Law

CHOICE OF APPROACH

Because, theoretically, an administrative agency can exercise legislative-type functions through its rulemaking authority and judicial-type functions through its adjudicatory authority, the question of how administrative agencies were to choose between the two processes quickly arose. There are competing considerations.

On the one hand, it is simple and efficient to set forth a general rule that applies to unknown parties in future activities. On the other hand, until the agency has had experience with the subject matter and has dealt with a number of individual cases, it may lack sufficient information to proceed with rulemaking.

In some cases, Congress will require the agency to enact a regulatory program and will provide a deadline for the issuance of final regulations. In the absence of congressional direction, administrative agencies have a fundamental right to decide whether to proceed on a case-by-case basis or by rule.[11] Such a right is necessary because an administrative agency cannot anticipate every problem it might encounter; problems could arise that are so specialized and varying in nature

as to be impossible to capture within the boundaries of a general rule.

AUTHORITY TO ACT

Administrative agencies resemble large corporations in size, structure, and, to some extent, function. Agencies provide benefits, sign contracts, and produce products. In the private arena, a person acting on behalf of an organization may bind the organization in accordance with both the person's actual authority and the person's apparent authority (concepts discussed in Chapter 5). Under the rules for government agencies, there is only actual authority.

In 1917, the Supreme Court held that the United States was not bound by acts of its officials who, on behalf of the government, entered into an agreement that was not permitted by law.[12] The Court rejected the argument that the neglect of duty by officers of the government was a defense to the suit by the United States to enforce a public right to protect a public interest. The Court has repeatedly upheld the fundamental principle that government employees acting beyond their authority cannot bind the government. The basic purpose of this rule is to prevent personal actions from circumventing Congress and the formal process of law. The negative effect of the rule, however, is to take away incentive for the government to make sure that its officials know the law and administer it properly.

The uninitiated naturally rely on the word of a government employee who explains the scope of his or her authority. This is a mistake. In fact, it is incumbent upon those dealing with governmental agencies to make sure that the person they are dealing with is authorized to act and that the proposed actions are permitted by law.

 Judicial Review *of* Agency Actions

If the courts control agency action with too heavy a hand, an agency can grind to a halt. If too little oversight is exercised, agencies can run roughshod over individual rights.

Congress or the appropriate state legislature sets the standards for judicial review of agency actions. Some agency actions are not reviewable because they are com-

10. *See* Wickmire v. Reinecke, 275 U.S. 101 (1927); NLRB v. Jones & Laughlin Steel Corp., 301 U.S. 1 (1937).
11. Securities & Exch. Comm'n v. Chenery Corp., 332 U.S. 194 (1947).
12. Utah Power Light Co. v. United States, 243 U.S. 389 (1917).

HISTORICAL PERSPECTIVE

From Revolutionary War Vets *to the* Environment

Administrative agencies date back to the country's earliest days. The first Congress established three administrative agencies, including one for the payment of benefits to Revolutionary War veterans. The Patent Office was created in 1790, and ten other federal administrative agencies were created before the Civil War.

At three critical junctures in U.S. history, Congress made extensive use of administrative agencies. During the Progressive Era, from 1885 until 1914, Congress turned to agencies such as the Interstate Commerce Commission, the

Federal Reserve Board, the Federal Trade Commission, and the Food and Drug Administration to solve problems concerning railroads and shipping, banks, trade, and food and drugs. In response to the stock market crash in 1929

and the subsequent Depression, Congress created many agencies to deal with the crisis and delegated broad authority to them. The Securities and Exchange Commission was given broad powers to regulate the offer and sale of securities, the brokerage industry, and the securities exchanges. Finally, during the dawn of the environmental era in the 1970s, Congress turned extensively to federal administrative agencies, especially the Environmental Protection Agency, to regulate health and restrict pollution.

---

mitted at the discretion of the agency. Most agency actions are reviewable by the courts, however, but the basic standard of review is highly deferential to the agency.

REVIEW OF RULEMAKING AND INFORMAL DISCRETIONARY ACTIONS

Courts will generally uphold an agency's action unless it is arbitrary and capricious. Under the *arbitrary and capricious standard,* if the agency chose from among several courses of action, the court will presume the validity of the chosen course unless it is shown to lack any rational basis.

In *Thorson v. Gemini,*[13] the U.S. Court of Appeals for the Eighth Circuit considered whether regulations enacted by the Department of Labor (DOL) properly construed the Family and Medical Leave Act (FMLA). Under the FMLA, an employee is entitled to twelve weeks of unpaid leave if he or she has a "serious health condition" that prevents the employee's return to work. By regulation, the DOL defined "serious health condition" as a period of incapacity requiring absence from work that exceeds three calendar days, during which the employee has continuing treatment by a health-care provider. The court upheld the DOL regulation, reasoning that although

it is possible that some absences from minor illnesses that Congress did not intend to be classified as 'serious health conditions' may qualify for FMLA protection . . . the DOL reasonably decided that such would be a legitimate trade-off for having a definition of 'serious health condition' that sets out an objective test that all employers can apply uniformly.[14]

In contrast, in *McGregor v. Autozone,*[15] the U.S. Court of Appeals for the Eleventh Circuit invalidated a DOL regulation that entitled an employee to an additional twelve weeks of leave if the employer failed to notify the employee that the twelve weeks of FMLA leave run concurrently with the thirteen weeks of employer-provided paid disability leave. The court ruled that DOL regulations may not grant entitlements that are beyond those of the statute and are inconsistent with the statute's purpose.

Courts will not defer to an agency action when Congress has not expressly delegated rulemaking authority to the agency. In the following case, the Supreme Court looked to the congressional history of regulating tobacco in order to determine whether the Food and Drug Administration had authority to regulate tobacco products.

---

13. 205 F.3d 370 (8th Cir. 2000).

14. *Id.* at 380.
15. 180 F.3d 1305 (11th Cir. 1999).

A CASE IN POINT

CASE 6.4

Food and Drug Administration v. Brown & Williamson Tobacco Corp.

Supreme Court of the United States
529 U.S. 120 (2000).

Summary

FACTS On August 28, 1996, the Food and Drug Administration (FDA) promulgated regulations entitled "Regulations Restricting the Sale and Distribution of Cigarettes and Smokeless Tobacco to Protect Children and Adolescents." The regulations targeted the promotion, labeling, and accessibility of tobacco products to children and adolescents. They prohibited the sale of cigarettes to persons younger than eighteen, required retailers to verify through photo identification the age of all purchasers younger than twenty-seven, and prohibited sales through self-service displays and vending machines except in adult-only locations. The regulations also prohibited advertising or distribution of promotional items such as T-shirts or hats within 1,000 feet of a playground or school. Finally, they required that the statement "A Nicotine-Delivery Device for Persons 18 or Older" appear on all tobacco product packages.

A group of tobacco manufacturers, retailers, and advertisers challenged the regulations on the grounds that the FDA lacked administrative authority to regulate tobacco products.

ISSUE PRESENTED Does the FDA have authority under the Food, Drug and Cosmetic Act (FDCA) to regulate tobacco products?

SUMMARY OF OPINION The Supreme Court began by acknowledging that its analysis was governed by *Chevron U.S.A., Inc. v. Natural Resources Defense Council, Inc.*[16] Under *Chevron,* a reviewing court must determine whether Congress has specifically addressed the question at issue. If so, the court "must give effect to the unambiguously expressed intent of Congress." However, if Congress has not specifically addressed the issue, the reviewing court must "respect the agency's construction of the statute so long as it is permissible."

The Court found that the FDCA was intended to exclude tobacco products from the FDA's jurisdiction. In enacting tobacco-specific legislation over the past thirty-five years, Congress acted against the backdrop of the FDA's consistent and repeated statements that it lacked authority under the FDCA to regulate tobacco absent claims of therapeutic benefit by the manufacturer. Indeed, even after the health consequences of tobacco use and nicotine's pharmacological effects had become well known, Congress considered and rejected bills that would have granted the FDA such jurisdiction.

The Court concluded:

[I]t is evident that Congress' tobacco-specific statutes have effectively ratified the FDA's long-held position that it lacks jurisdiction under the FDCA to regulate tobacco products.

. . .

Owing to its unique place in American history and society, tobacco has its own unique political history. Congress, for better or for worse, has created a distinct regulatory scheme for tobacco products . . . .

RESULT The U.S. Supreme Court struck down the FDA regulations on tobacco.

16. 467 U.S. 837 (1984).

REVIEW OF FACTUAL FINDINGS

An agency's factual findings are determinations that can be made without reference to the relevant law or regulation. The arbitrary and capricious standard of judicial review is not applied to the agency's factual findings. Instead, courts use a *substantial evidence standard* to review factual findings in formal adjudications. Under this standard, courts determine whether the evidence in the record could reasonably support the agency's conclusion.[17] Courts will defer to an agency's reasonable factual determinations, even if the record would support other factual conclusions. This standard of review is similar to an appellate court's review of jury verdicts in trial courts. Courts acknowledge that the agency's fact finder is generally in a better position to judge the credibility of witnesses and to evaluate evidence, especially if the evidence is highly technical or scientific.

In the following case, the Supreme Court considered whether the findings of the Patent and Trademark Office should be reviewed under the clearly erroneous standard used by an appellate court reviewing findings of fact by a trial judge or under the more deferential review standard set forth in the Administrative Procedure Act.

---

17. Consolidated Edison Co. v. NLRB, 305 U.S. 197 (1938).

A CASE IN POINT

CASE 6.5
Dickinson v. Zurko
*Supreme Court of the
United States
527 U.S. 150 (1999).*

Summary

FACTS Zurko applied for a patent on a method for increasing computer security. The Patent and Trademark Office (PTO) examiner denied the application after concluding that the method was obvious in light of prior art. The PTO's review board upheld the examiner's decision, and Zurko sought review in the U.S. Court of Appeals for the Federal Circuit. The appeals court treated the PTO's conclusion as a factual finding and ruled that it was "clearly erroneous." The Commissioner of Patents appealed.

ISSUE PRESENTED Are the PTO's factual findings subject to the clearly erroneous standard of review or the less stringent standard set forth in the APA?

SUMMARY OF OPINION The parties agreed that the PTO was an agency subject to the Administrative Procedure Act. As a result, the APA's less stringent review standard applied in the absence of an applicable exception. Section 559 of the APA provides that the APA does not limit or repeal additional requirements recognized by law. According to the Federal Circuit, at the time of the APA's adoption, the Court of Customs and Patent Appeals (a predecessor to the Federal Circuit) applied the clearly erroneous standard, thereby creating an "additional requirement" that under Section 559 trumps the requirements imposed by another section of the APA.

Recognizing the importance of maintaining a uniform approach to judicial review of administrative action, the Supreme Court stated that the existence of a grandfathered common law variation must be clear. After examining the eighty-nine cases that, according to Zurko, embodied the pre-APA standard of review, the Court concluded that those cases did not reflect a well-established stricter standard of judicial review for PTO fact-finding.

RESULT The Supreme Court held that the standard of review under the APA was the appropriate standard and reversed the judgment of the Federal Circuit.

COMMENTS Although the Court ruled that PTO findings of fact are reviewable under the APA rather than under the clearly erroneous standard, the Court failed to specify which APA standard applied—the arbitrary and capricious test (applied to agency rulemaking) or the substantial evidence test (used for findings of fact). The Federal Circuit subsequently addressed this issue in *In re Gartside*[18] and held that PTO findings of fact are reviewable under the APA's substantial evidence standard. The substantial evidence test, which is less deferential than the arbitrary and capricious test, asks "whether a reasonable fact finder could have arrived at the agency's decision."

---

18. 203 F.3d 1305 (Fed. Cir. 2000).

REVIEW OF STATUTORY INTERPRETATIONS

Courts will generally defer to an agency's *construction* (i.e., interpretation) of a statute within its area of expertise. This permits those with relevant practical experience to have the greatest influence in deciding how to implement a particular law. Although the Supreme Court's position on this issue has varied somewhat, its most recent cases have reinforced the rule of deference to administrative interpretation of law.

REVIEW OF PROCEDURES

For a number of years, the courts have endeavored to bring greater fairness to the administrative process. Some courts began to require agencies to follow procedures not specified by statutes or required by the Due Process Clause of the Fifth Amendment. This occurred most frequently in the rulemaking area, where rulemaking proceedings were often challenged as being fundamentally unfair and in need of greater public participation. These challenges were most often made by public interest groups battling large corporations with entrenched positions of influence with the agency.

In 1978, in a case involving a challenge by an environmental advocacy group to the licensing of a nuclear power plant, the Supreme Court held that the courts may not impose additional procedural requirements on agencies.[19] In the absence of extremely compelling circumstances, administrative agencies are free to fashion their own rules of procedure and to pursue their own methods of inquiry to discharge their broad and varied duties. A court is not free to impose on an agency its view as to what procedures the agency must follow; the court may only require the agency to comply with its own procedural rules and to conform to the requirements of the Due Process Clause.

19. Vermont Yankee Nuclear Power Corp. v. Natural Resources Defense Council, Inc., 435 U.S. 519 (1978).

"I'm sorry, sir, but F.A.A. rules forbid the wearing of Hawaiian shirts in the Business Class section."

From the *Wall Street Journal*. Reprinted by permission of Charles Almon. All Rights Reserved.

The reason for these highly deferential review standards is evident: the role of administrative agencies is to relieve the burden on the courts by having the agencies make their own adjudications. If the courts were to engage in searching inquiry on all factual questions and to exercise their own judgment on policy or procedural issues, the function of administrative agencies would be greatly diminished.

STANDING TO SUE

The Supreme Court has also significantly restricted standing to sue to obtain judicial review of federal agency action. In the following case, the Court held that members of an environmental organization could not challenge a federal action arguably violating the Endangered Species Act unless they could show a certain personal connection with the species affected.

A CASE IN POINT

CASE 6.6
Lujan v. Defenders of Wildlife
Supreme Court of the United States
504 U.S. 555 (1992).

In the Language of the Court

FACTS Section 7 of the Endangered Species Act of 1973 (ESA) is intended to protect species of animals against threats to their continuing existence caused by humans. The ESA instructs the secretary of the interior to promulgate a list of those endangered or threatened species and requires each federal agency, in consultation with the secretary of the interior, to ensure that any action authorized, funded, or carried out by such agency is not likely to jeopardize the continued existence of any endangered or threatened species.

(Continued)

(Case 6.6 continued)

In 1978, the Fish and Wildlife Service (FWS) and the National Marine Fisheries Service (NMFS), on behalf of the secretary of the interior and the secretary of commerce, respectively, promulgated a joint regulation stating that the obligations imposed by Section 7(a)(2) extend to actions taken in foreign nations. Thereafter, the Department of the Interior reinterpreted the section to require consultation only for actions taken in the United States or on the high seas.

Shortly thereafter, organizations dedicated to wildlife conservation and other environmental causes sued Manuel Lujan, the secretary of the interior, and sought an injunction requiring the secretary to promulgate a new regulation restoring the initial interpretation of the geographic scope. They claimed that U.S.-funded projects in Egypt and Sri Lanka would significantly reduce endangered and threatened species in these areas. Two members of the Defenders of Wildlife, Joyce Kelly and Amy Skilbred, submitted affidavits that they had traveled to foreign countries to observe endangered species (the endangered Nile crocodile in Egypt and the endangered Asian elephant and leopard in Sri Lanka) and that they planned to do so in the future.

The federal district court dismissed the case for lack of standing, and the court of appeals reversed. The secretary of the interior appealed.

OPINION SCALIA, J., writing for the U.S. Supreme Court:

Over the years, our cases have established that the irreducible constitutional minimum of *standing* contains three elements: First, the plaintiff must have suffered an "injury in fact"—an invasion of a legally protected interest which is (a) concrete and particularized, and (b) "actual or imminent, not 'conjectural' or 'hypothetical.'" Second, there must be a causal connection between the injury and the conduct complained of—the injury has to be "fairly . . . trace[able] to the challenged action of the defendant, and not . . . th[e] result [of] the independent action of some third party not before the court." Third, it must be "likely," as opposed to merely "speculative," that the injury will be "redressed by a favorable decision."

. . .

"[T]he 'injury in fact' test requires more than an injury to a cognizable interest. It requires that the party seeking review be himself among the injured." . . .

. . .

[The affidavits submitted by Kelly and Skilbred] plainly contain no facts . . . showing how damage to the species will produce "imminent" injury to Mss. Kelly and Skilbred. That the women "had visited" the areas of the projects before the projects commenced proves nothing. . . . And the [women's] profession of an "inten[t]" to return to the places they had visited before—where they will presumably, this time, be deprived of the opportunity to observe animals of the endangered species—is simply not enough.

. . .

. . . To say that the Act protects ecosystems is not to say that the Act creates (if it were possible) rights of action in persons who have not been injured in fact, that is, persons who use portions of an ecosystem not perceptibly affected by the unlawful action in question.

Respondents' other theories are called, alas, the "animal nexus" approach, whereby anyone who has an interest in studying or seeing the endangered animals anywhere on the globe has standing; and the "vocational nexus" approach, under which anyone with a professional interest in such animals can sue. Under these theories, anyone who

(Continued)

(Case 6.6 continued)

goes to see Asian elephants in the Bronx Zoo, and anyone who is a keeper of Asian elephants in the Bronx Zoo, has standing to sue. . . . This is beyond all reason.

RESULT The Supreme Court reversed the appeals court's ruling and held that the plaintiffs did not assert sufficiently imminent injury to have standing. Their claimed injury was not redressable.

QUESTIONS

1. Who, if anyone, would have standing to challenge the Department of the Interior's regulations?
2. In *Bennett v. Spear,*[20] the Supreme Court held that ranchers and irrigation districts that would be directly affected economically by a Fish and Wildlife finding that a waste-reclamation project might harm two endangered species of fish and its recommendation that minimum levels be maintained in certain reservoirs had standing to challenge the finding. Why did they have standing when Mss. Kelly and Skilbred did not?

20. 520 U.S. 154 (1997).

 # Limits *of* Review

NO RIGHT TO PROBE THE MENTAL PROCESSES OF THE AGENCY

One of the most critical points of administrative law concerns the extent to which a court can inquire into the process by which an administrative agency makes its decision. This issue was one of the first decided in the administrative law area. It was resolved in a case involving a decision of the secretary of agriculture that made news headlines at the end of the New Deal era.[21]

The Packers and Stockyards Act authorized the secretary of agriculture to determine reasonable rates for services rendered by cattle-marketing agencies. The marketing agencies of the Kansas Stockyards challenged the ultimate price set as too low. The federal district court had allowed the marketing agents to require the secretary to appear in person at the trial. He was questioned at length regarding the process by which he had reached his decision about the rates. The interrogation included questions as to what documents had been studied and the nature of consultations with his subordinates. The Supreme Court held that it was improper to permit this questioning relating to the mental processes of the secretary.

Today, formal federal review procedures limit judicial review of agency actions to the record compiled before

the agency. Thus, once an administrative process is complete, there is generally no judicial opportunity to inquire into the whys and wherefores of the decision-making process. Without this shield from judicial review, agency actions would be tied up in court and would lose their efficacy.

Nevertheless, the system of checks and balances is maintained in this area. Although a court may not inquire into the decision-making process, the legislature may. Congress regularly holds oversight hearings on how agencies are administering the law. Criticism from a key member of Congress or a congressional committee can lead to newspaper headlines and changed agency policies. Congress can also use the appropriation process to withhold funds from disfavored programs and to fund favored ones.

TIMING OF REVIEW

Two judicial doctrines are intended to prevent premature transfer of cases from the administrative arena to the courts: the doctrines of exhaustion of administrative remedies and of ripeness.

Exhaustion *Exhaustion of administrative remedies* concerns the timing and substance of the administrative review process. The general rule is that a court will not entertain an appeal to review the administrative process until the agency has had the chance to act and all possible avenues of relief before the agency have been fully

21. United States v. Morgan, 313 U.S. 409 (1941).

pursued. The purpose is to conserve judicial resources. However, a party is not required to exhaust all administrative avenues when that would be futile.

In *Harline v. Drug Enforcement Administration*,[22] the U.S. Court of Appeals for the Tenth Circuit considered when the exhaustion of remedies requirement may properly be waived. Harline brought suit in federal district court before satisfying the exhaustion of remedies requirement. Because he believed that the Drug Enforcement Administration's (DEA's) use of an administrative law judge employed by the DEA violated his procedural due process rights to a fair and impartial tribunal, Harline argued that the exhaustion requirement should be waived. The court stated that exhaustion is waivable either by the agency or at the court's discretion where the plaintiff's interest in prompt resolution is so great that it renders the doctrine of exhaustion inappropriate. This occurs when (1) the plaintiff asserts a colorable constitutional claim collateral to the substantive issues of the administrative law proceeding, (2) exhaustion would result in irreparable harm, and (3) exhaustion would be futile. The court concluded that Harline's general claims of due process violations were insufficient to justify waiver of the exhaustion requirement.

In reviewing an administrative agency's action, courts typically will not rule on issues that a party has failed to raise with the agency. In *Sims v. Apfel*,[23] however, the Supreme Court held that a party pursuing judicial review of denial of benefits by the Social Security Administration had not waived issues she failed to raise in administrative proceedings. Juatassa Sims had applied for disability and supplemental security income benefits under the Social Security Act. An administrative law judge denied her claim, and the Social Security Appeals Council denied her request for a review of that decision. Sims filed suit in district court contending that the ALJ (1) made selective use of the record, (2) posed defective questions to a vocational expert, and (3) should have ordered a consultative examination. The district court rejected all of these arguments. The appeals court affirmed but held that it could not consider the second and third contentions because Sims had not raised them in her request for review by the Appeals Council.

The Supreme Court reversed on the grounds that the reasons for requiring issue exhaustion were not present in Social Security proceeding. Although many administrative proceedings are adversarial, Social Security proceedings are primarily inquisitorial with the ALJ having the duty to investigate the facts and develop the arguments both for and against granting benefits. As a result, the Court ruled, the adversarial development of issues by the parties was not essential. Therefore, a party who exhausted administrative remedies available from the Social Security Appeals Council need not also exhaust issues in order to preserve judicial review of them.

Ripeness The *ripeness* doctrine helps ensure that courts are not forced to decide hypothetical questions. Courts will not hear cases until they are "ripe" for decision. The issue of ripeness most frequently arises in pre-enforcement review of statutes and ordinances; this occurs when review is sought after a rule is adopted but before the agency seeks to apply the rule in a particular case. The general rule is that agency action is ripe for judicial review when the impact of the action is sufficiently direct and immediate as to make review appropriate.[24]

 # Decision-Making Power *of* Agencies

There are a number of doctrines that limit administrative agencies' decision-making powers.

ONLY DELEGATED POWERS

The general rule is that an administrative agency may do only what Congress or the state legislature has authorized it to do. Agency action contrary to or in excess of its delegated authority is void.

The Iran-Contra controversy, to some extent, involved the question of whether Colonel Oliver North, a government official, exceeded the authority delegated to the National Security Agency (NSA) or contravened a congressional enactment. Congress had placed limits on the ability of specified government agencies to raise funds to supply rebels seeking to overthrow the government of Nicaragua. For many years, the NSA and the Central Intelligence Agency—two administrative agencies in the national security area—had been authorized to aid the rebels. When Congress withdrew this authority, North's alleged transgression was to continue providing such aid without proper authority. The drama of the North case is repeated daily on a smaller scale as administrative agencies seek to determine the scope of their authority to act.

22. 148 F.3d 1199 (10th Cir. 1998), *cert. denied,* 525 U.S. 1068 (1999).
23. 120 S. Ct. 2080 (2000).

24. *See* Abbott Lab. v. Gardner, 387 U.S. 136 (1967) (pre-enforcement review of FDA generic drug-labeling rule was appropriate because the issue was purely legal, the regulations represented final agency action, and the impact of the rules was direct and immediate).

OBLIGATION TO FOLLOW OWN RULES

Not only are agencies required to act within the authority delegated to them, but they are also required to follow their own rules and regulations. When an administrative agency adopts a regulation, it becomes binding on the public. It also binds the agency. For example, in *Service v. Dulles,*[25] the Supreme Court held that a State Department employee could not be discharged without being provided reasons because that would be contrary to the agency's regulations regarding discharges under the State Department's Loyalty Security Program.

At the federal level, one of the most prominent procedural obligations is the requirement to prepare an environmental impact statement before a major federal action can be approved. The National Environmental Policy Act (NEPA), passed in 1969, dramatically changed the way all federal agencies conduct their business.

Before 1969, an agency could focus exclusively on its substantive legal obligations (the legal rules that define the rights and duties of the agency and of persons dealing with it) and on its own duly adopted procedural obligations (the rules that define the manner in which these rights and duties are enforced). With NEPA's passage, each federal agency assumed a new procedural obligation to consider the environmental impacts of its proposed actions and the alternatives to those impacts. Each of the hundreds of thousands of federal agency actions must comply with NEPA. As a result, each agency attempts to document its compliance as a routine part of its procedures. The agencies have not found it easy to meet these procedural requirements. Hundreds of cases have invalidated agency actions as a result of the failure to meet this obligation.

EXPLANATION OF DECISIONS

As discussed earlier in this chapter, courts will not inquire into the mental processes of the decision maker. The corollary to this principle is that an agency must explain the basis for its decisions and must show that it has taken into account all relevant considerations as required by the statute. If an agency makes a decision and fails to provide an adequate explanation of why it acted, the courts will invalidate the agency's action.[26] In some instances, however, the court may permit the agency to explain deficiencies in the record and to add supplementary explanations of why it acted. The judiciary's insistence that an agency make a reasoned decision, supported by an explanation of why it acted, is a major restraint on improper agency action.

Finding *an* Agency's Rules *and* Procedures

In addition to rules and regulations set forth in officially published documents such as the *Federal Register* and the *Code of Federal Regulations,* federal agencies maintain internal guidance documents. For example, the U.S. Forest Service controls millions of acres of timber lands. Its formal rules are sparse, but it publishes a manual and a handbook that contain thousands of pages of guidance on such topics as how to conduct timber sales. The Forest Service's manual and handbook are not generally available and may be difficult to find, but they are an important source of law, agency practice, and policy. Reports of court cases provide equivalent information. Cases decided by agency adjudication usually are not reported.

Finding the rules is just a small part of the difficult task of complying with administrative rules and regulations. A small business typically must comply with more than two dozen regulatory procedures at the local, state, and federal levels in order to open.[27] This task is made even more difficult by the fact that relatively few places provide help to a small business trying to figure out the many regulations with which it must comply. Although the Small Business Administration, neighborhood economic development organizations, and banks may provide some guidance, few private small-business consultants specialize in the regulatory aspect of opening a business.

Obtaining Documents *from an* Agency

In court proceedings and formal agency adjudications, documents may be obtained by discovery. In other situations, individuals are entitled to obtain copies of government records pursuant to federal and state statutes. The federal statute authorizing this procedure is the Freedom of Information Act (FOIA).[28] Under FOIA, any citizen may request records of the government on any subject of interest. Unlike discovery, a FOIA request

25. 354 U.S. 363 (1957).
26. *See, e.g.,* Motor Vehicle Mfr. Ass'n v. State Farm Mut. Auto. Ins. Co., 463 U.S. 29 (1983).
27. Kenneth Howe, *Maze of Regulations,* San Francisco Chron., Oct. 29, 1997, at D1.
28. 5 U.S.C. § 552 (2000).

INTERNATIONAL CONSIDERATION

The development of the telecommunications and information technology industries has contributed substantially to economic growth, competitiveness, and job creation in Europe. Twenty-five percent of new jobs created in Europe are in Information Age industries. Due to their increasing importance to the European economy, in 2000 the European Commission was in the process of transforming its regulation of these industries. On December 3, 1997, the European Commission published the Green Paper on the Convergence of the Telecommunications, Media and Information Technology Sectors, and the Implications for Regulation Towards an Information Society Approach. The Green Paper discussed policy issues arising from the convergence of telecommunications, broadcast, and information technology. One of the issues was whether the current telecommunications regulatory scheme should be amended to create a new system covering both traditional telecommunications services and the new interactive information services.

The European Commission sought public comment on the Green Paper in two stages.[a] The first stage of public consultation, carried out from December 1997 to May 1998, was summarized in a Commission Working Document adopted in July 1998. Its main conclusion was that the convergence of technological platforms and network infrastructures was already a reality and that similar regulatory conditions should apply to all such infrastructures regardless of the types of services carried over them. The Commission Working Document launched the second stage of public consultation, from July to November 1998, by posting questions about three key areas: access to networks and gateway facilities; investment, innovation, and content production; and balancing regulation between public interest and competition considerations. More than eighty organizations responded.

On March 10, 1999, the European Commission adopted a Communication reporting on the results of the public consultation on the Green Paper.[b] The key message emerging from the consultation was that regulation needs to be transparent, clear, and proportional, which implies a more horizontal approach to regulation with a homogeneous treatment of all transport network infrastructures irrespective of the nature of the services carried. The Commission indicated that it intended to propose reforms in the regulation of infrastructure and associated services by the end of 1999 as part of the regulatory review.

On November 10, 1999, the Commission launched a review of the regulatory framework for electronic communications by adopting four Communications, including the Communication on a New Framework for Electronic Communications Infrastructure and Associated Services and the Communication Review.[c] The Commission stated that "[t]his process will be the cornerstone for maintaining and improving Europe's competitive position in the Information Society." The commissioner for the information society stated: "We should not rest on our laurels—more competition is still needed in particular at the local level where incumbent operators remain dominant. Only this way will we be able to grasp the full benefits of the development of the Internet in Europe." The Commission received more than 200 comments in response to the Communication Review.

On April 4, 2000, the Commission adopted a Communication setting out the results of its public consultation on the 1999 Communication Review. The key proposals include facilitating market entry by simplifying licensing conditions; rolling back regulations; giving national regulators greater flexibility to impose access and interconnection obligations according to national circumstances, balanced by strong coordination procedures at the European level to safeguard the single market; and ensuring that consumers are properly protected.[d] On May 10–11, the Commission held a public hearing on the new regulatory framework for electronic communications networks and services and indicated that it planned to issue legislative proposals by June. The Lisbon European Council called for these proposals to be adopted as soon as possible in 2001. Earlier, in April 2000, European leaders meeting at the council discussed the shift to a digital knowledge–based economy as a motor for growth, competitiveness, and employment.

a. European Commission's Web Site (visited May 23, 2000) <http://www.ispo.cec.be/convergencegp>.

b. European Commission Press Release, *Europe: Results of Consultation on Convergence in Media and Telecom Made Public*, BBC Worldwide Monitoring, Mar. 15, 1999.

c. European Commission Press Release, *The Commission Launches a Comprehensive Review of the Regulatory Framework for Electronic Communications*, Nov. 10, 1999, posted on the European Commission Web site at <http://www.ipso.cec.be/infosoc/telecompolicy/ press>.

d. European Commission Press Release, *Commission Outlines Results of Public Consultation on 1999 Telecom Review and Unveils Orientation of Forthcoming Proposals for New Regulatory Framework*, Apr. 26, 2000, posted on the European Commission Web site at <http:// www.ipso.cec.be/infosoc/telecompolicy/press>.

need not show the relevance of the documents to any particular legal proceeding or that the requester has any specific interest in the documents. It is sufficient that the requester seeks the documents.

In theory, FOIA provides an easy way to obtain documents from a government agency. The agency is required to respond to a document request within ten days. In practice, months, weeks, or even years may pass before the government responds to an FOIA request. Moreover, requesters are required to pay the cost of locating and copying the records. However, these costs are waived for public interest groups, newspaper reporters, and certain other requesters.

Not all documents in the government's possession are available for public inspection. FOIA exempts:

1. Records required by an executive order to be kept secret in the interest of national defense or foreign policy
2. Records related solely to the internal personnel rules and practice of an agency
3. Records exempted from disclosure by another statute
4. Trade secrets or confidential commercial and financial information
5. Interagency memorandums or decisions that reflect the deliberative process
6. Personnel files and other files that, if disclosed, would constitute a clearly unwarranted invasion of personal privacy
7. Information compiled for law enforcement purposes
8. Reports prepared on behalf of an agency responsible for the regulation of financial institutions
9. Geological information concerning wells

The government is not required to withhold information under any of these exemptions. It may do so or not at its discretion.

Frequently, regulated companies are required to submit confidential information to the government. From the perspective of a company submitting such information, FOIA presents a danger of disclosure to competitors. To protect information from disclosure, the company should mark each document as privileged and confidential so that government officials reviewing FOIA requests will not inadvertently disclose it.

From the perspective of those doing business with the government, FOIA provides an excellent opportunity to learn who is communicating with the agency and what the agency is thinking about a particular matter. FOIA can also be useful in obtaining government studies and learning generally about government activities.

Each federal agency has its own set of regulations relating to FOIA requests. These regulations must be complied with strictly, or consideration of the request may be greatly delayed.

IN BRIEF

Seven Basic Steps for Working Successfully with an Administrative Agency

STEP 1
Investigate the applicable standards that will govern the agency's actions.

STEP 2
Identify and evaluate the agency's formal structure.

STEP 3
Determine what facts are before the agency.

STEP 4
Identify the interests of others who may be involved in the decision-making process.

STEP 5
Adopt a strategy to achieve the desired goal.

STEP 6
Eliminate any adverse impacts on other interested parties.

STEP 7
Get involved in the administrative process early and stay involved.

THE RESPONSIBLE MANAGER
Working *with* Administrative Agencies

Administrative agencies are intended to be practical problem-solving entities. It is therefore easier for a non-lawyer to work with an administrative agency than to represent himself or herself in court. Most simple administrative matters do not require an attorney, but one may be necessary to handle more complicated matters. Seven basic recommendations for working successfully with an administrative agency are summarized in the "In Brief."

As recommended in Step 1, a manager working with an agency should first investigate the basic legal standards that will govern the agency's actions in the matter at hand. These include the agency's laws, regulations, and internal manuals and procedures. It is also important to investigate how the agency's administration of its laws and regulations is affected by its past history and by current political influences. Agencies, like any other bureaucracy, tend to have biases in how they carry out the applicable laws and regulations.

These investigations are important for three reasons. First, a manager needs to know what facts must be presented in order to prevail in a claim. Second, it is possible that the agency personnel may not know the applicable legal standard. Many administrative agencies have little access to legal advice and find it helpful to have a clear presentation of the law under which a person is proceeding. Third, it is important to know the law at the outset of an administrative proceeding because, under the doctrine of exhaustion of administrative remedies, issues not raised before the agency are generally deemed to be waived if the matter is later brought before a court.

The second step is for the manager to learn how the agency operates by identifying and evaluating its formal structure. Administrative agencies can have complicated structures. Because the power to make decisions may be vested in more than one official, it is important to know all of the decision maker's options before proceeding. A person can start at the top, the middle, or the bottom. The important point is to start at the right place. Finding out where that is takes some effort.

Next, the manager needs to determine what facts the agency already has (Step 3). In a judicial proceeding, the parties create the record by filing documents with the court. All parties have access to those documents and share the same factual record. The same is not true in an administrative agency proceeding. The factual record may be scattered about the agency in different files and offices. To function effectively before the agency, a manager must identify and locate this record.

Step 4 recommends that the manager identify the interests of other agencies or parties who may be involved in the decision-making process. In a court proceeding, all the parties to a case are known; in an administrative matter, the parties may not be designated formally. It helps to identify the people concerned at the outset and to determine how the proposed action will affect them.

Upon completing this background information, the manager should adopt a strategy to achieve the desired goal (Step 5). Investigation of an administrative matter could show that the agency lacks the authority to do what is proposed. In that case, the manager must persuade the agency to adopt new rules or go to the legislature to have new laws adopted. The most significant task, however, is to decide whether additional factual information should be gathered and presented to the agency. The record before the agency will normally be the record in court. The use of experts during the administrative process and the submission of key documents are important.

In reviewing a proposed action, the manager may find that the action would have undesirable impacts on other interested parties (Step 6). Elimination of those impacts is an effective way to avoid costly disputes.

Finally, as recommended in Step 7, the manager needs to participate in the administrative process at the earliest possible time and to continue participating throughout the proceedings. Once set in motion, agencies tend to stay in motion unless they are deflected by an outside force. The greater the momentum that has gathered, the harder it is to move the agency off the path it is pursuing. Therefore, it is important to participate early in the process in an effort to influence the agency before it makes up its mind rather than after.

OSHA Regulation *of* Home Offices

On November 15, 1999, the Occupational Safety and Health Administration (OSHA) posted a Letter of Interpretation (LI) on its Web site stating that employers that allow employees to work at home are responsible for federal health and safety violations that occur at the employee's home. The LI was posted in response to a request from CSC Credit Services, a unit of Computer Sciences Corporation, which sought advice from OSHA on setting up homes offices for ten workers in order to calculate its potential liability for OSHA violations in these home offices.[29] The LI indicated that ensuring safe and healthful working conditions for the employee should be a precondition for any home-based work assignments and further stated that "the employer is responsible for correcting hazards of which it is aware, or should be aware."[30] OSHA indicated that it would charge and fine employers who failed to provide safe workplaces for their employees who work at home.

OSHA stated that it did not intend to conduct inspections at private homes in the same way that it inspects employer work sites; nor would it require employers to inspect home work sites on a routine basis. OSHA would, however, hold employers responsible for any illnesses or injuries that occurred at home work sites. Although the LI did not set forth specifics, under OSHA regulations, an employer is normally responsible for making sure that offices have ergonomically correct furniture, proper lighting, and heating, cooling, and ventilation systems. In addition, the home work space must also have emergency medical plans and a first-aid kit.[31]

The LI had the potential of affecting a large number of employees. Nearly 20 million workers, a tenth of the workforce, regularly work from home. Millions more occasionally work at home for a variety of reasons, such as to tend a sick child or to finish work in the evening.

Business groups and lawmakers expressed strong disapproval of the LI. They claimed that making employers liable for home work sites would not only impose large costs on the employers, but would also prompt them to conduct home inspections, a possible violation of privacy. Critics argued that OSHA's position could result in companies refusing to allow their employees to work at home. In response to the harsh and widespread criticism, the secretary of labor, Alexis M. Herman, formally withdrew the LI because it had "caused widespread confusion and unintended consequences for others."[32] Stating that the letter was meant only to provide guidance for CSC Credit and was not intended as a broad new policy for all employers, Herman observed that the LI had raised an important issue and indicated that she planned to host a series of meetings to discuss the issue with business and labor groups.

On January 25, 2000, the Department of Labor (DOL) released a letter to the House Subcommittee on Employment, Safety, and Training clarifying its position on home work sites.[33] Specifically, the DOL stated that nothing in OSHA law excludes home work sites from regulations and that OSHA will hold employers responsible for work activities that involve hazardous materials and equipment or processes used in an employee's home. The DOL went on to state that "OSHA will not hold employers liable for work activities in employees' home offices; OSHA does not expect employers to inspect home offices; OSHA does not, and will not, inspect home offices."[34]

The incident prompted the DOL to investigate OSHA's procedures for issuing LIs. A report of that investigation revealed that no written OSHA procedures govern preparation of LIs, that OSHA's policies concerning the use of LIs are inconsistent and conflicting, and that no rules exist to guide OSHA staff in providing LIs as a means of interpreting the Occupational Safety and Health Act. In the case of the home office LI, no one involved in clearing the letter was charged with evaluating its policy ramifications, and not all documents and comments relevant to the LI were shared among OSHA employees responsible for clearing it for public release.[35] The report also set forth a

29. Sarah Lueck, *Business Groups Attack OSHA Advisory—Labor Secretary Retreats on Wide Interpretation of Home Work Safety*, WALL ST. J., Jan. 5, 2000, at A3.

30. *Firms Liable for Home Work Sites, U.S. Says*, L.A. TIMES, Jan. 4, 2000, at A-1.

31. *Id.*

32. Sarah Lueck, *Home Work-Safety Letter Is Rescinded—Industry, Lawmakers Force OSHA's About-Face; Herman Asks for Talks*, WALL ST. J., Jan. 6, 2000, at A2.

33. Bill Roberts, *About Face (Government Activity)*, ELECTRONIC BUS., Mar. 1, 2000, at 46.

34. *Id.*

35. *Sen. Bond: Faulty Process, Failed Supervision at OSHA Root of Home Office Inspection Fiasco*, U.S. NEWSWIRE, May 10, 2000.

number of recommended reforms. Senator Bond, chair of the Senate Committee on Small Business, and Senator Collins, chair of the Permanent Subcommittee on Investigations, urged the DOL to implement the report's recommendations as soon as possible. Bond commented that "[t]his report paints a picture of an agency completely adrift in its mission to help employers understand their responsibilities to comply with regulations."[36]

36. *Id.*

Despite the public outcry over this incident, there is no evidence of a major problem concerning safe working conditions for at-home workers. OSHA has never received a safety complaint from employees working at home, and few lawsuits have been filed over the issue.[37]

37. Sarah Lueck, *Home Workers Didn't File Any OSHA Protests,* WALL ST. J., Jan. 1, 2000, at A6.

KEY WORDS AND PHRASES

administrative law judge 171
arbitrary and capricious standard 177
codified 169
construction 180
de novo 171

exhaustion of administrative remedies 182
informal discretionary actions 172
record 171
regulatory negotiations (reg. neg.) 170

ripeness 183
standing 181
substantial evidence standard 178

QUESTIONS AND CASE PROBLEMS

1. Why are administrative agencies called the fourth branch of the U.S. government?

2. A statute gives the Department of the Interior the power to allow or to curtail mining within the national forests "as the best interests of all users of the national forest shall dictate." Is this a valid delegation of legislative power to the agency, or is it too broad a delegation of power?

3. In January 1998, the Occupational Safety and Health Administration (OSHA) issued a new regulatory standard for respiratory protection in the workplace. This represented a comprehensive revision of the portions of the old standard concerning the manner and condition of respirator use. The old standard reflected a preference for engineering controls over respirators in controlling employees' exposure to hazardous materials in the air (Hierarchy-of-Controls Policy). Although there were a number of changes, the new standard retained the Hierarchy-of-Controls Policy. After OSHA published its proposed new regulatory standard, it allowed a thirty-day comment period and held a public hearing regarding the new standard. The American Steel and Iron Institute (Steel) objected to the new standard because OSHA excluded the Hierarchy-of-Controls Policy from the rulemaking proceeding so that this policy was not open to comment or scrutiny. OSHA claimed that it did not

have to expose this policy to public commentary because the policy had not changed since it first came into effect in 1971. Steel argued that OSHA should not be permitted to selectively insulate favored aspects of the standard from public scrutiny and judicial review. In addition, Steel claimed that the facts had changed dramatically—now respirators may be as effective as engineering controls—since the Hierarchy-of-Controls Policy was adopted in 1971. Should the public be allowed to comment on the Hierarchy-of-Controls Policy, or should OSHA's decision be upheld? [*American Iron and Steel Institute v. OSHA*, 182 F.3d 1261 (11th Cir. 1999)]

4. The Federal Aviation Administration (FAA) issued an enforcement order to Captain Richard Merrell, a Northwest Airlines pilot whom the FAA determined had violated airline safety regulations. While Merrell was pilot-in-command of a commercial plane, the air traffic controller (ATC) instructed him to climb to an altitude of 17,000 feet. Merrell correctly repeated this instruction to the ATC, a standard procedure referred to as "readback." A minute later, the ATC transmitted an altitude clearance to another plane, directing it to climb to an altitude of 23,000 feet. Merrell mistakenly thought that this instruction was for him and repeated the instruction to the ATC. However, the ATC did not hear Merrell's readback because it overlapped with another pilot's message

sent at the same time. The ATC radio system can handle only one transmission at a time; if two transmissions overlap completely, the ATC will neither receive the pilot's readback nor be alerted by a noise that sounds when instructions somewhat, but not completely, overlap. Merrell, unaware that the ATC had not received his transmission, began to climb to the higher altitude. Before the ATC noticed Merrell was off course and alerted him to change his direction, he had lost the standard safety separation required between commercial flights.

FAA safety regulations obligate pilots to listen, hear, and comply with all ATC instructions except in an emergency. Under FAA regulations, inattention, carelessness, or an unexplained misunderstanding, including an error of perception, do not excuse a deviation from a clearly transmitted instruction. In response to claims that the FAA's interpretation of this regulation was arbitrary and capricious, the FAA stated that its apparently harsh regulation was justified in "the unforgiving environment of aviation, in which even good-faith error can lead to tragedy." Should a court reviewing the FAA's regulation uphold it? What is the applicable standard for review? [*FAA v. National Transportation Safety Board,* 190 F.3d 571 (D.C. Cir. 1999)]

5. The Food and Drug Administration (FDA), charged with implementation of the Food, Drug and Cosmetic Act, refused to approve the cancer-treatment drug Laetrile on the grounds that it failed to meet the statute's safety and effectiveness standards. Terminally ill cancer patients sued, claiming that the safety and effectiveness standards implemented by the FDA could have no reasonable application to drugs used by the terminally ill. The statute contained no explicit exemption for drugs used by the terminally ill. The case reached the court of appeals, which agreed with the plaintiffs and approved intravenous injections of Laetrile for terminally ill cancer patients. The United States appealed to the Supreme Court. Under what standard should the Supreme Court review the FDA's determination that an exemption from the Food, Drug and Cosmetic Act should not be implied for drugs used by the terminally ill? [*United States v. Rutherford,* 442 U.S. 544 (1979)]

6. In 1985, President Ronald Reagan signed into law the Gramm-Rudman-Hollings Act. The purpose of the Act was to reduce the federal deficit by setting a maximum deficit amount for fiscal years 1986 to 1991, progressively reducing the budget deficit to zero by 1991.

If the federal budget deficit were not reduced as the act required, an automatic budget process was to take effect. The comptroller would calculate, on a program-by-program basis, the amount of reductions needed to meet the target. He or she would then report that amount to the president, who was required to issue a sequestration order mandating these reductions. (A *sequestration order* directs spending levels to be reduced below the levels authorized in the original budget.) Unless Congress then acted to modify the budget to reduce the deficit to the required level, the sequestrations would go into effect.

The comptroller, unlike the employees of the executive branch and agency officials, does not serve at the pleasure of the president. He or she can be removed from office only by Congress.

Opponents of the Gramm-Rudman-Hollings Act argued that the comptroller's role in the automatic budget process was an exercise of executive functions. Because the comptroller was controlled by Congress, they argued that this role violated the constitutional requirement of separation of powers. Were they right? [*Bowsher v. Synar,* 478 U.S. 714 (1986)]

7. The Supreme Court has recognized that administrative inspections may be conducted without warrants in some situations where a company's business concerns an industry that has a history of government oversight and, as a result, has a reduced expectation of privacy. The Court held that a warrantless search would be held reasonable in the context of a pervasively regulated business if (1) there is a "substantial" government interest that underlies the regulatory scheme pursuant to which the search is made; (2) the warrantless inspection is necessary to further the regulatory scheme; and (3) the inspection program, in terms of the certainty and regularity of its application, provides a constitutionally adequate substitute for a warrant. Based on this standard, would the Court allow warrantless administration inspections to occur in the following industries: (a) firearms, (b) mining, (c) pharmaceutical, and (d) computer software design? [*In re Subpoenas Duces Tecum,* 51 F. Supp. 2d 726 (W.D. Va. 1999)]

8. In May 1995, the University Corporation for Atmospheric Research (UCAR), a research consortium funded in part by the National Science Foundation (NSF), a U.S. government agency, decided to purchase several supercomputers. UCAR solicited bids from three supercomputer manufacturers including NEC Corporation. UCAR needed NSF approval for the supercomputer acquisition,

and the NSF requested that UCAR obtain evidence that NEC's offer did not involve dumping, which is prohibited under the U.S. dumping laws. UCAR commissioned a study.

In April 1996, the Department of Commerce also decided to look into the matter. Commerce undertook a preliminary analysis of NEC's bid and determined that all the conditions for assessing an antidumping duty were present. Commerce transmitted a letter to the NSF from Acting Assistant Secretary Joffe setting forth its findings. The letter was equivocal, using words of qualification such as "estimated," "could," and "likely." Commerce also made a copy of the Joffe letter available to the press and public, including NEC's competitor Cray.

On June 5, 1996, Robert LaRussa succeeded Joffe as acting assistant secretary of commerce. Prior to that time, LaRussa had no involvement with the UCAR investigation although he was briefed on the investigation and provided with a copy of the Joffe letter. On June 5, three Commerce officials, including Joffe, met with staff members from the House of Representatives Ways and Means Committee to discuss the UCAR purchase. The Commerce officials indicated that the results were just an "estimate" taken from public information and other governmental sources, not from information supplied by NEC, and stressed that the department had not made a dumping determination.

On June 29, 1996, Cray filed an antidumping petition with Commerce and the International Trade Commission. Commerce responded on August 19, 1996, by initiating an investigation. NEC filed a suit in the Court of International Trade seeking to enjoin Commerce's investigation on the grounds that the department's conduct constituted prejudgment having the effect of denying NEC due process. The trial court denied NEC's claim, finding that it had failed to prove that Commerce's prior actions rendered the investigation a "hollow formality." Do you agree with the trial court's decision? Are there additional facts that you would need to know to make this determination? [*NEC Corp. v. U.S. Department of Commerce,* 151 F.3d 1361 (Fed. Cir. 1998), *cert. denied,* 525 U.S. 1139 (1999)]

9. James O'Hagan was a partner in the law firm of Dorsey & Whitney in Minneapolis, Minnesota. In July 1988, the London-based company Grand Metropolitan PLC (Grand Met) retained Dorsey & Whitney as local counsel for a potential tender offer for the common stock of the Pillsbury Company, headquartered in Minneapolis. Both Grand Met and Dorsey &

Whitney took precautions to protect the confidentiality of Grand Met's tender offer plans. O'Hagan, who was not working on the deal, began purchasing Pillsbury stock and call options for Pillsbury stock. When Grand Met announced its tender offer in October, the price of Pillsbury stock rose to $60 per share. O'Hagan sold his Pillsbury call options and stock, making a profit of more than $4.3 million.

The Securities and Exchange Commission (SEC) initiated an investigation into O'Hagan's transactions, culminating in a fifty-seven-count indictment, charging O'Hagan with, among other counts, violation of Rule 14e-3(a). Rule 14e-3(a) was adopted by the SEC pursuant to Section 14(e) of the Securities Exchange Act of 1934. Section 14(e) reads in relevant part:

> It shall be unlawful for any person . . . to engage in fraudulent, deceptive, or manipulative acts or practices, in connection with any tender offer . . . . The [SEC] shall, for the purposes of this subsection, by rules and regulations define, and prescribe means reasonably designed to prevent, such acts and practices as are fraudulent, deceptive, or manipulative.

Relying on Section 14(e)'s rulemaking authorization, the SEC promulgated Rule 14e-3(a) in 1980. A person violates Rule 14e-3(a) if he or she trades on the basis of material nonpublic information concerning a pending tender offer that he or she knows or has reason to know has been acquired "directly or indirectly" from an insider of the offeror or the target, or someone working on their behalf. Rule 14e-3(a) requires traders who fall within its ambit to abstain from trading or to disclose the nonpublic information, without regard to whether the trader owed a preexisting fiduciary duty to respect the confidentiality of the information. In contrast, courts have interpreted Section 14(e) to apply only to situations in which the person trading violated a fiduciary duty by trading. Did the SEC exceed its rulemaking authority by adopting Rule 14e-3(a) without requiring a showing that the trading at issue entailed a breach of fiduciary duty? [*United States v. O'Hagan,* 521 U.S. 642 (1997)]

MANAGER'S DILEMMA

10. Dora Reilly is the executive vice president of DNA in Combat, Inc., a genetic-engineering company based in Cambridge, Massachusetts. Eighteen months ago, she filed an application for FDA

approval of a promising anticancer drug, DBL. Two months ago, she met Gene Splice at an après-ski party and invited him to her room at the ski lodge to listen to her CD collection. After that night, Splice returned to his job as a senior specialist in the division of the FDA responsible for approving new drugs based on recombinant DNA, and Reilly returned to Cambridge. Two weeks after her return, Splice wrote Reilly a letter on FDA letterhead, saying, "It was nice to see your name cross my desk on your company's petition for approval of DBL. I'd really like to see you again—why don't you fly down this weekend?"

Reilly considered requesting that the petition be referred to another specialist at the FDA. However, she is concerned that that would delay the approval process by at least eighteen months. Her chief scientist has advised her that a key competitor is expected to have a similar drug on the market in four months. What should she do?

INTERNET SOURCES

The Federal Web Locator, a service of the Villanova Center for Information Law and Policy, offers users a chance to search for materials from and about the federal government, including its many agencies and their Web pages.	http://www.law.vill.edu/fed-agency/fedwebloc.html
The National Archives and Records Administration's page allows users to search the entire *Code of Federal Regulations*.	http://www.access.gpo.gov/nara/cfr/cfr-table-search.html
This page of the National Archives and Records Administration allows users to search the entire *Federal Register*.	http://www.access.gpo.gov/su_docs/aces/aces140.html
Cornell University's Legal Information Institute page provides the text of the entire U.S. Code, including the Administrative Procedure Act.	http://www.law.cornell.edu/uscode/5/ch5.html
Federal Communications Commission	http://www.fcc.gov
Equal Employment Opportunity Commission	http://www.eeoc.gov
Securities and Exchange Commission	http://www.sec.gov
Occupational Safety and Health Administration	http://www.osha.gov
The European Commission's Web site has information regarding the Green Paper on the Convergence of the Telecommunications, Media and Information Technology Sectors.	http://www.ispo.cec.be/convergencegp

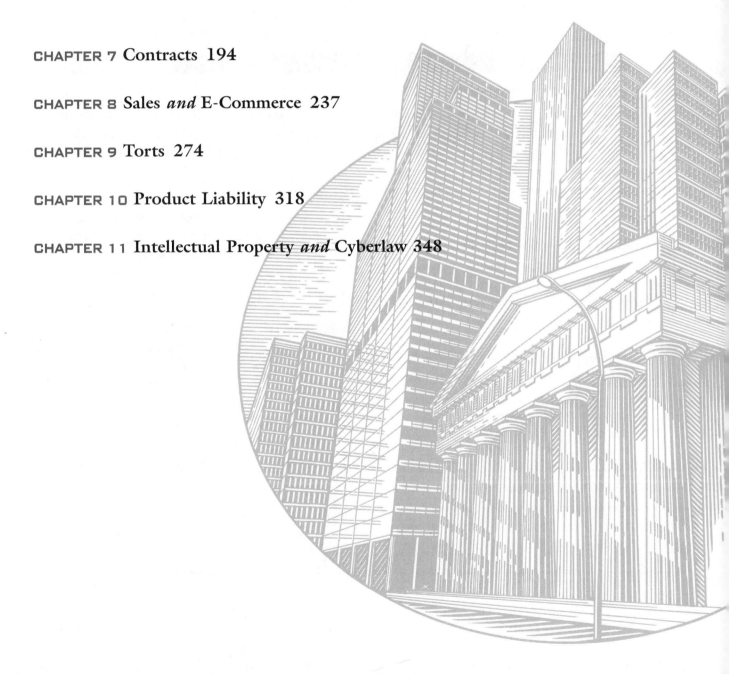

The Legal Environment

CHAPTER 7

Contracts

WHY CONTRACT LAW IS IMPORTANT

Contract law determines which agreements will be enforced by the courts and which will not. Contracts are central to the conduct of business both in the United States and internationally. Without contract law, a company could not make plans to move its offices into a new building knowing that the lease gives it an enforceable right to exclusive use of the space for the term of the lease at the specified rent. Similarly, an owner could not rent space knowing that the tenant must pay rent and comply with the other terms of the lease. Employees could not leave their current employers and begin work for a start-up company knowing that the new firm will grant the stock options promised by the founders when they were recruited. Each of these transactions is based on the parties' expectation that the promises made will be enforceable.

Contract law comes from case law, statutes, and tradition. It varies slightly from state to state. Many states follow the Restatement (Second) of Contracts, which is the basis for much of the discussion in this chapter. Common law contracts include employment agreements and other contracts involving services, leases and sales of real property, loan agreements, stock-purchase agreements, settlement agreements, and joint venture agreements. Commercial transactions involving the sale of goods, that is, movable personal property, are governed by Article 2 of the Uniform Commercial Code (UCC). Article 2, as well as the laws governing the sale of goods internationally and contracts for the

sale and licensing of software, is discussed in Chapter 8. The "In Brief" in Chapter 8 compares the common law, UCC, Convention on Contracts for the International Sale of Goods, and Uniform Computer Information Transactions Act.

CHAPTER OVERVIEW

This chapter discusses the elements necessary for a valid contract: agreement (formed by an offer and acceptance), consideration, contractual capacity, and legality. It explains the doctrine of promissory estoppel, which can, in certain circumstances, result in limited relief for a party who has relied on a noncontractual promise to his or her detriment. The need for genuine assent and the effects of fraud and duress are discussed, as are issues concerning misunderstanding or mistake about the meaning of a contract or the facts underlying the contract. The chapter explains the requirement that certain contracts be in writing and the rules for looking beyond the written terms of an agreement to discern the parties' intentions. It discusses damages for breach of contract and court orders for specific performance. The chapter then addresses precontractual liability, including the enforcement of an agreement to negotiate. It concludes with a look at the conflicts that may arise between a party's contractual obligations and its obligations to others and at liability for interference with a contract.

Basic Requirements *of a* Contract

A *contract* is a legally enforceable promise or set of promises. If the promise is broken, the person to whom the promise was made—the *promisee*—has certain legal rights against the person who made the promise—the *promisor*. If the promisor fails to carry out its promise, the promisee may be able to recover money damages, or it may be able to get an injunction or a court order forcing the promisor to perform the promise.

Formation of a valid contract requires four basic elements. First, there must be an agreement between the parties formed by an offer and acceptance. Second, the parties' promises must be supported by something of value, known as consideration. Third, both parties must have the capacity to enter into a contract. Fourth, the contract must have a purpose that is legal.

In addition, courts may invalidate contracts that do not reflect a true "meeting of the minds." For instance, if one party is induced into a contract by fraud, duress, or misrepresentation, courts may refuse to enforce the contract because both parties did not genuinely assent to its terms.

 # Agreement

A valid contract requires an offer and acceptance resulting in agreement between the two parties. Contract law has traditionally treated offer and acceptance as a rather sterile, step-by-step process. Despite its incongruity with the fluid nature of business deal making today, this narrow view continues to give the rules governing contract formation a formalistic flavor.

 # Offer

An *offer* is a manifestation of willingness to enter into a bargain that justifies another person in understanding that his or her assent to that bargain is invited and will conclude it. An offer is effective if (1) the *offeror* (the person making the offer) has an intention to be bound by the offer, (2) the terms of the offer are reasonably definite, and (3) the offer is communicated to the *offeree* (the intended recipient).

INTENTION

Courts will evaluate the offeror's outward expression of intent, not his or her secret intentions. Thus, if a reasonable person would consider an offeror's statement to be

a serious offer, an offer has been made. This means that offers made in obvious jest or in the heat of anger do not meet the intention requirement because a reasonable person would know the offer was not serious. This objective standard of contract interpretation makes it possible to plan one's business based on reasonable expectations of what the other party's words mean.

Most advertisements are treated not as offers but as invitations to negotiate. Sellers do not have an unlimited ability to provide services or an unlimited supply of goods. If advertisements were offers, then everyone who "accepted" could sue the seller for breach of contract if the seller's supply ran out. An advertisement will be treated as an offer only in the rare case where a seller makes a promise so definite that it is clearly binding the seller to the conditions stated. This can arise, for example, when the advertisement calls for some performance by the offeree, such as providing information that leads to the recovery of a lost or stolen article.

DEFINITENESS

An offer will form the basis for a contract if it is definite, meaning that essential terms are not left open. If essential terms (such as price, subject matter, duration of the contract, and manner of payment) are left open, then there is no contract.

COMMUNICATION

The offeror must communicate the offer to the offeree. For instance, a good Samaritan who returns a lost pet cannot claim a reward offered by the owner if he or she did not know about the reward beforehand.

TERMINATION OF OFFER

An offer can be terminated either by operation of law or by action of the parties.

Termination by Operation of Law An offer terminates when the time of acceptance specified by the offeror has elapsed or at the end of a reasonable period if the offeror did not specify a time. Death or incapacitation of either party terminates an offer, as does destruction of the subject matter.

Termination by Action of the Parties The offeror can *revoke* its offer—that is, cancel it—at any time before the offeree accepts. An offer is also terminated if the offeree rejects it. Merely inquiring into the terms of an offer, however, is not a rejection. For example, suppose

Cassandra offers Misha a managerial position at $105,000 per year, and Misha responds, "Does that include a five-week paid vacation?" This is an inquiry into terms, as distinguished from a counteroffer, and does not terminate the original offer.

A *counteroffer* is a new offer by the original offeree. A counteroffer constitutes a rejection of the original offer and has the effect of reversing the roles of the original offeror and offeree. Had Misha replied, "That salary is too low, but I'll take the job at $120,000 per year," he would have terminated the offer by making a counteroffer.

IRREVOCABLE OFFERS

Sometimes an offer cannot be revoked by the offeror. *Irrevocable offers* arise in two circumstances: (1) when an option contract has been created, and (2) when an offeree has relied on an offer to his or her detriment.

Option Contracts One type of irrevocable offer occurs when an offeror agrees to hold an offer open for a certain amount of time in exchange for some consideration from the other party. Such an agreement is known as an *option contract*. Under such an agreement, the offeror cannot revoke the offer until the time for acceptance has expired. For example, in exchange for a $200 payment by the offeree, a company might agree to keep the position of general manager open for ten days while the person offered the position decides whether to take the job.

Detrimental Reliance Another type of irrevocable offer can occur when an offeree has changed his or her position because of justifiable reliance on the offer. Sometimes courts will hold that such *detrimental reliance* makes the offer irrevocable.

Suppose Aunt Leila offers the use of her Maui condo during spring-break vacation to her niece Jaye in exchange for Jaye's promise to fix a hole in the condo roof during her stay. Under traditional contract law, Aunt Leila could revoke this offer at any time before Jaye accepts. But suppose Jaye relies on this offer, purchases a nonrefundable plane ticket to Maui, and passes up the opportunity to rent other condos for her stay. The modern view of this situation is quite different from traditional contract law. If Aunt Leila should reasonably have known Jaye would act to her detriment in reliance on Aunt Leila's offer, then the doctrine of promissory estoppel would make Aunt Leila's offer irrevocable. In other words, Aunt Leila would be estopped—or barred—from revoking her offer. The doctrine of promissory estoppel is described in more detail later.

 ## Acceptance

Acceptance is a response by the person receiving the offer that indicates willingness to enter into the agreement proposed in the offer. A typical example of an offer and acceptance is something like this: Nanci says to Jim, "I'll give you $100 to install my new computer software package and explain to me how it works," and Jim says, "Okay." A contract has been made. Nanci is now legally obliged to give Jim the money, and Jim is obliged to install the software and show Nanci how to use it.

Both offer and acceptance can be oral, written, or implied by conduct. For example, a manager offers a consultant $5,000 to develop a business plan for her company. The consultant begins interviewing key executives and drafting a business plan. By starting work on the business plan, he has accepted the offer. The acceptance is implied by his action, even though he did not actually say, "I accept your offer."

MODE OF ACCEPTANCE

The offeror is the "master of his offer" in that he or she can specify authorized and unauthorized means of acceptance. For example, the offeror could specify that the offer can be accepted only by a facsimile (fax) to a stated fax number and that the acceptance is not effective until actually received. In the absence of such a provision, acceptance is effective upon dispatch. Thus, if a person drops into the mailbox a properly addressed envelope with adequate postage containing a letter accepting an offer, a contract is formed when the letter is put in the mailbox; the offeror cannot thereafter revoke the offer.

Mirror Image Rule The traditional concept of contract formation requires that acceptance be unequivocal. In other words, what the offeree accepts must be a mirror image of what the offeror has offered. If it is not, the *mirror image rule* dictates that no contract has been formed.

For example, suppose Alyssa offers to rent to Victor 6,000 square feet of office space in Houston for $60 per square foot. Victor accepts the offer of office space but says he wants ten free underground parking spaces included as well. The requirements of the mirror image rule have not been met because Victor's acceptance is not unequivocal. Victor's request for the parking spaces is considered a counteroffer rather than an acceptance. Accordingly, there is no contract.

Intent to Be Bound Formalistic rules of contract formation often do not reflect the realities of how businesses enter into agreements. A joint venture agreement between contractors to build a hydroelectric dam, for example, can involve months of negotiations and a series of letters, memorandums, and draft contracts. As a result, it is sometimes difficult to determine exactly at what point the parties have entered into a valid legally binding contract.

At some point in negotiations, the parties will usually manifest an intention, either orally or in writing, to enter into a contract. Such *intent to be bound* can create an enforceable contract even if nonessential terms remain to be hammered out or a more definitive agreement is contemplated. The courts will look at the specific facts of each case when determining whether the parties regarded themselves as having completed a bargain.

In general, to determine the enforceability of preliminary agreements, courts examine (1) the intent of the parties to be bound and (2) the definiteness of the terms of the agreement. The great bulk of litigation concerning the enforceability of preliminary agreements with open terms has involved the problem of intent, as in the landmark case of *Pennzoil v. Texaco* discussed in the "Inside Story" for this chapter. In that case, the court ruled that Getty Oil, the Getty Trust, and the Getty Museum intended to be bound by a four-page "memorandum of agreement" calling for the sale of Getty Oil to Pennzoil, even though the memorandum was not expressly made binding, and the consummation of the multibillion dollar deal was subject to execution of a definitive agreement.

In deciding whether the parties to a preliminary agreement intended to be bound, courts look to a variety of factors, including (1) the degree to which the terms of the agreement are spelled out; (2) the circumstances of the parties (e.g., the importance of the deal to them); (3) the parties' prior course of dealing with each other, if any; and (4) the parties' behavior subsequent to the execution of the agreement (for example, issuing a press release may demonstrate intent).

The parties can make a preliminary agreement nonbinding by stating their intention not to be bound. However, courts will honor such an intent only if it is expressed in the clearest language. For example, titling an agreement a "letter of intent" or using the phrase "formal agreement to follow" might not be enough to prove to a court that the parties did not intend to be bound.

⚓ Consideration

A promise does not always constitute a valid contract. To form a valid contract, each side must provide something of value. The thing of value, known as *consideration,* can be money, an object, a promise, a service, or a giving up of the right to do something. For instance, an adult's promise to quit smoking for five years constitutes consideration because the promisor is giving up something he or she is legally entitled to do. A promise to take property off the market for thirty days constitutes consideration. So does a promise to do a midyear audit.

A promise to do something illegal, however, such as to pay for sexual favors in a state where prostitution is prohibited, does not constitute valid consideration. Likewise, a promise to fulfill a preexisting legal obligation, that is, to do something the promisor is already obligated to do—either by law or by contract—is not consideration.

For example, suppose Brett's Builders Corporation (BBC) has a contract to build a production facility for Hardware, Inc. for $15 million. Halfway through the project, BBC demands an additional $3 million to finish the project. Because it wants the project done as quickly as possible, Hardware promises to pay the additional $3 million. Hardware's promise is not enforceable by BBC because BBC's promise to "finish the project" did not constitute consideration. BBC was already contractually obligated to build the facility in its entirety. This type of situation is explored further in the discussion of contract modification below.

ADEQUACY OF CONSIDERATION

Generally, courts will not scrutinize the value of the consideration or the fairness of a contract. This means that courts will deem consideration adequate—and thus hold parties to their bargain—unless the courts feel the purported consideration is nothing more than a sham. Hence, the adage that even a peppercorn can be adequate consideration. The rare exception to this rule is the unconscionability doctrine discussed below.

BILATERAL AND UNILATERAL CONTRACTS

Consideration can be either a promise to do a certain act or the performance of the act itself.

A *bilateral contract* is a promise given in exchange for another promise. One party agrees to do one thing, and the other party agrees to do something in return. For example, Ibrahim promises to give Mercedes $10 if Mercedes promises to drive Ibrahim to business school. The exchange of promises represents consideration and makes the promises binding.

A *unilateral contract* is a promise given in exchange for an act. A unilateral contract is accepted by performing the specified act. For example, Ibrahim promises to give Mercedes $10 if Mercedes drives him to business school. Mercedes can accept the contract only by driving Ibrahim to business school, and no contract is performed until she does so.

MUTUALITY OF OBLIGATION IN BILATERAL CONTRACTS

The corollary of consideration in the case of bilateral contracts is the concept of *mutuality of obligation*. Unless both parties are obligated to perform their side of the bargain, neither will be. In other words, a bilateral contract must limit the behavior of both parties in some fashion for it to be enforceable. If one party has full freedom of action, there is no contract.

Mutuality of obligation applies only to bilateral contracts. In the case of a unilateral contract, the promisor becomes bound only after the promisee has performed the required act. Thus, in the example above, Ibrahim has no obligation to pay Mercedes $10 until Mercedes drives him to school.

ILLUSORY PROMISE

A promise that neither confers any benefit on the promisee nor subjects the promisor to any detriment is an *illusory promise*. Because there is no mutuality of obligation in such a case, the resulting agreement is unenforceable. For example, a classic case[1] involved a coal company, Wickham, that agreed to sell at a certain price all the coal that Farmers' Lumber, a lumber company, wanted to purchase from Wickham. The Iowa Supreme Court held that Farmers' Lumber's promise to purchase only what it wanted to purchase, which could be nothing at all, was illusory. Because there was no consideration flowing from Farmers' Lumber to Wickham, there was no contract. Farmers' Lumber could have avoided the finding of an illusory contract by agreeing to purchase all the coal it needed from Wickham. Such an agreement is called a requirements contract, which is further discussed below.

Sometimes a party may mischaracterize a unilateral contract as an illusory promise, as happened in the following case.

---

1. Wickham & Burton Coal Co. v. Farmers' Lumber Co., 179 N.W. 417 (Iowa 1920).

A CASE IN POINT

CASE 7.1

Dahl v. HEM Pharmaceuticals Corp.

United States Court of Appeals for the Ninth Circuit 7 F.3d 1399 (9th Cir. 1993).

In the Language of the Court

FACTS HEM Pharmaceuticals Corporation designed a new drug, Ampligen, to fight chronic fatigue syndrome. Typically, new medicines go through several phases of clinical evaluation before approval by the Food and Drug Administration (FDA) and general release onto the market. As part of that process, HEM began a clinical trial with ninety-two patients to evaluate the effectiveness, side effects, and risks of Ampligen.

Dahl and the other patients signed consent forms warning of the experimental nature of Ampligen and its possible side effects. The patients were free to withdraw from the clinical trial at any time, but if they remained in the study, they were required to accept the risks of treatment, to forgo other drugs, to not become pregnant, and to submit to intrusive and uncomfortable testing for one year. In return, after the testing ended they would be entitled to receive Ampligen for a full year at no charge.

At the end of the year-long study, HEM refused to provide the year's supply of the drug to the patients free of charge. The patients sued HEM for breach of contract.

ISSUE PRESENTED Is voluntary participation in clinical trials sufficient consideration to form a contract when the participants could have dropped out of the trials at any time?

OPINION KLEINFELD, J., writing for the U.S. Court of Appeals for the Ninth Circuit:

The arrangement with the experimental subjects was that they would participate in the double-blind study for a year. This was to facilitate evaluation of the safety and effectiveness of Ampligen. After the double-blind phase of testing ended, they would be entitled to receive Ampligen for a full year at no charge. . . .

(Continued)

(Case 7.1 continued)

...

HEM argues that as a matter of contract law, petitioners' probability of success on the merits was low, because its promise was not supported by consideration. This argument is without merit. The patients submitted themselves to months of periodic injections with an experimental drug or, unbeknownst to them, mere saline solution, combined with intrusive and necessarily uncomfortable testing to determine their condition as the tests proceeded. HEM sought to have them participate in its study so that it could obtain FDA approval for its new drug.

HEM argues that because petitioners participated voluntarily and were free to withdraw, they had no binding obligation and so gave no consideration. Somehow the category of unilateral contracts appears to have escaped HEM's notice. The deal was, "if you submit to our experiment, we will give you a year's supply of Ampligen at no charge." This form of agreement resembles that in the case taught in the first year of law school.[2] There, an uncle promised his nephew that if he would refrain from drinking, using tobacco, or playing cards and billiards until age 21, he would receive $5,000. The court held that consideration had been given because the nephew had refrained from the prohibited [but legally permissible] activities during the requisite period on the faith of his uncle's promise. He had accepted the offer by completing performance.

In this case, the petitioners performed by submitting to the double-blind tests. They incurred the detriment of being tested upon for HEM's studies in exchange for the promise of a year's treatment of Ampligen. Upon completion of the double-blind tests, there was a binding contract.

RESULT A binding contract was formed when the patients completed the trials, and the court ordered HEM to provide Ampligen to the participants who wanted it.

QUESTIONS

1. Given that a unilateral contract can be accepted only by performing the requested act, what would be the result if HEM had unilaterally terminated the trials two days before the first anniversary of their commencement and thereby made it impossible for the participants to complete the one-year trial?
2. Was it ethical for HEM to refuse to supply the drug or to require the participants to litigate?

2. Hammer v. Sidway, 27 N.E. 256 (N.Y. 1891).

CONDITIONAL PROMISES

Conditional promises often look illusory, but they are enforceable as long as the promisor is bound by conditions beyond his or her control. For example, Xerox promises to hire Diane as an inventor on condition that the Patent and Trademark Office issues a patent on her new photocopying process. Although the likelihood of obtaining a patent may be remote, the decision is out of the parties' hands. If the patent is issued, Xerox will be obligated to hire Diane. The contract is valid at the time it is agreed upon, but performance is not required until the condition is satisfied.

There are three types of conditions: (1) conditions precedent, (2) conditions concurrent, and (3) conditions subsequent. A *condition precedent* must be satisfied before performance under a contract is due. For example, if Martin agrees to buy Josie's house, provided he can obtain financing at less than 8 percent for thirty years within sixty days of signing the contract, then Martin's obtaining the specified financing is a condition precedent to his duty to buy the house. If the condition is satisfied, he must buy the house; if it is not, the contract will fail, and Martin will not be required to buy the house. When a condition is partially within the control of one party, that party will often have an implied-in-law duty to use best efforts to cause the condition to be satisfied.

Conditions concurrent occur when the mutual duties of performance are to take place simultaneously. For example, a buyer's obligation to pay for stock often does not become absolute until the seller tenders or delivers the stock certificates. Similarly, the seller's obligation to deliver the stock certificates does not become absolute until the buyer tenders or actually makes payment.

A *condition subsequent* is a contract term that operates to terminate an existing contractual obligation if that condition occurs. For example, a partner agrees to sell his share of the partnership for ten times the partnership's earnings unless an audit of the partnership's books shows earnings of less than $5 million. The parties have entered into a contract, but if the earnings of the partnership are less than $5 million (that is, if the condition subsequent occurs), then the partner will not be obligated to sell his share.

Conditional clauses must not be illusory promises. For example, courts usually disallow clauses that condition an agreement on the approval of a party's own lawyer.

REQUIREMENTS AND OUTPUT CONTRACTS

In a *requirements contract,* the buyer agrees to purchase all its requirements of a specified commodity, such as steel, from the seller, and the seller agrees to meet those requirements. The parties do not know how much steel the buyer will actually need, but whatever that amount is, the buyer will buy it all from that seller. The buyer is constrained from buying steel from another supplier.

In an *output contract,* the buyer promises to purchase all the output that the seller produces. Again, the parties do not how know many units that will be, but the seller must sell all its output to that buyer. The seller cannot sell any of its product to another buyer.

These types of contracts are not enforceable if the requirement or output is unreasonable or out of proportion to prior requirements or outputs. For example, the buyer cannot take advantage of the seller by increasing its requirement to triple the usual amount. The seller will not be required to sell anything over the reasonable or usual amount required by the buyer.

Promissory Estoppel

The primary exception to the rule that only promises supported by consideration will be enforced is the doctrine of promissory estoppel. *Promissory estoppel* (sometimes referred to as detrimental reliance) provides an exception to this rule only if the following four requirements are met:

- **Promise** There must be a promise. A statement of future intent is not sufficient, nor is an estimate or a misstatement of fact. For example, Hank asks Bart the time, and Bart mistakenly tells Hank it is two o'clock when it is actually three o'clock. As a result, Hank misses an important appointment. Hank relied on the information to his detriment, but there was no promise.

- **Justifiable reliance** The promise must cause the promisee to take an action that he or she would not otherwise have taken. When the niece Jaye buys the plane ticket to Hawaii, she is relying on Aunt Leila's promise. If Jaye had not bought the ticket, there would be no reliance, and her aunt would be free to take back her promise.

- **Foreseeability** The action taken in reliance on the promise must be reasonably foreseeable by the promisor. It is foreseeable that the niece would buy a plane ticket as a result of her aunt's promise. It is not foreseeable that she would quit her job to take a six-month vacation in Hawaii. Therefore, the aunt would probably have to pay for the plane ticket but not for the niece's lost wages.

- **Injustice** A promise that has been reasonably relied on will give rise to relief only if the failure to do so would cause injustice. The exact meaning of "injustice" has been debated in a variety of legal tracts, but a good rule of thumb is to ask whether the promisee has been harmed by his or her reliance on the promise. If the niece had made a plane reservation that could be canceled without penalty, there would be no injustice in letting the aunt take back her promise; thus, promissory estoppel would not apply.

The original interpretation of promissory estoppel was that it applied only to gifts, not to bilateral exchanges. A series of cases in the mid-1960s extended the doctrine of promissory estoppel to promises made in the course of contract negotiations. The leading case is set forth next.

CASE 7.2

Hoffman v. Red Owl Stores, Inc.

Supreme Court of Wisconsin
133 N.W.2d 267
(Wis. 1965).

In the Language of the Court

FACTS Hoffman negotiated with Red Owl Stores, Inc. to buy a franchise to open a Red Owl grocery store. The negotiations went through several stages and continued for more than two years before breaking down.

When Hoffman first approached Red Owl, he said he had only $18,000 to invest. Red Owl assured him that this amount would be sufficient. Hoffman already owned a bakery, and with Red Owl's encouragement, he bought a small grocery store to get more experience. The store was profitable, but Red Owl advised Hoffman to sell it because he would have a larger Red Owl store within a few months. A site in the nearby city of Chilton was soon found for the new store, and Hoffman paid the $1,000 deposit. Meanwhile, Hoffman also rented a residence for himself and his family near the new site.

Red Owl then told Hoffman that he had to sell his bakery before the franchise deal could go through. He sold it, and negotiations proceeded regarding the details of financing and leasing the new store. At this stage, Red Owl increased Hoffman's required investment from $18,000 to $24,100, and a few weeks later to $26,100. Hoffman requested money from his father-in-law, who agreed to put money into the business, provided he could come in as a partner. Negotiations broke down when Red Owl insisted that the father-in-law sign an agreement stating that the money he was advancing was an outright gift. Hoffman sued Red Owl for damages based on the defendant's failure to keep the promises that had induced him to act to his detriment.

ISSUE PRESENTED Can a party to failed negotiations successfully assert a claim for promissory estoppel based on precontractual negotiations and agreements and his acts taken in reliance thereon?

OPINION CURRIE, C.J., writing for the Wisconsin Supreme Court:

Many courts of other jurisdictions have seen fit over the years to adopt the principle of promissory estoppel, and the tendency in that direction continues. As Mr. Justice McFaddin, speaking in behalf of the Arkansas court, well stated, the development of the law of promissory estoppel "is an attempt by the courts to keep remedies abreast of increased moral consciousness of honesty and fair representations in all business dealings."[3]

...

The record here discloses a number of promises and assurances given to Hoffman by Lukowitz on behalf of Red Owl upon which plaintiffs relied and acted upon to their detriment.

Foremost were the promises that for the sum of $18,000 Red Owl would establish Hoffman in a store. After Hoffman had sold his grocery store and paid the $1,000 on the Chilton lot, the $18,000 figure was changed to $24,100. Then in November 1961, Hoffman was assured that if the $24,100 figure were increased by $2,000 the deal would go through. Hoffman was induced to sell his grocery store fixtures and inventory in June 1961, on the promise that he would be in his new store by fall. In November, plaintiffs sold their bakery building on the urging of defendants and on the assurance that this was the last step necessary to have the deal with Red Owl go through.

...

3. Peoples Nat'l Bank of Little Rock v. Linebarger Constr. Co., 240 S.W.2d 12, 16 (Ark. 1951).

(Continued)

(Case 7.2 continued)

There remains for consideration the question of law raised by defendants that agreement was never reached on essential factors necessary to establish a contract between Hoffman and Red Owl. Among these were the size, cost, design, and layout of the store building; and the terms of the lease with respect to rent, maintenance, renewal, and purchase options. This poses the question of whether the promise necessary to sustain a cause of action for promissory estoppel must embrace all essential details of a proposed transaction between promisor and promisee so as to be the equivalent of an offer that would result in a binding contract between the parties if the promisee were to accept the same.

. . . [It is not necessary for] the promise giving rise to the cause of action [to] be so comprehensive in scope as to meet the requirements of an offer that would ripen into a contract if accepted by the promisee.

Rather the conditions imposed are:

(1) Was the promise one which the promisor should reasonably expect to induce action or forbearance of a definite and substantial character on the part of the promisee?

(2) Did the promise induce such action or forbearance?

(3) Can injustice be avoided only by enforcement of the promise?

. . .

"The wrong is not primarily in depriving the plaintiff of the promised reward but in causing the plaintiff to change position to his detriment. It would follow that the damages should not exceed the loss caused by the change of position, which would never be more in amount, but might be less, than the promised reward."[4]

RESULT The Wisconsin Supreme Court awarded damages to the plaintiff for all items except one—damages for the loss, if any, on the sale of the grocery store, fixtures, and inventory—as to which a new trial was ordered to determine appropriate damages.

QUESTIONS

1. Assuming Hoffman relocated his family to be near the new store site, should the personal moving expenses of Hoffman's family be reimbursed? Should Hoffman be able to recover his opportunity costs, that is, the profits he would have earned if he had struck a deal with another franchise?

2. Suppose Hoffman made less money at his new job at the grocery store than he had previously made at the bakery. Given that Hoffman had taken on this job at the grocery store only to gain experience before owning a Red Owl store, should he be compensated for his lost profits?

4. Warren Seavey, *Reliance on Gratuitous Promises or Other Conduct,* 64 Harv. L. Rev. 913, 926 (1951).

⬙ Capacity

A valid contract requires that both parties possess the capacity to enter into an agreement. *Capacity* to contract is a legal term of art that refers to a person's ability to understand the nature and effect of an agreement. The widely accepted rule is that minors and mentally incompetent persons lack capacity.

The law's concern is that one party may take advantage of someone who is unable to protect his or her interests. As a result, the law generally gives minors and incompetent persons the power to repudiate their obligations under the contract. In other words, such contracts are *voidable,* or subject to being undone, at the option of the person lacking capacity: He or she can enforce the contract if it is favorable to him or her, or avoid the contract if it is not. Moreover, in some states minors not only have the power to avoid their contractual obligations, they are even entitled to retain any property they may have acquired under the voidable contract.

These voidability rules are subject to certain limitations. Both minors and mentally incompetent persons will be held to contracts for necessaries, such as food, clothing, and shelter. Otherwise, no one would be willing to provide the necessaries a minor or mentally incompetent person needs to survive. Both minors and mentally incompetent persons can ratify (agree to be bound by) contracts after they reach majority or gain competency. In many states, minors cannot repudiate their contractual obligations if they misrepresented their age to the other party.

Finally, it should be noted that contracts entered into by incompetent persons have the potential to be either void, voidable (at the option of the incompetent person), or valid. If a court has adjudged the party incompetent and appointed a guardian for him or her, the contract is void. If the party simply lacked mental capacity to comprehend the subject matter, the contract is voidable. If the party was able to understand the nature and effect of the agreement, however, then even if he or she lacked capacity to engage in other activities, the contract is valid, with no voidability option.

Legality

Contracts must have a purpose that is legal. Contracts that are either contrary to a statute or contrary to public policy are illegal and are generally considered void—that is, they are not valid contracts at all.

LICENSING STATUTES

Many states require licenses for the conduct of particular kinds of business, ranging from real estate and securities broker licenses to chauffeur licenses to contractor licenses. Many statutes provide that if a party fails to have a required license, the other party to the contract does not have to fulfill its side of the bargain, usually payment. This is true even if the unlicensed party performed the work perfectly and even if the other party knew that the person doing the work was unlicensed.

OTHER CONTRACTS CONTRARY TO STATUTE

Sometimes a statute will expressly make a contract illegal. For example, *usury statutes,* which limit the interest rate

on loans, usually provide that any loan agreement in violation of the statute is unenforceable. In some jurisdictions, this means that no amount of interest can be collected; in some states, the principal amount of the loan is not collectible either. Loans that violate the usury statutes also violate criminal law.

Other examples of *illegal contracts* include price-fixing agreements in violation of the antitrust laws, bribes, wagering contracts or bets in violation of applicable gambling laws, and unreasonable covenants not to compete. To be reasonable, a *covenant not to compete* entered into in connection with the sale of a business must be reasonable as to scope of activities, length of time, and geographic area and must be necessary to protect trade secrets or goodwill. The enforceability of covenants not to compete in the employment context is discussed in Chapter 14.

UNCONSCIONABILITY

A contract term is *unconscionable* if it is oppressive or fundamentally unfair. This concept is applied most often to consumer contracts when the consumer may have little or no bargaining power. The seller dictates the terms of the contract, and the buyer can take it or leave it.

A recent case presents the issue vividly. In August 1997, the State of Florida settled a suit against the tobacco industry for more than $11 billion. Florida had hired a group of outside attorneys to represent it in the case, in exchange for a 25 percent contingency fee. The settlement agreement with the tobacco industry called for attorneys' fees to be determined by an independent arbitrator. Several of the State's outside attorneys then went to court in an effort to enforce their 25 percent contingency-fee contract.

A Florida state judge denied their claim on unconscionability grounds. The court stated that a fee of tens of millions of dollars or perhaps even hundreds of millions could be reasonable, "but a fee of 2.8 *billion* dollars simply shocks the conscience of the court." The court calculated that if the twelve principal lawyers had worked around the clock beginning at the outset of negotiations in mid-1994 through the end of 1997, they would be paid the equivalent of $7,716 per hour if the contingency-fee agreement were upheld. The court found these figures to be "patently ridiculous" and "per se unreasonable."[5]

5. John McKinnon, *Florida Judge Blocks Lawyers' Bid to Collect Tobacco-Accord Fee,* WALL ST. J., Nov. 13, 1997, at B3.

ETHICAL CONSIDERATION

Envelopes for the processing of photographic film typically contain printed language on the outside of the envelope stating that in the event of loss, defect, or negligence in the processing, the purchaser's damages are limited to the replacement of the film and processing. Shortly before Mr. Sam Smoke died of a heart attack, his wife, Sara Smoke, took pictures of him playing with his new granddaughter. After his death, Mrs. Smoke took the film to Photo-Finish for processing. She gave the company her name but did not sign anything. Photo-Finish lost the film. Mrs. Smoke sued for negligence and claimed damages to compensate her for the emotional distress caused by the loss of the invaluable pictures. What is Photo-Finish legally required to do? What should it do?

Courts usually refuse to enforce contract terms that they find unconscionable. Unconscionability has both a procedural and a substantive element. When the term is central to the contract, the court can either rewrite the term (for example, by substituting a fair market price) or void (undo) the contract. As the Historical Perspective in this chapter describes further, the doctrine of unconscionability had its origins in Roman law.

Procedural Element The procedural element focuses on two factors: oppression and surprise. *Oppression* arises from an inequality of bargaining power that results in no real negotiation and an absence of meaningful choice for one party to the contract. *Surprise* arises when the terms of the contract are hidden in a densely printed form drafted by the party seeking to enforce these terms. Form contracts are usually drafted by the party with the superior bargaining position.

Substantive Element No precise definition of substantive unconscionability can be set forth. Courts have talked in terms of "overly harsh" or "one-sided" results. One commentator has pointed out that unconscionability turns not only on a "one-sided" result but also on an absence of justification for it. The most detailed and specific commentaries observe that a contract is largely an allocation of risk between the parties, and therefore a contractual term is substantively suspect if it reallocates the risk of the bargain in an objectively unreasonable or unexpected manner. But not all unreasonable risk allocations are unconscionable. The greater the unfair surprise or the inequality of bargaining power, the less likely the courts will tolerate an unreasonable risk allocation.

Releases Persons are sometimes asked to sign a general release, especially before embarking on a dangerous activity such as skydiving or race car driving. A *general release* purports to relieve the owner of the facility of any liability for injuries suffered by the person using the facility, including liability for negligence. A number of earlier cases held that the exculpatory language in a general release agreement was invalid because the agreement was unconscionable. There appears to be a trend toward honoring these releases, however, as demonstrated in the following case.

A CASE IN POINT

CASE 7.3
Kurashige v.
Indian Dunes, Inc.
California Court of Appeal
246 Cal. Rptr. 310
(Cal. Ct. App. 1988).

In the Language of the Court

FACTS Indian Dunes Park, owned by Indian Dunes, Inc., was used by the general public for motorcycle dirt-bike riding. On December 21, 1982, Kurashige was injured while riding his motorcycle on the park's trails. Before using the park, Kurashige had signed a general release agreement, which was printed in red ink with 10-point bold type and capital letters saying: "SINCE ALL MOTORBIKE RIDING IS DANGEROUS WE REQUIRE ALL RIDERS AND VISITORS TO ASSUME ALL RISK BY SIGNING THIS GENERAL RELEASE." At the bottom of the agreement, the words "MOTORCYCLING IS DANGEROUS" were printed in red in 17-point bold type. Below the agreement were three columns of 28 lines each for the riders to sign. Printed on each of the 84 lines were the words "THIS IS A RELEASE" in capital letters.

The agreement provided in pertinent part that each of the undersigned

Hereby Releases, Waives, Discharges and Covenants not to sue [defendants], all for purposes herein referred to as Releasees, from all liability to the Undersigned . . . for all loss or damage and any claim or demands therefor, on account of injury to the

(Continued)

(Case 7.3 continued)

person or property or resulting in death of the Undersigned, whether caused by the negligence of Releasees or otherwise while the Undersigned is upon the Park premises. . . .

Kurashige suffered injury and sued the owner of Indian Dunes. The trial court granted summary judgment in favor of Indian Dunes. By granting the motion for summary judgment, the court took the issue of liability away from the jury and decided as a matter of law that the defendant should prevail. Kurashige appealed.

ISSUE PRESENTED Is the exculpatory language in a general release agreement enforceable as a general matter and, more specifically, as against a claim of unconscionability?

OPINION SPENCER, J., writing for the California Court of Appeal:

[*Ed.:* The court began by considering whether any general release, regardless of terms, was valid. Relying on *Tunkl v. Regents of the University of California,*[6] the court held that an exculpatory provision may stand only if it does not involve "the public interest."]

. . . [T]he "General Release" agreement used here was printed legibly, contained adequate, clear and explicit exculpatory language and indicated defendants were to be absolved from the consequences of their own negligence. Furthermore, it did not involve the public interest: defendants' business was not generally thought to be suitable for public regulation; defendants did not perform a service of great importance to the public, and the business was not a matter of practical necessity for members of the public; and defendants' customers did not place their persons under defendants' control.

. . .

[The court then addressed the plaintiff's contention that the general release was unconscionable.] Turning to the procedural element of unconscionability, the first question is whether the "General Release" agreement was oppressive, whether there was "an inequality in bargaining power which result[ed] in no real negotiation and 'an absence of meaningful choice.'"[7] The record shows there was no real negotiation; the "General Release" agreement was preprinted and all users of Indian Dunes Park were required to sign it before using the park. However, the record does not show plaintiff had no meaningful choice in deciding to sign the agreement. . . . There is no evidence plaintiff could not have ridden his motorcycle elsewhere without the constraints imposed upon him by defendants.

The next question is whether plaintiff was surprised by supposedly agreed-upon terms hidden within a printed form drafted by defendants. The entire release agreement was printed at the top of the form signed by plaintiff. Warnings as to the dangers of motorcycling, the rider's assumption of the risk and the release and waiver of all liability stood out and the exculpatory provisions of the agreement were clearly set forth. Thus, the agreement was not procedurally unconscionable.

In examining the issue of substantive unconscionability, one question to be asked is whether the agreement was one-sided and, if so, whether the one-sidedness was justified. A further question is whether the agreement reallocated the risks of the bargain in an objectively unreasonable or unexpected manner. Risk reallocation which will be subjected to special scrutiny is that in which the risk shifted to a party is one that only the other party can avoid. Clearly, the agreement here was one-sided; all of

6. 383 P.2d 441 (Cal. 1963).
7. A & M Produce Co. v. FMC Corp., 186 Cal. Rptr. 114 (Cal. Ct. App. 1982).

(Continued)

(Case 7.3 continued)

the risk was reallocated to the Park's user, plaintiff. As previously discussed, the risk reallocation was not unexpected; the agreement clearly indicated the user assumed all risk of his use of the Park's facilities.

Was the risk reallocation objectively unreasonable? One signing the agreement warrants he knows "the present condition [of the Park and] that said condition may become more hazardous and dangerous during the time [he is] upon said premises." The agreement warned the user motorcycling is dangerous; implicit in the knowledge of the danger of motorcycling "is the knowledge that riding over rough, uneven terrain in an outdoor park poses a risk of injury from a fall" or other accident.[8] Moreover, to a certain extent, the risk of injury is conditioned upon the user's skill and experience as a motorcycle rider, factors over which the Park's owners and operators have no control. In view of the foregoing, the risk reallocation was not unreasonable and the "General Release" agreement was not substantively unconscionable.

RESULT The appeals court upheld the general release and affirmed the trial court's grant of summary judgment for the defendant, Indian Dunes.

COMMENTS It would appear that the court would limit the use of general releases in a county hospital. Would it matter if the hospital were private?

QUESTIONS

1. Would the result in this case have been any different if the plaintiff had been thrown off his bike after riding into a barbed-wire fence not visible from the hill he had just crested? What about a big hole on the other side of the hill?
2. What would the court consider a practical necessity for members of the public? A bus? A cosmetic surgery clinic? A public park for camping that charges a small fee?

8. Coates v. Newhall Land & Farming, Inc., 236 Cal. Rptr. 181 (Cal. Ct. App. 1987).

 # Genuineness *of* Assent

Even if a contract meets all the requirements of validity (agreement, consideration, capacity, and legality), it may not be enforceable if there was no true "meeting of the minds" between the two parties. In other words, a court will refuse to enforce a contract if it feels one or both of the parties did not genuinely assent to the terms of the contract. The discussion below examines a variety of problems that could prevent a true meeting of the minds, including fraud, duress, ambiguity, and mistake.

FRAUD

A contract is voidable if it is tainted with fraud. There are two types of fraud: fraud in the factum and fraud in the inducement. *Fraud in the factum* occurs when a party is persuaded to sign one document thinking that it is another. For example, if a person was given a deed to sign for the transfer of real property, after being told that the document was an employment agreement, the deed could be voided by the defrauded party.

The second type of fraud, *fraud in the inducement*, occurs when a party makes a false statement to persuade the other party to enter into an agreement. For example, if a jeweler told a customer that the stone in a ring was a diamond, when the jeweler knew it was zirconium, an agreement to purchase the ring would be fraudulent, and the purchaser would have the right to rescind, that is, cancel, the contract. A contract is not voidable due to fraudulent misrepresentation unless the misrepresentation was material to the bargain and relied on by the party seeking to void the contract.

Another variation of fraud in the inducement occurs when a party has a duty to disclose information to the other party but fails to do so. For example, a partner who knows the true value of a piece of property cannot sell it to a fellow partner without disclosing the true value. The duty to disclose often arises out of a special relationship

Unconscionability *and* Freedom *of* Contract

The principle of freedom of contract embodies the idea that the judicial system should give effect to the expressed intention of the parties to an agreement. It is difficult for a court to evaluate the fairness of a contract and to figure out the relative values of a business deal to the parties. Accordingly, courts observe the general principle that they should not substitute their judgment about the fairness of a contract for that of the parties.

Freedom of contract ensures that the law does not unduly restrict the ability of the competitive market to bring about productive and allocative efficiency. *Productive efficiency* exists when competition among parties seeking to earn profits results in resources flowing to lowest-cost producers of a good. *Allocative efficiency* exists when goods and services are produced up to the point at which their cost of production equals their price, which results in efficient allocation of scarce societal resources to the production of various goods.

Leaving the parties to define the contract terms as they see fit will result in greater maximization of profit, provided three conditions are met: (1) the parties to the contract are better informed than the courts about the conditions under which the benefits of the deal can be maximized; (2) the parties are equally well informed and enjoy roughly equal bargaining power; and (3) the legislature is unable to provide rules detailed enough to govern the particular business situation in which the contract was negotiated.

Naturally, these conditions are met more fully in some contexts than in others. Also, public policy concerns must be respected. Contracts that produce results contrary to public policy should not be

enforced, even if they enhance economic efficiency. Courts have therefore created exceptions to the principle of freedom of contract, voiding contracts of two types: (1) contracts that fail to meet the three conditions mentioned above, and (2) contracts where the purpose or result violates public policy.

The first type, in which the contract fails to meet the conditions necessary for freedom of contract to maximize economic efficiency, may be characterized as involving procedural unconscionability. The second type, in which the contract leads to a result that is against public policy, may be characterized as involving substantive unconscionability.

These concepts date back to Aristotelian theory and Roman law.[a] Under Roman law, each party to an exchange had to give something equal in value to what he or she received. Unequal exchanges were considered fundamentally unjust. In extreme cases, the law remedied the injustice through the doctrine of *laesio enormis*. This doctrine developed from language in the Code of Justinian that provided a remedy for those who sold land for less than half its "just price." *Laesio enormis* expanded this provision to cover contracts for goods whose contract price deviated by at least half from the just price. Under the Roman system, the just price was the market price for similar goods under sim-

ilar circumstances. The German and French laws that relieve a party from its obligations under a contract that is not for the just price have their roots in the Roman doctrine of *laesio enormis*.

In the United States and England, the general principle of freedom of contract, embodied in the common law rule that the judiciary will not examine the fairness of an exchange, has always been limited by the doctrine of unconscionability. In the eighteenth century, unequal exchanges were considered evidence of fraud in the making of the contract. Courts would refuse to enforce unconscionable contracts, which were generally defined as those involving harsh or oppressive terms of exchange.

The coming of the Industrial Revolution and the emergence of large corporations in the mid-1800s brought about fundamental changes in the mode of analysis of contract law. As goods became more complex, the seller typically had greater knowledge of them than the buyer, and the bargaining power of large corporations often greatly exceeded that of the individuals with whom they contracted. Thus, a greater number of contracts failed to satisfy the "equal footing" condition necessary to make freedom of contract efficiency enhancing. Consequently, courts became less hesitant to intervene to protect the party to a contract who was perceived to be weaker. The doctrine of unconscionability was expanded to cover situations where the parties were not on an equal footing.

a. The discussion of Roman, French, German, and English law and certain aspects of the discussion of U.S. law set forth above are based upon James Gordley, *Equality in Exchange*, 69 Cal. L. Rev. 1587 (1981), and the authorities cited therein.

between the parties (that is, a fiduciary relationship), such as between an officer and a corporation or between a trustee and a beneficiary. Parties engaged in arm's-length transactions cannot affirmatively misrepresent a fact, but,

as a general rule, they do not have a duty to disclose every fact that might be material to the other party.

Promissory fraud occurs when one party induces another to enter into a contract by promising to do something without having the intention to carry out the promise. Because a promise to do something necessarily implies the intention to perform, when a promise is made without such an intention, there is an implied misrepresentation of fact that can give the other party the right to rescind the contract.

DURESS

A contract is also voidable if one party was forced to enter into it through fear created by threats. Thus, inducing someone to sign a contract by blackmail or extortion is *duress*. Duress is present only if the threatened act is wrongful or illegal. Therefore, more subtle forms of pressure, such as an implied threat that at-will employees will lose their jobs unless they sign agreements waiving certain rights to employee benefits, do not constitute duress.

Economic duress is usually not enough to invalidate a contract. A contract may be invalidated on the basis of economic duress only if the party claiming economic duress can show that the other party caused the economic difficulty. Thus, many courts would uphold an agreement to sell a farm even if the owner had to sell it at a bargain price to avoid bankruptcy. Similarly, threats to withhold future business from a supplier unless more favorable terms are negotiated are not grounds to void a subsequent contract.

Under the related doctrine of *undue influence,* a court may invalidate an agreement if one party had sufficient influence and power over the other as to make genuine assent impossible. For example, if an invalid living alone, with few contacts with the outside world and dependent on a caregiver, agreed to sell her house to the caregiver at a bargain price, that agreement might be set aside based on undue influence.

AMBIGUITY

Misunderstandings may arise from ambiguous language in a contract or from a mistake as to the facts. If the terms of a contract are subject to differing interpretations, some courts will construe the ambiguity against the party who drafted the agreement. More often, courts will apply the following rule: The party who would be

adversely affected by a particular interpretation can void a contract when (1) both interpretations are reasonable, and (2) the parties either both knew or both did not know of the different interpretations. If only one party knew or had reason to know of the other's interpretation, the court will find for the party who did not know or did not have reason to know of the difference.

For example, in a case involving Mark Suwyn, an executive vice president of International Paper Company (the world's largest paper company), a federal court refused to prevent Suwyn from joining Louisiana-Pacific, a producer of wood products.[9] Suwyn had signed a broad covenant not to compete with International Paper after allegedly being assured by International Paper's chairman and chief executive officer John Georges that the covenant was aimed at preventing Suwyn from going to one of the big paper companies. Suwyn had attached to the signed agreement a note indicating that it was meant to prevent him from joining a major paper company such as Georgia-Pacific, Champion, or Weyerhauser. Because Louisiana-Pacific did not make paper and was not on the list, Suwyn argued that he was free to join the company. Georges responded that the noncompete agreement was broad and included wood products, such as plywood and lumber, that both companies produced. The judge ruled that Suwyn and Georges had such different meanings in mind that there had been no real agreement on the noncompete pact. As a result, there was no contract.

MISTAKE OF FACT

Like a misunderstanding due to ambiguity, a *mistake of fact* can make a contract voidable. A court's willingness to undo a contract based on a mistaken assumption of fact depends heavily on the particular circumstances. The court will look at three factors to determine if a mistake has been made: (1) the substantiality of the mistake, (2) whether the risks were allocated, and (3) timing.

Substantiality of the Mistake A court is more likely to void the contract when the mistake has a material effect on one of the parties. For example, in the classic case *Raffles v. Wichelhaus,*[10] two parties had signed a contract in which Wichelhaus agreed to buy 125 bales of cotton to be brought by Raffles from India on a ship named *Peerless*. There were, however, two ships named *Peerless,* both sailing out of Bombay during the same year. Raffles meant the *Peerless* that was sailing in December, and

9. William M. Carley, *CEO Gets Hard Lesson in How Not to Keep His Top Lieutenants,* WALL ST. J., Feb. 11, 1998, at A1.
10. 159 Eng. Rep. 375 (Exch. 1864).

Wichelhaus meant the *Peerless* that was sailing in October. When the cotton arrived on the later ship, Wichelhaus refused to complete the purchase, and Raffles sued for breach of contract. The English court held that the contract was voidable due to the mutual mistake of fact. The court described the situation as one of "latent ambiguity" and declared that there was no meeting of the minds and therefore no contract.

Note that the three-month delay made the cotton worthless to the buyer and thus the mistake was substantial. What if the delay had been only a few days? In that case, the court would probably have enforced the contract. On the other hand, even if the delay had been only a few days, if the buyer had planned to resell the cotton on the open market and the price of cotton had dropped sharply during that period, then the mistake would probably have been substantial enough to make the contract voidable.

Allocation of the Risks If one party accepts a risk, then this allocation of risk becomes part of the bargain even if it is doubtful the risk will materialize, and that party must bear the consequences. For example, suppose Gerald wants to sell Brandee a house. He says he is uncertain whether the house needs a retaining wall to bolster the foundation. Brandee does not want to pay for a report by a structural engineer. She says she doesn't think the house needs a retaining wall and that she is willing to take the risk of being wrong about that if Gerald will lower the selling price. They sign a contract to this effect. Structural damage is subsequently discovered. The parties have allocated the risk of a mistake about the need for a retaining wall, and the contract is valid.

If the parties have not expressly allocated a risk, sometimes a court will place the risk on the party who had access to the most information. In other cases, the court might impose the risk on the party better able to bear it.

Timing The party alleging a mistake of fact must give prompt notice when the mistake is discovered. If too much time passes before the other party is notified, undoing the contract might create more problems than letting it stand.

MISTAKE OF JUDGMENT

A *mistake of judgment* occurs when the parties make an erroneous assessment about some aspect of what is bargained for. For example, in a futures contract a seller agrees to sell a buyer a crop of sugar in three months at a price of fifty cents per pound. The seller is betting that the market price in three months will be less than fifty cents. The buyer is betting that the market price will be higher. One of them will be mistaken, but the futures contract will still be valid. This is a mistake of judgment. Such a mistake is not a valid defense to enforcement of the contract.

The line between judgment and fact can sometimes be unclear. In two recent cases, the courts found that parties had made mistakes of judgment despite their attempts to characterize their actions as mistakes of fact. In *CTA, Inc. v. United States*,[11] a company that entered into a contract to provide technical support services to the government included labor rates for its workers that were substantially lower than the market rates. After realizing this discrepancy, the company argued that it had made a mistake in the numbers contained in the labor rates set forth in its bid. The court rejected this argument after finding that the company had made an error in business judgment, not a mistake of fact. Similarly, in *Bissell, Inc. v. Oreck Corp.*,[12] the court rejected the plaintiff's argument that a settlement agreement had to be reformed because Bissell had made a mistake in the amount of equipment that Oreck had to purchase under the terms of the contract. The court found that the company had made a business judgment, not a mistake of fact, in providing an estimate rather than a more precise calculation of the amount of inventory to be purchased.

In a classic case, the Michigan Supreme Court held that a contract for the sale of a cow thought to be barren, but later found to be with calf, was a mistake of fact that made the contract unenforceable.[13] The court reasoned:

> If there is a difference or misapprehension as to the substance of the thing bargained for; if the thing actually delivered or received is different in substance from the thing bargained for, and intended to be sold, then there is no contract. . . . A barren cow is substantially a different creature than a breeding one.

A dissenting judge pointed out that the buyer had believed the cow could be made to breed, in spite of the seller's statements to the contrary, and had decided to take a chance on the purchase. He reasoned:

> There was no mistake of any material fact by either of the parties in the case as would license the vendors to rescind. . . . As to the quality of the animal, subsequently developed, both parties were equally ignorant, and as to this each party took his chances. If this were not the law, there would be no safety in purchasing this kind of stock.

---

11. 44 Fed. Cl. 684 (Fed. 1999).
12. 2000 U.S. Dist. LEXIS 3595 (W.D. Mich. Mar. 10, 2000).
13. Sherwood v. Walker, 33 N.W. 919 (Mich. 1887).

It is unclear whether the assumption that a cow is barren is an assumption of fact or of judgment. As the majority and dissenting opinions in the Michigan case demonstrate, different judges reach different conclusions.

Much of contract law comes down to the expectations of the parties involved. In the cow case, the seller did not consider the possibility that the cow was fertile. The buyer did not make known his secret belief that the cow could be made to breed. From the seller's point of view, the transaction was for a barren cow with no chance of breeding. However, the buyer did not see the transaction that way. The case might have come out differently if the buyer had explicitly said to the seller, "I know you believe the cow is barren, but I believe she can be made to breed, and I'm willing to take the chance in buying her."

Disclosing all expectations may make for firm contracts, but it is not the most effective negotiating technique. If the seller believes a cow is fertile, he or she will demand a higher price. Why pay the higher price when the vast majority of business transactions are completed without any need to do battle in the courtroom? One of the challenges of business is balancing the slim (but expensive) chances of litigation against the desire to capture value not apparent to the other party.

 ## Statute *of* Frauds

Although most oral contracts are enforceable, many states have statutes requiring certain types of contracts to be evidenced by some form of written communication. Such a statute is called a *statute of frauds*. If a contract covered by the statute is oral, it is still a valid contract, but the courts will not enforce it if the statute of frauds is raised as a defense. Therefore, if neither party raises the issue, the contract will be enforced. Similarly, even if the party seeking to enforce the contract has not signed anything, it can still enforce the contract against a party who has signed a writing embodying the essential terms of the deal.

There are four traditional justifications for requiring certain contracts to be evidenced by writing. First, requiring a written document avoids fraudulent claims that an oral contract was made. Second, the existence of a written document avoids fraudulent claims as to the terms of the contract. Third, putting agreements in writing reduces the risk of future misunderstandings. Fourth, the writing required by the statute has the psychological effect of reinforcing the importance of the parties' decision to enter into a contract.

TRANSACTIONS SUBJECT TO THE STATUTE OF FRAUDS

Contracts that must be evidenced by some writing include (1) a contract for the transfer of any interest in real property (such as a deed, lease, or option to buy); (2) a promise to pay the debt of another person; (3) an agreement that by its terms cannot be performed within a year; and (4) a *prenuptial agreement* (that is, an agreement entered into before marriage that sets forth the manner in which the parties' assets will be distributed and the support to which each party will be entitled in the event of divorce).

The statute-of-frauds issue that arises most often in litigation is whether a contract can by its terms be performed within one year. If it cannot—that is, if the contract is longer than one year in duration—then it must be put in writing to be enforceable.

A typical "performed within one year" case involves an oral promise of "lifetime employment." For example, *McInerney v. Charter Golf, Inc.*[14] involved a golf-apparel sales representative who received an offer to join a rival company, which promised to pay him an 8 percent commission. When notified of this offer, his employer orally promised to guarantee the sales rep a 10 percent commission "for the remainder of his life," subject to discharge only for dishonesty or disability. The sales rep accepted this offer and passed up the rival's offer. When he was fired three years later, he sued for breach of contract.

The Illinois Supreme Court ruled that a lifetime employment contract is intended to be permanent. It inherently anticipates a relationship of long duration—certainly longer than one year. Thus, the court found the contract subject to the statute of frauds and unenforceable because it was not put in writing.

Other courts have taken a contrasting approach and construe the words "cannot be performed" to mean "not capable of being performed within one year." Because, theoretically, an employee can die at any time, these courts reason that lifetime employment contracts are *capable* of being performed within one year. As a result, they deem such contracts to be outside the scope of the statute of frauds and valid even if not put in writing.

14. 680 N.E.2d 1347 (Ill. 1997).

 ETHICAL CONSIDERATION

Is it ethical for a manager to raise the defense of failure to comply with the statute to avoid enforcement of an oral promise that the manager knows he or she made?

The statute of frauds does not require the agreement to be embodied in a formal, legal-looking document. An agreement can be represented by an exchange of letters that refer to each other, even if no single letter is sufficient to reflect all essential terms. Details or particulars can be omitted; only the essential terms must be stated. What is essential depends on the agreement, its context, and the subsequent conduct of the parties. Under the *equal dignities rule,* if an agent acts on behalf of another (the principal) in signing an agreement of the type that must, under the statute of frauds, be in writing, the authority of the agent to act on behalf of the principal must also be in writing. Thus, an individual signs a written *power of attorney* to authorize a person, called an attorney-in-fact (who need not be a lawyer), to sign documents on the individual's behalf. Corporations authorize officers to sign through a combination of written authority specified in the bylaws of the corporation and the minutes of the governing body, the board of directors.

If there is clear evidence that a person made an oral promise, a court will strain to recharacterize the nature of the agreement so that it does not come within the statute of frauds.[15] One cannot count on such leniency, however; so the prudent manager will put any and all agreements that might fall within the statute of frauds in writing.

The Parol Evidence Rule

If a contract is in writing, when will a court go beyond the words of the contract and look to other evidence to ascertain the intent of the parties? Under the *parol evidence rule,* when there is a written contract that the parties intended to encompass their entire agreement, parol (that is, oral) evidence of prior or contemporaneous statements will not be permitted to alter the terms of the contract. Such extrinsic evidence is inadmissible in court and cannot be used to interpret, vary, or add to the terms of an unambiguous written contract that purports to be the entire agreement of the parties. A court usually will not look beyond the "four corners" of the document to discern the intentions of the parties.

For example, in *White v. Security Pacific Financial Services, Inc.,*[16] the borrower plaintiffs tried to intro-

duce evidence that the lender defendant had fraudulently induced them to execute a promissory note by assuring them that its sole recourse upon default would be under a deed of trust that collateralized the loan. The court found that this evidence could not be admitted because it contradicted the parties' written agreement.

CLARIFYING AMBIGUOUS LANGUAGE

The parol evidence rule does not prohibit showing what the contract means. Thus, courts are willing to look beyond the written agreement if its language is ambiguous. For example, if the contract stated that a party was to purchase a carload of tomatoes, it would not violate the parol evidence rule to present evidence showing that "carload" in the relevant commercial setting means a train carload, not a Chevy truckload. This evidence merely explains the ambiguous term "carload"; it does not vary the term. Parol evidence is also admissible to show mistake, fraud, or duress.

Changed Circumstances

Contracts often contain provisions for a variety of future events so that the parties involved can allocate the risks of different outcomes. It is not always possible to anticipate every occurrence, however. Three theories are used to address this situation: impossibility, impracticability, and frustration of purpose.

IMPOSSIBILITY

If Antonio signs a contract to sell Trevor computer chips of a special type manufactured only in Antonio's factory, which later burns down through no fault of Antonio's before he can manufacture the computer chips, it becomes impossible to perform the contract. The destruction of Antonio's factory is a changed circumstance that neither party contemplated when they made the contract.

Is Trevor entitled to money damages for Antonio's nonperformance? No. Because Antonio's performance has become impossible, he is discharged from his obligations under the contract due to *impossibility,* and Trevor is not entitled to damages. If, however, the computer chips could be manufactured in another factory, Antonio would have an obligation to have them manufactured there after his factory burned down. This is the case even if it costs Antonio more money to manufacture them at another facility.

---

15. *See, e.g.,* Wilson Floors Co. v. Sciota Park, Ltd., 377 N.E.2d 514 (Ohio 1978) (oral promise by construction lender to pay subcontractor if he returned to work served lender's own pecuniary interest so the agreement did not have to be in writing to be enforceable).
16. No. 5079754 (Cal. July 21, 1999), *cert. denied,* 120 S. Ct. 1172 (2000).

Electronic Contracts: *The* Uniform Electronic Transactions Act *and the* E-Sign Act

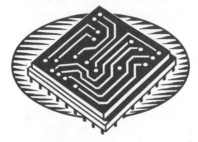

With the rise of e-commerce, more and more transactions have been taking place electronically. Until very recently, however, many states did not give contracts executed electronically the same legal effect as physical paper contracts. Moreover, laws governing electronic transactions varied widely from state to state.

In 1999, the National Conference of Commissioners on Uniform State Laws (NCCUSL) adopted the Uniform Electronic Transactions Act (UETA) to address the issue of whether electronic contracts and signatures are legal contracts. UETA serves as a model for state legislatures seeking to implement laws relating to electronic transactions, but adoption of UETA is not mandatory. As of October 2000, more than twenty states had enacted UETA. A majority of the states had already enacted some type of electronic legislation, and these states were also working to make their laws conform with UETA.[a]

UETA sets forth four basic rules regarding contracts entered into by parties that agree to conduct business electronically: (1) a record or signature may not be denied legal effect or enforceability solely because it is in electronic form; (2) a contract may not be denied legal effect or enforceability solely because an electronic record was used in its formation; (3) an electronic record satisfies a law that requires a record to be in writing; and (4) an electronic signature satisfies a law that requires a signature.[b]

Under UETA, almost any mark or process intended to sign an electronic record will constitute an electronic signature, including a typed name at the bottom of an e-mail message, a faxed signature, and a "click-through" process on a computer screen whereby a person clicks "I agree" on a Web page. The essential element necessary to determine the validity of an electronic signature is whether the person intended the process or mark provided to act as a signature and whether it can be attributed to that person.

In an effort to ensure more uniform treatment of electronic transactions across the United States, Congress enacted the Electronic Signatures in Global and National Commerce Act, more commonly known as the E-Sign Act, effective October 1, 2000. Consistent with UETA, the E-Sign Act provides that a signature, contract, or other record "may not be denied legal effect, validity, or enforceability solely because it is in electronic form."[c] The provisions of the E-Sign Act are very similar to those of UETA, except that UETA, where enacted, applies to intrastate and interstate transactions, whereas the E-Sign Act governs only transactions in interstate and foreign commerce. Moreover, the provisions of the E-Sign Act are mandatory.

The E-Sign Act resolves the problem of inconsistency among states that have or and have not enacted UETA by expressly preempting all state laws inconsistent with its provisions. For states that have adopted UETA, however, the E-Sign Act does allow state law "to modify, limit, or supersede" its provisions to the extent such variations are not inconsistent with the E-Sign Act. What variations will ultimately be considered "inconsistent" is not entirely clear and may have to be determined by the courts.

To protect those that choose not to conduct business electronically or do not have access to computers, the E-Sign Act and the UETA require that the use or acceptance of electronic records or electronic signatures be voluntary. Moreover, under the E-Sign Act, if a business is legally bound to provide information to a consumer in writing, electronic records may be used only if the business first secures the consumer's informed consent.

Notwithstanding the broad scope of the E-Sign Act and UETA, several classes of documents are not covered by their provisions and thus may not be considered fully enforceable if executed electronically. Both UETA and the E-Sign Act exclude:

- Wills, codicils, and trusts.
- Contracts or records relating to adoption, divorce, or other matters of family law.
- Contracts governed by certain provisions of the Uniform Commercial Code in effect in each state.

Unlike UETA, the E-Sign Act also excludes:

- Court orders and notices and other official court documents.
- Notices of cancellation or termination of utility services.
- Notices regarding credit agreements secured by, or rental agreements for, a primary residence (for example, eviction notices).
- Notices of cancellation or termination of health or life insurance benefits.
- Notices of recall.
- Documents required to accompany the transport of hazardous materials, pesticides, or other toxic materials.

Of course, a national standard governing electronic transactions does not resolve inconsistencies in laws of other countries. Some form of international coordination will be necessary to ensure that electronic transactions are consistently enforced across national borders. Toward that end, as of mid-2000, an effort was under way to encourage other countries to adopt similar standards.[d]

a. *Ohio Senate Passes Electronic Signature Bill*, Best's Ins. News, May 22, 2000.
b. David Schumacher, *U.S. Addresses Legal Issues Raised by Electronic Trading*, Int'l Fin. L. Rev., Apr. 1, 2000, at 19.
c. Electronic Signatures in Global and National Commerce Act, § 101(a)(2) (2000).
d. Office of the Press Secretary, the White House, "Statement by the President," June 30, 2000.

IMPRACTICABILITY

Closely related to impossibility is the concept of *impracticability,* where performance is possible but commercially impractical. As a rule, impracticability is difficult to prove.

Impracticability was invoked by several shipping companies after Egypt nationalized the Suez Canal in 1956, and the resulting political turmoil led to the temporary closing of the key waterway. A number of merchant ships had to detour around the Cape of Good Hope at the southern tip of Africa. The detour increased shipping costs so much that the shipping companies suffered substantial losses. Several of these companies sued to nullify the contracts they had entered into before the Suez Canal was closed. They claimed performance was im-

practical and sought to recover the full costs of sailing the longer route around the Cape of Good Hope. In only one case did the court grant relief. The other courts found that the added costs were not so great as to make performance impracticable. (Chapter 8 addresses impracticability in contracts for the sale of goods.)

When changed circumstances make performance of a contract more difficult, a party to the contract may wish to seek assurances that the other party can still perform despite the new difficulties. In the following case, the New York Court of Appeals considered whether one party can demand adequate assurances from the other party if there is reason to be concerned that the party may breach the contract.

A CASE IN POINT

CASE 7.4
Norcon Power Partners, L.P. v. Niagara Mohawk Power Corp.
Court of Appeals of New York
705 N.E.2d 656
(N.Y. 1998).

In the Language of the Court

FACTS In 1989, Norcon Power Partners, L.P., an independent power producer, entered into a contract with Niagara Mohawk Power Corporation, a public utility provider, whereby Niagara Mohawk agreed to purchase electricity generated at Norcon's Pennsylvania facility for a period of twenty-five years. There were three pricing periods under the contract. In the first period, Niagara Mohawk paid six cents per kilowatt-hour for electricity. In the second and third periods, the price paid by Niagara Mohawk was based on "avoided cost," which was calculated using the cost that Niagara Mohawk would incur to generate electricity itself or to purchase it from other sources. In the second period, Niagara Mohawk's payments were capped by a ceiling price. In the third period, the price paid by Niagara Mohawk was not subject to a cap or a floor. Payments made by Niagara Mohawk in the third period were adjusted to account for any balance existing in the adjustment account that operated in the second period.

In February 1994, Niagara Mohawk wrote to Norcon stating that, based on revised avoided cost estimates, substantial credits in Niagara Mohawk's favor would occur in the adjustment account during the second pricing period. As a result, the company's analysis indicated that the cumulative avoided cost account would exceed $610 million by the end of the second period. Concerned that Norcon would be unable to satisfy the escalating credits in the third period, Niagara Mohawk demanded that Norcon provide adequate assurance that it would duly perform all of its future repayment obligations. Norcon sued Niagara Mohawk, seeking a declaration that Niagara Mohawk had no contractual right to demand adequate assurance.

The district court found that New York common law recognizes the doctrine of demand for adequate assurance only when a promisor becomes insolvent or when the contract involves a sale of goods and is therefore governed by the Uniform Commercial Code. The decision was appealed to the U.S. Court of Appeals for the Second Circuit, which certified the question to the New York Court of Appeals for assistance in correct application of New York law.

ISSUE PRESENTED Can a party demand adequate assurance of future performance when reasonable grounds arise to believe that the other party will commit a breach by nonperformance of a contract governed by New York law, when the other party is solvent and the contract is not governed by the Uniform Commercial Code?

(Continued)

(Case 7.4 continued)

OPINION BELLACOSA, J., writing for the New York Court of Appeals:

This Court is . . . persuaded that the policies underlying the UCC 2–609 counterpart should apply with similar cogency for the resolution of this kind of controversy. [*Ed.:* Section 2-609 of the UCC provides that a party to a contract for the sale of goods has the right to demand assurances of future performance from the other party when grounds for insecurity exist. If no such assurances are provided, the party may assume that a repudiation has occurred.] A useful analogy can be drawn between the contract at issue and a contract for the sale of goods. If the contract here was in all respects the same, except that it was for the sale of oil or some other tangible commodity instead of the sale of electricity, the parties would unquestionably be governed by the demand for adequate assurance of performance factors in UCC 2–609. We are convinced to take this prudent step because it puts commercial parties in these kinds of disputes at relatively arms length equilibrium in terms of reliability and uniformity of governing legal rubrics. The availability of the doctrine may even provide an incentive and tool for parties to resolve their own differences, perhaps without the necessity of judicial intervention. Open, serious re-negotiation of dramatic developments and changes in unusual contractual expectations and qualifying circumstances would occur because of and with an eye to the doctrine's application.

The various authorities, factors and concerns, in sum, prompt the prudence and awareness of the usefulness of recognizing the extension of the doctrine of demand for adequate assurance, as a common law analogue. It should apply to the type of long-term commercial contract between corporate entities entered into by Norcon and Niagara Mohawk here, which is complex and not reasonably susceptible of all security features being anticipated, bargained for and incorporated in the original contract. Norcon's performance, in terms of reimbursing Niagara Mohawk for credits, is still years away. In the meantime, potential quantifiable damages are accumulating and Niagara Mohawk must weigh the hard choices and serious consequences that the doctrine of demand for adequate assurance is designed to mitigate.

RESULT The New York Court of Appeals found that the doctrine of adequate assurance of future performance should be incorporated into New York common law and applied to long-term commercial contracts between corporate entities.

QUESTIONS

1. Are there circumstances in which it would be appropriate to permit a party to demand adequate assurance of future performance under a contract for sale of goods but not under a contract for services?
2. Why did the court limit its holding to long-term commercial contracts between corporate entities?

FRUSTRATION OF PURPOSE

Frustration of purpose occurs when performance is possible, but changed circumstances have made the contract useless to one or both of the parties. A famous example is the King Edward VII coronation case.[17] Henry contracted to rent a room in London from Krell for the ac-

17. Krell v. Henry, 2 K.B. 740 (C.A. 1903).

knowledged purpose of viewing King Edward VII's coronation procession. Krell had advertised the room as one that would be good for viewing the coronation. When the King became ill with appendicitis and the coronation was postponed, Henry refused to pay for the apartment. Krell sued. The English court ruled that Henry did not have to pay because the entire reason for the contract had been "frustrated."

Note that performance of the contract was not impossible: Henry still could have rented the room. The outcome of the case would have been different if the room had not been rented for the express purpose of viewing the coronation. In that case, Krell would have won because the purpose of the contract would have just been for the rental of the room, not for the viewing of the coronation.

The contract defense of frustration requires that (1) the parties' principal purpose in making the contract is frustrated, (2) without that party's fault, (3) by the occurrence of an event, the nonoccurrence of which was a basic assumption on which the contract was made. For performance to be excused, this frustration of purpose must have occurred without the defendant's fault. The defense of frustration is unavailable if the defendant helped cause the frustrating event or if the parties were aware of the possibility of the frustrating event when they entered into the contract.

CONTRACTS WITH THE GOVERNMENT AND THE SOVEREIGN ACTS DOCTRINE

Changes in the law can also affect contracts. When a party's performance is made illegal or impossible because of a new law, performance of the contract is usually discharged, and damages are not awarded. But what happens when a party contracts with the government, and the government then promulgates a new law making its own performance impossible? If it no longer wishes to follow a contract, can the government simply change the law to make performance illegal, thereby discharging its obligations?

According to the *sovereign acts doctrine*, the government cannot be held liable for breach of contract due to legislative or executive acts. Because one Congress cannot bind a later Congress, the general rule is that subsequent acts of the government can discharge the government's preexisting contractual obligations.

This doctrine has limits, however. If Congress passes legislation deliberately targeting its extant contractual obligations, the defense otherwise provided by the sovereign acts doctrine is unavailable.[18] In that situation, the government is not prevented from changing the law, but it must pay damages for its legislatively chosen breach. On the other hand, if a new law of general application indirectly affects a government contract and makes the government's performance impossible, the sovereign acts doctrine will protect the government in a subsequent suit for breach of the contract.

18. United States v. Winstar, 518 U.S. 839 (1996).

 ## Contract Modification

Traditional contract law does not allow a contract to be modified if the modification would change the obligations of only one party. Under this view, no consideration has been given for the change. Over time, lawyers developed a variety of techniques to meet the formal requirements of consideration. One technique was *novation,* by which a new party is substituted for one of the old parties, and a new contract is written (with the consent of all old and new parties) effecting the desired change. Another technique was formal change, where the consideration for the desired modification is a formal but meaningless change, such as making the payment in cash rather than with a bank check. Similarly, if both parties agree to terminate the contract and enter into a new one, the new one will be valid.

Discharge *of* Contract

Once a manager has entered into a legally enforceable contract, his or her next concern is determining when the contractual obligations have been terminated or *discharged.* Most commonly, a contract is discharged when both parties have fully performed their obligations toward one another. But what happens when one party performs and the other does not? Or when one party performs only some of its obligations under the contract? These questions are answered under the rules on discharging contracts.

If one party fails to perform a contract according to its essential terms, such as by not performing a service after receiving payment, that party has *materially breached* the contract. Any material breach of a contract discharges the nonbreaching party from its obligations and provides grounds to sue for damages. A breach is minor if the essential terms and purpose of the contract have been fulfilled. In the case of a minor breach, the nonbreaching party still retains its contractual obligations but may suspend performance or sue for damages.

An *anticipatory repudiation* of a contract occurs when one party knows ahead of time (before performance is due) that the other party will breach the contract. Such a repudiation is treated as a material breach of the contract. By treating an anticipatory repudiation as a breach, the nonbreaching party can avoid having to wait until an actual breach before taking action.

Contracts may also be discharged by the failure or occurrence of certain conditions stipulated in the contract, such as a condition precedent or a condition subsequent,

IN BRIEF

Decision Tree for Contract Analysis

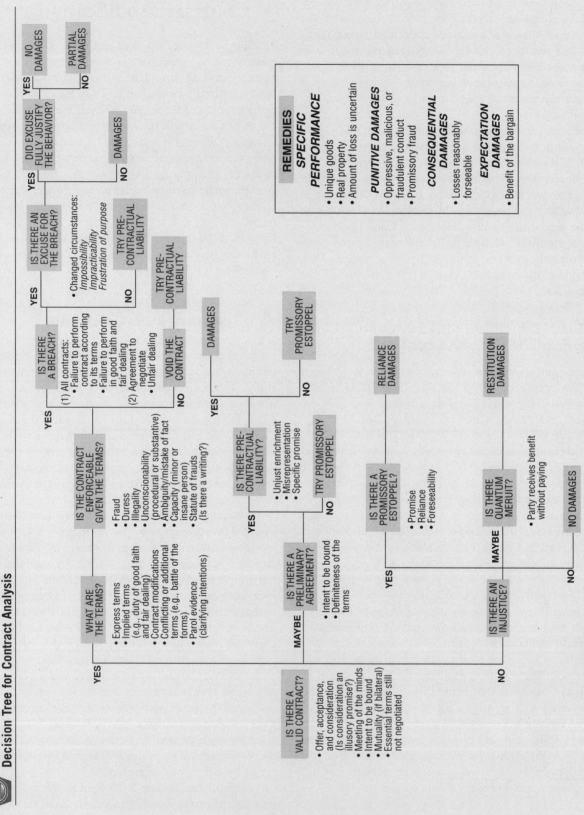

REMEDIES

SPECIFIC PERFORMANCE
- Unique goods
- Real property
- Amount of loss is uncertain

PUNITIVE DAMAGES
- Oppressive, malicious, or fraudulent conduct
- Promissory fraud

CONSEQUENTIAL DAMAGES
- Losses reasonably forseeable

EXPECTATION DAMAGES
- Benefit of the bargain

IS THERE A VALID CONTRACT?
- Offer, acceptance, and consideration (Is consideration an illusory promise?)
- Meeting of the minds
- Intent to be bound
- Mutuality (if bilateral)
- Essential terms still not negotiated

IS THERE A PRELIMINARY AGREEMENT?
- Intent to be bound
- Definiteness of the terms

IS THERE PRE-CONTRACTUAL LIABILITY?
- Unjust enrichment
- Misrepresentation
- Specific promise

IS THERE A PROMISSORY ESTOPPEL?
- Promise
- Reliance
- Foreseeability

IS THERE QUANTUM MERUIT?
- Party receives benefit without paying

IS THERE AN INJUSTICE?

WHAT ARE THE TERMS?
- Express terms
- Implied terms (e.g., duty of good faith and fair dealing)
- Contract modifications
- Conflicting or additional terms (e.g., battle of the forms)
- Parol evidence (clarifying intentions)

IS THE CONTRACT ENFORCEABLE GIVEN THE TERMS?
- Fraud
- Duress
- Illegality
- Unconscionability (procedural or substantive)
- Ambiguity/mistake of fact
- Capacity (minor or insane person)
- Statute of frauds (Is there a writing?)

IS THERE A BREACH?
(1) All contracts:
- Failure to perform contract according to its terms
- Failure to perform in good faith and fair dealing
(2) Agreement to negotiate
- Unfair dealing

IS THERE AN EXCUSE FOR THE BREACH?
- Changed circumstances:
  Impossibility
  Impracticability
  Frustration of purpose

DID EXCUSE FULLY JUSTIFY THE BEHAVIOR?

NO DAMAGES

PARTIAL DAMAGES

DAMAGES

TRY PRE-CONTRACTUAL LIABILITY

VOID THE CONTRACT

DAMAGES

TRY PROMISSORY ESTOPPEL

RELIANCE DAMAGES

RESTITUTION DAMAGES

NO DAMAGES

YES NO MAYBE

Source: This was prepared by Sheila Bonini with information and input from Constance E. Bagley. Used by permission.

as discussed above. If both parties agree, they may terminate the contract by *mutual rescission*. A mutual rescission is itself a type of contract and, as such, requires a valid offer, acceptance, and consideration. Often the consideration is simply the agreement by both parties not to enforce their legal obligations.

If one party prefers to retain the original contract but wants to contract with someone else, a third party may be substituted for one of the original parties. The third party will assume the original party's rights and responsibilities. All parties must agree to the substitution. Formally, a new contract is formed, with the same terms but with different parties.

An *accord and satisfaction* is any agreement to accept performance that is different from what is called for in the contract. For example, a contract involving a debt that is subject to a good faith dispute can be discharged by accord and satisfaction. Assume a creditor believes he is owed $100,000, but the debtor feels she owes only $75,000. An *accord* is formed when the creditor accepts the debtor's offer to settle the dispute for an amount less than the creditor claims is due (say, by cashing the debtor's check for $80,000 with "Full Payment" written on it). *Satisfaction* is the discharge of the debt.

Parties may sometimes have a valid contract that is discharged by operation of law. Certain types of changed circumstances, such as impossibility, impracticability, or frustration of purpose (described above), may discharge the contractual obligations of both parties. A bankruptcy proceeding by one party can also discharge its contractual obligations. Similarly, failing to file suit for breach of contract before the time specified in the statute of limitations has passed effectively discharges a contract because the courts will no longer enforce it. In many states, an action for breach of a written contract must be filed within four years after the breach occurs.

⚓ Duty *of* Good Faith *and* Fair Dealing

Every contract contains an implied covenant of good faith and fair dealing in its performance. This implied covenant imposes on each party a duty not to do anything that will deprive the other party of the benefits of the agreement. One court defined a lack of good faith as "some type of affirmative action consisting of at least . . . a design to mislead or to deceive another."[19] The covenant has been implied and enforced in a variety of contexts, including insurance contracts, agreements to

make mutual wills, agreements to sell real property, employment agreements, and leases. (Its application in the employment context is discussed in Chapter 14.)

Courts have long deemed the relationship between insurance companies and their insured a special relationship that calls for a careful examination of the faithfulness of contractual dealings. For example, suppose Reese is looking for an apartment. He comes upon Tara's apartment building and proceeds up the stairs to speak with the manager. Reese trips on a broken step, falls, and breaks his arm and leg. It is clear that the steps had not been maintained very well. Tara has insurance of $125,000 to cover this type of liability claim. Reese's lawyer originally demands $120,000, which includes a claim for punitive damages. Tara's insurance company refuses to pay the claim; the company does not believe that Tara was negligent and takes the case to trial. The jury awards Reese $180,000. Tara is liable for the full amount, although she was insured for only $125,000. Tara then brings an action against her insurance company for not settling the claim within the policy limits. Under the implied covenant of good faith and fair dealing, the insurance company will have the obligation to pay the full $180,000 judgment. An insurance company can refuse to settle within the policy limits. But once an insurance company refuses an offer to settle within the policy limits and instead goes to trial, the company becomes contractually responsible for paying whatever amount is awarded at trial.

In addition, claims that a party has complied with the terms of the contract may not be sufficient to satisfy its duty of good faith and fair dealing. In *Marsu B.V. v. Walt Disney Co.*,[20] Disney entered into an agreement with Marsu B.V. regarding a cartoon character "Marsupilami" owned by Marsu. Under the terms of the agreement, Disney was to create half-hour animated films for broadcast on television and to coordinate a merchandising campaign that would provide broad exposure for Marsupilami. Although Disney did some merchandising, the company's effort was halfhearted; among other things, junior employees were assigned to the project, and the merchandising campaign was not coordinated with the television broadcasts. A memo written by a Disney executive that was introduced as evidence of Disney's attitude toward the campaign stated that "we have neither the time nor the resources to do Marsu right" and "we have lots of other Disney priorities, more important both financially and strategically." The U.S. Court of Appeals for the Ninth Circuit rejected Disney's argument that it had fulfilled its express obligations under the terms of

---

19. Bunge Corp. v. Recker, 519 F.2d 449, 452 (8th Cir. 1975).

20. 185 F.3d 932 (9th Cir. 1999).

the contract and affirmed the district court's determination that Disney had breached the implied covenant of good faith and fair dealing.

The precise meanings of "good faith" and "fair dealing" are the subject of extended debate among legal scholars. The terms themselves are ambiguous, and the practical meanings may vary over time. What was considered fair dealing twenty years ago may be considered unfair today, and vice versa.

Two commonly used rules of thumb, though not precise, do offer guidance. Managers in doubt can ask themselves whether an action would embarrass them or their company if it became public. They can also consider whether they would follow the same course of action if they were dealing with a friend or relative. Although these questions address moral rather than legal issues, they can be useful in evaluating whether a contemplated action would meet the legal test of good faith. (Good faith in the context of negotiations is discussed more fully later in this chapter.)

 # Third-Party Beneficiaries

A person who is not a party to a contract can sometimes enforce the contract between the contracting parties. For example, suppose Sheila agrees to sell to Fernando a piece of real property in exchange for a $100,000 payment by Fernando to Jack. Fernando is the promisor, Sheila is the promisee, and Jack is the *third-party beneficiary* or intended beneficiary. A person is not a third-party beneficiary with legal rights to enforce the contract unless the contracting parties intended to benefit that party.

CREDITOR BENEFICIARY

If the promisee entered into the contract in order to discharge a duty he or she owed the third party, then the third party is a *creditor beneficiary* and has the right to enforce the contract between the promisor and the promisee. The third party must prove, however, that the promisee intended the contract to satisfy her obligation to him. For example, if Sheila owed Jack $100,000 and she and Fernando agree that she will sell land to Fernando in order to pay off that debt, Jack has enforceable rights under the contract as a creditor beneficiary. Jack can sue Fernando directly to compel performance. If the contract is not carried out, Jack also has the option of suing Sheila for the $100,000 she owes him.

 ETHICAL CONSIDERATION

Alejandro purchased a forty-foot-wide strip of land from a homeowner for a small sum of money. He then sold most of the land to the county, which laid down a road on the land. Alejandro kept a two-foot-wide strip of the land between the homeowner's property and the new road. When the homeowner crossed over this two-foot strip to get to the road, Alejandro threatened to sue for trespass. He then offered to sell back the two-foot strip for an extravagant sum. Should a court rescind the contract? On what theory? Was Alejandro's conduct ethical?

DONEE BENEFICIARY

A *donee beneficiary* is created when the promisee does not owe an obligation to the third party but rather wishes to confer a gift. For example, if Sheila agreed to sell her property to Fernando for $100,000 in order to make a $100,000 gift to Jack, Jack would be a donee beneficiary and could enforce the contract in most jurisdictions, but only against Fernando. Some jurisdictions, such as New York, require a family relationship between the donee beneficiary and the promisee before allowing the beneficiary to sue under the contract.

 # Damages

If one party breaches a contract, the other party is entitled to monetary damages or, in some instances, a court order requiring performance. The purpose of damages is to give the plaintiff the benefit of the bargain it contracted for, that is, to put the plaintiff in the position it would have been in had the contract been performed. A secondary purpose of damages is to discourage breaches of contract. However, recognizing that breaching a contract is sometimes economically efficient, the legal system generally does not punish a party for breach of contract alone. Punitive damages, traditionally a tort remedy, may be awarded if the court finds oppressive, malicious, or fraudulent conduct. For example, if one party enters into a contract knowing that it will not perform its obligations under the contract, that party may be liable for promissory fraud.

Over the years, a variety of methods have developed to measure appropriate monetary damages. The three standard measures are (1) expectation, (2) reliance, and (3) restitution. These measures may seem similar, but the resulting damage awards can be very different, as discussed below.

TYPES OF DAMAGES

Expectation Damages *Expectation damages* give the plaintiff the benefit of its bargain, putting the plaintiff in the cash position it would have been in if the contract had been fulfilled. For example, suppose an independent contractor agrees to work for $15 per hour. When the time comes to start working, the independent contractor reneges. The employer can find another independent contractor elsewhere, but the market price is now $20 per hour. This extra cost will cut into the profit margin on the product that the independent contractor was helping to manufacture. Instead of spending $600 for a forty-hour workweek, the employer must now pay $800. The employer's expectation damages are the difference between the two expenditures, that is, $200 per week.

Consequential Damages In addition to damages that compensate for the breach itself, the plaintiff is entitled to *consequential damages,* that is, compensation for losses that occur as a foreseeable result of the breach. For example, suppose the employer in the example above contracts with another person at $20 per hour, but the new independent contractor cannot start working until two weeks after the original independent contractor, so the employer has to hire a temporary employee at $21 per hour for two weeks. Thus, the employer faces an additional cost of $1 more per hour for two weeks, which results in $80 additional damages. This $80 is added to the $200 per week in expectation damages. If the two-week delay causes the employer to be late in delivering its product to one of its customers, any late fees the employer pays will also be added to the damages.

Consequential damages must be reasonably foreseeable. They will be awarded only if the breaching party knew, or should have known, that the loss would result from a breach of the contract.

For example, in *Hadley v. Baxendale,*[21] a mill owner sent a broken crankshaft by carrier to be repaired. Because this was the mill's only crankshaft, the mill was completely shut down until the carrier returned with the repaired crankshaft. The carrier did not deliver the shaft as quickly as promised. The mill owner sued the carrier for profits lost during the time the mill was closed. The English appellate court did not award damages for lost profits. The court observed that most mills had more

than one crankshaft, so the carrier had no way of knowing that the nondelivery of the crankshaft would mean the closure of the mill. In order for lost profits to have been awarded, the lost profits would have had to be reasonably foreseeable or a natural consequence of the breach. Neither was the case here.

In another case, a stove manufacturer paid a carrier $50 to ship a new model of stove to a major exhibition.[22] The stove did not arrive until the exhibition was over. The manufacturer sued for the value of all the lost business he had expected to get at the exhibition. The court found that the $50 was too small an amount to serve as insurance for the entire business. Moreover, the value of the lost business was too speculative to calculate with any certainty. Damages were limited to the shipping expenses of $50.

Uncertainty of Damages In the stove case just described, it was impossible to measure the consequential damages (the stove manufacturer's lost business). Sometimes it is not possible to know even what the benefit of the bargain would have been. For example, Publisher & Sons signs a contract to publish a book Rachel Author has written. It is her first book. Publisher later decides not to publish the book. To what damages is Rachel entitled? The benefit of her bargain would be the royalties from a published book, but the parties have no way to measure how much those royalties would have been. Because Rachel has the burden of proving the amount of her loss, she may collect very little in damages.

Similarly, new businesses have no record of past profits by which to estimate the loss caused by a breach. Traditionally, this prevented start-ups from collecting anything for lost profits. Today, however, new businesses are having more success recovering damages as more sophisticated methods are developed for projecting future profits.

Reliance Damages *Reliance damages* compensate the plaintiff for any expenditures it made in reliance on a contract that was subsequently breached. Instead of giving the plaintiff the benefit of the bargain, reliance damages return it to the position it was in before the contract was formed. For example, a seller agrees to sell a buyer a heavy drill press. The buyer invests in renovation work to strengthen the floor where the drill press will be placed. The buyer tells the seller of this work. The seller then sells the drill press to someone else. Reliance damages will require the seller to reimburse the buyer for the renovation expenses.

---

21. 156 Eng. Rep. 145 (1854).

22. Security Stove & Mfg. Co. v. American Ry. Express Co., 51 S.W.2d 572 (Mo. Ct. App. 1932).

Restitution and *Quantum Meruit* Restitution is similar to reliance damages, but whereas reliance damages look at what the plaintiff has lost, *restitution* looks at what the other party has gained from the transaction. The usual measure of restitution is the amount it would cost the receiver of the benefit to buy that benefit elsewhere.

A court will order restitution under the doctrine of *quantum meruit* when one party has received a benefit for which it has not paid and there was no contract between the parties. The obligation to give restitution is implied as a matter of law. For example, suppose a doctor provides medical service to an unconscious accident victim. The doctor normally charges $200 for the care rendered. The patient could have gotten the same care from another doctor for $100. The value of the care to the patient is therefore $100. Because the patient was unconscious, he was unable to bargain for the services and enter into a contract. In a situation like this, to prevent the patient from benefiting unfairly, a court will act as though a contract existed. The court will order the pa-

tient to make restitution by paying the doctor $100 for her services.

Similarly, suppose that an entrepreneur asks an advertising agency to place an advertisement. The agency contracts with an industry publication to place the ad but fails to pay for it. Under the doctrine of *quantum meruit*, the advertising agency's default on payment for the advertisement renders the entrepreneur liable to the publication for the value of the benefit the entrepreneur received (the advertisement). The entrepreneur must pay for the ad even though there was no contract between the entrepreneur and the publication.

In the following case, the U.S. Court of Federal Claims considered whether to award Glendale Federal Bank with expectation, reliance, or restitution damages as a result of the federal government's breach of contract. The bank suffered losses when the government passed the Financial Institutions Reform, Recovery and Enforcement Act.

A CASE IN POINT

CASE 7.5

Glendale Federal Bank, FSB v. United States

United States Court of Federal Claims
43 Fed. Cl. 390
(Fed. 1999).

In the Language of the Court

FACTS In 1981, Glendale Federal Bank, a savings and loan institution in California, entered into a supervisory merger with First Federal Savings and Loan Association of Broward County in Florida. At the time of the merger, the market value of First Federal's liabilities exceeded the market value of its assets by $734 million. Pursuant to its contract with the government, Glendale was permitted to treat First Federal's negative net worth as goodwill for regulatory capital purposes and to amortize it over a forty-year period. Otherwise, Glendale would immediately have become insolvent.

In 1989, eight years into the contract, Congress passed the Financial Institutions Reform, Recovery and Enforcement Act (FIRREA). The FIRREA eliminated Glendale's ability to count goodwill as regulatory capital by requiring an accelerated amortization schedule. The FIRREA also established new capital requirements. Glendale initially failed to meet these new requirements and was forced to engineer a massive recapitalization to satisfy them.

The U.S. Supreme Court had previously ruled in *United States v. Winstar*[23] that banks such as Glendale had an enforceable contract with the government to treat negative net worth in supervisory mergers as goodwill and to count such goodwill toward capital requirements. Because the government breached this contract, Glendale filed suit seeking damages.

ISSUE PRESENTED Under what contract measure of relief, expectancy, reliance, or restitution, is Glendale entitled to recover damages?

OPINION SMITH, J., writing for the U.S. Court of Federal Claims:

It is the court's view that restitution provides the clearest and best rule for allocating damages in this case. That is because the complexity, breadth, and length of the contract which was breached make it difficult to award expectancy damages, in-

23. 518 U.S. 839 (1996).

(Continued)

(Case 7.5 continued)

cluding Glendale's lost profits. . . . The difficulty, as plaintiff's model demonstrates, is the bank is operating in a dynamic market, making dynamic decisions, and responding to millions of stimuli in order to run a profitable enterprise. The government's breach fundamentally altered how the bank did these things, which makes it difficult to determine what plaintiff would have done to generate a return on their regulatory and regular capital. The extent of the breach, and the consequent difficulty in ascertaining lost profits, does not, and should not, however, immunize the government from paying appropriate damages.

Restitution provides a remedy, and a fair one. . . . Restitution, which is designed to return the parties to the position they would have been in had the contract not been made, would assign any benefits conferred on defendant at the time the contract was formed to plaintiff.

…

[T]he regulators who engineered the deal *at the time it was made* valued the benefit to the government at three-quarters of a billion dollars, or roughly what Glendale currently says was the immediate benefit to the government. . . .

Accordingly, the value of the benefit conferred by Glendale to the government, at the time the contract was made, is $798.291 million, which is comprised of the government's contemporaneous calculation of the total loss to FSLIC avoided by the merger through September 30, 1981, as well as additional losses of $14.5 million incurred by Broward between September 30 and November 19, 1981. The government does not dispute these numbers, only their relevance to any damage award, so the court accepts plaintiff's calculation.

[*Ed.:* The court also awarded nonoverlapping reliance damages, "wounded bank damages," caused by Glendale's failure to maintain capital compliance after the breach. Glendale provided evidence that it would not have fallen out of compliance but for its entry into the contract with the government and the breach by the government. The evidence showed that Glendale lost a historical advantage in cost of funds over its competitors because the government's breach ultimately forced Glendale out of capital compliance.]

RESULT Glendale was entitled to recover restitution damages and "nonoverlapping reliance damages" for a total of $908,498,000 in damages.

COMMENTS Glendale's former chief executive commented that the court's ruling "underscores the fact that the federal government must respect the sanctity of a contract."[24]

QUESTIONS

1. Why didn't Glendale receive expectation damages?
2. Given that the plaintiff bears the burden of proving damages, why was Glendale able to recover anything?

24. Richard B. Schmitt, *Judge Orders U.S. to Pay $908.9 Million to California Thrift Glendale Federal*, WALL ST. J., Apr. 12, 1999, at A4.

MITIGATION OF DAMAGES

When one party breaches a contract, the other party has a duty to use reasonable efforts to *mitigate,* or lessen, the amount of damages that flow from the breach. As a general rule, the nonbreaching party cannot recover damages that it could have reasonably avoided. This gives the nonbreaching party an incentive to make the best of a bad situation.

For example, suppose a manufacturing company and a hazardous-waste collection company enter into a contract whereby the collection company agrees to pick up hazardous waste for a fee of $500 per pickup. If the collection company fails to pick up the hazardous waste, the manufacturer should *cover*—find another hazardous-waste collection company at the current market price, say, $625 per pickup at the time of breach. The manufacturing company would still be entitled to expectation damages, measured by the difference between the market price at the time it learned of the breach ($625 per collection stop) and the contract price ($500 per collection stop), plus any consequential damages, such as extra storage fees, late fees, and expenses incurred in finding a substitute hazardous-waste collection company.

The manufacturing company could also elect not to cover. If it does not cover, however, the company is limited to expectation damages (as measured above) and cannot recover any consequential damages that could have been prevented by covering, such as late fees. If no cover is available, then the manufacturing company is entitled to foreseeable consequential damages resulting from the breach.

Additionally, the manufacturing company must avoid compounding damages from the breach. If hazardous waste collection services are available at both $625 and $650 per pickup and the quality is the same, then the manufacturing company will be required to purchase at the lower price. Thus, its expectation damages are limited to $125 per pickup. Any expenses incurred by the manufacturing company in reasonably attempting to mitigate damages, such as the costs of finding another collection company, are also recoverable under consequential damages, regardless of whether the efforts were successful.

From the seller's perspective, the duty to mitigate damages works similarly. For example, suppose a software company contracts to develop a customized program for a small architecture firm. The developer learns midway through the development process that the firm plans to breach the contract. The developer should cover by finding another buyer for the software, then charge the breaching firm for the difference between the contract price and the resale price (expectation damages), plus any consequential damages. If no other buyer is available, perhaps because the program is too customized, the developer should immediately stop its work and charge the breaching firm for expenses incurred plus the expected net profit.

Mitigation of damages is also important in the context of employment. If, for instance, an accountant is wrongfully terminated and files suit against her em-

ployer for lost wages, she cannot go away on vacation until the case is concluded and still collect all her lost wages. Her duty to mitigate her damages requires that she make reasonable efforts to obtain similar employment elsewhere, such as an accounting position in the same city. Unless the contract expressly provides otherwise, any recovery of lost wages under a wrongfully terminated employment contract will be reduced by what the employee earned or reasonably could have earned at a comparable job. Conversely, if the accountant had quit while under an employment contract, the employer would be required to make reasonable efforts to find a replacement for her. Courts will limit the employer's recovery to the difference between the cost of the replacement and the compensation specified in the original employment contract.

In *Boehms v. Crowell*,[25] concerning an employee's claim under the Age Discrimination in Employment Act, the court considered whether an employee is required to accept a position that involves less responsibility than his previous job in order to mitigate his damages. In this case, a manager lost his job following a reorganization and participated in the company's employee transition program, which allowed him to continue at the company for six months while he searched for another job. During those six months, he refused to accept a position that was inferior to his former position. The court found that his participation in the employee transition program and his search for new employment satisfied his duty to mitigate damages. The court, rejected the defendant's argument that the manager had an obligation to accept the inferior position: "We are unimpressed by this argument, as it would lead to the untenable result that a claimant in [the employee's] position must accept almost any position that becomes available while participating in a temporary employee assistance program. . . ."[26] However, the employee's refusal to take the inferior position did bar recovery of back pay beyond the date of his retirement without proof that his retirement constituted constructive discharge.

LIQUIDATED DAMAGES

The parties to a contract may include a clause that specifies the amount of money to be paid if one of them should later breach the agreement. Such *liquidated damages* clauses are frequently used in real estate and construction contracts. The amount of the liquidated

25. 139 F.3d 452 (5th Cir. 1998), *cert. denied,* 525 U.S. 1102 (1999).
26. *Id*. at 460.

damages should be the parties' best estimate of what the expectation damages would be. Courts will not enforce penalties. Thus, clauses that provide for damages that are substantially higher than the losses will not be enforced. The purpose of contract damages is to restore the aggrieved party to the position it would have been in had the contract been performed, not to punish the party who has committed the breach.

PENALTIES

Although parties may recover punitive damages in certain situations, courts will not force a party to pay multiple damages for the same contractual violation. In the following case, the court considered whether revocation of a license and payment of damages constituted double recovery.

A CASE IN POINT

CASE 7.6

MCA Television, Ltd. v. Public Interest Corp.
*United States Court of Appeals for the Eleventh Circuit
171 F.3d 1265
(11th Cir. 1999).*

In the Language of the Court

FACTS Public Interest Corporation (PIC) is a Florida corporation that owns and operates television station WTMV-TV in Lakeland, Florida. MCA Television (MCA) owns and licenses syndicated television programs. In 1990, MCA and PIC entered into a contract in which MCA agreed to license several television shows on a "barter basis" for advertising time on WTMV. MCA conditioned this exchange on PIC's agreement to license one other show, *Harry and the Hendersons,* for cash as well as barter. The two parties subsequently entered into additional licensing agreements for four other MCA television shows. These licensing agreements established a payment schedule and provided that late payment would constitute a default giving MCA the right to terminate the license. The agreements further contained a damages provision stating that, in the event of a default by PIC, MCA could (1) recover damages equivalent to the full value of the contract and (2) revoke PIC's broadcast licenses, recovering other available damages.

From the outset, PIC's payments were consistently behind schedule, but MCA did not object. PIC broadcast *Harry* and paid MCA with three minutes of advertising time, pursuant to the barter portion of the agreement. However, before payments in satisfaction of the cash portion of the agreement were scheduled to begin, PIC expressed its belief that it was not obligated under that portion of the contract. MCA demanded payment for *Harry* as well as late payments on the four other programs PIC had later licensed. After PIC denied any obligation to pay, MCA suspended PIC's broadcast rights and stated that any telecast of MCA programming by WTMV-TV would amount to copyright infringement. PIC continued to broadcast MCA's programs with the exception of *Harry.*

MCA filed suit against PIC alleging copyright infringement and breach of contract. Pursuant to the parties' damages provision, the trial court awarded MCA $804,538.65 for breach of contract and $1,060,000 for copyright infringement. PIC appealed.

ISSUE PRESENTED Did the award of damages for breach of contract as well as for copyright infringement, as permitted under the damages provision, constitute an improper double recovery?

OPINION BARKETT, J., writing for the U.S. Court of Appeals for the Eleventh Circuit:

Through the damages provision at issue here, MCA seeks to have it both ways. In demanding the full contract price in damages for the breach, MCA is effectively *ratifying* the contract, saying that the contract exists and that they are owed a recovery for its breach. But by revoking the broadcast licenses and suing in copyright, MCA is claiming to *rescind* the contract, thereby announcing that the rights established by the contract no longer exist. These statements cannot both be true—either the contract exists or it does not—but the damages provision at issue in this case would allow MCA to recover as if it were otherwise.

(Continued)

(Case 7.6 continued)

. . . [B]y incurring liability for the full contract price, PIC has, with MCA's consent, purchased the right to air the programs. Once a licensing contract has been reached between the parties, the realm of contract has been entered. And under no principle of contract law may a seller both recover the full price of the contract from a defaulting buyer *and* sue to repossess the goods that were the object of the contract. For when the buyer has paid the full contract price, whether up front or pursuant to a damages action, *the buyer owns the goods.*

The default provision at issue in this case allows MCA the equivalent of recovering the price of the goods and at the same time demanding their return: it requires PIC to pay the full licensing fees for the broadcast and at the same time wields the threat of damages in copyright infringement to prevent PIC from airing the programs for which it has already paid. This provision thus attempts to secure for MCA through the language of the contract the double recovery the election of remedies doctrine would otherwise forbid. Not only does this provision thus provide MCA a recovery for PIC's breach "disproportionate to the damages which could have been anticipated from breach of the contract," but it can only have been intended "to enforce performance of the main purpose of the contract by the compulsion of this very disproportion." It therefore establishes, not liquidated damages, but a penalty, and thus cannot be enforced.

RESULT MCA was not permitted both to recover for the full price of the contract, as if it were ratified and to sue for copyright infringement, as if the contract had been rescinded.

QUESTIONS

1. Under what circumstances will a court award punitive damages? How are these damages different from the double recovery sought by MCA?
2. How could MCA have structured the damages clause so that it would have had a right to terminate the license and also a right to some damages?

 # Specific Performance

Instead of awarding monetary damages, a court may order the breaching party to complete the contract as promised. *Specific performance* is ordered only when (1) the goods are unique (for example, an antique car or a painting), (2) the subject of the contract is real property, or (3) the amount of the loss is so uncertain that there is no fair way to calculate damages.

Courts never force an employee to provide services under an employment contract because that would constitute involuntary servitude in violation of the Thirteenth Amendment to the U.S. Constitution. For example, suppose a chief executive officer agrees to work for a corporation for five years. If she walks out after three years, the court will not force her to continue her employment. The court may, however, issue an injunction barring her from working for someone else. Similarly, if a professional baseball player with a seven-year contract

with the Boston Red Sox breaches his contract and starts playing for the Houston Astros, an injunction can be granted to prevent him from playing for the Astros.

 # Precontractual Liability

UNITED STATES

Under traditional contract law, the offeror is free to back out and revoke an offer at any time before a contract is made. A party entering negotiations does so at the risk of the negotiations breaking off. Courts typically will impose a duty to negotiate in good faith only if a letter of intent between the two parties specifically includes that duty. For example, in *Venture Associates Corp. v. Zenith Data Systems Corp.,*[27] a U.S. district court held that the two parties had entered into a preliminary

27. 887 F. Supp. 1014 (N.D. Ill. 1995).

agreement to negotiate in good faith on the basis of a letter of intent that Venture sent to Zenith Data stating, "this letter is intended to evidence the preliminary understanding which we have reached . . . and our mutual intent to negotiate in good faith to enter into a definitive Purchase Agreement." Similarly, in *Channel Home Centers v. Frank Grossman*,[28] the U.S. Court of Appeals for the Third Circuit found that Grossman had a duty to negotiate in good faith with Channel because the letter of intent signed by both parties expressly provided for their good faith negotiation of a leasing transaction.

One reason courts are reluctant to imply a common law duty to negotiate in good faith (and why some courts will not enforce an explicit promise to do so) is that determining the appropriate damages is difficult. Because negotiations failed, there is no contract to establish expectation damages. As a result, some courts will limit recovery to the out-of-pocket expenses (such as attorneys' fees) incurred by the nonbreaching party.

The parties to an agreement to negotiate should deal fairly. The standard of fair dealing ordinarily requires at least three things. First, each party must actually negotiate and refrain from imposing improper conditions on the negotiation. Second, each party must disclose enough about parallel negotiations to allow the other party to make a counterproposal. Third, each party must continue to negotiate until an impasse or an agreement has been reached.

In general, parties to a negotiation should describe as specifically as possible the duty of fair dealing to which they have agreed. Instead of simply pledging to use "best efforts" to negotiate fairly, the parties should specify whether the negotiations are to be exclusive, how long they must continue, and what must be held in confidence. Given the uncertain state of the law on these matters, no drafter should leave these items to a court to fill in.

In addition to imposing liability for a breach of the duty to negotiate, in narrow circumstances American courts will impose *precontractual liability* on theories of misrepresentation, promissory estoppel, or restitution.[29] For example, the Supreme Court of Washington found *misrepresentation* when the owner of a warehouse told the lessee that he intended to renew the lease for three years, when in fact the owner was negotiating the sale of the facility.[30]

28. 795 F.2d 291 (3d Cir. 1986).
29. For an excellent summary of the law in this area, *see* E. Allen Farnsworth, *Precontractual Liability and Preliminary Agreements: Fair Dealing and Failed Negotiations,* 87 COLUM. L. REV. 217 (1987).
30. Markov v. ABC Transfer & Storage Co., 457 P.2d 535 (Wash. 1969).

OTHER COUNTRIES

In general, other common law countries, such as the United Kingdom, do not impose liability on the theory of a common law duty to negotiate in good faith. However, civil law countries, such as France, Germany, the Netherlands, and Japan,[31] have been more willing to impose a good faith obligation during the negotiation of a contract. In 1994, the International Institute for the Unification of Private Law (Unidroit) published its Principles of International Commercial Contracts (Unidroit Principles), which set forth general rules for international commercial contracts for services. Article 2.15(2) provides that one who "breaks off negotiations in bad faith is liable for the losses caused to the other party." The Unidroit Principles, like the American Law Institute's Restatement of the Law, are not designed for legislative enactment and are primarily used in international arbitration. As a result, in many international agreements, there may be an expectation that the parties have a duty to negotiate in good faith and can be held liable if they fail to do so.

 # Mergers *and* Acquisitions

A corporation can acquire control of another corporation (the *target*) by merger, a sale of stock by the target's shareholders, or a sale of substantially all the assets of the target. A *merger agreement* is an agreement between two

31. *See* D. James Wan Kim Min v. Mitsui Bussan K.K., 1232 Hanrei Jihō (Tokyo High Court 1987), quoted in YUKO YANAGIDA ET AL., LAW AND INVESTMENT IN JAPAN, 223 (1994) (TRAN.).

 INTERNATIONAL CONSIDERATION

When doing business with companies in other nations, it is important to remember that although the law in the United States stems from a common law tradition, most non-English-speaking countries follow the civil law tradition. This system of jurisprudence was originally used in the Roman Empire, where it included institutes, codes, digests, and novels. Civil law countries rely primarily on codes (such as the Napoleonic Code in France) rather than case-by-case common law to develop rules for behavior. Therefore, it is prudent to include in multinational contracts a provision stating which country's law will apply (a choice-of-law provision) and in which jurisdiction a dispute must be brought (a choice-of-forum provision).

companies to combine into a single entity. Mergers and sales of substantially all the assets generally cannot be completed until the transaction is approved by the shareholders of both the acquiring and the target company.

Mergers and acquisitions are usually highly negotiated transactions that are governed by detailed acquisition agreements containing representations and warranties (statements about the entity being sold), covenants (promises to do or refrain from doing something), and conditions (events that must occur before either party has a duty to *close,* or consummate, the transaction, as well as events that will terminate a party's obligation to close). The seller's representations and warranties typically cover such matters as the proper organization of the entity as a corporation, the accuracy of its financial statements, title to its assets, the absence of undisclosed liabilities and undisclosed legal proceedings, and its compliance with all laws and contractual obligations by which it is bound. Covenants typically include promises to (1) conduct the business in the ordinary course until the closing date, (2) refrain from entering into any major new contracts, and (3) permit access to the business to enable the buyer to conduct due diligence.

Acquisition agreements in transactions involving private companies typically provide for indemnification by the seller for breaches of its representations, warranties, and covenants. The seller may also require the buyer to include indemnification provisions if the buyer is purchasing the company with shares of its stock. Public company acquisition agreements typically do not include indemnification clauses because the sellers consist of public shareholders and collecting indemnification from them would be virtually impossible.

The indemnification provisions often limit the seller's or buyer's exposure to some percentage of the total purchase price. In some agreements, different ceilings apply to different types of liabilities. In addition, the provisions may require that breaches of representations, warranties, or covenants be material before indemnification will be available. For example, the parties might agree that a claim must be worth at least $100,000 before the seller has an obligation to pay any damages to the buyer. If the parties decide to establish a dollar threshold, they must also decide whether the threshold should be a deductible amount or whether the indemnifying party should provide "dollar one" coverage. For example, under an agreement that uses the deductible approach, if the claim is $150,000 and the threshold is $100,000, the indemnifying party would be liable only for $50,000, the excess over $100,000. However, if the agreement uses the dollar one coverage approach, the party would be liable for the full amount of $150,000.

The issue of time limits on indemnification obligations is frequently one of the most controversial negotiating points in an acquisition agreement. The indemnifying party usually wants a shorter period than the applicable statute of limitations, and many acquisition agreements will place some time limit on indemnification obligations. The seller typically argues that after a certain period of time, the buyer, as the owner and operator of the business, should have discovered any misstatements. The buyer, however, often argues for longer time limits for tax claims, environmental claims, and capitalization matters as these problems may not surface for years.

CONFLICTING DUTIES

A merger agreement will frequently require the board of directors of the target to recommend the deal to the shareholders and to use its best efforts to consummate the transaction. Such a provision is called a *best-efforts clause.* What happens if a third party comes along and offers a higher price to the target company? May the directors of the target company negotiate with the third party? May they recommend the new deal to the shareholders? Has the third party incurred any liability by interfering with the previously signed merger agreement, or is the third party just being competitive by offering a better price?

In general, a third party is liable for *tortious interference with contract* if the following requirements are met: (1) there is a contract between the plaintiff and another; (2) the defendant has knowledge of that contract; (3) the defendant's actions cause the other party to breach that contract; (4) the plaintiff is damaged in some way; and (5) the defendant intentionally and wrongfully induces the other party to breach the contract.

Different courts have disagreed on what actions the target company's board of directors may or must take with regard to best-efforts clauses and what liability a competing bidder has if it succeeds in persuading the board of directors of the target company to breach the agreement with the first suitor and to recommend the second deal to the shareholders.

In *Jewel Cos. v. Pay Less Drug Stores Northwest, Inc.,*[32] the U.S. Court of Appeals for the Ninth Circuit held that the board of directors of a target company that had signed a merger agreement with one suitor could bind itself to refrain from negotiating or accepting a second merger proposal prior to the shareholder vote on the first proposal. The court stated:

32. 741 F.2d 1555 (9th Cir. 1984).

It is nowhere written in stone that the law of the jungle must be the exclusive doctrine governing parties within the world of corporate mergers. The legitimate exercise of the right to contract by responsible boards of directors can help bring some degree of much needed order to these transactions.

The court held that the third party, which offered a higher price, could be liable for tortious interference with contract if the target company and the first suitor intended by their agreement to preclude the target company from dealing with any other party until the first deal was put to the target company's shareholders for a vote.

In *ConAgra, Inc. v. Cargill, Inc.,*[33] the merger agreement between the target company and the first suitor stated that "nothing herein contained shall relieve either Board of Directors of their continuing duties to their respective shareholders." The Nebraska Supreme Court interpreted this clause to mean that the parties agreed that the target company was not contracting out of its duty to recommend the deal that would be best for its shareholders. The court held that the third party, which offered a higher price, could disrupt the merger with the first suitor without facing liability for tortious interference with contract.

The Delaware Supreme Court cited *ConAgra* with approval in *Paramount Communications, Inc. v. QVC Network, Inc.*[34] Paramount had entered into a friendly merger with Viacom. As part of the deal, Paramount granted Viacom an option to buy Paramount shares at a favorable price (a *lock-up option*) together with a termination fee payable if the merger did not go through. QVC made a hostile bid for Paramount and sought to invalidate the lock-up option, which was worth about $500 million. The Delaware Supreme Court held that because the directors of Paramount had violated their fiduciary duties by granting the option, Viacom had no enforceable contractual right to the option. This case is discussed further in Chapter 23.

FIDUCIARY OUTS

A merger agreement can be drafted to prevent the target company from soliciting other offers yet allow it to consider unsolicited offers. For example, in 2000, Warner-Lambert (WL) entered into a $72 billion merger agreement with American Home Products (AHP). The merger agreement allowed WL to consider merger proposals from other companies and provided for "cross options," which prohibited another bidder from using a favorable accounting method called "pooling of interests" to avoid goodwill write-offs against reported earnings. In addition, the agreement provided for a $2 billion breakup fee. A *breakup fee* is an agreed-on payment to a suitor if, through no fault of the suitor's, the merger is not consummated.

After the WL–AHP deal was announced, Pfizer made an $82.4 billion offer to buy WL. This was the largest unsolicited bid in corporate history. The agreement between AHP and WL gave the WL directors a *fiduciary out* because it allowed them to consider third-party merger proposals other than the AHP offer. A fiduciary out allows the target company's directors to remain faithful to their fiduciary duties to the corporation and its shareholders even after signing an agreement with a suitor. Pzifer won the battle for WL by agreeing to purchase WL in a stock swap valued at more than $90 billion and to pay AHP a $1.8 billion breakup fee.[35]

33. 382 N.W.2d 576 (Neb. 1986).
34. 637 A.2d 34 (Del. 1994).

35. Robert Langreth, *Pfizer, Warner-Lambert Agree on Terms,* Wall St. J., Feb. 7, 2000.

THE RESPONSIBLE MANAGER
Acting *in* Good Faith *and* Dealing Fairly

It is virtually always preferable to put the terms of an agreement or deal in writing. Memories of even the most well-intentioned parties fade over time. A manager should review any contract before signing it. If the terms are unfamiliar or unclear, the manager should consult an attorney. A manager should never sign a contract he or she does not understand.

It is rarely to a manager's advantage to try to slip a provision by the other party that the manager knows would be unacceptable if it were pointed out. It is far preferable to hash out any ambiguities at the negotiation stage while the parties are on good terms and in the mood to make a deal. Positions tend to polarize once the agreement is signed and a dispute arises.

Similarly, it is inappropriate and often unethical to bury offensive terms in a preprinted form contract in the hope that the other party will not spot them. Courts will sometimes refuse to enforce such terms, especially when they conflict with the position taken in the negotiations or are contrary to the spirit of the deal. It makes both legal and ethical sense to abide by the covenant of good faith and fair dealing in negotiating a contract. It is also good business. Contract litigation is expensive and time-consuming.

Managers should avoid signing a letter of intent unless they intend to be bound by its proposed terms. Many courts will let a jury decide whether there was intent to be bound, even when the letter of intent states that it is not meant to be binding. If a letter of intent is necessary to obtain financing or to begin due diligence, then the manager not intending to be bound if negotiations of the definitive agreement break down should consider doing the following: First, insert clear language into the letter stating that it is not binding, that there is no contract unless and until the parties execute a definitive written contract, and that the letter creates no obligation to negotiate in good faith and cannot be reasonably relied upon. Second, label the document "tentative proposal" or "status letter." Third, do not sign the document.[36]

36. *See* William G. Schopf et al., *When a Letter of Intent Goes Wrong,* 5 BUS. L. TODAY 31 (Jan.–Feb. 1996).

A manager should carefully consider whether there will be a conflict between the acts required by a contract and his or her fiduciary duties to the corporation and its shareholders. In general, a manager should not bind the directors to recommend a particular deal to the shareholders because it is always possible that a better offer will come along. The manager should reserve the right to recommend the best deal, even if to do so will require paying a breakup fee to the first bidder.

A manager should ensure that he or she is not tortiously interfering with the contract of another. As *Pennzoil v. Texaco,* discussed in the "Inside Story" below, demonstrates, even a very large company can be driven into bankruptcy if its executives guess wrong on either the question of whether there is a contract or the question of whether their deal tortiously interferes with it.

It is sometimes tempting to view the drafting and review of contracts as a necessary evil. However, astute managers realize that contract drafting and negotiation can provide opportunities to strengthen business relationships and to protect key assets such as trade secrets, which give a firm a competitive edge.

INSIDE STORY

Pennzoil v. Texaco

In 1983, Pennzoil Company and Getty Oil Company negotiated a memorandum of agreement for a merger. Their cadres of lawyers were in the process of drafting the final documents when Texaco, Inc. came along and offered a better price for Getty. Getty accepted Texaco's offer, and Pennzoil subsequently sued Texaco for tortious interference with a contract. To win, Getty had to prove (1) the existence of a contract, (2) Texaco's knowledge of the existence of the contract, (3) Texaco's intentional inducement of a breach of the contract, and (4) damages.[37] Texaco asserted that Pennzoil never had a contract because the parties had not yet agreed on every essential term of the deal. A Texas jury disagreed and awarded Pennzoil $10.5 billion in compensatory and punitive damages.

37. *See, e.g.,* Kronos, Inc. v. AVX Corp., 612 N.E.2d 289 (N.Y. 1993).

It took the two parties four and a half months to present all the facts and arguments to the jury. The published opinion of the Texas Court of Appeals summarizes the events in question.[38]

Excerpts from the Opinion of the Court of Appeals: Facts

For several months in late 1983, Pennzoil had followed with interest the well-publicized dissension between the board of directors of Getty Oil Company and Gordon Getty, who was a director of Getty Oil and also the owner, as trustee, of approximately 40.2% of the outstanding shares of Getty Oil. On December 28, 1983, Pennzoil announced an unsolicited, public tender offer for 16 million shares of Getty Oil at $100 each.

38. Texaco, Inc. v. Pennzoil Co., 729 S.W.2d 768 (Tex. Ct. App. 1987), *cert. dismissed,* 485 U.S. 994 (1988).

Soon afterwards, Pennzoil contacted both Gordon Getty and a representative of the J. Paul Getty Museum, which held approximately 11.8% of the shares of Getty Oil, to discuss the tender offer and the possible purchase of Getty Oil. In the first two days of January 1984, a "Memorandum of Agreement" was drafted to reflect the terms that had been reached in conversations between representatives of Pennzoil, Gordon Getty, and the Museum.

Under the plan set out in the Memorandum of Agreement, Pennzoil and the Trust (with Gordon Getty as trustee) were to become partners on a 3/7ths to 4/7ths basis, respectively, in owning and operating Getty Oil. Gordon Getty was to become chairman of the board, and Hugh Liedtke, the chief executive officer of Pennzoil, was to become chief executive officer of the new company. The plan also provided that Pennzoil and the Trust were to try in good faith to agree upon a plan to restructure Getty Oil within a year, but if they could not reach an agreement, the assets of Getty Oil were to be divided between them, 3/7ths to Pennzoil and 4/7ths to the Trust.

The Memorandum of Agreement stated that it was subject to approval of the board of Getty Oil, and it was to expire by its own terms if not approved at the board meeting that was to begin on January 2. Pennzoil's CEO, Liedtke, and Gordon Getty, for the Trust, signed the Memorandum of Agreement before the Getty Oil board meeting on January 2, and Harold Williams, the president of the Museum, signed it shortly after the board meeting began. Thus, before it was submitted to the Getty Oil board, the Memorandum of Agreement had been executed by parties who together controlled a majority of the outstanding shares of Getty Oil.

The Memorandum of Agreement was then presented to the Getty Oil board, which had previously held discussions on how the company should respond to Pennzoil's public tender offer.

The board voted to reject recommending Pennzoil's tender offer to Getty's shareholders, then later also rejected the Memorandum of Agreement price of $110 per share as too low. On the morning of January 3, Getty Oil's investment banker, Geoffrey Boisi, began calling other companies, seeking a higher bid than Pennzoil's for the Getty Oil shares.

When the board reconvened at 3 P.M. on January 3, a revised Pennzoil proposal was presented, offering $110 per share plus a $3 "stub" that was to be paid after the sale of a Getty Oil subsidiary ("ERC"), from the excess proceeds over $1 billion. Each shareholder was to receive a pro rata share of these excess proceeds, but in any case, a minimum of $3 per share at the end of five years. During the meeting, Boisi briefly informed the board of the status of his

inquiries of other companies that might be interested in bidding for the company. He reported some preliminary indications of interest, but no definite bid yet.

The Museum's lawyer told the board that, based on his discussions with Pennzoil, he believed that if the board went back "firm" with an offer of $110 plus a $5 stub, Pennzoil would accept it. After a recess, the Museum's president (also a director of Getty Oil) moved that the Getty board should accept Pennzoil's proposal provided that the stub be raised to $5, and the board voted 15 to 1 to approve this counterproposal to Pennzoil. The board then voted themselves and Getty's officers and advisors indemnity for any liability arising from the events of the past few months. There was evidence that during another brief recess of the board meeting, the counter-offer of $110 plus a $5 stub was presented to and accepted by Pennzoil. After Pennzoil's acceptance was conveyed to the Getty board, the meeting was adjourned, and most board members left town for their respective homes.

That evening, the lawyers and public relations staff of Getty Oil and the Museum drafted a press release describing the transaction between Pennzoil and the Getty entities. The press release, announcing an agreement in principle on the terms of the Memorandum of Agreement but with a price of $110 plus a $5 stub, was issued on Getty Oil letterhead the next morning, January 4, and later that day, Pennzoil issued an identical press release.

On January 4, Boisi continued to contact other companies, looking for a higher price than Pennzoil had offered. After talking briefly with Boisi, Texaco management called several meetings with its in-house financial planning group. . . .

On January 5, the *Wall Street Journal* reported on an agreement reached between Pennzoil and the Getty entities, describing essentially the terms contained in the Memorandum of Agreement. The Pennzoil board met to ratify the actions of its officers in negotiating an agreement with the Getty entities, and Pennzoil's attorneys periodically attempted to contact the other parties' advisors and attorneys to continue work on the transaction agreement.

The board of Texaco also met on January 5, authorizing its officers to make an offer for 100% of Getty Oil and to take any necessary action in connection therewith. Texaco first contacted the Museum's lawyer, Marty Lipton, and arranged a meeting to discuss the sale of the Museum's shares of Getty Oil to Texaco. Lipton instructed his associate, on her way to the meeting in progress of the lawyers drafting merger documents for the Pennzoil/Getty transaction, not to attend that meeting, because he needed her at his meeting with Texaco. At the meeting with Texaco, the Museum outlined various issues it wanted resolved in any transaction with Texaco, and then agreed to sell its 11.8% ownership in Getty Oil [for $125 per share].

At noon on January 6, Getty Oil held a telephone board meeting to discuss the Texaco offer. The board voted to withdraw its previous counterproposal to Pennzoil and unanimously voted to accept Texaco's offer. Texaco immediately issued a press release announcing that Getty Oil and Texaco would merge.

Soon after the Texaco press release appeared, Pennzoil telexed the Getty entities, demanding that they honor their agreement with Pennzoil. Later that day, prompted by the telex, Getty Oil filed a suit in Delaware for declaratory judgment that it was not bound to any contract with Pennzoil. The merger agreement between Texaco and Getty Oil was signed on January 6; the stock purchase agreement with the Museum was signed on January 6; and the stock exchange agreement with the Trust was signed on January 8, 1984.

In addition to the facts described in the excerpts from the opinion of the court of appeals, the Pennzoil lawyers emphasized several other events as evidence that both Pennzoil and Getty intended to be bound by the five-page memorandum of agreement.

At the conclusion of the January 3 Getty board meeting approving the Pennzoil merger, congratulations were exchanged, and many of the individuals present, including several Pennzoil representatives, shook hands. At trial, Texaco pointed out that, handshakes notwithstanding, the Getty board of directors left the meeting without signing the memorandum of agreement.

At trial, Pennzoil made this an issue of honor and the value of a man's word, asserting that a handshake could and often did seal a bargain. For its part, Texaco pointed to the fact that it had not made an offer until it was invited to do so by Getty. John McKinley, chairman of Texaco, repeatedly asked if Getty Oil was free to deal and was assured by Gordon Getty and by the Getty Museum that there was no contract with Pennzoil. In addition, under the law of New York, where all the deals were made, a contract does not exist until the parties have agreed on all the essential terms of the deal. Texaco argued that in a $5 billion deal involving four parties (Pennzoil, Getty Oil Company, the Sarah Getty Trust, and the Getty Museum), a five-page memorandum cannot possibly cover all the essential terms. Why else were some thirty lawyers working around the clock to draw up the merger documents?

Before going further into the many legal arguments involved, it is useful to look more closely at the memorandum of agreement reproduced in Exhibit 7.1.

Getty and Pennzoil had an agreement in principle, but did they have a contract? As soon as the board meeting adjourned on the evening of January 3, work began

on the legal documents and on the press release to announce the deal. Both were supposed to be completed by the next morning, but only the press release was ready. Typed on Getty Oil letterhead and dated January 4, 1984, it announced that Getty Oil and Pennzoil had "agreed in principle" to a merger. It further stated: "The transaction is subject to execution of a definitive merger agreement, approval by the stockholders of Getty Oil and completion of various governmental filing and waiting period requirements."

The Texaco deal was much simpler than the Pennzoil deal. Texaco simply bought out everyone at $125 a share. By 8 A.M. on January 6, a news release on Texaco letterhead had gone out. At 9 A.M., the Getty board of directors held another board meeting and approved the deal with Texaco. Texaco acquired Getty Oil, and Pennzoil was left out in the cold.

No one on Wall Street saw anything wrong with the deal, but the attitude in the Texas oil business was different. At the 1984 Pennzoil stockholder meeting, Hugh Liedtke described the decision to sue Texaco:

> It's one thing to play hardball. It's quite another thing to play foul ball. Conduct such as Texaco's is not made legal simply by protestations that the acts involved were, in fact, legal. All too often such assertions go unchallenged, and so slip into some sort of legal limbo, and become accepted as the norm by default. In this way, actions previously considered amoral somehow become clothed in respectability.[39]

On January 10, 1984, Pennzoil filed suit in Delaware against Getty Oil, Gordon Getty, the Getty Museum, and Texaco. Pennzoil wanted specific performance—that is, a court order that would give it back its deal with Getty. A few days later, Pennzoil discovered the indemnity clauses and added tortious interference with contract to its claims against Texaco.

The Delaware case was to be tried before a judge, not a jury. Through some legal maneuvering on Pennzoil's part and Texaco's failure to file an answer in the Delaware case right away, the case against Texaco ended up in a Texas court before a jury. (The suits against Getty, the Trust, and the Museum continued in Delaware.) For four and a half months, the two sides presented their evidence. Before the jury retired to the jury room, the judge instructed them how to apply the law to the facts they had heard. The word "contract" never appeared in the jury instructions. Instead, the judge used the word "agreement."

The jury deliberated and then returned a verdict in favor of Pennzoil. For Texaco's interference with a

39. Thomas Petzinger, Jr., Oil And Honor: The Texaco–Pennzoil Wars 275–76 (1987).

EXHIBIT 7.1 The Pennzoil–Getty Memorandum of Agreement

Memorandum of Agreement

January 2, 1984

The following plan (the "Plan") has been developed and approved by (i) Gordon P. Getty, as Trustee (the "Trustee") of the Sarah C. Getty Trust dated December 31, 1934 (the "Trust"), which Trustee owns 31,805,800 shares (40.2% of the total outstanding shares) of Common Stock, without par value, of Getty Oil Company (the "Company"), which shares as well as all other outstanding shares of such Common Stock are hereinafter referred to as the "Shares", (ii) The J. Paul Getty Museum (the "Museum"), which Museum owns 9,320,340 Shares (11.8% of the total outstanding Shares) and (iii) Pennzoil Company ("Pennzoil"), which owns 593,900 Shares through a subsidiary, Holdings Incorporated, a Delaware corporation (the "Purchaser"). The Plan is intended to assure that the public shareholders of the Company and the Museum will receive $110 per Share for all their Shares, a price which is approximately 40% above the price at which the Company's Shares were trading before Pennzoil's subsidiary announced its Offer (hereinafter described) and 10% more than the price which Pennzoil's subsidiary offered in its Offer for 20% of the Shares. The Trustee recommends that the Board of Directors of the Company approve the Plan. The Museum desires that the Plan be considered by the Board of Directors and has executed the Plan for that purpose.

1. Pennzoil agreement. Subject to the approval of the Plan by the Board of Directors of the Company as provided in paragraph 6 hereof, Pennzoil agrees to cause the Purchaser promptly to amend its Offer to Purchase dated December 28, 1983 (the "Offer") for up to 16,000,000 Shares so as:
   (a) to increase the Offer price to $110 per Share, net to the Seller in cash and
   (b) to increase the number of Shares subject to the Offer to 23,406,100 (being 24,000,000 Shares less 593,900 now owned by the Purchaser).

2. Company agreement. Subject to approval of the Plan by the Board of Directors of the Company as provided in paragraph 6 hereof, the Company agrees:
   (a) to purchase forthwith all 9,320,340 Shares owned by the Museum at a purchase price of $110 per Share (subject to adjustment before or after closing in the event of any increase in the Offer price or in the event any higher price is paid by any person who hereafter acquires 10 percent or more of the outstanding Shares) payable either (at the election of the Company) in cash or by means of a promissory note of the Company, dated as of the closing date, payable to the order of the Museum, due on or before thirty days from the date of issuance, bearing interest at a rate equivalent to the prime rate as in effect at Citibank, N.A. and backed by an irrevocable letter of credit (the "Company Note"),
   (b) to proceed promptly upon completion of the Offer by the Purchaser with a cash merger transaction whereby all remaining holders of Shares (other than the Trustee and Pennzoil and its subsidiaries) will receive $110 per Share in cash, and
   (c) in consideration of Pennzoil's agreement provided for in paragraph 1 hereof and in order to provide additional assurance that the Plan will be consummated in accordance with its terms, to grant to Pennzoil hereby the option, exercisable at Pennzoil's election at any time on or before the later of consummation of the Offer referred to in paragraph 1 and the purchase referred to in (a) of this paragraph 2, to purchase from the Company up to 8,000,000 Shares of Common Stock of the Company held in the treasury of the Company at a purchase price of $110 per share in cash.

3. Museum agreement. Subject to approval of the Plan by the Board of Directors of the Company as provided in paragraph 6 hereof, the Museum agrees to sell to the Company forthwith all 9,320,340 Shares owned by the Museum at a purchase price of $110 per Share (subject to adjustment before or after closing as provided in paragraph 2(a)) payable either (at the election of the Company) in cash or by means of the Company Note referred to in paragraph 2(c).

4. Trustee and Pennzoil agreement. The Trustee and Pennzoil hereby agree with each other as follows:
   (a) Ratio of Ownership of Shares. The Trustee may increase its holdings to up to 32,000,000 Shares and Pennzoil may increase its holdings to up to 24,000,000 Shares of the approximately 79,132,000 outstanding Shares. Neither the Trustee nor Pennzoil will acquire in excess of such respective amounts without the prior written agreement of the other, it being the agreement between the Trustee and Pennzoil to maintain a relative Share ratio of 4 (for the Trustee) to 3 (for Pennzoil). In connection with the Offer in the event that more than 23,406,100 Shares are duly tendered to the Purchaser, the Purchaser may (if it chooses) purchase any excess over 23,406,000; provided, however, (i) the Purchaser agrees to sell any such excess Shares to the Company (and the company shall agree to purchase) forthwith at $110 per Share and (ii) pending consummation of such sale to the Company the Purchaser shall grant to the Trustee the irrevocable proxy to vote such excess Shares.

(Exhibit 7.1 continues)

(Exhibit 7.1 continued)

(b) Restructuring plan. Upon completion of the transactions provided for in paragraphs 1, 2 and 3 hereof, the Trustee and Pennzoil shall endeavor in good faith to agree upon a plan for the restructuring of the Company. In the event that for any reason the Trustee and Pennzoil are unable to agree upon a mutually acceptable plan on or before December 31, 1984, then the Trustee and Pennzoil hereby agree to cause the Company to adopt a plan of complete liquidation of the Company pursuant to which (i) any assets which are mutually agreed to be sold shall be sold and the net proceeds therefrom shall be used to reduce liabilities of the Company and (ii) individual interests in all remaining assets and liabilities shall be distributed to the shareholders pro rata in accordance with their actual ownership interest in the Company. In connection with the plan of distribution, Pennzoil agrees (if requested by the Trustee) that it will enter into customary joint operating agreements to operate any properties so distributed and otherwise to agree to provide operating management for any business and operations requested by the Trustee on customary terms and conditions.

(c) Board of Directors and Management. Upon completion of the transactions provided for in paragraphs 1, 2 and 3 hereof, the Trustee and Pennzoil agree that the Board of Directors of the Company shall be composed of approximately fourteen Directors who shall be mutually agreeable to the Trustee and Pennzoil (which Directors may include certain present Directors) and who shall be nominated by the Trustee and Pennzoil, respectively, in the ratio of 4 to 3. The Trustee and Pennzoil agree that the senior management of the Company shall include Gordon P. Getty as Chairman of the Board, J. Hugh Liedtke as President and Chief Executive Officer and Blaine P. Kerr as Chairman of the Executive Committee.

(d) Access to Information. Pennzoil, the Trustee and their representatives will have access to all information concerning the Company necessary or pertinent to accomplish the transactions contemplated by the Plan.

(e) Press releases. The Trustee and Pennzoil (and the Company upon approval of the Plan) will coordinate any press releases or public announcements concerning the Plan and any transactions contemplated hereby.

5. Compliance with regulatory requirements. The Plan shall be implemented in compliance with applicable regulatory requirements.

6. Approval by the Board of Directors. This Plan is subject to approval by the Board of Directors of the Company at the meeting of the Board being held on January 2, 1984, and will expire if not approved by the Board. Upon such approval the Company shall execute three or more counterparts of the "Joinder by the Company" attached to the Plan and deliver one such counterpart to each of the Trustee, the Museum and Pennzoil.

IN WITNESS WHEREOF, this Plan, or a counterpart hereof, has been signed by the following officials thereunto duly authorized this January 2, 1984.

/s/ GORDON P. GETTY
_____
Gordon P. Getty as Trustee of the Sarah C. Getty Trust

The J. Paul Getty Museum

By /s/ HAROLD WILLIAMS
_____
Harold Williams, President

Pennzoil Company

By _____
J. Hugh Liedtke, Chairman of the Board and
Chief Executive Officer

Joinder by the Company

The foregoing Plan has been approved by the Board of Directors.

Getty Oil Company

By _____

January 2, 1984

contract, the jury awarded Pennzoil $7.53 billion compensatory damages and $3 billion punitive damages. (The punitive damages were eventually reduced to $1 billion. The compensatory damages were not changed.)

What did the judges for the Court of Appeals for the First Supreme Judicial District of Texas think of all this? In a lengthy opinion, excerpted below, they upheld the jury's verdict.

Excerpts from the Opinion of the Court of Appeals: Legal Analysis

Under New York law, if parties do not intend to be bound to an agreement until it is reduced to writing and signed by both parties, then there is no contract until that event occurs. If there is no understanding that a signed writing is necessary before the parties will be bound, and the parties have agreed upon all substantial terms, then an informal agreement can be binding, even though the parties contemplate evidencing their agreement in a formal document later.

Thus, under New York law, the parties are given the power to obligate themselves informally or only by a formal signed writing, as they wish. The emphasis in deciding when a binding contract exists is on intent rather than on form.

To determine intent, a court must examine the words and deeds of the parties, because these constitute the objective signs of such intent. Only the outward expressions of intent are considered—secret or subjective intent is immaterial to the question of whether the parties were bound.

Several factors have been articulated to help determine whether the parties intended to be bound only by a formal, signed writing: (1) whether a party expressly reserved the right to be bound only when a written agreement is signed; (2) whether there was any partial performance by one party that the party disclaiming the contract accepted; (3) whether all essential terms of the alleged contract had been agreed upon; and (4) whether the complexity or magnitude of the transaction was such that a formal, executed writing would normally be expected.

Although the magnitude of the transaction here was such that normally a signed writing would be expected, there was sufficient evidence to support an inference by the jury that the expectation was satisfied here initially by the Memorandum of Agreement, signed by a majority of shareholders of Getty Oil and approved by the board with a higher price, and by the transaction agreement in progress that had been intended to memorialize the agreement previously reached.

...

Texaco claims that even if the parties intended to bind themselves before a definitive document was signed, no binding contract could result because the terms that they intended to include in their agreement were too vague and incomplete to be enforceable as a matter of law. For a contract to be enforceable, the terms of the agreement must be ascertainable to a reasonable degree of certainty. The question of whether the agreement is sufficiently definite to be enforceable is a difficult one. The facts of the individual case are decisively important. The agreement need not be so definite that all the possibilities that might occur to a party in bad faith are explicitly provided for, but it must be sufficiently complete so that parties in good faith can find in the agreement words that will fairly define their respective duties and liabilities. . . .

Texaco's attempts to create additional "essential" terms from the mechanics of implementing the agreement's existing provisions are unpersuasive. The terms of the agreement found by the jury are supported by the evidence, and the promises of the parties are clear enough for a court to recognize a breach and to determine the damages resulting from that breach.

Burdened by the largest damages award in U.S. history, Texaco filed for bankruptcy in 1987 after its appeals in the Texas courts failed. As part of its reorganization plan, Texaco agreed to settle the case with Pennzoil for $3 billion.

This case had a tremendous impact on Wall Street, which the *Wall Street Journal* dubbed "the Texaco chill." Investment banker Alan Rothenberg summarized the new attitude: "No longer can we say, 'We stole a deal fair and square.'"[40] *Pennzoil v. Texaco* is still on the books and can be cited as precedent in similar cases. In legal circles, the arguments still continue as to whether the Texas judges properly understood New York contract law and the jury reached the correct verdict.

40. *Id.* at 459–60.

QUESTIONS AND CASE PROBLEMS

1. Leslie Landlord agreed to rent Ted Tenant an office for $3,000 per month for three years. Tenant encountered financial difficulties. Landlord agreed to reduce the rent to $2,200 per month, and Tenant agreed not to file for bankruptcy. Tenant had no plans to file for bankruptcy. Unbeknownst to both Landlord and Tenant, a promise not to file for bankruptcy is unenforceable under the Bankruptcy Code. Was the agreement to reduce the rent binding? Would it make a difference if Tenant had planned to file for bankruptcy if he couldn't get the rent reduction? Was Tenant's conduct ethical?

2. In the spring of 1999, the Mitchell Madison Group, after learning that it had low first quarter 1999 earnings, rescinded job offers to undergraduates and business school students. Mitchell Madison decided to rescind offers at schools where it felt that it could remain in good standing due to its prior strong relationship; the affected schools were pri-

marily elite undergraduate and business schools. The job offers had been extended to students during the fall and winter of the previous year. The majority of students who accepted the Mitchell Madison offers had rejected offers from other companies. Due to the late date of the rescission of the offers, the students anticipated that they would have difficulty obtaining jobs because other employers had already hired other students to satisfy their employment needs. Many of the students had already entered into apartment leases in New York, where they expected to be living and working after graduating. Can the students recover for breach of contract or promissory estoppel against Mitchell Madison Group? What damages would be avoidable? After reneging on its offers, Mitchell Madison realized it had made a mistake and decided to reinstate the offers. Can the students file a claim against the firm despite its decision to reinstate the offers?

[*See* Perry Bacon, *Consulting Firm Muddles Hiring, Angers Yale U. Students,* U-WIRE, Apr. 28, 1999.]

3. Andy Barstow, owner of a store, entered into a detailed letter of intent to negotiate in good faith the lease of the store with Zandra Ingalls, a prospective tenant. The letter included an outline of what terms needed to be negotiated, including rent. Barstow promised to withdraw the store from the marketplace during the negotiations. During the time of the negotiations, Ingalls spent money developing a marketing plan for her business. She also brought in a carpenter, who started building some furniture and cabinets specially designed for the new store. Barstow called Ingalls the following week, saying that he had decided to lease the store to his friend, Bob Burke. What damages, if any, can Ingalls recover?

4. Lanci was involved in an automobile accident with an uninsured motorist. Lanci and Metropolitan Insurance Company entered settlement negotiations and ultimately agreed to settle all claims for $15,000. Lanci's correspondence accepting the settlement offer clearly indicated his belief that his policy limit was $15,000. However, Lanci did not have a copy of his policy, and, in fact, his policy limit was $250,000. When Lanci learned the correct policy limit, he refused to accept the settlement proceeds of $15,000. Should Lanci be able to void the contract? On what basis? [*Lanci v. Metropolitan Insurance Co.,* 564 A.2d 972 (Pa. Super. Ct. 1989)]

5. Brooks filled out, signed, and submitted a job application at one of Circuit City's stores. The application stated:

> This agreement requires you to arbitrate any legal dispute related to your application for employment with Circuit City. Circuit City will not consider your application unless this agreement is signed. . . . I recognize that if I signed the Agreement and do not withdraw within three days of signing I will be required to arbitrate any and all employment-related claims I may have against Circuit City, whether or not I become employed by Circuit City.

Circuit City offered Brooks only seasonal part-time employment at the store where she wished to work. She rejected this offer and filed an employment-discrimination suit against Circuit City. Circuit City sought to remove the employment-discrimination suit from court and bring it to arbitration, pursuant to the "agreement" in Brooks's job application. What result? [*Brooks v. Circuit City Stores, Inc.,* 73 Fair Empl. Prac. Cas. (BNA) 1838 (D. Md. 1997)]

6. Hydrotech Systems, Inc., a New York corporation, agreed to sell wave-pool equipment to Oasis Waterpark, an amusement park in Palm Springs, California. Although Hydrotech was not licensed to install such equipment in California, it agreed to install the wave-pool equipment after Oasis promised to arrange for a California-licensed contractor to "work with" Hydrotech on any construction.

The contract between Hydrotech and Oasis called for Oasis to withhold a specific portion of the contract price pending satisfactory operation of the wave pool. Although the pool functioned properly after installation, Oasis continued to withhold payment for both the equipment and the installation services.

Section 7031 of the California Business and Professions Code states that one may not sue in a California court to recover compensation for any act or contract that requires a California contractor's license unless one alleges and proves that he or she was duly licensed at all times during the performance.

Can Hydrotech recover its compensation due under the contract? Does Hydrotech have a valid action against Oasis for fraud? Is it ethical for Oasis to use the California law to defend itself? [*Hydrotech Systems, Ltd. v. Oasis Waterpark,* 803 P.2d 370 (Cal. 1991)]

7. Emmett Employer called Sally Denoco and offered her a two-year employment contract. Denoco said, "Great, I accept," then quit her present job, forfeiting unvested stock options. After Denoco had worked for Employer for six months for a cash salary of $8,000 a month, Employer fired Denoco. She then sued. Who should win? Does it matter if Employer made a note to himself after the phone call: "Sally Denoco—two-year contract. Salary to be negotiated"? If Denoco were to win, what would be her damages? Would she be entitled to anything if she quit her old job but never started work for Employer? What should Employer and Denoco each have done to protect their rights?

8. In the course of their merger negotiations, Crane Company and Coltec Industries, Inc. entered into a confidentiality agreement providing, among other things, that the parties would notify each other if another company made a hostile takeover attempt or other attempt to gain control. Their agreement terminated on October 31, 1998. On November 23, 1998, Coltec and B.F. Goodrich Company announced that they had entered into a merger agreement. Crane sued Coltec and Goodrich alleging that Coltec breached the confidentiality agreement by failing to notify Crane when Goodrich contacted the company. What arguments can be made in support of Crane's claim? What arguments can be made to defend Coltec's decision not to inform Crane? [*Crane Co. v. Coltec Industries, Inc.,* 171 F.3d 733 (2d Cir. 1999)]

9. Mixed Nuts, Inc. hired an attorney, Christopher Bocci, to assist in obtaining a liquor license from the Oregon Liquor Control Commission (OLCC). Mixed Nuts had contracted to purchase a tavern, but the purchase was contingent on securing the license. In March 1994, after conducting an investigation, the OLCC recommended that the license be denied. Bocci assured the president of Mixed Nuts that if the OLCC ultimately denied the license, Mixed Nuts would "kick ass" before the Oregon Court of Appeals. The OLCC denied the license, and Bocci filed a petition for review by the Oregon Court of Appeals. The appeal was dismissed on the grounds that the petition was untimely. Mixed Nuts sued Bocci for breach of contract based on his guarantee that the company would prevail on its claim in the appeals court. How should the court rule? [*McComas v. Bocci*, 996 P.2d 506 (Or. 2000)]

MANAGER'S DILEMMA

10. As lawyers assembled closing documents for a refinancing of some of the outstanding debt of United States Lines (USL), a secretary working on "Amendment No. 1 to the First Preferred Ship Mortgage" omitted three zeros from the number representing USL's outstanding indebtedness to Prudential Insurance. As a result, the document showed the amount of Prudential's first mortgage as "$92,885.00" instead of "$92,885,000.00." No one noticed the error until eight months later when USL defaulted on the notes secured by the amended mortgage and went bankrupt.

When Prudential tried to foreclose its $92,885,000 first mortgage, USL's bankruptcy trustee objected, arguing that the mortgage should be limited to $92,885. In addition, General Electric Capital Corporation (GECC), which had lent money to USL secured by a second mortgage, brought suit for a declaration that Prudential's first mortgage was valid only to the extent of $92,885. Because GECC had lent money to USL secured by a mortgage junior to that of Prudential, GECC stood to gain by reducing the value of Prudential's first mortgage.

GECC had been intimately involved in USL's financing for some years and knew that Prudential had a $92,885,000 first mortgage. Neither GECC nor any other creditor of USL asserted that it had relied on erroneous information about the amount of USL's outstanding debt.

Is Prudential legally entitled to a $92,885,000 first mortgage?

If you had been the manager at GECC in charge of the USL account, what would you have done once the typo was discovered? What would be the ethical thing to do? [*See* Andrew Kull, *Zero-Based Morality: The Case of the $31 Million Typo*, 1 BUS. L. TODAY 11 (July–Aug. 1992).]

INTERNET SOURCES

The law firm of Fenwick and West supports a page offering information about contract issues relating to electronic commerce.	http://www.fenwick.com/pub/351684.html
The *Law Journal Extra* provides news and other information about commercial law.	http://www.ljx.com/practice/commercial/index.html
The Contract Law Information network page provides a variety of information about Australian contract law and related issues.	http://law.anu.edu.au
The Buyer's Resource home page provides an extensive glossary of contract and other business terminology.	http://homes.inresco.com/Bglossary.html
The 'Lectric Law Library page offers a variety of business contract forms.	http://www.lectlaw.com/formb.html
This site contains information about the Uniform Electronic Transactions Act including a draft of the act.	http://www.uetaonline.com
The National Conference of Commissioners on Uniform State Laws Web site contains information about the organization and legislative status of Uniform Acts.	http://www.nccusl.org

CHAPTER 8

Sales *and* E-Commerce

GOODS, SOFTWARE, AND ELECTRONIC COMMERCE

Virtually all commercial enterprises engage in the purchase or sale of goods. Sales of goods within the United States are governed by Article 2 of the Uniform Commercial Code (UCC); most international sales are governed by the Convention on Contracts for the International Sale of Goods. The UCC does not govern the rendering of services or the sale of land. Contracts for selling services or land are governed by common law contract principles, which are discussed in Chapter 7. The UCC has attempted to eliminate some of the legal formalities of traditional contract law to meet the needs and realities of the business world. Many provisions of the UCC can be changed by the express agreement of the parties. To the extent that the UCC is silent on a subject, the common law contract provisions described in Chapter 7 apply.

The Internet has transformed the way businesses and individuals conduct business in the United States and throughout the world. According to Forrester Research, Inc., Internet retail sales were $20 billion in 2000 and were expected to climb to between $130 billion and $180 billion by 2004. Commerce between businesses conducted over the Internet is even larger, totaling $176 billion in 1999 and estimated to increase to $1.3 trillion by 2003.[1] Due to the speed at which technology is developing and the range of novel issues it presents, state and national governments are scrambling to enact laws that both protect consumers and businesses and facili-

1. Ann Scott Tyson, *Should World Wide Web Be a Tax-Free Zone? E-Commerce Boosters Argue a Ban on Internet Taxes Is Critical for Growth, but States Worry They'll Lose Revenues,* CHRISTIAN SCI. MONITOR, Feb. 28, 2000, at 3.

tate electronic sales transactions using the Internet. In addition, the international reach of the Internet has required legal cooperation and collaboration by countries throughout the world.

CHAPTER OVERVIEW

This chapter begins by addressing contract formation under the UCC and the UCC approach to the *battle of the forms,* which occurs when the form accepting an offer contains terms different from those on the form that constitutes the offer. The special warranty provisions of the UCC are discussed, including express warranties and implied warranties of merchantability and fitness for a particular purpose. The chapter explains how the risk of loss is allocated and a buyer's right to reject nonconforming goods. The chapter then reviews excuses for nonperformance, including unconscionability and commercial impracticability, and remedies for unexcused nonperformance. Rules applicable to the international sale of goods are described and compared with those applicable to domestic sales transactions governed by the UCC.

The chapter also addresses laws regulating e-commerce such as the Uniform Computer Information Transactions Act, which provides a uniform commercial contract code for the licensing of computer software and other computer information transactions, and the Uniform Electronic Transactions Act. The chapter also discusses the issue of taxing e-commerce, particularly how sales taxes can be imposed on purchases made over the Internet. The "Inside Story" addresses the increasing problem of fraud at online auction houses and efforts by law enforcement agencies to regulate crime on the Internet where it is often difficult to identify the criminals.

When Does Article 2 *of the* UCC Apply?

Section 2-105 of the UCC defines *goods* as "all things (including specially manufactured goods) which are movable at the time of identification to the contract for sale." *Identification to the contract* means the designation—by marking, setting aside, or other means—of the particular goods that are to be supplied under the contract.

Sometimes it is not clear whether an activity should be characterized as a sale of goods or a sale of services. For example, when a hospital performs a blood transfusion, is it selling blood or rendering medical services? This distinction can be critical for purposes of both the UCC warranties and product liability in tort (discussed in Chapter 10). Many states have precisely addressed this issue by passing special amendments to their versions of the UCC. These so-called blood shield statutes define a blood transfusion as a provision of services, rather than a sale of goods, in order to limit hospital and blood bank liability for reasons of public policy.[2] In other states, the common law has led to the conclusion that such sales are incidental to the provision of medical services and are therefore outside the scope of the UCC.[3]

Similarly, there can be an issue as to whether something attached to land is considered goods or land. This gray area includes *fixtures,* which are items of personal property that are attached to real property and cannot be removed without substantial damage. Fixtures are not considered goods under Article 2. They are generally subject to the rules governing real property.

The UCC regulates sales of goods by both merchants and nonmerchants, to whom different rules may apply. Thus, for example, if Navrov were to sell a car to Jay, the UCC would dictate both parties' rights and obligations under the sales contract, whether Navrov was employed as a car dealer or was simply selling his personal possessions on his own behalf. Section 2-104 of the UCC defines a *merchant* as "a person who deals in goods of the kind or otherwise by his occupation holds himself out as having knowledge or skill peculiar to the practices or goods involved in the transaction."

Contract Formation

The UCC permits a contract to be enforced if the parties intended a binding contract, even though important terms may have been left open for later agreement. If a dispute later arises over a missing term, the court may simply use a "gap-filler" as provided by the UCC. The court will fill in missing terms, however, only if the party attempting to enforce the contract can prove that there was a genuine agreement, not a mere proposal or intention to continue negotiations. It must be apparent that an offer, acceptance, and consideration have occurred.

OFFER

Offer is not defined by the UCC, although it is used in several important sections. Therefore, traditional common law principles (discussed in Chapter 7) determine whether an offer has been made. Under the UCC, neither an invitation for bids nor a price quotation is an offer. Similarly, a proposal by a sales representative that is subject to approval by the home office is not an offer.

ACCEPTANCE

The UCC does not define *acceptance* either, except to state that an acceptance may contain terms additional to or different from those in the offer. This is different from the common law mirror image rule, which requires the acceptance to contain the exact same terms as the offer. Unless the offeror indicates unambiguously that his or her offer can be accepted only in a particular way, an offer may be accepted in any manner and by any medium that is reasonable in the circumstances.

In our heavily technological age, the issue of what constitutes acceptance can be murky, as the following case illustrates.

---

2. *See, e.g.,* Zichichi v. Middlesex Mem'l Hosp., 528 A.2d 805 (Conn. 1987); Garcia v. Edgewater Hosp., 613 N.E.2d 1243 (Ill. App. Ct. 1993).
3. *See, e.g.,* Lovett v. Emory Univ., Inc., 156 S.E.2d 923 (Ga. Ct. App. 1967).

CASE 8.1

ProCD, Inc. v. Zeidenberg
*United States Court of
Appeals for the
Seventh Circuit
86 F.3d 1447
(7th Cir. 1996).*

In the Language of the Court

FACTS ProCD compiled information from more than 3,000 telephone directories into a single database. The database cost more than $10 million to compile and was expensive to keep current. ProCD sold a version of this database, called SelectPhone, on CD-ROM. Each SelectPhone CD-ROM package contained within it a *shrink-wrap license,* that is, a license that customers could not read when they made their decision to purchase SelectPhone but were deemed to have accepted when they opened the wrapping around the envelope containing the disks or clicked on the "I Accept" box on the computer screen. Among other things, the shrink-wrap license prohibited the unauthorized resale of the SelectPhone database.

Zeidenberg purchased a SelectPhone in Wisconsin and opened the packaging, including the shrink wrap. He also clicked on the "I Accept" box on the computer screen but decided to ignore the terms of the license. Instead, he formed Silken Mountain Web Services, Inc. to resell the information in the SelectPhone database. Silken Mountain made the SelectPhone database available on the Internet to anyone willing to pay Silken Mountain's price, which was less than that charged by ProCD. Zeidenberg later purchased two updated versions of the database to make the latest SelectPhone information available via the Internet.

ProCD sued Zeidenberg and Silken Mountain for violating the license contained within the SelectPhone packages. The trial court found in favor of Zeidenberg and Silken Mountain on the grounds that the shrink-wrap license was not enforceable as a matter of Wisconsin contract law. ProCD appealed.

ISSUE PRESENTED Is a shrink-wrap or click-wrap license whose terms are unknown at the time of purchase binding on the buyer?

OPINION EASTERBROOK, J., writing for the U.S. Court of Appeals for the Seventh Circuit:

[C]onsider the purchase of an airline ticket. The traveler calls the carrier or an agent, is quoted a price, reserves a seat, pays, and gets a ticket, in that order. The ticket contains elaborate terms, which the traveler can reject by canceling the reservation. To use the ticket is to accept the terms, even terms that in retrospect are disadvantageous. Just so with a ticket to a concert. The back of the ticket states that the patron promises not to record the concert; to attend is to agree. A theater that detects a violation will confiscate the tape and escort the violator to the exit. One could arrange things so that every concert-goer signs this promise before forking over the money, but that cumbersome way of doing things not only would lengthen queues and raise prices but also would scotch the sale of tickets by phone or electronic data service.

Consumer goods work the same way. Someone who wants to buy a radio set visits a store, pays, and walks out with a box. Inside the box is a leaflet containing some terms, the most important of which usually is the warranty, read for the first time in the comfort of home. By Zeidenberg's lights, the warranty in the box is irrelevant; every consumer gets the standard warranty implied by the UCC in the event the contract is silent; yet so far as we are aware no state disregards warranties furnished with consumer products. Drugs come with a list of ingredients on the outside and an elaborate package insert on the inside. The package insert describes drug interactions, contraindications, and other vital information—but, if Zeidenberg is right, the purchaser need not read the package insert, because it is not part of the contract.

Next consider the software industry itself. Only a minority of sales take place over the counter, where there are boxes to peruse. A customer may place an order by

(Continued)

(Case 8.1 continued)

phone in response to a line item in a catalog or a review in a magazine. Much software is ordered over the Internet by purchasers who have never seen a box. Increasingly software arrives by wire. There is no box; there is only a stream of electrons, a collection of information that includes data, an application program, instructions, many limitations . . . and the terms of sale. The user purchases a serial number, which activates the software's features. On Zeidenberg's arguments, these unboxed sales are unfettered by terms—so the seller has made a broad warranty and must pay consequential damages for any shortfalls in performance, two "promises" that if taken seriously would drive prices through the ceiling or return transactions to the horse-and-buggy age.

According to the [trial] court, the UCC does not countenance the sequence of money now, terms later. . . .

What then does the current version of the UCC have to say? We think that the place to start is § 2-204(1): "A contract for sale of goods may be made in any manner sufficient to show agreement, including conduct by both parties which recognizes the existence of such a contract." A vendor, as master of the offer, may invite acceptance by conduct, and may propose limitations on the kind of conduct that constitutes acceptance. A buyer may accept by performing the acts the vendor proposes to treat as acceptance. And that is what happened. ProCD proposed a contract that a buyer would accept by using the software after having an opportunity to read the license at leisure. This Zeidenberg did. He had no choice, because the software splashed the license on the screen and would not let him proceed without indicating acceptance. So although the district judge was right to say that a contract can be, and often is, formed simply by paying the price and walking out of the store, the UCC permits contracts to be formed in other ways. ProCD proposed such a different way, and without protest Zeidenberg agreed. Ours is not a case in which a consumer opens a package to find an insert saying "you owe us an extra $10,000" and the seller files suit to collect. Any buyer finding such a demand can prevent formation of the contract by returning the package, as can any consumer who concludes that the terms of the license make the software worth less than the purchase price. . . .

. . .

Some portions of the UCC impose additional requirements on the way parties agree on terms. . . . Zeidenberg has not located any Wisconsin case—for that matter, any case in any state—holding that under the UCC the ordinary terms found in shrink-wrap licenses require any special prominence, or otherwise are to be undercut rather than enforced. In the end, the terms of the license are conceptually identical to the contents of the package. Just as no court would dream of saying that SelectPhone must contain 3,100 phone books rather than 3,000, or must have data no more than 30 days old, or must sell for $100 rather than $150—although any of these changes would be welcomed by the customer, if all other things were held constant—so, we believe, Wisconsin would not let the buyer pick and choose among terms. Terms of use are no less a part of "the product" than are the size of the database and the speed with which the software compiles listings. Competition among vendors, not judicial revision of a package's contents, is how consumers are protected in a market economy. ProCD has rivals, which may elect to compete by offering superior software, monthly updates, improved terms of use, lower price, or a better compromise among these elements. As we stressed above, adjusting terms in buyers' favor might help Matthew Zeidenberg today (he already has the software) but would lead to a response, such as a higher price, that might make consumers as a whole worse off.

(Continued)

(Case 8.1 continued)

RESULT The appeals court reversed the decision of the trial court and ruled that the terms of a shrink-wrap license are binding on the buyer unless the terms are objectionable on grounds applicable to contracts in general.

COMMENTS *ProCD* was decided before the promulgation of the Uniform Computer Information Transactions Act discussed below.

QUESTIONS

1. Would the result have been different if the terms had included restrictions on the number of hours per day the buyer could use the software? Restrictions on the number of different users allowed to use the software? Restrictions on the use of the information, for example, no fund-raising for gay rights?
2. Even though shrink-wrap licenses are most common in the software industry, are there limits to the types of products to which such licensing terms may be applied?

CONSIDERATION

Contracts for the sale of goods ordinarily must have consideration to be enforceable. However, a *firm offer,* that is, a signed offer by a merchant that indicates that the offer will be kept open, is not revocable for lack of consideration. The offer must be kept open during the time stated or, if none is stated, for a reasonable period of time, up to a maximum of three months. This rule is just one example of how the UCC provides more stringent standards for merchants than for non-merchants.

Under the UCC, an agreement to modify a contract is binding even if there is no consideration for the modification as long as the modification was made in good faith. However, if the original contract was required to be in writing to satisfy the statute of frauds (discussed later in this chapter), then the agreement to modify the contract must be in writing also.

Battle *of the* Forms

In a battle of the forms, the parties negotiate the essential terms of the contract (for example, quantity, quality, and delivery date) but neglect to bargain over items that are less immediately important (for example, whether disputes will be subject to arbitration, for how long a period after delivery the buyer may assert complaints of defects, or on whom the risk of loss during shipment falls). The parties then exchange standard printed forms, each of which is filled with fine print listing all kinds of terms advantageous to the party that drew up the form.

Often goods are shipped, received, and paid for before both parties have expressly accepted the same document as their contract. As a result of these exchanges, two questions arise: (1) Is there a contract? (2) If so, what are its terms?

The UCC calls a truce in the battle of the forms by effectively abolishing the mirror image rule. It is not necessary for an offer and acceptance to match exactly in order for a contract for the sale of goods to exist.

 ETHICAL CONSIDERATION

Devon Cartagena, an antique dealer, sees a desk for sale for $50 at a garage sale and recognizes it as a Louis XV desk worth $15,000. Does he have a legal or ethical obligation to disclose the true value to the person holding the garage sale? Should it matter that difficult financial circumstances forced the homeowner to sell the desk? Should Cartagena get some reward for the effort he has made to become an expert in antiques and for the time he has spent pawing through junk at countless garage sales?

A person recently sold a map for $3 that later turned out to be worth more than $19 million. Is there a moral duty to share the windfall with the seller? Would the seller have a moral duty to share the loss if the buyer paid $19 million for a map worth only $3?

What if a framed picture sold for $25 turned out to have an original copy of the U.S. Constitution behind the picture? Is this a mistake of judgment or of fact? What, if anything, is the buyer's ethical responsibility to the seller in such a case?

Adding to or modifying terms in the offer does not make the acceptance a counteroffer, as is true under common law.

DEFINITE RESPONSE

A definite and timely assent to an offer constitutes an acceptance. The presence of additional or different terms is not a bar to contract formation. The crucial inquiry is whether the parties intended to close a deal. Under Section 2-207, a contract exists whenever the parties act as if there is a contract between them. It is not necessary to determine which document constitutes the offer and which the acceptance. If the offeree's response manifests the intent to enter into a deal, the offer has been accepted. For example, if additional or different terms merely appear in the standard printed language of a form contract, it is likely that the offeree intended to close a deal. Once the contract is formed, the only issue to be decided is what are its terms.

If, however, the response indicates only a willingness to continue negotiations, it is not an acceptance but a counteroffer. For example, an additional or different term that directly pertains to one of the negotiated terms, such as price or quantity, is evidence that the parties are still negotiating and have not reached an agreement.

CONDITIONAL RESPONSE

If the offeree wants to make a counteroffer rather than an acceptance, he or she should state clearly that acceptance is conditioned on the offeror's agreement to the additional or different terms. The safest course is to use the language of the UCC: "This acceptance is expressly made conditional on offeror's assent to all additional or different terms contained herein. Should offeror not give assent to said terms, there is no contract between the parties." Less direct language (such as "The acceptance of your order is subject to the conditions set forth herein" and "Acceptance of this order is expressly limited to the condition of purchase printed on the reverse side") has been held to be an acceptance rather than a counteroffer.

ACCEPTANCE WITH MISSING TERMS

What happens when the parties ship, receive, and pay for goods without first agreeing on all material terms? In that case, Section 2-207(3) provides that the terms of the contract will be those on which the writings exchanged by the parties agree, supplemented by the UCC's gap-fillers where needed.

ACCEPTANCE WITH ADDITIONAL TERMS

What is the effect of additional terms in an acceptance when the contract is not expressly made subject to the offeror's agreeing to those terms? The answer depends on whether the parties are merchants. Under Section 2-207(2), if any of the parties is not a merchant, additional terms are construed as proposals for additions to the contract that the acceptance has created. Unless the offeror expressly agrees to the added provisions, they do not become part of the contract. If all parties are merchants, on the other hand, the additional provisions in the acceptance automatically become part of the contract, unless (1) the offer expressly limits acceptance to the terms of the offer, (2) the new terms materially alter the original offer, or (3) the party making the original offer notifies the other party within a reasonable time that it objects to the new terms. If one of these exceptions applies, the additional terms serve as proposals requiring the express consent of the offeror to become part of the contract.

ACCEPTANCE WITH DIFFERENT TERMS

What is the effect of different—as opposed to additional—terms in an acceptance when the acceptance is not expressly made subject to the offeror's agreeing to those terms? As in the case of additional terms in a response to an offer, different terms neither defeat the acceptance nor impede the formation of the contract. But do the different terms become part of the contract? Surprisingly, the language of Section 2-207 does not address this situation. There are generally three possible answers: (1) as with additional terms governed by Section 2-207(2), the different terms could become part of a contract between merchants unless one of the three conditions discussed previously is met; (2) the additional terms could be ignored or treated as separate offers to modify the accepted contract; and (3) the opposing terms could "knock out" each other, and UCC gap-fillers could be put in their place.

The following case illustrates how most courts deal with the situation in which the parties have sent conflicting forms, transacted their business, and then realized that they disagree about the terms of their contract.

A CASE IN POINT

CASE 8.2

Ionics, Inc. v. Elmwood Sensors, Inc.

United States Court of Appeals for the First Circuit
110 F.3d 184
(1st Cir. 1997).

Summary

FACTS Elmwood Sensors manufactures and sells thermostats, and Ionics makes hot- and cold-water dispensers, which it leases to its customers. On three separate occasions in 1990, Ionics purchased thermostats from Elmwood for use in its water dispensers. On each occasion, Ionics sent Elmwood a purchase order form that contained, in small type, various conditions.

Condition 18, entitled "Remedies," provided: "The remedies provided Buyer herein shall be cumulative, and in addition to any other remedies provided by law or equity. A waiver of a breach of any provision hereof shall not constitute a waiver of any other breach."

Condition 19, entitled "Acceptance," provided:

Acceptance by the Seller of this order shall be upon the terms and conditions set forth in items 1 to 17 inclusive, and elsewhere in this order. Said order can be so accepted only on the exact terms herein and set forth. No terms which are in any manner additional to or different from those herein set forth shall become a part of, alter or in any way control the terms and conditions herein set forth.

Before placing its first order, Ionics sent Elmwood a letter stating:

The information preprinted, written and/or typed on our purchase order is especially important to us. Should you take exception to this information, please clearly express any reservations to us in writing. If you do not, we will assume that you have agreed to the specified terms and that you will fulfill your obligations according to our purchase order. If necessary, we will change your invoice and pay your invoice according to our purchase order.

Following receipt of each order, Elmwood prepared and sent an "Acknowledgment" form containing the following language in small type:

This will acknowledge receipt of buyer's order and state seller's willingness to sell the goods ordered but only upon the terms and conditions set forth herein and on the reverse side hereof as a counteroffer. Buyer shall be deemed to have accepted such counteroffer unless it is rejected in writing within ten (10) days of the receipt hereof, and all subsequent action shall be pursuant to the terms and conditions of this counteroffer only; any additional or different terms are hereby objected to and shall not be binding upon the parties unless specifically agreed to in writing by seller.

For each of its three orders, Ionics received Elmwood's Acknowledgment prior to receiving the thermostats. Among the terms and conditions listed on the back of Elmwood's form was the following warranty term:

All goods manufactured by Elmwood Sensors, Inc. are guaranteed to be free of defects in material and workmanship for a period of ninety (90) days after receipt of such goods by Buyer or eighteen months from the date of manufacturer [sic] (as evidenced by the manufacturer's date code), whichever shall be longer. There is no implied warranty of merchantability and no other warranty, expressed or implied, except such as is expressly set forth herein. Seller will not be liable for any general, consequential or incidental damages, including without limitation any damages from loss of profits, from any breach of warranty or for negligence, seller's liability and buyer's exclusive remedy being expressly limited to the repair of defective goods f.o.b. the shipping point indicated on the face hereof or the repayment of the purchase price upon

(Continued)

(Case 8.2 continued)

the return of the goods or the granting of a reasonable allowance on account of any defects, as seller may elect.

Several of the Ionics dispensers subsequently caused fires, which allegedly resulted from defects in the Elmwood sensors. In an effort to recover costs incurred in the wake of the fires, Ionics sued Elmwood for breach of the implied warranty of fitness. Elmwood moved for partial summary judgment limiting its exposure to the warranty in its Acknowledgment. The trial court held that the conflicting terms would be stricken and that UCC warranty terms would apply in their place. As a result, a warranty of fitness attached to the thermostats. Elmwood appealed.

ISSUE PRESENTED If there has been an acceptance of an offer, but the offer and acceptance are on printed forms that contain contradictory terms, is there a contract? If so, what are its terms?

SUMMARY OF OPINION The U.S. Court of Appeals for the First Circuit began with a literal reading of Section 2-207, which addresses additional terms made in acceptance or confirmation of an order between merchants. Under Section 2-207, the additional terms become part of the contract unless (1) the offer expressly limits acceptance to the terms of the offer, (2) the terms materially change the contract, or (3) notification of objection is given within a reasonable time after the terms are received. The section goes on to state that conduct by both parties recognizing a contract will establish the contract, the terms of which will consist of the terms on which the writings of the parties agree and any supplementary terms provided by the UCC.

A case decided thirty-five years earlier by the same court, however, held that an acceptance with conflicting terms was outside the scope of Section 2-207. In *Roto-Lith, Ltd. v. F.P. Bartlett & Co.,*[4] the court applied the first part of Section 2-207 and ruled that a response to an offer that includes a term "materially altering the obligation solely to the disadvantage of the offeror" is an acceptance conditional on agreement to the new term. The *Roto-Lith* court then reverted to common law and concluded that the buyer had accepted the seller's terms by accepting the goods. Hence, the new terms were part of the contract.

The *Ionics* court then turned to the final part of Section 2-207, allowing conduct between merchants to establish a contract whose disputed terms are filled in by the UCC. Comment 6 to that section squarely addressed the issue:

> If no answer is received within a reasonable time after additional terms are proposed, it is both fair and commercially sound to assume that their inclusion has been assented to. Where clauses on confirming forms sent by both parties conflict, each party must be assumed to object to a clause of the other. . . . As a result, the requirement that there be notice of objection . . . is satisfied and the conflicting terms do not become part of the contract. The contract then consists of the terms originally expressly agreed to, terms on which the confirmations agree, and terms supplied by [the UCC].

[*Ed.:* The official comments to the UCC help courts to understand the drafters' intentions, but they are not binding. If a judge believes there is a conflict between the statute and the comment, the judge will follow the statute.]

Facing the stark contradiction between *Roto-Lith's* clear precedent and "the clear dictates of the [UCC]," the court had to make a choice. Noting the majority view in favor of the UCC comment, extensive criticism of the *Roto-Lith* approach, and the intent of

---

4. 297 F.2d 497 (1st Cir. 1962).

(Continued)

(Case 8.2 continued)

Section 2-207 to modify the mirror image rule, the court overturned *Roto-Lith*. In conclusion, the court noted: "The reality of modern commercial dealings, as this case demonstrates, is that not all participants read their forms. To uphold Elmwood's view would . . . fly in the face of good sense."

RESULT The appeals court affirmed the trial court's decision to strike the contradictory terms and to use the UCC implied warranty of fitness as a gap-filler. Hence, Elmwood's thermostats were sold subject to the implied warranty of fitness.

COMMENTS By formally adopting the knockout rule instead of the old approach under *Roto-Lith,* the appeals court made it much harder to game the system by exchanging preprinted forms with boilerplate rejection of the other party's terms. With conflicting terms simply thrown out and replaced by UCC gap-fillers, managers using such forms should be aware of which UCC provisions might replace their standard terms.

PROPOSED REVISIONS TO SECTION 2-207

Drafting committees appointed by the sponsoring organizations of the UCC have proposed changes to Article 2, which as of October 2000 had yet to be approved. The proposed draft of Article 2 awaiting approval by the American Law Institute thoroughly revises and simplifies the rules governing contract formation.[5] Section 2-206(c) of the 2000 draft version states that unless otherwise unambiguously indicated by the language or circumstances, "[a] definite and seasonable expression of acceptance in a record operates as an acceptance even if it contains terms additional to or different from the offer." This language was adapted from Section 2-207(1) of the original UCC. Revised Section 2-207 in the proposed 2000 draft specifies the terms of all contracts of sale, regardless of whether there was a "battle of the forms." Under Section 2-207, the terms of the contract are "(1) terms that appear in the records of both parties; (2) terms, whether in a record or not, to which both parties agree; and (3) terms supplied or incorporated under any provision of [the Uniform Commercial Code]." In effect, when two forms conflict, the conflicting terms are knocked out, and the UCC's standard provisions are applied.

 Statute *of* Frauds

Section 2-201 of the UCC is a *statute of frauds.* It provides that a contract for the sale of goods for $500 or more is unenforceable unless it is at least partly in writing. It states:

1. There must be some writing evidencing the sale of goods.
2. The writing must be signed by the party against whom enforcement is sought.
3. The writing must specify the quantity of the goods sold.

"SOME WRITING"

Statutes of frauds generally require all the essential terms of the contract to be in writing; the UCC's requirement for "some writing" is relatively lenient. The official comments to Section 2-201 state: "All that is required is that the writing afford a basis for believing that the offered oral evidence rests on a real transaction. It may be written in lead pencil on a scratch pad." The comments go on to state: "The price, time and place of payment or delivery, the general quality of the goods, or any particular warranties may all be omitted."

The only term that must appear in the writing is the quantity of goods to be sold. This term is necessary to provide a basis for awarding monetary damages in the case of a breach. The contract is not enforceable beyond the quantity of goods shown in the writing. If no quantity is specified, the contract is unenforceable unless (1) the goods were specially manufactured for the buyer and are not suitable for resale to others in the ordinary course of the seller's business, (2) the defendant admits in a judicial proceeding that there was an agreement; or (3) payment for the goods was made and accepted or the goods were received and accepted.

5. American Law Institute and the National Conference of Commissioners on Uniform State Laws, *Revision of Uniform Commercial Code, Article 2* <http://www.law.upenne.du/bll/ulc/ucc2/ucc20600.htm>.

SIGNATURE

The writing must be signed by the party against whom enforcement is sought unless the sale is between merchants and (1) a confirmation of the contract has been received, (2) the party receiving it has reason to know its contents, and (3) that party has not made a written objection within ten days after the confirmation was received. For example, an invoice that a seller sent to a buyer would be a contract enforceable against the buyer if the buyer did not respond within ten days after receiving the invoice.

THE E-SIGN ACT AND UNIFORM ELECTRONIC TRANSACTIONS ACT

As more business is being conducted electronically, state and federal statutes recognizing electronic signatures are being enacted. On June 30, 2000, President Bill Clinton signed the Electronic Signatures in Global and National Commerce Act (the E-Sign Act), which validates many transactions that take place electronically. The E-Sign Act states that "a signature, contract, or other record relating to such transaction may not be denied legal effect, validity, or enforceability solely because it is in electronic form."[6] Similarly, the Uniform Electronic Transactions Act (UETA), versions of which have been adopted by more than twenty states, provides that an electronic contract may not be denied legal effect simply because it is in electronic form. Under the E-Sign Act and UETA, almost any mark or process intended to sign an electronic contract or record (including a name typed at the bottom of an e-mail message and a "click-through" process on a computer screen whereby a person clicks "I agree" on a Web page) will constitute a valid electronic signature. (The E-Sign Act and the UETA are discussed more fully in Chapter 7.)

Digital Signatures Although the terms are frequently used interchangeably, there is a distinction between "electronic signatures" and "digital signatures."[7] A "digital signature" refers to a type of electronic signature that uses an information security measure, typically cryptography, to authenticate the identity of the person providing the electronic signature and to ensure the integrity and authenticity of the information.[8]

Digital signature technology provides a variety of options: a signature can be a smart card, thumbprint, retinal scan, or voice-recognition test.[9] This range of options will provide companies with varying levels of security for their transactions. The E-Sign Act does not require the use of any particular technology, and a number of companies have developed technology to capitalize on the growing market created by the Act.[10]

 ## Duty *of* Good Faith *under the* UCC

Section 1-203 of the UCC states that "[e]very contract or duty within this Act imposes an obligation of good faith in its performance and enforcement." This section imposes on each party a duty not to do anything that will deprive the other party of the benefits of the agreement. One court defined "good faith" as "a compact reference to an implied undertaking not to take opportunistic advantage in a way that could not have been contemplated at the time of drafting, and which therefore was not resolved explicitly by the parties."[11] Good faith in the case of a merchant has

9. Dan Briody, *Digital Signatures Create Market Potential; How Will Companies Make Consumers Feel Secure Enough to Sign on the Digital Line?*, INFOWORLD, July 24, 2000.
10. Lizette Alvarez & Jeri Clausing, *Senate Approves Bill That Allows Online Contracts*, N.Y. TIMES, June 17, 2000, at 1.
11. Brooklyn Bagel Boys, Inc. v. Earthgrains Refrigerated Dough Products, Inc., 212 F.3d 373 (7th Cir. 2000).

 INTERNATIONAL CONSIDERATION

On November 30, 1999, the European Commission approved a directive on a new legal framework for the recognition of electronic signatures throughout the European Union (EU). The directive was to be incorporated into the national laws of the EU's fifteen member states by April 2001. Although in the past only handwritten signatures were recognized as legally valid, the new directive recognizes electronic signatures as valid and provides that they can be used as evidence in legal proceedings. All products and services related to electronic signatures can circulate freely within the EU and are subject to legislation and control only by the country of origin. In addition, the directive defines the responsibilities of certification authorities and outlines the requirements for secure signature-creation devices. The directive also includes provisions for recognition of electronic signatures that emanate from outside the EU.

6. Electronic Signatures in Global and National Commerce Act, Pub. L. No. 106–229, § 101(a)(2) (2000).
7. Tom Melling, *Digital Signatures v. Electronic Signatures,* E-BUSINESS ADVISOR, Apr. 1, 2000, at 48.
8. Robert G. Ballen & Thomas A. Fox, *Sign of the Times: Electronic Disclosures, Contracts and Signatures,* J. INTERNET L., Sept. 1998, at 12.

*"I got my ticket for three dollars over the Internet.
Are you going to eat that salmon?"*

been interpreted as the observance of reasonable commercial standards of fair dealing in the trade.

The UCC applies to the enforcement, performance, or modification of a contract for the sale of goods, but not to the formation or procurement of a contract. For example, the Texas Supreme Court refused to invalidate a mutual release of liabilities for violation of good faith after characterizing the mutual release as the formation, not the modification, of a contract.[12]

 ## Warranties

Goods delivered pursuant to a contract may not live up to the buyer's expectations. In many such cases, the buyer can sue the seller for breaching an express or implied warranty that the goods sold would have certain qualities or would perform in a certain way.

The UCC's warranty provisions attempt to determine which attributes of the goods the parties have agreed on.

12. El Paso Natural Gas Co. v. Minco Oil & Gas, Inc., 8 S.W.3d 309 (Tex. 1999).

The UCC allows a great deal of flexibility in determining which warranties apply, permitting consideration of the description of the goods, the seller's words, common uses in the trade, the price paid, and the extent to which the buyer has communicated particular needs to the seller. As a result, the seller of goods may find itself bound, perhaps unintentionally, by one of the three warranties provided by the UCC: express warranty, implied warranty of merchantability, and implied warranty of fitness for a particular purpose.

EXPRESS WARRANTY

An *express warranty* is an explicit guarantee by the seller that the goods will have certain qualities. Section 2-313 of the UCC has two requirements for the creation of an express warranty. First, the seller must (1) make a statement or promise relating to the goods, (2) provide a description of the goods, or (3) furnish a sample or model of the goods. Second, this statement, promise, description, sample, or model must become a "part of the basis of the bargain" between the seller and the buyer. This second requirement is intended to

HISTORICAL PERSPECTIVE

From Medieval Guilds *to* Online Arbitration

The increased use of the Internet by businesses and individuals, combined with the lack of established legal rules, has resulted in the development of private legal institutions. For example, individuals doing business on the Internet are devising ways to ensure that the information they transmit to each other will remain confidential and be used only in an authorized manner. In addition, as noted in Chapter 4, Internet companies have established online mediation and dispute resolution sites allowing consumers to resolve their disputes without filing claims in courts. Although these private legal regimes may be revolutionary in that they are being used in connection with a new technology, private legal regimes have developed at other times in history when individuals needed to protect their rights and the existing legal regime was unable to do so.

In medieval Europe, the nation-state had not yet developed, so merchants and traders could not rely on a central government to enforce laws or contracts to protect their trading activities. As long-distance trade became more common, traders and merchants began to venture beyond the protection of a local ruler or entrusted agents to carry and deliver their goods to fairs and markets in other countries and collect payment for these goods. As a result, the merchants needed to create mechanisms to protect their interests. Accordingly, they developed private organizations, or guilds, and courts enforced by groups of merchants. To determine whether an unknown trader or agent was trustworthy, merchants turned to each other for information about the stranger's reputation. Merchants refused to trade with parties who breached commitments to pay or to perform services, and they organized guildwide embargoes to freeze out members of the guild who violated its rules. By developing these institutions, the merchants made long-distance trade safer and more secure and contributed significantly to the economic expansion of the period.

In modern society, members of private organizations often agree to be governed by a legal regime created and enforced by the organization. For example, a number of trade associations have rules that govern the relationships among the members and establish a procedure for resolving disputes that arise from breaches of these rules. Although these associations' rules are based upon public law, such as contract law, these legal regimes typically rely upon simple rules, which they interpret and apply literally.

Stock exchanges, such as the New York Stock Exchange and NASDAQ, also operate under quasi-private legal regimes. Members of these exchanges must comply with the exchanges' rules and are subject to their monitoring, investigation, and enforcement mechanisms. Once again, these exchanges are not subject just to a set of private rules. Their private rules are subject to review by the Securities and Exchange Commission and the courts, and they also incorporate public laws.

The Digital Revolution and the rapid development of e-commerce are acting as an engine to drive the development of a private legal regime. Not only is the Internet essentially unregulated, but with its innovative technology and ability to reach billions of consumers all over the world, it presents enormous challenges for legal regulation. Some early efforts to regulate the Internet reflect the introduction of privatization into this new electronic market. In addition to the domain-name dispute procedures described in the "Inside Story" for Chapter 4, companies have used private law regimes to deal with consumer concerns about privacy on the Internet and secure transmissions of sensitive data (such as credit card numbers) by establishing "Seal" programs. For example, TRUSTe is a nonprofit corporation founded by Online Privacy Alliance (a group of leading Internet firms), the Electronic Frontier Foundation (a public interest group), and the Boston Consulting Group (a management consulting firm). TRUSTe has established a set of practices regarding user privacy to which a company wishing to display the TRUSTe seal must adhere. TRUSTe enforces its policies by several methods including a dispute resolution process.

Source: This discussion is based upon Gillian K. Hadfield, *Privatizing Commercial Law: Lessons from the Middle and Digital Ages* (Mar. 2000) <http://aei-brookings.org/publications/related/hadfield.htm>.

---

ensure that the buyer actually relied on the seller's statement when making a purchasing decision. For example, if a car dealer asserts that a car will reach 130 mph, and the buyer's response is "I'm never going to take it above 55," it is unlikely that the buyer could claim breach of warranty if the car failed to go over 70 mph.

Puffing Section 2-313(2) provides that a warranty may be found even though the seller never used the word "warranty" or "guarantee" and had no intention of making a warranty. The seller has the burden of proving that the buyer did not rely on his or her representations. However, if a seller is merely *puffing*—that is, expressing an opinion about the quality of the goods—he or she has not made a warranty. For example, a car salesperson's statement that "this is a top-notch car" is puffing, whereas a factual statement such as "it will get 25 miles to the gallon" is an express warranty.

Unfortunately, the line between opinion and fact is not always easy to draw. Much turns on the circumstances surrounding the representation, including the identities and relative knowledge of the parties involved.

A number of courts employ a two-prong test to distinguish warranty language from opinion. The first prong is whether the seller asserted a fact of which the buyer was ignorant. If so, the assertion may be a warranty. The second prong is whether the seller merely stated a view on something about which the buyer could be expected to have formed his or her own opinion and whether the buyer could judge the validity of the seller's statement. In this second instance, the seller's statement is an opinion, not a warranty. The following case illustrates the distinction between sales talk and a warranty.

A CASE IN POINT

CASE 8.3
**Connor, Inc. v.
Proto-Grind, Inc.**
*Court of Appeal of Florida
761 So. 2d 426
(Fla. App. 2000).*

In the Language of the Court

FACTS Doug Connor, the president of Connor, Inc., a land-clearing business, became interested in purchasing a large commercial grinding machine manufactured by Proto-Grind, Inc., called the Proto-Grind 1200. Proto-Grind's brochure described the machine as the toughest grinder on the market and stated that the machine could grind timber, stumps, and railroad ties into mulch. Connor attended a demonstration of the machine during which a large log was reduced to mulch. During the demonstration, he spoke to Protos, the president of Proto-Grind, and told him that he needed a machine that would grind palmettos, palm trees, oak trees, and other trees. Protos assured him that the machine was capable of doing this work.

Connor purchased a Proto-Grind 1200 for $226,000 pursuant to a contract that provided for a two-week trial period during which he could use the machine and, only if satisfied, be committed to purchase it. However, Protos also offered an incentive that eliminated Connor's first installment payment of $5,500 in exchange for elimination of the trial period. Connor accepted this offer and gave up the two-week trial period.

Connor experienced problems with the new machine, including its inability to discharge mulch from cabbage palm trees and palmettos. Connor wrote several letters to Protos complaining about the deficiencies. After Proto-Grind failed to resolve the problems, Connor sued for breach of express oral warranties that the machine would grind organic materials effectively, that the machine would be free from defects for a period of six months, and that Proto-Grind would fix the machine. The case went to trial, and the trial court granted Proto-Grind's motion for a directed verdict at the conclusion of Connor's case on the grounds that Connor had waived the express warranty in exchange for elimination of the first installment payment of $5,500. Connor appealed.

ISSUE PRESENTED When do oral statements by a seller about the capability of a commercial grinding machine constitute an express warranty? Is a warranty claim waived if the buyer agrees to eliminate a trial period?

OPINION PETERSON, J., writing for the Florida Court of Appeal:

[*Ed:* The Florida Court of Appeal first found that only implied warranties, not express warranties, may be waived when the buyer refuses an opportunity to inspect the product prior to purchase.]

Proto-Grind argues that the oral affirmations made by the Proto-Grind agents merely constituted puffing, sales talk, or otherwise non-actionable opinion and that in order to satisfy the threshold of an affirmation of fact, the statement must be detailed

(Continued)

(Case 8.3 continued)

and specific. In *Miles*,[13] the court found that a seller of an airplane, by reference to his log-book, had warranted the accuracy of the information contained in the book. Proto-Grind states that the principle of that case is that the threshold of making a factual affirmation is that the statement be specific and detailed. Contrarily, *Miles* seems to support the opposite conclusion by providing a broad definition of an express warranty. The Court wrote:

> An express warranty need not be by words, but can be by conduct as well, such as the showing of a blueprint or other description of the goods sold to the buyer.

We believe that the statements made by Proto-Grind could amount to more than puffing or sales talk. Proto-Grind specifically understood the buyer's needs and represented to Connor that the Proto-Grind 1200 would meet those needs.

Proto-Grind further argues that an express warranty generally arises only where the seller asserts a fact of which the buyer is ignorant prior to the beginning of the transaction, and on which the buyer reasonably relies as part of the basis of the bargain. It is not clear from the record, however, that when Connor purchased the Proto-Grind 1200 he was aware that it was ill-equipped to mulch palm trees and palmetto brush.

On a similar note, Proto-Grind argues that because Doug knew that a competitor was, at times, quite dissatisfied with his Proto-Grind 1200, Connor was on equal footing with Proto-Grind with respect to knowledge of the machine's capability. Doug testified that the Proto-Grind was the first grinder that Connor ever purchased. Even if Doug was more savvy then he acknowledged, the manufacturer of an expensive product should be well aware of the product's attributes and deficiencies before it offers it to the public. We conclude that the relative knowledge of the parties is a matter for the jury to consider, not a complete bar to recovery by Connor. . . . [T]he finder of fact could reasonably conclude that the alleged oral promises made were more than mere puffing, that the product failed to meet the promise that it would sufficiently grind palm trees and palmettos, that Connor relied on these affirmations, and that because the deficiency of the product was not cured, Proto-Grind breached this express warranty.

RESULT The Florida Court of Appeal vacated the directed verdict in favor of Proto-Grind and remanded the case to the trial court for further proceedings.

COMMENTS Whether a statement about a product is an express warranty or merely an opinion depends on the context in which it is made, the degree to which the buyer is ignorant of the subject matter of the statement, the extent to which the seller was merely puffing, the time when the statement was made, and other factors concerning the relationship between the two parties.

QUESTIONS

1. Why doesn't elimination of a trial period waive any express warranties?
2. How could Connor have relied on Proto-Grind's statements when he knew that a competitor was quite dissatisfied with his Proto-Grind 1200?

13. 350 So. 2d 1090 (Fla. App. 1977).

IMPLIED WARRANTY OF MERCHANTABILITY

The *implied warranty of merchantability* guarantees that the goods are reasonably fit for the general purpose for which they are sold and that they are properly packaged and labeled. The warranty applies to all goods sold by merchants in the normal course of business. It does not depend on the seller's statements or use of a sample or model. Rather, it depends on the identity of the seller as a merchant who deals in goods of a certain kind.

To be merchantable under Section 2-314(2) of the UCC, goods must (1) pass without objection in the trade under the contract description; (2) be fit for the ordinary purposes for which such goods are used; (3) be within the variations permitted by the agreement and be of even kind, quality, and quantity within each unit and among all units involved; (4) be adequately contained, packaged, and labeled as the agreement may require; and (5) conform to the promises or affirmations of fact made on the container or label, if any. Fungible goods, such as grain, must be of average quality within the contract description.

Reasonable Expectations The key issue in determining merchantability is whether the goods do what a reasonable person would expect of them. The contract description is crucial. Goods considered merchantable under one contract may be considered not to be merchantable under another. A bicycle with a cracked frame and bent wheels is not fit for the ordinary purpose for which bicycles are used, but it will pass under a contract for the sale of scrap metal.

When no contract description exists, the most frequent claim on which breach is based is that the goods are not fit "for the ordinary purposes for which such goods are used." Proof that the goods are imperfect or flawed is often insufficient to succeed on this claim. Even imperfect goods can be fit for their ordinary purposes.

In *Lescs v. William R. Hughes, Inc.*,[14] a homeowner filed a claim against Dow Chemical Company when she became ill after moving into a home that had been sprayed with insecticide manufactured by Dow. The homeowner argued that Dow had breached the implied warranty of merchantability by marketing an unreasonably dangerous product. The U.S. Court of Appeals for the Fourth Circuit rejected her claim that the insecticide failed to meet consumer expectations because the warning label on the pesticide had been approved by the Environmental Protection Agency. The court reasoned that "it would be anomalous to hold 'that a consumer is entitled to expect a product to perform more safely than its government mandated warnings indicate.'"

IMPLIED WARRANTY OF FITNESS FOR A PARTICULAR PURPOSE

The *implied warranty of fitness for a particular purpose* is set forth in Section 2-315 of the UCC. It guarantees that the goods are fit for the particular purpose for which the seller recommended them. Broad in its scope, it may apply to merchants and nonmerchants alike. A "particular purpose" differs from the ordinary purpose for which a good is used in that "particular purpose" contemplates a specific use by the buyer that is peculiar to the buyer or the buyer's business. By contrast, the ordinary purpose is that contemplated by the concept of merchantability. For example, dress shoes are generally used for the purpose of walking on ordinary ground and are not warranted for mountain climbing, but a seller may know that a particular pair was selected for mountain climbing.

Unlike the implied warranty of merchantability, the implied warranty of fitness for a particular purpose does not arise in every sale of goods. It will be implied only if four elements are present: (1) the buyer had a particular purpose for the goods; (2) the seller knew or had reason to know of that purpose; (3) the buyer relied on the seller's expertise; and (4) the seller knew or had reason to know of the buyer's reliance. Although the warranty usually arises when the seller is a merchant with some level of skill or judgment, it is not restricted to such circumstances.

Reliance To prove that the buyer did not in fact rely on the seller's expertise, the seller may try to show that (1) the buyer's expertise was equal to or superior to the seller's, (2) the buyer relied on the skill and judgment of persons hired by the buyer, or (3) the buyer supplied the seller with detailed specifications or designs that the seller was to follow.

Identifiable patents and trademarks can play an interesting role in this area of the law. If the buyer insists on a particular brand and style, he or she cannot be relying on the seller's skill or judgment. Hence, no warranty results. The mere fact that a good has an identifiable patent or trade name, however, does not prove nonreliance, especially if the seller recommended the product to the buyer.

Managers must provide adequate instruction and training to salespersons and agents about express and implied warranties. An aggressive salesperson willing to say what it takes to close a deal may unwittingly cause his or her company to be held liable under an implied warranty of fitness for a particular purpose when it never intended to make any such warranty at all.

14. 48 Env't Rep. Cas. (BNA) 1144 (4th Cir. Jan. 14, 1999), *cert. denied*, 120 S. Ct. 942 (2000).

LIMITING LIABILITY

The seller can avoid responsibility for the quality of the goods under any of these warranties. First, the seller need not make any express warranties. This may be difficult to do, however, because even a simple description of the goods may constitute a warranty. Second, a seller may disclaim any warranties of quality if it follows specifically delineated rules in the UCC designed to ensure that the buyer is aware of, and assents to, the disclaimers. For example, Section 2-316 allows a seller to exclude all implied warranties by using "expressions like 'AS IS,' 'WITH ALL FAULTS' or other language which in common understanding calls the buyer's attention to the exclusion of warranties and makes plain that there is no implied warranty." This language means that the buyer takes the entire risk as to the quality of the goods involved. Third, the seller can refrain from professing expertise with respect to the goods and leave the selection to the buyer.

More commonly, the seller limits its responsibility for the quality of the goods by limiting the remedies available to the buyer in the event of breach. A typical method is the inclusion of a provision limiting the seller's responsibility for defective goods to repair or replacement. Some states limit a seller's right to limit liability especially for personal injury.

Under the UCC, a seller is not an absolute insurer of the quality of goods sold. To recover for breach of warranty, a buyer must prove that (1) the seller made an express or implied warranty under the UCC; (2) the goods were defective at the time of the sale; (3) the loss or injury was caused by the defect rather than the buyer's negligent or inappropriate use of the goods; and (4) the seller has no affirmative defenses, such as a disclaimer of warranty.

As an alternative to suing for breach of warranty, the plaintiff may sue in tort for strict product liability. A product liability claim may succeed where a breach-of-warranty claim would not. This may happen when there is no contractual relationship between the buyer and the seller. Chapter 10 discusses this issue.

Magnuson-Moss Warranty Act

The Magnuson-Moss Warranty Act[15] is a federal law that protects consumers against deception in warranties. It gives a consumer purchaser of a product the right to sue a manufacturer or retailer for failing to

---

comply with the Act or the terms of a written or implied warranty arising from the Act. The Act was adopted "in order to improve the adequacy of information available to consumers, to prevent deception, and to improve competition in the marketing of consumer products."[16]

Nothing in the Act requires a supplier of consumer products to give a written warranty; the Act applies only when a seller chooses to do so. If the seller does make a written promise or affirmation of fact, however, then it must also state whether the warranty is a full or a limited warranty. A *full warranty* gives the consumer the right to free repair or replacement of a defective product. A *limited warranty* might restrict the availability of free repair or replacement. These designations inform the average consumer about the level of protection provided by the warranty. In order for a warranty to earn the designation of "full warranty," it must meet minimum standards provided in the Act. This Act is discussed further in Chapter 20.

---

15. 15 U.S.C. §§ 2301–12 (1997).

16. 15 U.S.C. § 2302(a) (1994).

VIEW FROM CYBERSPACE

Taxing E-Commerce

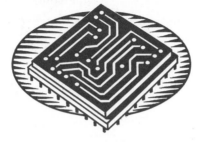

The issue of whether to tax electronic commerce has generated great controversy at the state and federal levels. In 1998, Congress enacted the Internet Tax Freedom Act, which declared a three-year moratorium on new taxes on the Internet but allowed states to enforce existing tax laws. Congress also created the Advisory Commission on Electronic Commerce to study federal, state, local, and international taxation of transactions using the Internet. The commission included executives of America Online, AT&T, Charles Schwab, Gateway, MCI Worldcom, and Time Warner as well as representatives of government at various levels.[a]

In March 2000, the Advisory Commission narrowly approved its report to Congress on continuing the tax moratorium, but the group was too divided to reach the two-thirds majority required for any "findings and recommendations" to Congress. Under the report, activities not triggering an obligation to collect state sales and use taxes would include the solicitation of orders, the presence of Web sites, the use of the Internet to create a Web site, the use of an Internet service provider, and the use of a telecommunications carrier.[b]

Taxation of Internet sales transactions raises issues regarding the existing maze of state sales taxes. Many feel the existing state tax regime should be amended. In *Quill v. North Dakota*,[c] the U.S. Supreme Court ruled that businesses selling goods through catalogs are required to collect sales taxes only on purchases made by consumers within the states where the business has a physical presence.

Under this ruling, an Internet company that sells to customers in states all over the country has no obligation to collect sales tax on sales to persons in states where it is not physically located. Many online retailers have sited their sales operations in the five American states that do not levy a sales tax so that

they have no obligation to collect sales taxes from any of their customers.[d] Consumers buying goods from outside their state of residence are supposed to pay a "use tax" in their home state equal to what the sales tax would have been, but they rarely do so.

Should the existing state tax regime be amended to address Internet sales? Regular "brick and mortar" retailers are opposed to the current system on the grounds that it gives Internet retailers an unfair advantage by allowing them to charge lower prices. As Governor John Engler of Michigan, testifying before Congress for the National Governors Association in February 2000, stated, "It is, in essence, a two-tiered system: good for clicks, bad for bricks."[e]

States are heavily dependent on sales taxes, which on average account for one-third of state tax revenues and one-quarter of the total state and local take. In some states, such as Texas, which has no income tax, the sales tax represents more than half of all revenues.[f] As of March 2000, retail sales on the Internet were less than 1 percent of all retail sales; according to Forrester Research, Inc., in 1999, states lost only $525 million, 0.3 percent of all sales-tax revenue.[g] Studies have predicted, however, that, by 2003, state and local governments could lose an estimated $3.5 billion to $10 billion a year in revenues if taxes are not collected on Internet sales.[h] Other commentators predict that the losses could be as high as $20 billion to $25 billion.[i]

In April 2000, more than thirty-six governors, including many with a reputation for cutting taxes, signed a letter

stating that Congress should not interfere with the right of states to determine their tax policies, claiming that such efforts by Congress "would substantially interfere with state sovereignty."[j] In addition, the governors delivered to Congress a scathing bipartisan attack on the Internet tax commission, characterizing it as a forum for businesses seeking tax breaks that would deprive states of money to fund education, state law enforcement agencies, and other services.[k]

Opponents of taxes on Internet sales argued that the growth of Internet businesses should not be slowed down by the imposition of taxes. According to a study by an economist at the University of Chicago, Internet sales in 1998 would have been 25 to 30 percent lower if sales taxes had been charged.[l]

a. David Cay Johnston, *Agreement on Internet Taxes Eludes Deeply Divided Commission*, N.Y. TIMES, Mar. 21, 2000, at 1.
b. *Panel Passes E-Commerce Report 10–8, Administration Officials All Vote Against Plan*, 68 U.S.L.W. 2601 (2000).
c. 504 U.S. 298 (1992).
d. *The Happy E-Shopper: How Feasible Is It to Tax Internet Spending?*, ECONOMIST, Jan. 29, 2000.
e. Ann Scott Tyson, *Should World Wide Web Be a Tax-Free Zone? E-Commerce Boosters Argue a Ban on Internet Taxes Is Critical for Growth, but States Worry They'll Lose Revenues*, CHRISTIAN SCI. MONITOR, Feb. 28, 2000, at 3.
f. Howard Gleckman, *The Great Internet Tax Debate: Should the States Get a Slice of Every E-Commerce Dollar or Should Cyber-Sales Be Free of Any Tax Burden?*, BUS. WK., Mar. 27, 2000, At 228.
g. *Id.*
h. Tyson, *supra* note e.
i. *Panel Passes E-Commerce Report 10–8*, *supra* note b.
j. David Cay Johnston, *Governors Criticize Internet Tax Panel*, N.Y. TIMES, Apr. 12, 2000, at 6.
k. *Id.*
l. *The Happy E-Shopper*, *supra* note d.

Right *to* Reject Nonconforming Goods

Generally, a buyer that has contracted to purchase goods from a seller must fulfill its obligation and pay for those goods. A buyer has the right to reject nonconforming goods, however. Under Section 2-601 of the UCC, if the goods or the tender of delivery fails to conform to the contract in any respect, the buyer may reject any or all of the goods. Section 2-602 requires that any rejection be made within a reasonable time after the goods are delivered. After such a rejection, the buyer may not treat the goods as if it owned them. To the contrary, if the buyer has taken possession of the goods before rejecting them, then it must hold the goods with reasonable care for a time sufficient to permit the seller to remove them. As the following case illustrates, the right to reject can be waived inadvertently by a buyer who accepts goods with knowledge of their nonconformity.

A CASE IN POINT

CASE 8.4

Moore & Moore General Contractors, Inc. v. Basepoint, Inc.
Supreme Court of Virginia
485 S.E.2d 131 (Va. 1997).

Summary

FACTS In late 1990, General Mills Restaurants, Inc. made plans to build a Red Lobster restaurant in Spotsylvania, Virginia. After requesting bids from various subcontractors for the elements of the project, general contractor Moore & Moore awarded a millwork subcontract to Basepoint. The subcontract called for Basepoint to provide custom-made cabinets of "melamine" for use throughout the restaurant. Even in the industry, the meaning of that term was unclear. Some evidence suggested that "melamine" referred to a composite product with a particular type of hard finish; other evidence suggested that it referred only to a finish and did not imply use of composite material.

In March and April of 1991, Basepoint delivered its cabinets to the job site, where they were received by Moore & Moore. Allen Lyle, Moore & Moore's field superintendent, and Donnie Hall, Lyle's subordinate, inspected the cabinets and noticed they were made of particle board instead of sturdier plywood, as called for in the master plans prepared by the project's architects. Believing that General Mills Restaurants would not know the difference and that he would be saving money by accepting delivery of the particle-board cabinets, Lyle directed the installation of all the cabinets.

On May 1, an inspector from General Mills Restaurants examined the installed millwork and rejected the cabinets as not conforming to the plans and specifications. The next day, Moore & Moore sent Basepoint a letter stating, "On Wednesday, May 1, 1991, it was discovered that most of your casework is constructed of particle board. Since the plans . . . we provided you for the above referenced job . . . call for plywood, all of the casework that has particle board does not conform and must be replaced." In the letter, Moore & Moore set the following Tuesday as the deadline for delivery of the replacement material, noting that Basepoint already had notified Lyle it could not meet the deadline. Upon removal of the cabinets made of particle board, Moore & Moore immediately procured plywood replacements from another subcontractor. The new cabinets were installed promptly, and the project was completed nearly on time.

Subsequently, Moore & Moore refused to pay Basepoint for the cabinets it had delivered. Basepoint then sued Moore & Moore for the $28,080 price of the cabinets. Moore & Moore denied any indebtedness to Basepoint, claiming that the materials supplied were defective. In addition, Moore & Moore filed a cross-complaint against Basepoint for the $47,000 cost of removing the particle-board casework, rebuilding the casework with plywood, and finishing the remaining work under the contract.

The trial court found for Basepoint and rejected Moore & Moore's cross-claim. Moore & Moore appealed.

(Continued)

(Case 8.4 continued)

ISSUE PRESENTED Can a buyer's acceptance of goods be revoked because of their nonconformity? If not, is the buyer entitled to recover from the seller the cost of substitute goods?

SUMMARY OF OPINION The Virginia Supreme Court first noted that as a sale of goods between merchants, the dispute was controlled by the UCC. Section 2-601 provides that if goods fail to conform to the contract, the buyer may (1) reject the whole, (2) accept the whole, or (3) accept any commercial unit or units and reject the rest. Section 2-606(1)(c) provides that acceptance of goods occurs when the buyer performs any act that is inconsistent with the seller's ownership of the goods. Because Moore & Moore's installation of the cabinets was an act inconsistent with Basepoint's ownership, the court found that Moore & Moore had accepted the goods. Even though Moore & Moore could have rejected any or all of the cabinets at delivery, its installation of them served as its acceptance.

Moore & Moore did not dispute this conclusion but instead contended that it had revoked its acceptance of the cabinets because of their nonconformity. The court, however, turned to Section 2-607(2), which provides that a buyer's acceptance of goods precludes their rejection and that acceptance cannot be revoked if it was given with knowledge of the nonconformity. Lyle and Hall's awareness that the cabinets were made of particle board amounted to such knowledge. Therefore, Moore & Moore could not revoke its acceptance.

Regardless of its liability to Basepoint for the cost of the cabinets, Moore & Moore pointed to Section 2-607(2), which provides that acceptance by a buyer "does not of itself impair any other remedy provided by this title for nonconformity." By its argument, Moore & Moore was entitled to an award based on the cover remedy of Sections 2-711 and 2-712, which allow a buyer to recover for procurement of substitute goods. The court noted, however, that under Section 2-711, the cover remedy is available in only four situations: (1) when the seller fails to make delivery, (2) when the seller repudiates the contract, (3) when the buyer rightfully rejects the goods, and (4) when the buyer justifiably revokes its acceptance of the goods. Here, Basepoint did make delivery and did not repudiate the contract. Moreover, Moore & Moore accepted the goods, thereby precluding rejection, and accepted with knowledge of nonconformity, making any revocation unjustified. With none of the four situations applicable, the court rejected Moore & Moore's cross-claim.

RESULT The trial court's decision was affirmed. Moore & Moore was required to pay for the cabinets.

Allocation *of* Risk *of* Loss

Goods can be lost in transit due to such events as fire, earthquake, flood, and theft. In the absence of an agreement to the contrary, Section 2-509 of the UCC places the risk of loss on the party controlling the goods at the time loss occurs because that party is better able to insure against loss and to take precautions to protect the goods. Section 2-319 expressly authorizes the buyer and seller to allocate risk of loss between them as they see fit and provides shorthand symbols, such as "FOB" (free on board), with defined meanings to facilitate the expression of such an agreement between the parties.

GOODS SHIPPED BY CARRIER

If a sales contract requires or authorizes the seller to ship the goods by carrier, the risk of loss passes to the buyer (1) at the time the goods are properly delivered to the carrier, if the contract does not require delivery at a particular destination; or (2) at the time the carrier tenders the goods to the buyer at the specified destination, if the contract specifies one. If nothing is said about delivery, the contract is not a delivery contract and does not require delivery to the destination.

If the parties indicate that shipment is to be made "FOB seller's place of business," delivery at a particular place is not required, so the risk of loss shifts to the buyer once the goods are properly placed in the possession of the carrier. An indication in the contract that shipment is to be made "FOB buyer's place of business" means that delivery at a particular place is required, so the risk of loss will not shift to the buyer until the goods are tendered to the buyer at its place of business. The parties' selection of an FOB term in a sales contract controls the allocation of the risk of loss even if contrary language exists elsewhere in the contract.

GOODS HELD BY INDEPENDENT WAREHOUSE

When the goods are in the possession of an independent warehouse and the seller provides the buyer with a document enabling it to pick up the goods at the warehouse, the risk of loss passes to the buyer when the buyer receives the document entitling it to pick up the goods.

ALL OTHER CASES

When the goods are neither to be shipped by carrier nor held by an independent warehouse, the allocation of the risk of loss in transit depends on whether the seller is a

INTERNATIONAL CONSIDERATION

The international mercantile community, acting through the International Chamber of Commerce, has elaborated a set of definitions of the most important trade terms now in use. Revised every ten years, the latest edition of these terms is INCOTERMS 2000. Traders of all countries commonly incorporate INCOTERMS into their international sales contracts.

INCOTERMS 2000 contains thirteen main trade terms, including FAS, FOB, CTF, and CIF, as well as several secondary terms. The CIF term, for example, requires a seller to procure, at its own cost and in a transferable form, a marine insurance policy against the risk of carriage involved in the contract.

merchant. (As mentioned earlier, a seller is a merchant if he or she possesses experience and special knowledge relating to the goods in question.) If the seller is a merchant, the risk of loss passes to the buyer only when the buyer receives physical possession of the goods. If the seller is not a merchant, the risk passes to the buyer when tender of delivery is made. Tender of delivery occurs when the seller notifies the buyer that it has the goods ready for delivery.

The following case deals with the question of when a buyer has physical possession of the goods and thus bears the risk of loss.

A CASE IN POINT

CASE 8.5
Lynch Imports, Ltd. v. Frey
Appellate Court of Illinois
558 N.E.2d 484
(Ill. App. Ct. 1990).

Summary

FACTS On October 22, 1987, the buyers agreed to purchase a 1987 Volkswagen automobile from the seller for the price of $8,706. The agreement was set forth in a purchase order in which the following phrases were handwritten on the purchase contract: "Car to be in totally acceptable condition or money will be refunded to the customer" and "Acceptance subject to inspection."

On October 24, the buyers took possession of the vehicle and paid the seller $4,706 as partial payment of the purchase price. The balance of the purchase price was to be financed. It was understood that the car was to come with air-conditioning, but at the time of delivery it was not yet installed. One of two riders attached to the purchase contract provided that the buyer was responsible for having the vehicle fully covered under liability and collision automobile insurance from the instant that the buyer took possession. The rider also stated that the buyer was not authorized to return the vehicle without the seller's authorization and that no vehicle was to be sold with the condition that the buyer might later return it.

Two to three days thereafter, the buyers brought the vehicle to the seller so the air conditioner could be installed. When they returned in the evening to pick up the vehicle,

(Continued)

(Case 8.5 continued)

the buyers were informed that the air conditioner had been installed but that the vehicle had sustained body damage in an accident. The buyers refused to take delivery of the automobile because of the damage and demanded that a new and undamaged car be substituted. When the seller refused, the buyers stopped payment on the check and canceled their application for financing the balance of the purchase price.

The car dealership sued the automobile purchasers for damages of $8,706 for breaching the sales contract and $4,706 for wrongfully stopping the check. The buyers filed a counterclaim for the seller's breach of contract in failing to deliver an acceptable car and sought damages of $1,330.35, representing the difference between the price paid by the buyers when they subsequently purchased a similar automobile and the contract price of the Volkswagen. The trial court granted summary judgment to the seller. The buyers appealed.

ISSUE PRESENTED When a buyer takes possession of a car, but it is understood that the buyer will return the car to have air-conditioning installed per the purchase order, has the buyer fully accepted the car and assumed complete responsibility for it?

SUMMARY OF OPINION The Illinois Appellate Court stated that there was an issue of material fact as to whether the buyers "accepted" the vehicle on October 24. The buyers argued that they did not accept the vehicle and therefore had the right to reject it, which they properly did, when it was damaged upon its return to the seller to install the air conditioner.

Under the provisions of Section 2-606 of the UCC, acceptance is deemed to have occurred when the buyer either signifies that the vehicle is conforming or "takes or retains" the vehicle in spite of its nonconformity. It was unclear to the court what the agreement was on October 24, 1987, just prior to the buyers' taking the vehicle. This uncertainty as to what transpired between the parties when the buyers took possession of the vehicle was of particular significance because the original purchase order contained the handwritten phrases: "Car to be in totally acceptable condition or money will be refunded to the customer" and "Acceptance subject to inspection."

Section 1-202 of the UCC provides that the effect of the provisions of the UCC may be varied by agreement. The court concluded that the handwritten notations in the purchase agreement were sufficient to raise an inference that the buyers did not intend to waive their right to defer acceptance until the vehicle was brought to full conformity, even though they took interim possession of the vehicle.

Under Section 2-509 of the UCC, the risk of loss does not pass to the buyer until the buyer accepts the goods, even though the buyer obtains an insurable interest under Section 2-501 after the goods are identified to the purchase contract. Thus, Rider 2, which required the buyer to obtain insurance, was not conclusive on its face to pass the risk of loss to the buyer.

RESULT The Illinois Appellate Court reversed the lower court's grant of summary judgment for the seller. There were material issues of disputed fact precluding summary judgment. The case was remanded to determine whether the buyers had accepted the vehicle on October 24 and whether they had the right to reject it when they later discovered it had been damaged during its return to the seller for the installation of air-conditioning.

 Unconscionability

A party is normally bound by the terms of a contract he or she enters into. However, if the contract is so unfair as to shock the conscience of the court, the judge may decline to enforce the offending terms or the entire contract.

Section 2-302(1) of the UCC provides procedural guidelines for judicial review of unconscionable clauses in contracts for the sale of goods, but it does not define "unconscionable." The official comments, however, do provide some guidance. For example, comment 1 to Section 2-302 states:

> The basic test is whether, in the light of the general background and the commercial needs of the particular trade or case, the clauses involved are so one sided as to be unconscionable under the circumstances existing at the time of the making of the contract. . . . The principle is one of the prevention of oppression and unfair surprise . . . and not of disturbance of allocation of risks because of superior bargaining power.

In deciding whether a contract is unconscionable, the court considers evidence in addition to the contractual language, particularly (1) whether the contractual obligation was bargained for and (2) whether the parties understood and accepted the obligation. As under common law (discussed in Chapter 7), unconscionability can be either procedural, (relating to the bargaining process) or substantive (relating to the provisions of the contract).

PROCEDURAL UNCONSCIONABILITY

A contract is procedurally unconscionable when one party is induced to enter the contract without having any meaningful choice. For example, in highly concentrated industries with few competitors, all the sellers may offer the same unfair contracts on a "take it or leave it" basis. Such contracts are known as *adhesion contracts.* They are most prevalent in consumer transactions where bargaining power is unequal.

It is also procedurally unconscionable for a seller to tuck oppressive clauses into the fine print or for high-pressure salespersons to mislead illiterate consumers. In commercial transactions, however, it is presumed that the parties have the sophistication to bargain knowledgeably. Procedural unconscionability is therefore more difficult to prove in the commercial setting.

SUBSTANTIVE UNCONSCIONABILITY

A contract is substantively unconscionable if its terms are unduly harsh or oppressive or unreasonably favorable to one side, such as in the case of an excessive price or an unreasonable limitation of one party's rights and remedies. The courts have not agreed on any well-defined test for determining when a price is so excessive as to be unconscionable. However, prices that were two to three times the price of similar goods sold in the same area have been held unconscionable.

Similarly, parties to a contract are allowed to limit the remedies available for breach but only to a certain extent. If, for example, consumer goods are involved, a provision that limits the purchaser's ability to recover monetary damages for personal injury is *prima facie* (or on its face) evidence of unconscionability. In the following case, the Supreme Court of Idaho considered whether a limitation of liability provision on a label was procedurally and substantively unconscionable.

A CASE IN POINT

CASE 8.6

Walker v. American Cyanamid Co.
Supreme Court of Idaho
948 P.2d 1123
(Idaho. 1997).

In the Language of the Court

FACTS Walker Farms purchased an herbicide, ASSERT, manufactured by American Cyanamid Company (Cyanamid) to use on crops of grain and potatoes grown in rotation on its fields. A Cyanamid representative told Walker that ASSERT was safe and posed no risk to potatoes even if sprayed directly on the plants. The label stated that potatoes could be planted in rotation after applying ASSERT on certain grain crops. A disclaimer on the label further provided:

> Any damages arising from breach of this warranty shall be limited to direct damages and shall not include consequential commercial damages such as loss of profits or values or any other special or indirect damages. American Cyanamid Company makes no express or implied warranty, including other express or implied warranty of FITNESS or of MERCHANTABILITY.

Walker applied Assert to grain crops in 1988 and 1989 and then harvested potato crops on those same fields in 1989 and 1990. The potato crops were irregular and substandard, so Walker planted grain on these fields in 1990 in order to avoid potato crop injury in 1991. Walker sued Cyanamid for damages on numerous theories, including

(Continued)

(Case 8.6 continued)

breach of express warranty. Walker claimed that the limitation of liability provision on the ASSERT label was unconscionable.

The trial court ruled that the limitation of liability provision was unconscionable, and the jury awarded Walker $3,428,703 in damages for potato crop losses and increased expenses. The trial court reduced the award by $315,333, the amount of crop insurance Walker received. Cyanamid appealed.

ISSUE PRESENTED Is an ambiguous provision limiting liability to "direct damages" unconscionable?

OPINION JOHNSON, J., writing for the Idaho Supreme Court:

Unconscionability has procedural and substantive components. Procedural unconscionability relates to the bargaining process leading to the agreement and is characterized by a "great disparity in the bargaining positions of the parties, by extreme need of one party to reach some agreement (however unfavorable), or by threats short of duress."

Substantive unconscionability focuses on the agreement itself and is a "narrow exception to the general principle that full force and effect must be given to a valid contract even though its provisions appear unwise or its enforcement may seem harsh." "The elements of one-sidedness, oppression and unfair surprise are commonly cited in analyses of unconscionability."

In making an unconscionability determination under I.C. Section 28-2-302, the court must consider the purpose and effect of the clause at issue, the commercial setting in which the contract was executed, and the reasonableness of the clause at the time of contracting.

. . .

In the present case, the trial court found that Cyanamid's representative advised Walker that ASSERT was safe for Walker's operation, that Walker's course of conduct proceeded under this premise, and that although Walker's knowledge concerning ASSERT grew as time passed, Walker's assessment of the risks was influenced by Cyanamid's representations. Although the trial court did not make an explicit finding concerning Cyanamid's superior knowledge, it is implicit in the trial court's findings that Cyanamid had superior knowledge concerning the effects of ASSERT.

. . .

There is uncontradicted evidence that Walker had knowledge of the limitation. Walker's employees testified that it is their practice to read pesticide labels. The trial court found, however, that the limitation of liability provision is not understandable. The limitation states:

> Any damages arising from breach of this warranty shall be limited to direct damages and shall not include consequential commercial damages such as loss of profits or values or any other special or indirect damages.

A contract provision is ambiguous if it is reasonably subject to conflicting interpretation and an ambiguous contract presents a question of fact regarding the parties' intent.

. . .

It is a reasonable interpretation that the damages that would naturally or ordinarily be expected to follow from the breach of the warranty in this case would be damages

(Continued)

(Case 8.6 continued)

to the potatoes that were planted after grain to which ASSERT was applied. The ambiguity is created because "direct damages" can reasonably be interpreted to cover the value of the potatoes, but the phrase "shall not include consequential commercial damages" can reasonably be interpreted to preclude recovery of the value of the potatoes. Because the limitation of liability provision is reasonably subject to conflicting interpretation, it is ambiguous. This ambiguity affects the commercial setting, purpose, and effect of the provision and is an appropriate consideration in determining unconscionability under I.C. Section 28-2-302.

The fact that Cyanamid had superior knowledge concerning ASSERT and made representations concerning its safety, coupled with the fact that the label is ambiguous and with the lack of Walker's bargaining power to negotiate concerning the limitation of liability, lead us to conclude that the limitation of liability provision is procedurally unconscionable.

Substantive unconscionability asks whether, at the time the contract was executed, and in light of the general background and commercial needs of a particular case, the clause is so one-sided as to oppress or unfairly surprise one of the parties.

The commercial setting, purpose, and effect of the clause are relevant in determining whether a contract is unconscionable. The risks contemplated by the parties at the time of the contract are relevant to the commercial setting, purpose, and effect of the parties. We conclude that it is this to which the trial court referred concerning the expectations of risk. It is clear that Walker contemplated there was a risk that ASSERT would harm the potato crops because Walker had discussions with Cyanamid representatives concerning this issue. The natural result of the breach of the warranty on the ASSERT label is damage to the potato crop. Therefore, it cannot be said that damage to the potato crop was not within Walker's contemplation.

The element of unfair surprise exists because of the ambiguity of the limitation of liability provision. A reasonable purchaser could interpret the provision not to limit the recovery of damages like those to Walker's potato crops.

Therefore, we conclude that the limitation of liability provision is substantively unconscionable because it constitutes unfair surprise.

RESULT The limitation of liability provision was procedurally and substantively unconscionable. Walker could recover for damage to his potato crops.

QUESTIONS

1. How might Cyanamid have worded its limitation of liability provision to defend successfully against claims of unconscionability?
2. Is it ethical for a company to represent that its product is safe for a particular use and then seek to limit its liability for damages resulting from that use?

 # Commercial Impracticability *under the* UCC

The UCC has adopted the doctrine of *commercial impracticability* rather than the common law doctrine of strict impossibility discussed in Chapter 7. Section 2-615 states that unless the contract provides otherwise, a failure to perform is not a breach if performance is made impractical by an event unforeseen by the contract. Section 2-615, the associated official comments, and the cases that have arisen under Section 2-615 establish certain criteria that a party seeking discharge from performance must show.

ETHICAL CONSIDERATION

Merchants selling goods on credit to low-income customers often charge a very high rate of interest. How should a manager balance the need for low-income persons to have credit to buy goods with the need for businesses to make a profit? Some businesspeople suggest that because low-income persons are statistically more likely to default on loans, creditors must charge a higher interest rate to cover themselves for the increased risk of default. They argue that if sellers are not allowed to charge higher interest rates or prices, low-income buyers will not be able to buy goods on credit. Are such higher rates and prices ethical? Should there be any limit to what a seller can charge for credit?

UNDERLYING CONDITION

First, a party must show that there was a failure of an underlying condition of the contract, that is, a condition that was not included in the parties' bargain. Certain occurrences are provided for fully in contracts, and the seller is assumed to have figured an appropriate "insurance premium" into the contract price. Other risks are deemed too remote and uncertain to be included in the contract price. The function of the court in applying the doctrine of commercial impracticability is to determine which risks were, or properly should have been, allocated to the buyer and which to the seller.

UNFORESEEN CONTINGENCY

In addition to showing that a condition was not reflected in the contract price, a seller seeking discharge must prove that the contingency that prevents performance was both unforeseen and unforeseeable. To some extent every occurrence is foreseeable—there is always some probability that a fire will destroy the anticipated source of supply, that a key person will die, or that various acts of God will occur. Legally, however, a foreseeable contingency is one that the parties should have contemplated in the circumstances surrounding the contracting. If there is a standard trade custom for allocating the risk, it is assumed that a particular contract follows that custom, unless it specifies differently.

Official comment 4 provides an illustrative, but not exhaustive, list of contingencies that are considered unforeseeable. Wars and embargoes are considered unforeseeable; market fluctuations are not.

IMPRACTICABLE PERFORMANCE

Even if a party is able to show that there was a failure of an underlying condition of the contract and that it did not implicitly assume the risk of this occurrence, the party still must prove that the performance was impracticable. Increased cost alone is not sufficient reason to excuse performance unless it is a marked increase. In one case, a ten- to twelvefold increase was considered sufficient. In another case, the court observed: "We are not aware of any cases where something less than a 100% cost increase has been held to make a seller's performance impracticable."[17] Transactions that have merely become unprofitable will not be excused. Sellers cannot rely on Section 2-615 to get them out of a bad bargain.

Some of the most famous cases concerning the issue of impracticability involved Westinghouse Electric Corporation, which argued unsuccessfully that the doctrines of *commercial impracticability* and *commercial impossibility* should relieve it of its obligation to supply uranium at a fixed price to utilities after a sharp increase in uranium prices.[18] On September 8, 1975, Westinghouse surprised and shocked the business and legal communities when it announced that it would not deliver about seventy million pounds of uranium under fixed-price contracts to twenty-seven utility companies. Westinghouse claimed that the potential loss of $2 billion made it commercially impractical to meet its obligations. In 1976, Westinghouse brought suit against its uranium suppliers, claiming that an international cartel had caused an unforeseen and precipitous increase in the price of uranium.

The judges involved in the ensuing litigation between Westinghouse and the utilities saw the conflict as primarily a business issue and pushed for settlement. Judge I. Martin Wickselman of the Court of Common Pleas in Pennsylvania stated:

> I am tired of pussyfooting and, more than that, I am tired of talking to lawyers when other, more powerful men, who have the ultimate power of decision, have not been here. The fiscal well-being, possibly the survival, of one of the world's corporate giants is in jeopardy. Any decision I hand down will hurt someone and, because of the potential damage, I want to make it clear that it will happen only because certain captains of industry could not together work out their problems so that the hurt might have been held to a minimum.

17. Publicker Indus., Inc. v. Union Carbide Corp., 17 U.C.C. Rep. Serv. 989 (E.D. Pa. 1975).
18. This discussion is based on William Eagan, *The Westinghouse Uranium Contracts: Commercial Impracticability and Related Matters,* 18 Am. Bus. L.J. 281 (1980).

On October 27, 1978, the U.S. District Court for the Eastern District of Virginia found that Westinghouse had not met its burden of establishing that it was entitled to be excused from its contractual obligations under Section 2-615 of the UCC. The court did not issue its supporting findings of facts and conclusions of law at the time, however, and instead urged the parties to settle as it was reluctant for the case to serve as legal precedent.

 ## Damages

The UCC generally tries to put the nonbreaching party in the same position it would have been in if the contract had been performed. This is usually done through the award of monetary damages.

SELLER'S REMEDIES

If a buyer wrongfully cancels a contract or refuses to accept delivery of the goods covered by the contract, the seller is entitled to damages under Section 2-708 of the UCC. The measure of damages is the difference between the market price at the time and place for delivery and the unpaid contract price, less expenses saved because of the buyer's breach. If this measure of damages is inadequate to put the seller in as good a position as performance would have, then the seller is entitled to recover the profit (including reasonable overhead) that it would have made from full performance by the buyer. Such a seller is called a *lost volume seller*.

BUYER'S REMEDIES

If a seller wrongfully fails to deliver the goods or repudiates the contract, or if the buyer justifiably rejects the tendered goods, then under Section 2-711 of the UCC the buyer has several choices. The buyer may cancel the contract and recover as much of the price as has been paid and then either (1) *cover,* that is, buy the goods elsewhere and be reimbursed for the extra cost of the substitute goods, or (2) recover damages for nondelivery.

If the buyer elects to cover under Section 2-712, it must make, in good faith and without reasonable delay, a reasonable purchase of substitute goods. The buyer may then recover from the seller the difference between the cost of covering and the contract price.

If the buyer elects not to cover, then under Section 2-713 the buyer is entitled to damages. The measure of damages is the difference between the market price at the time the buyer learned of the breach and the contract price. The buyer may also recover consequential

damages. Section 2-715 of the UCC permits the buyer to recover consequential damages for (1) any loss resulting from general or particular requirements and needs of the buyer that the seller at the time of contracting had reason to know and that could not reasonably be prevented by cover or otherwise and (2) injury to person or property proximately resulting from any breach of warranty.

 ## Specific Performance

If the promised goods are unique, then under Section 2-716 of the UCC a court may order the seller to deliver them. For example, if there is only one antique Mercedes–Benz of a certain vintage, then damages alone will not be adequate to remedy the loss suffered by the disappointed buyer. Only delivery of the promised car will suffice. On the other hand, if the car is one of thousands, monetary damages will suffice because an equivalent car can be purchased elsewhere.

Uniform Computer Information Transactions Act (UCITA)

In August 2000, the National Conference of Commissioners on Uniform State Laws (NCCUSL) adopted the final draft of the Uniform Computer Information Transactions Act (UCITA). The NCCUSL is a national organization of 350 lawyers, judges, and academics from the fifty states, the District of Columbia, Puerto Rico, and the U.S. Virgin Islands. UCITA was enacted to provide a uniform commercial contract code for software licenses and other computer information transactions. It essentially plays the same role for contracts dealing with information technology that the UCC plays for the sale of goods. As with the UCC, states may adopt UCITA with amendments.[19] As of January 2001, only two states (Maryland and Virginia) had adopted UCITA.

UCITA has provisions addressing all the standard contract issues that the UCC addresses for the sale of goods, including offer and acceptance of contract terms, warranties, transfer of contract interests, the rights and obligations of parties if a contract is breached, and remedies. In addition, it includes rules addressing issues unique to electronic contracts. As with the UCC, the parties can, with limited exceptions, vary the terms and effect of a contract from the default rules set forth in UCITA. UCITA follows Article 2 of the UCC in providing a standard of unconscionability for courts to employ in policing contract terms, but goes a step further and authorizes courts to strike down overreaching language that conflicts with fundamental public policy. UCITA also provides that common law doctrines, such as fraud and duress, remain effective.

SCOPE

UCITA covers transactions in *computer information,* defined as "information in electronic form which is obtained from or through the use of a computer or which is in a form capable of being processed by a computer." Under the terms of UCITA, a "computer information transaction" is an agreement to create, modify, transfer, or license computer information or informational rights

in computer information. UCITA therefore covers contracts to license or buy software, contracts to create computer programs, contracts for online access to databases, and contracts to distribute information over the Internet. It also governs custom software development and the acquisition of various rights in multimedia products.

If a contract involves more than computer information, UCITA will apply only to that part of the transaction that involves computer information, except when the remainder of the transaction does not concern goods and obtaining the computer information is the primary purpose of the transaction. If the transaction also concerns goods, UCC Article 2 or 2A will govern the goods while UCITA will govern the computer information. UCITA generally treats software embedded in goods, such as computerized braking systems, as goods.

STATUTE OF FRAUDS

Under the statute of frauds provision, a contract requiring payment of $5,000 or more is not enforceable unless there is an authenticated record of the existence of a contract. An authenticated record is sufficient even if it omits or incorrectly states a term. UCITA recognizes the validity of electronic signatures.

ASSENT AND CONTRACT FORMATION

The rules governing assent to a contract generally follow traditional common law. A contract may be formed in any manner sufficient to show agreement, including conduct by the parties or by operation of electronic agents that recognize the existence of a contract.[20] A contract may be formed by the interaction of electronic agents or the interaction of an electronic agent and an individual.[21] An acceptance of an offer will operate as an acceptance even if it contains terms that are different from the offer unless it materially alters the offer.[22] An acceptance materially alters an offer if it contains terms that materially conflict with or vary the terms of the offer or if it adds material terms not contained in the offer.

Unlike the common law, UCITA protects parties from inadvertent contracts. To be bound by the terms of an agreement, a party must have an opportunity to review the terms before manifesting assent.[23] Although it is not clear whether a failure to act will be sufficient to manifest assent, it appears that, at a minimum, continued

---

19. *UCITA Online* (visited Nov. 8, 2000)
<http://www.ucitaonline.com>.

20. UCITA § 202.
21. UCITA § 206.
22. UCITA § 204.
23. UCITA § 112(e).

use of the software by the consumer will be required to hold a license enforceable.[24] In the case of mass-market licenses, if a licensee does not have an opportunity to review the license prior to having the obligation to pay, then does not agree to the license after reviewing it, the licensee is entitled to return the product and receive a full refund plus reimbursement of reasonable expenses of returning the product and foreseeable costs of restoring the licensee's system.[25]

WARRANTIES

UCITA contains several implied and express warranties that usually are not recognized under common law:

1. Warranty of noninterference and noninfringement (applicable only to licensors who are merchants; the licensor warrants that the information will be delivered free of the rightful claim of any third person by way of infringement or misappropriation).
2. Implied warranty of merchantability of a computer program (applicable only to merchants; the licensor warrants to the end user that the computer program is fit for the ordinary purposes for which such computer programs are used).
3. Implied warranty of informational content (applicable only to merchants; a licensor that is in a special relationship of reliance with a licensee and collects or provides data warrants that there is no inaccuracy caused by the merchant's failure to perform with reasonable care).
4. Warranty of fitness for the licensee's particular purpose (if a licensor has reason to know of any particular purpose for which the information is required and that the licensee is relying on the licensor for expertise, the licensor warrants that the information will be fit for that purpose).
5. Implied warranty of system integration (if an agreement requires a licensor to provide a system consisting of computer programs and goods, and the licensor has reason to know that the licensee is relying on the licensor's skill or judgment to select the components, the licensor warrants that the components will function together as a system).

UCITA also requires a licensor to expressly warrant that the information furnished under the agreement will conform to any fact, promise, or description made by the licensor to the licensee. Advertising by the licensor may create an express warranty if it relates to the information and becomes part of the basis of the bargain.[26]

DAMAGES

One of the more controversial aspects of UCITA is a damages provision dealing with electronic self-help. In the software industry, "self-help" refers to the practice of placing disabling bugs or time bombs in software programs to disable them if the licensee refuses to pay for the product or services.[27] UCITA provides that upon cancellation of a license, the licensor has the right to possess all copies of the licensed information held by the licensee and to prevent the continued use of the licensed information by the licensee.[28] The licensor may exercise its rights using self-help measures if doing so will not breach the peace or risk personal injury or damage to property. In addition, electronic self-help must comply with procedures set forth in UCITA. These procedures include obtaining the licensee's assent to the term authorizing use of electronic self-help and providing notice to the licensee prior to exercising self-help.

SUPPORTERS AND CRITICS

Many sectors of the software industry strongly support UCITA and maintain that it will promote freedom of contract and bring predictability to licensing.[29] Many others, however, oppose UCITA, including consumer advocates, technology trade associations, law professors, the American Library Association, the Consumers Union, the Institute of Electrical and Electronics Engineers, and a long list of attorneys general.[30] These critics complain that UCITA provides too much protection for companies and not enough for consumers. Critics strongly oppose giving software vendors the right to monitor the use of their products by accessing computers remotely. Critics also argue that UCITA will weaken the warranty protection consumers receive under software licenses and make it more difficult to sue software vendors that have sold faulty programs.

---

24. Jessica Trivellini Toney, *Does Breaking the Seal Open Pandora's Box? Shrinkwrap Licensing and the UCITA*, J. Internet L., May 2000, at 17.
25. UCITA §§ 210, 112.
26. UCITA § 402.
27. Toney, *supra* note 24, at 19.
28. UCITA § 815.
29. Patrick Thibodeau, *UCITA Advances in Mid-Atlantic States*, Computerworld, May 1, 2000, at 4.
30. Neil Gross, *This Law Is User-Friendly*, Bus. Wk., Apr. 17, 2000, at 94.

IN BRIEF

Comparison of the UCC, Common Law, UCITA, and CISG

	Scope	Battle of the Forms	Warranties	Statute of Frauds
UCC	Sale of goods	Contract even if acceptance has additional or different terms	1. Implied warranties of merchantability and fitness for a particular purpose 2. Any express warranties made	Sales of $500 or more
Common Law	1. Provision of services 2. Contracts for sale of land or securities 3. Loan agreements	Mirror image rule	Any express warranties made	1. Transfer of real estate 2. Contract can't be performed within one year 3. Prenuptial agreement 4. Agreement to pay debt of another
UCITA	Computer information (including software, computer games, and online access)	Contract even if acceptance has additional or different terms unless acceptance materially alters the offer	1. Warranty of noninterference and noninfringement 2. Implied warranties of merchantability of computer program, informational content, fitness for licensee's particular purpose, and fitness for system integration 3. Any express warranties made	Contracts for $5,000 or more
CISG	Sale of goods by merchants in different countries unless parties opt out	In practice, mirror image rule	1. Implied warranties of merchantability and fitness for a particular use 2. Any express warranties made	None

 International Sale *of* Goods *and* CISG

The UCC's Article 2 largely unified the laws of the separate states in the United States governing the domestic sale of goods. International sales of goods, however, remain outside its scope. As international trade and the global economy grew throughout the twentieth century, the need for more uniform laws throughout the world became apparent. The Convention on Contracts for the International Sale of Goods (CISG), promulgated under the auspices of the United Nations, became effective in 1988. More than fifty countries have ratified the convention, including many of the world's largest economies: Canada, China, France, Germany, Russia, Singapore, and the United States.[31] Today, the signatories to CISG account for nearly two-thirds of the world's imports and exports.

31. For the most up-to-date information about the convention, including its signatories, *see* the UN Web site at <http://www.un.or.at/uncitral>.

SCOPE OF THE CONVENTION

CISG sets out substantive provisions of law to govern the formation of international sales contracts between merchants and the rights and obligations of buyers and sellers.[32] It applies to sales contracts between parties with places of business in different countries if those countries are bound by the convention, unless the parties have expressly opted out of CISG. Thus, CISG is the default provision that applies if a sales contract involving merchants from different countries is silent as to applicable law. As with the UCC, parties are free to specify applicable law and to vary the effect of CISG provisions.

CISG does not apply to sales (1) of goods bought for personal, family, or household use, unless the seller neither knew nor should have known that the goods were bought for such use; (2) by auction; (3) on execution of a judgment or otherwise by authority of law; (4) of stocks, shares, investment securities, negotiable instruments, or money; (5) of ships, vessels, hovercraft, or aircraft; and (6) of electricity. As for the distinction between goods and services, CISG does not apply to contracts in which goods are sold in conjunction with services unless the preponderance of the obligations of the seller consists of the supply of goods. Neither does it apply to liability of the seller for death or personal injury to any person caused by its goods.

CISG applies to oral as well as written contracts of sale. CISG contains no statute of frauds requiring certain contracts to be in writing, unless one party has its place of business in a country that has made a reservation to the convention in this regard. The United States did not make this reservation.

OFFER AND ACCEPTANCE

Under CISG, an offer becomes effective when it reaches the offeree, and it may be withdrawn if the withdrawal reaches the offeree before or at the same time as the offer. Until a contract is concluded, an offeror may revoke its offer if the revocation reaches the offeree before the offeree has dispatched its acceptance. An offer cannot be revoked, however, if the offer indicates that it is irrevocable or if the offeree reasonably relied on its irrevocability. Even if irrevocable, an offer is terminated when the offeree's rejection reaches the offeror.

A contract is concluded at the moment acceptance of an offer becomes effective. A statement made by the offeree indicating its assent is an acceptance. Conduct indicating assent is also acceptance, but silence or inactivity

32. For extensive materials relating to CISG, including international cases and commentary, *see* the Pace University School of Law's Web site on the convention at <http://www.cisg.law.pace.edu>.

does not in itself amount to acceptance. An acceptance becomes effective when it reaches the offeror, although an acceptance is not effective if it fails to reach the offeror within the time the offeror has specified. If the offeror has specified no time, then the acceptance must reach the offeror within a reasonable time. If the offer is oral, however, it must be accepted immediately unless circumstances indicate otherwise.

Recognizing the importance of custom and practice, CISG also provides that if the parties have established practices between themselves, the offeree may accept the offer by performing an appropriate act, such as sending the goods or paying the price, without notifying the offeror. In such a case, acceptance is effective as soon as the act is performed. Such acceptance by performance without notification differs from the UCC, which allows for acceptance by performance but requires notification.

BATTLE OF THE FORMS

An important difference between the UCC and CISG can be found in their respective approaches to the battle of the forms. Under CISG, a reply to an offer that purports to be an acceptance but contains additional terms or other modifications that materially alter the terms of the offer is a rejection of the offer and constitutes a counteroffer. Thus, there is no contract. If the modifications do not materially alter the terms of the offer and the offeror fails to object in a timely fashion, then there is a contract, which will include the terms of the offer with the modifications stated in the acceptance. CISG lists those categories of differences that are presumed to alter the terms of the offer materially: price, payment, quality and quantity of the goods, place and time of delivery, extent of one party's liability to the other, and settlement of disputes. The list leaves little for the sphere of "immateriality" and largely effects the old mirror image rule. As explained earlier, under the UCC, an acceptance with additional or conflicting terms may still result in a contract unless the offeree clearly specifies that there is no contract; even then, a contract may result if the offeror accepts the additions or modifications.

GOOD FAITH

CISG provides that in interpreting the convention there shall be regard for promoting "the observance of good faith in international trade." As noted earlier, Section 1-203 of the UCC provides: "Every contract or duty within this Act imposes an obligation of good faith in its performance and enforcement." At the most superficial level, the UCC provision is broader than the CISG principle, which literally applies only to the interpretation of the convention rather than to the conduct of merchants under it. Throughout CISG, however, are numerous requirements of "reasonableness," such as those for giving notice, making substitutions, relying, measuring inconvenience and expense, delaying performance, examining goods, incurring expenses, and making excuses.

Some commentators have suggested that the combination of CISG's requirements of good faith in interpretation and of reasonableness in so many areas of merchant behavior makes for a broad, albeit uncertain, duty for merchants to conduct themselves with good faith.[33] If that interpretation is correct, then, for example, if a seller requests additional time to deliver goods, a buyer would be required to act in good faith in deciding whether to grant that request. The buyer could not whimsically decide to enforce the letter of the contract to the seller's detriment. This contrasts with the UCC's *perfect tender rule,* which gives the buyer an absolute right to reject any goods not meeting all the contract requirements, including time of delivery. Nonetheless, managers are well advised to act in good faith rather than arbitrarily, both for their own long-term interests and reputation and to enhance their ability to attain a sympathetic hearing by possible legal decision makers.

33. *See, e.g.,* Phanesh Koneru, *The International Interpretation of the UN Convention on Contracts for the International Sale of Goods: An Approach Based on General Principles,* 6 MINN. J. GLOBAL TRADE 105 (1997).

IMPLIED WARRANTIES

Under CISG, the seller must deliver goods that are of the quantity, quality, and description required by the contract, and such goods must be packaged as specified by the contract. As with the UCC, the convention holds sellers liable for implied warranties of merchantability and fitness for particular use and for any express warranties they make. Under CISG:

> Unless the parties agree otherwise, goods do not conform unless they (a) are fit for the purposes for which goods of the same description would ordinarily be used; (b) are fit for any particular purpose expressly or impliedly made known to the seller at the time of the conclusion of the contract, except where the circumstances show that the buyer did not rely, or that it was unreasonable for him to rely, on the seller's skill and judgment; (c) possess the qualities of goods which the seller has held out to the buyer as a sample or model. . . .[34]

CISG makes clear, however, that the implied warranty of merchantability does not attach if the buyer knew that the goods were not fit for ordinary use.

34. 15 U.S.C. app. (1997), Convention on Contracts for the International Sale of Goods, art. 35.

THE RESPONSIBLE MANAGER
Operating *under* Varying Legal Regimes

Any manager who enters into contracts on behalf of a business should know which body of contract law will govern the transaction. In particular, the manager should determine whether the transaction is governed by Article 2 of the UCC, the common law rules concerning contracts, CISG, or UCITA. Article 2 applies only to the sale of goods, not services or land. Although some things are clearly designated as goods, others may be more difficult to categorize. CISG will apply to most international sales of goods unless the parties affirmatively opt out of its provisions. In states that have enacted the Uniform Computer Information Transactions Act, UCITA governs contracts to license or buy software, computer programs, multimedia products, computer games, and online access. A manager should obtain legal advice if there is any doubt as to which body of law controls in a particular situation.

Managers should be aware of the requirements that must be met for the valid formation of a contract under the different regimes. In particular, managers should focus on one of the key elements in creating a valid contract: the process of offer and acceptance. This knowledge is crucial to ensuring that the company can enforce the contracts it has entered into and wishes to uphold. In addition, a manager may have a valid reason to attempt to avoid an agreement that was not formed in the correct manner. Only if the manager knows the rules of contract formation can he or she assess whether a contract was validly created.

The manner of making an appropriate offer is the same under the UCC as it is under common law. However, a manager should note that Article 2 allows an offeree to accept an offer even if the offeree's acceptance contains terms additional to or different from those in the offer. In contrast, CISG in practice generally imposes the mirror image rule applied by the common law. The rules in this area and the corresponding case law are both complex and fact specific. Nonetheless, it is crucial that managers understand these rules before they engage in negotiations. Failure to develop this understanding can lead to adverse results. A manager or company may be legally bound to a contract even when there was no intention to be bound. Or a manager may inadvertently extinguish an offer by proposing modifications that ultimately the offeree might have been willing to forgo.

Article 2 of the UCC, CISG, and UCITA establish three types of warranties that buyers may rely upon when purchasing goods or computer information. Managers should be aware of how each warranty is created, how the warranties are applied, and how liability for products can be limited. These warranties also provide guidelines for managers regarding what is expected from a product in terms of quality and suitability for its intended use. It is essential that managers obtain legal advice in this area because lawsuits for breach of warranty can lead to large

awards of damages that are far in excess of the purchase price.

Managers should also be familiar with the legal doctrines that allow parties legally to back out of contracts. The doctrine of impracticability can protect a party when unexpected changes in circumstances make performance not literally impossible but commercially ruinous. The doctrine of unconscionability provides guidelines on the legal limits to one-sided contracts. Managers should keep in mind that sometimes more is less; extracting onerous concessions from a weaker party may backfire and cause a judge to declare a set of provisions invalid *in toto* when less onerous provisions might have passed judicial muster.

Both the UCC and CISG require the parties to act in good faith and in a commercially reasonable manner. Managers should avoid acting in an arbitrary manner and try to accommodate the reasonable requests of the other side (e.g., a seller's request to delay delivery when the delay would not have an adverse effect on the buyer's business).

INSIDE STORY

Caught *in the* Web *of* Internet Auction Fraud

According to the National Consumers League, a non-profit consumer organization, businesses and individuals lost $3.4 billion in 1999 as a result of Internet fraud.[35] Online auction fraud is the largest source of online consumer complaints, comprising 87 percent of all Internet fraud. The opportunity to defraud bidders has increased as the dollar amount of online auction sales doubled from $3 billion in 1999 to approximately $6 billion in 2000.

A variety of schemes, including high-tech fencing of stolen goods, have been used to defraud unsuspecting bidders at these cyberauctions. In June 2000, police arrested a group of thieves who had burglarized as many as 100 homes in Massachusetts and then sold their stolen goods on the eBay online auction site.[36] Similarly, in August 1999, two Michigan men were charged with racketeering and fraud after fencing thousands of dollars of

stolen property on online auction sites. In an interesting twist, law enforcement agencies in Oregon and California have started auctioning seized and recovered property online because it is more profitable than the traditional method of selling the goods through local auctions or sealed bids at a property warehouse.[37]

Other fraudulent online schemes have involved the sale of fake art and the use of "shill bidders" to enter multiple bids under different names in order to artificially inflate the auction price.[38] In June 2000, eBay suspended a seller who had entered bids on his own painting by using multiple screen names. Whereas Amazon.com's and Yahoo!'s auction sites require both bidders and sellers to enter their credit card numbers so that they can be traced, eBay currently requires only sellers to enter their credit card numbers. This makes it difficult to determine whether a bidder is

35. Dan Carney, *Business Week e.biz: Special Report: Internet Fraud,* Bus. Wk., Apr. 3, 2000, at EB58.
36. Marcella Bombardieri & John Ellement, *Stolen Goods Making Way to Internet, Fencing Schemes Use Online Auction Sites,* Boston Globe, June 1, 2000, at A1.
37. Mindy Sink, *Latest Items on eBay: Seized Loot,* N.Y. Times, May 11, 2000, at 11.
38. Judith Dobrzynski, *Spitzer Sues Gallery over Fake Art on eBay,* N.Y. Times, May 26, 2000, at 38.

in fact a seller using a different screen name to enter bids.[39] Online auction companies have been reluctant to prohibit the use of multiple names, claiming that many users depend on different names to establish identities better suited to different markets.[40]

Online auction site fraud has not been limited to the United States. In May 2000, a twenty-three-year-old Tokyo man was arrested for fraudulently acquiring seven million yen by posting a bogus advertisement for a popular game machine on an Internet auction site.[41] Even the National Police Agency in Japan became a victim of cyber-auction fraud when allegedly authentic police uniforms and badges were offered on Yahoo!Auction, a site opened in September 1999 by Yahoo!Japan Corporation.[42]

Online auction sites claim that they are under no legal obligation to determine whether goods auctioned on their sites are stolen. eBay's user agreement states:

> We are not involved in the actual transaction between buyers and sellers. As a result, we have no control over the quality, safety or legality of the items advertised, the truth or accuracy of the listings, the ability of sellers to sell items, or the ability of buyers to buy them.[43]

The company also claims that fraud affects only a tiny percentage of the sales at its site—one in 25,000.[44]

Although eBay has been criticized for failing to take enough steps to protect its customers, the company has made some effort to protect online bidders and sellers. A 100-member eBay fraud unit headed by a former federal prosecutor tracks down violators. eBay uses "shill hunter" software, although it has failed to detect some shill bidding schemes.[45] In addition, eBay offers an escrow service that allows a bidder to inspect the auctioned item before the seller is paid. eBay also insures goods up to $200, which the company claims covers approximately 85 percent of goods auctioned on the site.

In large part, eBay relies upon its customers to police its auction house Web site. For example, in May 2000, one victim of an eBay fraud organized an e-posse to track down the person who had swindled him out of $2,380 for two computers he won in an eBay auction. When he never received the computers, he went online to see whether any other people had tried to purchase computers from the same seller. His efforts resulted in a digital posse of other victims who provided clues to identify the criminal and enable the police to arrest him.[46]

Two recent incidents have raised questions about the liability of online auctions for goods sold on their sites. In May 2000, a French court ordered Yahoo! to find a way to prevent Internet users in France from accessing online auctions of Nazi memorabilia on its Web site because exhibiting or selling objects with racist overtones is illegal under French law.[47] After a special court-appointed panel of experts concluded that it was technologically feasible to keep 70 to 80 percent of all French Internet surfers out of banned Yahoo! auctions, the French court ordered Yahoo! to block access to the sites.[48] In January 2001, Yahoo! announced that it had changed its auctions policy to prohibit the auction of items that "promote or glorify hatred and violence," including Nazi and Ku Klux Klan-related items.

In contrast, the California Superior Court for San Diego County ruled in 2001 that eBay was not liable, under a California statute[49] requiring "dealers" selling collectibles with autographs to provide a certificate of authenticity, for fake sports memorabilia sold on its site.[50] Although the statute includes auctioneers of collectibles in its definition of dealers, the court concluded that eBay was neither an auctioneer nor a dealer. eBay provides a "trading venue" for buyers and sellers but the seller of the forged items, not eBay, selects the category and subcategory under which the items are listed.

In an attempt to combat Internet fraud, various agencies have set up Web sites where consumers can learn about cybercrime and file complaints. On May 8, 2000, the Federal Bureau of Investigation, jointly with the Department of Justice and the National White Collar Crime Center, announced the creation of the Internet Fraud Complaint Center where victims of Internet fraud can file a crime report online. In February 2000, the Federal Trade Commission launched Project Safebid, an effort to get local, state, and federal law enforcement to

39. Jim Carlton & Ken Besinger, *CEO Seeks to Reassure Public, but Use of Multiple Names by Bidders Poses Problems,* WALL ST. J., May 24, 2000, at B1.

40. Judith Dobrzynski, *The Bidding Game: A Special Report, in Online Auction World, Hoaxes Aren't Easy to See,* N.Y. TIMES, June 2, 2000, at 1.

41. *Suspected Net Auction Bilker Bagged,* YOMIURI SHIMBUN/DAILY YOMIURI, May 5, 2000.

42. *Police Goods Hawked on Internet Irks NPA,* YOMIURI SHIMBUN/DAILY YOMIURI, Apr. 15, 2000.

43. Bombardieri & Ellement, *supra* note 36.

44. Carlton & Besinger, *supra* note 39.

45. *Id.*

46. Julia Angwin, *How an E-Posse Led to Arrests in Online Fraud,* WALL ST. J., May 4, 2000, at B1.

47. *French Court Orders Yahoo! to Block Auctions of Nazi Memorabilia,* AGENCE FRANCE-PRESSE, May 22, 2000.

48. 5 Electronic Commerce & L. Rep. (BNA) 1165 (Dec. 6, 2000).

49. Cal. Civil Code § 1739.7.

50. Gentry v. eBay Inc., Calif. Supr. Ct., Case No. GIC 746980 (Jan. 18, 2001), 6 ELECTRONIC COMMERCE & L. REP. (BNA) 84 (Jan. 24, 2001).

address the problem of auction fraud cases.[51] The agency also created a database of online auction complaints.

Due to the global reach of the Internet, regulation of Internet auction sites will require international coopera-

tion. In December 2000, the Council of Europe (a non-European Union body) released a draft version of a document entitled Draft Convention on Cyber-crime, the first international treaty to address various types of criminal behavior directed against computer systems, networks, or data, including computer-related fraud and forgery.

51. Daniel Roth, *Fraud's Booming in Online Auctions, but Help Is Here Bidding Adieu*, FORTUNE, May 29, 2000, at 276.

KEY WORDS AND PHRASES

acceptance   238
adhesion contracts   258
battle of the forms   237
commercial impossibility   261
commercial impracticability   260
computer information   263
cover   262
express warranty   247
firm offer   241

fixtures   238
full warranty   252
goods   238
identification to the contract   238
implied warranty of fitness for a particular purpose   251
implied warranty of merchantability   250
limited warranty   252

lost volume seller   262
merchant   238
offer   238
perfect tender rule   267
prima facie   258
puffing   248
shrink-wrap license   239
statute of frauds   245

QUESTIONS AND CASE PROBLEMS

1. Paul Lewis, a sawmill operator, acquired a new hydraulic pump for his facility. In need of hydraulic fluid to operate the pump, Lewis contacted Mobil Oil Corporation's local representative, Frank Rowe. Lewis confessed his ignorance about the hydraulic pump, the type of fluid it required, and his necessary reliance on Mobil to supply the proper product. Without inquiring further, Rowe sold Lewis plain mineral oil without any chemical additives. Within a few days of using the oil, Lewis began to experience problems with the pump and asked Rowe several times if he was sure that the oil was appropriate for the pump. After several months, Lewis discovered that the oil he had bought from Mobil was improper for his pump. On what grounds could Lewis sue Mobil? What result? [*Lewis v. Mobil Oil Corp.*, 438 F.2d 500 (8th Cir. 1971)]

2. Hardie-Tynes Manufacturing Company subcontracted with Hunger United States Special Hydraulic Cylinders Corporation to manufacture two hydraulic cylinders to be used in construction of the Jordanelle Dam in Utah. After Hardie-Tynes sent a request for quotations for Hunger's best price for two cylinders, Hunger responded with a letter providing specific quantity, price, delivery, and payment terms. Both parties agreed that this constituted an offer to contract. A copy of Hunger's standard

terms and conditions, which included a provision attempting to specify a mode of acceptance and limiting acceptance to Hunger's terms, accompanied the offer. None of the terms related to payment of attorneys' fees in the event of a contract dispute.

Hardie-Tynes accepted Hunger's offer by sending a purchase order, which required payment of attorneys' fees in the event that Hardie-Tynes commenced litigation upon Hunger's default. Like Hunger, Hardie-Tynes limited the agreement to its own terms.

The cylinders manufactured by Hunger did not comply with government standards. Hardie-Tynes sued Hunger for breach of contract, and claimed that it was entitled to recover attorneys' fees. Did Hunger and Hardie-Tynes enter into a contract? If so, what were its terms? Would your answer differ if the proposed revisions to Article 2 were adopted? [*Hunger United States Special Hydraulic Cylinders Corp. v. Hardie-Tynes Manufacturing Co.*, 41 U.C.C. Rep. Serv. 2d 165 (10th Cir. 2000)]

3. The Essex Group manufactured aluminum wire products. In 1967, Essex entered into a contract with Aluminum Company of America (Alcoa), whereby Alcoa agreed, for a sixteen-year period (with a five-year renewable option at Essex's pleasure), to smelt Essex's aluminum into the molten aluminum Essex needed in its production process.

The contract contained an escalation clause that tied the price Alcoa charged Essex to the Wholesale Price Index–Industrial Commodities (WPI-IC). The WPI-IC is one of several indices available to measure inflation. Both parties agreed to the use of this index after concluding that its past record showed stability. Alcoa's objective was to achieve stable income of approximately four cents per pound of converted aluminum. Essex's objective was to ensure a long-term supply of aluminum.

Until 1972, the contract satisfied both parties' needs. Then, however, because of the energy crisis that began in 1973 and increased pollution control costs that were unanticipated in 1967, Alcoa's electricity costs increased at a rate far more rapid than the WPI-IC. Alcoa estimated that if it were to fulfill the terms of the contract, it would lose in excess of $60 million. Alcoa brought suit seeking reformation or equitable adjustment of the agreement. Essex counterclaimed seeking damages for breach of contract. Result? [*Aluminum Co. of America v. Essex Group, Inc.*, 499 F. Supp. 53 (W.D. Pa. 1980)]

4. Before deciding what remedies are available under Article 2 of the UCC, one must first determine whether the transaction involved the sale of goods. Consider the following cases:

a. An accounting firm, the Wahl firm, sold its business, including its list of customers, client files, and client contracts, to another accounting firm, the Serotta firm. On the afternoon of the sale, one of the principals of the Wahl firm decided that he wanted to start his own accounting firm. Toward that end, he used the list of customers that had been sold to the Serotta firm to contact and inform the clients that he would be starting his own firm. He also removed the contents of his desk, including computer backup tapes containing files with all of the firm's customer financial information. The Serotta firm brought a claim under the UCC against the Wahl firm. Does the claim involve the sale of goods or services? [*Crews v. Wahl*, 520 S.E.2d 727 (Ga. App. 1999)]

b. Palmetto Linen Service, Inc. operates a commercial laundry that supplies linens to hotels, restaurants, and hospitals. U.N.X., Inc. sold chemicals to Palmetto for use in the cleaning process. U.N.X. also installed a computerized pump system in Palmetto's washers to regulate the injection of the chemicals. Palmetto contracted for the chemicals supplied by U.N.X. and the installation of the chemical dispensing system by U.N.X. Palmetto later sued U.N.X., alleging

that the system malfunctioned and injected excessive amounts of chemicals into the washer. Was Palmetto's contract one for goods or services? [*Palmetto Linen Service, Inc. v. U.N.X., Inc.*, 205 F.3d 126 (4th Cir. 2000)]

c. Micro Data Base Systems (MDBS) entered into a contract with Dharma Systems, Inc., which provided that Dharma would customize its existing software program for use in a system that MDBS would provide to Unisys. The contract was for the program itself and the work of customizing the program. Was this a contract for the sale of a good or services? Would UCITA apply to such a contract? [*Micro Data Base Systems, Inc. v. Dharma Systems, Inc.*, 148 F.3d 649 (7th Cir. 1998)]

5. Charles Bowling Lanes, Inc., a company that owned and operated a bowling alley, entered into a lease agreement with AMF, Inc. for the installation of pinspotters in the building. The pinspotters were assembled in the bowling alley, placed in the alley lane that was redesigned to accommodate them, and then screwed, bolted, and riveted to the concrete floor. The lease agreement stated that the machines were to remain the sole and exclusive personal property of AMF despite the fact that they were attached to the bowling alley. The bowling alley was subsequently sold to Weber's St. Charles Lanes, Inc., but the price did not include consideration for the pinspotters as they were considered to be the property of AMF pursuant to the lease agreement.

Weber's purchase was financed in part by loans obtained from Boatmen's Bank. The promissory note was secured by a deed of trust and stated that it conveyed to the trustee both the real property and all buildings and fixtures on the property. Weber's executed a promissory note in favor of a different bank to finance the purchase of the pinspotters. Subsequently, Weber's defaulted on its loans, the banks foreclosed on the real property and the pinspotters, and an issue arose concerning whether the pinspotters were personal property or fixtures. How should the court rule? [*Rothermich v. Union Planters National Bank*, 10 S.W.3d 610 (App. Mo. 2000)].

6. Dalton Department Store sold Mary Walsh a television made by Dalton. With the television, Walsh received a warranty that covered all electric and electronic parts for ninety days and all other metal parts for one year. Walsh had the television for six weeks and then took it out of the box. She noticed that one leg was shorter than the others, the screen had several scratches on it, and the remote control

did not work. Walsh brought the television set back and demanded that Dalton repair all the problems at no charge. Dalton refused to do so. What rights does Walsh have? What if Mary had had the television for six months and then the glass screen suddenly shattered and the picture tube burned out?

7. Jordan Panel Systems Corp. is a construction subcontractor that contracted to install windows at an air cargo facility at John F. Kennedy Airport in New York City. Jordan entered into a contract to purchase custom-made windows from Windows, Inc., a fabricator and seller of windows located in South Dakota. The contract specified that the windows were to be shipped properly packaged and delivered to New York City. Windows, Inc. arranged to have the windows shipped to Jordan by common carrier and delivered the windows to the common carrier properly packaged. During the course of shipment, however, much of the glass was broken, and many of the window frames were gouged and twisted. Jordan refused to pay for the damaged windows, and Windows, Inc. sued to recover the full purchase price. Which company should win? [*Windows, Inc. v. Jordan Panel Systems Corp.*, 177 F.3d 114 (2d Cir. 1999)]

8. In 1969, Wayne, an American, bought a Ferrari originally commissioned by King Leopold III of Belgium. Lee, another Ferrari fan, made Wayne a series of offers for the car, culminating in an offer of $275,000, which was a price that Wayne had previously set to discourage offers. Lee, at Wayne's request, produced four checks, one of which was endorsed by Wayne's girlfriend. Wayne then wrote to Lee. The letter said, as Wayne had told Lee before, that the sale required Wayne's parents' consent. The letter also stated that, after talking with his parents, Wayne had decided the car would not be sold. Lee sued for breach of contract. Who should prevail? [*Lee v. Voyles*, 898 F.2d 76 (7th Cir. 1990)]

9. In July 1993, Werner Siebenmann sold a painting to David Rogath for $570,000. The piece, entitled *Self-Portrait*, was supposedly painted by Francis Bacon. In the bill of sale, Siebenmann warranted that he was the sole owner of the painting, that the piece was authentic, and that he was unaware of any challenges to its authenticity. Three months later, Rogath sold the piece to a New York art gallery for $950,000. The gallery soon learned of an existing challenge to *Self-Portrait*'s authenticity, first asserted in June by a London art dealer. The gallery asked Rogath to refund its money and take back the piece, which he did.

Rogath then sued Siebenmann for breach of contract and warranty. Siebenmann admitted that he knew of the challenge to *Self-Portrait* but claimed that he told Rogath about it, notwithstanding the language in the bill of sale. What result if (a) Siebenmann had said nothing about any challenge to Rogath? (b) Siebenmann had described the London art dealer's challenge to Rogath before concluding the sale? (c) Siebenmann had said nothing of any challenge but Rogath learned independently of the London art dealer's doubts the day before purchasing the piece? [*Rogath v. Siebenmann*, 129 F.3d 261 (2d Cir. 1997)]

MANAGER'S DILEMMA

10. Sandy Singlefather has two children and lives in a subsidized housing development in New City. He receives federal assistance to help raise his two children. Singlefather recently read an advertisement for household appliances. The advertisement stated that he could "rent to own" his appliances with no credit. Singlefather was in need of a washing machine but had a poor credit history, so he answered the advertisement. The appliance store was more than delighted to accommodate him. Singlefather now pays $30 a week for his washing machine and will own it after he makes seventy-eight payments. A washing machine usually sells for $350.

Has Singlefather entered into an unconscionable bargain? Should the manager of the rent-to-own business repossess the washing machine if Singlefather fails to pay the $30 weekly rent after possessing the machine and paying rent for fifty weeks?

Suppose that a rent-to-own business rents a large-screen television that retails for $3,000 for $100 a week with the right to own it after eighty weeks. The renter defaults after possessing the television and paying the $100 weekly rent for fifty weeks. Should the manager treat that transaction any differently from rental of the washing machine? How could the manager structure pricing to permit the transactions to withstand legal challenge yet still be profitable for the rent-to-own company? [*Murphy v. McNamara*, 416 A.2d 170 (Conn. Supp. 1979); *see also* Susan Lorde Martin & Nancy White Huckins, *Consumer Advocates vs. The Rent-to-Own Industry: Reaching a Reasonable Accommodation*, 34 AM. BUS. L.J. 385 (1997).]

INTERNET SOURCES

The Uniform Law Commissioners, who draft the UCC, have a Web site at the University of Pennsylvania Law School that contains the entire UCC, including Article 2, and its history and proposed changes, as well as other uniform laws.	http://www.law.upenn.edu/library/ulc/ulc.htm
This site provides an updated list of states that have adopted UCITA.	http://www.ucitaonline.com
The Communications Media Center at New York Law School sponsors a page addressing the use of disclaimers on the Web.	http://www.cmcnyls.edu/public/mlp/udsciwww.htm
This site provides a daily summary of Internet and technology law news stories, with links to the full-text stories.	http://www.GigaLaw.com
The United Nations Web site provides updated information about CISG, including its signatories.	http://www.un.or.at/uncitral
Pace University's Institute for International Consumer Law sponsors a page about the CISG.	http://www.cisg.law.pace.educial
The Justice Department sponsors this site, which provides information regarding computer crime and how to report it.	http://www.cybercrime.gov
These sites, maintained by international publisher Cameron May, provide information about international commercial law and useful links to other sites related to international trade and commerce.	http://www.lexmercatoria.org http://www.lexmercatoria.com
U.S. Advisory Commission on Electronic Commerce	http://www.ecommercecommission.org
Department of Commerce, Electronic Commerce Site	http://www.ecommerce.gov
National Conference of Commissioners on Uniform State Laws	http://www.nccusl.org
European Commission	http://www.europa.eu.int
United Nations Commission on International Trade Law	http://www.uncitral.org

CHAPTER 9

Torts

WHAT IS A TORT?

A *tort* is a civil wrong resulting in injury to a person or property. A tort case is brought by the injured party to obtain compensation for the wrong done. A crime, by contrast, is a wrong to society that is prosecuted by the state. (Criminal law is discussed in Chapter 17.) Even though a crime may be perpetrated against an individual, the victim is not a party to a criminal action. Criminal law generally is not concerned with compensating the victim but with protecting society and punishing the criminal.

The distinctions between tort and criminal law are not always as clear as they first appear, however. A criminal statute might call for the criminal to compensate the victim. The victim might sue the perpetrator of the crime in tort, using the violation of a criminal statute as a basis for the tort claim. In some cases, tort law purports, like criminal law, to protect society through the award of punitive damages.

CHAPTER OVERVIEW

This chapter first discusses intentional torts, which fall into three general categories: (1) torts that protect individuals from physical and mental harm, (2) torts that protect interests in property, and (3) torts that protect certain economic interests and business relationships. The chapter then addresses negligence (including an accountant's liability to third parties) and strict liability. Tortious activity by more than one individual or entity raises the issues of vicarious liability and apportioned responsibility. The chapter applies these various theories to the evolving law of toxic torts.

 # Elements *of an* Intentional Tort

To prevail in a tort action, the plaintiff must prove all elements of a claim. Intentional torts require the plaintiff to prove (1) actual or implied intent, (2) a voluntary act by the defendant, (3) causation, and (4) injury or harm. The act must be the actual and legal cause of the injury. The act required depends on the specific intentional tort.

INTENT

Intent is the subjective desire to cause the consequences of an act. *Actual intent* can be shown by evidence that the defendant intended a specific consequence to a particular individual. Intent is implied if the defendant knew that the consequences of the act were certain or substantially certain even if he or she did not actually intend any consequence at all.

As the degree of certainty of the result decreases, the defendant's conduct loses the character of intent and becomes recklessness. As the result becomes even less certain, the act becomes negligence, which is treated later in this chapter. For example, if Metro Corporation's custodian, Hal, dumped garbage out of Metro's third-floor office window onto a busy sidewalk and hit Alexis, the law would likely imply intent to hit Alexis. Even though Hal may have had no subjective intention of hitting Alexis with the garbage, throwing it onto a busy sidewalk was substantially certain to result in at least one pedestrian being hit. However, if late one night Hal put garbage in the middle of the sidewalk in front of the office building for morning pickup and Alexis tripped over it, the intent to cause harm is not so clear. If intent is not established, Hal will not be liable for the intentional tort of battery, which requires intent to bring about a harmful contact. Alexis might be able to establish negligence, however, if she can show that a reasonable person would not have left the garbage on the sidewalk.

Intent may be transferred. If the defendant intended to hit one person but instead hit the plaintiff, the intent requirement is met as to the plaintiff.

 Defenses

Even if a plaintiff has proved all elements of a tort, the defendant may raise a legal defense to absolve himself or herself of liability. The most frequently raised defense is consent. If the plaintiff consented to the act of the defendant, there is no tort. Even if the plaintiff did not explicitly consent, the law may imply consent. For example, a professional athlete injured during practice is deemed to have consented to the physical contact attendant to practice. The defendant may also be absolved of liability by a claim of self-defense or defense of others.

 Types *of* Intentional Torts

The intentional torts of battery, assault, false imprisonment, intentional infliction of emotional distress, defamation, and invasion of privacy are designed to protect individuals from physical and mental harm. The torts of trespass to land, nuisance, conversion, and trespass to personal property protect interests in property. Certain economic interests and business relationships are protected by the torts of disparagement, injurious falsehood, fraudulent misrepresentation, malicious prosecution, interference with contractual relations, interference with prospective business advantage, and bad faith. A single set of facts may give rise to claims under more than one theory.

 Intentional Torts *to* Protect Persons

BATTERY

Tort law recognizes a basic right to have one's body free from harmful or offensive contact. Battery is the violation of that right.

Battery is intentional, nonconsensual, harmful, or offensive contact with the plaintiff's body or with something in contact with it. Offensive contact, such as dousing a person with water or spitting in his or her face, may be a battery, even though the plaintiff has suffered no physical harm. The contact may be by the defendant directly or by something the defendant has set in motion. For example, putting poison in someone's food is a battery.

Another example of battery occurred when a company president spanked an employee with a carpenter's level in a hazing ritual while other employees watched.[1] The jury awarded $6,000 for pain and loss of consortium and $1 million in punitive damages. The trial court reduced the punitive damages award to $130,000 after finding the original award excessive.

ASSAULT

The tort of assault also protects the right to have one's body left alone. Unlike battery, however, assault does not require contact. *Assault* is an intentional, nonconsensual act that gives rise to the apprehension (though not necessarily fear) that a harmful or offensive contact is imminent.

Generally, assault requires some act, such as a threatening gesture, and the ability to follow through immediately with a battery. A punch thrown from close range that misses its target may be an assault, but a threat to punch someone out of punching range is not. For example, if someone makes a threatening gesture and says, "I would hit you if I weren't behind this desk," and the person is in fact behind the desk, there is no assault. The immediacy requirement has not been met. Similarly, the threat "I'll beat you up if you come to class next week" is not immediate enough to be an assault.

FALSE IMPRISONMENT

The tort of false imprisonment protects the right to be free from restraint of movement. *False imprisonment* is intentional, nonconsensual confinement by physical barriers or by physical force or threats of force. It requires that the plaintiff either knew he or she was confined or suffered harm as a result of the confinement.

False imprisonment has been found when the plaintiff's freedom of movement was restricted because of force applied to the plaintiff's valuable property. For example, if a store clerk grabs a package from a customer walking out the door, this is false imprisonment because the customer cannot be expected to abandon the package to leave the store.

---

1. Smith v. Phillips Getschow Co., 616 N.W.2d 526 (Wis. 2000).

Shopkeepers who detain and later release a person mistakenly suspected of shoplifting are sometimes sued for false imprisonment. Most states have legislation exempting shopkeepers from such claims if the shopkeeper has acted in good faith and the detention is made in a reasonable manner, is for a reasonable time, and is based on reasonable cause.

INTENTIONAL INFLICTION OF EMOTIONAL DISTRESS

The tort of *intentional infliction of emotional distress* protects the right to peace of mind. The law has been slow to redress purely mental injuries and is still evolving in this area. Jurisdictions differ sharply in their acceptance of this tort. In most jurisdictions, to prove intentional infliction of emotional distress, a plaintiff must show (1) outrageous conduct by the defendant; (2) intent to cause, or reckless disregard of the probability of causing, emotional distress; (3) severe emotional suffering; and (4) actual and proximate (or legal) causation of the emotional distress. The reluctance of the courts to accept intentional infliction of emotional distress as an independent tort most likely stems from the fear that plaintiffs will file false claims. Therefore, some jurisdictions also require a physical manifestation of the emotional distress.

The mental distress must be foreseeable. The defendant is liable only to the extent that the plaintiff's response is reasonably within the range of normal human emotions.

The acts of the defendant must be outrageous or intolerable. Insulting, abusive, threatening, profane, or annoying conduct is not in itself a tort. Everyone is expected to be hardened to a certain amount of abuse. In determining outrageousness, courts will consider the context of the tort, as well as the relationship of the parties. For example, an employee can expect to be subjected to evaluation and criticism in the workplace, and neither criticism nor discharge is in itself outrageous. On the other hand, sexual harassment by a supervisor in the workplace is less tolerated than it might be, for example, if done by a patron in a nightclub.

In *Ford v. Revlon, Inc.*,[2] the Supreme Court of Arizona found that Revlon was liable for intentional infliction of emotional distress after a Revlon employee, Leta Fay Ford, was harassed by her supervisor, the manager for the purchasing department. In addition to making vulgar and threatening remarks to Ford, the manager held her in a chokehold and fondled her at a company picnic. Ford repeatedly complained to management, but Revlon did not confront the manager for nine months. Indeed, one man-

ager to whom Ford complained told her that the complaint was too hot to handle and encouraged her to try not to think about her predicament. Ford not only suffered emotional distress but also developed physical complications, including high blood pressure and chest pains, as a result of her stressful work environment. The court found that Revlon had a specific policy and several guidelines for the handling of sexual harassment claims but recklessly disregarded these policies and guidelines.

DEFAMATION

Defamation is the communication (often termed *publication*) to a third party of an untrue statement, asserted as fact, that injures the plaintiff's reputation by exposing him or her to "hatred, ridicule, or contempt." *Libel* is written defamation, and *slander* is spoken defamation. The distinction between libel and slander is sometimes blurred with respect to modern communications.

Special rules apply to the requirement of injury to reputation. In an action for slander (spoken defamation), the plaintiff must prove that he or she has suffered actual harm, such as the loss of credit, a job, or customers, unless the statement is so obviously damaging that it falls into the category of slander *per se*. *Slander per se* means that the words are slanderous in and of themselves, for example, a statement that a person has committed a serious crime, is guilty of sexual misconduct, or is not fit to conduct business. In an action for libel (written defamation), the law presumes injury; that is, no actual harm need be shown unless the statement on its face is not damaging.

An opinion is defamation only if it implies a statement of objective fact. In *Sagan v. Apple Computer, Inc.*,[3] noted astronomer Carl Sagan sued Apple Computer for libel when Apple changed its code name for a new personal computer to "Butt-Head Astronomer" after Sagan demanded that the company cease using "Carl Sagan" as the code name. The court ruled that the dispositive question in determining whether a statement of opinion can form the basis of a libel action is whether a reasonable fact finder could conclude that the statement implies an assertion of fact. The court found that a reasonable fact finder would conclude that Apple Computer was not making a statement of fact about Sagan's competency as an astronomer in using the figurative term "Butt-Head" and would understand that the company was using the figurative term to retaliate in a humorous and satirical way for Sagan's reaction to Apple's use of his name. In addition, the court found that the statement that Sagan was a "Butt-Head Astronomer" could not rest on a core of objective evidence, so it could not be proved true or false.

2. 734 P.2d 580 (Ariz. 1987).

3. 874 F. Supp. 1072 (C.D. Cal. 1994).

In contrast, in *Flamm v. American Ass'n of University Women*,[4] the U.S. Court of Appeals for the Second Circuit found that a lawyer's libel claim against the American Association of University Women's Legal Advocacy Fund (AAUW) was based on a statement of fact not opinion. The AAUW compiles a directory of attorneys who are willing to consult with women involved in higher education who are considering bringing gender discrimination claims. The directory's entry on Mr. Flamm stated: "At least one plaintiff has described Flamm as an 'ambulance chaser' with interest only in 'slam dunk cases.'" The appeals court found that this statement contained in a "fact-laden" directory did not simply express an opinion but could reasonably be interpreted to imply a factual statement that Flamm engaged in the unethical solicitation of clients and took only easy cases.

The requirement of publication generally means that the statement must be made in the presence of a third person. Thus, the statement "You are a thief" made in a one-on-one conversation is not defamation. However, some courts have adopted the doctrine of *self publication* to give an employee a claim for defamation when, in firing the employee, the employer makes a false assertion that the employer could reasonably expect the employee to repeat to a prospective employer.

Defenses Defenses to defamation actions are framed in terms of privilege and may be asserted in a number of circumstances. An *absolute privilege* cannot be lost. A *qualified privilege* can be lost under certain conditions. If the defendant has an absolute privilege, he or she can publish with impunity a statement he or she knows to be false. The defendant can even do so with the most evil intention. Absolute privilege is limited to situations in which (1) the plaintiff has consented to the publication, (2) the statement is a political broadcast made under the federal "equal

4. 201 F.3d 144 (2d Cir. 2000).

ETHICAL CONSIDERATION

The damage done to a person's reputation by defamation can be instantaneous because the false statements frequently receive attention in the electronic and print media. The public, quick to latch on to the initial defamatory statements, is less likely to notice a court decision some years later that holds that the statements were, in fact, false.

Because of this phenomenon, someone determined to cast doubt on another person's reputation has a good chance of success. Once the damage is done, it is largely irreversible. Therefore, ethical restraint must sometimes take the place of legal restraint.

time" statute, (3) the statement is made by a government official in the performance of governmental duties, (4) the statement is made by participants in judicial proceedings, or (5) the statement is made between spouses.

In most jurisdictions, truth is an absolute defense to a defamation claim. The law will not protect a reputation the plaintiff does not deserve. However, the burden is on the defendant to prove that the derogatory statements are true. The law in most jurisdictions presumes that the plaintiff has a pristine reputation unless the defendant proves otherwise.

There is a qualified privilege to make statements to protect one's own personal interests, including statements to a peer review committee. There is also a qualified privilege to make statements to protect legitimate business interests, such as statements to a prospective employer, or to provide information for the public interest, such as credit reports. A qualified privilege can be lost if the person making the statement abuses the privilege.

In the following case, the New York Court of Appeals considered whether an Internet service provider was entitled to claim the same common law qualified privilege as a telephone company.

A CASE IN POINT

CASE 9.1

Lunney v. Prodigy Services Co.

Court of Appeals of New York
723 N.E.2d 539
(N.Y. App. 1999),
cert. denied,
120 S. Ct. 1832 (2000).

Summary

FACTS An impostor opened a number of accounts with Prodigy Services Company (Prodigy), an Internet service provider, using several variations of the false name Alexander Lunney. Lunney himself was actually a teenage Boy Scout. The impostor transmitted an e-mail message containing threatening and vulgar language to a local scoutmaster; he also posted two obscene messages on electronic bulletin boards. The scoutmaster who received the offensive e-mail alerted the police. The police investigating the story accepted Lunney's denial of authorship.

During the investigation, Prodigy notified Lunney that it was terminating one of his accounts due to the transmission of obscene and threatening material through the Prodigy service. Lunney informed Prodigy that an impostor had opened the account using his

(Continued)

(Case 9.1 continued)

name. The company apologized and informed him that it had located four additional accounts under his name and closed all of those.

Lunney sued Prodigy claiming that Prodigy was negligent in allowing accounts to be opened in his name and was responsible for his having been defamed. The trial court denied Prodigy's motions for summary judgment. The appeals court reversed, holding that (1) the messages did not concern Lunney and did not defame him; (2) although the messages were in very poor taste, the stigma associated with them did not amount to defamation; and (3) Prodigy was not the publisher of the messages, but even if it were, it was entitled to a qualified privilege sheltering it from liability. Lunney appealed.

ISSUE PRESENTED Is an Internet service provider, like the telephone and telegraph companies, entitled to a common law qualified privilege with respect to defamation claims?

SUMMARY OF OPINION The New York Court of Appeals began its analysis by stating that e-mail is the "evolutionary hybrid of traditional telephone line communications and regular postal service mail." In looking to New York common law on torts for guidance, the court found that the telephone company could not be considered a publisher of statements transmitted over the phone because it does not participate in preparing the message, it exercises no discretion or control over its communication, and it assumes no responsibility for it. In addition, even if the telephone company could be characterized as a publisher, it is entitled to a qualified privilege. The court found that Prodigy's role in transmitting e-mail was similar to that of a telephone company's role in transmitting messages over telephone lines; it was merely a conduit for the message. As a result, Prodigy was entitled to the common law qualified privilege accorded to telephone and telegraph companies. In support of its decision, the court commented that "[t]he public would not be well served by compelling an [Internet service provider] to examine and screen millions of e-mail communications, on pain of liability for defamation."

RESULT The New York Court of Appeals found that the qualified privilege applied to the defamation claim and Prodigy was not liable.

COMMENTS Prodigy also argued that the Communications Decency Act, discussed at greater length below, which states that an Internet service is not a publisher, should govern the case by retroactive application. However, the court rejected this argument: "At this point, we decline the invitation to come down on either side of this debate. This case does not call for it."

In addition to common law privileges, statutory devices may protect "speakers." For instance, under the Communications Decency Act of 1996, an Internet service provider will not be treated as the publisher of information provided by a third party.[5] Applying this statute, the U.S. Court of Appeals for the Fourth Circuit refused to hold America Online (AOL) liable for defamation when an unidentified user posted offensive (and false) messages related to the Oklahoma City bombing and attributed these messages to the plaintiff.[6]

Similarly, in *Ben Ezra, Weinstein, & Co. v. America Online, Inc.*,[7] AOL was sued for defamation for allegedly publishing inaccurate information about the price and share volume of a company's publicly traded stock. Because AOL did not create or develop the stock quote in-

5. 47 U.S.C. § 230 (2000).

6. Zeran v. America Online, Inc., 129 F.3d 327 (4th Cir. 1997), *cert. denied*, 524 U.S. 937 (1998).
7. 206 F.3d 980 (10th Cir. 2000), *cert. denied*, 148 L. Ed. 2d 33 (2000).

formation displayed, the U.S. Court of Appeals for the Tenth Circuit held that AOL was not the publisher of the information provided and was protected under the Communications Decency Act.

Public Figures and Media Defendants When commenting on a public official or public figure, the media, such as newspapers, television, or radio, have a qualified privilege that is almost absolute. Public officials include legislators, judges, and police officers. The definition of a public figure is addressed below.

The U.S. Supreme Court, in applying the First Amendment right of freedom of the press, has held that in order for a public official or public figure to recover damages for defamation by a media defendant, there must be a showing of *actual malice*. That means the statement must have been made with the knowledge that it was false or with a reckless disregard as to whether it was false. (Other aspects of the First Amendment are discussed in Chapter 2.)

Because it is difficult to prove actual malice, a corporation that anticipates that the press may publish an unfavorable story about its business may take proactive steps to counteract that negative publicity rather than try to initiate a defamation action after the fact in court. In October 1999, the diet product company Metabolife International, Inc. became concerned that ABC would broadcast an unfair report on the medical risks of a dietary supplement sold by Metabolife. The company therefore posted on the Internet a complete, unedited videotaped interview between an ABC News correspondent and Metabolife's chief executive. Although ABC said that Metabolife's decision to post the interview on the Internet would not affect the interview that it broadcast, television executives indicated that in the future networks might ask interviewees to agree not to make public material from the interview until after it is broadcast on television.

Public figures are those who, by reason of the notoriety of their achievements or the vigor and success with which they seek the public's attention, are injected into the public eye. In *Wells v. Liddy*,[8] the U.S. Court of Appeals for the Fourth Circuit made it clear that a private individual does not automatically become a public figure simply because she is involved in a public event. The event at issue in *Wells* was the Watergate burglary scandal, which ultimately resulted in President Richard Nixon's resignation. G. Gordon Liddy, the former self-described "political intelligence chieftain" and general counsel of the Committee to Reelect the President, publicly offered an alternative theory to explain the purpose of the June

17, 1972 Watergate break-in. He claimed that the burglars' objective was to determine whether the Democrats had information embarrassing to John Dean, former legal counsel to President Nixon. Specifically, Liddy claimed that the burglars were searching the desk of Ida Wells, secretary of the Democratic National Committee, to find a compromising photograph of Dean's fiancée among other photographs of women used to offer prostitution services to out-of-town guests. After Liddy claimed that Wells was involved in setting up these guests with prostitutes, Wells sued for defamation. The court found that Wells was a private figure, even though she had become involved in a public matter, and commented:

> There is a great temptation when evaluating a controversy as longstanding and significant as Watergate to allow the controversy itself to take precedence in the analysis and let it convert all individuals in its path into public figures. The Supreme Court has admonished us strongly against allowing the public event with which the individual is connected to be the determinative factor governing an individual's public figure designation.[9]

If the plaintiff suing a media defendant is not a public figure, he or she need not prove malice. A private plaintiff can sue for defamation if the defendant acted with knowledge, acted in reckless disregard of the facts, or was negligent in failing to ascertain the facts. If the plaintiff proceeds on a negligence theory, he or she must prove actual damages, such as loss of business or out-of-pocket costs. If the plaintiff proves malice, damages are presumed, meaning no proof of damages is required.

INVASION OF PRIVACY

Invasion of privacy is a violation of the right to keep personal matters to oneself. It can take several forms.

Intrusion is objectionable prying, such as eavesdropping or unauthorized rifling through files. Injunctions or court orders are usually available to prevent further intrusion. There must be a reasonable expectation of privacy in the thing into which there is intrusion. For example, courts have held that there is no legitimate expectation of privacy in conversations in a public restaurant. The tort of intrusion does not require publication of the information obtained.

In the following case, the U.S. Court of Appeals for the Ninth Circuit considered whether an individual could claim that his privacy had been violated when a reporter secretly tape-recorded an interview to which he had consented.

8. 186 F.3d 505 (4th Cir. 1999), *cert. denied*, 120 S. Ct. 939 (2000).

9. *Id.*

A CASE IN POINT

CASE 9.2

Alpha Therapeutic Corp. v. Nippon Hoso Kyokai

United States Court of Appeals for the Ninth Circuit
199 F.3d 1078
(9th Cir. 1999).

In the Language of the Court

FACTS Clyde McAuley was the medical director of Alpha Therapeutic (Alpha), a California corporation that produces blood plasma derivatives. Nippon Hosos Kyokai (NHK), Japan's only public broadcasting corporation, broadcast two television programs about Alpha and McAuley, an hour-long program broadcast in Japan and a four-minute program broadcast in Japan and the United States. In these programs, NHK claimed that Alpha and McAuley knowingly shipped blood products to Japan that were contaminated with the AIDS virus, falsified documents about their investigation of a blood donor, and reported false information about the donor to the Food and Drug Administration.

To produce the programs, an NHK reporter unexpectedly arrived at McAuley's home. When McAuley answered the door, the reporter started asking him questions, which McAuley answered. The reporter secretly recorded the interview with a microphone hidden on his tie, and the recording was included in NHK's hour-long program. McCauley sued NHK for, among other things, invasion of his privacy. The district court dismissed McAuley's claim, and he appealed.

ISSUE PRESENTED Does a reporter violate an individual's right of privacy when he secretly records an interview with an individual without that person's knowledge or consent?

OPINION PREGERSON, J., writing for the U.S. Court of Appeals for the Ninth Circuit:

McAuley's action for invasion of privacy has two elements: (1) intrusion into a private place, conversation, or matter, (2) in a manner highly offensive to a reasonable person.

. . .

"[T]o prove actionable intrusion, the plaintiff must show the defendant penetrated some zone of physical or sensory privacy surrounding, or obtained unwarranted access to data about, the plaintiff." The nature of intrusion may include "unwarranted sensory intrusions such as eavesdropping, wiretapping, and visual or photographic spying." But a claim for invasion of privacy can survive only if the plaintiff had an "objectively reasonable expectation of seclusion or solitude in the place, conversation, or data source."

"[A] person may reasonably expect privacy against the electronic recording of a communication, even though he or she had no reasonable expectation as to confidentiality of the communication's content." Moreover, although "one who imparts private information risks the betrayal of his confidence by the other party, a substantial distinction has been recognized between the secondhand repetition of the contents of a conversation and its simultaneous dissemination to an unannounced second auditor, whether that auditor be a person or a mechanical device." "Such secret monitoring denies the speaker an important aspect of privacy of communication—the right to control the nature and extent of firsthand dissemination of his statements."

RESULT The appeals court held that McAuley had stated a claim for invasion of privacy and reversed the district court's dismissal of his claim.

COMMENTS In *Sanders v. American Broadcasting Co.,*[10] the Supreme Court of California considered another claim of invasion of privacy based on a reporter's covert videotaping of a conversation. In that case, an ABC reporter obtained employment as a "telepsychic" with the Psychic Marketing Group and wore a small video camera hidden in her hat in order to covertly videotape conversations with coworkers. One of her

---

10. 978 P.2d 67 (Cal. 1999).

(Continued)

(Case 9.2 continued)

coworkers sued the reporter and ABC for invasion of privacy. The Supreme Court of California held that a person who lacks a reasonable expectation of complete privacy in a conversation because it could be seen and overheard by coworkers, but not the general public, may still have a claim for invasion of privacy by intrusion based on a reporter's videotaping of that conversation. However, the court noted that in circumstances where a workplace is regularly open to entry or observation by the public or press, any expectation of privacy against press recording is less likely to be deemed reasonable. Thus, whether a reasonable expectation of privacy is violated by recording depends on the nature of the circumstances.

Public disclosure of private facts requires publication, for example, by stating in a newspaper that the plaintiff does not pay debts or posting such a notice in a public place. The matter made public must not be newsworthy. The matter must be private, such that a reasonable person would find publication objectionable. Unlike in a defamation case, truth is not a defense.

Appropriation of a person's name or likeness may be an invasion of privacy. Often this tort is committed for financial gain. For example, using a fictitious testimonial in an advertisement, or using a person's picture in an advertisement or article with which he or she has no connection, would be a tort. In *Brown v. Ames,*[11] a group of blues musicians, songwriters, and music producers sued a music producer and record label for distributing cassettes, CDs, posters, and other products using the names and likenesses of the performers. The U.S. Court of Appeals for the Fifth Circuit ruled in the plaintiffs' favor by applying Texas state law, which allows recovery for unauthorized appropriation of names or likenesses if the plaintiff can prove that (1) the defendant misappropriated the plaintiff's name or likeness for the value associated with it and not in an incidental manner or newsworthy purpose, (2) the plaintiff can be identified from the publication, and (3) the defendant derived some advantage or benefit.

11. 201 F.3d 654 (5th Cir. 2000), *cert. denied,* 121 S. Ct. 299 (2000).

Intentional Torts That Protect Property

TRESPASS TO LAND

The previously described torts have involved interference with personal rights. *Trespass to land* is an interference with a property right. It is an invasion of property without consent of the owner. The land need not be injured by the trespass. The intent required is the intent to enter the property, not the intent to trespass. Thus, a mistake as to ownership is irrelevant.

Trespass may occur both below the surface and in the airspace above the land. Throwing something, such as trash, on the land, or shooting bullets over it, may be trespasses, even though the perpetrator was not standing on the plaintiff's land.

Refusing to move something that at one time the plaintiff permitted the defendant to place on the land may be a trespass. For example, if the plaintiff gave the defendant permission to leave a forklift on the plaintiff's land for one month, and it was left for two, the defendant may be liable for trespass.

Trespass may also occur if an individual permitted access to property commits a wrongful act in excess of and in abuse of the authorized entry. In *Food Lion, Inc. v. Capital Cities/ABC, Inc.,*[12] two ABC reporters used false résumés to obtain jobs at Food Lion, Inc. supermarkets in order to videotape unsanitary meat-handling practices at the markets. Food Lion sued, alleging that the reporters had committed trespass by secretly videotaping while working at the supermarkets. The U.S. Court of Appeals for the Fourth Circuit found that the two reporters had breached their duty of loyalty to the company as employees by videotaping in nonpublic areas, thereby nullifying Food Lion's consent for them to enter the property. Accordingly, the court found that

12. 194 F.3d 505 (4th Cir. 1999).

the reporters had committed trespass. The court rejected, however, Food Lion's argument that misrepresentation on a job application nullifies the consent given to an employee to enter the employer's property and thereby turns the employee into a trespasser.

NUISANCE

Nuisance is a nontrespassory interference with the use and enjoyment of property, for example, by an annoying odor or noise.

Public nuisance is unreasonable and substantial interference with the public health, safety, peace, comfort, convenience, or utilization of land. An action for public nuisance is usually brought by the government. It may also be brought by a private citizen who experiences special harm different from that experienced by the general public.

Private nuisance is interference with an individual's use and enjoyment of his or her land. Destruction of crops by flooding, the pollution of a stream, or playing loud music late at night in a residential neighborhood can constitute a private nuisance.

For example, the Wisconsin Supreme Court held that stray voltage that reduced a dairy herd's milk production was actionable on a private nuisance theory.[13] The court noted that the common law doctrine of private nuisance was broad enough to meet a wide variety of possible invasions and flexible enough to adapt to changing social values and conditions.

The focus of both public and private nuisance claims is on the plaintiff's harm, not on the degree of the defendant's fault. Therefore, even innocent behavior on the part of the defendant is actionable—that is, it may be the basis for a claim—if that behavior resulted in unreasonable and substantial interference with the use and enjoyment of the plaintiff's property. To determine whether the defendant's conduct is unreasonable, the court will balance the utility of the activity creating the harm and the burden of preventing it against the nature and the gravity of the harm. For example, hammering noise during the remodeling of a house may be easier to justify than playing loud music purely for recreation.

CONVERSION

Conversion is the exercise of dominion and control over the personal property, rather than the real property (that

is, land), of another. This tort protects the right to have personal property left alone. It prevents the defendant from treating the plaintiff's property as if it were his or her own. It is the tort claim a plaintiff would assert to recover the value of property stolen, destroyed, or substantially altered by the defendant.

The intent element for conversion does not include a wrongful motive. It merely requires the intent to exercise dominion or control over goods, inconsistent with the plaintiff's rights. The defendant need not know that the goods belonged to the plaintiff.

TRESPASS TO PERSONAL PROPERTY

When personal property is interfered with but not converted—that is, taken, destroyed, or substantially altered—there is a *trespass to personal property* (sometimes referred to as *trespass to chattels*). No wrongful motive need be shown. The intent required is the intent to exercise control over the plaintiff's personal property. For example, an employer who took an employee's car on a short errand without the employee's permission would be liable for trespass to personal property. However, if the employer damaged the car or drove it for several thousand miles, thereby lowering its value, he or she would be liable for conversion.

The tort of trespass to chattels can include demonstrations that involve private property on private land. For example, in an Oregon case a logging company sued six members of an environmental group who climbed on and chained themselves to the company's logging equipment.[14] The members of the environmental group had to pay punitive damages for demonstrating against government policies while on private property. The court ruled that the enforcement of these tort punitive damages did not violate the protesters' First Amendment rights.

In the following case, the court considered whether an Internet trading site could prevent another company from accessing its computer system through use of an automated querying program on the grounds that the program was trespassing on its property.

14. Huffman & Wright Logging Co. v. Wade, 857 P.2d 101 (Or. 1993).

13. Vogel v. Grant-LaFayette Elec. Coop., 548 N.W.2d 829 (Wis. 1996).

A CASE IN POINT

CASE 9.3

**eBay, Inc. v.
Bidder's Edge, Inc.**

*United States District Court
for the Northern District
of California
100 F. Supp. 2d 1058
(N.D.Cal. 2000).*

In the Language of the Court

FACTS eBay is the largest consumer-to-consumer online auction site. Users of eBay must agree to the eBay User Agreement, which prohibits the use of "any robot, spider, other automatic device, or manual process to monitor or copy our web pages or the content contained therein without our prior expressed written permission."

Bidder's Edge, Inc. (BE) is an auction aggregation site that allows online auction buyers to search for items across numerous online auctions without having to search each site individually. In April 1999, eBay agreed to permit BE to crawl the eBay site for ninety days, in order to collect information for the BE site, while the two companies negotiated a license. When those license negotiations failed, eBay requested that BE stop crawling the eBay site. BE initially complied. In November 1999, however, BE resumed accessing the eBay site, without authorization, to include eBay auction listings on its site. Once again, the parties failed to agree on a license, and eBay attempted, unsuccessfully, to block BE's unauthorized entries onto its site. eBay sued to enjoin BE from accessing eBay's computer systems based on nine causes of action including trespass to chattels.

ISSUE PRESENTED Is BE's entry onto eBay's Web site with an automated querying program a trespass to chattels?

OPINION WHYTE, J., writing for the U.S. District Court for the Northern District of California:

Trespass to chattels "lies where an intentional interference with the possession of personal property has proximately caused injury." Trespass to chattels . . . was recently applied to cover the unauthorized use of long distance telephone lines. Specifically, the court noted "the electronic signals generated by the [defendant's] activities were sufficiently tangible to support a trespass cause of action." Thus, it appears likely that the electronic signals sent by BE to retrieve information from eBay's computer system are also sufficiently tangible to support a trespass cause of action.

In order to prevail on a claim for trespass based on accessing a computer system, the plaintiff must establish: (1) defendant intentionally and without authorization interfered with plaintiff's possessory interest in the computer system; and (2) defendant's unauthorized use proximately resulted in damage to plaintiff.

a. BE's Unauthorized Interference

. . .

BE argues that it cannot trespass eBay's web site because that site is publicly accessible. BE's argument is unconvincing. eBay's servers are private property, conditional access to which eBay grants the public. eBay does not generally permit the type of automated access made by BE. In fact, eBay explicitly notifies automated visitors that their access is not permitted. "In general, California does recognize a trespass claim where the defendant exceeds the scope of the consent."

Even if BE's web crawlers were authorized to make individual queries of eBay's system, BE's web crawlers exceeded the scope of any such consent when they began acting like robots by making repeated queries. . . . Moreover, eBay repeatedly and explicitly notified BE that its use of eBay's computer system was unauthorized. . . .

. . .

(Continued)

(Case 9.3 continued)

b. Damage to eBay's Computer System

A trespasser is liable when the trespass diminishes the condition, quality or value of personal property. The quality or value of personal property may be "diminished even though it is not physically damaged by defendant's conduct."

...

BE argues that its searches represent a negligible load on plaintiff's computer systems, and do not rise to the level of impairment to the condition or value of eBay's computer system required to constitute a trespass. However, it is undisputed that eBay's server and its capacity are personal property, and that BE's searches use a portion of this property. Even if, as BE argues, its searches use only a small amount of eBay's computer system capacity, BE has nonetheless deprived eBay of the ability to use that portion of its personal property for its own purposes. The law recognizes no such right to use another's personal property.

RESULT The court found that eBay had made a strong showing that it was likely to prevail on the merits of its trespass claim and issued an injunction preventing BE from using any automated query program to access eBay's computer systems or networks for the purpose of copying any part of eBay's auction database.

QUESTIONS

1. Would BE have committed trespass to chattels if it had hired workers to access eBay's sites and manually prepare a list of the items available for auction?
2. What weight, if any, should a court give to BE's failed licensing negotiations with eBay?

Intentional Torts That Protect Certain Economic Interests *and* Business Relationships

DISPARAGEMENT

Disparagement is the publication of statements derogatory to the quality of the plaintiff's business, to the business in general, or even to the plaintiff's personal affairs, in order to discourage others from dealing with him or her. To prove disparagement, the plaintiff must show that the defendant made false statements about the quality or ownership of the plaintiff's goods or services, knowing that they were false or with conscious indifference as to their truth. The plaintiff must also prove that the statements caused him or her actual harm; damages will not be presumed.

INJURIOUS FALSEHOOD

False statements that are knowingly made, although they may not be disparaging of the plaintiff's business, may nevertheless give rise to an *injurious falsehood* claim. For example, a false statement that the plaintiff has gone out of business or does not carry certain goods is a tort if the statement results in economic loss to the plaintiff.

The range of damages for injurious falsehood is more restricted than for defamation. Injurious falsehood permits recovery of only pecuniary (that is, monetary) losses related to business operations, whereas defamation permits recovery for loss of reputation, including emotional damages, as well as pecuniary losses.

Defenses The defenses available to the defendant in a defamation action apply to injurious falsehood. In the case of comparison of goods, the privilege is even broader than the privilege available in defamation. For example, a defendant who favorably compares his or her own goods to those of a competitor is privileged, even

 ETHICAL CONSIDERATION

If a person knows that his or her goods are inferior, is it ethical to claim that they are better than a competitor's?

VIEW FROM CYBERSPACE

Stamping Out Spam

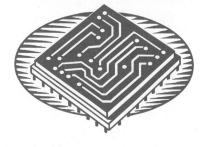

Frustrated by the proliferation of unsolicited e-mail advertisements (known as "spam") clogging its servers, online service provider CompuServe sued a prominent Internet junk mailer, Cyber Promotions, to prevent it from sending unsolicited e-mail to CompuServe subscribers.[a] The court found that CompuServe had a viable claim of trespass to personal property and was entitled to an injunction preventing Cyber Promotions from sending e-mail advertisements to CompuServe subscribers.

The court commented:

To the extent that defendants' multitudinous electronic mailings demand the disk space and drain the processing power of plaintiff's computer equipment, those resources are not available to serve CompuServe subscribers. Therefore, the value of that equipment to CompuServe is diminished even though it is not physically damaged by defendants' conduct.

Moreover, the messages were largely unwanted by CompuServe customers, many of whom terminated their accounts specifically because of the unabated receipt of bulk e-mail messages. Thus, insofar as Cyber Promotions' mailings diminished the capacity of CompuServe's equipment and harmed CompuServe's business reputation and goodwill with its customers, those mailings were actionable as a common law trespass to chattels.

Similarly, America Online (AOL) sued Over the Air Equipment for sending unsolicited e-mail messages promoting adult entertainment sites to AOL members. Perhaps fearing a repeat of Cyber Promotions' defeat, Over the Air settled the suit for an undisclosed sum and agreed to cease sending messages to AOL members. Officials at AOL estimate that 30 percent of e-mail sent through its system is "spam."[b]

Several states have considered and passed anti-spam laws, although several of these have been challenged as unconstitutional violations of the Commerce Clause.[c] In May 2000, Senator Conrad Burns of Montana introduced a bill, Controlling the Assault of Non-Solicited Pornography and Marketing (CAN-SPAM), in the U.S. Senate (S. 2542). The bill requires marketers who send spam to give an e-mail return address that would enable the Internet user to request the marketer to stop sending the junk e-mail. Under the bill, Internet companies could refuse to transmit messages that violate these conditions and could sue marketers that violate these rules and seek fines against them.[d] In July 2000, the U.S. House of Representatives passed the Unsolicited Electronic Mail Act (H.R. 3113). The bill allows Internet service providers to establish junk e-mail policies and to sue violators in state or federal court for damages; it also requires spam e-mailers to provide a return address and an opt-out provision for recipients who wish to stop receiving spam. As of February 2001, neither bill had been enacted into law.

a. CompuServe, Inc. v. Cyber Promotions, Inc., 962 F. Supp. 1015 (S.D. Ohio 1997).
b. Greg Wright, *Junk E-mail Bill Seeks to Can Spam*, GANNETT NEWS SERVICE, May 12, 2000.
c. Kelly Hearn, *Will US Crack Down on Rising Volume of E-mail "Spam"?*, CHRISTIAN SCIENCE MONITOR, Apr. 17, 2000, at 13.
d. Conrad Burns, *Burns Introduces Anti-spam Bill CAN-SPAM Establishes New Guidelines, Stiff Penalties for Spammers*, FED. DOC. CLEARING HOUSE, May 11, 2000.

---

though the defendant may not honestly believe in the superiority of his or her own goods.

FRAUDULENT MISREPRESENTATION

The tort of *fraudulent misrepresentation,* also called *fraud* or *deceit,* protects economic interests and the right to be treated fairly and honestly. Fraud requires proof that the defendant either (1) intentionally misled the plaintiff by making a material misrepresentation of fact upon which the plaintiff relied or (2) omitted to state a material fact when the defendant had a duty to speak because of a special relationship with the plaintiff. For example, a shareholder who has relied to his or her detriment upon an intentionally misleading accountant's opinion regarding the company's financial statements might sue the accountant for fraud.

Intent can be constructive—in other words, a court will sometimes impute a fraudulent intent to the defendant if the defendant showed reckless disregard for the truth.[15] (Negligent misrepresentation is discussed later in this chapter.)

Everyone has a duty to refrain from affirmatively misrepresenting the facts, that is, lying. But, as explained in Chapter 5, as a general rule, parties dealing at arm's length are not required to disclose all facts that might be

15. *See, e.g.,* Citizens Nat'l Bank of Wisner v. Kennedy & Co., 441 N.W.2d 180 (Neb. 1989); and Software Design & Application, Ltd. v. Price Waterhouse, LLP, 57 Cal. Rptr. 2d 36 (Cal. Ct. App. 1996).

relevant to the other party's decision. If, however, one party is a fiduciary (a person entrusted to protect the interests of another), then the fiduciary must disclose all relevant facts to the other party even if that party has not asked any questions. For example, if an executive is negotiating to buy a piece of property from the corporation, the executive must volunteer all information known to him or her that might affect the terms (such as the price) on which the corporation would be willing to sell the property.

Occasionally, a court will impose a duty to disclose even if the party required to disclose is not a fiduciary. For example, in *Brass v. American Film Technologies, Inc.,*[16] the defendant (AFT) convinced Brass and other plaintiffs to buy warrants that could be used to acquire common stock but failed to reveal that the underlying stock was restricted and could not be freely traded for a period of two years. Upon discovering the omission, the plaintiffs sued for fraud. The court held that, because AFT had superior knowledge about the restrictions on its securities, it had a duty to reveal those restrictions. Its failure to do so amounted to fraudulent concealment.

However, in *Albany Urology Clinic PC v. Cleveland,*[17] the Supreme Court of Georgia held that physicians do not have a common law or statutory duty to disclose to their patients personal factors that might adversely affect their professional performance. Cleveland sued his urologist for negligently performing unnecessary surgery on him and for fraudulently concealing his illegal use and abuse of cocaine. The court found that although a doctor has a common law duty to answer a patient's questions regarding medical or procedural risks, the doctor does not have the duty to disclose personal factors such as illicit drug use. The court found that the patient could sue the doctor for professional negligence but could not base a claim of fraud on the physician's failure to disclose his drug use.

A mere expression of an opinion generally is not a valid basis for a fraud claim. Although statements as to future actions are generally deemed opinions and therefore not actionable, they can constitute fraud when (1) the defendant held itself out to be specially qualified and the plaintiff acted reasonably in relying upon the defendant's superior knowledge; (2) the opinion is that of a fiduciary or other trusted person; and (3) the defendant stated its opinion as an existing fact or as implying facts that justify a belief in its truth.

To state a claim of fraud, a plaintiff must establish that he or she suffered damages as a result of the fraud. In *Maio v. Aetna, Inc.,*[18] a class of persons enrolled in Aetna's health maintenance organization (HMO) plan filed a claim alleging that the company had engaged in a fraudulent scheme to induce individuals to enroll in the HMO plan by representing that Aetna's primary commitment was to maintain and improve the quality of health care given to its members. The class alleged that, in fact, Aetna was driven primarily by financial and administrative considerations. The U.S. District Court for the Eastern District of Pennsylvania ruled that the plaintiffs' vague allegation that "quality of care" might suffer in the future was too hypothetical an injury to confer standing. The court also found that general assertions about Aetna's commitment to "quality of care" were "mere puffery" and could not serve as the basis for a fraud claim.

MALICIOUS PROSECUTION AND DEFENSE

A plaintiff can successfully sue for *malicious prosecution* if he or she shows that a prior proceeding was instituted against him or her maliciously and without probable cause or factual basis. In addition, the earlier case must have been resolved in the plaintiff's favor. This tort originated in the misuse of the criminal process but has been adapted to redress malicious civil prosecution as well. A victorious plaintiff can recover damages for attorneys' fees paid in connection with the prior action, injury to reputation, and psychological distress.

Courts frequently state that the malicious prosecution action is disfavored under the law. Because the action has the potential to produce a chilling effect that discourages legitimate claims, courts have been reluctant to expand its reach.

Nevertheless, one state expanded the doctrine to recognize an action for *malicious defense.* In *Aronson v. Schroeder,*[19] the defendant allegedly created false material evidence while serving as defense counsel in a prior case and then gave false testimony advancing the evidence. In a ruling for the plaintiff, the New Hampshire Supreme Court said:

> [The ruling] merely recognizes that when a defense is based upon false evidence and perjury or is raised for an improper purpose, the litigant is not made whole if the

16. 987 F.2d 142 (2d Cir. 1993).
17. 272 Ga. 296 (2000).
18. 1999 WL 800315 (E.D. Penn. Sept. 29, 1999), *aff'd,* 221 F.3d 472 (3d Cir. 2000).
19. 671 A.2d 1023 (N.H. 1995).

"We cannot write a life policy for your husband, Mrs. Blaine, because he is already dead. In insurance terms, that is considered a preëxisting condition."

© The New Yorker Collection 1997 J. B. Handelsman from cartoonbank.com. All Rights Reserved.

only remedy is reimbursement of counsel fees. It follows that upon proving malicious defense, the aggrieved party is entitled to the same damages as are recoverable in a malicious prosecution claim.

INTERFERENCE WITH CONTRACTUAL RELATIONS

The tort of *interference with contractual relations* protects the right to enjoy the benefits of legally binding agreements. It provides a remedy when the defendant intentionally induces another person to breach a contract with the plaintiff. The basis of interference with contractual relations is intent to interfere. Thus, courts usually require that the defendant induce the contracting party to breach, rather than merely create the opportunity for the breach. The defendant must know of the existence of the contract between the plaintiff and the other person, or there must be sufficient facts that would lead a reasonable person to believe there was such a contract.

Interference with contractual relations also requires an unacceptable purpose in some jurisdictions. If good grounds exist for the interference, the defendant is not liable. For example, if a manager of a corporation is incompetent, a stockholder of the corporation may be able to induce breach of the employment agreement between the manager and the corporation. The stockholder's motive would be to protect his or her investment. On the other hand, a defendant may not interfere with another person's contract in order to attract customers or employees away from that person. Similarly, a defendant that knowingly participates in or induces a breach of *fiduciary duty* (a duty to act with integrity) by another commits the tort of *participation in a breach of fiduciary duty.*

Perhaps the most famous case involving tortious interference with contract was *Pennzoil v. Texaco,* discussed in the "Inside Story" in Chapter 7. In 1983, Pennzoil and Getty Oil Company negotiated an agreement for a merger. During the process of drafting the final merger documents, Texaco offered a better price for Getty and agreed to indemnify Getty for any claims that might be asserted by Pennzoil. After Getty accepted Texaco's offer, Pennzoil sued Texaco for tortious interference with contract. Under New York law, Pennzoil had to prove (1) the existence of a valid contract, (2) Texaco's knowledge of the existence of the contract, (3) Texaco's intentional inducement of breach of that contract, and (4) damages incurred by Pennzoil as a result of the breach of contract. A jury decided against Texaco and awarded $10.5 billion to Pennzoil. The case was ultimately settled for $3 billion.

Defenses As in defamation, truth is a defense to a claim for interference with contractual relations. There is no liability if a true statement was made to induce another to break relations with the plaintiff.

INTERFERENCE WITH PROSPECTIVE BUSINESS ADVANTAGE

Courts are less willing to award damages for interference with prospective contracts than they are to protect existing contracts. To prove *interference with prospective business advantage,* the plaintiff must prove that the defendant interfered with a relationship the plaintiff sought to develop and that the interference caused the plaintiff's loss. The interference must be intentional. In rare cases, however, courts have permitted recovery when the defendant was merely negligent.

In one case,[20] Baum Research and Development Company, a manufacturer of wooden baseball bats, filed a claim of tortious interference with prospective economic advantage against several manufacturers of aluminum baseball bats, a trade association of bat manufacturers, and the National Collegiate Athletic Association. Baum claimed that the defendants had prevented the company from establishing relationships with amateur baseball teams and had disrupted its sale of bats to these teams by, among other things, disseminating false information about the Baum Hitting Machine manufactured by Baum, inducing baseball teams to terminate arrangements with Baum for the use of its wooden bats, and removing and destroying Baum bats and replacing them with aluminum bats. The court established that the necessary elements of tortious interference with economic relations are (1) the existence of a valid business relationship or expectancy, (2) knowledge of the relationship or expectancy on the part of the interferor, (3) intentional interference inducing or causing a breach or termination of a relationship or expectancy, and (4) damages. Concluding that the company "had more than a mere hope for business opportunities or the innate optimism of a salesman,"[21] the court ruled that Baum had a valid claim of tortious interference with economic relations.

Defense Most jurisdictions recognize a privilege to act for one's own financial gain. In some jurisdictions, the plaintiff has the burden of showing that the defendant acted from a motive other than financial gain, such as revenge. In others, the defendant has the burden of proving that he or she acted only for financial gain. Any purpose sufficient to create a privilege to disturb existing contractual relations will also justify interference with prospective business advantage.

20. *In re* Baseball Bat Antitrust Litig., 75 F. Supp. 2d 1189 (D. Kan. 1999).
21. *Id.*

ETHICAL CONSIDERATION

Is it ethical to refuse to deal with the plaintiff, to secretly negotiate with the plaintiff's customers, or to refuse to deal with third parties unless they agree to refuse to deal with the plaintiff?

As in defamation and interference with contractual relations, truth is a defense. Some jurisdictions have applied the First Amendment defenses available in defamation cases.

Interference with prospective business advantage is usually done by a competitor or at least by one who stands to benefit from the interference. However, it is not a tort to compete fairly. For the purposes of competition, a defendant may attempt to increase its business by cutting prices, allowing rebates, refusing to deal with the plaintiff, secretly negotiating with the defendant's customers, or refusing to deal with third parties unless they agree not to deal with the plaintiff.

BAD FAITH

Bad faith conduct by one party to a contract to the other party may serve as the basis for a claim of bad faith. This tort claim is separate and independent from a breach-of-contract claim. Typically, a claim of bad faith is brought by an insured against an insurance company for breaching its duty to act in good faith in the handling and payment of claims. The plaintiff must show that the insurer failed to exercise good faith in the processing of a claim and that its refusal to pay the claim was not predicated upon a reasonable justification. In the following case, the Supreme Court of Wisconsin considered whether the tort of bad faith should be applied to HMOs, as well as insurance companies, that deny medical coverage.

A CASE IN POINT

CASE 9.4
McEvoy v. Group Health Cooperative of Eau Claire
Supreme Court of Wisconsin
570 N.W.2d 397
(Wis. 1997).

In the Language of the Court

FACTS In 1991, Angela McEvoy, a thirteen-year-old girl, was diagnosed with anorexia nervosa (a potentially fatal eating disorder) by her primary physician, Dr. McFarlane of Group Health Cooperative of Eau Claire (GHC). GHC was a health maintenance organization (HMO) that insured Angela as a dependent of her mother, Susan McEvoy, the health care benefits policyholder.

(Continued)

(Case 9.4 continued)

After diagnosing anorexia, McFarlane approached GHC's administration about referring Angela to an inpatient eating disorder program at the University of Minnesota Hospital (UMH). When GHC was unable to care adequately for patients, it referred them to out-of-network providers. Neither GHC nor its network affiliates had experience treating a patient with anorexia nervosa. Dr. Lancer, the GHC's medical director responsible for its cost containment programs and medical management, approved Angela's referral for a two-week period of inpatient treatment. Subsequently, he approved an additional four weeks of inpatient care. After six weeks of treatment, Lancer decided to discontinue coverage of Angela's care at UMH and to refer her to a newly formed, in-network outpatient group therapy session for compulsive overeaters. Angela's treating physician and psychiatrist opposed Lancer's decision. At the time, approximately four weeks of inpatient psychological care benefits remained under the McEvoys' contract with GHC.

After being discharged from the inpatient program, Angela relapsed almost immediately and was readmitted to the inpatient program approximately two months later when she weighed seventy-four pounds. The McEvoys commenced an action against GHC, alleging that the HMO had breached the policy and in bad faith denied Angela coverage for her treatment. The court granted GHC's motion for summary judgment and dismissed the McEvoys' complaint on the grounds that application of the tort of bad faith to HMOs would be an "unwarranted extension of the bad faith doctrine." The appeals court reversed, and GHC appealed.

ISSUE PRESENTED Can HMOs be sued by subscribers under the common law tort of bad faith?

OPINION BRADLEY, J., writing for the Wisconsin Supreme Court:

To properly resolve this issue, we must consider the rationale underlying our previous adoption of the common law tort of bad faith, the nature and purpose of HMOs, the legislature's pronouncements concerning the regulation and organization of HMOs, and the policy implications behind labeling HMOs as insurers under bad faith tort. These considerations convince us that for purposes of the application of the common law doctrine of bad faith, HMOs making out-of-network benefit decisions are insurers.

...

The rationale underlying a bad faith cause of action is to encourage fair treatment of the insured and penalize unfair and corrupt insurance practices. By ensuring that the policyholder achieves the benefits of his or her bargain with the insurer, a bad faith cause of action helps to redress a bargaining power imbalance between parties for an insurance contract.

...

In the course of the contractual relationship between the HMO and subscriber, a power imbalance similar to that between a classical insurer and policyholder exists. An HMO subscriber has little effective negotiating power since policy terms, like those in insurance contracts, are usually prepackaged and subject to a significant number of regulations and rules. When faced with a problem, HMO subscribers, like many insurance policyholders, may encounter bureaucratic or procedural hurdles in asserting their contractual health care rights.

A review of legislative declarations in the Wisconsin statutes specifically applicable to GHC supports our general characterization of HMOs as insurers for bad faith purposes. . . .

...

(Continued)

(Case 9.4 continued)

Public policy also supports our decision to equate HMOs and insurers for purposes of applying bad faith tort to HMOs. Through contractual arrangements with physicians and patients, HMOs are able to exert significant influence on, if not outright control over, the costs of treatment regimens administered to patients, thereby limiting waste. The fears attendant with such arrangements, however, revolve around the economic model of health care financiers focusing on reducing aggregate costs while failing to recognize and to protect adequately the medical needs of individual subscribers.

This fear is particularly acute in the present high-cost medical economy where an adverse benefits ruling means not just that the financier will not provide payment, but also that the medical care itself is effectively denied. The tort of bad faith was created to protect the insured from such harm. . . . Because HMO subscribers are in an inferior position for enforcing their contractual health care rights, application of the tort of bad faith is an additional means of ensuring that HMOs do not give cost containment and utilization review such significant weight so as to disregard the legitimate medical needs of subscribers.

. . .

An HMO . . . may be liable in bad faith when it has denied a request for out-of-network care or coverage without a reasonable basis. Such a bad faith cause of action may arise when an HMO refuses to consider a patient or physician request for care or coverage, if the HMO makes no reasonable investigation of a request for care or referral put to it, if the HMO conducts its evaluation of a care or coverage request in such a way as to prevent it from learning the true facts upon which the plaintiff's claims are based or if, as the plaintiffs allege in this case, the HMO conducts its evaluation of a request and bases its decision primarily on internal cost-containment mechanisms, despite a demonstrated medical need and a contractual obligation.

RESULT The McEvoys were permitted to sue the HMO for the common law tort of bad faith. That tort applies to all HMOs making out-of-network benefit decisions.

QUESTIONS

1. Would a claim for bad faith against an HMO stand in the absence of serious medical consequences?
2. When is it proper for an HMO to reject a request for out-of-network benefits?

 # Elements *of* Negligence

An essential element of every intentional tort is the mental element of intent. Negligence does not include a mental element. Rather, the focus is on the conduct of the defendant. The law of negligence requires that all people act as reasonable persons, taking appropriate care in any given situation. It does not require that the defendant intended, or even knew, that his or her actions would harm the plaintiff. In fact, even if the defendant was full of concern for the safety of the plaintiff, the defendant's conduct may still be negligent. It is enough that the defendant acted carelessly or, in other words, that his or her conduct created an unreasonable risk of harm.

Negligence is defined as conduct that involves an unreasonably great risk of causing injury to another person or damage to property. To establish liability under a negligence theory, the plaintiff must show that (1) the defendant owed a duty to the plaintiff to act in conformity with a certain standard of conduct, that is, to act reasonably under the circumstances; (2) the defendant breached that duty by failing to conform to the standard; (3) a reasonably close causal connection exists between the plaintiff's injury and the defendant's breach; and (4) the plaintiff suffered an actual loss or injury.

DUTY

A person with a *legal duty* to another is required to act reasonably under the circumstances to avoid harming the other person. The required standard of care is what a reasonable person of ordinary prudence would do in the circumstances. It is not graduated to include the reasonably slow person, the reasonably forgetful person, or the reasonable person of low intelligence. In determining duty, the law allows reasonable mistakes of judgment in some circumstances. In emergency situations, the duty is to act as a reasonable person would act in the circumstances. The defendant is expected to anticipate emergencies. Drivers must drive defensively. Innkeepers must anticipate fires and install smoke alarms and, in some cases, sprinkler systems and must provide fire escapes and other fire-safety features. Owners of swimming pools in subdivisions with children must fence their property.

As explained further below, most states take a formalistic approach to duty and alter the scope of the defendant's liability depending on the court's characterization of the injured party (e.g., trespasser versus business guest). In 1993, the New Jersey Supreme Court articulated a more general framework: "Whether a person owes a duty of reasonable care toward another turns on whether the imposition of such a duty satisfies an abiding sense of basic fairness under all of the circumstances in light of considerations of public policy."[22] For that court, the analysis involves balancing many factors, including the relationship between the parties, the nature of the attendant risk, the opportunity and ability to exercise care, and the public interest in the proposed solution.

Duty to Rescue The law does not impose a general duty to rescue. However, once one undertakes a rescue, the law imposes a duty to act as a reasonable person and not to abandon the rescue effort unreasonably. Thus, if Ciril Wyatt sat on a river shore and watched Edward Donnelly drown, she would not be liable in negligence for Donnelly's death. However, if Wyatt saw Donnelly drowning, jumped in her boat, sped to him, tried to pull him into the boat and then changed her mind and let him drown, she would be liable.

A special relationship between two people may create a duty to rescue. If Donnelly were Wyatt's husband or child or parent, Wyatt would have a duty to rescue him. Other relationships that create a duty to rescue are employer and employee; innkeeper and guest; teacher and student; employee of a bus, train, or other common carrier and passenger; and possibly team members, hunting partners, or hiking partners.

22. Hopkins v. Fox & Lazo Realtors, 625 A.2d 1110 (N.J. 1993).

INTERNATIONAL CONSIDERATION

Some countries do impose a general duty to rescue. For example, France and Brazil require bystanders to try and help those in danger if trying to help will not put the bystanders at risk.

There is a duty to rescue those whom one has placed in peril. For example, if Wyatt had been driving her boat in a negligent manner, thereby causing Donnelly to fall overboard, she would have a duty to rescue him.

 ## Negligence: Duty *of* Landowner *or* Tenant

A possessor of land (such as a tenant) or its owner has a legal duty to keep the property reasonably safe. Such a person can be liable for injury that occurs outside, as well as on, the premises. For example, a landowner may be liable for harm caused when water from a cooling tower covers the highway; or when sparks from a railroad engine, which is not properly maintained, start a fire on adjacent property; or when snow slides from a roof onto the highway.

A landowner must exercise care in the demolition or construction of buildings on his or her property and in the excavation of his or her land. Landowners have been held liable when a pole on a landowner's property collapsed after it was hit by a car and injured a pedestrian and when a landowner erected a sign that obstructed the view and caused an accident.

In a few jurisdictions, landowners have a duty to maintain sidewalks that abut (are right next to) their property. In all jurisdictions, a landowner has a general duty to inspect his or her property and keep it in repair, and he or she may be liable if a showroom window, a downspout, a screen, or a loose sign falls and injures someone.

TRADITIONAL APPROACH TO LIABILITY FOR INJURIES ON PREMISES

Traditionally, the liability associated with injury on the premises of another has hinged on the distinctions between trespassers, licensees, and invitees. The landowner's duty is least for the trespasser and greatest for the invitee.

Duty to Trespassers In general, a landowner owes no duty to an undiscovered trespasser. If a substantial number of trespassers are in the habit of entering at a particular place, however, then the possessor has a duty to take reasonable care to discover and to protect the trespassers from activities he or she carries on. Some courts have also established a duty to protect such trespassers from dangerous conditions, such as concealed high-tension wires, that do not result from the possessor's activities. Some jurisdictions require the possessor to exercise reasonable care once he or she knows of the trespasser's presence.

Trespassing children are owed a higher level of duty. The *attractive nuisance* doctrine imposes liability for physical injury to child trespassers caused by artificial conditions on the land if (1) the landowner knew or should have known that children were likely to trespass; (2) the condition is one the landowner would reasonably know involved an unreasonable risk of injury to such children; (3) the children, because of their youth, did not discover the condition or realize the risk involved; (4) the utility to the possessor of maintaining the condition is not great; (5) the burden of eliminating the risk is slight compared with the magnitude of the risk to the children; and (6) the possessor fails to exercise reasonable care to protect the children.

Duty to Licensees A *licensee* is anyone who is on the land of another person with the possessor's express or implied consent. The licensee enters for his or her own purposes, not for those of the possessor. Social guests and uninvited sales representatives are licensees.

The possessor must exercise reasonable care for the protection of the licensee. This duty differs from that to a trespasser because the possessor is required to look out for licensees before they enter the land. However, he or she is not required to inspect for unknown dangers. The duty arises only when the possessor has actual knowledge of a risk.

Duty to Invitees An *invitee*, or business visitor, is someone who enters the premises for purposes of the possessor's business. The possessor owes a higher duty to an invitee than to a licensee. The possessor must protect invitees against known dangers and also against those dangers that he or she might discover with reasonable care.

The invitee is of particular importance to a manager. There are thousands of "slip and fall" cases each year due to wet floors, icy sidewalks, or broken steps. A customer is clearly an invitee and is accordingly owed a higher duty of care than a licensee such as a social guest.

Invitees of a landowner, such as contractors, may also have a duty to other persons admitted onto the property by the owner. Contractors who create a dangerous condition while working at a construction site may be held liable for injury caused by the dangerous condition after the contractor leaves the site and turns its work over to the property owner. In *Brent v. Unocal*,[23] ARCO Alaska, Inc.

hired Unocal, Inc., an independent contractor, to perform excavation and install sheet piling as part of a bridge construction project. After Unocal had finished its work and turned over the property to ARCO, construction worker William Brent was injured while working on the site when he fell into a hole created by Unocal. The Supreme Court of Alaska found that Unocal was liable under Section 385 of the Restatement (Second) of Torts, which states that "a contractor is held to the standard of reasonable care for the protection of third parties who may foreseeably be endangered by his negligence, even after acceptance of the work by the contractor." Section 385 reflects the rule of the majority of courts that have considered this issue.

A business's duty to invitees may even include an obligation to protect invitees from criminal conduct by third parties. States have been mixed in their application of this standard. The New Jersey Supreme Court held a supermarket liable when a 79-year-old woman was abducted from its parking lot and later killed.[24] Although there had never been an abduction or similar incident on the property, the court ruled that Food Circus was negligent in failing to provide any security or warning signs in its parking lot. Employing an analysis that considered the "totality of the circumstances," the court concluded that it was foreseeable that over the course of time an individual would enter the supermarket's parking lot and assault a customer.

The Washington Supreme Court has also held that businesses have a duty to take reasonable steps to protect invitees from criminal conduct by third parties but has indicated that this general duty does not necessarily include a duty to provide security personnel. In *Nivens v. 7-11 Hoagy's Corner*,[25] the court denied a claim by an assaulted convenience store patron. Its rationale was that imposing a requirement that businesses provide guards in all cases would unfairly shift responsibility for policing from the government to the private sector. In *dicta*, the court said that a duty to provide security guards may arise if "the construction or maintenance of the premises brings about a . . . peculiar temptation . . . for criminal misconduct" by third parties, but such facts were not present in *Nivens*. The issue of a landowner's duty to protect parties from criminal conduct by third parties also arises in the landlord–tenant relationship.

REASONABLE CARE APPROACH

The traditional approach of classifying one who enters a tenant's or landowner's property as either trespasser, licensee, or invitee has fallen into disfavor in several juris-

---

23. 969 P.2d 627 (Alaska 1998).

24. Clohesy v. Food Circus Supermarkets, Inc., 694 A.2d 1017 (N.J. 1997).

25. 943 P.2d 286 (Wash. 1997).

dictions due to the approach's potential for confusion and conflict. The process of determining the proper classification of an injured plaintiff is often difficult, sometimes requiring courts and juries to sift through hundreds of pages of testimony. Moreover, the status of a person on a landowner's property could change over the course of a day or a transaction. For example, an intruder would be deemed a trespasser, but if the intruder was spotted and permitted to remain, the trespasser's status could shift to licensee. The New York Court of Appeals put it this way: "[I]t remains a curiosity of the law that the duty owed to a plaintiff on exit may have been many times greater than that owed him on his entrance, though he and the premises all the while remained the same."[26]

To eliminate this potential for confusion, several jurisdictions have opted to abandon the traditional "trichotomy" in favor of a standard of *reasonable care under the circumstances*. Under this new standard, courts require all landowners to act in a reasonable manner with respect to entrants on their land, with liability hinging on the foreseeability of harm. Some jurisdictions, such as New York, have collapsed all three of the old standards into a single reasonable care standard. Other jurisdictions, such as North Carolina, have eliminated the distinction between licensees and invitees but continue to treat trespassers differently because they had no right to enter the land. In determining whether the landowner has exercised reasonable care, courts will consider the identity of the person entering the property and the reasons why that person entered. The New York Court of Appeals explained that "this standard of reasonable care should be no different than that applied in the usual negligence action."[27]

DUTY OF LANDLORD TO TENANT

In general, a landlord has a duty to take steps to provide adequate security to protect tenants from foreseeable

26. Basso v. Miller, 40 N.Y.2d 233 (1976).
27. *Id.*

criminal acts of a third party. Relevant issues are whether (1) the area was a high crime area, (2) there had been earlier criminal acts, (3) there was a failure to maintain locks, and (4) the landlord had knowledge of prior criminal acts.

In *Sharon P. v. Arman, Ltd.*,[28] the plaintiff, who was sexually assaulted in an underground commercial parking garage below her office building, sued the garage owner for failing to take measures to prevent criminal acts in the garage. The California Supreme Court found that a commercial landlord has a duty to take reasonable steps to secure common areas against *foreseeable* criminal acts of third parties that are likely to occur in the absence of such precautionary measures. Under this standard, a court must balance the foreseeability of the harm against the burden to be imposed on the landlord in taking precautionary measures. The court found that the garage had a ten-year history with no assaults and "absent any prior similar incidents or other indications of a reasonably foreseeable risk of violent criminal assaults in that location, we cannot conclude defendants were required to secure the area against such crime."

Negligence: Duty *of* Accountants *and* Other Professionals *to* Third Parties

The issue of duty takes on special significance when the plaintiff asserts a claim of professional negligence, or malpractice, against a lawyer, an architect, or an accountant. Although a professional clearly owes a duty to his or her client, a professional may not have a duty to a third party with whom he or she does not have a contractual relationship.

In the following case, the court considered an accountant's obligation to its broker–dealer client's customers.

28. 989 P.2d 121 (Cal. 1999), *cert. denied*, 120 S. Ct. 2689 (2000).

A CASE IN POINT

CASE 9.5

Securities Investor Protection Corp. v. BDO Seidman, LLP
United States Court of Appeals for the Second Circuit
222 F.3d 63 (2d Cir. 2000).

In the Language of the Court

FACTS The Securities Investor Protection Corporation (SIPC) is a private, nonprofit membership corporation formed pursuant to the Securities Investor Protection Act of 1970 (SIPA) to monitor the activities of broker–dealers and insure customer accounts in the case of a broker–dealer's liquidation. The SIPA requires broker–dealers to file annual audit reports with the Securities and Exchange Commission (SEC) and one of the self-regulatory bodies within the broker–dealer industry. Broker–dealers must employ an independent public accountant to file reports.

(Continued)

(Case 9.5 continued)

A.R. Baron & Company, Inc., a registered securities broker–dealer, retained BDO Seidman to serve as its independent certified public accountant and auditor from 1992 through 1995, as required by the SIPA. During that time, some of Baron's managers engaged in illegal activities including fraud in the sale of securities and manipulation of initial public offerings. Thirteen Baron employees pleaded guilty to or were convicted of crimes, and Baron also pleaded guilty to enterprise corruption. Baron filed for bankruptcy in 1996. On July 11, 1996, the U.S. District Court for the Southern District of New York found that Baron's customers were in need of the protection of the SIPA and directed the appointment of a trustee to oversee Baron's liquidation.

The trustee and SIPC brought a claim against Seidman, alleging that Seidman's inadequate performance as Baron's certified public accountant allowed Baron's management's misconduct to go undetected and ultimately to result in the firm's precarious financial condition. The plaintiffs claimed that Seidman failed to follow proper audit procedures and neglected to disclose Baron's inadequate internal fraud controls. They also alleged that Seidman negligently misrepresented Baron's financial condition in its audit reports to the SEC and the National Association of Securities Dealers (NASD).

The district court found that the plaintiffs could not state a claim for negligent misrepresentation because they had not established the privity-like relationship between Baron's customers and Seidman required for a negligent misrepresentation claim. The plaintiffs appealed.

ISSUE PRESENTED Does a broker–dealer's accountant have a duty to the broker–dealer's customers so that it can be held liable to them for negligent misrepresentation?

OPINION SOTOMAYOR, J., writing for the U. S. Court of Appeals for the Second Circuit:

In New York, a plaintiff claiming negligent misrepresentation against an accountant with whom he has no contractual relationship faces a heavy burden. To prevail, the plaintiff must establish three elements: 1) the accountant must have been aware that the reports would be used for a particular purpose; 2) in furtherance of which a known party was intended to rely; and 3) some conduct by the accountant "linking" him or her to that known party. The New York Court of Appeals has described these three factors as establishing a relationship "approaching that of privity" between the accountant and the third party claiming negligence. This strict limitation on the class of potential plaintiffs represents a policy determination by the New York courts that accountants will not, merely by contracting with a particular client, expose themselves "to a liability in an indeterminate amount for an indeterminate time to an indeterminate class."

. . .

To qualify as "known parties" under New York law, plaintiffs must be members of "a known group possessed of vested rights, marked by a definable limit and made up of certain components." Applying this standard, the New York Court of Appeals in [*White v. Guarantee*]²⁹ deemed the plaintiff a known party because the defendant accounting firm knew, when it agreed to perform an audit, that a group of limited partners, including the plaintiff, would rely on that audit in preparing their tax returns. Because the plaintiff thus was part of an identifiable, particularized group rather than "a faceless or unresolved class of persons," the court found that the accountant owed him a duty of care with respect to services performed for purposes of that group's reliance.

29. 372 N.E.2d 315 (N.Y. 1977).

(Continued)

(Case 9.5 continued)

By contrast, absent some evidence that he or she comprises part of such a specific class, a plaintiff generally will be unable to satisfy the "known party" requirement.

. . . [P]laintiffs do not allege that Seidman prepared its audit reports for Baron's customers; rather, Seidman prepared those statements for filing with the SEC and the NASD, as required under the SIPA. Even if Baron's customers relied indirectly on the material contained in those reports—specifically, information indicating that Baron was financially healthy—in deciding to invest or maintain accounts with Baron, the complaint does not allege that Seidman ever knew those investors' identities, or even of the number of customers Baron had at any one time. At best, therefore, the plaintiffs can establish that Baron's customers constitute an unknown class of investors, each of whom potentially would rely on Seidman's representations. These circumstances are insufficient to render the customers "known parties" under New York law.

The plaintiffs nonetheless urge this Court to find that Baron's customers meet this requirement on the ground that any accountant knows, when contracting for services with a broker-dealer, that customers will rely on its audit reports to ensure the financial viability of the dealers with whom they invest. . . . We reject this contention. Under New York law, the mere knowledge that some customers will rely on an accountant's work does not establish negligence liability. Rather, the accountant must have known when preparing the audit that the particular plaintiffs bringing the action would rely on its representations. . . . Because the plaintiffs here have not alleged that Seidman knew of any particular customers who would rely on its work for Baron, they have not satisfied the "known party" element of their negligent misrepresentation claim.

The plaintiffs also fail to allege "linking conduct" between Seidman and Baron's customers sufficient to impose negligent liability on Seidman. To demonstrate linking conduct, a plaintiff generally must show some form of direct contact between the accountant and the plaintiff, such as a face-to-face conversation, the sharing of documents, or other "substantive communication" between the parties.

Where direct contact between the accountant and the plaintiff has been nonexistent or even minimal, however, the plaintiff cannot recover for negligence.

. . . [W]e have little difficulty concluding that the plaintiffs have not shown such a link between Seidman and Baron's customers. The complaint in this case alleges no direct contact whatsoever between the customers and the defendant. At best, it alleges contact between Seidman and the SIPC regulators, who themselves operate at least one step removed from Baron's investors. The plaintiffs therefore cannot establish the direct nexus necessary to give the customers—or, by extension, the SIPC and the Trustees suing on their behalf—a cause of action against Seidman for negligent misrepresentation.

RESULT The court affirmed the district court's finding that Baron's customers could not recover for negligent misrepresentation against Seidman. The court did not decide whether SIPC could sue Seidman for negligent misrepresentation and certified that question for the New York state court to resolve.

COMMENTS Courts have developed three main approaches to the duty owed by a public accountant to third parties who rely on the accountant's reports. New York's "near privity" approach, which several states have followed, is the most restrictive. The most liberal approach, which few jurisdictions have adopted, extends an accountant's liability to all persons whom the accountant should reasonably foresee might obtain and rely on the accountant's report. States adopting the foreseeability approach compare defective audits with defective products and refuse to insulate auditors with a privity requirement

(Continued)

(Case 9.5 continued)

when manufacturers of defective products are strictly liable regardless of their relationship with the end user.[30] The majority view is set forth in the Restatement (Second) of Torts Section 552 (1977):

> [U]nder the Restatement, an accountant's duty is limited to the client and third parties whom the accountant or client intends the information to benefit. The Restatement approach recognizes that an accountant's duty should extend beyond those in privity or near-privity with the accountant, but is not so expansive as to impose liability where the accountant knows only of the possibility of distribution to anyone, and their subsequent reliance.[31]

QUESTIONS

1. Why should accountants be held to a lesser standard of liability than manufacturers?
2. Are there any circumstances under which Seidman would be liable to Baron's customers?

30. ML-Lee Acquisition Fund, L.P. v. Deloitte & Touche, 463 S.E.2d 618 (S.C. Ct. App. 1995).
31. *Id.*

In a case of intentional misrepresentation or fraud, if an accountant expects a person to rely on his or her opinion, then the accountant is liable to that person. Suit can also be brought by any person whom the accountant reasonably should have foreseen would rely upon the intentional misrepresentation. Thus, the greater the defendant's degree of fault, the wider the scope of potential plaintiffs.

The issues surrounding auditor liability to third parties closely parallel those surrounding the liability of investment bankers who issue fairness opinions in leveraged buyouts. Should shareholders be able to sue the investment bankers directly for negligent misrepresentation? Do investment bankers owe shareholders a duty? The actual client of the investment banker is the board of directors of the target company. However, some courts have upheld negligent misrepresentation actions by shareholders against investment bankers on a foreseeability basis.

Attorneys may also be liable to third parties for their negligence. In 1995, the New Jersey Supreme Court held a property seller's attorney liable to the buyer for providing incomplete inspection reports in the course of a sale of land.[32] Although the attorney claimed he had no duty to the purchaser and therefore could not be liable, the court disagreed. To the contrary, the court held, when an attorney knows or should know that a

32. Petrillo v. Bachenberg, 139 N.J. 472 (1995).

nonclient buyer will rely on his or her professional capacity, the attorney owes a duty to the third party and may be liable for breaching that duty.

 INTERNATIONAL CONSIDERATION

In *Hercules Managements Ltd. v. Ernst & Young,*[a] the shareholders of Northguard Acceptance Ltd. and Northguard Holdings Ltd. sued Ernst & Young, claiming that the accountants had negligently prepared audit reports that the shareholders relied upon in making their personal investment decisions. In its analysis, the Supreme Court of Canada focused on whether the shareholders used the audit reports for the specific purpose for which they were prepared. The Court found that the accountants had prepared the audit reports to help the shareholders in overseeing management of the companies, not to assist the shareholders in making personal investment decisions. In reaching its decision that Ernst & Young was not liable, the Court stated that "[t]he only purpose for which the reports could have been used so as to give rise to a duty of care on the part of the respondents, therefore, is as a guide for the shareholders, as a group, in supervising or overseeing management."

a. 2 S.C.R. 165 (1997).

Negligent Hiring *and* Liability *for* Letters *of* Recommendation

Employers face potential liability for negligently hiring incompetent employees and for harm caused by former employees for whom the prior employer wrote a favorable letter of recommendation.

NEGLIGENT HIRING

An employer may be held liable for the negligent or tortious conduct of its employee if the employer breached its duty to use care in hiring competent employees. Under the theory of negligent hiring, the proximate cause of the plaintiff's injury is the employer's negligence in hiring the employee, rather than the employee's wrongful act. A plaintiff must prove that (1) the employer was required to make an investigation of the employee and failed to do so, (2) an investigation would have revealed the unsuitability of the employee for the employment, and (3) it was unreasonable for the employer to hire the employee in light of the information it knew or should have known. In addition, the plaintiff must prove that (1) the employee was "unfit" for the employment position, (2) the employer knew or should have know that the employee was unfit for the position, and (3) the employee's particular unfitness proximately caused the plaintiff's injury.

In *Van Horne v. Evergreen Media Corp.,*[33] the Supreme Court of Illinois considered whether a radio station and its owner could be held liable for negligently hiring a disc jockey who allegedly made defamatory remarks during his radio show. The plaintiff argued that the defendants knew or should have known that the disc jockey was likely to make defamatory comments because of his prior outrageous conduct. The court rejected this argument, finding

33. 705 N.E.2d 898 (Ill. 1998), *cert. denied,* 120 S. Ct. 43 (1999).

that the fact that the disc jockey had engaged in offensive and outrageous conduct did not establish that he had a propensity to make false, defamatory statements. The court said that adopting the defendants' argument as its holding would have a "chilling effect on free speech, as media employers would be reluctant to hire controversial broadcasters or reporters" who are likely to engage in defamatory speech. The court declined, however, to decide whether First Amendment concerns would preclude all attempts to state a cause of action for negligent hiring based on an employee's defamatory statement.

DUTY OF EMPLOYERS TO THIRD PARTIES BASED ON LETTERS OF RECOMMENDATION

In recent years, employers have backed away from providing letters of recommendation, primarily because of the fear of lawsuits. A 1996 survey by the Society for Human Resource Management found that 63 percent of personnel managers refused to provide reference information about former employees to prospective employers.[34]

Employers have chosen this route—to issue "no comment" or "name, rank and serial number" reference letters—largely because writing a substantive reference puts them in a "damned if you do, damned if you don't" legal conundrum. On the one hand, employers who disclose "too much" information that might be deemed negative may be subject to a defamation suit by the former employee. On the other hand, employers who disclose "too little" negative information may be held liable to injured third parties for negligent misrepresentation.[35]

The following negligent misrepresentation case was widely publicized among human resource professionals and gave further resolve to their "no comment" approach.

34. *Note: Addressing the Cloud over Employee References: A Survey of Recently Enacted State Legislation,* 39 WM. & MARY L. REV. 177 (1997).
35. For a clever way a prospective employer may be able to finesse this issue, *see* PIERRE MORNELL, HIRING SMART 124 (1999).

A CASE IN POINT

CASE 9.6
Randi W. v. Muroc Joint Unified School District
*Supreme Court of California
929 P.2d 582 (Cal. 1997).*

Summary

FACTS Robert Gadams was a school administrator at Livingston Middle School. Randi W. was a thirteen-year-old student at Livingston. On February 1, 1992, Gadams allegedly molested and "engaged in sexual touching of" Randi.

The administrators at Livingston based their decision to hire Gadams in part on recommendation letters written by officials from three other school districts that had employed Gadams between 1985 and 1991. Gadams had been accused of sexual

(Continued)

(Case 9.6 continued)

misconduct with female students at each of these districts and at two of them was forced to resign on account of such accusations. The officials who wrote Gadams's recommendation letters were aware of these incidents. Nevertheless, each district provided a "detailed recommendation" that glowingly reviewed Gadams's work. One letter writer concluded: "I wouldn't hesitate to recommend Mr. Gadams for any position!" Another stated he "would recommend [Gadams] for almost any administrative position." A third recommended Gadams "for an assistant principalship or equivalent position without reservation." None of the letters made any reference to the allegations of Gadams's sexual misconduct.

Randi alleged that the letters constituted negligent misrepresentations and that the letter writers should have foreseen that these misrepresentations would cause injury to children at public schools. As a result, Randi argued that the letter writers owed a duty not only to the recipients of their letters but also to the children at public schools who were injured as a result of the misrepresentations.

The trial court dismissed Randi's claim on the basis that the defendants owed no duty to Randi. The court of appeal reversed. It relied on Sections 310 and 311 of the Restatement (Second) of Torts in imposing liability on one who intentionally or negligently gives false information to another person that results in physical injury to the recipient or another person. The school district appealed.

ISSUE PRESENTED Can an employer who writes a favorable recommendation letter that omits known, material, negative information be held liable to a third party who suffered physical injury as a result of the employer's omission?

SUMMARY OF OPINION The California Supreme Court first addressed the question of whether the defendants owed Randi a duty, which hinged on the foreseeability of the actual harm. The court found that while "the chain of causation leading from defendants' statements and omissions to Gadams's alleged assault on [Randi] is somewhat attenuated," the assault was reasonably foreseeable. Specifically, the defendants could foresee that (1) Livingston's officers would read and rely on the defendants' letters in hiring Gadams; (2) had they not unqualifiedly recommended Gadams, Livingston would not have hired him; and (3) Gadams, after being hired by Livingston, might molest or injure a Livingston student such as Randi.

Two other important factors were the availability of an alternative course of action and the balance of public policies. The defendants could just as easily have written "full disclosure" letters that revealed all relevant facts about Gadams's background or "no comment" letters that offered no affirmative representations about his background but simply verified basic employment dates and details. In addition, the court recognized that its ruling might discourage employers from writing full recommendation letters for fear of tort liability but felt that this effect was outweighed by the high priority society places on protecting children from physical and sexual abuse.

Having established the existence of a duty, the court went on to reject the defendants' alternative argument that their letters represented "mere nondisclosure," not "misleading misrepresentation." The court ruled that the defendants, having undertaken to provide some information about Gadams's ability and character, were obliged to disclose all other facts that would "materially qualify" the limited facts disclosed. Instead, the defendants completely omitted the materially qualifying facts surrounding Gadams's alleged sexual misconduct. Thus, their letters were "misleading half-truths," upon which liability for negligent misrepresentation could be founded.

RESULT The California Supreme Court affirmed the court of appeal's decision. The defendants were liable to Randi for negligent misrepresentation.

(Continued)

(Case 9.6 continued)

COMMENTS State legislatures have recognized that the beneficial free exchange of employment references is significantly stifled by the "damned if you do, damned if you don't" conundrum. In an effort to respond to this problem, more than thirty states had by 2000 enacted some type of statutory immunity for employers when they provide a reference.[36]

36. Wendy Bliss, *The Do's and Don'ts of Reference Checks,* COMPENSATION & BENEFITS OF LAW OFFICES, Oct. 2000.

 # Negligence: Breach *of* Duty, Causation, *and* Injury

Once it is determined that the defendant owed the plaintiff a duty, the next issue in a negligence case is whether the defendant breached that duty.

STANDARD OF CONDUCT

In many cases, the required standard of conduct will be that of a reasonable person. However, a person who is specially trained to participate in a profession or trade will be held to the higher standard of care of a reasonably skilled member of that profession or trade. For example, the professional conduct of a doctor, architect, pilot, attorney, or accountant will be measured against the standard of the profession. A specialist within a profession will be held to the standard of specialists.

The court will also look to statutes and regulations to determine whether the defendant's conduct amounted to a breach of duty. Some jurisdictions merely allow the statute to be introduced into evidence to establish the standard of care. In other jurisdictions, however, once the plaintiff shows that the defendant violated a statute and the violation caused the injury, the burden shifts to the defendant to prove that he or she was not negligent. This is often an impossible burden to satisfy. This rule, sometimes referred to as *negligence per se,* applies only if the statute or regulation was designed to protect a class of persons from the type of harm suffered by the plaintiff and if the plaintiff is a member of the class to be protected.

Courts will also look to the custom or practice of others under similar circumstances to determine the standard of care. Although the custom in the industry may be given great weight, it is not ordinarily dispositive or conclusive.

Res Ipsa Loquitur The doctrine of *res ipsa loquitur* ("the thing speaks for itself") allows the plaintiff to prove breach of duty and causation (discussed below) indirectly. *Res ipsa loquitur* applies when an accident has occurred and it is obvious, although there is no direct proof, that the accident would not have happened without someone's negligence. For example, if a postoperative X-ray showed a surgical clamp in the plaintiff's abdomen, even if no one testifies as to how the clamp got there, it can reasonably be inferred that the surgeon negligently left it there.

Res ipsa loquitur has three requirements. First, the plaintiff's injury must have been caused by a condition or instrumentality that was within the exclusive control of the defendant. This requirement eliminates the possibility that other persons, not named as defendants, were responsible for the condition that gave rise to the injury. Second, the accident must be of such a nature that it ordinarily would not occur in the absence of negligence by the defendant. Third, the accident must not be due to the plaintiff's own negligence.

Once *res ipsa loquitur* is established, jurisdictions vary as to its effect. In some jurisdictions, it creates a presumption of negligence, and the plaintiff is entitled to a directed verdict (whereby the judge directs the jury to find in favor of the plaintiff), unless the defendant can prove he or she was not responsible. This rule has the effect of shifting the burden of proof, normally with the plaintiff, to the defendant. Other jurisdictions leave the burden of proof with the plaintiff, requiring the jury to weigh the inference of negligence and to find the defendant negligent only if the preponderance of the evidence (including the *res ipsa* inference) favors such a finding.

CAUSAL CONNECTION

In addition to establishing duty and breach, a plaintiff claiming negligence must prove that the defendant's breach of duty caused the injury. The causation requirement has two parts: actual cause and proximate (or legal) cause.

Actual Cause To establish *actual cause,* the plaintiff must prove that he or she would not have been harmed but for the defendant's negligent conduct. The defendant is not liable if the plaintiff's injury would have occurred in the absence of the defendant's conduct. For example, if George Broussard put a garbage can out on the sidewalk for morning pickup and Anna Chang came along and broke her ankle, Broussard's conduct would not be the actual cause of Chang's injury if it were established that Chang had caught her heel in the sidewalk, turned her ankle, and then bumped into Broussard's garbage can.

When the plaintiff names more than one defendant, the actual-cause test may become a substantial-factor test: Was the defendant's conduct a substantial factor in bringing about the plaintiff's injury?

A further problem may arise if more than one individual could possibly have been the negligent party. A classic case involved two hunters shooting quail on an open range.[37] Both shot at exactly the same time, using identical shotguns. A shot from one of the guns accidentally hit another hunter. Clearly, only one of the two

37. Summers v. Tice, 199 P.2d 1 (Cal. 1948).

defendants caused the injury, but there was no way to determine which one it was. The court imposed the burden on each defendant to prove that he had not caused the injury. Because neither could do so, both were held liable for the whole injury.

Proximate Cause Once the plaintiff has proved that the defendant's conduct is an actual cause of the plaintiff's injury, he or she must also prove that it is the *proximate cause,* that is, that the defendant had a duty to protect the particular plaintiff against the particular conduct that injured him or her. Through the requirement of proximate cause, the law places limits on the defendant's liability.

In the following case involving the highly publicized bombing of a federal building in Oklahoma City, the court considered whether the negligence of the manufacturer of the fertilizer used to manufacture the bomb was the proximate cause of the injuries suffered by the bombing victims.

A CASE IN POINT

CASE 9.7

Gaines-Tabb v. ICI Explosives USA, Inc.
United States Court of Appeals for the Tenth Circuit
160 F.3d 613
(10th Cir. 1998).

Summary

FACTS On April 19, 1995, a bomb exploded in a federal building in Oklahoma City killing 168 people and injuring hundreds of others. Individuals injured by the bomb filed a suit for negligence against ICI Explosives (ICI), its parent company Imperial Chemical Industries, and a subsidiary of the parent. ICI manufactures ammonium nitrate that can be either "explosive grade" or "fertilizer grade." "Explosive-grade" ammonium nitrate can absorb sufficient amounts of fuel to allow detonation.

The plaintiffs alleged that ICI sold explosive-grade ammonium nitrate mislabeled as fertilizer-grade ammonium nitrate to Farmland Industries, which then sold it to Mid-Kansas Cooperative Association. Either Timothy McVeigh or Terry Nichols purchased eighty fifty-pound bags of the mislabeled ammonium nitrate from Mid-Kansas and used it to make a bomb. The plaintiffs claimed, among other things, that ICI was negligent in making explosive-grade ammonium nitrate available to the men who bombed the federal building.

The district court dismissed the plaintiffs' claims against ICI, finding that ICI did not have a duty to protect the plaintiffs and that ICI's actions were not the proximate cause of their injuries. The plaintiffs appealed.

ISSUE PRESENTED Was ICI's sale of explosive-grade ammonium nitrate mislabeled as fertilizer-grade ammonium nitrate the proximate cause of injuries to the Oklahoma bombing victims?

SUMMARY OF OPINION The U.S. Court of Appeals for the Tenth Circuit began its analysis by stating that under Oklahoma law, "the causal nexus between an act of negligence and the resulting injury will be deemed broken with the intervention of a new, independent and efficient cause which was neither anticipated nor reasonably foreseeable." This intervening cause (known as a *supervening cause*) must (1) be independent of the original act, (2) be adequate to bring about the injury, and (3) not be reasonably foreseeable. If the intervening act is intentionally tortious or criminal, then

(Continued)

(Case 9.7 continued)

the court must determine whether the negligent party realized or should have realized that his or her negligent conduct created a situation that afforded an opportunity to the third party to commit the tort or crime. The court looked to Section 448 of the Restatement (Second) of Torts for assistance in determining whether the criminal acts at issue in the case constituted a supervening cause of harm: "[U]nder comment b, the criminal acts of a third party may be foreseeable if (1) the situation provides a temptation to which a 'recognizable percentage' of persons would yield, or (2) the temptation is created at a place where 'persons of a peculiarly vicious type are likely to be.'" The court found no indication that a peculiarly vicious type of person was likely to frequent the Mid-Kansas Co-op; then the court considered the first alternative.

After finding no guidance as to the meaning of the term "recognizable percentage" as used in Section 448, comment b, the court held that:

[T]he term does not require a showing that the mainstream population or the majority would yield to a particular temptation; a lesser number will do. Equally, it does not include merely the law-abiding population. In contrast, we also believe that the term is not satisfied by pointing to the existence of a small fringe group or the occasional irrational individual, even though it is foreseeable generally that such groups and individuals will exist.

The plaintiffs were able to identify only two successful terrorist attacks using ammonium nitrate in the last twenty-eight years—a 1970 bombing at the University of Wisconsin–Madison and the Oklahoma City bombing at issue in this case. Due to the apparent complexity of manufacturing an ammonium nitrate bomb, including the difficulty of acquiring the correct ingredients (many of which are not widely available), mixing them properly, and triggering the resulting bomb, only a small number of persons would be able to create a bomb using ammonium nitrate. The court concluded that this group did not rise to the level of a "recognizable percentage" of the population.

RESULT The appeals court ruled as a matter of law that it was not foreseeable to the defendants that the ammonium nitrate that they distributed to the Mid-Kansas Co-op would be used to blow up the federal building. The criminal activities of the bombers were a supervening cause of the plaintiffs' injuries. Because ICI's negligence was not the proximate cause of the victims' injuries, the case was dismissed.

The defendant is not required to compensate the plaintiff for injuries that were unforeseeable, even if the defendant's conduct was careless. Courts apply the foreseeability requirement in two different ways. Some courts limit the defendant's liability to those consequences that were foreseeable. Others look to whether the plaintiff was a foreseeable plaintiff, that is, whether the plaintiff was within the *zone of danger* caused by the defendant's careless conduct.

INJURY

Finally, the plaintiff must prove that he or she or his or her property was injured. Even if a defendant is negli-

gent, the plaintiff cannot recover unless he or she can show some harm suffered as a result of the defendant's conduct.

This requirement is often the controlling factor in actions for *negligent infliction of emotional distress*. The traditional rule is that a plaintiff cannot recover for negligent infliction of emotional distress unless he or she can show some form of physical injury. However, in recent cases involving exposure to human immunodeficiency virus (HIV), courts have permitted plaintiffs to recover for emotional distress (over the fear of contracting HIV) without requiring that they actually have contracted the virus. Courts have set forth objective standards that prevent someone basing an action on an irrational fear that he or she contracted HIV. In *Bain v. Wells,*[38] the Tennessee Supreme Court ruled that a plaintiff must actually have been exposed to HIV in order to recover for emotional distress. Presumably, this means the plaintiff must demonstrate some medically sound channel of transmission. In *Williamson v. Waldman,*[39] the New Jersey Supreme Court held that a plaintiff can recover if a reasonable person would have experienced emotional distress over the prospect of contracting HIV under the circumstances. However, this hypothetical reasonable person would be presumed to have "then-current, accurate, and generally available" knowledge concerning the transmission of HIV. Again, an irrational fear of catching the virus would not be a valid basis for an emotional distress suit.

Defenses *to* Negligence

In some jurisdictions, the defendant may absolve itself of part or all of the liability for negligence by proving that the plaintiff was also negligent.

CONTRIBUTORY NEGLIGENCE

Under the doctrine of *contributory negligence,* if the plaintiff was also negligent in any manner, he or she cannot recover any damages from the defendant. Thus, if a plaintiff was 5 percent negligent and the defendant was 95 percent negligent, the plaintiff's injury would go unredressed. To address this inequity, most courts have replaced the doctrine of contributory negligence with that of comparative negligence.

COMPARATIVE NEGLIGENCE

Under the doctrine of *comparative negligence,* the plaintiff may recover the proportion of his or her loss attributable to the defendant's negligence. For example, if the plaintiff was 5 percent negligent and the defendant 95 percent, the plaintiff can recover 95 percent of the loss. Comparative negligence may take two forms: ordinary and pure. In an *ordinary comparative negligence* jurisdiction, the plaintiff may recover only if he or she is less culpable than the defendant. Thus, if the plaintiff is found 51 percent negligent and the defendant 49 percent negligent, the plaintiff cannot recover. In a *pure comparative negligence* state, the plaintiff may recover for any amount

of the defendant's negligence, even if the plaintiff was the more negligent party. For example, if the plaintiff was 80 percent negligent and the defendant was 20 percent negligent, the plaintiff may recover 20 percent of his or her loss.

ASSUMPTION OF RISK

The *assumption of risk* defense requires that the plaintiff (1) knew the risk was present and understood its nature and (2) voluntarily chose to incur the risk. It applies when the plaintiff, in advance of the defendant's wrongdoing, expressly or impliedly consented to take his or her chances of injury from the defendant's actions. Such consent, like consent to an intentional tort, relieves the defendant of any liability. For example, the plaintiff assumes the risk if he or she, knowing that a car has faulty brakes, consents to take the chance of injury by riding in the car, or if he or she voluntarily chooses to walk where the defendant has negligently scattered broken glass.

In those jurisdictions that have adopted the comparative negligence doctrine, there is a strong trend to abolish assumption of risk as a defense. Sometimes courts use duty to determine the viability of the defense of assumption of risk. In *Mosca v. Lichtenwalter,*[40] a man who was injured when he went ocean fishing and was accidentally struck in the eye by the sinker of another man's fishing pole sued the other fisherman for negligence. The California Court of Appeal found that the injury arose from a risk inherent in the activity of sportfishing and that imposing a duty on the other fisherman would alter the fundamental nature of the sport.

The California Supreme Court extended the doctrine of assumption of risk to skiing in *Cheong v. Antablin,*[41] when it held that a skier is not liable for injury to a fellow skier unless the defendant intentionally caused the injury or engaged in conduct that was so reckless as to be totally outside the range of ordinary activity involved in the sport.

COUNTERVAILING FEDERAL IMPERATIVES

In the following case, the court considered whether an employer's duty under federal law to investigate and remedy claims of sexual harassment precluded holding the employer liable to the alleged harasser under state law for negligent infliction of emotional distress resulting from the employer's investigation.

---

38. 936 S.W.2d 618 (Tenn. 1997).
39. 696 A.2d 14 (N.J. 1997).

40. 68 Cal. Rptr. 2d 58 (Cal. Ct. App. 1997).
41. 946 P.2d 817 (Cal. 1997).

CASE 9.8

Malik v. Carrier Corp.
*United States Court of
Appeals for the
Second Circuit
202 F.3d 97 (2d Cir. 2000).*

In the Language of the Court

FACTS Rajiv Malik joined Carrier Corporation as an associate in its executive training program, which was administrated by Regina Kramer, Carrier's manager of professional recruitment. The program provided associates with the opportunity to work in different divisions of the company, after which they could expect to be offered an executive position in one of these divisions.

While Malik was working in the program, several female workers complained that he made inappropriate sexual comments to them. These comments included inquiries as to whether a female employee was a virgin when she was married, whether she would go out with Malik if he were terminally ill, and whether her husband would "share" her with Malik if he visited their home. Another female employee complained that Malik had made inappropriate remarks to her and was "highly prone to turning the subject matter of every conversation to sex." Carrier investigated the sexual harassment claims. Although Malik was not disciplined, a Letter of Record regarding the complaints was placed in his personnel file.

Malik's employment with Carrier was eventually terminated after he failed to secure a final placement at the conclusion of the program. After his termination, Malik sued Carrier for negligent infliction of emotional distress as a result of the sexual harassment investigation. The jury returned a verdict for Malik. Carrier appealed.

ISSUE PRESENTED Can an employer investigating charges of sexual harassment against an employee be liable for negligent infliction of emotional distress resulting from the investigation?

OPINION WINTER, J., writing for the U.S. Court of Appeals for the Second Circuit:

The crux of [Malik's] negligence claim . . . is the quite credible emotional harm caused by Kramer's pressing of the sexual harassment investigation and the placing of the Letter of Record in his personnel file.

However, an employer's investigation of a sexual harassment complaint is not a gratuitous or optional undertaking; under federal law, an employer's failure to investigate may allow a jury to impose liability on the employer. . . . [I]t goes without saying that an employer's obligations in this regard do not cease because the alleged harasser denies inappropriate conduct.

. . . The issue is how to ensure that federal policies are not undermined by imposing on employers legal duties enforceable by damages that reduce their incentives to take reasonable corrective action as required by federal law.

Viewed in that perspective, corrective actions that a risk-averse employer might take to comply with federal law may not give rise to a negligence action, whether the rationale is couched in terms of breach, legal duty, or privilege. . . .

[Investigations of sexual harassment] forseeably produce emotional distress—often in copious amounts—in alleged harassers, whether guilty or innocent. As with any investigation into potentially embarrassing personal interactions, confidentiality is difficult or impossible to maintain if all pertinent information is to be acquired from all possible sources. . . . Even if the charge proves demonstrably baseless, the very existence of the investigation may give the charge temporary or even permanent credibility among some persons. . . .

. . .

. . . [T]he placing of the Letter of Record in Malik's file cannot be the basis for liability without undermining federal policy. . . .

(Continued)

(Case 9.8 continued)

. . . An employer simply cannot be diligent in carrying out an investigation if it must weigh every sentence or question with an eye to whether a jury might later conclude that it unreasonably injured an alleged harasser's psyche. . . . Malik's emotional distress claim therefore fails as a matter of law. Because the events upon which his claim rests are common to investigations into sexual harassment allegations under federal law, we need not describe with precision the kind of egregious or outrageous acts that might legitimately support a state law claim in such circumstances.

RESULT The U.S. court of appeals reversed the district court's order denying judgment as a matter of law to Carrier. Malik's suit was dismissed.

QUESTIONS

1. What conduct by an employer investigating a claim of sexual harassment might give rise to a valid claim for negligent infliction of emotional distress?
2. Given that Carrier did not discipline Malik, why did it put a Letter of Record regarding the complaints in his personnel file?

 # Vicarious Liability *and Respondeat Superior*

It is possible for one person to be held vicariously liable for the negligent, or in some cases the intentional, conduct of another.

RESPONDEAT SUPERIOR

Under the doctrine of *respondeat superior* ("let the master answer"), a "master" or employer is vicariously liable for the torts of the "servant" or employee if the employee was acting within the scope of his or her employment. The doctrine of *respondeat superior* may also apply when the person is not paid but acts on behalf of another person out of friendship or loyalty.

Underlying the doctrine of *respondeat superior* is the policy of allocating the risk of doing business to those who stand to profit from the undertaking. Because the employer benefits from the business, it is deemed more appropriate for the employer to bear the risk of loss than for the innocent customer to do so. The employer is in a better position to absorb such losses or to shift them, through liability insurance or price increases, to customers and insurers and, thus, to the community in general.

Liability for Torts Committed within the Scope of Employment An employer is directly liable for his or her own negligence in supervising or hiring an employee. In addition, the employer may also be vicariously liable for his

or her employee's wrongful acts, even if the employer had no knowledge of them and in no way directed them, provided the acts were committed while the employee was acting within the scope of employment. Activities within the scope of employment are activities closely connected to what the employee is employed to do or reasonably incidental to it. Whether an act was in the scope of employment is an issue for the jury to decide. (Scope of employment is discussed in greater detail in Chapter 5.)

Courts have held employers vicariously liable for an accident caused by an employee's negligence in driving while intoxicated after drinking alcohol at a company function on the grounds that the injury-producing event—the consumption of alcohol—occurred while the employee was acting within the scope of his employment by attending a company function.[42] In *Dickinson v. Edwards,*[43] the Washington Supreme Court found that an employer hosting a banquet may be sued under *respondeat superior* if the plaintiff establishes that (1) the employee consumed alcohol at a party hosted by the employer at which the employee's presence was requested or required by the employer; (2) the employee caused the accident while driving from the banquet; (3) the proximate cause of the accident (the intoxication) occurred at the time the employee negligently consumed the alcohol; and (4) because the banquet was beneficial

42. *See, e.g.,* Chastain v. Litton Systems, Inc., 694 F.2d 957 (4th Cir. 1982), *cert. denied,* 462 U.S. 1006 (1983); Wong-Leong v. Hawaiian Indep. Refinery, 879 P.2d 538 (Haw. 1994).
43. 716 P.2d 814 (Wash. 1986).

to the employer who required the employee's attendance, the employee negligently consumed the alcohol during the scope of his employment.

The employer may also be responsible for the safe passage home of an employee who was not intoxicated but was tired from working too many consecutive hours. In *Robertson v. LeMaster*,[44] LeMaster was an employee of the Norfolk and Western Railway Company. He was doing heavy manual labor, including lifting railroad ties and shoveling coal. After thirteen hours at work, he told his supervisor that he was tired and wanted to go home. The supervisor told him to continue working. This happened several times, until finally LeMaster said that he could no longer work because he was too tired. His supervisor told him that if he would not work, he should get his bucket and go home. LeMaster had been at work a total of twenty-seven consecutive hours. On his way home, he fell asleep at the wheel and was involved in an accident, causing injuries to Robertson. Robertson sued the railroad.

The Supreme Court of Appeals of West Virginia concluded that requiring LeMaster to work such long hours and then setting him loose on the highway in an obviously exhausted condition was sufficient to sustain a claim against the railroad. The court regarded the issue in this case as not the railway's failure to control LeMaster while he was driving on the highway but rather whether the railroad's conduct prior to the accident created a foreseeable risk of harm. The court concluded that the railway's actions created such a foreseeable risk.

44. 301 S.E.2d 563 (W. Va. 1983).

As explained in Chapter 5, courts are split on whether to impose liability on an employer who sends home an intoxicated employee who then injures a third party en route. The Court of Appeals of Arizona refused to impose vicarious liability for injury caused by an employee who had been using cocaine before and during work and had been ordered to leave the premises.[45] In contrast, the Supreme Court of Texas imposed a duty on employers to act with the degree of care a reasonably prudent employer would use to prevent injury to third parties.[46]

If intentional conduct caused the plaintiff's injury, courts will look to the nexus, or connection, between the conduct and the employment. In general, an employer is liable for its employee's intentional torts if the wrongful act in any way furthered the employer's purpose, however misguided the manner of furthering that purpose. Often intentional torts do not further the employer's business and therefore are outside the scope of employment. For example, a security company was found not liable when one of its security guards raped a worker in a client's building, even though the guard used his position to create the circumstances for the rape.[47]

In the following case, the Supreme Court of Oregon held that an employer could be vicariously liable for intentional torts outside the scope of employment that resulted from acts within the scope of employment.

45. Riddle v. Arizona Oncology Services, Inc., 924 P.2d 468 (Ariz. 1996) (Case 1.2).
46. Otis Eng'g Corp. v. Clark, 668 S.W.2d 307 (Tex. 1983).
47. Rabon v. Guardsmark, Inc., 571 F.2d 1277 (4th Cir. 1978), *cert. denied*, 439 U.S. 866 (1978).

A CASE IN POINT

CASE 9.9

Fearing v. Bucher
Supreme Court of Oregon
977 P.2d 1163 (Or. 1998).

In the Language of the Court

FACTS From 1970 through 1972, Bucher, a priest employed by the Franciscan Friars of California, Inc. and the Archdiocese of Portland in Oregon, acted as youth pastor, friend, confessor, and priest to Fearing and his family. Bucher gained the trust and confidence of Fearing's family and was a frequent guest in their home. Bucher began to spend substantial periods of time alone with Fearing, who was a minor, and committed a series of sexual assaults upon him.

Many years later, Fearing filed claims against the Archdiocese on theories of vicarious liability through application of the doctrine of *respondeat superior* and of negligent retention, supervision, and training of Bucher. The court of appeals affirmed the trial court's dismissal, and Fearing appealed.

ISSUE PRESENTED Can an employer be held vicariously liable for an employee's sexual assault on a minor based on the doctrine of *respondeat superior*?

OPINION GILLETTE, J., writing for the Oregon Supreme Court:

(Continued)

(Case 9.9 continued)

Bucher's alleged sexual assaults on plaintiff clearly were outside the scope of his employment, but our inquiry does not end there. The Archdiocese still could be found vicariously liable, if acts that were within Bucher's scope of employment "resulted in the acts which led to injury to plaintiff."

. . .

Bucher used his position as youth pastor, spiritual guide, confessor, and priest to plaintiff and his family to gain their trust and confidence, and thereby to gain the permission of plaintiff's family to spend large periods of time alone with plaintiff. By virtue of that relationship, Bucher gained the opportunity to be alone with plaintiff, to touch him physically, and then to assault him sexually. . . . [T]hose activities were committed in connection with Bucher's employment as youth pastor and priest, . . . they were committed within the time and space limitations of Bucher's employment, . . . they were committed out of a desire, at least partially and initially, to fulfill Bucher's employment duties as youth pastor and priest, and . . . they generally were of a kind and nature that he was required to perform as youth pastor and priest.

. . .

This is not a case . . . in which the *only* nexus alleged between the employment and the assault was that the employment brought the tortfeasor and the victim together in time and place and, therefore, gave the tortfeasor the "opportunity" to commit the assaults. . . . A jury reasonably could infer that Bucher's performance of his pastoral duties with respect to plaintiff and his family were a necessary precursor to the sexual abuse and that the assaults thus were a direct outgrowth of and were engendered by conduct that was within the scope of Bucher's employment.

RESULT The Supreme Court of Oregon found that the allegations of the amended complaint were sufficient to state a claim of vicarious liability against the Archdiocese based on the doctrine of *respondeat superior.* The plaintiff was permitted to proceed with his lawsuit.

COMMENTS On the same day, in *Lourim v. Swensen,*[48] the Supreme Court of Oregon found that the Boy Scouts of America could be vicariously liable for the actions of a volunteer leader who sexually assaulted a Boy Scout. The court stated: "[A] jury could infer that [the leader's] contact with the plaintiff was the direct result of the relationship sponsored and encouraged by the Boy Scouts, which invested [the Boy Scout leader] with authority to decide how to supervise minor boys under his care." Rejecting the Boy Scouts' argument that the organization could not be held liable because the Boy Scout leader was a volunteer, not an employee, the court found that a master–servant relationship may exist even if the servant is doing work gratuitously; the relevant inquiry is whether the master has the right to control the actions of the servant.

QUESTIONS

1. What, if anything, could the Archdiocese have done to avoid liability for the priest's sexual assault?
2. Based on the Oregon Supreme Court's reasoning in *Fearing,* would the owner of an appliance store be liable if one of its repairmen raped a customer while in her house for a service call?

48. 977 P.2d 1157 (Or. 1998).

Some courts apply the *aided-in-the-agency doctrine* (discussed in Chapter 5) and look beyond the scope of employment to determine whether the employee exercised authority conferred by, or abused assets provided by, his or her employer. Thus, one court held a county vicariously liable for battery, among other things, when one of its law enforcement officers stopped a woman, placed her in his patrol car, drove to an isolated place, and threatened to rape and murder her.[49]

 ## Successor Liability

As explained further in Chapter 10, under the doctrine of *successor liability,* individuals or entities that purchase a business may be held liable for the tortious acts of the previous owner. For example, if a company buys the assets of a ladder manufacturer and continues in the same line of business, the acquiring company may be liable for defective ladders manufactured and sold before the acquisition. Successor liability may also apply in the area of toxic torts, discussed later in this chapter.

 ## Liability *of* Multiple Defendants

The plaintiff may name numerous defendants. In some cases, the defendants may ask the court to join, or add, other defendants. As a result, when a court determines what liability exists, it must grapple with the problem of allocating the damages among multiple defendants.

JOINT AND SEVERAL LIABILITY

Under the doctrine of *joint and several liability,* multiple defendants are jointly (that is, collectively) liable and also severally (that is, individually) liable. This means that once the court determines that multiple defendants are at fault, the plaintiff may collect the entire judgment from any one of them, regardless of the degree of that defendant's fault. Thus, it is possible that a defendant who played a minor role in causing the plaintiff's injury must pay for all the damages. This is particularly likely when only one defendant is solvent, that is, when only one has money to pay the damages.

Many states have adopted statutes to limit the doctrine of joint and several liability for tort defendants.

49. White v. County of Orange, 212 Cal. Rptr. 493 (Cal. Ct. App. 1985).

Most states that have abolished joint and several liability have moved to a contributory regime. Under a joint and several liability regime, a defendant can be liable for all of a plaintiff's damages, even if the defendant was only 1 percent responsible for causing the plaintiff's injuries. This would be the result if the other defendants (those 99 percent responsible for causing the injuries) lacked funds to pay the judgment. Under contributory rules, the same defendant would under no circumstances be liable for more than 1 percent of the total damage award.

CONTRIBUTION AND INDEMNIFICATION

The doctrines of contribution and indemnification can mitigate the harsh effects of joint and several liability. *Contribution* distributes the loss among several defendants by requiring each to pay its proportionate share to one defendant; by doing so, they discharge their joint liability. *Indemnification* allows a defendant to shift its individual loss to other defendants whose relative blame is greater. The other defendants can be ordered to reimburse the one that has discharged a joint liability. It is important to keep in mind, however, that the right to contribution and the right to indemnification are worthless to a defendant if all the other defendants are insolvent or lack sufficient assets to contribute their share.

 ## Strict Liability

Strict liability is liability without fault, that is, without either intent or negligence. Strict liability is imposed in two circumstances: (1) in product liability cases (the subject of Chapter 10) and (2) in cases involving abnormally dangerous activities.

ULTRAHAZARDOUS ACTIVITIES

If the defendant's activity is ultrahazardous, the defendant is strictly liable for any injuries that result. An activity is *ultrahazardous* if it (1) necessarily involves a risk of serious harm to persons or property that cannot be eliminated by the exercise of utmost care and (2) is not a matter of common usage.

Courts have found the following activities to be ultrahazardous: (1) storing flammable liquids in quantity in an urban area, (2) pile driving, (3) blasting, (4) crop dusting, (5) fumigating with cyanide gas, (6) constructing a roof so as to shed snow onto a highway, (7) emission of noxious fumes by a manufacturing plant located in a settled area, (8) locating oil wells or refineries in populated communities, and (9) test-firing solid-fuel rocket motors. However, courts have considered parachuting, drunk driving, maintaining power lines, and letting water escape from an irrigation ditch not to be ultrahazardous. Discharging fireworks is not ultrahazardous because the risk of serious harm could be eliminated by proper manufacture. In most jurisdictions, liability does not attach until the court determines that the dangerous activity is inappropriate to the particular location.

Under strict liability, once the court determines that the activity is abnormally dangerous, it is irrelevant that the defendant observed a high standard of care. For example, if the defendant's blasting injured the plaintiff, it is irrelevant that the defendant took every precaution available. Although evidence of such precautions might prevent the plaintiff from recovering under a theory of negligence, it does not affect strict liability. Evidence of due care would, however, prevent an award of punitive damages. Adequate liability insurance is particularly important for companies engaged in ultrahazardous activities.

 # Damages

Tort damages generally attempt to restore the plaintiff to the same position he or she was in before the tort occurred. (In contrast, contract damages try to place the plaintiff in the position he or she would have been in had the contract been performed, as explained in Chapter 7.) Tort damages may include punitive as well as compensatory damages.

ACTUAL DAMAGES

Actual damages, also known as *compensatory damages,* measure the cost to repair or replace an item or the decrease in market value caused by the tortious conduct. Actual damages may also include compensation for medical expenses, lost wages, and pain and suffering.

PUNITIVE DAMAGES

Punitive damages, also known as *exemplary damages,* may be awarded to punish the defendant and deter others from engaging in similar conduct. Punitive damages are awarded only in cases of outrageous misconduct. The amount of punitive damages may properly be based on the defendant's wealth and, in most jurisdictions, must be proportional to the actual damages. Several states have limited punitive damages awards to situations in which the plaintiff can prove by clear and convincing evidence that the defendant was guilty of oppression, fraud, or malice.

As discussed in the "Political Perspective," the size and nature of some punitive damages awards have aroused controversy and led to calls by business leaders for legal reform to cap or eliminate punitive damages. Such enthusiasm, however, is largely limited to product liability cases, where businesses are defendants but rarely plaintiffs. In other areas, where businesses tend to be plaintiffs as well as defendants (such as contracts, unfair competition, and misleading advertising), reform of punitive damages appears to be less of a priority.[50]

 # Equitable Relief

If a monetary award cannot adequately compensate for the plaintiff's loss, courts may apply *equitable relief.* For example, the court may issue an *injunction,* that is, a court order, to prohibit the defendant from continuing a certain course of activity. This remedy is particularly appropriate for torts such as trespass or nuisance, when the plaintiff does not want the defendant's conduct to continue. The court may also issue an injunction ordering the defendant to take certain action. For example, a newspaper could be ordered to publish a retraction. In determining whether to grant injunctive relief, the courts will balance the hardship to the defendant against the benefit to the plaintiff.

 # Toxic Torts

Since the 1970s, tort law has been evolving in response to sustained social and political concerns over toxic substances and their potential for personal injury and environmental and property damage. When courts have been asked to adjudicate the disputes arising from the widespread use of toxic substances, the traditional tort rules for determining liability, measuring damages, and allocating them among the parties have not always provided ready answers. The resulting pressure for change has caused some courts to modify these rules and even to recognize new categories of damages.

DEFINITION

A *toxic tort* is a wrongful act that causes injury by exposure to a harmful, hazardous, or poisonous substance.

50. Richard B. Schmitt, *Why Businesses Sometimes Like Punitive Awards,* WALL ST. J., Dec. 11, 1995, at B1.

The Changing Tide *of* Tort Reform

The Traditional Arguments

For years, supporters and critics of the U.S. tort system have advanced largely unchanged arguments about the perceived need for tort reform.[a] Critics claim that the present tort system is unfairly expensive for defendants. Large and unpredictable jury awards have resulted in sharply higher liability insurance prices, which in turn (1) increase the cost of vital products and services, (2) stifle innovation in valuable but potentially dangerous products, and (3) render U.S. firms less equipped to compete with rivals abroad. Moreover, claim the critics, attorneys' fees and administrative costs are so extensive that less than half of the amount awarded by verdict or settlement is paid to injured plaintiffs.[b]

Supporters of the present tort system respond that it is the one place where the average citizen can battle the powerful on nearly equal terms. They claim that without the threat of lawsuits and their accompanying discovery process, large corporations would have every incentive to conceal harmful information about the effects of their products. The supporters believe that if any reform of the system is necessary, judicial review and self-policing would be more effective tools than legislation at either the state or the federal level.

Punitive Damages: Horror Stories and Calmer Studies

In recent years, the critics have asserted that the tort system has a random, Russian roulette flavor to it. To buttress this claim, they point to several recent cases in which juries have granted multimillion-dollar punitive damages awards to injured plaintiffs. These well-publicized horror stories include a $2.7 million award to a woman who spilled scalding-hot McDonald's coffee on her lap; a $4 million award against BMW for selling as new a car that had been damaged by acid rain and repainted;[c] and a $100 million award against General Motors in a case where the plaintiff, who was injured in a single-car accident, had admittedly consumed at least one beer and was not wearing a seatbelt.

Separate studies, however, have found that punitive damages awards are both

extremely rare and closely related to the size of compensatory damages. In a 1995 survey of the country's seventy-five most populous counties, the Department of Justice found that only 2 percent of the 762,000 cases even reached a jury. Plaintiffs won just over half of those cases, received punitive damages in just 6 percent of the cases they won, and received more than $50,000 in only half of all punitive awards.[d]

A similar study of forty-five populous counties found that punitive damages are not only less prevalent but also less random than often alleged.[e] The study found that when compensatory damages were $10,000, punitives averaged $10,860; when compensatory damages were $100,000, punitives averaged $65,720; and when compensatory damages were $1 million, punitives averaged $397,810.

Indeed, none other than the *Wall Street Journal* defended the multimillion-dollar award against McDonald's for its scalding coffee.[f] The *Journal* faulted McDonald's for serving its coffee at a significantly higher temperature than its competitors, for failing to respond to prior scalding incidents, and for mishandling the plaintiff's complaints by not apologizing.

Congressional Proposals Stalled

The movement to reform the tort system from the federal level gained momentum when the Republicans won control of both houses of Congress in 1994. House Republicans listed tort reform as Tenet Nine in their Contract with America. Although the House passed bills calling for a variety of tort reforms, they were significantly watered down by the Senate. Even the watered-down bill eventually approved by Congress was vetoed by President Bill Clinton in May 1996. Neither house was able to muster a two-thirds

vote to override. Not surprisingly, the veto proved an effective damper on the movement to reform tort law from Washington, especially after President Clinton won reelection in 1996. Advocates of reform expect President George W. Bush to be more supportive of future reform initiatives.

Reform at the State Level Proceeds

Interestingly, at the same time tort reform was stumbling in Washington, the states were actively passing legislation to curb perceived abuses. By August 1997, nearly all fifty states had some type of tort reform statute in place.

Thirty-four states had taken steps to eliminate joint and several liability for tort defendants.[g] Thirty-one states had either placed a cap on punitive damages or imposed evidentiary standards restricting their availability. State reforms, however, are not beyond challenge because they must comport with both state and federal constitutional requirements. At least seventy state courts have struck down attempts at reform on constitutional grounds.

a. *See, e.g.,* George Melloan, *Rule of Law or Rule of Lawyers?,* WALL ST. J., Nov. 21, 2000, at A27.
b. Philip Shuchman, *It Isn't That the Tort Lawyers Are So Right, It's Just That the Tort Reformers Are So Wrong,* 49 RUTGERS L. REV. 485 (1995).
c. The Alabama Supreme Court subsequently reduced this award to $2 million. BMW of North America, Inc. v. Gore, 646 So. 2d 619 (Ala. 1994). The U.S. Supreme Court then declared the $2 million award void as "grossly excessive" and unconstitutional. BMW of North America, Inc. v. Gore, 517 U.S. 559 (1996). On remand, the Alabama Supreme Court further reduced the award to $50,000. BMW of North America, Inc. v. Gore, 701 So. 2d 507 (Ala. 1997).
d. Richard C. Reuben, *Plaintiffs Rarely Win Punitives, Study Says,* 81 A.B.A. J. 26 (1995).
e. Edward Felsenthal, *Punitive Awards Are Called Modest, Rare,* WALL ST. J., June 17, 1996, at B2.
f. Andrea Gerlin, *A Matter of Degree: How a Jury Decided That a Coffee Spill Is Worth $2.9 Million,* WALL ST. J., Sept. 1, 1994.
g. The data in this paragraph are derived from information published by the American Tort Reform Association, <http://atra.org/atra/atri2c.htm>.

Modern industrial and consumer societies utilize these substances in a variety of ways, creating countless opportunities for toxic tort claims.

Potential toxic tort defendants include those manufacturers (1) that utilize substances that may injure an employee, a consumer, or a bystander; (2) whose processes emit hazardous by-products into the air or discharge them into a river; (3) whose waste material goes to a disposal site where it may migrate to the groundwater and contaminate nearby wells; or (4) whose product itself contains or creates substances that can injure. Liability is not limited to manufacturers, however. Everyday activities of governmental agencies, distribution services, and consumers may provide a basis for toxic tort claims. Some substances once thought safe, such as asbestos, have resulted in ruinous litigation when it was later established that they were harmful. Businesses and employers face lawsuits by their customers and employees for failure to provide premises free of harmful substances. Even financial institutions can be caught in the toxic tort net by becoming involved in the operations of a business handling hazardous materials or by buying contaminated land at a foreclosure sale.

EXPENSIVE TO DEFEND

Toxic tort claims are among the most difficult and expensive of lawsuits to defend or prosecute. Expert witness costs alone can run into the millions for a single case. Toxic tort claims are also difficult to evaluate and, as a consequence, often cannot be insured against at a reasonable cost. Cause-and-effect relationships are difficult to establish because of disagreement within the medical and scientific communities. Nonetheless, plaintiff attorneys are introducing new medical studies, such as a recent article in the *New England Journal of Medicine* that found a link between urban air pollution and higher mortality rates among people with heart disease and respiratory illnesses, as evidence to establish a relationship between diseases suffered by claimants and long-term exposure to environmental contaminants. Lawyers are also looking to strategies used in the tobacco litigation to prove their cases, such as introducing evidence that the manufacturers knew about harm caused to human health by the pollutants they were producing.

When illness or injury does occur, it often arises years after exposure began. Because exposures causing the injury can accumulate from a multitude of sources, including food, air, water, and skin contact, it is difficult to allocate blame among the various possible sources.

Open-ended claims for punitive damages are commonplace in toxic tort cases. For example, in June 2000, the city of Santa Monica filed a property damage suit against eighteen oil companies seeking more than $200 million in compensatory and punitive damages for contamination of groundwater used for drinking by the gasoline additive methyl tertiary butyl ether.[51] The city alleged negligence, trespass, nuisance, and unfair competition.

STRICT LIABILITY

Some courts have held hazardous-waste disposal to be an ultrahazardous activity and have imposed strict liability for injuries resulting from it. For instance, in *Sterling v. Velsicol Chemical Corp.*,[52] the Sixth Circuit Court of Appeals held that the operator of a waste-burial site for toxic material will be responsible for all resulting contamination under the doctrine of strict liability for ultrahazardous activities.

The federal Comprehensive Environmental Response, Compensation and Liability Act of 1980 (CERCLA) embodies this strict liability doctrine, as do many state statutes that largely mirror the provisions of CERCLA. CERCLA imposes strict liability for cleanup costs on (1) the current owner or operator of the property, (2) the owner or operator at the time the hazardous substance was discharged, and (3) the parties responsible for transporting and disposing of the waste.

In *Farm Bureau Mutual Insurance Co. v. Porter & Heckman, Inc.*,[53] the Court of Appeals of Michigan considered whether Porter & Heckman, the company that serviced an outdoor, aboveground heating-oil tank, was liable for the water and soil contamination caused by oil leaking from the tank. The plaintiff argued that because Porter & Heckman was in the business of servicing equipment containing a hazardous substance (the heating oil), it should be strictly liable for any damage attributable to the oil.

The Michigan Court of Appeals analyzed Farm Bureau's claim under Michigan's Environmental Response Act, which states that a defendant will be held strictly liable for contamination damage if (1) it is an operator of a facility that deals in hazardous substances or (2) it otherwise arranges for the disposal of a hazardous substance. As for the "operator" claim, the court ruled that a defendant is an operator only if it has authority to control the area where the hazardous substances are located. One who services a system does not automatically control the operation of the system. Thus, Porter & Heckman was

51. Santa Monica v. Shell Oil Co., Cal. Super. Ct., San Francisco, No. 313004, June 20, 2000.
52. 855 F.2d 1188 (6th Cir. 1988).
53. 560 N.W.2d 367 (Mich. Ct. App. 1996).

not liable as an "operator" merely because it serviced the heating-oil tank. Nor was it liable as an "arranger for disposal." The court ruled that this portion of the statute required an intent to dispose of the hazardous substance, as well as some ownership of or authority to control the actual substance. Here, Porter & Heckman had the intent and authority only to repair the heating-oil tank, not to dispose of or control the oil itself.

NEW THEORIES OF DAMAGES

Under traditional tort principles, toxic tort plaintiffs who prove exposure to a toxic substance and a defendant's liability for that exposure may still not receive a damage award because the rules require proof of an actual injury. The plaintiffs may be at risk of developing cancer or some other disease in the future, but tort law generally has not allowed recovery for risk of future disease unless some precursor symptom is present, or unless the plaintiffs prove they are more likely than not to get the disease. In the face of these limitations on damages, courts are being asked to allow awards for emotional distress in the absence of either physical symptoms or an intentional tort.

In *Sterling*, the trial judge who found Velsicol Chemical strictly liable also awarded compensatory damages to individuals who had consumed contaminated well water. The trial court awarded damages for physical symptoms caused by drinking the well water and also gave awards for increased risk of cancer, fear of increased risk of cancer, impairment of the immune system, and a psychological ailment known as posttraumatic stress disorder. The trial judge also awarded damages for impairment of the residents' quality of life, under the traditional tort of nuisance, and punitive damages.

Applying Tennessee law, the U.S. Court of Appeals for the Sixth Circuit disallowed the award for increased risk of cancer because no expert had testified that there was more than a 50 percent chance the plaintiffs would develop cancer. The awards for impairment of the immune system and for posttraumatic stress disorder were also thrown out on the ground that the medical evidence was insufficient. The award for fear of increased risk of cancer was allowed but was reduced to a fixed annual sum multiplied by the number of years of exposure. This limited measure of damages for fear of future cancer is unusual and may not be applied in other states.

Another novel remedy that is being urged is the award of damages to cover the future cost of medical monitoring in order to detect the disease at the onset, when treatment may be more effective.

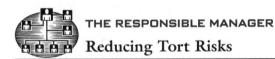

THE RESPONSIBLE MANAGER
Reducing Tort Risks

Managers should implement ongoing programs of education and monitoring to reduce the risks of tort liability. Because torts can be committed in numerous ways, the programs should cover all possible sources of liability. For example, the management of a company that does not respond satisfactorily to an allegation of sexual harassment may be liable for intentional infliction of emotional distress. Statements made by representatives of a company about some individual or product can constitute defamation.

In addition to preventing intentional torts, managers should work to prevent their employees from committing acts of negligence, which can lead to large damage awards against the company. Any tort-prevention program must recognize that under the principle of *respondeat superior,* employers will be held liable for any torts their employees commit in the scope of their employment. It is crucial, therefore, to define the scope of employment clearly.

Managers should use care to avoid committing torts that are related to contractual relations and competition with other firms. For example, a company may be held liable for interference with contractual relations if a court finds that the company intentionally tried to induce a party to breach a contract. Also, although competition itself is permissible, intentionally seeking to sabotage the efforts of another firm is not. Managers may need to consult counsel when they are unsure whether their activity has crossed the line from permissible competition to tortious interference with a prospective business advantage.

The prudent manager should keep abreast of developments in the emerging area of toxic tort law and strive to reduce the risk of liability for toxic substances used or distributed in his or her enterprise. Managers should adopt a long-term policy to protect employees, customers, and the environment from excess toxic exposure. They should identify any hazardous toxic substances used in their business activities or products or released into the environment. Where appropriate, managers should test and monitor to determine levels of exposure. Often it is necessary to obtain an expert assessment of the hazards of toxicity of these substances. Managers should develop a plan to control and reduce toxic exposure. This can be done by reducing the quantity of toxic substances used, by recycling, by seeking less toxic alternatives, and by educating and training employees. Managers should implement a plan by assigning responsibilities, allocating resources, and auditing compliance. The waste-management plan should include criteria for choosing third-party contractors. Insurance should be obtained, if available, and coverage should be reviewed periodically. Management should adopt a contingency plan for responding to toxic accidents and develop a public relations plan both for routine (that is, safe) use of toxic substances and for possible toxic accidents.

A program of overall risk management and reduction is essential to limit the potential of tort liability. It is often desirable to designate one person to be in charge of risk management. That person should keep track of all claims and determine what areas of the business merit special attention. The head of risk management should be free to report incidents and problems to the chief executive officer and the board of directors, in much the same way as an internal auditor reports directly to the independent directors on the audit committee. This enhances independence and reduces the fear of reprisals if the risk manager blows the whistle on high-ranking managers.

INSIDE STORY

Genetically Modified Food Litigation

When Monsanto first introduced genetically modified (GM) seeds to the market in 1996, they seemed to be a solution to the problem of using environmentally harmful pesticides to grow crops. With ordinary seeds, farmers must plow and spray for weeds and pests three or four times a year—twice that often for cotton. Not only is plowing labor intensive, but it also damages the topsoil. In addition, every weed requires a separate chemical, so spraying insecticide is both expensive and environmentally harmful because toxic runoff from the farms pollutes rivers and streams. With Monsanto's Roundup Ready seeds, which are resistant to Monsanto's herbicide Roundup, a farmer can spray Roundup only once, and it will kill all the weeds and pests without harming the Roundup Ready seeds. Monsanto also invented and patented Yieldgard, which causes corn to produce its own internal pesticide.[54]

Monsanto's GM seeds were initially popular with farmers, particularly in the United States, which, as of early 2000, accounted for approximately 75 percent of worldwide GM crops. From 1997 to 1998, use of Monsanto's GM seeds increased from 18 million to 57 million acres. More acres were sown with Monsanto's GM seeds than with the seeds of all of its competitors combined.[55] In 1999, GM crop acreage grew by 44 percent throughout the world. As of early 2000, 55 percent of U.S. soybeans and 33 percent of U.S. corn were genetically modified; most of these crops were grown from Monsanto seeds and sprayed with Monsanto's Roundup herbicide.[56]

After the initial excitement about Monsanto's biotech breakthrough, concerns arose about the safety of bioengineered food. Results from a Cornell University study showed that monarch butterfly caterpillars died after eating pollen from genetically modified corn. Environmentalists and consumers became concerned that GM foods could have a destructive impact on the environment and people's health. Critics argued that GM food could produce mutant pollens that would be harmful to beneficial insects and neighboring plants and also aggravate human allergies.[57] European consumers were the first to protest against the use of GM foods, but American consumers soon followed in boycotting products made from GM foods.

On December 14, 1999, five farmers from Iowa and Indiana, an organic farmer from France, the Foundation on Economic Trends, and the National Family Farm Coalition filed a class-action suit against Monsanto in the U.S. District Court in Washington D.C., alleging that Monsanto introduced GM crops without ensuring that they were safe for the environment and consumers. The National Farmers Union, the American Soybean Associ-

---

54. Peter Huber, *Ecological Eugenics*, WALL ST. J., Dec. 21, 1999, at 12.
55. Alex Lightman, *Monsanto: Reversal of Fortune*, RED HERRING, Mar. 1, 2000.

56. *Id.*
57. Mitchel Benson, *Foods Altered Genetically Face Labeling*, WALL ST. J., Dec. 22, 1999, at CA1.

ation, and the American Farm Bureau Federation (several of the biggest U.S. farm organizations) chose not to participate in the suit. The director of production of the National Corn Growers Association commented that "this [lawsuit] doesn't represent mainstream farmers."[58] Several months after the class action was initiated, twenty law firms were involved in representing the class and were seeking millions in damages in at least thirty countries in which GM seeds were sold.[59]

The class-action complaint alleges that

> Monsanto's lack of sufficient testing of GM seed for human health and environmental safety has caused the rejection of GM crops at market, and has thus reduced the value of farmers' crops and threatened the economic vitality of farmers' businesses, especially those of the American family farmer and small farmers in developing countries.[60]

The complaint also alleges that Monsanto should have tested its genetically modified corn in other countries to determine if the bioengineered corn could be harmful in different climates and soil types. It also accuses Monsanto of fraud on the grounds that the company allegedly made deceptive statements or omissions concerning the testing and approval of GM foods.

Plaintiffs may have difficulty proving that Monsanto performed insufficient testing. In 1992, the Food and Drug Administration ruled that GM foods pose no risk to human health and do not need to be specially labeled. In fact, several studies suggest that GM corn may be safer to eat than ordinary corn because insect pests are less likely to pierce GM corn kernels; this reduces the risk of infestation by a fungus that produces aflatoxin, a natural carcinogen.[61] Even if GM food is not a danger to human health, however, it may be disruptive to the environment. (Monsanto is now part of Pharmacia Corporation, having merged with Pharmacia & Upjohn in March 2000.)

Before the class action is resolved, consumers' fears regarding GM foods may ultimately put an end to their widespread use. Major food companies, such as Gerber (the baby-food maker) and Kirin (the Japanese brewer), have stopped using GM foods.[62] PepsiCo's Frito Lay unit has told farmers who supply corn for its products to plant seeds that have not been genetically modified. Archer Daniels Midland, the world's largest grain producer, has begun paying farmers more for grain that is not genetically modified.[63] The two largest natural-food chains, Wild Oats Markets and Whole Foods Market, have also stopped using GM ingredients in their brands.[64]

In November 1999, legislation was introduced in Congress to require mandatory labeling of genetically engineered food.[65] Efforts were also under way in California to introduce legislation that would require labeling of GM food. The California Farm Bureau Federation opposed mandatory labeling on the grounds that it would increase the costs of food and unnecessarily frighten consumers.[66]

58. Scott Kilman, *Monsanto Is Sued over Genetically Altered Crops*, WALL ST. J., Dec. 15, 1999, at A3.
59. Lightman, *supra* note 55.
60. Kathleen Hart, *Six Farmers File Class-Action Lawsuit Against Monsanto over Genetically Engineered Corn and Soybeans*, FOOD CHEMICAL NEWS, Dec. 20, 1999.

61. David Stipp, *Is Monsanto's Biotech Worth Less than a Hill of Beans?*, FORTUNE, Feb. 21, 2000, at 157.
62. *Id.*
63. Lightman, *supra* note 55.
64. Stipp, *supra* note 61.
65. Benson, *supra* note 57.
66. *Id.*

KEY WORDS AND PHRASES

absolute privilege 277
actual cause 299
actual damages 308
actual intent 274
actual malice 279
aided-in-the-agency doctrine 307
appropriation of a person's name or
   likeness 281
assault 275
assumption of risk 302
attractive nuisance 292
battery 275

comparative negligence 302
compensatory damages 308
contribution 307
contributory negligence 302
conversion 282
deceit 285
defamation 276
disparagement 284
equitable relief 308
exemplary damages 308
false imprisonment 275
fiduciary duty 287

fraud 285
fraudulent misrepresentation 285
indemnification 307
injunction 308
injurious falsehood 284
intent 274
intentional infliction of emotional
   distress 276
interference with contractual relations
   286
interference with prospective business
   advantage 287

QUESTIONS AND CASE PROBLEMS

1. Linda was sole proprietor of Clowntown USA, a successful amusement park. The main attraction of the amusement park was a very steep and fast rollercoaster. Although Linda maintained the rollercoaster meticulously, she knew that it was unsafe for riders under four feet tall. Accordingly, she instructed her employee, Oliver, not to permit anyone less than four feet tall to ride on the rollercoaster. On a particularly busy day in June, Oliver forgot his instructions and allowed several children below four feet tall to ride on the rollercoaster. The children were thrown from the ride and suffered serious bodily injury.

   a. Under what doctrine could the children's parents sue Linda for damages? What would Linda's lawyer assert as a defense? Who would be likely to prevail?

   b. Would your answer change if Linda had merely told Oliver to be careful in operating the rollercoaster, without specifically telling him not to permit anyone under four feet tall to ride it?

   c. What additional defense could Linda assert if she could prove that the children's parents had read and understood a conspicuous sign posted at the rollercoaster ticket booth stating that the ride was dangerous for those under four feet tall and that anyone under that height rode at their own risk?

2. Williams, a 25-year-old owner of a Buick dealership who had worked his way up from lot boy, had relied on Security Pacific Bank for several years for financial advice. When Williams wanted to purchase a new dealership, Security Pacific suggested he purchase Viking. Viking was losing money and owed Security Pacific money. In the meantime, Security Pacific was seeking a bailout from its financial obligations. The bank withheld all of this information from Williams. Williams then suffered great financial hardship and eventually lost both dealerships after the bank refused to extend financing. Did Security Pacific commit a tort? Why or why not? [*Security Pacific Nat'l Bank v. Williams*, 262 Cal. Rptr. 260 (Cal. Ct. App. 1989)]

3. Joe, Alice, and their baby, Pearl, live in a house next to a closed city dump. Since they moved in five years ago, the only source of water for drinking, cooking, and bathing has been a well under the house. Last month, Joe discovered that the well was contaminated by small amounts of waste solvents leaking from the dump. Joe and Alice show no symptoms but worry that the contamination will eventually make them sick. Baby Pearl has a condition that may become leukemia, and Joe and Alice are concerned that future children may be harmed as well. As a result of stress caused by worrying about the effects of the contamination on themselves and their family, Joe and Alice begin to smoke and do so even while Alice is nursing Pearl. Joe and Alice learn that Big Corporation sent 5 percent of the solvents to the dump. Big has $10 million in insurance. Last year, Big shut down its local plant, laying off 2,000 employees. Ten percent of the solvents came to the dump from Small Company. Small dissolved last year. Its former owner, Bill Small, is worth $3 million. The other 85 percent of the solvents came from thousands of separate households and small

businesses throughout the city, all of which paid the city trash-collection fees.

Joe and Alice's lawyer discovers that ten years ago Big Corporation and Small Company received copies of federal regulations classifying the solvent wastes as hazardous. No one at Small Company bothered to read the regulations, and the solvents continued to be disposed of at the city dump. At Big Corporation, however, the environmental engineer issued orders that the solvents be sent to a hazardous-waste site instead of the city dump. However, no one was assigned to police the order, and about once a month some solvent went to the city dump by mistake. The environmental engineer reissued the orders twice after hearing of the mistakes, but occasional violations continued until the plant closed.

   a. What claims are likely to prevail in a suit against the city? Big Corporation? Small Company? Bill Small? The local dry cleaner?

   b. What torts can Pearl claim if she develops leukemia and lung cancer thirty years later? Against whom?

   c. Can Joe and his family recover punitive damages against any of the defendants?

   d. What additional facts would improve the chances of securing a large punitive damages award?

4. A golfer was struck by lightning during a golf game and suffered serious injuries. He sued the golf course for negligence, alleging that it had breached a duty of care to him by not protecting him from lightning strikes. The golf course had advised its members that it monitored weather channels and had procedures in place to notify golfers of inclement weather. What result under the traditional analysis? Under the reasonable care approach? [*Maussner v. Atlantic City Country Club, Inc.,* 691 A.2d 826 (N.J. Super. 1997)]

5. During one of his typical end-of-the-show presentations on *60 Minutes,* Andy Rooney discussed the many products that manufacturers send to him in the mail. While lamenting the vast amount of junk mail he receives, he mentioned Rain-X, a product that was sent to him by its inventor and manufacturer. The product was sent after Rooney had complained in another episode that he thought cars needed larger windshield wipers. Rooney then, on the air, said that he had tried the sample of Rain-X on his windshield and that it didn't work. Should the inventor/manufacturer be able to sue Andy Rooney for business disparagement? How about defamation? [*Unelko Corp. v. Rooney,* 912 F.2d 1049 (9th Cir. 1990), *cert. denied,* 499 U.S. 961 (1991)]

6. Drew Keys was vice president of sales for Broadcasters Media Service, Inc. On June 9, 1997, Keys took a medical leave of absence from the company, stating that he was having surgery and would not be able to work during his recuperation. During his medical leave, Broadcasters Media Service paid his full salary and maintained his benefits package. While on medical leave, Keys started his own company and used his knowledge of potential customers of Broadcasters Media to solicit and divert them to his new business. Broadcasters Media Service sued Keys for tortious interference with prospective business advantage. How should the court rule? [*Broadcasters Media Service, Inc. v. Keys,* 1999 U.S. Dist. LEXIS 16195 (N.D. Ill. Sept. 30, 1999)]

7. Mindis Metals sold acid-filled batteries to a battery-recycling facility. During the recycling process, lead from the batteries escaped from the facility. The resulting lead contamination caused both personal injuries and property damage to the facility's immediate neighbors. A neighbor sued Mindis under a theory of strict liability, arguing that because battery recycling is an ultrahazardous activity, Mindis was liable for all injuries and damages resulting therefrom. What result? [*Thompson v. Mindis Metals, Inc.,* 692 So. 2d 805 (Ala. 1997)]

8. Bruce Marecki, an employee of Crystal Rock Spring Water Company, attended a seminar sponsored by the company at a Ramada Inn. At the seminar, he drank several beers. After the seminar ended, he was planning to go to happy hour at the hotel but at a separate location from the seminar room. Instead, he left the motel to purchase cigarettes after discovering that the cigarette machine in the hotel was broken. While he was driving to a store to buy cigarettes, he rear-ended another car and caused injuries to the driver. The driver sued Crystal Rock Spring Water Company under the doctrine of *respondeat superior.* Should the company be liable for the injuries the driver suffered? What if Crystal Rock Spring Water did not supply the liquor at the seminar but allowed it to be served? What if Marecki had nothing to drink at the seminar but then drank at the happy hour with his coworkers and had an accident when he was driving home after the happy hour? What if the seminar was optional and Marecki had no obligation to attend? [*Sheftic v. Marecki,* 1999 Conn. Super. LEXIS 2953 (Conn. Oct. 22, 1999)]

9. Harold Tod Parrot was employed as vice president of sales by Capital Corporation, a privately held investment adviser. Parrot purchased 40,500 shares of Capital stock pursuant to a stock-purchase agreement

that provided that upon termination of Parrot's employment, the company would buy back these shares at fair market value. The fair market value was to be determined by the accounting firm Coopers & Lybrand, which had been retained by Capital Corporation. Several years after the stock purchase, Parrot was terminated; Capital Corporation sought to repurchase his shares at fair market value as established by Coopers & Lybrand in the company's most recent biannual report. Parrot objected to the price of the shares and sued both the company and its accountant. His complaint alleged professional negligence and negligent misrepresentation against Coopers & Lybrand. He argued that the accountants had changed the valuation methodology, at Capital's request, in order to reduce the price of the shares and, as a result, Parrot was induced to accept a lesser value for his stock. Did Coopers & Lybrand owe a duty to Parrot? [*Parrot v. Coopers & Lybrand, LLP,* 702 N.Y.S.2d 40 (2000)]

 MANAGER'S DILEMMA

10. *The New Yorker* published an article detailing a falling out among professors working on the Sigmund Freud archives. Masson, one of the professors, sued *The New Yorker* and the article's author for defamation, after the article quoted him referring to himself as an "intellectual gigolo." The author attributed the following quotation to Masson:

> Then I met a rather attractive older graduate student, and I had an affair with her. One day, she took me to some art event, and she was sorry afterward. She said, "Well, it is very nice sleeping with you in your room, but you're the kind of person who should never leave the room—you're just a social embarrassment anywhere else, though you do fine in your own room." And you know, in their way, if not in so many words, Eissler and Anna Freud told me the same thing. They like me well enough "in my own room." They loved to hear from me what creeps and dolts analysts are. I was like an intellectual gigolo—you get your pleasure from him, but you don't take him out in public. . . .

Tape recordings contained the substance of Masson's reference to the graduate student but no suggestion that Eissler or Anna Freud considered him, or that he considered himself, an "intellectual gigolo." Instead, on the tapes, Masson said:

> They felt, in a sense, I was a private asset but a public liability. . . . They liked me when I was alone in their living room, and I could talk and chat and tell them the truth about things, and they would tell me. But that I was, in a sense, much too junior within the hierarchy of analysts, for these important training analysts to be caught dead with me.

The author of the article argued that not all of the conversations were recorded. She explained that at times her tape recorder was broken. In addition, she claimed to have taken notes (which she later typed up) during conversations between the two of them while walking or traveling by car.

Assume that the author faithfully captured the substance of Masson's comments but that he never said the exact words in quotation marks attributed to him. Does the author's alteration or reconstruction of the actual language used rise to the level of "actual malice"? If so, do all such alterations, except technical corrections of grammar or syntax, demonstrate actual malice? How much proof should a manager/editor demand from his or her authors or reporters to substantiate direct quotations? [*Masson v. The New Yorker Magazine, Inc.,* 501 U.S. 496 (1991)]

INTERNET SOURCES

The Northern Illinois University page provides access to its 1995 study of the costs of the U.S. tort system.	http://www.icjl.org/data2/niu.htm
The Law Journal Extra page provides the text of recent judicial decisions dealing with tort law and a searchable database of verdicts and settlements.	http://www.ljextra.com/practice/intentionaltorts/
The Worldwide Legal Information Association page provides information about tort law around the world.	http://www.wwlia.org/tort2.htm
The British law firm of Sweet & Maxwell provides a collection of reports on professional negligence.	http://www.smlawpub.co.uk/journal/pnlr/
The New York law firm of Queller & Fisher maintains a page dedicated to issues of negligence, including recent decisions and publications, descriptions of legislation, and links to other Web sites.	http://www.quellerfisher.com/negli.html
The Alexander Law Firm of San Jose, California, maintains the Consumer Law Page to disseminate information about torts, especially personal injury.	http://consumerlawpage.com
The American Tort Reform Association hosts a page addressing various issues about tort reform, including information about states that have enacted tort reform measures and facts about the impact of tort liability on the economy.	http://www.atra.org
The Association of Trial Lawyers of America, a group of attorneys who represent plaintiffs in tort and consumer protection lawsuits, maintains a site with articles and news clippings regarding recent developments in tort litigation and reform.	http://www.atla.org

CHAPTER 10

Product Liability

DEFINITION OF PRODUCT LIABILITY

Product liability is the legal liability manufacturers and suppliers have for defective products that cause injury to the purchaser, a user or bystander, or their property. Liability extends to anyone in the chain of distribution: manufacturers, distributors, wholesalers, and retailers.

Today, most states in the United States have adopted strict product liability, whereby an injured person may recover damages without showing that the manufacturer was negligent or otherwise at fault. No contractual relationship between the manufacturer and the injured person is necessary. The injured person merely needs to show that the product was sold in a defective or dangerous condition and that the defect caused his or her injury.

CHAPTER OVERVIEW

This chapter discusses the evolution of the strict liability doctrine, beginning with its origin in warranty and negligence theories. It then focuses on the bases for strict liability, including manufacturing defect, design defect, and failure to warn. The chapter examines who may be held liable for defective products and the allocation of liability among multiple defendants. Defenses to a product liability claim are discussed, along with legislative reforms designed to correct perceived abuses in the system. Finally, the chapter describes the law of product liability in the European Union.

 Theories *of* Recovery

The primary theories on which a product liability claim can be brought are breach of warranty, negligence, and strict liability.

BREACH OF WARRANTY

In a warranty action, the reasonableness of the manufacturer's actions is not at issue. Rather, the question is whether the quality, characteristics, and safety of the product were consistent with the implied or express representations made by the seller. A buyer may bring a warranty action whenever the product fails to meet the standards that the seller represents to the buyer at the time of purchase.

UCC Warranties As explained in Chapter 8, a warranty may be either express or implied. An express warranty is an affirmation made by the seller relating to the quality of the goods sold. An implied warranty is created by law and guarantees the merchantability and, in some circumstances, the fitness for a particular purpose of the goods sold.

Privity of Contract A breach-of-warranty action is based on principles of contract law. In order to recover, an injured person must be in a contractual relationship with the seller. This requirement is known as *privity of* *contract.* It necessarily precludes recovery by those persons, such as bystanders, who are not in privity with the seller.

NEGLIGENCE

MacPherson, which follows, is the landmark case in which the defendant manufacturer was found liable for negligence even though there was no contractual relationship between the manufacturer and the plaintiff. Thus, one of the obstacles posed in breach-of-warranty actions—the requirement of privity of contract—was removed. Although liability was still based on the negligence principles of reasonableness and due care, *MacPherson*'s abandonment of the privity requirement made it an important forerunner to the doctrine of strict product liability.

A CASE IN POINT

CASE 10.1

MacPherson v. Buick Motor Co.

Court of Appeals of New York 111 N.E. 1050 (N.Y. 1916).

Summary

FACTS MacPherson purchased a new Buick car with wooden wheels from a Buick Motor Company dealer who had previously purchased the car from its manufacturer, Buick Motor Company. MacPherson was injured when the car ran into a ditch. The accident was caused by the collapse of one of the car's wheels due to defective wood used for the spokes. The wheel had been made by a manufacturer other than Buick.

MacPherson sued Buick Motor Company directly. He proved that Buick could have discovered the defects by reasonable inspection and that such an inspection had not been conducted. No claim was made that the manufacturer knew of the defect and willfully concealed it. After the trial court found in favor of MacPherson, Buick appealed.

ISSUE PRESENTED Can a consumer who purchases a product from a retailer sue the manufacturer directly for negligent manufacture of the product even though there is no contract *per se* between the consumer and the manufacturer?

SUMMARY OF OPINION The New York Court of Appeals held that Buick could be held liable for negligence. As a manufacturer, it owed a duty to any person who could foreseeably be injured as a result of a defect in an automobile it manufactured. A manufacturer's duty to inspect was held to vary with the nature of the thing to be inspected. The more probable the danger, the greater the need for caution. Because the action was one in tort for negligence, no contract between the plaintiff and the defendant was required.

RESULT The court of appeals affirmed the lower court's finding that the manufacturer, Buick Motor Company, was liable for the injuries sustained by the plaintiff. Buick was found negligent in not inspecting the wheels and was responsible for the finished product.

COMMENTS This case established the rule, still applicable today, that a manufacturer can be liable for failure to exercise reasonable care in the manufacture of a product when such failure involves an unreasonable risk of bodily harm to users of the product. This rule is embodied in Sections 1 and 2(a) of the Restatement (Third) of Torts: Product Liability (1997).[1]

1. This rule also appeared in the Restatement (Second) of Torts (1977) in Section 395.

To prove negligence in a products case, the injured party must show that the defendant did not use reasonable care in designing or manufacturing its product or in providing adequate warnings. This can be quite difficult to prove. Moreover, injured persons are often negligent themselves in their use or misuse of the product. This precludes recovery in a contributory negligence state and reduces recovery in a comparative negligence state.

A manufacturer can be found negligent even if the product met all regulatory requirements because, under some circumstances, a reasonably prudent manufacturer would have taken additional precautions.[2] As discussed later in this chapter, the only exception is when a federally mandated standard is deemed to have preempted state product liability law.[3]

Courts will not permit a plaintiff to prove negligence by introducing evidence of subsequent remedial measures taken by a defendant to improve a product. The public policy behind this rule is to encourage companies to continually strive to improve the safety of their products. If such safety measures could be used to establish legal liability, companies would be deterred from improving their products.

STRICT LIABILITY IN TORT

Strict liability in tort allows a person injured by an unreasonably dangerous product to recover damages from the manufacturer or seller of the product. Negligent conduct on the part of the manufacturer or seller is not required. Because the defect in the product is the basis for liability, the injured person may recover damages even if the seller has exercised all possible care in the manufacture and sale of the product.

In 1963, the California Supreme Court became the first state supreme court to adopt strict product liability. In *Greenman v. Yuba Power Products, Inc.,*[4] a consumer sued the manufacturer of a Shopsmith combination power tool that could be used as a saw, drill, and wood lathe after he was injured while using the machine. He also sued the retailer who had sold the power tool to his wife. Claiming that the tool was defective and not suitable to perform the work for which it was intended, Greenman sued the manufacturer and retailer for breach of express and implied warranties and for negligent construction of the tool. The California Supreme Court ruled that a manufacturer is strictly liable in tort when it places an article on the market, knowing that the article is to be used without inspection for defects, and the article proves to have a defect that causes injury to a human being.

Rationale The legal principle of strict product liability is grounded in considerations of public policy. The rationale has three basic parts: (1) the law should protect consumers against unsafe products; (2) manufacturers should not escape liability simply because they typically do not sign a formal contract with the end-user of their product (or with nonusers who might be injured by their product); and (3) manufacturers and sellers of products are in the best position to bear the costs of injuries caused by their products, because they can pass these costs on to all consumers in the form of higher prices. In short, the goal of strict product liability is to force companies to internalize the costs of product-caused injuries. The crafters of the doctrine recognized that it would give manufacturers an incentive to improve the safety of their products.

Elements of a Strict Liability Claim For a defendant to be held strictly liable, the plaintiff must prove that (1) the plaintiff, or his or her property, was harmed by the product; (2) the injury was caused by a defect in the product; and (3) the defect existed at the time it left the defendant and did not substantially change along the way. Most states have followed the formulation of Section 402A of the Restatement (Second) of Torts, which states:

1. One who sells any product in a defective condition unreasonably dangerous to the user or consumer or to his property is subject to liability for physical harm thereby caused to the ultimate user or consumer, or to his property, if
   a. the seller is engaged in the business of selling such a product, and
   b. it is expected to and does reach the user or consumer without substantial change in the condition in which it is sold.
2. The rule stated in Subsection (1) applies although
   a. the seller has exercised all possible care in the preparation and sale of his product, and the user or consumer has not bought the product from or entered into any contractual relation with the seller.

As discussed later in this chapter, the American Law Institute (ALI) promulgated the Restatement (Third) of Torts: Product Liability in 1997. The ALI is a body of lawyers and law professionals that periodically produces a restatement of various areas of the law (such as agency, contracts, and property). These restatements provide judges and lawyers with a comprehensive view of the status of American case law (drawn from a survey of courts throughout the country) and the rationale behind it. The restatements are, of course, infused with their drafters' vision of the way that a particular area of the law should evolve.

The Restatement (Third) imposes strict liability for manufacturing defects but not for design defects and defects based on inadequate instructions or warnings; instead, it opts for a standard that is predicated on

---

2. *See, e.g.,* Hasson v. Ford Motor Co., 650 P.2d 1171 (Cal. 1982).
3. *See, e.g.,* Kemp v. Medtronic, Inc., 231 F.3d 216 (6th Cir. 2000).
4. 377 P.2d 897 (Cal. 1963).

negligence. Although judges often regard the most recent restatement as persuasive authority and an accurate depiction of present case law, courts are free either to follow or to ignore the restatement's formulation. Because a majority of states still follow the Restatement (Second), the discussion that follows is, except as otherwise noted, based on that restatement. It remains to be seen whether in the future courts will broadly adopt the Restatement (Third) standard for defects in design, instructions, and warnings.

Strategy and Punitive Damages Although negligence and breach of warranty are alleged in most product liability cases, they play a secondary role compared to strict liability. Under strict liability, the injured person does not have the burden of proving negligence and does not have to be in privity with the seller. Thus, strict liability is easier to prove than either negligence or breach of warranty.

Nonetheless, plaintiffs' attorneys usually try to prove negligence as well as strict liability. Proof of negligence will often stir the jury's emotions, leading to higher damages awards and, in some cases, punitive damages. For example, in August 1999, the Florida Supreme Court upheld a $31 million punitive damages award against Owens-Corning Fiberglass Corporation, the manufacturer of an asbestos-containing product, after finding that the company showed "blatant disregard for human safety."[5] The plaintiff suffered from a rare lung disease following asbestos exposure. The trial court found that Owens-Corning had intentionally and knowingly misrepresented and concealed the dangers of asbestos for more than thirty years. The company had intentionally contaminated a new product with asbestos despite knowing that slight exposure to asbestos could cause the lung disease. Similarly, in May 2000, an Illinois jury found Shell Oil liable for asbestos exposure and awarded $34.1 million in compensatory and punitive damages to a former union worker who contracted lung disease after exposure.[6]

On the other hand, once the plaintiff has raised the issue of negligence, the defense can introduce evidence that its products were "state-of-the-art" and manufactured with due care. Such evidence would be irrelevant to the issue of strict liability and hence inadmissible.

Employee Memos and Testimony In a product liability case against General Motors Corporation (GM), internal documents written by a GM engineer in 1973 were key to the jury's award of $4.9 billion, one of the largest ever in a product liability case. Six people were burned when their 1979 Chevrolet Malibu exploded after its fuel tank was ruptured in an accident, and they sued GM. The plaintiffs introduced evidence revealing that GM had been aware of problems with the fuel tank but chose not to redesign it due to economic considerations. In one GM memo, an engineer estimated that each death from burns from a fuel-related fire in a GM vehicle would cost $200,000. Using that figure, the company calculated that claims for fuel tank–related deaths would cost GM $2.40 for every vehicle on the road. The memo concluded that "a human fatality is really beyond value, subjectively." The company also calculated that redesigning the car to reduce the fire risk would cost an additional $8.95, a greater cost than paying claims for deaths. Thus, the internal memos reflected that GM had made a business decision to put people at risk rather than correct the design problem at a higher cost to the company. GM tried to prevent the memo from being introduced at trial and, when it was produced, argued that it was irrelevant.

In another case, the U.S. Supreme Court permitted Robert Elwell, a former GM engineer, to testify in a product liability lawsuit brought against GM in Missouri, even though Elwell had previously agreed as part of an employment settlement with GM not to testify in any product liability suits against GM without the company's consent.[7] Missouri was not required to honor an injunction issued by a Michigan judge that prohibited Elwell from testifying against GM in any case. The Supreme Court held that Michigan had no authority to control other states' courts "by precluding them, in actions brought by strangers to the Michigan litigation, from determining for themselves what witnesses are competent to testify and what evidence is relevant and admissible in their search for the truth."

Defective Product

An essential element for recovery in strict liability is proof of a defect in the product. The injured party must show that (1) the product was defective when it left the hands of the manufacturer or seller and (2) the defect made the product unreasonably dangerous. Typically, a product is dangerous if it does not meet the consumer's expectations as to its characteristics. For example, a consumer expects that a stepladder will not break when someone stands on the bottom step. A product may be dangerous because of a manufacturing defect; a design

5. *$31 Million Punitive Award Upheld in Asbestos Case,* CORP. COUNS. WKLY., Oct. 6, 1999, at 7.
6. *Illinois Jury Awards Former Roofer $34 Million,* MEALEY'S LITIG. REP.: INSURANCE, May 23, 2000.

7. Baker v. General Motors Corp., 522 U.S. 222 (1998).

defect; or inadequate warnings, labeling, or instructions. It may also be an unavoidably unsafe product.

MANUFACTURING DEFECT

A *manufacturing defect* is a flaw in a product that occurs during production, such as a failure to meet the design specifications. A product with a manufacturing defect is not like the others rolling off the production line. For example, suppose the driver's seat in an automobile is designed to be bolted to the frame. If a worker forgets to tighten the bolts, the loose seat will be a manufacturing defect.

DESIGN DEFECT

A *design defect* occurs when, even though the product is manufactured according to specifications, its inadequate design or poor choice of materials makes it dangerous to users. Typically, there is a finding of defective design if the product is not safe for its intended or reasonably foreseeable use. In a highly publicized example, a jury found that the Ford Pinto was defectively designed because the car's fuel tank was too close to the rear axle, causing the tank to rupture when the car was struck from behind.

INADEQUATE WARNINGS, LABELING, OR INSTRUCTIONS

To avoid charges of *failure to warn*, a product must carry adequate warnings of the risks involved in the normal

use of the product. For example, the manufacturer of a ladder must warn the user not to stand on the top step. A product must also be accompanied by instructions for its safe use. For example, sellers have been found liable for failing to provide adequate instructions about the proper use and capacity of a hook and the assembly and use of a telescope and sun filter.

Although a warning can shield a manufacturer from liability for a properly manufactured and designed product, it cannot shield the manufacturer from liability for a *defectively* manufactured or designed product. For example, an automobile manufacturer cannot escape liability for defectively designed brakes merely by warning that "under certain conditions this car's brakes may fail." As will be explained later, however, some products, such as certain prescription drugs, are unavoidably unsafe. In cases involving such products, the adequacy of the warning determines whether the product, known to be dangerous, is also "defective."

Causation Requirement To prevail on a failure-to-warn claim, a plaintiff must show both that the defendant breached a duty to warn and that the defendant's failure to warn was the proximate cause (or legal cause) of the plaintiff's injuries. The question of proximate cause is one for the jury to determine. As a result, the vast majority of courts will not disturb jury findings that a failure to warn was the proximate cause of an injury. However, in an extreme case—one in which the court believes no reasonable person could have deemed the failure to warn a proximate cause of the plaintiff's injury—the court may set aside a verdict on causation grounds.

© 1996 Ted Goff

VIEW FROM CYBERSPACE

Jurisdiction *of* E-Commerce Disputes *in the* EU

As of November 2000, a fierce debate was under way in the European Union (EU) as to whether and under what circumstances consumers could bring suit in their national courts against companies based elsewhere selling products through Web sites. In 1968, the EU adopted the Brussels Convention, which determines which country has jurisdiction (that is, in which country suit may be brought) in cross-border disputes. With the rise of e-commerce and the resulting blurring of national boundaries toward a single market, the reach of the Brussels Convention became unclear.

By late 2000, the EU was in the process of trying to agree on the circumstances under which a consumer could sue a foreign Web site in national court.

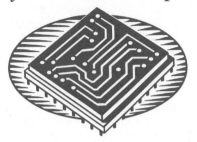

Some proponents argued that the ability to sue in national court would promote e-commerce growth by increasing consumer confidence. Opponents argued that fear of suit in other countries would discourage small and medium-sized businesses from setting up Web sites, thereby hindering growth in e-commerce. The European Parliament voted in September 2000 that jurisdiction in disputes be-

tween online buyers and sellers should be granted to the country of destination rather than the country of origin.[a] In November 2000, the European Commission approved the plan, making it EU policy to try e-commerce cases in the country of the purchaser.[b] Although consumer activists welcomed the action, one critic complained that the ruling "means we will still have 15 separate markets in the EU rather than one unified internal market, which I thought was the aim."[c]

a. Thomas Neyr, *European Parliament Deals E-Commerce a Blow*, DM News, Oct. 9, 2000.
b. Paul Meller, *Jurisdiction Dispute Heats Up in Europe*, Standard, Nov. 22, 2000.
c. Paul Meller, *Buyers Gain Online Rights in Europe, Effort Made to Lift Confidence in Web*, N.Y. Times, Dec. 1, 2000.

Bilingual Warnings The United States is a heterogeneous country. Diversity is one of its great strengths. With diversity can come challenges, however. Misunderstandings may arise due to differences in culture or language. Legislatures in states with substantial non-English-speaking populations have recognized the need for bilingual or multilingual documents in such areas as voting and public services. The following case addresses the need for bilingual warnings on nonprescription drugs.

A CASE IN POINT

CASE 10.2
Ramirez v. Plough, Inc.
Supreme Court of California
863 P.2d 167 (Cal. 1993).

Summary

FACTS In March 1986, when he was less than four months old, plaintiff Jorge Ramirez exhibited symptoms of a cold or similar upper respiratory infection. To relieve these symptoms, Ramirez's mother gave him St. Joseph's Aspirin for Children (SJAC), a nonprescription drug manufactured and distributed by Plough, Inc. The product label stated that the dosage for a child under two years old was "as directed by doctor." Moreover, the package displayed this warning:

> Warning: Reye Syndrome is a rare but serious disease which can follow flu or chicken pox in children and teenagers. While the cause of Reye Syndrome is unknown, some reports claim aspirin may increase the risk of developing this disease. Consult doctor before use in children or teenagers with flu or chicken pox.

The warnings were provided in English, although Plough was aware that Hispanics purchase the product. Ramirez's mother, who could read only Spanish, did not consult a doctor before using SJAC to treat Ramirez's condition. After two days, Ramirez's mother took him to a hospital, where the doctor advised her to administer Dimetapp or Pedialyte

(Continued)

(Case 10.2 continued)

(nonprescription medications that do not contain aspirin); she disregarded the advice and continued to treat Ramirez with SJAC. He thereafter developed the potentially fatal Reye syndrome, resulting in severe neurological damage, including cortical blindness, spastic quadriplegia, and mental retardation.

The plaintiff sued Plough, alleging that he contracted Reye syndrome as a result of ingesting SJAC. The plaintiff sought compensatory and punitive damages on, among other things, a theory of product liability. The complaint alleged that SJAC was defective when it left the defendant's control and that the product's reasonably foreseeable use involved a substantial and not readily apparent danger of which the defendant failed to warn adequately.

In finding no duty to warn and no causal relation between the defendant's actions and the plaintiff's illness, the trial court granted summary judgment for the defendant. On appeal, the court of appeal reversed because it found a duty to warn and felt that a jury question existed as to the adequacy of the necessary warning. The defendant appealed.

ISSUE PRESENTED May a manufacturer of nonprescription drugs that can lead to a deadly illness when taken as normally expected incur tort liability for distributing its products with warnings only in English despite the fact that the manufacturer knows that there are non-English-reading users?

SUMMARY OF OPINION The California Supreme Court began by noting that a manufacturer of nonprescription drugs has a duty to warn purchasers about dangers of its products. The issue under consideration was whether the defendant's duty to warn required it to provide label or package warnings in Spanish.

The court acknowledged that the Food and Drug Administration (FDA) encourages labeling that meets the needs of non-English speakers but only requires manufacturers to provide full labeling in English for all nonprescription drugs except those distributed solely in Puerto Rico or another territory where the predominant language is not English.

The court also emphasized that although the California legislature has enacted laws to protect non-English speakers in certain circumstances, there is no law in California requiring labeling in a foreign language. Because the state and federal statutes expressly require only English labeling, the court decided not to intrude upon a matter best handled by the legislature and adopted the existing legislative and administrative standard of care on the issue.

RESULT Because both state and federal laws require warnings in English but not in any other language, a manufacturer is not liable in tort for failing to label a nonprescription drug with warnings in a language other than English. Ramirez's case was dismissed.

COMMENTS The California Supreme Court was influenced by the experience of FDA-mandated Spanish inserts for prescription drugs. Recognizing that "the United States is too heterogeneous to enable manufacturers, at reasonable cost and with reasonable simplicity, to determine exactly where to provide alternative language inserts," the FDA for a time required manufacturers, as an alternative to multilingual or bilingual inserts, to provide Spanish-language translations of their patient package inserts to doctors and pharmacists on request. The FDA later concluded that manufacturers were having difficulty obtaining accurate translations, and eventually it abandoned altogether the patient package insert requirement for prescription drugs.

QUESTIONS

1. Should the result be different if the nonprescription medicine is for an illness particular to a certain non-English-speaking group residing in the United States?
2. Does it make a difference if a particular medicine is advertised in a language other than English?

UNAVOIDABLY UNSAFE PRODUCT

If the societal value of using an inherently dangerous product outweighs the risk of harm from its use, the manufacturer may be exonerated from liability for sale of such an *unavoidably unsafe product*. For example, certain drugs are generally beneficial but are known to have harmful side effects in some cases. The authors of the Restatement (Second) of Torts recognized that there should be a separate concept of product liability for manufacturers of prescription drugs. Nearly every jurisdiction in the United States has followed the reasoning of the Restatement (Second) in some form or another.[8]

For example, in a 1986 case, the plaintiff had contracted polio from the Sabin oral polio vaccine. The odds of contracting polio from the vaccine are one in a million. The Kansas Supreme Court held that harm resulting from the use of a drug would not give rise to strict liability if it was "unavoidably unsafe," that is, if its benefits outweighed its dangers, and if proper warnings were given.[9]

Comment b to Section 6 of the Restatement (Third) of Torts reflects a similar view of product liability for manufacturers of prescription drugs:

> The traditional refusal by courts to impose tort liability for defective designs of prescription drugs and medical devices is based on the fact that a prescription drug or medical device entails a unique set of risks and benefits. What may be harmful to one patient may be beneficial to another. Under Subsection (c) [of Section 6] a drug is defectively designed only when it provides no net benefit to any class of patients. . . . [M]anufacturers must have ample discretion to develop useful drugs and devices without subjecting their design decisions to the ordinary test applied to products generally.[10]

DEFINITION OF PRODUCT

Strict liability in tort applies only to products, not services. What qualifies as a *product* is sometimes not clear. In some cases, it is unclear whether an injury was caused by a defective product or a negligently performed service. For example, a person may be injured by a needle used by a dentist or the hair solution used by a beautician. Some courts apply strict liability in these situations. Other courts will not go so far down the chain of distribution.

ETHICAL CONSIDERATION

Do publishers have an ethical obligation to warn readers that information in a book is not complete and should not be relied on?

Courts that have addressed the definition-of-product question have required that the thing giving rise to liability be a tangible item. In *Winter v. G.P. Putnam's Sons*,[11] the plaintiffs were mushroom enthusiasts who purchased a book entitled *The Encyclopedia of Mushrooms*, which was published by the defendant. The plaintiffs relied on descriptions in the book to determine which wild mushrooms were safe to eat, then became critically ill after eating a poisonous variety. The court rejected the plaintiffs' strict product liability claim because the "product" involved was a collection of ideas and expressions, not a tangible item. The court reasoned that a high value should be placed on the unfettered exchange of ideas and that the threat of strict liability on the contents of books could seriously inhibit that exchange.

Massachusetts extended this "tangible item" requirement to the promotion of a sport or game. The plaintiff in *Garcia v. Kusan, Inc.*[12] was an elementary school student who was hit in the eye by a wayward stick in a floor hockey game in a physical education class. He claimed that Kusan marketed the sport of floor hockey to elementary schools and then sold them the equipment necessary to play. Garcia did not argue that the stick was defective; instead he argued that the game of floor hockey itself (as marketed by Kusan) was defective. Garcia referred the court to an old Kusan floor hockey instruction manual, which stated that the game required no protective equipment. The court, citing the rationale of *Winter*, entered summary judgment for Kusan. It reasoned that a game—the concept and instructions—could not constitute a "product" that would give rise to product liability; the necessary "tangible item" was lacking.

In the following case, the court considered whether a telephone pole installed in the ground was a product.

11. 938 F.2d 1033 (9th Cir. 1991).
12. 655 N.E.2d 1290 (Mass. App. Ct. 1995).

8. *See* RESTATEMENT (SECOND) OF TORTS § 402A cmt. k (1997).
9. Johnson v. American Cyanamid Co., 718 P.2d 1318 (Kan. 1986).
10. RESTATEMENT (THIRD) OF TORTS: PRODUCT LIABILITY § 6 cmt. b (1997).

A CASE IN POINT

CASE 10.3

Bell v. T.R. Miller Mill Co.
*Supreme Court of Alabama
Prod. Liab. Rep. (CCH) ¶15,
743 (Feb. 4, 2000).*

In the Language of the Court

FACTS On August 12, 1995, Jasmine Bell and her two children, Jasmarie and Jason, were driving in their car on a highway. A van parked on a driveway near the highway rolled down a hill and struck a guy-wire attached to a telephone pole. The telephone pole broke, causing the telephone lines to sag down over the highway and strike Bell's car. The lines lifted Bell's car into the air. When the car landed on its back, Jasmarie was ejected; she subsequently died.

Jasmine Bell filed a wrongful-death action under the Alabama Extended Manufacturer's Liability Doctrine (AEMLD) against T.R. Miller Mill Company, the manufacturer of the telephone pole, claiming that the pole had been defective and unreasonably dangerous. At the end of Bell's case at trial, Miller filed a motion for directed verdict, which the court granted. Bell appealed.

ISSUE PRESENTED Is a telephone pole installed in the ground a "product" for purposes of establishing product liability?

OPINION MADDOX, J., writing for the Alabama Supreme Court:

We first consider whether a telephone pole that has been installed in the ground is a "product" for purposes of the AEMLD. Miller, citing *Wells v. Clowers Constr. Co.*,[13] argues that, because the telephone pole was installed in the ground and was securely attached to the land, it was a structural improvement and, as such, cannot be classified as a "product." . . . The plaintiff states that since it decided the *Wells* case this Court has decided several cases, under the AEMLD doctrine, that involved products that had a more permanent connection to real estate than did the telephone pole in this case. She cites *Beam v. Tramco, Inc.*[14] (involving a conveyor belt installed in a grain-storage facility); *Sears, Roebuck & Co. v. Harris*[15] (gas water heater in a home); *McDaniel v. French Oil Mill Mach. Co.*[16] (cylindrical rotary soybean conditioner located in a soybean extraction facility); and *King v. S.R. Smith, Inc.*[17] (diving board that had been installed with an in-ground, vinyl-lined swimming pool).

Although we note that a number of jurisdictions adhere to the general rule upon which Miller's argument is based, namely that structural improvements to real property are not considered products for purposes of products-liability actions, we believe that a review of our cases applying AEMLD law involving products that have been affixed to real property shows that the policies underlying the application of the AEMLD doctrine have little relation to the policies underlying the fixtures doctrine, and that the application of products-liability law should not be totally dependent upon the intricacies of real-property law. Consequently, based upon the facts of this case, we hold that, although the telephone pole here was installed in the ground and was attached to the property, it did not by that fact lose its character as a "product" for purposes of the AEMLD.

RESULT The Supreme Court of Alabama found that a telephone pole was a "product." The directed verdict in favor of the defendant was reversed.

QUESTIONS

1. What are the policies underlying extended manufacturer liability?
2. Should the builder of a house be strictly liable for any defects?

13. 476 So. 2d 105 (Ala. 1985).
14. 655 So. 2d 979 (Ala. 1995).
15. 630 So. 2d 1018 (Ala. 1993).
16. 623 So. 2d 1146 (Ala. 1993).
17. 578 So. 2d 1285 (Ala. 1991).

Who May Be Liable

In theory, each party in the chain of distribution may be liable: manufacturers, distributors, wholesalers, and retailers. Manufacturers of component parts are frequently sued as well.

MANUFACTURERS

A manufacturer will be held strictly liable for its defective products regardless of how remote the manufacturer is from the final user of the product. The only requirement for strict liability is that the manufacturer be in the business of selling the injury-causing product. The manufacturer may be held liable even when the distributor makes final inspections, corrections, and adjustments of the product.

WHOLESALERS

Wholesalers are usually held strictly liable for defects in the products they sell. In some jurisdictions, however, a wholesaler is not liable for latent or hidden defects if the wholesaler sells the products in exactly the same condition it received them.

RETAILERS

A retailer may also be held strictly liable. For example, in the automobile industry, retailers have a duty to inspect and care for the products. In several jurisdictions, however, a retailer will not be liable if it did not contribute to the defect and played no part in the manufacturing process.

SELLERS OF USED GOODS AND OCCASIONAL SELLERS

Sellers of used goods are usually not held strictly liable because they are not within the original chain of distribution of the product. In addition, the custom in the used-goods market is that there are no warranties or expectations relating to the quality of the products (although some jurisdictions have adopted rules requiring warranties for used cars). A seller of used goods is, however, strictly liable for any defective repairs or replacements he or she makes. Occasional sellers, such as people who host garage sales, are not strictly liable.

A maker of component parts to manufacturer's specifications is not liable if the specifications for the entire product are questioned; instead, such a shortcoming is considered a design defect. For example, the maker of a car's fuel-injection system will not be liable if the automaker's specifications for the fuel-injection system

turn out to be defective because the engine provides insufficient power to change lanes safely on a freeway. Makers of component parts are liable for manufacturing defects, however.

SUCCESSOR LIABILITY

A corporation purchasing or acquiring the assets of another is liable for its debts if there is (1) a consolidation or merger of the two corporations or (2) an express or implied agreement to assume such obligations. Successor liability also exists in situations where (1) the purchasing corporation is merely a continuation of the selling corporation or (2) the transaction was entered into to escape liability.[18]

Thus, the acquiring corporation can be liable to a party injured by a defect in the transferor corporation's product. For example, a corporation that acquired all of a truck manufacturing company's assets was held liable for an injury caused by a defect in one of that company's trucks.[19] The court reasoned that the new company was essentially a continuation of the predecessor corporation and that the acquiring corporation was in a better position to bear and allocate the risk than the consumer.

MARKET-SHARE LIABILITY

When there are multiple manufacturers of identical products, the injured party may not be able to prove which of the defendant manufacturers caused the injury. In certain cases, particularly those involving prescription drugs, the court may allocate liability on the basis of each defendant's share of the market. This doctrine of *market-share liability* was developed by the California Supreme Court in *Sindell v. Abbott Laboratories*[20] to address the specific problem of DES litigation.

Women whose mothers took the drug diethylstilbestrol (DES) during pregnancy alleged that they were injured by the DES, which, among other things, increased their likelihood of developing cancer. They sought damages from a number of DES manufacturers. Many of the plaintiffs could not pinpoint which manufacturer was directly responsible for their injuries.

A number of factors made it difficult to identify particular DES manufacturers. All manufacturers made DES from an identical chemical formula. Druggists typically filled prescriptions from whatever stock they had on hand. During the twenty-four years that DES was sold

18. Conway *ex rel.* Roadway Express, Inc. v. White Trucks, 639 F. Supp. 160 (M.D. Pa. 1986).
19. *Id.*
20. 607 P.2d 924 (Cal. 1980), *cert. denied*, 449 U.S. 912 (1980).

for use during pregnancy, more than three hundred companies entered and left the market. The harmful effects of DES were not discovered until many years after the plaintiffs' mothers had used the drug.

By the time the lawsuit was filed, memories had faded, records had been lost, and witnesses had died. Given the difficulty of pinpointing the defendant responsible for each plaintiff, the court held that the fairest way was to apportion liability based on each manufacturer's national market share.

The New York Court of Appeals followed California's lead in *Hymowitz v. Eli Lilly & Co.*[21] The *Hymowitz* court stressed that "the DES situation is a singular case, with manufacturers acting in a parallel manner to produce an identical, generally marketed product, which causes injury many years later." Given this unusual scenario, the court reasoned, it was more appropriate that the loss be borne by those who produced the drug than by those who suffered injury.

In *Brenner v. American Cyanamid Corp.*,[22] the Supreme Court of New York, Appellate Division, refused to apply market-share liability in a lead poisoning case when the manufacturer of the lead pigment that caused the lead poisoning could not be determined. Twenty percent of the lead pigments found in the paints could have been manufactured by defendants not named in the litigation. In addition, the plaintiffs were unable to identify the particular years in which paint was applied to their house, making it impossible to determine which defendants manufactured paint during the relevant time period. Furthermore, lead-based paint was not a fungible product; different paints contained varying amounts of lead pigments—unlike DES, all of which had an identical chemical composition. Finally, the court found that there was no signature injury in lead poisoning cases, making it impossible to determine whether the plaintiff's injuries were caused by some other source besides lead. Thus, market-share liability was considered an inappropriate basis for recovery.

Market-share liability has been rejected in many jurisdictions. It has been criticized for being a simplistic response to a complex problem and for implying that manufacturers must be the insurers of all their industry's products. Market-share liability has also been challenged on the constitutional ground that it violates a defendant's right to due process of law because it denies the defendant

the opportunity to prove that its individual products did not cause the plaintiff's injury.

PREMISES LIABILITY

Recently, courts have recognized liability for asbestos-related diseases on a *premises liability* theory. Under this theory, a building owner may be found liable for violating its general duty to manage the premises and warn of asbestos dangers.[23]

Defenses

The defendant in a product liability case may raise the traditional tort defenses of assumption of risk and, in some jurisdictions, a variation of comparative negligence known as comparative fault. Other defenses, such as obvious risk, unforeseeable misuse of the product, the statute of limitations, the government-contractor defense, and the state-of-the-art defense, apply only to product liability cases. Acceptance of these defenses varies from state to state. Finally, under certain circumstances state product liability law is preempted by federal law.

ASSUMPTION OF RISK

Under the doctrine of *assumption of risk,* when a person voluntarily and unreasonably assumes the risk of a known danger, the manufacturer is not liable for any resulting injury. For example, if a ladder bears a conspicuous warning not to stand on the top step, but a person steps on it anyway and falls, the ladder manufacturer will not be liable for any injuries caused by the fall.

In a leading case in this area, a Washington appellate court found no assumption of risk when a grinding disc exploded and hit a person in the eye.[24] The court reasoned that although the injured person should have been wearing goggles, he could not have anticipated that a hidden defect in the disc would cause it to explode. By not wearing goggles, the injured person assumed only the risk of dust or small particles of wood or metal lodging in his eyes.

In the following case, the court addressed the issue of when an employee will be deemed to have assumed the risk of injury while working on the job.

21. 539 N.E. 2d 1069 (N.Y. 1989), *cert. denied,* 493 U.S. 944 (1989).
22. 263 A.D.2d 165 (N.Y. 1999).

23. *CA App. Ct. Reverses Exxon Nonsuit Ruling,* ASBESTOS LITIG. REP., July 16, 1999.
24. Haugen v. Minnesota Mining & Mfg. Co., 550 P.2d 71 (Wash. Ct. App. 1976).

CASE 10.4

Crews v. Hollenbach

Court of Appeals of Maryland
751 A.2d 481 (Md. 2000).

Summary

FACTS John Hollenbach, an employee of Honcho & Sons, Inc., was excavating land for Honcho in its role as a subcontractor of Excalibur Cable Communications. Maryland Cable Partners, L.P. had hired Excalibur to carry out a cable installation project. During his work, Hollenbach struck a buried natural-gas line owned by Washington Gas Light Company and caused a leak in the line. Gas escaped into the air, and, as a result, the neighborhood where the gas line was located had to be evacuated. The fire department notified Washington Gas, which dispatched a repair crew to the scene of the leak. Lee James Crews, an employee of Washington Gas for over twenty years, was the foreman of the gas-line repair team dispatched to repair the leak. While he and his crew worked to repair the leak, the gas ignited and an explosion occurred, seriously injuring Crews.

Crews sued Hollenbach, Honcho & Sons, Excalibur Cable Communications, Maryland Cable Partners, and Byers Engineering Company (which marked the utility lines), claiming negligence and strict liability. The trial court dismissed the case on the grounds that Crews assumed the risk as part of his job. The Court of Special Appeals affirmed the judgment. Crews appealed.

ISSUE PRESENTED Is assumption of risk a viable defense against a suit by an employee hired to repair gas leaks who was injured during the process of repair?

SUMMARY OF OPINION The Court of Appeals of Maryland found that under the assumption of risk analysis applicable to this case, it had to determine whether the plaintiff (1) had knowledge of the risk of danger, (2) appreciated the risk, and (3) voluntarily exposed himself to that risk. The court found that Crews had knowledge of the risk because he was aware of the heavy smell of gas near the leak.

With respect to an appreciation of the risk, the court found that Crews, a gas-line repairman with over twenty years of experience, noticed the smell of gas in the area and knew that a ruptured gas line could cause an explosion.

"... [T]here are certain risks which anyone of adult age must be taken to appreciate: the danger of slipping on ice, of falling through unguarded openings, of lifting heavy objects, ... of inflammable liquids, ... and doubtless many others." The evident risk of an explosion following the rupture of a gas line is among the risks we will recognize as being understood by anyone of an adult age and competency.

The appeals court next considered whether Crews had voluntarily exposed himself to the risk. Crews argued that he had to repair the leak to prevent serious harm to the people and property of the surrounding neighborhood. While "commending Mr. Crew's apparent initiative here," the court found no evidence that he was forced to make those efforts or what the larger implications might have been had he not acted. Instead, the court reasoned that "the danger Mr. Crews encountered [at the gas leak] is the very danger that he accepted the risk of confronting when he became an employee of Washington Gas some twenty years earlier."

RESULT The appeals court affirmed the judgment of the Court of Special Appeals and held that assumption of risk was a valid defense.

COMMENTS Other jurisdictions have handled this issue differently. For example, in *Van Coppenolle v. Kamco Industries,*[25] the Ohio Court of Appeals considered whether an employee injured on the job had assumed the risk of injury. The court stated that assumption of risk is not a valid defense when an employee is injured by a defective product if

25. 1997 WL 679631 (Ohio Ct. App. Oct. 31, 1997).

(Continued)

(Case 10.4 continued)

the job requires the employee to encounter the risk and the employee is injured while engaging in normal job-related tasks. In this case, however, because the plaintiff was injured while using a machine improperly, she had voluntarily exposed herself to, and therefore assumed, the risk.

COMPARATIVE FAULT

Contributory negligence by the plaintiff is not a defense in a strict liability action. However, the plaintiff's damages may be reduced by the degree to which his or her own negligence contributed to the injury. This doctrine is known as *comparative fault*.

OBVIOUS RISK

If the use of a product carries an *obvious risk*, the manufacturer will not be held liable for injuries that result from ignoring the risk. Although a plaintiff will argue that the manufacturer had a duty to warn of the dangers of a foreseeable use of the product, courts often apply the standard that a manufacturer need not warn of a certain danger if that danger is generally known and recognized.

For example, in *Maneely v. General Motors Corp.*,[26] two men who rode in the cargo bed of a pickup truck sued GM after sustaining serious injuries in a collision. The men argued that GM failed to warn of the dangers of riding in a cargo bed. The court rejected their claims, noting that a manufacturer should not bear the paternalistic responsibility of warning users of every possible risk that could arise from use of its product. As the public generally recognizes the dangers of riding unrestrained in the cargo bed of a moving pickup truck, GM had no duty to warn of those dangers.

UNFORESEEABLE MISUSE OF THE PRODUCT

A manufacturer or seller is entitled to assume that its product will be used in a normal manner. The manufacturer or seller will not be held liable for injuries resulting from abnormal use of its product. But an unusual use that is reasonably foreseeable may be considered a normal use.

For example, operating a lawn mower with the grass bag removed was held to be a foreseeable use, and the manufacturer was liable to a bystander injured by an object that shot out of the unguarded mower.[27] How-

ever, the creation of a bomb through the alteration and misuse of fertilizer was not considered to be an "objectively foreseeable" result.[28] Thus, the owner of the World Trade Center could not hold fertilizer manufacturers liable for damages resulting from the 1993 terrorist bombing on grounds that they failed to use additives to make it more difficult to turn their products into explosives.

STATUTE OF LIMITATIONS AND REVIVAL STATUTES

A *statute of limitations* defines a time limit, within which a lawsuit must be brought. Ordinarily, the statute of limitations starts to run at the time a person is injured. There are exceptions, however. In many cases of injuries caused by exposure to asbestos, for example, the plaintiff did not become aware of the injury until after the statute of limitations had run out. This led to the adoption of *discovery-of-injury statutes,* which generally provide that the statute of limitations for asbestos cases does not begin to run until the person discovers the injury from exposure to asbestos.

For prenatal injuries caused by the drug DES, *revival statutes* have been enacted to permit plaintiffs to file lawsuits that had previously been barred by the running of the statute of limitations. DES manufacturers argued that the revival statutes violated their right to due process of law. The manufacturers also argued that their right to equal protection of the laws had been violated because the revival statutes typically apply to only a few substances, such as DES or asbestos, but not to other dangerous chemical substances. The manufacturers claimed that this categorization was without sufficient basis and that it was the result of political compromise. Most courts have rejected these arguments and held that state revival statutes have a rational basis and that legislatures enacting such statutes are acting within their broad discretion.[29] More recently, revival statutes have

---

26. 108 F.3d 1176 (9th Cir. 1997).
27. LaPaglia v. Sears Roebuck & Co., 531 N.Y.S.2d 623 (N.Y. App. Div. 1988).

28. Port Authority of New York & New Jersey v. Arcadian Corp., 991 F. Supp. 309 (D.N.J. 1998), *aff'd,* 189 F.3d 305 (3d Cir. 1999).
29. *See, e.g.,* Hymowitz v. Eli Lilly & Co., 539 N.E.2d 1069 (N.Y. 1989), *cert. denied,* 493 U.S. 944 (1989).

been enacted to extend the time in which women may sue for injuries caused by silicone breast implants.

Many statutes of limitations have been amended to define more precisely when a cause of action arises. For example, the Ohio statute provides:

- An asbestos cause of action arises when the claimant learns or should have realized that he was injured by exposure to asbestos, whichever is earlier.
- An Agent Orange type cause of action involving exposure of a veteran to chemical defoliants or herbicides arises when the claimant learns that he was injured by the exposure.
- A DES cause of action arises when the claimant learns from a physician that her injury might be related to DES exposures or when she should have realized she had such an injury, whichever is earlier.[30]

GOVERNMENT-CONTRACTOR DEFENSE

Under the *government-contractor defense,* a manufacturer producing products under contract to the government can avoid product liability if (1) the product was produced according to government specifications, (2) the manufacturer possessed less knowledge about the specifications than did the government agency, (3) the manufacturer exercised proper skill and care in production, and (4) the manufacturer did not deviate from the specifications. The rationale for this immunity is that the manufacturer is acting merely as an agent of the government; to hold the manufacturer liable would unfairly shift the insurance burden from the government to the manufacturer.

STATE-OF-THE-ART DEFENSE

The *state-of-the-art defense* shields a manufacturer from liability if no safer product design is generally recognized as being possible. State courts have split over how to analyze this defense on two grounds. First, states have differed in their definition of "state of the art." Some states have defined "state-of-the-art" to mean complying either with industry custom (e.g., Alaska and New Jersey) or with existing governmental regulations (e.g., Illinois).[31] The majority of states, however, deem "state-of-the-art" to refer to what is technologically feasible at the time of design. Accordingly, a manufacturer may have a duty to make products pursuant to a safer design even if the custom of the industry is not to use that alternative.[32]

States have also split on whether the state-of-the-art defense is available in design defect cases. Some courts have ruled that state-of-the-art evidence is irrelevant in strict product liability cases because it improperly focuses the jury's attention on the reasonableness of the manufacturer's conduct. Other courts have made state-of-the-art evidence a complete defense to a design defect claim. The overwhelming majority of states, though, hold that state-of-the-art evidence is simply relevant to determining the adequacy of the product's design. As the Connecticut Supreme Court concluded, "state of the art is a relevant factor in considering the adequacy of the design of a product and whether it is in a defective condition unreasonably dangerous to the ordinary consumer."[33]

The contours of the state-of-the-art defense are often first laid down by judges, then codified by state legislatures. This is especially true with respect to failure-to-warn claims. For example, an Arizona statute provides a defense "if the plans or designs for the product or the methods and techniques of manufacturing, inspecting, testing and labeling the product conformed with the state of the art at the time the product was first sold by defendant."[34] A Missouri statute provides that if the defendant can prove that the dangerous nature of the product was not known and could not reasonably have been discovered at the time the product was placed in the stream of commerce, then the defendant will not be held liable for failure to warn.[35]

PREEMPTION DEFENSE

Perhaps the most significant and controversial of the defenses to product liability is the *preemption defense.* Certain federal laws and regulations set minimum safety standards for products. For example, the National Traffic and Motor Vehicle Safety Act sets standards for auto manufacturers, and the Safe Medical Devices Act sets standards for the manufacture of medical devices. Manufacturers that meet those standards will sometimes be granted immunity from product liability claims made under state law on grounds of preemption. The rationale for deferring to the federal regulatory scheme is that allowing the states to impose fifty different sets of requirements would frustrate the purpose of a uniform federal scheme.

Manufacturing groups want preemption to serve as a "silver bullet" defense, effectively eliminating the possibility of state law product liability claims in any sphere governed by federal safety law and regulation. Commenting

---

30. OHIO REV. CODE ANN. § 2305.10 (Anderson 2000).
31. *See* Potter v. Chicago Pneumatic Tool Co., 694 A.2d 1319, 1345–46 (Conn. 1997).
32. *Id.* at 1347.

33. *Id.*
34. ARIZ. REV. STAT. § 12-683(1) (2000).
35. MO. REV. STAT. § 537.764 (1999).

on a medical-device case before the U.S. Supreme Court, one of the manufacturers' most vocal representatives put the argument this way: "What it boils down to is whether we want to have the experts at the FDA tells us what is a safe pacemaker, or do we want each jury designing its own pacemaker—one doing it one way in Brooklyn and one doing it another way in Missouri?"[36]

In practice, the preemption defense is not the sweeping tool manufacturing groups want it to be. Instead, its availability depends largely on the language and context of the federal statute at issue. In recent years, courts have struggled to determine whether federal safety statutes preempt state product liability claims involving tobacco, faulty medical devices, and automobiles without air bags. For example, in *Consolidated Cigar Corp. v. Reilly*,[37] the U.S. Court of Appeals for the First Circuit upheld a state's ban on cigarette advertising, notwithstanding the existence of the Federal Cigarette Labeling and Advertising Act covering similar subject matter. The court concluded that the state regulations did not interfere with the scheme established by Congress.

In *Cipollone v. Liggett Group, Inc.* (a 1992 decision), the U.S. Supreme Court concluded that Congress intended the Public Health Cigarette Smoking Act of 1969 to have a broad preemptive effect.[38] In particular, the Court held that the act preempted claims based on a failure to warn and on the neutralization of federally mandated warnings through advertising techniques to the extent that those claims relied on omissions or inclusions in a tobacco company's advertising or promotions. However, the Court ruled that the act did not preempt claims based on express warranty, intentional fraud and misrepresentation, or conspiracy.

Four years later, in *Medtronic, Inc. v. Lohr*, the Court examined similar statutory language in the Medical Device Amendments of 1976 and found no preemption.[39] *Medtronic* involved a pacemaker that the Food and Drug Administration (FDA) had cleared for distribution under a statutory provision requiring premarket notification for some types of medical devices. *Medtronic* makes it clear that compliance with a regulatory scheme is not always a valid defense. However, the more rigorous the regulatory process, the more likely that product liability claims will be preempted. In *Medtronic*, the FDA had not closely scrutinized the pacemaker: it had received an exemption from thorough review because it was deemed "substantially equivalent" to pacemakers already on the market. The fact that the pacemaker had not undergone rigorous regulatory examination was an important factor in the Court's decision not to preempt product liability claims against Medtronic.[40]

In the following case, the Supreme Court resolved the question of whether state product liability "no air bag" claims were preempted by federal requirements for passive restraints in automobiles.

---

36. Paul M. Barrett, *Lora Lohr's Pacemaker May Alter Liability Law*, WALL ST. J., Apr. 9, 1996, at B1 (quoting Victor Schwartz).
37. 218 F.3d 30 (1st Cir. 2000).
38. 505 U.S. 504 (1992).

39. 518 U.S. 470 (1996).
40. This interpretation is supported by the FDA's recent proposal of regulations that serve to clarify its position.

A CASE IN POINT

CASE 10.5

Geier v. American Honda Motor Co.

Supreme Court of the United States
529 U.S. 861 (2000).

In the Language of the Court

FACTS While driving a 1987 Honda Accord, Alexis Geier crashed into a tree and was seriously injured. Although the car had manual shoulder and lap belts that Geier was using at the time of the accident, it had no air bags or other passive restraint devices. Geier and her parents sued American Honda under state law for failing to include a driver's side air bag.

The Federal Motor Vehicle Safety Standard (FMVSS) 208, promulgated pursuant to the National Traffic and Motor Vehicle Safety Act, required auto manufacturers to equip 10 percent of their national fleet of cars with passive restraints but did not require air bags. The district court dismissed the plaintiff's claim on the grounds that it was preempted by federal law. The U.S. court of appeals affirmed, and the Geiers appealed.

ISSUE PRESENTED Does the Safety Act preempt state tort claims based upon a manufacturer's failure to equip a vehicle with air bags?

OPINION BREYER, J., writing for the U.S. Supreme Court:

(Continued)

(Case 10.5 continued)

The basic question . . . is whether a common-law "no airbag" action like the one before us actually conflicts with FMVSS 208. We hold that it does.

. . . [The Department of Transportation's] comments, which accompanied the promulgation of FMVSS 208, make clear that the standard deliberately provided the manufacturer with a range of choices among different passive restraint devices. Those choices would bring about a mix of different devices introduced gradually over time; and FMVSS 208 would thereby lower costs, overcome technical safety problems, encourage technological development, and win widespread consumer acceptance—all of which would promote FMVSS 208's safety objectives. . . .

. . .

[P]etitioners' tort action depends upon its claim that manufacturers had a duty to install an airbag when they manufactured the 1987 Honda Accord. Such a state law— i.e., a rule of state tort law imposing such a duty—by its terms would have required manufacturers of all similar cars to install airbags rather than other passive restraint systems, such as automatic belts or passive interiors. It thereby would have presented an obstacle to the variety and mix of devices that the federal regulation sought. It would have required all manufacturers to have installed airbags in respect to the entire District-of-Columbia-related portion of their 1987 new car fleet, even though FMVSS 208 at that time required only that 10% of a manufacturer's nationwide fleet be equipped with any passive restraint device at all. It thereby also would have stood as an obstacle to the gradual passive restraint phase-in that the federal regulation deliberately imposed. In addition, it could have made less likely the adoption of a state mandatory buckle-up law. Because the rule of law for which petitioners contend would have stood "as an obstacle to the accomplishment and execution of" the important means-related federal objectives that we have just discussed, it is preempted.

RESULT The Supreme Court held that the state product liability claims asserted by Geier conflicted with the objectives of FMVSS 208 and were preempted by the Act. The claims were dismissed.

QUESTIONS

1. Why were state mandatory buckle-up laws not preempted by federal standards?

2. Must a conflict between state and federal law exist for preemption to occur?

⚖ Legislative Developments

Legislative reforms have been enacted in response to larger jury awards, perceived inconsistent treatment of litigants, and the insurance crisis of the 1980s, which made it prohibitively expensive or impossible to obtain product liability insurance in some industries.

STATUTES OF REPOSE

A *statute of repose* cuts off the right to assert a cause of action after a specified period of time from the delivery of the product or the completion of the work. A statute of repose is different from a statute of limitations, in which the time period is measured from the time the injury occurred. Thus, if a statute of repose sets a repose period of ten years, a person injured eleven years after the product was delivered would be time-barred from suing by the statute of repose, though not by the statute of limitations.

For example, the General Aviation Revitalization Act, enacted in 1994, creates an eighteen-year statute of repose limiting an aircraft manufacturer's liability for performance of an aircraft after the first eighteen years of the aircraft's life. Because the average aircraft was thirty years old in 1994, the Act significantly limited the product liability exposure of aircraft manufacturers.[41]

41. Allen Michel et al., *Protecting Future Product Liability Claimants,* AM. BANKR. INST. J., Dec. 1999, at 3–4.

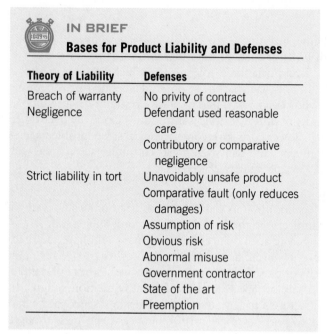

IN BRIEF

Bases for Product Liability and Defenses

Theory of Liability	Defenses
Breach of warranty	No privity of contract
Negligence	Defendant used reasonable care
	Contributory or comparative negligence
Strict liability in tort	Unavoidably unsafe product
	Comparative fault (only reduces damages)
	Assumption of risk
	Obvious risk
	Abnormal misuse
	Government contractor
	State of the art
	Preemption

(such as clear and convincing evidence rather than a mere preponderance of evidence) before punitives will be awarded. For example, in 1997, North Dakota passed a law requiring plaintiffs to prove oppression, fraud, or actual malice before claiming punitive damages. Other states have placed outright caps on punitive damages (Georgia, for instance, caps punitives at $250,000) or have tied punitive damages to compensatory damages (such as Florida's limitation that punitives cannot exceed three times compensatory damages). Finally, a few states (such as New Hampshire) have banned punitive awards altogether.

The constitutionality of legislative limits on punitive damages has recently come under scrutiny. For example, in *Smith v. Schulte*,[42] the Alabama Supreme Court struck down a statute that limited punitive damages awards against health care providers in an effort to reduce health care costs. The court held that the statute impermissibly isolated a class of victims—those suffering injuries from health care providers—for less favorable treatment and thus violated the constitutional guarantee of equal protection.

CODIFICATION OF DEFENSES

As discussed in the previous section, an injured person's conduct can be the basis for a defense to a strict liability action. Several states have enacted statutes to codify such defenses, that is, to add them to the code of laws that courts must follow.

Plaintiff's Negligence Michigan law provides that the negligence of the plaintiff does not bar recovery, but damages are reduced by his or her degree of fault—that is, the negligence attributed to the plaintiff.[43] Under Illinois law, if the jury finds that the degree of the plaintiff's fault exceeds 50 percent, then the plaintiff cannot recover damages. If the jury finds that the degree of the plaintiff's fault is less than 50 percent, the plaintiff can recover damages, but the damages will be reduced in proportion to the plaintiff's fault.[44]

Assumption of Risk Under Ohio law, if the claimant's express or implied assumption of risk is the direct and proximate cause of the harm, recovery is completely barred.[45]

Misuse of Product Unforeseeable misuse of a product is a defense under Indiana law if it is the proximate cause

Statutes of repose have usually been upheld on the ground that they serve some legitimate state purpose, such as encouraging manufacturers to upgrade their products. Absent a statute of repose, a manufacturer might not upgrade, out of fear that upgrading might be seen as an admission that the earlier version was inadequate.

LIMITATIONS ON PUNITIVE DAMAGES

Large awards of punitive damages have been criticized for providing windfalls to injured parties far in excess of their actual losses and for motivating plaintiffs and their lawyers to engage in expensive and wasteful litigation rather than settling the case.

In response to these criticisms, between 1986 and 1989, twenty-five states enacted legislation limiting punitive damages awards. By August 1997, the number of states with such legislation had increased to thirty-one. These reforms have typically taken three basic forms. Some states have placed limits on when punitive damages are available or have required a higher standard of evidence

ETHICAL CONSIDERATION

Given that an upgrade of a product can be construed as an admission of a prior defect, what is the ethical responsibility of a manager contemplating an upgrade needed to improve safety?

42. 671 So. 2d 1334 (Ala. 1995), *cert. denied*, 517 U.S. 1220 (1996).
43. MICH. COMP. LAWS § 600.2959 (2000).
44. 735 ILL. COMP. STAT. ANN. 5/2-1116 (West 2000).
45. OHIO REV. CODE ANN. § 2315.20 (Anderson 2000).

of the harm and the misuse is not reasonably expected by the seller at the time the seller conveys the product to another party.[46]

LIMITATIONS ON NONMANUFACTURER'S LIABILITY

Rather than holding all companies in the chain of distribution liable, many states limit the liability of nonmanufacturers. For example, a Minnesota statute provides that once an injured person files a claim against the manufacturer of the product, the court must dismiss the strict liability claim against any other defendants. A nonmanufacturer can be held strictly liable, however, if it was involved in the design or manufacture of the product or provided instructions or warnings about the defect, or if it knew of or created the defect. The nonmanufacturer may also be held strictly liable if the manufacturer is no longer in business or if it cannot satisfy a judgment against it.[47]

An Illinois statute provides that an action against a defendant other than the manufacturer will be dismissed unless the plaintiff can show that the defendant (1) had some control over the design or manufacture of the product or instructed or warned the manufacturer about the alleged defect, (2) actually knew of the defect, or (3) created the defect.[48]

LIMITATIONS ON JOINT LIABILITY

Traditionally, all defendants in a strict liability action were held jointly and severally liable. Each defendant was held liable not only for the injuries it severally—that is, individually—caused but also for all of the injuries caused by all of the defendants jointly.

At least thirty-eight states have placed limits on joint and several liability, with many abolishing joint liability altogether.[49] For example, an Oregon statute limits joint and several liability as follows:

> Liability of each defendant for non-economic damages is several, not joint. Liability of a defendant who is less than 15% at fault for economic damages is several only. Liability of a defendant who is 15% or more at fault for the economic damages is joint and several, except that a defendant whose fault is less than the plaintiff's is liable only for that percentage of the recoverable economic damages.[50]

PENALTIES FOR FRIVOLOUS SUITS

Some states have enacted penalties to deter frivolous lawsuits. For example, a Wisconsin statute provides that if a claim or defense is found to be frivolous, the prevailing party can be awarded its legal costs and attorneys' fees.[51] Minnesota and South Dakota passed similar legislation in 1997.

Tobacco *and* Guns

One of the most dramatic applications of product liability law has been the lawsuits against tobacco companies for illness, death, and medical expenses resulting from the use of tobacco or from secondhand smoke. In November 1998, forty-six states that had filed claims to recover billions they had spent in health care costs related to smoking settled with the tobacco industry for $206 billion—the largest civil settlement in U.S. history.[52] Four other states had previously entered into settlements with the tobacco companies totaling $40 billion. In September 1999, the federal government filed a similar suit to recover the more than $20 billion that the government spends every year to care for individuals who have health problems caused by smoking and use of tobacco.[53]

Class actions by private parties against the tobacco industry seem likely to result in huge damages paid by the tobacco companies. In the first smokers' class-action case to go to trial, a jury in Florida awarded $12.7 million in compensatory damages, and $145 billion in punitive damages, to three of the named plaintiffs with cancer.

Litigation against the tobacco industry is not limited to the United States. The governments of Bolivia, Guatemala, Nicaragua, and Venezuela have filed claims in the federal district court in Washington, D.C., in an effort to recover health care expenses related to smoking.[54] Similar suits have been filed in the courts of other countries as well. In addition, individual suits have been brought against the tobacco industry in a number of countries including Argentina, Canada, Germany, Ireland, Israel, Japan, Sri Lanka, Thailand, and Turkey.

Gun-control advocates have begun using a strategy similar to the states' strategy against the tobacco industry in an effort to hold gun manufacturers liable for violence

46. IND. CODE ANN. § 34-20-6-4 (West 2000).
47. MINN. STAT. § 544.41 (2000).
48. 735 ILL. COMP. STAT. ANN. 5/2-621 (West 2000).
49. David Olsen, *Minnesota: Key Reform Bills Head for State Senate*, METROPOLITAN CORP. COUNS., Feb. 2000.
50. OR. REV. STAT. § 18.485 (1999).

51. WIS. STAT. § 814.025 (1999).
52. Milo Geyelin, *States Agree to $206 Billion Tobacco Deal*, WALL ST. J., Nov. 23, 1998, at B13.
53. *Tobacco Industry Hits Home on Federal Lawsuit*, DOW JONES INT'L, June 24, 2000.
54. Richard A. Daynard, *Litigants Worldwide Blaming then Branding Big Tobacco in Court*, WORLDPAPER, June 1, 2000.

involving guns.[55] The "Inside Story" in this chapter discusses litigation by cities, counties, and states against the gun industry.

Litigation by private individuals against gun companies has had mixed results. The U.S. Court of Appeals for the Second Circuit dismissed a negligence case against Olin Corporation by victims of the December 7, 1993 shooting on a Long Island Railroad commuter train.[56] The shooter killed six people and wounded nineteen others using a 9mm handgun loaded with Olin's Black Talon ammunition, which has razor-sharp edges designed to rip and tear through a victim's body. The court rejected the plaintiffs' arguments that Olin was negligent in marketing the Black Talon bullets to the general public. However, dissenting judge Guido Calabresi believed there was no question that Olin's marketing of Black Talons created an unreasonable risk to the public and was the legal cause of the victims' severe injuries.

In contrast, the California Court of Appeal reinstated a suit brought by survivors and families of individuals killed in a San Francisco high rise in 1993 by a gunman armed with two TEC-DC9 semiautomatic assault weapons manufactured by Navegar, Inc.[57] The court dismissed the claims against the manufacturer for negligence *per se* and strict liability for ultrahazardous activities but permitted the plaintiffs to proceed with their suit for ordinary negligence. The court ruled that "Navegar owed [the plaintiffs] a duty to exercise reasonable care not to create risks above and beyond those inherent in the presence of firearms in our society and that there are triable issues of fact as to whether it breached that duty." The court reasoned that imposing such a duty was warranted because (1) the use of the TEC-DC9s in violent assaults of the type carried out in San Francisco was foreseeable; (2) Navegar engaged in "morally blameworthy conduct" by marketing the weapons in such a way as to bring them to the attention of violent persons likely to use the weapons for criminal purposes; and (3) imposing

such a duty would help prevent future harm and would not unduly interfere with a societal interest in keeping the guns on the market. Similarly, a federal court in Ohio permitted product liability and tort claims to proceed against seventeen gun makers and three trade associations because they refused to incorporate safety devices in their guns.[58] All other appellate courts that have considered the issue have refused to impose on gun manufacturers a duty of care to persons injured and the survivors of others killed by criminal misuse of their products.[59]

Product Liability Class Actions

Product liability cases are frequently resolved through class actions, a procedural device that allows a large number of plaintiffs to recover against a defendant in a single case. Lawsuits involving the tobacco industry, asbestos, silicone breast implants, and harmful diet drugs were all resolved through class actions.

In *Amchem Products, Inc. v. Windsor*,[60] the U.S. Supreme Court set forth the elements necessary for certification of a class of plaintiffs suing asbestos manufacturers. The proposed class included individuals who had not previously sued asbestos manufacturers and either (1) had been exposed to asbestos by the asbestos manufacturers through their occupations or the occupation of a household member or (2) had a spouse or family member who had been exposed to asbestos. The Court denied the class certification because the class members had different interests. For example, those individuals who were currently injured would seek immediate payment, whereas those who had been exposed and were anticipating future injury would seek a fund for future compensation. The Court identified additional differences as well to support its denial of class certification. In general, *Amchem* established more stringent standards for class certification and settlement.

Rule 23(b)(1)(B) of the Federal Rules of Civil Procedure provides a mechanism to resolve class actions in which the total of the aggregated liquidated claims exceeds the fund available to satisfy them (*limited-fund class actions*). In *Ortiz v. Fibreboard Corp.*,[61] another asbestos class action, the Supreme Court made it clear that

55. Many of the arguments for holding gun manufacturers liable are set forth in the Web page for the Center to Prevent Handgun Violence's Legal Action Project, <http://www.handguncontrol.org>.
56. McCarthy v. Olin Corp., 119 F.3d 148 (2d Cir. 1997).
57. Merrill v. Navegar, Inc., 89 Cal. Rptr. 2d 146 (Cal. Ct. App. 1999), *reh'g. granted*, Jan. 19, 2000 (5083466). The plaintiffs were precluded from suing based on strict product liability by Section 1714.4 of the California Civil Code, which provides that, in a product liability action, (1) no firearm shall be deemed defective in design because the benefits do not outweigh the risk of injury; (2) the potential of a firearm to cause serious injury does not make the product defective in design; and (3) injuries resulting from discharge of a firearm are not proximately caused by its potential to cause injury but are proximately caused by the actual discharge of the product.

58. *Cleveland Suit Against Gun Makers Survives Motion to Dismiss*, CONSUMER PROD. LITIG. REP., May 2000.
59. *See, e.g.*, Valentine v. On Target, Inc., 727 A.2d 947 (Md. 1999).
60. 521 U.S. 591 (1997).
61. 527 U.S. 815 (1999).

the trial court must itself determine whether the fund is limited. Thus, it was improper for the trial court to simply accept an agreement between the lead plaintiffs, the insurance companies, and the manufacturer as to the maximum amount the insurance companies could be required to pay tort victims.

In some class actions, the class may base its suit on the anticipation of illness or physical injury resulting from drug ingestion or exposure to a toxic product. In other words, no actual injury or illness has yet emerged. In *Petito v. A.H. Robins Co.*[62] the Florida Court of Appeal recognized a cause of action for "medical monitoring" for plaintiffs who had been prescribed the weight-loss drugs Fenfluramine and Phentermine. Although they had no physical injuries, the class members argued that taking the drugs had placed them at a substantially increased risk of developing serious cardiac and circulatory damage, including heart valve damage. Therefore, the class sought to require the drug manufacturers and sellers to pay for a court-supervised medical monitoring program that would provide for medical testing, monitoring, and study of the class. The court found for the plaintiffs and commented: "[O]ne can hardly dispute that an individual has just as great an interest in avoiding expensive diagnostic examinations as in avoiding physical injury."[63]

Problems *with the* Product Liability System *and the* Restatement (Third)

The product liability scheme that has evolved has increasingly been criticized because of the financial burden it imposes on industry. The cornerstone of the scheme is the assumption that manufacturers are in the best position to insure against loss or to spread the risk of loss among their customers. Nevertheless, the costs to manufacturers—huge jury awards and high insurance premiums—have been enormous. Moreover, manufacturers often find it difficult to obtain an insurance policy that does not include a substantial deductible, which the manufacturer must pay. Sometimes insurance is not available at all, and companies have to pay all claims themselves. This leads to higher manufacturing costs.

The product liability scheme also takes its toll on industry efficiency and competitiveness. Companies have become unwilling to invest in product creation or modification because this may be seen as an admission of guilt.

62. 750 So. 2d 103 (Fla. Dist. Ct. App. 1999).
63. *Id.* at 105.

In most jurisdictions, product modification is admissible as evidence of the product's prior defective condition. Companies find themselves in a no-win situation: failure to remedy a defect may expose the company to punitive damages, but remedying the defect may expose the company to compensatory damages in subsequent suits.

RESTATEMENT (THIRD) OF TORTS: PRODUCT LIABILITY

Informed by these concerns, the American Law Institute (ALI) completed its five-year effort to synthesize the current case law of product liability and approved the Restatement (Third) of Torts: Product Liability in 1997. The new restatement proposes bold changes in the doctrine of product liability. Most importantly, it requires that any claim of design defect be supported by a showing of a reasonable alternative design. The effect of this change is to move away from strict liability for defectively designed products. (The new restatement avoids using the term *strict liability* altogether.) Instead, the reasonable-alternative-design requirement forces plaintiffs to prove that the defendant acted wrongly or negligently in choosing an improper design.

In many respects, those who failed in their ardent attempts to push tort and product liability reform through Congress saw their ideas embodied in the new restatement. Indeed, the most vocal critics of the Restatement (Third) charged that the effort had been captured by defense attorneys seeking to accomplish through the ALI what they could not on Capitol Hill.

ETHICAL CONSIDERATION

Although there is a movement toward reducing companies' strict liability for injuries caused by their products, one commentator has warned that the trend may be reversed if companies do not act responsibly:

> The law can be said always to be moving toward some point of equilibrium. Perhaps it is at that point now for products. However, should it become apparent in the future that corporations are abusing their current degree of protection or that more persons are being injured by hazardous substances than society can justify, then one may expect to see a return to the trend of increasing the liability of the suppliers of such substances.[a]

How can managers help prevent an adverse shift in the law?

a. Paul D. Rheingold, *The Future of Product Liability: The Plaintiff's Perspective*, 17 PROD. SAFETY & LIAB. REP. (BNA) 711 (1989).

As noted earlier, no court is bound by the restatement's formulation of product liability law. As of the middle of 2000, only a minority of states had adopted the Restatement (Third) approach, either in whole or in part. In the following case, the Supreme Court of Connecticut explicitly rejected the "reasonable-alternative-design" provision.

A CASE IN POINT

CASE 10.6

Potter v. Chicago Pneumatic Tool Co.
Supreme Court of Connecticut
694 A.2d 1319
(Conn. 1997).

In the Language of the Court

FACTS John Potter and his fellow plaintiffs were shipyard workers injured in the course of their employment at a General Dynamics Corporation electric-boat facility as a result of using pneumatic tools manufactured by the defendants. The plaintiffs used the tools to chip, grind, and smooth metal surfaces at General Dynamics for approximately twenty-five years. They developed permanent vascular and neurological impairment of their hands, which caused blanching of their fingers, pain, numbness, reduction of grip strength, and intolerance of cold. Consequently, the plaintiffs were unable to continue their employment as grinders, and their ability to perform other activities was restricted.

The plaintiffs claimed that (1) the tools were defectively designed because they exposed the plaintiffs to excessive vibration and (2) the defendants failed to provide adequate warnings about the potential danger of excessive vibration.

The jury found for the plaintiffs. The defendants appealed.

ISSUE PRESENTED Are plaintiffs in a defective-design suit required to support their claim by demonstrating the existence of a reasonable alternative design?

OPINION KATZ, J., writing for the Connecticut Supreme Court:

We first address the defendants' argument that the trial court improperly failed to render judgment for the defendants notwithstanding the verdicts because there was insufficient evidence for the jury to have found that the tools had been defectively designed. Specifically, the defendants claim that, in order to establish a prima facie design defect case, the plaintiffs were required to prove that there was a feasible alternative design available at the time that the defendants put their tools into the stream of commerce. We disagree.

...

Although courts have widely accepted the concept of strict tort liability, some of the specifics of strict tort liability remain in question. In particular, courts have sharply disagreed over the appropriate definition of defectiveness in design cases. As the Alaska Supreme Court has stated: "Design defects present the most perplexing problems in the field of strict products liability because there is no readily ascertainable external measure of defectiveness. While manufacturing flaws can be evaluated against the intended design of the product, no such objective standard exists in the design defect context."[64]

Section 402A [of the Restatement (Second) of Torts] imposes liability only for those defective products that are "unreasonably dangerous" to "the ordinary consumer who purchases it, with the ordinary knowledge common to the community as to its characteristics." Under this formulation, known as the "consumer expectation" test, a manufacturer is strictly liable for any condition not contemplated by the ultimate consumer that will be unreasonably dangerous to the consumer.

---

64. Caterpillar Tractor Co. v. Beck, 598 P.2d 871, 880 (Alaska 1979).

(Continued)

(Case 10.6 continued)

[Some jurisdictions apply a competing approach:] a balancing test that inquires whether a product's risks outweigh its benefits. Under [this test], otherwise known as the "risk-utility" test, the manufacturer bears the burden of proving that the product's utility is not outweighed by its risks in light of various factors. . . .

With this history in mind, we turn to the development of strict products liability law in Connecticut. . . .

This court has long held that in order to prevail in a design defect claim, "the plaintiff must prove that the product is unreasonably dangerous." We have derived our definition of "unreasonably dangerous" from comment (i) to § 402A, which provides that "the article sold must be dangerous to an extent beyond that which would be contemplated by the ordinary consumer who purchases it, with the ordinary knowledge common to the community as to its characteristics." This "consumer expectation" standard is now well established in Connecticut strict products liability decisions.

The defendants propose that it is time for this court to abandon the consumer expectation standard and adopt the requirement that the plaintiff must prove the existence of a reasonable alternative design in order to prevail on a design defect claim. We decline to accept the defendants' invitation.

In support of their position, the defendants point to the second tentative draft of the Restatement (Third) of Torts: Products Liability (1995) (Draft Restatement [Third]), which provides that, as part of a plaintiff's prima facie case, the plaintiff must establish the availability of a reasonable alternative design. Specifically, § 2(b) of the Draft Restatement (Third) provides: "[A] product is defective in design when the foreseeable risks of harm posed by the product could have been reduced or avoided by the adoption of a reasonable alternative design by the seller or other distributor, or a predecessor in the commercial chain of distribution, and the omission of the alternative design renders the product not reasonably safe." The reporters to the Draft Restatement (Third) state that "very substantial authority supports the proposition that [the] plaintiff must establish a reasonable alternative design in order for a product to be adjudged defective in design."

We point out that this provision of the Draft Restatement (Third) has been a source of substantial controversy among commentators. . . . Contrary to the rule promulgated in the Draft Restatement (Third), our independent review of the prevailing common law reveals that the majority of jurisdictions do not impose upon plaintiffs an absolute requirement to prove a feasible alternative design.

. . . Our research reveals that, of the jurisdictions that have considered the role of feasible alternative designs in design defect cases: (1) six jurisdictions affirmatively state that a plaintiff need not show a feasible alternative design in order to establish a manufacturer's liability for design defect; (2) sixteen jurisdictions hold that a feasible alternative design is merely one of several factors that the jury may consider in determining whether a product design is defective; (3) three jurisdictions require the defendant, not the plaintiff, to prove that the product was not defective; and (4) eight jurisdictions require that the plaintiff prove a feasible alternative design in order to establish a prima facie case of design defect.

In our view, the feasible alternative design requirement imposes an undue burden on plaintiffs that might preclude otherwise valid claims from jury consideration. Such a rule would require plaintiffs to retain an expert witness even in cases in which lay jurors can infer a design defect from circumstantial evidence. Connecticut courts, however, have consistently stated that a jury may, under appropriate circumstances, infer a defect from the evidence without the necessity of expert testimony.

(Continued)

(Case 10.6 continued)

Moreover, in some instances, a product may be in a defective condition unreasonably dangerous to the user even though no feasible alternative design is available. In such instances, the manufacturer may be strictly liable for a design defect notwithstanding the fact that there are no safer alternative designs in existence. . . . Accordingly, we decline to adopt the requirement that a plaintiff must prove a feasible alternative design as a sine qua non to establishing a prima facie case of design defect.

RESULT Though the Connecticut Supreme Court did not require the plaintiffs to support their claim by demonstrating the existence of a reasonable alternative design, it vacated the jury verdict and ordered a new trial on separate grounds. Specifically, it found that General Dynamics, the plaintiffs' employer, had substantially modified the pneumatic tools prior to their use by the plaintiffs.

QUESTIONS

1. Would the adoption of the reasonable-alternative-design standard eviscerate strict liability for defective products and replace it with a negligence standard?
2. Should a plaintiff injured by a defective product be prevented from reaching a jury until he or she can provide an expert who outlines an alternative way to design that product?

 # Product Liability *in the* European Union

Differences among the product liability laws of the various countries within the European Union (EU) created two major problems. First, there was uncertainty as to what law would apply to cross-border disputes. This uncertainty was harmful to both the consumer and the manufacturer of the product. Second, competition within the EU was distorted because liability and the severity of financial repercussions varied from one nation to another. Thus, the need for a uniform product liability directive was recognized.

In July 1985, after nearly a decade of debate, the Council of Ministers of the EU adopted a product liability directive. The directive was intended to provide increased consumer protection and to harmonize competitive conditions within the EU.[65] In 1995, the European Commission decided to leave the directive unchanged, rejecting the urging of consumer groups to strengthen the liability provisions.[66]

The directive's basic purpose is to hold manufacturers strictly liable for injuries caused by defects in their products. This represents a fundamental change for manufacturers of products marketed in Europe. Traditionally, in most of the twelve member states, an injured consumer had to prove both negligence and privity of contract in order to recover damages from the producer of a defective product. Only France had previously imposed strict product liability.

COMPARISON WITH U.S. STRICT LIABILITY

The EU product liability directive is quite similar to the strict liability doctrine prevalent in the United States. To recover damages, an injured party has to prove the existence of a defect, an injury, and a causal relationship between the defect and the injury. (Plaintiffs may also sue under the traditional negligence and contract laws of the EU member states.) In determining whether a product is defective, the courts in the EU countries, like those in the United States, consider such factors as the product's foreseeable uses and the instructions and warnings provided by the manufacturer.

In June 1999, in light of separate outbreaks of mad cow disease, *E. coli,* and salmonella, the commission adopted an amendment to the 1985 directive that extended product liability to cover agricultural products.[67] The directive does not apply to services, which remain governed solely by national law.

65. 1985 O.J. (L 210) 29.
66. Robert Rice, *Business and the Law: A Question of Safety—The European Union's Product Liability Legislation,* FINANCIAL TIMES, Jan. 16, 1996, at 13.

67. John R. Schmertz, Jr. & Mike Meier, *EU Amends Product Liability Directive to Include Agricultural Products,* INT'L L. UPDATE, June 1999.

The available defenses are similar to those available in the United States. For example, a manufacturer will not be liable if (1) the manufacturer did not put the product into circulation, (2) the defect did not exist when the product went into circulation, (3) the product was a component that was neither manufactured nor distributed by the manufacturer of the overall product, or (4) the defect was due to compliance of the product with mandatory regulations. The manufacturer of a component part will not be liable if the defect was attributable to the design of the product into which the component was fitted.

The directive includes a statute of limitations and a statute of repose. An injured person must sue within three years of when he or she knew, or should have known, of the injury, the defect, and the manufacturer's identity. A manufacturer's liability will be extinguished ten years after the product was put into circulation, unless the injured party has commenced proceedings in the meantime. Thus, as in some states in the United States, a defect that does not become apparent until eleven years after the product went into circulation may leave the injured person without a remedy. Most EU member states previously had statutes of repose with a thirty-year period.

Unlike in the United States, a supplier or wholesaler is not strictly liable unless the injured party is unable to identify the manufacturer. In such an instance, the supplier can escape liability by informing the injured person of the manufacturer's identity.

The directive provides for a "development risks" or state-of-the-art defense. A producer can escape liability by proving that the state of scientific knowledge when the product went into circulation was insufficient to allow it to discover the defect. This provision is controversial because it introduces an element of fault, which is precisely what the strict liability doctrine attempts to exclude. The initial directive required the Council of Ministers to consider whether to repeal the state-of-the-art defense in 1995; as stated above, the council chose to leave this defense, as well as the remainder of the directive, unchanged. By 2000, however, elimination of the state-of-the-art defense was once again under consideration.

It should be noted that importers of products into the EU are strictly liable under the directive. Thus, U.S. exporters may be required to indemnify overseas importers. U.S. exporters should carry product liability insurance and adhere to EU safety standards.

 THE RESPONSIBLE MANAGER
Reducing Product Liability Risk

Managers have the responsibility to minimize their company's exposure to liability in the design, manufacture, assembly, and sale of its products. They should implement a product-safety program to ensure that the products are sold in a legally safe condition. They also have an obligation to discover and correct any defects in the products. The goal should be to prevent accidents. If an accident does occur, evidence of a product-safety program is crucial for limiting the manufacturer's liability for punitive damages. To protect against potential liabilities, managers should implement internal loss-control procedures, obtain insurance protection, and seek the advice of product liability counsel from the earliest stages of product development.

Managers should check the safety of their products both in their intended use and in reasonably foreseeable misuse. Managers should develop adequate instructions and comprehensive warnings. They should consider the reasonably foreseeable risks of using the product, ways to avoid those risks, and the consequences of ignoring the risks. Managers may find it helpful to follow industry standards, but sometimes a company must break

new ground and go beyond what the industry has done in the past.

Managers should have a thorough understanding of all statutes, regulations, and administrative rulings to which a product must conform. Failure of the product to comply with any of these rules will typically be deemed a product defect. Mere conformance with these rules is considered a minimum requirement, however, and does not automatically release a manufacturer from liability.

Managers should keep internal records of their product engineering and manufacturing decisions. These records should include design specifications, design-failure tests, and safety reviews. Managers should monitor the product at every stage of production. The records must indicate that the design process was carefully considered; the records must include more than the mere suggestions or ruminations of employees.

Companies should be careful how they advertise and warrant their products. In product liability litigation, the overall impression of such representations may be criticized by opposing counsel. Careless advertising may even lead to product misuse, resulting in an injury for which the manufacturer will be liable.

Managers should continuously monitor field reports of injuries caused by both use and misuse of their company's products. Appropriate reaction to such information may bear on the issue of punitive damages.

Managers have a postsale duty to warn of any hazards of which they have become aware, even if the product was initially thought to be safe. This duty may simply require sending a letter to purchasers of the product. Or it may require providing the purchaser with a corrective device. In addition to updating consumers on product-safety concerns, some jurisdictions require management to inform consumers of technological advances or safety improvements. Section 15 of the Consumer Product Safety Act[68] imposes substantial product-safety reporting requirements. It requires management to notify an administrative agency if a product does not comply with applicable product-safety rules or if it contains a defect that could create a "substantial risk of injury to the public."

Managers should ensure that their products are performing as intended over the lives of the products and that the products have as little adverse effect on the environment as possible under current technology. It is helpful to establish a product-safety committee and to conduct regular safety audits to identify and correct problems. The advice of experienced counsel can be helpful in this area.

68. 15 U.S.C. § 2064 (2000).

INSIDE STORY

Taking Aim *at the* Gun Industry

Highly publicized incidents of shootings at public schools and in the workplace, including the Columbine incident in Colorado and the shooting of a six-year-old girl by a six-year-old boy in Michigan, have focused public attention on gun control and the gun industry's responsibility for violence resulting from the abuse of guns. On average, twelve children are killed by guns every day, making the issue of gun control and gun safety devices an important matter of public safety. In the last few years, litigation by local, state, and federal governments, rather than legislation enacted by Congress, has been responsible for major efforts to change the regulation of the gun industry.

After the enormously successful litigation against the tobacco industry that resulted in a $206 billion settlement, cities and counties launched a similar attack against the gun industry. However, unlike the tobacco companies, which have deep pockets and many assets to satisfy damage claims, gun companies are small, mostly privately held companies with annual sales of only $2.5 billion.[69]

In October 1998, New Orleans sued gun manufacturers and distributors to recover millions of dollars in medical and other costs caused by gun violence. New Orleans alleged that guns were "unreasonably dangerous" because the gun makers had not included enough safety elements on the weapons.[70] Shortly thereafter, Chicago filed a public nuisance lawsuit seeking $433 million in damages; the suit alleged that gun manufacturers and distributors were selling their guns through suburban gun shops in an effort to circumvent the city's strict gun laws. A number of other cities and counties followed the lead of New Orleans and Chicago. By October 2000, thirty-two cities and counties (including New York, Chicago, Atlanta, the District of Columbia, and Miami) had initiated actions against the gun industry.[71]

In 1999, the cities and counties suing the industry entered into settlement negotiations with executives of the gun manufacturers. The federal government also joined the negotiations. President Bill Clinton announced that he was sending aides to assist with the negotiations; if that failed, he threatened to organize a class-action suit on behalf of thousands of federally subsidized housing projects where many shootings occur.[72]

In early 2000, two Clinton administration lawyers—the deputy general counsel of Housing and Urban De-

69. Paul Barrett, *As Lawsuits Loom, Gun Industry Presents a Fragmented Front*, WALL ST. J., Dec. 9, 1998, at A1.

70. Yvonne Zipp, *Who Pays Cost of Gun Violence? A Growing Cadre of Big Cities Sues Gunmakers in an Effort to Recoup Losses Associated with Treating Shooting Victims*, CHRISTIAN SCIENCE MONITOR, Nov. 23, 1998, at 1.

71. Richard Perez-pena, *New York Suit on Guns to Be First by a State*, N.Y. TIMES, June 26, 2000, at 1.

72. *Behind the Gun Pact: Mixing Legal Hardball with Personal Bonds*, N.Y. TIMES, Mar. 21, 2000, at 1.

velopment and the general counsel at the Treasury Department, which helps oversee the Bureau of Alcohol, Tobacco and Firearms—presented a list of gun-control demands to Ed Schultz, the chief executive officer of Smith & Wesson Corporation. Smith & Wesson, a unit of Britain's Tomkins PLC, is America's largest maker of handguns. Schultz initially responded by asking one of the lawyers how old he was. When the lawyer replied that he was thirty-four years old, Schultz said, "If you live a good long life, you will not live to see this proposal happen." Two months later, however, Smith & Wesson agreed to a settlement based upon that initial proposal.

Smith & Wesson agreed to make a number of changes, including the following:

- All guns would be shipped with external child safety locks.
- Within two years, all pistols would be manufactured with internal safety locks.
- Within one year, all firearms would be made child-proof.
- Handguns would have to pass a stringent performance test.
- The company would devote 2 percent of its gross revenues to developing a "smart" gun that can be fired only by its owner.

The company also agreed to develop a code of conduct for its dealers and distributors that would require background checks on purchasers and would forbid sale to anyone who had not passed a safety exam or taken a training class.

At least fifteen of the cities and countries agreed to drop their suits against Smith & Wesson after the company signed the settlement agreement. In addition, the states of New York and Connecticut and the Clinton administration agreed not to name Smith & Wesson in the lawsuits they had been threatening to commence.[73] Federal, state, and local governments also agreed to make Smith & Wesson firearms their "preferred" choice when buying guns for law enforcement officers, thereby providing a financial incentive for other gun companies to agree to the terms of the settlement. As of the end of June 2000, at least 411 communities had agreed to this pact. However, Smith & Wesson was the only manufacturer to do so.[74]

After the settlement was announced, two other gun companies, the U.S. subsidiary of Austria's Glock GmbH and Brazil's Forjas Taurus SA, also indicated a willingness to require stringent new sales restrictions.[75] However, other companies, such as Sturm, Ruger & Company and the U.S. unit of Italy's Beretta SpA, indicated that they did not intend to change their position in light of Smith & Wesson's settlement.

Smith & Wesson's settlement has been compared by commentators to Liggett Group's decision to break ranks with the other tobacco companies and settle its tobacco cases. But whereas Liggett was a small tobacco company, Smith & Wesson is one of the most powerful gun companies in the industry. Eliot Spitzer, New York State's attorney general, who was involved in designing the Smith & Wesson settlement, commented, "The idea all along was that one responsible company would break away from the rest of the industry and that would be leverage to use against the rest."[76]

The gun industry sharply criticized Smith & Wesson. The head of the National Shooting Sports Foundation, which represents all major gun makers, stated that Smith & Wesson's decision to settle "violated a trust with their consumers and with the entire domestic firearms industry." He also charged that the company had "run off and cut their own deal" in a manner that "fractures the unity we had since the first lawsuit was filed in October 1998."[77] Some claimed that Smith & Wesson's settlement amounts to an admission that guns can be made safer, thus undermining the industry's long-held position that companies have no obligation to make naturally dangerous products safer.

Commentators outside the gun industry also criticized the Smith & Wesson deal on grounds that it represented an undemocratic way of making public policy.[78] They argued that the Clinton administration, frustrated with the partisan gridlock in Congress preventing the enactment of gun-control legislation, used litigation to establish new regulations for the gun industry.[79] "This is backdoor gun control through coercion and through threat of litigation," said one member of Congress.[80] Indeed, Representative Bob Barr of Georgia, who is also a member of the National Rifle Association board of directors, introduced

---

73. Paul M. Barrett, Vanessa O'Connell, & Joe Mathews, *Glock May Accept Handgun Restrictions—Austrian Firm May Follow Lead of Smith & Wesson to Avoid U.S. Sanctions,* WALL ST. J., Mar. 20, 2000, at A3.
74. Alan Fram, *House Kills Effort to Scuttle Safety Pact with Smith & Wesson,* ASSOCIATED PRESS NEWSWIRE, June 27, 2000.
75. Vanessa O'Connell, *Glock Plans to Change How It Sells Guns; Taurus Unit Echoes Call on Restrictions,* WALL ST. J., Mar. 21, 2000, at A3.
76. Barrett, O'Connell, & Mathews, *supra* note 73.
77. Sharon Walsh, *Gun Industry Views Pact as Threat to Its Unity,* WASH. POST, Mar. 18, 2000, at A10.
78. Stuart Taylor, *Guns and Tobacco: Government by Litigation,* NAT'L L. J., Mar. 25, 2000.
79. Walter K. Olson, *Plaintiffs' Lawyers Take Aim at Democracy,* WALL ST. J., Mar. 21, 2000, at A26.
80. Fram, *supra* note 74.

legislation in Congress to ban lawsuits against the gun industry. Others applauded the ability of private litigation to succeed in an area where Congress, locked in partisan gridlock, had failed.[81]

On June 26, 2000, New York became the first state to sue the gun industry. The suit was commenced after the failure of negotiations aimed at requiring gun manufacturers to adopt a code of conduct to reduce the number of guns that end up in the hands of criminals. New York sued the gun industry under a public nuisance law (in contrast to many of the previous actions brought by cities and counties on grounds of negligence and product liability).[82] Under New York state law, guns possessed illegally are a public nuisance. The gun industry contributes to the nuisance by designing and distributing weapons in a manner that ultimately leads to criminal possession. The suit named nine gun manufacturers, three importers, and twelve wholesalers as defendants in the action and sought to require the gun industry to change the way it distributes and sells guns. No damages were sought.

Litigation by cities and counties against gun companies has had mixed results. As of October 2000, six courts across the country had refused to dismiss lawsuits brought by eighteen cities and counties (including Boston; New Orleans; Detroit; Wayne County, Michigan; and twelve cities and counties in California). Judges dismissed actions by Bridgeport, Connecticut; Cincinnati; and Miami–Dade County, Florida.[83]

81. *Id.*
82. Paul Barrett, *New York State Files Suit Against Gun Firms*, WALL ST. J., June 27, 2000, at B8.

83. Paul M. Barrett, *New York City Intends to Sue 25 Gun Makers*, WALL ST. J., June 20, 2000, at A4.

KEY WORDS AND PHRASES

assumption of risk   328
comparative fault   330
design defect   322
discovery-of-injury statute   330
failure to warn   322
government-contractor defense   331
limited-fund class action   336

manufacturing defect   322
market-share liability   327
obvious risk   330
preemption defense   331
premises liability   328
privity of contract   318
product liability   318

revival statute   330
state-of-the-art defense   331
statute of limitations   330
statute of repose   333
unavoidably unsafe product   325

QUESTIONS AND CASE PROBLEMS

1. A product may be deemed unreasonably dangerous as a result of a manufacturing defect, a design defect, or a failure to warn. Explain how the three types of defects differ.

2. Roy Mercurio drove his Nissan Altima into a tree in the middle of the night at a speed of approximately thirty-five miles per hour. When the car struck the tree, the passenger compartment collapsed, and Mercurio was seriously injured. He was driving while intoxicated with a blood alcohol content that was at least .18 percent. He brought a product liability action against Nissan on the grounds that the car was not crashworthy. Nissan argued that the claim should be dismissed, asserting as defenses assumption of risk and unforeseeable misuse of the car due to the fact that Mercurio was driving while intoxicated. Mercurio argued that evidence of his blood alcohol level at the time of the accident was irrelevant and should be excluded. How should the court rule? [*Mercurio v. Nissan Motor Corp.*, 81 F. Supp. 2d 859 (N.D. Ohio 2000)]

3. Pamela Murray had spinal fusion surgery to treat severe back pain. Her physician used two stainless steel Dynamic Compression Plates to stabilize her spine and also used six screws during the surgery to secure the plates to her spine. The plates and four of the screws were manufactured by Synthes (U.S.A.), Inc. The other two screws were manufactured by two other companies. At the time of the surgery, the Food and Drug Administration had not approved the use of bone screws to attach an internal fixation device. When Murray learned that the process had not been approved by the FDA, she filed suit in district court in Pennsylvania, alleging design defect

and manufacturing defect against the manufacturers. Under Pennsylvania state law, strict liability is imposed on manufacturers of products sold "in a defective condition unreasonably dangerous to the user or consumer." However, state law also denies application of strict liability to "unavoidably unsafe products" such as prescription drugs. Should Murray be entitled to sue the manufacturers in strict liability? Are there other theories under which she could recover against the companies? [*Murray v. Synthes (U.S.A.), Inc.,* WL 672937 (E.D. Penn. Aug. 23, 1999)]

4. Terrell Redman, senior vice president of Alligator Corporation, is evaluating a potential acquisition for the company. The entity he wishes to acquire has several divisions, two of which manufacture chemicals and industrial tools.
   a. What risks does the acquisition present to Alligator Corporation under product liability law?
   b. Are there ways to limit the company's exposure?
   c. To the extent that product liability law will expose the company to liability for the acquired company's prior conduct, what steps must be taken at the time of the acquisition to ensure the ability to defend potential claims? [*Tolo v. Wexco,* 993 F.2d 884 (9th Cir. 1993)]

5. Rochelle Black's husband worked as an auto mechanic in the Air Force from 1971 to 1986. When he died of lung cancer in 1991, Mrs. Black sued forty-eight asbestos manufacturers, alleging that her husband's death had been caused by his exposure to asbestos-containing products while working as an auto mechanic. She based her claims on market-share liability. Although she conceded that market-share liability would be inappropriate if she were alleging injury from exposure to many different types of asbestos products, she argued that she should be allowed to proceed in her market-share claims against four manufacturers of asbestos-containing "friction products," including brake and clutch products. These four companies produced friction products that contained between 7 and 75 percent asbestos fibers. How should the court rule? What if the range of asbestos fibers in the products produced by the four companies was 40 to 60 percent? [*Black v. Abex Corp.,* 603 N.W.2d 182 (N.D. 1999)]

6. Laura Hollister was a business student at Northwestern University. She attended a business school party with her friend and then returned to her apartment. When Hollister left the party, she was intoxicated. She woke the next morning with no memory of subsequent events after she had re-

turned to her apartment, but she had third-degree burns over 55 percent of her body. From the evidence, police determined that she had been cooking; when she reached for the cupboard over the stove, her shirt brushed against the hot burner and caught fire. Hollister brought an action against the department store where her mother had purchased the shirt on the grounds that the shirt was defective because it lacked a warning regarding its extreme flammability. The department store argued that the danger inherent in having clothing come into contact with a hot stove is "open and obvious." How should the court rule? [*Hollister v. Dayton Hudson Corp.,* 201 F.3d 731 (6th Cir. 2000)]

7. Many states have laws regulating sales that impose an implied warranty of merchantability to the effect that the merchandise is fit for consumer use. Should the same durational limit that is provided to buyers by the manufacturers' express warranties be applied to implied warranties? [*Carlson v. General Motors Corp.,* 883 F.2d 287 (4th Cir. 1989), *cert. denied,* 495 U.S. 910 (1990)]

8. Richard Welge loves to sprinkle peanuts on his ice cream sundaes. One day Karen Godfrey, with whom Welge boards, bought a 24-ounce vacuum-sealed plastic-capped glass jar of peanuts at a convenience store in Chicago. In order to obtain a $2 rebate that the manufacturer was offering to anyone who bought a "party" item, such as peanuts, Godfrey needed proof of her purchase from the jar of peanuts. Using an Exacto knife, she removed the part of the label that contained the bar code. She then placed the jar on top of the refrigerator. About a week later, Welge removed the plastic seal from the jar, uncapped it, took some peanuts, replaced the cap, and returned the jar to the top of the refrigerator, all without incident.

   A week later, Welge took down the jar, removed the plastic cap, spilled some peanuts into his left hand to put on his sundae, and replaced the cap with his right hand. But as he pushed the cap down on the open jar, the jar shattered. His hand was severely cut and is now, he claims, permanently impaired.

   Welge has brought suit and has named three defendants: the convenience store, the manufacturer of the peanuts, and the manufacturer of the jar itself.
   a. From whom will Welge be able to recover?
   b. What defenses, if any, are available to the defendants? [*Welge v. Planters Lifesavers Co.,* 17 F.3d 209 (7th Cir. 1994)]

9. Darleen Johnson was driving her Ford car under rainy conditions on a two-lane highway through

Missouri. The car's front tires had a reasonable amount of tread remaining on them, but the back tires were nearly bald. For an undetermined reason, Johnson lost control of the car, spun into the other lane, and collided with a pickup truck driven by Kathyleen Sammons. Johnson was killed instantly.

Johnson's father claimed that the inboard C.V. joint boot on the front axle was torn, which allowed debris to contaminate the joint. (The boot is a covering that contains the grease that lubricates the joint.) This contamination allegedly made the joint act like a brake on the left front wheel and caused Johnson's car to pivot around that wheel and into the path of the oncoming pickup truck.

Ford admits that the joint boot can become torn, which will allow contamination of the joint. In its manuals, Ford recommends periodic inspection of the boots. However, Ford contends that the joint on Johnson's car was contaminated during or after the accident. Ford also contends that contamination of the joint could not result in the joint seizing and creating a loss of steering control, and that the worst that could result from contamination would be some vibration and noise. According to Ford, Johnson's accident was caused by road conditions and driving error.

The case is submitted to the jury on theories of strict liability and negligent design and manufacture.

a. Is Ford liable for Johnson's death?

b. Are there any additional arguments that Ford can raise in its defense?

c. Who will prevail in this case? [*Johnson v. Ford Motor Co.,* 988 F.2d 573 (9th Cir. 1993)]

MANAGER'S DILEMMA

10. You are a product manager at Beak, Inc., a company that manufactures construction equipment. The head of your department, Kimura Kim, recently received a visit from the company's CEO, who described for Kim a problem with the performance of Beak's Titan cranes. Apparently, the hook portion of the crane has broken off on several occasions, resulting in the release of the object being moved. As yet, no serious injuries have resulted from the accidents. Research by the company's engineering department indicates that the problem occurs only when the cranes are used at full capacity on windy days and could be eliminated by reinforcing certain joints on the crane. The CEO is considering various alternatives, including doing nothing; sending a letter to all owners of the crane, warning them not to use the crane at full capacity on windy days; recalling the cranes to make the adjustment; and changing the design of the cranes to incorporate the reinforcements. Recalling the cranes would involve a cost to Beak of approximately $100 million. Changing the design of the cranes would require retooling a significant portion of the company's equipment at a cost of $50 million.

Kim asks you to draft a memo outlining Beak's possible liability for injuries resulting from operation of the cranes and recommending a course of action designed to minimize that liability. Draft that memo, paying particular attention to the liability implications of each alternative course of action and the company's ethical responsibilities to its customers.

INTERNET SOURCES

The U.S. Consumer Product Safety Commission's Web site provides information about recent recalls and other agency activity.	http://www.cpsc.gov
The Federal Trade Commission's Web site provides information about its enforcement actions, consumer protection, and its regional offices.	http://www.ftc.gov
The Better Business Bureau's Web site provides consumers with information about its private regulation of business, including recent warnings and local offices.	http://www.bbb.org
The International Organization for Standardization's Web site provides information about its attempt to create various technical and product standards for business and government.	http://www.iso.ch
This site, maintained by the tobacco industry, links to various tobacco companies' Web sites regarding tobacco litigation.	http://tobaccoresolution.com/
The Association of Trial Lawyers of America, a group of attorneys who represent plaintiffs in tort and consumer protection lawsuits, maintains a site with articles and news clippings regarding recent product liability cases and developments.	http://www.atla.org

CHAPTER 11

Intellectual Property *and* Cyberlaw

STRATEGIC IMPORTANCE OF INTELLECTUAL PROPERTY

Intellectual property has risen to a position of prominence on the strategic agenda of today's managers. *Intellectual property* is any product or result of a mental process that is given legal protection against unauthorized use. Representing somewhere in the range of 70 percent of an average firm's value (up from less than 40 percent in the past),[1] intellectual property is now recognized as one of the most important revenue-generating assets held by a company. As observed by the *New York Times,* "Intellectual property has been transformed from a sleepy area of law and business to one of the driving engines of a high technology economy."[2]

There are four basic types of intellectual property: patents, copyrights, trademarks, and trade secrets. Different types of intellectual property are protected in different ways.

A *patent* is a government-granted right to exclude others from making, using, or selling an invention. The patent holder need not personally make use of the invention. After a period of time (twenty years from the application date for utility patents and fourteen years for design patents in the United States), the patent expires and the invention is dedicated to the public.

A *copyright* is the legal right to prevent others from copying or displaying an original expression embodied in a literary work, musical work, sound recording, audiovisual work, sculptural work,

pictorial work, computer program, or any other work of authorship fixed in a tangible medium. The protection also extends to derivative works, that is, works based upon the protected work. It is the expression that is protected, not the ideas underlying the expression. The owner also has exclusive rights to distribute, display, and perform the work. Protection is provided for at least seventy years. The layout or topography of an integrated circuit may be protectable as a registered mask work under the Semiconductor Chip Protection Act of 1984.

Trademarks—that is, words or symbols (such as brand names) that identify the source of goods or services—are also given legal protection. Because trademarks tend to embody or represent the goodwill of the business, they are not legally transferable without that goodwill. Trademarks are protected for an indefinite time. They can be valuable marketing and business assets. The packaging or dressing of a product may also be protected under the trademark laws as *trade dress.*

Trade secrets are another valuable form of intellectual property in today's world economy. A *trade secret* is information that gives a business an advantage over its competitors that do not know the information. Plans, formulas, customer lists, research and development results, sales data, pricing information, computer programs, marketing techniques, and production techniques can all qualify as trade secrets. The classic example of a trade secret is the formula for Coca-Cola. Trade secrets are protected for an indefinite time.

Know-how—that is, detailed information on how to make or do something—can be a trade secret, or it can be show-how. *Show-how* is nonsecret information used to teach someone how to make or do something. It is generally not legally protectable.

---

1. Kevin G. Rivette & David Kline, *Discovering New Value in Intellectual Property,* HARV. BUS. REV. (Jan.–Feb. 2000), at 58.
2. KEVIN G. RIVETTE & DAVID KLINE, REMBRANDTS IN THE ATTIC: UNLOCKING THE HIDDEN VALUE OF PATENTS 2 (2000) (quoting Sabra Chartrand, *Patents,* N.Y. TIMES, Apr. 5, 1999).

CHAPTER OVERVIEW

This chapter describes the law of patents, copyrights, trademarks, and trade secrets in detail. It also discusses technology licensing, that is, the selling of permission to use a patented invention, a copyrighted work, a trade secret, or a trademark.

Patents

Patents are one of the oldest recognized forms of intellectual property. Their importance has increased as our society has become more technologically advanced. Patents have formed the basis for whole businesses, such as the production of instant cameras, and industries, such as high-engineering plastics and biotechnology. Patent disputes have become one of the battlegrounds on which high-technology battles are fought.

Patent protection is specifically authorized by Article I of the U.S. Constitution. The Constitution grants Congress the power "to promote the Progress of Science and useful Arts, by securing for limited times to . . . Inventors the exclusive Right to their . . . Discoveries." The Patent and Trademark Office (PTO), an agency of the U.S. Department of Commerce, is responsible for issuing patents.

The PTO issued its first patent in 1790.[3] Since that time, the PTO has issued over six million patents. It is-

3. Brigid Quinn & Maria V. Hernandez, *PTO Announces First Patent and Trademark of New Millennium*, U.S. Patent & Trademark Office press release, Jan. 13, 2000.

sued 169,094 patents in 1999 alone, a 36 percent increase from the number issued in 1997. The types of patents issued by the office have changed dramatically over the years, particularly in the last century. The first patent issued in 1900 was for an early version of the washing machine. The first patent issued in 2000 was for a sun visor/eye shield for athletes participating in "extreme" sports. The top ten private-sector patent recipients for the 2000 calendar year (based on a preliminary count) are identified in Exhibit 11.1.

UTILITY PATENTS

U.S. patent law provides for three types of patents: utility patents, design patents, and plant patents. Utility patents are the most frequently issued type of patent. A *utility patent* protects any novel, useful, and nonobvious process, machine, manufacture, or composition of matter, or any novel, useful, and nonobvious improvement thereof. To be approved, a patent application must satisfy the *utility requirement;* that is, the invention must have a practical or real-world benefit. If the PTO issues a patent, the patent owner has the exclusive right to

EXHIBIT 11.1	Top Ten U.S. Patent Recipients in 2000			
Preliminary Rank in 2000	Preliminary Number of Patents in 2000	Organization	Final Rank in 1999	Final Number of Patents in 1999
1	2,886	International Business Machines Corporation	1	2,756
2	2,020	NEC Corporation	2	1,842
3	1,890	Canon Kabushiki Kaisha	3	1,795
4	1,441	Samsung Electronics Company, Ltd.	4	1,545
5	1,411	Lucent Technologies, Inc.	9	1,152
6	1,385	Sony Corporation	5	1,410
7	1,304	Micron Technology, Inc.	14	933
8	1,232	Toshiba Corporation	6	1,200
9	1,196	Motorola, Inc.	7	1,192
10	1,147	Fujitsu Limited	7	1,192

Source: *USPTO Releases Annual List of 10 Organizations Receiving Most Patents,* U.S. Patent & Trademark Office press release, Jan. 10, 2001.

make, use, sell, and import for use the invention for a nonrenewable period of twenty years from the date on which the patent application was filed.

An invention is *novel* if it was not anticipated, that is, if it was not previously known or used by others in the United States and was not previously patented or described in a printed publication in any country. Even if the invention is novel, it will be denied patent protection if its novelty merely represents an obvious development over *prior art,* that is, existing technology. That was the concern of two New Yorkers who applied for a patent for their device to remove garbage bags blown into tree branches. Although similar to the fruit picker, invented in 1869, the "bag-snagger" was found sufficiently different to warrant a separate patent.

The inventor must be diligent in his or her effort to file for patent protection. A *statutory bar* precludes protection in the United States if, prior to one year before the inventor's filing, the invention was described in a printed publication in the United States or a foreign country or if it was publicly used or sold in the United States. In most other countries, a patent application must be filed *before* the invention is described in a publication, publicly used, or sold.

Even when the inventor files promptly for protection of a novel, useful, and nonobvious invention, he or she may still be denied a patent. There is no protection for nonstatutory subject matter, such as abstract ideas (rather than specific applications of ideas), mental processes, naturally occurring substances, arrangements of printed matter, scientific principles, or laws of nature.

BIOTECHNOLOGY

In *Diamond v. Chakrabarty,*[4] a microbiologist sought patent protection for his invention of a live, human-made, genetically engineered bacterium capable of breaking down crude oil. The patent examiner rejected the patent application for the bacterium. On appeal, the U.S. Supreme Court held that living organisms, if they are human-made, can be patented. The Supreme Court stated that patent statutes should include "anything under the sun that is *made* by man." Thus, patent protection was extended to the new organism.

The Supreme Court prophetically noted that its decision in *Chakrabarty* could determine whether research efforts would be accelerated by the hope of reward or slowed by the want of incentives. In fact, the *Chakrabarty* decision spurred investment in commercial genetic-engineering re-

search and spawned a whole new industry. It allowed small biotechnology firms to attract venture capitalists and other investors. The very existence of some biotechnology firms can be traced to the *Chakrabarty* decision.

In 1987, then-PTO Commissioner Donald Quigg confirmed that nonnaturally occurring, nonhuman multicellular living organisms (including animals) are patentable subject matter. The PTO issued a patent in 1988 on a transgenic mouse that was engineered to be susceptible to cancer. It issued three more mouse patents in 1993.

More recently, the patent laws have been applied even more broadly to include patents on human and other genes. According to the PTO, gene sequences are patentable subject matter. Specifically, a gene patent covers "the genetic composition isolated from its natural state and processed through purifying steps that separate the gene from other molecules naturally associated with it."[5] Close to 6,000 gene patents have been issued to date, and about one-sixth of those are for human genes.[6] Many gene patents have been associated with research leading to the treatment of disease. Exhibit 11.2 shows the top ten holders of U.S. patents on human, animal, plant, and microbial gene sequences.

Gene patenting (which has always been controversial) sparked new controversy when a patent was issued to Human Genome Sciences, Inc. for a gene that was discovered to serve as a platform from which the AIDS virus can infect cells of the body. Questions arose as to the legal and moral right to own a human gene. Perhaps

5. 66 Fed. Reg. 4 (Jan. 5, 2001).
6. Jenna Greene, *PTO to Rein in Gene Patents,* LEGAL TIMES, July 24, 2000.

EXHIBIT 11.2 Top Ten Holders of Gene Patents

This exhibit lists the top holders of all gene-related patents issued by the U.S. Patent and Trademark Office as of June 28, 2000.

Holder	Patents
Incyte Genomics	397
University of California	253
Glaxo SmithKline	248
U.S. government	205
Novo Nordisk	196
Genentech	165
Isis Pharmaceuticals	146
Chiron	135
American Home Products	130
Novartis	128

Source: U.S. Patent & Trademark Office, *as reported in* Antonio Regalado, *The Great Gene Grab,* MIT TECH. REV. (Sept.–Oct. 2000).

4. 447 U.S. 303 (1980).

ETHICAL CONSIDERATION

What legal and ethical issues are raised by efforts to patent the process for creating a chimera, a two-species mixture created by combining human and animal embryo cells? Should an inventor be allowed to patent the process for making human clones?

INTERNATIONAL CONSIDERATION

In late 2000, the European Union elected not to extend patent protection to software for fear that it would stifle innovation. Software can be copyrighted in Europe, but that protects against actual copying of the code, not reverse engineering.

more significantly, concerns arose over the effect of giving one company the ability to control medical research related to a life-threatening disease, especially when that company may not appreciate the medical value of the gene.[7] In response to these concerns, on December 29, 2000, the PTO issued new guidelines for examination of gene applications for compliance with the utility requirement. The PTO had been faulted for issuing patents on genes before the inventors had ascertained the gene's function. By requiring a stronger showing of utility, these guidelines will make it more difficult for genes to be patented. Nonetheless, the propriety of gene patents remains the subject of intense controversy.

COMPUTER SOFTWARE

The law's embrace of software patenting began in 1981, when the Supreme Court held that if a "claim containing a mathematical formula implements or applies that formula in a structure or process, which when considered as a whole, is performing a function which the patent laws were designed to protect (e.g., transforming or reducing an article to a different state or thing), then the claim [may be patentable]."[8] Since then, software patents have been sought by developers and granted by the PTO at a quickening pace.

7. For an excellent collection of articles on the pros and cons of gene patents, see MIT Tech. Rev. (Sept.–Oct. 2000).
8. Diamond v. Diehr, 450 U.S. 175, 176 (1981).

Many experts believed that the PTO was issuing software patents too readily. Most software code is not published, so much of the relevant prior art is not accessible to the PTO examiners. In addition, U.S. patent applications are not published until and unless a patent is issued. As a result, the PTO has been issuing patents for computer programs that many believe are not novel or are merely obvious improvements of existing programs.

In March 1994, partly in response to charges from intellectual property lawyers that the patent was overly broad, the PTO took the unusual step of reversing a patent granted to Compton's New Media and Encyclopedia Britannica. The patent (which covered virtually all ways of storing and retrieving text, sound, and images stored on compact discs) appeared to give Compton's a dominant position in the fast-growing multimedia market. The fact that the patent was issued in the first place was cited by the Interactive Multimedia Association as evidence of the need to improve the training of the PTO's software examiners.

BUSINESS METHOD PATENTS

In recent years, the PTO has been overwhelmed with applications for patents on "business method" inventions, particularly in connection with the Internet and electronic commerce. This wave of applications was spurred largely by the following decision, which granted a patent on a computerized system for managing mutual fund investments.

A CASE IN POINT

CASE 11.1

State Street Bank & Trust Co. v. Signature Financial Group, Inc.

United States Court of Appeals for the Federal Circuit
149 F.3d 1368 (1998).

Summary

FACTS Signature Financial Group was the assignee of U.S. Patent No. 5,193,056, entitled "Data Processing System for Hub-and-Spoke Financial Services Configuration" (the hub-and-spoke patent). The system was designed for use in Signature's business as administrator and accounting agent for "fund of funds" mutual funds. Through this system, mutual funds (the spokes) pool their assets into an investment portfolio (the hub), which is organized as a partnership. Signature then can enjoy economies of scale in managing the investments, along with the tax benefits of partnership status.

(Continued)

(Case 11.1 continued)

State Street sought to license the hub-and-spoke patent from Signature, but negotiations broke down. State Street then sought a summary judgment ruling that the patent was invalid. The district court granted summary judgment for State Street, and the case was appealed.

ISSUE PRESENTED Is a computerized data-processing system patentable?

SUMMARY OF OPINION The U.S. Court of Appeals for the Federal Circuit observed that three categories of subject matter are not patentable: laws of nature, natural phenomena, and abstract ideas. As clarified by the U.S. Supreme Court, mathematical algorithms, formulas, or calculations are considered abstract unless they are reduced to a useful and practical application. Based on this precedent, the Federal Circuit ruled that "the transformation of data, representing discrete dollar amounts by a machine through a series of mathematical calculations into a final share price constitutes a practical application of a mathematical algorithm, formula or calculations."

The court then went on to consider whether the patent was invalid under the judicially created business method exception. The court concluded that the business method exception was no longer an "applicable legal principle," and it took "this opportunity to lay this ill-conceived exception to rest."

RESULT The patent was upheld, and the summary judgment ruling was reversed.

Following the decision in *State Street,* the number of applications for business method patents rose dramatically. The PTO granted 301 business method patents in 1999, compared to 30 in 1997.[9] In response to criticism that it was granting business method patents too readily, with an inadequate review of prior art, the PTO announced in March 2000 that it was adding a second layer of review for applications seeking protection for e-commerce-based business methods.[10]

DESIGN PATENTS

A *design patent* protects any novel, original (rather than nonobvious), and ornamental (rather than useful) design for an article of manufacture. Design patents protect against the copying of the appearance or shape of an article such as a computer terminal cabinet, a perfume bottle, a typeface, or the icons and screen displays used in computer programs. A design dictated by function rather than aesthetic concerns cannot be protected by a design patent, but it may be protectable by a utility patent. A design patent has a duration of fourteen years from the date on which the patent application was filed, compared to twenty years for utility and plant patents.

9. Anandashankar Mazumdar, *PTO to Add Additional Layer to Reviews of Electronic-Commerce Business Methods,* 68 U.S.L.W. 2603 (Apr. 11, 2000).
10. *Id.*

Traditionally, design patents have rarely been used in the United States; other forms of protection, such as unfair competition law, have been relied upon instead. Recently, however, the use of design patents has been increasing.

PLANT PATENTS

Plant patents protect any distinct and new variety of plant that is asexually reproduced (that is, not reproduced by means of seeds). The variety must not exist naturally. Thus, a plant patent will not be issued to someone who merely discovers a wild plant not previously known to exist. Once a plant patent is granted, the patent owner has the exclusive right to exclude others from asexually reproducing, using, or selling the plant. Currently, the Senate is reviewing the Omnibus Patent Act, which would widen the scope of patents related to proprietary, specially bred plants to include fruit and flowers.

Filing *for* Patent Protection

To obtain patent protection in the United States, the inventor must file a patent application with the PTO. Each patent application contains four parts: the specifications, the claims, the drawings (except in chemical cases), and a declaration by the inventor.

E-Commerce Patents

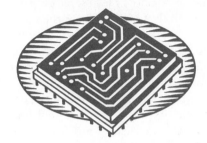

One of the most famous business method patents was issued for Amazon.com's "one-click" feature (U.S. Patent No. 5,960,411). Visitors to the Amazon.com Web site can input their name, address, and credit card data once and thereafter purchase items with one click of the mouse button. The company received a patent on this method of ordering online in September 1999. Amazon promptly sued Barnes & Noble for patent infringement, claiming that Barnesandnoble.com had instituted a similar one-click ordering procedure in its online "Express Lane." The trial court granted Amazon a preliminary injunction, after finding that it was likely to prove infringement of its patent. In a closely watched decision, the Federal Circuit overturned the preliminary injunction, after concluding that Barnesandnoble.com had "mounted a serious challenge to the validity of Amazon's patent,"[a] based on prior art.

Priceline.com received a patent for its Internet version of an old auction technique, the name-your-price "reverse" auction used to sell tulips in Amsterdam since the sixteenth century. Priceline sued Microsoft Corporation and its online travel spin-off Expedia for allegedly violating that patent. The suit was settled for an undisclosed sum when Microsoft and Expedia agreed to pay royalties to Priceline for a license to use its invention.[b]

a. Amazon.com, Inc. v. Barnesandnoble.com, Inc., 239 F.3d 1343 (Fed. Cir. 2001).
b. Bloomberg News, *Priceline, Expedia Settle Patent Infringement Suit*, CNET NEWS, Jan. 9, 2001.

The *specifications* must describe the invention (as defined by the claims) in its best mode and the manner and process of making and using the invention so that a person skilled in the relevant field could make and use it. The *best mode* must be the best way the inventor knows of making the invention at the time of filing the application. All descriptions must be clear, concise, and exact.

The *claims* (the numbered paragraphs at the end of the patent) describe those elements of the invention that will be protected by the patent. Any element not specifically set forth in the claims is unprotected by the patent. Thus, the drafting of the claims is crucial in obtaining adequate protection.

The *drawings* must show the claimed invention. The *declaration by the inventor* must state that the inventor has reviewed the application and believes that he or she is the first inventor of the invention. The inventor is also required to make a full disclosure of any known relevant prior art, that is, of developments that relate to the claimed invention. Knowing the prior developments assists the patent attorney in drafting the claims to avoid the prior art; it also permits the patent examiner to determine whether the invention is novel or whether it would have been obvious to those familiar with the relevant field.

The patent examiner may initially reject the application as being precluded by prior inventions or otherwise failing to meet the statutory requirements. (Ninety-nine percent of all patent applications are initially rejected by the PTO.) The inventor may then present arguments (and in extreme cases, evidence) to contest the examiner's rejection or may seek to amend the application to overcome the rejection. If the application is finally rejected, the inventor can either refile the application as a continuation application or appeal to the Patent Office's Board of Appeals and subsequently to either the U.S. District Court for the District of Columbia or the U.S. Court of Appeals for the Federal Circuit. Once the examiner agrees that a patent should be issued, and the examiner and applicant agree on the precise language of the claims, a patent may be issued.

Patent Infringement

TYPES

A patent may be infringed in three ways: directly, indirectly, or contributorily. The patent law defines *direct infringement* as the making, use, or sale of any patented invention within the United States during the term of the patent. When an accused device or process does not have precisely each element of a particular claim of a patent (that is, the patent is not literally infringed), but the patented invention is replicated in a product or process that works in substantially the same way and accomplishes substantially the same result, a direct infringement can be found under the *doctrine of equivalents*.

In 1996, the U.S. Supreme Court held that construction of the words in the claims is a matter of law for the court, not the jury, to decide.[11] The Court reasoned that "[t]he construction of written instruments is one of those things that judges often do and are likely to do better than jurors unburdened by training in exegesis."

Indirect infringement is defined as the active inducement of another party to infringe a patent. *Contributory infringement* occurs when one party knowingly sells an item that has one specific use that will result in the infringement of another's patent. For example, if a company sells a computer add-on card for a specific use that will infringe another's patent, the sale is a contributory infringement even though the add-on card itself does not violate any patent. Direct infringement can be committed innocently and unintentionally; indirect and contributory infringement require some knowledge or intent that a patent will be infringed.

DEFENSES

A defendant to a patent-infringement action may assert a variety of defenses to a patent-infringement claim, including (1) noninfringement of the patent, (2) invalidity of the patent, or (3) misuse of the patent.

Noninfringement The defense of *noninfringement* asserts that the allegedly infringing matter does not fall within the claims of the issued patent. Under this defense, the specific language of the patent claims is compared with the allegedly infringing matter. If the allegedly infringing matter is not described by the patent claims, then the defense of noninfringement is successful. The patent owner may not assert any claim interpretation at odds with the application on file with the PTO. This doctrine is known as *file-wrapper estoppel*. Because the patent holder has previously negotiated the scope of the invention with the PTO, he or she may not renegotiate that scope in a subsequent court proceeding.

Invalidity A patent is presumed to be valid, but a court may find it invalid if (1) the invention was not novel, useful, or nonobvious when the patent was issued; (2) the patent covers nonstatutory subject matter such as an abstract idea, a scientific principle, a mental process, or a method of doing business; (3) a statutory bar was created by a publication or sale of the invention more than one year prior to the filing of the patent application; or (4) any other requirement of the patent law was not met.

11. Markman v. Westview Instruments, Inc., 517 U.S. 370 (1996).

Patent Misuse A defense based on *patent misuse* asserts that although the defendant has infringed a valid patent, the patent holder has abused his or her patent rights and therefore has lost, at least temporarily, the right to enforce them. Patent misuse is not statutorily defined, but courts have found misuse when a patent holder has conditioned the granting of a patent license upon the purchase of other, unrelated goods or technologies. The patent holder will be barred from recovering for any infringement of the patent during the period of misuse. If the patent holder later "purges" himself or herself of the misuse, however, the patent holder may recover for any subsequent infringement.

REMEDIES

If a valid patent has been infringed, the patent holder has a variety of remedies: (1) preliminary and permanent injunctive relief, (2) damages, (3) court costs, and (4) attorneys' fees.

Injunctive Relief A preliminary injunction may be used to prevent any further infringement of the patent pending the court's ultimate decision. Most courts, however, are reluctant to grant injunctive relief before they have determined that a valid patent has actually been infringed. Once such a determination has been made, the patent holder is entitled to permanent injunctive relief.

Damages Damages may also be awarded, based on a reasonable royalty for the infringer's use of the invention. Court costs, as fixed by the court, may be added. The

---

ETHICAL CONSIDERATION

Some inventors have made fortunes by turning out a steady stream of blueprints and drawings for new or improved devices without bothering to develop them into commercial products or even to create prototypes. Instead, they design their claims on top of existing products in order to create infringements by current manufacturers; then they delay filing their applications as long as possible to maximize their patents' value and longevity.[a] Is it ethical to use the patent system simply as a means of collecting revenue rather than as a spur to innovation?

a. For an example of such a controversy, see Bernard Wysocki, Jr., *How Patent Lawsuits Make a Quiet Engineer Rich and Controversial*, WALL ST. J., Apr. 9, 1997, at A1.

court also has discretion to increase the award of damages by up to three times for intentional or willful infringement and to award attorneys' fees in exceptional cases.

The instant-camera litigation between Polaroid Corporation and Eastman Kodak Company illustrates the potential for large damages awards for patent infringement. Kodak sought a license from Polaroid to produce instant cameras and film. The parties never reached an agreement, but Kodak nonetheless began to develop an instant camera and film, which were introduced in 1976. Polaroid sued Kodak for patent infringement. A federal district court held that Kodak had infringed twenty claims of seven Polaroid patents and enjoined Kodak from any further infringements. The injunction terminated Kodak's instant-camera business and left it with $200 million worth of useless manufacturing equipment and losses of $600 million.[12] Kodak was later ordered to pay $910 million in damages to Polaroid for infringing its patents, including $454.2 million in lost profits and royalties and $455.3 million in interest. This is the largest award ever granted in a patent-infringement suit. Even so, the award "disappointed Polaroid and heartened Kodak."[13]

In 2001, a unanimous U.S. Court of Appeals for the Federal Circuit held that Intel Corporation had no right to use patented "Clipper" technology owned by Intergraph Corporation.[14] Intergraph, which first sued Intel in November 1997, indicated that it would seek royalties from Intel for use of its patented technology in Intel's Pentium processors.

It can be difficult for small companies to recover from larger firms because the cost of patent litigation can be prohibitive. In fact, some corporations may purposely lengthen and complicate the discovery process in order to strain the resources of their smaller challengers. Nonetheless, intellectual property rights, such as a patent or trademark, can provide a David with an effective means to strike down a Goliath. For example, Stac Electronics successfully sued Microsoft for patent infringement of its data compression technology. Aware of the danger that Microsoft could make the litigation process very expensive, Stac significantly narrowed its claims and limited its requests for discovery. As a result, the case went to trial only one year after the complaint was filed.

In 1994, a jury awarded Stac a $120 million judgment against Microsoft for infringing two of Stac's patents.[15] Similarly, in the trademark area, GoTo.com was successful in forcing Walt Disney Company to abandon the use of a logo for its Go.com service that was infringingly similar to GoTo's trademarked logo.

 # International Patent Protection

With increased globalization, many companies are seeking patent protection abroad as well as in their home country. Almost two hundred countries grant some form of patent protection.

Several multinational treaties seek to harmonize the application of the intellectual property laws of various jurisdictions. These treaties do not alter the differing criteria that each jurisdiction applies to determine whether an application for protection merits acceptance; instead, they seek to coordinate the registration and recognition process among signatory countries.

In most countries, if two entities file for protection of the same patented invention or trademark, protection is granted to the entity that filed first. This can be a problem for an inventor or a trademark owner who files for protection in one country and later discovers that another person has subsequently filed for protection of the same invention or trademark in another country. The International Convention for the Protection of Industrial Property Rights (popularly known as the Paris Convention) seeks to avoid this type of problem by encouraging reciprocal recognition of patents, trademarks, service marks, and similar forms of intellectual property rights among signatory nations (of which there are more than eighty, including the United States). Each signatory nation agrees to grant to nationals of other signatory nations a grace period after filing in their home country within which to file corresponding patent or trademark applications in other signatory countries. These grace periods are six months for trademarks and one year for most patents; they give the filers a reasonable time to complete the filing and registration formalities in foreign countries.

The Paris Convention does not alter the substantive requirements of the laws of signatory countries, so patent or trademark protection in one signatory country does not necessarily translate into protection in another

12. Polaroid Corp. v. Eastman Kodak Co., 789 F.2d 1556 (Fed. Cir. 1986), *cert. denied,* 479 U.S. 850 (1986).

13. Lawrence Ingrassia & James S. Hirsch, *Polaroid's Patent-Case Award, Smaller than Anticipated, Is a Relief for Kodak,* Wall St. J., Oct. 15, 1990, at A3.

14. Intergraph Corp. v. Intel Corp., 2001 U.S. App. LEXIS 2929 (Fed. Cir. Mar. 1, 2001).

15. *A Giant-Killer Should Limit Scope of Attack,* Nat'l L.J. Mar. 13, 1995.

signatory country. Differing rules governing eligibility may mean that actions in the original jurisdiction that do not compromise protection there may forfeit protection in others (for example, disclosure or sale of inventions prior to filing for a patent). Seeking the appropriate expertise or advice in this area can help a manager avoid irreparable mistakes.

Rather than having to apply for separate patents in many different countries, the Patent Cooperation Treaty (PCT) allows an inventor to file a single international patent application in order to seek patent protection in each contracting country.[16] The international patent application can be filed either with the national patent office (e.g., the PTO for U.S. inventors) or the International Bureau of the World Intellectual Property Organization.

Every international patent application is subject to an "international search" by an International Searching Authority. The results of this search include a list of citations of prior art relevant to the claims of the international patent application and information regarding the possible relevance of the citations to the questions of novelty and nonobviousness. This information enables the applicant to evaluate the chances of obtaining patents in the countries designated. An applicant may also have an international preliminary examination of the application, which provides even more information about the patentability of the invention than the international search.

The laws regarding statutory bars in foreign jurisdictions are radically different from U.S. patent law. A rule of thumb is that any public disclosure of an invention prior to filing the patent application will bar an inventor's ability to obtain foreign patent protection.

The patent practice of other countries is often different from that of the United States. Some jurisdictions are more receptive to certain types of patents than others. A number of countries do not permit invention patents for pharmaceuticals, although they may be entitled to some protection under process patents. Given the differences in patent practice, it is important to discuss the rules that apply in the foreign country with an attorney prior to disclosure or sale of any patentable invention.

⚜ Copyrights

Best-selling novels, award-winning films, off-the-shelf software packages, and compact discs are all copyrightable works. So are restaurant menus, digital videodiscs, designer linens, plush toy animals, and cereal boxes. The United States Copyright Act of 1976 requires that the material for which copyright protection is sought be original (not copied) and fall within one of the following categories: (1) literary works; (2) musical works; (3) dramatic works; (4) pantomimes and choreographic works; (5) pictorial, graphic, and sculptural works; (6) motion pictures and other audiovisual works; and (7) sound recordings.

The act further requires that the work be fixed in a tangible medium from which it can be perceived, reproduced, or communicated. For example, stories may be fixed in written manuscripts, computer software on floppy disks, recordings of songs on compact discs, and staging of a play recorded on videotape. Protection is automatic. Neither registration nor the use of a copyright notice is required. However, it is usually helpful for a growing company to register so that statutory damages and attorneys' fees are available. Otherwise, the company can recover only its actual damages, which can often be difficult to prove for a company with a limited track record or a new product with uncertain prospects.

TERM

The duration of a copyright depends upon the identity of the author. If the author is a known individual, the term is the life of the author plus seventy years. For a work made for hire or for an anonymous or pseudonymous work, the term is the lesser of ninety years after first publication or one hundred years after creation of the work.

ORIGINALITY AND COMPILATIONS

Copyright protection extends only to original works of authorship evidencing some degree of creativity. Facts are not copyrightable. A compilation of facts may be eligible for copyright protection, but only if the selection, coordination, or arrangement of the facts is original. As explained by the Supreme Court, "[t]he sine qua non of copyright is originality."[17] The Supreme Court further explained:

> Facts, whether alone or as part of a compilation, are not original and therefore may not be copyrighted. A factual compilation is eligible for copyright if it features an original selection or arrangement of facts, but the copyright is limited to the particular selection or arrangement. In no event may copyright extend to the facts themselves.

16. U.S. Patent & Trademark Office (visited Feb. 11, 2000), <http://www.uspto.gov/web/offices/pac/dapps/pct/wipo.htm>.

17. Feist Publications, Inc. v. Rural Tel. Serv. Co., 499 U.S. 340, 345 (1991).

Applying this standard, the Supreme Court held that a directory of telephone numbers and addresses, arranged alphabetically, was not copyrightable, even though the creator had expended considerable time and money compiling the directory.

In *Warren Publishing, Inc. v. Microdos Data Corp.,*[18] the U.S. Court of Appeals for the Eleventh Circuit held that a directory of cable television operators (which included number of subscribers, channels offered, prices, and types of equipment used), organized by community, was not sufficiently creative to be copyrightable. Attorney Rebecca Edelson distilled the following principles about the copyrightability of compilations from the *Warren* opinion:

1. A selection of data is not copyrightable when the entire universe is "selected," even if the compiler is the first to think of compiling the information and even if the compilation is commercially useful.
2. A selection is not copyrightable when it is not the result of the compiler's own judgment, even if the compiler is the first to think of making the selection in the particular manner.
3. A "system" of selecting is not subject to copyright protection even if it is creative and original.
4. Organizing principles and discovery techniques are not subject to copyright protection no matter how commercially useful, novel, or industrious they are.[19]

Database publishers have been pressuring Congress to pass legislation to strengthen database protection in the United States. Databases are already afforded greater protection in the European Union. Several bills have been introduced in Congress that would provide varying degrees of protection. For example, the proposed Consumer and Investor Access to Information Act of 1999 (H.R. 1858) would have prohibited the duplication and sale or distribution of a database compiled by another person. A competing proposal, the Collections of Information Antipiracy Act (H.R. 354), would have created a new cause of action under copyright law for the mere misappropriation of compiled information, irrespective of whether that information was later sold or distributed. As of February 2001, no consensus had emerged in Congress as to the appropriate scope of database protection.

EXPRESSION VERSUS IDEA

The Copyright Act prohibits unauthorized copying of the *protected expression* of a work, but the underlying ideas embodied in the work remain freely usable by others. Section 102 of the Act excludes from copyright protection any "idea, procedure, process, system, method of operation, concept, principle or discovery, regardless of the form in which it is described, explained, illustrated, or embodied."

The U.S. Court of Appeals for the First Circuit held that the menu-command structure of the Lotus 1-2-3 computer spreadsheet program, taken as a whole—including the choice of command terms, the structure, sequence, and organization of these terms, their presentation on the screen, and the long prompts—was a method of operation and therefore not protectable.[20] The court reasoned that Lotus 1-2-3's use of commands labeled "Print" and "Copy" was no different from buttons on a videocassette recorder (VCR) labeled "Play" and "Fast Forward." That such VCR buttons are arranged and labeled does not make them an expression of the abstract method of operating a VCR. Rather, the buttons *are* the method of operating the VCR. To the extent there was expression in Lotus 1-2-3's choice of terms such as "Exit" or "Save," the court deemed it part of the method of operation and therefore not copyrightable either. Quoting the U.S. Supreme Court's *Feist*[21] decision, the court noted that "copyright assures authors the right to their original expression, but encourages others to build freely upon the ideas and information conveyed by that work." An evenly divided U.S. Supreme Court affirmed.

When an idea and its expression are inseparable, the *merger doctrine* dictates that the expression is not copyrightable. If it were, this would confer a monopoly over the idea. Thus, a manufacturer of a karate video game cannot keep a competitor from producing another video game based on standard karate moves and rules. The idea of a karate game (including game procedures, karate moves, background scenes, a referee, and the use of computer graphics) is not protected expression. The manufacturer can, however, keep a competitor from copying any original graphics it has used in the game so long as they are not inseparable from the idea of karate or of a karate video game.

18. 115 F.3d 1509 (11th Cir. 1997), *cert. denied,* 522 U.S. 963 (1997).
19. Rebecca "Bec" Edelson, *Another Factual Compilation Bites the Dust Under the Copyright Laws: Warren Publishing, Inc. v. Microdos Data,* 22 NEW MATTER 9–11 (Fall–Winter 1997).
20. Lotus Dev. Corp. v. Borland Int'l, Inc., 49 F.3d 807 (1st Cir. 1995), *aff'd,* 516 U.S. 233 (1996).
21. Feist Publications, Inc. v. Rural Tel. Serv. Co., 499 U.S. 340 (1991).

USEFUL ARTICLES DOCTRINE

Under the *useful articles doctrine,* copyright protection does not extend to a useful article, that is, the useful application of an idea. The application of ideas is considered to be within the province of patent law. The act defines pictorial, graphic, and sculptural works to include "works of artistic craftsmanship insofar as their form but not their mechanical or utilitarian aspects are concerned." For example, blank forms, which are used to record information rather than convey information, are considered articles of use and are not copyrightable.

If the expression of a pictorial, graphic, or sculptural work cannot be identified separately from and exist independently of such utilitarian aspects, copyright protection will be denied to the whole work. An example of an article whose expression is separable from its utilitarian aspects would be a lamp that incorporates a statue of a woman in its base. An example of an article whose expression is not separable from its utilitarian aspects is the layout of an integrated circuit. Although a drawing of the circuit is copyrightable, the actual circuitry is not copyrightable because it is impossible to separate the utilitarian aspect of the circuit from its expression or layout. It is the layout of the circuit that enables the circuit to operate correctly. The circuit may be patentable, however. In addition, the layout or topography of the circuit may be protectable as a registered mask work under the Semiconductor Chip Protection Act of 1984.

COPYRIGHT OWNERSHIP

The author of a work is the original owner of the copyright. The author is either the creator of the work or, in the case of a work made for hire, the party for whom the work was prepared. A *work made for hire* is either (1) a work created by an employee within the scope of his or her employment or (2) a work in one of nine listed categories that is specially commissioned through a signed writing that states that the work is a "work made for hire."

The author can transfer ownership by an assignment of copyright. Assignments are often sought by parties that commission independent contractors to produce works that fall outside the nine categories of the Act, such as computer programs. Thus, if commissioning a work or preparing a work as an independent contractor, one should consult with an experienced copyright attorney to ensure that the desired party obtains copyright ownership.

The advent of nonprint media, such as CD-ROMs and electronic databases, has given rise to disputes between freelance writers and photographers on one side and newspapers and magazines buying their work on the other about who owns the electronic or digital rights. For example, in 1997, a group of freelance writers sued the newspapers to which they sold their stories, alleging that the newspapers' publishing of their work in nonprint media exceeded the newspapers' rights to the material. The U.S. Court of Appeals for the Second Circuit agreed. Although the owner of a copyright for a collective work (in this case, the publisher of the newspaper or magazine) has the right to revise the individual works, that does not include the right to republish them in an electronic database.[22] The U.S. Supreme Court agreed to review the Second Circuit's ruling, but regardless of how the case is ultimately decided, it underscores the importance of negotiating a clear assignment of rights applicable to any known or future media.

EXCLUSIVE RIGHTS

To encourage the production of new works, copyright owners are given certain exclusive economic rights in the work. Any of these rights can be conveyed to others. The copyright owner owns the exclusive rights (1) to reproduce the copyrighted work, (2) to prepare derivative works based on the copyrighted work, (3) to distribute copies or phonorecords of the copyrighted work to the public, (4) to perform the work publicly, and (5) to display the copyrighted work publicly.

Fair Use Doctrine Under the *fair use doctrine,* embodied in Section 107 of the Copyright Act, a person may infringe the copyright owner's exclusive rights without liability in the course of such activities as literary criticism, social comment, news reporting, education, scholarship, or research. In deciding what constitutes fair use, the courts balance the public benefit of the defendant's use against the effect on the copyright owner's interests. The factors they consider are the purpose of the use (including whether it was for profit), the economic effect of the use on the copyright owner, the nature of the work used, and the amount of the work that is used.

In *Campbell v. Acuff-Rose Music, Inc.,*[23] the U.S. Supreme Court held that the commercial use of the copyrighted Roy Orbison song "Pretty Woman" in a parody by rap group 2 Live Crew did not presumptively constitute unfair use with respect to either the character and purpose of use of the copyrighted work or the harm caused by that use to the potential market for the copyrighted work. The Court ruled that a parody that uses no

---

22. *Tasini v. New York Times,* 192 F.3d 356 (2d Cir. 1999), *cert. granted,* 121 S. Ct. 425 (2000).
23. 510 U.S. 569 (1994).

more of the lyrics and music of the original work than is necessary to make it recognizable does not de facto copy an unreasonable part of the copyrighted work, even if the copied part is the heart of the original work.

In a 1994 case,[24] the U.S. Court of Appeals for the Second Circuit held that internal copying by Texaco scientists of articles from copyrighted scientific and technical journals purchased by Texaco was not fair use under the Copyright Act. The scientists were making copies of helpful articles from the circulating library copy to keep in their personal files or in the laboratory.

In a more recent case, the U.S. Court of Appeals for the Sixth Circuit considered fair use in the academic environment.[25] In this case, a Michigan photocopy shop was in the business of preparing course readers for university professors. The professors selected excerpts from a variety of copyrighted works belonging to authors and publishers. The copy shop then compiled and numbered the excerpts, created a table of contents, photocopied the compilation, and sold copies of the assembled reader to students for use in the course. Neither the professor nor the copy shop sought permission to use the excerpts.

One publisher sued the copy shop in federal district court for copyright infringement.

The copy shop argued that its photocopying was fair use because of the ultimately educational use of the course readers by university students, the transformative value of the compilation over the separate copyrighted works, the insubstantial portion of each excerpt compared to the larger copyrighted work, and the lack of displacement for demand of the copyrighted works. The appeals court rejected these arguments. The copy shop's motivation was commercial profit, not education; the "transformative" value was slight at best; the excerpts were substantial; and the market value of the larger, copyrighted works was harmed. Without its defense of fair use, the copy shop was liable for copyright infringement and enjoined from further infringement. The U.S. District Court for the Southern District of New York had reached the same result five years earlier in a case with nearly identical facts involving the copy shop Kinko's.[26]

In the following case, the court considered whether copying software for the purpose of reverse engineering was fair use.

24. American Geophysical Union v. Texaco, Inc., 60 F.3d 913 (2d Cir. 1994).
25. Princeton Univ. Press v. Michigan Document Serv., 99 F.3d 1381 (6th Cir. 1996), *cert. denied,* 520 U.S. 1156 (1997) (mem.).

26. Basic Books, Inc. v. Kinko's Graphics, Inc., 758 F. Supp. 1522 (S.D.N.Y. 1991).

A CASE IN POINT

CASE 11.2

Sony Computer Entertainment, Inc. v. Connectix Corp.
United States Court of Appeals for the Ninth Circuit
203 F.3d 596
(9th Cir. 2000).

Summary

FACTS Sony Computer Entertainment, Inc. produces and markets the Sony PlayStation console, a small computer with hand controls that connects to a television for game playing. The console contains hardware components and software. Sony owns the copyright on the basic input-output system (BIOS), which is the software that operates the PlayStation.

Connectix Corporation makes and sells a software program called "Virtual Game Station." The Virtual Game Station software allows PlayStation game disks to be used on a regular computer. Although the Virtual Game Station does not contain any of Sony's copyrighted material, Connectix made use of Sony's copyrighted BIOS while it was producing it. Specifically, Connectix "reverse engineered" the BIOS to find out how the Sony PlayStation worked. During this process, Connectix made several copies of the BIOS. The BIOS was also copied and otherwise used during the debugging phase.

Sony sued Connectix for copyright infringement. The district court concluded that Connectix's "intermediate copying" was not "fair use" protected under copyright laws and enjoined Connectix from selling the Virtual Game Station or from copying or using the BIOS code in the development of other Virtual Game Station products. Connectix appealed.

ISSUE PRESENTED Were the intermediate copies made by Connectix during the course of its reverse engineering of the Sony BIOS protected by the fair use doctrine?

(Continued)

(Case 11.2 continued)

SUMMARY OF OPINION The U.S. Court of Appeals for the Ninth Circuit began by acknowledging that intermediate copying may constitute copyright infringement even though the final product does not actually contain the copyrighted material. The court also noted that intermediate copying could be protected as a fair use if it was necessary in order to access the "fundamental elements" of the software. This distinction was important because "the Copyright Act protects expression only, not ideas or the functional aspects of a software program."

The court found that the Sony BIOS deserved only a limited level of protection because it contained unprotected elements that could be accessed only through copying. Moreover, the court determined that the methods used by Connectix to reverse engineer the Sony BIOS were necessary to gain access to the unprotected elements. Accordingly, Connectix's intermediate copying of the Sony BIOS constituted a fair use within the meaning of the Copyright Act.

RESULT The appeals court reversed the trial court and remanded with instructions to dissolve the injunction. Connectix did not infringe Sony's copyright.

First Sale Doctrine Under the *first sale doctrine,* codified in Section 109(a) of the Copyright Act, once the copyright owner sells the copyrighted item and thereby puts it in the stream of commerce, the owner has exhausted his or her exclusive statutory right to control distribution of the item. In 1998, the U.S. Supreme Court held that the first sale doctrine applies even when the product is sold outside the United States with the expectation that it will not be resold in the United States.[27]

The Supreme Court decision dealt a blow to U.S. companies trying to combat the gray market, that is, a market where products are sold outside the normal channel of distribution, often at a discounted price.[28] According to sellers of so-called premium brands, consumers will be less willing to pay higher prices for high-quality products if they are sold by discounters. Thus, companies, such as high-end hair-product manufacturer L'anza, try to maintain a list of authorized retailers. By contrast, big retailers, such as Costco and Wal-Mart, favor application of the first sale doctrine to imports so that their customers can buy brand name products at discounted prices.

PREEMPTION OF STATE LAW

Because the Copyright Act is a federal statute, it preempts any state law that conflicts with it. Nonetheless, it may not preclude application of all state laws. For example, in *National Basketball Ass'n v. Motorola, Inc.,*[29] the

National Basketball Association (NBA) sued Motorola and STATS for federal copyright infringement as well as for unfair competition under state law when Motorola began marketing its SportsTrax paging device, which displayed information on NBA games in progress with only a two- to three-minute lag. STATS reporters, who watched the games on television or listened to them on the radio, provided the data feed for SportsTrax.

The U.S. Court of Appeals for the Second Circuit began by noting that the Copyright Act provides protection for simultaneously recorded broadcasts of live performances, including sports events.[30] Although the event itself is not an "original [work] of authorship" and is therefore not copyrightable, broadcast of the event is entitled to copyright protection. State law claims that enforce rights "equivalent" to the federal copyright are therefore preempted. The court, however, recognized an exception for "hot news." The *hot-news exception* applies in cases where (1) the plaintiff generates or gathers the information at a cost; (2) the information is time-sensitive; (3) the defendant's use of the information amounts to a free ride on the plaintiff's efforts; (4) the defendant is in direct competition with the plaintiff; and (5) the availability of other parties to free ride on the plaintiff's efforts would so reduce the plaintiff's incentive to provide the product or service that its existence or quality would be threatened. Applying these requirements to the facts at hand, the court held that the hot-news exception did not apply because the NBA had failed to show that SportsTrax's free riding had any competitive effect on the NBA's incentive to provide a high-quality product. As a

27. Quality King Distrib., Inc. v. L'anza Research Int'l, Inc., 523 U.S. 135 (1998).
28. *See* Edward Felsenthan, *Copyright Scope Limited for Some Firms,* WALL ST. J., Mar. 10, 1998, at B5.
29. 105 F.3d 841 (2d Cir. 1997).

30. 17 U.S.C. § 101 (1997).

"Any intellectual property yet, honey?"

result, the state misappropriation claim was preempted by federal copyright law. Because federal copyright law did not preclude STATS from collecting its data from television or radio broadcasts, the NBA's case was dismissed.

In contrast, in *Brown v. Ames,*[31] the Fifth Circuit ruled that state tort claims for misappropriation of the names and likenesses of music artists were not preempted by federal copyright law. The defendants had allegedly marketed compact discs and cassettes of musical performances by the plaintiff artists without obtaining copyright permission and had used the artists' names and likenesses to assist in the illegal marketing effort. The artists sued both for copyright infringement and for misappropriation. In deciding that the misappropriation claim was not preempted, the court emphasized that names and likenesses are not copyrightable and therefore could not be the subject of a federal copyright claim.

INTERNATIONAL COPYRIGHT PROTECTION

The United States is a party to a number of international copyright treaties, including the Berne Convention for the Protection of Literary and Artistic Works and the Universal Copyright Convention. American works receive the same protection that is afforded to the works of a national in foreign countries that are signatories of the same treaties. Before distributing a copyrightable work outside the United States, it is important to discuss with an attorney what, if any, copyright protection is available for the work in the relevant foreign jurisdictions and what steps are necessary to obtain such protection.

Digital Millennium Copyright Act

In October 1998, President Clinton signed the Digital Millennium Copyright Act (DMCA)[32] into law. The DMCA implemented two recent digital copyright treaties, the World Intellectual Property Organization (WIPO) Copyright Treaty and the WIPO Performances and Phonograms Treaty. The DMCA is designed to provide copyright protection for books, music, videos, software,

E-COMMERCE

31. 201 F.3d 654 (5th Cir. 2000).

32. 17 U.S.C. § 512.

and other creative works transmitted in digital form over the Internet.[33] The DMCA outlaws the manufacture, sale, or distribution of devices used to illegally copy software and makes it a crime to circumvent the antipiracy measures that are part of most commercial software.[34] The DMCA does, however, permit the cracking of copyright protection devices to conduct encryption research, to test computer security systems, and to assess products.

Scientists, librarians, and university professors opposed the original draft of the DMCA because it made it a crime to use copyright works in digitized research papers and classroom materials and thus eroded the fair use doctrine. In response, specific language providing exemptions for fair use, particularly for libraries and educational institutions, was added to the draft of the bill that was passed by Congress. Despite these changes, the American Library Association argued that the DMCA could create a "pay-per-use-intellectual universe" that would prohibit persons from making legal copies of material for private use.[35] The DMCA established a two-year period during which the government was to study how it could affect fair use laws.

In *Kelly v. Arriba Soft Corp.,*[36] a photographer claimed that Arriba, which operates a "visual search engine" on the Internet, violated the DMCA and infringed his copyright when it made his photographs available in "thumbnail" (reduced) form to users of the search engine. Arriba's search engine allowed a user to obtain a list of Web sites in response to a search request, but, instead of retrieving text, the search engine produced a set of thumbnail pictures related to the search request. Approximately thirty-five of the photographer's images were indexed and put in Arriba's image database. The district court held that the company's display of thumbnail versions of copyrighted images was a fair use because the images served a functional rather than an aesthetic purpose. The court rejected the photographer's argument that Arriba had violated the DMCA by displaying the thumbnails of the photographs without displaying copyright management information including the author and title of the work. By clicking on the thumbnail image, users of the search engine could obtain a full-sized version of the picture together with information about the Web site where associated copyright management information was available. Arriba had also posted information instructing its users to check with the originating Web sites before copying and using the reduced images.

The DMCA added a safe-harbor provision shielding an Internet service provider (ISP) from liability for copyright infringement for storing material on the system at the direction of a user, if the service provider:

> (A) (i) does not have actual knowledge that the material or an activity using the material on the system or network is infringing;
>
> (ii) in the absence of such actual knowledge, is not aware of facts or circumstances from which infringing activity is apparent; or
>
> (iii) upon obtaining such knowledge or awareness, acts expeditiously to remove, or disable access to, the material;
>
> (B) does not receive a financial benefit directly attributable to the infringing activity, in a case in which the service provider has the right and ability to control such activity; and
>
> (C) upon notification of claimed infringement as described in paragraph (3), responds expeditiously to remove, or disable access to, the material that is claimed to be infringing or to be the subject of infringing activity.

In *ALS Scan, Inc. v. Remarq Communities, Inc.,*[37] the U.S. Court of Appeals for the Fourth Circuit held that an ISP was not entitled to rely on the safe-harbor defense because it failed to respond properly and expeditiously to notice of infringement that was imperfect but still adequate to enable the ISP to locate the information.

 # Copyright Formalities

Using proper copyright notices and registering copyrighted works afford the copyright owner substantial benefits.

COPYRIGHT NOTICE

Copyright notices are not mandatory for works first published after March 1, 1989, but the use of a notice is advisable because it prevents an infringer from claiming innocent infringement. For works first published prior to March 1, 1989, most copyright authorities agree that notices should still be used to avoid the risk of releasing the work into the public domain. A proper U.S. copyright notice for works distributed within the United States includes these elements: "Copyright" or "Copr." or "©," the year of first publication, and the name of the copyright owner.

REGISTRATION

Registration with the U.S. Copyright Office is a prerequisite for filing an infringement suit for a work of U.S. origin. Statutory damages and attorneys' fees are available only if the work was registered within ninety days after the first

33. John Simons, *Congress Passes Copyright Law for Internet Items,* WALL ST. J., Oct. 13, 1999, at B13.
34. UCLA Online Institute for Cyberspace Law and Policy (visited Aug. 2, 2000) <http://www.gseis.ucla/edu/iclp>.
35. John Schwartz, *House Presses Copyright Bill, Clinton Says He'll Sign Measure Addressing Online Issues,* WASH. POST, Oct. 13, 1998, at C3.
36. 77 F. Supp. 2d 1116 (C.D. Cal. 1999).
37. 239 F.3d 619 (4th Cir. 2001).

INTERNATIONAL CONSIDERATION

In December 1997, the European Commission proposed a copyright directive that would update and harmonize member state copyright laws to bring them into conformity with the WIPO Treaty and the WIPO Performances and Phonograms Treaty. The proposal identified four areas that required legislative action if the European Union were to achieve harmony in its copyright laws: (1) a reproduction right, (2) a communication to the public right, (3) a distribution right, and (4) protection against circumvention of abuse and protection systems. An amended version of the proposed directive was approved by the European Union Council of Ministers in June 2000 and by the European Parliament in February 2001. The Directive on Copyright is intended to complement the Directive on Electronic Commerce enacted on June 8, 2000.[a]

Once enacted, the Directive on Copyright will outlaw the manufacture of devices that facilitate circumvention of copyright-protection technology. The Directive will also provide authors with the exclusive right to authorize or prohibit communication of their work to the public, by wire or wireless means, including interactive Internet sites that offer such works without the author's permission.

a. Directive 2000/31/EC, O.J. (L 178) (July 17, 2000).

publication or was registered prior to the infringement at issue. The availability of statutory damages (generally $100,000 per willful violation) is particularly important for a start-up or a more established company selling a new product because, as noted earlier, the absence of historical sales can make it very difficult to prove actual damages. In addition, registration creates a legal presumption of ownership and copyright validity, which can be extremely helpful to a plaintiff in a copyright-infringement suit. Because the timing of registration is critical to obtaining some of the related benefits, it is important to consult with a copyright attorney before beginning to publicly distribute a work.

◢ Copyright Infringement

Copyright infringement is the copying, modification, display, performance, or distribution of a work without the permission of the copyright owner. The plaintiff in a copyright-infringement suit must show substantial similarity of the protected expression, not merely substantial similarity of the ideas contained in the work. In addition, the plaintiff must prove that the alleged infringer had access to the plaintiff's work.

PIRACY

Private companies in industries ranging from software to designer clothing, cosmetics, toys, liquor, and audiocassettes are increasingly forming alliances to work with government officials in many countries to combat piracy. For example, sixty companies doing business in Mexico (including Levi Strauss, Reebok, Hard Rock Café, Walt Disney, and Tequila Herradura) banded together in 1998 to fight piracy.

Software companies are losing billions of dollars each year due to the illegal copying or pirating of software. According to a recent study by International Planning and Research, about 25 percent of the software sold in the United States is pirated. Lost jobs, wages, and tax revenues attributable to the manufacturing and sale of counterfeit software amount to about $2.8 billion per year in the United States and close to $13 billion globally.[38]

The rapid growth of the Internet has facilitated piracy and created new problems for copyright holders. In 2000, Microsoft announced actions against 7,500 Internet sites in thirty-three countries.[39] In addition to software publishers, music publishers are being challenged by the new technology. According to Frank Creighton, vice president of the Recording Industry Association of America (RIAA), "Technology has created this animal, and technology will need to fix it."[40] One such "fix" is the use of Web robots, programs that search and index the Internet for specific content by visiting Web sites, requesting documents based on certain criteria, and following up with requests for documents referenced in those documents already retrieved. Encryption and watermarking can also be used. Creighton estimates that his association focuses at least three-fourths of its antipiracy resources on the Internet and new technology. Those resources include lawsuits against online music archives that serve as distribution points for hundreds of unauthorized copies of digital sound recordings. The RIAA's suit against Napster is the "Inside Story" for this chapter.

REMEDIES

Civil A plaintiff is entitled to recover his or her actual damages and the defendant's profits attributable to the infringement as well as attorneys' fees under certain circumstances, to the extent that these are not duplicative

38. Microsoft press release, *Microsoft Works Hand-in-Hand with Government Agencies in Combating a $2.8 Billion per Year Piracy Industry* (Nov. 29, 2000) <http://www.microsoft.com/presspass/features/ 2000/nov00/11-29piracy.asp>.
39. Rebecca Buckman, *Microsoft Steps Up Software-Piracy War,* WALL ST. J., Aug. 2, 2000.
40. *Copyright Owners Learning to Police Online Sales, Performance of Musical Works,* 66 U.S.L.W. 2483 (1998).

Intellectual Property Rights *and* Incentives *to* Innovate

A basic tenet of neoclassical economic theory is that productive efficiency and allocative efficiency will be achieved through free competition by private parties interested in maximizing their own welfare. Productive efficiency exists when competition among individual producers drives all but the lowest-cost producers of goods or services out of the market. Allocative efficiency exists when scarce societal resources are allocated to the production of various goods and services up to the point at which the cost of producing each good or service equals the benefit society reaps from its use.

In general, the economic policy of the United States is to foster the functioning of free markets in which individuals may compete. For example, the antitrust laws, discussed in Chapter 20, are designed to protect competition by prohibiting any individual entity or group of entities from monopolizing an industry.

The area of intellectual property is a seeming exception to the general free-market orientation of the U.S. economy. Patent laws provide inventors with the opportunity to gain a legally enforceable monopoly to prevent the manufacture, use, and sale of their inventions for a limited time.

The economic rationale for granting monopolies to inventors is based on the high value of innovation to society and the need to give inventors an incentive. Technological advances are crucial to a growing economy. Development of new techniques increases productive effi-

ciency, thereby expanding the quantity of goods and services that can be produced with a given level of societal resources. Development of new products meeting previously unfulfilled needs increases the welfare of society as a whole. In the past decade, such innovation has taken on increasing importance for the United States in the international context. Although countries with lower-cost labor have a competitive advantage in the manufacture of goods with established production techniques, the United States' competitive advantage lies in its ability to develop new technologies.

Individuals will produce innovations only up to the point at which the rewards they reap equal their costs. Without legal rules protecting the ownership of inventions, whenever a valuable new product or cost-saving technique was introduced, others would become free riders and immediately copy it and profit from it, even though they bore none of the costs of its creation. To ensure that innovation is produced fully up to the point at which its social cost equals its social benefit (that is, to ensure allocative efficiency), the law must guarantee to innovators a

significant part of the benefit from their innovations. The U.S. solution to this problem is to provide inventors whose inventions meet the requirements for a patent with a limited monopoly to exclude others from the manufacture, use, and sale of their inventions. This system ensures that inventors will be able to capture the full benefit of their inventions during the period of their monopoly and that the innovation will be freely available to others thereafter. The stringent requirements for patents prevent unnecessary restrictions on free competition.

An important secondary objective is to give the scientific community access to state-of-the-art technology. Without a legal monopoly, innovators would keep their advances secret to prevent others from copying them. Such secrecy would result in waste of scarce societal resources, as other researchers would struggle to discover what is already known.

The World Bank has identified property rights, including intellectual property rights, as one of the keys to energizing countries in transition to market-based economies. Many developing and transitioning economies have already adopted intellectual property laws similar to those of the developed nations, but, as the World Bank acknowledges, these laws are difficult to enforce. Nevertheless, enforcement of these laws will encourage development of intellectual property and the foreign investment needed to spur growth.

---

of each other. Alternatively, if the copyright is registered within three months of first publication or prior to the alleged infringement, a plaintiff may elect to recover statutory damages, which can be up to $100,000 for willful infringement, and attorneys' fees under certain circumstances. Injunctive relief, seizure of the infringing copies, and exclusion of infringing copies from import into the United States are also available under certain circumstances.

In some cases, an apology by the party that infringed another party's copyright may be either imposed by a court or included as a term of a settlement agreement. Exhibit 11.3 shows the acknowledgment of copyright infringement that the Pine Group published in a quarter-page ad in the *Wall Street Journal* on January 13, 2000.

Although the Copyright Act does not provide a statutory right to a jury trial, a defendant in a copyright-infringement suit in which the copyright holder seeks

---

EXHIBIT 11.3 **Pine Group's Acknowledgment of Copyright Infringement**

ACKNOWLEDGEMENT OF COPYRIGHT INFRINGMENT [sic]
THE PINE GROUP

The Pine Group, through its group companies Pineview Industries Limited ("Pineview") and Pine Technology Limited ("Pine Technology"), makes and sells sound cards for use with computers. On October 26, 1999, Yamaha Corporation brought an action in the Hong Kong Court of First Instance against Pineview and Pine Technology to cease and desist the use of Yamaha's sound software, including S-YXG50, S-YG20, Midplug, XG studio, Visual Arranger and 20 MIDI files. The remedies sought were granted as requested.

The Pine Group, Pineview and Pine Technology acknowledge that each such party has infringed on Yamaha's Software since May 1998 through late October 1999. We sell sound cards under the "IDEMA" trademark in North America. . . .

We sincerely apologize to our customers for supplying unauthorized software. As part of the settlement among Yamaha, Pineview and Pine Technology, we will provide a certificate of authenticity from Yamaha if you can provide a proof of purchase. We sincerely regret our mistake in the infringement and we are determined not to repeat this mistake again. We hereby apologize to Yamaha Corporation for our described actions and for any damages we have caused Yamaha.

This statement is made pursuant to a settlement agreement entered into among Pineview, Pine Technology and Yamaha Corporation.

Date: January 13, 2000
THE PINE GROUP
PINEVIEW INDUSTRIES LIMITED
PINE TECHNOLOGY LIMITED

Source: The Pine Group, Pineview Industries Limited, Pine Technology Limited, *Acknowledgement of Copyright Infringment* [sic], WALL ST. J., Jan. 13, 2000, at B21.

---

statutory damages is entitled to a jury trial under the Seventh Amendment to the U.S. Constitution.[41] The defendant also has the right to have the jury determine the amount of statutory damages.

Criminal Infringers may face criminal penalties. For example, Adrian Frederick Herr, a thirty-year-old who recently pled guilty to two felony counts of copyright infringement and false labeling, faced up to ten years in prison and up to $500,000 in fines for selling as much as $30,000 worth of Microsoft software out of his house.

Before 1997, criminal penalties applied only to willful copyright violations for commercial gain; those who stole copyrighted works and gave them away were immune to criminal prosecution. In December 1997, this immunity was eliminated when President Clinton signed into law the No Electronic Theft Act.[42] This law punishes with fines and prison those who copy compact discs, videocassettes, or software worth more than $1,000 without permission

41. Feltner v. Columbia Pictures Television, Inc., 523 U.S. 340 (1998).
42. The law (Pub. L. No. 105-145) amends the copyright-infringement sections of Titles 17 and 18 of the U.S. Code.

of the copyright holder. No proof that the defendant commercially gained from the infringement is required.

TYPES OF INFRINGEMENT

Direct Infringement In the Michigan and New York copyshop cases discussed above, publishers had accused the shops of *direct copyright infringement;* that is, one party was alleged to have violated at least one of the five exclusive rights of the copyright holder by its own actions. Its alleged infringement was directly against one of the exclusive rights.

Contributory Infringement A party may also be liable for *contributory copyright infringement*—inducing, causing, or materially contributing to the infringing conduct of another with knowledge of the infringing activity.

In 1995, the Church of Scientology sued Internet service provider Netcom On-Line Communications Services, Inc. for contributory infringement. The church based its claim on an ex-member's posting of copyrighted works by the church's founder to a Usenet news group. To post the works, the ex-member allegedly uploaded them to an electronic bulletin board service (BBS) that used Netcom to access the Internet. The federal district court in California concluded that Netcom could be held liable for contributory infringement if it knew or should have known of the infringement but did nothing to remove the posting.[43] Similarly, in 1997, a federal district court in Ohio found a BBS liable for contributory infringement of *Playboy* magazine's copyright in its adult photographs by encouraging BBS subscribers to upload electronic versions of the pictures so that other subscribers could then download them.[44]

In an earlier case, the U.S. Supreme Court considered whether Sony Corporation of America had contributed to the infringement of copyrights held by Universal City Studios, Inc.[45] Universal alleged that Sony, by manufacturing and selling the Betamax videocassette recorder (VCR), had contributed to the infringement of Universal copyrights on programs that were broadcast over the public airwaves, which viewers would copy by means of Sony's device. The Court held that the sale of copying equipment does not constitute contributory infringement if the product has substantial noninfringing uses. In Sony's case, the trial court had found that time-shifting of television programs by private, noncommercial viewers so that the programs could be viewed later was harmless and that many other copyright holders would not object to viewers so shifting their viewing times. Hence, the Court held that Sony's manufacture and sale of VCRs did not contributorily infringe on Universal's copyrights. The concept of contributory infringement has also been applied to trademark law.[46] As explained in the "Inside Story," Napster unsuccessfully argued that its service constituted permissible space-shifting under *Sony*.

Vicarious Infringement Liability also extends to vicarious infringement of copyrights. A defendant may face *vicarious liability* for the actions of the direct infringer if the defendant (1) had the right and ability to control the infringer's acts and (2) received a direct financial benefit from the infringement. Unlike contributory infringement, vicarious infringement does not require that the defendant know of

the primary infringement. Although "direct financial benefit" certainly includes a percentage of the value of each illegal sale, it is not limited to such per unit arrangements.

In 1996, the U.S. Court of Appeals for the Ninth Circuit held that a swap-meet organizer could be held vicariously liable for creating and administering a market where bootleg music was bought and sold.[47] Although the swap-meet organizer did not receive a percentage of sales, it did receive daily rental fees from the infringing vendors, admission fees from customers purchasing the illegally copied music, and incidental payments for parking, food, and other services. Furthermore, the availability of such bootleg music was a significant attraction of the swap meet. The court held that such a financial benefit could satisfy the second prong of the test for vicarious liability.

Registered Mask Work

The Semiconductor Chip Protection Act of 1984 created a highly specialized form of intellectual property, the *registered mask work*. Semiconductor masks are detailed transparencies that represent the topological layout of semiconductor chips. The mask work was the first significant new intellectual property right introduced in the United States in nearly one hundred years. The act gives the owner exclusive rights in the mask for a period of ten years and proscribes copying or use by others. The act specifically allows reverse engineering, however. The law was aimed primarily at counterfeiters who would replicate the semiconductor masks for a chip already on the market and produce the chips without having to expend their own resources on development. The remedies for infringement are an injunction, damages, and the impoundment of the infringing mask and chips.

Trademarks

Most people associate a particular trademark with the product to which it is applied without considering how this association has been generated. For example, when consumers purchase Apple computers, they usually do not think about how the word for a type of fruit has become representative of that particular brand of personal computer. Trademark law concerns itself with just such questions: how trademarks are created, how trademark rights arise, how such rights can be preserved, and why certain marks are given greater protection than others.

---

43. Religious Tech. Ctr. v. Netcom On-Line Communications Servs., Inc., 907 F. Supp. 1361 (N.D. Cal. 1995). In 1996, the parties settled the case. The settlement included an agreement by Netcom to establish a protocol on its home page for handling future intellectual property disputes. The protocol can be found at <http://www.netcom.com/about/protectcopy.html>.

44. Playboy Enters., Inc. v. Russ Hardenburgh, Inc., 982 F. Supp. 503 (N.D. Ohio 1997).

45. Sony Corp. of Am. v. Universal City Studios, Inc., 464 U.S. 417 (1984).

46. Hard Rock Café Licensing Corp. v. Concession Serv., Inc., 955 F.2d 1143 (7th Cir. 1992).

47. Fonovisa, Inc. v. Cherry Auction, Inc., 76 F.3d 259 (9th Cir. 1996).

STATUTORY DEFINITION

The federal trademark act, otherwise known as the Lanham Act, and the 1988 Trademark Law Revision Act[48] define a trademark as "any word, name, symbol, or device or any combination thereof adopted and used by a manufacturer or merchant to identify and distinguish his goods, including a unique product, from those manufactured or sold by others, and to indicate the source of the goods, even if that source is unknown."

This definition has been interpreted as recognizing four different purposes of a trademark: (1) to provide an identification symbol for a particular merchant's goods, (2) to indicate that the goods to which the trademark has been applied are from a single source, (3) to guarantee that all goods to which the trademark has been applied are of a constant quality, and (4) to advertise the goods.

Basically, a trademark tells a consumer where a product comes from and who is responsible for its creation. A trademark also implies that all goods sold under the mark are of a consistent level of quality. A consumer purchasing french fries at a McDonald's restaurant, for instance, can reasonably expect them to taste as good as those sold at any other McDonald's. The trademark does not necessarily reveal the product's manufacturer. For example, the trademark Sanka identifies a brand of decaffeinated coffee. We may not know whether the manufacturer is a company called Sanka, but we know that all coffee products bearing the Sanka mark are sponsored by a single company (or its licensees).

For producers, a trademark represents the goodwill of a business, that is, an accumulation of satisfied customers who will continue buying from that business. Trademark rights are determined predominantly by the perceptions and associations in the minds of the buying public, so maintaining a strong trademark is essential to preserving the success of a business.

Exhibit 11.4 lists the fifteen most valuable brand names in the world in 1995, according to a survey by *Financial World* magazine, and the percentage change in value from 1994.

The first trademark issued in 1900, which is still in use, was for Cream of Wheat and its design. The first trademark registered in the new millennium was issued to a cosmetic company, Origins Natural Resources, Inc., for its name and design. The PTO registered 104,000 trademarks in 1999 alone.

Although most trademarks are verbal or graphic, trademark law also protects distinctive shapes, odors, packaging, and sounds. For instance, there is trademark protection for the unique shape of the Coca-Cola bottle and NBC's three chimes. Color may also qualify as a trademark.

In *Qualitex Co. v. Jacobson Products Co.,*[49] the Supreme Court articulated two principal criteria for determining

48. 15 U.S.C. §§ 1051–72 (1994).

49. 514 U.S. 159 (1995).

EXHIBIT 11.4 **Most Valuable Brand Names**

Rank	Brand	Company	Value (Billions)	Percentage Change (From Prior Year)
1.	Coca-Cola	Coca-Cola Company	$39.05	14%
2.	Marlboro	Philip Morris Companies	38.71	13
3.	IBM	International Business Machines Corporation	17.15	*
4.	Motorola	Motorola, Inc.	15.28	73
5.	Hewlett-Packard	Hewlett-Packard Company	13.17	74
6.	Microsoft	Microsoft Corporation	11.74	31
7.	Kodak	Eastman Kodak Company	11.59	(6)
8.	Budweiser	Anheuser-Busch Companies	11.35	6
9.	Kellogg's	Kellogg Company	11.00	2
10.	Nescafe	Nestle, SA	10.34	(2)
11.	Intel	Intel Corporation	9.71	55
12.	Gillette	Gillette Company	9.67	12
13.	Pepsi	PepsiCo, Inc.	7.81	3
14.	GE	General Electric Company	7.42	25
15.	Levi's	Levi Strauss & Company	6.92	10

*Change not meaningful.

whether trademark protection is available for a color: (1) whether the color has attained secondary meaning and thus identifies and distinguishes a particular brand; and (2) whether the functionality doctrine applies, that is, whether the color serves a useful function and thus addresses a competitive, rather than mere reputational, need.[50] If the color has attained secondary meaning and does not address a functional need, trademark protection is available.

OTHER MARKS

Trademarks should not be confused with other forms of legally protected identifying marks, such as service marks, trade names, and certification marks.

Service Marks A trademark is used in connection with a tangible product; a *service mark* is used in connection with services. The law concerning service marks is almost identical to that of trademarks.

Trade Names While a trademark is used to identify and distinguish products, a *trade name* or a corporate name identifies a company, partnership, or business. Trade names cannot be registered under federal law, unless they are also used as trademarks or service marks. The use of a trade name—evidenced by the filing of articles of incorporation or a fictitious business name statement—gives the company using the name certain common law rights, however.

Certification Marks A *certification mark* placed on a product indicates that the product has met the certifier's standards of safety or quality. An example is the "Good Housekeeping" seal of approval placed on certain consumer goods.

 ## Choosing *a* Trademark

To get a sense of how one chooses a trademark, consider a hypothetical entrepreneur who has developed a new form of computer software. This entrepreneur's program takes personal information—such as place and date of birth and daily biorhythms—and processes it to give the user predictions as to what may happen in the future (on the basis of "the past," that is, on the basis of the inserted information). He has chosen three possible names for his software: Viron, Venus, and Gypsy in a Disc.

The entrepreneur wants to be certain that the trademark he chooses for his software is protectable. Under trademark law, the degree of protection is determined by where a trademark can be classified on a scale of distinctiveness. The more distinctive a mark is, the less likelihood of confusion with other marks. Hence, the most distinctive marks are given, at least initially, the greatest legal protection. The policy is to reward originality in the creation of a mark.

INHERENTLY DISTINCTIVE

Inherently distinctive marks are marks that need no proof of distinctiveness. They are often called strong marks because they are immediately protectable. Fanciful, arbitrary, or suggestive marks are all inherently distinctive.[51]

Fanciful Marks A *fanciful mark* is a coined term having no prior meaning until used as a trademark in connection with a particular product. Fanciful marks are usually made-up words, such as Kodak for camera products and Exxon for gasoline. In the preceding hypothetical, "Viron" is an example of a fanciful, made-up mark.

Arbitrary Marks *Arbitrary marks* are real words whose ordinary meaning has nothing to do with the trademarked product, for example, Camel for cigarettes and Shell for gasoline. In the hypothetical, "Venus" is an example of an arbitrary mark.

Suggestive Marks A *suggestive mark* suggests something about the product without directly describing it. After seeing the mark, a consumer must use his or her imagination to determine the nature of the goods. For instance, Chicken of the Sea does not immediately create an association with tuna fish; it merely suggests some type of seafood. In the hypothetical, "Gypsy in a Disc" is an example of a suggestive mark. It merely suggests a future-predicting software program.

NOT INHERENTLY DISTINCTIVE

Marks that are not inherently distinctive are not immediately protectable. Granting trademark rights for a description of a product that may apply equally to different products would frustrate the fundamental distinguishing purpose of a trademark.

---

50. To grant trademark protection in this circumstance would amount to a grant of monopoly control.

51. Distinctiveness refers to the inherent qualities of a mark and is a completely different concept from fame. Indeed, a famous mark may be so ordinary or descriptive as to be notable for its lack of distinctiveness. Nabisco, Inc. v. PF Brands, Inc., 191 F.3d 208 (2d Cir. 1999).

Descriptive Marks *Descriptive marks* specify certain characteristics of the goods, such as size or color, proposed uses, the intended consumers of the goods, or the effect of using the goods. Laudatory terms, such as First Rate or Gold Medal, are also considered descriptive marks.

Geographic Terms Geographic descriptive terms are usually considered nondistinctive unless secondary meaning (discussed below) has been established. Geographic terms used in an arbitrary manner are inherently distinctive, however, for example, Salem for cigarettes and North Pole for bananas.

Personal Names Personal first names and surnames are not inherently distinctive. But an arbitrary use of a historical name, such as Lincoln for a savings bank, does not require secondary meaning.

Often even judges do not agree on whether a proposed trademark is distinctive. For example, in 1998, America Online (AOL) registered "Buddy List" as a trademark for its Buddy Chat function, which lets AOL users know when friends and family are online, thereby permitting real-time instant exchange of e-mails. After AOL sued AT&T to prevent it from using the term "Buddy List" on its WorldNet online service, the trial court held in 1999 that the mark was not distinctive enough to warrant protection and dismissed the suit. In 2001, the U.S. Court of Appeals for the Fourth Circuit reversed after concluding that the trial judge had failed to give proper weight to the PTO's finding that the "Buddy List" phrase was sufficiently distinctive.[52] It remanded the case for a trial to determine whether "Buddy List" is a protectable trademark. The appeals court agreed, however, with the trial court's ruling that "You've Got Mail" and "IM" were too generic to warrant trademark protection.

SECONDARY MEANING

Marks that are initially unprotectable can still become protectable if they acquire *secondary meaning,* that is, a mental association by the buyer that links the mark with a single source of the product. Through secondary meaning, a mark obtains distinctiveness. Once this occurs, the mark is granted trademark protection. Secondary meaning is necessary to establish trademark protection for descriptive marks, geographic terms, and personal names.

Establishment of secondary meaning depends on a number of factors, such as the amount of advertising, the type of market, the number of sales, and consumer recognition and response. The testimony of random buyers or of product dealers may be required to prove that a mark has acquired secondary meaning. Although its application was denied initially, Microsoft Corporation succeeded in registering the mark "Windows" five years later after it presented studies demonstrating that users associated the mark with Microsoft's operating system for personal computers.

GENERIC

No protection is given to generic terms, such as "spoon" or "software," because doing so would permit a producer to monopolize a term that all producers should be able to use equally. It would be ridiculous to permit one manufacturer to obtain the exclusive right to use the word "computer," for example, and thereby force all competitors to come up with a new word, rather than a brand name, for the same type of product. Generic terms are not protected even when they acquire secondary meaning.

Many terms that were once enforceable trademarks have become generic. For example, "escalator" was once the brand name of a moving staircase, and "cellophane" was a plastic wrap developed by DuPont. Due to misuse or negligence by the owners, these marks lost their connection with particular brands and became ordinary words (see Exhibit 11.5). That is the reason Xerox Corporation spends more than $100,000 a year explaining that you don't "Xerox" a document, you "copy" it on a Xerox copier.[53]

53. Weigel, *Whatever You Do with This Article, Don't "Xerox" It,* CHICAGO SUN-TIMES, Oct. 7, 1990, at 57.

INTERNATIONAL CONSIDERATION

In 1997, Japan enacted a trademark law to harmonize its trademark procedures with the international community and to bring itself into compliance with the Trademark Law Treaty. The 1997 law also addressed the accumulation of unused registered trademarks by allowing anyone to petition for the cancellation of a mark that has gone unused and by making it more difficult to defend against such petitions. The law also shortened the time required to approve trademark applications. Observers expected the new trademark regime to make it easier for non-Japanese to register and protect their marks in Japan. Among its many provisions, the law allowed for the registration of three-dimensional marks for the first time.

52. America Online, Inc. v. AT&T Corp., 2001 U.S. App. LEXIS 2866 (4th Cir. Feb. 28, 2001).

EXHIBIT 11.5 Attempts to Preserve a Trademark

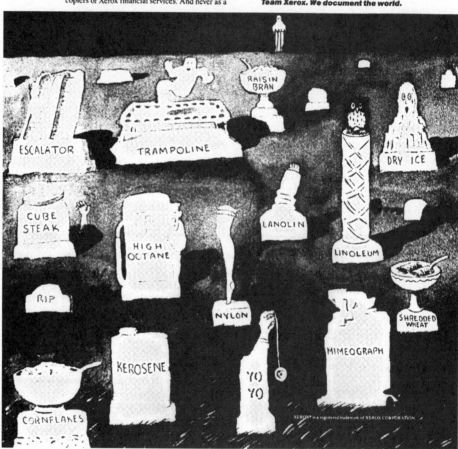

Used by permission.

For terms that describe products made by only one company, the problem of *genericism*—the use of the product name as a generic name—is acute. Without competitive products, buyers may begin to think of the trademark as indicative of what the product is rather than where the product comes from. Manufacturers can try to avoid this problem by always using the trademark as an adjective in conjunction with a generic noun. It is all right to say "Sanka decaffeinated coffee" or "a Kleenex tissue," but not "a cup of Sanka" or "a Kleenex." Once the buying public starts using the mark as a synonym for the product, rather than as a means of distinguishing its source, loss of the trademark is imminent.

INTERNATIONAL CONSIDERATION

India, the world's most populous democracy, is paying increased attention to intellectual property rights as it attempts to attract foreign investment and expand its role in international trade. Although the Indian legal system is notoriously slow, its courts are acting with relative speed to issue injunctions and search-and-seize orders to halt the sale of fake goods. Still, trademark applications, which rose fourfold between 1992 and 1997, take five to seven years to process. Violations of software copyrights have also fallen. Such pirating accounted for 89 percent of the software market in 1991 but for only 60 percent in 1996. The fall is the result of stronger copyright laws, elimination of duties on software imports, and aggressive litigation by copyright holders and support from international business associations.[a]

a. Jonathan Karp, *India's Laws a Mixed Blessing for Investors,* WALL ST. J., July 11, 1997, at A10.

 # Creating Rights *in a* Trademark

Trademark rights initially are obtained in the United States through use of the mark in commerce or the filing of an intent to use application with the PTO. Following use in interstate commerce, additional rights may be obtained by federal registration. State registration requires only intrastate use.

USE

A trademark is used in commerce if it is physically attached to goods that are then sold or distributed. Each subsequent use of a trademark creates greater rights because increased sales and advertising generate greater customer awareness of the mark as representing the product. Nonetheless, advertising and promotional activities in the United States by a foreign restaurant bearing a foreign trademark, but providing no restaurant services in the United States, was held not to constitute sufficient "use" of that trademark in commerce to merit protection in the United States.[54] As noted earlier, for marks that are not inherently distinctive, use is also necessary to establish secondary meaning.

54. Buti v. Impressa S.R.L., 139 F.3d 98 (2d Cir. 1998).

For inherently distinctive marks in the United States, ownership is governed by priority of use. The first person to sell the goods under a mark becomes the owner and senior user of the mark. The mark is protected immediately, provided the adoption and use of the mark are done in good faith and without knowledge, actual or constructive, of any superior rights in the mark.

There is an exception to the rule of first use. If a subsequent, or junior, user establishes a strong consumer identification with its mark in a separate geographic area, the junior user may be granted superior rights for that area. The senior user, by failing to expand its business to other parts of the country, takes the risk that a junior user may be permitted to use the same or a confusingly similar mark in a distant area. The junior user's use must be in good faith; that is, the junior user must take reasonable steps to determine whether any preexisting mark is confusingly similar to the one it plans to use.

This geographic rule is inapplicable, however, if the senior user has applied for or obtained federal registration. Once the senior user has filed an application or has obtained federal registration, it is permitted to claim nationwide constructive notice of the mark. This precludes any use of the mark—even a good faith use—by a junior user. Even with an application pending or registration, however, the senior user may not take any action against the junior user in a geographically removed area until the senior user is likely to expand into that area.

TRADEMARK SEARCHES

A company about to use a new trademark needs first to conduct a trademark search. Without conducting a search, the company has no way of knowing whether use of the proposed mark will constitute an infringement. The time, money, and effort spent on promotion and advertising will be wasted if use of the mark is ultimately prohibited.

There are various ways of searching a mark. The records of the PTO provide information on federally registered marks; the office of the secretary of state usually can provide relevant data for state marks. Both state and federal registrations describe the mark and the goods it identifies, the owners of the mark, the date of registration, and the date on which the mark was first used. Most of this registration material has been computerized and can be accessed by an attorney.

Searching for unregistered marks is more difficult. Trade and telephone directories are often a good source of common law uses of marks. Some searches can be done by anyone using the Internet. There are also several professional trademark search firms that search databases for customers. Although there is always the risk that a new mark or a common law user may be untraceable, any search is better than no search. Searching is evidence of a good faith effort to determine whether any other entity has preexisting rights in a mark.

FEDERAL REGISTRATION

Although not a requirement for obtaining U.S. rights in a mark, registration on the federal Principal Register provides many legal advantages. Such registration provides constructive notice of a claim of ownership in all fifty states. This makes it easier to enjoin subsequent users because unauthorized use of a federally registered mark cannot be in good faith. Other benefits of registration on the Principal Register include (1) *prima facie* evidence of ownership; (2) the "incontestable" right (subject to certain defenses) to use the mark, obtainable after five years of continuous use following registration; and (3) the right to prevent importation into the United States of articles bearing an infringing mark.

Registration on the Principal Register makes strategic sense. It deters others from using the mark, as they are on constructive notice of the mark's ownership. It also gives the owner the right to preempt junior users if the owner expands into their territories.

Certain marks that do not qualify for registration on the Principal Register may be registered on the Supplemental Register. Such registration does not afford the owner any of the above benefits, however, and should be pursued only upon the advice of counsel.

Federal registration of trademarks is conducted by the PTO. An applicant may file either an "actual use" application or an "intent to use" application. For the latter, the applicant must state a bona fide intent to use the mark, then commence use, and provide the PTO with a statement of use within six months of receiving notice that the application is entitled to registration. The six-month period can be extended for up to thirty months, giving applicants a total of three years from the date of the notice of allowance in which to file the statement of use. Registration is postponed until the applicant actually uses the mark. The applicant has priority rights, however, against any party who neither used the same mark nor filed an application for it before the application filing date.

The registration process can be complex and confusing, and consultation with legal counsel is strongly advised before proceeding. It is also time-consuming. After an application is filed, it can take up to eighteen months for a federal registration to be issued. Most state registrations take less time. Consequently, a company waiting on federal registration may simultaneously register the mark on the state level to ensure more immediate protection.

STATE REGISTRATION

State registration does not provide as much protection as federal registration, but it does offer certain benefits. In most states, registration can be obtained within a few weeks of filing and is proof of ownership of the mark. For marks that are not eligible for federal registration, state registration usually provides at least a modicum of protection, as long as there has been sufficient use of the mark. The degree of protection is determined by the relevant state statute.

State registration cannot preempt or narrow the rights granted by federal registration. For example, a junior user with a state registration predating a senior user's federal registration gains exclusive rights in the mark only in the geographic area of continuous usage preceding the federal registration, and not the entire state. A state trademark law that purported to reserve the entire state for the junior user would be preempted by the Lanham Act.

INTERNATIONAL PROTECTION

The United States is one of the few countries where a trademark can be created by use rather than registration. In virtually every other country, the right to use a mark belongs to the first person to file an application for trademark registration.

As noted earlier, however, the Paris Convention provides for a six-month grace period from the date a trademark registration application is filed in the home country to file in other signatory countries. As long as the foreign filing is made within that grace period, it is treated as if it had been filed in the foreign jurisdiction on the date it was filed in the home country.

The Madrid Agreement Concerning the International Registration of Trademarks allows for centralized international registration of trademarks. The owner of a trademark in its home country can file at the International Bureau of the World Intellectual Property Organization in Geneva for registration of its trademark in those signatory countries that it specifies.

The Pan American Convention recognizes the right of a trademark owner in one signatory country to successfully challenge the registration or use of that same trademark in another country. The issue is whether persons using or applying to register the mark had knowledge of the existence and continuous use of the mark in any of the member states on goods of the same class.

⚓ Loss *of* Trademark Rights

Failure to use one's mark—known as *abandonment*—may result in the loss of rights. A federally registered mark that has been abandoned can be used by a junior user. A trademark search can reveal whether a previously registered trademark has lost its enforceability. There are two types of abandonment: actual and constructive.

ACTUAL ABANDONMENT

Actual abandonment occurs when an owner discontinues use of the mark with the intent not to resume use. Mere nonuse for a limited period does not result in loss of protection. There is, however, a presumption of abandonment after two years of nonuse. Because protection for federally registered marks is nationwide, the abandonment must be nationwide for loss of rights to result.

CONSTRUCTIVE ABANDONMENT

Constructive abandonment results when the owner does something, or fails to do something, that causes the mark to lose its distinctiveness. Constructive abandonment can result from a mark lapsing into genericism through improper use, such as using "thermos" as a noun rather than a brand name. It can also result from the failure of an owner to adequately control companies licensed to use its mark. Thus, a licensor should carefully exercise quality controls and approval procedures for its licensees' products to ensure a consistent quality level.

 ## Trademark Infringement

Every trademark owner runs the risk either of having a mark infringed or of being the infringer of someone else's mark. A trademark can be infringed whether or not it is registered; the test for determining infringement in both cases is similar. To establish infringement, a trademark owner must prove (1) the validity of the mark

(note that a federally registered mark is *prima facie* valid), (2) priority of usage of the mark, and (3) a likelihood of confusion in the minds of the purchasers of the products in question.

Proving validity and priority of usage is fairly straightforward if the mark is registered. Even if the mark is not registered, proof is a factual matter. Establishing likelihood of confusion, on the other hand, involves subjectively weighing a variety of factors, including (1) the similarity of the two marks with respect to appearance, sound, connotation, and commercial impression; (2) the similarity of the goods; (3) the similarity of the channels of trade in which the goods are sold; (4) the strength of the marks, as evidenced by the amount of sales and advertising and the length of use; (5) the use of similar marks by third parties with respect to related goods and services; (6) the length of time of concurrent use without actual confusion; and (7) the extent and nature of any actual confusion of the two marks in the marketplace.[55]

Taking advantage of trademark confusion, however, does not necessarily amount to infringement. In 1996, the U.S. Court of Appeals for the Sixth Circuit ruled that a travel agency had not infringed Holiday Inns' trademark in its vanity toll-free telephone number by using a similar number.[56] To promote itself, Holiday Inns had widely publicized its toll-free reservation line as 1-800-HOLIDAY, which translates to 1-800-465-4329 on a numeric keypad. Perhaps anticipating that dialers would mistake Holiday Inns' letter "O" for the number zero, the travel agency reserved the toll-free number 1-800-405-4329 for its own use. Acknowledging the potential for confusion, the court rejected Holiday Inns' claim of trademark infringement. The travel agency did not create the confusion; it merely took advantage of it.

Under the Federal Trademark Dilution Act of 1995,[57] owners of famous trademarks are entitled to sue for damages and injunctive relief from parties whose commercial use of a mark "begins after the mark has become famous and causes dilution of the distinctive quality of the mark." Damages are available only if the defendant willfully intended to trade on the reputation of the famous mark owner or to cause dilution of the famous mark. Relief is available even if the other mark does not cause consumer confusion as to the source of the product. Dilution can result from "blurring" or "tarnishment." Blurring occurs when the nonfamous mark reduces the strong association between the owner of the famous mark and its products. Tarnishment occurs when use of the famous mark in

55. *See, e.g.,* Brookfield Communications, Inc. v. West Coast Enter. Corp., 174 F.3d 1036 (9th Cir. 1999).
56. Holiday Inns, Inc. v. 800 Reservation, Inc., 86 F.3d 619 (6th Cir. 1996), *cert. denied*, 519 U.S. 1093 (1997).
57. 15 U.S.C. §§ 1125, 1127 (Supp. 1996).

connection with a particular category of goods or goods of an inferior quality reduces the positive image associated with the products bearing the famous mark. For example, use of candyland.com for a child pornography Web site tarnished the value of Hasbro's popular trademarked "Candy Land" children's game.

FIRST SALE DOCTRINE

As with copyrighted items, under the first sale doctrine, the right of a producer to control the distribution of a trademarked product extends only to the first sale of the product. Resale of the original product by the first purchaser is neither trademark infringement nor unfair competition. The first sale doctrine attempts to strike a balance among (1) the trademark law's goal of allowing producers to reap the benefits of their reputation, (2) consumers' desire to receive the genuine product they bargain for, and (3) the maintenance of competitive markets by limiting producer control of resale.

In 1995, Sebastian International, a consumer products manufacturer, attempted to get around the first sale doctrine by affixing a special mark to its products. The mark read "Sebastian Collective Salon Member" and referred to an organization of professional hair salons and distributors that Sebastian created and controlled. When drugstore discounter Longs Drug Stores, which was not a member of the group, attempted to sell Sebastian products with the mark, Sebastian sued for trademark infringement and unfair competition. Although a trial court preliminarily enjoined Longs from selling Sebastian products, the U.S. Court of Appeals for the Ninth Circuit relied on the first sale doctrine to reverse that decision and allow Longs to continue selling the products.[58]

58. Sebastian Int'l, Inc. v. Longs Drug Stores Corp., 53 F.3d 1073 (9th Cir. 1995), *cert. denied*, 516 U.S. 914 (1995) (mem.).

REMEDIES

The remedies for trademark infringement include injunctive relief, an accounting for lost profits due to customer confusion, and damages. The type of relief granted is determined on a case-by-case basis.

DOMAIN NAMES AND CYBERSQUATTING

Internet addresses are called *domain names.* The top-level domain is the domain name's suffix, which characterizes the type of organization. For example ".edu" is used by educational organizations, and ".com" by commercial organizations. Country codes, such as ".fr" for France, also serve as top-level domain names. The secondary-level domain identifies the specific organization. For example, in the domain name "cnn.com," the "cnn" identifies Cable News Network. As the Internet is increasingly used to conduct business, companies seek domain names that easily identify their Web locations.

The regulatory body that oversees the Internet's address system is the Internet Corporation for Assigned Names and Numbers (ICANN). Until very recently, only a limited number of top-level domain names were available through ICANN, forcing companies to compete for the treasured .com address. In November 2000, ICANN approved the use of seven new top-level domain names, thereby dramatically increasing the number of possible Internet addresses available. Exhibit 11.6 lists the new domain names and their permitted uses.

Domain names are registered on a first-come, first-served basis. Because the registrar does not check whether use of the name by the person seeking registration would violate someone else's trademark, a practice developed, dubbed "cybersquatting," whereby persons

EXHIBIT 11.6 New Top-Level Domains

Domain	Permitted Uses
.aero	Registration limited to entities providing services related to the air transport industry.
.biz	General commercial top-level domain.
.coop	Initial registration limited to National Cooperative Business Association members.
.info	General commercial top-level domain.
.museum	Registration limited to museums accredited by the Museum Domain Management Association (Internet Council of Museums and J. Paul Getty Trust).
.name	Registration limited to personal names for personal use.
.pro	Registration limited to individuals or entities that can prove membership in legal, medical, and accounting professions (perhaps other fields as well).

would register famous trademarks as domain names, then offer to sell them to the trademark owner for a "ransom."[59] ICANN defines *cybersquatting* as the registration of a domain name that is confusingly similar or identical to a protected trademark, where the person registering the domain name has no legitimate interest in that particular domain name and registers and uses it in bad faith.

As explained in the "Inside Story" for Chapter 4, ICANN developed a uniform domain name dispute resolution policy (UDRP) and authorized dispute resolution service providers to handle such disputes. The first such authorized provider was WIPO's Mediation and Arbitration Center. Under the UDRP, a complaint will be successful only if it demonstrates that:

59. *See, e.g.*, Panavision Int'l, L.P. v. Toeppen, 141 F.3d 1316 (9th Cir. 1998).

1. The domain name is identical or misleadingly similar to a trademark to which the complainant has rights;
2. The respondent has no legitimate rights in the domain name; and
3. The domain name is being held and used in bad faith. Bad faith is established by showing that the respondent registered the domain name in order to:
   a. Later sell it to the owner of the trademark to extract profit;
   b. Prevent a trademark owner from using the domain name;
   c. Interfere with the business of a competitor; or
   d. Extract profit due to the likelihood of confusion with the complainant's trademark.

In late November 1999, the Lanham Act was amended to include the Anticybersquatting Consumer Protection Act (ACPA).[60] The ACPA creates a federal remedy for cybersquatting. Under the ACPA, a person is liable in an action by the owner of a distinctive or famous mark if, with a bad faith intent to profit from that mark, he or she registers, traffics in, or uses a domain name that (1) in the case of a mark that is distinctive at the time of the registration of the domain name, is identical or confusingly similar to that mark, or (2) in the case of a mark that is famous at the time of the registration of the domain name, is identical or confusingly similar to or dilutive of that mark. The ACPA definition of cybersquatting is broader than the ICANN definition in that it makes bad faith alone actionable, regardless of use. The standard is whether there was "bad faith intent to profit."

The following case was the first ACPA case decided by a U.S. court of appeals.

60. Pub. L. No. 106-113 (1999).

A CASE IN POINT

CASE 11.3
Sporty's Farm LLC v. Sportsman's Market, Inc.
United States Court of Appeals for the Second Circuit
202 F.3d 489
(2d Cir. 2000), cert. denied, 120 S. Ct. 2719 (2000).

In the Language of the Court

FACTS Sportsman's is a mail-order catalog company that is well known to pilots who purchase its products. Sportsman's expanded its catalog business into tools and home accessories. In the 1960s, Sportsman's began using the logo "Sporty" to identify its products and catalogs; in 1985, Sportsman's registered it as a trademark with the U.S. Patent and Trademark Office. The company spends approximately $10 million per year advertising the Sporty logo.

Omega is a mail-order company that sells scientific process measurement and control instruments. In 1994 or 1995, the owners of Omega, Arthur and Betty Hollander,

(Continued)

(Case 11.3 continued)

decided to enter the aviation catalog business and formed a wholly owned subsidiary, Pilot's Depot, LLC. Omega registered the domain name sportys.com with Network Solutions, Inc., the organization responsible for registering domain names. At the time, Arthur Hollander was aware that Sportsman's used the Sporty trademark.

Nine months after registering sportys.com, Omega formed a subsidiary called Sporty's Farm, which grows and sells Christmas trees, and sold to it the rights to sportys.com. Sporty's Farm began advertising its Christmas trees on a sportys.com Web page. Ralph S. Michael, the CEO of Omega and manager of Sporty's Farm, claimed that he selected the name "Sporty's Farm" because of a dog named Spotty that he owned when he was young. Spotty strayed and was therefore sent to live on Michael's uncle's farm, the current site of the Christmas tree farm. After the dog went to live on the uncle's farm, Michael referred to the farm as Spotty's Farm; Sporty's Farm was a subsequent derivation. There was no evidence that Hollander was ever acquainted with Michael's dog Spotty or that Hollander was considering starting a Christmas tree business when he registered sportys.com.

In March 1996, Sportsman's learned that Omega had registered sportys.com as a domain name. Sporty's Farm filed a declaratory action seeking the right to continue to use sportys.com. Sportsman's claimed that Omega had committed trademark infringement and dilution pursuant to the Federal Trademark Dilution Act.

OPINION CALABRESI, J., writing for the U.S. Court of Appeals for the Second Circuit:

[The court began by concluding that "Sporty's" was a distinctive mark and that the domain name "sportys.com" was identical or confusingly similar to the registered mark.]

We next turn to the issue of whether Sporty's Farm acted with a "bad faith intent to profit" from the mark *sporty's* when it registered the domain name sportys.com. The statute lists nine factors to assist courts in determining when a defendant has acted with a bad faith intent to profit from the use of a mark. But we are not limited to considering just the listed factors when making our determination of whether the statutory criterion has been met. The factors are, instead, expressly described as indicia that "may" be considered along with other facts.

These factors are:

(I) the trademark or other intellectual property rights of the person, if any, in the domain name;

(II) the extent to which the domain name consists of the legal name of the person or a name that is otherwise commonly used to identify that person;

(III) the person's prior use, if any, of the domain name in connection with the bona fide offering of any goods or services;

(IV) the person's bona fide noncommercial or fair use of the mark in a site accessible under the domain name;

(V) the person's intent to divert consumers from the mark owner's online location to a site accessible under the domain name that could harm the goodwill represented by the mark, either for commercial gain or with the intent to tarnish or disparage the mark, by creating a likelihood of confusion as to the source, sponsorship, affiliation, or endorsement of the site;

(VI) the person's offer to transfer, sell, or otherwise assign the domain name to the mark owner or any third party for financial gain without having used, or having an intent to use, the domain name in the bona fide offering of any goods or services, or the person's prior conduct indicating a pattern of such conduct;

(Continued)

(Case 11.3 continued)

(VII) the person's provision of material and misleading false contact information when applying for the registration of the domain name, the person's intentional failure to maintain accurate contact information, or the person's prior conduct indicating a pattern of such conduct;

(VIII) the person's registration or acquisition of multiple domain names which the person knows are identical or confusingly similar to marks of others that are distinctive at the time of registration of such domain names, or dilutive of famous marks of others that are famous at the time of registration of such domain names, without regard to the goods or services of the parties; and

(IX) the extent to which the mark incorporated in the person's domain name registration is or is not distinctive and famous . . . .

We hold that there is more than enough evidence in the record below of "bad faith intent to profit" on the part of Sporty's Farm. . . . First, it is clear that neither Sporty's Farm nor Omega had any intellectual property rights in sportys.com at the time Omega registered the domain name. . . . Second, the domain name does not consist of the legal name of the party that registered it, Omega. . . .

The third factor, the prior use of the domain name in connection with the bona fide offering of any goods or services, also cuts against Sporty's Farm since it did not use the site until after this litigation began, undermining its claim that the offering of Christmas trees on the site was in good faith. . . .

The most important grounds for our holding that Sporty's Farm acted with a bad faith intent, however, are the unique circumstances of this case, which do not fit neatly into the specific factors enumerated by Congress but may nevertheless be considered under the statute. . . . Omega planned to enter into direct competition with Sportsman's in the pilot and aviation consumer market. As recipients of Sportsman's catalogs, Omega's owners, the Hollanders, were fully aware that *sporty's* was a very strong mark for consumers of those products. It cannot be doubted, as the court found below, that Omega registered sportys.com for the primary purpose of keeping Sportsman's from using that domain name. . . . Given these facts . . . there is ample and overwhelming evidence that, as a matter of law, Sporty's Farm's acted with a "bad faith intent to profit" from the domain name sportys.com as those terms are used in the ACPA.

RESULT The appeals court ordered Omega and Sporty's Farm to release their interest in sportys.com and to transfer it to Sportsman's.

QUESTIONS

1. Why do you think Omega started the Christmas tree farm and named it "Sporty's Farm"?
2. Do you agree that Omega registered sportys.com with bad faith intent to profit from it?

Trade Dress

In addition to protecting registered marks, courts have extended the protections of the Lanham Act to include *trade dress,* that is, the packaging or dressing of a product. In the following case, the Supreme Court considered whether product design constituted trade dress and thus could be protected.

A CASE IN POINT

CASE 11.4

Wal-Mart Stores, Inc. v. Samara Brothers, Inc.

Supreme Court of the United States
529 U.S. 205 (2000).

Summary

FACTS Samara Brothers, Inc. designs and manufactures children's clothing. Its main product is a line of one-piece seersucker outfits decorated with hearts, flowers, and fruits. A number of retail stores, including J.C. Penney, sold this line of clothing. Wal-Mart, one of the nation's largest retailers, contracted with one of its suppliers, Judy-Philippine, Inc., to manufacture a line of clothes similar to Samara's line. Wal-Mart sent photographs of Samara's line to Judy-Philippine, which then copied sixteen of Samara's garments with only minor modifications.

Subsequently, a buyer for J.C. Penney recognized Samara's designs selling at Wal-Mart for a lower price than J.C. Penney was allowed to charge under its contract with Samara. Because it had no contract with Wal-Mart, Samara launched an investigation and discovered that knockoffs of its outfits were being sold at various retailers. Samara sued Wal-Mart, Judy-Philippine, and others on several grounds, including infringement of unregistered trade dress. Samara won a jury trial, and Wal-Mart moved for a judgment that there was insufficient evidence to establish infringement of unregistered trade dress under the Lanham Act. The Second Circuit affirmed the district court's denial of Wal-Mart's motion, and an appeal to the Supreme Court followed.

ISSUE PRESENTED Is product design protectable in an action for infringement of unregistered trade dress?

SUMMARY OF OPINION The U.S. Supreme Court held that unregistered trade dress is not entitled to protection unless it is distinctive or has acquired secondary meaning. Recognizing that design is similar to color in that it is not inherently distinctive, the Court ruled that design could be protected only upon a showing of secondary meaning. The Court explained:

> The attribution of inherent distinctiveness to certain categories of work marks and product packaging derives from the fact that the very purpose of attaching a particular word to a product, or encasing it in a distinctive packaging, is most often to identify the source of the product. . . . In the case of product design, as in the case of color, we think customer predisposition to equate the feature with the source does not exist. Consumers are aware of the reality that, almost invariably, even the most unusual of product designs—such as a cocktail shaker shaped like a penguin—is intended not to identify the source, but to render the product itself more useful or more appealing.

RESULT The Supreme Court held that in an action for infringement of unregistered trade dress under the Lanham Act, a product's design is protectable as distinctive only upon a showing of secondary meaning.

COMMENT Although product design is protected under the Lanham Act only upon a showing of secondary meaning, product packaging may be protected if it is inherently distinctive or has acquired secondary meaning.[61] In November 2000, the U.S. Supreme Court heard oral arguments in a case concerning whether federal trade dress protection extends to a product configuration covered by an expired utility patent.[62]

61. *See* Two Pesos, Inc. v. TacoCabana, Inc., 505 U.S. 763 (1992).
62. Traffix Devices, Inc. v. Marketing Displays, Inc., 200 F.3d 929 (6th Cir. 1999), *cert. granted*, 120 S. Ct. 2715 (2000).

In *Leatherman Tool Group, Inc. v. Cooper Industries,*[63] the U.S. Court of Appeals for the Ninth Circuit considered whether the design of a multipurpose pocket knife was entitled to trade dress protection under the Lanham Act. Leatherman created a knife called the "Pocket Survival Tool" that improved on the "Swiss army knife" by adding a number of additional features, including full-size pliers. A competitor released a nearly identical knife called the "Toolzall," which differed from the Pocket Survival Tool in only a few relatively minor features. Leatherman sued the competitor for trade dress infringement, arguing that the overall appearance of the knife was protected by the Lanham Act. The Ninth Circuit disagreed, holding that the physical details and design of a product may be protected under the trademark laws only if they are nonfunctional. The court stated that "where the whole is nothing other than the assemblage of functional parts, and where even the arrangement and combination of the parts is designed to result in superior performance, it is semantic trickery to say that there is still some sort of separate 'overall appearance' which is non-functional." In 2000, the U.S. Supreme Court agreed to hear an appeal of the Ninth Circuit's decision.

Trade Secrets

In our free-market system, the value of many types of information decreases with availability. With a highly mobile workforce, the demand for modern technologies and innovation may lead to unauthorized disclosure of sensitive information. Trade-secret law is necessary to protect the owners of such information.

The increased value of trade-secret information has fueled a growing trend of litigation in this area. Volkswagen AG of Germany paid General Motors Corporation (GM) $100 million in 1997 as part of its settlement of GM's allegations that its purchasing chief stole trade secrets, including plans for future GM models and car-building techniques, when he left GM to join Volkswagen. The settlement also called for Volkswagen to purchase $1 billion of auto parts from GM over seven years, sever all business ties with the ex-employee in question, and return documents belonging to GM. As explained more fully later in this chapter, under the emerging doctrine of *inevitable disclosure,* an employer can challenge a former employee's decision to work for a competitor, even in the absence of a covenant not to compete, if the new position

63. 199 F.3d 1009 (9th Cir. 1999), *cert. granted,* 121 S. Ct. 297 (2000).

would result in the inevitable disclosure or use of the former employer's trade secrets.

The term "trade secret" is difficult to define due to the fact-specific nature of the case law. Trade secrets can take almost any form. Anything that makes a company unique, or that a competitor would like to know because the information gives a competitive advantage, may be a trade secret.

Trade-secret law is primarily the province of the states. Until recently, the law of trade secrets was developed on a case-by-case basis as the courts applied the laws of the relevant state. The decisions were based on tort theories when the cases involved theft or *misappropriation* of trade secrets and on contract theories when a special relationship or duty was present. Many trade-secret cases involved a combination of the two theories.

COMMON LAW

Under the common law, the definition of "trade secret" most widely accepted by the courts is contained in the Restatement (Second) of Torts. Section 757(b) provides:

> A trade secret may consist of any formula, pattern, device, or compilation of information which is used in one's business, and which gives him an opportunity to obtain an advantage over competitors who do not know or use it. It may be a formula for a chemical compound, a process of manufacturing, treating or preserving materials, a pattern for a machine or other device, or a list of customers.

The courts have developed a number of factors to determine whether specific information qualifies as a trade secret. These factors include (1) the extent to which the information is known outside the business, (2) the extent to which measures are taken to protect the information, (3) the value of the information, (4) the amount of money or time spent to develop the information, and (5) the ease of duplicating the information.

Unfortunately, even with this formal definition and set of factors, a certain amount of guesswork is still required to determine whether a particular type of information qualifies as a trade secret under the common law. The courts have classified identical types of information differently when the factual settings were only slightly different.

THE UNIFORM TRADE SECRETS ACT

In 1979, the Uniform Trade Secrets Act (UTSA) was promulgated in an attempt to provide a coherent framework for trade-secret protection. The drafters of the

UTSA hoped to eliminate the unpredictability of the common law by providing a more comprehensive definition of trade secrets. In particular, the drafters expanded the common law definition by adding the terms "method," "program," and "technique" to the Restatement's list of types of information that are protected. The intention was to specifically include know-how, that is, technical knowledge, methods, and experience. In addition, the common law definition was broadened by deleting the requirement that the secret be continuously used in a business. Accordingly, the UTSA defines a trade secret as:

> Information, including a formula, pattern, compilation, program, device, method, technique, or process, that (1) derives independent economic value, actual or potential, from not being generally known to, and not being readily ascertainable by proper means by, other persons who can obtain economic value from its disclosure or use, and (2) is the subject of efforts that are reasonable under the circumstances to maintain its secrecy.

Although the common law does not protect information unless it is in use, the UTSA definition is broad enough to include (1) information that has potential value from being secret; (2) information regarding one-time events; and (3) negative information, such as test results showing what will not work for a particular process or product.

The most significant difference between the UTSA and the common law definitions is in the overall approach to determining whether information is protectable as a trade secret. As discussed above, at common law a fairly objective five- or six-part test was developed. Although many courts adopted a reasonableness standard when interpreting the individual factors of the test, the focus was on objectivity, as delineated in this test. The UTSA uses a more flexible test, indicating that the steps taken to preserve the information as a trade secret must be reasonable and that the owner must derive independent economic value from secrecy. The latter is a somewhat subjective determination; there are not yet enough cases interpreting the "independent economic value" factor to indicate whether it will become significant over time.

Adopted, at least in part, in forty states, the UTSA has only partially fulfilled its goal of standardizing trade-secret law. States have tended to incorporate only those parts of the UTSA that embody the existing common law of the particular state. Consequently, in states that have adopted the UTSA, the courts rely on a combination of the common law and the UTSA.

While the UTSA seems to have fallen short of its goal of establishing consistent protection for trade secrets, it may provide broader protection to owners of trade secrets in the states where it has been adopted. Its definition of the term "trade secret" is broader than the common law definition, so the burden of proof on the owner is reduced. In addition, the UTSA provides more effective remedies.

The UTSA did not improve on the common law definition in all areas, however. For example, the UTSA adopted separate definitions of the terms "trade secret" and "misappropriation"; but, because the definitions overlap, it is almost impossible to apply them separately. In addition, the protection of unique trade secrets, such as customer lists, may have been undermined because the UTSA does not directly address this controversial type of trade secret.

In a recent California case under the UTSA, however, the California Appeal Court ruled that departing employees of a roofing company had misappropriated trade secrets by taking with them their collection of business cards representing 75 percent of the company's customers.[64] Morlife, Inc. was in the business of inspecting, maintaining, and repairing roofs for commercial properties. Lloyd Perry, a sales representative employed by Morlife, signed an agreement not to use, duplicate, or disclose information about the company's customers if he terminated his employment. In October 1993, Perry and Carl Bowersmith, a Morlife production manager, resigned from Morlife to form Burlingame Buildings, Inc., a competitor of Morlife. Perry took with him his collection of business cards. Perry then used the business cards to solicit business from Morlife's customers.

Morlife filed a suit charging Perry, Bowersmith, and their company with misappropriation of trade secrets in violation of California's Uniform Trade Secrets Act. Considering whether a customer list qualifies as a trade secret under the UTSA, the court emphasized that the list must have economic value. In other words, the secrecy of the information must provide the business with a "substantial business advantage."[65] Moreover, the company must have taken reasonable steps to protect the information from disclosure. The court found that the customer names were not readily ascertainable as it is difficult to ascertain the decision makers with authority to purchase roofing services. Moreover, the company tried to protect the information by allowing only restricted access and requiring employees to sign confidentiality agreements. Thus, in this case, the customer names were entitled to trade-secret protection. The court noted that

---

64. Morlife, Inc. v. Perry, 66 Cal. 2d 731 (Cal. Ct. App. 1997).
65. *Id.*

customer lists need not take any specific form and that the standard for protection is flexible: the more difficult and expensive information is to obtain, the more worthy it is of protection by the court as a trade secret.

ECONOMIC ESPIONAGE ACT

The federal Economic Espionage Act,[66] enacted in 1996, imposes criminal liability (including fines and prison sentences) on any person who intentionally or knowingly steals a trade secret or knowingly receives or purchases a wrongfully obtained trade secret. The act's definition of trade secret is substantially similar to the definition in the Uniform Trade Secrets Act.

Although the act was prompted by a desire to remedy perceived problems created by foreign thefts of trade secrets from U.S. businesses, it applies to any products placed in interstate commerce. Organizations (other than foreign instrumentalities) can be fined up to $5 million (or two times either the defendant's gain or the trade-secret owner's loss, if greater). Foreign instrumentalities, defined as entities substantially owned or controlled by a foreign government, can be fined up to $10 million; individuals knowingly benefiting a foreign instrumentality can be fined up to $500,000 and imprisoned up to fifteen years.

The act has extraterritorial application: it applies to any violation outside the United States by a U.S. citizen or resident alien or by an organization organized in the United States. It also applies to violations outside the United States if any act in furtherance of the offense was committed in the United States.

COMPARISON WITH OTHER FORMS OF PROTECTION

Unlike the more formal procedures for patent and copyright protection, there are no lengthy application and filing procedures for trade-secret protection. No review or approval by a governmental agency is required. To create and protect a trade secret, one need only develop and maintain a trade-secret protection program. When the information being protected has a short shelf life, trade-secret protection may be a more practical solution than copyright or patent protection.

Trade secrets are immediately protectable. Unlike patents or copyrights, there is no fixed length of time for ownership. As long as the protected information remains confidential and is not developed independently by

someone else, a trade secret will continue to be protectable under the law.

Another advantage of trade-secret protection is that material that would not qualify for patent or copyright protection is often protectable as a trade secret. A trade secret need not be as unique as a patentable invention or as original as a copyrightable work. It need only provide a competitive advantage. It may be merely an idea that has been kept secret, such as a way to organize common machines in an efficient manner, a marketing plan, or a formula for mixing the ingredients of a product.

Finally, obtaining patent and copyright protection usually requires disclosure of trade-secret information. Patent law requires the disclosure of the best method of making the invention, and copyright law requires a deposit of the copyrightable work, with certain exceptions. There is always a risk that after the sensitive information has been revealed, the reviewing agency will not grant the protection. To avoid this risk, trade-secret protection may be the safest course of action.

There are two disadvantages to utilizing trade-secret protection, however. First, the confidentiality procedures must be continuously and rigidly followed in order to preserve trade-secret status. The cost of a full-fledged program to protect trade secrets can be substantial. Second, trade-secret protection provides no protection against reverse engineering or independent discovery. The uncertainty of protection may limit the productive uses of the trade secret.

Protecting *a* Trade Secret

To properly protect trade-secret information, the owner must develop a program to preserve its confidentiality. In almost every jurisdiction, the test of a trade-secret program's adequacy may be reduced to the question of whether the owner has taken reasonable precautions to preserve the confidentiality of his or her trade secrets.

The most common forms of *misappropriation* of trade secrets are inadvertent disclosure and disclosure by employees. A program to protect against such disclosures should contain the elements discussed below. This outline, however, should not be relied upon to develop an actual policy. An attorney knowledgeable in the area should always be consulted.

A trade-secret program should be in writing, with a statement explaining its purpose. It should cover four areas in detail: (1) notification, (2) identification, (3) security, and (4) exit interviews. The program must then be properly implemented and maintained.

66. Pub. L. No. 104-294, 110 Stat. 3488 (1996).

NOTIFICATION

A written indication that all employees are aware of the trade-secret program is critical; at a minimum, a written notice should be posted. Ideally, the company's trade-secret policy should be explained to each new employee during orientation, and each new employee should sign a confidentiality agreement. The agreement should specify how long confidentiality will be required. The duration of the agreement should not be so long, however, that a court would view it as overly restrictive and thus unreasonable.

Labeling is another means of notification. A rubber stamp denoting confidential material and the posting of signs in areas containing sensitive materials will in most cases satisfy the reasonableness requirement. Some authorities, however, believe that labeling may actually hurt the trade-secret status of information because in practice it can be difficult to ensure consistent and continuous labeling procedures. These authorities claim that failure to label some of the documents may be seen as evidence that the information in those documents should not be afforded trade-secret status. More advanced kinds of labeling, such as passwords, lend additional support for a finding of reasonableness.

The company should also provide written notice to any consultant, vendor, joint venturer, or other party to whom a trade secret must be revealed. The notice should take the form of a confidentiality agreement that describes the protected information and limits the receiving party's rights to use it. Without such notice, the receiving party may be unaware of the nature of the information and unwittingly release it into the public domain.

A nondisclosure agreement (NDA) can serve as the basis of recovery if it is subsequently determined that the party who gained access to trade secrets later used or disclosed them in violation of the agreement. For example, in *Celeritas Technologies, Ltd. v. Rockwell*,[67] the parties entered into negotiations for the licensing of Celeritas's "de-emphasis technology," a method for reducing high-frequency noise in cellular communications. Prior to gaining access to information, Rockwell was asked to sign an NDA. The licensing negotiations ultimately failed, and Rockwell subsequently developed its own modem chips that incorporated de-emphasis technology. The same engineers who had access to Celeritas's technology under the NDA worked on Rockwell's de-emphasis technology project. Celeritas brought suit claiming, among other things, breach of the NDA. Because the technology was not readily ascertainable in the

public domain and was found to have come directly from Celeritas, the court concluded that a breach of the NDA had occurred. Celeritas was entitled to damages.

Sometimes an NDA may contain a "residuals" provision, which permits either party to use and exploit any information retained in the minds of the representatives of the nondisclosing party that they learned in the course of the subject negotiations or engagement. This can create a very large loophole in the strictures on nondisclosure.

IDENTIFICATION

There is some controversy concerning the appropriate method of identifying trade secrets. One view is that everything in the workplace, or pertaining to the business, is a trade secret. The problem with this umbrella approach is that a court will most likely deem it overly restrictive of commerce and therefore against public policy. Such a finding could undermine the company's trade-secret program, exposing all of its trade secrets to unrecoverable misappropriation.

At the other extreme is a program that attempts to specify each trade secret of the company. This approach may be too narrow because any legitimate trade secrets that are not specified will not be protected. Also, it is often difficult to pinpoint all of a company's potential trade secrets. For example, although it may be easy to designate all research and development projects as trade secrets, gray areas such as sales data, customer lists, or marketing surveys may cause problems. The best solution may be a program that specifies as much information as possible while also including a limited number of catchall categories.

SECURITY

Measures must be taken to ensure that trade-secret information remains secret, at least from the public. The disclosure of a trade secret, whether intentional (for example, as part of a sale) or by mistake, destroys any legal protection.

Access to confidential information should be limited to those who truly have a need to know. Hard copies of confidential information should be locked up in secure filing cabinets or a secure room. Photocopying machines should be placed as far as possible from confidential files. Digital confidential information should be encrypted.

A company should also guard against the unintentional disclosure of a trade secret during a public tour of its facilities. An offhand remark in the hall overheard by a visitor, or a formula left written on a chalkboard in plain view of a tour group, is all that is needed. The best

---

67. 150 F.3d 1354 (Fed Cir. 1998).

way to avoid this situation is to keep all trade secrets in areas restricted from public access. If such physical barriers are not possible, visitors' access should be controlled through a system that logs in all visitors, identifies them with badges, and keeps track of them while they are on the premises.

Trade secrets may also be inadvertently disclosed by employees participating in trade groups, conferences, and conventions and through publication of articles in trade journals and other periodicals. To avoid this problem, an employer should consistently and continuously, as part of its trade-secret program, remind its employees and contractors of when and how to talk about the company's business activities.

EXIT INTERVIEWS

When an employee who has had access to trade secrets leaves the company, he or she should be given an exit interview. The exit interview provides an opportunity to reinforce the confidentiality agreement that the employee signed on joining the company. If no confidentiality agreement exists, the exit interview is even more important. It will provide the notice and possibly the identification necessary to legally protect a trade secret. The exit interview also lets the departing employee know that the company is serious about protecting its trade secrets and that any breach of confidentiality could result in legal proceedings against him or her. After such a warning, any misappropriation would be deliberate and could therefore result in punitive damages.

In some states, posttermination restrictions on competition imposed on a departing employee may be unenforceable. In California, for example, a provision in an employment contract that prohibits an employee based in California from later working for a competitor is void as an unlawful business restraint, except to the extent necessary to prevent the misappropriation of trade secrets. It is therefore important to consult with local counsel concerning the permissible scope of posttermination restrictions.

Misappropriation of Trade Secrets

An individual misappropriates a trade secret when he or she (1) uses or discloses the trade secret of another or (2) learns of a trade secret through improper means. The UTSA defines "improper means" by a list of deceitful actions. The list, however, is not exclusive, and anything

INTERNATIONAL CONSIDERATION

The North American Free Trade Agreement requires the United States, Canada, and Mexico to protect trade secrets from unauthorized acquisition, disclosure, or use, as does the Trade-Related Aspects of Intellectual Property Rights (TRIPS) Agreement, adopted in 1994 and administered by the World Trade Organization. The United Kingdom, Canada, France, Germany, and Italy all provide strong trade-secret protection and entitle private litigants to recover damages and obtain injunctive relief.[a] From 1977 until 1991, approval of foreign investments by the Indian government often required the disclosure of trade secrets (prompting Coca-Cola and IBM to withdraw from India), but since 1991, the situation has improved. Japan enacted a national trade-secret law effective June 15, 1991. China's first trade-secret law, Article 10 of the Law of the People's Republic of China Against Unfair Competition, became effective on December 1, 1993.

a. This discussion of international trade-secret protection is based on R. Mark Halligan, *International Protection of Trade Secrets* (visited Mar. 20, 2001) <http://execpc.com/~mhalligan/intern.html>.

that strikes a court as improper would probably qualify as an improper means.

INEVITABLE DISCLOSURE DOCTRINE

Courts have begun to recognize a form of threatened misappropriation by employees under the inevitable disclosure doctrine. In essence, the doctrine recognizes that former employees who go to work for a competitor in a similar capacity may inevitably rely on and disclose the trade secrets gained in their former employment.

The inevitable disclosure doctrine was first recognized by a U.S. court of appeals in *Pepsico, Inc. v. Redmond*.[68] William Redmond, Jr. worked as a senior marketing manager for PepsiCo in its Pepsi-Cola North America division. Redmond had just completed work on the strategic marketing plans for AllSport (a sports drink that competed against Gatorade) and PepsiCo's powdered teas (which competed against, among others, Snapple). In November 1994, Redmond accepted an offer from Quaker Oats to work as the vice president of field operations in Quaker's combined Gatorade and Snapple drinks subsidiary. PepsiCo sued to enjoin Redmond from working at Quaker Oats on grounds of threatened misappropriation.

68. 54 F.3d 1262 (7th Cir. 1995).

The Seventh Circuit held that a company may prove trade-secret misappropriation by demonstrating that the employee's new position will inevitably lead him to rely on his ex-employer's trade secrets. Because of the competition between AllSport and Gatorade, the court concluded that Redmond could not help but rely on PepsiCo trade secrets as he plotted Gatorade's course. Specifically, Quaker Oats would have a substantial advantage by knowing how PepsiCo would price, distribute, and market its sports drinks. The Seventh Circuit likened the situation to that faced by a football team whose key player leaves to play for the other team and takes the play book with him.

By recognizing the notion of inevitable disclosure within the UTSA's provision of "threatened disclosure," the *PepsiCo* case gives employers greater leverage over departing employees and a powerful weapon against competitors who would lure away valuable employees. A number of other courts have accepted the doctrine. Nonetheless, some courts have shown some hesitation in applying the inevitable disclosure doctrine except in rare circumstances. For example, in *Earthweb, Inc. v. Schlack,*[69] the U.S. District Court for the Southern District of New York refused to apply the inevitable disclosure doctrine in circumstances where a noncompete agreement was considered overbroad and thus unenforceable. The court reasoned that the inevitable disclosure doctrine "treads an exceedingly narrow path through judicially disfavored territory. Absent evidence of actual misappropriation by an employee, the doctrine should be applied in only the rarest of cases."

According to CNET, "Intellectual property suits based on employee recruiting are a staple of the high-tech industry, but are often difficult to win."[70] The same might be said of non-high-tech industries. For example, after initiating a lawsuit, Campbell Soup Company agreed to let the former head of its U.S. soup business join Heinz's tuna and pet-food businesses on the condition that he stay out of Heinz's soup business for one year. In November 2000, Intel and Broadcom settled on undisclosed terms litigation sparked by Broadcom's hiring of three former Intel workers.[71] The trial court had ruled in May 2000 that Broadcom could hire the workers but had appointed a monitor to ensure that no Intel trade secrets were divulged. In February 2001, Compaq Computer sued RLX Technologies, a server start-up run by a number of former Compaq executives, for alleged misappropriation of trade secrets in connection with RLX's recruitment of two former Compaq vice presidents. RLX's vice president of business development called the suit groundless and characterized it as "a move to de-focus our management team."[72]

REMEDIES

Once a trade secret has been misappropriated, the law provides a choice of remedies. These are not mutually exclusive, and the typical trade-secret case involves more than one form of relief.

Injunction A court may issue an injunction ordering the misappropriator to refrain from disclosing or using the stolen trade secret. An injunction is desirable because it preserves the confidentiality of the trade secret.

An injunction is available only to prevent irreparable harm, however. If the secret has already been disclosed, an injunction may no longer be appropriate to protect the secret. The court may, however, still enjoin the misappropriator from using the information in order to deny the misappropriator the benefits of his or her misappropriation. In this situation, the injunction is often combined with an award of damages. In *General Electric Co. v. Iljin Corp.,*[73] the court enjoined Iljin from selling a new product created using misappropriated trade secrets for a period of time equal to what it would have taken Iljin to develop the product on its own had it not misappropriated resources from General Electric.

The owner may also be able to seek an injunction or damages from anyone receiving the misappropriated trade secret or anyone hiring the individual who misappropriated it. Finally, an injunction may also be appropriate when an individual threatens to use or disclose a trade secret, although the real damage has not yet occurred. In the PepsiCo inevitable disclosure case, for example, the former PepsiCo employee was not permitted to work for Quaker Oats until the information he had in his head about PepsiCo's marketing strategy was stale and lacked competitive value.

Damages Monetary damages are often awarded when the owner of the trade secret has suffered financial harm. The situations in which monetary damages are received are fact-specific. Damages may be awarded based upon either a contract theory or a tort theory. The technical

69. 71 F. Supp. 2d 299 (S.D.N.Y. 1999), *aff.d*, 205 F.3d 1322 (2d Cir. 2000).

70. Michael Kanellos, *Compaq Files Recruitment Lawsuit Against RLX*, CNET News.com, Feb. 23, 2001.

71. Ian Fried, *Intel, Broadcom Settle Trade Secret Lawsuits*, CNET News.com, Nov. 21, 2000.

72. Kanellos, *supra* note 70.

73. 27 U.S.P.Q.2d (BNA) 1372 (D. Mass. 1993).

differences between the two measures of damages make little practical difference. Most courts will attempt to fairly compensate the owner of a misappropriated trade secret regardless of how the case is characterized.

Under the tort theory of trade secrets, the purpose of the damages is not only to make the owner whole but to disgorge any profits the misappropriator may have made due to his or her wrongful act. The key to the tort measure of damages is that there was either a harm or an unjust gain, or both.

The contract theory of trade secrets, on the other hand, measures damages by the loss of value of the trade secret to the owner as a result of a breach of contract. The loss of value is determined by adding the general loss to any special losses resulting from the breach and subtracting any costs avoided by the owner as a result of the breach.

Punitive Damages Punitive damages are available when the misappropriation was willful and wanton. A misappropriation that can be characterized only as a breach of contract does not warrant punitive damages. In some states, attorneys' fees are also recoverable by the prevailing party if the misappropriation was willful and malicious.

Technology Licensing

Technology licensing is big business worldwide. The volume of commercial technology transfers has increased dramatically since World War II and is accelerating. Whereas revenues from patent licensing amounted to approximately $15 billion in 1990, by 1998 they exceeded $100 billion and were still increasing.[74]

One way for a technology owner to benefit from its technology is to use it itself. Another is to license others to use it. Conversely, a potential acquirer of technology may choose either to develop the technology itself or to obtain it under license from another. Depending upon the circumstances of the parties and the market, a commonality of interest may develop that leads to a license transaction.

Until very recently, the market for intellectual property remained highly fragmented and inefficient. Sales and licensing occurred on an infrequent basis and often took place between parties that already had a preexisting relationship, whether formal or informal. Finding an interested and qualified buyer or seller of intellectual property was a time-consuming and difficult task. As a result, many potential revenue sources remained untapped. Indeed, according to *Fortune*, only 2 percent of the worldwide

market for new intellectual property (estimated at $5 trillion) was licensed in 1998.[75] Recognizing the inadequacies of the current market for intellectual property, several companies recently emerged to offer a solution.

One such company, the Patent and License Exchange (or pl-x.com) based in Pasadena, California, provides an Internet-based forum that introduces potential buyers and sellers of intellectual property and facilitates the valuation process while offering risk-minimizing services. The exchange focuses on patents, but trademarks, trade secrets, and know-how are included as well. Nir Kossovsky, the chairman and CEO of pl-x.com, points out that "inventors have a great opportunity to transform their underutilized technologies into new revenue opportunities through a sale or license on the exchange."[76] Other similar exchanges, most notably, Yet2.com, based in Cambridge, Massachusetts, offer related solutions to the fragmented market. If these new exchanges work according to plan, they will eliminate the most significant barriers to an efficient market for intellectual property. These companies are still in the starting phase and thus have yet to prove whether an Internet-based marketplace of intangible assets is a viable concept.

ADVANTAGES TO THE LICENSOR

From a licensor's perspective, there are a variety of reasons to license technology. One obvious reason is to generate revenue. License transactions constitute a substantial source of income for many technology-based companies. Licensing may be a way for a licensor to exploit its older technology. Often a somewhat dated technology is what a licensee can best use.

Licensing is often an inexpensive way to gain a presence in a target market. In essence, through the mechanism of a license, a licensor may be able to push many of the costs of market development onto the licensee in exchange for a share of the profits from the venture. A licensor seeking new technology may condition its license upon a cross-license of the licensee's existing technology or may require a grant-back of any future technology developed by the licensee.

A license transaction may also give the licensor an inexpensive source of supply of the licensed product. When the licensee is operating in a low-cost labor market, such product-purchase rights may be highly valued by the licensor.

74. RIVETTE & KLINE, *supra* note 2, at 5.

75. Tyler Maroney, *The New Online Marketplace for Ideas*, FORTUNE, Apr. 17, 2000.

76. *The Patent & License Exchange Offers Unprecedented Opportunity to Independent Inventors to Sell Innovations Online Quickly and Safely*, BUS. WIRE, June 6, 2000.

E-COMMERCE

IN BRIEF

Intellectual Property Protection: Comparative Advantages

	Trade Secret	Copyright	Patent	Trademark
Benefits	Very broad protection for sensitive, competitive information; very inexpensive	Prevents copying of a wide array of artistic and literary expressions, including software; very inexpensive	Very strong protection; provides exclusive right to exclude others from making, using, and selling an invention; protects the idea itself	Protects marks that customers use to identify a business; prevents others from using confusingly similar identifying marks
Duration	So long as the information remains valuable and is kept confidential	Life of author plus 70 years; for corporations, 90 years from date of first publication or 100 years from date of creation, whichever is shorter	20 years from date of filing utility or plant patent application; 14 years from date of filing design patent application	As long as the mark is not abandoned and steps are taken to police its use
Weaknesses	No protection from accidental disclosure, independent creation by a competitor, or disclosure by someone without a duty to maintain confidentiality	Protects only particular way an idea is expressed, not the idea itself; hard to detect copying in digital age	Must meet high standards of novelty, utility, and nonobviousness; often expensive and time-consuming; must disclose invention to public	Limited scope; protects corporate image and identity but little else; can be costly if multiple overseas registrations are needed
Required Steps	Take reasonable steps to protect—generally a trade-secret protection program	None required; however, notice and filing can strengthen rights, and filing is required before an action for infringement can be filed	Detailed filing with U.S. Patent and Trademark Office that requires search for prior art and hefty fees	Only need to use mark in commerce; however, filing with U.S. Patent and Trademark Office is usually desirable to gain stronger protections
International Validity of U.S. Rights?	No. Trade-secret laws vary significantly by country, and some countries have no trade-secret laws.	Generally, yes	No. Separate patent filings are required in each country unless file international patent application or file in the European Patent Office for the EU countries	No. Separate filings are required in foreign jurisdictions, and a mark available in the U.S. may not be available overseas.

Source: Adapted from Constance E. Bagley & Craig E. Dauchy, The Entrepreneur's Guide to Business Law 471–72 (1998). *Used by permission.*

INTERNATIONAL CONSIDERATION

If either the licensee or the licensor is located outside the United States, careful compliance with U.S. export-control laws is essential to avoid potential liability. Unfortunately, such compliance may result in undue expense or delay. Also, it should be borne in mind that other countries may not offer the same intellectual property protection as the United States.

ADVANTAGES TO THE LICENSEE

There are also several reasons why a licensee might wish to license technology. By taking a license, a licensee can obtain immediate access to new technology and can avoid the research and development costs that would be necessary to duplicate the technology. A license may enable the licensee to penetrate its target market sooner or to get a head start on its competitors.

A licensee may be seeking a long-term relationship with its licensor, which will enable it to graduate to higher and higher levels of the licensor's technology (including future developments). A licensee may seek to share in the goodwill of its licensor through the license transaction. If the licensor has strong trademarks or is otherwise the beneficiary of substantial goodwill, the licensee may be able to benefit in its local market.

DISADVANTAGES TO THE LICENSOR

There are also a variety of reasons why a licensor may choose not to license its technology. By far the greatest risk for a licensor is that its licensee may become its future competitor. Numerous examples of this phenomenon abound.

A licensor that relies exclusively upon its licensee for the manufacture of the licensed product may find that it loses the ability to manufacture the product efficiently itself. Licensors may be reluctant to undertake the service obligations that often arise in license transactions. A licensee may require a lot of training and assistance if the license transaction is to be successful. The licensor may ultimately be unable to recoup such costs.

The managements of the licensor and licensee may differ on fundamental aspects of the license transaction, such as commitment, strategy, and marketing, thereby making success improbable. If language and cultural differences are added, the licensor may well decide that a proposed transaction is not worthwhile.

DISADVANTAGES TO THE LICENSEE

A licensee, too, may decide that its differences with the licensor make the transaction not worthwhile. There are several other reasons why a potential licensee may choose not to carry through a license transaction.

A licensee may have concerns about technology transfer problems. Just because a licensor can operate its technology at a certain level does not necessarily mean it can effectively teach the licensee to use it at the same level. Licensees are often bitterly disappointed by the technology they have paid so dearly to acquire. In addition, continuing royalty payments can become burdensome to a licensee, particularly if competitors who are not paying a comparable royalty enter the market.

INTELLECTUAL PROPERTY DISPUTE SETTLEMENT

A license may be utilized as a means of settling an intellectual property dispute. Patent litigation, for example, is risky both for the defendant, who may face a treble damages award, and for the plaintiff, who may find his or her patent invalidated. To minimize such risks, the parties may enter into a license agreement. Two biotechnology companies, Cetus Corporation and Amgen, Inc., took such an approach. Amgen had brought an action against Cetus claiming that certain of Cetus's patents relating to Interleukin-2 were invalid; Cetus had counterclaimed that Amgen was infringing Cetus's patents. Rather than letting a court determine their fate, the parties settled the suit through an agreement whereby certain of Amgen's patent rights were assigned to Cetus and Cetus granted Amgen a license to use Cetus's patents.

THE RESPONSIBLE MANAGER
Protecting Intellectual Property Rights

Some of a company's most important assets may be intangible forms of intellectual property. Consider the formula for Coke, never registered as a patent but kept as a trade secret by generations of executives at the Coca-

Cola Company. An effective trade-secret policy is essential to almost all forms of business today. This chapter has provided suggestions regarding the implementation of such a policy.

Problems can arise when a manager leaves the employment of one company to assume a position at another. It is critical that the manager and the new employer ensure that no confidential information, including trade secrets, is conveyed to the new employer, either in the form of documents or as information in the manager's head. At the time of hire, the employer should determine whether the potential employee is bound by a restrictive covenant. Moreover, a company should provide written notice to all employees that it has a policy against receiving, using, or purchasing any trade secrets belonging to third parties. Misappropriation of trade secrets is a civil and criminal offense. During the exit interview, employees should be reminded of their obligations, and materials and computers being removed from the employer's premises should be inspected.

If the manager cannot fulfill all the duties of his or her new job without using trade secrets, it is necessary to scale back the manager's activities and responsibilities. This can be accomplished by having the former employer and the new employer agree that the manager will not assume responsibility for certain product lines that compete with his or her former employer's until a date when the strategic and other confidential information known by the manager is stale. If at all possible, the departing manager should address this issue up front and negotiate it as part of his or her severance arrangements, rather than wait for a costly lawsuit to be brought by the former employer.

In addition to trade secrets, intellectual property is given legal protection through patents, copyrights, and trademarks. Patents are extremely important to high-technology companies and some e-commerce firms. In fact, patents have formed the basis for whole businesses, such as biotechnology. A manager should strive to protect his or her company's patents from infringement by others. Royalties from patents can add tens or even hundreds of millions of dollars to a company's revenues.

Patents also have an important strategic use as a defensive measure in the event that another company claims patent infringement. In such a case, it is very helpful for a manager to have patents that can be used as bargaining chips to negotiate a settlement, which often takes the form of cross-licenses.

A manager should develop a global patent strategy because 179 different jurisdictions grant patents, each of which gives the holder exclusive rights only in the granting jurisdiction. Moreover, few countries share the U.S. system. For instance, only one other country, the Philippines, uses a "first-to-invent" instead of "first-to-file" approach in issuing patents. Furthermore, many countries do not share the U.S. practice of keeping patent applications confidential until the patent is issued; thus, an applicant risks revelation of trade secrets if the patent is denied.

Copyrights prevent others from copying literary work, musical work, sound recordings, computer software, and other forms of expression fixed in a tangible medium. A manager should be aware that copyright registration with the U.S. Copyright Office is a prerequisite for filing an infringement suit for a work of U.S. origin. Statutory damages and attorneys' fees are available only to owners who have registered the work within ninety days of first publication or prior to the infringement that forms the basis of the infringement suit.

Trademarks that identify brands of goods or services are protected for an indefinite time. Managers must work to preserve trademarks, however. Once the buying public starts using the trademark as a synonym for the product, rather than as a means of distinguishing its source, loss of the trademark is imminent.

A manager should not only protect his or her company's own intellectual property but should also ensure that the company does not infringe the intellectual property rights of others, whether they be patents, copyrights, trademarks, or trade secrets.

A company may benefit from technology licensing. Such arrangements offer advantages and disadvantages for both the licensor and licensee.

Finally, managers should evaluate the adequacy of the company's insurance coverage for losses and claims related to intellectual property and electronic commerce.[77] In light of the importance of computers, it is important to ensure that policies for property damage and business interruption cover damage to hardware and software, loss of data, and business disruptions caused by a virus, hacker attack, or other electronic assault. Commercial general liability policies, which provide coverage for the liability a company may face for harm to third parties, usually cover bodily injury, property damage, personal injury, and advertising injury. Emerging issues include whether data are tangible property, whether the insertion of a defective computer part or software into a larger system causes property damage, and whether any company with a Web site is in the business of advertising and therefore not covered by the standard advertising injury provisions, which can cover intellectual property infringement and defamation claims. Some insurance companies are attempting to eliminate coverage for cyberspace and e-commerce claims from traditional policies, often in the hope of selling specialty policies to cover cyber-risks. Although the new specialty policies are "potentially valuable," policyholders

---

77. For an excellent discussion of this issue (from which this discussion is drawn), see Matthew J. Schlesinger & Paul R. Cassell, *Cyberspace Liabilities: Are You Covered?*, 5 Electronic Commerce & L. Rep. 1184 (Dec. 6, 2000).

must be careful to assess the gaps in coverage that can result if traditional "all-risk" liability coverage is replaced with a "patchwork of specialty policies."[78] Also, the language of the new policies can vary widely, so managers need to ensure that the coverage chosen matches the risks. Finally, managers should be aware that the new language used in these policies will inevitably result in disputes about its meaning.

78. *Id.*

Napster Ordered *to* Face *the* Music

E-COMMERCE

On February 12, 2001, a three-judge panel of the U.S. Court of Appeals for the Ninth Circuit held that Napster, Inc., the popular Internet system used for swapping audio recordings stored as digital MP3 files, should be enjoined from participating in copyright infringement.[79] The Ninth Circuit had temporarily stayed a preliminary injunction issued by the district court on July 26, 2000, which had enjoined Napster from facilitating others in copying, downloading, uploading, transmitting, or distributing the plaintiffs' copyrighted musical compositions and sound recordings without express permission.[80] In its 2001 decision, the Ninth Circuit confirmed that a preliminary injunction against Napster's participation in copyright infringement was "not only warranted but required." However, the appeals court ordered the trial court to modify the injunction (1) to put the burden on the plaintiffs to identify the copyrighted works available on the Napster system before imposing on Napster the duty to disable access to the offending content; and (2) to recognize that Napster has the duty to police the system only within the technological limits of the system, which currently does not allow Napster access to users' MP3 files but rather relies on users to name the files.

NAPSTER SYSTEM

Napster facilitates transmission of MP3 files between its users through a process commonly called "peer-to-peer" file sharing. Napster's MusicShare software (available free from Napster's Web site) and its network servers and server-side software enable its users to (1) make MP3 music files stored on individual computer hard drives available for copying by other Napster users, (2) search for MP3 music files stored on other users' computers, and (3) transfer exact copies of the contents of other users' MP3 files from one computer to another via the Internet.

If a registered user wants to make files stored on his or her hard drive available for others to access, the user can upload the names assigned to the MP3 files from his or her computer to the Napster servers. The contents of the MP3 files remain stored in the user's computer, but once Napster confirms that the files are properly formatted, the user's MP3 file names are stored in Napster's server-side "library" and become part of a "collective directory" of files available for transfer while the user is logged onto the Napster system. Napster software permits users to search the collective directory by song or artist name. The "hot list" function permits a user to create a list of other users from whom the user has obtained MP3 files in the past; when the user is logged onto Napster's service, the system alerts him or her whenever someone on the hot list is also logged on. The system can also generate an index of all MP3 file names in a particular hot-listed user's library.

To transfer a copy of the contents of a requested MP3 file, the Napster server software obtains the Internet address of both the requesting user and the user with the available files (the host user), then communicates the host user's address to the requesting user. The requesting user's computer uses this information to establish a connection with the host user and then downloads a copy of the contents of the requested MP3 file onto the requesting user's computer hard drive.

DIRECT INFRINGEMENT

Because there can be no secondary liability for copyright infringement without direct infringement by a third party, the Ninth Circuit first considered whether Napster's users were engaged in direct infringement. Based on the trial court's finding that as many as 87 percent of

79. A & M Records, Inc. v. Napster, 239 F.3d 1004 (9th Cir. 2001).
80. A&M Records, Inc. v. Napster, Inc., 114 F. Supp. 2d 896 (N.D. Cal. 2000).

STAGE
DOOR

"*Wow, thanks. I'm a big fan. I've downloaded all your stuff.*"

the files available on Napster may be copyrighted and more than 70 percent may be owned or administered by the plaintiff record companies, the Ninth Circuit concluded that the Napster users infringe at least two of the copyright holders' five exclusive rights: the rights of reproduction and distribution.

NO FAIR USE

Napster contended that its users did not directly infringe the record companies' copyrights because the users were engaged in a fair use of the material. Napster alleged three fair uses: (1) "sampling," where users make temporary copies of songs before purchasing the compact disc (CD); (2) "space shifting," where users use the Napster system to access sound recordings that they already own in CD format; and (3) permissive distribution of recordings by both new and established artists.

The Ninth Circuit applied the four-prong test for fair use (purpose and character of use, nature of use, portion used, and effect of use on market) and concluded that the Napster users were not engaged in fair use. Because Napster users "get something for free they would nor-

mally have to buy," their use was "commercial." The copied works were "creative in nature," not "factual." Napster's users engaged in "wholesale copying" of entire works. Finally, Napster had a "deleterious effect on the present and future digital download market."

The Ninth Circuit rejected Napster's argument that space shifting was a fair use. In *Recording Industry Ass'n of America v. Diamond Multimedia System, Inc.*,[81] the Ninth Circuit had ruled that use of the Rio portable MP3 player to render portable, or space shift, music files that already resided on a user's hard drive was "paradigmatic noncommercial personal use" within the precedent set by the U.S. Supreme Court in the Sony Betamax case.[82] But the *Napster* court found these cases "inapposite because the methods of shifting in these cases did not also simultaneously involve distribution of the copyrighted material to the general public; the time or space-shifting of copyrighted material exposed the material only to the original user."

81. 180 F.3d 1072, 1079 (9th Cir. 1999).
82. Sony Corp. of Am. v. Universal City Studios, Inc., 464 U.S. 417 (1984).

NAPSTER'S SECONDARY LIABILITY

The Ninth Circuit then affirmed the lower court's determination that Napster was secondarily liable for the direct infringement by its users. Napster was liable for contributory copyright infringement because it knowingly encouraged and assisted its users' direct infringement.

The court also affirmed the district court's finding of vicarious liability. The requirement for a direct financial benefit was satisfied because the availability of the infringing material acted as a draw to customers, thereby increasing the user base on which Napster's future revenues were dependent. Napster's ability to control access to its system was sufficient to give it the requisite right and ability to supervise the infringing activity.

The court then rejected two statutory defenses raised by Napster: the Audio Home Recording Act of 1992[83] and the Digital Millennium Copyright Act.[84] The court found that the Audio Home Recording Act does not cover the downloading of MP3 files and that the plaintiffs had raised serious doubts as to whether Napster was a service provider protected by the Digital Millennium Copyright Act and otherwise entitled to its safe-harbor protection from copyright infringement suits.

83. 17 U.S.C. § 1008.
84. 17 U.S.C. § 512.

In October 2000, Napster had surprised many when it agreed to give entertainment giant Bertelsmann equity rights in exchange for a $60 million loan. Within a week of the adverse Ninth Circuit ruling, executives of Napster and Bertelsmann called on other record companies to suspend legal hostilities and agree to permit their copyrighted music to be traded on Napster in exchange for $1 billion payable over five years.[85] They also announced plans to convert Napster from a free service to a tiered paid subscription model by July 2001. The head of the Recording Industry Association of America dismissed Napster's offer and called on Napster to "[s]top the infringements, stop the delay tactics in court, and redouble your efforts to build a legitimate system."[86]

In March 2001, U.S. District Judge Marilyn Hall Patel modified her injunction to require Napster to remove any unauthorized song from its system within three days of receiving from the music labels the song title and artist name together with certification that they controlled the copyright to the song. To prevent new songs from becoming available on the service, Judge Pabel permitted the record labels also to provide Napster with lists of songs not yet released.

85. John Borland, *Napster Offers Recording Industry $1 Billion,* CNET News.com, Feb. 20, 2001.
86. *Id.*

KEY WORDS AND PHRASES

abandonment 372
actual abandonment 373
arbitrary marks 368
best mode 353
certification mark 368
claims 353
constructive abandonment 373
contributory copyright infringement 365
contributory infringement 353
copyright 348
cybersquatting 375
declaration by the inventor 353
descriptive marks 369
design patent 352
direct copyright infringement 365
direct infringement 353
doctrine of equivalents 353
domain names 374

drawings 353
fair use doctrine 358
fanciful marks 368
file-wrapper estoppel 354
first sale doctrine 360
genericism 370
hot-news exception 360
indirect infringement 354
inevitable disclosure doctrine 379
inherently distinctive marks 368
intellectual property 348
know-how 348
merger doctrine 357
misappropriation 379
noninfringement 354
novel 350
patent 348
patent misuse 354
prior art 350

protected expression 357
registered mask work 366
secondary meaning 369
service mark 368
show-how 348
specifications 353
statutory bar 350
suggestive marks 368
trade dress 348
trademark 348
trade name 368
trade secret 348
useful articles doctrine 358
utility patent 349
utility requirement 349
vicarious liability 366
work made for hire 358

1. Gerald Banks, an optical engineering expert, was hired to work for Burroughs Corporation in 1987. Banks was never asked to sign an agreement to assign inventive rights to the company's parent, Unisys, although such agreements were standard procedure. Two years later, Unisys filed a number of patent applications derived from Banks's engineering work. Banks was listed as co-inventor on only three of them.

    As to these three applications, Banks was asked to sign assignment agreements in return for payment. Banks later discovered that three other patent applications were based on his work, although his name was not listed as co-inventor. Unisys refused to pay Banks for assignment rights, and Banks sued. At the time of the suit, who had the right to the inventions? [*Banks v. Unisys Corp.*, 228 F.3d 1357 (Fed. Cir. 2000)]

2. Lucent Technologies registered "Lucent" as a trademark with the PTO in November 1995. Thereafter, Lucent manufactured, marketed, and sold telecommunications equipment under the Lucent and Lucent Technologies marks. Various Lucent marks for goods and services were registered with the PTO.

    Lucent argues that it has spent considerable time and effort promoting its goods and services and has created valuable goodwill in the marks. In August 1998, Russell Johnson registered the domain name lucentsucks.com. The Web site sells pornographic photographs and services. Lucent brought suit claiming trademark infringement and dilution of trademark and sought a transfer of the lucentsucks.com domain name. What result? [*Lucent Technologies, Inc. v. Lucentsucks.com*, 95 F. Supp. 2d 528 (E.D. Va. 2000)]

3. E.I. duPont de Nemours & Company has developed a new and very efficient process for manufacturing automobiles. You work for McKivex Company and are writing a consultant's report for another firm about the manufacturing processes of its competitors including DuPont. DuPont has a new plant, but the roof has not yet been built over it. You want to learn about the process without getting sued.

    Can you take aerial photographs of the plant? Can you go through the garbage cans on the company's grounds looking for information that would describe the process? Can you go through DuPont's garbage at the city dump? Can you interview the manufacturing manager on the telephone and in-

clude her comments in your report? What if you did consulting for DuPont and knew the process—could you then include it in your report for its competitor? What is ethical? [*E.I. duPont de Nemours & Co. v. Christopher*, 431 F.2d 1012 (5th Cir. 1970), *cert. denied*, 400 U.S. 1024 (1971)]

4. Virgil Richards conceived a way to regulate the translation of heterologous DNA in bacteria. He worked on this invention with three other people. Richards conceived of the idea in May 1998, reduced it to practice on May 14, 1999, and filed a patent application on June 1, 2000. Richards is being sued by the co-inventors for not including their names on the application.

    On May 3, 1999, Richards published an article in Japan that explained his idea in detail. Clyde Taylor reduced this idea to practice on May 14, 1999, making only minor changes to the procedure disclosed in the article. He applied for a patent on June 1, 1999.

    Can Richards or Taylor obtain a patent for the technology? The process includes some basic scientific principles. Does that mean that both patent applications will be rejected? [*In re O'Farrell*, 853 F.2d 894 (Fed. Cir. 1988)]

5. Best Cellars operated retail wine stores where it used its "wine by style" concept, which categorized wine by taste and weight rather than by grape type or place of origin. By reducing the world of wine to eight taste categories, Best Cellars demystified wine for unsophisticated purchasers. Best Cellars also used a "wall of wine" racking system and other distinctive visual displays in its stores. Grape Finds began using the same "wine by style" categories and the "wall of wine" racking system in its stores. Does Best Cellars have any basis for obtaining an injunction to prohibit Grape Finds from using the "wine by style" categories and "wall of wine" racking system? [*Best Cellars, Inc. v. Grape Finds at Dupont, Inc.*, 90 F. Supp. 2d 431 (S.D.N.Y. 2000)]

6. A hypothetical new communications product is described below. After reading the product description, think up three trademarks for this product: one that is inherently distinctive; one that is potentially, but not inherently, distinctive; and one that is nondistinctive.

    New Product Description

    This new product incorporates global positioning technology into a multifunctional device that is worn like a watch. Not only does the device provide the time, but it also allows others to determine the location of the device and thus the location of the person. Moreover, the device is equipped to send and receive simple e-mail messages. The device may be especially suited for parents hoping to track remotely the whereabouts of their children. The location of the device can be determined through an online site that requires input of an identifying password.

7. Dan Parisi registered the domain names lockheed-sucks.com and lockheedmartinsucks.com to provide Web sites for individuals to criticize Lockheed Martin Corporation's practices in particular and corporate America in general. Lockheed Martin, a well-known aerospace and electronics manufacturer, filed a complaint under the uniform domain name dispute resolution policy to require transfer of the names to it. How should the WIPO arbitration panel rule? [*Lockheed Martin Corp. v. Parisi*, WIPO, Case No. D2000-1015 (Jan. 23, 2001), available at <http://arbiter.wipo.int/domains/decisions/html/2000/d2000-1015.html>. *See also Bally Total Fitness v. Faber*, 29 F. Supp. 2d 1161 (C.D. Cal. 1998).]

8. Free Republic is a "bulletin board" Web site. Its members post news articles, and they, as well as visitors to the site, add remarks or commentary to the articles. Members usually post the entire text of articles including verbatim copies of articles from the *Los Angeles Times* and *Washington Post* Web sites. The Los Angeles Times and The Washington Post have sued Free Republic, alleging that the unauthorized copying and posting of the articles constitute copyright infringement. Free Republic argues that the copying of newspaper articles onto its Web site is protected by the fair use doctrine and the First Amendment. How should the court rule? Would it make any difference if, instead of posting the articles, Free Republic provided "deep links" to them, which bypassed the subject newspaper's home page? Could Free Republic legally link to an article but delete the newspaper's advertising and frame the article with its own advertisements and logo? [*Los Angeles Times v. Free Republic*, 2000 U.S. Dist. LEXIS 5669 (C.D. Cal. Apr. 5, 2000)]

9. Monsanto sold a polymer to CaMac, knowing that CaMac was using the polymer to produce a certain nylon fiber product. Monsanto became aware that the nylon product was covered by a patent owned by DuPont but continued to supply the polymer to CaMac while it looked for other noninfringing recipes. Is Monsanto liable under 35 U.S.C. § 271, which provides that "Whoever actively induces infringement of a patent shall be liable as an infringer"? [*E.I. duPont de Nemours & Co. v. Monsanto Co.*, 903 F. Supp. 680 (D. Del. 1995)]

MANAGER'S DILEMMA

10. You are the vice president for sales at QuickGifts, Inc., a small start-up headquartered in Chicago, Illinois. QuickGifts specializes in supplying on short notice a variety of inexpensive gifts for all occasions, including cards, flowers, perfume, gift baskets, wine, books, and compact discs. Since QuickGifts' launch six months ago, the bulk of its revenue has come from catalog-driven telephone sales, often to frantic procrastinators calling the day before a spouse or parent's birthday. For a premium fee, QuickGifts arranges immediate delivery of a tasteful gift, usually overnight, but often within hours.

Recently, QuickGifts hired a Web designer to create an Internet outlet for its products. The designer has nearly completed his work on the site but has asked you about meta-tagging the site. Meta-tagging, he explains, is the labeling of your site with terms and phrases so that search engines, such as Yahoo, can identify it to users as they surf the Web. He recommends numerous conventional tags, including "gifts," "cards," and "flowers," but warns that many companies have already established a name in this business. Without quite recommending it, the designer notes that using the names of your competitors will at least give prospective customers the chance to see your Web site when they search for a specific rival. For instance, you could use meta-tags like "Hallmark," "FTD," "Amazon," and "CDnow." Is it legal to use these names as mega-tags? Would it be ethical? [*Playboy Enterprises, Inc. v. Calvin Designer Label*, 985 F. Supp. 1220 (N.D. Cal. 1997)]

INTERNET SOURCES

The United Nations site includes the full text of the Berne Convention on Artistic and Literary Works, including the signatories.	http://www.un.or.at/uncitral
The World Intellectual Property Organization's Web site contains full text versions of the WIPO Copyright Treaty and the WIPO Performers and Phonograms Treaty.	http://www.wipo.int
U.S. Patent and Trademark Office	http://www.uspto.gov/
U.S. PTO Guidelines on Domain Names as Trademarks	http://www.uspto.gov/web/offices/tac/domain/tmdomain.htm
U.S. Copyright Office	http://lcweb.loc.gov/copyright/
Japanese Patent Office	http://www.jpo-miti.go.jp
The European Union On-Line site is a searchable collection of official documents (such as Directives), news releases, the Official Journal of the European Communities, and case law of the European Court of Justice, with links.	http://www.europa.eu.int
National Telecommunications and Information Administration	http://www.ntia.doc.gov
The U.S. House of Representatives Internet Law Library site contains a variety of links to useful intellectual property articles and resources on the Web.	http://law.house.gov/105.htm
"Thomas": The U.S. Congress's Official Legislative Information Page is an extremely well-organized page describing pending bills, committee information, and Internet sources.	http://thomas.loc.gov
The President's Information Infrastructure Task Force	http://www.iitf.nist.gov
World Intellectual Property Organization's Arbitration and Mediation Center	http://arbiter.wipo.int/
Internet Corporation for Assigned Names and Numbers (ICANN)	http://www.icann.org
Foreign and International Law Resources on the Internet: Annotated from Cornell Law Library (International)	http://www.law.cornell.edu/library/guides/forin
Franklin Pierce Law Center's Intellectual Property "Mall"	http://www.ipmall@fplc.edu
American Bar Association Section of Intellectual Property Law	http://www.aipla.org
Intellectual Property Owners Association	http://www.ipo.org
Emory Law Library Federal Courts Finder	http://www.law.emory.edu/FEDCTS/
Internet Law Wire from the University of Pittsburgh Law School	http://jurist.law.pitt.edu/internet_law.htm
The filter, which is operated by the Berkman Center for Internet and Society at Harvard Law School, offers free monthly newsletters.	http://cyber.law.harvard.edu/filter/intro.html
Cyberspace Law Subject Index from the John Marshall Law School	http://www.jmls.edu/cyber/index/index.html

Syracuse University's Digital Convergence Center	http://dcc.syr.edu/
New York Times Cyber Law Journal	http://www.nytimes.com/pages-technology/cybertimes/cyberlaw/
Tech Law Journal	http://www.techlawjournal.com/
KuesterLaw—The Technology Resource Center	http://www.kuesterlaw.com/
Law.com—Tech Law Practice Center	http://www.law.com/professionals/techlaw.html
BNA's Internet Law News provides free daily e-mail updates.	http://ecommercecenter.bna.com/
The law firm of Baker & McKenzie provides a free weekly e-mail on developments in electronic commerce and cyberlaw throughout the world.	http://www.bakerinfo.com/elaw/
The GigaLaw.com site provides legal information for Internet professionals, including a free daily e-mail update on breaking developments and articles of interest.	http://www.gigalaw.com
The Law Engine site provides lots of useful links for federal and state statutes, rules, and court opinions.	http://www.fastsearch.com/law
This site includes free sources of the law of any state.	http://www.azstarnet.com/~frey/fed.htm
FindLaw Cyberspace Law News	http://news.findlaw.com/legalnews/scitech/cyber/
Yahoo!–Copyright Law	http://dir.yahoo.com/Government/Law/Intellectual_Property/Copyrights
Legal Information Institute: Copyright Law Copyrights	http://www.law.cornell.edu/topics/copyright.html
FindLaw Copyright Index	http://www.findlaw.com/01topics/23intellectprop/01copyright/index.html
Yahoo!–Patent Law	http://dir.yahoo.com/Government/Law/Intellectual_Property/Patents/
Legal Information Institute: Patent Law	http://www.law.cornell.edu/topics/patent.html
FindLaw Patent Index	http://www.findlaw.com/01topics/23intellectprop/02patent/index.html
Yahoo!–Trademark Law	http://dir.yahoo.com/Government/Law/Intellectual_Property/Trademarks/
Legal Information Institute: Trademark Law	http://www.law.cornell.edu/topics/trademark.html
FindLaw Trademark Index	http://www.findlaw.com/01topics/23intellectprop/03trademark/index.html
The Trade Secrets Home Page, maintained by R. Mark Halligan, a principal in the Chicago intellectual property firm of Welsh & Katz, provides case summaries and articles about trade-secret protection.	http://www.execpc.com/~mhallign/
Recording Industry Association of America	http://www.riaa.org

International Business

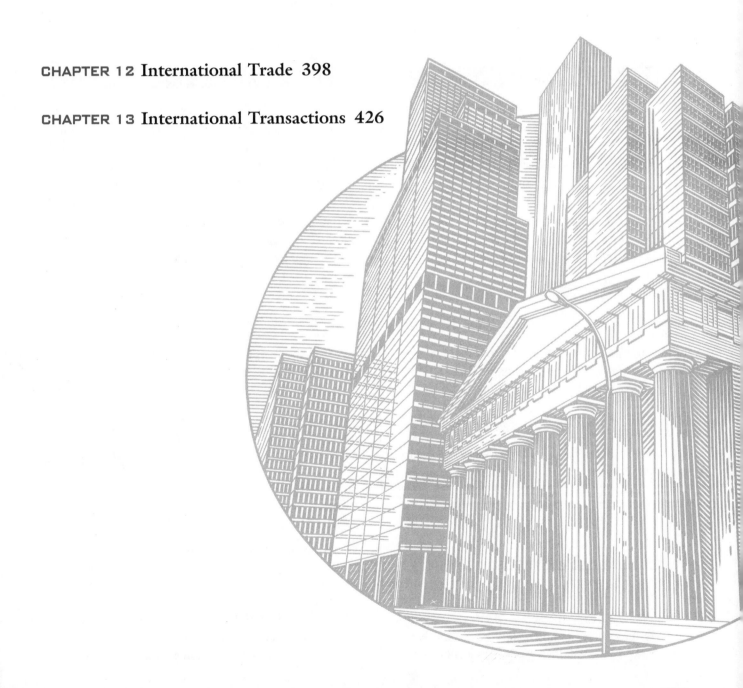

CHAPTER 12

International Trade

HIGH-PRIORITY CONCERN FOR GLOBAL MANAGERS

The Asian financial crisis of the late 1990s and its impact on the U.S. economy underscored the existence of a global economy and the importance of international trade. Total U.S. trade in goods reached $1.7 trillion in 1999, representing $695.8 billion in exports and $1 trillion in imports. Because far more countries are exporting goods to the United States than ever before, domestic products are facing increased competition. Indeed, the U.S. trade deficit has more than doubled since 1997, reaching a record $369.69 billion in 2000.

Dealing with import competition and opening foreign markets for U.S. exports are the traditional objectives of U.S. international trade policy and trade law. For corporate managers, having a basic knowledge of this law and the domestic and international policy considerations that affect its enactment and implementation is more important than ever.

ter turns to highlighting certain aspects of U.S. trade law and policy, including a discussion of how U.S. trade policy is made and the role played by Congress, the president, and federal administrative agencies in promulgating and implementing trade agreements and regulations. The chapter then explains the U.S. laws affecting imports (including tariffs and import relief laws), as well as U.S. laws affecting exports. Next, the chapter discusses international trade regimes, ranging from the bilateral U.S.–Israel Free Trade Agreement to the regional North American Free Trade Agreement and the multilateral World Trade Organization. The final section looks at the European Union and explains how a group of countries that originally came together to form a common market for the sale of goods evolved into a union of member states with the ultimate objective of complete economic, monetary, and political integration.

CHAPTER OVERVIEW

This chapter begins by presenting a framework for understanding U.S. trade law and policy. With this framework in place, the chap-

---

 ## U.S. Trade Policy: Three Perspectives

U.S. trade policy in the modern age of rapid global business integration is most easily understood with the help of a conceptual framework. Trade policy can be

viewed from at least three perspectives, namely, (1) economic theory, (2) practical and political considerations, and (3) legal reality.

ECONOMIC THEORY

From an economic theoretical perspective, the consensus is that the objective of U.S. trade policy should continue to be the promotion of "free" and "fair" trade. Stated differently, U.S. trade policy ought to focus on eliminating government-controlled or -induced regulatory rules or practices (such as tariffs, quotas, or discriminatory practices) that distort trade flows in goods and services. The purpose of eliminating such regulatory advantages is to ensure that market outcomes reflect the real costs of goods and services and the resources used to produce them. Accordingly, protectionist measures to limit imports and shield domestic industries from foreign competition should be employed only on a temporary basis. In addition, the purpose of these safeguard restrictions should be to provide the domestic economy an opportunity to reallocate resources away from noncompetitive sectors to those where domestic firms are relatively more competitive.

PRACTICAL AND POLITICAL PERSPECTIVE

From a practical and political perspective, U.S. trade policy can be seen as an amalgam of competing and sometimes conflicting sets of interests. Traditionally, the major divide has been between *export-intensive* industries, which derive the bulk of their revenues from sales outside the United States, and *import-competing* industries, which derive their revenues primarily from U.S. sales and face significant competition from foreign firms. In recent times, a slight variation on this theme has arisen within both types of industries, as the outsourcing of traditional manufacturing and other labor-intensive work to facilities outside the United States has become a matter of contention between U.S. workers and managers, who are responsible for maximizing the returns to shareholders.

Beyond these traditional import–export and labor–management divides, more recent clashes have emerged over trade policies affecting the environment and human health. While some are concerned that trade and economic-based interests are being promoted over those of the environment and human health, others believe that environmental and human health issues are improperly being used to hijack the global trade discussions among governments that are essential to further trade liberalization. By most accounts, lurking behind this divide is a growing chasm between two groups: (1) those who support the objective of creating a global rules-based trade system by delegating the regulation of international trade to a multilateral institution, specifically, the World Trade Organization (WTO); and (2) those who believe that this delegation threatens national sovereignty, borders on usurpation, and places at risk traditional domestic policy prerogatives. To get a sense of the

mounting tension over the WTO and international trade issues more generally, one need only look at the demonstrations that took place during the WTO summit in Seattle, Washington, in December 1999, the subject of the "Inside Story" for this chapter.

LEGAL PERSPECTIVE

The legal perspective reflects the academic discussions that take place at the theoretical level and the policy debates that involve the myriad interests that have a stake in U.S. trade policy. Put differently, from the domestic policy-making process (which encompasses both the theoretical and the more practical political perspectives) come the U.S. laws that either (1) provide private individuals with rights vis-à-vis the executive branch and its regulation of U.S. foreign trade or (2) authorize, compel, or even expressly prohibit certain governmental action.

These laws also determine how the United States will implement the international trade agreements it enters into. Thus, it is U.S. law, rather than treaty language, that governs the force and effect that international trade agreements will have domestically. This reflects the important legal principle that international agreements (even treaties ratified by the U.S. Senate) are not "self-executing" under U.S. law unless Congress makes clear that it intends the provisions of an agreement to take effect directly as a matter of U.S. public law.

 # Developments *in* Trade Policy

The U.S. government has given trade policy increasingly higher priority over the last few decades. The Office of U.S. Trade Representative has cabinet-level rank. Meanwhile, although there is some discussion over which department or agency within the executive branch should take the lead on trade policy, there is no dispute over its importance to the nation.

 # Structure *of* U.S. Governmental Regulation *of* Trade

U.S. trade laws are enacted by Congress pursuant to the Commerce Clause of the U.S. Constitution, and they are

The Past *as a* Warning *for the* Future

As the following article demonstrates, U.S. trade policy can have a dramatic effect on business:

Economists Are Right for a Change, 1930

PRESIDENT HERBERT HOOVER, ignoring the pleas of 1,028 economists to veto it, signed with six gold pens the Smoot–Hawley Tariff Act on June 17, 1930. It was a hollow celebration.

The day before, anticipating the signing, the stock market suffered its worst collapse since November 1929, and the law quickly helped push the Great Depression deeper.

Its tariffs, which by 1932 rose to an all-time high of 59 percent of the average value of imports (today it's 5 percent), were designed to protect U.S. farm and textile products from foreign competition. Economists

warned that angry nations would retaliate, adding that foreigners would also have fewer dollars to buy U.S. goods as well as to settle their World War I debts.

Within two years, Great Britain and more than 20 other nations raised their tariffs and reduced buying of U.S. imports. Within the U.S., prices and output continued their fast fall.

From 1930 to 1931, U.S. imports dropped 29 percent, but U.S. exports fell

even more, 33 percent, and continued their collapse to a modern-day low of $2.4 billion in 1933.

One long-lasting effect of the act: The definition of "ornamental apparel," which has braid or lace, has stuck over the years and still adds to the duty paid. But in 1930, it was 90 percent; now it's 30 percent. In the 1930s it was another reason for women to use plainer lingerie.

In 1934, Congress passed the Reciprocal Trade Agreements Act to empower the president to reduce tariffs by half the 1930 rates in return for like cuts in foreign duties on U.S. goods. The "beggar thy neighbor" policy was dead.

Source: WALL ST. J., Apr. 28, 1989, at B1. Reprinted with permission of the *Wall Street Journal,* © 1989 Dow Jones & Company, Inc. All Rights Reserved Worldwide.

administered by the federal government and its administrative agencies.

THE ROLE OF CONGRESS

Congress has the power to regulate all aspects of foreign commerce, including imports and exports, foreign investment, licensing of technology, and other commercial activities. This chapter focuses primarily on international trade laws, that is, laws governing imports and exports. The trade laws may affect other aspects of foreign commerce as well, however.

Trade laws are generally designed to restrict or to facilitate imports and exports. Imports are restricted primarily by means of tariffs and quantitative limitations. Conversely, imports may be facilitated through exemption from U.S. tariffs. Exports are controlled by means of export licenses. Exports may be facilitated by federal subsidies, tax breaks, and other legislation, including Section 301 of the Trade Act of 1974, discussed later in this chapter.

Laws passed by state and local governments can also affect U.S. trade, although as the following case makes clear, the authority of states and localities in this area is very limited.

A CASE IN POINT

CASE 12.1
Crosby v. National Foreign Trade Council
Supreme Court of the United States
530 U.S. 363 (2000).

In the Language of the Court

FACTS In 1996, the Commonwealth of Massachusetts passed a law barring governmental entities in Massachusetts from buying goods or services from companies doing business with Burma (Myanmar). Subsequently, the U.S. Congress enacted federal legislation imposing mandatory and conditional sanctions on Burma. The Massachusetts law was inconsistent with the new federal legislation. The National Foreign Trade Council sued on behalf of its several members, claiming that the Massachusetts law unconstitutionally infringed on federal foreign affairs power, violated the Foreign Commerce Clause of the U.S. Constitution, and was preempted by the subsequent federal legisla-

(Continued)

(Case 12.1 continued)

tion. The district and appeals courts ruled in favor of the Council, and the Commonwealth appealed.

ISSUE PRESENTED Did Massachusetts exceed the scope of its authority by passing a law barring state entities from purchasing goods or services from companies doing business in Burma?

OPINION SOUTER, J., writing for the U.S. Supreme Court:

The Massachusetts law is preempted, and its application unconstitutional under the Supremacy Clause of the U.S. Constitution. State law must yield to a congressional act if Congress intends to occupy the field, or to the extent of any conflict with a federal statute. This is the case even where the relevant congressional act lacks an express preemption provision. This Court will find preemption where it is impossible for a private party to comply with both state and federal law and where the state law is an obstacle to the accomplishment and execution of Congress's full purposes and objectives. In this case, the state Act is an obstacle to the federal Act's delegation of discretion to the President of the United States to control economic sanctions against Burma. Within the sphere defined by Congress, the statute has given the President as much discretion to exercise economic leverage against Burma, with an eye toward national security, as law permits. It is implausible to think that Congress would have gone to such lengths to empower the President had it been willing to compromise his effectiveness by allowing state or local ordinances to blunt the consequences of his actions—exactly the effect of the state Act.

In addition, the Massachusetts law interferes with Congress's intention to limit economic pressure against the Burmese Government to a specific range. . . . Finally, the Massachusetts law conflicts with the President's authority to speak for the United States among the world's nations to develop a comprehensive, multilateral Burma strategy. In this respect, the state Act undermines the President's capacity for effective diplomacy.

RESULT The Supreme Court affirmed the rulings of the lower courts. The Massachusetts law was struck down.

COMMENTS By limiting the basis of its ruling to the theory of federal preemption and the Supremacy Clause doctrine, the Supreme Court did not address whether the Massachusetts law would have violated the Constitution in the absence of a federal law concerning Burma sanctions.

QUESTIONS

1. Is it ever appropriate for states to adopt laws that affect international trade?
2. How should a manager of a U.S. company handle seemingly inconsistent state and federal laws related to international trade?

THE ROLE OF THE PRESIDENT

The president administers U.S. trade laws pursuant to the authority delegated to the president by Congress. As chief executive, the president has broad power to negotiate trade agreements but cannot regulate trade without congressional delegation or approval. Nevertheless, as the following case shows, the president can negotiate nonbinding, voluntary undertakings.

A CASE IN POINT

CASE 12.2

Consumers Union, Inc. v. Kissinger

United States Court of Appeals for the District of Columbia

506 F.2d 136 (D.C. Cir. 1974), cert. denied, 421 U.S. 1004 (1975).

In the Language of the Court

FACTS In order to assist the U.S. steel industry, President Richard Nixon (through his secretary of state, Henry Kissinger) sought to reduce steel imports from Japan and Europe by convincing foreign producers to limit their exports to the United States. The undertakings to do so were voluntary, and the United States made no attempt to enforce them legally.

Consumers Union, believing that U.S. consumers were hurt by this restriction on supplies of foreign steel, sued the secretary of state. It argued that the president had, in effect, regulated foreign commerce without any specific statutory delegation of authority from Congress and, thus, had exceeded his authority.

ISSUE PRESENTED Did President Nixon act within his powers in negotiating nonbinding, voluntary undertakings with foreign producers to reduce their exports to the United States?

OPINION McGOWAN, J., writing for the U.S. Court of Appeals for the District of Columbia Circuit:

The steel import restraints do not purport to be enforceable, either as contracts or as governmental actions with the force of law; and the executive has no sanctions to invoke in order to compel observance by the foreign producers of their self-denying representations. They are a statement of intent on the part of the foreign producer associations. The signatories' expectations, not unreasonable in light of the reception given their undertakings by the executive, are that the executive will consult with them over mutual concerns about the steel import situation, and that it will not have sudden recourse to the unilateral steps available to it under the Trade Expansion Act to impose legal restrictions on importation. The President is not bound in any way to refrain from taking such steps if he later deems them to be in the national interest, or if consultation proves unavailing to meet unforeseen difficulties; and certainly the Congress is not inhibited from enacting any legislation it desires to regulate by law the importation of steel.

RESULT The export restraints by the foreign producers were upheld. The president did not exceed his constitutional authority because the export restraints were accomplished through an informal, voluntary agreement. The restraints were not legally binding on the foreign exporters, and they were not enforced by U.S. authorities.

COMMENTS Congress later approved the steel restraints. President Ronald Reagan negotiated new steel-export restraints with foreign governments in 1984, and President George Bush extended them in 1988; Congress approved both actions.

QUESTIONS

1. What incentives do foreign exporters have to voluntarily refrain from exporting their goods to the United States?
2. Could the U.S. Customs Service have enforced this agreement by excluding imports in excess of the agreed limits?

The President's Power to Restrict Trade Over the years, Congress has authorized the president to regulate or restrict trade and other economic activity when necessary to protect the U.S. national security, foreign policy, or economy. The International Emergency Economic Powers Act,[1] passed in 1977, limited the president's au-

thority to restrict trade and other commercial transactions to instances when a national emergency had been declared in response to an "unusual and extraordinary threat, which has its source in whole or substantial part outside the United States, to the national security, foreign policy or economy of the United States."

The economic sanctions imposed under these laws are administered by the Office of Foreign Assets Control in

1. 50 U.S.C. §§ 1701–06 (1998).

the Department of the Treasury, which issues appropriate regulations. To varying degrees, the regulations apply not only to transactions in the United States but also to transactions by foreign affiliates of U.S. companies and to transactions abroad involving U.S. property. The application of the regulations to foreign subsidiaries or operations of U.S. companies has caused considerable difficulty, particularly for companies subjected to conflicting requirements imposed by foreign governments on their foreign affiliates.[2]

ADMINISTRATIVE AGENCIES

The agencies primarily responsible for administrating the trade laws are the U.S. Trade Representative (USTR), the Department of Commerce, the Department of State, the Department of the Treasury, the U.S. International Trade Commission, and the U.S. Customs Service (which is part of the Treasury Department).

The USTR, assisted by the other agencies, is responsible for developing U.S. trade policy and negotiating trade agreements with other countries. The USTR makes all policy decisions concerning the operation of these agreements. The Commerce Department is generally responsible for implementing U.S. trade policy, enforcing certain import relief laws and export controls, and promoting U.S. exports. The State Department administers controls on munitions exports and defends U.S. economic interests through U.S. embassies abroad.

The Treasury Department administers embargoes imposed on U.S. trade with countries such as Iraq, Cuba, and Libya. The International Trade Commission is an independent agency with a variety of responsibilities, including investigating the effect of imports on U.S. industries. The Customs Service enforces all U.S. customs laws and import restrictions and collects U.S. tariffs. With the assistance of the Customs Service, other agencies, such as the U.S. Department of Agriculture, administer restrictions on U.S. trade falling in their particular areas of responsibility.

The Interagency Committee The president makes trade policy decisions based on the recommendations of an interagency committee headed by the USTR. In addition to the agencies listed above, the committee includes the

2. *See, e.g.,* Dresser Indus. v. Baldridge, 549 F. Supp. 108 (D.D.C. 1982). (French subsidiary of U.S. company unsuccessful in enjoining application of sanctions by U.S. Department of Commerce for failure to honor U.S. prohibition on exports of certain types of equipment to the Soviet Union even though the French subsidiary had been ordered by the French government to honor the contractual commitments to ship the equipment.)

Department of Labor, the Council of Economic Advisers, and other agencies interested in trade policy. Private interests are typically given the opportunity to express their views to any of these agencies or to the interagency committee directly. For example, tariffs on a particular product are rarely changed without first consulting the affected industry. Government officials at all the agencies are generally receptive to requests and comments from U.S. companies. In many cases, public hearings are held before decisions are made.

THE EXPORT–IMPORT BANK

The Export–Import Bank of the United States (Eximbank) was created more than fifty years ago to provide financing for the purchase of U.S. exports. The Eximbank is the U.S. government's response to foreign governments' export subsidies. By offering financing at below-market interest rates, the Eximbank allows U.S. exporters to compete with foreign companies.

Major Programs The major programs of the Eximbank have traditionally been direct long-term loans at fixed interest rates to foreign buyers and financial guarantees. Long-term loans or guarantees are generally reserved for exports of turnkey projects, such as manufacturing, electric power, and petrochemical plants. Short-term and medium-term bank guarantees and short-term and medium-term export credit insurance are also provided. Over the years, other programs have been introduced, including the I-Match Program, which authorized the Eximbank to pay interest subsidies to private lenders when necessary to compete with foreign subsidized financing. Another program is the Tied Aid Credit War Chest, which authorized $300 million to be used to subsidize exports and fight mixed credit financing by foreign governments. This program is part of the Treasury Department's effort to negotiate a comprehensive agreement among the industrialized countries to limit the practice of mixing foreign aid with export credit, which distorts trade.

U.S. Laws Affecting Imports

TARIFFS

Tariffs are the basic tool for limiting imports to protect domestic industries. Today, most tariffs are *ad valorem tariffs,* meaning that the importer must pay a percentage of the value of the imported merchandise. For instance, a 10 percent tariff on a shipment of imports valued at

$10,000 would result in a *duty,* that is, a required payment, of $1,000.

U.S. tariffs are established by federal law. They can be changed only by statute or by administrative action authorized by statute. Congress frequently changes U.S. tariffs. In addition, under the auspices of the Trade Agreements Program initiated by Congress in 1934, Congress has periodically delegated to the president the authority to reduce U.S. tariffs in exchange for tariff concessions by other nations. Congress has also for many years delegated to the president the power to increase tariffs temporarily in order to protect domestic industries in certain specified situations. These import relief laws are discussed later in this chapter.

THE HARMONIZED TARIFF SCHEDULE

The United States has accepted an internationally harmonized tariff system. Current tariffs are found in a document entitled the *Harmonized Tariff Schedule of the United States (HTS).*[3] The HTS lists the tariffs on goods imposed by Congress and by the president pursuant to the Trade Agreements Program, based on their country of origin.

For each product category, there are two basic rates of duty. One column applies to most countries (column 1), and the second applies to several less-favored countries, such as Cuba and North Korea (column 2), with whom the United States does not have normal trade relations. These columns reflect tariffs imposed by Congress or negotiated by the president. Column 1 is subdivided into general and special tariffs. Special tariffs reflect preferential rates for certain countries on certain products; these are described later in this chapter. Temporary increases in U.S. tariffs are listed in Chapter 99 of the HTS.

COUNTRY OF ORIGIN

U.S. tariffs vary depending on the country of origin. A good is considered the product of the country from which it was first exported, unless it has been substantially transformed into a new article of commerce. If such a *substantial transformation* occurs, the country of origin is considered to be the country in which the transformation took place.

TARIFF CLASSIFICATION

Tariffs also vary depending on the article's *tariff classification,* that is, where it is best described in the HTS. Determining an article's classification is often a simple

3. Published by the U.S. International Trade Commission.

matter because many articles are described exactly in the schedules. For example, mineral waters are classified under item 2201.10. Articles are not always as clearly described, however, and disagreements may occur. This is especially true of newly developed products.

CUSTOMS VALUATION AND LAWS

The duty paid on an imported article depends on the value assigned to it by the Customs Service, that is, on the *customs valuation* of the article. The lower the valuation, the lower the duty.

The basic rule of customs valuation in the United States is that the value of an article for customs purposes is the *transaction value,* which is the price indicated on the sales invoice. Following this rule makes customs valuation for most imports a simple matter. There are exceptions to this rule, however. For example, if the importer and the foreign seller are related, the Customs Service is authorized to determine whether the invoice reflects a price negotiated by the two parties at arm's length.

There are further rules to keep in mind. For example, the cost of foreign inland freight is not *dutiable* (subject to duty) if charged separately from the invoice price. If, however, the cost of foreign inland freight is included in the invoice price, then it is included in the valuation and becomes dutiable. Careful customs planning can avoid such needless extra duties. Proper customs planning can not only minimize the import duties paid but can also help to avoid violations of the customs laws. Penalties can be severe and may involve forfeiture of the imported articles, along with heavy fines.

The U.S. customs laws are administered by the Customs Service. Its headquarters are in Washington, D.C., but the service has a district office at every U.S. port. Tariff rulings by the district offices can be appealed to headquarters and then to the U.S. Court of International Trade. Appeals from this court are to the U.S. Court of Appeals for the Federal Circuit and then to the U.S. Supreme Court. The customs laws are found in Title 19 of the U.S. Code. The regulations of the Customs Service are in Title 19 of the Code of Federal Regulations.

TARIFF PREFERENCES

Pursuant to authority delegated by Congress, the president has established preferential tariffs for imports from certain developing countries. The most important are embodied in the Generalized System of Preferences (GSP).

The Generalized System of Preferences The Generalized System of Preferences, which was agreed to multilaterally, is a program developed by the industrialized countries to assist developing nations by improving their ability to export. The GSP has been used to integrate developing countries into the international trade system and to encourage beneficiary countries to eliminate or reduce barriers to trade and to enforce intellectual property rights. Under the GSP, which was adopted in Title V of the Trade Act of 1974,[4] the president has designated certain products as eligible for duty-free treatment if they are produced in developing countries designated as eligible beneficiaries of the program.

Under the GSP, an eligible product receives duty-free treatment only if 35 percent or more of the value of the product was added in an eligible country. There are also limitations on the volume of eligible articles that may be imported from a single country. If the volume limitation is exceeded, the product is automatically removed from the category of eligible imports from that country.

If a country is found to be sufficiently competitive, the president can remove it from the program, either entirely or with respect to individual products. This process is referred to as "graduation." In 1989, Singapore, South Korea, and Taiwan were graduated from the program entirely. Countries can also be removed from the GSP program for policy reasons, such as failure to protect intellectual property rights. The program is reviewed annually to determine which countries and products should be removed from or added to the program. The program is administered for the president by the U.S. Trade Representative.

Import Relief Laws

In a series of laws, known collectively as the *import relief laws,* Congress has authorized the president to raise U.S. tariffs on specified products and to provide other forms of import protection to U.S. industries. These laws vary as to the nature of the unfair practice (if any) to which they are directed, the degree of injury required in order to obtain relief, the nature of the relief authorized, the agencies authorized to provide the relief, and the amount of discretion given to the president in determining whether to grant relief.

SECTION 201

Section 201 of the Trade Act of 1974 (*Section 201*)[5] provides for temporary relief to domestic industries seriously

injured by increasing imports, regardless of whether unfair practices are involved. It is sometimes called the *fair trade law.* The relief is designed to give the U.S. industry a few years (normally no more than five) to adjust to import competition.

The U.S. International Trade Commission (ITC) investigates petitions filed by U.S. industries. If the ITC makes an affirmative finding of injury from imports, it recommends specific import relief, such as higher duties or quantitative limits on imports. The president must provide the recommended relief unless he or she finds that it would not be in the national economic interest, as defined in the law. Because import relief always has economic costs, such as inflationary effects, the president may decide not to provide relief. As a result, the president may be the target of aggressive lobbying on the part of foreign governments, purchasers of the challenged imports, and the domestic industry.

The Omnibus Trade and Competitiveness Act of 1988[6] encourages petitioning industries to submit plans illustrating how they would use Section 201 relief to adjust to import competition. It further provides that the ITC should recommend relief that not only addresses the injury caused by imports but will also facilitate the domestic industry's adjustment to import competition. As a complement to that, the law provides that the president can grant either import relief or other appropriate relief within his or her legal authority.

Thus, the law encourages making relief conditional on the ability of the domestic industry to meet the competition or to transfer its resources elsewhere. The ITC has recommended relief in approximately 50 percent of the investigations made under Section 201. The president has granted relief in approximately half of those cases.

An excellent example of the use of Section 201 is provided by the U.S. steel industry. In 1984, when President Reagan negotiated the new set of voluntary steel-export restraints (discussed earlier in this chapter), he did so after the steel industry had filed a Section 201 petition. The ITC recommended relief, but President Reagan decided not to impose higher tariffs or mandatory quotas under this law. Instead, he negotiated voluntary bilateral agreements with most of the major steel-producing countries.

In another case, the ITC refused to recommend relief under Section 201 for the automobile industry. A majority of the commission found that the injury being suffered by the industry was not primarily caused by imports.

In the following case, the Clinton administration accepted a recommendation by the ITC for trade restrictions on lamb imports.

---

4. 19 U.S.C. §§ 2461–66 (1998).
5. 19 U.S.C. § 2251 (1998).

6. 15 U.S.C. §§ 78dd-1, 78dd-2, 78ff. (1998).

A CASE IN POINT

CASE 12.3

Presidential Decision under Section 201: Lamb Imports
Statement by the President, July 7, 1999.

Summary

FACTS When the U.S. lamb industry lodged a complaint that a surge in cheap lamb imports, mostly from Australia and New Zealand, was causing serious injury to the U.S. lamb market, the International Trade Commission (ITC) launched a thorough investigation of lamb imports under Section 201 of the Trade Act of 1974. The ITC determined that lamb imports had increased nearly 50 percent between 1993 and 1997 and had continued to increase at a rapid rate through 1999. The ITC concluded that the increase in lamb imports had caused serious injury to the domestic industry, and it unanimously recommended that trade restrictions be imposed on lamb imports for four years.

ISSUE PRESENTED Would imposing trade restrictions on lamb imports be detrimental to the national economic interest?

DECISION The Clinton administration agreed with the ITC that temporary trade restrictions were necessary to preserve the U.S. lamb industry and give it time to become more competitive.

RESULT The ITC's recommendation to provide relief was accepted.

THE ANTIDUMPING LAW

The antidumping law, codified in the Tariff Act of 1930, as amended,[7] is the most frequently used import relief law. If a U.S. industry is materially injured by imports of a product being *dumped* in the United States (that is, sold below the current selling price in the exporter's home market or below the exporter's cost of production), then the law imposes an antidumping duty on the dumped product. The amount of the duty is equal to the amount of the *dumping margin,* that is, the difference between the U.S. price and the price in the exporting country. If the ITC determines that dumping has occurred and caused material injury, the Commerce Department is required to impose duties on the imports sold at less than fair value.

In determining what constitutes dumping of imports, the law applies a different standard to countries with nonmarket economies (such as socialist countries). This is done on the theory that prices in such countries do not reflect market forces and are, therefore, not a reasonable basis for determining whether price discrimination exists.

The U.S. steel industry has generated approximately 46 percent of the unfair trade complaints filed with the ITC in the last two decades even though steel accounts for less than 5 percent of U.S. imports.[8] Even though steelmakers have lost approximately 54 percent of the dumping and unfair subsidy cases filed with the ITC in recent years, companies have learned that the mere fact of filing a complaint can cause imports from the target companies to drop.[9]

THE COUNTERVAILING DUTY LAW

The countervailing duty law[10] provides that, if a U.S. industry is materially injured by imports of a product benefiting from a foreign subsidy, a *countervailing duty* must be imposed on those imports, that is, an import duty that offsets the amount of the benefit conferred by the subsidy. *Countervailable subsidies* are benefits provided by a government to stimulate exports. They can take many forms, including direct grants and loans to industry at below-market interest rates. For certain countries, injury to the U.S. industry is not a prerequisite; the existence of a countervailable subsidy suffices to trigger relief. As under the antidumping law, if a subsidy and (where applicable) injury are found to exist, relief is mandatory.

SECTION 337

Section 337 of the Tariff Act of 1930 (*Section 337*)[11] provides that if a U.S. industry is injured (or if there is a restraint or monopolization of trade in the United States) by reason of unfair acts in the importation of articles into the United States, an order must be issued requiring the exporters and importers to cease the unfair

7. 19 U.S.C. §§ 1673–77 (1998).
8. Chris Adams, *U.S. Steelmakers Win Even When They Lose an Unfair-Trade Case,* WALL ST. J., Mar. 27, 1998, at A1.

9. *Id.*
10. 19 U.S.C. §§ 1303, 1671a–h (1998).
11. 19 U.S.C. § 1337 (1998).

acts or, if necessary, excluding imports of the offending articles from all sources. This law applies to unfair competition of all kinds not covered in other import relief laws, but it is most commonly used in cases involving patent or trademark infringement. Relief is mandatory unless the president disapproves the ITC decision, which seldom happens.

The Omnibus Trade and Competitiveness Act eliminated the requirement to show economic injury in cases involving intellectual property rights (infringement of patents, trademarks, and copyrights). The Act affected most Section 337 cases and made it significantly easier for U.S. companies to obtain relief under this statute.

SECTION 406

Section 406 of the Trade Act of 1974 (*Section 406*)[12] is similar to Section 201. It provides for import relief if a U.S. industry is suffering material injury by reason of rapidly increasing imports from a communist country. Relief is discretionary.

SECTION 232

Section 232 of the Trade Expansion Act of 1962 (*Section 232*)[13] provides for relief from imports threatening to impair U.S. national security. It has been used very rarely. Relief is discretionary.

THE BUY AMERICAN ACT

Under the Buy American Act,[14] federal agencies, when procuring supplies and equipment, must give a preference to products made in the United States unless their price is a certain percentage higher than the price of the equivalent foreign product. Products are deemed to be American made, and therefore eligible for the preference, if they are manufactured in the United States and at least 50 percent of the components are American made.

As explained later in this chapter, preferences to domestic industry in government procurement are a common form of nontariff barrier to imports that was addressed in one of the GATT codes. Pursuant to that code (the Agreement on Government Procurement),[15] many U.S. agencies have joined foreign agencies in eliminating this preference. Defense-related articles are not subject to the agreement, however, and still receive the Buy American Act preference.

12. 19 U.S.C. § 2436 (1998).
13. 19 U.S.C. § 1862 (1998).
14. 41 U.S.C. §§ 10a–d (1998).
15. 18 I.L.M. 1052 (1979).

 # Foreign Trade Zones

Foreign trade zones are special areas within or adjacent to a U.S. port of entry that have been designated as such by the Foreign Trade Zones Board at the U.S. Department of Commerce.[16] Merchandise may be imported into the United States directly to a foreign trade zone; the import duties normally due on entry into the United States are not due until the merchandise is withdrawn from the zone.

Foreign trade zones provide several advantages. Merchandise may be imported to a foreign trade zone for demonstration purposes only; if it is reexported from the zone, no duties are owed. Merchandise may also be imported to a foreign trade zone and manufactured into a new article of commerce. In that case, duties are owed on the new article of commerce when it is withdrawn from the zone for consumption in the United States. This is advantageous to the importer if the duty is lower on the manufactured product than on the imported intermediate product.

 # U.S. Laws Affecting Exports

Several U.S. laws serve to facilitate or, in some cases, control exports.

SECTION 301

Section 301 of the Trade Act of 1974 (*Section 301*)[17] is the principal U.S. statute addressing unfair foreign practices affecting U.S. exports of goods or services. Section 301 may be used to enforce U.S. rights under international trade agreements. It may also be used to respond to unreasonable, unjustifiable, or discriminatory foreign government practices that burden or restrict U.S. commerce. Specifically, Section 301 authorizes the U.S. Trade Representative (USTR) to investigate alleged unfair practices of foreign governments that impede U.S. exports of both goods and services. Subject to the five exceptions listed below, the USTR must take action in response to foreign government practices that (1) violate trade agreements with the United States or (2) are unjustifiable (that is, in violation of the international legal rights of the United States) and burden or restrict U.S. commerce. The USTR has discretionary authority to take action if he or she determines that an act or policy of a foreign country is unreasonable or discriminatory and burdens or restricts U.S. commerce.

16. Foreign Trade Zones Act of 1934, 19 U.S.C. §§ 81a–u (1998).
17. 19 U.S.C. § 2411 (1998).

Section 301 has been used with growing aggressiveness by the U.S. government. Since 1993, the USTR has initiated twenty-nine Section 301 investigations, some of which were resolved through the World Trade Organization (WTO) dispute settlement process (discussed in detail later in the chapter).[18] In practice, the United States uses Section 301, along with "Super 301" and "Special 301" (discussed below), in conjunction with bilateral and WTO mechanisms to promote compliance and to address problems that are outside the scope of the WTO and the North American Free Trade Agreement.

The USTR is not required to take action if (1) a WTO panel concludes that there is no unfair trade practice, (2) the USTR believes the foreign government is taking steps to solve the problem, (3) the foreign government agrees to provide compensation, (4) the action could adversely affect the American economy disproportionately to the benefit to be achieved, or (5) the national security of the United States could be harmed through action.

The Omnibus Trade and Competitiveness Act of 1988 created a program known as *Super 301,* which required the USTR to draw up a list of the foreign governments whose practices pose the most significant barriers to U.S. exports and to commence immediate Section 301 investigations with respect to these practices. Similarly, under the *Special 301 provisions* in U.S. trade law, the USTR identifies those countries that deny adequate and effective protection for intellectual property rights or deny fair and equitable market access for persons who rely on intellectual property protection. Countries that have the most onerous or egregious practices and whose practices have the greatest adverse impact on the relevant U.S. products are designated as "priority foreign countries" and are subject to Section 301 investigations. Other countries with less severe problems protecting intellectual property rights are placed on a "watch list" or "priority watch list" and are monitored closely for progress.[19] Brazil and Thailand were designated as priority foreign countries in 1993, China was similarly designated in 1994 and 1996, and Paraguay in 1997.[20]

THE EXPORT ADMINISTRATION ACT

The Export Administration Act of 1979[21] is the primary restriction on U.S. exports. It authorizes the secretary of commerce to prohibit exports when necessary to protect national security, carry out U.S. foreign policy, enforce U.S. nuclear nonproliferation policy, or prevent the export of goods that are in short supply. Some controls are imposed unilaterally by the United States. Others are imposed jointly with U.S. allies on exports to communist countries. These restrictions are agreed on and administered through an informal arrangement known as CoCom.

The Act's most significant restrictions are those that control high technology and its products. The explosion of high-technology industries has resulted in a radical increase in the volume of U.S. exports that are controlled under this law. This restriction has had serious adverse consequences for U.S. exporters competing for business abroad.

One particularly controversial application of the Act relates to encryption software. Several U.S. companies claim that their inability to sell software with so-called strong encryption puts them at a competitive disadvantage with respect to foreign companies offering such security.

The Omnibus Trade and Competitiveness Act of 1988, reflecting the importance attached to the trade deficit and the need to promote U.S. exports, removed many controls on exports, particularly to friendly countries. The United States and its allies are further reducing controls on exports to Eastern Europe and former republics of the Soviet Union in the light of the reduced military threat now posed by those countries. Restrictions on encryption software have also been eased.

Export Licenses The export controls are enforced by a system of export licenses. Certain categories of commodities and technical data may not be exported without an export license from the Commerce Department's Bureau of Export Administration. The bureau reviews all applications and determines whether to issue licenses. Its decision in each case is based on a number of factors, including the nature of the item to be exported, the country to which it is to be shipped, the foreign consignee, and the use to which the item will be put. The restrictions vary with all of these factors.

Managers should be aware of these controls when planning export transactions and negotiating with foreign buyers and should take steps to ensure that the rules are followed. The rules are complex and easily misunderstood, and the civil and criminal penalties for violations are severe.

Three points are often overlooked by exporters. First, U.S. restrictions apply not only to exports of goods but also to exports of technology (referred to as technical data). Second, U.S. restrictions apply not only to exports

18. *Monitoring and Enforcing Trade Laws and Agreements,* U.S. TRADE REPRESENTATIVE FACT SHEET, May 1, 2000.
19. *Id.*
20. *Id.*
21. 50 U.S.C. App. § 2401 *et seq.* (1982 & Supp. 1987).

from the United States but also to many reexports of U.S.-origin goods and technology to third countries by other countries. The restrictions also apply to exports from other countries of certain foreign-made articles that are direct products of U.S. technology. Third, the transfer of technical data to a foreign citizen in the United States is generally considered to be an export, which means that an export license is required. Such transfers include verbal exchanges of technology on U.S. soil and visits by foreign nationals to U.S. plants.

THE ARMS EXPORT CONTROL ACT

The Arms Export Control Act[22] authorizes the U.S. secretary of state to prohibit exports of munitions and munitions technology from the United States. The act is administered by the Office of Munitions Control of the State Department, which issues the International Traffic in Arms Regulations (ITARs) and operates a licensing system, similar to that of the Commerce Department, based on the United States Munitions List.[23] The Commerce and State Departments both issue advisory opinions to exporters concerning the applicability of export controls to specific transactions.

EXPORT TRADING COMPANIES

Before 1982, U.S. companies complained that their efforts to compete abroad by pooling their resources were hindered by the U.S. antitrust laws. The Export Trading Company Act of 1982[24] sought to address these concerns.

Under this law, the Commerce Department may certify an export trading company formed by two or more independent companies exclusively for export purposes. If a certificate is issued (with the concurrence of the Department of Justice), the participants in the export trading company are protected from private treble damage actions and government criminal and civil suits under federal and state antitrust laws for the export activities specified in the certificate. The law does not, however, protect them from private antitrust actions for actual damages. Certification is authorized for export activities that do not restrain competition in the United States and do not constitute unfair competition in the U.S. export trade.

The act also permits the Export–Import Bank of the United States to guarantee loans to export trading companies and other exporters. This provision, however, applies only to short-term loans, generally with a term of

twelve months or less. The intention is to make available to exporters loans that would not otherwise be available.

 # International Trade Regimes

In order to achieve its trade goals with respect to both the regulation of imports and the facilitation of exports, the United States engages its trade partners in a wide array of bilateral, regional, and multilateral trade agreements. Bilateral agreements tend to be limited in subject matter, covering matters such as tariffs, taxes, and intellectual property rights. To the extent disputes arise under these agreements, they are resolved at the mutual desire of the parties through negotiated settlement. In the regional and multilateral contexts, the North American Free Trade Agreement and the World Trade Organization are remarkable for their dispute settlement mechanisms, which were negotiated as part of each agreement.

U.S.–ISRAEL FREE TRADE AGREEMENT

The U.S.–Israel Free Trade Agreement[25] is an example of a bilateral agreement between the United States and one of its trade partners. Under this agreement, all tariffs between the United States and Israel were eliminated in 1995. As a bilateral agreement, the tariff preferences apply only to trade between the two countries and not to imports from other countries.

THE TRADE AND DEVELOPMENT ACT OF 2000

The Trade and Development Act of 2000[26] (the 2000 Trade Act) includes the Africa Growth and Opportunity Act and the U.S.–Caribbean Basin Trade Partnership Act. The 2000 Trade Act provides the foundation for expanded trade between the United States and the countries of sub-Saharan Africa and the countries of the Caribbean Basin and replaces the Caribbean Basin Initiative enacted in 1983.[27]

Beyond provisions specifically applicable to countries in sub-Saharan Africa and the Caribbean Basin, the 2000 Trade Act also contains far-reaching workers' rights provisions. These include (1) specific prohibitions on imports of

---

22. 22 U.S.C. §§ 2751–96 (1998).
23. 22 C.F.R. pt. 121 (1990).
24. 15 U.S.C. §§ 4001–21 (1998).

25. Free Trade Agreement, Apr. 22, 1985, United States–Israel, U.S.T. __, T.I.A.S. No. __, 24 I.L.M. 653 (1985). This agreement was approved by Congress in the United States–Israel Free Trade Area Implementation Act of 1985. 19 U.S.C. §§ 2701–07 (1988).
26. *See* Trade and Development Act of 2000, Pub. L. No. 106-200.
27. Caribbean Basin Economic Recovery Act of 1983. 19 U.S.C. §§ 2461–66 (1998).

goods made using forced child labor, (2) new eligibility criteria for GSP status based on compliance with certain child labor provisions promulgated by the International Labor Organization (ILO), and (3) a general requirement that a country's human rights practices be considered when determining eligibility for trade preferences.

THE NORTH AMERICAN FREE TRADE AGREEMENT

The trilateral North American Free Trade Agreement (NAFTA)[28] provides for the gradual elimination of all barriers to trade between the United States, Canada, and Mexico and for the free cross-border movement of goods and services between the territories of the three signatories. Designed to improve all three countries' economies and to benefit 390 million consumers with lower-priced goods and increased investment opportunities, NAFTA established the world's largest free trade zone. Congress approved the agreement on November 17, 1993, and it went into effect on January 1, 1994.

Under NAFTA, Mexico is eliminating tariffs on U.S. capital goods in stages based on three categories: "A," "B," and "C." Tariffs on Category A goods, which include automobiles, were eliminated in January 1994. Category B goods, which include textile and apparel goods, became duty-free in 1998. Category C goods, which include the majority of capital goods, will be duty-free in 2003. The United States eliminated the majority of its tariffs on Mexican goods on January 1, 1994.

In addition to eliminating its custom duties, each country is required to accord national treatment to the goods of the other nations in accordance with Article III of the General Agreement on Tariffs and Trade (GATT) (discussed below). The agreement also substantially reduced the barriers to government procurement and effectively results in totally open procurement by the year 2004.

NAFTA prohibits new restrictions on investment and on trade in services among the three countries. It includes major provisions relating to specific industries, such as agriculture, telecommunications, and energy. In addition, it established special rules of origin to ensure that only products originating in the United States, Canada, or Mexico enjoy duty-free treatment. Certificates of origin are required on all goods being exported between the three countries to certify that the good qualifies as an "originating" good.

The pact also provides for the adequate protection and enforcement of intellectual property rights and at-

tempts to ensure that these rights do not become barriers to trade. Each country was required to implement several international agreements regarding intellectual property rights, such as the Berne Convention for the Protection of Literary and Artistic Works (dealing with copyrights) and the Paris Convention for the Protection of Industrial Property Rights (dealing with patents).

NAFTA explicitly protects the continued enforceability of U.S. environmental regulations and includes a mechanism for sanctions if Mexico fails to enforce its own environmental laws. In addition, a side agreement set up a three-nation mechanism, the Commission on Environmental Cooperation, to address environmental disputes. Any country or private interest group that believes that a nation is not enforcing its environmental laws may complain. If the commission determines that a violation has occurred, it can impose a fine up to $20 million or impose trade sanctions on the offending country. Since 1992, Mexico has enacted five major environmental statutes and numerous regulations (often modeled on U.S. environmental laws) and has drastically improved its environmental enforcement regime.[29] Even so, some environmentalists have faulted the commission for not demanding more, especially in the area of transboundary cleanup and remediation.[30]

The North American Agreement on Labor Cooperation, a side agreement that established panels in the United States, Mexico, and Canada to hear complaints about worker abuse, has had little impact.[31] The panels have restricted themselves to fact-finding. They cannot levy fines or impose trade sanctions unless there is a persistent lack of enforcement of existing child labor, safety and health, or minimum employment standards.[32] Several U.S. unions have argued that violations relating to freedom of association, collective bargaining, and strikes should also give rise to fines and trade sanctions, not just the high-level ministerial consultations called for in the side agreement.[33] In the words of counsel for the International Labor Rights Fund, who litigated the five cases filed in Mexico: "[I]n all of these cases workers are left with a piece of paper that says 'you were right.' Not a single worker was ever reinstated, not a single employer was sanctioned, no union was ever recognized."[34]

---

28. North American Free Trade Agreement, Dec. 17, 1992, United States–Canada–Mexico, U.S.T. __, T.I.A.S. No. __, 32 I.L.M. 605 (1993).

29. Richard H. Steinberg, *Trade-Environment Negotiations in the EU, NAFTA, and WTO: Regional Trajectories of Rule Development,* 91 Am. J. Int'l L. 231 (1997).

30. Joel Millman, *Nafta's Do-Gooder Side Deals Disappoint,* Wall St. J., Oct. 15, 1997, at A19.

31. *Id.*

32. *Labor, Business Say Labor Side Accord Misses the Mark; Suggest Major Changes,* 66 U.S.L.W. 2515 (May 3, 1998).

33. *Id.*

34. Millman, *supra* note 30.

Primarily to protect fruit, vegetable, and sugarcane growers in Florida, NAFTA phases out U.S. agricultural tariffs over fifteen years. In addition, during that period, any dramatic increases in Mexican fruit and vegetable imports will trigger temporary "snap-back" tariffs to protect U.S. growers.

FREE TRADE AREA OF THE AMERICAS (FTAA)

In September 1998, the thirty-four democratically elected governments of the Western Hemisphere initiated negotiations over the creation of a Free Trade Area of the Americas (FTAA) as a way to build on NAFTA. The ultimate goal of the FTAA is to achieve a comprehensive free trade agreement by 2005. Nine FTAA negotiating groups have been established to address market access; agriculture; services; investment; government procure-

ment; intellectual property; subsidies, antidumping, and countervailing duties; competition policy; and dispute settlement.

Fast-Track Negotiating Authority According to some observers, the first step for the George W. Bush administration toward meeting the 2005 target will be a strong push to reenact fast-track authority for the president.[35] *Fast-track negotiating authority* allows the president to negotiate trade agreements and then submit them for an up-or-down vote by Congress with no amendments permitted. As explained in the "Political Perspective," the Congress denied President Clinton fast-track authority in 1997.

35. Anthony DePalma, *Latin America Is Priority on Bush Trade Agenda,* N.Y. TIMES, Dec. 23, 2000, at C23.

POLITICAL PERSPECTIVE

Denial *of* Fast-Track Authority *for* President Clinton

For the first time since President Franklin Delano Roosevelt began cutting tariffs in 1934, a U.S. president lost a significant vote in Congress for trade liberalization when Congress denied President Bill Clinton fast-track negotiating authority in 1997. Organized labor fought ferociously against fast track based on its belief that expanded trade undermines job security and wages in the United States. Unions have insisted that future trade agreements contain labor safeguards enforceable by trade sanctions, a demand rejected by U.S. businesses and their Republican allies in Congress and by Clinton as well.

Since 1973, the wage gap between skilled and unskilled workers in the United States has widened. In 1973, a college graduate made $1.48 for every dollar earned by a high school graduate; that had increased to $1.63 per dollar by the end of 1995. Trade has played a role in widening the wage gap, but there is no consensus as to how significant that role has been. William Cline, chief economist at the Institute of International Finance, an association of large financial service companies, estimated that 10.1 percent of wage inequality is due to trade, compared

to 3.7 percent attributable to technological change, 4.4 percent to the decline of unions, and 2.9 percent to immigration.[a]

Since NAFTA took effect in January 1994, approximately 150,000 U.S. garment workers (about 16 percent of the garment industry's workforce) have lost their jobs, largely because of import competition from Mexico and other low-wage nations.[b] Free trade has also created jobs by increasing exports, however, so, on balance, it appears to have been a wash.[c] Even so, a 1997 poll showed that a majority of Americans believe that trade agreements, such as NAFTA, destroy jobs in the United States.

In some ways, the fast-track vote became a referendum on NAFTA, which was itself negotiated using fast-track authority. Vintners and cattle ranchers in California claimed that the Clinton ad-

ministration had failed to live up to its promises to open up markets in Mexico, Canada, and Europe and to reduce tariffs on U.S. goods. The California wine industry was particularly concerned that Clinton would use his fast-track authority to expand NAFTA to include Chile, a major competitor.[d]

Denial of fast-track authority weakens the president's ability to create a Free Trade Area of the Americas. This has assumed new importance in light of the creation of the South American trading bloc—Mercosur—which includes Argentina, Brazil, Paraguay, and Uruguay. Members of Mercosur enjoy reduced tariffs when trading with other Mercosur countries, and they are in the process of negotiating a reciprocal free trade pact with the European Union.

a. Bob Davis, *At the Heart of the Trade Debate: Inequity,* WALL ST. J., Oct. 31, 1997, at A2.
b. *Id.*
c. Helene Cooper, *Expert's View of NAFTA's Economic Impact: It's a Wash,* WALL ST. J., June 17, 1997, at A20.
d. Greg Hitt, *To California Vintners, Promised a Rose Garden, Fast-Track Bill Is Wreathed in Grapes of Wrath,* WALL ST. J., Oct. 6, 1997.

⚜ *The* World Trade Organization *and the* GATT

Besides negotiating bilateral and regional preferential agreements, the United States participates in the World Trade Organization (WTO), the successor to the General Agreement on Tariffs and Trade (GATT). The WTO was created by agreement of the GATT members in 1994 (GATT 1994) and came into existence on January 1, 1995,[36] after the conclusion of the Uruguay Round of GATT multilateral trade negotiations.

The WTO oversees all the agreements reached in the Uruguay Round,[37] and it is the principal multilateral mechanism devoted to the regulation of international trade. As of 2001, the WTO had 135 members, and at least another thirty countries (including Russia and China) were waiting to join.

The WTO is especially notable as an emerging international institution similar to, albeit less well funded than, the World Bank and the International Monetary Fund. It is this institutional aspect of the WTO, along with its large membership and broad scope, that draws attention to the organization, both positive and negative. Protests surrounding the WTO's 1999 ministerial meeting in Seattle are described in the "Inside Story" for this chapter.

The GATT had a profound effect on world trade.[38] Tariffs today are, on average, a small fraction of what they were when the GATT was formed in 1947. The Uruguay Round, the eighth in the history of the GATT, was the most ambitious GATT round ever held. The 117 participating nations agreed to reduce their tariffs by an average of one-third over six years. In addition, agricultural tariffs were reduced by 36 percent in industrial na-

36. Agreement Establishing the World Trade Organization, Apr. 15, 1994, LEGAL INSTRUMENTS—RESULTS OF THE URUGUAY ROUND vol. 1 (1994), 33 I.L.M. 1132 (1994).

37. Final Act Embodying the Results of the Uruguay Round of Multilateral Trade Negotiations, Apr. 15, 1994, LEGAL INSTRUMENTS—RESULTS OF THE URUGUAY ROUND vol. 1 (1994), 33 I.L.M. 1140 (1994).

38. General Agreement on Tariffs and Trade, opened for signature Oct. 30, 1947, T.I.A.S. No. 1700, 55 U.N.T.S. 187.

"The prince married the princess, they got most favored nation status and lived happily ever after."

The WTO Tackles Electronic Commerce

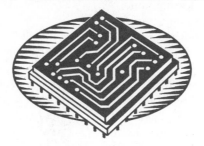

In July 2000, members of the World Trade Organization agreed to revive the WTO's e-commerce work program, which had been stalled for almost two years.[a] AOL Time Warner and other U.S. companies have been urging the United States to promote e-commerce outside the United States by using the ongoing WTO negotiations on liberalizing trade in services to address issues related to e-commerce, such as the inability of customers to pay directly for goods purchased online and the inability of companies to deliver products in a timely manner.[b]

In a paper distributed to WTO members on November 30, 2000, the European Union (EU) called on governments to (1) address the proper classification of products delivered electronically and the applicable customs duties; (2) improve e-commerce infrastructure services, including computer applications, payment services, advertising, and physical distri-

bution; and (3) discuss claims by some governments that the provisions in the WTO's decision requiring the liberalization of access to and use of public telecommunications networks and services do not necessarily apply to Internet access and network services.

The EU has taken the approach that e-commerce is still commerce and, as such, should be governed by the existing WTO rules and obligations. It asserts that all products delivered electronically should be classified as services and therefore be governed by the WTO's General Agreement on Trade in Services.

In May 1998, the WTO imposed a moratorium on customs duties applicable to electronic information sent over the Internet. Although the WTO had been expected to decide in its 1999 Seattle meeting whether to extend the moratorium, the meeting collapsed without a decision after the members were unable to agree on the agenda for the next multilateral round of trade talks. The United States has taken the position that the moratorium is still in effect, but Mexico and Pakistan claim that it expired when it was not extended at the Seattle meeting. The EU indicated in November 2000 that it would support continuation of the moratorium.

a. *EU Offers Paper for WTO Work Program on Electronic Commerce, Customs Duties,* 5 ELECTRONIC COM. & L. REP. (BNA) 1200 (Dec. 13, 2000).
b. *U.S. Plans Proposal at WTO in December to Spur E-Commerce in Europe, Elsewhere,* 5 ELECTRONIC COM. & L. REP. (BNA) 1175 (Dec. 6, 2000).

---

tions and by 24 percent in developing nations. For the first time, agriculture, services, textiles, and investment services were covered by international rules of fair trade, as was the protection of intellectual property rights. The agreement, also for the first time, protected the right of service-sector companies to operate on foreign soil free of discriminatory laws.

The WTO agreement requires member states to participate in the Multilateral Trade Agreements, including (1) fourteen Agreements on Trade in Goods (including GATT 1994); (2) the General Agreement on Trade in Services (GATS); (3) the Agreement on Trade-Related Aspects of Intellectual Property Rights (TRIP); (4) the Understanding on Rules and Procedures Governing the Settlement of Disputes (DSU); and (5) the Trade Policy Review Mechanism (TPRM). These agreements are binding on all members of the WTO.

BASICS PRINCIPLES

Three basic principles undergird the GATT and its successor, the WTO: (1) most favored nation treatment, (2) bound tariffs, and (3) national treatment.

Most Favored Nation Treatment The *most favored nation (MFN)* principle is the foundation of the current world trading system. Article I of the GATT states that each member of the WTO must accord to all other member countries tariff treatment no less favorable than it provides to any other country. In other words, if the United States agrees to lower its tariff on imports of a product from a certain country, it must grant the same treatment to all other WTO members. (The GSP and other preferential agreements discussed above are exceptions to the MFN principle and are authorized by the GATT.) The theory behind the MFN principle is that world trade will be enhanced if countries avoid discriminating among themselves and creating trading blocs that expand trade within the blocs but restrict trade between them.

The GATT encourages regional economic integration and participation in free trade areas and customs unions, however. A *free trade area* is created when a group of states reduce or eliminate tariffs between themselves but maintain their own individual tariffs as to other states. A *customs union* is similar but involves the establishment of a common tariff for all other states.

Once a free trade area or customs union is established, the GATT rules apply to the area or union as a whole and not to the constituent states. Members of the WTO may participate in free trade areas or customs unions only if the area or union does not establish higher duties or more restrictive commercial regulations for other WTO countries.

Bound Tariffs A second basic principle of the GATT is that of *bound tariffs*. Each time tariffs are reduced, they become bound; that is, they may not be raised again. If any country raises its bound tariffs, it must compensate the other WTO members, normally through other tariff concessions. This principle is set out in Article II of the GATT.

National Treatment A third basic principle, set out in Article III of the GATT, is that of *national treatment*. WTO members may not discriminate against imported products in favor of domestically produced "like products." Thus, for example, special taxes on imported goods are illegal if not applied equally to domestic products. The determination of what is a "like product" is done on a case-by-case basis by examining such factors as (1) the product's end uses in a given market; (2) consumers' tastes and habits, which vary from country to country; and (3) the product's properties, nature, and quality.[39]

NONTARIFF BARRIERS

Tariffs are not the only barrier to trade. *Nontariff barriers (NTBs)* in some cases have replaced tariffs as a means of protecting domestic industries threatened by import competition. For example, the preference often given to domestic products in government procurement can reduce the volume of imports. International codes designed to reduce nontariff barriers were negotiated during the Tokyo Round of the GATT (which occurred from 1973 to 1979). Further efforts to reduce NTBs, specifically those arising from regulatory measures that explicitly or effectively protect domestic industries, are reflected in the Agreement on Technical Barriers to Trade and the Agreement on the Application of Sanitary and Phytosanitary Measures.

39. *See, e.g.*, World Trade Organization: Report of the Appellate Body in Japan—Taxes on Alcoholic Beverages, WTO Docs. WT/DS8/AB/R, WT/DS10/AB/R and WT/DS11/AB/4, 1997 BDIEL AD LEXIS 27 (Oct. 4, 1996) (shochu and vodka are like products, so Japan could not tax imported vodka at a higher rate than domestic shochu).

 ETHICAL CONSIDERATION

France and other European countries have typically restricted American-made programs to a maximum of 50 percent of the total television broadcasts and have imposed a series of taxes on movie tickets, television movies, and videocassettes. The money generated from the taxes has been used to underwrite French films.

For years, Quebec has been concerned that the U.S. media would turn Canada into a mini–United States. In April 1998, federal regulators in Ottawa adopted a requirement that at least 35 percent of music played on local radio stations after January 1999 be Canadian, up from 25 to 30 percent in 1998. Similar restrictions on Canadian ads in publications with less than 60 percent Canadian content were also proposed to bolster local Canadian magazines, as were restrictions on the distribution of movies in Canada by U.S. movie companies. In 1997, 95 percent of the movies screened in Canada were foreign films.[a] Sheila Copps, Canadian heritage minister, claimed that these measures are necessary to ensure "a dynamic forum for the expression of Canadian ideas and interests."[b] Cultural policies were exempted in part from NAFTA.

An earlier attempt by Canada to impose an 80 percent excise tax on advertisements in split-run editions of periodicals was struck down by the WTO as a violation of Article III's requirement of national treatment.[c] A split-run edition of a magazine is one that both (1) contains advertisements primarily directed to a market in Canada and (2) does not appear in identical form in all editions of an issue distributed in that periodical's country of origin.

To what extent should media companies worry about protecting local culture? Should popular tastes prevail, as in the song "I Want My MTV!"?

a. Rosanna Tamburri, *Canada Considers New Stand Against American Culture*, Wall St. J., Feb. 4, 1998, at A18.
b. Joseph Weber, *Does Canadian Culture Need This Much Protection?*, Bus. Wk., June 8, 1998, at 37.
c. World Trade Organization: Report of the Appellate Body in Canada—Certain Measures Concerning Periodicals, WTO Doc. WT/DS31/AB/R, 1997 BDIEL AD LEXIS 12 (June 30, 1997).

ENVIRONMENTAL AND HEALTH EXCEPTIONS AND THE SPS AGREEMENT

Article XX of the GATT gives member states the right to adopt and enforce measures "relating to the conservation of exhaustible natural resources" as well as measures "necessary to protect human, animal or plant life or health." Such measures cannot be applied in an arbitrary or unjustifiably discriminatory manner, however; nor may they be used as a disguised restriction on trade.

To date, this exception to national treatment has been construed very narrowly.[40] A GATT dispute resolution panel declared a U.S. embargo on tuna caught by fishing methods causing high dolphin mortality to be illegal.[41] Similarly, the U.S. reformulated gasoline standards (adopted as part of the Clean Air Act Amendments in 1990), which imposed tougher baselines for foreign producers and refiners, were successfully challenged by Venezuela and Brazil.[42] The Committee on Trade and Environment, established under the auspices of the WTO to make recommendations on the need for rules to enhance the positive interaction between trade and environmental measures for the promotion of sustainable development, has to date done little.

The Agreement on the Application of Sanitary and Phytosanitary Measures (SPS Agreement), adopted as part of the Uruguay Round, deals with additives, contaminants, toxins, and disease-carrying organisms in food. The SPS Agreement gives WTO member states the right to take sanitary and phytosanitary measures that are "necessary" for the protection of human, animal, or plant life and health. In addition to not being discriminatory or used as disguised restrictions on trade, the measures cannot be more trade restrictive than required to achieve their appropriate level of protection. A measure is more trade restrictive than required if there is a reasonably available and feasible alternative that would accomplish the same result.

The European Union unsuccessfully tried to defend its ban on hormone-treated imported meat as a health-related measure in the following case.

---

40. *See* Thomas J. Schoenbaum, *International Trade and Protection of the Environment: The Continuing Search for Reconciliation,* 91 AM. J. INT'L L. 268 (1997).
41. United States—Restrictions on Imports of Tuna, 30 I.L.M. 1598 (1992).
42. United States—Standards for Reformulated and Conventional Gasoline, 35 I.L.M. 274 (1996).

A CASE IN POINT

CASE 12.4

EC Measure Concerning Meat and Meat Products (Hormones)

World Trade Organization Appellate Body
WTO Docs. WT/DS26/AB/R,
WT/DS46/ABR
(Jan. 16, 1998).

Summary

FACTS The European Union (EU) banned the import of all meat from cattle treated with any of six growth hormones. The United States and Canada claimed that the hormone ban was not based on convincing scientific evidence and conflicted with the SPS Agreement.

ISSUE PRESENTED Under what circumstances can a WTO member set a level of consumer protection higher than international health standards?

SUMMARY OF OPINION The WTO Appellate Body held that WTO members have a sovereign and autonomous right to set a level of sanitary protection for their own consumers that exceeds international health standards, but only if the sanitary measures are based on a scientific risk assessment. The risk assessment for human health is not a quantitative scientific analysis, but it must cover risk in human societies as they actually exist. Responsible and representative governments may act in good faith on the basis of a divergent scientific view coming from qualified and respected scientists. But, in this case, the EU scientific reports did not support the ban because the studies on which the reports were based did not focus specifically on the effects in humans of residues in meat from hormone-treated cattle.

RESULT The EU ban was inconsistent with the requirements of the SPS Agreement.

COMMENTS The deadline for compliance with the WTO ruling was set for May 13, 1999. When compliance was not reached by that date, the United States sought permission to retaliate by suspending tariff concessions on EU goods. Arbitrators determined that the amount of trade lost to the United States because of the EU's noncompliance was $116.8 million. The United States was given discretion as to which products from the EU would bear the significant increase in tariffs.

In January 2000, ministers from more than 130 countries meeting in Montreal, Canada, adopted a new "Biosafety Protocol" to address concerns about what *The Economist* characterized as "the most controversial issue in international trade—genetically modified organisms (GMOs)." To allay widespread fears that GMOs pose risks to biodiversity and health, the Protocol requires exporters to label shipments that "may contain" bio-engineered commodities (such as maize and soybeans) and permits countries to block imports of GMOs on a "precautionary" basis unless the exporter can show that its products are safe. The Protocol does not supercede WTO law but would appear to be consistent with WTO rules permitting countries to take provisional measures "on the basis of available pertinent information" when there is insufficient scientific evidence of a possible health risk.

WTO DISPUTE SETTLEMENT PROCEDURES

The United States has used the WTO dispute settlement process both as a means of vindicating rights in particular cases and as a way to communicate to U.S. trading partners that the United States expects them to take seriously compliance with the WTO rules. In fact, according to U.S. government figures, the United States has been the world's most active user of the WTO dispute settlement process, having elected to use it in fifty-three cases from January 1995 to May 2000.[43]

Although the United States has for the most part been successful in pursuing these matters, both by prevailing in cases it has brought and by negotiating settlement agreements, the United States has also lost its share of cases. The United States lost its first case before the WTO in December 1997, when the WTO rejected Eastman Kodak Company's claims that Fuji Photo Film and the Japanese government had erected internal barriers to trade in Japan. Until then, the United States had won outright or obtained concessions in all fourteen of the other cases it had brought at the WTO. The Kodak ruling sparked criticism of the WTO. In the words of then Senator John Ashcroft (R-Missouri), the ruling "raises serious questions about the credibility of this international body and of the U.S. trade representatives' capacity to secure and defend free-trade agreements."[44]

As of June 2000, the United States had lost eight cases initiated by other WTO member countries. These included the WTO's decision concerning reformulated gasoline, a case concerning provisions of the U.S. tax code giving preferred treatment to U.S. foreign sales corporations (FSCs),[45] and a case challenging the operation of the U.S. Revenue Act of 1916.[46]

A significant concern of the United States, as reflected in executive branch testimony before Congress and writings of academics and trade professionals,[47] involves implementation of WTO decisions. Before the establishment of the WTO, the defendant in a GATT dispute could, in effect, block dispute settlement procedures because the GATT Council could only adopt a panel report unanimously. The WTO's Understanding on Rules and Procedures Governing the Settlement of Disputes improved that process. Under the WTO, a panel of experts will be established at the request of a complaining party. Panel reports will be adopted virtually automatically unless they are rejected by consensus of the WTO members (including the member–complainant that filed the case in question).

The nature of the WTO as an international institution raises issues that do not arise in the context of implementing domestic judicial decisions. In the domestic setting, a court order has the force of law, and compliance with such orders is ultimately backed by the physical power of governmental authorities. By contrast, a WTO member can respond to losing a case before a panel or appellate body of the WTO by: (1) implementing the rec-

43. *U.S. Interests and Experience in the WTO Dispute Settlement System: Hearings before the Trade Subcomm. of the Senate Comm. on Finance,* 106th Cong. (June 20, 2000) (testimony of Ambassador Charlene Barshefsky).
44. Robert S. Greenberger et al., *WTO's Kodak Ruling Heightens Trade Tensions,* WALL ST. J., Dec. 8, 1997, at A3.
45. FSCs are offshore corporations possessing special tax attributes allowing them to exempt from U.S. income taxation a portion of revenue earned on sales of U.S.-origin goods outside the United States. The WTO ruled in February 2000 that these exemption provisions constituted an illegal export subsidy under WTO rules. U.S.—Tax Treatment for "Foreign Sales Corporations," WTO Docs. WT/DS108/AB/R (WTO App. Body Feb. 24, 2000).
46. In August 2000, a WTO Appellate Body upheld a dispute settlement panel finding that the U.S. Revenue Act of 1916 is inconsistent with WTO antidumping rules. The Appellate Body upheld the panel's findings that WTO antidumping rules are applicable to the 1916 Act and that the 1916 Act is inconsistent with these rules because the Act allows for treble damages and criminal penalties against importers of products sold below market value. In addition, according to the WTO, the 1916 Act impermissibly allows duties to be imposed against imports without first requiring a finding of material injury with respect to the import-competing industry. The United States had argued that the 1916 Act was more akin to U.S. antitrust laws and, as such, should not be considered subject to the WTO antidumping rules. The WTO ruling did not affect the antidumping law contained in the Tariff Act of 1930, which is consistent with the WTO Antidumping Agreement.
47. *See, e.g.,* Symposium on the First Three Years of the WTO Dispute Settlement System, 32 INT'L LAW. (Fall 1998).

ommendations and rulings, (2) providing compensation, or (3) accepting suspension of concessions by the winning party or parties. To date, the express preference of the United States has been for members to comply with WTO rulings and implement such changes to national law and policy as are necessary to achieve compliance with the applicable WTO agreement.

This strong preference—and the U.S. willingness to act on it—helps explain why the United States moved expeditiously to comply with a February 2000 WTO decision that required a change in U.S. tax law relating to foreign sales corporations.[48] It also helps explain the strong trade tensions that have erupted between the United States and the EU over EU's implementation of WTO decisions in the so-called bananas and beef hormone cases. In the "bananas case," the United States, along with Ecuador, Guatemala, Honduras, and Mexico, successfully challenged the EU banana regime in WTO dispute settlement proceedings.[49] The WTO panel found that the regimen was designed, among other things, to take away a major part of the banana distribution business of U.S. companies. Nonetheless, on January 1, 1999, the EU adopted a regime that, from the U.S. perspective, perpetuated the violations identified by the WTO panel and the appellate body. In consequence, the United States sought WTO authorization to suspend concessions (i.e., retaliate) with respect to certain products from the EU, whose value was equivalent to the trade damage sustained by the United States. WTO arbitrators determined the level of damage to be $191.4 million. On April 19, 1999, the WTO authorized the United States to suspend concessions, and the United States imposed 100 percent *ad valorem* duties on a list of EU products with an annual trade value of $191.4 million. As of March 2001, discussions with the EU to resolve the bananas case were ongoing.

The beef hormones case was presented earlier in this chapter as Case 12.4. As described earlier, in response to the EU's position on implementation in these two cases, the United States sought and obtained WTO approval to retaliate by imposing duties on EU exports to the United States worth $308 million. The beef hormones case was important both as a test of the integrity of the WTO dispute settlement system and as the first completed WTO case interpreting the SPS Agreement.

Timetable The WTO Understanding on Rules and Procedures Governing the Settlement of Disputes sets forth the procedures and the timetable for resolving disputes. The agreed limits are flexible, but normally a case should not take more than one year (fifteen months if the case is appealed) to run the full course from consultation among the countries involved in the dispute (with mediation by the WTO director–general if the parties cannot resolve the dispute themselves) to a ruling by the Dispute Settlement Body. Exhibit 12.1 presents the timetable for resolution of the reformulated gasoline cases brought by Venezuela and Brazil against the United States.

Relationship between Section 301 and the WTO Dispute Settlement Process Whether Section 301 gives the president (acting through the USTR) the ability to take unilateral action to penalize countries whose trade practices threaten American interests without going through the WTO dispute settlement process is a matter of some debate. On their face, the provisions of Section 301 do seem to allow for this result, and the legislative history of the U.S. bill implementing the Uruguay Round and creating the WTO suggests that Congress did not intend for the WTO dispute resolution process to displace the unilateral power vested in the USTR by Section 301.[50] On the other hand, the President's Statement of Administrative Action, issued by President Bill Clinton, provided that the United States will use Section 301 only in a WTO "compliant manner"; that is, it will retaliate against other WTO members under Section 301 only after such retaliation is authorized by the WTO. In practice, the United States has largely stuck to this policy, perhaps because taking action under Section 301 without authorization by the WTO could greatly weaken the WTO and subject the United States to criticism for taking a pick-and-choose approach to trade disputes.[51]

Nonetheless, the United States has not always awaited WTO authorization before retaliating under Section 301. For example, the United States was strongly criticized when it bypassed the WTO and unilaterally imposed sanctions on Japan in in 1995 in a dispute over automobiles.[52]

In March 2000 a WTO panel ruled that Section 301 was not invalid on its face because the USTR had discretion to ensure that implementation of Section 301 is WTO compliant. But that same WTO panel ruled that the United States had used Section 301 in an impermissible

48. *See United States Trade Representative Press Release,* Sept. 30, 2000 (announcing that the United States and the EU had reached an agreement regarding procedures for reviewing whether replacement legislation for the current FSC regime is WTO compliant and urging Congress to complete this action as expeditiously as possible).
49. European Communities—Regime for the Importation, Sale and Distribution of Bananas, WTO Doc. WT/DS27/15 (Jan. 7, 1998).

50. A. Lynne Puckett & William L. Reynolds, *Current Development: Rules, Sanctions and Enforcement under Section 301: At Odds with the WTO?,* 90 Am. J. Int'l L. 675, 687 (1996).
51. *Id.* at 688–89.
52. *See, e.g.,* Nathaniel E. Nash, *The Lonely Americans: Isolated in a Trade War,* N.Y. Times, May 26, 1995, at D2.

| EXHIBIT 12.1 | **Timetable for WTO Dispute Settlement Process in Practice: Reformulated Gasoline Decision** |

On January 23, 1995, Venezuela complained to the WTO Dispute Settlement Body that, pursuant to amendments to the U.S. Clean Air Act adopted in 1990, the United States applied stricter rules on the chemical characteristics of imported gasoline than it did for domestically refined gasoline. Brazil joined the case in April 1996. The following chart shows the actual timetable for resolution of the dispute.[a]

Time (0 = start of case)	Target Period	Date	Action
−5 years		1990	U.S. Clean Air Act amended.
−4 months		September 1994	U.S. restricts gasoline imports under Clean Air Act.
0		January 23, 1995	Venezuela complains to Dispute Settlement Body, asks for consultation with U.S.
+1 month	60 days	February 24, 1995	Consultations take place. Fail.
+2 months		March 25, 1995	Venezuela asks Dispute Settlement Body for a panel.
+2 1/2 months	30 days	April 10, 1995	Dispute Settlement Body agrees to appoint panel. U.S. does not block. (Brazil starts complaint, requests consultation with U.S.)
+3 months		April 28, 1995	Panel appointed. (On May 31, panel assigned to Brazilian complaint as well.)
+6 months	6+ months	July 10–12 and 13–15, 1995	Panel meets.
+11 months	(actual = 9 months)	December 11, 1995	Panel gives interim report to U.S., Venezuela, and Brazil for comment.
+1 year		January 29, 1996	Panel circulates final report to Dispute Settlement Body.
+1 year, 1 month	60 days	February 21, 1996	U.S. appeals.
+1 year, 3 months		April 29, 1996	Appellate Body submits report.
+1 year, 4 months	30 days	May 20, 1996	Dispute Settlement Body adopts panel and appeal reports.
+1 year, 10½ months		December 3, 1996	U.S. and Venezuela agree on what U.S. should do (implementation period is 15 months from May 20).
+1 year, 11½ months		January 9, 1997	U.S. submits first monthly report to Dispute Settlement Body on status of implementation.
+2 years, 7 months		August 19–20, 1997	U.S. signs new regulation (19th). End of agreed implementation period (20th).

a. *Settling Disputes; Case Study: The Timetable in Practice,* <http://www.wto.org/english/thewto_e/whatis_e/tif_e/disp3_e.htm> (visited Mar. 13, 2001).

manner by imposing sanctions against EU goods before obtaining WTO authorization.

CHINA'S WTO ACCESSION

In October 2000, the United States approved *Permanent Normal Trade Relations (PNTR)* for China, relegating to

history the annual vote on whether to afford China MFN status. Granting China PNTR status was viewed as a necessary, if not sufficient, step in bringing China into the WTO. Indeed the second part of the bill approving China for PNTR status also approved China's accession to the WTO, providing that it did so on terms at least equivalent to those agreed to between the United States and China in their 1999 bilateral agreement. That agreement required China to reduce both tariff and nontariff barriers to Chinese markets for agricultural and industrial goods.

Although some experts expected China to join the WTO by the end of 2000, by February 2001 it was readily apparent that China's accession would not proceed as rapidly as had been hoped. In fact, as of early 2001, speculation was that China would not accede to the WTO until as late as 2002. The process apparently was slowed by last-minute wrangling over agricultural subsidies. In particular, China maintained that it should be classified as a developing country in the area of agriculture, a characterization that would entitle China to subsidize its farmers at a rate of up to 10 percent of their agricultural production; the United States, in particular, was unlikely to accept this result.[53] In addition, China also seemed to be taking a go-slow approach to obtain additional time to adjust to the changes it had committed to in its bilateral agreements.[54] Finally, some speculated that as it seemed unlikely that a new multilateral round of trade negotiations would begin soon, China felt no pressure to rush to join the WTO as a means of influencing those discussions.

Whatever the reasons for the delay, China's accession to the WTO still appears to be a question of when, not if. Even then, however, China's accession to the WTO seems unlikely to resolve the continued tension between U.S. economic ties to China and U.S. concerns about China's human rights policies.

The Future Direction *of* U.S. Trade Policy

At the dawn of a new millennium, the United States faces several issues regarding the direction of its trade policy. One issue is whether to pursue a rules-based multilateral trading regime administered by international institutions such as the WTO. If the United States and its trade allies continue to support the development of multilateral trade regimes, then steps must be taken to recover some of the ground lost at the Seattle WTO summit, where failure to agree on the agenda for future multilateral trade talks postponed for more than a year any serious consideration of additional multilateral trade negotiations.

A second issue is whether and how to incorporate nontraditional considerations, such as protection of the environment, workers' rights, and human rights, into the trade agenda. Models for incorporating such considerations are being developed as the Trade and Development Act of 2000 demonstrates. Nevertheless, much work remains to be done in this area; in February 2001, for example, U.S. business leaders rejected a U.S.–Jordan trade agreement due to concern about provisions on workers' rights.

A final issue is whether to expand the jurisdiction of international trade agreements and institutions into areas such as investment and rules on competition. There is a growing consensus that improved international coordination and consultation on issues such as competition policy are required. It is not clear, however, whether such coordination will be conducted outside the international trade rules. Much perhaps will depend on the ultimate direction of international trade regulation and whether time lost following the setback in Seattle can be regained.

 ## The European Union

The European Union (EU), formally known and still often referred to as the European Community (EC), is an intergovernmental organization of fifteen states in Europe. Founded in 1951 with the intention of creating a common market, the EU is now well down the path to economic, monetary, and political union. The EU was established through the following treaties: the European Coal and Steel Community (established in 1951); the European Atomic Energy Commission (Euratom, established in 1957); the Treaty of Rome, which established the European Economic Community (EEC) in 1957;[55] the Single European Act (1987); and the Treaty on European Union[56] (also known as the Maastricht Treaty), which established the European Union in 1993. As of 2001, the member states were Austria, Belgium, Denmark, Finland, France, Germany, Greece, Ireland, Italy, Luxembourg, the Netherlands, Portugal, Spain, Sweden, and the United Kingdom, with several Eastern European countries poised to join.

Goods, services, people, and capital can move almost as freely within the EU as within one country. There are no tariff barriers between the states, and all states apply a single set of tariffs (called the *common customs tariff*) on goods imported from outside the EU.

The creation of the single EU market has had profound effects on U.S. businesses. It has facilitated the formation

53. David Murphy, *China Nears WTO Entry Slowly; Buys Time to Adapt,* FAR EAST ASIAN ECON. REV. (Feb. 14, 2001) (Dow Jones Newswires ed.).
54. *Id.*

55. Treaty Establishing the European Economic Community, Mar. 25, 1957, 298 U.N.T.S. 11.
56. Treaty on European Union, Feb. 7, 1992, 1992 O.J. (C 224) 1, 31 I.L.M. 247 (1992).

of larger European companies with a bigger home market and has increased large-scale research and development in Europe. At the same time, the single market has created a larger market for American goods and has made the EU a more attractive place in which to invest.

The EU negotiates international trade agreements on behalf of the member states, but all agreements (including negotiations with the WTO) must be approved by the individual states. The EU has the exclusive power to take action against dumping in its market by companies in nonmember countries. Agriculture is centrally coordinated through the Common Agricultural Policy, which supports prices of agricultural products and promotes the modernization of agriculture throughout the EU.

EU competition law, based on U.S. antitrust principles, has been used to prevent companies from engaging in private restraints of trade affecting the member states. For example, the European Commission required Boeing to abandon certain exclusive contracts it had with American Airlines as a condition to obtaining European approval of its acquisition of McDonnell–Douglas. The agreements adversely affected European aircraft company Airbus Industries by locking American Airlines into purchases of Boeing aircraft for a period of twenty years. The EU also required America Online and Time-Warner to make certain concessions as a condition to approving their merger.

Five main institutions have the responsibility for governing the EU: (1) the European Commission, (2) the Council of Ministers, (3) the European Parliament, (4) the European Court of Justice, and (5) the European Central Bank.

THE EUROPEAN COMMISSION

The European Commission is the executive branch of the EU. It comprises twenty individuals appointed by the governments of the member states (with France, Germany, Italy, Spain, and the United Kingdom appointing two members each and the remaining ten states appointing one member each). Commissioners are expected to act independently of their national governments. With a staff of approximately 15,000 civil servants, the Commission is at the heart of the EU's policy-making process.

The Commission formulates recommendations, addresses opinions to members, and may bring member states before the European Court of Justice for failure to carry out their obligations under the Maastricht and Rome Treaties.

THE COUNCIL OF MINISTERS

The Council of Ministers, officially known as the Council of the European Union, is the legislative body of the EU. It enacts legislation based on proposals referred to it by the Commission. Members of the Council are appointed by the governments of the member states, but, unlike the Commission members, they represent the interests of their respective states.

EU legislation may be in the form of *regulations,* which are directly applicable in the member states without the need for national measures to implement them. Legislation may also take two other forms. One is the *directive,* which is a law directing member states to enact certain laws or regulations. Directives are binding with respect to the objective to be achieved but allow national authorities to choose the form and means of implementation. The third form of legislation is the *decision,* which is an order directed at a specific person or member state.

THE EUROPEAN PARLIAMENT

The 626 members of the European Parliament (EP) are elected directly by the citizens of the member states (it is the only community body directly elected), generally in proportion to the population of each state. The Parliament must be consulted twice on each legislative proposal. First, it considers the proposed law at the committee level; then it expresses its opinion by a vote in plenary session. If the EP rejects a proposal, the law can be enacted only by a unanimous Council vote. The EP can also amend Commission proposals; in that case, if the Commission supports the amendment, the amended proposal can be defeated only by a unanimous Council vote. Finally, the Parliament has the power to dismiss the Commission with a two-thirds vote and to reject the Commission's annual budget.

THE EUROPEAN COURT OF JUSTICE

The European Court of Justice (ECJ) is the judicial branch of the EU. Its role is to interpret the treaties establishing the EU and to determine whether national laws, as applied by the national courts, are consistent with those obligations. The ECJ has been a major force in affirming the powers of community institutions and the development of the single market.

The ECJ comprises up to fifteen judges and nine advocates general appointed by the national governments. In 1999, the ECJ decided 378 cases from a total of 534 brought before it. There are five primary avenues to the ECJ:[57]

1. *Failure to comply.* The Commission advises a company or country that it has failed to comply with a directive or regulation. If the company or country contests the Commission's ruling, then the matter is brought before the ECJ.
2. *Annulment.* Any member state or EU institution (i.e., Commission, Council, or Parliament) may ask the ECJ to annul an EU decision as contrary to the Rome Treaty.
3. *Failure to act.* Member states of EU institutions may ask the ECJ to declare that a country, the Council, or the Commission has failed to take required action. Individuals who are personally and directly concerned may intercede in the proceeding.
4. *Civil liabilities.* National courts and individuals may ask the ECJ for a ruling that the EU or a national government is liable for damages for an act or failure to act.
5. *Preliminary rulings.* National courts can ask for an opinion as to whether a national law conflicts with one or more articles of the Rome or Maastricht Treaties and request guidance as to how EU law should be interpreted and applied to the matter at hand. Most of the ECJ's cases fall into this category.

Court of First Instance In an effort to reduce a two-year backlog, a junior court—the Court of First Instance—was created in 1989. It hears administrative cases, competition cases, dumping suits involving countries outside the EU, and intellectual property cases. Appeals from the Court of First Instance to the ECJ can be made only on matters of law, not matters of fact.

THE EUROPEAN CENTRAL BANK AND THE EMU

The Maastricht Treaty required all member states to converge their economic and monetary policies with the goal of creating a single European currency, the *euro*. The convergence criteria called for the member states to harmonize their budget deficits, inflation levels, public-sector debt, and long-term interest rates at specific target levels and to achieve exchange-rate stability. These efforts culminated in the creation of the European Monetary Union (EMU) on January 1, 1999. Eleven European Union members qualified for participation in the euro: Austria, Belgium, Finland, France, Germany, Ireland, Italy, Luxembourg, the Netherlands, Portugal, and Spain. Greece will not meet the convergence criteria for some time; the United Kingdom, Sweden, and Denmark were eligible but adopted a wait-and-see approach. By giving up their national currencies, members of the EMU relinquished control of their exchange rates and monetary policy to the independent European Central Bank (ECB) based in Frankfurt, Germany, which came onstream on July 1, 1998. The ECB's primary duty is to maintain price stability, usually by lowering or raising interest rates.

On January 1, 1999, all currencies of participating member states were irrevocably locked together at a specified conversion rate, and the euro became official currency. National currency units became denominations of the euro. Until June 30, 2002, national currencies will remain legal tender in participating states, but both the euro and national banknotes will be used simultaneously, with prices posted in both denominations. On June 30, 2002, the French franc, the German mark, the Dutch guilder, and other European currencies (very likely including the British pound) will cease to exist, and the euro will become the sole currency for much of Europe.

CHALLENGES

Notwithstanding the tremendous progress toward European integration, challenges remain. There is no European citizenship—a nonnational can vote in local but not national elections. There is no European company law or Europe-wide insurance. Rules for pension plans are not coordinated, and plans cannot hold nonnational shares of stock. There is no tax harmonization; national varieties include value-added, income, company, capital gains, wealth, and inheritance taxes.

The EU administrative structure is top-heavy and will become even more unwieldy when new members are added. As of 2001, entry negotiations were under way with Poland, Hungary, the Czech Republic, Estonia, Slovenia, Cyprus, Lithuania, Latvia, Bulgaria, Romania, Slovakia, and Malta. Two particularly thorny issues are whether votes in the Council will be weighted by population and whether veto rights will be limited so that a small member cannot block action favored by all of the larger members.

---

57. The author gratefully acknowledges the assistance of Professor Claude Mosséri-Marlio in the preparation of this discussion of the ECJ.

THE RESPONSIBLE MANAGER

Engaging *in* International Trade

It is important to plan in advance for import and export operations. Many restrictions and other important rules may affect the operation. Failure to plan can lead to inadvertent violations of law. A common mistake by exporters is providing technology to foreign persons without obtaining the prerequisite export licenses. Traveling abroad with a laptop computer loaded with strong encryption software could violate applicable law. Assigning an incorrect value to imported goods for customs purposes is another violation. Lack of planning can also cause the company to miss benefits such as duty-free treatment under the North American Free Trade Agreement and other international agreements.

Managers need to take the rapid changes occurring in world trade into account. Barriers to trade with Eastern European countries have been removed. Significant reductions of barriers to trade with other countries are being negotiated. New markets and new opportunities are arising with great speed. At the same time, these changes carry new risks for managers. They will cause increased competition not only overseas, but also in the United States. Government regulation of trade will change, but not as rapidly as the world is changing. Managers should keep abreast of regulatory changes but also be sensitive to gaps between the new realities of world trade and the government's efforts to regulate.

INSIDE STORY

The New Trade War: Seattle 1999

Opponents of globalisation wreaked havoc at a big trade summit in Seattle this week. Their long-term impact will be less dramatic.[58]

The World Trade Organization summit, launching a new round of talks to liberalise trade, was meant to be a chance for Seattle to show off. Instead, Sea Town became siege town. A furious rag-bag of anti-globalisation protesters brought the city to a standstill. Hordes of angry activists blocked off the city centre, trapping (among others) Kofi Annan, the United Nations' secretary-general, and Madeleine Albright, America's secretary of state, in their hotels. The opening of the summit was delayed. Police in full riot gear with armoured personnel carriers fired tear gas and rubber bullets at protesters who refused to move. Masked youths rampaged through the streets, smashing shop windows. Seattle was put under curfew as the mayor declared a civil emergency and the governor sent in the National Guard.

Yet most of the protests were peaceful. Long before the WTO summit started on November 30th [1999], 2,500 campaigners attended a packed teach-in on the evils of globalisation (held, ironically, in a plush symphony hall whose benefactors had made their money from exports). By the time the delegates arrived, the city was teeming with protesters, banners ("The WTO is a hazardous waste") and chants ("Hey, hey, ho, ho. WTO has got to go"). Tens of thousands of trade unionists attended a protest rally and march organised by the AFL–CIO. Environmentalists donned sea-turtle outfits. Human-rights activists conducted a "people's tribunal" that indicted Union Carbide, the Gap and other firms for crimes against humanity. Students carrying Japanese cameras and drinking foreign coffee railed that trade should be local, not global. José Bové, a French farmers' leader who gained fame by attacking his local McDonald's, was mobbed by fans when he appeared with his own Roquefort cheese outside a Seattle McDonald's that had just been vandalised.

Unsurprisingly, Pat Buchanan, a conservative protectionist demagogue and presidential hopeful for the Reform Party [in 2000] who was also in Seattle this week, revelled in the controversy. "There is something higher than commerce," he declared. "It's called country, and we're joining the battle in Seattle to ensure that someone still stands for ours." . . .

. . .

. . . The fact is that the WTO has become the magnet for a myriad of often contradictory complaints about the perceived ills of globalisation. Old-fashioned protectionists, such as trade unionists, are making common cause with an unruly alliance of greens, human-rights campaigners, consumer-rights groups, sovereignty-obsessed nationalists and others. Trade unionists talk about fair trade, not free trade (in other words, they want to curb competition for jobs from workers in poor countries). Development lobbies, such as Oxfam, think poor countries get a raw deal out of the world trading system. Green groups, such as the Sierra Club or Friends of the Earth, claim that the WTO wrecks the environment. Consumer groups argue that the WTO foists genetically modified (GM) food on them and promotes the interests of big business at the expense of the little guy. As for Mr. Buchanan, he is enraged by the constraint on American unilateralism that WTO rules impose.

Many of these concerns are not new. But they have assumed greater importance for many people as America luxuriates in an unprecedented peacetime boom, and as free trade's contribution to that prosperity is forgotten. They have, moreover, found a new focus in the WTO, which enforces the rules for a globalising economy. It is a convenient target: a multilateral institution, based in a faraway place (Geneva), whose rulings, though based on rules that have been ratified by Congress, are uniquely binding on America.

. . .

Less obvious is what impact the protests will have. Certainly, the protesters failed in their immediate aim of derailing the talks entirely. They caused havoc, and massively delayed proceedings. They angered delegates, though many of those were also quick to identify the protesters with their own agenda (the French, for instance, claimed the protests proved how much people hate GM food). But behind the grandstanding the protests have, if anything, steeled the resolve of WTO governments to bridge their differences, notably over agriculture and developing countries' demands for better access to rich-country markets. Mike Moore, the head of the WTO, was in fighting spirit. "To those who argue that we should stop our work, I say: 'Tell that to the poor, to the marginalised around the world who are looking to us to help them'."

KEY WORDS AND PHRASES

ad valorem tariff 403
bound tariffs 414
common customs tariff 419
countervailable subsidies 406
countervailing duty 406
customs union 413
customs valuation 404
decision 420
directive 420
dumped 406
dumping margin 406
dutiable 404
duty 404

euro 421
export extensive 399
fair trade law 405
fast-track negotiating authority 411
foreign trade zones 407
free trade area 413
Harmonized Tariff Schedule (HTS) 404
import competing 399
import relief laws 405
most favored nation (MFN) 413
national treatment 414
nontariff barriers (NTBs) 414

Permanent Normal Trade Relations (PNTR) 418
regulations 420
Section 201 405
Section 232 407
Section 301 407
Section 337 406
Section 406 407
Special 301 provisions 408
substantial transformation 404
Super 301 408
tariff classification 404
transaction value 404

QUESTIONS AND CASE PROBLEMS

1. A fast-growing U.S. beverage company wishes to import mineral water and has asked you, its vice president for purchasing, to recommend foreign sources. You know that sources exist in France, Canada, and Australia. What U.S. trade laws should you consider in choosing among these sources?

2. Assume the facts in Question 1. Suppose that you determine that the best source of mineral water for your purposes is France, but the tariff makes imports from that country noncompetitive. How could you seek a reduction in this tariff?

3. You are the vice president for marketing at a U.S. manufacturer of electric shavers. Imports of electric shavers have been increasing rapidly in the last year, undercutting your prices and taking significant market share from your company. The shavers are coming from five countries. You know that exporters in two of these countries are selling in the United States at prices below their home market prices and that exporters in two other countries are receiving export subsidies. The single exporter in the fifth country appears to be infringing on a patent that your company holds on a particular type of electric shaver, but your lawyers have said it is not a strong patent. Which U.S. import relief laws might be available to you to relieve the competitive pressure from these imports?

4. You are the president of a U.S. engineering company. You have made a competitive bid to help design a new airport to be built by the Japanese government, but your bid has not been accepted. You believe that the government is reserving all significant engineering work on this project for Japanese companies. You are concerned that future projects will also be reserved for local companies. Does U.S. law provide for any relief?

5. In each of the following situations, name the U.S. government agency to which a request for assistance or petition for relief would be most appropriately addressed:
   a. You believe that your company's domestic sales are being damaged by increasing imports from country X. Country X is not employing any unfair trade practices.
   b. You believe that your company's export business to country Y is limited by unfair practices of that country's government.
   c. Your company specializes in research and development. New technologies developed by your firm often have important military applications. The government of country Z makes your company a very attractive offer to purchase a recently developed technology. You would like to accept the offer, but you are unsure whether export of the technology is prohibited under the Arms Export Control Act.

6. Your company is U.S.-based and has a subsidiary in France. The French government is encouraging companies to do business in Shangri-la, a country with colonial ties to France but with a Marxist dictatorship. The United States has imposed an embargo on all U.S. trade with that country. Can your French subsidiary sell its products to Shangri-la? Should it?

7. You are discussing the possibility of licensing know-how to a Vietnamese company for the manufacture of personal computers. A delegation is coming to visit your company in Massachusetts to negotiate the terms of the license, to see your plant, and to discuss your technology. What laws and regulations might be applicable to this meeting?

8. The Thailand Tobacco Acts of 1966 prohibited the importation of tobacco except by license of the director–general. No licenses for cigarettes had been issued for more than ten years. The United States argued that this violated the GATT's prohibition on import-license restrictions on the import of products of other GATT members. Thailand argued that its ban on the importation of cigarettes came within the GATT's exception for measures necessary to protect human life or health. Result? [*Thailand—Restrictions on Importation of and Internal Taxes on Cigarettes*, GATT Doc. D510/R (Nov. 7, 1990)]

9. The European Commission brought an action against the United Kingdom for failure to adopt national laws necessary to implement Council Directive 85/374/EEC (OJ 1985 L 210, p. 29) on product liability. Article 1 of the Directive provides that "the producer shall be liable for damage caused by a defect in his product." Because achieving "a fair apportionment of risk between the injured person and the producer implies that the producer should be able to free himself from liability if he furnishes proof as to the existence of certain exonerating circumstances," the Article sets forth a number of defenses. The producer is not liable if he proves "that the state of scientific and technical knowledge at the time when he put the product into circulation was not such as to enable the existence of the defect to be discovered."

The United Kingdom adopted the Consumer Protection Act of 1987 (the UK Act), which said that it was designed to comply with the Directive and should be construed accordingly. Section 4(1)(e) of the UK Act provided that it is a defense for the producer to show:

> that the state of scientific and technical knowledge at the relevant time was not such that a producer of products of the same description as the product in question might be expected to have discovered the defect if it had existed in his products while they were under his control.

The Commission claimed that the UK Act had broadened the defense to a considerable degree and converted the strict liability imposed by Article 1 into mere liability for negligence. How should the ECJ rule? [*Commission of the European Communities v. United Kingdom,* Case C-300/95, 1997 E.C.R. I-2649]

MANAGER'S DILEMMA

10. Your company imports electronic parts from China for use in its finished products. If China is not admitted to the WTO, you will have to buy these parts elsewhere at a much higher price. This will reduce your profits on your most important products by one-fourth. Some, but not all, of your competitors will be similarly affected. Your trade association is considering lobbying the president and Congress to promote China's entry into the WTO. Several human rights' groups have called on Congress to deny China WTO status until it stops using prison labor and grants greater rights to its citizens. To what extent, if at all, should you, as a manager of a private company, take into account China's human rights record when deciding whether to buy products made there and when considering whether to support liberalized trading relations? Consider whether trade with the United States will help or hinder the development of democracy in China.

INTERNET SOURCES

International Trade Law	http://itl.irv.uit.no/trade_law
U.S. Department of Commerce	http://www.doc.gov
U.S. International Trade Commission	http://www.usitc.gov
U.S. Trade Representative	http://www.ustr.gov
World Trade Organization	http://www.wto.org
A Summary of the Final Act of the Uruguay Round is available at this site.	http://www.wto.org/wto/legal/ursum_wp.htm
This site is maintained by Transparency International, a nongovenmental organization formed in 1993 to raise global awareness of corruption. It publishes an annual Corruption Index, which measures perceptions of corruption around the world.	http://www.transparency.de
This site for the International Law Section of the Academy of Legal Studies in Business provides extensive and useful links to international business law–related sites on the Internet.	http://www.wsu.edu/~legal/alsb_ils
This is the site for the *International Business Law Journal,* an online journal containing professional articles relating to public and private international law edited by the International Law Section of the Academy of Legal Studies in Business.	http://www.wsu.edu:8080/~legal/ijrnl/
United Nations Commission on Sustainable Development	http://www.un.org/esa/sustdev

CHAPTER 13

International Transactions

MANAGING IN A GLOBAL ECONOMY

Managers in today's global economy can expect to engage in one or more types of international business transactions, including (1) sales and leasing of goods and services, (2) transfers of technology, (3) equity investments, and (4) international lending. The variety of types of transactions, potentially complex transaction structures, and diverse legal and business environments involved in international transactions create a wealth of issues and risks, but also opportunities, that may not be seen in many domestic transactions.

CHAPTER OVERVIEW

This chapter begins with a discussion of buying and selling goods abroad, focusing primarily on the international sales contract but also reviewing leasing, compensation trade, and processing operations. It then discusses the use of letters of credit and guaranties to secure the buyer's payment for goods and the borrower's repayment of loans. The chapter then shifts to issues involved with international transfers of technology through licensing and franchising. The threads of sales and technology transfer issues are drawn together in the context of overseas investment, which often involves multilayered cross-border relationships. The discussion of overseas investment focuses first on the planning stage, including the need to set investment goals, obtain accurate information dealing with economic and political conditions in the host country, and evaluate site options properly. The chapter then addresses operational concerns and language and cultural considerations, as well as the laws governing doing business with and litigating against foreign governments. The discussion concludes with a review of the process of managing international transactions from a U.S. perspective.

 Buying *and* Selling Abroad

The most common form of international business involves the buying and selling of tangible goods. Importers of foreign products to the United States must be aware of regulations governing U.S. businesses (in addition to the U.S. tariffs and trade laws discussed in Chapter 12). Exporters of U.S. products are also affected by laws (also discussed in Chapter 12) regulating export of products or information and providing benefits to certain exporters. Such U.S. regulations may apply even to transactions entirely outside the United States among non-U.S. parties.

The laws and regulations of other countries involved in a transaction may also apply, and they may impose restrictions or requirements different from or occasionally even entirely incompatible with those that exist under U.S. law. Customs and usages of international and domestic trade in other countries, as well as local industry practices, add yet another layer of complexity. Some of these are reflected in multilateral and bilateral treaties, but many other restrictions are less formal or even unwritten. By dealing through a knowledgeable agent or distributor with a presence abroad, a U.S. importer or exporter can reduce some of the risk from unforeseen foreign laws and practices. Local bankers, accountants, and lawyers can also play a valuable role. When issues have been identified, they can be addressed and risks reapportioned in the relevant agency contract, distributorship agreement, or direct international sales contract.

 ## *The* International Sales Contract

An international contract, like a domestic one, may reallocate rights, obligations, and risks in a way different from what they would be in the absence of the contract under applicable law. In an international context, however, the practices common to the parties may be fewer, their assumptions and expectations more divergent, and the risks greater. There is, in short, more ground to be covered to ensure a true meeting of the minds—and more risk and uncertainty in proceeding without one.

APPLICABLE LAW

The substantive terms of a contract are typically subject to the laws of a single jurisdiction. Those laws will clar-ify, modify, or even render voidable the provisions of a contract. If a contract leaves an issue open, the applicable law may fill the gap, disregarding the parties' unwritten intentions. Certain provisions may be included to address requirements of laws of other jurisdictions (for example, U.S. export controls may affect non-U.S. contracts). Even if the written contract addresses an issue, that provision may be affected by what is allowed or required under the relevant local law. It is important, therefore, to understand clearly not only what the parties wish to do but also what they are permitted to do.

On both these levels, achieving understanding can be difficult. Familiar legal terms in one jurisdiction may have a different meaning and effect in another. Only a small proportion of the businesspeople, lawyers, accountants, and other advisers in each jurisdiction will understand the relevant differences between that jurisdiction and another sufficiently to fully address the intricacies of cross-border transactions (although an approximation is often sufficient in practice). Having advisers with this capability is important.

One technique of reducing risk is to provide that the laws of a familiar jurisdiction will govern interpretation and implementation of the contract (for example, California law might be used for an Asian–European contract). This option is available, at least in part, in most

"There. Now it's all on paper. Feel better?"

international transactions involving sales, leasing, or the licensing of goods. Explicit choice-of-law and choice-of-forum provisions are advisable in order to avoid later disputes over which law applies and which country's courts have jurisdiction. (A lawsuit brought in one country may be tried under the law of another country.)

It is important to remember, however, that under certain circumstances a court will not honor the parties' choice-of-law provision. As explained further in Chapter 3, this is most likely to occur when application of the chosen law would violate the public policy of the jurisdiction in which the lawsuit is brought. For example, an Indian court would not enforce a postemployment covenant not to compete against an Indian employee living in India even if the employer is based in Massachusetts and the employment contract specified that the law of the Commonwealth of Massachusetts (which will enforce reasonable covenants not to compete) will govern the contract and employment relationship. To enforce the covenant would violate India's strong public policy in favor of employees' right to ply their trade.

When jurisdiction and choice of law are not specified in the contract and are disputed, the court in which the suit is filed will apply *conflict-of-law* principles. Although these usually focus on the significance of each country's relationship to the contract, these principles (sometimes referred to as principles of private international law) vary in some respects from country to country, and the process of litigating these issues can be extended and expensive. Consequently, addressing these issues in advance is prudent.

As explained in Chapter 8, if both parties to an international sales contract are nationals of countries that are signatories to the United Nations Convention on Contracts for the International Sale of Goods (CISG), the rules of that convention may apply, unless the parties opt out of the CISG rules. CISG rules are also applicable if the country whose law applies (as determined by the contract or by conflict-of-law principles) is a signatory to CISG.

DISPUTE RESOLUTION

The choice of a forum and a procedure for resolution of contract disputes is distinct from the choice of substantive law. A contract party may be willing to accept the substantive law of the other party's country but prefer that it be applied by a neutral body. When a neutral forum is desired, an international arbitral organization is commonly specified. Arbitration is preferable for several reasons. International arbitral bodies are often more experienced in dealing with international commercial disputes than their judicial counterparts. Many argue that arbitration is typically a more flexible, less costly, and speedier method of resolving disputes than litigation. Arbitral awards in many cases are enforceable pursuant to treaty in many countries where a foreign court's judgment would not be. Another benefit is that arbitral bodies, unlike courts, can keep the nature and the outcome of the dispute confidential, and they may provide a more level playing field than some judicial systems.

Commonly selected international arbitral forums include the International Chamber of Commerce (ICC) in Paris, the International Center for the Settlement of Investment Disputes (ICSID), the Arbitration Institute of the Stockholm Chamber of Commerce, and the Arbitration Institute of the Zurich Chamber of Commerce. Each international arbitral body has its own procedural rules. Internationally accepted arbitration rules, such as those adopted by the United Nations Commission on International Trade Law (UNCITRAL), may also be used in conjunction with the parties' own methods of selecting an arbitral panel. This latter type of arrangement is referred to as *ad hoc* arbitration. If there is no mutually convenient venue for the arbitration, often the parties will designate a place that is comparably distant and inconvenient for both parties.

It is common for the parties to stipulate that an arbitration decision is final and binding and not subject to review by any courts. Absent such a stipulation, the dispute could be reviewed by a court without reference to the arbitration (*de novo* review), rendering the arbitration decision unenforceable. The purpose of the 1958 United Nations Convention on the Recognition and Enforcement of Foreign Arbitral Awards (often referred to as the New York Convention) is "to unify standards by which agreements to arbitrate are observed and arbitral awards are enforced in signatory countries." More than sixty countries, including the United States and most of the major trading nations, are parties to the convention. In some countries, one cannot necessarily escape the court system just by agreeing to arbitration. Arbitration abroad or execution of the contract abroad may be necessary to escape local courts.

PAYMENT AND LETTERS OF CREDIT

Because the parties to an international sale may not be well known to each other, the buyer may be unwilling to pay for the goods before delivery, and the seller may be unwilling to ship the goods without certainty of payment. As a result, the most common payment mechanism for international sales transactions is the opening (that is, the establishment) of a documentary credit, commonly known as a letter of credit. Letters of credit are discussed further in a following section.

OVERSEAS OFFICES AND SUBSIDIARIES

U.S. businesses can establish a presence in a foreign country to supervise or manage sales with little or no investment by setting up a liaison, representative, or branch office in the host country. The scope of permissible activities, capital requirements, and tax liabilities of each of these forms of representation varies with the legal scheme of the host jurisdiction.

Typically, the greater the scope of permissible activities, the more stringent the capitalization and taxation rules. In Taiwan, for example, a liaison office may not engage in any business activity other than quotation, bidding, negotiating, executing contracts, and procurement on behalf of a home office, nor may it deliver or accept any goods or cash remuneration. A liaison office has no tax obligations (because the permitted activities incur no revenue) but is still required to register with the Taiwanese government.

Thus, representative and liaison offices are generally limited to providing services on behalf of a home office. They cannot engage in manufacturing operations, and the nature of the sales support and marketing activities they can conduct typically is limited. In countries with very limited or no provision for such operations, companies may be forced to choose between use of an agent or distributor on the one hand and a branch or subsidiary on the other.

A branch office can perform certain kinds of services, such as import and export, provided it is formally capitalized, registers with local government authorities, and pays income and other required taxes. Legally, the lack of local limited liability protection is one reason not to use a branch office. Many companies have subsidiaries that are entirely separate legal entities, with their own capital structure, boards of directors, and officers. Different tax treatment is a second reason to favor a subsidiary rather than a foreign office when establishing an overseas presence. Another issue that should not be overlooked is the burden of disclosing and possibly restating company financials under local regulations.

⚓ Documentary *and* Standby Letters *of* Credit *and* Guaranties

Letters of credit and guaranties are frequently used to secure payment for goods and repayment of loans in international transactions. The buyer or borrower (the *applicant*) enters into a contract with the issuing bank, which is usually in the buyer's or borrower's jurisdiction. The issuing bank issues a *letter of credit (L/C)* in favor of the seller or lender (the *beneficiary*). The *documentary letter of credit* provides for payment by the issuing bank to the beneficiary upon tender by the beneficiary (or its agent or assignee) of specified documents. The nature of these specified documents is based on the terms of the contract between the applicant and the beneficiary.

UCC ARTICLE 5 AND THE UCP

Two sets of rules can apply to L/Cs in international transactions. The first is Article 5 of the Uniform Commercial Code (UCC), which was revised in 1995 and varies slightly from state to state. The second set of rules is set forth in the International Chamber of Commerce's UCP, the most recent version of which is contained in a document often cited in bank L/C forms as *Uniform Customs and Practice for Documentary Credits,* 1993 Revision, ICC Publication No. 500.

There are significant differences between UCC Article 5 and the UCP. For example, UCC Article 5, as interpreted by most U.S. courts, provides that, once established, an L/C is irrevocable unless otherwise agreed. The UCP, by its terms, establishes the opposite presumption: an L/C is revocable at the issuing bank's option and without prior notice to or agreement of the beneficiary unless the contract and the L/C expressly state that the L/C is irrevocable. These rules, as much as the terms of the underlying sales contract, can determine the outcome of a payment dispute.

The parties can elect to have their L/C governed by UCC Article 5 or by the UCP, and they should be specific about their choice.[1] It is also prudent to expressly specify in the L/C whether it is revocable or irrevocable.

USE OF LETTERS OF CREDIT IN SALES TRANSACTIONS

In a transaction involving the sale of goods, the most common document to be tendered is a bill of lading, which the carrier (the transporter) of the goods issues to the seller. A *bill of lading* describes the goods received from the seller, the loading location, the name of the carrying vessel, and the destination; it also passes title to the buyer. A typical L/C requires the beneficiary to present to the issuing bank a *clean bill of lading,* that is, one with no notations indicating defects or damage to the goods

---

1. Certain provisions in revised Article 5 cannot be varied by agreement; but as a practical matter, the nonvariable rules are unlikely to conflict with any UCP rule.

when they were received for transport. When the seller presents the bill of lading (and any other documents specified by the L/C), the issuing bank makes payment. The issuing bank will then give the bill of lading to the buyer, which uses it to claim the goods from the carrier upon arrival.

Other typical documents that sales contracts often require to be tendered under the L/C include (1) an invoice, (2) a packing list, (3) a certificate of inspection issued by a designated organization confirming that the quality or condition of the goods at the time of shipment complies with the contract terms, (4) a certificate of origin (for customs purposes), (5) a certificate of insurance establishing that the goods are properly insured prior to shipment, and (6) a draft drawn on the issuing bank in the amount of the purchase price.

A *confirming bank* may also be involved in the transaction. This is a bank located in the seller's jurisdiction that confirms (makes a legal commitment) to the seller that it will honor the terms of the L/C issued by the issuing bank. By making a more familiar local bank the paying entity, this commitment gives the seller a greater sense of security. The fee for a confirmation is usually a fraction of the original L/C fee.

A seller can use the L/C as security for its own issuing bank to issue a second L/C to finance its purchase of products or materials from its supplier. This is known as a *back-to-back letter of credit*.

It is important to recognize that the purpose of documentary L/Cs is to allow the issuing bank to pay based solely on the tender of particular documents without requiring it to examine any extraneous facts, including the parties' compliance with their sales contract. Article 15 of the UCP states:

Banks assume no liability or responsibility for the form, sufficiency, accuracy, genuineness, falsification or legal effect of any document(s), or for the general and/or particular conditions stipulated in the document(s) or superimposed thereon; nor do they assume any liability or responsibility for the description, quantity, weight, quality, condition, packing,

delivery, value or existence of the goods represented by any document(s), or for the good faith or acts and/or omissions, solvency, performance or standing of the consignor, the carriers, the forwarders, the consignees, or the insurers of the goods, or any other person whomsoever.[2]

As a result, a sale of goods pursuant to an L/C involves two separate contracts. The first is the sales contract between the buyer and the seller whereby the seller agrees to deliver goods meeting the requirements of the contract of sale and the buyer agrees to pay for conforming goods. The second is an independent contract whereby the issuing bank, at the request of the buyer–applicant, promises to pay the seller–beneficiary the purchase price upon delivery of the documents specified in the L/C. This is shown graphically in Exhibit 13.1.

A breach of the first contract will not relieve the bank of its obligations under the second contract unless the buyer proves actual material fraud in the transaction.[3] This fraud exception is construed very narrowly. An injunction against payment will be issued only if (1) the beneficiary has "no colorable right"[4] to draw, (2) the beneficiary's demand has "absolutely no basis in fact,"[5] or (3) the beneficiary's wrongdoing has "vitiated the entire transaction."[6] For example, the U.S. District Court for the Southern District of New York enjoined the Bank of India from drawing on a standby L/C (discussed below) issued by a German bank to secure payment for naphtha that was

2. Uniform Customs and Practice for Documentary Credits, 1993 Revision, Int'l Chamber of Commerce Publication No. 500.
3. *See* U.C.C. § 5-114(2). Under New York law, U.C.C. Section 5-114(2) prohibits honoring facially valid documents in a transaction involving fraud even if the letter of credit is governed by the UCP, because the UCP does not itself address fraud (*Brenntag International Chemicals, Inc. v. Norddeutsche Landesbank GZ,* 70 F. Supp. 2d 399 (S.D.N.Y. 1999)).
4. Itek Corp. v. First Nat'l Bank of Boston, 730 F.2d 19, 25 (1st Cir. 1984).
5. Dynamics Corp. of America v. Citizens & S. Nat'l Bank, 356 F. Supp. 991, 999 (N.D. Ga. 1973).
6. Intraworld Indus. v. Girard Trust Bank, 336 A.2d 316, 324–25 (Pa. 1925).

EXHIBIT 13.1 **Letter of Credit Parallel Contracts**

Contract 1:	Buyer–Applicant	and	Seller–Beneficiary
	Payment of purchase price for conforming goods	→	
		←	Delivery of conforming goods
Contract 2:	Issuing Bank	and	Seller–Beneficiary
	Payment of purchase price	→	
		←	Delivery of specified documents

to have been shipped from Indonesia to India on the M/T *Crystal River.*[7] The beneficiary presented an undated default letter and fraudulent invoice for goods that in fact were never shipped. Indeed, the M/T *Crystal River* was en route from Saudi Arabia to Alaska at the time the shipment allegedly occurred. The court concluded both that there was fraud in the transaction and that the Bank of India was not a holder in due course.

As a result of this narrowly construed exception for fraud, even if the goods delivered are defective, the buyer will not have the authority to stop the issuing bank from making a payment if the seller presents the documents specified in the L/C. In other words, payment on an L/C is conditioned on tender of conforming documents, not on performance of the underlying contract. Specifying the appropriate documents is critical for both parties.

Sellers in international transactions typically require irrevocable L/Cs when dealing with unfamiliar parties. An *irrevocable letter of credit* can be amended or canceled only with the consent of the beneficiary and the issuing bank. If the buyer learns of defects in the goods that do not prevent tender of the required documents, its only recourse under an irrevocable L/C is to sue the seller for breach of the underlying sales contract.

GUARANTIES AND STANDBY LETTERS OF CREDIT IN FINANCING TRANSACTIONS

Guaranties are often used to provide security for those providing financing for a major construction project in another country. If the political or credit risks of a country are perceived to be especially great, an entity in the host country, often an instrumentality of the host country government, may be called upon to act as the guarantor. Under a *guaranty* arrangement, a local financial institution guarantees, for the benefit of the project owners, that the lender will be repaid if the project principals are unable to pay, as long as the parties to the project have adhered to the contracts. The choice of law for enforcement of the guaranty may be subject to negotiation. The local financial institutions authorized to issue guaranties, especially if they involve repayment in hard currencies, may be subject to a variety of local regulations that, if not adhered to, could result in the guaranty becoming unenforceable and therefore worthless.

A standby L/C may also be used to secure financing or other obligations. A *standby letter of credit* is a form of documentary L/C, but unlike the traditional L/C in a sales transaction, which requires payment based on evidence of the seller's performance, a standby L/C requires payment only if the applicant has failed to perform its obligations. Thus, payment is usually conditioned upon a brief statement, in language previously agreed on by the applicant and the beneficiary and set forth verbatim in the L/C, that the applicant is in default or has failed to perform an obligation to the beneficiary under the project contract and that the beneficiary is therefore entitled to payment from the issuing bank. Unlike the common form of guaranty, the creditor need only tender the specified document and need not establish that the debtor breached its obligations in the underlying contract, which could involve extended litigation or arbitration.

This distinction is critical. A guarantor is liable under the guaranty only when the primary obligor is liable for the underlying obligation. The guarantor can raise any defenses that the primary obligor could raise before having to make payment to the beneficiary. In contrast, a standby L/C constitutes the primary obligation of the issuing bank to the beneficiary to pay upon the presentation of specified documents.

As with commercial L/Cs used in connection with the sale of goods, the issuing bank cannot inquire into the underlying transaction or assert the defenses the applicant might have. It must generally pay within seven business days following presentation of the specified documents, which means that the beneficiary has the funds while the dispute between the applicant and the beneficiary is worked out or litigated.

U.S. law prohibits U.S. banks from issuing guaranties, so the standby L/C mechanism is a useful way to provide payment or repayment comfort, especially to a party with superior bargaining power. As with L/Cs generally, however, the applicant should enter into such arrangements only with a clear understanding of how the mechanism works. Because the documentary L/C transaction is independent of the underlying contract, applicants should clearly establish what the documentary conditions for payment are, in addition to establishing the terms of the underlying contract.

Letters of credit cost money and, in an ongoing relationship, the buyer usually presses for more favorable payment terms. In the multinational-corporation context, having a well-known parent company guarantee a local affiliate's obligations is a fairly common cost-saving alternative to L/Cs.

International Leasing

Under a true lease, the owner of the leased goods expects to recover them at the end of the lease term. Under a *financing lease,* commonly used to finance the acquisition of expensive capital equipment and vehicles (such as

7. Brenntag Int'l Chems., Inc. v. Norddeutsche Landesbank GZ, 70 F. Supp. 2d 399 (S.D.N.Y. 1999).

airplanes, locomotives, and ships), the parties expect the lessee to purchase the leased equipment at the end of the lease term at an agreed-on residual value. Typical finance-lease transactions range from $100,000 to several million dollars.

A financing lease offers several advantages over a direct purchase. In a financing lease, the owner retains legal title to the goods until the lessee pays all or most of the purchase price. In countries with an undeveloped law of secured transactions (which establishes creditors' rights to collateral for loans), this alternative offers greater comfort to the owner of the transferred goods.

For foreign banks, leasing offers a way to establish a local presence in countries that may not allow bank branches. As equipment lessors, banks operate as lenders, factoring interest charges into the lease payments, while nominally serving a commercial function, namely, the sale of equipment. Foreign banks should consult local counsel to determine whether there are any nondisclaimable lessor obligations under local laws and whether retention of title creates any tort or other liability risks under local law.

In many countries, lessors, as owners of the leased goods, can fully depreciate those goods during the lease term, thereby gaining substantial tax benefits. Many countries allow the lessee to deduct all or a portion of its lease payments.

Some countries impose restrictions on the purchase of expensive imports, particularly where foreign-exchange expenditures are carefully monitored or restricted. Lease payments may escape these limitations, however, either because there is no up-front sale or because the payments can be spread out in acceptable installments. Sometimes, the installment payments can even be made from earnings generated by the leased goods.

International leasing may be subject to a wide range of other foreign laws. Local tax and accounting regulations will determine tax benefits for the owner and user of the leased goods. The creditor's rights, if any, will be determined by local laws. If creditor–debtor laws exist, there may be limitations on the lessor's rights in the event of a default by the lessee. Foreign-exchange laws may substantially affect how lease payments are calculated and made, particularly in countries where the local currency is not freely convertible or is undergoing high rates of inflation.

COMPENSATION TRADE

Compensation trade is a variation on the simple sale or lease transaction. The foreign party transfers usage and/or eventual ownership of a good, usually equip-

ment, to the local party, who then repays the foreign party with products produced using the foreign party's equipment. The foreign party may also supply the materials for the production process. This is known as a *processing operation*. Both types of transactions are simpler than full-scale direct investments but may still be subject to local laws involving foreign exchange, customs, tax, and creditors' rights.

 # International Transfers *of* Technology

The transfer of technology across national boundaries involves many of the same legal and commercial issues as the sale of goods: the choice of applicable law, the form of payment, and the method of resolving disputes. Protecting the owner's rights in the transferred technology is a prime concern, usually accomplished by appropriate license terms and by taking the actions necessary to protect proprietary rights under local laws.

LICENSING

Technology is protected by intellectual property laws, which vary from country to country. These laws are discussed in more detail in Chapter 11. Transfers of technology can be accomplished by sale or by operation of law as part of an acquisition. In many cases, however, technology is transferred pursuant to a licensing agreement whereby the owner of the technology (the licensor) transfers it so that the user (the licensee) can manufacture specified products, normally in exchange for an ongoing royalty that is typically based on production quantity or sales of the products.

Developing countries encourage the licensing of technology to upgrade local manufacturing capabilities and expertise. This policy goal may come into conflict with the licensor's desire to restrict the use of the technology or to keep it confidential. Foreign licensors need to be especially sensitive to the nature of the host country's patent, trademark, copyright, and trade-secret laws and its actual enforcement practices in dealing with foreign-owned intellectual property.

Because a technology transfer involves intangible property, its dissemination is harder to control than the sale of tangible products. This presents problems for both licensor and licensee. The licensee will be concerned with the scope of the rights it has been granted, including whether it has the exclusive right to use the licensed technology.

The licensor, which typically has invested substantial time and money in creating its technology, wants to be certain that the licensee will not disclose or use the technology without the licensor's consent. For technology that the licensor protects as a trade secret, contract provisions requiring confidentiality and restrictions on the employees who will have access to the technology are essential. In many developing countries, however, dissemination of technology is a policy objective, and technology-licensing laws or administrative policies may expressly limit the terms of a license agreement and its confidentiality or enforcement provisions. These limitations may be unacceptable to a licensor.

If the licensor is also a manufacturer and exporter of products produced by the licensed technology, it will be concerned about the effect of the licensee's prospective sales on its own markets. Outside the European Union, this issue can usually be resolved by imposing restrictions on the geographic markets available to the licensee. As noted in Chapter 12, members of the European Union are prohibited from restricting the resale of goods into any other member state. In developing countries, local technology transfer laws may also prohibit certain types of geographic market limitations. In addition, local antitrust laws may be used to challenge such limitations. In one common resolution to such disputes, selling efforts outside the territory are prohibited, but unsolicited sales are permitted. These issues are all central to the transfer and use of technology, and they must be carefully negotiated in the context of local requirements.

The licensing of technology frequently involves the licensing of rights in special types of intellectual property, such as copyrights, trademarks, service marks, patents, and trade secrets. The confidentiality of trade-secret technology can generally be protected, as between the contract parties, by a well-drafted, enforceable licensing contract with strong nondisclosure provisions. To protect its ownership and use rights in trademarks, service marks, copyrights, and patents against third parties in foreign countries, the licensor generally must perfect its ownership in compliance with local requirements. Obtaining protection under local patent and trademark laws can be a technical, extended process; nevertheless, the protection available under those laws is essential to preserving the value of the owner's intellectual property.

INTERNATIONAL INTELLECTUAL PROPERTY PROTECTION

The scope and duration of patent and trademark protection vary from country to country. Many countries have less stringent intellectual property laws than the United States (or laws that are less rigorously enforced). For example, a number of countries in the Middle East have been very reluctant to grant patent protection for pharmaceuticals because that would make it impossible for local companies to produce patented drugs and sell them at a fraction of the price charged by the patent holder in other countries. As a result, the production of counterfeit goods that infringe intellectual property rights is more prevalent in such countries. U.S. trade laws (discussed in Chapter 12) may prevent the entry of such counterfeit goods into the United States, but they can only indirectly restrict the production and sale of such goods in countries other than the United States. As explained in Chapter 11, several multinational treaties seek to harmonize the application of the intellectual property laws of various jurisdictions.

INTERNATIONAL FRANCHISING

Franchising has become an increasingly common form of international licensing. A typical *franchise agreement* involves a package of licensed rights, including the right of the franchisee to use the franchisor's trademarks, service marks, patents, and confidential, unpatented know-how (including trade secrets). The franchisor may or may not also contribute an equity investment, but its major contribution is usually its goodwill—the value of the customers' recognition of a popular enterprise. If the franchisor does not properly register its trademarks and service marks locally, it can effectively lose control of its most valuable assets.

The concept of franchising as a method of doing business and the corresponding rights and obligations between the parties are still in a state of flux in many countries. Protection of marketing and operations methods, designs, trade dress, quality control systems, and other benchmarks of franchise businesses that are well understood domestically are often limited or unavailable internationally.

Investment Abroad

Before investing outside the United States, U.S. firms should (1) assess their investment goals; (2) consider the economic, political, geographic, legal, and labor conditions in the host country; and (3) address any financial issues, such as currency considerations, project capitalization, and taxation.

INVESTMENT GOALS

A business plan for investing abroad must begin with an assessment of the investor's goals. The attractiveness of a prospective investment in a given host country can vary greatly, depending on these goals.

Local Market Penetration For legal or business reasons, some markets are almost inaccessible to U.S. manufacturers wishing to sell their products. Developing countries may lack hard currency—that is, convertible foreign exchange—and these shortages may limit their purchase of imports. Applicable laws may restrict imports of certain products but grant benefits to foreign investors wishing to manufacture those products locally. The only practical way to penetrate such markets may be to invest in a local manufacturing facility. As another example of how foreign companies may be prevented from competing in certain markets, certain Asian countries permit only local companies to establish retail businesses.

Regional Base U.S. businesses that wish to compete in Europe or Asia may need to establish manufacturing, marketing, and/or service centers in the relevant region to gain credibility with local customers. U.S. businesses may also need to be on-site to sustain their local sources of supplies for operations elsewhere. Regional bases can reduce transportation costs, enhance time-to-market responses, help avoid cultural difficulties, and generally help the home office monitor the business pulse of the region. They also avoid potential problems with distributors or agents not 100 percent committed to the products or not aligned with the foreign parent. The challenge of integrating an expatriate with the local business environment is the corollary of this issue of aligning locally hired managers with the overall corporate mission and goals.

Cheaper Production Costs Developing countries typically offer cheaper labor and raw materials than more industrialized countries. These reduced costs are often the primary reason for U.S. business investment in foreign manufacturing operations. As discussed below, however, the assessment of true production costs is not limited to a line item comparison of the costs of each element of production. Intangible issues such as labor efficiency, reliability of supplies, local labor law requirements, and political stability can affect the true costs of production.

HOST COUNTRY CONDITIONS

Prospective investors need to consider the economic, political, geographic, legal, and labor conditions in the host country.

Economic Conditions The host country's economic condition is usually a high-profile issue in the investment-evaluation process. Per capita income, for example, may determine whether a particular country is a realistic market for a particular product or whether it is a likely source of inexpensive labor. Economic growth trends can suggest both a growing consumer market and increasing labor costs. The monetary system is also important. Existence of a readily convertible currency and the nature of the currency-exchange laws will determine whether profits can be easily repatriated (that is, transferred abroad). In a country with a high inflation rate, local suppliers may be reluctant to perform on long-term contracts, and capital and working loans may be more expensive.

The U.S. Department of Commerce, the U.S. Foreign Commercial Service, and the U.S. Department of State regularly publish reports on the economic condition of various countries. These agencies can offer a good introduction for a prospective foreign investor. The U.S. Foreign Commercial Service has a wide-ranging network of commercial officers stationed at U.S. embassies and consulates throughout the world. They collect and analyze economic data and are available on-site to U.S. businesses to interpret data that may be relevant to an investment project.

Political Conditions Political instability inevitably leads to some degree of legal and economic instability. Such instability is a matter of degree. Investors are generally concerned mainly with the reliability and stability of the local legal institutions that enforce contracts and protect property rights. Changes of government in Western democracies can lead to changes in the legal and policy environment that dramatically affect the economic results of foreign investments but do not undermine the rule of law. Other political systems may have a stable regime but with a corrupt judicial and legislative system that does not offer effective legal recourse for investors. At the outer extreme, violent political or civil divisions can lead to a situation where the rule of law completely collapses. Business can still be done in such an environment, but the written contractual terms become insignificant next to practical considerations of power, possession, and protection.

A prospective foreign investor must, therefore, look beyond the reasonableness of the contract, the competence of its foreign business counterpart, and the desirability of the site to determine whether the existing government and its policies are aligned with the needs of the project and whether that government or its policies are likely to change in adverse ways. Managers should analyze both (1) political risks, such as expropriation, partial nationalization, and serious operational restrictions, which often stem from a change in the overall political orientation; and (2) legal risks, such as changes in tax, customs, employment, and other laws, that do not represent an inherent shift against private ownership or against foreign investment.

The Overseas Private Investment Corporation (OPIC), a U.S. government agency, specializes in providing eligible U.S. investors with insurance against certain defined risks, including political risks such as expropriation. To be eligible for OPIC insurance, an investor must be (1) a U.S. citizen, (2) a U.S. partnership or corporation substantially owned by U.S. citizens, or (3) a foreign business at least 95 percent owned by a U.S. citizen or by a U.S. partnership or corporation. OPIC insures U.S. investors' interests only in "friendly" countries—that is, those that have investment-protection agreements (bilateral treaties of friendship, navigation, and commerce, or FNCs, or bilateral investment treaties, or BITs) with the United States. Coverage is also available for inconvertibility of foreign-currency remittances and losses due to hostile action during civil unrest.[8]

Geographic Conditions Climatic and geographic conditions can directly affect the production and transportation of products. Severe weather in certain seasons can affect delivery schedules. Consequently, it is important to ascertain the breadth and reliability of the transportation system and other infrastructure available. A manager needs to keep all these conditions in mind when selecting a manufacturing site and supplier and making service and sales contract commitments for production and shipment.

The nature, cost, and development status of a prospective site are major considerations. In some countries (such as China, Indonesia, the Philippines, and Thailand), foreign investors are not permitted to own land but can, often with the assistance of a local partner, obtain long-term land-use rights. If the capital investment will be large relative to the parent company's assets, a foreign investor may want to consider investing only in countries that offer guaranties concerning expropriation or in friendly developing countries where U.S. investors are eligible for OPIC insurance. Sometimes, a country may seek to attract investment to certain areas by offering attractive land-use terms and new infrastructure.

Mistaken assumptions about land rights and use, flood control, power supply, fire protection, utility service, legal and informal employee protections, and the like can present the most significant hidden operational hazards in foreign direct investment. It is critical for the investor and its legal and business advisers to probe these areas aggressively in their due diligence.

Legal Conditions Managers should ask whether local laws and courts offer predictability, uniformity, and even-handed enforcement. Also, is the judicial system speedy, efficient, and inexpensive? Beyond the letter of the laws, their effectiveness depends on political conditions and the nature of the legal and administrative organs that interpret and enforce them. A reliable court system or comparable dispute resolution forum (such as an established arbitration system) is essential; without it, the investor will have little leverage to enforce contracts or invoke commercial laws.

Although trade or licensing contracts may allow for choice of the law of a jurisdiction other than the host country, in foreign-investment projects the substantive laws of the host country will apply. In some instances, however, rules of interpretation and dispute resolution procedures may be governed by the rules of a third jurisdiction.

Sources of necessary supplies should be secure, and their transportation and storage not subject to rampant theft. The existence of a reasonably diligent and fair law enforcement network is a factor to be considered in this regard.

Foreign investors must develop a working knowledge of the applicable host country laws and acceptable forums for dispute resolution, and they should obtain professional advice from local attorneys. These professionals can also assist in providing accurate translations of contracts where required. It is not uncommon for a country to require that the definitive text of a contract be in the local language (for example, Mexico requires contracts to be in Spanish), but an accurate English version is critical.

Many countries offer a variety of vehicles for foreign investment. A foreign investor can select the investment format most appropriate to its project in a foreign country, just as a U.S. business can choose to operate domestically as a sole proprietorship; a general, limited, or limited liability partnership; a limited liability company; or a corporation. Each form is subject to its own set of laws, which affect the management structure, equity investment requirements, limitation of investor liabilities, and taxation.

Often, though, businesses have less structural flexibility in foreign jurisdictions. In some countries, unlike in the United States, more prestige is attached to specific entity forms (for example, in some European countries, the private limited company form may be perceived as a less serious commitment than the public limited company form). Country handbooks published by international

---

8. OPIC publishes a number of handbooks that describe its programs and services. They are available from the Information Officer, Overseas Private Investment Corporation, 1129 20th Street, N.W., Washington, DC 20527.

accounting firms, local law firms, and the U.S. government contain useful information on such issues.

The licensing or contribution of technology by the U.S. business to the foreign business is often a component of an equity investment project. Some countries' investment laws or policies may limit the portion of the foreign party's equity investment that can be attributable to intellectual property (such as patents, trademarks, or know-how) as compared with cash or equipment, for example. Certain restrictions on technology use may be invalid under local technology-licensing laws.

A would-be investor should also check for the existence of bilateral tax or investment treaties that grant reciprocal rights to businesses from the host and investor countries. These treaties may offer significant benefits, such as avoidance of double taxation (that is, taxation by both the host and investor countries) and guaranties against uncompensated expropriation by the host government.

The U.S. State Department compiles records of ratified treaties and their signatories. A quick review of this information can provide a sense of the relative involvement of various nations in international conventions that affect foreign investment. Attorneys familiar with how these treaties apply locally can best advise investors in a particular jurisdiction.

Labor Conditions A leading reason for investing abroad is to take advantage of relatively low labor costs in a foreign country. The true cost of labor, however, is more than the hourly or daily wage. It includes labor efficiency, trainability, reliability, and adherence to quality control standards. In addition, the labor and foreign-investment laws of some countries, particularly those with socialist economies, require employers to fund a wide range of employee benefits that are not expected by U.S. investors. These benefits include housing, travel, education, and food subsidies, as well as the more common retirement, health insurance, and maternity benefits. Many nations do not permit employers to terminate an employee without just cause, which can make it difficult to terminate inefficient or redundant workers. Local labor laws may limit the degree to which employees may be treated differently, thus restricting flexibility in incentive compensation.

FINANCIAL ISSUES

Several common financial concerns for an equity investor in a foreign project include currency considerations, project funding and capitalization, and taxation.

Currency Considerations The currency in which the foreign entity does business and in which its assets and obligations are denominated can be a major concern for a U.S. investor in many developing countries. The ideal is an open economy (1) without currency and other monetary restrictions and (2) with a currency tied directly to the dollar or at least to another stable major currency such as the euro (which is discussed in Chapter 12). This minimizes fluctuations in investment results due solely to currency issues relative to those inherent in the fundamental economics of the business. In the second-best case, the prices of inputs and outputs are primarily denominated in hard currency, even though the local currency is the unit of account (a common requirement). This is most typical in export and processing operations. In many cases, however, the investor will find local currency controls and financing restrictions a significant issue. Then, hedging contract commitments and planning capital allocations across currencies and in view of governmental restrictions will be essential to establishing and implementing a successful financial plan.

Local financial institutions often are restricted in offering foreign-currency loans. Conversely, foreign banks outside the host country may be reluctant to offer capital loans if local currency profits may not be freely convertible for loan repayment. Project proceeds or even host country project properties may not offer sufficient security for a loan from a foreign financial institution. The foreign investor may be required to obtain and provide security entirely outside the host jurisdiction for any loans it desires.

The availability and cost of hard currency can be a major issue when the host country currency is not freely convertible. It may be of less concern to a foreign investor that expects to earn hard currency through exports of either the project's products or other local products purchased with its local currency profits. This latter arrangement is known as *countertrade*.

Cash-flow hedging methods are increasingly common in countries that maintain restrictive foreign-exchange controls. For example, a company with both import and export activities might structure import payments to match hard-currency inflows in order to reduce potential exchange-rate losses. If the local currency is depreciating rapidly, inflows of hard-currency earnings may lag behind offsetting import payments. As a currency is devalued, import costs rise. Potential exchange-rate losses can be avoided by delaying the conversion of export receivables into local currency until imported goods are paid for.

The currency denomination also affects the capitalization of an investment project. For example, a foreign partner in a joint venture may agree to contribute a specified amount of U.S. dollars over time, with the host country partner making an equal contribution in local currency. If the local currency depreciates against the U.S. dollar, the foreign partner will end up making a greater than 50 percent contribution to the joint venture in local currency terms. Some reconciliation of paid-in capital and share pricing may be needed under local law. Unequal contributions may also arise where local law requires foreign-currency capital contributions to be valued at an official exchange rate that fails to reflect the local currency's true value. These currency risks can be addressed by careful contract drafting and, where possible, through currency swaps and hedging.

Project Capitalization The foreign business to which the investor is committing an investment typically requires fixed capital (often for construction costs) and working capital for daily operations. Local laws and practices may not permit the flexibility in capital structure available in the United States. The reliability and attractiveness of a host nation in this regard may be affected by factors such as political risk, currency-convertibility laws, profit-repatriation restrictions, local banking laws and practices, and the enforceability of guaranties or security agreements. As noted earlier, the lenders will usually require the borrower to secure its repayment obligations by providing a standby letter of credit.

Taxation Tax planning is an essential part of any foreign investor's business plan. Careful pre-planning can minimize the risk of withholding taxes and double income taxation and take advantage of local tax benefits. One simple way of addressing tax risks is a *gross-up clause,* whereby the local partner or licensee is obligated to pay all taxes other than those specifically allocated to the foreign partner. In this way, the foreign party avoids the risk of tax increases or unknown taxes. Some countries prohibit such reallocation of responsibility for the payment of certain taxes, however, and will not recognize gross-ups. As a result, a gross-up, though simple in concept, often is not the most efficient way of addressing certain tax issues.

The United States has bilateral tax treaties with more than fifty countries. The treaties seek to avoid double taxation of U.S.-based businesses and individuals. Some treaties also impose tax ceilings on certain types of income; for example, one treaty imposes a 10 percent tax ceiling on passive income such as royalties from technology licenses or rental income. Bilateral tax treaties may not affect all the taxes applicable to a foreign-investment project or to an individual expatriate employee's income; but, when a tax treaty provision is applicable and offers more favorable tax treatment than the comparable domestic tax rule, the treaty rule will generally apply.

Tax credits may be available to U.S. businesses engaged in foreign projects that are taxed by the host country. Such credits are available for the amount of foreign taxes paid up to a certain limit, which is derived by dividing the foreign-source taxable income by the total taxable income (which includes all foreign- and domestic-source income) and multiplying that fraction by the U.S. tax liability on the total taxable income. (Thus, if foreign tax rates exceed U.S. rates, no credit is available for the excess in the current year.) Foreign tax credits for any one year cannot exceed the amount of foreign income taxes that have been paid or accrued, but taxes in excess of the limitation can be carried back two years and forward five years, subject to each year's tax credit limit.

Operational Concerns

Many noncommercial issues can affect the desirability of operating a business abroad. Some of the most common factors include language and cultural customs, ease of communication and transportation, and amenities for expatriate staff.

LANGUAGE AND CULTURAL CUSTOMS

Knowledge of the language and customs of the host country, or the use of proficient interpreters, is essential to the success of a business venture abroad. Stories abound concerning the gaffes of U.S. investors who, because of language difficulties or cultural misunderstandings, offended their foreign partners, misinterpreted contract negotiations, miscalculated the effect of their business operations, or simply could not maintain effective working relationships with their foreign counterparts. A sound fundamental business concept can be undermined by deficient communication.

Contract terms, both legal and technical, require accurate translation to ensure effective implementation. Product marketing and trademark and trade-name registration require sophisticated language skills and cultural sensitivity to ensure appropriateness for a foreign culture.

Other business customs of a host country can have a substantial impact on local business operations on very basic levels. A frank and direct management style may be welcomed in some countries; in others, it may be viewed as arrogant and gauche. Gift giving may be appropriate, even expected, behavior in certain circumstances; in other situations, it may be regarded as unethical and possibly illegal.

COMMUNICATIONS

International direct-dial land phones, cellular phones, fax machines, and electronic mail are common business tools in some regions but may not be available in some developing countries (whose natural resources, labor skills, and markets attract foreign investors). Even postal or courier services may be unreliable. Such infrastructural deficiencies need to be reflected in contract provisions requiring timely notice or delivery of documents. Expatriate managers without quick access to headquarters may have to be more creative and self-reliant in making decisions than their colleagues in more developed countries.

TRANSPORTATION

Without reliable transportation, products and the people responsible for production cannot effectively reach their destinations. Transportation problems can affect the delivery of raw materials within a host country. Inadequate port facilities can lead to delayed shipments abroad and lost sales. Inefficient or corrupt customs officials can have similar effects in delaying business transactions and increasing their cost. These concerns must be addressed in contracts that hinge on timely delivery of equipment or products. Some of these weaknesses in the transportation infrastructure may not be readily evident; special investigation may be required.

EXPATRIATE AMENITIES

In many developing countries, an expatriate manager and staff may be essential to provide needed skills. In addition, expatriate managers are often needed to proselytize the corporate culture and goals to local staff and maintain consistency with the home office's overall strategy. To attract qualified personnel to hardship posts, a company must usually offer a compensation package that includes income premiums and benefits. If expatriate staff must pay additional income tax under the laws of the host country, further additional compensation may have to be paid to counteract this disadvantage.

Expatriate packages often pose a problem for local personnel policy. Local managers may resent the higher compensation of their expatriate counterparts, and local laws may require that local managers receive comparable compensation. Ignoring this issue in the planning stage may prove expensive later in terms of both cash and local management goodwill.

Substantial start-up costs may be incurred while expatriate personnel acclimatize. In addition, some companies have found that expatriates may eventually become too acclimatized, engaging in local practices inconsistent with home office or industry practice.

Personal safety may be an issue in some countries, effectively precluding the assignment of personnel with families. It may be difficult to extend comparable company health and life insurance benefits to expatriate employees.

 # Factors *to* Consider When Going International

Before expanding into international markets, a firm must consider not only market conditions but also the laws and mores of the foreign country. Examples of substantive laws that may affect a foreign business are import/export regulations, employment law, tax law, securities law, and antitrust law. A company that follows the correct form of doing business but fails to recognize or understand local law may reduce its profitability. A company considering foreign investments should therefore carefully analyze the sociopolitical and economic climate of the prospective host country; obtain a clear understanding of the legal, regulatory, and administrative regimes; and anticipate foreseeable future changes in relevant conditions.

One way that companies typically expand into the international marketplace is through direct sales to customers. Direct sales pose special problems, however, including export regulations, international contract law, letters of credit, import regulations, and the use of local representatives.

If costs do not justify opening a local office, a firm will often retain a local representative to oversee the sale of its products. If the transaction is not correctly structured, however, the company may find that it has a dependent agent in the foreign country—that it has, under local law, opened an office in the foreign country. Transactions thought to be tax-free will, in fact, be subject to corporate tax, and the local agent may have acquired additional rights and protections under local employment law.

A company can also conduct business in a foreign country by acquiring an existing company. Such transactions are governed by the laws regulating foreign investment in the country. Tax issues will play a predominant role in determining the form of the acquisition and the method of future operation.

A firm may also choose to create a new entity distinct from the parent corporation. This entity could be a corporation with 100 percent foreign ownership or a joint venture in the form of a corporation or partnership. Local law will define the regulations and restrictions to be imposed on the firm. Common restrictions include requiring majority local ownership or that a majority of the board be resident directors. In many countries, the foreign investor may specify whether the entity is to be treated as a partnership or corporation for U.S. tax purposes. Every jurisdiction seems to have some unique wrinkles in the areas of formation and administration; matters taken for granted by locals that may occasion surprise and delays for foreign investors.

Local advisers experienced in dealing with foreign investors can help smooth the process and minimize surprises on both practical issues and matters of substantive and procedural law. Special attention should be paid to coordinating tax/accounting and legal advice within the context of the investor's business goals. The investor must recognize, though, that sometimes foreign lawyers and accountants take a compartmentalized rather than interdisciplinary approach—they normally perform only a technical role and do not act as general business advisers. It is important that the investor's point person, the transaction manager, actively set expectations and coordinate the advisory process.

This is perhaps nowhere more important than in the tax area. Even similar tax systems will differ in significant respects, and only rarely can one find a single individual who is thoroughly versed in the laws of two jurisdictions and their interrelations. It is important to coordinate carefully and start early in the planning stage to uncover potential problem areas. Obtaining tax credits is relatively obvious. More subtle issues can arise in many contexts. An agreement, exchange of assets, or other transaction that creates no tax liability or is not deemed a tax event in one country may create income tax liability in another. For example, stock dividends and splits are not taxable in the United States and other major economies because there is no change of economic substance. Thus, it might not occur to a U.S. manager, tax lawyer, or accountant to inquire and discover that they may be taxable in other countries.

Corporate laws also vary by jurisdiction. The U.S. system of corporate law and procedure is relatively flexible. Most other jurisdictions have less permissive rules regarding capital structure, dissolution, corporate formalities, and officers and directors, as well as different penalties for noncompliance. An investor may not be able to form, operate, and close down the entity how and when it wants, and achieving the desired management structure may prove impossible or impractical.

If the company employs workers in the host country, it is subject to a system of employment laws, regulations, and customs that is, in most cases, more restrictive and more protective of workers than U.S. law. Employment laws are highly politicized and seek to protect local workers, particularly against foreign "exploitation." They need not make sense to U.S. managers. Restricted use of foreign personnel, required proportions of local workers, prescribed terms of employment, and difficulty in terminating unsatisfactory employees are all common issues. The foreign investor may have to compromise its employment policies to satisfy local requirements.

IN BRIEF
Thinking Internationally

Market Conditions and Competition

- Product/service market fundamentals
- Distribution/operational realities
- Personnel and management
- Location
- Currency
- Competitors
- Achieving "local touch"

Legal Mores of Foreign Country

- Rule of law
- Corruption
- Judicial integrity

Substantive Foreign Law

- Exchange controls
- Import/export costs and controls
- Employment law
- Taxes, both foreign and domestic
- Securities
- Antitrust
- Formation, governance, and dissolution of foreign entity

Sociopolitical and Economic Climate of Host Country

- Long-term economic stability
- Stable pro-market consensus
- Attitude toward foreign investors

In some areas, such as environmental law, many developing countries are far less regulated than the United States, but the investor should expect to see these countries' legal regimes eventually catch up. Legal advantages, like business advantages, are often transitory. The investor needs to evaluate and understand both areas to develop the knowledge of and sensitivity to local conditions needed to make the right investment decision.

 # Extraterritorial Application *of* Domestic Law *and Forum Non Conveniens*

Under certain circumstances, a country will seek to apply its law to conduct that occurred outside its borders. For example, as explained in Chapter 20, the United States applies its antitrust laws to activities occurring outside the United States if they have substantial effects on U.S. exports or imports.

A related issue arises when a foreign national seeks to invoke another country's laws and use its courts to obtain relief that is not available under domestic law. Most courts will not exercise jurisdiction unless the country in which the court sits has some interest in the transaction. The following case addressed the right of an English citizen to sue an English company in the United States for securities fraud under U.S. law.

A CASE IN POINT

CASE 13.1

Robinson v. TCI/U.S. West Communications, Inc.

United States Court of Appeals for the Fifth Circuit
117 F.3d 900
(5th Cir. 1998).

Summary

FACTS Alan Robinson, an English citizen and resident, was a founder of Croydon Cable Television Limited (CCTV), one of the first cable franchises in England. Through a series of joint ventures and other investment agreements, Robinson's interest in CCTV became an interest in an English company called United Artists Communications (London South), PLC. United Artists was controlled by Tele Communications, Inc. (TCI) and U.S. West, Inc.

Robinson had sued United Artists in England after representatives of that company tried to force him to trade in his voting stock for nonvoting stock. TCI and U.S. West considered Robinson a thorn in their side, and by 1993, they had decided to negotiate a way to buy him out. Robinson negotiated directly with Stephen Davidson, finance director of TeleWest Communications, PLC, an English company formed by TCI and U.S. West. Robinson alleged that he was directed to negotiate with Davidson by Gary Bryson, a U.S. West executive in Denver, Colorado, and that Davidson was acting on Bryson's authority.

After lengthy negotiations, Robinson and Davidson reached a settlement. Robinson agreed to sell all his stock in United Artists to TCI/U.S. West (a Colorado corporation) in exchange for two payments, one to occur at the time the shares were transferred and one to occur later. Under the first payment, Robinson would receive £790,000. Robinson's second payment was to be based on a valuation of TeleWest at the time its shares were offered to the public.

Robinson's primary concern was that he be paid the full value of his stock. To that end, he said he liked this scheme because Davidson told him that the valuation used to calculate his payment would be the same one used in preparing for the public offering. Thus, because it would be in TCI's and U.S. West's interests to get a high valuation, Robinson felt he was protected from an artificially low estimate.

Robinson received his £790,000 as promised. Then, in preparation for its initial public offering, TeleWest requested a valuation from an English bank. The bank valued TeleWest at $540 million. Robinson alleged that under this valuation his second payment should have been worth $9 million. TeleWest then requested that the bank prepare a second valuation for the purposes of determining the value of Robinson's payments under the settlement. When plugged into the formula, this alternative valuation resulted in a value of zero for the second payment to Robinson.

Robinson alleged that the letter instructing the English bank to do a second valuation was actually drafted by, and faxed from the legal department of, U.S. West. Only later, he alleged, was it put on TeleWest letterhead.

In 1995, Robinson sued TCI, U.S. West, and their affiliated companies, claiming they had defrauded him in violation of Section 10(b) of the Securities Exchange Act of 1934 (the 1934 Act) and Rule 10b-5. The district court dismissed the case for lack of subject matter jurisdiction. Robinson appealed.

ISSUE PRESENTED Does the 1934 Act give U.S. federal courts jurisdiction over a case in which an English citizen alleged securities fraud on the part of an English company when a central act in the alleged fraud was conducted in the United States by an American affiliate of that English company?

(Continued)

(Case 13.1 continued)

SUMMARY OF OPINION The U.S. Court of Appeals for the Fifth Circuit first commented that Robinson's allegations forced it to confront the "rather nebulous issue" of the extent to which the U.S. securities laws may be applied extraterritorially. With one small exception, the 1934 Act does nothing to address the circumstances under which U.S. courts have subject matter jurisdiction to hear suits involving foreign transactions. That exception did not apply in this case. Thus, the court found itself faced with the task of "filling the void" created by a combination of congressional silence and the growth of international commerce since the 1934 Act was passed.

Courts that have previously addressed this problem created two basic tests for jurisdiction: (1) the *effects test,* which asks whether conduct outside the United States has had a substantial adverse effect on American investors or securities markets; and (2) the *conduct test,* which in essence asks whether the fraudulent conduct occurred in the United States. Courts employing the conduct test have advanced two competing strains: the restrictive conduct test states that the domestic conduct must have been of "material importance" to or have "directly caused" the fraud complained of; a more relaxed conduct test requires only that the conduct be significant to the fraud rather than a direct cause of it.

The court applied the restrictive version of the conduct test. It reasoned that because federal courts have limited jurisdiction, "unless a contrary intent appears, [legislation] is meant only to apply within the territorial jurisdiction of the United States." Moreover, the court said, "what little guidance we can glean from the securities statutes indicates that they are designed to protect American investors and markets as opposed to the victims of any fraud that somehow touches the United States."

Applying this restrictive conduct test to the facts at hand, the court found that Robinson's complaints provided a sufficient basis for subject matter jurisdiction. It rejected the district court's rationale, which reasoned that the "lone mailing" of the instruction letter (drafted and initially faxed by U.S. West), "an event occurring months after the allegedly fraudulent inducement, cannot justify the heaving of an entire cause of action . . . across the Atlantic Ocean."

Instead, the court noted that the heart of Robinson's allegation (which the district court ignored) was that the entire scheme was directed and controlled from the United States by TCI and U.S. West. Robinson's basic claim was that the defendants duped him into selling his stock by telling him there would be only one valuation. As a result, the court said, it is self-evident that the act of requesting the second valuation (an act nominally performed by TeleWest, but allegedly directed by U.S. West) was a substantial act in furtherance of the scheme. Thus, the drafting of the instruction letter was more than just tangential to the alleged fraud; "it directly triggered the injury of which Robinson now complains."

RESULT The district court's dismissal of Robinson's claim was reversed, and the case was remanded to the district court. Robinson could sue in a U.S. court for violation of the 1934 Act.

The U.S. Court of Appeals for the Second Circuit reached a different result in a case involving a sale of unregistered foreign securities by an English account manager in the London branch of a French bank to a Panamanian corporation with offices in Monaco that was owned by a Canadian.[9] The account manager had proposed the investment to the Canadian owner while he was in London. The sale was consummated via a series of telephone calls and faxes to the Canadian while he was at his vacation home in Florida. When the investment soured, the Panamanian corporation sued the French bank, a Luxembourg bond fund and its Bahamian manager, and the English account manager in federal district court in New York, asserting violations of the Securities Act of 1933 (the 1933 Act) and the 1934 Act.

9. Europe & Overseas Commodity Traders, S.A. v. Banque Paribas London, 147 F.3d 118 (2d Cir. 1998).

The Second Circuit modified the conduct and effects tests used in extraterritorial securities fraud cases under the 1934 Act by requiring a higher level of activity to support jurisdiction over a case under the 1933 Act. The court held that the 1933 Act's registration provisions should apply only to those offers of unregistered securities that tend to have the effect of creating a market for unregistered securities in the United States.

The court acknowledged that phone calls into the United States conveying an offer to sell securities ordinarily would be sufficient to support jurisdiction for a fraud case. Nonetheless, the court held that "a series of calls to a transient foreign national in the United States is not enough to establish jurisdiction under the conduct test without some additional factor tipping the scales in favor of our jurisdiction." Although reliance on the misrepresentations may have taken place in the United States, "there is no U.S. party to protect or punish." In contrast, the Second Circuit permitted a securities fraud case against a Canadian company to proceed in a U.S. court because the company sold and listed the securities on U.S. stock exchanges and sold a majority of the securities to citizens in the United States.[10]

FORUM NON CONVENIENS

In addition to arguing that a court lacks subject matter jurisdiction because the laws of the nation in which the court sits do not apply outside its borders, defendants often invoke the doctrine of *forum non conveniens,* claiming that the forum chosen by the plaintiff is not convenient. To prevail on a motion to dismiss a case under this doctrine, the defendant must first show that an adequate forum exists. On "rare occasions" the remedy available in the alternative forum may be so unsatisfactory that the forum is inadequate, but the "mere fact that the foreign and home fora have different laws does not ordinarily make the foreign forum inadequate."[11] Indeed, the U.S. Court of Appeals for the Second Circuit has explained:

> Even if particular causes of action or certain desirable remedies are not available in the foreign forum, that forum will usually be adequate so long as it permits litigation of the subject matter of the dispute, provides adequate procedural safeguards and the remedy available in the alternative forum is not so inadequate as to amount to no remedy at all.[12]

Thus, England was deemed an adequate forum even though the Sherman Act and certain common law claims were not available and even though English courts had never awarded money damages in an antitrust case;[13] and Trinidad was adequate despite the likelihood that the plaintiff, who potentially could recover $8 million in the United States, was limited to $570,000 in Trinidad.[14]

After showing the adequacy of the alternative forum, the defendant must demonstrate that the ordinarily strong presumption favoring the plaintiff's chosen forum is countered by public and private interest factors identified by the U.S. Supreme Court in *Gulf Oil Corp. v. Gilbert.*[15] In *Gilbert,* the Supreme Court outlined four public interest factors for courts to weigh in the *forum non conveniens* inquiry: (1) the administrative difficulties associated with court congestion, (2) the unfairness of imposing jury duty on a community with no relation to the litigation, (3) the "local interest in having localized controversies decided at home," and (4) the difficulties inherent in deciding conflict-of-law issues and applying foreign law. The private interest factors enumerated in *Gilbert* include (1) ease of access to evidence; (2) the availability of compulsory process to compel the attendance of unwilling witnesses; (3) the cost of willing witnesses' attendance; (4) if relevant, the possibility of a view of premises; and (5) all other factors that might make a trial quicker or less expensive.

Suing Foreign Governments

Sovereign immunity and the act-of-state doctrine are international legal principles that affect the rights of private commercial parties when a government becomes involved in or interferes with an international commercial transaction.

SOVEREIGN IMMUNITY

The doctrine of *sovereign immunity* prevents the courts of one country from hearing suits against the governments of other countries. The rationale underlying this rule is that all sovereign states are equal, and none may subject others to its laws.

The needs of commerce have gradually tempered this rule. Because private entities often enter into commercial transactions with foreign governments, it became apparent

10. DiRienzo v. Philip Servs. Corp., 232 F.3d 49 (2d Cir. 2000).
11. *Id.*
12. *Id.* at 57.

13. Capital Currency Exch., N.V. v. National Westminster Bank PLC, 155 F.3d 603 (2d Cir. 1998), *cert. denied,* 526 U.S. 1067 (1999).
14. Alcoa S.S. Co. v. M/V Nordic Regent, 654 F.2d 147 (2d Cir. 1980) (en banc).
15. 330 U.S. 501 (1947).

that allowing a government to have complete immunity from all suits was not desirable. Thus, the concept of absolute immunity yielded to the restrictive theory of sovereign immunity, which allows immunity for a government's public activities but not for its commercial activities.

The Foreign Sovereign Immunities Act of 1976 (FSIA) is the U.S. codification of the restrictive theory of immunity. The FSIA was designed to eliminate the inconsistencies associated with politically initiated decisions to grant or withhold sovereign immunity in particular cases. It empowered the courts to determine when sovereign immunity applies, "by reference to the nature of the course of conduct or particular transaction or act."

The FSIA is the sole basis for obtaining jurisdiction over a foreign government in U.S. courts. The FSIA grants a blanket immunity to foreign states except in cases in which (1) the foreign state expressly or impliedly waives its immunity; (2) the foreign state engages in commercial activities; (3) the foreign state expropriates property in violation of international law (that is, seizes it without proper compensation); (4) property in the United States that is immovable or was acquired by gift or succession is at issue; (5) the foreign state commits certain noncommercial torts; (6) suit is brought to enforce a maritime lien under admiralty (that is, maritime) law; and (7) the defendant wishes to file a counterclaim in a suit initiated by the foreign state.

The *commercial activity exception* to sovereign immunity provides that a foreign sovereign or its agencies and instrumentalities shall not be immune from the jurisdiction of the courts of the United States or of the states in any case in which the action is based upon an act (1) outside the territory of the United States in connection with a commercial activity of the foreign sovereign elsewhere (2) that causes a direct effect in the United States. As the U.S. Court of Appeals for the Second Circuit explained: "If the sovereign's activity is commercial in nature and has a direct effect in the United States, then the jurisdictional nexus is met, no immunity attaches, and a district court has the authority to adjudicate disputes based on that activity."[16] For example, in *Argentina v. Weltover*,[17] the U.S. Supreme Court held that Argentina's unilateral rescheduling of bond payments had a "direct effect" in the United States because New York was the place of payment.

The FSIA is particularly relevant to U.S. companies that do or intend to do business with state-owned or state-managed enterprises, such as those in China and Vietnam. The exception from immunity for the commercial activities of these entities may not always be clear. In addition, if the contract is between a foreign, wholly owned subsidiary of a U.S. company and a foreign, state-owned enterprise, the fact that the U.S. parent is affected by a breach of the contract may not give rise to any remedial rights under U.S. law. If the nature of the foreign party to a contract or the subject matter of a contract is not clearly commercial, it may be advisable to require the foreign government to waive sovereign immunity in the contract.

ACT-OF-STATE DOCTRINE

The *act-of-state doctrine* applies to the noncommercial acts of a government that affect foreign business interests within that government's territory. The doctrine was most clearly expressed by the U.S. Supreme Court in *Underhill v. Hernandez*,[18] when it stated that "the courts of one country will not sit in judgment on the acts of the government of another, done within its own territory." Pursuant to this doctrine, U.S. courts are extremely reluctant to provide a legal remedy under U.S. law for the public acts of a foreign government. As a result, U.S. businesses generally cannot look to the U.S. courts for protection from or compensation for acts such as expropriation unless there is a bilateral treaty between the United States and the foreign country that specifies the procedural and substantive rights of a U.S. investor in that country. As mentioned earlier, however, OPIC (the Overseas Private Investment Corporation) will insure U.S. businesses against certain host government acts, such as expropriation or restrictions on the conversion of local currency earnings.

 # U.S. Domestic Considerations

A number of U.S. laws and business practices directly or indirectly affect U.S. investment abroad.

TRADE LAWS

If a U.S. investor in a foreign manufacturing facility wishes to market its foreign-manufactured products in the United States, it will face many of the same trade restrictions that are imposed on other foreign manufacturers seeking to export to the United States. In addition, if exports to the United States are a primary goal, the U.S. investor abroad should consider the advantages of preferential programs

16. Commercial Bank of Kuwait v. Rafidain Bank, 15 F.3d 238 (2d Cir. 1994).
17. 504 U.S. 607 (1992).

18. 168 U.S. 250, 252 (1897).

such as the North American Free Trade Agreement. (Trade laws are discussed in Chapter 12.)

PRODUCT-SAFETY STANDARDS

Exports to the United States may have to originate in facilities certified by the U.S. government or be produced according to U.S. government standards. For example, pharmaceutical products exported to the United States must be produced in facilities that adhere to the manufacturing practices established by the U.S. Food and Drug Administration. Airplanes built abroad for use in U.S. airspace must be built according to Federal Aviation Administration (FAA) standards in FAA-certified facilities. Investment contracts for such export projects need to reflect the production standards required by U.S. law.

Foreign-based U.S. manufacturers, like domestic U.S. manufacturers, need to be aware of U.S. product liability law (discussed in Chapter 10) and product standards (discussed in Chapter 21). Developing countries are increasingly enacting manufacturing safety standards and rules of manufacturer liability. Events such as the Bhopal disaster in India (discussed in Chapter 1) have shown that foreign-based U.S. investors cannot avoid liability solely by compliance with local standards.

EXPORT LICENSING

Foreign-investment projects that involve U.S. technology may be subject to licensing and reexport restrictions imposed by the Export Administration Act or the Arms Export Control Act (both discussed in Chapter 12). These restrictions can extend to the technical training of foreign technicians in the United States. Noncompliance penalties can be severe.

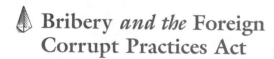

Bribery *and the* Foreign Corrupt Practices Act

As discussed in Chapter 1, bribery of public officials to secure favorable treatment is widespread.

FOREIGN CORRUPT PRACTICES ACT

Following the discovery that more than 400 American corporations had paid bribes or made questionable payments abroad, the United States enacted the Foreign Corrupt Practices Act (FCPA)[19] in 1977 as an amend-

19. 15 U.S.C. §§ 78a–78LLL (1988).

ment to the Securities Exchange Act of 1934 (the 1934 Act). The bribes in question were often given to high-ranking foreign officials to secure contracts with the foreign government. Bribes were also given to low-ranking officials to expedite the granting of routine requests, such as applications for permission to import or export.

Prohibited Payments The FCPA prohibits any payment by a company, its employees, or its agents directly or indirectly to a foreign government official or a foreign political party for the purpose of improperly influencing government decisions in order to obtain business abroad. The statute is violated even if the bribe is only offered but never paid. It is also violated if the payment is made to a private company or individual with the knowledge that it will be funneled to the government.

An exception is made for payments to low-ranking officials who merely expedite the nondiscretionary granting of a permit or license. If any of the allegedly nondiscretionary tasks paid for are in fact discretionary, however, the American company will be in violation of the FCPA. A second exception is made for payments to foreign businesses, as long as they are not acting as conduits for the money to pass to the foreign government.

A troublesome clause of the FCPA prohibited payments to third persons (such as local agents) with "reason to know" that the payment would be passed on to a government official or political party. This standard was considered by many to be unacceptably vague for a criminal statute. The Omnibus Trade Act amended this clause to prohibit such payments only when they are made with actual knowledge or a willful disregard of the fact that they will be used in violation of the law.

Directors, officers, employees, or agents of the corporation who willfully violate this portion of the FCPA are subject to a $100,000 fine and up to five years in prison; the corporation can be fined up to $2 million or, if greater, twice its profits from the illegal activity. The FCPA is administered by both the Department of Justice and the Securities and Exchange Commission.

Record-Keeping Requirements The record-keeping requirements of the FCPA apply to all public companies that file periodic reports with the Securities and Exchange Commission under the 1934 Act. A purely domestic public company that is not engaged in foreign trade must still comply with the FCPA's record-keeping requirements.

The FCPA requires each corporation to keep records that accurately reflect the dispositions of the company's assets and to implement internal controls to ensure that the corporation's transactions are completed as authorized by management. Periodic reports must be filed.

VIEW FROM CYBERSPACE

French Court Orders Yahoo! *to* Block Access *to* Nazi Memorabilia

A case decided by Judge Jean-Jacques Gomez of the Superior Court of Paris on November 20, 2000, sparked new debate about which country's laws should govern the inherently global reach of the Internet. The lawsuit was brought by two groups in France, the International League Against Racism and Anti-Semitism and the Union of French Jewish Students, against California-based Yahoo! Inc. They claimed that Yahoo! had violated the French law against exhibiting or selling objects with racist overtones by hosting online auctions of Nazi memorabilia such as Nazi uniforms and SS badges. The French-language portal www.yahoo.fr did not carry the auctions, but Web surfers in France could easily access the U.S. site and view the Nazi items for sale.

Judge Gomez called the auctions "an offence to the collective memory of the country,"[a] and on May 22, 2000, he ordered Yahoo! to block French surfers from the English-language auctions. After Yahoo! claimed that it was technologically impossible to block access, the French court appointed a panel of experts to report on the feasibility of blocking access. The experts advised the French court that no system was fail-safe but that it was possible to block up to 90 percent of French surfers. The November 20 court order gave Yahoo! three months to find and implement a technological means to prevent Web surfers in France from accessing the Web pages featuring Nazi memorabilia or face fines of $13,000 for each day past the deadline it failed to comply.[b]

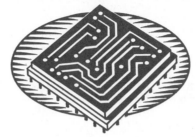

The sites are protected under U.S. law by the First Amendment's guarantee of free speech. Critics of the decision argue that it "is an alarming example of a foreign court's willingness to impose its national law on the activities of a U.S.-based Web site"; they claim that under Judge Gomez's logic, "any Web site with global reach could be subject to the jurisdiction of every nation on earth."[c] Supporters of the court's ruling called it "perfectly reasonable under the circumstances" and a "welcome harbinger of things to come."[d]

Yahoo! faced similar charges in Germany in connection with alleged sales of *Mein Kampf,* Adolf Hitler's manifesto, which is banned in Germany.[e] In January 2001, Yahoo! announced that it was banning the auction of items associated with racial hatred, including Nazi, neo-Nazi, and Ku Klux Klan materials.

On December 12, 2000, the Bundesgerichtshof, Germany's highest court, ruled that German legislation enacted in the wake of World War II that bans the Nazi party and its glorification—including denial of the Holocaust—can be applied to non-Germans who post content on the Web in other countries if that content can be accessed by people inside Germany.[f] The Court found Frederick Töben guilty

of spreading "Auschwitz lies." Töben, who emigrated from Germany to Australia when he was ten years old, used the Web site of his Australian-based Adelaide Institute to challenge the historical basis of the Holocaust. Töben could face up to five years in prison if he returned to Germany. Andy Mueller-Maguhn, a leader of Berlin's Chaos Computer hacker collective, who is regarded as a technology visionary in Germany, characterized the ruling as "the worst Internet-dependent court decision so far," and warned, "If other countries would take this as an orientation and start to apply their laws on the citizens of other countries acting in their countries, the worldwide free flow of information could lead very fast to an unfree situation in the real world."[g] Rabbi Abraham Cooper, Associate Dean of the Simon Wiesenthal Center in Los Angeles, commended the German authorities "for sticking to their commitment," saying, "It was their blood that was shed. What's theoretical for us is very real over there . . . the Internet community is going to have to address these issues in a less contentious way."[h]

a. *France Could Block Most Nazi Web Sites—Experts,* YAHOO! NEWS, Nov. 6, 2000.
b. Carl S. Kaplan, *Ruling on Nazi Memorabilia Sparks Legal Debate,* N.Y. TIMES, Nov. 24, 2000.
c. *Id.*
d. *Id.*
e. Steve Gold, *Germany Probes Yahoo Sale of 'Mein Kampf,'* NEWSBYTES, Nov. 28, 2000.
f. Steve Kettmann, *German Hate Law: No Denying It,* WIRED NEWS (Dec. 15, 2000).
g. *Id.*
h. *Id.*

Failure to maintain the appropriate records and procedures is a violation, whether or not a bribe is paid. This portion of the FCPA was designed to prevent companies from developing a slush fund and then accounting for questionable payments as legitimate business expenses. The record-keeping provisions of the FCPA do not contain any specific penalties. Violations are punished in accordance with the basic criminal and civil sanctions under the 1934 Act, discussed in Chapter 17.

OECD Convention Since 1977, when the United States became the first major industrial country to ban bribes, it has encouraged other countries to adopt similar prohibitions. The United States scored a major victory when it helped persuade the Organization for Economic Cooperation and Development (OECD) and its members to adopt the international convention on bribery, discussed in Chapter 1.

THE RESPONSIBLE MANAGER
Managing International Business Transactions

Managing an international business transaction, whether it be a sale, a license of intellectual property, or an equity investment, requires all the skills needed for a comparable domestic transaction and more. A broad range of foreign and domestic factors—legal, economic, social, and political—complicates the transaction. Managers in a multinational business environment must keep these factors in mind but cannot afford to suspend their critical objectivity and commitment to the underlying goals of the transaction. The transaction manager should be inquisitive but tactful, broad in scope of analysis but focused in attention.

A U.S. business entity is subject to the business and ethical expectations of its management, shareholders, and customers. It is also subject to both U.S. and foreign laws. All of these may constrain the extent to which the transaction manager can achieve the project goals.

Buying, selling, and investing abroad begin with identification of the project goals, which are often broader than those for transactions in the home market. "Penetrating new markets," "establishing a presence," and "going international" are fine-sounding goals that need to be embodied in a concrete business and operational plan. Without sound and achievable goals, transnational ventures can quickly go wrong, incurring significant costs in the process. Financial goals can be defeated by unexpected costs and efficiency problems. Profit repatriation can be frustrated by currency inconvertibility or foreign-exchange restrictions. Historically successful marketing strategies can fail under local conditions. Expectations for labor productivity can prove sadly optimistic. The objectives of local agents, management, or partners can diverge from those of the U.S. company.

In many countries, a business does not have the freedom of crafting a contract within the broad field of permissible business terms that businesses in the United States enjoy. Developing countries, in particular, impose restrictions on issues that most U.S. businesses are used to treating as freely negotiable. The laws of these countries are not merely default rules that need only be consulted to fine-tune a done deal or fill in gaps. They are often intended to define the principal parameters of an acceptable transaction. At the same time, they often provide incentives for certain types of transactions.

A manager will often begin with an analysis of the foreign-investment laws of the host country. Provisions of bilateral investment and tax treaties with the United States will also be relevant to crafting permissible project terms, incentives, and remedies. The manager cannot stop there, however, but must pursue the due-diligence investigation of host country conditions by inquiring into the full range of potential legal and practical issues that might arise. Failure to do so can lead to embarrassment, costlier and more extended negotiations, and failure of project goals. The transaction manager is often the *only* person whose responsibility is broad enough to discover and address some of the complications that may arise.

Early use of professional services, such as those offered by legal counsel, accountants, and banking advisers with experience in the industry and the appropriate culture, can reduce negotiation costs, minimize the risk of disputes, and help prevent later surprises. Although reliable advice is needed in the domestic context as well, it is far more critical in the international context, where physical and cultural separation, travel burdens, linguistic differences, and different sets of default expectations can more easily lead to misunderstandings and disputes. Advisers can help frame the early discussion goals so as to avoid early commitments that later prove regrettable and perhaps suggest other terms that are easier to nail down favorably in the early stages of negotiation.

The choice of governing language and the selection of the party who will draft and revise the agreements to reflect the negotiations are often critical. Even if both sides negotiate the deal points thoroughly, the party who controls the documents obtains an incremental benefit that is well known to every experienced lawyer. Managers should not allow the other side to assume control of the drafting as if it were a matter of little importance. By involving the firm's lawyer early in the process, a manager can propose that the lawyer prepare the first draft, which is often a negotiating advantage.

The applicable substantive law and the choice of a forum for resolving disputes are two legal questions that managers should try to resolve favorably early on rather than later, when the other side may treat these issues as major rather than minor concessions. By preparing the first draft, a party can get its preferred terms into the contract and not let the other side take the local law and forum for granted (although one may ultimately have to concede the point under local law or for other reasons). Arbitration of disputes by a specialized forum may be more efficient and offer more confidentiality than litigation in a public court, but it may not adhere to judicial precedents, and an award may not be easily enforceable (although arbitration awards can be more easily enforceable than court judgments in countries that are signatories to the New York Convention).

In U.S. domestic business transactions, various vehicles are available to ensure that each party will perform the contract or will compensate the other party for failure to perform. U.S. laws offer a relatively sophisticated array of contractual and statutory remedies. Foreign laws may offer fewer established options. Even when effective remedies are nominally available, their use may not be practical under the legal and administrative system of the foreign country. The capable international manager needs to know the legal and practical remedies available in the host country if the other party fails to perform. Fortunately, third-party alternatives such as guaranties and L/Cs are also available.

Managers or their advisers should be thoroughly familiar with all applicable exchange controls and restrictions, and the transaction manager should fully understand the effect of exchange-rate fluctuations from both the economic and the accounting perspectives. These fluctuations affect product pricing, capital contribution and distribution formulas of the respective parties, and financial results. It is also crucial to know what repatriable earnings are available from a foreign investment, a licensing transaction, or even the sale of products or services abroad.

Although the manager's focus will be on conditions in the host country, he or she will probably also be responsible for evaluating the impact of U.S. laws, ranging from tax and product liability laws to administrative regula-

tions governing the certification of imported products. Some U.S. laws, such as the Foreign Corrupt Practices Act and the antitrust laws, affect the conduct of transactions occurring outside the United States. Having legal counsel with experience in the relevant types of international transactions available in at least a consultative capacity is indispensable.

The manager may be put in the unenviable position of having to reconcile the sometimes conflicting ethical standards of two or more cultures. For example, in some cultures, offering a gift—ranging from a token company lapel pin to an expensive automobile—is an expected courtesy. In other cultures (and under the U.S. Foreign Corrupt Practices Act), gift giving, however innocently intended, may be viewed as an improper attempt to influence a business decision. A U.S. business may feel hamstrung by its inability, for legal or ethical reasons, to match a competitor's gift or offer of "training"—in effect an all-expenses-paid vacation abroad—for employees of its foreign counterpart. The existence of relevant company policies or U.S. laws barring such actions, however, can give a manager a face-saving, nonoffensive way to decline to engage in unethical behavior.

Under pressure to make the deal happen, a manager may be tempted to go beyond what is legally permissible and accept the "practical" solution on the grounds that everyone does it. As foreign visitors, however, U.S. companies and their personnel are at particular risk of being held up as public examples of unacceptable behavior if there is a political, and perhaps business, reason for doing so. Behavior acceptable for locals is not necessarily acceptable for Americans. Nationalism, regionalism, and competitive advantage are all reasons for focusing a spotlight on U.S. businesses.

Responsibly fulfilling all of these roles ultimately requires sensitivity, flexibility, and creativity. It requires familiarity with the technical needs of the project as well as practical business skill and experience. It also requires strength of character and maturity. Strength of character is needed to keep centered on the goals of the transaction rather than being swept away by deal momentum and the pressure of participants with narrower interests. Strength of character permits a manager to be receptive to foreign ways of doing things without compromising the standards of the home company or the manager's own professionalism and integrity. Maturity provides the flexibility and security needed to recognize one's own limitations and to accept advice and other input from a wide range of professionals and other participants.

Restructuring *the* Socialist Economies *of* Eastern Europe

Postsocialist Eastern European societies had no historical models for the transition from a command economy to a fully functioning market economy, although the experiences of Chile, Taiwan, and Korea provided some guidelines. As a consequence of the lack of models and local political cross-currents generated by the unsettling effect of change on existing social and economic structures, the transformation process was one of experimentation and proceeded at a sometimes slow and uneven pace. Nonetheless, on the whole, the transformation occurred with startling speed and thoroughness. The states of Eastern Europe (other than many of the republics of the former Soviet Union) have more or less reached Western standards in terms of legal and regulatory frameworks and have achieved an economic level roughly comparable to that of less affluent Western countries. Hungary, Poland, and the Czech Republic have joined the North Atlantic Treaty Organization (NATO) and are serious candidates for European Union (EU) membership early in the twenty-first century. Estonia is now one of the freest markets in Europe and, with Slovenia, has been mentioned as a potential EU member.

These economies can be evaluated on terms similar to those used for other European countries, but special attention should be paid to the degree of internal consensus and commitment to free markets. One must also ask how well they are coping with the negative aspects of postsocialist transition. These include widespread corruption, excessive influence of Mafia-type organizations, weak environmental protections, weak and inequitable tax-collection systems, rapidly evolving laws and regulations, and loose norms of social and business behavior.

State subsidization and at least indirect control of some portions of the economy remain typical. Price controls and exchange controls exist in some countries, but these were common in other European countries as well prior to the EU taking hold in earnest after 1992. Political instability, in terms of which political party is in power and whether it tends toward capitalism or social welfarism, is also familiar elsewhere in Europe. Unemployment is another trans-European issue. Nowhere, except perhaps in Belarus and Ukraine, are there prospects of a change of power that would turn back the clock to communism.

The former Soviet Union has encountered the most difficulty in making the transition toward a market economy. It has greater ethnic diversity, greater geographic distances with which to contend, greater diversity of political opinion, and less historical familiarity with the workings of a market economy than the Eastern European nations. Often preoccupied with political issues, Russia has lagged behind in the transition but has still made enormous progress. Substantial privatization has occurred (though not without controversy). However, the devaluation of the ruble and the Russian stock market crash in August 1998 caused a financial and political crisis. Elected in the wake of that crisis, President Vladimir Putin has slowed Russia's transformation into a capitalist market economy and could, in the future, steer it closer to its communist past.

Nevertheless, the material wealth of Russia and the other republics of the former Soviet Union makes them attractive for investors looking for bargains in undervalued assets. It is a matter of business judgment as to how much of any perceived discount represents a true bargain and how much reflects the inherent risks.

KEY WORDS AND PHRASES

QUESTIONS AND CASE PROBLEMS

1. Voest-Alpine Trading USA Corporation entered into a contract with Jiangyin Foreign Trade Corporation (JFTC) to sell JFTC 1,000 metric tons of styrene monomer at a total price of $1.2 million. To finance the transaction, JFTC obtained a letter of credit for the benefit of Voest-Alpine through the Bank of China. The L/C required payment to Voest-Alpine once the goods had been shipped to Zhangjiagang, China, upon presentation to the Bank of China of the paperwork described in the L/C. The L/C indicated that the transaction would be subject to the UCP. By the time the product was ready to ship, the market price of styrene monomer had dropped significantly from the original contract price between Voest-Alpine and JFTC. JFTC requested a price concession from Voest-Alpine in light of the change in market conditions, but Voest-Alpine declined and went ahead with the shipment.

   In addition to numerous other typographical errors, the L/C listed Voest-Alpine's name as "Voest-Alpine USA Trading Corp." instead of "Voest-Alpine Trading USA Corp." The destination port was also misspelled in one place as "Zhangjiagng," missing the third "a." After JFTC proved unwilling to waive the discrepancies, the Bank of China refused to honor the L/C. Was the Bank of China's dishonor proper? Was JFTC's conduct ethical? Should Voest-Alpine have reduced the contract price when the market price dropped? [*Voest-Alpine Trading USA Corp. v. Bank of China*, 2000 U.S. Dist. LEXIS 8223 (S.D. Tex. 2000). *Compare Hanil Bank v. Pt. Bank Negara Indonesia (Per sero)*, 2000 U.S. Dist. LEXIS 2444 (S.D.N.Y. 2000).]

2. The New England Petroleum Corporation (NEPCO), a U.S. corporation, obtained refined oil from its wholly owned Bahamas subsidiary refinery, PETCO. In 1968, PETCO entered into a long-term contract to purchase crude oil from Chevron Oil Trading (Chevron), a branch of a petroleum company that held 50 percent of an oil concession in Libya. In 1973, Libya nationalized several foreign-owned oil concessions, including Chevron's. As a result, Chevron terminated its contract with PETCO.

   PETCO then entered into a new contract with the National Oil Corporation, which was wholly owned by the Libyan government. One month after execution of the contract, Libya imposed an oil embargo on the United States, and National canceled its contract with PETCO. Three months later, after a dramatic increase in oil prices, PETCO executed a new contract with National. National allegedly breached that contract as well.

   PETCO's assignee, Carey, brought suit against National, seeking to recover damages for National's breach of the two contracts. National raised the defense of sovereign immunity. Carey claimed that there was no sovereign immunity under the Foreign Sovereign Immunities Act because the breach of contract was an act outside the territory of the United States in connection with a commercial activity that caused a direct effect in the United States. Who should prevail? [*Carey v. National Oil Corp.*, 592 F.2d 673 (2d Cir. 1979)]

3. Heatwave, Inc. is a New York corporation that manufactures a highly advanced electronic instrument to measure the heat generated by electric motors operating at high speeds. The instrument has a variety of civilian and military applications. Although it can be run with different software packages available in the market, Heatwave has developed special software that it feels is superior to that of its competitors and that Heatwave claims gives a more accurate reading on the instrument. Heatwave's management is extremely proud of the company's reputation as the world leader in this type of instrument and vigilantly guards against infringement of its proprietary technology and its trade name. Heatwave has a number of U.S. patents on both the instrument and the software. In addition, it uses a federally registered trademark on all its products.

   Heatwave would like to expand the production and sale of the instrument overseas. It is looking at a number of countries in both Europe and the Far East as possible markets, and it is considering using one of the following vehicles for its overseas activities: (1) licensing its technology to a foreign entity in exchange for a royalty, (2) setting up a branch in the foreign country to produce and sell the products locally, (3) establishing a wholly owned foreign subsidiary to produce and sell the products locally, or (4) establishing a joint venture with a local company to produce and sell the products locally.

Heatwave wants to protect its market in the United States and in certain foreign countries in which it is currently making direct sales. It is also concerned about maintaining the instrument's reputation for high quality. Therefore, Heatwave would like to restrict sales of the instrument to the local market and to require that a copy of its software be sold with each sale of the instrument. Regardless of the investment vehicle used, all rights to the software would remain with Heatwave.

a. What U.S. laws may have an impact on whether and how Heatwave expands overseas?

b. What local foreign laws may have an impact on Heatwave's decision on the type of vehicle it chooses to conduct its overseas activities and on the country into which it may expand?

4. Optomagic, Inc. is a U.S. corporation that produces optomagic gizmos. Production of optomagic gizmos involves a confidential gizmo-processing technique (which is described in printed confidential Optomagic manuals), labor-intensive processing, and inclusion of an optomagic component for which Optomagic was granted a U.S. patent six months ago. The optomagic component has widespread uses in the space, aviation, and medical industries.

Eight months ago, in the African country of Varoom, a relatively peaceful popular uprising resulted in the removal of the "old guard" leaders, who had favored a strong, centrally planned economy. The new provisional government called for free elections in one year, began taking immediate steps to reform the economy, and promised to liberalize foreign-investment laws to attract foreign investors.

Because the government bureaucracy is still in some disarray, it is extremely helpful, as a practical matter, to have close contacts with a government official who can speed the review and approval process for applications for foreign investment. During a recent official tour of the United States, Dr. Segun Ayantuga, the Varoomian minister of health and welfare, visited Optomagic's manufacturing facility in Boston, Massachusetts. Ayantuga is an eminent surgeon and a strong proponent of bringing advanced medical technology to his developing country so that the best medical care can be made available to the public. In addition, to earn badly needed foreign exchange for Varoom, he is interested in finding labor-intensive U.S. industries that may be able to produce products in Varoom for export to the more developed countries. Optomagic is very interested in the newly emerging markets of Africa, and in Varoom in particular. Optomagic would also like to obtain gizmonium, a raw material necessary for the production of optomagic gizmos, which is found in great abundance in the mountains of Varoom, but which, under Varoomian law, is available only to Varoomian enterprises.

Two weeks after his visit to Optomagic, Ayantuga wrote to the chief executive officer of Optomagic to make the following proposal. Ayantuga and a state-owned medical clinic, Varoom Medical, are interested in establishing a joint venture in Varoom with Optomagic. Current Varoomian law limits foreign-investment interests in Varoomian enterprises to 50 percent of the total investment. Ayantuga states that, although under local law the Varoomian partners would share equal responsibility for the management of the venture, they would in fact defer to Optomagic in all material matters related to the operation of the manufacturing facility. In addition, Ayantuga assures Optomagic that the foreign-investment law is likely to be liberalized within the year. As his investment in the venture, Ayantuga offers to contribute his lease interest in certain property in Varoom and to ensure that all the necessary government permits for the construction and licensing of the facility are obtained. Ayantuga expresses his confidence in being able to obtain all the government approvals for the proposed project because "our government has recently issued a decree emphasizing the national importance of upgrading our health care industries."

The father of Optomagic's CEO emigrated from Varoom sixty years ago. He is excited about the developments in Varoom and finds Ayantuga to be a delightful, dynamic man. He is convinced that Optomagic should move into Varoom now, before its competitors do.

Your assignment is to put together a business plan for the proposed joint venture, assuming that it's going to cost something up front but will be worth the expense in the long run. The CEO wants a preliminary report in two weeks to take to the board of directors, which will be considering establishing a wholly owned subsidiary in Cairo to operate prospective sales and manufacturing facilities in Africa. He also wants a comprehensive report to follow in another four weeks.

a. You have full access to your expert in-house legal counsel, who has experience in international projects. How can you best use her to assist in putting your plan together? What issues of particular importance should be addressed by counsel for inclusion in the preliminary report?

b. Given the uncertainty in the development of Varoom's foreign-investment laws (and its government), what types of terms or conditions do you think should be included in the contract for the proposed joint venture to protect against unexpected changes in the laws or government policies? What is your evaluation of the desirability of other forms of protection?

5. Assume the facts in Question 4. Are there any legal problems with including Ayantuga as an investor in the project? As a paid consultant?

6. Upon further general inquiry on behalf of Optomagic, you learn the following facts in addition to those set forth in Question 4. First, Varoom has a patent law and a trademark-registration law and is a signatory of the Paris and Madrid Conventions, but it has no copyright law. Second, Varoomian law provides that licenses of foreign technology cannot (1) unreasonably restrict the geographic market for such exports, (2) require that the Varoomian party purchase components or raw materials from the foreign party, or (3) restrict use of the technology by the Varoomian licensee beyond a term of ten years without approval from the supervising ministry (which in this case is the Ministry of Health).

What other information do you need to determine how best to protect Optomagic's intellectual property rights in the proposed venture? Based on what you do know, what steps should be taken to maximize protection of Optomagic's intellectual property rights? What U.S. laws will apply to the contribution, licensing, or other transfer of optomagic gizmo components by Optomagic to the joint venture? What license and joint venture contract terms are important to obtain?

7. Assume the facts in Question 4. Varoom Medical is prepared to invest 950 million baninis (U.S. $1 = 1,000 baninis) over the first five years of the project. Its commitment will be backed by a standby letter of credit to be issued by the National People's Bank of Varoom, a state-owned bank.

a. What more do you need to know about the proposed capital contribution to be made by Varoom Medical and the standby L/C from the bank? Would you impose any additional conditions or requirements on the proposed contribution and the L/C?

b. What do you propose Optomagic contribute as its share of capital to the proposed joint venture?

What factors do you need to consider to make that decision?

8. Assume the facts in Question 4. You begin to consider the labor force that the joint venture will need. Ayantuga suggests that the venture technicians should make regular technical training visits to Optomagic's facility in Boston, Massachusetts. Ayantuga also suggests that he can arrange to select the Varoomian technicians for the joint venture. Monthly salaries in Varoom for the relevant types of workers are 70 percent lower than in the United States. However, Varoom's labor laws require that all enterprises (1) provide employees with housing and health insurance subsidies equal to 50 percent of their salaries; (2) engage in mandatory arbitration with the local labor bureau prior to termination of any employee for any reason; and (3) in the case of foreign-invested enterprises, pay local managers salaries and benefits comparable to those of the expatriate management personnel of the foreign-invested enterprise.

a. How would you assess the legal and economic advantages and disadvantages of the employees that Ayantuga proposed be hired?

b. Is there another way to structure the workforce?

c. What U.S. laws may apply to the training of joint venture technicians at Optomagic's U.S. facilities?

d. Would you recommend that resident expatriate management personnel, or just visiting technicians, be assigned to the prospective project? Why? What qualities do you think an expatriate employee in Varoom should have?

9. In addition to the facts covered in Questions 4 through 8, you learn that the banini is not freely convertible into dollars. The Varoom foreign-exchange and tax laws provide that a foreign-invested joint venture can repatriate up to 50 percent of its foreign-exchange earnings, subject to a repatriation tax of 15 percent (in addition to the tax imposed on the joint venture's income). Banini profits can be exchanged only upon prior approval by the supervising ministry (each ministry is allocated a quota of baninis for which it can approve an exchange into foreign currencies). In addition, Varoom's foreign-investment law requires that foreign-invested enterprises export a minimum of 50 percent of their products.

a. What alternatives exist to repatriating foreign-currency earnings in the prospective venture?

b. What U.S. laws, if any, might apply to exports of optomagic gizmos to the United States from Varoom?

10. Domingo Castro Alfaro, a Costa Rican resident and employee of Standard Fruit Company, and eighty-one other Costa Rican employees and their wives brought suit against Dow Chemical Company and Shell Oil Company. The employees claimed that while they were working on a banana plantation in Costa Rica for Standard Fruit Company, they suffered personal injuries as a result of exposure to dibromochloropropane (DBCP). DBCP is a pesticide manufactured by Dow and Shell, which allegedly was furnished to Standard Fruit. Standard Fruit is an American subsidiary of Dole Fresh Fruit Company, headquartered in Boca Raton, Florida. The employees exposed to DBCP allegedly suffered several medical problems, including sterility.

After the U.S. Environmental Protection Agency (EPA) banned DBCP in the United States, Shell and Dow apparently shipped several hundred thousand gallons of the pesticide to Costa Rica for use by Standard Fruit. Alfaro sued Dow and Shell in Texas in April 1984, alleging that their handling of DBCP caused the employees serious personal injuries for which Shell and Dow were liable under the theories of product liability, strict liability, and breach of warranty. Under the doctrine of *forum non conveniens,* the defendants argued that Texas was not a convenient forum in which to litigate this case. Should the court grant the defendant's motion to dismiss? Was the conduct of Dow Chemical and Shell Oil ethical? Was Standard Fruit's use of the U.S.-banned pesticide ethical? Were the defendants arguing inconvenient forum to avoid a jury trial and Texas laws regarding personal injury and wrongful death? If so, is that ethical? If goods are not consistent with some sets of standards but are basically OK, is it ethical to sell them? If they are dangerous, how dangerous is too dangerous? Should it matter that consumers in a developing country may not be able to afford products meeting higher but more expensive Western standards? [*Dow Chemical Co. v. Alfaro,* 786 S.W.2d 674 (Tex. 1990)]

INTERNET SOURCES

The full text of the European Commission's proposed electronic signatures directive is available on the European Union's Web site.	http://europa.eu.int/comm/dg15/en/media/ infso/sign.htm
This site, maintained by Professor Ray August at Washington State University, provides updates on international business law.	http://www.wsu.edu:8080/~legal/ibl
This site, maintained by C. Matthew Schulz of Baker & McKenzie, includes a "What's New?" link to information on visas and immigration.	http://www.schulzlaw.com
The International Trade Law Monitor site offers search potential and links to a comprehensive array of documents.	http://itl.irv.uit.no/trade_law
LawCrawler provides international law searching by country domains.	http://www.lawcrawler.com
The International Chamber of Commerce site provides information about doing business internationally and news alerts.	http://www.iccwbo.org/

Human Resources *in the* Legal *and* Regulatory Environment

CHAPTER 14

The Employment Agreement

EMPLOYEE RIGHTS, POWERS, AND PROTECTION

Over the past seventy years, there has been an explosion in laws regulating the employment relationship. As a result of the union movement, employees acquired economic and political power in their dealings with employers. With the emergence of the civil rights movement and the antidiscrimination legislation of the 1960s, employers began to examine their hiring and other employment practices more closely with respect to the treatment of women, minorities, and other protected groups. New laws concerning worker safety and employee pensions and other benefit plans challenged employers to make the workplace safer and the receipt of promised benefits more certain. Federal and state *whistle-blower statutes* prohibited retaliation against employees who complained to a governmental agency about working conditions that they believed violated the law.

The courts developed new doctrines that limit the employer's traditional right to discharge an employee. These judicial decisions recognized implied contractual obligations to show just cause for a discharge. Indeed, under the current law, an employer may be bound by contracts with its employees without even knowing it. Managers must devote an ever-increasing amount of attention and resources to complying with the sometimes bewildering array of statutes, regulations, and common law principles that bear upon their relations with their employees.

CHAPTER OVERVIEW

This chapter discusses the traditional rule that employees can be terminated at will and the exceptions that have developed in recent years, including wrongful termination based on a violation of public policy, breach of an implied contract, and breach of the implied covenant of good faith and fair dealing. It also examines the tort of fraudulent inducement and the enforceability of covenants not to compete. The laws relating to drug testing, genetic testing, lie detector tests, and certain hiring practices are also addressed. The chapter explains the employer's responsibility for worker safety and the system of workers' compensation, including the minimum wage and overtime payments.

The chapter then discusses the Employee Retirement Income Security Act of 1974 (ERISA), which governs employer-sponsored pensions and employee benefit plans (including employer-sponsored health maintenance organizations). It concludes with a brief discussion of the federal laws regarding the continuation of employee benefit plan coverage after an employee leaves, the eligibility of new employees for health coverage without an exception for preexisting conditions, and the advance notice required for plant closings and mass layoffs. Chapter 15 describes the major pieces of civil rights legislation that prohibit discrimination. Chapter 16 outlines the labor-relation laws applicable to unionized workers and their employers.

At-Will Employment

Most nonunionized American workers have no written employment contract. They are hired for a job without any express agreement as to how long the job will last. For at least the last hundred years, the American rule has been that an employment agreement of indefinite duration is an *at-will contract;* that is, the employee can quit at any time, and the employer can discharge the employee at any time, for any or no reason, with or without notice. Whether by statute or judicial decision, all states originally followed this rule. The courts reasoned that denying the employer the right to discharge its employee, while the employee was at liberty to quit at any time for any reason, would deprive the employer of property without due process of law. Today, however, in many states, the at-will rule has been largely buried under its exceptions. Although some courts have declined to recognize these exceptions to the at-will doctrine, the trend is toward some level of protection against discharge in certain circumstances. Employers are well advised to consider whether the reasons for any termination will pass muster as "good cause."

EMPLOYEES NOT SUBJECT TO THE AT-WILL RULE

Public employees and employees who negotiated express contracts with their employers have generally not been subject to the at-will rule.

Public Employees Most employees of federal, state, and local government agencies have long worked under civil service or merit systems that provide for tenure, require just cause for discharge, and guarantee administrative procedures to determine whether there is just cause for discharge.

Employees with Individual Contracts A private-sector employee can avoid at-will status by negotiating a contract that provides for a specific term of employment and defines how the contract can be terminated. Employers will almost always reserve the right to fire an employee, but the employment contract will usually require the employer to provide some level of severance pay if the termination was without cause. For example, a contract might give an employee with a three-year contract, who is fired without cause at the end of the first year, the right to salary and benefits for the remaining two years. In some cases, but not all, the

amount due is reduced by any monies the employee receives from another employer. Negotiated contracts requiring just cause for termination by the employer usually provide some level of payment and benefits if the employee quits "for good reason." This is often defined to include being required to move more than fifty miles from the original place of employment or having one's duties and responsibilities substantially changed or reduced. Persons in professional or managerial positions are more likely to be able to negotiate individual contracts with such provisions.

Union Contracts Other employees rely on union contracts, which almost universally require just cause for termination and establish arbitration procedures whereby an employee can challenge his or her discharge.

 Wrongful Discharge

Beginning in the early 1970s, courts in a number of states began to recognize new causes of action for *wrongful discharge,* that is, termination of employment without good cause. Wrongful discharge is a common-law-based claim supported by three theories: public policy, implied contract, and implied covenant of good faith.

These causes of action are based on both contract and tort law. Although the line between wrongful discharge and fraud is not always clear, each claim receives different damages. The former gives rise only to contract damages, whereas the latter gives rise to personal-injury and punitive damages. However, even this distinction is hazy. Thus, some wrongful-discharge plaintiffs may be able to collect damages for emotional distress and punitive damages, not simply lost wages.

THE PUBLIC POLICY EXCEPTION

One of the earliest exceptions to the at-will rule was the *public policy exception.* Even if an individual is an at-will employee, in most states, the employer is prohibited from discharging the employee for a reason that violates public policy. The greatest protection is given to an employee discharged due to a refusal to commit an unlawful act, such as perjury or price-fixing, at the employer's request. Indeed, an employer's request that an employee violate a criminal statute—or even a statute that is not criminal—is almost always deemed against public policy and is thus not a valid ground for discharge.

Although most states recognize a public policy exception to at-will employment, several states do not. These include New York,[1] Alabama,[2] Mississippi,[3] and Florida.[4] The Georgia Supreme Court held in *Reilly v. Alcan Aluminum Corp.*[5] that an at-will employee could not sue in tort for wrongful discharge based on age discrimination. Reilly filed a claim against Alcan, alleging that the company used a "grade-age matrix" in making personnel decisions and that his age influenced the company's decision to terminate his employment. The court ruled that since the Georgia age discrimination law provided no civil remedy and another state statute merely set forth general

1. Murphy v. American Home Products Corp., 448 N.E.2d 86 (N.Y. 1983).
2. Salter v. Alfa Ins. Co., 561 So. 2d 1050 (Ala. 1990).
3. Perry v. Sears, Roebuck & Co., 508 So. 2d 1086 (Miss. 1987).
4. Smith v. Piezo Tech. & Prof. Adm'rs, 427 So. 2d 182 (Fla. 1983).
5. 528 S.E.2d 238 (Ga. 2000).

principles of tort law, the court had no authority to create an exception to the state's at-will doctrine.

Remedies In *Tameny v. Atlantic Richfield*,[6] the California Supreme Court held that an employee may maintain both tort and contract actions if the employee's discharge violated fundamental principles of public policy. As a result, damages for pain and suffering and possibly punitive damages were available.

Sources of Public Policy The following case addressed the issue of whether termination for refusal to violate a professional code of ethics constituted wrongful termination contrary to public policy.

6. 610 P.2d 1330 (Cal. 1980).

A CASE IN POINT

CASE 14.1
Rocky Mountain Hospital and Medical Service v. Mariani
Supreme Court of Colorado
916 P.2d 519 (Colo. 1996).

Summary

FACTS Diana Mariani was a certified public accountant employed for three years by the defendant, Rocky Mountain Hospital and Medical Service. She began as the general manager of the human resources department and later became the manager of special projects. In these capacities, Mariani objected to questionable accounting practices by Rocky Mountain. In particular, she discovered expense-allocation practices that enabled otherwise unprofitable enterprises to appear profitable and, as a result, benefit from artificially high solvency ratings. In response to these observations, Mariani's supervisor told her that the allocation of expenses was a business decision.

Later, Mariani was assigned to draft materials regarding a proposed merger of regional insurance companies. Properly adjusting for the improper accounting, Mariani could not discern any benefits of the proposed merger. After she reported this to her supervisor, her supervisor told her that if she did not find any benefits, she would be fired. Questionable practices continued, including inappropriate tax breaks, misstated liabilities, and omissions in various reports that Mariani considered material.

Mariani was fired. She considered this to be the direct result of her objections to Rocky Mountain's irregular accounting practices. Rocky Mountain claimed that Mariani was an at-will employee whose position was eliminated due to financial restructuring. Mariani sued for wrongful discharge. She argued that dismissal of an accountant for refusing to violate the Colorado State Board of Accountancy Rules of Professional Conduct, which prohibit an accountant from knowingly misrepresenting facts or subordinating her judgment to others, constituted wrongful termination contrary to public policy. The district court judge found for the employer. The appeals court reversed and remanded part of the case. Mariani appealed.

ISSUE PRESENTED Can an at-will employee state a claim for wrongful discharge under the public policy exception based on a professional code of ethics?

SUMMARY OF OPINION In a bold move, the Colorado Supreme Court held that the rules of professional conduct for accountants do embody principles of public policy and, as a result, can be the source of a wrongful-termination claim. The court began by outlining the public policy exception to the at-will rule, noting that the sources of public policy in previous cases had been specific statutory mandates. Nevertheless, the court held

(Continued)

(Case 14.1 continued)

that to the extent the ethical codes of a profession serve a public purpose greater than mere professional advancement and are sufficiently specific so as to create a clear mandate, courts may look to ethical codes of conduct for sources of public policy.

The court found that the accountants' code of professional ethics serves the public by creating a standard ensuring the accurate computation and reporting of financial information. The requirements of the ethical code were also sufficiently specific to specify the rights and responsibilities of an accountant. As a result, Rocky Mountain violated Colorado public policy when it dismissed Mariani for refusing to violate the Colorado State Board of Accountancy Rules of Professional Conduct.

RESULT The Colorado Supreme Court ruled that Mariani had been wrongfully discharged in violation of Colorado's public policy.

The Colorado Supreme Court acknowledged that jurisdictions are split as to whether to recognize nonlegislative sources of public policy. Some jurisdictions, including California and Michigan, limit the sources of public policy to statutory or constitutional provisions designed to protect society at large.[7] Others have recognized that nonlegislative sources, including professional ethical codes, may provide the basis for a public policy claim.[8]

A federal Occupational Safety and Health Administration (OSHA) regulation may not necessarily reflect the public policy of the state and satisfy the public policy exception under state law. In *McLaughlin v. Gastrointestinal Specialists,*[9] Mary McLaughlin, who managed a medical office, complained to her employer about fumes in her workplace. She sent a sample of the air to a testing laboratory, which verified that it violated OSHA regulations. She complained several more times to her employer, which failed to remedy the situation and then fired her. McLaughlin sued for wrongful discharge, but the Supreme Court of Pennsylvania found that she could not recover under the public policy exception because the OSHA regulation was not the public policy of the state. The court held that "a bald reference to a violation of a federal regulation, without any more articulation of how the public policy of this Commonwealth is implicated, is insufficient to overcome the strong presumption in favor of the at-will employment relation."[10] (As noted below, OSHA itself prohibits, as a matter of federal law, discharge in retaliation for exercising rights under the act.)

Courts have also considered whether attorneys, who have professional ethical codes of conduct, may recover for retaliatory discharge. In *Jacobson v. Knepper & Moga,*[11] the Illinois Supreme Court held that an attorney, who had been fired by his firm after discovering that it was violating federal law, could not recover for retaliatory discharge. Alan Jacobson, an associate at the law firm Knepper & Moga, discovered that the firm was filing consumer debt-collection actions in violation of the Fair Debt Collection Practices Act. After speaking several times to one of the principal partners of the firm with no change in the firm's practice, he was terminated. Jacobson filed a claim against the firm, alleging that he had been discharged in retaliation for his insistence that the firm cease violating the federal law. In order to recover, Jacobson had to establish that his discharge was in contravention of a clearly mandated public policy. The court found that the public policy to be protected by the Fair Debt Collection Practices Act (protecting debtors' property and ensuring them due process) was adequately safeguarded by the ethical obligations imposed by the rules of professional conduct, making it unnecessary to expand the tort of retaliatory discharge to employee attorneys.

In contrast, in *General Dynamics Corp. v. Rose,*[12] the California Supreme Court held that an attorney could recover against his corporate employer for retaliatory discharge. Andrew Rose was in-house counsel at General Dynamics. After he was abruptly fired, he filed a claim for retaliatory discharge, claiming that he had been fired

---

7. *See, e.g.,* Green v. Ralee Eng'g Co., 960 P.2d 1046 (Cal. 1998); Suchodolski v. Michigan Consol. Gas Co., 316 N.W.2d 710 (Mich. 1982).
8. *See, e.g.,* Winkelman v. Beloit Memorial Hosp., 483 N.W.2d 211 (Wis. 1992) (administrative rules); Pierce v. Ortho Pharm. Corp., 417 A.2d 505 (N.J. 1980) (legislation; administrative rules, regulations, or decisions; judicial decisions; and, in certain instances, a professional code of ethics).
9. 750 A.2d 283 (Pa. 2000).
10. *Id.* at 290.
11. 706 N.E.2d 491 (Ill. 1998).
12. 876 P.2d 487 (Cal. 1994).

because he (1) had spearheaded an investigation of drug use at the company that resulted in the termination of more than sixty employees; (2) had protested the company's failure to investigate the bugging of the office of the chief of security, a criminal offense; and (3) had advised company officials that General Dynamics' salary policy might be in violation of the Fair Labor Standards Act, which could potentially expose the company to several hundred million dollars in backpay claims. The court held that an attorney could base a claim of retaliatory discharge on allegations that he was terminated for refusing to violate a mandatory ethical duty embodied in the rules of professional conduct or other relevant statutes.

A body of law related to the law governing retaliation for refusing to commit an illegal act recognizes a tort cause of action for discharge in retaliation for exercising a statutory right or privilege. For example, an employee claimed he was discharged by the Central Indiana Gas Company for filing a workers' compensation claim. Although no state statute prohibited such a discharge, the Indiana Supreme Court recognized a tort cause of action for retaliatory discharge.[13] In another case, an employee of Firestone Tire and Rubber Company was discharged for refusing to take a lie detector test; a Pennsylvania statute prohibited employers from requiring such tests. The U.S. Court of Appeals for the Third Circuit found that the termination gave rise to a tort claim—not just a claim under the statute—because the statute represented a public policy.[14]

Employees who are discharged for carrying out important civic duties are also usually protected by the courts under the public policy doctrine. For example, the Oregon Supreme Court held that an employee could not be fired for performing jury duty.[15] The court reasoned that jury duty was an important civic duty and that the will of the community and the effectiveness of the jury system would be thwarted if employers were allowed to discharge employees for fulfilling such an obligation.

13. Frampton v. Central Indiana Gas Co., 297 N.E.2d 425 (Ind. 1973).
14. Perks v. Firestone Tire & Rubber Co., 611 F.2d 1363 (3d Cir. 1979).
15. Nees v. Hocks, 536 P.2d 512 (Or. 1975).

Statutory Protections The judicially created cause of action for discharge contrary to public policy exists alongside specific statutory provisions prohibiting retaliatory discharge. For example, the National Labor Relations Act prohibits discharge for union activities or for filing charges under the act.[16] The Fair Labor Standards Act (FLSA) prohibits discharge for exercising rights guaranteed by the minimum-wage and overtime provisions of that act.[17] In *Valerio v. Putnam Associates, Inc.,*[18] the U.S. Court of Appeals for the First Circuit extended the anti-retaliation provisions of the FSLA to retaliatory discharge as a result of internal complaints lodged by employees with employers as well as legal proceedings commenced by the employee. In that case, the court held that a worker, who was fired after complaining to her employer that it was not properly paying her overtime pursuant to the FSLA, could sue under the anti-retaliation provisions of the FSLA. The U.S. courts of appeals are split on this issue: the majority allow employees to sue if they are discharged after filing internal complaints with their employers, but a minority of courts require the employee to have initiated a formal, legal proceeding.

The Occupational Health and Safety Act prohibits discharge of employees in retaliation for exercising rights under the act, such as complaining about work procedures or about health and safety violations in the workplace.[19] Many state statutes contain similar provisions.

In the following case, the U.S. Supreme Court considered whether an at-will employee, who alleged that his employer had fired him in retaliation for obeying a federal grand jury subpoena and to deter him from testifying in an upcoming trial concerning charges that his employer had committed Medicare fraud, could recover damages under the Civil Rights Act of 1871. Section 1985(2) provides relief for anyone "injured in his person or property" by witness tampering.

16. 29 U.S.C. § 158(a) (1), (3), and (4) (1994).
17. 29 U.S.C. §§ 215(a) (3), 216(b) (1994).
18. 173 F.3d 35 (1st Cir. 1999).
19. 29 U.S.C. § 660(c) (1988).

A CASE IN POINT

CASE 14.2

Haddle v. Garrison

Supreme Court of the United States

525 U.S. 121 (1999).

Summary

FACTS A federal grand jury indicted Healthmaster, Inc. and two of its officers (Jeanette Garrison and Dennis Kelly) for Medicare fraud. Michael Haddle was an at-will employee of Healthmaster who cooperated with the federal agents in the investigation that preceded the indictment. He also appeared in response to a subpoena to testify before the grand jury but did not testify. Haddle was expected to testify as a witness in the criminal trial resulting from the indictment.

(Continued)

(Case 14.2 continued)

Garrison and Kelly conspired with G. Peter Molloy, another officer of Healthmaster, to terminate Haddle's employment. They terminated him in order to intimidate him and also to retaliate against him for attending the federal court proceedings. Haddle filed claims under the Civil Rights Act and state law. Pursuant to the requirements of Section 1985 of the Civil Rights Act of 1871, he alleged that he had been "injured in his person or property" and was entitled to recover damages. The district court dismissed his claim on the grounds that as an at-will employee, he had no constitutionally protected interest in continued employment. The appeals court affirmed, and Haddle appealed.

ISSUE PRESENTED Was Haddle "injured in his property or person" when Garrison and Kelly induced Healthmaster to terminate his at-will employment as part of a conspiracy prohibited by the Civil Rights Act?

SUMMARY OF OPINION The U.S. Supreme Court rejected the assertion that a person must suffer an injury to a "constitutionally protected property interest" to state a claim for damages under Section 1985(2). The Court explained that the gist of the wrong at which Section 1985(2) is directed is not deprivation of property but intimidation or retaliation against witnesses in federal court proceedings. The terms "injured in his person or property" define the harm that the victim may suffer as a result of the conspiracy to intimidate or retaliate. Thus, the fact that at-will employment is not "property" for purposes of the Due Process Clause does not mean that loss of at-will employment may not injure the plaintiff in his person or property for purposes of Section 1985(2).

RESULT The Supreme Court reversed the appeals court on the grounds that the harm alleged by Haddle—third-party interference with an at-will employment relationship—was a basis for relief under the Civil Rights Act. Haddle was permitted to proceed with his suit.

A more recent development has been the adoption of *whistle-blower statutes.* For example, the New York state statute[20] protecting private-sector whistle-blowers provides:

An employer shall not take any retaliatory personnel action against an employee because such employee does any of the following:

(a) discloses, or threatens to disclose to a supervisor or to a public body an activity, policy or practice of the employer that is in violation of law, rule or regulation which violation creates and presents a substantial and specific danger to the public health or safety;

(b) provides information to, or testifies before, any public body conducting an investigation, hearing or inquiry into any such violation of a law, rule or regulation by such employer; or

(c) objects to, or refuses to participate in any such activity, policy or practice in violation of a law, rule or regulation.

The rationale behind the protection of whistle-blowing is that it is in the public interest to promote compliance with law. It would be irresponsible to blindly protect all employee disclosures, however, because some disclosures may be intended merely to harass the employer. Courts must balance the public interest in the enforcement of laws, the whistle-blower's interest in being protected from reprisal, and the employer's interest in managing its workforce. Consequently, the courts have established standards of review by which to judge the actions of both employers and employees. For example, when a dismissed employee seeks reinstatement, the U.S. Court of Appeals for the Federal Circuit requires a showing of a "genuine nexus" (or connection) between the whistle-blowing and the employee's dismissal.[21] Proving this connection is often difficult.

IMPLIED CONTRACTS

The second judicial exception to the at-will rule arises out of the willingness of courts to interpret the parties' conduct as implying a contract limiting the employer's right to discharge, even though no written or express oral contract exists. Such a contract is known as an *implied*

---

20. N.Y. LAB. LAW § 740 (McKinney 1989).

21. Warren v. Department of Army, 804 F.2d 654, 656 (Fed. Cir. 1986).

contract. Some factors that can give rise to an implied obligation to discharge the employee only for good cause are that the person (1) has been a long-term employee; (2) has never been formally criticized or warned about his or her conduct; (3) has received raises, bonuses, and promotions throughout his or her career; (4) has been assured that his or her employment would continue if he or she did a good job or that the company did not terminate employees at his or her level except for good cause; and (5) has been assured before by the company's management that he or she was doing a good job. Other relevant factors include the personnel policies or practices of the employer and the practices of the industry in which the employee is engaged.

A personnel manual stating that it was the employer's policy to release employees for just cause only, together with oral assurances that the employee would be with the company as long as he or she did his or her job properly, can give rise to a reasonable expectation that an employee will not be terminated except for good cause. In so holding, the Michigan Supreme Court stated in *Toussaint*[22] that there could be a contractual obligation binding on the employer without negotiations or any meeting of the minds, or even any communication of the policies to the employee:

> No pre-employment negotiations need take place and the parties' minds need not meet on the subject; nor does it matter that the employee knows nothing of the particulars of the employer's policies and practices or that the employer may change them unilaterally. It is enough that the employer chooses, presumably in its own interest, to create an environment in which the employee believes that, whatever the personnel policies and practices, they are established and official at any given time, purport to be fair, and are applied consistently and uniformly to each employee. The employer has then created a situation "instinct with an obligation."

Although few courts have been willing to go as far as the Michigan Supreme Court went in *Toussaint,* some courts have agreed that a personnel manual given to employees may give rise to contractual obligations. The Oklahoma Court of Appeals held that the manual constitutes an offer of terms and conditions and that the employee's continuing to work is deemed an acceptance of the offer.[23]

The California Supreme Court, which had previously held that an implied contract not to terminate without good cause could be based on the employee's reasonable reliance on the company's personnel manual or policies,[24] applied the same principles to a claim of wrongful demotion.[25] Two engineers employed by Pacific Gas and Electric Company (PG&E) for twenty-four and twenty years, respectively, who were senior managers in the technical and ecological service unit, were demoted, stripped of all supervisory authority, and had their pay cut by 25 percent. PG&E had a progressive discipline policy embodied in a document entitled "Pacific Gas and Electric Company: Positive Discipline Guidelines," which provided for progressively more serious, but constructively oriented, responses to employee misconduct. Demotion was discussed as an intermediate disciplinary step short of discharge, particularly appropriate when the employee showed an "ability deficiency." A PG&E personnel manager testified that PG&E expected employees to rely on company discipline policies so that the employees would know what the company expected and what they could expect from the company. The California Supreme Court held that the progressive discipline policy gave rise to an implied contractual agreement prohibiting demotion without good cause, which PG&E had breached. The court upheld a jury award for both engineers of $1,325,000 in damages for past and anticipated future lost earnings from the decreased salary and benefits as a result of the demotion and noneconomic damages of $150,000 for emotional distress.

Other courts have been unwilling to treat written personnel policies as contracts. For example, an employee of Citibank based his claim that he was entitled not to be discharged except for cause on provisions of a personnel manual. A New York appellate court rejected this argument and held that the manual did not create any legal obligation upon the employer because the employee was still free to terminate the relationship at will.[26] Similarly, in a case involving Westinghouse Electrical Corporation, the North Carolina Court of Appeals held that unilaterally implemented employment policies are not part of the employment contract unless expressly included in it.[27]

Even when there is an implied contract not to terminate except for good cause, an employer may legally terminate an employee suspected of misconduct if, acting in good faith and following an investigation that was appropriate under the circumstances, the employer

22. Toussaint v. Blue Cross & Blue Shield of Mich., 292 N.W.2d 880 (Mich. 1980).

23. Langdon v. Saga Corp., 569 P.2d 524 (Okla. Ct. App. 1976).

24. Foley v. Interactive Data Corp., 765 P.2d 373 (Cal. 1988).

25. Scott v. Pacific Gas & Elec. Co., 904 P.2d 834 (Cal. 1995).

26. Edwards v. Citibank, N.A., 74 A.D.2d 553, *appeal dismissed,* 414 N.E.2d 400 (N.Y. 1980).

27. Walker v. Westinghouse Elec. Corp., 335 S.E.2d 79 (N.C. Ct. App. 1985), *review denied,* 341 S.E.2d 39 (1986).

had reasonable grounds for believing that the employee had engaged in misconduct. For example, in one case,[28] a male manager was terminated following charges of sexual harassment by two female employees. The employer conducted a thorough investigation, which included interviews with the manager, the two accusers, and twenty-one other people who had worked with the manager. The investigation was inconclusive, however; the employer could not determine with certainty whether the acts of harassment had actually taken place. The company felt that the accusers were credible, and its investigator concluded that, more likely than not, the harassment had occurred. Fearing a suit by the two women, the company terminated the male manager. He sued for wrongful termination; the jury awarded him $1.78 million, after apparently finding that the charges against him were false. The California Supreme Court reversed and sent the case back for retrial so that the jury could determine whether the company had a good faith belief, following a reasonable investigation, that the manager had engaged in sexual harassment. If so, the company would not be liable for wrongful termination.

IMPLIED COVENANT OF GOOD FAITH AND FAIR DEALING

The third prong in the developing law of wrongful discharge is the recognition of an *implied covenant of good faith and fair dealing* in the employment relationship. For example, the Supreme Judicial Court of Massachusetts held that a twenty-five-year employee of National

---

28. Cotran v. Rollins Hudig Hall Int'l, 948 P.2d 412 (Cal. 1998).

IN BRIEF
Limits on At-Will Employment

The employer's right to terminate an employee without cause may be subject to and restricted by:

- civil service systems
- union contracts
- express employment contracts (must be in writing if for longer than one year)
- the public policy exception
- whistle-blower statutes
- implied contracts
- the implied covenant of good faith and fair dealing.

Cash Register Company, with a written contract providing for at-will employment, could sue for wrongful termination when the employer discharged him to deprive him of $46,000 in commissions.[29]

Courts in Texas, New Mexico, Florida, and Wisconsin have expressly declined to recognize an implied covenant of good faith and fair dealing in employment cases. California, like Massachusetts, recognizes such an implied covenant but provides only contract remedies for breach of the implied covenant; tort remedies, such as damages for pain and suffering and punitive damages, are not available.[30]

Right *to* Fair Procedure *and* Managed Care

The California courts have acknowledged a common law right to fair procedure protecting individuals from arbitrary exclusion or expulsion from private organizations that control important economic interests. Individuals having this right must be given notice of the charges against them and an opportunity to respond to those charges. They cannot be expelled from membership for reasons that are arbitrary, capricious, or contrary to public policy, notwithstanding provisions to the contrary in the organization's bylaws. Organizations can exercise their sound business judgment when establishing standards for membership, but any removal must be "both substantively rational and procedurally fair."[31] This right has become increasingly important for health care providers belonging to managed-care networks.

For example, in *Potvin v. Metropolitan Life Insurance Co.*,[32] the California Supreme Court applied the common law doctrine of fair procedure to an insurance company's decision to remove a physician from its preferred provider lists even though the contract between the physician and the insurer provided that the listing could be terminated by either party at any time with or without cause. The court declined to extend its holding to every insurer wishing to remove a doctor from one of its preferred provider lists, however: "The [fair procedure]

---

29. Fortune v. Nat'l Cash Register Co., 364 N.E.2d 1251 (Mass. 1977).
30. Foley v. Interactive Data Corp., 765 P.2d 373 (Cal. 1988).
31. Pinsker v. Pacific Coast Soc'y. of Orthodontists, 526 P.2d 253 (Cal. 1974).
32. 997 P.2d 1153 (Cal. 2000). *See also* Harper v. Healthsource New Hampshire, Inc., 674 A.2d 962, 966 (N.H. 1996) ("the public has a substantial interest in the relationship between health maintenance organizations and their preferred provider physicians").

obligation . . . arises only when the insurer possesses power so substantial that the removal significantly impairs the ability of an ordinary, competent physician to practice medicine or a medical specialty in a particular geographic area, thereby affecting an important, substantial economic interest."[33]

33. *Id.* at 1071.

 # Fraudulent Inducement

During difficult economic times, a business may engage in puffery and exaggeration to keep and attract highly qualified personnel. The following case serves as a warning that a company may be held liable for overzealous sales pitches under a theory of fraudulent inducement.

A CASE IN POINT

CASE 14.3

Lazar v. Rykoff-Sexton, Inc.

Supreme Court of California
909 P.2d 981 (Cal. 1996).

In the Language of the Court

FACTS Andrew Lazar was employed as president of a family-owned restaurant equipment company in New York where he lived with his wife and two children. In September 1989, a vice president of Rykoff-Sexton, Inc. (Rykoff) contacted Lazar and asked him to move to Los Angeles to work as Rykoff's West Coast general manager for contract design. The company intensively recruited Lazar through February 1990. During this process, Lazar expressed concern to Rykoff about relinquishing a secure job with a family business, moving his children far away from their friends, and leaving his home of forty years. As a condition of agreeing to relocate, Lazar required Rykoff's assurance that his job would be secure and involve significant pay increases.

Rykoff represented that Lazar would become part of Rykoff's "family," would enjoy continued advancement, and would have security and a long-term relationship with the company. The company told Lazar that it would employ him as long as he performed his job and achieved goals. Rykoff also implied that the current head of the department in which Lazar would work had plans to retire and that Lazar would be groomed for that position. In addition, Rykoff represented that the company was very strong financially and anticipated profits and growth in the future. Lazar was assured that he would receive annual reviews and raises.

In fact, Rykoff's representations were false as the company had just experienced its worst economic performance in recent history and its financial outlook was pessimistic. Rykoff was planning an operational merger that would eliminate Lazar's position, and the company had no intention of retaining him. The company knew that promised compensation increases would not be forthcoming as company policy limited increases to only 3 percent a year.

Based on Rykoff's false representations, in May 1990, Lazar resigned from his job in New York, relocated his family to Los Angeles, and commenced employment at Rykoff. He performed his job in an exemplary manner, obtaining sales increases for his assigned regions and lowering operating costs within his department. In April 1992, Rykoff failed to pay Lazar bonus compensation to which he was entitled. Several months later, Rykoff told Lazar his job was being eliminated owing to management reorganization. After being terminated, Lazar was unable to find comparable employment.

Lazar sued Rykoff on a number of theories including fraudulent inducement for inducing his relocation to Los Angeles by making false representations. The trial court dismissed most of Lazar's claims, but the appeals court vacated this order. Rykoff appealed.

OPINION WERDEGAR, J., writing for the California Supreme Court:

An action for promissory fraud may lie where a defendant fraudulently induces the plaintiff to enter into a contract. . . . In such cases, the plaintiff's claim does not depend upon whether the defendant's promise is ultimately enforceable as a contract.

(Continued)

(Case 14.3 continued)

"If it is enforceable, the [plaintiff] . . . has a cause of action in tort as an alternative at least, and perhaps in some instances in addition to his cause of action on the contract.". . . Recovery, however, may be limited by the rule against double recovery of tort and contract compensatory damages. . . .

Lazar's allegations, if true, would establish all the elements of promissory fraud. As detailed above, Lazar alleges that, in order to induce him to come to work in California, Rykoff intentionally represented to him he would be employed by the company so long as he performed his job, he would receive significant increases in salary, and the company was strong financially. Lazar further alleges that Rykoff's representations were false, and he justifiably relied on them in leaving secure New York employment, severing his connections with the New York employment market, uprooting his family, purchasing a California home and moving here.

. . .

. . . Lazar's reliance on Rykoff's misrepresentations was truly detrimental, such that he may plead all the elements of fraud. Lazar's employer, Rykoff, did not have the power to compel Lazar to leave his former employment. Rykoff's misrepresentations were made before the employment relationship was formed, when Rykoff had no coercive power over Lazar and Lazar was free to decline the offered position. Rykoff used misrepresentations to induce Lazar to change employment, a result Rykoff presumably could not have achieved truthfully (because Lazar had required assurances the Rykoff position would be secure and would involve significant increases in pay). Moreover, Lazar's decision to join Rykoff left Lazar in worse circumstances than those in which he would have found himself had Rykoff not lied to him. (Allegedly, Lazar's secure living and working circumstances were disrupted, and Lazar became the employee of a financially troubled company, which intended to treat him as an at-will employee.)

. . .

. . . Because of the extra measure of blameworthiness inhering in fraud, and because in fraud cases we are not concerned about the need for "predictability about the cost of contractual relationships," fraud plaintiffs may recover "out-of-pocket" damages. . . .

. . .

Consistent with the foregoing, as to his fraud claim Lazar may properly seek damages for the costs of uprooting his family, expenses incurred in relocation, and the loss of security and income associated with his former employment in New York. On the facts as pled, however, Lazar must rely on his contract claim for recovery of any loss of income allegedly caused by wrongful termination of his employment with Rykoff. Moreover, any overlap between damages recoverable in tort and damages recoverable in contract would be limited by the rule against double recovery.

RESULT The court affirmed the appeals court's decision, finding that Lazar had stated a cause of action for fraudulent inducement.

COMMENTS In reaching its decision, the court distinguished *Hunter v. Up-Right, Inc.,*[34] an earlier case in which the California Supreme Court had held that an at-will employee who was induced to resign by being falsely told that his job was being eliminated could not state a valid tort claim for fraud. The *Lazar* court reasoned that the employer in *Hunter* had used deception when it could have directly fired the employee. In contrast, the employer in

34. 864 P.2d 88 (Cal. 1993).

(Continued)

(Case 14.3 continued)

Lazar did not have the power to force the executive to leave his company in New York. As a result, the executive's reliance on the employer's representations was truly detrimental.

QUESTIONS

1. What is the difference between breach of contract and fraudulent inducement?
2. Why was it necessary for the plaintiff to couch his claim in terms of fraudulent inducement?

In *Rodowicz v. Massachusetts Mutual Life Insurance Co.*,[35] certain retired MassMutual employees sued the company, alleging that it had failed to reveal that a more favorable retirement option was forthcoming at the time they were considering retiring. As a result, they retired under terms that were less favorable than those in a special offer made to employees shortly after they retired. Under Massachusetts fraud law, plaintiffs had to demonstrate (1) that MassMutual made false statements of material fact to induce them to retire when they did, and (2) that the plaintiffs reasonably relied on those statements to their detriment. In contrast, the Employee Retirement Income Security Act (ERISA) requires employers to disclose information to employees about possible changes in benefits only if those changes reach a level of "serious consideration." The First Circuit ruled that the retired employees could sue for fraudulent inducement under state law based upon MassMutual's misrepresentation that its board of directors was not considering changing its retirement package.

 ## Noncompete Agreements

A *covenant not to compete* is a device, ancillary to another agreement (such as an employment contract), designed to protect a company's interests by limiting a former employee's ability to use trade secrets in working for a competitor or setting up a competing business. Enforcing a noncompete agreement can be difficult because rules vary by jurisdiction. For example, California, Texas, and Florida severely limit the enforceability of noncompetes.

Due to these differences in state laws, disputes can arise regarding which law to apply to noncompete agreements. In *International Business Machines Corp. v. Bajorek*,[36] the U.S. Court of Appeals for the Ninth Circuit upheld provisions in a noncompete agreement requiring Dr. Bajorek, an executive to whom IBM had granted stock options worth more than $500,000, to return any profits he obtained from the options if he worked for a competitor within six months after exercising the options. After Bajorek left IBM to work for one of its competitors, IBM notified him that his stock options had been canceled. Although the stock option agreement stated that New York law should apply to any disputes, Bajorek sued IBM in federal district court in California and argued that California law should apply. The district court agreed, after finding that applying New York law would violate California public policy against both recoupment of wages paid to employees and employee noncompetition agreements. The appeals court reversed on the grounds that these California policies were inapplicable. In addition to finding that stock options were not wages, the appeals court ruled that California restricts only agreements that completely restrain an individual from pursuing his or her profession. The court commented:

> It is one thing to tell a man that if he wants his pension, he cannot ever work in his trade again, . . . and quite another to tell him that if he wants a million dollars from his stock options, he has to refrain from going to work for a competitor for six months.[37]

Even if an employment agreement does not contain an express noncompetition clause, any provisions having

35. 192 F.3d 162 (1st Cir. 1999), *reh'g denied*, 195 F.3d 65 (1st Cir. 1999).

 ETHICAL CONSIDERATION

What role, if any, should the law play in penalizing an employer who lies to its employee about the reason for termination in order to persuade the employee to resign? What role do ethics play in this situation?

36. 191 F.3d 1033 (9th Cir. 1999).
37. *Id.* at 1041.

a similar effect will be unenforceable in a jurisdiction banning noncompetes. For example, Dean Witter's employment agreement forced brokers in Los Angeles to repay training costs if they left the company within two years. In a settlement of a class-action suit in October 1997, Dean Witter agreed to return $540,000 collected from thirty-four former brokers and to pay another $1.2 million in legal fees for "involuntary servitude" in violation of California's ban on noncompetes unrelated to the sale of a business.[38]

Even in states permitting noncompete agreements, courts will enforce only reasonable restrictions on competition. Unreasonableness can be found on many grounds, including duration of limitation, geographic scope, scope of activities prohibited, and the employer's relation to the interests being protected. For example, the Nevada Supreme Court invalidated a noncompete agreement restricting a lighting-retrofitting employee from competing with his former employer within a 100-mile radius of the former employer's site for five years.[39] The duration placed a great hardship on the employee and was not necessary to protect the former employer's interests.

Thus, care must be taken when drafting noncompete agreements to ensure that they are not unduly restrictive. Corporate managers should keep the following guidelines in mind:[40]

- Know the relevant state laws. Given that different states apply different standards for reviewing noncompetes, be sure to structure each agreement in a way that courts will recognize and uphold.
- Be specific. Clarify the specific roles and responsibilities of a given employee so that the noncompete is not overly restrictive, thereby reducing the risk of judicial invalidation.
- Provide consideration for the noncompete. The noncompete may be a condition of employment; but for existing employees, be sure to provide something in exchange, such as a bonus or a promotion.

To protect trade secrets, a New York court imposed noncompete obligations in the absence of a written agreement. Former employees of DoubleClick, Inc. who had not signed noncompete agreements were enjoined from working in the same industry for six months.[41] The court reasoned that the similarity in the two businesses and positions made it inevitable that the employees would use the former employer's trade secrets in their work for the new company. Trade-secret protection and the inevitable disclosure doctrine are discussed further in Chapter 11.

The majority of states recognize an employer's investment of time and money to develop customer and client relationships as a legitimate employer interest that can justify a noncompete agreement. In the following case, the New York Court of Appeals considered whether the protection of customer and client relationships was a rationale for enforcing a noncompete agreement.

---

38. Patrick McGeehan, *Attempting to Dun a Former Broker Costs Dean Witter $1.8 Million*, WALL ST. J., Oct. 23, 1997, at B12.
39. Jones v. Deeter, 913 P.2d 1272 (Nev. 1996). *See also* Rollins Burdick Hunter of Wis., Inc. v Hamilton, 304 N.W.2d 752 (Wis. 1981).
40. *See* Christopher Caggiano, *Think All Noncompetes Stink? Think Again,* INC., Oct. 1997, at 114.

41. Frances A. McMorris, *Judge Restricts Two Executives Despite Lack of Noncompete Pacts*, WALL ST. J., Nov. 25, 1997, at B10.

A CASE IN POINT

CASE 14.4
BDO Seidman v. Hirshberg
Court of Appeals of New York
712 N.E.2d 1220
(N.Y. 1999).

In the Language of the Court

FACTS Jeffrey Hirshberg was employed in the Buffalo, New York office of BDO Seidman, a national accounting firm. As a condition of receiving a promotion to the position of manager, Hirshberg was required to sign a "Manager's Agreement." Paragraph SIXTH of the agreement provided that if, within eighteen months following the termination of his employment, Hirshberg served any former client of BDO Seidman's Buffalo office, he would be required to compensate BDO Seidman "for the loss and damages suffered" in an amount equal to one-and-a-half times the fees BDO Seidman had charged that client over the last fiscal year of the client's patronage.

After Hirshberg resigned from BDO Seidman, the accounting firm claimed that it lost 100 former clients to Hirshberg who were billed a total of $138,000 in the year Hirshberg left the firm. Hirshberg denied serving some of the clients; claimed that a substantial number of them were personal clients he had brought to the firm through his own contacts; and claimed, with respect to some clients, that he had not been the primary BDO Seidman employee working on their accounts.

(Continued)

(Case 14.4 continued)

The trial court invalidated the reimbursement clause on the grounds that it constituted an overbroad and unenforceable anticompetitive agreement. BDO Seidman appealed.

ISSUE PRESENTED Is an agreement requiring a former employee to reimburse the employer for any loss sustained by losing clients to the employee enforceable?

OPINION LEVINE, J., writing for the New York Court of Appeals:

The modern, prevailing common-law standard of reasonableness for employee agreements not to compete applies a three-pronged test. A restraint is reasonable only if it: (1) is no greater than is required for the protection of the legitimate interest of the employer, (2) does not impose undue hardship on the employee, and (3) is not injurious to the public. . . . A violation of any prong renders the covenant invalid.

. . .

. . . Close analysis of paragraph SIXTH of the agreement under the first prong of the common-law rule, to identify the legitimate interest of BDO and determine whether the covenant is no more restrictive than is necessary to protect that interest, leads us to conclude that the covenant as written is overbroad in some respects. BDO claims that the legitimate interest it is entitled to protect is its entire client base, which it asserts a modern, large accounting firm expends considerable time and money building and maintaining. However, the only justification for imposing an employee agreement not to compete is to forestall unfair competition. . . . If the employee abstains from unfair means in competing for those clients, the employer's interest in preserving its client base against the competition of the former employee is no more legitimate and worthy of contractual protection than when it vies with unrelated competitors for those clients.

. . . Protection of customer relationships the employee acquired in the course of employment may indeed be a legitimate interest. . . . "The risk to the employer reaches a maximum in situations in which the employee must work closely with the client or customer over a long period of time, especially when his services are a significant part of the total transaction.". . . The employer has a legitimate interest in preventing former employees from exploiting or appropriating the goodwill of a client or customer, which had been created and maintained at the employer's expense, to the employer's competitive detriment. . . .

. . .

To the extent, then that paragraph SIXTH of the Manager's Agreement requires defendant to compensate BDO for lost patronage of clients with whom he never acquired a relationship through the direct provision of substantive accounting services during his employment, the covenant is invalid and unenforceable. . . . Indeed, enforcement of the restrictive covenant as to defendant's personal clients would permit BDO to appropriate goodwill created and maintained through defendant's efforts, essentially turning on its head the principal justification to uphold any employee agreement not to compete based on protection of customer or client relationships.

Except for the overbreadth in the foregoing two respects, the restrictions in paragraph SIXTH do not violate the tripartite common-law test for reasonableness. The restraint on serving BDO clients is limited to eighteen months, and to clients of BDO's Buffalo office. The time constraint appears to represent a reasonably brief interlude to enable the firm to replace the client relationship and goodwill defendant was permitted to acquire with some of its clients. Defendant is free to compete immediately for new business in any market and, if the overbroad provisions of the

(Continued)

(Case 14.4 continued)

covenant are struck, to retain his personal clients and those clients of BDO's that he had not served to any significant extent while employed at the firm. . . .

Moreover, given the likely broad array of accounting services available in the greater Buffalo area, and the limited remaining class of BDO clientele affected by the covenant, it cannot be said that the restraint, as narrowed, would seriously impinge on the availability of accounting services in the Buffalo area from which the public may draw, or cause any significant dislocation in the market or create a monopoly in accounting services in that locale. These factors militate against a conclusion that a reformed paragraph SIXTH would violate the third prong of the common-law test, injury to the public interest.

RESULT The New York Court of Appeals found that the agreement was reasonable and enforceable except to the extent that it required Hirshberg to compensate BDO Seidman for fees paid by his personal clients or by clients with whom he had never acquired a relationship through his employment at BDO Seidman.

COMMENTS Six weeks before *BDO Seidman v. Hirshberg* was decided, the U.S. Court of Appeals for the Second Circuit reached a similar conclusion on the issue of recognizing relationships with customers as a basis to enforce a noncompete agreement. In *Ticor Title Insurance Co. v. Cohen*,[42] the Second Circuit Court of Appeals affirmed enforcement of a noncompete agreement between a title insurance company and one of its most successful salespeople. The noncompete agreement prohibited the salesman from competing for six months after leaving Ticor to afford the company an opportunity to fairly compete to retain the business of the customers with whom the former employee had maintained relationships on Ticor's behalf. The salesman's relationships with Ticor clients qualified as unique services because competition for title insurance business relied heavily on personal relationships with salespeople. In addition, because Ticor's potential clients were limited and well known throughout the industry, maintaining current clients from this established group was crucial to the company.

QUESTIONS

1. Could Hirshberg be required to reimburse BDO for fees paid by a client for whom he had not worked while at BDO if the firm could prove that he was aware of the client only because the name was on BDO's client list?
2. Should Hirshberg be excused from paying fees to BDO in connection with a client that testifies that it was dissatisfied with BDO's services and had planned to move its account elsewhere even before knowing that Hirshberg had left?

42. 173 F.3d 63 (2d Cir. 1999).

Employers may attempt to prevent other companies from luring away their employees. In May 2000, PaineWebber Group, Inc. sued Morgan Stanley Dean Witter & Co. to prevent it from hiring top talent away from J.C. Bradford & Co., a Nashville-based regional brokerage house that PaineWebber was acquiring.[43]

43. Charles Gasparino, *Paine Webber Alleges in Lawsuit That Morgan Stanley Lured Staff,* WALL ST. J., May 5, 2000, at B8.

PaineWebber accused Morgan Stanley "of a carefully planned, broadbased campaign to raid Bradford personnel and interfere with the merger agreement between PaineWebber and Bradford." Morgan Stanley had previously made a losing bid for Bradford before PaineWebber successfully purchased it.

In October 1994, PaineWebber had filed similar suits against Donaldson Lufkin & Jenrette Securities, Inc. and Dean Witter Reynolds, accusing the two firms of raiding

ETHICAL CONSIDERATION

Companies can require their employees to sign a noncompete agreement as a condition of employment. In *Tatge v. Chambers & Owen, Inc.,*[a] a company asked an at-will employee to sign a noncompete agreement that provided that he would not work for one of the company's competitors for a period of six months after termination of his employment. Tatge refused to sign the agreement, and the company terminated him. He sued the company, alleging several claims including wrongful discharge. The Supreme Court of Wisconsin dismissed his claim, after concluding that the company's requirement that he sign the noncompete agreement was not a violation of public policy. The court noted that signing the agreement would not have prevented Tatge from arguing that its terms were unreasonable if the company had tried to enforce it. Although it was legal for the employer to fire Tatge for failing to sign the noncompete agreement, was it ethical? Does it matter whether the employer knows the agreement is overbroad?

a. 579 N.W.2d 217 (Wis. 1998).

brokers after PaineWebber purchased Kidder Peabody.[44] The suit, which sought millions of dollars in punitive damages, was a success. After it was filed, the two firms stopped attempting to hire PaineWebber brokers; PaineWebber dropped the suits in early 1995.

At-Will Employment *and* Preemployment Practices

In deciding whether there is an express or implied contractual right not to be fired except for cause, a court may consider statements made during preemployment interviews and on application forms. Consequently, if an employer wants to preserve the traditional legal right to discharge employees at will, it should see that limitations on this right are not inadvertently created.

To illustrate, an application form might include the following language above the employee signature line: "I understand that, if hired, my employment can be terminated with or without cause, at either my employer's or my option." Inclusion of such language reminds the employee that his or her employment is at will—and

verifies that he or she was so informed—and lessens the likelihood that the employee will be able to establish an implied contractual right to be discharged only for cause. Additionally, no statements should be made during interviews that could create an impression that the applicant would not be fired without good cause. "Employees are never fired from here without good reason," "Your job will be secure, as long as you do your work," and "We treat our employees like family" are examples of such statements. In short, the employer should not mislead an applicant about the security of the job offered.

In some states, it may be difficult to maintain an at-will relationship except by an express contract or by a disclaimer in the employment application or the personnel manual stating that nothing in the employment relationship and no personnel policy or benefit shall create a right to continued employment. If such a disclaimer is plainly contrary to the company's stated policy, however, it may be rejected by a court. For example, a statement on an application form that employment is at will probably will not be upheld if the company's written personnel policy expressly provides that employees will be given progressive discipline and will not be fired without just cause.

Second, if an employer chooses to have a written personnel policy, care should be taken to see that the language expressly reserves those rights that the employer wishes to maintain, especially with respect to discharge. Also, if employees are given handbooks that purport to summarize the official personnel manuals, the handbook and the manuals must be consistent. Otherwise, courts and juries are likely to uphold the policy that is most favorable to the employee.

Third, if an employer chooses to have a policy of progressive discipline, it is essential that supervisors and managers, as well as the human resources staff, be trained to administer the policy. In particular, they

INTERNATIONAL CONSIDERATION

Before making a decision to move abroad, a manager should check to see whether the company will have flexibility in hiring. Many countries do not permit employers to terminate employees without good cause. A business should also make sure that its workers can get necessary visas to work abroad. Many countries have quotas requiring that a certain percentage of a foreign company's labor force be nationals of the host country.

44. *Id.*

should be trained to document performance problems and to counsel employees about the need to improve.

Fourth, an employer can enter into an agreement with the employee that any dispute shall be subject to arbitration. Most courts will enforce an evenhanded arbitration clause in a fairly negotiated written contract; however, a *boilerplate clause*—that is, standardized, nonnegotiable language—in an employment application form may be found invalid. As discussed in Chapters 4 and 15, mandatory arbitration of discrimination claims can pose special concerns.

Fifth, an employer should decide whether to establish an internal grievance procedure. Such a procedure can result in fewer lawsuits. If established, however, a grievance procedure must be followed. Otherwise, the employer may face claims for failure to follow its own procedure, especially when the procedure is elaborate.

The bottom line is that the employer should have in place a system of checks and balances to ensure that the company's policies are properly communicated and followed. Discharges should be well documented and handled in accordance with these policies. Employees should be treated in a fair and consistent manner.

Recommendations *for* Former Employees

Employers are often asked to give references regarding former employees to prospective employers. An employee always hopes that a reference will be favorable, but that is not always the case. At any rate, the employee expects the reference to be fair. If the reference is not fair and the employer has impugned the individual's reputation, he or she can sue the employer for defamation.

In *Deutsch v. Chesapeake Center*,[45] a reverend, who was hired as director of an overnight lodging and meeting facility for church groups, was terminated as a result of accusations of racism and sexual harassment. When he applied for a position as a church pastor in another community, his former employer told the prospective employer of the charges that had resulted in termination of his employment. The reverend sued his former employer for defamation, but the U.S. District Court for the District of Maryland dismissed his claim, finding that the

45. 27 F. Supp. 2d 642 (Md. 1998).

ECONOMIC PERSPECTIVE

Record Layoffs *at a* Time *of* Record Employment

Although the United States was experiencing an economic boom with low unemployment at the end of the twentieth century and the beginning of the new millennium, companies were laying off workers in record numbers. U.S. companies laid off 675,000 workers in 1999 and 678,000 in 1998, the highest number for the decade. In contrast, only 111,285 employees were laid off in 1989. At the same time that companies were laying off some workers, they were actively hiring others. According to a recent survey by the American Management Association, during the year ending in June 1999, 36 percent of the 2,000 companies interviewed reported that they had created new jobs at the same time that they eliminated jobs, a 27 percent increase from the previous year. The report concluded "more hiring, more firing, and more companies doing both."

This trend represents "creative destruction," an economic theory that received attention in the 1930s as a result of Austrian economist Joseph Schumpeter. Under this theory, the churning of the labor force, with lots of job destruction and creation, is a sign of progress because capitalism tends to reinvent itself through chaotic change.

Today, many managers, concerned about keeping current with new technologies and promoting efficiency in the quickly changing economy, feel less guilt than their predecessors about laying off employees rather than trying to retrain them. In the past, managers were reluctant to lay off workers because of the bad publicity and trauma layoffs created; now many see layoffs as simply another management tool. At the same time, however, because companies are hiring as much as they are firing, less stigma is associated with layoffs than previously. Indeed, most workers are able to find new employment. How to deal with workers unable to find comparable jobs in the new economy is an ethical challenge both for the managers firing them and for society as a whole.

Source: This discussion is based on Patrick Barta, *Zero-Sum Gain; In Current Expansion, As Business Booms, So, Too, Do Layoffs*, WALL ST. J., Mar. 13, 2000, at A1.

former employer's statements were protected by a conditional privilege to communicate information concerning a former employee to a prospective employer.

In contrast, in *MacCord v. Christian Academy*,[46] the U.S. District Court for the Eastern District of Pennsylvania concluded that a principal's comments regarding a teacher's poor performance during a faculty meeting were not protected by the privilege. The principal had abused the privilege by publishing the defamatory statements to the entire faculty and including allegedly defamatory matter not reasonably believed to be necessary for the purpose of informing the faculty that some teachers' contracts would not be renewed.

Traditionally, defamation law requires publication, meaning that the communicator of the defamatory information tells the information to a third party, such as a prospective employer. Some jurisdictions, however, recognize an exception in the employment context. Under the *doctrine of self-publication*, a defamatory communication by an employer to an employee may constitute publication if the employer could foresee that the employee would be required to repeat the communication, for instance, to a prospective employer. The doctrine is designed to provide a cause of action to the job-seeking employee who is forced to self-publicize the former employer's defamatory statement. To keep disgruntled former employees from overusing the doctrine, most jurisdictions require a showing of abuse on the part of the former employer and some reasonable degree of foreseeability of a compelled future self-publication.

An employer may be protected against liability for defamation claims by a former employee if the employee signs a waiver and release form releasing potential claims. In *Bardin v. Lockheed Aeronautical Systems Co.*,[47] Bethany Bardin had worked for Lockheed from 1987 until 1993. After she was laid off by the company, she applied for a job as a police officer with the Los Angeles Police Department. As part of the application process, she signed a "Release and Waiver" form, which authorized a background investigation and provided that former employers were cleared "from any and all liability for damage of whatever kind." The police department notified Bardin that her application was suspended because she had failed to disclose employment problems at Lockheed, including a complaint related to her drinking. Bardin sued Lockheed, but the court found the language in the waiver and release form sufficiently broad to protect Lockheed from liability.

Fear of a defamation claim may tempt an employer to give an overly positive recommendation. This is not prudent. As explained in Chapter 9, an employer giving an untrue assessment of a former employee may be liable not only to the new employer who relies on the recommendation but also to third persons physically harmed as a foreseeable result of the recommendation.

Employee Drug *and* Genetic Testing

Many employers have adopted drug-screening programs for their employees and applicants to avoid the decreased productivity, quality control problems, absenteeism on the job, accidents, and employee theft that can result from drug and alcohol abuse. According to the American Management Association, 77 percent of large companies in the United States test their employees for drugs.[48] Some employers use drug testing in conjunction with a comprehensive drug program that provides education and assistance to an employee with a drug or alcohol problem.

The issue of drug testing generally comes before the courts in the context of discipline or discharge of an employee for refusing to take a test. Whether testing will be deemed permissible in a particular situation depends on four factors: (1) the scope of the testing program, (2) whether the employer is a public or private employer, (3) any state constitutional guarantees of a right to privacy, and (4) any state statutes regulating drug testing.

The first major factor, scope, concerns who is being tested: all employees (random testing); only employees in a specific job where it is felt that there is a legitimate job-related need (for example, nuclear power plant employees); groups of employees (for example, all employees in one facility because there is a general suspicion of drug use within that group); or specific individuals who are believed to be using drugs. The smaller the group to be tested and the more specific the reason for testing, the more likely a court will uphold the test. Random testing is the most difficult to defend. The final three factors are discussed in more detail below.

An employee may challenge a drug test in many ways. The employee may claim that (1) the test breached his or her employment contract; (2) there was no justification for the test; (3) it violated the public policy that protects privacy; (4) he or she was defamed by false accusations of drug use based on an erroneous test; (5) he or she suffered emotional distress, especially if the test result was in

46. 1998 U.S. Dist. LEXIS 19412 (E.D. Penn. Dec. 4, 1998).
47. 82 Cal. Rptr. 2d 726 (1999).
48. *Who's Watching?* UFCW ACTION, Jan.–Feb. 1998, at 16.

"Maybe zero tolerance is setting the bar too high."

error; or (6) the testing disproportionately affects employees of one race or sex and therefore is discriminatory.

PUBLIC EMPLOYEES

Because public employees are protected by the U.S. Constitution's Fourth Amendment prohibition against unreasonable searches and seizures and by the right to privacy, there are greater limitations on testing public employees than on testing private-sector employees. It has long been recognized that urine tests and blood tests are a substantial intrusion upon bodily privacy and are therefore searches subject to regulation. With some exceptions, there is no federal constitutional limitation on drug testing in the private sector.

In *Skinner v. Railway Labor Executives' Ass'n*[49] the U.S. Supreme Court held that railroads can be required to test public employees involved in a major train accident and have the authority to test employees who violate certain safety rules. The Court reasoned that any intrusion upon individual privacy rights in the railroad context was outweighed by the government's compelling interest in public and employee safety.

The Supreme Court also upheld mandatory drug testing of U.S. Customs Service employees in line for transfer or promotion to certain sensitive positions involving drug interdiction or the handling of firearms.[50] Although there was no perceived drug problem among Customs employees, the Court held that the program was justified by the need for national security and by the extraordinary safety hazards attendant to the positions involved.

In *Knox County Education Ass'n v. Knox County Board of Education*,[51] the U.S. Court of Appeals for the Sixth Circuit held that subjecting public school teachers to drug and alcohol testing was not an unconstitutional violation of their right to privacy. Of primary importance in the court's decision was the unique role teachers play by accepting *in loco parentis* (in place of the parents) obligations to ensure the safety of children and to serve as role models. The court commented that "teachers must expect with this extraordinary responsibility, they will be subject to scrutiny to which other civil servants or professionals might not be subjected, including drug testing."[52]

50. National Treasury Employees Union v. Von Raab, 489 U.S. 656 (1989).
51. 158 F.3d 361 (6th Cir. 1998).
52. *Id.* at 384.

49. 489 U.S. 602 (1989).

Health Screening and Genetic Testing Health screening has become an important issue and involves many of the same issues that arise in the context of drug testing. In *Norman–Bloodsaw v. Lawrence Berkeley Laboratory,*[53] the U.S. Court of Appeals for the Ninth Circuit held that it was illegal for a government laboratory to test blood and urine samples for syphilis, sickle-cell anemia, and pregnancy without an employee's knowledge. The tests violated both the U.S. and California constitutions and Title VII. The court explained: "One can think of few subject areas more personal and more likely to implicate privacy interests than that of one's health or genetic makeup."

In February 2000, President Bill Clinton signed an executive order prohibiting the federal government from using genetic testing in hiring or promotion decisions.[54] At that time, the majority of states had already passed genetic-privacy laws. Thirty-nine states had laws preventing insurance companies from denying coverage based on a patient's genetic predispositions, and fifteen states had passed similar laws on employment practices.[55] Only five states had no laws on the matter.[56] In June 2000, the Senate voted to endorse a law preventing insurers from raising premiums or denying coverage to people in group health plans or individual plans based on genetic testing. The Senate rejected a proposal that would have prohibited employers from making hiring, salary, or other decisions related to employment on the basis of genetic information.[57] The following month, the head of the Human Genome Project testified before the Senate Health, Education, Labor and Pensions Committee that Congress should enact legislation before the end of the year to prevent genetic discrimination both by insurance companies and by employers because current protections were inadequate.[58] As of December 2000, however, Congress had failed to enact any legislation banning genetic testing.

PRIVATE EMPLOYERS

The right to privacy guaranteed by the U.S. Constitution protects against invasions of privacy by public actors (e.g., state and federal governments or agencies) but does not protect against invasions by private (i.e., nongovernmental) actors. Similarly, the Fourth Amendment ban on unreasonable searches and seizures applies only to governmental activity. Many state constitutions also guarantee the right to privacy, however. Some states extend this to private invasions of privacy; others limit it to governmental invasions.

In *Luddtke v. Nabors Alaska Drilling, Inc.,*[59] the Alaska Supreme Court held that the right to privacy in the state constitution applied only to governmental intrusions, not to alleged violations by private entities. Therefore, the state constitution did not shield its citizens from drug tests by a private employer. Moreover, even if there was a right, the company's interest in maintaining the health, safety, and welfare of its workers would outweigh any privacy interest.

In contrast, the California Court of Appeal held that a pupillary-reaction test given to all employees of Kerr–McGee Corporation at its chemical plant in Trono, California, might violate the California Constitution's right to privacy, depending on the intrusiveness of the test and the employer's safety needs.[60] The test consisted of shining a light in the person's eye and observing how much the pupil contracted. Although the court acknowledged that the pupillary test was less intrusive than urine, blood, or breath tests, it held that the trial court needed more facts to determine just how intrusive the test was.

Statutory Limitations A number of states have adopted legislation regarding drug testing by private employers. Such legislation often sets forth the notice procedures an employer must follow before asking an employee to submit to a drug test. In Vermont, for example, before administering the test, the employer must give the employee a copy of a written policy setting forth the circumstances under which persons may be tested, the drugs that will be screened, the procedures involved, and the consequences of a positive result.

A number of states have comprehensive drug- and alcohol-testing laws that require reasonable suspicion or probable cause before an employer may test. The requirements for establishing reasonable suspicion or probable cause vary from state to state. For instance, Connecticut's law permits testing when "the employer has reasonable suspicion that the employee is under the influence of drugs or alcohol which adversely affects or could adversely affect such employee's job performance."[61]

53. 135 F.3d 1260 (9th Cir. 1998).
54. Francine Kiefer, *Amid Genetic Discoveries, a Nod to Privacy. As Science Advances, Clinton Bars Use of Genetic Information in Hiring for Federal Jobs,* CHRISTIAN SCI. MONITOR, Feb. 10, 2000, at 2.
55. *Id.*
56. *Id.*
57. Aaron Zitner, *Senate Votes to Bar Insurance Denials Based on Genes Health: Measure, Milder Than What Democrats Wanted, Extends Current Protections to Individual Policies. Bill Would Also Prevent Premium Hikes,* L.A. TIMES, June 30, 2000, at A-18.
58. *Congress Told to Protect Against Genetic Discrimination,* CONGRESS DAILY, July 20, 2000.

59. 768 P.2d 1123 (Alaska 1989).
60. Semore v. Pool, 217 Cal. App. 3d 1087 (Cal. Ct. App. 1990).
61. CONN. GEN. STAT. ANN. § 31-51x (West Supp. 1993).

Although private employers, as well as public employers, may face some limits on implementing a drug-testing program, it should be noted that employers have the right to make and enforce rules prohibiting drug use or possession on work premises, as well as rules prohibiting employees from being under the influence of drugs while at work. When an employee exhibits visible signs of intoxication or impairment or inadequate performance, the employer may take disciplinary action. Because of the inadequacy of drug tests and the uncertainty about the scope of employees' rights, the employer may wish instead to develop programs that provide assistance and drug education and to counsel employees about the performance problems that drug abuse can cause.

 ## Polygraph Testing *of* Employees

Polygraph testing is another area where employees' right to privacy may limit employers' investigative rights. The Employee Polygraph Protection Act of 1988 (EPPA)[62] generally makes it unlawful for employers to (1) ask an applicant or employee to take a polygraph exam or other lie detector test; (2) rely on or inquire about the results of a lie detector test that an applicant or employee has taken; (3) take or threaten to take any adverse action against an applicant or employee because of a refusal to take, or on the basis of the results of, any lie detector test; or (4) take or threaten to take any adverse action against an employee or applicant who has filed a complaint or participated in a proceeding relating to the polygraph law.

The EPPA does not completely ban the use of polygraph exams. Employers may test employees who are reasonably suspected of conduct injurious to the business, as well as applicants or employees in certain businesses involving security services or the handling of drugs.

These rights cannot be waived by the employee in advance. For example, a federal district court held that although a bartender signed a release form stating that her employer had reasonable suspicion of theft before requesting that she take a polygraph test, the bartender could still sue for violation of the EPPA.[63] The court held that an employee can waive rights or procedures under the EPPA only pursuant to a written settlement of a pending lawsuit.

The EPPA does not restrict federal, state, or local government employers from administering polygraph exams. However, several states have laws restricting or prohibiting the use of polygraph examinations. For example, in Massachusetts, an employer cannot request that an applicant or employee take a lie detector test as a condition of employment.[64] Rhode Island,[65] Delaware,[66] and Pennsylvania[67] have similar statutes. Even when lie detector tests are permitted, no question should be asked during the test that could not lawfully be asked on an application form or during an interview.

 ## Employee Surveillance

According to a 1997 survey by the American Management Association, 35 percent of businesses in the United States surveyed said that they use various strategies to check up on employees, including listening in on employees' voicemail and phone calls, inspecting their computer files, and using video surveillance.[68] Of those, 25 percent indicated that they conducted these activities without the consent or awareness of employees.

Employers have a legitimate interest in observing their employees to ensure quality control and productivity, but under certain circumstances surveillance may transgress the employees' privacy rights. The watershed case in this area was *O'Connor v. Ortega*.[69] In that case, the U.S. Supreme Court ruled that a public employee may, in certain circumstances, enjoy a reasonable expectation of privacy in the workplace. However, the employee's privacy interest is to be balanced by the "operational realities" of the workplace. Since *Ortega*, lower courts have looked to (1) whether the employee was provided exclusive working space, (2) the nature of the employment, and (3) whether the employee was on notice that parts of the workplace were subject to employer intrusions. For example, in *Vega-Rodriguez v. Puerto Rico Telephone Company,*[70] the U.S. Court of Appeals for the First Circuit held that governmental security operators, sitting in an open, undifferentiated work area, who monitored computer banks to detect alarm-system signals, had no reasonable expectation of privacy. As a result, the public employer's soundless video surveillance of the workplace did not violate the employees' Fourth Amendment rights.

62. 29 U.S.C. §§ 2001–2009 (1988).
63. Long v. Mango's Tropical Café, Inc., 958 F. Supp. 612 (S.D. Fla. 1997).

64. Mass Gen. Laws Ann.. ch. 149, § 19B (West 1996).
65. R.I. Gen. Laws § 28-6.1-1 (1996).
66. Del. Code Ann. tit. 19, § 704 (1997).
67. 18 Pa. Cons. Stat. Ann. § 7321 (West 1998).
68. *Who's Watching?, supra* note 48.
69. 480 U.S. 709 (1987).
70. 110 F.3d 174 (1st Cir. 1997).

Big Brother Is Reading Your E-Mail

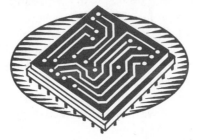

A 1998 Ernst & Young survey reported that electronic mail had become the primary business communication tool: 36 percent of respondents used e-mail more than the telephone or face-to-face meetings.[a] Employee use of the Internet and e-mail has raised a number of new issues in the workplace. Employers are increasingly concerned that employees are wasting company time by using the Internet for personal reasons during working hours. In addition, employees' use of the Internet and e-mail could subject their employers to liability or disrupt business within the company. Despite employers' concerns, a survey by the Society for Human Resource Management revealed that 51 percent of companies do not train employees on proper and improper use of e-mail, although 52 percent do have formal written policies addressing its use.[b]

An American Management Association survey found that in 1999, 27 percent of major U.S. firms checked employee e-mail, up from 15 percent from 1997.[c] In 1999, the New York Times Company fired more than twenty employees for sending e-mail that was "inappropriate and offensive"; Xerox Corporation fired forty workers, including those who visited pornographic Web sites from office computers, for violating its company policy on Internet use; and investment firm Edward Jones & Co. terminated nineteen employees when it discovered they were using the company's e-mail system to send inappropriate material.[d] Most courts have upheld the right of employers to monitor and regulate workplace e-mail and use of computers on the grounds that the employees could not prove that they had a reasonable expectation of privacy in workplace e-mails or computer use.[e] Because the Internet and e-mail are used for union-organizing activities, the National Labor Relations Board has placed more restrictions than the courts on employers' monitoring and regulation of employee use of the Internet and e-mail.[f]

Even former employees' abuse of a company's e-mail system can raise problems. In 1998, a California state court ruled that a former employee of Intel Corporation, Kenneth Hamidi, trespassed on Intel property when he sent seven mass e-mailings criticizing the company to as many as 30,000 Intel employees.[g] After Hamidi was fired by Intel, he began a campaign of criticizing its human resource policies; in addition to his mass e-mailings, he established a Web site critical of the company. Rejecting Hamidi's argument that his e-mails were protected by the First Amendment, the court barred Hamidi from sending mass e-mailings in the future. The American Civil Liberties Union took up Hamidi's case and filed an *amicus* brief in 2000 supporting his appeal.[h]

As more people buy and sell stock over the Internet, online trading on company time has also increased. From December 1998 to March 1999, the number of employees who visited financial Web sites while at work increased 37 percent.[i] In fact, people spend 70 percent more time visiting financial Web sites on the job than they do at home.[j] As well as taking time away from work, large losses or profits from financial trading often create additional stress and distract employees from their work. In addition, companies could potentially face liability if an employee claimed that an investment decision was based on old information from a cached site that the employer did not update. (Some employers "cache" Web sites, which involves copying them and displaying them over the company's electronic system. However, companies do not always update these sites; as a result, employees may trade on outdated information.)

To avoid problems and resolve conflicts with employees, companies should draft Internet, e-mail, and computer use policies.[k] These policies should prohibit the sending of unlawful, offensive, and defamatory statements via the corporate e-mail system. In addition, companies should establish security measures and educate their employees about the policies and the manner in which the employer will enforce them.

a. Susan R. Hobbs, *Most Companies Need to Train Workers in E-Mail Use Policy to Avoid Exposure to Litigation and Waste of Employees' Time,* CORP. COUNS. WKLY., Apr. 14, 1999, at 8.
b. *Id.*
c. Nick Wingfield, *More Companies Monitor Employees' E-Mail,* WALL ST. J., Dec. 2, 1999, at B8.
d. *Id.*
e. Susan E. Gindin, *Employee E-Mail and Internet Use Raises Many Legal Issues,* CORP. COUNS. WKLY., Sept. 15, 1999, at 8.
f. *Id.*
g. Tom Abate, *Corporate America Is Eyeing the Outcome of Intel's E-Mail Case,* SAN FRANCISCO CHRON., Dec. 14, 1998, at B1.
h. Sherman Fridman, *ACLU Accuses Intel of Violating Free Speech,* NEWSBYTES, May 12, 2000.
i. Simon J. Nadel, *Employers Have Good Reason to Be Bearish, As Online Trading by Their Employees Increases Thirty Seven Percent During Company Time,* CORP. COUNS. WKLY., Oct. 13, 1999, at 6.
j. *Id.*
k. Gindin, *supra* note e.

⬧ Responsibility *for* Worker Safety

Both federal and state laws require employers to provide a reasonably safe workplace.

OCCUPATIONAL SAFETY AND HEALTH ACT

The Occupational Safety and Health Act of 1970 (OSHA)[71] was enacted to require employers to establish safe and healthful working environments. The federal agency responsible for enforcing the provisions of OSHA is the Occupational Safety and Health Administration (also called OSHA). This agency is authorized by Congress to govern additional workplace issues, including exposure to hazardous chemicals, protective gear, fire protection, and workplace temperatures and ventilation.

An employer governed by OSHA must provide a place of employment that is free from *recognized hazards* that are causing or are likely to cause death or serious physical harm to employees. What constitutes a recognized hazard is not entirely clear. However, its reach is broad and includes anything from sharp objects to radiation. Conditions that are obviously dangerous or are considered by the employer or other employers in the industry to be dangerous are considered recognized hazards. OSHA also imposes on employers a "general duty" to abate workplace hazards.[72]

In March 2000, OSHA announced that approximately 13,000 employers needed to correct workplace safety and health hazards or face comprehensive safety and health inspections.[73] OSHA identified the employers based on data reported in a 1998 OSHA survey of lost workday injury and illness rates of 80,000 workplaces. The identified employers had eight or more injuries and illnesses resulting in lost workdays for every one hundred workers, substantially higher than the national average of three incidents per one hundred workers.

OSHA inspectors are allowed to conduct surprise inspections at work sites when (1) OSHA believes an imminent danger is present, (2) an employee has filed a complaint, or (3) a fatality or catastrophe has occurred. During the inspection, the OSHA investigator may review company records, check for compliance with the relevant OSHA standards, inspect fire-protection and other safety equipment, examine the company's safety and health-management programs, interview employees, and walk through the facility.

When the inspection has been completed, the inspector meets with the employer and the employee representative, if any. The inspector discusses the results of the inspection and, if appropriate, issues a written citation for violations. There are five types of violations: (1) de minimis (that is, unimportant) violations, for which no notice is posted and no penalty is imposed; (2) nonserious violations, which present hazards that are not likely to cause death or serious bodily harm, for which a fine of up to $7,000 for each violation may be imposed; (3) serious violations, which have a substantial likelihood of resulting in death or serious bodily harm, for which a fine of up to $7,000 for each violation may be imposed; (4) willful violations, which are deliberate or intentional, for which a fine of at least $5,000 and up to $70,000 may be imposed for each violation; and (5) repeated violations, which occur within three years of a previously cited violation, for which a fine of up to $70,000 for each violation may be imposed. Courts may also impose criminal sanctions for health and safety infractions (see Chapter 17).

For purposes of sanctioning violations, the U.S. Court of Appeals for the Fifth Circuit held that the hazardous condition is the proper unit of prosecution, rather than the number of employees exposed to the hazardous condition.[74] Thus, if eighty-seven employees are threatened by a chemical explosion, then one violation (the explosion), rather than eighty-seven (the number of individuals exposed to the risk of heat, burns, and flying debris as a result of the explosion), may be cited.

If OSHA finds a violation, the employer is required to remedy the problem immediately. If remedial action is not taken, OSHA will seek a court order to ensure compliance. The employer may either settle the violation or seek review of the OSHA decision by the Occupational Safety and Health Review Commission. OSHA may penalize egregious violations by imposing a separate fine for each violation rather than an overall fine for a group of violations. Additionally, punitive damages are available, and the courts have upheld their application in extreme cases. For example, a federal district court recently permitted punitive damages in a suit against a nursing home that "blatantly" retaliated against a nurse for filing a complaint with OSHA regarding the lack of latex gloves at the site.[75]

71. Pub. L. No. 91-596, 84 Stat. 1590 (1970) (codified as amended at 29 U.S.C. §§ 651–678 (2000)).

72. Reich v. Pepperidge Farm, 66 U.S.L.W. 2095 (OSHRC 1997).

73. *13,000 Employers Must End Hazards; 4,200 Could Face Inspections,* CORP. COUNS. WKLY., Apr. 5, 2000.

74. Reich v. Arcadian Corp., 110 F.3d 1192 (5th Cir. 1997).

75. Reich v. Skyline Terrace Inc., 977 F. Supp. 1141 (N.D. Okla. 1997).

In January 1999, OSHA imposed a $1.6 million fine on Tomasco Mulciber, Inc., an Ohio company that builds car frames for Honda of America.[76] The company had failed to protect workers from unguarded machinery that resulted in more than sixty accidents. OSHA issued citations alleging twenty-eight willful violations of machine-guarding requirements and seventeen serious violations of standards. OSHA's inspection revealed eighty instances of machine-guarding deficiences over a four-year period.

OSHA also requires employers to maintain certain records, including the OSHA Form 200, which lists and summarizes all work-related injuries and illnesses. (Certain industries, such as retail, finance, and insurance, are exempt from this record-keeping requirement.) A summary of these records must be posted annually at the job site. In addition, employers must post in a conspicuous place (1) OSHA's official Job Safety Poster; (2) any OSHA citations for violations; and (3) notices of imminent danger to employees, including exposure to toxic substances.

A 1999 OSHA survey revealed that more than 85 percent of employers conduct voluntary self-audits of safety and health conditions at their work sites as part of an effort to reduce workplace injury and illness rates, to ensure compliance with OSHA regulations, and because it is the "right thing" to do.[77]

Ergonomics Regulations and Repetitive-Stress Injuries In November 2000, OSHA adopted highly controversial ergonomics regulations designed to combat repetitive-stress disorders caused by having workers do the same task repeatedly.[78] The agency had been developing the regulations since 1989. Under the new rules, companies where at least one injury has been reported must initiate training, implement engineering and equipment changes in the workplace to eliminate or sharply reduce hazards, and provide injured employees time off for up to ninety days with 90 percent of wages and 100 percent of benefits.[79] Although OSHA estimated that it would cost businesses $4.8 billion a year to comply, cost estimates from industry ranged from $18 billion a year (by the National Association of Manufacturers) to $125.6 billion a year (by the Employment Policy Foundation, a think tank). United Parcel Service estimated that compliance would cost the company $20 billion initially and $5 billion a year thereafter.[80]

The regulations characterize a variety of tasks as hazardous, including using a keyboard and/or computer mouse "in a steady manner for more than four hours total in a workday," using certain vibrating equipment (such as chainsaws) for more than thirty minutes a day, and lifting more than seventy-five pounds once a day. Companies are required to provide all employees deemed to be at risk for repetitive-stress injuries free access to a physician or other health care professional.

Within two weeks after the final adoption of OSHA's ergonomics regulations, business and labor groups had already filed a flurry of lawsuits across the United States challenging the new rules.[81] Corporations, including steel manufacturers, attacked the regulations as too onerous, while unions challenged them for being too weak. A lawyer for the National Association of Manufacturers called the rules "the biggest regulation in the history of the republic." He lamented, "This deals with sitting, the angle of your neck and whether you can lift ten pounds. What doesn't it deal with?"[82]

In March 2001, the Senate and the House of Representatives adopted, and President George W. Bush signed, legislation that rescinded the regulations.

Criminal Prosecutions The number of criminal prosecutions of employers for OSHA violations is increasing. In March 2000, for example, the Department of Labor's Mine Safety and Health Administration launched a criminal probe of Kaiser Aluminum Corporation in response to a huge explosion in 1999 that bathed workers in boiling lye.[83] Although the word "employer" has not been defined, it appears to include those corporate officers who are responsible for ensuring compliance with OSHA standards.

State Analogues to OSHA Many states have enacted laws similar to OSHA to ensure employees' safety in the workplace. In 1999, the state of Michigan fined Ford Motor Company $1.5 million for safety violations under Michigan's OSHA, as a result of a boiler explosion that killed six employees and injured fourteen others. The

76. *OSHA Hits Plant with $1.6 Million Fine for Unguarded Machines,* Corp. Couns. Wkly., Feb. 10, 1999.

77. *More Than 85 Percent of Employers Do Self-Audits of Work Site Safety, Health Conditions, OSHA Says,* Corp. Couns. Wkly., Dec. 1, 1999.

78. Yochi J. Dreazen, *Ergonomic Rules Are the First in a Wave of Late Regulations,* Wall St. J., Nov. 14, 2000 at A4.

79. Yochi J. Dreazen & Phil Kuntz, *New OSHA Proposal Enrages Business: Ergonomics Plan Is Tougher Than One That Caused Big Budget Stalemate,* Wall St. J., Nov. 8, 2000, at A2.

80. *Id.*

81. Cindy Skrzycki, *The Regulators: Repetitive-Lawsuit Syndrome,* Wash. Post, Nov. 28, 2000, at E1.

82. *Id.*

83. Gardiner Harris & Robert Guy Matthews, *Criminal Probe of Kaiser Blast Is Begun,* Wall St. J., Mar. 22, 2000, at A2.

fine was the largest monetary sanction ever levied by the state of Michigan under its OSHA act.[84] Ford also agreed, as part of the settlement, to spend $5.5 million for workplace safety training and research, inspections of the work site, and donations to hospitals for burn care.[85]

STATE CRIMINAL PROSECUTIONS

Recognizing OSHA's financial and staff limitations, prosecutors in at least fourteen states have charged employers with crimes ranging from assault and battery to reckless homicide for ignoring warnings to correct workplace safety hazards.[86] In addition, California and Maine have enacted laws specifically providing for criminal penalties for employers who endanger their employees.

Prosecutors have criminally charged a number of managers and officers of corporations in connection with serious violations that led to the death of employees. These prosecutions have had mixed results. For example, in 1990, the Michigan Court of Appeals held that a supervisor was not guilty of involuntary manslaughter because he did not own the equipment that caused the accident.[87] In 1992, after twenty-five workers died in a fire at a chicken plant in North Carolina because fire-exit doors were locked, allegedly to prevent employees from stealing chickens, the plant owner pled guilty to involuntary manslaughter and was sentenced to nearly twenty years, the stiffest prison term to date.[88]

In 1996, Massachusetts charged two metal-processing companies and their owners with assault and battery with a dangerous weapon: lead dust that workers inhaled while standing over giant kettles, stirring molten metals. The vacuum device that was supposed to suck up the vapors was broken. The Massachusetts attorney general claimed that this was not an accident: "They knew that they had created illegal conditions which were dangerous."[89] The former president of one of the companies, Tewksbury Industries, pled guilty in 1998 to misdemeanor assault and battery charges and was sentenced to three years' probation and four hundred hours of community service.[90]

TORT LIABILITY FOR VIOLENCE IN THE WORKPLACE

Employers also face potential liability for violence in the workplace perpetrated by employees or their former lovers or spouses. A survey of security professionals for Fortune 1000 companies, released in April 2000, revealed that workplace violence was the most significant security concern for U.S. businesses. Workplace violence results in three deaths daily and thousands of injuries yearly, costing employers $36 billion annually.[91]

According to the 1999 Workplace Violence Survey (conducted by the Society for Human Resource Management), 68 percent of the organizations that responded to the survey have written policies addressing workplace violence, and 79 percent have written policies regulating weapons on their premises.[92] To help prevent domestic violence from spilling over into the workplace, some companies hold seminars on domestic-violence issues on company time, provide a twenty-four-hour telephone counseling service for employees and their partners, and tap the phones of women who fear an attack and provide them with escorts to and from parking lots. Sometimes, the employer seeks restraining orders in its name to keep alleged abusers from potential victims' work sites.[93]

Once an employer is informed about the risk of violence or takes an interest in the case, it exposes itself to liability for negligence if it fails to take reasonable steps to prevent injury. For example, in 1995, both the employer of a woman killed in her Houston office by a former boyfriend and the office-building manager agreed to pay more than $350,000 to settle a case brought by the woman's family. The woman had told them that the former boyfriend was subject to a restraining order and that she feared he would kill her. According to her mother, "They didn't believe her story."[94]

In contrast, in *Holdervaum v. Itco Holding Co.*,[95] the Florida Appeals Court held that the employer was not liable in tort for the murder of a supervisor by an employee he laid off. When the supervisor informed the employee that he had lost his job, the employee threatened the supervisor's life in front of other employees. Later that day, he used a pistol other employees knew that he kept at the workplace to murder the supervisor. The court held that

84. Todd Nighswonger, *Rouge Settlement Sparks Safety Initiative at Ford*, Occupational Hazards, Oct. 1, 1999, at 101.
85. *Ford Pays $7 Million to Settle State Probe of Plant Explosion*, Wall St. J., Sept. 3, 1999, at B6.
86. Ann Davis, *Treating On-the-Job Injuries as True Crimes*, Wall St. J., Feb. 26, 1997, at B1.
87. Michigan v. Hegedus, 451 N.W.2d 861 (Mich. Ct. App. 1990), *appeal denied*, 435 Mich. 860 (1990).
88. Davis, *supra* note 86.
89. *Id.*
90. *Officer Pleads Guilty for Two Workplace Deaths*, Corp. Couns. Wkly., Oct. 7, 1998, at 5.

91. *On-Job Violence Costs Three Deaths Daily, $36 Billion Annually*, Corp. Couns. Wkly., Apr. 19, 2000.
92. *As Reports of Workplace Violence Rise, Employers Step Up Security Measures, Training*, Corp. Couns. Wkly., Nov. 24, 1999.
93. *Id.*
94. *Id.*
95. 753 So. 2d 699 (Fla. App. 2000).

AT THE TOP

A manager can be held criminally responsible for serious workplace safety violations. Diligent oversight of health and safety aspects of the workplace can reduce both the chance that an employee will suffer serious injury or death in the first place and the likelihood that an individual manager will be found criminally liable if, despite his or her diligence, a fatal accident does occur.

the company was protected by the immunity granted employers under the state workers' compensation act. Even though the company may have been grossly negligent in not taking the laid-off employee's threats seriously, its actions did not exhibit a deliberate intent to injure nor were they so substantially certain to result in injury or death as to constitute an intentional tort.

Similarly, in *Jarrell v. Englefield*,[96] the Ohio Court of Appeals did not hold a gas station/convenience store operator responsible when a cashier was murdered at one of its stores. The court found that the company did not know of the existence of a dangerous condition nor of a high probability that an employee would be injured there because there was no history of violence at the store. In addition, the store contained security devices (including a closed-circuit camera, a silent alarm, and signs indicating there was a camera), and the employee had been trained in handling himself during a robbery. Thus, the employer had taken adequate measures to protect its employees.

Workers' Compensation

State workers' compensation statutes provide for coverage of income and medical expenses for employees who suffer work-related accidents or illnesses.[97] The statutes are based on the principle that the risks of injury in the workplace should be borne by industry. The system is no-fault, and an employee is entitled to benefits regardless of the level of safety in the work environment and the degree to which the employee's carelessness contributed to the incident. However, the monetary awards are generally lower than those that might be obtained in lawsuits for negligence or other torts. Independent contractors are generally excluded from workers' compensation.

Workers' compensation can be provided through (1) self-insurance, (2) insurance purchased through a state fund, or (3) insurance purchased through a private company. A properly implemented workers' compensation insurance program for all employees enables the employer to argue against other, more expensive remedies an injured employee may seek, such as tort damages. For example, the California Supreme Court ruled that a firefighter's claim of intentional infliction of emotional distress was barred by the workers' compensation statutes.[98]

Some courts have recognized exceptions to the general rule that workers' compensation is the sole remedy available for workplace injuries. For example, the Washington Supreme Court permitted a suit involving employee exposure to toxic chemicals in a fiberglass cloth used in airplane construction to continue.[99] The court ruled that the employer's conduct amounted to deliberate intent to injure. As a result, the suit was not barred by the workers' compensation remedy.

Minimum Wage, Overtime, *and* Child Labor

The federal Fair Labor Standards Act (FLSA),[100] enacted in 1938 and amended many times thereafter, was established primarily to regulate the minimum wage, overtime pay, and the use of child labor. Many, if not all, states have established wage and hour regulations as well. In general, when the federal and state laws vary, employers must abide by the stricter law. Because of the wide variance in state laws, this discussion focuses on the federal law.

WHO IS COVERED

The FLSA applies to employees who individually are engaged in interstate commerce or in the production of goods for interstate commerce, or who are employed by employers that engage in interstate commerce. As a practical matter, employers of any size that participate in interstate commerce or in the production of goods for interstate commerce are covered by the FLSA.

The FLSA does not apply to independent contractors. Proper characterization of workers can be hotly contested. Chapter 5 outlines the factors courts use in deciding whether a worker is an employee or an independent contractor.

96. 2000 Ohio App. LEXIS 1076 (Ohio Ct. App. Mar. 17, 2000).
97. *See* CONSTANCE E. BAGLEY & CRAIG E. DAUCHY, THE ENTREPRENEUR'S GUIDE TO BUSINESS LAW 378–89 (1998).

98. Cole v. Fair Oaks Fire Protection Dist., 729 P.2d 743 (Cal. 1987).
99. Birklid v. Boeing Co., 904 P.2d 278 (Wash. 1995).
100. 29 U.S.C. §§ 201–219 (1998 & Supp. 1992).

HOURS WORKED

The FLSA does not limit the number of hours that an employee may work in a workweek or workday, as long as the employee is paid appropriate overtime. (But, as noted in Chapter 9, if an employer forces an employee to work too many hours, the employer may be liable under common law negligence for injury to a third party resulting from the employee's fatigue.)

In 1985, Congress amended the FLSA to permit state and local governments to comply with the statute's overtime provisions by giving employees compensatory time (comp time) in lieu of overtime pay. *Comp time* is extra paid vacation time granted instead of extra pay for overtime work. In the following case, the Supreme Court considered whether public employers can require employees to use their accrued comp time when the amount reaches a certain level.

A CASE IN POINT

CASE 14.5

Christensen v. Harris County
*Supreme Court of the
United States
120 S. Ct. 1655 (2000).*

Summary

FACTS Sheriff Tommy B. Thomas of Harris County, Texas, and 127 deputy sheriffs agreed to accept compensatory time, instead of cash, as compensation for overtime. As they accumulated comp time, Harris County became concerned that it lacked the financial resources to pay employees who (1) worked overtime after reaching the statutory cap on comp time accrual or (2) left their jobs with large amounts of accrued time.

To address these concerns, Harris County implemented a policy setting the maximum number of hours of comp time that could be accumulated. After an employee's hours had reached the maximum, the employee was asked to reduce his or her comp time; if the employee did not do so, a supervisor could order the employee to use the comp time at specified times. The sheriffs sued, claiming that the policy violated the FLSA.

ISSUE PRESENTED Can a state or its subdivision require employees to use accrued comp time?

SUMMARY OF OPINION The U.S. Supreme Court began its analysis by noting that both parties conceded that nothing in the FLSA expressly prohibits a state or subdivision thereof from compelling employees to use accrued comp time. The sheriffs argued, however, that the FLSA implicitly prohibits this practice in the absence of an agreement authorizing compelled use, because the statute requires an employer to reasonably accommodate employee requests to use comp time. The Court found this argument unpersuasive. The Court read this provision as a safeguard to ensure that an employee will receive timely compensation for working overtime rather than as setting forth the exclusive *method* by which compensatory time can be used. Thus, the statute imposes a restriction upon an employer's efforts to *prohibit* the use of comp time when employees request to do so, but it says nothing about restricting an employer's efforts to *require* employees to use comp time.

RESULT The Supreme Court upheld Harris County's policy requiring use of comp time.

COMPENSATION

The FLSA requires that employees be compensated for all hours worked. In the case of professional or off-site employees, the number of hours worked may be hotly contested. In general, the hours that an employer knows or has reason to know that an employee has worked, even though the employee has not been requested to work, are deemed hours worked. If an employee is asked to be on

standby—that is, available to return to work while off duty—the hours spent on standby will not be counted as hours worked if the employee is free to use the time for his or her own purposes. Workers will also not be compensated for their time spent traveling to or from the job. In *Kavanagh v. Grand Union Co.,*[101] a supermarket employee who worked as a mechanic traveling to different

101. 192 F.3d 269 (2d Cir. 1999).

job sites sought overtime compensation for his commute. Although the U.S. Court of Appeals for the Second Circuit held that he was entitled to compensation for travel between the different sites during his workday between 8:00 A.M. and 4:30 P.M., he was not entitled to overtime compensation for time spent traveling between his home and the first job of the day or the time between the last job of the day and home.

MINIMUM WAGE AND OVERTIME

In 1938, the FLSA first established the minimum wage at 25 cents per hour. The federal minimum wage in December 2000 was $5.15 per hour. The FLSA also requires that, with some exceptions, every nonexempt employee be paid one and one-half times the regular rate of pay for hours worked in excess of forty in a workweek. In May 2000, the FLSA was amended to permit employers to exclude profits from certain employer-provided stock options, stock appreciation rights, and bona fide stock purchases from the calculation of regular pay rates when calculating overtime pay.[102]

Exempt Employees Certain types of employees are exempt from the minimum-wage and overtime requirements of the FLSA, including salespersons and executive, administrative, and professional employees.[103] In 1999, Nabisco, Inc. agreed to pay $5 million to settle a suit brought by the Department of Labor against the company for its failure to pay overtime to 3,130 of its retail sales employees.[104] Nabisco had classified these employees as retail sales representatives, a classification exempt from overtime pay, when, in fact, they spent most of their time delivering and stocking products, which was work compensated for on an hourly basis.

The regulations of the Wage and Hour Division of the Department of Labor define the characteristics of executive, administrative, and professional employees in terms of salary and work duties. In general, an *exempt employee* is paid a minimum salary per week or month, while *nonexempt employees* are often paid an hourly wage. In *Auer v. Robbins,*[105] the U.S. Supreme Court held that police officers could be exempt employees even though their compensation could theoretically be reduced due to variations in the quality or quantity of their work. The

Court ruled that the salary test is met if an employee's compensation may not, as a practical matter, be reduced due to work-product variations. If, however, there is either an actual practice of making deductions or a significant likelihood of such deductions, then the employees are covered by the overtime provisions of the FLSA.

The U.S. Court of Appeals for the Ninth Circuit held that subjecting an employee's pay to deductions for absences of less than a day was antithetical to the concept of a salaried employee.[106] In *In re Wal-Mart Stores, Inc.,*[107] a federal district court held that Wal-Mart had violated the FLSA when it failed to pay overtime as a result of improperly characterizing pharmacists as exempt employees when they were actually hourly employees. Because Wal-Mart cut the base salaries of the pharmacists after the company reduced store hours by one or two hours due to slow business, the court concluded that the pharmacists' salaries were based on the number of hours that they worked. The Ninth Circuit has accepted the Department of Labor's position that additional compensation in the form of hourly overtime payment does not defeat exempt status under the salary-basis test.[108]

For a person to qualify as an *executive,* his or her primary duty must consist of the management of the enterprise where he or she is employed or of a customarily recognized department or subdivision of the enterprise. The person must also (1) customarily and regularly direct the work of two or more other full-time employees, (2) have the authority to hire or fire other employees, (3) customarily or regularly exercise discretion, and (4) not devote more than 20 percent of his or her time to other types of duties.

To qualify as an *administrative employee,* a person's primary duty must consist of nonmanual work directly related either to management policies or to the general business operations of the employer or the employer's customers. The person's primary duty must require the exercise of discretion and independent judgment. For example, the U.S. Court of Appeals for the First Circuit held that insurance company marketing representatives qualify as administrative employees and are therefore exempt from the FLSA's overtime provisions.[109] The court rejected the Department of Labor's argument that the representatives were not given discretion in "matters of consequence." Instead, the court looked to the nature of the work and held that the discretion and independent judgment involved, in addition to its substantial eco-

102. Simon J. Nadel, *FLSA: The Law Employers Love to Hate Is Scrutinized in Light of the New Economy,* 68 U.S.L.W. 49, June 27, 2000, at 2771.
103. 29 U.S.C. § 213(a) (1).
104. *Nabisco Will Pay $5 Million to Settle Overtime Violations,* Corp. Couns. Wkly., Oct. 13, 1999, at 5.
105. 519 U.S. 452 (1997).

106. Abshire v. County of Kern, 908 F.2d 483 (9th Cir. 1990), *cert. denied,* 498 U.S. 1068 (1991).
107. 58 F. Supp. 2d 1219 (D. Colo. 1999).
108. Boykin v. Boeing Co., 128 F.3d 1279 (9th Cir. 1997).
109. Reich v. John Alden Life Ins. Co., 126 F.3d 1 (1st Cir. 1997).

nomic consequences, satisfied the requirements of an administrative employee.

For a person to qualify as a *professional employee,* he or she must have a position requiring advanced knowledge in a field of science or learning customarily acquired by a prolonged course of specialized intellectual instruction and study. In *Freeman v. National Broadcasting Co.,*[110] the U.S. Court of Appeals for the Second Circuit held that writers and producers for a national television news program were exempt from the overtime provisions of the FLSA. The court reasoned that the workers were artistic professionals and could not be considered nonexempt employees.

Similarly, in *Fazekas v. Cleveland Clinic Health Care Ventures, Inc.,*[111] the U.S. Court of Appeals for the Sixth Circuit held that nurses who made home-care visits were employed in a professional capacity and, as a result, were exempt from the FLSA's overtime requirements. The court found that the nurses' work required advanced knowledge and the exercise of discretion and judgment. In addition, they were compensated on a per-visit fee basis regardless of the time spent at each visit.

In September 1999, the General Accounting Office recommended that the Department of Labor revise the FLSA regulations so that the "white-collar exemption" would more accurately reflect the realities of the contemporary workplace.[112] According to the report, the regulations had been updated only in a piecemeal fashion over the past forty-five years. Employers complained that the regulations were outdated and too complex, and employees claimed that they did not sufficiently restrict the exemptions. The director of governmental affairs at the Society for Human Resource Management commented that the FLSA regulations were drafted when "employees were brought on more for their brawn than their brains."[113] He added, "There is a new type of worker out there," and "that gray area [between white- and blue-collar workers] is becoming larger with technology workers."

Who Is Liable for Violations Individuals as well as corporations may be held liable for violations under the FLSA. In *Herman v. RSR Security Services,*[114] the U.S. Court of Appeals for the Second Circuit ruled that Murray Portnoy, a principal in a labor relations firm, exercised enough control over a security company's employees to be held liable as an employer for violations of the FLSA's minimum-wage, overtime, and record-keeping requirements. Portnoy partially owned the security company, he funded its start-up costs, and he chaired its board of directors. The appeals court affirmed a judgment of $160,000 against Portnoy.

In *Luder v. Endicott,*[115] a federal district court held that individual employees of a state government could also be liable under the FLSA. In this case, hourly employees at a Wisconsin state penitentiary brought a claim alleging that the warden and other supervisors violated the FLSA by altering time sheets and not compensating them for their work. The court held that individuals who do not pay employees' wages may still qualify as employers under the FLSA if they have substantial control over the terms and conditions of the employees' work. The court also ruled that the supervisors were not protected by Eleventh Amendment immunity when sued in their individual capacities for violating the FLSA.

CHILD LABOR

The FLSA child-labor provisions were enacted to stop the early twentieth-century abuses of many employers who employed children at minimal wages. Under federal law, it is illegal to employ anyone under the age of fourteen, except in specified agricultural occupations. Children aged fourteen or fifteen may work in some occupations, but only if the employment occurs outside school hours and does not exceed daily and weekly hour limits. Individuals aged sixteen to eighteen may work in manufacturing occupations, but they may not work in jobs that the secretary of labor has declared to be particularly hazardous, such as operating a power-driven woodworking machine, a hoisting apparatus, a metal-forming machine, or a circular or band saw. Jobs entailing exposure to radioactive materials are also deemed to be hazardous.

MODERN-DAY SLAVERY

Responding to several cases, including one involving a farm labor contractor who pled guilty to coercing migrant workers in South Carolina to harvest cucumbers against their will, U.S. Attorney General Janet Reno established the Worker Exploitation Task Force in April 1998 to investigate and prosecute cases of "modern-day slavery" in the United States. She cited one case involving Thai garment workers in California who were forced by armed guards to work twenty-hour shifts in sweatshop conditions and another case involving sixty deaf

110. 80 F.3d 78 (2d Cir. 1996).
111. 204 F.3d 673 (6th Cir. 2000).
112. *DOL Advised to Update Regs on "White Collar" Exemptions,* CORP. COUNS. WKLY., Oct. 20, 1999, at 3.
113. Nadel, *supra* note 102.
114. 172 F.3d 132 (2d Cir. 1999).
115. 86 F. Supp. 2d 854 (W.D. Wis. 2000).

Mexicans forced to peddle key chains in the streets and subways of New York City.

 # Employee Retirement Income Security Act

For several decades before 1974, the number of pension plans, the number of employees covered by those plans, and the annual benefits paid to retirees from these plans grew tremendously. Despite these increases, many employees who expected to receive pension payments upon retirement received either no benefits or far fewer benefits than they had anticipated. Plan officials made ill-advised investments; employees quit or were discharged with few or no vested benefits; or the employer terminated an underfunded plan with insufficient assets to cover its obligations. To help remedy these problems, Congress enacted the Employee Retirement Income Security Act of 1974 (ERISA).[116]

COVERAGE

With few exceptions, ERISA applies to all pension plans and to many other types of employee benefit plans, established by employers engaged in interstate commerce. With regard to pension plans, ERISA (1) establishes minimum funding requirements and participation and vesting standards; (2) imposes fiduciary obligations on pension plan administrators; (3) requires detailed disclosure and reporting of certain pension plan information; (4) restricts substantially the investment of pension plan assets; and (5) calls for pension plan administrators to provide annual, audited financial statements to the government and participants. An employer must also maintain records of each employee's years of service and vesting percentage.

Nonpension benefit plans (such as medical, dental, and disability plans) are also subject to ERISA's reporting, disclosure, and fiduciary-responsibility rules. For example, employees must be provided with documents such as a summary plan description, a summary annual report, and a summary of any material modifications to the plan. Further, the employer or plan administrator must maintain sufficient records, usually including age, hours worked, salary, and employee contributions, to calculate each employee's benefits.

Other employee benefits (which may not be part of a formal plan) are covered by ERISA if a reasonable person could determine from the surrounding circumstances the

existence of the intended benefits, the beneficiaries, the financing for the benefits, and the procedures for receiving the benefits. Many types of group severance pay plans are deemed to be either pension plans or welfare plans and are thus regulated by ERISA. However, individually negotiated severance agreements are not.

PENSION PLANS

ERISA provides that officers and trustees of a pension plan are fiduciaries, required to act solely in the interest of the plan's participants and beneficiaries in providing benefits and defraying expenses.[117] ERISA expressly requires private pension plans to use the "prudent person" investment standard. The rule requires trustees to employ "the care, skill, prudence and diligence under the circumstances then prevailing that a prudent man acting in a like capacity and familiar with such matters would use in the conduct of an enterprise of a like character and with like aims."[118]

In *Hughes Aircraft Co. v. Jacobson*,[119] the U.S. Supreme Court held that Hughes Aircraft Company did not violate ERISA when it amended a contributory defined benefit pension plan and used the surplus assets in that plan to provide a new noncontributory plan and retirement program. In 1985, Hughes provided a defined benefit plan for employees to which both the company and employees made contributions. (In a *defined benefit plan,* the employer guarantees the employee a specific payment regardless of the total contributions made to the plan or the plan's investment performance. In contrast, in a *defined contribution plan,* the employer agrees only to make specific contributions, usually a percentage of salary, so the payout is dependent on both the total contributions and the plan's investment performance.) In 1987, Hughes stopped making contributions to the plan when it had surplus assets of almost $1 billion. In 1989, Hughes amended the plan to include an early retirement program with additional benefits to certain eligible employees. Two years later, the company amended the plan to provide that new participants could not contribute to the plan and would receive fewer benefits. A class of retirees claimed that Hughes had violated ERISA by amending the plan.

The Supreme Court rejected the retirees' claim. The Court explained that a defined benefit plan consists of a general pool of assets rather than individual dedicated ac-

116. 29 U.S.C. §§ 1001–1461 (1988 & Supp. 1992).

117. Richard H. Koppes & Maureen L. Reilly, *An Ounce of Prevention: Meeting the Fiduciary Duty to Monitor an Index Fund Through Relationship Investing,* 20 Iowa CORP.. L. 414, 426 (1995).
118. *Id.* citing to 29 U.S.C. § 1104 *et seq.* (1988 & Supp. 1992).
119. 525 U.S. 432 (1999).

counts. Although employees can contribute to the plan, the employer assumes the entire investment risk. The members of the plan have a right to their accrued benefits but not to any particular asset that is part of the plan's general asset pool. As a result, the plan's performance does not affect their statutory entitlement. The Court stated that "[s]ince a decline in the value of a plan's assets does not alter accrued benefits, members similarly have no entitlement to share in a plan's surplus—even if it is partially attributable to the investment growth of their contribution." The Court also rejected the claims that Hughes violated its fiduciary duties, finding that ERISA's fiduciary provisions did not apply to the amendments.

In *Bins v. Exxon Co. U.S.A.*,[120] the U.S. Court of Appeals for the Ninth Circuit addressed the issue of whether an employer considering a specific proposal to alter employee benefits presented by managers empowered to implement the changes has a fiduciary duty to disclose the proposed modification to the potentially affected employees. Ernest Bins, who had worked for Exxon for fifteen years, heard rumors in the months before his retirement that the company was considering offering a lump-sum retirement incentive under the employee benefit plan covered by ERISA. In response to his inquiries, a benefits counselor and human resources adviser told

120. 189 F.3d 929 (9th Cir. 1999), *reh'g en banc granted*, 198 F.3d 1191 (9th Cir. 2000).

Bins that they knew nothing about whether the rumor was true. Less than two weeks after Bins retired, Exxon publicly announced the very retirement incentive about which he had inquired. Bins sued, claiming that the company had breached its duties as an ERISA fiduciary in not disclosing the potential change in ERISA benefits to all employees who might be affected. The appeals court agreed, ruling that an employer "seriously considering" a proposal to implement a change in ERISA benefits must disclose information about the proposal to all plan participants or beneficiaries to whom the employer knows, or has reason to know, the information is material. An employer "seriously considers" a proposal when (1) a specific proposal (2) is being discussed for purposes of implementation (3) by senior management with authority to implement the change. The U.S. courts of appeals are split on the issue of whether an ERISA fiduciary has an affirmative duty to disclose proposed changes in benefits in the absence of employee inquiries.

ERISA AND HMOs

The U.S. Supreme Court considered the fiduciary duties imposed by ERISA in the context of health maintenance organizations (HMOs) providing care pursuant to employer-sponsored health plans in the following case.

A CASE IN POINT

CASE 14.6

Pegram v. Herdrich
*Supreme Court of the
United States
120 S. Ct. 2143 (2000).*

In the Language of the Court

FACTS Carle Clinic Association P.C., Health Alliance Medical Plans, Inc., and Carle Health Insurance Management Company, Inc. (collectively Carle) constitute a health maintenance organization. Cynthia Herdrich was covered by Carle through State Farm Insurance Company, her husband's employer. In the course of a physical exam prompted by Herdrich's complaint of pain in her groin, Dr. Lori Pegram, a Carle doctor, discovered an inflamed mass in Herdrich's abdomen. Instead of ordering an immediate ultrasound at the local hospital, Dr. Pegram decided that she should wait eight more days for an ultrasound at a facility staffed by Carle. Prior to the scheduled ultrasound, Herdrich's appendix ruptured, causing peritonitis.

Herdrich sued Pegram and Carle in state court for medical malpractice and fraud. Carle and Pegram argued that ERISA preempted the fraud counts and removed the case to federal court. Herdrich argued that the provision of medical services under the Carle HMO, which rewarded its physicians for limiting medical care to cut costs, was a breach of Carle's fiduciary duty under ERISA because it created an incentive to make decisions in the physicians' self-interest rather than in the exclusive interests of patients. The district court dismissed the ERISA count on the grounds that Carle was not acting as an ERISA fiduciary in this situation. The appeal court reversed, and Carle appealed.

ISSUE PRESENTED Are treatment decisions made by a physician employed by an HMO providing services pursuant to an employer-sponsored medical plan fiduciary acts within the meaning of ERISA?

(Continued)

(Case 14.6 continued)

OPINION SOUTER, J., writing for the U.S. Supreme Court:

The nub of the claim . . . is that when State Farm contracted with Carle, Carle became a fiduciary under the plan, acting through its physicians. . . . The pleadings must . . . be parsed very carefully to understand what acts by physician owners acting on Carle's behalf are alleged to be fiduciary in nature. It will help to keep two sorts of arguably administrative acts in mind. What we will call pure "eligibility decisions" turn on the plan's coverage of a particular condition or medical procedure for its treatment. "Treatment decisions," by contrast, are choices about how to go about diagnosing and treating a patient's condition: given a patient's constellation of symptoms, what is the appropriate medical response?

. . .

These decisions are often practically inextricable from one another. . . .

The kinds of decisions mentioned in Herdrich's ERISA count and claimed to be fiduciary in character are just such mixed eligibility and treatment decisions: physicians' conclusions about when to use diagnostic tests; about seeking consultations and making referrals to physicians and facilities other than Carle's; about proper standards of care, the experimental character of a proposed course of treatment, the reasonableness of a certain treatment, and the emergency character of a medical condition.

. . .

. . . [W]e think Congress did not intend Carle or any other HMO to be treated as a fiduciary to the extent that it makes mixed eligibility decisions acting through its physicians. . . . [T]he common law trustee's most defining concern historically has been the payment of money in the interest of the beneficiary.

Mixed eligibility decisions by an HMO acting through its physicians have, however, only a limited resemblance to the usual business of traditional trustees. To be sure, the physicians (like regular trustees) draw on resources held for others and make decisions to distribute them in accordance with entitlements expressed in a written instrument. . . . Traditional trustees administer a medical trust by paying out money to buy medical care, whereas physicians making mixed eligibility decisions consume the money as well. Private trustees do not make treatment judgments, whereas treatment judgments are what physicians reaching mixed decisions do make, by definition. . . . Thus, it is at least questionable whether Congress would have had mixed eligibility decisions in mind when it provided that decisions administering a plan were fiduciary in nature.

RESULT The Supreme Court held that mixed eligibility decisions by HMO physicians are not fiduciary decisions under ERISA, so Herdrich could not sue Carle for breach of fiduciary duty under ERISA.

QUESTIONS

1. Does an HMO have a duty under ERISA to disclose financial incentive arrangements between the HMOs and doctors that cause doctors to keep testing, referrals, and use of health care to a minimum?[121]
2. Should an employer selecting an HMO for employees be required to disclose any financial incentives the HMO might have to restrict patient care?

121. *See* Ehlmann v. Kaiser Found. Health Plan of Tex., 198 F.3d 552 (5th Cir. 2000), *reh'g denied*, 210 F.3d 365 (5th Cir. 2000), *petition for cert. filed* (May 15, 2000).

Federal Preemption Although patients can assert claims of medical malpractice against the physicians providing medical care through HMOs, most courts have prevented patients from suing the HMOs themselves for any state law claims, such as fraud. Instead, courts have held that ERISA provides the sole remedies for claims arising out of the administration of employee welfare plans. As a result, most courts have dismissed cases brought under state law against HMOs or their administrators based on the HMO's denial of benefits. The Supreme Court's decision in *Pegram v. Herdrich* dealt another blow to patients' rights activists because it precluded patients from suing HMOs for breach of fiduciary duty arising out of the denial of benefits. Although both houses of Congress have considered legislation that would amend ERISA to provide enrollees in health plans governed by ERISA with the right to sue plan administrators for injury or death caused by administrative decisions that denied or restricted health care, as of December 2000, none of the bills had been enacted into law.

Although ERISA preempts many state laws, it does not preempt all of them. In *Unum Life Insurance Co. v. Ward*,[122] Unum had issued a long-term group disability policy to Management Analysis Company (MAC) as a benefit plan governed by ERISA. The policy provided that proof of claims must be furnished to Unum within a certain limited period of time. Ward, a MAC employee, became disabled and qualified for state disability benefits. Upon inquiry, MAC informed Ward that its long-term disability plan covered his condition, and Ward submitted a benefits application. MAC processed the application and forwarded it to Unum, which advised Ward that his claim was untimely. Under California's notice-prejudice rule, an insurer cannot avoid liability where proof of claim is untimely unless the insurer can show that it suffered actual prejudice from the delay. Under California's agency rule, a California employer that administers an insured group health plan should be deemed to act as the agent of the insurance company. Ward argued that under this rule, his notice to MAC, acting as Unum's agent, sufficed to supply timely notice to the insurance company.

The issue before the U.S. Supreme Court was whether ERISA preempted the two California state law rules. The Court concluded that the notice-prejudice rule regulates insurance, an area traditionally governed by state law, and was not preempted by ERISA. By allowing a longer period to file than the minimum filing terms mandated by federal law, the state law complemented rather than contradicted ERISA. With respect to the agency rule, the Court ruled that it related to an employee benefit plan and was, therefore, preempted by ERISA.

In an effort to avoid the HMOs' traditional defense that claims regarding quality of care should be filed under ERISA, a group of chronically ill and disabled patients, who claim that they were denied quality medical care, have filed a case alleging violations of the Americans with Disabilities Act by two HMOs, Humana Health Plans of Texas and PacifiCare of Texas, and a physicians' group, HealthTexas Medical Group.[123] A doctor who previously worked for HealthTexas and was fired after refusing to follow the cost-driven policy of the physicans' group is also a plaintiff in the case.[124] The Texas Medical Association, which is also involved in the suit, alleges that the HMOs violated the federal disabilities law by "limiting care for chronically ill patients because they are more costly to treat."[125]

PENALTIES

ERISA imposes various penalties for failure to conform to requirements. Plan participants or beneficiaries may sue for lost benefits and for loss of the plan's tax benefits. Any fiduciary of a plan who breaches a duty is personally liable for the losses resulting from the breach. ERISA also provides for civil penalties for breach of its prohibited transaction rules (which bar many transactions between an ERISA plan and a fiduciary of that plan) of up to 100 percent of the amount of the prohibited transaction.[126]

To minimize costs and maximize benefit levels, many employers belong to multiemployer pension plans. Under the Multiemployer Pension Plan Amendments Act of 1980, withdrawal from such a plan may result in stiff penalties.

 # Other Laws Affecting *the* Employment Relationship

Federal legislation concerning employee benefits and layoffs indirectly affects employee relations. These laws, which apply regardless of whether employees belong to a union, are discussed below.

---

122. 526 U.S. 358 (1999).

123. Milo Geyelin, *Unhealthy Bias? A Disabled Attorney Puts Civil-Rights Spin on HMO Litigation*, WALL ST. J., Jan. 26, 2000, at A2.
124. David Koenig, *Texas Lawyer Claims HMOs Discriminate Against Chronically Ill Patients*, ASSOCIATED PRESS, Apr. 2, 2000.
125. *Managed Care Monitor—Managed Care: ADA Law Places "Civil Rights Spin" on Suit*, AM. HEALTH LINE, Jan. 27, 2000.
126. 29 U.S.C. §§ 1106, 1132 (1988 & Supp. 1992).

CONSOLIDATED OMNIBUS BUDGET RECONCILIATION ACT

The Consolidated Omnibus Budget Reconciliation Act (COBRA)[127] was enacted in 1986 to allow group health, dental, and visual benefits to continue for employees who are terminated voluntarily or involuntarily (unless the discharge was for gross misconduct) and for employees whose hours are reduced to the point that coverage would normally cease. COBRA applies to employers of twenty or more workers that sponsor a group health plan. Churches and federal government agencies are exempt. Employers must notify employees of their rights when they begin participation in a group health plan or when coverage has been threatened by an event such as termination or reduced hours. Under the Technical and Miscellaneous Revenue Act of 1988,[128] employers who fail to comply with COBRA's requirements are subject to adverse tax consequences.

Under COBRA, eligible employees must be given at least sixty days from the date their coverage ceases to elect to have their coverage continued. If coverage continuation is elected, the employer is required to extend, for up to eighteen months, coverage identical to that provided under the plan for similarly situated employees or spouses. The eligible employee may be required to pay all or part of the premium. Disabled employees are eligible for continued coverage for up to twenty-nine months. If the employee declines to continue coverage, the employer has no further coverage obligations.

An employer may discontinue coverage for any one of five reasons: (1) the employer ceases to provide group health coverage to any of its employees; (2) the premium for the coverage is not paid; (3) the employee, or former employee, becomes insured under another group plan; (4) the employee, or former employee, becomes eligible for Medicare; or (5) a spouse of the employee, or former employee, is divorced, remarries, and becomes covered under the new spouse's plan.

HEALTH INSURANCE PORTABILITY AND ACCOUNTABILITY ACT

The Health Insurance Portability and Accountability Act of 1996 (HIPAA)[129] is an employee health care reform law that provides special protection for individuals with

 ETHICAL CONSIDERATION

The elimination or reduction of insurance agent commissions for sales to HIPAA-eligible individuals is a circumvention of HIPAA, but it may not rise to the level of a failure to offer coverage under federal law. Is it ethical for a manager to adopt a policy of withholding commissions when it is not clearly illegal to do so?

lifelong illnesses who change jobs. The principal provisions of HIPAA cover all companies with fifty or more employees and went into effect on January 1, 1998.

HIPAA requires that new employees and their dependents be eligible for health insurance coverage by the new employer without an exclusion (or higher premiums) for preexisting conditions if they had health insurance for at least eighteen months provided by the previous employer and joined the new company within sixty-three days of leaving the previous employer. The previous employer must provide a certificate to a leaving employee documenting the previous coverage.

HIPAA also provides that the duration of an employee's previous coverage may be applied to fulfilling a new employer's waiting period. It also extends COBRA for up to twenty-nine months for individuals who leave work as a result of illness or disability, provided that they apply within sixty days of leaving. In addition, HIPAA requires companies to offer the same health coverage whether the illness is physical or mental; it also provides greater health-related tax deductions for self-employed individuals.

Despite its multiple provisions, HIPAA has not resolved all issues related to health insurance reform. For example, HIPAA did not include insurance pools for small businesses nor did it raise the lifetime caps on insurance benefits.

WORKER ADJUSTMENT AND RETRAINING NOTIFICATION ACT

The Worker Adjustment and Retraining Notification Act of 1988 (WARN Act)[130] requires an employer to provide timely notice to its employees of a proposal to close a plant or to reduce its workforce permanently. The act applies to employers with 100 or more employees, either all working full-time or working an aggregate of at least 4,000 hours per week.

127. Pub. L. No. 99-272, 100 Stat. 82 (1986) (codified as amended in scattered sections of 29 U.S.C.).
128. Pub. L. No. 100-647, 102 Stat. 3342 (1989) (codified as scattered sections of 26 U.S.C.
129. Pub. L. No. 104-191, 110 Stat. 1936 (1996) (codified in scattered sections of 18, 26, 29, 42 U.S.C.).

130. Pub. L. No. 100-379, 102 Stat. 890 (1988) (codified at 29 U.S.C. §§ 2101-2109 (1988).

The WARN Act attempts to strike a balance between the employer's interest in maintaining employee productivity and efficiency and the employee's interest in being forewarned of a mass layoff or plant closing. It requires employers to give employees sixty days' advance notice of any plant closing that will result in a loss of employment during any thirty-day period for fifty or more employees. A shutdown of a product line or operation within a plant is included within the act's definition of a plant closing. The act also requires sixty days' notice for layoffs during any thirty-day period that affect at least 500 employees, or at least fifty employees if they comprise one-third of the workforce. Employers are required to give written notice of the plant closing or layoff to each representative of the affected employees or, if there is no representative, to each affected employee. Employers are also required to give written notice to the state and local governments where the layoff or plant closing will occur.

The WARN Act permits an employer to order the shutdown of a plant before the conclusion of the sixty-day notice period if (1) at the time notice would have been required, the employer was actively seeking capital or business that would enable it to avoid or postpone the shutdown, and the employer reasonably and in good faith believed that giving the required notice would preclude it from obtaining the needed business or capital; or (2) the plant closing or mass layoff was caused by a natural disaster or by business circumstances that were not reasonably foreseeable at the time notice would have been required. The terms "actively seeking capital" and "business circumstances that were not reasonably foreseeable" remain largely undefined.

The WARN Act does not apply to the closing of a temporary facility. It also does not apply to a closing or mass layoff that results from the completion of a particular project if the affected employees were hired with the understanding that their employment would not continue beyond the duration of the project. Finally, it does not apply to a closing or layoff that results from a strike or lockout that is not intended to evade the requirements of the act.

The WARN Act includes several enforcement provisions. Aggrieved employees are entitled to receive back wages and benefits for each day that the employer is in violation. The court has discretion to award the prevailing party reasonable attorneys' fees. In addition, an employer who violates the act may be subject to a civil penalty of up to $30,000, to be paid to the affected communities.

THE RESPONSIBLE MANAGER
Avoiding Wrongful-Discharge Suits

Many courts appear to be moving toward providing all employees the protection against discharge without good cause that traditionally was offered only by union contracts or by individually negotiated contracts. As a result, employers often find themselves in costly litigation, attempting to convince a jury that a discharge was justified. A survey released by the Society for Human Resource Management in 1999 found that 53 percent of the member organizations had been named as a defendant in at least one employment-related suit during the past five years.[131] Forty-six percent of the organizations reported that they had received federal or state Equal Employment Opportunity Commission demand letters or charges.

An employer needs to develop a human resource approach that takes into account the statutory rights of employees, its own business needs, and the evolving common law of the state.[132] This need is particularly acute in the new economy where busy employers, under pressure from rapidly changing conditions and intense competition, may neglect to devote sufficient attention to compliance with employment laws and regulations.

An employer can do many things to limit its exposure to unwanted contractual obligations.[133] First, the employer should articulate the kind of contractual relationship it wishes to have with its employees. That relationship may not be the same for every employee or job classification. In some instances, it may be appropriate to maintain an at-will relationship. In other cases, the employer may prefer to have a written contract that specifies the terms and conditions of employment, including the circumstances under which the employment relationship may be terminated by either party.

If the company has a code of conduct (as discussed in Chapter 1), violations of the code may be good cause for termination, particularly if the employee has signed an agreement to comply with it. For example, American Express Company requires each of its approximately

---

131. *Employers Taking More Steps to Prevent Employee Lawsuits*, Corp. Couns. Wkly., July 14, 1999, at 6.
132. *See* Jeffrey Pfeffer, Competitive Advantage Through People 137–48 (1994).

133. *See* Bagley & Dauchy, *supra* note 97, at 389–97.

15,000 managers to sign an agreement to abide by the policies set forth in the company's code of conduct.

Recently, companies have been exploring the viability of peer review of employment conflicts rather than judicial review. For example, Darden Restaurants (the company that owns the Red Lobster and Olive Garden chains of restaurants) has been using peer review of employee complaints since 1994.[134] The company has found that peer review (1) reduces the quantity, and therefore the costs, of litigation; (2) reduces tensions in the workplace; and (3) often avoids the costs of hiring and training a new person by facilitating reconciliation rather than conflict.

Red Lobster takes peer review seriously. Employees who have been fired or disciplined may seek a peer review. The decision of the peer review panel is binding and can overturn management's decision. The panels can even award damages. The program has reduced annual legal fees by $1 million.

The Society for Human Resource Management survey reported that 62 percent of the respondents provided training on employment-related litigation matters for their employees. Twenty-nine percent of the organizations also reported that they had purchased employment practices liability insurance.

With respect to potential violations of the FLSA, employers should consider several issues.[135] For example, employers should make sure that nonexempt employees required to work through lunch are compensated. For salaried employees, employers cannot deduct wages for late arrivals or disciplinary suspensions. Employers should factor in bonus payments, prorated to a weekly rate of pay, when calculating overtime payments. Although commuting time to and from work is not compensable, employers must consider whether they should compensate for commuting time if the employee travels from home directly to a client's site rather than to the employer's site. Although outside sales people are exempt, sales people within the workplace are not exempt. Perhaps the best defense against a lawsuit is to create a corporate culture where employees feel appreciated, which includes compensating them fairly and providing honest feedback about job requirements and performance.

134. Margaret A. Jacobs, *Red Lobster Tale: Peers Decide Fired Waitress's Fate,* WALL ST. J., Jan. 20, 1998, at B1.

135. Nadel, *supra* note 102.

INSIDE STORY

Working "Off *the* Clock"

The FLSA requires all nonexempt employees working more than forty hours per week to receive overtime, that is, pay for one and one-half times the hours worked. However, many businesses are finding ways to avoid this requirement. Called "off the clock," it is the phenomenon of not compensating workers for the time they put in. Ways used to avoid paying overtime include (1) not marking the hours employees work on their time cards, (2) having employees come to work at different hours, (3) rolling one week's overtime to another week, (4) encouraging a work atmosphere where everyone puts in extra time, and (5) even qualifying promotions and social acceptance upon working the extra hours without pay.

The practice is surprisingly pervasive. The Department of Labor estimated that 142,468 workers were owed more than $82 million in overtime pay in 1999. Analysts attribute the rise in off-the-clock work to employers seeking to cut costs and workers' ignorance and fear that they will lose their jobs if they complain. But as workers learn their rights and news about the practice spreads, more cases are appearing.

For example, the U.S. Court of Appeals for the Second Circuit held that workers required to remain at outdoor work sites over their lunch break were providing a valuable service and were entitled to compensation for that time.[136] The court upheld the lower court's award of $5 million in overtime pay and almost $10 million in damages for 1,500 telecommunications employees.

Many other cases have settled. For instance, a Taco Bell in Seattle settled a class-action lawsuit alleging that workers were systematically denied proper compensation. Perhaps as many as 16,000 people will receive compensation for work done before and after the official work shift. Nordstrom's department stores also settled a suit that alleged that the company required employees to deliver packages

136. Reich v. Southern New Eng. Telecomm. Corp., 121 F.3d 58 (2d Cir. 1997).

to customers' homes off the clock. Albertson's, a grocery chain based in Idaho, is being sued in federal court for allegedly not recording the time employees worked on their time cards.

Captain D's, a division of Shoney's, Inc., provides a good example of inappropriate reclassification of workers as exempt employees to avoid having to pay overtime. Managers of 370 stores who spend more than 80 percent of their time preparing food challenged their classification as salaried managerial employees. This is the third suit against the parent company in a relatively short period of time.

Not all claims of off-the-clock work have been successful, however. The U.S. Court of Appeals for the Eleventh Circuit rejected a claim by police officers that physical training necessary to pass mandatory physical fitness tests constitutes work under the FLSA.[137] The court reasoned that the officers' exercise time was not compensable because it was undertaken outside regular working hours and was neither compulsory nor productive work. Moreover, the court found that the exercise provided benefits that transcended the employment requirements and, as a result, the exercise was not directly related to the police officers' jobs. Thus, although claims of off-the-clock work are increasingly brought by disgruntled employees, courts do not blindly accept the plaintiffs' charges.

137. Dade County v. Alvarez, 124 F.3d 1380 (11th Cir. 1997), *cert. denied,* 523 U.S. 1122 (1998).

KEY WORDS AND PHRASES

administrative employee 480
at-will contract 455
boilerplate clause 469
comp time 479
covenant not to compete 464
defined benefit plan 482
defined contribution plan 482

doctrine of self-publication 470
executive 480
exempt employee 480
implied contract 459
implied covenant of good faith and fair dealing 461
nonexempt employee 480

professional employee 481
public policy exception 455
recognized hazard 475
whistle-blower statutes 459
wrongful discharge 455

QUESTIONS AND CASE PROBLEMS

1. In 1986, Pacific Bell unilaterally adopted a "Management Employment Security Policy," providing that the company would "offer all management employees who continue to meet our changing business expectations employment security through reassignment to and retraining for other management positions, even if their present jobs are eliminated." The policy went on to state that it "will be maintained so long as there is no change that will materially affect Pacific Bell's business plan achievement." Pacific Bell unilaterally discontinued the policy in 1992, even though there was no change materially affecting its business plan achievement. Can a management employee who was terminated after his position was eliminated, without the option of reassignment and retraining, successfully assert a claim of wrongful discharge? On what theory? [*Asmus v. Pacific Bell,* 999 P.2d 71 (Cal. 2000)]

2. In March 1991, 43-year-old Peter Barnes read an ad in the *Chicago Tribune* that Pentrix was seeking experienced word processors to work in its Chicago office. Pentrix is a national corporation specializing in the design and manufacture of hand-held computers. The ad stated that Pentrix was looking for "experienced word processors seeking a career in a stable and growing company." On March 8, 1991, Barnes interviewed with Renee Thompson, the head of Pentrix's word processing department in Chicago. Thompson was impressed with Barnes's prior experience and reassured him that although Pentrix is a national corporation, the employees in Pentrix are like a family and look after one another. Thompson offered Barnes a job at the end of the interview, and Barnes began work on March 15, 1991.

Barnes received an updated policy manual from the personnel department every year that he worked for Pentrix. In addition to discussing such things as vacation, salary, and benefits, the policy manual described Pentrix's progressive discipline system.

Pentrix's progressive discipline system consisted of three basic steps. First, an employee's supervisor must discuss the employee's deficiencies with the employee and suggest ways for the employee to improve his or her work performance. Second, the employee must receive written notice of his or her poor performance with suggestions of how the performance can improve. Third, the employee must receive a written warning that if the employee's performance does not improve, he or she will be terminated.

The manual provided that in cases of "material misconduct" a supervisor had the discretion to decide whether to follow the progressive discipline procedures. The policy manual also provided that Pentrix had complete discretion to decide who will be discharged in the event of a company layoff.

In 1993, the following language was added to the policy manual:

> These policies are simply guidelines to management. Pentrix reserves the right to terminate or change them at any time or to elect not to follow them in any case. Nothing in these policies is intended or should be understood as creating a contract of employment or a guarantee of continued employment with Pentrix. Employment at Pentrix remains terminable at the will of either the employee or Pentrix at any time for any reason or for no reason.

Barnes signed an acknowledgment of receipt of the 1993 policy manual.

Barnes received several good performance reviews during the time he worked at Pentrix. On a few occasions, Thompson discussed with Barnes the importance of arriving at work on time, but no record was kept of the times that Barnes was late. Thompson noted in Barnes's 1998 and 1999 performance evaluations that Barnes should proofread his work more carefully.

In October 2000, Barnes received an offer to work as a word processor for Lintog, another computer manufacturing corporation in Chicago. Barnes discussed this offer with Thompson. Thompson persuaded Barnes to remain at Pentrix by suggesting that he might be promoted to day-shift word processing supervisor when the current day-shift supervisor resigned. The day-shift supervisor has yet to resign from Pentrix.

Barnes was discharged from Pentrix on July 1, 2001. Thompson told Barnes that he was being fired because Pentrix was experiencing a slowdown and that two word processors were being let go in each of Pentrix's twenty offices across the country. Thompson wrote on the separation notice placed in Barnes's personnel file that Barnes was being dis-

charged as a result of a workforce reduction. Before leaving on July 1, Barnes saw Olga Svetlana, Pentrix's vice president of computer design, getting into her car. Svetlana said to Barnes, "Too bad about your job, but maybe this will teach you to stop leaking our computer designs to other companies."

Barnes had trouble sleeping and felt depressed after being fired from Pentrix. He waited three weeks before he began looking for another job. He then submitted an application to Lintog, the company that had offered him a job in 2000. Rob Grey, the head of the word processing department at Lintog, called Renee Thompson at Pentrix to find out why Barnes had left. Thompson responded that Barnes had worked in Pentrix's word processing department for more than ten years and was discharged as a result of a slowdown. Barnes interviewed with Grey on July 26, 2001. During the interview, Grey asked Barnes why he had left his job at Pentrix. Barnes responded that although he was officially told that he was being discharged because of a reduction in force, he was fired because he was wrongly suspected of leaking the corporation's computer designs. Barnes was not hired by Lintog.

a. What claims might Barnes bring against Pentrix, Inc.?

b. If you were investigating whether Barnes could successfully sue Pentrix, what information would you want to know?

c. What damages might Barnes be entitled to recover?

3. In the following cases, should the court find that the employee was an exempt employee who received a salary or an hourly employee entitled to overtime pay?

a. Heather Hagadorn joined M.F. Smith & Associates, Inc. as a computer consultant in August 1994 and worked thirteen months on a project. A month after the project ended, she was furloughed for lack of work. Hagadorn sued under the FLSA, claiming that she was an hourly employee and seeking pay for approximately 500 hours for which she was not paid overtime. M.F. Smith contends that she was a salaried employee paid a predetermined amount each pay period but paid straight time on an hourly basis for time she worked that exceeded the minimum 37.5 hours required each pay period. Documents produced during the litigation include pay statements that reflect the number of hours for which Hagadorn was paid; these statements do not separate the regular minimum required hours (37.5 hours per week) from any overtime hours. A memorandum indicating a base annual salary of $48,500 contains the handwritten notation "$24.88/hr." M.F. Smith argues that it computed this hourly amount by dividing the annual salary by fifty weeks and then by 37.5 hours to determine Hagadorn's regular salary rate on an hourly basis. It claims it used this rate to pay Hagadorn for hours worked that exceeded the standard 37.5-hour workweek. [*Hagadorn v. M.F. Smith & Associates, Inc.*, 172 F.3d 878 (10th Cir. 1999)]

b. Anthony Piscione worked as a consultant at Ernst & Young LLP from 1991 until September 1996. During that time, he was promoted from staff consultant to senior staff consultant and then to manager. He was paid straight overtime for the hours he worked in excess of forty hours per week during the first eight months of his employment, but after that he did not receive any overtime pay. After resigning from the firm in 1996, Piscione filed a claim, alleging that Ernst & Young violated the FLSA by classifying him as an exempt employee and not paying him overtime. Ernst & Young argued that Piscione fell within the FLSA's administrative or professional exemption and thus was not entitled to overtime pay. The firm contended that he was a salaried employee and that his duties required the exercise of discretion and independent judgment and related to the general business operations of the firm. Piscione argued that his work did not require independent thought or creativity, as he was simply plugging numbers into formulas; that his supervision of employees involved only a small amount of his time; and that his work was more similar to the work of a cashier in a retail store than that of a professional or administrative employee. In addition, he claimed that Ernst & Young docked his pay if he did not work for eight hours each day. [*Piscione v. Ernst & Young, LLP*, 171 F.3d 527 (7th Cir. 1999)]

4. Robinson was the branch manager of one of Smith Barney's brokerage offices. One of his most important duties was to recruit experienced brokers. He contracted annually with Smith Barney in 1991, 1992, and 1993 under three separate but identical agreements. The 1993 agreement provided that:

> [I]n consideration of payment of the 1993 Incentive Compensation to me, I agree that should my employment with Smith Barney terminate for any reason and I become employed at a competitor organization, I will not for a one-year period directly or indirectly solicit or induce any Smith Barney employee to resign from either (a) the Smith Barney branch office at which I worked; or (b) any other Smith Barney office within a 50-mile radius of the competitor organization's office at which I work in order for that employee to accept employment at the competitor organization at which I work.

Robinson made this promise in return for a promise from Smith Barney to allow him to participate in the firm's 1993 incentive compensation program. The exact amount of Robinson's incentive compensation was to be calculated after Smith Barney's 1993 profits were determined. He was to receive quarterly advances toward the compensation that he would ultimately be paid. In the event that Robinson were to resign or were to be terminated for cause during 1993, he would be required to return any advances received in that year. In April 1993, Robinson received a $7,000 advance, which he did not repay after he voluntarily left Smith Barney's employ on June 17, 1993.

Robinson conceded that during 1993 he left Smith Barney's employ, began to work for a competitor organization, and, having been advised that the nonsolicitation agreement was unenforceable, knowingly breached the agreement by actively recruiting Smith Barney's employees. Will Robinson succeed in challenging the validity of the nonsolicitation agreement? [*Smith, Barney, Harris Upham & Co., Inc. v. Robinson*, 12 F.3d 515 (5th Cir. 1994)]

5. Susan Weissman sued her former employer, Crawford Rehabilitation, for breach of implied contract based on Crawford's failure to abide by the termination procedures set forth in the employee manual. Thereafter, Crawford discovered that Weissman had made fraudulent representations on her application for employment. Does this after-acquired evidence provide a complete defense? [*Crawford Rehabilitation Services, Inc. v. Weissman*, 938 P.2d 540 (Colo. 1997)]

6. IBP, Inc., which operates a meat processing plant, hired DCS Sanitation Management, Inc. as an independent contractor to clean the plant's machinery after the close of production each day. The DCS contract gave IBP the right to terminate the agreement if DCS violated IBP's contractor safety policy. IBP's employees pointed out numerous safety violations by DCS's employees to DCS supervisors and management, but IBP did not terminate the contract. Is IBP liable under the Occupational Safety

and Health Act (OSHA) for the failure of DCS's employees to comply with OSHA safety procedures? Was IBP's conduct ethical? [*IBP, Inc. v. Herman,* 144 F.3d 861 (D.C. Cir. 1998)]

7. Luellen Datar married Roger Salt in 1995 while he was finishing his Ph.D. in electrical engineering at Rensselaer Polytechnic Institute. Upon graduation, Salt began work on a personal digital assistant. When the Internet gained in popularity, he started a new company to develop a device that could be used both as a wireless telephone and as a means of accessing the Internet. He used money he had inherited from his great-aunt to finance the company until his first round of venture capital financing. When the company went public in the dot.com frenzy of the late 1990s, he owned 30 percent of the outstanding stock.

Luellen did not own any stock in her own name but served as vice president of business development. She had never gotten around to negotiating an employment contract and thus served as an at-will employee. Roger was chief executive officer and chair of the board. After a series of nasty fights regarding the state of their marriage, Roger asked his wife to sign a postnuptial agreement confirming that, in the event of a divorce, she would have no right to any of Roger's stock in the company. When she refused to sign, Roger fired her. She sued the company for wrongful termination. How should the court rule?

8. Victoria A. Stewart was an attorney who was employed in the environmental law department of a New York law firm. In October 1988, Ronald Herzog, a partner of the law firm Jackson & Nash, contacted Stewart regarding employment at his firm. Herzog represented to Stewart that Jackson had recently secured a large environmental law client, that Jackson was in the process of establishing an environmental law department, and that Stewart would head the department and be expected to service the firm's substantial existing environmental law client. Stewart accepted employment at Jackson. Upon her arrival, she was primarily assigned general litigation matters, but Herzog repeatedly assured her that the promised environmental work would be forthcoming and that she would be promoted to a position as head of Jackson's environmental law department. Finally, in May 1990, a Jackson & Nash partner informed Stewart that Jackson never did environmental work, nor had it secured an environmental law client. Jackson & Nash dismissed Stewart on December 31, 1990. Stewart filed suit, alleging that

Jackson & Nash fraudulently induced her to enter into and remain in its employment. How should the court rule? [*Stewart v. Jackson & Nash,* 976 F.2d 86 (2d Cir. 1992)]

9. Have any of the employers in the following cases terminated an employee in violation of public policy? Has the employer acted ethically?

   a. A long-time at-will employee was fired by his supervisor after the supervisor found out that the employee had told management about the supervisor's history of embezzlement. [*Foley v. Interactive Data Corp.,* 765 P.2d 373 (Cal. 1988)]

   b. An employee was fired in retaliation for supporting a coworker's sexual harassment claim. [*Gantt v. Sentry Insurance,* 824 P.2d 680 (Cal. 1992)]

   c. An employee was forced to resign after complaining to management about violations of internal operating practices and the company's collective bargaining agreements. [*Turner v. Anheuser-Busch, Inc.,* 876 P.2d 1022 (Cal. 1994)]

   d. A quality control inspector in his fifties at Ralee Engineering, a company engaged in manufacturing fuselage and wing components for aircraft, was fired after complaining on several occasions over a two-year period to supervisory personnel and the company's president that the company was shipping some aircraft parts that had failed his team's safety inspections. The Federal Aviation Act delegates to the Federal Aviation Administration (FAA) the duty to promote safe flight by establishing minimum standards for the construction of aircraft. FAA regulations require prime manufacturers (such as Boeing) seeking FAA certification to ensure that their subcontractors (such as Ralee Engineering) establish quality control systems to make sure that each component conforms to the design and is in a condition for safe operation. [*Green v. Ralee Engineering Co.,* 960 P.2d 1046 (Cal. 1998)]

MANAGER'S DILEMMA

10. Chelsea Lamar joins your high-tech start-up in 1999, immediately after graduating from Carnegie-Mellon University. She forgoes better-paying consulting and investment banking opportunities to get in on the ground floor of a young, fast-growing company. As compensation, Lamar receives a nominal salary and stock options. Because the company's

product will require three years to bring to market, the options do not vest for three years. This means that Lamar forfeits all of the stock options if she leaves the company before 2002.

In 2001, the company begins having serious problems. Even though the project is on schedule and is anticipated to be a huge success, costs are skyrocketing, and your investors demand a significant reduction in operating expenses.

You are considering firing Lamar. Although she has performed well, Lamar was the most recent person hired. She is an at-will employee, but, con-sidering that she has less than one year to go until she can exercise her stock options, you fear a lawsuit, especially given the company's close-knit character. At this critical stage, the legal fees alone from a wrongful-termination lawsuit could bankrupt the company.

a. Should you fire Lamar to reduce operating expenses?

b. If Lamar is terminated, on what basis could she sue the company? Would she prevail?

c. How could you have structured the relationship to avoid this potential lawsuit?

INTERNET SOURCES

The Department of Labor site includes information about Bureau of Labor statistics; OSHA data on occupational injuries; and laws and regulations administered and enforced by DOL agencies.	http://www.dol.gov
This site provides an index of laws and articles on employment law and the Labor and Employment Law Web Guide.	http://www.findlaw.com/01topics/27labor
The United Food and Commercial Workers International site provides news and information about employment cases and issues, particularly workers' rights.	http://www.ufcw.org
The AFL-CIO site includes information regarding safety on the job, workers' rights, and unequal pay.	http://www.aflcio.org
OSHA	http://www.osha.gov

CHAPTER 15

Civil Rights *and* Employment Discrimination

LAWS DESIGNED TO ELIMINATE EMPLOYMENT DISCRIMINATION

The abolition of slavery after the American Civil War and the civil rights movement of the 1960s were two great forces behind modern civil rights legislation. From the Civil Rights Act of 1866 to that of 1991, the law has been moving in a direction to eliminate discrimination based on race, sex, color, religion, national origin, age, or disability. Civil rights laws help ensure that every member of society has the opportunity to reach his or her full potential.

Managers who fail to enact and enforce policies to ensure compliance with federal legislation prohibiting employment discrimination put their companies at risk of being penalized by large fines and judgments. In 1999 and 2000, corporations paid millions of dollars in settlements or judgments as a result of racial or sexual discrimination lawsuits brought by their employees: as described further in the "Inside Story" for this chapter, the Coca-Cola Company agreed to pay $192.5 million to settle racial discrimination charges; Kodak paid $13 million in retroactive and current pay raises to female and minority workers; Hyundai Elec-

tronics America, Inc. paid $10 million to an executive recruiter who alleged that the company had told him that its Korean managers did not want him to refer African-American or female candidates to them; and Mazda North America, Inc. paid $4.1 million to a female employee who had been sexually harassed and then fired by a male supervisor when she rejected his overtures.

CHAPTER OVERVIEW

This chapter provides an overview of federal legislation barring employment discrimination, with special attention to Title VII, the Age Discrimination in Employment Act, the Americans with Disabilities Act, and the Family and Medical Leave Act. It also illustrates the various legal theories pursued under each piece of legislation and shows how those theories relate to legal and appropriate behavior by managers in a business environment. It concludes with an application of discrimination laws to pre-employment practices and a brief discussion of how these laws apply to persons hiring contingent or temporary workers.

 Overview *of* Civil Rights Legislation

The federal statutes that forbid various kinds of discrimination in employment are summarized in Exhibit 15.1. Many states have passed their own fair employment acts, which in some instances provide greater protection than their federal counterparts. For example, Florida's Civil

Rights Act prohibits discrimination on the basis of marital status.[1]

The federal statutes discussed here apply only to employees, not independent contractors. As explained in Chapter 5, there is no bright-line distinction between the two categories. The courts tend to use two primary criteria to distinguish independent contractors from employ-

1. Donato v. AT&T, 767 So. 2d 1146 (Fla. 2000).

ees. First, independent contractors control the outcome of a piece of work and the means and manner of achieving the outcome. Second, independent contractors offer services to the public at large, not just to one business.

Although the statutes described in Exhibit 15.1 have created a far more level playing field for all workers, progress can be slow. For example, the Equal Pay Act was enacted in 1963, but as of 1998, men in full-time executive, administrative, and managerial positions still earned an average of $17,000 a year more than women in these positions.[2]

DEFINITION OF ADVERSE EMPLOYMENT ACTION

In most discrimination and retaliation cases, the employee must establish that his or her employer subjected him or her to an adverse employment action. The federal appeals courts are split as to what constitutes an adverse employ-

ment action. Six of the circuits have taken an expansive view. Under this interpretation, demotions, refusals to hire or promote, unwarranted negative job evaluations, disadvantageous transfers or assignments, depriving an employee of support services, cutting off challenging assignments, moving an employee from a spacious office to a dingy closet, forcing an employee to jump through hoops in order to obtain severance benefits, making and soliciting from coworkers negative comments about an employee, needlessly delaying authorization for medical treatment, requiring an employee to work without a lunch break, and changing an employee's schedule without notification have all been characterized as adverse employment actions.[3] Two of the circuits have held that an adverse action is something that materially affects the terms and conditions of employment, such as employee compensation or privileges. The last two circuits have adopted the most restrictive test, holding that only actions affecting hiring, firing, promoting, and demoting are adverse employment actions.

2. *Women Rise in Workplace but Wage Gap Continues,* Wall St. J., Apr. 25, 2000, at A12.

3. Ray v. Henderson, 217 F.3d 1234 (9th Cir. 2000).

EXHIBIT 15.1 Major Pieces of Federal Civil Rights Legislation

Statute	Major Provisions	Employers Subject to Statute	Comments
Civil Rights Act of 1866[a] (Section 1981)	Prohibits racial discrimination by employers of any size in the making and enforcement of contracts, including employment contracts.	All public and private employers.	The bar against racial discrimination applies not only to hiring, promotion, and termination but also to working conditions, such as racial harassment, and to breaches of contract occurring during the term of the contract.
Equal Pay Act of 1963[b]	Mandates equal pay for equal work without regard to gender.	All public and private employers with twenty or more employees (including federal, state, and local governments).	
Title VII of the Civil Rights Act of 1964[c] (Title VII)	Prohibits discrimination in employment on the basis of race, color, religion, national origin, or sex. Later amended to provide that discrimination on the basis of sex includes discrimination on the basis of pregnancy, childbirth, or related medical conditions.	All public and private employers with fifteen or more employees.	

(Exhibit 15.1 continues)

| EXHIBIT 15.1 | Major Pieces of Federal Civil Rights Legislation—continued |

Statute	Major Provisions	Employers Subject to Statute	Comments
Age Discrimination in Employment Act of 1967[d] (ADEA)	Protects persons forty years and older from discrimination on the basis of age. The ADEA was amended in 1990 by the Older Workers' Benefit Protection Act, which prohibits age discrimination in providing employee benefits and establishes minimum standards for waiver of one's rights under the ADEA.	All public and private employers with twenty or more employees.	
The Vietnam Era Veterans' Readjustment Assistance Acts of 1972 and 1974[e]	Require affirmative action to employ disabled Vietnam-era veterans.	Employers holding federal contracts of $10,000.	Enforced by U.S. Department of Labor.
Vocational Rehabilitation Act of 1973[f]	Prohibits discrimination against the physically and mentally disabled. Imposes affirmative-action obligations on employers having contracts with the federal government in excess of $2,500.	Employers receiving federal financial assistance of any amount.	Enforced by U.S. Department of Labor. This legislation was the precursor to and guided the development of the Americans with Disabilities Act.
Veterans Re-Employment Act of 1974[g]	Gives employees who served in the military at any time the right to be reinstated in employment without loss of benefits and the right not to be discharged without cause for one year following such reinstatement.	All public and private employers.	
Immigration Reform and Control Act of 1986[h] (IRCA)	Prohibits discrimination against applicants or employees based on national origin or citizenship status.	All private employers with four or more employees.	If employer has fifteen or more employees, plaintiff must file national-origin discrimination claims under Title VII.
Americans with Disabilities Act of 1990[i] (ADA)	Prohibits discrimination in employment on the basis of a person's disability. Also requires businesses to provide "reasonable accommodation" to the disabled,	All private employers with fifteen or more employees.	The ADA is the most sweeping civil rights measure since the Civil Rights Act of 1964.

(Exhibit 15.1 continues)

| EXHIBIT 15.1 | Major Pieces of Federal Civil Rights Legislation—continued | | |

Statute	Major Provisions	Employers Subject to Statute	Comments
	unless such an accommodation would result in "undue hardship" on business operations.		
Civil Rights Act of 1991[j]	Legislatively overruled several parts of recent Supreme Court rulings that were unfavorable to the rights of plaintiffs in employment-discrimination cases. Also extended coverage of the major civil rights statutes to the staffs of the president and the Senate.	Varies.	
Family and Medical Leave Act of 1993[k]	Designed to allow employees to take time off from work to handle domestic responsibilities, such as the birth or adoption of a child or the care of an elderly parent. Employees are guaranteed job security despite familial responsibilities.	Private employers with fifty or more employees at work sites within seventy-five miles of each other.	Part-time employees are excluded from the act's coverage and are not counted in calculating the fifty employees necessary for an employer to be covered by the act.

a. 42 U.S.C. § 1981 (1994).
b. 29 U.S.C. § 206(d) (1994).
c. 42 U.S.C. §§ 2000e–2000e-17 (1994).
d. 29 U.S.C. §§ 621–634 (1994).
e. 38 U.S.C. § 4100 *et seq.* (1994).
f. 29 U.S.C. §§ 701–797 (1994).
g. 38 U.S.C. §§ 4301–4307 (1994).
h. Pub. L. No. 99-603, 100 Stat. 3359 (1986) (codified as amended in scattered sections of the U.S.C.)
i. 42 U.S.C. §§ 12101–12213 (1994).
j. Pub. L. No. 102-106, 105 Stat. 1071 (1991) (codified in scattered sections of the U.S.C.).
k. 29 U.S.C. §§ 2601–2654 (1994).

 # Enforcement

The Equal Employment Opportunity Commission (EEOC) is the primary enforcer of civil rights legislation in the United States. A part of the Department of Justice, the EEOC processes hundreds of complaints, investigating and evaluating their merit. If a claim is unfounded, it is dismissed. If the claim withstands initial inquiry and the EEOC is unable to pursue the case due to staff and resource constraints, the agency will provide a right-to-sue letter to the private party. Without this administrative permission, private litigants cannot initiate suits under various statutes, including Title VII and the ADA.

The EEOC has recently become more proactive in its approach to enforcing antidiscrimination laws. In early 1998, the EEOC began contracting with private organizations to use "testers" to identify employers that discriminate.[4] In employment-discrimination testing, pairs of equally qualified individuals are sent to apply for entry-level positions in an effort to determine whether

4. *EEOC Contracts with Private Testers to Uncover Employers' Discriminatory Hiring,* 66 U.S.L.W. 2391–92 (Jan. 8, 1998).

impermissible factors such as race, gender, national origin, or disability influence employment decisions. In 2000, the U.S. Court of Appeals for the Seventh Circuit held that testers had standing to bring employment-discrimination cases under Title VII even though they had no real desire to work for the companies where they applied.[5] In contrast, the D.C. Circuit held that testers lack standing to sue under Section 1981 of the Civil Rights Act of 1866 for employment discrimination.[6]

 # Title VII

SCOPE

Title VII bans discrimination based on an individual's race, color, religion, national origin, or sex. The racial discrimination suits against Texaco and Coca-Cola, discussed in the "Inside Story," were initiated under Title VII.

LEGAL THEORIES UNDER TITLE VII

Litigation under Title VII has produced two distinct legal theories of discrimination: (1) disparate treatment and (2) disparate impact.

Disparate Treatment A plaintiff claiming *disparate treatment* must prove that the employer intentionally discriminated against him or her by denying a benefit or privilege of employment because of his or her race, religion, sex, or national origin. The U.S. Supreme Court has established a systematic approach for providing proof of these claims.[7] First, the employee must prove a *prima facie* case, which entails proving (1) that the employee is a member of a class of persons protected by Title VII and (2) that the employee was denied a position or benefit he or she sought, for which he or she was qualified, and which was available. If the employee proves the *prima facie* case, the employer then must present evidence, but need not prove, that it had legitimate, nondiscriminatory grounds for its decision. If the employer meets this burden of producing evidence, the employee then must prove that the grounds offered by the employer were only a pretext for intentional discrimination.

The Supreme Court held in *St. Mary's Honor Center v. Hicks*[8] that a showing of pretext is insufficient, in and of itself, to compel judgment for the employee as a mat-

ter of law. In *Reeves v. Sanderson Plumbing Products, Inc.*,[9] the Supreme Court reiterated its holding that the plaintiff bears the burden of proving that the employer intentionally discriminated but made it clear that a jury, as the trier of fact, could "infer the ultimate fact of discrimination from the falsity of the employer's explanation." As a result, "a plaintiff's prima facie case, combined with sufficient evidence to find that the employer's asserted justification is false, may permit the trier of fact to conclude that the employer unlawfully discriminated" without the need for additional, independent evidence of discrimination.

In a disparate-treatment case, for example, an African-American employee might claim that he was fired because of his race. He would show in the first instance that he is an African American, was fired, and possessed at least the minimum qualifications for the job. Some courts may require that he also show that his job was not eliminated but was filled by someone else after his termination. Once he proves this, his employer might present evidence that the employee was terminated for excessive absenteeism. The employer might produce the employee's attendance records and a supervisor's testimony that his attendance was unacceptable. The employee could attempt to prove pretext in a number of ways. He might show that his em-

5. Kyles v. J. K. Guardian Security Servs., Inc., 222 F.3d 289 (7th Cir. 2000).
6. Fair Employment Council of Greater Washington, Inc. v. BMC Mktg. Corp., 28 F.3d 1268 (D.C. Cir. 1994).
7. *See* McDonnell Douglas Corp. v. Green, 411 U.S. 792 (1973).
8. 509 U.S. 502 (1993).
9. 530 U.S. 133 (2000).

ployer's attendance policy requires a written warning about poor attendance before the employee can be terminated on that ground, and that he received no such warning. He might show that white employees with similar attendance records were not fired. He might show that his supervisor uttered racial slurs from time to time. In any event, the employee has the burden of proving that his employer fired him because of his race.

For example, in *Frank v. United Airlines, Inc.*,[10] the U.S. Court of Appeals for the Ninth Circuit held that United Airlines' use of different weight policies for male and female flight attendants was illegal disparate treatment on the basis of sex. The airline required female flight attendants to meet weight limits based on suggested weights for medium body frames but permitted male flight attendants to meet weight limits based on large body frames. The court held that United failed to show that having thinner female than male flight attendants affected the flight attendants' ability to greet passengers, move luggage, push carts, or provide physical assistance in emergencies. In fact, the court found that the discriminatory weight requirement may have hindered female employees' job performance.

When an employee proves that the employer's decision was motivated in part by impermissible discrimination, the employer has engaged in an illegal employment practice. But if the employer demonstrates that it would have taken the same action in the absence of the impermissible motivating factor, then the court cannot award damages or order reinstatement, hiring, or promotion. In such a case, declaratory relief is still available, as is an award of attorneys' fees and costs.

Disparate Impact The *disparate-impact* theory arose out of Title VII class actions brought in the 1970s against large employers. These suits challenged testing and other selection procedures, claiming that they systematically excluded women or particular ethnic groups from certain types of jobs. It is not necessary to prove intentional discrimination to prevail in a disparate-impact case. Dis-

10. 216 F.3d 845 (9th Cir. 2000).

INTERNATIONAL CONSIDERATION

Managers should be aware of civil rights laws of foreign countries when exploring globalization strategies and managing the workforce of foreign subsidiaries or joint ventures. A foreign jurisdiction's interpretations of acceptable behavior, in addition to the country's regional or international commitments, should be researched.

crimination can be established by proving that an employment practice, although neutral on its face, had a disparate impact on a protected group.

For example, suppose an employer has a policy that it will hire for security guard positions only persons who are at least 5 feet 8 inches tall, weigh at least 150 pounds, and can pass certain agility tests. This policy would seem to be neutral, in that it does not expressly exclude women or some Asian males. However, if the number of qualified women or Asian males who are refused employment is proportionately greater than the number of white males refused employment, then that policy has a disparate impact.

To prove disparate impact, the plaintiff must demonstrate that the specific employment practice, policy, or rule being challenged has caused a statistically significant disproportion between the racial or other composition of the persons holding the jobs at issue and the racial or other composition of the *qualified* persons in the relevant labor market.[11] The employer then has the burden to demonstrate that the challenged practice is job related for the position in question and consistent with business necessity.

If a job requires no special skills, then all members of the labor pool are considered when doing the statistical analysis necessary to determine whether a facially neutral policy has a disparate impact. For example, in *EEOC v. Steamship Clerks Union, Local 1066*,[12] a labor union representing the individuals who check cargo passing through the port of Boston against inventory lists had adopted a membership sponsorship policy (MSP) that required union applicants to be sponsored by an existing member. When the union adopted the MSP, there were no African-American or Hispanic members. Over the next six years, the union accepted thirty new members, all of whom were Caucasian. After 1986, the union closed its membership rolls.

In 1991, the EEOC sued the union for disparate-impact discrimination. Although African Americans and Hispanics constituted between 8 and 27 percent of the relevant labor pool in the Boston area, none was hired by the union. Because the jobs required no special skills, all members of the labor pool were deemed qualified and therefore included in the calculation of qualified applicants. The union claimed that its MSP was merely a form of nepotism, not racial discrimination, because every member admitted between 1980 and 1986 was closely related to an existing member of the union. The First Circuit disagreed, holding that the union's membership policy was discriminatory: by its very nature, it created a strong likelihood that no nonwhite face would ever appear in the union's ranks.

11. *Wards Cove Packing Co. v. Atonio,* 490 U.S. 642 (1989).
12. 48 F.3d 594 (1st Cir. 1995), *cert. denied,* 516 U.S. 814 (1995).

Historically, disparate-impact analysis has been limited to objective selection criteria, such as tests and degree requirements. However, the Supreme Court has indicated that this analysis may also apply to subjective bases for decisions, such as interviews and supervisor evaluations.

In *Bullington v. United Air Lines*,[13] a female ground school academic instructor for United Airlines claimed that the company's interviewing process violated Title VII because it had a disparate impact on women. Bullington presented evidence that 27.9 percent of women versus 46.6 percent of men passed the airline's interview for flight officer positions. The Tenth Circuit refused to dismiss the case, holding that a pass rate for women that was equal to only 60 percent of the pass rate for men raised a genuine issue of material fact regarding the existence of a significant disparate impact on a protected group.

The business justification offered by the employer to justify the disparate impact must relate to job performance. Inconvenience, annoyance, or expense to the employer will not suffice. For example, a Latina applicant who is denied employment because she failed an English-language test might challenge the language requirement. If she has applied for a sales job, the employer might justify the requirement on the ground that ability to communicate with customers is an indispensable qualification. On the other hand, if she has applied for a job on the production line, that justification would probably not suffice unless her duties included communicating with others in English. As under disparate-treatment analysis, the ultimate burden of persuasion rests with the plaintiff.

HOSTILE ENVIRONMENT

The courts have long recognized that creation of a hostile working environment for an employee because of his or her race, color, national origin, or religion violates Title VII. An example of *hostile-environment harassment* would be continually subjecting an African-American employee to ridicule and racial slurs. To be actionable, the alleged

harassment must have been so severe or pervasive that it altered the working environment. Hostile-environment sexual harassment is discussed later in this chapter.

Although some courts have held that a onetime incident is not enough to create a hostile environment, the trend appears to be to find hostile environment if the incident is severe enough and involves a supervisor. In one case,[14] for example, an African-American female county employee alleged that, while she was training at a police academy firing range, her direct supervisor (the sheriff) turned to a deputy and said, "There's the jungle bunny." The New Jersey Supreme Court identified several factors that made the incident severe enough to create actionable hostile-environment discrimination under the New Jersey Law Against Discrimination (patterned after Title VII): (1) the derogatory term used by the sheriff was "patently a racial slur, and [was] ugly, stark and raw in its opprobrious connotation"; (2) the sheriff was the plaintiff's ranking supervisor, effectively closing her avenue for redress; (3) the sheriff was the chief law enforcement officer; and (4) the remark was made not only in the plaintiff's presence but in front of the deputy.

DUTY TO ACCOMMODATE RELIGIOUS BELIEFS

The EEOC reported in 1999 that religious discrimination claims under Title VII had increased in each of the previous five years, with 1,786 claims filed in fiscal 1998.[15] These claims included not just refusals to hire or promote based on religious prejudice but also allegations that employers would not give employees flexible schedules to allow them to attend religious ceremonies or flexibility in workplace dress codes to accommodate clothing mandated by the employee's religion.

In the following case, the Ninth Circuit considered whether an employer had met its duty under Title VII to reasonably accommodate an employee who due to her religious beliefs was unable to work between sundown Friday and sundown Saturday.

13. 186 F.3d 1301 (10th Cir. 1999).

14. Taylor v. Metzger, 706 A.2d 685 (N.J. 1998).
15. Sam McManis, *Culture Clash on the Job*, SAN FRANCISCO CHRON., Oct. 22, 1999, at E1.

A CASE IN POINT

CASE 15.1

Balint v. Carson City
United States Court of Appeals for the Ninth Circuit
180 F.3d 1047
(9th Cir. 1999).

Summary

FACTS Lisette Balint was required by her membership in the Worldwide Church of God to observe the Sabbath from sundown Friday to sundown Saturday. All types of secular work were prohibited during the Sabbath. In 1995, Balint was offered a job in the detention department of the Carson City Sheriff's Department. When she informed the department that she could not work during the Sabbath and requested that her schedule accommodate her religious beliefs, she was informed that her schedule would not be

(Continued)

(Case 15.1 continued)

changed. Balint withdrew her application for employment and filed a claim of religious discrimination in violation of Title VII.

The department argued that its seniority-based, shift-bidding system prevented it from accommodating Balint. The twelve or thirteen deputies assigned to the jail bid for shifts in order of seniority. Only one deputy had both Saturday and Sunday off, and an unwritten rule prohibited deputies from trading shifts on a regular basis. The trial court held that given the department's bona fide shift-bidding system, changing the schedule to accommodate Balint's religious beliefs would be an undue hardship. Balint appealed.

ISSUE PRESENTED Does an employer's neutral seniority system relieve it of its duty under Title VII to accommodate an employee's religious beliefs?

SUMMARY OF OPINION The U.S. Court of Appeals for the Ninth Circuit applied a two-part framework to review claims of religious discrimination under Title VII. First, the employee has the burden to establish a *prima facie* case of religious discrimination. Second, the employer has the burden to show either that it attempted to reasonably accommodate the employee's religious beliefs or that any accommodation of the employee's needs would result in undue hardship. The inquiry in this case focused on whether accommodation would pose an undue hardship on the department.

The court rejected the department's argument that a bona fide seniority system was a complete defense to Balint's claim. A seniority system is no defense if reasonable accommodation can be made without impact on the seniority system and at only a de minimis cost to the city. Thus, both the seniority system and the reasonable accommodation could coexist without transgressing the seniority system.

The court suggested that implementing split shifts would accommodate Balint's religious beliefs without harming the seniority system. A split-shift system would still allow senior employees to bid for their shift preferences and thus would not create a direct conflict with the seniority system. As there was limited evidence regarding whether implementing a split-shift schedule would create an undue hardship for the city, there was a genuine question of material fact regarding this issue.

RESULT The appeals court reversed and remanded the case for trial after finding that there was a genuine issue of material fact as to whether the department could reasonably accommodate the plaintiff's religious practices.

DEFENSES UNDER TITLE VII

Title VII sets forth several statutory defenses to claims of discriminatory treatment. Of these defenses, the one most frequently cited is the defense of bona fide occupational qualification.

Bona Fide Occupational Qualification Title VII provides that an employer may lawfully hire an individual on the basis of religion, sex, or national origin if religion, sex, or national origin is a *bona fide occupational qualification (BFOQ)* reasonably necessary to the normal operation of that particular business. This is known as the *BFOQ defense.* The BFOQ defense is not available when discriminatory treatment is based on a person's race or color. Because

BFOQ is an affirmative defense, the employer has the burden of showing a reasonable basis for believing that the category of persons (for example, women) excluded from a particular job was unable to perform that job.

The BFOQ defense has been narrowly construed. Regulations promulgated by the Equal Employment Opportunity Commission provide that gender will not qualify as a BFOQ where a gender-based restriction is based on (1) assumptions of the comparative employment characteristics of women in general (such as the assumption that women have a higher turnover rate than men); (2) stereotyped characterizations of the sexes (for example, that men are less capable of assembling intricate equipment than women); or (3) the preferences of coworkers, employers, or customers for one sex or the other.[16] Gender will be considered a BFOQ when physical attributes are important for authenticity (as with actors) or when a gender-based restriction is necessary to protect the rights of others to privacy (as with restroom attendants).

Seniority and Merit Systems Bona fide seniority and merit systems are expressly excluded from Title VII, as long as such systems do not result from intentional discrimination. This is considered an exemption rather than an affirmative defense. Consequently, the plaintiff has the burden of proving a discriminatory intent or illegal purpose. Moreover, although a disproportionate impact may be some evidence of discriminatory intent, such an impact is not, in itself, sufficient to establish discriminatory intent.

After-Acquired Evidence

When an employee initiates a suit under Title VII, sometimes over the course of discovery an employer will learn that the individual violated company rules. Under these circumstances, employers have argued that the plaintiff's discrimination claim should fail because, had the employer known of the employee misconduct, the employee would have been discharged anyway.

In *McKennon v. Nashville Banner Publishing Co.*[17] the U.S. Supreme Court held that after-acquired evidence of misconduct does not bar a discrimination claim. But the employee misconduct is not ignored: remedies available to plaintiffs in cases involving misconduct are limited to back pay and should not include reinstatement or front pay. Lower courts have further refined the *McKennon* standard. For example, the Ninth Circuit held that in a discrimination suit in which the employer relies on after-acquired evidence, the employer must prove by a preponderance of the evidence that it would have made the disputed employment decision once it had the after-acquired evidence.[18]

Sexual Harassment

As more women have entered the workforce and risen to positions previously dominated by men, courts have recognized sexual harassment as a form of sexual discrimination. Sexual harassment, which can be asserted by

ETHICAL CONSIDERATION

Civil rights legislation has done more than simply prohibit intentional discrimination against minority groups and women. It has fostered a major shift in public attitudes about the capabilities of individuals and contributed to the breakdown of stereotypes regarding ethnic and gender groups. As a result, many longstanding stereotypes held by employers and society in general have been challenged. What obligations do managers have to identify and redress group-based animus within their organization? What can a manager do to change racist or sexist attitudes?

male or female employees, is one of the more complex and emotional issues in antidiscrimination law.

TYPES

Early on, the courts recognized that a specific, job-related adverse action, such as denial of a promotion, in retaliation for a person's refusal to respond to his or her supervisor's sexual advances is a violation of Title VII. Such retaliation is referred to as *quid pro quo harassment*. The employer is always liable in cases of *quid pro quo* harassment regardless of whether it knew or should have known about the supervisor's conduct.

A threat of adverse job action in retaliation for rebuffing sexual advances does not constitute *quid pro quo* harassment, however, if the threat is not carried out. Instead, it is a form of hostile-environment harassment.[19]

In *Meritor Savings Bank v. Vinson*,[20] the U.S. Supreme Court first ruled that creation of a hostile environment by sexual harassment is a form of sex discrimination barred by Title VII, even if there is no retaliatory employment action against the employee. Thus, it is not necessary for the employee to show a concrete economic effect on employment, such as discharge or denial of a raise or promotion, to establish a violation. The Supreme Court noted that not every sexually offensive comment or act constitutes actionable sexual harassment; the conduct must be sufficiently offensive to give rise to a pervasively hostile atmosphere. This determination should be based on the totality of the circumstances.

In *Harris v. Forklift Systems, Inc.*,[21] the Supreme Court held that no showing of a serious effect on an employee's psychological well-being, or other injury, is necessary for a hostile-environment claim under Title VII, reasoning

16. 29 C.F.R. § 1604.2(a)(1)(i)–(iii) (1997).
17. 513 U.S. 352 (1995).
18. O'Day v. McDonnell–Douglas Helicopter Co., 79 F.3d 756 (9th Cir. 1996).

19. Burlington Indus. v. Ellerth, 524 U.S. 742 (1998).
20. 477 U.S. 51 (1986).
21. 510 U.S. 17 (1993).

that "Title VII comes into play before the harassing conduct leads to a nervous breakdown." The Court ruled in favor of a female manager of an equipment-rental company who was harassed for two years by its president. In the presence of other employees, the president said such things as, "You're a woman, what do you know?" and "We need a man as the rental manager," and called her a "a dumb-ass woman." The president also made sexual innuendos, suggesting that they "go to the Holiday Inn to negotiate her raise," and occasionally asked female employees to get coins from his front pants pocket. Despite complaints, the sexual comments continued.

SAME-SEX SEXUAL HARASSMENT

In *Oncale v. Sundowner Offshore Services, Inc.,*[22] the U.S. Supreme Court held that same-sex harassment involving heterosexuals or homosexuals may be actionable under Title VII. Although same-sex harassment was not the evil Congress sought to remedy when it passed Title VII, the Court saw "no justification in the statutory language or our precedents for a categorical rule excluding same-sex harassment claims from the coverage of Title VII." To be actionable under Title VII, the conduct need not be motivated by sexual desire, but it must constitute discrimination because of sex. The Court explained that "the statute does not reach genuine but innocuous differences in the ways men and women routinely interact with members of the same sex and of the opposite sex." It requires "neither asexuality nor androgyny in the workplace." Workplace harassment is not automatically sexual discrimination merely because the words used have sexual content or connotations. Title VII prohibits only "behavior so objectively offensive as to alter the 'conditions' of the victim's employment." The Court called on courts and juries to use "common sense" to differentiate sex discrimination from horseplay, saying that a pat on the bottom by a football coach to a player running onto the field may not constitute sex discrimination, but similar touching of a secretary might.

DEFINING A HOSTILE WORK ENVIRONMENT

To determine whether there is a hostile or abusive environment, courts must look at all the circumstances, including (1) the frequency and severity of the discriminatory conduct; (2) whether it is physically threatening or humiliating, or merely an offensive utterance; and (3) whether it unreasonably interferes with an employee's work performance.

22. 523 U.S. 75 (1998).

To be actionable under Title VII, sexual harassment must be so severe or pervasive as to alter the conditions of the victim's employment and create an abusive working environment.[23] The U.S. Supreme Court has ruled that "'simple teasing,' offhand comments, and isolated incidents (unless extremely serious) will not amount to discriminatory changes in the terms and conditions of employment." The conduct must be "extreme." The standards for judging hostility are sufficiently demanding to prevent plaintiffs from converting Title VII into a "general civility code"; they are intended to filter out "complaints attacking 'the ordinary tribulations of the workplace, such as the sporadic use of abusive language, gender-related jokes, and occasional teasing.'"

In *Schmitz v. ING Securities, Futures & Options, Inc.,*[24] a case reminiscent of the film *Erin Brockovich,* the court considered whether repeated comments made by the employer's chief financial officer to the receptionist regarding her risqué clothing constituted sexual harassment. The CFO told her that her skirts and blouses were too tight, too short, and too revealing. He called her an "exhibitionist" and once summoned her into his office to reprimand her for dressing so provocatively that any "hot-blooded male" in the office would be aroused and distracted from his work. After she complained to ING's director of human resources, her workload increased and the CFO became openly hostile to her. Six weeks later, she was terminated for inadequate work performance. The court dismissed her claim for sexual discrimination and retaliatory harassment, and the Seventh Circuit affirmed on the grounds that the receptionist had failed to establish that she was subject to sexual advances or requests for sexual favors. The court also held that the receptionist had failed to show that her work environment was hostile or abusive. Commenting on the CFO's behavior, the court said that "[his] failings 'to treat a female employee with sensitivity, tact, and delicacy'" are "too commonplace . . . to be classified as discriminatory."[25]

How often the conduct must occur to constitute a hostile environment has not been completely resolved. In *Faragher v. City of Boca Raton,*[26] the Supreme Court seemed to acknowledge that an "extremely serious" isolated incident might give rise to a finding of hostile environment. In *Burlington Industries v. Ellerth,*[27] however, the Court reserved the issue of whether a single unfulfilled threat by a supervisor of adverse job action is sufficient.

23. Faragher v. City of Boca Raton, 524 U.S. 775 (1998).
24. 191 F.3d 456 (7th Cir. 1999).
25. *Id.* quoting Minor v. Ivy Tech State College, 174 F.3d 855, 858 (7th Cir. 1999).
26. 524 U.S. 775 (1998).
27. 524 U.S. 742 (1998).

The Supreme Judicial Court of Maine ruled that a supervisor's request for sexual favors in exchange for money over the course of a business lunch was sufficiently severe to state a hostile work environment under *Meritor* and *Harris*.[28] By contrast, the U.S. Court of Appeals for the Second Circuit held that suggestive, nude male pictures posted on an office bulletin board did not create a hostile work environment because the pictures did not produce an atmosphere of "intimidation, ridicule and insult" that altered the terms of the plaintiff's employment.[29] In *Brooks v. San Mateo, California*,[30] the Ninth Circuit held that a single incident in which a male coworker touched a female employee's breast and stomach while she was answering a 911 emergency call was not sufficient to establish a hostile work environment. The employee suffered no physical injury, and the employer took prompt steps to remove the male employee from the workplace. The court acknowledged that a single incident involving a supervisor was more likely to result in employer liability for hostile environment than comparable conduct by a coworker.

Recently, several large multinational corporations with offices in the United States paid millions of dollars to settle claims of sexual harassment. For example, in 1998, Astra USA, a unit of the pharmaceutical giant Astra AB of Sweden, agreed to pay $9.85 million to at least seventy-nine women and one man who were punished for speaking out.[31] An investigative report by *Business Week* had uncovered a corporate culture at Astra in which female employees were regularly groped, expected to go to executives' hotel rooms and have drinks, sexualized at work, and regularly subjected to sexual advances by the president and other members of top management.[32] Those who complained suffered retaliation by being discredited, passed up for promotion, and even discharged. After an internal probe, the president was fired.[33]

VICARIOUS LIABILITY FOR HOSTILE ENVIRONMENT

As explained in Chapter 5, employers are vicariously liable under the doctrine of *respondeat superior* for all torts

---

28. Nadeau v. Rainbow Rugs, Inc., 675 A.2d 973 (Me. 1996).
29. Brennan v. Metropolitan Opera A'ssn, 192 F.3d 310 (2d Cir. 1999).
30. 229 F.3d 917 (9th Cir. 2000).
31. Associated Press, *Drug Firm to Pay Record $9.85 Million*, SAN FRANCISCO CHRON., Feb. 6, 1998, at A3.
32. Mark Maremont, *Abuse of Power: The Astonishing Tale of Sexual Harassment at Astra USA*, BUS. WK., May 13, 1996, at 86.
33. Laura Johannes, *Astra USA Fires Bildman from Top Post*, WALL ST. J., June 27, 1996, at A3.

INTERNATIONAL CONSIDERATION

Japan experienced a surge in the number of sexual harassment claims during the 1990s. Most of these cases were tort claims resulting from physical contact or sexual assaults. With respect to sexual harassment due to a hostile working environment, one district court held that a coworker's rumor concerning the plaintiff's promiscuity was an actionable tort because it was an infringement on her human dignity and caused her working conditions to deteriorate.[a]

In June 1997, Japan's Equal Employment Opportunity Law of 1985 (EEOL) was drastically revised to provide more protection for women in the workplace. The 1997 amendment includes a new provision imposing on employers a duty to prevent sexual harassment.

The EEOL also prohibits discrimination against women in employment recruitment, hiring, assignment, promotion, training, education, fringe benefits, and termination. The 1997 amendment includes sanctions, which were not present in the original law, to enforce these new provisions. In addition, when an employer violates the EEOL, the labor minister can publicize the fact.

Although twelve women were successful in procuring a court order upholding a $1.6 million award against a company for systematically discriminating against them in pay and promotions, most of the recent job seekers, labor lawyers, economists, and women's rights advocates interviewed by a *New York Times* reporter said that the new law "had little real impact, and the old patterns of consignment of women to noncareer positions continued unabated."[b]

a. Andrew Pollack, *In Japan, It's See No Evil; Have No Harassment*, N.Y. TIMES, May 7, 1996, at C1.
b. Howard W. French, *Diploma in Hand, Japanese Women Find Glass Ceiling Reinforced with Iron*, N.Y. TIMES, Jan. 1, 2001.

---

committed by employees acting within the scope of employment. As a result, if a supervisor fails to promote a woman because of her gender, the employer is liable for sexual discrimination because the supervisor was acting within the scope of employment when deciding whom to promote. But when a supervisor harasses an employee (either by demanding sexual favors or by creating a hostile environment), the supervisor is rarely acting for the benefit of the employer.

The U.S. Supreme Court reviewed general principles of agency law to determine when an employer is liable for the creation of a hostile environment. Under Section 219(2) of the Restatement (Second) of Agency, an employer is liable for torts of employees not acting in the scope of employment if (1) the employer intended the

IN BRIEF

Elements of a Sexual Harassment Claim

Unwelcome sexual advances, requests for sexual favors, and other verbal or physical conduct of a sexual nature constitute sexual harassment when:

1. an individual's employment depends on submission to such conduct;
2. submission to or rejection of such conduct is used as the basis of employment decisions; or
3. such conduct unreasonably interferes with the individual's work performance or creates an intimidating, hostile, or offensive working environment.

To establish a claim of hostile-environment sexual harassment under Title VII, the plaintiff must show that:

1. the harassment created an abusive working environment;
2. the harassment was based on sex; and
3. the harassment was so severe or pervasive as to alter the conditions of the victim's employment.

conduct, (2) the employee's high rank makes him or her the employer's alter ego, (3) the employer was negligent, or (4) the employee was aided in accomplishing the tort by the existence of the agency relation.[34]

Negligence The employer is negligent with respect to sexual harassment if it knew or should have known of the harassment but failed to stop it by taking appropriate corrective measures. This negligence standard would govern hostile environment by coworkers (and probably customers with whom the employee must deal as part of his or her job).

Aided-in-the-Agency Relation and Supervisor Harassment
In *quid pro quo* and hostile-environment cases, the employer is always vicariously liable under the aided-in-the-agency-relation standard when a supervisor takes a tangible employment action against a subordinate (such as firing, failing to promote, reassignment with significantly different responsibilities, or reducing benefits). Thus, in such cases, the employer is vicariously liable for the hostile environment created by a supervisor with immediate (or successively higher) authority over the victimized employee regardless of whether the employer knew or should have known about the supervisor's conduct.

In *Faragher v. City of Boca Raton*,[35] the U.S. Supreme Court applied the aided-in-the-agency-relation standard to a case brought by an ocean lifeguard, involving the creation of a hostile environment by supervisors, in which tangible employment action was threatened but not taken. The Court acknowledged that in a sense a harassing supervisor is always assisted in his or her conduct by the supervisory relationship: "When a fellow employee harasses, the victim can walk away or tell the offender where to go, but it may be difficult to offer such responses to a supervisor" with the power to hire, fire, and set work schedules and pay raises.

Even so, the Court felt constrained by its holding in *Meritor* that the employer is not automatically liable for harassment by a supervisor. It also noted that the primary objective of Title VII is to avoid harm. To implement that statutory policy, the Court considered it appropriate "to recognize the employer's affirmative obligation to prevent violations and give credit here to employers who make reasonable efforts to discharge their duty." At the same time, the Court acknowledged an employee's duty to avoid or mitigate harm. If the employee unreasonably failed to avail himself or herself of the employer's preventive or remedial apparatus, the employee should not recover damages that could have been avoided if he or she had done so.

Accordingly, the Court held that if the supervisor's harassment does not culminate in a tangible employment action (such as discharge, demotion, or undesirable assignment), then the employer may raise an affirmative defense to liability or damages. To establish the defense, the employer must prove two things: (1) it exercised reasonable care to prevent and correct promptly any sexually harassing behavior; and (2) the employee unreasonably failed to take advantage of any preventive or corrective opportunities provided by the employer or to avoid harm otherwise. For example, if an employer has provided a proven, effective mechanism for reporting and resolving complaints of sexual harassment that is available to the employee without undue risk or expense, then the employee's unreasonable failure to use that complaint procedure will normally suffice to satisfy the employer's burden under the second element of the defense.

Applying these principles to the facts of the case at hand, the Court ruled as a matter of law that the City of Boca Raton did not exercise reasonable care to prevent the supervisors' harassing conduct. The City had failed to disseminate its policy against sexual harassment among the beach employees. The City's policy

34. *See* Burlington Indus. v. Ellerth, 524 U.S. 742 (1998).

35. 524 U.S. 775 (1998).

VIEW FROM CYBERSPACE

Harassment *in the* Virtual Office

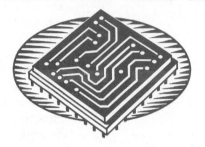

Employers face new challenges as company electronic networks provide a new venue for sexual and other types of harassment. A recent case[a] involving a female pilot at Continental Airlines illustrates the issues involved.

In December 1989, Tammy Blakey became the first female captain at Continental to fly an Airbus 300 widebody jet. Soon thereafter, she began complaining to Continental about a hostile working environment, based on conduct and comments directed at her by male coworkers. These included placing pornographic photographs in her plane's cockpit and other work areas and directing vulgar gender-based comments at her. After she sued Continental for sexual discrimination in 1993, a number of Continental's male pilots posted derogatory and insulting remarks about Blakey on the pilots' online computer bulletin board, the Crew Members Forum. Although employees using the Forum, not Continental, paid the Internet service provider (CompuServe) an hourly fee to access the Forum, the Forum was an option on the Continental Airlines Home Access program, which crew members were required to access to learn their flight schedules.

In analyzing Continental's potential liability for the retaliatory comments posted on the Forum, the New Jersey Supreme Court began by stating that if a bulletin board in a lounge at an airport used exclusively by the pilots and crew members of an airline contained similar comments by the pilots, then there would be "little doubt" that if management had notice of the messages that created a hostile environment, the airline would be liable for hostile-environment harassment, if it failed to take prompt corrective action. Similarly, if senior management, pilots, and crew frequented some nearby place where one of the crew was subjected to sexually offensive insults that continued a pattern of harassment in the workplace, then an employer with notice of the harassment "would not be entirely free to ignore it." The court then reasoned that the fact that an electronic bulletin board is located outside the workplace does not mean that the employer has no duty to correct off-site harassment by cowork-

ers.[b] The court noted the importance of extensions of the workplace where "the relations among employees are cemented or sometimes sundered" and asked "what exactly is the outsider (whether black, Latino, or woman) to do" when the belittling conduct continues in an after-hours setting: "Keep swallowing the abuse or give up the chance to make the team?"

The court was careful to explain that employers have no duty to monitor employees' mail, given the "[g]rave privacy concerns" implicated. But, the court suggested, employers may not disregard the posting of offensive messages on company or state agency e-mail systems when the employer knows or has reason to know that this is part of a pattern of harassment that is taking place in the workplace and in settings related to the workplace. Otherwise, the employer "sends the harassed employee the message that the harassment is acceptable and that the management supports the harasser."

---

a. Blakey v. Continental Airlines, Inc., 751 A.2d 6538 (N.J. 2000).
b. *See, generally,* Diana J.P. McKenzie, *Information Technology Policies: Practical Protection in Cyberspace*, 3 STAN. J. L. BUS. & FIN. 84 (1997).

---

did not include a sensible complaint procedure because it did not provide any assurance that the harassing supervisors could be bypassed in registering complaints. Its officials made no attempt to keep track of the conduct of supervisors, even though the supervisors were given virtually unchecked authority over subordinates who were completely isolated from the City's higher management.

The Court stated that the promulgation of an antiharassment policy with a complaint procedure was not necessary as a matter of law, but that the need for a stated policy suitable to the employment circumstances would be relevant to determining whether the employer acted reasonably. Although the Court raised the possibility that an employer with a small workforce might be able to prevent harassing behavior by acting informally, it is clear that every employer, regardless of the size of its workforce, is well advised to adopt, disseminate, and enforce a written policy prohibiting harassment and providing a reasonable complaint procedure.

In the following case, the court considered whether the employer had taken adequate steps to prevent and correct harassing behavior and was, therefore, able to establish the affirmative defense provided in *Faragher*.

A CASE IN POINT

CASE 15.2

Hill v. American General Finance, Inc.

*United States
Court of Appeals
for the Seventh Circuit
218 F.3d 369
(7th Cir. 2000).*

Summary

FACTS Louise Hill worked as a lending/collection administrator in the Alton, Illinois office of American General Finance, Inc. (AGF). She was the only African American working in the office. Within a month of her arrival, her supervisor Darin Brandt started to racially and sexually harass her. For example, he said, "I like a woman with a big ass, like Louise's," and he made reference to the size of his penis. On one occasion, he rubbed his pelvis against her buttocks and said, "Boy that feels good." He also said, "Once you go black, you never go back." In addition to the sexual comments, he made offensive racial comments such as, "Don't come into this office talking black, because this ain't no Aunt Jemima office." He also told her that he was "sick of black people getting food stamps and having those black babies."

On two separate occasions, Hill wrote a letter to AGF's chief executive officer complaining about Brandt's behavior. Rather than signing her own name, she signed the letters with a pseudonym, pretending to be a customer. The human resources officer conducted an investigation, including an interview with Hill. Although no other employees confirmed the harassment, some said that conversations of a sexual nature did occur in the office. Gary English, the director of operations, issued Brandt a letter warning him for allowing these conversations to occur.

Subsequently, Hill wrote a letter to English describing the harassment, but this time she signed her name. The company's human resource attorney and outside counsel promptly commenced an investigation and decided to issue a written warning to Brandt, provide him with additional training, transfer and demote him with a $10,000 reduction in salary, and transfer Hill to prevent retaliation from her coworkers.

Hill complained that her transfer was to a high-crime area and claimed that the company was retaliating against her. She resigned and filed a claim for sexual and racial harassment under Title VII. The district court dismissed the case after finding both that the plaintiff had failed to take advantage of her employer's policies and procedures regarding harassment and that the company had promptly taken appropriate corrective action after learning of the harassment. Hill appealed.

ISSUE PRESENTED What actions constitute reasonable care by an employer to prevent and correct sexually harassing behavior?

SUMMARY OF OPINION The U.S. Court of Appeals for the Seventh Circuit began by stating that a defendant employer can raise an affirmative defense to a charge of harassment by establishing that (1) the employer exercised reasonable care to prevent and correct promptly any sexually harassing behavior, and (2) the plaintiff employee unreasonably failed to take advantage of any corrective or preventive opportunities provided by the employer.

With respect to the first prong of the defense, the court found that the company took immediate corrective action after receiving Hill's letter by launching an investigation regarding the allegations. As a result of this investigation, the company punished Brandt for his conduct and transferred him so that he could no longer harass Hill.

In determining whether the company took corrective action, the court also considered whether the company had policies or procedures to help employees deal with harassment. AGF had several policies in place at the time of these incidents. It had an equal employment policy and a sexual harassment policy. In addition, the company had established a complaint procedure with four levels. Employees could report to their immediate supervisor or manager. Alternatively, the employee could speak with the field relations consultant, the associate director for employee relations and benefits, or the director of

(Continued)

(Case 15.2 continued)

human resources and systems management. The third level of complaint was to the fair employment practices compliance officer. Employees were provided with a phone number so that they could communicate complaints. Finally, the fourth level was the Personnel Administration Committee through the director of human resources and system management.

Although Hill claimed that she did not receive AGF's policies, the policies were kept in a set of notebooks available to the public within each branch office. In addition, Hill testified that she knew that the human resources group in the company had the responsibility to prevent sexual and racial harassment. She testified that she knew that she could talk to that group or to English about any complaints she had.

The court stated that Hill's signed letter reporting Brandt's conduct was a reasonable step taken to correct the situation, but it found that she did not notify the company of the harassment until she sent this letter. The two previous letters signed with false names of customers were not a reasonable form of notice.

RESULT The court of appeals affirmed the lower court's decision. The adequacy of AGF's policies and procedures and Hill's failure to take reasonable steps to notify the company of the harassment established a defense against her discrimination claims.

COMMENTS As exemplified by *Hill v. American General Finance,* the affirmative defense the U.S. Supreme Court articulated in *Faragher* provides companies a powerful shield in hostile-environment cases. By being proactive, employers can reduce the likelihood that harassment will occur, mitigate the harm caused if it does occur, and limit or eliminate their vicarious liability.

APPROPRIATE PREVENTIVE AND CORRECTIVE ACTION

Supervisors and nonsupervising employees should be taught that all forms of sexual conduct and sexual talk in the workplace are inappropriate. This should be stated clearly in a written policy. The management of a company, whether through its human resource staff or otherwise, must be familiar with the atmosphere of its workplace and be vigilant in maintaining an appropriate environment in which employees can work comfortably.

It is also important to develop an atmosphere in which the employee feels free to bring a complaint. This has two components. First, victims of sexual harassment should be given information and support to identify and report sexual harassment.[36] Second, because the harasser is often the employee's supervisor, an effective

procedure should provide more than one resource person to whom the employee can complain. Persons of both genders should be available so that the employee has a choice; sexual harassment is not a problem for female employees only.

The company should also ensure that all complaints are thoroughly investigated. The employer should meet with the complaining employee at the employee's earliest convenience and immediately interview the accused person, coworkers, and other witnesses. If the investigation reveals a problem, then the employer should consider whether termination or reassignment of the harasser or a reprimand is in order. Any reprimand should be in writing and be put in the harasser's personnel file. The reprimand should make it clear to the harasser that his or her conduct is unacceptable and warn that any recurrence will be grounds for severe discipline (including termination). The harasser should also be instructed to avoid having contact with the victim or talking about him or her. The employer should follow up with the victim to ensure that there are no continuing problems and to assure him or

36. *See* Bernice R. Sandler, *Handling Sexual Harassment,* WOMEN IN MED. AND THE MED. SCI., Fall 1997, at 1 (discussing strategies that victims may use to address workplace sexual harassment).

her that it will do whatever it can to support the victim's career goals.[37] Even if the investigation is inconclusive, it may be appropriate for the employer to offer the alleged victim a reassignment.

If an employer does not take appropriate action in response to claims or evidence of sexual harassment, then the company is exposing itself to potentially astronomical jury awards. For example, Baker & McKenzie, the world's largest law firm with 1,670 lawyers in thirty countries, learned the hard way in September 1994 about an employer's liability for sexual harassment by a manager. A California jury awarded legal secretary Rena Weeks $50,000 compensatory damages and $6.9 million punitive damages from Baker & McKenzie for its failure to provide a harassment-free workplace. Martin Greenstein, a former Baker & McKenzie partner who allegedly grabbed Weeks's breasts and buttocks and dropped M&M candies in her blouse pocket, was ordered to pay $225,000 in punitive damages. At trial, Weeks presented evidence that for several years before Baker & McKenzie hired her, Greenstein had engaged in similar conduct with other female employees. The incidents were reported to the firm's management, but the firm did little in response other than to speak to Greenstein and document the reports in the women's personnel files. Each time the firm spoke to him, Greenstein denied the accusation, and the firm warned him not to engage in such conduct but never took further action.

In assessing punitive damages equal to 10 percent of Baker & McKenzie's net worth, jurors were, according to juror Frank Lewis, "highly cognizant of the fact that we were sending a message not only to Baker & McKenzie but to corporate America."[38] The trial court reduced the punitive damage award to $3.5 million.

The California Court of Appeal upheld the award under Section 3294 of the California Civil Code, which permits a punitive damage award against an employer for its employee's acts of oppression, fraud, or malice if the employer, through its managing agents, had advance knowledge of the employee's unfitness and employed him or her with a conscious disregard of the rights and safety of others.[39] The court held that an employer may not employ or continue to employ a harasser without taking action reasonably designed to protect others. The court rejected Baker & McKenzie's argument that an employer is left in the impossible situation of either terminating every accused harasser or facing punitive damage liability for the employee's later acts. Although an employer is not required to terminate a harassing employee, it is required to take reasonable measures to prevent a known harasser from committing future acts of harassment.

In light of such liabilities, some companies have acted quickly to fire individuals accused of sexual harassment. However, as discussed in Chapter 14, without a full investigation and a good faith belief that harassment occurred, the employer may find itself sued for wrongful termination by a discharged employee.[40]

Although employers are clearly liable if they know of a hostile work environment and do nothing, in certain limited circumstances an employer that does not immediately act on a claim of sexual harassment may not be liable. In *Torres v. Pisano*,[41] the U.S. Court of Appeals for the Second Circuit ruled that a supervisor who did not act on an employee's sexual harassment claim in order to honor the victim's request for confidentiality did not expose the employer to liability for that victim's harassment. The court reasoned that the supervisor's failure to act did not violate his duty to take reasonable steps to eliminate the sexual harassment because of the victim's specific instructions that he not share the information with anyone else. Although the employer won this case, promising confidentiality is a dangerous approach. If the alleged harasser goes on to harass someone else, and that person discovers that the employer knew of previous harassment claims against the alleged harasser but did nothing, the employer's failure to act could be used against it in a suit by the second victim. For this reason, managers should rarely, if ever, agree to keep the matter confidential.

 ## Retaliatory Harassment

Employers may also be held liable for retaliation against employees who have complained to the company or the EEOC about sexual harassment or other types of discrimination banned by Title VII. In the following case, the Sixth Circuit addressed the issue of an employer's responsibility for retaliatory harassment of an employee.

---

37. *See* Casenas v. Fujisawa USA, Inc., 58 Cal. App. 4th 101 (1997) (describing the employer's timely investigation of, and response to, the sexual harassment allegations as "a textbook example of how to respond appropriately to an employee's harassment complaint").
38. Rachel Gordon, *Amount of Award Split Harassment Jury,* SAN FRANCISCO EXAMINER, Sept. 3, 1994, at A1.
39. Weeks v. Baker & McKenzie, 74 Cal. Rptr. 2d 510 (Cal. Ct. App. 1998).

40. Howard Mintz, *Proving Sex Harassment: Firms Struggle over Employee Rights vs. Workplace Protection,* SAN JOSE MERCURY NEWS, Oct. 20, 1997, at A1.
41. 116 F.3d 625 (2d Cir. 1997), *cert. denied,* 522 U.S. 997 (1997).

A CASE IN POINT

CASE 15.3

Morris v. Oldham County, Kentucky, Fiscal Court

United States Court of Appeals for the Sixth Circuit 201 F.3d 784 (6th Cir. 2000).

Summary

FACTS Judy Morris was employed as a clerk and secretary by the Oldham County Road Department. Her supervisor, Brent Likins, told jokes with sexual overtones in front of her, commented on her clothes, and indicated that if Morris performed sexual favors for him, he would give her a more favorable job evaluation. Morris complained to the defendant, County Judge Black, who wrote a letter to Likins reprimanding him for his behavior. After receiving this reprimand, Likins became overly critical of Morris's work. After Morris made further complaints to Judge Black about Likins's behavior, he transferred her to another location. Likins continued to harass Morris: (1) he called her on the phone over thirty times and visited her new office fifteen times despite Black's orders prohibiting communication with her; (2) he followed Morris home from work one day, pulled his car up beside her, and gave her "the finger"; (3) he threw nails onto her home driveway; and (4) he destroyed the television set that Morris watched at work.

As a result of this behavior, Morris started having anxiety attacks and, ultimately, left work on sick leave. She sued the County, Black, and Likins, alleging sexual discrimination and retaliation under Title VII and the Kentucky Civil Rights Act. The district court dismissed the claims on the grounds that Morris had not been subjected to any adverse employment action by the defendants and thus her retaliation claim was without merit. Morris appealed.

ISSUE PRESENTED Is retaliatory harassment by a supervisor actionable under Title VII?

SUMMARY OF OPINION The U.S. Court of Appeals for the Sixth Circuit held that severe or pervasive supervisor harassment that results from an individual opposing any practice made an unlawful employment practice by Title VII constitutes discrimination. To establish a *prima facie* case of Title VII retaliation, the plaintiff must prove that (1) her activity was protected by Title VII; (2) the defendant knew of her exercise of protected rights; (3) the defendant took adverse employment action against the plaintiff, or she was subjected to severe or pervasive retaliatory harassment by a supervisor; and (4) there was a causal connection between the protected activity and the adverse employment action or harassment.

The court also ruled that the defendant could assert as a defense that there was a legitimate, nondiscriminatory reason for his actions. The employer could also establish an affirmative defense by demonstrating (1) that the employer exercised reasonable care to prevent and correct any harassing behavior, and (2) that the plaintiff unreasonably failed to take advantage of any preventive or corrective opportunities provided by the employer to avoid harm.

RESULT The appeals court held that Likins had engaged in severe or pervasive retaliatory harassment. The district court's decision was reversed, and the case was remanded to the district court for further proceedings, during which the County would be given the opportunity to prove an affirmative defense.

In 1997, the U.S. Supreme Court unanimously ruled that both current and former employees can sue for retaliation.[42] The case involved an employer who allegedly gave a former employee a negative reference because he had filed a claim of racial discrimination against the company.

Actions allegedly taken to prevent further harassment may be deemed retaliatory under Title VII if they harm the employee's employment situation. In *DiIenno v. Goodwill Industries of Mid-Eastern Pennsylvania,*[43] the Third Circuit found that transferring an employee to a

---

42. Robinson v. Shell Oil Co., 519 U.S. 377 (1997).

43. 162 F.3d 235 (3d Cir. 1998).

job that the employer knew she could not perform in retaliation for her complaint that her manager was sexually harassing her violated Title VII. Prior to the transfer, the employee had complained to Goodwill's human resource director and sales manager that she was being sexually harassed. Following her complaint, she was transferred from her job of tagging and pricing clothing to a job requiring her to sort through clothes contributed to Goodwill. The employee's phobia of "critters," such as the mice, insects, and bugs found in these bags of clothing, prevented her from performing the job. The court found that "[i]t is important to take a plaintiff's job-related attributes into account when determining whether a lateral transfer was an adverse employment action."

SEXUAL STEREOTYPING

In *Price Waterhouse v. Hopkins*,[44] Ann Hopkins had been denied partnership in the Big Five accounting firm Pricewaterhouse Cooper. She claimed that the firm had discriminated against her on the basis of sex. She produced evidence that the policy board had advised her that, to improve her chances for partnership, she should "walk more femininely, talk more femininely, dress more femininely, wear make-up, have her hair styled, and wear jewelry."

The U.S. Supreme Court concluded that the evidence produced by Hopkins was sufficient to establish that sexual stereotyping played a part in the firm's decision not to promote her and held that it constituted discrimination based on sex. With respect to sexual stereotyping, the Court stated: "An employer who objects to aggressiveness in women but whose positions require this trait places women in an intolerable and impermissible Catch-22: out of a job if they behave aggressively and out of a job if they

44. 490 U.S. 228 (1989).

 ETHICAL CONSIDERATION

A rule that no employee should be subjected to requests for sexual favors is not sufficient. Sexual harassment may include overt or subtle sexual advances, even if there is no retaliation when such advances are rebuffed; sexual joking; leering; or any unwelcome touching. A workplace where physical familiarity has come to be accepted, or where sexual comments are laughed at or tolerated, presents a difficult situation. If management appears to condone such conduct, employees may feel compelled to go along with it, even if they find it intimidating or if it interferes with their ability to work.

don't. Title VII lifts women out of this bind."[45] In addition, although the case dealt with gender discrimination, the Court expressly stated that all references to gender and all principles announced in the opinion "apply with equal force to discrimination based on race, religion, or national origin."

Special Applications *of* Title VII

Civil rights legislation was founded on the fundamental premise that people ought not to be denied a job or an opportunity on the job because of their race, religion, or sex. The law has expanded beyond that basic premise to reach more subtle forms of discrimination.

PREGNANCY DISCRIMINATION

In 1976, the U.S. Supreme Court held that denying a woman disability insurance benefits for a temporary disability caused by pregnancy was not sex discrimination, even though the employer provided men unlimited temporary disability benefits.[46] The Supreme Court reasoned that the denial of benefits was based not on being female but on being pregnant, and that a distinction between pregnant persons (albeit all female) and nonpregnant persons was not sex discrimination.

Congress responded by passing the Pregnancy Discrimination Act, which provides that discrimination on the basis of pregnancy is, on its face, a form of sex discrimination under Title VII.[47] Employers must provide the same compensation for disabilities related to pregnancy and childbirth as they provide for any other disability. Many states have followed suit, and, as in other areas of discrimination law, some provide greater protection than is required under federal law.

These protections are not absolute, however. The U.S. Court of Appeals for the First Circuit, for example, ruled that an employer could discharge a manager who was on maternity leave, when it realized the company could function effectively without her.[48] The court reasoned that discharge is an ordinary risk of employment, whether or not one is pregnant, and it ruled that the

45. *Id.*
46. General Elec. Co. v. Gilbert, 429 U.S. 125 (1976).
47. 42 U.S.C. § 2000e(k) (1994).
48. Smith v. F.W. Morse & Co., 76 F.3d 413 (1st Cir. 1996). *Accord* Rhett v. Carnegie Ctr. Assoc., 129 F.3d 290 (3d Cir. 1997), *cert. denied*, 524 U.S. 938 (1998).

ETHICAL CONSIDERATION

Shayne Kahn worked as an executive recruiter for Objective Solutions International (OSI) and was considered an exemplary employee of the company. While she was working at OSI, she had an affair with Steven B. Wolfe, the president of the company. After Wolfe's wife found out about the affair, Kahn was fired. She filed a sexual harassment and sexual discrimination claim under Title VII. The U.S. District Court for the Southern District of New York dismissed her claim, stating: "Participation in a consensual office affair does not constitute actionable gender discrimination when the termination of the affair results in discharge. It may constitute unfair and certainly unchivalrous behavior, but not discrimination because of gender."[a] Although the court did not find that Wolfe had violated the law, was his behavior ethical? Should the company discipline Wolfe for his action either in having the affair or in firing Kahn?

a. Kahn v. Objective Solutions Int'l, 865 F. Supp. 2d 377 (S.D.N.Y. 2000).

employer had demonstrated that it would have eliminated her position regardless of her pregnancy.

FETAL-PROTECTION POLICIES

Certain substances used in manufacturing are harmful to the fetus being carried by a pregnant woman. In an effort to avoid such harm, and related lawsuits for unsafe working environments, some companies adopted so-called fetal-protection policies. A *fetal-protection policy* bars a woman from certain jobs unless her inability to bear children is medically documented. In *Automobile Workers v. Johnson Controls, Inc.*,[49] the Supreme Court struck down Johnson Controls' policy, which precluded women with childbearing capacity from working at jobs in which lead levels were defined as excessive.

The Court held that the fetal-protection policy was a facially discriminatory policy forbidden under Title VII and that women cannot be excluded from certain jobs because of their childbearing capacity. The Court stated that "[d]ecisions about the welfare of future children must be left to the parents who conceive, bear, support, and raise them rather than to the employers who hire those parents." The Court went on to say that "[i]t is no more appropriate for the courts than it is for individual employers to decide whether a woman's reproductive role is more important to herself and her family than her economic role."

49. 499 U.S. 187 (1991).

In the wake of *Johnson Controls,* employers have been forced to walk a fine line between not limiting the positions available to female employees and limiting or reducing potential workplace hazards. Indeed, in eight states employers may be liable for not providing a safe work environment for a pregnant employee's fetus.[50] Employers have been held liable for falling machines, triggering premature birth and brain damage to the child, and requiring pregnant employees to work beyond their doctor's orders, resulting in premature birth and later death of the fetus.[51]

ENGLISH-ONLY LAWS

The national origin provisions of Title VII have been used to challenge English-only workplace rules, which prohibit employees from speaking any language other than English at work. The EEOC has taken the position that language is closely linked to national origin, so English-only laws can have a disparate impact on Hispanic employees and others whose native language may not be English.[52] The U.S. Supreme Court agreed to review during its 2000–2001 term a case in which the U.S. Court of Appeals for the Eleventh Circuit ruled that the Alabama Department of Public Safety's policy of administering driver's license examinations only in English violated Title VII because it had a disproportionately adverse impact on Alabama residents of foreign descent.[53] A federal court in Texas refused to dismiss an EEOC disparate-impact lawsuit against two telecommunications providers (Premier Operator Services, Inc. and Digital Network Services, Inc.), in which the EEOC argued that Hispanic workers were barred from speaking the language in which they were best able to communicate and faced a disproportionate risk of termination for violating the policy.[54]

DRESS CODES

Although employers have the right to enact and enforce dress codes, these codes can result in legal claims involving religious and sexual discrimination and harassment. The trend toward allowing employees to wear casual clothing has the potential to further complicate this matter.

50. Sue Shellenbarger, *Work and Family: Recent Suits Make Pregnancy Issues Workplace Priorities,* WALL ST. J., Jan. 14, 1998, at B1.
51. *Id.*
52. *At Panel Discussion on National Origin Bias EEOC Says English-Only Challenges Are Rising,* 66 U.S.L.W. 2375 (Dec. 23, 1997).
53. Sandoval v. Hagan, 197 F.3d 484 (11th Cir. 1999), *cert. granted,* 121 S. Ct. 28 (2000).
54. EEOC v. Premier Operator Servs., Inc. (N.D. Tex. 1999).

Employees have based claims of religious discrimination on their employer's refusal to let them wear turbans rather than protective headgear. In response, the Occupational Health and Safety Administration amended its regulations to exempt persons wearing a turban from its hard-hat requirements.

Remedies *under* Title VII

Remedies available under Title VII include compensation for lost salary and benefits, reinstatement or "front pay" equal to what the employee would have received had the individual not been discharged, and injunctive relief to stop prohibited discriminatory actions. Front pay is awarded when reinstatement is inappropriate because the position is unavailable or hostility raises a practical barrier.

The plaintiff may also recover compensatory damages for future pecuniary losses, emotional pain and suffering, inconvenience, mental anguish, loss of enjoyment of life, and other nonpecuniary losses. While front pay is limited in duration because it compensates for the immediate effects of discrimination, lost future earnings compensate an employee for a lifetime of diminished earnings resulting from the reputational harm suffered as a result of discrimination. Therefore, an employee may be awarded both front pay and damages for lost future earnings.[55] Punitive damages are also available and can be awarded even if the jury awarded no compensatory damages.[56]

CAPS ON LIABILITY

The compensatory and punitive damages available for discrimination based on sex or religion are capped at $50,000 for employers of 100 or fewer employees, $100,000 for employers with 101 to 200 employees, $200,000 for employers with 201 to 500 employees, and $500,000 for employers with more than 500 employees. But the compensatory caps do not apply to intentional racial or ethnic discrimination.

Any party to a case for damages can demand a jury trial, but the court may not inform the jury of the caps on damage awards. The majority of federal appeals courts have held that, when front pay is awarded as a substitute for reinstatement because reinstatement is not available, then the award of front pay is an equitable remedy not subject to the cap on compensatory dam-

ages.[57] The U.S. Supreme Court agreed to review in its 2000–2001 term a case[58] in which the Sixth Circuit held that the caps do apply to front pay.

PUNITIVE DAMAGES

In *Kolstad v. American Dental Association*,[59] the Supreme Court considered the circumstances under which punitive damages may be awarded under Title VII. The Court began by noting that punitive damage awards are available only in cases of "intentional discrimination," that is, cases that do not rely on the disparate-impact theory of discrimination. To recover punitive damages, the complaining party must demonstrate that the employer engaged in a discriminatory practice or practices *with malice or with reckless indifference to the federally protected rights of an aggrieved individual.* (Punitive damages are not available in suits against a government, government agency, or political subdivision.) To prevail in obtaining punitive damages, the employee is not required to show that the employer engaged in egregious misconduct. Instead, the Court explained:

> The terms "malice" and "reckless" ultimately focus on the actor's state of mind. While egregious misconduct is evidence of the requisite mental state, §1981a does not limit plaintiffs to this form of evidence, and the section does not require a showing of egregious or outrageous discrimination independent of the employer's state of mind.

Even if the employee can show the requisite malice or indifference, the employer may still not be liable for punitive damages. The Court held that if the employer has engaged in "good-faith efforts" to comply with Title VII, then it is not vicariously liable for punitive damages based on discriminatory employment decisions by managerial agents when those decisions are contrary to the employer's good faith efforts. To hold otherwise, the Court reasoned, would reduce the incentive for employers to implement antidiscrimination programs.

In *EEOC v. Wal-Mart Stores, Inc.*,[60] the U.S. Court of Appeals for the Tenth Circuit held that Wal-Mart's written antidiscrimination policy was not sufficient to establish a "good faith" defense preventing an award of punitive damages for discriminatory conduct prohibited under the Americans with Disabilities Act. The appeals

55. Williams v. Pharmacia, Inc., 137 F.3d 944 (7th Cir. 1998).
56. Timm v. Progressive Steel Treating, Inc., 137 F.3d 1008 (7th Cir. 1998).
57. *See, e.g.,* Kramer v. Logan County Sch. Dist., 157 F.3d 620 (8th Cir. 1998); EEOC v. W & O, Inc., 213 F.3d 600 (11th Cir. 2000).
58. Pollard v. E.I. DuPont de Nemours Co., 213 F.3d 933 (6th Cir. 2000), *cert. granted,* 121 S. Ct. 756 (2001).
59. 527 U.S. 526 (1999).
60. 187 F.3d 1241 (10th Cir. 1999).

court highlighted the language in *Kolstad* requiring employers both to adopt antidiscrimination policies and to educate employees on federal discrimination laws. Although Wal-Mart did establish a written policy, it did not "demonstrate an implemented good faith policy of educating employees on the Act's accommodation and nondiscrimination requirements."

⚖ Age Discrimination

The principal federal law prohibiting discrimination in employment on the basis of age is the Age Discrimination in Employment Act (ADEA). The ADEA prohibits age discrimination in employment with respect to individuals aged forty years or older. Because the ADEA protects only persons aged forty or above, individuals under age forty have no protection from discrimination based on age. Courts have held that the employer, not the individual making the discriminatory decision, is liable for age discrimination.[61]

The substantive provisions of the ADEA are similar to those of Title VII. The ADEA generally prohibits age discrimination with respect to hiring, firing, and compensating employees, as well as with respect to the terms, conditions, and privileges of employment. As with Title VII, creation of a hostile environment because of age is a form of age discrimination.[62] The ADEA also prohibits retaliation against an individual aged forty or older because of the individual's opposition to unlawful age discrimination or because he or she has made a charge or testified or assisted in an investigation, proceeding, or litigation under the ADEA.

The U.S. Court of Appeals for the Second Circuit ruled that members of Johnson & Higgins' board of directors who were retired officers were considered employees and therefore were protected from mandatory retirement from the board if they continued to perform their previous duties and reported to a senior board member.[63] The case was subsequently resolved when Johnson & Higgins paid $28 million to settle the EEOC suit brought on behalf of thirteen former company directors compelled to retire at age sixty-two.[64]

The ADEA also prohibits unlawful age discrimination among persons within the protected age group. Thus, for example, if two individuals aged forty-one and fifty-three apply for the same position, the employer may not lawfully reject either applicant on the basis of age. In other words, an employer may still have engaged in age discrimination even if it hires a person who is over forty.

In *O'Connor v. Consolidated Coin Caterers Corp.*,[65] a unanimous Supreme Court explained that age discrimination cannot be inferred simply because the replacement employee is outside the protected class. In other words, replacing a forty-year-old employee with a thirty-nine-year-old employee does not give rise to a stronger inference of discrimination than replacing a fifty-two-year-old employee with a forty-year-old employee. Rather, "the fact that a replacement is substantially younger than the plaintiff is a far more reliable indicator of age discrimination." Thus, the Court suggested that there is no age discrimination unless the person hired is substantially younger than the person fired.

Differences in treatment between older and younger employees will not always serve as the basis for a claim under the ADEA. In *Stokes v. Westinghouse Savannah River Co.*,[66] the Fourth Circuit ruled that an employer had not violated the ADEA when, during a layoff, the company offered older employees the option of receiving either severance pay or a special retirement option. The court concluded that laid-off persons over fifty were treated better than younger employees because they were given the option of choosing between severance pay and the special retirement option whereas younger employees could receive only less valuable severance benefits.

As noted earlier, the Supreme Court established in *Reeves v. Sanderson Plumbing Products, Inc.*[67] that a finding of liability for intentional discrimination under the ADEA could be based solely on the plaintiff's *prima facie* case of discrimination together with sufficient evidence for a reasonable fact finder to reject the employer's nondiscriminatory explanation for its decision. In *Reeves*, a fifty-seven-year-old worker established a *prima facie* case and offered evidence showing that he had properly maintained attendance records to dispute the employer's claim that he was fired for failing to discipline late and absent employees due to shoddy record keeping. Reeves also introduced evidence that the supervisor responsible for his firing was motivated by age-based animus. The supervisor told Reeves that he was old enough to have

61. Stults v. Conoco, Inc., 76 F.3d 651 (5th Cir. 1996).
62. Crawford v. Medina Gen. Hosp., 96 F.3d 830 (6th Cir. 1996) (finding the hostile-work-environment claim a "relatively uncontroversial proposition").
63. EEOC v. Johnson & Higgins, Inc., 91 F.3d 1529 (2d Cir. 1996), *cert. denied*, 522 U.S. 808 (1997).
64. EEOC v. Johnson & Higgins, Inc., 1999 U.S. Dist. LEXIS 11396 (S.D.N.Y. July 26, 1999).

65. 517 U.S. 308 (1996).
66. 206 F.3d 420 (4th Cir. 2000).
67. 530 U.S. 133 (2000).

"We have no mandatory retirement age, Dave, but under certain conditions we tend to encourage people to die."

come over on the *Mayflower* and said that he was just "too damn old" for the job. The Court found that this was sufficient evidence for the jury to conclude that the employer had intentionally discriminated and therefore reinstated the jury verdict in favor of Reeves.

In contrast, the U.S. Court of Appeals for the First Circuit held that Ramon Suarez, the fifty-nine-year-old president of CaribAd (a subsidiary of Pueblo International), was not constructively discharged based on age when Pueblo was restructured and most of CaribAd's employees were relocated to corporate headquarters, leaving Suarez alone in an office with a receptionist.[68] Although Suarez was told that the in-house advertising for which he had been responsible was being transferred to someone else and that he would be responsible for bringing in new clients, he maintained his position as president and continued to be paid his salary of $190,000 a year. The court stated that "[i]n that rarified financial atmosphere . . . an increase in work requirements that does not surpass reasonable expectations" cannot sustain a constructive discharge claim. Even if Pueblo was attempting to marginalize Suarez, the "unpleasantness, hurt feelings, and wounded pride" that resulted did not create working conditions that were "so

onerous, abusive or unpleasant that a reasonable person in the employee's position would have felt compelled to resign." In short, the ADEA does not guarantee workplaces "free from the ordinary ebb and flow of power relations and inter-office politics."

The federal circuit courts are split on the issue of whether a disparate-impact cause of action can be brought under the ADEA.[69] In refusing to recognize a disparate-impact claim brought by the EEOC on behalf of a group of laid-off employees over fifty-five, the Eighth Circuit argued that if disparate-impact claims on behalf of subgroups were cognizable under the ADEA, an employer would be forced to attempt "to achieve statistical parity among the virtually infinite number of age subgroups in its work force."[70]

OLDER WORKERS' BENEFIT PROTECTION ACT

The Older Workers' Benefit Protection Act[71] (OWBPA) prohibits age discrimination in providing employee benefits. It also establishes minimum standards for employees who waive their rights under the ADEA.

To meet the minimum standards, the waiver must be "knowing and voluntary." The employee must be given at least twenty-one days to consider whether to enter into an agreement waiving rights under the ADEA. This period is extended to forty-five days when the waiver is in connection with an early retirement or exit-incentive plan offered to a group or class of employees. The agreement must also give the employee a period of at least seven days following execution of the agreement during which the employee may revoke it. An employee who has accepted a severance payment in exchange for waiving his or her rights under the ADEA can still sue the employer for violation of the ADEA without having to return the payment if the waiver was not made in accordance with the OWBPA.[72]

Employers may revoke a proposed early retirement agreement during the time frame that the OWBPA gives employees to act on it. For example, in *Ellison v. Premier Salons International, Inc.,*[73] the Eighth Circuit held that an employer could revoke a separation agreement containing a waiver of claims under the ADEA and provide a new, less valuable agreement, after learning that the employee had made defamatory statements about the company.

---

68. Suarez v. Pueblo Int'l, Inc., 229 F.3d 49 (1st Cir. 2000).

69. *See* Smith v. Xerox Corp., 196 F.3d 358, 367 n.6 (2d Cir. 1999).
70. EEOC v. McDonnell Douglas Corp., 191 F.3d 948 (8th Cir. 1999).
71. 29 U.S.C. § 623(f) (1994).
72. Oubre v. Entergy Operations, Inc., 522 U.S. 422 (1998).
73. 164 F.3d 1111 (8th Cir. 1999).

ECONOMIC PERSPECTIVE

Bias *against* Older Workers *at* High-tech Firms: Myth *or* Reality?

A number of high-technology firms, including many in Silicon Valley, have successfully lobbied Congress to increase the number of visas available for skilled foreign workers to remedy a claimed critical shortage of engineers and programmers. Yet a number of older, skilled American workers claim that they have been unable to get high-tech jobs because of companies' erroneous assumptions about older workers and their abilities. Although some companies assume older workers will not take the time to learn a new computer language, it often takes longer for a company to find and hire a foreign worker than to train an older worker in the United States.

There are few reported legal cases alleging age discrimination by high-tech companies, and many argue that there is less bias than has been claimed. In *Sheehan v. Daily Racing Form*,[a] the Seventh Circuit dismissed a fifty-four-year-old assistant editor's claim that he was laid off after the employer converted to a computerized publishing system. The court ruled that an employer can assess workers' job skills when determining whom to lay off, and it found that the plaintiff had not presented sufficient evidence of age discrimination. However, the court stated: "Everyone knows that younger people are more comfortable with computers than older people are, just as older people are on average more comfortable with manual-shift cars

than younger people are." In another case, a former vice president at an information technology management consulting firm alleged that he was fired because of his age under the company's "promote and eliminate" policy regarding top executives.[b] Dismissing the fifty-five-year-old's claim, the court stated: "[He] earned well into the six-figure range, and, as a highly-paid executive, was held to a higher standard— a standard that younger people in the company would someday hope to achieve. He apparently did not meet that standard . . . and thus was fired."

Analysts of high-tech companies believe that these firms employ fewer older workers because many of the current employees interviewing applicants are young and have difficulty connecting with people who are as old as their parents. The younger employees tend to want to hire people like themselves. Thus, the problem has been characterized as a "culture clash" rather than age bias.[c]

Other observers argue that many high-tech firms are run by entrepreneurs

in their late twenties and early thirties who appear to be under the misperception that employment laws and policies do not apply to them. One attorney commented that "the greed and unwillingness to follow any kind of law among these dot-coms is just flabbergasting" and added that there are a "bunch of mini-Bill Gateses out there."[d] One particularly pernicious practice used by start-ups is to hire older workers as "window dressing" to give the company the appearance of legitimacy. Although the employee is given a high salary, stock options, and a two-year contract, the firm has no intention of maintaining a long-term relationship with the employee and fires him or her within six months. One employment lawyer at a Silicon Valley law firm commented on this practice: "Somewhere along the way, young entrepreneurs heard about the doctrine of at-will employment and decided that they could hire and fire without regard to civil rights and anti-discrimination laws."[e]

a. 104 F.3d 940 (7th Cir. 1997), *cert. denied*, 521 U.S. 1104 (1997).
b. Ransom v. CSC Consulting, Inc., 217 F.3d 467 (7th Cir. 2000), *cert. denied*, 121 S. Ct. 628 (2000).
c. *Perception of Age Bias by High-Tech Firms Fueled by Anecdotal, Not Legal, Evidence*, 69 U.S.L.W. 2197 (Oct. 10, 2000).
d. *Id.*
e. *Id.*

DEFENSES

An employer faced with an age discrimination claim may assert in its defense that (1) age is a BFOQ reasonably necessary to the normal operation of the business (extremely difficult to prove); (2) the differential treatment is based on reasonable factors other than age; (3) the employer's action is based on a bona fide seniority system or employee benefit plan—such as a retirement, pension, or insurance plan—that is not invoked as a subterfuge to evade the purposes of the ADEA; or (4) the discharge of or discipline of a protected individual was

for good cause.[74] Although these defenses are set forth in the ADEA itself, employers should proceed with caution because the courts construe them strictly.

 ## Disability Discrimination

Title I of the Americans with Disabilities Act (ADA) prohibits employers from discriminating against a qualified individual because of a disability in regard to job-application

74. 29 U.S.C. § 623(f) (1994).

procedures, hiring, advancement, discharge, compensation, job training, and other terms, conditions, and privileges of employment. Such discrimination includes the use of selection criteria to screen out individuals with disabilities unless the criteria are job related and consistent with business necessity. The employer may not exclude a disabled individual if that individual, with some "reasonable accommodation," could perform the essential functions of the position, unless the accommodation would impose an "undue hardship" upon the employer. The EEOC has indicated that employers may ask preemployment questions about reasonable accommodations, but employers are barred from asking about disabilities or requiring medical tests that are not a business necessity.[75]

The employee must be able to attend work to be considered a "qualified individual" within the meaning of the ADA. In *Corder v. Lucent Technologies*,[76] the court found that an employee diagnosed with depression who was unable to come to work could not qualify for protection under the ADA.

The ADA also extends to employee benefit packages. In March 2000, the U.S. Court of Appeals for the Second Circuit agreed with six other federal circuits in holding that the ADA does not bar employers from providing less coverage for mental and emotional disabilities than for physical disabilities under long-term disability plans.[77]

IMPERMISSIBLE DISCRIMINATION

Under the ADA, employers are prohibited from intentionally discriminating against disabled persons and from engaging in employment practices that are not intentionally discriminatory, but have the effect of discriminating against disabled persons or perpetuating the past effects of such discrimination. The term *discriminate* as construed under the ADA includes the following prohibited practices:

1. Limiting, segregating, or classifying an applicant or employee because of his or her disability so as to adversely affect his or her opportunities or status.
2. Entering into a contractual relationship with an employment or referral agency, union, or other organization that has the effect of subjecting employees or applicants with a disability to prohibited discrimination.
3. Utilizing standards, criteria, or methods of administration that have the effect of discriminating or perpetuating the effects of discrimination because of disability.

4. Denying equal job benefits to a qualified individual because of the known disability of a person with whom the qualified individual is known to have a relationship or association.
5. Not making reasonable accommodations to the known physical or mental limitations of an otherwise qualified employee or applicant with a disability unless to do so would impose undue hardship on the employer.
6. Denying job opportunities to an otherwise qualified employee or applicant with a disability in order to avoid having to make reasonable accommodations for that disability.
7. Using qualification standards or employment tests that tend to screen out individuals with disabilities, unless the qualification standards or employment tests are shown to be job related and are consistent with business necessity.
8. Failing to select and conduct job testing in such a way as to ensure that when the test is administered to an applicant or employee with a disability that impairs his or her sensory, manual, or speaking skills, the results of the test accurately reflect the skills or aptitude that test is designed to measure, rather than reflecting the sensory, manual, or speaking impairment.

DEFINITION OF DISABILITY

The ADA codifies existing law developed under the Vocational Rehabilitation Act of 1973 by defining a person with a *disability* as (1) a person with a physical or mental impairment that substantially limits one or more of that person's major life activities, (2) a person with a record of a physical or mental impairment that substantially limits one or more of that person's major life activities, or (3) a person who is regarded as having such an impairment. Because working is included among the major life activities, any impairment that limits an individual's ability to work, or that the employer perceives as limiting those abilities, is considered a disability.

Physical or Mental Impairment The first prong of the ADA's definition of a disability is functional; that is, it focuses upon how and to what extent the individual is impaired. This has led to considerable confusion and conflicting outcomes.

One example is the status of cancer as a disability. The U.S. Court of Appeals for the Fifth Circuit has ruled that a woman with breast cancer who was discharged from her job after undergoing radiation treatment was not disabled.[78] The court held that she had a

75. Asra Q. Nomani, *EEOC Eases Question Limits for Disabled*, Wall St. J., Oct. 11, 1995, at A5.
76. 162 F.3d 924 (7th Cir. 1998).
77. EEOC v. Staten Island Savings Bank, 207 F.3d 144 (2d Cir. 2000).

78. Ellison v. Software Spectrum, Inc., 85 F.3d 187 (5th Cir. 1996).

physical impairment, but that none of her major life activities were limited. The serious side effects of her treatment were not sufficient to trigger protection under the ADA. The U.S. Court of Appeals for the Eleventh Circuit came to a similar conclusion.[79] By contrast, the Federal District Court for the Southern District of New York held that an individual discharged while diagnosed with cancer and undergoing chemotherapy was disabled under the ADA due to his cancer-related hospitalizations.[80]

79. Gordon. v. E.L. Hamm & Assocs., Inc., 100 F.3d 907 (11th Cir. 1996), *cert. denied,* 520 U.S. 1030 (1997).
80. Mark v. Burke Rehabilitation Hosp., No. 94-3596, 1997 U.S. Dist. WL 189124 (S.D.N.Y. Apr. 17, 1997).

Regarded as Disabled The third prong of the definition of a disability is based on the notion that societal stereotypes and prejudice may constrain individuals with disabilities more than their actual limitation. As a result, an employer may not discriminate against an individual based on the effects of a disease on others because their reactions may be based on stereotypes, misinformation, and long-held misconceptions of handicapped individuals. In other words, an individual might be "regarded as" disabled (and therefore protected under the ADA), even if he or she does not actually have a disability, if the employer treats him or her as if the condition constituted a disability.

In the following case, the Supreme Court considered the issue of whether correctable myopia is a "disability" under the ADA.

A CASE IN POINT

CASE 15.4
Sutton v. United Air Lines, Inc.
Supreme Court of the United States
527 U.S. 471 (1999).

In the Language of the Court

FACTS Karen Sutton and Kimberly Hinton were twin sisters who had severe myopia. Although their myopia prevented them from conducting numerous activities, they could, with the help of glasses or contact lenses, function in the same way as individuals with normal vision. They applied to United Air Lines to become commercial airline pilots but were told that they did not meet the airline's minimum vision requirements (uncorrected vision of 20/100 or better). The sisters filed a suit, alleging that United had discriminated against them on the basis of their disability in violation of the ADA.

ISSUE PRESENTED Is myopia that is correctable with glasses or contact lenses a "disability" under the ADA?

OPINION O'CONNOR, J., writing for the U.S. Supreme Court:

A "disability" exists only where an impairment "substantially limits" a major life activity, not where it "might," "could," or "would" be substantially limiting if mitigating measures were not taken. A person whose physical or mental impairment is corrected by medication or other measures does not have an impairment that presently "substantially limits" a major life activity. To be sure, a person whose physical or mental impairment is corrected by mitigating measures still has an impairment, but if the impairment is corrected it does not "substantially limit" a major life activity.

. . .

. . . Had Congress intended to include all persons with corrected physical limitations among those covered by the Act, it undoubtedly would have cited a much higher number of disabled persons in the findings. That it did not is evidence that the ADA's coverage is restricted to only those whose impairments are not mitigated by corrective measures.

. . .

. . . Under subsection (C), individuals who are "regarded as" having a disability are disabled within the meaning of the ADA. . . .

. . .

(Continued)

(Case 15.4 continued)

Assuming without deciding that working is a major life activity and that the EEOC regulations interpreting the term "substantially limits" [to mean "unable to perform" or "significantly restricted"] are reasonable, petitioners have failed to allege adequately that their poor eyesight is regarded as an impairment that substantially limits them in the major life activity of working. They allege only that respondent regards their poor vision as precluding them from holding positions as a "global airline pilot." Because the position of global airline pilot is a single job, this allegation does not support the claim that respondent regards petitioners as having a *substantially limiting* impairment. Indeed, there are a number of other positions utilizing petitioners' skills, such as regional pilot and pilot instructor to name a few, that are available to them. Even under the EEOC's Interpretative Guidance, to which petitioners ask us to defer, "an individual who cannot be a commercial airline pilot because of a minor vision impairment, but who can be a commercial airline co-pilot or a pilot for a courier service, would not be substantially limited in the major life activity of working."

RESULT The appeals court's decision dismissing the case was affirmed. The sisters were not disabled and therefore were not protected by the ADA.

QUESTIONS

1. Would a person with diabetes that can be controlled with insulin be disabled if he or she elected not to take insulin and, as a result, could not work?
2. Could an employer terminate an employee with high cholesterol to avoid having to pay for expensive cholesterol-lowering drugs? Would the result be the same if the employee were HIV-positive and was taking very expensive drugs to control the condition?

Exclusions Although the definition of a disability under the ADA is relatively vague, the statute does clearly exclude many things. For example, the ADA specifically excludes homosexuality, bisexuality, sexual-behavior disorders, compulsive gambling, kleptomania, and pyromania from the definition of a disability.

Psychoactive-substance-use disorders resulting from current illegal use of drugs, including the use of alcohol in the workplace against the employer's policies, are also excluded from the ADA's definition of a disability. Although "current use" is not specifically defined in the statute, it has been interpreted to include drug use weeks or months before discharge.[81] An employee or applicant who is no longer engaged in the illegal use of drugs or alcohol on the work site, but who is involved in or has completed a supervised rehabilitation program, may be regarded as a disabled person. Also, although an individual may not be fired on the basis of his or her alcoholism, an employer may discharge the person based upon behavior related to the alcoholism.[82] In 2000, the EEOC issued an informal guidance letter stating that an employer that excludes injuries or diseases that result from chronic alcoholism or drug addiction from its disability retirement plan could be required to justify the exclusion by the risks or costs of coverage or as necessary for the viability of the plan.[83]

DEFINITION OF MAJOR LIFE ACTIVITY

The U.S. Supreme Court resolved a split in the circuits when it ruled in *Bragdon v. Abbott*[84] that reproduction is a major life activity. The Ninth Circuit ruled that an employee who took medication for an anxiety disorder that made him drowsy and sexually impotent was entitled to relief under the ADA on the grounds that sleeping, engaging in sexual relations, and interacting with

81. Shafer v. Preston Mem'l Hosp. Corp., 107 F.3d 274 (4th Cir. 1997).

82. James Podgers, *Disability and DUIs: ADA Claims by Fired or Demoted Alcoholic Employees Fail*, A.B.A. J., Feb. 1996, at 46.
83. *EEOC Says Alcohol-Related Disabilities May Not Be Excluded from Employer Plan*, 69 U.S.L.W. 2089 (Aug. 15, 2000).
84. 524 U.S. 624 (1998).

others were major life activities.[85] In *Weber v. Strippit, Inc.*,[86] the Eighth Circuit held that a sales manager with a heart condition had no claim under the ADA because having a "fully functioning cardiovascular system" was not a major life activity. In *Pack v. Kmart Corp.*,[87] the Tenth Circuit held that although a pharmacy technician's depression was a mental impairment that limited her ability to concentrate at work, concentration was not a "major life activity" under the ADA.

In terms of work performance, courts have given employers greater leeway. For example, the U.S. Court of Appeals for the Seventh Circuit ruled that an employee who was discharged due to low performance immediately following a heart attack was not protected under the ADA because the employment decision was based only on reasons related to the disability, not the disability itself.[88]

ENFORCEMENT AND REMEDIES

Title I of the ADA is enforced in the same manner as Title VII of the Civil Rights Act of 1964, and the same remedies are available. Compensatory and punitive damages are subject to the same caps as those applicable to discrimination based on sex or religion.

Disability-related claims now account for about 20 percent of all discrimination charges filed by the EEOC.[89] The number of cases filed under the ADA declined during the last several years, however, after peaking in 1995.[90] The EEOC has successfully litigated many cases, including a $5.5 million jury award.[91]

REASONABLE ACCOMMODATION

The ADA requires employers to make reasonable accommodations to an employee's disability, as long as doing so does not cause the employer "undue hardship." Thus, even if a disability precludes an individual from performing the essential functions of the position or presents a safety risk, the employer is required to assess whether there is a reasonable accommodation that will permit the individual to be employed despite the disability.

Title I sets forth a nonexhaustive list of what might constitute "reasonable accommodation." These include (1) making work facilities accessible; (2) restructuring jobs or modifying work schedules; (3) reassigning the individual to another job; (4) acquiring or modifying equipment or devices; (5) modifying examinations, training materials, or policies; and (6) providing qualified readers or interpreters or other similar accommodations for individuals with disabilities.

To establish liability under the ADA, the employee must have requested an accommodation from his or her employer; it is the employee's initial request for an accommodation that triggers the employer's obligation to provide one.[92] An employee who fails to provide the employer with necessary medical information is precluded from claiming that the employer failed to provide reasonable accommodation.[93] Employers must train supervisors to recognize when a reasonable request for accommodation has been made.[94] For example, a request for accommodation could be a doctor's note advising an employer that an employee has work restrictions or an employee's statement that he or she is depressed and needs a modification in work duties.

Six federal appeals courts have found that an employer must be proactive and make a reasonable effort to determine the appropriate accommodation once a request for accommodation is made.[95] The U.S. Court of Appeals for the Ninth Circuit went a step further and held that employers have a mandatory obligation to work interactively with individuals requesting accommodation, reasoning that without such an obligation, "employers would have less incentive to engage in a cooperative dialogue and to explore fully the existence and feasibility of reasonable accommodations."[96]

A minimum requirement seems to be that the employer discuss potential accommodations with a disabled

---

85. McAlindin v. County of San Diego, 192 F.3d 1226 (9th Cir. 1999), *cert. denied*, 120 S. Ct. 2689 (2000).
86. 186 F.3d 907 (8th Cir. 1999), *cert. denied*, 528 U.S. 1078 (2000).
87. 166 F.3d 1300 (10th Cir. 1999), *cert. denied*, 528 U.S. 811 (1999).
88. Matthews v. Commonwealth Edison Co., 128 F.3d 1194 (7th Cir. 1997).
89. Lisa J. Stansky, *Opening Doors*, A.B.A. J., Mar. 1996, at 66.
90. Susan B. Garland, *Protecting the Disabled Won't Cripple Business*, Bus. Wk., Apr. 26, 1999, at 73.
91. *Federal Jury Hands Victory to the EEOC in Disabilities Case*, Wall St. J., Jan. 7, 1997, at B10.
92. Jovanovic v. In-Sink-Erator Div. of Emerson Elec. Co., 201 F.3d 894 (7th Cir. 2000).
93. Templeton v. Neodata Servs., 162 F.3d 617 (10th Cir. 1998).
94. *Employers Should Train Supervisors in ADA Accommodation Duty, EEOC Official Advises*, 69 U.S.L.W. 2254–55 (Oct. 31, 2000).
95. *See, e.g.*, Loulseged v. Akz. Nobel, Inc., 178 F.3d 731 (5th Cir. 1999) (an interactive process is a "means to the end of forging reasonable accommodation"); Mengine v. Runyon, 114 F.3d 415 (3d Cir. 1997) (an employer that fails to work with the employee requesting accommodation "may not discover a way in which the employee's disability could have been reasonably accommodated, thereby risking violation"). A jury awarded a systems engineer at Microsoft Corporation with Hepatitis C $2.3 million under the Washington state discrimination law for failure to do enough to help him find a job he could do in a forty-hour week. Manny Frishberg, *Microsoft Loses Disability Case*, Wired. Com (Nov. 7, 2000).
96. Barnett v. U.S. Air, Inc., 228 F.3d 1105 (9th Cir. 2000) (en banc).

employee and not make unilateral decisions regarding the adequacy of potential accommodations.[97] Courts have not been receptive to claims that a reasonable accommodation includes transferring the individual to a new supervisor.[98]

The circuits are split on whether an employer is required to reassign a disabled employee to a new job if the employee is not qualified, even with reasonable accommodation, for the job he or she currently holds or from which he or she was terminated.[99] However, reassignment can be used as a means of accommodating a disabled employee when accommodating the employee in the current position is possible but difficult for the employer.

In *Smith v. Midland Brake, Inc.,*[100] the U.S. Court of Appeals for the Tenth Circuit found that the employer, Midland Brake, could have reassigned employee Robert Smith to another job within the company after he became unable to perform his job because of a chronic skin condition. The court argued that the ADA's reasonable accommodation requirement would be transformed into a "hollow promise" if it merely extended the right "to compete equally with the rest of the world for a vacant position" to disabled workers.

In contrast, in *EEOC v. Humiston-Keeling, Inc.,*[101] the Seventh Circuit held that the employer did not violate the ADA by refusing to reassign a warehouse picker to a vacant cleric position for which she was minimally qualified when there were other applicants who were better qualified for the position. The court ruled that the ADA does not require an employer to reassign a disabled employee to a job for which a better qualified applicant exists, provided the employer's consistent and honest policy is to hire the best applicant for the job. The court rejected the argument that a disabled employee is entitled to more consideration than a nondisabled employee, saying that would amount to a policy of requiring employers to give bonus points to people with disabilities.

An employer does not have to accommodate a disabled employee if doing so would conflict with seniority rules under the employer's collective bargaining agreement.[102] Yet the Ninth Circuit held that an employer's unilaterally imposed seniority system (not embodied in a collective bargaining agreement) that conflicts with a reassignment that is a reasonable accommodation under the ADA will not necessarily serve to bar the reassignment. In *Barnett v. U.S. Air, Inc.,*[103] an employee who suffered a serious back injury while working asked his employer to reassign him to another job in the company's mail room. Two employees with greater seniority planned to exercise their seniority right to transfer to jobs in the mail room, thereby preventing the disabled employee from working there. The court found that a seniority system is not a *per se* bar to reassignment as a reasonable accommodation under the ADA. Instead, the seniority system is one factor that a company should consider in its undue hardship analysis to determine whether it can accommodate the disabled employee.

A 1998 survey by the Job Accommodation Network, sponsored by the President's Committee on Employment of People with Disabilities, found that the mean cost of providing accommodations to disabled workers was $935 per person.[104] The fear that the ADA would be inordinately expensive to businesses has not materialized.

Undue Hardship A reasonable accommodation is not required if it would impose an undue hardship on the employer. The ADA defines "undue hardship" to mean an activity requiring significant difficulty or expense when considered in light of (1) the nature and cost of the accommodation needed; (2) the overall financial resources of the facility, the number of persons employed at the facility, the effect on expenses and resources, or any other impact of the accommodation on the facility; (3) the overall financial resources of the employer and the overall size of the business with respect to the number of employees and the type, number, and location of its facilities; and (4) the type of operation of the employer, including the composition, structure, and functions of the workforce, and the geographic separateness and administrative or fiscal relationship of the facility in question to the employer.

An example of an accommodation that was deemed unreasonable involved an employee with various mental impairments that made it impossible for him to work in

97. Bultemeyer v. Fort Wayne Community Schs., 100 F.3d 1281 (7th Cir. 1996).

98. Frances A. McMorris, *Employee's Transfer Plea Rejected in Another Disabilities-Act Ruling,* WALL ST. J., Jan. 21, 1997, at B5.

99. *Compare* Barnett v. U.S. Air, Inc., 228 F.3d 1105 (9th Cir. 2000) (en banc) (reassignment must be provided to disabled employee who can no longer perform essential functions of his or her current position unless the employer shows undue hardship) *with* Dalton v. Subaru-Isuzu Auto., Inc., 141 F.3d 667, 679–80 (7th Cir. 1998) (no duty to reassign "to virtually every other job in a company, from the president to the janitors. Nothing in the ADA requires an employer to abandon its legitimate, nondiscriminatory company policies defining job qualifications, prerequisites, and entitlements to intra-company transfers").

100. 180 F.3d 1154 (10th Cir. 1999).

101. 227 F.3d 1024 (7th Cir. 2000).

102. *See, e.g.,* Davis v. Florida Power & Light Co., 205 F.3d 1301 (11th Cir. 2000).

103. 228 F.3d 1105 (9th Cir. 2000) (en banc).

104. Garland, *supra* note 90.

an unduly stressful environment. The employee asked for a transfer out of the stressful work environment and later sued when the employer did not honor his request. The U.S. Court of Appeals for the Third Circuit ruled that transferring the employee away from the stressful work environment was not a reasonable accommodation because it would impose extraordinary administrative costs on the employer.[105]

Business Necessity Employers may also argue that they had to discriminate against an applicant or employee with a disability due to a business necessity. In *Belk v. Southwestern Bell Telephone Co.*,[106] the Eighth Circuit ruled that employment tests, qualification standards, and other selection criteria are acceptable under the ADA if they are related to the job and consistent with business necessity. Southwestern Bell had argued that it had job-related reasons for not accommodating a worker who wore a leg brace during a physical performance test for a technician job.

In *EEOC v. Exxon Corp.*,[107] the Fifth Circuit analyzed Exxon's policy, adopted in response to the 1989 *Exxon Valdez* oil spill disaster, of permanently removing any employee who had undergone treatment for substance abuse from certain safety-sensitive positions. The EEOC sued, arguing that Exxon had to prove that the class of individuals posed a "direct threat" to the health or safety of others. The Fifth Circuit rejected this argument, stating that Exxon could justify its policy as a business necessity. Whereas the "direct threat" test focuses on the individual employee and the specific risk posed by the employee's disability, the "business necessity" defense concerns whether a safety policy is addressed to all employees of a given class. The court further ruled that in evaluating whether a safety policy constitutes a business necessity, both the magnitude of possible harm and the probability of harm must be evaluated.

In *Sullivan v. River Valley*,[108] the Sixth Circuit held that a school district did not violate the ADA by ordering post-hiring mental and physical examinations of a teacher who engaged in disruptive and abusive verbal outbursts, a dramatic change from his typical behavior during his seventeen years of teaching. The court cautioned, however, that an employer's discretion to order employees to undergo examinations and tests was lim-

ited: "Post-hiring demands for examinations can only be made where shown to be 'job-related and consistent with business necessity.' . . . [T]here must be significant evidence that could cause a reasonable person to inquire as to whether an employee is still capable of performing his job."

PERMISSIBLE EXCLUSION

If an applicant or employee is disabled, he or she may be excluded from the employment opportunity only if, by reason of the disability, he or she (with or without reasonable accommodation) cannot perform the essential functions of the job or if his or her employment poses a significant risk to the health or safety of others.

Inability to Perform Essential Functions In determining whether a job function is essential, the ADA requires that consideration be given to the employer's judgment as to which functions are essential, but it also looks to any written job description prepared *before* advertising or interviewing for the job commenced. The applicant or employee does not have to prove his or her ability to perform all the functions of the job, only the essential functions.[109]

Direct Threat An employer cannot deny a job due to risk of future injury unless, given the person's current condition, there is a probability of substantial harm. For example, the U.S. Court of Appeals for the Sixth Circuit ruled that a hospital acted lawfully when it laid off an HIV-positive surgical technician after concluding that he posed a direct threat to the health and safety of others. His job included, on an infrequent basis, engaging in invasive, exposure-prone activities, such as inserting his fingers into a patient's incision during surgery.[110] The presence of sharp instruments on which the technician could prick his hand increased the risk of HIV transmission. Employers cannot rely on their own physician's opinion, however; risk of injury must be based upon generally accepted medical opinion.

In the following case, the Ninth Circuit considered whether the "direct threat" defense under the ADA applies to employees who pose a direct threat to their own health or safety, but not to other persons in the workplace.

105. Gaul v. Lucent Techs., Inc., 134 F.3d 576 (3d Cir. 1998).
106. 194 F.3d 946 (8th Cir. 1999).
107. 203 F.3d 871 (5th Cir. 2000).
108. 224 F.3d 840 (6th Cir. 1999), *cert. denied*, 528 U.S. 1019 (1999).
109. Deane v. Pocono Med. Ctr., 142 F.3d 138 (3d Cir. 1998) (en banc).
110. Estate of Mauro v. Borgess Med. Ctr., 137 F.3d 398 (6th Cir. 1998), *cert. denied*, 525 U.S. 815 (1998).

A CASE IN POINT

CASE 15.5

Echazabal v. Chevron USA, Inc.

United States Court of Appeals for the Ninth Circuit 226 F.3d 1063 (9th Cir. 2000).

Summary

FACTS Mario Echazabal worked for various maintenance contractors at Chevron's oil refinery in El Segundo, California. In 1992, he applied to work directly for Chevron. Chevron offered him a job contingent on his passing a physical examination. The exam revealed that Echazabal's liver was releasing certain enzymes at an abnormally high level. Chevron concluded that his liver might be damaged by exposure to solvents and chemicals in the refinery, so it rescinded the offer. Echazabal continued to work for a maintenance contractor operating at the refinery.

Subsequently, Echazabal was diagnosed with asymptomatic chronic active hepatitis C. His physicians did not advise him to stop working at the refinery because of his medical condition. In 1995, Echazabal applied again to Chevron for a position in the refinery. After making him an offer, Chevron again rescinded it after learning about Echazabal's liver disease. Chevron also wrote to the maintenance contractor who employed him and requested that it remove Echazabal from the refinery or place him in a position that eliminated his exposure to solvents and chemicals. As a result, Echazabal could no longer work at the refinery. He filed a complaint against Chevron, alleging that it violated the ADA. The district court dismissed his claim, and he appealed.

ISSUE PRESENTED Does the "direct threat" defense apply to employees who pose a direct threat to their own health or safety, but not to the health or safety of other persons?

SUMMARY OF OPINION The U.S. Court of Appeals for the Ninth Circuit began its analysis by looking at the legislative history of the ADA. The term "direct threat" was used hundreds of times throughout the legislative history, but in nearly every instance, the term was accompanied by a reference to the threat to other individuals in the workplace. The term was never accompanied by a reference to threats to the disabled persons themselves.

The court also emphasized that, in general, courts have interpreted federal employment statutes to prohibit paternalistic employment policies (citing, among other cases, the *Automobile Workers v. Johnson Controls* fetal-protection plan case). Title VII allows individuals to decide for themselves whether to put their own health and safety at risk, and the court concluded that the same freedom of choice should be given to disabled individuals.

The court rejected Chevron's argument that performing work at the refinery without posing a threat to one's own health or safety was an "essential function" of the refinery job. The court also dismissed Chevron's argument that hiring individuals who pose a risk to their own health or safety would expose employers to tort liability; in that event, said the court, state tort law would be preempted by federal antidiscrimination law.

RESULT Reversing the district court's decision, the court held that the ADA's direct threat defense does not permit employers to shut disabled individuals out of jobs on the ground that they may put their own health at risk.

HIV DISCRIMINATION

A major issue today is the employer's relationship with an employee who has HIV disease, that is, an individual who has been infected with the human immunodeficiency virus (HIV). Due to recent advances in drug treatments, more individuals are living healthy, productive lives while infected with HIV. This is called asymptomatic HIV disease. When an individual's immune system is compromised and the person becomes ill due to HIV-related complications, the individual is considered symptomatic. Acquired immune deficiency syndrome (AIDS) refers to the most serious stage of symptomatic HIV disease.

Although the ADA does not specifically list HIV disease as a disability, in *Bragdon v. Abbott*,[111] the Supreme Court held that asymptomatic HIV-positive individuals are disabled within the meaning of the ADA.[112] The Court concluded that infection with HIV constitutes a physiological disorder with a constant and detrimental effect on the infected person's hemic and lymphatic systems from the moment of infection. This physical impairment substantially limits the major life activity of reproduction. Although the HIV infection did not make it impossible for Abbott to reproduce, it substantially limited her ability to reproduce by (1) imposing on the man a significant risk of becoming infected and (2) creating a risk that the child would be infected during gestation and childbirth. The Court rejected Bragdon's attempt to limit the phrase "major life activity" to those aspects of a person's life that have a public, economic, or daily character.

In the context of HIV disease, courts have narrowly construed the direct threat exception in accordance with medical evidence that HIV cannot be transmitted through casual contact. Thus, only those professions that could lead to the transmission of bodily fluids, such as health care workers, are given closer analysis under the direct threat exception.

In *McNeil v. Time Insurance Co.*,[113] the U.S. Court of Appeals for the Fifth Circuit considered whether health insurance policies with lower coverage limits for AIDS than for other diseases violate the public accommodation provisions of Title III of the ADA. Title III provides that no individual shall be discriminated against on the basis of disability in the full and equal employment of goods, services, or accommodations of any place of public accommodation. The district court dismissed this claim on the grounds that Time's provision of insurance did not constitute a "public accommodation" under the ADA and that Title III of the ADA applied only to physical use of the services of a place of public accommodation. The Fifth Circuit affirmed this decision.

The case did not involve an employer-sponsored insurance plan subject to Title I of the ADA. Exclusions for certain diseases in insurance plans offered by an employer would probably be more difficult to justify.

Dealing with HIV Disease in the Workplace An employer cannot justify discrimination against a person with AIDS on the basis of coworker or customer preference. Similarly, the fact that the employment of someone with

AIDS will increase group health insurance costs or cause absenteeism does not make discrimination permissible.

Many states recognize either a common law or a constitutional right to privacy. This protects individuals from improper communication of their HIV status, even though the information is true and was properly obtained for a specific purpose. Communication of such personal information might be protected by the qualified-privilege defense as long as it is confined only to those people who have a legitimate need to know. General communication of someone's HIV status among coworkers is probably not protected by the privilege. Statutes prohibiting disclosure of medical information, specifically HIV-related information, may also be a source of employer liability. Thus, HIV-related information should be kept in confidence among individuals who need to know.

The employer also runs the risk of being sued for libel or slander if careless statements are made about employees. For example, falsely accusing an employee of having AIDS could be grounds for a defamation suit. Truth, however, is a complete defense.

A number of employers, especially larger corporations, have aggressively developed and utilized HIV-education programs for all employees. They show videotapes, circulate pamphlets and articles in employee newsletters, and invite medical professionals to give presentations. Companies strive to give employees accurate medical information about how HIV is transmitted, to assure employees that the employer is not going to discriminate against an employee infected with HIV, and to assure all employees that attention will be given to their health needs.

GENETIC DISCRIMINATION

The Council for Responsible Genetics, a bioethics group based in Cambridge, Massachusetts, estimates that at least 200 people have suffered employment discrimination based on genetic information. For example, a job applicant who mentioned to the interviewer that her father had Huntington's disease, a fatal genetic disorder, was told that the company would not hire her because it could not afford the 50–50 chance that she, too, might develop Huntington's.[114] University of Washington professor Phil Bereano argues that using genetic tests to predict who will get sick creates a class of people who are considered "damaged goods," making them especially vulnerable to discrimination by employers and insurers.[115]

---

111. 524 U.S. 624 (1998).
112. John Gibeaut, *Filling a Need*, A.B.A. J., July 1997, at 48.
113. 205 F.3d 179 (5th Cir. 2000).

114. Carol Smith, *Other Perspectives: Some Cases of Genetic Discrimination*, SAN FRANCISCO SUNDAY EXAMINER & CHRON., Feb. 22, 1998, at CL 15.
115. *Id.*

Employees tend to take their cue from the conduct of their employer. For example, if the employer discriminates in its hiring, retention, and promotion policies, employees may be more likely to believe that such conduct is acceptable. The employees may take the employer's behavior as an indication of not only how they can act in the workplace but also how they should act.

Approximately eighteen states have enacted laws banning genetic discrimination by insurers and employers. In 1996, Congress passed legislation prohibiting group health plans from using information obtained from genetic tests as a basis for denying or limiting coverage or for charging more for coverage. In 2000, President Clinton signed an executive order prohibiting federal departments and agencies from using genetic information in personnel decisions.

In April 2000, the EEOC commissioner announced that the ADA prohibits genetic discrimination pursuant to a 1995 policy guidance adopted by the EEOC. Although the ADA does not specifically refer to genetic discrimination, the statute's "regarded as disabled" prong includes discrimination on the basis of a diagnosed genetic predisposition toward an asymptomatic condition or illness.[116]

Sexual-Orientation Discrimination

Discrimination in employment based on sexual orientation is not barred by Title VII or other federal laws but is prohibited by many local and several state statutes. Legislation to amend Title VII to include sexual orientation has been introduced in every term of Congress since 1975 but has not passed. In 2000, the European Union adopted a directive banning employment discrimination based on sexual orientation.

Civil Rights Act of 1991

This chapter has described, in context, many of the provisions and effects of the Civil Rights Act of 1991. Other provisions not yet covered are discussed below.

The act overturned *Lorance v. AT&T Technologies*[117] by providing that a seniority system adopted for an intentionally discriminatory purpose can be challenged under Title VII when the seniority system is adopted, when an individual becomes subject to the system, or when a person aggrieved is injured by application of the seniority system.

The act provides that Title VII and the Americans with Disabilities Act, like the Age Discrimination in Employment Act, apply to U.S. citizens employed in foreign countries by American-owned or American-controlled companies unless compliance with Title VII or the ADA would cause the employer to violate the law of the foreign country where it is located.

The 1991 act also expanded the categories for which compensatory and punitive damages can be recovered to include intentional religious, disability, and sex discrimination. Under prior law, recovery of damages was limited to victims of intentional racial or ethnic bias.

In addition, the act banned so-called *race norming of employment tests,* which is a device designed to ensure that a minimum number of minorities and women are in the application pool. The act prohibits an employer, in connection with the selection or referral of applicants or candidates for employment or promotion, from adjusting the scores of, using different cutoff scores for, or otherwise altering the results of employment-related tests on the basis of race, color, religion, sex, or national origin.

Family *and* Medical Leave Act *of* 1993

The Family and Medical Leave Act of 1993[118] (FMLA) has a number of specific and rather straightforward guidelines regarding employee eligibility and employer obligations. The employee must have worked at the place of employment for at least twelve months and have completed at least 1,250 hours of service to the employer during that twelve-month period to be eligible for a family leave.

Eligible employees are entitled to twelve weeks of unpaid leave per year. An employee may use leave under the act in four situations: (1) the birth of a child; (2) the placement of an adopted or foster-care child with the employee; (3) care of a child, a parent, or a spouse; or (4) a serious health condition that renders the employee unable to do his or her job.

116. *EEOC Commissioner Says ADA Bans Genetic Discrimination,* Corp. Couns. Wkly, Apr. 12, 2000.

117. 490 U.S. 900 (1989) (holding that the period for filing a challenge began with the date the system was adopted).
118. 29 U.S.C. §§ 2601–2654 (1994).

To vindicate rights under the FMLA, a plaintiff may sue both the employer and his or her supervisor individually.[119] This interpretation is distinctive because a supervisor cannot be sued in his or her individual capacity under Title VII, the ADEA, or the ADA.

The act should be considered a floor, not a ceiling, to what employers can provide their employees in terms of leave. Even if employers provide for more generous leave, however, they must provide employees with notice regarding the consequences of taking the extra leave.[120]

An employee cannot contract out of his or her right to leave time under the act. But the employer may require, or an employee may choose, to substitute any or all accrued paid leave for the leave time that is provided for under the act. Employers have no obligation to give employees advance notice that their paid leave will be counted toward the unpaid leave provided by the FMLA.[121]

In general, the employer is required to restore the employee to the same position, or one with equivalent benefits, pay, and other terms and conditions of employment, following the expiration of the leave. But the employer is not required to reinstate key employees to their previous position if the employer determines that "such denial is necessary to prevent substantial and grievous economic injury to the operations of the employer." "Key employee" is defined as a salaried employee who is among the highest-paid 10 percent of the employees located within seventy-five miles of the facility where the subject employee is employed. The EEOC regulations require the employer to notify an employee, at the time the leave is requested, of his or her status as a key employee and of the consequence of taking a leave.[122]

In *O'Connor v. PCA Family Health Plan, Inc.*,[123] the Eleventh Circuit held that an employee taking leave under the FMLA does not have an absolute right to reinstatement if his or her employment is terminated during the leave as part of a general reduction in force (RIF) by the employer. The court explained: "An employee has no greater right to reinstatement or to other benefits and conditions of employment than if the employee had been continuously employed during the FMLA leave period." The burden of proof is on the employer denying reinstatement to show that it would have discharged the employee even if he or she had not been on FMLA leave.

Unfortunately, studies have indicated that many companies are not complying with the law.[124] A significant minority of businesses either are not guaranteeing the jobs of people who take leaves or are not providing health benefits during the leave. Many more companies do not provide for an appeals process and do not have formal written policies regarding the FLMA.

 # Affirmative Action

Affirmative-action programs are generally viewed as a means to remedy past acts of discrimination. Such programs are usually established pursuant to court orders, court-approved consent decrees, or federal and state laws that impose affirmative-action obligations on government contractors.

Executive Order 11246 requires federal government contractors to include in every government contract not exempted by the order provisions whereby the contractor agrees (1) not to discriminate in employment on the basis of race, color, religion, sex, or national origin; (2) to take affirmative steps to prevent discrimination; and (3) to file equal opportunity surveys every other year.[125] In some cases, a contractor's affirmative-action plan must be put in writing. Although individuals have no private right of action based on an alleged violation of the order, the Department of Labor, through its Office of Federal Contract Compliance Programs, has a wide range of sanctions available to it, including terminating a government contract and disqualifying the contractor from entering into any future government contracts.[126] Government contractors are subject to affirmative-action obligations under other federal laws as well, including the Vocational Rehabilitation Act of 1973 and the Vietnam Era Veterans' Readjustment Assistance Act of 1972.

As explained in Chapter 2, the U.S. Supreme Court held in *Adarand Constructors, Inc. v. Peña*[127] that government-mandated affirmative-action plans are subject to strict scrutiny under the Equal Protection Clause. In reinstating a reverse-discrimination claim by a white-owned construction company that lost a contract to a

119. Freeman v. Foley, 911 F. Supp. 326 (N.D. Ill. 1995).
120. Fry v. First Fidelity Bancorp., No. 95-6019, 1996 U.S. Dist. WL 36910 (E.D. Pa. Jan. 30, 1996).
121. McGregor v. Autozone, 180 F.3d 1305 (11th Cir. 1999).
122. Panza v. Grappone Cos., Civil No. 99-221-M, Opinion No. 2000 DNH 224 (D.N.H. Oct. 20, 2000).
123. 200 F.3d 1349 (11th Cir. 2000).
124. *Family-Leave Compliance Is Falling Short,* WALL ST. J., Mar. 16, 1994, at B1.
125. Exec. Order No. 11246, 3 C.F.R. § 339 (1964–1965), *reprinted in* 42 U.S.C. § 2000e (1994).
126. The Office of Federal Contract Reliance Programs' new regulations overhauling the thirty-year-old requirements for affirmative action under Executive Order 11246 were published in the November 13, 2000 issue of the *Federal Register,* 65 Fed. Reg. 68,021, and took effect on December 13, 2000.
127. 515 U.S. 200 (1995).

minority-owned business, the Court held that benign and invidious racial classifications should be subject to the same standards. This ruling was significant because it required the government to show a specific history of discrimination in order to justify preferential treatment of minority-owned businesses in government contracts.

The Department of Justice has since revised its approach to assessing minority set-aside programs. If the percentage of minority-owned firms receiving government contracts in a given industry is sufficiently smaller than the percentage of minority-owned firms in the industry as a whole, then this will be presented as evidence of discrimination and will justify the implementation of flexible benchmarks that identify targets, rather than rigid quotas, for contract dispersal. When the disparity between the total number of minority-owned firms and the number of government contracts they win decreases, the Department of Commerce will eliminate the benchmarks.[128]

In 2000, the Tenth Circuit upheld the use in federal highway procurement contracts of a clause offering contractors additional compensation if they hired subcontractors certified as "disadvantaged business enterprises."[129] Disadvantaged business enterprises (DBEs) are small businesses with 51 percent ownership by socially and economically disadvantaged individuals such as minorities. The court found that the Department of Transportation had narrowly tailored the program to advance the government's compelling interest in remedying racial discrimination. The program limited the duration of a DBE's certification to ten and a half years and required contractors to use race-neutral means for certifying DBE status.

In 1998, in *Lutheran Church–Missouri Synod v. FCC*,[130] the U.S. Court of Appeals for the District of Columbia Circuit struck down the Federal Communications Commission's affirmative-action requirements for radio and television broadcast licenses The court held that *Adarand's* requirement of strict scrutiny applied not just to racial preferences in hiring but to any race-conscious decision making that affects employment opportunities even if it does not establish preferences, quotas, or set-asides. The court explained:

> [W]e do not think it matters whether a government hiring program imposes hard quotas, soft quotas, or goals. Any one of these techniques induces an employer to hire with

an eye toward meeting the numerical target. As such, they can and surely will result in individuals being granted a preference because of their race.

The court also held that the FCC's interest in fostering diverse programming was not compelling. Even if the diversity goal could be deemed a compelling state interest, the court concluded that the FCC's equal employment opportunity rules were not narrowly tailored to foster diverse programming.

In January 2000, in response to *Lutheran Church*, the FCC adopted new rules to promote employment of women and minorities in the broadcast and cable television industries. The rules require broadcast licensees to disseminate information about job openings to all members of the community to ensure that all applicants have the opportunity to compete for jobs. The FCC chair stated that the rules were designed to advance the goals of prohibiting discrimination in hiring and promoting diversity in broadcasting.[131]

Although government programs have been struck down by the courts, some affirmative-action programs by private employers have been accepted. For example, the U.S. Supreme Court upheld a collective bargaining agreement containing an affirmative-action plan giving preference to African-American employees entering into skilled-craft training positions.[132] Concluding that Title VII did not preclude all private, voluntary, race-conscious affirmative-action programs, the Court noted that the plan (1) like Title VII, was designed to break down patterns of racial segregation and hierarchy; (2) "did not unnecessarily trammel the interests of white employees"; and (3) was a temporary measure intended to attain rather than maintain racial balance. The EEOC has promulgated regulations regarding voluntary affirmative-action plans.[133]

In *Taxman v. Board of Education*,[134] the U.S. Court of Appeals for the Third Circuit struck down a school board's affirmative-action plan as a violation of Title VII. The plan gave preference to minority teachers over nonminority teachers in layoff decisions when teachers were equally qualified. The court read the Supreme Court's ruling in *United Steelworkers v. Weber* to permit race-based employment decisions only when they are necessary to remedy past discrimination. A mere desire to promote

128. Rochelle Sharpe, *Who Benefits? Asian-Americans Gain Sharply in Big Program of Affirmative Action*, Wall St. J., Sept. 9, 1997, at A1.
129. Adarand Constructors, Inc. v. Slater, 228 F.3d 1147 (10th Cir. 2000).
130. 141 F.3d 344 (D.C. Cir 1998).

131. *FCC Votes to Adopt New Rule on Equal Employment Opportunity*, 68 U.S.L.W. 2443 (Feb. 1, 2000).
132. United Steelworkers of America v. Weber, 443 U.S. 193 (1979).
133. *See* 29 C.F.R. § 1608.1–12 (1997).
134. 91 F.3d 1547 (3d Cir. 1996) (en banc), *cert. dismissed*, 522 U.S. 1010 (1997).

diversity in education was not sufficient to warrant a discriminatory policy. The U.S. Supreme Court granted the petition for *certiorari* and heard oral arguments; before it ruled, however, the parties settled the case. Several civil rights groups feared that the Supreme Court would use this case as an occasion to ban all affirmative-action programs, so they contributed the bulk of the money paid in the settlement.[135]

The Civil Rights Act of 1991 limited the ability to challenge affirmative-action litigated judgments and consent decrees. A person cannot challenge a judgment or consent decree if any of the following three conditions is applicable: (1) the person had actual notice of the proposed judgment or order sufficient to let that person know that the judgment or decree might adversely affect his or her interests and legal rights and had an opportunity to present objections; (2) the person had a reasonable opportunity to present objections to the judgment or order; or (3) the person's interests were adequately represented by another person who had previously challenged the judgment or order on the same legal grounds and with a similar factual situation.

⬥ Mandatory Arbitration *of* Employment Disputes

As explained in Chapter 4, a key issue in employment law today is the enforceability of agreements to arbitrate future discrimination claims. Employees often prefer to go to court where they are entitled to extensive discovery, a jury, witnesses of their own choosing, and possible punitive damages.

In 1974, in *Alexander v. Gardner-Denver Co.*,[136] the U.S. Supreme Court struck down an arbitration clause in a collective bargaining agreement (CBA), holding that arbitration cannot provide an adequate substitute for a judicial proceeding in protecting federal statutory rights under Title VII. Yet, in 1991, in *Gilmer v. Interstate/Johnson Lane Corp.*,[137] the Supreme Court held that brokerage employees who had signed individual agreements to arbitrate could be required to arbitrate age discrimination claims under the ADEA. In *Wright v. Universal Maritime Service Corp.*,[138] the Supreme Court commented on its rulings in *Gilmer* and *Gardner-Denver* and acknowledged that "there is obviously some tension be-

tween these two lines of cases," but it did not resolve this tension. In *Wright,* the Court held that an arbitration clause in a collective bargaining agreement is not enforceable if it does not contain a "clear and unmistakable" waiver of employees' right to litigate employment-discrimination claims.

In cases subsequent to *Wright,* courts have held that a waiver of statutorily conferred rights is sufficiently clear and unmistakable if either of two conditions is met:

> First, a waiver is sufficiently explicit if the arbitration clause contains a provision whereby employees specifically agree to submit all federal causes of action arising out of their employment to arbitration. . . .
>
> Second, a waiver may be sufficiently clear and unmistakable when the CBA contains an explicit incorporation of the statutory anti-discrimination requirements in addition to a broad and general arbitration clause.[139]

Creating a split in the circuits, the Ninth Circuit held in *Circuit City Stores, Inc. v. Adams*[140] that the Federal Arbitration Act (FAA) did not apply to any employment contracts. The court relied on Section 1 of the FAA,[141] which exempts from FAA enforcement "contracts of employment of seamen, railroad employees, or any other class of workers engaged in foreign or interstate commerce."[142] In 2001, the U.S. Supreme Court reversed the Ninth Circuit and held that only contracts involving transportation workers are excluded from the FAA's provisions requiring judicial enforcement of arbitration agreements.[143] The Court also reiterated its position that employees can be required to arbitrate claims based on federal discrimination statutes.

It is clear that under *Wright* an arbitration clause in a collective bargaining agreement will not be enforced if there is no clear waiver of the employee's statutory rights. The circuits are split on whether individual agreements to arbitrate are subject to the same requirement. Both the First[144] and the Ninth Circuits[145] have refused to enforce arbitration clauses that did not contain express waivers. In

135. Eva M. Rodriguez, *Rights Group's Settlement Settles Little,* Wall St. J., Nov. 24, 1997, at A3.
136. 415 U.S. 36 (1974).
137. 500 U.S. 20 (1991).
138. 525 U.S. 70 (1998) (Case 4.2).

139. Rogers v. New York University, 220 F.3d 73 (2d Cir. 2000), *cert. denied,* 121 S. Ct. 626 (2000).
140. 194 F.3d 1070 (9th Cir. 1999), *rev'd,* 121 S. Ct. 1302 (2001).
141. 9 U.S.C. § 1.
142. This conflicted with the conclusion reached by every other U.S. Court of Appeals (nine *in toto*) to have addressed the question.
143. Circuit City Stores, Inc. v. Adams, 121 S. Ct. 1302 (2001).
144. Rosenberg v. Merrill Lynch, Pierce, Fenner & Smith, Inc., 170 F.3d 1 (1st Cir. 1999).
145. Prudential Ins. Co. of America v. Lai, 42 F.3d 1299 (9th Cir. 1994), *cert. denied,* 516 U.S. 812 (1995).

contrast, the Sixth Circuit expressly rejected the First Circuit's approach and enforced a clause in a Form U-4 signed by a securities broker in which the broker agreed to arbitrate any dispute with his firm "that is required to be arbitrated under the rules . . . of the organizations with which [he] register[ed]."[146] The broker registered with the National Association of Securities Dealers (NASD), which at that time required arbitration of all employment disputes. The Sixth Circuit applied general principles of contract law and held that a contractual agreement to arbitrate is enforceable "absent a showing of fraud, duress, mistake, or some other ground upon which a contract may be voided." The court ruled that "ignorance as to the terms of the U-4 Form is no defense."

The circuits are also split on the issue of whether an employee's agreement to arbitrate statutory discrimination claims precludes the EEOC from suing the employer. In *EEOC v. Waffle House, Inc.,*[147] the Fourth Circuit held that an agreement to arbitrate does not preclude the EEOC from suing for injunctive relief but does preclude it from seeking monetary relief. However, in *EEOC v. Frank's Nursery & Crafts, Inc.,*[148] the Sixth Circuit ruled that an arbitration agreement does not affect the EEOC's ability to seek monetary or injunctive relief.

 Preemployment Practices

From both a legal and a practical standpoint, the employer–employee relationship begins at the start of the application process. Recent years have seen an increase in litigation concerning preemployment practices, such as job advertising, employment applications, job interviewing, and testing. Employers must take care to avoid unlawful discrimination in these activities.

Obviously, a policy or a particular decision not to hire an applicant because the person is a woman, an African American, or a Jew would be subject to challenge under disparate-treatment analysis. A policy or decision must not treat some applicants differently from others simply because of their gender, race, or religion.

A more common problem in today's business environment concerns hiring practices and policies that appear to be race- or gender-neutral but that have a disparate impact on one race or gender. As noted earlier, where a hiring practice or policy is found to have a disparate impact on a protected class of persons, the employer must show that the policy is a business necessity. The business necessity must be related to job performance and not to inconvenience, annoyance, or expense.

JOB ADVERTISEMENTS

Many employers begin the recruitment process by posting or publishing a Help Wanted notice. Title VII and the ADEA prohibit employers from publishing or printing job notices that express a preference or limitation based on race, color, religion, sex, national origin, or age, unless such specifications are based on good faith occupational qualifications. For example, an advertisement for a "waitress" implies that the employer is seeking a woman for the job. If there is no bona fide reason why the job should be filled by a woman rather than a man, the advertisement might be considered discriminatory. Similarly, terms such as "young woman" or "girl" should never be used because they discourage job candidates from applying for positions because of their sex or age.

Many state laws also prohibit discriminatory advertisements. For example, Massachusetts and Ohio prohibit notices that express, directly or indirectly, any limitations or specifications concerning race, color, religion, national origin, sex, age, ancestry, or disability. Word-of-mouth recruitment practices, which normally involve current employees informing their family and friends of job openings, can also be discriminatory. When information is disseminated in this way, it may reach a disproportionate number of persons of the same race or ethnicity as the employer's current employees.

Employers advertising for jobs should avoid placing advertisements in publications with sex-segregated help-wanted columns. The advertisements should indicate that the employer is an equal opportunity employer and should be placed in media designed to reach people in both minority and nonminority communities.

APPLICATIONS AND INTERVIEWS

Employers use the application and interview process to gain information about an individual's personal, educational, and employment background. Unless it has a valid defense, an employer should avoid making inquiries on an application form, during a preemployment interview, or in some other manner that identify the protected characteristics of a job candidate. Although federal laws do not expressly prohibit preemployment inquiries concerning an applicant's race, color, national origin, sex, marital status, religion, or age, such inquiries are disfavored because they

---

146. Haskins v. Prudential Ins. Co. of America, 230 F.3d 231 (6th Cir. 2000).

147. 193 F.3d 805 (4th Cir. 1999), *cert. granted,* 121 S. Ct. 1401 (2001).

148. 177 F.3d 448 (6th Cir. 1999).

create an inference that these factors will be used as selection criteria. These inquiries may be expressly prohibited under state law.

Often the line between permissible and impermissible areas of inquiry is not clear. It is crucial that recruiters, interviewers, and supervisors understand which questions should and should not be asked. As a general rule, recruitment personnel should ask themselves, "What information do I really need to decide whether an applicant is qualified to perform this job?"

Sex and Marital/Family Status

Any preemployment inquiry that explicitly or implicitly indicates a preference or limitation based on an applicant's sex is unlawful unless the inquiry is justified by a bona fide occupational qualification. In general, questions concerning an applicant's sex, as well as marital/family status, should be avoided. For example, application forms and interviewers should not ask:

1. whether an applicant is male or female;
2. the number or ages of an applicant's children;
3. how an applicant will arrange for child care;
4. an applicant's views on birth control;
5. whether an applicant is pregnant or plans to become pregnant;
6. whether a female applicant prefers to be addressed as Mrs., Miss, or Ms.; or
7. the applicant's maiden name.

In addition, an interviewer should not direct a particular question, such as whether the applicant can type, only to female or only to male applicants.

Some of the above information eventually will be needed for benefits, tax, and EEOC profile purposes, but it can be collected after the applicant is employed. There are exceptions to this general rule, however. For example, state law or federal contracting regulations may require employers to collect data regarding the race, sex, and national origin of each applicant and the job for which he or she has applied. Certain government contractors are also obligated to collect applicant-flow data. Such data are collected for statistical and record-keeping purposes only and cannot be considered by the employer in its hiring decision. In general, if an employer is required to collect such data, the employer should ask applicants to provide self-identification information on a form that is separate or detachable from the application form.

Age

Application forms and interviewers should not try to identify applicants aged forty and older. Accordingly, job candidates generally should not be asked their age, their birth date, or the date that they completed elementary or secondary school. An employer can inquire about age only if (1) age is a bona fide job requirement, as for a child actor; or (2) the employer is trying to comply with special laws, such as those applying to the employment of minors. The claim that it may cost more to employ older workers as a group does not justify differentiating among applicants based on age.

Race

Employers should not ask about an applicant's race. Questions concerning complexion or skin, eye, or hair color should be avoided, and applicants should not be asked to submit photographs.

National Origin

An applicant should not be asked about his or her nationality or ancestry. The Immigration Reform and Control Act of 1986 (IRCA) makes it unlawful for an employer to discriminate against applicants or employees on the basis of either their national origin or their citizenship status.

The IRCA also makes it unlawful for an employer of any size to knowingly hire an individual who is not authorized to work in the United States. Violators can be subject to civil and criminal penalties. Employers must not, however, discriminate against persons solely because they appear to be foreign or speak a foreign language. The act specifies the correct procedure for determining whether an applicant is authorized to work.

INTERNATIONAL CONSIDERATION

In *Estados Unidos Mexicanos v. DeCoster*,[a] the U.S. Court of Appeals for the First Circuit held that the Mexican government lacked standing to sue U.S employers for discrimination against Mexican workers. Fourteen migrant workers of Mexican descent sued an egg farm in Maine, claiming that they were treated worse than non-Mexican workers. The government of Mexico joined the suit, alleging that it was appearing in its *parens patriae* capacity to protect its citizens and its own quasi-sovereign interests. The court denied Mexico *parens patriae* status, stating: "By definition, a foreign nation has no cognizable interests in our system of federalism. And such interests are a critical element of *parens patriae* standing." The court rejected Mexico's argument that it should be treated like one of the fifty states because the justification for *parens patriae* standing "derives from important principles underlying [the U.S.] federal system." The court also indicated that it was reluctant to act on an issue of foreign affairs because it might impinge on the powers of Congress and the executive branch.

a. 229 F.3d 322 (1st Cir. 2000).

Under the act, any newly hired employee is required to complete a Form I-9 certifying that he or she is authorized to work in the United States and has presented documentation of work authorization and identification to the employer. After examining the documents presented, the employer must complete the remainder of the form, certifying that the documents appear genuine, relate to the employee, and establish work authorization. The Form I-9 must be completed within a prescribed period of time.

Religion An employer generally should not ask questions about an applicant's religion. An employer can tell an applicant what the normal work schedule is but should not ask which religious holidays the applicant observes or whether the applicant's religion will interfere with his or her job performance.

An employer can ask about a candidate's religious beliefs if they are a bona fide occupational qualification. For example, a school that is owned, supported, or controlled by persons of a particular religion can require that its employees have a specific religious belief. In an extreme case, a federal district court ruled that a helicopter pilot could be required to convert to Islam, the Muslim religion, in order to fly over certain areas of Saudi Arabia that are closed to non-Muslims.[149] The court ruled that the requirement was a BFOQ justified by safety considerations because Saudi Arabian law prohibits non-Muslims from entering Mecca; non-Muslims risk being beheaded if caught entering this area.

Disabilities and Physical Traits Applicants should not be questioned about their general medical condition. After an employer has described a job's requirements, the employer can ask the applicant if he or she can perform the job. If the applicant answers no, the employer should ask if there is any way to accommodate the applicant's limitation. An applicant can also be told that the job offer is contingent on passing a job-related medical exam (discussed further below).

Applicants generally should not be asked questions about their height or weight. Height and weight requirements have been deemed unlawful when such standards disqualify physically disabled persons, women, and members of certain ethnic or national-origin groups, and the employer could not establish that the requirements were directly related to job performance.

Conviction Record Although an employer can ask applicants if they have ever had a criminal conviction, this

149. Kern v. Dynalectron Corp., 577 F. Supp. 1196 (N.D. Tex. 1983), aff'd, 746 F.2d 810 (5th Cir. 1984).

question should be followed by a statement that the existence of a criminal record will not automatically bar employment. Because in many geographic areas a disproportionate number of minorities are convicted of crimes, the use of conviction records to automatically exclude applicants may have a disparate effect on minorities and therefore may be unlawful. In general, consideration of a criminal record is lawful if the conviction relates to the requirements of the particular job. For example, an employer may be justified in rejecting an applicant convicted of theft for a hotel-security position.

Employers should not ask applicants if they have ever been arrested. Some states, such as Washington and Illinois, prohibit or restrict employers from asking applicants about arrests or detentions that did not result in conviction.

Education Employers can ask applicants questions regarding their education and work experience, but all requirements, such as possession of a high school diploma, must be job related. Inflated standards of academic achievement, language proficiency, or employment experience may be viewed as a pretext for unlawful discrimination against women and members of minority groups.

Credit References Rejection of an applicant because of a poor credit rating may be unlawful unless the employer can show that the decision not to hire the applicant was due to business necessity. Because the percentage of minority-group members with poor credit ratings generally is higher than that of nonminority-group members, rejection of applicants on this basis can have a disparate impact on minority groups.

PREEMPLOYMENT TESTS

Many employers use preemployment tests as a screening mechanism. Title VII prohibits employers from using any test that is designed, intended, or used to disqualify applicants in one of the protected groups. In addition, there are restrictions on the use of tests that have the effect of screening out protected-group members. An employer considering a test as a means to select employees must (1) determine if the test will have an adverse effect on a protected group of applicants and (2) have the test validated in accordance with procedures specified by the EEOC.

A test has an adverse effect on members of a protected group if the pass rate of any sex, race, or ethnic group is less than 80 percent of the pass rate for the highest group passing the test. For example, if 100 percent of whites and only 79 percent of African Americans pass a particular test, the test is presumed to be unlawful because it has an adverse effect on African Americans.

A test that has an adverse impact on a protected group must be validated under the Uniform Guidelines on Employee Selection Procedures, published by the EEOC. Validation is expensive and complicated. Even if a test is job related, it may still be challenged if alternative, less discriminatory selection procedures would equally aid the employer in making hiring decisions. In 1999, the Sixth Circuit held that Ford Motor Company could use a test that had a disparate impact on African Americans in its hiring process because the test related to job requirements and predicted how well applicants would perform on the job.[150]

PHYSICAL EXAMINATIONS

The ADA prohibits preemployment medical examinations or inquiries concerning the existence, nature, or extent of the disability of an applicant unless the inquiries relate directly to that individual's general ability to perform job-related functions and a tentative offer of employment has been made. Medical examinations may be required only after a definite employment offer has been made and before the employee begins his or her employment duties. The offer of employment may be conditioned on the job-related results of the medical

150. Williams v. Ford Motor Co., 187 F.3d 533 (6th Cir. 1999).

examination only if all entering employees are subject to such an examination. Moreover, the results of such an examination must be treated as confidential medical records and kept separate from other personnel information.

Applicability *of* Civil Rights Laws *to* Temporary Workers

The EEOC has responded to the growth in the number of temporary or contingent workers by extending potential liability for discrimination against such workers to both the employment agencies or temporary staffing firms and their client-employers.[151] If both the staffing firm and its client have the right to control the worker, then they are treated as joint employers and subject to liability for both back and front pay as well as compensatory and punitive damages. If the staffing firm learns that one of its clients has discriminated against a temporary employee, the firm should not assign other workers to that work site unless the client has taken the necessary corrective and preventive measures to ensure that the discrimination will not recur. Otherwise, the staffing firm will be liable along with the client if a worker later assigned to that client is subjected to similar misconduct.

151. Text of the EEOC's guidance on application of the employment-discrimination laws to contingent workers is available at <http://www.eeoc.gov/press/12-8-97.html>.

 THE RESPONSIBLE MANAGER
Honoring Employees' Civil Rights

Managers must be diligent in preventing and correcting any unlawful discrimination either in the preemployment process or during employment. Management should develop a written policy, which (1) clearly outlines discriminatory acts prohibited by federal, state, and local statutes; and (2) prohibits retaliation against employees who complain about discrimination. Employees should be advised that any form of discrimination is inappropriate. The policy should have an enforcement mechanism and should clearly state that violations of the policy will result in poor performance reviews or termination. Such a policy will not only curb discriminatory acts but will demonstrate that management diligently attempted to prevent such behavior in the event that litigation should arise.

The firm should also create a working environment where employees feel comfortable bringing complaints

against fellow workers and supervisors. Each complaint should be thoroughly investigated, and, if necessary, the violator should be punished. In addition, the company should designate at least two individuals, a male and a female, to whom such complaints may be brought. Because supervisors are often the discriminators, an employee should not be required to first complain to his or her supervisor.

Although the establishment of a comprehensive policy is one way to prevent unlawful discriminatory practices, it is not sufficient in itself. Managers must also abide by the policy and comply with all federal, state, and local statutes prohibiting unlawful discrimination. If management participates in discriminatory acts, its employees will have little incentive to abide by the firm's policy against discrimination and will hesitate to bring a claim for discriminatory treatment.

It is crucial that employers make sure that they do not retaliate against employees who have filed discrimination claims. Although employers often perceive discrimination claims by an employee as an act of disloyalty, retaliation will make it more likely that the employer will be found liable by a jury or judge even if the initial claim would not have supported liability.

Employers should also create nondiscriminatory policies and procedures for hiring new employees, including training employees in interviewing to ensure that interviewers ask proper questions and use objective criteria. Employers can use interview teams staffed by diverse interviewers in the hiring process. When advertising vacant positions, employers should use a job posting system that promotes an open and fair application process.

Employers may also want to purchase employment practice liability insurance (EPLI) to protect against discrimination claims. When introduced in the early 1990s, these insurance plans were expensive, did not offer broad coverage, and excluded punitive damages, but by the late 1990s, more carriers had entered the market, resulting in lower prices and expanded coverage.

With respect to the ADA, employers should be proactive and engage in an interactive process with employees requesting accommodation. According to David Fram, director of equal employment opportunity and ADA services at the National Employment Law Institute, "Lack of communication is a big cause of lawsuits. If you share with someone how hard you're trying, he or she is likely to be less mad."[152] If an employer explores every option but still cannot find a way to provide an accommodation, the employer should inform the individual and ask if he or she has any suggestions.[153] The employer should create a paper trail to document the actions it took to find an accommodation. While focusing on finding an accommodation, the employer should refrain from determining whether the employee is actually disabled and allow the courts to make that determination.

Dating and romantic relationships between employees at a company can lead to discrimination and sexual harassment claims, particularly when there is a significant power and age gap between the partners. Such relationships are very perilous. If the parties have a falling out, the subordinate may claim that the relationship was not consensual and that he or she feared adverse employment consequences for rebuffing the manager's advances. To address this problem, IBM instituted a policy that a manager may become involved with a subordinate as long as the manager transfers to another job within or outside the company so that he or she is not supervising or evaluating the performance of the subordinate involved.

152. *Interactive Process Helps Employers Prevail, but Isn't Required,* CORP. COUNS. WKLY., Jan. 10, 2001, at 12.
153. *Id.*

INSIDE STORY

Texaco *and* Coca-Cola Pay Hundreds *of* Millions *to* Settle Racial Discrimination Lawsuits

In March 1994, six African-American employees of oil giant Texaco, Inc. filed a class-action lawsuit on behalf of 1,500 current and former employees, charging Texaco with racial discrimination. Within a week after a dismissed Texaco executive provided plaintiffs' attorneys with clandestine tape recordings he had made of high-ranking Texaco officials disparaging African-American workers, Texaco settled the lawsuit at a total cost of $176 million, including cash payments, salary raises, and the design and implementation of new diversity programs.[154] Most of the executives involved were suspended with pay and eventually fired.

The Texaco settlement served as a model for the settlement reached by the Coca-Cola Company and African-American employees in November 2000—the largest settlement ever in a racial discrimination case. The Coca-Cola lawsuit, filed in April 1999, accused Coke of providing fewer opportunities for advancement and paying lower salaries to African-American employees than to white employees. According to the complaint, the company's African-American managers were excluded from the global marketing and finance divisions (the most powerful departments offering the most potential for advancement) and were relegated instead to low-profile divisions, such as human resources and corporate affairs.[155] A 1995 report

154. Allanna Sullivan & Peter Fritsch, *Texaco Is Trying to Reach a Settlement in 1994 Racial-Discrimination Lawsuit,* WALL ST. J., Nov. 11, 1996, at A3; Anne Reifenberg, *Texaco Settlement in Race-Bias Case Endorsed by Judge,* WALL ST. J., Mar. 26, 1997, at B9.

155. Davan Maharaj, *Coca-Cola to Settle Racial Bias Lawsuit: Soft Drink Giant Agrees to Pay $192.5 Million over Allegations It Treated Blacks Unfairly,* L.A. TIMES, Nov. 17, 2000, at A-1.

by African-American executives to Coke's president stated that the company had created an atmosphere in which African-American employees felt "humiliated, ignored, overlooked, or unacknowledged" and criticized the lack of African Americans in top management.[156]

The $192.5 million settlement included $113 million in cash to the class members, $43.5 million to adjust salaries to employees over ten years, and $36 million for various diversity initiatives. In addition, the company agreed to donate $50 million to the Coca-Cola Foundation for community programs related to advancing diversity.[157]

The settlement also provided that an outside panel, appointed by Coke and the plaintiffs' lawyers, will monitor the company's employment practices. Plaintiffs' lawyers and the company will each appoint three members of the task force and jointly select the chair. The seven members will include experts in civil rights, labor employment, business, and diversity issues. During their term of four years, they will oversee a review of the company's human resource policies and practices and prepare an annual report of its compliance with the settlement. In addition, two industrial psychologists with expertise in business systems will review the company's policies with the task force.[158] Coke's chairman and chief executive officer Douglas N. Daft explained, "We need to have outside people helping us. We would be foolish to cut ourselves off from the outside world."[159]

Months prior to the settlement, in March 2000, Daft distributed an e-mail announcing that in the future his compensation and that of other senior managers would be tied to diversity goals.[160] Daft added, "Diversity, in its broadest sense, is a clear business imperative for our company and its future, and it is a top priority for me."[161]

At the time of the settlement, Coca-Cola indicated it planned to hire an ombudsperson to report directly to Daft to investigate claims of discrimination and to monitor the company's response to these claims. In addition, the company's board said it would form a committee on diversity to review its equal employment opportunity performance. The settlement also requires Coke to address the issue of the diversity of its board members; at the time of the settlement, the twelve-member board included only one African American and two women.

The settlement does not resolve all of Coke's legal problems, however. Four plaintiffs from the original lawsuit opted to join a second racial bias suit on behalf of former employees. This group of employees, represented by high-profile lawyers Johnnie Cochran and Willie Gary, is seeking $1.5 billion in damages from Coca-Cola.[162]

156. Greg Winter, *Coca-Cola Settles Racial Bias Case,* N.Y. TIMES, Nov. 17, 2000, at 1.
157. Betsy McKany, *Coca-Cola Agrees to Settle Bias Suit for $192.5 Million—Outside Panel Will Monitor Company's Activities; 'Painful Chapter' Closes,* WALL ST. J., Nov. 17, 2000, at A3.
158. *Id.*

159. Winter, *supra* note 156.
160. Mary Helen Gillespie, *Coca-Cola Case Sets Example,* BOSTON GLOBE, Nov. 26, 2000, at G15.
161. *Coca-Cola Head Plans Link Between Executive Pay, Diversity,* CORP. COUNS. WKLY., Mar. 22, 2000, at 7.
162. McKany, *supra* note 157.

KEY WORDS AND PHRASES

bona fide occupational qualification
  (BFOQ) defense   501
disability   517
discriminate   517

disparate impact   499
disparate treatment   498
fetal-protection policy   512
hostile-environment harassment   500

quid pro quo harassment   502
race norming of employment tests
  525

QUESTIONS AND CASE PROBLEMS

1. Pam Armstrong was employed by Flowers Hospital as a nurse in the Home Care Services division; her duties involved visiting and treating patients in their homes. On December 12, 1990, Armstrong was informed that she had been assigned a patient who was diagnosed as HIV-positive. He was further diagnosed as having cryptococcal meningitis, an infectious disease common among AIDS patients.

That same day, Armstrong informed Cheryl Wynn, her supervisor at Home Care Services, that she did not believe that she should treat this patient because she was in the first trimester of pregnancy. Armstrong stated that it was not the AIDS that concerned her as much as the opportunistic infections commonly present with AIDS. She further stated that she was not concerned about her own health because she, as a healthy adult, would be capable of recovering from most of these infections. Her primary concern was the health of her unborn baby.

Wynn informed Armstrong that the policy of Home Care Services was not to allow reassignment of patients to other nurses. Home Care's policy on the treatment of AIDS patients stated that the "Universal Precautions" provided by the Centers for Disease Control (CDC) were to be followed by all nurses in treating patients with infectious diseases. Any nurse who refused to treat a patient was subject to termination. After Armstrong refused to treat the AIDS patient, she was terminated. Did Flowers Hospital violate Title VII? Did Wynn act in an ethical manner? [*Armstrong v. Flowers Hosp.,* 812 F. Supp. 1183 (M.D. Ala. 1993), *aff'd,* 33 F.3d 1208 (11th Cir. 1994)]

2. Marianne Stanley was hired as head coach of the University of Southern California's women's basketball team in 1989. She had a four-year contract that paid a salary of $62,000 and provided a $6,000 annual housing allowance. During negotiations to renew her contract in 1993, she sought a salary equivalent to the one paid to George Raveling, the men's basketball coach. USC refused to pay her this amount and terminated Stanley when she did not accept a lower salary.

   Stanley sued USC for sex discrimination and retaliatory discharge. USC argued that the men's coach received a higher salary because he had greater responsibility for generating revenues; he did generate more revenue for the university, and he was subject to more pressure by the fans and media to win games. Stanley argued that this greater responsibility was due to the university's history of disparate treatment of the men's and women's teams: USC had invested more in the men's team and had promoted it more heavily than the women's team. Should the court consider this history in reaching a decision? [*Stanley v. University of Southern California,* 178 F.3d 1069 (9th Cir. 1999), *cert. denied,* 528 U.S. 1022 (1999)]

3. Charles Nesser, a customer service agent at Trans World Airlines, was excessively absent from work because he suffered from Crohn's disease, a chronic intestinal disease. He sought the accommodation of working from home in order to avoid being fired for missing excessive amounts of work, but TWA refused to permit him to work at home. Should a company have to accommodate an employee who must work from home due to a chronic illness? [*Nesser v. Trans World Airlines, Inc.,* 160 F.3d 442 (8th Cir. 1998)]

4. Rosalie Cullen was forty-nine years old and had worked as a manager of marketing administration for Olin Corporation for over twenty-five years. She was terminated in February 1996 because, according to Olin, it was downsizing due to an economic downturn. Cullen filed a suit against Olin under the ADEA, alleging that she was fired due to her age. She presented evidence that Doug Cahill, the president of the Winchester Division of Olin, where Cullen worked, had remarked at a meeting that some employees were "old fashioned" and that "older people have trouble with change and that they were gonna have to learn to go with the change or conform or they were going to be out." In addition, she introduced evidence that after she was fired, all of her duties were taken over by employees ranging in age from thirty-two to forty-three years old. Olin argued that Cahill was so far removed from the selection process that his comments did not motivate the decision to discharge her. Cullen argued that Cahill was the person who decided that personnel cutbacks were necessary, set the parameters for the layoffs, and reviewed the vice president's personnel decisions. Did Olin violate the ADEA? [*Cullen v. Olin Corp.,* 195 F.3d 317 (7th Cir. 1999), *cert. denied,* 120 S. Ct. 1423 (2000)]

5. Red Mendoza worked in the accounting department of Borden, Inc. Daniel Page, the controller and highest-ranking employee at the plant where Mendoza worked, was her supervisor. After Mendoza was fired for being absent from work for three consecutive days without calling in to explain her absence, she filed a sexual harassment claim under Title VII. Mendoza testified at trial that Page constantly watched her and followed her around at work. In addition, she testified that on two occasions, he "looked me up and down, and stopped in my groin area and made a . . . sniffing motion." She testified further that while she was standing at a fax machine, Page passed by her and rubbed his hip up against her hip, touched her shoulder, and smiled. When Mendoza confronted Page about his harassing behavior by stating to him, "I came in here to work, period," he replied, "Yeah, I'm getting fired up, too." After a trial in which Mendoza presented this evidence, the court granted judgment as a matter of law to Borden. Was the court's decision correct? [*Mendoza v. Borden, Inc.,* 195 F.3d 1238 (11th Cir. 1999), *cert. denied,* 120 S. Ct. 1674 (2000)]

6. Vincent Krocka began working as a police officer for the Chicago Police Department in the early 1980s and received good performance evaluations. In

1990, he began taking Prozac after being diagnosed with severe depression. The medication improved his psychological condition, and he continued to perform his job and receive good evaluations. In 1992, the department learned that Krocka was taking Prozac and placed him on medical leave while it conducted physical and psychological evaluations to determine his ability to continue performing his job. After determining that Krocka had no symptoms of psychological illness, he was allowed to return to his regular duties, but, pursuant to departmental policy, he had to participate in the department's Personnel Concerns Program (PCP). Many of the officers in the PCP had disciplinary problems and were closely monitored; as a result, a negative stigma was associated with being placed in the program. Krocka filed a complaint, alleging that placing him in the PCP because he was taking Prozac was a violation of the ADA. What result? [*Krocka v. Chicago,* 203 F.3d 507 (7th Cir. 2000)]

7. Joseph Mondzelewski was a fifty-five-year-old man with a sixth-grade education who worked for thirty-five years as a bagger and meat cutter at Pathmark Stores, Inc. He injured his back lifting boxes of meat and subsequently was restricted by the company's doctor from lifting objects weighing more than fifty pounds and carrying objects weighing more than twenty-five pounds.

Mondzelewski claimed that Pathmark retaliated against him for asserting his right under the ADA to obtain reasonable accommodation for a disability. He claimed that the company assigned him to a new schedule with bad hours that were considered "punishment shifts" by workers. In addition, he claimed that he received retaliatory reprimands when he refused to lift a weight that exceeded the weight restrictions established by his doctor. Mondzelewski filed a claim against Pathmark, alleging that it had failed to provide him reasonable accommodation for his lifting restrictions and had retaliated against him for requesting accommodation. What result? [*Mondzelewski v. Pathmark Stores,* 162 F.3d 778 (3d Cir. 1998)]

8. Rena Lockard worked as a waitress during the evening shift at a Pizza Hut in Atoka, Oklahoma. On November 6, 1993, two crude and rowdy male customers came into the restaurant. The two men had eaten at the restaurant several times in the past and had made offensive comments to Lockard, such as "I would like to get into your pants." Lockard had informed her manager, Micky Jack, that she did not like waiting on them but had not repeated to

him the comments they had made. On November 6, Jack ordered Lockard to wait on the two men after other wait staff, including young men, argued over who would serve them because no one wanted to wait on them. While Lockard was waiting on the men, one of them commented to Lockard that she smelled good and asked what kind of perfume she was wearing. When she responded that it was none of his business, her grabbed her by the hair. Lockard informed Jack of the incident and said that she did not want to continue waiting on them. Jack responded, "You wait on them. You were hired to be a waitress. You waitress." When Lockard returned to the table with a pitcher of beer, one of the customers pulled her to him by the hair, grabbed her breast, and put his mouth on it. Lockard told Jack that she was quitting and left.

Lockard sued Pizza Hut, Inc. and its owner A&M Food Service, Inc., alleging sexual harassment under Title VII and intentional infliction of emotional distress. Should Pizza Hut be held responsible for its customers' actions? [*Lockard v. Pizza Hut, Inc.,* 162 F.3d 1062 (10th Cir. 1998)]

9. Connie Lynn Madray and Melody Holden were employed as clerks at Publix Super Markets, Inc. in Okeechobee, Florida. The manager of their store and their supervisor, Ronald Selph, had a practice of hugging and patting his employees, including Madray and Holden. Subsequently, this behavior escalated to groping; full-body hugs; rubbing his body against theirs in such a way that his genitals made contact with their body; kissing; blowing in their ear; wetting his finger in his mouth and sticking it in their ears; rubbing their hips, legs, backs, and shoulders; and making provocative comments. The two female employees commented upon this inappropriate behavior to several mid-level managers at the store, who had observed Selph's behavior on several occasions, but they did not lodge a formal complaint. Eventually, at the urging of an assistant manager, they called the district manager and made a formal complaint regarding Selph's behavior. The district manager was very upset that he had not learned of the problem earlier and indicated that the managers should have informed him of Selph's conduct. After promptly investigating the complaint, he issued a written warning to Selph, demoted him, and transferred him to a store in another city so that the women no longer had any contact with him.

At the time of these incidents, Publix had a written sexual harassment policy that it disseminated to employees. The policy directed employees to file complaints with persons in company management by first discussing their problem with their immediate supervisor and then proceeding to the next highest level of management. Although Selph was a designated manager, there were other designated company representatives accessible to Publix's store employees, including the district manager who visited the store at least once each week. In addition, the company provided employees with phone numbers of other company representatives, including a toll-free number, that employees could use to file sexual harassment complaints. Did Publix exercise reasonable care to prevent and correct sexual harassment? If not, what should it have done differently? [*Madray v. Publix Super Markets, Inc.*, 208 F.3d 1290 (11th Cir. 2000), *cert. denied*, 121 S. Ct. 303 (2000)]

MANAGER'S DILEMMA

10. Catherine Van Order is a manager at American Eagle's hangar at the Miami International Airport. The hangar's workforce consists of eighty mechanics, including a small number of African Americans, Latinos, and white ex-strikers from Eastern Air Lines who are earning half as much as they did at their old employer. American Eagle has been struggling to regain the public's confidence after two of its planes suffered fatal crashes. Although the airline is downsizing in two other cities in the South, it wants to increase its business to Latin America and the Caribbean so it has hired more staff at the Miami airport. Workers were assigned heavy workloads at low pay and have to work with aging equipment in run-down facilities, leading to a great deal of tension at the Miami hangar.

Employees have tried to ease the tension by playing practical jokes on each other and making wisecracks. These jokes included sexual and ethnic jokes along with comments about people's appearance, including weight, and their religion. Employees posted cartoons depicting black mechanics as gorillas or starving Somalis on the bulletin board. When Van Order suggested to one of the mechanics that the joking was getting out of control, he told her that people were just making fun of stereotypes and that nobody was trying to be personally offensive to their coworkers.

Although no employees complained to her about the joking, Van Order issued a memo setting forth the company's policy on discrimination and harassment. Several employees then told her that the memo had affected morale; without the joking, workers seemed tense and anxious and were less productive. Within several weeks, the joking commenced again and escalated when a poster of a black basketball player with a mop on his head and a watermelon in his hand was posted in the locker room. Van Order spoke to several African-American workers about the incident, but both seemed reluctant to talk about it. She senses that they were quiet for fear of either losing their jobs or becoming the victims of hostile treatment by their coworkers. What should Van Order do?

INTERNET SOURCES

Equal Employment Opportunity Commission	http://www.eeoc.gov
U.S. Department of Labor	http://www.dol.gov
The site for the International Labour Organization, a United Nations–sponsored agency, provides excellent reports on employment issues throughout the world.	http://www.ilo.org
This site, maintained by a nonprofit organization founded to disseminate information about disabilities in the workplace, provides a searchable guide, with links, to disability resources on the Internet and the Disability Resources Monthly reports.	http://www.disabilityresources.org/

(Continued on next page.)

(Internet Sources continued)

The Small Business Advisor maintains a searchable site with links to articles and sites concerning employment issues.	http://www.isquare.com/
American Civil Liberties Union	http://www.aclu.org/
This is the corporate home page for the Coca-Cola Company.	http://www.thecoca-colacompany.com/default.asp?pass=on
This site, maintained by the National Employment Law Institute (a nonprofit organization providing training and information for human resources professionals and managers), provides articles and links relating to employment issues.	http://www.neli.org
The AHI Employment Law Resource Center publishes articles, provides links to government sites and other information, and offers free biweekly e-mail updates on employment law.	http://www.ahipubs.com/

CHAPTER 16

Labor–Management Relations

UNIONS IN THE TWENTY-FIRST CENTURY

Managers are likely to encounter organized labor in a variety of industries, ranging from automakers (e.g., General Motors), aircraft manufacturers (e.g., Boeing), heavy equipment manufacturers (e.g., Caterpillar), aerospace companies (e.g., Lockheed Martin), and telecommunications firms (e.g., Verizon) to airlines (e.g., United Airlines). Yet unions are also cropping up in new places: hospitals and medical offices where physicians, tired of being pushed around by health maintenance organizations, are seeking to form unions; legal departments, where attorneys are organizing to get better compensation, computers, and paralegal help; and Internet companies, bastions of the New Economy, where dot.com workers hope that unions will help them negotiate higher wages, fewer hours of forced overtime, and more opportunities for promotion. (Organizing efforts at Amazon.com and other New Economy companies are described further in the "Inside Story" for this chapter.) Managers in the twenty-first century will need to be sensitive to the signs of worker alienation that often spark efforts to

unionize, as well as familiar with the laws governing organizing efforts, collective bargaining, and labor disputes.

CHAPTER OVERVIEW

This chapter discusses the coverage and application of the National Labor Relations Act (NLRA), which governs labor relations in the United States. The chapter explains who is eligible to be a member of a union, and it outlines the procedure whereby eligible employees can decide whether they wish to be represented by a particular union. The chapter identifies the types of employer conduct that are unlawful under the NLRA, including interference with union-organizing activities and failure to bargain in good faith. It compares lawful and unlawful strikes and outlines the rights of strikers to reinstatement. The chapter concludes with a discussion of unlawful union conduct, including coercing employees to join a union or to remain on strike.

History

Congress has comprehensively regulated labor–management relations in an attempt to balance equitably the economic power of employers, individual employees, and unions. Before the mid-1930s, attempts by employees to band together and demand better wages and working conditions were largely ineffective. Organized economic actions, such as strikes and picketing, were enjoined as unlawful conspiracies. Employers squelched

attempts to organize by lawfully discharging union organizers.

In 1932, Congress enacted the Norris–La Guardia Act,[1] which regulated and largely prohibited the issuance of injunctions or court orders in labor disputes. Through the Wagner Act[2] in 1935 and the Taft–Hartley Act[3] in 1947, Congress sought to provide employees with

1. 29 U.S.C. §§ 101–115 (1988).
2. 29 U.S.C. §§ 151–169 (1994).
3. 29 U.S.C. §§ 141–144 (1994).

greater economic bargaining power by allowing them to organize but also sought to curb perceived union excesses. The Landrum–Griffin Act was enacted in 1959 primarily to address problems created by corruption within union leadership. These laws are known collectively as the National Labor Relations Act.

Exhibit 16.1 shows the number of workers in unions in the United States from 1930 to 1999 as a percentage of the total nonagricultural workforce.

EXHIBIT 16.1   **U.S. Union Membership, 1930–1999**

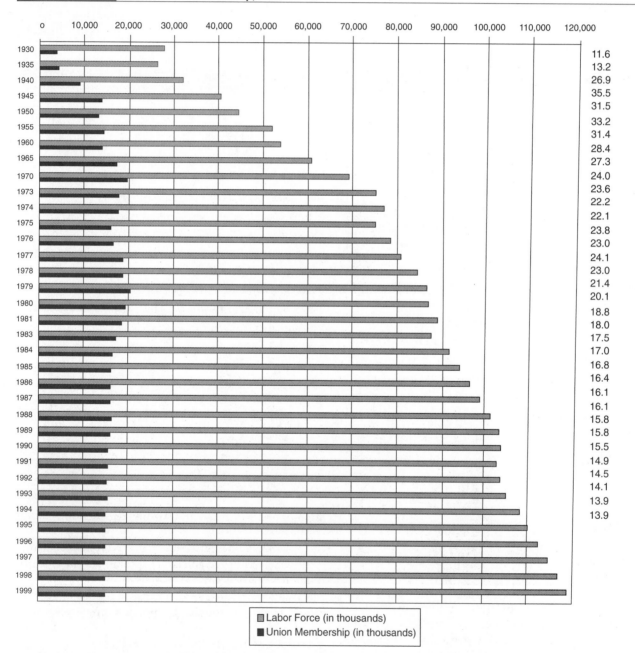

Percentage of Union Members to Labor Force

Year	Percentage
1930	11.6
1935	13.2
1940	26.9
1945	35.5
1950	31.5
1955	33.2
1960	31.4
1965	28.4
1970	27.3
1973	24.0
1974	23.6
1975	22.2
1976	22.1
1977	23.8
1978	23.0
1979	24.1
1980	23.0
1981	21.4
1983	20.1
1984	18.8
1985	18.0
1986	17.5
1987	17.0
1988	16.8
1989	16.4
1990	16.1
1991	16.1
1992	15.8
1993	15.8
1994	15.5
1995	14.9
1996	14.5
1997	14.1
1998	13.9
1999	13.9

■ Labor Force (in thousands)
■ Union Membership (in thousands)

Source: U.S. Department of Labor, Bureau of Labor Statistics.

Coverage *of the* National Labor Relations Act

The National Labor Relations Act covers all enterprises whose operations affect interstate or foreign commerce. With court approval, however, the National Labor Relations Board (NLRB), which administers the act, has limited its jurisdiction to enterprises having a substantial effect on commerce. The dollar volume of an employer's revenues or purchases determines whether its impact on commerce is sufficiently substantial to bring it within the NLRB's jurisdiction. In 1974, Congress extended the NLRB's jurisdiction to employees of all health care institutions, including nonprofit hospitals.

In general, the NLRA covers only employees located within the territorial United States, not U.S. employees located elsewhere. The NLRB has ruled, however, that its jurisdiction extends to non-U.S. employers doing business within the United States that would otherwise be under the NLRB's jurisdiction.

SUPERVISORS

Section 7 of the NLRA grants rights only to employees, not to supervisors. The NLRB defines *supervisor* to mean:

> Any individual having authority, in the interest of the employer, to hire, transfer, suspend, lay off, recall, promote, discharge, assign, reward or discipline other employees, or responsibility to direct them, or to adjust their grievances, or effectively to recommend such action, if in connection with the foregoing the exercise of such authority is not of a merely routine or clerical nature, but requires the use of independent judgment.

In the following case, the court considered whether nurses are supervisors of nursing assistants and, therefore, ineligible to join a union.

A CASE IN POINT

CASE 16.1

Beverly Enterprises, Virginia, Inc. v. National Labor Relations Board
United States Court of Appeals for the Fourth Circuit
165 F.3d 307
(4th Cir. 1999).

Summary

FACTS Beverly Enterprises, Virginia, Inc. operated Carter Hall Nursing Home in Dryden, Virginia, which served fifty patients. Direct patient care was provided by six licensed practical nurses (LPNs) and twenty-one nursing assistants. The LPNs assigned the nursing assistants to patients, directed their work, and taught them nursing procedures; the nursing assistants reported directly to the LPNs. The LPNs implemented the schedule formulated by the director and assistant director of nursing and filled out daily assignment sheets for the nursing assistants. The LPNs did not directly discipline the nursing assistants, but they could send them home for misbehavior and provide input for disciplinary decisions made by the director and assistant director. For two-thirds of the time during the week, the LPNs were the most senior representatives of Beverly Enterprises present at Carter Hall and, therefore, were responsible for ensuring the operation of the nursing home.

The United Mine Workers of America petitioned the NLRB to allow the union to represent a unit of approximately forty employees at Carter Hall, including the six LPNs. Beverly Enterprises objected to the inclusion of the LPNs, asserting that they were supervisors. After concluding that the LPNs' functions were routine and essentially clerical in nature, the NLRB ordered Beverly Enterprises to begin bargaining with the union, but Beverly Enterprises refused.

ISSUE PRESENTED Are LPNs who direct the work of nursing assistants "supervisors" under the NLRA and, as a result, not entitled to bargain collectively?

SUMMARY OF OPINION The U.S. Court of Appeals for the Fourth Circuit began by setting forth the test for determining whether an employee is a supervisor under the NLRA. To be a supervisor, an employee must meet the following criteria: (1) the employee must be authorized to perform or recommend at least one of the twelve duties enumerated in the statute; (2) the employee's authority must promote the interest of the

(Continued)

(Case 16.1 continued)

employer; and (3) the exercise of the employee's authority must require the use of independent judgment.

With respect to the first prong, the court found that the LPNs did perform several of the duties itemized in the statute: they assigned and directed the nursing assistants to work tasks, filled out their daily assignment sheets, and instructed them about the work they needed to accomplish. In addition, the LPNs were responsible for the continued operation of the nursing home and could discipline nursing assistants by sending them home and recommending their discharge. In terms of the second prong, the LPNs' duties were undertaken in the interest of their employer, Beverly Enterprises.

The court disagreed with the Board's ruling that the third prong of the test was not satisfied. The court set forth a list of findings that demonstrated that the LPNs exercised independent judgment, including the fact that the LPNs were the most senior staff at Carter Hall during almost two-thirds of the time that Beverly Enterprises operated the facility. During this time, they faced decisions that required independent judgment, including deciding which nursing assistants should provide treatment for which patients and whether to discipline a particular nursing assistant. Finding that these were not the decisions of a "night watchman" but required "sensitive and nuanced" judgment, the court concluded that the LPNs did exercise judgment. The court further concluded that these judgments were independent because they were made without guidelines or established criteria from Beverly Enterprises.

RESULT The court reversed the NLRB's decision. Because the LPNs were supervisors, they could not be included in the proposed union.

The NLRB will not allow supervisors to vote in union elections. In most cases, the NLRB does not have the authority to find that supervisors have been treated unlawfully under the NLRA.

INDEPENDENT CONTRACTORS

Independent contractors are not covered by the NLRA because they are not employees. In determining whether an individual is an independent contractor, the NLRB invokes the common law right-to-control test (which is discussed in Chapter 5). A person is deemed to be an *independent contractor* if the employer exercises no control over either the means of performing the work or the end result of the work.

AGRICULTURAL LABORERS

The NLRA specifically excludes from its coverage any individual employed as an agricultural laborer. An agricultural laborer is one who performs work primarily in connection with (1) an agricultural operation or (2) an operation that is both an integral part of ordinary agricultural production and an essential step before the products can be marketed in normal outlets.

PROFESSIONAL WORKERS

In the 1990s, professionals, including doctors and lawyers, made efforts to gain the right to unionize. Despite the interest in organizing, health care providers must first overcome several legal obstacles. In the past, doctors have been held to be independent contractors, rather than rank-and-file employees, and therefore not capable of forming a bargaining unit.[4] Alternatively, health maintenance organizations (HMOs) may argue that health care providers are supervisors.[5] Supporters of unionizing retort that managed care companies have transformed autonomous health care providers into employees with little decision-making authority. They cite HMO-mandated working conditions and influence over medical and office procedures. State medical associations have supported bills to grant physicians power to bargain collectively with health plans. By early 2000, physician-bargaining bills had

---

4. *See, e.g.,* Andrea Adelson, *Physician, Unionize Thyself: Doctors Adapt to Life as HMO Employees,* N.Y. TIMES, Apr. 5, 1997, at 35. A physician-bargaining unit consisting of employee physicians was recognized by the NLRB. Thomas–Davis Medical Centers, 324 N.L.R.B. 15 (1997).

5. *See, e.g., Physician Organizing Continuing Despite Legal, Political Obstacles,* 66 U.S.L.W. 2608 (Apr. 7, 1998).

"Sorry, but I don't do stitches anymore. All stitches are now handled by Local 405 over at Bellevue."

been introduced in Delaware, New York, New Jersey, Pennsylvania, Texas, and the District of Columbia.[6]

Lawyers have also tried to engage in collective bargaining. In 1999, the Florida Supreme Court held that public-sector attorneys had the right to form unions.[7] The decision permitted 800 to 900 attorneys who work in Florida's comptroller's office, cabinet, and Departments of Transportation, Insurance, and Business and Professional Regulation to bargain collectively for better compensation and benefits and access to better computers, libraries, paralegal help, and law clerks. The ruling did not cover assistant state attorneys general or public defenders.

TEMPORARY WORKERS

In 2000, the NLRB released a decision permitting temporary workers to form their own unions or to join existing unions if (1) the company to which they are assigned supervises them and (2) they do the same work, and are employed beside, full-time workers.[8] Workers meeting these requirements are deemed employees of the firm where they are assigned, and they do not need permission from their staffing firm or other employer to join in collective bargaining at the firm to which they are assigned. A February 1999 survey cited by the NLRB indicated that 5.6 million workers (4.3 percent of all employees) were contingent workers or subject to some other alternative employment arrangement.

Representation Election Procedure

The five-member NLRB has established a number of regional offices throughout the country to handle the day-to-day tasks of overseeing *representation elections,* that is,

6. Chad Bowman & Kurt Fernandez, *More Physicians-Bargaining Bills Expected as MDs Seek Strength Through State Action,* 68 U.S.L.W. 2461 (Feb. 8, 2000).

7. Carol Marbin Miller, *Fla. Attorneys Clear Way for Collective Bargaining,* FLORIDA DAILY BUS. REV., May 28, 1999.

8. Stephanie Armour, *Labor Ruling Lets Temps Join Union,* USA TODAY, Sept. 1, 2000, at 2B.

elections among employees to decide whether they want a union to represent them for collective bargaining.

FILING A PETITION

The procedure for conducting a representation election is initiated by filing a petition with a regional office of the NLRB. The vast majority of those petitions are filed by labor organizations.

To call an election, a union must make a *showing of interest;* that is, it must prove that a sufficient number of employees have an interest in an election. This is nearly always done by submitting to the NLRB *union authorization cards* from at least 30 percent of the employees in an appropriate collective bargaining unit. Each card generally contains a statement that the individual signing it wishes to be represented for purposes of collective bargaining by a certain union. If the union cannot provide a showing of interest, the NLRB will dismiss the petition.

An individual employee may file a petition to decertify an incumbent union if at least 30 percent of the employees in the bargaining unit sign a statement that they no longer wish to be represented for collective bargaining by their union. Petitions may also be filed by employers at certain intervals to test the union's continuing support. To do so, an employer must show objectively that a majority of the employees in the collective bargaining unit no longer wish to be represented by the union.

APPROPRIATE UNIT

Regardless of whether the union, the employer, or an employee files the petition for election, the election procedures are essentially the same, except that in the case of an initial organizing campaign, the parties or the NLRB may have to determine which employees should be allowed to vote in an election. The NLRB will hold elections only in appropriate collective bargaining units. An *appropriate collective bargaining unit* is one in which the employees share a community of interest; that is, they have similar compensation, working conditions, and supervision, and they work under the same general employer policies. The NLRB also looks at the (1) kind of work performed, (2) similarity in the qualifications and skills of employees, (3) frequency of contact among employees, (4) geographic proximity of employees, and (5) wishes of affected employees.

SCOPE OF UNIT

With certain limitations, the union and the employer are free to agree on the scope of the unit in which an elec-

 INTERNATIONAL CONSIDERATION

During the last forty years, unions in Scandinavian countries have grown in strength and numbers while unions in the United States and other countries have lost members and power. Three factors have contributed to making Sweden, Denmark, Finland, and Norway the four Organization for Economic Cooperation and Development (OECD) countries with the strongest unions. First, unions in these countries have political strength because they were involved in founding political parties that are still in power. Second, they have national bargaining power, which enables the unions to negotiate nationwide agreements with employer associations. Third, unions traditionally administer unemployment insurance. This practice makes it difficult for employers to recruit strikebreakers from the unemployed. Four other OECD countries where labor unions are struggling—Japan, Switzerland, the United States, and France—are weak in these three factors: unions have little political power; there is weak or no national bargaining; and governments, rather than unions, administer unemployment insurance.[a]

Unions in other European countries, such as Germany and the United Kingdom, have not fared as well as unions in Scandinavia. As a result, many of the European unions that have lost members are merging to create mega-unions. For example, in November 1999, five German unions formed a committee to create the world's largest union with 3.2 million members. The same year, three British banking unions merged to create a 200,000-member organization called Unifi.[b] It is not clear whether these larger unions will be better at positioning themselves in a rapidly changing labor market that emphasizes the individual rather than groups of workers. Many are planning to attract new members by offering services directed at individual workers, such as legal counseling and career advice. Yet, after four Dutch unions merged in February 1998, the resulting superunion ran into financial difficulties as it tried to offer services such as career advice and personal finance.

a. *Labor Unions Under Stress*, Sci. Am., May 1999, at 30.
b. Konstantin Richter, *European Super-Unions Face Challenges*, Wall St. J., Jan. 11, 2000, at A23.

tion should be conducted. If the proposed unit will include both professional and nonprofessional employees, however, the consent of the professional employees must be obtained. In addition, Section 9(b)(3) of the NLRA prohibits a labor organization from representing security guards if that organization admits nonguards to membership or is affiliated with a labor organization that admits nonguards to membership. These special rules for security guards are necessary to prevent guards from having conflicts during strikes between their responsibility as employees and their loyalty as union members.

If the employer and the union cannot agree on the scope of the unit, the NLRB will conduct a hearing to resolve the issue. A common issue at a representation hearing is whether a certain position is supervisory. The director of the regional office in which the petition is filed makes such determinations, which are appealable to the NLRB.

CONDUCT OF ELECTION

Following an agreement between the parties for an election or a decision from the regional director over disputed unit issues, the regional office will conduct an election. An NLRB agent travels to the employer's location, erects a portable voting booth, and oversees the election process. The employer and the union agree on the specific place and time for the election.

The NLRB agent hands out ballots to the employees and ensures that no irregularities occur during the election. Each employee enters the place of voting and indicates by placing a mark in an appropriate square on the ballot whether he or she wishes to be represented for collective bargaining by the specified union. The employee then deposits the marked ballot in a ballot box, which is opened at the close of the election by the NLRB agent. The NLRB agent then tallies the election results and signs a ballot count. With a unit of previously unrepresented employees, the union needs 50 percent plus one of the valid votes cast in the election to win.

OBJECTIONS

The party losing the election may file objections to it. Objections typically allege misconduct either by the other party before or during the election or by the NLRB agent at the election. For example, a union that has lost an election may allege that, just before the election, the employer unlawfully threatened employees with reprisals if they voted for the union. If the objections are deemed without merit, the election will be certified by the NLRB. If they are deemed meritorious, the NLRB will conduct a new election. If an employer's misconduct was so serious that a free and fair election is impossible, the NLRB will order the employer to bargain with the union, even without an election.

Unfair Labor Practices *by* Employers

Section 8(a) of the NLRA prohibits employers from engaging in specified activities against employees or their unions. Such activities, known as *unfair labor practices,* are investigated and prosecuted by the general counsel of the NLRB and his or her representatives.

Unfair labor practice charges may be filed in the NLRB's regional offices. Ordinarily, the time limit for filing a charge is six months. A charge is usually investigated by a field examiner or a field attorney of the local office. The regional director then decides whether, based on evidence disclosed by the investigation, the charge has merit.

If the charge is meritorious, the local office will attempt to arrange a settlement. If the matter cannot be settled at the local level, it will be tried before an administrative law judge (ALJ). The decision of the ALJ is reviewable by the NLRB, which may adopt, modify, or reverse the decision. The NLRB's decision is in turn appealable to a federal appellate court and, ultimately, to the U.S. Supreme Court.

INTERFERENCE WITH PROTECTED ACTIVITIES

Section 8(a)(1) of the NLRA makes it illegal for an employer to interfere with, restrain, or coerce employees in the exercise of their Section 7 rights to organize and bargain collectively and to engage in other protected, concerted activities. This prohibition covers a wide range of employer conduct, including (1) threatening employees with any adverse action for organizing or supporting a union, (2) promising employees any benefits if they abandon support for a union, (3) interrogating employees about union sentiment or activity, and (4) engaging in surveillance of employees' union activities. For example, an employer may not threaten to shut down its business or to take away benefits if the union wins a representation election. Similarly, an employer may not interrogate employees about whether they have signed a union representation card or ask about the union activities of other employees.

In 2000, the NLRB held the world's largest pork-processing plant liable for "egregious and pervasive" violations of the labor laws after managers threatened and improperly interrogated employees about their involvement with a union during two unionizing campaigns.[9] The illegal actions included trying to scare the many Hispanic workers by claiming that the union would report workers to the Immigration and Naturalization Service and warning of layoffs and a possible plant closing if the employees joined the union. The plant's general manager had positioned county sheriff deputies in the plant parking lot on the day of the union

---

9. Smithfield Packing Co., Inc. v. United Food & Commercial Workers Union, 2000 N.L.R.B. LEXIS 905 (Dec. 15, 2000).

election to intimidate workers, and one employee was assaulted in retaliation for his effort to unionize.[10]

Section 8(a)(1) also prohibits an employer from enforcing an overly broad rule against soliciting other employees (perhaps for union support) or distributing literature on company premises. In general, an employer may prohibit solicitation or distribution of literature by employees on company property only during work time. It is not yet clear whether an employer must give employees access to the employer's electronic mail system for solicitation and distribution of information.

Nonemployee union organizers do not have the same rights as employees to solicit and distribute literature. The U.S. Supreme Court held in *Lechmere, Inc. v. NLRB*[11] that, except in very limited circumstances, nonemployee union organizers have no right to trespass on an employer's private property for the purpose of communicating with and organizing employees. *Lechmere* involved the efforts of a union to gain access to a parking lot partially owned by a retail store. The Court reasoned that although employees have an unrestricted right to organize themselves, nonemployees are not afforded the same protection unless the employees are inaccessible because they live on the employer's property. Because the employees did not live on the store's property, the store could ban nonemployee labor organizers from its parking lot.

Sometimes a union will pay individuals to seek work with a nonunion employer with the intent of having them organize the other workers once hired. This practice is often referred to as *salting*. In *NLRB v. Town & Country Electric, Inc.*,[12] the U.S. Supreme Court upheld the

10. Kevin Sack, *Judge Finds Labor Law Broken at Meat-Packing Plant*, N.Y. TIMES, Jan. 4, 2001.
11. 502 U.S. 527 (1992).

12. 516 U.S. 85 (1995).

VIEW FROM CYBERSPACE

Union Access *to the* Cyber Water Cooler

In general, companies can restrict employee access to their computer networks, but unions may deserve an exception if a company's electronic mail system is deemed equivalent to the physical work spaces to which unions have historically been allowed access. In 1997, the NLRB's general counsel office issued a memo stating that a company cannot issue a complete ban on all nonbusiness use of e-mail that would include employee messages protected by federal labor law. Comparing an e-mail to the telephone, the NLRB memo stated that, "e-mail allows a reader to talk back. This ability to exchange ideas and discuss what action to take collectively is the key to effective preservation of labor rights and the equalization of bargaining power." The NLRB declared that Pratt & Whitney's policy of banning use of its e-mail system for nonbusiness activities was overly broad and illegal;[a] the company then issued a memo stating that employees could use e-mail to discuss the "terms and conditions of employment and the employee's interest in self-organization."[b]

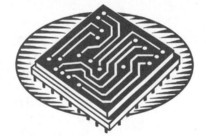

An NLRB case pending in February 2001 may shed further light on this issue. In September 2000, the employee newspaper guild of the *Washington Post* sent an e-mail bulletin to its 1,300 members, arguing that *Post* employees should receive compensation for their work on the newspaper's Web site. The *Post* wrote a letter to the guild, ordering it to cease distributing literature via e-mail and to distribute material only on designated bulletin boards and other sites. The guild filed an unfair labor practice charge against the newspaper on December 13, 2000, arguing that the *Post*'s computer network is a gathering place for *Post* workers—a cyber water cooler where employees exchange information.[c] A decision was expected in 2001.

In similar disputes, the NLRB has supported employees' rights to use a company's e-mail system for voicing complaints about their employer. In *Timekeeping Systems, Inc.*,[d] the NLRB ruled that an employee who criticized the employer's new vacation policy in an e-mail sent via the company's system was engaged in activity protected under the NLRA, even though the company had no union and the employee was not trying to start one.[e]

a. *Electronic Communication Raises Issues over Rights of Workers, Unions, Employers*, 68 U.S.L.W. 2488 (Feb. 22, 2000).
b. Michael J. McCarthy, *Sympathetic Ear, Your Manager's Policy on Employees' E-Mail May Have a Weak Spot*, WALL ST. J., Apr. 25, 2000, at A1.
c. Greg Miller, *Guild Pushes to Use Paper's E-Mail System to Reach Workers: Labor Union Leader Calls Computer Network a 'Modern-Day Water Cooler.' Management Sees Violation of Contract*, WALL ST. J., Dec. 25, 2000, at C1.
d. 323 N.L.R.B. No. 30 (1997).
e. McCarthy, *supra* note b.

NLRB's position that such job applicants are employees protected by the NLRA despite their union affiliation and intentions. In response to the employer's claim that under agency law a servant cannot have two masters, the Court reasoned that as long as service to one does not lead to the abandonment of obligations owed to another, there is no conflict. The Court also rejected the employer's assertion that a worker being paid by a union is, by definition, disloyal, because there was no indication that salted employees were any more likely to undermine the interests of the company than other employees. As a result, the employer had violated the NLRA by firing and refusing to interview individuals paid by a union solely on the basis of their union activities.

Town & Country was a blow to nonunion contractors, who have since been lobbying Congress to pass anti-salting legislation.[13] Although legislation to amend the NLRA to prohibit salting abuses was introduced into Congress in 1998 and thereafter, as of early 2001, no anti-salting legislation had been enacted into law.[14]

Even though a salted worker is considered an employee for purposes of the NLRA, an employer may still refuse to hire a full-time union organizer on the basis of a general company rule against hiring individuals with full-time jobs. Refusing to hire individuals with full-time jobs constitutes a legitimate, nondiscriminatory reason for refusing to hire an applicant, provided the rule is applied and was promulgated in a nondiscriminatory manner.[15]

Section 8(a)(1) also protects employees who engage in concerted activities for mutual aid and protection. For example, an employer may not retaliate against a group of employees who approach management and complain about some aspect of their working conditions, such as poor lighting or uncomfortable temperatures in the workplace. For an activity to be *concerted*, it must be "engaged in with or on the authority of other employees, and not solely by and on behalf of the employee himself."[16] The NLRB will find a violation of the NLRA only when (1) the employer knows of the concerted nature of the employee's activity; (2) the concerted activity is protected by the NLRA; and (3) the discipline at issue is in retaliation for the employee's protected, concerted activity.

13. *Supreme Court Speaks,* 66 U.S.L.W. 2292 (Nov. 18, 1997).
14. *See* John E. Higgins, *Firms Can Take Protective Measures Against 'Salting,'* KANSAS CITY BUS. J., Nov. 5, 1999, at 14.
15. Architectural Glass & Metal Co. v. NLRB, 107 F.3d 426 (6th Cir. 1997).
16. Meyers Indus., 268 N.L.R.B. 493, 497 (1984), *remanded sub nom.* Prill v. NLRB, 755 F.2d 941 (D.C. Cir. 1985), *cert. denied,* 474 U.S. 971 (1985).

ETHICAL CONSIDERATION

Should a manager honor a request by a nonunion employee to have another individual present at an investigatory interview?

In *NLRB v. Weingarten, Inc.,*[17] the U.S. Supreme Court held that an employer may not deny a union employee's request that a union representative be present at an investigatory interview. The Court ruled that an employee's seeking the assistance of a union representative at a confrontation with the employer clearly falls within the literal wording of Section 7, which gives employees the right to engage in concerted activities for the purpose of mutual aid and protection. The employee sought "aid or protection" against a perceived threat to her employment security.

DOMINATION OF A LABOR ORGANIZATION

Under Section 8(a)(2) of the NLRA, an employer may not dominate or assist a labor organization. The employer may not instigate, encourage, or directly participate in the formation of a labor organization, nor may it give financial support to a labor organization. An employer also may not attempt to influence the making of union policy. Supervisors may not serve as union officials or on a union bargaining team. An employer may not recognize a union as the bargaining representative of a unit of employees when a majority of its employees do not support the union. These provisions were enacted to prevent an employer from helping a compliant organization become the representative of its employees and then imposing a "sweetheart" collective bargaining contract— that is, a contract unduly favorable to the employer.

The U.S. Court of Appeals for the Seventh Circuit held that an employer that created and maintained employee "action committees" violated the NLRA because they constituted representational labor organizations dominated by management.[18] Management created the committees to develop solutions to employee dissatisfaction with attendance and pay policies. Unlike independent employee participation organizations, the committees at issue had their structures, duration, and subject matter defined by management, and they included at least one member of management. Similarly, the U.S. Court of Appeals for the Sixth Circuit upheld a determination by the NLRB that an employer-created "plant council," with

17. 420 U.S. 251 (1975).
18. Electromation, Inc. v. NLRB, 35 F.3d 1148 (7th Cir. 1997).

ETHICAL CONSIDERATION

The law prevents an employer from attempting to escape its collective bargaining obligation by shutting down a unionized operation and moving the functions of that former operation to a nearby site. This violation, known as a *runaway shop,* is to be distinguished from an employer's decision to close a unionized facility permanently without transferring its functions elsewhere. Is this a fair distinction?

three of eight members representing management, which met on company property during working hours, was a company-dominated labor organization.[19]

DISCRIMINATION AGAINST UNION SUPPORTERS

Section 8(a)(3) prohibits employers from discriminating against any employee to encourage or discourage membership in any labor organization. If an employee has been unlawfully discharged, the NLRB may order that the employee be reinstated and given full back pay.

A common Section 8(a)(3) allegation is that a worker was discharged for attempting to organize fellow employees. To prove a violation of Section 8(a)(3), the NLRB must prove that the employee's Section 7 conduct was a substantial motivating factor in the discharge. To escape liability, the employer must then show by a preponderance of the evidence that the employee would have been discharged for legitimate reasons regardless of the protected activity.[20] If the alleged business reason is a pretext, intended to cover up an unlawful discharge, then the employer has violated Section 8(a)(3).

Section 8(a)(3) permits a union and an employer to incorporate a *union security clause* into a collective bargaining contract. Such a clause requires, as a condition of employment, that employees in the collective bargaining unit either become members of the union after a certain period of time or pay fees to the union equivalent to the periodic union dues. The laws of a number of states forbid union security clauses.

In *Communications Workers of America v. Beck,*[21] the U.S. Supreme Court held that employees in a represented unit who are not union members need pay only those fees necessary for the union to perform its activities related to collective bargaining, contract administra-

tion, and grievance adjustment. Thus, a union cannot use a union security clause to require nonunion employees to pay fees expended on (1) organizing employees of other employers; (2) lobbying for labor legislation; or (3) participating in social, charitable, and political events. In contrast, union members (as opposed to nonmembers) may be required to pay the entire dues amount.[22] The union is required to inform employees of their rights under *Beck.* If the union does not provide an employee with notice of his or her rights, it commits an unfair labor practice.[23]

DISCRIMINATION AGAINST EMPLOYEES WHO FILE CHARGES

Under Section 8(a)(4) of the NLRA, it is an unfair labor practice for an employer to discharge or otherwise discriminate against an employee because he or she has filed charges with, or given testimony to, the NLRB, either in a representation proceeding or pursuant to an unfair labor practice charge.

FAILURE TO BARGAIN IN GOOD FAITH

Section 8(a)(5) of the NLRA imposes upon unionized employers a duty to bargain collectively. For example, the employer must be willing to meet union representatives at reasonable times to bargain over the conditions of employment. A related provision, Section 8(d), requires employers to bargain in good faith, that is, to approach negotiations with an honest and serious intent to engage in give-and-take bargaining in an attempt to reach an agreement. The obligation to bargain in good faith does not, however, compel either party to agree to a proposal or to make concessions. The examination of whether an employer has bargained in good faith is difficult because it involves determining the employer's subjective frame of mind. The NLRB will look at all of the surrounding circumstances, including the employer's willingness to negotiate and its conduct at the bargaining table.

In *NLRB v. General Electric Co.,*[24] the U.S. Court of Appeals for the Second Circuit held that General Electric did not bargain in good faith when it adopted a take-it-or-leave-it posture, announcing when it made its offer to the union that it would hold nothing back, but also saying that it would hold firmly to its offer and not engage

19. Webcor Packaging, Inc. v. NLRB, 118 F.3d 1115 (6th Cir. 1997), *cert. denied,* 522 U.S. 1108 (1998).
20. NLRB v. Transportation Mgt. Corp., 462 U.S. 393 (1983).
21. 487 U.S. 735 (1988).

22. Monson Trucking, Inc., 324 N.L.R.B. 933 (1997).
23. *NLRB Renews Support for* Beck *Notice, but Gould Favors Broad Nationwide Remedy,* 66 U.S.L.W. 2329 (Dec. 2, 1997).
24. 418 F.2d 736 (2d Cir. 1969), *cert. denied,* 397 U.S. 965 (1970).

in give-and-take bargaining. The court concluded that GE's well-publicized policy of firmness tended to back the company into an inflexible position and to establish in the minds of employees the idea that the union was unnecessary.

If an employer does not bargain in good faith, a union may seek an injunction against unfair labor practices from the NLRB. During the Reagan and Bush administrations, injunctions were rarely issued. Under the Clinton administration, the NLRB was more active and much more willing to issue injunctions to jump-start collective bargaining efforts.[25] Indeed, during the Clinton administration the number of injunctions jumped from 35 per year to approximately 140.

25. Richard C. Reuben, *Baseball Strike Teaches Legal Lessons: Lawyers Should Reassess Strategies, Avoid Animosities in Negotiations*, A.B.A. J., June 1995, at 42.

Implementation after Impasse The duty to bargain collectively in good faith prohibits an employer from unilaterally changing some term or condition of employment unless, after bargaining with the union to an impasse, the employer makes unilateral changes that are "reasonably comprehended" within its pre-impasse proposals and are consistent with the offers the union has rejected. Thus, the employer cannot implement changes that are substantially different from any it had proposed during its negotiations.[26] This is the *implementation-after-impasse doctrine.*

In the following case, the court analyzed an employer's attempt to unilaterally implement several specific terms and conditions of employment when the parties had reached an impasse on a particular issue but not on the collective bargaining agreement as a whole.

26. *See, e.g.,* Loral Defense Sys.–Akron v. NLRB, 200 F.3d 436 (6th Cir. 1999).

A CASE IN POINT

CASE 16.2

Visiting Nurses Services of Western Massachusetts, Inc. v. National Labor Relations Board

United States Court of Appeals for the First Circuit 177 F.3d 52 (1st Cir. 1999), cert. denied, 528 U.S. 1074 (2000).

Summary

FACTS The Visiting Nurses Services of Western Massachusetts, Inc. (VNS) provides home-based nursing services. After the collective bargaining agreement between VNS and the Service Employees International Union expired on October 31, 1992, the parties attempted to negotiate a successor agreement. VNS offered several written proposals, but they were only partially accepted by the union. Specifically, the union objected to VNS's proposal for a change from a weekly to a biweekly payroll system.

On June 18, 1996, VNS presented another proposal that included a 2 percent wage increase and a job classification change previously proposed by the union. The proposal also included three new provisions: (1) the transformation of three scheduled holidays into "floating" holidays, (2) the implementation of a "clinical ladders" program, and (3) the adoption of an enterostomal therapist classification and program. The VNS also offered an alternative proposal, the mini package, which included many of the same changes as the other proposal. The parties were unable to reach an agreement on either of these proposals.

On August 20, 1996, VNS advised the union that it was contemplating implementing the mini package. The union responded by stating that it opposed the unilateral implementation of these proposals. Despite this protest, VNS sent a memorandum to the bargaining unit employees, but not to the union, informing them that it had implemented the mini package. VNS argued that all of the changes in the proposal were positive terms that would enhance the staff's economic conditions while bargaining continued.

The union filed a charge with the NLRB, which found that VNS had violated the NLRA by unilaterally implementing the proposed changes while it was still bargaining with the union and without reaching a general impasse. VNS appealed.

ISSUE PRESENTED Can an employer that has not reached a general impasse on a package of collective bargaining issues take unilateral action on particular issues after declaring an impasse was reached on those specific issues?

SUMMARY OF OPINION The U.S. Court of Appeals for the First Circuit began by stating that when parties are engaged in negotiations for a collective bargaining

(Continued)

(Case 16.2 continued)

agreement, an employer's obligation to refrain from making unilateral changes encompasses a duty to refain from implementing changes absent an overall impasse on bargaining for the agreement as a whole. The two exceptions to this rule are (1) when a union, in response to an employer's diligent and earnest efforts to engage in bargaining, insists on continually avoiding or delaying bargaining; or (2) when economic exigencies or business emergencies compel prompt action.

The court rejected VNS's position that the parties were at an impasse because the union did not accept the employer's position on a particular issue. If an employer could implement changes based on impasse as to one issue, then the employer would be able to remove issues from the table, one by one, and thereby impair the parties' ability to reach an overall agreement through compromise on particular items. Ultimately, an employer could implement all of the changes it desired regardless of the state of negotiations between the company and the union. The court also stated that such a process would undermine the union's role by implying that the union lacked the power to keep issues on the table. The court did acknowledge that there may be situations where one or two issues dominate and drive the collective bargaining negotiations to such an extent that the NLRB would be justified in finding that impasse on those one or two issues amounts to a bargaining deadlock, but the court concluded that that was not the situation here.

RESULT Because the parties had not reached an impasse on the agreement as a whole, VNS had to bargain to impasse before making a unilateral change. The NLRB's decision was upheld.

Bargaining Subjects The duty to bargain in good faith also requires employers to bargain over certain subjects. There are three categories of bargaining subjects: mandatory, permissible, and illegal. Employers must bargain over mandatory subjects—those that vitally affect the terms and conditions of employment, such as wages and work hours. Employers may, but are not obligated to, bargain over permissible subjects. Employers must not bargain over illegal subjects.

There has been much litigation over which subjects are mandatory. In the following case, the Supreme Court considered whether an employer must bargain over a decision to close part of its operations.

A CASE IN POINT

CASE 16.3

First National Maintenance Corp. v. National Labor Relations Board
Supreme Court of the United States
452 U.S. 666 (1981).

Summary

FACTS First National Maintenance Corporation was engaged in the business of providing housekeeping, cleaning, maintenance, and related services for commercial customers. Following a dispute with a nursing home over fees, First National terminated its contract with that customer and discharged the employees who worked there. The union representing those employees requested bargaining over the decision to terminate the contract. After First National refused, the union claimed that the employer's refusal breached its duty to bargain in good faith.

ISSUE PRESENTED Does an employer need to bargain over a decision to shut down part of its business for purely economic reasons?

SUMMARY OF OPINION The U.S. Supreme Court stated that Congress did not intend that the union would become an equal partner with the employer in the running of the business enterprise. An employer must bargain over a decision only if bargaining would "promote the fundamental purpose of the Act by bringing a problem of vital con-

(Continued)

(Case 16.3 continued)

cern to labor and management within the framework established by Congress as most conducive to industrial peace." An employer needs to make certain decisions fundamental to its operation without the encumbrance of the collective bargaining obligation. The Court concluded that bargaining over management decisions that have a substantial impact on the continued availability of employment should be required only if the benefit, for labor–management relations and the collective bargaining process, outweighs the burden placed on the conduct of the business.

RESULT The Supreme Court ruled that an employer is not required to bargain over every business decision that it makes.

COMMENTS Even though an employer may not be required to bargain over a decision to close part of its operations for economic reasons, the employer will be required to bargain with the union over the effects of such a decision on employees represented by the union. Moreover, the Supreme Court in *First National Maintenance* explicitly limited its holding to "partial closings" accomplished for economic reasons and stated that it was not expressing a view as to other management decisions, including plant relocations, sales, or other kinds of subcontracting or automation. Finally, bargaining over a management decision to close or modify operations may be required when the decision hinges on labor costs over which the union has some control.

In 1989, the NLRB ruled that drug testing of current employees injured while on the job is a mandatory subject of bargaining.[27] By requiring testing, an employer could change the method by which it would investigate possible employee responsibility for accidents and the character of proof on which an employee's job security might depend.

In a companion case, *Star Tribune*,[28] the NLRB ruled that the employer, a daily newspaper, did not violate the NLRA by failing to bargain over the implementation of a mandatory drug- and alcohol-testing policy for job applicants. The NLRB noted that such testing would not vitally affect either workplace safety or the terms and conditions of employment for current employees represented by the union. Thus, preemployment testing of applicants was not a mandatory subject of bargaining.

In *Air Line Pilots Ass'n v. Northwest Airlines, Inc.*,[29] the D.C. Circuit considered whether imposition of an arbitration clause, requiring that airplane pilots submit all claims against the airline arising from the employment relationship to binding arbitration, was a mandatory subject of bargaining. The Air Line Pilots Association (ALPA) is the union that represents Northwest pilots in collective bargaining. When a new pilot first begins training, he or she is not represented by the ALPA or any other union. The pilot becomes a member of the union when he or she completes training and becomes a probationary employee. Northwest had unilaterally required training pilots to agree to certain conditions as part of their employment contracts. Some of these conditions continued to apply even after the pilots became members of the ALPA. As one of these conditions, the pilots agreed to arbitrate any employment disputes. When the ALPA learned of this condition imposed by Northwest, it filed suit against the company, alleging that Northwest had unilaterally implemented the condition, a mandatory subject of bargaining, without first negotiating with the union. The court disagreed and ruled that Northwest could propose the arbitration clause directly to each individual employee because the employment contract was not inconsistent with the collective bargaining agreement with the ALPA and did not constitute an unfair labor practice.

PUBLIC POLICY

Courts will not enforce a collective bargaining agreement that is contrary to public policy.[30] Any such policy must be explicit, well defined, and dominant, and it must

27. Johnson-Bateman Co., 295 N.L.R.B. 180 (1989).
28. 295 N.L.R.B. 63 (1989).
29. 199 F.3d 477 (D.C. Cir. 1999), *cert. denied*, 121 S. Ct. 565 (2000).

30. W.R. Grace v. Rubber Workers, 461 U.S. 757 (1983).

be "ascertained by reference to the laws and legal precedents, not from general considerations of supposed public interests."[31] In the following case, the U.S. Supreme

31. *Id.* at 766.

Court considered whether enforcement of an arbitrator's decision requiring reinstatement of an employee who twice tested positive for marijuana was barred by public policy.

A CASE IN POINT

CASE 16.4

Eastern Associated Coal Corp. v. United Mine Workers of America
Supreme Court of the United States
121 S. Ct. 462 (2000).

In the Language of the Court

FACTS Eastern Associated Coal Corporation and the United Mine Workers of America were parties to a collective bargaining agreement requiring binding arbitration of disputes. The agreement provided that Eastern could not discharge employees without "just cause."

James Smith was employed as a truck driver for Eastern. In that position, he was subject to the Department of Transportation (DOT) regulations requiring random drug testing of workers performing "safety-sensitive" tasks. After Smith tested positive for marijuana in March 1996, Eastern sought to terminate his employment. The union challenged Eastern's right to fire Smith, and the dispute was submitted to binding arbitration. The arbitrator determined that Smith's positive drug test was not just cause to fire him and ordered that Smith be suspended without pay for thirty days, be compelled to participate in a substance-abuse program, and undergo drug testing by Eastern for the next five years.

Between April 1996 and January 1997, Smith passed four random drug tests. In July 1997, he again tested positive for marijuana, and Eastern again attempted to fire him. The union went to arbitration, and once again, the arbitrator concluded that there was not just cause to fire Smith. The arbitrator ordered that Smith (1) be suspended without pay for approximately three months, (2) continue to participate in a substance-abuse program, (3) undergo random drug testing, (4) provide Eastern with a signed letter of resignation to take effect if he tested positive within the next five years, and (5) reimburse Eastern for the costs of the arbitration.

Eastern sought to vacate the decision on the grounds that it violated the public policy against the operation of dangerous machinery by workers who test positive for drugs.

ISSUE PRESENTED Is an arbitration award ordering an employer to reinstate an employee truck driver who twice tested positive for marijuana unenforceable as a violation of public policy?

OPINION BREYER, J., writing for the U.S. Supreme Court:

Eastern asserts that a public policy against reinstatement of workers who use drugs can be discerned from an examination of . . . the Omnibus Transportation Employee Testing Act of 1991 and DOT's implementing regulations. The Testing Act embodies a congressional finding that "the greatest efforts must be expended to eliminate the . . . use of illegal drugs, whether on or off duty, by those individuals who are involved in [certain safety-sensitive positions, including] the operation of . . . trucks." . . .

In Eastern's view, these provisions embody a strong public policy against drug use by transportation workers in safety-sensitive positions and in favor of random drug testing in order to detect that use. Eastern argues that reinstatement of a driver who has twice failed random drug tests would undermine that policy—to the point where a judge must set aside an employer-union agreement requiring reinstatement.

Eastern's argument, however, loses much of its force when one considers further provisions of the Act that make clear that the Act's remedial aims are complex. The

(Continued)

(Case 16.4 continued)

Act says that "rehabilitation is a critical component of any testing program," that rehabilitation "should be made available to individuals, as appropriate," and that DOT must promulgate regulations for "rehabilitation programs." The DOT regulations specifically state that a driver who has tested positive for drugs cannot return to a safety-sensitive position until (1) the driver has been evaluated by a "substance abuse professional" to determine if treatment is needed; (2) the substance-abuse professional has certified that the driver has followed any rehabilitation program prescribed; and (3) the driver has passed a return-to-duty drug test. In addition, (4) the driver must be subject to at least six random drug tests during the first year after returning to the job. Neither the Act nor the regulations forbid an employer to reinstate in a safety-sensitive position an employee who fails a random drug test once or twice. The congressional and regulatory directives require only that the above-stated prerequisites to reinstatement be met.

...

We believe that these expressions of positive law embody several relevant policies. As Eastern points out, these policies include Testing Act policies against drug use by employees in safety-sensitive transportation positions and in favor of drug testing. They also include a Testing Act policy favoring rehabilitation of employees who use drugs. And the relevant statutory and regulatory provisions must be read in light of background labor law policy that favors determination of disciplinary questions through arbitration when chosen as a result of labor-management negotiation.

The award before us is not contrary to these several policies, taken together. The award does not condone Smith's conduct or ignore the risk to public safety that drug use by truck drivers may pose. Rather, the award punishes Smith by suspending him for three months, thereby depriving him of nearly $9,000 in lost wages; it requires him to pay the arbitration costs of both sides; it insists upon further substance-abuse treatment and testing; and it makes clear (by requiring Smith to provide a signed letter of resignation) that one more failed test means discharge.

...

. . . Neither Congress nor the Secretary [of Transportation] has seen fit to mandate the discharge of a worker who twice tests positive for drugs. We hesitate to infer a public policy in this area that goes beyond the careful and detailed scheme Congress and the Secretary have created.

RESULT The Supreme Court held that considerations of public policy did not require the Court to refuse to enforce the arbitration award. Eastern did not have just cause to terminate Smith.

QUESTIONS

1. What public policy is served by enforcing the arbitrator's decision?
2. What could Eastern have done differently to avoid having to retain an employee who had twice tested positive for drugs?

PRESUMPTION OF MAJORITY SUPPORT

A union certified by the NLRB as the bargaining agent for a unit of employees enjoys an *irrebuttable presumption* of majority support for one year. The union's support may not be questioned during that time, and the employer may not refuse to bargain with it. Such a refusal is a *per se violation* of the NLRA, that is, a violation in itself, without the need for proof of any further misconduct. After the first year, the employer may rebut the presumption of majority support by showing either that (1) the union does not in fact have majority support or that (2) the employer has a good faith doubt of the union's majority support.

When an employer replaces striking employees, the question arises as to whether the replacements support or oppose the incumbent union. The NLRB has followed a no-presumption approach and ruled that the replacements' union sentiments should be decided on a case-by-case basis. The U.S. Supreme Court approved that approach in *NLRB v. Curtin Matheson Scientific, Inc.*,[32] in which it found that the NLRB need not assume that workers who replace striking workers are anti-union. The Court noted that an anti-union presumption could allow an employer to eliminate the union entirely merely by hiring a sufficient number of replacement employees. The Court concluded that the NLRB's adoption of a case-by-case approach was rational, was consistent with the NLRA's policy of maintaining

32. 494 U.S. 775 (1990).

INTERNATIONAL CONSIDERATION

Managers with operations outside the United States need to consider the labor-relations laws of the foreign countries where they have employees. Trade unions, often more active than in the United States, commonly work more closely with management. For example, at Germany's Volkswagen plants, trade union representatives sit on special work councils that approve or reject company changes in production. Work councils typically represent all workers in an establishment, whether or not they are unionized.

Indeed, Germany's co-determination laws require most large German corporations to have a supervisory board elected by both the shareholders and the employees and union representatives. The supervisory board in turn selects the management board, which consists of the officers responsible for managing the corporation. DaimlerChrysler, the German corporation that resulted from the merger of Big Three automaker Chrysler Corporation in the United States and Daimler-Benz AG in Germany, has such a corporate governance structure.

By contrast, Chile provides very little protection for labor organizing. Workers must organize within individual companies, rather than across industries, and many blatant anti-union tactics outlawed in the United States are perfectly legal.[a]

a. Matt Moffett, *Pinochet's Legacy: Chile's Labor Law Hobbles Its Workers and Troubles the U.S.*, WALL ST. J., Oct. 15, 1997, at A1.

industrial peace, protected the bargaining process, and preserved employees' rights to engage in protected activity.

Lawful *and* Unlawful Strikes

Lawful strikes are of two kinds: economic strikes and unfair labor practice strikes. Other types of strikes violate the NLRA.

ECONOMIC STRIKES

Unions often strike employers when they are unable to extract acceptable terms and conditions of employment through collective bargaining. An employer subjected to an *economic strike* is permitted to hire permanent replacements for the striking employees. If it does so, the employer need not rehire striking employees who offer to return to work, unless the departure of the replacements creates vacancies. If vacancies are later created by the departure of strike replacements, then the company must reinstate striking workers who make unconditional offers to return to work.[33]

The U.S. Court of Appeals for the District of Columbia Circuit upheld an employer's right to replace striking employees without adverse consequences, even against an executive order by President Bill Clinton barring federal agencies from contracting with employers that permanently replace striking workers.[34] The court held that the executive order illegitimately impinged upon the NLRB's specific policy provision to the contrary.

Even when a vacancy occurs, an employer may not be required to reinstate a striking employee, if (1) the former striker has secured regular and equivalent employment elsewhere; or (2) the employer has legitimate and substantial business reasons, such as the striker's lack of necessary skills; or (3) the striker has committed sufficiently serious misconduct during the strike.

UNFAIR LABOR PRACTICE STRIKES

Workers sometimes strike an employer wholly or partly to protest an unfair labor practice. For example, a union may strike because it believes that the employer is not bargaining in good faith. Workers who engage in such an

33. Laidlaw Corp. v. NLRB, 414 F.2d 99 (7th Cir. 1969), *cert. denied*, 397 U.S. 920 (1970).
34. Chamber of Commerce v. Reich, 74 F.3d 1322 (D.C. Cir. 1996).

"O.K. guys, now lets go and <u>earn</u> that four hundred times our workers' salaries."

unfair labor practice strike have a right to be reinstated to their former positions if they make an unconditional offer to return to work. If the employer refuses to rehire them, the NLRB may award them reinstatement plus back pay. This difference between the rights of economic strikers and those of unfair labor practice strikers can give rise to disputes as to whether the employer committed an unfair labor practice and whether the strike was called to protest that practice.

UNLAWFUL STRIKES

The NLRA prohibits certain kinds of *organizational strikes* or picketing (whose purpose is to organize employees) and certain kinds of *recognitional strikes* (whose purpose is to force the employer to recognize the union as a collective bargaining agent for its employees). It also outlaws certain *secondary boycotts,* strikes called against an outside company to induce it to put pressure (usually by withholding business) on the employer with whom the union has a dispute.

In *Warshawsky & Co. v. NLRB,*[35] the U.S. Court of Appeals for the District of Columbia Circuit held that Ironworkers Local 386 engaged in a secondary boycott when its members distributed handbills, which stated that a subcontractor paid substandard wages and benefits, to employees of a neutral contractor and subcontractor as they drove into the construction site. The court rejected the argument that barring the union from distributing the handbill violated its First Amendment rights. Language in the handbill, stating that the union was "appealing only to the general public. We are not seeking any person to cease work or to stop making deliveries," was inadequate to keep the distribution from being deemed a secondary boycott.

A strike may also be unlawful if it is unduly disruptive. In the following case, the court considered whether a walkout by employees was a reasonable means of protesting the firing of their well-liked supervisor.

35. 182 F.3d 948 (D.C. Cir. 1999), *cert. denied,* 120 S. Ct. 1267 (2000).

A CASE IN POINT

CASE 16.5

Bob Evans Farms, Inc. v. National Labor Relations Board

United States Court of Appeals for the Seventh Circuit 163 F.3d 1012 (7th Cir. 1998).

In the Language of the Court

FACTS Diane Gorrell was first assistant manager at the Bob Evans restaurant in East Peoria, Illinois. She was in charge of the night shift and had a close relationship with the employees she supervised. Mark Weaver, a second assistant manager, was in charge of the night shift on Gorrell's days off. On October 15, 1995, Weaver was having difficulty supervising the shift, and two of the employees telephoned Gorrell for assistance. She came in, took over, and restored order. Shortly before closing time for the restaurant, Gorrell initiated a pizza party, which turned into a raucous food fight. At aproximately 4:00 A.M., the party moved to Gorrell's house. Two hours later, an inebriated Gorrell left to attend a management meeting with Dave Ward, the Bob Evans area director.

At Gorrell's next scheduled shift, she was fired for her behavior on the evening of October 15. As she left the restaurant, she told several employees that her employment had just been terminated. Within a few minutes, fifteen employees had walked off the job and gathered outside the restaurant to encourage prospective customers to dine elsewhere. Subsequently, all but one of the employees offered to return to work. Bob Evans refused to reinstate them because they had abandoned their jobs, leaving the restaurant in dire straits on what was characteristically one of its busiest shifts. In addition, two employees, fed up with the difficult working conditions resulting from the walk-out, quit, thereby exacerbating an already chaotic situation.

Gorrell filed an unfair labor practice charge with the NLRB on behalf of the employees who had gone on strike. The NLRB ordered Bob Evans to offer the employees full reinstatement to their former positions, to compensate them for any losses sustained, and to remove any evidence of the incident from their files. Bob Evans appealed.

ISSUE PRESENTED Was the walkout a reasonable means of protest protected by the NLRA?

OPINION CUDAHY, J., writing for the U.S. Court of Appeals for the Seventh Circuit:

Concerted activity is generally protected under the Act provided it is conducted "for the purpose of mutual aid and protection." This has been interpreted to mean that the underlying dispute must relate to the terms and conditions of work. . . . [I]t is generally accepted that the hiring and firing of supervisory personnel is a managerial action unrelated to the terms and conditions of the work of non-supervisory employees. . . .

In holding that Gorrell's termination was a special case, the Board relied on a narrow but well recognized exception to the general rule: concerted activity over the firing of a supervisor is protected when the identity and capabilities of the supervisor have a direct impact on the employees' own job interests and work performance. . . .

. . .

. . . [T]he right to disrupt is not unbridled and is tempered by an inherent proportionality requirement. Common sense dictates that an employer cannot object to a strike on grounds of mere inconvenience but that, at the other extreme, employees cannot run an employer out of business solely to make known a minor grievance. . . .

. . . [W]e reject the Board's contention that concerted activities can take any form and reassert the approach adopted by the majority of the courts which have confronted the issue, namely, that the reasonableness of the means of protest is one of a variety of factors that are examined in order to determine whether employee activity is protected. . . . [T]he Act does not protect employees who protest a legitimate grievance by recourse to unduly and disproportionately disruptive or intemperate means.

. . . When they walked out of the restaurant en masse at the start of a busy Friday evening shift, Gorrell's underlings surely strayed into the realm of unprotected ac-

(Continued)

(Case 16.5 continued)

tivity. The walkout had the immediate effect of crippling the restaurant's ability to function at what was characteristically a particularly busy time. The employees must have been aware of the consequences that were likely to flow from their actions and could have resorted to less disruptive forms of concerted action in order to register their dissatisfaction over Gorrell's dismissal. . . . There is substantial evidence to suggest that their unduly disruptive walkout bore no reasonable relation to their grievance and necessarily lost them the protection of the Act.

RESULT The court denied enforcement of the Board's order. Bob Evans had no obligation to reinstate the employees to their jobs.

QUESTIONS

1. Would a strike ever be a proper response to the firing of a supervisor?
2. Would it be legal for an insurance company to discharge two insurance sales representatives for drafting a letter recommending that management promote the assistant cashier to the post of cashier?[36]

36. *See* NLRB v. Phoenix Mut. Life Ins. Co., 167 F.2d 983 (7th Cir. 1948).

Organizational Strikes Section 8(b)(7) of the NLRA prohibits organizational or recognitional strikes or picketing when (1) the employer has already lawfully recognized another labor organization as the representative of its employees unless the union can properly raise a question concerning that representation; (2) the NLRB has conducted a representation election under the NLRA within the preceding twelve months; or (3) the union has not filed a petition for a representation election within a reasonable period of time, not to exceed thirty days, from the date picketing commenced.

Recognitional Strikes Section 8(b)(4)(i)(C) of the NLRA makes it unlawful for a labor organization to induce employees (for example, through picketing) to engage in a work stoppage to force the employer to recognize a labor organization if another labor organization has been certified as the employees' representative.

Secondary Boycotts Section 8(b)(4) of the NLRA was enacted primarily to address the problem of a union unfairly involving neutral employers, with whom the union has no quarrel, in a labor dispute. Section 8(b)(4)(B) makes it illegal for a union to engage in or encourage a strike with the object of forcing any person to cease handling the products of an employer or to cease doing business with that employer.

Section 8(b)(4)(B) allegations arise quite commonly in the construction industry, where a number of employers often work on a single construction site. A union

that has a dispute with one of those employers may picket the entire job site, hoping to shut down the work completely and thereby put maximum pressure on that employer. Employers have countered this tactic by directing the employees and vendors of the *primary employer,* that is, the employer with whom the union has a dispute, to use a gate that is physically separated from the gate to be used by all other persons. Under this arrangement, known as the *neutral-gate system,* the union may picket only at the gate reserved for the employees and vendors of the primary employer.

⚘ Non-Strike-Related Unfair Labor Practices *by* Unions

Section 8(b) of the NLRA specifies several activities, besides unlawful strikes, in which unions may not engage.

COERCION OF EMPLOYEES

Section 8(b)(1)(A) of the NLRA prohibits unions from coercing employees to join the union or to support its activities. For example, a union may not attempt to intimidate employees into voting for it in a representation election. A union is also prohibited from coercing employees to join, or refrain from abandoning, a strike.

Unions—and employers—are also prohibited from influencing election results by offering monetary or

ECONOMIC PERSPECTIVE

Decline *of* Pattern Bargaining

Pattern bargaining is a type of collective bargaining that tries to achieve uniform contract terms for firms throughout an industry. Although pattern bargaining was used frequently in the 1950s and 1960s when unions were strong, its use has declined with the weakening of unions in the past few decades.

One of the most significant factors contributing to the decline in pattern bargaining is the decline in union membership. When an industry is only approximately 50 percent unionized, it does not make sense for a company to pay the pattern wage because it can negotiate a lower wage with the large number of employees who are not unionized.

The use of pattern bargaining has also been affected by changes in particular industries. For example, the trucking industry changed dramatically when it was deregulated in the 1980s. Prior to deregulation, the industry was dominated by a few large companies that paid wages established by the National Master Freight

Agreement. After deregulation, smaller companies that paid lower wages entered the industry. By offering fewer benefits to younger workers who were willing to work for less than older workers, these smaller companies were able to compete with the larger companies for trucking business.

The contract dispute between Caterpillar, Inc. and the United Auto Workers in 1991 involved pattern bargaining. Caterpillar refused to agree to pattern terms accepted by Deere & Co. Despite the union's decision to strike, Caterpillar was able to earn record profits because it had a large market share and could rely upon

manufacturers around the world to do the work of the striking employees. As a result, the union's bargaining power was weakened, and the terms of the settlement ultimately reached between the union and the company favored Caterpillar.

Despite the decline in pattern bargaining, it is still used in industries where labor costs comprise only a small fraction of total costs. For example, pattern bargaining is used in the brewing industry where labor is only 10 percent of operating costs. Communications and manufacturing also use pattern bargaining due to the relatively low labor costs in these industries.

Unions now are generally more flexible about pattern bargaining than in the past. Unions tend to negotiate uniformity on a limited number of key issues, leaving the remaining issues to be negotiated locally. For example, a contract recently negotiated between IBT and Pony Express included a price floor, allowing local unions to negotiate the actual wage rates.

---

nonmonetary benefits to employees. For example, the U.S. Court of Appeals for the Fifth Circuit ruled that a union's promise to throw "the biggest party in the history of Texas" if the union won the election was a conditional inducement that invalidated the election results.[37] The court reasoned that the only motivation for the promise was to encourage employees to vote for the union, as opposed to attempts to cultivate good employee–management relations. Thus, like employer promises of a Christmas party[38] or union promises of a raffle made before an election,[39] the union's promise interfered with and therefore invalidated the election.

As the employees' exclusive bargaining representative, the union has a statutory duty under Section 8(b)(1) to represent all employees fairly when engaging in collective bargaining (without regard to their union affiliation) and

when enforcing the collective bargaining agreement.[40] Under this doctrine, the union has an obligation to represent all members of a designated unit without hostility or discrimination toward any employees. It must exercise its discretion with complete good faith and honesty and avoid arbitrary conduct.

INDUCING EMPLOYER DISCRIMINATION AGAINST NONUNION WORKERS

Under Section 8(b)(2) of the NLRA, a union may not cause or attempt to cause an employer to discriminate against an employee on the basis of union affiliation or activities. For example, a union may not encourage an employer to discharge someone because he or she does not belong to the union. In addition, a union may not cause or attempt to cause an employer to discriminate against an

37. Trencor v. NLRB, 110 F.3d 268 (5th Cir. 1997).
38. NLRB v. Lou Taylor, Inc., 564 F.2d 1173 (5th Cir. 1977).
39. Crestwood Manor, 234 N.L.R.B. 1097 (1978).

40. Vaca v. Sipes, 386 U.S. 171 (1967).

IN BRIEF
Unfair Labor Practices

By Employers

1. Interfering with employees' rights to organize and bargain collectively, including:
   - Threatening employees with any adverse action for organizing or supporting a union.
   - Promising employees any benefits if they fail to support a union.
   - Questioning employees regarding union activity.
   - Engaging in surveillance of employees' union activities.
2. Enforcing an overly broad rule against soliciting other employees for union support or distributing union literature.
3. Punishing employees for engaging in concerted activities for mutual aid and protection.
4. Dominating or assisting a labor organization.
5. Discriminating against any employee to encourage or discourage membership in any labor organization.
6. Discharging or otherwise discriminating against an employee because he or she has filed charges with the NLRB.
7. Failing to bargain collectively and in good faith, including:

- Changing some term or condition of employment, unless bargaining with the union has come to an impasse and the changes are consistent with the pre-impasse proposal.
- Failing to bargain over mandatory subjects.
8. Refusing to reinstate workers who engage in an unfair labor practice strike.

By Unions

1. Unlawful strikes.
2. Coercing employees to join the union or support its activities.
3. Failing to fairly and honestly represent all of the employees in a collective bargaining unit without regard to their union affiliation.
4. Inducing employer discrimination against nonunion workers.
5. Failing to bargain in good faith.

employee who has been denied union membership for any reason other than failure to pay union dues.

FAILURE TO BARGAIN IN GOOD FAITH

Section 8(b)(3) requires the union to bargain in good faith with the employer. The union must meet with the employer at reasonable times. Section 8(d) requires the union to approach bargaining with a serious and honest intent to conclude a collective bargaining contract. Employers rarely allege that a union has failed to bargain in good faith.

THE RESPONSIBLE MANAGER
Building Good Labor Relations

Managers should always be attentive to workplace morale and strive to keep open the lines of communication with employees. If faced with a union-organizing effort, managers must, at a minimum, observe the restrictions that the NLRA places upon employer activity. They should not threaten adverse treatment if employees support a union, interrogate employees about their union activities, promise employees benefits if they abandon the union, or spy on union activities.

Managers are, however, permitted by law to discuss certain matters with employees. They may tell employees that the company opposes a union. A manager may review with employees the disadvantages of unionism, such as the possibility of strikes and the payment of union dues and initiation fees. Managers may also discuss with employees their current benefits and the company's history of favorable treatment of employees, which has occurred without a union. Managers may also tell employees that it is unlawful for the union to attempt to harass or intimidate them into supporting it.

Most managers in the United States have a visceral negative reaction to attempts to unionize their workers, believing that unions interfere with management control in the workplace and hinder efforts to achieve competitive levels of costs, quality, and productivity.[41] For example, after meat cutters at Wal-Mart's store in Jacksonville, Texas, voted to join a union in 2000, Wal-Mart announced that it would stop cutting meat in its stores and, instead, would purchase beef and pork prepackaged by the meatpacker. Although the meat cutter employees could keep their jobs in the stores' meat departments, they were left with little to do but stock shelves. When Wal-Mart announced this change, it claimed that the new policy had been planned before the union vote. The timing seemed more than coincidental, however, particularly in light of the company's philosophy, originally established by founder Sam Walton, that unions are unnecessary and divisive.[42]

Some academics argue that there is systemic empirical evidence indicating that unions are positively associated with higher training expenditures, successful employee involvement, and successful quality-improvement programs and organizational innovation.[43] Indeed, many of the best-known examples of high-performance production systems occur at unionized plants, such as those at Saturn, Xerox, Corning, Levi Strauss, NUMMI, and AT&T.[44] Thus, it behooves managers to consider carefully the potential benefits, as well as the potential disadvantages, of unionization when deciding whether to oppose efforts to unionize.

When a union lawfully represents a unit of employees, management is required to meet at reasonable times with the union and to confer in good faith with respect to wages, hours, and other terms and conditions of employment. The law does not specify how many times or for how long the employer must meet with the union. At a minimum, the employer cannot refuse to meet with the union at all or meet on so few occasions that it is almost impossible to attain an agreement. If a union accuses an employer of unlawfully attempting to delay bargaining, the NLRB will look at all of the surrounding circumstances, including the number and length of meetings, the reasons given by the employer for any delays, and any conditions placed upon bargaining by the employer. Some courts have held that an employer must approach collective bargaining with the same seriousness as it would approach the negotiation of a commercial contract.

The NLRA also requires management to give the union the information it needs to discharge its collective bargaining duties adequately. The general rule is that management must disclose all relevant information, such as employees' wages, overtime hours, surveys leading to changes in working conditions, layoffs resulting from subcontracting, and seniority lists. Some courts have ruled, however, that the employer need disclose only information that is both relevant and necessary. Thus, management may not be required to disclose particularly sensitive employee data, such as the results of employee aptitude or intelligence tests.

Management must be careful about withdrawing any proposals it has made during bargaining. An employer's reneging may be evidence of bad faith, although it normally is not a *per se* violation of the law. In determining whether withdrawing an offer amounts to bad faith, the NLRB considers such factors as the subjects on which the offer was withdrawn, the number of times the employer reneged, and the reasons offered by the employer for reneging.

If management questions the validity of union activities relating to an election, then it may challenge the election in court. Although this may be an effective tool to address unfair labor practices by a union, management should not abuse the process by needlessly delaying the implementation of election results.[45] Moreover, management should abide by the directives of the NRLB and court orders. One poultry producer in Texas delayed implementation of a successful organizing effort through litigation for ten years; then it refused to respond to court and administrative orders to comply. The NLRB sought a contempt order against the poultry producer. Such intransigence engenders distrust and resentment by workers and is fundamentally disrespectful to the judiciary and the NLRB.

In most circumstances, managers should make every possible effort to avoid a strike as it can have longstanding impacts on the company. For example, both morale and business at Boeing Company suffered in 2000 when the company experienced a forty-day strike by 17,000 white-collar workers belonging to the Society of Professional Engineering Employees in Aerospace union. The walkout disrupted the company's commercial-jet unit and its military programs. The resulting delays in deliveries of dozens of jets reduced Boeing's earnings. In retrospect, several members of the Boeing board of directors regretted how the company had handled labor talks; many managers regarded the incident as

---

41. *See* Jeffrey Pfeffer, The Human Equation: Building Profits by Putting People First 226 (1998).

42. Ann Zimmerman, *Carved Out, Pro-Union Butchers at Wal-Mart Win a Battle, Lose War,* Wall St. J., Apr. 11, 2000, at A1.

43. Pfeffer, *supra* note 41, at 248.

44. *Id.*

45. *See* G. Pascal Zachary, *Long Litigation Often Holds Up Union Victories,* Wall St. J., Nov. 17, 1995, at B1.

expensive and unnecessary; and analysts characterized it as "the strike that didn't need to be."[46] The three-year

labor agreements ultimately ratified included significant concessions by Boeing.

46. Jeff Cole, *Boeing Board Encounters Some Dissent over Firm's Handling of Recent Strike,* WALL ST. J., Apr. 14, 2000, at B4.

Union Organizing *in the* New Economy

E-COMMERCE

The first year of the twenty-first century introduced several mainstays of the Old Economy—unions and financial difficulties—to the dot.com Internet companies of the New Economy. Customer service employees at Amazon.com, who are increasingly concerned about job security, low compensation, long hours of forced overtime, limited opportunities for promotion, and poor communcation with management, have enlisted the aid of the Washington Alliance of Technology Workers (WashTech). Washtech, an affiliate of the Communications Workers of America, previously helped contractors at software giant Microsoft organize to demand better working conditions.[47]

WashTech began a drive to gather 400 signatures from Amazon.com's Seattle-based employees to force a union election. The United Food and Commercial Workers Union and the Prewitt Organizing Fund, an independent organizing group, have attempted to organize the 5,000 warehouse workers who work in Amazon.com's eight warehouses located in Nevada, Georgia, Kansas, and Kentucky.[48]

Amazon's management launched its own campaign to discourage its employees from becoming unionized. The company posted anti-union material on its internal Web site, stating that unions would cause conflict and strikes and could not guarantee improved wages or benefits. The Web site advised managers to be aware of warning signs that a union was trying to organize, such as an increase in employee complaints, a decrease in work quality, "hushed conversations," and "small group huddles breaking up in silence on the approach of the supervisor."[49] The Web site also stated: "Unions actively foster distrust toward supervisors. They also create an uncooperative attitude among associates by leading them to

think they are 'untouchable' with a union." The site further claimed that "[U]nions limit associate incentives. Merit increases are contrary to union philosophy."[50]

Amazon's chief executive officer, Jeffrey Bezos, explained: "I think unions have an important role in society. I think they're not needed at Amazon. All our employees are owners."[51] During a pep talk to employees working long hours of overtime during the 2000 holiday period, he reiterated that Amazon.com didn't need unions because all of its employees were owners of the company.[52]

Yet, as the once lofty prices at which dot.coms traded in the late 1990s deflated in 2000, this argument may have become less persuasive as many employees saw the value of their stock options and employer stock plummet.

In 1999, IBM employees formed Alliance@IBM, an informal organization affiliated with the Communications Workers of America, in response to a dispute over pension rights. Alliance does not have the power to collectively bargain for IBM workers, but it takes credit for successfully pressuring the company to make changes in its pension plan that affected roughly 65,000 workers.[53]

According to David Moffat, who develops instructional software for the University of North Carolina at Chapel Hill, "[a]ssemblers, information workers, and many other segments of the 'Information Economy' are in a position similar to that of industrial workers at the turn of the last century. Corporations have the upper hand in determining when, where and for how much employees will work."[54]

47. Carolyn Said, *Union Movement Taking Shape at Amazon.com,* SAN FRANCISCO CHRON., Dec. 3, 2000, at B3.
48. *Id.*
49. Steven Greenhouse, *Amazon Fights Union Activity,* N.Y. TIMES, Nov. 29, 2000.

50. *Id.*
51. Nick Wingfield & Yochi J. Dreazen, *Your Career Matters: Dot-Com Rout Is a Mixed Blessing for Unionizers,* WALL ST. J., Jan. 2, 2001, at A9.
52. *Unions Pushing to Organize Thousands of Amazon.com Workers,* N.Y. TIMES, Nov. 23, 2000.
53. Troy Wolverton, *Will High-Tech Chaos Finally Give Birth to Unions?,* CNET NEWS.COM, Jan. 16, 2001.
54. *Id.*

In January 2001, customer service employees at etown.com, a division of Collaborative Media that provides consumer electronics information, were scheduled to vote on whether to join the Communications Workers of America. Etown was the first dot.com faced with an NLRB-sanctioned union election.[55] The vote was postponed after the union submitted claims of unfair labor practices by management to the NLRB. Robert Heimblem, etown.com's CEO, blamed workers for naively believing that they would make a quick buck working at a dot.com and being unprepared for the economic crunch: "They came to work with stars in their eyes."[56]

A customer service representative at etown.com was fired after he organized a sickout to protest employees' salaries and management's failure to honor promised raises and promotions. The worker argued that he was fired because he had backed a union. Management claimed that he was terminated because he was unhappy in the job and had refused to promise not to take part in another sickout.[57] Several weeks later, two other workers connected to union organizing were fired when etown.com laid off twenty-eight more workers. Etown's president denied that the layoffs resulted from union activity, claiming that the employees were terminated for economic reasons.[58] Indeed, a slowdown in the American economy in 2000 and 2001 would appear likely to chill union-organizing efforts as increasing layoffs make employees more concerned about job security.

Nonetheless, labor organizers seem confident that Amazon.com and etown.com are just the first of many Internet companies that will soon be unionized. Amy Dean, the executive officer of the AFL–CIO Labor Council in San Jose, California, commented in December 2000: "What's happening in Silicon Valley or Seattle isn't an aberration. It's a foreshadowing of what's to come for the rest of the country."[59] In fact, many jobs at Internet companies are positions that are frequently represented by unions. For example, labor experts estimate that appoximately 35,000 workers are unloading trucks and assembling and packing shipments at companies such as Amazon, Peapod, inc., and online subsidiaries of large retail stores, such as Wal-Mart and J.C. Penney.[60] A spokesman for the Teamsters commented: "There is absolutely no difference between a warehouse or shipping worker for Amazon or Webvan and their counterparts at traditional companies. When you look past the glamour of the Internet, you find that the New Economy is actually full of Old Economy jobs."[61]

55. Michelle R. Smith, *Etown.com Employees First Dot-commers to Seek Union Elections,* ASSOCIATED PRESS, Dec. 15, 2000; Steven Greenhouse, *The First Unionization Vote by Dot-Com Workers Is Set,* N.Y. TIMES, Jan. 9, 2001, at 4.
56. *Id.*
57. *Id.*
58. Carrie Johnson, *The Uniting Geeks of America? Unrest at a Calif. Site Spotlights Tech's Emerging Labor Problem,* WASH. POST, Dec. 9, 2000, at E01.
59. *Id.*
60. Wingfield & Dreazen, *supra* note 51.
61. *Id.*

KEY WORDS AND PHRASES

appropriate collective bargaining unit   544

concerted activity   547

economic strike   554

implementation-after-impasse doctrine   549

independent contractor   542

irrebuttable presumption   553

neutral-gate system   557

organizational strikes   555

pattern bargaining   558

per se violation   553

primary employer   557

recognitional strike   555

representation elections   543

runaway shop   548

salting   546

secondary boycott   555

showing of interest   544

supervisor   541

unfair labor practices   545

unfair labor practice strike   555

union authorization cards   544

union security clause   548

QUESTIONS AND CASE PROBLEMS

1. Terry Spence, a computer trainer at Compuware Corporation, was discharged after he threatened to tell Compuware's client about work-related problems. Although Spence was the only employee who threatened to complain, he had consulted with other employees before threatening to speak out. Did Spence's discharge violate the NLRA? Does it matter whether Compuware knew that Spence had

consulted with other employees? [*Compuware Corp. v. NLRB,* 134 F.3d 1285 (6th Cir. 1998), *cert. denied,* 523 U.S. 1123 (1998)]

2. For some time, the Acme Dye Company suspected that a union was attempting to organize its production and maintenance workers. The employer's suspicions were confirmed when Local 123 of the Teamsters Union filed a petition with the NLRB, asking it to hold a union representation election. Because Acme believed that its employees were unhappy with their relatively low wages, the company sent a memorandum to all employees immediately after the filing of the petition. The memo thanked them for their hard work and announced an immediate 5 percent pay increase for all employees.

   Did the announcement of the pay increase, which came as a complete surprise to the employees, violate the NLRA? Would it make any difference if the employer could demonstrate that it had planned for several weeks before the filing of the petition to grant a wage increase and that it was merely coincidence that the announcement came on the heels of the union petition? Would the answer be the same if the employer made the announcement just before the filing of the petition? [*NLRB v. Exchange Parts Co.,* 375 U.S. 405 (1964)]

3. During a union's organizing drive at a General Electric Company plant in West Virginia, GE employees distributed anti-union handbills, which stated: "The company and the union organizers are MILES APART! Are you willing to see this site possibly become another victim in *long, bitter negotiations?* Are you willing to face the possibility of a *long and ugly strike?* VOTE NO!" The union claimed that GE's distribution of the handbill was an unfair labor practice because its language was used to threaten and coerce workers. The union also claimed that GE committed an unfair labor practice when the plant's general manager warned in a speech to employees that "we won't have a business here ten years from now" and suggested that GE might withhold further investment in the plant if the employees chose the union. Did GE violate the NLRA? [*General Electric Co.,* 332 N.L.R.B. 91 (2000)]

4. Teamsters Local Union 122 was engaged in a labor dispute with August A. Busch & Company, a beer distributor. On three occasions, numerous union members descended on the employer's stores, bought small items (such as packs of bubble gum or bags of potato chips), and paid for them with large-denomination bills. These shopping expeditions, involving between 50 and 125 participants, crowded the employer's stores and created long checkout lines, full parking lots, and delays for regular customers on days that were usually particularly lucrative for the employer. The activity was not presented to the general public as an official union activity. The employer filed a complaint with the NLRB that the associational shopping constituted a secondary boycott insofar as it aimed to deter retailers from purchasing the employer's beverages. Are the "shop-ins" a secondary boycott that should be enjoined as an unfair union practice? [*Pye v. Teamsters Local Union No. 122,* 61 F.3d 1013 (1st Cir. 1995)]

5. In May 1990, the United Food and Commercial Workers Local 400 started organizing the workers of approximately thirty Be-Lo grocery stores in southern Virginia. Less than one year later, the union informed management that a majority of its workers had signed authorization cards, indicating that they supported collective representation by the union. An election was scheduled for late March 1991. Between February and March, the company initiated a campaign to dissuade its workers from voting for the union. Its tactics included videos, memoranda, meetings, and the dissemination of flyers in the form of a mock "pink slip" describing stores that had been forced to close after unionization. The company focused on the potential harms that could result from a union win. In March, the union lost the election by a vote of 377 to 220. Did Be-Lo engage in any unfair labor practices before the election? If so, what is the appropriate remedy? If not, does the union have the right to picket at a number of Be-Lo grocery stores? Why or why not? [*Be-Lo Stores v. NLRB,* 126 F.3d 268 (4th Cir. 1997)]

6. In the course of collective bargaining negotiations, the union and the employer are far apart on the question of proposed wage increases. The union has demanded a wage increase of $1.00 per hour; the employer has offered three increases of 25 cents per hour over the next three years. The employer tells the union that it simply cannot afford the union's wage demands and that, if it grants them, it will no longer be competitive. The union believes that the employer can easily afford its requested wage increases. The union asks to inspect the company's financial records so that it can determine for itself whether the employer is in a position to afford its wage demands. The employer refuses, telling the union that those records are highly confidential and that their disclosure to competitors would be extremely damaging.

May the company lawfully refuse to disclose the requested records? Would it make any difference if the union agreed to keep the records confidential? Should it make a difference if the company refused to accede to the union's wage demands, not on the ground that it cannot afford them, but on the ground that those demands are out of line with the collective bargaining agreements its competitors have recently accepted? [*NLRB v. Truitt Manufacturing Co.*, 351 U.S. 149 (1956)]

7. Graduate teaching assistants at New York University signed union authorization cards for the United Auto Workers' Technical, Office and Professional Department in order to organize as a union. The university argued that the NYU graduate assistants were students, not employees, and that they received financial assistance rather than pay for their work. The university compared graduate teaching assistants to hospital residents and interns and argued that none of these individuals were employees because their work was a fundamental part of their education. Are the NYU graduate teaching assistants employees covered by the NLRA? Would it make a difference if they received academic credit, financial assistance, or tuition remission for their work? [*New York University*, 332 N.L.R.B. 111 (Oct. 31, 2000)]

8. Colgate–Palmolive Company installed hidden cameras throughout the work environment, including the restrooms and fitness area, in order to reduce workplace theft and employee misconduct. The International Chemical Workers Union, Local 15, issued a bargaining demand letter to Colgate–Palmolive. It argued that the video surveillance was a mandatory subject of bargaining because employees could be discharged on the basis of misconduct documented by the camera. Colgate–Palmolive refused to bargain, and the union filed a complaint with the NLRB. Who should prevail? [*Colgate-Palmolive Co.*, 323 N.L.R.B. 82 (1997)]

9. Diamond Walnut Growers, Inc. processes and packages walnuts. In September 1991, approximately 500 of Diamond's workers went on strike after failed collective bargaining between management and the Cannery Workers, Processors, Warehousemen and Helpers, Local 601, of the International Brotherhood of Teamsters, AFL–CIO. A bitter strike ensued. Diamond hired replacement workers to carry on business. The union engaged in acts of violence, an international economic boycott, and a public relations campaign to discredit Diamond.

This campaign included a national bus tour distributing information describing Diamond as employing "scabs" and packaging walnuts contaminated with "mud, dirt, oil, worms and debris."

Before a union election, six striking workers unconditionally offered to return to work. Three returning strikers were unable to resume their previous positions. One individual, Miller, had been a quality control supervisor before the strike but was given a seasonal packing position upon returning. The NRLB filed a complaint alleging violation of Section 8(a)(1) and (3) of the NLRA for unlawfully discriminating against Miller for her protected union activities. How should the court rule? [*Diamond Walnut Growers, Inc. v. NLRB*, 113 F.3d 1259 (D.C. Cir. 1997) (en banc), *cert. denied*, 523 U.S. 1020 (1998)]

MANAGER'S DILEMMA

10. The EFCO Corporation formed four employee participation committees in an effort to increase employee involvement and productivity. The committees were designed to educate and involve employees in order to increase their productivity, assist management in making policy and benefit decisions, and keep the management committee informed. Three of the four committees were composed of employees selected by the company's chief financial officer, personnel director, and plant facilitator, respectively. The fourth committee was initially chosen by the company, but subsequently members of the committee selected their own replacements. Three of the four committees—the benefit, policy, and safety committees—evaluated existing plans, policies, and conditions; solicited ideas from other employees; and made recommendations to management that were either accepted or rejected. The fourth committee performed clerical duties by screening suggestions but did not formulate proposals or recommend any to management. Are these four committees "labor organizations" under the NLRA? Does EFCO's relationship with these committees violate any provision of the NLRA? If so, how can managers involve employees in their efforts to increase productivity and improve morale without running afoul of the NLRA? [*EFCO Corp. & United Brotherhood of Carpenters & Joiners of America*, 327 N.L.R.B. 372 (Dec. 31, 1998), 215 F.3d 1318 (4th Cir. 2000)]

INTERNET SOURCES

Department of Labor	http://www.dol.gov
National Labor Relations Board	http://www.nlrb.gov
This site provides an index of laws and articles on labor law.	http://www.findlaw.com/01topics/27lab
The National Right to Work Legal Defense Foundation site provides links to articles, cases, and laws applicable to compulsory unionism, union violence, and use of union dues for political lobbying.	http://www.nrtw.org
The Association of Labor Relations Agencies is an association of impartial government agencies in the United States and Canada responsible for administering labor-management relations laws or services.	http://www.alra.org
United Food and Commercial Workers International Union	http://www.ufcw.org
AFL–CIO	http://www.aflcio.org
Teamsters Union	http://www.teamster.org
The nongovernmental consulting firm Labor Relations Institute, Inc. assists employers in resisting union organization, and is, according to their website, "the nation's most active firm conveying the overwhelming disadvantages of union membership."	http://www.lrionline.com/

The Regulatory Environment

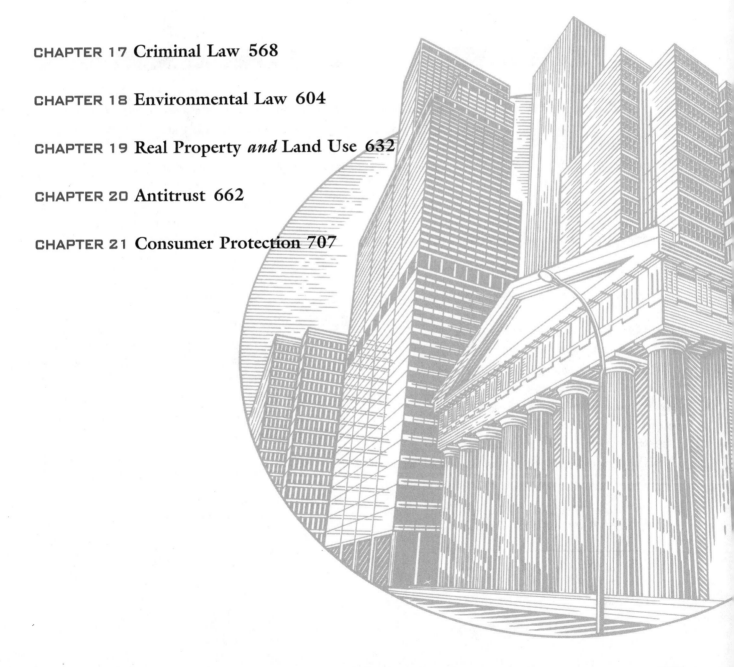

CHAPTER 17

Criminal Law

IMPACT ON CORPORATE BEHAVIOR

Criminal law is a powerful tool for controlling corporate behavior and ensuring ethical conduct. Companies devote significant resources to preventing and defending criminal law violations. Areas of concern for many managers include bribery, compliance with environmental laws, worker safety, government contracts, securities fraud, antitrust law compliance, and securities trading by officers and directors.

Violations of criminal laws often result in the imposition of substantial monetary penalties for the companies involved. For example, LifeScan, a subsidiary of Johnson & Johnson, pled guilty in December 2000 to criminal misdemeanor charges and agreed to pay $60 million in fines for selling defective blood glucose monitoring devices and failing to report the defects to regulators at the Food and Drug Administration (FDA).[1] LifeScan's director of clinical evaluations told management in May 1997 that he believed the company was required to tell the FDA about some of the most serious complaints and he recommended an immediate recall, but LifeScan did not report the problems to the FDA until June 1998, when the agency had begun its criminal investigation.

Prosecutors often seek (and obtain) severe prison sentences for white-collar criminals. For example, Donald Ferrarini, the for-

mer chief executive officer (CEO) of Underwriters Financial Group, was sentenced to twelve years and one month for accounting fraud.[2] In price-fixing or financial fraud cases, the government frequently offers lower-level employees immunity or leniency in exchange for testimony implicating senior management.

Criminal liability may be imposed in several ways. Individuals are always responsible for their own criminal acts, even when they are working under orders from top management. Supervisors may also be vicariously liable for the acts of their subordinates. Corporations (and other business entities) may also be found guilty of crimes based on the illegal conduct of their employees.

CHAPTER OVERVIEW

This chapter defines the elements necessary to create criminal liability. It discusses the statutory sources of criminal law and the Federal Sentencing Guidelines. It describes criminal procedure—the mechanics of a criminal action, the plea options, and the trial. Constitutional issues include search warrant requirements and the privilege against self-incrimination. The chapter continues with a discussion of the Racketeer Influenced and Corrupt Organizations Act, wire and mail fraud, computer crime, and other white-collar crimes.

---

1. Melody Petersen, *Guilty Plea by Division of Drug Giant: Monitors for Diabetes Found to Be Defective*, N.Y. TIMES, Dec. 16, 2000.

2. Carol J. Loomis, *Lies, Damned Lies, and Managed Earnings*, FORTUNE, Aug. 2, 1999, at 77. His sentence is on appeal.

⟁ Definition *of a* Crime

A *crime* is an offense against the public at large. It may be defined as any act that violates the duties owed to the community, for which the offender must make satisfaction to the public. An act is criminal only if it is defined as criminal in a federal or state statute or in a local ordinance enacted by a city or county.

Two elements are necessary to create criminal liability: (1) an act that violates an existing criminal statute, and (2) the requisite state of mind.

THE CRIMINAL ACT

The term *actus reus* (guilty act or wrongful deed) is often used to describe the act in question. A crime is not committed unless some overt act has occurred. Merely thinking about a criminal activity is not criminal.

THE STATE OF MIND

Generally, a crime is not committed unless the criminal act named in the statute is performed with the requisite state of mind, known as *mens rea* (guilty mind). Under some statutes, however, a person can be guilty regardless of his or her state of mind or degree of fault. This is known as *strict liability.*

Strict Liability Strict liability statutes are generally disfavored. Most courts will require clear legislative intent to impose strict liability before they will construe a statute as imposing strict liability. The U.S. Supreme Court has stated that the requirement of "a relation between some mental element and punishment for a harmful act is almost as instinctive as the child's familiar exculpatory 'But I didn't mean to.'"[3] Typically, strict liability statutes address issues of public health and safety. (Strict liability statutes that provide for vicarious criminal liability are discussed later in the chapter.)

Mens Rea The three forms of *mens rea* are negligence, recklessness, and intention to do wrong. Negligence is the least culpable state of mind, and intention to do wrong is the most culpable. The statute that defines the criminal act also defines the requisite state of mind. Generally speaking, crimes associated with a higher degree of culpability are punished more severely. Convictions for intentional homicide, for instance, bring penalties far more harsh than those for negligent homicide.

Negligence is the failure to see the possible negative consequences that a reasonable person would have seen. Someone may be negligent even if that individual did not know of the possible harm of his or her act. All that is necessary is that a reasonable person would have known of the possible harm. A reasonable person is often thought of as a rational person using ordinary care under the circumstances. *Recklessness* in the criminal context is conscious disregard of a substantial risk that the individual's actions will result in the harm prohibited by the statute. Recklessness is found when the individual knew of the possible harm of his or her act but ignored the risk. A person has an *intention to do wrong* when he or she consciously intends to cause the harm prohibited by the statute, or when he or she knows such harm is substantially certain to result from his or her conduct.

Merely being able to define these terms, however, often does not provide an answer to more complex questions of real-world guilt. Consider the intention-to-do-wrong requirement in the context of the federal false-statement statute.[4] The statute makes it a crime to "knowingly and willfully" make any false statement or representation "in any manner within the jurisdiction of any department or agency of the United States." Suppose a defendant made a statement to a federal agent that she knew was false. However, she did not know that the person to whom she directed the statement was a federal agent. Would this defendant be convicted?

In *United States v. Yermian*,[5] the U.S. Supreme Court ruled that she would be. The Court applied the "intention to do wrong" requirement only to the "false statement" portion of the statute. In other words, it required only that a defendant knowingly lie to a person who is in fact a federal agent, rather than that she knowingly lie to a person she knows is a federal agent.

A commonly invoked platitude is "ignorance of the law is no excuse." Although true as a general principle, this is an imprecise rule that, taken alone, does not tell courts how to apply the *mens rea* requirements of particular criminal statutes. There is often substantial room for interpretation and debate as to the meaning of certain statutes and the *mens rea* required under them. For example, in *Liparota v. United States*,[6] the Supreme Court addressed the *mens rea* required by the federal food stamp fraud statute, which provides that "whoever knowingly uses, transfers, acquires, alters or possesses coupons or authorization cards in any manner not authorized by [the statute] or the regulations" is subject to

---

3. Morissette v. United States, 342 U.S. 246, 250–51 (1952).

4. 18 U.S.C. § 1001 (2000).
5. 468 U.S. 63 (1984).
6. 471 U.S. 419 (1985).

a fine and imprisonment. Acknowledging that it was unclear how far down the sentence the word "knowingly" traveled, the Court set forth the rule that when statutory language is ambiguous, the traditional assumption is that some *mens rea* is required. As a result, the Court held that the defendant could not be convicted under the statute unless he knew that he was acquiring food stamps in an unauthorized or illegal manner.

In *Bryan v. United States*,[7] the Supreme Court held that, as a general matter, a "willful" act is "one undertaken with a 'bad purpose.' In other words, in order to establish a 'willful' violation of a statute, 'the Government must prove that the defendant acted with knowledge that his conduct was unlawful.'" The defendant does not need to know which particular law he or she is breaking, however, only that some law is being violated. In contrast, the term "knowingly" merely requires proof of knowledge of the facts that constitute the offense, not knowledge of unlawfulness, unless (as in *Liparota*) the text of the statute dictates a different result.

Criminal *versus* Civil Liability

Many regulatory statutes provide for both criminal and civil sanctions if they are violated. An individual or a corporation may therefore be sued under both criminal and civil law for a single act.

Civil law, particularly tort law (discussed in Chapter 9), compensates the victim for legal wrongs committed against the person or his or her property. Criminal law protects society by punishing the criminal. It does not compensate the victim. However, the victim of a crime may bring a civil suit for damages against the perpetrator. Violation of a criminal statute is *negligence per se;* this means that in a subsequent civil suit, the court will accept the criminal conviction as sufficient proof that the accused was negligent, that is, that the defendant did not act with the care a reasonable person would have used under the same circumstances. Consequently, defendants must carefully review their criminal defense strategy in light of possible future civil litigation.

BURDEN OF PROOF

Criminal trials differ from civil trials in imposing a much heavier *burden of proof.* Generally, to prevail in a civil trial, the plaintiff need only establish the facts by a *preponderance of the evidence.* If the evidence tips the scales only slightly in favor of the plaintiff, he or she wins. In a

criminal case, the accused is presumed innocent until proven guilty beyond a reasonable doubt.

This difference in the degree of proof required is typical of the procedural and constitutional safeguards protecting defendants' rights throughout criminal proceedings. In a criminal case, the formidable resources of the state are focused on an individual. In this contest of unequal strength, it seems only fair to require the state to meet a higher standard of proof. Moreover, the deprivation of personal liberty and the lifelong stigma of criminal conviction are at stake in a criminal prosecution, whereas in a civil lawsuit only monetary damages are at stake.

Sources *of* Criminal Law

Conviction of a crime can lead to a substantial fine, a prison sentence, or even the death penalty. Because the results of a criminal conviction can be so serious, all criminal liability is specifically defined in statutes, which are binding on a court. In contrast, much of civil law was developed by the courts without applicable statutes.

A criminal charge and prosecution are brought by either the state or the federal government. Under most federal and state laws, crimes are divided into two categories. A *felony* is a crime punishable by death or by imprisonment for more than one year. A *misdemeanor* is a less serious crime, punishable by a fine or a jail sentence of one year or less.

EX POST FACTO CLAUSE

Under the *Ex Post Facto Clause* of the U.S. Constitution,[8] a person can be convicted of a crime only if the person's actions constituted a crime at the time they occurred. In *Lynce v. Mathis*,[9] the U.S. Supreme Court explained: "To fall within the ex post facto prohibition, a law must be retrospective—that is, it must apply to events occurring before its enactment—and it must disadvantage the offender affected by it, by altering the definition of criminal conduct or increasing the punishment for the crime."

The Ex Post Facto Clause also prevents a person from having to bear legal consequences for an act when such legal consequences did not exist at the time the act was committed. For example, in *Carmell v. Texas*,[10] Carmell was charged with several sexual offenses against his stepdaughter. At the time the offenses occurred, Texas law

---

7. 524 U.S. 184.

8. U.S. Const., art. 1, § 10, cl. 1.
9. 519 U.S. 433, 441 (1997).
10. 529 U.S. 513 (2000).

provided that a victim's testimony could serve as the basis for a conviction for sexual offenses only if supported by corroborating evidence. Prior to Carmell's trial, however, Texas law was amended to permit conviction for sexual offenses based solely on the victim's testimony. Carmell was convicted on the basis of his stepdaughter's testimony alone. The Supreme Court held that it was unconstitutional to apply the less strict proof requirements in the amended law to establish Carmell's conviction. The U.S. Court of Appeals for the Tenth Circuit has held that the Ex Post Facto Clause also applies to an agency regulation that is legislative in nature, but the court acknowledged that there was a split in the circuits over this issue.[11]

THE MODEL PENAL CODE

The criminal statutes of the individual states and the federal government are similar but not exactly the same. This is because most states have adopted the Model Penal Code but have modified it to meet their own needs. The Model Penal Code is a set of criminal law statutes that were proposed by the National Conference of Commissioners of Uniform State Laws for adoption by the states.

 The Federal Sentencing Guidelines

State and federal criminal statutes normally specify penalties that include both prison time and monetary fines. The length of a prison sentence usually falls within a specified range. In a state court, if the defendant is found guilty, the judge generally has sentencing discretion within that range. In a federal court, the judge has considerably less discretion and must follow the Federal Sentencing Guidelines.

FEDERAL SENTENCING GUIDELINES FOR INDIVIDUALS

The U.S. Sentencing Commission is an independent agency in the judicial branch charged with monitoring criminal-sentencing practices in the federal courts. In establishing the commission, Congress sought to create an honest, fair, and effective federal sentencing system that would impose reasonably uniform sentences for similar criminal offenses committed by similar offenders.

The Sentencing Commission established sentencing guidelines, which create categories of "offense behavior" and "offender characteristics." A sentencing court must select a sentence (up to the maximum authorized by statute for each federal crime) from within the guideline ranges specified by the combined categories. In unusual cases, a court may depart from the guidelines, but it must specify the reasons for its departure.

Congress abolished federal parole in 1984. Rather than permit a parole commission to decide how much of a sentence an offender actually serves, an offender serves the full sentence imposed by the court under the sentencing guidelines, less approximately 15 percent for good behavior.

The average length of prison sentences imposed for offenders in federal district courts in 1998 was 112.8 months for murder, 74.5 months for rape, 18.6 months for tax law violations, 21.2 months for bribery, 23.3 months for fraud, and 15.7 months for embezzlement.[12]

FEDERAL SENTENCING GUIDELINES FOR ORGANIZATIONS

The Federal Sentencing Guidelines for Organizations, enacted in 1991, specify stiff fines for companies convicted of fraud, antitrust violations, and most types of corporate wrongdoing. According to the Sentencing Commission, the guidelines for organizations were "designed so that the sanctions imposed upon organizations and their agents . . . will provide just punishment, adequate deterrence, and incentives for organizations to maintain internal mechanisms for preventing, detecting and reporting criminal conduct."[13]

The guidelines take a carrot-and-stick approach. The "stick" is that organizations are held liable for the criminal actions of all their employees and agents. The "carrot" is that a company's maintenance of a meaningful voluntary compliance program is deemed a mitigating factor that will reduce otherwise applicable fines. A company can also achieve significant mitigation of fines by cooperating with or self-reporting misconduct to authorities.

In determining the sentence for a particular crime, the first step is to determine the base fine, which is set according to the severity of the crime. For instance, money laundering is considered a more serious offense than price-fixing; thus, the base fine for price-fixing is $20,000

11. Smith v. Scott, 223 F.3d 1191 (10th Cir. 2000). *Accord* United States v. Bell, 991 F.2d 1445 (8th Cir. 1993) (subjecting Federal Sentencing Guidelines to *ex post facto* analysis). *Contra* Dominique v. Weld, 73 F.3d 1156 (1st Cir. 1996).

12. Bureau of Justice Statistics, Sourcebook of Criminal Justice Statistics Online (2000).
13. Itamar Sittenfeld, *Federal Sentencing Guidelines,* Internal Auditor, Apr. 1996, at 58.

(offense level 10), whereas the base fine for laundering money instruments (such as checks) is $1.6 million (offense level 23). If the base fine is exceeded by either the organization's gain or the plaintiff's loss from the crime, then that amount will supplant the base fine.

The second step is to adjust the base fine to reflect the culpability of the organization. A variety of factors come into play, including whether (1) the organization itself was convicted of a crime, (2) management condoned or willfully ignored the criminal misconduct, (3) management assisted authorities in their investigation, and (4) the organization had an effective compliance program in place at the time of the misconduct. The possibility of fine mitigation serves as a strong incentive for organizations to adopt and maintain compliance programs.

Misgivings about the Guidelines The Federal Sentencing Guidelines for Organizations have been credited with encouraging corporations to self-police their own misconduct and to assist authorities in their criminal investigations. Yet the vice-chair of the U.S. Sentencing Commission recently acknowledged that, in many cases, organizational compliance programs exist only on paper.[14] A recent KPMG survey revealed that employees believe that significant corporate misconduct continues and that existing compliance programs are ineffective in halting such misconduct. Thus, the commission may need to revise the guidelines to require explicitly that organizations engage in "ongoing auditing and testing" of their compliance programs.

In addition, most experts argue that the guidelines need to be updated to reflect new types of cyber-crime, such as transmission of computer viruses, computer theft of trade secrets, hacking into secure sites to access credit card information and other confidential data, and denying people access to certain sites. The existing guidelines often fail to provide clear guidance on how to calculate the dollar amount of the harm or the gain in such cases.

Letting Employees Take the Rap When facing a criminal probe, corporations have increasingly responded to the guidelines' encouragement to cooperate with authorities by winning leniency for themselves at the expense of their employees. Because the guidelines call on corporations to apply "adequate discipline" to employees deemed responsible for criminal violations, a company has an incentive to isolate a small group of "fall guys,"

14. *U.S. Sentencing for Organizations May Need to Mandate Compliance Program Audits, Commissioner Says,* Corp. Couns. Wkly., May 3, 2000.

AT THE TOP

To take advantage of the provisions in the Federal Sentencing Guidelines that reduce culpability for a company with an effective compliance program, a company must:

1. Establish compliance standards and procedures reasonably capable of reducing the prospect of criminal activity. A viable code of conduct is a good starting point.
2. Assign high-level personnel the responsibility for overseeing the compliance effort. It is often appropriate for the audit committee of the board of directors to oversee the program.
3. Use due care in delegating authority. Don't give substantial discretionary authority to individuals with a propensity to engage in illegal activities. The fox can't guard the hen house.
4. Effectively communicate the standards to all employees and other agents. A well-designed video can help ensure ongoing training about the standards.
5. Adopt mechanisms for monitoring compliance with the standards and reporting criminal misconduct. An anonymous toll-free hotline can help encourage reporting of misconduct.
6. Consistently enforce the standards through investigation and adequate discipline.
7. Adopt procedures for feedback and correction. After an offense has been detected, the organization must take all reasonable steps to respond adequately to the offense and to prevent further offenses—including any necessary modifications to its compliance program.

Source: This summary of the seven-step program is drawn from Itamar Sittenfeld, *Federal Sentencing Guidelines,* Internal Auditor, Apr. 1996, at 58, and 18 U.S.C. § 8A1.2 cmt. 3(K)(1)–(7) (2000).

---

fire them, and cooperate with the federal government in their prosecution. This pattern frequently occurs even though it can often be difficult to determine who is really responsible for corporate crimes.[15]

15. *See, e.g.,* Dean Starkman, *More Firms Let Employees Take the Rap,* Wall St. J., Oct. 9, 1997, at B3.

 ETHICAL CONSIDERATION

Is it ethical for a corporation to turn in some but not all of the managers who may have participated in criminal wrongdoing?

Criminal Procedure

A criminal action begins with the arrest of the person suspected of a crime and proceeds through a preliminary hearing to plea bargaining and trial.

ARREST

After a person is *arrested* (taken into custody against his or her will for criminal prosecution or interrogation), he or she is taken to a police station and *booked,* that is, the charges against him or her are written in a register. The arresting police officer must then file a report with the prosecutor. Based on this report, the prosecutor must decide whether to press charges against the arrested person. If charges are to be pressed, many states require that the accused be taken before a public judicial official, usually a justice of the peace or magistrate, to be informed of the charges. Bail is often determined during this initial appearance before the public official.

PLEA

If the accused is charged with only a misdemeanor, the person will be asked at this initial appearance whether he or she pleads guilty or not guilty. In the case of a felony, the next step in many states is a *preliminary hearing,* at which the prosecutor must present evidence demonstrating probable cause that the defendant committed the felony. Following this hearing, formal charges are usually filed either by the prosecutor through an *information,* a document filed with the court, or by a grand jury through an *indictment.* The accused will then be arraigned before a trial court judge. At the arraignment, the accused will be informed of the charges against him or her and be asked to enter a *plea* of guilty or not guilty. If the defendant enters a plea of not guilty, the case is set for trial.

The accused can also plead *nolo contendere,* which means that he or she does not contest the charges. For the purpose of the criminal proceedings, this plea is equivalent to a guilty plea. Unlike a guilty plea, however, a plea of *nolo contendere* cannot be introduced at a subsequent civil trial. Therefore, a *nolo contendere* plea may be used by corporate defendants who anticipate civil suits based on the same activity for which they face criminal charges.

PLEA BARGAINING

Very few cases ever reach trial. Most cases are resolved through plea bargaining between the accused and the prosecutor. *Plea bargaining* is the process whereby the prosecutor agrees to reduce the charges in exchange for a guilty plea from the accused.

Frequently, a lower-ranking member of a criminal conspiracy will "cop a plea," that is, provide the prosecutor with testimony incriminating his or her criminal superiors, in exchange for a reduced sentence or immunity from prosecution. The immunity granted may be either use immunity or transactional immunity. *Use immunity* prohibits the testimony of the witness from being used against him or her in any way. *Transactional immunity,* which is broader, prohibits any criminal prosecution of the witness that relates to any matter discussed in his or her testimony.

Some courts have challenged the offer of leniency in exchange for testimony as a violation of the federal statute forbidding the exchange of "anything of value" for testimony. However, a majority of U.S. courts of appeals allow the government to offer leniency.[16]

Consent decrees are common in the corporate context. A *consent decree* is a court order based on an agreement by the defendant corporation to take measures to remedy the problem that led to criminal charges. Like a plea of *nolo contendere,* a consent decree cannot be introduced as evidence of guilt in a subsequent civil trial.

TRIAL

A criminal trial proceeds in much the same way as civil trials, which were discussed in Chapter 3. There are opening statements, direct examination and cross-examination of witnesses, and closing arguments. The jury then deliberates to reach a verdict of guilty or not guilty.

 Fourth Amendment Protections

The Fourth Amendment to the U.S. Constitution provides:

> The right of the people to be secure in their persons, houses, papers, and effects, against unreasonable searches and seizures, shall not be violated, and no Warrants shall issue, but upon probable cause, supported by Oath or affirmation, and particularly describing the place to be searched, and the persons or things to be seized.

The Fourth Amendment applies only to actions by government officials, unless a private person is acting on behalf of the government. This provision was intended to

---

16. *See, e.g.,* United States v. Singleton, 165 F.3d 1297 (10th Cir. 1999).

prevent the arbitrary and intrusive searches that had characterized British rule during the American colonial period. Courts have struggled, however, to strike the appropriate balance between the individual's expectation of privacy and the government's legitimate need to secure evidence of wrongdoing to prevent criminal acts and apprehend criminals.

THE ARREST WARRANT REQUIREMENT

An arrest is a Fourth Amendment seizure. No arrest is valid unless there is probable cause. *Probable cause* for arrest is defined as a reasonable belief that the suspect has committed a crime or is about to commit a crime. The Fourth Amendment does not require that a warrant be obtained prior to an arrest in a public place when the officer has reasonable suspicion to believe a felony has been committed by the individual or when a misdemeanor has been committed in the officer's presence. In general, an arrest warrant is required only for arrests in the suspect's own home or in another person's home. In determining what is "reasonable suspicion," the Supreme Court has deemed nervous, evasive behavior on the part of the suspect to be relevant. For example, in *Illinois v. Wardlow*,[17] the Court held that an arrest made by police officers patrolling a high-crime area was reasonable when the suspect fled after spotting the officers. Stating that headlong flight is a "consummate act of evasion," the Court reasoned that "determination of reasonable suspicion must be based on commonsense judgments and inferences about human behavior."

SEARCHES AND SEIZURES AND REASONABLE EXPECTATIONS OF PRIVACY

Before conducting any search or seizure that would be deemed unreasonable under the Fourth Amendment, a law enforcement agent must obtain a warrant. The touchstone of the Supreme Court's analysis in Fourth Amendment search warrant cases has been whether the individual has a reasonable expectation of privacy under the circumstances. In the Court's landmark Fourth Amendment case, *United States v. Katz*,[18] Justice John Marshall Harlan's concurring opinion framed the issue as follows: Has government action intruded upon an individual's subjective expectation of privacy? If so, is that expectation one that society deems reasonable? If an individual did not have a subjective privacy expectation, or if he or she had an expectation that society would not

deem reasonable, then the police were entitled to conduct a search without a warrant.

In applying this framework, courts have held that a citizen's interest in freedom from governmental intrusions is very strong in his or her private home—an expectation of privacy there is quite reasonable. In places open to the public (such as a business office), law enforcement has been given broader scope. For instance, the Supreme Court permitted warrantless searches of business offices when the government agent entered during business hours and observed what was visible to customers or the public from the public areas of the premises. Similarly, the Court permitted a warrantless search of garbage cans placed at curbside for collection where the garbage was readily accessible to animals and other persons, including the trash haulers who could have sorted through it before commingling it with garbage collected from other dwellings.

No search warrant is required for government officials to search an individual's bank deposit records. An individual lowers the expectation of privacy by revealing his or her affairs to the bank, and he or she assumes the risk that the information will be revealed to the government.

Some stops and searches may be justified without a showing of probable cause (e.g., brief questioning when police observe unusual conduct that leads to a reasonable suspicion of criminal activity). In fact, most police searches are not conducted pursuant to a warrant. These searches are permissible either (1) because they are deemed not "unreasonable searches" under the *Katz* test or not "searches" within the meaning of the Fourth Amendment,[19] or (2) because they fall within one of six established exceptions to the search warrant requirement. The six exceptions are (1) search incident to a lawful arrest; (2) search of an automobile when there is probable cause to believe evidence of a crime will be found; (3) anything discovered by police in plain view when the officers are legitimately on the premises; (4) stop and frisk of a suspect when the officer reasonably believes the suspect is dangerous; (5) search when the owner or a person who appears to have authority voluntarily and intelligently consents to the search; and (6) instances when the police are in "hot pursuit" or when the evidence may disappear before a warrant can be obtained (e.g., blood samples containing alcohol). If a person is validly arrested, the officer has the authority to search the arrestee and the area immediately within the arrestee's control to protect the safety of the officer.

---

17. 528 U.S. 119 (2000).
18. 389 U.S. 347 (1967).

19. *See* United States v. Karo, 468 U.S. 705, 712 (1984) (a "search" occurs "when an expectation of privacy that society is prepared to consider reasonable is infringed").

The Supreme Court has drawn a line between visual inspection and tactile examination. A border patrol officer cannot touch or squeeze a bus passenger's carry-on bag placed in the overhead rack, even though other passengers might also be expected to touch the bag.[20]

The Supreme Court has given police broad scope to stop motorists suspected of traffic violations. If a police officer makes a traffic stop that is justified objectively by probable cause to believe a traffic violation has occurred, then it is irrelevant that the police officer might have used the violation only as a pretext to stop the car.[21] Police officers need not inform detained drivers that they are "legally free to go" before asking for consent to search their vehicles.[22] A police officer may order passengers out of a vehicle during the course of a traffic stop,[23] but the police cannot conduct a full car search after issuing a routine traffic citation unless the driver consents.[24]

SUSPICIONLESS AND ADMINISTRATIVE SEARCHES AND SEIZURES

In general, a search or seizure is unreasonable "in the absence of individualized suspicion of wrongdoing."[25] Nonetheless, the Supreme Court has upheld "certain regimes of suspicionless searches where the program was designed to serve 'special needs, beyond the normal need for law enforcement.'"[26] These include the random drug testing of student-athletes,[27] U.S. Customs Service employees seeking transfer or promotion to certain positions,[28] and railway employees involved in train accidents or found to be in violation of particular safety regulations.[29]

The Court has also upheld suspicionless searches for certain administrative purposes, including inspections of the premises of a "closely regulated" business,[30] fire-damaged structures to determine the cause of a blaze,[31] and buildings to ensure compliance with a city housing code.[32] A warrantless inspection of a closely regulated business will be reasonable only if (1) there is a "substantial" government interest that informs the regulatory scheme pursuant to which the inspection is made; (2) the warrantless inspections are necessary to further the regulatory scheme; and (3) the inspection program, in terms of the certainty and regularity of its application, provides a constitutionally adequate substitute for a warrant.[33]

Recognizing the government's interest in policing the nation's borders, the Court upheld brief, suspicionless seizures of motorists at two fixed Border Control checkpoints that were designed to intercept illegal aliens and were located on major U.S. highways less than one hundred miles from the Mexican border.[34] The Supreme Court also upheld highway sobriety checkpoints designed to detect signs of intoxication and to remove impaired drivers from the road.[35]

But the Court struck down highway checkpoints aimed at the discovery and interdiction of illegal narcotics: "When law enforcement authorities pursue primarily general crime control purposes at checkpoints . . . , stops can only be justified by some quantum of individualized suspicion."[36] The Court distinguished between sobriety checkpoints to protect the public from an "immediate, vehicle-bound threat of life and limb" and narcotics stops "justified only by the generalized and ever-present possibility that interrogation and inspection may reveal that any given motorist has committed a crime." The Court made it clear that sobriety checkpoints, border searches, searches at airports and government buildings, and "roadblocks set up to thwart imminent terrorist attack or to catch a dangerous criminal who is likely to flee by way of a particular route" were not prohibited. The Court left open the legality of a checkpoint program with the primary purpose of checking driver's licenses and a secondary purpose of interdicting narcotics.

SEARCHES EMPLOYING NEW TECHNOLOGY

The framers of the Fourth Amendment protections could not have conceived of the technological tools at the disposal of today's law enforcement agencies. As a result, it has been the duty of the courts to apply those protections in a modern, technologically sophisticated context. The seminal *Katz* decision involved the government's use of an electronic bug on the outside of a pay-phone booth.

20. Bond v. United States, 529 U.S. 334 (2000).
21. Whren v. United States, 517 U.S. 806 (1996).
22. Ohio v. Robinette, 519 U.S. 33 (1996).
23. Maryland v. Wilson, 519 U.S. 408 (1997).
24. Knowles v. United States, 525 U.S. 113 (1998).
25. City of Indianapolis v. Edmond, 121 S. Ct. 447 (2000).
26. *Id.*
27. Veronia Sch. Dist. 47J v. Acton, 515 U.S. 646 (1995).
28. Treasury Employees v. Von Raab, 489 U.S. 656 (1989).
29. Skinner v. Railway Labor Executives' Ass'n, 489 U.S. 602 (1989).
30. New York v. Burger, 482 U.S. 691 (1987).
31. Michigan v. Tyler, 436 U.S. 499 (1978).
32. Camara v. Municipal Court of City and County of San Francisco, 387 U.S. 523 (1967).

33. United States v. Argent Chem. Lab., Inc., 93 F.3d 572 (9th Cir. 1996).
34. United States v. Martinez-Fuerta, 428 U.S. 543 (1976).
35. Michigan Dep't of State Police v. Sitz, 496 U.S. 444 (1990).
36. City of Indianapolis v. Edmonds, 121 S. Ct. 447 (2000).

The Court ruled this mode of surveillance unconstitutional without a warrant.

Thermal-Image Scanners One technology now in widespread use by law enforcement agencies is the infrared thermal-image scanner. The scanner is commonly used to investigate homes of suspected marijuana cultivators. "Hot spots" that show up on the scanner indicate artificial heat sources, such as heat being released from grow lights for hidden marijuana crops.

Police generally use thermal-image scanners without a warrant as part of their effort to compile enough information to obtain a warrant for a physical search of the premises. This warrantless use of scanners has given rise to a heated legal debate about their constitutionality, which the U.S. Supreme Court may resolve during its 2000–2001 term in deciding *United States v. Kyllo.*[37] In *Kyllo,* the Ninth Circuit joined the Fifth, Seventh, Eighth, and Eleventh Circuits in holding that thermal-image scanners may be used without a warrant.[38] The Washington[39] and Montana[40] state supreme courts have ruled that the use of thermal-image scanners unconstitutionally infringes on the reasonable expectation of privacy in the home guaranteed by their state constitutions.

Two theories are typically set forth to support the use of thermal-image scanners without a warrant. Under one theory, the scanner is viewed simply as a tool for measuring "waste heat," for which the individual defendants have no subjective expectation of privacy. In this view, searches using scanners are analogous to garbage searches, which have been ruled constitutional, and dog-sniff searches, which have been held constitutional because individuals have no subjective expectation of privacy in the odors they give off. Under the other theory, the use of the scanner is considered so minimally intrusive that society would not deem that privacy expectation reasonable. This rationale compares thermal imaging to the use of a mapping camera on a high-altitude surveillance flight or to a pen register, which discloses only the telephone numbers that have been dialed and not the content of communications. The crucial factor, under this analysis, is that the government's surveillance was too imprecise to reveal "intimate details" about the defendant or his or her property.

Cordless and Cellular Phones and E-Mail No search warrant is required for a search of the phone numbers a person has called. A search warrant is required to listen to or record conversations conducted on traditional land-based telephones (wiretapping) but not on cordless[41] or cellular telephones.[42] Users of cordless and cellular phones have no reasonable expectation of privacy because communications on those phones could be overheard by other users.

Similarly, a user of a commercial online service was deemed to have lacked a reasonable expectation of privacy in e-mail messages and chat room "conversations."[43] Accordingly, the Fourth Amendment was not violated when a federal agent lurking in a chat room collected e-mail and chat messages containing child pornography from the defendant.

A more contested issue is whether police may obtain, without a warrant, the names and electronic addresses of the persons to whom a defendant has sent e-mail. Law enforcement personnel argue that this is equivalent to obtaining a pen register for telephone calls. Defense lawyers and privacy advocates claim that it is far more intrusive and revealing because the names and addresses convey much more information than a series of telephone numbers.

OBTAINING A SEARCH WARRANT

When a law enforcement agent needs to obtain a search warrant, the agent must persuade a "neutral and detached" magistrate that a search is justified. The rights of private citizens are protected by the requirement that a magistrate, rather than a law enforcement agent, determine whether probable cause exists for a search.

A valid search warrant must (1) be based on probable cause, (2) be supported by an oath or affirmation, and (3) describe in specific detail (with particularity) what is to be searched or seized. Probable cause is to be determined by the totality of the circumstances, balancing the privacy rights of the individual against the government's law enforcement needs.

37. 190 F.3d 1041 (9th Cir. 2000), *cert. granted,* 121 S. Ct. 29 (2000).
38. *See, e.g.,* United States v. Real Property Located at 15324 County Highway E, 219 F.3d 602 (7th Cir. 2000); United States v. Ishmael, 48 F.3d 850 (5th Cir. 1995); United States v. Myers, 46 F.3d 668 (7th Cir. 1995); United States v. Robinson, 62 F.3d 1325 (11th Cir. 1995); United States v. Pinson, 24 F.3d 1056 (8th Cir. 1994). *See also* State v. Cramer, 851 P.2d 147 (Ariz. Ct. App. 1992); LaFollette v. Commonwealth, 915 S.W.2d 747 (Ky. 1996); State v. McKee, 510 N.W.2d 807 (Wis. Ct. App. 1993).
39. State v. Young, 867 P.2d 593 (Wash. 1994).
40. State v. Siegal, 934 P.2d 176 (Mont. 1997).

41. Tyler v. Berodt, 877 F.2d 705 (8th Cir. 1989).
42. *See, e.g.,* Edwards v. State Farm Ins. Co., 833 F.2d 535 (5th Cir. 1987).
43. *See* United States v. Charbonneau, 979 F. Supp. 1177 (S.D. Ohio 1997).

When government authorities obtain a warrant to conduct a physical search of a business, the scope of the search typically must have some limits. To obtain a broad warrant to conduct a sweeping raid of a company, the government must show that the company is "pervaded by fraud."[44] The U.S. Court of Appeals for the Ninth Circuit denied a request for a sweeping warrant by federal officials investigating Solid State Devices, Inc. on charges that the company sold dozens of inexpensive, commercial-grade semiconductors as "high-reliability" devices suitable for premier weapons and space applications.[45] The court stated that it would be very difficult for the government to obtain a sweeping warrant as long as the company was "engaged in some legitimate activity." The "pervaded by fraud" exception applies only to companies that are little more than "boiler room" sales operations engaged only negligibly in legitimate business activities.

 ## *The* Exclusionary Rule

The *exclusionary rule* is virtually unique to the U.S. legal system. In many circumstances, it prohibits a prosecutor from introducing evidence at a criminal trial as proof of guilt when that evidence was obtained by an illegal search or seizure in violation of the Fourth Amendment (or in violation of the Fifth Amendment's ban on self-incrimination, discussed below). Illegal evidence includes evidence found when the search went beyond the scope of the warrant, evidence gathered without a warrant when a warrant was required, and evidence acquired directly or indirectly as a result of an illegal search or arrest or interrogation (called *fruit of the poisonous tree*).

The exclusionary rule is often criticized in the media as simply a device to set guilty criminals free on a technicality. Supporters of the rule argue that it is necessary to protect personal freedom.

EXCEPTIONS TO THE EXCLUSIONARY RULE

After a shift in its composition during the 1980s, the U.S. Supreme Court began to sharply limit the application of the exclusionary rule. The two most important limitations the Court has elaborated are the good faith exception and the inevitable discovery exception.

Under the *good faith exception,* evidence obtained by police in good faith will not be excluded from trial, even

if it was obtained in violation of the Fourth Amendment.[46] Because the exclusionary rule was designed to deter police misconduct, the Court reasoned that no deterrent purpose would be served by excluding evidence the police acquired while acting in good faith. The Court extended the good faith exception to cover errors made by court personnel. As a result, if police conduct an unconstitutional search relying on erroneous information from a court employee, the exclusionary rule will not apply.

The *inevitable discovery exception* provides that illegally obtained evidence can lawfully be introduced at trial if it can be shown that the evidence would inevitably have been found by other legal means.[47] For example, *United States v. Pimentel*[48] concerned Duroyd Manufacturing Company, a defense contractor that falsified documents and charges to the Defense Department. Evidence of this fraud was contained in a letter to Duroyd from one of its subcontractors, which the government obtained in an illegal search. Duroyd sought to exclude the letter from evidence. Because the contract gave the Defense Department's auditors the right to examine all "books, records, documents and other evidence . . . sufficient to reflect properly all direct and indirect costs . . . incurred for the performance of this contract," the court held that this letter would inevitably have been discovered and therefore refused to apply the exclusionary rule.

 ## Fifth Amendment Protections

The Fifth Amendment prohibits forced self-incrimination, double jeopardy, and criminal conviction without due process of law.

SELF-INCRIMINATION

The Fifth Amendment provides that no person "shall be compelled in any criminal case to be a witness against himself." This protection against self-incrimination extends to the preliminary stages in the criminal process as well as the trial itself. In a landmark self-incrimination case, *Miranda v. Arizona,*[49] decided in 1966, the Supreme Court laid down what has become known as the *Miranda* rule: a statement made by a defendant in custody is admissible only if the defendant was informed

44. *In re* Grand Jury Investigation Concerning Solid State Devices, Inc., 130 F.3d 853 (9th Cir. 1997).
45. *See* Andy Pasztor, *U.S. Appeals Panel Ruling Clouds Probe of Faulty Electronic Parts,* WALL ST. J., Jan. 5, 1998, at B10.

46. United States v. Leon, 468 U.S. 897 (1984).
47. See Nix v. Williams, 467 U.S. 431 (1984).
48. 810 F.2d 366 (2d Cir. 1987).
49. 384 U.S. 436 (1966).

"*You have the right to remain silent, you are a child of the universe, no less than the trees and the stars. You have the right to be here. And, whether or not it is clear to you, no doubt the universe is unfolding as it should.*"

prior to police interrogation of his or her constitutional right to remain silent and to have counsel present. In the case that follows, the Supreme Court revisited the valid- ity of the *Miranda* rule and rejected attempts by Congress to overrule it.

A CASE IN POINT

CASE 17.1

Dickerson v. United States
Supreme Court of the United States
120 S. Ct. 2326 (2000).

Summary

FACTS Charles Dickerson was indicted for bank robbery, conspiracy to commit bank robbery, and using a firearm in the course of committing a crime. Before trial, Dickerson moved to *suppress* (i.e., prevent the prosecution from introducing into evidence) a confession he made to the FBI because he had not been given the required *Miranda warnings.* The district court granted Dickerson's motion to suppress, but the appeals court reversed, holding that Congress had effectively overruled *Miranda* when it adopted a statute (18 U.S.C. § 3501) that required only a showing that the statement was made voluntarily. According to Section 3501, voluntariness is to be determined through an examination of the "totality of circumstances." Dickerson appealed.

ISSUE PRESENTED Does *Miranda* continue to govern the admissibility of statements made during police interrogations?

SUMMARY OF OPINION The U.S. Supreme Court acknowledged that Section 3501 represented an attempt by Congress to overrule the longstanding *Miranda* rule but held that "*Miranda,* being a constitutional decision of this Court, may not be in effect overruled by an Act of Congress . . . ."

(Continued)

(Case 17.1 continued)

While recognizing that the *Miranda* rule has some drawbacks that Congress was attempting to address, the Court declined to alter the rule:

> The disadvantage of the *Miranda* rule is that statements which may be by no means involuntary, made by a defendant who is aware of his "rights," may nonetheless be excluded and a guilty defendant go free as a result. But experience suggests that the totality-of-the-circumstances test which §3501 seeks to revive is more difficult than *Miranda* for law enforcement officers to conform to, and for courts to apply in a consistent manner.

RESULT The judgment of the appeals court was reversed. Because the police did not read Dickerson his rights before questioning him, his motion to suppress his statement was granted.

The Fifth Amendment privilege against self-incrimination applies only to compelled testimonial evidence. Requiring defendants to provide tangible evidence such as fingerprints, body fluids (urine and blood), or voice or handwriting samples does not violate the Fifth Amendment prohibition against self-incrimination. Requiring a person to appear in a lineup also does not violate the privilege.

Business Records and Papers and the Collective Entity Doctrine The Fifth Amendment protection for business records and papers is very limited. Corporations (and other business entities) enjoy no protection. Under the *collective entity doctrine,* the Supreme Court has held that the custodian of records for a collective entity (such as a corporation) may not resist a subpoena for such records on the ground that the act of production will incriminate him or her.[50] Nonetheless, the custodian cannot be compelled to testify as to the contents of the documents if that testimony would incriminate him or her personally.

The Fifth Amendment privilege may not be invoked to resist compliance with a regulatory regime, as long as that regime is designed with a public purpose unrelated to the enforcement of criminal laws.[51] Thus, records that government regulations require a business to keep can be used against the reporting individual in a criminal prosecution.

The business records compiled by a sole proprietor may have some protection. Courts must at least assess the Fifth Amendment rights at issue when the business records of a sole proprietor are subpoenaed.[52] This analysis is not concerned with the content of the documents, however. Rather, a privilege may be invoked only if the government cannot authenticate the documents without the proprietor; in that case, the act of furnishing documents may have the qualities of self-incriminating testimony.

In the following case, the Supreme Court emphasized that, while a person can be required to hand over specified documents, he or she cannot be required to assist in identifying sources of information.

---

50. *See* Braswell v. United States, 487 U.S. 99 (1988).

51. *See* Shapiro v. United States, 335 U.S. 1 (1948).
52. *See* Fisher v. United States, 425 U.S. 391 (1976). *See also* Braswell v. United States, 487 U.S. 99 (1988).

A CASE IN POINT

CASE 17.2
United States v. Hubbell
Supreme Court of the United States
120 S. Ct. 2037 (2000).

Summary

FACTS During an independent counsel investigation of possible violations of federal law by former president Bill Clinton, his wife Hillary, and their Arkansas law partners in connection with the Whitewater Development Corporation, Webster Hubbell entered into a plea bargain. Hubbell pled guilty to charges of mail fraud and tax evasion, was sentenced to twenty-one months in prison, and promised to provide full information relating to the Whitewater investigation. The independent counsel later served Hubbell with a

(Continued)

(Case 17.2 continued)

subpoena for eleven categories of Whitewater documents. Hubbell attempted to invoke the Fifth Amendment privilege against self-incrimination but was required to provide 13,120 pages of documents and records with the assurance that he would be granted immunity "to the extent allowed by law." The contents of the documents provided the basis for a second grand jury prosecution of Hubbell in which he was indicted on ten counts of tax-related crimes and mail and wire fraud. Hubbell challenged the indictment on the grounds that it was based on the documents he produced under a grant of immunity in violation of his privilege against self-incrimination.

ISSUE PRESENTED Does the Fifth Amendment privilege against self-incrimination protect a witness from having to testify about the existence and sources of potentially incriminating information?

SUMMARY OF OPINION The U.S. Supreme Court initially set forth the well-established rule that "a person may be required to produce specific documents even though they contain incriminating assertions of fact or belief because the creation of these documents was not 'compelled' within the meaning of the privilege." However, the Court also acknowledged that the act of making documents available in response to a subpoena may implicitly communicate statements of fact in violation of a witness's rights under the Fifth Amendment.

Pointing out that the prosecution needed Hubbell's assistance in identifying the sources of information and in producing those sources, the Court concluded that the subpoena was tantamount to requiring Hubbell to answer a series of questions about the existence and location of particular documents falling under a broad description. Answers to these questions could provide a prosecutor "a link in the chain of evidence needed to prosecute." Concluding that just such a link was provided in this case, the Court held that "the constitutional privilege against self-incrimination protects the target of a grand jury investigation from being compelled to answer questions designed to elicit information about the existence of sources of potentially incriminating evidence."

RESULT The prosecutor violated Hubbell's privilege against self-incrimination, and the ten-count indictment was dismissed.

Foreign Prosecutions A witness in a U.S. proceeding who is not facing prosecution in the United States may not invoke the privilege to avoid having to give testimony that might incriminate the witness in another country, unless the sovereign that the witness fears will prosecute him or her is itself bound by the privilege.[53] The Supreme Court has left open the question of whether the privilege against self-incrimination may be asserted if the cooperation between the United States and another country has reached a point at which prosecution in the other country could not fairly be characterized as "foreign."

53. United States v. Balsys, 524 U.S. 666 (1998).

DOUBLE JEOPARDY

The *Double Jeopardy Clause* of the Fifth Amendment protects criminal defendants from multiple prosecutions for the same offense. If the defendant is found not guilty, the defendant is cleared of all charges, and the prosecutor may not appeal the verdict. If the defendant is found guilty, however, the defendant can appeal. Double jeopardy does not bar a second prosecution if there was a hung jury in the first proceeding.

There are important limitations on the double jeopardy protection. A single criminal act may result in several statutory violations for which the defendant may be prosecuted even if each prosecution is based on the same set of facts. For example, a prosecutor could bring criminal charges against a defendant operating a securities scam for securities law violations, wire and mail fraud, false statements, and tax evasion. The Double Jeopardy Clause also does not protect against prosecutions by different governments (such as state and federal) based on the same underlying facts. Thus, after two police officers who beat Rodney King in 1991 were acquitted on California state criminal charges, spawning the 1992 Los Angeles riots, they could still be tried and convicted one year later on federal charges of violating King's civil rights.

Finally, the prohibition against double jeopardy does not preclude a civil suit against a criminal defendant by the victim. Thus, although O.J. Simpson was acquitted on criminal murder charges in 1996, the families of his alleged victims were still able to secure multimillion-dollar judgments against Simpson in a 1997 civil trial.

Civil and Criminal Prosecutions by the Government A vital issue for the prosecutors and perpetrators of business crimes has been whether the government could seek both civil sanctions (such as fines) and criminal punishment for the same illegal conduct. The U.S. Supreme Court clarified the law in this area in a case decided in 1997 that made it far more difficult for defendants to argue that a civil sanction implicates the Double Jeopardy Clause. In *Hudson v. United States,*[54] the Court emphasized that the Double Jeopardy Clause protects only against the imposition of multiple *criminal* punishments for the same offense. Legislative intent is the guiding factor in determining whether a particular penalty is "civil" or "criminal." When the legislature has indicated an intention to establish a civil sanction, courts should rarely transform it into a criminal penalty for double jeopardy purposes.

DUE PROCESS AND VOLUNTARY CONFESSIONS

When the conduct of law enforcement officials in obtaining a confession is outrageous or shocking, the *Due Process Clauses* of the Fifth and Fourteenth Amendments bar the government from using the involuntary confession, even if the *Miranda* warnings were given. For example, physical coercion or brutality invalidates a confession. However, the courts have usually held that misleading or false verbal statements that induce the suspect to confess are not grounds for invalidating the confession, unless the statements rise to the level of unduly coercive threats.

A Florida appeals court invalidated a confession elicited through the use of fabricated (and false) labora-

tory reports linking the defendant to the crime.[55] Other courts, however, have said that there is no "bright line" that dictates that all uses of false documents are unconstitutional. These courts have held that after considering the "totality of the circumstances," confessions similarly obtained were in fact "voluntary."[56]

Before a confession of guilt will be admitted into evidence, the trial judge must determine whether the confession was voluntarily made, as required by the Due Process Clauses. Nonetheless, the erroneous admission at trial of a coerced confession will not always automatically require that the conviction be overturned.[57]

 # Sixth Amendment Protections

The Sixth Amendment grants the criminal defendant a number of procedural protections, including a right to counsel and to a trial by jury.

ASSISTANCE OF COUNSEL

The defendant in most criminal prosecutions has the right "to have the Assistance of Counsel." This means, first, that the accused has the right to his or her own attorney. If the defendant cannot afford an attorney, he or she is entitled to a court-appointed attorney. Second, once taken into custody, the accused must be informed of his or her right to counsel as part of the *Miranda* warnings. Third, the assistance of counsel must be effective, that is, within the range of competence required of attorneys in criminal cases. In practice, counsel is presumed effective and only in outrageous cases is counsel considered ineffective. Fourth, an attorney must be appointed for an appeal of a verdict.

JURY TRIAL

Most defendants in criminal cases have the right to a jury trial. Jury trials are not required in cases in which the authorized punishment for the charged offense is six months or less. A jury is also not required in juvenile proceedings. State court juries consist of six to twelve individuals, with a minimum of six jurors. Federal courts have twelve jurors. To render a verdict in a federal criminal

---

54. 522 U.S. 93 (1997).

55. Florida v. Cayward, 552 So. 2d 971 (Fla. Dist. Ct. App. 1989).
56. *See, e.g.,* Sheriff, Washoe County v. Bessey, 914 P.2d 681 (Nev. 1996); Arthur v. Virginia, 480 S.E.2d 749 (Va. Ct. App. 1997).
57. *See* Arizona v. Fulminante, 499 U.S. 279 (1991) (harmless error test applies to determine whether conviction must be overturned).

trial, the jury must reach a unanimous decision. Juries of six in state courts must also be unanimous in order to reach a verdict in a criminal case, but the U.S. Supreme Court has not ruled on juries of seven or more.

OTHER PROCEDURAL RIGHTS

The Sixth Amendment also guarantees the right to a speedy trial and the right to confront and cross-examine witnesses.

 # Nonconstitutional Protections

In a criminal prosecution, the prosecutor is obligated to show the defendant all evidence that the defendant specifically requests. In addition, certain items (such as any exculpatory evidence) must be turned over regardless of whether the defendant requests them. The accused may also be required to reveal certain information to the prosecutor, such as statements made by witnesses who have testified in a sworn statement.

More requirements to reveal evidence are imposed on the prosecutor than on the defendant. The rationale for this protection is the need to neutralize the natural advantage of the state against the individual defendant.

ATTORNEY–CLIENT PRIVILEGE

When criminal charges are brought against a corporate employee who is represented by a lawyer paid by the corporation, it may be unclear to whom the attorney–client privilege belongs. Is the client the employee charged with the offense, the corporation that is paying the lawyer, or both? In general, a client must establish a relationship with the attorney for the attorney–client privilege to apply. Thus, if the employee wants to be treated as the client, the employee should obtain an engagement letter from the attorney that expressly states that the employee is the client even though the employer is paying the attorney's fees. In general, in-house counsel investigating possible violations of law represent the corporation and its directors, not the individual employees who might be questioned by counsel. (The attorney–client privilege is discussed in Chapter 3.)

 # Liability *for* Criminal Actions

Liability may be imposed on the person who actually committed the crime, on that person's supervisors as individuals, and on the corporation (or other entity) that employs the person.

INDIVIDUAL LIABILITY

Individuals may commit a criminal act either against a corporation for their own gain or on behalf of the corporation. If an officer, director, or employee commits a crime against the corporation (such as theft, embezzlement, or forgery), that person will be prosecuted as an individual.

Officers, directors, or employees who commit crimes will be prosecuted as individuals even if they were trying to benefit the corporation. As discussed below, the person's supervisor may also be held responsible.

If a supervisor asks an employee to commit an act that the employee suspects is criminal, the employee should bear two things in mind. First, if there is a criminal prosecution, it is not a valid defense for the employee to state that he or she was just following the orders of upper-level officers or directors of the corporation. Second, as discussed in Chapter 14, an employee cannot be terminated for refusing to commit a criminal act.

INDIVIDUAL VICARIOUS LIABILITY

Vicarious liability (also called *imputed liability*) is the imposition of liability on one party for the wrongs of another. Under the theory of vicarious liability, officers, directors, and managers may be found guilty of a crime committed by employees under their supervision. Criminal statutes that provide for the vicarious liability of corporate officers usually require that the officer commit some wrongful act. This requirement can typically be fulfilled simply by the officer's failure to provide adequate supervision or failure to satisfy a duty imposed by the statute. In other words, the wrongful act need not always be an affirmative act.

The more delicate issue is what kind of *mens rea*, or mental state, is required to find a corporate officer vicariously liable for a crime. In cases involving criminal vicarious liability, the crucial questions are most often "How much did the manager know?" and "How much does the statute require that the manager know before he or she can be held criminally liable?"

Responsible Corporate Officer Doctrine The *responsible corporate officer doctrine* addresses these questions. It is important to note at the outset that two different but interwoven issues are involved. The first is a vicarious liability issue: whether an officer bears responsibility for the actions of his or her subordinates. The second is a *mens* *rea* issue: whether the officer must have known about or intended the violation before he or she can be held criminally liable.

The Supreme Court applied the responsible corporate officer doctrine in *United States v. Park.*[58] John Park was the CEO of Acme Markets, a national retail food chain that employed 36,000 people and operated 874 retail outlets. Despite this enormous size and the multiple layers of authority between Park and the employees who had been instructed to eliminate rodents in Acme's warehouses, Park was found guilty as an individual of distributing "adulterated" food in violation of the Food, Drug and Cosmetic Act (FDCA). The Court noted that "Congress has seen fit to enforce the accountability of responsible corporate agents dealing with products which may affect the health of customers" by enacting "rigorous" penal sanctions. Corporate officers have a "duty to implement measures that will insure that violations will not occur"; in other words, the FDCA imposed "requirements of foresight and vigilance."

The Food and Drug Administration (FDA) had on two separate occasions advised Park that the company was storing food in rodent-infested warehouses. Although Park had been told by a vice president that the problem had been taken care of after the first FDA visit, he failed to personally investigate the problems even after the FDA visited a second time and again complained of rats in the warehouse.

At first glance, the Supreme Court established a sweeping precedent for the criminal prosecution of corporate officers. Seemingly, under *Park,* any corporate officer could be found guilty of a crime if he or she bore a "responsible relation" to a violation of a statute dealing with "products which may affect the health of customers."

This is not, however, how the responsible corporate officer doctrine has been applied. Courts of appeals have recognized an important limitation on the doctrine: it should be applied in criminal cases only when the statute at issue is a public welfare statute lacking an express knowledge or other *scienter* requirement. The FDCA, the statute involved in *Park,* was a strict liability misdemeanor statute. After being found guilty, Park was subject only to a fine and not incarceration. Courts generally have not applied the responsible corporate officer doctrine in cases involving felony statutes, though the government has often attempted to prosecute felonies under the doctrine. But appellate courts have used the responsible corporate officer doctrine to impose monetary penalties (though not imprisonment) under the Occupational Safety and Health Act (OSHA)[59] and the Radiation Control for Health and Safety Act.[60]

When a statute requires that a defendant "knowingly" commit a wrongful act, courts have ruled that the responsible corporate officer doctrine cannot be used to convict officers absent direct or circumstantial proof of knowledge.[61] For example, the Federal Meat Inspection Act and environmental statutes such as the Comprehensive Environmental Response, Compensation, and Liability Act and the Resource Conservation and Recovery Act (discussed in Chapter 18) all require that defendants knowingly commit wrongful acts before being found guilty. Even though these statutes clearly concern public health and safety, the appellate courts refused to affirm convictions under the responsible corporate officer doctrine.[62]

Nonetheless, appellate courts have held that knowledge may be inferred for responsible corporate officers in appropriate circumstances.[63] For example, in *United States v. Self,*[64] the U.S. Court of Appeals for the Fifth Circuit stated: "[W]hile knowledge of prior illegal activity is not conclusive as to whether a defendant possessed the requisite knowledge of later illegal activity, it most certainly provides circumstantial evidence of the defendant's later knowledge from which the jury may draw the necessary inference."

---

58. 421 U.S. 658 (1975). *See also* United States v. Dotterweich, 320 U.S. 277 (1943) (criminal sanctions can be imposed on the corporate officers who have a "responsible relation" to the offending acts of the corporation even in the absence of proof that the officers were conscious of the wrongdoing).

59. *See, e.g.,* United States v. Doig, 950 F.2d 411 (7th Cir. 1991).

60. *See, e.g.,* United States v. Hodges X-Ray, Inc., 759 F.2d 557 (6th Cir. 1985).

61. *See, e.g.,* United States v. MacDonald & Watson Waste Oil Co., 933 F.2d 35 (1st Cir. 1991) ("in a crime having knowledge as an express element, a mere showing of official responsibility . . . is not an adequate substitute for direct or circumstantial proof of knowledge"). Similarly, the U.S. District Court for the Western District of Missouri held that "something more than a mere status should be required before civil penalties are assessed against corporate officers for knowing violations of the [Federal Hazardous Substances Act]." United States v. Shelton Wholesale, Inc., 1999 U.S. Dist. LEXIS 15980 (W.D. Mo. Sept. 21, 1999). *But see* United States v. International Minerals & Chem. Corp., 402 U.S. 558 (1971) (officers of chemical company were "under a species of absolute liability for violation of the regulations [proscribing knowing failure to record shipment of chemicals] despite the 'knowingly' requirement").

62. *See, e.g.,* United States v. Agnew, 931 F.2d 1397 (10th Cir. 1991).

63. *See, e.g.,* United States v. Johnson & Towers, Inc., 741 F.2d 662, 669–70 (3d Cir. 1984) ("knowledge" in a Resource Conservation and Recovery Act criminal prosecution "may be inferred by the jury as to those individuals who hold the requisite responsible positions with the corporate defendant").

64. 2 F.3d 1071, 1087–88 (5th Cir. 1993).

Impossibility Defense to Strict Liability A corporate officer might not be held strictly (and vicariously) liable if he or she did everything possible to ensure legal compliance, yet the company was still unable to comply with the applicable standards. In these circumstances, the officer can argue the defense of impossibility. According to the U.S. Court of Appeals for the Second Circuit: "To establish the *impossibility defense*, the corporate officer must introduce evidence that he exercised extraordinary care and still could not prevent violations of the Act."[65]

CORPORATE LIABILITY

A corporation (or other business entity) can be held liable for criminal offenses committed by its employees if the acts were committed within the scope of their employment (whether actual or apparent). This form of vicarious liability is known as *respondeat superior*, which means "let the superior give answer." (The doctrine of *respondeat superior* in civil cases is discussed in Chapters 5 and 9.)

For example, the Pennsylvania Superior Court held a bus company criminally liable for homicide by vehicle when a low-level employee, the driver of a school bus owned by the corporation, ran over and killed a six-year-old who was crossing in front of the bus.[66] The bus driver could not see the child because mirrors that were required by state statute were missing.

In cases involving misdemeanor offenses or regulatory crimes, the well-established rule is that a corporation is criminally liable for all violations committed by any of its agents or employees.[67] Although a small minority of courts have held that a corporation cannot be guilty of a non-strict liability crime—that is, a crime requiring a guilty mental state such as "knowledge" or "intent"—it is now the generally accepted rule that a corporation may be indicted for a crime (such as negligent homicide) for which a specific guilty mental state is essential. In such cases, the knowledge or intent of the employees and agents is imputed to the corporation.[68] In many cases, the legislature has clearly indicated (either in the language of the statute or in legislative history) a desire to

INTERNATIONAL CONSIDERATION

Many European nations do not recognize corporate criminal liability because (1) the corporation does not possess a guilty mind, (2) the corporation is not viewed as the real offender when a crime is committed, and (3) the corporation is not considered well suited for either punishment or rehabilitation. For example, the German constitution prohibits imposition of criminal liability on corporations. These countries focus instead on identifying and punishing the individuals responsible for the criminal acts.

impose criminal liability on corporations; courts consistently enforce such legislative intent.[69]

The corporation will almost always be vicariously liable if upper management or the board of directors adopts a policy or issues instructions that cause an employee to violate the law. Even if an agent acted contrary to a corporate policy or express instructions, the corporation may still be criminally liable if the agent was acting within his or her apparent authority (and, in some states, at least in part for the benefit of the corporation).[70] As a practical matter, courts have been willing to impose liability upon the corporation if the agent's actions were at least "tolerated" by management.[71] Typically, courts make this determination based on the totality of the circumstances surrounding the agent's actions.

For example, one case[72] involved Edwin Clancy, the president of defendant Penn Valley Resorts, who agreed to provide dinner and an open bar for sixty undergraduate students from the State University of New York. A twenty-year-old minor became noticeably intoxicated, and en route back to the university, he caused an automobile accident in which he was killed. At the time of death, his blood alcohol content was .23; a level of .10 is normally considered sufficient to make a person intoxicated.

The Pennsylvania court held that a corporation could be found criminally liable even if the corporation's board of directors did not condone the action. If the illegal conduct is performed or tolerated by a high managerial agent acting on behalf of the corporation within the

---

65. United States v. Gel Spice Co. 773 F.2d 427 (2d Cir. 1985) (quoting United States v. New England Grocers Co., 488 F. Supp. 230 (D. Mass. 1980)). (Emphasis added.)
66. Commonwealth v. McIlwain Sch. Bus Lines, 423 A.2d 413 (Pa. Super. 1980).
67. *See* 18 Am. Jur. 2d *Corporations* § 2136 (1985).
68. *See, e.g.*, Boise Dodge v. United States, 406 F.2d 771 (9th Cir. 1969); Vaughn & Sons, Inc. v. State, 737 S.W.2d 805 (Tex. Crim. App. 1987); 18 Am. Jur. 2d *Corporations* § 2137 (1985).

69. *See, e.g.*, Hanlester Network v. Shalala, 51 F.3d 1390 (9th Cir. 1995); People v. Mattiace, 568 N.E.2d 1189 (N.Y. 1990).
70. *See, e.g.*, United States v. Beusch, 596 F.2d 871 (9th Cir. 1979); State v. Hy Vee Food Stores, Inc., 533 N.W.2d 147 (S.D. 1995). *See also* State v. Pinarfville Athletic Club, 594 A.2d 1284 (N.H. 1991).
71. *See* Minnesota v. Christy Pontiac–GMC, Inc., 354 N.W.2d 17 (Minn. 1984).
72. Commonwealth v. Penn Valley Resorts, Inc., 494 A.2d 1139 (Pa. Super. 1985).

scope of his or her office or employment, the corporation can be held criminally liable. The appellate court found that the defendant corporation was properly convicted of criminal involuntary manslaughter, reckless endangerment, and furnishing liquor to minors and visibly intoxicated persons.

White-Collar Crime

White-collar crime is violation of the law by a corporation (or other business entity) or one of its managers. White-collar employees—that is, managers or professionals—may be either the victims or the perpetrators of crime. Many white-collar criminal statutes do not have a *mens rea* requirement. It is, therefore, possible to commit a crime in the corporate setting without having the intention of breaking the law.

CRIME AGAINST THE EMPLOYER

Examples of crimes committed by an employee against his or her employer include theft, embezzlement, fraud, and acceptance of a bribe.

ETHICAL CONSIDERATION

The line between accepting gifts and taking bribes is not always clear. For instance, if a data-processing manager will make the decision on the purchase of a mainframe computer, it is unethical and illegal for him or her to accept a percentage of the sales price of the computer from the seller. Some data-processing managers accept expensive meals, sports tickets, and other "perks" from computer salespersons. Is acceptance of such gifts ethical?

Theft, technically known as *larceny*, is simply the taking of property without the owner's consent. White-collar theft ranges from taking home pens and paper from the office to stealing money through the company's computer system.

Embezzlement is the taking of money or property that is lawfully in the employee's possession by reason of his or her employment. For example, a company's treasurer who takes money that belongs to the company by writing checks to dummy accounts is guilty of embezzlement.

Fraud is any deception intended to induce someone to part with property or money. Fraud may involve a

IN BRIEF

Liability for Criminal Actions

Type of Defendant	Standard for Liability
Individual	The individual must have performed *actus reus* (criminal act) with *mens rea* (guilty mind). An individual can perpetrate a crime against the corporate employer (e.g., embezzlement) or for the benefit of the corporation (e.g., price-fixing).
Corporate officers	Officers can be directly liable for failing to supervise subordinates. In addition to individual liability for their own acts, officers may be vicariously liable for crimes committed by other employees. Under the responsible corporate officer doctrine, officers can be liable for criminal actions of their subordinates if the officer bore a "responsible relation" to the violation of law. Typically, the doctrine is used to impose criminal liability only for violations of strict liability statutes involving public health where the officer is charged with a misdemeanor or the prosecution proves, through direct or circumstantial evidence, that the officer knew of the violation.
Corporations (and other business entities)	*Respondeat superior* liability. A corporation is criminally liable for (1) all misdemeanor offenses and regulatory crimes committed by any of its agents or employees; (2) all crimes committed pursuant to top management's corporate policy or express instructions; and (3) all crimes committed by employees if the acts (a) were committed within the scope of their employment (whether actual or apparent and, in some states, also in furtherance of the corporation's business interests) or (b) were tolerated by top management.

false representation of fact, whether by words or by conduct, or concealment of something that should have been disclosed. Examples of fraud include the padding of an expense account, the submission of falsely inflated insurance reimbursement bills, and the doctoring of financial statements to influence stock price.

Acceptance of a bribe may also be a crime against the employer. For example, a sales representative cannot legally accept a kickback from a purchaser of his or her employer's products. Similarly, a purchasing agent for a corporation must not accept a bribe from an outside salesperson.

CRIME BY THE CORPORATION

Examples of crimes perpetrated by corporations (and other business entities) and employees or agents acting on their behalf include consumer fraud, securities fraud, tax evasion, and environmental pollution. Corporations can also commit crimes against other corporations. Examples include price-fixing (discussed in Chapter 20) and misappropriation of trade secrets or violations of copyright or patent laws (discussed in Chapter 11).

Most white-collar crime is nonviolent and is committed either against a business or the government or by a business against a large group of individuals. Although there is no precise definition of white-collar crime, government estimates put the cost of nonviolent fraud and commercial crime at more than $100 billion a year. The balance of this chapter is devoted to a description of the most common types of white-collar crimes.

The Racketeer Influenced and Corrupt Organizations Act

The Racketeer Influenced and Corrupt Organizations Act (RICO)[73] was originally designed to combat organized crime and to provide an enforcement mechanism against syndicate bosses and masterminds who might otherwise escape liability. Today, the criminal provisions of RICO are a prosecutor's most powerful weapon to fight classic white-collar crimes.

RICO prohibits (1) the investment in any enterprise of income derived from racketeering, (2) the acquisition of an interest in an enterprise through a pattern of racketeering activity, (3) participation in an enterprise through a pattern of racketeering activity involving at least two related predicate acts in a ten-year period, and (4) conspiring to engage in any of these activities.

73. 18 U.S.C.A. §§ 1961–68 (West 1984 and Supp. 1998).

INTERNATIONAL CONSIDERATION

The inbred financial world of Japan has generated a series of scandals involving corporate extortion. By threatening to disclose unsavory information through magazines or at shareholder meetings, elements of Japan's mobster class (referred to as the *sokaiya*) have squeezed payoffs from some of Japan's biggest companies, including Nomura Securities, retailer Ajinmoto, and Dai–Ichi Kangyo Bank. No other industrialized economy has lived with a comparable level of corporate blackmail. Extortion has thrived in Japan because in its corporate culture, public information is given out sparingly and a tight web of cross-shareholdings among companies excludes individual stockholders.

Official tolerance of corporate blackmail has been waning ever since the mob began taking a higher profile in the booming economy of the late 1980s. Moreover, the current Japanese government is cracking down on extortion as part of its broader effort to reform Japan's financial markets. The specter of mobster-backed blackmail cannot help Japan's attempts to woo global investors interested in trading securities or effecting mergers and other capital-raising transactions.

Source: The information in this section is drawn from Brian Bremmer & Emily Thornton, *Blackmail!*, Bus. Wk., July 21, 1997, at 42.

RICO REQUIREMENTS

Section 1961(4) of RICO broadly defines an *enterprise* as "any individual, partnership, corporation, association, or other legal entity, and any union or group of individuals associated in fact although not a legal entity." *Racketeering activity* is defined to include various state and federal offenses, specifically including mail and wire fraud and fraud in the sale of securities. Consequently, almost any business fraud can serve as the basis for a criminal RICO violation.

In order to demonstrate a pattern of racketeering activity, a plaintiff must show that at least two related predicate acts have occurred within a ten-year period. Two isolated acts are not considered sufficient.

USE OF RICO

RICO has proved particularly effective against groups of traders, brokers, and others who have developed a continuous relationship of passing and trading on inside information. In July 1988, for example, Alfred Elliot was charged with making $680,000 in illegal profits from trading on confidential information he had acquired while a partner at a Chicago law firm.

Although RICO is generally given a liberal construction to ensure that Congress's intent is not frustrated by an overly narrow reading of the statute, the reach of the statute is not unlimited. In *Reves v. Ernst & Young*,[74] purchasers of demand notes from a farmer's cooperative brought a securities fraud and RICO action against the cooperative's auditors. The U.S. Supreme Court held that the accountants hired to perform an audit of the cooperative's records did not exert control over the company and did not "participate in the operation or management" of the cooperative's affairs. Such a finding of participation would have been necessary to find the accountants liable under RICO for failing to inform the cooperative's board of directors that the cooperative was insolvent. As clarified by the U.S. Court of Appeals for the Seventh Circuit, "participation" requires that one "knowingly agree to perform the services of a kind which facilitate the activities of those who are operating the enterprise in an illegal manner."[75]

Reves is an important case for accountants, underwriters, attorneys, and others who work with a company that is issuing securities. Such persons can no longer be found liable under RICO just because they were involved in the offering process. Instead, some involvement in the management of the issuer of the securities is required.

PENALTIES UNDER RICO

Persons convicted of criminal RICO violations are subject to a fine and imprisonment for up to twenty years (or life if the violation is based on a racketeering activity for which the maximum penalty includes life imprisonment).

Civil Actions In addition to criminal penalties, the statute grants a private right of action that permits individuals to recover treble damages (that is, three times their actual damages) and also their costs and attorneys' fees in a civil action. The private right of action apparently was intended as a tool against businesses fueled by funds generated through organized crime. The statute contains no explicit requirement that organized crime be involved, however, and RICO has been used in numerous civil suits against legitimate businesses.

To prevail in a civil case under RICO, the plaintiff must demonstrate that the defendant committed an "overt act . . . in furtherance of a RICO conspiracy."[76] Thus, a president fired for reporting activity that violated RICO did not have a private cause of action against his former employer because the termination of his employment was not a racketeering activity. In 1995, Congress foreclosed the use of the RICO private right of civil action against alleged perpetrators of securities fraud. Denying the potential for RICO-based shareholder lawsuits was one of the many measures in the Private Securities Litigation Reform Act,[77] which was designed to curb abusive shareholder litigation. Criminal RICO charges can still be based on securities fraud.

The Wire *and* Mail Fraud Acts *and the* False Statements *and* Claims Acts

WIRE AND MAIL FRAUD

Next to RICO, the Wire and Mail Fraud Acts[78] may be the prosecutor's most powerful weapon against white-collar criminal defendants. Chief Justice Warren Burger characterized the Mail Fraud Act as a "stopgap" provision that criminalizes conduct that a court finds morally reprehensible but that is not mentioned in any other criminal statute.

To establish *mail fraud* or *wire fraud* under the Acts, the prosecutor must demonstrate (1) a scheme intended to defraud or to obtain money or property by fraudulent means, and (2) the use of the mails or of interstate telephone lines in furtherance of the fraudulent scheme. Exactly what constitutes a fraudulent scheme has never been established. It remains a factual question determined on a case-by-case basis. The Supreme Court has broadly construed "fraud" to encompass "everything designed to defraud by representations as to the past or present, or suggestions and promises as to the future."[79]

Violations of the Acts are punishable by a fine not to exceed $1,000 and a prison sentence not to exceed five years. If the violation affects a financial institution, the violator may be fined up to $1 million or imprisoned up to thirty years, or both.

Federal prosecutions under these Acts have involved such diverse activities as defense procurement fraud, insurance fraud, false financial statements fraud, medical advertising fraud, tax fraud, divorce mill fraud, and securities fraud. Indeed, it is rare for a white-collar criminal prosecution to be brought without alleging a violation of

---

74. 507 U.S. 170 (1993).
75. Brouwer v. Raffensperger, 199 F.3d 961 (7th Cir. 2000).
76. Beck v. Prupis, 529 U.S. 494 (2000).

77. Pub. L. No. 104-67, § 107, 109 Stat. 737, 758 (codified at 18 U.S.C.A. § 1964(c) (West Supp. 1998)).
78. 18 U.S.C. §§ 1343, 1341 (1994).
79. Durland v. United States, 161 U.S. 306, 313 (1896).

the Wire and Mail Fraud Acts. Also, violation of these Acts can trigger RICO liability; as a result, wire and mail fraud and RICO prosecutions often proceed in tandem.

The Wire and Mail Fraud Acts can be used to prosecute a broad array of fraudulent activity. For example, in *Schmuck v. United States,*[80] the Supreme Court upheld an indictment for mail fraud although the actual mailings were merely incidental to the scheme to defraud. Wayne T. Schmuck, a used-car distributor, purchased used cars, rolled back their odometers, and sold them to Wisconsin retail dealers at prices artificially inflated by the low-mileage readings. The unwitting dealers, relying on the altered readings, resold the cars to customers at inflated prices. The dealers consummated these transactions by mailing title-application forms to the state authorities on behalf of the buyers. The U.S. Supreme Court held that the mailings at issue satisfied the mailing element of the crime of mail fraud.

A prosecution for wire and mail fraud can be brought in addition to other prosecutions based on the same events. Thus, the defendant may be charged with violation of the securities laws, the bankruptcy laws, the tax laws, or the Truth in Lending Act, as well as with wire or mail fraud.

A prosecutor can choose under which statutes to charge the defendant. This prosecutorial discretion increases the plea-bargaining power of the government. Additionally, by presenting multiple statutory violations to the jury, the prosecutor increases the chances of conviction and the likelihood of a stiffer sentence.

THE FALSE STATEMENTS ACT

The False Statements Act provides that:

> Whoever, in any manner within the jurisdiction of any department or agency of the United States knowingly and willfully
>
> 1. falsifies, conceals or covers up by any trick, scheme, or device a material fact;
> 2. makes any false, fictitious or fraudulent statements or representations, or
> 3. makes or uses any false writing or document knowing the same to contain any false, fictitious or fraudulent statement or entry, shall be fined [not more than $5,000] or imprisoned not more than five years, or both.[81]

Although not used as frequently as the Wire and Mail Fraud Acts, the False Statements Act has become an effective tool for criminal prosecutions of businesses and employees who deal dishonestly with governmental administrative agencies. For example, in *United States v. Yermian,*[82] an employee of Gulton Industries, a defense contractor, was convicted of making false statements to the Department of Defense in connection with his application for a security clearance.

THE FALSE CLAIMS ACT

Since the late 1980s, the U.S. government has used a civil statute, the False Claims Act (FCA),[83] to attack defense-contract and health care fraud. Both the federal government and private parties (usually whistle-blowers) acting on the government's behalf (*qui tam* plaintiffs) can bring civil suits to recover treble damages and penalties of up to $10,000 per knowing false claim from persons who submit false claims for government funds knowingly or with recklessness or deliberate ignorance of their truth or falsity. The *qui tam* plaintiffs receive up to 25 percent of the recovery. By February 2000, the United States had recovered more than $3.5 billion through FCA *qui tam* cases, of which $550 million was paid to the whistle-blowers who brought the cases.[84] In 2000, the U.S. Supreme Court rebuffed a challenge to the *qui tam* provisions when it held that whistle-blowers have standing under Article III of the U.S. Constitution to sue on the government's behalf.[85]

Computer Crime

White-collar crime often involves computers. Many computer-related crimes are likely to go undetected because computer offenses generally involve little or no visible physical activity. The computer may be used not only to commit the offense but also to hide or destroy the evidence. Because most computer crime is perpetrated by insiders, the individuals who are in the best position to discover the crime are often the ones who committed it.

Even if computer crime is detected, it often goes unreported. Most businesses, especially financial institutions, do not want it publicly known that an employee or an outsider used the company's computer system to steal from the company. In some cases, the affected company,

80. 489 U.S. 705 (1989).
81. 18 U.S.C. § 1001 (1994).
82. 581 F.2d 595 (7th Cir. 1978).
83. 31 U.S.C. § 3729 et seq. (2000).
84. Shelley R. Slade & Thomas A. Colhurst, *Health-Care Fraud and the False Claims Act: The Supreme Court Supports a Federal Weapon,* Bus. L. Today, Sept.–Oct. 2000, at 24, 26.
85. Vermont Agency of Natural Resources v. United States *ex rel.* Stevens, 120 S. Ct. 1858 (2000).

instead of prosecuting the computer criminal, has hired him or her as a computer security consultant.

Even when computer crimes are reported, the perpetrators are not always prosecuted and punished. Many prosecutors are overworked, and their offices understaffed; as a result, they give low priority to nonviolent crimes.

COMPUTER FRAUD

Computer fraud is the use of a computer to steal company or government funds. This type of theft generally involves improper or unauthorized access to the computer system and the creation of false data or computer instructions. The computer system then generates fraudulent transfers of funds or bogus checks that are cashed by the wrongdoer.

More than forty different sections of the federal criminal code may apply to thefts by computer, ranging from embezzlement from an Indian tribal organization to wire fraud. The Computer Fraud and Abuse Act (CFAA), discussed below, broadly addresses the general problem of theft by computer. Most computer-aided thefts can also be prosecuted under traditional state larceny laws.

THE COMPUTER FRAUD AND ABUSE ACT

The Computer Fraud and Abuse Act[86] prohibits (1) accessing a computer without authorization, if by such access the user obtains information from any protected computer and if the conduct involves an interstate or foreign communication; or (2) knowingly transmitting a program, information, code, or command that results in intentionally causing "damage" without authorization to a protected computer. "Damage" is defined as "any impairment to the integrity or availability of data, a program, a system, or information." Although the CFAA originally

86. 18 U.S.C.A. § 1030 (West Supp. 1998).

applied only to "federal interest computers" (computers of the federal government and certain financial institutions), Congress amended the Act in 1996 to substitute the phrase "protected computer" in place of "federal interest computer." "Protected computer" is defined as a computer used in interstate or foreign commerce.

The Act makes illegal the knowing transmission of computer viruses (discussed below). If the computer fraud perpetrated by a defendant was committed for commercial advantage or private gain, or if the value of information obtained by the fraud exceeds $5,000, the defendant is subject to up to five years imprisonment and a fine of up to $250,000, or up to twice the amount of the defendant's gross gain or the victim's gross loss for the offense. Persons who intentionally break into, or abuse their authority to use, a computer and thereby obtain information worth less than $5,000 are guilty of a misdemeanor.

A *computer virus* is a computer program that can replicate itself into other programs without any subsequent instruction, human or mechanical. A computer virus may destroy data, programs, or files, or it may prevent user access to a computer (*denial-of-service attacks*). A computer virus need not be destructive. It may be benign and temporary.

The proliferation of personal computers networked together has created millions of entry points for viruses. A virus can be concealed in any software and then passed on to other computers through attachments to electronic mail, information services, disks, or other means.

The following case demonstrates how certain amendments to the CFAA enacted in 1996 have, together with the explosive growth in the use of the Internet, greatly expanded the types of activities covered by the Act. (Although this case involved civil claims, the sections of the CFAA the court analyzed also provide the basis for a criminal prosecution.)

A CASE IN POINT

CASE 17.3

Shurgard Storage Centers, Inc. v. Safeguard Self Storage, Inc.

United States District Court for the Western District of Washington
119 F. Supp. 2d 1121 (W.D. Wash. 2000).

In the Language of the Court

FACTS Shurgard Storage Centers, the industry leader in full- and self-service storage facilities in both the United States and Europe, sued a competitor, Safeguard Self Storage, for allegedly embarking on a "systematic" scheme to hire away key employees for the purpose of obtaining trade secrets. Shurgard claimed that Eric Leland, one of its employees subsequently hired by Safeguard, used Shurgard's computers to access various trade secrets and proprietary information belonging to Shurgard and to send e-mails containing the information to Safeguard. Leland was still employed by Shurgard at the time he sent the e-mails.

(Continued)

(Case 17.3 continued)

Shurgard alleged misappropriation of trade secrets, conversion, unfair competition, tortious interference with a business expectancy, and violations of the Computer Fraud and Abuse Act. Safeguard moved to dismiss the CFAA claims.

ISSUE PRESENTED Does the CFAA apply to an employee's use of his employer's computer to e-mail misappropriated trade secrets to a competitor?

OPINION ZILLY, J., writing for the U.S. District Court for the Western District of Washington:

Under § 1030(a)(2)(C), "whoever . . . intentionally accesses a computer without authorization or exceeds authorized access, and thereby obtains . . . information from a protected computer if the conduct involved an interstate or foreign communication . . . shall be punished . . . . " [Section 1030(g) creates a private right of action for persons who suffer damage or loss because of a violation.]

. . . [T]he defendant asserts that the plaintiff has not alleged that the employees in question accessed the trade secrets without authorization. . . .

. . .

The plaintiff responds by arguing that the authorization for its former employees ended when the employees began acting as agents for the defendant. . . .

. . .

Under the Restatement (Second) of Agency:

Unless otherwise agreed, the authority of an agent terminates if, without knowledge of the principal, he acquires adverse interests or if he is otherwise guilty of a serious breach of loyalty to the principal.[87]

Under this rule, the authority of the plaintiff's former employees ended when they allegedly became agents of the defendant. . . .

. . .

. . . [T]he defendant maintains the CFAA is limited to those industries whose computers contain vast amounts of information, which if released, could significantly affect privacy interests in the public at large. The defendant also maintains the CFAA is limited to "outsiders" or "hackers," and not "insiders" (employees). Though the original scope of the CFAA was limited to the concerns addressed by the defendant, its subsequent amendments have broadened the scope sufficiently to cover the behavior alleged in this case.

. . .

. . . [T]he CFAA was intended to control interstate computer crime, and since the advent of the Internet, almost all computer use has become interstate in nature.

RESULT The defendant's motion to dismiss was denied. Shurgard had stated valid claims under the CFAA.

COMMENTS Section 1030(e)(8)(A) defines "damage" as "any impairment to the integrity or availability of data, a program, a system or information, that causes loss aggregating at least $5,000 in value during any one-year period to one or more individuals."[88] The court held that the defendant's collection and dissemination of confidential informa-

---

87. Restatement (Second) of Agency § 112 (1958).
88. In *United States v. Middleton*, 231 F.3d 1207 (9th Cir. 2000), the U.S. Court of Appeals for the Ninth Circuit held that "individuals" include corporations and other artificial entities.

(Continued)

(Case 17.3 continued)

tion constituted an impairment of its integrity even though no data were physically damaged or erased. The court also held that the plaintiff had stated a claim under Section 1030(a)(4), which prohibits any person from knowingly and with intent to defraud accessing a protected computer without authorization. The court held that a plaintiff need not prove the common law elements of fraud, but only that the defendant engaged in wrongdoing or employed dishonest methods.

QUESTIONS

1. Is a computer or its information "damaged" within the meaning of the CFAA when intruders alter existing log-on programs to copy user passwords to a file that the hackers can retrieve later if, after retrieving the newly created password file, the intruders restore the altered log-in file to its original condition?

2. Does a computer user with authorized access to a computer and its programs act without authorization if he or she uses the program in an unauthorized way?

COMPUTER PIRACY

Computer piracy is the theft or misuse of computer software. (With the increasing value and decreasing size of computer equipment, the theft of computer hardware is increasing. This is larceny, however, not computer piracy.)

Concerned about the increase in computer software theft, Congress amended the Copyright Act in 1980 to cover computer software. (Copyright law is discussed further below and in Chapter 11.) Most states have made the theft of computer software a crime. For example, Sections 156.30 and 156.35 of the New York Penal Law define six crimes related to computer misuse. The statute makes it a felony to duplicate a computer software program without authorization if the software has a value in excess of $2,500 or if the duplication is done in connection with another felony. The legislation also prohibits the possession of unlawfully duplicated materials with a value in excess of $2,500.

 ## Crimes Involving Intellectual Property

In 1997, U.S. companies lost $200 billion due to worldwide copyright, trademark, and trade secret infringement.[89] Congress has adopted a series of statutes to address this growing problem.

THE COPYRIGHT ACT AND NO ELECTRONIC THEFT ACT

Section 506 of the Copyright Act criminalizes the willful infringement of copyrights for commercial gain.[90] Any person who willfully infringes a copyright is subject to a maximum prison term of five years and a maximum fine of $250,000. Section 506 also criminalizes fraudulent use of a copyright notice, fraudulent removal of a notice, and false representations in connection with a copyright application.

The No Electronic Theft Act[91] permits federal prosecution of willful copyright infringement, even if the infringer has not acted for his or her commercial advantage or private financial gain, if the infringer reproduced or distributed one or more copies of a copyrighted work with a retail value in excess of $1,000. If such an infringer also made ten or more illicit copies with an aggregate value in excess of $2,500, he or she may be imprisoned for up to five years and fined $250,000.

THE ECONOMIC ESPIONAGE ACT

In 1996, Congress passed the Economic Espionage Act, which made theft of trade secrets a federal crime for the first time. The Act was passed in response to a dramatic rise in the incidence of industrial espionage,

---

89. *PBF Looks at What's Being Done to Arrest Cyberfraud,* Preventing Bus. Fraud, Apr. 2000, at 1.

90. 17 U.S.C.A. § 506(a) (West Supp. 1998); 18 U.S.C.A. § 2319 (West Supp. 1997).
91. 18 U.S.C. § 2319(b) (2000).

VIEW FROM CYBERSPACE

Fighting Cyber-Crime

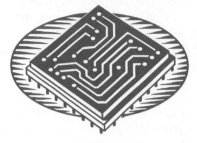

The ability of computer hackers to access protected financial and governmental records is one of the primary concerns spawned by increased use of the Internet. A 1996 study by the General Accounting Office estimated that, in 1995 alone, the two million computers on the 10,000 networks of the Defense Department were broken into as many as 250,000 times.[a] The private sector has been equally afflicted. Hackers have stolen credit card numbers, transmitted highly destructive viruses, and shut down popular online sites.[b] In 1999, 273 companies used the Federal Bureau of Investigation's (FBI's) InfraGuard program to report losses from computer crime totaling $265 million.[c]

In 2000, a presidential working group established to analyze the applicability of the existing federal legal framework to the rising problem of Internet crimes released its report, "The Electronic Frontier: The Challenge of Unlawful Conduct Involving the Use of the Internet."[d] The report concluded that existing laws are adequate to address Internet crime and recommended that the lawfulness of Internet-based conduct be evaluated in the same manner as more traditional communications. The goal should be consistent legal rules regardless of medium. The report did, however, call for laws and rules governing enforcement to be updated to ensure that legal authorities are able to adequately investigate and prosecute cyber-crime.

The Council of Europe, which comprises fifty-one member states (including the fifteen states of the European Union), has been engaged since 1998 in drafting a proposed treaty—the Convention on Cyber-Crime—aimed at promoting uniform computer crime laws throughout the world and facilitating international cooperation in preventing and prosecuting computer crime through extradition and mutual assistance across national borders. The November 19, 2000 redraft called on signatory nations to amend their substantive criminal laws to (1) prohibit unauthorized access to a computer system, interception of computer data transmissions, and interference with computer data; (2) establish criminal laws relating to computer-related forgery and fraud; (3) prohibit child pornography on computer systems (including virtual depictions of minors engaged in sexually explicit conduct); (4) prohibit copyright infringements; and (5) make corporate officers criminally, civilly, or administratively liable for offenses attributable to corporations along with the person who actually committed the offense.[e] Procedural provisions would give law enforcement authorities the power to order the search and seizure of computer systems and data.

The FBI has developed an Internet surveillance system, Carnivore, to access e-mail transmissions and track Internet usage by tapping into the computer servers of Internet service providers. Although the FBI obtains a warrant before using Carnivore, privacy advocates claim that there are inadequate protections to prevent the FBI from accessing the e-mail of any person using the same Internet service provider.[f]

In December 2000, McConnell International released a report based on its examinations of ten types of computer crime in fifty-two countries. McConnell found that thirty-three of the countries studied had no laws specifically covering cyber-crime, ten had partially updated their laws, and eight (including the United States) had substantially updated their laws. The only country with fully updated cyber-crime legislation was the Philippines, which adopted comprehensive legislation outlawing most forms of cyber-crime after being unable to prosecute the Filipino student responsible for the I LOVE YOU virus in early 2000, because he had not specifically violated any existing provision of Filipino law.[g]

a. *See* Jon Jefferson, *Deleting Cybercrooks,* A.B.A. J., Oct. 1997, at 68.
b. For an excellent discussion of the computer crime laws applicable to different types of cyber-crime, *see* Eric J. Sinrod & William P. Reilly, *Hacking Your Way to Hard Time: Application of Computer Crime Laws to Specific Types of Hacking Attacks,* 4 J. INTERNET L. 1 (2000).
c. *FBI Using Several Initiatives to Get Ahead of Wave in Rising Tide of Computer Crime,* Computer Tech. L. Rep. (BNA) 227 (Oct. 20, 2000).
d. A REPORT OF THE PRESIDENT'S WORKING GROUP ON UNLAWFUL CONDUCT ON THE INTERNET (Mar. 2000).
e. *Draft Proposed Treaty on Computer Crime to Be Completed by End of December,* ELECTRONIC COM. & L., Dec. 13, 2000, at 1195.
f. The report issued by the Illinois Institute of Technology Research Institute, an independent review team engaged by the Department of Justice to review Carnivore's capabilities, outlining problems and potential solutions is available at <http://www.usdoj.gov/jmd/publications/carniv_entry.htm>.
g. *Worldwide Lack of Cyber-Crime Legislation Forces Private Firms to Protect Themselves,* ELECTRONIC COM. & L., Dec. 13, 2000, at 1196.

which resulted in an estimated loss to U.S. companies of $25 billion in 1995 alone.[92]

92. *See* Stan Crock & Jonathan Moore, *Corporate Spies Feel a Sting,* BUS. WK., July 14, 1997, at 76.

The Act targets theft of trade secrets both by foreigners and by domestic spies. For foreign defendants, it defines economic espionage as knowingly stealing, or by fraud or deception obtaining, a trade secret with the intention that it will benefit a foreign government or agent. On the domestic side, the test is whether the defendant (1) intends to convert a trade secret to the economic benefit of anyone other than the trade-secret owner and (2) intends or knows that this act will injure the owner. In order for information to be considered a trade secret, the owner must have taken "reasonable measures to keep such information secret," and the value of the information must stem from its proprietary nature.[93]

Within a year of the Economic Espionage Act's enactment, the FBI had conducted a number of high-profile sting operations under its authority. One sting nabbed two Taiwanese businesspersons who were attempting to buy stolen data about Bristol-Myers Squibb's blockbuster cancer drug, Taxol.[94] Another involved a contract worker for PPG Industries, Inc., who attempted to sell secret fiberglass formulas to Owens–Corning.[95]

Penalties under the Act can reach fifteen years imprisonment and fines of up to $10 million, depending on the value of the trade secrets stolen.[96] Critics have already complained that sentencing is not severe enough to adequately deter the immensely profitable industry of industrial espionage. They note that because many white-collar corporate spies are first-time offenders, the Federal Sentencing Guidelines are lenient. For instance, the defendant in the Owens–Corning case was sentenced to only fifteen months in jail, even though PPG estimated the value of the information stolen at up to $20 million.[97]

⚖ Tax *and* Antitrust Laws

Certain violations of the Internal Revenue Code are subject to criminal penalties. The strictest penalties are found in Section 7201,[98] which prohibits willful attempts to evade any tax imposed under the code, including employee withholding requirements. Anyone convicted under this provision is subject to a fine not to exceed $100,000 ($500,000 for a corporation) plus all costs of the prosecution and/or a prison term not to exceed five years. Section 7206 forbids any false statements in a tax return and is punishable with the same fine structure but with a maximum prison sentence of three years. Under Section 7207, willful delivery of a fraudulent return to the secretary of the treasury is punishable with up to one year in jail and a fine of $10,000 ($50,000 in the case of a corporation).

A tax fraud prosecution must allege willful misconduct on the part of the accused. Consequently, prosecutors in tax fraud cases often add a mail fraud charge, which can result in a conviction even if willful misconduct is not proved. Moreover, mail fraud, unlike tax fraud, can be the basis for a RICO claim.

Section 6672 imposes civil liability for a penalty equal to the amount of a corporation's unpaid federal employment taxes on "those with the power and responsibility within the corporate structure for seeing that the taxes withheld from various sources are remitted to the Government."[99] The U.S. Court of Appeals for the Ninth Circuit has ruled that a person cannot be held liable for failure to pay over taxes unless the party (1) was the person required to collect, truthfully account for, and pay over the tax; and (2) willfully refused to pay the tax.[100]

THE SHERMAN ACT

The antitrust laws are designed to encourage active business competition. (These laws are discussed in detail in Chapter 20.)

Criminal prosecutions under the antitrust laws occur most frequently in actions brought under Sections 1 and 2 of the Sherman Act.[101] Section 1 of the Sherman Act prohibits, among other things, all agreements in restraint of trade, including price-fixing. Section 2 prohibits monopolization, that is, the willful acquisition or maintenance of monopoly power coupled with the intent to monopolize.

Penalties under the Sherman Act Criminal prosecutions under the Sherman Act are initiated under the direction of the U.S. attorney general through the Antitrust Division of the Department of Justice or the appropriate U.S. attorney. Individuals who violate the act are subject to a statutory maximum of three years in prison and/or a $350,000 fine per violation. Corporations that violate the Sherman Act are subject to a fine of up to $10 million per violation, and the fine can be increased under other statutes to twice the gain to the violators or twice the loss to the victims, whichever is greater.

Because the Sherman Act contains both criminal and civil sanctions, the government must always determine whether to bring a criminal action, a civil action, or both. In making this determination, the government continues

93. *See* 18 U.S.C.A. §§ 1831, 1832 (West Supp.1998).
94. Crock & Moore, *supra* note 92.
95. Dan Gottlieb, *Justice Enforces "Spy Act" of 1996,* PURCHASING, Apr. 1997, at 18.
96. *See* 18 U.S.C.A. § 1831 (West Supp.1998).
97. Crock & Moore, *supra* note 92.
98. 26 U.S.C. § 7201 (1998).

99. Monday v. United States, 421 F.2d 1210, 1214 (7th Cir. 1970).
100. Teel v. United States, 529 F.2d 903 (9th Cir. 1976).
101. 15 U.S.C §§ 1–2 (1998).

to rely on a report issued by the U.S. attorney general in 1955, under which the criminal sanction has generally been limited to particularly egregious conduct, such as price-fixing or group boycotts, or has been applied to individuals previously convicted of an antitrust offense.

 ## Securities Law Violations

The offer and sale of securities are governed by a complex set of federal and state laws and regulations.

FEDERAL SECURITIES LAWS

The two main federal securities laws are the Securities Act of 1933[102] (1933 Act) and the Securities Exchange Act of 1934[103] (1934 Act). Both of these statutes were drafted in the wake of the stock market crash of 1929 as a way to restore investor confidence in the nation's securities markets. The Securities and Exchange Commission (SEC) administers both the 1933 Act and the 1934 Act. These acts are discussed more fully in Chapters 24 and 25 but are briefly described here. The SEC's crackdown on accounting fraud and earnings manipulation is the "Inside Story" for this chapter.

The 1933 Act The 1933 Act covers the initial distribution of a security from the issuer to the public. Unless an exemption applies, the issuer must file a registration statement (including a detailed prospectus) with the SEC. To encourage proper disclosure of all information demanded by the statute, Section 24 of the Act provides for criminal penalties in addition to civil sanctions.

Any person or entity that willfully violates the 1933 Act or any regulation promulgated by the SEC is subject

102. 15 U.S.C.A. § 77a *et seq.* (West 1997).
103. 15 U.S.C.A. § 78a *et seq.* (West 1997).

to a maximum fine of $10,000 and/or a five-year prison sentence. The U.S. attorney, not the SEC, decides whether to bring criminal charges.

The 1934 Act The 1934 Act focuses on the need for public companies (that is, those with securities trading in the public markets) to periodically update disclosures initially made under the 1933 Act. The 1934 Act requires public companies to file annual reports, quarterly reports, and additional reports to reflect any material change in the company, such as a merger or sale of substantially all of its assets. The 1934 Act regulates, among other things, insider transactions, proxy solicitations, tender offers, brokers and dealers, and the securities exchanges. The 1934 Act also contains a general prohibition on securities fraud and on *insider trading,* that is, trading based on material nonpublic information.

The 1934 Act provides for criminal penalties for willful violations of the Act or the related SEC rules. Violators can be punished with a fine not to exceed $1 million and/or a ten-year prison sentence, except that if the violator is a person other than a natural person (such as a corporation), a fine up to $2.5 million may be imposed. Violators who prove they had no knowledge of the rule or regulation will not be subject to imprisonment, however. The penalties for insider trading are set forth in Chapter 25.

BLUE SKY LAWS

In addition to the regime of federal securities regulation established by the 1933 Act and the 1934 Act, the states have also enacted laws governing securities violations within their borders. These laws are known as *blue sky laws.* As demonstrated in the following case, blue sky laws can be more restrictive than their federal counterparts.

A CASE IN POINT

CASE 17.4
Mueller v. Sullivan
United States Court of Appeals for the Seventh Circuit
141 F.3d 1232 (1998).

Summary

FACTS Mark Mueller and James Stopple controlled Farm Loan Services, an auction house for the sale of securities. Mueller and Stopple persuaded their clients to accept payment for monies owed them in Farm Loan Services corporate notes rather than in cash, but they prohibited their staff from revealing that Farm Loan Services had significant debt and cash-flow problems and was unprofitable with no available assets.

They were charged with violating Wisconsin's version of the Uniform Securities Act, which provides that the willful omission of material facts in connection with the purchase or sale of securities is a crime. The trial judge instructed the jury that Mueller and

(Continued)

(Case 17.4 continued)

Stopple could be convicted under the act if the prosecution proved that they knew that the investors were not being told relevant information that was objectively material. Mueller and Stopple were subsequently convicted.

Mueller and Stopple challenged their convictions, claiming that the Due Process Clause of the Fourteenth Amendment required a more stringent showing of mental state, specifically, the intent to deceive, which is required in cases under Section 10(b) of the Securities Exchange Act of 1934 (1934 Act), on which many sections of the Uniform Securities Act were modeled.

ISSUE PRESENTED Does the Due Process Clause permit conviction for violation of state securities laws when the defendants knew what they were doing but did not know that it was illegal?

SUMMARY OF OPINION The U.S. Court of Appeals for the Seventh Circuit pointed out that few criminal statutes require proof that the defendant knew the wrongfulness of his or her acts. Rather, most statutes require only a showing that the defendant intended to bring about the forbidden consequence. The court concluded that states have a legitimate interest in penalizing conduct even if the defendant did not know that the conduct was unlawful:

> States are entitled to give corporate managers incentives to learn the law. No one with half a brain can offer "an opportunity to invest in our company" without knowing that there is a regulatory jungle out there. To say that the Constitution entitles entrepreneurs to propagate deceptive half-truths about their securities unless they have the same level of legal understanding as a practitioner of securities law . . . is to create a powerful incentive to go buccaneering. Regulatory statutes . . . serve to induce caution and consultation.

The court recognized that such a standard may have the effect of penalizing someone who had no idea the conduct was wrongful but concluded, after weighing the relative hardships, that the burden should be placed on those who are engaging in the regulated activity, not on the innocent public.

RESULT The convictions of Mueller and Stopple were upheld.

 Other Federal Criminal Regulatory Laws

A large number of federal regulatory laws provide for criminal as well as civil penalties for their violation. Several of the more important are discussed in this section.

THE ENVIRONMENTAL LAWS

During the past several decades, Congress has passed new legislation or significantly modified existing laws to protect the environment (see Chapter 18). These laws provide for criminal sanctions against both the corporation and its employees. The Wire and Mail Fraud Acts and the False Statements Act supplement the criminal sanctions included in the environmental statutes. As explained in Chapter 18, the Environmental Protection Agency (EPA) offers more lenient treatment for those who self-report violations.

Two examples of environmental laws that impose criminal sanctions are the Clean Water Act and the Resource Conservation and Recovery Act.

The Clean Water Act The Clean Water Act[104] requires all industrial and municipal entities to obtain a permit from the EPA prior to discharging specified pollutants into a water source. Detailed records of all discharges and

104. 33 U.S.C. § 1351 *et seq.* (1994).

periodic testing of sample discharges are required. Criminal penalties under the Act vary, depending on whether the violation was negligent, knowing, or knowing and endangered others. First-time violators are subject to prison terms ranging from one to fifteen years and fines ranging from $2,500 to $100,000 per day. Organizations that knowingly endanger others can be fined up to $1 million. For second and subsequent violations, prison terms and fines are doubled.

Any person who knowingly falsifies any records required to be maintained under the Act may be fined $10,000 and imprisoned for up to two years. Prison terms and fines are also doubled for subsequent violations.

The Resource Conservation and Recovery Act The Resource Conservation and Recovery Act (RCRA) of 1976, as amended in 1984,[105] provides for cradle-to-grave monitoring of hazardous-waste material. This statute and the accompanying regulations set out procedures and record-keeping requirements for the transportation, storage, and treatment of hazardous waste. Criminal penalties can be levied both against the corporation and against individual employees who dispose of hazardous waste without the appropriate RCRA permit.

THE OCCUPATIONAL SAFETY AND HEALTH ACT

The Occupational Safety and Health Act (OSHA)[106] applies to all employers engaged in a business affecting interstate commerce. OSHA is discussed in Chapter 14.

OSHA Requirements OSHA requires employers to provide a place of employment free from recognized hazards that are likely to cause death or serious physical harm. Employers are also required to comply with many detailed safety regulations.

Penalties under OSHA Most violations of OSHA are punished by civil penalties. The penalties are mandatory when the employer receives a citation for a serious violation, discretionary when the violation is nonserious. More severe civil penalties (that is, fines up to $70,000) are imposed for willful or repeated violations. The terms "serious," "nonserious," "willful," and "repeated" are all defined in the Act.

Section 666(e) of the Act provides for even harsher penalties if the employer commits a willful violation that results in the death of an employee. In this case, the employer may suffer a fine, imprisonment, or both. If the employer has not previously been convicted of a violation, he or she may be punished by a fine of not more than $10,000 or by imprisonment of up to six months, or both. For a second conviction, the punishment can be a fine of up to $20,000 or imprisonment of up to one year, or both.

State Law Prosecutions of Workplace Safety Hazards As noted in Chapter 14, state prosecutors have taken an aggressive approach toward workplace safety hazards that result in injuries. Employers have defended against such charges by claiming that OSHA preempts state prosecutions based on failure to maintain workplace safety. The U.S. Court of Appeals for the First Circuit has rejected this argument,[107] however, and several other courts have adopted the First Circuit's reasoning.[108]

THE FOREIGN CORRUPT PRACTICES ACT

The Foreign Corrupt Practices Act,[109] discussed further in Chapter 13, makes it a crime for any U.S. firm to make payments to an official of a foreign government in an attempt to influence the official's actions. The Act also requires detailed record-keeping and internal control measures by all public companies, whether international or purely domestic.

---

105. 42 U.S.C. § 6901 *et seq.* (1994).
106. 29 U.S.C. § 651 *et seq.* & 29 U.S.C.A. § 651 *et seq.* (West Supp. 1997).

107. *See* Pedraza v. Shell Oil Co., 942 F.2d 48 (1st Cir. 1991).
108. *See, e.g.,* Wickham v. American Tokyo Kasei, Inc., 927 F. Supp. 293 (N.D. Ill. 1996); Donovan v. Beloit Co., 655 N.E.2d 313 (Ill. App. Ct. 1995).
109. 15 U.S.C. § 78dd-2 (1994).

THE RESPONSIBLE MANAGER
Ensuring Criminal Law Compliance

Senior management can take various actions to encourage criminal law compliance. First, the company should develop a code of ethics, as discussed in Chapter 1. All criminal acts should be outlawed by the code. The code of ethics should have an enforcement mechanism, and it should clearly state that violations of the code will result in sanctions such as salary reductions, poor performance ratings, and, in extreme cases, termination of employment. Some corporations require that employees sign a yearly statement saying that they have read the code of ethics.

The corporation should develop a comprehensive program to ensure compliance with laws and regulations. Senior management, with guidance from the audit committee of the board of directors, should oversee the program. A good reporting structure is a crucial feature of such a compliance program. Prosecutors and courts are very inclined to mitigate the punishment of a corporation if it consistently reports the criminal misconduct of its employees. The corporation should also have educational procedures to remind all employees about the provisions of the compliance program.

It should be clear throughout the company that ethical behavior is expected. A policy of honesty should be stressed. What top management does when it sees criminal law–related problems will influence all employees. It is much harder for employees to justify committing criminal acts against the corporation when they cannot claim that top management is also guilty of criminal acts.

Experts note that criminal misconduct within a corporation is often a function of goal setting and performance measures that induce people to do what they should not do. Managers should be careful to avoid sending mixed signals that reward (or demand) performance at all costs regardless of compliance with the law.

Corporate in-house counsel should be independent and report directly to the board of directors. They should not succumb to pressure from a division manager to give the go-ahead to an action that they believe may violate a criminal statute.

Outside firms can be hired to audit the corporation's methods of ensuring criminal law compliance. These firms can also make suggestions to improve the corporation's methods.

The corporation should also focus on the continuing education of its employees. All employees need to know the criminal law that affects them. In-house training can keep corporate employees abreast of changes in the criminal law and can help ensure that employees do not forget their obligations under criminal law.

If the corporation is faced with a possible criminal investigation, quickness of action is important, as the corporation could be facing severe fines and harmful publicity that could prove damaging to future business. When there is some indication of possible criminal conduct by company employees, the corporation should seek the immediate advice of outside counsel and conduct an internal investigation prior to contacting the authorities. The fact of the internal investigation should not be widely publicized within the corporation. If employees are interviewed in connection with the investigation, outside counsel should make it clear that they are representing the company, and not the employee. Managers should be careful when turning over information about internal investigations to prosecutors because they might inadvertently waive the attorney–client privilege applicable to notes prepared by outside counsel.

INSIDE STORY

Cooking *the* Books: *The* SEC Cracks Down *on* "Managed Earnings"

In a speech given to certified public accountants, lawyers, and academics in September 1998, Arthur Levitt, chairman of the Securities and Exchange Commission, declared war on the "accounting hocus-pocus" used by companies to manage the numbers in their financial statements or to "smooth out" earnings. As reported by *Fortune* magazine, "Levitt left no doubt that he intends to keep the heat on. . . . For those who can't get with the program, the punishment increasingly could be criminal prosecution."[110]

Levitt's campaign was sparked by what *Fortune* described as "the continual eruption of accounting frauds."[111] *Fortune* asserted: "The accumulation of cases, in fact, keeps suggesting that beneath corporate America's uncannily disciplined march of profits during this decade lie great expanses of accounting rot, just waiting to be revealed."

The SEC is directing its attacks primarily at five accounting practices: revenue recognition, "big-bath" restructuring charges, acquisition accounting, "cookie-jar reserves," and materiality. Revenue-recognition abuses range from the outright fraud of reporting sales that never occurred to the more subtle—but still illegal—booking

110. Loomis, *supra* note 2, at 74.

111. *Id.* at 77.

of sales with an implied (and unreported) right of return. Roughly 50 percent of the two hundred alleged frauds carried out by publicly owned companies in the eleven years ended in 1997 had a revenue-recognition component.[112]

Exhibit 17.1 is a partial list of chief executive officers convicted of accounting fraud from 1994 to 1999, together with a summary of their crimes and sentences. Mary Jo White, the U.S. attorney in New York's Southern District, has brought a series of accounting-fraud cases, with more in the pipeline. Her district has several significant criminal cases stemming from managed earnings, but she has also prosecuted smaller cases for their deterrence value, claiming that "'significant jail time' for a white-collar executive is apt to give others of his ilk severe shakes."[113]

112. *Id.* at 74.
113. *Id.*

"I never should have tried to take my accounting to the next level."

 EXHIBIT 17.1   **The CEO as Felon**

The CEO	What He Did	Conviction/Plea	The Outcome
Donald Ferrarini, 71 Underwriters Financial Group	Reported nonexistent revenues; made losing company look like profit maker.	Convicted, 2/99.	Sentenced to twelve years, one month. Is appealing.
Richard Rubin, 57 Donnkenny	Concocted false invoices and revenues to meet earnings goals.	Pled guilty, 2/99.	Sentence pending; faces maximum of five years.
Chan Desaigoudar, 61 California Micro Devices	Led staff to record sales for products not shipped—or even manufactured.	Convicted, 7/98.	Serving sentence of three years.
Clifford Hotte, 51 Health Management	Altered books well after the 1995 year ended to get nearer Street estimates.	Convicted, 5/98.	Sentence of nine years is on appeal.
Paul Safronchik, 35 Home Theater Products International	Invented customers and sales; showed profits when red ink was the reality.	Pled guilty, 12/96.	Serving sentence of three years, one month.
Earl Brian, 57 FNN	Spun companies he controlled into an elaborate plot that inflated FNN's sales.	Convicted, 10/96.	Serving sentence of five years.
Eddie Antar, 51 Crazy Eddie	Fabricated inventory data, overstated income, got PR firms to issue lies.	Pled guilty, 5/96.	Serving sentence of six years, ten months.
Steven Hoffenberg, 54 Towers Financial	Ran Ponzi scheme that defrauded Towers investors of $450 million.	Pled guilty, 4/95.	Serving sentence of twenty years.
Q.T. Wiles, 79 Miniscribe	Falsified books to "make numbers"; shipped bricks instead of disk drives.	Convicted, 7/94.	Served sentence of two years, six months.

Source: Carol J. Loomis, *Lies, Damned Lies, and Managed Earnings,* FORTUNE, Aug. 2, 1999, at 82.

According to *Fortune:*

Levitt is threatening a practice many CEOs regard as part of their bill of rights. The former communications director of a prominent *Fortune* 500 company remembers the blast his CEO once let loose at the financial managers and lawyers trying to tell him that the quarterly earnings he proposed to announce weren't accurate. Roared the CEO: "Stop fooling around with my numbers! The No. 1 job of management is to smooth out earnings."[114]

Smoothed earnings come at the expense of market transparency, however, by obscuring the true value of a business. Investors may not be aware of foreboding trends until too late.

For example, on May 17, 2000, Emanuel Pinez, former CEO of Centennial Technologies, Inc., was sentenced to five years in prison and ordered to pay $150 million in restitution after federal authorities discovered that he had been cooking the books from 1994 to 1997 and inflating the stock price. According to Donald K. Stern, U.S. attorney in Boston, Pinez "directed an extremely sophisticated fraud on the public, transforming the company's stock into one of the hottest on Wall Street in 1996." The *Boston Globe* reported that "Pinez caused Centennial to overstate earnings by more than $32 million. Pinez was also accused of fabricating dozens of phony sales transactions and directing subordinates to falsify company books."[115]

114. *Id.*
115. Beth Healy, *Former Centennial Chief Gets Jail Term*, Boston Globe, May 18, 2000.

In early 2001, a federal grand jury indicted Walter A. Forbes, former chair of Cendant Corp., and E. Kirk Shelton, former vice chair, for one count of wire fraud and one count of criminal conspiracy based on their alleged role in directing massive accounting fraud at Cendant, which, when revealed, caused Cendant's stock to drop $14 billion in one day. The indictment charged that Forbes and Shelton, the highest ranking executives of Cendant at the time the fraud occurred, "were directly involved in knowingly and fraudulently overstating the earnings of CUC [a firm that merged with HFS Inc. to create Cendant in 1997] and Cendant, in violation of accounting standards and their company's own internal policies."[116] Each count carries a maximum prison term of five years and a $250,000 fine, plus possible additional restitution for their profits from selling millions of shares of Cendant's stock.

The former chief financial officer, controller, and accountant in charge of external reporting of Cendant each pled guilty in mid-2000 to conspiring to transfer amounts from special merger reserves and other sources to artificially inflate earnings. As of March 2001, all three awaited sentencing. The former CFO, who cooperated with government investigators, testified that the practice of fraudulent reporting "was ingrained by our superiors."[117]

116. Ann Davis, *Former Cendant Top Executives Are Indicted in Accounting Case*, Wall St. J., Mar. 1, 2001.
117. *Id.*

KEY WORDS AND PHRASES

actus reus 569
arrest 573
blue sky laws 594
booked 573
burden of proof 570
collective entity doctrine 579
computer fraud 589
computer piracy 591
computer virus 589
consent decree 573
crime 569
denial-of-service attacks 589
Double Jeopardy Clause 580
Due Process Clauses 581
embezzlement 585
enterprise 586

exclusionary rule 577
Ex Post Facto Clause 570
felony 570
fraud 585
fruit of the poisonous tree 577
good faith exception 577
impossibility defense 584
imputed liability 582
indictment 573
inevitable discovery exception 577
information 573
insider trading 594
intention to do wrong 569
larceny 585
mail fraud 587
mens rea 569

Miranda warnings 577
misdemeanor 570
negligence 569
negligence *per se* 570
nolo contendere 573
plea 573
plea bargaining 573
preliminary hearing 573
preponderance of the evidence 570
probable cause 574
qui tam plaintiff 588
racketeering activity 586
recklessness 569
respondeat superior 584
responsible corporate officer doctrine 582

QUESTIONS AND CASE PROBLEMS

1. Argent Chemical Laboratories manufactures and repackages veterinary drugs. Food and Drug Administration (FDA) agents inspected Argent without a warrant several times between the summer of 1993 and May 1994 to ensure compliance with the Food, Drug and Cosmetic Act. The FDA cited Argent for certain deficiencies. Several months after the last inspection, FDA agents and U.S. marshals seized over $100,000 worth of veterinary drugs from Argent's premises. Did the seizure of Argent's veterinary drugs without a warrant violate the Fourth Amendment? [*United States v. Argent Chemical Laboratories, Inc.*, 93 F.3d 572 (9th Cir. 1996)]

2. Dow Chemical Company operated a 2,000-acre chemical-manufacturing facility with numerous covered buildings in Midland, Michigan. Dow maintained extensive security around the facility. Security measures around the perimeter of the facility prevent ground-level public viewing, and Dow also investigates any low-level aircraft flights over the facility.

   The Environmental Protection Agency (EPA) sought to inspect two of Dow's power plants in the facility for violations of federal air-quality standards. Without obtaining a search warrant to enter the property and despite Dow's refusal to voluntarily agree to a search, the EPA employed a commercial airplane with precision aerial-camera mapping equipment to photograph Dow's large manufacturing and research facilities from the air. The powerful equipment allowed power lines as small as 0.5 inches in diameter to be observed. Yet, at all times, the aircraft stayed within navigable airspace.

   Dow became aware of the EPA's actions and claimed that its Fourth Amendment rights had been violated. Did the EPA's photographs constitute an unreasonable search in violation of the Fourth Amendment? [*Dow Chemical Co. v. United States*, 476 U.S. 227 (1986)]

3. Cronic and two associates were indicted on mail fraud charges involving the transfer of more than $9 million in checks between banks in Tampa, Florida, and Norman, Oklahoma, over a four-month period. Right before the trial was to begin, the attorney for the defendants withdrew. The court-appointed substitute counsel turned out to be an attorney who specialized in real estate and had never argued before a jury.

   Once counsel was appointed, the court allowed the attorney only twenty-five days of pretrial preparation, even though it had taken the government more than four years to investigate the case and review all the documents. Cronic's two codefendants ended up testifying for the government. Cronic was convicted and received a twenty-five-year sentence.

   On appeal, Cronic claimed that the conviction cannot stand because he did not have effective assistance of counsel. Is he correct? [*United States v. Cronic*, 466 U.S. 648 (1984)]

4. Bert's Sporting Goods, Inc., with stores located throughout the state of Lys, sells a wide variety of sporting goods, including guns. Section 123.45 of the Lys Penal Code requires sellers of guns to verify that the purchaser has not committed a felony within the last five years. If the purchaser has committed a felony within that period, the seller is not allowed to make the sale. "Willfully" selling a gun to a recent felon is considered a misdemeanor and is punishable by up to one year in jail and/or a maximum $10,000 fine.

   Jim Dandy, who was convicted of a felony under Lys's penal code four years ago, went to purchase a gun at one of the Bert's Sporting Goods stores. Joe Mountain, a salesman at Bert's, sold Dandy the gun without asking for identification or checking to see whether Dandy was a convicted felon.

   As a matter of fact, Mountain never checked whether any of the customers to whom he sold guns were felons. Mountain did not know of the Lys law requiring that he check on the customer's prior criminal history. However, Jay Lake, Mountain's supervisor, knew of the law and also knew that Mountain never checked whether a customer was a felon. Bert, the sole shareholder and director of Bert's Sporting Goods, Inc., knew about the law but did not know that Mountain did not check on his customers' prior criminal history.

   Dandy used the gun in a robbery and shot two police officers during his getaway. He was never captured. Can Mountain be punished under Section 123.45 of the penal code? What about Lake? Bert?

Bert's Sporting Goods, Inc.? What penalties should be assessed?

5. Barry Engel was president of Gel Spice Company, which imported, processed, and packaged spices. As president he was responsible for the purchasing and storing of spices in the company's warehouse in Brooklyn, New York. In June 1972, the FDA inspected the Gel Spice warehouse and found widespread rodent infestation. Upon reinspection in August 1972, the FDA found evidence of continuing infestation. Following the two 1972 inspections, the FDA considered a criminal prosecution against Gel Spice. Before referring the case to the Department of Justice, however, an additional inspection was performed. At that July 1973 inspection, no evidence of rodent infestation was found, and the criminal prosecution was dropped. Three years later, in July 1976, the FDA inspected Gel Spice and again found active rodent infestation. Four additional inspections were performed from 1977 to 1979, each of which revealed continuing infestation. Thereafter, the government instituted criminal proceedings against Gel Spice and its president, Barry Engel. Under what theory of criminal liability could Engel be held liable for violating the Food, Drug and Cosmetic Act? Can Engel successfully assert any defense? [*United States v. Gel Spice Co.,* 773 F.2d 427 (2d Cir. 1985)]

6. An employee of Ladish Malting Company was killed when he fell from a dilapidated fire-escape platform that collapsed. Ladish was charged and indicted under a provision of the Occupational Safety and Health Act (OSHA) that imposes criminal penalties on any employer that "willfully violates" any occupational safety or health standard and thereby causes the death of an employee.

At trial, the government did not prove that Ladish had actual knowledge that the fire-escape platform was hazardous. The trial judge's instruction to the jury permitted the conclusion that Ladish "willfully" violated the applicable regulation if it "should have known" that the fire escape was in disrepair. The jury found Ladish guilty of "willfully violating" a safety standard and thereby causing the death of an employee, and the judge imposed a $450,000 fine. On appeal, should the verdict be upheld? [*United States v. Ladish Malting Co.,* 135 F.3d 484 (7th Cir. 1998)]

7. Bermel Enterprises, Inc. is a supplier of computer programming consulting services to the federal government. In completing their time reports, Alex and Margot Frankel, two Bermel systems analysts, have consistently overstated the time they spent working

on the government projects. These time reports determine how much money the government pays the company. Additionally, Michelle Laff, a manager at Bermel, has falsified the results of tests conducted on the computer systems installed for the government. As a result, the systems appear to be bug-free when, in fact, they contain many errors.

What criminal charges may the government bring against the employees? Against Larry Bermel, owner of Bermel Enterprises, Inc.? Against Bermel Enterprises, Inc. itself?

8. Anthony Viola was the proprietor of Blue Chip Coffee, a wholesale coffee company in Brooklyn, New York. Michael Formisano performed odd jobs for Viola, mostly consisting of light cleanup and maintenance work. Viola, Formisano, and other defendants were convicted under the Racketeer Influenced and Corrupt Organizations Act (RICO) (and other statutes) for their involvement in a drug-and-stolen-property importation and distribution ring.

The government alleged that the defendants assisted narcotics dealers in their efforts to import drugs into the United States through the Brooklyn waterfront. The drug owners would contact Viola who, in turn, would use his influence and access to information to locate the drugs and remove them from the pier, thereby circumventing the U.S. Customs agents' inspections of imported goods. The government also alleged that the defendants purloined cargo from the waterfront and sold the goods on the black market.

The government established at trial that Formisano was employed by Viola to perform menial tasks and that, on two occasions, Formisano agreed to sell goods for Viola knowing they were stolen. Also, the government showed that Formisano once was present when Viola ordered another employee to load stolen goods on a delivery truck. However, in the wealth of evidence presented at trial to show the existence and scope of the Viola enterprise, Formisano was hardly ever mentioned. Formisano argued that he could not be convicted under RICO because he had no part in the operation or management of the Viola enterprise. Should Formisano's RICO conviction be upheld on appeal? [*United States v. Viola,* 35 F.3d 37 (2d Cir. 1994)]

9. Joseph Russo and Everett James Garner entered into an agreement to establish a building materials manufacturing business, Panel Building Systems, Inc. (PBS). To obtain capital to fund the development of the new company, Russo applied for a $630,000 loan from the U.S. Small Business Administration (SBA). On the loan application, Russo

stated that he was the president and 100 percent owner of PBS. PBS subsequently defaulted on the loan, and the SBA suffered losses of about $474,000. The SBA's investigation of the default revealed that the actual president of PBS was Garner, not Russo, and that Garner had a poor financial record. Russo later admitted that he knew the information supplied on the loan application was false and that the false information was supplied in order to secure a loan from the SBA. Russo was sued for knowingly and willfully making a false statement to the federal government under 18 U.S.C. § 1001, which requires willful intent to deceive.

Russo claims that although he knew the information supplied on the loan application was false, he lacked willful intent to deceive the federal government because he always intended to be president and CEO of PBS. Russo also argued that he thought Garner was a wealthy man and did not know Garner had a poor financial record. Did Russo have willful intent to deceive the federal government? [*United States v. Russo,* 202 F.3d 283 (10th Cir. 2000)]

MANAGER'S DILEMMA

10. You are the chief financial officer of X-Ray Corporation, the largest subsidiary of Medtech, a publicly traded medical-imaging firm. When you report to Medtech's CEO that X-Ray had better-than-expected earnings for the quarter ended June 30, 2001, the CEO asks you to "hold some of them back" as a cushion in case other subsidiaries report lower-than-expected earnings in future quarters. How would you respond? Suppose that you tell the CEO that you can't do that because this "cookie-jar reserve" would violate Generally Accepted Accounting Principles, but the CEO then warns that failure to create the reserve would be a career-limiting move. What would you do?

What if, instead of higher-than-expected earnings, X-Ray Corporation had lower-than-expected earnings due to unforeseen bugs in the software for its new suite of imaging equipment? How would you respond to a request from the CEO to book sales in the quarter ending June 30, 2001, that would not actually be finalized until July 2001, which is when X-Ray's engineers predict that the bugs will be worked out? [This question is based, in part, on a scenario described in Carol J. Loomis, *Lies, Damned Lies, and Managed Earnings,* FORTUNE, Aug. 2, 1999, at 92.]

INTERNET SOURCES

This site for Corporate Compliance, Ltd. provides information on establishing and testing criminal compliance systems.	http://www.corporatecompliance.com
This FindLaw site, when searched using the word "criminal," provides links to a variety of cases and sites dealing with federal and state criminal law.	http://www.findlaw.com
This site provides information about the Federal Bureau of Investigation's InfraGuard program.	http://www.nipc.gov/infragard.htm
This site contains information about the Internet Fraud Complaint Center.	http://www.ifccfbi.gov
The Council of Europe Directorate General for Legal Affairs Treaty Office site provides the text of the proposed Convention on Cyber-Crime.	http://conventions.coe.int/
This site, maintained by the U.S. Department of Justice Criminal Division's Computer Crime and Intellectual Property Section, provides information about cyber-crime.	http://www.cybercrime.gov

McConnell International, a computer security consulting firm in Washington, D.C., maintains a site that includes the text of its report, "Cyber Crime . . . and Punishment? Archaic Law Threatens Global Information."	http://www.mcconnellinternational.com
The U.S. Sentencing Commission site provides a copy of the sentencing guidelines and related information.	http://www.ussc.gov/

CHAPTER 18

Environmental Law

ROLE IN BUSINESS MANAGEMENT

Environmental law consists of numerous federal, state, and local laws with the common objective of protecting human health and the environment. These laws are of great concern to businesses, many of which may not have considered environmental liability when they first undertook an activity.

Some industries (such as petroleum, mining, and chemical manufacturing) are well accustomed to intense government regulation of the environmental effects of their operations. In recent years, however, the scope and impact of environmental laws have grown steadily. Today, real estate owners and investors, developers, insurance companies, and financial institutions find that their operations, too, are often affected by laws and regulations intended to protect the environment.

For example, railroads have become one of the country's most serious pollution problems. Railroads began transporting and storing hazardous chemicals before the end of the nineteenth century—long before environmental laws were enacted to regulate the transport and disposal of dangerous substances. As a result, toxic waste was routinely dumped at railroad sites.[1] As of the end of 1999, more than 300 rail yards had been identified as contaminated, and approximately $1.5 billion had been spent to clean them up. Many more railroad sites still need to be cleaned of dangerous pollutants.

Failure to comply with environmental laws can result in large judgments and punitive fines for companies, as well as criminal

penalties (including imprisonment) for the corporate executives responsible for these violations. In 1999, more than $166 million in civil penalties were paid to resolve violations of environmental laws.[2] The same year, an executive received a prison sentence of thirteen years, the longest sentence ever issued under federal environmental laws, after pleading guilty to felony charges that he ordered employees of his firm to illegally discharge hazardous waste into the city storm sewer system that emptied into a bay in Tampa, Florida.[3]

CHAPTER OVERVIEW

This chapter introduces four federal environmental laws that illustrate the importance of environmental regulation for an expanding range of business activities. The Clean Air Act, the Clean Water Act, and the Resource Conservation and Recovery Act are discussed as examples of environmental statutes that control the release of pollutants into the air, water, and land. The Comprehensive Environmental Response, Compensation, and Liability Act is discussed as an example of a remedial statute with broad application to all kinds of businesses and individuals. The chapter also addresses the potential liability of shareholders, directors, officers, and managers, as well as affiliated companies and lenders, under the environmental laws. It outlines the key elements of effective compliance programs and audits, and it concludes with a discussion of international considerations.

---

1. Daniel Machalaba, *Local Ties, Decades of Mishandling Hazardous Cargo Leave Railroads a Toxic Legacy*, WALL ST. J., Feb. 3, 1999, at A1.

2. *Penalties Increase for Environmental Violations*, CORP. COUNS. WKLY., Feb. 9, 2000.
3. United States v. Benkovitz, 229 F.3d 1168 (11th Cir. 2000).

⚜ Environmental Laws

COMMON LAW NUISANCE

Historically, public officials relied primarily on the common law theory of nuisance (discussed in Chapter 9) to control industrial and agricultural activities that interfered with the health or comfort of the community. Thus, industrial odors, noise, smoke, and pollutants of all kinds were the subjects of numerous lawsuits that attempted to balance the legitimate business interests of the polluter with the private interests of the surrounding community. The need to file a lawsuit in each case and the complexity of the common law made nuisance a cumbersome way to control environmental pollution in an industrial society. Moreover, a lawsuit could not prevent pollution; it could only provide a remedy after the fact. Today, state and federal regulatory programs have largely replaced common law nuisance as a means of pollution control.

STATUTES

Environmental statutes establish policy, set goals, and authorize the executive branch or one of its administrative agencies to adopt regulations specifying how the law will be implemented. The statutes and regulations are interpreted and applied in administrative and judicial proceedings. Thus, environmental laws consist of the statutes, the regulations, and the administrative and judicial interpretations of their meaning. In addition, the administrative agency often issues policy statements and technical guidance that, while not having the force of law, guide enforcement efforts or provide assistance to the regulated community.

Three Categories Environmental laws can be divided into three broad categories. The largest category consists of laws that regulate the release of pollutants into the air, water, or ground. These laws usually authorize the government to issue and enforce permits for releases of pollutants. They may also authorize emergency responses and remedial action if, for example, improper waste disposal or accidental chemical spills threaten human health or the environment. Statutes in this category include the Clean Air Act; the Federal Water Pollution Control Act, as amended by the Clean Water Act; the Solid Waste Disposal Act, as amended by the Resource Conservation and Recovery Act (RCRA); the Comprehensive Environmental Response, Compensation, and Liability Act (CERCLA or Superfund), as amended by the Superfund

Amendments and Reauthorization Act of 1986; and similar state laws. These four pollution-control laws are discussed in this chapter.

A second category includes laws that govern the manufacture, sale, distribution, and use of chemical substances as commercial products. This category includes (1) the Federal Insecticide, Fungicide and Rodenticide Act, which applies to pesticide products; and (2) the Toxic Substances Control Act, which applies to all chemical substances both manufactured in and imported into the United States, excluding certain substances that are regulated under other federal laws. The Safe Drinking Water Act, which governs the quality of drinking water served by public drinking-water systems, can also be included in this category.

A third category includes laws that require government decision makers to take into account the effect of their decisions on the quality of the environment. This category includes the National Environmental Policy Act (NEPA) and similar laws adopted by most states. NEPA, discussed in Chapters 6 and 19, affects all business activities that require governmental authorizations, permits, or licenses.

NATURAL RESOURCES LAWS

Although environmental law contributes to the protection of natural resources, it generally does not include wilderness preservation, wildlife protection, coastal zone management, energy conservation, national park designation, and the like. Those laws are commonly referred to as *natural resources laws*. Nor does environmental law cover land-use regulation and zoning. Such laws, which are generally administered by local governments, are commonly referred to as land-use laws. They are discussed in Chapter 19.

INDUSTRY PARTICIPATION

Environmental laws and regulations are constantly changing as new threats to human health and the environment become apparent and new ways are discovered to manage such threats safely and economically. Congressional or administrative agency staff may be unaware of how a proposed law or regulation may affect a particular industry and usually welcome constructive industry participation in the law- and rule-making process. This is particularly the case when a company can propose alternative ways to accomplish the same legislative goals.

ETHICAL CONSIDERATION

Environmental laws establish minimum standards to which companies must adhere. Companies also have fiduciary duties to their shareholders, and many labor activists argue that companies have similar duties to their employees. Is it ethical for a manager to adhere to stricter standards than mandated by law when such adherence will raise costs, reduce shareholder returns, and possibly jeopardize existing jobs? Is it more ethical, or less, to do so when the standards are to be implemented in a developing country with no environmental laws?

 # Administration *of* Environmental Laws

All the federal laws that set national goals and policies for environmental protection are administered by the Environmental Protection Agency (EPA), except for the National Environmental Policy Act, which is administered by the Council on Environmental Quality. State programs administer state laws and, with the authorization of the EPA, federal laws as well.

THE ENVIRONMENTAL PROTECTION AGENCY

The *Environmental Protection Agency (EPA)* was created in 1970 by an executive order and operates under the supervision of the president. The EPA administrator and assistant administrators are appointed by the president with the advice and consent of the Senate. The EPA is, however, neither an independent agency nor a cabinet-level department.

Several of the assistant administrators are responsible for administering the agency's regulatory programs; others have internal administrative functions. These national program managers share responsibility with the ten regional administrators who head each of the ten EPA regional offices. The national managers at headquarters develop policy and set goals for the regional offices. The regional administrators take responsibility for day-to-day program operation.

STATE PROGRAMS

State environmental laws and programs often predate the comparable federal programs. Moreover, many states have laws that are more stringent and more comprehensive than the federal laws. For example, California's

hazardous-waste-management laws, water-quality-control laws, underground-tank regulations, and ban on land disposal of certain hazardous wastes all predate and in some cases provided the model for subsequent federal legislation.

When a state already has an environmental program, the EPA may reduce its own administrative burden by authorizing or approving the state program in lieu of the federal program in that state. The EPA does not delegate its federal authority; it merely approves a state program as "equivalent to or more stringent than" the federal program and then refrains from implementing the federal program in that state. The EPA generally provides oversight, however. It retains its enforcement authority and may revoke its authorization if the state program fails to meet federal requirements.

 # *The* Clean Air Act

The Clean Air Act, as amended by the Clean Air Act of 1990,[4] sets four types of air quality goals. First, it requires the EPA to establish *national ambient air quality standards, (NAAQS),* that is, the maximum levels of pollutants in the outdoor air that, with adequate margins of safety, are compatible with public health. Standards have been set for six pollutants: (1) particulate matter, (2) sulfur dioxide, (3) ozone, (4) nitrogen dioxide, (5) carbon monoxide, and (6) lead. Every state and locality must seek to achieve and maintain these national air quality standards, which are revised periodically.

Second, the Clean Air Act requires that air quality not be allowed to deteriorate in those areas that already meet the national ambient air quality standards. Third, the Act requires the natural visibility to be preserved within the major national parks and wilderness areas. Fourth, it requires the EPA to establish emission standards that protect public health, with an ample margin of safety, from hazardous air pollutants.

The law also requires reductions in vehicle tail-pipe emissions of certain pollutants and the use of reformulated gasoline. It mandates that fleets use clean, low-emission fuels in some nonattainment areas. Major sources of some 200 hazardous air pollutants are required to meet new emission limits based on maximum achievable control technology. Electric power plants must reduce emissions that lead to the formation of acid rain. Finally, the law phases out methylchloroform and chlorofluorocarbons and places limitations on the production of certain substitute chemicals.

4. *42 U.S.C. § 7401 et seq.* (1995).

NATIONAL AMBIENT AIR QUALITY STANDARDS

The national ambient air quality standards are to be achieved through (1) state implementation plans approved by the EPA; (2) technological controls, including new source performance standards, set by the EPA; and (3) mobile-source controls set by the EPA. The *state implementation plans (SIPs)* prescribe emission-control measures for motor vehicles and for stationary sources existing prior to 1970. The SIPs also establish programs for state regulation of the "modification, construction, and operation of any stationary source." The SIPs include special programs for areas in each state that have not yet attained the national ambient air quality standards. For those areas that have attained the standards, the SIPs contain a program to prevent significant deterioration. The content and procedures of the SIPs vary considerably from state to state.

For new sources, the EPA establishes performance standards based on the best control technology available for a category of similar sources. The idea is that by requiring new sources to utilize the best control technology available, the sources of pollution will gradually be eliminated. Also, it is hoped that adherence to the performance standards will ensure roughly equal treatment of similar sources throughout the nation.

Before major sources of emissions can be constructed in areas that have achieved national ambient air quality goals, a case-by-case determination of the *best available control technology (BACT)* is required. BACT is defined as an emission limitation that the permitting authority determines achieves the maximum reduction of pollutants, taking into account energy, environmental, and economic considerations. The permitting authority may consider the cost of the technology only in relation to the reduction of pollutants it achieves. Before construction of major sources of emissions in nonattainment areas, case-by-case determinations of the *lowest achievable emission rate (LAER)* for the sources are required. New sources include not only new plants but also modifications of existing plants if these cause a significant increase in emissions.[5] By affecting land-use decisions and transportation changes, as well as imposing emission controls, the law helps determine which areas of the country and which industrial sectors will be able to grow over the next twenty years or more.

The law also provides deadlines for attaining ambient air quality standards and puts pressure on those areas of the country that do not yet meet the national standards. If a nonattainment area fails to develop an adequate plan to attain the national standards, the federal government is required to impose penalties, such as bans on construction of new sources of pollution, limits on the use of federal highway funds, limits on drinking-water hookups, and withholding of federal funds for air-pollution control.

In *Whitman v. American Trucking Ass'ns,*[6] the U.S. Supreme Court unanimously upheld Congress's broad delegation of authority to the EPA under the Clean Air Act to set ambient air quality standards that, in the judgment of the EPA Administrator, "allowing an adequate margin of safety, are requisite to protect the public health." The Supreme Court overturned the court of appeals decision that had faulted the EPA for failing to provide an intelligible principle to determine how much is too much. The Supreme Court held:

> Section 109(b)(1) of the [Clean Air Act], which to repeat we interpret as requiring the EPA to set air quality standards at the level that is "requisite"—that is, not lower or higher than is necessary—to protect the public health with an adequate margin of safety, fits comfortably within the scope of discretion permitted by our precedent.

After determining that the language and legislative history of the Clean Air Act make it clear that economic considerations are to play no part in the promulgation of the standards, the Court also held that the EPA cannot consider the cost of compliance as a factor in revising the standards.[7]

 The Clean Water Act

The Federal Water Pollution Control Act[8] was adopted in 1972 and was substantially amended by the Clean Water Act of 1977 and by the Water Quality Act of 1987. The act, as amended, is commonly referred to as the Clean Water Act. The principal goal of the Clean Water Act is to eliminate the discharge of pollutants into the navigable waters of the United States. *Navigable waters* are all "waters of the United States which are used in interstate commerce," including "all freshwater wetlands that are adjacent to all other covered waterways."

---

5. 42 U.S.C. §§ 7408, 7479, and 7511 (1995).

6. 121 S. Ct. 903 (2001) (Case 6.3).

7. In *Michigan v. EPA,* 213 F.3d 663 (D.C. Cir. 2000), the U.S. Court of Appeals for the District of Columbia Circuit ruled that the EPA could require states to adopt state implementation plans to reduce their nitrogen oxide levels by "highly cost-effective controls," which it described as removing nitrogen oxides at a cost of $2,000 or less per ton. The court held that the EPA could incorporate these cost considerations into its rule designed to reduce interstate transport of ozone.

8. 33 U.S.C. § 1251 *et seq.* (1998).

In *Solid Waste Agency of Northern Cook County v. Army Corps of Engineers,*[9] the U.S. Supreme Court ruled that an abandoned sand and gravel pit in northern Illinois that provided habitat for migratory birds did not constitute "navigable waters" within the meaning of the Clean Water Act. The Court held that the Act does not apply to ponds that are not adjacent to open water. The Court reasoned that the term "navigable" in the statute reflected Congress's intention to limit the application of the Clean Water Act to waters that are or had been navigable in fact or that could reasonably be made so. Permitting federal jurisdiction over ponds and mudflats would impinge on the states' traditional power over land and water use.

NATIONAL POLLUTANT DISCHARGE ELIMINATION SYSTEM

The principal regulatory program established by the Clean Water Act is the *National Pollutant Discharge Elimination System (NPDES),* which requires permits for the discharge of pollutants from any point source to navigable waters. EPA regulations establish *national effluent limitations,* which impose increasingly stringent restrictions on pollutant discharges, based on the availability of economic treatment and recycling technolo-

gies. More stringent restrictions are imposed on new sources through the setting of national standards of performance. General and specific industry pretreatment standards are set for discharges to *publicly owned sewage treatment works (POTWs).* The pretreatment standards are designed to ensure the effective operation of the POTW and to avoid the pass-through of pollutants. The POTW, in turn, must comply with its own NPDES permit for the discharge of treated waters. The NPDES program is administered largely through approved state programs, although the EPA maintains NPDES authority in areas not within the jurisdictions of states having EPA-approved programs.

INDIVIDUAL LIABILITY OF CORPORATE OFFICERS

A corporate officer can be held responsible under the Clean Water Act if he or she had authority to exercise control over the corporation's activity that caused the unlawful discharge. A corporate officer can also be held criminally liable if he or she knowingly violated the Act.

In *United States v. Iverson,*[10] the U.S. Court of Appeals for the Ninth Circuit upheld a one-year prison sentence for the president and chairman of the board of CH20, Inc., a manufacturer of acid cleaners and alkaline compounds, after finding that he had actual authority to

9. 121 S. Ct. 675 (2001).

10. 162 F.3d 1015 (9th Cir. 1998).

prevent the company's dumping of industrial waste into a sewer. The executive was also fined $75,000 and received an additional sentence of three years of supervised release. Similarly, two business partners received criminal sentences after violating the Clean Water Act by illegally dumping sewage sludge on a California farm. One partner was sentenced to fifty-one months in prison after being convicted of violating the federal environmental law, and the other served a six-month sentence after pleading guilty. The court justified the fifty-one-month sentence on the grounds that (1) the businessman was a leader, manager, and supervisor in the offense; (2) he owned half the company and oversaw its day-to-day operations; and (3) he found the farmer who agreed to accept the sludge.[11]

 The Resource Conservation *and* Recovery Act

The Solid Waste Disposal Act, as amended by the Resource Conservation and Recovery Act (RCRA) of 1976 and the Hazardous and Solid Waste Amendments of 1984,[12] governs the management of hazardous wastes. The act authorizes the EPA to identify and list hazardous wastes, to develop standards for the management of hazardous wastes by generators and transporters of wastes, and to set standards for the construction and operation of hazardous-waste treatment, storage, and disposal facilities.

CRADLE-TO-GRAVE RESPONSIBILITY

RCRA imposes "cradle-to-grave" responsibility on generators of hazardous waste. Each generator must obtain an EPA identification number and use a transportation manifest when transporting wastes for treatment or disposal. This allows the EPA to track the hazardous wastes from the generator's facility to the final disposal site. A manifest is also required to transport hazardous wastes to an authorized storage facility.

Under RCRA, hazardous wastes must be treated to render them less hazardous before being disposed of on land. To comply with the EPA's disposal requirements, companies that generate hazardous waste may have to make substantial capital investments in treatment systems or incur increased costs for having wastes treated elsewhere prior to disposal.

Generators of hazardous waste must certify that they have a program in place to reduce the quantity and toxicity of their wastes. They must also certify that they are disposing of their wastes in a manner that, to the extent practicable, minimizes future threats to human health and the environment.

Owners and operators of hazardous-waste facilities must obtain permits and comply with stringent standards for the construction and operation of their facilities. These standards include maintaining certain liability insurance coverage and providing financial assurances that show the owner/operator has the financial wherewithal to close the facility at the appropriate time and to maintain it properly after closure.

Even though hazardous-waste facilities are closely regulated, companies that generate hazardous wastes must select treatment, transportation, and disposal facilities carefully. Liability may be imposed on persons who "own or operate" the facility or who have used the facility for the storage, treatment, or disposal of wastes. Under RCRA, as under most environmental laws, *person* includes both corporations and individuals and does not exclude officers and shareholders. Moreover, persons who "contributed" to the improper waste disposal can include persons who had no direct involvement but had the authority to control the corporation's actions and failed to do so.

CRIMINAL LIABILITY

Although RCRA imposes strict civil liability, a criminal violation requires some sort of knowledge. In particular, RCRA provides criminal sanctions for any person who "knowingly transports any hazardous waste identified or listed under this subchapter to a facility which does not have a permit."[13] As explained in Chapter 17, it is not always clear how far down the sentence the word "knowingly" travels.

The U.S. Court of Appeals for the Eleventh Circuit held in *United States v. Hayes International Corp.*[14] that knowledge of the regulation banning transport of hazardous waste to an unlicensed facility is not an element of the offense. Furthermore, the defendants could be found guilty even if they did not know that the substance being disposed of (a mixture of paint and solvents) was a hazardous waste within the meaning of the regulations. It was enough that they knew that what was being disposed of was a mixture of paint and solvents. The court distinguished *Liparota v. United States,*[15] which required

11. United States v. Cooper, 173 F.3d 192 (9th Cir. 1999).
12. 42 U.S.C. § 6901 *et seq.* (1995).
13. 42 U.S.C. § 6928(d)(1).
14. 786 F.2d 1499 (11th Cir. 1986).
15. 471 U.S. 419 (1985).

Corporate Environmentalism

Although the use of laws, regulations, and standards (referred to as "command and control" policy) is still an important tool for ensuring that companies' operations do not pollute the environment, many corporations have gone beyond simply complying with the laws.[a] The second era of corporate environmentalism began in response to the Union Carbide plant explosion in Bhopal, India, in 1984, which killed and injured thousands of people. (The Bhopal incident is described in detail in Chapter 1.) In response to that disaster, the U.S. Chemical Manufacturers Association imposed as a condition of membership a requirement that companies implement a program, called Responsible Care, to improve environmental performance.

Two years later, Congress enacted the Superfund Amendments and Reauthorization Act (SARA), which required companies to publish emission levels for hundreds of chemicals. This opened corporate books to the public's scrutiny and prompted many companies to try to reduce emissions. For example, in 1988, Monsanto announced a plan to reduce its emissions by 90 percent. Other companies, such as Polaroid and AT&T, made similar commitments to go beyond simply complying with the legal limits.

As part of this movement, corporations' began to broaden their focus to include the materials they used in production, as well as the pollutants they generated. After scrutinizing both their inputs and outputs, companies began to implement principles of "eco-efficiency" by using less energy, fewer new materials, and more reused and recycled materials in their operations. For example, Lockheed reduced the amount of energy it used in its 600,000-square-foot building by using sunlight rather than electrical lighting. This required an initial investment of $2 million, but saved the company $500,000 per year thereafter. Lockheed's use of sunlight also increased employee productivity.

As Lockheed's example indicates, corporations also began to look for pollution-prevention and eco-efficiency strategies that would produce economic savings, as well as environmental benefits. Harvard Business School Professor Michael E. Porter maintains that firms can remain competitive and, in fact, gain competitive advantage through innovation offsets. Porter and his colleague Claas van der Linde use the term *innovation offsets* to describe technological advantages gained by companies that meet the challenge of environmental regulations and discover lower costs and better-quality products as a result. Corporations started implementing the concept of *strategic environmental management,* which advocates placing environmental management on the profit side of the corporation rather than the cost side. This represented a profound shift in how companies viewed their relationship with the environment.

Another era of corporate environmentalism began in the 1990s and continues in the twenty-first century, as companies they try not just to reduce waste but to eliminate it altogether. This process involves looking at whole systems rather than the individual parts to create designs that take advantage of feedback loops within the company's operations. Some companies have begun to sell services rather than products, for example, by providing a rug or copying machine to a corporation for a period of time before recycling it for continued use.

Companies are also looking for ways to work with other firms for both economic and environmental benefit. For example, *industrial ecology* advocates a systems approach to eco-efficiency and applies it to groups of corporations working together. The best-known application of this approach is in Kalundborg, Sweden, where a refinery, power plant, pharmaceutical company, and fish farm located next to each other reduce costs by using each other's waste as resource inputs. For example, heat generated by one operation is used in another company's manufacturing operations.

Finally, corporations have begun to exploit the opportunities created by environmental problems. Car manufacturers, such as DaimlerChrysler, Honda, and Toyota, are racing to manufacture fuel cell and hybrid vehicle cars with reduced emissions and increased gas mileage. Energy companies are also investing in developing alternative sources of energy, as reflected in BP Amoco's advertising that its corporate initials stand for "Beyond Petroleum."

Harvard Business School Professor Forest Reinhardt has identified five approaches that companies can take to incorporate environmental issues into their business model: (1) differentiate their products by making them environmentally friendly and, as a result, command high prices; (2) "manage" competitors by imposing a set of private regulations or helping government write rules; (3) cut costs by implementing environmental practices; (4) manage risk and reduce lawsuits and accidents; and (5) make systemic changes concerning environmental issues that will redefine competition in their markets.[b]

a. This "Economic Perspective" is based, in substantial part, on CARL FRANKEL, IN EARTH'S COMPANY: BUSINESS, ENVIRONMENT, AND THE CHALLENGE OF SUSTAINABILITY (1998).
b. See FOREST REINHARDT, DOWN TO EARTH: APPLYING BUSINESS PRINCIPLES TO ENVIRONMENTAL MANAGEMENT (2000).

knowledge that the purchase of food stamps was illegal, on the grounds that (1) the food stamp law required "knowing violation of a regulation"; and (2) RCRA, unlike the food stamp law, was a public welfare statute involving a heavily regulated area with great ramifications for the public health and safety. The court concluded that it was fair to charge those who chose to operate in such an area with knowledge of the regulatory provisions.

The court held, however, that the government did have to prove that the defendants knew that the facility to which the waste was sent did not have a permit. Thus, even if the transporters did not know a permit was required, as long as they knew the facility did not have one or knew they had not inquired, that would be sufficient knowledge for a conviction. Such knowledge can be shown circumstantially. For example, given that it is common knowledge that properly disposing of wastes is an expensive task, if someone is willing to take away wastes at an unusually low price or under unusual circumstances, then a juror could infer that the transporter knew that the wastes were not being taken to a licensed facility.

The court did acknowledge that mistake of fact would be a defense if the defendants had a good faith belief that the materials were being recycled. The regulations applicable at the time provided an exemption from the permit requirement for waste that was recycled. The court distinguished a case in which the U.S. Supreme Court had held that a person who believed in good faith that he was shipping distilled water, when in fact he was shipping dangerous acid, did not "knowingly" ship dangerous chemicals in violation of applicable regulations.[16] Unlike the defendant in that case, the defendants in *Hayes* knew what was being shipped—a combination of waste and solvents—and they did not have a good faith belief that the materials were being recycled. Therefore, the convictions were upheld.

The Federal Superfund Law (CERCLA)

More than any other environmental law, the Comprehensive Environmental Response, Compensation, and Liability Act (CERCLA) of 1980, as amended by the Superfund Amendments and Reauthorization Act of 1986,[17] has affected individuals and businesses that do not themselves produce environmental pollutants. CERCLA authorizes

the federal government to investigate and take remedial action in response to a release or threatened release of hazardous substances to the environment. CERCLA established the *Hazardous Substance Superfund* to finance federal response activity. Since its creation, the Superfund has been replenished with tax revenue numerous times, for a total of more than $15 billion.

How federal Superfund money will be spent is determined in part by the EPA's National Priorities List, which identifies sites that may require remedial action. The sites are listed by the EPA in a rulemaking proceeding based on a *hazard ranking score,* which represents the degree of risk that the site presents to the environment and public health.

STRICT LIABILITY

The courts have interpreted CERCLA's liability provisions broadly in order to effectuate the remedial policies of the statute. With few exceptions, CERCLA imposes strict liability, meaning that the responsible parties are liable regardless of fault. It is now well established, for example, that the present owner of the land is liable for the cleanup of hazardous substances disposed of on the land by another person (usually a previous owner or tenant), unless the owner can establish the third-party defense (also called the innocent landowner defense), discussed later in this chapter.

The law permits the imposition of joint and several liability, which means that any one responsible party can be held liable for the total amount of response (cleanup) costs and natural resource damage even though others may also be responsible for the release. A responsible party that incurs costs in cleaning up a toxic-waste site can seek cost recovery or contribution from other responsible parties. In resolving contribution claims, the court may allocate response costs among liable parties using such equitable factors as the court determines are appropriate.[18] Of course, the right of contribution is of value only if the other parties are still in existence and able to pay. Many times they are not. Thus, joint and several liability allows the government to select financially sound parties from whom to collect response costs and puts the burden of recovering these costs from other responsible parties on the selected defendants.

---

16. United States v. International Minerals, 402 U.S. 558 (1971).
17. 42 U.S.C. § 9601 *et seq.* (1998).

18. In *Browning-Ferris Industries v. Ter Maat,* 195 F.3d 953 (7th Cir. 1999), *cert. denied,* 120 S. Ct. 1832 (2000), the U.S. Court of Appeals for the Seventh Circuit held that if one party has been required to pay the entire cost of cleaning up a site to which several other parties also contributed hazardous waste, the other parties can be held jointly and severally liable for contribution.

A party may escape joint and several liability if it can prove that it contributed to only a divisible portion of the harm or that it was the source of waste that, when mixed with other hazardous waste, did not contribute to the release and cleanup costs that followed. The party bears the burden of establishing a reasonable basis for apportioning liability.[19]

RESPONSIBLE PERSONS

The EPA may undertake remedial action itself or require responsible persons to do so. If the EPA performs the remedial work, it can recover its costs from the responsible

19. United States v. Alcar Aluminum Corp., 990 F.2d 711 (2d Cir. 1993).

persons. The *responsible persons* include (1) the present owner or operator of the facility, (2) the owner or operator at the time of disposal of the hazardous substance, (3) any person who arranged for treatment or disposal of hazardous substances at the facility, and (4) any person who transported hazardous substances to and selected the facility.[20] CERCLA allows recovery for cleanup costs but does not permit punitive damages unless recklessness is found.

Lessee as Owner In the following case, the court considered whether a lessee of contaminated property may be held liable as an "owner" under CERCLA.

20. 42 U.S.C. § 9607 (1998).

A CASE IN POINT

CASE 18.1

Commander Oil Corp. v. Barlo Equipment Corp.
United States Court of Appeals for the Second Circuit
215 F.3d 321
(2d Cir. 2000), cert. denied,
121 S. Ct. 427 (2000).

Summary

FACTS Commander Oil Corporation was the owner of two lots of land in Nassau County, New York, which contained office and warehouse space and housed twelve petroleum storage tanks. Commander leased some of the office and warehouse space to Barlo Equipment Corporation, which was in the business of buying, manufacturing, and distributing equipment for handling petroleum. Commander leased the other lot to Pasley Solvent & Chemicals, Inc., which used the property to reclaim, revitalize, and repackage solvents. Subsequently, Commander Oil consolidated the leases and rented both lots to Barlo, which subleased one of the lots to Pasley. Approximately ten years later, contamination was discovered on the property subleased to Pasley, which then agreed to remove the solvents and vacate the premises.

Six years later, the EPA ordered Commander Oil to determine the extent of contamination and propose a remediation plan. The EPA also sought reimbursement from Commander Oil for costs incurred in remediating the site. Commander agreed to reimburse the EPA and subsequently filed an action demanding contribution or indemnification from Barlo and Pasley. The district court found that Barlo was an "owner" under CERCLA due to its "authority and control" over the lot it leased from Commander Oil. At trial, the court held that Commander Oil could recover 25 percent of its costs from Barlo. Barlo appealed.

ISSUE PRESENTED When are lessees/sublessors liable as "owners" under CERCLA?

SUMMARY OF OPINION Although the U.S. Court of Appeals for the Second Circuit acknowledged that most district courts that have considered the issue have held that site control is a sufficient indicator of ownership to impose owner liability on lessees or sublessors, the Second Circuit rejected this approach. It held that site control is not a proper basis for imposing owner liability because it confuses the two statutorily distinct categories of owner and operator under CERCLA. Instead, the Second Circuit ruled, the critical question is whether the lessee's status is that of a de facto owner. In determining whether a lessee is an "owner," important factors to consider are (1) the length of the lease and whether it allows the owner/lessor to determine how the property is used; (2) whether the owner has the power to terminate the lease before it expires; (3) whether the lessee can sublet the property without notifying the owner; (4) whether the lessee

(Continued)

(Case 18.1 continued)

must pay taxes, insurance, assessments, and operation and maintenance costs; and (5) whether the lessee is responsible for making structural repairs.

Applying these factors to the relationship between Commander and Barlo, the court found that although Barlo possessed some attributes of ownership (such as an obligation to secure insurance and make repairs), it did not possess sufficient attributes of ownership to be characterized as an owner for purposes of establishing liability under CERCLA. Commander Oil had retained many of the rights and obligations of ownership, including the right to enter the lot, the right to use storage tanks located on the property, an option to use office space on the property, and responsibility for making structural repairs.

RESULT The appeals court reversed the district court's decision. Because Barlo lacked most of the bundle of rights that come with ownership of property, it could not be held liable as an owner under CERCLA.

Owner at Time of Disposal In the following case, the court considered whether a person was the owner at the time of disposal if the contamination was due to the passive movement of substances without any human intervention.

A CASE IN POINT

CASE 18.2

United States v. 150 Acres of Land

United States Court of Appeals for the Sixth Circuit 204 F.3d 698 (6th Cir. 2000).

Summary

FACTS Three generations of the Bohaty family had owned approximately 150 acres of real estate in three parcels in Medina County, Ohio, where they operated a farm-equipment repair business. The present generation had inherited the property except for one member of the family who had purchased part of the land from relatives. On March 30, 1997, the local fire department notified the Ohio Environmental Protection Agency that they had noticed fifty-five-gallon drums on the property. The agency visited the property and found approximately 3,000 drums containing nontoxic laboratory chemicals, paint waste, and red sludge, but it did not instruct the Bohaty family to remove the materials. After the agency inspected the property again seventeen months later, it concluded that the drums had been placed there from the mid-1950s through the early 1970s.

On October 1991, the federal EPA conducted an inspection, took soil samples, and determined that the soil was contaminated. The government presented evidence that the husband of one of the owners, Ethel Bohaty, knew of the dumping and may have profited from it. The surviving Bohatys presented unrebutted evidence that they did not know of the presence of the drums, which were hidden by heavy vegetation.

The EPA removed the drums and sued the Bohaty family to recover the removal costs. The family asserted a number of defenses, including a claim that no "disposal" of hazardous substances had occurred while they owned the property, as the drums had been deposited on the land before they inherited it.

ISSUE PRESENTED Does "disposal" of hazardous substances under CERCLA include passive movement of substances involving no human activity?

SUMMARY OF OPINION The U.S. Court of Appeals for the Sixth Circuit began by examining the distinction between "disposal" and "release," after determining that this distinction was important to its resolution of the case. With respect to the definition of "disposal," CERCLA refers to the Solid Waste Disposal Act, which provides that "the

(Continued)

(Case 18.2 continued)

term 'disposal' means the discharge, deposit, injection, dumping, spilling, leaking, or placing of any solid waste or hazardous waste into or on any land or water."

Although earlier courts have interpreted "disposal" to include passive movement of substances, two circuit courts recently ruled that "disposal" was limited to spills caused by human interventions. The court found that this interpretation was the better of the two for several reasons. First, the court argued that because "disposal" was defined primarily in terms of active words, such as "injection," "deposit," and "placing," the potentially passive words "spilling" and "leaking" should be interpreted actively. The court also found that "release" must be broader than "disposal" because disposal was included within release. Finally, the court found that it made sense with respect to the statutory scheme to define "disposal" as activity that precedes the entry of a substance into the environment and to define "release" as the actual entry of substances into the environment. On the basis of this analysis, the court found that because the Bohatys had not moved the hazardous substances during the time they owned the property, they had not disposed of the substances on the property.

RESULT The court affirmed the court's decision with respect to the issue of "disposal." The surviving Bohatys were not the owners at the time of disposal.

LIABILITY FOR AFFILIATED COMPANIES AND PIERCING THE CORPORATE VEIL

Corporate relatives must also worry about CERCLA liability. In every state, corporations have limited liability, so shareholders risk only their invested capital. Hence, a plaintiff suing a corporation may go after that company's assets but not the assets of its shareholders, including a parent corporation. To protect plaintiffs against corporate schemes that use this protection to inappropriately evade responsibility, courts may "pierce the corporate veil" that separates a firm from its subsidiary. Such a collapsing of the legal distinction between parent and subsidiary is appropriate only if the corporation is merely a sham or if the distinction is a fiction meant simply to protect shareholders from illegal activity.

In *United States v. Bestfoods*,[21] the U.S. Supreme Court outlined the responsibility a parent corporation has for the hazardous-waste-disposal activities of a subsidiary. The Court held that under CERCLA there are two bases for imposing liability on parent corporations for operating facilities ostensibly under the control of their subsidiaries. First, a parent corporation will have derivative CERCLA liability as an owner for its subsidiary's actions when (but only when) the corporate veil may be pierced. Piercing is appropriate when the corporate form would otherwise be misused to accomplish certain wrongful purposes, such as fraud. Second, a par-

ent corporation may have direct liability as an operator for its own actions in operating a facility owned by its subsidiary. The Court held that "an operator must manage, direct, or conduct operations specifically related to pollution, that is, operations having to do with the leakage or disposal of hazardous waste, or decisions about compliance with environmental regulations." Thus, the question is not whether the parent operates the subsidiary, but rather whether it operates the facility.

The Court acknowledged that it is common for directors of the parent to serve as directors of its subsidiary. Directors and officers holding positions with a parent and its subsidiary can and do "change hats" to represent the two corporations separately. Courts generally presume that the directors are wearing their "subsidiary hats," and not their "parent hats," when acting for the subsidiary. As a result, the parent is not liable just because dual officers and directors made policy decisions and supervised activities at the facility.

The parent company may, however, be held directly liable if (1) the parent operates the facility in the stead of its subsidiary or alongside the subsidiary in some sort of joint venture; (2) a dual officer or director departs so far from the norms of parental influence exercised through dual officeholding as to serve the parent, even when ostensibly acting on behalf of the subsidiary, in operating the facility; or (3) an agent of the parent with no hat to wear but the parent's hat manages or directs activities at the facility. Activities involving the facility that are consistent with the parent's investor status (such as moni-

21. 524 U.S. 51 (1998).

toring the subsidiary's performance, supervising the subsidiary's finance and capital budget decisions, and articulating general policies and procedures) should not give rise to direct operator liability for the parent.

In its initial ruling in *Bestfoods*, the U.S. Court of Appeals for the Sixth Circuit had turned to Michigan corporate law in deciding whether to pierce the Michigan firm's corporate veil. Other courts have turned to federal common law, that is, the principles that the courts have developed for interpreting federal statutes like CERCLA. Under federal common law, courts may give less respect to the corporate form than under the common law of many states.

Bestfoods involved a corporate parent–subsidiary relationship. In the following case, the court considered the potential liability of an individual who was both president and the major shareholder of a corporation that had not properly handled its hazardous waste.

A CASE IN POINT

CASE 18.3

Browning-Ferris Industries v. Ter Maat

United States Court of Appeals for the Seventh Circuit 195 F.3d 953 (7th Cir. 1999), cert. denied, 120 S. Ct. 1832 (2000).

In the Language of the Court

FACTS In 1971, the owners of a landfill leased it to a predecessor of Browning-Ferris Industries, which operated it until 1975. Between 1975 and 1988, M.I.G. Investments, Inc. and AAA Disposal Systems, Inc. operated the landfill. Richard Ter Maat was the president and principal shareholder of these two corporations. In 1988, Ter Maat sold AAA and moved to Florida. M.I.G., an Illinois corporation, abandoned the site without properly covering it. M.I.G. had operated with little capital and, as a result, did not have funds to cover the landfill.

Two years after the site was abandoned, the EPA placed the property on the National Priorities List. Browning-Ferris and several other companies, which shared responsibility for the pollution at the site, agreed to clean it up. Subsequently, these companies brought a suit under CERCLA against Ter Maat, AAA, and M.I.G. for contribution for the cost of remediation. The district court held that Ter Maat was not a potentially liable person because he had done nothing that would subject him to liability on a "piercing the corporate veil" theory for the actions of the two corporations. Browning-Ferris and the other companies appealed.

ISSUE PRESENTED When is a corporate officer and major shareholder individually liable as an operator of a hazardous-waste facility under CERCLA?

OPINION POSNER, J., writing for the U.S. Court of Appeals for the Seventh Circuit:

Two issues are relatively simple and we address them first. One is whether an individual can shield himself from liability for operating a hazardous-waste facility merely by being an officer or shareholder of a corporation that also operates the facility. The answer is no. The principle of limited liability shields a shareholder from liability for the debts (including debts arising from tortious conduct) of the corporation in which he owns shares (with the exception discussed later for "veil piercing" situations), but not for his personal debts, including debts arising from torts that he commits himself. In other words, the status of being a shareholder does not immunize a person for liability for his, as distinct from the corporation's, acts. There is no liability shield at all for an officer. If he commits an act that is outside the scope of his official duties, his employer may not be liable; but he is whether or not the act was within that scope. Which is not to say, however, that the officer is automatically liable for the acts of the corporation; there is no doctrine of "superiors' liability," comparable to the doctrine of *respondeat superior*, that is, the employer's strict liability for torts of the employee committed within the scope of his employment.

So if Ter Maat operated the landfill personally, rather than merely directing the business of the corporations of which he was the president and which either formally, or jointly with him (as well as with each other), operated it, he is personally liable.

(Continued)

(Case 18.3 continued)

The line between a personal act and an act that is purely an act of the corporation (or of some other employee) and so not imputed to the president or to other corporate officers is sometimes a fine one, but often it is clear on which side of the line a particular act falls. If an individual is hit by a negligently operated train, the railroad is liable in tort to him but the president of the railroad is not. Or rather, not usually; had the president been driving the train when it hit the plaintiff, or had he been sitting beside the driver and ordered him to exceed the speed limit, he would be jointly liable with the railroad. If Ter Maat did not merely direct the general operations of M.I.G. and AAA, or specific operations unrelated to pollution, but supervised the day-to-day operations of the landfill—for example, negotiating waste-dumping contracts with the owners of the wastes or directing where the wastes were to be dumped or designing or directing measures for preventing toxic substances in the wastes from leaching into the ground and thence into the groundwater—then he would be deemed the operator, jointly with his companies, of the site itself.

. . .

[The court then considered whether there was a basis for piercing the corporate veil and holding Ter Maat derivatively liable for M.I.G.'s debt to Browning-Ferris and the other companies seeking contribution.] . . . [W]e can think of only two arguments for piercing the corporate veil. The first is that the owners may have so far neglected the legal requirements . . . for operating in the corporate form that they should be taken to have forfeited its protections. . . . [I]f the formalities have been flouted, it becomes hard to see how the investors could reasonably have relied on the protections of limited liability; they would have known they were skating on thin ice.

. . .

Second, it could be argued that enterprises engaged in potentially hazardous activities should be prevented from externalizing the costs of those activities, by being required to maintain or at least endeavor to maintain a sufficient capital cushion to be answerable in a tort suit should its activities cause harm for which liability would attach, on pain of its shareholders' and affiliates' losing their limited liability should the corporation fail to do this. This argument has not carried the day in any jurisdiction that we are aware of . . . .

There is no evidence that either M.I.G. or AAA failed to comply with the legal requirements for operating in the corporate form, except with regard to keeping minutes of their corporate meetings—not a failure significant enough to warrant forfeiture of limited liability, given that penalties should be proportioned to the gravity of the misconduct being penalized. The plaintiffs further argue, however, that M.I.G. was undercapitalized. . . .

. . . [T]he fact that M.I.G. might have been "undercapitalized" for tax reasons is not a reason for piercing the corporate veil. The cases in which undercapitalization has figured in the decision to pierce the corporate veil are ones in which the corporation had so little money that it could not and did not actually operate its nominal business on its own. . . . Undercapitalization is rarely if ever the sole factor in a decision to pierce the corporate veil, and we think it is best regarded simply as a factor helpful in identifying a corporation as a pure shell, which M.I.G. was not.

RESULT The appeals court reversed the trial court's decision and remanded the case for a determination of whether Ter Maat individually operated the landfill personally rather than merely directed the business of the corporations. The appeals court also held that there was no basis for piercing the corporate veil.

(Continued)

(Case 18.3 continued)

COMMENTS The appeals court applied Illinois state law to determine whether to pierce the corporate veil. Some states, including California, will pierce the corporate veil solely on the grounds of undercapitalization. On remand, the trial court held Ter Maat jointly liable as an operator for $4.1 million in clean-up costs, after finding that he exerted direct control over the day-to-day operations of the landfill.

QUESTIONS

1. Would Ter Maat be liable as an operator if, as president of M.I.G., he knew that there were no waste-dumping contracts with the owners of the wastes and no measures in place to keep wastes from leaching into the groundwater?
2. Would a company operating a landfill be deemed so undercapitalized as to warrant piercing the corporate veil if it retained no funds to pay for closing the landfill and covering it?

SUCCESSOR LIABILITY

Another important issue is *successor liability*, that is, the responsibility of an acquirer of corporate assets for the liabilities of the corporation that sold its assets. Ordinarily, a purchaser of corporate assets—as opposed to a purchaser of all the stock of a corporation—does not assume any liabilities from the seller. The doctrine of successor liability arose out of attempts by companies to evade liability by selling the bulk of their business or assets. In such a scheme, a corporation expecting liability might sell off everything but its corporate name and then distribute the proceeds to shareholders, thereby leaving its creditors with no assets to collect against. Although this aspect of corporate law is a province of state common law, CERCLA has raised the specter of a federal common law of successor liability regarding environmental cleanup under CERCLA.

The majority of circuits, the Second, Third, Fourth, Seventh, and Eighth Circuits, have adopted the position that the doctrine of successor liability should be fashioned by reliance on federal common law. For example, in 1998, the Seventh Circuit argued that resort to federal common law was warranted because of the need for national uniformity in interpreting CERCLA and the possibility that parties would frustrate the statute's aims by choosing to merge under the laws of states that restricted successor liability.[22] The First, Sixth, and Eleventh Circuits have relied on state common law to determine successor liability.

LENDER LIABILITY

Lenders also face liability under CERCLA because foreclosure of a contaminated property potentially makes a lender the owner and, therefore, liable. In 1996, Congress passed the Asset Conservation, Lender Liability, and Deposit Insurance Protection Act of 1996, which modified CERCLA's definition of "owner or operator" to limit the potential exposure of lenders that foreclose on real property.[23]

The definition now excludes from "owner or operator" a lender that did not participate in the management of a facility prior to foreclosure. Participation in management means "actually participating in the management or operational affairs" of the facility; mere capacity to influence management is not a sufficient basis for imposing operator liability on a lender. Although a lender may take steps to sell the property or buy it at the foreclosure sale, the lender must attempt to sell or lease the property as soon as practicable for a commercially reasonable price. This definition also allows a lender to hold "indicia of ownership," such as a deed of trust, to protect its security interest without facing liability.

Under the amended law, a fiduciary's liability is limited to the assets held in trust. There is also a safe harbor for fiduciaries that undertake lawful response actions, but the safe harbor does not protect against negligence that causes or contributes to the release or threatened release of hazardous substances.[24]

RETROACTIVE APPLICATION

As the following case demonstrates, owners can be held liable for hazardous waste disposed of before CERCLA became law.

22. North Shore Gas Co. v. Salomon, Inc., 152 F.3d 642 (7th Cir. 1998).

23. 42 U.S.C. § 9601(20) (Supp. 1997).
24. 42 U.S.C. § 9607(n) (Supp. 1997).

A CASE IN POINT

CASE 18.4

United States v. Olin Corp.

*United States
Court of Appeals for the
Eleventh Circuit
107 F.3d 1506
(11th Cir. 1997).*

In the Language of the Court

FACTS For nearly fifty years, Olin Corporation operated a chemical-manufacturing facility in McIntosh, Alabama. During its first thirty years, the plant produced mercury- and chlorine-based commercial chemicals that contaminated significant segments of the company's property. As a result, groundwater and soil pollution on one part of the property made it unfit for future residential use. The United States sued Olin under CERCLA, seeking a cleanup order against it and reimbursement for response costs. After negotiations with the government, Olin agreed to a consent decree calling for it to pay all costs associated with remediation of the site. The decree also resolved Olin's liability for contamination caused by disposal activities before and after CERCLA's effective date of December 11, 1980.

Olin contended that CERCLA was not intended to impose liability for conduct predating the statute's enactment. Agreeing with Olin, the district court rejected the consent decree and dismissed the government's complaint against Olin. The government appealed.

ISSUE PRESENTED Does CERCLA liability apply retroactively to disposals occurring prior to its enactment?

OPINION KRAVITCH, J., writing for the U.S. Court of Appeals for the Eleventh Circuit:

[E]ven absent explicit statutory language mandating retroactivity, laws may be applied retroactively if courts are able to discern "clear congressional intent favoring such a result." . . .

We examine first CERCLA's language. . . . [T]he statute contains no explicit statement regarding retroactive application of its cleanup liability provisions. Olin mistakenly contends that CERCLA's text therefore offers no insight into Congress's intent on this subject. CERCLA imposes liability for response costs upon "owners and operators" of "any site or area where a hazardous substance has been deposited. . . ." Its reach also extends to "any person who at the time of disposal of any hazardous substance owned or operated" such a facility. Congress thus targeted both current and former owners and operators of contaminated sites. By imposing liability upon former owners and operators, Congress manifested a clear intent to reach conduct preceding CERCLA's enactment.

. . .

An analysis of CERCLA's purpose, as evinced by the statute's structure and legislative history, also supports the view that Congress intended the statute to impose retroactive liability for cleanup. . . . Congress's twin goals of cleaning up pollution that occurred prior to December 11, 1980, and of assigning responsibility to culpable parties can be achieved only through retroactive application of CERCLA's response cost liability provisions.

RESULT The appeals court reversed the district court's dismissal of the government's complaint and remanded the case for further proceedings. Olin was liable for waste disposed of before CERCLA became law.

COMMENTS Subsequent to the Eleventh Circuit's decision in this case, the U.S. Supreme Court held in *Eastern Enterprises v. Apfel* [25] that retroactive application of the Coal Industry Retiree Health Benefit Act of 1992 to a company that had abandoned its coal business in 1965 violated the Takings Clause of the Fifth Amendment of the U.S. Constitution. (This is discussed further in Chapter 2.) Although defendant firms have argued in several cases that *Eastern Enterprises* overrules all previous decisions holding

25. 524 U.S. 498 (1998).

(Continued)

(Case 18.4 continued)

that CERCLA could constitutionally be applied retroactively, three federal district courts (the Eastern District of Virginia, the Northern District of New York, and the Western District of Arkansas)[26] have rejected this argument and upheld the retroactive application of CERCLA.

QUESTIONS

1. Given that Congress can pass environmental laws that penalize actions previously thought innocuous, or at least quite legal, what should a manager do when making decisions that may affect the environment?
2. How would the court have analyzed the issue if the legislative history had contained no references to retroactive liability?

26. Combined Properties/Greenbriar Ltd. Partnership v. Morrow, 58 F. Supp. 2d 675 (E.D. Va. 1999); United States v. Alcan Aluminum Corp., 49 F. Supp. 2d 96 (N.D.N.Y. 1999); United States v. Vertac Chem. Corp., 33 F. Supp. 2d 769 (W.D. Ark. 1998).

DEFENSES

CERCLA provides only three defenses to liability. The defendant must show that the release of hazardous substances was caused solely by (1) an act of God (that is, an unavoidable natural disaster, such as an earthquake); (2) an act of war; or (3) the act or omission of a third party, provided that certain other requirements are met.

Third-Party or Innocent Landowner Defense To assert the *third-party defense* (also referred to as the *innocent landowner defense*), a defendant must show that the third party was not an employee and had no contractual relationship with the person asserting the defense. If the facility was acquired from the third party, the written instrument of transfer is deemed to create a contractual relationship, unless the purchaser acquired the facility after the hazardous substances were disposed of and without any knowledge or reason to know that hazardous substances had previously been disposed of at the facility. To establish that the purchaser had no reason to know that hazardous substances were disposed of at the facility, the purchaser must show that, prior to the sale, it undertook "all appropriate inquiry into the previous ownership and uses of the property consistent with good commercial or customary practice in an effort to minimize liability."[27]

Recyclers The 1999 Superfund Recycling Equity Act exempts recyclers from liability in private party actions under CERCLA. They remain liable in suits brought by

27. 42 U.S.C. § 9601(35)(B) (Supp. 1997).

a state or the federal government. Under the statute, a person "who arranged for recycling of a recyclable material shall not be liable under [CERCLA's cost recovery and contribution sections] with respect to such material." The term "recyclable material" includes lead-acid and nickel-cadmium used in batteries. The act applies retroactively to private actions that were pending on the date of its enactment, November 29, 1999.[28]

 # Enforcement *of* Environmental Laws

Enforcement includes the monitoring of regulated companies' compliance with the environmental laws and the correction or punishment of violations.

28. Gould, Inc. v. A&M Battery & Tire Serv., 232 F.3d 162 (3d Cir. 2000).

 ETHICAL CONSIDERATION

An action that is cost-effective in the short term may not be in the long term, particularly when the environment and human health are concerned. Given the possibility of retroactive liability, managers should consider not just what the law requires of them at the time but also any effects their actions now might have on the environment in the future. But, if there were no possibility of retroactive liability, would it be ethical for managers to ignore those possible but uncertain future effects?

AGENCY INSPECTIONS

The environmental laws give broad authority to the administering agencies to conduct on-site inspections of plant facilities and their records. Many laws authorize the agency to collect samples for analysis. Inspections may be conducted routinely or in response to reports or complaints from neighbors or employees. If criminal violations are suspected, the agency may choose to conduct an inspection under the authority of a search warrant. Violations observed during the inspection may be the subject of civil or criminal enforcement actions.

SELF-REPORTING AND AUDITS

Many statutes and regulations require regulated companies to report certain facts to the EPA, such as the concentrations and/or the amounts of pollutants discharged from a facility. These reports may indicate a violation and may therefore prompt an enforcement action by the agency. There are severe penalties for filing false reports, including criminal sanctions for knowingly providing false information to a government agency.

The EPA may reduce or eliminate fines for civil or administrative violations by companies that discover such violations through their own systematic compliance reviews, report them to the EPA within twenty-one days of discovery by a responsible party, and remedy them. A company may also qualify under the policy if, after having been found liable for violations at one facility, it discloses similar violations at other facilities. The EPA may also recommend against criminal prosecution by the Department of Justice if the company cooperates with the EPA.[29]

Any protection against criminal prosecution gained by voluntary disclosures under the audit policy applies only to the company. Officers and employees may still be subject to criminal liability based on information disclosed by the company.

The voluntary disclosure policy has been widely used. As of March 2000, 670 companies owning or operating 2,700 facilities had made voluntary disclosures, resulting in the resolution of claims at 1,300 facilities. American Airlines used the policy to avoid paying $1.4 million in penalties as a result of alleged violations of the Clear Air Act. The company paid only $95,000 in penalties after discovering and disclosing to the EPA that it was improperly using aviation fuel, rather than diesel fuel, in

29. *EPA May Recommend Not Prosecuting Companies That Uncover, Report Crimes*, 66 U.S.L.W. 2520 (1998). *See* <http://es.epa.gov/oeca/oceft/audpol2.html> for the official EPA memo on the policy.

ETHICAL CONSIDERATION

Would it be a breach of fiduciary duty or unethical for top management to decide not to voluntarily disclose violations to the EPA due to fear of criminal prosecution of corporate employees? Who within the corporation should make the decision of whether to self-report?

ground vehicles and equipment at its facilities across the country.[30]

ENFORCEMENT ACTIONS

Because the environmental laws are intended to accomplish such important societal goals and violations of the laws may cause serious harm or injury, environmental regulatory agencies generally are given strong enforcement powers. For a first violation, the agency might issue a warning and impose a schedule for compliance. If the schedule is not met or the violations are repeated, more aggressive enforcement action will likely follow. Such action may take the form of an administrative order to take specified steps to achieve compliance or a formal administrative complaint containing an assessment of administrative penalties. The penalties vary. Be-

30. Peyton Sturges, *Revisions to EPA Audit Policy Dovetail with Enforcement Initiatives, Official Says*, 68 U.S.L.W. 2576 (Mar. 28, 2000).

INTERNATIONAL CONSIDERATION

Although internal environmental audits in the United States may be protected through the attorney–client privilege, that may not be the case in other countries where the privilege is either not recognized or provides more limited protection than in U.S. courts. For example, in many countries in Latin America, the attorney–client privilege does not extend to attorney memos that a company has in its files. Internal environmental audit documents, including attorney memos, may be obtained in most Latin American countries through a court order. As a result, foreign citizens can use these documents to file claims in U.S. courts against domestic companies for their actions outside the United States.[a]

a. *U.S. Business Documents Can Be Used in Suits by Foreign Citizens, Attorney Says*, 69 U.S.L.W. 2251 (Oct. 31, 2000).

cause they can be assessed for each day of each violation, they can be substantial for repeated, multiple, or long-standing violations.

In more egregious cases, the enforcing agency may initiate a civil lawsuit and/or a criminal prosecution. Courts are authorized in most instances to impose penalties of $25,000 to $100,000 per day of violation and to sentence individuals to prison terms of one year or more.[31] (See also the discussion of penalties in Chapter 17.) In some cases, the agency may have authority to close down the violator's operations. In 2000, the EPA's enforcement efforts resulted in the assessment of $122 million in criminal fines for environmental violations and $102 million in civil penalties.

31. *See, e.g.,* 33 U.S.C. § 1319 (1995) and 42 U.S.C. § 6928 (1995).

 INTERNATIONAL CONSIDERATION

Although pollution laws are often not enforced in India, in November 1999, the Supreme Court of India ordered New Delhi authorities to comply with its 1996 order to close approximately 90,000 small factories that were polluting residential areas in the capital city or to relocate them to areas outside the city. The businesses at issue included leather, fertilizer, chemical, food-processing, and paint plants that polluted the city's air and water sources. After the India Supreme Court issued the order, thousands of workers violently protested closure of the factories by torching buses, blocking major roads, and throwing stones.[a] These protests essentially shut down the capital for a week. Opponents of the closure argued that shutting down the small factories, which employed approximately one million people and generated business worth more than $1 billion annually, would cripple the city's economy.[b] The India Supreme Court argued that closure of the polluting industries was necessary for public health reasons and stated that it would not be influenced by the protests: "The court will not withdraw its orders just because hooligans have taken to the streets."[c] The governments of the rapidly industrializing states of Haryana and Uttar Pradesh, New Delhi's neighbors to the north, issued advertisements encouraging factories to relocate there.[d]

a. Celia W. Dugger, *A Cruel Choice in New Delhi: Jobs vs. a Safer Environment,* N.Y. TIMES, Nov. 24, 2000.
b. Ranjit Devrai, *Development—India: Thousands of Jobless Question Green Concerns,* INTER PRESS SERVICE, Dec. 29, 2000.
c. Dugger, *supra* note a.
d. Kartik Goyal, *India: Neighbouring States Gain as Delhi Shuts Polluting Units,* REUTERS ENGLISH NEWS SERVICE, Dec. 29, 2000.

ENVIRONMENTAL JUSTICE

A relatively new area of enforcement addresses so-called environmental justice. *Environmental justice* is the notion that decisions with environmental consequences (such as where to locate incinerators, dumps, factories, and other sources of pollution) should not discriminate against poor and minority communities. Because such decisions usually require state or municipal permits, environmental justice concerns are often enforced by the federal government against states, cities, and counties.

In 1992, the EPA created the Office of Environmental Justice and began integrating environmental justice into the agency's policies, programs, and activities. Between 1993 and 1998, the EPA received fifty-one environmental justice complaints, most of which addressed the granting of state and local permits.

In August 2000, the National Environmental Justice Advisory Council issued its recommendations to the EPA with respect to environmental justice. The report set forth approximately eighty recommendations, including (1) that federal environmental laws and policies should be fairly and equitably enforced in communities so that environmental justice concerns can be fully integrated into federal environmental programs; (2) that the EPA's Office of General Counsel should provide guidance on the extent to which permit issuers can deny an environmental permit on environmental justice grounds; and (3) that public participation requirements should be strengthened to ensure that permit issuers consult with affected communities in the decision-making progress.

Management *of* Environmental Compliance

Knowledgeable corporate officials today recognize the need to adopt corporate policies and create management systems to ensure that company operations are protective of human health and the environment. These programs generally include several key elements.

CORPORATE POLICY

A strong corporate policy of environmental protection, adopted and supported at the highest levels of management, is usually the keystone of an effective program. Mere compliance with environmental laws may not be enough. A practice that is lawful today could nevertheless lead to environmental harm and future liability. For example, underground storage of flammable materials was once considered a sound practice and was actually required by many local fire codes. Little thought was given to the possibility of leaks or spillage around the tanks, with resulting harm to underground water supplies. If the risks had been perceived properly, double containment could have been provided when the tanks were first installed. This lack of foresight caused many companies to incur substantial costs for groundwater restoration.

The corporate policy should require every employee to comply with environmental laws. It should encourage management to consider more stringent measures than those required by law if such measures are necessary to protect human health and the environment. Finally, the policy should encourage a cooperative and constructive relationship with government agency personnel and should support active participation in legislative and administrative rulemaking proceedings.

WELL-DEFINED ORGANIZATION AND CRISIS-MANAGEMENT PLAN

Management of environmental compliance requires a well-defined organization with clear responsibilities and reporting relationships. The complex and technical nature of environmental laws and regulations requires a highly trained professional staff with legal and technical expertise.

Every company should have a crisis-management plan in place that designates someone other than the CEO to coordinate the response. That response, in turn, should include immediate stabilization of the situation, objective inquiry into it, and some immediate action to assure the company's constituencies that things are being put under control. For that reason, constituencies must receive information as the response continues. To the extent crises are at least foreseeable, more detailed plans should be developed ahead of time.[32]

PERIODIC ENVIRONMENTAL AUDITS

An important step in comprehensively managing environmental liability and reducing penalties for noncompliance is to conduct periodic environmental audits. Such candid, internal self-assessments document and measure (1) compliance with occupational health and safety requirements; (2) compliance with federal, state, and local emissions limits and other requirements of a company's licensing, if any; (3) current practices for the generation, storage, and disposal of hazardous wastes; and (4) potential liability for past disposal of hazardous substances. Audits should also test the effectiveness of

AT THE TOP

A corporation can be held liable for the malfeasance of its employees acting within the scope of employment, even if they acted contrary to company policies. At the same time, an employee involved in illegal conduct can be held personally criminally liable, even if he or she was just following orders from a supervisor. In addition, as explained in this chapter and in Chapter 17, under certain circumstances, the corporate executive officer responsible for operating or overseeing the operation of facilities or activities involving hazardous waste can be civilly and criminally liable for illegal conduct by the employees under his or her supervision. It is critical for a corporation to conduct an education program designed to make its employees and managers aware of their environmental responsibilities.

the management system and ensure that all instances of noncompliance are corrected. According to a mid-1990s study by Price Waterhouse, 75 percent of firms have environmental auditing programs.

Although such programs can generate valuable information for management, they may also be self-incriminating. A thorough audit that reveals contaminated properties, shoddy disposal practices, and lax compliance with regulations will certainly aid a company seeking to improve its environmental compliance. If the results of such an audit were publicly available, however, plaintiffs in the discovery stage of litigation could use the audit results to further their case. For that reason, several states have enacted laws making such information privileged in order to motivate companies to produce and use it. At least one court has established a qualified privilege for certain self-critical analyses.[33]

LONG-TERM STRATEGIES

The company should develop strategies for reducing the costs of compliance and the risk of liability over the long term. Corporate strategies might include minimizing the amounts and kinds of pollutants produced, developing ways to recycle waste products, and investing in new technologies to render wastes nonhazardous. If the company cannot avoid producing hazardous wastes that must be disposed of, it should have procedures for evaluating and selecting well-managed and well-constructed disposal facilities.

---

32. Stanley Sporkin, *A Plan for Crisis Management and Avoidance,* Address at Nonprofit Risk Management Institute (Nov. 12, 1997).

33. Reichhold Chems., Inc. v. Textron, Inc., 157 F.R.D. 522 (N.D. Fla. 1994).

RECORD KEEPING AND ACCOUNTING

Good record-keeping and cost-accounting systems are also essential. Many environmental laws require certain records to be developed and maintained for specified periods of time. These laws need to be consulted when a company develops a record-retention policy. Cost-accounting procedures need to be developed that allow the company to forecast and report the costs of environmental compliance.

Publicly traded companies must carefully evaluate the costs of compliance and potential environmental liabilities for purposes of Securities and Exchange Commission (SEC) disclosure and reporting requirements. The SEC requires disclosure of environmental enforcement proceedings and litigation, as well as estimated costs of environmental compliance, including capital expenditures and any effects of compliance on earnings and competitive position that may be material. The SEC uses information provided by the EPA in enforcing these reporting requirements.

REPORTING POLICIES AND PROCEDURES

The company should have policies and procedures for reporting environmental law violations to corporate management and for managing the company's reporting obligations to government agencies. Top management needs to ensure that whistle-blowers are not subject to retaliation.

AGENCY INSPECTION POLICIES AND PROCEDURES

Government agencies may undertake inspections with little or no advance notice. The company should be prepared for such an event by having a protocol for handling the inspection. Individuals trained in company protocol should accompany the inspector to ensure that the inspection is conducted properly and within the inspector's authority. The person who accompanies the inspector should prepare a report to management and make sure that any instances of noncompliance identified during the inspection are corrected.

EDUCATION AND TRAINING

The most essential component of good environmental management is comprehensive education and training. Every employee must know about and understand the company's environmental policy and recognize his or her responsibilities in carrying it out.

PUBLIC AND COMMUNITY RELATIONS

As popular sentiment increasingly favors environmental sensitivity and protection, companies must pay attention to the public relations consequences of their environment-affecting actions. Dissatisfaction with a company's environmental record can lead to adverse publicity, activist protests, consumer boycotts, and more stringent regulation.

The way a company handles an environmental problem can have an important impact on its relationship with the community where it is located, as well as on the economic damages it will suffer. A company can gain credibility and respect by handling an environmental accident in a proactive and fair manner.

For example, Eastman Kodak's handling of an environmental problem increased its standing in the city of Rochester, where it is headquartered. When the local newspaper reported that toxic chemicals from Kodak had seeped into the bedrock beneath the soil and were moving underground toward homes, panic erupted and the homes' values plummeted. The company instituted a series of homeowner relief programs to assure homeowners that they would lose no money as a result of the decline in value of their homes. Kodak offered discounted refinanced mortgages and home improvement grants to encourage people to stay in their homes rather than sell them. For those who wanted to sell, the company agreed to pay the difference between the selling price and the home's market value before the environmental problem was discovered. If a house took longer than three months to sell, Kodak supplied an interest-free bridge loan so the owners could move into their new home before their old home was sold. The president of the neighborhood association that represented 5,000 Rochester households commented, "The program was a perfect example of a company being proactive in their interactions with the community. Everyone I know [from the polluted area] felt they were given a good deal. I've not heard any objections."[34]

DuPont took a different tack when the company's disposal of toxic chemicals polluted groundwater in the city of Wilmington, Delaware. The company sent out letters to homeowners, promising each of them $5,000 in return for an agreement not to sue for property damages. The letter infuriated the community. As a result, 1,808 residents filed a lawsuit alleging that the values of their homes had been diminished due to contamination by DuPont.[35] Although DuPont argued that the toxic groundwater would not lessen the value of the homes, the litigation continues.

---

34. *Uncivil Action,* 9 Treasury & Risk Mgmt. 25 (Jan.–Feb. 1999).
35. *Id.*

IN BRIEF

Developing an Environmental Compliance Program

In evaluating or developing an environmental compliance program, a manager should consider the following areas and ask the following questions:

1. Achieving and maintaining compliance
   - What laws and regulations affect the company's facilities?
   - What procedures effectively balance compliance costs with liability?
   - How can those procedures be communicated to those responsible for their implementation?
   - How can employees be persuaded they have a stake in the program's success?
2. Obtaining timely notice of new requirements
   - What is being done to keep abreast of new requirements?
   - Will management receive notice early enough to make necessary changes cost-effectively?
3. Influencing future requirements
   - What environmental laws and regulations are on the horizon?
   - How are they being tracked?
   - What is being done to influence their wording and enactment?
4. Monitoring compliance accurately
   - What kind of monitoring is required?
   - Who will perform that monitoring?
   - How will the results be assessed?
5. Timely and accurate reporting
   - When must a manager report information to regulators?
   - What procedures ensure that reportable incidents are brought to management's attention?
   - Does the company have databases for tracking chemical use and other technical information?
6. Responding to emergencies
   - What systems are in place to respond to emergencies?
   - Are responsible employees trained to respond appropriately?
7. Maintaining community relations
   - How strong is the company's relationship with the surrounding community?
   - What kind of programs are in place to maintain and expand that relationship?
   - How would management expect the community to respond to emergencies?

Source: Based on Steven J. Koorse, *When Less Is More—Trouble,* Bus. L. Today, Sept.–Oct. 1997, at 24.

 International Aspects

The National Environmental Policy Act of 1970 was the first element of the new environmental regulatory regime in the United States. Other countries have also promulgated environmental policy acts. Central to each of these acts is the requirement that the government expressly consider environmental values in its decision making and that it document this consideration in written environmental impact reports that can be reviewed by the public. These requirements are especially important when the government itself is responsible for major development projects.

A fundamental element of the U.S. scheme is the policy that the polluter pays. The European Union (EU) has also adopted this policy: "The cost of preventing and eliminating nuisances must, as a matter of principle, be borne by the polluter."[36] The EU's environmental policy includes the following objectives: preserving, protecting, and improving the quality of the environment; protecting human health; prudent and rational utilization of natural resources; and promoting measures at the international level to deal with regional or worldwide environmental problems. In general, European countries,

36. Objective 17, Restatement of the Objectives and Principles of a Community Environment Policy, 1977 O.J. (C 139).

particularly Scandinavian countries, have been leaders in enacting and implementing environmental laws and in developing innovative approaches to addressing environmental problems.

This concept is also being introduced in Asia. Taiwan, for example, has enacted an environmental law modeled, in part, on CERCLA, with modifications to address the local culture, issues, and concerns.

When the laws of other nations are closely patterned on U.S. laws, compliance may be easier for U.S. companies operating in those countries. U.S. companies must be careful, however, to note the differences between the U.S. laws and the laws of their host countries.

SUSTAINABLE DEVELOPMENT

An environmental issue of increasing importance is the concept of sustainable development. *Sustainable development* "holds that future prosperity depends on preserving 'natural capital'—air, water, and other ecological treasures—and that doing so will require balancing human activity with nature's ability to renew itself. It also recognizes that growth is necessary to eliminate poverty, which leads to the plunder of resources."[37] This concept is politically controversial because it entails significant changes in national regulatory and economic policies. Increased cooperation among industrialized and developing nations, the possibility of industrialized nations scaling back their transformation of the world's resources into wealth, and the use of new technology to preserve the earth's environment and prevent pollution would also be important.

KYOTO PROTOCOL AND GLOBAL WARMING

In November 2000, representatives of approximately 170 countries met at The Hague for the Sixth Conference of the Parties (COP-6) to the United Nations Framework Convention on Climate Change in an effort to work out the details of the international treaty on global climate change originally agreed to in Kyoto, Japan, in 1997. The Kyoto Protocol requires developed countries to cut their levels of greenhouse gas emissions by 5 percent, using 1990 emissions as the baseline. After two weeks of intensive talks at The Hague, the negotia-

tions broke down because the United States and the European Union were unable to reach an agreement on the issue of whether developed countries should be allowed to count the effect of forests and other carbon "sinks" toward meeting the emission levels.[38] Trees and other plants in forests act as "sinks" by absorbing carbon dioxide, the main greenhouse gas, from the atmosphere. In early 2001, President George W. Bush announced that the United States—the world's largest producer of greenhouse gases—was abandoning the Kyoto Protocol.

Some industrialized countries are also interested in purchasing unused quotas of other nations to meet their quotas under the Kyoto Protocol. When quotas were originally set in 1990, former members of the Soviet Union negotiated permissible emission levels comparable to those of other industrialized countries. After industrial production in the former Soviet republics plummeted due to changes in their governments and economies, their actual emissions were only 40 percent of their levels at the time the quotas were set. As a result, these countries want to sell their unused quotas to other industrialized countries to reap huge profits. Analysts predict that Russia could potentially earn more than $12 billion annually (and Kazakhstan $4 billion) by selling its rights to emit greenhouse gases to other countries.[39] A number of countries are opposed to this arrangement because it would allow some industrialized countries to meet their obligations by simply buying unused quotas of other nations rather than reducing their fuel use.

ROLE OF BUSINESS

As the attempts to curb greenhouse gases demonstrate, efforts at negotiating international treaties and adopting national laws to implement them are insufficient to prevent the extensive and irreversible destruction to the environment that is currently occurring. In an award-winning *Harvard Business Review* article, Professor Stuart Hart called on business leaders to step into the breach:

> Like it or not, the responsibility for ensuring a sustainable world falls largely on the shoulders of the world's enterprises, the economic engines of the future. Clearly, public

37. Emily T. Smith, *Growth vs. Environment,* Bus. Wk., May 11, 1992, at 66. *See also* Mathis Wackernagel & William Resse, Our Ecological Footprint: Reducing Human Impact on the Earth (1996) (if everybody lived like the average American, we would need at least three planets to live sustainably).

38. Andrew C. Revkin, *The Tree Trap: Envoys Could Not Agree on Value of Forests to World Environment,* N.Y. Times, Nov. 26, 2000.
39. Steve LeVine, *Ex-Soviet States Sit on a Gold Mine of Greenhouse Gases,* Wall St. J., Nov. 21, 2000, at A23.

policy innovations (at both the national and international levels) and changes in individual consumption patterns will be needed to move towards sustainability. But corporations can and should lead the way, helping to shape public policy and driving change in consumers' behavior. In the final analysis, it makes good business sense to pursue strategies for a sustainable world.[40]

40. Stuart L. Hart, *Beyond Greening: Strategies for a Sustainable World,* Harv. Bus. Rev. (Jan.–Feb. 1997).

THE RESPONSIBLE MANAGER
Managing Risks *of* Environmental Liability

Several sources of potential environmental liability present risks to the parties in business transactions. In evaluating a company for purposes of acquisition, investment, or financing, a manager must consider that the company's earnings may be affected by the costs of compliance with environmental laws. The value of its equipment assets may be affected by regulatory limitations that make the equipment obsolete. Its ability to expand in existing locations may be impaired as a result of limitations on new sources of air emissions or the lack of nearby facilities for waste treatment or disposal. A company's cash flow may be affected by additional capital investments or by increased operating costs necessitated by environmental regulations. Failure to comply with existing regulations may lead to the imposition of substantial penalties, also affecting cash flow. Small companies or companies that are highly leveraged may not be able to meet these additional demands for cash.

Similarly, a small company may not be able to survive the imposition of liability for response costs under CERCLA or similar state laws. Potential liabilities may not be properly reflected in the company's financial statements. Finally, a company's operations or the condition of its properties may present risks of injury to other persons and their property, giving rise to possible tort claims.

The most important element in managing the risk of these potential liabilities is *due diligence,* that is, a systematic and ongoing process for determining whether property contains or emits hazardous substances and whether the company is in compliance with environmental laws. The object of environmental due-diligence investigations is to identify and characterize the risks associated with the properties and operations involved in the business transaction. Such investigations have become highly sophisticated undertakings, often requiring the use of technical consultants and legal counsel with special expertise. Although much of the effort focuses on the review of company documents and available public records, it may also involve physical inspections of the properties, including soil and groundwater sampling and analysis. Care should be taken to avoid negligent soil investigations, which can create liability for disposal of hazardous waste. Environmental due-diligence efforts may represent a significant cost of the transaction and may take much longer to complete than traditional due-diligence efforts.

The scope of the due-diligence effort will depend on the nature of the assets and the structure of the transaction. For example, if the transaction is a simple purchase and sale of real estate, then the due diligence can be limited to the property to be acquired and its surroundings. If the transaction involves the acquisition of a business with a long history of operations in many locations, however, then the due-diligence investigation must cover not only the current operating locations but also prior operating locations and the sites used for off-site disposal of wastes. This is particularly true in the case of an acquisition by merger because the surviving company takes over all of the liabilities of the disappearing company.

Allocation of the risk of liability under CERCLA and other environmental laws has become a significant issue in the negotiation of business transactions. The parties can, by contract, allocate the identified risks of environmental liability by undertaking specified obligations, assuming and retaining contingent liabilities, adjusting the purchase price, making representations and warranties, giving indemnities, and the like. But care must be exercised when the identified risks are not yet quantifiable. For example, if liability for response costs is accepted in return for a reduction in the purchase price, the buyer should bear in mind that response costs often exceed by a wide margin the initial estimate provided by a consultant or government agency.

It is also important to remember that contractual arrangements to shift environmental liability are not binding on federal or state governments. Thus, even if the seller of a piece of property agrees to indemnify the purchaser for any environmental claims arising out of the seller's activities, the EPA can still recover response costs from the present owner. The present owner could sue the seller for indemnification and contribution, but the present owner will bear the entire cleanup cost if the previous owner is insolvent or has insufficient assets.

Under CERCLA, secured lenders, and in some cases equity investors, may be held liable for response costs as present operators if they participate in the day-to-day management of the borrower. If a lender takes title at foreclosure, it may also be found liable for response costs as a present owner unless it attempts to dispose of the property reasonably quickly. Thus, the risk of hazardous-substance releases on the subject property should be carefully evaluated in connection with the loan application. The operations of the borrower should also be carefully reviewed in order to evaluate the risks they present during the life of the loan. If a release of hazardous substances occurs on the property, its value as collateral is impaired. Upon default, the lender may not be able to recover the outstanding amount of the debt.

In trying to protect against diminishment of the value of collateral, a lender must be careful not to participate in management, however. Overly strict loan covenants that involve the lender in making decisions (such as approval of major capital expenditures) may create operator liability for the lender.

In addition, some states have adopted *superlien* provisions, which secure recovery of response costs incurred by state agencies. Where a superlien exists, it may take priority over existing security interests.

When an owner leases property, it must take care to evaluate the environmental risks of the tenant's operations. Use of the property should be carefully limited to prevent any unauthorized activities. If the tenant's activities present significant risks, financial assurances in the form of parent corporation guaranties, letters of credit, or performance bonds might be obtained to ensure that any damage caused by the tenant will be remedied. Tenants also should be cautious in taking possession of property formerly occupied by others. Many tenants perform *baseline assessments* to establish the environmental condition of the property at both the commencement and the termination of the lease. These assessments may provide some protection from liability for conditions caused by prior or succeeding tenants.

INSIDE STORY

City *and* Businesses *in* Rockford Craft *an* Innovative Solution *for a* Superfund Cleanup

When property is placed on the Superfund National Priorities List (NPL), thereby indicating that it is one of the nation's hazardous-waste sites most in need of remediation, it can create nightmares for the community.[41] Property values and local tax revenues plummet; the economy stagnates as businesses close, jobs are lost, and development ceases; and endless lawsuits, countersuits, and negotiations between businesses and municipal authorities create rifts in the community. When property in Rockford, Illinois, was declared a Superfund site, local business and government leaders negotiated an innovative settlement with the federal EPA and the Illinois Environmental Protection Agency (IEPA) to avoid these nightmares and preserve the economic health of their community.

In March 1989, after groundwater pollution was discovered, a one-square-mile site in Rockford was declared

a Superfund site and placed on the NPL. Additional studies indicated that an area of approximately ten square miles, representing 20 percent of the city (including its principal industrial corridor), was contaminated. The EPA investigated potential sources for the contamination but determined that most sources were no longer ongoing contributors to the problem, except for one heavily contaminated site, designated Source Area 7, which had been an open dump for waste materials.

The EPA named seven potentially responsible parties, all of which were manufacturers with facilities located within the boundaries of the contaminated area. The seven companies all denied responsibility for the contamination. Other companies in the area also fell under a cloud of suspicion, even though they had not been identified as potentially responsible parties. Community and business leaders feared that the environmental problems would disrupt the city's economic livelihood. The Rockford area has more than 1,000 manufacturers and leads Illinois in industrial growth, export sales, and job creation.

---

41. This "Inside Story" is based in its entirety on Peggy Morrissette, *A Local Solution to Superfund Cleanup: Case Study of the Southeast Rockford Site,* published by Manufacturers Alliance (1998).

As a result, the Chamber of Commerce started investigating how it could resolve the environmental problem without protracted litigation. In early 1993, the mayor of Rockford proposed to the EPA, the Department of Justice, and the IEPA that the city would facilitate an innovative settlement to finance remediation of the pollution and resolve legal liability. Three years later, the mayor announced the terms of the final agreement that had been reached between the city and the federal and state environmental agencies. He characterized it as "a reasonable solution designed to avoid a potential crisis not only for property owners in this area, but also for the entire community. It's an opportunity to meet a responsibility we have under the law without triggering the need for massive, costly litigation which could span decades."

As part of a consent decree, the city agreed to pay $9 million in costs incurred by the federal and state governments for remediation of the groundwater and to provide a cash-out of $5 million for remediation of soil contamination in Source Area 7. The city also agreed to connect 240 additional homes to the municipal water supply at its expense and to continue to monitor the quality of the city's groundwater. All of the property owners, except for the city of Rockford, were to be released from liability for groundwater contamination.

The city proposed to finance the cost of groundwater remediation with a bond issue. The bonds would be retired by creating a Special Service Area taxing district within the industrially zoned property located in the groundwater study area. The tax rate would be increased 11 percent for a twenty-year period, resulting in an extra $0.82 per $100 of assessed valuation each year. Five area businesses and the local park district volunteered to fund the $5 million remediation of Source Area 7. The city planned to issue water revenue bonds to cover the cost of hooking up additional homes to the municipal water supply. To make up for any shortfalls, the city planned to issue an additional $3 million in water revenue bonds, which would be retired by increasing water rates for large users by approximately 5 percent.

The final settlement offered numerous benefits. The EPA agreed to accept $9 million from the city even though its expenses had been $14 million. The $5 million cash-out for Source Area 7 was lower than similar cleanups, which typically cost five times that amount. The city was the only named party, which shielded the business community from any legal liability. The terms of the settlement preserved property market values and the tax base. The Special Service Area tax was assessed according to the size of the property, so 20 percent of the property owners paid 80 percent of the assessment. The settlement also allowed the city to maintain local control over the environmental cleanup.

Perhaps most importantly, the settlement resolved the situation without harming the local economy or involving the business community in protracted litigation. One business owner commented, "The idea of putting this behind the city and moving forward, instead of the threat of litigation and the stigma of being under the Superfund cloud, makes this solution a preferred option."

KEY WORDS AND PHRASES

baseline assessments   627
best available control technology
   (BACT)   607
due diligence   626
environmental justice   621
environmental law   604
Environmental Protection Agency
   (EPA)   606
hazard ranking score   611
Hazardous Substance Superfund   611
industrial ecology   610

innocent landowner defense   619
innovation offsets   610
lowest achievable emission rate
   (LAER)   607
national ambient air quality standards
   (NAAQS)   606
national effluent limitations   608
National Pollutant Discharge Elimination System (NPDES)   608
natural resources laws   605
navigable waters   607

person   609
publicly owned sewage treatment works
   (POTWs)   608
responsible persons   612
state implementation plans (SIPs)   607
strategic environmental management
   610
successor liability   617
superlien   627
sustainable development   625
third-party defense   619

QUESTIONS AND CASE PROBLEMS

1. Northeastern Pharmaceutical and Chemical Company (NEPACCO) had a manufacturing plant in Verona, Missouri, that produced various hazardous and toxic by-products. The company pumped the by-products into a holding tank, which a waste hauler periodically emptied. Michaels founded the

company, was a major shareholder, and served as its president. In 1971, a waste hauler named Mills approached Ray, a chemical-plant manager employed by NEPACCO, and proposed disposing of some of the firm's wastes at a nearby farm. Ray visited the farm and, with the approval of Lee, the vice president and a shareholder of NEPACCO, arranged for disposal of wastes at the farm.

Approximately eighty-five 55-gallon drums were dumped into a large trench on the farm. In 1976, NEPACCO was liquidated, and the assets remaining after payment to creditors were distributed to its shareholders. Three years later the EPA investigated the area and discovered dozens of badly deteriorated drums containing hazardous waste buried at the farm. The EPA took remedial action and then sought to recover its costs under RCRA and other statutes. From whom and on what basis can the government recover its costs? [*United States v. Northeastern Pharmaceutical and Chemical Co.*, 810 F.2d 726 (8th Cir. 1986), *cert. denied*, 484 U.S. 848 (1987)]

2. George Lu has been named the executive director of the Cornell University Foundation, a nonprofit association organized to support the university. As part of its efforts, the foundation has begun a program to preserve open-space land and ecologically sensitive environments near the university's campus in upstate New York. The foundation plans to buy or receive gifts of land, especially from alumni, and then sell the land to public entities for permanent preservation. The difference between the purchase price and the sale price will be used to finance the association's efforts and to support Cornell generally. One of Lu's first tasks is to develop a protocol and prepare model agreements for making acquisitions.

   a. As a nonprofit, educational organization, does the association have potential liability under the environmental laws?

   b. What procedures should Lu establish to protect the association from potential environmental law liabilities in connection with its acquisitions?

   c. What kinds of contractual arrangements should be considered to protect the association from environmental law liabilities? [*United States v. Alcan Aluminum Corp.*, 34 E.R.C. 1744 (N.D.N.Y. 1991)]

3. RCRA regulations defining solid waste state that a "solid waste is any discarded material." The EPA issued a new regulation classifying reclaimed mineral-processing materials destined for recycling as regulated "solid waste." These reclaimed materials are stored in tanks and containers before they are re-

cycled. Industry groups representing most U.S. producers of steel, metal, and coal and most industrial miners challenged the new regulations. They argued that, by allowing the materials stored before recycling to be considered waste, the rule conflicts with RCRA's definition of waste as discarded material. How should the court rule? [*Association of Battery Recyclers, Inc. v. EPA*, 208 F.3d 1047 (D.C. Cir. 2000)]

4. The City of Florence, a municipal corporation organized under the laws of Alabama, purchased property for the purpose of encouraging industrial development within the county where the city was located. Florence leased the property to Stylon, a corporation that planned to construct and operate a ceramic tile manufacturing factory on the property. Florence issued bonds to finance the purchase of the property and mortgaged the property to First National Bank of Florence, pledging that Stylon's rent payments for the property would be used to secure the repayment on the bonds held by the bank.

   Stylon operated a tile manufacturing facility on the property for approximately twenty years until it went bankrupt. During that time, it discharged hazardous substances, which contaminated the property. After Stylon went bankrupt, Monarch Tile, Inc. leased the property for fifteen years from the City of Florence, with the city retaining title. Subsequently, Monarch purchased the property from the city.

   After Monarch discovered the contamination, it notified the EPA and was directed to remediate pursuant to CERCLA. Monarch brought suit against the City of Florence for contribution under CERCLA. The City of Florence argued that it was not liable because it held ownership of the property primarily to protect its security interest. How should the court rule? Should the First National Bank of Florence or the former Stylon shareholders be forced to contribute to the cost of remediation? [*Monarch Tile, Inc. v. City of Florence*, 212 F.3d 1219 (11th Cir. 2000)]

5. Johanna Landing has been hired by Newco Corporation to identify possible sites for construction of a major new manufacturing facility. Newco's operations will involve the production of substantial quantities of hazardous waste and constitute a major new source of air emissions.

   a. How will these facts affect Landing's consideration of possible construction sites?

   b. How will these facts and the location affect Newco's analysis of its costs of construction and operation?

6. Gregg Entrepreneur is organizing a small company to manufacture a new biotechnology product. Entrepreneur will be a principal shareholder and president of the company. What measures should Entrepreneur take to ensure that his company operates in compliance with environmental laws?

Despite all the measures Entrepreneur has taken to ensure environmental law compliance, his vice president of operations reports that the production manager has been disposing of wastes into the sewer in violation of national pretreatment standards and that she has been submitting false reports to the publicly owned sewage treatment works (POTW) to cover up the violations. All of the reports have been signed by the vice president of operations, who had no knowledge that they contained false statements. What steps should Entrepreneur take? Should he report the violations to the POTW even if doing so could result in personal civil or criminal liability? What about the vice president? The production manager? What is Entrepreneur's ethical responsibility? [*United States v. Alley,* 755 F. Supp. 771 (N.D. Ill. 1990)]

7. American Widgets is a manufacturing company that has gained a large share of the international widget market, largely because of high quality and competitive pricing. The disposal of the company's wastes has become increasingly expensive, however. Due to a new ban on land disposal, one of the company's largest waste streams will have to be incinerated. Plants of competitors located in Southeast Asia and South America are subject to increasing environmental regulation modeled after the laws in the United States, but they can still use land disposal and thus will have a significant competitive advantage over plants located in the United States. Jimmy Tsai, an American Widgets manager, is considering the possibility of locating a new plant in Southeast Asia. What factors should he take into account? What alternatives are there besides relocation?

8. An enterprising young Texas MBA graduate, Nancy Schmidt, purchased land near Houston from Winetka Development, Inc. for $12 million. Schmidt was speculating that the demands, and consequently the inflated prices, of Houston suburbia would soon reach her property. Within two years, Schmidt formed a joint venture with a developer and broke ground on her subdivision plan, expending $1.4 million on streets, plumbing, and irrigation for a planned championship golf course designed by Arnold Palmer. Much to her chagrin, an EPA investigation identified this parcel of land as a former municipal waste landfill and a source of groundwater pollution. The EPA notified Schmidt and her partner that, as the present owners and operators of the property, they were "potentially responsible parties," jointly and severally liable for all of the costs of cleanup, with cleanup costs estimated to be upwards of $29 million.

Who will be liable for the cleanup costs? Is the developer liable? Is it relevant that Schmidt knew or did not know about the landfill prior to the purchase? Does it matter that this was a municipal waste landfill? If a vice president of Winetka Development lied to Schmidt about the prior uses of the land, is Winetka liable for the cleanup costs? For the purchase price and development costs? If a lower-level manager of Winetka is the person who lied to Schmidt, does the analysis change? Does the analysis change if Winetka and all of its employees had not known about the waste? Can Schmidt just give the property back to Winetka in order to free herself from any legal entanglements? [*Tanglewood East Homeowners v. Charles–Thomas, Inc.,* 849 F.2d 1568 (5th Cir. 1988)]

9. In 1979, IBC Manufacturing Company purchased all of the outstanding stock of Chemwood Corporation. Chemwood had operated a wood-preservative blending site in Arlington, Tennessee, until 1976, three years before it was purchased by IBC. After IBC purchased it, Chemwood continued doing business at other locations until 1988, when it shut down. At that time, Chemwood's net worth was $282,000 in accounts receivables, primarily due from its parent corporation IBC. In 1983, the EPA began investigating contamination at the Arlington site; in 1993, the EPA ordered Chemwood to clean up the site. Chemwood agreed to contribute money for the cleanup, but by 1995, its assets were depleted, and it could no longer contribute to the remediation costs. IBC sought a court order declaring that it was not liable for the costs to remediate the Arlington site. How should the court rule? [*IBC Manufacturing Co. v. Velsicol Chemical Corp.,* 187 F.3d 635 (6th Cir. 1999)]

MANAGER'S DILEMMA

10. You are the CEO of a Brazilian real estate company that owns several hundred thousand acres of rain forest. A representative of a large American hamburger chain approaches you with an offer to buy a portion of the land at a very attractive price. The revenue from the sale of the land would permit your

company to undertake a large development project in Rio de Janeiro, which would both provide new jobs and increase the amount of low-cost housing in the city. You are aware that the hamburger chain intends to convert the rain forest acreage into grazing lands for cattle. What should you do? Discuss the trade-offs between environmental preservation and economic development. Describe sustainable development. How do environmental laws affect national policy with regard to industrial growth and economic development in the United States? Competition in international markets? How do state environmental laws affect competition between states for industrial development?

INTERNET SOURCES

Environmental Protection Agency	http://www.epa.gov
National Environmental Defense Council	http://www.nedc.org
The Chemical Scorecard Web site, developed by the Environmental Defense Fund, combines more than 150 government and university databases to allow users to locate polluters in their community, research the dangers of common household products, and compile sophisticated pollution rankings.	http://www.scorecard.org
This is the site for the Environmental Defense Fund, which has joined with the Pew Charitable Trusts to form the Alliance for Environmental Innovation, an organization that has worked with McDonald's, Starbucks, SC Johnson, and other large corporations to reduce the environmental impact of their operations.	http://www.edf.org
Sierra Club	http://www.sierraclub.org
The World Resources Institute Web site has reports and publications, including a library of business school case studies focusing on environmental issues, and information regarding its annual Bell Conference and other events.	http://www.wri.org
The World Business Council for Sustainable Development is a Geneva-based coalition of 150 international companies from thirty countries and twenty major industrial sectors (including Sony, AOL Time Warner, Ford, and AT&T) united by a commitment to sustainable development. Its Web site includes publications and information regarding conferences addressing issues on business and the environment such as eco-efficiency.	http://www.wbcsd.org
The Global Environmental Management Initiative's Web site includes publications and tools to help companies assess and improve their environmental performance. GEMI sponsors a conference on business and environmental issues.	http://www.gemi.org
CERES is a U.S. coalition of environmental, investor, and advocacy groups. CERES has developed a ten-point code of environmental conduct. Its Web site includes information on environmental reporting.	http://www.ceres.org

CHAPTER 19

Real Property *and* Land Use

IMPORTANCE

It is difficult to imagine any business enterprise that does not involve real property in some way. From the global company with factories or retail outlets on several continents to a mail-order business operated out of a rented apartment, real estate is important to the successful functioning of most businesses.

Real estate law finds its roots in both English common law and Spanish civil law. Many of the laws are determined by municipalities, others by the state. In recent years, the federal government has played an increasingly active role through tax policy and environmental regulations. The federal government is also interested in the safety of real estate (through the Occupational Safety and Health Administration), physical accessibility to commercial facilities (under the Americans with Disabilities Act), foreign investment in U.S. real estate, and the preservation of parklands.

CHAPTER OVERVIEW

This chapter discusses the forms of real estate ownership and the transfer of ownership, including the different types of deeds and the effect of recording statutes. It explains the role of brokers and the effect of express and implied warranties concerning the condition of the property. The chapter outlines the alternatives to acquiring real property for cash, including tax-deferred exchanges, sales and leasebacks, and real estate investment trusts. Certain types of preliminary agreements, including option contracts, rights of first refusal, and letters of intent, are then described. Methods of financing are also addressed, as are leasing and lease terms. The chapter outlines governmental regulation of the use of real property by the exercise of police and condemnation powers and the circumstances in which government restrictions on land use are deemed "takings," requiring compensation of the owner under the U.S. Constitution. The chapter closes with a discussion of the application of the Americans with Disabilities Act to construction and places of public accommodation.

Forms *of* Ownership

Real property can be held in a variety of ways. A business will normally own real estate in the name of the business. Whether that business is organized as a partnership (general or limited), a corporation, or a limited liability company will depend on tax, financial, securities, and liability factors. The choice of the proper entity for owning real estate is particularly important at the beginning of an investment or development. It may be difficult to make a change at a later date without adverse tax consequences. The issue of choice of entity is discussed further in Chapter 22.

INDIVIDUAL OWNERSHIP

In the simplest type of ownership, property is owned by a single individual. From a business perspective, individual ownership is often undesirable because the individual owner may be liable in tort for any accidents occurring on the property. The risk of unlimited personal liability can, however, be reduced by obtaining liability insurance.

TENANCY IN COMMON

Tenants in common each own an undivided fractional interest in a parcel of real property. For example, one tenant in common may have a two-thirds interest and another a one-third interest. Two or more persons can hold property as tenants in common. Regardless of the percentage ownership interest, each tenant in common has an equal right to possession of the property, and no co-tenant has the right of exclusive possession of the property against any other co-tenant. But a co-tenant does have the right to exclude any third party. Co-tenants share the income and burdens of ownership. The interest of a tenant in common is assignable and inheritable without the consent of any other co-tenant.

JOINT TENANCY

In a *joint tenancy,* property is owned in equal shares by two or more individuals. The key characteristic of a joint tenancy is the right of survivorship. If a joint tenant dies, his or her interest passes automatically to the remaining joint tenant or tenants. However, an attempt by a single joint tenant to convey separately his or her interest in the property will destroy the joint tenancy and convert it to a tenancy in common. Use of joint tenancy property in a business may also terminate the joint tenancy.[1]

TENANCY BY THE ENTIRETY

Historically, English common law recognized a special type of co-ownership of real property between husband and wife called *tenancy by the entirety.* Like joint tenancy, tenancy by the entirety includes a right of survivorship. Unlike a joint tenancy, however, neither spouse can convey an individual interest to a third party and thereby terminate the right of survivorship. Additionally, unlike joint tenancy, where joint tenants have equal rights to possession of the property, tenancy by the entirety entitled only the husband to possession, use, and enjoyment of the property. In effect, he acted as a guardian over the wife's interest.

Approximately twenty-two states recognize some form of tenancy by the entirety. Most states have retained the indestructible right of survivorship, but they give the husband and wife equal rights to the possession,

use, and revenues of the property. Additionally, the modern view is that divorce converts a tenancy by the entirety to a tenancy in common.[2]

COMMUNITY PROPERTY

In Arizona, California, Idaho, Louisiana, Nevada, New Mexico, Texas, and Washington, property acquired by either spouse during marriage is considered to be *community property;* that is, each spouse owns an undivided one-half interest in the property. Alaska permits spouses to elect community property status if they so choose. Property acquired prior to the marriage or by gift or inheritance during the marriage is *separate property,* belonging solely to the spouse who acquired it before marriage or received it by gift or inheritance, unless the spouse owning the property has converted it to community property. Separate property is converted into community property when (1) one spouse gifts separate property to the other spouse; (2) the parties treat the separate property in such a manner that a presumption of a gift arises; or (3) the separate and common property have been commingled, or mixed together.

Conveyance Community property cannot be conveyed unless both spouses execute the instrument by which the conveyance is effected. It should be noted, however, that when one spouse does not sign the instrument, but both spouses were present during negotiations and were fully aware of the terms and conditions, the nonsigning spouse may not claim that the transaction is void due to the absence of a signature.[3]

The community-property interest of a spouse may be separately willed upon death. In the absence of a will, community property passes to the other spouse.

Divorce Most of the cases interpreting what is or is not community property arise in the divorce context. Community-property laws vary from state to state. Complicated issues can arise, for example, when one spouse inherits land from his or her family (which is separate property at the date of inheritance), but subsequently one or both spouses improve or develop the property. In this case, some or all of the inherited property may turn into community property. Similarly, if one spouse uses separate property as seed capital for a business that he or she operates during the marriage, then part of the value of the business will be separate property and part will be community property.

---

1. Williams v. Dovell, 96 A.2d 484 (Md. 1953).
2. Markland v. Markland, 21 So. 2d 145 (Fla. 1945).
3. Calvin v. Salmon River Sheep Ranch, 658 P.2d 972 (Idaho 1983).

TRUST

Property may be held in a *trust,* whereby the property is owned and controlled by one person, the *trustee,* for the benefit of another, the *beneficiary.* The duration of the trust, the powers of the trustee and the trustor (the person creating the trust), and the express rights of the beneficiary are set forth in a trust agreement.

GENERAL PARTNERSHIP

When property is held in a general partnership, the partners have rights similar to those of co-tenants, and each partner is liable for all the debts of the partnership. A general partner has no right to possess partnership property for other than partnership purposes. In addition, a general partner may not assign his or her individual interest in specific partnership property. On the other hand, a general partner can effectively convey the entire partnership property to a bona fide purchaser who has no knowledge of any restriction that might exist on the general partner's authority to convey partnership property.

LIMITED PARTNERSHIP

Real property may be held in a limited partnership, consisting of one or more general partners, who manage the property, and one or more limited partners. The liability of a limited partner is usually restricted to the amount of capital he or she has contributed to the partnership. Typically, limited partners will indemnify the general partners with the indemnity secured by the value of the real estate assets. The authority of the general partner to convey the property is determined by the limited partnership agreement and the jurisdiction's limited partnership law.

CORPORATE OWNERSHIP

A corporation may own real property. Corporate authority to convey the property is governed by the corporation's articles of incorporation and bylaws, as well as the jurisdiction's corporate law. The board of directors must authorize most transfers of real property.

LIMITED LIABILITY COMPANY

Generally, the preferred form of ownership for real property is now the limited liability company or LLC (whereas previously limited partnerships were more popular). Authority to convey property is governed by the operating agreement, as well as the jurisdiction's LLC law. The board of managers must authorize most transfers of real property.

Transfer *of* Ownership

Ownership of land is transferred by a document known as a *deed,* which is recorded at a public office, typically the office of the county recorder in the county where the real property is located. Any document transferring an interest in real estate, such as a deed or a lease, is called a *conveyance.* The person conveying the property is the *grantor,* and the person to whom the property is conveyed is the *grantee.* Occasionally, but seldom in business, ownership is obtained through an installment sales contract, with the deed to follow when payment for the real estate has been completed. Ownership of property subject to probate is transferred by a court order from the probate court.

In most purchases of real estate, the type of interest conveyed is a *fee simple* interest, that is, absolute ownership of the property. However, many other transactions, such as a lease, convey less than an absolute ownership interest in the property.

TITLE

A seller of real estate is generally required to convey *marketable title,* that is, a fee simple interest free from defects. Defects that make a title unmarketable include any cloud on the title that would cause the buyer to receive less than a fee simple interest. For example, the existence of a lien on the property would constitute a defect of title sufficient to make the title unmarketable.

The type of interest (usually fee simple) and the quality of title (that is, whether it is marketable) are set forth in a deed executed by the party conveying the property. The type of deed determines the scope of warranties granted.

TYPES OF DEEDS

An interest in real property can be conveyed only by a signed deed that specifically describes that interest and is delivered to and accepted by a named grantee. There are three basic types of deeds: grant deeds, quitclaim deeds, and warranty deeds. These differ in the specific warranties they contain.

Grant Deed A *grant deed* contains two implied warranties: (1) the grantor has not previously conveyed the same property or any interest in it to another person, and (2) the title is marketable. A grant deed also conveys *after-acquired title*. This means that if at the date the deed is executed the grantor does not have title to the real property referred to in the grant deed, but subsequently acquires it, the title will be automatically transferred to the grantee.

Quitclaim Deed A *quitclaim deed* contains no warranties, and the grantor only conveys whatever right, title, and interest it holds, if any, at the time of execution. A quitclaim deed does not convey after-acquired title.

Warranty Deed A *warranty deed* contains the implied warranties of a grant deed; in addition, the grantor expressly warrants the title to and the quiet possession of the property. Warranty deeds may also contain other express warranties.

 Recording Statutes

Deeds and other instruments of conveyance must be recorded with a government official in a public office, where copies will be available to anyone. The documents must be in *recordable form*. The requirements vary from state to state but typically include legibility and some type of notarization by a notary public. The record in the public office is the principal basis for determining the state of title of real estate.

Recording statutes establish an orderly process by which claims to interests in real property can be resolved. There are three types of recording statutes: (1) race statutes, (2) pure notice statutes, and (3) race–notice statutes.[4]

Under *race statutes*, recording is a race—the rule is "first in time is first in right." The first to record a deed has superior rights, regardless of whether he or she knew that someone else had already bought the property but had failed to record the deed.

Under *pure notice statutes*, a person who has notice that someone else has already bought the property cannot validate his or her deed by recording it first. Notice may be *actual* or constructive. Courts may find *constructive notice* if a reasonable inquiry (for instance, inspection of the property) would have disclosed the prior interest. A pure notice statute protects good faith subsequent purchasers. A *good faith subsequent purchaser* is one who purchases for value, in good faith, without knowledge of a prior outstanding interest. Thus, if a subsequent purchaser acquires a deed and has no notice (actual or constructive) of a prior deed at that time, then he or she will have superior rights.

Race–notice statutes protect only those good faith subsequent purchasers who record their deed before the prior purchaser records its deed.

 Title Insurance

Despite the existence of recording statutes, the condition of title to a specific property and the priority of any claims against the property are often difficult to ascertain. In some states, title is searched by attorneys, in others by title abstract companies on which attorneys rely, and in still others by title insurance companies. Title insurance companies may also insure the condition of title or the priority of one's interest. In some states, lawyers' opinions are still used rather than title insurance.

EXTENT OF COVERAGE

A title insurance policy insures against loss as a result of (1) undisclosed liens or defects in title to the property or (2) errors in the abstraction of the title, that is, in the summary of the relevant recorded deeds and liens. Generally, the policy limit is the purchase price of the property or the amount of the *encumbrance*, that is, the claim against the property.

It is important to review a title report or insurance policy carefully before acquiring title to property. The exceptions listed in the report may be defects in title.

ESCROW

In addition to issuing title insurance policies, title companies often hold the purchase money in *escrow*, that is, in a special account, until the conditions for the sale have all been met. The money is then paid to the seller. If the sale does not go through, the money is returned to the would-be purchaser. Banks also perform this service, and in some jurisdictions there are separate escrow companies.

The *escrow agent* acts as a neutral stakeholder, allowing the parties to close the transaction without the physical difficulties of passing instruments and funds between the parties. Additionally, it is the duty of the escrow agent to coordinate the closing with the recording of

---

4. Only two states (Delaware and North Carolina) use race statutes. Usage in other states is split about evenly between pure notice statutes and race–notice statutes.

documents, the issuance of title insurance, and other activities that take place concurrently with the closing.

Neutral Party As a neutral party, the escrow agent is an agent of all parties to the transaction and must follow their specific instructions. Because an escrow agent has a fiduciary duty to all of the parties, it cannot act when the parties have submitted conflicting instructions. Generally, if conflicts between instructions are not resolved by the parties, the escrow agent will go to court for a resolution of the conflict.

The following case addressed the scope of an escrow agent's fiduciary duty to one of its principals.

A CASE IN POINT

CASE 19.1

Schoepe v. Zions First National Bank

United States District Court for the District of Utah 750 F. Supp. 1084 (D. Utah 1990).

Summary

FACTS In October 1980, Lion Hill, a Nevada partnership, contracted to sell Nevada mining property to Pacific Silver Corporation. In February 1981, Lion Hill and Pacific Silver signed an escrow agreement whereby Pacific Silver agreed to pay the purchase price in installments to Zions First National Bank, which, as escrow agent, would deliver the payments to Lion Hill.

In March 1984, Zions lent $1.6 million to Pacific Silver without the knowledge or consent of Lion Hill. In January 1985, again without the knowledge or consent of Lion Hill, Zions lent $700,000 to Pacific Silver.

Later in 1985, Lion Hill agreed to extend Pacific Silver's payment schedule by decreasing current payments and increasing later payments. This 1985 extension was also made part of the escrow agreement.

After making the 1986 payment on the loan, Pacific Silver defaulted. Lion Hill claimed that it would not have agreed to the 1985 extension had it known of the $2.3 million in loans that Zions had made to Pacific Silver. Lion Hill sued Zions, alleging that Zions, acting as escrow agent, breached its fiduciary duty to disclose these loans.

ISSUE PRESENTED Does an escrow agent have a fiduciary duty to disclose dealings with principals that fall outside the scope of the escrow agreement?

SUMMARY OF OPINION The U.S. District Court for the District of Utah first noted that the duties of an escrow agent do not reach the level of common law agency duties. The scope of an escrow agent's fiduciary duty is limited by the terms of the escrow agreement. An escrow agent's primary obligation is to exercise reasonable skill and ordinary diligence in following the escrow instructions.

It was uncontested that Zions exercised reasonable skill and ordinary diligence in following the escrow instructions. It also was uncontested that the escrow agreement contained no language imposing a duty on Zions to disclose any information to its principals. Finally, Lion Hill did not allege that Zions was engaged in fraud or that it had knowledge of a third party committing a fraud upon Lion Hill.

Lion Hill argued that Zions' knowledge of the loans it made to Pacific Silver constituted "knowledge of material facts" that gave rise to a duty to disclose. The court disagreed, holding that, regardless of whether the existence of the loans was "material" to Lion Hill, Zions had no duty to disclose them because it did not acquire the knowledge "in the course of its agency." Instead, Zions was acting outside the scope of the escrow agreement when it made the loans to Pacific Silver.

RESULT The court dismissed Lion Hill's claim.

COMMENTS The court noted that Lion Hill could have avoided this result by requiring Pacific Silver to submit a financial statement before it agreed to extend the payments or by imposing a duty to disclose on the escrow agent in the escrow agreement.

ETHICAL CONSIDERATION

Was it ethical for Zions First National Bank, the defendant in *Schoepe v. Zions First National Bank* (Case 19.1), to lend money to Pacific Silver without disclosing that fact to a party (Lion Hill) for whom it was acting as an escrow agent?

Brokers

The market for real estate is imperfect, and brokers serve to maintain that market by putting together buyers and sellers.

COMPENSATION

Brokers are customarily retained by the seller through a listing agreement that, to be enforceable, must be in writing. Generally, brokers are compensated by a payment based on a percentage of the gross selling price (or aggregate rental income). To the extent that the buyer's or lessee's broker is compensated, it is usually by sharing the commission paid by the seller.

LISTING AGREEMENTS

There are several types of listing agreements: open, exclusive, and net.

Open Listing In an *open listing,* the listing broker will receive a commission only if he or she procures a ready, willing, and able buyer. It is understood that the seller will be contracting with more than one broker, so the first broker to procure a buyer is the one who will receive a commission. Because of the uncertainty of earning a commission even if a buyer is found, it is hard to get a broker to work diligently to sell a commercial property with an open listing.

Exclusive Listing An *exclusive listing* grants the broker the right to sell the property; any sale of the property during the term of the listing will entitle the broker to a commission. If a seller has dealt with particular potential buyers before signing an exclusive listing agreement, he or she may wish to exclude them from the agreement.

Net Listing A *net listing* involves a completely different compensation scheme: the broker will receive any sales proceeds in excess of the net listing amount specified by the seller. Net listings are uncommon.

REGULATION OF BROKERS

In most states, real estate brokers are heavily regulated. They are generally required to have a license to perform brokerage activities, which are broadly defined to include effecting or negotiating (1) any sale or offer to sell or purchase real property or a business opportunity and (2) any leases, loans secured by real property, or real property sales contracts. Anyone who engages in brokerage activities without a license will not be able to sue successfully to recover his or her fee. A mere finder, who does nothing more than introduce two parties for a fee, does not need a broker's license.

In many states, real estate brokers must report and keep records of their transactions. Brokers may also be required to meet continuing education requirements and maintain knowledge regarding the particulars of real estate loans.

AGENCY RELATIONSHIP

Brokers may also be subject to regulations concerning the disclosure of the agency relationship between the broker and the parties to the transaction. Brokers are fiduciaries. As a general rule, a broker may not act for more than one person in a transaction without the knowledge and consent of all parties to the transaction. When a broker acts for both the buyer and the seller, the relationship is characterized as a *dual agency.* In most instances, a dual agent is prohibited from disclosing to the buyer, without the consent of the seller, that the seller is willing to sell the property for less than the listing price. Similarly, a dual agent may not disclose to the seller that the buyer is willing to pay a price greater than the listing price. Agency issues are discussed further in Chapter 5.

Acquisitions *and* Dispositions

Acquisitions and dispositions of real estate interests are contracted for in the same manner as most commercial transactions. Although standardized contracts are often used in relatively simple transactions (such as the conveyance of a single-family residence or a small commercial property), most large transactions require custom-drafted contracts.

Generally, contracts for the sale of an interest in real property are the result of protracted negotiations between the parties. In addition to essential terms such as price, time, and method of payment, common areas of negotiation include types of acceptable financing, the condition of title, closing costs, taxes, and compliance with zoning laws, building codes, and environmental regulations. In many purchase and sale agreements, the most heavily negotiated provisions are the seller's representations and warranties concerning the condition of the property.

REPRESENTATIONS AND WARRANTIES

In the past, real estate transactions were governed by the traditional rule of *caveat emptor* ("let the buyer beware"). Under this rule, the seller of a home or other property made no warranties to the buyer other than those expressly included in the deed or contract of sale. Current law is more protective of the buyer, especially when a person is buying a home.

Implied Warranty of Habitability A majority of the states impose on builders of houses an implied warranty of habitability. Under this modern approach, the seller of a home is in effect a guarantor of the home's fitness. As with the Uniform Commercial Code's implied warranty of merchantability for sales of goods (discussed in Chapter 8), under the *implied warranty of habitability* the seller warrants that the house is in reasonable working order and is of reasonably sound construction.

In 2000, the California Supreme Court held that homeowners could not recover tort damages from negligent builders for construction defects—deviations from the applicable building codes or industry standards—that have not caused property damage or ripened into out-of-pocket losses.[5] Homeowners were therefore precluded from recovering from the contractors the cost of repairs or the decline in value of their homes attributable to construction defects.

5. Aas v. Superior Court of San Diego, 12 P.3d 1125 (Cal. 2000).

"On the Internet, nobody knows you're a dog."

Seller's Duty to Disclose The traditional rule of *caveat emptor* is also giving way to a duty on sellers to disclose defects in real property transactions. In most states, sellers have an obligation to disclose any known defect that (1) materially affects the value of the property and (2) could not reasonably be discovered by the buyer. As the following case illustrates, sellers (and their brokers) can be liable for nondisclosure of certain off-site conditions that materially affect the value of the property.

A CASE IN POINT

CASE 19.2
Strawn v. Canuso
Supreme Court of New Jersey
657 A.2d 420 (N.J. 1995).

In the Language of the Court

FACTS The plaintiffs are more than 150 families who purchased new homes in Voorhees Township. The homes were developed and marketed by companies controlled by the Canuso family. The homebuyers sought damages against the Canusos and their companies because—unbeknownst to the buyers—the new homes they purchased had been constructed near the Buzby Landfill, a hazardous-waste dumpsite.

Between 1966 and 1978, large amounts of hazardous materials and chemicals were dumped at the Buzby Landfill. Toxic materials escaped, contaminating the groundwater and air. The federal Environmental Protection Agency recommended that the site be considered for a Superfund cleanup.

The homebuyers alleged (1) that the developers and brokers knew of the Buzby Landfill before they considered the site for residential development; and (2) that, although specifically aware of the existence and environmental hazards of the landfill, they failed to disclose those facts to the families when they purchased their homes. The representa-

(Continued)

(Case 19.2 continued)

tives of the Canuso brokerage and development companies were instructed never to disclose the existence of the Buzby Landfill, even when asked about such conditions.

ISSUE PRESENTED Do the developers of new homes and the real estate brokers marketing those homes have a duty to disclose to prospective buyers that the homes have been constructed near an abandoned hazardous-waste dump?

OPINION O'HERN, J., writing for the New Jersey Supreme Court:

[A] seller of real estate or a broker representing the seller would be liable for nondisclosure of on-site defective conditions if those conditions were known to them and unknown and not readily observable by the buyer. Such conditions, for example, would include radon contamination and a polluted water supply. . . .

. . . [T]he principal factors shaping the duty to disclose have been the difference in bargaining power between the professional seller of residential real estate and the purchaser of such housing, and the difference in access to information between the seller and the buyer. Those principles guide our decision in this case.

The first factor causes us to limit our holding to professional sellers of residential housing (persons engaged in the business of building or developing residential housing) and the brokers representing them. . . . Hence, we believe that it is reasonable to extend to such professionals a similar duty to disclose off-site conditions that materially affect the value or desirability of the property.

. . . Defendants used sales-promotion brochures, newspaper advertisements, and a fact sheet to sell the homes in the development. That material portrayed the development as located in a peaceful, bucolic setting with an abundance of fresh air and clean lake waters. Although the literature mentioned how far the property was from malls, country clubs, and train stations, "neither the brochures, the newspaper advertisements nor any sales personnel mentioned that a landfill [was] located within half a mile of some of the homes.". . .

. . .

We hold that a builder-developer of residential real estate or a broker representing it is not only liable to a purchaser for affirmative and intentional misrepresentation, but is also liable for nondisclosure of off-site physical conditions known to it and unknown and not readily observable by the buyer if the existence of those conditions is of sufficient materiality to affect the habitability, use, or enjoyment of the property and, therefore, render the property substantially less desirable or valuable to the objectively reasonable buyer.

RESULT The verdict in favor of the homebuyers was affirmed. The defendants had violated their duty to disclose the existence of the landfill.

QUESTIONS

1. Would the court have reached a different result if the sellers had not touted the development's bucolic setting, fresh air, and clean lake waters?
2. Why should a seller of commercial property have a lesser obligation to disclose adverse off-site conditions than a seller of houses?

Contractual Protections and Due Diligence A skillful buyer will request express contractual representations and warranties from the seller as to the condition of the property.

This is particularly important in commercial transactions because courts are less willing to impose implied warranties and a duty to disclose when the buyer is a commercial entity, rather than an individual. From the seller's perspective, the representations and warranties are a potential source of liability. From the buyer's perspective, the representations and warranties provide some assurance that the buyer is getting what it expected. If nothing else, the negotiation of representations and warranties frequently leads to additional disclosures regarding the physical condition of the property.

The buyer should not rely on representations and warranties as an alternative to its own careful investigation of the condition of the property, however. Although the seller is generally required to indemnify the buyer against liability arising from the inaccuracy of any of its representations and warranties, the right to indemnification is not worth much if the seller does not have the resources to back it up. Perhaps more important, defects in the property can seriously disrupt the buyer's operations and business.

ENVIRONMENTAL CONSIDERATIONS

Due diligence is particularly necessary with respect to environmental issues (discussed in Chapter 18). Because liability under federal and state environmental laws and regulations can be so large as to overshadow any other economic aspect of the property, the buyer should diligently investigate whether there are toxic or hazardous substances on or under the property.

Under the Comprehensive Environmental Response, Compensation, and Liability Act (CERCLA), the current owner or operator of a contaminated facility is jointly and severally liable for the costs associated with cleaning up the facility. This liability attaches even if the current owner purchased the property with no knowledge of the prior contamination, unless it can show that it made all due inquiry and still had no reason to know about the contamination.

To establish this *innocent landowner defense,* the purchaser must do extensive due diligence in the form of environmental tests of the water and soil and research into prior uses of the property and any adjacent property from which waste might have spread. Because it is so difficult to establish the requisite level of due diligence, one commentator has observed that "the innocent landowner defense provides effectively no reliable defense to a purchaser of real estate today."[6]

In the absence of the innocent landowner defense, CERCLA holds present owners or operators and the owners or operators at the time of waste disposal jointly and severally liable for cleanup costs. As a result, if the prior owner is insolvent or nonexistent, the current owner can be responsible for the entire cleanup.

As the following case illustrates, courts tend to apply the innocent landowner defense strictly, particularly in commercial transactions.[7]

6. *See* L. Jager Smith, *CERCLA's Innocent Landowner Defense: Oasis or Mirage?,* 18 Colum. J. Envtl. L. 155, 157 (1993).
7. *See* Eva M. Fromm et al., *Allocating Environmental Liabilities in Acquisitions,* 22 Iowa J. Corp. L. 429 (1997).

A CASE IN POINT

CASE 19.3

New York v. DelMonte

United States District Court for the Western District of New York 2000 U.S. Dist. LEXIS 5147 (W.D.N.Y. Mar. 31, 2000).

Summary

FACTS Samuel DelMonte had been in the demolition business for many years. In February 1992, DelMonte acquired a piece of property (including an old run-down building) from Behringer Bros., Inc. DelMonte paid nothing for the property but signed an agreement accepting the property "as is."

Based on tests of the property performed in 1991, the New York Department of Environmental Conservation (DEC) concluded that an impermissible amount of lead had been released at the site. Although DelMonte was aware that the area where the site was located was contaminated, he claimed that he was unaware that the site itself was contaminated when he acquired it.

In March 1993, the DEC classified the site as a significant threat to the public health and environment. DelMonte was aware that people were trespassing on his property, but even after learning of the contamination, he failed to limit access to or clean up the site. In June 1995, the DEC discovered that excavation had taken place at the site. Because of the potential for public exposure to hazardous lead levels and because DelMonte failed to prevent public access to the site, the DEC initiated an emergency cleanup of the lead. The total cost of the cleanup was $161,773.10. New York sued DelMonte for the recovery of these costs and moved for summary judgment.

(Continued)

(Case 19.3 continued)

ISSUE PRESENTED Is CERCLA's innocent landowner defense available to a current owner if he was unaware of the environmental hazards present at the site when he acquired the property?

SUMMARY OF OPINION The U.S. District Court for the Western District of New York concluded that DelMonte had failed to perform an appropriate pre-purchase investigation of the site and thus was unable to take advantage of the innocent landowner defense. Because DelMonte had been in the business of demolition for several years and knew the area was contaminated, he should have known the site was contaminated. Even if there were a genuine question as to whether DelMonte's level of pre-purchase inquiry were appropriate, DelMonte failed to exercise due care as required under CERCLA. "One cannot be an 'innocent landowner' under CERCLA if, after learning of the contamination, he fails to take 'precautions to prevent the "threat of release" or other foreseeable consequences arising from the pollution on the site.' "

RESULT The plaintiff's motion for summary judgment was granted, and DelMonte was ordered to pay the cleanup costs of $161,773.10.

TAX-DEFERRED EXCHANGES

An alternative to acquiring real property for cash is a *tax-deferred exchange,* whereby the seller exchanges its property for another piece of property. Such transactions can have favorable tax consequences. In particular, the capital gains tax owed by the seller may be deferred if the seller (1) is disposing of a property held for investment or for productive use in a trade or business and (2) is acquiring a property that qualifies under the Internal Revenue Code. Tax-deferred exchanges take many forms. In the most common—the three-party exchange—the buyer purchases a piece of property designated by the seller and exchanges it for the seller's property. Because these exchanges can be complex, it is prudent to consult an attorney specializing in tax and real estate issues when acquiring real property through a tax-deferred exchange.

SALE AND LEASEBACK

A *sale and leaseback* arrangement involves a simultaneous two-step transaction. In the first step, an institutional lender with funds to invest, such as a life insurance company or a pension fund, purchases real property from a corporation. In the second step, or often simultaneously, the property is leased back to the corporation for its use. The term of the lease is long, often ranging from twenty to forty years. The length of the term influences how the lease will be accounted for on the balance sheet. A longer-term lease may be capitalized as an asset on the balance sheet, whereas an *operating lease* (typically shorter term) will not appear on the balance sheet at all.

The tenant may have the option of repurchasing the property on or before the termination date of the lease.

The amount of rent payable is structured so that during the term of the lease, the lessor will recoup the purchase price of the property and realize an acceptable return on its investment. The lessee pays all taxes and maintenance and operating costs.

SYNTHETIC LEASES

Today, synthetic leases are commonly used to take advantage of the dichotomy between tax and accounting rules governing leases. In a *synthetic lease,* the transaction is treated as a conventional operating lease for accounting purposes, so it does not appear on the balance sheet. Payments under the lease are treated merely as rent. At the same time, for tax purposes, the lessee of the property treats the transaction as though he or she had purchased the property and obtained a loan from the seller. Thus, payments under the lease are treated as debt service on the loan, and the lessee may take favorable interest payment deductions as well as depreciation write-offs.[8]

REAL ESTATE INVESTMENT TRUSTS (REITs)

Real estate investment trusts, commonly referred to as *REITs,* can provide a good tax vehicle for investors seeking to invest in a portfolio of real property. REITs sell beneficial shares that are traded in the stock markets, and

8. Gerard R. Boyce, *Synthetic Leases: The Hard Facts,* N.Y.L.J. (Jan. 13, 2000).

they permit small investors to invest in a diversified portfolio of real estate, similar to an investment in common stocks through a mutual fund.

As long as at least 95 percent of a REIT's net income is distributed to shareholder–beneficiaries, the REIT itself pays no income tax; taxes are paid at the shareholder–beneficiary level only. REITs are limited in the types of operations they may conduct. Ownership concentration is also limited: no five persons can own more than 50 percent of the REIT's beneficial interests; often the proportion of shares any shareholder can own is limited to 9.8 percent or less.[9]

TRANSACTIONS WITH FOREIGNERS

Sales of real property interests to nonresident aliens are regulated by the federal government. Under the Foreign Investment in Real Property Tax Act (FIRPTA), the purchaser of a U.S. real property interest from a foreign person is required to withhold 10 percent of the purchase price to ensure that U.S. capital gains tax is paid on the sale. Additionally, the Agricultural Foreign Investment Disclosure Act requires foreign acquirers of U.S. agricultural land to file an informational report with the U.S. secretary of agriculture.

Preliminary Agreements

Often the parties to a real estate transaction are able to reach a general agreement on terms and conditions but need more time either to negotiate specific representations and warranties or to investigate the sale further. A number of alternatives to the traditional contract for the sale of real property have been developed. Examples of alternative methods of acquiring rights in real estate include option contracts, rights of first refusal, and letters of intent.

OPTION CONTRACT

In an *option contract,* the potential buyer pays the seller for the right, but not the obligation, to purchase the property during a given time period. The option gives the buyer time to conduct investigations, determine whether the purchase of the property is economically feasible, and obtain financing. The seller receives payment for taking the property off the market for a specified period of time.

To be enforceable, an option contract must be in writing and consideration must be paid to the seller. Addi-

9. David M. Einhorn, et al., *REIT M&A Transactions—Peculiarities and Complications,* BUS. LAW. (Feb. 2000).

INTERNATIONAL CONSIDERATION

Many countries do not allow foreigners to own land. Therefore, in these countries, a foreigner must obtain a long-term lease on the property.

Mexico's laws restricting foreign ownership offer a complex example. Foreigners cannot buy title to any property within thirty-one miles of the ocean or within sixty-two miles of the U.S. or Guatemalan borders. All a foreigner can legally acquire near the beach or border is the right to use the land for up to fifty years through a Mexican bank trust called a *fideicomiso translativo de dominio.*[a]

Even these trusts can be invalidated if the title to the land is not clear. Mexican title records are not thorough, and title insurance is rare. Public notaries in Mexico can search for liens against property title, but they typically search back no more than a decade.[b]

In any country where foreign ownership is permitted, an investor should be cautious when purchasing property. Many countries do not have adequate means for searching the title of property. In addition, many countries allow for *squatter's rights,* whereby ownership of property that is not occupied by its owner for a certain period of time will be transferred to those who have been unlawfully occupying it. Such a transfer is usually not reflected in the official land records.

a. *See* Bob Ortega, *Quirky Laws for Americans Buying Mexican Property,* WALL ST. J., Oct. 17, 1997, at B1.
b. *See id.*

tionally, the option contract must state the major terms of the proposed purchase agreement and must specify the manner in which the option may be exercised. It is also advisable to record the option to provide constructive notice to third parties and thereby prevent the sale of the property to a third party before the option has expired.

RIGHT OF FIRST REFUSAL

A *right of first refusal* is the right, conferred by a written contract, to purchase the property on the same terms offered by or to a third party. It is probably used most frequently with a tenant of a leasehold interest. The holder of the right of first refusal should require that it be recorded.

A right of first refusal can chill the owner's ability to sell the property. Few buyers will want to start investigations and negotiations knowing that they could lose the deal if the party with the right of first refusal exercises its right.

Consequently, the owner will often want to modify the right of first refusal, giving the holder only the right to negotiate the purchase of the property before the seller enters negotiations with another party. This is sometimes called a *right of first negotiation.* Another method of accommodating the needs of the seller is to provide for a very short time, such as seventy-two hours, for the holder to exercise its right of first refusal.

LETTER OF INTENT

A letter of intent may create the right to acquire an interest in a specific property. A *letter of intent* sets forth the general terms and conditions of a proposed purchase until a formal acquisition agreement can be signed. Letters of intent are often viewed as unenforceable by the parties, but courts have increasingly treated them as enforceable contracts. In one case, the court focused on the conduct of the parties to determine whether an enforceable agreement was intended despite express written statements to the contrary in the letter of intent.[10] Consequently, if the parties do not wish to be bound by their letters of intent, they must ensure that the terms and conditions are not set forth so specifically that a binding legal obligation is created; they must also conduct themselves consistently with the absence of a binding contract.

When properly utilized, letters of intent allow the parties to investigate the proposed transaction to determine whether it is worth pursuing. Although letters of intent are generally not as effective as options or rights of first refusal in removing property from the market, they can create an ethical commitment to consummate the transaction. In some states, the execution of a letter of intent creates an implied covenant of good faith and fair dealing between the parties, requiring good faith negotiation of a formal acquisition agreement.

Financing

Financing the purchase of real estate may involve borrowing funds for a long or short term. The loan is usually secured by a lien on the property, known as a *mortgage* or *deed of trust.*

Most large lenders use standard documents for loan agreements, although changes are sometimes made. In substantial transactions, it is essential that all documents be reviewed and negotiated by all parties to a transaction and their counsel.

The availability of financing depends on the intrinsic value of the property or on both its value and its poten-

10. Computer Sys. of Am. v. International Bus. Machs. Corp., 795 F.2d 1086 (1st Cir. 1986).

tial for the production of income. There are an almost unlimited number of types of financing. Some of the more common forms are discussed in this section.

PERMANENT LOANS

The most common type of real estate loan is the *permanent loan.* This is usually a long-term loan, repaid over five, ten, or sometimes up to twenty years.

Fixed-Interest Loans Traditionally, permanent loans have had a fixed interest rate; that is, the rate of interest does not change over the term of the loan. The lender assumes the risk of losing the benefit of any increase in interest rates, and the borrower assumes the risk of losing the benefit of any decrease.

In order to benefit from any increases in market interest rates, many lenders reserve the right to call (that is, demand repayment of) fixed-interest loans after a specified period, often after five, ten, or fifteen years. Conversely, to prevent borrowers from refinancing their obligation when market interest rates fall below the fixed interest rate of the loan, some lenders may insert a lock-in clause to prohibit prepayments of principal, or they may impose a penalty, called a *prepayment penalty,* if the loan is paid off early. Usually, the penalty declines with time.

Variable-Interest Loans Variable-interest loans allow lenders to avoid the risk of fluctuating interest rates. In a *variable-interest loan,* the rate of interest is often set at a fixed number of percentage points over a specified standard or base rate (often the *prime rate,* i.e., the rate at which major financial institutions offer to lend to their most creditworthy customers). Over the term of the loan, the interest rate fluctuates with changes in the base rate or index. The interest rate is usually adjusted annually or semiannually. The total amount of the change over the term of the loan is generally subject to some cap or maximum top rate. A floor may also be established to ensure that the interest rate does not fall below a specified percentage.

Points In addition to interest, real estate lenders often charge a loan fee, called *points.* The fee is the amount funded, multiplied by a fixed percentage. Each 1 percent is a point. For example, a 2½-point fee on a $100,000 loan would be $2,500. Points are usually paid at the time the loan is made.

CONSTRUCTION LOANS

Construction loans generally have a term slightly longer than the estimated construction period. Upon completion of construction, the developer obtains either permanent (take-out) financing or interim (gap) financing and repays the construction lender. If the construction loan becomes due before permanent financing is available, the developer obtains *interim* or *gap financing* to pay off the loan. Permanent financing is provided by someone other than the construction lender and is longer term. A *take-out commitment* is an agreement by a lender to replace the construction loan with a permanent loan, usually after certain conditions, such as the timely completion of the project, have been met.

DEVELOPMENT LOANS

Developers use construction loans for the acquisition and improvement of commercial properties and *development loans* for the acquisition, subdivision, improvement, and sale of residential properties. Funds are advanced by the lender as development progresses. The lender normally requires that the developer obtain performance bonds and personal guaranties by his or her principals. From the lender's perspective, development loans are riskier than construction loans because repayment of the development loan depends on the developer's ability to sell parcels of the development.

EQUITY PARTICIPATION BY LENDER

Many lenders attempt to increase their yield from real estate projects by participating in the *equity,* or ownership, of the property. The developer can benefit from the higher loan-to-value ratio, lower interest rates, and slower repayment terms that a participating lender will accept.

Equity participation by lenders is a relatively recent phenomenon. Historically, federal and state statutes prohibited banks and other lenders from owning real estate. In recent years, however, these statutory restraints have been substantially liberalized.

 # Wraparound Financing

Occasionally, an owner will require financing in addition to an existing loan secured by a deed of trust or mortgage on the property. Unless the second lender is willing to take a position subordinate to the holder of the first loan with respect to rights to the property, the owner will need to obtain a second loan sufficient to satisfy (pay off) the first loan and still provide sufficient funds to meet its financing requirements.

Paying off the first loan may not be economically attractive, however, because of prepayment penalties or because the interest rate on the first loan may be lower than on a new loan. In such instances, wraparound financing can provide additional funds without requiring the owner to first pay off the original loan.

In a *wraparound financing* transaction, the second lender lends the owner the additional funds and agrees to take over the servicing of the first loan. In exchange, the owner executes a deed of trust or mortgage and an all-inclusive note, covering the combined amount of the first and second loans. The new lender benefits because the rate charged on the all-inclusive note is higher than the weighted-average interest rates of the first and second loans. The owner benefits because the interest rate on the all-inclusive note is lower than the rate it would have to pay if it paid off the first loan and took out a new loan to cover the entire amount.

 # Appraisal Methods

The value of an income-producing property may be appraised by (1) the cost approach, whereby the construction cost of building a given improvement on the property is added to the value of the unimproved land; (2) the market approach, which looks at the selling prices in recent sales of properties with similar income-producing characteristics; or (3) the income approach, which establishes the present value of the estimated annual cash flow over the anticipated holding period. The income approach is generally favored because it provides a basis for comparison; the cost approach is rarely used.

The appraisal of property is an inexact science and is relatively unregulated by state governments. Because the funds available to a developer, and the financial institution's loan fees, are based upon the property's appraised value, the appraiser may be pressured to inflate the appraisal. Although increased loan fees and increased funds for development may provide short-term benefits, inflated appraisals can have disastrous long-term effects. For example, the savings and loan crisis in the 1980s (which cost taxpayers in excess of $300 billion) was in part caused by inflated appraisals that induced savings and loan associations to make reckless loans.

 # Protective Laws *for* Borrowers

Every jurisdiction has laws regulating the conduct of lenders and borrowers, especially in the areas of the interest rate that can be charged *(usury laws)* and the remedies that are available if a borrower fails to pay on time or is otherwise in default. Both sets of laws are designed primarily to protect individuals rather than businesses. Many of the default laws originated during the Great Depression to protect farmers.

In recent years, usury laws have tended to disappear because an out-of-date usury law (e.g., limiting the interest rate to 8 percent when the prevailing rate is 12 percent) will simply cause loan money to go to a more liberal jurisdiction. In some states, however, the usury laws still apply unless the title to the property is held by a corporation. In other states, equity participation by a lender may result in an illegally high interest rate. The penalties for violating the usury laws can be severe, and treble damages are sometimes available. A borrower cannot effectively agree to waive the benefits of a usury law; such a waiver is considered contrary to public policy.

Fair lending laws prohibit racial discrimination in lending practices. The Department of Housing and Urban Development (HUD) is active in enforcing these laws.

FORECLOSURE

The legal process by which a mortgagee may put up a piece of property for sale in the public arena to raise cash in order to pay off a debt owed by the mortgagor to the mortgagee is known as *foreclosure*. The property is sold to the highest bidder; the proceeds are then first used to satisfy the debt obligation (plus interest) of the unpaid mortgage and court costs. Any remainder is given to any other secured creditors holding a mortgage or deed of trust on the property. The mortgagor receives nothing until all creditors with a security interest in the property are paid in full.

In some states, the lender can bid the amount of the outstanding indebtedness at the foreclosure sale. If the lender is the highest bidder, it acquires the property, and the debt is extinguished.

The exact details of the foreclosure process differ from state to state. Some states allow *rights of redemption,* which give the mortgagor and certain other categories of interested persons the right to redeem (reacquire) the property within a statutory limited period, ranging from two months to two years after the sale. If the foreclosure amount plus interest is not paid by the expiration of the redemption period, the purchaser at the foreclosure sale receives the deed and clear ownership of the property.

◭ Commercial Leasing

A *commercial lease* is not only a conveyance of an interest in real property from the landlord to the tenant but also

a contract that governs the respective rights and obligations of the parties during the lease term. Because most businesses do not own the premises where their business operations are conducted, the availability and the terms and conditions of commercial leasing can be crucial factors in determining the success or failure of a business. There are four types of commercial leases: office leases, retail leases, industrial leases, and ground leases.

OFFICE LEASES

Most office premises occupy only a portion of an office building. Unless the tenant is to occupy a substantial portion of the building, the landlord will ordinarily present a standard lease form used for all of the tenants of the building. Because the landlord is more interested in obtaining occupants than in having any particular tenant as an occupant, it is often unwilling to negotiate each lease provision separately or to permit the tenant to prepare the lease. In a tight market for tenants, however, more negotiation is possible.

Assignments and Subleases An *assignment* of a lease is a permanent transfer of the lease to a third party. The third party acquires the tenant's rights under the lease; however, the tenant remains liable for the rent if the third party defaults unless the lessor has agreed to look only to the third party. A *sublease* is a temporary transfer of the lease to a third party.

If the premises fail to meet the tenant's needs, or if the tenant can no longer afford the lease, it may wish to assign or sublease. Landlords, on the other hand, may be hesitant to grant the right to assign or sublease. In an escalating market, a lease may develop a substantial bonus value if market rents exceed the rent due under the lease. Therefore, the landlord may condition the assignment or subleasing of space on the tenant's paying over any bonus value or splitting it with the landlord. Moreover, landlords are often concerned about the financial wherewithal of any assignees or sublessees. Therefore, most leases require the landlord's written consent for an assignment or a sublease. Most landlords are willing to provide in the lease that they will not withhold consent unreasonably.

RETAIL LEASES

In the negotiation of retail leases, the focus is on the operation of the tenant's business. Retail leases frequently contain a *percentage rent clause* that requires the tenant to pay, in addition to a base monthly rent, a percentage of its gross sales to the landlord.

Environmental concerns are significant in retail leases. Having a paint store or a dry cleaner as a tenant can impose liability upon the landlord under federal and state environmental laws and regulations.

INDUSTRIAL LEASES

Industrial leases tend to have a five-year term with renewal options. They usually contemplate substantial capital improvements by the tenant in the form of plant and equipment. Industrial leases are almost always *triple net*, which means the tenant pays all taxes, insurance, and operating maintenance expenses. Additionally, because the industrial use tends to be very site-specific, assignments of industrial leases are usually allowed only upon the sale of a tenant's business, and subleasing is usually strictly prohibited.

GROUND LEASES

A *ground lease* is a very long-term lease, sometimes as long as ninety-nine years. Ground leases are used when a landowner desires to obtain a steady return of income from undeveloped commercial property without the expense of improving or managing the property. Alternatively, a ground lease may be proposed by a tenant that does not wish to invest its own funds in the land but is willing to erect improvements for its own use and at its own risk.

 # Government Regulation *of* Land Use

Land use is most heavily regulated at the local level, although several states regulate at least some aspects of land use on a regional or statewide level. For example, the state of Florida has preempted the authority of local jurisdictions to regulate land use. Federal and state laws concerning environmental matters, such as air and water quality and the protection of wetlands and endangered species, can also affect the permitted uses of property.

The discussion that follows first outlines federal and state regulations, then explains general principles of local land-use regulation. Each state has its own scheme for land-use regulation at the local level. Local regulatory systems operating under a state's scheme may vary from city to city, although some states require more uniformity than others ("city" is used here to refer to both cities and counties unless otherwise noted). The specific laws and regulations applicable in each state and local jurisdiction must be consulted in order to understand how land use in that local jurisdiction is regulated.

THE NATIONAL ENVIRONMENTAL POLICY ACT

The National Environmental Policy Act (NEPA)[11] requires all federal agencies to preserve and enhance the environment so that "man and nature can exist in productive harmony, and fulfill the social, economic, and other requirements of present and future generations of Americans." To implement this goal, NEPA requires all agencies of the federal government to consider the environmental consequences of their actions. As part of any proposal for legislation or other major federal action that may significantly affect the quality of the environment, the government must include an *environmental impact statement (EIS)*. The EIS considers (1) the environmental impact of the proposed action, (2) any adverse environmental effects that the proposed action would unavoidably have, (3) alternatives to the proposed action, (4) the relationship between the short-term uses of the environment and the maintenance and enhancement of long-term productivity, and (5) any irretrievable commitments of resources that the proposed action would involve.

EIS Requirement Some federal actions are categorically exempt from the EIS requirement because they do not have any environmental impact. If the action is not categorically exempt, an *environmental assessment (EA)* is prepared, which identifies any significant impact on the environment. If the EA indicates that the action will not have significant impact on the environment, no EIS is prepared. If there may be significant impact, an EIS is required. In some cases, courts have determined that an EIS may not be required when the agency proposing the action performs an environmental review substantially equivalent to an EIS.

State Law Counterparts Most states have adopted environmental quality laws similar to NEPA, which require state and local agencies to consider the environmental impact of their decisions. NEPA and its state law counterparts are enforced mainly through litigation by persons who wish to challenge a government agency decision. NEPA and state law complaints have been used extensively by groups opposing real estate developments and federal leases of public lands for private use. Such litigation can delay projects for many years.

Planning Planning for compliance with NEPA or its state law counterparts is an important part of planning for any business project that requires state or federal decisions, approvals, or permits. This means not only preparing an EIS, if required, but also planning the project to minimize adverse effects on the environment.

11. 42 U.S.C. § 4321 *et seq.* (1994).

Taking *to the* Rooftops

Over the past few years, the Federal Communications Commission (FCC) has actively pursued a policy aimed at making advanced telecommunications services available to all Americans. To this end, the FCC has adopted a variety of regulations designed to increase competition among telecommunications providers. On October 12, 2000, the FCC adopted a rule requiring building owners to allow telecom providers nondiscriminatory access to building roofs so that antennas and satellite dishes can be placed there. The rule does not require a building owner to make its rooftop available to telecom providers, but it provides that, if access is granted to one provider, it must be made available to other providers on equal terms.

Opponents of the rule argue that a nondiscriminatory access requirement amounts to a regulatory taking from the

owners of the buildings in violation of the Fifth Amendment. Others question whether any violation of the U.S. Constitution has occurred because the building owners have not been required to provide access, only prohibited from providing discriminatory access.

The FCC rejected constitutional challenges to the new rule. In its October 12, 2000 decision, the FCC emphasized that the only "taking" involved in this rule "is from utilities, who are deprived of the power to exclude others from con-

duits or rights-of-way to the extent of their ownership or control. This taking, however, is compensated under statute and our rules, and thus is fully consistent with constitutional requirements."[a]

a. In the Matter of Promotion of Competitive Networks in Local Telecommunications Markets; Wireless Communications Association International, Inc. Petition for Rulemaking to Amend Section 1.4000 of the Commission's Rules to Preempt Restrictions on Subscriber Premises Reception or Transmission Antennas Designed to Provide Fixed Wireless Services; Implementation of the Local Competition Provisions in the Telecommunications Act of 1996; Review of Sections 68.104, and 68.213 of the Commission's Rules Concerning Connection of Simple Inside Wiring to the Telephone Network, WT Docket No. 99-217; CC Docket No. 96-98; CC Docket No. 88-57, 2000 FCC LEXIS 5672 (Oct. 12, 2000).

THE POLICE POWER

The legal basis for land-use planning and regulation is the *police power,* that is, the inherent authority of a city or county to protect the health, safety, and welfare of its residents. The scope of the police power has been given wider and wider interpretation. Its exercise is no longer limited to addressing immediate threats to the public health and safety, such as fires or unsanitary conditions. The U.S. Supreme Court explained:

> The concept of the public welfare is broad and inclusive. . . . The values it represents are spiritual as well as physical, aesthetic as well as monetary. It is within the power of the Legislature to determine that the community should be beautiful as well as healthy, spacious as well as clean, well-balanced as well as carefully patrolled.[12]

Under this broad reading of public welfare, regulations as varied as architectural review, rent control, limitations on condominium conversions, and restrictions on off-site advertising signs have all been upheld as being appropriate uses of a city's police power.

Rent Control In 1999, the California Supreme Court upheld the City of Santa Monica's rent control law, which, among other things, established maximum allowable rents, provided for adjustments of allowable rents, and prohibited evictions except in specified circumstances.[13] The law's stated purpose was to prevent owners from exploiting a growing shortage of affordable housing units by charging unreasonably high rents. A landlord challenged the rent control law, arguing that it did not accomplish its stated purpose but rather caused "gentrification" in Santa Monica.

The California Supreme Court "recogniz[ed] the well-established case law of the United States Supreme Court and of this court holding that ordinary rent control statutes are generally constitutionally permissible exercises of governmental authority," but the court also noted that particular decisions of public agencies charged with administering rent control may be deemed to be unconstitutional if they deprive landlords of a fair rate of return. In addition, rent control laws must possess certain structural features that safeguard against confiscatory results. The Fifth Amendment is violated when

12. Berman v. Parker, 348 U.S. 26, 33 (1954).

13. SMB, Ltd. v. Superior Court of Los Angeles County, 968 P.2d 993 (Cal. 1999).

a land-use regulation "does not substantially advance legitimate state interests."

The court found that the prevention of "excessive and unreasonable rent increases" was a legitimate government interest, regardless of whether the primary beneficiaries of this protection were tenants with low or merely moderate incomes. The court concluded: "[W]ith rent control, as with most other such social and economic legislation, we leave to legislative bodies rather than the courts to evaluate whether the legislation has fallen so far short of its goals as to warrant repeal or amendment."

REGULATORY TAKINGS

Although the range of activities a city can engage in is broad, there are limitations to the police power. A land-use regulation will be upheld if it is reasonably related to the public welfare, but the city may not act arbitrarily or capriciously in enacting or applying land-use regulations. In addition, regulations are sometimes challenged on the ground that they amount to a taking of the property without just compensation, in violation of the Fifth Amendment to the U.S. Constitution (made applicable to the states by the Fourteenth Amendment).

The U.S. Supreme Court has stated that a *regulatory taking* (sometimes referred to as *inverse condemnation*) has occurred if the regulation either (1) does not substantially advance legitimate state interests or (2) denies the owner all economically viable use of its land.[14]

14. Agins v. Tiburon, 447 U.S. 255, 260 (1980).

INTERNATIONAL CONSIDERATION

Nation–states have the right to expropriate or nationalize foreign property under the power of eminent domain. Western countries tend to consider expropriation or nationalization proper as long as (1) it is for a legitimate public purpose, (2) it does not discriminate against a particular class of foreigners, and (3) the state promptly pays fair compensation. Many emerging countries object to having to pay fair market value for expropriated property, citing, among other things, the history of European imperialism and colonialism.

In *Penn Central Transportation Co. v. City of New York*,[15] the Supreme Court held that the City of New York did not effect a taking requiring just compensation when it denied Penn Central permission to build a fifty-story office building over Grand Central Terminal. New York City had designated Grand Central a landmark under the Landmarks Preservation Law, which restricts the owner's right to substantially alter the building. Although the application for the construction of the building met all local zoning requirements, Penn Central was denied permission under the landmarks law. Rejecting Penn Central's claim that the application of the landmarks law had deprived it of its property without just compensation, the Supreme Court emphasized that application of the law did not interfere with "Penn Central's primary expectation concerning the use of the parcel" or prevent Penn Central from earning a "reasonable return" on its investment.

15. 438 U.S. 104 (1978).

POLITICAL PERSPECTIVE

States Take Initiative *in* Protecting Property Rights

Land-use regulation, especially the restrictions imposed by environmental laws in the mid-1980s (particularly the Endangered Species Act[a] and wetlands regulations[b]), spawned a political movement devoted to the protection of private-property rights. The Republican "Contract With America," promulgated in 1994, called for federal legislation to give property owners a right to compensation for any reduction in the value of their property greater than 10 percent. In 1995, the Clinton administration estimated that implementation of these pro-

visions would have cost taxpayers $28 million over seven years.

The first state law protecting real property rights was adopted in 1991. Since then, property rights legislation has been

proposed in every state and in Congress. As of 2000, more than half of the states had enacted some sort of property rights protection. At least seventeen states had adopted *assessment statutes,* which require state and local governments to consider, before imposing conditions on development, whether the restriction will constitute a taking under federal or state constitutional law. Four states (including Texas and Florida) currently have *compensation statutes* in place, which require the

(Political Perspective continues)

(Political Perspective continued)

government agency adopting a regulation to pay the landowner for the loss in property value if the regulation causes the value of the property to decline beyond a certain percentage (for example, in Texas, by 25 percent or more). Two states (Florida and Maine) have adopted the latest innovation in property rights legislation—*conflict resolution statutes,* which set up formal procedures for negotiation between state agencies and property owners.

In other states, however, efforts to introduce property rights legislation have failed. Property rights statutes enacted by the Arizona and Washington legislatures were overturned by popular referendum. In Colorado and Oregon, governors vetoed property rights statutes passed by the state legislatures.

Citing John Locke's *Two Treatises on Government,* "[p]roponents of this legislation argue that current land use policy and regulation erode private property rights and threaten the very foundation of U.S. democratic society by undermining the fundamental social contract upon which the country was founded."[c] Opponents "reject these statutes as politically-driven measures that force taxpayers to pay property owners not to create harm for others."[d]

a. 16 U.S.C. §§ 1531–44 (1994).
b. *See* Section 404 of the Clean Air Act, 33 U.S.C. § 1344 (1988 & Supp. 1997).
c. Lynda J. Oswald, *Property Rights Legislation and the Police Power,* 37 AM. BUS. L.J. 527, 535 (2000).
d. *Id.*

Source: This discussion is based on an excellent article by Associate Professor Lynda J. Oswald of the University of Michigan Business School, entitled *Property Rights Legislation and the Police Power,* 37 AM. BUS. L.J. 527 (2000).

In *Lucas v. South Carolina Coastal Council,*[16] the U.S. Supreme Court considered whether South Carolina's desire to prevent harmful or noxious uses could justify its promulgation of the Beachfront Management Act in 1988. The Act effectively barred Lucas, the owner of two residential lots purchased in 1986 for $975,000, from erecting any permanent structure on his parcels. The U.S. Supreme Court held that if the Act did no more than duplicate the result under the state's common law nuisance law, then no compensation would be required. But, if the Act prohibited an activity not prohibited by common law nuisance and denied the owner all economically viable use of his land, then compensation may be required. The Court put the burden of proof on the state to show that its regulation was not a taking.

In the following case, the U.S. Court of Appeals for the Ninth Circuit considered whether a temporary moratorium on development may constitute a taking.

16. 505 U.S. 1003 (1992).

A CASE IN POINT

CASE 19.4

Tahoe-Sierra Preservation Council, Inc. v. Tahoe Regional Planning Agency
United States Court of Appeals for the Ninth Circuit
216 F.3d 764
(9th Cir. 2000).

Summary

FACTS The plaintiffs owned property in the Lake Tahoe Basin. Due to rapid development of the basin, the nutrients being washed into Lake Tahoe increased significantly. This encouraged the growth of algae, which caused the lake to become more and more green and opaque. In an effort to halt the increasing environmental damage, Congress approved the bi-state Tahoe Regional Planning Compact in 1969. The Compact created the Tahoe Regional Planning Agency (TRPA) and set goals for preserving Lake Tahoe and the surrounding basin.

The 1969 Compact was amended in 1980 to provide for the adoption of a new regional plan. The 1980 Compact directed the TRPA to review all projects and to establish temporary restrictions on development in the basin pending formulation of a new regional land-use plan. To comply with the 1980 Compact, the TRPA enacted an ordinance that temporarily prohibited construction in several classes of land in the basin, with some possibility of exception. The moratorium continued for about thirty-two months between 1981 and 1984 until a new land-use plan was issued. Because that plan was challenged as too lenient, development permits were withheld for several more years.

The landowners whose rights to develop property were suspended during the moratorium sued the TRPA claiming, among other things, that the moratorium constituted an unconstitutional taking for which compensation was due. The district court ruled that certain property owners in the basin were entitled to compensation, and the TRPA appealed.

(Continued)

(Case 19.4 continued)

ISSUE PRESENTED Did the temporary moratorium on property development in the Lake Tahoe Basin constitute an unconstitutional taking of property?

SUMMARY OF OPINION The U.S. Court of Appeals for the Ninth Circuit first pointed out that the U.S. Supreme Court has identified two circumstances where it will find that a government regulation constitutes an unconstitutional taking: (1) regulations that compel a property owner to suffer a permanent physical invasion or occupation of his or her property, and (2) regulations that deny all economically beneficial or productive use of land. The issue on appeal was whether the moratorium fell within the second category.

The landowners argued that, for purposes of determining whether a taking has occurred, the court should not look to the entire interest in the property, but rather should consider the "temporal slice" of the property interest covered during the time span in which the moratorium was in effect. The court rejected this approach, specifically relying on *Penn Central*'s ruling that a court should look to the nature and extent of the interference with the rights in the "parcel as a whole" rather than divide a single parcel into discrete segments.

The court emphasized that acceptance of the concept of temporal severance would raise the possibility that every temporary planning moratorium would be treated as an unconstitutional taking. Such a result would conflict with the Supreme Court's explanation in *Lucas* that it is "relatively rare" for government regulation to deny all economically beneficial or productive use of land. Moreover, such a ruling would impair the state's ability to engage in land-use planning. The court went on to conclude that considering the parcel as a whole, the temporary moratorium did not eliminate all present value of the property's future use.

RESULT The temporary moratorium was not an unconstitutional taking, and the ruling of the district court was reversed.

COMMENTS Takings questions also arise when a regulatory agency imposes a condition that must be satisfied before a building permit or other land-use approval is granted. This is addressed later in this chapter as part of the discussion of regulatory schemes.

Regulatory Schemes

The fundamental components of most land-use regulatory schemes are a general plan, a zoning ordinance, and a subdivision ordinance. Some jurisdictions also employ more specialized planning documents, often called specific plans or community plans, that function somewhere between the general plan and the zoning ordinances.

THE GENERAL PLAN

Many cities have a general development plan, known variously as the general plan, city plan, master plan, or comprehensive plan. (All such plans are referred to as the general plan in this chapter.) A *general plan* is a long-range planning document that addresses the physical development and redevelopment of a city. It is comprehensive in that it addresses the entire city and a wide range of concerns, such as housing, natural resources, public facilities, transportation, and the permitted locations for various land uses. It includes goals, objectives, policies, and programs related to these concerns.

The practical effect of the general plan varies from state to state. In some states, a general plan is not required at all. In certain states, the general plan is strictly an advisory document that need not be adhered to when planning decisions are made. In other states, the plan functions as the "constitution" for development, and, by law, planning decisions (such as zoning, subdivision approval, and road and sewer construction) must be consistent with it. When the general plan has this significance, anyone contemplating development of a specific piece of property should determine what the general plan says about the allowed uses for that property. The general plan may also include important information about the city's policies regarding growth, where and when public services and facilities will be provided, and whether developers will be expected to provide or pay for needed infrastructure.

If development of the type contemplated is not authorized by the general plan, a general plan amendment will be required. The general plan may also be amended to preclude a contemplated development. Authorization of a type of development in the general plan is not, however, a guarantee that a specific development will be permitted. The development must also be authorized by the zoning ordinance, and other land-use approvals could be required.

OTHER PLANNING DOCUMENTS

Some jurisdictions employ other planning documents in addition to the general plan. Called *specific plans, special plans, community plans, area plans,* and a number of other names, these plans usually encompass just a portion of the city's geographic area. They may focus on areas in particular need of planning, such as a downtown area slated for redevelopment, an environmentally sensitive area, a transportation corridor, or an area facing unusual development pressure. Typically, these plans are more detailed than the general plan.

ZONING

Zoning is the division of a city into districts and the application of specific land-use regulations in each district. Zoning regulations are divided into two classes: (1) regulations regarding the structural and architectural design of buildings (such as height or bulk limitations); and (2) regulations regarding the uses, such as commercial or residential, to which buildings within a particular district may be put. These types of regulations are employed both in traditional zoning systems and in more recently developed approaches to zoning.

Traditional Zoning Traditional zoning separates different land uses. For example, residential areas are separate from commercial and industrial areas, and residential areas of varying densities are separate. This approach to zoning finds its roots in the earliest land-use regulations, which promoted health and safety by separating residences from certain types of manufacturing and service industries. Early zoning also protected property values by preventing apartments from being built near more desirable single-family dwellings.

Planned Unit Development Although many cities still employ some form of traditional zoning, others have adopted different approaches. For example, under *planned unit development (PUD) zoning,* the land-use regulations for a given piece of property reflect the proposed development plans for that property. These plans may include a mixture of uses, such as residential, office, and retail commercial, which could not be accommodated under the separation of uses required by traditional zoning. Residential development may be clustered on a portion of the property, creating densities higher than what would be permitted under traditional zoning but also providing larger areas of open space. Planned offices or industrial parks may be subject to covenants and restrictions such as regulated setbacks or signage. Many feel that this more flexible approach to zoning allows greater creativity and shows greater sensitivity to environmental and aesthetic concerns. The "Inside Story" in this chapter discusses the problem of sprawl and mechanisms communities have used to revitalize their urban centers.

Zoning Relief Variances and conditional-use permits may create exceptions to a zoning ordinance. A *variance* allows a landowner to construct a structure or to carry on an activity not otherwise permitted under the zoning regulations. It allows the property owner to use the property in a manner basically consistent with the established regulations, with such minor variations as are necessary to avoid inflicting a unique hardship on that property owner. In some states, variances may be granted to allow uses not authorized by the zoning regulations. In other states, variances are limited to sanctioning deviations from regulations governing physical standards, such as the minimum lot size, the maximum number of square feet that may be developed, and off-street parking requirements.

A *conditional-use permit* allows uses that are not permitted as a matter of right under the zoning ordinance. The permit imposes conditions to ensure that the use will be appropriate for the particular situation.

Nonconforming Uses A *nonconforming use* is an existing use that was originally lawful but that does not comply with a later-enacted zoning ordinance. A zoning ordinance may not compel immediate discontinuance of a nonconforming use (unless it constitutes a public nuisance). A city can, however, require that nonconforming uses be eliminated within a reasonable time or upon application for a building permit to modify the premises.

SUBDIVISION

Frequently, development requires the division of land into separate parcels. This process is known as *subdivision.* It is a necessary step in residential development and often in industrial or commercial development.

The subdivision process allows the city to regulate new development and to limit harm, deterioration of water quality, soil erosion, and building in areas subject to earth movement. The subdivider may also be required to address, for example, the impact of the subdivision on scenic views and other aesthetic concerns or on traffic circulation.

Subdivision approval frequently requires that the subdivider install streets, utilities, sewers, drainage facilities, and other infrastructure to serve the subdivision. It may be required to dedicate land for parks, schools, libraries, and fire stations and to pay impact fees to offset the increased burden on public facilities and services resulting from the subdivision. The conditions may include constructing on-site or off-site facilities or paying fees for purposes as varied as acquiring parkland or providing day-care centers, public art, or low-income housing.

CONDITIONS

Conditions to a land-use approval will be upheld if they are reasonably related to the burdens on the community created by the development being approved. Thus, if the development will result in an influx of residents or employees, a fee to fund traffic improvements made necessary by that influx will be upheld. In the absence of the legally required relationship between a condition to an approval and the impacts of the development being approved (the *nexus*), the condition may be struck down as an unconstitutional taking.

For example, in the case of *Nollan v. California Coastal Commission,*[17] James and Marilyn Nollan sought a permit from the California Coastal Commission to demolish their existing single-story beachfront house and replace it with a two-story, three-bedroom house approximately three times larger than the existing structure. Public beaches were located within one-half mile to the north and south of the Nollans' property. Finding that the new house would further obstruct the ocean view, increase private use of the beach, and establish a "psychological barrier" to access to the nearby public beaches, the commission approved the construction subject to the condition that the Nollans dedicate an easement for public access across the portion of their property lying between the high-water mark and a sea wall approximately ten feet inland. The Nollans challenged this condition.

The U.S. Supreme Court held that the dedication condition amounted to an unconstitutional taking because it did not substantially advance a legitimate governmental interest. The Court found no nexus between the requirement of an easement for public access and the stated interest of reducing obstacles to the ocean view as well as "psychological barriers" to using the beach. The Court concluded by saying that if the government wanted an easement across the Nollans' property, "it must pay for it."

In *Dolan v. City of Tigard,*[18] the Supreme Court held that there has to be a showing of "rough proportionality" between the conditions imposed on a permit and the nature and extent of the proposed development's impact. The Court held that a city could not require Dolan to dedicate a portion of her property to a pedestrian/bicycle pathway as a condition to permitting the expansion of her retail sales facility. The Court acknowledged that the enlarged retail sales facility would increase traffic on the streets of the central business district by roughly 435 additional trips per day. The Court also noted that dedications for streets, sidewalks, and other public ways are generally reasonable exactions to avoid excessive congestion for a proposed property use. The Court concluded, however, that the city had not met its burden of demonstrating that the additional number of vehicle and bicycle trips generated by Dolan's development was reasonably related to the city's requirement for dedication of the pedestrian/bicycle easement. Thus, the exaction amounted to an unconstitutional taking.

In *Monterey v. Del Monte Dunes at Monterey, Ltd.,*[19] the U.S. Supreme Court held that *Dolan's* rough proportionality test applied only to exactions and not to outright denials of permission to develop. The Court explained:

> Although in a general sense concerns for proportionality animate the Takings Clause, we have not extended the rough proportionality test of *Dolan* beyond the special context of exactions—land-use decisions conditioning approval of development on the dedication of property to public use. The rule applied in *Dolan* considers whether dedications demanded as conditions of development are proportional to the development's anticipated impacts. It was not designed to address, and is not readily applicable to, the much different questions arising where, as here, the landowner's challenge is based not on excessive exactions but on denial of development. We believe, accordingly, that the rough proportionality test of *Dolan* is inapposite to a case such as this one.

A city's imposition of a condition on the grant of a permit can also be evaluated under the Equal Protection Clause. In a case decided in 2000, the U.S. Supreme Court recognized that a valid claim for relief existed when a village "intentionally demanded a 33-foot ease-

17. 483 U.S. 825 (1987).

18. 512 U.S. 374 (1994).
19. 526 U.S. 687 (1999).

ment as a condition to connecting [one property owner's] property to the municipal water supply where the village required only a 15-foot easement from similarly situated property owners."[20]

ENVIRONMENTAL ASSESSMENT

Some states, before approving a development project, require a detailed evaluation of the effects of the project on the environment. The state may also require the developer to discuss alternatives to the proposed project and identify measures that would mitigate adverse environmental effects.

VESTED DEVELOPMENT RIGHTS

Until a developer obtains a *vested right*—that is, a fully guaranteed right—to develop a property, the regulations governing that property may be changed. In other words, a developer has no claim to the land-use regulations in effect when the property was acquired, when preliminary steps to development were taken, or at any other time prior to the vesting of the right to develop. A change in the land-use regulations prior to vesting may, therefore, preclude a development that would have been permissible under the regulations in force at the time the property was acquired.

In some states, the right to develop vests when substantial work is done and substantial liabilities are incurred in reliance on a building permit. In other states, vesting is tied to obtaining the "last discretionary approval" required for development. States differ on what constitutes the last discretionary approval.

Early Vesting Mechanisms to allow early vesting are available in several states. One such mechanism is a development agreement, which is authorized in Arizona, California, Colorado, Florida, Hawaii, and Nevada. The development project is governed by the regulations in effect when the agreement is entered into and is immune from subsequent changes in the land-use regulations.

Physical Accessibility *to* Commercial Facilities

Under the Americans with Disabilities Act (ADA),[21] any new renovations or alterations to commercial facilities must be accessible to disabled persons, including those in wheelchairs. "Commercial facilities" are defined under

IN BRIEF
Limits on Land-Use Regulation

1. Regulation must be reasonably related to the public welfare.
2. Regulation cannot deny the owner all economically viable use of its land.
3. Regulation must substantially advance legitimate state interests.
4. Conditions to a land-use approval must be reasonably related to the burdens on the community created by the development being approved (nexus).
5. There must be rough proportionality between the conditions imposed and the nature and extent of the proposed development's impact.

the Act as all structures except those intended for residential use. This accessibility rule applies, however, only to the areas being renovated, and it requires compliance only to the extent feasible. New construction, on the other hand, is subject to more complex accessibility rules. In building new structures, architects and builders must comply with regulations established by the U.S. attorney general regarding accessibility.

In general, new structures must be designed and constructed so that they are "readily accessible to and usable by individuals with disabilities," unless it is structurally impossible to do so. Violation of the physical-accessibility rules for renovations and new construction can result in a private lawsuit or action by the U.S. attorney general. Violators may be required to pay damages as well as civil penalties of up to $50,000 for a first violation and $100,000 for subsequent violations.

The ADA also requires minor physical changes to existing workplaces to accommodate disabled workers. For example, the ADA mandates removal of architectural barriers in existing stores, offices, and firms where the removal is "readily achievable." Modifications are readily achievable if they are easy to accomplish and can be made without significant expense. Readily achievable changes might include ramping a few steps or lowering a public telephone for wheelchair users, installing grab bars in rest rooms, putting raised letters and numerals on elevator controls, and rearranging office furniture to provide increased accessibility.

The ADA also prohibits discrimination on the basis of disability by public entities. In *Bay Area Addiction Research & Treatment, Inc. v. Antioch*,[22] the U.S. Court

---

20. Village of Willowbrook v. Olech, 528 U.S. 562 (2000).
21. 42 U.S.C. § 12101 *et seq.* (1994).

22. 179 F.3d 725 (9th Cir. 1999).

of Appeals for the Ninth Circuit reviewed an "urgency ordinance" prohibiting the operation of a methadone clinic within 500 feet of residential areas. The city of Antioch, California, adopted the ordinance to block the planned relocation of a methadone clinic to the city after Antioch residents expressed concerns about a possible increase in crime and drug use if the clinic were located in the area. Acting on behalf of heroin addicts, the clinic brought a class action against Antioch to enjoin enforcement of the ordinance under the ADA and the Vocational Rehabilitation Act. The court held that the ADA's prohibitions against discrimination on the basis of disability apply to zoning and stated that the ADA protections are available to disabled individuals unless the individuals pose a significant risk to the health or safety of others that cannot be mitigated by reasonable modifications. The court emphasized that the goal of the ADA is to protect disabled individuals from deprivations based on prejudice, stereotypes, or unfounded fears. Thus, when determining whether a significant risk exists, a court must distinguish legitimate concerns from mere expressions of prejudice, stereotypes, and unfounded fears.

Whether a significant risk exists turns on an individualized assessment of the nature, duration, and severity of the risk and the probability that the potential injury will actually occur. If a significant risk is present, then to be qualified for protection under the ADA, a party must show that the risk can be ameliorated by reasonable modifications. If it cannot be ameliorated, ADA protections are unavailable.

The ADA also requires full and equal enjoyment of accommodation in any place of public accommodation. "Public accommodation" is defined to include, among other things, a restaurant, place of lodging, place of entertainment, place of public gathering, and place of exercise or recreation. In *Stevens v. Premier Cruises*,[23] the plaintiff, who was confined to a wheelchair, sued Premier Cruises for failing to make all areas of the cruise ship wheelchair accessible. The U.S. Court of Appeals for the Eleventh Circuit held that "those portions of the cruise ship that come within the statutory definition of 'public accommodation' are subject to the public accommodation provisions" of the ADA. In contrast, the Third Circuit ruled that arenas subject to the ADA do not have to provide spectators in wheelchairs with sightlines over standing spectators.[24]

23. 215 F.3d 1237 (11th Cir. 2000).
24. Caruse v. Blockbuster-Sony Music Enter. Ctr. at the Waterfront, 193 F.3d 730 (3d Cir. 1999).

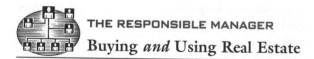

THE RESPONSIBLE MANAGER
Buying *and* Using Real Estate

The typical manager who does not manage real estate full-time will probably find that there are more laws, administrative regulations, and governmental practices associated with real estate than with many other management activities. The manager will not always be able to rely on common sense in managing real estate because the laws and administrative practices can have surprising effects.

Before acquiring real estate, the manager should (1) determine whether the property is properly located for the company's operations; (2) determine whether the improvements, if already built, comply with applicable building codes and are suitable for the company; (3) determine whether the facility complies with physical-accessibility regulations under the Americans with Disabilities Act; (4) determine whether previous owners have fully complied with federal, state, and local environmental and hazardous-waste laws and confirm that the company will not be liable under any of those laws; (5) decide whether the company should lease or buy the property; (6) decide, if the property is rental property, for how long and under what terms it should be leased; (7) decide, if the property is for sale, how best to negotiate the purchase contract and finance the purchase; and (8) keep senior executives and/or the board of directors informed about the manager's actions and decisions throughout the process.

The magnitude of the investment and the permanence of the acquisition render these decisions some of the most important that a manager will make. Although large corporations generally have a department for facilities management, smaller organizations do not. The manager will need to have access to responsible professionals, including knowledgeable commercial/industrial real estate brokers, attorneys who specialize in real estate, environmental consultants, and attorneys specializing in environmental law. If the company is acquiring bare land and building its own improvements, the manager will also need to have available expertise in planning and land use. With the heavy use of outside consultants comes the responsibility of managing the consultants and controlling the costs.

Similar responsibilities accompany the occupancy of real estate. If a company occupies premises under a full-service lease, which requires the lessor to maintain the property, the tenant's responsibilities may be limited to seeing that the services provided are adequate. Most manufacturing companies, however, do not occupy leased premises on a full-service basis. Hence, management may be responsible for continuing maintenance, repairs, and compliance with laws, including environmental laws. In any type of occupancy, management must always plan ahead to ensure that the facilities will continue to be adequate for present and future operations. It is often difficult to anticipate needs, and it is easy to overspend or, conversely, to fail to anticipate a new demand.

Finally, the manager is likely to find that he or she has less control than desired over real estate decisions. For example, building or other occupancy permits may need to be obtained from several agencies, such as building departments and fire departments. Those agencies may not be responsive to a company's urgent demands, and the official involved may have a great deal of discretion in both the timing and the interpretation of the applicable laws. Delays beyond the company's control frequently try managers' patience and cause inconvenience and downtime. In either the acquisition or the disposition phase, a manager is well advised to allow considerable extra time for delays.

INSIDE STORY

Smart Growth, Not Sprawl

In the five-year period from 1992 to 1997, sixteen million acres of forests and agricultural land were developed into new suburbs and communities outside urban centers, double the rate of development in the previous ten years. Wetlands are currently being converted into residential and commercial areas at a rate of 54,000 acres per year.[25] The result—*sprawl*—has contributed to the decline of cities and inner suburbs, the loss of affordable housing, and environmental degradation, including pollution and loss of natural habitats. Sprawl can contribute to economic decline as more employees elect to leave areas plagued by traffic congestion and other problems related to uncontrolled development.

From 1980 to 2000, the U.S. population grew by 1 percent per year, but miles driven increased at approximately three times that rate.[26] The increased use of cars for commuting from outlying communities to the urban centers where most people work places more pressure on infrastructure, such as highways and road maintenance. It also increases the stress on both the environment and the commuters (with an attendant increase in road rage).

A 2000 survey by the Pew Center for Civil Journalism identified sprawl as one of the top problems facing communities.[27] Not surprisingly, politicians are making increased efforts to address the issue in an attempt to convert unrestrained development into "smart growth." More than half of state governors have addressed issues relating to sprawl, including traffic congestion.[28] In 1998, voters approved 70 percent of the 240 initiatives to combat sprawl that appeared on ballots in thirty-one states.[29]

Smart growth measures have included development fees that increase with the distance from urban centers; urban growth boundaries; revision of building codes to encourage development in certain areas; priority for state funding to regional planning commissions; and tiered growth systems designating some land as urban and other as rural, agricultural reserve, and glade.[30]

Sprawl is particularly a problem in the western United States, and many of the most intense efforts to control it have occurred there. Oregon was the first state to draw growth boundaries around its urban centers.[31] In November 2000, some of the strictest growth control measures in the country were proposed in two ballot initiatives in Arizona and California. Arizona has grown

25. John J. Fialka, *Campaign 2000: Campaign Against Sprawl Overruns a County in Virginia, and Soon Perhaps Much of Nation*, WALL ST. J., Jan. 4, 2000, at A24.
26. *Id.*

27. Peter Grant, *The Debate over Sprawl Has Only Just Begun—Various Ballot Initiatives in the West Illustrated Growing Rift in the U.S.*, WALL ST. J., Nov. 8, 2000, at B14.
28. *Id.*
29. Williak C. Smith, *The Brawl over Sprawl*, A.B.A. J., Dec. 1, 2000, at 48–52.
30. *Id.*
31. Grant, *supra* note 27.

by 30 percent since 1990—an increase of a million people, primarily in Phoenix and Tucson.[32]

Arizona's Proposition 202 would have required municipalities with more than 2,500 people to set boundaries on growth and builders of developments located miles from other developments to pay fees to build public infrastructure. Colorado's Amendment 28 proposed that counties and cities with more than 25,000 people obtain voter approval of future development.[33]

The propositions in Arizona and Colorado initially received strong support, but it was subsequently weakened by a real estate industry media blitz warning that efforts to limit growth would lead to higher housing costs, the loss of jobs, and crowded communities.[34] Opponents of the Colorado proposition raised $5.7 million to prevent its passage, making it the most expensive race in that state's history. Both propositions were defeated: the Colorado proposal failed by 70 percent to 30 percent, and the Arizona proposal failed by a two-to-one margin.[35]

Eco-terrorists, not content to await a political solution to sprawl, have begun taking matters into their own hands. On New Year's Eve 2000, the radical environmental group Earth Liberation Front firebombed luxury houses under construction in the town of Mount Sinai on Long Island in New York. They left graffiti messages: "Stop Urban Sprawl" and "If You Build It We Will Burn It."[36] This group has claimed responsibility for two dozen other acts of arson and vandalism, including a fire that destroyed a $12 million restaurant and ski-lift facility in the ski resort of Vail, Colorado.[37] Another eco-terrorist group, CSP, has set nine fires causing $5 million in damage to stop developments in Phoenix.[38]

32. Peter Grant, *Raising Arizona: A Sprawling Batter Nears Vote—Polls Show Strong Support for Measure to Limit Growth Around Cities,* WALL ST. J., Sept. 20, 2000, at B12.
33. Matt Kelley, *Home Builders Celebrate Defeat of Growth-Limitation Initiatives in Colorado, Arizona,* ASSOC. PRESS NEWSWIRES, Nov. 16, 2000.
34. Grant, *supra* note 27.

35. Kelley, *supra* note 33.
36. Al Baker, *"Eco-Terrorism," and Nary a Redwood in Sight,* N.Y. TIMES, Jan. 14, 2001, at 1.
37. *Burning Suburbia,* NEWSWEEK INT'L, Jan. 15, 2001.
38. *Id.*

KEY WORDS AND PHRASES

actual notice   635
after-acquired title   635
area plan   651
assessment statute   648
assignment   645
beneficiary   634
caveat emptor   638
commercial lease   645
community plan   651
community property   633
compensation statute   648
conditional-use permit   651
conflict resolution statute   649
constructive notice   635
conveyance   634
deed   634
deed of trust   643
development loans   644
dual agency   637
encumbrance   635
environmental assessment (EA)   646
environmental impact statement (EIS)   646
equity   644
escrow   635

escrow agent   635
exclusive listing   637
fair lending laws   645
fee simple   634
foreclosure   645
gap financing   644
general plan   650
good faith subsequent purchaser   635
grant deed   634
grantee   634
grantor   634
ground lease   646
implied warranty of habitability   638
innocent landowner defense   640
interim financing   644
inverse condemnation   648
joint tenancy   633
letter of intent   643
marketable title   634
mortgage   643
net listing   637
nexus   652
nonconforming use   651
open listing   637
operating lease   641

option contract   642
percentage rent clause   645
permanent loan   643
planned unit development (PUD) zoning   651
points   643
police power   647
prepayment penalty   643
prime rate   643
pure notice statutes   635
quitclaim deed   635
race–notice statutes   635
race statutes   635
real estate investment trust (REIT)   641
recordable form   635
recording statutes   635
regulatory taking   648
right of first negotiation   643
right of first refusal   642
rights of redemption   645
sale and leaseback   641
separate property   633
special plan   651
specific plan   651

QUESTIONS AND CASE PROBLEMS

1. Miller granted his neighbor a *view easement,* that is, an interest in Miller's property that entitled the neighbor to an unobstructed view. The easement was recorded. Miller later contracted to sell the property and disclosed the existence of the view easement to the buyer, Gazzo. A preliminary title report issued by Fidelity National Title Insurance Company failed to disclose the existence of the easement. Gazzo then requested that Fidelity investigate the possible existence of the easement. Fidelity assured Gazzo that the easement did not exist and maintained that, except for those items set forth in Fidelity's title report, Miller had free title. Miller executed a grant deed conveying the property to Gazzo.

   Gazzo later found out that the easement had in fact been recorded, and he recovered $125,000 from Fidelity for the diminution in the property's value as a result of the easement. Gazzo assigned any claim that he had against Miller to Fidelity, and Fidelity sued Miller for breach of warranty. Fidelity claimed that by executing the grant deed Miller had implicitly warranted that title to the property was being conveyed free of any encumbrances. Does Miller's prior disclosure of a recorded encumbrance to Gazzo prevent Fidelity from relying on the warranty against encumbrances that is typically implied in a seller's grant deed? [*Fidelity National Title Insurance Co. v. Miller,* 264 Cal. Rptr. 17 (Cal. Ct. App. 1989)]

2. Ace owns Blueacre, a forty-acre parcel of unimproved real estate on the outskirts of a burgeoning city in the state of Calvada. In June 1988, the legislature of Calvada approved the construction of a freeway adjacent to Blueacre. Shortly after the completion of the freeway in 1995, Ace was approached by Greenhorn, who desired to construct an apartment building on Blueacre. Greenhorn is a licensed general contractor previously employed by several large apartment building developers. Although Greenhorn could not arrange financing to purchase Blueacre outright, he was able to negotiate a sixty-year ground lease from Ace on the express condition that Greenhorn complete construction of the apartment building before July 1, 2000. The lease was duly executed by both Ace and Greenhorn, and a memorandum of the lease was legally recorded.

   Greenhorn obtained a $10 million loan at 10 percent interest that was due and payable on or before July 1, 2000, from Construction Lender. To secure repayment of the construction loan, Greenhorn executed a leasehold mortgage in favor of Construction Lender and legally recorded it.

   Concurrently with the funding of the construction loan, Greenhorn obtained a standby commitment from Permanent Lender to advance $10 million at 8 percent interest contingent on (1) the issuance of certificates of occupancy for 80 percent of the apartment building and (2) the leasing of 60 percent of the total rentable space of the apartment building to tenants acceptable to Permanent Lender. Greenhorn contracted with various subcontractors for the construction of the apartment building. Certificates of occupancy for 80 percent of the apartment building were issued on or before May 31, 2000. Certificates of occupancy for the remaining units were not obtained until July 3, 2000. The leasing of units was hampered by the availability of apartments at a lower cost in competing complexes. As of May 31, 2000, Permanent Lender had approved leases for only 45 percent of the rentable space.

   Fearful of defaulting on the construction loan, Greenhorn approached both Construction Lender and Permanent Lender and was successful in negotiating a letter of intent between Greenhorn, Construction Lender, and Permanent Lender, whereby it was agreed in principle that the term of the construction note would be extended to December 31, 2000, subject to approval by counsel for both Construction Lender and Permanent Lender. Upon the execution of the letter of intent, the officer of Construction Lender negotiating it exclaimed that he was glad that an agreement had been reached to extend the construction loan. The officer representing

Permanent Lender replied that he should receive a memento to mark the occasion.

Subsequently, the prime interest rate rose from 8 percent to 13 percent in a two-month period, the lending policies of Permanent Lender were scrutinized by the federal regulatory authorities, and its reserve requirements were substantially increased. Permanent Lender, unbeknownst to Greenhorn and Construction Lender, was no longer in a position to fund the permanent loan because of its increased reserve requirements.

Prior to December 31, 2000, Greenhorn submitted executed leases to Permanent Lender sufficient to meet the 60 percent lease contingency. The financial condition of the tenants who signed these leases was equal to or greater than that of the tenants previously approved by Permanent Lender. Recognizing the tight position that it was in, Permanent Lender's attorneys uncovered an ancient deed restriction that precluded the sale or lease of Blueacre or any portion thereof to any person of Chinese descent, and Permanent Lender refused to approve several leases to individuals with Chinese surnames. As a result, Greenhorn was unable to fulfill the 60 percent lease contingency prior to December 31, 2000, and Permanent Lender refused to fund the permanent loan.

On January 5, 2001, Construction Lender sent a notice of default to Greenhorn and announced its intent to foreclose the leasehold mortgage. What are the legal rights and obligations of Ace, Greenhorn, Construction Lender, and Permanent Lender? Has each of the parties acted ethically?

3. The Rocking K Ranch is located in state X, which utilizes a race–notice recording system. Although the ranch had been operated for many years by Abel, record title was actually held by Abel's reclusive uncle, Meier. After a number of years of unexpectedly low cattle prices, Abel encountered severe cash-flow difficulties. In an attempt to solve his financial problems, Abel entered into the following transactions:

a. On January 1, 2001, Abel sold the ranch to Baker for $250,000. Abel delivered a duly executed and acknowledged grant deed to Baker, but the grant deed was not recorded by Baker until August 2, 2001.

b. On February 1, 2001, Abel leased the ranch to his neighbor, Carter, for a period of five years. Carter immediately removed the fences surrounding the Rocking K and operated his ranch and the Rocking K as a single outfit.

c. On February 26, 2001, Abel sold the ranch to Dalton for $250,000, delivering a duly executed and acknowledged quitclaim deed to Dalton. The quitclaim deed was duly recorded by Dalton on March 5, 2001.

d. Meier died on March 10, 2001. Under the terms of Meier's will, Abel inherited the ranch. A grant deed (the Meier deed) was delivered to Abel by the executor of Meier's estate on July 10, 2001.

e. On July 25, 2001, with the Meier deed in his back pocket, Abel approached his other neighbor, Everready, offering to sell the ranch for $240,000. Everready was reluctant to purchase it because he knew that Carter had recently been operating the Rocking K. After talking with Carter and determining that Carter's only interest in the ranch was a leasehold interest, Everready agreed to purchase the ranch from Abel for $220,000. At the consummation of the sale, Everready received the Meier deed and a grant deed executed by Abel in favor of Everready. On August 3, 2001, Everready first recorded the Meier deed and then recorded the grant deed executed by Abel.

As of August 4, 2001, who is the lawful owner of the Rocking K Ranch?

4. Patricia and Bobby Star were married in New Mexico in July 1992. They had been living together since 1989. In July 1999, they separated. They had purchased a residence as joint tenants in April 1991. Bobby made the down payment from his separate funds. The mortgage payments were made out of commingled funds before and after marriage.

In August 1993, Patricia founded BioGene Corporation, a biotechnology firm, with $20,000 that she received as an inheritance from her grandmother. All of the stock of BioGene was issued in Patricia's name, and Patricia worked full-time for BioGene. Bobby retained his job with another employer and was not involved in the operations of BioGene. Due to limited financial resources, Patricia did not draw a salary from BioGene until August 1999. In September 1999, BioGene's first product was approved by the Food and Drug Administration. Shortly thereafter, Patricia sold all of her BioGene stock to a large pharmaceutical concern for $30 million. Two days after the sale of the stock, Patricia filed for dissolution of the marriage.

You are the judge in the Family Law Court. Is the residence that Patricia and Bobby acquired community property or property held in joint tenancy?

Would it matter if after marriage they had written a document stating that they wanted to hold the property as community property? In joint tenancy? Does Bobby have any interest in the proceeds from the sale of the BioGene stock?

5. In 1984, Occidental Chemical Corporation sold a warehouse to BCW Associates, Ltd. The sales contract provided that BCW would purchase the warehouse "as is." The contract also provided that BCW would have forty-five days to inspect the warehouse and could terminate the sale during this period. BCW formally waived this termination right and acquired the property. BCW subsequently leased the warehouse to Knoll International, Inc., which used the warehouse to store and distribute inventory from its office-furniture business.

Both BCW and Knoll had noticed a significant amount of dust in the warehouse, but viewed the dust as merely a nuisance. Three different consulting firms evaluated the warehouse and reported to BCW and Knoll that there were no environmental hazards at the facility. In addition, Occidental gave comfort letters to BCW in which Occidental represented that no hazardous materials were stored in the warehouse.

In the fall of 1985, Knoll's activity in the warehouse caused dust to "rain down" from the rafters. When the dust was analyzed, Knoll learned that the dust showed dangerous levels of lead.

Before Occidental acquired the warehouse, it had been owned and operated by Firestone Tire and Rubber Company from 1952 to 1980. The dust in the warehouse was created by the grinding phase of Firestone's production of white sidewall tires. Firestone conducted these operations throughout its occupation of the warehouse.

Knoll and BCW jointly undertook a thorough cleaning of the warehouse. BCW paid for the cleanup of the warehouse structure, in part because Knoll's lease required BCW to indemnify Knoll for costs associated with cleaning the dust. Knoll paid for the cost of cleaning its inventory and equipment, and it incurred costs to provide its employees with personal protective equipment. Is the innocent landowner defense available to BCW and Knoll under the Comprehensive Environmental Response, Compensation, and Liability Act? [*BCW Associates, Ltd. v. Occidental Chemical Corp.*, 1988 WL 102641 (E.D. Pa. Sept. 29, 1988)]

6. Plaintiff owns a 150-acre tract of land in the town of Mamaroneck, which has been leased by a private country club since 1921. In 1922, the area where the country club was located became the subject of a zoning ordinance and was rezoned for residential use. The area surrounding the country club has been subject to similar zoning rules. In 1994, the town of Mamaroneck enacted a local law that rezoned the area where the country club was located so that it could be developed only for recreational use. The purpose of the law was to slow down the process of urbanization, preserve recreational opportunities for the town, and prevent increased flooding in the area due to residential development. Just months prior to the passage of this law, plaintiff had submitted a plan for developing the property into 71 residential lots while leaving 112 acres of standing open space. Because of the plan to rezone the area, the town denied plaintiff's development proposal. Did the local law effect an unconstitutional taking of plaintiff's property without just compensation? [*Bonnie Briar Syndicate, Inc. v. Town of Mamaroneck*, 721 N.E.2d 971 (N.Y. 1999)] [*See also Palazzola v. Rhode Island*, 746 A.2d 707 (R.I. 2000), *cert. granted*, 121 S.Ct. 296 (2000).]

7. In 1978, California voters staged a so-called property tax revolt when they approved Proposition 13. This statewide ballot initiative amended the California state constitution and limited the rate at which real property was taxed within the state and the rate at which real property assessments could be increased. Proposition 13 raised questions of equity and fairness because two very similar pieces of property could have drastically different tax consequences depending on when the properties were last transferred. Property was reassessed when it was sold, so the new buyer often paid substantially more property tax than a neighbor with a comparable house who had owned the property for a number of years. Is Proposition 13's acquisition-value scheme for assessing property tax a violation of the Equal Protection Clause of the Fourteenth Amendment? [*Nordlinger v. Hahn*, 505 U.S. 1 (1992)]

8. Lucy Dunworth, developer of a shopping mall, entered into an easement and operating agreement with three major department stores. One of the covenants in the agreement was that each occupant promised to operate its store area as a first-class department store under its trade name for a twenty-year period. The occupants each purchased their commercial space in fee (that is, they actually purchased the land) from the developer. Kaufman–Straus Company, one of the

tenants, sold its place to a discount store two years later. The other two first-class department stores bring an action against the discount store because it is not a first-class operation. What is the result? [*Net Realty Holding Trust v. Franconia Properties, Inc.,* 544 F. Supp. 759 (E.D. Va. 1982)]

9. A group of disabled individuals brought suit against the owners of the televised quiz show *Who Wants to Be a Millionaire?* on the grounds that they were subjected to discrimination in violation of the Americans with Disabilities Act. In order to qualify to become a participant on the show, contestants must call a toll-free number and answer a series of questions. The initial qualifying round includes time limitations and the use of an automated telephone system requiring touch-tone phones. Plaintiffs claim that these requirements prevent them from being able to compete on an equal basis in the qualifying round. What would the plaintiffs have to prove to win their suit? What result? Should PGA Tour be required to permit a disabled golfer to use a golf cart between holes, instead of being required to walk the course? [*Rendon v. Valleycrest Productions,* 119 F. Supp. 2d 1344 (S.D. Fla. 2000); *Martin v. PGA Tour, Inc.,* 204 F.3d 994 (9th Cir. 2000), *cert. granted,* 121 S.Ct. 30 (2000)]

MANAGER'S DILEMMA

10. John Hardy, the general manager of a large retail home improvement chain, has been looking for new locations for expansion. When Hardy learns that a large plot of land near a residential development is available for sale to commercial entities, he enters into negotiations with the property owner to purchase a majority of the land. Eventually, a letter of intent is signed, which sets forth the general terms and conditions of the negotiated purchase. Although both parties intend to sign a formal acquisition agreement at the closing, neither expresses any doubt that the purchase will be successfully concluded. Moreover, it is well known that Hardy's company has the necessary financial backing to complete the transaction.

A few days later, however, Hardy hears a rumor that the City Planning Commission is considering a new zoning ordinance that would reserve certain open lands for residential development. If passed, the ordinance would prevent Hardy's company from building a retail store on the tract of land that is the subject of the signed letter of intent. The proposed zoning ordinance has many opponents, and it is unclear how the Commission will ultimately resolve the issue. What should Hardy do?

INTERNET SOURCES

National Association of Realtors	http://nar.realtor.com
This site includes home listings and information and offers a finance center with a featured lender (GMAC Mortgage).	http://www.realtor.com
The American Real Estate and Urban Economics Association site includes a biannual newsletter for professionals and academics interested in real estate and urban policy.	http://www.areuea.org
This site provides advice on buying and selling as well as home listings.	http://www.realty.com
The National Association of Real Estate Investment Trusts site includes information regarding legal issues affecting REITs.	http://www.nareit.com
The Web site for Case Shiller Weiss, a Cambridge, Massachusetts company mainly serving mortgage lenders and investors, offers an analysis of the current value of a residential property, with a "confidence level" grade on its accuracy (one free sample, then $35/report).	http://www.cswcasa.com
This site, the oldest e-commerce residential site (created July 1998) is an all-purpose site with home listings, mortgages, and other tools.	http://homeadvisor.msn.com
This site uses Digital Handshake technology to transact home purchases online.	http://www.ilumin.com
This site provides free real estate legal forms and a dictionary of legal terms.	http://www.kaktus.com
This site provides natural hazard, environmental risk, and community information.	http://www.nearmyhome.com
This site provides information on pest control.	http://www.pestweb.com
This site provides market analysis reports, including information on neighborhoods.	http://www.RealEstate.com
This site offers closeyourdeal.com, which allows agents, lenders, and appraisers to collaborate and manage the transaction process online.	http://www.realtyplusonline.com
This site provides one of largest databases of location-specific real estate, environmental, and underwriting information in the United States.	http://www.vistainfo.com
This site provides mortgage-market reports, mortgage calculators, and advice.	http://www.bankrate.com
This provides a state-by-state comparison of mortgage rates and names of lenders.	http://www.HSH.com
Both of these sites provide weekly e-mail updates on real property matters.	http://www.dispatch@pikenet.com http://circulation@iren.com

CHAPTER 20

Antitrust

FIRMS PAY RECORD FINES

In 1998, Ucar International was fined what at the time was a record $110 million for rigging prices and squelching competition in the international market for graphite electrodes, an essential component in furnaces used to produce steel.[1] Two years earlier, the U.S. Justice Department fined Archer–Daniels–Midland (ADM—self-described "Supermarket to the World") $100 million for fixing prices in the markets for citric acid and lysine, a livestock-feed additive.[2] In 2000, the European Commission fined ADM and its four Asian co-conspirators $105 million, bringing ADM's total legal tab to more than $250 million for criminal fines and civil settlements.[3] Michael D. Andreas, former ADM executive vice president, was fined $350,000 and sentenced to three years in prison. Both Ucar and ADM violated the *antitrust laws,* which prohibit monopolistic combinations of companies *(trusts)* and other unreasonable restraints on trade and competition, such as price-fixing among competitors.

The Ucar and ADM fines were dwarfed by the $862 million fines levied in 1999 against five vitamin manufacturers (F. Hoffman La Roche of Switzerland, BASF AG of Germany, and Eisaid Company, Daichi Pharmaceutical Company and Takeda Chemical Industries Ltd. of Japan) for participating in a cartel to fix prices for wholesale vitamins. Hoffman LaRoche alone paid a $500 million fine, the largest fine the U.S. Department of Justice had ever

obtained in any criminal case. Two Swiss nationals and two German nationals, who were high officers at Hoffman LaRoche or BASF, were sentenced to prison and fined a total of $625,000. The five companies, together with Rhone-Poulenc SA of France (which was not prosecuted because it provided key evidence against the other members of the cartel), agreed in November 1999 to pay $1.05 billion to settle the private class-action litigation brought in federal court on behalf of direct purchases of vitamins and vitamin premix.[4]

The basic principle of antitrust law is that the economy functions best when firms are free to compete vigorously but fairly with one another. A competitive economy allows the consumer to enjoy better goods at lower prices, or, as economists say, it maximizes consumer wealth. If, however, competition is decreased or eliminated by firms seeking jointly or independently to wield monopoly power, consumers suffer and the performance of the economy declines.

The antitrust statutes contain certain very general prohibitions on business conduct. These general prohibitions often have little content until courts apply them to the particular facts of a case. Thus, bright lines that clearly separate lawful from unlawful conduct are rare in this field. A business practice that harms competition in one market setting might not harm competition in another. The courts and agencies that enforce the antitrust laws must distinguish between the pernicious and the benign.

1. Gordon Fairclough, *Ucar to Pay Record Fine in Antitrust Case,* WALL ST. J., Apr. 8, 1998, at B15.
2. Bryan Gruley, *ADM's $100 Million Price-Fixing Fine Blows Lid off Usual Maximum Penalty,* WALL ST. J., Oct. 16, 1996, at A4.
3. Scott Kilman, *European Commission Sets ADM Fine,* WALL ST. J., June 8, 2000, at A4.

4. Harry First, *Antitrust at the Millennium (Part II): The Vitamins Case: Cartel Prosecutions and the Coming of International Competition Law,* 68 ANTITRUST L.J. 711 (2001).

CHAPTER OVERVIEW

This chapter offers a general overview of the federal antitrust laws, pointing out which aspects are settled and which are not. It begins with a discussion of Sections 1 and 2 of the Sherman Act, then addresses the Clayton Act provisions relating to mergers and combinations. The chapter then outlines the Robinson–Patman Act's prohibitions on price discrimination, and it concludes with a discussion of the international application of the U.S. antitrust laws.

Agreements *in* Restraint *of* Trade: Section 1 *of the* Sherman Act

Section 1 of the Sherman Act provides that "[e]very contract, combination in the form of trust or otherwise, or conspiracy, in restraint of trade or commerce among the several States, or with foreign nations, is declared to be illegal."[5] On its face, Section 1 appears to prohibit all concerted activity that restrains trade. Almost every business transaction, even a contract for the purchase of goods or services, restrains trade to a certain extent, however. A contract, for example, restrains the parties from doing things that would constitute a breach, such as selling goods to someone else. Read literally, Section 1 would outlaw every type of business transaction involving more than one party.

In order to avoid an unworkable construction of the Sherman Act, the courts have construed Section 1 to prohibit only those restraints of trade that *unreasonably* restrict competition. This chapter explores in some detail the circumstances under which conduct unreasonably restrains trade.

TRADE AND COMMERCE

The Sherman Act applies only to "trade or commerce" among the states or with foreign nations. The phrase "commerce among the several States" extends the reach of the Sherman Act as far as constitutionally allowed under the Commerce Clause.[6] The resulting scope of antitrust jurisdiction is therefore broad and encompasses more than restraints on trade that are motivated by a desire to limit interstate commerce or that have their sole impact on interstate commerce. The commerce requirement of the act may be satisfied when the defendant's conduct (1) directly interferes with the flow of goods in the stream of commerce or (2) has a substantial effect on interstate commerce.

In 1997, a fraternity at Hamilton College in New York argued that the school's new policy of requiring all students to live in college-owned facilities and to purchase college-sponsored meal plans was an attempt to monopolize the housing and dining markets in that area in violation of Section 2 of the Sherman Act (discussed below). The fraternity alleged substantial effects on interstate commerce, including Hamilton's out-of-state student population (56 percent) and its annual revenue for room and board from those students ($4 million). The district court dismissed the complaint on the grounds that the provision of residential services under the new policy did not involve "trade or commerce." The appeals court reversed the dismissal, however, and ruled that such a question was suitable for trial.[7]

ENFORCEMENT

The Sherman Act is enforced in a number of ways. First, violations of Section 1 may be prosecuted as felonies. Corporations can be fined up to $10 million for each violation under the Sherman Act, and the fine can be increased under other statutes to twice the gain to the violator or twice the loss to the victim, whichever is greater. Individuals can be fined up to $350,000 for each violation and imprisoned for up to three years. Second, the Justice Department may bring civil actions to enforce the Sherman Act. Third, private plaintiffs, sometimes called private attorneys general, are entitled to recover three times the damages they have sustained as a consequence of the Sherman Act violation. Finally, state attorneys general may bring civil actions for injuries sustained by residents of their respective states. In these *parens patriae actions*, treble damages may also be recovered. (In addition to the federal antitrust laws, there are state antitrust laws giving causes of action both to private persons and to state attorneys general.)

---

5. 15 U.S.C. § 1 (1997).
6. Summit Health, Ltd. v. Pinhas, 500 U.S. 322, 329 n.10 (1991).

7. Hamilton Chapter of Alpha Delta Phi, Inc. v. Hamilton College, 128 F.3d 59 (2d Cir. 1997).

Politics *and* Economics

The first antitrust law, the Sherman Act, was passed by Congress in 1890 as fear of corporate power grew during the Progressive Era. It was part of a populist movement to combat the rise of powerful trusts in such basic industries as oil and steel. "You must heed [the voters'] appeal or be ready for the socialist, the communist, and the nihilist," Senator John Sherman declared during the debate over his bill. The Sherman Act's general prohibitions have evolved over the past century through judicial decisions. This rather ad hoc development of the law has led to some seemingly confused results. For example, business practices forbidden under the Sherman Act in the early twentieth century are often permissible in today's changed economic environment.

More than a century after the Sherman Act was passed, the United States finds itself in the midst of a world economy in which many industries compete on an international scale. Often the United States is no longer the dominant economic power. In this changed environment, a new generation of academics, lawyers, and judges has challenged their predecessors' conclusions that certain business practices or market conditions are inherently anticompetitive. This school of thought, known as Law and Economics, concludes that market forces defeat most anticompetitive practices. Its proponents question the efficacy of the government's regulation of commerce and markets, arguing that instead of promoting competition, attempts at regulation often increase the anticompetitive structure of markets.

As economics continues to inform legal decisions and market-based arguments are made and refined, antitrust law continues to evolve. To many, this evolutionary process is antitrust's greatest strength and the reason it has entered its second century.

 ## Violation *of* Section 1

For liability to attach under Section 1, a plaintiff must demonstrate that (1) there is a contract, combination, or conspiracy among separate entities; (2) it unreasonably restrains trade; (3) it affects interstate or foreign commerce (this requirement is of little practical import, because the Supreme Court has interpreted interstate commerce as including virtually all commerce); and (4) it causes an antitrust injury.

A CONTRACT, COMBINATION, OR CONSPIRACY

Section 1 does not prohibit unilateral activity in restraint of trade. Acting by itself, an individual or firm may take any action, no matter how anticompetitive, and not violate Section 1. (Section 2 of the Sherman Act, discussed later in this chapter, does prohibit some forms of unilateral conduct, however.)

This threshold requirement of concerted action is one of the most frequently litigated issues in antitrust cases. In 1984, the Supreme Court ruled that a parent corporation and its wholly owned subsidiary cannot "agree" within the concerted-action requirement of Section 1.[8] Whether sister corporations or corporations that are less than wholly owned can impermissibly agree remains an open issue.

Conspiracies, especially illegal conspiracies, are inherently secretive. Most price-fixers do not keep minutes of their meetings or send confirming letters. Consequently, requiring direct proof of a conspiracy would likely permit many undesirable activities to escape Section 1 liability. On the other hand, because unilateral behavior is not a violation, courts must be careful in relaxing the requirement that conspiracy be proved. Courts have struggled to develop mechanisms that allow lawsuits under Section 1 to go forward without direct proof of a conspiracy or agreement while ensuring that only the truly guilty are convicted.

One such mechanism is the distinction between horizontal and vertical agreements. *Horizontal agreements* are those between firms that directly compete with each other, such as retailers selling the same range of products. *Vertical agreements* are those between firms at different levels of production or distribution, such as a retailer and its supplier.

8. Copperweld Corp. v. Independence Tube Corp., 467 U.S. 752 (1984).

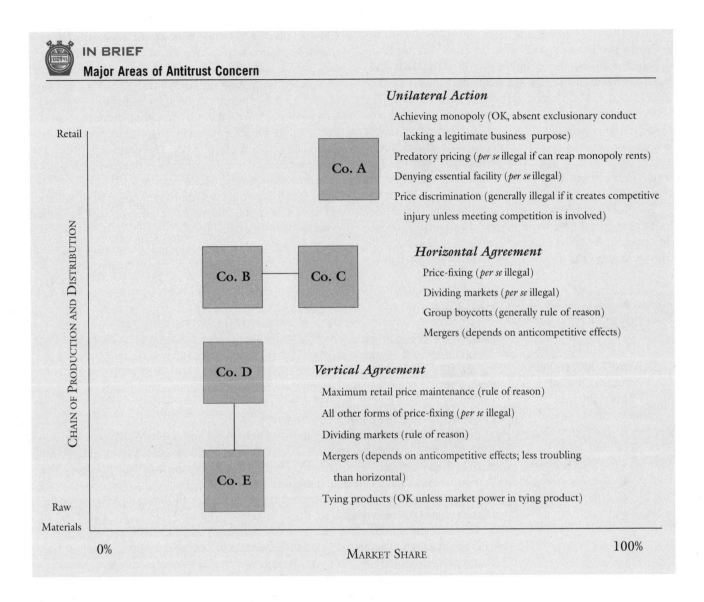

IN BRIEF
Major Areas of Antitrust Concern

Unilateral Action

Achieving monopoly (OK, absent exclusionary conduct
    lacking a legitimate business purpose)

Predatory pricing (*per se* illegal if can reap monopoly rents)

Denying essential facility (*per se* illegal)

Price discrimination (generally illegal if it creates competitive
    injury unless meeting competition is involved)

Horizontal Agreement

Price-fixing (*per se* illegal)

Dividing markets (*per se* illegal)

Group boycotts (generally rule of reason)

Mergers (depends on anticompetitive effects)

Vertical Agreement

Maximum retail price maintenance (rule of reason)

All other forms of price-fixing (*per se* illegal)

Dividing markets (rule of reason)

Mergers (depends on anticompetitive effects; less troubling
    than horizontal)

Tying products (OK unless market power in tying product)

Co. A

Co. B — Co. C

Co. D

Co. E

CHAIN OF PRODUCTION AND DISTRIBUTION

Retail

Raw
Materials

0%   MARKET SHARE   100%

The judicial characterization of an agreement as horizontal or vertical has dramatic consequences. A horizontal agreement may be proved by *circumstantial evidence,* that is, evidence of the parties' actions from which an agreement may be inferred. A vertical agreement, on the other hand, can be proved only by direct evidence that there was an agreement or by circumstantial evidence that tends to exclude the possibility of independent action.

Proving a Horizontal Conspiracy Because an agreement between horizontal competitors, such as two automakers, almost invariably reduces interbrand competition, such agreements are generally disfavored under the antitrust laws. *Interbrand competition* is competition between companies producing the same type of product. For example, Ford Motor Company and General Motors engage in interbrand competition for trucks and automobiles.

The classic definition of conspiracy, whether horizontal or vertical, focuses on whether the alleged conspirators had a meeting of the minds in a scheme that violates the law. The courts will not require evidence of an explicit agreement to violate the law. As the U.S. Court of Appeals for the Ninth Circuit has stated with respect to a horizontal conspiracy, a "knowing wink can mean more than words."[9]

9. Esco Corp. v. United States, 340 F.2d 1000, 1007 (9th Cir. 1965).

Plaintiffs often attempt to infer a horizontal conspiracy from evidence of parallel behavior by ostensibly independent firms, for example, by showing that they consistently set prices at the same levels and change prices at the same time *(conscious parallelism)*. The problem with this type of evidence (particularly when a homogeneous product or service is involved) is that it is ambiguous as an indicator of anticompetitive behavior. Parallel pricing of similar products or services can result either from illegal price-fixing or from vigorous competition.

To infer an agreement or conspiracy from parallel behavior, the courts have required that the plaintiff show additional facts or "plus factors." Under the standard set in *Theatre Enterprises, Inc. v. Paramount Film Distributing Corp.,*[10] parallel behavior that would appear to be contrary to the economic interests of the defendants, were they acting independently, will support an inference of conspiracy. On the other hand, if the defendants can produce reasonable business explanations for the behavior, a court will not infer a conspiracy. Other circumstantial evidence of an agreement, such as a meeting between two defendants, may be a plus factor. Increasing prices and persistent profits despite a decline in demand for the good or service may also be plus factors.

In the following case, the court considered whether producers of potash, a mineral used in fertilizers, had conspired to fix prices.

10. 346 U.S. 537 (1954).

A CASE IN POINT

CASE 20.1

Blomkest Fertilizer, Inc. v. Potash Corp. of Saskatchewan

United States Court of Appeals for the Eighth Circuit
203 F.3d 1028
(8th Cir. 2000), cert. denied,
121 S. Ct. 50 (2000).

Summary

FACTS The Canadian province of Saskatchewan founded the Potash Corporation of Saskatchewan (PCS), which produces 38 percent of the potash in North America. During the 1980s, PCS suffered huge losses after it mined potash in quantities that far exceeded demand and thereby caused the price of potash to fall dramatically. In 1986, shortly after Saskatchewan elected to privatize PCS, the new company reduced its output, which caused the price of potash to rise.

In 1986, the New Mexico Potash Corporation (NMPC) and another American potash company filed a complaint with the U.S. Department of Commerce, alleging that Canadian producers had dumped potash in the United States at prices below fair market value. The Commerce Department agreed and negotiated an agreement with the Canadian producers that raised the price of Canadian potash in the United States by setting a minimum price. After the agreement was negotiated, PCS and other producers raised their price on potash.

A class of potash consumers filed a claim, alleging that the potash producers had colluded to increase the price of potash in violation of Section 1 of the Sherman Act. The producers argued that the price increase was due to the interdependent nature of the industry and its reaction to the privatization of PCS and the agreement entered into by the U.S. Commerce Department and the Canadian potash producers. The district court agreed with the producers and dismissed the claim. The class appealed.

ISSUE PRESENTED Did the potash producers engage in price-fixing in violation of Section 1 of the Sherman Act?

SUMMARY OF OPINION The U.S. Court of Appeals for the Eighth Circuit began by stating that evidence that a business has met the pricing of its competitors does not prove a violation of the antitrust laws, unless certain "plus factors" are present. The class argued that it had established the necessary "plus factors" by providing evidence of (1) communications between the firms that produced potash, (2) the companies' acts against self-interest, and (3) an econometric model that allegedly proved that the price of potash would have been lower in the absence of collusion. The court concluded that this evidence did not support the plaintiff's claims.

With respect to the first factor, the court found that the evidence presented was far too ambiguous to support an inference of conspiracy. The evidence of interfirm communications did not exclude the possibility of independent action by the different firms.

(Continued)

(Case 20.1 continued)

As for the second factor, the only evidence that the potash producers acted against their economic interest was their participation in the agreement with the Department of Commerce. The court found that there was no evidence to contradict the conclusion that ending the Commerce Department dumping investigation with a settlement that required the artificially low potash prices to rise was a legitimate business decision for the low-tariff producers. By entering into the settlement, they avoided the cost of litigation and the risk of penalties and benefited from increased revenues. The court concluded that their decision to enter into the settlement could not be characterized as an act against self-interest.

Finally, the court found that the econometric model failed to take into account the privatization of PCS and the antidumping proceedings. The model heavily relied on evidence, such as the producers' common membership in trade associations and their publication of price lists to consumers, that was not probative of collusion as a matter of law.

RESULT The appeals court affirmed the decision of the district court. The suit was dismissed.

Proving a Vertical Conspiracy Vertical agreements, such as those between an automaker and its local dealers, may reduce *intrabrand competition,* that is, price competition between local dealers selling the same manufacturer's products. But they often enhance *interbrand competition,* that is, competition between dealers selling different manufacturers' products. It is in the best interests of both the automaker and its dealers to provide the most marketable product so as to receive the greatest possible share of available consumer dollars. Courts look more favorably on reductions in intrabrand than interbrand competition when there is vigorous interbrand competition that can prevent the reduction in intrabrand competition from harming consumers.

Since the mid-1980s, the courts have generally been unwilling to allow proof of vertical conspiracies by circumstantial evidence alone. The Supreme Court has held that firms in a vertical arrangement, unlike competitors, have many legitimate reasons to communicate with each other. Therefore, a plaintiff seeking to prove an unlawful conspiracy must introduce evidence that tends to exclude the possibility that the firms acted independently.[11] Evidence of action that could be either concerted or independent is insufficient to prove a Section 1 violation under this test. Few plaintiffs lacking direct evidence of a conspiracy have been successful in asserting a Section 1 claim based on a vertical restraint.

UNREASONABLE RESTRAINT OF TRADE

There are two approaches to analyzing the reasonableness of a restraint: the *per se* rule and the rule of reason.

11. Monsanto Co. v. Spray-Rite Serv. Corp., 465 U.S. 752 (1984).

***Per se* Violations** *Per se analysis* condemns practices that are considered completely void of redeeming competitive rationales. This is appropriate when the practice always or almost always tends to restrict competition and decrease output. Once identified as *illegal per se,* a practice need not be examined further for its impact on the market, and its procompetitive justifications will not be considered.

Law and Economics scholars have argued that very few practices are inherently anticompetitive. Because this scholarship has been accepted by many courts, the number of truly *per se* violations of the antitrust laws has declined.

The Rule of Reason If the plaintiff has not proved a *per se* violation, the activity will be evaluated under the *rule of reason.* The objective of this rule is to determine whether, on balance, the activity promotes or restrains competition, or to put it differently, whether it helps or harms consumers. In making this determination, the court will consider the structure of the market as well as the defendant's action. The court will analyze the anticompetitive and procompetitive effects of the challenged practice. Activity that has a substantial net anticompetitive effect is deemed an unreasonable restraint of trade and hence is unlawful.

 Types *of* Horizontal Restraints

Unlawful horizontal restraints, that is, restraints between direct competitors, include price-fixing, market division, and some kinds of group boycotts. These have traditionally been treated as *per se* violations of Section 1 of the Sherman Act. Trade associations may also be found to be acting unlawfully under the rule of reason in some circumstances.

Some products, such as sporting events, may require horizontal restraints in order to exist at all. Economists suggest that a sporting league comprising the different teams (such as the National Football League) should be viewed as a single firm in the business of providing competition. Hence, constraints on teams are simply attempts to put "departments" within the firm on an equal footing so that customers can enjoy balanced contests among them. Courts, however, take a more formalistic view but make allowances for the needed horizontal constraints.

HORIZONTAL PRICE-FIXING

Horizontal price-fixing, such as an agreement between retailers to set a common price for a product, is the classic example of a *per se* violation of Section 1. *Horizontal price-fixing* agreements include (1) setting prices (including maximum prices); (2) setting the terms of sale, such as customer credit terms; (3) setting the quantity or quality of goods to be manufactured or made available for sale; or (4) rigging bids (agreements between or among competitors to rig contract bids).

In 1999, federal prosecutors charged a former purchasing manager for Lorillard Tobacco Company with conspiring to rig bids in exchange for $300,000 in kickbacks. He was one participant in a large bid-rigging and kickback scheme devised by sellers of promotional materials for tobacco companies; the scheme undermined corporate bidding policies and inflated costs for seven companies including Philip Morris and Warner–Lambert Company. Two groups of vendors rigged bids and divided up contracts worth more than $100 million by bribing purchasing managers with cash, vacations, plane tickets, and other goods and services.[12] Federal prosecutors have been investigating the scheme for a decade; eighteen individuals and nine small makers of promotional materials have already pled guilty to the illegal activity.

The Justice Department views price-fixing as "hard crime," to be punished by prison sentences whenever possible. Many executives have been imprisoned for price-fixing. Indeed, under the Federal Sentencing Guidelines, some term of confinement is mandatory for individuals convicted of horizontal price-fixing, bid rigging, or market-allocation agreements; in most cases, first-time offenders serve a minimum of six to twelve months in prison.

Multimillion-dollar fines against corporations convicted of price-fixing are the rule rather than the exception. But civil actions, in particular class actions (which inevitably follow criminal prosecutions), can have even more drastic financial consequences. Liability for antitrust damages is joint and several among all of the conspirators, so each conspirator is potentially liable for treble damages for the losses caused by all of the defendants.

The world's leading auction houses, Christie's International PLC and Sotheby's Holding, colluded to enter into economic agreements, including identical sliding-scale fee commission structures. Christie's and Sotheby's agreed to pay $537 million to settle civil suits by former sellers. Sotheby's chief executive, Diana D. Brooks, pled guilty to one felony count of conspiring to fix prices, which carried a possible prison sentence. Alfred Taubman, Sotheby's former chairman, and the former chairman of Christie's, Sir Anthony J. Tennant, were indicted in May 2001 in the U.S. District Court for the Southern District of New York. Taubman pled not guilty; Tennant refused to appear, prompting the judge to issue a bench warrant for his arrest.[13] Tennant will probably avoid prosecution because he lives in Britain, where only companies, not individuals, can be charged with price-fixing.

 INTERNATIONAL CONSIDERATION

In October 1996, Archer–Daniels–Midland (ADM) was fined $100 million by the U.S. government for criminally fixing the price of lysine, a livestock-feed additive. The conspiracy involved agreements between ADM and at least three Asian firms: Kyowa Hakko Kogyo Company, Ltd. and Ajinomoto Company of Japan and Sewon Company of South Korea. The government's case against ADM was helped by the cooperation of the Asian firms, which pled guilty earlier that year and accepted fines of $20 million. In turn, the corporate convictions gave the government leverage against three of the executives at the Asian firms who pled guilty for their individual roles in the scheme. In exchange for relatively light sentences—fines of no more than $75,000—they then assisted the Justice Department in its prosecution of executives at ADM.[a]

a. *Asian Businessmen Enter Pleas in ADM Price-Fixing*, WALL ST. J., Jan. 15, 1997, at B2.

---

12. Frances A. McMorris, *Bid-Rigging, Kickbacks Inflated Costs for Many Companies, Prosecutors Find*, WALL ST. J., Feb. 1, 1999, at B8.
13. *Sotheby's Ex-Chief Pleads Not Guilty*, NEW YORK TIMES, May 5, 2001, at B12.

HORIZONTAL MARKET DIVISION AND NONPRICE HORIZONTAL RESTRAINTS

The Supreme Court considers market divisions so inherently anticompetitive as to constitute *per se* violations of Section 1. *Horizontal market division* can take various forms. For instance, competitors might divide up a market according to class of customer or geographic territory or restrict product output. In 1972, the U.S. Supreme Court considered the legality of an agreement among members of an association of supermarket chains to divide the grocery market.[14] The association's members, twenty-five small- and medium-size independent supermarket chains, each agreed to sell a particular trademarked brand only in an assigned area. They also agreed not to sell the brand's products to other retailers. Although the association argued that exclusive territories were necessary to encourage local advertising of the fledgling brand, the Court ruled that market division is prohibited even if it is intended to enable small competitors to compete with larger companies and to foster interbrand competition. More recently, the Supreme Court has emphasized that horizontal market division by potential as well as actual competitors is *per se* illegal.[15]

Horizontal agreements among competitors not to compete on nonprice matters may also violate Section 1. For example, in *Continental Airlines, Inc. v. United Air Lines, Inc.,*[16] the trial court held that an agreement involving an association of airlines serving Dulles Airport to install X-ray screening devices at airport security checkpoints that would restrict the size of carry-on bags was a naked restraint on the airlines' ability to engage in nonprice competition on the basis of carry-on luggage capacity. Continental had spent approximately $15 million to install oversized overhead bins in its aircraft to accommodate larger carry-on bags and had adopted a liberal "gate-checking" policy on commuter flights in order to compete with other airlines. Safety concerns were not compromised by Continental's policy. The agreement to restrict the size of carry-on bags had been adopted at the urging of United Air Lines, which was the dominant carrier at Dulles and in charge of operating the security checkpoints. The court concluded that the agreement was analogous to other horizontal agreements that had been held *per se* illegal.

GROUP BOYCOTTS

It is a fundamental principle of liberty and freedom of contract that an individual may choose to do business with

AT THE TOP

Any communications by a company's employees with competitors regarding price-fixing, or any direct involvement in such activities, may subject the company to potential liability in the form of civil damages and criminal penalties. Education is key. The code of conduct from Dun & Bradstreet excerpted in Exhibit 20.1 is an excellent example of the type of information that companies should provide all their employees. A code of conduct is not sufficient in itself, however. It simply provides a solid foundation from which compliance values are imparted to employees on an ongoing basis. An adequate supervisory mechanism is needed as well.

whomever he or she wants. Nevertheless, an agreement among competitors to refuse to deal with another competitor—a *group boycott*—has traditionally been treated as a *per se* violation of Section 1. An agreement between or among competitors that deprives another competitor of something it needs to compete effectively is considered so inherently anticompetitive that no economic motivation for the action may be offered as a defense.

For example, the U.S. Supreme Court held that manufacturers of appliances could not agree with a distributor's competitors to refrain from selling to the distributor or to do so only at higher prices. Such an agreement was treated as a *per se* violation of Section 1 even though there was no agreement on the exact price, quantity, or quality of the appliances to be sold.[17]

More recently, the U.S. Supreme Court has begun to distinguish some forms of group boycotts that it believes are not so inherently anticompetitive as to merit *per se* treatment. For instance, in 1985, the Court found no Sherman Act violation when a purchasing cooperative of office-supply retailers expelled a member for violating a cooperative bylaw requiring notification of changes in ownership.[18] As a result, the remaining members would not transact business with the expellee, but it had alternative suppliers available to it. Although concerted boycotts cutting off a competitor from necessary supplies justify *per se* treatment, some boycotts involving restraints and exclusions encourage competition and call for analysis under the rule of reason. Using such a rule of reason, the Court held that the cooperative had not violated the Sherman Act.

14. United States v. Topco Assocs., Inc., 405 U.S. 596 (1972).
15. Palmer v. BRG of Ga., Inc., 498 U.S. 46 (1990).
16. 120 F. Supp. 2d 556 (E.D. Va. 2000).

17. Klor's, Inc. v. Broadway–Hale Stores, Inc., 359 U.S. 207 (1959).
18. Northwest Wholesale Stationers, Inc. v. Pacific Stationery & Printing Co., 472 U.S. 284 (1985).

EXHIBIT 20.1 | **Excerpts on Antitrust and Competition from the *Dun & Bradstreet Policy of Business Conduct***

Dun & Bradstreet will not tolerate any business transaction or activity that violates the letter or spirit of the antitrust and competition laws of any country that apply to the Company's business.

...

The antitrust laws are deliberately broad and general in their language. They contain sweeping provisions against restraints that threaten a competitive business economy, but they provide no definitive list of those activities. This means D&B associates must pay careful attention to possible antitrust implications of the Company's business activities. The Legal Department should be contacted in all cases of doubt.

...

Social Discussions and Company Communications

. . . Any kind of casual understanding between two companies that a business practice adopted by one would be followed by the other may be used in court to prove an illegal agreement.

Even social conversations can be used as evidence that an agreement existed. Memos and other written communications that use casual or inappropriate language might some day be examined by a government agency or opposing lawyers. Using loose language may raise questions about conduct that is entirely legal and may undermine all our efforts to comply with the antitrust and competition laws.

Example: Sales managers of two competing information companies met socially after work. After a few drinks, they agreed that it would be great if they reduced their workload by not chasing after the same customers. The bartender overheard the conversation.

In actuality, neither sales manager stopped selling to particular customers. Later, one company won most of the information business from law firms in the region, while the other company won most of the business from newspapers. This led to an investigation into market allocation of both companies, and the bartender's testimony was used against them.

But aren't my files and memos confidential?

No! Except for certain "privileged" communications with lawyers, all Company documents and computer files, including the most casual note or electronic-mail message, may be disclosed to government enforcement organizations or private parties in lawsuits against the Company. You should also know that stamping documents "restricted" or "confidential" does not protect them from being disclosed in court.

How can I avoid being tripped up by my own memos?

Follow these general guidelines:

- Report facts, be concise and objective, and indicate where information came from to establish that there is no cooperation with competitors.
- Do not draw legal conclusions.
- Avoid expressions that may imply guilt, such as "Please destroy after reading" or, "We stole this customer from Acme Widget Corp."
- Do not refer to "industry policies," "industry price," or similar expressions that imply a common course of action exists even though it does not.
- Do not use language that would suggest a false intent to harm competitors, such as, "This new program will 'destroy' the competition" or "establish a dominant position."
- Do not overstate your share of the market or refer to a market that is unreasonably narrow in order to make your market share appear larger.
- Consult with the Legal Department about when communications with a lawyer can be "privileged."

Questions and Answers

I work in sales and am friendly with a sales representative from one of our competitors. Our kids are on the same soccer team, so we see each other every week. Last weekend, we talked about a new sales promotion my company is offering. This promotion is no secret; we ran a big advertisement in the trade magazines. Did I do anything wrong?

Yes. You should never discuss price or other terms of sale with competitors under any circumstances. It is too easy for others to misinterpret any conversations you have, however innocent you believe them to be.

(Exhibit 20.1 continues)

(Exhibit 20.1 continued)

My boss asked me how a sales call to a prospective customer went. I mentioned that the customer seemed very interested, but was locked into a three-year contract with one of our competitors that still had two years to go. My boss told me to follow up immediately. I was supposed to convince the customer that no contract was "written in stone" and he shouldn't be so timid about walking away from the other contract. I do not feel comfortable telling the customer what to do about his contract.

You are correct to feel uncomfortable. It is against Company policy to interfere with the contracts of competitors. You might suggest that the customer review his contract to see if he has a right to terminate early, but never advise a customer to violate a contract or offer advice on how to interpret a competitor's contract.

Our main service is so popular that it almost sells itself. We are definitely the industry leaders in this field, and our sales show it. However, some of our other services are a bit stagnant and haven't moved much lately. So, I started to offer the main service only as a partner service to a couple of the slow movers. The customers want the main service so badly they don't seem to care. Isn't this a great idea?

No. If a product with a dominant market share is sold only to customers if they also agree to buy another product, this could be an illegal tying arrangement. While there are exceptions, any such plan should be cleared by your Legal Department.

At a trade association meeting, a few of us from competing companies met for drinks and the talk turned to what we each charge our customers. This seemed wrong but I didn't know how to deal with the situation.

You should say forcefully that you can't participate in price or similar discussions. If the talk continues, walk out and make a show of it (such as spilling your drink) so your protest will be remembered. Discussions like these are frequently used as evidence of illegal agreements, even against people who participated unwillingly but silently.

Source: From *The Dun & Bradstreet Corporation's Policy of Business Conduct* (1998). Used by permission.

In *NYNEX Corp. v. Discon, Inc.,*[19] the Supreme Court held that a corporation that switched from one supplier to another that allegedly offered an under-the-table rebate as part of a scheme to defraud regulators had not engaged in a *per se* illegal boycott. Even though there was no legitimate business reason for the decision to switch suppliers, the Court held that the *per se* rule in the boycott context was limited to cases involving horizontal agreements among direct competitors. As a result, the plaintiff had to allege and prove harm, not just to a single competitor, but to the competitive process, that is, to competition itself. The Court reasoned:

> To apply the *per se* rule here—where the buyer's decision, though not made for competitive reasons, composes part of a regulatory fraud—would transform cases involving business behavior that is improper for various reasons, say, cases involving nepotism or personal pique, into treble-damages antitrust cases. And that *per se* rule would discourage firms from changing suppliers—even where the competitive process itself does not suffer harm.

> The freedom to switch suppliers lies close to the heart of the competitive process that the antitrust laws seek to

encourage. At the same time, other laws, for example, "unfair competition" laws, business tort laws, or regulatory laws, provide remedies for various "competitive practices thought to be offensive to proper standards of business morality."

TRADE ASSOCIATIONS AND GROUP BOYCOTTS

Courts do not look favorably upon attempts at self-regulation by trade and professional associations that result in group boycotts. For example, an American Medical Association rule of ethics that forbade salaried practice and prepaid medical care was struck down as a violation of the Sherman Act.[20]

In the following case, the court considered whether rules of the California Dental Association forbidding all advertising that referred to "low" or "reasonable" prices, offered volume discounts, or made any claims about quality of service had an anticompetitive effect in violation of Section 5 of the Federal Trade Commission Act, which prohibits unfair methods of competition and unfair or deceptive practices.

19. 525 U.S. 128 (1998).

20. American Med. Ass'n v. United States, 317 U.S. 519 (1943).

CASE 20.2

California Dental Association v. Federal Trade Commission

United States Court of Appeals for the Ninth Circuit
224 F.3d 942
(9th Cir. 2000).

In the Language of the Court

FACTS The California Dental Association (CDA) is a trade association for California dentists; approximately 19,000 of the 26,000 licensed dentists in California are CDA members. The CDA provides a variety of services, including marketing, public relations seminars on practice management, continuing education, lobbying, and an administrative procedure for handling patients' complaints. It also has subsidiaries that provide liability insurance, discounts on long-distance calling, and financing for equipment. The CDA has a code of ethics by which members must abide. The code includes a section that prohibits dentists from advertising or soliciting patients with any communication that is false and misleading. The guidelines forbid advertising that refers to "low" or "reasonable" prices, offers volume discounts, or makes any claims about quality of service. The CDA objected to claims regarding quality of service on the grounds they could imply superiority over other dentists' services, which was unverifiable.

The U.S. Court of Appeals for the Ninth Circuit affirmed the finding of the Federal Trade Commission (FTC) that the CDA had prevented its members from engaging in truthful, nonmisleading advertising offering discounts or claims about service quality. On appeal, the U.S. Supreme Court held that the appeals court had erred by engaging in an abbreviated rule-of-reason analysis and had failed to consider a number of theories under which the restrictions might prove procompetitive. The case was then remanded to the appeals court.

OPINION HALL, J., writing for the U.S. Court of Appeals for the Ninth Circuit:

Are the Restrictions Procompetitive?

The Supreme Court's opinion focuses on the question of whether the presumptive economic benefits resulting from CDA's advertising restrictions outweigh their economic harms. The Court noted that "it seems to us that the CDA's advertising restrictions might plausibly be thought to have a net procompetitive effect, or possibly no effect at all on competition."

. . . Specifically, the Court pointed to several aspects of the advertising restrictions that might cause them to have a net procompetitive effect:

(1) Misleading advertising for professional services might be particularly harmful to consumers because of inherent difficulties in obtaining accurate information about service quality (i.e., information asymmetries).

(2) Consumers are relatively loyal to the professionals who have treated them previously.

(3) The restrictions at issue here were much less severe than a complete ban on advertising.

(4) Some advertising methods prohibited by the restrictions might, in the long run, drive consumers away from dentists.

(5) The advertising restrictions might prevent consumers from being misled into believing that they are receiving more of a bargain than they are actually receiving.

(6) The advertising restrictions might amount to no more than a procompetitive ban on puffery.

. . .

We now consider the record evidence bearing on the six factors identified above.

Information Asymmetries

. . . We conclude from the record that dentists are far better at evaluating the quality of dental services than patients are, i.e., that there is an informational asymmetry in the market. . . .

(Continued)

(Case 20.2 continued)

. . . A dentist can determine what his fellow dentists charge for services more easily than a consumer can. . . .

...

CDA . . . has made a strong case that the advertising restrictions at issue here correct for some of the informational asymmetries inherent in the market for dental services. . . . It appears that CDA's policies would require . . . dentists [who want to advertise a discounted rate] to disclose the regular and discounted rates, thereby allowing a price-conscious consumer to determine from the ads which of the . . . dentists is actually offering a lower fee. . . . As a result, a consumer's costs of searching for the less expensive service would be reduced. . . .

...

Consumer Loyalty
. . . We understand the Court's guidance as encouraging us to consider the view that restricting advertising in the dental market may be much less detrimental than restricting advertising in a market where consumers are much more likely to switch brands. . . .
. . . [W]e conclude that an analysis of the consequences of consumers' heightened loyalty in the dental market therefore does not cut in either party's favor.

Partial versus Complete Advertising Ban
...

If CDA's advertising restrictions amount to something approximating an absolute ban on price advertising, it may be appropriate to treat them as an absolute ban. An examination of the testimonial evidence cited by the FTC in support of this point, however, leaves us convinced that substantial evidence does not support such a conclusion. . . .
. . . For example, it appears that a dentist could advertise: "Root canals formerly $7500, now $6000" without violating the guidelines on their face or as enforced.

...

The FTC marshals an overwhelming quantum of evidence indicating that quality of service is a very important variable in patients' decisions about which dentist to choose. But there is no evidence that dentists who advertise that their services are of high quality in fact offer high-quality service, an assumption upon which the assertion that CDA's restrictions are anticompetitive at least implicitly relies. . . . Notably, there is no evidence that CDA prevents members from making objectively verifiable quality claims in their advertisements. Thus, if an independent, respected publication such as Consumer Reports were to rank the quality of various dentists in a community, we see nothing that would prevent those CDA members who performed well in such a survey from trumpeting their high rankings.

...

Misleading Advertising Driving Consumers Away
...

. . . This consideration . . . does not alter our view of the case in either party's favor.

Do the Restrictions Prevent Consumers from Being Misled?
...

. . . [U]nverifiable advertising may, by making a consumer less discerning, cause a patient to stay with a dentist longer than she otherwise might, thereby reducing the
(Continued)

(Case 20.2 continued)

ability of other (possibly superior) dentists to compete for her business. It should be noted, however, that while this argument has some plausibility, CDA has not put forth rigorous psychological evidence supporting its assertion. . . . Thus, we view this argument as slight additional support for the procompetitive tendencies of CDA's policies.

The Restrictions as a Ban on Puffery

...

While CDA argues that its policies only prohibit advertisements that it considers false or misleading, CDA does not argue that its policies are no more than a prohibition on puffery. . . .

...

In order to prevail under rule-of-reason analysis, the FTC must show that CDA's restrictions engendered a net harm to competition in the California dental service market. After weighing the evidence summarized in the discussion above, we conclude that the FTC has not met that burden, and that substantial evidence therefore does not support the Commission's determination.

...

. . . [B]ecause CDA's advertising restrictions do not harm consumer welfare, there is no antitrust violation.

RESULT The CDA's limitations on advertising were not a violation of Section 5 of the Federal Trade Commission Act because they did not have an anticompetitive effect.

QUESTIONS

1. How might misleading discount advertising drive consumers away from dentists?
2. Would the CDA rules permit a dentist to advertise a guarantee to replace for free any filling or crown that fails within one year?

Trade and professional associations often disseminate information among their members. Association agreements rarely state goals that violate the Sherman Act, so courts must draw inferences about the probable effects of the information exchanged. Courts will consider the structure of the market and the type of information exchanged to ensure that the exchange of information does not facilitate anticompetitive behavior, such as price-fixing or market division.

A large *cartel,* or group of competitors that agrees to do something, is inherently unstable. Conversely, the fewer the companies, the more likely they will agree and be able to enforce the agreement. Therefore, the more concentrated the industry, the more closely courts will scrutinize trade-association activity.

An example of an extremely effective cartel is the one controlled by De Beers of South Africa, which has dominated the world's diamond market for decades. In the 1950s, the company controlled the sale of more than 80 percent of all diamonds and frequently used more than market power to maintain its hold. Although the opening of new mines in Australia and Canada, increased smuggling in Central and West Africa, and Russia's unwillingness to cooperate with De Beers after the breakup of the Soviet Union have loosened the South African company's iron grip on the diamond market, it still produced more than 40 percent of the world's diamonds in 2000. Despite its recent stumbles, De Beers has been remarkably successful in maintaining a cartel for one hundred years—much longer than other companies have been able to maintain cartels in other industries.[21]

The type of information exchanged within a trade association plays an even more critical role than market structure in the analysis. For example, a weekly report disseminated by a hardwood manufacturers' trade asso-

21. James Surowiecki, *The Diamond Market vs. the Free Market,* New Yorker, July 31, 2000, at 27.

ciation listed the names of companies that sold lumber and the prices at which they sold it. Additionally, monthly reports discussed future price trends and provided future estimates of production. The U.S. Supreme Court held that this exchange of information violated Section 1 of the Sherman Act, as members could utilize the information to police secret agreements setting uniform prices or terms.[22] Another manufacturers' association disseminated information on average costs and the terms of past transactions, but it did not identify individual sellers or buyers and did not discuss future pricing. The Supreme Court found no violation of Section 1.[23]

Information that does not involve prices or terms of sale receives less scrutiny by the courts. Activities such as cooperative industrial research, market surveys, and joint advertising concerning the industry have been upheld. The exchange of information concerning contractors whose payments were two months in arrears was upheld

22. American Column & Lumber Co. v. United States, 257 U.S. 377 (1921).
23. Maple Flooring Mfrs. Ass'n v. United States, 268 U.S. 563 (1925).

as a reasonable way to help members avoid contractor fraud.[24]

 # Types *of* Vertical Restraints

Unlawful *vertical restraints,* that is, restraints between firms at different levels in the chain of distribution, include price-fixing, market division, tying arrangements, and some franchise agreements.

VERTICAL PRICE-FIXING

The Supreme Court has determined that agreements on price between firms at different levels of production or distribution can be as anticompetitive as agreements between direct competitors at the same level of production or distribution. Thus, for many years, vertical price-fixing— also known as *resale price maintenance (RPM)* when the

24. Cement Mfrs. Protective Ass'n v. United States, 268 U.S. 588 (1925).

B2B Electronic Marketplaces

The Internet has provided an opportunity for companies to conduct business electronically by creating Web sites where buyers and sellers can meet to transact business. Business-to-business (B2B) exchanges have raised concerns about whether companies may be using the exchange of information as a way to form agreements in violation of antitrust laws. Specifically, B2B exchanges may increase the risk of "coordinated interaction"—an antitrust term referring to action by a group of firms that is profitable for the group as a result of the concerted actions of the group members. If this concerted action involves collusion, it could violate antitrust laws. For example, a B2B exchange may allow sellers to view the prices of other sellers and thus encourage price-fixing or price stabilization without an express agreement. Alternatively, it could enable buyers to form a group to drive down the prices they will pay to suppliers or the wages they will pay to employees.

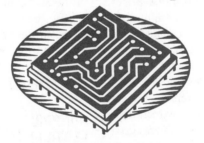

In June 2000, the Federal Trade Commission (FTC) sponsored a workshop on B2Bs, entitled "Competition Policy in the World of B2B Electronic Marketplaces," where businesspeople, policymakers, and attorneys discussed issues raised by conducting business over the Internet.[a] Following the conference, the FTC issued the report *Entering the 21st Century: Competition Policy in the B2B Electronic Marketplaces;* the report discusses antitrust issues raised during the workshop and outlines a framework for addressing antitrust issues in the B2B context.[b]

In September 2000, the FTC closed its investigation of Covisint, a plan by major

auto manufacturers Ford, General Motors, Nissan, Toyota, Renault, and DaimlerChrysler to build an e-marketplace for trading auto components and materials. The companies estimated that they will eventually spend $300 billion annually at this Web site. The FTC commenced its investigation to determine whether the exchange would violate Section 7 of the Clayton Act. Although the FTC found that no violation had occurred, it indicated that it would keep a close eye on Covisint as it develops.

In the summer of 2000, the European Commission (EC) permitted a joint venture designed to provide B2B business for aerospace companies, MyAircraft.com, to proceed. The EC's investigation revealed that the new joint venture would face strong competition from other similar Web sites in the same sector.

a. William M. Hannary, *Traditional Rules Still Apply to Nontraditional Commerce,* 69 U.S.L.W. 2243 (Oct. 31, 2000).
b. *Id.*

agreement fixes minimum prices—has been held to be a *per se* violation of the Sherman Act. RPM agreements have been challenged by consumers claiming overcharges, by competitors claiming loss of sales, and by dealers or retailers terminated by the manufacturer for offering discounts from list or suggested prices. As discussed later in this chapter, however, a competitor cannot successfully challenge RPM unless it can show antitrust injury.

Resale price maintenance has been unlawful *per se* since 1911, when the U.S. Supreme Court held that an agreement between a drug manufacturer and its distributors setting both wholesale and retail prices violated Section 1 of the Sherman Act. Such restrictions impermissibly limited the freedom of choice of other drug distributors and retailers. As a result, society was deprived of the benefits that it would have received from unrestricted distribution of the drugs.[25]

Some academics and jurists have challenged the treatment of RPM as a *per se* violation. They argue that most vertical price restrictions do not limit competition among competitors or give them power to restrict output or to raise prices. They contend that vertical price restrictions ensure economic efficiencies and maximize consumer welfare by preventing price competition that forces retailers to cut back on nonprice items such as consumer service.

The Supreme Court has so far rejected these arguments with regard to maintenance of *minimum* prices and has retained the *per se* rule against vertical minimum price-fixing. It has, however, greatly increased the plaintiff's burden of proof by requiring evidence of an agreement on specific price levels. Many antitrust lawyers believe that this change in the analysis has dealt a fatal blow to attempts by terminated discounters to invoke the *per se* rule in cases alleging RPM. Very few manufacturers are clumsy enough to insist that their dealers agree on specific minimum prices.

In *State Oil Co. v. Khan*,[26] the Supreme Court held that "vertical maximum price fixing, like the majority of commercial arrangements subject to the antitrust laws, should be evaluated under the rule of reason." In so ruling, the Court overturned *Albrecht v. Herald Co.*,[27] which had held that maximum vertical price-fixing was *per se* illegal. Reiterating that "the primary purpose of the antitrust laws is to protect interbrand competition," the Court explained that low prices "benefit consumers regardless of how those prices are set, and so long as they are above predatory levels, they do not threaten competition." The Court did not deem vertical maximum price-fixing legal *per se* but ruled only that it should be analyzed under a rule of reason "to identify those situations in which [it] amounts to anticompetitive conduct." But the Court was careful to point out that vertical *minimum* price-fixing remains illegal *per se*, although it did not offer a new rationale for that prohibition.

As noted earlier, Section 1 of the Sherman Act addresses only concerted action. Because unilateral action is not prohibited, a manufacturer or distributor can announce list prices to dealers, and the dealers may decide independently to follow those suggestions. Similarly, manufacturers and distributors may advertise suggested retail prices. Indeed, a manufacturer or distributor may (absent any intent to create or maintain a monopoly) announce that it will terminate any dealer that does not charge its suggested list prices and then terminate those who do not do so (because the conduct is entirely unilateral).[28] Most manufacturers and distributors do not want to terminate dealers that violate the policy, however. They, therefore, frequently use termination as a threat to coerce agreement. Once there is agreement, there is a violation of Section 1. Any threats of sanctions that interfere with a retailer's freedom to set its own minimum price for the goods or services that it sells will constitute an unreasonable restraint of trade in violation of the Sherman Act. Similarly, if the manufacturer or distributor becomes a clearinghouse for dealers' complaints about another dealer's failure to charge the suggested list price and the manufacturer or distributor agrees to police the prices charged by the other dealer, then concerted action has occurred.

NONPRICE VERTICAL RESTRAINTS AND VERTICAL MARKET DIVISION

Vertical market division is an arrangement imposed by a manufacturer on its distributors or dealers that limits their freedom to market the manufacturer's product. Such an agreement may establish exclusive distributorships, territorial or customer restrictions, location clauses, areas of primary responsibility, and the like. These nonprice vertical restrictions are not illegal *per se*. Rather, they are judged under the rule of reason.

The central inquiry is whether the reduction in intrabrand competition is justified by interbrand competition. The higher the market share of a particular manufacturer's product, the greater the likelihood that a decline in intrabrand competition will violate the rule of reason.

---

25. Dr. Miles Medical Co. v. John D. Park & Sons Co., 220 U.S. 373 (1911).
26. 522 U.S. 3 (1997).
27. 390 U.S. 145 (1968).

28. United States v. Colgate & Co., 250 U.S. 300 (1919).

For example, suppose that Pixel Unlimited controls 80 percent of the market for high-definition television (HDTV) screens in Atlanta, Georgia, and sells its products through five independent retail outlets. Pixel agrees with three of its dealers to terminate the other two. Although a reduction in competition among Pixel dealers might arguably increase interbrand HDTV competition, given Pixel's high market share, that increase would not offset the anticompetitive effect of the decrease in Pixel intrabrand competition. Accordingly, the reduction in the number of Pixel dealers might violate Section 1.

Exclusive Distributorships In an *exclusive distributorship*, a manufacturer limits itself to a single distributor in a given territory or, perhaps, line of business. As long as a manufacturer does not have dominant market power, it may allocate different geographic areas to its distributors and refuse to sell to other potential distributors in those areas. Exclusive distributorships have been upheld under the rule of reason when there is some competitive pressure that limits the market power of the retailers holding them. Exclusive automobile dealerships for particular geographic regions are the classic example. This restriction on intrabrand competition is permissible because of the intense interbrand competition among U.S. and foreign automobile manufacturers.

In the following case, the court considered the legality of exclusive distributorships in the provision of supplemental news to Chicago's newspapers.

A CASE IN POINT

CASE 20.3

Paddock Publishing, Inc. v. Chicago Tribune Co.
United States Court of Appeals for the Seventh Circuit
103 F.3d 42 (7th Cir. 1996), cert. denied, 520 U.S. 1265 (1997).

In the Language of the Court

FACTS The two largest newspapers in Chicago are the *Chicago Tribune* and the *Sun–Times*. In addition to printing the work of its own staff, the *Tribune* prints stories from the New York Times News Service, a supplemental news service to which it subscribes. The New York Times News Service, which provides news and other material of interest to newspapers around the world, is one of many supplemental news providers that offer exclusive contracts to newspapers in each metropolitan area. The *Sun–Times* subscribes to the Los Angeles Times/Washington Post News Service. As a result, stories provided by the Los Angeles Times/Washington Post News Service to the *Sun–Times* are not available to the *Tribune* or any other Chicago newspaper, and stories provided by the New York Times News Service to the *Tribune* are not available to the *Sun–Times* or any other newspapers in Chicago.

Because the news providers charge their subscribers according to circulation, they strive to sign up the largest paper in each market. Similarly, newspapers prefer exclusive licensing because printing the same stories as their competitors would make them less distinctive and valuable to readers. As a result, the larger newspapers subscribe to the more popular services, and the smaller newspapers are left to subscribe to the less popular services for their supplemental news. Chicago's third-largest newspaper, the *Daily Herald,* was further disadvantaged because the third most popular provider was owned by the *Tribune,* which refused to license its stories to a competitor in its home market.

The *Daily Herald* challenged the pattern of exclusive distributorships as a violation of Section 1 of the Sherman Act, because it effectively denied the *Herald* the opportunity to subscribe to the best supplemental news services. The trial court dismissed the *Daily Herald's* complaint for failure to state a claim. The paper appealed.

ISSUE PRESENTED Does a pattern of exclusive distributorships in a market violate the Sherman Act?

OPINION EASTERBROOK, J., writing for the U.S. Court of Appeals for the Seventh Circuit:

The *Herald* does not contend that the *Tribune* has conspired with the *Sun–Times* to bring about this state of affairs. Nor does it contend that the supplemental news services and features syndicators (or their contributing papers and authors) have agreed among themselves. It concedes that each has adopted its method of doing business

(Continued)

(Case 20.3 continued)

independently; they take the same approach to distribution because each has discovered that it is the most profitable way to do business. All of the contracts between services and newspapers are terminable at will or on short notice (usually 30 days, although some features require a year's notice). . . .

This is fundamentally an "essential facilities" claim—but without any essential facility. There are three supplemental news services that the *Herald* is willing to acknowledge as major competitors (and others besides, though the *Herald* denigrates them). There are hundreds, if not thousands, of opinion and entertainment features; a newspaper deprived of access to the *New York Times* crosswords puzzles can find others, even if the *Times* has the best known one. . . . [T]his case does not involve a single facility that monopolizes one level of production and creates a potential to extend the monopoly to others. We have, instead, competition at each level of production; no one can "take over" another level of production by withholding access from disfavored rivals. . . . [T]he existence of three competing facilities not only means that none is an "essential facility" but also means that each of the three is entitled to sign an exclusive contract with a favored user. Other firms that want to enter the market can do so by competing at intervals for these contracts.

Competition-for-the-contract is a form of competition that antitrust laws protect rather than proscribe, and it is common. Every year or two, General Motors, Ford, and Chrysler invite tire manufacturers to bid for exclusive rights to have their tires used in the manufacturers' cars. Exclusive contracts make the market hard to enter in mid-year but cannot stifle competition over the longer run, and competition of this kind drives down the price of tires, to the ultimate benefit of consumers. Just so in the news business—if smaller newspapers are willing to bid with cash rather than legal talent. In the meantime, exclusive stories and features help the newspapers differentiate themselves, the better to compete with one another. A market in which every newspaper carried the same stories, columns, and cartoons would be a less vigorous market than the existing one. And a market in which the creators of intellectual property (such as the *New York Times*) could not decide how best to market it for maximum profit would be a market with less (or less interesting) intellectual property created in the first place. No one can take the supply of well researched and written news as a given; legal rulings that diminish the incentive to find and explicate the news (by reducing the return from that business) have little to commend them.

In what way could the news services' practices harm consumers? Tacit collusion (economists' term for "shared monopoly") could be a source of monopoly profits and injury to consumers even if none of the stages of production is monopolized. Some distribution arrangements might be objectionable because they facilitate tacit collusion. But collusion, tacit or express, requires some horizontal cooperation, or at least forbearance from vigorous competition among rivals. Although the newspaper market is concentrated on the readers' side, the inputs to newspaper production are unconcentrated and therefore do not facilitate tacit collusion in the more concentrated market. The New York Times News Service competes for column inches of ink not only with other supplemental news services but also with the Associated Press, Reuters, and the reporters of the subscribing papers. . . .

What the *Herald* does argue is that a mixture of fewness of firms, exclusive contracts, and relations between suppliers and users of news that endure despite short contract terms, hampers the growth of small rivals even though each market is competitive. Such an argument does not come within any of the economic approaches to tacit collusion—but it does, the *Herald* insists, come within the holding of [previous cases].

(Continued)

(Case 20.3 continued)

...

[The case relied on by the *Daily Herald*] involved exclusive dealing, while this case involves exclusive distributorships. Despite the similarity in nomenclature, there is a difference. . . . An exclusive dealing contract obliges a firm to obtain its inputs from a single source. . . . None of the newspapers in Chicago (or anywhere else) has promised by contract to obtain all of its news from a single source—and the sources have not locked all of their output together. . . . A new entrant to the supplemental news service business could sell to every newspaper in the United States, if it chose to do so. . . .

[In *Theatre Enterprises, Inc. v. Paramount Film Distributing Corp.*, the] FTC and the Supreme Court concluded that even exclusive dealing contracts are lawful if limited to a year's duration. The Commission saw that exclusivity can promote competition by making it feasible for firms to invest in promoting their products—for these costs would not be recoverable if the contracts were of very short terms, or if rivals could exhibit the same films and obtain the benefit of this promotional activity. Moreover, with year-long contracts, the entire market is up for grabs. A new entrant can sell to a twelfth of the theaters in the first month, a sixth of all theaters by the end of the second month, and so on; competition for the contract makes it possible to have the benefits of exclusivity and rivalry simultaneously. Things work similarly in the newspaper business. Contract terms are short, so competition for the contract can flourish. Meanwhile, exclusive distribution of news or features through a single paper in a city helps the paper distinguish itself from, and compete with, its rivals. The *Sun–Times* will not promote a readership for a particular columnist if the *Tribune* and the *Herald* carry the same column; free-riding would spoil the investment and thwart this aspect of competition.

RESULT The trial court's dismissal of the case was affirmed. The exclusive distribution agreements were not unreasonable restraints on trade.

COMMENTS In addition to rejecting the *Daily Herald*'s claim, the court showed its contempt for the paper's attempt to use antitrust law against its successful competitors by noting that the *Herald* had never even tried to outbid the *Tribune* or *Sun–Times* for their supplemental news service subscriptions. In its conclusion, the court sharply offered the paper some advice: "The *Herald* has never tried to make a better offer, and we conclude that it has come to the wrong forum. It should try to outbid the *Tribune* and *Sun–Times* in the marketplace, rather than to outmaneuver them in court."

QUESTIONS

1. If the publishers of the *Tribune* and the *Sun–Times* had agreed with each other to subscribe to supplemental news services only on an exclusive basis, how would the court have viewed the *Daily Herald*'s claim?
2. How would the market for news have been affected if the *Daily Herald* had succeeded in eliminating exclusive distribution agreements?

Territorial and Customer Restrictions *Territorial* and *customer restrictions* prevent a dealer or distributor from selling outside a certain territory or to a certain class of customers. For example, a Dow representative selling industrial chemicals might be permitted to sell only to hardware stores, and only in a specified area. The Supreme Court has held that vertical territorial or customer restrictions are not *per se* violations of Section 1. Such restrictions often increase interbrand competition; thus, an accompanying reduction of intrabrand competition may be permissible.

A manufacturer cannot disguise an agreement to maintain minimum resale prices as a territorial restriction, however. A court will look beyond the form of the transaction to the substance and will use the *per se* rule to strike down what is in reality a vertical minimum price restraint. Similarly, where a number of retailers combine to force a manufacturer to impose an ostensibly vertical agreement on its retailers, the agreement is in reality horizontal and will be deemed a *per se* violation of Section 1.

Dual Distributors A manufacturer that sells its goods both wholesale and at retail is called a *dual distributor*. Early decisions held that such an arrangement was unlikely to create the efficiencies and increased competition created by permissible forms of vertical nonprice agreements. Accordingly, restraints imposed by dual distributors were considered illegal *per se*. The trend in recent decisions, however, is to analyze such restraints under the rule of reason (as long as they originate with the manufacturer, not the retailers), because they can have beneficial economic effects.

TYING ARRANGEMENTS

Tying arrangements can be challenged under Section 1 of the Sherman Act or Section 3 of the Clayton Act. The Clayton Act specifically prohibits tying arrangements in commodities, while the Sherman Act prohibits tying arrangements generally. The legal analysis applied under the two statutes has converged; thus, the following analysis applies to both Clayton Act and Sherman Act claims.

In a *tying arrangement*, the seller will sell product A (the *tying*, or desired, product) to the customer only if the customer agrees to purchase product B (the *tied* product) from the seller. A tying arrangement is a way of forcing a buyer to purchase a product or service it would not buy on the product's or service's own merits.

For example, suppose that Metro Cable expands its cable-television service into a new town. The public utilities commission grants Metro the exclusive right to provide cable service in the new town. Metro is a subsidiary of Moviemax, a company that provides a cable-television movie channel for subscribers. To improve Moviemax's profit margin, the marketing vice president decides to require all of Metro's customers to subscribe to Moviemax. In this example, the tying product is the basic cable service. The tied product is the Moviemax television channel.

Tying arrangements unreasonably restrain trade by preventing competitors from selling their goods to customers obliged to buy the tied product. In the Moviemax example, the tying arrangement would make it more difficult for other movie channels, such as HBO, to sell their product to cable customers in the new town.

Tying arrangements also restrict the freedom of choice of purchasers who are forced to buy the tied product.

Tying arrangements have traditionally been held to be *per se* violations, provided that (1) the tying and tied products are separate products, (2) the availability of the tying product is conditioned upon the purchase of the tied product, (3) the party imposing the tie has enough market power in the tying product market to force the purchase of the tied product, and (4) a "not insubstantial" amount of commerce in the tied product is affected.

Separate Products Whether there are separate products may be difficult to determine. Firms often label or market a combination of goods and services as a single product. The courts attempt to determine whether there are two economically distinct products by considering whether a separate demand exists for each product. For example, in one case the Supreme Court found that below-market financing that was provided to buyers of prefabricated metal homes was a separate product from the homes themselves. A key issue in the Justice Department's case against Microsoft Corporation, discussed in this chapter's "Inside Story," is whether Microsoft's Internet Explorer Web browser is a separate product from Microsoft's Windows operating system.

Condition of Sale If the tying product can be purchased on nondiscriminatory terms, without the tied product, there is no tie. It has been suggested that a manufacturer should not make a second product technologically interdependent with the purchased product such that technology, rather than contract terms, forces customers to buy both. To date, however, these technological ties have been found lawful as long as there is no separate demand for the products involved, or the interdependent products provide functionalities not available if each product is purchased separately.

Market Power The nature and extent of the market power required are frequently litigated. As the Supreme Court defines it, *market power* is "the power to force a purchaser to do something that he would not do in a competitive market."[29] It is ordinarily inferred from a firm's predominant share of the market, but in tying claims the issue is how power in one market translates into power in another. The extent to which power in one market allows a producer or seller to exploit another market depends on the *cross-elasticity of demand,* that is, the sensitivity of consumer demand for one good to the

29. Eastman Kodak Co. v. Image Technical Servs., Inc., 504 U.S. 451 (1992).

price of another good. The lower the cross-elasticity of demand between, say, gasoline and cars, the less sensitive is consumers' demand for cars to the price of gasoline. Hence, a car dealership with dominant market power in cars would be better able to leverage that power to dominate the gasoline market. The higher the cross-elasticity, the more sensitive the demand for cars is to the price of gasoline and the less able the dealership is to translate its market power in cars to market power in gasoline. Hence, the first dealership would be better able to dominate the gasoline market by requiring its car customers to purchase its gasoline even as it raises the cost of that gasoline.

A firm's ability to translate power in one market to power in another is often a function of product complementarity. If product B is needed to make product A work, then the firm controlling the market for product A will have a good shot at forcing consumers to buy the complementary product (B) from it. Courts have not fashioned any precise formula using market share and cross-elasticity of demand by which firms can discern ahead of time the line between antitrust violation and shrewd business.

Effect on Commerce A "not insubstantial" amount of commerce is affected if more than a trifling dollar amount is involved.

Business Justification Unlike other *per se* violations, a tying arrangement may be upheld if there is a business justification for it. In a Ninth Circuit decision,[30] Mercedes–Benz's policy of requiring its dealers to sell only factory-made parts was upheld. The court ruled that this tying arrangement was justified by the assurance it provided to Mercedes that service on its automobiles, important in preserving their high-quality image, would not be performed with substandard parts.

Some lower courts have allowed tying arrangements in fledgling industries. For example, one court upheld a tying arrangement that required purchasers of cable-television satellite antennas to purchase service contracts to ensure proper functioning of the antennas.[31]

Thus, although the courts continue to say that tying arrangements are *per se* illegal, they apply a flexible *per se* rule that considers market power and business justifications. Tying arrangements are in effect judged under a type of rule of reason.

FRANCHISE AGREEMENTS

A *franchise* is a business relationship in which one party (the franchisor) grants to another party (the franchisee) the right to use the franchisor's name and logo and to distribute the franchisor's products from a specified locale. (Franchises are discussed further in Chapter 22.) The franchise agreement may provide that the franchisor will not grant another franchise within a specified distance of the franchisee's business location. The Supreme Court has held that under the rule of reason, vertical market division between a franchisor and a franchisee may be lawful when interbrand competition is enhanced by the limitation on intrabrand competition.[32] Such division may take the form of limits on the number of franchisees in a geographic region and restrictions on the sale of franchisor products to specifically franchised locations.

Antitrust issues are also raised when a franchisor, in an effort to promote uniformity and name recognition, imposes certain types of limitations on the franchisee. For example, a McDonald's hamburger franchisee might be required to have all employees wear an approved uniform and to decorate the restaurant in an approved fashion. Requirements for the franchisee to purchase goods or equipment from the franchisor have been challenged as illegal tying arrangements. For example, ice cream manufacturer Baskin Robbins was accused of imposing an illegal tying arrangement when it required all franchisees to buy their ice cream from Baskin Robbins. The tying claim was rejected because Baskin Robbins had no market power over the tying product; ice cream franchises, like automobile franchises, face intense interbrand competition. No one franchisor had the ability to dominate the market even if it did require all of its franchisees to buy its products.

Several recent cases suggest, however, that a franchisor might have market power if the franchisor keeps the purchase requirement secret from the would-be franchisee and the franchisee cannot easily recoup its investment in the franchise. In such a case, the franchisee could be "locked in" and not be free to acquire a different franchise on more favorable terms.

⚖ Antitrust Injury

To recover damages, a plaintiff must establish that it sustained an *antitrust injury,* that is, a loss due to a competition-reducing aspect or effect of the defendant's violation of the Sherman Act. A plaintiff may not recover

30. The Mozart Co. v. Mercedes–Benz of North Am., Inc., 833 F.2d 1342 (9th Cir. 1987), *cert. denied,* 488 U.S. 870 (1988).

31. United States v. Jerrold Elecs. Corp., 187 F. Supp. 545 (E.D. Pa. 1960), *aff'd,* 365 U.S. 567 (1961).

32. Continental T.V., Inc. v. GTE Sylvania, Inc., 433 U.S. 36 (1977).

under the antitrust laws for losses that resulted from competition as such.

In 1990, the Supreme Court considered whether resale price maintenance (RPM) gives rise to an antitrust injury in the absence of predatory pricing. USA Petroleum, an independent gasoline retailer, claimed that Atlantic Richfield Company (ARCO), an integrated oil company, conspired with retail service stations selling ARCO-brand gasoline to fix prices at below-market levels. USA Petroleum argued that this was an illegal maximum RPM scheme whereby the competition that would otherwise exist among ARCO-brand dealers was eliminated by agreement. As a result, the retail price of ARCO-brand gasoline was maintained at artificially low and uncompetitive levels. This allegedly drove many independents in California out of business.

The U.S. Supreme Court held that USA Petroleum could not recover damages for ARCO's RPM because there was no showing of predatory pricing, that is, pricing below cost designed to drive competitors out of the market.[33] The Court reasoned that when the prices under an RPM program are set at nonpredatory levels, there is generally no anticompetitive effect, even though such pricing may reduce the market share of competitors or the price that they may charge consumers. Without doubt, those competitors are injured as a result of the practice, but there is nothing anticompetitive about that in and of itself. Indeed, such a result benefits the consumer. In such a case, the Court held, the competitor may not recover damages under the antitrust laws. (The *ARCO* case was decided seven years before the Court's decision in *State Oil Co. v. Khan* eliminating *per se* treatment of maximum RPM and in many ways laid the groundwork for that decision.)

Limitations *on* Antitrust Enforcement

The courts have limited the private enforcement rights of individual citizens and states by invoking the doctrine of standing. They have also limited the liability of state governments by applying state-action exemptions.

STANDING

To prevent private parties from jumping on the treble-damages bandwagon, the Supreme Court requires that a private plaintiff have *standing* to sue; that is, the plaintiff must have suffered an injury from the defendant's viola-

ETHICAL CONSIDERATION

False disparaging statements about a rival may rise to the level of antitrust violation only when they have significant and enduring anticompetitive effects.[a] Is it ethical to make such statements before they rise to the level of an antitrust violation? Is it ethical to threaten antitrust litigation to quiet a competitor's accurate but disparaging remarks about one's products?

a. American Prof. Testing Serv. Inc. v. Harcourt Brace Jovanovich Legal & Prof. Pub., Inc., 108 F.3d 1147 (9th Cir. 1997).

tion of the antitrust law. Thus, a consumer buying goods from an innocent middleman does not have standing to recover from a manufacturer that was a member of a price-fixing cartel.

More complicated standing issues arise when a company alleges that its competitors are violating the antitrust laws. For example, suppose that Connaught Gin complains that its competitor, Profumo Gin, has imposed an illegal exclusive dealing agreement on Connaught's former dealer, Liquor World. At first, Connaught's injury appears indirect compared with that of Liquor World. However, the central reason that the antitrust law is concerned with exclusive dealing agreements is their impact on the market opportunities of competitors. Accordingly, Connaught is granted standing because it has suffered injury of the kind that the antitrust laws are designed to prevent (and is a more likely plaintiff than Liquor World). The courts thus hold substance over form to promote the primary goal of the antitrust laws—fostering competition.

STATE-ACTION EXEMPTION

More than fifty years ago, the Supreme Court declared that the antitrust laws apply to anticompetitive actions by private parties, not to anticompetitive actions by state legislatures or administrative bodies. Thus, state action is exempt as long as (1) there is a clear state purpose to displace competition, and (2) the state provides adequate public supervision. For example, the California legislature passed a law designed to limit the production, and consequently raise the price, of raisins. Given that California produced nearly one-half of the world's raisins, the effect of this statute on interstate commerce was substantial. Nevertheless, the U.S. Supreme Court enunciated and applied the state-action exemption in this case.[34]

33. Atlantic Richfield Co. v. USA Petroleum Co., 495 U.S. 328 (1990).

34. Parker v. Brown, 317 U.S. 341 (1943).

The courts have refused to extend the exemption to local municipalities except in certain limited circumstances. The Local Government Antitrust Act of 1984, enacted to allay municipalities' fears of treble damages, eliminated local governments' liability for antitrust damages but preserved equitable remedies, such as injunctions. The act extended immunity from damages to all officials or employees acting in an official capacity.

Monopolies: Section 2 of the Sherman Act

Section 2 of the Sherman Act provides that "[e]very person who shall monopolize, or attempt to monopolize, or combine or conspire with any other person or persons, to monopolize any part of the trade or commerce among the several States, or with foreign nations, shall be deemed guilty of a felony."[35]

As under Section 1 of the Sherman Act, corporations can be fined up to $10 million (or double the gain to the violator or double the loss to the victim if that is more than $10 million) for each violation, and individuals can be fined up to $350,000 for each violation and imprisoned for up to three years. As a practical matter, however, violators of Section 2 are not prosecuted criminally.

A firm that possesses monopoly power is able to set prices at noncompetitive levels, harming both consumers and competitors. Consequently, Section 2 condemns actual or attempted monopolization of any market. Unlike Section 1, Section 2 does not require proof of an agreement or any other collective action; unilateral conduct may violate Section 2.

Section 2 does not, however, prohibit the mere possession of monopoly power. The offense of monopolization has two elements. The plaintiff must first show that the defendant has monopoly power in a relevant market and then that the defendant willfully acquired or maintained that power through anticompetitive acts. A firm that has monopoly power thrust upon it by circumstances or attains it by superior performance does not violate Section 2. Thus, a violation involves both a status element (the defendant must be an entity with monopoly power) and a conduct element (the defendant must commit anticompetitive acts).

MONOPOLY POWER

Courts define *monopoly power* (also called market power) as the power to control prices or exclude competition in a

35. 15 U.S.C. § 2 (1997).

 INTERNATIONAL CONSIDERATION

Article 85(1) of the Treaty of Rome, which created the European Economic Community (precursor to the European Union), prohibits agreements whose object or effect is to restrict competition in the European Union (EU). Agreements that violate Article 85(1) are automatically void under Article 85(2) and unenforceable before the national courts in the EU member states.

Article 85(2) prohibits abuse of an entity's dominant position. The question of what constitutes a dominant position is complex and depends on a number of factors, such as the firm's market share in the relevant market, the competitive pressures it faces, its ability to control price, and barriers to entry to its market.

For example, in 1980 the European Commission opened a proceeding against IBM, the world's largest computer manufacturer. The commission claimed that IBM had abused its dominant position in the supply of two key products (the central processing unit and the operating system) for its most powerful range of computers, System/370, in an effort to control the markets for the supply of all products compatible with System/370. The alleged abuses included (1) failing to supply other manufacturers in sufficient time with the technical interface information needed to permit competitive products to be used with System/370, (2) not offering System/370 central processing units (CPUs) without main memory included in the price, (3) not offering System/370 CPUs without the basic software included in the price, and (4) refusing to supply certain software installation services to users of non-IBM CPUs.

In 1984, IBM entered into an undertaking in which it agreed to offer its System/370 CPUs either without main memory or with only such capacity as was strictly required for testing and to disclose, in a timely manner, sufficient interface information to enable competitors to attach both their hardware and software products to System/370. IBM had previously advised the Commission that it had taken steps to make installation services available to all users of its software and was in the course of unbundling all software.[a]

a. Commission of the European Communities, *Fourteenth Report on Competition Policy* (1984).

relevant market. Monopoly power is marked by supracompetitive prices (that is, prices that are higher than they would be in a competitive market) over an extended period of time and the unavailability of substitute goods or services. The determination of whether a particular corporation has monopoly power usually requires complex

INTERNATIONAL CONSIDERATION

In a case brought in France by Orangina against Coca-Cola of France for abuse of dominant position, the French court ruled in 1997 that the relevant product market was all colas, not all soft drinks as Coca-Cola had asserted.[a]

a. David Buchan, *Orangina Takes Some Fizz Out of Coke*, FIN. TIMES, Jan. 30, 1997, at 2.

economic analysis. Presumptions based on market share and other structural characteristics of markets are used to simplify the analysis; but in practice, each case turns on its unique (and usually disputed) facts.

Defining the Relevant Market Competition takes place in discrete markets. Therefore, the existence of monopoly power can be determined only after the relevant market for the product is determined. Markets have two components: a product component and a geographic component.

Multiple-Brand Product Market The *multiple-brand product market* is made up of product or service offerings by different manufacturers or sellers that are economically interchangeable and may therefore be said to compete. Sometimes it is easy to identify substitutes. No one would deny that Coca-Cola competes against Pepsi. Frequently, the question is more complex. Does Coca-Cola compete against Dr Pepper? Almost certainly. Against powdered iced tea? That is harder to say.

These questions are important because the power of a seller to set prices above competitive levels is limited by the ability of purchasers to substitute other types of products. If purchasers are unable to substitute other goods in the face of a price increase, the seller can set prices at monopoly levels. The product market is that collection of goods or services that customers deem to be practically substitutable.

Single-Brand Product Market The Supreme Court in *Eastman Kodak Co. v. Image Technical Services, Inc.* held that "[b]ecause service and parts for Kodak equipment are not interchangeable with other manufacturers' service and parts, the relevant market from the Kodak-equipment owner's perspective is composed of only those companies that service Kodak machines."[36] The Court rejected Kodak's argument that the relevant market was all copy machines and that Kodak could not have market power as

36. 504 U.S. 451 (1992).

to Kodak parts and service for copy machines because it did not have market power in copy machines. Evidence in the case showed that Kodak controlled nearly 100 percent of the Kodak parts market and 80 to 95 percent of the Kodak service market, so Kodak-equipment owners had no readily available substitutes. Because of the high costs of switching to another brand, consumers could not readily change copy-machine manufacturers if Kodak unilaterally raised its service fees. Thus, in some cases, a single brand of a product or service may constitute a separate market in a Section 2 analysis.

Geographic Market Competition is also affected by geographic restraints on product movement. If a firm in Michigan is the only maker of widgets in the Midwest, it has the potential to exercise monopoly power unless widget makers from other parts of the country can profitably ship their products to that area. Some markets are national or even international in scope, for example, the markets for long-distance telephone service, supercom-

INTERNATIONAL CONSIDERATION

The European Commission has taken an approach similar to that used in the *Eastman Kodak* case in deciding whether a nondominant manufacturer of a primary product can be dominant with respect to a secondary market consisting solely of replacement parts, consumables, and maintenance services that must be technically compatible with the primary product. Relevant factors include the price and life of the primary product, the transparency of prices of secondary products, the prices of secondary products as a proportion of the primary product value, and information costs.

Applying these factors, the Commission rejected in 1995 the complaint of Pelikan, a German manufacturer of toner cartridges for printers, against Kyocera, a Japanese manufacturer of computer printers, including toner cartridges for those printers. The Commission found that Kyocera did not have a dominant position in the market of consumables. Purchasers were well informed about the price charged for consumables and appeared to take it into account in making their decision to buy a printer. Life-cycle costs of consumables (mainly toner cartridges) represented a very high proportion of the value of a printer. Therefore, if the prices for consumables of a particular brand were raised, consumers were not locked into a particular brand of toner and would have a strong incentive to buy another brand of printer.[a]

a. European Commission, *Twenty-fifth Report on Competition Policy 1995* (1996), at 41–42.

puter sales, and nuclear power plant designs. Other markets are localized, for example, markets for products that are expensive to transport, such as wet cement. The contours of geographic markets may also be affected by government regulations that confine firms to certain regions.

By defining the geographic market, antitrust courts try to separate firms that affect competition in a given region from those that do not. The geographic market encompasses all firms that compete for sales in a given area at current prices or would compete in that area if prices rose by a modest amount.

Market Share Once the relevant market is determined, the plaintiff must show that, within this market, the defendant possessed monopoly power. The Supreme Court has held that monopoly power may be inferred from a firm's predominant share of the market because a dominant share of the market often carries with it the power to control output across the market and thereby control prices. In determining market share, the initial definition of the relevant market is crucial. For example, Perrier mineral water could be considered part of the market for imported mineral water. Perrier's competitors would include other imported mineral-water sellers like Pellegrino. Perrier has a major share of that market. On the other hand, if the market is defined as all mineral water (including, for example, Calistoga and Poland Springs), then Perrier's market share would be considerably smaller. Consequently, how a relevant market is defined often determines whether a particular firm has a dominant share of the market.

In one case, the Supreme Court found that 87 percent of the market was a predominant share sufficient to create a presumption of monopoly power. As a general proposition, firms with market shares in excess of 60 percent are especially vulnerable to Section 2 litigation. When a single brand of a product or service constitutes the relevant market, market share may be 100 percent.

Barriers to Entry Market shares do not, however, conclusively establish monopoly power. Market share must be analyzed in the context of other characteristics of the market in question. The plaintiff must show that new competitors face high market barriers to entry and that current competitors lack the ability to expand their output to challenge a monopolist's high prices. Common entry barriers include patents, governmental licenses or approvals, control of essential or superior resources, entrenched buyer preferences, economies of scale, and, according to some authorities, high initial capital requirements. Courts will also look at profit levels, market trends, pricing patterns, product differentiation, and government regulation. Es-

sentially, the court is trying to determine the likelihood that another company will become a viable competitor in the relevant market if there is a small but significant nontransitory increase in price levels.

MONOPOLISTIC INTENT

Once the presence of monopoly power is established, the defendant's intent may be relevant. Some cases hold that the plaintiff must prove that the defendant's conduct lacks a legitimate business purpose. Other cases hold that the initial burden is on the defendant to prove a legitimate business purpose; if it does so, the plaintiff must then prove a monopolistic intent. It is possible to prove intent through evidence of statements by the monopolist's executive expressing a desire to eliminate competition. Hostility between competitors is commonplace, however, and may even be beneficial to vigorous competition. Therefore, the courts often require that *monopolistic intent* be proved by evidence of conduct (not merely statements) that is inherently anticompetitive.

A defendant may rebut allegations of monopolistic intent by showing that its success in the marketplace is the result of "superior skill, foresight, and industry." A monopoly earned by superior performance is not unlawful. Indeed, the law recognizes that the possibility of attaining such a monopoly may be a powerful incentive to vigorous competition, which benefits consumers. Therefore, a key issue in Section 2 litigation is whether the defendant acquired or maintained its monopoly by procompetitive acts or by anticompetitive acts. Anticompetitive acts include predatory pricing and, under certain circumstances, refusal to deal.

PREDATORY PRICING

The courts have not settled on a single definition of *predatory pricing,* that is, the attempt to eliminate rivals by undercutting their prices to the point that they lose money and go out of business, leaving the monopolist unrestrained by competition and thus able to raise its prices. The courts have struggled to develop principles that distinguish between such anticompetitive pricing and the procompetitive pricing that occurs when a more efficient firm competes vigorously yet fairly against its rivals. In the latter case, the more efficient firm could undercut its rivals, forcing them out of business, and a lawful monopoly would result.

When prices are above average variable cost but below average total cost and the company has excess capacity, courts will usually find the pricing legal. (*Variable cost* is the cost of producing the next incremental unit; *total*

E C O N O M I C   P E R S P E C T I V E

The Regulation *of* Natural Monopolies

In the imagined world of perfect competition, *productive efficiency* (an equilibrium in which only the lowest-cost producers of goods and services survive) and *allocative efficiency* (an equilibrium in which scarce societal resources are allocated to the production of various goods and services up to the point where the cost of the resources equals the benefit society reaps from their use) would go hand in hand. In the real world, however, this is not always so. For example, the most cost-efficient way to provide telephone connections to homes is to link all of the homes to one central station, using one set of lines. Competition would require duplication of this expensive infrastructure; productive efficiency is best served by a monopoly. But the pricing policy of a monopolist is not controlled by competition. Consequently, the unregulated price of local telephone service would rise above the socially efficient level, and allocative efficiency would be impaired (see Exhibit 20.2). This can be remedied only

by regulation of such industries, which are known as natural monopolies.

For many years, the American Telephone and Telegraph Company (AT&T) enjoyed a regulated monopoly in both local and long-distance telecommunications. The provision of long-distance service is not a natural monopoly because more than one network of intercity telephone lines can be profitably operated. Nonetheless, there was no competition in long-distance service because AT&T controlled access to the lines to individual homes.

In 1974, the U.S. government brought an antitrust suit against AT&T, charging

monopolization of the telecommunications industry in violation of Section 2 of the Sherman Act. The case was decided in 1983.[a] In 1984, AT&T signed a consent decree to enable competition to flourish in the long-distance market. The decree provided for (1) the breakup of AT&T's monopoly over local service by creating seven regional telecommunications companies, known as the Baby Bells, and (2) a complex set of rules to ensure that both AT&T and other companies providing long-distance service, such as MCI and Sprint, would have equal access to the local networks. The Baby Bells would, of course, be subject to regulation because each of them would still enjoy a monopoly in the provision of local telephone service.

a. United States v. American Tel. & Tel. Co., 552 F. Supp. 131 (D.D.C. 1982), *aff'd sub nom.*, Maryland v. United States, 460 U.S. 1001 (1983).

---

cost includes variable cost and fixed costs, such as rent and overhead.) If a company does not have excess capacity, the legality of the pricing depends on the company's intent; the cases are very fact-specific. Prices below average variable cost are presumptively illegal unless the business can demonstrate that the pricing is an introductory offer or that costs will fall dramatically as the company progresses along the learning curve. At some point, pricing below cost becomes economically irrational unless the predator is anticipating the long-term gains that would result from destroying its rivals.

Some academics have argued that predatory pricing is self-defeating in all but a few market scenarios. Having eliminated its rivals, the predator needs to keep its old rivals, and new entrants, out of the market when it raises its prices to recoup its losses. That will be difficult as the high prices—and high profits—can be expected to attract new entrants. Thus, predatory pricing is an irrational strategy unless the market, because of barriers to entry or other factors, is structurally conducive to monopolization.

The Supreme Court has accepted this argument. In 1986, the Court rejected a claim brought by U.S. television manufacturers against their Japanese counterparts.[37] It held that some allegations of predation are inherently implausible because the marketplace cannot be successfully monopolized. In such cases, there is no Sherman Act violation, whatever monopolistic intent the defendant may have had. This has been referred to as the *rule of impossibility.*[38]

In 1999, the California Supreme Court considered whether a cellular company's predatory pricing violated California's Unfair Practices Act.[39] The Los Angeles Cellular Telephone Company was one of two companies licensed by the federal government to provide cellular telephone service in the Los Angeles area. In addition to

37. *See, e.g.,* Matsushita Elec. Indus. Co. v. Zenith Radio Corp., 475 U.S. 574 (1986).
38. *See, e.g.,* Brooke Group, Ltd. v. Brown & Williamson Tobacco Corp., 509 U.S. 209 (1993).
39. Cel-Tech Communication, Inc. v. L.A. Cellular Tel. Co., 973 P.2d 527 (Cal. 1999).

EXHIBIT 20.2 Welfare Loss from Monopoly

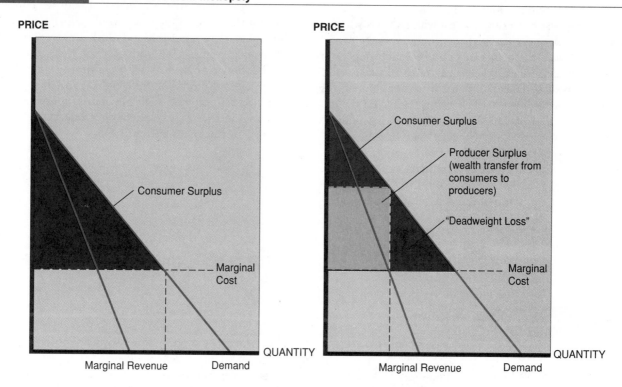

COMPETITIVE MARKET   MONOPOLY

DEFINITION OF TERMS

Consumer surplus The difference between the value of a good to consumers (measured by the price they would be willing to pay for the good) and the price they actually must pay to obtain the good.

Producer surplus The difference between the cost to producers of producing a good (measured by the minimum price at which they would sell a given quantity of the good) and the price they actually receive in the market.

Total surplus The sum of producer and consumer surplus. Total surplus represents the difference between the cost to society of the inputs used to make a good, including raw materials and labor, and the value of the finished good to society. Total surplus measures the overall increase in societal wealth attributable to production of a good.

Deadweight loss The difference between total surplus in a competitive market and total surplus in a monopolized market.

selling cellular service, the company also sold cellular telephones. L.A. Cellular sold the telephones below cost and recouped the losses in its cellular service. A group of companies that sold only cellular telephones, not service, sued L.A. Cellular, alleging that its business practice of selling telephones below cost was a violation of the Unfair Practices Act. The court ruled that the plaintiffs could not recover treble damages under the statute because L.A. Cellular did not intend to harm its competitors by selling phones below cost; the statute requires a showing that a company acted with the purpose of injuring competitors or destroying competition. The court did, however, hold that the companies could recover limited damages against L.A. Cellular for its below-cost sales.

REFUSAL TO DEAL

As a general proposition, the antitrust laws do not prevent a firm from deciding with whom it will or will not deal. Yet the courts have long recognized that in certain circumstances a unilateral refusal to deal may allow a firm to acquire or maintain monopoly power.

A monopolist has a duty to deal with its rivals when it controls an *essential facility,* that is, some resource necessary to its rivals' survival that they cannot feasibly duplicate. A court considers four elements in an essential-facility case: (1) whether the defendant prevents would-be competitors from using the facility; (2) whether it is feasible for the defendant to permit access to the facility by its would-be competitors; (3) whether the defendant has monopoly power and control of the facility; and (4) most critically, whether the competitors are able to duplicate the essential facility. This approach was followed in the *AT&T*[40] case, which led to the breakup of the Bell Telephone System.

40. United States v. American Tel. & Tel. Co., 552 F. Supp. 131 (D.D.C. 1982), *aff'd sub nom.,* Maryland v. United States, 460 U.S. 1001 (1983).

The essential-facility doctrine does not require a firm to share resources that are merely useful. A company need not share technology that would allow competitors to compete more effectively and need not share resources that the competitors could duplicate on their own.

The following case deals with the thorny issue of how to reconcile the monopoly-type rights granted to owners of intellectual property, such as patents, as incentives to innovate and the limits on refusals to deal imposed by Section 2 of the Sherman Act.

A CASE IN POINT

CASE 20.4

CSU, LLC v. Xerox Corp.

United States Court of Appeals for the Federal Circuit

203 F.3d 1322 (Fed Cir. 2000), cert. denied, 121 S. Ct. 1077 (2001).

Summary

FACTS In 1984, Xerox Corporation established a policy of not selling parts for its series 10 copiers to independent service organizations (ISOs), including CSU, unless they were end-users of the copiers. Several years later, Xerox expanded the policy to include other products. In 1989, Xerox refused to sell restricted parts to CSU and implemented an "on-site end-user verification" procedure to ensure that parts ordered by certain ISOs, including CSU, were actually for their use as an end-user.

In order to continue its business of servicing Xerox equipment, CSU used parts obtained from other ISOs, which were purchased through customers or from Xerox. CSU also purchased parts from a European affiliate of Xerox until Xerox forced the company to stop selling to CSU.

In 1994, Xerox settled an antitrust lawsuit with a class of ISOs and agreed to suspend its restrictive parts policy for six and a half years. CSU opted out of the settlement and filed a suit, alleging that Xerox had violated the Sherman Act by setting prices on its patented products higher for ISOs than for end-users, thereby forcing ISOs to raise their prices to noncompetitive levels and eliminating them from the service markets for high-speed copiers and printers. Xerox counterclaimed for patent and copyright infringement. The district court dismissed CSU's claims, finding that if a patent or copyright is lawfully acquired, the holder of the intellectual property right can refuse to sell or license its patented invention or copyrighted expression even if by doing so it affects the market. CSU appealed.

ISSUE PRESENTED Is a patent or copyright's holder's refusal to sell or license its patented invention or copyrighted expression to ISOs anticompetitive conduct prohibited by the antitrust laws?

SUMMARY OF OPINION The U.S. Court of Appeals for the Federal Circuit began by stating that although intellectual property rights do not confer a privilege to violate antitrust laws, antitrust laws also do not prevent the owner of intellectual property rights from excluding others from its patented property. A patent owner who brings a suit to exclude others from making, using, or selling the claimed invention is exempt from an-

(Continued)

(Case 20.4 continued)

titrust laws unless (1) the patent was obtained through knowing and willful fraud, or (2) the infringement suit is a mere sham to disguise an attempt to interfere directly with the business relationships of a competitor. Neither of these two exceptions was at issue in the case.

The court rejected CSU's reliance on the U.S. Supreme Court's decision in *Eastman Kodak Co. v. Image Technical Services, Inc.*,[41] in which the Court had held that it was an antitrust violation for a seller to exploit its dominant position in one market to expand into another market. Whereas the *Kodak* case was a tying case, CSU had made no claims that Xerox had tied the sale of its patented parts to unpatented products. The court also declined to inquire into the subjective motivation behind Xerox's refusal to sell or license its patented works, finding that if a patent infringement suit is not objectively baseless, then the antitrust defendant's subjective motivation is immaterial. In the absence of illegal tying, fraud on the Patent or Trademark Office, or sham litigation, the patent holder could enforce its statutory intellectual property rights without violating the antitrust laws.

With respect to Xerox's refusal to license its manuals and software, the court acknowledged that property rights granted by copyright law cannot be used to extend power into the marketplace beyond what Congress intended. The court agreed with the First Circuit's holding that an author's desire to exclude others from use of its copyrighted work is a presumptively valid business justification for any immediate harm to consumers resulting from the exclusionary conduct, however. The antitrust plaintiff bears the burden to overcome this presumption. The court declined to examine Xerox's subjective motivation in asserting its right to exclude under the copyright laws in the absence of evidence introduced by CSU that Xerox had obtained the copyrights by unlawful means or used them to gain monopoly power beyond the statutory copyright granted by Congress.

RESULT Xerox's refusal to sell or license patented or copyrighted work was within the rights granted by Congress and did not constitute a violation of antitrust laws.

41. 504 U.S. 451 (1992).

In *Image Technical Services, Inc. v. Eastman Kodak Co.*,[42] the Ninth Circuit held on remand that Section 2 of the Sherman Act prohibits refusal to deal in order to create or maintain a monopoly unless there is a legitimate business justification. The court acknowledged that intellectual property rights may create such a justification. In particular, a monopolist's desire to exclude others from its protected work is a presumptively valid business justification for any immediate harm to consumers caused by a monopolist's unilateral refusal to license a patent or copyright or to sell its patented or copyrighted work. That presumption may be rebutted, however, by evidence that the intellectual property protection was acquired unlawfully or that its use as a business justification was merely pretext.

The Ninth Circuit held that Kodak's refusal to sell replacement copier parts to independent service organiza-

tions was not justified by a desire to exploit its patents or copyrights. Although Kodak's equipment required thousands of parts, only sixty-five were patented. Yet Kodak refused to sell both protected and unprotected parts. In addition, Kodak's parts manager testified that patents "did not cross [his] mind" at the time Kodak began refusing to sell its parts to the ISOs. This evidence of pretext rebutted Kodak's presumption of valid business justification for its refusal to sell parts.

The Ninth Circuit noted the tension between antitrust law's concerns about monopoly as a threat to competition and copyright and patent law's goal of granting limited monopolies as an incentive to innovate. While acknowledging that patent and copyright holders may refuse to sell or license protected work, the court stated that a monopolist that acquires a dominant position in one market through patents and copyrights may violate Section 2 if the monopolist exploits that dominant position to extend the lawful monopoly into a separate market.

42. 125 F.3d 1195 (9th Cir. 1997), *cert. denied,* 523 U.S. 1094 (1998).

DERIVATIVE MARKETS

Ordinarily, Section 2 liability is restricted to monopolistic behavior within the specific market in which the firm has monopoly power. Through leveraging, however, a firm with monopoly power in one market can use that power to gain an advantage in a separate market. It is clear that when such an advantage amounts to monopoly power in the second market, the firm has violated Section 2. It is less clear whether a firm can use its monopoly power in one market to gain a competitive advantage, short of actual monopolization, in another market. A federal appeals court explored this issue in a case involving Kodak's pocket-sized camera.

Kodak had introduced a pocket-sized camera with a new type of film, which was capable of producing photographs that could previously be taken only by much larger cameras. For eighteen months after the introduction of the camera system, only Kodak produced the new type of film, which required special photo-processing equipment to develop. Kodak possessed a monopoly in the film market.

In *Berkey Photo, Inc. v. Eastman Kodak Co.,*[43] Berkey Photo, a seller and processor of film, challenged the introduction of the new camera system. It accused Kodak of attempting to use its monopoly power in the film market to gain leverage in the photo-finishing equipment and services markets in violation of Section 2 of the Sherman Act. In rejecting Berkey's claim, the court concluded that Kodak's invention resulted from its superior business skill, product, and foresight. Thus, the failure to disclose the product innovation prior to introduction of the new product did not constitute willful maintenance of monopoly power in violation of the Sherman Act.

Underlying the decisions under Section 2 is the conflict between the goal of preventing anticompetitive behavior and the goal of promoting consumer welfare by encouraging innovation. In certain cases, firms are permitted to adopt practices that, though they might exclude competition, also foster innovation.

For example, a firm is entitled to introduce technological innovations that adversely affect competitors, even if, in order to do so, it erects barriers to other firms' entry into the market. Consumers pay for such exclusion in the form of higher prices. Nevertheless, the courts and legislators have decided that, as a matter of policy, these higher prices are acceptable as the cost of technological change. If firms were denied the right to act as Kodak did, there would be no incentive to innovate. Technological innovation, in the long run, increases social welfare.

The *Berkey Photo* court did, however, suggest that the use of monopoly power in one market to obtain a competitive advantage in another market might violate Section 2. Recent Supreme Court decisions tend to undercut this suggestion, but they do not do so decisively. More specifically, in another case,[44] the Supreme Court held that the plaintiff in every Section 2 case involving unilateral conduct must prove a dangerous probability that the defendant's conduct will create or maintain monopoly power in a market. That holding seems to suggest that "leveraging" that confers only a "competitive advantage" in a market cannot violate Section 2.

The U.S. Court of Appeals for the Ninth Circuit adopted this approach when it held that two airlines that had developed the two largest proprietary computerized airline reservation systems did not violate Section 2 merely because the systems gave them a competitive advantage in the air-transportation market by listing their flights first.[45] The court held that unless the monopolist uses its power in the first market to acquire and maintain a monopoly in the second market, or to attempt to do so, there is no Section 2 violation. The plaintiffs had conceded that the two airlines did not have a monopoly in the leveraged, downstream air-transportation market and that there was no dangerous probability that either defendant would acquire such a monopoly. Therefore, their Section 2 claims were rejected.

On the other hand, some language in *Eastman Kodak Co. v. Image Technical Services, Inc.* suggests that leveraging monopoly power in one market to create a competitive advantage in another market can be a Section 2 violation. Therefore, the Supreme Court's position on monopoly leveraging that confers only a competitive advantage is not yet totally clear.

Other Anticompetitive Acts Other practices that have been held to indicate the presence of monopolistic intent include the allocation of markets and territories, price-fixing, fraudulently obtaining a patent, or engaging in sham litigation against a competitor. Firms can also incur Section 2 liability by acquiring or maintaining monopoly power through corporate mergers or acquisitions.

Mergers: Section 7 of the Clayton Act

If a merger or acquisition unreasonably restrains trade, it violates Section 1 of the Sherman Act. If it results in monopolization, it violates Section 2. These statutes, however, are rarely invoked to challenge mergers. Dissatisfied

43. 603 F.2d 263 (2d Cir. 1979), *cert. denied,* 444 U.S. 1093 (1980).
44. Spectrum Sports, Inc. v. McQuillan, 506 U.S. 447 (1993).
45. Alaska Airlines, Inc. v. United Airlines, Inc., 948 F.2d 536 (9th Cir. 1991).

with the ability of the government to attack mergers under the Sherman Act, Congress amended the Clayton Act in 1950 to prohibit mergers that threaten to harm competition. Section 7 of the Clayton Act provides:

> No person engaged in commerce or in any activity affecting commerce shall acquire, directly or indirectly, the whole or any part of the stock or other share capital and no person subject to the jurisdiction of the Federal Trade Commission shall acquire the whole or any part of the assets of another person engaged also in commerce or in any activity affecting commerce, where in any line of commerce or in any activity affecting commerce in any section of the country, the effect of such acquisition may be substantially to lessen competition, or to tend to create a monopoly.[46]

Two types of mergers are covered by Section 7: *horizontal mergers* between actual or prospective competitors at the same level of distribution and *vertical mergers* between firms at different points along the chain of production and distribution. In recent years, challenges to vertical mergers have been rare.

Unlike the Sherman Act, the Clayton Act does not provide criminal sanctions for violations of its terms. The Justice Department, through the courts, and the Federal Trade Commission (FTC), through its own administrative proceedings, may seek (1) divestiture of acquired stock or assets; (2) sale of particular subsidiaries, divisions, or lines of business; (3) compulsory sale of needed materials to a divested firm; (4) compulsory sharing of technology; or (5) temporary restrictions upon the defendant's own output or conduct.

In contrast to the Sherman Act, which is often enforced by private plaintiffs, the Clayton Act is enforced mainly by the federal agencies. Justice Department or FTC action can delay, if not abort, a corporate merger or acquisition.

Private parties, such as competitors of the merging firms, may also bring actions for injunctive relief. Recently, however, some courts have come to look with disfavor upon such actions, fearing that they might halt mergers that would actually intensify competition. State attorneys general may enforce Section 7, and they have begun to do so with increasing frequency.

HART–SCOTT–RODINO ANTITRUST IMPROVEMENTS ACT

The Hart–Scott–Rodino Antitrust Improvements Act amended Section 7 in 1976 to provide a premerger notification procedure whereby the FTC and Justice Department can review the anticompetitive effects of proposed mergers meeting certain size-of-party and size-of-transaction tests, which were raised in 2000. A premerger notification must be filed if (1) one party to the transaction has assets or annual sales of at least $10 million, (2) the other has assets or annual sales of at least $200 million, and (3) the transaction involves a purchase of at least $50 million or 15 percent of the voting securities of the acquired company. Failure to notify can result in fines and reversals of transactions.

In 1997, the FTC fined German auto-parts maker Mahle GmbH $5.1 million for failing to alert authorities to its $40 million purchase of 50.1 percent of a Brazilian rival's voting stock. Because both companies have U.S. subsidiaries, the FTC had authority to intervene.[47] In 1996, Sara Lee Corporation paid a fine of $3.1 million after the FTC challenged its failure to notify authorities of its purchase of $26 million of assets from a company in the United Kingdom in 1991. Sara Lee had counted the deal as two transactions: $13.1 million for the company's U.S. assets and $12.7 million for its U.K. assets. In addition to the fine, the FTC forced Sara Lee to sell one of the brands it had acquired from the U.K. company and another brand it had acquired previously.[48]

In general, parties to a merger must give the FTC and Justice Department thirty days to review their filings (fifteen days in the case of a tender offer). Either period can be extended if the government requests additional information. Requests for additional information should be avoided, if possible, because they cause further delays before the merging parties know whether the Justice Department will challenge the proposed merger.

MERGER GUIDELINES

In connection with their enforcement obligations, the FTC and the Justice Department have together developed a series of guidelines as to the kinds of transactions that are likely to be challenged as violations of the Clayton Act. Under the merger guidelines, the FTC and the Justice Department (the reviewing agencies) seek to determine whether a proposed corporate combination will more likely than not reduce competition; to make this determination, they use basically the same analysis that the courts use in applying Section 2 of the Sherman Act (discussed earlier in this chapter). The reviewing agency first determines the relevant geographic and product markets. Then, it calculates the market shares of the companies proposing to merge. Finally, it determines the effect of the merger on the relevant market.

---

46. 15 U.S.C. § 18 (1997).

47. John R. Wilke & Bryan Gruley, *Fines Grow for Evading Antitrust Review,* WALL ST. J., Feb. 28, 1997, at A2.
48. *Id.*

If the merger appears to increase the concentration in the relevant market by a certain amount, the reviewing agency will ordinarily challenge the transaction. However, the question of whether to challenge a combination is left to the discretion of the agency.

As an aid to the interpretation of market data, the Justice Department uses the *Herfindahl–Hirschman Index (HHI)* of market concentration. The HHI is calculated by summing the squares of the individual market shares of all the firms in the market. For example, in a market with four competitors having market shares of 35 percent, 25 percent, 25 percent, and 15 percent, the HHI is 2,700 ($35^2 + 25^2 + 25^2 + 15^2 = 1,225 + 625 + 625 + 225 = 2,700$).

When the postmerger HHI is less than 1,000, the Justice Department characterizes the market as unconcentrated. In such cases, the department will not challenge the merger or other combination.

When the postmerger HHI is between 1,000 and 1,800 and the merger will produce an HHI increase of 100 points or more, the 1992 merger guidelines state that the merger will possibly raise significant competitive concerns.

When the postmerger HHI is above 1,800, the department considers the market to be highly concentrated. In such cases, an increase in the HHI of 100 points or more creates a rebuttable presumption of anticompetitive effects. For example, a merger between firms with market shares of 5 percent and 10 percent will result in a 100-point increase in the HHI ($15^2 = 225$, $5^2 + 10^2 = 125$), whereas a merger between firms with market shares of 7 percent and 8 percent will result in a 112-point increase ($15^2 = 225$, $7^2 + 8^2 = 113$).

When the increase in the HHI is less than 50 points, Justice Department action is unlikely. When the increase is between 50 and 100 points, the department will challenge the transaction if it determines, based on a broad-ranging analysis of the market, that the effect of the merger is "substantially to lessen competition." The department will consider such factors as changing market conditions, the relative strength or weakness of the firms in the market, and barriers to entry into the relevant market. It should be noted that even if the Justice Department or the FTC approves the merger, it may still be challenged in court by another party.

Litigation *under* Section 7

Although the Justice Department's merger guidelines are of considerable persuasive value, the standards applied by the courts differ in several significant respects. Moreover, a court's analysis may vary depending on the type of merger or corporate combination that has been challenged.

HORIZONTAL MERGERS

A horizontal merger is the combining of two or more competing companies at the same level in the chain of production and distribution. The first step in determining the lawfulness of such a merger is to identify the relevant product and geographic markets. The same standards discussed in connection with Section 2 of the Sherman Act are used.

Once the market is defined, the court will look primarily at three factors: (1) the market shares of the firms involved in the transaction, (2) the level of concentration in the market, and (3) whether the market is structurally conducive to anticompetitive behavior.

The case of *United States v. Philadelphia National Bank*[49] illustrates this method of analysis. In the early 1960s, Philadelphia National Bank (PNB) was the second largest bank in the Philadelphia market, which consisted of forty-two commercial banks in the metropolitan area of Philadelphia, Pennsylvania, and its three contiguous counties. When PNB signed a merger agreement with Girard Bank, the third largest bank in the same market, the United States sued to enjoin the merger on the grounds that it would violate Section 7 of the Clayton Act.

The merger would have resulted in PNB's controlling at least 30 percent of the commercial banking business in the four-county Philadelphia metropolitan area, which the U.S. Supreme Court viewed as a threat to competition. After the merger, the two largest banks would control 59 percent of the market, whereas the two largest banks before the merger controlled only 44 percent. This increase in concentration also worried the Court. Neither the high level of government regulation of the banking business nor the banks' provision of services and intangible credit, rather than tangible products, made the banking industry immune from the anticompetitive effects of undue concentration. Because of these three elements, the Court directed the district court to enter judgment enjoining the merger. The Court explained:

> [A] merger which produces a firm controlling an undue percentage share of the relevant market, and results in a significant increase in the concentration of firms in that market is so inherently likely to lessen competition substantially that it must be enjoined in the absence of evidence clearly showing the merger is not likely to have such anticompetitive effects.

49. 374 U.S. 321 (1963).

The 30 percent market share that the Court held to be excessive has been taken by many lower courts to create a presumption of illegality. The Supreme Court has insisted, however, that no single numerical standard can be applied to all markets. In one case, the Supreme Court enjoined a merger between competing grocery stores when the acquiring grocery store had a 4.7 percent market share and the acquired grocery store had a 4.2 percent market share.[50] The top four firms in the relevant market controlled only 24.4 percent of the market. (This decision, however, has been relentlessly criticized.) Most courts today require that, in the absence of a highly concentrated market, the merging firms have a combined market share of at least 30 percent before a Section 7 violation will be found.

In a more recent case, the FTC challenged the merger of office-supply retailers Office Depot, Inc. and Staples, Inc., the first and second largest operators of office-supply superstores, respectively. In 1996, the two firms agreed to merge their operations (with more than $8 billion in combined revenues), joining their more than 1,000 stores. Although Staples and Office Depot did not compete with each other in many geographic markets, the FTC contended that the merger would hurt consumers on balance by reducing competition in the markets where the two companies did compete.

To satisfy the regulators, the companies negotiated a consent decree with the FTC staff to permit the merger on the condition that the companies sell sixty-three stores to OfficeMax, the third-largest office-supply superstore retailer, in those markets where the FTC most feared a reduction in competition. Nonetheless, the FTC commissioners again ruled against the merger and asked the district court to enjoin the companies from joining.

Defining the relevant product market as consumable office supplies sold through office-supply superstores,

the court rejected the argument that Wal-Mart and other retailers compete in the same market with Staples, Office Depot, and OfficeMax. The court relied heavily on pricing data that indicated, among other things, that prices were on average 13 percent higher in geographic markets where Staples was the only office superstore than in markets where all three superstores competed, even though retail and discount chains selling consumable office supplies were present in both markets. Turning then to market concentration, the court noted that before the merger, the least concentrated market had an HHI of 3,597 and the most concentrated had an HHI of 6,944. After the proposed merger, those figures would rise to 5,003 and 10,000, respectively. Thus, these markets were already "highly concentrated" and would see an average increase of 2,715 HHI points. Furthermore, the industry's large economies of scale meant that new entrants would have to open many large stores nationally in order to compete. The large amount of capital necessary to do this would be a barrier to entry. Ultimately, the district court sided with the FTC and, in 1997, issued an injunction, killing the $3.4 billion deal.[51]

Even if a merger or combination is determined to be presumptively illegal on the basis of market shares, the defendants may still show that the transaction is not likely to decrease competition. For example, if there are no barriers to entry in the relevant market, any transitory increase in concentration will be quickly eroded by the entry of new competitors into the market. If one of the combined firms is failing, the proposed transaction may be the only alternative to that failure. In either of these cases, Section 7 liability can be avoided.

In the following case, the court considered whether the merger of the number two and number three baby food producers would violate Section 7 of the Clayton Act.

50. United States v. Von's Grocery Co., 384 U.S. 270 (1966).

51. Federal Trade Comm'n v. Staples, Inc., 970 F. Supp. 1066 (D.D.C. 1997).

A CASE IN POINT

CASE 20.5

Federal Trade Commission v. H.J. Heinz Company
*United States Court of Appeals for the District of Columbia Circuit
2001 U.S. App.
LEXIS 7735
(D.C. Cir. Apr. 27, 2001).*

Summary

FACTS Gerber Products Company, Heinz, and Beech-Nut are the only significant manufacturers and distributors of baby food in the United States. Gerber is the largest company, with a market share of approximately 65 percent. Heinz has a market share of 17 percent, and Beech-Nut's market share is 15 percent. As the dominant firm in the market (with brand loyalty greater than that of any other product sold in the United States including Coca-Cola and Nike), Gerber generally is the first to increase its prices. Beech-Nut and Heinz follow Gerber's prices, but Heinz markets its baby food at a slightly lower price as a "value brand."

(Continued)

(Case 20.5 continued)

On February 28, 2000, Heinz and Beech-Nut entered into a merger agreement providing for Heinz to acquire Beech-Nut's voting securities for $185 million. On July 14, 2000, the FTC sued to enjoin the proposed merger.

After defining the relevant market as jarred baby food in the United States, the trial court found that the baby food industry was highly concentrated and that the proposed merger would significantly increase market concentration. The total HHI for the baby food industry was 4,775, which would rise to 5,285 as a result of the merger. This increase is five times the 100-point threshold established in the merger guidelines. As a result, the FTC had established a *prima facie* case supporting a preliminary injunction. Nonetheless, the trial court concluded that the cost savings and efficiencies resulting from the merger would allow the firm to compete more effectively with Gerber for the benefit of consumers, and it refused to enjoin the merger. The FTC appealed.

ISSUE Will a merger between two of the three main manufacturers of baby food lessen competition in violation of Section 7 of the Clayton Act?

SUMMARY OF OPINION The U.S. Court of Appeals for the District of Columbia Circuit reversed the district court, after concluding that the district court's finding that there was no significant pre-merger competition between Heinz and Beech-Nut was clearly erroneous. Even though generally only one of the two brands is available on any given store's shelves, they compete aggressively at the wholesale level for the "second shelf" position.

As for the claimed post-merger efficiencies, the court noted that the U.S. Supreme Court "has not sanctioned the use of the efficiencies defense in a section 7 case," but indicated that "the trend among lower courts is to recognize the defense." Indeed, the 1997 amendments to the 1992 merger guidelines recognize that mergers may generate significant efficiencies. The guidelines require, however, that such claims be substantiated so that the government "can verify by reasonable means the likelihood and magnitude of each asserted efficiency, how and when each would be achieved (and any costs of doing so), how each would enhance the merged firm's ability and incentive to compete, and why each would be merger-specific." Beech-Nut and Heinz failed to demonstrate the "extraordinary efficiencies" that would be required to rebut the presumption of lessened competition given the high market concentration levels. Finally, the appeals court found no structural barriers to collusion between Gerber and the proposed Heinz—Beech-Nut merged entity, concluding instead that "[t]he combination of a concentrated market and barriers to entry is a recipe for price coordination."

RESULT The appeals court issued a preliminary injunction enjoining the merger pending the FTC's administrative adjudication of the merger's legality.

VERTICAL MERGERS

A vertical merger is the acquisition by one company of another company at a higher or lower level in the chain of production and distribution. For example, the merger of an airplane manufacturer and an airplane-engine manufacturer would be a vertical merger. In vertical merger cases, the courts tend to focus on whether the merger has excluded competitors from a significant sector of the market. For example, when competing suppliers were denied access to approximately 25 percent of the highly concentrated automobile market, Section 7 was held to be violated. When the market is less concentrated, however, the courts will analyze the market more thoroughly to determine whether the transaction has any anticompetitive effects.

CONGLOMERATE MERGERS

In the 1960s and 1970s, many academics and government prosecutors favored expanding Section 7 prohibitions to cover mergers that were neither horizontal nor vertical in the traditional sense. This effort to prohibit *conglomerate mergers*—that is, the acquisition of a company by another company in a different line of business—has now largely been abandoned. Because the merging companies are in different markets, there is no threat to competition.

One theory advanced during this period has endured, although it has rarely been applied. A merger between firms that are not competitors at the time of the acquisition but that might, without the merger, have become competitors may be held to violate Section 7. This is because potential competition is useful in keeping prices at competitive levels. When prices rise above competitive levels, potential competitors will have an incentive to enter the market and charge competitive prices. When there is no such potential entrant into the market, there is no pressure to keep prices at competitive levels. Monopoly pricing may result.

Consequently, it can be argued that a merger violates Section 7 if a plaintiff proves that (1) the market is highly concentrated; (2) one of the merging firms is an actual, substantial competitor in the market and the other is one of a small number of firms that might have entered the market; (3) entry of that firm *de novo,* or anew, or by a "toehold" acquisition into the market would be reasonably likely to have procompetitive effects; and (4) without the merger, entry by that firm would have been likely. Some attorneys argue that a merger does not have to eliminate an actual potential entrant in order to violate Section 7. Under this theory, it is sufficient if the merger eliminates a perceived potential entrant.

 Price Discrimination: *The* Robinson–Patman Act

Section 2 of the Clayton Act, as amended by the Robinson–Patman Act, prohibits *price discrimination,* that is, selling the same product to different purchasers at the same level of distribution at different prices. By outlawing price discrimination, the legislators believed that they could protect independent businesses by preventing the formation of monopolies. It was assumed that price discrimination was the means by which trusts were built and that discriminatory price concessions were the means by which large retail chains expanded at the expense of smaller independent retailers.

Today, enforcement of the Robinson–Patman Act is a low priority of the Federal Trade Commission; the Justice Department does not enforce the act at all. Private enforcement through civil litigation continues, however.[52]

ELEMENTS OF A ROBINSON–PATMAN CASE

To establish a price-discrimination case under the Robinson–Patman Act, six elements must be established. First, there must be discrimination in price, that is, a difference in the price at which goods are sold, or in the terms and conditions of sale, or in such items as freight allowances or rebates.

Second, some part of the discrimination must involve sales in interstate commerce; that is, at least one sale must be across state lines or involve the instrumentations of interstate commerce. A seller may discriminate in price as long as no sale across state lines occurs.

Third, the discrimination must involve sales for use, consumption, or resale within the United States. Fourth, there must be discrimination between different purchasers. In other words, there must be at least two sales. Fifth, the discrimination must involve sales of tangible commodities of like grade and quality.

Finally, there must be a probable injury to competition. The probable injury to competition is assessed at three levels: (1) the seller level, (2) the buyer level, and (3) the customer level.

DEFENSES

Even if a plaintiff has shown the elements of a Robinson–Patman violation, a number of defenses are available.

Meeting Competition Discriminatory prices are not prohibited if the seller acted in "good faith to meet an equally low price of a competitor."[53] As defined by the FTC, good faith is "a flexible and pragmatic, not a technical or doctrinaire, concept. The standard of good faith is simply the standard of the prudent businessman responding fairly to what he reasonably believes is a situation of competitive necessity."[54]

---

52. *See* Meyerowitz, *Beware of Price-Discrimination Pitfalls,* Bus. Marketing, June 1986, at 136.
53. 15 U.S.C. § 13(b) (1997).
54. Continental Baking Co., 63 F.T.C. 2071, 2163 (1963).

Cost Justification Price differentials that would otherwise be prohibited by the Robinson–Patman Act are not prohibited if the differentials "make only due allowance for differences in the cost of manufacture, sale or delivery resulting from the differing methods or quantities" in which the goods are sold and delivered.[55] To establish this defense, the defendant must show actual cost savings, not merely generalized assertions of cost savings, to justify the price reduction. Defendants may show savings not only in manufacturing costs but also in selling and delivery costs (such as costs of billing; credit losses; costs of advertising, promotion, and selling; and freight and delivery charges). The FTC interprets this defense restrictively, and it is expensive to compile the necessary paper trail.

Changing Conditions Section 2(a) does not prohibit price changes

> from time to time where in response to changing conditions affecting the market for or the marketability of the goods concerned such as but not limited to actual or imminent deterioration of perishable goods, obsolescence of seasonal goods, distress sales under court process, or sales in good faith in discontinuance of business in the goods concerned.[56]

In the few cases where this defense has been raised, the issue was whether the price discrimination was a response to one of the conditions listed in the statute. The changing-conditions defense has generally been confined to situations caused by the physical characteristics of the product, such as the perishable nature of fruit. For example, a court

55. 15 U.S.C. § 13(a) (1997).
56. *Id.*

permitted price differentials on bananas from a single shipload because they reflected the perishable nature of bananas.

 # International Application *of the* Antitrust Laws

SOVEREIGN IMMUNITY

To avoid antitrust disputes with foreign governments, the U.S. courts apply a *sovereign immunity* doctrine. This doctrine protects foreign governments from applications of U.S. laws. (The sovereign immunity doctrine is discussed further in Chapter 13.) Much litigation turns on whether a foreign firm's anticompetitive activity was directed by its government or was merely tolerated. If the foreign government tolerates but does not require the anticompetitive acts, the U.S. antitrust laws apply.

EXTRATERRITORIAL APPLICATION OF U.S. LAW

The Supreme Court has interpreted the Sherman Act to apply extraterritorially when (1) the intent of parties is to affect commerce within the United States, and (2) their conduct actually affects commerce in the United States. This relatively straightforward statement of the law obscures, however, the complex issues involved in applying U.S. antitrust laws to activities occurring outside U.S. borders.

The following case dealt with the question of whether conduct by a non-U.S. company outside the United States but having an effect on commerce in the United States could form the basis for a criminal antitrust case.

A CASE IN POINT

CASE 20.6
United States v. Nippon Paper Industries Co.
United States Court of Appeals for the First Circuit
109 F.3d 1 (1st Cir. 1997),
cert. denied,
525 U.S. 1044 (1998).

Summary

FACTS In 1995, a federal grand jury indicted Nippon Paper Industries Company, Ltd. (NPI), a Japanese manufacturer of facsimile (fax) paper, for criminally violating Section 1 of the Sherman Act. The indictment alleged that in 1990 NPI and certain unnamed co-conspirators held meetings in Japan during which they agreed to fix the price of thermal fax paper throughout North America. To achieve this goal, NPI and other manufacturers purportedly sold the paper in Japan to unaffiliated trading houses on the condition that the houses charge inflated prices for the paper when they resold it in North America. The trading houses then shipped and sold the paper to their subsidiaries in the United States, which in turn sold it to American consumers at artificially high prices.

NPI moved to dismiss the indictment, in part because the alleged conduct took place entirely in Japan and was, therefore, beyond the reach of the Sherman Act in a criminal

(Continued)

(Case 20.6 continued)

case. Accepting this argument, the district court dismissed the case. The government appealed.

ISSUE PRESENTED May a criminal antitrust prosecution be based on conduct that took place entirely outside the United States?

SUMMARY OF OPINION The U.S. Court of Appeals for the First Circuit began by noting that the courts presume that congressional legislation applies only within the territorial jurisdiction of the United States unless contrary intent appears. The first Supreme Court case to address extraterritorial application of the Sherman Act found that it did not apply to a civil action concerning conduct wholly outside the United States that had no discernible effect on imports to the United States.[57] Since then, however, the Court has upheld civil liability under the Sherman Act for conduct outside the United States that had substantial anticompetitive effects in the United States.[58] The issue of criminal liability for extraterritorial conduct has never been addressed.

In this case, however, the same language of the same section of the same statute (Section 1 of the Sherman Act) governs both civil and criminal liability: "Every contract, combination in the form of trust or otherwise, or conspiracy, in restraint of trade or commerce among the several States, or with foreign nations, is declared to be illegal." Common sense suggests that courts should interpret the same language uniformly, whether the impetus for interpretation is civil or criminal. Such understanding flows from the basic canons of statutory interpretation and Supreme Court interpretation of other statutes.

Although there is no direct precedent for antitrust criminal liability for wholly extraterritorial conduct, the court reasoned that "[t]here is a first time for everything." The absence of earlier criminal actions is more a reflection of the relative unimportance of the global economy in previous periods and less of Section 1's limited reach. As well, there is precedent for application of state criminal laws to conduct occurring wholly outside the state.

The principle of lenity provides that when interpreting statutes in criminal cases, ambiguity should favor the accused. Here, however, there is no such ambiguity. Lenity applies when inquiry yields ambiguity, not simply because the meaning of a statute is not readily apparent without inquiry. Similarly, the principle of comity counsels forbearance when two sovereigns both have legitimate claims to jurisdiction in a dispute. More aspiration than fixed rule, comity in antitrust applies only when another sovereign's law mandates conduct that violates U.S. antitrust law. That was not the case here.

RESULT The decision of the trial court was reversed, and the indictment reinstated. NPI could be criminally prosecuted in the United States for fixing prices of products sold in the United States even though the meetings to fix prices took place in Japan.

COMMENTS As one commentator critically noted, "Inch by inch, for half a century the courts have given the Justice Department a longer and longer leash in allowing it to pursue antitrust cases abroad. A First Circuit Court of Appeals panel may have cut that leash entirely."[59] On the other hand, former Deputy Assistant Attorney General Diane P. Wood has pointed out the difficulties of effectively implementing international antitrust enforcement without taking into account events, transactions, and parties beyond the enforcing country's borders.

---

57. American Banana Co. v. United Fruit Co., 213 U.S. 347 (1909).
58. Hartford Fire Ins. Co. v. California, 509 U.S. 764 (1993).
59. John Gibeaut, *Sherman Goes Abroad,* A.B.A. J., July 1997, at 42.

In *Nieman v. Dryclean U.S.A. Franchise Co.*,[60] the Eleventh Circuit considered the issue of extraterritorial application of U.S. law when a citizen of Argentina tried to recover under the Federal Trade Commission Act against a U.S. company that allegedly failed to make certain disclosures required by the FTC's franchise rule. The U.S. corporation refused to return a $50,000 deposit when the plaintiff was unable to raise capital to finance purchase of dry-cleaning franchises in Argentina. The court found that the FTC Act did not authorize extraterritorial application of the franchise rule and that the FTC did not intend the rule to apply to a U.S. franchisor in its dealings with foreign franchisees with respect to franchises located in a foreign country.

Foreign nations do not always accept the applicability of U.S. antitrust laws. For example, Canada, Australia, and South Africa all enacted laws forbidding their citizens to make available to U.S. courts any documents bearing on the nature and existence of an alleged uranium cartel. This action prevented U.S. courts from gathering the information necessary to ascertain whether an antitrust violation had occurred. (The alleged uranium cartel was one of the defenses Westinghouse Electric Corporation raised in the lawsuit discussed in the "Inside Story" in Chapter 8.)

Many countries do not accept treble damages as a remedy. For example, the United Kingdom does not allow any recovery in excess of single damages. Suppose a U.S. court awards a U.S. corporation, USCO, $15 million in damages, after trebling, in a suit against UKCO, a U.K. corporation. When USCO attempts to collect $15 million of UKCO's assets, the U.K. court will treat two-thirds of the $15 million award, or $10 million, as an illegal treble-damages award. Thus, USCO will be able to recover only $5 million in the U.K. court. Even when a U.S. court finds a foreign corporation in violation of the antitrust laws, any award of damages is meaningless without foreign enforcement of the award.

60. 178 F.3d 1126 (11th Cir. 1999), *cert. denied*, 528 U.S. 1118 (2000).

INTERNATIONAL CONSIDERATION

Invocation of another nation's antitrust laws can be an important strategy for international expansion. In recent years, Procter & Gamble (P&G) has successfully wielded antitrust laws against competitors to support its move into Latin America. After losing to Colgate–Palmolive in a bidding war to acquire a Brazilian toothpaste manufacturer with 52 percent market share, P&G contacted the Brazilian trade commission. P&G pointed out that Colgate already controlled 27 percent of the market, whereas P&G was simply trying to get its foot in the door. In 1996, after a two-year review, the agency ordered Colgate to pull the acquired Brazilian brand from the shelves for four years. Earlier that year, P&G complained to Mexican regulators about the likely effects of the merger between Kimberly–Clark and Scott Paper. Because the merger would give the new entity control over 90 percent of the Mexican tissue market, P&G supplied the Mexican officials with reams of data about the Mexican tissue business and pointed out that the earlier rulings on the merger by U.S. and European officials required Kimberly to sell off its worldwide baby-wipes operation. As a result, Mexican regulators required Kimberly to divest itself of a popular brand of tissue with 20 percent market share. P&G has used similar tactics against Unilever Group in Argentina, where charges that Unilever used unfair trade practices in the market for laundry detergent came under investigation.[a]

a. Tara Parker-Pope, *P&G Calls the Cops as It Strives to Expand Sales in Latin America*, WALL ST. J., Mar. 20, 1998, at A1.

As the global economy becomes more of an economic reality, the antitrust analysis of the relevant market will have to take into account foreign goods produced but not sold in the United States. Another issue that must be resolved in the future is how the antitrust laws will apply to U.S. companies purchasing foreign entities that have potentially valuable national security or technology applications in highly concentrated markets.

THE RESPONSIBLE MANAGER
Avoiding Antitrust Violations

Although it is impossible for a manager to eliminate all possible antitrust violations, there are a number of steps that should be implemented. The underlying purpose of the antitrust statutes is to benefit consumers by promoting competition. The economy functions best when firms compete vigorously, but fairly, with one another. In antitrust, however, the line between legal and illegal conduct is often blurry. Consequently, there are few rules that a manager can give his or her employees. Rather, the manager must identify the activities or conditions that most often trigger antitrust liability, such as discussions with competitors, discussions with buyers about their future prices, and activities that may increase concentration in any market that is already highly concentrated.

Discussions among competitors receive the highest degree of antitrust scrutiny. Trade and professional associations are particularly vulnerable. If they disseminate information that identifies parties to individual transactions and the prices of even past or current individual transactions, the antitrust laws may be violated. Equally hazardous is the dissemination of information that may result in market division or output restriction. As a general rule, any trade-association information concerning prices should be immediately forwarded to in-house or outside counsel to address potential antitrust concerns.

Antitrust scrutiny is also heightened whenever price is discussed, even between manufacturers and retailers. A corporation must make clear to its salespersons that they cannot coerce the retailer regarding the minimum price it charges the end consumer. Such conduct will raise the specter of treble-damages liability.

Finally, antitrust scrutiny is heightened where markets are highly concentrated. The fewer the entities that compete in a particular market, the more likely that agreements among them can be effectuated and that mergers can lead to unlawful monopolies. Consequently, corporations operating in concentrated markets should be particularly cautious. A manager can obtain rough approximations of market concentration from company counsel.

Employees should be encouraged, through an appropriate award system, to inform the manager whenever any of the above "red flags" appear. A manager should not hesitate to seek assistance from counsel in analyzing any activity that might violate the antitrust laws. The manager should also be careful to avoid any situations that could be interpreted as evidence of illegal activity. If a manager attending a trade show, for example, hears competitors discussing price or other terms of sale, the manager should leave the room, preferably in a manner that calls attention to his or her departure.

Common sense and education are the keys. Actions that don't seem fair usually are not. Continuing education programs will keep corporate employees aware of potential antitrust problems. A manager should always stress that short-term gains through unethical or illegal behavior are always outweighed by longer-term losses, particularly in the area of antitrust with its treble-damages awards.

INSIDE STORY

An Operating System *by* Any Other Name Would Browse *as* Sweetly

In 1994, the U.S. Department of Justice's Antitrust Division charged Microsoft Corporation, the largest software company in the world, with unlawful monopoly and restraint of trade under Sections 1 and 2 of the Sherman Act. Among other things, the regulators alleged that Microsoft had engaged in anticompetitive marketing practices directed at personal computer (PC) manufacturers that preinstall operating system software on the PCs they produce for retail sale. These practices included charging per processor royalties, whereby PC manufacturers were offered a discount if they agreed to pay a royalty to Microsoft for each computer processor sold, regardless of whether the unit was shipped with the Microsoft operating system or a competitor's operating system.

After a year of legal wrangling, Microsoft signed a consent decree on August 21, 1995. Microsoft agreed not to charge per processor royalties. The decree also prohibited Microsoft from conditioning the licensing of its operating system software to original equipment manufacturers (OEMs) on their agreement to license other Microsoft products. Microsoft retained the right to develop integrated products, however.

The government based its demand on the notion of "network economies," a condition in which the value of owning a product rises as other consumers own the same product. Facsimile machines are an obvious example. Having the only fax machine in the world is worthless, but having one of a million fax machines is quite valuable because it allows the owner to communicate with 999,999 other fax-machine owners. Much of the value of the product arises from being part of the network.

Networks can be physical or virtual. Physical networks include telephones and railroads; virtual networks include most shared technologies and standards. For instance, there are networks of VHS video recorders and Macintosh computers that enable members of the network to interact with each other in valuable ways, such as by exchanging videotapes or computer files. The interaction is possible because users share a common technology or standard. Computer operating system software is another example; software developers generally prefer to invest their resources in designing applications for platforms in widespread, rather than limited, use. Once there are many applications for an operating system, that system becomes more attractive to consumers as well.

For this reason, Microsoft's stunning success in the market for PC operating system software worried the regulators. Because most PC owners used Microsoft's operating system, the regulators argued, Microsoft could coerce them into buying other products simply by tying the two together. For instance, Microsoft might condition the sale of Windows on the purchase of its word-processing software Word. By so tying the products together, Microsoft would force PC users to combine, rather than separate, their choices for operating systems and word processors. As a result, consumers of PCs would end up buying Microsoft's operating system and its word processor even if they would prefer Microsoft's operating system and a non-Microsoft word processor. Of course, consumers could still purchase the non-Microsoft word processor, but the additional purchase price and switching costs would probably deter some.

Microsoft argued, however, that operating systems are dynamic and must respond to consumer demand and technological advances. Microsoft reasoned that operating systems initially did not include modules for data compression, memory management, file backup, or device driving. Such "extras" were provided separately. Over time, these functions were integrated into the operating system as consumers began to expect them as standards rather than options.

While the antitrust guardians were battling Microsoft and hammering out the consent decree, the World Wide Web came into being and promised to give everyone access to everything. In April 1994, Microsoft founder, chair, and CEO Bill Gates publicly announced Microsoft's intention to include Internet-browsing software in Windows 95. Soon after, Microsoft unveiled Internet Explorer (IE) to compete with Netscape Communications Corporation's wildly popular Navigator browser. By the time Microsoft signed the consent decree in 1995, Microsoft had already supplied to manufacturers a version of Windows 95 bundled with Explorer at no additional cost. OEMs were prohibited from disassembling the package.

Historically, PC operating systems have always served to coordinate a user's access to various sources of infor-

mation, including internal hard drives, floppy disk drives, random access memory, and CD-ROM drives. With the birth of the Internet, Microsoft reasoned, it was time for operating systems to provide access to this next, great source of information. By its logic, integration of Web browsers was the natural next step in operating system evolution.

Within two years, Internet Explorer had garnered more than 40 percent of the Web browser market, largely at Netscape's expense. No doubt, Internet Explorer's rapid success arose in part from Microsoft's provision of the browser with Windows for the same price. Its functionality, however, made it a worthy rival to Navigator. Many critics concluded that Internet Explorer 4.0, released in 1997, was a better product than Netscape Navigator.[61] Dell Computer Corporation chair Michael Dell claimed that his customers would demand Windows with Internet Explorer even if the products were not bundled.[62]

On October 20, 1997, the Justice Department petitioned the U.S. District Court for the District of Columbia to find Microsoft in contempt of court for violating the 1995 consent decree and to fine the company $1 million per day until it complied by unbundling Windows and Internet Explorer.

The case was assigned to Judge Thomas Penfield Jackson, a pro-business conservative Republican appointed by President Reagan. Judge Jackson did not find Microsoft in contempt, but he did issue a preliminary injunction prohibiting Microsoft from further conditioning its licensing of PC operating system software (including Windows 95 or any successor version) on the licensing of any Microsoft browser pending development of the record.

On May 12, 1998, the U.S. Court of Appeals for the District of Columbia stayed the injunction insofar as it applied to Windows 98 (which further integrated Internet Explorer into the operating system).[63] The court held that "[t]he United States presented no evidence suggesting Windows 98 was not an 'Integrated Product' and thus exempt from the prohibitions of Section IV (E)(I)." The court ruled that, at least for purposes of deciding whether products were integrated within the meaning of the consent decree, the test was whether the integrated product provided functionalities and advantages that consumers could not themselves achieve by buying both products and using them together. The

61. For a list of product reviews, see <http://www.microsoft.com/ie/press/>.
62. David Bank, *Why Software and Antitrust Law Make an Uneasy Mix*, WALL ST. J., Oct. 22, 1997, at B1.
63. Microsoft Corp. v. United States, 147 F.3d 935 (D.C. Cir. 1998).

court also questioned the competency of judges to dictate what features should be included in an operating system.

Faced with the imminent launch of Windows 98 and perhaps believing that it was now or never, the Justice Department filed a wide-ranging complaint against Microsoft on May 18, 1998. The attorneys general of twenty states filed similar suits the same day. The Justice Department alleged that Microsoft's restrictive agreements with Internet and online service providers (such as America Online) and Internet content providers, whereby those companies agreed not to license, distribute, or promote non-Microsoft products (or to do so only on terms that materially disadvantaged such products), and Microsoft's agreements with OEMs restricting modification or customization of the PC boot-up sequence and screen unreasonably restricted competition in violation of Section 1. The complaint also alleged that Microsoft had engaged in a series of anticompetitive practices (including tying and unreasonably exclusionary agreements) with the purpose and effect of maintaining its PC operating system monopoly and extending that monopoly to the Internet browser market in violation of Section 2. The case was assigned to Judge Jackson.

The trial began on October 19, 1998, and concluded on February 26, 1999. On November 5, 1999, the district court issued a 207-page finding of fact that strongly and clearly rejected Microsoft's version of the facts.[64] Subsequent to issuing the findings of fact, but before issuing his conclusions of law, Judge Jackson asked Judge Richard Posner to mediate a resolution of the case. Judge Posner is the chief judge of the U.S. Court of Appeals for the Seventh Circuit and has an outstanding reputation as an antitrust expert.

For four months, Judge Posner went back and forth trying to negotiate a settlement between the two teams of lawyers representing the Justice Department and Microsoft. Posner spent hours talking to Bill Gates, who described Judge Posner as "super-smart." The negotiations resulted in eighteen drafts of proposed settlements, but Microsoft refused to accept the Justice Department's last offer. Draft 18 would have (1) required Microsoft to set a uniform price list for Windows; (2) prohibited Microsoft from entering into exclusive contracts with Internet service and content providers; (3) forced Microsoft to open its application programming interfaces; (4) given PC makers the right to receive versions of Windows without new features added by Microsoft; and (5) given PC makers the right to license the Windows source code so

that they could modify the desktop, integrate rival software, or add their own features.[65]

On April 3, 2000, the district court entered its conclusions of law. The court held that Microsoft had violated Section 1 by tying Internet Explorer to Windows and had attempted to monopolize the browser market in violation of Section 2. The court rejected the Justice Department's exclusive dealing claim under Section 1 on the grounds that Microsoft's promotion and distribution agreements for Internet Explorer did not foreclose enough of the relevant market to constitute a violation.

On June 7, 2000, the district court ordered that Microsoft be split into two companies, with one selling the Window's operating system and the other selling Microsoft's Office suite of word-processing, spreadsheets, and other applications. Microsoft immediately appealed.

After issuing his decision, Judge Jackson agreed to be interviewed, an extremely unusual act by a sitting federal judge. During the interview, he made it clear that Microsoft's lack of credibility undermined its arguments. Quoting the Latin expression *"Falsus in uno, falsus in omnibus,"* which means "Untrue in one thing, untrue in everything," he commented, "I don't subscribe to that

65. John Heilemann, *The Truth, the Whole Truth, and Nothing but the Truth,* WIRED, Nov. 2000.

© Ingram Pinn/Financial Times.

64. United States v. Microsoft Corp., 84 F. Supp. 2d 9 (D.D.C. 1999).

as absolutely true. But it does lead one to suspicion. It's a universal human experience. If someone lies to you once, how much else can you credit as the truth?"[66] The judge also referred to his lack of trust in Microsoft in his written decision explaining his order to break up the company:

> Microsoft has proved untrustworthy in the past. In earlier proceedings in which a preliminary injunction was entered, Microsoft's purported compliance with that injunction while it was on appeal was illusory and its explanation disingenuous. If it responds in similar fashion to an injunctive remedy in this case, the earlier the need for enforcement measures becomes apparent the more effective they are likely to be.[67]

In its brief appealing the decision, Microsoft criticized Judge Jackson's decision to speak to the press about the case: "The district judge's public comments about the merits of the case, together with this improper handling of the litigation, undermine all confidence in the integrity of the proceedings." Microsoft also argued that the court's decision reflected a "profound misunderstanding" of antitrust laws. The company argued that, contrary to the court's finding, its conduct was procompetitive and helped, rather than harmed, consumers.

During the oral arguments that took place in the U.S. Court of Appeals for the Federal Circuit at the end of February 2001, the judges were extremely critical of Judge Jackson's conduct and accused him of violating a judicial canon restricting judges from making comments on pending cases. The judges' questions also appeared to reflect skepticism about the theory that Microsoft maintained a monopoly in computer software. In addition, they suggested that the trial court should have held a hearing to allow for the presentation of evidence before issuing a decision to break Microsoft into two separate companies. At the end of the hearing, the *New York Times* predicted that much of the lower court's decision would be overturned or that the case would be remanded to a different district court judge for further proceedings.[68]

Other large high-tech companies have already learned from Microsoft's mistakes. In 1997, Cisco Systems chose to cultivate antitrust regulators by opening an office in Washington, D.C., and hiring lobbyists to jawbone decision makers in the federal government.[69] The company uses a legal training tool delivered over the company's internal Web site to educate and caution salespeople about bid-rigging, price-fixing, and collusion with competitors. Cisco has also instructed its salespersons and marketers to avoid using inflammatory language in e-mail and paper memos, citing the *Microsoft* case as an example of how these communications can be used against the company in legal actions.

Intel Corporation had already begun training its executives and sales staff in antitrust law back in 1987. When the company was later sued by the FTC, its compliance program allowed it to avoid large exposure and receive only minor sanctions. As of 2000, Intel included antitrust training as part of its annual sales conference.[70]

---

66. John R. Wilke, *For Antitrust Judge, Trust, or Lack of It, Really Was the Issue,* WALL ST. J., June 8, 2000, at A1.
67. *Judge Orders Microsoft Breakup and Restrictions,* WALL ST. J., June 8, 2000, at A12.
68. Stephen Labaton, *Judges Voice Doubt on Order Last Year to Split Microsoft,* N.Y. TIMES, Feb. 28, 2001, at 1.
69. Scott Thurm, *Safe Conduct, Microsoft's Behavior Is Helping Cisco Learn How to Avoid Trouble,* WALL ST. J., June 1, 2000, at A1.
70. *Id.*

KEY WORDS AND PHRASES

allocative efficiency 686
antitrust injury 681
antitrust laws 662
cartel 674
circumstantial evidence 665
conglomerate merger 695
conscious parallelism 666
cross-elasticity of demand 680
customer restrictions 679
dual distributor 680
essential facility 688
exclusive distributorship 677

franchise 681
group boycott 669
Herfindahl–Hirschman Index (HHI) 692
horizontal agreement 664
horizontal market division 669
horizontal merger 691
horizontal price-fixing 668
illegal *per se* 667
interbrand competition 665
intrabrand competition 667
market power 680

monopolistic intent 685
monopoly power 683
multiple-brand product market 684
parens patriae action 663
per se analysis 667
predatory pricing 685
price discrimination 695
productive efficiency 686
resale price maintenance (RPM) 675
rule of impossibility 686
rule of reason 667
sovereign immunity 696

QUESTIONS AND CASE PROBLEMS

1. Gerber, Heinz, and Beech-Nut, manufacturers of baby food, account for essentially the entire market in the United States. A number of retail stores filed an antitrust class action against the companies alleging that they had violated Section 1 of the Sherman Act by engaging in an unlawful conspiracy to fix prices. The class presented evidence that sales representatives employed by the three companies exchanged price information about their products, including, on occasion, sending each other advanced notice of price increases. The class of store owners also introduced evidence of e-mails indicating that the companies were aware of anticipated price increases before they were announced in the market. One memo stated that Heinz would not try to secure a majority base of distribution in a sales area because it had agreed to a "truce" with Gerber. Did the companies violate the antitrust laws? Is there any additional evidence that you would need to know to make this determination? [*In re Baby Food Antitrust Litigation,* 166 F.3d 112 (3d Cir. 1999)]

2. A manufacturer of electronics in New Orleans, Louisiana, authorized Hayman Electronics and Radio World to sell its products in the New Orleans area. Hayman had been a retailer of these products for several years; Radio World's relationship with the manufacturer was more recent. Hayman complained to the manufacturer that Radio World was price cutting and requested that the manufacturer terminate Radio World as a retailer. The manufacturer did so. Radio World comes to you, the company attorney, asking you what Radio World can do about the termination. What additional information would you like to know, and how will you respond?

3. Queen City Pizza is a franchisee of Domino's Pizza, Inc. By Domino's standard franchise agreement, all pizza ingredients, beverages, and packaging materials used by Queen City must conform to standards set by Domino's. The agreement also gives Domino's sole discretion to require franchisees to purchase these items only from Domino's or approved suppliers. As a result, Domino's supplies 90 percent of the $500 million in ingredients used by

its 3,500 franchisees each year. Except for fresh dough, Domino's purchases the ingredients from approved suppliers and then resells them to franchisees at a markup.

Queen City claims that Domino's has monopolized the market in pizza supplies and ingredients for use in Domino's stores in violation of Section 2 of the Sherman Act. Analyze the merits of this claim. [*Queen City Pizza, Inc. v. Domino's Pizza, Inc.,* 124 F.3d 430 (3d Cir. 1997), *cert. denied,* 523 U.S. 1059 (1998)]

4. The National Collegiate Athletic Association (NCAA) is an association of approximately 1,100 educational institutions that coordinates the intercollegiate athletic programs of its members. As part of that coordination, the NCAA adopts and promulgates playing rules, standards of amateurism, standards for academic eligibility, student-recruitment regulations, and rules governing the sizes of athletic squads and coaching staffs. The rules vary based on division status, which reflects differences in program size and scope.

Concerned with rapidly rising program costs at Division I schools in the 1980s, the NCAA promulgated new rules in 1991 to limit the number of basketball coaches at those schools to four—one head coach, two assistant coaches, and one entry-level coach. The new rules also restricted the annual salary of an entry-level coach to $16,000 but allowed these so-named restricted-earnings coaches (RECs) to receive additional compensation for performing duties in other departments of the institutions.

A group of RECs from Division I schools for the 1992–1993 academic year challenged the compensation limit as an illegal attempt to restrain trade under Section 1 of the Sherman Act. The NCAA argued that some horizontal restraints were necessary to provide its product, namely competition. Furthermore, it argued that these limits were reasonable and procompetitive. How should the court rule? [*Law v. NCAA,* 134 F.3d 1010 (10th Cir. 1998)]

5. U.S. manufacturers want to bring a suit against Japanese manufacturers, alleging a conspiracy to take over the U.S. automobile industry by exporting low-priced products to the United States while keeping the prices artificially high in Japan. The U.S. manufacturers tell you, their attorney, that the Japanese manufacturers have formed an association in which they discuss market conditions in the United States, potential or actual import restrictions, surcharges, and simplification of export procedures, as well as other topics.

a. In light of these facts, what are the chances of successfully bringing an antitrust suit against these manufacturers? Assume that there are no conflict-of-law or other procedural problems due to the manufacturers being in another country.

b. What if, instead of discussing the topics listed above, they discussed the details of individual sales, production, inventories, current price lists, and future price trends?

c. What if they discussed average costs, freight rates, and terms of past transactions without identifying buyers or sellers? [*Matsushita Electrical Industrial Co. v. Zenith Radio Corp.*, 475 U.S. 574 (1986)]

6. Lillian Alexander worked for Western Propane Company in Colorado. After becoming disgruntled with the company, she left and opened her own propane company, which competed directly with Western Propane. The two companies fought for the same customers. Within two years, Alexander's company went from 0 to 25 percent of the market, and Western Propane's share dropped from 75 to 50 percent. Alexander comes to you, her attorney, wanting to bring suit against Western Propane for predatory pricing. She tells you that during a recent price war Western Propane priced its product below average total cost. What must you prove to show predatory pricing, and what are your chances of success? [*McGahee v. Northern Propane Gas Co.*, 858 F.2d 1487 (11th Cir. 1988), *cert. denied*, 490 U.S. 1084 (1989)]

7. Digital Equipment Corporation (DEC) manufactured hardware ranging from personal computers to mainframes. In April 1994, DEC introduced a new line of mid-range servers that were more powerful and versatile than their predecessors and included a three-year warranty as part of the package. Although multiyear warranties for personal computers had become standard, a three-year warranty, rather than a one-year warranty, was uncommon in the mid-range server market. SMS Systems Maintenance Services was an independent service organization that specialized in servicing particular brands of equipment,

including DEC equipment. SMS alleged that DEC's inclusion of a three-year warranty with its mid-range servers was anticompetitive and violated Section 2 of the Sherman Act. As a result, SMS alleged, the DEC warranty functioned as a vehicle for aftermarket monopolization by creating a disincentive for computer purchasers to consult service firms other than the manufacturer itself. How should the court rule? [*SMS Systems Maintenance Services, Inc. v. Digital Equipment Corp.*, 188 F.3d 11 (1st Cir. 1999), *cert. denied*, 528 U.S. 1188 (2000)]

8. The Aspen Skiing Company (Aspen Ski) owned three of the four mountain skiing facilities in Aspen, Colorado. The fourth facility was owned by the Aspen Highlands Skiing Corporation (Highlands). Between 1962 and 1977, Aspen Ski and Highlands jointly offered a six-day ticket providing skiers with unlimited access to all four facilities. Revenues from the "all-Aspen" ticket, which was very popular with skiers, were divided on the basis of usage. In 1976–1977, Aspen Ski's share of the market for downhill-skiing services in Aspen was approximately 80 percent.

In the late 1970s, Aspen Ski's management came to believe that Aspen Ski could expand its market share if it discontinued the all-Aspen ticket. For the 1977–1978 season, Aspen Ski refused to market the all-Aspen ticket unless Highlands accepted a fixed share of the revenue, rather than a share based on usage. In 1978–1979, Aspen Ski refused to market the all-Aspen ticket unless Highlands accepted an extremely low fixed share of the revenue, which Highlands declined to do. An Aspen Ski official admitted that Aspen Ski intended to make Highlands an offer that it could not accept. In addition, Aspen Ski took affirmative steps to make it difficult for Highlands to market its own all-Aspen ticket. This included refusing to sell lift tickets for Aspen Ski's facilities to Highlands and refusing to accept guaranteed Highlands vouchers in exchange for lift tickets to Aspen Ski's facilities.

As a result of these actions, Highlands's share of the market for downhill-skiing facilities in Aspen steadily declined, reaching 11 percent in 1980–1981. In 1979, Highlands sued Aspen Ski for monopolization of the downhill-skiing market in Aspen.

a. What elements are required to prove a charge of monopolization?

b. Did Aspen Ski enjoy monopoly power in the relevant market?

c. Could the all-Aspen ticket be fairly characterized as an essential facility? If so, did Aspen Ski's refusal to provide Highlands with access to the all-Aspen ticket constitute evidence of intent to monopolize? [*Aspen Skiing Co. v. Aspen Highlands Skiing Corp.*, 472 U.S. 585 (1985)]

9. Honeywell, Inc. manufactures and sells industrial equipment that controls the manufacturing processes at various refineries and factories. The equipment depends heavily on printed circuit boards, which contain many components. These components periodically fail, which in turn often causes the circuit board and the industrial control equipment also to fail. When a circuit board fails, Honeywell will replace it with a new or refurbished board, charging its customer 50 percent of the list price, as long as the customer returns the defective board.

   Roughly 95 percent of the components on the circuit boards can be purchased either from the component manufacturer or from a component distributor. The other 5 percent are designed specifically for Honeywell by third-party manufacturers. Honeywell has restrictive agreements with these manufacturers whereby the manufacturers agree not to sell these components to either Honeywell equipment owners or service organizations. Honeywell also has a stated policy of not selling its components to anyone. When a circuit board fails, equipment owners usually cannot identify which component caused the failure. As a result, equipment owners essentially must return the circuit boards to Honeywell to obtain an entire replacement board.

   PSI Repair Services offers circuit-board repair services to owners of industrial control equipment. PSI provides board services for customers that own systems manufactured by Honeywell's competitors by purchasing the necessary components from either the equipment or the component manufacturer. It is also able to obtain any firmware and documentation necessary for the nongeneric components either from the manufacturer's marketing information or by purchasing this information from the manufacturer. Because PSI is unable to obtain any of the components manufactured exclusively for Honeywell, it is, for all practical purposes, unable to compete in the market for repair of Honeywell boards. What legal claims does PSI have against Honeywell? Will PSI prevail? [*PSI Repair Services, Inc. v. Honeywell, Inc.*, 104 F.3d 811 (6th Cir. 1997), *cert. denied*, 520 U.S. 1265 (1997)]

MANAGER'S DILEMMA

10. You are the vice president for marketing at Lucky Liquor, a manufacturer of liquor. During a meeting with your staff, several pricing proposals are made with strong arguments to support each proposal:

    a. The manufacturer sets a minimum price per ounce that the wholesalers can charge.

    b. The manufacturer sets a maximum price per ounce that the wholesalers can charge.

    c. The wholesalers can charge any price they want within a certain range; if they charge a higher price, they must give the customer a rebate coupon for the differential.

    d. The wholesalers can charge any price they want, but if they advertise a price that is less than Lucky Liquor's specified minimum advertised price, the wholesalers are not entitled to receive the marketing funds that Lucky Liquor provides wholesalers that do not advertise prices that are less than the specified minimum advertised price.

    After the meeting, you are considering the pros and cons of each plan so that you can make a recommendation to the president. Although each plan has different marketing advantages, your staff estimates that each will result in approximately the same level of sales. What other factors should you consider before making your recommendation? What are the legal pros and cons of each proposal? What else do you need to know before calculating the legal trade-offs among the proposals?

INTERNET SOURCES

Department of Justice, Antitrust Division	http://www.usdoj.gov/atr
Federal Trade Commission	http://www.ftc.gov
Microsoft Corporation	http://www.microsoft.com
The European Union On-Line	http://europa.int
The Competition Online site, maintained by the editors of *Competition Journal* in Dublin, Ireland, is a gateway to numerous U.S., European, and other antitrust sites.	http://www.clubi.ie/competition/WorldsBiggestAntiTrustSitesList.html
FindLaw—Antitrust and Trade Regulation	http://www.findlaw.com/01topics/01antitrust/index.html
AOL Time Warner	http://www.aoltimewarner.com/index_flash.shtml

CHAPTER 21

Consumer Protection

ROLE OF CONSUMER PROTECTION LAW IN BUSINESS

Historically, consumers had little recourse in the event of a dispute with a vendor, manufacturer, producer, service provider, or creditor. The words commonly associated with consumer transactions were *caveat emptor* ("let the buyer beware"). Now many federal and state laws protect consumers from unsafe or harmful consumer products, unfair and deceptive trade practices, fraud, and misleading and discriminatory credit requirements. Managers must, of course, comply with the law. In addition, by being proactive and promoting industry self-regulation, managers may be able to forestall burdensome new regulatory restrictions.

CHAPTER OVERVIEW

This chapter examines four primary areas of consumer protection law and the agencies, departments, and commissions that admin-

ister and enforce them: (1) consumer health and safety (including the regulation of food, drugs, medical devices, alcohol, tobacco, smoking, gambling, firearms, automobiles, broadcasting, and the Internet); (2) consumer privacy; (3) unfairness, deception, and fraud (including the regulation of advertising, packaging and labeling, pricing, warranties, and certain sales practices); and (4) consumer credit. The chapter focuses primarily on federal legislation, although numerous state law topics are discussed. In general, state consumer protection laws are more stringent than federal law. Consumer bankruptcy under Chapter 13 of the Bankruptcy Code is discussed in Chapter 26.

 ## Commissions *and* Agencies

Federal regulatory agencies involved in consumer protection are either independent commissions or executive branch agencies. Independent commissions include the Federal Trade Commission, the Federal Communications Commission, the Securities and Exchange Commission, the Federal Reserve System, and the Consumer Product Safety Commission. The Federal Trade Commission, for example, has five commissioners appointed by the president and confirmed by the Senate for seven-year terms. No more than three of them can be from the

same political party. The commissioners make decisions by majority vote and issue rules.

Executive branch regulatory agencies are located in cabinet departments. Examples include the Food and Drug Administration (in the U.S. Department of Health and Human Services), the Office of Interstate Land Sales Registration (U.S. Department of Housing and Urban Development), and the National Highway Traffic Safety Administration (U.S. Department of Transportation).

The "In Brief" identifies the key commissions and agencies charged with administering major consumer protection laws.

IN BRIEF
Consumer Protection Laws and Their Administration

Agency, Department, or Commission	Consumer Credit	Unfairness, Deception, and Fraud	Consumer Health and Safety
Federal Trade Commission Established: 1914 Commissioners: 5	Credit advertising; Fair Credit Reporting Act; Fair Debt Collection Practices Act	Advertising; sales practices	
Food and Drug Administration (U.S. Department of Health and Human Services Established: 1930 Commissioners: 1		Labeling of food (except meat, poultry, and eggs), drugs, and cosmetics	Adulterated food and cosmetics; approval of drugs and medical devices
U.S. Department of Agriculture Established: 1862		Labeling of meat, poultry, and eggs	Inspection of meat, poultry, and egg processing facilities
Federal Communications Commission Established: 1934 Commissioners: 5		Telemarketing	Broadcast standards
U.S. Postal Service Established: 1775 Reorganized: 1970		Fraudulent mail schemes	
Office of Interstate Land Sales Registration (U.S. Department of Housing and Urban Development) Established: 1969		Interstate land sales	
Securities and Exchange Commission Established: 1934 Commissioners: 5		Securities fraud	
Federal Reserve Board Established: 1913 Governors: 7	Truth-in-Lending Act (Regulation Z); Consumer Leasing Act (Regulation M); Equal Credit Opportunity Act (Regulation B); Electronic Fund Transfer Act (Regulation E)		
National Highway Traffic Safety Administration (NHTSA) (U.S. Department of Transportation) Established: 1970 Administrators: 1			Automobile safety standards; driver safety
Consumer Product Safety Commission (CPSC) Established: 1972 Commissioners: 3			Consumer Product Safety Act (CPSA); consumer product safety
U.S. Department of Labor Established: 1913	Garnishment of wages		
State law, departments, and commissions	Installment sales; loans to consumers; Uniform Consumer Credit Code (UCCC)	State labeling laws; state deceptive practices statutes; insurance regulation; lemon laws; Uniform Commercial Code (UCC)	State departments of consumer affairs
Other federal law	Chapter 13 consumer bankruptcy		

Consumer Health *and* Safety

Consumers' health and safety is protected by a number of federal, state, and local regulatory agencies, including the Food and Drug Administration (FDA), the Department of Agriculture, the Department of Transportation's National Highway Traffic Safety Administration, and the Consumer Product Safety Commission. For example, under the Food, Drug and Cosmetic Act,[1] the FDA monitors the production and sale of $1 trillion worth of food and medical products each year. In addition to regulating food, drug, medical device, and cosmetic labeling to prevent *misbranding,* the FDA also oversees the process for approving new drugs. The Federal Trade Commission also regulates the packaging and labeling of some products.

At the state level, consumer health and safety laws cover a wide variety of areas, such as food, drugs, medical devices, cosmetics, clothing and the availability of alcohol, tobacco, and gambling. State and local provisions also address no-smoking regulations, restaurant inspections, and the competency of professional workers through the granting of various occupational licenses.

Consumer protection law should not be confused with product liability law, discussed in Chapter 10. Product liability law provides a common law remedy enforced by private action, whereas consumer protection law provides a statutory remedy enforced by the government (and, in some cases, also by private parties).

Food Safety *and* Labeling

PRODUCT DEFINITION: FOOD OR DRUG?

Drugs, as defined by the Food, Drug and Cosmetic Act, include (1) articles intended for use in the diagnosis, cure, mitigation, treatment, or prevention of disease; and (2) articles (other than food) intended to affect the structure or any function of the body. Thus, many things that are, in fact, food may fit this definition. For example, orange juice might be used to prevent disease. Under the Act, *foods* include (1) articles used for food or drink, (2) chewing gum, and (3) articles used for components of either.

Because the distinction between drugs and food is important in the application of both the mislabeling and the adulteration provisions of the Act, as well as in the drug-approval process, the FDA must categorize each product. In general, the FDA looks at the intended use of a product in determining how to categorize it. Intent may be apparent from the manufacturer's purpose or from consumers' reasons for using the product, or it may be inferred from labels, promotional material, or advertisements.

FDA STANDARDS FOR FOOD CONDEMNATION

The FDA also protects consumer health and safety through the confiscation of contaminated or adulterated foods. The standards for condemnation differ depending on whether the product is a natural food or contains additives. An *additive* is anything not inherent in the food product, including pesticide residue, unintended environmental contaminants, and unavoidably added substances from packaging. If an additive (in the quantity present in the food product) is injurious to any group in the general population, then the product will be deemed adulterated.

A natural food is adulterated if it "consist[s] in whole or in part of any filthy, putrid or decomposed substance, or if it is otherwise unfit for food." All foods contain some level of unavoidable natural defects, so the FDA sets minimum tolerance standards for defects that will be permitted. Articles that exceed those minimum levels are deemed adulterated and seized by the FDA. In some cases, a seized product may be rehabilitated by a manufacturer and released by the FDA for sale.

In other cases, a manufacturer may be required to recall a contaminated food. In the largest recall of its kind, Hudson Foods recalled 25 million pounds of hamburger meat contaminated with a virulent strain of *E. coli* bacteria in 1997. Tainted food causes an estimated 6.5 million to 33 million illnesses and 9,000 deaths annually in the United States.

ROLE OF THE U.S. DEPARTMENT OF AGRICULTURE

The U.S. Department of Agriculture (USDA) also plays a major role in food safety. The USDA's primary consumer protection activities all involve food and include inspecting facilities engaged in slaughtering or processing meat, poultry, and egg products; preventing the sale of mislabeled meat or poultry products; and offering producers a voluntary grading program for various agricultural products.

PESTICIDES

Under the Food, Drug and Cosmetic Act, the FDA shares with the Environmental Protection Agency (EPA) the responsibility for regulating pesticide residues on

---

1. 21 U.S.C. § 321 *et seq.* (Supp. 1998).

INTERNATIONAL CONSIDERATION

Recent trade treaties have made the U.S. food market one of the most open in the world. Food imports doubled in the 1990s and now amount to 30 billion tons annually. The importation of fresh fruits and vegetables, gourmet cheeses, meats, and shellfish present new challenges for regulators. For example, raspberries imported from Guatemala carried a food-borne parasite that struck hundreds of people in 1996.

To allay concerns in the United States, authorities in Mexico (which ships 90 percent of its $4.5 billion in annual food exports to the United States) are encouraging produce exporters to have their operations certified by private U.S. laboratories that inspect the fields, irrigation water and packing conditions, and the bathrooms workers use. Mexican growers of mangoes destined for the United States employ sixty inspectors from the U.S. Department of Agriculture. Still experts argue that the ultimate burden of ensuring safe food may fall on the globalized food industry.[a]

a. Paul Magnusson et al., *News: Analysis & Commentary,* Bus. Wk., Sept. 8, 1997, at 30–32.

food. The EPA registers pesticides and establishes tolerances under the Act. The FDA enforces the tolerance levels and deems a food to be adulterated if it does not conform to the established tolerance levels.

GENETICALLY MODIFIED FOOD

In April 2000, the National Academy of Science issued a report advising the federal government to increase its regulation of genetically modified foods. Although the report did not find that genetically modified food was unsafe, it urged scientists to develop better methods for identifying potential allergens and called on the regulatory agencies to monitor the environmental impact of genetically modified organisms (GMOs). The report also concluded that the EPA, USDA, and FDA should do a better job of coordinating their work and informing the public about GMOs.[2]

European consumers have vehemently opposed the sale of genetically modified foods and launched a major campaign against Monsanto's efforts to market GMOs

2. Scott Kilman, *Government Is Advised to Tighten Regulation of Bioengineered Crops,* WALL ST. J., Apr. 6, 2000, at B2.

"Today's objective is the genetically modified corn in this quadrant!"

AT THE TOP

A chief executive officer of a food company may be held vicariously and strictly liable for introducing adulterated articles into interstate commerce.[a] The CEO should ensure that top managers have adequate policies and checks in place to ensure the proper handling and storage of food. If a problem is brought to a manager's attention, he or she should immediately report it to a supervisor and personally ensure that it is remedied.

a. United States v. Park, 421 U.S. 658 (1975).

in European countries. In 1998, the European Union approved legislation that required its member countries to label all food that contained genetically modified ingredients.[3] In 2001, the European Parliament approved legislation that requires continuous monitoring of GMOs. The law calls for labeling and monitoring of genetically modified foods, seeds, feeds, and pharmaceuticals and requires governments to maintain a registry of where genetically modified plants are being grown.[4]

As noted in the "Inside Story" for Chapter 10, opposition to GMOs has spread to the United States where consumers have protested GMOs because of both health safety and environmental concerns. Due to the potential enormous benefits of genetically modified foods, particularly for developing countries, the debate over regulating genetically engineered crops is far from over.

IRRADIATED FOODS

In December 1997, the FDA authorized the irradiation of fresh and frozen red meat as a means to kill food-borne bacteria (including *E. coli*) and lengthen shelf life. During irradiation, food is passed through a sealed chamber, where it is exposed to gamma ray radiation from cobalt 60 or cesium 137 or to an electron beam. FDA regulations require irradiated foods to be prominently and conspicuously labeled with the radura symbol (a stylized green flower) and the words "Treated with Radiation" or "Treated by Irradiation."

For many consumers, irradiation conjures up images of mushroom clouds and Chernobyl.[5] Some activists have threatened to organize consumer boycotts of companies selling irradiated foods and to launch media campaigns against irradiation. Nevertheless, experts predict that consumers will be won over by irradiation's safety and effectiveness in protecting against bacteria and other microbes. Former FDA commissioner Dr. David Kessler draws parallels to the public's shunning of pasteurized milk in the early twentieth century and the initial distrust of microwave ovens in the 1970s.[6]

ORGANIC FOODS

The U.S. market for organic foods increased by more than 20 percent during each year of the 1990s. Sales from organic products amounted to approximately $6 billion in 2000 and accounted for 1 to 2 percent of total food sales.[7] In December 2000, the USDA issued uniform standards for organic food, which are being implemented over an eighteen-month period beginning in February 2001. The standards ban the use of pesticides, genetic engineering, growth hormones, and irradiation, and they require dairy cattle to have access to pasture. Foods grown and processed according to the standards will bear the seal "USDA Organic."[8]

FOOD LABELING

The FDA has primary responsibility for regulating the packaging and labeling of food (except meat, poultry, and eggs, which are under the jurisdiction of the USDA), drugs, medical devices, and cosmetics. In 1966, Congress passed the Fair Packaging and Labeling Act[9] in response to the surge in prepackaged items available at supermarkets and the perceived subtle deceptions some manufacturers employed.

Under the Act, a food label must contain the name and address of the manufacturer, packer, or distributor; the net quantity on the front panel, placed in a uniform location; the quantity given in servings, with the net quantity of

3. Steve Stecklow, *Foodstuff, Genetically Modified on the Label Means . . . Well, It's Hard to Say*, WALL ST. J., Oct. 26, 1999, at A1.
4. *Genetic Engineering: Euro Parliament Approves Guidelines*, Feb. 14, 2001, at <http://www.eenews.net>.
5. Martha Groves, *Less-Than Glowing Image Hampers Food Irradiation*, L.A. TIMES, Mar. 15, 1998, at A1.

6. Joanna Ramey, *Food Industry Groups Near Start of Irradiation Campaign*, SUPERMARKET NEWS, Apr. 17, 1998, at 23.
7. Betsy Block, *What You Need to Know About Organic Food*, BOSTON GLOBE, Mar. 29, 2000, at E1.
8. Frederick J. Frommer, *Some Worry New USDA Label Will Change Organic Farming*, ASSOCIATED PRESS, Jan. 13, 2001.
9. 15 U.S.C. § 1451 *et seq.* (1998).

 INTERNATIONAL CONSIDERATION

Manufacturers of goods that are to be exported need to consider foreign labeling requirements, such as language translations, country of origin disclosures, and weight conversions.

each serving stated; and the quantity listed in certain ways, depending on how the product is classified. This last provision requires dual declarations of sizes (for example, one quart and thirty-two ounces) and forbids the use of terms such as "jumbo quart" and "super ounce."

Another area of concern for Congress was the proliferation of various package sizes, making price comparison extremely difficult for consumers. For example, a "jumbo" size of one product might contain the same amount as the "large" size of another. Similarly, the terms "small, medium, and large" have often been embellished with terms like "ketchup-lover size," "family size," and "fun size." The 1966 Act gave the FDA authority to add requirements concerning the use of such terms, as well as terms associated with value claims such as "economy size." Many supermarkets now provide unit-pricing information so that consumers can more easily compare the prices of competing products.

Nutrition Facts The Nutrition Labeling and Education Act of 1990[10] (1) requires nutrition labeling of almost all foods through a nutrition panel entitled "Nutrition Facts"; (2) imposes expanded ingredient labeling requirements; and (3) restricts nutrient content claims and health claims. The FDA regulations also govern the use of nutrient claims, such as "light," "fat free," and "low calorie," and provide uniform definitions so that these terms mean the same for any product on which they appear.

Approximately 90 percent of processed foods must carry nutrition information. Some exceptions include plain coffee and tea, delicatessen items, and bulk food. The Nutrition Facts panel must include the amount per serving of saturated fat, cholesterol, dietary fiber, sodium, and other nutrients. These panels also provide information on how the food fits into an overall daily diet. Under the Act, point-of-purchase nutrition information is voluntary for many raw foods including meat, poultry, raw fish, and fresh produce. Such information may be shown in a poster or chart at a butcher's counter or a produce stand.

Prior to 1984, the FDA took the position that a statement that consumption of a food could prevent a particular disease was "tantamount to a claim that the food was a drug . . . and therefore that its sale was prohibited until a new drug application has been approved."[11] The Nutrition Labeling and Education Act of 1990 permits health claims on foods to be made without FDA approval as a new drug, or the risk of sanctions for issuing a "misbranded" product, if the claim has been certified by the FDA as being supported by significant scientific

agreement. The FDA has approved several health claims on foods, including the relationship between calcium and osteoporosis, fiber-containing products and cancer, fruits and vegetables and cancer, folate and neural tube defects, and soluble fiber and coronary heart disease.

Drugs *and* Medical Devices

FDA STANDARDS FOR DRUG APPROVAL

The FDA has authority to require that certain drugs be available only by prescription. If a drug authorized only for prescription use is sold over-the-counter, then it is misbranded and the FDA will halt its sale. In general, the FDA will require prescription use only when a drug is, for example, toxic, requires a physician's supervision for safe use, or is addictive.

The first step in the approval process for new drugs is their classification by the Drug Enforcement Agency (DEA) into one of five schedules based on potential for abuse and currently accepted medical use. Only Schedule I drugs, those with the highest potential for abuse and no currently accepted medical use, cannot be approved by the FDA.

The drug-approval process for non–Schedule I drugs begins with preclinical research (which includes animal testing) aimed at the discovery and identification of drugs that are sufficiently promising to study in humans. The drugmaker then submits this preclinical research, along with a document called "Claimed Exemption for Investigational New Drug," to the FDA. The FDA can then permit or deny continued research. If approved for investigational purposes, a drug will be tested in humans in three separate phases, with FDA review at the end of each phase. This framework is designed to protect the safety of the human subjects used in the study, to develop necessary data on the drug, and to ensure that all studies are done properly. Once all of the testing data are assembled, they are submitted to the FDA, which may approve or deny the drug. Approval is based on a drug's safety and effectiveness; the approval may require marketing restrictions; and it can be contested by anyone. The FDA must also approve the description of a drug (for example, labels and package inserts).

Drugs with a high potential for therapeutic gain and no satisfactory alternative may be given priority (expedited) review by the FDA. In addition, through open protocols, such drugs may be available during the investigational stage to people not within the clinical test group. For example, people with AIDS may have access to new drugs under investigation if preliminary evidence of effectiveness exists.

10. 21 U.S.C.A. §§ 301, 321, 337, 343, 371 (1972 & Supp. 1998).
11. H.R. REP. NO. 538, at 9 (1990), *reprinted in* 1990 U.S.C.C.A.N. 3336, 3338.

Congress passed the Food and Drug Administration Modernization Act of 1997 to speed up the approval of new drugs and medical devices by permitting the FDA to use outside reviewers to evaluate medical devices and make it easier for seriously ill patients to obtain experimental drugs.[12] This Act also includes provisions governing drug manufacturers' distribution of information concerning "off-label" uses of their drugs. Off-label uses are uses other than those for which a drug was approved. A physician can prescribe a drug to serve any purpose that he or she thinks is appropriate regardless of whether the drug was initially approved for that use. In 2000, the U.S. Court of Appeals for the District of Columbia Circuit held that the FDA's policies regarding the dissemination of information about off-label uses did not violate the First Amendment after the FDA conceded that it had no authority to ban dissemination of information about off-brand uses.[13]

In *Western States Medical Center v. Shalala*,[14] the D.C. Circuit struck down the provisions of the Food and Drug Administration Modernization Act[15] that exempted compounded drugs from the FDA's approval requirements only if the compounding pharmacy refrained from advertising particular compounded drugs. Compounding is a process whereby a pharmacist, pursuant to a physician's prescription, mixes ingredients to create a medication for a particular patient, usually because the patient is allergic to an ingredient in a mass-produced product. The court held that the ban violated the Free Speech Clause of the First Amendment, as construed by the U.S. Supreme Court in *Central Hudson Gas & Electric Corp. v. Public Service Commission*.[16] The prohibited commercial speech was neither unlawful nor misleading. The government failed to demonstrate a substantial interest in preventing widespread compounding and offered no evidence that the restrictions would reduce the type of con-

sumption of compounded drugs that is harmful. In addition, the restrictions were more extensive than necessary to achieve the government's asserted goal of maintaining the integrity of the drug-approval process.

LABELING OF MEDICAL DEVICES

Labeling of medical devices is also under the jurisdiction of the FDA. As noted in Chapter 10, even if a manufacturer provides the FDA-mandated warnings, it still could be found liable under state product liability law for failure to warn if reasonable manufacturers would have done more. For example, the U.S. Court of Appeals for the Tenth Circuit upheld a $10 million punitive damage award against International Playtex for failure to adequately warn users about the risk of fatal toxic shock syndrome from use of high-absorbing tampons.[17] The court concluded that Playtex had shown reckless indifference to consumer safety by deliberately disregarding studies and medical reports linking high-absorbency tampon fibers with increased risk of toxic shock at a time when other tampon manufacturers were responding to this information by modifying or withdrawing their high-absorbency products.

DRUG ADVERTISING

In 1997, the FDA, which regulates drug advertising, eased the restrictions on the advertising of prescription drugs on television and radio. Drug companies can now tout a drug's benefits without listing all of the side effects and explaining how to properly use the drug. Television ads must, however, warn of major risks and provide a quick way (such as a toll-free telephone number, Web address, or magazine advertisement) for consumers to obtain full information about the drug. In response to a dramatic increase in drug advertising, the FDA announced in 2001 that it was reviewing its policies in this area.

 Health Claims *and* Labeling *of* Dietary Supplements

Under the Dietary Supplement Health and Education Act of 1994,[18] the sale of dietary supplements is regulated only when the supplement contains a new dietary ingredient or poses a safety risk. Dietary supplements include products such as vitamins, minerals, herbs, and amino acids. As with food, however, health claims on dietary supplements can cause them to be characterized as

12. Food and Drug Administration Modernization Act of 1997, Pub. L. No. 105-115 (1997).
13. Washington Legal Found. v. Henney, 202 F.3d 331 (D.C. Cir. 2000).
14. 238 F.3d 1090 (D.C. Cir. 2001).
15. 21 U.S.C. § 353a.
16. 447 U.S. 557 (1980).

17. Ogilvie v. International Playtex, Inc., 821 F.2d 1438 (10th Cir. 1987), *cert. denied*, 486 U.S. 1032 (1988).
18. 21 U.S.C.A. §§ 350b, 342(f) (Supp. 1998).

drugs. The Nutrition Labeling and Education Act created a safe harbor for health claims on dietary supplements akin to that provided for food but delegated to the FDA the task of establishing a procedure and standard regarding the validity of health claims.

The FDA issued regulations providing that it would authorize a health claim only if there was substantial scientific agreement among experts that the claim was supported by the totality of publicly available scientific evidence.[19] In *Pearson v. Shalala,*[20] the U.S. Court of Appeals for the District of Columbia Circuit curtailed the FDA's right to ban health-related claims made by sellers of nutritional supplements. Two dietary supplement marketers sought permission from the FDA to place health claims on their products. The FDA denied the request on the grounds that there was no significant scientific agreement concerning the claims. The FDA refused to allow the marketers to make the claims even if they also included disclaimers from the FDA. The court ruled that the FDA's refusal to permit the health claims with disclaimers violated the marketers' First Amendment rights and held that marketers may put health claims on the labels of dietary supplements as long as these labels also include disclaimers saying that the FDA considers the evidence supporting the claims inconclusive.

In 2000, the FDA published a final rule clarifying the types of claims that manufacturers of dietary supplements can make without prior review by the FDA and identifying those that require prior authorization.[21] The FDA also issued a ten-year strategic plan outlining its strategy for regulating dietary supplements under the 1994 Dietary Supplement Health and Education Act. The agency's goals include improving the capability of its reporting system, taking action against unsafe products, strengthening the scientific base for dietary supplement review, and enhancing outreach efforts.

19. 21 C.F.R. § 101.14(c) (1998).
20. 164 F.3d 650 (D.C. Cir. 1999).

21. *FDA Regulates Statements Made on Effects of Dietary Supplements,* 68 U.S.L.W. 2392–93 (Jan. 11, 2000).

HISTORICAL PERSPECTIVE

Food *and* Drug Regulation

Thalidomide Tragedy Spurs New Laws, 1962

[T]he thalidomide tragedy of the 1960s, though Americans were spared its worst effects, produced the still-stronger drug-testing laws of 1962.

Thalidomide, developed in Germany, had been hailed as the greatest sleeping pill in history. After it became a bestseller in Germany, Britain and Canada, the century-old William Merrell Company asked the U.S. Food and Drug Administration in September 1960 for approval to sell it in the United States. The application, backed by four telephone-book-sized volumes of data, was assigned to Frances Kelsey, a Canadian-born physician and pharmacologist who had just joined the FDA.

Dr. Kelsey thought thalidomide looked "peculiar." For one thing, the sleeping pill didn't make test animals sleepy. Despite constant—and angry—pressure from Merrell, she blocked approval, asking Merrell for more and more data.

Meanwhile, German and other European doctors were puzzling over an epidemic of phocomelia, children born with flipper-like appendages instead of proper arms and legs. In November 1961, Widiking Lenz, a Hamburg

pediatrician, discovered the link: Mothers of the deformed babies had been using thalidomide. The drug was withdrawn that month and Merrell dropped its application for FDA approval.

When the thalidomide story hit the United States, it caused shudders that had seismic effects in Congress. Sen. Estes Kefauver, whose tough drug-regulating bill had been gutted on Capitol Hill, now saw it revived, strengthened and sped on its way to President Kennedy's desk. He signed it into law in October 1962, two months after he had awarded Dr. Kelsey the Distinguished Federal Civilian Service Award.

Source: WALL ST. J., Sept. 6, 1989, at B1. Reprinted by permission of the *Wall Street Journal,* © 1989, Dow Jones & Company, Inc. All Rights Reserved Worldwide.

Update

In a strange historical twist, this birth-defect-causing drug came back in vogue in the 1990s as a possible treatment for the effects of AIDS. In 1995, the FDA gave Celgene Corporation permission to conduct clinical trials of thalidomide to counteract the severe weight loss and deterioration that often accompany AIDS.[a] In the following year, Celgene applied for federal permission to use thalidomide to treat an especially painful form of leprosy.[b] In 1997, the FDA Advisory Committee recommended approval of thalidomide for this treatment, signaling a newfound respect for this scourge of the 1960s.[c]

a. *Once-Feared Thalidomide to Be Offered AIDS Patients,* SEATTLE POST-INTELLIGENCER, Aug. 29, 1995, at A3.
b. *Company Applies to Use Thalidomide for Leprosy,* ORLANDO SENTINEL, Dec. 24, 1996, at A8.
c. *FDA Approves Thalidomide's Use Against ENL,* ECN—EUR. CHEM. NEWS, Sept. 15, 1997, at 51.

Labeling *of* Other Products

CLOTHING

The Federal Trade Commission (FTC) has primary responsibility for regulating the packaging and labeling of commodities other than food, drugs, medical devices, and cosmetics. For example, numerous federal laws regulate the labeling of clothing. Among these are the Wool Products Labeling Act,[22] the Fur Products Labeling Act,[23] the Flammable Fabrics Act,[24] and the Textile Fiber Products Identification Act.[25] Each of these laws is intended to protect distributors and consumers against misbranding and false advertising.

ALCOHOL

In 1989, a congressionally mandated warning label began to appear on bottles, cans, and packages of wine, beer, and spirits. The label states that alcohol consumption increases the risks of birth defects, warns that consuming alcoholic beverages can impair one's ability to drive a car, and cautions against the use of alcohol when operating machinery.[26]

The Bureau of Alcohol, Tobacco and Firearms (BATF), a branch of the Treasury Department, regulates everything that appears on packages of alcoholic beverages and bottles of wine. BATF regulations attach legal meanings to various statements made on wine labels, including the vintage year, grape variety, producer, and alcohol content. Warnings are also required to alert those who are allergic to sulfites that wine contains trace amounts of the substances, which may be used as a preservative and are also produced naturally during fermentation.

MADE IN USA

The FTC has adopted guidelines specifying when manufacturers and marketers can label their products "Made in USA". Under the FTC's Made in USA policy, "all or virtually all" of the product must be made in the fifty states, the District of Columbia, or the U.S. territories and possessions. "All or virtually all" means that all significant parts and processing that go into the product must be of U.S. origin. A manufacturer or marketer must have a reasonable basis, based on competent and reliable evidence, to support its claim that the product was made in the USA.[27]

STATE LABELING LAWS

Many states have enacted labeling laws aimed at protecting consumers from dangerous products. Historically, these laws have sought to protect consumers from the danger of imminent bodily harm. Recently, however, some states have enacted more extensive labeling laws. Notable among these statutes is California's Safe Drinking Water and Toxic Enforcement Act of 1986, better known as Proposition 65. Proposition 65 provides that "no person . . . shall knowingly and intentionally expose any individual to a chemical known to the state to cause cancer or reproductive toxicity without first giving clear and reasonable warning to such individual."[28]

The law requires the governor to compile a list of the chemicals requiring warnings and to update the list annually. The current list includes ingredients such as alcohol and saccharin, as well as potential contaminants such as lead and mercury. The labeling requirements apply to manufacturers, producers, packagers, and retail sellers and may be in the form of product labels, signs at retail outlets, or public advertising. An example of a Proposition 65 warning is: "Warning: This product contains a chemical known to the State of California to cause birth defects or other reproductive harm." The FDA has the authority to issue regulations that would preempt state labeling requirements, such as Proposition 65, but so far the FDA has chosen not to do so.

Broadcasting *and the* Internet

BROADCASTING

Regulation of broadcasting by the Federal Communications Commission (FCC) seeks to ensure that broadcast media are competitive and operate for the public's benefit and use. Enforcement of FCC policies is achieved primarily through its ability to withhold license renewals. Licenses cannot be transferred or assigned without the FCC's permission and a finding that such a transfer will serve the public interest. As explained in Chapter 2, FCC regulation of the content of broadcast programming raises First Amendment issues.

---

22. 15 U.S.C. § 68 *et seq.* (1998).
23. 15 U.S.C. § 69 *et seq.* (1998).
24. 15 U.S.C. § 1191 *et seq.* (1998).
25. 15 U.S.C. § 70 *et seq.* (1998).
26. Dan Berger, *Modern Wine Industry Still Fears the "Feds" but for Labeling Reasons*, L.A. TIMES, Nov. 24, 1989, at H2.

27. *Complying with the Made in the USA Standard*, FTC Bureau of Consumer Protection publication posted on the FTC's Web site at <http://www.ftc.gov/bcp/conline/pubs/buspubs/madeusa/htm>.
28. CAL. HEALTH & SAFETY CODE § 25,249.6 (West 1997).

ETHICAL CONSIDERATION

On average, an American child sees about 8,000 murders on television before reaching high school. How should programming managers respond if scientific evidence shows that television violence leads to more violent behavior by children? Can content-based regulation of broadcasting protect consumer health and safety? What additional precautions (such as time, place, and manner restrictions), if any, should be taken to protect children?

As explained in Chapters 9 and 17, the Internet has spawned new types of fraudulent schemes, such as online auction fraud, pyramid schemes, and securities fraud. The FTC, the U.S. Department of Justice, and the Securities and Exchange Commission are active in prosecuting offenders.

The Consumer Product Safety Commission

Congress created the Consumer Product Safety Commission (CPSC), an independent regulatory agency, in 1972. Its purposes include protecting the public against unreasonable risks of injury associated with consumer products and assisting consumers in evaluating the comparative safety of such products. Under the Consumer Product Safety Act[29] (which created the CPSC), the CPSC is authorized to set consumer product safety standards, such as performance or product-labeling specifications.

The statute provides a detailed scheme governing the adoption of such a standard. Any interested person may petition the CPSC to adopt a standard and may resort to judicial remedies if the commission denies the petition. The CPSC itself can begin a proceeding to develop a standard by publishing a notice in the *Federal Register* inviting any person to submit an offer to do the development. Within a specified time limit, the CPSC can then accept such an offer, evaluate the suggestions submitted, and publish a proposed rule. The issuance of the final standard is subject to notice and comment by interested persons.

The penalty provisions of the Act make it unlawful to manufacture for sale, offer for sale, distribute in commerce, or import into the United States a consumer product that does not conform to an applicable standard. Violators are subject to civil penalties, criminal penalties, injunctive enforcement and seizure, private suits for damages, and private suits for injunctive relief. This means

29. 15 U.S.C. § 2051 *et seq.* (1998).

that if a product cannot be made free of unreasonable risk of personal injury, the CPSC may ban its manufacture, sale, or importation altogether. The supplier of any already-distributed products that pose a substantial risk of injury may be compelled by the CPSC to repair, modify, or replace the product or refund the purchase price.

Before implementing a mandatory safety standard, the CPSC must find that voluntary standards are inadequate. One obvious concern for the commission is that producers motivated solely by short-term profits may not be willing or able to self-regulate. Any standards that the CPSC issues must also be reasonably necessary to eliminate an unreasonable risk of injury that the regulated product presents. To determine whether a standard is reasonably necessary, the commission weighs the standard's effectiveness in preventing injury against its effect on the cost of the product.

The CPSC administers several consumer protection acts, including the Flammable Fabrics Act, the Federal Hazardous Substances Act,[30] the Poison Prevention Packaging Act (child-resistant bottle caps), and the Refrigerator Safety Act. The CPSC currently has no jurisdiction over tobacco products, firearms, pesticides, motor vehicles, food, drugs, medical devices, or cosmetics.[31] These products are regulated by other entities, such as the FDA, or are unregulated. In addition to its other duties, the CPSC maintains an Injury Information Clearinghouse to collect and analyze information relating to the causes and prevention of death, injury, and illness associated with consumer products.

One of the CPSC's areas of responsibility is ensuring the safety of infant products and toys. In 1999, approximately $4.9 billion was spent on cribs, car seats, high chairs, strollers, and other products for infants, but many of these products were dangerous. The CPSC recalled

30. This Act is a composite of three significant acts: the Hazardous Substances Labeling Act, the Child Protection Act, and the Child Protection and Toy Safety Act. 15 U.S.C. § 2052 (1988).
31. *Id.*

INTERNATIONAL CONSIDERATION

Under Section 2067 of the Consumer Product Safety Act, goods produced in the United States that are manufactured for export only are exempt from compliance with U.S. product-safety standards. Goods declared "banned hazardous substances" by the CPSC are also exempt from regulation as long as they are intended for export. Exporters of such goods must file a notifying statement with the CPSC thirty days before shipping the product, however, so that the CPSC can notify the government of the foreign country of the shipment and the basis for the applicable U.S. safety standard.

Exporting unsafe products to foreign markets raises serious ethical concerns. Should U.S. managers sell products determined to be hazardous by the CPSC in countries where government regulations are less stringent? Consider silicone breast implants (regulated by the FDA, not the CPSC). As recently as 1992, three of the four manufacturers of silicone-filled breast implants were continuing to export the devices, which were subject to a sales moratorium imposed in the United States earlier that year.[a] Is that more or less defensible than selling a heater without the extra safety features that would be required in the United States but would make the heater prohibitively expensive in some poorer countries?

a. Robert L. Rose, *Breast Implants Still Being Sold Outside U.S.*, WALL ST. J., Mar. 4, 1992, at B1.

Suppose that you are the product manager for your company's portable infant playpen. Two infants suffocated after their caregiver failed to properly latch the sides open, permitting the playpen to collapse. The CPSC orders a recall of the playpens but requires only minimal publicity about the recall. Should you do more to publicize the recall than the CPSC requires? What if you elect not to and three more infants die the same way? Would you do the extra publicity then? Suppose the parents of the fourth infant to die sue your company. Is it ethical to settle the case on the condition that the settlement be kept confidential?[a]

a. Thanks to Professor Michael Wheeler of the Harvard Business School for this hypothetical.

ninety-five toys and infant products in 1999, amounting to tens of millions of items. Despite these recalls, more than 65,000 children visited emergency rooms as a result of injuries associated with products for infants. Frequently, companies, reluctant to generate negative publicity about their product, try to negotiate with the CPSC to issue press releases that use language that minimizes the hazards. For example, the company may issue a press release that announces a "recall for repair" rather than a straight recall. These vaguely worded press releases are designed to attract less attention and, consequently, may not reach parents to inform them of potential dangers.[32]

In addition to the federal Consumer Product Safety Act, several states have enacted laws to protect children from dangerous products. Two University of Chicago professors, whose son died when his Playskool Travel-Lite portable crib collapsed while he was napping, initiated the Children's Product Safety Act in Illinois. The act was signed into law in August 1999. Michigan followed suit and enacted the same law in June 2000.[33]

 ## Automobiles

Automobile safety has seen enormous gains since Ralph Nader first brought the issue to the nation's attention in the 1960s.[34] Air bags (for the driver and

front passenger) and antilock brakes have become popular safety features and are standard equipment on many new cars.

The National Highway Traffic Safety Administration (NHTSA), created in 1970, is an agency of the U.S. Department of Transportation. By law, the NHTSA has the power to establish motor vehicle safety standards,[35] establish a National Motor Vehicle Safety Advisory Council, engage in testing and development of motor vehicle safety, prohibit the manufacture or importation of substandard vehicles, and promote tire safety.[36] In addition, the NHTSA is charged with developing national standards for driver safety performance, accident reporting, and vehicle registration and inspection. States refusing to comply with established federal standards are denied federal highway funds.[37]

35. Boats are subject to safety regulation under the Federal Boat Safety Act of 1971 (46 U.S.C. § 4301 *et seq.* (1998)), and aircraft safety is regulated by the Federal Aviation Act of 1958 (49 U.S.C. § 1421 *et seq.* (1998)).
36. Motor Vehicle Safety Act of 1966, 15 U.S.C. § 1381 *et seq.* (1998).
37. Highway Safety Act of 1966, 23 U.S.C. § 401 *et seq.* (1998).

32. E. Marla Felcher, *Children's Products and Risk*, ATLANTIC MONTHLY (Nov. 2000).
33. *Id.*
34. RALPH NADER, UNSAFE AT ANY SPEED (1965) (criticizing in particular General Motors Corporation's Corvair model). For a critique of Ralph Nader's consumer activist activities, see DAN BURT, ABUSE OF TRUST (1982).

Adding new safety requirements for automobiles can increase product cost and shut some consumers out of the market. Should governments coerce individuals into paying for unwanted safety features, or should individual consumers be allowed to choose which features they are willing to pay for?

Privacy Protections

Technological developments, especially the Internet, have made it possible to amass large amounts of detailed personal information about consumers, causing Scott McNealy, chief executive officer of Sun Microsystems, to quip, "Privacy is gone. Get over it." Nevertheless, consumers are putting increased pressure on government to find ways to protect their privacy.

States have taken the lead in formulating consumer privacy policy. In 2000 alone, more than one hundred privacy bills were introduced in forty-one states.[38] The bills fell into three general categories: (1) bills to prohibit or limit the financial industry's use of account-related information; (2) bills to regulate the use of information collected by online service providers and Web sites; and (3) bills to prevent state agencies from selling information about people who do business with the state, including obtaining driver's licenses.[39] As noted in Chapter 2, Congress passed legislation banning the sale of driver's license information.

California has been one of the most active states; in 2000 alone, it enacted six new laws aimed at protecting consumers' privacy. One of these laws created the first statewide Office of Privacy Protection in the nation. Two others require (1) businesses to destroy customer records that contain personal information and (2) credit card companies to provide their customers with the opportunity to "opt out" of having their personal information disclosed to third parties.[40] In 1999, California passed a law that limits the information that supermarkets can demand from customers as a condition of signing up for grocery club discount cards. Some supermarkets had been selling data about their customers' purchases of items such as liquor and tobacco to insurance companies. Under the new law, consumers do not have to provide their Social Security numbers and driver's license numbers to obtain these cards.[41]

Opponents of states' efforts to protect consumers' privacy argue that the different states are creating a patchwork of conflicting rules, and undermining efforts to enact federal legislation on privacy. But some consumer privacy advocates hope that enacting strong state privacy laws will put pressure on Congress to enact federal privacy legislation.[42] Congress was expected to pass some type of national privacy legislation in 2001.

FINANCIAL INSTITUTIONS

State attorney generals are also investigating and prosecuting claims against financial institutions for violations

---

42. Michael Schroeder, *Business Targets State Privacy Initiatives*, WALL ST. J., Feb. 10, 2000, at A2.

INTERNATIONAL CONSIDERATION

A law allowing Russia's intelligence agency, the Federal Security Bureau (FSB), to eavesdrop on all cellular telephone conversations, pager communications, and Internet traffic went into effect in September 2000. Regulations covering only telephone calls were enacted in 1995 but were updated in 1998 to include the Internet. The law entitled the "System of Operational and Investigative Measures" requires all Russian Internet service providers to equip their networks with an FSB monitor, costing $15,000 to $25,000, and a high-speed fiber-optic link with FSB headquarters. Failure to install the bugging devices will result in loss of the service provider's operating license. Approximately 4.8 percent of Russia's 145 million population are connected to the Internet. Like the rest of the world, Russians use the Internet to air grievances about the government as well as for business. Russian civil rights groups have protested the law, characterizing it as Soviet-style political repression. The founder of a Russian political Web site commented that with the law, "The resistance movement is as good as dead."[a]

In contrast, a French court ruled on November 2, 2000, that e-mail is covered by French privacy laws.[b] Three staff members at the School of Industrial Physics and Chemistry in Paris were fined for tapping into a Kuwaiti student's e-mail, after suspecting him of using the school's e-mail service for personal activities.

In October 2000, Britain adopted regulations empowering employers to monitor employees' e-mails and Internet activity.[c] In April 2000, the American Management Association published a study revealing that 74 percent of U.S. companies conducted some form of active electronic monitoring of their employees; 38 percent monitored e-mail.[d]

---

a. Margaret Coker, *Big Comrade Is Watching*, COX NEWS SERVICE, Sept. 9, 2000.
b. Agence France-Presse, *Intercepting E-Mail Illegal, French Court Rules*, Globetechnology.com (Nov. 3, 2000).
c. *Id.*
d. Jeffrey Benner, *Privacy at Work? Be Serious*, WIRED NEWS, Mar. 1, 2001.

---

38. Rachel Zimmerman & Glenn R. Simpson, *Lobbyists Swarm to Stop Tough Privacy Bills in States*, WALL ST. J., Apr. 21, 2000, at A16.
39. *Id.*
40. Derrick Cain, *California Governor Signs Six Laws Aimed at Protecting Consumer Privacy*, 5 ELECTRONIC COM. & L. REP. 1079 (Nov. 1, 2000).
41. James Glave, *The Safeway to Shop*, WIRED NEWS, Oct. 8, 1999.

of their customers' privacy rights. In 2000, the New York state attorney general's office entered into a settlement with Chase Manhattan Corporation to prohibit Chase from sharing information about its depositors with non-affiliated businesses unless it receives clear permission to do so. Even if it receives permission, Chase may provide only customers' names, addresses, and telephone numbers—no financial information. The settlement resulted from a New York inquiry into Chase's practices, following a similar investigation of U.S. Bankcorp in Minneapolis by Minnesota state and federal authorities.[43]

In 1999, Congress enacted the Gramm–Leach–Bliley Act, requiring financial institutions to provide privacy protections to consumers. The Act requires financial institutions to give notice before sharing personal information with other entities, restricts the institutions right to give out personal information, and requires them to disclose their privacy policy annually and to give customers the right to opt out of disclosures to third parties. The law applies to banks, debt collectors, credit counselors, retailers, and travel agencies. The Federal Trade Commission and seven other financial regulatory agencies (including the Federal Deposit Insurance Corporation, the Federal Reserve Board, and the Securities and Exchange Commission) are required to issue regulations to implement the privacy protections provided by the statute.[44] The Gramm–Leach–Bliley Act does not preempt states from implementing stricter privacy regulations, and by early 2000, seventeen states had introduced or were planning to introduce their own financial privacy legislation.[45]

In 2001, Congress was considering a bill to amend the Gramm–Leach–Bliley Act. The new bill would require financial institutions to disclose their privacy policies and practices to customers before the relationship is established rather than at the time the relationship is established, which is the standard under the Gramm–Leach–Bliley Act. In addition, the proposed law would require customer

43. Jathon Sapsford, *Chase, New York Reach Accord on Privacy*, WALL St. J., Jan. 26, 2000, at A4.
44. Eileen Canning, *FDIC, OTS Issue Privacy Proposals Under Financial Modernization Law*, 68 U.S.L.W. 2469 (Feb. 15, 2000).
45. Eileen Canning, *States Legislating Financial Privacy Before Federal Regulators Even Issue Draft*, 68 U.S.L.W. 2453 (Feb. 8, 2000).

INTERNATIONAL CONSIDERATION

In January 2001, Canada enacted the Personal Information Protection and Electronics Act, an online privacy law that requires foreign firms doing business in Canada to adhere to a strict set of privacy rules. The law, known as C-6, regulates the collection of, access to, and use and disclosure of personal information in the private sector. The law is taking effect in stages over a three-year period. Businesses in federally regulated industries (including telecommunications, financial services, and airlines) must comply with its provisions immediately. In the subsequent twelve months, medical information services must comply with the law. In the third stage, all remaining commercial businesses that handle information must be in compliance by January 1, 2004. Prior Canadian federal legislation protected personal information in the public sector but not in the private sector.[a]

a. Martin Stone, *Canada Privacy Law Impacts Foreign Firms*, NEWSBYTE NEWS NETWORK, Jan. 5, 2001.

consent to share personal financial information with affiliated companies; existing law requires consent only for sharing with nonaffiliated third parties.[46]

SAFE-HARBOR PROVISION IN U.S. AGREEMENT WITH THE EU

The 1988 European Union (EU) Directive on Privacy Protection requires companies that transport personal data concerning citizens in the EU to non-European nations to comply with strict privacy laws that protect Europeans.[47] Companies in the EU may not collect personal information that identifies the individual involved without the individual's consent. Some member states, such as Germany, require individuals to affirmatively opt in to the collection of the information; others, such as the United Kingdom, require only that individuals have the ability to opt out.

U.S. companies objected to the high price of complying with these strict laws. After years of negotiations, the EU agreed to a "safe-harbor" provision, which establishes a set of guidelines that U.S. companies can follow to avoid prosecution under the EU privacy law.[48]

46. *Even with Gramm-Leach-Bliley, Congress Introducing More Privacy-Related Bills*, BEST'S INS. NEWS, Feb. 7, 2001.
47. Kenneth Neil Cukier, *Will the Safe Harbor Rule Help U.S. Firms Comply with European Privacy Law?*, REDHERRING.COM, Jan. 18, 2001.
48. Thomas E. Weber, *Europe and the U.S. Reach Truce on Net Privacy but What Comes Next?*, WALL St. J., June 19, 2000, at B1.

ETHICAL CONSIDERATION

When, if ever, does an advertiser possess too much information about a consumer's preferences and buying habits? What implications might interactive television have for consumer privacy?

VIEW FROM CYBERSPACE

Privacy *in the* Electronic Age

The increasing use of the Internet to conduct personal and commercial transactions, as well as to provide access to information, raises a number of privacy issues. Some concerns, such as fears that credit card numbers will be used without the consumer's consent, have hampered electronic commerce. A study by Forrester Research found that e-commerce companies lose $14.4 billion each year because consumers are afraid to shop online.[a] A 1999 survey by the Pew Internet and American Life Project, a nonprofit group that studies the impact of the Internet on society, found that more than 84 percent of U.S. consumers worried about businesses and strangers obtaining their personal information.[b]

Consumers' fears appear to be well-founded. Less than 20 percent of the companies PricewaterhouseCooper audits for privacy policy adherence are in compliance. Approximately 30 percent could pass the audit if they addressed a few problems, but some 50 percent would fail outright.[c]

The Federal Trade Commission does not impose substantive privacy requirements, but it treats any company's failure to abide by its own stated privacy policies as a deceptive practice in violation of Section 5 of the Federal Trade Commission Act. One of the most publicized cases concerning privacy on the Internet involved the online advertising firm DoubleClick, Inc.'s use of "cookie technology" to track consumers' use of the Internet. A "cookie" is a small piece of software transferred from a Web site to a consumer's hard drive via the Internet browser. The cookie records "click stream data," which are the consumer's movements through a Web site, to see which sites are viewed, the time spent viewing, and the site visited next. Internet ad-tracking companies put "cookies" on Web-surfers' computer hard drives without notifying or obtaining the consent of the user. Web sites usually request personal information when a user registers to gain access to the services (such as a product warranty) and information provided at the site. Companies use this information to tai-

lor their marketing pitches to the tastes of the individual consumer.

In the summer of 1999, DoubleClick announced its intention to acquire Abacus Direct, a company that tracks the buying habits of consumers, which had compiled a repository of names, addresses, and information about millions of consumers.[d] DoubleClick planned to merge its click stream data with the consumer database in order to put names and addresses together with data about Web site visits. Both the FTC and consumers were alarmed that DoubleClick's business strategy would violate individuals' rights to privacy without providing them with sufficient notice to block surveillance of their travels through the Web. Although DoubleClick argued that it did provide notice to consumers who could then disable the cookie, consumers filed class-action lawsuits, and the FTC and state attorneys general commenced investigations into the company's practices.[e] In March 2000, in response to the public outcry and negative publicity, DoubleQuick announced that it would not combine the two businesses. In January 2001, the FTC dropped its investigation of the company's online advertising practices, after concluding the DoubleClick had not violated its stated privacy policies. In March 2001, the U.S. District Court for the Southern District of New York dismissed, with prejudice, a class action alleging that DoubleClick's use of cookies to collect data violated the Electronic Communications Privacy Act (18 U.S.C. § 2701 *et seq.*), the Federal Wiretap Act (18 U.S.C. § 2510 *et seq.*), and the Computer Fraud and Abuse Act (18 U.S.C. § 1030 *et seq.*).[f]

In an effort to prevent government from imposing costly restrictions, the

high-tech industry has made some attempts to police itself. For example, seal-of-approval programs, whereby a third party establishes an oversight privacy program and provides a "trustmark" seal to indicate that a particular Web site participates in the program, have been used to identify corporations that comply with privacy regulations.[g] One of these programs, TRUSTe, reported at the end of 1999 that all of the major Internet portal sides (including America Online, Microsoft, Yahoo!, Lycos, and Netscape) had joined the TRUSTe program.

In September 2000, the Office of the Information and Privacy Commissioner of Ontario and the Office of the Federal Privacy Commissioner of Australia issued a report evaluating the three leading online Web seal programs, BBBOnLine, TRUSTe, and WebTRust, to determine whether they complied with three key components of an effective program: sufficient privacy principles to which participating Web sites must adhere, a method for resolving disputes between consumers and Web sites, and a mechanism for ensuring that "sealed" Web sites complied with the seal's standards. The report concluded that although the three seals addressed privacy protection, dispute resolution, and compliance, none of them did so completely satisfactorily.[h]

Faced with an onslaught of proposed legislation, some companies have shifted their strategy from opposing legislation to helping influence the type of legislation adopted. For example, the AeA (the trade group formerly known as the American Electronics Association) originally proposed voluntary controls by industry. In 2001, the group, whose members include Microsoft and Intel, presented Congress with eight principles for developing Internet privacy legislation. The AeA called on Congress to enact federal legislation that builds upon the groundwork already established by industry and that is "explicitly and solely designed to preempt the enactment of a

(View From Cyberspace continues)

(View From Cyberspace continued)

crazy quilt of onerous, contradictory new state laws."[i] Commenting on the association's change in policy, an AeA senior vice president said, "Quite frankly, there's a knife to our throats and that's the threat of state legislation. I don't think there's a company in this country that can tolerate ten different state bills, much less fifty different state bills."[j]

Although the Information Technology Industry Council (ITI), which represents the thirty largest information technology companies in the United States, had stated that it would prefer to rely on industry self-regulation, it too recently indicated that it preferred federal legislation to a confusing patchwork of state laws. In November 1997, the ITI had issued voluntary guidelines regarding privacy to its member organizations. The guidelines, *The Protection of Personal Data in Electronic Commerce,* set forth eight principles intended to apply to both data collection practices and electronic database use over the Internet. The principles included (1) providing information on data protection policies, (2) notifying and empowering the consumer, (3) limiting collection of personal data to information needed for valid business reasons, (4) ensuring data accuracy, (5) enabling informed choice, (6) educating the marketplace, and (7) adapting private practices to electronic and online technologies.

Internet privacy bills, many of them bipartisan, were among the first pieces of legislation introduced in the 107th Congress at the beginning of 2001. The Online Privacy Protection Act would give consumers access to their personal data; the Internet Integrity and Critical Infrastructure Protection Act of 2000 would impose a criminal penalty for fraudulent access to personal information.[k] Another bill, the Consumer Internet Privacy Enhancement Act (H.R. 237), would require Web sites and e-businesses to disclose to consumers how the sites use and secure the personal information they collect and compel them to provide ways to prevent inappropriate use of this information for marketing and other activities.[l]

Two of the bills, SR 2928 (proposed by Senators John McCain and John Kerry) and SR 2606 (proposed by Senator Ernest Hollings), differ on one of the most contentious issues in the area of privacy law: whether companies should have to comply with an opt-out or an opt-in requirement. Opt-in means that consumers are notified of a company's privacy policy before entering the Web site and then are given the option to continue. Opt-out means that viewers must search for the policy on their own and then inform the company that they do not agree to it. Companies argue that an opt-in procedure makes it overly difficult for consumers to access a site. Supporters of opt-in provisions counter that companies have greater ability to confuse consumers with opt-out provisions.[m] Although it is not clear which bill will be enacted, experts predicted that some form of federal legislation would be enacted during 2001.

Children's Online Privacy Protection Act

The Children's Online Privacy Protection Act (COPPA) of 1998 went into effect in April 2000. The federal law prevents Web sites from collecting personal information from children under age thirteen without parental consent. Parental consent can be in the form of a note, credit card number, or e-mail with a password. Web sites must disclose what personal information they collect from children and how they use it, including whether they share it with third parties.[n] The FTC may fine Web sites up to $11,000 for failing to obtain parental consent.[o]

In *FTC v. Toysmart.com,*[p] the U.S. District Court for the District of Massachusetts precluded Toysmart.com, a Web toy vendor in dire financial straits, from selling the personal information it had collected from consumers. Toysmart had created family profiles with the names and birth dates of children, shopping preferences, names, addresses, and billing information. The company's privacy policy stated that personal information collected would never be shared with third parties. The complaint filed by the FTC also alleged that the company had violated COPPA by collecting information from children

under thirteen without obtaining parental consent. The court ordered Toysmart to delete or destroy any information collected in violation of the COPPA.

In 2001, the FTC approved the self-regulatory program of the Children's Advertising Review Unit of the Council of Better Business Bureaus as the first "safe-harbor" program under the COPPA. Companies that comply with these self-regulatory programs are deemed to have complied with the COPPA.[q]

a. Lisa Burden, *Report Says Privacy Laws Cost Big Bucks Without Calming Customer Fears,* Fin. News, Jan. 29, 2001.
b. Carrie Kirby, *Spotlight on Privacy/Tech Industry, Consumer Advocates Set to Grapple with Congress over Pressing Internet Security Issues,* San Francisco Chron., Jan. 29, 2001, at B1.
c. L. Scott Tillett, *The Push For Netprivacy—Companies Take Action as Government Weighs Legislation,* Internetweek, Feb. 5, 2001, at 12.
d. Andrea Petersen, *DoubleClick Reverses Course After Privacy Outcry,* Wall St. J., Mar. 3, 2000, at B1.
e. *Lawsuits, Bad Publicity Halt Company's Plan to Fully Exploit Net's Data Gathering Power,* 68 U.S.L.W. 2552 (Mar. 21, 2000).
f. *In re* DoubleClick Inc. Privacy Litig., 2001 U.S. Dist. LEXIS 3498 (Mar. 29, 2001). *See also* Bob Tedeschi, *DoubleClick Is Seeking Ways to Use Online and Offline Data and Protect Users' Anonymity,* N.Y. Times, Jan. 29, 2001, at 9.
g. 67 U.S.L.W. 2396 (Jan. 12, 1999).
h. Ann Cavoukian & Malcolm Crompton, Web Seals: A Review of Online Privacy Programs, Sept. 2000.
i. Tillett, *supra* note c.
j. Mitchel Benson & Glenn R. Simpson, *Privacy Measures for U.S. Is Backed by Trade Group,* Wall St. J., Jan. 18, 2001, at B6.
k. Luc Hatlestad, *Online Privacy Matters,* Red Herring, Jan. 16, 2001.
l. Wayne Rash, *Bill Would Set Right Privacy Balance for the Internet,* Internetweek, Feb. 5, 2001, at 26.
m. Hatlestad, *supra* note k.
n. *New Children's Privacy Rules Pose Obstacles for Some Sites,* Wall St. J., Apr. 14, 2000, at B8.
o. Robert H. Williams, *Protecting Kids Online,* Boston Globe, Apr. 20, 2000, at A27.
p. *See FTC Sues Failed Website, Toysmart.com, for Deceptively Offering for Sale Personal Information of Website Visitors,* FTC press release, July 10, 2000, available at <http://www.ftc.gov/opa/2000/07/toysmart.htm>.
q. *First "Safe Harbor" Approved for Children's Online Privacy Protection Act,* M2 Presswire, Feb. 2, 2001.

Under the safe-harbor agreement, American companies must still comply with guidelines that protect Europeans' privacy, but these safeguards are enforced less stringently than within Europe. In particular, data may be used only after obtaining the individual's consent, cannot be resold without prior user consent, and must be destroyed once they are no longer needed. In addition, companies must provide individuals with notice and choice about the prospective uses of their data and access to the information so they can confirm its accuracy. Before a U.S. company can take advantage of the safe harbor, it must enact a privacy policy that complies with the safe-harbor principles. The Federal Trade Commission, not EU authorities, is responsible for enforcing violations of the safe-harbor guidelines under the Federal Trade Commission Act.[49]

In April 2000, a group of large U.S. companies (including General Electric, Fidelity Investments, Home Depot, and Seagram Company) objected to the privacy agreement in a letter to the Commerce Department. The group (which called itself the National Business Coalition on E-Commerce and Privacy) characterized the agreement as a nontariff trade barrier that would put U.S. businesses at a disadvantage and argued that it raised serious questions about national sovereignty.[50]

As of early 2001, fewer than a dozen U.S. firms had signed up to take advantage of the safe harbor, with Dun & Bradstreet being the largest. Many other companies, particularly technology firms, were still considering whether to attempt to reach separate agreements with regulators in the European countries where they do business, change their information-sharing polices, or simply stop transferring data about Europeans outside the countries where they reside. The executive vice president of the Software & Information Industry Association commented upon the companies' wait-and-see attitude, "It's like an eighth-grade dance. Everyone's standing around the punch bowl, but no one wants to be the first one on the floor."[51]

 ## State Occupational Licensing

State departments of consumer affairs protect the public by examining and licensing firms and individuals who possess the necessary education and demonstrated skills to perform their services competently. Among the occupations generally regulated are accountants, architects, barbers, contractors, cosmetologists, dentists, dry cleaners, marriage counselors, nurses, pharmacists, physical therapists, physicians, and social workers.[52] Attorneys are regulated by state bar associations and the courts. State departments of consumer affairs also investigate and resolve consumer complaints and hold public hearings involving consumer matters.

Unfairness, Deception, *and* Fraud

A number of regulatory agencies, both federal and state, are involved in the area of unfair and deceptive trade practices and consumer fraud. They include the Federal Trade Commission, the Food and Drug Administration, the Federal Communications Commission, the U.S. Post Office, the U.S. Department of Housing and Urban Development, and the Securities and Exchange Commission. (Securities fraud is discussed in Chapter 25.) These federal agencies regulate advertising, packaging and labeling, pricing, warranties, and numerous sales practices. State attorneys general and state departments of consumer affairs are also involved in protecting consumers through their administration of various state labeling laws, state warranty provisions (such as "lemon laws"), state deceptive sales practices statutes, and state privacy laws.

52. As noted in Chapter 7, any person required to be licensed who is in fact not licensed cannot enforce a promise to pay for unlicensed work.

 INTERNATIONAL CONSIDERATION

At the end of 1999, the Organization for Economic Cooperation and Development issued Guidelines for Consumer Protection in Electronic Commerce reflecting agreement among twenty countries on general policies for protecting consumers shopping online. The guidelines describe fair business, marketing, and advertising practices and identify information companies should disclose to consumers so that they can make informed choices. In addition, the guidelines point to the need for companies to establish procedures and mechanisms for confirming transactions and ensuring secure payment. The guidelines call for cooperation between countries on law enforcement, recognition of cross-border legal judgments, and development of alternative dispute resolution procedures.[a]

a. Bureau of Consumer Protection, FTC, *Consumer Protection in the Global Electronic Marketplace*, Sept. 2000, <http://www.ftc.gov/bcp/icpw/lookingahead/lookingahead.htm>

49. John Reynolds & Amy Worlton, *Safe Harbor Agreement*, 5 ELECTRONIC COM. & L. REP. 1092 (Nov. 1, 2000).

50. Glenn R. Simpson, *Businesses Criticize U.S.–E.U. Privacy Pact as Hurdle to Global E-Commerce Efforts*, WALL ST. J., Apr. 6, 2000, at A24.

51. Edmund Sanders, *U.S. Firms Abstain from EU Privacy Pact Trade: Companies Aren't Convinced 'Safe-Harbor' Agreement Would Protect Them from Europe's Data-Protection Laws*, L.A. TIMES, Jan. 5, 2001, at C-3.

E-COMMERCE

⚖ Advertising *and* Warranties

Consumers are bombarded daily with the competing claims of various advertisers trying to generate new sales. From billboards to television to banner ads on Web sites and even the back of grocery receipts, advertisers vie for the consumer's attention. In this competitive environment, companies sometimes make claims that are deceptive or false. Legal solutions to this problem have historically involved three separate approaches: the common law, statutory law, and regulatory law. Regulatory law, enacted and enforced through the Federal Trade Commission (FTC), has proved to be the most effective vehicle for combating false advertisements.

COMMON LAW

A traditional common law approach provides two remedies for a consumer who has been misled by false advertising. First, a consumer can sue for breach of contract. In this instance, however, it may be difficult to prove the existence of a contract because the courts usually consider advertisements to be only an offer to deal. Second, a consumer might sue for the tort of deceit. Deceit requires the proof of several elements, including knowledge by the seller that the misrepresentation is false. In addition, the misrepresentation must be one of fact and not opinion, a difficult distinction to make in the context of advertising. (Deceit, also called fraudulent misrepresentation, is discussed in Chapter 9.)

STATUTORY LAW

The Uniform Commercial Code (UCC) and the Lanham Trademark Act are two statutes that may protect consumers from false advertising. As noted in Chapter 8, under Section 2-313 of the UCC, any statement, sample, or model may constitute an *express warranty* if it is part of the basis of the bargain. Thus, an advertising term may be construed as an express warranty for a product. If the product does not conform to the representation made, the warranty is breached. Express warranties can be disclaimed in a sales contract, however, so the UCC generally does not provide a strong response to false advertising claims.

The Lanham Trademark Act forbids the use of any false "description or representation" in connection with any goods or services and provides a private cause of action for any competitor injured by any other competitor's false claims. The purpose of the Act is to ensure truthfulness in advertising and to eliminate misrepresentations of quality regarding one's own product or the product of a competitor. Neither consumers nor retailers have standing to sue for violations of the Lanham Act. Only direct commercial competitors or surrogates for direct commercial competitors have standing to pursue claims under the Act.[53]

For example, the Coca-Cola Company, maker of Minute Maid orange juice, successfully sued Tropicana Products, Inc. in the early 1980s under the Lanham Trademark Act. At issue was a television commercial in which athlete Bruce Jenner squeezed an orange while saying, "It's pure, pasteurized juice as it comes from the orange," and then poured the juice into a Tropicana carton. Coca-Cola claimed the commercial was false because it represented that Tropicana contains unprocessed, fresh-squeezed juice when in fact the juice is heated (pasteurized) and sometimes frozen before packaging. The court agreed that the representation was false because it suggested that pasteurized juice comes directly from oranges. The court enjoined Tropicana from continuing to use the advertisement.[54]

In the following case, the court considered whether a manufacturer of baby formula violated the Lanham Act when it advertised its product as the "1st Choice of Doctors."

53. Conte Bros. Automotive, Inc. v. Quaker State-Slick, 50, Inc., 165 F.3d 221 (3d Cir. 1998).
54. Coca-Cola Co. v. Tropicana Prods., Inc., 690 F.2d 312 (2d Cir. 1982).

A CASE IN POINT

CASE 21.1

Mead Johnson & Co. v. Abbott Laboratories
United States Court of Appeals for the Seventh Circuit
201 F.3d 883
(7th Cir. 2000), cert. denied,
121 S. Ct. 276 (2000).

Summary

FACTS The Ross Pediatrics division of Abbott Laboratories manufactures the infant formula Similac and advertises it as the "1st Choice of Doctors." Mead Formula, which manufactures a competing infant formula (Enfamil), sued Abbott, alleging that its claim that Similac was the first choice of doctors was misleading and violated the Lanham Act. In support of its claims, Mead Johnson introduced evidence from a survey of women who had recently purchased or contemplated purchasing formula to demonstrate how consumers interpreted the claim "1st Choice of Doctors."

The district court relied upon Mead Johnson's survey to conclude that the claim conveyed to consumers the message that at least a majority of doctors preferred Similac on

(Continued)

(Case 21.1 continued)

grounds of qualitative superiority. The district court then analyzed surveys of physicians to see whether Abbott's claim, as understood by consumers, had been substantiated. The district court acknowledged that there were surveys showing that a majority of physicians preferred Similac, but it concluded that the surveys were not designed to ensure that the preference was based on Similac's superiority: surveys that limited the grounds of preference did not show majority support for Similac. In addition, the district court ruled that Abbott could not claim that its product was the first choice because a majority of doctors did not prefer it. Accordingly, the court held that "1st Choice of Doctors" violated the Lanham Act. Abbott appealed.

ISSUE Did Abbott's claim that its infant formula was the first choice of doctors violate the Lanham Act?

SUMMARY OF OPINION The U.S. Court of Appeals for the Seventh Circuit held that Mead Johnson's survey of women who had recently purchased formula should not have been used to define the meaning of the phrase "1st Choice of Doctors." The court also rejected the assertion that Abbot could use the word "first" only if a majority of doctors preferred the product. Instead, the court ruled that "first" denoted rank in a series rather than a particular ratio or percentage of doctors.

RESULT The case was dismissed. Abbott did not violate the Lanham Act, so it could continue to advertise Similac as the first choice of doctors.

FTC REGULATORY LAW

The Federal Trade Commission is charged with preventing unfair and deceptive trade practices, including false advertising. Among the areas that the FTC has addressed under Section 5 of the Federal Trade Commission Act are deceptive price and quality claims and false testimonials and mock-ups.

If the FTC believes a violation of Section 5 exists, it will attempt to negotiate a consent order with the alleged violator. A *consent order* is an agreement to stop the activity that the FTC has found illegal. If an agreement cannot be reached, the matter will be heard by an administrative law judge. The judge's decision can be appealed to the full commission, and the full commission's decision can be appealed to a U.S. court of appeals.

Deceptive Price One example of deceptive pricing practices involves the sale of advertised items at higher prices to customers unaware of the advertised price. In one case, a person purchased a blue 1986 Chevrolet Celebrity with 29,000 miles from an automobile dealer for $8,524.[55] Unbeknownst to the buyer, the dealership was currently advertising a blue 1986 Celebrity with 29,000 miles for $6,995 in a local newspaper. When he

returned home, the buyer saw the ad and telephoned the dealership to demand that the deal be renegotiated. The salesman refused, claiming that the advertised car had been sent to auction. The customer sued under the Illinois Consumer Fraud Act, which forbids false misrepresentations as well as omission of material facts. The trial court held that the dealership had a duty to inform the customer of the advertised price and awarded him the difference in prices, plus costs.

ETHICAL CONSIDERATION

Publication of a newspaper article entitled "A Car Buyer's Guide to Sanity," which taught consumers how to negotiate lower prices, so angered car dealers that they pulled at least $1 million worth of advertising from the newspaper. The FTC challenged the dealers' action under the antitrust laws, claiming that they had deprived consumers of essential price information in the form of newspaper advertising and had chilled the newspaper from publishing similar stories in the future.[a] Should the government become embroiled in an advertiser's decision to pull advertising from a news publication? Was the advertisers' conduct ethical?

a. Anthony Ramirez, *Car Dealers to Stop Ad Threat*, SAN FRANCISCO CHRON., Aug. 2, 1995, at B3.

55. Affrunti v. Village Ford Sales, Inc. 597 N.E.2d 1242 (Ill. App. Ct. 1992).

Deceptive pricing practices also include offers of free merchandise with a purchase or two-for-one deals in which the advertiser recovers the cost of the free merchandise by charging more than the regular price for the merchandise bought. Another example of deceptive pricing, bait and switch advertising, is regulated by the FTC. An advertiser violates the FTC's *bait and switch advertising* rules if it refuses to show an advertised item, fails to have a reasonable quantity of the item in stock, fails to promise to deliver the item within a reasonable time, or discourages employees from selling the advertised item.

Quality Claims Advertisements often include quality claims. Under the FTC's general view, quality claims made without any substantiation are deceptive. For example, the marketers of Doan's pills were held to have disseminated false and deceptive statements when they claimed the pills were more effective at relieving back pain than other over-the-counter pain relievers without any reasonable basis for substantiating the representations.[56]

56. *In re* Novartis Corp., FTC Docket No. 9279 (Mar. 9, 1998), 66 U.S.L.W. 2582 (Mar. 31, 1998).

On the other hand, obvious exaggerations and vague generalities are considered *puffing* and are not considered deceptive because they are unlikely to mislead consumers. (Puffing is discussed in Chapter 8.) To determine whether an advertiser has made a deceptive quality claim, the FTC must first identify the claim and then determine whether the claim is substantiated.

Testimonials and Mock-ups Testimonials and endorsements in which the person endorsing a product does not, in fact, use or prefer it are considered to be deceptive and therefore in violation of the Federal Trade Commission Act. It is also deceptive for the endorser to imply falsely that he or she has superior knowledge or experience. The use of comparative advertising is illustrated by the following case.

A CASE IN POINT

CASE 21.2

L&F Products v. Procter & Gamble Co.
United States Court of Appeals for the Second Circuit
45 F.3d 709 (2d Cir. 1995).

Summary

FACTS L&F Products, a division of Sterling Winthrop, Inc., manufactures and markets Lysol cleaning products, including Lysol Basin Tub & Tile Cleaner (a bathroom cleanser) and Lysol Deodorizing Cleaner (an all-purpose product often employed for bathroom cleaning). Procter & Gamble Company (P&G) manufactures and sells several Spic and Span household cleaning products, including Spic and Span Basin–Tub–Tile Cleaner, Spic and Span Bathroom Cleaner, and Ultra Spic and Span, a general cleanser.

In July 1993, P&G began a television advertising campaign in which its products were compared to those of an unnamed competitor obviously intended to be Lysol Deodorizing Cleaner. In three different commercials, a Spic and Span product and Lysol Deodorizing Cleaner were used by two custodians on identical soiled shower stalls, tubs, or tile floors set in a large, white room. The surfaces are visibly dirty when the custodians begin their tasks, and each custodian is shown making one swipe across the dirty surface. The screen then "dissolves," and the custodians leave, looking pleased with their work. Two new characters enter, and each contrives to casually pass a white cloth over the just-cleaned surfaces. The surface cleaned with Lysol is ultimately revealed to have been left with a residue that sullies the cloth. The white cloth passed over the surface cleaned with Spic and Span is not similarly dirtied.

Two of the commercials employed templates made of the same materials that formed the tubs and showers. Like other manufacturers, P&G developed its own soap scum for use in testing its products. Its formula includes carbon black, a dark pigment used as a laboratory marker. To mimic the tenacity of household soap scum, the laboratory-developed product is baked onto a test surface at high temperatures. Because of the impossibility of baking an entire shower stall or tub, templates are used. P&G did not need to bake the laboratory version into the test surface for the third commercial, which addressed floor grime.

(Continued)

(Case 21.2 continued)

The soiled templates were wiped with the competing products off-screen an equal number of times with a comparable degree of force. They were later inserted into the shower and steambath sets; then, on-screen, white cloths were rubbed against them. The initial swipe across the shower and tub tiles by the custodians was performed on tiles dirtied with ordinary soil, rather than the laboratory-developed scum.

L&F sued P&G, alleging that the commercials were false or misleading. The district court dismissed the lawsuit, and L&F appealed.

ISSUE PRESENTED Is it a deceptive trade practice (1) to add substances to make cleaning residue more easily filmed or (2) to simulate without disclosure the wiping of ordinary soil with the actual wiping of laboratory-developed soil?

SUMMARY OF OPINION The U.S. Court of Appeals for the Second Circuit began by noting that the Lanham Act forbids the use of a "false designation of origin, or any false description or misrepresentation, including words or other symbols tending falsely to describe or represent the same." To successfully sue under this act, a plaintiff must demonstrate that the challenged advertisement either is literally false or, although literally true, is still likely to mislead or confuse consumers.

L&F claimed that the use of carbon black and tile templates constituted false advertising *per se*. Carbon black, however, exists in many household items and is thus a natural component of organic soap scum. Stating that "[t]he inescapable fact is that Lysol products sometimes leave a residue," the court held that P&G was entitled to make the residue camera-registerable by using carbon black. As for the use of tile templates, the court found nothing inherently misleading about simulating cleaning on-screen while conducting the actual cleaning off-screen, nor did the court find anything deceptive in showing the custodians wiping ordinary soil rather than the laboratory-developed scum that was used for the actual test results.

RESULT The appeals court affirmed the dismissal of the complaint. P&G's ads were not misleading.

COMMENTS Not all advertisements withstand challenge so easily. In the mid-1960s, the FTC successfully challenged a series of three television commercials involving Colgate–Palmolive Company's Rapid Shave shaving cream.[57] Each of the commercials featured a sandpaper test, in which the announcer informed the audience that "[t]o prove Rapid Shave's super-moisturizing power, we put it right from the can onto this tough, dry sandpaper. It was apply . . . soak . . . and off in a stroke." While the announcer was speaking, Rapid Shave was applied to a substance that appeared to be sandpaper, and immediately thereafter a razor was shown shaving the substance clean. The FTC charged that the commercials were false and deceptive. Evidence disclosed that sandpaper of the type depicted in the commercials could not be shaved immediately after the application of Rapid Shave but required a soaking period of approximately eighty minutes. The evidence also showed that the substance resembling sandpaper was in fact a simulated prop, or "mock-up," made of plexiglass to which sand had been applied. Ultimately, the U.S. Supreme Court agreed with the FTC and held that the commercials were unlawfully deceptive.

57. FTC v. Colgate–Palmolive Co., 380 U.S. 374 (1965).

The FTC has the authority to issue cease and desist orders to advertisers who violate Section 5 of the Federal Trade Commission Act, such as those who employ deceptive price or quality claims or false testimonials. A *cease and desist order* instructs the advertiser to stop using the methods deemed unfair or deceptive. In one case, the FTC required the maker of Listerine to cease and desist from making the claim that Listerine prevented colds and sore throats or lessened their severity. Testing performed by the FTC revealed that this claim, which the company had made for more than fifty years, was false. To counteract years of false claims, the FTC required the company to disclose in any future advertisements for Listerine that, contrary to prior advertising, Listerine did not help prevent colds or sore throats or lessen their severity. The order applied only to the next $10 million of Listerine advertising.[58]

FTC remedies include civil damages, affirmative advertising (advertiser required to include specific information), counter or corrective advertising (as with Listerine), and multiple product orders (advertiser required to cease false claims regarding all of its products).

INFOMERCIALS

Infomercials, also known as long-form marketing programs or direct response television, are advertisements generally presented in the format of half-hour television talk shows or news programs. Their very format, however, may present problems by blurring the line between advertising and regular television programming.[59] Some infomercials, called "sitcommercials," are full-length shows resembling family sitcoms. For example, Bell Atlantic filmed "The Ringers," a sitcom intended to show off and sell telephone equipment.

58. Warner–Lambert Co. v. FTC, 562 F.2d 749 (D.C. Cir. 1977), *cert. denied*, 435 U.S. 950 (1978).
59. Karen Zagor & Gary Mead, *Illumination from the Stars: A Look at the New-Found Respectability of So-Called "Infomercials,"* FIN. TIMES, Nov. 5, 1992, at 18.

In response to numerous complaints alleging deceptive advertising in infomercials, the infomercial industry established an internal watchdog agency, the National Infomercial Merchandising Association, in 1990. The association offers guidelines to combat deceptive practices, endorses legitimate infomercial producers, and reports violations to the FTC.

UCC WARRANTIES

As noted earlier, an advertisement may create an express warranty. Article 2 provides a buyer of goods with a remedy for a seller's breach of an express or implied warranty. UCC warranties are discussed in Chapter 8.

MAGNUSON–MOSS WARRANTY ACT

In addition to the statutory protections provided by the UCC, the federal government has passed a law that is designed to inform consumers about the products they buy. This law, which applies only when a seller offers a written warranty, is the Magnuson–Moss Warranty Act.[60] The Act does not require any seller to provide a written warranty, but if a seller does offer one, the Act requires certain disclosures. In addition, it restricts disclaimers for implied warranties and permits consumers to sue violators of the Act and to recover damages plus costs, including reasonable attorneys' fees.

A manufacturer or seller that offers a written warranty on goods costing more than $15 must "fully and conspicuously disclose in simple and understandable language the terms and conditions of the warranty." The FTC has issued various rules relating to this provision, including one that requires consumer notification that

60. 15 U.S.C. § 2301 *et seq.* (1998).

some states do not allow certain manufacturer exclusions or limitations.

A manufacturer or seller that offers a written warranty on goods costing more than $10 must also state whether the warranty is full or limited. Under the Act, for a warranty to be "full," it must meet the following minimum federal standards. First, a full warranty must give the consumer the right to free repair of the product within a reasonable time or, after a reasonable number of failed attempts to fix the product, permit the customer to elect a full refund or replacement. Second, the warrantor may not impose any time limit on the warranty's duration. Lastly, the warrantor may not exclude or limit damages for breach of warranty unless such exclusions are conspicuous on the face of the warranty. Any warranty that does not meet these minimum federal standards must be designated as "limited."

Also, under the Act, a seller that offers a written warranty may not disclaim *implied warranties,* such as the implied warranty of merchantability. These implied warranties may be limited to the duration of the written warranty, but then the written warranty must be designated as "limited." Still, a seller may disclaim all implied warranties by not offering any written warranty or service contract at all and selling a product "as is."

FTC rules allow a seller to establish an informal dispute resolution procedure and to require consumers to use this procedure before filing a lawsuit under the Act. The Act also requires that the warrantor be given an opportunity to remedy its noncompliance before a lawsuit is filed. In *Southern Energy Homes, Inc. v. Ard,*[61] an Alabama state court held that the Magnuson–Moss Warranty Act does not invalidate arbitration provisions in a written warranty.

STATE LEMON LAWS

A majority of states have laws dealing with warranties on new cars and new mobile homes. These *lemon laws* are designed to protect consumers from defective products that cannot be adequately fixed. The statutes vary considerably from state to state, but there are several common features. In general, a new car must conform to the warranty given by the manufacturer. This means that if, after a reasonable number of attempts (usually four), the manufacturer or dealer is unable to remedy a defect that substantially impairs the value of the car, the car must be replaced or the purchase price refunded. Lemon laws also typically require replacement or refund if a new car has been out of service ("in the shop") for thirty days during the statutory warranty period.

61. 772 So. 2d 1131 (Ala. 2000).

INTERNATIONAL CONSIDERATION

Taiwan adopted its Consumer Protection Law in 1994. The law covers consumer contracts, warranties, door-to-door sales, installment sales, product safety, and mechanisms for the resolution of consumer disputes.

In addition to permitting the revocation of a new car sales contract, state lemon laws (like the Magnuson–Moss Warranty Act) are designed to encourage informal resolution of disputes concerning defective new cars. Lemon laws achieve this objective by requiring that a consumer use a manufacturer's arbitration program before litigating, as long as the manufacturer has established an informal dispute resolution program that complies with FTC regulations. Some states, including New York, have adopted their own standards for these dispute resolution programs.

Sales Practices

Laws designed to protect consumers from unfair and deceptive trade practices often require disclosure of specific forms of sales practices. Such regulations may apply to all industries or be industry specific, such as the FTC's rules for sellers of used cars or state insurance regulations. A number of state and federal agencies currently regulate sales practices, including the FTC, the FCC, the Postal Service, and the Department of Housing and Urban Development.

Sometimes laws of general application can be invoked to protect consumers. For example, a lawyer in Washington, D.C., won two state court judgments totaling $11.6 million against affiliates of Tele-Communications, Inc. for charging excess late fees on monthly cable-television bills.[62] He successfully argued that the fees violated the general principle of contract law that damages assessed for breach of contract cannot be disproportionate to the actual harm caused by the breach.

By 2000, Prudential Insurance Company of America had paid approximately $2.7 billion to settle claims that its agents had engaged in illegal sales tactics. These tactics included tricking policyholders into cashing in old policies with accrued cash-surrender value to purchase new expensive ones with no surrender value, making false promises that dividends would build up quickly enough to pay for premiums, and disguising insurance policies as retirement programs.

62. Eben Shapiro, *Attorney Finds a Way to Battle Bills' Late Fees,* WALL ST. J., Oct. 6, 1997, at B1.

STATE DECEPTIVE PRACTICES STATUTES

Most state consumer protection laws are directed at deceptive trade practices and prohibit sellers from providing false or misleading information to consumers. Although there is considerable variation among state laws, they often provide more stringent protections than federal laws.

UCC UNCONSCIONABILITY PRINCIPLE

Also on the state level, the Uniform Commercial Code protects consumers from unfair sales practices through the unconscionability principle contained in Section 2-302 of the UCC, as discussed in Chapter 8. This section prohibits the enforcement of any contracts for the sale of goods that are so unfair and one-sided that they shock the conscience of the court.

DOOR-TO-DOOR SALES

Door-to-door sales are initiated and concluded at a buyer's home. They pose special risks because individuals may feel more pressure to buy something from someone standing at their door, or they may make a purchase just to get rid of a persistent salesperson. As a result, the FTC has mandated a three-day cooling-off period during which a consumer may rescind a door-to-door purchase. Under FTC rules, the seller must also notify a buyer of the right to cancel. Laws in some states provide longer periods during which consumers can cancel a sale.

REFERRAL SALES AND PYRAMID SALES

A number of states have enacted legislation restricting referral and pyramid sales. In a *referral sale,* the seller offers the buyer a commission, rebate, or discount for furnishing the seller with a list of additional prospective customers. The discount is usually contingent on the seller actually making later sales to the prospects provided by the original customer. In a *pyramid selling* scheme, a consumer is recruited as a product "distributor" and receives commissions based on the products he or she sells and on the recruitment of additional sellers (or even receives commissions on the sales of the recruits). The problem with both referral and pyramid sales is that unless the buyer or "distributor" becomes involved early in the chain, the supply of prospective recruits is quickly exhausted.

TELEMARKETING

Aggressive telemarketing sales practices, particularly the use of autodialers and "900" telephone numbers, have

ETHICAL CONSIDERATION

Is it ethical for telemarketers to use caller ID to identify and create a database of the individuals who call their 800 or 900 telephone numbers?

prompted congressional intervention. For example, the Telephone Consumer Protection Act (TCPA) of 1991[63] directed the FCC to adopt rules and regulations to curb telemarketing abuses. In general, the TCPA prohibits the use of either autodialers or simulated or prerecorded voice messages to deliver calls to emergency telephone lines, health care facilities, radio telephone services, and other services where the called party will incur some charge for the call. The only exception is for calls to a person who has given prior consent to such calls. A second provision prohibits the use of prerecorded messages when calling residential telephone numbers, except with the prior consent of the called party or in an emergency. Although enforcement of this second provision was initially enjoined by a federal court in Oregon on free speech grounds, the provision was later upheld by the U.S. Court of Appeals for the Ninth Circuit.[64]

In July 1993, the FCC and the FTC adopted final rules regulating the advertising, operation, and billing of 900 numbers. The rules require that (1) calls to 900 numbers in excess of two minutes include a preamble disclosing the name of the information provider and a brief description of the service, (2) any advertisements include the cost of the call adjacent to and in a type size no less than one-half the size of the 900 number, and (3) the cost per minute and any minimum charges be disclosed to consumers.

In 1997, the North American Securities Administrators Association and the FTC announced that their six-month "Field of Schemes" crackdown on investment-related telemarketing fraud had resulted in sixty-one enforcement actions. The schemes ranged from ostrich ranching in Idaho to digital fingerprint identification in Indiana and worthless oil and gas programs in Kentucky.

MAIL-ORDER SALES

Unscrupulous mail-order sales practices have led to a high incidence of consumer complaints with resultant state and federal regulation. Sellers must respond to

63. 47 U.S.C. § 227 (1998).
64. Moser v. FCC, 46 F.3d 970 (9th Cir. 1995), *cert. denied,* 515 U.S. 1161 (1995).

consumer mail orders by shipping merchandise or offering refunds within a reasonable time. Unsolicited or unordered merchandise sent by U.S. mail may be kept or disposed of by the recipient without incurring any obligation to the sender. Book and record clubs are generally legal as long as they comply with state law provisions requiring sellers to provide consumers with forms or announcement cards that may be used to instruct the seller not to send the offered merchandise. The U.S. Postal Service has authority to assess criminal and civil penalties for fraudulent mail schemes that injure consumers.

INDUSTRY-SPECIFIC SALES PRACTICES

Since the early 1980s, the FTC has become more involved in regulating the sales practices of specific industries. For example, in 1985 the FTC began to require used-car sellers to affix a Buyer's Guide label to the cars that they sell.[65] The Buyer's Guide is intended to disclose to potential buyers information about the car's warranty and any service contract provided by the dealer. If the car is sold without a warranty, the label must state that the car is being sold "as is."

A related and well-developed area of state and federal consumer law concerns restrictions on tampering with car odometers. Consumers purchasing a motor vehicle rely heavily on the odometer reading as an indication of a car's safety and reliability. The Motor Vehicle Information and Cost Savings Act[66] makes it a crime to change a car's odometer.

On the state level, industry-specific regulation covers the insurance industry. State insurance commissioners both establish regulations regarding the disclosure of information to perspective policyholders and set maximum rates within a state.

REAL ESTATE SALES

A number of state and federal laws, including the Federal Real Estate Settlement Procedures Act and the Interstate Land Sales Full Disclosure Act, protect consumers in real estate transactions. Certain disclosure requirements of the Truth-in-Lending Act apply to real estate credit transactions as well. In some transactions, real estate buyers have the right to cancel the purchase contract if certain information is not disclosed to them or if other procedures are not properly followed.

The Real Estate Settlement Procedures Act and revisions made to it in 1976 are designed to assist home buyers by requiring disclosure of any requirements for settlement proceedings, which may include title insurance, taxes, and fees for attorneys, appraisers, and brokers. In general, lenders must give an estimate of settlement costs, identify service providers the applicant is required to use, and provide a statement showing the annual percentage rate for the mortgage.

In response to fraudulent practices in the sale of subdivided land for investment purposes or for second or retirement homes, Congress passed the Interstate Land Sales Full Disclosure Act[67] in 1968. It is administered by the secretary of the Department of Housing and Urban Development (HUD). Under the Act, the secretary created the Office of Interstate Land Sales Registration and imposed federal disclosure requirements on the sale of 100 or more lots of undeveloped subdivided land akin to the disclosures required for the offer of securities under the Securities Act of 1933. The Act gives the secretary of HUD the power to bring suit in federal district court to enjoin sales by developers who have not registered in accordance with the Act. Purchasers affected by a promoter's wrongdoing have a private cause of action and may cancel the purchase contract.

⚠ Consumer Credit *and the* Consumer Credit Protection Act

Because credit plays an important role in many consumer transactions, a range of consumer protection laws address this area. Federal consumer credit law can be confusing because many of the acts have similar names. These complex acts and regulations are all part of the lengthy Consumer Credit Protection Act (CCPA),[68] which was initially passed by Congress in 1968. Since 1968, several additional acts (or titles) have been added to the original legislation. Exhibit 21.1 provides an overview of the CCPA.

TRUTH-IN-LENDING ACT

Title I, the Truth-in-Lending Act (TILA), is intended "to assure a meaningful disclosure of credit terms so that the consumer will be able to compare more readily the vari-

---

65. 16 C.F.R. § 455 (1998) (Used Motor Vehicle Trade Regulation Rule).
66. 15 U.S.C. § 1901 *et seq.* (1998).

67. 15 U.S.C. § 1701 *et seq.* (1998).
68. 15 U.S.C. § 1601 *et seq.* (1998).

EXHIBIT 21.1 Consumer Credit Protection Act (CCPA)

Title	Consumer Credit Protection Act
I.	Truth-in-Lending Act (TILA)
	Chapter 1: General Provisions*
	Chapter 2: Credit Transactions
	Chapter 3: Credit Advertising
	Chapter 4: Fair Credit Billing Act
	Chapter 5: Consumer Leasing Act
II.	Extortionate Credit Transactions
III.	Restrictions on Garnishment
IV.	National Commission on Consumer Finance*
V.	General Provisions*
VI.	Fair Credit Reporting Act
VII.	Equal Credit Opportunity Act
VIII.	Fair Debt Collection Practices Act
IX.	Electronic Fund Transfer Act

*Not discussed in this chapter.

ous credit terms available and avoid the uninformed use of credit."[69] In particular, the Act makes uniform the actuarial method for determining the rate charged for consumer credit. TILA is not a usury statute, however, and nowhere in the Act are interest rates set. TILA applies only to credit transactions (for example, sales, loans, and leases[70]) between creditors and consumers, not to credit transactions between two consumers. Debtors must be natural persons, so corporations and other entities are not protected by the Act.

Consumers can be required to arbitrate their claims if they agreed to do so when applying for or procuring credit. For example, in 2000, a U.S. district court ruled that a claim that a lender's consumer loan agreement violated TILA by failing to disclose the annual percentage rate, finance charge, and financing for rollover loans was subject to mandatory arbitration.[71] The loan agreement stated that any dispute regarding the loan was subject to arbitration. The court rejected the borrowers' argument that TILA gave them a statutory right to seek relief through a class action.

69. 15 U.S.C. § 1601 (1998).
70. Under federal law, consumer lessees are also protected by the 1976 Consumer Leasing Act, which is Chapter 5 of the TILA. The Federal Reserve Board has issued regulations (known collectively as Regulation M) to implement the Act. Under these regulations, consumer leases are defined to include leases that last more than four months and do not exceed $25,000. The Act and accompanying regulations control both advertising and disclosure in connection with these consumer leases.
71. Thompson v. Illinois Title Loans, Inc., 2000 U.S. Dist. LEXIS 232 (Jan. 6, 2000).

TILA draws a distinction between open-end credit and closed-end credit. With *open-end credit,* the parties intend the creditor to make repeated extensions of credit (for example, Visa or MasterCard); *closed-end credit* involves only one transaction (for example, a car or house loan). Open-end consumer credit plans must make certain disclosures at three separate times: (1) in an initial disclosure statement when the account is opened, (2) in subsequent periodic billing statements, and (3) annually when a consumer must be notified of his or her rights under the Fair Credit Billing Act. In general, the required information includes finance and other charges, security interests (collateral), previous balance and credits, identification of transactions, closing date and new balance, and annual percentage rates and period rates.

Closed-end credit plans must disclose at least the following for each transaction: identity of creditor, amount financed, finance charge, annual percentage rate, variable rate, payment schedule, total of payments, total sale price, prepayment provisions, late payment fee, security interest, credit insurance, loan assumption policy, and required deposit. Special rules apply for certain residential mortgages and adjustable rate transactions.

In *Williams v. Chartwell Financial Services Ltd.,*[72] the Seventh Circuit ruled that under TILA, the annual percentage rate a lender must disclose is based on the face amount of the loan reduced by the amount of cash collateral on the loan, when the collateral is used to reduce the amount of the loan rather than to serve as a security

72. 204 F.3d 748 (7th Cir. 2000).

 ETHICAL CONSIDERATION

In 2000, the Departments of Treasury and Housing and Urban Development issued a report, entitled *Curbing Predatory Home Mortgage Lending,* showing that predatory lending practices are concentrated in the subprime mortgage market. Subprime lending tends to be concentrated in low-income communities. A majority of the mortgages in the subprime market are used for consumer debt rather than housing purposes. Should subprime lenders provide additional information and explanations concerning the loan to borrowers who due to lack of experience or education may not understand the loan terms? Would the cost of providing the additional information be a factor in your decision, or is it the province of government to dictate the required disclosure?[a]

a. *HUD–Treasury Predatory Lending Report Seeks New Legislation, Tougher Enforcement,* 68 U.S.L.W. 2777 (June 27, 2000).

interest. In reaching its decision, the court emphasized the importance of substance over form in TILA litigation. It concluded that rather than reducing the lender's risk by providing it with property to sell upon default, the cash collateral reduced the amount of money the bank initially loaned.

In 2000, the FTC settled a claim against providers of short-term, high-interest-rate "payday loans" for alleged violations of TILA and the FTC's Telemarketing Sales Rule.[73] Two companies used direct mail and telemarketing to market the MoneyMarketCard. They offered consumers, regardless of their credit history, a credit line of $5,500 at a 14.99 percent interest rate. After consumers paid $149 to $169 to receive the MoneyMarketCard, they discovered that they could use the credit only to buy items from one of the company's catalogs and that the cash advance privileges were short-term payday loans of $20 to $40 with annual interest rates of 360 percent or more. The FTC alleged that although the companies collected membership fees of more than $12 million between 1996 and 1999, less than 8 percent of the customers ever purchased even one catalog product or took out a cash loan. The settlement required the companies to stop their deceptive practices, to disgorge $350,000 received from consumers, and to forgive $1.6 million in outstanding consumer debts.

Regulation Z Congress directed the Federal Reserve Board (FRB) to interpret and enforce TILA. To that end, the FRB issued regulations, known collectively as *Regulation Z*.[74] The FRB has also produced model disclosure forms for use with credit sales and loans.

Regulation Z applies to any transaction (in which both parties are subject to TILA) that involves an installment contract where payment is to be made in more than four installments and the credit is primarily for personal, family, or household purposes. The two most important terms in a TILA disclosure statement are the finance charge (interest over the life of the loan expressed as a dollar amount) and the annual percentage rate, or APR (interest expressed as a percentage), both as defined in Regulation Z. Typical transactions include car loans, student loans, home improvement loans, and certain real estate loans in which the amount financed is less than $25,000. Regulation Z also contains provisions dealing with disclosure of the terms of any credit or mortgage insurance offered in connection with a loan.

Credit and Charge Cards Although Regulation Z is usually triggered by credit arrangements in which a finance charge is imposed, TILA and Regulation Z were amended in 1970 to include regulation of both credit cards (such as Visa or MasterCard, which permit deferred payment over a period of time) and charge cards (such as American Express, which require payment of the full balance upon receipt of the bill).

In 2000, the Federal Reserve Board published a rule revising Regulation Z to require more explicit disclosures on credit card applications. The new rule requires marketing material to prominently display a table that clearly states the annual percentage rate and other critical information (including the annual fee). The annual percentage rate for purchases and the variable rate information, grace period, minimum finance charge, method of computing the balance, cash advance fee and over-limit fee, and any other fees that vary by state must be printed in the box in at least eighteen-point type to prevent efforts to hide information in the "fine print." In addition, the overall disclosure statement must be printed in at least twelve-point type and be in a "reasonably understandable form."[75]

TILA limits the liability of credit card holders to $50 per card for unauthorized charges made before a card issuer is notified that the card has been lost or stolen. Once a card issuer has been notified, a card holder incurs no liability from unauthorized use. A credit or charge card company also cannot bill a consumer for unauthorized charges if the card was improperly issued by the card company.

Home Equity Lending Plans TILA provides specific protections for consumers who use their home as collateral for a second mortgage or open-end line of credit. Because losing one's home has such significant consequences, Congress felt special disclosure requirements were in order. TILA provides consumers with a *right of rescission* (that is, a right to cancel the contract) whenever their home is used as collateral except for original construction or acquisition. These cancellation rights are generally available for three days if all procedures are properly followed by the lender, three years if they are not. TILA also mandates disclosure of up-front costs, repayment schedules, and the annual percentage rate and its method of calculation.

Credit Advertising Chapter 3 of TILA includes specific provisions that regulate credit advertising. The idea be-

---

73. FTC v. Consumer Money Mkts., Inc., D. Nev. CVS001071 (Sept. 6, 2000).
74. 12 C.F.R. § 226 (1998).
75. *Fed Issues Final Regulation Under TILA Requiring New Clarity for Card Disclosures*, 69 U.S.L.W. 2200 (Oct. 10, 2000).

Should businesses serving communities with largely non-English-speaking populations provide written translations of written documents? Should businesses provide oral translations, perhaps on voice recording cassettes, of important terms in consumer transactions, such as home equity loans and door-to-door sales, so that illiterate consumers can understand important terms of the transaction?

hind these provisions is that consumers equipped with complete and accurate credit information will be able to find the best terms. Regulation Z requires that any advertised specific credit terms actually be available and that any credit terms (for example, finance charge or annual percentage rate) mentioned in the advertisement be explained fully. The FTC enforces the advertising provisions of Regulation Z. Unlike the other sections of TILA, Chapter 3 does not give consumers a private cause of action to sue credit advertisers directly.

Credit Billing By 1974, Congress had become concerned about the problems consumers were having in getting creditors to respond to their complaints. In response, Congress enacted the Fair Credit Billing Act (Chapter 4 of TILA), which requires creditors, such as credit card companies, to respond to consumer complaints by first acknowledging the complaint and then conducting a reasonable investigation to determine whether the complaint is justified. Companies cannot evade this requirement by canceling a cardholder's account.

For example, in 1982, American Express Company canceled a cardholder's account during a dispute about incorrect billings. American Express argued that its contract with the cardholder allowed it to revoke a credit card at any time for any reason, but the U.S. Court of Appeals for the District of Columbia ruled that the Fair Credit Billing Act's protections were not waivable.[76] As the court explained:

> The rationale of consumer protection legislation is to even out the inequalities that consumers normally bring to the bargain. To allow such protection to be waived by boiler plate language of the contract puts the legislative process to a foolish and unproductive task. A court ought not impute such nonsense to a Congress intent on correcting abuses in the market place.

76. Gray v. American Express Co., 743 F.2d 10 (D.C. Cir. 1984).

Hence, the Fair Credit Billing Act protected the cardmember despite the provisions of the Cardmember Agreement that purported to waive the protections of the Act.

EXTORTIONATE CREDIT TRANSACTIONS

Title II of the CCPA prohibits any *extortionate extension of credit,* that is, the extension of credit where the parties expect nonpayment to result in bodily harm.

RESTRICTIONS ON GARNISHMENT

Garnishment is the legal procedure by which a creditor may collect a debt by attaching a portion of the debtor's weekly wages. Title III of the CCPA puts limits on the ability of creditors to garnish wages. In particular, the Act restricts the amount of a debtor's wages that is available for garnishment to the lesser of (1) 25 percent of the "disposable earnings" for that week (defined by the Act as the amount remaining after deductions required by law) or (2) the amount by which "disposable earnings" for that week exceed thirty times the current federal minimum hourly wage. The secretary of labor enforces the provisions of this title. Some states prohibit garnishment of wages altogether.

FAIR CREDIT REPORTING ACT

Qualifying for credit is important because of the widespread use of credit in consumer transactions. Almost everyone over the age of eighteen has a credit report on file somewhere. Lenders look to the various reporting agencies for information on an individual's creditworthiness. Because negative information in a credit report can make obtaining credit considerably more difficult, it is helpful for consumers to be able to access their credit reports and to correct any false information before it is reported to lenders or shared with any other reporting agency's computer.

In response to concerns about potential injury to consumers through errors in credit reports, Congress passed the Fair Credit Reporting Act (FCRA) in 1970. Under the FCRA, consumers can request all information (except medical information) on themselves, the source of the information, and any recent recipients of a report. The FCRA also gives consumers a right to have corrected copies of their credit reports sent to creditors. The FTC has primary responsibility for the enforcement of the FCRA.

Credit bureaus must investigate disputed information in credit reports and resolve consumer complaints within thirty days. The credit-reporting agency must go beyond the original source of the information to determine whether it is accurate. Thus, when a consumer notified the agency that she had never held the credit cards her report showed as being delinquent, the agency could not just rely on the credit card companies' statements that the applications for the cards contained the correct information; instead, the agency should have checked the handwriting on the credit applications and determined whether the applications were obtained by fraud.[77] Credit bureaus must give consumers written notice of the results of the investigation within five days after it is completed.

The FCRA also imposes duties on persons who furnish information regarding unpaid bills to credit-reporting

agencies. When a consumer tells a credit-reporting agency that he or she disputes a charge, the agency is required to notify the furnisher of the information that the information provided is in dispute. The creditor must then conduct an investigation and review all relevant information to determine whether it is accurate. Any inaccurate or incomplete information must be reported to all national credit bureaus. The FCRA also contains restrictions on *investigative consumer reporting* (reports that contain information on character and reputation, not just credit history), including the requirement that, in most cases, a consumer be notified in writing that such a report may be made. In the following case, the court considered whether consumers can sue companies that furnish information to a credit-reporting agency if they fail to reinvestigate credit information that has been disputed.

77. Cushman v. Trans Union Corp., 115 F.3d 220 (3d Cir. 1997).

A CASE IN POINT

CASE 21.3

Dornhecker v. Ameritech Corp.

United States District Court for the Northern District of Illinois 99 F. Supp. 2d 918 (N.D. Ill. 2000).

Summary

FACTS Scott Dornhecker, José Sanchez, and Carolyn Johnson received letters from collection agencies attempting to collect, on Ameritech's behalf, unpaid balances for phone services. The three claimed that they had never opened accounts with Ameritech and that Ameritech had opened phone service accounts on behalf of third persons who had fraudulently used their names and falsely incurred the debt in their names.

The plaintiffs alleged that Ameritech violated its duties as a furnisher of information by inadequately investigating the information after being notified that it was disputed. Ameritech moved to dismiss the complaint on the grounds that the FCRA creates no duties enforceable by consumers.

ISSUE PRESENTED Can a furnisher of credit information be held civilly liable to a consumer under the FCRA for failing to comply properly with the investigation duty once it has received notice of a dispute from a credit-reporting agency?

SUMMARY OF OPINION The U.S. District Court for the Northern District of Illinois began by noting that the FCRA makes no explicit reference to a private right of action for enforcement. When considering whether there was an implied private right of action, the court looked to the U.S. Supreme Court decision in *Cort v. Ash*[78] for guidance. In that case, the Court set forth four factors to consider in determining whether a private remedy is implicit in a statute that does not explicitly provide a remedy: (1) whether the plaintiff is a member of the class for whose benefit the statute was enacted, (2) whether the legislative history reflects any explicit or implicit intent to create or deny a remedy, (3) whether the implication of a private remedy would frustrate the purpose of the statute, and (4) whether the cause of action is traditionally relegated to state law.

Applying these four factors, the court concluded that the plaintiffs were members of the class of people sought to be protected by the FCRA. The legislative history suggests that Congress did not intend to limit civil liability. A private remedy would not frustrate the purpose of the FCRA scheme as other provisions of the statute provide consumers

78. 422 U.S. 66 (1975).

(Continued)

(Case 21.3 continued)

with a private right of action. Finally, Congress expressly intended for the FCRA to coexist with state consumer protection laws. As a result, implication of a private right of action under the federal statute was appropriate.

RESULT The court concluded that individual consumers may bring a private lawsuit against a furnisher of information for failing to comply with the FCRA. Ameritech's motion to dismiss was denied.

Use of Credit Reports in Employment Decisions Before asking a credit bureau for a report on an applicant or employee, an employer must notify the individual in writing that a report may be used and obtain the individual's consent. An employer may not rely on a credit report to take adverse action (defined as denying a job applicant a position, reassigning or terminating an employee, or denying a promotion), unless it first provides the individual with a "pre–adverse action disclosure," which includes a copy of the credit report and the FTC's "A Summary of Your Rights Under the Fair Credit Reporting Act."

Employers who fail to get permission before requesting a credit report or to provide the pre–adverse action disclosures are subject to suits for damages (including punitive damages for deliberate violations) by individuals and civil penalties by the FTC.

After an employer has taken adverse action, it must give the individual notice—orally, in writing, or electronically—that the action has been taken. The notice must include (1) the name, address, and phone number of the credit bureau that supplied the credit report; (2) a statement that the credit bureau did not make the decision to take the adverse action and cannot give specific reasons for it; and (3) a notice of the individual's right to dispute the accuracy or completeness of any information the bureau furnished and the individual's right upon request to an additional free credit report from the credit bureau within sixty days.

EQUAL CREDIT OPPORTUNITY ACT

Passed by Congress in 1974, the Equal Credit Opportunity Act (Title VII of the CCPA) was originally intended to address the difficulty many women faced in obtaining credit; it prohibited discrimination in the granting of credit on the basis of sex or marital status. The current list of protected categories includes race, color, religion, national origin, sex or marital status, age (except that older applicants may be given favorable treatment), applicants whose income derives from public assistance,

and applicants who have exercised in good faith any right under the CCPA.

The Federal Reserve Board has issued regulations (known collectively as Regulation B) to implement the Act. Unlike most of the other acts covered so far, the Equal Credit Opportunity Act applies to business credit as well as consumer credit. In general, the rejection of an application for credit triggers the Act and various compliance steps, which include written notification of the reasons for denial. The regulations also establish methods for evaluating the creditworthiness of an applicant.

FAIR DEBT COLLECTION PRACTICES ACT

Prior to enactment of the Fair Debt Collection Practices Act in 1978 (Title VIII of the CCPA), the common law was used to protect debtors from outrageous collection practices. For example, if a loan shark broke a debtor's kneecaps, the debtor would have an action for battery. Defamation and invasion of privacy actions were also common.

Since 1978, the Fair Debt Collection Practices Act (which is enforced by the FTC) has regulated debt collectors and debt collection practices and provided a civil remedy for anyone injured by a violation of the statute. The Act covers only third-party debt collectors (for example, collection agencies) or someone pretending to be a third-party collector. First-party debt collectors (for example, retail store collection departments) are not covered under the Act, although the FTC can reach these individuals under its duty to address "unfair and deceptive trade practices" under Section 5 of the Federal Trade Commission Act.

 ETHICAL CONSIDERATION

Is it ethical for a lender to call a friend in the police department to see whether a loan applicant has a criminal record? Should the applicant be notified of that investigation?

ETHICAL CONSIDERATION

The Fair Debt Collection Practices Act specifically forbids a debt collector to engage in certain practices, including contacting a debtor at any time if that debtor is represented by an attorney. What self-imposed limits, if any, might a debt collector adopt, and what role should a debtor's personal circumstances (for example, unemployment or terminal illness) play in how aggressive a debt collector chooses to be?

The U.S. Court of Appeals for the Seventh Circuit held that a letter from an attorney on behalf of a landlord demanding that a tenant pay back rent (within three days) or face eviction was subject to the Fair Debt Collection Practices Act.[79] The court held that rent past due is a debt and that the lawyer's letter was a debt collection "communication" within the meaning of the statute.

79. Romea v. Helberger & Assocs., 163 F.3d 111 (2d Cir. 1998).

People who write bad checks for goods and services are protected from abusive debt collection practices by the Fair Debt Collection Practices Act. The Seventh,[80] Eighth,[81] and Ninth Circuits[82] have each held that the payment obligation that arises from a bounced check is "debt" within the meaning of the Act even though the transaction involved no offer of credit or extension of credit.

In general, FTC guidelines require collectors to tell the truth and not use any deceptive means to collect a debt or locate a debtor. For example, a collector may not give the impression that it is a government agency or credit bureau. As the following case illustrates, debt collectors have serious obligations toward those from whom they attempt to collect.

80. Bass v. Stolper, Koritzinsky, Brewer & Neider, 111 F.3d 1322 (7th Cir. 1997).
81. Duffy v. Landberg, 133 F.3d 1120 (8th Cir. 1998), *cert. denied*, 525 U.S. 821 (1998).
82. Charles v. Lundgren & Assoc., P.C., 119 F.3d 739 (9th Cir. 1997), *cert. denied*, 522 U.S. 1028 (1997).

A CASE IN POINT

CASE 21.4

Bartlett v. Heibl

United States Court of Appeals for the Seventh Circuit
128 F.3d 497
(7th Cir. 1997).

In the Language of the Court

FACTS Micard Services, a credit card company, hired attorney John Heibl to collect a consumer credit card debt of approximately $1,700 from Curtis Bartlett. Heibl sent Bartlett a letter, which Bartlett received but did not read, in which Heibl told him that "if you wish to resolve this matter before legal action is commenced, you must do one of two things within one week of the date of this letter": (1) pay $316 toward the satisfaction of the debt, or get in touch with Micard (the creditor), or (2) "make suitable arrangements for payment. If you do neither, it will be assumed that legal action will be necessary." Under Heibl's signature appeared a near-verbatim description of Section 1692g(a) of the Fair Debt Collection Practices Act. The section advised Bartlett that he had thirty days to dispute the debt, in which case Heibl would mail him a verification of it. At the end of the paraphrase, Heibl added that "suit may be commenced at any time before the expiration of this thirty (30) days."

Alleging that Heibl's letter violated the Act by stating the required information in a confusing manner, Bartlett filed suit against the debt collector. The trial court found for Heibl, and Bartlett appealed.

ISSUE PRESENTED Does a dunning letter violate the Fair Debt Collection Practices Act by describing the debtor's and collector's respective rights in a way that confuses the debtor about his rights?

OPINION POSNER, C.J., writing for the U.S. Court of Appeals for the Seventh Circuit:

The Fair Debt Collection Practices Act provides that within five days after a debt collector first duns a consumer debtor, the collector must send the debtor a written notice containing specified information. The required information includes the amount of the debt, the name of the creditor, and, of particular relevance here, a statement that unless the debtor "disputes the validity of the debt" within thirty days the debt

(Continued)

(Case 21.4 continued)

collector will assume that the debt is valid but that if the debtor notifies the collector in writing within thirty days that he is disputing the debt, "the debt collector will obtain verification of the debt [from the creditor] . . . and a copy of [the] verification . . . will be mailed to the consumer." A similar provision requires that the debtor be informed that upon his request the debt collector will give him the name and address of his original creditor, if the original creditor is different from the current one. If the debtor accepts the invitation tendered in the required notice, and requests from the debt collector either verification of the debt or the name and address of the original creditor, the debt collector must "cease collection of the debt . . . until the [requested information] is mailed to the consumer." These provisions are intended for the case in which the debt collector, being a hireling of the creditor rather than the creditor itself, may lack first-hand knowledge of the debt.

If the statute is violated, the debtor is entitled to obtain from the debt collector, in addition to any actual damages that the debtor can prove, statutory damages not to exceed $1,000 per violation, plus a reasonable attorney's fee. . . .

The letter is said to violate the statute by stating the required information about the debtor's rights in a confusing fashion. . . . The defendant . . . contends that even if the letter is confusing this is of no moment because Bartlett didn't read it. That would be a telling point if Bartlett were seeking actual damages, for example as a consequence of being misled by the letter into surrendering a legal defense against the credit-card company. . . . But he is not seeking actual damages. He is seeking only statutory damages, a penalty that does not depend on proof that the recipient of the letter was misled. . . .

The main issue presented by the appeal is whether the district judge committed a clear error in finding that the letter was not confusing. The statute does not say in so many words that the disclosures required by it must be made in a nonconfusing manner. But the courts, our own included, have held, plausibly enough, that it is implicit that the debt collector may not defeat the statute's purpose by making the required disclosures in a form or within a context in which they are unlikely to be understood by the unsophisticated debtors who are the particular objects of the statute's solicitude.

Most of the cases put it this way: the implied duty to avoid confusing the unsophisticated consumer can be violated by contradicting or "overshadowing" the required notice. . . .

As with many legal formulas that get repeated from case to case without an effort at elaboration, "contradicting or overshadowing" is rather unilluminating—even, though we hesitate to use the word in this context, confusing. . . .

It would be better if the courts just said that the unsophisticated consumer is to be protected against confusion whatever form it takes. A contradiction is just one means of inducing confusion; "overshadowing" is just another; and the most common is a third, the failure to explain an apparent though not actual contradiction—as in this case. . . . On the one hand, Heibl's letter tells the debtor that if he doesn't pay within a week he's going to be sued. On the other hand, it tells him that he can contest the debt within thirty days. This leaves up in the air what happens if he is sued on the eighth day, say, and disputes the debt on the tenth day. He might well wonder what good it would do him to dispute the debt if he can't stave off a lawsuit. The net effect of the juxtaposition of the one-week and thirty-day crucial periods is to turn the required disclosure into legal gibberish. That's as bad as an outright contradiction.

. . . The cases . . . leave no room to doubt that the letter to Bartlett was confusing; nor as an original matter could we doubt that it was confusing—we found it so,

(Continued)

(Case 21.4 continued)

and do not like to think of ourselves as your average unsophisticated consumer. So the judgment must be reversed. But we should not stop here. Judges too often tell defendants what the defendants cannot do without indicating what they can do, thus engendering legal uncertainty that foments further litigation. . . .

. . . We here set forth a redaction of Heibl's letter that complies with the statute without forcing the debt collector to conceal his intention of exploiting his right to resort to legal action before the thirty days are up. We are not rewriting the statute; that is not our business. We are simply trying to provide some guidance to how to comply with it. We commend this redaction as a safe harbor for debt collectors who want to avoid liability for the kind of suit that Bartlett has brought and now won. . . .

Dear Mr. Bartlett:

I have been retained by Micard Services to collect from you the entire balance, which as of September 25, 1995, was $1,656.90, that you owe Micard Services on your Master-Card Account No. 5414701617068749.

If you want to resolve this matter without a lawsuit, you must, within one week of the date of this letter, either pay Micard $316 against the balance that you owe (unless you've paid it since your last statement) or call Micard at 1-800-221-5920 ext. 6130 and work out arrangements for payment with it. If you do neither of these things, I will be entitled to file a lawsuit against you, for the collection of this debt, when the week is over.

Federal law gives you thirty days after you receive this letter to dispute the validity of the debt or any part of it. If you don't dispute it within that period, I'll assume that it's valid. If you do dispute it—by notifying me in writing to that effect—I will, as required by the law, obtain and mail to you proof of the debt. And if, within the same period, you request in writing the name and address of your original creditor, if the original creditor is different from the current creditor (Micard Services), I will furnish you with that information too.

The law does not require me to wait until the end of the thirty-day period before suing you to collect this debt. If, however, you request proof of the debt or the name and address of the original creditor within the thirty-day period that begins with your receipt of this letter, the law requires me to suspend my efforts (through litigation or otherwise) to collect the debt until I mail the requested information to you.

Sincerely,

John A. Heibl

We cannot require debt collectors to use "our" form. But of course if they depart from it, they do so at their risk. . . .

RESULT The appeals court reversed the trial court's decision and ordered judgment for the plaintiff and computation of statutory damages, costs, and attorneys' fees.

QUESTIONS

1. How would the court have analyzed the case if Bartlett had been a consumer rights attorney and, in spite of Heibl's letter, had been well aware of his rights and Heibl's corresponding obligations under the Fair Debt Collection Practices Act?

2. What are the arguments for and against statutory damages that allow a debtor who did not read a dunning letter to challenge it based on the letter's confusing, but never read, text?

ELECTRONIC FUND TRANSFER ACT AND DEBIT CARDS

Online Debit Cards and Preauthorized Fund Transfers The Electronic Fund Transfer Act (Title IX of the CCPA), passed by Congress in 1978, covers online debit cards issued by banks for use with automatic teller machines (ATMs) and point-of-sale transactions, as well as preauthorized electronic fund transfers or automatic payments from a consumer's account. As with credit cards, banks are prohibited from sending out debit cards except in response to a consumer's request.

The Federal Reserve Board (FRB) has issued regulations (called collectively Regulation E) and model forms for banks to use to satisfy disclosure requirements under the Act. In general, the FRB forms ensure disclosure regarding contract terms, potential customer liability for unauthorized use (as with credit cards, customer liability is usually limited to no more than $50), and consumer complaint procedures. Banks are also required to issue a receipt with every ATM transaction and to mail periodic statements showing electronic fund transfer activity on a consumer's account during the period. For preauthorized transfers or automatic payments, banks are required to provide either (1) written or oral notice within two days of the scheduled transaction date that the transaction did or did not occur or (2) a telephone line for consumers to call and ascertain whether the transfer occurred. Most financial institutions have adopted the latter approach.

Off-Line Debit Cards Online debit cards are PIN-protected; that is, cash cannot be withdrawn from an ATM and a deduction cannot be made at a point-of-sale terminal unless the holder uses a personal identification number (PIN). In contrast, off-line debit cards (which may bear the Visa or MasterCard logo) have the characteristics of both an ATM card and a credit card, and they can be used without a PIN. For example, the holder of an off-line debit card can authorize a deduction from his or her bank account by signing a charge slip at a restaurant. Visa and MasterCard voluntarily agreed in August 1997 to impose a $50 cap on liability for their debit cards.

State Laws Regulating Consumer Credit

U–TRIPLE C

All states have statutes regulating consumer credit. Two types of consumer credit transactions are addressed primarily at the state level: installment sales and loans to consumers. The state statutes vary widely, however, and an attempt to create uniform state laws on consumer credit through adoption of the Uniform Consumer Credit Code (UCCC, called the U–Triple C) has been largely unsuccessful. Only a handful of states have adopted the UCCC, and each of them has altered it so significantly that little uniformity remains. The UCCC is intended to replace a state's consumer credit laws, including those that regulate usury, installment sales, consumer loans, truth in lending, and garnishment.

INSTALLMENT SALES

State installment sales laws set caps on the legal interest rate and permissible charges such as late charges and deferral charges. In addition, the state statutes discuss remedies and attorneys' fees, as well as any party's right to assign the sales contract.

CONSUMER LOANS

Most states also have a statute (or several statutes) pertaining to consumer loans. In general, these statutes require compliance with the state's *usury statute,* which may set the maximum interest rate permissible, although often a lender may be granted an exemption from the usury statute by obtaining a specified license in the state. If a lender is exempted from coverage of the usury laws, it can charge whatever rate of interest the market will bear.

STATE CREDIT CARD REGULATION

State usury statutes are also of concern to the credit card industry. In the early 1980s, in response to New York State's particularly stringent usury statute and credit card fee limits, Citibank moved its entire credit card operations from New York to South Dakota, a state with virtually no credit card regulations. The U.S. Supreme Court had previously ruled that the usury statutes and credit card fee limits in effect in the state where the credit card operations are located apply to all customers, regardless of where they live.[83] Thus, a bank with credit card operations in a state such as South Dakota or Delaware can charge a resident of Massachusetts the high interest rates and fees permitted in that state even though they are in excess of the Massachusetts limits.

---

83. Marquette Nat'l Bank of Minneapolis v. First of Omaha Serv. Corp., 439 U.S. 299 (1978).

THE RESPONSIBLE MANAGER
Complying *with* Consumer Protection Laws

Managers have a responsibility to make sure that current and potential customers are treated fairly and in a manner that will not subject them to injury, economic or physical. In that regard, managers must take steps to ensure that employees are aware of, and in compliance with, various federal and state consumer protection regulations. Because both managers and employees can be held legally accountable for their actions (and criminally liable in some cases), specific procedures should be in place to educate employees about important consumer law topics.

Managers in a manufacturing setting must recognize that product recalls may be necessary to correct a defective product. These recalls may be voluntary, or the government may, under consumer protection laws, order a company to remedy a potentially hazardous situation. A company has an ethical obligation to issue a warning about a product defect it discovers after its product is sold.

Managers should consider establishing an internal product-safety committee to conduct regular product-safety inspections. Production-line employees and others should be empowered to make suggestions on how to improve product safety and thereby protect consumers. Also critical is some form of whistle-blower protection for an employee who brings possible consumer protection law violations to the attention of a manager. Concealment or inaction on the part of a manager may subject him or her to criminal prosecution and a possible prison sentence.

In a competitive marketplace, managers often feel the need to be aggressive in advertising products or services.

Nonetheless, managers must refrain from making claims that may be deceptive or false. The FTC aggressively pursues companies that make false advertising claims. FTC remedies can include civil damages and corrective advertising campaigns, which can cost millions of dollars.

Managers should not be satisfied merely to meet minimum government standards with respect to consumer protection. Mere compliance may not be sufficient to release a manager or his or her company from liability when the manager has superior product information and should have taken additional precautions.

Managers whose companies extend credit to customers need to be aware that many discriminatory practices in the extension of credit are illegal. In particular, the Equal Credit Opportunity Act covers the following protected categories: race, color, religion, national origin, sex, marital status, age (except that older applicants may be given favorable treatment), and applicants whose income derives from public assistance. Some states also prohibit discrimination in credit based on sexual orientation.

Managers should embrace the opportunity to self-regulate or, at least, work closely with a regulatory agency to establish industry standards that meet the concerns of both the agency and the company. A good example of a self-regulating industry is the infomercial industry. Faced with possible government regulation, the industry established its own watchdog agency. In doing so, it was able to avert government involvement and the possibility of more restrictive regulation.

Firestone's Massive Tire Recall

In August 2000, the tire manufacturer Firestone, a unit of Japan's Bridgestone Corporation, issued a recall for 6.5 million tires, the industry's second largest recall ever. The tires had been linked to accidents resulting in 148 deaths in the United States and 48 in other countries. By the beginning of 2001, the number of deaths in the United States attributed to the defective tires had risen to 174.[84] Many of these accidents involved Firestone tires installed as original equipment on the Ford Explorer sport-utility vehicles (SUVs) and other light trucks. The tires allegedly have a tread-separation defect, which causes the tread to separate from the body of the tire.[85]

An onslaught of lawsuits were filed against Bridgestone/Firestone and Ford Motor Company. As of the end of 2000, 180 federal class-action and personal-injury suits had been consolidated in federal court in Indianapolis[86] and assigned to Chief U.S. District Judge Sarah Evans Barker for resolution in one forum.[87]

Bridgestone Corporation has rejected suggestions that the legal claims could bankrupt Firestone and says it has set aside $450 million to cover possible damage claims. The company spent $450 million in 2000 replacing the recalled tires with new tires, bringing the estimated total costs relating to the recall to $900 million.[88]

The recall prompted a congressional investigation to determine how long the companies had been aware of the problems with the tires. Investigators claimed that Firestone documents reflected that tests conducted in 1996 indicated that approximately 10 percent of the tires experienced tread-separation defects. In September 2000, the Senate Commerce Committee voted unanimously to pass a measure that would impose criminal penalties on manufacturers that knowingly make defective products that result in injuries or death. Members of the industry objected to the imposition of criminal penalties, arguing that it would discourage companies from informally sharing information with officials at the National Highway Traffic Safety Administration (NHTSA). A General Motors Corporation vice president commented, "We hope the Congress will ensure that careful deliberation is not sacrificed for speed in responding to a tragic yet extraordinary set of circumstances."[89] In any event, several auto industry officials told the *Wall Street Journal* that "they are increasingly resigned to the likelihood that public outrage over the Firestone recall will lead to new regulations that the industry has long lobbied against."[90] One official lamented, "A misstep by one leads to a punishment for all."[91]

During the congressional hearings, Ford and Firestone blamed each other for the injuries and deaths resulting from accidents of the Ford Explorer. Ford's president and chief executive officer testified, "First, this is a tire issue, not a vehicle issue." A Firestone executive vice president countered, "We firmly believe that the tire is only part of the overall safety problem." Typically, corporations present a united front as part of a legal strategy to avoid paying large sums to settle with plaintiffs. One prominent product liability lawyer commented, "It's a plaintiffs' lawyer's dream when co-defendants are fighting among themselves." Another plaintiffs' lawyer commented, "Now I've got the Goliaths fighting each other, instead of David fighting Goliath."[92]

Bridgestone's CEO Yoichiro Kaizaki's handling of the tire recall contributed to Firestone's problems. He was accused of stonewalling when he refused to disclose information regarding the recall and insisted that there were no problems with the tires. In January 2001, he resigned as CEO but remained with the company as a full-time adviser. When his resignation was announced, he denied that it symbolized his acceptance of responsibility for the recall. He told the press he had achieved his goals despite "a bit of trouble" during his last year—a reference to the tire recall.[93]

84. Stephen Power, *More Fatalities Are Associated with Tires from Firestone,* WALL ST. J., Feb. 7, 2001, at A6.

85. Stephen Power, *Update Needed for Tire Rules, Activists Argue,* WALL ST. J., Sept. 8, 2000, at B1.

86. Milo Geyelin & Timothy Aeppel, *Ford, Firestone Face Major Suits as Firms Seek to Allay Tire Issue,* WALL ST. J., Dec. 21, 2000, at A4.

87. Milo Geyelin & Timothy Aeppel, *Tire Suits Consolidated as Others Are Disclosed,* WALL ST. J., Oct. 26, 2000, at A3.

88. Todd Zaun et al., *Firestone Parent Will Set Aside Cash for Claims—Bridgestone Says Lawsuits Won't Force U.S. Unit into Bankruptcy Court,* WALL ST. J., Dec. 6, 2000, at A6.

89. Stephen Power, *Battered Auto Firms Seem Resigned to New Rules,* WALL ST. J., Sept. 21, 2000, at A3, A10.

90. *Id.* at A10.

91. *Id.*

92. Milo Geyelin, *Squabbles Between Ford and Firestone May Hurt Their Legal Defense,* WALL ST. J., Oct. 9, 2000, at B1.

93. Phred Dvorak & Michael Williams, *Bridgestone's CEO Kaizaki Is Resigning,* WALL ST. J., Jan. 12, 2001, at A15.

Firestone announced a series of measures designed to prevent future tire failures. These included (1) setting up three top-level committees to review the company's quality controls, production processes, and tire design; (2) having quality control report directly to the chief executive and chair; (3) improving its tracking of safety problems with tires installed on vehicles shipped outside the United States; (4) using data on tire-related deaths in its quality reviews; and (5) conducting a review of the materials and techniques used in making tires.[94]

As a result of Firestone's recall, consumers began putting pressure on the NHTSA to change its manner of regulating tires. The NHTSA requires tire manufacturers

to meet speed and endurance tests and to rate tires according to these criteria. The Uniform Tire Quality Grading System does not apply to "deep-tread" tires that are used on pickup trucks and SUVs, however. These vehicles either did not exist or were rarely used as passenger cars in the 1960s when the National Motor Vehicle Safety Act was enacted.

The NHTSA has agreed that it needs to update its standards and is working with agencies in other countries to develop a global tire standard. As of 2001, the NHTSA had rejected a proposal before the United Nations/Economic Commission for Europe because it did not address another type of tire failure created by the tire breaking away from the rim.[95]

94. Keith Bradsher, *Advertising: 2 Different Approaches in Aftermath of Tire Recall*, N.Y. TIMES, Apr. 5, 2001.

95. Power, *supra* note 89.

KEY WORDS AND PHRASES

additive 709
bait and switch advertising 725
caveat emptor 707
cease and desist orders 726
closed-end credit 731
consent order 724
drug 709
express warranty 723

extortionate extension of credit 733
food 709
garnishment 733
implied warranties 728
infomercial 727
investigative consumer reporting 734
lemon laws 728
misbranding 709

open-end credit 731
puffing 725
pyramid selling 729
referral sale 729
Regulation Z 732
right of rescission 732
usury statute 739

QUESTIONS AND CASE PROBLEMS

1. On March 19, 1997, Gulender Ozkaya wrote a check for $1,041.55 to pay an automobile dealership for repairs to her car. When she realized that her car had not been properly repaired, Ozkaya stopped payment on the check. The canceled check was then purchased by Telecheck Services, Inc., which sent Ozkaya a form dunning letter attempting to collect payment. In the letter, Telecheck said, "Until this is resolved, we may not approve your checks or the opening of a checking account at over 90,000 merchants and banks who use Telecheck nationally." It also warned, "We have assigned your file to our Recovery Department where it will be given to a professional collection agent. Please be aware that we may take reasonable steps to contact you and secure payment of the balance in full." To resolve the issue and update her record quickly, Ozkaya was instructed to send a cashier's check or money order for the amount due in a return enve-

lope that was provided. Telecheck added a $25 service charge, listed as a "fee" at the top of the letter, to the amount of the original check. Finally, it cautioned that "[a]ny delay, or attempt to avoid this debt, may affect your ability to use checks."

At the bottom of the page, the reader was referred to the back "for important legal notice and corporate address." The reverse side of the letter contained a standard debt validation notice, which indicated that if the consumer disputed the debt, she should contact Telecheck in writing within thirty days.

Ozkaya filed suit against Telecheck. What claims under the Fair Debt Collection Practices Act could she make against the company, and what are Telecheck's strongest defenses? [*Ozkaya v. Telecheck Services., Inc.,* 982 F. Supp. 578 (N.D. Ill. 1997)]

2. Americans consume an estimated 80 billion aspirin tablets a year, and more than fifty over-the-counter drugs contain aspirin as the principal active ingredi-

ent. Yet aspirin labeling intended for the general public does not discuss its use in arthritis or cardiovascular disease because treatment of these conditions—even with a common over-the-counter drug—has to be medically supervised. The consumer labeling contains only a general warning about excessive or inappropriate use of aspirin and specifically warns against using aspirin to treat children and teenagers who have chicken pox or the flu because of the risk of Reye's syndrome, a rare but sometimes fatal condition. In 1993, the FDA proposed a new label for aspirin products that would read, "IMPORTANT: See your doctor before taking this product for your heart or for other new uses of aspirin because serious side effects could occur with self treatment." As new uses for old drugs are discovered, how should the FDA respond to protect consumers from possible injury?

3. In 1989, John M. Stevenson began receiving phone calls from bill collectors regarding overdue accounts that were not his. After Stevenson obtained a copy of his credit report from TRW, Inc., a credit-reporting agency, he discovered many errors in the report. The report included information on accounts that belonged to another John Stevenson; it also included accounts belonging to his estranged son, John Stevenson, Jr., who had fraudulently obtained some of the disputed accounts by using the senior Stevenson's Social Security number. In all, Stevenson disputed sixteen accounts, seven inquiries, and much of the identifying information.

   TRW investigated the complaint; on February 9, 1990, it told Stevenson that all disputed accounts containing negative credit information had been removed. Inaccurate information, however, either continued to appear on Stevenson's reports or was reentered after TRW had deleted it. Stevenson then filed suit, alleging both common law libel and violations of the Fair Credit Reporting Act. Did TRW violate the Fair Credit Reporting Act in its handling of Stevenson's dispute? [*Stevenson v. TRW, Inc.,* 987 F.2d 288 (5th Cir. 1993)]

4. Rehavem and Eleanor Adiel entered into a contract with Lakeridge Associated, Ltd. to purchase a townhouse to be built by Lakeridge. Thereafter, Lakeridge executed and delivered a mortgage application to Chase Federal Savings & Loan Association. The loan was approved, and Lakeridge executed a promissory note payable to Chase. The funds were used by Lakeridge to construct the townhouse. Under the terms of the Adiels' purchase agreement, the Adiels were required to submit a mortgage loan application to Chase for the same amount as the Lakeridge loan. The Adiels' application to Chase was for a residential consumer loan. Once approved, the Adiels were to assume the Lakeridge loan.

   Chase did not provide a truth-in-lending statement in connection with the original loan to Lakeridge or when the Adiels assumed the Lakeridge mortgage. Was the original loan a commercial loan or a consumer loan? Does the Truth-in-Lending Act apply to both? Can an argument successfully be made that if Chase was aware of the prearrangement it should have provided truth-in-lending documents with the original loan? [*Adiel v. Chase Federal Savings & Loan Ass'n,* 810 F.2d 1051 (11th Cir. 1987)]

5. You lose your purse or wallet, which contains all of your credit cards, checkbook, automatic teller machine (ATM) card, Visa debit card, and numerous personal items. You later learn that someone found it and charged several thousand dollars on your credit cards before you had the opportunity to notify your credit card companies. He or she also forged a $500 check. This person used the Visa debit card to purchase a $10,000 home theater system, resulting in a $10,000 deduction from your checking account. In addition, he or she found your personal identification number (PIN) and was able to withdraw $400 from your checking account at an ATM. What are your liabilities to the credit card companies and your bank under the Truth-in-Lending Act and the Electronic Fund Transfer Act? Can you force your bank to return the $10,400 deducted from your checking account? Assume the finder uses your Social Security number to obtain new credit accounts in your name and then never pays the bills. What are your remedies under the Fair Credit Reporting Act?

6. In 1974, a flood caused by storm-driven waves from the Bering Sea swept through the city of Nome, Alaska. The floodwaters caused extensive damage to the commercial district of Nome, including the Bering Sea Saloon. The floodwaters burst through the back door of the saloon, resulting in merchandise being thrown to the ground and being exposed to various amounts of seawater and possibly to raw sewage. As a result, the FDA ordered the destruction of 1,638 cases of alcoholic beverages. On what basis can the FDA seize contaminated food or beverages? What criteria does it employ? Might it be possible for the Bering Sea Saloon to recondition the seized articles? [*United States v. 1,638 Cases of Adulterated Alcoholic Beverages and Other Articles of Food,* 624 F.2d 900 (9th Cir. 1980)]

7. From 1934 to 1939, Charles of the Ritz Distributors sold more than $1 million worth of its "Rejuvenescence Cream." Advertisements for the cosmetic product typically referred to "a vital organic ingredient" and certain "essences and compounds" that the cream allegedly contained. Users were promised that the cream would restore their youthful appearance, regardless of the condition of their skin. How might the FTC analyze the representations made by Charles of the Ritz? What evidence might the FTC consider to determine whether the advertisements are deceptive? Is it important that consumers actually believe that the product will make them look younger? How might the product's name affect the FTC's analysis? [*Charles of the Ritz Distributors Corp. v. FTC,* 143 F.2d 676 (2d Cir. 1944)]

8. In a 1991 attempt to persuade soft drink bottlers to switch from 7UP to Sprite, Coca-Cola Company, the distributor of Sprite, developed a promotional campaign entitled "The Future Belongs to Sprite." In its presentation, Coca-Cola used charts and graphs to compare the two drinks' relative sales and market share during the previous decade. The campaign was especially targeted at seventy-four "cross-franchise" bottlers that distributed 7UP along with Coca-Cola products other than Sprite. After Coca-Cola made the presentation to eleven of these cross-franchise bottlers, five decided to switch from 7UP to Sprite. In response, Seven-Up Company filed suit against Coca-Cola, alleging that the presentation violated the Lanham Act's prohibition on misrepresentations "in commercial advertising or promotion." Coca-Cola argued that its presentation was not sufficiently disseminated to the public to constitute advertising under the statute. Was Coca-Cola's presentation "advertising" and therefore subject to the Lanham Act? [*Seven-Up Co. v. Coca-Cola Co.,* 86 F.3d 1379 (5th Cir. 1996)]

9. Mr. Begala obtained a sixty-month car loan from PNC Bank, which provided the disclosures required under the Truth-in-Lending Act. During the life of the loan, on nine occasions, the bank set him a letter offering him a payment holiday. During this holiday, he could pay a small fee, skip his monthly payment, and add that month onto the rest of the loan. The letters did not state that additional finance charges would be added to the loan as a result of his deferral of monthly payments. Mr. Begala agreed to all of these payment holidays. When he made his final payment on the loan, PNC told him that he owed an additional $1,000 due to his deferrals of the monthly payments. He filed a class action, alleging that the bank had violated its duty under the Truth-in-Lending Act to disclose the additional finance charges assessed on his loan due to the payment holidays. How should the court rule? [*Begala v. PNC Bank,* 163 F.3d 948 (6th Cir. 1998), *cert. denied,* 528 U.S. 868 (1999)]

THE MANAGER'S DILEMMA

10. Your company manufactures recreational all-terrain vehicles (ATVs). The Consumer Product Safety Commission (CPSC) has expressed concern that ATVs may be unnecessarily dangerous. As a result, the CPSC is contemplating regulations regarding their sale and use. How might your company respond to the CPSC? In what way might your company work with other ATV manufacturers to avert governmental involvement? What powers does the CPSC have over your business? [*Consumer Federation of America v. CPSC,* 990 F.2d 1298 (D.C. Cir. 1993)]

INTERNET SOURCES

Federal Trade Commission	http://www.ftc.gov
Food and Drug Administration	http://www.fda.gov
Federal Communications Commission	http://www.fcc.gov
U.S. Postal Service	http://www.usps.gov
Securities and Exchange Commission	http://www.sec.gov
National Highway Traffic Safety Administration	http://www.nhtsa.dot.gov
Consumer Product Safety Commission	http://www.cpsc.gov
This site, maintained by the FTC's Bureau of Consumer Protection, provides consumer news on product recalls, tips for avoiding scams, smart shopping suggestions, and contacts for lodging consumer complaints, as well as links to other Web sites containing consumer information.	http://www.consumer.gov
The *Georgia Institute of Technology Survey* on Internet privacy is available at this site.	http://www.epic.org/privacy/survey
Position of the American Dietetic Association on Food Irradiation is available at this site.	http://www.eatright.org/airradi.htm
The Privacy Information page on the FTC's Web site contains information on how to protect personal information from public access, including sample "opt-out" letters for consumers to send to credit bureaus and the Direct Marketing Association requesting that their personal information not be sold, shared with third parties, or used for marketing purposes.	http://www.ftc.gov/privacy
This site, maintained by the Association of Trial Lawyers of America, provides information and links relating to product safety, including recalls.	http://www.atla.org/famsafe/index.ht
The Privacy Forum site provides an online compendium of privacy-related topics.	http://www.vortex.com/privacy

Ownership *and* Control

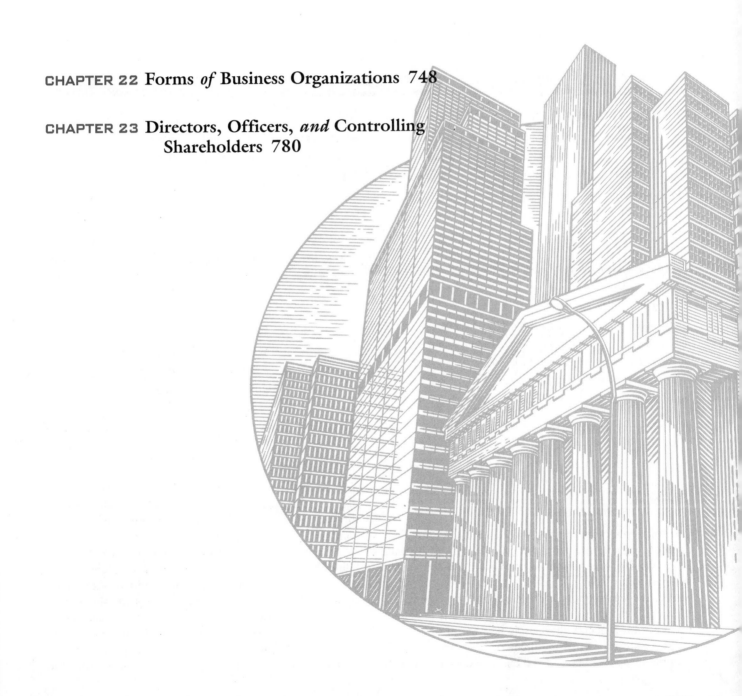

CHAPTER 22

Forms *of* Business Organizations

CHOOSING THE PROPER FORM

One of the first questions facing any entrepreneur wishing to start a business is which form of business organization will best suit the enterprise. In weighing the advantages and disadvantages associated with the various forms, four considerations take on primary importance. First, to what extent will the personal assets of the founders and investors be exposed to the liabilities of the business? Second, how can taxes be minimized? Third, which format will make the business most attractive to potential investors, lenders, and employees? Finally, what costs are associated with creating and maintaining the organization?

Entrepreneurs selecting a form of entity enjoy a broad range of options. This decision comes in the earliest stages in the life of a business, but it is nonetheless a crucial one. Changing the form of organization can be very costly—not only will administrative and legal fees be incurred, but a change may also give rise to tax lia-

bility or cause a business opportunity to be lost. Thus, at the outset of their venture, entrepreneurs should carefully consider its expected evolution and choose the form of organization accordingly. In addition, once the form of entity is chosen, its managers must be diligent in complying with all statutory requirements.

CHAPTER OVERVIEW

This chapter begins with a description of the most frequently used forms of business organizations: sole proprietorships, partnerships (both general and limited), corporations (including S corporations), limited liability companies, and limited liability partnerships. It examines their advantages and disadvantages. Next, the chapter summarizes the basic tax treatment of these different entities. The remainder of the chapter offers a more detailed discussion of how partnerships and corporations are structured and operated.

Sole Proprietorship

The sole proprietorship is the simplest and most prevalent form of business enterprise in the United States. In a *sole proprietorship,* one person owns all of the assets of the business and is solely liable for all of its debts. In other words, the sole proprietor is the business; therefore, any individual who does business without creating a separate organization is operating as a sole proprietorship.

There are no formal requirements for forming a sole proprietorship. However, if the business operates under a

fictitious business name—that is, a name other than the name of the owner—that name must be registered with the state. A sole proprietorship ends upon either the discontinuation of the business or the death of the proprietor.

Advantages of a sole proprietorship include the flexibility afforded by having one person in complete control of the business. Also, because a sole proprietorship can be created without formal agreements or state filings, it is the easiest and least costly form of business organization to set up. Sole proprietorships pay only one level of income tax—the proprietor reports income from the business on his or her personal tax returns. Finally, the proprietor receives all of the profits generated by the business.

If the business loses money, however, the proprietor alone bears liability for the losses. This element of risk is the major disadvantage of the sole proprietorship. In addition, it is more difficult for sole proprietorships to raise capital. A sole proprietor can tap only personal funds and the funds of those willing to lend money.

General Partnership

A *general partnership* is created when two or more persons agree to place their money, efforts, labor, or skills in a business and to share the profits and losses. Their agreement can be express or implied, but they must share in real profits, not just receive wages or compensation. Indeed, the association of two or more persons to carry on as co-owners a business for profit forms a partnership, whether or not the persons intend to form a partnership.[1] In some respects, a partnership is like a marriage or a family. Its members share both the benefits and the burdens of the relationship. Absent an express agreement to the contrary, each partner has some control over the business, and each may have the authority to bind the partnership with respect to third parties. Thus, a partnership is, in many respects, a mutual agency relationship. (See Chapter 5 for a discussion of agency principles.) Property acquired by a partnership, by transfer or otherwise, becomes property of the partnership and belongs to the partnership as an entity, rather than to the individual partners.

One of the key advantages of a partnership is that it allows for a wide variety of operational and profit-sharing arrangements. In essence, partners may agree to any terms in forming a partnership as long as they are not illegal or contrary to public policy. As an example of this flexibility, partners may make contributions to the business in the form of either capital or services. Suppose Pro and Ron decide to form a partnership, called Rad Waves, to manufacture windsurfing equipment. Ron contributes the start-up and operating capital, and Pro contributes only his management services. Even though Pro has not contributed capital to the partnership, he is an equal partner with Ron in Rad Waves (unless the partners agree otherwise).

Like a sole proprietorship, a partnership has the advantage of being subject to only one level of tax. Though

1. *See* Sections 101(6) and 202(a) of the Uniform Partnership Act (1997).

an informational return must be filed with the Internal Revenue Service (IRS), a partnership does not pay income taxes as a separate entity. Instead, the profit earned by the partnership (whether distributed or not) "passes through" to the individual partners, who report it as income on their individual returns. Thus, a partnership is a *pass-through entity.*

General partnerships face a disadvantage similar to sole proprietorships in that individual partners are subject to joint and several personal liability for all obligations of the partnership. Thus, if the partnership is unable to pay its debts, creditors of the partnership have claims against the assets of individual partners. Because partners have joint and several liability, one partner could be required to pay all of the partnership's obligations if the other partners fail to pay their share.

JOINT VENTURE

A *joint venture* is a onetime partnership of two or more persons for a specific purpose, such as the construction of a hydroelectric dam or a cogeneration plant. Like a general partnership, a joint venture requires that the parties (1) share a community of interest; (2) have the mutual right to direct and govern; (3) share the partnership's profits and losses; and (4) combine their property, money, efforts, skill, or knowledge in the undertaking. Unlike a general partnership, a joint venture is not a continuing relationship; it terminates when the project is completed.

In a joint venture, there is no mutual agency relationship, unless the partners specifically provide for it. Thus, the authority of one member to bind the others is more limited than in a general partnership. To avoid inadvertently conferring apparent authority to bind the other members, a joint venture should make clear in its dealings with third parties that it is a joint venture and not a partnership. This distinction should be reflected in the entity's name and in the recitation of its legal status in its contracts.

UNIFORM PARTNERSHIP ACT OF 1997

The preceding discussion of general partnerships is based on the Uniform Partnership Act of 1997 (UPA), which has been adopted by more than thirty states. The remaining states (except Louisiana) have adopted the predecessor statute, the Uniform Partnership Act of 1994. Exhibit 22.1 outlines several significant changes the 1997 UPA makes to the 1994 version.

EXHIBIT 22.1

Significant Changes the 1997 Uniform Partnership Act Makes to the Provisions in the 1994 Version

- Generally, the 1997 Uniform Partnership Act shifts emphasis from protecting partners against the unauthorized acts of their fellow partners toward protecting the rights of third parties that deal with the partnership in good faith.
- A partnership is treated as an entity distinct from its partners.
- A partner is not a co-owner of partnership property; the concept of "tenancy in partnership" is eliminated.
- Property that is not acquired in the name of the partnership is nonetheless partnership property if the instrument transferring title refers to either (1) the person taking title as a partner or (2) the existence of the partnership.
- The 1997 UPA codifies specific fiduciary duties owed by a partner to the partnership and the other partners.
- A partnership is not automatically dissolved upon a partner's bankruptcy, death, or withdrawal; instead, the partners holding a majority of the partnership interests may elect to continue the general partnership within ninety days after the occurrence of such events.

Source: This information is drawn from Jack S. Johal et al., *Practicing Under California's Revised Uniform Partnership Act,* Bus. L. News, Winter 1997, at 3.

Limited Partnership

The basic form of partnership described above is called a general partnership. A *limited partnership* is a special type of partnership consisting of general partners and limited partners. General partners of a limited partnership remain jointly and severally liable for partnership obligations (just like partners in a general partnership), and they are responsible for the management of the partnership. *Limited partners,* however, assume no liability for partnership debts beyond the amount of capital they have contributed, and they have no right to participate in the management of the partnership.

Limited partnerships are often used to raise capital—the limited liability for limited partners makes them attractive to investors. Returning to the Rad Waves example, suppose that the general partners desire to raise capital to finance a sportswear line to promote their other products. To do so, they restructure their partnership as a limited partnership with Ron and Pro remaining as general partners. They can now offer an investor a limited partnership interest in the business, renamed Rad Waves, L.P. If Olivia contributes

$1,000 to the partnership, she becomes a limited partner in Rad Waves (assuming compliance with the relevant state statute), and her personal liability for Rad Waves' obligations is limited to her $1,000 original investment.

This ability to attract investors with the assurance of limited liability is the main advantage of a limited partnership. A limited partnership is more difficult to create than a general partnership, however. Unlike a general partnership, a limited partnership does not come into existence until a certificate of limited partnership has been filed with the appropriate state agency. Moreover, courts are generally strict about enforcing the formal requirements of limited partnership status. If a partnership runs afoul of those requirements, courts will treat it as a general partnership instead.

Corporations

A *corporation* is an organization authorized by state law to act as a legal entity distinct from its owners. As a separate legal entity, the corporation has its own name and operates with limited powers to achieve specific purposes. Corporations are owned by shareholders, who have purchased an ownership stake in the business. The board of directors, which is elected by the shareholders, has central decision-making authority. The board of directors typically employs officers to manage the day-to-day operations of the business.

One of the most attractive features of a corporation is that the liability of its shareholders is limited to their investments. Only the corporation itself is responsible for its liabilities. (An important exception to this general rule, the piercing the corporate veil theory, is discussed later in this chapter.) This cap on liability permits entrepreneurs and investors to undertake risky ventures without the worry of losing personal assets if things go badly.

Another benefit of a corporation is that it has the ability to raise significant capital by selling ownership shares of corporate stock (also known as equity) to investors. Finally, corporations have the advantage of perpetual life. Thus, if a key investor dies or decides to sell his or her interest in the business, the corporation as an entity continues to exist and to conduct business.

The main disadvantage of the corporate form of organization is that it is subject to two levels of taxation: both corporate and shareholder. The corporation pays tax on the income generated by the business, and shareholders pay tax on that same income when it is distributed as dividends.

S CORPORATIONS

Some small corporations can avoid this double taxation by electing to be treated as S corporations under Subchapter S of the Internal Revenue Code. An *S corporation* is taxed as a pass-through entity. In other words, the corporation itself is not taxed on its income; rather, shareholders pay tax on their pro rata share of the corporation's income. An election to be taxed under Subchapter S does not affect the status of the organization as a corporation for state corporate law purposes. Any corporation that has not elected to be an S corporation is called a *C corporation* because it is governed by the tax rules in Subchapter C of the Internal Revenue Code.

To qualify for S corporation status, a corporation must satisfy the following requirements:

1. The corporation must have no more than seventy-five shareholders, all of whom must be individuals who are citizens of the United States or U.S. resident aliens, or certain types of tax-exempt organizations, trusts, or estates.
2. The corporation must have only one class of stock.
3. The corporation generally may not own 80 percent or more of any other corporation.
4. The corporation must file a timely election to be treated as an S corporation.

CLOSE CORPORATIONS

Some states have enacted laws that give close corporations extra operating flexibility. A *close corporation* is one whose shares are held by a small number of persons, often members of a family. The statutory limit on the number of shareholders a close corporation may have is typically thirty. A corporation must elect close corporation status by stating in its certificate of incorporation that it is a close corporation; otherwise, the corporation will not be treated as a close corporation regardless of the number of shareholders. State close corporation laws can permit significant departures from formalities imposed on traditional corporations, such as the requirements that the corporation conduct annual shareholder and board meetings, adopt bylaws, and maintain formal records of board and shareholder decisions.

 Limited Liability Companies

The limited liability company is a relatively new form of business organization that is rapidly gaining popularity in the United States. A *limited liability company (LLC)* combines the tax advantages of a pass-through entity with the limited liability advantages of a corporation. Like corporations and limited partnerships, the LLC is a creature of state law. To form an LLC, a charter document must be filed with the appropriate state agency (usually the office of the secretary of state). This LLC charter document is typically called the *articles of organization* (as in California) or the *certificate of formation* (as in Delaware). The name of the business must include the initials L.L.C. or the words Limited Liability Company.

The rights, obligations, and powers of the owners of the company (the *members*), the managers, and the officers are set forth in an *operating agreement*. The members elect the *managers* who, like a board of directors, are responsible for managing the business, property, and affairs of the company. The managers appoint the officers of the company.

In 1997, the IRS issued regulations that clarified the status of LLCs as entities that are not taxed at the firm level (unless they elect to be taxed as corporations). In effect, these new "check the box" regulations permit the founders to decide whether an entity—other than a corporation under state law or a publicly held entity—is to be taxed as a corporation or a pass-through entity. State-law corporations and publicly traded entities are taxed as corporations.

The LLC form of business organization offers the advantages of both the limited partnership and the S corporation without their respective drawbacks. Properly formed LLCs are taxed as partnerships, but unlike the general partners in limited partnerships, even the controlling persons in LLCs can limit their liability to the amount invested. Moreover, all owners of an LLC can participate fully in the management of the business. An LLC (like a partnership) can also have flexible allocations of profits and losses. The main advantage of the LLC form over the S corporation is the lack of restrictions on shareholders and the ability to have more than one class of securities. Specifically, there is no limit on the number of members an LLC can have; and, in contrast with an S corporation, its investors can be corporations, partnerships, and foreigners.

One disadvantage of the LLC form of business organization is the cost of preparing a customized operating agreement. As LLCs have become more common, however, standardized forms have started to emerge.[2] They provide a good starting point for drafting but must be tailored to the individual company and the needs of its members.

---

2. *See, e.g.,* Guide to Organizing and Operating a Limited Liability Company in California (Allan B. Duboff ed., Partnerships and Unincorporated Business Organizations Committee of the Business Law Section of the State Bar of California, 1995). This guide includes annotated sample short-form and long-form operating agreements and other useful exemplars.

Limited Liability Partnerships

The *limited liability partnership (LLP)* is an even more recently developed form of business organization. The LLP has features similar to those of the LLC and is designed primarily for professionals who typically do business as a partnership. The main function of an LLP is to insulate its partners from *vicarious liability* for certain partnership obligations, such as liability arising from the malpractice, that is, negligent or wrongful conduct, of another partner. Partners in an LLP usually have unlimited liability for their own malpractice.

LLPs are created by filing appropriate forms with a central state agency. A major advantage of the LLP form for existing partnerships, such as law firms or accounting firms, is that attaining LLP status requires no significant modification of the business's partnership agreement. Difficulties relating to negotiating and drafting the agreements required to convert an existing partnership to a limited liability entity such as a corporation or LLC were often cited as major obstacles to such a conversion.[3] In addition, like other forms of partnerships, LLPs retain pass-through taxation treatment.

LLP statutes are not uniform. Most statutes provide limited liability at least for debts and obligations arising from the malpractice of other partners. However, a few states, such as Minnesota and New York, protect partners from commercial liabilities (such as trade debt) as well.[4] This type of expanded protection further narrows the distinction between an LLP and an LLC. In fact, the trend in LLP statutes enacted after 1995 has been to provide the broader type of liability protection exemplified by Minnesota and New York.[5]

Income Tax Considerations

The analysis that follows is concerned solely with federal income tax consequences under the Internal Revenue Code of 1986, as amended and in force as of January 1, 2001. Many state income tax provisions follow the federal rules. Because provisions in the tax laws change often, it is more important to understand the general issues than to strive for a detailed knowledge of the tax laws for any given year.

---

3. *See* Elizabeth G. Hester, *Keeping Liability at Bay,* Bus. L. Today, Jan.–Feb. 1996, at 59.
4. *See id.* at 60.
5. *Id.*

COMPARING SEPARATE TAXABLE ENTITIES WITH PASS-THROUGH ENTITIES

The tax treatment of a C corporation differs from that of pass-through entities (such as partnerships, S corporations, and LLCs) in several respects. Each may have favorable or unfavorable tax consequences depending on the circumstances.

Property Transfers Because a C corporation is a separate taxable entity, a transfer of cash or any other kind of property between the corporation and its owners is a taxable transaction unless it comes within one of the statutory exceptions in Subchapter C. It is easier to transfer property to and from a partnership or an LLC on a tax-free basis than it is with either a C corporation or an S corporation. For example, a transfer of property to either type of corporation in exchange for stock is tax-free only if the persons transferring the property own, immediately after the transaction, 80 percent or more of the stock of the corporation to which the property is transferred. In contrast, an exchange of property for an interest in a partnership is tax-free regardless of the percentage interest in the partnership.

Similarly, property that has appreciated in value may be more easily distributed tax-free from a partnership or an LLC than from a corporation. Neither the partnership nor the LLC is subject to tax on the appreciated property, and the partner receiving the property is not taxed until he or she subsequently sells the property. This can be particularly important for venture capital funds that often make distributions of illiquid stock in the portfolio companies in which the fund has invested. If the fund is organized as a partnership or an LLC, these securities can be distributed to the partners or members tax-free, with no tax due until the partner or member sells the securities. In contrast, a corporation will be taxed on the appreciation in value just as if it had sold the property for cash, and the shareholders will be taxed on the fair market value of the property they have received. Thus, in the case of a C corporation, there will be both a corporate-level tax and a shareholder-level tax on the distribution. For an S corporation, the taxable income is passed through and will be taxed only at the shareholder level.

Cash Distribution The income of a C corporation is taxed at the corporate level, and it is taxed again at the individual level when it is distributed. This double taxation does not occur with the other forms of business organizations. This difference alone may make a pass-through entity preferable to a C corporation as the chosen form of business organization.

Double taxation can be reduced in two ways. First, the tax liability of the corporation can be reduced to the extent that corporate income can be offset by tax-deductible payments to shareholders. For example, if personal services are a major source of the corporation's income, payment of employee compensation to shareholders active in the business will reduce the corporation's taxable income. If capital investment is a major source of income, payment of interest or rent to shareholders may provide similar relief. Second, the tax liability of the shareholders can be reduced to the extent that the business income is retained by the corporation and not distributed to shareholders. However, the accumulated earnings of a corporation may be taxed if they are not being retained for a legitimate business purpose of the corporation.

Cash distributions from partnerships and S corporations are tax-free to the recipients, up to the amount of their previous capital contributions less any income previously passed through to them. Distributions from C corporations, on the other hand, generally result in taxable dividend income to the shareholders.

Operating Losses If the business operations of a C corporation produce a loss, as is frequently the case with start-up companies and real estate investments in their early years, the operating loss is recognized at the corporate level. This means that the shareholders receive no tax benefits from the operating loss, and the corporation receives no benefit until it has operating income against which its prior losses can be deducted.

On the other hand, if the same business is operated by a partnership, LLC, or S corporation, the operating loss each year is passed through to the individual partners or shareholders. They may, if certain tax law requirements are satisfied, deduct the operating loss from their other income. Passive-loss limitations allow only owners who materially participate in the business to deduct its losses from other ordinary income (such as wages or interest), however. Passive investors may not deduct such losses from ordinary income, but they can use passive losses to offset passive gains (such as capital gains on the sale of stock).

Capitalization The tax law imposes no restrictions on a C corporation's capitalization. As business needs require, the corporation may issue common stock, preferred stock, bonds, notes, warrants, options, and other instruments. These instruments may confer the right to varying degrees of control and varying shares of earnings and may be convertible, redeemable, or callable. The tax treatment of each type of capital instrument is not always the same as its classification by the corporation, however. For example, shareholder debt may be treated as stock if the corporation has too little *equity capital,* that is, capital received in exchange for shares in the ownership of the corporation. As a consequence, tax-deductible "interest" payments may be recast as nondeductible "dividends."

Allocation of Losses Items of partnership (or LLC) income or loss generally can be allocated to specific partners (or members) at specific times as long as these allocations have a substantial economic effect apart from tax considerations. Thus, an LLC can allocate a disproportionate amount of losses or depreciation to a particular member in the early years and allocate a disproportionate amount of later income to the same member until the loss is recovered. This form of allocation may generate a valuable tax deferral for that member.

No comparable allocation can be made by a C corporation, except to a limited extent by capitalizing the corporation with different classes of stock and debt. An S corporation is even more limited in this respect. It may have only one class of stock, and all income and losses must be allocated strictly in proportion to stock ownership.

Ability to Raise Venture Capital Although pass-through entities (such as partnerships, LLCs, and S corporations) offer many tax advantages, they are rarely used for a business that intends to raise money from venture capitalists. Instead, the C corporation is usually used for two reasons. First, most venture capital firms raise money from large institutional investors, such as pension funds, university endowments, and the like. Nonprofit entities such as these can invest in securities and receive their income and capital gains tax-free only if the issuer of the securities is not a pass-through entity. Otherwise, the nonprofits will be deemed to have received unrelated business income, which is fully taxable. Second, most start-ups want the ability to sell securities to outside investors at a significantly higher price than was paid by the founders at the outset. To justify the price differential, and avoid having some of the value of the founders' shares treated as employee compensation, companies issue two classes of stock: common stock to the founders and preferred stock to the outside investors. Because an S corporation cannot have more than one class of stock, the C corporation is usually the easiest vehicle to use.

IN BRIEF

Choice of Business Entity: Pros and Cons

The following chart lists the principal considerations in selecting the form of business entity and applies them to the C corporation, S corporation, general partnership, limited partnership, limited liability company, and limited liability partnership. The considerations are listed in no particular order, in part because their importance will vary depending on the nature of the business, its sources of financing, and the plan for providing financial returns to the owners (for example, distributions of operating income, a public offering, or a sale of the business). Other factors that are not listed will also influence the choice of entity. In addition, the "yes or no" format oversimplifies the applicability of certain attributes.

	C Corporation	S Corporation	General Partnership	Limited Partnershp	Limited Liability Company	Limited Liability Partnership
Limited liability	Yes	Yes	No	Yes[a]	Yes	Yes[b]
Flow-through taxation	No	Yes	Yes	Yes	Yes	Yes
Simplicity/low cost	Yes	Yes	No	No	No	No
Limitations on eligibility	No	Yes	No	No	No	No
Limitations on capital structure	No	Yes	No	No	No	No
Ability to raise venture capital	Yes	No	No	No	No	No
Ability to take public	Yes	Yes[c]	No[d]	No[d]	No[d]	No[d]
Flexible charter documents	No	No	Yes	Yes	Yes	Yes
Ability to change structure without tax	No	No	Yes	Yes	Yes	Yes
Favorable employee incentives (including incentive stock options)	Yes	Yes/No[e]	No[f]	No[f]	No[f]	No[f]
Qualified small business stock exclusion for gains	Yes[g]	No	No	No	No	No
Special allocations	No	No	Yes	Yes	Yes	Yes
Tax-free in-kind distributions	No	No	Yes	Yes	Yes	Yes

[a] Limited liability for limited partners only; a limited partnership must have at least one general partner with unlimited liability.

[b] Partners in LLPs generally are protected from liability for malpractice and other wrongful conduct of fellow partners; states are split on whether LLP partners can be held individually liable for other partnership liabilities, such as commercial debt.

[c] An S corporation would convert to a C corporation upon a public offering because of the number of shareholders.

[d] Although the public markets are generally not available for partnership offerings, partnerships (including LLPs) and LLCs can be incorporated without tax and then taken public.

[e] Although an S corporation can issue incentive stock options (ISOs), the inability to have two classes of stock limits favorable pricing of the common stock offered to employees.

[f] Although partnership and LLC interests can be provided to employees, they are poorly understood by most employees. Moreover, ISOs are not available.

[g] A special low capital gains rate is available for stock of U.S. C corporations with not more than $50 million in gross assets at the time the stock is issued if the corporation is engaged in an active business and the taxpayer holds the stock for at least five years.

Agency Law *and* Limited Liability

It is critical for individuals acting on behalf of any business entity to make it clear whether they are acting on their own or as agents of a separate legal entity. The following case demonstrates how failure to do this can result in personal liability for the manager involved.

A CASE IN POINT

CASE 22.1

Water, Waste & Land, Inc. v. Lanham

Supreme Court of Colorado
955 P.2d 997
(Colo. 1998) (en banc).

In the Language of the Court

FACTS Water, Waste & Land, Inc. was a land development and engineering company doing business under the name "Westec." Donald Lanham and Larry Clark were managers and also members of Preferred Income Investors, L.L.C. (P.I.I.), a limited liability company organized under the Colorado Limited Liability Company Act.

In March 1995, Clark contacted Westec about the possibility of hiring Westec to perform engineering work in connection with the construction of a fast-food restaurant known as Taco Cabana. In the course of preliminary discussions, Clark gave his business card to representatives of Westec. The business card included Lanham's address, which was also the address listed as P.I.I.'s principal office and place of business in its articles of organization filed with the secretary of state. Although the name Preferred Income Investors, L.L.C. was not on the business card, the letters "P.I.I." appeared above the address on the card. There was, however, no indication as to what the acronym meant or that P.I.I. was a limited liability company.

Although Westec never received a signed contract from Lanham, in mid-August it did receive verbal authorization from Clark to begin work. Westec completed the engineering work and sent a bill for $9,183.40 to Lanham. When no payments were made on the bill, Westec filed a claim in county court against Clark and Lanham individually as well as against P.I.I.

The county court found in favor of Westec. The district court reversed and held that Lanham was not personally liable. The court reasoned that Westec was put on notice that it was dealing with a limited liability company because the business card contained the letters "P.I.I." and Section 7-80-208 of the LLC Act provides that the filing of the articles of organization serves as constructive notice of a company's status as an LLC.

ISSUE PRESENTED May a member of a limited liability company claim protection for amounts owing for services rendered if the existence of the LLC was not disclosed at the time the services were requested or performed?

OPINION SCOTT, J., writing on behalf of the Colorado Supreme Court:

Under the common law of agency, an agent is liable on a contract entered on behalf of a principal if the principal is not fully disclosed. In other words, an agent who negotiates a contract with a third party can be sued for any breach of the contract unless the agent discloses both the fact that he or she is acting on behalf of a principal and the identity of the principal.

...

In light of the partially disclosed principal doctrine, the county court's determination that Clark and Lanham failed to disclose the existence as well as the identity of the limited liability company they represented is dispositive under the common law of agency. Still, if the General Assembly has altered the common law rules applicable to this case by adopting the LLC Act, then these rules must yield in favor of

(Continued)

(Case 22.1 continued)

the statute. We conclude, however, that the LLC Act's notice provision was not intended to alter the partially disclosed principal doctrine.

...

... [S]ection 7-80-208 places third parties on constructive notice that a fully identified company—that is, identified by a name such as "Preferred Income Investors, LLC," or the like—is a limited liability company provided that its articles of organization have been filed with the secretary of state. Section 7-80-208 is of little force, however, in determining whether a limited liability company's agent is personally liable on the theory that the agent has failed to disclose the identity of the company.

RESULT Clark and Lanham were personally liable for the monies owed by P.I.I.

QUESTIONS

1. Would the court have reached the same result if Lanham's business card had indicated "Preferred Income Investors, L.L.C." instead of just "P.I.I."?
2. Does the undisclosed principal theory require a showing that the individual was engaged in wrongful conduct before personal liability will be imposed?

Partnership Mechanics

This section describes in more detail how partnerships are formed, operated, and terminated.

FORMATION OF A GENERAL PARTNERSHIP

A general partnership can be created with nothing more than a handshake and a general understanding between the partners. For example, students agree to work together on a business plan; a baker and a chef agree to open a restaurant together; an engineer and a mechanic agree to design bicycles together—in each case, a partnership is formed. The intention of one party alone, however, cannot create a partnership. There must be a meeting of the minds to carry on a business as co-owners. Hence, in the Rad Waves example, if Ron viewed his agreement with Pro as forming a partnership, while Pro contemplated a mere employee–employer relationship, a partnership would not be formed.

A partnership does not require a minimum of capital in order to be formed. Partners usually contribute cash or property, or agree to provide personal services to the partnership. In some instances, a partnership interest may be received as a gift. The partnership need not be given a name. There may or may not be a written partnership agreement.

Without a Written Agreement If there is no written partnership agreement, the laws in the state where the par-

ties are doing business will determine whether the relationship is to be treated as a partnership or some other relationship, such as an agency. If the relationship is recognized as a partnership, state partnership laws will govern the partnership and prescribe the rights of the partners if there is no written agreement. Some provisions of those laws could lead to undesirable business results, so it is almost always best to have a written partnership agreement.

In the Rad Waves example, Pro and Ron could form a partnership with a simple oral agreement. Under state partnership law, however, Pro and Ron will be required to share the profits and losses equally. Furthermore, until the partnership is terminated, neither partner may withdraw capital without the consent of the other.

With a Written Agreement A written partnership agreement can prevent future misunderstandings. It can also provide for a dispute resolution mechanism, such as arbitration. A written partnership agreement can override many of the provisions of partnership statutes that could turn out to be undesirable to the partners.

A partnership agreement usually includes (1) the term of the partnership's existence, (2) the capital characteristics of the partnership, (3) the division of profits and losses between the partners, (4) partnership salaries or withdrawals, (5) the duties of the partners, and (6) the consequences to the partnership if a partner decides to sell his or her interest in the partnership or becomes incapacitated or dies. Also included are the name of the partnership, the names and addresses of the partners, the type of business to be conducted, and the location of the business.

Drafting a partnership agreement focuses the partners' attention on matters that they might not consider with a less formal arrangement.[6] For example, will all partners have an equal voice in management? What limits will be placed on the managing partners? How will disputes be settled? May a partner be expelled? May new partners be admitted? If so, by what process?

OPERATION OF A GENERAL PARTNERSHIP

The operation of a general partnership may be informal. Decisions may be made by consensus rather than by formal votes. Lack of formality should not be equated with lack of responsibility for the fortunes, or misfortunes, of the partnership, however. For example, if Pro and Ron form Rad Waves as a general partnership, they will each be responsible for the full amount of any liabilities incurred by the partnership or by either partner acting within the scope of his authority as a partner. Hence, Ron's personal assets can be seized if Rad Waves' partnership assets are insufficient to satisfy a judgment against Rad Waves. Ron's personal assets might also be seized if Rad Waves breaches a contract entered into by Pro on behalf of the partnership.

Each partner is an agent of the partnership for the purpose of its business unless the partnership has filed

6. *See* Eleena de Lisser, *Partnership Prenuptials,* WALL ST. J., Sept. 25, 1999, at 12.

INTERNATIONAL CONSIDERATION

Before a business decides to incorporate abroad, its management should consult a lawyer in the country under consideration to be advised of the country's laws governing tax, labor, and corporate issues. Parties contemplating a partnership or joint venture should note that civil law jurisdictions usually do not recognize common law–style partnerships. They instead look through the partnership to the partners and view the partners as the legal owners.

with the secretary of state a statement specifying which partners have authority for entering into certain transactions on behalf of the partnership, as specified in Sections 105 and 303 of the Uniform Partnership Act (1997). Each partner in a general partnership is liable for the debts incurred by another partner acting in the name of the partnership if that partner had express authority to assume the debt or was carrying on the business of the partnership in the usual way.

FIDUCIARY DUTY

Partners owe one another certain fiduciary duties, in particular, a duty of loyalty and a duty of care. Partners must also discharge their duties to the partnership and to one another in accordance with the obligation of good faith and fair dealing. The following case explores the scope of such duties under the common law of Texas.

A CASE IN POINT

CASE 22.2

Bohatch v. Butler

Supreme Court of Texas

977 S.W.2d 543

(Tex. 1998).

Summary

FACTS In February 1990, Collette Bohatch was named a partner in the Washington, D.C. office of Butler & Binion, a Houston-based law firm. John McDonald was then the managing partner of the firm's D.C. office, which worked almost exclusively for Pennzoil. Bohatch soon became privy to internal firm reports showing the number of hours each attorney worked, billed, and collected. After reviewing such reports, she became concerned that McDonald was overbilling Pennzoil.

On July 15, 1990, Bohatch met with Louis Paine, Butler & Binion's managing partner, to report her concerns about McDonald's billing practices. Paine told Bohatch he would investigate. The following day, McDonald met with Bohatch and informed her that Pennzoil was not satisfied with her work and wanted her work to be supervised. Bohatch later testified that this was the first time she had ever heard criticism of her work for Pennzoil.

After looking into Bohatch's complaint and discussing the allegations with Pennzoil's in-house counsel, who said that Pennzoil believed the firm's bills were reasonable, Paine informed Bohatch in August that he found no basis for her contentions. Paine also told her she should begin to look for other employment. In June 1991, she was informed that that month's partnership distribution would be her last. She was asked to leave by November.

(Continued)

(Case 22.2 continued)

Bohatch filed suit for breach of fiduciary duty and other claims in October 1991. The firm voted to expel her three days later. At trial, a jury found that the firm had breached its fiduciary duty to Bohatch. The court of appeals reversed, holding that the firm's only duty to Bohatch was not to expel her in bad faith. Bohatch appealed.

ISSUE PRESENTED Can a partnership expel a whistle-blowing partner merely for reporting in good faith the alleged misconduct of another partner?

SUMMARY OF OPINION The Texas Supreme Court first recognized that the relationship between partners "is fiduciary in character, and imposes upon all the participants the obligation of loyalty . . . and the utmost good faith, fairness, and honesty in their dealings with each other." Nevertheless, partners have no obligation to remain partners—"at the heart of the partnership concept is the principle that partners may choose with whom they wish to be associated."

Thus, the question the court addressed was whether, in this case, the fiduciary relationship between and among partners gave rise to a duty not to expel a partner who in good faith reported suspicions of overbilling by another partner. The court concluded that there should be no such whistle-blower exception to the basic at-will nature of partnerships. Although the public policy arguments in favor of the exception were "not without force," courts had consistently held that a partnership may expel a partner for "purely business reasons."

An allegation such as Bohatch's can create a fundamental schism in a partnership, severely damaging the personal confidence and trust essential to the partner relationship. Once such charges are made, partners may find it impossible to continue to work together. In these circumstances, expulsion of the accusing partner may be the only way to preserve the partnership. As a result, the court concluded that the fiduciary duty that partners owe one another "does not encompass a duty to remain partners or else answer in tort damages."

RESULT The Texas Supreme Court affirmed the appellate court decision that Butler & Binion did not breach any fiduciary duty it owed to Bohatch.

COMMENTS Members of a professional corporation also have fiduciary duties to fellow members. The Illinois Supreme Court held that two lawyers who resigned from the law firm of Dowd & Dowd, a professional corporation, violated their fiduciary duties if they surreptitiously solicited the firm's clients before resigning.[7] The New York Court of Appeals characterized the loyalty owed partners as what "distinguishes partnerships (including law partnerships) from bazaars."[8]

7. Dowd & Dowd, Ltd. v. Gleason, 693 N.E.2d 358 (Ill. 1998).
8. Graubard Mollen Dannett & Horowitz v. Moskovitz, 653 N.E.2d 1179, 1183 (N.Y. 1995).

DECISION MAKING IN A GENERAL PARTNERSHIP

Unlike a corporation, which has a centralized board of directors and a staff of hired executives for decision making, a general partnership is characterized by direct owner management and control of the business. Each partner's assets are vulnerable to the poor business decisions of the fellow partners. It is therefore important that each partner have a voice in the business decisions of the partnership.

A partnership may choose to cede managerial control of the business to one or more of its partners. Unless the partners expressly agree otherwise, partnership law requires unanimous agreement of all partners on all but the most ordinary matters. If the partners in an informal partnership cannot agree on a decision, they may disband the partnership, distribute its assets, and terminate it.

DISSOLUTION OF A GENERAL PARTNERSHIP

Dissolution of a general partnership occurs when the partners no longer carry on the business together. A partnership may be dissolved for many reasons. The agreed term for the partnership may expire, or the partners may decide to dissolve the partnership prior to the expiration of the agreed term. A particular undertaking specified in the partnership agreement may be completed. One or more partners may desire to dissolve the partnership. (Unless there is an agreement to the contrary or the remaining partners elect not to dissolve the partnership, withdrawal or death of a general partner results in the dissolution of the partnership.) A partner may be expelled, and the remaining partners may thereafter agree to terminate the partnership. A partner may die or go bankrupt, and the remaining partners may not want to continue the partnership.

A partnership will also be dissolved if the business for which the partnership was formed becomes unlawful—for example, if there is a war between the countries of two or more of the partners. In such a case, the partnership will be dissolved regardless of the wishes of the partners. If a partner becomes disabled, insane, or otherwise unable to perform as a partner, a court may issue a decree of dissolution. Courts also have the power to dissolve a partnership when a partner willfully breaches the agreement or performs in such a manner as to make it impractical to carry on the partnership. Because the purpose of partnerships is to make a profit, a partnership may be dissolved by court decree if it becomes apparent that the entity is unprofitable and lacks any real prospect of success. If the partnership has reasonable prospects of earning money in the future, however, it may not be dissolved by court decree despite recent losses.

WINDING UP THE GENERAL PARTNERSHIP

Upon dissolution, all of the partners' authority ceases except their authority to complete transactions begun but not yet finished and to wind up the partnership. *Winding up* involves settling the accounts and liquidating the assets of the partnership for the purpose of making distributions and terminating the concern. The liabilities and obligations of the partners do not end at dissolution; the partnership continues throughout the winding-up period.

During the winding-up process, the partners' fiduciary duties to one another continue. The winding-up partners may not run the business for their own benefit but must account as trustees to the withdrawing partners or to the estate of a deceased partner.

TERMINATION OF THE GENERAL PARTNERSHIP

Termination occurs when all the partnership affairs are wound up and the partners' authority to act for the partnership is completely extinguished. A dissolved partnership may terminate or may be continued by a new partnership formed by the remaining partners (including perhaps the estate or heirs of a deceased partner).

Limited Partnership Requirements

The basic rules that govern formation, operation, and termination of general partnerships apply to limited partnerships as well. Some additional requirements placed on limited partnerships are discussed below.

FORMAL REQUIREMENTS

In addition to the requirement that a certificate of limited partnership be filed with the appropriate state authority, most states' statutes require that the partnership agreement clearly designate the limited partners as such. Any partnership that does not substantially meet this and other statutory requirements will be treated as a general partnership, with mutual liability and apparent authority attaching to each partner. A person who intended to be only a limited partner may face unlimited personal liability for all of the partnership's debts if there has not been substantial compliance in good faith with the formal requirements.

Section 11 of the Uniform Limited Partnership Act provides, however, that persons who contributed capital to a business erroneously believing that they became limited partners in a limited partnership will not be liable as general partners if, upon ascertaining the mistake, they promptly renounce their interest in the profits of the business.[9] The Revised Limited Partnership Act provides that a person who believed in good faith that he or she had become a limited partner is liable only to third parties that both transacted business with the purported limited partnership before the certificate of limited partnership was filed and reasonably believed that the person was a general partner at the time of the transaction.[10]

LIMITED PARTICIPATION

A limited partner's liability is limited unless he or she takes part in the control of the business. Thus, if limited partners have a voice in the business decisions of the partnership, they are opening themselves up to the possibility of

9. If such a renunciation is not effectuated, the putative limited partner faces liability in an individual capacity for debts of the partnership. Reiman v. International Hospitality Group, Inc., 614 A.2d 925 (D.C. 1992).
10. *See, e.g.,* Section 15633 of the California Revised Limited Partnership Act.

liability beyond their original capital investment. Furthermore, a limited partner may contribute money or property to the partnership but generally not services. Hence, in the Rad Waves example, if Olivia assists with the design of the sportswear line, in most states her liability could exceed her original $1,000 capital contribution. Therefore, limited partners should not take part in any partnership activity beyond monitoring the progress of their investment and exercising such statutory rights as the right to vote on the removal of a general partner. Moreover, the limited partner's name cannot appear in the name of the partnership without incurring unlimited liability.

Incorporation

Incorporation is the process by which a corporation is formed. The corporate statutes of each state set forth the steps that must be taken to establish a corporation in that state. Many states' statutes are based in whole or in part on the Model Business Corporation Act, an annotated uniform statute prepared by academics and practitioners. The state under whose laws a corporation is formed is called the corporation's *corporate domicile.* A corporation is not limited to doing business in its corporate domicile. It can conduct business as a foreign corporation in other states. Typically, in order to do so, it must file a statement of *foreign corporation* with the appropriate secretary of state and state taxing authority.

WHERE TO INCORPORATE

Corporations may incorporate in any state; it need not be the state where most of their business is located. Two important factors affect the decision of where to incorporate: (1) the costs of incorporation in a given state, and (2) the relative advantages and disadvantages of that state's corporation laws. If the corporation is privately held and its business will be conducted largely within one state, incorporation in that state is probably the best choice. If the corporation will be large from the outset or will be engaged in substantial interstate business, however, then incorporation in a jurisdiction with the most advantageous corporate statutes and case law should be considered.

Corporation laws may be favorable either to management or to the shareholders. Some states, such as Delaware, are considered to be pro-management because their statutes and court decisions tend to give control on a wide range of issues to the officers and directors. Other states, such as California, make it difficult for corporate managers to do certain things without

the approval and participation of the shareholders. These states are regarded as pro-shareholder.

A discussion of the Delaware statutes helps highlight some of the key corporate governance choices. The power to elect the board of directors is the primary way shareholders exercise control, and it is provided for in all jurisdictions. Delaware permits, but does not require, cumulative voting (discussed further below), which allows a minority shareholder greater opportunity to elect someone to the board. Delaware also permits a *staggered* (or *classified*) *board,* whereby directors serve for specified terms, usually three years, with only a fraction of them up for reelection at any one time. A classified board makes it more difficult to replace the entire board at once. In Delaware, classified boards are the norm. Delaware prohibits the removal of directors on a classified board without cause, unless the certificate of incorporation provides otherwise. In contrast, all corporations incorporated in California, except publicly traded companies, must have cumulative voting and cannot have a staggered board. In addition, as explained further in Chapter 23, Delaware permits broader limitations on directors' personal monetary liability than California.

Close to 60 percent of the corporations that make up the *Fortune* 500 (300,000 corporations total) are incorporated in Delaware. The Delaware General Corporation Law is a dynamic statute designed to give corporations maximum flexibility in ordering their affairs. The Delaware Court of Chancery, established in 1792, hears (without juries) all cases involving corporate law issues and has rendered thousands of written opinions interpreting virtually every provision of the Delaware General Corporation Law.[11] When deciding whether to incorporate in the local state or Delaware, entrepreneurs must weigh the advantages Delaware provides for managers against the expense of paying Delaware corporate franchise taxes, the expense of hiring lawyers familiar with Delaware law, and the possibility of having to defend a lawsuit in Delaware. Businesses incorporated in their local state often reincorporate in Delaware once they have grown large enough to justify the effort and expense of reincorporation.

HOW TO INCORPORATE

To create a corporation, one or more incorporators must prepare a document called the *certificate* or *articles of incorporation* (or the *corporate charter*). This document must be filed with the appropriate state governmental

---

11. *See* Lewis S. Black, Jr., *Why Delaware? A Practitioner Gives Reasons for Incorporation,* CORP. COUNS. WKLY., Oct. 20, 1999, at 8.

agency, usually the secretary of state for the jurisdiction that will become the corporate domicile.

The articles of incorporation are generally quite short. For example, the Pennsylvania Business Corporation Law specifies that the articles need set forth only the name of the corporation, the location and mailing address of the corporation's registered office in Pennsylvania, a brief statement of the purpose of the corporation, the term for which the corporation is to exist (which may be perpetual), the total number of shares that the corporation is authorized to issue, the name and mailing address of each of the incorporators, and a statement of the number of shares to be purchased by each.

Section 204 of the Pennsylvania Business Corporation Law, like most modern corporation statutes, goes on to provide that the purpose clause "may consist of or include a statement that the corporation shall have unlimited power to engage in and to do any lawful act concerning any or all lawful business for which corporations may be incorporated under this act." Pennsylvania's corporate law goes on to specify corporate powers, so there is no need to have a long purpose clause in the articles of incorporation. Indeed, to do so invites trouble, because one might inadvertently exclude an activity in which the corporation may later want to engage.

After the articles of incorporation are filed, the incorporators adopt the *bylaws,* that is, the rules governing the corporation (including the number of authorized directors), and elect the initial board of directors. This can be done either at an organizational meeting or by unanimous written consent. The incorporators are exclusively empowered to place the directors in office. After electing the board of directors, the incorporator signs a written resignation. The directors then have an organizational meeting at which they (1) ratify the adoption of the bylaws by the incorporators or adopt new bylaws, (2) appoint officers, (3) designate a bank as depository for corporate funds, (4) authorize the sale of stock to the initial shareholders, and (5) determine the consideration to be received in exchange for such shares—cash, other property, or past (but not future) services rendered to the corporation.

Exhibit 22.2 outlines the steps required to form a corporation.

DEFECTIVE INCORPORATION

Because a corporation exists only by statute, not by common law, any defect in the incorporation process can have the effect of denying corporate status. A business organization that was intended to function as a corporation but has failed to comply with the statutory require-

---

EXHIBIT 22.2 **Steps Required to Form a Corporation**

- Select a corporate name and agent for service of process.
- File certificate of incorporation (also known as articles of incorporation or charter in some jurisdictions) signed by incorporator(s).
- Sign action by incorporator(s) that:
  - adopts bylaws, and
  - specifies initial directors.
- Obtain written resignation of incorporator(s).
- Hold first directors' meeting or take action by unanimous written consent of the directors. Among other items of business,
  - ratify the adoption of the bylaws by the incorporator(s) or adopt new bylaws,
  - elect officers,
  - issue stock, and
  - authorize corporate bank account.

---

ments is in fact a partnership or, if there is only one shareholder, a sole proprietorship. The owners will not enjoy the protection of limited liability and can be held personally responsible for all debts of the enterprise. The courts have, however, developed several doctrines to avoid this result if it would be unfair.

De Jure Corporation When incorporation has been done correctly, a *de jure corporation* is formed. This means that the entity is a corporation by right and cannot be challenged. Most jurisdictions will find de jure corporate status as long as the incorporators have substantially complied with the incorporation requirements. For example, substantial compliance will be found even if the incorporators failed to obtain a required signature or submitted an improper notarization.

De Facto Corporation If the incorporators cannot show substantial compliance, a court may treat the entity as a *de facto corporation,* that is, as a corporation in fact even though it is not technically a corporation by law. For the court to find a de facto corporation, the incorporators must demonstrate that they were unaware of the defect and that they made a good faith effort to incorporate correctly. For example, if a clerk for the secretary of state delayed filing the articles, the business would not be a corporation de jure but would probably be a corporation de facto.

Corporation by Estoppel An entity that is neither a de jure nor a de facto corporation may be a *corporation by estoppel.* If a third party, in all of its transactions with the enterprise, acts as if it were doing business with a corporation, the third party is *estopped,* or prevented, from claiming that the enterprise is not a corporation.[12] It is considered unfair to permit the third party to reach shareholders' personal assets when all along it had believed it was dealing with a corporation whose shareholders had limited liability.

 # Piercing *the* Corporate Veil

The corporation is built around the central premise of limited liability. Under certain circumstances, however, courts will deny this central premise and hold the shareholders liable for claims against the corporation. A court will *pierce the corporate veil* in this way if necessary to prevent the evasion of statutes, the perpetration of fraud, or other activities against public policy. The need to pierce arises only if the corporation is unable to pay its own debts.

Courts have used the same approach to decide whether to pierce the veil of a limited liability company and hold its members personally liable. For example, the Court of Appeal of Louisiana held that Insulation Sales and Service, Inc. (ISS), the majority owner of AAI Ventures, L.L.C., was liable for monies owed under a contract between AAI and Patrick Hamilton, an individual hired to provide general management services to AAI in connection with its subcontract to remove asbestos from a casino.[13] AAI, which was formed to do asbestos removal work at the casino, was undercapitalized; the separate corporate existence of AAI and its affiliated companies was disregarded; individuals associated with the casino project were unsure of co-workers' job titles or employers of record; employees of one organization were housed at the offices of other organizations; and AAI had no employees—its accounting was handled by employees of ISS.

There are two legal approaches to piercing the corporate veil. The *alter ego theory* applies when the owners of a corporation have so mingled their own affairs with those of the corporation that the corporation does not exist as a distinct entity—instead, it is an alter ego of its owners. The *undercapitalization theory* applies when the corporation is a separate entity, but its deliberate lack of adequate capital allows it to skirt potential liabilities. Such undercapitalization constitutes a fraud upon the public.

Courts usually apply some combination of these theories. If a court suspects wrongdoing or bad faith on the part of shareholders, it will be more inclined to pierce

the corporate veil. Because a publicly traded corporation generally does not have one controlling shareholder, attempts to pierce the veil of such corporations are rare. Usually, the cases involve small, closely held corporations, including subsidiaries of larger corporations.

ALTER EGO THEORY

A court will consider several factors when deciding whether a corporation is merely the alter ego of a shareholder.

Domination by Controlling Shareholder If an individual or another corporation owning most of the stock of the corporation exerts a great deal of control, such that the standard corporate decision-making mechanisms are not in operation, the courts may find that the corporation has no separate mind, will, or existence of its own.

Commingling of Assets The courts will also examine whether the books and funds of the corporation and of the controlling shareholder have been commingled; for example, whether the shareholder uses company checks to make personal purchases or payments.

Bypassing Formalities If an action that requires approval by the board proceeds without a board meeting being held, or if other procedural rules (such as the requirement of an annual shareholders meeting) are consistently broken, the courts will be inclined to view the corporation as the instrument of the controlling shareholder.

Close Corporation Recognizing that small businesses are run in a more informal manner than large ones, legislators have created the statutory category of the *close corporation.* As mentioned earlier, a close corporation has a limited number of shareholders and must be explicitly designated as a close corporation in its charter. Under some close corporation statutes, if a close corporation's shareholders agree not to observe corporate formalities relating to meetings of directors or shareholders in connection with the management of its affairs, the bypassing of these formalities may not be considered a factor in deciding whether to pierce the corporate veil. In addition, many statutes permit the management of a close corporation to reside in the shareholders as long as a certain percentage of the shareholders agree to this in writing.

UNDERCAPITALIZATION THEORY

In deciding whether a corporation is undercapitalized, a court will consider whether the founders should have

12. *See, e.g.,* Cranson v. International Bus. Machs. Corp., 200 A.2d 33 (Md. 1964).
13. Hamilton v. AAI Ventures, L.L.C., 768 So. 2d 298 (La. Ct. App. 2000). *See also* Litchfield Asset Management v. Howell, 2000 Conn. Super. LEXIS 2991 (Nov. 14, 2000).

reasonably anticipated that the corporation would be unable to pay the debts or liabilities it would incur. (Of course, the amount of capital invested does not have to guarantee business success—if it did, all failed businesses would be deemed undercapitalized.)

For example, assume a new corporation is formed to build airplanes, an activity that requires large expenditures and entails substantial risks of liability for third-party injury. The corporation has raised only $1,000 in capital. It is obvious that the corporation will run out of funds quickly and be unable to pay its bills. It will not have money to buy adequate product liability insurance or to self-insure against claims for injuries caused by defective airplanes. A court may, because of the undercapi-

talization, ignore the corporate form and hold the owners of the corporation personally liable for its debts and liabilities.

The above example is an exaggerated case. In reality, it is often difficult for a court to decide how much capital is enough. Two judges examining the same facts may come to different conclusions as to whether the owner should have reasonably anticipated that the corporation would need more capital. Judges may also disagree as to whether undercapitalization alone is sufficient grounds to pierce the corporate veil. In the following classic case, the majority opinion and the minority dissent reflect two sides of this issue.

A CASE IN POINT

CASE 22.3
Walkovszky v. Carlton
Court of Appeals of New York
223 N.E.2d 6 (N.Y. 1966).

In the Language of the Court

FACTS The plaintiff was severely injured in New York City when he was run down by a taxicab owned by the defendant, Seon Cab Corporation. The individual defendant, Carlton, was a shareholder of ten corporations, including Seon, each of which had two cabs registered in its name. Each cab was covered by only the minimum $10,000 per cab automobile liability insurance required by New York law.

Although seemingly independent of one another, these corporations were, according to the plaintiff, "operated . . . as a single entity, unit and enterprise" with regard to financing, supplies, repairs, employees, and garaging, and all were named as defendants. The plaintiff also asserted that the multiple corporate structures constituted an unlawful attempt "to defraud members of the general public" who might be injured by the cabs. He therefore sought to hold their sole shareholder personally liable for his injury.

ISSUE PRESENTED May the corporate veil be pierced solely because the corporation is undercapitalized?

OPINION FULD, J., writing for the New York Court of Appeals:

The law permits the incorporation of a business for the very purpose of enabling its proprietors to escape personal liability but, manifestly, the privilege is not without its limits. Broadly speaking, the courts will disregard the corporate form, or, to use accepted terminology, "pierce the corporate veil," whenever necessary "to prevent fraud or to achieve equity."

. . .

The individual defendant is charged with having "organized, managed, dominated and controlled" a fragmented corporate entity but there are no allegations that he was conducting business in his individual capacity. . . . The corporate form may not be disregarded merely because the assets of the corporation, together with the mandatory insurance coverage of the vehicle which struck the plaintiff, are insufficient to assure him the recovery sought. . . . [I]f the insurance coverage required by statute "is inadequate for the protection of the public, the remedy lies not with the courts but with the Legislature." It may very well be sound policy to require that certain corporations must take out liability insurance which will afford adequate compensation to their potential tort victims. However, the responsibility for imposing conditions on the privilege of incorporation has been committed by the Constitution to the Legislature and

(Continued)

(Case 22.3 continued)

it may not be fairly implied, from any statute, that the Legislature intended, without the slightest discussion or debate, to require of taxi corporations that they carry automobile liability insurance over and above that mandated by the Vehicle and Traffic Law.

DISSENTING OPINION KEATING, J., dissenting from the majority opinion:

From their inception these corporations were intentionally undercapitalized for the purpose of avoiding responsibility for acts which were bound to arise as a result of the operation of a large taxi fleet having cars out on the street 24 hours a day and engaged in public transportation. And during the course of the corporations' existence all income was continually drained out of the corporations for the same purpose.

The issue presented by this action is whether the policy of this State, which affords those desiring to engage in a business enterprise the privilege of limited liability through the use of the corporate device, is so strong that it will permit that privilege to continue no matter how much it is abused, no matter how irresponsibly the corporation is operated, no matter what the cost to the public. I do not believe that it is.

[Judge Keating then cited with approval a California Supreme Court case[14] holding that the corporate veil could be pierced based on undercapitalization alone.]

...

What I would merely hold is that a participating shareholder of a corporation vested with a public interest, organized with capital insufficient to meet liabilities which are certain to arise in the ordinary course of the corporation's business, may be held personally responsible for such liabilities. Where corporate income is not sufficient to cover the cost of insurance premiums above the statutory minimum or where initially adequate finances dwindle under the pressure of competition, bad times or extraordinary and unexpected liability, obviously the shareholder will not be held liable.

RESULT In New York, the corporate veil may not be pierced solely because the corporation is undercapitalized. Accordingly, plaintiff Walkovszky cannot sue Carlton in his individual capacity.

COMMENTS In *Walkovszky,* the court rejected the argument that undercapitalization alone constituted fraud. The court suggested, however, that the plaintiff amend the complaint to allege that the individual defendants were "shuttling . . . personal funds in and out of the corporation 'without regard to formality and to suit their immediate convenience,'" thus stating a valid cause of action under the alter ego theory.

As indicated in Chapter 18, the U.S. Court of Appeals for the Seventh Circuit held that undercapitalization alone did not justify piercing the corporate veil of an Illinois corporation operating a garbage dump.[15]

QUESTIONS

1. From a public policy standpoint, with which opinion do you agree, the majority or the dissent?
2. Would the result have been different if defendant Carlton's name had been conspicuously displayed on the sides of all of the taxis owned by the various corporations of which Carlton was the sole shareholder and if Carlton actually serviced, inspected, repaired, and dispatched the taxis?

14. Minton v. Cavaney, 364 P.2d 473 (Cal. 1961).
15. Browning–Ferris Indus. v. Ter Maat, 195 F.3d 953 (7th Cir. 1999), *cert. denied,* 120 S. Ct. 1832 (2000) (Case 18.3).

TORT VERSUS CONTRACT

A tort plaintiff's contact with the corporation (for example, being hit by a taxi) may be completely involuntary. Many courts are therefore more sympathetic to the tort victim who faces an undercapitalized corporate defendant than to a plaintiff seeking to pierce the corporate veil in a breach-of-contract case. Why should someone who voluntarily contracted to provide credit to a weakly capitalized corporation, perhaps charging a premium interest rate in so doing, later be entitled to reach the owner's personal assets? After all, the creditor had, or could have negotiated, access to the corporation's financial statements. The voluntary decision to do business with the undercapitalized company contrasts quite sharply with the plight of a party who is a victim of a tort committed by an officer or employee of the corporation. If, however, a shareholder misrepresents the financial condition of the corporation when negotiating a contract, then courts will pierce the corporate veil.

Management *of the* Corporation

Corporate control is apportioned among the directors, officers, and shareholders. The directors are the overall managers and guardians of the corporation. The officers are the day-to-day managers. The shareholders, as the owners of the corporation, do not participate directly in management, but they elect the directors. The shareholders also must approve certain major transactions.

DIRECTORS

Most state statutes provide that the business and the affairs of the corporation shall be managed, and all corporate powers shall be exercised, by or under the direction of the board of directors. The board may delegate the management of the day-to-day operations of the business of the corporation to a management company or to other persons, such as officers. A member of the board may also serve as an officer. Such a person is called an *inside director*. A director who is not also an officer is

called an *outside director*. An understanding of the dynamics between the board and the officers is essential to comprehend the workings of a corporation.

OFFICERS

The officers appointed by the board of directors are agents of the corporation and have the power to act on its behalf. A corporation will normally have a chief executive officer (often called president), a secretary, a chief financial officer, and other officers as designated in the bylaws or determined by the board.

Any number of offices may be held by the same person, unless the articles or bylaws provide otherwise. Officers are chosen by the board and serve at the pleasure of the board. If an officer is terminated in violation of a contract of employment, the officer cannot sue to get his or her job back but can sue for damages. An officer may resign at any time upon written notice to the corporation. The corporation can sue for damages if an officer's resignation breaches his or her employment contract.

SHAREHOLDERS

The shareholders elect the directors. The courts have held that directors have no inherent right to remain in office. In some states, directors can be removed by the shareholders with or without cause at any time. In other states, such as Delaware, a director who is elected to a staggered board (where directors serve for designated terms) may not be removed without cause, unless the certificate of incorporation provides otherwise. The shareholders might be able to accomplish the same result by first eliminating the charter or bylaw provision requiring the staggered board, then voting to remove the director. In addition, certain transactions, such as a merger or the sale of substantially all of the corporation's assets, can be approved only by a vote of the shareholders.

Exhibit 22.3 provides a graphic depiction of the relationship among the shareholders, directors, and officers of a corporation.

 ## Shareholder Voting Rules

Shareholders can act by voting at a meeting or by written consent. A shareholder who cannot be present at a meeting can vote by *proxy,* that is, by a written authorization for another person to vote on his or her behalf. Only *shareholders of record,* that is, persons whose names appear on the corporation's shareholder list on a specified date, are entitled to vote.

No action can be taken at a shareholders meeting unless there is a *quorum;* the quorum requirements are set forth in each state's corporate statute. In most jurisdictions, there is no quorum unless the holders of at least 50 percent of the outstanding shares are present in person or by proxy.

EXHIBIT 22.3 **The Corporate Governance Triangle**

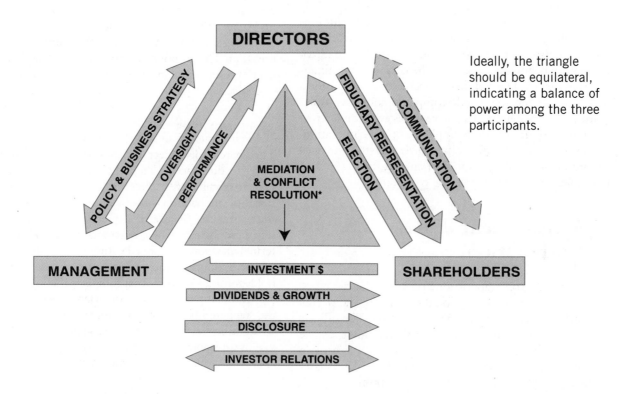

*The Board is responsible for resolving the structural conflicts that arise between the conflicting but equally valid goals of management and shareholders on the following issues:
- Control
- Capital structure
- Compensation of senior management
- Nomination of directors
- Shareholders rights

CUMULATIVE VOTING

In the election of directors, shareholders can cast one vote per share for each director. A shareholder's total number of votes is thus equal to the number of directors to be elected multiplied by the number of shares owned by the shareholder. Some states permit, and some require, *cumulative voting*, whereby each shareholder may cast all of his or her votes for one nominee or allocate them among nominees as the shareholder sees fit.

In an election permitting cumulative voting, the number of shares, *x*, required to elect a given number of directors, *y*, may be calculated by the following formula:

$$x = \frac{y \times z}{1 + d} + 1$$

where *z* is the total number of shares voting, and *d* is the total number of directors to be elected.

To illustrate, assume a shareholder wants to elect three directors ($y = 3$) to a board with five members up for election ($d = 5$). The corporation has 100 shares outstanding, and they are all voted ($z = 100$). Then

$$x = \frac{3 \times 100}{1 + 5} + 1$$

$$x = 51$$

With cumulative voting, a shareholder would need 51 shares to elect three directors.

 # Shareholders' Right *of* Inspection

INSPECTION RIGHTS AND SHAREHOLDER PROPOSALS

Shareholders have a common law right to inspect the corporate books and records, including the stock register and/or shareholder list, the minutes of board meetings and shareholder meetings, the bylaws, and books of account. In making the examination, shareholders are permitted the assistance of an accountant, lawyer, or other expert.

In most states, the right of inspection is limited, however, by the requirement that the inspection be conducted for a proper purpose. States vary in their interpretation of this limit. Some jurisdictions construe "proper purpose" liberally, leaving shareholder inspection rights virtually unfettered. These states reason that inspection rights should be broad because everything that affects a corporation eventually has an effect on its shareholders. Other states, more concerned with the potential for the inspection right to be an abusive tool, protect against "fishing expeditions" by requiring more than a vague allegation of mismanagement to establish a proper purpose.

Many of the most intense shareholder inspection battles involve access to the list of shareholders. Shareholders seeking to change a corporate policy or gain control of the board of directors want to identify and target their message to the holders of large blocks of stock. In order to do this, the insurgents need a copy of the shareholder list. Precisely because the list is so valuable to its shareholder critics, incumbent managers are likely to resist efforts to obtain it.

Acknowledging that access to the shareholder list can be vital to a successful corporate power struggle, some jurisdictions allow such access without requiring a proper purpose, provided that the shareholder owns a substantial block of shares. For example, Section 1600(a) of the California Corporations Code provides that any 5 percent shareholder can inspect and copy the record of shareholders' names, addresses, and shareholdings during usual business hours upon five business days' written notice.

Most states still require a proper purpose to obtain a shareholder list, however. The following case considers which motivations will qualify as a proper purpose under Delaware law.

A CASE IN POINT

CASE 22.4

State *ex rel.* Pillsbury v. Honeywell, Inc.
Supreme Court of Minnesota
191 N.W.2d 406
(Minn. 1971).

Summary

FACTS Charles Pillsbury opposed the Vietnam War. On July 3, 1969, he attended a protest meeting where he learned that Honeywell, Inc. (a Delaware corporation) had a large government contract to produce antipersonnel fragmentation bombs for use in the war. Upset that such bombs were being produced in his own community by a company that he knew and respected, Pillsbury resolved to stop Honeywell's munitions production.

On July 14, 1969, Pillsbury purchased 100 shares of Honeywell. He admitted that the sole purpose of the purchase was to give himself a voice in Honeywell's affairs so that he could persuade the company to cease producing munitions. Pillsbury submitted two

(Continued)

(Case 22.4 continued)

formal demands to Honeywell, requesting that it produce its current shareholder list and all corporate records dealing with weapons and munitions manufacture. Honeywell refused.

Pillsbury filed suit to force Honeywell to comply with his inspection request. The trial court dismissed his suit, holding that Pillsbury's purpose was not proper. Pillsbury appealed.

ISSUE PRESENTED Does a shareholder whose desire to change a corporate policy is motivated by social or political concerns have the proper purpose required to gain access to a shareholder list?

SUMMARY OF OPINION The Minnesota Supreme Court reasoned that the act of inspecting a corporation's shareholder list must be viewed in its proper perspective. In the context of a large firm, inspection can be more akin to a weapon in corporate warfare. "Considering the huge size of many modern corporations and the necessarily complicated nature of their bookkeeping, it is plain that to permit thousands of stockholders to roam at will through their records would render impossible . . . the proper carrying on of their business." Because the power to inspect may be the power to destroy, the court reasoned, it is important that only those with a bona fide interest in the corporation enjoy that power.

The court determined that a proper purpose under Delaware law (which governed the case because Honeywell was incorporated in Delaware) contemplated a concern with investment return. Pillsbury had "utterly no interest" in Honeywell's affairs before he learned of its production of fragmentation bombs. His avowed purpose in buying Honeywell was to place himself in a position to try to impress his social and political opinions upon Honeywell's management and its other shareholders. Such an interest, the court concluded, could hardly be deemed a proper purpose germane to his economic interest as a shareholder.

RESULT The Minnesota Supreme Court affirmed the trial court's denial of Pillsbury's petition to compel Honeywell to provide corporate records for inspection.

COMMENTS Under the rules adopted by the Securities and Exchange Commission (SEC) for the solicitation of proxies, publicly traded companies must either mail the proxy materials for the insurgents seeking to elect their own directors (or to effect another corporate transaction) or provide a shareholder list. Most companies elect to mail the materials, so insurgents must generally continue to rely on state inspection statutes to gain access to the shareholder list.[16]

16. *See generally* Constance E. Bagley & David Berger, Proxy Contests: Strategic Considerations (1998).

SHAREHOLDER PROPOSALS

The SEC requires publicly traded companies to include certain shareholder proposals in the proxy statement management sends to shareholders to solicit proxies for the election of directors. Shareholder activists have used shareholder proposals extensively to raise social or political issues. Early examples asked that companies stop doing business in South Africa to protest the policy of apartheid (mandated segregation of blacks and whites) or adopt the CERES Principles, a ten-point code of environmental conduct.

More recently, activists have focused on issues such as doing business in China. For example, in 2000, the staff of the SEC's Division of Corporate Finance advised Microsoft Corporation that it could not exclude a proposal requesting that it endorse a list of principles on human rights for workers in China.[17] Microsoft had unsuccessfully argued that the proposal could be excluded under the exceptions for proposals that (1) involve ordinary business operations, (2) contain impermissibly vague and

17. *Microsoft Can't Exclude China Human Rights Request*, Corp. Couns. Wkly., Oct. 25, 2000, at 3.

misleading statements, or (3) are so vague that the company lacks the power or authority to implement them. Although proposals raising social or political concerns usually do not receive majority support, they still provide a forum for socially minded shareholders to advance their agendas.

Since the mid-1990s, shareholder proposals have focused more on corporate governance issues. These include proposals (1) to eliminate a classified board and provide for the annual election of all directors; (2) to eliminate or modify antitakeover provisions, such as poison-pill plans; and (3) to have a majority of the directors independent of management. Although shareholder proposals rarely won majority support in the late 1980s and early 1990s, in 1999 alone, more than fifty shareholder proposals (all addressing corporate governance issues) were approved by a majority of the votes cast.[18]

Structural Changes

State laws establish mechanisms by which the fundamental structure of the corporation can be changed. These changes can range from a reorganization of the enterprise to the end of the corporation as a separate entity. Because structural changes have far-reaching consequences, they cannot be made easily.

State corporation law prohibits certain changes, such as a merger or the sale of substantially all of the corporation's assets, unless they are approved by both the board of directors and the shareholders. Approval by the shareholders usually means approval by a simple majority of the outstanding shares, but the articles of incorporation may require approval by a larger majority, such as two-thirds of the shareholders. Such a requirement for supermajority approval reflects the importance of structural changes.

MERGER

A *merger* is the combination of two or more corporations into one. The *disappearing corporation* no longer maintains its separate corporate existence but becomes part of the *surviving corporation*. The surviving corporation assumes, that is, becomes responsible for, all of the liabilities and debts of the disappearing corporation and automatically acquires all of its assets by operation of law. The new corporation may take on the name of one of the

parties to the merger, or a new corporate name may be chosen.

An agreement of merger, negotiated between the two companies, will specify such crucial matters as who will comprise the management team of the new enterprise. A merger generally cannot occur unless the boards and the shareholders of both companies approve the transaction. Once the requisite approval is given, the agreement of merger is filed with the secretary of state.

In a noncash merger, the shares in the disappearing corporation are automatically converted into shares in the surviving corporation. Shareholders are required to surrender their old stock certificates for new certificates representing the stock of the surviving corporation. If a shareholder does not surrender the old certificate, it is deemed by operation of law to represent shares of the surviving corporation.

In a cash merger, some shareholders (usually the public shareholders) are required to surrender their shares in the disappearing corporation for cash. They retain no interest in the surviving corporation. Hence, such a merger is also called a *freeze-out merger*.

If a proposed merger meets certain size-of-party and size-of-transaction tests, a premerger notification must be filed with the Federal Trade Commission and the Department of Justice. This notification enables the federal agencies to review the anticompetitive effects of the proposed merger before the combination occurs. (Such Hart–Scott–Rodino filings and antitrust in general are covered in Chapter 20.)

SALE OF ASSETS

A company may want to acquire the assets of another company but not its liabilities. To achieve this goal, it can purchase all or most of the other company's assets without merging with the other company. The proceeds of the sale of assets can be distributed to the selling company's shareholders as part of a dissolution of the corporation. Alternatively, the selling company may choose to continue its corporate existence and invest the proceeds of the sale of assets in a new business.

A sale of all or substantially all of the assets of a corporation must be approved by both the board and the shareholders of the selling company. Most states consider a sale of 50 percent or more of the assets of a company to be a sale of substantially all of the assets. Some states do not require that the transaction be approved by the shareholders of the acquiring company, on the theory that the acquisition of assets is a routine management decision, in which the shareholders should not be involved.

---

18. Bruce A. Babcock, *'Shareholder Proposals Have Come of Age in Recent Years': More Than 50 Received Majority Support in 1999, ISS Says,* Corp. Couns. Wkly., Jan. 19, 2000, at 8.

"Don't anybody move: this is a merger."

APPRAISAL RIGHTS

In a merger or a sale of assets, dissenting shareholders—those who voted against the transaction—are frequently granted *appraisal rights,* that is, the right to receive in cash the fair value of the shares they were forced to give up as a result of the transaction. This right is available only if the transaction was subject to shareholder approval and if the dissenting shareholder complies with certain statutory procedures.

In *M.P.M. Enterprises, Inc. v. Gilbert,*[19] the Delaware Supreme Court held that for purposes of calculating the amount due shareholders exercising appraisal rights, "fair value" is "the value of the company to the stockholder as a going concern, rather than its value to a third party as an acquisition." Using projected revenue growth, terminal value in five years, and an appropriate discount rate, the court determined that the equity value of M.P.M. Enterprises was $156.33 million, even though Cookson Group PLC had agreed to buy M.P.M. for $65

19. 731 A.2d 790 (Del. 1999).

million plus up to $73.6 million in subsequent payments, contingent upon earnings.

Ownership Changes

One company may gain control of another by buying a majority of its voting shares, rather than by merging with it or purchasing its assets.

TENDER OFFERS

A *tender offer* is a public offer to all the shareholders of a corporation to buy their shares at a stated price, usually higher than the market price. The party making the offer is called a *bidder,* or sometimes a raider because of the hostile nature of the bid. The bidder may offer either cash or other securities in exchange for the stock it seeks to acquire. The bidder is often a new corporation formed for the purpose of making the offer.

The shareholders are free to reject or accept the tender offer without the approval of the board of the target. If shareholders sell sufficient stock to the bidder, it will acquire control of the *target corporation*. Hence, the term *takeover* is commonly used to describe this transaction. Because the corporate structure of the target is almost certain to change substantially as a result of the takeover, tender offers are the subject of much regulation by federal statutes, as well as by the laws of the individual states. (Takeovers and the defensive tactics that boards can use to thwart them are discussed more fully in Chapter 23.)

An example of a takeover that results in a major change in corporate structure is the *second-step back-end merger*. First, the bidder acquires more than 50 percent of the shares of a company through a tender offer, then replaces the target company's board of directors with its own people. The new board then approves the merger of the target company into a company owned by the bidder, with the shareholders of the target company receiving cash or securities for their stock. As the majority shareholder of the target company, the bidder can outvote any dissenters and provide the required shareholder approval. The remaining shareholders are thus frozen out of the new company, and the bidder ends up with all the equity interest.

LEVERAGED BUYOUTS

Any tender offer can be structured as a *leveraged buyout (LBO)*, that is, a stock purchase financed by debt. In many LBOs, the group of investors seeking to gain control of a corporation includes members of corporate management. The debt financing an LBO is typically secured by the assets of the target company (such as real estate or plant and equipment), and it may take the form of the issuance of bonds, a commercial bank loan, or a loan from an investment bank. An LBO often results in a high debt load, which requires the company to make a series of substantial interest payments. Bankruptcy risks associated with LBOs are discussed in Chapter 26.

THE RESPONSIBLE MANAGER
Choosing *the* Appropriate Business Organization

The individuals who participate in the creation of a business organization will often go on to become its managers. These managers have a strong incentive to maximize the new enterprise's potential for success. To do this, several concerns must be addressed during the entity-selection process.

First, the founders should define and clarify the business goals of the enterprise in a business plan. For example, if the enterprise will need capital from a large number of individuals, it will be necessary to ensure limited liability for some or all of these investors. A general partnership would not be suitable, as there would be no limited liability for passive investors. A related concern is clarifying the goals of the individual participants in the enterprise. For example, experienced managers who have developed a new product that requires little capital outlay would probably want exclusive control of the new business. A general partnership might be best suited to their needs.

If a general partnership is chosen, there are additional concerns. For example, it is important to put the partnership agreement in writing. A written partnership agreement forces people to think through their business objectives and relationships before they begin working together. It also avoids the imposition of certain statutory partnership rules that apply when there is no written agreement.

If several persons work together on an informal basis with a common business objective, and then one leaves, the *forgotten founder* problem can arise. The person who left may have ownership rights in the enterprise. Such rights can be based on the laws of intellectual property if the person leaving created a protectable piece of property, such as a patentable invention or computer software that is protected by copyright law. (Intellectual property is discussed in Chapter 11.) Even if a founder created no protectable intellectual property before leaving, he or she may have been a partner in an informal oral general partnership if the parties had been sharing profits and losses. As such, that founder would be entitled to a share of the partnership assets.

One way to mitigate the forgotten founder problem is to incorporate early and issue shares that are subject to vesting over time. A common vesting schedule provides that if a person leaves in the first year, he or she forfeits all rights to any stock. Under this approach, called *cliff vesting*, one-quarter of the stock is often vested at the end of the first year. The remainder is vested monthly over the next three to four years.

If early incorporation is not feasible or is otherwise undesirable, it is important to spell out in writing at the beginning of a joint project what will happen if someone leaves. Otherwise, those who remain could find themselves sued years down the road for a share of the company that finally is formed, a partnership interest, or royalties for use of intellectual property.

Tax considerations play a major role in the choice of a business entity. Because tax law is constantly changing, its impact on a particular business form cannot be predicted with certainty. Nonetheless, the larger issues, such as whether taxation will be at both the entity and the owner level or only at the owner level, must be considered. In addition, optimal tax planning does not necessarily mean tax minimization. When deciding how to organize a business, the company must weigh the tax advantages against the agency costs, which can arise when ownership is separated from management.

If the founders decide that incorporation is the best course, they should obtain competent legal advice. State statutes vary in their requirements for incorporation. As a practical matter, founders should always request that their lawyer send them a certified copy of the articles of incorporation to confirm that the articles were in fact filed with the secretary of state on the specified date.

Even if a corporation is formed in accordance with the appropriate legal requirements, a court may still disregard the corporate form. In some jurisdictions, the corporate veil may be pierced solely because the corporation is undercapitalized. The founders should consult with counsel as to the capital requirements in the jurisdiction of incorporation. Courts may also pierce the corporate veil if the shareholders fail to respect the corporate form in their execution of daily activities or if they commingle personal and corporate funds. Managers should make it clear in all of their dealings with third parties that they are acting on behalf of a corporation. All firm stationery and agreements should indicate corporate status.

Once the corporation has been established, the managers will oversee the process of capitalization. To decide what percentages of debt and equity are to be used in financing the operation, managers should have a realistic idea of the existing demand and the distinct markets for both types of financing. In addition, managers must be aware of the rates at which the corporation can borrow money and the terms that debt and equity holders will require. Tax considerations are crucial to this process.

The final capital structure can take a variety of forms, and much creativity can be employed in this area. Managers will often seek assistance from attorneys specializing in finance and tax law, as well as from accountants and investment bankers. The more the managers understand about capitalization, however, the better they can utilize the information provided by lawyers, bankers, and accountants to achieve a suitable capital structure.

The officers of a corporation are empowered by the board to manage the day-to-day operations of the business. They are also agents for the corporation and must be concerned with the impact of agency law on their actions. First, a manager must be certain that he or she is acting with actual authority (such as a resolution from the board of directors, passed in a procedurally correct manner, that approves a proposed action). Second, a manager has the power to delegate authority to subordinates to bind the corporation. Accordingly, the manager should clearly define the scope of employment for all employees of the corporation and clearly indicate to third parties the extent of each employee's authority.

Managers are often directors, as well as officers. As board members, they should ensure that the board acts in accordance with the articles of incorporation and the applicable corporate law. Board actions are valid only if the directors act in their collective role and not in their individual capacities. The duties of board members to act in an informed manner and to make decisions based on the best interests of the corporation are discussed in Chapter 23.

Focus *on* Franchises

Although franchises are not a separate form of business entity in the traditional sense, they are a common business arrangement, subject to regulation by both the Federal Trade Commission (FTC) and the states. Well-known franchisors include McDonald's, Taco Bell, Realty World America, and Dunkin' Donuts.

The word "franchising" is commonly understood to refer to an arrangement whereby the franchisor receives cash up front, followed by monthly payments based on a reseller's gross receipts, in exchange for granting the franchisee the right to use the franchisor's trademarks and marketing plan. Yet some state statutes define the term far more broadly and may bring within their ambit product distribution arrangements between manufacturers and dealers that many managers would not have considered to be franchises.[20] Because franchise laws can override the parties' contractual arrangements (for example, by prohibiting termination of the relationship without good cause), a manufacturer's ability to alter its supply chains to take advantage of new distribution channels, such as the Internet, may be constrained.

DEFINITION OF "FRANCHISE"

State franchise statutes tend to use either a marketing plan or a community of interest definition, with the marketing plan definition being the more prevalent. The definition used by the FTC is broad enough to encompass relationships that would be included under either state definition.

Marketing Plan Definition The California Business and Professions Code, which is representative of statutes using a marketing plan definition, defines a franchise as a

> . . . contract or agreement, either expressed or implied, whether oral or written, between two or more persons by which:
> (a) a franchisee is granted the right to engage in the business of offering, selling, or distributing goods or services under a marketing plan or system prescribed in substantial part by a franchisor; and

> (b) The operation of the franchisee's business pursuant to that plan or system is substantially associated with the franchisor's trademark, service mark, trade name, logotype, advertising, or other commercial symbol designating the franchisor or its affiliate; and
> (c) The franchisee is required to pay, directly or indirectly, a franchise fee.[21]

The courts have construed the requirement for a marketing plan very liberally. It can be as little as a quota of copiers to sell in a specific territory, coupled with a requirement that the distributor's personnel participate in mandatory product training,[22] or an agreement with a boat manufacturer specifying that the dealer is to advertise intensively, conduct a variety of promotions, and carry the boat manufacturer's array of accessory sales devices.[23]

Similarly, it takes very little to satisfy the requirement for a franchise fee. Although many states exclude payments for goods at a bona fide wholesale price, payments for videocassettes, posters, and brochures to promote the manufacturer's product have been viewed as franchise fees when they were required by the manufacturer or recommended as essential for the successful operation of the business.

Community of Interest Definition The New Jersey definition of "franchise" is representative of state statutes using the community of interest definition:

> "Franchise" means a written arrangement for a definite or indefinite period, in which a person grants to another person a license to use a trade name, trade mark, service mark, or related characteristics, and in which there is a community of interest in the marketing of goods or services at wholesale, retail, by lease, agreement, or otherwise.[24]

Some states, including Hawaii and Minnesota, also require payment of a franchise fee.

---

20. Thomas J. Collin, *State Franchise Laws and the Small Business Franchise Act of 1999: Barriers to Efficient Distribution*, 55 Bus. Law. 1699 (2000). This "Inside Story" is based entirely on this article.

21. Cal. Bus. & Prof. Code § 20001(a)–(c) (West 1997).
22. Wright–Moore Corp. v. Ricoh Corp., 908 F.2d 128 (7th Cir. 1990).
23. Boat & Motor Mart v. Sea Ray Boats, Inc., 825 F.2d 1285 (9th Cir. 1987).
24. N.J. Stat. Ann. § 56:10-3(a) (West 1989).

"Yes, I know the meaning of life, but I've decided to franchise it."

Reprinted with permission.

The supplier is deemed to have given the requisite license if the distributor has the right to identify itself as an authorized dealer even if the distributor does not have the right to use the supplier's name as part of its own business name. A community of interest in the marketing of goods is also easily shown, and it is present in most supplier–dealer arrangements. For example, courts found a community of interest to exist when (1) a "consultant" was required to pay an information services firm 1 percent of the proceeds received from each loan placed by the consultant using the information, and (2) a dealer made significant investments that were specific to the supplier's goods or services and therefore were not fully recoverable upon termination of the relationship.[25]

STATE FRANCHISE LAWS: NO TERMINATION WITHOUT GOOD CAUSE

In the 1960s and early 1970s, a number of state legislatures adopted laws to protect local businesses investing in franchises from the superior bargaining power of large franchisors. These statutes typically prohibit termination or nonrenewal except where there is good cause, such as (1) failure by the franchisee to comply with any material

and reasonable obligation under the franchise agreement, or (2) conduct by the franchisee that substantially impairs the franchisor's trademark or trade name.

Although manufacturers may feel justified in terminating a distribution arrangement if the franchisee's performance is sub-par, according to Thomas J. Collin of Thompson Hine & Flory LLP, "[c]ases finding that sub-par performance constitutes good cause for termination are scarcer than hen's teeth . . . ."[26] As a result, a franchisor that seeks to terminate a dealer for lack of market penetration or performance "faces a steep uphill climb."[27] In some states, such as New Jersey and Indiana, the franchisor cannot terminate the franchise even if it has bona fide business reasons for doing so, such as a desire to eliminate distributors' exclusive territories or to terminate distributors in order to sell directly to end-users.

STATE REGISTRATION AND DISCLOSURE REQUIREMENTS

Some states (including California, Illinois, Michigan, and Wisconsin) require franchisors to register before they can sell franchises in that state and to provide a

25. Collin, *supra* note 20, at 1722.

26. *Id*. at 1731–32.
27. *Id*. at 1732.

prospectus or other disclosure document to prospective franchisees. Most of these states also have broad antifraud provisions that prohibit any person from making any untrue statement of material fact, or a material omission, in connection with the offer or sale of a franchise.

FTC'S FRANCHISE DISCLOSURE RULE

Effective October 21, 1979, the FTC adopted a regulation requiring franchisors to give a prospective franchisee the detailed written disclosures specified in the rule.[28] The FTC enforces the rule, and there is no implied private right of action for its violation.

SMALL BUSINESS FRANCHISE ACT OF 1999

The Small Business Franchise Act of 1999 (the Bill)[29] would, if enacted, provide uniform federal standards of conduct for franchise contracts. The Bill would (1) re-

quire good cause for termination, (2) give franchisees more freedom in choosing where they buy their supplies, and (3) prohibit encroachment. *Encroachment* occurs "when a franchisor sells a franchisee an outlet in a certain location, and then a few months later, sells another outlet a few blocks away to someone else."[30] The new establishment diverts customers and revenues away from the original franchisee, but the franchisor is often still better off because it is receiving its percentage royalty from two stores. According to Susan Kezios, president of the American Franchisee Association, "McDonald's wants to have a Big Mac five minutes away from every man, woman, and child. . . . They don't give a rat's ass if they devalue your asset [in the process]."[31] Matthew Shay, vice president and chief counsel of the rival International Franchise Association (which counts McDonald's and Kentucky Fried Chicken among its members), claims that the Bill would "rewrite every condition and every term in a franchise agreement" and "impose such extreme restrictions on franchising that it would basically kill the business."[32]

28. Disclosure Requirements and Prohibitions Concerning Franchising and Business Opportunity Ventures, 16 C.F.R. § 436.1–.3 (2000).
29. H.R. 3308, 106th Cong. (1999), reproduced as Appendix I to the *Report of the American Bar Association Section of Antitrust Law on Proposed Small Business Franchise Act*, available at <http://www.abanet.org/antitrust/final.html>.

30. Deidre Shesgreen, *Franchisees Seek Protection on the Hill*, LEGAL TIMES, Jan. 4, 1999, at 1.
31. *Id.*
32. *Id.*

KEY WORDS AND PHRASES

1. Amy Rockwell was a brilliant but penniless electrical engineer. She had designed a new type of cogeneration plant that she believed had great commercial potential. On January 15, she approached Benjamin Furst, a successful and experienced manager in the energy field, with the idea of starting Cogen, Inc., a corporation devoted to building a plant based on this new design. Furst was enthusiastic. On January 28, he enlisted the support of Clyde Pfeffer, a well-known venture capitalist who had retired from venture capital work but was looking to invest the proceeds of his past endeavors. On Februrary 16, Pfeffer gave the green light to establish the new enterprise.

Furst retained the law firm of Fumble & Botchem to handle the details of incorporation. Fumble, one of the partners, drafted the articles of incorporation, signed them as the incorporator, and filed them with the secretary of state on February 28. He then advised his clients that the articles had been filed. Because of a typographical error, the articles of incorporation filed with the secretary of state referred to the company as Cogene, not Cogen.

Rockwell, Furst, and Pfeffer decided that they would save further expense by completing the incorporation process without any more assistance from Fumble & Botchem. On March 3, they held what they called the meeting of incorporators to elect the directors and proceeded to elect themselves to the board. As board members, they appointed themselves as the company's officers. They typed up the minutes of this meeting.

On March 4, the daily operations of Cogen, Inc. commenced. In all of their transactions with third parties, the officers represented themselves as doing business for the corporation. One of these transactions was with Firstloan Bank, which lent the company $5 million. The representations in the loan agreement stated that the corporation had been duly formed, that it existed as a valid corporation under Texas law, and that the shares of stock owned by the various shareholders had been duly authorized and were fully paid.

On May 5, the corporation began building its cogeneration plant. Three months later, energy prices dropped drastically, and there was no longer a need for a cogeneration facility in that location. The corporation was forced to default on the bank loan. The lawyers for the bank, upon being informed that it would not receive any more loan payments, reviewed the original loan documents, the articles of incorporation, and the minutes of the first meeting of the incorporators. Upon reviewing these documents, they initiated an action directly against the three founders in their individual capacities for liability on the bank loan.

a. What arguments can the lawyers for the bank make in their effort to hold the founders personally liable for the debt of the corporation? Should their arguments prevail?

b. What counterarguments can the founders make to avoid such liability?

2. Roberto Herrara was the sole force behind In Over Our Heads, Inc., a corporation designed to run a year-round community swimming pool. The enterprise was incorporated in the correct manner in January, with Herrara as the sole director and shareholder. Herrara contributed $100,000 of starting capital, which was just enough to purchase the pool, finance initial advertising, and leave a reserve of $10,000. The corporation had no liability insurance.

On March 10, the pool opened for business. The corporation operated with a profit over the next few months. In June, Herrara took a two-week vacation in Europe and used a check from the company bank account to purchase his airline ticket. In November, he decided to have the pool repainted. Because business had slowed and the corporation's bank account did not have sufficient funds, Herrara wrote a personal check for this job.

Herrara feared he would not make enough money through the winter to turn a profit, so he decided to take a part-time job as a telephone salesperson for a real estate company. He used the swimming pool's office phone to make his calls and made a substantial profit.

On February 11, a child drowned in the pool. The parents brought suit for wrongful death against the corporation and against Herrara in his individual capacity as owner. At the time of the suit, the corporation had the $10,000 reserve and less than $1,000 in its bank account. Because of these limited funds, the child's parents hoped to recover most of their damages directly from Herrara.

What arguments can be made to hold Herrara liable for any debt of the corporation arising from this death? Should they prevail? How could Herrara have protected himself against such potential liability? Can an owner–manager of a small corporation guarantee that he or she will not be held liable for the corporation's debts?

3. Sullivan purchased an American Football League (AFL) franchise for a professional football team for $25,000. Several months later, he organized a corporation, the American League Professional Football Team of Boston. Sullivan contributed his AFL franchise, and nine other people contributed $25,000. In return, each of the ten investors received 10,000 shares of voting common stock in the corporation. Approximately four months later, the corporation sold 120,000 shares of nonvoting common stock to the public at $5 per share.

In 1975, Sullivan obtained control of all 100,000 voting shares of the corporation. He immediately used his control to vote out the other directors and elect a friendly board. To finance the purchase of the voting shares, Sullivan borrowed approximately $5 million. As a condition of the loan, Sullivan was to use his best efforts to organize the corporation so that its income could be devoted to the payment of the personal loan and its assets pledged to secure the loan. To accomplish this goal, Sullivan had to eliminate the interests in the nonvoting shares.

In 1976, Sullivan organized a new corporation. The boards of directors of the new and old company executed a merger agreement for the two corporations, providing that after the merger the voting stock of the old corporation would be extinguished and the nonvoting stock would be exchanged for cash at $15 per share.

David Coggins owned 10 shares of nonvoting stock in the old corporation. He voted against the merger and brought suit against what he alleged was an unfair and illegal transaction. Was the transaction unfair to the nonvoting shareholders? Should Coggins be able to obtain an injunction to stop the merger? [*Coggins v. New England Patriots Football Club*, 492 N.E.2d 1112 (Mass. 1986)]

4. While attending Georgia Tech, Alan, Brian, Cathy, and Diane conceived of an innovative design for a hospital management software system, but they did not actually write the code. At the time, there was some talk among them of starting a business after graduation, but there was no formal agreement. Four months after graduation, Alan, Brian, and Cathy formed a company to develop the system. They initially took the position that Diane was not entitled to share in the new enterprise because of the enormous amount of work that would be required to develop the code and make it commercially viable.

Their lawyer suggested reaching an agreement with Diane, whereby she would receive a 5 percent equity interest in the new company in exchange for any rights she might have in the technology.

Should Alan, Brian, and Cathy accept their lawyer's advice? What risks do they face if they do not?

5. Francis McQuade was the manager of the New York Giants baseball team. Charles Stoneham (father of Horace Stoneham, who acquired the baseball franchise in 1936 and moved it from New York to San Francisco in 1958) owned a majority of the stock of the company that owned the Giants and sold shares in that company to McQuade and John McGraw. As part of this transaction, these three shareholders each agreed to use his best efforts to continue to keep each of the others as directors and officers of the company at their present salaries. Stoneham and McGraw subsequently failed to use their best efforts to continue to keep McQuade as a director and treasurer of the company. McQuade sued for specific performance of the agreement. What result? [*McQuade v. Stoneham*, 189 N.E. 234 (N.Y. 1934)]

6. Smith Construction contracted with Wolman, Duberstein & Thompson (WBT), a general partnership, to build two homes. The partnership then failed to pay the balance due on the homes (approximately $107,000), thereby breaching the contract. Smith Construction obtained a judgment against WBT for the balance due but received only about $2,000 of that judgment, which was garnished from WBT's bank account. WBT had no other assets.

Can Smith Construction execute the remainder of its judgment against the assets of the individual partners of WBT? If so, are the individual partners jointly and severally liable, or are they only jointly liable for this business debt? (Joint and several liability means that each partner is potentially liable for the entire debt of the partnership; joint liability means that each is liable only for a portion of the debt.) Will the terms of the WBT partnership agreement affect the outcome? [*Wayne Smith Construction Co. v. Wolman, Duberstein & Thompson*, 604 N.E.2d 157 (Ohio 1992)]

7. In 1987, William Myers injured his hand while operating a cement pump. The pump had been manufactured in 1981 by Thomson Equipment. In 1982, Putzmeister, Inc. purchased the assets of Thomson Equipment but did not expressly assume the liabilities. Is Putzmeister liable to Myers for product liability? What factors would the court consider in determining whether Putzmeister must assume

Thomson Equipment's liability for wrongfully manufactured products? [*Myers v. Putzmeister, Inc.*, 596 N.E.2d 754 (Ill. App. Ct. 1992)]

8. Mary Doting was a partner in the Frank J. Trunk and Son Partnership. In 1988, Doting successfully petitioned the court to order a dissolution of the partnership. The court concluded that the partnership could not be wound up until its affairs were completed. At the time, the partnership still had receivables under contract that would not be payable until 1997 at the earliest and 2001 at the latest.

   Frank and Mary Trunk wanted the partnership to continue and succeeded in preventing its termination through October 1992. At that time, Doting filed a second petition to terminate the partnership. The Trunks argued that the partnership could not be terminated until the last receivable had been received. Must all partnership receivables be received by a partnership before a court can order its termination? [*Doting v. Trunk*, 856 P.2d 536 (Mont. 1993)]

9. Ernie Jameson is a design engineer with a proven track record in the field of electronic musical instruments. He recently designed a new VLSI (very large scale integrated) chip. This chip is meant to be the heart and soul of a digital sampling keyboard to be called Echo. Jameson believes the Echo will set a new industry standard. He wishes to organize a business enterprise to build and market it. He has a meeting with his lawyer and conveys to her the following bits of information:

   a. It will take approximately two years to turn the VLSI chip into a marketable product.

   b. Jameson has more than $200,000 in savings from previous ventures. He does not want any of that money at risk in this new venture. However, he wants a part of the ownership; he is unsure what percentage he wants.

   c. Currently, five private investors are willing to put money into this venture. Only two of the five want to play an active role in the enterprise. Jameson is willing to give these two some limited control.

   d. Jameson knows that he is not qualified to manage the new endeavor. Nonetheless, he wants a significant say in how it proceeds.

   e. Five more investors could be attracted to this project, but only if they could be guaranteed some fixed return on their money or could realize immediate tax benefits from investing.

   f. Jameson would like Bernie Lord, a manager much in demand in the electronics field, to be his CEO. It would take significant incentives to attract him to the enterprise.

   Jameson is not committed to using any particular type of business organization; he is interested in weighing the alternatives. What possible types of business organizations could accommodate the needs of the various players? What are the advantages and disadvantages of each alternative? Which one should Jameson choose?

MANAGER'S DILEMMA

10. Entrepreneurs starting a new business often are strapped for cash. Because experienced lawyers are expensive, some entrepreneurs may be tempted to avoid seeking counsel until they have a commitment for their first round of outside financing. This often means putting off incorporating the business until later. What are the pitfalls with this approach?

    Some law firms will ask to invest in the start-ups they help set up, particularly if they have agreed to defer payment of their fees until the first round of financing closes. In some cases, firms will ask only for the right to invest in the first round on the same terms and conditions as the outside investors. Some firms, however, demand the right either to receive a piece of equity (often 1 to 3 percent of the company) free or for the very low price paid by the founders. What factors should an entrepreneur take into account when deciding whether to permit counsel to invest in the start-up? [For a discussion of the ethical considerations an attorney must take into account when investing in clients, see Association of the Bar of the City of New York Committee on Professional and Judicial Ethics, Formal Op. 2000-3 (2000); American Bar Association, Committee on Ethics and Professional Responsibilty, Formal Op. 00-418 (2000); and Edward H. Cohen, *Lawyers Investing in Their Clients: The Rules of Professional Responsibility*, 14 INSIGHTS 2 (Aug. 2000).]

The National Conference of Commissioners on Uniform State Laws, in association with the University of Pennsylvania Law School, makes available drafts and revisions to finalized versions of the Uniform Partnership Act, the Uniform Limited Partnership Act, the Uniform Limited Liability Partnership Act, and the Uniform Limited Liability Company Act.	http://www.law.upenn.edu/bll/ulc/ulcframe.htm
The site for the National Conference of Commissioners on Uniform State Laws provides an updated list of which states have adopted various uniform acts.	http://www.nccusl.org/
Implications of California's Adopted Revised Uniform Partnership Act	http://www.taxlawsb.com/resources/BusTax/ptshp.htm
The Small Business Administration's site provides valuable information about starting and financing small businesses, a searchable online library, and links to other sites of interest (including the home pages for each state's department of corporations).	http://www.sbaonline.sba.gov/
This site for Richards, Layton & Finger, the largest law firm in Delaware, contains excellent articles on Delaware corporate and partnership law and provides links to other legal-related sites.	http://www.rlf.com/
LLC-USA.com operates a Web site dedicated to issues surrounding limited liability companies.	http://www.llc-usa.com
The Harvard Business School Publishing site provides the Entrepreneurs Resource Center with searchable bibliographies and materials and very useful links to sites of interest to persons starting a business.	http://www.hbsp.harvard.edu/ideasatwork/entrep/

CHAPTER 23

Directors, Officers, *and* Controlling Shareholders

FIDUCIARY DUTIES

Directors and officers are agents of the corporation and owe a fiduciary duty to the corporation and its shareholders. Under certain circumstances, a majority or controlling shareholder owes a fiduciary duty to other shareholders as well.

These duties take two basic forms: a duty of care and a duty of loyalty. Generally, the *duty of care* requires fiduciaries to make informed and reasonable decisions and to exercise reasonable supervision of the business. The *duty of loyalty* mandates that fiduciaries act in good faith and in what they believe to be the best interest of the corporation, subordinating their personal interests to the welfare of the corporation. As then Judge Benjamin Cardozo stated, many forms of conduct permissible in the business world for those acting at arm's length are forbidden to those bound by fiduciary ties. A trustee, he said, is held to something stricter than the morals of the marketplace. Not mere honesty, but a "punctilio of honor the most sensitive" is the standard of behavior with which fiduciaries must comply.[1]

CHAPTER OVERVIEW

This chapter outlines the duties of directors, officers, and, in certain situations, controlling shareholders. First, it analyzes the duty of care in terms of the most applicable judicial doctrine, the business judgment rule. Next, it addresses issues arising under the duty of loyalty, including corporate opportunities. The chapter discusses the fiduciary duties of directors that arise when the directors must decide whether to sell the company or resist a corporate takeover bid. Legislative responses to these issues are also described. Finally, the chapter looks at the duties of controlling shareholders in connection with sales of corporate control and squeeze-out mergers.

1. Meinhard v. Salmon, 164 N.E. 545, 546 (N.Y. 1928) (Case 1.1).

 The Business Judgment Rule *and the* Duty of Care

In cases challenging board decisions for breach of the duty of care, the courts generally defer to the business judgment of the directors, acknowledging that courts are ill equipped to second-guess directors' decisions at a later date. Thus, under the *business judgment rule,* as long as certain standards are met, a court will presume that the directors have acted in good faith and in the honest belief that the action taken was in the best interest of the company. The court will not question whether the action was wise or whether the directors made an error of judgment or a business mistake.

In order to take advantage of the rule, the directors must have made an informed decision with no conflict between their personal interests and the interests of the corporation and its shareholders. If the business judgment rule does not apply to a transaction, courts generally shift to the directors the burden of proving that their acts were not grossly negligent (or in cases involving transactions in which the directors are interested, that the transaction was fair and reasonable).

INFORMED DECISION

The business judgment rule is applicable only if the directors make an informed decision. The general corporation law of most jurisdictions authorizes directors to rely on the reports of officers and certain outside experts. However, passive reliance on such reports may result in an insufficiently informed decision, as in the following case.

CASE 23.1
Smith v. Van Gorkom
Supreme Court of Delaware
488 A.2d 858 (Del. 1985).

Summary

FACTS Trans Union Corporation was a publicly traded, diversified holding company engaged in the railcar-leasing business. Its stock was undervalued, largely due to accumulated investment tax credits. Jerome W. Van Gorkom, the chairman of the board of Trans Union, was reaching retirement age. He asked the chief financial officer, Donald Romans, to work out the per-share price at which a leveraged buyout could be done, given current cash flow. Romans came up with $55, based on debt-servicing requirements. He did not attempt to determine the intrinsic value of the company. Van Gorkom later met with Jay Pritzker and worked out a merger at $55 per share. Trans Union stock was then trading at about $37 per share.

Van Gorkom called a board meeting for September 20, 1980, on one day's notice, to approve the merger. All of the directors were familiar with the company's operations as a going concern, but they were not apprised of the merger negotiations before the board meeting on September 20. They were also familiar with the current financial status of the company; a month earlier they had discussed a Boston Consulting Group strategy study. The ten-member board included five outside directors who were CEOs or board members of publicly held companies, as well as a former dean of the University of Chicago Business School.

Copies of the merger agreement were delivered to the directors, but too late for study before or during the meeting. The meeting began with a twenty-minute oral presentation by chairman Van Gorkom. The chief financial officer then described how he had arrived at the $55 figure. He stated that it was only a workable number, not an indication of a fair price. Trans Union's president stated that he thought the proposed merger was a good deal.

The board approved the merger after a two-hour meeting. Board members later testified that they had insisted that the merger agreement be amended to ensure that the company was free to consider other bids before the closing; however, neither the board minutes nor the merger documents reflected this clearly.

Plaintiff Smith sued to challenge the board's action, arguing that the merger price was too low. The Delaware Court of Chancery held that, given the premium over the market value of Trans Union stock, the business acumen of the board members, and the effect on the merger price of the prospect of other bids, the board was adequately informed and did not act recklessly in approving the Pritzker deal. In making its findings, the court relied in part on actions taken by the board after the meeting on September 20, 1980, that were intended to cure defects in the directors' initial level of knowledge.

ISSUE PRESENTED Were directors who accepted and submitted to the shareholders a proposed cash merger without determining the intrinsic value of the company grossly negligent in failing to inform themselves adequately before making their decision?

SUMMARY OF OPINION The Delaware Supreme Court reversed the lower court and held that the directors were grossly negligent in failing to reach a properly informed
(Continued)

(Case 23.1 continued)

decision. They were not protected by the business judgment rule even though there were no allegations of bad faith, fraud, or conflict of interest. The court found that the directors could not reasonably base their decision on the inadequate information presented to the board. They should have independently valued the company.

The court found that the directors had inadequate information as to (1) the role of Van Gorkom, Trans Union's chairman and chief executive officer, in initiating the transaction; (2) the basis for the proposed purchase price of $55 per share; and, most importantly, (3) the intrinsic value of Trans Union, as opposed to its current and historical stock price. The court held that in the absence of any apparent crisis or emergency, it was grossly negligent for the directors to approve the merger after a two-hour meeting, with eight of the ten directors having received no prior notice of the proposed merger.

The court stated:

> None of the directors, management or outside, were investment bankers or financial analysts. Yet the board did not consider recessing the meeting until a later hour that day (or requesting an extension of Pritzker's Sunday evening deadline) to give it time to elicit more information as to the sufficiency of the offer, either from inside management (in particular Romans) or from Trans Union's own investment banker, Salomon Brothers, whose Chicago specialist in mergers and acquisitions was known to the Board and familiar with Trans Union's affairs.
>
> Thus, the record compels the conclusion that on September 20 the Board lacked valuation information adequate to reach an informed business judgment as to the fairness of $55 per share for sale of the Company.

The court additionally held that the directors' subsequent efforts to find a bidder willing to pay more than Pritzker were inadequate to cure the infirmities of their uninformed exercise of judgment.

The court rejected the directors' argument that they properly relied on the officers' reports presented at the board meeting. The court stated that a pertinent report may be relied on in good faith, but not blindly. The directors were duty bound to make reasonable inquiry of Van Gorkom (the chief executive officer) and Romans (the chief financial officer). If they had done so, the inadequacy of those officers' reports would have been apparent. Van Gorkom's summary of the terms of the deal was inadequate because he had not reviewed the merger documents and was basically uninformed as to the essential terms. (Indeed, he had signed the merger agreement at the opening of the Chicago Lyric Opera without first reading it.) Romans's report on price was inadequate because it was not a valuation study, just a cash flow–cash feasibility study.

The court also held that the mere fact that a substantial premium over the market price was being offered did not justify board approval of the merger. A premium may be one reason to approve a merger, but sound information as to the company's intrinsic value is required to assess the fairness of an offer. In this case, there was no attempt to determine the company's intrinsic value.

RESULT The Delaware Supreme Court held that the Trans Union directors were grossly negligent in making an uninformed decision regarding the proposed merger agreement. Their decision was not protected by the business judgment rule. The case was remanded to the Delaware Court of Chancery for an evidentiary hearing to determine the fair value of the shares based on Trans Union's intrinsic value on September 20, 1980, the day of the board's meeting at which the Pritzker offer was considered. If the chancellor found that value to be higher than $55 per share, the directors would be liable for the difference.

(Continued)

(Case 23.1 continued)

COMMENTS The case was settled for $23.5 million—$13.5 million in excess of the directors' liability insurance coverage. Although the purchasers, the Pritzker family, ultimately paid the amount by which the settlement exceeded the directors' coverage, they were not legally obligated to do so.

Smith v. Van Gorkom was one of the most highly debated corporate law cases ever decided. Three years after the decision, one of the key defendants—Trans Union's CEO, Jerome W. Van Gorkom—wrote an article giving the defendants' side of the story. The article makes it clear that the defendants and the Delaware Supreme Court had very different views about what the directors actually did and what their options really were.

In his article, Van Gorkom stated that at the September 20 meeting:

The directors, all broadly experienced executives, realized that an all-cash offer with a premium of almost 50 percent represented an unusual opportunity for the shareholders. They also knew, however, that $55 might not be the highest price obtainable. At the meeting, therefore, there was considerable discussion about seeking an outside "fairness opinion" that might shed further light on the ultimate value of the company.[2]

Furthermore, Van Gorkom explained that:

Acceptance of the offer was not a decision by the directors that the company should be sold for $55 a share. The acceptance was the only mechanism by which the offer could be preserved for the shareholders. *They* would make the ultimate decision as to the fairness of the price and they would do so only after the free market had had ample time in which to determine if $55 was the top value obtainable. The market's opinion would be definitive and worth infinitely more to the shareholders than any theoretical evaluation opinion that the directors could obtain in 39 hours or even longer. On this reasoning the offer was accepted.

Following the meeting, the Trans Union directors hired Salomon Brothers to conduct an intensive search for a higher bidder. In addition, Van Gorkom stated that once the $55 offer became a matter of public knowledge, an auction occurred in the market with Trans Union's stock sometimes selling above $56 on the New York Stock Exchange. After three months of the intensive search and the public auction, no higher bid was ever received. "[T]he market had proven beyond a shadow of a doubt that $55 was the highest price obtainable."

Van Gorkom believed that he and the other Trans Union directors wholeheartedly fulfilled their fiduciary obligations. He concluded that their actions clearly should have been protected under the business judgment rule.

Reliability of Officers' Reports As underscored by *Van Gorkom,* not every statement of an officer can be relied on in good faith, and no statement is entitled to blind reliance. The passivity of the Trans Union directors in *Van Gorkom* unquestionably influenced the court's finding of gross negligence. When the chief financial officer, Romans, told the board that the $55 figure was within a "fair price range" for a leveraged buyout,

no director sought any further information from Romans. No director asked him why he put $55 at the bottom of his range. No director asked Romans for any details as to his study, the reason why it had been undertaken or its depth. No director asked to see the study; and no director asked Romans whether Trans Union's finance department could do a fairness study within the remaining 36-hour period available under the Pritzker offer. . . . [If he had been asked,] Romans would have presumably . . . informed the Board of his view, and the widespread view of Senior Management, that the timing of the offer was wrong and the offer inadequate.[3]

When the CEO, Van Gorkom, told the board that $55 per share was fair, no questions were asked.

The Board thereby failed to discover that Van Gorkom had suggested the $55 price to [the bidder] Pritzker and, most crucially, that Van Gorkom had arrived at the $55 figure based on calculations designed solely to determine the feasibility of a leveraged buy-out. No questions were raised either as to the tax implications of a cash-out merger or how the price for the one million share option granted Pritzker was calculated.[4]

---

2. J. W. Van Gorkom, *Van Gorkom's Response: The Defendant's Side of the Trans Union Case,* reprinted in Mergers & Acquisitions, Jan.–Feb. 1988. Excerpts reprinted by permission.

3. Smith v. Van Gorkom, 488 A.2d 858, 876 (Del. 1985).

4. *Id.*

Reliability of Experts' Reports Two principles regarding the use of experts' reports emerge from the cases. First, a board should engage a reputable investment banking firm, aided if necessary by an outside appraiser, (1) to prepare a valuation study and (2) to give a written opinion as to the financial fairness of the transaction and of any related purchase of assets or options.

Second, directors have a duty to pursue reasonable inquiry and to exercise reasonable oversight in connection with their engagement of investment bankers and other advisers. A conclusory fairness opinion (that is, an opinion that merely states a conclusion without giving the factual grounds for that conclusion) of an investment banker, however expert, is not a sufficient basis for a board decision, particularly if the investment banker's conclusion is questionable in light of other information known to the directors. As the directors of SCM Corporation learned in *Hanson Trust PLC v. ML SCM Acquisition, Inc.*,[5] an expert's opinion must be in writing and be reasoned.

SCM was the subject of a hostile tender offer by a British conglomerate, Hanson Trust PLC. SCM's board negotiated a friendly management leveraged buyout led by "white knight" Merrill Lynch. As part of this agreement, SCM granted Merrill Lynch an *asset lock-up option* to purchase two divisions of SCM, considered to be SCM's key assets or *crown jewels*. The option would be exercisable if Merrill Lynch was not successful in acquiring control of SCM. A lock-up option is a kind of consolation prize for the loser in a bidding war; depending on how it is priced, a lock-up option can have the effect of deterring other bids. Merrill Lynch represented in negotiations that it would not proceed with its leveraged buyout offer without the lock-up.

5. 781 F.2d 264 (2d Cir. 1986).

SCM's investment banker, Goldman Sachs, issued a written fairness opinion on the overall deal, stating that the sale of SCM to Merrill Lynch was fair to the shareholders of SCM from a financial point of view. A partner at Goldman Sachs also orally advised SCM's directors that the option prices were "within the range of fair value." However, the directors did not inquire what the range of fair value was or how it was calculated. Unfortunately for the directors, the banker had not in fact calculated the fair value of the two divisions. Although the directors knew that the two divisions generated more than two-thirds of SCM's earnings, they never asked the investment banker why the divisions were being sold for less than half the total purchase price. The U.S. Court of Appeals for the Second Circuit held that the SCM directors' "paucity of information" and "their swiftness of decision-making" strongly suggested a breach of the duty of care. The asset lock-up was struck down. As in the case of officers' reports, blind reliance on the reports of experts creates a risk that the directors will not receive the protection of the business judgment rule.

REASONABLE SUPERVISION

As fiduciaries, directors have a responsibility to exercise reasonable supervision over corporate operations. Because the prescribed role of the corporate director is to establish broad policies and then rely on managers to implement them, the question of what constitutes reasonable supervision is necessarily one of degree. The outcome in reasonable supervision cases depends heavily on particular facts. The Delaware Court of Chancery refined and clarified the reasonable supervision doctrine in the following case.

A CASE IN POINT

CASE 23.2

In re **Caremark International Derivative Litigation**
Court of Chancery
of Delaware
698 A.2d 959
(Del. Ch. 1996).

Summary

FACTS After the Department of Health and Human Services and the Department of Justice conducted an extensive four-year investigation of alleged violations by Caremark employees of federal and state laws and regulations applicable to health care providers, Caremark was charged with multiple felonies. It thereafter entered into a number of plea agreements in which it agreed to pay civil and criminal fines and to make payments to various private and public parties. In all, Caremark agreed to pay approximately $250 million.

A shareholder derivative suit was filed in 1994, in which the plaintiff initially sought to recover these losses from the individual members of the Caremark board of directors. The complaint charged that the directors had allowed a situation to develop and continue that exposed the corporation to enormous legal liability and, in so doing, had violated a duty to be active monitors of corporate performance. The complaint did not charge either director with self-dealing or the breach of the duty of loyalty. The parties sought court approval of a proposed settlement that included no payment by individual

(Continued)

(Case 23.2 continued)

board members but outlined a series of procedures the company would implement to promote future compliance with applicable laws and regulations.

ISSUE PRESENTED What is the scope of a director's duty to exercise reasonable supervision over corporate operations?

SUMMARY OF OPINION The Delaware Chancery Court began by noting that director liability for a breach of the duty to exercise appropriate attention may, in theory, arise in two distinct contexts. First, such liability may follow from a board decision that results in a loss because that decision was ill advised or negligent. Second, liability may arise from an unconsidered failure of the board to act in circumstances in which due attention would, arguably, have prevented a loss to the corporation.

Most of the decisions that a corporation, acting through its human agents, makes are not the subject of director attention. Legally, the board itself will be required only to authorize the most significant corporate acts or transactions: mergers, changes in capital structure, fundamental changes in business, appointment and compensation of the CEO, and the like. However, ordinary business decisions that are made by officers and employees deeper in the interior of the organization can vitally affect the welfare of the corporation and its ability to achieve its various strategic and financial goals. This raises the question: What is the board's responsibility with respect to the organization and monitoring of the enterprise to ensure that the corporation functions within the law to achieve its purposes?

The court noted an increasing tendency, especially under federal law, to employ the criminal law to ensure corporate compliance with external legal requirements, including environmental, financial, employee, and product safety, as well as assorted other health and safety regulations. The federal Organizational Sentencing Guidelines offer powerful incentives for corporations to have in place compliance programs to detect violations of law, to promptly report violations to appropriate public officials when discovered, and to take prompt, voluntary remedial efforts.

In light of these developments, the court held that directors cannot satisfy their obligation to be reasonably informed concerning the corporation unless they assure themselves that appropriate information and reporting systems exist in the organization. These systems must be reasonably designed to provide to senior management and to the board itself timely and accurate information sufficient to allow management and the board to reach informed judgments concerning both the corporation's compliance with law and its business performance.

The level of detail that is appropriate for such an information system is a question of business judgment. The court acknowledged that no rationally designed information and reporting system will remove the possibility that the corporation will violate laws or regulations. But the board is required to exercise a good faith judgment that the corporation's information and reporting system is in concept and design adequate to assure the board that appropriate information will come to its attention in a timely manner as a matter of ordinary operations, so that it may satisfy its responsibility.

Thus, the court ruled that a director's obligation includes a duty to attempt in good faith to ensure that there is a corporate information and reporting system that the board concludes is adequate. Failure to do so under certain circumstances may, in theory at least, render a director liable for losses caused by noncompliance with applicable legal standards.

RESULT The court concluded that the settlement was fair and reasonable and, therefore, approved it.

COMMENTS The court noted that if the shareholders are not satisfied with the informed good faith judgment of the directors, their recourse is to elect different directors.

In 1997, the Securities and Exchange Commission (SEC) issued a release emphasizing the affirmative responsibility of officers and directors under the federal securities laws to ensure the accuracy and completeness of public company filings with the SEC, such as annual and quarterly reports and proxy statements.[6] They are required to conduct a full and informed review of the information contained in the final draft of the filings. If an officer or director knows or should have known about an inaccuracy in a proposed filing, he or she has an obligation to correct it. An officer or director may rely on the company's procedures for determining what disclosure is required only if he or she has a reasonable basis for believing that those procedures are effective and have resulted in full consideration of those issues.

If a director or officer is aware of facts that might have to be disclosed, he or she must go beyond the established procedures to inquire into the reasons for nondisclosure. Officers and directors cannot blindly rely on legal counsel's conclusions about the need for disclosure if they are aware of facts that seem to suggest that disclosure is required. They must then discuss the issue specifically with disclosure counsel, telling counsel ex-

actly what they know and asking specifically whether disclosure is required. If they are not satisfied with the answers provided, they should insist that the documents be revised before they are filed with the SEC.

DISINTERESTED DECISION

Even when the board makes an informed decision, the business judgment rule is not applicable if the directors have a financial or other personal interest in the transaction at issue. For example, if a board of inside directors (that is, directors who are also officers of the corporation) sets executive compensation, they can be required to prove to a court that the transaction was fair and reasonable. To be disinterested in the transaction normally means that the directors can neither have an interest on either side of the transaction nor expect to derive any personal financial benefit from the transaction (other than benefits that accrue to all shareholders of the corporation, which are not considered self-dealing).

Even if one or more individual directors have an interest in the transaction, the board's decision may still be entitled to the protection of the business judgment rule if the transaction is approved by a majority of the disinterested directors. However, if the board delegates too much of its authority or is too much influenced by an interested party, then the entire board may be tainted with

6. Report of Investigation Pursuant to Section 21(a) of the Securities Exchange Act of 1934 concerning the Conduct of Certain Former Officers and Directors of W.R. Grace & Co., Exchange Act Release No. 39,157 (Sept. 30, 1997).

VIEW FROM CYBERSPACE

Shareholder Meetings *in* Cyberspace

On July 1, 2000, a number of amendments to the Delaware General Corporation Law that were designed to permit corporations to take advantage of evolving technology went into effect. Section 228(d), for example, permits a shareholder's written consent to be effected by electronic transmission (including e-mail), facsimile (fax), or other reliable methods of reproducing a consent. Section 212(c) already authorized electronic transmission of proxies and the use of copies and faxes. New Section 232 permits the electronic delivery of notice to a shareholder if the shareholder has consented to delivery of notice in such form. A revamped Section 211(a) gives directors the power to authorize shareholders who are not physi-

cally present at a meeting to participate by means of remote communication, such as a conference call. Indeed, directors are given sole discretion to hold shareholder meetings either partially or totally by remote communication, without any physical location.

Amendments to Section 141 permit director action by unanimous consent

that is effected by electronic transmission; previously, consent had to be in writing. Although the drafters considered authorizing board meetings by remote communication, it was determined that "considerations of collegiality precluded 'chat room' or similar formats, and that the current practice of holding meetings by telephone conference calls provided sufficient flexibility."[a]

a. Frederick H. Alexander, *Amendments to Delaware Corporation Law Allow for Evolving Technology*, 69 U.S.L.W. 2051, 2052 (Aug. 1, 2000).

that individual's personal motivations and lose the protection of the business judgment rule.

In some jurisdictions, a relevant factor in determining whether a board is disinterested is whether the majority of the board consists of outside directors. The fact that outside directors receive directors' fees but not salaries is viewed as heightening the likelihood that the directors were not motivated by personal interest. Application of these rules in the context of takeovers, mergers, and acquisitions is discussed later in this chapter.

DISCLOSURE VIOLATIONS

When requesting shareholder action, directors have a duty to disclose all material facts. In *Malone v. Brincat,*[7] the Delaware Supreme Court went a step further and held that whenever directors disseminate information to shareholders, the fiduciary duties of care, loyalty, and good faith apply, even if no shareholder action is sought. As a result, the court held that "directors who knowingly disseminate false information that results in corporate injury or damage to an individual stockholder violate their fiduciary duty, and may be held accountable in a manner appropriate to the circumstances."

 ## Statutory Limitations *on* Directors' Liability *for* Breach *of* Duty *of* Care

Cases such as *Van Gorkom* significantly increased the cost of directors' and officers' liability insurance and had a devastating impact on the availability of qualified outside directors. In response, Delaware adopted legislation in 1986 to allow shareholders to limit the monetary liability of directors for breaches of the duty of care in any suit brought by the corporation or in a *shareholder derivative suit,* that is, a suit by a shareholder on behalf of the corporation. Most other states followed suit. Most statutes require that the limitation be contained in the original articles of incorporation or in an amendment approved by a majority of the shareholders.

The statutes do not affect directors' liability for suits brought by third parties; they merely allow the shareholders to agree that, under certain circumstances, they will not seek monetary recovery against the directors. The directors' liability for breach of the duty of loyalty may not be limited. Also, most states do not allow offi-

cers to be exonerated from liability for breach of the duty of care or the duty of loyalty.

DELAWARE'S STATUTE

Section 102(b)(7) of the Delaware General Corporation Law permits the certificate of incorporation to include a provision limiting or eliminating the personal liability of directors to the corporation or to its shareholders for monetary damages for breach of fiduciary duty. (Delaware law is especially relevant because many large public companies are incorporated there.) Such a provision cannot, however, eliminate or limit the liability of a director for (1) any breach of the director's duty of loyalty to the corporation or its shareholders, (2) acts or omissions that are not in good faith or that involve intentional misconduct or knowing violation of law, (3) unlawful payments of dividends or stock purchases, or (4) any transaction from which the director derived an improper personal benefit.

CALIFORNIA'S STATUTE

Section 204(a)(10) of the California Corporation Code, which applies to corporations organized under California law, is more restrictive. In addition to the four exceptions in the Delaware statute, California prohibits elimination or limitation of director liability for (1) acts or omissions that show a reckless disregard for the director's duty to the corporation or its shareholders in circumstances in which the director was aware, or should have been aware, of a risk of serious injury to the corporation or its shareholders; and (2) an unexcused pattern of inattention that amounts to an abdication of the director's duties to the corporation or its shareholders.

Although other states apply their corporate governance rules only to corporations incorporated there, California imposes its pro-shareholder provisions on so-called privately held *quasi-foreign corporations,* that is, corporations incorporated elsewhere with (1) more than 50 percent of their stock owned by California residents and (2) more than 50 percent of their sales, payroll, and property tax derived from activities in California. As a result, a quasi-foreign corporation will be subject to California's more restrictive limits on monetary liability even though the state of incorporation (such as Delaware) is more permissive.

 ## Duty *of* Loyalty

To comply with their duty of loyalty, directors and managers must subordinate their own interests to those of the corporation and its shareholders. As a result, when a

7. 722 A.2d 5 (Del. 1998).

shareholder attacks a transaction in which managers or directors are engaged in self-dealing or have a self-interest other than that of corporate fiduciaries, courts will closely review the merits of the deal. Traditionally, such a transaction has been voidable unless its proponents could show that it was fair and reasonable to the corporation.

CORPORATE OPPORTUNITIES

One central corollary of the fiduciary duty of loyalty is that officers and directors may not take personal advantage of a business opportunity that rightfully belongs to the corporation. This is known as the *corporate opportunity doctrine*. For example, suppose that a copper-mining corporation is actively looking for mining sites. If an officer of the corporation learns of an attractive site in the course of his or her business for the corporation, the officer may not buy it for himself or herself. If the officer attempts to do so, a shareholder can block the sale or impose a *constructive trust* on any profits the officer makes from the acquisition, that is, force the officer to hold such profits for the benefit of the corporation and pay them over to it on request.

The courts have devised several tests for determining whether an opportunity belongs to a corporation. Perhaps the most widely used is the *line-of-business test*. Under this test, if an officer, director, or controlling shareholder learns of an opportunity in the course of his or her business for the corporation and the opportunity is in the corporation's line of business, a court will not permit the officer, director, or controlling shareholder to keep the opportunity for himself or herself.

For example, the Delaware Supreme Court ruled that the president and director of Loft, Inc., a company engaged in the manufacturing of candies, syrups, beverages, and foodstuffs, could not set up a new corporation to acquire the secret formula and trademarks of Pepsi Cola.[8] He had unsuccessfully sought a volume discount for Loft's purchases of syrup from Coca-Cola Company and was contemplating substituting Pepsi for Coke.

If the officer or director develops an idea on company time using company resources, then a court will be more likely to find a breach of fiduciary duty if the officer or director then leaves to pursue the idea. If the officer or director has signed an assignment of inventions, then the idea usually will belong to the company under the terms of that agreement. Even without such an agreement, use of company time or resources may restrict the ability of the officer or director to define the line of business narrowly.

For example, the Georgia Court of Appeals estopped three ex-officers of the Atlanta-based commuter airline Metro Express, who had left to form a company offering commuter services in Memphis, from claiming that Metro Express was incorporated solely to provide services from the Atlanta hub and was therefore not interested in the Memphis route.[9] They had developed the idea on company time and using company resources.

Other courts have considered whether (1) it would be fair for the fiduciary to keep the opportunity, (2) the corporation has an expectancy or interest growing out of an existing right in the opportunity, or (3) the interference by the fiduciary will hinder the corporation's purposes. Because different states apply different tests, it is important for a corporate fiduciary to consult local counsel if there is any question of the fiduciary's actions interfering with a corporate opportunity.

An officer or director presented with a corporate opportunity is expected to disclose it to disinterested directors, who then may accept or reject the opportunity. The adequate disclosure of a corporate opportunity will provide defendants with a safe harbor from liability for breach of fiduciary duty.

The Delaware Supreme Court held that corporate officers and directors who usurp a corporate opportunity must disgorge to the corporation any gains obtained through their breach of loyalty, even though they, acting in their capacity as controlling shareholders, could have prevented the corporation from taking advantage of the opportunity. In *Thorpe v. CERBCO, Inc.*,[10] two brothers were officers, directors, and controlling shareholders of CERBCO. When a potential acquirer brought up the possibility of buying one of CERBCO's subsidiaries, the brothers instead proposed to sell their own shares to the acquirer. Because the brothers (in their capacity as shareholders) could have blocked every viable sale of the subsidiary, CERBCO was not in fact able to take advantage of the opportunity. Thus, CERBCO suffered no damages as a result of this lost opportunity because there was zero probability of the sale occurring (due to the brothers' lawful right to vote against it). Nevertheless, the brothers were fiduciaries of CERBCO and, as such, had the duty to present the sale opportunity to CERBCO. The court held that the brothers were not entitled to the profit gained by their breach of this duty. As a result, they were not entitled to keep the profit they had made on the sale of their stock to the potential acquirer of CERBCO's subsidiary.

---

8. Guth v. Loft, Inc., 5 A.2d 503 (Del. 1939).

9. Phoenix Airline Servs., Inc. v. Metro Airlines, Inc., 403 S.E.2d 832 (Ga. Ct. App. 1991).
10. 703 A.2d 645 (Del. 1997).

Executive Compensation

One of the most controversial issues in corporate governance today is the high level of executive compensation, which can add up to tens or hundreds of millions of dollars for chief executive officers with a substantial number of stock options. In the period from 1990 to 1999, CEO pay increased by more than 500 percent while the average worker's pay increased by only 80 percent. Institutional investors stress the need for pay for performance. This is often achieved with stock options, which are usually exercisable at the market price at the time of grant for up to ten years.

Options are designed to align the incentives of management and shareholders—if the stock price goes up, the executive can exercise the option and sell his or her stock at a premium over the exercise price. In a rising stock market, however, such as the bull market in the mid-to-late-1990s, an executive could be rewarded not for company-specific performance but simply because the broader market had gone up—the rising-tide-lifts-all-boats phenomenon.

Worse yet, sometimes the company's stock price goes down and drops below the exercise price; so the board agrees to reprice the options, making them exercisable at the lower price. With repricing, the executive can earn additional compensation even though all the shareholders have lost money. Under rules adopted by the Financial Accounting Standards Board in the late 1990s, corporations that reprice are subject to adverse accounting treatment, but repricing is not prohibited.

To date, the SEC and institutional investors have sought to address the issue of executive compensation through (1) disclosure of executive compensation and company performance compared to its peer group to shareholders in the proxy statement for the election of directors, (2) the establishment of compensation committees consisting solely of independent directors, (3) shareholder proposals to prohibit repricing of options, and (4) the adoption of other measures designed to improve corporate governance.[11] Other popular proposals include separating the roles of CEO and chair (or appointing an independent director as lead director)[12] and having a majority of the board be independent of management.

11. *See, e.g., The California Public Employees Retirement System Principles of Corporate Governance for U.S. Companies,* available at <http://www.calpers.ca.gov/site/invest.htm#CORPORATE>.
12. *See, e.g.,* Constance E. Bagley & Richard H. Koppes, *Leader of the Pack: A Proposal for Disclosure of Board Leadership Structure,* 34 SAN DIEGO L. REV. 149 (1997).

As this chapter's "Inside Story" dealing with Walt Disney Company explains, however, sometimes a company does very well and rewards its shareholders with a high stock price even though executive compensation is very high and the board is not very independent. This raises the proverbial "If it ain't broke, don't fix it." To which institutional investors respond, it may not be broken yet, but it will break in the future, with often disastrous results, unless a proper governance structure is put in place before there is a crisis (such as the death of the CEO with no clear succession plan for training and selecting his or her successor).

 # Duties *in the* Context *of* Takeovers, Mergers, *and* Acquisitions

In deciding whether to sell a company, directors should consider seven key factors: (1) the company's intrinsic value, (2) nonprice considerations, (3) the reliability of officers' reports to the board, (4) the appropriateness of delegating negotiating authority to management, (5) the reliability of experts' reports, (6) the investment banker's fee structure, and (7) the reasonableness of any defensive

 INTERNATIONAL CONSIDERATION

It is quite common for the CEOs of publicly traded companies in the United States to be granted *golden parachutes,* lucrative severance payments or stock awards made in the event the CEO loses control of the company due to a takeover or other change of control. Golden parachutes arrived in Germany on February 4, 2000, when the supervisory board of Mannesmann granted a $16.04 million "appreciation award" to CEO Klaus Esser in connection with the takeover of Mannesmann AG by Vodafone AirTouch PLC.[a] The CEOs of several French companies (including Philippe Jaffre of Elf Aquitaine and Andre Levy-Lang of Paribas) had already received severance payments ranging between 100 million and 250 million francs. Because the German Stock Corporation Act requires compensation to a member of the management board to be reasonable, supervisory boards in Germany can be expected to be reluctant to grant golden parachutes in advance of an agreement to sell the company.[b]

a. *See* Anita Raghavan & G. Thomas Sims, *'Golden Parachutes' Emerge in European Deals,* WALL ST. J., Feb. 14, 2000, at A17.
b. *Id.*

tactics. As explained earlier, the directors must act in good faith and be adequately informed.

THE COMPANY'S INTRINSIC VALUE

The ability to make an informed decision as to the acceptability of a proposed buyout price requires knowledge of the company's intrinsic value. Determining intrinsic value entails more than an assessment of the premium of the offering price over the market price per share of the company's stock. When, as in *Van Gorkom*, it is believed that the market has consistently undervalued the company's stock, evaluating the offered price by comparing it with the market price is, according to the Delaware Supreme Court, "faulty, indeed fallacious."

Thus, the directors must do more than assess the adequacy of the premium and compare it with those paid in other takeovers in the same or similar industries. They must also assess the intrinsic or fair value of the company (or division) as a going concern and on a liquidation basis.

Practitioners have read *Van Gorkom* as virtually mandating participation by an investment banker if directors are to avoid personal liability. However, the *Van Gorkom* court expressly disclaimed such an intention:

> We do not imply that an outside valuation study is essential to support an informed business judgment; nor do we state that fairness opinions by independent investment bankers are required as a matter of law. Often insiders familiar with the business of a going concern are in a better position than are outsiders to gather relevant information; and under appropriate circumstances, such directors may be fully protected in relying in good faith upon the valuation reports of their management.[13]

For all practical purposes, however, directors should look to both internal and external sources for guidance. The most reliable valuation information will consist of financial data supplied by management and evaluated by investment bankers knowledgeable about the industry and recent merger and acquisition activity.

The *Hanson Trust* decision makes it clear, however, that the mere presence of investment bankers in the target's boardroom will not shield its directors from personal liability. In that case, the Goldman Sachs partner's oral opinion that the option prices were "within the range of fair value" did not withstand the scrutiny of the Second Circuit on appeal.

DELEGATION OF NEGOTIATING AUTHORITY

If members of management are financial participants in the proposed transaction, the delegation of negotiation responsibilities to management or inside directors will expose the board to greater risks of liability. The Second Circuit observed in *Hanson Trust:*

> SCM's board delegated to management broad authority to work directly with Merrill to structure an LBO proposal, and then appears to have swiftly approved management's proposals. Such broad delegations of authority are not uncommon and generally are quite proper as conforming to the way that a Board acts in generating proposals for its own consideration. However, when management has a self-interest in consummating an LBO, standard post hoc review procedures may be insufficient. SCM's management and the Board's advisers presented the various agreements to the SCM directors more or less as faits accompli, which the Board quite hastily approved. In short, the Board appears to have failed to ensure that negotiations for alternative bids were conducted by those whose only loyalty was to the shareholders.[14]

NONPRICE CONSIDERATIONS

In evaluating a buyout proposal, directors have a fiduciary duty to familiarize themselves with any material nonprice provisions of the proposed agreement. Directors are duty bound to consider separately whether such provisions are in the best interest of the company and its shareholders or, if not, whether the proposal as a whole, notwithstanding such provisions, is in the best interest of their constituencies.

In *Van Gorkom*, for example, several outside directors maintained that Pritzker's merger proposal was approved with the understanding that "if we got a better deal, we had a right to take it." The directors also asserted that they had "insisted" upon an amendment reserving to Trans Union the right to disclose proprietary information to competing bidders. However, the court found that the merger agreement reserved neither of these rights to Trans Union. In the court's view, the directors had "no rational basis" for asserting that their acceptance of Pritzker's offer was conditioned upon a market test of the offer or that Trans Union had a right to withdraw from the agreement in order to accept a higher bid.

Directors should therefore ensure not only that they correctly understand the nonprice provisions of a pro-

13. Smith v. Van Gorkom, 488 A.2d 858, 876 (Del. 1985) (Case 23.1).

14. Hanson Trust PLC v. ML SCM Acquisition, Inc., 781 F.2d 264, 277 (2d Cir. 1986).

posed merger agreement but also that the provisions find their way into the definitive agreement. They should verify this by reading the documents prior to execution.

No-Talk Provisions Delaware courts are highly skeptical of agreements that purport to limit directors' ability to fulfill what they in good faith perceive their fiduciary duties to be. For example, the Court of Chancery refused to enforce a no-solicitation clause in a stock-for-stock merger agreement between Capital Re Corporation and Ace Limited. The clause permitted Capital Re Corporation to engage in discussions with and provide information to other bidders only if the board concluded, based on the written opinion of outside legal counsel, that engaging in discussions or providing information was required to prevent the board from breaching its fiduciary duties to its stockholders.[15] Although Capital Re's counsel opined that negotiating with other bidders was consistent with the board's fiduciary duties, counsel did not state that the board was *required* to discuss an offer by another bidder. The court indicated that a provision that purports to prevent a board from talking with other bidders even if the directors determine that they have a fiduciary duty to do so is "particularly suspect when a failure to consider other offers guarantees the consummation of the original transaction, however more valuable an alternate transaction may be and however less valuable the original transaction might have become since the merger agreement was signed."

The court did suggest that a no-solicitation clause with no *fiduciary out* (a clause permitting the board of directors to negotiate with other bidders or to terminate the merger agreement) might be permissible if (1) the shareholders could freely vote for or against the existing merger agreement and choose among the present merger, a subsequent merger, or no merger at all; or (2) the board agreed to the provision as a way to end an auction for sale of the company after a thorough canvass of the market. While acknowledging the tension between a vested contract right and the board's duty to determine what its own fiduciary duties require, the court concluded that a contract right must give way when (1) "the acquirer knew, or should have known, of the target board's breach of fiduciary duty"; (2) the "transaction remains pending"; and (3) "the board's violation of fiduciary duty relates to policy concerns that are especially significant."

Breakup Fees In exchange for providing a fiduciary out, a bidder will usually demand that it be paid some prede-

termined amount of money if the deal fails to close because the target terminates the agreement. *Termination* or *breakup fees* are sometimes characterized as liquidated damages provisions, and they are often 2 to 3 percent of the value of the deal. They are usually intended to help make the bidder whole for its out-of-pocket expenses (for attorneys, investment bankers, and the like) and lost opportunity costs.

For example, in 2000, American Home Products Corporation was paid a termination fee of $1.8 billion when its merger partner Warner–Lambert Company walked away from their $72 billion deal and agreed to be acquired by Pfizer, Inc. In mergers of equals, where there is no clear buyer or seller, there are often reciprocal termination fee provisions. For example, the agreement for the $131.49 billion merger of America Online, Inc. and Time–Warner, Inc. provided that if AOL backed out of the deal under certain conditions, it would have to pay Time–Warner a $5.37 billion breakup fee (2.75 percent of AOL's market capitalization); if Time–Warner walked away, it would have to pay AOL $3.9 billion.[16] Although courts in Delaware and elsewhere have upheld termination fees in the 1 to 3 percent range under either the business judgment rule or the standard of reasonableness applied to liquidated damages provisions, fees that are so large as to constitute "show-stoppers" are much more likely to be struck down.[17]

TAKEOVER DEFENSES

The business judgment rule creates a powerful presumption in favor of actions taken by the directors of a corporation. As noted earlier, however, the business judgment rule does not apply if the directors have an interest in the transaction being acted upon. If a hostile raider is successful, it is probably going to replace the company's management and board of directors as its first step after assuming control. A successful defense against the takeover has the effect of preserving the positions of current management and directors. Thus, the directors arguably have a personal interest whenever a board opposes a hostile takeover.

Unocal Corp. v. Mesa Petroleum Co.[18] established the principle that the business judgment rule applies to

---

15. Ace Ltd. v. Capital Re Corp., 747 A.2d 95 (Del. Ch. 1999).

16. Nikhil Deogun & Nick Wingfield, *Stock Drops Spur Questions on AOL Deal*, WALL ST. J., Jan. 13, 2000, at A3.
17. For an interesting empirical analysis of deals involving breakup fees and other forms of lock-ups, see John C. Coates IV & Guhan Subramanian, *A Buy-Side Model of M&A Lockups: Theory and Evidence*, 53 STAN. L. REV. 307 (2000).
18. 493 A.2d 946 (Del. 1985).

INTERNATIONAL CONSIDERATION

The laws of Germany and several Scandinavian countries require union and employee representation on the boards of directors of most public corporations. These representatives participate in all of the basic decisions related to investment policy, choice of product and technology, marketing, employee relations, and other matters of managerial concern. When Germany's Daimler–Benz AG merged with Chrysler Corporation in 1998, the combined entity, DaimlerChrysler, was organized under German law. As required by Germany's codetermination laws, half of the members of the supervisory board were elected by the employees and union leaders; half were elected by the shareholders. Under Germany's two-tier board system, the supervisory board consists solely of non-employee directors, and it is often chaired by a representative of the corporation's main bank. The supervisory board appoints the management board, which consists solely of inside directors and reports to the supervisory board.[a]

a. Greg Steinmetz & Gregory L. White, *Chrysler Pay Draws Fire Overseas*, WALL ST. J., May 26, 1998, at B1, B4.

takeover defenses, provided that the directors can show that they had reasonable grounds for believing that the unwelcome suitor posed a threat to corporate policy and effectiveness and that the defense was a reasonable response to that threat. This enhanced judicial scrutiny is designed to guard against "the omnipresent specter that a board may be acting primarily in its own interests, rather than those of the corporation and its shareholders."

The Delaware Supreme Court further explained:

If a defensive measure is to come within the ambit of the business judgment rule, it must be reasonable in relation to the threat posed. This entails an analysis by the directors of the nature of the takeover bid and its effect on the corporate enterprise. Examples of such concerns may include: inadequacy of the price offered, nature and timing of the offer, questions of illegality, the impact on "constituencies" other than shareholders (that is, creditors, customers, employees, and perhaps even the community generally), the risk of nonconsummation, and the quality of securities being offered in the exchange. While not a controlling factor, it also seems to us that a board may reasonably consider the basic stockholder interests at stake, including those of short term speculators, whose actions may have fueled the coercive aspect of the offer at the expense of the long term investor.

If the directors succeed in making this initial showing, then they are entitled to the protection of the business judgment rule. Under those circumstances, the Delaware Supreme Court stated:

[U]nless it is shown by a preponderance of the evidence that the directors' decisions were primarily based on perpetuating themselves in office, or some other breach of fiduciary duty such as fraud, overreaching, lack of good faith, or being uninformed, a court will not substitute its judgment for that of the board.

Applying these standards to the hostile bid for Unocal by Mesa Petroleum and its CEO, T. Boone Pickens, the court upheld a discriminatory self-tender by Unocal for its own stock, whereby all of the shareholders, except Mesa Petroleum, Pickens, and their affiliates, could exchange their Unocal stock for debt securities worth $18 per share more than the $54 per share offered by Pickens in the first stage of his two-tier front-loaded tender offer. Pickens's offer was deemed coercive because he was acquiring just enough shares in the first stage to get control. Hence, even if shareholders considered the price inadequate, they might well feel coerced into tendering in the first stage for fear of receiving securities of even less value in the second stage, when Unocal was merged with a Mesa-controlled corporation. The Unocal board viewed the threat as a grossly inadequate two-tier coercive tender offer coupled with the threat of greenmail. (*Greenmail* occurs when a raider acquires stock in a target company and then threatens to commence a hostile takeover unless the target repurchases its stock at a premium over the market price.)

The strategy used in *Unocal* is no longer available because of the SEC's "all holders rule." According to the rule, a selective stock repurchase plan is deemed a tender offer in which all holders of securities of the same class must be allowed to participate. Nonetheless, this case remains a key Delaware precedent for the analysis of defensive tactics, including shareholder rights plans (also called poison pills), which can have much the same effect as a discriminatory self-tender.

Once the judgment is made that a sale or breakup of the corporation is in the best interests of the shareholders or is inevitable, directors have a fiduciary duty to obtain the best available price for the shareholders. This rule was first articulated in a case involving a hostile takeover bid for Revlon, Inc. by Pantry Pride.[19]

After initially resisting the takeover attempt, the Revlon board elected to go forward with a friendly buyout from another company at a lower price than that offered by the

19. Revlon, Inc. v. MacAndrews & Forbes Holdings, Inc., 506 A.2d 173 (Del. 1986).

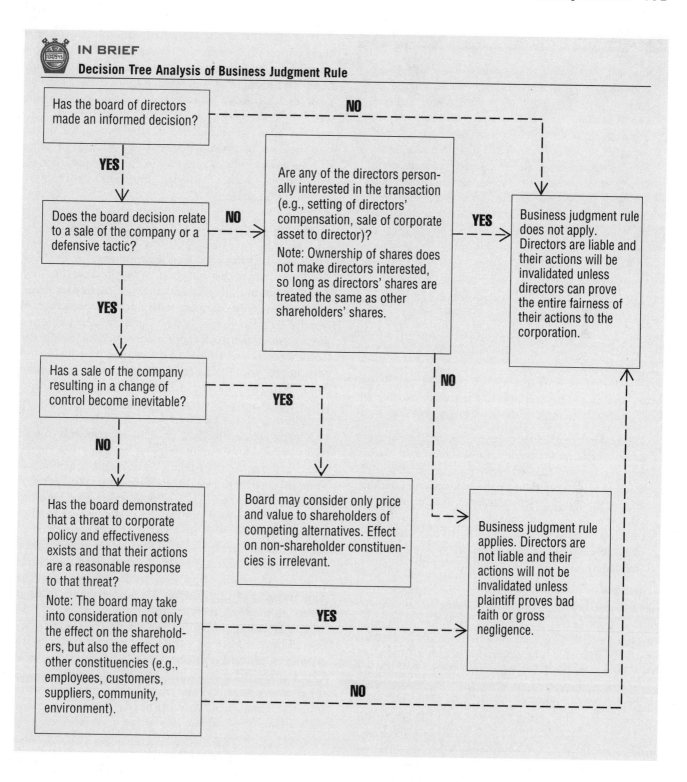

IN BRIEF

Decision Tree Analysis of Business Judgment Rule

Has the board of directors made an informed decision?

NO

YES

Does the board decision relate to a sale of the company or a defensive tactic?

NO

Are any of the directors personally interested in the transaction (e.g., setting of directors' compensation, sale of corporate asset to director)?

Note: Ownership of shares does not make directors interested, so long as directors' shares are treated the same as other shareholders' shares.

YES

Business judgment rule does not apply. Directors are liable and their actions will be invalidated unless directors can prove the entire fairness of their actions to the corporation.

YES

Has a sale of the company resulting in a change of control become inevitable?

YES

NO

NO

Board may consider only price and value to shareholders of competing alternatives. Effect on non-shareholder constituencies is irrelevant.

Has the board demonstrated that a threat to corporate policy and effectiveness exists and that their actions are a reasonable response to that threat?

Note: The board may take into consideration not only the effect on the shareholders, but also the effect on other constituencies (e.g., employees, customers, suppliers, community, environment).

YES

Business judgment rule applies. Directors are not liable and their actions will not be invalidated unless plaintiff proves bad faith or gross negligence.

NO

hostile bidder. The Revlon board sought to justify the lower price by pointing out the benefits of the friendly buyout for other corporate constituencies, such as the Revlon noteholders. The hostile bidder sued to enjoin the friendly buyout.

The Delaware Supreme Court required the Revlon board to seek the highest price for the shareholders. The court defined the duty of the directors as follows:

> The Revlon board's authorization permitting management to negotiate a merger or buyout with a third party was a recognition that the company was for sale. The duty of the board had thus changed from the preservation of Revlon as a corporate entity to the maximization of the company's value at a sale for the stockholders' benefit. . . . The directors' role changed from defenders of the corporate bastion to auctioneers charged with getting the best price for the stockholders at a sale of the company.

In *Barkan v. Amsted Industries,*[20] the Supreme Court of Delaware held that the basic teaching of cases such as *Revlon* is simply that directors of corporations must act in accordance with their fundamental duties of care and loyalty. The court ruled, however, that acting in accordance with these duties does not mean that every change of corporate control necessitates an auction. If fairness to shareholders and the minimizing of conflicts of interest can be demonstrated, the added burden of having an auction may not be necessary. The court in *Barkan* declined to make a specific rule for determining when a market test (or "market check") is required. The court simply stated: "[I]t must be clear that the board had sufficient knowledge of relevant markets to form the basis for its belief that it acted in the best interests of the shareholders."[21]

It is doubtful that a failure of directors to consider every conceivable alternative would in itself amount to a breach of fiduciary duty. Such a rule would be unduly harsh. In hindsight, a complaining shareholder could almost always conjure up at least one alternative that the directors failed to consider. On the other hand, the failure of a board to consider any alternatives at all, or the unwillingness of a board to negotiate with anyone other than its chosen white knight (or with the initial offeror), would be a breach of fiduciary duty unless there were special circumstances.

WHEN IS A COMPANY IN *REVLON* MODE?

The case of *Paramount Communications, Inc. v. Time, Inc.*[22] examined the question of what constitutes an event triggering the *Revlon* duty to maximize shareholder value. (A company with such an obligation is deemed to be in *Revlon mode*.) Time had entered into a friendly stock-for-stock merger agreement with Warner Communications. Under that agreement, roughly 60 percent of the stock of the new combined entity Time–Warner would be held by former public shareholders of Warner. The merger agreement was subject to the approval of Time's shareholders.

Shortly before the Time shareholder vote was to take place, Paramount Communications made a hostile, unsolicited cash tender offer for all Time shares. In response, Time proceeded with its own highly leveraged cash tender offer to acquire 51 percent of Warner, to be followed by a back-end, second-step merger of the two companies. This tender offer, which would preclude acceptance of the Paramount tender offer, did not require approval by the Time shareholders. Paramount challenged the actions of Time's directors in opposing its offer, arguing that the Time board had put Time in the *Revlon* mode when it agreed to the stock merger with Warner.

The Delaware Supreme Court held that this transaction did not trigger *Revlon* duties because there was no change in control. Majority control shifted from one "fluid aggregation of unaffiliated shareholders" to another and remained in the hands of the public. As a result, the Time board could properly take into account such intangibles as the desire to preserve the Time culture and journalistic integrity in deciding to reject Paramount's hostile tender offer, which was arguably worth more to shareholders than the Time–Warner combination. The court considered this to be a strategic alliance, not a sale of Time to Warner, which would have triggered the *Revlon* duty to maximize shareholder value.

20. 567 A.2d 1279 (Del. 1989).
21. *Id* at 1288.

22. 571 A.2d 1140 (Del. 1990).

Relying heavily on the precedent established by the *Time–Warner* case, Paramount entered into a friendly merger agreement with Viacom, Inc. in September 1993. When QVC Network, Inc. made a hostile unsolicited offer for Paramount at a price worth $1.3 billion more than what Viacom was offering, the Paramount board refused to negotiate with QVC and instead stood by its merger agreement with Viacom. In the following case, the Delaware Supreme Court examined the propriety of the Paramount board's action, especially in light of the fact that Viacom was controlled by a single individual, Sumner Redstone.

A CASE IN POINT

CASE 23.3

Paramount Communications, Inc. v. QVC Network, Inc.

Supreme Court of Delaware 637 A.2d 34 (Del. 1994).

In the Language of the Court

FACTS Beginning in the late 1980s, Paramount Communications, Inc., which owned and operated a diverse group of entertainment businesses, investigated the possibility of acquiring or merging with other companies in the entertainment, media, or communications industry. Paramount considered such transactions to be desirable, and perhaps necessary, in order to keep pace with competitors in the rapidly evolving field of entertainment and communications.

In April 1993, Martin Davis, chairman and CEO of Paramount, met with Sumner Redstone, CEO, chairman, and majority owner of Viacom, a communications company that owned MTV and Showtime Networks. After five months of discussions, they entered into a friendly merger agreement between Paramount and Viacom, along with other related agreements. Under these merger agreements, the Paramount shareholders would receive a combination of stock and cash that was then valued at $69.14 per share. In addition, Paramount amended its poison pill so that it would not be triggered by the Viacom deal.

Viacom and Paramount both made public statements to the effect that outside bids were unwelcome. However, in September 1993, QVC Network, Inc., the owner of a television shopping channel, proposed to Davis that QVC would offer cash and stock worth approximately $80 per share to acquire Paramount. In response to the hostile QVC offer, Viacom increased its bid to $80 cash per share at the front end, to be followed by a second-step stock-for-stock merger of equivalent value. In the next two months, QVC and Viacom each continued to enter competing bids. Paramount repeatedly rebuffed QVC, although QVC often submitted offers of higher value than those of Viacom.

QVC then sued the Paramount directors, arguing that the Paramount board had put Paramount in the *Revlon* mode when it committed to a transaction that would shift control of Paramount from the public shareholders to Redstone. The Delaware Court of Chancery agreed, and Paramount appealed the decision.

ISSUE PRESENTED Does a board of directors have an obligation to consider an unsolicited tender offer from one corporation when the board has expressed a desire not to receive competing bids because it is engaging in a friendly merger agreement with another corporation?

OPINION VEASEY, J., writing for the Delaware Supreme Court:

II. Applicable Principles of Established Delaware Law

...

A. The Significance of a Sale or Change of Control

...

In the case before us, the public stockholders (in the aggregate) currently own a majority of Paramount's voting stock. Control of the corporation is not vested in a

(Continued)

(Case 23.3 continued)

single person, entity, or group, but vested in the fluid aggregation of unaffiliated stockholders. In the event the Paramount–Viacom transaction is consummated, the public stockholders will receive cash and a minority equity voting position in the surviving corporation. Following such consummation, there will be a controlling stockholder. . . . Irrespective of the present Paramount Board's vision of a long-term strategic alliance with Viacom, the proposed sale of control would provide the new controlling stockholder with the power to alter that vision.

. . . Once control has shifted, the current Paramount stockholders will have no leverage in the future to demand another control premium.

...

C. Enhanced Judicial Scrutiny of a Sale or Change of Control Transaction

...

The key features of an enhanced scrutiny test are: (a) a judicial determination regarding the adequacy of the decisionmaking process employed by the directors, including the information on which the directors based their decision; and (b) a judicial examination of the reasonableness of the directors' action in light of the circumstances then existing. The directors have the burden of proving that they were adequately informed and acted reasonably.

...

. . . Accordingly, a court applying enhanced judicial scrutiny should be deciding whether the directors made a reasonable decision, not a perfect decision. . . .

D. *Revlon* and *Time–Warner* Distinguished

...

Under Delaware law there are, generally speaking and without excluding other possibilities, two circumstances which may implicate *Revlon* duties. The first, and clearer one, is when a corporation initiates an active bidding process seeking to sell itself or to effect a business reorganization involving a clear break-up of the company. However, *Revlon* duties may also be triggered where, in response to a bidder's offer, a target abandons its long-term strategy and seeks an alternative transaction involving the break-up of the company.

The Paramount defendants have misread the holding of *Time–Warner.* Contrary to their argument, our decision in *Time–Warner* expressly states that the two general scenarios discussed in the above-quoted paragraph are not the only instances where "*Revlon* duties" may be implicated. The Paramount defendants' argument totally ignores the phrase "without excluding other possibilities. . . ."

...

Accordingly, when a corporation undertakes a transaction which will cause: (a) a change in corporate control; or (b) a break-up of the corporate entity, the directors' obligation is to seek the best value reasonably available to the stockholders. This obligation arises because the effect of the Viacom–Paramount transaction, if consummated, is to shift control of Paramount from the public stockholders to a controlling stockholder, Viacom. Neither *Time–Warner* nor any other decision of this Court holds that a "break-up" of the company is essential to give rise to this obligation where there is a sale of control.

III. Breach of Fiduciary Duties by Paramount Board

...

(Continued)

(Case 23.3 continued)

A. The Specific Obligations of the Paramount Board

...

Since the Paramount directors had already decided to sell control, they had an obligation to continue their search for the best value reasonably available to the stockholders. This continuing obligation included the responsibility, at the October 24 board meeting and thereafter, to evaluate critically both the QVC tender offers and the Paramount–Viacom transaction to determine if: (a) the QVC tender offer was, or would continue to be, conditional; (b) the QVC tender offer could be improved; (c) the Viacom tender offer or other aspects of the Paramount–Viacom transaction could be improved; (d) each of the respective offers would be reasonably likely to come to closure, and under what circumstances; (e) other material information was reasonably available for consideration by the Paramount directors; (f) there were viable and realistic alternative courses of action; and (g) the timing constraints could be managed so the directors could consider these matters carefully and deliberately.

B. The Breaches of Fiduciary Duty by the Paramount Board

...

Throughout the applicable time period, and especially from the first QVC merger proposal on September 20 through the Paramount Board meeting on November 15, QVC's interest in Paramount provided the opportunity for the Paramount Board to seek significantly higher value for the Paramount stockholders than that being offered by Viacom. QVC persistently demonstrated its intention to meet and exceed the Viacom offers, and frequently expressed its willingness to negotiate possible further increases.

...

V. Conclusion

The realization of the best value reasonably available to the stockholders became the Paramount directors' primary obligation under these facts in light of the change of control. That obligation was not satisfied, and the Paramount Board's process was deficient. The directors' initial hope and expectation for a strategic alliance with Viacom was allowed to dominate their decisionmaking process to the point where the arsenal of defensive measures established at the outset was perpetuated (not modified or eliminated) when the situation was dramatically altered. QVC's unsolicited bid presented the opportunity for significantly greater value for the stockholders and enhanced negotiating leverage for the directors. Rather than seizing those opportunities, the Paramount directors chose to wall themselves off from material information which was reasonably available and to hide behind the defensive measures as a rationalization for refusing to negotiate with QVC or seeking other alternatives. Their view of the strategic alliance likewise became an empty rationalization as the opportunities for higher value for the stockholders continued to develop.

RESULT The Paramount board of directors, in order to fulfill its fiduciary duties to its shareholders, must entertain competing merger bids because the board had already agreed to a change in control in the attempted friendly merger deal with Viacom.

QUESTIONS

1. Why was it relevant that the acquiring company, Viacom, had such a large shareholder in Redstone?
2. Could Paramount and Viacom have structured their deal in a different way to avoid putting Paramount in *Revlon* mode?

In *In re Lukens, Inc. Shareholders Litigation*,[23] the Delaware Court of Chancery concluded that a merger of Lukens with Bethlehem Steel triggered *Revlon* duties even though more than 30 percent of the merger consideration consisted of shares of common stock of Bethlehem, a widely held company with no controlling stockholder. Because 62 percent of the consideration was cash, the court concluded that "for a substantial majority of the then-current shareholders, 'there is no long run.'"

⚓ Allocation *of* Power *between the* Directors *and the* Shareholders

A key issue that emerges from cases involving hostile takeovers and defensive tactics is who gets to decide whether the corporation should be sold—the board of directors or the shareholders. Theoretically, the board of directors is the guardian of the shareholders' interests, but the interests and obligations of the two groups sometimes conflict.

Frequently, a hostile takeover attempt presents such a conflict. Sometimes the proposed terms are attractive to the shareholders because the acquiring corporation offers to pay a substantial premium for their stock. The board of directors, however, may believe that the acquiring company's plans for the corporation are ultimately destructive, as in the case of a bust-up takeover, in which the acquired corporation is taken apart and its assets sold piecemeal. The directors may have legitimate concerns about the effect of such a takeover on the company's employees or on the community where the corporation is located. Or the directors might believe that the long-term value of the company is greater than the price being offered. Of course, directors might oppose a transaction just so they can remain on the corporation's board in violation of their legal obligation to put the corporation's interests before their own.

POISON PILLS

In one of the first cases addressing the allocation of power between the directors and the shareholders in deciding whether the corporation should be sold, a board of directors, without shareholder approval, had adopted a *poison pill* or *shareholder rights plan*, that is, a plan that would make any takeover not approved by the directors

prohibitively expensive.[24] In 1984, the directors of Household International, fearing that Household might be taken over and busted up, adopted a poison pill in the form of a Preferred Share Purchase Rights Plan. This plan provided that, under certain triggering circumstances, common shareholders would receive a "right" per every common share of Household. In the event of a merger in which Household was not the surviving corporation, the holder of each common share of Household would have the right to purchase $200 of the common stock of the acquiring company for only $100. If this right were triggered and exercised, it would dilute the value of the stock of the acquiring company, making a takeover prohibitively expensive for the acquirer.

The Delaware Supreme Court upheld the board's power to adopt the plan. The court found that the plan did not usurp the shareholders' ability to receive tender offers and to sell their shares to a bidder without board approval of the sale. Household's poison pill left "numerous methods to successfully launch a takeover." For example, a bidder could make a tender offer on the condition that the board redeem the rights, that is, buy them back for a nominal sum before they were triggered. A bidder could set a high minimum of shares and rights to be tendered; it could solicit consents to remove the board and replace it with one that would redeem the rights; or it could acquire 50 percent of the shares and cause Household to self-tender for the rights. In a self-tender, the company would agree to buy back the shareholders' rights for a fair price.

The court also found that the plan did not fundamentally restrict the shareholders' right to conduct a proxy contest. In a *proxy contest,* someone wishing to replace the board with his or her own candidates must acquire a sufficient number of shareholder votes to do so. Such votes are usually represented by *proxies,* or limited written powers of attorney entitling the proxy holder to vote the shares owned by the person giving the proxy. The court found that a proxy contest could be won with an insurgent ownership of less than 20 percent (the threshold for triggering distribution of the rights), and that the key to success in a proxy contest is the merit of the insurgent's arguments, not the size of his or her holdings.

The court concluded that the decision to adopt the poison-pill plan was within the board's authority. Moreover, because the directors "reasonably believed Household was vulnerable to coercive acquisition techniques and adopted a reasonable defensive mechanism to protect itself," the court held that the board had discharged

---

23. 757 A.2d 720 (Del. Ch. 1999), *aff'd*, 757 A.2d 1278 (Del. 2000).

24. Moran v. Household Int'l, Inc., 500 A.2d 1346 (Del. 1985).

its fiduciary duty appropriately under the business judgment rule. As of 2000, more than 2,300 poison-pill plans were in effect.

Although the Delaware Supreme Court upheld the adoption of a poison-pill plan in *Moran,* it reserved judgment on how such a plan would operate in practice. In particular, it left open the question of when directors must redeem the poison-pill rights to permit shareholders to tender their shares to a bidder.

The question of whether a board must redeem a pill is fact-specific—a court will look at all of the circumstances in making its decision. Certain factors will favor keeping the pill in place. These include (1) a tender offer that is only slightly above the market price of the stock; (2) a tender offer for less than all of the shares; (3) an active attempt by the board to solicit other offers; (4) a conscious effort by the board to allow its outside directors, deemed more disinterested, to make the decisions in this area; and (5) the fact that the tender offer is only in its early stages. The *Time–Warner* case made it clear that, under certain circumstances, a board faced with a hostile takeover bid can "Just Say No."

The Delaware Court of Chancery struck down a so-called dead-hand pill, which could be redeemed only by the directors in office before the hostile bidder gained control or their designated successors.[25] The court held that the dead-hand provision violated the requirement under Section 141 of the Delaware General Corporation Law that the directors manage the business and affairs of the corporation because it gave distinctive voting rights to one category of directors that were not shared by the other directors. Although the Delaware statute permits different directors to be given distinctive voting rights, those rights must be set forth in the certificate of incorporation, which was not the case here.

The court also held that the dead-hand feature violated the directors' duty of loyalty for two reasons. First, it failed to meet the more exacting *Blasius*[26] standard (after the case of the same name in which the Delaware Court of Chancery first articulated this standard) applicable to defensive tactics touching upon issues of control. The dead-hand feature failed this test because it purposefully disenfranchised the company's shareholders (that is, interfered with their right to elect directors) without any compelling justification. In particular, "even in an election contest fought over the issue of the hostile bid, the shareholders will be powerless to elect a board that is both willing and able to accept the bid." Instead, the shareholders "may be forced to vote for [incumbent] directors whose policies they reject because only those directors have the power to change them." Second, it failed to satisfy *Unocal's* requirement that the defense be proportionate to the threat because it was preclusive: it eliminated the use of a proxy contest as a possible means to gain control.

In the following case, the Delaware Supreme Court examined the validity of a so-called no-hand pill, which could not be redeemed for six months even if the insurgent's slate of directors were elected and wanted to redeem it.

---

25. Carmody v. Toll Bros., Inc., 723 A.2d 1180 (Del. Ch. 1998).

26. Blasius Indus. v. Atlas Corp., 564 A.2d 651 (Del. Ch. 1988).

A CASE IN POINT

CASE 23.4

Quickturn Design Systems, Inc. v. Shapiro

Supreme Court of Delaware 721 A.2d 1281 (Del. 1998).

In the Language of the Court

FACTS Mentor Graphics Corporation (an Oregon-based corporation engaged in the manufacture, marketing, and support of electronic design automation software and hardware) launched a hostile bid for Quickturn Design Systems, the market leader in the sale of logic emulation technology used to verify the design of complex silicon chips and electronics systems. On August 12, 1998, Mentor announced an unsolicited cash tender offer for all outstanding common shares of Quickturn at $12.125 a share, a price representing a 50 percent premium over Quickturn's pre-offer price. Consummation of the tender offer would be followed by a second-step cash merger in which Quickturn's nontendering shareholders would receive the same $12.125 per share. Mentor also announced its intent to solicit proxies to replace the Quickturn board at a special meeting.

The Quickturn board concluded that Mentor's offer was inadequate and recommended that Quickturn shareholders reject it. The board also amended Quickturn's shareholder rights plan to add a Deferred Redemption Provision, under which no newly elected board could redeem the rights plan for six months after taking office if the redemption would

(Continued)

(Case 23.4 continued)

facilitate a transaction with the person who proposed the election of the new directors. The board also amended Quickturn's bylaws to provide that any special shareholders' meeting requested by shareholders must take place not less than ninety nor more than one hundred days after the receipt of the shareholders' request. The combined effect of the two defensive measures would be to delay any acquisition of Quickturn by Mentor for at least nine months, even if Mentor received tenders of shares that, together with the shares Mentor already owned, represented more than 51 percent of Quickturn's outstanding stock. Mentor sued to invalidate the defenses.

ISSUE PRESENTED Are defensive measures (including a "no-hand" pill) designed to prevent a hostile bidder from acquiring control of a Delaware corporation for at least nine months valid?

OPINION HOLLAND, J., writing for the Delaware Supreme Court:

One of the most basic tenets of Delaware corporate law is that the board of directors has the ultimate responsibility for managing the business and affairs of a corporation. . . .

...

The Delayed Redemption Provision would prevent a new Quickturn board of directors from managing the corporation by redeeming the Rights Plan to facilitate a transaction that would serve the stockholders' best interests, even under circumstances where the board would be required to do so because of its fiduciary duty to the Quickturn stockholders. Because the Delayed Redemption Provision impermissibly circumscribes the board's statutory power under Section 141(a) [to manage the business and affairs of the company] and the directors' ability to fulfill their concomitant fiduciary duties, we hold that the Delayed Redemption Provision is invalid.

RESULT The Delayed Redemption Provision was invalid.

COMMENTS At the time Mentor launched its hostile tender offer, Quickturn permitted any person owning at least 10 percent of its stock to call a special meeting of shareholders at which new directors could be elected. The Chancery Court upheld the bylaw amendment that permitted the board to delay holding a special shareholders' meeting for up to 120 days, and Mentor did not contest this ruling on appeal.

QUESTIONS

1. Why did the court let the bylaw amendment stand but strike down the no-hand pill?
2. If Mentor succeeded in electing its slate of new Quickturn directors, what factors and whose interests would those directors have to take into account in deciding whether to redeem the poison pill?

ISSUES OF CONTROL AND THE *BLASIUS* STANDARD

A number of takeover cases have drawn a distinction between the exercise of two types of corporate power: (1) the power over the assets of the corporation, and (2) the power relationship between the board and the shareholders.[27] As explained earlier, directors have broad power over the assets of the corporation. Such decisions are generally protected by the business judgment rule or subjected to *Unocal*'s proportionality analysis if they relate to defensive

27. *See* Hilton Hotels Corp. v. ITT Corp., 978 F. Supp. 1342 (D. Nev. 1997).

tactics. As the Delaware Chancellor William Allen explained in *Paramount Communications, Inc. v. Time, Inc.,* "The corporation law does not operate on the theory that directors, in exercising their powers to manage the firm, are obligated to follow the wishes of a majority of shares."[28] Thus, the Time directors had the power to acquire Warner Communications even though the holders of a majority of Time's stock would have preferred to take Paramount's offer.

If a board's unilateral decision to adopt a defensive measure touches on issues of control, however, then further judicial scrutiny is required to protect the shareholder franchise essential for corporate democracy. In particular, the court must decide whether the board purposefully disenfranchised its shareholders. If so, then under the *Blasius* standard, the action is strongly suspect and cannot be sustained without a compelling justification.[29]

For example, in *Chesapeake Corp. v. Shore,*[30] the Delaware Court of Chancery held that a supermajority bylaw provision adopted by the board of Shorewood Packing Corporation to thwart a hostile bid by Chesapeake Corporation was "a preclusive, unjustified impairment of the Shorewood stockholders' right to influence their company's policies through the ballot box." The provision increased from a simple majority to 60 percent the number of Shorewood shares needed to amend the bylaws. Because Shorewood's management controlled almost 24 percent of its stock, the supermajority provision made it virtually impossible for Chesapeake to garner enough votes to amend the bylaws to eliminate the classified board so that it could unseat the current directors and install a new board amenable to its offer.

The Shorewood board claimed that Chesapeake's offer posed two threats: (1) the price was grossly inadequate, so Shorewood shareholders faced great harm if they sold their stock at that price; and (2) "there was a danger that Shorewood stockholders would be confused about the intrinsic value of the company, fail to understand management's explanation as to why the market was undervaluing their stock, and mistakenly tender consents to Chesapeake to facilitate its unfair offer." The court found the threat of confusion "at best quite a weak one" in light of (1) the fact that more than 80 percent of Shorewood's shares were held by management and insti-

AT THE TOP

Protecting the shareholder franchise is critical because the business judgment rule provides the directors and officers great latitude in managing the day-to-day affairs of the corporation. As a result, shareholders who are displeased with the business performance generally have only two options: sell their shares or vote to replace the incumbent board members. The corporate governance system loses a key control if unhappy shareholders cannot vote the directors out of office.

tutional holders, (2) the ability of the board to engage in a more vigorous communications campaign, and (3) the fact that reputable analysts were already tracking the stock. Although the court acknowledged that the price offered might be inadequate, it held that the supermajority bylaw was "an extremely aggressive and overreaching response to a very mild threat." Instead, if the board truly believed that price inadequacy was the problem, it could have taken Chesapeake up on its offer to negotiate price and structure.

The court acknowledged that several cases have stated that a corporate board may consider a fully financed all-cash, all-shares, premium-to-market tender offer a threat to stockholders "when the board believes that the company's present strategic plan will deliver more value than the premium offer, the stock market has not yet bought that rationale, the board may be correct, and therefore there is a risk that 'stockholders might tender . . . in ignorance or based upon a mistaken belief.'" Yet the court noted that this threat of *substantive coercion*[31] can be invoked in almost every situation, given that "[t]here is virtually no CEO in America who does not believe that the market is not valuing [his or] her company properly," so it called on courts to ensure that the threat is real and that the board is not imagining or exaggerating it.

The court also pointed out that:

[O]ne of corporate management's functions is to ensure that the market recognizes the value of the company and that the stockholders are apprised of relevant information about the company. This informational responsibility would include, one would think, the duty to communicate the company's strategic plans and prospects to stockholders as clearly and understandably as possible.

28. Fed. Sec. L. Rep. (CCH) ¶ 94,514 (Del. Ch. July 14, 1989), *aff'd,* 571 A.2d 1140 (Del. 1990).
29. *See* Stroud v. Grace, 606 A.2d 75 (Del. 1992); Unitrin, Inc. v. American Gen. Corp., 651 A.2d 1361 (Del. 1995); Blasius Indus. v. Atlas Corp., 564 A.2d 651 (Del. Ch. 1988).
30. 2000 Del. Ch. LEXIS 20 (2000).

31. *See* Ronald J. Gilson & Reiner Kraakman, *Delaware's Standard for Defensive Tactics: Is There Substance to Proportionality Review?,* 44 Bus. Law. 247, 267 (1989).

Duty *of* Directors *to* Disclose Preliminary Merger Negotiations

Directors can face a difficult decision when determining whether they must disclose an offer to buy the company or the company's participation in merger negotiations. As is discussed more fully in Chapter 25, disclosure can be required even if the parties have not reached an agreement in principle on the price and structure of the transaction. The U.S. Supreme Court held in *Basic, Inc. v.*

Levinson[32] that such "soft information" can be material. Yet directors may fear that disclosure of negotiations will put the company in *Revlon* mode.

Managers planning a management buyout (MBO) of a company have a real conflict of interest in deciding whether to disclose their offer to the public because disclosure will often bring forth competing bidders. Prudent directors, like the independent directors of RJR Nabisco when faced with CEO Ross Johnson's bid in 1988, will often require public announcement of the bid even if it puts the company "in play."

32. 485 U.S. 224 (1988).

The Pennsylvania Antitakeover Statute

The nation's toughest state antitakeover statute, Pennsylvania Senate bill 1310, also known as Act 36, was signed into law by Governor Bob Casey (a Democrat) on April 27, 1990.[a] This controversial statute illustrates how state legislatures may attempt to shape the law to protect corporations based in their states from hostile takeovers.

Background
The impetus for the statute came from the Belzberg family's hostile takeover bid for Armstrong World Industries, Inc., then a *Fortune* 500 company specializing in flooring and furnishings, headquartered in Lancaster, Pennsylvania. After Armstrong's board rejected the Belzbergs' offer to buy the company, the Belzbergs' holding company, First City Financial Corporation, initiated a proxy fight for control of four directors' seats on the board. The shareholders' meeting, at which the results of the proxy fight were to be announced, was scheduled for April 30, 1990.

Noah W. Wenger (a Republican), the state senator from the Lancaster district, introduced a comprehensive antitakeover bill while the Belzbergs and Armstrong were in the midst of their conflict. The bill, drafted in part by the Pennsylvania Chamber of Business and Industry, was designed not only to throw a wrench in the plans of corporate raiders in general

but perhaps also to impede the Belzberg bid in particular.

The Statute
The Pennsylvania statute attacks hostile bids for corporate control on three major fronts. First, it requires controlling persons (defined as those who own, or control proxies for, 20 percent of a company's stock) to disgorge—that is, give back to the company—any profits they make by selling stock of the company within eighteen months after becoming a controlling person. Such disgorgement is required if stock acquired within twenty-four months before or within eighteen months after becoming a controlling person is sold by the controlling person within eighteen months after becoming a controlling person.

This provision is aimed at those who, after failed takeover attempts, attempt to reap short-term profits by selling acquired stock at a premium. Institutional investors and other shareholders who launch proxy fights for purposes other than gaining control of a majority of the

board are exempted from the disgorgement provision.

Second, the statute expands the directors' ability to consider other constituencies when making change-of-control decisions. Subsection (d) of Section 511 provides an expansive list of constituencies that a director may consider when exercising his or her duty to the corporation:

In discharging the duties of their respective positions . . . directors may, in considering the best interests of the corporation, consider to the extent they deem appropriate:

(1) The effects of any action upon *any or all groups affected by such action,* including shareholders, employees, suppliers, customers and creditors of the corporation, and upon communities in which offices or other establishments of the corporation are located.
(2) The short-term and long-term interests of the corporation, including benefits which may accrue to the corporation from its long-term plans and the *possibility that these interests may be best served by the continued independence of the corporation.*
(3) The resources, intent and conduct (past, stated and potential) of person seeking to acquire control of the corporation.
(4) *All other pertinent factors.* [Emphasis added.]

In addition, the directors are not required to regard any particular corporate interest or the interest of any group as "a

(Political Perspective continues)

(Political Perspective continued)

dominant or controlling interest or factor." The implication is clear. A director's duty when considering a proposal for a change of control is not simply to maximize shareholder value.

Third, like some other states' antitakeover statutes, the Pennsylvania law deprives a shareholder of its voting rights when it crosses certain ownership lines, placed at 20 percent, 33 percent, and 50 percent of the company's stock. The voting rights can be regained only if the holders of a majority of the shares—excluding holders of shares acquired in the previous twelve months—give their approval at a special shareholders' meeting.

The statute also protects the employees of a company that is taken over. Existing labor contracts must be honored, and a successful bidder must pay severance benefits to employees who lose their jobs within two years of the takeover.

Corporations are allowed to opt out of various provisions of the antitakeover statute. Within two years after its enactment, more than 66 corporations (including the former Westinghouse Electric) of the estimated 200 corporations affected by the statute had opted out of at least one of its subchapters.[b]

Recent Use

In 1998, the Pennsylvania statute may have helped Mellon Bank (a Pennsylvania corporation) thwart a hostile bid by the Bank of New York.[c] In rejecting the Bank of New York's $23.6 billion offer (which represented a premium of 28 percent over Mellon's closing stock price the day before the offer was announced and a premium of 34 percent over Mellon's average closing stock price over the last thirty trading days), the chairman of Mellon's board seemed to be invoking the Pennsylvania statute when he criticized the proposed merger as not benefiting "our shareholders, employees, customers and—in particular—the communities we serve."[d]

a. The independent sections are codified as 15 PA. CONS. STAT. ANN. §§ 511, 512, 1721, 2502 (1990); 15 PA. CONS. STAT. ANN. §§ 2561–67, 2571–74, 2581–83, 2585–88 (1990).
b. Jeffrey L. Silberman, *How Do Pennsylvania Directors Spell Relief? Act 36*, 17 DEL. J. CORP. L. 115 (1992).
c. *See* Bloomberg News, *In Pennsylvania, Watch Out What You Try to Take Over: Thanks to Tough Rules, Mellon Bank Is Able to Flatly Reject an Offer from Bank of New York*, L.A. TIMES, Apr. 23, 1998, at D7.
d. Associated Press, *Mellon Bank Sues Bank of New York to Avoid Takeover; $23 Billion Bid Was Rejected*, STAR TRIB. (Minneapolis), Apr. 24, 1998, at 1D.

 # Duties *of* Controlling Shareholders

A shareholder who owns sufficient shares to outvote the other shareholders, or to otherwise set corporate policy, and thus to control the corporation is known as a *controlling shareholder*. A person owning a majority of the outstanding shares is almost always a controlling shareholder, but persons owning a lower percentage (30 percent, for example) may still be deemed controlling if the shares are widely dispersed and there are no other large holders. In certain situations, controlling shareholders owe a fiduciary duty to the corporation and to its other shareholders. Generally, controlling shareholders have a responsibility to minority shareholders to control the corporation in a fair, just, and equitable manner. They may not engage in a bad faith scheme to drain off the corporation's earnings, ensuring that minority shareholders are frozen out of all financial benefits.[33]

SALE OF CONTROL

The obligation not to exercise control in a manner that intentionally harms the corporation and minority shareholders spills over into a sale of control. For instance, if a controlling shareholder knows or has reason to believe

33. Sugarman v. Sugarman, 797 F.2d 3 (1st Cir. 1986).

 INTERNATIONAL CONSIDERATION

Because European banks are not subject to the regulatory strictures applicable to U.S. banks, they are much more important institutional investors and exert a more powerful force on how a company is run than comparable U.S. banks. For example, German banks exercise extraordinary control over company access to capital. By law, the banks can represent shareholders who deposit their shares with the banks. Because only the banks are allowed to trade on the floor of the German stock exchanges and therefore have the best knowledge of stock performance, most shareholders take advantage of this service.

In 1986, German banks held proxies for an average of 65 percent of the shares present at the shareholder meetings at 100 of the largest German companies. For example, at the 1986 shareholder meeting of Siemens, approximately 61 percent of the outstanding shares were present at the meeting. Of the shares voted, Deutsche Bank voted 18 percent, Dresdner Bank 11 percent, and Commerzbank 4 percent. All banks taken as a group voted approximately 80 percent of the shares voted at the meeting.[a] Banks are also permitted to purchase directly up to 100 percent of the shares of a company, although it is considered imprudent for them to invest substantial portions of their capital in any single company.

a. Theodor Baums, *Corporate Governance in Germany: The Role of Banks*, 40 AM. J. COMP. L. 503, 524 (1992).

that the purchaser of its shares intends to use controlling power to the detriment of the corporation, the controlling shareholder has a duty not to transfer the power of management to such a purchaser.

A controlling interest in a corporation usually commands a higher price per share than a minority interest. Does this control premium belong to the corporation or to the majority shareholder? The widely accepted rule is that controlling shareholders normally have a right to derive a premium from the sale of a controlling block of stock.[34] For instance, in *Zetlin v. Hanson Holdings, Inc.*,[35] the New York Court of Appeals commented:

> In this action plaintiff Zetlin contends that minority stockholders are entitled to an opportunity to share equally in any premium paid for a controlling interest in the corporation. This rule would profoundly affect the manner in which controlling stock interests are now transferred. It would require, essentially, that a controlling interest be transferred only by means of an offer to all stockholders, that is, a tender offer. This would be contrary to existing law and if so radical a change is to be effected it would be best done by the Legislature.

In extreme circumstances, however, courts may be willing to characterize the control premium as a corporate asset, thus entitling minority shareholders to a portion. The U.S. Court of Appeals for the Second Circuit took such an approach in *Perlman v. Feldmann*.[36] *Perlman* involved Newport Steel Corporation, whose mills produced sheets of steel for sale to manufacturers of steel products. C. Russell Feldmann was the chairman of the board of directors and president of the corporation; he

was also the controlling shareholder. In August 1950, when the supply of steel was tight due to the Korean War, Feldmann and some other shareholders sold their stock to a syndicate of end-users of steel who were interested in securing a source of supply.

Minority shareholders brought a shareholder derivative suit to compel the controlling shareholders to account for, and make restitution of, their gains from the sale. The court held that the consideration received by the defendants included compensation for the sale of a corporate asset, namely the ability of the board to control the allocation of the corporation's product in a time of short supply.

Note that the court did not seek to prohibit majority shareholders from ever selling their shares at a premium; it was careful to circumscribe its holding with an emphasis on the extreme market conditions:

> We do not mean to suggest that a majority stockholder cannot dispose of his controlling block of stock to outsiders without having to account to his corporation for profits or even never do this with impunity when the buyer is an interested customer, actual or potential, for the corporation's product. But when the sale necessarily results in a sacrifice of this element of corporate good will and consequent unusual profit to the fiduciary who has caused the sacrifice, he should account for his gains. So when in a time of market shortage, where a call on a corporation's product commands an unusually large premium, in one form or another, we think it sound law that a fiduciary may not appropriate to himself the value of this premium.

The following case involved elements of abuse of control and sale of control. The dominant shareholders took a series of steps to ensure that they participated in the financial benefits of the company without letting the minority shareholders also participate.

34. *See, e.g.,* Essex Universal Corp. v. Yates, 305 F.2d 572 (2d Cir. 1962).
35. 397 N.E.2d 387 (N.Y. 1979).
36. 219 F.2d 173 (2d Cir. 1955), *cert. denied,* 349 U.S. 952 (1955).

A CASE IN POINT

CASE 23.5

**Jones v.
H.F. Ahmanson & Co.**

*Supreme Court of California
460 P.2d 464 (Cal. 1969).*

Summary

FACTS The shares of the United Savings and Loan Association were not actively traded due to their high book value, the closely held nature of the association, and the failure of its management to provide information to shareholders, brokers, or the public.

In 1958, investor interest in shares of savings and loan associations and holding companies increased. Savings and loan stocks that were publicly marketed enjoyed a steady increase in market price. The controlling shareholders of the United Savings and Loan Association decided to create a mechanism by which the association, too, could attract investor interest. They did not, however, attempt to render the association's shares more readily marketable.

(Continued)

(Case 23.5 continued)

Instead, a holding company, the United Financial Corporation of California, was incorporated in Delaware on May 8, 1959. On May 14, pursuant to a prior agreement, certain association shareholders owning a majority of the association's stock exchanged their shares for those of United Financial.

After the exchange, United Financial held 85 percent of the association's outstanding stock. The former majority shareholders of the association had become the majority shareholders of United Financial and continued to control the association through the holding company. They did not offer the minority shareholders of the association an opportunity to exchange their shares.

The first public offering of United Financial stock was made in June 1960. An additional public offering in February 1961 included a secondary offering (that is, an offering by selling shareholders) of 600,000 shares. There was active trading in the United Financial shares. Sales of the association shares, however, decreased from 170 shares per year before the formation of United Financial to half that number by 1961. United Financial acquired 90 percent of the association's shares that were sold.

A shareholder of the association brought suit, on behalf of herself and all other similarly situated minority shareholders, against United Financial and the individuals and corporations that had set up the holding company. The plaintiff contended that the defendants' course of conduct constituted a breach of fiduciary duty owed by the majority shareholders to the minority. She alleged that they had used their control of the association for their own advantage and to the detriment of the minority when they created United Financial, made a public market for its shares that rendered the association's stock unmarketable except to United Financial, and then refused either to purchase the minority's association stock at a fair price or to exchange the stock on the same terms afforded to the majority. She further alleged that they had created a conflict of interest that might have been avoided had they offered all association shareholders the opportunity to participate in the initial exchange of shares.

ISSUE PRESENTED Did majority shareholders who transferred their shares to a holding corporation, then took it public without allowing the minority to exchange their shares, breach their fiduciary duty to the minority shareholders?

SUMMARY OF OPINION The California Supreme Court began its analysis by stating that the majority shareholders, acting either singly or in concert, have a fiduciary responsibility to the minority and to the corporation. They must use their ability to control the corporation fairly. They may not use it to benefit themselves alone or in a manner detrimental to the minority. Any use to which they put their power to control the corporation must benefit all shareholders proportionately and must not conflict with the proper conduct of the corporation's business. The court summarized the rule as one of "inherent fairness from the viewpoint of the corporation or those interested therein."

The court noted that the controlling shareholders of the association could have taken advantage of the bull market in savings and loan stock in two other ways. They could have caused the association to effect a stock split, thereby increasing the number of outstanding shares, or they could have created a holding company and permitted all shareholders to exchange their shares before offering the holding company's shares to the public. Either course would have benefited all of the shareholders alike, although the majority shareholders would have had to relinquish some of their control shares. Instead, however, the defendants chose to set up a holding company that they controlled and did not allow minority shareholders to exchange association shares for shares of the holding company. Moreover, the market created by the defendants for United Financial shares would have been available for association shares had the defendants chosen a stock split of the association's shares.

(Continued)

(Case 23.5 continued)

The court stated that when a controlling shareholder sells or exchanges his or her shares, the transaction is subject to close scrutiny, particularly if the majority receives a premium over market value for its shares. If the premium constitutes payment for what is properly a corporate asset, all shareholders are entitled to a proportionate share of the premium (citing *Perlman v. Feldmann*). The defendants' exchange of association stock for United Financial stock was an integral part of a scheme that the defendants could have reasonably foreseen would destroy the potential public market for association stock. The remaining association shareholders would thus be deprived of the opportunity to realize a profit from those intangible characteristics that attach to publicly marketed stock.

RESULT The majority shareholders who transferred their shares to a holding corporation, then took it public without allowing the minority to exchange their shares, breached their fiduciary duty to the minority shareholders. The minority shareholders were awarded damages that placed them in a position at least as favorable as the position the majority shareholders created for themselves.

FREEZE-OUTS

The Delaware Supreme Court has held that a majority shareholder may *freeze out* the minority, that is, force the minority to convert their shares into cash, as long as the transaction is fair.[37] Sometimes a freeze-out is effected by merging a subsidiary into its parent, as in *Rosenblatt v. Getty Oil Co.*[38] In this case, Skelly Oil Company and Mission Corporation merged into Getty Oil Company, which was indirectly the majority shareholder of both Skelly and Mission. All three corporations were in the oil business. At issue was the fairness of the exchange ratio in the merger, that is, the ratio that would be used to convert the minority shareholders' stock into cash.

The Delaware Supreme Court stated that the concept of fairness in parent–subsidiary mergers has two aspects: fair dealing and fair price. Both must be examined together in resolving the ultimate question of entire fairness.

As to fair dealing, a court will look at the timing of the transaction; how it was initiated, structured, negotiated, and disclosed to the board; and how director and shareholder approval was obtained. The court cited a number of factors, including the adversarial nature of the negotiations between the parties to the merger, that led to a conclusion of fair dealing by Getty.

Regarding fair price, a court will look at economic factors, such as asset value, market value, earnings, and future prospects, and at any other elements that affect the intrinsic value of a company's stock. Both Getty and Skelly believed that the real worth of an oil company is centered in its reserves. Therefore, the court was especially impressed with the fact that they had employed D & M, a petroleum consulting engineering firm with a worldwide reputation and nearly thirty-seven years of experience, to estimate Getty's and Skelly's respective oil and natural gas reserves. The court concluded that Getty had dealt fairly with the Skelly minority shareholders in the merger.

Although the controlling shareholder may be permitted to negotiate a deal for the sale of the entire company, the board of directors of the target must still determine the intrinsic value of the company and the maximum shareholder value reasonably attainable so that the board has an informed basis for recommending the proposed deal to the minority stockholders or for suggesting that the minority stockholders vote against the deal and exercise their appraisal rights.[39] The representatives of the controlling shareholder on the target board owe the target's minority shareholders "an uncompromising duty of loyalty."

Greenmail

In 1984, Saul Steinberg, through a syndicate called MM Acquisition Corporation (MM for Mickey Mouse), took a run at Walt Disney Productions. Within twelve hours of threatening a cash tender offer for Disney, Steinberg was bought out for $325.4 million ($297.4 million for the stock he had acquired and $28 million for the esti-

37. Weinberger v. UOP, Inc. 457 A.2d 701 (Del. 1983).
38. 493 A.2d 929 (Del. 1985).
39. McMullin v. Beran, 2000 Del. LEXIS 481 (Del. 2000).

mated cost of preparing the tender offer), giving him a profit of about $60 million. Several Disney shareholders sued the Disney directors for paying greenmail. Before the trial, the plaintiffs sought to impose a constructive trust on the greenmail proceeds received by Steinberg. (A constructive trust is used to secure any assets misappropriated by a fiduciary and make them available to their rightful owners.) The trial court imposed a con-

structive trust, and an appellate court affirmed. (In 1989, after three weeks of trial, the case was settled for $89.5 million.) The case presented here, which deals with an aspect of the Steinberg affair, addresses the extent to which a shareholder who receives greenmail from a company's board of directors is an aider and abettor of that board's breach of duty to the company.

A CASE IN POINT

CASE 23.6

Heckmann v. Ahmanson

Court of Appeal of California
214 Cal. Rptr. 177
(Cal. Ct. App. 1985).

Summary

FACTS In March 1984, a group headed by Saul Steinberg purchased more than two million shares of stock of Walt Disney Productions, the owner of Disneyland. Disney responded by announcing that it would acquire the Arvida Corporation for $200 million in newly issued Disney stock and would assume Arvida's $190 million debt. The Steinberg group countered with a shareholder derivative suit in federal court, seeking to block the Arvida transaction. All of the proceeds of a shareholder derivative suit (less expenses) go to the corporation for the benefit of all of its shareholders.

While the shareholder derivative suit was pending, the Steinberg group proceeded to acquire two million additional shares of Disney stock, increasing its ownership position to approximately 12 percent of the outstanding Disney shares. On June 8, 1984, the Steinberg group advised Disney's directors of its intention to make a tender offer for 49 percent of the outstanding shares at $67.50 a share and its intention to later tender for the balance at $72.50 a share.

As described above, the Disney directors responded by repurchasing all the Disney stock held by the Steinberg group, leaving the group with a profit of about $60 million. In return, the Steinberg group agreed not to purchase any more Disney stock and to drop the Arvida litigation. The group did not actually drop the derivative claims, but it agreed not to oppose a motion to dismiss made by Disney.

After the repurchase of the Steinberg group's shares was announced, several Disney shareholders, as described above, brought an action seeking to rescind Disney's purchase agreement with the Steinberg group. At a preliminary hearing, the trial court granted the constructive trust sought by the shareholders. The Steinberg group appealed.

ISSUES PRESENTED Was a shareholder who induced the board of directors to pay greenmail liable as an aider and abettor of the board's breach of its duty to the company? Was the shareholder, who (as part of the greenmail transaction) abandoned a derivative suit against the company, also liable to the other shareholders for breaching his fiduciary duty to them?

SUMMARY OF OPINION The California Court of Appeal concluded that the plaintiffs had demonstrated a reasonable probability of success at trial and upheld the trial court's imposition of a constructive trust.

First, the court found that the plaintiffs had made a sufficient showing of personal interest on the part of the directors to shift the burden onto the board to show that the transaction was fair. The court held that the directors had not sustained that burden merely by making a vague assertion that their objective in repurchasing the stock was to avoid the damage to Disney and its shareholders that would have resulted from the Steinberg tender offer. Thus, the directors were not given the protection of the business judgment rule.

(Continued)

(Case 23.6 continued)

The court further found that the Steinberg group could be held liable as an aider and abettor of the board in its alleged breach of fiduciary duty. The court noted that the Steinberg group knew it was reselling its stock at a price considerably above market value to enable the Disney directors to retain control of the corporation. It also knew or should have known that Disney was borrowing the $325 million purchase price. From its previous dealings with Disney, including the Arvida transaction, it knew that the increased debt load would adversely affect Disney's credit rating and the price of its stock.

Second, the court found that the plaintiff shareholders had adequately demonstrated a breach of the fiduciary duty owed directly by the Steinberg group to the Disney shareholders. When the Steinberg group filed the derivative suit against Disney to block Disney's purchase of Arvida, it assumed a fiduciary duty to the other shareholders. It could not abandon the suit for its own financial advantage. The plaintiff's duty in a derivative action is analogous to the duty of care owed by a volunteer rescuer to the rescuee. The court stated that the members of the Steinberg group "are like the citizens of a town whose volunteer fire department quits fighting the fire and sells its equipment to the arsonist who set it (who obtains the purchase price by setting fire to the building next door)." Thus, the plaintiffs had demonstrated a reasonable probability that the Steinberg group breached its fiduciary duty to the other Disney shareholders by abandoning the Arvida litigation two weeks after it was filed.

RESULT The shareholder who induced the board to pay greenmail was liable as an aider and abettor of the board's breach of its duty to the company. He was also liable for his breach of fiduciary duty to his fellow shareholders when he abandoned the shareholder derivative suit.

Delaware courts analyze the payment of greenmail in the same way that they analyze other defensive tactics under *Unocal*. If the board demonstrates that the shareholder to be bought out poses a threat to corporate policy and effectiveness and the repurchase of shares at a premium is a reasonable response to that threat, then the payment will be protected by the business judgment rule.

HUSHMAIL

The Delaware Supreme Court coined the term *hush-mail*—that is, a combination of greenmail and hush money—to refer to a repurchase of shares at a premium over the market price to ensure silence. The term was first used in *Grobow v. Perot*.[40]

The case arose after General Motors Corporation (GM) agreed in 1986 to pay nearly $745 million to repurchase certain GM stock and contingent notes owned by H. Ross Perot (later a presidential candidate) and his close associates. Perot himself said that his securities were repurchased at a "giant premium."

Perot resigned immediately from GM's board. He also resigned as chairman of GM's subsidiary Electronic Data Systems (EDS), which he had founded and of which he was the largest shareholder. Perot further agreed (1) to stop criticizing GM management, in default of which he agreed to pay GM damages of up to $7.5 million; (2) not to purchase GM stock or engage in a proxy contest against the board for five years; and (3) not to compete with EDS for three years or recruit EDS executives for eighteen months. The commitment by Perot not to criticize the GM board was later characterized as the hushmail feature of the agreement.

The GM repurchase came at a time when GM was experiencing financial difficulty and was engaged in cost cutting. Public reaction to the announcement ranged from mixed to adverse. The repurchase was sharply criticized by people in the auto industry, including several GM managers. The criticism focused on the size of the premium over the market price of the repurchased stock and on the hushmail provision. A shareholder derivative suit ensued.

The Delaware Supreme Court ruled that the plaintiffs' complaints regarding the hushmail provision failed to sup-

---

40. 539 A.2d 180 (Del. 1988).

port a conclusion that the primary purpose of the board's payment of the premium was to buy Perot's silence. To the contrary, the plaintiffs themselves stated in their complaints two legitimate business purposes for the GM board's decision to sever its relationship with Perot: (1) the board's determination that it would be in GM's best interest to retain control over its wholly owned subsidiary EDS, and (2) the desire to rid itself of the principal cause of the growing internal policy dispute over EDS's management direction. In addition, GM secured significant covenants from Perot besides the hushmail provision: (1) not to compete or hire EDS employees, (2) not to purchase GM stock or engage in proxy contests, and (3) to stay out of GM's and EDS's affairs. Moreover, Perot agreed to pay liquidated damages should he breach his no-criticism covenant. The court found that the plaintiffs' effort to measure the fairness of the premium paid by GM was flawed by their inability to place a dollar value on Perot's promises, particularly his covenant not to compete with EDS or attempt to hire EDS employees.

The court concluded that, although the board of directors might be subject to criticism for the premium paid Perot and his associates for the repurchase of their interest in GM, on the present record the repurchase could only be seen legally as an exercise of business judgment by the GM board with which a court may not interfere. In the spring of 1990, in response to continuing shareholder pressure, GM adopted a bylaw prohibiting the payment of greenmail.

THE RESPONSIBLE MANAGER
Carrying Out Fiduciary Duties

Officers, directors, and controlling shareholders are fiduciaries. They owe their principal (the corporation and its shareholders) undivided loyalty. They must act in good faith. They may not put their own interests before those of the corporation and its shareholders. They cannot, for example, fight off a hostile takeover just to keep their jobs. They cannot use the company's confidential information for their personal gain.

Officers and directors also owe the corporation and its shareholders a duty of care. They should act with the care reasonable persons would use in the management of their own property. They have a duty to make only informed decisions. They cannot rely blindly on the advice of other people, even experts.

The duty to make informed decisions, which is a part of the duty of care, takes various forms. In the context of takeovers, board members cannot reject an offer without taking sufficient time to analyze its merit. Managers must be able to demonstrate that they made their decisions only after sufficient deliberation and after review of all relevant information. They should consider the possible effects of both the monetary and the nonmonetary aspects of the transaction.

A manager should never sign a document without reading it first. Ideally, each director should read the document the board is asked to approve. If that is not practical, the directors should demand and read a written summary prepared by counsel. They should also make sure that the officers who are authorized to sign the agreement have read it before signing it.

A manager should be informed as to the rules regarding the duty of care in the company's state of incorporation. Some jurisdictions permit the shareholders to amend the articles of incorporation to relieve directors of any financial liability for violations of the duty of care. But even with such provisions in place, directors must still act in good faith and in what they honestly believe is the best interest of the corporation. Otherwise, they will breach their duty of loyalty. Such a breach can not only result in monetary liability but can also demoralize the shareholders and employees of the corporation, making it difficult to maintain a high level of ethical behavior among them.

In a situation involving a potential conflict of interest, a manager should excuse himself or herself and leave the decision to others who do not have a conflict. It is common, for example, to establish special independent committees of the board of directors, either to examine the fairness of a management offer to acquire the company or to review the merits of shareholder litigation against the directors or officers.

A repurchase of stock at a premium from a dissident (or unhappy) shareholder may violate both the directors' duty to the corporation and the shareholder's duty to the other shareholders. Different courts view such repurchases differently, and local counsel should always be consulted. It is often appropriate for the board not only to obtain a written opinion from counsel that such a repurchase is permissible but also to convene a special independent committee of directors to decide whether the consideration that will be paid for the stock is fair.

Any controlling shareholder engaging in a transaction such as a merger with the company it controls must be able to prove that the transaction is fair both procedurally and substantively. The use of independent committees, advised by independent financial consultants and counsel, helps show procedural fairness, as does a willingness to negotiate the proposed transaction with such a committee on an arm's length basis. Paying a fair price for corporate assets or for shares of a corporation shows substantive fairness. The fairness of a price can be demonstrated by evidence of competing offers or independent appraisals or evaluations. The appraiser or investment banker should not be compensated in a manner that gives that person an interest in the outcome of the appraisal or of the transaction. It is often preferable to pay the appraiser or investment banker a flat fee regardless of whether the deal goes through, rather than an incentive fee based on the value of the deal struck.

Certain acts of directors, officers, and controlling shareholders are both illegal and unethical, such as the seizing of a corporate opportunity by an officer. Other conduct may be legal yet ethically questionable, such as the payment of hushmail or, in some circumstances, greenmail.

Some situations present conflicting ethical concerns. The Delaware Supreme Court has held that the directors must maximize shareholder value, that is, get the best price available, if they decide to sell control of the corporation. Yet a sale to a bust-up artist who will sell the company's assets, or to a union buster, might adversely affect the corporation's other constituencies, such as employees, suppliers, and the community in which the corporation does business.[41] A manager should try to select a course of action that protects the corporation's constituencies without sacrificing the shareholders' right to the best price. If the management team itself bids for the company, the board may find itself forced to become an auctioneer whose sole goal is to get the best price for the shareholders.

A board of directors can use various defensive measures to prevent a hostile takeover, provided that the

41. *See* Constance E. Bagley & Karen Page, *The Devil Made Me Do It: Replacing Corporate Directors' Veil of Secrecy with the Mantle of Stewardship*, 36 SAN DIEGO L. REV. 4 (1999), for a discussion of the legal, economic, and organizational behavioral aspects of directors' consideration of factors other than simply shareholder return when acting on behalf of the corporation.

"I, too, hate being a greedy bastard, but we have a responsibility to our shareholders."

measures are reasonable in relation to the threat posed and that the board considers it in the best interests of the company and its constituencies for the company to remain independent. Any measures designed to interfere with the shareholder franchise require proof by the directors of a compelling justification.

Similarly, if the board adopts a strategy resulting in a change of control of a corporation, it cannot use defensive tactics, such as no-shop provisions (whereby the board agrees not to consider other offers) or large asset or stock lock-ups, to deter competing bidders. In short, if the board agrees to a change of control, it breaches its fiduciary duties if it makes competing offers impossible by adopting a scorched-earth policy that leaves the successful bidder with a depleted target. Although legal counsel will advise managers and directors in this area, a knowledge of the rules of the game is essential to good management.

No Mickey Mouse Pay *at* Disney

As with the saying from Walt Disney Co.'s "Toy Story" films, Michael Eisner's compensation used to seem like it soared to infinity and beyond, especially since it reached $576 million one year.[42]

Not so anymore. In a reflection of the Burbank-based entertainment giant's sagging financial performance and lackluster stock price, the Disney chief executive and three other top corporate officers were shut out when it came to bonuses for the fiscal year that ended Sept. 30, according to proxy materials the company filed Wednesday with the Securities and Exchange Commission.

Eisner received only his $750,000 salary, the annual pay he agreed to when he was hired in 1984 from Paramount Pictures to turn Disney around. Eisner also failed to receive any new stock option grants.

Not that Eisner's hurting. In addition to reaping more than $1 billion over the last 15 years from bonuses and stock option grants, Eisner exercised an additional $50 million worth of stock options last year. Those options had been granted to Eisner in 1989 and were due to expire.

42. This "Inside Story" is adapted from James Bates, *Company Town; No Bonuses for Eisner, 3 Other Disney Execs,* L.A. Times, Jan. 6, 2000, at C1. Reprinted with permission. Copyright © 2000 Times Mirror Company. All rights reserved worldwide.

Nonetheless, Eisner's goose egg on the bonus scoreboard says a lot about Disney's fortunes last year and how his performance-based compensation formula has a downside as well as the extraordinarily lucrative upside he's previously enjoyed.

"He took his lumps, which is what he should have done. He didn't wimp out and give the standard excuse: 'It's not my fault,'" said executive compensation specialist Graef Crystal, who designed Eisner's early pay formulas but no longer consults for the company.

...

"With a lot of companies, the profits are high and the stock is up, so the CEO gets rich," Crystal said. "When the stock goes down and profits are down, then it's all Fed Chairman Alan Greenspan's fault and the board gives the CEO a lot of money as a consolation prize." During Disney's previous fiscal year, Eisner's bonus was slashed 49%, but it still came to $5 million. That year was his most spectacular compensation period because he exercised $569.8 million in stock options in December 1997.

The disclosure about Eisner's lack of a bonus comes as Disney's stock—for the first time in nearly a year—is showing some life, with some investors finally turning hopeful.

KEY WORDS AND PHRASES

QUESTIONS AND CASE PROBLEMS

1. Lee Gray was a director, president, and treasurer of HMG/Courtland Properties, Inc. (HMG), a publicly held real estate investment trust, and of its investment adviser Courtland Group, Inc. As such, he negotiated the terms of a joint venture with Norman Fieber, another HMG director, for the development of a portfolio of properties located in the northeastern United States. During the course of the negotiations, Gray told Fieber that Martine Avenue Associates, a general partnership controlled by Gray and his sister, would be interested in co-investing with Fieber in buying an interest in the properties. Neither Gray nor Fieber disclosed that possibility to HMG. Martine did ultimately join a group of investors on Fieber's side of the transaction in May 1986, but HMG did not learn of Gray's economic interest in Martine until October 1996. Did either Gray or Fieber violate his fiduciary duties to HMG? [*HMG/Courtland Properties, Inc. v. Gray,* 749 A.2d 94 (Del. Ch. 1999)]

2. Bell Atlantic Corporation entered into merger negotiations with NYNEX Corporation to create one of the nation's largest telecommunications companies. NYNEX stated that it would execute a binding merger agreement only if the agreement included a liquidated damages provision under which either company would be forced to pay the other $550 million if its shareholders did not approve the deal. The termination fee arguably reflected each company's costs for negotiating and structuring the merger; however, it also clearly gave shareholders a disincentive to reject the merger. As a Bell Atlantic director who otherwise favored the NYNEX merger, would you approve the agreement with the fee provision?

    Assume the merger was approved by the shareholders of both companies. A dissenting Bell Atlantic shareholder sues the company's directors for breach of fiduciary duty, claiming that the termination fee impaired shareholder voting rights by inequitably coercing shareholders into voting for the merger. Was the Bell Atlantic board's adoption of the merger agreement (including the $550 million termination fee) a valid exercise of its business judgment? [*Brazen v. Bell Atlantic Corp.,* 695 A.2d 43 (Del. 1997)]

3. Missouri Fidelity Union Trust Life Insurance Company stock was trading at $2.63 per share. Eight directors sold their stock for $7.00 per share, conditioned on the resignation of eleven of the fifteen directors of the corporation and the provision that five nominees of the buyer be elected as a majority of the executive and investment committees. Did the directors violate their fiduciary duty? Would the answer be different if the directors had controlled a majority of the voting stock? [*Snyder v. Epstein,* 290 F. Supp. 652 (E.D. Wis. 1968)]

4. The After-School Care Corporation owned more than forty day-care centers specializing in providing care to elementary-school-aged children in the afternoons. The president of the company, Clark Holmes, received a phone call at work one day from Marney Stein, the owner and sole proprietor of Pro Providers, a firm that owned six nursery schools for children aged two to four. Stein indicated that she wanted to sell Pro Providers for $1 million and asked if After-School was interested. Holmes proposed the purchase to the After-School board of directors. The directors were divided on the issue because they were not certain that branching out into nursery care would be a smart move. However, as funds were not available, there was no need to vote on the issue at that time.

    Holmes decided that he would try to purchase Pro Providers on his own. After securing a loan, Holmes entered into negotiations with Stein. They agreed on a price of $900,000, and the sale went through. Holmes did not inform the board of his activity until after the transaction was completed.

    A shareholder sues Holmes, alleging that he is taking for himself a corporate opportunity that belongs to the corporation. What kinds of arguments will the shareholder make? Will she be successful? Would the result be different if Holmes expands one of the Pro Provider nursery schools into a nursery/after-school center?

5. The Engulf Corporation is a large media and entertainment conglomerate with its stock trading on the New York Stock Exchange. Engulf is a major producer of films and videos and also publishes several magazines. The company has a shareholder rights plan (that is, a poison pill), which would make any hostile takeover financially prohibitive unless the pill is redeemed by Engulf's board of directors. On January 10, the Megaclout Corporation, in a move designed to gain control of Engulf, announced a tender offer for 51 percent of Engulf's shares at $140, an $11 premium over the market price.

   On January 14, in a meeting that lasted more than thirteen hours, the Engulf board of directors considered Megaclout's offer. Engulf's lawyers and investment bankers attended and made detailed presentations on the adequacy of the offer. The next day, the directors officially announced that they believed the Megaclout offer was unacceptable for two reasons: (1) the long-term value of the Engulf stock ranged from $160 to $170, so $140 was financially inadequate; and (2) Engulf had a distinct corporate culture that included special ways of doing business, an outstanding record of management–employee relations, and strong support for community projects in the towns where Engulf businesses were located. Acceptance of Megaclout's tender offer would pose a direct threat to this corporate culture. For these reasons, the board refused to redeem the poison pill.

   Megaclout brought suit as an Engulf shareholder against the Engulf board of directors, demanding that the board redeem the poison pill, which would allow all the shareholders to decide whether they wanted to accept the offer by tendering their shares.
   a. Must the Engulf board of directors redeem the poison pill at this time?
   b. The board argues that the offer, which is $11 over the market price of the stock, is financially inadequate. Is the argument convincing? Why or why not?
   c. Should managers be concerned about corporate constituencies other than shareholders, such as employees or communities where businesses are located? What if these different concerns conflict?
6. Shlensky is a minority shareholder of Chicago National League Ball Club, Inc., which owns and operates the Chicago Cubs baseball team. The defendants are directors of the club. Shlensky alleges that since 1935, when the first night baseball game was played, every major league team except the Cubs had scheduled most of its home games at night. This has allegedly been done for the specific purpose of maximizing attendance, thereby maximizing revenue and income.

   The Cubs have sustained losses from their direct baseball operations. Shlensky attributes the losses to inadequate attendance at the Cubs' home games, which are played at Wrigley Field. He feels that if the directors continue to refuse to install lights at Wrigley Field and schedule night baseball games, the Cubs will continue to sustain similar losses.

   Shlensky further alleges that Philip Wrigley, the president of the corporation, has refused to install lights not, as Wrigley claims, for the welfare of the corporation, but because of his personal opinion that "baseball is a daytime sport." Additionally, Shlensky alleges that the other directors have acquiesced in Wrigley's policy.

   In his complaint, Shlensky charges that the directors are acting for reasons contrary to the business interests of the corporation and that such acts constitute mismanagement and waste of corporate assets. Does the directors' decision fall within the scope of their business judgment? Have the directors failed to exercise reasonable care in managing the corporation's affairs? [*Shlensky v. Wrigley,* 237 N.E.2d 776 (Ill. App. Ct. 1968)]
7. McDonald, a potential buyer of financial institutions, visited Halbert at the Tulane Savings and Loan Association. Halbert was president, manager, and chairman of the board, and, along with his wife, he was the owner of 53 percent of the stock of the association. McDonald asked if the association was for sale. Halbert replied that it was not for sale but that he and his wife would sell their controlling stock for $1,548 per share. Halbert did not tell the association's board of directors or its shareholders about McDonald's interest in acquiring the association.

   In addition to agreeing to sell his stock, Halbert also agreed to cause the association to withhold the payment of dividends. After Halbert's shares were purchased, Halbert, who had not yet relinquished his corporate offices, helped McDonald solicit the minority shareholders' shares and even advised them that, because McDonald was going to withhold dividends for ten to twenty years, they ought to take his offer of $300 per share. McDonald bought some of the minority shares at $300 and others for between $611 and $650.

   Did Halbert owe the minority shareholders a fiduciary duty? If so, what was his duty in selling his minority stock position? Was his conduct ethical? [*Brown v. Halbert,* 76 Cal. Rptr. 781 (Cal. App. Ct. 1969)]

8. In early 1993, Joseph Bydalek and Robert M. Fox formed a corporation to buy and run the "Fill-Er-Up Club." Fox owned 51 percent of the stock and was the sole officer and director; Bydalek owned 49 percent. On July 20, 1993, the club opened and Fox died in a car accident. Jeannine Willis, Fox's sister, became administrator. Five months later, she and two attorneys were elected officers and directors. Bydalek continued to run the club and his wife Laura tended bar and kept the books until July 18, 1994, when Willis had the club's locks changed to lock them out of the premises. Prior to the lockout, the Bydaleks were salaried, at-will employees. Willis never took a salary. The club lost $10,000 in its first year, never generated a profit, and never paid dividends. Willis closed the club in February 1996 because it was losing money and could not renew its liquor license. In October 1995, the Bydaleks sued Willis for conversion, breach of fiduciary duty, and shareholder oppression. Result? [*Willis v. Bydalek,* 997 S.W.2d 798 (Tex. Ct. App. 1999)]

9. The board of directors of ITT Corporation adopted a reorganization plan to thwart a hostile tender offer and proxy contest by Hilton Hotels Corporation. The plan called for the breakup of ITT into three new entities, the largest of which (ITT Destinations) would hold more than 90 percent of ITT's current assets. The board of directors of ITT Destinations would consist of the current directors of ITT, but, unlike the current ITT board, the ITT Destinations board would be classified or staggered. The board would be divided into three classes with each class of directors serving for a term of three years and with one class to be elected each year. A shareholder vote of 80 percent would be required to remove the directors without cause or to repeal the classified board.

The ITT board proposed to implement this plan prior to ITT's annual meeting and without obtaining shareholder approval. The net effect of the plan was to make it impossible for the ITT shareholders at the 1997 annual meeting to elect a majority of the directors nominated under Hilton's proxy contest. Was ITT's adoption of the reorganization plan a valid exercise of business judgment? [*Hilton Hotels Corp. v. ITT Corp.,* 978 F. Supp. 1342 (D. Nev. 1997)]

10. Many old economy businesses, such as United Technologies Corporation and Prudential Insurance Company of America, do not permit employees to receive stock options from or invest in customers, suppliers, or other business partners. In contrast, senior executives at Internet switching equipment dynamo Cisco Systems, Inc. frequently invest in or accept stock options from Cisco's customers, suppliers, and partners. For example, Deborah Traficante, a Cisco vice president who led a team that sold $16 million worth of Cisco networking gear to a small Internet service provider called MysINet and helped arrange for Cisco's financing arm to lend money to MysINet to finance the purchase, earned $200,000 in profits on her MysINet stock when the company was sold. She also received allocations of "friends and family" shares in the initial public offerings of three Cisco customers.

Cisco characterized such purchases as proper because the executives disclosed their investments to the company and disqualified themselves from decisions involving companies in which they invested. Cisco executives are in high demand to sit on boards of directors and advisory boards, where they receive stock options in start-ups that are, or may become, Cisco customers or suppliers. Having a Cisco executive as an investor or board member gives a young company invaluable credibility, opening doors to potential customers and other investors. If you were the CEO of Cisco, would you continue to permit executives to invest in Cisco's customers, suppliers, or partners? Why or why not? What would you recommend if you were Cisco's largest shareholder? [*See* Glenn R. Simpson & Scott Thurm, *Web of Interests: At Cisco, Executives Accumulate Stakes in Clients, Suppliers,* WALL ST. J., Oct. 3, 2000, at A1.]

INTERNET SOURCES	
This site for Richards, Layton & Finger, the largest law firm in Delaware, contains excellent articles on Delaware corporate and partnership law and provides links to other legal-related sites.	http://www.rlf.com
The California Public Employees Retirement System (CalPERS) is the largest public pension fund in the United States and a very active institutional investor. Its site contains detailed recommendations for corporate governance practices in the United States, Europe, and Japan.	http://www.calpers.ca.gov/site/invest.htm#CORPORATE
The AFL–CIO Web site on executive pay—Executive Pay Watch—tracks executive compensation, highlights shareholder proposals dealing with excessive executive compensation, and identifies directors on compensation committees who have conflicts of interest with the executives they are overseeing.	http://www.paywatch.org

Securities *and* Financial Transactions

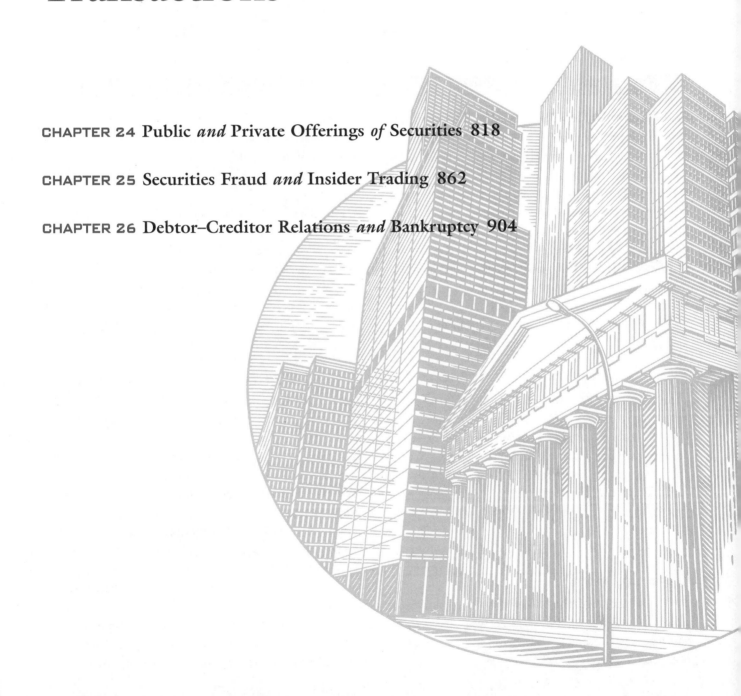

CHAPTER 24

Public *and* Private Offerings *of* Securities

RAISING CAPITAL THROUGH SECURITIES OFFERINGS

Most businesses reach a certain point at which the founders' initial capital investment and ongoing bank loans are insufficient for continued growth. At this juncture, the directors and managers of the company must decide whether to rein in the company's growth consistent with its existing capital asset base or to sell an interest in the company to raise capital for continued expansion. Although entrepreneurs often turn first to family and friends and wealthy individual investors *(angels),* then to venture capitalists, many companies eventually seek to raise capital through an initial public offering of the company's shares. Even those companies that can internally generate the cash flow for growth may decide to sell securities to spread the concentration of risk in the business venture and to give the founders and early investors liquidity.

Because registered public offerings are very expensive (often costing more than $900,000 in out-of-pocket expenses alone), sales of securities to private investors or venture capitalists are almost always structured to be exempt from the federal registration requirements. Whether the directors and managers of a company seek an exemption or go through the public offering process, they must understand and comply with federal and state securities laws. Penalties for noncompliance include damages, fines, and imprisonment.

CHAPTER OVERVIEW

This chapter first provides an overview of the federal statutory scheme that regulates the offer and sale of securities. It then defines the key terms "security," "offer," and "sale" under the Securities Act of 1933 (the 1933 Act).

Next, the chapter describes the public offering process, including the registration of securities, the role of an underwriter, the importance of due diligence, and the preparation of the registration statement, and provides a managerial timeline for a public offering.

The chapter then outlines some of the most relied-on exemptions from registration for offerings by the issuer, including the private offering and small business exemptions. A table that lists the key elements of certain exemptions is also provided.

The chapter goes on to discuss exemptions for secondary offerings by shareholders, the restrictions on the resale of registered and unregistered securities, offerings outside the United States under Regulation S, and sales to qualified institutional buyers under Rule 144A. The periodic reporting and certain other requirements under the Securities Exchange Act of 1934 (the 1934 Act) are identified.

The chapter then highlights liability for failure to meet the registration and prospectus-delivery requirements under Section 12(1) of the 1933 Act and for misstatements or omissions in the registration statement. The discussion focuses on Section 11, under which issuers are strictly liable for misstatements or omissions in a registration statement and certain officers, all directors, accountants, and underwriters are liable if they fail to act with due diligence. The chapter explains who may sue, who may be sued, the elements of liability, the available defenses, and the calculation of damages and provides guidelines for due diligence.

Section 12(a)(2) of the 1933 Act, which provides a remedy for any person who purchases a registered or unregistered security in a public offering by means of a misleading prospectus or oral communication, is then discussed. The broader antifraud provisions contained in Section 10(b) of the 1934 Act and Rule 10b-5 (which apply to both registered and exempt offerings of securities) are discussed in Chapter 25. This chapter concludes with a discussion of criminal penalties for violations of the 1933 Act.

Federal Statutory Scheme

The two principal federal acts that regulate securities transactions and issuers, the Securities Act of 1933 and the Securities Exchange Act of 1934, were adopted during the depths of the Great Depression. These and subsequent acts embodied three important beliefs: (1) investors should be provided with all essential information prior to investing in speculative ventures, (2) corporate insiders should not be allowed to abuse their position and use nonpublic information concerning their companies to their own financial advantage, and (3) injured investors should receive adequate relief even in the absence of common law fraud.

THE 1933 ACT

In adopting the 1933 Act, the U.S. Congress sought to ensure adequate disclosure to investors of material information about the issuer and the offering. The Act requires that promoters of securities offerings register them with the Securities and Exchange Commission (SEC), an agency of the U.S. government, and provide to prospective purchasers a prospectus containing material information about the issuer and the offering, unless the security or the type of transaction is exempt from registration.

Congress rejected suggestions that it also regulate the content or quality of securities offerings. As a result, investors are not protected from making highly speculative or foolish investments. The 1933 Act requires only that they be advised of all material facts before they invest their money.

In addition to requiring registration, the 1933 Act expressly creates private rights of action for certain violations of its provisions. This means that in addition to public enforcement by the SEC or criminal proceedings by the U.S. Attorney's Office, any investor can bring a private suit for damages.

THE 1934 ACT

The 1934 Act sought to build upon the 1933 Act by implementing a policy of continuous disclosure. Companies

---

HISTORICAL PERSPECTIVE

Genesis *of the* 1933 Act

Regulations governing securities offerings in the United States stem from the public and governmental outrage at and distrust of the nation's financial markets that followed the stock market crash of 1929. According to Representative (later Speaker of the House) Sam Rayburn:

Millions of citizens have been swindled into exchanging their savings for worthless stocks. The fraudulent promoter has taken an incredible toll from confiding people. . . .

These hired officials of our great corporations who permitted, who promoted, who achieved the extravagant expansion of the financial structure of their respective companies today present a pitiable spectacle. Five years ago they arrogated to themselves the greatest privileges. They scorned the interference of the Government. They dealt with their stockholders in the most arbitrary fashion. They called upon the people to bow down to them as the real rulers of the country. Safe from the pitiless publicity of Government supervision, unrestrained by Federal statute, free from any formal control, these few men, proud, arrogant, and blind, drove the country to financial ruin. Some of them are fugitives from justice in foreign lands; some of them have committed suicide; some of them are under indictment; some of them are in prison; all of them are in terror of the consequences of their own deeds.[a]

a. House Consideration, Amendment and Passage of H.R. 5480, May 5, 1932, *77* CONG. REC. 2910, 2918 (1933), *reprinted in* 1 FED. SEC. L. LEGIS. HIST. 1933–1982, at 2948 (1983).

of a certain size and with a certain number of shareholders or whose stock is traded on a national securities exchange are required to file periodic reports with the SEC. The 1934 Act also contains stringent antifraud provisions and implements filing requirements for insiders dealing in their own company's stock. In addition, the 1934 Act established a framework for the self-regulation of the securities industry under the ultimate supervision of the SEC.

All of the securities acts have been amended numerous times since their adoption. Exhibit 24.1 briefly describes the main sections of the 1933 and 1934 Acts. More detailed excerpts from both acts and the SEC regulations adopted thereafter can be found in Appendixes J and K of this book.

THE PRIVATE SECURITIES LITIGATION REFORM ACT OF 1995

The Private Securities Litigation Reform Act of 1995 (the Reform Act)[1] was designed to correct perceived

1. Pub. L. No. 104-67, 109 Stat. 737 (1995) (codified in scattered sections of 15 U.S.C.). The complete text of the act is available at <http://thomas.loc.gov/c104/h1058.enr.txt>.

EXHIBIT 24.1	Important Sections of the 1933 and 1934 Acts

1933 Act

- *Section 2*—defines terms, including security, offer, sale, and underwriter.
- *Sections 3 and 4*—list exempt securities and describe exempt transactions.
- *Section 5*—requires the registration of all securities offered and sold in the United States (unless an exemption from registration is available) and the delivery of a prospectus.
- *Sections 6–8 and 10*—outline the general procedures of the registration process and detail the guidelines for the registration statement and the accompanying prospectus.
- *Sections 11 and 12*—describe the penalties, elements of liability, damages, and parties held liable for violation of the 1933 Act.

1934 Act

- *Section 10*—regulates the use of manipulative and deceptive devices in the purchase or sale of securities.
- *Section 12*—lists the reporting requirements for registered public companies.
- *Section 16*—provides the reporting requirements for insiders including directors, officers, and principal shareholders and the limitations on insider transactions.

abuses in private securities litigation, particularly class actions that coerced settlements and thereby increased the cost of raising capital and chilled corporate disclosure to investors. The Reform Act included a variety of procedural provisions designed to prevent the filing of frivolous suits by so-called professional plaintiffs who often owned a limited number of shares in many companies and stood ready to lend their names to class-action complaints they often had not even read. The Act introduced the idea that the "most adequate plaintiff" should be the lead plaintiff and should select counsel to represent the class. There is a rebuttable presumption that the plaintiff with the largest financial interest in the relief being sought by the class is the most adequate.

The Reform Act limited discovery to prevent "fishing expedition" lawsuits designed to force the defendants to settle frivolous claims to avoid the cost of discovery. Except in extraordinary circumstances, courts must stay discovery pending a ruling on a motion to dismiss. Stricter and uniform pleading requirements require the investors to specify each statement alleged to be misleading and the reason or reasons the statement is misleading. The plaintiffs also must plead and then prove that the misstatement or omission alleged in the complaint actually caused their loss. They must also specifically allege facts giving rise to a "strong inference" that the defendant acted with the required state of mind. Thus, in securities fraud cases under Section 10(b), which require *scienter*, the plaintiffs must allege facts giving rise to a strong inference of fraudulent intent on the part of the defendant. The combination of the stricter pleading requirements and the staying of discovery pending a decision on a motion to dismiss makes it more likely that defendants will be able to resolve frivolous claims more quickly and cheaply by winning motions to dismiss before incurring the time and expense of extensive discovery.

The Reform Act generally eliminates joint and several liability in cases under Section 10(b) of the 1934 Act for defendants who did not commit knowing violations and requires such defendants to pay only their "fair share" of the damages, that is, the portion attributable to their percentage of responsibility. Outside directors are given the same protection for suits under Section 11 as a way to encourage capable outsiders to serve on corporate boards.

The Reform Act also imposes new requirements for independent public accountants auditing the financial statements of publicly traded companies. These requirements, which are designed to result in early detection and disclosure of fraud, are discussed more fully in Chapter 25.

Finally, the Reform Act created a new statutory safe harbor for written and oral forward-looking statements by issuers and certain persons retained or acting on behalf of the issuer. This provision is discussed further in the sections dealing with liability under Sections 11 and 12(2) of the 1933 Act. Its application to fraud cases under Section 10(b) of the 1934 Act and Rule 10b-5 is discussed in Chapter 25.

In 1998, Congress passed the Securities Litigation Uniform Standards Act[2] to limit a plaintiff's ability to bring a securities fraud case involving a publicly traded company in state court. State court proceedings had become more prevalent since the passage of the Reform Act because most state laws do not provide the protections it afforded to companies and their officers and directors. By eliminating this possible end run around the Reform Act, Congress sought to create national standards for fraud cases brought against companies traded on the national securities exchanges (such as the New York Stock Exchange and the Nasdaq Stock Market). The so-called Delaware carve-out permits shareholders to bring a state law class-action suit against a corporation and its directors for breach of preexisting common law fiduciary disclosure obligations, however. Because directors of a Delaware corporation have a fiduciary duty to disclose fully and fairly all material information within their control and to avoid misleading partial disclaimers, shareholders of USA Networks, Inc. were permitted to bring a class action in New York state court based on the allegation that the company had advised shareholders that it was going into television merchandising in Italy but failed to advise them of the risks involved.[3]

SEC RULES AND REGULATIONS

Since Congress adopted the 1933 Act and the 1934 Act, the SEC has used its power as an administrative agency to adopt a number of rules and regulations. The SEC uses these rules and regulations to address some of the ambiguity of the securities acts, make case-specific exemptions, carry out informal discretionary actions, and conduct investigations regarding compliance with the securities acts.

For instance, in 1972, the SEC adopted Rule 144 to clarify the definition of the term "underwriter." In 1982, the SEC adopted Regulation D with rules that outlined the requirements and limitations for exempt private offerings and offerings by small businesses. Subsequently, it adopted Rule 701 to exempt offers and sales of securities pursuant to employee benefit plans. Regulation A was revised to make it easier for small businesses to raise capital without going through a public offering.

BLUE SKY LAWS

In addition to the federal securities laws, state statutes called *blue sky laws* also regulate offerings and sales of securities. An issuer selling securities must comply not only with the federal securities laws but also with the securities laws of all of the states where the securities are offered or sold. Fortunately, many states, the District of Columbia, and Puerto Rico have adopted the Uniform Securities Act, so there is some consistency among state laws. Other states, including New York and California, have retained their own version of securities regulatory schemes. As explained in Chapter 17, in some respects the state laws are stricter than their federal counterparts, yet as the U.S. Court of Appeals for the Seventh Circuit noted in *Mueller v. Sullivan,*[4] ignorance of those laws is no excuse.

Like the federal statutes, the Uniform Securities Act emphasizes disclosure as the primary means of protecting investors. Some states, however, authorize the securities administrator to deny a securities selling permit unless he or she finds that the issuer's plan of business and the proposed issuance of securities are fair, just, and equitable. Even if the state statute does not specifically include this provision, a state securities commissioner can usually deny registration or qualification to sell in that state until he or she is satisfied that the offering is fair. This process is referred to as *merit review.*

In late 1996, Congress passed the Capital Markets Efficiency Act of 1996,[5] which was designed in part to provide more uniformity between federal and state securities regulation. Under this law, states cannot require more than the type of filing required by the SEC (including any amendments), a consent to service of process, and a filing fee for transactions involving only accredited investors that are exempt pursuant to Rule 506 under Regulation D. Accordingly, pre-offer and pre-sale notice filings and merit review requirements of the states have been preempted in connection with Rule 506 offerings. The law similarly preempts state registration requirements and merit review in connection with most initial public offerings registered with the SEC. The law also provides federal preemption for the issuance of securities to "qualified purchasers," a category of investors to be defined by the SEC at a later time.

---

2. 15 U.S.C. § 77 p(d).
3. Lalondriz v. USA Networks, Inc., No. 99 Civ. 1711 (RO) (S.D.N.Y. June 30, 1999). *Accord* Gibson v. PS Group Holdings, Inc., No. 00-CV-0372 W (RBB) (S.D. Cal. Mar. 8, 2000).
4. 141 F.3d 1232 (7th Cir. 1998) (Case 17.4).
5. Pub. L. No. 104-290, 110 Stat. 3416 (1996).

INTERNATIONAL CONSIDERATION

On most U.S. stock exchanges, foreign securities are traded in the form of American Depository Receipts (ADRs). The securities themselves are held by a financial institution called a depository, which issues the ADRs traded by investors and handles any foreign-exchange transactions. This structure allows the foreign securities to trade at a per-share price level customary in the U.S. market. In addition, it allows investors to trade interests in foreign securities in compliance with U.S. clearance and settlement requirements.

 # Definition *of* Terms

It is necessary to define three basic terms used in the 1933 Act—security, offer, and sale. Their meanings in a securities law context may be different from their everyday meanings.

SECURITY

The meaning of *security* for purposes of the 1933 Act—and most other securities statutes—is much broader than the common conception of the term. Section 2(1) of the 1933 Act defines a security as:

> any note, stock, treasury stock, bond, debenture, evidence of indebtedness, certificate of interest or participation in any profit-sharing agreement, collateral-trust certificate, pre-organization certificate or subscription, transferable share, investment contract, voting-trust certificate, certificate of deposit for a security, fractional undivided interest in oil, gas, or other mineral rights, any put, call, straddle, option, or privilege on any security, certificate of deposit, or group or index of securities (including any interest therein or based on the value thereof), or any put, call, straddle, option, or privilege entered into on a national securities exchange relating to foreign currency, or, in general, any interest or instrument commonly known as a "security," or any certificate of interest or participation in, temporary or interim certificate for, receipt for, guarantee of, or warrant or right to subscribe to or purchase, any of the foregoing.

Because security is defined so broadly, the circumstances of a particular transaction must be analyzed to determine whether it does, in fact, involve a security and is subject to regulation.

Certain investments that are commonly agreed to be securities include the stock and bonds of public and private companies. However, some investments, which by their name fall into the definition of securities, are not necessarily considered securities. An example is stock in a cooperative association owning an apartment building, whereby an occupant of the building owns shares of stock that are inextricably linked to the lease of a particular unit of the building. In *United Housing Foundation v. Forman,*[6] the U.S. Supreme Court held that because the dwelling was used as a place of habitation, the inducement to purchase was solely to acquire living space and not to invest for profit. Consequently, the Court ruled that the shares of stock were not securities under the 1933 Act.

Investment Contract The scope of the law goes further than just the category of commonly agreed-on securities. Under federal law, one type of security—an *investment contract*—is present if the transaction involves an investment of money in a common enterprise with profits to come solely from the efforts of others. This test was first enunciated in the following landmark case.

6. 421 U.S. 837 (1975).

A CASE IN POINT

CASE 24.1
SEC v. W.J. Howey Co.
Supreme Court of the United States
328 U.S. 293 (1946).

Summary

FACTS The W.J. Howey Company owned large tracts of citrus acreage in Lake County, Florida. Expansion of the citrus acreage was financed, in part, by the sale of strips of land bearing citrus trees to persons living in various parts of the United States. Each prospective investor was offered both a land sale contract and an optional service contract (with a ten-year term) after being told that it was not feasible to invest in a grove unless service arrangements were made. Although investors were free to use any service company, approximately 85 percent of the acreage sold was serviced by a company affiliated with Howey.

(Continued)

(Case 24.1 continued)

Most of the investors were unskilled in agriculture. Their primary motivation for investing was the expectation of substantial profits, projected to be 10 percent annually over a ten-year period.

ISSUE PRESENTED Does the offer and sale of parcels of land bearing citrus trees, coupled with optional management contracts pursuant to which the promoter cares for the trees, constitute an investment contract and hence a security under Section 2(1) of the 1933 Act?

SUMMARY OF OPINION The U.S. Supreme Court held that the transactions in this case clearly involved investment contracts as listed in Section 2(1). The plan involved a scheme "whereby a person invests his money in a common enterprise and is led to expect profits solely from the efforts of the promoter or a third party." The persons buying the land were not skilled in the cultivation, harvesting, or marketing of citrus fruits; they had no intent to occupy the land and develop it for themselves; and they were attracted solely by the prospect of a return on their investment.

The Court held that the critical elements in the transaction were the large-scale cooperative nature of the enterprise and the managerial efforts of the promoters. The transfer of real property rights was purely incidental. Accordingly, there was no question that an investment contract was involved. The fact that some investors chose not to accept the optional service contract was immaterial, the Court concluded, because the 1933 Act prohibits the offer, as well as the sale, of unregistered, nonexempt securities.

RESULT Howey had offered and sold securities.

COMMENTS This case makes it clear that a security can be present even in schemes that are not purely speculative or promotional in nature and that involve investments in tangible assets having intrinsic value. The Supreme Court shifted the focus of the analysis for determining whether a security was involved from the surface appearance of a transaction to the expectations of the parties. Subsequent cases have expanded the *Howey* test and have held that Section 2(1) is not to be read literally because Congress intended the application of the federal securities laws to turn on the economic realities underlying a transaction and not on the name attached to it.

There is a split in the circuits as to whether the "common enterprise" element of the *Howey* test can be met simply by showing "vertical commonality" between the promoter and the investor or whether these must be "horizontal commonality," that is, multiple investors who usually pool their funds and receive a pro rata share of the profits.[7] The majority view is that horizontal commonality is required.

Although the *Howey* test required that the investor rely solely on the efforts of others for the expectation of profits, subsequent decisions have established that there can be an investment contract, and thus a security, even if the investor participates in the generation of profits.[8] For example, an interest in a general partnership is generally held not to be a security because each partner by law has the right to exercise control in the operation of the partnership. But the courts have found a general partnership interest to be a security if it meets any of the following three tests:

1. The partnership agreement leaves so little power to the partners that the arrangement is tantamount to a limited partnership.
2. The investor is so inexperienced in business affairs that he or she is incapable of intelligently exercising his or her partnership powers.

---

7. *See* SEC v. Unique Fin. Concepts, Inc., 196 F.3d 1195 (11th Cir. 1999) (vertical commonality sufficient) and the cases cited therein.

8. SEC v. Glenn W. Turner Enters., Inc., 474 F.2d 476 (9th Cir. 1973), *cert. denied*, 414 U.S. 821 (1973).

3. The investor is so dependent on the unique management ability of the promoter or manager that he or she cannot replace the manager or exercise meaningful partnership powers.[9]

A limited partnership interest is almost always held to constitute a security because limited partners, in order to protect their limited liability, are prohibited by law from assuming any control over the partnership business. An interest in real estate is not in itself considered a security, though it may be a security if it is combined with a management contract, as in *Howey*.

The SEC and at least thirty-five state securities regulators have taken the position that interests in a limited liability company (LLC) are securities. Regulators base their conclusion on either of two theories: that LLC interests constitute investment contracts under *Howey* or

that they have all the characteristics of stock. The U.S. Supreme Court has not yet ruled on this issue.

A controversy arose as to whether the sale of an entire business through the sale of its corporate stock involved the sale of a security. Under the *sale-of-business doctrine*, certain courts held that compliance with federal securities laws was not necessary because the economic reality of the transaction was that a business, rather than securities, was being sold. The U.S. Supreme Court rejected this doctrine in *Landreth Timber Co. v. Landreth*,[10] holding that the sale of a business through a stock transaction is a securities transaction if the stock sold possesses all of the characteristics traditionally associated with common stock.

Family Resemblance Test Promissory notes and other evidences of indebtedness may or may not constitute securities, depending on the factual context. In the following case, the Supreme Court set forth the family resemblance test for determining which types of notes are securities.

---

9. The test to determine whether a general partnership constitutes a security was set forth in *Williamson v. Tucker*, 645 F.2d 404 (5th Cir. 1981), *cert. denied*, 454 U.S. 897 (1981), and later applied in *Holden v. Hagopian*, 978 F.2d 1115 (9th Cir. 1992).

10. 471 U.S. 681 (1985).

◀ A CASE IN POINT ▶

CASE 24.2

Reves v. Ernst & Young
*Supreme Court of the
United States
494 U.S. 56 (1990).*

Summary

FACTS Farmers' Cooperative of Arkansas and Oklahoma, Inc. (the Co-op) was an agricultural cooperative of approximately 23,000 members. To raise money to support its general business operations, the Co-op sold demand notes, that is, promissory notes payable at any time the holder of the note requested payment. The notes were not collateralized and were uninsured; they paid a variable rate of interest that was adjusted monthly to keep it higher than the rate paid by local financial institutions. The Co-op offered the notes to both members and nonmembers, marketing the scheme as a safe and secure "investment program."

Despite such assurances, the Co-op filed for bankruptcy, leaving approximately $10 million in demand notes unpaid. A group of note holders sued the Co-op's auditors under Section 10(b) of the 1934 Act, claiming that the auditors intentionally failed to follow generally accepted accounting principles in evaluating the financial condition of the Co-op.

The note holders prevailed at the trial level, receiving a $6.1 million judgment. The auditors appealed, claiming that the demand notes were not securities under the 1934 Act. (The definition of "security" under Section 3(a)(10) of the 1934 Act is virtually identical to the definition under Section 2(1) of the 1933 Act.) The appeals court reversed, and the note holders appealed.

ISSUE PRESENTED Are demand notes issued by a farmers' cooperative to its members securities?

SUMMARY OF OPINION The U.S. Supreme Court adopted a *family resemblance test* to use in determining whether a promissory note is a security. Under this test, a promissory note is initially presumed to be a security based upon the literal language of the securities acts ("The term 'security' means any note . . ."). This presumption may be

(Continued)

(Case 24.2 continued)

rebutted, however, by a showing that the note bears a "strong resemblance" (in terms of four specific factors) to an enumerated category of instruments commonly held not to constitute securities, such as notes delivered in connection with consumer financing, notes secured by a home mortgage, and short-term notes secured by accounts receivable. The four specific factors used in evaluating an instrument are:

1. the motivations that would prompt a reasonable seller and buyer to enter into the transaction;
2. the plan of distribution of the instrument;
3. the reasonable expectations of the investing public; and
4. whether some factor, such as the existence of another regulatory scheme, significantly reduces the risk of the instrument, thereby rendering application of the federal securities laws unnecessary.

Applying these four factors to the case at hand, the Court observed the following: (1) the Co-op sold the notes in an effort to raise capital for its general business operations, and the purchasers bought them in order to earn a profit in the form of interest; (2) the notes were distributed to a wide group of people over an extended period; (3) the notes were characterized to the public as investments, and it is likely that the public perceived them as such; and (4) there was no risk-reducing factor making application of the federal securities laws unnecessary (for example, the notes were not federally insured certificates of deposit). Because the notes bore no family resemblance to the types of notes commonly held not to constitute securities and, in fact, resembled the types of instruments the federal securities laws were designed to regulate, the Court held that the notes were securities.

In reaching its decision, the Court expressly rejected the use of the *Howey* test in determining whether a note constitutes a security. It stated that the *Howey* test is useful in determining whether an instrument that does not come within any of the categories listed in the statutory definition of security constitutes an investment contract, but is not helpful in determining whether an instrument is a note or other instrument listed in the statutory definition.

The Court also expressly rejected the use of an investment-versus-commercial test, which previously had been used by the majority of circuits in determining whether a note constituted a security. Under this test, notes issued in a commercial or consumer context were held not to be securities, but those issued in an investment context were held to be securities.

The Court lastly rejected the auditor's argument that because the notes were demand notes, they fell within the literal terms of Section 3(a)(10) of the 1934 Act ("the term 'security' . . . shall not include . . . any note . . . which has a maturity at the time of issuance of not exceeding nine months"). The Court held that a demand note does not necessarily mature in nine months. In light of this patent ambiguity and Congress's broad purposes in enacting the federal securities laws, the Court chose not to interpret the exclusion in Section 3(a)(10) to cover the Co-op's demand notes.

RESULT The demand notes issued by the farmers' cooperative to its members were securities.

COMMENTS The holding in *Reves v. Ernst & Young* removed much of the uncertainty regarding the status of promissory notes for securities law purposes. Prior to this decision, the courts were widely split as to the proper test to use in evaluating promissory notes.

The "In Brief" provides a decision tree for determining whether an instrument is a security and for analyzing the securities registration requirements discussed below.

OFFER

Section 2(3) of the 1933 Act defines an *offer* as "every attempt or offer to dispose of, or solicitation of an offer to buy, a security or interest in a security, for value." This definition is much broader than that in contract law. An offer that is unacceptably vague for contract law purposes may well constitute an offer for federal securities law purposes. Section 2(3) expressly provides, however, that preliminary negotiations or agreements between an issuer and an underwriter or among underwriters do not constitute an offer to sell.

SALE

A *sale* is defined by Section 2(3) to include "every contract of sale or disposition of a security or interest in a security, for *value*." The crucial term in this definition is value. It has been defined by the courts very broadly—more broadly, for example, than in state corporations statutes, which require that stock can be issued for "value" only in the form of cash, property, or compensation for past services.

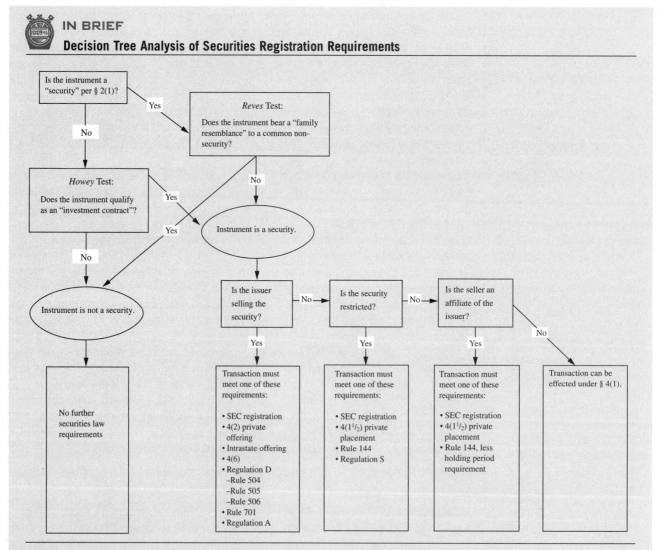

IN BRIEF

Decision Tree Analysis of Securities Registration Requirements

Source: This decision tree was created by John Lee based on information provided by Constance E. Bagley. Copyright © 1998 by Constance E. Bagley. Used by permission.

The Public Offering

Once it is determined that an investment offering does, in fact, involve a security, the issue of registration must be addressed.

REGISTRATION OF SECURITIES

Section 5 of the 1933 Act requires the registration of all securities offered and sold in the United States, unless an exemption from registration is available. Section 5 can be summarized as follows:

1. Section 5(a) prohibits the sale of a security before a registration statement has been filed with the SEC. The *registration statement* consists of filing forms and the *prospectus,* the disclosure document that an issuer of securities provides to prospective purchasers. Section 5(c) prohibits the use of any means of interstate commerce to offer to sell or buy any security during this time.
2. During the waiting period between the filing of the registration statement and the date the registration statement becomes effective with the SEC, written and oral offers to sell the security may be made, but all written offers must meet the standards required of a prospectus.
3. Once the registration becomes effective with the SEC (referred to as *going effective*), offers and sales of securities may be made. However, Section 5(b) continues to require that any written offer or sale of a security be preceded or accompanied by a prospectus meeting the requirements of the 1933 Act.

In general, every public offering of securities must be registered with the SEC. The registration requirement is designed to ensure that certain information is filed with the SEC and distributed to potential investors by means of a prospectus. Unlike certain state securities authorities, the SEC does not have statutory authority to approve or disapprove an offering on its merits. Instead, the registration process is designed to ensure that the information provided to investors is accurate and complete. The general procedures to be followed in the registration process are found in Sections 6 and 8 of the 1933 Act.

The registration of a public offering is an expensive and time-consuming affair. The process includes the preparation of the registration statement—that is, the document filed with the SEC—and of the prospectus, which must be included in the registration statement and provided to prospective investors. Securities lawyers, independent accountants, investment bankers, a printer,

and an engraver all become involved in the process. The out-of-pocket fees and expenses for an initial public offering, excluding compensation for the investment bankers who underwrite the offering, can easily exceed $900,000. All such fees must be paid by the issuer of the securities (or, in the case of offerings by persons other than the issuer, by the seller of the securities).[11]

THE ROLE OF THE UNDERWRITER

A public offering of securities is typically, though not necessarily, underwritten by one or more broker–dealers or investment banking firms.

Firm Commitment Underwriting In a *firm commitment underwriting,* the underwriters agree to purchase the entire offering, thus effectively shifting the risk of the offering from the issuer to the underwriters. The lead underwriter is responsible for negotiating with the issuer the terms of the offering and compensation and for putting together an underwriting group (the *syndicate*). Each member of the underwriting group agrees to purchase a certain number of the securities of the issuer once the offering is declared effective by the SEC.

In theory, such a commitment places the underwriters in a risky position. In practice, the lead underwriters will not go forward with the offering unless they have tentative offers from buyers for as much as three times the number of shares being offered. Accordingly, the underwriting agreement between the issuer and the lead underwriter as representative of the underwriting group and the agreements among the members of the underwriting group are typically not signed until immediately before the offering is declared effective by the SEC. The price at which the securities will be offered and the underwriters' commission are usually not formally determined until the evening before the offering goes effective.

Once the offering becomes effective, the underwriters attempt to sell the securities that they are obligated to purchase. Most firm underwriting agreements are of short duration. Usually, the sale closes within two days of the date the agreement is signed. As of the closing date, the underwriters are obligated to purchase any securities that remain unsold.

Because a firm commitment underwriting will provide the issuer with a predetermined amount of money within a specified period, it is attractive to issuers. A firm commitment underwriting is also attractive to

11. The process of doing an initial public offering is discussed in detail in Constance E. Bagley & Craig E. Dauchy, The Entrepreneur's Guide to Business Law 494–540 (1998).

investors because it implies that the underwriters themselves are willing to take a risk on the offering. Because it places the members of the underwriting group at risk for the amount of the offering, broker–dealers and investment bankers will usually agree to a firm underwriting only if they are certain that they will be able to sell the offered securities quickly. Such certainty will depend on a variety of factors, including the amount of money being sought, the performance and prospects of the company, whether the company is seasoned or relatively new, and the condition of the public securities market.

Best-Efforts Underwriting In a *best-efforts underwriting*, the underwriters do not agree to purchase the securities being offered. Instead, they agree to use their best efforts to find buyers at an agreed-on price. Best-efforts underwritings are often used for initial public offerings or for companies that are unseasoned.

A best-efforts offering leaves the risks of the offering entirely with the issuer. Some established, successful companies may prefer a best-efforts offering, however, because the cost of distribution is lower than for a firm commitment underwriting.

THE REGISTRATION STATEMENT

Sections 7 and 10 of the 1933 Act and the rules promulgated by the SEC under the Act contain detailed guidelines as to what must be included in the registration statement and the accompanying prospectus. Regulations C and S–K, adopted by the SEC pursuant to the 1933 Act, list the general information required in connection with most public registrations.[12] In addition, the SEC has issued a variety of forms that list the information required in connection with particular types of transactions.

Forms Securities offered in an initial public offering are registered in a registration statement meeting the requirements of *Form S–1* (or if the issuer is a small business, *Form SB–1*). The registration statement must include a complete description of the securities being offered, the business of the issuer, the risk factors, the management, and the major shareholders. It must also include audited financial statements.

Companies that have been filing periodic reports under the 1934 Act, but are not followed so widely that the SEC can be confident that information previously filed will be disseminated in the marketplace, file on

12. 17 C.F.R. § 230.400 *et seq.* (1997); 17 C.F.R. § 229 (1997).

Form S–2. *Form S–2* allows these companies to present certain information in a streamlined form and to incorporate previous filings by reference so that investors can obtain more information if desired. This is part of the SEC's integrated disclosure system, which is designed to integrate the reporting requirements under the 1934 Act with the prospectus delivery requirement under the 1933 Act.

Form S–3 applies to a category of companies that have filed periodic reports under the 1934 Act for at least three years and have a widespread following in the marketplace. An issuer can use Form S–3 for an offering of common stock only if the aggregate market value of the voting stock held by nonaffiliates is $150 million or more or, alternatively, if the aggregate market value of the voting stock held by nonaffiliates is $100 million or more and the issuer has an annual trading volume of three million shares or more. (*Affiliates* include officers, directors, and controlling shareholders. The SEC has a rebuttable presumption that any shareholder with 10 percent of the issuer's stock is an affiliate.)

For companies filing on Form S–3, information about the registrant that has been reported in annual and quarterly reports filed under the 1934 Act need not be provided to investors in the prospectus, unless there has been a material change in the registrant's affairs or financial statements. However, such reports are incorporated by reference and are deemed a part of the prospectus for liability purposes.

As part of the Small Business Initiatives (SBI) designed to ease the cost of raising capital for small businesses, the SEC adopted new registration forms, Forms SB–1 and SB–2, to simplify the offering methods for small business issuers. *Small business issuers* are defined as companies with revenues less than $25 million whose market value of publicly held securities (other than those held by affiliates) is less than $25 million. Other aspects of the SBI changes that affect exemptions from registration and reporting requirements are discussed later in this chapter.

Nonreporting and transitional small business issuers can use Form SB–1 to offer up to $10 million annually. *Form SB–2* has no limit on the amount of offerings by small business issuers. Both forms can be used for initial and repeat offerings as well as for primary and secondary offerings. In addition, the SB forms require less extensive audited financial statements than are required under Form S–1. Only the last fiscal year's audited balance sheet and the previous two years' audited income statements are required under Forms SB–1 and SB–2. Exhibit 24.2 compares some of the requirements of registered offerings on Forms S–1, SB–1, and SB–2.

EXHIBIT 24.2	**Comparison of Public Offering Requirements**		
	Form S–1 Offering	**Form SB–1 Offering**	**Form SB–2 Offering**
Amount of offering	No limit	Up to $10 million in any fiscal year	No limit
Type of issuer	Any issuer	Must be a nonreporting or a transitional small business issuer	Must be a small business issuer
Type of offering	No limitations	No limitations	No limitations
Type of disclosure required	S–1 basic registration form for most offerings. S–1 items referenced in Regulation S–K.	Offering statement with three models: 1. Q&A, Form U–7 2. Form 1–A, old form 3. Form SB–2, part I	Simplified Form SB–2. SB–2 items referenced in Regulation S–B, a simplified version of Regulation S–K.

Prospectus The prospectus is the document provided to prospective purchasers of an issuer's securities. It is contained within the registration statement.

The tone of a prospectus frequently strikes nonlawyers as dry, bleak, and confusing. This perception arises out of the conflicting purposes of the prospectus. On the one hand, it is a selling document, designed to present the best possible view of the investment and the issuing company. On the other hand, it is a disclosure document, an insurance policy against claims of securities fraud. This second function usually predominates. The prospectus usually contains only provable statements of fact, with numerous disclaimers regarding the future success of the issuer. Businesspeople, accustomed to presenting their company in the best possible light, frequently have difficulty adjusting to the somber tone of the prospectus.

Effective October 1, 1998, companies selling securities to the public in the United States were required to use plain English in the design and language of the cover page, summary, and risk factors sections of the prospectus. In these sections, companies must (1) use short sentences with everyday words, (2) avoid legal jargon and highly technical business terms, (3) use the active voice, (4) not use multiple negatives, and (5) use bulleted lists for complex information, if possible. Companies are encouraged, but not required, to use plain English throughout the prospectus. On January 24, 2000, as part of Regulation M–A, the SEC extended the plain English requirements to the summary sheet for tender offers, mergers, and going-private transactions. As of early 2001, "most observers agree that prospectuses have become more understandable and useful documents."[13]

A sample cover page of a prospectus appears as Exhibit 24.3.

DUE DILIGENCE

A key step in preparing the registration statement is the process of *due diligence,* whereby the company, the underwriters, and their respective counsel assemble and review the information about the company in the registration statement. The company must be prepared to back up every claim it makes in the prospectus. Even if the claim is stated as an opinion (such as "The company believes that it is the industry leader"), the company must be able to demonstrate the reasonableness of the belief.

Underwriters cannot simply rely on the representations of issuers or the officials of issuers but must perform their own independent due diligence investigation. They should go beyond the corporate documents provided by the issuer and examine information in press releases and news reports concerning key competitors and others important to the issuer's business. Underwriters should also monitor relevant Web sites and public agency filings.

Exhibit 24.4 provides a long but useful list of tasks that should be undertaken by officers, directors, underwriters, and counsel engaged in the offering of securities.

REGISTRATION PROCEDURE

The registration statement must be filed with the SEC. Section 8 of the 1933 Act provides that the registration automatically becomes effective on the twentieth day after filing, unless the SEC fixes an earlier date. Virtually all registrants file their registration statement with language stating that it will not become effective until declared

---

13. Pankaj K. Sinha & C. Grace Campnell, *'Plain English' Rules Have Generally Been Successful,* CORP. COUNS. WKLY., Mar. 14, 2001, at 88.

EXHIBIT 24.3 | Sample Prospectus Cover Page

PROSPECTUS

600,000,000 Shares

agere systems

CLASS A COMMON STOCK

Agere Systems Inc. is offering 600,000,000 shares of its Class A common stock. This is our initial public offering and no public market currently exists for our shares.

Our Class A common stock has been approved for listing on the New York Stock Exchange under the symbol "AGR.A," subject to official notice of issuance.

Investing in our Class A common stock involves risks. See "Risk Factors" beginning on page 8.

PRICE $6 A SHARE

	Price to Public	Underwriting Discounts and Commissions	Proceeds to Agere Systems
Per Share..............	$6.00	$.234	$5.766
Total..................	$3,600,000,000	$140,400,000	$3,459,600,000

Lucent Technologies Inc., as selling stockholder, has granted Morgan Stanley & Co. Incorporated the right to purchase up to an additional 90,000,000 shares of Class A common stock to cover over-allotments. Under federal securities laws, Lucent is the selling stockholder of any shares of our Class A common stock that Morgan Stanley acquires from Lucent in the exchange for Lucent indebtedness held by Morgan Stanley, as described in "Underwriters — Over-allotment Option," and sells in this offering. We will not receive any proceeds from the sale of shares of our Class A common stock by the selling stockholder.

The Securities and Exchange Commission and state securities regulators have not approved or disapproved these securities, or determined if this prospectus is truthful or complete. Any representation to the contrary is a criminal offense.

Morgan Stanley & Co. Incorporated, in its capacity as lead underwriter, expects to deliver the shares to purchasers on April 2, 2001.

MORGAN STANLEY DEAN WITTER

BEAR, STEARNS & CO. INC.

JPMORGAN

SALOMON SMITH BARNEY

DEUTSCHE BANC ALEX. BROWN

ABN AMRO ROTHSCHILD LLC

SG COWEN

BLAYLOCK & PARTNERS, L.P.

March 27, 2001

Source: *Courtesy of Agere Systems.*

EXHIBIT 24.4 **Due Diligence Checklist**

The Product

1. Examine and operate each product, particularly new products, to assess appearance, function, design, and so on.
2. Assess the threat of obsolescence for each significant product line.
3. Review new product and service plans and development progress.
4. Compare the product with those of competitors and assess the threat from new competitors.
5. Perform an analysis of unproven technology, using experts if necessary.

The Industry

1. Estimate the size of the industry, present and projected, in each significant product line, and compare company growth projections with anticipated market size for consistency.
2. Review government and trade reports and trade literature regarding the company's market segments to check for consistency with the representations and unstated premises in the prospectus.
3. Analyze competitors' SEC filings for unanticipated trends or developments.
4. Evaluate the importance of proprietary products, copyrights, and trademarks within the industry.
5. Interview trade association personnel concerning trends of relevance to the prospectus.
6. Assess the effect of macroeconomic trends (for example, interest rate fluctuations, inflation rates, and economic growth rates) on the issuer's prospects for success.
7. Assess the comparative strengths and weaknesses of competitors in terms of the dominant competitive factors in the industry (price, service, performance, and so on).
8. Compare the company's financial performance with that of its competitors.
9. Determine whether research and development (R&D) expenditures are consistent with industry practice.

Marketing and Distribution

1. Evaluate the importance of original equipment manufacturers (OEMs), present and future.
2. Interview principal customers regarding the company's products and services, complaints, anticipated future needs, and so on.
3. Analyze each significant contract regarding contingencies, extent of warranties and other service obligations, rights of cancellation, and so on. Check contracts with customers for completeness and to determine the existence of side written or oral commitments or other terms that materially vary company contracts. Evaluate the quality of the backlog.
4. Evaluate the adequacy of the distribution network, the degree of control over distribution, and the like.
5. Evaluate the effectiveness of marketing personnel.
6. For new products, estimate the cost of introduction, and determine whether the cost is adequately reflected in cash-flow projections.
7. Assess the likelihood of discontinuation of products or services and whether the prospectus should disclose this information.

Technology

1. Review the company's R&D plans to determine whether any radical changes in product direction are anticipated and what cost burden will be imposed on the company in coming years.
2. Evaluate the effectiveness of R&D personnel and organization to assess the company's capacity for technological innovation.
3. Evaluate the company's patent position and the enforceability of its technology licenses.
4. Analyze any litigation regarding technology rights.
5. Review royalty contracts for contingencies and the like, and contact the licensees to determine the existence of any agreement or understanding that varies the terms of the contract.
6. With regard to government contracts, determine what interest, if any, the government asserts or may assert in company technology.
7. Review employee and independent contractor nondisclosure agreements, assignments of inventions, and noncompete agreements.
8. Evaluate other professional affiliations of management or R&D personnel (such as academic affiliations) to assess the likelihood of competing claims on company technology.
9. Evaluate the effectiveness of the company's efforts to police its patents, preserve its trade secrets, maintain its copyrights and marks, and other intellectual property; assess the company's resources to perform these tasks.
10. Determine whether the company's exports are consistent with export-control laws.

(Exhibit 24.4 continues)

(Exhibit 24.4 continued)

Management

1. Investigate the prior experience of management and directors in the same industry and the same size company, their experience with large firms, and so on. Also, investigate the backgrounds of officers and directors (including any criminal complaints or lawsuits), their standing in the community, their reputation in the industry, and so on.
2. Evaluate the responsiveness of management to previous auditors' management letters.
3. Assess the effectiveness of management through interviews with outside customers and suppliers, bankers, auditors, and so on.
4. Review prior transactions between the company and insiders for fairness, propriety, full disclosure, and so on.
5. Assess the effectiveness of the board of directors, and identify any gaps in expertise or independence.
6. Determine whether any significant defections from management or the board are imminent, and assess the effect on company competitiveness.

Employees

1. Compare the company's stock option plans, pension plans, salaries, and other executive compensation with those of competitors to assess the company's ability to attract and retain skilled employees.
2. Consider whether the public offering is likely to result in the loss of key employees to retirement.
3. Review employee contracts for terms, unrecorded benefit obligations, contingencies, and the like. Interview key employees to determine whether unrecorded written or oral commitments have been made to them.
4. Determine whether compensation obligations have been properly accounted for in the company's books.
5. Assess the adequacy of the labor supply for each operating division.
6. Evaluate the company's labor relations history, union contracts, prospects of union activity, and so on.

Production

1. Assess the ability of production facilities to handle anticipated volumes and whether the cost of new plant and equipment is consistent with anticipated cash flow.
2. Evaluate product and process obsolescence, and compare production facilities to those of industry competitors to determine future competitiveness, both technical and economic.
3. Inquire into anticipated plant closings as well as plans for new facilities, and consider whether disclosure in the prospectus would be advisable.
4. Evaluate the adequacy of management information systems and inventory-control programs.
5. Assess the exposure to single-source suppliers, and evaluate the company's contingency plan for responding to an interruption to supplies.
6. Contact major suppliers to determine their satisfaction with the company and their plans to retire, reduce, or raise the price of key supplies and components.

Accounting

1. Determine whether intangible expenses, such as R&D expenditures, are being or should be expensed.
2. Analyze company finances, including supporting work papers where necessary, for prior years.
3. Review budgets and projections in order to determine material changes in the company's financial position, and compare past budgets and projections with actual experience in order to assess the accuracy of management's estimates.
4. Compare the company's revenue-recognition policy and other accounting conventions with those of the industry.
5. Evaluate the effect of customer financing practices on present and future revenues.
6. Evaluate the effect of changes in tax laws and the company's position with respect to open tax years.
7. Verify that the use of proceeds matches financial needs quantitatively and qualitatively.
8. Determine whether inventory turns are consistent with industry ratios.
9. Assess the accuracy of the inventory reported and the adequacy of the inventory obsolescence reserve, and determine the suitability of the mix of materials inventory.
10. Review aging receivables for consideration of reserve or write-off, and assess the adequacy of the bad-debt reserve and other reserves against income.
11. Obtain a report as to the adequacy of the company's accounting controls.
12. Ascertain that the preeffective auditor's "cold comfort" letter is complete.

(Exhibit 24.4 continues)

(Exhibit 24.4 continued)

Legal

1. Identify and assess the effect of new and proposed governmental regulations on operations, expenses, and the like.
2. Check company property and equipment for title, title insurance, encumbrances, liens, and so on.
3. Review incorporation documents, bylaws, and minutes of all shareholder, board, and board committee meetings for several years, both to confirm regularity and to identify events that might require further investigation.
4. Review stock transfer records for regularity, and check for agreements affecting ownership or control of shares.
5. Evaluate pending litigation, review the terms of significant concluded litigation, and investigate the existence of threatened claims or future exposure for statutory or regulatory violations.
6. Determine whether any acquisitions, mergers, reorganizations, and the like are impending or likely and what effect they will have on the company.
7. Review all press releases, promotional literature, company reports, news accounts, and the like for consistency with the prospectus.
8. Review company banking, leasing, factoring arrangements, and the like, and assess the likelihood and effect of disruption or termination.
9. Determine that all insurable risks have been adequately insured against and that policies do not have material adverse exclusions or omissions.

Source: Derived from Robert Alan Spanner, *Limiting Exposure in the Offering Process,* REV. SEC. & COMMODITIES REG. 64–66 (Apr. 8, 1987). Copyright © 1987, Standard & Poor's Corporation. Reprinted by permission.

effective by the SEC so that the SEC staff has the necessary time (which usually exceeds the statutory twenty-day period) to review the filing.

Each amendment to the registration statement filed prior to the effective date starts the twenty-day period running again; however, if the SEC has consented to the amendment, the waiting period may be accelerated. If the SEC finds that the registration statement is materially defective in some respect, it may, after notice and a hearing, issue a stop order suspending the effectiveness of the offering.

Review Registration statements received by the SEC are subject to review by the SEC staff. The extent of the review is usually affected by the nature of the offering and the number of filings that the SEC must review. In general, all first-time registrants receive a complete review. Most repeat registrants receive a more limited review, and some receive no review.

Comments of the SEC staff are conveyed through a letter of comment, which is either read over the telephone to the issuer's counsel or, less often, mailed to counsel directly. The members of the SEC staff are usually available to discuss these letters of comment either by telephone or in person. Although the comment letters contain only suggestions without force of law, they generally result in the filing of an amendment to the registration statement. Acceding to the staff's reasonable suggestions is less expensive and less time-consuming than fighting an issue in an administrative hearing and in

court. The amended registration statement is usually filed with a letter from counsel answering, item by item, the issues raised by the staff.

Waiting Period The time between the filing of the registration statement and the time it becomes effective is called the *waiting period* or the *quiet period* because the law severely limits what the issuer and underwriters can say or publish during this time. No sale of securities can occur prior to the effectiveness of the registration statement; however, the underwriters may assemble selling groups, distribute copies of the preliminary prospectus, and even solicit offers to buy the securities.

In September 2000, the SEC announced that it was examining the increasingly common practice of start-ups selling cheap stock or granting warrants to corporate customers that place big orders to determine whether this activity results in an overstatement of revenues. This is the topic of the "Inside Story" for this chapter.

The preliminary prospectus—sometimes referred to as a *red-herring prospectus* because a notice on the cover states in red ink that it is not final and is subject to revision—is an incomplete version of the final prospectus. It sets forth the proposed range for the selling price and omits the underwriters except for the lead underwriters, whose names appear on the cover page. The preliminary prospectus usually is not distributed until all changes needed to respond to SEC staff comments are incorporated.

Selling efforts during the waiting period must be done in strict compliance with the securities laws. They

ETHICAL CONSIDERATION

During the roadshow, large institutional investors are frequently shown earnings projections by the lead underwriter's industry analyst, the assumptions underlying the company's business model, and industry comparisons. This information should not be provided in writing unless the underwriters gather it up after the meeting. Nonetheless, it sometimes finds its way into "cheat sheets" that, although meant for the underwriters' internal use, are given to favored clients. Is it fair to give additional information—beyond that contained in the prospectus—to certain favored investors?

usually include *roadshows,* that is, oral presentations to large institutional investors in key cities in the United States, Europe, and Asia. Any offers to buy can be accepted only after the registration statement is declared effective by the SEC and only after each prospective investor is provided with a copy of the final prospectus. Notice of a proposed offer can be circulated by means of a *tombstone ad,* so named because of its appearance and somewhat somber tone.

The issuing company and its lead underwriter must be careful about the information they release to the public during the waiting period. Conditioning the market with a news article or press release about the company and its upcoming offering is referred to as *gun-jumping.* In such circumstances, the company may be in violation of the 1933 Act, and the SEC may require the issuer to postpone the offering. For example, the SEC required Web Van, the Internet grocer, to postpone its initial public offering after it released significant information not contained in its prospectus during a conference call as part of its roadshow.

Going Effective Once a registration statement has been informally cleared by the SEC staff or the registrant has received notice that the registration statement will not be reviewed, a preeffective amendment will be filed with the SEC. This is typically accompanied by a request that the waiting period be accelerated so that the registration statement will become effective at a particular date and time. Without the request for acceleration, the registration statement would not become effective until the expiration of an additional twenty-day period.

Once an offering is declared effective, sales of the securities may be consummated, provided that each purchaser is given a copy of the final prospectus. Information concerning the price of the securities and underwriting arrangements is filed with the SEC as part of the final

prospectus. Supplemental sales literature, which in most cases need not be reviewed by the SEC, may be provided to prospective purchasers. Such sales literature must be preceded or accompanied by the final prospectus. Often the underwriters will run a tombstone ad to publicize their involvement in the offering.

Exhibit 24.5 suggests a timeline for managers who are considering a public securities offering.

SHELF REGISTRATION

Rule 415 under the 1933 Act provides for the *shelf registration* of securities, that is, the registration of a number of securities at one time for issuance later. The securities can then be issued over a period of time, for example, in connection with continuous acquisition programs or employee stock-benefit plans, or they can be issued at a later date, for example, when interest rates or market conditions are more favorable to the issuance of securities. Shelf registration can result in reduced legal, accounting, and printing expenses and increased competition among potential underwriters. Moreover, the issuer can respond more flexibly to rapidly changing market conditions by varying the structure and terms of the securities on short notice.

Registration is intended to ensure that current information is available to prospective underwriters and purchasers of securities. Accordingly, shelf registration is restricted to offerings in which the information contained in the registration statement will not become stale or inaccurate after some months or years.

EXHIBIT 24.5	Managerial Timeline for a Public Securities Offering
Day 1	Decide upon a public offering of securities to raise capital, and choose a securities underwriting firm.
Day 30–60	With the aid of the underwriter, prepare the forms and prospectus for the registration statement.
Day 61–90	File the registration statement with the SEC for review, and submit any amendments to the filing.
Day 91–120	During the quiet period, the underwriter can assemble selling groups, distribute copies of the preliminary prospectus, and solicit offers to sell the securities.
Day 121 +	Once the offering is declared effective and the pricing amendment is filed, sales of the company's securities may begin.

Rule 415 limits the availability of shelf registration to ten types of offerings, which can be broken down into two basic categories: (1) traditional shelf offerings, and (2) offerings of securities of certain large, publicly traded companies that are eligible to use short-form registration procedures such as Form S–3.

Traditional shelf offerings include (1) securities offered pursuant to employee benefit plans; (2) securities offered or sold pursuant to dividend or interest reinvestment plans; (3) warrants, rights, or securities to be issued upon conversion of other outstanding securities; (4) mortgage-related securities; and (5) securities issued in connection with business combination transactions. With respect to offerings by certain large, publicly traded companies, the SEC has decided that because the market receives a steady stream of high-quality information concerning these issuers, the risks of stale information are minimal.

REORGANIZATIONS AND COMBINATIONS

When securities holders are asked to approve a corporate reorganization or combination—such as a reclassification of securities, a merger involving an exchange of securities, or a transfer of assets of one corporation in exchange for the securities of another—they are in effect faced with an investment decision. In recognition of this fact, the SEC adopted Rule 145, which expressly provides that the protections provided by the 1933 Act's registration requirements are applicable to certain types of business reorganizations and combinations. An offer, offer to sell, or sale occurs when a plan of reorganization is submitted to shareholders for approval. Transactions that fall within the guidelines specified in Rule 145 should be registered with the SEC in a combined registration statement and proxy statement on *Form S–4,* unless an exemption from registration is available.

Because shareholder approval of mergers and other combinations necessarily involves communications between a corporation and its shareholders, Rule 145 also contains specific rules as to when such communications will be deemed to be a prospectus or an offer to sell for purposes of the 1933 Act.

Rule 145 also provides that under certain circumstances affiliates of the acquired company, such as officers, directors, or controlling shareholders, are deemed *underwriters,* that is, persons selling securities on behalf of the issuer or a person who controls or is under common control with the issuer. Such affiliates cannot resell their securities without compliance with certain resale restrictions, which include limitations on the amount of securities sold in a three-month period.

SECONDARY OFFERINGS

A principal advantage of registering a securities offering with the SEC and the appropriate state securities authorities is that the securities may be traded relatively freely following the initial public offering. A *secondary offering,* that is, a subsequent offering by a person other than the issuer, must either be registered with the SEC or be exempt from registration. If the secondary offering is of nonrestricted securities and is made by a nonaffiliate, there are no limitations on the size of the offering or the number of offerees.

 # Exemptions *for* Offerings *by the* Issuer

In adopting the 1933 Act registration provisions, Congress provided exemptions from registration when there is no practical need for it or the public benefits from it would be too remote. Exemptions from registration fall into two categories: exempt securities and exempt transactions.

Exempt securities, listed in Section 3 of the 1933 Act, include the following:

1. Any security issued or guaranteed by the United States or any state of the United States.
2. Any security issued or guaranteed by any national bank.
3. Any security issued by a charitable organization.
4. Any security that is part of an issue offered and sold only to persons residing within a single state or territory, if the issuer is a resident of the same state or territory. (*Note:* Even though the intrastate offering exemption is listed under Section 3, the SEC treats it as a transactional exemption under Section 4.)

Exempt transactions are described in Section 4 of the 1933 Act. They include the following:

1. "Transactions by any person other than an issuer, underwriter or dealer" (Section 4(1)).
2. "Transactions by an issuer not involving any public offering" (Section 4(2), the private-offering exemption).

Most state blue sky laws have exemptions from registration that roughly correspond to the federal exemptions.

PRIVATE OFFERINGS UNDER SECTION 4(2)

Because of the expense and burdens of public offerings, companies trying to raise money usually attempt to qualify for an exemption from registration. They most frequently rely on the exemption for private offerings. A *private offering,* often called a *private placement,* is directed to selected qualified investors, rather than to the public. A private offering can be consummated more quickly and with far less expense than a public offering.

Because securities offered under the private-offering exemption are unregistered, their subsequent transfer is restricted, and their price will be discounted accordingly. In addition, purchasers of privately offered securities may demand a greater voice in the operation of the business or sweeteners such as dividend preferences or mandatory redemption privileges, which force the company to re-purchase the stock upon the occurrence of certain events.

Under Section 4(2), an offering is exempt from regis-tration if it does not involve a "public offering." This term is not defined in the 1933 Act and thus has been the sub-ject of much judicial interpretation. The SEC originally took the position that "under ordinary circumstances an offering to not more than twenty-five persons is not an of-fering to a substantial number and presumably does not involve a public offering."[14] This guideline was rejected by the Supreme Court in the following landmark case.

14. Securities Act Release No. 285 (1935).

A CASE IN POINT

CASE 24.3
SEC v. Ralston Purina Co.
Supreme Court of the United States
346 U.S. 119 (1953).

Summary

FACTS Ralston Purina, a feed and cereal company, offered common stock at market prices to the employees of the company. Among those employees responding to the offer were artists, bake-shop foremen, chow-loading foremen, clerical assistants, clerks, stenographers, and at least one veterinarian. Between 1947 and 1951, the company sold a total of $2 million worth of stock to 2,000 of its employees. The employees lived in various locations throughout the United States. Ralston Purina took the position that because the stock was offered only to "key employees" of the company, it was a private offering exempt from registration under the 1933 Act.

ISSUE PRESENTED Does the determination of whether a transaction is a public or private offering depend primarily on the number of offerees or the sophistication of the offerees?

SUMMARY OF OPINION The U.S. Supreme Court held that the offering was not ex-empt from registration. The Court stated that absent a showing of special circum-stances, employees are indistinguishable from other members of the investing public as far as the securities laws are concerned.

The Supreme Court also rejected a strict numerical test. Instead, the Court held that the critical consideration is whether the class of persons offered the securities needs the protection of the 1933 Act: "An offering to those who are shown to be able to fend for themselves is a transaction not involving any public offering." If, as in the present case, an offering is made to those who are not able to fend for themselves, the transaction is a public offering. The Court noted that an important factor affecting this determination is whether the offerees have access to the same kind of information that the 1933 Act would make available through a registration statement.

RESULT Ralston Purina's offer of stock to its employees was not exempt from registration.

COMMENTS The Supreme Court's ruling in *Ralston Purina* refocused attention under Section 4(2) from a strict numerical test to the sophistication of the offerees. The ruling did little to clarify the private-offering exemption, and reliance on Section 4(2) therefore remained an uncertain and somewhat risky proposition.

REGULATION D: SAFE-HARBOR EXEMPTIONS

Responding to the need for greater certainty in connec-tion with the private-offering exemption, the SEC adopted Regulation D in 1982. Regulation D offers a safe harbor for those seeking exemption from registration. An issuer that fails to comply with all of the requirements of the applicable rule will not necessarily fail to have an ex-emption, however, because the transaction may still meet the more general conditions of Section 4(2).

Regulation D contains three separate exemptions from registration, defined by Rules 504, 505, and 506. Rules 501–503 define terms and concepts applicable to one or more of the exemptions.

Accredited Investors The concept of an accredited investor, derived from earlier federal regulations and state securities laws, is based on the idea that certain investors are so financially sophisticated that they do not need all the protections afforded by the securities laws. Rule 501 defines an *accredited investor* as any one of the following:

1. Any national bank.
2. Any corporation, business trust, or charitable organization with total assets in excess of $5 million.
3. Any director, executive officer, or general partner of the issuer.
4. Any natural person who had individual income in excess of $200,000 in each of the two most recent years, or joint income with that person's spouse in excess of $300,000 in each of those years, and who has a reasonable expectation of reaching the same income level in the current year.
5. Any natural person whose individual net worth, or joint net worth with that person's spouse, at the time of the purchase exceeds $1 million.

Integration of Sales If an issuer makes successive sales within a limited period of time, the SEC may *integrate* the successive sales; that is, it may deem them to be part of a single sale. Integrating two or more offerings may increase the number of unaccredited investors beyond acceptable limits, resulting in the loss of a private-offering exemption. The SEC and the courts look at a variety of factors to determine whether offerings should be integrated. If the offerings (1) are part of a single plan of financing, (2) are made at or about the same time, (3) involve the same type of consideration, and (4) are made for the same purpose, then the SEC may recommend integration of the offerings.

Rule 502(a) provides an integration safe harbor for Regulation D offerings. Under Rule 502(a), offers and sales made more than six months before the start of a Regulation D offering or more than six months after its completion will not be considered part of the Regulation D offering, provided that the same issuer makes no offers or sales of a similar class of securities during those six-month periods.

Rule 504 Rule 504 exempts offerings of up to $1 million within a twelve-month period. There may be an unlimited number of purchasers under Rule 504. Rule 504 is not available to issuers registered under the 1934 Act—known as public companies—or to investment companies such as mutual funds. It is also not available to *blank check companies,* which are development-stage companies that have no specific business plan or have a business plan to acquire a currently unknown business. The issuer must file a notice on Form D with the SEC within fifteen days after the first sale of securities.

Rule 505 Rule 505 exempts offerings of up to $5 million within a twelve-month period. General solicitations and advertising are not permitted in connection with a Rule 505 offering, and the issuer must reasonably believe that there are not more than thirty-five unaccredited investors. Rule 505 is not available to investment companies. Rule 505 requires that certain specified information be provided to purchasers (unless all are accredited investors). This information is generally compiled in a private-placement memorandum (described later) or offering circular. Rule 505 also requires that purchasers have the opportunity to ask questions and receive answers concerning the terms of the offering. A notice on Form D must be filed with the SEC within fifteen days of the first sale of securities.

Rule 506 Rule 506 (adopted by the SEC under Section 4(2)) exempts offerings that in the issuer's reasonable belief are limited to no more than thirty-five unaccredited investors, provided that the issuer reasonably believes immediately prior to making any sale that each unaccredited investor, either alone or with his or her purchaser representative, has enough business experience to evaluate the merits and risks of the prospective investment. There can be an unlimited number of accredited investors. General solicitations and advertising are not permitted, however.

Like Rule 505, Rule 506 requires that certain specified information be provided to purchasers (unless all purchasers are accredited investors) and that purchasers have the opportunity to ask questions and receive answers concerning the terms of the offering. A notice on Form D must be filed with the SEC within fifteen days of the first sale of securities.

SECTION 4(6) EXEMPTION

Section 4(6) of the 1933 Act exempts offers and sales by any issuer to an unlimited number of accredited investors, provided that the aggregate offering price does not exceed $5 million and there is no public solicitation or advertising in connection with the offering. The Section 4(6) definition of "accredited investor" is almost identical to that of Regulation D. The availability of this exemption does not depend upon the use of any type of disclosure document, nor is the issuer required to make any filing with the SEC.

REGULATION A

The 1992 SEC Small Business Initiatives expanded the previously largely unused Regulation A exemption and included the adoption of a "testing the waters" provision, which permits issuers to solicit indications of interest before filing any required disclosure documents.

Size of Offering and Eligible Companies Under Regulation A, $5 million of securities can be offered and sold in a twelve-month period, of which up to $1.5 million may be sold by the selling security holders. Only U.S. and Canadian companies that are not required to report under the 1934 Act can qualify to use Regulation A. In addition, the regulation cannot be used by an investment company, a company issuing oil and gas rights, or a blank check company.

Under Rule 262, the "bad boy" provision, Regulation A is unavailable if the issuer or its officers, directors, principal shareholders, or affiliates have been subject to specified proceedings, convictions, injunctions, or disciplinary orders from the SEC or other regulatory agencies arising from the securities business or postal fraud. To disqualify the company from using Regulation A, the misconduct must have occurred within five years preceding the filing, or within ten years for officers, directors, and principal shareholders.

Testing the Waters Regulation A issuers can determine interest in a proposed offering prior to filing an offering statement. The issuer need only file a solicitation of interest document with the SEC, along with copies of any written or broadcast media ads. There is no prohibition on general solicitation or advertising. Radio and television broadcasts and newspaper ads are permitted to determine investor interest in the offering.

No sales may be made or payment received during the testing-the-waters period. To move forward, the company must file Form 1–A with the SEC, and the Regulation A offering statement must be qualified by the SEC. Once the offering statement is filed, testing-the-waters activity ceases. Sales can be made only after the passage of a required twenty-day waiting period from the time of the last solicitation of interest.

OFFERINGS TO EMPLOYEES

Nonpublic companies that are not registered pursuant to the 1934 Act often face a problem when instituting employee stock plans. If the company relies on Rule 504, it can issue only $1 million in one twelve-month period. Because employee offerings are usually continuous, the issuer may face serious integration problems. It is seldom practical to shut a stock plan down for six months to take advantage of Regulation D's integration safe harbor.

In response to these problems, the SEC adopted Rule 701 and temporary Rules 702T and 703T. Rule 701 exempts offers and sales of securities made (1) pursuant to a written compensatory benefit plan for employees, directors, general partners, trustees (if the issuer is a business trust), officers, consultants, or advisers; or (2) pursuant to a written contract relating to the compensation of such persons. If the benefit plan is for consultants or advisers, they must render bona fide services not connected with the offer and sale of securities in a capital-raising transaction. Exempt compensatory benefit plans include purchase, savings, option, bonus, stock-appreciation, profit-sharing, thrift-incentive, and pension plans. The issuer must provide each plan participant with a copy of the plan and each contractor with a copy of his or her contract, but no other disclosure document is required by Rule 701.

Rule 701 applies only to securities offered and sold in an amount not more than the greatest of (1) $500,000, (2) 15 percent of the total assets of the issuer, or (3) 15 percent of the outstanding securities of the class being offered and sold. Moreover, the aggregate offering price of securities subject to outstanding offers made in reliance on Rule 701 plus securities sold in the preceding twelve months in reliance on Rule 701 may not exceed $5 million.

Rule 701 provides additional integration relief for issuers that sell both under Rule 701 and under Rule 504 or 505 of Regulation D. Offerings under Rule 701 are not integrated with those under Rules 504 and 505, and vice versa.

Rule 702T requires that a Form 701 be filed not later than thirty days after the first sale that brings the aggregate sales under Rule 701 above $100,000 and thereafter annually within thirty days following the end of the issuer's fiscal year. Rule 703T makes Rule 701 unavailable to issuers subject to injunctions for failure to file Form 701.

Exhibit 24.6 summarizes the key elements of certain exemptions from registration discussed in this chapter.

THE PRIVATE-PLACEMENT MEMORANDUM

The *private-placement memorandum* is the private-offering counterpart to the prospectus. Like the prospectus, the private-placement memorandum is both a selling document and a disclosure document. The disclosure function is usually primary, so the memorandum may not be as upbeat as the issuer might like.

EXHIBIT 24.6 **Key Elements of Certain Federal Exemptions from Registration**

Type of Exemption	Dollar Limit of the Offering	Limits on the Number of Purchasers	Purchaser Qualifications	Information Delivery Requirement	Issuer Qualifications
Section 4(2)	No limit	Generally limited to small number of sophisticated offerees able to understand and bear risk	Offerees and purchasers must have access to information and be sophisticated investors	No specific requirement but must answer questions from prospective investors and give access to information	No limitations
Regulation D: Rule 504[a]	Up to $1 million in twelve months	No limit	No requirements	None	Not a 1934 Act public-reporting company or an investment or blank check company
Regulation D: Rule 505[a]	Up to $5 million in twelve months	No limit on the number of accredited investors, but limited to thirty-five unaccredited investors and no general institution	No requirements for unaccredited investors	Disclosure documents meeting requirements of Regulation D if any are unaccredited investors	Not an investment company
Regulation D: Rule 506[a]	No limit	No limit on the number of accredited investors but limited to thirty-five unaccredited investors and no general institution	Unaccredited investors must have sufficient experience to evaluate the investment	Disclosure documents meeting requirements of Regulation D if any are unaccredited investors	No limitations
Section 4(6)	Up to $5 million	No limit on the number of accredited investors	All purchasers must be accredited—no unaccredited investors allowed	None	No limitations
Regulation A	$5 million in twelve months, with a maximum of $1.5 million sold by the selling security holders	No limit	No requirements	Offering statement qualified by SEC	A U.S. or Canadian company, but not a 1934 Act public-reporting company, or an investment company, or a blank check company, or a company issuing oil/gas/mineral rights, or disqualified under "bad boy" Rule 262
Rule 701[b]	The greatest of $500,000 or 15 percent of the total assets of the issuer of 15 percent of the outstanding securities of the same class, up to a limit of $5 million over twelve months	No limit on the number of employees, directors, officers, advisers, or consultants	Advisory and consulting services must not be connected with the offer and sale of securities in a capital-raising transaction	None	Not a 1934 Act public-reporting company or an investment company

a. All issuers relying on these exemptions are required to file a notice on Form D with the SEC within fifteen days after the first sale of securities.
b. Must be pursuant to written compensatory benefit plans or written contracts relating to compensation, and all issuers relying on this exemption must file Form 701 with the SEC within thirty days after the sale of more than $100,000 worth of securities and annually thereafter.

The content of the private-placement memorandum is determined by the exemption on which the issuer relies. For example, Rule 502(b) under Regulation D provides that if an issuer is selling securities under Rule 505 or 506 to any purchaser that is not an accredited investor, certain specified information, including certain additional financial statements, must be provided to the purchaser. On the other hand, if the issuer is offering securities under Rule 504, or only to accredited investors, or in reliance upon the general Section 4(2) exemption, the issuer is not required to provide any specific information. State blue sky laws may also influence the content and format of a private-placement memorandum.

In many circumstances, no private-placement memorandum is technically required. However, an issuer is well advised to create such a document in order to clearly demonstrate the disclosure made to prospective investors. Such disclosure is important to rebut claims of securities fraud, a topic discussed in Chapter 25.

Exemptions *for* Secondary Offerings

A principal advantage of registering a securities offering with the SEC and the appropriate state securities authorities is that the securities may be traded relatively freely following the initial public offering. However, securities issued in a private placement cannot be sold in a secondary offering, that is, a subsequent offering by a person other than the issuer, unless they are either registered or exempt from registration. Securities issued in a private placement are thus called *restricted securities.*

Exhibit 24.7 summarizes the definitions of certain key terms from the 1933 Act and the SEC regulations promulgated under it.

SECTION 4(1) EXEMPTION

Section 4(1) of the 1933 Act provides that "transactions by any person other than an issuer, underwriter, or dealer" are exempt from registration. Section 2 of the 1933 Act defines an *issuer* as any person "who issues or proposes to issue any security." A *dealer* is defined as "any person who engages either for all or part of his time, directly or indirectly, as agent, broker, or principal, in the business of offering, buying, selling, or otherwise dealing or trading in securities issued by another person."

An "underwriter" is defined as "any person who has purchased from an issuer with a view to, or offers or sells for an issuer in connection with, the distribution of any security." As used in the definition of an underwriter, the term "issuer" includes "any person directly or indirectly controlling or controlled by the issuer, or any person under direct or indirect common control with the issuer." For example, the sale of securities to the public by a controlling shareholder is a transaction involving an underwriter. Thus, the Section 4(1) exemption is unavailable.

If the person desiring to sell unrestricted securities is not an issuer, underwriter, or dealer, he or she may sell the securities without registration under Section 4(1). There is no limit to the size of the offering or the number of offerees. Section 4(1) is the exemption most often relied on by persons who sell securities in the secondary market in an ordinary transaction involving a broker.

RULE 144

Because of the uncertainty in the definition of the term "underwriter," the SEC adopted Rule 144 in 1972. Rule 144 is intended merely to provide objective criteria for deciding whether a person is an underwriter; it is not meant to be the exclusive means through which restricted securities may be sold. Under Rule 144, a person is *not an underwriter* if the following conditions are met.

1. Adequate current public information must be available concerning the issuer. This requirement effectively means that the issuer is a publicly traded company that has complied with the periodic reporting requirements imposed by the 1934 Act (discussed later in this chapter).
2. The securities must have been beneficially owned—with all economic rights belonging to the owner—and fully paid for at least one year prior to the date of sale.
3. In any three-month period, the seller must not sell more than the greater of (a) 1 percent of the outstanding securities of the class or (b) the average weekly trading volume in the securities during the four calendar weeks preceding the filing of the notice of sale on Form 144.
4. The securities must be sold in "broker's transactions," as defined in the 1933 Act, or directly to a "market maker," as defined in the 1934 Act. Solicitation of offers to buy is not permitted, and no com-

EXHIBIT 24.7	**Key Terms of the Securities Act of 1933 and SEC Regulations**

Security	Most commonly used criteria under federal law:
	1. Instrument listed in statutory definition (e.g., stock, note, bond, option) that does not bear family resemblance to instrument commonly understood not to be a security (Reves)
	2. Investment contract (Howey)
	   a. Investment of money
	   b. Common enterprise
	   c. Profits derived "solely" from efforts of others [Section 2(1)]

Offer	"Every attempt or offer to dispose of, or solicitation of an offer to buy, a security or interest in a security, for value." [Section 2(3)]
Sale	"Every contract of sale or disposition of a security or interest in a security, for value." [Section 2(3)]
Accredited investor	As defined by Rule 501 under Regulation D: 1. National bank, savings and loan, registered broker–dealer, insurance company, investment company, SBIC (small business investment company), employee benefit plan if the investment decision is made by a "plan fiduciary" 2. Charitable organization, corporation, or business trust with total assets greater than $5 million 3. Any director, executive officer, or general partner of the issuer 4. Any natural person with individual income greater than $200,000 in each of the two most recent years, or joint income with spouse greater than $300,000 in each of those years, with a reasonable expectation of the same income level in the current year 5. Natural person with individual net worth, or joint net worth with spouse, greater than $1 million at time of purchase 6. Entity owned by any of the above 7. Trust with assets greater than $5 million with purchases directed by a sophisticated investor 8. Private development company (as defined)
Restricted securities	"Securities issued in a transaction not involving a public offering." [Rule 144]
Issuer	"Every person who issues or proposes to issue any security," including, for purposes of definition of underwriter, "any person directly or indirectly controlling or controlled by the issuer, or any person under direct or indirect common control with the issuer." [Section 2(4)]
Affiliate	Any officer, director, or major shareholder (generally presumed to include one holding at least 10 percent of issuer's stock). Someone who controls, or is controlled by, or co-controls with the issuer. [Rule 144]
Underwriter	"Any person who has purchased from an issuer with a view to, or offers or sells for an issuer in connection with, the distribution of any security." [Section 2(11)]
"Not an underwriter"	"Not an underwriter" safe-harbor requirements of Rule 144: 1. Adequate public information available 2. One-year holding period (unless affiliate sells unrestricted securities) 3. Sales limitations for any three-month period: the greater of 1 percent of the outstanding securities of the class, or the average weekly trading volume for the preceding four weeks 4. Must sell through a broker or directly to a market maker 5. Form 144 filing if more than 500 shares or greater than $10,000 aggregate price in three months 6. Must have bona fide intention to sell within a reasonable amount of time after filing Form 144
Rule 144(k)	A nonaffiliate who has held the security for more than two years may resell without restriction.
Rule 144A	A nonaffiliate may resell without restriction to a "qualified institutional buyer."

missions for the sale may be paid to any person other than the broker who executes the order or sale.

5. If the amount of the securities sold during any three-month period will exceed 500 shares or have an ag-

gregate sale price in excess of $10,000, a notice on Form 144 must be filed with the SEC and with the principal stock exchange (if any) on which the securities are traded.

6. The person filing the Form 144 must have a bona fide intention to sell the securities within a reasonable time after the filing of the notice.

Rule 144(k) provides that a person who is not an affiliate of the issuer, and has not been an affiliate for three months preceding the sale, may sell restricted securities without regard to items 1, 3, 4, and 5 above if he or she has owned the securities for at least two years prior to their sale. This is of particular importance for privately held companies that do not file 1934 Act reports. Affiliates include officers, directors, and major shareholders. The SEC has a rebuttable presumption that anyone owning at least 10 percent of the issuer's stock is an affiliate.

If the requirements of Rule 144 are met, restricted securities may be sold publicly without registration. Usually, restricted securities are identified as such by legends appearing on the face or back of their stock certificates. Accordingly, an opinion from the issuer's attorney may be required before a transfer agent is willing to consummate a transaction involving restricted securities. Certificates issued following a sale pursuant to Rule 144 may be issued without restrictive legends.

If an affiliate of the issuer wants to sell stock, he or she must sell in accordance with Rule 144 (except for the one-year holding period requirement, which is inapplicable if the securities being sold were acquired in a registered offering) or use another available exemption. The most common is the *Section 4(1½) exemption* for private offerings by an affiliate. These offerings could qualify as private placements under Section 4(2) if made by the issuer. Thus, the securities can be offered only to persons who are capable of bearing and understanding the risk of the investment and who acquire the securities for investment purposes only and not with a view to distribution.

Exhibit 24.8 depicts the alternatives available for resales by affiliates and nonaffiliates.

Rule 144A *and* Regulation S

In 1990, the SEC adopted two new regulations governing the resale of unregistered securities and the offering of securities outside the United States. The rules were designed to liberalize primary and secondary trading of private-placement securities.

RULE 144A

Rule 144A permits the resale of unregistered securities to *qualified institutional buyers*—that is, institutional investors holding and managing $100 million or more of se-

EXHIBIT 24.8 Alternatives for Resale

Securities		Seller	
		Affiliate	**Nonaffiliate**
Issued in public offering		Register Section 4(1½) Rule 144 (without holding period requirement)	Section 4(1)
Not issued in public offering		Register Section 4(1½) Rule 144 (including holding period requirement)	Register Rule 144A Rule 144 (including holding period requirement) Rule 144(k)—if held for more than two years

curities—if the securities are not of the same class as any securities of the issuer listed on a U.S. securities exchange or quoted on an automated interdealer quotation system (such as Nasdaq Stock Market). The rule creates a safe harbor for trading unregistered securities that are often issued to institutional investors in private placements and are generally subject to Rule 144's holding periods. The creation of a secondary market for eligible unregistered securities has increased the liquidity and value of these securities and reduced the private offering discount for them.

If a transaction meets the terms of Rule 144A, it is deemed not to be a distribution. Therefore, the seller is not an underwriter as defined in the 1933 Act. If the seller is also not an issuer or dealer, it may rely on the Section 4(1) exemption for transactions by persons who are not issuers, underwriters, or dealers, so long as it resells only to other qualified institutional buyers.

Dealers may also take advantage of Rule 144A. Under Section 4(3) of the 1933 Act, dealers are entitled to an exemption from registration, unless they are participants in a distribution or in a transaction taking place within a specified period after securities have been offered to the public. If a transaction complies with Rule 144A, the dealer will be deemed not to be a participant in a distribution, and the securities will be deemed not to have been offered to the public. Accordingly, the transaction will be exempt from registration.

Rule 144A is a nonexclusive exemption. If the requirements of Rule 144A cannot be met, the parties to the transaction may still rely on the facts-and-circumstances analysis commonly associated with nonpublic transfers of unregistered stock. For example, the Section 4(1½) exemption for private resales of restricted securities may apply.

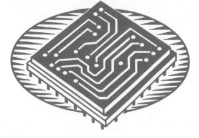

Offerings *on the* Internet

In 1995, Spring Street Brewing Company became the first company to conduct an initial public offering over the Internet.[a] Spring Street raised $1.6 million in an offering exempt under Regulation A. The securities were qualified under the blue sky laws of eighteen states on the assumption that the majority of potential purchasers resided in those states.

Other small companies have done offerings of up to $1 million under Rule 504 of Regulation D, which does not prohibit general solicitation for offerings of up to $1 million. Rule 505 (with its $5 million limit) and Rule 506 (with no dollar limit) do prohibit general solicitation. The SEC has taken the position that offerings on the Internet violate that ban unless access to offering materials is restricted to prequalified, accredited investors. This is normally done by making the sites offering the securities accessible only by password and only to investors shown by questionnaire to be accredited.[b]

Companies doing registered offerings can post the registration statement on their Web site. In addition, NETRoadshow and other firms have begun to make audiovisual transmissions of live investor roadshows to authorized investors via the Internet. The transmission is not edited for content and contains the oral presentations by management, questions and answers, and charts and graphics presented at the roadshow.[c] Access to the online versions of the roadshow is generally password protected and limited to the analysts, securities professionals, institutional investors, and others typically invited to attend roadshows.[d]

In April 2000, the SEC issued an interpretive release providing guidance on the electronic delivery of documents, Web site content, and online offerings.[e]

The release made it clear that a hyperlink embedded within a prospectus causes the hyperlinked information to be treated as part of the prospectus.

But the fact that information on a Web site is close to the prospectus does not, by itself, make the information an offer within the meaning of the securities laws. For issuers in the process of registering, however, Web site contents qualify as communications subject to Section 5 of the 1933 Act and so can constitute gun-jumping if they condition the market.

a. *See* Constance E. Bagley & John Arledge, *SEC Could Ease Offerings of Securities via the Web,* NAT'L L.J., Jan. 13, 1997, at B9.
b. *See* Constance E. Bagley & Robert J. Tomkinson, *Internet Is Seeing Its Share of Securities Offerings,* NAT'L L.J., Feb. 2, 1998, at C3.
c. *Id.* at C4.
d. *See, e.g.,* Activate.net corp., SEC No-Action Letter, available Sept. 21, 1999.
e. Available at <http://www.sec.gov/rules/concindx.htm#int>.

REGULATION S

Regulation S clarifies the general rule that any offer or sale outside the United States is not subject to the federal registration requirements. The SEC has long held the view that the Section 5 registration requirements do not apply to offers and sales effected in a manner that would result in the securities coming to rest abroad. Transactions meeting the requirements of certain safe harbors for the issuance and resale of securities set forth in Regulation S will be deemed to occur outside the United States.

All offers and sales of any security under Regulation S must be made in *offshore transactions,* defined as those in which no offer is made to a person in the United States and either (1) the buyer is outside the United States at the time the buy order is originated; or (2) the transaction is executed in, on, or through the facilities of a designated offshore securities market. No directed selling efforts may be made in the United States.

The combination of Rule 144A and Regulation S has expanded the private-placement market by increasing the liquidity of privately placed securities. The clear exemptions from registration and its related expenses have made the U.S. market more attractive to both U.S. and foreign companies. Additionally, Regulation S has enabled U.S. companies to offer securities abroad with greater certainty that such securities are exempt from registration.

Exhibit 24.9 provides a flow chart of the registration and exemption requirements applicable to primary and secondary offerings of securities.

 ## Reporting Requirements *of* Public Companies

The completion of a public offering does not terminate the issuer's relationship with the SEC. Under Section 15(d) of the 1934 Act, a company with registered securities in a

| **EXHIBIT 24.9** | **An Outline of Registration and Exemption Requirements** |

Initial Offerings of Securities

Nonexempt Securities
- must be registered with the SEC, or
- offered in exempt transactions

Exempt Securities
- issued or guaranteed by the U.S. or any state government
- issued by a national bank or a charitable organization
- issues offered and sold only to persons resident in the same state as the issuer (SEC treats as transactional—resale restrictions apply)
- others
  - ▶ *nonrestricted, unregistered securities so no resale restrictions apply, except as noted above*

Exempt Transactions

SEC Registration
- file registration statement forms and prospectus
- SEC review
- quiet period
- going effective
  - ▶ *nonrestricted, registered securities*

Section 4(2)
- private offering limited to sophisticated investors
  - ▶ *restricted, unregistered securities*

Section 4(6)
- accredited investors
- sell up to $5 million
  - ▶ *restricted, unregistered securities*

Regulation D
Safe Harbors
- Rule 504
- Rule 505
- Rule 506
  - ▶ *restricted, unregistered securities (except 504— nonrestricted, unregistered securities)*

Regulation A
Small Business
- "testing-the-waters" provision
  - ▶ *nonrestricted, unregistered securities*

Secondary Offering of Securities

Restricted Securities
- SEC registration
- Section 4(1½) for private placements
- Section 4(1) exemptions
  - – Rule 145(d)
  - – Rule 144, "not an underwriter" safe harbor
  - – Rule 144(k), not available to affiliates

Nonrestricted Securities
- Section 4(1) exemption for persons ". . . other than an issuer, underwriter or dealer": no limitations on the size of offering or number of offerees, provided sale is by a nonaffiliate
- Affiliates must rely on Rule 144 or Section 4(1½)
  - ▶ *nonrestricted, unregistered securities*

public offering must file periodic reports. Usually, under Section 12 of the 1934 Act, the company must also register the class of equity securities offered to the public.

SECTION 12

Under Section 12 of the 1934 Act, an issuer engaged in interstate commerce and having total assets exceeding $5 million must register with the SEC each nonexempt class of security that (1) is listed on a national stock exchange or (2) is an equity security held of record by at least 500 persons. Registration subjects the issuer to various reporting requirements and to certain rules and regulations concerning proxies, tender offers, insider trading, and so on. A company registered with the SEC under Section 12 is commonly referred to as a public or *reporting company*. Registration under the 1934 Act is intended to supplement the 1933 Act registration and to ensure that current information concerning the issuer is available to the public, enabling investors to make informed decisions about securities purchases and sales.

The following are some of the significant requirements associated with becoming a registered company under Section 12 of the 1934 Act:

- *10–Q* An unaudited quarterly statement of operations and financial condition must be filed with the SEC on Form 10–Q within forty-five days after the end of each fiscal quarter.
- *10–K* An annual audited report must be filed with the SEC on Form 10–K within ninety days after the end of the issuer's fiscal year.
- *8–K* Certain events, including changes in control, acquisitions or dispositions of key assets, and resignation of directors or auditors, require a report to be filed with the SEC on Form 8–K within fifteen days of the event.

Small business issuers that are required to file periodic reports under the 1934 Act can do so with simplified forms under Regulation S–B. These abbreviated forms include *Form 10–KSB* for annual reports and *Form 10–QSB* for quarterly reports.

OTHER SECTIONS OF THE 1934 ACT

Other sections of the 1934 Act regulate such activities as proxy solicitations, insider trading, and tender offers.

Proxy Solicitations The proxy regulation provisions of Section 14 of the 1934 Act apply to all public companies. They govern the solicitation of written powers of attorney, or *proxies,* that give the proxy holder the right to vote the shares owned by the person who signs the

proxy card. Proxy solicitations relate not just to the board of directors but to shareholder proposals as well.

Insider Trading Section 16 of the 1934 Act requires that reports be filed with the SEC listing securities holdings of officers, directors, and persons holding more than 10 percent of the issuer's equity securities, as well as any changes in such holdings. Form 5 states that these reports must be filed "both initially and on an annual basis." (These reports are described more fully in Chapter 25.) Insiders of companies not registered under the 1934 Act need not file regular reports with the SEC. Trading by insiders is also subject to Section 10(b)'s antifraud provisions, which are discussed in Chapter 25.

Tender Offers Any person making a *tender offer* to shareholders, whereby shareholders are asked to sell their shares to that person for a stated price, must comply with the tender offer rules found in Section 14 of the 1934 Act. Some rules, such as the requirement that a tender offer be left open for at least twenty business days, apply even if the company is not registered under the 1934 Act if it has a significant number of shareholders. Other rules, such as the rule giving shareholders the right to withdraw their shares once they are tendered, and the rule requiring proration if the offer is oversubscribed, apply only if the company is registered under the 1934 Act.

Schedule 13D Under Section 13, any person acquiring at least 5 percent of the shares of a reporting company must file a Schedule 13D within ten days of that acquisition. The Schedule 13D must disclose the number of shares acquired and the intentions of the person acquiring them. Often the person acquiring the shares will state that he or she is buying the shares for investment purposes only. Sometimes, however, the company suspects an ulterior motive, such as preparation for a hostile takeover attempt.

 ## Selective Disclosure *and* Regulation FD

Effective October 23, 2000, the SEC adopted a broad prohibition on the practice of *selective disclosure,* whereby issuers of publicly traded securities disclose material nonpublic information, such as advance warnings of earnings results, to securities analysts or selected institutional investors before making full disclosure of the same information to the general public. Those privy to the information are able to make a profit or avoid a loss at the expense of those kept in the dark. According to the SEC, this "leads to a loss of investor confidence in the integrity of our capital markets. Investors who see a security's price change dramatically and only later are given access to the information responsible for that move rightly question whether they are on a level playing field with market insiders."[15] Selective disclosure also threatens the integrity of the securities markets by creating "the potential for corporate management to treat material information as a commodity to be used to gain or maintain favor with particular analysts or investors."[16] Analysts may feel pressure to report favorably about a company for fear of being excluded from calls and meetings to which other analysts are invited. Finally, the SEC reasoned, "Whereas issuers may once have had to rely on analysts to serve as information intermediaries, issuers now can use a variety of methods to communicate directly with the market." These methods include Internet webcasting and teleconferencing. Accordingly, the SEC concluded, "Technological limitations no longer provide an excuse for abiding the threats to market integrity that selective disclosure represents."[17]

Regulation FD (Fair Disclosure) provides that whenever an issuer, or a person acting on its behalf, discloses material nonpublic information to securities market professionals or holders of the issuer's securities who may well trade on the basis of the information, the issuer must make public disclosure of that same information simultaneously (for intentional disclosures) or promptly (for nonintentional disclosures). Disclosure is considered intentional only if the person knows, or is reckless in not knowing, that the information he or she is communicating is both material and nonpublic. In cases of unintentional disclosure, the issuer must disclose the information to the public as soon as practical (but no later than twenty-four hours) after a senior official learns of the disclosure and knows (or is reckless in not knowing) that the information disclosed was both material and nonpublic. Market professionals include broker–dealers, investment advisers and investment managers, investment companies and hedge funds, and officials thereof.

No public disclosure is required for communications (1) made to a person who owes the issuer a duty of trust or confidence (such as an investment banker, accountant, or attorney), (2) made to any person who expressly agrees to maintain the information in confidence, (3) with a credit rating agency, or (4) made in connection with most offerings of securities registered under the 1933 Act.

Information is material if there is a substantial likelihood that a reasonable shareholder would consider it important in making an investment decision. Types of information or events likely to be considered material include (1) earnings information; (2) mergers, acquisitions, tender offers, or changes in assets; (3) new products or developments regarding customers or suppliers; (4) changes in control or management; (5) changes in auditors; (6) defaults on senior securities, repurchase plans, or stock splits; and (7) bankruptcies. The SEC cautioned that an official who engages in a private discussion with an analyst seeking guidance about earnings estimates "takes on a high degree of risk under Regulation FD."[18] On the other hand, an issuer is not prohibited from disclosing a nonmaterial piece of information to an analyst, even if, unbeknownst to the issuer, that piece of information helps the analyst complete a "mosaic" of information that, taken together, is material.

To avoid creating a chilling effect on issuers' willingness to communicate with outsiders, the SEC expressly provided that private parties cannot sue issuers for violations of Regulation FD. It is not an antifraud rule, and no failure to make a public disclosure required solely by Regulation FD is deemed to be a violation of Rule 10b–5. The SEC is empowered to bring an enforcement action if an issuer failed to comply with Regulation FD and could seek an injunction and/or civil money penalties.

 # Violation *of the* Registration *and* Prospectus Delivery Requirements *of the* 1933 Act: Section 12(1)

As explained above, Section 5 of the 1933 Act provides that, absent an exemption, all securities must be registered and may be sold only after delivery of a prospectus meeting the requirements of the 1933 Act. The penalty for violation of Section 5 is simple and severe. Section 12(1) provides that, absent an exemption, anyone who offers or sells a security without an effective registration statement or by means of a noncomplying prospectus is liable to the purchaser for rescission or damages. In effect, the purchaser is given a put: if the investment proves successful, the investor can keep the shares, but if, within one year from the date of purchase, the investment proves unprofitable, the investor can get his or her money back.

---

15. Selective Disclosures and Insider Trading, SEC Release Nos. 33-7881, 34-43154, SC-24599; 17 C.F.R. pts. 240, 243, 249 (Aug. 15, 2000).

16. *Id.*

17. *Id.*

18. *Id.*

ELEMENTS OF LIABILITY

To establish a Section 12(1) claim, the plaintiff must show that the defendant sold or offered securities without an effective registration statement or by means of a noncomplying prospectus, through the use of interstate transportation or communication. A plaintiff typically satisfies the interstate transportation or communication requirement by proving that the mails, telephone, or other interstate means were used in the offer or sale to that particular plaintiff. The plaintiff must file suit within one year from the date the securities were offered or sold.

Section 12(1) imposes a standard of strict liability. The plaintiff need not show that the defendant acted willfully or negligently, only that the defendant committed the act of selling unregistered securities.

DAMAGES

If the plaintiff still owns the securities, he or she is entitled to rescind the purchase. To rescind, the plaintiff returns the securities, together with any income (such as dividends) he or she received from them, in exchange for the price paid for the securities, plus interest. If the plaintiff has sold the securities, he or she is entitled to recover damages—usually the difference between what was paid and what was received for the securities.

WHO MAY BE SUED

The severity of the remedy under Section 12(1) has naturally led to a great deal of interest as to just who may be considered to have offered or sold securities within the meaning of the statute. It clearly includes the issuer. But what about others involved in an unregistered securities transaction, such as attorneys, accountants, underwriters, and investment bankers?

Before the U.S. Supreme Court decided the following case, many courts had held that a defendant had seller status under Section 12(1) if it engaged in actions that were a substantial factor in bringing about the plaintiff's securities purchase. The Supreme Court rejected the substantial-factor test in this case.

A CASE IN POINT

CASE 24.4

Pinter v. Dahl

Supreme Court of the United States
486 U.S. 622 (1988).

In the Language of the Court

FACTS Maurice Dahl was a California real estate broker and investor. Dahl purchased unregistered securities in the form of oil and gas interests from B.J. Pinter, an oil and gas producer and registered securities dealer in Texas. Enthusiastic about his investment, Dahl successfully encouraged his friends and family to purchase additional securities from the defendant. When the investment failed, the purchasers sued Pinter for violation of Section 12(1) of the Securities Act of 1933.

Pinter claimed that Dahl, who encouraged his friends and family to invest, was a substantial factor in those sales. Pinter therefore contended that Dahl was a seller and should be held liable under Section 12(1).

ISSUE PRESENTED Is a person with no financial interest in an offering of unregistered securities a seller under Section 12(1) of the 1933 Act?

OPINION BLACKMUN, J., writing for the U.S. Supreme Court:

In determining whether Dahl may be deemed a "seller" for purposes of 12(1), such that he may be held liable for the sale of unregistered securities to the other investor-respondents, we look first at the language of 12(1). That statute provides, in pertinent part: "Any person who . . . offers or sells a security in violation of the registration requirement of the Securities Act shall be liable to the person purchasing such security from him." This provision defines the class of defendants who may be subject to liability as those who offer or sell unregistered securities. But the Securities Act nowhere delineates who may be regarded as a statutory seller, and the sparse legislative history sheds no light on the issue. The courts, on their part, have not defined the term uniformly.

At the very least, however, the language of 12(1) contemplates a buyer–seller relationship not unlike the traditional contractual privity. Thus, it is settled that 12(1) imposes liability on the owner who passes title, or other interest in the security, to

(Continued)

(Case 24.4 continued)

the buyer for value. Dahl, of course, was not a seller in this conventional sense, and therefore may be held liable only if 12(1) liability extends to persons other than the person who passes title.

...

Although we conclude that Congress intended 12(1) liability to extend to those who solicit securities purchases, we share the Court of Appeals' conclusion that Congress did not intend to impose rescission based on strict liability on a person who urges the purchase but whose motivation is solely to benefit the buyer. When a person who urges another to make a securities purchase acts merely to assist the buyer, not only is it uncommon to say that the buyer "purchased" from him, but it is also strained to describe the giving of gratuitous advice, even strongly or enthusiastically, as "soliciting." Section 2(3) defines an offer as a "solicitation of an offer to buy . . . for value." The person who gratuitously urges another to make a particular investment decision is not, in any meaningful sense, requesting value in exchange for his suggestion or seeking the value the titleholders will obtain in exchange for the ultimate sale. The language and purpose of 12(1) suggest that liability extends only to the person who successfully solicits the purchase motivated at least in part by a desire to serve his own financial interests or those of the securities owner. If he had such a motivation, it is fair to say that the buyer "purchased" the security from him and to align him with the owner in a rescission action.

...

We are unable to determine whether Dahl may be held liable as a statutory seller under 12(1). The District Court explicitly found that "Dahl solicited each of the other plaintiffs in connection with the offer, purchase and receipt of their oil and gas interests." We cannot conclude that this finding was clearly erroneous. It is not clear, however, that Dahl had the kind of interest in the sales that make him liable as a statutory seller. We do know that he received no commission from Pinter in connection with the other sales, but this is not conclusive. Typically, a person who solicits the purchase will have sought or received a personal financial benefit from the sale, such as where he "anticipat[es] a share of the profits," or receives a brokerage commission. But a person who solicits the buyer's purchase in order to serve the financial interests of the owner may properly be liable under 12(1) without showing that he expects to participate in the benefits the owner enjoys.

The Court of Appeals apparently concluded that Dahl was motivated entirely by gratuitous desire to share an attractive investment opportunity with his friends and associates. This conclusion, in our view, was premature. The District Court made no findings that focused on whether Dahl urged the other purchases in order to further some financial interest of his own or of Pinter. Accordingly, further findings are necessary to assess Dahl's liability.

RESULT The Supreme Court vacated the judgment of the appeals court and remanded the case for further proceedings consistent with its opinion.

QUESTIONS

1. Was Dahl partially responsible for the failure to register the securities? If so, should he have been liable for violating Section 5?
2. What facts do you need to know to determine whether Dahl was a seller within the meaning of Section 12(1)?

WHO MAY SUE

Anyone who purchases shares issued in violation of the registration requirements can bring suit. If the securities were sold to a number of persons, then a plaintiff could bring a class-action suit on behalf of all persons who have allegedly been harmed by the acquisition of the illegally issued securities.

 # Section 11 *of the* 1933 Act

Section 11 provides a remedy for a person who purchases a security pursuant to a misleading registration statement. Note that Section 11 applies only to registered securities. The section is the most lengthy and detailed civil liability provision in the 1933 Act, spelling out who may sue, who may be sued, the elements of the offenses, the permitted defenses, and the damages that may be awarded. Under Section 11, an issuer of securities is liable for its false statements even if they were not made with intent to defraud.

WHO MAY SUE

Tracing Requirement Any person who has purchased a registered security may sue under Section 11. But the purchaser must prove that the security at issue was actually one of those sold with the misleading registration statement. Although this requirement does not present a problem for direct purchasers of an initial public offering, open-market purchasers may find it difficult to trace their securities back to a sale made under the defective registration statement.

Class Actions Plaintiffs in a Section 11 case will typically bring a class action, in which the named plaintiffs act on behalf of themselves and "all others similarly situated." The advantage to the plaintiffs (and their attorneys) of proceeding in this manner is that the individual plaintiffs' claims, worth only a few hundred or a few thousand dollars, together amount to millions of dollars.

WHO MAY BE SUED

Section 11 lists, and thereby limits, the entities and persons who may be sued: (1) the issuer offering the security; (2) the underwriters; (3) any member of the board of directors at the time of the offering; (4) persons who gave their consent to be named in the registration statement as future directors; (5) every person who signed the registration statement (under Section 6(a) of the 1933 Act, it must be signed by the issuer, its principal executive officer, its principal financing officer, and its principal accounting officer); and (6) experts who consented to give authority to the "expertized" portion of the registration statement, such as accountants who audited the financial statements contained in it. No person can be named in the registration statement as an expert unless that person has consented in writing to being named.

All defendants in a Section 11 case have joint and several liability for violations, meaning that one defendant can be held responsible for all the damages awarded the plaintiff, even if that defendant was only partially responsible for the violation. The one exception is that outside directors who did not commit knowing violations are generally liable only for the portion of the damages attributable to their percentage of responsibility.

Plaintiffs often allege that persons or entities other than those specified in Section 11 are liable under a theory of secondary liability, such as aiding and abetting or conspiracy. Most (but not all) courts reject such attempts to expand liability under Section 11. In 1994, the U.S. Supreme Court held that a private plaintiff may not maintain an aiding and abetting suit under Section 10(b).[19]

ELEMENTS OF LIABILITY

The elements of a Section 11 offense are straightforward. The plaintiff must show that at the time the registration statement became effective it either (1) contained a false or misleading statement of a material fact or (2) omitted to state a material fact that is required to be stated in the registration statement or is necessary to make the statements contained in the registration statement not misleading.

The Supreme Court has defined a *material fact* as one that a reasonable investor would most likely have considered important in deciding whether to buy or sell— that is, what a reasonable hypothetical investor would have considered important, not necessarily what the actual investor considered important. The Supreme Court has held that an omitted fact is material if there is "a substantial likelihood that the disclosure of the omitted fact would have been viewed by the reasonable investor as

---

19. Central Bank of Denver, N.A. v. First Interstate Bank of Denver, N.A., 511 U.S. 164 (1994).

having significantly altered the 'total mix' of information made available."[20]

The plaintiff does not have to establish that he or she relied upon the misstatement or omission except in the following instance: A plaintiff who purchases a security on the open market after the issuing company has released its income statements for the year following the registration statement must show that the misrepresentation influenced his or her decision to buy.

DEFENSES

Section 11 sets forth several defenses to a claim under its provisions. The defenses of no reliance and no causation focus on the effects of the misstatements on the behavior of investors and the market, while the defense of due diligence looks to the culpability of the defendants.

No Reliance The defense of no reliance relates to the investor's knowledge. An investor who knows that there was a misstatement or omission cannot claim to have relied on it; he or she is presumed to have acted despite the misstatement or omission. Thus, if the defendant can establish that the plaintiff knew that a statement was false or that there was an omission, there is no liability under Section 11.

No Causation The defense of no causation focuses on the link between the misstatement and the investor's loss. Even if there was a misstatement or omission of material fact, a defendant will not be liable if it can show that the misstatement or omission did not actually cause the plaintiff to suffer any loss. In other words, the plaintiff may have lost money on a trade, but that loss may not have been due to the defendant's conduct. This showing typically consists of an expert analysis of the various factors that influenced the price movements of the securities in question.

Due Diligence The defense of due diligence focuses on the behavior of the defendants. It is available to all defendants except the issuing company. A defendant is not liable for a misrepresentation or omission if it acted with due diligence; that is, it (1) conducted a reasonable investigation and (2) reasonably believed (a) that the statements made were true, and (b) that there were no omissions that made those statements misleading. A reasonable investigation is what a prudent person managing his or her own property would conduct.

20. TSC Indus. v. Northway, Inc., 426 U.S. 438, 449 (1976).

ETHICAL CONSIDERATION

Plaintiffs have an incentive to urge the courts to broadly construe the guidelines as to who may be a defendant—particularly when the plaintiff is looking for a "deep pocket" defendant who can pay large damages. A plaintiff has every right to use the securities laws to their fullest extent to redress a wrong covered by one of the statutes. However, some commentators believe that certain plaintiffs attempt to recover losses beyond the scope of the statutes. Although some claim that plaintiffs cannot be faulted for trying, the better view is that plaintiffs should proceed only if they believe in good faith that the suit is justified under the legal guidelines.

Indeed, Rule 11 of the Federal Rules of Civil Procedure, which is designed to deter bad faith claims, provides for sanctions against an attorney who signs a complaint that he or she does not reasonably believe has merit. The Reform Act gave Rule 11 new teeth by requiring courts to include in the record, at the conclusion of the action, specific findings as to whether all parties and all attorneys complied with each requirement of Rule 11(b). If the action was brought for an improper purpose, was unwarranted by existing law, was legally frivolous, or was not supported by facts, then the Act creates a presumption that the appropriate sanction is an award to the prevailing party of all attorneys' fees and costs incurred in the case.

The primary wrinkle in the due diligence defense arises in connection with the expertized portions of the registration statement, such as audit reports on the company's financial statements, appraisal reports, or engineering reports. Nonexpert defendants are entitled to rely on the experts. They can establish due diligence by showing that they had no reasonable basis to believe that the experts' reports were misleading and in fact did not believe them to be misleading. Significantly, the defendants need not show that they undertook any investigation of those reports.

The experts are, of course, responsible for their own reports, provided that the reports are identified as having been prepared by them and that the experts have given their consent to the use of their reports in the registration statement. The experts are generally not responsible under Section 11 for portions of the registration statement other than their reports.

The case that follows was the first to articulate the due diligence standards applicable to the various participants in the offering process.

A CASE IN POINT

CASE 24.5

Escott v. BarChris Construction Corp.

United States District Court for the Southern District of New York
283 F. Supp. 643 (S.D.N.Y. 1968).

In the Language of the Court

FACTS BarChris was in the business of building bowling alleys. It obtained capital through a public offering in May 1961. Due to financial problems, the company filed for protection under the Bankruptcy Act in October 1962. A class action followed, alleging Section 11 claims against the company, its officers and directors, and its underwriters.

ISSUE PRESENTED When is the due diligence defense available to the principal officers or the inside directors of the issuer? May a chief financial officer rely on the audited financial statements if he had reason to believe those statements were incorrect? Have outside directors and underwriters, who relied on management's statements and made no independent investigation, acted with due diligence?

OPINION McLEAN, J., writing for the U.S. District Court for the Southern District of New York:

[The court first found that both the expertized and the nonexpertized portions of the registration statement were misleading. Every defendant raised the defense of due diligence except the issuer, to whom the defense was not available.]

[The court applied the most stringent standards to the company's principal officers and inside directors. It first noted that principal officers and inside directors (directors who are also officers of the corporation) who sign a registration statement have a significant burden. Because of their extensive knowledge of the company's affairs, they rarely can establish a successful due diligence defense. The court held that the chief financial officer was not entitled to rely on the outside auditors as to the accuracy of the financial statements because he had reason to believe that those statements were incorrect. The court concluded that the liability of principal officers and inside directors approaches that of the company itself. They cannot escape liability for the nonexpertized portions of the statement even if they did not read the statement, did not understand it, and relied on assistants and lawyers to make adequate disclosures.]

[The court then considered the liability of two outside directors who had become directors a month before the offering. Neither had read the registration statement in final form, and both relied on assurances from the officers that everything was in order.]

Section 11 imposes liability in the first instance upon a director, no matter how new he is. He is presumed to know his responsibility when he becomes a director. He can escape liability only by using that reasonable care to investigate the facts which a prudent man would employ in the management of his own property. In my opinion, a prudent man would not act in an important matter without any knowledge of the relevant facts, in sole reliance upon representations of persons who are comparative strangers and upon general information which does not purport to cover the particular case. . . .

[The court then considered whether the underwriters had established the due diligence defense.] [I]t is clear that no effectual attempt at verification was made. The question is whether due diligence required that it be made. Stated another way, is it sufficient to ask questions, to obtain answers which, if true, would be thought satisfactory, and to let it go at that, without seeking to ascertain from the records whether the answers in fact are true and complete?

...

The underwriters say that the prospectus is the company's prospectus, not theirs. Doubtless this is the way they customarily regard it. But the Securities Act makes no

(Continued)

(Case 24.5 continued)

such distinction. The underwriters are just as responsible as the company if the prospectus is false. And prospective investors rely upon the reputation of the underwriters in deciding whether to purchase the securities.

...

In a sense, the positions of the underwriter and the company's officers are adverse. It is not unlikely that statements made by company officers to an underwriter to induce him to underwrite may be self-serving. They may be unduly enthusiastic. As in this case, they may, on occasion, be deliberately false.

The purpose of Section 11 is to protect investors. To that end the underwriters are made responsible for the truth of the prospectus. If they may escape that responsibility by taking at face value representations made to them by the company's management, then the inclusion of underwriters among those liable under Section 11 affords the investors no additional protection. To effectuate the statute's purpose, the phrase "reasonable investigation" must be construed to require more effort on the part of the underwriters than the mere accurate reporting in the prospectus of "data presented" to them by the company. It should make no difference that this data is elicited by questions addressed to the company officers by the underwriters, or that the underwriters at the time believe that the company's officers are truthful and reliable. In order to make the underwriters' participation in this enterprise of any value to the investors, the underwriters must make some reasonable attempt to verify the data submitted to them. They may not rely solely on the company's officers or on the company's counsel. A prudent man in the management of his own property would not rely on them.

RESULT None of the defendants could rely on the due diligence defense, except the outside directors, who were permitted to rely on the opinion of the auditors as to the audited financial statements.

COMMENTS The degree of reliance a participating underwriter may place on a principal underwriter remains unclear. The court in *BarChris* summarily noted that the participating underwriters who relied solely on the primary underwriters did not establish due diligence. An SEC release has since suggested that a participating underwriter has met its due diligence requirements if it satisfies itself that the managing underwriter has made the kind of investigation the participant would have performed were it the manager.

QUESTIONS

1. Why were the underwriters not permitted to take management's representations at face value?
2. Should accountants be held to the standard of their profession or that of a reasonable person?

BESPEAKS CAUTION DOCTRINE

According to the *bespeaks caution doctrine*, a court may determine that the inclusion of sufficient cautionary statements in a prospectus renders immaterial any misrepresentations and omissions contained therein. The doctrine stands for the proposition that a statement or omission must be considered in context, so accompanying statements may render it immaterial as a matter of law.

In 1993, Trump Castle Funding issued a prospectus conveying to potential investors the risks inherent in the proposed venture, the financing of the Taj Mahal casino. The prospectus alerted potential investors that there was a chance that the partnership would be unable to repay the bondholders. The court held that the extensive cautionary statements, tailored to the specific risks involved, negated any potentially misleading effect that the optimistic projections in the prospectus might have on a reasonable investor. Trump was therefore not liable for violating Rule 10b–5.[21]

Not all courts have adopted the bespeaks caution doctrine. In addition, cautionary language may render an alleged omission or misrepresentation immaterial, but only if the cautionary statements are substantive and tailored to specific future projections, estimates, or opinions in the prospectus.

In 1994, the Fifth Circuit stated:

> . . . cautionary language is not necessarily sufficient, in and of itself, to render predictive statements immaterial as a matter of law. . . . The appropriate inquiry is whether, under all the circumstances, the omitted fact or the prediction without a reasonable basis "is one [that] a reasonable investor would consider significant in [making] the decision to invest, such that it alters the total mix of information available about the proposed investment." Inclusion of cautionary language . . . is, of course, relevant to the materiality inquiry. . . . Nevertheless, cautionary language as such is not dispositive of this inquiry.[22]

REFORM ACT SAFE HARBOR FOR FORWARD-LOOKING STATEMENTS

The Reform Act provides a statutory safe harbor for certain forward-looking statements by issuers subject to the 1934 Act's reporting requirements and persons acting on their behalf. It is not available for initial public offerings or offerings by a blank check company, a partnership, a limited liability company, or a direct participation investment program, however. The safe harbor also does not apply to any forward-looking statement included in a financial statement prepared in accordance with generally accepted accounting principles.

The safe harbor provides two independent and alternative grounds for precluding liability. Under the first prong, liability for a written or oral forward-looking statement is precluded if it was identified by the speaker as a forward-looking statement and was accompanied by meaningful cautionary statements that identify important factors that could cause actual results to differ materially from those in the statement. Even if the statement does not satisfy these criteria, a second prong precludes liability for a forward-looking statement unless the person who made the statement did so with actual

knowledge that the statement was false or misleading. A company is not liable for a forward-looking statement it issues unless the plaintiff proves that the statement was made by, or with the approval of, an executive officer who had actual knowledge that the statement was false or misleading. This safe harbor is discussed further in Chapter 25.

DAMAGES

Section 11 sets forth the damages recoverable for violation of its provisions. If the plaintiff has not sold the securities in question, the recoverable damages are the amount paid for each security minus its value at the time the plaintiff brings the claim. The value at the time the plaintiff brings the claim is usually the market price, unless the market price has been affected by the misrepresentation or omission. If the securities have been sold before the plaintiff brings the claim, the recoverable damages are the amount paid for the security minus the amount received at sale.

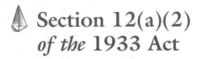 **Section 12(a)(2) of the 1933 Act**

Section 12(a)(2) provides a remedy for any person who purchases a security by means of a misleading prospectus or oral communication. To establish a Section 12(a)(2) claim, the plaintiff must prove that (1) through the mails or other means of interstate commerce, (2) the defendant offered or sold a security, (3) by means of a prospectus or oral communication, (4) that included a material misrepresentation or omission. Materiality under Section 12(a)(2) is the same as materiality under Section 11. The purchaser may rescind the purchase unless the defendant proves that the depreciation in the value of the security resulted from factors unrelated to the alleged misstatement or omission. If the purchaser has sold the security, he or she generally may recover damages equal to the difference between what was paid and what was received for the security. If the defendant demonstrates that part or all of the decline in the value of the security was caused by factors other than the misstatement or omission alleged in the complaint, then the plaintiff may not recover damages based on that portion of the decline.

Section 12(a)(2) does not require the plaintiff to prove that he or she relied on the misrepresentation or that the defendant acted with *scienter,* that is, an intent to deceive. On the other hand, Section 12(a)(2) applies only to those who offer or sell a security. Under Section 12(a)(2), the

21. *In re* Donald J. Trump Casino Sec. Litig., 7 F.3d 357 (3d Cir. 1993), *cert. denied,* 510 U.S. 1178 (1994). *See also* Grossman v. Novell, Inc., 120 F.3d 1112 (10th Cir. 1997); Moorhead v. Merrill Lynch, 949 F.2d 243 (8th Cir. 1997); *In re* Worlds of Wonder Sec. Litig., 35 F.3d 1407 (9th Cir. 1994), *cert. denied,* 516 U.S. 909 (1995).
22. Rubinstein v. Collins, 20 F.3d 160 (5th Cir. 1994).

plaintiff must bring the action within one year from when he or she discovered or should have discovered the fraud, or three years after the sale, whichever is the shorter.

The Supreme Court interpreted Section 12(a)(2) to apply only to public offerings in the following case.

A CASE IN POINT

CASE 24.6
Gustafson v. Alloyd Co.
Supreme Court of the United States
513 U.S. 561 (1995).

Summary

FACTS Three individuals (Sellers), who owned all of the stock of Alloyd Company, a corporation engaged in the manufacture of clear plastic blister-packaging and automatic heat-seal packaging equipment, entered into a stock-purchase agreement, whereby they agreed to sell their stock to Wind Point Partners II, L.P., an experienced and sophisticated venture-capital investment partnership. Sellers represented that they had estimated Alloyd's inventory and that the interim financial statements fairly presented Alloyd's financial condition. The stock-purchase agreement expressly stated that there would be an adjustment in the purchase price to take account of any variance between the inventory estimates in the interim financials and the year-end audit. Wind Point also expressly waived any right it had to seek rescission.

When the year-end audit revealed a substantial inventory shortfall, Wind Point sought to rescind the transaction under Section 12(a)(2). Wind Point claimed that the stock-purchase agreement was a prospectus in which Sellers had materially misrepresented Alloyd's financial condition as of the date of the interim financials. Because Section 14 of the 1933 Act renders invalid waivers of the Act's protections, the contractual agreement to waive rescission would not apply to a Section 12(a)(2) claim.

The district court granted Sellers' motion for summary judgment, but the appeals court reversed. Sellers appealed.

ISSUE PRESENTED Does Section 12(a)(2) apply to misrepresentations in a stock-purchase agreement in connection with a private offering of stock?

SUMMARY OF OPINION The U.S. Supreme Court first focused on Section 10, which provides that a "prospectus" is a document, related to a public offering by an issuer or its controlling shareholders, that must contain the information contained in a registration statement. Although Section 10 does not define what a prospectus is, the Court reasoned that it does indicate what a prospectus cannot be if the 1933 Act is to be interpreted as a symmetrical and coherent regulatory scheme.

There was no dispute that the stock-purchase agreement was not required to contain the information contained in a registration statement. The sale was a private placement exempt under Section 4(2). Therefore, the Court held that the stock-purchase agreement was not a prospectus under Section 10 and thus not a prospectus for purposes of Section 12(a)(2) either.

The Court limited Section 12(a)(2) to transactions involving a Section 10 statutory prospectus (and transactions involving exempt securities that are exempt from that requirement by reason of Section 3). A document can still be a prospectus if it omits a required piece of information, but it is not a prospectus if it need not comply with Section 10's requirements in the first place.

RESULT Wind Point's claim under Section 12(a)(2) was dismissed.

COMMENTS *Gustafson* makes it clear that Section 12(a)(2) liability extends to fraudulent statements or omissions in statutory prospectuses (those contained in the registration statement) used in a registered public offering but does not extend to fraudulent documents used in connection with secondary market transactions, at least those not involving resales by affiliates. Resales by affiliates under Rule 144 or 144A should not

(Continued)

(Case 24.6 continued)

fall within the scope of Section 12(a)(2). However, resales by affiliates that would constitute a distribution under traditional Section 2(11) analysis are probably public offerings subject to Section 12(a)(2).[23]

23. *See* Stephen M. Bainbridge, *Securities Act Section 12(2) After the Gustafson Debacle,* 50 Bus. Law. 1231, 1258 (1995).

Section 12(a)(2) liability would appear to extend to selling documents, such as a brochure sent to investors along with the statutory prospectus, used in connection with registered offerings. Section 12(a)(2) clearly applies to oral communications made in connection with a registered public offering. Although the *Gustafson* opinion is not clear on this point, Section 12(a)(2) probably would not apply to oral communications made in connection with a private placement.[24]

The Supreme Court did not define what it meant by public offerings. Private placements under Section 4(2) are clearly not public offerings. But what about sales under Regulation D? The SEC did not adopt Rules 504 and 505 of Regulation D under Section 4(2); instead, they were adopted under its authority in Section 3(b) to exempt offerings of less than $5 million. The SEC relied on Section 4(2) for its statutory authority to adopt Rule 506, but the rule's safe harbor is far more liberal than the case law under Section 4(2). It is not yet clear whether the term "public offering" applies to (1) all offerings not exempted under Section 4(2) or (2) all offerings that must be registered under Section 5 and all offerings of securities exempted under Section 3. The latter reading would exclude offerings under Regulation D from Section 12(a)(2)'s reach.

WHO MAY BE SUED

Section 12(a)(2)'s language relating to who may be liable is identical to that of Section 12(1): anyone who "offers or sells" a security by means of a misleading prospectus or oral communication. Accordingly, most courts treat Sections 12(1) and 12(a)(2) as the same for the purposes of identifying potential defendants. In *Pinter v. Dahl,*[25] the Supreme Court considered only Section 12(1) and declined to extend its holding to Section 12(a)(2). Some subsequent cases in the lower courts, however, have applied *Pinter* to Section 12(a)(2), hold-

ing that only those in privity with the plaintiff or those who solicit the securities sale for financial gain face liability under Section 12(a)(2). Those in privity would include underwriters, brokers, and dealers having a direct contractual relationship with the plaintiff.

REASONABLE CARE DEFENSE

Section 12(a)(2) provides a defense of reasonable care. A defendant will not be liable for a Section 12(a)(2) violation if it can prove that it did not know, and in the exercise of reasonable care could not have known, about the misrepresentations or omissions. In contrast to the due diligence defense of Section 11, the defense of reasonable care is not spelled out in detail. Commentators have suggested that reasonable care may require a defendant to undertake an investigation. In *Sanders v. John Nuveen & Co.,*[26] the U.S. Court of Appeals for the Seventh Circuit held that there is no difference between the duties imposed on an underwriter by Section 11, which requires a reasonable investigation, and Section 12(a)(2). An underwriter, the Seventh Circuit held, must look beyond published data and undertake some investigation of that part of the data that is verifiable. Because the underwriter in *Sanders* did not examine the issuing company's records, contracts, or tax returns, the underwriter did not act with reasonable care.

Liability *of* Controlling Persons

Section 15 imposes liability on anyone who "controls any person liable under Section 11 or 12." The term "control" is not defined in the 1933 Act. Congress left this issue for the courts to decide:

It was thought undesirable to attempt to define the term. It would be difficult if not impossible to enumerate or to anticipate the many ways in which actual control may be

---

24. *See* Ballay v. Legg Mason Wood Walker, Inc., 925 F.2d 682 (3d Cir. 1991), *cert. denied,* 502 U.S. 820 (1991).
25. 486 U.S. 622 (Case 24.4).

26. 619 F.2d 1222 (7th Cir. 1980), *cert. denied,* 450 U.S. 1005 (1981).

exerted. A few examples of these methods used are stock ownership, lease, contract, and agency. It is well known that actual control sometimes may be exerted through ownership of much less than a majority of the stock of a corporation either by the ownership of such stock alone or through such ownership in combination with other factors.[27]

Unsurprisingly, the courts do not agree as to when there is *controlling-person liability*. Some courts will find control if the defendant had the power to directly or indirectly control or influence corporate policy or the power to control the general affairs of an entity.[28] Other courts require that the person must have actually participated in the securities violation.[29] Most courts will find liability if a person merely possesses the power to control the specific activity that is the basis for the securities violation, regardless of whether that power was exercised, provided that the person did actually exercise some degree of general control or influence over the Section 11 defendant.

A controlling person is usually an officer, director, or major shareholder of the company. In *Metge v. Baehler*,[30] the plaintiff claimed that the company's bank was a controlling person and therefore liable under the securities laws. The U.S. Court of Appeals for the Eighth Circuit applied the following two-prong test to determine whether Banker's Trust was a controlling person. A plaintiff must establish both (1) that the defendant actually participated in (that is, exercised control over) the company's operations in general, and (2) that the defendant possessed the power to control the specific transaction or activity upon which the primary violation was predicated. Because the court found no actual exercise of control by Banker's Trust, the court concluded that the bank had no controlling-person liability.

The case illustrates the flexibility of the securities laws and the creativity of plaintiffs. Had the bank obtained

more restrictive covenants in its lending agreements, the court might have found that it was liable as a controlling person even though it did not participate in the specific violations of the securities laws. A lender that overprotects itself via restrictive covenants and control of its borrower may thus create a problem for itself.

Section 15 does not impose strict liability on controlling persons. Controlling persons are not liable if they had no knowledge of the facts giving rise to the controlled person's alleged liability and had no reasonable ground to believe in the existence of such facts. The majority view is that the defendant bears the burden of establishing the defenses of "no knowledge" and no "reasonable ground to believe." This is normally done by proving that the defendant acted in good faith and took reasonable measures, in light of the situation, to prevent the securities violation.[31]

Criminal Penalties

In addition to buying back the securities or paying damages, defendants also face criminal penalties that include fines and imprisonment for violations of state or federal securities laws. Under Section 24 of the 1933 Act, any person who willfully violates the provisions of the Act shall upon conviction be fined not more than $10,000 or imprisoned for up to five years, or both. A violation can be willful even if the defendant did not know that the transaction at issue involved securities or that the law was being violated. In cases claiming false statements or omissions of material facts, the government need show only that the defendant knew what investors were and were not being told, accompanied by proof that the statements or omissions were objectively material.[32]

---

27. H.R. REP. No. 1383, 73d Cong., 2d Sess. § 19 at 26 (1934).
28. *See, e.g.*, Abbott v. Equity Group, Inc., 2 F.3d 613 (5th Cir. 1993).
29. *See, e.g.*, Sharp v. Coopers & Lybrand, 649 F.2d 175 (3d Cir. 1981) (interpreting identical language in Section 20(a) of the 1934 Act to require culpable participation in the securities violation).
30. 762 F.2d 621 (8th Cir. 1985), *cert. denied*, 474 U.S. 1057 (1986).

31. *See* Lewis D. Lowenfels & Alan R. Bromberg, *Controlling Person Liability Under Section 20(a) of the Securities Exchange Act and Section 15 of the Securities Act*, 53 BUS. LAW. 1, 26–27 (1997).
32. United States v. English, 92 F.3d 909 (6th Cir. 1996).

THE RESPONSIBLE MANAGER
Complying *with* Registration Requirements

Any person offering securities must comply with the registration requirements of the 1933 Act as well as any applicable blue sky laws. This includes start-up companies, as well as large, publicly traded companies. Failure to

comply gives the purchaser of the security the right to keep the proceeds if the investment is successful or to return the security to the seller if the investment does not turn out as hoped. Moreover, as was explained in Chapter 17, a willful failure to comply is a criminal offense. Even if a security is exempt from registration, it is not exempt from the antifraud provisions of the 1934 Act, as discussed in Chapter 25.

Managers, particularly those of small firms, should be familiar with the four-part *Howey* test. They should be aware that certain contracts that are not normally thought of as securities may run afoul of the 1933 and 1934 Acts.

Furthermore, securities held by officers, directors, and other affiliates cannot be freely resold. They must be sold under Rule 144, subject to its volume and public information requirements, or in a private offering to sophisticated, eligible buyers. Companies must put legends on affiliates' share certificates, issue stop-transfer orders to the transfer agent, or take other such steps as may be reasonable to ensure compliance with these rules.

The preparation of a private-placement memorandum is an involved process that requires an intimate knowledge of the statutory requirements. Managers face considerable liability for incorrect or misleading statements in these documents.

Any person involved in a public offering of securities has a legal and ethical duty to ensure that the prospectus contains no misleading statements or omissions. Experts, such as accountants, have a particularly heavy responsibility. The underwriters and outside directors cannot rely passively on the representations of management. Violations of these rules give rise to both civil and criminal liability.

Managers should work closely with counsel during the waiting period to ensure that there are no gun-jumping problems due to eagerness of the underwriter or the company's public relations department. It is very important that the company not issue an abnormal number of press releases or increase the amount of its advertising prior to the registration going effective. In other words, the manager should make sure that the company remains quiet and does not depart from its ordinary routine.

In addition, a manager should ensure that there are no material misstatements or omissions in any public disclosures (for example, Form 10–K or Form 10–Q). Once a disclosure is made, even if there was no legal obligation to disclose, the statements contained in it must be truthful and are subject to securities law.

INSIDE STORY

SEC Scrutinizes Sales *of* Cheap Stock *to* Customers

In 2000, the SEC staff required several companies seeking to go public to take a charge against revenues for the value of warrants or cheap stock they issued to customers that placed large orders for the companies' products. Dubbed a "unique marriage of convenience" by the *Wall Street Journal*,[33] the practice is particularly prevalent in the highly competitive telecommunications industry, where new companies seek an edge when battling industry giants such as Nortel Networks, Lucent Technologies, and Cisco Systems. In turn, the network operators have an incentive to buy the products because their firms can make far more on their investments in the start-up after it goes public than they spent on the equipment. To avoid overstating the start-up's revenues, Brooke Seawell, a general partner at Technology Crossover Ventures, argues that the revenue from sales to warrant-holding customers "should be offset by the value of the warrants."[34]

The SEC staff appears to have required CoSine Communications, Inc. to do just that. CoSine, which priced its initial public offering on September 26, 2000, amended its financial statements to reduce revenues from $11.3 million to $7.6 million to reflect "non-cash charges related to equity" issuances. Six of CoSine's eight customers hold stock or warrants.

The practice of issuing cheap stocks or warrants in exchange for orders also raises the specter of a pyramid-type scheme where the purchasers buy the new equipment not due to faith in the product but as a way to inflate the value of the start-up so that it can go public at an unrealistically high valuation. Public investors stand to get hurt when sales to nonaffiliated purchasers (that is, purchasers that received neither the cheap stock nor warrants) fail to materialize.

33. Scott Thurm, *SEC Questions Start-Ups' Cheap Stock Sales to Customers*, WALL ST. J., Sept. 26, 2000, at C1.

34. *Id*. at C18.

KEY WORDS AND PHRASES

accredited investor   837
affiliate   828
angel   818
bespeaks caution doctrine   852
best-efforts underwriting   828
blank check companies   837
blue sky laws   821
controlling-person liability   856
dealer   840
due diligence   829
family resemblance test   824
firm commitment underwriting   827
Form S–1   828
Form S–2   828
Form S–3   828
Form S–4   835
Form SB–1   828
Form SB–2   828
Form 8–K   845
Form 10–K   845
Form 10–KSB   845

Form 10–Q   845
Form 10–QSB   845
going effective   827
gun-jumping   834
integration   837
investment contract   822
issuer   840
material fact   849
merit review   821
not an underwriter   840
offer   826
offshore transactions   843
private offering   835
private placement   835
private-placement memorandum   838
prospectus   827
proxy   845
qualified institutional buyer   842
quiet period   833
red-herring prospectus   833
registration statement   827

reporting company   845
restricted securities   840
roadshow   834
sale   826
sale-of-business doctrine   824
scienter   820
secondary offering   835
Section 4(1½) exemption   842
security   822
selective disclosure   845
shelf registration   834
small business issuers   828
syndicate   827
tender offer   845
tombstone ad   834
traditional shelf offerings   835
underwriter   835
value   826
waiting period   833

QUESTIONS AND CASE PROBLEMS

1. Life Partners, Inc. is the leading promoter of interests in viatical settlements, whereby investors purchase at a discount interests in a pool consisting of life insurance benefits of terminal AIDS patients. Is Life Partners engaged in the sale of securities? [*SEC v. Life Partners Inc.*, 87 F.3d 536 (D.C. Cir. 1996)]

2. Rock Corporation proposes to merge with Quarry, Inc. Quarry will first obtain the approval of its shareholders; then, by operation of law, the Quarry shares will become shares of the survivor corporation, Rock Quarry, Inc. Is it necessary to register the Rock Quarry shares?

   Suppose that prior to the merger Feldon Flintstone owns 30 percent of Quarry's stock that she acquired three years before in a private placement, but after the merger she will own only 2 percent of the Rock Quarry shares (and will not be an officer or director of Rock Quarry). May she freely resell the Rock Quarry shares? Does it matter whether they were registered in connection with the merger?

3. LaserVision Technologies, Inc. developed a camera system to create souvenirs for fans at sporting events, then formed SurroundVision Advanced

Imaging, LLC (SAIL) to finance the marketing of the technology. Adrian Gluck was LaserVision's president and also served as CEO, president, and a director of SAIL. Donald Williams, a LaserVision director, served as a manager of SAIL, and Raymond Kelly had no connection to SAIL except through his role as a LaserVision outside director. In October 1997, Richmond Dellastatious purchased $261,000 in SAIL stock, relying at least in part on an offering memorandum provided by SAIL. SAIL ceased operations in 1998, and its shares are now worthless.

Dellastatious and another investor sued SAIL, certain SAIL officers, LaserVision, and two of LaserVision's outside directors—Williams and Kelly. The plaintiffs alleged that the offering memorandum (1) materially misrepresented the closeness of the relationship between SAIL—essentially a shell corporation—and LaserVision, and (2) grossly overstated SAIL's projected revenues and misrepresented the nature of its assets. The plaintiffs further alleged that Williams and Kelly were liable as "control persons" under Section 20 of the 1934 Act. The trial court granted Kelly and Williams's summary judgment motion, concluding that neither was a control person of any liable party and that both lacked the requisite culpability for controlling person liability. What facts do the plaintiffs have to prove to hold Williams and Kelly liable? [*Dellastatious v. Williams,* 242 F.3d 191 (4th Cir. 2001).

4. Ventura Corporation of Denver, Colorado, made a private offering of its common stock on January 1 and additional offerings on March 1, August 1, and November 1. All of the private placements are with the same group of fifty individuals and pension funds. Do these separate private offerings constitute one continuous public offering by Ventura?

5. Susan Newton, thirty-eight, founded her own software firm at age fifteen and acquired her stock in an offering under Rule 505 of Regulation D. Newton grew her firm to $20 million in revenues before EBM Corporation purchased it in exchange for EBM common stock in a private placement under Section 4(2). Newton no longer is an officer or active in the day-to-day management of her business. She does, however, sit on the board of directors of EBM Corporation and owns 15 percent of its outstanding common stock. She proposes to sell her interest in EBM to the public. The stock is actively traded on the Nasdaq Stock Market. Are there any restrictions on Newton's ability to sell her EBM shares?

6. Integrated Resources obtained short-term loans from Security Pacific National Bank through a line of credit the bank had extended. Participations in these loans were sold to various institutional investors under a master agreement containing a disclaimer stating that each investor participated in the loans without relying on Security Pacific. Integrated later defaulted on the loans and declared bankruptcy. Several investors sued Security Pacific, arguing that the loan participations were securities under the 1933 Act and seeking to rescind their purchase agreement. Did Security Pacific sell securities? [*Banco Español de Crédito v. Security Pacific National Bank,* 973 F.2d 51 (2d Cir. 1992), *cert. denied,* 509 U.S. 903 (1993)]

7. In January, Arbor Corporation, a paper company with annual sales of more than $2 billion and assets of more than $5 billion, issued four million registered common shares at an average price of $50 per share. In preparing the registration statement, Charles Controller relied on a report by Acme Appraisers, which stated that the company's woodlands were worth $900 million. Acme's report was not included in the registration statement, and Acme was

not mentioned. Ollie Olson, the company's newly elected outside director (and Controller's brother-in-law) questioned whether the woodland estimate might be too high. Controller reassured him that "if the numbers are good enough for our CPAs, they're good enough for me."

In February, the company discovered that the woodland appraisal was overstated by $150 million. Management and the directors are livid about the error. To add to Arbor's problems, a major competitor shocked the industry by announcing that it will double its paper production capacity. Arbor's stock price is now $20 per share.

Do the shareholders have a basis for a suit? Who can they sue? What problems or defenses will they likely encounter? Assuming that the suit is otherwise successful, how will damages be determined?

8. Duke Distribution, Inc. recently had a public offering of its shares. The company's attorneys, its CPAs, and the underwriter's attorneys worked diligently to meet a tight deadline that management had imposed. Unfortunately, in its haste to meet the deadline, Duke's team failed to include several items in the registration statement. The prospectus failed to mention that while Duke's inventory-to-sales ratio was constant over the past few years, most competitors' ratios had declined significantly over the same period. It also failed to mention that the company leases warehouses from a partnership consisting of three of its directors. The leases require rent that is about 8 percent higher than the market rate for equivalent facilities. After the initial public offering, the company engaged in additional transactions with insiders.

Now the economy has softened and competition has increased. The price of Duke stock has fallen from $15 to $10. Is there a cause of action? Against whom? What are the defenses?

9. Gateway 2000, Inc., a leading direct marketer of personal computers in the United States, issued 11.7 million shares of common stock at a price of $15 per share in an initial public offering in December 1993. The prospectus included the following language: "Although the company anticipates significant growth in the future, it does not expect its growth to continue at the rates previously experienced." The prospectus also identified sixteen risk factors, including (1) "Short Product Life Cycles," which warned that there could be no assurance that the new products and features introduced in 1993 will be successful or that the introduction of new products will not materially and adversely affect the

sale of the company's existing products; (2) "Management of Growth," stating that the company has experienced and may continue to experience problems with its management information systems and inventory controls; (3) "Potential for Fluctuating Operating Results," noting that the personal computer industry generally has been subject to seasonality and to significant quarterly and annual fluctuations in operating results; (4) "Potential Liability for Sales, Use or Income Taxes," stating that the company does not collect or remit sales or use taxes with respect to its sales in any state other than South Dakota, where its physical plant and employees are located, and warning that in the future the company may be required to collect sales and use taxes in states other than South Dakota; and (5) "Absence of Public Market and Possible Volatility of Stock Price," warning that the market price for the company's common stock may be highly volatile.

The per share earnings for the first quarter of 1994 declined, triggering a drop in Gateway's stock price from $20.44 to $15.50 per share. Earnings dropped again during the second quarter of 1994, and the stock price plummeted to $9.25 per share on June 23, 1994. Gateway attributed the reduced earnings to product transitions, unanticipated sales mix, and technical problems with a new line of portable computers.

The plaintiffs, who had purchased Gateway stock soon after the stock was publicly offered, sued under Sections 11 and 12(a)(2) of the 1933 Act and Section 10(b) and Rule 10b–5 of the 1934 Act. They alleged that the prospectus (1) overstated earnings in 1993 and 1994 by failing to adequately reserve for uncollectible accounts receivable and product returns; (2) misrepresented Gateway's prospect for growth; (3) misrepresented the existence and extent of obsolete and defective inventories; (4) misrepresented the adequacy of Gateway's reserves for doubtful accounts, thereby overstating Gateway's assets by $6.8 million; (5) misrepresented the quality of Gateway's new portable computers; (6) misrepresented serious deficiencies in Gateway's purchasing and inventory control systems, management information and order systems, and management and forecasting procedures; and (7) misrepresented Gateway's obligations to pay sales taxes to states other than South Dakota.

Should any of the plaintiffs' claims be dismissed? On what theory? [*Parnes v. Gateway 2000, Inc.*, 122 F.3d 539 (8th Cir. 1997)]

MANAGER'S DILEMMA

10. Shares in "hot" initial public offerings (IPOs) are by definition in high demand. Most shares are allocated to large institutional investors. In a practice dubbed "spinning," the investment bank may allocate shares to the personal accounts of executives of the bank's corporate clients or would-be corporate clients. Because hot deals usually trade at a premium over the IPO price, the executives can sell the shares on the day of the IPO for quick profits.

Cristina Morgan, Hambrecht & Quist's managing director of investment banking, defends the practice of allocating IPOs to the personal brokerage accounts of clients who direct corporate-finance business to the firm, saying, "Is it appropriate? Well, yeah." She reasons: "If you sell doughnuts, you do everything you can to enhance the image and service of your doughnut shop to customers. You're just doing your job. That's what we all are doing." Morgan points out that the amounts involved, often 500 to 1,000 shares, are small compared to the net worth of her clients, and she asserts that there is no way that the IPO allocations could influence the corporate decisions made by the executives who receive the allocations.[35]

Regina Taoka is the newly appointed head of investment banking at an old-line Wall Street investment banking firm that is eager to shake off its stodgy image and to increase its share of high-technology IPOs. Taoka knows that the firm's personal clients include venture capitalists owning substantial shares in privately owned companies that are contemplating going public and officers and directors of public companies that may engage in secondary offerings or mergers and acquisitions.

The manager in charge of business development has proposed that the firm give these individuals "a taste" of future hot IPOs, in hopes that "they will remember who their friends are" when selecting a lead underwriter or financial adviser for their companies. He tells Taoka that "everyone is doing it." He also recommends adopting a policy of allocating extra IPO shares to investment funds and other institutional investors that agree to buy additional shares after the IPO in the after-market.

---

35. Morgan is quoted in Michael Siconolfi, *Hambrecht & Quist Goes on Offensive on 'Spinning,'* WALL ST. J., Nov. 26, 1997, at C1, C20. *See also* Michael Siconolfi, *SEC, NASD Begin Probes of IPO 'Spin' Accounts,* WALL ST. J., Nov. 13, 1997, at A3.

Of course, IPO shares do not always go up, especially in the bear market that began in 2000. For example, shares of Imagic TV fell from its November 2000 $11.00 offering price to $6.75 in its first two days of trading. The *New York Times* quipped in late 2000: "Now that investors have little appetite for new stocks, people with the connections to the next hot offering may be left wondering: with friends and family like these, who needs enemies?"[36]

36. *Initial Offerings: Once Hot, but Now Hot Potatoes*, N.Y. TIMES, Nov. 26, 2000.

What restrictions, if any, should Taoka put on spinning? Is allocation to the personal account of a private company executive more or less defensible than allocation to the account of an executive of a publicly traded company? Would a policy of allocating additional shares in an IPO based on the fund's willingness to commit to buy on the after-market raise any legal or ethical issues? [*See* Susan Pulliam & Randall Smith, *Seeking IPO Shares, Investors Offer to Buy More in After-Market*, WALL ST. J., Dec. 6, 2000, at A1.]

INTERNET SOURCES

Securities and Exchange Commission	http://www.sec.gov
The SEC's guidance on how to comply with the plain English requirements—*A Plain English Handbook: How to Create Clear SEC Disclosure Documents*—is posted on this site.	http://www.sec.gov/consumer/plaine.htm
This site provides free access to electronic filings with the SEC.	http://www.freeedgar.com
Nasdaq Stock Market	http://www.nasdaq.com
New York Stock Exchange	http://www.nyse.com
This site maintained by Houlihan Smith & Company, a specialized investment banking firm, includes a helpful article on due diligence entitled *The Investment Banker's Perspective on Due Diligence for Mergers, Acquisitions and Securities Offerings*.	http://www.houlihansmith.com
The National Association of Corporate Directors publishes a variety of Blue Ribbon reports as well as *Director's Monthly*.	http://www.nacdonline.org

CHAPTER 25

Securities Fraud *and* Insider Trading

MAINTAINING THE INTEGRITY OF THE SECURITIES MARKETS

The principal antifraud provisions of the federal securities laws are Sections 11 and 12(a)(2) of the Securities Act of 1933 (the 1933 Act), discussed in Chapter 24, and Section 10(b) of the Securities Exchange Act of 1934 (the 1934 Act). As explained in Chapter 24, Section 11 applies only to registered offerings, and Section 12(a)(2) applies only to public offerings not exempt from the 1933 Act's registration requirements. In contrast, Section 10(b) applies to all purchases and sales of securities, regardless of whether they are registered or exempt from registration.

Under Section 10(b) and Rule 10b–5, promulgated by the Securities and Exchange Commission (SEC) pursuant to the 1934 Act, it is unlawful for any person to use a fraudulent, manipulative, or deceptive device in connection with the purchase or sale of any security. Rule 10b–5 also prohibits *insider trading,* that is, trading securities based on material nonpublic information in violation of a duty to the corporation or its shareholders or the source of the information. SEC Rules 10b5–1 and 10b5–2 clarify certain aspects of insider trading.

Section 16(b) of the 1934 Act regulates "short-swing" trading by insiders. In particular, it allows a public corporation to recover the profits if any officer or director of the corporation or any person who owns more than 10 percent of the corporation's securities purchases and sells, or sells and purchases, securities of the corporation within a six-month period.

Many attribute the size and success of the U.S. capital markets to the transparency and perceived fairness of the securities markets, which is a direct result of the 1933 Act's registration requirements, the 1934 Act's periodic reporting requirements, and the antifraud provisions in both acts. As the U.S. Supreme Court intimated in *Basic, Inc. v. Levinson,*[1] no one "would knowingly roll the dice in a crooked crap game."

CHAPTER OVERVIEW

This chapter focuses on Section 10(b) and Rule 10b–5. It sets forth the seven elements necessary in a Rule 10b–5 securities fraud case and the fraud-on-the-market theory of liability. The safe harbor for certain forward-looking statements is discussed. Section 17(a) of the 1933 Act, under which the U.S. government can bring fraud claims, is briefly discussed. The chapter defines insider trading and discusses in detail the legal elements of an insider-trading case. Short-swing trading is then defined, and the rules for calculating the recoverable profits are discussed, as well as the requirements for reporting by insiders.

1. 485 U.S. 224 (1988).

Section 10(b) *of the* 1934 Act

Section 10(b) gives the SEC power to prohibit individuals or companies from engaging in securities fraud by authorizing the SEC to prescribe specific rules for the protection of investors.

RULE 10b–5

The SEC promulgated Rule 10b–5 to encourage disclosure of information relevant to the investing public, to protect investors, and to deter fraud in the securities industry. Rule 10b–5 states:

> It shall be unlawful for any person, directly or indirectly, by the use of any means or instrumentality of interstate commerce, or of the mails, or of any facility of any national securities exchange,
>
> (1) to employ any device, scheme, or artifice to defraud,
>
> (2) to make any untrue statement of a material fact or to omit to state a material fact necessary in order to make the statements made, in the light of the circumstances under which they were made, not misleading, or
>
> (3) to engage in any act, practice, or course of business which operates or would operate as a fraud or deceit upon any person, in connection with the purchase or sale of any security.

The SEC has broad power to investigate apparent violations of Rule 10b–5 and to order that the violator stop its wrongful conduct or to recommend criminal prosecution for willful violations.

More suits are brought under Rule 10b–5 than under any other securities law provision, including those, such as Sections 11 and 12(a)(2) of the 1933 Act, that explicitly create private rights of action. Although there is some overlap, Rule 10b–5 extends to misconduct not covered by other securities laws. Under Rule 10b–5, managers could be liable for misleading statements contained in any document—such as a press release or a letter to shareholders—or even a speech to a trade association as long as the statements were made in a manner reasonably calculated to influence the investing public.

Since 1946, courts have held that Rule 10b–5 also creates an implicit private right of action, giving individual investors the right to sue a violator for damages. Although the Supreme Court has lately shown increasing hostility toward implied rights of action under other provisions of the securities laws, most commentators do not expect it to abrogate the private right of action under Rule 10b–5.

Controlling Persons Section 20(a) imposes joint and several liability on every person who, directly or indirectly, controls any person liable under the 1934 Act, unless the controlling person acted in good faith and did not directly or indirectly induce the acts constituting the violation. This provision is generally interpreted in the same way as Section 15 of the 1933 Act, which is discussed in Chapter 24.

Aiding and Abetting In *Central Bank of Denver, N.A. v. First Interstate Bank of Denver, N.A.,*[2] the Supreme Court ruled that a private plaintiff may not maintain an aiding and abetting suit under Section 10(b). In that case, the plaintiff had attempted to hold the bank that was the indenture trustee for a municipal bond issue secondarily liable as an aider and abettor of the fraud perpetrated by the issuers of the bonds.

In reaching its decision, the Supreme Court noted the vexatious nature of Rule 10b–5 suits and the fact that it requires secondary actors to expend large sums for pretrial defense and the negotiation of settlements. The Court went on to state:

> This uncertainty and excessive litigation can have ripple effects. For example, newer and smaller companies may find it difficult to obtain advice from professionals. A professional may fear that a newer or smaller company may not survive and that business failure would generate securities litigation against the professional, among others. In addition, the increased costs incurred by professionals because of the litigation and settlement costs under 10b–5 may be passed on to their client companies, and in turn incurred by the company's investors, the intended beneficiaries of the statute.

The SEC can still bring aider-and-abettor cases seeking injunctive relief or damages under Section 10(b). To prove that a person is an *aider and abettor,* it is necessary to show (1) the existence of a primary violation of Section 10(b) or Rule 10b–5, (2) the defendant's knowledge of (or recklessness as to) that primary violation, and (3) substantial assistance of the violation by the defendant.

Conspiracy In *Dinsmore v. Squadron, Ellenoff, Plesent, Sheinfeld & Sorkin,*[3] the U.S. Court of Appeals for the Second Circuit applied *Central Bank's* reasoning to a claim of conspiracy to fraudulently buy or sell securities and held that there is no private implied cause of action for conspiracy under Section 10(b).

---

2. 511 U.S. 164 (1994).
3. 135 F.3d 837 (2d Cir. 1998).

Primary Liability for Secondary Actors Both the Supreme Court in *Central Bank* and the Second Circuit in *Dinsmore* took pains to make it clear that secondary actors (such as an accountant, lawyer, or bank) can be liable in private suits if their conduct satisfies the requirements for primary liability, as happened in the following case.

A CASE IN POINT

CASE 25.1

McGann v. Ernst & Young
United States Court of Appeals for the Ninth Circuit
102 F.3d 390
(9th Cir. 1996), cert. denied,
520 U.S. 1181 (1997).

Summary

FACTS Ernst & Young was the outside auditor for Community Psychiatric Centers (CPC), a publicly traded corporation. The plaintiffs alleged that Ernst & Young failed to disclose that CPC had a major accounts receivable problem and thereby issued a false and misleading audit opinion regarding CPC's financial statements for the fiscal year ending in November 1990.

Moreover, the plaintiffs alleged that Ernst & Young knew that CPC would include this audit opinion in its annual report on Form 10–K filed with the SEC. The plaintiffs claimed that the suppression of this information caused CPC's stock price to be artificially inflated. In September and November 1991, when CPC announced a major drop in earnings due to $37 million in uncollectible debts, the value of CPC's stock declined precipitously.

The plaintiffs were the class of persons who purchased CPC between the time Ernst & Young published its audit opinion for CPC's 1990 fiscal year and the time CPC announced its bad debts. They alleged that Ernst & Young, by producing a fraudulent audit report with the knowledge that its client would disseminate the report to the securities market, committed fraudulent acts "in connection with" the trading of securities and thus violated Section 10(b) of the 1934 Act. The district court dismissed the claim, and the plaintiffs appealed.

ISSUE PRESENTED Is an accounting firm subject to primary liability under Section 10(b) of the 1934 Act when it prepares a fraudulent audit report that it knows its client will include in a Form 10–K?

SUMMARY OF OPINION The U.S. Court of Appeals for the Ninth Circuit began by noting that accountants have no aider-and-abettor liability under Section 10(b) per *Central Bank of Denver.*[4] The court held, however, that *Central Bank* did not undercut *SEC v. Texas Gulf Sulphur Co.,*[5] which stands for the proposition that any false and misleading assertions made "in a manner reasonably calculated to influence the investing public" are made "in connection with" the purchase or sale of securities within the meaning of Section 10(b). The language of Section 10(b) does not limit liability to those who actually trade securities. One who "introduces fraudulent information into the securities market does no less damage to the public because that party did not trade stocks." Therefore, Ernst & Young could be liable for a primary violation of Section 10(b) if the plaintiff could prove that Ernst & Young made a misleading statement in the audit opinion, knowing that the opinion would be included in CPC's Form 10–K.

RESULT The appeals court reversed the district court's judgment in favor of Ernst & Young and remanded the case to the district court. The allegations survived the motion to dismiss.

COMMENTS Similarly, the Second Circuit held that a securities broker could be held primarily liable for market manipulation in violation of Section 10(b) and Rule 10b–5 when he followed a stock promoter's directions to execute stock trades designed to create the appearance of an actual market for a company's shares and thereby artificially

4. 511 U.S. 164 (1994).
5. 401 F.2d 833 (2d Cir. 1968) (Case 25.2).

(Continued)

(Case 25.1 continued)

raise the stock price.[6] The court stated that the broker would be liable if he knew, or was reckless in not knowing, that the trades were manipulative, even if he did not share the promoter's specific overall purpose of manipulating the market for the stock.

6. SEC v. U.S. Environmental, Inc., 155 F.3d 107 (2d Cir. 1998).

McGann involved an alleged failure to disclose that caused the audit opinion to be false and misleading. Accountants are generally not responsible for misrepresentations or omissions in other parts of a document that they did not certify.[7] The Second Circuit applies a "bright-line" rule that a secondary actor will not have primary liability for a material misstatement unless (1) the person actually made the false or misleading statement; and (2) the misrepresentation was attributed to that specific person at the time of public dissemination, that is, in advance of the investment decision.[8] The Ninth Circuit uses a more lenient standard and will find a secondary actor liable for "substantial participation" in the misrepresentation.

Accountants must sign a written consent before their audited report can be included in a registration statement. Before doing so, they should do an *S–1 review,* which is a review of events subsequent to the date of the certified balance sheet in the registration statement to ascertain whether any material change has occurred in the company's financial position that should be disclosed to prevent the balance sheet figures from being misleading. This review includes comparing recent financial statements to earlier ones, reading minutes of the shareholders' and directors' meetings, and investigating changes in material contracts, bad debts, and newly discovered liabilities.

7. *See* Shapiro v. Cantor, 123 F.3d 717 (2d Cir. 1997).
8. Winkler v. Wigley, 2000 U.S. App. LEXIS 31332 (2d Cir. Dec. 6, 2000). *See also* Wright v. Ernst & Young LLP, 152 F.3d 169 (2d Cir. 1998). *Accord* Anixter v. Home-Stake Prod. Co., 77 F.3d 1215 (10th Cir. 1996).

 ETHICAL CONSIDERATION

Suppose that, in the course of the S–1 review, the accountants learn that the company's earnings have dropped dramatically from earnings for the comparable periods included in the registration statement. Should the accountants refuse to sign the consent for inclusion of their opinion on the financial statements for the previous period unless the adverse results are disclosed in the prospectus?

Statute of Limitations Suits under Section 10(b) must be brought within one year of the date the plaintiff discovered or should have discovered the fraud or within three years of the date of the violation, whichever is shorter.[9]

Elements *of a* Rule 10b–5 Cause *of* Action

In order to recover damages from a defendant under Rule 10b–5, a plaintiff must show each of the following elements:

1. The defendant used either an instrumentality of interstate commerce or the mails or a facility of a national securities exchange.
2. The defendant made a statement that either misrepresented or omitted a fact.
3. The fact was of material importance.
4. The misrepresentation or omission was made with *scienter* (culpable state of mind).
5. The statement or omission was made in connection with the purchase or sale of securities.
6. The plaintiff acted in reliance either on the defendant's misrepresentation or on the assumption that the market price of the stock accurately reflected its value.
7. The defendant's misrepresentation or omission caused the plaintiff to suffer losses.

Each of these seven elements is described in more detail below.

INTERSTATE COMMERCE

The requirement that the defendant used interstate commerce, the mails, or a national securities exchange gives Congress the power to regulate the defendant's conduct under the U.S. Constitution. The requirement is usually easy to satisfy. Use of interstate commerce includes use

9. Lampf, Pleva, Lipkind, Prupis & Petigrow v. Gilbertson, 501 U.S. 350 (1991).

VIEW FROM CYBERSPACE

Securities Fraud Moves *from the* Boiler Room *to the* Internet

In early 2001, the SEC announced that it had filed charges against twenty-three companies and individuals who used phony Internet press releases, false message board postings, and spam e-mails to pump up stock prices and defraud investors. One case involved a company that used a promotional Web site and spam to promote an upcoming initial public offering (IPO) for its online eyewear sales business. In fact, the IPO was never registered, and the company had no office, inventory, or products. The promoter used the investors' money to pay for trips to casinos and strip clubs and other personal expenses.[a]

Mark S. Jacobs, a twenty-three-year-old former community college student, pled guilty in December 2000 to one count of wire fraud and two counts of securities fraud in connection with his distribution of a bogus press release that caused Emulex shareholders to lose $110 million after trading on the phony news.[b] The press release falsely stated that Emulex was being investigated by the SEC, that it had overstated its reported earnings figures for the preceding quarter, and that its CEO had resigned. The plea agreement recommended that Jacobs be sentenced to thirty-seven to forty-six months in prison and pay $330 million in government fines and restitution to the Emulex shareholders.

In 2000, the Massachusetts Securities Division launched an Internet securities fraud unit to combat fraudulent securities trading on the Web. Secretary of State William F. Galvin reported "a continuing migration of bad brokers from the 'boiler room' to the Internet" and indicated that 25 percent of the division's cases now involved the Internet.[c]

a. Joanna Glasner, *SEC Attacks Online Scammers,* WIRED NEWS, Mar. 1, 2001.
b. Bloomberg News, *Guilty Plea Expected in Emulex Fraud Case,* CNET News.com, Dec. 28, 2000.
c. Beth Healy, *State Launches Web Securities Fraud Unit,* BOSTON GLOBE, Apr. 20, 2000, at C4.

---

of a radio broadcast heard in more than one state; use of a newspaper advertisement in a newspaper delivered to more than one state; or use of a telephone wired for interstate calls, even if no interstate calls were actually made. Use of the mails includes sending a letter within a state because the mail is an instrumentality of interstate commerce. Use of a national securities exchange includes use of any facility of such an exchange.

MISSTATEMENT OR OMISSION

A *misstatement* is a misrepresentation of a fact; in other words, a lie. An *omission* is a fact left out of a statement, such that the statement becomes misleading.

Misstatement In the following case, a company's attempts to dispel rumors were found to misrepresent the facts.

A CASE IN POINT

CASE 25.2

SEC v. Texas Gulf Sulphur Co.

United States District Court for the Southern District of New York

312 F. Supp. 77 (S.D.N.Y. 1970), aff'd, 446 F.2d 1301 (2d Cir. 1971), cert. denied, 404 U.S. 1005 (1971).

Summary

FACTS On November 12, 1963, Texas Gulf Sulphur Company (TGS) drilled a test hole, which indicated the possible discovery of copper. TGS did not immediately disclose the results of its drill hole or undertake further drilling because it wanted to acquire property in the surrounding area and did not want to drive up the price of the property.

On April 12, 1964, in response to rumors about the copper discovery, TGS issued a press release. By this time, the company had confirmed the discovery of copper. Preliminary tests indicated that the discovery was significant. The press release, however, minimized the importance of the discovery. It said (in part):

For Immediate Release

TEXAS GULF SULPHUR COMMENT ON TIMMINS, ONTARIO, EXPLORATION NEW YORK, April 12—The following statement was made today by Dr. Charles F. Fogarty,

(Continued)

(Case 25.2 continued)

executive vice president of Texas Gulf Sulphur Company, in regard to the company's drilling operations near Timmins, Ontario, Canada. Dr. Fogarty said:

During the past few days, the exploration activities of Texas Gulf Sulphur in the area of Timmins, Ontario, have been widely reported in the press, coupled with rumors of a substantial copper discovery there. These reports exaggerate the scale of operations, and mention plans and statistics of size and grade of ore that are without factual basis and have evidently originated by speculation of people not connected with TGS.

The facts are as follows. TGS has been exploring in the Timmins area for six years as part of its overall search in Canada and elsewhere for various minerals—lead, copper, zinc, etc. During the course of this work, in Timmins as well as in Eastern Canada, TGS has conducted exploration entirely on its own, without the participation by others. Numerous prospects have been investigated by geophysical means and a large number of selected ones have been core-drilled. These cores are sent to the United States for assay and detailed examination as a matter of routine and on advice of expert Canadian legal counsel. No inferences as to grade can be drawn from this procedure.

Most of the areas drilled in Eastern Canada have revealed either barren pyrite or graphite without value; a few have resulted in discoveries of small or marginal sulfide ore bodies.

Recent drilling on one property near Timmins has led to preliminary indications that more drilling would be required for proper evaluation of this prospect. The drilling done to date has not been conclusive, but the statements made by many outside quarters are unreliable and include information and figures that are not available to TGS.

The work done to date has not been sufficient to reach definite conclusions and any statement as to size and grade of ore would be premature and possibly misleading. When we have progressed to the point where reasonable and logical conclusions can be made, TGS will issue a definite statement to its stockholders and to the public in order to clarify the Timmins project.

The SEC contended that TGS's April 12 release was a misstatement because the impression it left with investors was contrary to the known facts at the time.

ISSUE PRESENTED Does a press release giving a misleading impression about the results of a drilling operation violate Rule 10b–5?

SUMMARY OF OPINION The U.S. District Court for the Southern District of New York acknowledged that the timing of disclosure is a matter for the business judgment of the corporate officers. When a company chooses to issue a press release to respond to spreading rumors regarding its activities, it must, however, describe the true picture at the time of the press release. This should include the basic facts known, or which reasonably should be known, to the drafters of the press release. Such facts are necessary to enable the investing public to make a reasonable appraisal of the existing situation.

Because the press release misled reasonable investors to believe either that there was no ore discovery, or that any discovery was not a significant one, TGS violated Section 10(b) and Rule 10b–5.

RESULT TGS violated Section 10(b) and Rule 10b–5.

COMMENTS A company may have excellent reasons to attempt to dispel rumors. TGS, for example, had an interest in keeping the find quiet in order to keep down the acquisition costs of land. Or consider a company involved in merger negotiations that is asked by the press whether there is any reason for unusual trading in its stock. The company

(Continued)

(Case 25.2 continued)

may well want to keep the negotiations under wraps for a variety of legitimate reasons. Yet, if it says that it is unaware of any corporate developments, it runs the risk of Rule 10b–5 liability. The SEC has indicated that it considers such a statement in these circumstances to be a violation of Rule 10b–5. The Supreme Court addressed this issue in *Basic, Inc. v. Levinson,* discussed further below.

A prediction about the future can be a misstatement, but only if the person making the prediction does not believe it at the time. A prediction is not a guarantee, and it does not become a misstatement simply because the facts do not develop as predicted. If there is no reasonable basis for a prediction, however, then it is a misstatement, because the person who made it could not have honestly believed it.[10] The Private Securities Litigation Reform Act of 1995 (the Reform Act) contains a safe harbor for certain forward-looking statements. It is discussed later in this chapter.

Omission It is clear that a company must be careful if it chooses to speak. What if it chooses not to speak?

The general rule is that a company has no duty under Rule 10b–5 to reveal corporate developments unless the company or its insiders trade in its securities, recommend trading to someone else, or disclose the information as a *tip*—that is, a disclosure made to an individual and withheld from the general public. The fact that information is material does not, in itself, give rise to a duty to disclose.[11]

Silence or a "no comment" statement in response to rumors will not lead to liability if the company has not previously spoken on the subject and insiders are not trading or tipping. There is a caveat, however: A policy of not commenting on rumors must be adhered to in the face of both true and untrue rumors. If the company always says "no comment" when the rumor is true but provides facts to dispel untrue rumors, then the "no comment" acts as an admission that the rumor is true.

Although keeping silent may be safer under Rule 10b–5, in many cases it will be hard to do. If a corporation's stock is traded on rumors of some major development, silence may contribute to disorderly market activity, distrust of company management, and possible abuse by those with access to inside information. More-

over, a blanket "no comment" policy makes it impossible to dispel false but damaging rumors. Once the silence is broken, of course, the company must be exceedingly careful in its statements even as to speculative events.[12]

Stock exchange rules require that issuers promptly reveal material developments unless there is a business reason not to do so, and the securities laws require that certain information be disclosed in registration statements, annual and quarterly reports, and proxy solicitations. In particular, Management's Discussion and Analysis of Financial Condition and Results of Operations must disclose any known material event or uncertainty that would cause reported financial information not to be necessarily indicative of future operating results or financial condition.[13]

---

12. *See* Dale E. Barnes, Jr. & Constance E. Bagley, *Great Expectations: Risk Management Through Risk Disclosure,* 1 Stan. J.L., Bus. & Fin. 155 (1994).
13. *See* Item 303 of SEC Regulation S-K, Management's Discussion and Analysis of Financial Condition and Results of Operations, 17 C.F.R. § 229.303(a)(3)(ii) (1996).

INTERNATIONAL CONSIDERATION

Under the London Stock Exchange rules, if a listed company's share price moves significantly on the basis of rumor and the rumor is true, then the company must disclose the existence of the rumored event. For example, in January 1998, drug powerhouse SmithKline Beecham PLC was required to disclose that it was engaged in merger negotiations with American Home Products after rumors of a deal sent shares of both companies rising.[a] Although there is no numerical threshold for disclosure, a rule of thumb is that a 10 percent move in the stock triggers the duty to disclose the accuracy of truthful rumors. On the other hand, if the rumors are not true, then the company can continue to say "no comment."

a. Steven Lipin & Sara Calian, *Did U.K.'s Strict Rules Spur Deal?,* Wall St. J., Feb. 2, 1998, at C1.

---

10. *See* Virginia Bankshares v. Sandberg, 501 U.S. 1083 (1991) (holding that a statement as to beliefs or opinions may be actionable if the opinion is known by the speaker at the time it is expressed to be untrue or to have no reasonable basis in fact).
11. Backman v. Polaroid Corp., 893 F.2d 1405 (1st Cir. 1990).

Once the company has said something about a particular topic, it has a duty to disclose enough relevant facts so that the statement is not inaccurate, incomplete, or misleading. The statement may be an obligatory one. Or the statement may be voluntary; for example, a company may choose to publicize information about favorable new developments or to respond to unfavorable rumors.

Whether the statement is obligatory or voluntary, the company's officials must tell the whole truth with respect to that topic or risk being sued later for a misleading omission.

The following case addressed the issue of whether a company has a duty to update or correct statements that have become misleading in light of subsequent events.

A CASE IN POINT

CASE 25.3

Weiner v. Quaker Oats Co.
United States Court of Appeals for the Third Circuit
129 F.3d 310
(3d Cir. 1997).

In the Language of the Court

FACTS On November 2, 1994, the Quaker Oats Company and Snapple Beverage Corporation announced that Quaker would acquire Snapple in a tender offer and merger transaction for $1.7 billion in cash. The market disapproved of the deal. Subsequent to the announcement, Quaker's stock price fell $7.375 per share—approximately 10 percent of the stock's value.

To finance the acquisition, Quaker had obtained $2.4 billion of credit from a banking group led by NationsBank Corporation. The Snapple acquisition nearly tripled Quaker's debt, from approximately $1 billion to approximately $2.7 billion. The acquisition also increased Quaker's total debt-to-total capitalization ratio to approximately 80 percent.

Over the course of the year prior to its acquisition of Snapple, Quaker had announced in several public documents the company's guideline for debt-to-equity ratio and its expectations for earnings growth. The announcements formed the basis for the plaintiffs' action.

In its 1993 Annual Report (dated October 4, 1993), Quaker stated that "our debt-to-total capitalization ratio at June 30, 1993 was 59 percent, up from 49 percent in fiscal 1992. For the future, our guideline will be in the upper-60 percent range." Quaker's president reiterated this "guideline" in a letter contained in the same Annual Report. Quaker's Form 10–Q for the quarter ended September 30, 1993 (filed with the SEC in November 1993) repeated the total debt-to-total capitalization ratio guideline.

In its 1994 Annual Report (dated September 23, 1994), Quaker stated that "we are committed to achieving real earnings growth of at least 7 percent over time." In addition, the report noted that Quaker's total debt-to-total capitalization ratio was 68.8 percent, "in line with our guideline in the upper-60 percent range."

Negotiations between Quaker and Snapple apparently began in the spring of 1994. By early August 1994, Quaker had advised Snapple that it was interested in pursuing a merger of the two companies and had commenced a due diligence investigation. As noted, the merger was completed in November of that year.

The gist of the plaintiffs' complaint was that, even if Quaker's announcements about its total debt-to-total capitalization ratio and projected earnings growth were true at the time they were made, Quaker still had a duty to update or correct those statements if it knew they had become materially misleading in light of subsequent events. The plaintiffs alleged that (1) Quaker knew those statements were materially misleading as soon as it was reasonably certain the Snapple merger would be finalized, and (2) Quaker had such certainty at least sometime prior to its formal announcement of the merger on November 2, 1994.

The district court dismissed both portions of the plaintiffs' claim, on the basis that neither Quaker's statements relating to its total debt-to-total capitalization ratio nor its statements relating to its projected earnings growth were material. The plaintiffs appealed.

ISSUE PRESENTED Under what circumstances do a corporation and its officers have a duty to update, or at least not to repeat, particular projections regarding the corporation's

(Continued)

(Case 25.3 continued)

financial condition (for example, total debt-to-total capitalization ratio or earnings growth projections)?

OPINION POLLAK, J., writing for the U.S. Court of Appeals for the Third Circuit:

Rule 10b–5, promulgated pursuant to § 10(b) of the [1934] Act, provides the framework for a private cause of action for violations involving false statements or omissions of material fact. To establish a valid claim of securities fraud under Rule 10b–5, plaintiffs must prove that the defendant: (1) made misstatements or omissions of material fact, (2) with *scienter,* (3) in connection with the purchase or sale of securities, (4) upon which plaintiffs relied, and (5) that plaintiffs' reliance was the proximate cause of their injury.

In the present litigation, the plaintiffs allege that . . . they purchased shares in reliance on statements made by Quaker . . . about (1) Quaker's guideline for the ratio of total debt-to-total capitalization (in the upper 60 percent range) governing the company's financial planning and (2) Quaker's expected earnings growth in fiscal 1995.

The statements about expected earnings growth were made in August and September of 1994 . . . and it is plaintiffs' contention that, at a point when Quaker was in active pursuit of Snapple, Quaker and Smithburg must have known that the projections were illusory.

Plaintiffs' central complaint with respect to [the statements regarding the guideline for the ratio of total debt-to-total capitalization] is that, when the Snapple negotiations went into high gear, Quaker . . . had to have known that a . . . ratio in the high 60 percent range was no longer a realistic possibility. At that point, plaintiffs contend, defendants had a duty publicly to set the guidelines record straight.

...

A. The Total Debt-to-Total Capitalization Ratio Guideline

...

Plaintiffs' claims under this heading are claims of nondisclosure. "When an allegation of fraud under Section 10(b) is based upon a nondisclosure, there can be no fraud absent a duty to speak." In general, Section 10(b) and Rule 10b–5 do not impose a duty on defendants to correct prior statements—particularly statements of intent—so long as those statements were true when made. However, "[t]here can be no doubt that a duty exists to correct prior statements, if the prior statements were true when made but misleading if left unrevised." To avoid liability in such circumstances, "notice of a change of intent [must] be disseminated in a timely fashion." Whether an amendment is sufficiently prompt is a question that "must be determined in each case based upon the particular facts and circumstances."

...

1. Materiality

...

In *Basic,* the Court adopted in the context of § 10(b) and Rule 10b–5 the standard of materiality set forth in *TSC Industries.* The *Basic* Court approved . . . the principle that "[a]n omitted fact is material if there is a substantial likelihood that a reasonable shareholder would consider it important in deciding how to [proceed]."

...

Therefore, "[o]nly if the alleged misrepresentations or omissions are so obviously unimportant to an investor that reasonable minds cannot differ on the question of

(Continued)

materiality is it appropriate for the district court to rule that the allegations are inactionable as a matter of law."

...

In sum, in the present case, we find that a trier of fact could conclude that a reasonable investor reading the 1993 Annual Report published on October 4, 1993, and then the 1994 Annual Report published on September 23, 1994, would have no ground for anticipating that the total debt-to-total capitalization ratio would rise as significantly as it did in fiscal 1995. There was after all no abjuration of the "upper 60-percent range" guideline. The company had predicted the rise from 59 percent to the "upper 60-percent range" in the 1993 report and that rise had occurred by and was confirmed in the 1994 report. Therefore, it was reasonable for an investor to expect that the company would make another such prediction if it expected the ratio to change markedly in the ensuing year.

...

B. Earnings Growth Projections

...

Quaker's 1994 Annual Report—issued on September 23, 1994, more than five weeks prior to the November 2 merger announcement—contained the statement that "we are committed to achieving a real earnings growth of at least 7 percent over time." We conclude that the phrase "over time" in this second statement inoculates Quaker from any claims of fraud that point to a decline in earnings growth in the immediate aftermath of the Snapple acquisition. No reasonably careful investor would find material a prediction of seven-percent growth followed by the qualifier "over time." Therefore, we hold that no reasonable finder of fact could conclude that the projection influenced prudent investors.

RESULT The claim relating to Quaker's total debt-to-total capitalization ratio guideline was reinstated and remanded to the district court; the dismissal of the claim relating to Quaker's earnings growth projections was affirmed.

QUESTIONS

1. Given that a wealth of data compiled by market analysts demonstrates that, over the long run, stock prices follow corporate earnings, which piece of information would you find more important to your investment decision to buy or sell Quaker stock: (a) forecasts relating to the company's total debt-to-total capitalization ratio, or (b) forecasts relating to the company's real earnings growth?
2. Would an announcement by Quaker that it was contemplating increasing its total debt-to-total capitalization ratio have "tipped the market" to a pending acquisition? What result might that have brought?

An omission can occur when a company makes a statement that is true at the time but becomes misleading in light of later events. There is a duty to correct when "a company makes a historical statement [of a material fact] that at the time made, the company believed to be true, but as revealed by subsequently discovered information actually was not."[14] In contrast, the duty to

update—which may arise when a statement, reasonable at the time it is made, becomes misleading due to a subsequent event—is more limited.[15] There is no duty to update if the original statement was not material,[16] or "when the original statement was not forward looking

14. Stransby v. Cummins Engine Co., 51 F.3d 1329 (7th Cir. 1995).

15. *See, e.g., In re* Time Warner, Inc. Sec. Litig., 9 F.3d 259 (2d Cir. 1993).

16. Hillson Partners Ltd. Partnership v. Adage, Inc., 42 F.3d 204 (4th Cir. 1994).

and does not contain some factual representation that remains 'alive' in the minds of investors as a continuing representation."[17] On the other hand, if investors are reasonably relying on the previous statements, the company can be held liable for failing to disclose the new information. For example, a company incurs a duty to update its financial projections when a projection changes or the company discovers that the projection was incorrect from the outset.

There is a duty to disclose the results of product-safety tests, if they make previously disclosed test results false. For example, A.H. Robins Company, a pharmaceutical manufacturer, reported in 1970 that its Dalkon Shield intrauterine contraceptive device was safe and effective. In 1972, internal studies indicated that the Dalkon Shield was not as safe or effective as originally reported.[18] The U.S. Court of Appeals for the Second Circuit held that Robins's omission of the new information rendered its earlier statements misleading. Because investors were still relying on the statement that the Dalkon Shield was safe, the company had a duty to correct once it learned that the statement was inaccurate.

In contrast, in *Oran v. Stafford*,[19] the U.S. Court of Appeals for the Third Circuit held that reports that the diet pill combination fen-phen (made by American Home Products Corporation—AHP) caused heart-valve abnormalities were not material because they did not definitively establish a link between the two drugs and heart-valve disorders. As a result, AHP's failure to disclose this data did not render its statements about the inconclusiveness of the relationship materially misleading. The court also ruled that the data were not material because when they were eventually released, they had no adverse effect on AHP's stock.

Statements by Third Parties and Entanglement Even if the company itself did not publish the misleading projection, or make the statement, or start the rumor, it may nevertheless have a duty to reveal all of the facts regarding the issue. This is the case when the company is so entangled with the third party's statement that the statement can be attributed to the company; the company is then responsible for making sure that the statement is accurate. For example, if a company makes it a practice to review and correct drafts of analysts' forecasts, then the company implicitly represents that the corrected forecast is in

ETHICAL CONSIDERATION

If there is no legal obligation to disclose bad news, is there ever an ethical duty to disclose it?

accord with the company's view, and it has a duty to reveal all facts necessary to ensure that the analyst's report is not misleading.[20] Similarly, a company's distribution of copies of an analyst's report to investors or other members of the public or the posting of an analyst's report on the company's Web site may be construed as an implied representation that the information in the report is accurate or reflects the company's views.

MATERIAL FACT

A buyer or seller of stock cannot recover damages just because an executive misrepresented or omitted a fact about the company. The fact must be material. As explained in Chapter 24, a fact is material if a reasonable investor would consider it important in deciding how to act. Materiality is judged at the time of the misstatement or omission. Materiality is not affected by the intent of the party making the statement. There can be liability even if the manager did not know the omitted or misrepresented fact came within the legal definition of a material fact.

Although it is not always possible to predict which facts a court will consider material, some issues are nearly always considered material. For example, any statements about the earnings, distributions, or assets of a company (unless the misrepresentation is inadvertent and concerns a minor amount) are material. In August 1999, the SEC accounting staff cautioned companies and their auditors against using "rules of thumb" to determine whether errors in the financial statements are material.[21] Even if two errors net out to zero, they can still be material. For example, an overstatement of revenues can be material even if it is accompanied by an overstatement of cost of goods sold. The SEC staff also stated that any intentional misstatement of a number in the financial statements is, by definition, material.

Significant facts about a parent or a subsidiary are usually material. These include the discovery of embezzlement or falsification of financial statements, an impending tender offer, or the loss of a manufacturer's

17. *In re* International Bus. Machs. Corp. Sec. Litig., 163 F.3d 102 (2d Cir. 1998). *See also In re* Burlington Coat Factory Sec. Litig., 114 F.3d 1410 (3d Cir. 1997).
18. Ross v. A.H. Robins Co., 607 F.2d 545 (2d Cir. 1979), *cert. denied*, 446 U.S. 946 (1980).
19. 226 F.3d 275 (3d Cir. 2000).

20. *See, e.g.*, Stack v. Lobo, 903 F. Supp. 1361 (N.D. Ca. 1995).
21. Staff Accounting Bulletin No. 99, 1999 WL 1123073 (SEC Aug. 12, 1999).

major customer. Other facts that are probably material include inability to obtain supplies, increased costs of supplies, a decision to close a plant, information regarding the outlook in the industry, an intention to market a new product or cease marketing an old one, potential liability for damages in a lawsuit, a major discovery or product development, cost overruns, a change in management or compensation of corporate officers, and an increase in real estate taxes. As this list illustrates, a material fact is any fact that is likely to affect the market value of the company's stock.

The Supreme Court has recognized that for contingent or speculative events, such as negotiations regarding a potential merger, it is difficult to tell whether a reasonable investor would consider the omitted fact material at the time. The Court has declined to adopt a bright-line rule, however; materiality is a fact-specific determination.[22] If a misstatement or omission concerns a future event, such as a potential merger, its materiality will depend on a balancing of the probability that the event will occur and the anticipated magnitude of the event in light of the totality of the company's activity.

Thus, the materiality of preliminary merger discussions in any particular case depends on the facts. Generally, to assess the probability that the event will occur, a fact finder will need to look to indicia of interest in the transaction at the highest corporate levels. Without attempting to catalog all such possible factors, the Court noted by way of example that board resolutions, instructions to investment bankers, and actual negotiations between principals or other intermediaries may serve as indicia of interest. To assess the magnitude of the transaction to the issuer of the securities allegedly manipulated, a fact finder will need to consider such facts as the size of the two corporate entities and of the potential premiums over market value. No particular event or factor short of closing the transaction need be either necessary or sufficient by itself to render merger discussions material.

Vague statements of corporate optimism that are not capable of objective verification and mere puffing are immaterial as a matter of law because reasonable investors do not rely on them in making investment decisions.[23]

For example, the Second Circuit characterized a statement made on October 15, 1992, by Jim Clippard, the director of investor relations of International Business Machines Corporation (IBM), that "we're not—despite your anxiety—concerned about being able to cover the dividend for quite a foreseeable time" as an immaterial expression of optimism, not a guarantee, because he qualified it by noting that "this is a relatively short-term period of economic difficulty we're going through. And we think that we can ride through this with no problem [whatsoever] as far as [the] dividend is concerned."[24] The court held that there was no duty to *correct* the statement when the chief financial officer concluded in late November 1992 that the dividend was likely to be cut because, at the time the statement was made (October 15, 1992), IBM did not have a plan or need to alter the dividend. The court also held that "there is no duty to *update* vague statements of optimism or expressions of opinion." (Emphasis added.) In another case, however, a prediction that the company "expects . . . a net income of approximately $1.00 a share" for the fiscal year to close in two months was held to be a material statement.[25]

Bespeaks Caution Doctrine As explained in Chapter 24, under the judicially developed *bespeaks caution doctrine,* a court may determine that the inclusion of sufficient cautionary statements in a document renders immaterial any misrepresentation and omission contained therein. The doctrine applies only to projections, estimates, and other forward-looking statements that are accompanied by precise cautionary language that adequately discloses the risks involved. The cautionary language must relate to the specific information that the plaintiffs allege is misleading.[26] Unlike the safe harbor provided in the Reform Act, the bespeaks caution doctrine applies to forward-looking statements in any context, including initial public offerings. The legislative history of the Reform Act makes it clear that Congress did not intend its statutory safe-harbor provisions to replace the judicial bespeaks caution doctrine or to foreclose further development of that doctrine by the courts.

SCIENTER

Rule 10b–5 does not impose liability for innocent misstatements or omissions. The misstatements or omissions must be made with *scienter,* that is, a mental state

22. Basic, Inc. v. Levinson, 485 U.S. 224 (1988).
23. *See, e.g.,* Raab v. General Physics Corp., 4 F.3d 286 (4th Cir. 1993) (statements in annual report that company expected 10 percent to 30 percent growth rate over the next several years and was "poised to carry the growth and success of 1991 well into the future" held to be immaterial puffing); San Leandro Emergency Med. Group Profit Sharing Plan v. Philip Morris Cos., 75 F.3d 801 (2d Cir. 1996) (statement that company was "optimistic" about its earnings in 1993 and that it should deliver income growth consistent with its historically superior performance was mere puffery and lacked the sort of definite positive projections that might require later correction).

24. *In re* International Bus. Machs. Corp. Sec. Litig., 163 F.3d 102 (2d Cir. 1998).
25. Marx v. Computer Sciences Corp., 507 F.2d 485 (9th Cir. 1974).
26. *See, e.g.,* Kaplan v. Rose, 49 F.3d 1363 (9th Cir. 1994).

embracing the intent to deceive, manipulate, or defraud. Intent to deceive means that the defendant says something he or she believes is untrue with the expectation that others will rely on the statement, or that the defendant omits a fact in the hope that the omission will cause others to misunderstand what he or she does say. The Supreme Court has made clear that *scienter* is more than mere neg-ligence or lack of care. The Reform Act requires the plain-tiff to plead with particularity specific facts giving rise to a strong inference that the defendant acted with *scienter*.

As indicated in the following case, there is currently a split in the circuits as to whether the allegations of the defendant's motive and opportunity to commit fraud are sufficient to meet the strict pleading requirement.

A CASE IN POINT

CASE 25.4

Kasaks v. Novak

United States Court of Appeals for the Second Circuit 216 F.3d 300 (2d Cir. 2000).

In the Language of the Court

FACTS The plaintiffs sued AnnTaylor Stores Corporation—which, through its wholly owned subsidiary, defendant AnnTaylor, Inc., is a specialty retailer of women's clothing, shoes, and accessories—and several of its top officers for violation of Section 10(b) and Rule 10b–5. They alleged that the defendants knowingly and intentionally issued finan-cial statements that overstated AnnTaylor's financial condition by accounting for inven-tory that they knew to be obsolete and nearly worthless at inflated values and by deliberately failing to adhere to the company's publicly stated markdown policy. The plaintiffs focused on AnnTaylor's so-called Box and Hold practice, whereby a substantial and growing quantity of out-of-date inventory was stored in several warehouses without being marked down. Ultimately, the defendants were forced to publicly acknowledge se-rious inventory problems—that is, that inventories were too high and that liquidation would result in much lower fiscal 1995 earnings than expected—at which point AnnTay-lor's stock price fell precipitously. The district court granted the defendants' motions to dismiss the complaint for failure to plead *scienter* and fraud with sufficient particularity. The plaintiffs appealed.

ISSUE PRESENTED Are allegations of motive and opportunity sufficient to meet the heightened pleading standards for *scienter* under the Reform Act (the PSLRA)? Can fraud be pleaded with sufficient particularity if the plaintiff relies on unnamed confiden-tial sources?

OPINION WALKER, J., writing for the U.S. Court of Appeals for the Second Circuit:

In order "to curtail the filing of meritless lawsuits," the PSLRA imposed stringent procedural requirements on plaintiffs pursuing private securities fraud actions. . . .

B. The Pleading Standard for Scienter

1. The Second Circuit's Pre-PSLRA Pleading Standard
We can easily summarize the pleading standard for scienter that prevailed in this cir-cuit prior to the PSLRA:

Plaintiffs must allege facts that give rise to a strong inference of fraudulent intent. "The requisite 'strong inference' of fraud may be established either (a) by alleging facts to show that defendants had both motive and opportunity to commit fraud, or (b) by alleging facts that constitute strong circumstantial evidence of conscious mis-behavior or recklessness."

. . .

. . . Plaintiffs could not proceed based on motives possessed by virtually all cor-porate insiders, including: (1) the desire to maintain a high corporate credit rating, or otherwise sustain "the appearance of corporate profitability, or of the success of

(Continued)

(Case 25.4 continued)

an investment"; and (2) the desire to maintain a high stock price in order to increase executive compensation, or prolong the benefits of holding corporate office. Rather, plaintiffs had to allege that defendants benefited in some concrete and personal way from the purported fraud. This requirement was generally met when corporate insiders were alleged to have misrepresented to the public material facts about the corporation's performance or prospects in order to keep the stock price artificially high while they sold their own shares at a profit. Accordingly, in the ordinary case, adequate motive arose from the desire to profit from extensive insider sales.

. . .

2. Implications of the PSLRA for the Pleading Standard for Scienter in this Circuit

Courts have disagreed on the proper interpretation of the new pleading requirement imposed by . . . the PSLRA . . . . They have generally come to one of two conclusions:

(1) The statute effectively adopts the Second Circuit's pleading standard for *scienter* wholesale, and thus plaintiffs may continue to state a claim by pleading either motive and opportunity or strong circumstantial evidence of recklessness or conscious misbehavior.[27] (2) The statute strengthens the Second Circuit's standard by rejecting the simple pleading of motive and opportunity.[28]

Our own review of the text and legislative history leads us to a middle ground. We conclude that the PSLRA effectively raised the nationwide pleading standard to that previously existing in this circuit and no higher (with the exception of the "with particularity" requirement). At the same time, however, we believe that Congress's failure to include language about motive and opportunity suggests that we need not be wedded to these concepts in articulating the prevailing standard. . . .

. . .

Accordingly, we hold that the PSLRA adopted our "strong inference" standard: In order to plead *scienter*, plaintiffs must "state with particularity facts giving rise to a strong inference that the defendant acted with the required state of mind." . . . Although litigants and lower courts need and should not employ or rely on magic words such as "motive and opportunity," we believe that our prior case law may be helpful in providing guidance as to how the "strong inference" standard may be met. . . . These cases suggest that the inference may arise where the complaint sufficiently alleges that the defendants: (1) benefited in a concrete and personal way from the purported fraud; (2) engaged in deliberately illegal behavior; (3) knew facts or had access to information suggesting that their public statements were not accurate; or (4) failed to check information they had a duty to monitor. . . .

3. Strong Inference of Fraudulent Intent on the Part of the AnnTaylor Defendants

. . .

By refusing to mark down inventory they knew to be "worthless," "obsolete," and "unsellable," the defendants acted "intentionally and deliberately" to artificially inflate AnnTaylor's reported financial results. They discussed the need to mark down inventory but refused to do so because that would damage the Company's financial

27. *See In re* Advanta Corp. Sec. Litig., 180 F.3d 525 (3d Cir. 1999).
28. *See* Bryant v. Avado Brands, Inc., 187 F.3d 1271 (11th Cir. 1999); *In re* Silicon Graphics, Inc. Sec. Litig., 183 F.3d 970 (9th Cir. 1999); *In re* Comshare, Inc. Sec. Litig., 183 F.3d 542 (6th Cir. 1999).

(Continued)

(Case 25.4 continued)

prospects. Further, in approving the inventory management practices of "Box and Hold," the defendants knowingly sanctioned procedures that violated the Company's own markdown policy, as stated in the Company's public filings. . . . In short, the Complaint alleges that the defendants engaged in conscious misstatements with the intent to deceive. . . .

C. Particularity of the Facts Pleaded

...

In order to survive at this stage, the Complaint must state with particularity sufficient facts to support the belief that the "Box and Hold" inventory was of limited value, and accordingly that the defendants' positive public statements concerning inventory growth were false and misleading. The district court concluded that the plaintiffs had failed to meet these particularity requirements, in substantial part because they failed to reveal their confidential sources for some of the facts on which their belief in the essential worthlessness of the "Box and Hold" inventory was based. . . .

...

[A] January 22, 1996 Weekly Report showed that even six months after the Class Period [February 3, 1994 to May 4, 1995], substantial amounts of "Box and Hold" inventory still dated from 1993 and 1994, which supports the inference that inventory during the Class Period was similarly dated.

Thus, the complaint identifies with particularity several documentary sources that support the plaintiffs' belief that serious inventory problems existed during the Class Period itself.

...

[T]here is nothing in the case law of this circuit that requires plaintiffs to reveal confidential sources at the pleading stage.

RESULT The dismissal of the case was vacated. The case was remanded to the trial court with instructions that the plaintiffs be permitted to replead their claims in light of the Second Circuit's opinion.

QUESTIONS

1. What weight, if any, should a jury give to the fact that a top executive sold a large block of stock shortly before a negative earnings announcement?
2. Why shouldn't the plaintiffs be required to disclose the names of their confidential sources in the complaint?

Recklessness There is also a split in the circuits as to the effect, if any, of the Reform Act's heightened pleading standards on whether recklessness is sufficient for a finding of *scienter*. The Second Circuit made it clear in *Kasaks v. Novak*[29] that in its view, recklessness continues to be sufficient for a showing of *scienter*. It defined reckless conduct as:

conduct which is "highly unreasonable" and which represents "an extreme departure from the standards of ordinary care . . . to the extent that the danger was either known to the defendant or so obvious that the defendant must have been aware of it." . . . "[A]n egregious refusal to see the obvious, or to investigate the doubtful, may in some cases give rise to an inference of . . . recklessness."

...

[S]ecurities fraud claims typically have sufficed to state a claim based on recklessness when they have specifically

29. 216 F.3d 300 (2d Cir. 2000) (Case 25.4).

alleged defendants' knowledge of facts or access to information contradicting their public statements. . . .

Under certain circumstances, we have found allegations of recklessness to be sufficient where plaintiffs alleged facts demonstrating that defendants failed to review or check information that they had a duty to monitor, or ignored obvious signs of fraud. . . .

At the same time, however, we have identified several important limitations on the scope of liability for securities fraud based on reckless conduct. First, we have refused to allow plaintiffs to proceed with allegations of "fraud by hindsight." . . . Corporate officials need not be clairvoyant; they are only responsible for revealing those material facts reasonably available to them. . . .

Second, as long as the public statements are consistent with reasonably available data, corporate officials need not present an overly gloomy or cautious picture of current performance and future prospects. . . .

Third, there are limits to the scope of liability for failure adequately to monitor the allegedly fraudulent behavior of others.

The Ninth Circuit reached a contrary conclusion in a case involving Silicon Graphics[30] and held that the Reform Act precludes liability under Section 10(b) for mere recklessness. Instead, a "heightened form of recklessness, i.e., deliberate or conscious recklessness, at a minimum, is required to establish a strong inference of intent."

The Sixth Circuit held that allegations giving rise to a strong inference of recklessness are sufficient to pass muster but that facts showing a mere motive and opportunity to commit fraud do not.[31] The court concluded that Congress changed the pleading, but not the state of mind, requirements applicable to Section 10(b) and Rule 10b–5 cases. The First Circuit also held that the Reform Act did not alter preexisting *scienter* requirements for securities fraud cases.[32]

To avoid liability, the officers should, before making any statement, investigate what the facts are. Managers should make no statement unless they in good faith believe it to be true. The investigation must be fairly thorough. At least in the Second Circuit, an officer may be liable for misrepresenting facts that he or she should have been aware of, even if the officer was not in fact aware of them. For example, directors may be deemed to have knowledge of facts in the corporate books regardless of whether they have actually examined the books.

These tough pleading requirements make it more important than ever for insiders to avoid trading while in possession of material nonpublic information. Plaintiffs can be expected to claim that insiders who sold before the announcement of bad news knew of the impending negative developments and sold their stock while the market price was artificially high, thereby "cashing in" on their alleged misrepresentations and omissions.[33] This arguably creates an inference of fraud.

The U.S. Court of Appeals for the Ninth Circuit rejected this argument in the *Silicon Graphics* case and held that the fact that company executives sold an unusually large amount of Silicon Graphics stock months before the announcement of disappointing news was insufficient to show fraud. It is not yet clear how the U.S. Supreme Court will rule on this issue, but until there is a definitive ruling, managers and companies would be well advised to assume that insider trading shortly before the announcement of bad news will create an inference of fraud sufficient to satisfy the Reform Act's pleading requirements.

IN CONNECTION WITH THE PURCHASE OR SALE OF ANY SECURITY

Rule 10b–5 requires that the conduct occur "in connection with the purchase or sale of any security." This requirement defines both those who can sue and those who can be sued under Rule 10b–5.

The Supreme Court has made it clear that only persons who actually purchase or sell securities can sue under Rule 10b–5. Persons who have not purchased (or sold) cannot sue on the theory that they would have purchased (or sold) had they known the true facts. Thus, liability under Rule 10b–5 does not extend to the whole world of potential investors but only to those who actually buy or sell stock after a misstatement or omission.

Parties that can be sued under Rule 10b–5 are those that make or are responsible for misstatements and omissions in connection with the purchase or sale of securities. Statements are made "in connection with" the purchase or sale of securities if they were made in a manner reasonably calculated to influence the investing public or if they were of the sort upon which the investing public might reasonably rely.

For example, the U.S. Court of Appeals for the Third Circuit held that fraudulent financial statements issued by Cendant during the course of its tender offer for American Bankers Insurance Group (ABI) were misrepresentations

---

30. *In re* Silicon Graphics, Inc. Sec. Litig., 183 F.3d 970 (9th Cir. 1999).

31. *In re* Comshare, Inc. Sec. Litig., 183 F.3d 542 (6th Cir. 1999).

32. Greebel v. FTP Software, Inc., 194 F.3d 185 (1st Cir. 1999).

33. *See* Dale E. Barnes, Jr. & Karen Kennard, *Greater Expectations: Risk Disclosure under the Private Securities Litigation Reform Act of 1995—An Update,* 2 STAN. J.L., BUS. & FIN. 331, 347–48 (1996).

made "in connection with" the plaintiffs' purchase of ABI shares during the tender offer even though the plaintiffs had neither purchased any Cendant shares nor tendered shares of ABI stock to Cendant.[34] The plaintiffs had alleged that Cendant's misrepresentations artificially inflated the price at which they purchased their ABI shares, and that they suffered a loss when those misrepresentations were disclosed to the public and the merger agreement between Cendant and ABI was terminated.

In summary, a company must be careful to monitor its public statements, such as those made in periodic reports, press releases, proxy solicitations, and annual reports. Even when addressing noninvestors, such as creditors or labor union representatives, a manager should exercise caution if the statements can reasonably be expected to reach investors.

RELIANCE

To establish liability under Rule 10b–5, investors must show that they relied either directly or indirectly on the

34. Semerenko v. Cendant Corp., 223 F.3d 165 (3d Cir. 2000).

misrepresentation or omission. If the investors did not rely on the misstatement or omission in deciding to buy or sell stock, then any loss they incurred cannot be blamed on the company that made the misrepresentation or omission.

Direct Reliance A plaintiff may show reliance by showing that he or she actually read the document, such as a press release or prospectus, that contained the misstatement. In the case of an omission, the U.S. Supreme Court has ruled that the plaintiff will be presumed to have relied on the omission, if it was material. That presumption of reliance can be rebutted—that is, shown to be not true—by a showing that the plaintiff would have bought (or sold) the stock even if the omitted fact had been included.

In the following case, the buyer of stock was able to avoid liability for allegedly deceptive oral statements made to the seller based on a nonreliance clause in the stock-purchase contract.

A CASE IN POINT

CASE 25.5

Rissman v. Rissman
United States Court of Appeals for the Seventh Circuit
213 F.3d 381
(7th Cir. 2000).

In the Language of the Court

FACTS Randall Rissman owned two-thirds of the stock of Tiger Electronics, a toy and game company founded by his father. His brother Arnold owned the balance. Randall managed the business while Arnold worked as a salesperson. Arnold did not elect himself to the board of directors of Tiger, although he could have done so because Tiger permitted cumulative voting. After the brothers had a falling out, Arnold sold his shares to Randall for $17 million. Thirteen months later, Tiger sold its assets to toymaker Hasbro for $335 million. Arnold sued Randall, claiming that Randall had deceived him into thinking that he would never take Tiger public or sell it to a third party. Believing that his stock would remain illiquid and not pay further dividends, Arnold sold his shares for whatever Randall was willing to pay. Arnold then sought the extra $95 million he would have received had he retained his stock until the sale to Hasbro.

During the negotiation of the sale of his shares to Randall, Arnold asked Randall to represent in writing that Tiger would never be sold. Randall refused; instead, he warranted (accurately) that he was not aware of any offers to purchase Tiger and was not engaged in negotiations for its sale. Arnold and Randall also agreed that if Tiger were sold before Arnold had received all installments of the purchase price, then payment of the principal and interest would be accelerated. Arnold represented in the stock-sale agreement that "this Agreement is executed by [Arnold] freely and voluntarily, and without reliance upon any statement or representation by Purchaser, the Company, any of the Affiliates or O.R. Rissman or any of their attorneys or agents . . . ."

The trial court granted Randall's motion to dismiss the federal securities law claims, and Arnold appealed. For purposes of the appeal, the appeals court assumed the accuracy of Arnold's allegations that Randall had told Arnold that he was determined to keep

(Continued)

(Case 25.5 continued)

Tiger a family firm and that Randall secretly had planned to sell Tiger after acquiring Arnold's shares.

ISSUE PRESENTED Does a nonreliance clause in a written stock-sale agreement preclude a seller of stock from recovering damages under the federal securities laws for prior oral statements?

OPINION EASTERBROOK, J., writing for the U.S. Court of Appeals for the Seventh Circuit:

Arnold does not contend that any representation in the stock-purchase agreement is untrue or misleading; his entire case rests on Randall's oral statements. Yet Arnold assured Randall that he had not relied on these statements. Securities law does not permit a party to a stock transaction to disavow such representation—to say, in effect, "I lied when I told you I wasn't relying on your prior statements" and then to seek damages for their contents. . . .

Two courts of appeals have held that non-reliance clauses in written stock-purchase agreements preclude any possibility of damages under the federal securities laws for prior oral statements. . . .

Memory plays tricks. Acting in the best of faith, people may "remember" things that never occurred but now serve their interests. Or they may remember events with a change of emphasis or nuance that makes a substantial difference to meaning. Express or implied qualifications may be lost in the folds of time. A statement such as "I won't sell at current prices" may be recalled years later as "I won't sell." Prudent people protect themselves against the limitations of memory (and the temptation to shade the truth) by limiting their dealings to those memorialized in writing, and promoting the primacy of the written word is a principal function of the federal securities laws. . . .

Negotiation could have avoided this litigation. Instead of taking the maximum Randall was willing to pay unconditionally, Arnold could have sought a lower guaranteed payment (say, $10 million) plus a kicker if Tiger were sold or taken public. . . .

Arnold calls the no-reliance clauses "boilerplate," and they were; transactions lawyers have language of this sort stored up for reuse. But the fact that language has been used before does not make it less binding when used again. Phrases become boilerplate when many parties find that the language serves their ends. That's a reason to enforce the promises, not to disregard them.

RESULT The dismissal of Arnold's securities laws claims was affirmed.

QUESTIONS

1. How could Arnold have avoided this result?
2. Arnold claimed that he signed the stock-sale agreement under duress because (a) Randall threatened to fire him; (b) his stock was illiquid and worthless unless Randall could be persuaded to buy it (or sell Tiger), which Randall threatened not to do if Arnold caused trouble; (c) Arnold feared Randall would cause Tiger to breach its agreement to distribute dividends equal to the shareholders' tax obligations (Tiger had elected Subchapter S treatment); and (d) Randall threatened to "drag [Arnold] through the courts forever" unless Arnold sold his stock. How should the court rule? Are there any other theories Arnold could have used to recover the extra $95 million from Randall? Did Randall act ethically?

Fraud on the Market In the securities market, direct reliance is rare because transactions usually are not conducted on a face-to-face basis. The market is interposed between the parties, providing important information to them in the form of the market price. As the U.S. District Court for the Northern District of Texas said in the *LTV Securities Litigation*: "The market is acting as the unpaid agent of the investor, informing him that, given all the information available to it, the value of the stock is worth the market price."

Economists refer to the theory underlying this view as the *efficient-market theory*. It holds that in an open and developed securities market, the price of a company's stock equals its true value. The market is said to evaluate information efficiently and to incorporate it into the price of a company's securities.

Against this background, the courts have approved the *fraud-on-the-market theory:* If the information available to the market is incorrect, then the market price will not reflect the true value of the stock. Under this theory, an investor who purchases or sells a security is presumed to have relied on the market, which has in turn relied on the misstatement or omission when it set the price of the security. In *Basic, Inc. v. Levinson,* the Supreme Court affirmed this theory. Quoting one of the earlier lower court decisions, the Supreme Court noted that "[i]t is hard to imagine that there ever is a buyer or seller who does not rely on market integrity. Who would knowingly roll the dice in a crooked crap game?"

Thus, plaintiffs do not have to show that they read or heard a defendant's misstatement in order to recover damages from that defendant. Instead, reliance is presumed if the investor shows (1) that the defendant made a public material misrepresentation that would have caused reasonable investors to misjudge the value of the defendant's stock and (2) that the investor traded shares of the defendant's stock in an open securities market after the misrepresentations were made and before the truth was revealed.

A defendant can rebut the fraud-on-the-market presumption by showing that the plaintiff traded or would have traded despite knowing the statement was false. For example, an insider who is aware of nonpublic information that results in the stock being undervalued, but who sells for other reasons, cannot be said to have relied on the integrity of the market price.

Lower courts have declined to apply the fraud-on-the-market presumption in cases that lack efficient, open, and developed market. The courts have identified at least five factors to consider in identifying an efficient market: (1) sufficient weekly trading volume, (2) sufficient reports and analyses by investment professionals, (3) the presence of market makers and arbitrageurs, (4) the existence of issuers eligible to file Form S–3 short-form registration statements, and (5) a historical showing of immediate price response to unexpected events or financial releases. In short, for a market to be open and developed, it must have a large number of buyers and sellers and a relatively high level of trading activity and frequency. It also must be a market where prices rapidly reflect new information.

Truth on the Market Defendants have also used the efficient-market theory to their advantage. For example, even if the defendant misrepresents that it is not involved in merger negotiations, if the market makers were privy to the truth, there is no fraud on the market. In the following case, an appellate court found that the market was aware of one set of facts undisclosed by the defendants but was not aware of another set of undisclosed facts.

A CASE IN POINT

CASE 25.6

In re **Apple Computer Securities Litigation**

United States Court of Appeals for the Ninth Circuit

886 F.2d 1109

(9th Cir. 1989), cert. denied, 496 U.S. 943 (1990).

Summary

FACTS In late 1982 and early 1983, Apple Computer, Inc. made several optimistic public statements concerning its newly developed office computer, the Lisa. For example, in a January 31, 1983 *Business Week* article, Apple's chairman of the board, Steven Jobs, was quoted as saying: "I don't think we will have any problem selling all the Lisa's we can build." In an April 14, 1983 *Wall Street Journal* article, he was quoted as stating: "Lisa is going to be phenomenally successful in the first year out of the chute."

Many of the risks and problems associated with Lisa were also widely publicized, however. The same *Business Week* article quoting Jobs as saying that Apple would have little trouble selling the Lisa also stated: "One indication of how uncertain Apple's prospects are is that expert estimates of how many Lisa's the company will sell are all over the lot—from 2,000 to 30,000." The article also questioned whether vendors would

(Continued)

(Case 25.6 continued)

write software to support the Lisa and whether its price was too high. Similarly, the *Wall Street Journal* article in which Jobs predicted the Lisa's great success was captioned: "Some Warm Up to Apple's 'Lisa,' but Eventual Success Is Uncertain." The article discussed the Lisa's incompatibility with IBM products, its difficulties in attracting software suppliers, and its high price tag.

The Lisa was a commercial failure and was discontinued shortly after its introduction. As a result of this disappointing news, Apple's stock price fell by almost 75 percent.

The plaintiffs, purchasers of Apple stock, brought a Section 10(b) fraud-on-the-market suit against Apple and its officers and directors, alleging that they failed to disclose problems with the Lisa that would have contradicted their earlier, optimistic public statements.

ISSUE PRESENTED Was there fraud on the market when a manufacturer made optimistic predictions about a new product, even though analysts and others following the company discounted the predictions and publicized the true state of affairs?

SUMMARY OF OPINION The U.S. Court of Appeals for the Ninth Circuit held that in a fraud-on-the-market case a defendant's failure to disclose material information may be excused if that information has been made credibly available to the market by other sources. As the court explained, "individuals who hear [only good news or only bad news] may receive a distorted impression . . . , and thus may have an actionable claim. But the market, and any individual who relies only on the price established by the market, will not be misled."

The press portrayed the Lisa as a risky gamble. At least twenty articles explored the risks Apple was taking. Moreover, many of the optimistic statements challenged by the plaintiffs appeared in those same articles. In the words of the court, "The market could not have been made more aware of Lisa's risks." Therefore, the defendants were not liable, as a matter of law, for failing to disclose those risks. Accordingly, the defendants' motion for summary judgment on the claims related to the Lisa was granted.

The court reached a different conclusion with respect to two optimistic statements Apple made concerning Twiggy, the new disk drive to accompany the Lisa computer. In a November 29, 1982 press release, Apple had claimed that Twiggy "represents three years of research and development and has undergone extensive testing and design verification during the past year." The release went on to state that Twiggy "ensures greater integrity of data than the other high density drives by way of a unique, double-sided mechanism designed and manufactured by Apple."

The court concluded that certain technical problems relating to Twiggy had not been revealed to the market. Neither the press nor anyone else disclosed that (1) the internal tests conducted by Apple indicated that Twiggy was slow and unreliable; (2) the Apple division responsible for the production of the Lisa warned top executives that Twiggy's unreliability could delay the introduction of the Lisa by several months; and (3) Jobs expressed "virtually zero confidence" in the division that was responsible for the design and development of Twiggy. Accordingly, the court concluded that if Twiggy's technical problems were material facts tending to undermine the optimism of the two statements, the defendants could be liable for failing to reveal those facts. Materiality was thus left as a triable issue of fact, and the defendants' motion for summary judgment on the claims related to Twiggy was denied.

RESULT The plaintiffs' claims relating to the Lisa computer were dismissed as a matter of law. The claims related to the Twiggy disk drive were not dismissed because they raised questions of fact for a jury to decide. In 1991, after two former executives were found guilty of making "materially misleading statements," Apple agreed to set up a $16 million fund to settle the suit.

(Continued)

(Case 25.6 continued)

COMMENTS The Ninth Circuit pointed out that a defendant is not relieved of its duty to disclose material information unless that information has been transmitted to the public with a degree of intensity and credibility sufficient to counterbalance any misleading impression created by the defendant. A brief mention of the omitted fact in a few poorly circulated or lightly regarded publications would be insufficient.

CAUSATION

A plaintiff must prove that the defendant's misstatement or omission caused him or her to suffer losses. Increasingly, this is an economic question—what factors influence the price of a stock in the securities market?

In a securities case involving Nucorp Energy, for example, investors claimed that the company's misrepresentation of the value of its oil reserves caused them to suffer losses. The claim was based on the contention that the stock price was maintained at an artificially high level as a result of the misrepresentation. The investors attributed the later drop in the stock price to the revelation of the true facts. At trial, the defendants presented the testimony of an economist that the drop in the price of the stock was not attributable to any misrepresentation of the value of the oil reserves but rather was caused by a drop in the price of oil. The jury found that the plaintiffs had failed to prove their claim.

As a result of these developments in the area of causation, proponents of the efficient-market theory may be right when they predict that in the future an entire Rule 10b–5 case may boil down to one question: Did the misleading statement artificially affect the market price?

Reform Act Safe Harbor *for* Forward-Looking Statements

The Reform Act provides issuers subject to the 1934 Act's reporting requirements and persons acting on their behalf a two-prong safe harbor for certain forward-looking state-

ments.[35] *Forward-looking statements* include (1) a statement containing a projection of revenues, income, earnings per share, capital expenditures, dividends, capital structure, or other financial items; (2) a statement of management's plans and objectives for future operations, including plans relating to the issuer's products and services; (3) a statement of future economic performance, including any such statement in management's discussion and analysis (MD & A) of financial condition or in the results of operations required to be included by the SEC; and (4) any statement of the assumptions underlying or relating to any such statement.

The safe harbor does not apply to forward-looking statements in connection with (1) an initial public offering; (2) an offering of securities by a blank check company; (3) a rollup or going-private transaction; (4) a tender offer; or (5) an offering by a partnership, limited liability company, or direct participation investment program. The safe harbor also does not apply to any forward-looking statement included in (1) a financial statement prepared in accordance with generally accepted accounting principles or (2) a report of beneficial ownership on Schedule 13D.

As explained in Chapter 24, the statutory safe harbor for forward-looking statements was designed to promote market efficiency by encouraging companies to disclose projections and other information about their future prospects. Anecdotal evidence indicated that corporate counsel were advising their clients to say as little as possible due to fear that if a company failed to satisfy its announced earning projections—perhaps due to an industry downturn or the timing of a large order or release of a new product—the company would automatically be sued.

Under the first prong of the safe harbor, a person is protected from liability for a misrepresentation or omission based on a written forward-looking statement as long as the statement (1) is identified as forward-looking and (2) is accompanied by meaningful cautionary statements identifying important factors that could cause ac-

ETHICAL CONSIDERATION

Managers of companies frequently act as promoters, describing the company's products to the press and the public in an aggressive, upbeat manner. It is reasonable to expect them to engage in a certain amount of puffing and exaggeration. Are these exaggerations ethically justifiable as long as they do not violate the securities laws?

35. 15 U.S.C. § 77z-2.

tual results to differ materially from those projected in the statement. The safe harbor also protects forward-looking oral statements if the person making the statement (1) identifies the statement as forward-looking, (2) states that results may differ materially from those projected in the statement, and (3) identifies a readily available written document (such as a document filed with the SEC) that contains factors that could cause results to differ materially.

The stated factors must be relevant to the projection and of a nature that could actually affect whether the forward-looking statement is realized. Boilerplate warnings will not suffice. Failure to include the particular factor that ultimately causes the forward-looking statement not to come true will not mean that the statement automatically is not protected by the safe harbor. The company must disclose all important factors, not all factors. In this respect, the safe harbor provides greater protection than the bespeaks caution doctrine.

For example, in *Harris v. Ivax Corp.*,[36] the U.S. Court of Appeals for the Eleventh Circuit held that a generic drug manufacturer was not liable for securities fraud despite its failure to disclose the possibility of a $104 million reduction in the carrying value of goodwill for several of its businesses. The company's cautionary language was adequate even though it did not explicitly mention the factor that ultimately belied the forward-looking statement. The court explained: "When an investor has been warned of risks of a significance similar to that actually realized, she is sufficiently on notice of the danger of the investment to make an intelligent decision about it according to her own preferences for risk and reward."

In ruling on a motion to dismiss based on this prong of the safe harbor, the state of mind of the person making the statement is not relevant. The court looks only at the cautionary language accompanying the forward-looking statement.

Even if a person cannot rely on this first prong, there is an independent prong based on the state of mind of the person making the statement. A person or business entity will not be liable in a private lawsuit involving a forward-looking statement unless the plaintiff proves that the person or business entity made a false or misleading forward-looking statement with actual knowledge that it was false or misleading. A statement by a business entity will come within the safe harbor unless it was made by or with the approval of an executive officer of the entity with actual knowledge by that officer that the statement was false or misleading.

 ## Auditor Disclosure *of* Corporate Fraud

The Reform Act added a new Section 10A to the 1934 Act to promote disclosure by independent public accountants of illegal acts committed by their publicly traded audit clients. Each audit must include, in accordance with generally accepted auditing standards, (1) procedures designed to provide reasonable assurance of the detection of illegal acts that would have a direct and material effect on the determination of financial statement amounts, (2) procedures designed to identify material related-party transactions (such as those involving officers, directors, and controlling shareholders of the company being audited), and (3) an evaluation of whether there is substantial doubt about the ability of the company to continue as a going concern during the ensuing fiscal year.

If, in the course of the audit, the independent public accountant detects or otherwise becomes aware of information indicating that an illegal act has or may have occurred (regardless of whether it is perceived to have a material effect on the financial statements), then the accountant must (1) determine whether it is likely that an illegal act has occurred and, if so, determine and consider the possible effect on the financial statements; and (2) inform the appropriate level of the management of the company. The accountant must ensure that the audit committee, or the board of directors in the absence of such a committee, is adequately informed with respect to the illegal act, unless the illegal act is clearly inconsequential. If, after informing the audit committee or board, the accountant concludes that (1) the illegal act has a material effect on the company's financial statements, (2) senior management has not taken timely and appropriate remedial actions with respect to the illegal act, and (3) the failure to take remedial action is reasonably expected to warrant departure from a standard audit report or the resignation of the accountant, then the accountant must, as soon as practicable, directly report its conclusions to the board of directors. The board is then required to notify the SEC within one business day after receiving the report. If the board fails to do so, the accountant must furnish the SEC with a copy of its report (or documentation of any oral report given).

 ## Accounting Fraud Is Top SEC Enforcement Priority

In March 1999, Stephen M. Cutler, deputy director of the SEC's Division of Enforcement, reported an "alarming increase in financial reporting failures," including

36. 182 F.3d 799 (11th Cir. 1999).

large restatements by large well-known companies.[37] He cited a recent *Business Week* survey in which 67 percent of the sixty-five chief financial officers responding indicated that they had been asked by top management to misrepresent financial results and 12 percent responded that they had done so.

As noted in the "Inside Story" in Chapter 17, the SEC has focused its enforcement efforts on fighting accounting fraud—cooking the books. It has adopted a multi-prong approach. First, in August 1999, the SEC accounting staff warned auditors that any intentional misstatement in the financial statements is material and that using mechanical rules of thumb to classify certain errors as immaterial is inappropriate.[38] Second, in October 2000, the SEC tightened the rules for auditor independence to reduce the conflict of interest that can arise, for example, when an accounting firm acts both as an auditor of management and as a consultant hired by and working for management.[39] The SEC noted that the intense pressure on public company executives to meet earnings expectations has led to "enhanced pressure on auditors to enable their clients to meet expectations."[40] The tougher independence standards are designed both (1) to "foster high quality audits by minimizing the possibility that any external factors will influence an auditor's judgements"[41] and (2) "to promote investor confidence in the financial statements of public companies" by ensuring that investors perceive the outside auditor as an independent and objective professional, not as "an advocate for the corporate client."[42] Third, the SEC announced in November 2000 its intention to crack down on accountants who turn a blind eye toward fraud.[43]

Fourth, the SEC brought enforcement actions against the directors of W.R. Grace and other companies with accounting irregularities to underscore the directors' responsibility for accurate financial reporting. Fifth, in 1999 and 2000, the SEC adopted new regulations governing the audit committees of publicly traded companies. Audit committees must now be comprised solely of independent directors and must play an active role in overseeing the company's auditors.[44] They must also issue a report to shareholders in the company's proxy statement about auditor independence,[45] including disclosure as to whether the audit committee "has considered whether the provision of non-audit services is compatible with maintaining the principal accountant's independence."[46] The SEC originally proposed that the audit committee be required to certify that, to the best of its knowledge, the company's financial statements were prepared in accordance with generally accepted accounting principles and contain no material misstatements. Critics of the proposal charged that it unfairly made the directors—who are rarely certified public accountants—responsible for professional judgment calls beyond their reasonably expected expertise.

Damages *for* Violation *of* Rule 10b–5

The measure of damages in a Rule 10b–5 case is typically the out-of-pocket loss, that is, the difference between what the investor paid (or received) and the fair value of the stock on the date of the transaction. Alternatively, investors can elect to rescind the transaction, returning what they received and getting back what they gave. In the court's discretion, *prejudgment interest*—that is, interest on the amount of the award between the date the securities were purchased and the date of the judgment—may also be awarded. Punitive damages are not available.

In theory, damages must be proved with reasonable certainty. In practice, however, damages are awarded on the basis of expert testimony, which can be highly conjectural. For example, a claim that a company's failure to reveal negative information about its new product artificially inflated the price of its stock is quite difficult to evaluate with any scientific certainty because even the experts do not agree to what extent any particular piece of information affects the price of a company's securities.

In addition, the number of traders who can claim damage can only be estimated. For example, in-and-out traders' trades are included in the total volume of trading; but such traders who buy, then quickly sell, suffer no damage if they sell the securities before the price drop.

37. *Microcap, Financial Fraud, Reporting Violations at Top of List of Enforcement Priorities, SEC Says,* CORP. COUNS. WKLY., Mar. 24, 1999, at 5.
38. Staff Accounting Bulletin No. 99, *supra* note 21.
39. Revision of the Commission's Auditor Independence Requirements, Securities Act Release No. 7919, 2000 SEC LEXIS 2717 (Nov. 21, 2000).
40. *Id.*
41. *Id.*
42. *Id.* (quoting United States v. Arthur Young & Co., 465 U.S. 805 (1984)).
43. *Enforcement Staff to Target Auditors Who Ignore Fraud,* CORP. COUNS. WKLY., Nov. 15, 2000, at 4.

44. *See* Order Approving Proposed Rule Change by the New York Stock Exchange, Exchange Act Release No. 42233, 1999 SEC LEXIS 2645 (Dec. 14, 1999).
45. *See* Audit Committee Disclosure, Exchange Act Release No. 42266, 1999 SEC LEXIS 2713 (Dec. 22, 1999).
46. Revision of the Commission's Auditor Independence Requirements, *supra* note 39.

Evidence of damages is therefore often presented on the basis of a comparison with industry or market performance, on the assumption that the industry or the market was not subject to the same artificial inflation. This clearly remains a fertile field for argument and future litigation.

Section 17(a)

Section 17(a) of the 1933 Act prohibits fraud in connection with the sale of securities. It is similar in scope to Section 10(b) of the 1934 Act, which prohibits fraud in both the sale and the purchase of securities. Unlike Section 10(b), Section 17(a) does not require proof of *scienter*. The SEC and the U.S. Attorney's Office can use Section 17(a) to prosecute securities fraud, but private parties cannot sue based on it.

Definition *of* Insider Trading

Insider trading refers in general terms to trading by persons (often insiders, such as officers and directors) based on material nonpublic information. The Supreme Court has held, however, that not every trade made while in possession of material nonpublic information violates Section 10(b). Because there is no statutory definition of insider trading, the law in this area has developed on a piecemeal basis. This lack of a clear definition has caused enforcement problems for the SEC and federal prosecutors. It can also make it difficult for investors to know whether their actions constitute prohibited insider trading.

The safest course is never to trade while in possession of material nonpublic information; however, such a premise is unduly restrictive. The nature of insider trading can best be understood by examining the purposes underlying the laws that prohibit it.

Two fundamental goals of the securities laws in general are to protect the investing public and to maintain fairness in the securities markets. Allowing a party who knows that the market is incorrectly pricing a security to exploit another party's ignorance of that fact is fundamentally unfair. Yet, if an efficient market is to be maintained, market professionals, such as securities analysts, must be given an incentive to ferret out the truth about companies and their prospects. There would be no incentive if the persons who expended the time and effort to piece together the truth were precluded from either trading on that information or selling it to others in the form of a tip or analyst report.

In light of this need to promote an efficient market and the language of Section 10(b), which refers to fraudulent and manipulative practices, the Supreme Court has held that a trade based on material nonpublic information is illegal only if there is a breach of duty by the person trading; or if the person trading is the recipient of a tip—a piece of inside information—there must be a breach of duty by the person who gave the tip. The person giving the tip is known as the *tipper;* the person receiving it is known as the *tippee.*

Insider-trading cases focus specifically on the duty to disclose, before trading, material information that is not publicly known (that is, not commonly available to the investing public). An insider must either disclose material nonpublic information in his or her possession or refrain from trading. The fundamental question in an insider-trading case is whether this obligation should be imposed on a particular trader.

For example, corporate officers and directors have specific legal duties to the corporation and shareholders they serve, which prohibit them from engaging in insider trading. As corporate fiduciaries, these individuals are required to subordinate their self-interests to the interests of the shareholders, as discussed in Chapter 23.

In 2000, the SEC sought to clarify several aspects of insider trading by promulgating Rules 10b5–1 and 10b5–2 (which are set forth in Appendix L). Rule 10b5–1 provides that any person who purchases or sells securities of any issuer on the basis of material nonpublic information about the security or issuer violates Section 10(b) if the purchase or sale was in breach of a duty of trust or confidence owed directly, indirectly, or derivatively to (1) the issuer or its security holders or (2) any other person who is the source of the material nonpublic information. A trade is "on the basis of" material nonpublic information if the person trading was aware of the information at the time of the trade, unless the person can demonstrate that:

1. before becoming aware of the information, he or she (a) entered into a binding contract to purchase or sell, (b) gave instructions for the trade, or (c) adopted a written plan to trade; *and*
2. the contract, instruction, or plan either (a) specified the amount of securities to be traded and the price, or (b) included a written formula or algorithm for determining the amount and price, or (c) did not permit the person to exercise any subsequent influence over how, when, and whether to trade; *and*
3. the trade was pursuant to the contract, instruction, or plan.

Thus, Rule 10b5–1 creates a presumption that persons who trade while in possession of material nonpublic information trade on the basis of that information unless the trade is pursuant to a preexisting plan. The rule was adopted in response to several cases in which the court held that a person who trades while in possession of inside information violates Rule 10b–5 only if he or she decided to trade based on that information.[47]

The affirmative defense is designed to cover situations in which the person trading can demonstrate that the material nonpublic information was not a factor in the trading decision. It permits those who would like to plan securities transactions in advance, at a time when they are not aware of material nonpublic information, to carry out those preplanned transactions at a later time, even if they later become aware of material nonpublic information. Rule 10b5–2, discussed further later, creates certain presumptions about the existence of a duty of trust or confidence in certain nonbusiness relationships, such as marriage.

Classical Theory *of* Insider Trading

An *insider* is a person with access to confidential information and an obligation of disclosure to other traders in the marketplace. Insiders include not only traditional insiders—such as officers and directors—but also temporary insiders, such as outside counsel and financial consultants.

TRADITIONAL INSIDERS

Traditionally, only persons closely allied with the corporation itself were considered insiders. They are true insiders because they acquire information by performing duties within or on behalf of the issuer corporation. Persons or entities traditionally considered insiders include (1) officers and directors, (2) controlling shareholders, (3) employees, and (4) the corporation itself.

Officers and Directors Officers and directors have a fiduciary obligation of loyalty and care to the corporate

47. *See, e.g.*, SEC v. Adler, 137 F.3d 1325 (11th Cir. 1998).

shareholders. They also have the greatest access to sensitive information regarding corporate events.

Controlling Shareholders Because of their majority stock ownership, controlling shareholders are generally in a position to control the activities of the corporation. They are therefore likely to be aware of impending corporate events.

Employees As agents or servants of a corporation, employees have a duty of loyalty. They may not personally profit from confidential information that they receive in the course of their employment.

The Corporation Often a corporation (or other issuer) will engage in the purchase or sale of its own securities. Under these circumstances, the corporation and those acting on its behalf are insiders and must not trade while in possession of material nonpublic information.

TEMPORARY INSIDERS

Outside attorneys, accountants, consultants, and investment bankers who are not directly employed by the corporation, but who acquire confidential information through the performance of professional services, are also considered insiders. The Supreme Court extended liability under Section 10(b) to such *temporary insiders* in footnote 14 to the *Dirks* case, which is presented as Case 25.7.

Tippees *of* Insiders

Tippees—that is, persons who receive information from a traditional or temporary insider—may also be subject to liability under Rule 10b–5, but only if they can be considered derivative insiders. In most cases, a tippee has no independent duty to the shareholders of the corporation whose shares he or she is buying or selling and with which he or she may have little or no connection. Tippees will not be held liable as *derivative insiders* unless the insider's duty of disclosure can somehow be imposed upon them. This rule was established in the following landmark case.

CASE 25.7

Dirks v. SEC

Supreme Court of the United States
463 U.S. 646 (1983).

Summary

FACTS Raymond Dirks, an officer of a New York broker–dealer firm, specialized in providing investment analysis of insurance company securities to institutional investors. Dirks was contacted by Ronald Secrist, a former employee of Equity Funding of America, who was seeking aid in exposing the fraudulent activities of that corporation. These fraudulent activities had resulted in an overvaluation of Equity Funding's assets. Dirks

(Continued)

(Case 25.7 continued)

was thus the potential tippee, with Secrist the tipper. After corroborating Secrist's story, Dirks advised certain clients that they should sell their shares in Equity Funding. When the corporate fraud was later revealed, the price of the company's stock went down.

The SEC brought proceedings against Dirks on the theory that he had constructively breached a fiduciary duty. In effect, the SEC maintained that anyone receiving information from an insider stands in the insider's shoes and should be held to the same standards and be subject to the same duties as that insider.

ISSUE PRESENTED Is a tippee liable when the tipper has not violated a fiduciary duty?

SUMMARY OF OPINION The U.S. Supreme Court rejected the argument that anyone receiving information from an insider should be held to the same standards as the insider. The Court held instead that a tippee is not liable unless the tippee and the tipper join in a co-venture to exploit the information. Only in such a case will the fiduciary duty of the tipper be derivatively imposed on the tippee. For the tippee to be liable, therefore, the tipper must have a duty to the corporation not to disclose the information and must breach this duty by seeking to benefit personally from the disclosure of the information. The benefit sought by the tipper can be either tangible or intangible. Intangible benefits might include an enhanced reputation or the intangible benefit received through the giving of gifts.

In this case, the insider was motivated solely by a desire to expose fraudulent conduct. He did not breach any fiduciary duties because it was in the interests of the corporation that this information be disclosed.

RESULT Without a breach of duty on the part of the insider/tipper, no derivative duty could be imposed on Dirks, the tippee. Dirks was not guilty of illegal insider trading.

The requirement that the tipper be seeking some benefit implies that the tipper must desire that the tippee trade on the information, but it is unclear whether such a showing is necessary. For example, the tipper could derive a benefit merely from impressing the tippee with his or her access to confidential information. Such a desire could stem from social or career aspirations of the tipper and could have nothing to do with the stock-trading ramifications of the information.

BREACH OF FIDUCIARY DUTY

In addition to seeking some benefit, the tipper must also be breaching a fiduciary duty to the corporation (or to another under the misappropriation theory, discussed later in this chapter) by disclosing the information to the tippee. The information must be nonpublic at the time it is divulged, and it must be in the interests of the corporation (or the other party in a misappropriation case) to keep the information confidential.

The tippee is liable only if he or she knew or should have known that the tipper's disclosure of the confidential information constituted a fiduciary breach. If the tippee has reason to know that the insider's disclosure was wrong or against the interests of the corporation, the tippee's actual knowledge will be irrelevant.

In *United States. v. Chestman*,[48] the U.S. Court of Appeals for the Second Circuit held that the nephew-in-law of a controlling shareholder and family patriarch did not violate Rule 10b-5 when he passed on inside information to his broker, who traded on the information. The nephew-in-law was not in the inner circle of the family, and the court held that the fact of marriage, taken alone, did not create a fiduciary relationship. Rule 10b5-2 creates a presumption that spouses, parents, children, and siblings are bound by fiduciary ties. The presumption can be rebutted only by a showing that their past dealings (with respect to securities or any other matter) did not involve an implied obligation of confidentiality.

REMOTE TIPPEES

Remote tippees—that is, the tippees of tippees—may be found to have violated Section 10(b) and Rule 10b–5 even if they are completely unacquainted with and are removed

48. 947 F.2d 551 (2d Cir. 1991) (en banc), *cert. denied*, 503 U.S. 1004 (1992).

from the original insider tipper. However, remote tippees are not liable unless they knew or should have known that the first-tier tipper was breaching a fiduciary duty in passing on the nonpublic information.[49] The phrase "should have known" is key to this formulation. It means that tippees cannot insulate themselves from liability merely by failing to inquire as to the source of the information. If a tippee has reason to suspect that the information was wrongfully acquired, such conscious avoidance of knowledge will not prevent a finding of *scienter.*

 ## Misappropriation Theory *of* Insider Trading

From time to time, the SEC has unsuccessfully attempted to impose liability on anyone who trades while

in possession of material nonpublic information. In *Chiarella v. United States,*[50] the Supreme Court rejected the argument that every trade based on material nonpublic information should be held to violate the securities laws.

Under the *misappropriation theory,* a Rule 10b–5 violation occurs if a person breaches a fiduciary duty owed to the source of nonpublic information by trading on that information after misappropriating it for his or her own use. No independent duty of disclosure to the person from whom the securities were bought or sold or the issuer is required. Liability is imposed because the trader converted the confidential information to his or her own use. The U.S. Supreme Court embraced this theory in the following case.

50. 445 U.S. 222 (1980).

49. SEC v. Musella, 678 F. Supp. 1060 (S.D.N.Y. 1988).

A CASE IN POINT

CASE 25.8
United States v. O'Hagan
*Supreme Court of the
United States
521 U.S. 642 (1997).*

In the Language of the Court

FACTS Attorney James Herman O'Hagan purchased stock and options for stock in Pillsbury Company prior to the public announcement of a tender offer for Pillsbury's stock by Grand Met PLC. O'Hagan possessed material nonpublic information about Grand Met's intentions, which he had obtained as a partner of the law firm representing Grand Met in connection with its acquisition of Pillsbury. O'Hagan realized a profit in excess of $4 million on his Pillsbury-related transactions.

O'Hagan was convicted of fifty-seven counts of securities fraud, mail fraud, and money laundering. [The counts under Rule 14e–3(a), which prohibits a person with nonpublic information about a tender offer from buying stock in the target company, are discussed in Chapter 6 (Case 6.2).] The appeals court reversed, and the United States appealed.

ISSUE PRESENTED Is a person who trades in securities for personal profit, using confidential information misappropriated in a breach of fiduciary duty to the source of the information, guilty of violating Section 10(b) and Rule 10b–5?

OPINION GINSBURG, J., writing for the U.S. Supreme Court:

In pertinent part, § 10(b) of the Exchange Act provides:

> It shall be unlawful for any person, directly or indirectly, by the use of any means or instrumentality of interstate commerce or of the mails, or of any facility of any national securities exchange—
>
> ...
>
> b. To use or employ, in connection with the purchase or sale of any security registered on a national securities exchange or any security not so registered, any manipulative or deceptive device or contrivance in contravention of such rules and regulations as the [Securities and Exchange] Commission may prescribe as necessary or appropriate in the public interest or for the protection of investors.

(Continued)

(Case 25.8 continued)

The statute thus proscribes (1) using any deceptive device (2) in connection with the purchase or sale of securities, in contravention of rules prescribed by the Commission. The provision, as written, does not confine its coverage to deception of a purchaser or seller of securities; rather, the statute reaches any deceptive device used "in connection with the purchase or sale of any security."

Pursuant to its § 10(b) rulemaking authority, the Commission has adopted Rule 10b–5, which, as relevant here, provides:

> It shall be unlawful for any person, directly or indirectly, by the use of any means or instrumentality of interstate commerce, or of the mails or of any facility of any national securities exchange,
>
> (a) To employ any device, scheme, or artifice to defraud, [or]
>
>   ...
>
> (c) To engage in any act, practice, or course of business which operates or would operate as a fraud or deceit upon any person, in connection with the purchase or sale of any security.

Liability under Rule 10b–5, our precedent indicates, does not extend beyond conduct encompassed by Section 10(b)'s prohibition.

Under the "traditional" or "classical theory" of insider trading liability, § 10(b) and Rule 10b–5 are violated when a corporate insider trades in the securities of his corporation on the basis of material, nonpublic information. . . .

The "misappropriation theory" holds that a person commits fraud "in connection with" a securities transaction, and thereby violates § 10(b) and Rule 10–5, when he misappropriates confidential information for securities trading purposes, in breach of a duty owed to the source of the information. Under this theory, a fiduciary's undisclosed, self-serving use of a principal's information to purchase or sell securities, in breach of a duty of loyalty and confidentiality, defrauds the principal of the exclusive use of that information. In lieu of premising liability on a fiduciary relationship between company insider and purchaser or seller of the company's stock, the misappropriation theory premises liability on a fiduciary turned trader's deception of those who entrusted him with access to confidential information.

   ...

B

We agree with the Government that misappropriation, as just defined, satisfies § 10(b)'s requirement that chargeable conduct involve a "deceptive device or contrivance" used "in connection with" the purchase or sale of securities. We observe, first, that misappropriators, as the Government describes them, deal in deception. A fiduciary who "[pretends] loyalty to the principal while secretly converting the principal's information for personal gain" . . . defrauds the principal.

   ...

We turn next to the § 10(b) requirement that the misappropriator's deceptive use of information be "in connection with the purchase or sale of [a] security." This element is satisfied because the fiduciary's fraud is consummated, not when the fiduciary gains the confidential information, but when, without disclosure to his principal, he uses the information to purchase or sell securities. The securities transaction and the breach of duty thus coincide. This is so even though the person or entity defrauded is not the other party to the trade, but is, instead, the source of the nonpublic information. A misappropriator who trades on the basis of material, nonpublic information, in short, gains his advantageous market position through

(Continued)

(Case 25.8 continued)

deception; he deceives the source of the information and simultaneously harms members of the investing public.

...

In sum, considering the inhibiting impact on market participation of trading on misappropriated information, and the congressional purposes underlying § 10(b), it makes scant sense to hold a lawyer like O'Hagan a § 10(b) violator if he works for a law firm representing the target of a tender offer, but not if he works for a law firm representing the bidder. The text of the statute requires no such result.

RESULT O'Hagan's conviction was upheld. He violated § 10(b) and Rule 10b–5 by trading on material nonpublic information in violation of his duty to his partners and the firm's client.

QUESTIONS

1. Would the misappropriation theory apply to a case in which a person defrauded a bank into giving him a loan or embezzled cash from another and then used the proceeds of the misdeed to purchase securities?

2. If the fiduciary disclosed to the source of the nonpublic information that she planned to trade on the basis of that information, would her trading constitute a Section 10(b) violation? Would it violate any other laws? Would it be ethical?

Liability under the misappropriation theory requires that the defendant's trading threaten some injury to the defrauded party or the source of the information. Actual injury need not be demonstrated. The threatened injury need not be pecuniary; it may be reputational or intangible.

Rule 10b5–2 sets forth a nonexclusive list of three situations in which a person has a duty of trust or confidence for purposes of the misappropriation theory. First, a duty of trust or confidence exists whenever a person agrees to maintain information in confidence. Second, this duty exists when two people have a history, pattern, or practice of sharing confidences such that the recipient of material nonpublic information knows or reasonably should know that the person communicating the information expects that the recipient will maintain its confidentiality. Third, as noted earlier, the duty exists when a person receives or obtains material nonpublic information from a spouse, parent, child, or sibling unless the recipient can demonstrate that, under the facts and circumstances of that family relationship, no duty of trust or confidence existed.

The misappropriation theory widens the class of persons who can be found liable for insider trading, but the requirement that there be a fiduciary duty remains a limiting factor. For instance, someone who merely overhears a conversation relating to confidential information has no fiduciary duty and therefore no liability. Similarly,

someone who infers from the movements of corporate executives that an event will likely take place owes no duty to the corporation or its employees.

The Supreme Court upheld the conviction of R. Foster Winans, author of the *Wall Street Journal* column "Heard on the Street," under the Mail and Wire Fraud Acts, thereby providing an additional way to prosecute insider trading.[51] Winans had misappropriated the content of his soon-to-be-published columns and tipped the information to two stockbrokers, who used the information to make trades based on the anticipated positive market response to the column's publication. The Court held that if a business generates confidential information and has the right to control the use of that information prior to public disclosure, then use of that information to trade can be prohibited under the wire and mail fraud statutes.

⚜ RICO

A securities fraud claim cannot be used as a predicate act in a civil case under the Racketeer Influenced and Corrupt Organizations Act (RICO) (discussed in Chapter 17) unless the defendant has been criminally convicted in connection with the fraud. Similarly, a criminal conviction under the

---

51. Carpenter v. United States, 484 U.S. 19 (1987).

IN BRIEF
Decision Tree Analysis of Insider-Trading Laws

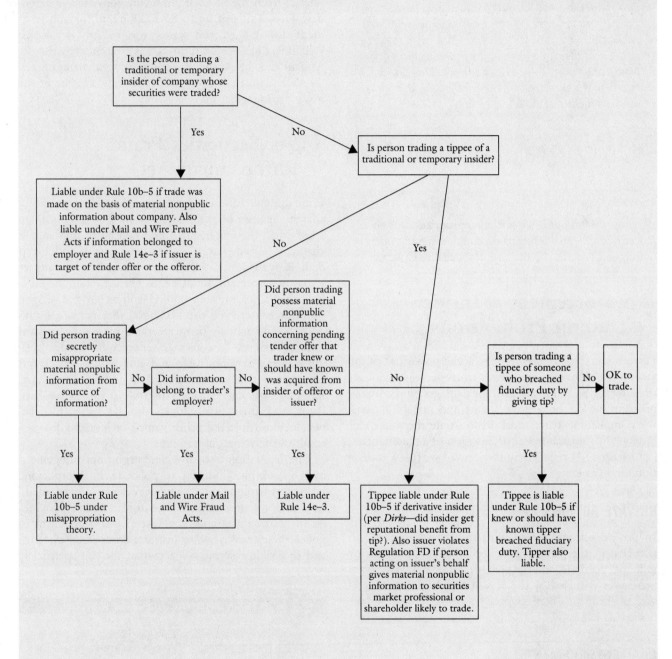

INTERNATIONAL CONSIDERATION

Germany's insider-trading laws prohibit directors from selectively divulging nonpublic information without issuing a broad public announcement. For example, in June 1997, the Federal Securities Regulatory Office began investigating whether Daimler–Benz AG board member Eckhard Cordes had illegally given a profit forecast to a handful of reporters at a dinner during the Geneva Motor Show when he told them that Daimler's 1996 net profits would likely "have a 2 before the decimal point," thereby signaling that profits would be more than two billion marks.[a]

a. Brandon Mitchener, *Daimler Official Is the Subject of Investigation,* WALL ST. J., June 6, 1997, at A9A.

Wire and Mail Fraud Acts for misappropriation of an employer's confidential information could, assuming other requirements are met, be the basis for a civil RICO case.

Enforcement *of* Insider-Trading Prohibitions

Persons who violate the insider-trading provisions of the federal securities laws are subject to civil enforcement actions by the SEC, private suits for damages, and criminal prosecution. In both government and private actions, the complaining party must demonstrate these five elements: (1) a misstatement or omission of a material fact, (2) *scienter*, (3) reliance by the injured party, (4) causation, and (5) loss.

PRIVATE ACTIONS

In private actions, the plaintiff must have standing to sue; that is, the plaintiff must be an actual purchaser or seller of securities, and the plaintiff's loss must have been proximately caused by the acts of the defendant. A private plaintiff may recover only his or her actual out-of-pocket damages.

CIVIL ENFORCEMENT

In an SEC civil enforcement action, the defendant may be liable for treble damages and disgorgement of profits and may be subject to an injunction prohibiting future trading.

CRIMINAL PROSECUTIONS

The SEC itself has no criminal enforcement power. Criminal prosecutions are brought by the Department of Justice through the U.S. Attorney's Office, often on referral from the SEC. If criminally convicted, a defendant faces a fine of up to $1 million and/or imprisonment for up to ten years for willful violations. Willfulness has been interpreted as awareness by the defendant that he or she was committing a wrongful act; the defendant need not specifically know that he or she was violating a statute.

The Securities Fraud Enforcement Act

Immediately following the massive insider-trading charges against Michael Milken and Drexel Burnham Lambert in the late 1980s (discussed more fully in this chapter's "Inside Story"), Congress passed and President Reagan signed the Insider Trading and Securities Fraud Enforcement Act of 1988. The act raised the maximum penalty for insider trading from five to ten years in prison and increased the likelihood that persons found guilty would actually be incarcerated for some period of time. (Previously, the average sentence for insider trading was less than one year, and community service was often ordered in lieu of prison.) In addition, the maximum fine was raised from $100,000 to $1 million. Violators and their firms could also be liable for civil penalties of triple the profit gained or loss avoided as a result of the wrongful trading.

The legislation also provided strong encouragement to the brokerage industry to police itself. A brokerage house can be fined if it "knew or recklessly disregarded" information that would indicate insider-trading activities on the part of its employees. Intended to force firms to police their employees, to institute compliance systems, and to monitor suspicious activities, the Act specifically

INTERNATIONAL CONSIDERATION

The European Commission's Insider-Trading Directive requires each member state in the European Union to enact its own penalties. Many nations with less active trading markets impose civil rather than criminal sanctions. Since 1993, however, Britain, France, and Germany have all instituted criminal sanctions against persons engaging in insider trading.

sold securities of the same class at the same time the insider was trading. The total amount of damages that may be recovered is limited to the amount of the profit gained or loss avoided in the unlawful transaction. Any amounts disgorged pursuant to court order or at the instance of the SEC will offset the amount of recoverable damages by contemporaneous traders. Of significance to potential tippers and tippees is the provision that makes tippers and all direct and remote tippees jointly and severally liable. That means that any individual in the chain can be found liable for all of the profits gained or losses avoided in every transaction within the chain of information.

"What's your exit strategy?"

requires registered brokers and dealers to maintain and enforce reasonably designed written policies and procedures to prevent the misuse of material nonpublic information. The maximum criminal penalty that can be imposed on brokerage firms was raised from $500,000 to $2.5 million.

Although this legislation does not explicitly require it, many commentators have suggested that it is prudent for other companies not in the brokerage business to implement such policies and procedures in light of their potential liability.

BOUNTY PAYMENTS

Under the Act, individuals whose tips result in insider-trading prosecutions can receive bounty payments, similar to the payments provided by the Internal Revenue Service in tax cases. These bounties can be as high as 10 percent of any revenues recovered from a defendant through penalties or settlement.

PRIVATE RIGHT OF ACTION

The Act also provides a private right of action for contemporaneous traders, that is, persons who purchased or

 ## Short-Swing Trading

Section 16(b) of the 1934 Act governs *short-swing trading*—the purchase and sale, or the sale and purchase, of equity securities of a public company within a six-month period by the company's officers, directors, and greater-than-10 percent shareholders. Unlike Section 10(b), which requires *scienter* (that is, a showing of bad intent), liability is imposed under Section 16(b) regardless of the insider's state of mind.

Although the purpose of Section 16(b) is to prevent insiders of publicly held companies from exploiting information not generally available to the public in order to secure quick profits, it need not be proved that the insider actually possessed any material nonpublic information at the time he or she traded in the securities. To establish liability under Section 16(b), it is sufficient to prove that an insider purchased and then sold, or sold and then purchased, equity securities within a period of six months.

 ETHICAL CONSIDERATION

A number of brokerage houses have investigated whether any of their employees were involved in insider trading. Most of these firms turned over their trading records to the New York Stock Exchange for computer analysis. Persons suspected of illicit activities could be subject to SEC enforcement actions and criminal prosecutions. Such investigations send a stern message to employees and encourage ethical behavior and compliance with the insider-trading laws. They also improve the public's perception of the brokerage industry. How stringently should managers of brokerage houses follow these procedures?

Section 16(a) of the 1934 Act imposes certain reporting obligations on officers and directors and shareholders owning more than 10 percent of a public company's equity securities. Section 16(c) prohibits such persons from *selling securities short*, that is, from selling securities they do not yet own.

DEFINITIONS

Section 16(b) of the 1934 Act provides that each officer, director, and greater-than-10 percent shareholder of an issuer that has registered any class of its equity securities under the 1934 Act must surrender to the issuer "any profit realized by him from any purchase and sale, or any sale and purchase, of any equity security of such issuer (other than an exempted security) within any period of less than six months."

Equity Security An *equity security* includes (1) any stock or similar security; (2) any security that is convertible, with or without consideration, into such a security; (3) any security carrying any warrant or right to subscribe to or purchase such a security; (4) any such warrant or right; and (5) any other security that the SEC deems to be of a similar nature and that, for the protection of investors or in the public interest, the SEC considers appropriate to treat as an equity security. Thus, equity securities may include hybrids that are not ordinarily considered equity securities, such as convertible debt securities that have not been registered under the 1934 Act.

Special problems can arise in connection with the grant and exercise of stock options and other derivative securities. A set of complicated rules embodied largely in Rule 16b–3 (adopted by the SEC under Section 16(b) of the 1934 Act) governs this area. Before becoming an officer or director, a person should consult counsel to avoid inadvertent Section 16(b) liability.

Matching The shares that are sold need not be the same shares that were purchased. Any purchase and any sale will incur liability if they occur less than six months apart, regardless of whether the transactions involve the same shares. For example, if on January 1 an officer of XYZ Corporation sold 100 shares of XYZ common stock that he had held for ten years, then on February 1 purchased 200 shares of XYZ common stock at a lower price, he would be liable for the short-swing profits on 100 of the shares. The January 1 sale would be matched with the February 1 purchase, even though the officer had held the securities for ten years before he sold them.

Profit Calculation To calculate the profits recoverable under Section 16(b), the sale price is compared with the purchase price. If several purchases and sales occur within a six-month period, the lowest purchase price will be matched with the highest sale price; then the next lowest purchase price with the next highest sale price; and so on, regardless of the order in which the purchases and sales actually occurred. By matching purchases and sales in this manner, the recoverable profit is maximized.

Short-swing profits cannot be offset by trading losses that were incurred in the same period. Thus, there may be recoverable profits under Section 16(b) even though the officer or director suffered a net loss on the trading transactions.

The following example illustrates the "lowest-in, highest-out" matching principle just described. Assume that an officer made purchases and sales, each of 100 shares, as follows:

Date	Transaction	Price
Jan. 1	Purchase	$ 9
Jan. 30	Sale	10
Feb. 15	Sale	15
Feb. 28	Purchase	12
March 15	Purchase	6
March 30	Sale	4

These transactions result in a recoverable short-swing profit of $1,000, calculated as follows. The February 15 sale is matched with the March 15 purchase, for a profit of $15 − $6 = $9 per share, or $900. Then the January 30 sale is matched with the January 1 purchase, for a profit of $10 − $9 = $1 per share, or $100. Even though the February 28 purchase at $12 per share and the subsequent sale at $4 per share resulted in a loss of $8 per share, or $800, that loss will not be taken into account. The officer will have to surrender $900 + $100 = $1,000, even though she in fact realized only $200 of net profit in the trading transactions (total sales of $2,900 less purchases of $2,700).

Six Months To result in recoverable short-swing profits, the purchase and sale, or sale and purchase, must have occurred "within any period of less than six months." That period commences on the day on which the first purchase or sale occurred and ends at midnight two days before the corresponding date in the sixth succeeding month. For example, for a transaction on January 1, the six-month period ends at midnight on June 29, two days before July 1.

Officer or Director A person may be liable under Section 16(b) if he or she was an officer or director at the time of either the purchase or the sale; it is not necessary that both transactions occur during the person's tenure.

For example, if an officer purchased 100 shares of XYZ Corporation common stock at $10 per share on January 1, resigned as an officer on February 1, then sold 100 shares of XYZ common stock at $20 per share on March 1, she would be liable for $1,000 of short-swing profits because she was an officer when she made the January 1 purchase. Similarly, if a person purchased 100 shares of XYZ Corporation at $10 per share on January 1, became an officer of XYZ Corporation on February 1, and sold the shares at $20 on March 1, that person would be liable for $1,000 of short-swing profits because he was an officer at the time of the sale. On the other hand, if an officer who had not traded for more than six months before March 1 resigned on March 1, bought 100 shares of XYZ Corporation at $10 on April 1, then sold them at $20 on April 2, she would not have recoverable profits because she was not an officer or director at the time of either the purchase or the sale.

Greater-than-10 Percent Shareholder The rule is different for persons who are not officers or directors but are owners of more than 10 percent of the issuer's equity securities. Such persons are liable under Section 16(b) only if they hold more than 10 percent of the securities at both the time of the purchase and the time of the sale. The transaction whereby the person becomes a 10 percent shareholder does not count.

For example, if a person purchased 10.5 percent of XYZ Corporation's common stock at $10 on January 1, then sold those shares at $20 on March 1, he would have no recoverable short-swing profits. However, if the same person had purchased another 2 percent of XYZ common stock in February, then the February purchase could be matched against the March sale because he owned more than 10 percent of the stock at the time of the February purchase and also at the time of the March sale.

Beneficial Ownership of Shares Officers, directors, and greater-than-10 percent shareholders can be liable for purchases and sales of shares they do not own of record but are deemed to beneficially own. Under Section 16(b), a person will be considered the *beneficial owner* of any securities held by his or her immediate family—his or her spouse, any minor children, or any other relative living in his or her household. There is a rebuttable presumption that a person is the beneficial owner of any securities over which he or she has the practical power to

vest title in himself or herself, or from which he or she receives economic benefits (such as sales proceeds) substantially equal to those of ownership.

Purchases and sales of securities held beneficially by an officer, director, or greater-than-10 percent shareholder will be attributed to that person in determining his or her liability for short-swing trading. For example, the purchase of securities by an officer's wife could be matched under Section 16(b) with the sale of other securities by the officer himself within six months of his wife's purchase, thereby resulting in liability for short-swing profits. Thus, any officer, director, or greater-than-10-percent shareholder planning a purchase or sale must consider not only his or her own trading record but also the record of those persons whose securities he or she is deemed to beneficially own.

UNORTHODOX TRANSACTIONS

If a purchase or sale by an officer, director, or greater-than-10 percent shareholder that would otherwise result in recoverable short-swing profits was involuntary and did not involve the payment of cash, and if there was no possibility of speculative abuse of inside information, then a court may hold that it was an *unorthodox transaction* to which no liability will attach. These situations generally arise in the context of exchanges in mergers and other corporate reorganizations, stock conversions, stock reclassifications, and tender offers in which securities are sold or exchanged for consideration other than cash. On the other hand, in a tender offer or acquisition, an exchange of securities for cash by an officer, director, or greater-than-10 percent shareholder would almost certainly be deemed a sale for which the person receiving the cash could be liable under Section 16(b).

BENEFICIAL-OWNERSHIP REPORTS

Section 16(a) of the 1934 Act requires that officers, directors, and greater-than-10 percent shareholders of companies that have registered any class of equity securities under the 1934 Act file beneficial-ownership reports with the SEC and with any national securities exchange on which their company's equity securities are listed. Within ten days of becoming an officer or director, a person must file an initial ownership report on Form 3, even if the person does not beneficially own any securities of the company at that time. In the case of greater-than-10 percent shareholders, a Form 3 must be filed within ten days of the date a greater-than-10 percent interest is acquired. (In addition, as noted in Chapter 24, any person who acquires more than 5 percent of the voting securities of a public company must file a Schedule 13D within ten days of the date he or she acquires that interest. An amendment to the Schedule 13D must be filed promptly after any material change in beneficial ownership or investment purpose.)

Subsequently, an officer, director, or greater-than-10-percent shareholder must file a Form 4 within ten days after the end of each month in which any change in beneficial ownership occurs. In the initial Form 3, an officer or director must report all purchases or sales that occurred within the previous six months, even if those transactions were effected before the person became an officer or director. A Form 5 showing changes in beneficial ownership during the preceding year must be filed annually. However, if there were no changes in beneficial ownership during the year, an officer or director may instead present to the company a certificate stating that there were no reportable events. The company must keep this certificate on file.

A person who ceases to be an officer or director must continue to report any changes in beneficial ownership that occur within six months of the last reportable transaction while he or she was an officer or director.

Acquisitions of shares through reinvestment of cash dividends under a qualifying dividend reinvestment plan do not require the filing of a Form 4. Participation in the plan and the ownership of shares under the plan must be disclosed in Form 4 reports that are otherwise required to be filed, however.

The SEC has brought enforcement actions to force executives to file these ownership reports within the required time frame. Publicly traded companies must disclose in their proxy statements and in their annual reports on Form

INTERNATIONAL CONSIDERATION

In response to a series of financial-market scandals in Germany, Finance Ministry officials announced in March 2001 that Germany was considering enacting new regulations to curb stock manipulation and insider trading. The proposed legislation would require members of the supervisory board and top corporate executives of publicly traded companies to report sales of their own company's stock within fourteen days. It would also punish companies that make false statements on the Frankfurt Stock Exchange's corporate newswire.[a]

a. Alfred Keuppers & Jonathan Stearns, *Germany Considers Tighter Rules to Ensure Transparency for Investors,* WALL ST. J., Mar. 28, 2001, at A18.

10–K whether their officers and directors have complied with their Section 16(a) reporting obligations.

PROHIBITION ON SELLING SHORT

As mentioned earlier, Section 16(c) of the 1934 Act prohibits officers or directors from selling any of their company's equity securities short. If the officer or director owns the security being sold, he or she must deliver it within twenty days after the sale, or deposit it in the mails or other usual channels of delivery within five days. If the officer or director fails to do this, he or she will be liable under Section 16(c) unless (1) he or she acted in good faith and was unable to make the delivery or deposit within the specified time, or (2) he or she acted in good faith and satisfying the time requirements would have caused undue inconvenience or expense.

THE RESPONSIBLE MANAGER
Preventing Securities Fraud *and* Insider Trading

Each company that takes advantage of the capital markets has a legal and ethical duty to ensure the integrity of those markets. Securities fraud, in any form, erodes investor confidence and makes it more difficult and expensive for honest businesses to raise capital.

Managers have an obligation not to mislead investors in company public announcements, periodic reports, or speeches. Although a company can remain silent about material developments if neither the company nor insiders are trading, early disclosure is often the better

course. This gives all investors equal access to current information about the company. There is a trade-off here, however. Sometimes the company's business or transactions may be in a state of flux. For example, a party with no visible source of financing may have made an offer to buy the company's assets. In this case, it may be worse to disclose the offer and get the market's hopes up than to wait and see if the offer is real. Managers, together with their lawyers, must make these judgment calls.

Another reason for early disclosure is to avoid illegal insider trading. A company must make disclosure if it knows its insiders, such as officers or directors, are trading in the company's securities.

Any forward-looking statements should be identified as such and be accompanied by meaningful cautionary language identifying important factors that could cause actual results to differ materially from those in the forward-looking statement. It is often helpful to (1) prioritize the order of risk factors, (2) state the risk in the first sentence, (3) be specific, (4) convey the magnitude of the risk, and (5) focus risk factors on the negatives without softening them by including positives.

Trading by a manager while in possession of material nonpublic information is illegal. It violates the manager's fiduciary duty to subordinate his or her personal interests to the interests of the corporation and shareholders he or she serves. A manager is given access to nonpublic information not for the manager's own personal gain but to better enable the manager to serve his or her principal—the corporation and its shareholders. Violation of those rules erodes both shareholder confidence and the confidence of investors generally in the capital markets. It is also unethical.

A manager cannot give tips to others in exchange for money or even just to enhance his or her reputation as "someone in the know." A manager should carefully guard the information given in confidence by his or her employer or client. Managers must also instill these values in their subordinates. Everyone, from the person who empties the trash or runs the copy machine to the person who occupies the largest office in the executive suite, must be told to follow these rules or risk dismissal. This edict should be made clear in the corporation's code of ethics and in its personnel manual. All corporations, and especially brokerage firms, without adequate procedures in place to prevent illegal insider trading face potential liability for their insiders' illegal trades.

A company cannot disclose material information only to certain favored analysts. This is unfair to the public investors and can result in liability for the company and for the manager who tips an analyst whose clients then trade based on the tip. It also violates Regulation FD, discussed in Chapter 24.

A company's policy on insider trading[52] should prohibit any person associated with the company from trading in any security, whether it was issued by the company or another company, based on material nonpublic information. The policy should also ban passing on material nonpublic information to outsiders who may trade (tipping). It should require persons who are likely to obtain material nonpublic information on a regular basis to pre-clear all purchases and sales of the company's securities. The policy should also (1) describe the legal penalties for insider-trading and the company's potential liability for the insider-trading violations of its employees and (2) provide that any employee who violates the policy may be terminated.

An officer or director of a public company who buys and sells securities within a six-month period has a legal and ethical responsibility to come forward and pay all profits over to the corporation. This is true even if the short-swing trade was inadvertent, as might happen if an officer sold securities not realizing that his or her spouse had bought securities less than six months before. A corporation that discovers a short-swing trade must try to persuade the insider to voluntarily turn the profits over to the corporation. If the insider refuses to do so, the corporation has an obligation to bring suit to recover the profits from the short-swing trading. If a corporation fails to bring suit, any shareholder has the right to sue on behalf of the corporation.

Officers and directors of public companies must report their security holdings and their trades in a timely manner. Disregard of these filing requirements breeds contempt for the law and encourages illegal or unethical behavior by others in the organization.

Each manager has a role to play in preventing securities fraud and insider trading. As with preventing the other types of criminal behavior described in Chapter 17, a manager leads by example. If the manager permits his or her company to engage in unlawful or unethical conduct, the manager exposes himself or herself and the company to considerable risk of civil and criminal liability. Such a manager is also likely to encourage illegal behavior by subordinates.

52. This discussion is drawn from *Effective Company Policy May Avoid Violations, ABA Told,* Corp. Couns. Wkly., Aug. 11, 1999, at 2.

INSIDE STORY

Insider-Trading Scandals *of the* 1980s

Inquiries into insider trading tend to focus on high-volume trading that occurs before major corporate announcements. Enforcement agencies generally watch organized trading rings and well-known public figures because of their high profiles. However, ordinary investors and isolated violations are also detected and prosecuted. Surveillance groups monitor daily trading and investigate any suspicious activity. One such group, the American Exchange Stock Watch Group, was instrumental in breaking the "Heard on the Street" case discussed earlier.

DENNIS LEVINE AND IVAN BOESKY

Prosecutors and enforcement agencies also rely heavily on information gathered from informers and persons already under indictment. For example, the arrest and prosecution of Dennis Levine and Ivan Boesky in 1986 set off the most comprehensive investigation of securities-trading practices in the history of federal regulation. Levine, a former managing director of Drexel Burnham Lambert, was initially charged with illegal trading in approximately fifty-four stocks. An investment banker, Ira B. Sokolow, then pled guilty to passing stolen information to Levine. As a result of cooperation by Levine, the SEC was able to bring insider-trading charges against one of Wall Street's richest and most active speculators, Ivan Boesky.

Boesky, the son of an immigrant restaurateur, made his career and fortune as a risk arbitrageur who concentrated on the purchase and sale of stock in target corporations that were the subject of tender offers. Generally, the acquiring corporation pays a premium for the stock of the target corporation; thus, people who invest prior to the announcement of the acquisition are in a position to make swift and substantial profits. The SEC alleged that Levine, who worked on mergers and acquisitions, passed on information to Boesky, who was able to purchase shares in the target prior to the public announcement of the impending takeover. It is further believed that Boesky offered Levine a 5 percent commission for any information leading to an initial stock purchase and a 1 percent commission for information pertaining to stocks already owned by Boesky.

In 1985, Levine allegedly passed to Boesky information received from Sokolow regarding the merger of Nabisco and R.J. Reynolds. Use of this information resulted in approximately $4 million in profits for Boesky. In all, Boesky was alleged to have made approximately $50 million through these insider-trading activities. Both Levine and Boesky pled guilty to criminal charges. Boesky settled the SEC's civil charges by agreeing to pay $100 million and to cooperate with the government in future prosecutions of others. Both men were sentenced to prison for their actions.

DREXEL BURNHAM LAMBERT

Approximately two years later, with the cooperation of Ivan Boesky, the SEC brought dramatic charges against Drexel Burnham Lambert and four of its prominent employees, including the head of its junk-bond department, Michael Milken. According to the SEC, Drexel had entered into a secret agreement with Boesky to defraud its clients and drive up the price of target-company stocks. The complaint, filed in September 1988, alleged that Drexel utilized Boesky to engage in *stock parking*—the temporary sale of shares to another entity or individual so as to hide the true ownership of the shares in order to avoid tax-reporting requirements or the net-margin requirements of the securities laws applicable to brokerage firms. Drexel, which assisted companies interested in acquisitions, was also accused of advising Boesky to purchase massive amounts of shares in certain companies in order to give the appearance of active trading in them and to drive up the takeover price.

In December 1988, Drexel agreed to plead guilty to six felony counts, pay a $680 million fine, and submit to SEC oversight, contingent upon its settlement of civil charges (which occurred in April 1989). As a part of both settlements, Drexel was required to terminate the employment of Michael Milken.

MICHAEL MILKEN

In 1999, Milken pled guilty to six felony counts, ranging from securities and mail fraud to tax evasion and conspiracy.[53] He agreed to pay a fine of $200 million and to put $400 million into a fund for restitution to defrauded investors. Milken was sentenced to ten years in prison

---

53. Laurie P. Cohen, *Public Confession: Milken Pleads Guilty to Six Felony Counts and Issues an Apology*, WALL ST. J., Apr. 25, 1990, at A1.

but was released after serving only twenty-two months. He was banned for life from acting as a securities broker or dealer. A 2001 *New Yorker* article questioned, however, whether he had violated that prohibition by orchestrating major corporate mergers and acquisitions after his release from prison.[54]

U.S. Attorney General Richard Thornburgh characterized Milken's crimes as "some of the most serious ef-

forts undertaken to manipulate and subvert Wall Street's securities markets,"[55] But Thornburgh also observed that the case sends a strong message to those involved in "crime in the suites: those white-collar criminals are never so powerful or clever that they cannot be caught by diligent and persistent law enforcement efforts."[56]

54. *See* James B. Stewart, *The Milken File,* NEW YORKER, Jan. 22, 2001, at 47.

55. Cohen, *supra* note 53.
56. *Id.*

KEY WORDS AND PHRASES

aider and abettor   863
beneficial owner   895
bespeaks caution doctrine   873
derivative insider   886
efficient-market theory   880
equity security   894
forward-looking statement   882
fraud-on-the-market theory   880
insider   886

insider trading   862
misappropriation theory   888
misstatement   866
omission   866
prejudgment interest   884
remote tippees   887
S–1 review   865
scienter   865
selling securities short   894

short-swing trading   893
stock parking   898
temporary insiders   886
tip   868
tippee   885
tipper   885
unorthodox transaction   895

QUESTIONS AND CASE PROBLEMS

1. During a session with her psychiatrist, Dr. Robert Willis, Joan Weill mentioned in confidence the imminent merger of the company headed by her husband, Sanford Weill, with another company. Willis, upon hearing of the merger, communicated the information to Martin Sloate, who traded in the company's securities for his own account and for his customers' accounts.

    Did Willis or Sloate engage in illegal insider trading? Was the conduct of the parties ethical? [*SEC v. Willis,* 777 F. Supp. 1165 (S.D.N.Y. 1991)]

2. Gallop, Inc. is a toy manufacturer specializing in games for boys and girls aged eight to twelve. Gallop had predicted first-quarter earnings of $.20 per share on March 30. On April 15, Gallop received a fax from its key distributor reporting a $10 million claim for personal injury of a nine-year-old child who was allegedly injured by a design defect in Gallop's most popular product line, the Spartan Warriors. Gallop's outside counsel was instructed to prepare a press release describing the claim. Before the press release was sent to the copy center at Gal-

lop's executive office, the vice president of marketing, one director, and the outside counsel sold all of their Gallop shares at the prevailing market price of $25.25 per share.

    Collin Copier, who ran the photocopying machine at Gallop's executive office, saw the draft press release; called his broker, Barbara Broker; told her about the press release; and ordered her to sell the 500 shares of Gallop that Copier had acquired in Gallop's initial public offering. Broker then called her best client, Charleen Client, and suggested that she sell her 100,000 shares of Gallop stock but did not tell her why. Client agreed, and Broker sold Copier's and Client's stock at $25.25 a share right before the market closed on April 17.

    The press release was publicly announced and was reported on the Business Wire after the market closed on April 17. The next day, Gallop's stock dropped to $20.75 per share. A class action suit has been brought, and the SEC has commenced enforcement proceedings. Criminal prosecution is threatened by the U.S. Attorney's Office.

What are the bases on which each proceeding could be brought? Who is potentially liable? For how much?

3. Ann Boland, a freelance writer, called her mother to boast about a press release that she was writing for Empire Corporation. The assignment called for the strictest confidence because it involved the announcement of a takeover.

   Later in the day, Ann's mother casually tells her son Tim, a business student, about his sister's press release. She does not mention the name of the takeover target, but she naively provides Tim with enough details that he is almost certain who it is.

   Tim calls his rich buddy, Carl Consultant, and tells him the story. They decide to buy options on the target company's stock and to split any profits 50–50. In a week, the two have made a small fortune. Are there any Rule 10b–5 violations? If so, who may be required to disgorge profits?

4. American Banknote Corporation (ABN) spun off its wholly owned subsidiary American Bank Note Holographics (ABNH) in an initial public offering. Morris Weissman was the founder of ABN and also the chair and CEO of both ABNH and ABN. Plaintiff purchasers of ABNH's stock sued Weissman, among others, for securities fraud under Sections 11, 12(a)(2), and 10(b). In two press releases, Weissman stated:

   > Our most important goal in 1998 is to enhance shareholder value. We hope to prove to the market that inherent values of our underlying operating subsidiaries, not apparent when evaluating American Banknote on the basis of traditionally consolidated earnings per share, are indeed significant.
   >
   > This IPO is a win–win for both companies. . . . ABNH can now concentrate on continuing the profitable growth of its core security holography business as well as explore business and market expansion opportunities.

   In fact, ABNH was neither a valuable company nor profitable. Is Weissman liable under Section 10(b) and Rule 10b–5? What would be the best argument in his defense? [*In re American Bank Note Holographics, Inc. Securities Litigation,* 93 F. Supp. 2d 424 (S.D.N.Y. 2000)]

5. National Industries acquired 34 percent of TSC Industries' voting stock from TSC's founder and principal shareholder and his family. After the sale, the TSC founder resigned from TSC's board of directors. Subsequently, five National nominees, including National's president and CEO, were placed on TSC's board. Several months later, TSC's board, with the National nominees abstaining, approved a proposal to liquidate and sell all of TSC's assets to National. One month later, the two companies issued a joint proxy statement to their shareholders, recommending approval of the proposal. The proxy solicitation was successful, TSC was liquidated, and the exchange of shares was effected.

   A TSC shareholder brought an action against the two companies claiming that their joint proxy statement was materially misleading. The basis of the claim was that the proxy statement omitted material facts relating to the degree of National's control over TSC. Were the omitted facts material? [*TSC Industries v. Northway, Inc.,* 426 U.S. 438 (1976)]

6. On November 8, 1990, the *Wall Street Journal* reported rumors of a possible merger of AT&T and NCR. AT&T declined to comment on the rumors. That same day, Charles Brumfield, vice president of labor relations for AT&T, called his friend Joseph Cusimano and told him that he believed the contents of the newspaper article were true and that "AT&T was going to be attempting to acquire NCR." Cusimano made a series of trades in NCR securities on November 9, 12, and 15 through 20. The AT&T board authorized the acquisition of NCR on November 14 and publicly announced its interest on December 2.

   Did either Brumfield or Cusimano violate Section 10(b) and Rule 10b–5? On what theory? Was Brumfield's information nonpublic and material? [*United States v. Mylett,* 97 F.3d 663 (2d Cir. 1996); *United States v. Cusimano,* 123 F.3d 83 (2d Cir. 1997), *cert. denied,* 522 U.S. 1133 (1998)]

7. Texas International Speedway, Inc. (TIS) filed a registration statement for $4,398,900 in securities with the proceeds to be used to construct an automobile racetrack called the Texas International Speedway. The entire issue was sold on the offering date, October 30, 1969. On November 30, 1970, TIS filed for bankruptcy.

   The prospectus stated that the speedway was under construction. It also included a pro forma balance sheet showing that, upon completion of the public offering and application of the proceeds to the construction costs of the speedway, TIS would have $93,870 in cash on hand on the speedway's opening date.

   The TIS prospectus warned that "THESE SECURITIES INVOLVE A HIGH DEGREE OF RISK" and that the construction costs might be underestimated. If the plaintiff investors present evidence from which a jury could infer that, on the effective date of the registration statement, the two officers and directors of TIS and its accountant knew that the cost of construction was understated and that consequently TIS's working capital position would not be as favorable as the prospectus reflected, will the plaintiff win a suit under Section 10(b) and Rule 10b–5? What would be the result if the Reform Act applied? [*Huddleston v. Herman & MacLean*, 640 F.2d 534 (5th Cir. 1981), *rev'd in part and aff'd in part,* 456 U.S. 914 (1982)]

8. On June 24, 1994, Novell, Inc., a leading provider of network operating software, merged with Word-Perfect in a stock-for-stock exchange registered under the 1933 Act pursuant to a registration statement initially filed on April 22, 1994, and last amended on June 23, 1994.

The registration statement included a warning that the integration of Novell and WordPerfect could be difficult due to intense competition in WordPerfect's market sector and the company's declining financial performance. It further cautioned that the acquisitions of WordPerfect and the Quattro Pro spreadsheet software program from Borland, Inc. in the first part of 1994 could be difficult because they were large acquisitions in new markets where Novell did not have management or marketing experience. The registration statement warned that no assurance could be given that the various businesses could be successfully integrated. Also, the dominant competition expected from Microsoft was stressed. In addition, Novell warned that the merger and acquisition would lead to higher expenditures in sales, marketing, and support and higher other costs. Novell predicted that its future earnings and stock price could be subject to "significant volatility, particularly on a quarterly basis" and warned that WordPerfect's market was "characterized by severe competitive pressure" that could "materially adversely affect Novell." The June 10 amendment to the registration statement advised that "disruptions associated with the merger and the acquisition of Quattro Pro have resulted in declines in sales of Quattro Pro in recent periods." Also, significant deterioration in the sales and profitability of WordPerfect was disclosed.

The merger was completed five weeks before the end of the third quarter. On August 19, 1994, Novell announced that its consolidated third-quarter earnings would be between 15 and 20 percent lower than analysts' projections and that the company would recognize a $120 million charge against earnings for the quarter related to its acquisition of Quattro Pro. The next business day, August 22, Novell's stock price fell from $15.12 per share to $14.00 per share, a 7 percent drop.

The plaintiff class members purchased shares of Novell stock during the period between April 27, 1994, and August 19, 1994. They alleged that beginning on April 27, 1994, Novell issued to the press and to financial analysts a series of false and misleading statements that omitted material facts regarding the effect of the WordPerfect merger on Novell's operations and near-term earnings potential. They did not claim that the registration statement itself was misleading.

In particular, the plaintiffs alleged that the following statements had inflated the price of Novell stock during the class period: (1) a statement by defendant Wise (Novell's senior vice president for finance) on April 27, 1994, that there were "indications" that WordPerfect was "gaining market share . . . from less than 20% in 1992 to more than 40% today" and that "the combination wouldn't dilute future earnings"; (2) a statement by defendant Frankenberg (Novell's CEO, president, and chair) on June 27, 1994, that Novell had experienced substantial success in integrating the sales forces and operations of WordPerfect and that the merger process had been moving "faster than we thought it would"; (3) Frankenberg's statement in the same June 27, 1994 publication that "we have not slowed down the effort to create new products, we've accelerated it" and that he believed there was "a compelling set of opportunities" available to the new Novell; (4) a statement by Rietveld (CEO of WordPerfect and later the president of Novell's WordPerfect/Novell applications group) on June 28, 1994, that the merger had been "perhaps the smoothest of mergers in recent history"; (5) Frankenberg's statement on June 28, 1994, that "he was pleased with the accelerating pace of product development since the acquisition was completed in March"; and (6) Novell's statement on July 20, 1994, that "[b]y moving rapidly to a fully integrated sales force, we are leveraging our combined knowledge of the expanding scope of network solutions," and "Novell expects that network applications will quickly reshape customer expectations and expand the role of our channel partners in supporting end-user network solutions."

Novell and the other defendants made a motion to dismiss the complaint. Result? Should Novell's officers have done anything differently? Was their conduct ethical? [*Grossman v. Novell, Inc.,* 120 F.3d 1112 (10th Cir. 1997)]

9. EchoCath was a small New Jersey research and development company engaged in developing, manufacturing, and marketing medical devices to enhance and expand the use of ultrasound technology for medical applications and procedures. EchoCath consummated its initial public offering on January 17, 1996, and issued a lengthy prospectus, which cautioned that "an investment in the securities offered . . . is speculative in nature and involves a high degree of risk." It also set forth several pages of risk factors. In particular, EchoCath cautioned investors that the company "intended to pursue licensing, joint development and other collaborative arrangements with other strategic partners . . . but there can be no assurance . . . that the Company will be able to successfully reach agreements with any strategic partners, or that other strategic partners will ever devote sufficient resources to the Company's technologies."

More than six months after the public offering, MedSystems began to consider a sizable investment in EchoCath. Frank DeBernardis, the CEO of EchoCath, orally represented to MedSystems that EchoCath had engaged in lengthy negotiations to license its products and was on the verge of signing contracts with a number of prominent medical companies, which he identified as including UroHealth, Johnson & Johnson, Medtronic, and C.R. Bard, Inc., to develop and market EchoCath's women's health products. Throughout the negotiations and until the closing in February 1997, EchoCath's CEO continued to represent to MedSystems officials that the contracts with these companies to develop these products were "imminent." In the fifteen months after MedSystems made its investment, EchoCath failed to enter into a single contract.

MedSystems filed suit under Section 10(b) and Rule 10b–5, alleging that EchoCath intentionally or recklessly made misrepresentations to MedSystems in connection with the sale of securities in an effort to induce MedSystems to purchase its securities. MedSystems alleged that EchoCath was not on the verge of signing contracts with any company to develop its line of women's health products in August 1996, or any other time up to the closing on February 27, 1997. EchoCath moved to dismiss the complaint on the grounds that the CEO's statements were not material. Result? [*ER MedSystems v. EchoCath, Inc.,* 235 F.3d 865 (3d Cir. 2000)]

 MANAGER'S DILEMMA

10. In 1984, several individuals (including David Greenberg) formed seven limited partnerships to develop and operate a chain of 100 "Video USA" video rental stores. One hundred and sixteen limited partners, who had invested $13 million in three private placements, sued Touche Ross, among others, for securities fraud. They alleged that Touche Ross (1) had failed to disclose that David Greenberg was a convicted felon; that his twelve-year-old son was the sole officer, director, and shareholder of one of the corporations that served as a general partner; and that the principals used fraudulent invoices and made fraudulent claims against insurance companies; and (2) had prepared the materially misleading financial projections attached as exhibits to the offering memoranda. Touche Ross did not issue an opinion or certification as to any part of the offering documents. Attached to each of the projections that Touche Ross issued was a letter stating that the projection was based on management's "knowledge and belief" and cautioning that the projection "does not include an evaluation of the support for the assumptions underlying the projections." Is Touche Ross liable under Section 10(b) to the limited partners? If you were the account manager at Touche Ross and learned about Greenberg's felony conviction and the existence of fraudulent invoices, what would you have done? [*Shapiro v. Cantor,* 123 F.3d 717 (2d Cir. 1997)]

INTERNET SOURCES

Securities and Exchange Commission	http://www.sec.gov
Investors can register complaints by e-mail with the Securities and Exchange Commission by following the instructions at this site.	http://www.sec.gov/consumer/reachus.htm.
Milberg Weiss is perhaps the largest (and in Silicon Valley the most feared and hated) law firm specializing in representing plaintiffs in securities fraud suits and class actions.	http://securities.milberg.com http://www.milberg.com
The brainchild of Stanford Law School professor (and former SEC commissioner) Joseph Grundfest, the Securities Class Action Clearinghouse site has been called the "Mecca for the securities lawyer." This is the first Designated Internet Site for required electronic posting of court documents in the United States.	http://securities.stanford.edu
The Securities Law Home Page provides access to many important securities law cases and useful links to other law-related sites.	http://www.seclaw.com
The National Investor Relations Institute Web site includes the results of a survey on the effect of Regulation FD.	http://www.niri.org/cdps2001.pdf

CHAPTER 26

Debtor–Creditor
Relations *and* Bankruptcy

SALVAGING A BUSINESS IN FINANCIAL TROUBLE

The reasons for borrowing money, and the uses to which the loan proceeds are applied, are many and varied. A business will generally decide to borrow when it needs funds and believes it is in a position to pay interest for the use of such funds. Although lenders sometimes take equity positions in a borrower, whereby they receive returns based on the profits or losses of the borrower, lenders in a loan transaction are entitled only to interest at a stated rate on the amount borrowed (generally called the *principal*) and the return of the principal at the end of the term.

When a business is in trouble, because of external events or internal miscalculations or misdeeds, it will inevitably run short of cash and fall behind in its payments. Creditors may be temporarily appeased; but those with collateral will ultimately pursue foreclosure, and others will file lawsuits in a race for the remaining assets. Defending against these actions can absorb resources and hamper management's ability to cure the company's underlying ills. Successful collection can cripple or kill the business.

Predatory dismemberment may destroy a company's real economic value. This loss in value will ultimately hurt creditors if there are not enough assets to go around. Even if all debts can be paid, the equity holders in the company will suffer. The collapse of a large enterprise could leave many unemployed and send disruptive waves through related industries.

The legal tools used to stem this potentially destructive tide are found mainly in the Bankruptcy Code.[1] The U.S. Constitution gives Congress the power to enact bankruptcy laws. A successful reorganization under Chapter 11 of the Bankruptcy Code results in the restructuring of financial relationships among the owners and creditors of a business and, ideally, the preservation of a viable going concern. Even when reorganization is not possible, the bankruptcy system is designed to realize the maximum value from the available assets, to provide equitable distribution among claimants, and to foster fair and efficient administration through a collective or multiparty process.

CHAPTER OVERVIEW

This chapter categorizes commercial loans according to the type of lender, the purposes to which the loan proceeds will be applied, and whether the loan is secured or unsecured. This discussion is followed by a summary of the typical terms of a loan agreement. Methods for securing a loan under Article 9 of the Uniform Commercial Code are discussed, and the terms of a typical security agreement are described. Equipment leasing, guaranties, and subordination are addressed. This is followed by a discussion of business bankruptcies under Chapter 7 and Chapter 11 of the Bankruptcy Code and consumer bankruptcy under Chapter 7 and Chapter 13. The chapter concludes with a discussion of workouts and lender liability.

---

1. Codified in scattered sections of 11 U.S.C.

Loans Categorized *by* Lender

Commercial loans are most commonly made by banks, insurance companies, and purchasers of *commercial paper,* that is, short-term corporate indebtedness. Both banks and insurance companies are highly regulated. Extensive federal and state legislation prescribes the types of entities that may call themselves banks, who may own them, and, once they become banks, what they may or may not do. Similarly, insurance companies are restricted by state legislation in connection with their business of insuring against risk. The regulatory framework within which banks, insurance companies, and other types of lenders operate affects the sources and availability of their funds; these factors in turn affect the terms on which they will offer to lend money. Insurance companies commonly offer medium- to long-term loans at fixed interest rates. Banks generally are more flexible in the length of the terms of their loans, their interest-rate formulas, and the mechanics of their loan administration. Whether a lender is a bank or an insurance company, it may have particular expertise in the industry in which the borrower does business or in making loans for particular purposes.

Loans Categorized *by* Purpose

A borrower may require funds to meet everyday working capital needs, to finance an acquisition of assets or a business, or to finance a real estate construction project or an engineering project. Under regulations promulgated by the board of governors of the Federal Reserve System, lenders and borrowers may not enter into transactions whereby secured credit will be used to acquire stock, unless certain requirements are met. Apart from these basic restrictions and additional restrictions that apply to borrowers in regulated industries, borrowers may borrow money for a wide variety of reasons. These reasons will dictate whether the loan will be a term loan or a revolving loan.

TERM LOANS

Funds required for a specific purpose, such as an acquisition or a construction project, are generally borrowed in the form of a *term loan.* A specified amount is borrowed, either in a lump sum or in installments. It is to be repaid on a specified date (known as the *maturity date*) or *amortized* (paid off over a period of time). For exam-

ple, in an acquisition the buyer may be required to pay the purchase price up front and thus will require a lump-sum loan. By contrast, the owner of a construction project will require a loan that is disbursed in installments as scheduled progress payments become due. Amounts repaid under a term loan cannot be reborrowed.

REVOLVING LOANS

A business may project its working capital needs for a given period but desire flexibility as to the exact amount of money borrowed at any given time. A *revolving loan* or *revolving line of credit* allows the business to borrow whatever sums are required, up to a specified maximum amount. The borrower may also reborrow amounts it has repaid (hence the term "revolving"). The lender will require a *commitment fee* as consideration for its promise to keep the commitment available, as it receives no interest on amounts not borrowed.

Secured Loans

In making a loan, the lender relies on the borrower's cash flow, the borrower's assets, or the proceeds of another loan as sources of repayment. If the lender relies solely on the borrower's promise to repay the loan, the lender's recourse for nonpayment is limited to suing the borrower. Moreover, even if the lender does sue, it stands in no better position than other general creditors of the borrower and has no special claim to any specific assets of the borrower as a source of repayment. Because of this risk, lenders are often unwilling to make loans unless the borrower provides more than a promise to repay. Lenders usually require *collateral,* that is, property belonging to the borrower that will become the lender's if the loan is not repaid. A loan backed up by collateral is known as a *secured loan.* Unsecured loans, if available at all, are priced at a higher rate to reflect the greater credit risk to the lender.

If the borrower fails to repay a secured loan, the lender, in addition to suing for return of the monies lent, may *foreclose* on—that is, take possession of—the collateral and either sell it to pay off the debt or keep it in satisfaction of the debt. It should be noted that under some *antideficiency* and *one-form-of-action laws* lenders seeking remedies against real property security may be restricted from suing the borrower personally. In cases in which a lender has recourse to the borrower or to other property of the borrower and exercises such rights, the lender may be precluded from foreclosing on real estate mortgaged by the borrower. These laws, which date back to the Great Depression, are designed to protect borrowers from forfeiting their properties to overzealous lenders.

 # Loan Agreements

Given the variety of loans described above, the basic structure of loan agreements is surprisingly standard. Lenders are concerned about the administration of their loans, their ongoing relationship with the borrowers, and the rights they have if the borrowers breach their promises. At times, these concerns must be addressed in specially tailored documentation; generally, however, banks use a collection of standard forms, which are distributed to loan officers along with instructions for their use. This section discusses the basic features common to all loan agreements.

PARTIES TO THE AGREEMENT

The parties to a loan agreement are the lender and the borrower. There may be more than one lender and more than one borrower. If the lender is an insurance company, the loan agreement will be called a *note purchase agreement*.

Lenders When two or more lenders, usually banks, together make one loan to a borrower, it is called a *syndicated loan*. In a syndicated loan, the lenders enter into concurrent direct obligations with the borrower to make a loan, typically on a pro rata basis. The loan is coordinated by a lead lender who serves as agent for all of the lenders in disbursing the funds, collecting payments of interest and principal, and administering and enforcing the loan.

In a *participation loan,* the original lender sells shares to other parties, called participants. Each participant acquires an undivided interest in the loan. The sale may be made without the borrower's involvement.

Borrowers Multiple borrowers are usually related entities, such as a parent corporation and its subsidiaries. It is important to remember that corporate law recognizes each corporation as a separate entity. From the lender's point of view, the parent and its subsidiaries are one economic entity; from the subsidiaries' point of view, however, if each subsidiary is jointly and severally liable for the entire debt, the obligation may outweigh the economic benefit a subsidiary receives from the loan. (To the extent that the loan is used by the parent rather than the subsidiary, the transaction may be invalidated as a

fraudulent transfer under state law and the federal Bankruptcy Code, as discussed below.)

Additional Parties In more complicated transactions, additional parties may become involved in the negotiations for a loan, even though they are not parties to the loan agreement. For example, in a leveraged buyout, the acquisition of a company is financed largely by debt secured by its assets. The lender will want assurances from the seller that the assets being sold to the borrower are free and clear of all liens, and this concern may affect the structure of the buyout; or, if the seller is taking a note from the buyer for part of the purchase price, the lender will want to negotiate with the seller an agreement setting forth their relative rights to repayment. In a construction loan, the construction lender will advance sufficient funds to complete the construction project with the expectation of being repaid when a permanent, long-term lender steps in. In such a situation, the construction lender will negotiate with the permanent lender as well as the borrower.

In certain types of project financings, a limited partnership may be formed for the sole purpose of constructing, say, a power plant. The general partner's liability is normally unlimited; however, for tax and other reasons, a lender may agree that it will look only to the partnership's assets for repayment of a loan. In such a case, the lender would need to assure itself that the limited partnership has sufficient resources to repay the loan. For example, if the partnership's primary resources are fees from the sale of goods or services, the lender will be interested in the nature of the partnership's contracts for those sales.

In all of these examples, the lender has a legitimate interest in seeing that the borrower's relationships with third parties will not adversely affect the loan.

COMMITMENT TO MAKE A LOAN

A loan agreement may be preceded by a *term sheet,* which is a letter outlining the terms and conditions on which the lender will lend. A commitment to make a loan need not be in writing to be enforceable, but an oral promise may be difficult to enforce because reasonable people may honestly differ in their recollections of what was said. A jury may, however, award damages for breach of an oral loan commitment.[2]

Several state legislatures have proposed, and at least one has adopted, legislation specifically requiring loan

2. *See, e.g.,* Landes Constr. Co. v. Royal Bank of Canada, 833 F.2d 1365 (9th Cir. 1987).

commitments that exceed a threshold dollar amount to be in writing to be enforceable. Even in the absence of such legislation, a prudent lender will use a written term sheet or commitment letter to specify the terms of a proposed loan (including the amount, interest rate, fees, and repayment provisions) and to disclaim any obligation to lend until the investigation is completed, additional terms and conditions are negotiated, and formal documentation is signed.

DESCRIPTION OF THE LOAN

A loan agreement contains the lender's promise to lend a specified amount of money. Frequently, this will be the only promise that the lender makes in the agreement. The agreement also describes the mechanics by which funds will be disbursed, the rate of interest to be charged, the manner of computing such interest, and the repayment terms.

Mechanics of Funding The funds are usually sent by wire transfer to an account specified by the borrower. If the timing is important, the borrower should discuss with the lender the logistical details of the loan agreement, such as the lender's deadline for sending wire transfers. The logistics may become critical if the lender and the borrower are in different time zones or if there are multiple lenders, as in a syndicated loan.

Interest Rates Interest rates may be fixed or *floating,* that is, fluctuating throughout the life of the loan according to the interest rate that the lender would pay if it borrowed the funds in order to relend them. Insurance companies commonly make fixed-rate term loans; banks generally prefer a floating rate. The floating rate may be pegged to the bank's *prime rate,* that is, the lowest published rate of interest at which the bank lends to its best

and most creditworthy commercial customers. Because a bank may lend money at a rate below its so-called prime rate, banks often use the terms *base rate* or *reference rate.* Some banks include in their definition an explicit statement that the prime (or base or reference) rate is not the bank's best or lowest rate. The floating rate may be expressed either as a percentage of the prime rate (such as 110 percent of the prime rate) or, more commonly, as the sum of the prime rate and a specified number of percentage points (such as the prime rate plus 10 percent).

Alternatively, the floating rate may be pegged to the London Interbank Offered Rate (LIBOR) or to the certificate of deposit (CD) rate. These rates are based on the theoretical cost that a bank incurs to obtain, for a given period of time, the funds it will lend. To this cost is added a spread (or margin) to arrive at the actual interest rate. Frequently, a loan agreement will offer prime-rate, LIBOR, and CD-rate options that the borrower can select during the life of the loan.

The *London Interbank Offered Rate (LIBOR)* is based on the cost of borrowing offshore U.S. dollars in the global interbank market, which nowadays is centered in several locations in addition to London. Deposits made through the interbank offering market are generally for periods of one, two, three, six, nine, or twelve months; LIBOR loans are made for corresponding periods. At the end of an interest period, the borrower may elect to (1) roll over the LIBOR loan, that is, to continue it for another interest period; (2) repay the loan; or (3) convert it to a loan based on a different interest rate.

The *certificate of deposit (CD) rate* is based on the average of the bid rates quoted to the bank by dealers in the secondary market for the purchase at face value of the bank's CDs in a given amount and for a given term. CD-rate loans are commonly available for interest periods of 30, 60, 90, or 180 days.

Computation of Interest Interest is generally computed on a daily basis according to one of several methods. Under the *365/360 method,* the nominal annual interest rate is divided by 360, and the resulting daily rate is then multiplied by the outstanding principal amount and the actual number of days in the payment period. Thus, for a year of 365 or 366 days, the actual rate of interest will be higher than the nominal annual rate.

Under the *365/365 method,* the daily rate is determined by dividing the nominal annual interest rate by 365 (or 366, in leap years); then this daily rate is multiplied by the outstanding principal amount and the actual number of days in the payment period. Under the *360/360 method,* it is assumed that all months have thirty days; thus, the monthly interest amounts are always the same.

 ETHICAL CONSIDERATION

Managers should be careful not to make oral promises that they cannot, or will not, perform. The business environment is always changing, and it is better to qualify one's statements than to make a strong commitment today that may be regretted tomorrow.

Managers should recognize that many types of oral contracts are binding. When there is no independent witness to an oral contract, a contracting party may be tempted to alter his or her version of the facts, leading to a contest of "your word against mine." This type of behavior is clearly unethical.

The method used to compute interest is significant when large principal amounts are involved. It may also be significant if the lender or the loan is subject to state *usury* laws, which limit the maximum rate of interest that may be charged. National banks and other specified classes of lenders are subject to federal legislation that preempts state usury laws; and many states permit higher interest rates for exempt commercial transactions over a given dollar amount. Unless a state or federal exemption applies, lenders and borrowers should analyze whether a loan is usurious by virtue of its terms and conditions. For example, compensation paid for a loan, such as commitment fees, expenses, and prepayment penalties, may be treated as interest.

Repayment Terms A revolving loan may be repaid from time to time at the borrower's discretion, subject to a final maturity date when all sums outstanding become due and payable. In a term loan, the lender may require the entire principal to be repaid in one lump sum upon maturity or in equal or unequal installments.

Agreements for term or revolving loans may also specify mandatory prepayment when certain events occur. For example, in a receivables and inventory line of credit, a prepayment will be required if the level of receivables and/or inventory supporting the outstanding borrowings drops. A sale of assets outside the ordinary course of business or financial earnings below a specified level may also mandate a prepayment.

Asset-Based Loans In structuring a loan agreement, the fact that a loan is secured or unsecured is not particularly significant, except in certain types of asset-based financing in which the amount lent is based on the level of assets available from time to time. One example of an asset-based loan is a revolving line of credit based on receivables, inventory, or both. Subject to certain criteria as to what inventory or receivables are eligible—that is, acceptable to the lender—the borrower borrows against such assets and repays the loan on a revolving basis out of collections of the receivables generated from the sale of inventory. Sometimes payments are made directly to the lender through such mechanisms as a locked-box or blocked account, which allows the lender to take the outstanding loan repayments out of the collected proceeds before they are distributed to the borrower.

REPRESENTATIONS AND WARRANTIES

Before committing to make a loan, a lender will investigate the potential borrower's financial condition and creditworthiness. The lender will also require the borrower to confirm:

- Its legal status, including, in the case of a corporation, its proper incorporation and good standing.
- That corporate and other actions have authorized the proposed borrowing.
- That regulatory and other approvals that might be required for the borrowing have been obtained.
- That there are no court orders or contracts that would be in conflict with the loan agreement.
- Whether the borrower is involved in any litigation.
- That the borrower has good and marketable title to all of its assets, including any assets that constitute collateral for the loan.
- That the loan agreement is legal, valid, and binding.
- That no default has occurred or would result from entering into the loan agreement.

The purpose of these representations and warranties is to specify the assumptions on which the lender is willing to lend. In the negotiation process, the representations and warranties serve as a checklist of major areas of investigation by the lender. They also provide a framework for the borrower to examine its legal and financial position.

Qualifications Often a borrower will state that a representation is true to the best of its knowledge. The borrower will want to be held accountable only for what it knows, not for what it does not know. The lender will want the borrower to take steps to ascertain the accuracy of its representations. The risk of a representation proving to be untrue is usually placed on the borrower rather than the lender. Any qualification based on the borrower's knowledge is therefore likely to be phrased in terms of what the borrower either knows or should know after diligent inquiry. It may include a definition of the appropriate standard of diligence.

In the loan agreement, the borrower states that the representations and warranties are true and complete as of the date of the agreement. They do not apply prospectively. However, the loan agreement may provide that if advances are to be made, the representations and warranties will be updated as of the time of the advances.

Truthfulness of Representations Before a disbursement is made under the loan agreement, the lender will require an opinion of counsel and a certification by an independent public accountant, confirming the representations made by the borrower. The lender's obligation to continue to lend will likewise be conditioned upon the continuing truthfulness of the representations in the loan agreement.

CONDITIONS TO CLOSING

Authority to Approve the Loan The lender will require evidence that the borrower's internal requirements for approving the loan have been met. It may require copies of the relevant corporate resolutions certified by the corporate secretary. It may also require certification of the incumbency of the officers authorized to execute the loan agreement.

Completion of Documents The loan agreement is typically only one of several documents that must be signed in connection with a loan. The lender will also require a promissory note and, if the loan is secured, a security agreement and financing statements.

Payment of Fees Some fees, such as commitment fees, must be paid before any funds are disbursed.

Other Conditions Other conditions may apply in certain circumstances. For example, in the case of a term loan to finance a merger or acquisition, the lender will condition any disbursement on the consummation of the transaction.

Regulatory approval may be required because of the nature of the borrower's business. In such cases, the lender will specify the permits and approvals that must be obtained or issued before it will disburse any funds.

As explained in Chapter 18, lenders have become increasingly concerned about the liability they may face if real property they hold, either as security or outright after a foreclosure, is required to comply with environmental cleanup laws. The lender may, therefore, require an opinion of environmental counsel, an environmental audit by qualified consultants and engineers, and indemnity agreements with the borrower and with any third parties that may be responsible for the environmental condition of the property.

CONDITIONS PRECEDENT

If the basic assumptions and facts upon which the lender has relied change materially after a commitment to lend has been made, the lender will need to reevaluate the loan. It may (1) refuse to advance the funds committed, (2) refuse to advance additional funds if some disbursements have already been made, or (3) accelerate the maturity of the loan. The loan agreement will specify the conditions that must be met before the lender's obligations arise under the agreement. These are known as *conditions precedent.*

COVENANTS

Covenants are the borrower's promises to the lender that it will or will not take specific actions as long as either a commitment or a loan is outstanding. If a covenant is breached, the lender is free to terminate the loan.

Whereas the lender's obligation is simply to make the loan once the stated conditions are met, the list of obligations imposed upon the borrower can be quite lengthy. The borrower's obligations may also affect nonparties to the loan agreement. For example, the lender may require that the borrower and its subsidiaries maintain a specified net worth, computed on a consolidated basis. Because the subsidiaries are not parties to the loan agreement, that agreement cannot directly impose such an obligation on them. However, the borrower may be required to cause its subsidiaries to comply with the covenant. Such a covenant assumes that the borrower is in a position to influence the nonparties' actions.

Affirmative Covenants *Affirmative covenants* state what the borrower undertakes to do, for example, maintain its corporate existence, pay taxes, maintain insurance, and comply with applicable laws.

The borrower is usually required to keep the lender informed of its financial condition and to submit unaudited financial reports monthly or quarterly and audited financial reports annually. Financial tests relating to income statement and balance sheet items may be imposed. A catchall covenant will require the borrower to inform the lender of any material adverse change in its operations or financial condition.

Negative Covenants *Negative covenants* state what the borrower undertakes not to do, for example, not to incur additional debt beyond a specified amount and not to grant liens other than those specifically enumerated or those arising in the ordinary course of business. (A *lien* is a claim on property that secures a debt owed by the owner of the property.)

Scope Covenants are generally heavily negotiated. Financial covenants, because they are based on projections of future financial results, require flexibility in long-term loans. The borrower will resist any covenants that appear to interfere with its control and operation of its business. A lender sensitive to borrowers' fears of lender control will draft its covenants carefully to impose no more control than is needed to protect its right to be repaid. For example, a provision that effectively gives the lender the right to select the borrower's management may be difficult to justify. Lawsuits, some resulting in multimillion-dollar punitive judgments against unduly interfering lenders, have alerted lenders to the need for caution in drafting and enforcing such provisions.

EVENTS OF DEFAULT

The loan agreement lists the events that will trigger the lender's right to terminate (or *call*) the loan, accelerate the repayment obligations, and, if the loan is secured, take possession of the property securing the loan. The parties to the loan agreement may define these *events of default*. They usually include (1) failure to pay on time any amounts due under the loan agreement, (2) making false or misleading representations or warranties in connection with the loan, and (3) failing to live up to any covenant in the loan agreement. In addition, if the borrower, any subsidiary, or a guarantor enters into bankruptcy, the lender will want to put its obligations on hold while it considers the next course of action.

Some events of default are outside the control of the borrower. For example, if a corporation obtains a loan on the strength of the lender's confidence in a particular individual's management ability, his or her death may be included as an event of default. Similarly, involuntary liens or legal judgments against the borrower, although more or less outside the borrower's control, change the fundamental bases on which a loan was originally made. A loan agreement cannot require the borrower to take or not take actions that are outside its control. Nevertheless, because the consequences of certain events, regardless of how they are caused, are of concern to the lender, the lender will want to include these events in the default section.

Cross-Default A *cross-default* provision provides that any breach by the borrower under any other loan agreement constitutes an event of default under this loan agreement. A borrower will want to limit the provision to apply only to a serious breach of a loan agreement covering a loan larger than a specified minimum. The borrower may also want the lender to agree that the borrower's breach of another agreement will not constitute an event of default under this agreement unless the other lender terminates its loan on account of the breach.

The lender, on the other hand, will want to define the events of default broadly. It will want the right to join with other creditors to negotiate some form of protection for its position as soon as the borrower's financial condition deteriorates.

Provided the borrower does not seek bankruptcy, the lender and borrower are free to renegotiate the terms and conditions on which the loan will remain outstanding. For example, the lender may agree to continue the loan in exchange for new or additional collateral, new guaranties, or a higher rate of interest. Such negotiations are a practical alternative to the more drastic measure of calling the loan. (If the borrower seeks bankruptcy, the lender's efforts to restructure the loan will be subject to the jurisdiction of the bankruptcy court.)

REMEDIES FOR DEFAULT

The default section sets forth the remedies for default. These remedies are optional for the lender. If the lender *waives* a default—that is, decides not to exercise any of its remedies—it may exact additional consideration from the borrower in the form of a higher interest rate or additional security.

It is prudent to put a waiver in writing to avoid any misunderstanding as to its scope and the terms and conditions on which it is being granted, including any additional obligations of the borrower. In lender liability lawsuits, express terms in a loan agreement have been found to be superseded by oral or written communications between the lender and the borrower or by the actions of the borrower or lender. Reducing understandings to writing and avoiding actions that may be inconsistent with the written documents will avoid surprises and failed expectations on both sides.

 Secured Transactions *under the* UCC

The mechanics of taking a security interest in personal property and fixtures, and the consequences of taking such a security interest, are governed by Article 9 of the Uniform Commercial Code (UCC). Except where otherwise noted, the following discussion is based on the Revised Article 9 approved by the National Conference for Uniform State Laws in 1999. Before Article 9 was adopted, such common law security devices as the pledge, the chattel mortgage, the conditional sale, the trust receipt, and the factor's lien were all governed by different rules. Article 9 of the UCC was intended to provide a unified, comprehensive scheme for all types of *secured transactions*, that is, loans or other transactions secured by collateral put up by the borrower. Article 9 applies to (1) a transaction (regardless of its form) that creates a security interest in personal property or fixtures, including goods; (2) an agricultural lien; (3) a sale of accounts, chattel paper, payment intangibles, or promissory notes; and (4) a consignment.

TERMINOLOGY

Part 1 of Article 9 defines terms. In place of the various common law security devices, the UCC uses the single term *security interest* to signify any interest in personal property or fixtures that is used as collateral to secure payment or the performance of an obligation. The parties to a secured transaction are (1) the *debtor,* that is, the person who owes payment or other performance of the obligation secured, whether or not that person owns or has rights in the collateral; and (2) the *secured party,* that is, the lender, seller, or other person in whose favor there is a security interest. The agreement that creates or provides for a security interest is a *security agreement.*

FORMAL REQUISITES

Part 2 of Article 9 prescribes the formal requisites for creating an enforceable security interest and describes the rights of the parties to a security agreement. If the secured party takes possession of the collateral, an oral agreement is sufficient to create a security interest; otherwise, a security agreement authenticated by the debtor containing a description of the collateral is required. Under the UCC, for a security interest to be enforceable, value must have been given in exchange for it, and the debtor must have rights in the collateral or the power to transfer rights in the collateral. These requirements do not have to be fulfilled in any particular order. When all of the requirements have been met, a security interest is said to have *attached.*

RIGHTS AND REMEDIES

The remainder of Article 9 sets forth the rights of the secured party against other creditors of the debtor; the rules for perfecting a security interest, that is, making it valid against other creditors of the debtor; and the remedies available to a secured party when a debtor defaults.

SCOPE OF ARTICLE 9

Article 9 covers most consensual security interests, but some security interests are outside its scope. The article does not apply to liens on real property. Various state and federal laws preempt the UCC in the areas of ship mortgages, mechanic's liens, and aircraft liens. Notices of security interests in trademarks are commonly filed in the Patent and Trademark Office in addition to being perfected as general intangibles under the UCC. Article 9 does not apply to security interests subject to a landlord's lien, to a lien given by statute or other rule of law for

services or materials, or to a right of setoff. (With a *right of setoff,* one party may automatically deduct amounts due to it from payments due to the other party.) Security interests in securities are governed by Article 8 of the UCC.

 # Security Agreements

A security agreement identifies the parties and the property to be used as collateral. It may also specify the debtor's obligations and the lender's remedies in case of default.

PARTIES TO THE AGREEMENT

Security agreements typically use the UCC terminology to identify the parties. In a loan transaction, the secured party is the lender. The debtor is the borrower, if it owns the collateral or if the owner has authorized it to use the property for collateral. If the third-party owner acts as a guarantor of the borrower's obligation, it may also be referred to as the debtor. (Guaranties are discussed later in this chapter.)

GRANTING CLAUSE

Unless the security interest is a possessory interest (traditionally called a *pledge*), the security agreement must be authenticated by the debtor and must expressly grant a security interest in some specified property. The standard operative words are: "The debtor hereby grants to the secured party a security interest in . . . ." The UCC does not require a precise form, but the collateral must be described. The debtor may authenticate the agreement by signing it or by executing a record that is stored in an electronic or other medium and is retrievable in perceivable form.

DESCRIPTION OF THE COLLATERAL

The description of the collateral need not be specific, as long as it reasonably identifies the property. Loans to finance the purchase of specific property, such as an equipment loan, will typically be secured by the property purchased; the security agreement will contain a specific description of such property.

For example, a working capital loan may be secured by receivables and inventory, with the inventory described as "any and all goods, merchandise, and other personal property, wherever located or in transit, that are held for sale or lease, furnished under any contract of service, or held as raw materials, work in process, supplies, or materials used

E-COMMERCE

or consumed in the debtor's business." Frequently, a secured party will take a security interest in all of the debtor's assets—not only fixed assets, inventory, and receivables but also trademarks, trade names, goodwill, licenses, books, and records. In such cases, the collateral may be described as all tangible and intangible property that, taken together, is intended to preserve the value of the debtor as a going concern.

After-Acquired Property *After-acquired property* is property that the debtor acquires after the execution of the security agreement. After-acquired assets may be included in the security agreement either in addition to, or as replacements of, currently owned assets. A security interest in after-acquired collateral will attach when the debtor acquires rights in the collateral, assuming that the other prerequisites for attachment have previously been met.

Proceeds The UCC provides that, unless otherwise agreed, a security agreement gives the secured party a security interest in the proceeds if the collateral is sold, exchanged, collected, or otherwise disposed of. The security interest is equally effective against cash, accounts, or whatever else is received from the transaction. This feature makes a security interest created under Article 9 a *floating lien*.

DEBTOR'S OBLIGATIONS

The debtor is obligated to repay the debt and to pay interest and related fees, charges, and expenses. In addition, the debtor will have nonmonetary obligations, such as obligations to maintain prescribed standards of financial well-being, measured by net worth, cash flow, and debt coverage (the ratio of debt to equity). These obligations are typically set forth in detail in a loan agreement or a promissory note, although occasionally they are included in a security agreement.

CROSS-COLLATERALIZATION

The collateral for one loan may be used to secure obligations under another loan. This is done by means of a *cross-collateralization* provision—sometimes called a *dragnet clause*—in the security agreement. For example, a lender extending an inventory and receivables line of credit to a borrower may insist that the line be secured not only by inventory and receivables but also by equipment owned by the borrower and already held by the lender as collateral for an equipment loan. Thus, if the lender forecloses on the equipment, any proceeds in excess of the amounts owed under the equipment loan will

be available to pay down the inventory and receivables line of credit. Similarly, if the equipment loan is cross-collateralized with collateral for the inventory and receivables line of credit, any proceeds realized from foreclosure of the inventory and receivables will be available to pay down the equipment loan.

REMEDIES FOR DEFAULT

The remedies described in a security agreement track the rights and procedures set forth in Article 9. After default, the secured party has the right to take possession of the collateral without judicial process if this can be done without breach of the peace. The secured party must then dispose of the collateral at a public or private sale. If there is a surplus from the sale of the collateral, the secured party is required to return it to the debtor. If there is a deficiency, the debtor remains liable for that amount. The proceeds from the sale must be applied in this order: (1) to the reasonable expenses of foreclosure and, if provided for in the agreement, reasonable attorneys' fees and legal expenses; (2) to the satisfaction of the obligations secured; and (3) to the satisfaction of indebtedness secured by a subordinate security interest, if a written demand for such satisfaction is timely received.

Although the UCC establishes a framework for the exercise of the lender's remedies, some details must be provided for by contract. For example, the parties may agree to apply the proceeds of a foreclosure sale to attorneys' fees and legal expenses, or they may agree that the debtor will assemble the collateral and make it available to the secured party at a designated place. All such provisions are subject to the requirement that the secured party's disposition of the collateral must be commercially reasonable. This term is not defined in the UCC, but it is generally interpreted to require conformity with prevailing standards and to prevent one party from taking undue advantage of another. However, the secured party and the debtor are free to fashion a mutually acceptable standard of commercial reasonableness, and security agreements typically contain a description of such standards.

Perfecting *a* Security Interest

To protect its rights in the collateral, a lender must ensure that its security interest is *perfected,* that is, valid against other creditors of the debtor and against a trustee in bankruptcy of the debtor. The UCC does not define perfection; instead, it describes the situations in which an unperfected security interest will be subordinated to the rights of third parties. For example, a security interest is subordinate to the rights of a person who becomes a lien creditor before the security interest is perfected. Subordination to lien creditors means in effect that the security interest is not valid against the debtor's trustee in bankruptcy.

METHODS OF PERFECTION

Security interests can be perfected by taking possession of the collateral, by taking control of the collateral, by filing a financing statement, or automatically.

By Possession A security interest in goods, instruments (other than certificated securities, which are covered by Article 8 of the UCC—see below), negotiable documents, or tangible chattel paper may be perfected by the secured party's taking possession of the collateral. A security interest in money may be perfected only by possession.

By Control A security interest in a deposit account or a letter-of-credit right may be perfected only by control.

By Filing For all types of collateral (other than money, deposit accounts, and letter-of-credit rights), perfection may be accomplished by filing a financing statement. Standard printed forms, known as *UCC-1 forms,* are widely available for this purpose.

Automatic Perfection Some security interests require neither possession nor filing for perfection. For example, a *purchase-money security interest* in consumer goods (created when the seller of consumer goods lends the buyer the money with which to buy them) is automatically perfected. Under certain circumstances, a security interest in a certificated security or an instrument is temporarily perfected without filing or possession. Automatic perfection is of limited duration, however, and it must be followed by possession or filing if perfection is to survive for a longer period.

Uncertificated Securities The once fundamental distinction between possessory and nonpossessory security interests became blurred by the introduction of uncertificated, or book-entry, securities. Article 8 of the UCC, which governs investment securities, was revised in 1977 to provide for the creation and perfection of security interests in certificated and uncertificated securities. These topics were then removed from Article 9, except for cross references to the applicable sections of Article 8.

FILING PROCEDURE

The purpose of perfection by filing is to provide notice "to the world" that assets of one person are subject to the security interest of another. If a security interest is not perfected by possession, the collateral remains in the debtor's possession and control. This occurs, for example, when the collateral is intangible (such as accounts), or when possession by the secured party is impractical (as in the case of inventory). A centralized system gives effective public notice that property in the possession and under the apparent control of the debtor is actually subject to the rights of another. The filing system enables a prospective creditor to determine whether in claiming its rights to such assets it will be competing with other creditors or with a trustee in bankruptcy. It also enables a purchaser of goods to determine whether the seller's creditors have any claims against the goods. (Under certain circumstances, a purchaser of goods is protected from liens on the goods created by the seller; for example, consumers are protected from inventory liens on a seller's goods.)

What to File To perfect a nonpossessory security interest in personal property, a financing statement must be filed. The financing statement merely gives notice that a financing transaction is being or is about to be entered into but does not describe the transaction. It need contain only the names of the debtor and secured party, and an indication of the collateral in which a security interest has been or may be granted. If a financing statement covers crops grown or to be grown or goods that are or are to become fixtures, the UCC also requires a legal description of the land concerned.

Where to File The financing statement must be filed in the office of the secretary of state in the state where the debtor is located. A security interest in collateral closely associated with real property, such as fixtures, growing crops, timber, or minerals, must be filed in the state where the real property is located, in the office in which a mortgage on real estate would be recorded; this is usually the county recorder's office in the county where the real property is located.

When to File A financing statement may be filed in advance of the transaction or the security agreement. This is important because, under the UCC, a security interest is perfected when the statement is filed. Thus, the first secured party to file has priority over other parties with security interests in the same debtor's property, unless special priority rules apply, as in the case of purchase-money security interests.

Equipment Leasing

To conserve its working capital, a company may decide to lease, rather than purchase, the equipment it needs. Leasing sometimes offers an attractive alternative to borrowing funds to purchase the equipment because a leasing company may provide more lenient terms than a bank or other lender. A leasing company may also be willing to accept a greater credit risk than a bank, but it will probably charge higher interest rates as a result. A newer enterprise may sometimes be asked for a security deposit or personal guaranty in connection with an equipment lease.

When equipment is leased, three parties are involved: the seller of the equipment, the leasing company, and the user of the equipment. The user determines its needs and negotiates a purchase price for the equipment, then engages a leasing company to purchase the equipment and lease it to the user. The manufacturer or seller of the equipment may lease it to the user, either directly or through a leasing subsidiary, but third-party leasing companies are more frequently used.

DIFFERENCES FROM TRUE LEASE

An equipment lease that serves the purpose of financing is known as a *finance lease*. A finance-lease agreement is a lengthy document that differs from a true lease in several ways. It gives the lessor some degree of control over the use, alteration, and location of the equipment. It prohibits major changes in the user's business operations without the consent of the lessor, unless the lessee first repays the lessor in full. The lessee is required to keep the equipment in good repair and to insure it against loss or damage. The lessor is given a security interest in the equipment, and it may foreclose and sell the equipment in the event of default by the user. In addition to the terms of the lease agreement, the rights and remedies of the lessor and lessee are governed by Article 9 of the UCC

For accounting purposes, a finance lease is treated as a long-term debt of the lessee, which is deemed to own the leased equipment; the lessee may therefore enjoy tax benefits such as depreciation deductions. The lessee may have the right to purchase the equipment at the end of the lease term. In this case, the lease will often provide that the purchase price will be the fair market value of the equipment at that time.

Guaranties

A *guaranty* is an undertaking by one person, the *guarantor,* to become liable for the obligation of another person, the *primary debtor.* A guaranty allows the party that is to receive payment to look to the guarantor in the event the primary debtor fails to pay. The guarantor can be an individual, a corporation, a partnership, a limited liability company, or any other type of entity willing to lend its credit support to another's obligation. The most common form of guaranty is a guaranty that indebtedness or other payment obligations of another will be paid when due. A less common form is a guaranty that specified nonpayment obligations will be performed; this is sometimes referred to as a *guaranty of performance.* The type of guaranty and the duties of the guarantor will be determined by the language of the guaranty instrument. The statute of frauds requires that a guaranty be in writing to be enforceable.

Lenders often require a guaranty when a credit analysis indicates that the borrower's credit is not sufficient to support the requested loan. The lender will then evaluate the credit of each guarantor and decide whether to make the loan based on the combined credit of the borrower and the guarantors. Also, a lender may require guaranties from officers, directors, or shareholders of a borrower, especially when the borrower is a closely held corporation. To protect its position under a guaranty, a lender may require that the guarantor refrain from incurring additional debt or granting liens on its assets.

PAYMENT VERSUS COLLECTION

Under a *guaranty of payment,* the guarantor's obligation to pay the lender is triggered, immediately and automatically, when the primary debtor fails to make a payment when due. In contrast, under a *guaranty of collection,* the guarantor becomes obliged to pay only after the lender has attempted unsuccessfully to collect the amount due from the primary debtor. With a collection guaranty, the lender generally must commence a lawsuit and take other steps to collect a debt before calling on the guarantor to pay (unless the primary debtor is insolvent or is otherwise clearly unable to pay). Enforcing collection guaranties is so cumbersome and expensive that lenders almost always require payment guaranties.

LIMITED VERSUS UNLIMITED

A guarantor's liability under a guaranty may be either limited or unlimited. With a *limited guaranty,* the maximum amount of the guarantor's liability is expressly stated in the guaranty instrument. Usually, this maximum is a specific dollar amount, although it can be expressed in other ways, such as a percentage of the primary debtor's total indebtedness to the lender.

RESTRICTED VERSUS CONTINUING

A *restricted guaranty* is enforceable only with respect to a specified transaction or series of transactions. A guaranty that covers all future obligations of the primary debtor to the lender is referred to as a *continuing guaranty*. The objective of the continuing guaranty is to make the guarantor liable for any debt incurred at any time by the primary debtor, regardless of whether the debt was contemplated at the time the guaranty was entered into. Lenders naturally favor continuing guaranties over restricted guaranties.

Revocation In many jurisdictions, a continuing guaranty may be revoked by the guarantor during his or her lifetime. Such a revocation prevents the guarantor from becoming liable for debts incurred by the primary debtor in connection with transactions not yet entered into. The death of the guarantor also revokes a guaranty, but the guarantor's estate remains liable for debts incurred by the primary debtor prior to the guarantor's death.

Discharging the Guarantor A lender that makes a guaranteed loan must avoid any actions that would have the effect of discharging the guarantor, such as altering the terms of the agreement with the primary debtor (for example, increasing the interest rate on the loan or the amount of the scheduled payments), extending the time for payment of the loan or renewing the indebtedness, or releasing or impairing the lender's rights with respect to collateral pledged by the primary debtor. A well-drafted guaranty can alleviate some of these potential pitfalls. The best approach, however, is for the lender to obtain the consent of the guarantor before making any material change to the arrangement with the primary debtor.

GUARANTIES VERSUS LETTERS OF CREDIT

As explained in Chapter 13, a standby letter of credit can often be used in place of a guaranty. Uniform standards for standby letters of credit can be incorporated into the letter of credit by reference to the International Chamber of Commerce's International Standby Practices (ISP98).[3]

FRAUDULENT CONVEYANCES

A guaranty may be attacked as a fraudulent conveyance under the federal Bankruptcy Code or state fraudulent transfer statutes. In a *fraudulent conveyance,* assets are directly or indirectly transferred to a third party so as to hinder, delay, or defraud creditors by putting the assets out of their reach; the conveyance is fraudulent whether the transfer was made with actual intent to thwart the creditors or merely has that effect. A guaranty may be a fraudulent conveyance if it confers no benefit on the guarantor but makes the guarantor's assets unavailable to creditors other than the party receiving the guaranty. For example, if the guarantor did not receive fair value in exchange for giving its guaranty and was insolvent at the time it gave its guaranty, or if the guarantor was rendered insolvent or left with unreasonably small capital as a result of giving its guaranty, the party receiving the guaranty may have an unfair advantage over other creditors of the guarantor. In such a case, the other creditors would be able to invalidate the guaranty. A lender must carefully examine these issues before accepting a guaranty.

Upstream Guaranty With an *upstream guaranty,* subsidiaries guarantee the parent company's debt or pledge their assets as security for the parent's debt. An upstream guaranty may be found fraudulent if the guarantor received none of the loan proceeds or received an inadequate amount compared to the liability it incurred. Other creditors of the subsidiary (and the subsidiary's minority shareholders, if the subsidiary is less than wholly owned by the parent) may claim that the lender, as the beneficiary of the guaranty, received an unfair advantage at the other creditors' expense.

Leveraged Buyouts Leveraged buyouts, in which the acquisition of a company is financed largely through debt, may be subject to attack as fraudulent conveyances. For example, if a leveraged buyout is structured so that a newly formed corporation will acquire the stock of the target company using proceeds from a loan, the lender's source of repayment will be dividends paid from the target company to the borrower. To ensure that such funds will be available, the lender may require the target company to give a guaranty, which may or may not be secured by the target's assets. Alternatively, the lender may require a merger between the target company and the borrower. Such guaranties or mergers will be invalidated if the target company both (1) failed to receive a reasonably equivalent value and (2) was left insolvent, with assets that were unreasonably small in relation to its business, or with insufficient working capital.

PREFERENCES

A transfer from a debtor to an outsider creditor that results in a reduction in the guaranty liability of an insolvent insider may be a voidable preference if it occurs

3. ICC Publication No. 590 (1998).

within one year of the date the insider files bankruptcy.[4] For example, suppose that on February 1, 2000, ABC Corporation borrows $1 million from Friendly Bank and that Henri-Claude, a major shareholder of ABC Corporation, guarantees the loan. ABC Corporation makes a $100,000 payment to Friendly Bank on March 1, 2001. On October 1, 2001, Henri-Claude files bankruptcy. Henri-Claude's creditors will be able to set aside the $100,000 payment because it reduced his guarantor liability dollar for dollar and thereby preferred Friendly Bank by paying off part of his debt to the bank with funds not available to his other creditors.

Subordination

A *debt subordination* is an agreement whereby one or more creditors of a common debtor agree to defer payment of their claims until another creditor of the same debtor is fully paid. The indebtedness that is subordinated under the agreement is referred to as the subordinated or *junior debt*. The indebtedness that benefits from the subordination is called the *senior debt*.

The primary purpose of a debt subordination is to protect the senior creditor in the event of the debtor's insolvency. As long as the debtor is solvent, both the junior debt holder and the senior debt holder can expect to be paid. If the debtor becomes insolvent, there will be insufficient assets to satisfy all of its creditors. In such circumstances, creditors can expect to receive only a partial payment on their claims. In subordinating its claim, the holder of the junior debt agrees to yield its right of payment to the senior creditor until the senior creditor has been paid in full.

Corporations frequently use subordinated debt as a means of raising capital. The use of subordinated notes or subordinated debentures (long-term secured bonds) may have certain advantages over equity financing. For example, the interest payable on subordinated debt will be tax-deductible. In addition, the interest rate payable on subordinated debt is often less than the dividend rate that would have to be offered on comparable preferred stock.

INDEBTEDNESS TO INSIDERS

When a borrower seeks a short-term loan from a bank or other commercial lender, the lender will often require that the borrower's indebtedness to insiders, such as officers, directors, and shareholders, be subordinated. This

is especially the case when the borrower is a closely held corporation and the insider debt is significant in relation to the amount of the lender's loans.

LIEN SUBORDINATION

A *lien subordination* is an agreement between two secured creditors whose respective security interests, liens, or mortgages attach to the same property. The subordinating party agrees that the lien of the other creditor will have priority notwithstanding the relative priorities that the parties' liens would otherwise have under applicable law. Unlike debt subordination, a lien subordination does not limit the right of the subordinating party to accept payment from the debtor. Instead, the lien subordination has the effect of limiting the subordinating party's recourse to the collateral until the prior secured party's claim has been satisfied.

EQUITABLE SUBORDINATION

A creditor's claim may be involuntarily postponed through application of the doctrine of *equitable subordination*. This doctrine was developed in bankruptcy law to prevent one creditor, through fraud or other wrongful conduct, from increasing its recovery at the expense of other creditors of the same debtor. The court will order that the creditor that acted wrongfully receive no payment from the debtor until the claims of all other creditors have been fully paid.

Business Bankruptcies

There are two major types of business bankruptcies: liquidation under Chapter 7 and reorganization under Chapter 11. The good faith requirements for bankruptcy are discussed in this section. Later sections examine the pros and cons of filing bankruptcy under Chapters 7 and 11 from the perspectives of the debtor and the creditors, and discuss out-of-court resolutions, called workouts.

GOOD FAITH REQUIREMENTS

The bankruptcy law[5] specifically authorizes the court to convert a case under Chapter 11 to a case under Chapter 7 or to dismiss a case for cause. The following case addressed the propriety of a financially healthy company's decision to file for Chapter 11 protection in the face of civil antitrust litigation.

---

4. *See, e.g.,* Levit v. Ingersoll Rand Fin. Corp. (*In re* V.N. Deprizio Constr. Co.), 874 F.2d 1186 (7th Cir. 1989).

5. 11 U.S.C. § 1112(b).

CASE 26.1

In re **SGL Carbon Corp.**
*United States Court of
Appeals for the Third Circuit
200 F.3d 154
(3d Cir. 1999).*

In the Language of the Court

FACTS SGL Carbon manufactures and sells graphite electrodes used in steel production and is part of the SGL Carbon Group. In 1997, the U.S. Department of Justice commenced an investigation of alleged price-fixing by graphite electrode manufacturers, including the SGL Carbon Group.

In June 1998, SGL Carbon's German parent SGL AG recorded a charge in deutschmarks of approximately $240 million as its "best estimate" of the SGL Carbon Group's potential liability in the criminal and civil antitrust litigation. On December 16, 1998, at the direction of SGL AG, SGL Carbon filed a voluntary Chapter 11 bankruptcy petition in the U.S. District Court for Delaware. In its Disclosure Statement, in a section addressing "Factors Leading to [the] Chapter 11 Filing," SGL Carbon discussed only the antitrust litigation. The bankruptcy filing contained a proposed reorganization plan under which only one type of creditor would be required to accept less than full cash payment for its account, namely the antitrust plaintiffs that obtained judgments against SGL Carbon. Under the plan, potential antitrust judgment creditors would receive credits against future purchases of SGL Carbon's product valid for thirty months following the plan's confirmation. The proposed plan also barred any claimant from bringing an action against SGL Carbon's affiliates, including its parent SGL AG, "based on, relating to, arising out of, or in any way connected with" their claims against SGL Carbon.

On December 17, in a press release, SGL Carbon explained that it had filed for bankruptcy "to protect itself against excessive demands made by plaintiffs in civil antitrust litigation and in order to achieve an expeditious resolution of the claims against it." In the press release, Wayne T. Burgess, SGL Carbon's president, stated: "SGL Carbon Corporation is financially healthy. . . . We expect to continue our normal business operations."

ISSUE PRESENTED May a Chapter 11 petition be dismissed if it is not filed in good faith? What constitutes bad faith?

OPINION SCIRICA, J., writing for the U.S. Court of Appeals for the Third Circuit:

At the time SGL Carbon filed its Chapter 11 petition, the $240 million reserve was in place and untouched.

The Official Committee of Unsecured Creditors (eight of nine members of which were antitrust plaintiffs) filed a motion to dismiss SGL Carbon's bankruptcy petition on the grounds that it was a "litigation tactic designed to frustrate the prosecution of the civil antitrust claims against SGL Carbon and preserve its equity from those claims."

The threshold issue is whether Chapter 11 petitions may be dismissed for "cause" under 11 U.S.C. § 1112(b) if not filed in good faith. . . .

Four factors guide our adoption of a good faith standard—the permissive language of § 112(b), viewed in light of its legislative history; the decisions of our sister courts of appeals; the equitable nature of bankruptcy; and the purposes underpinning Chapter 11. [The Fifth, Sixth, Eighth, Ninth, and Eleventh Circuits have held that the absence of good faith constitutes cause to dismiss a Chapter 11 petition. The Third Circuit quoted with approval an opinion from the Fifth Circuit[6] holding that the "requirement of good faith prevents abuse of the bankruptcy process by debtors whose overriding motive is to delay creditors without benefiting them in any way. . . ."]

We conclude a Chapter 11 petition is subject to dismissal for "cause" under 11 U.S.C. § 1112(b) unless it is filed in good faith.

6. Little Creek Dev. Co. v. Commonwealth Mortgage Corp. (*In re* Little Creek Dev. Co.), 779 F.2d 1068, 1072 (5th Cir. 1986).

(Continued)

(Case 26.1 continued)

Having determined that § 1112(b) imposes a good-faith requirement . . . , we consider whether SGL Carbon's Chapter 11 petition was filed in good faith.

...

[T]he District Court found SGL Carbon's Chapter 11 petition was filed in good faith for two reasons: first, because the distractions caused by the antitrust litigation "posed a serious threat to [SGL Carbon's] continued successful operations," and second, because the litigation might result in a judgment that could cause the company "financial and operational ruin," SGL was required to file when it did. . . . [W]e believe each of these findings of fact was clearly erroneous. . . .

Although there is some evidence that defending against the antitrust litigation occupied some officers' time, there is no evidence this "distraction" posed a "serious threat" to the company's operational well being. . . .

There is no evidence that the possible antitrust judgments might force SGL Carbon out of business. . . .

Whether or not SGL Carbon faces a potentially crippling antitrust judgment, it is incorrect to conclude it had to file when it did. As noted, SGL Carbon faces no immediate financial difficulty. All the evidence shows that management repeatedly asserted the company was financially healthy at the time of the filing. . . . [A] debtor need not be insolvent before filing for bankruptcy protection. . . .

...

We do not hold that a company cannot file a valid Chapter 11 petition until after a massive judgment has been entered against it. Courts have allowed companies to seek the protections of bankruptcy when faced with pending litigation that posed a serious threat to the companies' long-term viability. In those cases, however, debtors experienced serious financial and/or managerial difficulties at the time of filing. . . .

...

[S]everal cases hold that a Chapter 11 petition is not filed in good faith unless it serves a valid reorganizational purpose. . . .

Courts . . . have consistently dismissed Chapter 11 petitions filed by financially healthy companies with no need to reorganize under the protection of Chapter 11. . . .

The absence of a valid reorganizational purpose and the consequent lack of good faith by SGL Carbon is evident here. SGL Carbon's financial disclosure documents give no indication the company needed to reorganize under Chapter 11 protection. Prior to filing, SGL Carbon had assets of $400 million and liabilities of only $276 million, or a net worth of $124 million. In addition, there is no evidence that SGL Carbon had difficult meeting its debts as they came due, that it had any overdue debts, or that it had defaulted on any debts. Nor is there any evidence that SGL had any difficulty raising or borrowing money, or otherwise had impaired access to the capital markets.

The [reorganization] plan's differing treatment of creditors suggests SGL Carbon's petition was not filed to reorganize the company but rather to put pressure on antitrust plaintiffs to accept the company's settlement terms.

RESULT SGL Carbon's bankruptcy petition was dismissed.

QUESTIONS

1. Texaco filed for bankruptcy after a $10.5 billion judgment was rendered against it in its litigation with Pennzoil over the acquisition of Getty Oil (this is the subject of the

(Continued)

(Case 26.1 continued)

"Inside Story" in Chapter 7). How would you distinguish what Texaco successfully did from what SGL Carbon tried to do?

2. Would pending litigation ever provide a good faith reason for filing for bankruptcy?

Chapter 7 Liquidations

A bankruptcy case is initiated by filing a petition. The filing of a bankruptcy petition automatically creates a *bankruptcy estate,* which consists of virtually all the debtor's existing assets. A trustee is appointed to administer the estate. In a Chapter 7 bankruptcy, sometimes called a *straight bankruptcy,* the trustee liquidates the estate and distributes the proceeds, first to secured creditors (to the extent of their collateral) and then in a prescribed order and pro rata within each level. The unencumbered funds are applied in this order: (1) to pay priority claims, such as bankruptcy administrative expenses, wages or benefits up to $2,000 per employee, consumer deposits up to $900, and most unsecured taxes; (2) to pay general unsecured creditors (with timely filed claims coming before tardy ones); (3) to pay noncompensatory fines or penalties; and (4) to pay legal interest on unsecured claims. In practice, the estate is rarely adequate to pay unsecured creditors even fifty cents on the dollar; no-asset cases are quite common.

INDIVIDUAL DEBTORS

Individual debtors normally are *discharged*—that is, relieved—from bankruptcy (also called prepetition) obligations, except for nondischargeable debts such as (1) taxes; (2) educational loans (unless repayment would constitute an undue hardship); (3) spousal or child support; (4) fines or penalties; (5) drunk-driving liabilities; and (6) claims arising from fraud, theft, or willful and malicious injury. Punitive damages awarded on account of the debtor's fraudulent acquisition of money, property, services, or credit are also nondischargeable.[7]

In assessing undue hardship in the student loan context, the most widely used criteria are (1) whether the debtor can maintain a minimal standard of living for most of the loan repayment period, given his or her current income and expenses; and (2) whether the debtor has made good faith repayment efforts. Other relevant considerations include the amount of the debt, the accu-

mulation of interest, and the debtor's claimed expenses and current standard of living. A bankruptcy court may partially discharge student loans when full repayment would impose undue hardship on a debtor who could nonetheless manage partial payment.

A Chapter 7 discharge is not available to debtors who have received a discharge in a bankruptcy filed in the preceding six years. It will also be denied if the debtor has mistreated his or her creditors or abused the system, such as by fraudulently transferring or concealing property, destroying or falsifying financial information, or disobeying lawful court orders. (Unlike in Chapter 7, a debtor's prior misconduct or discharge within the past six years will not bar Chapter 13 discharge.)

Under Chapter 7, individuals are permitted to retain exempt property. *Exempt property,* which is excluded from the bankruptcy estate, is intended to provide for the individual's future needs and generally includes such things as a homestead, one or more motor vehicles, household or personal items, tools of the debtor's trade, health aids, personal-injury awards, alimony or support payments, disability or retirement benefits (including individual retirement accounts), life insurance or annuities, and some special deposits or cash. Available exemptions vary from state to state and are usually limited to a maximum dollar amount or by a necessity standard.

The Bankruptcy Code permits debtors to nullify involuntary liens that impair their allowable exemptions. They can even invalidate consensual liens on most household items, tools of the trade, or health aids, unless the secured creditor financed the debtor's purchase of the property or was given possession of it. To take full advantage of the exemptions, debtors often convert assets from nonexempt to exempt forms before filing their bankruptcy cases. They must be careful not to take steps that could be considered fraudulent, however, because fraudulent conduct could jeopardize the right to discharge existing debts.

An individual who has filed under Chapter 7 can enter into a contract with a creditor (a *reaffirmation agreement*), whereby the debtor agrees to repay a debt even though the debt would otherwise be discharged in the debtor's bankruptcy case. The creditor must file the reaffirmation agreement with the bankruptcy court, which

---

7. Cohen v. de la Cruz, 523 U.S. 213 (1998).

"The sharp quills protect me from creditors."

has the power to disapprove the agreement if the court finds that it is not in the debtor's best interests.

From 1985 to 1997, Sears, Roebuck & Company unlawfully dunned more than 200,000 consumers who had outstanding debt on Sears credit cards and had filed for bankruptcy protection. Sears persuaded them to sign reaffirmation agreements but failed to file the agreements with the bankruptcy courts. In June 1997, Sears entered into a settlement with the Federal Trade Commission, whereby it agreed to refund $100 million to consumers for its improper credit card collection practices.[8] Sears also agreed to write off the unpaid portion of the balances on the invalid reaffirmation agreements.[9]

There is a split in the circuit courts of appeals as to whether an individual debtor who has filed for protection under Chapter 7 may retain property that secures a loan if the debtor remains current on the loan payments without having to reaffirm the debt. The U.S. Court of Appeals for the Ninth Circuit held that a Chapter 7 debtor who was current on his car payments could retain a car financed by a credit union by making the loan payments specified in the loan agreement without having to reaffirm the debt.[10] The Second, Fourth, and Tenth Circuits reached the same result. In contrast, the Fifth, Seventh, and Eleventh Circuits have held that once a debtor decides to retain rather than surrender the property, the debtor must claim an exemption, redeem the property by paying off the debt, or reaffirm the debt.

8. Robert Berner & Bruce Ingersoll, *Sears to Repay Card Holders $100 Million*, WALL ST. J., June 5, 1997, at A3.
9. The Seventh Circuit has held that there is no private right of action for damages for a creditor's failure to file debt discharge agreements with the bankruptcy court. Cox v. Zale Delaware, Inc., 239 F.3d 910 (7th Cir. 2001).

10. McClellan Fed. Credit Union v. Parker (*In re* Parker), 139 F.3d 668 (9th Cir. 1998).

NONINDIVIDUAL DEBTORS

Chapter 7 does not provide a discharge for corporations, partnerships, or similar business entities. Once their assets are sold, these debtors essentially become defunct shells whose unpaid obligations have no significance. Thus, from the vantage point of the debtor firm's management, the only virtue of a liquidation may be that the task of selling property and paying creditors falls to a trustee. The principals of closely held companies are often better advised to avoid bankruptcy and to handle these chores themselves. Rather than adhering to the pro rata distribution model, they may wish to prefer some creditors by channeling funds first to those who are most likely to pursue them personally (such as holders of guaranties). Also, they may not want to expose earlier transactions (such as preferential payments) to scrutiny by a trustee, who can become a more troublesome foe than any of the company's creditors by invoking the avoiding powers discussed below.

 Consumer Bankruptcy *under* Chapter 13

Chapter 13 (consumer bankruptcy) of the Bankruptcy Code deals with adjustments to the debt of an individual or married couple with regular income. Although an individual may also be the subject of a Chapter 7 liquidation or a Chapter 11 reorganization, only individuals or small proprietorships are eligible under Chapter 13.

CHAPTER 13 REQUIREMENTS

Individuals with regular income, including wage earners and individuals engaged in business, may qualify for Chapter 13 status if their unsecured debts do not exceed $100,000 and their secured debts do not exceed $350,000. Chapter 13 is similar to a reorganization in that it provides for a plan for repaying creditors.

Chapter 13 plans can be proposed only by debtors and usually are quite simple. The plan ordinarily allows the debtor to retain all of his or her assets, not just those that would be exempt under Chapter 7. However, his or her future disposable income (which would be the debtor's to keep in a Chapter 7 or 11 bankruptcy) must be paid to a disbursing trustee for the next three to five years. Creditors holding claims secured by a mortgage, deed of trust, or security interest are entitled to the equivalent of the present value of their lien rights, except that Chapter 13 plans cannot modify home mortgage loans unless they provide for payments to cure default.

Unlike under Chapter 11, creditors do not vote on Chapter 13 plans. They can, however, object to confirmation if the plan is proposed in bad faith, is not feasible, or offers them less than they would get in a Chapter 7 liquidation.

A Chapter 13 plan may be either a composition plan or an extension plan. In a *composition plan,* creditors receive a percentage of the indebtedness, and the debtor is discharged of the remaining obligation, meaning that the debtor is no longer legally liable for that amount. In an *extension plan,* creditors receive the entire indebtedness, but the period for payment is extended beyond the original due date.

After completing all plan payments, the debtor obtains a Chapter 13 discharge. An earlier discharge may be granted in hardship cases if the creditors have received at least as much as they would get under Chapter 7. Apart from the hardship situation, this fresh start (sometimes called *super discharge*) will extinguish otherwise nondischargeable debts (such as claims for fraud, theft, willful and malicious injury, or drunk driving), but not spousal or child support.

ADVANTAGES OF CHAPTER 13

Chapter 13 has many advantages for overextended consumers. For example, the filing of a bankruptcy petition stops all creditor collection activity other than the filing of a claim in the bankruptcy proceeding. In addition, unlike in a Chapter 7 liquidation, a Chapter 13 debtor does not surrender any assets. A good faith effort to pay creditors can preserve goodwill and future credit prospects. Unfortunately, Chapter 13 debtors are often unable to make the payments outlined in their plan and eventually convert from Chapter 13 to Chapter 7. After conversion, the debtor's nonexempt property is liquidated, and the debtor receives a Chapter 7 discharge.

 Consumer Bankruptcy Reform

In 2001, the Bankruptcy Abuse Prevention and Consumer Protection Act of 2001 (BAPCPA H.R. 333 and S. 420), which would represent the most sweeping changes in the bankruptcy code in twenty years, was passed by both houses of Congress. The legislation was virtually the same as the Gekas–Grassley Bankruptcy Reform Act of 2000, which was passed by the House and Senate and then pocket vetoed by President Bill Clinton at the end of 2000.

The BAPCPA is designed to reduce the number of individual bankruptcy filings and balance the needs of both debtors and creditors in contrast to the existing law, which favored debtors. The bill establishes a flexible formula that will allow judges to channel debtors who are capable of repaying their debt to file under Chapter 13, which requires some repayment to creditors, rather than Chapter 7, which essentially erases a consumer's debt. The bill was prompted in part by a study that estimated that financial losses resulting from bankruptcy filings exceeded $44 billion in 1997.[11] President Clinton vetoed the bill because he said it was unfair to moderate-income debtors while providing protection, such as homestead exemptions for lavish homes, for wealthy individuals.[12]

Although President George W. Bush has supported bankruptcy reform and appeared likely to sign the BAPCPA into law, the reform effort appeared to have stalled as of March 2001 when the Senate approved amendments to the original bill that would limit the homestead exemption to $125,000.[13] While governor of Texas, Bush voiced strong opposition to any limits on the unlimited homestead exemptions provided by several states, including Texas and Florida.

Chapter 11 Reorganizations

Chapter 11 is designed for reorganizing troubled businesses, from single-asset limited partnerships and joint ventures (such as Dow Corning, manufacturer of silicon breast implants) to huge publicly held corporations, such as the oil giant Texaco, the pharmaceutical manufacturer A.H. Robins, the retailer Federated Department Stores, and the building materials supplier Johns–Manville. The treatment of the debtor's creditors and holders of ownership interests and the future of its business are set forth in a plan developed by one or more of the parties. If the plan meets the statutory requirements and is confirmed by the court, it becomes a master contract that redefines the legal relationships among all who have claims against (or interests in) the debtor; it binds even those who do not consent to its terms.

THE PLAN

All plans divide claims and equity interests into separate classes according to their legal attributes. For example, lienholders' claims are classified by collateral and rank

11. *House, Senate Reintroduce Bankruptcy Reform Bill,* CARD NEWS, Feb. 7, 2001.
12. *Legislation to Overhaul Laws on Bankruptcy Dies as President Fails to Sign It,* N.Y. TIMES, Dec. 20, 2000, at 32.
13. *Senate Passes Bankruptcy Bill with Controversial Homestead Cap,* 69 U.S.L.W. 2558 (Mar. 20, 2001).

(often resulting in one claim per class, because each lien confers distinct rights and usually secures only one claim). Relevant priority claims (such as wages or consumer deposits) are put into discrete classes, separate from general unsecured claims. Holders of preferred shares are grouped separately from common shareholders.

A plan must also prescribe treatment for the claims and interests in each class. Some plans simply extend the time for repaying debts; others reduce the amounts payable. A reduction in the amount payable is known as a *composition*. In many cases, creditors exchange all or part of their claims for preferred or common stock or other ownership interests in the business, thereby diluting or extinguishing the rights of the prebankruptcy shareholders. Sometimes, the entire business will be sold free of claims, with creditors dividing the sale proceeds. A plan can even call for liquidation and distribution comparable to the Chapter 7 process. Unless they agree otherwise, priority claimants usually are entitled to full payment when the plan becomes effective, except that prepetition unsecured taxes may be paid in installments over six years from the assessment date, with interest at the market rate.

In addition, the plan must explain the intended means for its execution. Plans often provide for payments from cash on hand, future earnings, asset sales, new capital contributions, or some combination of sources.

CONFIRMATION

To be confirmed, a plan must meet numerous statutory requirements. Some of the less technical requirements are discussed below.

Feasibility The plan must be feasible. There is no point in replacing the debtor's existing obligations with a new set of obligations that the debtor cannot meet.

Best Interests of Creditors Unless accepted unanimously, the plan must pass the *best interests of creditors test*. Dissenters must be given a bundle of rights with a current value at least as great as the distribution they would receive through a Chapter 7 liquidation.

Reorganization Bonus It should be relatively easy to satisfy the fixed minimum standards for confirmation if the business has significant value as a going concern. In that case, the viability of a plan often turns on how it proposes to split what might be labeled the reorganization bonus. This bonus or premium is the difference between the aggregate liquidation value of the assets and the worth of the business as an operating whole. Ordinarily, the bonus must be distributed according to existing priorities. Unless a creditor class accepts less favorable treatment, each class is paid fully before any distribution is made to any junior class. Similarly, creditors are paid in full (with postconfirmation interest) before equity holders receive anything.

Disclosure Statement Before deciding whether to accept the plan, creditors and shareholders are entitled to receive a disclosure statement that the court has found contains adequate information to enable them to make an informed judgment. This disclosure process largely displaces otherwise applicable laws and regulations governing the issuance and sale of securities, including the requirements of the Securities Act of 1933, described in Chapter 24.

Acceptance A creditor class accepts the plan if the affirmative ballots constitute a simple majority and represent two-thirds of the total claim amounts of those voting. An equity class accepts if the favorable ballots represent two-thirds of the voted interests.

Impaired Claims If a plan impairs any class of claims, it cannot be confirmed unless at least one impaired class accepts it (excluding favorable votes cast by insiders). Claims are considered *impaired* if the plan does not provide for full cash payment on its effective date and if it alters the creditors' legal, equitable, or contractual rights in any way (except by curing defaults and reinstating the maturity of the claim).

If the basic requirements discussed above are met and all impaired classes accept the plan, the plan should be confirmed.

CRAMDOWN CONFIRMATION

Though rejected by a class, the plan can still be confirmed by a *cramdown,* that is, confirmed over the objections of creditors. A cramdown can occur, however,

only if the court finds that the plan does not discriminate unfairly and that it is fair and equitable. Although both phrases have technical meanings that are open to interpretation, the phrase "fair and equitable" is more frequently the subject of debate. If the rejecting class consists of secured claims, the plan ordinarily can be found fair and equitable only if creditors will retain their liens until they receive full payment in cash of the secured claims. The cash payments must have a present value at least as great as the present value of the collateral. If the debtor elects to retain and use the creditor's collateral, the value of the collateral (and thus the secured claim) is the replacement value, that is, what the debtor would have to pay for comparable property.[14] For other creditors and equity holders, the plan will be considered fair and equitable only if no class junior to the naysayers will receive anything under the plan or if the rejecting class is to receive value equivalent to immediate payment in full.

Thus, to cram down a plan that would distribute stock in satisfaction of claims, the proponent must show that the stock will neither overpay nor underpay those who receive it. The value of the stock turns on the going-concern value of the business, which is often a controversial issue. When classes have not accepted a debt-for-stock plan, the confirmation hearing can easily become a battle among expert witnesses arguing over whether higher or lower multiples or multipliers should be used to capitalize the reorganized debtor's expected earnings, which are themselves subject to competing projections.

In the following case, the U.S. Supreme Court considered whether former equity holders could, upon payment of new value, be granted the exclusive right to buy equity in the reorganized venture.

14. Associates Commercial Corp. v. Rash, 520 U.S. 953 (1997).

A CASE IN POINT

CASE 26.2

Bank of America National Trust & Savings Association v. 203 North Lasalle Street Partnership
Supreme Court of the United States
526 U.S. 434 (1999).

Summary

FACTS Bank of America National Trust and Savings Association was the major creditor of the debtor, 203 North LaSalle Street Partnership, an Illinois real estate limited partnership. The value of the partnership property mortgaged to the bank was less than the balance due, leaving the bank with an unsecured deficiency of $38.5 million. The partnership sought to cram down over the bank's objection a plan whereby (1) the bank's $38.5 million unsecured deficiency claim would be discharged for an estimated 16 percent of its present value; and (2) certain former partners of the partnership would contribute $6.125 million in new capital, over the course of five years, in exchange for the partnership's entire ownership of the reorganized debtor. The old equity holders were the only ones given the right to contribute new capital in exchange for equity.

(Continued)

(Case 26.2 continued)

ISSUE PRESENTED May a debtor's prebankruptcy equity holders, over the objection of a senior class of impaired creditors, contribute new capital and receive ownership interests in the reorganized equity, when that opportunity is given exclusively to the old equity holders under a plan adopted without consideration of alternatives?

SUMMARY OF OPINION The U.S. Supreme Court began by explaining that the objection of an impaired creditor class may be overridden only if the plan is fair and equitable. If the claims of the dissenting creditors are not paid in full, then a plan may be found to be "fair and equitable" only if the holder of any claim or interest that is junior to the claims of the impaired unsecured class will not receive or retain any property "on account of such junior claim or interest."[15] The Court characterized this requirement as the "core" of the *absolute priority rule.*

The Court rejected as "beset with troubles" the partnership's argument that property is received or retained "on account of" a junior interest only if the property was in exchange for the prior interest, without any significant new contribution. It instead concluded that "the better reading of subsection (b)(2)(b)(ii) recognizes that a causal relationship between holding the prior claim or interest and receiving or retaining property is what activates the absolute priority rule." At the same time, it criticized the "starchy position" advanced by the government, as *amicus curiae,* that an old equity holder simply cannot take any property under a plan if creditors are not paid in full, reasoning that a truly full-value transaction, whereby the old equity holders pay full value for the new property, would pose no threat to the bankruptcy estate not posed by any reorganization.

In this case, "the exclusiveness of the opportunity, with its protection against the market's scrutiny of the purchase price by means of competing bids or even competing plan proposals, rendered the partners' right a property interest extended 'on account of' the old equity position. . . ." The Court concluded:

> Whether a market test would require an opportunity to offer competing plans or would be satisfied by a right to bid for the same interest sought by old equity, is a question we do not decide here. It is enough to say, assuming a new value corollary, that plans providing junior interest holders with exclusive opportunities free from competition and without benefit of market valuation fall within the prohibitions of § 1129(b)(2)(B)(ii).

RESULT The plan could not be approved over the objections of the bank.

15. 11 U.S.C. § 1129(b)(2)(B)(ii).

PLAN NEGOTIATIONS

Because confirmation by cramdown is both difficult and uncertain, plan proponents frequently try to draft terms that will encourage broad acceptance. For the first 120 days (or for a longer or shorter time that the court may fix), only the debtor can propose a plan. After this exclusivity period expires, any party may propose a plan. Thus, a debtor that does not bargain reasonably may be faced with a competing plan that might be threatened or proposed by a major secured creditor or by the official committee that is appointed in Chapter 11 cases to represent the interests of unsecured creditors. Even if the debtor is the only party proposing a plan, an endorse-

ment from the creditors' committee can be essential to obtain the creditor support necessary to achieve confirmation without a cramdown. Taken together, these dynamics promote negotiation and accommodation among the interested parties. Most successful plans in large Chapter 11 cases reflect such compromises.

DISCHARGE

Just as a discharge under Chapter 7 can give individual debtors a fresh start, confirmation under Chapter 11 can give reorganized debtors a new financial beginning under the plan. For individual debtors, however, the same debts that would be nondischargeable under Chapter 7 are excluded from the Chapter 11 discharge. Also, a plan that calls for liquidation and cessation of business will afford a discharge only to individuals who would have been eligible for one in Chapter 7. Because entities such as corporations or partnerships are not eligible for a discharge under Chapter 7, they will similarly not be discharged under Chapter 11 in the event of a liquidation. If the business is rehabilitated, the debtor entity is liable for preconfirmation claims only insofar as they are expressly preserved by the plan. No bankruptcy discharge, whether under Chapter 11 or otherwise, protects the debtor's co-obligors, such as guarantors or joint tortfeasors.

 ## Other Chapters

In addition to Chapter 7 (which includes special subchapters for commodity and stockbroker liquidations), Chapter 11 (which includes a subchapter for railroad reorganizations), and Chapter 13 (consumer bankruptcy), the Bankruptcy Code contains two chapters that are more limited and three others of broader significance. Chapter 12, a hybrid of Chapters 11 and 13, provides debt adjustment, but not a super discharge, for family farmers (a technically defined term) whose aggregate debts do not exceed $1.5 million. Chapter 9, largely patterned after Chapter 11, provides debt adjustment for municipalities. Chapters 1, 3, and 5 apply to all bankruptcies. These chapters contain important provisions—discussed in the sections that follow—such as the automatic stay, rules for claim allowance and priority, the definition of the bankruptcy estate and framework for its administration, and the trustee's avoiding powers.

 ## Bankruptcy Procedures

Individuals can wipe the slate clean immediately through a Chapter 7 liquidation or obtain a super discharge by devoting their future earnings to creditors through a

Chapter 13 plan. Troubled business debtors that file under Chapter 11 may be able to preserve value for the benefit of shareholders or other equity interests. Bankruptcy also offers several other advantages for debtors.

AUTOMATIC STAY

The most immediate and dramatic advantage of any bankruptcy filing is the *automatic stay*, which instantly suspends most litigation and collection activities against the debtor, its property, or that of the bankruptcy estate. Many debtors file for bankruptcy on the eve of foreclosure to forestall the loss of crucial assets; others file primarily to stave off litigation or collection activities. The latter group includes such notable bankruptcy refugees as Dow Corning (facing 19,000 lawsuits involving 400,000 women claiming immune-system illness caused by silicon breast implants), Johns–Manville (sued for thousands of asbestos-related injuries), and Texaco (unable to post a bond while appealing the multibillion-dollar judgment against it for interfering with Pennzoil's efforts to acquire Getty Oil).

Though they may feel frustrated, creditors must honor the automatic stay. As the following case demonstrates, failure to do so can be costly.

A CASE IN POINT

CASE 26.3

In re **Computer Communications, Inc.**

United States Court of Appeals for the Ninth Circuit

824 F.2d 725

(9th Cir. 1987).

Summary

FACTS In April 1979, Codex Corporation, a designer and manufacturer of communications equipment and networks used for transmitting information between complex computer systems, entered into a joint marketing and development agreement with Computer Communications, Inc. (CCI), a manufacturer of computer equipment and software. Under the agreement, Codex agreed to make minimum quarterly purchases of equipment and software from CCI for incorporation in Codex's products. The agreement was amended on November 4, 1980, and its term was extended to four years commencing in

(Continued)

(Case 26.3 continued)

April 1979. The amended agreement required CCI to continue to provide technical support and spare parts. On November 6, 1980, two days after the parties executed the amended agreement, CCI filed a petition under Chapter 11.

On December 30, 1980, Codex notified CCI that it was terminating the agreement pursuant to a clause in the amended agreement that expressly permitted termination in the event of a filing in bankruptcy. Codex failed to make its minimum purchases for the quarter ending December 31, 1980, and failed to make any of its quarterly minimum purchases after that.

CCI filed suit in bankruptcy court on January 30, 1981, alleging that Codex's termination of the agreement violated the automatic-stay provision of the Bankruptcy Code. On February 23, 1981, Codex notified CCI that it was terminating purchases of equipment from CCI pursuant to a clause in the amended agreement that permitted unilateral notice of termination by Codex upon payment of not more than $400,000.

The bankruptcy court held that Codex had willfully violated the automatic stay. The court awarded general damages of $4,750,000 (apparently based on loss of projected profits), plus $250,000 in punitive damages. Codex appealed.

ISSUE PRESENTED Does unilateral termination of an agreement with a debtor that has filed for bankruptcy violate the automatic-stay provision?

SUMMARY OF OPINION The U.S. Court of Appeals for the Ninth Court upheld the award, holding that Codex violated the automatic-stay statute by terminating its contract unilaterally, rather than applying for relief from the bankruptcy court. According to the legislative history, the purpose of the automatic stay is to give the debtor a "breathing spell" from creditors, stop all collection efforts, and permit the debtor to attempt repayment or reorganization.

Codex argued that the contract was not property of the bankrupt estate and was therefore not automatically stayed. The court rejected this argument, finding that the contract did fall within the definition of "property of the estate."

RESULT Codex violated the automatic stay and was liable for the debtor's loss of projected profits and for punitive damages.

COMMENTS This case makes it clear that even if a party to a contract has a unilateral right to terminate it, the contract cannot be terminated once the other party is in bankruptcy, unless the bankruptcy court orders relief from the automatic stay. Willful violations of the automatic stay may also constitute contempt of court and warrant punitive damages.

 ETHICAL CONSIDERATION

In *In re Computer Communications, Inc.* (Case 26.3), CCI extended its agreement with Codex only two days before filing for bankruptcy. It seems clear that Codex would not have renewed the agreement if it had known that CCI was going to declare bankruptcy. The managers of CCI locked in a favorable contract by concealing their intentions from Codex. Was the CCI managers' conduct unethical or just good business?

The U.S. Supreme Court ruled that a bank could, without violating the automatic stay, put a temporary administrative hold on the portion of the bankrupt debtor's checking account that the bank claimed was subject to setoff.[16] The bank refused to pay withdrawals from the bankrupt's account that would reduce the balance below the sum the bank claimed was due on its loan to the bankrupt party. The bank then filed a motion for relief from the automatic stay in the bankruptcy court. The Court ac-

16. Citizens Bank of Maryland v. Strumpf, 516 U.S. 16 (1995).

knowledged that a bankruptcy filing gives rise to an automatic stay of various types of activities by creditors, including "the setoff of any debt owing to the debtor that arose before the commencement of the [bankruptcy case] against any claim against the debtor." The Court held that a setoff has not occurred, however, until three steps have been taken: (1) a decision to effectuate a setoff, (2) some action accomplishing the setoff, and (3) a recording of the setoff. Thus, there is no setoff unless the creditor intends to permanently settle accounts.

The Court reasoned that a bank account is not money belonging to the depositor but rather represents a promise by a bank to pay the depositor an amount equal to the money in the account. Therefore, by imposing an administrative hold, the bank does not exercise dominion over the bankrupt's property. Rather, the hold represents a temporary refusal of a creditor to pay a debt that is subject to setoff against a debt owed by the bankrupt.

By stopping creditors in their tracks, the automatic stay provides a breathing spell that can enable a Chapter 11 debtor to focus on the operation of the business and the reorganization of its financial affairs. The stay is not a permanent shield, however. The court may authorize creditors to resume collection efforts, most often foreclosure on collateral, for cause—that is, if there is inadequate protection of the creditors' property interests, such as when the value of collateral declines with use and no replacement security is provided. Relief from the stay will also be granted if the debtor has no equity in the property and a stay is not necessary for effective reorganization. Such relief from the automatic stay becomes more likely as time passes without progress toward reorganization. The automatic stay is rarely lifted to permit garden-variety litigation against the debtor, however.

ADMINISTRATION OF CLAIMS

Instead of lawsuits, creditors file a relatively simple *proof of claim*. This serves to centralize the administration of most claims in the bankruptcy court, where the process is streamlined. The proof-of-claim requirement in a Chapter 11 bankruptcy is deemed satisfied for claims listed in the debtor's schedules as uncontingent and undisputed (unless the creditor wishes to claim more than the debtor acknowledges is due).

Filed claims are deemed valid or allowed unless and until someone objects. Except for personal-injury or wrongful-death claims, which are triable to a jury in the district court, disputed claims normally are resolved through a quick hearing before the bankruptcy judge. If resolution would unduly delay administration of the

bankruptcy case (such as when a claim is contingent upon a future event), the bankruptcy court will estimate the allowable amount of certain claims.

Some claims are limited in bankruptcy. For example, a landlord's damages claim for termination of a lease cannot exceed rent for the greater of one year or 15 percent (but not to exceed three years) of the remaining term. Similarly, a terminated employee's damages claim may not exceed one year's compensation. Unless the estate can pay all claims in a liquidation, postpetition interest is allowed only to secured creditors that can recover it from their collateral.

CONTROL

Though handling claims effectively is important, preserving value to pay them is more important. The debtor's track record for good management may be uneven. Nevertheless, based upon the debtor's presumed knowledge of the business and incentive to save it for the benefit of all concerned, Chapter 11 leaves the debtor in possession of the bankruptcy estate. A *debtor in possession (DIP)* has basically the same powers and duties as a trustee. (Because of this general congruity, references to the DIP below should be understood to apply equally to a duly appointed trustee unless the context clearly indicates otherwise.)

Under Chapter 11, an independent trustee normally will not be appointed to displace the DIP without proof that current management is either dishonest or clearly incompetent. Thus, subject to the constraints discussed below, Chapter 11 usually permits the debtor to operate in the ordinary course of business. This, together with the automatic stay and the initial exclusive right to propose a plan, may represent the distressed debtor's best opportunity to exercise control over its fate.

The following case dealt with the question of whether acrimony between the debtor and the creditors is sufficient cause to justify appointment of a bankruptcy trustee in a Chapter 11 case.

A CASE IN POINT

CASE 26.4

In re **Marvel Entertainment Group, Inc.**
United States Court of Appeals for the Third Circuit
140 F.3d 463
(3d Cir. 1998).

Summary

FACTS After Marvel Entertainment Group filed for bankruptcy protection under Chapter 11, tensions arose between several of the creditors. Eventually, one creditor acquired control of Marvel, thereby assuming the roles of DIP and creditor. The new DIP and the other creditors attempted to settle their claims against the estate, but negotiations broke down. The new DIP then commenced adverse litigation against the other creditors. The other creditors petitioned for the appointment of a trustee, arguing that the new DIP was incapable of neutrality. The district court appointed a trustee, and the new DIP appealed.

ISSUE PRESENTED Is acrimony between the DIP and certain creditors sufficient cause to justify appointment of a trustee?

SUMMARY OF OPINION The U.S. Court of Appeals for the Third Circuit began by noting that appointment of a trustee should be the exception rather than the rule. Nonetheless, a court does have the power to appoint a trustee "for cause, including fraud, dishonesty, incompetence, or gross mismanagement of the affairs of the debtor by current management" or "if such an appointment is in the interests of the creditors, any equity security holders, and other interests of the estate." Because the new DIP's dual role had caused extreme acrimony, the court concluded that the appointment of a trustee was not an abuse of discretion by the district court.

The court explained that the determination of what kind of acrimony would rise to the level of cause was within the district court's discretion and should be made on a case-by-case basis "when the inherent conflicts extend beyond the healthy conflicts that always exist between debtor and creditor, or . . . when the parties 'begin working at cross purposes.'"

RESULT The appointment of a trustee was affirmed.

OBTAINING CREDIT

The DIP's first priority often is to stay in business and continue (or resume) providing goods and services to customers at a profit. Yet, as observed at the outset, poor cash flow often paves the way to Chapter 11. Although the bankruptcy system does not manufacture money, it may enhance or create some funding possibilities.

Customer Payments The debtor's liquidity crisis sometimes stems from a secured lender's insistence that all encumbered customer payments be applied to the loan, leaving little or no cash to operate. If a bankruptcy petition is filed, customer payments on prebankruptcy accounts will remain the lender's cash collateral, but the court may authorize the DIP to use the funds if the lender's position is adequately protected. Such protection might be found in surplus collateral that gives the lender an ample equity cushion, or it might be provided by granting the lender a substitute lien on postpetition inventory and receivables. Of course, the court may underestimate the need for protection, and this risk often

prods an otherwise recalcitrant lender to negotiate terms for use of its cash collateral.

Extension of Unsecured Credit Filing for reorganization may encourage suppliers (and perhaps other lenders) to extend unsecured credit. During the debtor's prebankruptcy decline, conventional trade terms (such as payment due thirty days after invoice) often become unavailable as the debtor falls behind on accounts payable and word of its shaky condition spreads. Fearful that they may recover only pennies on the dollar from credit sales if the debtor collapses, vendors typically begin requiring cash on delivery or even in advance. This only aggravates the debtor's problems. Ironically, the same suppliers, particularly those that are sophisticated and value the debtor's patronage most, may be willing to resume regular credit transactions with the DIP.

Flexibility returns because postpetition debts incurred in the ordinary course of doing business are allowable as administrative expenses, which are accorded priority over virtually all other unsecured claims. Thus, vendors that extend postpetition credit expect full payment on those transactions. In so doing, they may strengthen the debtor's business and promote a greater recovery on their prepetition claims.

Secured Borrowings The debtor's ability to borrow on a secured basis can be similarly enhanced in a Chapter 11 reorganization, mainly because collateral may be more available. For example, assets acquired after the bankruptcy petition is filed (other than those derived directly from prebankruptcy collateral) will not be subject to prepetition security agreements designed to cover such after-acquired property. Therefore, a debtor that can produce inventory or generate accounts receivable after the bankruptcy filing may have enough unencumbered property to support new secured loans. Moreover, if credit is not otherwise available, the court can authorize borrowing that is secured by a priming lien, provided that the preexisting lienholder is adequately protected. A *priming lien* is a lien that is senior to a previously granted security interest. Thus, for example, a first mortgage on raw land might be involuntarily subordinated to a new lien that will secure a DIP–developer's construction financing.

Court Oversight On occasion, the bankruptcy court's oversight alone may help the debtor arrange new secured loans. By obtaining court approval after giving appropriate notice to other creditors, lenders can virtually immunize their repayment rights and security interests from the attacks by other creditors that sometimes undermine prebankruptcy loans.

Turnover of Debtor's Property Though usually less expeditious than borrowing, other bankruptcy tools can also help the DIP obtain funds for operations and enhance the value of the estate. Almost anyone can be compelled to turn over property of the estate that could be used by the DIP. Thus, if adequate protection is provided, a lender that has frozen the debtor's deposit accounts at the banking institution or a taxing authority that has seized them may be required to relinquish these funds.

AVOIDING POWERS

Still more striking is the DIP's ability to invoke the potent *avoiding powers* that trustees can use to invalidate or reverse certain prebankruptcy transactions.

Strong-Arm Clause Under the *strong-arm clause,* the DIP is granted the rights of a hypothetical creditor that extended credit to the debtor at the time of bankruptcy and, as a result, either obtained a judicial lien on all property in which the debtor has an interest or obtained

an execution against the debtor that was returned unsatisfied. The DIP also has the rights that a bona fide purchaser of real property from the debtor would have if the transfer was perfected. The DIP has these powers and rights regardless of whether a judgment-lien creditor or a bona fide purchaser actually exists.

Thus, if a deed of trust or mortgage was not properly recorded before bankruptcy or a security interest in personal property was not duly perfected against third-party claims under applicable law (typically, Article 9 of the Uniform Commercial Code), the DIP can establish superior rights to the affected property for the benefit of the estate. This is the case even if the debtor could not have recovered such assets outside bankruptcy. In addition, the DIP can avoid—that is, invalidate—any transactions that an existing unsecured creditor could invalidate. These might include unauthorized dividends to shareholders, procedurally defective bulk sales, or transfers considered fraudulent as to creditors under nonbankruptcy laws such as a state fraudulent transfer statute.

The scope of the DIP's strong-arm powers usually depends on state property law, so it may differ from case to case. For example, in many states, the rights of a creditor holding a judicial lien against real property are superior to those of a party with an unrecorded mortgage against the same property. Using the strong-arm powers, a DIP can avoid the unrecorded lien. Similarly, where a judicial creditor's lien would have priority over an unperfected security interest, the DIP may use its hypothetical status to invalidate a security interest that was not perfected by filing or possession but would otherwise be valid between a debtor and its creditor. If state law permits, the DIP may reverse other transfers of the debtor's property and void otherwise valid obligations of the debtor. Any value the DIP recovers pursuant to the strong-arm clause inures to the benefit of the creditors of the bankruptcy estate.

Fraudulent Transfers The DIP may invoke the Bankruptcy Code to avoid fraudulent transfers or obligations. In general, these arise from transactions that occurred within a year before bankruptcy (1) that are actually intended to hinder, delay, or defraud creditors or (2) that provide less than reasonably equivalent value in exchange and leave the debtor insolvent or without sufficient capital to engage in business or to pay expected debts. Thus, a leveraged buyout that leaves a company with insufficient capital and high debt leverage after the payouts to equity holders may be voidable as a fraudulent conveyance.[17] Most states have roughly parallel fraudulent transfer laws, but the

17. *See, e.g.,* United States v. Tabor Court Realty Corp., 803 F.2d 1288 (3d Cir. 1987), *cert. denied,* 483 U.S. 1005 (1987).

HISTORICAL PERSPECTIVE

From Mosaic Law *to* Vulture Capitalists

The principle that debtors should be permitted to discharge certain debts has ancient roots. As early as 1400 B.C., Mosaic law required unconditional forgiveness of debts every seven years to encourage a proper focus on social relationships. The word "bankruptcy" is believed to have evolved from the Latin words "banca" and "rupta," referring to the broken bench or moneychangers' table left behind by failed merchants fleeing from their creditors. In A.D. 1542, lawmakers under King Henry VIII passed a Bankruptcy Act to regulate failing English merchants. Over the centuries, strong sanctions for insolvency, including imprisonment, generally made bankruptcy a remedy for creditors rather than a relief for debtors.

The roots of the American bankruptcy system can be traced to the experiences of colonists who were refugees from debtors' prisons in Europe. The drafters of the Constitution, recognizing the importance of debtor relief, gave Congress the exclusive right to establish national bankruptcy laws and thereby override the states' treatment of debtors and creditors. The first bankruptcy enactments, early in the nineteenth century, contained no provisions for voluntary bankruptcy. Not until 1898, when a severe depression forced many railroads into receivership, did Congress use its bankruptcy power to allow troubled enterprises to reorganize. The Bankruptcy Act of 1898 enabled failing railroads and other businesses to continue operating while reorganizing, generally stripping shareholders of their interests.

Financier J.P. Morgan reorganized so many busted railroads that his work in this area became known as "Morganization." Fifty years after Morgan, the trustee for the estate of Alfred I. du Pont obtained control of the Florida East Coast Railway by holding 56 percent of its defaulted mortgage bonds. Astute purchases of defaulted rail bonds in the 1940s provided the start for a number of Wall Street fortunes.[a]

In 1978, Congress enacted the Bankruptcy Reform Act, which created the Bankruptcy Code. That legislation, the result of nearly a decade of intensive study and debate about problems in the bankruptcy system and proposed reforms, made sweeping changes in the law, most of them favorable to debtors.

In light of the massive defaults on junk bonds in 1989 and the early 1990s, some questioned whether Congress gave debtors too much relief under the Bankruptcy Code. The lead-in to a *Forbes* article on the subject summarized the state of affairs as of 1990: "In the old days, a debt was an obligation and bankruptcy was a disgrace. Nowadays bond issuers concoct ever more ways to stiff investors."[b]

In the *Forbes* article, commentator Matthew Schifrin compared the debtor-lenient U.S. system with the systems of other Western countries, where a debtor's property is auctioned off if it can't pay its debts: "That's why Australian conglomerator Alan Bond is scrambling to save his highly leveraged empire. The bankruptcy laws in Australia have scant provision for reorganization. If you owe and you can't pay, your creditors can liquidate your company."[c] In the United States, the debtor usually retains control of the enterprise while it is being reorganized.

Even in the United States, however, bond holders are fighting back. A new breed, called vulture capitalists, has arisen. They buy up bonds at depressed prices and then seek to throw out existing management. Or, as happened to Chapter 11 debtor R.H. Macy & Company in 1994, a competitor—in this case, Federated Department Stores—can buy up senior debt and promise bond holders more than they might otherwise receive if the debtor stays independent. Then the competitor forces a merger of the two companies as part of the plan of reorganization needed for the debtor to emerge from bankruptcy.[d]

a. Matthew Schifrin, *Enough Already!*, FORBES, May 28, 1990, at 126.
b. *Id.*
c. *Id.* at 128.
d. Patrick M. Reilly & Laura Jereski, *Macy, Federated Reach Accord in Merger Talks*, WALL ST. J., July 15, 1994, at A3.

Bankruptcy Code's version may be broader. For example, the state laws may be inapplicable to distressed foreclosure sales that are noncollusive and procedurally proper; bankruptcy law has been applied to invalidate such sales if the proceeds are less than 70 percent of the collateral's fair market value. Thus, although a good faith buyer should have a lien for the value given (which is usually the amount of the secured debt), the DIP may be able to reverse the foreclosure and recapture equity.

Preferences The avoiding power used most extensively is the ability to recover preferences. *Preferences* are transfers to (or for the benefit of) creditors on account of antecedent debts that are made from an insolvent debtor's property within ninety days before bankruptcy and that enable the creditors to receive more than they would through a Chapter 7 liquidation. (The preference window is enlarged to a year before bankruptcy if the benefited creditor is an insider—that is, someone in a position to control the debtor's conduct, such as a relative, partner, director, officer, or substantial shareholder.) Preferences are made avoidable in bankruptcy both to discourage creditors from dismembering a troubled business in their race for its assets and to foster equal distribution among similarly situated claimants. Subject to limited exceptions, the DIP can recover voluntary or involuntary preferential payments and strip away preferential security interests or collection liens, all for the benefit of the bankruptcy estate.

A payment is a preference only if it is for an antecedent (or preexisting) debt. To avoid penalizing creditors that continue to deal in a customary fashion with the debtor during its slide into bankruptcy, current payments in the ordinary course of business cannot be recovered as preferences.[18] In *Union Bank v. Wolas,*[19] the U.S. Supreme

18. 11 U.S.C. § 547(c)(2).
19. 502 U.S. 151 (1991).

Court held that payments on long-term debt, as well as payments on short-term debt, may qualify for the ordinary course of business exception to the DIP's power to avoid preferential transfers if (1) the loan was incurred in the ordinary course of the debtor's business and of the bank's business, (2) the payments were made in the ordinary course of business, and (3) the payments were made according to ordinary business terms.

The following case addressed the scope of the *earmarking doctrine,* whereby a payment to a preexisting creditor may not be recoverable as a preference if the funds for the repayment were provided by some other creditor and not by the debtor.

A CASE IN POINT

CASE 26.5

Adams v. Anderson (*In re Superior Stamp & Coin Co.*)
United States Court of Appeals for the Ninth Circuit
223 F.3d 1004
(9th Cir. 2000).

In the Language of the Court

FACTS Superior Stamp & Coin operated as a full-service auction house specializing in the auction of coins, sports and Hollywood memorabilia, and related goods. In 1992, Carolyn Adams and Superior entered into an auction consignment agreement, whereby Superior agreed to auction Adams's coin collection and pay her the net proceeds within thirty days after receiving the funds. After Superior failed to remit the $374,125.57 of net proceeds, Adams and Superior negotiated a repayment schedule in April 1994, which called for Superior to remit the proceeds in six equal $62,355 payments.

In early 1994, Superior was under severe financial strain, and its largest creditor, the Bank of California, was actively involved in Superior's day-to-day management. In an effort to preserve Superior's business, the bank agreed to fund certain repayments, including the $62,355 installments owed to Adams.

Superior issued a $62,355 check to Adams on May 27, 1994. When the check was presented to the bank, it was subjected to a "special review" process and then approved by the bank. The bank then advanced to Superior's account the funds necessary to clear the check—in this case, the full amount of the $62,355 payment—and simultaneously electronically transferred the funds to Adams. Superior issued a second $62,355 check to Adams on July 7, 1994. The bank again approved the payment and advanced the funds necessary to cover the check. This time, because Superior's General Account already contained $42,439.10, the bank advanced only $19,915.90—the amount required to fund the shortfall.

In spite of the efforts to save Superior, the company failed. On August 26, 1994, Superior filed an involuntary petition for Chapter 11 bankruptcy. The trustee sought to recover the payments to Adams on the grounds that they were voidable preference transfers. Adams argued that the bankruptcy doctrine of earmarking immunized the transfers funded by the bank from avoidance.

ISSUE PRESENTED Does the earmarking doctrine apply when a debtor requests a loan to pay a particular creditor, and the lender does not pay the creditor directly but advances the funds to the debtor for payment to the selected creditor?

(Continued)

(Case 26.5 continued)

OPINION REINHARDT, J., writing for the U.S. Court of Appeals for the Ninth Circuit:

Under § 574(b) of the Bankruptcy Code, a trustee may recover certain transfers made by the debtor within ninety days before the bankruptcy petition was filed. A transfer by the debtor constitutes an avoidable preference if six elements are shown: (1) a transfer of an interest of the debtor in property; (2) to or for the benefit of a creditor; (3) for or on account of an antecedent debt; (4) made while the debtor was insolvent; (5) made on or within ninety days before the date of the filing of the petition; and (6) one that enables the creditor to receive more than such creditor would receive in a Chapter 7 liquidation of the estate. Adams concedes that five of those elements exist and disputes only the bankruptcy court's conclusion as to the first element. . . .

In order to determine whether property that is transferred belongs to the debtor for purposes of § 547, we apply the "diminution of estate" doctrine. Under this doctrine, a transfer of an interest of the debtor in property occurs where the transfer "diminishes directly or indirectly the fund to which creditors of the same class can legally resort for the payment of their debts, to such an extent that it is impossible for other creditors of the same class to obtain as great a percentage as the favored one." Adams concedes that, generally, transfers by a debtor of borrowed funds constitute transfers of the debtor's property because the borrowed funds, had they not been transferred, would have been available in bankruptcy to satisfy the claims of other creditors.

There is an exception (or perhaps a corollary) to this general rule, however, known as the earmarking doctrine. . . .

The earmarking doctrine applies "when a third party lends money to a debtor for the specific purpose of paying a selected creditor." . . .

If the debtor controls the disposition of the funds and designates the creditor to whom the monies will be paid independent of a third party whose funds are being used in . . . payment of the debt, then the payments made by the debtor to the creditor constitute a preferential transfer. . . .

The [bankruptcy] court suggested that Superior "controlled" the borrowed funds because the advances from the bank were deposited in Superior's account rather than paid directly to Adams by the bank. This gave Superior "control," the court stated, because possession of the funds gave it the power (though not the right) to divert the loan to another use. . . . The fact that Superior may have had the power to divert the loan after it was deposited into Superior's account does not amount to "control" of the funds by Superior. . . .

Accordingly, the proper inquiry is not whether the funds entered the debtor's account, but whether the debtor had the right to disburse the funds to whomever it wished, or whether their disbursement was limited to a particular old creditor or creditors under the agreement with the new creditor. . . .

Here, the bank advanced the funds for the specific purpose of paying a specific creditor, namely Adams. The bank agreed to fund the payments to the extent necessary but only on the express condition that the amounts involved be paid to Adams. . . . Where there is an agreement between a new lender and the debtor that the funds will be used to pay a specified antecedent debt, a debtor has not exercised control over the funds by "designating the creditor to whom the monies will be paid independent of a third party whose funds are being used in . . . in payment of the debt." Because the bank disbursed the funds pursuant to such an antecedent agreement, Superior did not exercise "control" over the money even though Superior requested the loan to pay Adams and the funds were placed in Superior's account rather than being paid directly to Adams by the bank.

(Continued)

(Case 26.5 continued)

RESULT The $82,270.90 in payments made by the bank to fund the checks to Adams fell within the earmarking doctrine and were not voidable preferences.

QUESTIONS

1. Was the $42,439.10 paid to Adams out of Superior's existing funds a voidable preference?
2. Why would a bank advance additional funds to a debtor already in financial trouble? How does the earmarking doctrine affect a bank's willingness to advance new funds?

Setoff Rights A creditor exercising a setoff right automatically deducts what the debtor owes the creditor from what the creditor owes the debtor. By analogy to the preference provision, creditors who exercise setoff rights within ninety days before bankruptcy can be required to disgorge such offsets to the extent that they decreased their obligations to the debtor within the ninety-day period.

Statutory Liens The DIP can avoid certain statutory liens, including those that first arise upon insolvency or that would not have been enforceable against a bona fide purchaser of the encumbered property when the bankruptcy was filed. This prevents state law from creating hidden priorities that would distort the federal bankruptcy distribution scheme.

Collective Bargaining Agreements The rules for avoiding collective bargaining agreements changed after Frank Lorenzo, the CEO of Continental Airlines, used Chapter 11 to avoid the company's collective bargaining agreements. In the early 1980s, when labor rejected his demands for sizable wage concessions, Lorenzo took Continental into a Chapter 11 proceeding and repudiated its collective bargaining agreements. Continental emerged from bankruptcy a nonunion carrier with a reduced wage structure.

Organized labor protested the use of the Bankruptcy Code by Lorenzo (and, increasingly, others) to break unions. In 1984, Congress responded, amending the Bankruptcy Code so that a debtor no longer has broad discretion to unilaterally abrogate its labor contracts. Instead, a debtor may reject collective bargaining agreements over the objection of its unions only if (1) it has presented labor with a proposal showing that rejection is economically necessary and fair to the affected parties; (2) it has bargained to impasse; and (3) the bankruptcy court finds that, on balance, fairness clearly favors rejection.

EXECUTORY CONTRACTS AND LEASES

The DIP has the option of assuming or rejecting prebankruptcy *executory contracts*—that is, contracts that have not yet been performed—or unexpired leases. Assumption preserves the debtor's rights and duties under the existing relationship, whereas rejection terminates them.

If an executory contract or unexpired lease is a valuable asset, the DIP will want to assume it so that it can be preserved for the reorganizing business or sold at a profit. For example, assumption is advantageous when it allows the debtor to sell or buy goods at a favorable price or to lease space or equipment at better-than-market rents. Even a contract or lease in default can be assumed, provided that the DIP cures and compensates for the breach and gives adequate assurance of future performance. Once assumed, the contract or lease obligations are allowable as administrative expenses, as with other authorized postpetition transactions. Even if a contract or lease contains contractual restrictions barring assignment, any assumed contract or lease can be sold and assigned intact if the prospective assignee's future performance is adequately assured.

On the other hand, by rejecting a disadvantageous contract or lease, the DIP can escape burdensome performance obligations. The nondebtor party to the contract or lease will be deemed to have a prepetition damages claim for breach and thus will be treated like others whose claims arose from prebankruptcy transactions.

The following case addressed the issue of whether an option to buy property is an executory contract.

A CASE IN POINT

CASE 26.6

Unsecured Creditors Committee of Robert L. Helms Construction & Development Co. v. Southmark Corp.
(*In re* Robert L. Helms Construction & Development Co.)

United States Court of Appeals for the Ninth Circuit
139 F.3d 702
(9th Cir. 1998) (en banc).

In the Language of the Court

FACTS Southmark, a Texas corporation, sold the Double Diamond Ranch in Nevada to the Double Diamond Ranch Limited Partnership (Double Diamond), retaining an option to buy back part of the ranch. Southmark later filed for bankruptcy in Texas. As part of its Chapter 11 reorganization plan, it assumed various executory contracts by filing a notice of assumption. The plan provided that all executory contracts not listed were deemed rejected. The notice did not list the option to buy back the ranch; therefore, the option would have been deemed rejected if it was an executory contract.

Double Diamond then itself filed for bankruptcy in Nevada. The committee administering the Double Diamond bankruptcy decided to sell the ranch to South Meadows Properties Limited Partnership. The committee asked the bankruptcy court to allow sale of the ranch free and clear of Southmark's option. A free-and-clear sale was appropriate only if the option was no longer valid because it had been stripped away in the Texas bankruptcy proceeding. The Nevada bankruptcy court held that the option was an executory contract that had been rejected in Southmark's bankruptcy. Therefore, it allowed Double Diamond to sell the ranch to South Meadows free and clear of Southmark's option. Southmark appealed.

ISSUE PRESENTED Is an option to buy property an executory contract?

OPINION KOZINSKI, J., writing for the U.S. Court of Appeals for the Ninth Circuit:

An executory contract is one "on which performance remains due to some extent on both sides." More precisely, a contact is executory if "the obligations of both parties are so unperformed that the failure of either party to complete performance would constitute a material breach and thus excuse the performance of the other."

A paid-for but unexercised option presents a puzzle. Is it executory or isn't it? Each side may have unperformed obligations, but they are contingent on the optionee's decision to exercise the option. If it does, the optionor has a duty to deliver the property, and the optionee may have a duty to tender payment, depending on the mechanics of the option. But if the option is not exercised, nothing happens and neither party commits a breach. The contingent nature of the obligations has troubled courts. Some have said that these are contingent obligations, but obligations nonetheless, hence options are executory. Other courts have held that the optionee has fulfilled its only true obligation under the option by paying for it; the creation of further obligations lies within the optionee's sole discretion, so the contract isn't executory.

. . .

A better approach . . . is to ask whether the option requires further performance from each party at the time the petition is filed. Typically the answer is no, and the option is therefore not executory. The optionee need not exercise the option—if he does nothing, the option lapses without breach. The contingency which triggers potential obligations—exercising the option—is completely within the optionee's control. While some options may be executory, *Easebe*[20] is overboard in holding that they all are.

. . .

We therefore reject *Easebe*'s broad rule that all options are executory contracts. Instead, we look to outstanding obligations at the time the petition for relief is filed and ask whether both sides must still perform. Performance due only if the optionee chooses at his discretion to exercise the option doesn't count unless he has chosen

20. Gill v. Easebe Enters. (*In re* Easebe Enters.), 900 F.2d 1417 (9th Cir. 1990).

(Continued)

(Case 26.6 continued)

to exercise it. An option may on occasion be an executory contract, for instance, where the optionee has announced that he is exercising the option, but not yet followed through with the payment at the option price.

The question thus becomes: At the time of filing, does each party have something it must do to avoid materially breaching the contract? Typically, the answer is no; the optionee commits no breach by doing nothing.

It appears likely that the option here wasn't executory when Southmark filed its petition, but the record is not entirely clear.

RESULT The case was remanded to the bankruptcy court with instructions to determine the effect of the confirmed Southmark reorganization plan. If the plan did not resolve the question, the bankruptcy court was instructed to apply the legal test described above to determine whether the option contract was executory at the time of filing and to fashion a remedy if it found that the option was not an executory contract and remained an asset of the Southmark estate.

QUESTIONS

1. If Southmark had given written notice of its intent to exercise the option, but had not yet paid the purchase price, before filing for bankruptcy, would the option have been an executory contract?
2. The option agreement expressly provided that the option was for a period of fifteen years "provided, however, that the option granted herein shall terminate in the event Southmark files for protection under Chapter 11 of the Bankruptcy Code." Why wasn't the option automatically terminated when Southmark filed under Chapter 11?

Section 365(c) provides an exception to the debtor's usual right to assume, assign, or reject executory contracts and unexpired leases. It provides that the debtor may not assume or assign an executory contract or unexpired lease if "applicable laws excuse a party . . . to such contract or lease from accepting performance from or rendering performance to an entity other than the debtor" unless the other party consents to the assignment or assumption. In *Perlman v. Catapult Entertainment, Inc.*,[21] the Ninth Circuit held that a debtor in Chapter 11 may not assume a nonexclusive patent license even when the debtor, not a third-party assignee, would in fact continue to be the licensee. The parties agreed that the licenses were executory contracts. Nonetheless, the court held that because federal patent law provides that nonexclusive patent licenses are personal and assignable only with the consent of the licensor, the licenses could not be assumed over the objection of the licensor.

The court rejected Catapult's argument that the statute should be read to bar assumption only where the

reorganization in question results in the nondebtor actually having to accept performance from a third party (the "actual test"). Under the actual test, the debtor would be permitted to assume any executory contract as long as no assignment was contemplated. The Ninth Circuit acknowledged that Catapult had "marshaled considerable authority to support this reading," including the fact that the literal reading would appear to be incompatible with legislative history and contrary to sound bankruptcy policy, but concluded that "Congress is the policy maker, not the courts." Thus, the Ninth Circuit joined the Third,[22] Fourth,[23] and Eleventh Circuits[24] in interpreting the plain statutory language to bar assumption if assignment is prohibited by nonbankruptcy law. It rejected the actual test, which in the view of the First Circuit[25] better accomplished the intent of Congress. Given this split in the circuits, the issue of whether

---

21. *In re* Catapult Enter., Inc., 165 F.3d 747 (9th Cir. 1999), *cert. dismissed*, 528 U.S. 924 (1999).

22. *In re* West Elec., Inc., 852 F.2d 79 (3d Cir. 1988).
23. *In re* Catron, 158 B.R. 629 (E.D. Va. 1993), *aff'd without op.*, 25 F.3d 1038 (4th Cir. 1994).
24. *In re* James Cable Partners, 27 F.3d 534 (11th Cir. 1994).
25. Institut Pasteur v. Cambridge Biotech Corp., 104 F.3d 489 (1st Cir. 1997), *cert. denied*, 521 U.S. 1120 (1997).

patent licenses may be assumed by the debtor will not be definitively decided until the U.S. Supreme Court rules.

SALE OF PROPERTY

Bankruptcy can facilitate favorable sales of assets other than contracts or leases. For example, if partition or division of property jointly owned by the debtor and another is impractical and if separate sale of the debtor's undivided interest would yield significantly less for the estate, the DIP can sell both interests and disburse the net proceeds proportionately, as long as the resulting benefit would outweigh the detriment to the other owner. Similarly, the DIP may sell property free and clear of liens or other interests (which normally will be shifted to the proceeds) if the price will exceed all encumbrances or if the nondebtor's interest is in bona fide dispute. Thus, although the debtor's sale before bankruptcy might be stymied, the DIP can sometimes break the logjam and pass clear title under Chapter 11.

This cleansing power of bankruptcy extends beyond specific property. It can be the key to successful reorganization through the sale of the entire business or through new capital infusions. When a business is troubled and its future is in doubt, potential investors may shy away, despite the venture's intrinsic worth. Similarly, the price a prospective going-concern purchaser will pay may be seriously depressed by the fear that acquiring all of the assets will also subject the buyer to the debtor's obligations under doctrines of successor liability (discussed in Chapter 10). The same investors or buyers are often less jittery, and hence more willing to recognize the true value of the debtor's business, if the transaction proceeds under a confirmed plan or other court order that quantifies or cuts off preexisting claims. Subject to possible constitutional due process protections for unknown future claimants, Chapter 11 can dispel uncertainties that would otherwise prevent the debtor from realizing the equity in its business.

 ## Workouts

Because the high transaction costs and the adverse publicity of a Chapter 11 bankruptcy can be disadvantageous for debtors and creditors alike, the parties often try to negotiate an out-of-court settlement. Such an agreement, called a *workout*, restructures the debtor's financial affairs in much the same way that a confirmed plan would, but it can bind only those who expressly consent.

The foundation of any successful workout is trust. Creditors will not sign an agreement that leaves the busi-

ness in the hands of managers they consider to be dishonest or incompetent. If the debtor has lost credibility by misleading creditors or evading their reasonable inquiries (a common problem), its management may need to recruit and defer to a turnaround specialist in order to restore confidence. Full disclosure and candor are especially important when creditors are agreeing to accept partial payment in full satisfaction of undisputed debts. The debtor's misrepresentation or concealment of material facts probably would invalidate an otherwise binding release.

Workouts are forged in the shadow of bankruptcy, and the parties measure their concessions against the obvious alternative. The debtor and major creditors may be willing to accept something less than unanimity (for example, to preclude dissenters from extorting preferred treatment), but the deal will unravel if there are too many holdouts. When this risk is apparent from the outset, the workout agreement can be drafted in the form of a Chapter 11 plan. If necessary, and provided the information disclosed in soliciting assent to the agreement was adequate, the debtor can then file for reorganization and use the prepetition votes to transform the workout into a confirmed plan that binds dissenters. This is called a *prepackaged bankruptcy*.

Regardless of its terms, a workout agreement cannot stop the debtor from taking refuge in Chapter 11 if the restructured obligations prove too great. The right to file bankruptcy cannot be waived. Sometimes, however, creditors have strategic reasons to defer the debtor's filing, perhaps to buttress their positions with new guaranties or to season transfers against the avoiding powers. In any event, if the debtor has broken faith with the workout pact, the court may consider previous creditor concessions in deciding whether to lift the stay, to allow creditors to propose a plan at the outset, to appoint a trustee, or to convert the case to a Chapter 7 liquidation.

 # Lender Liability

A series of court decisions expanded the recoveries available to borrowers against lenders, and, as a consequence, lenders have become more aware of the risks of lender liability. This section describes several theories on which lender liability claims may be based.

BREACH OF CONTRACT

A breach of contract results from a lender's failure to act or to refrain from acting as required by the terms of a loan document or other agreement. As noted earlier, a

IN BRIEF

Advantages and Disadvantages of Bankruptcy

Category	Advantages	Disadvantages
Debtors	*Automatic Stay* • Instantly suspends most litigation and collection activities against the debtor, its property, or the bankruptcy estate. *Control* • Debtor retains possession of the bankruptcy estate (unless a trustee is appointed). • Chapter 11 permits the debtor to operate in the ordinary course of business. *Contracts, Leases, and Property* • Debtor in possession (DIP) has option of assuming or rejecting prebankruptcy executory contracts or unexpired leases. • DIP may (in certain circumstances) sell property free and clear of liens or other interests.	*Administrative Costs* • Legal and accounting expenses. • Official creditors' committee fees. *Reduction in Autonomy* • Creditor oversight. • Management's ability to make and implement decisions rapidly and autonomously is curtailed. *Stigma of Bankruptcy* • Morale or confidence problems among staff, vendors, or customers. • Customer anxiety regarding future warranty claims or product support.
Creditors	*Enhanced Value and Participation* • Preserves going-concern value of an insolvent business. • DIP more accountable due to bankruptcy reporting and notice requirements. *Equitable Distribution* • When inequitable conduct by any creditor (typically, an insider) has prejudiced others, bankruptcy court has authority to subordinate all or part of transgressor's claim to payment of other creditors. *Involuntary Petitions* • Creditors may file an involuntary petition for relief under Chapter 7 or (more rarely) Chapter 11 and force the debtor into bankruptcy.	*Suspension of Individual Remedies* • Automatic stay stalls foreclosure. • Nondebtor parties to executory contracts and unexpired leases are left in limbo. *Unequal Effects* • Some bankruptcy procedures affect various creditors unequally (e.g., avoiding actions, claim caps, equitable subordination). *Reduced Distribution* • Only a small fraction of Chapter 11 cases filed result in a successful reorganization. Continued operation results in less funds to distribute at liquidation.

lender's failure to honor a promise to make a loan may give rise to a breach-of-contract claim. Compensatory damages will be awarded to place the borrower in the same position it would have been in if the lender had properly performed the agreement.

BREACH OF DUTY OF GOOD FAITH

Some cases have imposed an implied obligation of good faith and fair dealing on lenders. This duty requires the lender to act reasonably and fairly in dealing with the borrower and in exercising its rights and remedies under the loan documents and under applicable law.

When there is a fiduciary relationship between the lender and borrower or when the parties are of unequal bargaining strength, punitive damages may be recoverable for breach of the implied duty of good faith and fair dealing. For example, the U.S. Court of Appeals for the Sixth Circuit affirmed a judgment of $1.5 million compensatory damages and punitive damages against the Irving Trust Company. The company was found to have breached an implied covenant of good faith and fair dealing when it failed to give notice to the borrower before refusing to make further advances under a discretionary line of credit.[26]

FRAUDULENT MISREPRESENTATION

A lender may be liable for making false statements if, for example, it represents that it will make a loan facility available to a borrower when, in fact, it has decided not to extend any credit to the borrower. If a fiduciary relationship exists between the lender and the borrower, the lender may have an additional duty to disclose information if nondisclosure would result in injury to the borrower. Both compensatory and punitive damages may be recovered for fraudulent misrepresentation.

ECONOMIC DURESS

Economic duress is the coercion of the borrower by threatening to do an unlawful act that might injure the borrower's business or property. If the lender pressures the borrower into doing something that the borrower is not required to do under the loan documents, a court may find that the lender's action constitutes economic duress. For example, a threat by the lender to accelerate the loan unless the borrower provides additional collateral may constitute economic duress if there is no default under the loan documents. Compensatory and punitive damages may be recovered for economic duress.

TORTIOUS INTERFERENCE

The lender was found liable for wrongful or tortious interference with the borrower's corporate governance in *State National Bank of El Paso v. Farah Manufacturing Co.*,[27] which set a precedent for claims of this kind. In that case, the loan agreement between the bank lenders

and the borrower prohibited any change in the borrower's management "which any two Banks shall consider, for any reason whatsoever, to be adverse to the interests of the Banks." The lenders threatened to accelerate the loan if a certain individual, of whom the lenders disapproved, was reappointed as chief executive officer of the borrower. In response to this threat, the borrower appointed a series of CEOs proposed by the lenders. After the financial position of the borrower seriously deteriorated during the tenure of these chief executives, the borrower sued the banks for tortious interference.

The Texas Court of Appeals held that the banks had wrongfully interfered with the borrower's right to have its affairs managed by competent directors and officers who would maintain a high degree of undivided loyalty to the company. The interference compelled the election of directors and officers whose particular business judgment, inexperience, and divided loyalty proximately resulted in injury to the borrower. The banks were liable for the losses suffered by the borrower while under the bank-imposed management, resulting in a judgment against the banks in excess of $18 million.

INTENTIONAL INFLICTION OF EMOTIONAL DISTRESS

A lender was found liable for intentional infliction of emotional distress when, after deciding not to make any additional advances to the borrower, bank officials publicly ridiculed him, pointing at him, using profanities, and laughing about his financial difficulties. To recover for intentional infliction of emotional distress, the lender's conduct must be extreme and outrageous and must intentionally or recklessly cause emotional distress to the borrower. Compensatory and punitive damages may be recovered.

NEGLIGENCE AND GENERAL TORT LIABILITY

Claims that do not fall into one of the other established categories may be characterized as negligence or general tort liability. Negligence is the failure to exercise reasonable care, resulting in injury to the borrower. General tort liability arises from conduct that intentionally causes injury to a borrower.

STATUTORY BASES OF LIABILITY

A lender may be liable to the borrower if it violates a statutory standard of conduct. For example, the federal Racketeering Influenced and Corrupt Organizations Act

26. K.M.C. Co. v. Irving Trust Co., 757 F.2d 752 (6th Cir. 1985).
27. 678 S.W.2d 661 (Tex. App. 1984).

(RICO) has been used by private litigants in lender liability cases. Although RICO was adopted by Congress as a tool for fighting organized crime, the definition of a "pattern of racketeering activity" is arguably broad enough to encompass fraud or misrepresentation by banks or other lenders. The treble damages available under RICO provide an incentive for borrowers to claim RICO violations in their lender liability suits.

The federal antitying statutes prohibit banks and thrifts from conditioning a loan or other financial service on the borrower's purchase of an unrelated property or service from the lender or on the borrower's providing to the lender a product or service unrelated to the original loan. A lender may be subject to penalties in cases brought by the Securities and Exchange Commission for aiding or abetting a borrower in violating federal securities laws if it knew, or should have known, that a violation was taking place or if it is found to be a controlling person with respect to the borrower.

Under the federal Comprehensive Environmental Response, Compensation and Liability Act (CERCLA, discussed in Chapter 18) and state law counterparts, if the lender falls within the statutory definition of an owner or operator of a site contaminated by hazardous wastes and does not come within the statutory safe harbor for lenders, it may find itself liable for all the costs of cleanup even if they exceed the amount of the loan.

Special Defenses Available *to the* Federal Insurers *of* Failed Banks *and* Savings *and* Loans

When a bank or savings and loan has failed and federal banking agencies have taken control, a common law principle known as the *D'Oench, Duhme* doctrine[28] has been used by the Federal Depository Insurance Corporation (FDIC)—and during the savings and loan debacle of the 1980s by the Resolution Trust Corporation (RTC)—to increase the value of the failed institution by easing the federal agencies' ability to collect on loans. *D'Oench, Duhme* bars many claims and defenses against conservators and receivers that might have been valid against the failed bank itself. In particular, the doctrine bars enforcement of any agreements (including secret agreements) unless those agreements are in writing and have been approved contemporaneously by the bank's board or loan committee and recorded in the bank's written records. This permits federal and state bank examiners to rely exclusively on the bank's written records in evaluating the worth of the bank's assets.[29] *D'Oench, Duhme* applies only to banking transactions engaged in by federally insured institutions. It does not apply to nonbanking transactions or to transactions engaged in by a bank's nonbank subsidiaries. Congress partially codified the holding of *D'Oench, Duhme* in the Federal Deposit Insurance Act of 1950, as modified by the Financial Institutions Reform, Recovery, and Enforcement Act (FIRREA).[30]

As a result of this doctrine, the federal agencies are often victorious over borrowers in cases in which a borrower asserts certain common law defenses to escape a loan obligation assumed by the FDIC or RTC. It has also been used as a defense to breach-of-contract and torts claims based on oral promises or arrangements.[31]

Support for the common law doctrine may be eroding, however. In 1995, the U.S. Court of Appeals for the District of Columbia Circuit held that the U.S. Supreme Court's reasoning in *O'Melveny & Myers v. FDIC*[32] leads "inelectably" to the conclusion that the common law *D'Oench, Duhme* doctrine has been preempted by the FIRREA.[33] The Ninth Circuit reached a similar conclusion in 1997 when it relied on the U.S. Supreme Court's decisions in *O'Melveny & Myers* and *Atherton v. FDIC*[34] to support its ruling that the *D'Oench, Duhme* doctrine does not protect the FDIC as a receiver of a failed bank.[35] In contrast, the Eleventh Circuit held in 1997 and again in 2000 that the FDIC, acting as a receiver of a failed bank, was still protected by the common law doctrine.[36] The Eleventh Circuit discerned "no indications that *D'Oench* is ripe for overruling." The U.S. Supreme Court may resolve the split in the circuits when it reviews the Eleventh Circuit's ruling in *Murphy v. FDIC*, which was contrary to the District of Columbia Circuit's prior ruling in the same case.

---

28. From the Supreme Court case of the same name, *D'Oench, Duhme & Co. v. FDIC*, 315 U.S. 447 (1942).

29. Alexandria Assocs. v. Mitchell Co., 2 F.3d 598 (5th Cir. 1993).

30. 12 U.S.C. § 1823(e)(1).

31. *See, e.g.,* Murphy v. FDIC, 208 F.3d 959 (11th Cir. 2000), *cert. granted,* 2000 U.S. LEXIS 4866 (2000).

32. 512 U.S. 79 (1994).

33. Murphy v. FDIC, 61 F.3d 34 (D.C. Cir. 1995).

34. 519 U.S. 213 (1997).

35. Ledo Fin. Corp. v. Summers, 122 F.3d 825 (9th Cir. 1997). *Accord* DiVall Insured Income Fund Ltd. Partnership v. Boatmen's First Nat'l Bank, 69 F.3d 1398 (8th Cir. 1995).

36. Motorcity of Jacksonville Ltd. v. Southeast Bank, N.A., 120 F.3d 1140 (11th Cir. 1997) (en banc), *cert. denied,* 523 U.S. 1093 (1998); Murphy v. FDIC, 208 F.3d 959 (11th Cir. 2000), *cert. granted,* 2000 U.S. LEXIS 4866 (2000). *Accord* Young v. FDIC, 103 F.3d 1180 (4th Cir. 1997), *cert. denied,* 522 U.S. 928 (1997).

THE RESPONSIBLE MANAGER
Managing Debtor–Creditor Relations

A responsible manager must understand lender liability risks. The following steps will help lenders minimize those risks.

In negotiating loan terms, the lender should indicate clearly that any commitment must be in writing and approved by the loan committee or other appropriate officials of the lender. The lender's written communications to the borrower should disclaim any commitment if none is intended.

The lender should avoid provisions in loan documents giving it a broad right to control the borrower's management decisions or day-to-day business activities. The lender should refrain from using its financial leverage to influence such activities as the selection of management, the hiring or firing of employees, or the payment of other creditors.

The loan documents should contain a merger clause stating that the written loan documents supersede any prior oral understandings and that the borrower is not relying on any prior oral promise or representation by the lender. The loan documents should provide that any amendment, modification, or waiver of the terms of the documents or of the rights of the parties must be in writing and signed by both the lender and the borrower.

The lender may ask the borrower to insert in the loan documents a waiver of its right to a jury trial. Juries are often perceived as sympathetic to borrowers; a judge may be less likely to award large compensatory or punitive damages to the borrower. The lender may want to specify in the loan documents that any legal action by the borrower must be brought in a court in a specific state or city to avoid the possible disadvantage the lender may have as a defendant in a court in the borrower's home territory. The lender may want to add an arbitration clause to the loan documents, stating that any disputes arising under the loan documents will be resolved through binding arbitration instead of litigation in a court.

The lender should maintain accurate and complete credit files supporting all the actions it takes. Virtually all of the documents in the lender's files may be subject to legal discovery; it is wise to assume that any entry in the credit files may someday be read to a judge or jury in a lender liability case.

The lender should not threaten to take actions that are not yet authorized or that it does not actually intend to take. The lender should give reasonable warning and, if possible, written notice to the borrower before terminating a line of credit, changing an established course of conduct, accelerating a loan, or exercising any remedies. In a workout situation, when the borrower is trying to renegotiate a loan it cannot pay, or when it becomes apparent that the borrower may be preparing a lender liability suit, the lender should consult with legal counsel.

Except when acting as a trustee or other fiduciary, the lender should refrain from giving any legal, financial, or investment advice to the borrower that might create a fiduciary relationship between the lender and the borrower. The lender should be cautious about giving other creditors the financial history of the borrower or opinions as to the borrower's creditworthiness.

At all times the lender's loan officers should behave professionally, regardless of their level of frustration with the borrower. Any personality conflicts with the borrower should be avoided. If a personality conflict does develop, the matter should be transferred to other loan officers.

It has become fashionable in some circles to view Chapter 11 as a strategic option for creative business planning. Apart from the fresh start granted to individual debtors, however, the bankruptcy system generally respects a debtor's obligations existing under state or other federal law; it merely provides a forum for dealing fairly, efficiently, and flexibly with the rights of all the creditors and equity holders. Thus, although insolvency is not a prerequisite for relief, a bankruptcy filing is generally not appropriate unless the business is in serious financial difficulties.

If those difficulties are present, the bankruptcy system can be an effective mechanism for overcoming them while preserving a productive enterprise. Yet for each celebrated success, there are countless failed Chapter 11 cases, in which no plan is confirmed and creditors are left with less than they would have received through prompt liquidation. This is partly the price of giving depressed businesses the chance to rebound, but it also reflects fundamental problems.

Many debtors, most of them single-asset or other small businesses, file Chapter 11 cases without any realistic prospect for reorganization. In some instances, the principals refuse to recognize and deal with financial ills until the business is too weak to survive. Continuing their ostrichlike pattern, they then file a Chapter 11 petition, awash in a sort of terminal euphoria, not recognizing that liquidation is inevitable. Other debtors see the writing on the wall but file to buy time, hoping for a miracle cure. Still others file merely to postpone the management's impending unemployment.

Congress gave creditors the means to protect their interests, however. If management acts improperly, a trustee can be appointed; if reorganization is improbable, the case can be dismissed or converted to a Chapter 7 liquidation. Unfortunately, these remedies are rarely invoked before the creditors' interests are seriously prejudiced. Not surprisingly, individual unsecured creditors tend to be reluctant to throw good money after bad by policing the debtor's conduct. For the same reason (though with less justification), they frequently decline to serve or participate actively on the official creditors' committee, so this watchdog may be somnolent or nonexistent in smaller cases. Thus, unless a secured creditor is motivated to overcome this inertia, a Chapter 11 case may have a bleak outcome.

Unless prompted by an interested party, the bankruptcy judge ordinarily will not intervene until the situation becomes egregious, as when the DIP does not comply with the rules, such as those requiring regular financial and tax reporting. Because the court is not well equipped to investigate the progress of each Chapter 11

debtor, an abusive case can languish for considerable time before the court itself initiates corrective action.

The effectiveness of the bankruptcy system depends largely upon knowledgeable and responsible conduct by the interested parties. In general, both debtors and creditors benefit by addressing financial problems early and pursuing a constructive workout. Because the charged emotional climate often makes this difficult, it is important to obtain objective and practical advice from counsel. If a workout is not possible, the debtor's management should consider whether a reorganization is plausible before filing for relief under Chapter 11. If the case is filed, creditors must recognize that meaningful participation, ideally through the official creditors' committee, is usually necessary to protect their interests.

Directors of a corporation in financial trouble assume new responsibilities to protect not only shareholders but the entire community of interests represented by creditors, employees, and other parties with a stake in the continued viability of the corporation. Once a corporation becomes insolvent or files for bankruptcy, the directors owe a fiduciary duty to creditors as well as shareholders.

INSIDE STORY

RJR Nabisco Leveraged Buyout

From time to time, a company may incur long-term indebtedness in the form of bonds. The proceeds of such debt will generally be used for long-term purposes, such as the acquisition of machinery or the construction of a new plant. Bonds are usually negotiable and are available for purchase and sale by investors in the public market. The company that sells the bonds, called the issuer, will normally sell them to an underwriter that, in turn, markets them to the public.

The agreement governing a bond issue is contained in a written document called an *indenture*. Like a loan agreement or a note purchase agreement, an indenture contains a description of the terms, or characteristics, of the bonds. Such terms include the interest rate; the security, if any, for the bonds; and the terms for repayment of the principal and retirement of the bonds. In addition, the issuer will make certain representations and warranties about itself, the bonds, and certain promises (or covenants) with respect to what it will or will not do while the bonds are outstanding. Because a public market exists for

bonds, many of the terms found in indentures have become standardized.

In the past, the standard indenture did not contain protections against changes in corporate structure, such as leveraged buyouts, mergers, or hostile takeovers. Such events, called *event risks,* cause the prices of high-grade investments to plummet. For example, in a leveraged buyout (LBO), in which the buyer acquires the stock or assets of a company by borrowing large sums of debt and using little equity, the company's assets must be pledged as security for the debt. Frequently, after the LBO is consummated, the acquired company's assets are sold off to reduce the debt burden.

The case of *Metropolitan Life Insurance Co. v. RJR Nabisco, Inc.*[37] arose when two institutional bondholders found themselves holding bonds whose values had declined after the issuer's LBO. They sued the issuer in the U.S. District Court for the Southern District of New

37. 716 F. Supp. 1504 (S.D.N.Y. 1989).

York. Even though the indentures did not expressly prohibit an LBO, the bond holders argued that the issuer was required to repurchase the bonds because it had breached an implied covenant of good faith and fair dealing when it entered into the LBO. The court held that, because the written agreement did not contain an express LBO prohibition, to imply a covenant of good faith and fair dealing that prohibited the LBO would add to the indenture a term that was neither bargained for nor contemplated by the parties.

BACKGROUND

On October 20, 1988, F. Ross Johnson, then the CEO of RJR Nabisco, Inc., proposed a $17 billion leveraged buyout of the company. A bidding war began, and Kohlberg Kravis Roberts and Company (KKR) submitted the successful bid. KKR's proposal called for a $24 billion buyout valued at approximately $109 per share.

Even before the company had accepted KKR's proposal, the bond holders, Metropolitan Life Insurance Company (MetLife) and Jefferson Life Insurance Company, filed suit. They alleged that the company's actions drastically impaired the value of the bonds they held by "misappropriating" the value of those bonds to help finance the acquisition, thereby creating a windfall for the company's shareholders. The plaintiffs argued that the acquisition contradicted the understandings of the market on which the plaintiffs had relied. They also said that RJR had actively solicited, and had received, investment-grade ratings for its bonds; and, because the ratings would be adversely affected by the LBO, the LBO contradicted a basic premise for their investment.

MetLife and Jefferson were sophisticated investors in the bond market, having held approximately $350 million in bonds issued by RJR between July 1975 and July 1988. MetLife had assets exceeding $88 billion and debt holdings exceeding $49 billion. Jefferson had more than $3 billion in total assets and $1.5 billion in debt securities. The court acknowledged that the plaintiffs, like other holders of public bond issues, had acquired the bonds after the indentures had been negotiated and memorialized. Nevertheless, the court noted, the underwriters that ordinarily negotiate the terms of the indentures with the issuers must then sell the bonds; thus, they must negotiate with the interests of the buyers in mind. Moreover, the plaintiffs presumably reviewed the indentures carefully before lending large sums to any company.

The indentures all contained the same basic provisions. None restricted the creation of unsecured debt or the payment of dividends by RJR. All permitted mergers as long as the surviving corporation assumed existing debt. Two of the indentures had previously included restrictions on incurring the type of debt contemplated by the LBO, but these restrictions had been deleted in subsequent negotiations unrelated to the LBO. In one case, MetLife had bargained for a guarantee from RJR's predecessor, R.J. Reynolds, in exchange for its agreement to delete the restrictive covenants. In the other case, MetLife had bargained for a new rate and different maturity in exchange for such deletion.

THE COURT'S DECISION

The plaintiffs had argued that the company, explicitly or implicitly, had agreed with the bond holders' premise that the bonds would maintain their investment ratings. However, the court determined that the indentures contained no explicit prohibition against the LBO with KKR and that they unambiguously permitted the LBO. Because the indentures were unambiguous, the court said, the plaintiffs could not introduce extrinsic evidence— that is, evidence outside the indenture language—to show that the intention of the parties was to prohibit the LBO. Thus, documents indicating that MetLife had recognized the risk of an LBO to public debt (but had not taken any steps to protect against such risk) were inadmissible as evidence.

The court said that under certain circumstances, courts will consider extrinsic evidence to evaluate the scope of an implied covenant of good faith. However, the court noted that under applicable precedents, a different rule applied in interpreting boilerplate provisions of indentures used in the securities market. The court explained that boilerplate provisions do not result from the relationship of particular borrowers and lenders and thus do not depend upon the particularized intentions of the parties. Because the efficiency of capital markets relied upon uniform interpretation of indentures, the meaning of boilerplate provisions in such indentures was not subject to case-by-case determination.

The court noted that, even though the plaintiffs had not alleged that an express covenant had been breached, a covenant of good faith and fair dealing could be implied if the "fruits of the agreement" between the parties had been "spoiled." In this analysis, the court determined that the "fruits" guaranteed by the indentures included the periodic and regular payment of interest and the eventual repayment of principal. Yet interest payments had been continuing, and there was no indication that the principal would not be paid when due. The court said that a restriction against incurring new debt would be an additional "fruit" or benefit that the parties had not bargained for. The court added that it had no reason to believe that the market, in evaluating bonds, did not discount for the possibility that the issuer might engage in a debt-financed buyout. Thus, the loss in bond value was a market risk that public bond holders accepted.

The court noted that the indentures contained provisions for adding new covenants on the mutual agreement of RJR and the bond holders, and it suggested that these provisions could be used to add restrictions against LBO debt. While acknowledging that huge, sophisticated companies like RJR might not accept such new covenants, the court said that multibillion-dollar investors like MetLife and Jefferson presumably had some say in the terms of the investments they make and continue to hold. If the issuers were to need new infusions of capital, for example, the bond holders would have an opportunity to impose new covenants. Because of the plaintiffs' and RJR's relatively equal bargaining positions, the court concluded that the contract between them was not inequitable.

PROTECTING AGAINST EVENT RISK

In response to bond purchasers' concern about event risk, underwriters have begun to include new, express covenants. In one recent bond issue, the indenture included a provision granting bond holders the right to sell their bonds back to the issuer in the event of a change of control or leveraged buyout. Some lenders have devised debts in which the interest rate is adjusted if the issuer's debt rating is downgraded.

Standard and Poor Corporation responded by introducing a rating system called "event risk covenant rankings." Bonds are ranked on a scale of "E–1, strong protection" to "E–5, insignificant or no protection," based on the degree of covenant protection provided in a bond indenture.

KEY WORDS AND PHRASES

absolute priority rule 924
affirmative covenants 909
after-acquired property 912
amortized 905
antideficiency laws 905
attached 911
automatic stay 925
avoiding powers 929
bankruptcy estate 919
base rate 907
best interests of creditors test 922
call 910
certificate of deposit (CD) rate 907
collateral 905
commercial paper 905
commitment fee 905
composition 922
composition plan 921
conditions precedent 909
continuing guaranty 915
covenants 909
cramdown 923
cross-collateralization 912
cross-default 910
debt subordination 916
debtor 911
debtor in possession (DIP) 927

discharged 919
D'Oench, Duhme doctrine 939
dragnet clause 912
earmarking doctrine 931
economic duress 938
equitable subordination 916
event risk 941
events of default 910
executory contracts 933
exempt property 919
extension plan 921
finance lease 914
floating 907
floating lien 912
foreclose 905
fraudulent conveyance 915
guarantor 914
guaranty 914
guaranty of collection 914
guaranty of payment 914
guaranty of performance 914
impaired claim 923
indenture 941
junior debt 916
lien 909
lien subordination 916
limited guaranty 914

London Interbank Offered Rate (LIBOR) 907
maturity date 905
negative covenants 909
note purchase agreement 906
one-form-of-action laws 905
participation loan 906
perfected 911
pledge 911
preferences 930
prepackaged bankruptcy 936
primary debtor 914
prime rate 907
priming lien 929
principal 904
proof of claim 927
purchase-money security interest 913
reaffirmation agreement 919
reference rate 907
restricted guaranty 915
revolving line of credit 905
revolving loan 905
right of setoff 911
secured loan 905
secured party 911
secured transactions 910
security agreement 911

QUESTIONS AND CASE PROBLEMS

1. You have just graduated from business school, but the economy has taken a turn for the worse and you are unable to find a job. While looking for work, you decide to move back in with your parents. Although your parents are willing to feed and shelter you temporarily, they tell you that your student loans are your own responsibility. After you have missed several months of loan payments, a friend of yours who went to law school suggests that you file for bankruptcy under Chapter 13 and attempt to get your loans discharged under the "hardship" exception because you are unemployed and have no income. What is the likely result in the bankruptcy court? Is the result different under Chapter 7? Is it ethical to file for bankruptcy if you expect to get a good job once the economy improves? [*In re Claxton,* 140 B.R. 565 (N.D. Okla. 1992); *In re Coveney,* 192 B.R. 140 (W.D. Tex. 1996)]

2. ABC Food Corporation, a food company with annual sales of more than $1 billion, operated a paper division that supplied ABC with packaging for its food products. ABC's management determined that the company should concentrate on its core business of manufacturing food products and recommended to the board of directors that the assets of the paper division be sold.

   Newcorp, Inc. is a newly formed corporation with two shareholders who have experience in the timber industry. Those two shareholders also jointly own Lumber Corporation, which operates two lumber mills in the state of Washington. Newcorp was formed specifically to acquire the assets of ABC's paper division.

   On February 1, 2000, ABC and Newcorp signed a letter of intent specifying a closing no later than July 1, 2000, subject to Newcorp obtaining satisfactory financing. The letter of intent provided that ABC and Newcorp would enter into a long-term contract whereby Newcorp would supply specified quantities of paper packaging to ABC.

   On February 15, 2000, Newcorp approached the Bank of Hope to request a term loan to acquire the assets of ABC's paper division and a revolving line of credit to meet its day-to-day working capital requirements. On March 31, 2000, the Bank of Hope delivered to Newcorp a letter stating that it would agree to extend a credit facility to Newcorp on the terms and conditions described in a term sheet attached to the letter.

   The Bank of Hope required, as a condition to its credit facility, that the credit be secured by all fixed and current assets of Newcorp. Carlos Banker, the account officer for the bank, took all steps necessary to give the Bank of Hope a valid first-priority lien on all collateral.

   A major source of revenue for Newcorp will be the long-term supply contract with ABC. The Bank of Hope is requiring an assignment of the supply contract. The assignment would prohibit ABC and Newcorp from making any amendments to the contract without the bank's consent.

   a. You are a manager of Newcorp. What objections would you have to such an assignment?

   b. You are a manager of ABC. Any objections?

3. Assume the facts in Question 2. One of the terms of the Bank of Hope's loan is a guaranty from each shareholder and from Lumber Corporation.

   a. You are Sylvia Daily, president of Newcorp. As president, you will be involved in the day-to-day operations of Newcorp. What arguments might you make against giving such a guaranty?

   b. You are Joe Lucre. You own 51 percent of the stock of Newcorp, and you made loans to Newcorp during the initial stages of its existence. You have since left the running of Newcorp to Sylvia Daily and other managers. What arguments could you make against giving such a guaranty?

   c. You are the Bank of Hope's attorney. What advice would you give the bank about taking a guaranty from Lumber Corporation?

4. Assume the facts in Questions 2 and 3. On June 1, 2000, Revolving Credit Bank takes over the revolving line of credit from the Bank of Hope and acquires the Bank of Hope's security interest in

Newcorp's accounts receivable and inventory. Beginning in early 2001, due to a combination of internal and external conditions, Newcorp's business failed to generate sufficient revenue to meet its debt obligations. The loan agreement between Newcorp and Revolving Credit Bank contains an advance clause, which states that the bank may, at its discretion, advance up to $2 million based on eligible accounts receivable and inventory. Revolving Credit Bank informed Newcorp that Newcorp had failed to maintain certain financial covenants contained in their credit agreement. Without declaring a default, Revolving Credit Bank then required Newcorp to establish a locked-box arrangement with the bank, so that all payments made to Newcorp could be used first to repay any advances outstanding. On March 1, 2001, Newcorp's treasurer called Valerie Lender, Revolving Credit Bank's account officer, and asked for a $350,000 advance to cover checks that would be presented to the bank that day. Revolving Credit Bank refused to lend the full amount requested but did advance $200,000 to pay certain suppliers.

You are the manager of one of Newcorp's trade creditors that has not been paid. Do you have any rights against Revolving Credit Bank?

5. Assume the facts in Questions 2 through 4. In April 2001, Newcorp began to have difficulty meeting its monthly repayment obligations on the term loan from the Bank of Hope. Although Newcorp never missed a payment, the payments were all a few days late. In May 2001, Carlos Banker called Newcorp's treasurer, assuring him that the Bank of Hope "would stand by the company" and that Newcorp should do whatever it could to keep the payments current. In September 2001, Revolving Credit Bank, concerned about continuing deteriorating conditions, decided to initiate foreclosure proceedings. The Bank of Hope followed suit only when Revolving Credit Bank began foreclosure proceedings. When the Bank of Hope began foreclosure proceedings against the paper plant, it discovered that the nearby Temecula River was polluted due to wastewater discharged from the plant.

a. You are a manager of Newcorp. What defenses would you raise against Revolving Credit Bank's foreclosure? Against the Bank of Hope's foreclosure?

b. You are a manager of Revolving Credit Bank. How would you respond to Newcorp's arguments?

c. You are a manager of the Bank of Hope. How would you respond to Newcorp's arguments?

Should the Bank of Hope proceed to foreclose against the plant? Should it require Newcorp to clean up the river? What recourse does the Bank of Hope have against Newcorp if it does not foreclose? Does it have any recourse against any other party?

d. You are a manager of ABC and hold a junior deed of trust on the property. How would you react to the Bank of Hope's latest action?

e. Was the Bank of Hope's foreclosure ethical?

6. Boo.com North America, Inc., an Internet retailer of brand name sportswear, filed a voluntary petition under Chapter 11 on October 31, 2000. Its primary asset was an unexpired lease for 9,043 square feet of office space in New York City at a rent of $27.50 per square foot. Given that the market rent had risen to $50 a square foot, Boo.com sought to assume the lease and assign it to Radical Media for $350,000. The lease provided that the lessee could not sublet or assign the lease without the lessor's prior consent and that, even if consent were given, the lessee was required to pay over to the lessor any profit realized on the sublet or assignment. Can the lessor prevent Boo.com from assigning the lease to Radical Media? If not, can it require Boo.com to pay over to it the $350,000 profit? [*In re Boo.com North America Inc.*, 2000 Bankr. LEXIS 1559 (Bankr. S.D.N.Y. Dec. 15, 2000)]

7. Rembert ran up gambling losses of between $18,000 and $24,000. She obtained a second mortgage on her house and repaid some of her credit card debt, but she continued gambling and incurred further losses. When she filed bankruptcy under Chapter 7, the two credit card companies from which she had received cash advances claimed that her debts (totaling $11,000) were procured by fraud and therefore were nondischargeable. They argued that by using the credit cards, she represented that she had the ability to repay the debt when in fact her financial condition made repayment impossible. Rembert countered that there was fraud only if, at the time she used the cards, she had no intent to repay the debt incurred. Who is correct? Is it ethical to incur debt without knowing how one will be able to repay it? [*Rembert v. AT&T Universal Card Service*, 141 F.3d 277 (6th Cir. 1998); *Citibank (South Dakota) N.A. v. Eashai (In re Eashai)*, 87 F.3d 1082 (9th Cir. 1996)]

8. In August 1989, Bruce G. Murphy invested $515,672 in a limited partnership interest in Orchid Island Associates Limited Partnership, which was developing the Orchid Island Golf and Beach Club

E-COMMERCE

Project in Florida. The general partner had projected a 6.1 multiple return on investments. In the period from the fall of 1988 until the beginning of 1991, Southeast Bank provided loans for the project totaling $50 million. Orchid eventually defaulted on its loans, and Southeast foreclosed on the property. Southeast itself was declared insolvent in September 1991 and placed in FDIC receivership. Ultimately, after all of Southeast's creditors had been paid, there was a $150 million surplus available for distribution to its shareholders.

In 1992, Murphy sued the FDIC, as receiver for Southeast, alleging that Southeast asserted extensive control over the project and that Southeast knew about and participated in the general partner's fraudulent misrepresentation that projections by Arthur Anderson & Company reflected a "6.1 multiple return" on his investment. Murphy claimed that Southeast acted in concert with Orchid in making decisions pertaining to the Orchid development, and that these decisions were separate and apart from Southeast's role as a mere lender to Orchid. Murphy sued for breach of fiduciary duty, breach of contract, accounting deficiencies, fraud, negligent misrepresentation, and securities violations. What facts would Murphy have to prove to establish his claims against Southeast's receiver, the FDIC? What defenses are available to the FDIC? Who is likely to prevail? [*Murphy v. FDIC*, 208 F.3d 959 (11th Cir. 2000), *cert. granted*, 2000 U.S. LEXIS 4866 (2000); *Murphy v. FDIC*, 61 F.3d 34 (D.C. Cir. 1995)]

9. Koenig Sporting Goods, Inc. was the lessee under a ten-year lease that required it to pay the landlord $8,500 on the first day of each month for that month's rent. On August 18, 1997, Koenig filed a Chapter 11 petition for bankruptcy. On November 25, 1997, Koenig notified the landlord that it was rejecting the lease effective December 2, 1997, which was the date Koenig in fact vacated the property. Is the landlord entitled to the full month's rent or rent for only December 1 and 2? [*Koenig Sporting Goods, Inc. v. Morse Road Co.* (*In re Koenig Sporting Goods, Inc.*), 203 F.3d 986 (6th Cir. 2000)]

MANAGER'S DILEMMA

10. MNVA was a Minnesota corporation engaged in operating a short-line freight railroad. Larry and Diane Wood were officers and directors and major shareholders of MNVA, and DMVW was a wholly

owned subsidiary of MNVA. In August 1994, MNVA agreed in principle to the terms of a letter of intent with Pioneer Railcorp under which Pioneer agreed to acquire MNVA's operating assets by purchasing MNVA's stock. MNVA decided to spin off DMVW to the MNVA shareholders as part of the reorganization in connection with the sale to Pioneer. In October 1994, the deal between MNVA and Pioneer was restructured as a sale of assets. On November 21, 1994, after determining that the company would be able to pay its debts in the ordinary course of business after the proposed distribution of DMVW stock to the MNVA shareholders, the MNVA board of directors approved the distribution of DMVW stock to the existing MNVA shareholders in proportion to the percentage of stock they owned in MNVA. No consideration was paid to MNVA for the distribution of DMVW stock. After the distribution, DMVW became an independently operated entity. In December 1994, MNVA sold its assets to Pioneer in exchange for $1 and the assumption of certain secured debts; it thereafter ceased operations.

In May 1996, Helm Financial obtained a state court judgment against MNVA for railcar leasing fees in the amount of $96,028, plus interest and attorneys' fees and costs, but MNVA had insufficient assets to pay them. According to MNVA, during the course of winding up its affairs, it was unable to pay all of its creditors in full because it experienced an "unexpected shortfall" after losing several substantial claims, including one against the Minnesota Department of Transportation for reimbursement of track rehabilitation expenses.

In June 1997, Helm sued MNVA, DMVW, and the individual officers and directors of MNVA, alleging that the distribution of DMVW stock to the MNVA shareholders defrauded MNVA's creditors in violation of the Minnesota Uniform Fraudulent Transfer Act and constituted an unlawful preference of the defendant officers, directors, and shareholders over MNVA's creditors in breach of their fiduciary duty to the creditors. Helm alleged that the spinoff left MNVA insolvent because DMVW was MNVA's most valuable asset.

Was the distribution of the DMVW stock a fraudulent transfer? Did the Woods violate their fiduciary duty to creditors, such as Helm? Under the Minnesota corporation law, a distribution to shareholders is permitted only when "the corporation will be able to pay its debts in the ordinary course of business after making the distribution and the board does not know before the distribution is made that the determination was or has become erroneous." Did the Woods and their fellow officers and directors act ethically? Would your answer be any different if instead of distributing shares of a subsidiary as a dividend, the board had voted to repay preexisting loans from the Woods to MNVA? [*Helm Financial Corp. v. MNVA Railroad, Inc.*, 212 F.3d 1076 (11th Cir. 2000)]

INTERNET SOURCES	
This site provides links to bankruptcy journals and publications and to law firm Web sites providing bankruptcy information.	http://findlaw.com/01topics/03bankruptcy
This site, maintained by the American Bankruptcy Institute, includes legislative updates.	http://www.abiworld.org/legis
The Bankruptcy Lawfinder site, maintained by the law offices of Warren E. Agin in Massachusetts, provides answers to frequently asked bankruptcy questions.	http://www.agin.com/bkfaq
This site, maintained by Cornell Law School, contains a full-text version of UCC Article 9.	http://www.law.cornell.edu/ucc/9

Appendices

PREAMBLE

We the People of the United States, in Order to form a more perfect Union, establish Justice, insure domestic Tranquility, provide for the common defence, promote the general Welfare, and secure the Blessings of Liberty to ourselves and our Posterity, do ordain and establish this Constitution for the United States of America.

ARTICLE I

Section 1. All legislative Powers herein granted shall be vested in a Congress of the United States, which shall consist of a Senate and House of Representatives.

Section 2. The House of Representatives shall be composed of Members chosen every second Year by the People of the several States, and the Electors in each State shall have the Qualifications requisite for Electors of the most numerous Branch of the State Legislature.

No Person shall be a Representative who shall not have attained to the Age of twenty five Years, and been seven Years a Citizen of the United States, and who shall not, when elected, be an Inhabitant of that State in which he shall be chosen.

Representatives and direct Taxes shall be apportioned among the several States which may be included within this Union, according to their respective Numbers, which shall be determined by adding to the whole Number of free Persons, including those bound to Service for a Term of Years, and excluding Indians not taxed, three fifths of all other Persons. The actual Enumeration shall be made within three Years after the first Meeting of the Congress of the United States, and within every subsequent Term of ten Years, in such Manner as they shall by Law direct. The Number of Representatives shall not exceed one for every thirty Thousand, but each State shall have at Least one Representative; and until such enumeration shall be made, the State of New Hampshire shall be entitled to chuse three, Massachusetts eight, Rhode Island and Providence Plantations one, Connecticut five, New York six, New Jersey four, Pennsylvania eight, Delaware one, Maryland six, Virginia ten, North Carolina five, South Carolina five, and Georgia three.

When vacancies happen in the Representation from any State, the Executive Authority thereof shall issue Writs of Election to fill such Vacancies.

The House of Representatives shall chuse their Speaker and other Officers; and shall have the sole Power of Impeachment.

Section 3. The Senate of the United States shall be composed of two Senators from each State, chosen by the Legislature thereof, for six Years; and each Senator shall have one Vote.

Immediately after they shall be assembled in Consequence of the first Election, they shall be divided as equally as may be into three Classes. The Seats of the Senators of the first Class shall be vacated at the Expiration of the second Year, of the second Class at the Expiration of the fourth Year, and of the third Class at the Expiration of the sixth Year, so that one third may be chosen every second Year; and if Vacancies happen by Resignation, or otherwise, during the Recess of the Legislature of any State, the Executive thereof may make temporary Appointments until the next Meeting of the Legislature, which shall then fill such Vacancies.

No Person shall be a Senator who shall not have attained to the Age of thirty Years, and been nine Years a Citizen of the United States, and who shall not, when elected, be an Inhabitant of that State for which he shall be chosen.

The Vice President of the United States shall be President of the Senate, but shall have no Vote, unless they be equally divided.

The Senate shall chuse their other Officers, and also a President pro tempore, in the Absence of the Vice President, or when he shall exercise the Office of President of the United States.

The Senate shall have the sole Power to try all Impeachments. When sitting for that Purpose, they shall be on Oath or Affirmation. When the President of the United States is tried, the Chief Justice shall preside: And no Person shall be convicted without the Concurrence of two thirds of the Members present.

Judgment in Cases of Impeachment shall not extend further than to removal from Office, and disqualification to hold and enjoy any Office of honor, Trust, or Profit under the United States: but the Party convicted shall nevertheless be liable and subject to Indictment, Trial, Judgment, and Punishment, according to Law.

Section 4. The Times, Places and Manner of holding Elections for Senators and Representatives, shall be prescribed in each State by the Legislature thereof; but the Congress may at any time by Law make or alter such Regulations, except as to the Places of chusing Senators.

The Congress shall assemble at least once in every Year, and such Meeting shall be on the first Monday in December, unless they shall by Law appoint a different Day.

Section 5. Each House shall be the Judge of the Elections, Returns, and Qualifications of its own Members, and a Majority of each shall constitute a Quorum to do Business; but a smaller Number may adjourn from day to day, and may be authorized to compel the Attendance of absent Members, in such Manner, and under such Penalties as each House may provide.

Each House may determine the Rules of its Proceedings, punish its Members for disorderly Behavior, and, with the Concurrence of two thirds, expel a Member.

Each House shall keep a Journal of its Proceedings, and from time to time publish the same, excepting such Parts as may in their Judgment require Secrecy; and the Yeas and Nays of the Members of either House on any question shall, at the Desire of one fifth of those Present, be entered on the Journal.

Neither House, during the Session of Congress, shall, without the Consent of the other, adjourn for more than three days, nor to any other Place than that in which the two Houses shall be sitting.

Section 6. The Senators and Representatives shall receive a Compensation for their Services, to be ascertained by Law, and paid out of the Treasury of the United States. They shall in all Cases, except Treason, Felony and Breach of the Peace, be privileged from Arrest during their Attendance at the Session of their respective Houses, and in going to and returning from the same; and for any Speech or Debate in either House, they shall not be questioned in any other Place.

No Senator or Representative shall, during the Time for which he was elected, be appointed to any civil Office under the Authority of the United States, which shall have been created, or the Emoluments whereof shall have been increased during such time; and no Person holding any Office under the United States, shall be a Member of either House during his Continuance in Office.

Section 7. All Bills for raising Revenue shall originate in the House of Representatives; but the Senate may propose or concur with Amendments as on other Bills.

Every Bill which shall have passed the House of Representatives and the Senate, shall, before it become a Law, be presented to the President of the United States; If he approve he shall sign it, but if not he shall return it, with his Objections to the House in which it shall have originated, who shall enter the Objections at large on their Journal, and proceed to reconsider it. If after such Reconsideration two thirds of that House shall agree to pass the Bill, it shall be sent together with the Objections, to the other House, by which it shall likewise be reconsidered, and if approved by two thirds of that House, it shall become a Law. But in all such Cases the Votes of both Houses shall be determined by Yeas and Nays, and the Names of the Persons voting for and against the Bill shall be entered on the Journal of each House respectively. If any Bill shall not be returned by the President within ten Days (Sundays excepted) after it shall have been presented to him, the Same shall be a Law, in like Manner as if he had signed it, unless the Congress by their Adjournment prevent its Return in which Case it shall not be a Law.

Every Order, Resolution, or Vote to which the Concurrence of the Senate and House of Representatives may be necessary (except on a question of Adjournment) shall be presented to the President of the United States; and before the Same shall take Effect, shall be approved by him, or being disapproved by him, shall be repassed by two thirds of the Senate and House of Representatives, according to the Rules and Limitations prescribed in the Case of a Bill.

Section 8. The Congress shall have Power To lay and collect Taxes, Duties, Imposts and Excises, to pay the Debts and provide for the common Defence and general Welfare of the United States; but all Duties, Imposts and Excises shall be uniform throughout the United States;

To borrow Money on the credit of the United States;

To regulate Commerce with foreign Nations, and among the several States, and with the Indian Tribes;

To establish an uniform Rule of Naturalization, and uniform Laws on the subject of Bankruptcies throughout the United States;

To coin Money, regulate the Value thereof, and of foreign Coin, and fix the Standard of Weights and Measures;

To provide for the Punishment of counterfeiting the Securities and current Coin of the United States;

To establish Post Offices and post Roads;

To promote the Progress of Science and useful Arts, by securing for limited Times to Authors and Inventors the exclusive Right to their respective Writings and Discoveries;

To constitute Tribunals inferior to the supreme Court;

To define and punish Piracies and Felonies committed on the high Seas, and Offenses against the Law of Nations;

To declare War, grant Letters of Marque and Reprisal, and make Rules concerning Captures on Land and Water;

To raise and support Armies, but no Appropriation of Money to that Use shall be for a longer Term than two Years;

To provide and maintain a Navy;

To make Rules for the Government and Regulation of the land and naval Forces;

To provide for calling forth the Militia to execute the Laws of the Union, suppress Insurrections and repel Invasions;

To provide for organizing, arming, and disciplining, the Militia, and for governing such Part of them as may be employed in the Service of the United States, reserving to the States respectively, the Appointment of the Officers, and the Authority of training the Militia according to the discipline prescribed by Congress;

To exercise exclusive Legislation in all Cases whatsoever, over such District (not exceeding ten Miles square) as may, by Cession of particular States, and the Acceptance of Congress, become the Seat of the Government of the United States, and to exercise like Authority over all Places purchased by the Consent of the Legislature of the State in which the Same shall be, for the Erection of Forts, Magazines, Arsenals, dock-Yards, and other needful Buildings;—And

To make all Laws which shall be necessary and proper for carrying into Execution the foregoing Powers, and all other Powers vested by this Constitution in the Government of the United States, or in any Department or Officer thereof.

Section 9. The Migration or Importation of such Persons as any of the States now existing shall think proper to admit, shall not be prohibited by the Congress prior to the Year one thousand eight hundred and eight, but a Tax or duty may be imposed on such Importation, not exceeding ten dollars for each Person.

The privilege of the Writ of Habeas Corpus shall not be suspended, unless when in Cases of Rebellion or Invasion the public Safety may require it.

No Bill of Attainder or ex post facto Law shall be passed.

No Capitation, or other direct, Tax shall be laid, unless in Proportion to the Census or Enumeration herein before directed to be taken.

No Tax or Duty shall be laid on Articles exported from any State.

No Preference shall be given by any Regulation of Commerce or Revenue to the Ports of one State over those of another: nor shall Vessels bound to, or from, one State be obliged to enter, clear, or pay Duties in another.

No Money shall be drawn from the Treasury, but in Consequence of Appropriations made by Law; and a regular Statement and Account of the Receipts and Expenditures of all public Money shall be published from time to time.

No Title of Nobility shall be granted by the United States: And no Person holding any Office of Profit or Trust under them, shall, without the Consent of the Congress, accept of any present, Emolument, Office, or Title, of any kind whatever, from any King, Prince, or foreign State.

Section 10.   No State shall enter into any Treaty, Alliance, or Confederation; grant Letters of Marque and Reprisal; coin Money; emit Bills of Credit; make any Thing but gold and silver Coin a Tender in Payment of Debts; pass any Bill of Attainder, ex post facto Law, or Law impairing the Obligation of Contracts, or grant any Title of Nobility.

No State shall, without the Consent of the Congress, lay any Imposts or Duties on Imports or Exports, except what may be absolutely necessary for executing its inspection Laws: and the net Produce of all Duties and Imposts, laid by any State on Imports or Exports, shall be for the Use of the Treasury of the United States; and all such Laws shall be subject to the Revision and Controul of the Congress.

No State shall, without the Consent of Congress, lay any Duty of Tonnage, keep Troops, or Ships of War in time of Peace, enter into any Agreement or Compact with another State, or with a foreign Power, or engage in War, unless actually invaded, or in such imminent Danger as will not admit of delay.

ARTICLE II

Section 1.   The executive Power shall be vested in a President of the United States of America. He shall hold his Office during the Term of four Years, and, together with the Vice President, chosen for the same Term, be elected, as follows:

Each State shall appoint, in such Manner as the Legislature thereof may direct, a Number of Electors, equal to the whole Number of Senators and Representatives to which the State may be entitled in the Congress; but no Senator or Representative, or Person holding an Office of Trust or Profit under the United States, shall be appointed an Elector.

The Electors shall meet in their respective States, and vote by Ballot for two Persons, of whom one at least shall not be an Inhabitant of the same State with themselves. And they shall make a List of all the Persons voted for, and of the Number of Votes for each; which List they shall sign and certify, and transmit sealed to the Seat of the Government of the United States, directed to the President of the Senate. The President of the Senate shall, in the Presence of the Senate and House of Representatives, open all the Certificates, and the Votes shall then be counted. The Person having the greatest Number of Votes shall be the President, if such Number be a Majority of the whole Number of Electors appointed; and if there be more than one who have such Majority, and have an equal Number of Votes, then the House of Representatives shall immediately chuse by Ballot one of them for President; and if no Person have a Majority, then from the five highest on the List the said House shall in like Manner chuse the President. But in chusing the President, the Votes shall be taken by States, the Representation from each State having one Vote; A quorum for this Purpose shall consist of a Member or Members from two thirds of the States, and a Majority of all the States shall be necessary to a Choice. In every Case, after the Choice of the President, the Person having the greater Number of Votes of the Electors shall be the Vice President. But if there should remain two or more who have equal Votes, the Senate shall chuse from them by Ballot the Vice President.

The Congress may determine the Time of chusing the Electors, and the Day on which they shall give their Votes; which Day shall be the same throughout the United States.

No person except a natural born Citizen, or a Citizen of the United States, at the time of the Adoption of this Constitution, shall be eligible to the Office of President; neither shall any Person be eligible to that Office who shall not have attained to the Age of thirty five Years, and been fourteen Years a Resident within the United States.

In Case of the Removal of the President from Office, or of his Death, Resignation or Inability to discharge the Powers and Duties of the said Office, the same shall devolve on the Vice President, and the Congress may by Law provide for the Case of Removal, Death, Resignation or Inability, both of the President and Vice President, declaring what Officer shall then act as President, and such Officer shall act accordingly, until the Disability be removed, or a President shall be elected.

The President shall, at stated Times, receive for his Services, a Compensation, which shall neither be increased nor diminished during the Period for which he shall have been elected, and he shall not receive within that Period any other Emolument from the United States, or any of them.

Before he enter on the Execution of his Office, he shall take the following Oath or Affirmation: "I do solemnly swear (or affirm) that I will faithfully execute the Office of President of the United States, and will to the best of my Ability, preserve, protect and defend the Constitution of the United States."

Section 2.   The President shall be Commander in Chief of the Army and Navy of the United States, and of the Militia of the several States, when called into the actual Service of the United States; he may require the Opinion, in writing, of the principal Officer in each of the executive Departments, upon any Subject relating to the Duties of their respective Offices, and he shall have Power to grant Reprieves and Pardons for Offenses against the United States, except in Cases of Impeachment.

He shall have Power, by and with the Advice and Consent of the Senate to make Treaties, provided two thirds of the Senators present concur; and he shall nominate, and by and with the Advice and Consent of the Senate, shall appoint Ambassadors, other public Ministers and Consuls, Judges of the supreme Court, and all other Officers of the United States, whose Appointments are not herein otherwise provided for, and which shall be established by Law; but the Congress may by Law vest the Appointment of such inferior Officers, as they think proper, in the President alone, in the Courts of Law, or in the Heads of Departments.

The President shall have Power to fill up all Vacancies that may happen during the Recess of the Senate, by granting Commissions which shall expire at the End of their next Session.

Section 3. He shall from time to time give to the Congress Information of the State of the Union, and recommend to their Consideration such Measures as he shall judge necessary and expedient; he may, on extraordinary Occasions, convene both Houses, or either of them, and in Case of Disagreement between them, with Respect to the Time of Adjournment, he may adjourn them to such Time as he shall think proper; he shall receive Ambassadors and other public Ministers; he shall take Care that the Laws be faithfully executed, and shall Commission all the Officers of the United States.

Section 4. The President, Vice President and all civil Officers of the United States, shall be removed from Office on Impeachment for, and Conviction of, Treason, Bribery, or other high Crimes and Misdemeanors.

ARTICLE III

Section 1. The judicial Power of the United States, shall be vested in one supreme Court, and in such inferior Courts as the Congress may from time to time ordain and establish. The Judges, both of the supreme and inferior Courts, shall hold their Offices during good Behaviour, and shall, at stated Times, receive for their Services a Compensation, which shall not be diminished during their Continuance in Office.

Section 2. The judicial Power shall extend to all Cases, in Law and Equity, arising under this Constitution, the Laws of the United States, and Treaties made, or which shall be made, under their Authority;—to all Cases affecting Ambassadors, other public Ministers and Consuls;—to all Cases of admiralty and maritime Jurisdiction;—to Controversies to which the United States shall be a Party;—to Controversies between two or more States;—between a State and Citizens of another State;—between Citizens of different States;—between Citizens of the same State claiming Lands under Grants of different States, and between a State, or the Citizens thereof, and foreign States, Citizens or Subjects.

In all Cases affecting Ambassadors, other public Ministers and Consuls, and those in which a State shall be a Party, the supreme Court shall have original Jurisdiction. In all the other Cases before mentioned, the supreme Court shall have appellate Jurisdiction, both as to Law and Fact, with such Exceptions, and under such Regulations as the Congress shall make.

The Trial of all Crimes, except in Cases of Impeachment, shall be by Jury; and such Trial shall be held in the State where the said Crimes shall have been committed; but when not committed within any State, the Trial shall be at such Place or Places as the Congress may by Law have directed.

Section 3. Treason against the United States, shall consist only in levying War against them, or, in adhering to their Enemies, giving them Aid and Comfort. No Person shall be convicted of Treason unless on the Testimony of two Witnesses to the same overt Act, or on Confession in open Court.

The Congress shall have Power to declare the Punishment of Treason, but no Attainder of Treason shall work Corruption of Blood, or Forfeiture except during the Life of the Person attainted.

ARTICLE IV

Section 1. Full Faith and Credit shall be given in each State to the public Acts, Records, and judicial Proceedings of every other State. And the Congress may by general Laws prescribe the Manner in which such Acts, Records and Proceedings shall be proved, and the Effect thereof.

Section 2. The Citizens of each State shall be entitled to all Privileges and Immunities of Citizens in the several States.

A Person charged in any State with Treason, Felony, or other Crime, who shall flee from Justice, and be found in another State, shall on Demand of the executive Authority of the State from which he fled, be delivered up, to be removed to the State having Jurisdiction of the Crime.

No Person held to Service or Labour in one State, under the Laws thereof, escaping into another, shall, in Consequence of any Law or Regulation therein, be discharged from such Service or Labour, but shall be delivered up on Claim of the Party to whom such Service or Labour may be due.

Section 3. New States may be admitted by the Congress into this Union; but no new State shall be formed or erected within the Jurisdiction of any other State; nor any State be formed by the Junction of two or more States, or Parts of States, without the Consent of the Legislatures of the States concerned as well as of the Congress.

The Congress shall have Power to dispose of and make all needful Rules and Regulations respecting the Territory or other Property belonging to the United States; and nothing in this Constitution shall be so construed as to Prejudice any Claims of the United States, or of any particular State.

Section 4. The United States shall guarantee to every State in this Union a Republican Form of Government, and shall protect each of them against Invasion; and on Application of the Legislature, or of the Executive (when the Legislature cannot be convened) against domestic Violence.

ARTICLE V

The Congress, whenever two thirds of both Houses shall deem it necessary, shall propose Amendments to this Constitution, or, on the Application of the Legislatures of two thirds of the several States, shall call a Convention for proposing Amendments, which, in either Case, shall be valid to all Intents and Purposes, as part of this Constitution, when ratified by the Legislatures of three fourths of the several States, or by Conventions in three fourths thereof, as the one or the other Mode of Ratification may be proposed by the Congress; Provided that no Amendment which may be made prior to the Year One thousand eight hundred and eight shall in any Manner affect the first and fourth Clauses in the Ninth Section of the first Article; and that no State, without its Consent, shall be deprived of its equal Suffrage in the Senate.

ARTICLE VI

All Debts contracted and Engagements entered into, before the Adoption of this Constitution shall be as valid against the United States under this Constitution, as under the Confederation.

This Constitution, and the Laws of the United States which shall be made in Pursuance thereof; and all Treaties made, or which shall be made, under the Authority of the United States, shall be the supreme Law of the Land; and the Judges in every State shall be bound thereby, any Thing in the Constitution or Laws of any State to the Contrary notwithstanding.

The Senators and Representatives before mentioned, and the Members of the several State Legislatures, and all executive and judicial Officers, both of the United States and of the several States, shall be bound by Oath or Affirmation, to support this Constitution; but no religious Test shall ever be required as a Qualification to any Office or public Trust under the United States.

ARTICLE VII

The Ratification of the Conventions of nine States shall be sufficient for the Establishment of this Constitution between the States so ratifying the Same.

AMENDMENT I [1791]

Congress shall make no law respecting an establishment of religion, or prohibiting the free exercise thereof; or abridging the freedom of speech, or of the press; or the right of the people peaceably to assembly, and to petition the Government for a redress of grievances.

AMENDMENT II [1791]

A well regulated Militia, being necessary to the security of a free State, the right of the people to keep and bear Arms, shall not be infringed.

AMENDMENT III [1791]

No Soldier shall, in time of peace be quartered in any house, without the consent of the Owner, nor in time of war, but in a manner to be prescribed by law.

AMENDMENT IV [1791]

The right of the people to be secure in their persons, houses, papers, and effects, against unreasonable searches and seizures, shall not be violated, and no Warrants shall issue, but upon probable cause, supported by Oath or affirmation, and particularly describing the place to be searched, and the persons or things to be seized.

AMENDMENT V [1791]

No person shall be held to answer for a capital, or otherwise infamous crime, unless on a presentment or indictment of a Grand Jury, except in cases arising in the land or naval forces, or in the Militia, when in actual service in time of War or public danger; nor shall any person be subject for the same offence to be twice put in jeopardy of life or limb; nor shall be compelled in any criminal case to be a witness against himself, nor be deprived of life, liberty, or property, without due process of law; nor shall private property be taken for public use, without just compensation.

AMENDMENT VI [1791]

In all criminal prosecutions, the accused shall enjoy the right to a speedy and public trial, by an impartial jury of the State and district wherein the crime shall have been committed, which district shall have been previously ascertained by law, and to be informed of the nature and cause of the accusation; to be confronted with the witnesses against him; to have compulsory process for obtaining witnesses in his favor, and to have the Assistance of Counsel for his defence.

AMENDMENT VII [1791]

In Suits at common law, where the value in controversy shall exceed twenty dollars, the right of trial by jury shall be preserved, and no fact tried by jury, shall be otherwise re-examined in any Court of the United States, than according to the rules of the common law.

AMENDMENT VIII [1791]

Excessive bail shall not be required, nor excessive fines imposed, nor cruel and unusual punishments inflicted.

AMENDMENT IX [1791]

The enumeration in the Constitution, of certain rights, shall not be construed to deny or disparage others retained by the people.

AMENDMENT X [1791]

The powers not delegated to the United States by the Constitution, nor prohibited by it to the States, are reserved to the States respectively, or to the people.

AMENDMENT XI [1798]

The Judicial power of the United States shall not be construed to extend to any suit in law or equity, commenced or prosecuted against one of the United States by Citizens of another State, or by Citizens or Subjects of any Foreign State.

AMENDMENT XII [1804]

The Electors shall meet in their respective states, and vote by ballot for President and Vice-President, one of whom, at least, shall not be an inhabitant of the same state with themselves; they shall name in their ballots the person voted for as President, and in distinct ballots the person voted for as Vice-President, and they shall make distinct lists of all persons voted for as President, and of all persons voted for as Vice-President, and of the number of votes for each, which lists they shall sign and certify, and transmit sealed to the seat of the government of the United States, directed to the President of the Senate;—The President of the Senate shall, in the presence of the Senate and House of Representatives, open all the certificates and the votes shall then be counted;— The person having the greatest number of votes for President, shall be the President, if such number be a majority of the whole number of Electors appointed; and if no person have such majority, then from the persons having the highest numbers not exceeding three on the list of those voted for as President, the House of Representatives shall choose immediately, by ballot, the President. But in choosing the President, the votes shall be taken by states, the representation from each state having one vote; a quorum for this purpose shall consist of a member or members from two-thirds of the states, and a majority of all states shall be necessary to a choice. And if the House of Representatives shall not choose a President whenever the right of choice shall devolve upon them, before the fourth day of March next following, then the Vice-President shall act as President, as in the case of the death or other constitutional disability of the President.—The person having the greatest number of votes as Vice-President, shall be the Vice-President, if such number be a majority of the whole number of Electors appointed, and if no person have a majority, then from the two highest numbers on the list, the Senate shall choose the Vice-President; a quorum for the purpose shall consist of two-thirds of the whole number of Senators, and a majority of the whole number shall be necessary to a choice. But no person constitutionally ineligible to the office of President shall be eligible to that of Vice-President of the United States.

AMENDMENT XIII [1865]

Section 1. Neither slavery nor involuntary servitude, except as a punishment for crime whereof the party shall have been duly convicted, shall exist within the United States, or any place subject to their jurisdiction.

Section 2. Congress shall have power to enforce this article by appropriate legislation.

AMENDMENT XIV [1868]

Section 1. All persons born or naturalized in the United States, and subject to the jurisdiction thereof, are citizens of the United States and of the State wherein they reside. No State shall make or enforce any law which shall abridge the privileges or immunities of citizens of the United States; nor shall any State deprive any person of life, liberty, or property, without due process of law; nor deny to any person within its jurisdiction the equal protection of the laws.

Section 2. Representatives shall be apportioned among the several States according to their respective numbers, counting the whole number of persons in each State, excluding Indians not taxed. But when the right to vote at any election for the choice of electors for President and Vice President of the United States, Representatives in Congress, the Executive and Judicial officers of a State, or the members of the Legislature thereof, is denied to any of the male inhabitants of such State, being twenty-one years of age, and citizens of the United States, or in any way abridged, except for participation in rebellion, or other crime, the basis of representation therein shall be reduced in the proportion which the number of such male citizens shall bear to the whole number of male citizens twenty-one years of age in such State.

Section 3. No person shall be a Senator or Representative in Congress, or elector of President and Vice President, or hold any office, civil or military, under the United States, or under any State, who having previously taken an oath, as a member of Congress, or as an officer of the United States, or as a member of any State legislature, or as an executive or judicial officer of any State, to support the Constitution of the United States, shall have engaged in insurrection or rebellion against the same, or given aid or comfort to the enemies thereof. But Congress may by a vote of two-thirds of each House, remove such disability.

Section 4. The validity of the public debt of the United States, authorized by law, including debts incurred for payment of pensions and bounties for services in suppressing insurrection or rebellion, shall not be questioned. But neither the United States nor any State shall assume or pay any debt or obligation incurred in aid of insurrection or rebellion against the United States, or any claim for the loss or emancipation of any slave; but all such debts, obligations and claims shall be held illegal and void.

Section 5. The Congress shall have power to enforce, by appropriate legislation, the provisions of this article.

AMENDMENT XV [1870]

Section 1. The right of citizens of the United States to vote shall not be denied or abridged by the United States or by any State on account of race, color, or previous condition of servitude.

Section 2. The Congress shall have power to enforce this article by appropriate legislation.

AMENDMENT XVI [1913]

The Congress shall have power to lay and collect taxes on incomes, from whatever source derived, without apportionment among the several States, and without regard to any census or enumeration.

AMENDMENT XVII [1913]

Section 1. The Senate of the United States shall be composed of two Senators from each State, elected by the people thereof, for six years; and each Senator shall have one vote. The electors in each State shall have the qualifications requisite for electors of the most numerous branch of the State legislatures.

Section 2. When vacancies happen in the representation of any State in the Senate, the executive authority of such State shall issue writs of election to fill such vacancies: Provided, That the legislature of any State may empower the executive thereof to make temporary appointments until the people fill the vacancies by election as the legislature may direct.

Section 3. This amendment shall not be so construed as to affect the election or term of any Senator chosen before it becomes valid as part of the Constitution.

AMENDMENT XVIII [1919]

Section 1. After one year from the ratification of this article the manufacture, sale, or transportation of intoxicating liquors within, the importation thereof into, or the exportation thereof from the United States and all territory subject to the jurisdiction thereof for beverage purposes is hereby prohibited.

Section 2. The Congress and the several States shall have concurrent power to enforce this article by appropriate legislation.

Section 3. This article shall be inoperative unless it shall have been ratified as an amendment to the Constitution by the legislatures of the several States, as provided in the Constitution, within seven years from the date of the submission hereof to the States by the Congress.

AMENDMENT XIX [1920]

Section 1. The right of citizens of the United States to vote shall not be denied or abridged by the United States or by any State on account of sex.

Section 2. Congress shall have power to enforce this article by appropriate legislation.

AMENDMENT XX [1933]

Section 1. The terms of the President and Vice President shall end at noon on the 20th day of January, and the terms of Senators and Representatives at noon on the 3d day of January, of the years in which such terms would have ended if this article had not been ratified; and the terms of their successors shall then begin.

Section 2. The Congress shall assemble at least once in every year, and such meeting shall begin at noon on the 3d day of January, unless they shall by law appoint a different day.

Section 3. If, at the time fixed for the beginning of the term of the President, the President elect shall have died, the Vice President elect shall become President. If the President shall not have been chosen before the time fixed for the beginning of his term, or if the President elect shall have failed to qualify, then the Vice President elect shall act as President until a President shall have qualified; and the Congress may by law provide for the case wherein neither a President elect nor a Vice President elect shall have qualified, declaring who shall then act as President, or the manner in which one who is to act shall be selected, and such person shall act accordingly until a President or Vice President shall have qualified.

Section 4. The Congress may by law provide for the case of the death of any of the persons from whom the House of Representatives may choose a President whenever the right of choice shall have devolved upon them, and for the case of the death of any of the persons from whom the Senate may choose a Vice President whenever the right of choice shall have devolved upon them.

Section 5. Sections 1 and 2 shall take effect on the 15th day of October following the ratification of this article.

Section 6. This article shall be inoperative unless it shall have been ratified as an amendment to the Constitution by the legislatures of three-fourths of the several States within seven years from the date of its submission.

AMENDMENT XXI [1933]

Section 1. The eighteenth article of amendment to the Constitution of the United States is hereby repealed.

Section 2. The transportation or importation into any State, Territory, or possession of the United States for delivery or use therein of intoxicating liquors, in violation of the laws thereof, is hereby prohibited.

Section 3. This article shall be inoperative unless it shall have been ratified as an amendment to the Constitution by conventions in the several States, as provided in the Constitution, within seven years from the date of the submission hereof to the States by the Congress.

AMENDMENT XXII [1951]

Section 1. No person shall be elected to the office of the President more than twice, and no person who has held the office of President, or acted as President, for more than two years of a term to which some other person was elected President shall be elected to the office of President more than once. But this Article shall not apply to any person holding the office of President when this Article was proposed by the Congress, and shall not prevent any person who may be holding the office of President, or acting as President, during the term within which this Article becomes operative from holding the office of President or acting as President during the remainder of such term.

Section 2. This article shall be inoperative unless it shall have been ratified as an amendment to the Constitution by the legislatures of three-fourths of the several States within seven years from the date of its submission to the States by the Congress.

AMENDMENT XXIII [1961]

Section 1. The District constituting the seat of Government of the United States shall appoint in such manner as the Congress may direct:

A number of electors of President and Vice President equal to the whole number of Senators and Representatives in Congress to which the District would be entitled if it were a State, but in no event more than the least populous state; they shall be in addition to those appointed by the states, but they shall be considered, for the purposes of the election of President and Vice President, to be electors appointed by a state; and they shall meet in the District and perform such duties as provided by the twelfth article of amendment.

Section 2. The Congress shall have power to enforce this article by appropriate legislation.

AMENDMENT XXIV [1964]

Section 1. The right of citizens of the United States to vote in any primary or other election for President or Vice President, for electors for President or Vice President, or for Senator or Representative in Congress, shall not be denied or abridged by the United States, or any State by reason of failure to pay any poll tax or other tax.

Section 2. The Congress shall have power to enforce this article by appropriate legislation.

AMENDMENT XXV [1967]

Section 1. In case of the removal of the President from office or of his death or resignation, the Vice President shall become President.

Section 2. Whenever there is a vacancy in the office of the Vice President, the President shall nominate a Vice President who shall take office upon confirmation by a majority vote of both Houses of Congress.

Section 3. Whenever the President transmits to the President pro tempore of the Senate and the Speaker of the House of Representatives his written declaration that he is unable to discharge the powers and duties of his office, and until he transmits to them a written declaration to the contrary, such powers and duties shall be discharged by the Vice President as Acting President.

Section 4. Whenever the Vice President and a majority of either the principal officers of the executive departments or of such other body as Congress may by law provide, transmit to the President pro tempore of the Senate and the Speaker of the House of Representatives their written declaration that the President is unable to discharge the powers and duties of his office, the Vice President shall immediately assume the powers and duties of the office as Acting President.

Thereafter, when the President transmits to the President pro tempore of the Senate and the Speaker of the House of Representatives his written declaration that no inability exists, he shall resume the powers and duties of his office unless the Vice President and a majority of either the principal officers of the executive department or of such other body as Congress may by law provide, transmit within four days to the President pro tempore of the Senate and the Speaker of the House of Representatives their written declaration and the President is unable to discharge the powers and duties of his office. Thereupon Congress shall decide the issue, assembling within forty-eight hours for that purpose if not in session. If the Congress, within twenty-one days after receipt of the latter written declaration, or, if Congress is not in session, within twenty-one days after Congress is required to assemble, determines by two-thirds vote of both Houses

that the President is unable to discharge the powers and duties of his office, the Vice President shall continue to discharge the same as Acting President; otherwise, the President shall resume the powers and duties of his office.

AMENDMENT XXVI [1971]

Section 1. The right of citizens of the United States, who are eighteen years of age or older, to vote shall not be denied or abridged by the United States or by any State on account of age.

Section 2. The Congress shall have power to enforce this article by appropriate legislation.

AMENDMENT XXVII [1992]

No law, varying the compensation for the services of the Senators and Representatives, shall take effect, until an election of Representatives shall have intervened.

APPENDIX B *The* Uniform Electronic Transactions Act [Excerpts]

Section 5. Use of Electronic Records and Electronic Signatures; Variation by Agreement.

(a) This [Act] does not require a record or signature to be created, generated, sent, communicated, received, stored, or otherwise processed or used by electronic means or in electronic form.

(b) This [Act] applies only to transactions between parties each of which has agreed to conduct transactions by electronic means. Whether the parties agree to conduct a transaction by electronic means is determined from the context and surrounding circumstances, including the parties' conduct.

(c) A party that agrees to conduct a transaction by electronic means may refuse to conduct other transactions by electronic means. The right granted by this subsection may not be waived by agreement.

(d) Except as otherwise provided in this [Act], the effect of any of its provisions may be varied by agreement. The presence in certain provisions of this [Act] of the words "unless otherwise agreed," or words of similar import, does not imply that the effect of other provisions may not be varied by agreement.

(e) Whether an electronic record or electronic signature has legal consequences is determined by this [Act] and other applicable law.

Section 6. Construction and Application.

This [Act] must be construed and applied:

(1) to facilitate electronic transactions consistent with other applicable law;

(2) to be consistent with reasonable practices concerning electronic transactions and with the continued expansion of those practices; and

(3) to effectuate its general purpose to make uniform the law with respect to the subject of this [Act] among States enacting it.

Section 7. Legal Recognition of Electronic Records, Electronic Signatures, and Electronic Contracts.

(a) A record or signature may not be denied legal effect or enforceability solely because it is in electronic form.

(b) A contract may not be denied legal effect or enforceability solely because an electronic record was used in its formation.

(c) If a law requires a record to be in writing, an electronic record satisfies the law.

(d) If a law requires a signature, an electronic signature satisfies the law.

. . .

Section 10. Effect of Change or Error.

If a change or error in an electronic record occurs in a transmission between parties to a transaction, the following rules apply:

(1) If the parties have agreed to use a security procedure to detect changes or errors and one party has conformed to the procedure, but the other party has not, and the nonconforming party would have detected the change or error had that party also conformed, the conforming party may avoid the effect of the changed or erroneous electronic record.

(2) In an automated transaction involving an individual, the individual may avoid the effect of an electronic record that resulted from an error made by the individual in dealing with the electronic agent of another person if the electronic agent did not provide an opportunity for the prevention or correction of the error and, at the time the individual learns of the error, the individual:

(A) promptly notifies the other person of the error and that the individual did not intend to be bound by the electronic record received by the other person;

(B) takes reasonable steps, including steps that conform to the other person's reasonable instructions, to return to the other person or, if instructed by the other person, to destroy the consideration received, if any, as a result of the erroneous electronic record; and

(C) has not used or received any benefit or value from the consideration, if any, received from the other person.

(3) If neither paragraph (1) nor paragraph (2) applies, the change or error has the effect provided by other law, including the law of mistake, and the parties' contract, if any.

(4) Paragraphs (2) and (3) may not be varied by agreement.

APPENDIX C Title VII *of the* Civil Rights Act *of* 1964 [Excerpts]

Title VII of the Civil Rights Act of 1964—
The Employment Discrimination Section

Section 703. Unlawful Employment Practices. (a) It shall be an unlawful employment practice for an employer—

(1) to fail or refuse to hire or to discharge any individual, or otherwise to discriminate against any individual with respect to his compensation, terms, conditions, or privileges of employment, because of such individual's race, color, religion, sex, or national origin; or

(2) to limit, segregate, or classify his employees or applicants for employment in any way which would deprive or tend to deprive any individual of employment opportunities or otherwise adversely affect his status as an employee, because of such individual's race, color, religion, sex, or national origin.

(b) It shall be an unlawful employment practice for an employment agency to fail or refuse to refer for employment, or otherwise to discriminate against, any individual because of his race, color, religion, sex, or national origin, or to classify or refer for employment any individual on the basis or his race, color, religion, sex, or national origin.

(c) It shall be an unlawful employment practice for a labor organization—

(1) to exclude or to expel from its membership, or otherwise to discriminate against, any individual because of his race, color, religion, sex, or national origin;

(2) to limit, segregate, or classify its membership or applicants for membership, or to classify or fail or refuse to refer for employment any individual, in any way which would deprive or tend to deprive any individual of employment opportunities, or would limit such employment opportunities or otherwise adversely affect his status as an employee or as an applicant for employment, because of such individual's race, color, religion, sex, or national origin; or

(3) to cause or attempt to cause an employer to discriminate against an individual in violation of this section.

(d) It shall be an unlawful employment practice for any employer, labor organization, or joint labor-management committee controlling apprenticeship or other training or retraining, including on-the-job training programs to discriminate against any individual because of his race, color, religion, sex, or national origin in admission to, or employment in, any program established to provide apprenticeship or other training.

(e) Notwithstanding any other provision of this subchapter—

(1) it shall not be an unlawful employment practice for an employer to hire and employ employees, for an employment agency to classify, or refer for employment any individual, for a labor organization to classify its membership or to classify or refer for employment any individual, or for an employer, labor organization, or joint labor-management committee controlling apprenticeship or other training

or retraining programs to admit or employ any individual in any such program, on the basis of his religion, sex, or national origin in those certain instances where religion, sex, or national origin is a bona fide occupational qualification reasonably necessary to the normal operation of that particular business or enterprise, and

(2) it shall not be an unlawful employment practice for a school, college, university, or other educational institution or institution of learning to hire and employ employees of a particular religion if such school, college, university, or other educational institution or institution of learning is, in whole or in substantial part, owned, supported, controlled, or managed by a particular religion or by a particular religious corporation, association, or society, or if the curriculum of such school, college, university, or other educational institution or institution of learning is directed toward the propagation of a particular religion.

(f) As used in this subchapter, the phrase "unlawful employment practice" shall not be deemed to include any action or measure taken by an employer, labor organization, joint labor-management committee, or employment agency with respect to an individual who is a member of the Communist Party of the United States or of any other organization required to register as a Communist-action or Communist-front organization. . . .

(g) Notwithstanding any other provision of this subchapter, it shall not be an unlawful employment practice for an employer to fail or refuse to hire and employ any individual for any position, for an employer to discharge any individual from any position, or for an employment agency to fail or refuse to refer any individual for employment in any position, or for a labor organization to fail or refuse to refer any individual for employment in any position, if—

(1) the occupancy of such position, or access to the premises in or upon which any part of the duties of such position is performed or is to be performed, is subject to any requirement imposed in the interest of the national security of the United States . . . and

(2) such individual has not fulfilled or has ceased to fulfill that requirement.

(h) Notwithstanding any other provision of this subchapter, it shall not be an unlawful employment practice for an employer to apply different standards of compensation, or different terms, conditions, or privileges of employment pursuant to a bona fide seniority or merit system, or a system which measures earnings by quantity or quality of production or to employees who work in different locations, provided that such differences are not the result of an intention to discriminate because of race, color, religion, sex, or national origin, nor shall it be an unlawful employment practice for an employer to give and act upon the results of any professionally developed ability test provided that such test, its administration or action upon the results is not designed, intended or used to discriminate because of race, color, religion, sex, or national origin. . . .

(j) Nothing contained in this subchapter shall be interpreted to require any employer, employment agency, labor organization, or joint labor-management committee subject to this subchapter to grant preferential treatment to any individual or to any group because of the race, color, religion, sex, or national origin of such individual or group on account of an imbalance which may exist with respect to the total number or percentage of persons of any race, color, religion, sex, or national origin employed by any employer, referred or classified for employment by any employment agency or labor organization, or admitted to, or employed in, any apprenticeship or other training program, in comparison with the total number or percentage of persons of such race, color, religion, sex, or national origin in any community, State, section, or other area, or in the available work force in any community, State, section, or other area.

Section 704. Other Unlawful Employment Practices. (a) It shall be an unlawful employment practice for an employer to discriminate against any of his employees or applicants for employment, for an employment agency, or joint labor-management committee controlling apprenticeship or other training or retraining, including on-the-job training programs, to discriminate against any individual, or for a labor organization to discriminate against any member thereof or applicant for membership, because he has opposed any practice made an unlawful employment practice by this subchapter, or because he has made a charge, testified, assisted, or participated in any manner in an investigation, proceeding, or hearing under this subchapter.

(b) It shall be an unlawful employment practice for an employer, labor organization, employment agency, or joint labor-management committee controlling apprenticeship or other training or retraining, including on-the-job training programs, to print or publish or cause to be printed or published any notice or advertisement relating to employment by such an employer or membership or any classification or referral for employment by such a labor organization, or relating to any classification or referral for employment by such an employment agency, or relating to admission to, or employment in, any program established to provide apprenticeship or other training by such a joint-labor-management committee, indicating any preference, limitation, specification, or discrimination, based on race, color, religion, sex, or national origin, except that such a notice or advertisement may indicate a preference, limitation, specification, or discrimination based on religion, sex or national origin when religion, sex, or national origin is a bona fide occupational qualification for employment.

APPENDIX D Americans *with* Disabilities Act *of* 1990 [Excerpts]

TITLE I—EMPLOYMENT

Sec. 101. Definitions.

As used in this title: . . .

(8) Qualified individual with a disability. The term "qualified individual with a disability" means an individual with a disability who, with or without reasonable accommodation, can perform the essential functions of the employment position that such individual holds or desires. For the purposes of this title, consideration shall be given to the employer's judgment as to what functions of a job are essential, and if an employer has prepared a written description before advertising or interviewing applicants for the job, this description shall be considered evidence of the essential functions of the job.

(9) Reasonable accommodation. The term "reasonable accommodation" may include—

(A) making existing facilities used by employees readily accessible to and usable by individuals with disabilities; and (B) job restructuring, part-time or modified work schedules, reassignment to a vacant position, acquisition or modification of equipment or devices, appropriate adjustment or modifications of examinations, training materials or policies, the provision of qualified readers or interpreters, and other similar accommodations for individuals with disabilities.

(10) Undue Hardship.

(A) *In general.* The term "undue hardship" means an action requiring significant difficulty or expense, when considered in light of the factors set forth in subparagraph(B).

(B) *Factors to be considered.* In determining whether an accommodation would impose an undue hardship on a covered entity, factors to be considered include—

(i) the nature and cost of accommodation needed under this Act;

(ii) the overall financial resources of the facility or facilities involved in the provision of the reasonable accommodation; the number of persons employed at such facility; the effect on expenses and resources, or the impact otherwise of such accommodation upon the operation of the facility;

(iii) the overall financial resources of the covered entity; the overall size of the business of a covered entity with respect to the number of its employees; the number, type, and location of its facilities; and

(iv) the type of operation or operations of the covered entity, including the composition, structure, and functions of the workforce of such entity; the geographic separateness, administrative, or fiscal relationship of the facility or facilities in question to the covered entity.

Sec. 102. Discrimination.

(a) General Rule. No covered entity shall discriminate against a qualified individual with a disability because of the disability of such individual in regard to job application procedures, the hiring, advancement, or discharge of employees, employee compensation, job training, and other terms, conditions, and privileges of employment.

(b) Construction. As used in subsection (a), the term "discriminate" includes—

(1) limiting, segregating, or classifying a job applicant or employee in a way that adversely affects the opportunities or status of such applicant or employee because of the disability of such applicant or employee;

(2) participating in a contractual or other arrangement or relationship that has the effect of subjecting a covered entity's qualified applicant or employee with a disability to the discrimination prohibited by

this title (such relationship includes a relationship with an employment or referral agency, labor union, an organization providing fringe benefits to an employee of the covered entity, or an organization providing training and apprenticeship programs);

(3) utilizing standards, criteria, or methods of administration—

(A) that have the effect of discrimination on the basis of disability; or

(B) that perpetuate the discrimination of others who are subject to common administrative control;

(4) excluding or otherwise denying equal jobs or benefits to a qualified individual because of the known disability of an individual with whom the qualified individual is known to have a relationship or association;

(5)(A) not making reasonable accommodations to the known physical or mental limitations of an otherwise qualified individual with a disability who is an applicant or employee, unless such covered entity can demonstrate that the accommodation would impose an undue hardship on the operation of the business of such covered entity; or

(B) denying employment opportunities to a job applicant or employee who is an otherwise qualified individual with a disability, if such denial is based on the need of such covered entity to make reasonable accommodation to the physical or mental impairments of the employee or applicant;

(6) using qualification standards, employment tests or other selection criteria that screen out or tend to screen out an individual with a disability or a class of individuals with disabilities unless the standard, test or other selection criteria, as used by the covered entity, is shown to be job-related for the position in question and is consistent with business necessity; and

(7) failing to select and administer tests concerning employment in the most effective manner to ensure that, when such test is administered to a job applicant or employee who has a disability that impairs sensory, manual, or speaking skills, such test results accurately reflect the skills, aptitude, or whatever other factor of such applicant or employee that such test purports to measure, rather than reflecting the impaired sensory, manual, or speaking skills of such employee or applicant (except where such skills are the factors that the test purports to measure). . . .

Sec. 104. Illegal Use of Drugs and Alcohol

(b) Rules of Construction. Nothing in subsection (a) shall be construed to exclude as a qualified individual with a disability an individual who—

(1) has successfully completed a supervised drug rehabilitation program and is no longer engaging in the illegal use of drugs, or has otherwise been rehabilitated successfully and is no longer engaging in such use;

(2) is participating in a supervised rehabilitation program and is no longer engaging in such use; or

(3) is erroneously regarded as engaging in such use, but is not engaging in such use; except that it shall not be a violation of this Act for a covered entity to adopt or administer reasonable policies or procedures, including but not limited to drug testing, designed to ensure that an individual described in paragraph (1) or (2) is no longer engaging in the illegal use of drugs. . . .

Sec. 107. Enforcement

(a) Powers, Remedies, and Procedures. The powers, remedies, and procedures set forth in sections 705, 706, 707, 709, and 710 of the Civil Rights Act of 1964 (42 U.S.C. 2000e-4, 2000e-5, 2000e-6, 2000e-8, and 2000e-9) shall be the powers, remedies, and procedures this title provides to the Commission, to the Attorney General, or to any person alleging discrimination on the basis of disability in violation of any provision of this Act, or regulations promulgated under section 106, concerning employment.

(b) Coordination. The agencies with enforcement authority for actions which allege employment discrimination under this title and under the Rehabilitation Act of 1973 shall develop procedures to ensure that administrative complaints filed under this title and under the Rehabilitation Act of 1973 are dealt with in a manner that avoids duplication of effort and prevents imposition of inconsistent or conflicting standards for the same requirements under this title and the Rehabilitation Act of 1973. The Commission, the Attorney General, and the Office of Federal Contract Compliance Programs shall establish such coordinating mechanisms (similar to provisions contained in the joint regulations promulgated by the Commission and the Attorney General at part 42 of title 28 and part 1691 of title 29, Code of Federal Regulations, and the Memorandum of Understanding between the Commission and the Office of Federal Contract Compliance Programs dated January 16, 1981 (46 Fed. Reg. 7435, January 23, 1981)) in regulations implementing this title and Rehabilitation Act of 1973 not later than 18 months after the date of enactment of this Act.

Sec. 108. Effective Date

This title shall become effective 24 months after the date of enactment.

APPENDIX E   National Labor Relations Act [Excerpts]

Section 3. National Labor Relations Board. (a) The National Labor Relations Board (hereinafter called the "Board") . . . as an agency of the United States, shall consist of five . . . members, appointed by the President by and with advice and consent of the Senate . . . for terms of five years each. . . . The President shall designate one member to serve as Chairman of the Board. Any member of the Board may be removed by the President, upon notice and hearing, for neglect of duty or malfeasance in office, but for no other cause.

Section 7. Rights of Employees. Employees shall have the right to self-organization, to form, join, or assist labor organizations, to bargain collectively through representatives of their own choosing, and to engage in other concerted activities for the purpose of collective bargaining or other mutual aid or protection, and shall also have the right to refrain from any or all of such activities except to the extent that such right may be affected by an agreement requiring membership in a labor organization as a condition of employment as authorized in section 8(a) (3).

Section 8. Unfair Labor Practice. (a) It shall be an unfair labor practice for an employer—

(1) to interfere with, restrain, or coerce employees in the exercise of the rights guaranteed in section 7;

(2) to dominate or interfere with the formation or administration of any labor organization or contribute financial or other support to it: Provide, that subject to rules and regulations made and published by the Board pursuant to section 6, an employer shall not be prohibited from permitting employees to confer with him during working hours without loss of time or pay;

(3) by discrimination in regard to hire or tenure of employment or any term or condition of employment to encourage or discourage membership in any labor organization: Provided, that nothing in this Act . . . shall preclude an employer from making an agreement with a labor organization . . . to require as a condition of employment membership therein . . . Provided further, that no employer shall justify any discrimination against an employee for nonmembership in a labor organization (A) if he has reasonable grounds for believing that such membership was not available to the employee on the same terms and conditions generally applicable to other members, or (B) if he has reasonable grounds for believing that membership was denied or terminated for reasons other than the failure of the employee to tender periodic dues and initiation fees uniformly required as a condition of acquiring or retaining membership;

(4) to discharge or otherwise discriminate against an employee because he has filed charges or given testimony under this Act;

(5) to refuse to bargain collectively with the representatives of his employees, subject to the provisions of section 9(a).

(b) It shall be an unfair labor practice for a labor organization or its agents—

(1) to restrain or coerce (A) employees in the exercise of the rights guaranteed in section 7: Provided, that this paragraph shall not impair the right of a labor organization to prescribe its own rules with respect to the acquisition or retention of membership therein; or (B) an employer in the selection of his representatives for the purposes of collective bargaining or the adjustment of grievances;

(2) to cause or attempt to cause an employer to discriminate against an employee in violation of subsection (a) (3) or to discriminate against an employee with respect to whom membership in such organization has been denied or terminated on some ground other than his failure to tender the periodic dues and the initiation fees uniformly required as a condition of acquiring or retaining membership.

(3) to refuse to bargain collectively with an employer, provided it is the representative of his employees subject to the provisions of section 9 (a).

(4) (i) to engage in, or to induce or encourage any individual employed by any person engaged in commerce or in an industry affecting commerce to engage in, a strike or a refusal in the course of his employment to use, manufacture, process, transport, or otherwise handle or work on any goods, articles, materials, or commodities or to perform any services; or, (ii) to threaten, coerce, or restrain any person engaged in commerce or in an industry affecting commerce, where in either case an object thereof is:

(A) forcing or requiring any employer or self-employed person to join any labor or employer organization or to enter into any agreement which is prohibited by section 8 (e);

(B) forcing or requiring any person to cease using, selling, handling, transporting, or otherwise dealing in the products of any other producer, processor, or manufacturer, or to cease doing business with any other person, or forcing or requiring any other employer to recognize or bargain with a labor organization as the representative of his employees unless such labor organization has been certified as the representative of such employees . . . Provided, that nothing contained in this clause (B) shall be construed to make unlawful, where not otherwise unlawful, any primary strike or primary picketing;

(C) forcing or requiring any employer to recognize or bargain with a particular labor organization as the representative of his employees if another labor organization has been certified as the representative of such employees. . . .

(D) forcing or requiring any employer to assign particular work to employees in a particular labor organization or in a particular trade, craft, or class. . . .

Provided, that nothing contained in this subsection (b) shall be construed to make unlawful a refusal by any person to enter upon the premises of any employer (other than his own employer), if the employees of such employer are engaged in a strike ratified or approved by a representative of such employees whom such employer is required to recognize under this Act: Provided further, that for the purposes of this paragraph (4) only, nothing contained in such paragraph shall be construed to prohibit publicity, other than picketing, for the purpose of truthfully advising the public, including consumers and members of a labor organization, that a product or products are produced by an employer with whom the labor organization has a primary dispute and are distributed by another employer, as long as such publicity does not have an effect of inducing any individual employed by any person other than the primary employer in the course of his employment to pick up, deliver, or transport any goods, or not to perform any services, at the establishment of the employer engaged in such distribution;

(5) to require of employees covered by an agreement authorized under subsection (a) (3) the payment, as a condition precedent to becoming a member of such organization, of a fee in an amount which the Board finds excessive or discriminatory. . . .

(6) to cause or attempt to cause an employer to pay or deliver or agree to pay or deliver any money or other thing of value, in the nature of an exaction, for services which are not performed or not to be performed; and

(7) to picket or cause to be picketed, or threaten to picket or cause to be picketed, any employer where an object thereof is forcing or requiring an employer to recognize or bargain with a labor organization as the representative of his employees, or forcing or requiring the employees of an employer to accept or select such labor organization as their collective bargaining representative, unless such labor organization is currently certified as the representative of such employees:

(A) where the employer has lawfully recognized in accordance with this Act any other labor organization and a question concerning representation may not appropriately be raised under section 9(c) of this Act,

(B) where within the preceding 12 months a valid election under section 9(c) of this Act has been conducted, or

(C) where such picketing has been conducted without a petition under section 9(c) being filed within a reasonable period of time not to exceed 30 days from the commencement of such picketing:

Provided, that when such a petition has been filed the Board shall forthwith, without regard to the provisions of section 9(c) (1) or the absence of a showing of a substantial interest on the part of the labor organization, direct an election in such units as the Board finds to be appropriate and shall certify the results thereof: Provided further, that nothing in this subparagraph (C) shall be construed to prohibit any picketing or other publicity for the purpose of truthfully advising the public (including consumers) that an employer does not employ members of, or have a contract with, a labor organization, unless an effect of such picketing is to induce any individual employed by any other person in the course of his employment, not to pick up, deliver or transport any goods or not to perform any services.

Nothing in this paragraph (7) shall be construed to permit any act which would otherwise be an unfair labor practice under this section 8(b).

(c) The expressing of any views, argument, or opinion, or the dissemination thereof, whether in written, printed, graphic, or visual form, shall not constitute or be evidence of an unfair labor practice under any of the provisions of this Act, if such expression contains no threat of reprisal or force or promise of benefit.

(d) For the purposes of this section, to bargain collectively is the performance of the mutual obligation of the employer and the representative of the employees to meet at reasonable times and confer in good faith with respect to wages, hours, and other terms and conditions of employment, or the negotiation of an agreement, or any question arising thereunder, and the execution of a written contract incorporating any agreement reached if requested by either party, but such obligation does not compel either party to agree to a proposal or require the making of a concession: Provided, that where there is in effect a collective bargaining contract covering employees in an industry affecting commerce, the duty to bargain collectively shall also mean that no party to such contract shall terminate or modify such contract, unless the party desiring such termination or modification—

(1) serves a written notice upon the other party to the contract of the proposed termination or modification 60 days prior to the expiration date thereof, or in the event such contract contains no expiration date, 60 days prior to the time it is proposed to make such termination or modification;

(2) offers to meet and confer with the other party for the purpose of negotiating a new contract or a contract containing the proposed modifications;

(3) notifies the Federal Mediation and Conciliation Service within 30 days after such notice of the existence of a dispute . . .

(4) continues in full force and effect, without resorting to strike or lockout, all the terms and conditions of the existing contract for a period of 60 days after such notice is given or until the expiration date of such contract, whichever occurs later.

(e) It shall be an unfair labor practice for any labor organization and any employer to enter into any contract or agreement, express or implied, whereby such employer ceases or refrains or agrees to cease or refrain from handling, using, selling, transporting, or otherwise dealing in any of the products of any other employer, or to cease doing business with any other person, . . . Provided, that nothing in this subsection (e) shall apply to an agreement between a labor organization and an employer in the construction industry relating to the contracting or subcontracting of work to be done at the site. . . .

Section 9. Representatives and Elections.

(a) Representatives designated or selected for the purposes of collective bargaining by the majority of the employees in a unit appropriate for such purposes, shall be the exclusive representatives of all the employees in such unit for the purposes of collective bargaining in respect to rates of pay, wages, hours of employment, or other conditions of employment: Provided, that any individual employee or a group of employees shall have the right at any time to present grievances to their employer and to have such grievance adjusted, without the intervention of the bargaining representative, as long as the adjustment is not inconsistent with the terms of a collective bargaining contract or agreement then in effect: Provided further, that the bargaining representative has been given opportunity to be present at such adjustment.

(b) The Board shall decide in each case whether, in order to assure to employees the fullest freedom in exercising the rights guaranteed by this Act, the unit appropriate for the purposes of collective bargaining shall be the employer unit, craft unit, plant unit, or subdivision thereof: Provided, that the Board shall not (1) decide that any unit is appropriate for such purposes if such unit includes both professional employees and employees who are not professional employees unless a majority of such professional employees vote for inclusion in such unit; or (2) decide that any craft unit is inappropriate for such purposes on the ground that a different unit has been established by a prior Board determination, unless a majority of the employees in the proposed craft unit vote against separate representation or (3) decide that any unit is appropriate for such purposes, if it includes, together with other employees, any individual employed as a guard to enforce against employees and other persons, rules to protect property of the employer or to protect the safety of persons on the employer's premises; but no labor organization shall be certified as the representative of employees in a bargaining unit of guards if such organization admits to membership, or is affiliated directly or indirectly with an organization which admits to membership, employees other than guards.

(c) (1) Wherever a petition shall have been filed, in accordance with such regulations as may be prescribed by the Board—

(A) by an employee or group of employees or any individual or labor organization acting in their behalf alleging that a substantial number of employees (i) wish to be represented for collective bargaining and that their employer declines to recognize their representative as the representative defined in section 9(a), or (ii) assert that the individual or labor organization, which has been certified or is being currently recognized by their employer as the bargaining representative as defined in section 9(a); or

(B) by an employer, alleging that one or more individuals or labor organizations have presented to him a claim to be recognized as the representative defined in section 9(a);

the Board shall investigate such petition and if it has reasonable cause to believe that a question of representation affecting commerce exists shall provide for an appropriate hearing upon due notice. Such hearing may be conducted by an officer or employee of the regional office, who shall not make any recommendations with respect thereto. If the Board finds upon the record of such hearing that such a question of representative exists, it shall direct an election by secret ballot and shall certify the results thereof.

(2) In determining whether or not a question of representation affecting commerce exists, the same regulations and rules of decision shall apply irrespective of the identity of the persons filing the petition or the kind of relief sought and in no case shall the Board deny a labor organization a place on the ballot by reason of an order with respect to such labor organization or its predecessor not issued in conformity with section 10(c).

(3) No election shall be directed in any bargaining unit or any subdivision within which, in the preceding twelve-month period, a valid election shall have been held. Employees engaged in an economic strike who are not entitled to reinstatement shall be eligible to vote under such regulations as the Board shall find are consistent with the purposes and provisions of this Act in any election conducted within twelve months after the commencement of the strike. In any election where none of the choices on the ballot receives a majority, a run-off shall be conducted, the ballot providing for a selection between the two choices receiving the largest and second largest number of valid votes cast in the election.

(4) Nothing in this section shall be construed to prohibit the waiving of hearings by stipulation for the purpose of a consent election in conformity with regulations and rules of decision of the Board.

(5) In determining whether a unit is appropriate for the purposes specified in subsection (b) the extent to which the employees have organized shall not be controlling.

(d) Whenever an order of the Board made pursuant to section 10(c) is based in whole or in part upon facts certified following an investigation pursuant to subsection (c) of this section and there is a petition for the enforcement or review of such order, such certification and the record of such investigation shall be included in the transcript of the entire record required to be filed under section 10(c) or 10(f), and thereupon the decree of the court enforcing modifying, or setting aside in whole or in part the order of the Board shall be made and entered upon the pleadings, testimony, and the proceedings set forth in such transcript.

(e)(1) Upon the filing with the Board, by 30 per centum or more of the employees in a bargaining unit covered by an agreement between their employer and a labor organization made pursuant to section 8(a)(3), of a petition alleging they desire that such authority be rescinded, the Board shall take a secret ballot of the employees in such unit, and shall certify the results thereof to such labor organization and to the employer.

(2) No election shall be conducted pursuant to this subsection in any bargaining unit or any subdivision within which, in the preceding twelve month period, a valid election shall have been held.

Section 19. Individuals with Religious Convictions.

Any employee who is a member of and adheres to established and traditional tenets or teachings of a bona fide religion, body, or sect which has historically held conscientious objections to joining or financially supporting labor organizations shall not be required to join or financially support any labor organization as a condition of employment; except that such employee may be required in a contract between such employee's employer and a labor organization in lieu of periodic dues and initiation fees, to pay sums equal to such dues and initiation fees to a nonreligious, nonlabor organization charitable fund exempt from taxation under section 501(c)(3) of title 26 of the Internal Revenue Code.

APPENDIX F Sherman Antitrust Act [Excerpts]

Section 1. Every contract, combination in the form of trust or otherwise, or conspiracy, in restraint of trade or commerce among the several States, or with foreign nations, is hereby declared to be illegal. Every person who shall make any contract or engage in any such combination or conspiracy shall be deemed guilty of a felony, and, on conviction thereof, shall be punished by fine not exceeding $10,000,000 if a corporation, or, if any other person, $350,000 or by imprisonment not exceeding three years, or by both said punishments in the discretion of the court.

Section 2. Every person who shall monopolize, or attempt to monopolize, or conspire with any other person or persons, to monopolize any part of the trade or commerce among the several States, or with foreign nations, shall be deemed guilty of a felony, and, on conviction thereof, shall be punished by fine not exceeding $10,000,000 if a corporation, or, if any other person, $350,000 or by imprisonment not exceeding three years, or by both said punishments, in the discretion of the court.

APPENDIX G Clayton Act *of* 1914 [Excerpts]

Section 3. That it shall be unlawful for any person engaged in commerce, in the course of such commerce, to lease or make a sale or contract for sale of goods, wares, merchandise, machinery, supplies, or other commodities, whether patented or unpatented, for use, consumption, or resale within the United States or . . . other place under the jurisdiction of the United States, or fix a price charged therefor, or discount from, or rebate upon, such price, on the condition, agreement, or understanding that the lessee or purchaser thereof shall not use or deal in the goods, wares, merchandise, machinery, supplies, or other commodities of a competitor or competitors of the lessor or seller, where the effect of such lease, sale, or contract for sale or such condition, agreement, or understanding may be to substantially lessen competition to tend to create a monopoly in any line of commerce.

Section 4. That any person who shall be injured in his business or property by reason of anything forbidden in the antitrust laws may sue therefor in any district court of the United States in the district in which the defendant resides or is found, or has an agent, without respect to the amount in controversy, and shall recover threefold the damages by him sustained, and the cost of suit, including a reasonable attorney's fee.

Section 4A. Whenever the United States is hereafter injured in its business or property by reason of anything forbidden in the antitrust laws it may sue therefor in the United States district court for the district in which the defendant resides or is found or has an agent, without respect to the amount in controversy, and shall recover actual damages by it sustained and the cost of suit.

Section 4B. Any action to enforce any cause of action under sections 4 or 4A shall be forever barred unless commenced within four years after the cause of action accrued. No cause of action barred under existing law on the effective date of this act shall be revived by this Act.

Section 6. That the labor of a human being is not a commodity or article of commerce. Nothing contained in the antitrust laws shall be construed to forbid the existence and operation of labor, agricultural or horticultural organizations, instituted for the purposes of mutual help, and not having capital stock or conducted for profit, or to forbid or restrain individual members of such organizations from lawfully carrying out the legitimate objects thereof; nor shall such organizations or the members thereof, be held or construed to be illegal combinations or conspiracies in restraint of trade, under the antitrust laws.

Section 7. That no person engaged in commerce shall acquire, directly or indirectly, the whole or any part of the stock or other share capital and no corporation subject to the jurisdiction of the Federal Trade Commission shall acquire the whole or any part of the assets of another corporation engaged also in commerce, where in any line of commerce in any section of the country, the effect of such acquisition may be substantially to lessen competition, or to tend to create a monopoly.

No person shall acquire, directly or indirectly, the whole or any part of the stock or other share capital and no corporation subject to the jurisdiction of the Federal Trade Commission shall acquire the whole or any part of the assets of one or more corporations engaged in commerce, where in any line of commerce in any section of the country, the effect of such acquisition, of such stocks or assets, or of the use of such stock by the voting or granting of proxies or otherwise, may be substantially to lessen competition, or to tend to create a monopoly.

This section shall not apply to persons purchasing such stock solely for investment and not using the same by voting or otherwise to bring about, or in attempting to bring about, the substantial lessening of competition . . . .

Section 8. . . . No person shall, at the same time, serve as a director or officer in any two or more corporations (other than banks, banking associations, and trust companies) that are—

(A) engaged in whole or in part in commerce; and

(B) by virtue of their business and location of operation, competitors, so that the elimination of competition by agreement between them would constitute a violation of any of the antitrust laws; if each of the corporations has capital, surplus, and undivided profits aggregating more than $10,000,000 as adjusted pursuant to paragraph (5) of this subsection.

APPENDIX H   Federal Trade Commission Act *of* 1914 [Excerpts]

Unfair Methods of Competition Prohibited

Section 5. Unfair methods of competition unlawful; prevention by Commission—declaration. Declaration of unlawfulness; power to prohibit unfair practices.

(a) (1) Unfair methods of competition in or affecting commerce, and unfair or deceptive acts or practices in or affecting commerce, are declared unlawful.

. . .

(b) Any person, partnership, or corporation who violates an order of the Commission to cease and desist after it has become final, and while such order is in effect, shall forfeit and pay to the United States a civil penalty of not more than $10,000 for each violation, which shall accrue to the United States and may be recovered in a civil action brought by the Attorney General of the United States. Each separate violation of such an order shall be a separate offense, except that in the case of a violation through continuing failure or neglect to obey a final order of the Commission, each day of continuance of such failure or neglect shall be deemed a separate offense.

APPENDIX I   Robinson-Patman Act [Excerpts]

Price Discrimination; Cost Justification; Changing Conditions

Section 2—Discrimination in price, services, or facilities. (a) Price; Selection of Customers.

It shall be unlawful for any person engaged in commerce, in the course of such commerce, either directly or indirectly, to discriminate in price between different purchases of commodities of like grade and quality, where either or any of the purchases involved in such discrimination are in commerce, where such commodities are sold for use, consumption, or resale within the United States or any Territory thereof or the District of Columbia or any insular possession or other place under the jurisdiction of the United States, and where the effect of such discrimination may be substantially to lessen competition or tend to create a monopoly in any line of commerce, or to injure, destroy, or prevent competition with any person who either grants or knowingly receives the benefit of such discrimination, or with customers of either of them; *Provided,* That nothing herein contained shall prevent differentials which make only due allowance for differences in the cost of manufacture, sale, or delivery resulting from the differing methods or quantities in which such commodities are to such purchasers sold or delivered: *Provided, however,* That the Federal Trade Commission may, after due investigation and hearing to all interested parties, fix and establish quantity limits, and revise the same as it finds necessary as to particular commodities or classes of commodities, where it finds that available purchasers in greater quantities are so few as to render differentials on account thereof unjustly discriminatory or promotive of monopoly in any line of commerce; and the foregoing shall then not be construed to permit differentials based on differences in quantities greater than those so fixed and established: *And provided further,* That nothing herein contained shall prevent persons engaged in selling goods, wares, or merchandise in commerce from selecting their own customers in bona fide transactions and not in restraint of trade: *And provided further,* That nothing herein contained shall prevent price changes from time to time where in response to changing conditions affecting the market for or the marketability of the goods concerned, such as but not limited to actual or imminent deterioration of perishable goods, obsolescence of seasonal goods, distress sales under court process, or sales in good faith in discontinuance of business in the goods concerned.

Meeting Competition

(b) Burden of rebutting prima-facie case of discrimination.

Upon proof being made, at any hearing on a complaint under this section, that there has been discrimination in price or services or facilities furnished, the burden of rebutting the prima-facie case thus made by showing justification shall be upon the person charged with a violation of this section, and unless justification shall be affirmatively shown, the Commission is authorized to issue an order terminating the discrimination: *Provided, however,* That nothing herein contained shall prevent a seller rebutting the prima-facie case thus made by showing that his lower price or the furnishing of services or facilities to any purchaser or purchasers was made in good faith to meet an equally low price of a competitor, or the services or facilities furnished by a competitor.

Brokerage Payments

(c) Payment or acceptance of commission, brokerage or other compensation.

It shall be unlawful for any person engaged in commerce, in the course of such commerce, to pay or grant, or to receive or accept, anything of value as a commission, brokerage, or other compensation, or any allowance or discount in lieu thereof, except for services rendered in connection with the sale or purchase of goods, wares, or merchandise, either to the other party to such transaction or to an agent, representative, or other intermediary therein where such intermediary is acting in fact for or in behalf, or is subject to the direct or indirect control, of any party to such transaction other than the person by whom such compensation is so granted or paid.

Promotional Allowances

(d) Payment for services or facilities for processing or sale.

It shall be unlawful for any person engaged in commerce to pay or contract for the payment of anything of value to or for the benefit of a customer of such person in the course of such commerce as compensation or in consideration for any services or facilities furnished by or through such customer in connection with the processing, handling, sale or offering for sale of any products or commodities manufactured, sold, or offered for sale by such person, unless such payment of consideration is available on proportionally equal terms to all other customers competing in the distribution of such products or commodities.

Promotional Services

(e) Furnishing services or facilities for processing, handling, etc.

It shall be unlawful for any person to discriminate in favor of one purchaser against another purchaser or purchasers of a commodity bought for resale, with or without processing, or by contracting to furnish or furnishing, or by contributing to the furnishing of, any services or facilities connected with the processing, handling, sale, or offering for sale of such commodity so purchased upon terms not accorded to all purchasers on proportionally equal terms.

Buyer Discrimination

(f) Knowingly inducing or receiving discriminatory price.

It shall be unlawful for any person engaged in commerce, in the course of such commerce, knowingly to induce or receive a discrimination in price which is prohibited by this section.

Predatory Practices

Section 3—Discrimination in rebates, discounts, or advertising service charges; underselling in particular localities; penalties. It shall be unlawful for any person engaged in commerce, in the course of such commerce, to be a party to, or assist in, any transaction of sale, or contract to sell, which discriminates to his knowledge against competitors of the purchaser, in that, any discount, rebate, allowance, or advertising service charge is granted to the purchaser over and above any discount, rebate, allowance, or advertising service charge available at the time of such transaction to said competitors in respect of a sale of goods of like grade, quality, and quantity; to sell, or contract to sell, goods in any part of the United States at prices lower than those exacted by said person elsewhere in the United States for the purpose of destroying competition, or eliminating a competitor in such part of the United States; or, to sell, or contract to sell, goods at unreasonably lower prices for the purpose of destroying competition or eliminating a competitor.

Any person violating any of the provisions of this section shall, upon conviction thereof, be fined not more than $5,000 or imprisoned not more than one year, or both.

APPENDIX J Securities Act *of* 1933 [Excerpts]

Prohibitions Relating to Interstate Commerce and the Mails

Sec. 5. (a) Unless a registration statement is in effect as to a security, it shall be unlawful for any person, directly or indirectly—

(1) to make use of any means or instruments of transportation or communication in interstate commerce or of the mails to sell such security through the use or medium of any prospectus or otherwise; or

(2) to carry or cause to be carried through the mails or in interstate commerce, by any means or instruments of transportation, any such security for the purpose of sale or for delivery after sale.

[Prospectus Requirements]

(b) It shall be unlawful for any person, directly or indirectly—

(1) to make use of any means or instruments of transportation or communication in interstate commerce or of the mails to carry or transmit any prospectus relating to any security with respect to which a registration statement has been filed under this title, unless such prospectus meets the requirements of section 10, or

(2) to carry or to cause to be carried through the mails or in interstate commerce any such security for the purpose of sale or for delivery after sale, unless accompanied or preceded by a prospectus that meets the requirements of subsection (a) of section 10.

[Prohibition Against Offers Prior to Registration]

(c) It shall be unlawful for any person, directly or indirectly, to make use of any means or instruments of transportation or communication in interstate commerce or of the mails to offer to sell or offer to buy through the use or medium of any prospectus or otherwise any security, unless a registration statement has been filed as to such security, or while the registration statement is the subject of a refusal order or stop order or (prior to the effective date of the registration statement) any public proceeding or examination under section 8.

Civil Liabilities on Account of False Registration Statement

Sec. 11. (a) In case any part of the registration statement, when such part became effective, contained an untrue statement of a material fact or omitted to state a material fact required to be stated therein or necessary to make the statements therein not misleading, any person acquiring such security (unless it is proved that at the time of such acquisition he knew of such untruth or omission) may, either at law or in equity, in any court of competent jurisdiction, sue—

[Signers of Registration Statement]

(1) every person who signed the registration statement;

[Directors and Partners]

(2) every person who was a director of (or person performing similar functions), or partner in, the issuer at the time of the filing of the part of the registration statement with respect to which his liability is asserted;

[Persons Named as Being, or About to Become, Directors or Partners]

(3) every person who, with his consent, is named in the registration statement as being or about to become a director, person performing similar functions, or partner;

[Accountants, Engineers, Appraisers, and Other Professional Persons]

(4) every accountant engineer, or appraiser, or any person whose profession gives authority to a statement made by him, who has with his consent been named as having prepared or certified any part of the registration statement, or as having prepared or certified any report or valuation which is used in connection with the registration statement, with respect to the statement in such registration statement, report, or valuation, which purports to have been prepared or certified by him;

[Underwriters]

(5) every underwriter with respect to such security.

[Purchase after Publication of Earning Statement]

If such person acquired the security after the issuer has made generally available to its security holders an earning statement covering a period of at least twelve months beginning after the effective date of the registration statement, then the right of recovery under this subsection shall be conditioned on proof that such person acquired the securities relying on such untrue statement in the registration statement or relying upon the registration statement and not knowing of such omission, but such reliance may be established without proof of the reading of the registration statement by such person.

[Defenses of Persons Other than Issuer]

(b) Notwithstanding the provisions of subsection (a) no person, other than the issuer, shall be liable as provided therein who shall sustain the burden of proof—

[Resignation before Effective Date]

(1) that before the effective date of the part of the registration statement with respect to which his liability is asserted (A) he had resigned from or had taken such steps as are permitted by law to resign from, or ceased or refused to act in, every office, capacity or relationship in which he was described in the registration statement as acting or agreeing to act, and (B) he had advised the Commission and the issuer in writing, that he had taken such action and that he would not be responsible for such part of the registration statement; or

[Statements Becoming Effective without Defendants Knowledge]

(2) that if such part of the registration statement became effective without his knowledge, upon becoming aware of such fact he forthwith acted and advised the Commission, in accordance with paragraph (1), and, in addition, gave reasonable public notice that such part of the registration statement had become effective without his knowledge; or

[Belief on Reasonable Grounds that Statements Were True]

(3) that (A) as regards any part of the registration statement not purporting to be made on the authority of an expert, and not purporting to be a copy of or extract from a report or valuation of an expert and not purporting to be made on the authority of a public official document or statement, he had, after reasonable investigation, reasonable ground to believe and did believe, at the time such part of the registration statement became effective, that the statements therein were true and that there was no omission to state a material fact required to be stated therein or necessary to make the statements therein not misleading; and

[Statement Made on Authority of Defendant as Expert]

(B) as regards any part of the registration statement purporting to be made upon his authority as an expert or purporting to be a copy of or extract from a report or valuation of himself as an expert, (i) he had, after reasonable investigation, reasonable ground to believe and did believe, at the time such part of the registration statement became effective, that the statements therein were true and that there was no omission to state a material fact required to be stated therein or necessary to make the statements therein not misleading, or (ii) such part of the registration statement did not fairly represent his statement as an expert or was not a fair copy of or extract from his report or valuation as an expert; and

[Statement Made on Authority of Expert Other than Defendant]

(C) as regards any part of the registration statement purporting to be made on the authority of an expert (other than himself) or purporting to be a copy of or extract from a report or valuation of an expert (other than himself), he had no reasonable ground to believe and did not believe, at the time such part of the registration statement became effective, that the statements therein were untrue or that there was an omission to state a material fact required to be stated therein or necessary to make the statements therein not misleading, or that such part of the registration statement did not fairly represent the statement of the expert or was not a fair copy of or extract from the report or valuation of the expert; and

[Statement Made by Official Person; Copy of Public Official Document]

(D) as regards any part of the registration statement purporting to be a statement made by an official person or purporting to be a copy of or extract from a public official document, he had no reasonable ground to believe and did not believe, at the time such part of the registration statement became effective, that the statements therein were untrue, or that there was an omission to state a material fact required to be stated therein or necessary to make the statements therein not misleading, or that such part of the registration statement did not fairly represent the statement made by the official person or was not a fair copy of or extract from the public official document.

["Reasonable" Investigation and "Reasonable" Grounds for Belief]

(c) In determining, for the purpose of paragraph (3) of subsection (b) of this section, what constitutes reasonable investigation and reasonable ground for belief, the standard of reasonableness shall be that required of a prudent man in the management of his own property.

[Person Becoming Underwriter after Effectiveness of Registration Statement]

(d) If any person becomes an underwriter with respect to the security after the part of the registration statement with respect to which his liability is asserted has become effective, then for the purposes of paragraph (3) of subsection (b) of this section such part of the registration statement shall be considered as having become effective with respect to such person as of the time when he became an underwriter.

[Amount of Damages; Bond for Costs of Suit]

(e) The suit authorized under subsection (a) may be to recover such damages as shall represent the difference between the amount paid for the security (not exceeding the price at which the security was offered to the public) and (1) the value thereof as of the time such suit was brought, or (2) the price at which such security shall have been disposed of in the market before suit, or (3) the price at which such security shall have been disposed of after suit but before judgment if such damages shall be less than the damages representing the difference between the amount paid for the security (not exceeding the price at which the security was offered to the public) and the value thereof as of the time such suit was brought: Provided, that if the defendant proves that any portion or all of such damages represents other than the depreciation in value of such security resulting from such part of the registration statement, with respect to which his liability is asserted, not being true or omitting to state a material fact required to be stated therein or necessary to make the statements therein not misleading, such portion of or all such damages shall not be recoverable. In no event shall any underwriter (unless such underwriter shall have knowingly received from the issuer for acting as an underwriter some bene-

fit, directly or indirectly in which all other underwriters similarly situated did not share in proportion to their respective interests in the underwriting) be liable in any suit or as a consequence of suits authorized under subsection (a) of this section for damages in excess of the total price at which the securities underwritten by him and distributed to the public were offered to the public. In any suit under this or any other section of this title the court may, in its discretion, require an undertaking for the payment of the costs of such suit, including reasonable attorney's fees, and if judgment shall be rendered against a party litigant, upon the motion of the other party litigant, such costs may be assessed in favor of such party litigant (whether or not such undertaking has been required) if the court believes the suit or the defense to have been without merit, in an amount sufficient to reimburse him for the reasonable expenses incurred by him, in connection with such suit, such costs to be taxed in the manner usually provided for taxing of costs in the court in which the suit was heard.

[Joint and Several Liability]

(f) (1) Except as provided in paragraph (2), All or any one or more of the persons specified in subsection (a) shall be jointly and severally liable, and every person who becomes liable to make any payment under this section may recover contribution as in cases of contract from any person who, if sued separately, would have been liable to make the same payment, unless the person who had become liable was, and the other was not, guilty of fraudulent misrepresentation.

(2)(A) The liability of an outside director under subsection (e) shall be determined in accordance with Section 21D(f) of the Securities Exchange Act of 1934.

[*Ed.*: Section 21D(f) provides that any person found liable shall be jointly and severally liable for all damages awarded the plaintiff only if the trier of fact specifically determines that the person knowingly committed a violation of the securities laws. Otherwise (except for uncollectible amounts, as described below), a person is liable solely for the portion of the judgment that corresponds to that person's percentage of responsibility (such percentage to be determined by considering both the nature of the person's conduct and the nature and extent of the causal relationship between the person's conduct and the damages incurred by the plaintiff). If part of the judgment owed by all defendants remains uncollectible, then each defendant has joint and several liability for the uncollectible share if the plaintiff is an individual with a net worth less than $200,000 and the recoverable damages represent more than 10 percent of that net worth. Otherwise, each defendant is liable for the uncollectible share in proportion to his or her percentage of responsibility up to a maximum of 50 percent of that person's proportionate share of liability.]

(B) For purpose of this paragraph, the term "outside director" shall have the meaning given such term by rule or regulation of the commission.

[Limitation on Amount of Damages]

(g) In no case shall the amount recoverable under this section exceed the price at which the security was offered to the public.

Civil Liabilities Arising in Connection with Prospectuses and Communications

Sec. 12. (a) *In General*—Any person who—

(1) offers or sells a security in violation of section 5, or

Offers or Sells by Use of Interstate Communications or Transportation

(2) offers or sells a security (whether or not exempted by the provisions of section 3, other than paragraph (2) of subsection (a) thereof), by the use of any means or instruments of transportation or communication in interstate commerce or of the mails, by means of a prospectus or oral communication, which includes an untrue statement of a material fact or omits to state a material fact necessary in order to make the statements, in the light of the circumstances under which they were made, not misleading (the purchaser not knowing of such untruth or omission), and who shall not sustain the burden of proof that he did not know, and in the exercise of reasonable care could not have known, of such untruth or omission, shall be liable, subject to subsection (b), to the person purchasing such security from him, who may sue either at law or in equity in any court of compe-

tent jurisdiction, to recover the consideration paid for such security with interest thereon, less the amount of any income received thereon, upon the tender of such security, or for damages if he no longer owns the security.

(b) *Loss Causation.*—In an action described in subsection (a)(2), if the person who offered or sold such security proves that any portion or all of the amount recoverable under subsection (a)(2) represents other than the depreciation in value of the subject security resulting from such part of the prospectus or oral communication, with respect to which the liability of that person is asserted, not being true or omitting to state a material fact required to be stated therein or necessary to make the statement no misleading, then such portion or amount, as the case may be, shall not be recoverable.

APPENDIX K   Securities Exchange Act *of* 1934 [Excerpts]

Regulation of the Use of Manipulative and Deceptive Devices

Sec. 10. It shall be unlawful for any person, directly or indirectly, by the use of any means or instrumentality of interstate commerce or of the mails, or of any facility of any national securities exchange—

. . .

[Use or Employment of Manipulative or Deceptive Devices]

(b) To use or employ, in connection with the purchase or sale of any security registered on a national securities exchange or any security not so registered, any manipulative or deceptive device or contrivance in contravention of such rules and regulations as the commission may prescribe as necessary or appropriate in the public interest or for the protection of investors.

. . .

[Directors, Officers, and Principal Stockholders]

Sec. 16. (a) Every person who is directly or indirectly the beneficial owner of more than 10 per centum of any class of any equity security (other than exempted security) which is registered pursuant to section 12 of this title, or who is a director or an officer of the issuer of such security, shall file, at the time of the registration of such security on a national securities exchange or by the effective date of a registration statement filed pursuant to section 12(g) of this title, or within ten days after he becomes such beneficial owner, director, or officer, a statement with the Commission (and, if such security is registered on a national securities exchange, also with the exchange) of the amount of all equity securities of such issuer of which he is the beneficial owner, and within ten days after the close of each calendar month thereafter, if there has been a change in such ownership during such month, shall file with the

Commission (and if such security is registered on a national securities exchange, shall also file with the exchange), a statement indicating his ownership at the close of the calendar month and such changes in his ownership as have occurred during such calendar month.

[Profits Realized from Purchase and Sales within Period of Less than Six Months]

(b) For the purpose of preventing the unfair use of information which may have been obtained by such beneficial owner, director, or officer by reason of his relationship to the issuer, any profit realized by him from any purchase and sale, or any sale and purchase, of any equity security of such issuer (other than an exempted security) within any period of less than six months, unless such security was acquired in good faith in connection with a debt previously contracted, shall inure to and be recoverable by the issuer, irrespective of any intention on the part of such beneficial owner, director, or officer in entering into such transaction of holding the security purchased or of not repurchasing the security sold for a period exceeding six months. Suit to recover such profit may be instituted at law or in equity in any court of competent jurisdiction by the issuer, or by the owner of any security of the issuer in the name and in behalf of the issuer if the issuer shall fail or refuse to bring such suit within sixty days after request or shall fail diligently to prosecute the same thereafter; but no such suit shall be brought more than two years after the date such profit was realized. This subsection shall not be construed to cover any transaction where such beneficial owner was not such both at the time of the purchase and sale, or the sale and purchase, of the security involved, or any transaction or transactions which the Commission by rules and regulations may exempt as not comprehended within the purpose of this subsection.

APPENDIX L   Rules 10b-5, 10b5-1, and 10b5-2 *from* Code *of* Federal Regulations

Regulations adopted by the Securities and Exchange Commission Pursuant to Section 10(b) of the Securities Exchange Act of 1934

§ 240.10b-5 Employment of manipulative and deceptive devices.

It shall be unlawful for any person, directly or indirectly, by the use of

any means or instrumentality of interstate commerce, or of the mails or of any facility of any national securities exchange,

(1) to employ any device, scheme, or artifice to defraud,

(2) to make any untrue statement of a material fact or to omit to state a material fact necessary in order to make the statements made,

in light of the circumstances under which they were made, not misleading, or

(3) to engage in any act, practice, or course of business which operates or would operate as a fraud or deceit upon any person,

in connection with the purchase or sale of any security.

[13 Fed. Reg. 8, 183 (Dec. 22, 1948), as amended at 16 Fed. Reg. 7, 928 (Aug. 11, 1951)]

§ 240.10b5–1 Trading "on the basis of" material nonpublic information in insider trading cases.

Preliminary Note to § 240.10b5–1: This provision defines when a purchase or sale constitutes trading "on the basis of" material nonpublic information in insider trading cases brought under Section 10(b) of the Act and Rule 10b–5 thereunder. The law of insider trading is otherwise defined by judicial opinions construing Rule 10b–5, and Rule 10b5–1 does not modify the scope of insider trading law in any other respect.

(a) General. The "manipulative and deceptive devices" prohibited by Section 10(b) of the Act (15 U.S.C. 78j) and § 240.10b–5 thereunder include, among other things, the purchase or sale of a security of any issuer, on the basis of material nonpublic information about that security or issuer, in breach of a duty of trust or confidence that is owed directly, indirectly, or derivatively, to the issuer of that security or the shareholders of that issuer, or to any other person who is the source of the material nonpublic information.

(b) Definition of "on the basis of." Subject to the affirmative defenses in paragraph (c) of this section, a purchase or sale of a security of an issuer is "on the basis of" material nonpublic information about that security or issuer if the person making the purchase or sale was aware of the material nonpublic information when the person made the purchase or sale.

(c) Affirmative defenses. (1)(i) Subject to paragraph (c) (1) (ii) of this section, a person's purchase or sale is not "on the basis of" material nonpublic information if the person making the purchase or sale demonstrates that:

(A) Before becoming aware of the information, the person had:

(1) Entered into a binding contract to purchase or sell the security,

(2) Instructed another person to purchase or sell the security for the instructing person's account, or

(3) Adopted a written plan for trading securities;

(B) The contract, instruction, or plan described in paragraph (c) (1) (i) (A) of this Section:

(1) Specified the amount of securities to be purchased or sold and the price at which and the date on which the securities were to be purchased or sold;

(2) Included a written formula or algorithm, or computer program, for determining the amount of securities to be purchased or sold and the price at which and the date on which the securities were to be purchased or sold; or

(3) Did not permit the person to exercise any subsequent influence over how, when, or whether to effect purchases or sales; provided, in addition, that any other person who, pursuant to the contract, instruction, or plan, did exercise such influence must not have been aware of the material nonpublic information when doing so; and

(C) The purchase or sale that occurred was pursuant to the contract, instruction, or plan. A purchase or sale is not "pursuant to a contract, instruction, or plan" if, among other things, the person who entered into the contract, instruction, or plan altered or deviated from the contract, instruction, or plan to purchase or sell securities (whether by changing the amount, price, or timing of the purchase or sale), or entered into or altered a corresponding or hedging transaction or position with respect to those securities.

(ii) Paragraph (c) (1) (i) of this section is applicable only when the contract, instruction, or plan to purchase or sell securities was given or entered into in good faith and not as part of a plan or scheme to evade the prohibitions of this section.

(iii) This paragraph (c) (1) (iii) defines certain terms as used in paragraph (c) of this Section.

(A) Amount. "Amount" means either a specified number of shares or other securities or a specified dollar value of securities.

(B) Price. "Price" means the market price on a particular date or a limit price, or a particular dollar price.

(C) Date. "Date" means, in the case of a market order, the specific day of the year on which the order is to be executed (or as soon thereafter as is practicable under ordinary principles of best execution). "Date" means, in the case of a limit order, a day of the year on which the limit order is in force.

(2) A person other than a natural person also may demonstrate that a purchase or sale of securities is not "on the basis of" material nonpublic information if the person demonstrates that:

(i) The individual making the investment decision on behalf of the person to purchase or sell the securities was not aware of the information; and

(ii) The person had implemented reasonable policies and procedures, taking into consideration the nature of the person's business, to ensure that individuals making investment decisions would not violate the laws prohibiting trading on the basis of material nonpublic information. These policies and procedures may include those that restrict any purchase, sale, and causing any purchase or sale of any security as to which the person has material nonpublic information, or those that prevent such individuals from becoming aware of such information.

[65 Fed. Reg. 51,716, 51,737 (Aug. 24, 2000)]

§ 240.10b5–2 Duties of trust or confidence in misappropriation insider trading cases.

Preliminary Note to § 240.10b5–2: This section provides a nonexclusive definition of circumstances in which a person has a duty of trust or confidence for purposes of the "misappropriation" theory of insider trading under Section 10(b) of the Act and Rule 10b–5. The law of insider trading is otherwise defined by judicial opinions construing Rule 10b–5, and Rule 10b5–2 does not modify the scope of insider trading law in any other respect.

(a) Scope of Rule. This section shall apply to any violation of Section 10(b) of the Act (15 U.S.C. 78j(b)) and § 240.10b–5 thereunder that is based on the purchase or sale of securities on the basis of, or the communication of, material nonpublic information misappropriated in breach of a duty of trust or confidence.

(b) Enumerated "duties of trust or confidence." For purposes of this section, a "duty of trust or confidence" exists in the following circumstances, among others:

(1) Whenever a person agrees to maintain information in confidence;

(2) Whenever the person communicating the material nonpublic information and the person to whom it is communicated have a history, pattern, or practice of sharing confidences, such that the recipient of the information knows or reasonably should know that the person communicating the material nonpublic information expects that the recipient will maintain its confidentiality; or

(3) Whenever a person receives or obtains material nonpublic information from his or her spouse, parent, child, or sibling; provided, however, that the person receiving or obtaining the information may demonstrate that no duty of trust or confidence existed with respect to the information, by establishing that he or she neither knew nor reasonably should have known that the person who was the source of the information expected that the person would keep the information confidential, because of the parties' history, pattern, or practice of sharing and maintaining confidences, and because there was no agreement or understanding to maintain the confidentiality of the information.

[65 Fed. Reg. 51,716, 51,738 (Aug. 24, 2000)]

APPENDIX M Rule 14e-3 *from* Code *of* Federal Regulations

§ 240.14e-3 Transactions in securities on the basis of material, nonpublic information in the context of tender offers. (a) If any person has taken a substantial step or steps to commence, or has commenced, a tender offer (the "offering person"), it shall constitute a fraudulent, deceptive or manipulative act or practice within the meaning of section 14(e) of the Act for any other person who is in possession of material information relating to such tender offer which information he knows or has reason to know is nonpublic and which he knows or has reason to know has been acquired directly or indirectly from:

(1) The offering person,

(2) The issuer of the securities sought or to be sought by such tender offer, or

(3) Any officer, director, partner or employee or any other person acting on behalf of the offering person or such issuer, to purchase or sell or cause to be purchased or sold any of such securities or any securities convertible into or exchangeable for any such securities or any option or right to obtain or dispose of any of the foregoing securities, unless within a reasonable time prior to any purchase or sale such information and its source are publicly disclosed by press release or otherwise.

(b) A person other than a natural person shall not violate paragraph (a) of this section if such person shows that:

(1) The individual(s) making the investment decision on behalf of such person to purchase or sell any security described in paragraph (a) of this section or to cause any such security to be purchased or sold by or on behalf of others did not know the material, nonpublic information; and

(2) Such person had implemented one or a combination of policies and procedures, reasonable under the circumstances, taking into consideration the nature of the person's business, to ensure that individual(s) making investment decision(s) would not violate paragraph (a) of this section, which policies and procedures may include, but are not limited to, (i) those which restrict any purchase, sale and causing any purchase and sale of any such security or (ii) those which prevent such individual(s) from knowing such information.

(c) Notwithstanding anything in paragraph (a) of this section to contrary, the following transactions shall not be violations of paragraph (a) of this section:

(1) Purchase(s) of any security described in paragraph (a) of this section by a broker or by another agent on behalf of an offering person; or

(2) Sale(s) by any person of any security described in paragraph (a) of this section to the offering person.

(d)(1) As a means reasonably designed to prevent fraudulent, deceptive or manipulative acts or practices within the meaning of section 14(e) of the Act, it shall be unlawful for any person described in paragraph (d)(2) of this section to communicate material, nonpublic information relating to a tender offer to any other person under circumstances in which it is reasonably foreseeable that such communication is likely to result in a violation of this section except that this paragraph shall not apply to a communication made in good faith:

(i) To the officers, directors, partners or employees of the offering person, to its advisors or to other persons, involved in the planning, financing, preparation or execution of such tender offer;

(ii) To the issuer whose securities are sought or to be sought by such tender offer, to its officers, directors, partners, employees or advisors or to other persons, involved in the planning, financing, preparation or execution of the activities of the issuer with respect to such tender offer; or

(iii) To any person pursuant to a requirement of any statute or rule or regulation promulgated thereunder.

(2) The persons referred to in paragraph (d)(1) of this section are:

(i) The offering person or its officers, directors, partners, employees or advisors;

(ii) The issuer of the securities sought or to be sought by such tender offer or its officers, directors, partners, employees or advisors;

(iii) Anyone acting on behalf of the persons in paragraph (d)(2)(i) of this section or the issuer or persons in paragraph (d)(2)(ii) of this section; and

(iv) Any person in possession of material information relating to a tender offer which information he knows or has reason to know is nonpublic and which he knows or has reason to know has been acquired directly or indirectly from any of the above.

[46 FR 60418 (SEPT. 12, 1980)]

Glossary

abandonment (of a trademark) The failure to use a mark after acquiring legal protection may result in the loss of rights, and such loss is known as abandonment.

absolute priority rule In a bankruptcy proceeding in which the claims of dissenting creditors are not paid in full, a plan may be found to be "fair and equitable" only if the holder of any claim or interest that is junior to the claims of the impaired unsecured class will not receive or retain any property "on account of such junior claim or interest."

absolute privilege In defamation cases, the right of the defendant to publish with impunity a statement known by the defendant to be false.

acceptance An agreement to the amount offered for certain services or products. Acceptance may be verbal, written, or implied by action.

accord *See* Accord and Satisfaction

accord and satisfaction An agreement to accept performance that is different from what is called for in the contract.

accredited investor Certain investors who are so financially sophisticated that they do not need all the protections afforded by the securities laws.

act-of-state doctrine The doctrine that states that the courts of one country will not sit in judgment on the acts of the government of another done within its own territory.

actionable Behavior that is the basis for a claim.

actual abandonment The result of an owner's discontinued use of a trademark with no intent to resume use.

actual authority The express or implied power of an agent to act for and bind a principal to agreements entered into by an agent.

actual cause Proof that but for the defendant's negligent conduct the plaintiff would not have been harmed.

actual damages The amount required to repair or to replace an item or the decrease in market value caused by tortious conduct. Actual damages restore the injured party to the position it was in prior to the injury. Also called compensatory damages.

actual intent The subjective desire to cause the consequences of an act, or the belief that the consequences are substantially certain to result from it.

actual malice A statement made with the knowledge that it is false or with a reckless disregard for the truth.

actual notice Concerning claims on title, actual notice refers to a claimant actually knowing of a prior interest in the real property.

***actus reus* (guilty deed)** A crime; a criminal act.

ad valorem (according to value) tariff An importer must pay a percentage of the value of the imported merchandise.

additive Anything not inherent in a food product—including pesticide residues, unintended environmental contaminants, and unavoidably added substances from packaging.

adhesion contract An unfair type of contract by which sellers offer goods or services on a take-it-or-leave-it basis, with no chance for consumers to negotiate for goods except by agreeing to the terms of said contract.

administrative employee An employee whose primary duty consists of nonmanual work directly related either to management policies or to the general business operations of the employer or the employer's customers.

administrative law judge The presiding official at an administrative proceeding who has the power to issue an order resolving the legal dispute.

adverse possession Ownership of property that is not occupied by its owner for a certain period of time may be transferred to those who have been unlawfully occupying it and openly exercising rights of ownership. Such a transfer is usually not reflected in the official land records. Also called squatter's rights.

affidavit A written or printed declaration or statement of facts, made voluntarily, and confirmed by the oath or affirmation of the party making it, taken before a person having authority to administer such oath or affirmation.

affiliate Any person who controls an issuer of securities, or is controlled by the issuer, or is under common control. Includes officers, directors, and major shareholders of a corporation.

affirmative covenant The borrower's promise to do certain things under the loan agreement.

affirmative defense The admission in an answer to a complaint that defendant has acted as plaintiff alleges, but denies that defendant's conduct was the real or legal cause of harm to plaintiff.

after-acquired property The property a debtor acquires after the execution of a security agreement.

after-acquired title If, at the date of execution of a grant deed, the grantor does not have title to the real property referred to in the grant deed but subsequently acquires it, such after-acquired title is deemed automatically transferred to the grantee.

agency A relationship in which one person (the agent) acts for or represents another person (the principal).

agency by estoppel When the principal leads a third party to believe that a person is his or her agent, the principal is estopped (prevented) from denying that the person is his or her agent.

agency by ratification An agency formed when a principal approves or accepts the benefits of the actions of an otherwise unauthorized agent.

agent A person who manages a task delegated by another (the principal) and exercises whatever discretion is given to the agent by the principal.

aided-in-the-agency doctrine *See* Aided-in-the-Agency-Relation Doctrine

aided-in-the-agency-relation doctrine An agency principle whereby the principal may be held vicariously liable for the wrongful acts of an agent acting outside of the scope of authority because the principal provided the instrumentability or created the circumstances that made it possible for the agent to commit the wrongful act.

aider and abettor A person with knowledge of (or recklessness as to) a primary violation who provides substantial assistance to the primary violation.

allocative efficiency An equilibrium in which scarce societal resources are allocated to the production of various goods and services up to the point where the cost of the resources equals the benefit society reaps from their use.

alter ego theory When owners have so mingled their own affairs with those of a corporation that the corporation does not exist as distinct entity, it is an alter ego (second self) of its owners, permitting the piercing of the corporate veil.

amortize To pay the principal over a period of time.

anchor tenant A key tenant of a shopping center, such as a supermarket or department store.

angels Wealthy individual investors to whom entrepreneurs often turn for equity capital after exhausting the funds available from family and friends.

answer The instrument by which defendant admits or denies the various allegations stated in the complaint against the defendant.

anticipatory repudiation If a party indicates before performance is due that it will breach the contract, there is an anticipatory repudiation of the contract.

antideficiency laws Statutes that restrict lenders seeking remedies against real property security from suing the borrower personally. If a lender has recourse to the borrower or to other property of the borrower, and exercises such rights, the lender may be precluded from foreclosing on real estate mortgaged by the borrower. Alternatively, if the holder of a mortgage or deed of trust secured by real property forecloses on the property, the lender may be precluded from suing the borrower personally to recover whatever is still owing after a foreclosure sale. Also called one-form-of-action laws.

antitrust injury The damages sustained by a plaintiff in an antitrust suit as a result of the defendant's anticompetitive conduct.

antitrust laws The laws that seek to identify and forbid business practices that are anticompetitive. Also called competition laws.

apartheid Prior to its abolition in the 1980s, an official policy of racial segregation in South Africa that relegated its black citizens to a second-class status in employment, housing, and opportunity.

apex deposition The deposition of the most senior executives of a corporation.

apparent authority A principal, by words or actions, causes a third party to reasonably believe that an agent has authority to act for or bind the principal.

appellant The person who is appealing a judgment or seeking a writ of certiorari. Also called a petitioner.

appellate jurisdiction The power of the Supreme Court and other courts of appeal to decide cases that have been tried in a lower court and appealed.

appellee The party in a case against whom an appeal is taken; that is, the party who has an interest adverse to setting aside or reversing the judgment. Also called respondent.

applicant Person (the buyer in a sales transaction) requesting an issuing bank to provide a letter of credit in favor of another party called the beneficiary (the seller in a sales transaction).

appraisal rights In a merger or sale of assets, shareholders who voted against the transaction have appraisal rights, that is, the right to receive the fair cash value of the shares they were forced to give up as a result of the transaction.

appropriate collective bargaining unit A collective bargaining unit in which the employees share a community of interest; that is, they have similar compensation, working conditions, and supervision, and they work under the same general employer policies.

appropriation of a person's name or likeness Unauthorized use of a person's name or likeness for financial gain.

arbitrary and capricious standard If an agency has a choice between several courses of action, the court will presume that the chosen course is valid unless the person challenging it shows that it lacks any rational basis.

arbitrary marks Real word used in connection with a product or service whose ordinary meaning has nothing to do with the trademarked product, for example, Camel for cigarettes and Shell for gasoline.

arbitration The resolution of a dispute by a neutral third party.

arbitration clause A clause that specifies that in the event of a dispute arising out of a contract, the parties will arbitrate specific issues in a stated manner.

arbitrator The neutral third party who conducts an arbitration to resolve a dispute.

area plan *See* Specific Plan.

arrest To deprive a person of his or her liberty by legal authority. Taking, under real or assumed authority, custody of another for the purpose of holding or detaining him or her to answer a criminal charge or civil demand.

articles of incorporation The basic document filed with the appropriate governmental agency upon the incorporation of a business. The contents are prescribed in the general corporation statutes but generally include the name, purpose, agent for service of process, authorized number of shares, and classes of stock of a corporation. It is executed by the incorporator(s). Also called the charter or the certificate of incorporation.

articles of organization The charter document for a limited liability company. Also called certificate of formation.

assault An intent to create a well-grounded apprehension of an immediate harmful or offensive contact. Generally, assault also requires some act (such as a threatening gesture) and the ability to follow through immediately with the battery.

assessment statute A state statute that requires state and local governments to consider, before imposing conditions on development, whether the restriction will constitute a taking under federal or state constitutional law.

asset lock-up option A lock-up option relating to assets of the target company.

assignment The transfer by a tenant of all or a portion of rented premises.

assumption of risk The expressed or implied consent by plaintiff to defendant to take the chance of injury from a known and appreciated risk.

at-will contract An employment relationship of indefinite duration.

attach If the three basic prerequisites of a security interest exist (agreement, value, and collateral), the security interest becomes enforceable between the parties and is said to attach. Also called attachment.

attorney-client privilege The common law rule that a court cannot force the disclosure of confidential communications between client and client's attorney.

attorney work-product doctrine A doctrine that protects information that an attorney prepares in the course of his or her work.

attractive nuisance Artificial conditions on land for which an owner is liable for physical injury to child trespassers if (1) the owner knew or should have known that children were likely to trespass; (2) the condition is one the owner would reasonably know involved an unreasonable risk of injury to such children; (3) the children, because of their youth, did not discover the condition or realize the risk involved; (4) the utility to the owner of maintaining the condition is not great; (5) the burden of eliminating the risk is slight compared with the magnitude of the risk to the children; and (6) the owner fails to exercise reasonable care to protect the children.

attractive nuisance rule The duty imposed on landowner for liability for physical injury to child trespassers caused by artificial conditions on the land.

authoritative decision A court decision that must be followed regardless of its persuasive power, by virtue of relationship between the court that made decision and the court to which decision is cited.

automatic conversion The exchange of preferred stock for common stock that is triggered by specified events at a specified ratio.

automatic stay Feature of bankruptcy filing that instantly suspends most litigation and collection activities against the debtor, its property, or property of the bankruptcy estate.

avoiding powers The powers trustees can use to invalidate or reverse certain prebankruptcy transactions.

back-to-back letter of credit A seller uses the letter of credit in its favor provided by the buyer to finance its purchase of products or materials from its supplier.

BACT (best available control technology) An emission limitation that the permitting authority determines achieves the maximum reduction of pollutants, taking into account energy, environmental, and economic considerations.

bait-and-switch advertising An area of deceptive pricing in which an advertiser refuses to show an advertised item, fails to have a reasonable quantity of the item in stock, fails to promise to deliver the item within a reasonable time, or discourages employees from selling the item.

bankruptcy estate Virtually all of a debtor's existing assets, less exempt property.

base rate The lowest rate of interest publicly offered by major lending institutions to their most creditworthy customers. Also called reference rate or prime rate.

baseline assessment The appraisal performed by a tenant that establishes the environmental condition of leased property at the commencement and termination of the lease.

battery The intentional, non-consensual harmful or offensive contact with an individual's body or with those things in contact with or closely connected with it.

battle of the forms An exchange of forms by a buyer and seller of goods in which each party claims that its own form represents the actual terms of the contract.

beneficial owner A person is considered to be a beneficial owner of any securities held by his or her immediate family, spouse, any minor children, and any other relative living in his or her household.

beneficiary An individual who is benefited by a trust or a will.

bespeaks caution doctrine A doctrine whereby a court may determine that the inclusion of sufficient cautionary statements in a prospectus or other document renders immaterial any misrepresentations and omissions contained therein.

best alternative to a negotiated agreement (BATNA) The outcome a person will choose if the negotiation fails.

best available control technology (BACT) An emission limitation that the permitting authority determines achieves the maximum reduction of pollutants, taking into account energy, environmental, and economic considerations.

best available technology economically achievable (BAT) For toxic pollutants, BAT represents the best economically achievable performance in the category.

best conventional pollutant control technology (BCT) For conventional pollutants, BCT is intended to prevent unnecessarily stringent treatment that might be required under BAT.

best-efforts clause The clause in a merger agreement that requires the board of directors of the target to recommend the deal to the shareholders and to use its best efforts to consummate the transaction.

best-efforts underwriting An agreement among underwriters of an offering to use their best efforts to find buyers at an agreed on price.

best interests of creditors test In a Chapter 11 bankruptcy case, dissenters must be given a bundle of rights the current value of which is at least as great as the distribution they would receive through a Chapter 7 liquidation.

best mode The best way the inventor knows of making an invention at the time of filing the patent application.

best practicable control technology currently available (BPT) The average of the best existing performances by industrial plants of various sizes and ages within a point source category.

BFOQ defense Civil Rights Act of 1964 provision that states that it is not an unlawful employment practice for an employer to hire and employ an individual on the basis of his or her religion, sex, or national origin where religion, sex, or national origin is a bona fide occupational qualification reasonably necessary to the normal operation of that particular business or enterprise.

bicameralism The state of being composed of two legislative chambers; in the case of the United States, the Congress consists of the House of Representatives and the Senate.

bid rigging An agreement between or among competitors to rig contract bids.

bidder The party who makes a tender offer.

bilateral contract A promise given in exchange for another promise.

bill of attainder A law enacted to punish individuals or an easily ascertainable member of a group. Prohibited by Article I, Section 9, of the U.S. Constitution.

bill of lading The document carrier issues to seller that indicates what goods the carrier has received from the seller, the loading location, the names of the carrying vessel, and the destination.

Bill of Rights The first ten amendments to the Constitution.

blank check company A development-stage company that has no specific business plan or whose business plan is to acquire a presently unknown business.

blue-sky laws A popular name for the state statutes that regulate and supervise offerings and sales of securities to persons in that state.

boilerplate clause Nonnegotiable standardized text.

bona fide occupational qualification (BFOQ) defense A defense against employment discrimination that allows an employer to hire an individual of a given religion, sex, or national origin if that characteristic is reasonably necessary to the normal operation of that particular business.

bond Long-term corporate indebtedness.

booked Having criminal charges against someone who has been arrested written in a register at a police station.

bound tariffs The WTO principle that holds that each time tariffs are reduced, they may not be raised again.

break-up fee An amount agreed to in a merger agreement to be paid to a friendly suitor company if the agreement with the target company is not consummated through no fault of the friendly suitor company.

burden of proof The requirement of a prosecutor in a criminal case to establish a defendant's guilt beyond a reasonable doubt.

business judgment rule In a case challenging a board decision, this rule holds that as long as directors have made an informed decision and are not interested in the transaction being considered, a court will not question whether the directors' action was wise or whether they made an error of judgment or a business mistake.

bust-up takeover A takeover in which the corporation, upon acquisition, is taken apart and its assets sold.

bylaws The internal rules governing a corporation.

C corporation A business organization that is taxed at both the entity level and the owner level.

call a loan To terminate a loan.

capacity The ability (requisite presence of mind) to enter into a binding contract.

cartel A group of competitors that agrees to set prices.

caveat emptor **(let the buyer beware)** This maxim summarizes the rule that a purchaser must examine, judge, and test for himself or herself. It does not apply where strict liability, warranty, or other consumer protection laws protect consumer-buyers.

cease and desist order An order of an administrative agency or court prohibiting a person or business firm from continuing a particular course of conduct.

cert. denied Indicates that a writ of certiorari was sought but denied by the Supreme Court.

certificate of deposit (CD) A bank deposit payable after a specified period of time.

certificate of deposit (CD) rate The CD rate is based on the average of the bid rates quoted to the bank by dealers in the secondary market for the purchase at face value of certificates of deposit of the bank in a given amount and for a given term.

certificate of formation The charter document for a limited liability company. Also called articles of organization.

certificate of incorporation *See* Articles of Incorporation.

certification mark A mark placed on a product or used in connection with a service that indicates that the product or service in question has met the standards of safety or quality that have been created and advertised by the certifier.

certiorari A writ of common law origin issued by a superior to an inferior court requiring the latter to produce a certified record of a particular case tried in the inferior court. The U.S. Supreme Court uses the writ as a discretionary device to choose the cases it wishes to hear.

choice-of-forum clause The clause in a contract wherein the parties agree in advance in which jurisdiction a dispute arising out of their agreement is to be litigated.

churning A practice whereby insurance agents write new policies for customers and pay for the new policies with the cash value of existing policies.

circumstantial evidence The indirect (not based on personal knowledge or observation) evidence of certain facts that, taken alone, do not prove a particular conclusion but, if taken as a whole, give a trier of fact a reasonable basis for asserting a certain conclusion is true.

cite The citation of a case.

civil procedure The methods, procedures, and practices that govern the processing of a civil lawsuit from start to finish.

claims (under patent law) The description of those elements of an invention that will be protected by the patent.

class action suit A suit filed on behalf of all persons who have allegedly been harmed by a defendant's conduct.

classified board A board on which directors serve for specified terms, usually three years, with only a fraction of them up for reelection at any one time. Also called staggered board.

clean bill of lading Bill of lading that has no notations indicating defects or damage to the goods when they were received for transport.

cliff vesting A common vesting schedule that provides that if a person granted stock options leaves in the first year of employment, he or she forfeits all rights to any stock.

close corporation A corporation owned by a limited number of shareholders, usually thirty, most of whom are actively involved in the management of the corporation, that elects close corporation status in its charter.

closed-end credit Credit that involves only one transaction, such as a car or house loan.

code of federal regulations (CFR) A multi-volume codification of federal regulations and rules.

codify To collect and arrange items, such as statutes or regulations, systematically.

collateral The property belonging to a borrower that will become the lender's if the loan is not repaid.

collective entity doctrine Under this doctrine, the custodian of records for a collective entity (such as a corporation) may not resist a subpoena for such records on the ground that the act of production will incriminate him or her.

commerce clause The constitutional clause that gives Congress the power to regulate commerce with other nations, with Indian tribes, and between states.

commercial activity exception An exception to the blanket immunity from suits provided by the Foreign Sovereign Immunity Act for cases in which the foreign state was engaged in commercial activities.

commercial impossibility An excuse for nonperformance of a contract because of dramatic changes in circumstances or the relative benefits and burdens of the contract to each party.

commercial impracticability Section 2-615 of the Uniform Commercial Code states that unless the contract provides otherwise, a failure to perform is not a breach if performance is made impractical by an event unforeseen by the contract.

commercial lease A contract that conveys an interest in real property from the landlord to the tenant and governs the respective rights and obligations of the parties during the lease term.

commercial paper Short-term corporate indebtedness.

commitment fee The fee payable to a lender in connection with a revolving loan as consideration for its promise to keep the commitment available.

common customs tariff A single set of tariffs applied by all European Union (EU) member states on goods imported from outside the EU.

common law The legal rules made by judges when they decide a case in which no constitution, statute, or regulation resolves the dispute.

common market The customs union in which there are no tariffs on trade among its members, and a single set of tariffs applies to goods imported from outside the union.

common stock Stock that subjects all the shareholders to the same rights and restrictions.

community plan *See* Specific Plan.

community property The property acquired during marriage with assets earned by either spouse during the marriage.

comp (compensatory) time Extra paid vacation time granted instead of extra pay for overtime work.

comparative fault The liability of an injured party because of misuse or abuse of manufacturer's product.

comparative negligence The doctrine by which courts decide amount of award to be given a plaintiff based on the amount (percentage) of negligence plaintiff demonstrated when injured by defendant.

compensation statute A state statute that requires the government agency adopting a land use regulation to pay the landowner for the loss in property value if the regulation causes the value of the property to decline beyond a certain percentage.

compensation trade An international transaction in which a foreign party transfers use and/or eventual ownership of a good, usually equipment, to the local party, who then repays the foreign party with products produced using the foreign party's equipment.

compensatory damages *See* Actual Damages.

compensatory justice Aims at compensating people for the harm done by another.

complaint The statement of plaintiff's grievance that makes allegations of the particular facts giving rise to dispute and states the legal reason why plaintiff is entitled to a remedy, the request for relief, the explanation why the court applied to has jurisdiction over the dispute, and whether plaintiff requests a jury trial.

composition A reduction in the amount payable to creditors pursuant to a composition plan.

composition plan An agreement between an insolvent debtor and his or her creditors whereby the creditors agree to accept a sooner payment of less than the whole amount in satisfaction of the whole amount.

computer fraud The unauthorized access of a computer used by the federal government, by various types of financial institutions, or in interstate commerce with the intent to alter, damage, or destroy information or to prevent authorized use of the such computers.

computer information Information in electronic form which is obtained from or through the use of a computer or which is in a form capable of being processed by a computer.

computer piracy The theft or misuse of computer software or hardware.

computer virus A computer program that can replicate itself into other programs without any subsequent instruction, human or mechanical.

concerted activity Under the National Labor Relations Act, the exercise by employees of their rights to band together for mutual aid and protection that is engaged in with or on the authority of other employees and not solely by and on behalf of one employee.

condition precedent A condition that must be met before a party's obligations arise under a contract.

condition subsequent In contracts, a provision giving one party the right to divest itself of liability and obligation to perform further if the other party fails to meet the condition.

conditional use permit A method of relief from the strict terms of a zoning ordinance that provides for other uses of real property that are not permitted as a matter of right, but for which a use permit must be obtained.

conditions concurrent Conditions that are mutually dependent and are to be performed at the same time or simultaneously.

conduct test A test for personal jurisdiction that asks in essence whether the fraudulent or wrongful conduct occurred in the United States.

confirming bank A bank located in the seller's jurisdiction that makes a legal commitment to the seller that it will honor the terms of the letter of credit issued by the issuing bank in the buyer's jurisdiction.

conflict-of-laws rules When choice of law is disputed, the court in which the suit is filed will apply conflict of laws principles to determine which state's or country's laws should govern the dispute. They usually focus on the significance of each country's relationship to the parties and the contract.

conflict resolution statute A state statute that sets up formal procedures for negotiation between state agencies and property owners about land use.

conglomerate merger A combination of firms that were not competitors at the time of the acquisition, but that may, absent the merger, have become competitors.

conscious parallelism In business, the act of consistently setting prices at the same levels and changing prices at the same time as competitors.

consent decree A judgment entered by the consent of the parties whereby the defendant agrees to stop the alleged illegal activity without admitting guilt or wrongdoing. Also called consent order.

consequential damages Compensation for losses that occur as a foreseeable result of a breach of contract. Actual damages represent the damage, loss, or injury that flows directly and immediately from the act of the other party; in contrast, consequential damages refer to damage, loss or injury flowing from some of the consequences or results of such act.

consideration A thing of value (money, services, an object, a promise, forbearance, or giving up the right to do something) exchanged in a contract.

construction (of a statute) Interpretation.

constructive abandonment The loss of a trademark's distinctiveness as the result of an owner's actions or failure to act, for instance, by allowing a mark to lapse into genericism or by not adequately controlling companies licensed to use that mark.

constructive notice Notice attributed by the existence of a properly recorded deed.

constructive trust A trust imposed on profits derived from an agent's breach of fiduciary duty.

continuing guaranty A guaranty that covers all future obligations of the primary debtor to the lender.

contract A legally enforceable promise or set of promises.

contribution The doctrine that provides for the distribution of loss among several defendants by requiring each to pay its proportionate share to one who has discharged the joint liability of the group.

contributory copyright infringement Inducing, causing, or materially contributing to the infringing conduct of another with knowledge of the infringing activity.

contributory patent infringement One party knowingly sells an item that has one specific use that will result in the infringement of another's patent.

contributory negligence Plaintiff was negligent in some manner when injured by defendant.

controlling-person liability A person (or other entity), usually an officer or director of a company, responsible and liable for a securities violation.

controlling shareholder A shareholder who owns sufficient shares to outvote the other shareholders, and thus to control the corporation.

conversion The exercise of dominion and control over the personal property, rather than the real property (land), of another. Term includes any unauthorized act that deprives an owner of his or her personal property permanently or for an indefinite time.

convertible debt instrument The document that permits conversion of debt principal into stock.

convertible preferred stock Preferred stock that may be converted into common stock at a specified exchange ratio.

conveyance An instrument transferring an interest in real estate, such as a deed or lease.

copyright The legal right to prevent others from copying the expression embodied in a protected work.

corporate charter The document issued by a state agency or authority granting a corporation legal existence and the right to function as a corporation. Also called the articles or certificate of incorporation.

corporate domicile The state under whose laws a corporation is formed.

corporate opportunity doctrine The doctrine that holds that a business opportunity cannot legally be taken advantage of by an officer, director, or controlling shareholder if it is in the corporation's line of business.

corporation An organization authorized by state law to act as a legal entity distinct from its owners.

corporation by estoppel When a third party, in all its transactions with an enterprise, acts as if it were doing business with a corporation, the third party is prevented or estopped from claiming that the enterprise is not a corporation.

counterclaim A legal claim by defendant in opposition to or as a deduction from claim of plaintiff.

counteroffer A new offer by the initial offeree that rejects and modifies the terms originally proposed by the offeror.

countertrade A foreign investor uses its local currency profits to purchase local products for sale abroad.

countervailing duty law The law that provides that if a U.S. industry is materially injured by imports of a product benefiting from a foreign subsidy, an import duty that offsets the amount of the benefit must be imposed on those imports.

countervailing subsidy The benefits provided by a government to stimulate exports.

covenant The borrower's promise to the lender that it will or will not take specific actions as long as either a commitment or a loan is outstanding.

covenant not to compete An agreement, generally part of a contract of employment or a contract to sell a business, in which the covenantor agrees for a specific period of time and within a particular area to refrain from competition with the convenantee. Also called a noncompete agreement.

cover In the case of a seller failing to make delivery of goods, cover refers to buyer's legal remedy of buying the goods elsewhere and recovering the difference between the cost of the substitute goods and the contract price.

cram down A bankruptcy relief plan confirmed over the objections of creditors.

creditor beneficiary Third party to a contract that the promisee enters into in order to discharge a duty to said third party.

crime An offense against the public at large; an act that violates the duties owed to the community, for which the offender must make satisfaction to the public.

cross-collateralization The collateral for one loan is used to secure obligations under another loan.

cross-default Any breach by the borrower under any other loan agreement will constitute an event of default under the subject loan agreement.

cross-elasticity of demand The extent to which consumers will change their consumption of one product in response to a price change in another.

crown jewels The most valuable assets or divisions of a target company in a takeover battle.

cumulative voting The process by which a shareholder can cast all its votes for one director nominee or allocate them among nominees as it sees fit.

customer restrictions Restrictions that prevent a dealer or distributor from selling to a certain class of customer.

customs union A group of countries that reduce or eliminate tariffs between themselves, but establish a common tariff for trading with all other states.

customs valuation The value assigned to an imported article by the U.S. Customs Service.

cybersquatting The registration of a domain name that is confusingly similar or identical to a protected trademark, where the person registering the domain name has no legitimate interest in that particular domain name and registers and uses it in bad faith.

D'Oench, Duhme doctrine A doctrine that bars many claims and defenses against conservators and receivers that might have been valid against the failed bank or savings and loan itself. It bars enforcement of agreements unless those agreements are in writing and have been approved contemporaneously by the bank's board or loan committee and recorded in the bank's written records.

de facto (in fact) corporation When incorporators cannot show substantial compliance with incorporation requirements, a court may find a corporation is a de facto corporation (corporation in fact) even though it is not technically a corporation by law, if the incorporators demonstrate that they were unaware of the defect and that they made a good faith effort to incorporate correctly.

de jure (by law) corporation When incorporators have substantially complied with incorporation requirements, the entity is a de jure corporation (a corporation by right).

de novo Anew; a de novo proceeding takes place when a case has been successfully appealed and will be litigated again from the beginning.

dealer Under the Securities Act of 1933, any person who engages either for all or part of his or her time, directly or indirectly, as agent, broker, or principal, in the business of offering, buying, selling, or otherwise dealing or trading in securities issued by another person.

debt securities The documents indicating that a corporation has incurred a debt by borrowing money from the holder of the document.

debt subordination An agreement whereby one or more creditors of a common debtor agree to defer payment of their claims until another creditor of the same debtor is fully paid.

debtor Under the Uniform Commercial Code, the person who owes payment or other performance of the obligation secured, whether or not that person owns or has rights in the collateral.

debtor in possession In a Chapter 11 bankruptcy, the debtor may, for the benefit of all concerned, be left in possession of the bankruptcy estate.

deceit See Fraudulent Misrepresentation.

decision A form of European Union legislation in which an order is directed at a specific person or member state.

declaration by the inventor Part of a patent application, the declaration by the inventor states that the inventor has reviewed the application and that he or she believes that he or she is the first inventor of the invention.

declaratory judgment action A lawsuit that seeks only a judicial order articulating the legal rights and responsibilities of the parties, rather than monetary damages.

deed A written document transferring an interest in real estate that is recorded at a public office where title documents are filed.

deed of trust A loan to buy real property secured by a lien on the real property. Also called a mortgage.

defamation The intentional communication to a third party of an untrue statement of fact that injures the plaintiff's reputation or good name, by exposing the plaintiff to hatred, ridicule or contempt.

default judgment A judgment that may be entered in favor of the plaintiff if the defendant does not file an answer within the time required.

defendant The person defending or denying; the party against whom relief or recovery is sought in an action or suit. The accused in a criminal case.

defined benefit plan An employee benefit plan in which the employer guarantees the employee a specific payment regardless of the total contributions made to the plan or the plan's investment performance.

defined contribution plan An employee benefit plan in which the employer agrees only to make specific contributions, usually a percentage of salary, so the payout is dependent on both the total contributions and the plan's investment performance.

Delaware Court of Chancery The trial court in Delaware that hears corporate law cases.

demand rights An investor's right to require an issuer to register a stated portion of the investor's shares in a public offering.

denial-of-service attacks Computer viruses that prevent user access to an Internet site.

deontological theory An ethical theory that focuses on the motivation behind an action rather than the consequences of an action.

depeçage A choice-of-law doctrine under which the court is permitted to apply the laws of different states to different issues when more than one state has an interest in the outcome of a case.

deposition The written or oral questioning of any person who may have helpful information about the facts of a case.

derivative insider A person, such as a tippee, upon whom the insider's duty of disclosure is imposed.

descriptive mark The identifying marks that directly describe (size, color, use of) the goods sold under the mark.

design defect A type of product defect that occurs when the product is manufactured according to specifications, but its inadequate design or poor choice of materials causes it to be defective.

design patent A patent that protects any novel, original, and ornamental design for an article of manufacture.

detour A temporary turning aside from a usual or regular route, course, or procedure, or from a task or employment. To be distinguished from a frolic, which is outside of an agent's scope of employment.

detrimental reliance Occurs when an offeree has changed his or her position because of justifiable reliance on an offer.

development loans Loans used for the acquisition, subdivision, improvement, and sale of residential properties.

direct copyright infringement Occurs when one party is alleged to have violated at least one of the five exclusive rights of the copyright holder by its own actions.

direct patent infringement The making, use, or sale of any patented invention in the jurisdiction where it is patented during the term of the patent.

directed verdict After the presentation of evidence in a trial before jury, either party may assert that other side has not produced enough evidence to support the legal claim or defense alleged. The moving party then requests that the judge take the case away from the jury and direct that a verdict be entered in favor of the moving party.

directive A form of European Union legislation that is a law directing member states to enact certain laws or regulations.

disability A physical or mental impairment that substantially limits one or more of a person's major life activities; having a history of such an impairment or being regarded as having one.

disappearing corporation In a merger of two corporations, the corporation that no longer maintains its separate corporate existence is the disappearing corporation.

discharge Relieve.

discovery The process through which parties to a lawsuit collect evidence to support their claims.

discovery of injury statutes Statutes that provide that the statute of limitations does not begin to run until the person discovers the injury.

discovery rule The statute of limitations period does not accrue until the injured party discovers or, by using reasonable diligence, should have discovered the injury.

discriminate To treat differently.

disparagement Untrue statements derogatory to the quality or ownership of a plaintiff's goods or services, that the defendant knows are false, or to the truth of which the defendant is consciously indifferent.

disparate impact The systematic exclusion of women, ethnic groups, or others in a protected class from employment through testing and other selection procedures.

disparate treatment Intentional discrimination against a person by employer by denying the person employment or a benefit or privilege of employment because of race, religion, sex, national origin, age, or disability.

dispute negotiation Backward looking negotiation that addresses past events that have caused disagreement.

dissolution The designation of the point in time when partners no longer carry on their business together.

distributive justice A theory of justice that looks to how the burden and benefits of a particular situation of a system are distributed.

distributive negotiations Negotiations in which the only issue is the distribution of the fixed pie. Also called zero-sum negotiations.

diversity jurisdiction The power of U.S. District Courts to decide lawsuits between citizens of two different states when amount in controversy, exclusive of interest and all costs, exceeds $50,000.

doctrine of equivalents The doctrine that holds that a direct infringement of a patent has occurred when a patent is not literally copied, but is replicated to the extent that the infringer has created a product or process that works in substantially the same way and accomplishes substantially the same result as the patented invention.

doctrine of self-publication A defamatory communication by an employer to an employee may constitute publication if the employer could foresee that the employee would be required to repeat the communication, for instance, to a prospective employer.

documentary letter of credit A letter of credit issued by a bank that provides for payment by the bank to the beneficiary upon tender by the beneficiary (or its agent or assignee) of specified documents; frequently used to secure payment for goods and repayment of loans in international transactions.

domain names Internet addresses.

donee beneficiary Third party to a contract to whom promisee does not owe an obligation, but rather wishes to confer a gift or a right of performance.

dormant commerce clause An implied constitutional limitation on state action affecting interstate commerce even in the absence of preempting federal legislation.

double jeopardy Fifth Amendment guarantee that protects against a second prosecution for the same offense after acquittal or conviction, and against multiple punishments for the same offense.

dragnet clause In a security agreement, a provision giving the secured party a security interest in all the debtor's property and in the proceeds from the sale of such property.

dram shop act A statute that makes a tavern liable for damage or injury caused by a drunk driver who was served drinks even though visibly intoxicated.

drawings The drawings (except in chemical cases) must show the claimed invention in graphic form.

drug Defined by the Food, Drug and Cosmetic Act to include (1) articles intended for use in the diagnosis, cure, mitigation, treatment, or prevention of disease; and (2) articles (other than food) intended to affect the structure or any function of the body.

dual agency In a real estate transaction, a broker acts for both the buyer and the seller.

dual distributor A manufacturer that sells its goods both at wholesale and at retail.

due diligence The identification and characterization of risks associated with property and operations involved in various business transactions. A defense available to a defendant (other than the issuer) in a securities violation case concerning a registration statement who (1) conducted a reasonable investigation, and (2) reasonably believed that (a) the statements made were true, and (b) that there were no omissions that made those statements misleading.

due process clause A clause in the Fourteen Amendment that provides that no state shall "deprive any person of life, liberty, or property without due process of law."

due process clauses Clauses of the Fifth and Fourteenth Amendments that bar the government from using involuntary confessions, even if the *Miranda* warnings were given, when the conduct of the law enforcement officials in obtaining a confession is deemed outrageous or shocking.

dumping Sale of imported products in the United States below the current selling price in the exporter's home market or below the exporter's cost of production.

dumping margin The difference between the U.S. price for foreign goods and the price of those goods in their country of origin.

duress Coercion.

dutiable Import articles subject to required payment.

duty (1) The obligation to act as a reasonably prudent person would act under the circumstances to prevent an unreasonable risk of harm to others. (2) The required payment on imports.

duty of care The fiduciary duty of agents, officers, and directors to act with the same care that a reasonably prudent person would exercise under similar circumstances. Sometimes expressed as the duty to use the same level of care a reasonably prudent person would use in the conduct of his or her own affairs.

duty of loyalty The fiduciary duty of agents, officers, and directors to act in good faith and in what they believe to be the best interest of the principal or the corporation.

early neutral evaluation (ENE) A dispute resolution mechanism whereby a neutral attorney familiar with the law in the area reviews the case and offers each side his or her evaluation of the strengths and weaknesses.

earmarking doctrine A bankruptcy doctrine whereby a payment to a preexisting creditor may not be recoverable as a preference if the funds for the repayment were provided by some other creditor and not by the debtor.

economic duress The coercion of the borrower, threatening to do an unlawful act that might injure the borrower's business or property.

economic strike A union strikes employers when they are unable to extract acceptable terms and conditions of employment through collective bargaining.

effects test A test for personal jurisdiction that asks whether conduct outside the United States has had a substantial adverse effect on American businesses, consumers, or investors or securities markets.

efficient-market theory The theory that holds that in an open and developed securities market, the price of a company's stock equals its true value.

effluent limitations The regulations designed to impose increasingly stringent limitations on pollutant discharges based on the availability of economic treatment and recycling technologies.

embezzlement The acquisition by an employee of money or property by reason of some office or position, which money or property the employee takes for personal use.

eminent domain The power of state and federal governments to take private property for government uses for which property owners are entitled to just compensation.

employer One who employs the services of others; one for whom employees work, and who pays their wages or salaries.

en banc (en banc) hearing A hearing at which all the judges of a court of appeals sit together to hear and decide a particularly important or close case.

encroachment Occurs when a franchisor sells a franchisee an outlet and later sells another outlet nearby to another franchisee.

encumbrance A claim against real property.

enterprise Any individual, partnership, corporation, association, or other legal entity, and any union or group of individuals associated in fact although not a legal entity.

entrenchment Entrenchment occurs when a director opposes a transaction in order to maintain a place on the corporation's board.

environmental assessment (EA) A document that identifies any significant impact of a development on the environment.

environmental impact statement (EIS) A required document for any proposal for legislation or other major governmental action that may significantly affect the quality of the environment.

environmental justice The notion that decisions with environmental consequences (such as where to locate incinerators, dumps, factories, and other sources of pollution) should not discriminate against poor and minority communities.

environmental laws The numerous federal, state, and local laws with the common objective of protecting human health and the environment.

Environmental Protection Agency (EPA) Federal agency that administers all of the federal laws that set national goals and policies for environmental protection, except for the National Environmental Policy Act, which is administered by the Council on Environmental Quality.

equal dignities rule Under this rule if an agent acts on behalf of another (its principal) in signing an agreement of the type that must under the statute of frauds be in writing, the authority of the agent to act on behalf of the principal must also be in writing.

equitable relief An injunction issued by the court to prohibit a defendant from continuing in a certain course of activity or to require a defendant to perform a certain activity.

equitable subordination The doctrine that prevents one creditor, through fraud or other wrongful conduct, from increasing its recovery at the expense of other creditors of the same debtor.

equity The value of real property that exceeds the liens against it.

equity capital The cash or property contributed to an enterprise in exchange for an ownership interest.

equity security An equity security includes (1) any stock or similar security; (2) any security that is convertible, with or without consideration, into such a security; (3) any security carrying any warrant or right to purchase such a security; (4) any such warrant or right; and (5) any other security that the Securities and Exchange Commission (SEC) deems to be of a similar nature and that, for the protection of investors or in the public interest, the SEC considers appropriate to treat as an equity security.

Erie doctrine In a diversity action in federal court, except as to matters governed by the U.S. Constitution and acts of Congress, the law to be applied in any case is the law of the state in which the federal court is situated.

escrow The system by which a neutral stakeholder (escrow agent) allows parties to a real property transaction to fulfill the various conditions of the closing of the transaction without the physical difficulties of passing instruments and funds between the parties.

escrow agent A neutral stakeholder who facilitates the transfer of real property between interested parties.

essential facility Some resource necessary to a company's rival's survival that they cannot economically or feasibly duplicate.

estopped A defendant is legally barred from alleging or denying a certain fact when the defendant's words and/or actions have been to the contrary.

euro The name of the currency for the European Monetary Union.

event risks Changes in the structure of a corporation such as leveraged buyouts, mergers, or hostile takeovers that affect the credit rating or riskiness of outstanding debt.

events of default The events contained in a loan agreement that will trigger the lender's right to terminate the loan, accelerate the repayment obligations, and, if the loan is secured, take possession of the property securing the loan.

ex post facto **clause (after the fact)** The laws prohibited by the U.S. Constitution that punish actions that were not illegal when performed.

exclusionary rule The evidence obtained in an unlawful search or interrogation cannot be introduced into evidence at trial against a defendant.

exclusive dealership (distributorship) An agreement in which a manufacturer limits itself to a single dealer or distributor in a given territory.

exclusive listing A listing that grants the real estate broker the right to sell the property; any sale of the property during the term of the listing will entitle the broker to a commission.

exclusivity clause Limits or prevents the operation of a competing store in a shopping center.

executive An employee whose primary duty consists of the management of the enterprise where he or she is employed or of a customarily recognized department or subdivision of the enterprise.

executive privilege The type of immunity granted the president against the forced disclosure of presidential communications made in the exercise of executive power.

executory contract Contracts that have not yet been performed and involve an exchange of promises.

exemplary damages Damages awarded to a plaintiff over and above what will fairly compensate it for its loss. They are intended to punish the defendant and deter others from engaging in similar conduct. Also called punitive damages.

exempt employee An employee that is exempt from the minimum-wage and overtime requirements of the Federal Labor Standards Act; such an employee is generally paid a salary instead of an hourly wage.

exempt property Excluded from a bankruptcy estate, and intended to provide for the individual's future needs. Generally includes a homestead, motor vehicles, household or personal items, tools of the debtor's trade, health aids, personal injury awards, alimony or support payments, disability or retirement benefits (including IRAs), life insurance or annuities, and some special deposits of cash.

exhaustion of administrative remedies A court will not entertain an appeal from the administrative process until an agency has had a chance to act and all possible avenues of relief before the agency have been fully pursued.

exit vehicle A way for investors to get their money back without liquidating a company, for example, through acquisition by a larger company or through an initial public offering of the company's securities.

expectation damages In the case of breach of contract, refers to remuneration that puts a plaintiff into the cash position the plaintiff would have been in if the contract had been fulfilled.

export extensive Used to describe industries that derive the bulk of their revenues from sales outside the United States.

express authority The power of an agent to act for a principal based on that agent's justifiable belief that the principal has authorized him or her to do so; may be given by the principal's actual words or by an action that indicates the principal's consent.

express ratification Express ratification occurs when the principal, through words or behavior, manifests an intent to be bound by the agent's act.

express warranty An explicit guarantee by the seller that the goods purchased by a buyer will have certain qualities.

extension plan A plan by which creditors are repaid the entire indebtedness, but the period for payment is extended beyond the original due date.

extortionate extension of credit Making a loan for which violence is understood by the parties as likely to occur in the event of nonpayment.

failure to warn Failure of a product to carry adequate warnings of the risks involved in the normal use of the product.

fair lending laws Laws that prohibit discrimination in lending practices.

fair trade law A federal law providing for temporary relief to domestic industries seriously injured by increasing imports, regardless of whether unfair practices are involved.

fair use doctrine The doctrine that protects from liability a defendant who has infringed a copyright owner's exclusive rights when countervailing public policies predominate. Activities such as literary criticism, social comment, news reporting, educational activities, scholarship, or research are traditional fair use domains.

false imprisonment The confinement of an individual without that individual's consent and without lawful authority.

family resemblance test A test for determining whether an instrument is a security by asking whether it bears a family resemblance to any nonsecurity.

fanciful marks Words that have no prior meaning until used as a trademark in connection with a particular product, for example, Kodak for camera products or Exxon for gasoline.

fast-track negotiating authority Legislation allowing the president to negotiate trade agreements and then submit them for an up or down vote by Congress with no amendments permitted.

Federal Arbitration Act (FAA) The federal law requiring courts to honor agreements to arbitrate and arbitration awards.

federal common law The judicial interpretations of federal statutes and administrative regulations.

federal question When a dispute concerns federal law, namely, a legal right arising under the U.S. Constitution, a federal statute, an administrative regulation issued by a federal government agency, federal common law, or a treaty of the United States, it is said to raise a federal question.

Federal Rules of Civil Procedure (FRCP) The procedural rules that govern civil litigation.

Federal Rules of Evidence (FRE) Federal rules governing the admissibility of evidence in litigation in federal court.

federalism The doctrine that serves to allocate power between the federal government and the various state governments.

fee simple Title to property that grants owner full right of disposition during his or her lifetime that may be passed on to owner's heirs and assigns forever.

felony An offense punishable by death or prison term exceeding one year.

fetal protection policy A company policy that bars a woman from certain jobs unless her inability to bear children is medically documented.

fictitious business name The name of a business that is other than that of the owner.

fiduciary A person having a duty to act primarily for the benefit of another in matters connected with undertaking fiduciary responsibilities.

fiduciary duty The obligation of a trustee or other fiduciary to act for the benefit of the other party.

fiduciary out The allowance in a merger agreement for directors of target company to remain faithful to their fiduciary duties to their shareholders (for example, by recommending other unsolicited offers) even after signing an agreement with a suitor company.

file-wrapper estoppel The doctrine that prevents a patent owner involved in infringement from introducing any evidence at odds with the information contained in the owner's application on file with the U.S. Patent and Trademark Office.

final-offer arbitration A form of arbitration used most notably in baseball salary disputes; each side submits its "best and final" offer to the arbitrator, who must choose one of the two proposals.

financing lease Under a financing lease (commonly used to finance the acquisition of expensive capital equipment and vehicles such as airplanes, locomotives, and ships), the parties expect the lessee to purchase the leased equipment at the end of the lease term at an agreed-upon residual value.

firm commitment underwriting The underwriters agree to purchase the entire offering, thus effectively shifting the risk of the offering from the issuer to the underwriters.

firm offer Under the Uniform Commercial Code, an offer signed by a merchant that indicates that the offer will be kept open is not revocable, for lack of consideration, during the time stated, or for a reasonable period of time if none is stated, but in no event longer than three months.

first sale doctrine Once the copyright or trademark owner places a copyrighted or trademarked item in the stream of commerce by selling it, the owner has exhausted its exclusive statutory right to control its distribution.

fixtures The items of personal property that are attached to real property and that cannot be removed without substantial damage to the item.

floating interest rate An interest rate that fluctuates throughout the life of the loan according to the interest rate that the lender would pay if it borrowed the funds in order to relend them.

floating lien In a security interest, if the collateral is sold, exchanged, collected, or otherwise disposed of, the security interest is equally effective against cash, account, or whatever else is received from the transaction.

food Defined by the Food, Drug and Cosmetic Act as (1) articles used for food or drink; (2) chewing gum; and (3) articles used for components of either.

foreclosure The legal process by which a mortgagee may put up a piece of property for sale in the public arena to raise cash in order to pay off a debt owed by the mortgagor to the mortgagee.

foreign corporation A corporation doing business in one state though chartered or incorporated in another state is a foreign corporation as to the first state.

foreign trade zone A special area within or adjacent to U.S. ports of entry, where import duties on merchandise normally due upon entry into the United States are not due until the merchandise is withdrawn from the zone.

forgotten founder A problem that can arise when several persons work together on an informal basis with a common business objective, and then one leaves. The person who left (the forgotten founder) may have ownership rights in the enterprise.

Form 8-K A form on which companies registered with the Securities and Exchange Commission (SEC) must report certain events, including changes in control, acquisitions or dispositions of key assets, and resignation of directors or auditors, to the SEC within fifteen days of the event.

Form 10-K A form on which companies registered with the Securities and Exchange Commission (SEC) must file their annual audited reports with the SEC within ninety days after the end of the issuer's fiscal year.

Form 10-KSB A simplified form that small businesses required to file periodic reports to the Securities and Exchange Commission (SEC) may use to file annual reports.

Form 10-Q A form on which companies registered with the Securities and Exchange Commission (SEC) must file their unaudited quarterly statements of operations and financial condition with the SEC within forty-five days after the end of each fiscal quarter.

Form 10-QSB A simplified form that small businesses required to file periodic reports to the Securities and Exchange Commission (SEC) may use to file quarterly reports.

Form S-1 The registration statement used in an initial public offering of securities.

Form S-2 A form of registration statement that allows public companies to present certain information in a streamlined form and to incorporate previous filings by reference.

Form S-3 An abbreviated form of registration statement that is available to companies that have filed periodic reports under the Securities Exchange Act of 1934 for at least three years and have a widespread following in the marketplace.

Form S-4 A combined securities registration statement and proxy statement.

Form SB-1 Allows nonreporting and transitional small business issuers to register up to $10 million of securities annually.

Form SB-2 A form for registration of any amount of securities by small business issuers.

forum non conveniens A doctrine whereby a suit is dismissed because an alternate, more convenient forum is available.

forum shopping A party to a lawsuit attempts to have a case tried in a particular court or jurisdiction where party feels the most favorable judgment or verdict will be received.

forward-looking statement A statement by a publicly traded company (1) containing a projection of revenues, income, earnings per share, capital expenditures, dividends, capital structure, or other financial items; (2) of management's plans and objectives for future operations, including plans relating to the issuer's products and services; (3) of future economic performance, including any such statement in management's discussion and analysis of financial condition or in the results of operations required to be included by the SEC; and (4) of the assumptions underlying or relating to any such statement.

franchise agreement A business relationship in which one party (the franchisor) grants to another party (the franchisee) the right to use the franchisor's name and logo and to distribute the franchisor's products from a specified locale.

fraud Any intentional deception that has the purpose of inducing another in reliance upon the deception to part with some property or money. Fraud may involve false representations of fact, whether by words or conduct; false allegations; omission (especially by fiduciary); or concealment of something that should have been disclosed.

fraud in the factum A type of fraud that occurs when a party is persuaded to sign one document thinking that it is another.

fraud in the inducement A type of fraud that occurs when a party makes a false statement to persuade the other party to enter into an agreement.

fraud on the market The theory that holds that if the information about a company available to the market is incorrect, then the market price will not reflect the true value of the stock.

fraudulent conveyance The direct or indirect transfer of assets to a third party with actual intent to defraud or have inadequate consideration in circumstances when the transferor is insolvent.

fraudulent misrepresentation Deceit; intentionally misleading by making material misrepresentations of fact that the plaintiff relied on that cause injury to the plaintiff.

free trade area A free trade area is created when a group of countries reduce or eliminate tariffs among themselves, but maintain their own individual tariffs as to other states.

freeze out In a merger with a controlling shareholder, some shareholders (usually the public shareholders) are required to surrender their shares in the disappearing corporation for cash.

frolic An activity by an employee that is entirely outside the employer's purpose. To be distinguished from a detour, which is within the scope of employment.

fruit of the poisonous tree Evidence acquired directly or indirectly as a result of an illegal search or arrest is generally inadmissible.

frustration of purpose Frustration of purpose occurs when performance is possible, but changed circumstances have made the contract useless to one or both of the parties.

full warranty The warranty that gives the consumer the right to free repair or replacement of a defective product.

gap financing Financing that a developer obtains to pay off a construction loan when it becomes due before the permanent financing is available. Also called interim financing.

garnishment The legal procedure by which a creditor may collect a debt by attaching a portion of a debtor's weekly wages.

general partnership A form of business organization between two or more persons in which the partners share in the profits or losses of a common business enterprise.

general plan A long-range planning document that addresses the physical development and redevelopment of a city.

general release An agreement by person engaging in a dangerous activity to assume all risks and hold the party offering access to said dangerous activity free of all liability.

genericism The use of a trademark as a generic name for the product, for example, "a Kleenex" for "tissue."

geographic market All firms that compete for sales in a given area at current prices, or would compete in that area if prices rose by a modest amount.

going effective Culmination of the securities registration process with the Securities and Exchange Commission. Sales can be legally consummated as of this date and time.

golden parachute A termination agreement that gives extra salary and other benefits to an executive upon a corporate change in control.

good faith exception An exception to the exclusionary rule that provides that evidence obtained by police in good faith will not be excluded from trial, even if it was obtained in violation of the Fourth Amendment.

good faith subsequent purchaser A person who acquires real property for fair value without being aware of a disputed claim to the property.

goods All things (including specially manufactured goods) that are movable at the time of identification to the contract for sale.

government-contractor defense The limited immunity available for manufacturers that produce products to the specifications of government contracts.

grant deed A deed that contains implied warranties that the grantor has not previously conveyed the same property or any interest in it to another person and that the title is marketable.

grantee A person to whom real property is conveyed.

grantor A person conveying real property.

greenmail Payment by a target company to buy back shares owned by a potential acquirer at a premium over market. The acquirer in exchange agrees not to pursue its hostile takeover bid.

gross-up clause The clause in foreign investment contracts by which local partner or licensee is obligated to pay all taxes other than those specifically allocated to the foreign partner.

ground lease A lease for land on which a building will be built.

group boycott An agreement among competitors to refuse to deal with another competitor.

guarantor The person who agrees to be liable for the obligation of another person.

guaranty An undertaking by one person to become liable for the obligation of another person.

guaranty of collection Under a guaranty of collection, the guarantor becomes obliged to pay only after the lender has attempted unsuccessfully to collect the amount due from the primary debtor.

guaranty of payment A provision that holds guarantor's obligation to pay the lender is triggered, immediately and automatically, if the primary debtor fails to make a payment when due.

guaranty of performance A guaranty that specified nonpayment obligations will be performed.

guardian *ad litem* (guardian for the suit) A person authorized to bring suit for a minor.

gun-jumping A violation of the securities laws that occurs when an issuer or underwriter conditions the market with a news article, press release, or speech about a company engaged in the registration of its securities.

harmonized tariff schedule (HTS) A U.S. government document that lists the tariffs on goods imposed by Congress and by the president pursuant to the Trade Agreements Program, based on the country of origin.

hazard ranking score The Environmental Protection Agency ranking that represents the risks presented by certain sites to the environment and public health.

hazardous substance superfund Finances federal activity to investigate and take remedial action in response to a release or threatened release of hazardous substances to the environment.

hearing The phase of arbitration that is similar to a trial.

Herfindahl-Hirschman Index (HHI) An aid to the interpretation of market data when determining the anticompetitive effect of a merger; the HHI of market concentration is calculated by summing the squares of the individual market shares of all the firms in the market.

horizontal agreement A conspiracy agreement between firms that compete with each other on the same level of production or distribution.

horizontal market division An agreement among competitors to divide a market according to class of customer or geographic territory; it violates antitrust law.

horizontal merger A corporate combination of actual or prospective competitors.

horizontal price fixing An agreement between competitors at the same level of distribution to set a common price for a product; it violates antitrust law.

hostile environment harassment The creation of a hostile working environment, such as continually subjecting an employee to ridicule and racial slurs, or unwanted sexual advances.

hostile takeover A transaction in which a third party (a raider) seeks to obtain control of a company (the target) over the objections of its management.

hot-news exception A state-law doctrine giving the plaintiff the right to preclude others from using information in cases where (1) the plaintiff generated or gathered the information at a cost; (2) the information is time-sensitive; (3) the defendant's use of the information amounts to a free ride on the plaintiff's efforts; (4) the defendant is in direct competition with the plaintiff; and (5) the availability of other parties to free ride on the plaintiff's efforts would so reduce the plaintiff's incentive to provide the product or service that its existence or quality would be threatened.

hushmail A repurchase of shares at a premium over market to ensure silence from a shareholder who has been critical of management.

identification to the contract Setting aside or otherwise designating the particular goods for sale under a contract.

identity theft Taking an individual's information (such as Social Security number and mother's maiden name) and using that information to fraudulently obtain credit or commit other financial crimes.

illegal contract A contract is illegal if its formation or performance is expressly forbidden by a civil or criminal statute, or if a penalty is imposed for doing the act agreed upon.

illegal *per se* A practice that is illegal regardless of its impact on the market or its procompetitive justifications.

illusory promise A promise that does not in fact confer any benefit on the promisee or subject the promisor to any detriment.

impaired claim A claim is considered impaired if the bankruptcy relief plan does not provide for full cash payment on its effective date and it alters the creditors' legal, equitable, or contractual rights in any way (except by curing defaults and reinstating the maturity of the claim).

implementation after impasse doctrine The duty to bargain collectively in good faith prohibits an employer from unilaterally changing a term or condition of employment unless, after bargaining with the union to an impasse, the employer's unilateral changes are consistent with the employer's pre-impasse proposal.

implied authority The power of an agent to do whatever is reasonable to complete the task he or she has been instructed to undertake.

implied contract An employment agreement—implied from such facts as long-term employment; receipt of raises, bonuses and promotions; and assurance from management that the employee was doing a good job—that the employee would not be terminated except for good cause.

implied covenant of good faith and fair dealing An implied covenant in every contract that imposes on each party a duty not to do anything that will deprive the other party of the benefits of the agreement.

implied intent If a person does not intend a particular consequence of an act, but knew that the consequence of the act was certain, or substantially certain, and does the act anyway, intent to cause the consequence is implied.

implied ratification Implied ratification occurs when the principal, by his or her silence or failure to repudiate the agent's act, acquiesces in it.

implied warranties Representations about the quality or suitability of a product that are implied, not explicitly stated. *See also* Implied Warranty of Fitness for a Particular Purpose and Implied Warranty of Merchantability.

implied warranty of fitness for a particular purpose The warranty whereby goods involving the following elements are judged satisfactory for the buyer's purpose: (1) the buyer must have a particular purpose for the goods; (2) the seller must have known or have had reason to know of that purpose; (3) the seller must have known or had reason to know that the buyer was relying on the seller's expertise; and (4) the buyer must have relied upon the seller.

implied warranty of habitability A warranty made by a commercial seller of houses in which the seller warrants that the house is in reasonable working order and is of reasonably sound construction.

implied warranty of merchantability The warranty by which all goods sold by merchants in the normal course of business must meet following criteria: (1) pass without objection in the trade under the contract description; (2) be fit for the ordinary purposes for which such goods are used; (3) be within the variations permitted by the agreement, of even kind, quality and quantity within each unit and among all units involved; (4) be adequately contained, packaged, and labeled as the agreement may require; and (5) conform to the promises or affirmations of fact made on the container or label, if any.

import competing Used to describe industries that derive their revenues primarily from U.S. sales and face significant competition from foreign firms.

import relief laws A series of laws through which Congress has authorized the president to raise U.S. tariffs on specified products and to provide other forms of import protection to U.S. industries.

impossibility An excuse for nonperformance based on the destruction of something vital to the performance of the contract or another unforeseen event that makes performance of the contract impossible.

impossibility defense A defense to strict liability in which a corporate officer might not be held strictly (and vicariously) liable if he or she did everything possible to ensure legal compliance to applicable standards, even though the company was still unable to comply.

impracticability A situation in which performance is possible but is commercially impractical.

improper means Deceitful actions through which party obtains trade secrets of another.

imputed liability The imposition of civil or criminal liability on one party for the wrongful acts of another. Also called vicarious liability.

in personam jurisdiction Personal jurisdiction based upon the residence or activities of the person being sued. It is the power that a court has over the defendant itself, in contrast to the court's power over the defendant's interest in property (*quasi in rem* jurisdiction) or power over the property itself (*in rem* jurisdiction).

in rem jurisdiction Jurisdiction over property based upon the location of the property at issue in the lawsuit.

incorporation The process by which a corporation is formed.

indemnification The doctrine that allows a defendant to recover its individual loss from a co-defendant whose relative blame is greater or who has contractually agreed to assume liability.

indenture The agreement governing a bond issue.

independent contractor A person is deemed to be an independent contractor only if the employer neither exercises control over the means of performing the work nor the end result of that work.

indictment Formal charges filed by a grand jury.

indirect patent infringement One party's active inducement of another party to infringe a patent.

industrial ecology A concept that advocates a systems approach to eco-efficiency and applies it to groups of corporations working together.

inevitable disclosure doctrine A doctrine that permits a former employer to prevent an employee from working for a competitor when the new position will require the employee to disclose or use the trade secrets of the former employer.

inevitable discovery exception An exception to the exclusionary rule that provides that illegally obtained evidence can lawfully be introduced at trial if it can be shown that the evidence would inevitably have been found by other legal means.

infomercial An advertisement generally presented in the format of half-hour television talk shows or news programs.

informal discretionary action The administrative agencies' decision-making process for repetitive actions that are inappropriate to litigate in courts.

information The formal charges filed with the court in a criminal case.

inherently distinctive mark Inherently distinctive marks (often called strong marks) are identifying marks that need no proof of distinctiveness.

initiative A formal petition generated by a certain percentage of the electorate to introduce legislative change.

injunction A remedy granted by the court that requires defendant to perform or cease from performing some activity.

injurious falsehood False statements knowingly made that lead to economic loss for a plaintiff.

innocent landowner defense In a case under the Comprehensive Environmental Responsibility, Contribution, and Liability Act, a potentially responsible current owner can assert this defense if the release or disposal of hazardous materials was by a third party who was not an employee and with whom the current owner had no contractual relationship. Also called the third-party defense.

innovation offsets Technological advantages gained by companies that met the challenge of environmental regulations and discovered lower costs and better quality products as a result.

inquiry notice Notice attributed when reasonable inquiry would have disclosed an adverse interest, for example, if inspection of a property would have revealed that some person other than the grantor was in possession or owned the property.

inside director A member of a board who is also an officer.

insider A person with access to confidential information and an obligation of disclosure to other traders in the marketplace.

insider trading Trading securities based on material nonpublic information, in violation of a duty to the corporation or its shareholders or others.

integrated disclosure system The system that seeks to eliminate duplicative or unnecessary disclosure requirements under the Securities Act of 1933 and the Securities Exchange Act of 1934.

integration When an issuer makes successive sales of securities within a limited period of time, the Securities and Exchange Commission may integrate the successive sales; that is, it may deem them to be part of a single sale for purposes of deciding whether there was an exemption from registration.

integrative negotiations Negotiations in which mutual gains are possible as parties trade lower valued resources for higher valued ones. Also called variable-sum negotiations.

intellectual property Any product or result of a mental process that is given legal protection against unauthorized use.

intelligent agents Semi-autonomous computer programs that can be dispatched by the user to execute certain tasks.

intent The actual, subjective desire to cause the consequences of an act, or the belief that the consequences are substantially certain to result from it.

intent to be bound The oral or written statement regarding intention of parties to enter into a contract.

intention to do wrong Subjective intent or desire to do wrong or intent to take action substantially certain to cause a wrong to occur.

intentional infliction or emotional distress Outrageous conduct by the individual inflicting the distress; intention to cause, or reckless disregard of the probability of causing, emotional distress; severe emotional suffering; and actual and proximate (or legal) causation of the emotional distress.

interbrand competition The price competition between a company and its competitors that sell a different brand of the same product.

interference with contractual relations A defendant intentionally induces another to breach a contract with a plaintiff.

interference with prospective business advantage Intentional interference by the defendant with a business relationship the plaintiff seeks to develop, which interference causes loss to the plaintiff.

interim financing Financing that a developer obtains to pay off a construction loan when it becomes due before the permanent financing is available. Also called gap financing.

interlocutory Something intervening between the commencement and the end of a suit that decides some point or matter, but is not a final decision regarding the whole controversy.

interrogatory Written question to a party to a lawsuit and its attorney.

intraband competition The price competition among the different dealers selling products produced by the same company.

intrusion Objectionable prying, such as eavesdropping or unauthorized rifling through files. It includes the act of wrongfully entering upon or taking possession of property of another.

invasion of privacy Prying or intrusion that would be objectionable or offensive to a reasonable person, including eavesdropping, rifling through files one has no authorization to see, public disclosure of private facts, or unauthorized use of an individual's picture in an advertisement or article with which that person has no connection.

inverse condemnation The unlawful taking of private real property by the government for a public use without just compensation. Also called regulatory taking.

investigative consumer reporting Report that contains information on character and reputation, not just credit history.

investment contract A type of security created by an investment of money in a common enterprise with profits to come solely from the efforts of others.

investors Persons putting up cash or property in exchange for an equity interest in an enterprise.

invitee A business visitor who enters a premises for the purposes of the possessor's business.

involuntary redemption rights The permission of a corporation, at its option, to redeem the shares for a specified price either after a given period of time or on the occurrence of a certain event.

irrebuttable presumption A presumption that cannot be disputed even through the introduction of contrary evidence.

irrevocable letter of credit A letter of credit that cannot be amended or canceled without the consent of the beneficiary and the issuing bank.

irrevocable offer Irrevocable offers arise in two circumstances: (1) when an option contract has been created, and (2) when an offeree has relied on an offer to its detriment.

issuer A company that offers or sells any security.

join In cases in which more than one defendant is liable for damages, named defendant(s) may ask the court to join or add other defendants.

joint and several liability In a case in which the court determines that multiple defendants are at fault, the doctrine whereby a plaintiff may collect the entire judgment from any single defendant, regardless of the degree of that defendant's fault.

joint tenancy A specialized form of co-ownership involving real property owned in equal shares by two or more persons who have a right of survivorship if one joint tenant dies.

joint venture A one-time group of two or more persons in a single specific business enterprise or transaction.

judgment notwithstanding the verdict (judgment N.O.V.) Reverses the jury verdict on the ground that the evidence of the prevailing party was so weak that no reasonable jury could have resolved the dispute in that party's favor. Also called judgment n.o.v. (*non obstante veredicto*, notwithstanding the verdict).

judicial review The power of federal courts to review acts of the legislative and executive branches of government to determine whether they violate the Constitution.

junior debt Indebtedness that is subordinated under a debt subordination agreement.

junk bond A form of high yield, high risk unsecured corporate indebtedness that is not investment grade.

juristic personality The characteristic of a business entity, such as a corporation, whereby the entity is treated as a legal entity separate from its owners.

Kantian theory An ethical theory that looks to the form of an action, rather than the intended result, in examining the ethical worth.

kicker A percentage of gross or net income in a real estate transaction payable to lender.

know-how Detailed information on how to make or do something.

laesio enormis A doctrine developed from language in the Code of Justinian that provided a remedy for those who sold land at less than half its just price.

larceny Theft. The taking of property without the owner's consent.

legal duty The requirement to act reasonably under the circumstances to avoid harming another person.

lemon laws Laws designed to protect consumers from defective products that cannot be adequately fixed, such as new cars and new mobile homes.

letter of credit (L/C) A payment mechanism for international sales transactions involving a bank in the buyer's jurisdiction that commits to pay the seller. Also called a documentary credit.

letter of intent An instrument entered into by the parties to a real estate or other transaction for the purpose of setting forth the general terms and conditions of a purchase and sale agreement until a formal legal commitment can be made through the execution of a formal acquisition agreement.

leveraged buyout (LBO) A takeover financed with loans secured by the acquired company's assets, in which groups of investors, often including management, use borrowed money along with some of their own money to buy back the company's stock from its current shareholders.

libel A written communication to a third party by a defendant of an untrue statement of fact that injures a plaintiff's reputation.

licensee Anyone who is privileged to enter upon land of another because the possessor has given expressed or implied consent.

lien A claim on a property that secures a debt owed by the owner of the property.

lien notice A written notice that property is subject to a claim by someone other than its owner for the payment of a debt.

lien subordination An agreement between two secured creditors whose respective security interest, liens, or mortgages attach to the same property. The subordinating party agrees that the lien of the other creditor shall have priority notwithstanding the relative priorities that the parties' liens would otherwise have under applicable law.

limited-fund class action A class action in which the total of the aggregated liquidated claims exceeds the fund available to satisfy them.

limited guaranty A guaranty in which the maximum amount of the guarantor's liability is expressly stated in the guaranty instrument.

limited liability company (LLC) A form of business entity authorized by state law that is taxed like a limited partnership and provides its members with limited liability, but like a corporation gives its members the right to participate in management without incurring unlimited liability.

limited liability partnership (LLP) A form of limited partnership designed primarily for professionals who typically do business as a partnership that insulates its partners from vicarious liability for certain partnership obligations.

limited partners The participants in a limited partnership whose liability for partnership business is limited to their capital contribution.

limited partnership A form of business organization in which limited partners must refrain from actively participating in the management of the partnership but are liable for the debts of the partnership only up to the amount they personally contributed to the partnership.

limited warranty The warranty that limits the remedies available to the consumer for a defective product.

line-item veto Allowed the president to sign a bill into law and then cancel any dollar amounts that he or she believed to be fiscally irresponsible. Declared unconstitutional by the U.S. Supreme Court.

line-of-business test If an officer, director, or controlling shareholder learns of an opportunity in the course of business for the corporation, and if the opportunity is in the corporation's line of business, a court will not permit that person to keep the opportunity for personal gain.

liquidated damages The amount of money stipulated in a contract to be paid to non-breaching party should one of the parties breach the agreement.

lock-up option An option to buy assets or stock of a target company; it is exercisable only if the recipient of the option is unsuccessful in acquiring control of the target company. Depending on how it is priced, a lock-up option can have the effect of deterring other bids.

London Interbank Offered Rate (LIBOR) An interest rate based on the cost of borrowing offshore U.S. dollars in the global interbank market, centered in several locations in addition to London.

long-arm statute A state statute that subjects an out-of-state defendant to jurisdiction when the defendant is doing business or commits a civil wrong in the state.

lost volume seller A seller that can be put in as good a position as performance would have only by permitting the seller to recover the profit (including reasonable overhead) that it would have made from full performance by the buyer.

lowest achievable emission rate (LAER) The lowest achievable emission rate using best available technology.

mail fraud A scheme intended to defraud or to obtain money or property by fraudulent means through use of the mails.

malicious defense A tort committed when a defendant creates false material evidence and gives false testimony advancing the evidence.

malicious prosecution A plaintiff can successfully sue for the tort of malicious prosecution if he or she shows that a prior proceeding was instituted against him or her maliciously and without probable cause or factual basis.

malpractice A claim of professional negligence.

managers Persons elected by the members (owners) of a limited liability company who, like a board of directors in a corporation, are responsible for managing the business, property, and affairs of the company.

mandatory arbitration One party will not do business with the other unless it agrees to arbitrate any future claims.

manufacturing defect A flaw in a product that occurs during production, such as a failure to meet the design specifications.

market power The power to control market prices or exclude competition in the relevant market. Also called monopoly power.

market-share liability The liability for damages caused by a manufacturer's products assessed based on a manufacturer's national market share.

marketable title Title to property that is fee simple and is free of liens or encumbrances.

marshaling assets Partnership creditors have first priority to partnership assets and, as to those assets, stand in front of creditors of individual partners themselves.

material breach A failure to perform a significant obligation under a contract, such as by not performing a service after receiving payment. A material breach discharges the nonbreaching party from its obligations and provides grounds to sue for damages.

material fact A fact that a reasonable investor would most likely have considered important in deciding whether to buy or sell his or her stock.

maturity date The date a term loan becomes due and payable.

med-arb The parties to a dispute enter mediation with the commitment to submit the dispute to binding arbitration if mediation fails to resolve the conflict.

mediation A form of dispute resolution whereby the parties agree to try to reach a solution themselves with the assistance of a neutral third party who helps them find a mutually satisfactory solution.

mediator The third party who helps the parties in mediation find a mutually satisfactory solution.

members The owners of a limited liability company.

mens rea **(guilty state of mind)** Criminal intent.

merchant A person who deals in goods of the kind or otherwise by its occupation holds itself out as having knowledge or skill peculiar to the practices or goods involved in the transaction.

merger The combination of two or more corporations into one.

merger agreement An agreement between two companies to combine those companies into one.

merger doctrine If an idea and its expression are inseparable, the merger doctrine dictates that the expression is not copyrightable.

merit review A review by a state securities commissioner to determine whether the issuer's plan of business and the proposed issuance of securities are fair, just, and equitable.

minimum contacts As long as the person has sufficient minimum contacts with a state, such that it is fair to require him or her to appear in a court of that state, the state has personal jurisdiction over that person.

minitrial A cross between arbitration and negotiation, truncated presentation of evidence conducted by lawyers, usually with business persons present.

Miranda **warnings** Once a person is placed in custody, he or she cannot be questioned by the police unless first advised of his or her constitutional rights to remain silent and to have counsel present.

mirror-image rule A traditional rule of contract formation that requires the offeree's acceptance to be a mirror image of what the offeror has offered.

misappropriation (of a trade secret) Learning through improper means or unauthorized use of the trade secret of another.

misappropriation theory (securities) A securities violation occurs when a person breaches a fiduciary duty to the owner of nonpublic information by trading on that information after misappropriating it for his or her own use.

misbranding False or misleading labeling prohibited by federal and state statutes. Includes claiming unsubstantiated medicinal benefits for a food, inadequate labeling for a drug, or selling over-the-counter a drug for which a prescription is required.

misdemeanor An offense lower than a felony, punishable by fine or imprisonment for less than one year (not in a penitentiary).

misrepresentation A misleading or false representation of the facts intended to deceive another party.

misstatement (Rule 10b–5) A misrepresentation of a fact; a lie.

mistake of fact A mistake about an underlying fact that may make a contract voidable.

mistake of judgment A mistake of judgment occurs when the parties make an erroneous assessment about the value of what is bargained for.

mitigate Lessen.

mitigation of damages After a breach of contract, the non-breaching party has a duty to take any reasonable actions that will lessen the amount of the damages.

monopolistic intent The maintenance or acquisition of monopoly power through anticompetitive acts.

monopoly power The power to control market prices or exclude competition in the relevant market. Also called market power.

mortgage A loan to buy real property secured by a lien on the real property. Also called deed of trust.

most favored nation (MFN) The principle that holds that each member country of the World Trade Organization (WTO) must accord to all other WTO members tariff treatment no less favorable than it provides to any other country.

motion for judgment on the pleadings A motion filed immediately after the complaint and answer have been filed. One party, usually the defendant, argues that the pleadings alone demonstrate that the action is futile.

motion for summary judgment A motion requesting the trial judge to decide a case as a matter of law, without a trial, when there are no material facts in dispute.

motion to dismiss The formal request that the court terminate lawsuit on the ground that plaintiff's claim is technically inadequate.

multiple-brand product market A market made up of product or service offerings by different manufacturers or sellers that are economically interchangeable and may therefore be said to compete.

mutual recission An agreement by both parties of a contract to terminate the contract. A mutual recission is itself a type of contract.

mutuality of obligation Both parties in a bilateral contract are obligated to perform their side of the bargain.

national ambient air quality standards The permissible levels of pollutants in the ambient or outdoor air that, with adequate margins of safety, are required to protect public health; set forth in the Clean Air Act.

national effluent limitations Increasingly stringent Environmental Protection Agency restrictions on pollutant discharges, based on the availability of economic treatment and recycling technologies.

national pollutant discharge elimination system (NPDES) The principal regulatory program established by the Clean Water Act; requires permits for the discharge of pollutants from any point source to navigable waters.

national treatment The World Trade Organization principle that holds that WTO members must not discriminate against imported products in favor of domestically produced products.

natural resource law The laws that govern wilderness protection, wildlife protection, coastal zone management, energy conservation, and national park designation.

navigable waters The waters of the United States and the territorial seas, as well as lakes and streams that are capable of being used for purposes of navigation.

negative commerce clause *See* Dormant Commerce Clause.

negative convenant The borrower's promise of what it undertakes not to do under the loan agreement.

negligence A breach of the requirement that a person act with the care a reasonable person would use in the same circumstances.

negligence *per se* Violation of a statute that shifts the burden to the defendant to prove the defendant was not negligent once the plaintiff shows that the defendant violated a statute and the violation caused an injury.

negligent-hiring theory An employer is negligent if the employer hires an employee who endangers the health and safety of other employees.

negligent infliction of emotional distress A tort committed when the defendant negligently inflicts emotional distress that causes the plaintiff some form of physical injury.

negotiation The give and take people engage in when coming to terms with each other.

net listing A real estate listing in which the broker receives any sales proceeds in excess of the net listing amount specified by the seller.

neutral gate system In a secondary boycott situation, the union may picket only at the gate reserved for the employees and vendors of the primary employer that is physically separated from the gate to be used by all other persons.

new source performance standards (NSPS) Require use of technology chosen as BAT for new sources of pollutants.

nexus The legally required relationship between a condition to a land-use approval and the impacts of the development being approved.

nolo contendere **(I will not contest it)** A plea that means the accused does not contest the charges.

non obstante veredicto Latin for "notwithstanding the verdict."

nonbinding arbitration Arbitration in which the parties are not bound by the arbitrator's decision.

nonconforming use An existing land use that was lawful but that does not comply with a later-enacted zoning ordinance.

nonexempt employee An employee that is not exempt from the minimum-wage and overtime requirements of the Federal Labor Standards Act; such an employee is often paid an hourly wage.

noninfringement In a patent dispute, the defense of noninfringement asserts that the allegedly infringing matter does not fall within the claims of the issued patent.

nontariff barriers (NTBs) Barriers to trade other than tariffs that have in some cases replaced tariffs as a means of protecting domestic industries threatened by import competition.

not an underwriter Under Rule 144, an affiliate or a person selling restricted securities is not an underwriter if certain conditions (e.g., holding period, volume limitations, manner of sale, filing of Form 144, and available public information) are met.

note purchase agreement The title of a loan agreement when the lender is an insurance company.

novation The method of contract modification by which the original contract is canceled and a new one is written with perhaps only one change, such as substitution of a new party.

novel An invention is novel if it was not anticipated; i.e., if it was not previously known or used by others in the United States and was not previously patented or described in a printed publication in any country.

nuisance A thing or activity that unreasonably and substantially interferes with an owner's use and enjoyment of owner's property.

obvious risk If the use of a product carries an obvious risk, the manufacturer will not be held liable for injuries that result from ignoring the risk.

offer (contracts) A proposal to enter into a contract. Proposal may be verbal, written, or implied by action.

offer (securities) Every attempt or offer to dispose of, or solicitation of an offer to buy, a security or interest in a security, for value.

offeree A person to whom an offer is made.

offeror A person making an offer.

offshore transaction A security transaction in which no offer is made to a person in the United States and either (1) at the time the buy order is originated, the buyer is outside the United States; or (2) the transaction is one executed in, on, or through the facilities of a designated offshore securities market.

ombudsperson A person who hears complaints, engages in fact finding, and generally promotes dispute resolution through information methods such as counseling or mediation.

omission (Rule 10b–5) A company or its managers fail to tell the whole truth about a fact to the investing public, and what the company does say makes it likely that reasonable investors will take away an impression contrary to the true facts.

one-form-of-action laws *See* Antideficiency Laws.

open-end credit Credit in which the creditor makes repeated extensions of credit (for example, Visa or MasterCard).

open listing A real estate listing in which the broker receives a commission only if he or she procures a ready, willing, and able buyer.

operating agreement A contract that sets forth the rights, obligations, and powers of the owners, managers, and officers of a limited liability company.

operating lease Typically a short-term lease that does not appear on the balance sheet.

oppression An inequality of bargaining power that results in no real negotiation and an absence of meaningful choice for one party to the contract.

option contract A contract in which the offeror promises to hold an offer open for a certain amount of time.

ordinary comparative negligence In an ordinary comparative negligence jurisdiction, the plaintiff may recover only if it is less culpable than the defendant.

organizational strike An unlawful strike whose purpose is to organize employees.

original jurisdiction The power of the U.S. Supreme Court to take cognizance of a case at its inception, try it, and pass judgment upon the law and facts. Distinguished from appellate jurisdiction.

output contract A contract under which a buyer promises to buy all the products that the seller produces.

outside director A member of a board who is not also an officer.

over-the-counter A drug for which a prescription is not required.

override The ability of Congress to annul a president's veto by a two-thirds vote of both the House of Representatives and the Senate.

***parens patriae* (parent of the country) action** Antitrust suits brought by state attorneys general for injuries sustained by residents of their respective states.

parol evidence rule If there is a written contract that the parties intended would encompass their entire agreement, oral evidence of prior or contemporaneous statements will not be permitted to vary or alter the terms of the contract.

partial summary judgment A summary judgment granted on some issues of a case while other issues proceed to trial.

participation in a breach of fudiciary duty A tort committed when the defendant induces another party to breach its fiduciary duty to the plaintiff.

participation loan A loan in which the original lender sells shares to other parties, called participants.

pass-through entity A business organization that is not a separate taxpayer; all its income and losses are passed through and taxed to its owner. S Corporations, partnerships, and limited liability companies are pass-through entities.

passive investor An investor in a business who does not materially participate in that business.

passive-loss limitation The rule enacted by the Tax Reform Act of 1986 under which only owners who materially participate in a business may deduct losses against their other ordinary income.

patent A government-granted right to exclude others for a stated period of time (usually 20 years) from making, using, or selling within the government's jurisdiction an invention that is the subject of the patent.

patent misuse In a patent dispute, a defense asserting that although the defendant has infringed a valid patent, the patent holder has abused its patent rights and therefore has lost, at least temporarily, its right to enforce them.

pattern An involvement in racketeering activity demonstrated by at least two predicate acts occurring within a ten-year period.

pattern bargaining In collective bargaining, a technique of matching agreements within an industry.

payoff table A diagram that illustrates the results the possible outcomes of various choices in game theory.

penumbra The peripheral rights that are implied by the specifically enumerated rights in the Bill of Rights.

***per se* analysis** A form of antitrust analysis that condemns practices that are completely void of redeeming competitive rationales.

***per se* violation** A violation without proof of anything more.

percentage rent clause A clause frequently contained in retail leases that requires the tenant to pay, in addition to a base monthly rent, a percentage of its gross sales to the landlord.

perfect tender rule A Uniform Commercial Code rule that gives the buyer an absolute right to reject any goods not meeting all the contract requirements, including time of delivery.

perfecting (under the UCC) In connection with security interests, perfection refers to making the security interest valid as against other creditors of the debtor.

permanent loan Usually a long-term loan used to acquire property that is repaid over five, ten, or sometimes up to twenty years.

person (under environmental law) A party who has contributed to imminent and substantial endangerment to human health or the environment

and therefore is required in a civil action to take remedial action. Person in this sense includes companies, individual employees, and officers, as well as shareholders if state law would mandate piercing the corporate veil.

personal jurisdiction The power of state court to hear (decide) a civil case based upon residence or location of activities of the person being sued.

persuasive decision A well-reasoned court decision that another court, not bound by the first decision, would, when confronted with a similar dispute, probably follow.

petitioner The person who is appealing a judgment or seeking a writ of certiorari. Also called appellant.

piercing the corporate veil When a court denies limited liability to a corporation and hold shareholders personally responsible for claims against the corporation, the court has pierced the corporate veil.

piggyback rights An investor's right to request registration of that investor's shares in a public offering initiated by the company.

placement agent A broker-dealer who distributes the private placement memorandum to suitable persons and assists in private placement of securities.

plaintiff A person who brings an action; the party who complains or sues in a civil action and is so named on the record. The prosecution in a criminal case (i.e., the state or the United States in a federal case).

planned unit development (PUD) The land use regulations for a given piece of property that reflect the proposed development plans for that property. PUD allows for mixture of uses for property not possible under traditional zoning regulations.

plea The response by a defendant in criminal case of guilty, not guilty, or nolo contendere.

plea bargaining The process by which the prosecutor agrees to reduce the charges in exchange for a guilty plea from the accused.

pleadings The formal allegations by the parties to a lawsuit of their respective claims and defenses.

pledge A type of security interest whereby the creditor or secured party takes possession of the collateral owned by the debtor.

points A one-time charge to a borrower buying real property (in addition to interest) computed by a lender by multiplying the amount funded by a fixed percentage.

poison pill A plan that would make any takeover of a corporation prohibitively expensive. Also called shareholder rights plan.

police power The general power granted state and city governments to protect the health, safety, welfare, or morals of its residents.

political question A conflict that should be decided by one of the political branches of government or by the electorate. A court will refuse to decide questions of a purely political character.

posthearing The final phase of arbitration in which the arbitrator renders his or her award after considering all the evidence presented in the prehearing and the hearing.

power of attorney A written instrument that authorizes a person, called an attorney-in-fact (who need not be a lawyer), to sign documents or perform certain specific acts on behalf of another person.

prayer The request for relief in a complaint.

precontractual liability The claims by the disappointed party if contract negotiations fail before a contract has been finalized.

predatory pricing The act of pricing below the producer's actual cost with the intent of driving other competitors out of the market, thus enabling the person engaging in predatory pricing to raise prices later.

preempt A federal law takes precedence when state law conflicts with federal law.

preemption defense (product liability) The immunity granted manufacturers if they meet minimum standards of conduct under certain regulatory schemes.

preferences Transfers to (or for the benefit of) creditors on account of antecedent debts that are made from an insolvent debtor's property within ninety days before bankruptcy (one year if creditor is insider) and that enable the creditors to receive more than they would through a Chapter 7 liquidation.

preferred return The legal right to have distributions made to the person entitled to a preferred return before any distributions are made to any other equity holder.

preferred stock Stock that has priority over common stock in the payment of dividends (and in the distribution of assets if the corporation is dissolved).

prehearing The first stage in arbitration in which parties may submit trial-like briefs, supporting documents, and other written statements making their case.

prejudgment interest The interest on the amount of an award from the date of the injury to the date of judgment.

preliminary hearing A hearing in which the prosecutor presents evidence demonstrating probable cause that the defendant committed the crime.

premises liability A theory under which a building owner may be found liable for violating its general duty to manage the premises and warn of dangers, such as asbestos.

prenuptial agreement An agreement entered into before marriage that sets forth the manner in which the parties' assets will be distributed and the support to which each party will be entitled, in the event the parties get divorced.

prepackaged bankruptcy A workout plan approved by key creditors and the debtor before the debtor files bankruptcy; it becomes the plan of reorganization in a Chapter 11 bankruptcy.

prepayment penalty A clause whereby a lender imposes a penalty if the loan is paid off early.

preponderance of the evidence The evidence offered in a civil trial that is more convincing than the evidence presented in opposition to it.

price amendment Information concerning the price of securities and underwriting arrangement filed with the Securities and Exchange Commission once the registration statement has been informally cleared by the SEC staff, or the registrant receives notice that the registration statement will not be reviewed.

price antidilution A provision that prevents a corporation from diluting a shareholder's interests by simply issuing shares of common stock at a price below the conversion price.

price discrimination Sellers charge different prices to purchasers in interstate sales for commodities of like grade and quality.

price fixing The cooperative setting of price levels or ranges by competing firms.

prima facie (on its face) A fact considered true until evidence is produced to the contrary.

primary debtor The person with an obligation for which the guarantor becomes liable.

primary employer In a secondary boycott situation, the employer with whom union has a dispute.

prime rate The lowest rate of interest publicly offered by major lending institutions to their most creditworthy customers. Better practice dictates using the terms base rate or reference rate because sometimes lenders offer a loan below prime.

priming lien A lien that is senior to a previously granted security interest.

principal A person who delegates a portion of his or her tasks to another person who represents the principal as an agent.

principal (of a loan) The amount borrowed.

prior art Developments or pre-existing art that relates to a claimed invention.

prior restraints Prohibitions barring speech before it occurs.

private nuisance Interference with a person's use and enjoyment of his or her land and water.

private offering An offering to selected individuals or entities who have the ability to evaluate and bear the risk of the investment; that is, they have the ability to fend for themselves.

private placement *See* Private offering.

private placement memorandum A booklet offered by entrepreneurs seeking financing from private individual investors that furnishes information about themselves and their enterprise.

privately held corporation A corporation whose shares are not bought and sold among the general public.

privileges and immunities clause A clause in the Fourteen Amendment that provides that no state "shall make or enforce any law which shall abridge the privileges or immunities of citizens of the United States."

privity of contract The necessity for a person injured by a product to be in a contractual relationship with the seller of the product in order for the injured person to recover damages.

probable cause As applied to an arrest or a search warrant, a reasonable belief that the suspect has committed a crime or is about to commit a crime. Mere suspicion or belief, unsupported by facts or circumstances, is insufficient.

procedural due process The parties whose rights are to be affected are entitled to be heard and, in order that they may enjoy that right, they must be notified before adverse action is taken.

procedural obligations The rules that define the manner in which rights and duties are enforced.

processing operation In a compensation trade arrangement, a processing operation refers to the foreign party supplying the materials that are processed by the local party using the foreign party's equipment.

product liability The liability of a manufacturer or seller of a product that because of a defect, causes injury to a purchaser, user, or bystander.

product market A product or service offering made by different manufacturers or sellers that are economically interchangeable and may therefore be said to compete.

productive efficiency An equilibrium in which only the lowest-cost producers of goods and services survive.

professional corporation An organization of professionals (such as doctors, lawyers, or architects) authorized by state law to act as a legal entity distinct from its owners.

professional employee An employee who holds a position requiring advanced knowledge in a field of science or learning customarily acquired by a prolonged course of specialized intellectual instruction and study.

promisee In contract law, the promisee is the person to whom the promise (contract) was made.

promisor In contract law, the promisor is the person who made the promise.

promissory estoppel A promise that the promisor should reasonably expect to induce action or forbearance on the part of the promisee or a third person and that does induce such action or forbearance can create liability for reliance damages if injustice can be avoided only by providing some relief when promise is broken.

promissory fraud A type of fraud that occurs when one party induces another to enter into a contract by promising to do something without having the intention to carry out the promise.

proof of claim A claim filed by creditors on uncontingent and undisputed debt.

prospectus Any document that is designed to produce orders for a security, whether or not the document purports on its face to offer the security for sale or otherwise to dispose of it for value. The descriptive document that an issuer of securities provides to prospective purchasers.

protected expression The part of a work that is subject to copyright protection.

proximate cause A reasonably foreseeable consequence of the defendant's negligence, without which no injury would have occurred.

proxy A written authorization by a shareholder to another person to vote on the shareholder's behalf.

proxy contest A battle for corporate control whereby someone wishing to replace the board with its own candidates seeks to acquire a sufficient number of shareholder votes to do so.

public disclosure of private facts The publication of a private fact that is not newsworthy. The matter must be private, such that a reasonable person would find publication objectionable. Unlike in a defamation case, truth is not a defense.

public figures Individuals, who, by reason of their achievements or the vigor and success with which they seek the public's attention, are injected into the public eye.

public nuisance Unreasonable and substantial interference with the public health, safety, peace, comfort, convenience, or utilization of land.

public policy exception An employer is prohibited from discharging an employee for a reason that violates public policy.

publication Communication to a third party.

publicly held corporation A corporation whose shares are traded on one of the national stock exchanges or the over-the-counter market.

publicly owned sewage treatment works (POTWs) General and specific industry pretreatment standards are set for discharges to publicly owned sewage treatment works (POTWs).

puffing The expression of opinion by a seller regarding goods; not a warranty.

punitive damages Damages awarded to a plaintiff over and above what will fairly compensate it for its loss. They are intended to punish the defendant and deter others from engaging in similar conduct. Also called exemplary damages.

purchase-money security interest A security interest created when a seller lends the buyer the money to buy the seller's goods.

pure comparative negligence A tort system in which the plaintiff may recover for the part of the injury due to the defendant's negligence, even though the plaintiff was the more negligent party.

pure notice recording statutes Under these statutes, a person who has notice that someone else has already bought the real property cannot validate his or her deed by recording it first.

pyramid selling A scheme whereby a consumer is recruited as a product "distributor" and receives commissions based on the products he or she sells and on the recruitment of additional sellers.

qualified institutional buyer Institutional investors holding and managing $100 million or more of securities.

qualified privilege In defamation cases, the right by a defendant to make statements to (1) protect one's own personal interests; (2) protect business interests, such as statements to a prospective employer; or (3) provide information for the public interest, such as credit reports.

quantum meruit A basis for equitable relief by a court when there was no contract between the parties, but one party has received a benefit for which it has not paid.

quash To declare invalid.

quasi-foreign corporation A corporation incorporated outside of California but with more than 50 percent of its stock owned by California residents and with more than 50 percent of its sales, payroll, and property tax derived from activities in California.

qui tam plaintiff A plaintiff suing on the government's behalf, often entitled to a share of the amount recovered.

"quick look" rule of reason The "quick look" rule of reason is used whenever the practice has obvious anticompetitive effects but is not illegal per se; it allows for immediate inquiry into procompetitive justifications.

quid-pro-quo (this for that) harassment The specific, job-related adverse action, such as denial of a promotion, in retaliation for a worker's refusal to respond to a supervisor's sexual advances.

quiet period The time between filing of securities registration statement and the date the registration statement becomes effective.

quitclaim deed A deed that contains no warranties; the grantor conveys only any right, title, and interest held by the grantor, if any, at the time of execution.

quorum The holders of more than 50 percent of the outstanding shares of a corporation.

race norming of employment tests A device designed to ensure that a minimum number of minorities and women are in an application pool by adjusting the scores or using different cutoff scores for employment related tests on the basis of race, color, religion, sex, or national origin.

race-notice recording statutes These statutes protect only a good faith subsequent purchaser who recorded its deed before the prior purchaser recorded its deed.

race recording statutes Under these statutes, recording is a race—the rule is "first in time is first in right." The first to record a deed has superior rights, regardless of whether he or she knew that someone else had already bought or claimed an interest in the real property.

racketeering activity The state and federal offenses involving a pattern of illegal acts, including mail and wire fraud.

raider In a hostile takeover, a third party who seeks to obtain control of a corporation, called the target, over the objections of its management.

ratification A principal affirms through words or actions a prior act of an agent that did not bind the principal.

rational basis test A test under which a discriminatory classification will be held valid if there is any conceivable basis upon which the classification might relate to a legitimate governmental interest; applies to all classifications that relate to matters of economics or social welfare.

Rawlsian moral theory A deontological line of thought that aims to maximize the utility of the worst off person in society.

reaffirmation agreement A contract with a creditor whereby an individual who has filed under Chapter 7 agrees to repay a debt even though the debt would otherwise be discharged in the debtor's bankruptcy case.

real estate investment trust (REIT) A tax-advantaged pool of real property.

reasonable care under the circumstances A standard requiring landowners to act in a reasonable manner with respect to entrants on their land, with liability hinging on the foreseeability of harm.

recklessness In the criminal context, conscious disregard of a substantial risk that an individual's actions would result in the harm prohibited by a statute.

recognitional strike An unlawful strike whose purpose is to force an employer to recognize the union as the collective bargaining agent for certain of its employees.

recognized hazard Workplace conditions that are obviously dangerous or are considered by the employer or other employers in the industry to be hazardous.

record The oral and written evidence presented at an administrative hearing.

recordable form The requirements established by the state regarding how title to real estate is filed and recorded. Requirements generally include legibility and notarization.

recording statutes Statutes that establish an orderly process by which claims to interests in real property can be recorded as part of the public record and resolved.

red-herring prospectus Preliminary prospectus; incomplete version of the final prospectus.

redemption The buying back of shares by a corporation from a shareholder.

reference rate The lowest rate of interest publicly offered by major lending institutions to their most creditworthy customers.

referral sale The seller offers the buyer a commission, rebate, or discount for furnishing the seller with a list of additional prospective customers.

registered mask work Highly detailed transparencies that represent the topological layout of semiconductor chips.

registration rights An investor's right to require a company to register under applicable federal and state securities laws the shares of common stock into which the preferred stock is convertible.

registration statement The registration statement consists of filing forms and the prospectus, the disclosure document that an issuer of securities provides to prospective purchasers.

Regulation Z Regulations issued by the Federal Reserve Board to interpret and enforce the federal Truth-in-Lending Act.

regulations The rules of order prescribed by superior or competent authority relating to action of those under its control.

regulatory negotiations (reg-neg) A style of administrative rulemaking in which representatives of major groups convene with an administrative agency and work out a compromise through negotiation on the substance of new regulations.

regulatory taking The taking by the government of private real property for a public use; requires payment of just compensation.

reliance damages The awards made to a plaintiff for any expenditures made in reliance on a contract that was subsequently breached.

remand The power of a court of appeal to send a case back to a lower court for reconsideration.

remote tippee Recipient of a tip from another tippee other than the original tippee.

reporter The published volumes of case decisions by a particular court or group of courts.

reporting company A company registered under Section 12 of the Securities Exchange Act of 1934 that subjects issuers to various reporting requirements and to certain rules and regulations concerning proxies, tender offers, and insider trading.

representation election An election among employees to decide whether they want a union to represent them for collective bargaining.

requests for production of documents Requests for documents such as medical records and personal files to be produced as part of the discovery process before a trial.

requirements contract A contract under which the buyer agrees to buy all of a specified commodity the buyer needs from the seller and the seller agrees to provide that amount.

res ipsa loquitur **(the thing speaks for itself)** The doctrine that allows a plaintiff to prove breach and causation indirectly.

resale price maintenance (RPM) An agreement on minimum price between firms at different levels of production or distribution that violates antitrust law.

rescind Void or make ineffective.

reservation price That price at which one is indifferent between the success and failure of the negotiation.

respondeat superior **(let the master answer)** The doctrine under which an employer may be held vicariously or secondarily liable for the negligent or intentional conduct of the employee that is committed in the scope of the employee's employment.

respondent The party in a case against whom an appeal is taken; the party who has an interest adverse to setting aside or reversing the judgment.

responsible corporate officer doctrine A criminal law doctrine that, under certain circumstances, imposes vicarious liability on an officer responsible for compliance based on the actions of subordinates.

responsible persons The responsible persons from whom the Environmental Protection Agency can recover the costs of remedial work include (1) the present owner or operator of the facility; (2) the owner or operator at the time of disposal of the hazardous substance; (3) any person who arranged for treatment or disposal of hazardous substances at the facility; and (4) any person who transported hazardous substances to and selected the facility.

restatement Former common law rules in a particular subject area (e.g., contracts, torts) integrated into formal collections that a judge or legislature is free to adopt.

restitution An award made to a plaintiff of a benefit improperly obtained by the defendant.

restricted guaranty A guaranty in which the guarantor's liability is enforceable only with respect to a specified transaction or series of transactions.

restricted securities Securities issued in a private placement; they cannot be resold or transferred unless they are either registered or exempt from registration. The most common exemption is pursuant to Securities and Exchange Commission Rule 144.

retributive justice A theory that states that every crime demands payment in the form of punishment.

reversibility An ethical theory that looks to whether one would want a rule applied to one's self.

revival statutes State and federal statutes that allow plaintiffs to file lawsuits that have been barred by the running of the statute of limitations.

Revlon **mode** A company is said to be in *Revlon* mode when a change of control or breakup of the company has become inevitable.

revoke To annul an offer by recission.

revolving line of credit A line of credit that allows a borrower to borrow whatever sums it requires up to a specified maximum amount and reborrow amounts it has repaid.

revolving loan A loan that allows a borrower to borrow whatever sums it requires up to a specified maximum amount and to reborrow amounts it has repaid.

right of first negotiation Gives the holder the right to negotiate the purchase of the property before the seller enters negotiations with another party.

right of first refusal A contract that provides the holder with the right to purchase property on the same terms and conditions offered by or to a third party.

right of redemption Gives the mortgagor and certain other categories of interested persons the right to redeem or get back foreclosed property within a statutorily limited period.

right of rescission A right to cancel a contract.

right of setoff Permits Party A to deduct automatically from payments due Party B amounts due from Party B to Party A.

ripeness A court will not hear agency cases if they are not ripe for decision, for example, after a rule is adopted but before the agency seeks to apply it to a particular case.

roadshow Oral presentations to large institutional investors in key cities in the United States, Europe, and Asia.

rule of impossibility The rule under which claims of predation are rejected because the marketplace in question cannot be successfully monopolized.

rule of reason The rule that takes into account a defendant's actions as well as the structure of the market to determine whether an activity promotes or restrains competition.

rules The legislative enactments that serve as general principles and guidelines for sensitive issues not governed by law.

runaway shop An illegal attempt by an employer to escape its collective-bargaining obligation by shutting down a unionized operation and moving the functions of that former operation to a nearby site.

S–1 review A review by the auditor of events subsequent to the date of the certified balance sheet in the registration statement to ascertain whether any material change has occurred in the company's financial position that should be disclosed to prevent the balance sheet figures from being misleading.

S Corporation A corporation meeting certain requirements and that is taxed only at the owner level.

sale (1933 Act) Every contract of sale or disposition of a security or interest in a security, for value.

sale and leaseback A simultaneous two-step transaction, whereby an institutional lender purchases real property from a company, and the property is leased back to the company for its use.

sale-of-business doctrine A doctrine the U.S. Supreme Court rejected that held that compliance with federal securities laws was not necessary when 100 percent of the stock of a company was sold.

salting The practice of paying individuals to seek work with a nonunion employer with the intent of having them organize the other workers once hired.

satisfaction *See* Accord and Satisfaction.

scienter An intent to deceive.

second-step, back-end merger The second step in a corporate takeover whereby the shareholders who did not tender their shares receive cash or securities in a subsequent merger.

secondary boycott A strike against an employer with whom a union has no quarrel in order to encourage it to stop doing business with an employer with whom it does have a dispute.

secondary meaning A descriptive trademark becomes protectable by acquiring secondary meaning, or sufficient consumer recognition through sufficient use and/or advertising of the goods under the mark.

secondary offering A securities offering by a person other than the issuer.

Section 4(½) exemption An exemption for a private offering of securities by an affiliate that would qualify as a private placement under Section 4(2) of the Securities Act of 1933 if made by the issuer.

Section 201 Provides for temporary relief to U.S. industries seriously injured by increasing imports, regardless of whether unfair practices are involved. It is sometimes called the fair trade law.

Section 232 Provides for relief from imports threatening to impair U.S. national security.

Section 301 Authorizes the U.S. Trade Representative to investigate alleged unfair practices of foreign governments that impede U.S. exports of both goods and services.

Section 337 Provides that if a U.S. industry is injured (or there is a restraint or monopolization of trade in the United States) by reason of unfair acts in the importation of articles into the United States, an order must be issued requiring the exporters and importers to cease the unfair acts or, if necessary, excluding imports of the offending articles from all sources.

Section 406 Provides for import relief if a U.S. industry is suffering material injury by reason of rapidly increasing imports from a communist country.

secured loan A loan backed up by collateral.

secured party The lender, seller, or other person in whose favor there is a security interest.

secured transaction A loan or other transaction secured by collateral put up by the borrower.

security Any note, stock, treasury stock, bond, debenture, evidence of indebtedness, certificate of interest or participation in any profit-sharing agreement, collateral trust certificate, pre-organization certificate or subscription, transferable share, investment contract, voting-trust certificate, certificate of deposit for a security, fractional undivided interest in oil, gas, or other mineral rights; any put, call, straddle, option, or privilege on any security, certificate of deposit, or group or index of securities (including any interest therein or based on the value thereof; or any put, call, straddle, option, or privilege entered into on a national securities exchange relating to foreign currency; or, in general, any interest or instrument commonly known as a "security," or any certificate of interest or participation in, temporary or interim certificate for, receipt for, guarantee, of, or warrant or right to subscribe to or purchase, any of the foregoing.

security agreement An agreement that creates or provides for a security interest.

security interest Any interest in personal property, fixtures or letters of credit and accounts that is used as collateral to secure payment or the performance of an obligation.

selective disclosure A practice whereby issuers of publicly traded securities disclose material nonpublic information, such as advance warnings of earnings results, to securities analysts or selected institutional investors before making full disclosure of the same information to the general public.

self-financing Generating capital by carefully managing a company's own funds.

self-publication A doctrine giving an employee a claim for defamation when the employer makes a false assertion in firing an employee, which the employer could reasonably expect the employee to repeat to a prospective employer.

self-tender An offer by a corporation to buy back its stock or shareholder rights for a fair price.

selling short The sale of securities the seller does not own.

senior debt Indebtedness that benefits from a debt subordination agreement.

separate property Property that belongs solely to the spouse who acquired it before marriage or received it by gift or inheritance.

separation of powers The distinct authority of governance granted the three branches of U.S. government (executive, legislative, and judicial) by the U.S. Constitution.

sequestration order A governmental order that requires spending levels to be reduced below the levels provided in the budget.

service mark A legally protected identifying mark connected with services.

settle When parties to a lawsuit go over claims and ascertain and agree on the balance due one another prior to taking case to trial, they have settled the lawsuit.

severability The ability to separate a clause in a contract from the remainder of the contract.

shareholder A holder of equity securities of a corporation. Also called stockholder.

shareholder derivative suit A lawsuit brought against directors or officers of a corporation by a shareholder on behalf of the corporation.

shareholder of record The persons whose names appear on a corporation's shareholder list on a specified date who are entitled to vote.

shareholder rights plan *See* Poison Pill.

shelf registration The registration of a number of securities at one time for issuance later.

short-swing trading The purchase and sale or sale and purchase by an officer, director, or greater-than-10 percent shareholders of securities of a public company within a six-month period.

show-how Nonsecret information used to teach someone how to make or do something; generally not legally protectable.

showing of interest A sufficient number of employees who express interest in a union representation election.

shrinkwrap license A license that customers cannot read when they purchase software but are deemed to have accepted when they open the wrapping around the envelope containing the discs or click on the "I Accept" button on the computer screen. Also called clickwrap agreement

slander A spoken communication to a third party by a defendant of an untrue statement of fact that injures a plaintiff's reputation.

slander *per se* Words that are slanderous in and of themselves. Only statements that a person has committed a serious crime, has a loathsome disease, is guilty of sexual misconduct, or is not fit to conduct business are slanderous *per se*.

small business issuers Companies with revenues less than $25 million whose market value of publicly held securities (other than those held by affiliates) is less than $25 million.

sole proprietorship One person owns all the assets of the business, has complete control of the business, and is solely liable for all the debts of the business.

sovereign acts doctrine The government cannot be held liable for breach of contract due to legislative or executive acts of general application.

sovereign immunity The doctrine that prevents the courts of one country from hearing a suit against the government of another country.

Special 301 Provisions Provisions in U.S. trade law under which the U.S. Trade Representative identifies countries that deny adequate and effective protection for intellectual property rights or deny fair and equitable market access for persons who rely on intellectual property protection.

special plan *See* Specific Plan.

specific performance A court order to a breaching party to complete the contract as promised.

specific plan A planning document in addition to a general plan that usually encompasses just a portion of a city's geographic area; typically more detailed than the general plan.

specifications The description of an invention in a patent application in its best mode and the manner and process of making and using the invention so that a person skilled in the relevant field may make and use the invention.

sprawl A condition that results from unchecked development; contributes to the decline of cities and inner suburbs as more people move away from the cities where they work.

squatter's rights *See* Adverse Possession.

staggered board A board on which directors serve for specified terms, usually three years, with only a fraction of them up for reelection at any one time. Also called classified board.

standby letter of credit A method of securing a party's performance, whereby an issuing bank undertakes to pay a sum of money to the person (the beneficiary) to which performance is due on presentation of certain documents specified in the letter of credit, usually a brief statement (in language agreed on by the two parties) that the other party is in default and the beneficiary is entitled to payment from the issuing bank.

standing A party to a lawsuit has standing if the person seeking relief is the proper party to advance the litigation, has a personal interest in the outcome of the suit, and will benefit from a favorable ruling.

stare decisis (to abide by) The doctrine that holds that once a court resolves a particular issue, other courts addressing a similar legal problem generally follow the initial court's decision.

state implementation plans (SIPs) The prescribed emission control measures for stationary sources existing prior to 1970 and on the use of motor vehicles as necessary to achieve national ambient air quality standards.

state-of-the-art-defense A defense against claims based on a manufacturer's compliance with the best available technology (that may or may not be synonymous with the custom and practice of the industry).

statute of frauds A statute that requires that certain contracts, such as contracts conveying an interest in real property, must be in a signed writing to be enforceable in a court.

statute of limitations A time limit, defined by the statute, within which a lawsuit must be brought.

statute of repose A time limit that cuts off the right to assert a cause of action after a specified period of time from the date the product is sold.

statutory bar An inventor is denied patent protection in the event that prior to one year before the inventor's filing, the invention was (1) patented; (2) publicly used or sold in the United States; or (3) described in a printed publication in the United States or a foreign country.

stock lock-up option A lock-up option relating to stock of the target company.

stock parking The temporary sale of shares to another entity or individual to avoid tax reporting requirements or the net margin requirements of the securities laws applicable to brokerage firms.

stockholder A holder of equity securities of a corporation. Also called shareholder.

straight bankruptcy A bankruptcy in which the trustee liquidates the estate and distributes the proceeds first to secured creditors (to the extent of their collateral) and then in a prescribed order, pro rata within each level.

strategic alliance A source of financing by which a collaborative arrangement is entered into between an established company that has business needs or objectives complementary to another company.

strategic environmental management A concept that advocates placing environmental management on the profit side of the corporation rather than on the cost side.

strict liability Liability without fault. The concept that sellers are liable for all defective products. Also imposed for abnormally dangerous (or ultrahazardous) activities and toxic torts.

strict scrutiny test Under this test, a discriminatory classification will be held valid only if it is necessary to promote a compelling state interest and narrowly tailored; applies to classifications based on race or religion.

strong arm clause The clause that grants a debtor in possession the rights of a hypothetical creditor who extended credit to the debtor at the time of bankruptcy and who, as a result, either obtained a judicial lien on all property in which the debtor has an interest or obtained an execution against the debtor that was returned unsatisfied.

structural antidilution A provision that adjusts the conversion ratio at which convertible preferred shares may be exchanged for shares of common stock, if the total number of shares of common stock is increased, for example, by a stock split.

structural barriers Barriers to negotiation that arise from the existing frameworks and institutions within which a manager operates.

subdivision A division of land into separate parcels for development purposes.

subject matter jurisdiction The specific types of cases enumerated under Article III of the U.S. Constitution to be decided by the Supreme Court and lower courts established by Congress.

sublease An act by a tenant of renting out all or a portion of property the tenant has rented from a landlord.

subordinated debt instrument The document providing that a holder's right to repayment is subordinate to that of other creditors of the debtor.

substantial evidence standard Under this standard, the courts defer to an administrative agency's factual determinations in formal adjudications even if the record would support other factual conclusions.

substantial transformation An article exported from its country of origin is changed into a new article of commerce in a different country.

substantive coercion A threat that shareholders may agree to sell their shares in an otherwise noncoercive tender offer out of ignorance about the target company's true value.

substantive due process The constitutional guarantee that no person shall be arbitrarily deprived of life, liberty or property; the essence of substantive due process is protection from arbitrary and unreasonable action.

substantive legal obligations The legal rules that define the rights and duties of the agency and of persons dealing with it.

successor liability Individuals or entities who acquire an interest in a business or in real property may be held liable for personal injury and property or environmental damage resulting from acts (including sale of products) of the predecessor entity or previous owner.

suggestive marks Terms that suggest something about the products they identify without directly describing them, for example, Chicken of the Sea for tuna.

summary judgment A procedural device available for disposition of a controversy without trial. A judge will grant summary judgment only if all of the written evidence before the court clearly establishes that there are no disputed issues of material fact and the party who requested the summary judgment is entitled to prevail as a matter of law.

summary jury trial (SJT) Parties to a dispute put their cases before a real jury, which renders a nonbinding decision.

summons The official notice to a defendant that a lawsuit is pending against the defendant in a particular court.

Super 301 A provision of the Omnibus Trade Act of 1988 that required the U.S. Trade Representative to draw up a list of the foreign governments whose practices pose the most significant barriers to U.S. exports, and to immediately commence Section 301 investigations with respect to these practices.

super discharge A type of discharge available under Chapter 13 that extinguishes otherwise nondischargeable debts such as claims for fraud, theft, willful and malicious injury, or drunk driving, but not spousal or child support.

superlien An instrument that secures recovery of environmental cleanup response costs incurred by state agencies.

supervening cause An intervening cause that serves to separate an act of negligence from the resulting injury when it is (1) independent of the original act, (2) adequate to bring about the injury, and (3) not reasonably foreseeable.

supervisor Anyone possessing specified personnel functions if the exercise of that authority is not of a merely routine or clerical nature, but requires the use of independent judgment.

suppress To prevent the prosecution from introducing evidence.

surprise The extent to which the supposedly agreed on terms of the bargain are hidden in a densely printed form drafted by the party seeking to enforce the disputed terms.

surviving corporation In a merger of two corporations, the corporation that maintains its corporate existence is the surviving corporation.

sustainable development A theory that holds that future prosperity depends on preserving natural capital: air, water, and other ecological resources.

syndicate An underwriting group in a public offering; each member agrees to purchase a certain number of the securities of the issuer once the offering is declared effective by the Securities and Exchange Commission.

syndicated loan In a syndicated loan, the lenders enter into concurrent direct obligations with the borrower to make a loan, typically on a pro rata basis. The loan is coordinated by a lead lender that serves as agent for all the lenders in disbursing the funds, collecting payments of interest and principal, and administering and enforcing the loan.

synthetic lease A lease that is treated as a conventional operating lease for accounting purposes (so does not appear on the lessee's balance sheet) but is treated as if the lessee had purchased the property and obtained a loan from the seller for tax purposes.

take-out commitment An agreement by a lender to replace the construction loan with a permanent loan, usually after certain conditions, such as the timely completion of the project, have been met.

takeover A bidder acquires sufficient stock from a corporation's shareholders to obtain control of the corporation.

target A corporation that is the subject of a tender offer.

tariff classification The tariff on articles imported to the United States is determined by their description on the Harmonized Tariff Schedule.

tax basis The amount of cash or the fair market value of property exchanged for another asset, such as a general partnership interest.

tax-deferred exchange A transfer of real property for an alternative piece of real property meeting certain requirements.

teleological theory An ethical theory concerned with the consequences of something. The good of an action is to be judged by the effect of the action on others.

temporary insiders Outside attorneys, accountants, consultants, or investment bankers who are not directly employed by a corporation, but who acquire confidential information through performance of professional services.

tenancy by the entirety A special type of co-ownership of real property between husband and wife; like joint tenancy, it includes a right of survivorship.

tenants in common The individuals who own undivided interests in a parcel of real property.

tender offer A public offer to all the shareholders of a corporation to buy their shares at a stated price, usually higher than the market price.

term loan A loan for a specified amount funded in a lump sum or in installments to be repaid on a specified maturity date or paid off over a period of time.

term sheet A letter that outlines the terms and conditions on which a lender will lend.

termination The point after the dissolution of a partnership when all the partnership affairs are wound up and partners' authority to act for the partnership is completely extinguished.

termination fee *See* Breakup Fee.

territorial restrictions Restrictions that prevent a dealer or distributor from selling outside a certain territory.

third-party beneficiary One who does not give consideration for a promise yet has legal rights to enforce the contract. A person is a third-party beneficiary with legal rights when the contracting parties intended to benefit that person.

third-party defense Under the Comprehensive Environmental Responsibility, Contribution, and Liability Act, a potentially responsible current owner can assert this defense if the release or disposal of hazardous materials was by a third party who was not an employee and with whom the current owner had no contractual relationship. Also called the innocent landowner defense.

360/360 Method A method for calculating interest whereby it is assumed that all months have 30 days; thus the monthly interest amounts are always the same.

365/360 Method A method for calculating interest whereby the nominal annual interest rate is divided by 360, and the resulting daily rate is then multiplied by the outstanding principal amount and the actual number of days in the payment period.

365/365 Method A method for calculating interest whereby the daily rate is determined by dividing the nominal annual interest rate by 365 (or 366, in leap years), then this daily rate is multiplied by the outstanding principal amount and the actual number of days in the payment period.

tip Disclosure of a fact made to an individual and withheld from the general public.

tippee A person who receives inside information.

tipper A person who gives inside information.

tombstone ad A newspaper advertisement surrounded by bold black lines identifying the existence of a public offering and indicating where a prospectus may be obtained.

tort A civil wrong resulting in injury to a person or a person's property.

tortious interference with contract A wrongful interference with a contract by a third party when (1) there is a contract between the plaintiff and another; (2) the defendant has knowledge of the contract; (3) the defendant's actions cause the other party to breach that contract; (4) the plaintiff is damaged in some way; and (5) the defendant intentionally and wrongfully induces the other party to breach the contract.

total-activity test A combination of tests used to determine where a company engaged in multistate operations is domiciled; considers all aspects of the corporate entity, including the nature and scope of the company's activities.

total cost Variable cost plus fixed costs, such as rent and overhead.

toxic tort Any wrongful injury that is caused by exposure to a harmful, hazardous, or poisonous substance.

trade dress A manifestation of trademark law, the concept of trade dress is to protect the overall look of a product as opposed to just a particular design.

trade name A trade name or a corporate name identifies and symbolizes a business as a whole, as opposed to a trademark, which is used to identify and distinguish the various products and services sold by the business.

trade secret Information that derives independent economic value from not being generally known and that is subject to reasonable efforts to maintain its secrecy.

trademark A word or symbol used on goods or with services that indicates their origin.

traditional shelf offerings The registration of (1) securities offered pursuant to employee benefit plans; (2) securities offered or sold pursuant to dividend or interest reinvestment plans; (3) warrants, rights, or securities to be issued upon conversion of other outstanding securities; (4) mortgage-related securities; and (5) securities issued in connection with business combination transactions.

transaction value The price of an imported article indicated on a sales invoice.

transactional immunity The prohibition from prosecution granted a witness that relates to any matter discussed in that person's testimony.

transactional negotiation Negotiation that is forward looking with concern for desired relationships.

trespass to chattels When personal property is interfered with but not taken, destroyed, or substantially altered (i.e., not converted), there is a trespass to chattels. Also called trespass to personal property.

trespass to land The intentional invasion of real property (below the surface or in the airspace above) without consent of the owner.

trespass to personal property When personal property is interfered with but not taken, destroyed, or substantially altered (i.e., not converted), there is said to be a trespass to personal property.

triple net lease A type of industrial lease that requires the tenant to pay all taxes, insurance, and maintenance expenses.

trust (1) A combination of competitors who act together to fix prices, thereby stifling competition. (2) A manner of holding property that is controlled by a trustee for the benefit of a beneficiary.

trustee An individual who controls property held in trust for the benefit of a beneficiary.

tying arrangement A business arrangement whereby a seller will sell product A (the tying or desired product) to the customer only if the customer purchases product B (the tied product) from the seller.

UCC-1 Form In most states, this is the form a secured creditor uses for a financing statement under the Uniform Commercial Code.

ultrahazardous activity Activity that is so dangerous that no amount of care could protect others from the risk of harm.

unavoidably unsafe product A product, such as a vaccine, that is generally beneficial but is known to have harmful side effects in some cases.

unconscionable A contract term that is oppressive or fundamentally unfair.

undercapitalization theory A corporation is a separate entity, but its lack of adequate capital may constitute a fraud on the public. May be a basis for piercing corporate veil.

underwriter Any person who has purchased any security from an issuer with a view to, or offers or sells for an issuer in connection with, the distribution of any security.

undisclosed principal Use of an agent so that the third party to an agreement does not know or have reason to know of a principal's identity or existence.

undue burden Under the U.S. Constitution, a state regulation creates an undue burden when the regulatory burden on interstate commerce outweighs the state's interest in the legislation.

undue influence Sufficient influence and power over another as to make genuine assent impossible.

unenforceable contract A contract having no legal effect or force in a court action. A contract is unenforceable if it is (1) illegal or (2) unconscionable. A contract is also unenforceable if some public policy interest dictates that the agreement should not be upheld, regardless of the desire of one or more of the parties.

unfair labor practice strike A union strikes an employer for the employer's failure to bargain in good faith.

unfair labor practices Unlawful misconduct by an employer to employees exercising union rights.

Uniform Customs and Practice for Documentary Credits (UCP) A document that contains a set of rules that applies to letters of credit in international transactions; contrasts with the set of rules in Article 5 of the Uniform Commercial Code (UCC).

unilateral contract A promise given in exchange for an act. Offer can be accepted only by performing the act.

union authorization cards Generally, these cards contain a statement that the individual signing it wishes to be represented for purposes of collective bargaining by a certain union.

union security clause The clause in a collective bargaining contract under which employees in a particular unit are required, after a certain period of time, to become members of a union as a condition of employment.

universalizability An ethical theory that asks whether one would want everyone to perform in this manner.

unjust enrichment The unfair appropriation of the benefits of negotiation of contracts for the party's own use.

unorthodox transaction The purchase or sale by an officer, director, or greater-than-10 percent shareholder that would otherwise result in recoverable short-swing profits but is involuntary and does not involve the payment of cash, and there is no possibility of speculative abuse of insider information.

unreasonable *per se* Unreasonable no matter what the circumstances.

upstream guaranty A guaranty whereby subsidiaries guarantee the parent corporation's debt, or pledge their assets as security for the parent corporation's debt.

use immunity The prohibition on the use of the testimony of a witness against that witness in connection with the case in which that person is testifying or another case.

useful article doctrine The doctrine that holds that copyrightable pictorial, graphic, and sculptural works include works of artistic craftsmanship insofar as their form but not their mechanical or utilitarian aspects are concerned.

usury Charging an amount of interest on a loan that is in excess of the maximum specified by applicable law.

usury laws State statutes that set legal caps on what interest rates lenders may charge.

utilitarianism A major teleological system of ethics that stands for the proposition that the ideal is to maximize the total benefit for everyone involved.

utility patent A patent that protects any novel, useful, and nonobvious process, machine, manufacture, or composition of matter; or any novel, useful, and nonobvious improvement of such process, machine, manufacture, or composition of matter.

utility requirement A requirement a patent application must satisfy that states that the invention has a practical application or real-world use.

vacate The power of a court of appeal to nullify a previous court's ruling.

value Cash, property, or compensation for past services.

variable cost The cost of producing the next incremental unit.

Variable-interest loan A loan in which the rate of interest is often set at a fixed number of percentage points over a specified standard or base rate (often the prime rate).

variable-sum negotiations Negotiations in which mutual gains are possible as parties trade lower valued resources for higher valued ones. Also called integrative negotiations.

variance A method of relief from the strict terms of a zoning ordinance that allows a landowner to construct a structure or carry on an activity not otherwise permitted under zoning regulations.

venture capital Money managed by professional investors for investment in new enterprises.

venue The particular county or geographical area in which a court with jurisdiction may hear and determine a case.

vertical agreement An agreement between firms that operate at different levels of production or distribution.

vertical market division An agreement between a company and a dealer or distributor that prevents the dealer or the distributor from selling outside a certain territory or to a certain class of customer.

vertical merger A combination between firms at different points along the chain of distribution.

vertical restraint Unlawful restraint between firms at different levels in the chain of distribution, including price-fixing, market division, tying arrangements, and some franchise agreements.

vested right The right of a developer to develop property sometimes, but not always, obtained when a building permit is issued, substantial work is done, and substantial liabilities are incurred in reliance of that permit.

veto power The power of the president to prevent permanently or temporarily the enactment of a law created by Congress that does not meet his or her approval.

vicarious liability The imposition of civil or criminal liability on one party (e.g., an employer) for the wrongful acts of another (e.g., an employee). Also called imputed liability.

view easement An interest in property owned by another by which an easement holder is guaranteed that a landowner will not obstruct the holder's view by making changes to said property.

voidable Unenforceable at the option of one party.

voir dire Questioning of potential jurors to determine possible bias.

voluntary conversion The exchange by a holder of preferred stock for common stock on the occurrence of certain events.

voluntary redemption rights The requirement of a corporation to redeem an investor's shares for cash at a specified price, provided that the corporation is not prohibited by law from buying back stock or making distributions to its shareholders.

waiting period The period between the filing of the registration statement and the date the registration statement becomes effective with the SEC. Also called the quiet period.

waive To refrain from exercising certain rights.

warrant A right, for a given period of time, to purchase a stated amount of a security (frequently, stock) at a stated price (often equal to the fair market value when the warrant is issued, permitting its holder to benefit from any increase in values of the securities).

warranty deed A warranty deed is similar to a grant deed. In addition to the implied warranties contained in a grant deed, the grantor of a warranty deed also expressly warrants the title to and the quiet possession of the property to grantee.

whistle-blower statutes Federal and state statutes that prohibit employers from discharging or retaliating against an employee who has exercised the right to complain to a supervisor or government agency.

white-collar crime Nonviolent violations of the law by companies or their managers.

winding up The process of settling partnership affairs after dissolution.

wire fraud A scheme intended to defraud or to obtain money or property by fraudulent means through use of telephone systems.

work letter agreement An agreement between a tenant and a landlord, often an exhibit to a lease, that covers issues regarding tenant's improvements to rented space.

work made for hire A copyrightable work created by an employee within the scope of his or her employment, or a work in one of nine listed categories that is specially commissioned through a signed writing that states that the work is a "work made for hire."

work-product doctrine Protects information, including the private memoranda and personal thoughts of the attorney, created by the attorney while preparing a case for trial.

workout An out-of-court settlement between debtors and creditors that restructures the debtor's financial affairs in much the same way that a confirmed plan would, but it can bind only those who expressly consent.

wrap-around financing The transaction in which a new lender lends the owner of mortgaged real property additional funds and agrees to take over the servicing of the first loan. In exchange, the owner executes a deed of trust or mortgage and an all-inclusive note, covering the combined amount of the first and new loans.

writ An order in writing issued under seal in the name of a court or judicial officer commanding the person to whom it is directed to perform or refrain from performing an act specified therein.

writ of certiorari An order written by the U.S. Supreme Court when it decides to hear a case, ordering the lower court to certify the record of proceedings below and send it up to the U.S. Supreme Court.

wrongful discharge An employee termination without good cause that (1) violates public policy; (2) breaches an implied contract; or (3) violates the implied covenant of good faith and fair dealing.

zero-sum negotiations Negotiations in which the only issue is the distribution of the fixed pie. Also called distributive negotiations.

zone of danger The area in which an individual is physically close enough to a victim of an accident as to also be in personal danger.

zoning The division of a city into districts and the application of specific land use regulations in each district.

Index